Encyclopedia of social work. 18th edition, 1987
    Silver Spring, Md., National Association of Social Workers.

    v. 25 cm.

    Decennial, 1977–
    The 17th– issues kept up to date between editions by annual supple-
ments, 1983–84—
    Continues: Social work year book.
    ISSN 0071-0237 = Encyclopedia of social work.

    Social service—Yearbooks.   I. National Association of Social Workers.
II. Supplement to the Encyclopedia of social work.
    DNLM: HV 35 E56

HV35.S6   361'.003   30-30948
ISBN 0-87101-141-7   MARC-S

Printed in U.S.A.

Designer: Steffie Kaplan

Encyclopedia of Social Work

EIGHTEENTH EDITION

Volume 1

BOARD OF EDITORS

Anne Minahan, *Editor-in-Chief*

Rosina M. Becerra

Scott Briar

Claudia J. Coulton

Leon H. Ginsberg

June Gary Hopps

John F. Longres

Rino J. Patti

William J. Reid

Tony Tripodi

S. K. Khinduka, *Ex Officio*

Jacqueline M. Atkins, Executive Editor

Kenneth R. Greenhall, Managing Editor

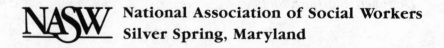 **National Association of Social Workers**
Silver Spring, Maryland

PREFACE TO THE EIGHTEENTH EDITION

The purpose of the *Encyclopedia of Social Work* is to provide an objective overview of social work in the United States—its history, its current concerns and interests, the state of its art, and its view of the future.

This edition is the eighteenth in a series that began in 1929 with the *Social Work Year Book*, which was published at two- or three-year intervals until 1960. Editions of the *Encyclopedia of Social Work* were published in 1965, 1971, and 1977. Originally, the National Association of Social Workers (NASW) had planned to publish the eighteenth edition in 1983 or 1984. However, in the early 1980s, the political, social, economic, and ideological environments in the United States appeared to shift sharply away from the past. These shifts produced changes in the economy; in employment; in governmental social policies; in public and voluntary social welfare services; in societal institutions; in social problems, causes, and issues; and in the lives of people. These changes affected the interactions between people and their environments and thus affected social work practice.

The NASW Publications Committee and the Board of Directors therefore concluded that the publication of a complete encyclopedia in the early 1980s would be premature and should be delayed until later in the decade, when the changes that were taking place could be better understood and described. Thus, instead of producing a complete encyclopedia, NASW decided to publish a 1983–1984 supplement to the 1977 edition. The supplement described some of the major changes taking place in social work and social policy, focusing on developments and trends in practice, research, social issues, political action, and technology; and on special population groups. A comprehensive section of statistical and demographic tables surveying social and demographic developments also was included.

In 1983, NASW's president appointed a Board of Editors to plan and develop the eighteenth edition of the encyclopedia. The board began its work by reading and evaluating past editions of the encyclopedia (as well as the 1983–1984 supplement) and by reviewing the findings and recommendations of the 1981 report from an NASW task force, chaired by Joseph Vigilante, set up to evaluate the seventeenth edition. The Board of Editors also reviewed surveys of the 1977 encyclopedia by the NASW membership and by purchasers of previous editions. In addition, the editors reflected on the purposes and objectives of the current practice of social work, on the institutional bases of most practice, on current social problems and issues, and on the environmental context of the mid-1980s in the United States.

Content of Articles

On the basis of their review and reflection, the board decided that the major criterion for selecting subject matter for the encyclopedia should be the relevance of each topic to social work practice in the United States. The editors also decided that the themes that should permeate the encyclopedia were the implications of the subject matter for social work practice, for ethnic, racial, and cultural minorities, and for women.

Discussions of article content highlighted the impact of the current social, political, economic, and ideological climate on all areas of concern to social work in the 1980s. Therefore, the editors decided that an article providing an overview of the current context for social work should be the first entry in the encyclopedia. Leon Ginsberg, a member of the Board of Editors, wrote the article.

In order to generate relevant subject matter and topics, the editors developed a working framework. This framework was not viewed as an elegant analytical scheme to conceptualize all the knowledge and interventions related to social work practice but as a commonsense device to guide the selection of articles that would reflect social work thinking, concerns, and practice in the mid-1980s and be relevant and useful to readers.

In developing the framework for generating topics for articles, and in outlining article content, the editors realized that inevitably there would be some duplication or overlapping of material. However, surveys of

Table 1. Framework Used To Develop Topics for the Eighteenth Edition

I.   Fields of Practice
II.   Populations
III. Social Issues and Problems
IV.   Social Work Practice
         A. Direct Frontline Practice
         B. Macro Practice
V.   Social Institutions and Human
         Development
VI.   Research
VII. Profession
VIII. Miscellaneous

users of previous editions indicated that most readers do not read the complete encyclopedia but choose articles of particular interest to them. Therefore the editors decided that each article should be able to stand on its own, should include material relevant to the subject even if some of the content was discussed elsewhere, and should conclude with cross-references to other articles.

The editors' thinking about the framework was influenced by statements of social work objectives and purposes contained in two "conceptual framework" special issues of the NASW journal *Social Work*, by the Council on Social Work Education Curriculum Policy Statement, and by other conceptual work on social work.[1] The framework was built pragmatically, block by block, in language that is familiar to social workers and that reflects their way of thinking about interventions focused on person-environment interactions.

Eight areas were identified in the framework, and each member of the Board of Editors took responsibility for developing certain topics and outlining the content of articles. The areas, which are summarized in Table 1, are as follows.

Fields of Practice. Fields of practice are the major delivery systems and programs through which services and resources are provided. Article content in this area includes description of delivery systems and services,

---

[1] See *Social Work*, 22(5), 1977; *Social Work*, 26(1), 1981; and Appendix 2 (CSWE Curriculum Policy Statement) in Volume 2 of this encyclopedia.

historical background and current trends and issues, relevant theory and research, financing, social policy affecting services, and the role of social work. The articles in this area include, for example, Child Welfare Services; Health Service System; Mental Health Services; Settlements and Neighborhood Centers; Sexual Assault Services; Aid to Families with Dependent Children; Juvenile Justice System; Hunger and Malnutrition; and Retirement and Pension Programs. Claudia J. Coulton and Leon H. Ginsberg were the editors responsible for the area.

Populations. Populations are groups identified by age, ethnicity, gender, sexual orientation or preference, physical and developmental disability, and other characteristics. Content of articles in this area includes definition of the population; demographic information; historical trends; special needs and risks; social policy relevant to the population; programs, if any, designed for the population; and the role of social work. Among the specific articles assigned are Aged; Blacks; Disabilities: Physical; Mexican Americans; and Women. Rosina M. Becerra was the editor for this area.

Social Issues and Problems. Social issues and problems are related to conditions and behavior that affect a significant number of people and create societal debate and response through programs, legislation, and other actions. Content of articles in this area includes definition of the problem or issue; discussion of its significance; demographic information; and coverage of historical trends, social policies, delivery systems, and the role of social work. Articles that were assigned include Child Support; Domestic Violence; Homelessness; and Poverty, among others. John F. Longres was the editor responsible for this area.

Social Work Practice. Almost every article in the encyclopedia emphasizes social work practice. In addition, the editors believed it was essential to include specific articles on perspectives, methods, and approaches that describe what social workers do in different fields of practice, in work with different populations, and in relation to different social problems and issues. Topics were generated that would be of primary interest to workers in direct practice—those who are doing frontline, or micro, practice—and to workers who are performing functions related primarily to administration, planning, and social policy—those who are engaged in macro practice.

Direct Frontline Practice. Content includes (1) overview articles on practitioner roles, functions, and trends and issues; (2) articles on practice approaches and perspectives that discuss theoretical foundations, strategies, interventions, adaptations, and research on effectiveness; and (3) articles on practice methods used in interventions with systems of different sizes. Specific articles include Advocacy; Crisis Intervention; Existential Approach; Generalist Perspective; and Termination in Direct Practice. William J. Reid was responsible for this area.

Macro Practice. Content includes (1) articles on social planning and community organizations that cover definition and purpose, philosophical bases and assumptions, history, and current methods and settings; (2) articles on administration that cover history of development, issues and trends, relevant research, and description and analysis of specific practitioner functions and methods; and (3) articles on social policy that discuss trends and issues, policy, techniques of policy analysis, and interventions. The assigned articles include Administration in Social Welfare; Community-Based Social Action; Organizations: Context for Social Service Delivery; Social Planning; Social Planning and Community Organization; and Social Welfare Policy: Trends and Issues. Rino J. Patti was the editor responsible for this area.

Social Institutions and Human Development. Content on social institutions includes articles on theory, research, and historical perspectives, and descriptions of family, group, formal organization, neighborhood, and community. Content on human development includes articles on the biological, sociocultural, and psychological perspectives on human development. Articles assigned in this area include Community Theory and Research; Family: Contemporary Patterns; Neighborhoods; and Organizations: Impact on Employees and Community. John F. Longres and Rino J. Patti were the editors responsible for this area.

Research. Article content includes the distinctive characteristics of social work research; history, development, and current trends; descriptions of different research methods and measures; applications and implications of research to practice; and technological developments. Among the specific articles are Computer Utilization; Ethical Issues in Research; Research in Social Work; and Research Measures and Indices in Direct Practice. Scott Briar was the editor responsible for this area.

Profession. Article content covers contemporary characteristics of the social work profession; professional social work organizations and their purpose, membership, historical background, major programs, and issues and debates; and professional trends. The assigned articles include Professional Associations: Council on Social Work Education; Professional Associations: National Association of Social Workers; Professional Associations: Special Interest; and Profession of Social Work: Contemporary Characteristics. June Gary Hopps was the editor responsible for this area.

Miscellaneous. The primary purpose of the framework described previously was to create a commonsense mechanism to generate topics for articles that would be of interest to readers. Realizing that not all topics related to social work would be identified through the use of the framework, the editors created a miscellaneous category to generate articles on other subjects germane to social work. Content of subjects in this area includes discussion of their definition, historical development, impact on society, and implications for social work, and of topics specifically relevant to the subject of the article. Among these articles are Mutual Help Groups; Private and Proprietary Services; Unions: Social Work; and Values and Ethics. Also included are three articles on aspects of international social welfare. Sarah Connell was the original editor of this area but had to withdraw early in the planning process. Tony Tripodi was then appointed as editor.

Biographies

Past editions of the encyclopedia have included biographies of deceased people who have had a significant impact on social work and social welfare in the United States. The editors decided to continue this practice and to make special efforts to include people who had made outstanding contributions to ethnic minorities and other populations. All the biographies are in a special section (see Volume 2). John F. Longres was the editor responsible for the biographies.

Statistical Tables

The editors also decided to continue the practice of including comprehensive statistical and demographic tables to illustrate and highlight social and economic trends and developments. These tables are presented in a separate volume, and is anticipated that they will be updated and published at intervals before publication of the next encyclopedia. Sumner M. Rosen and David Fanshel were commissioned to do the statistical tables. They were assisted by Mary Lutz.

Board of Editors

The Board of Editors held a series of meetings to make decisions on the content and organization of the encyclopedia, on selection of authors, and on other editorial policies. After formulating the framework discussed earlier to generate topics, each board member took responsibility for one or more areas. The editor in charge of an area recommended to the whole board for approval a proposed list of articles, outlines of content for articles, and names of suggested authors. To determine if any previous articles should be retained and updated, editors reviewed articles relevant to their areas in the 1983–1984 supplement to the seventeenth edition, the seventeenth edition itself, and other past editions of the encyclopedia. Because the new framework generated new types of articles and new content, only a few past articles were selected for retention. Thus, almost all the articles in this edition are new. The editors asked the board-approved authors to write articles, assigned a topical outline for each article, reviewed all articles in their area—suggesting revisions when appropriate—and then approved all entries in their area. The editor-in-chief reviewed all the encyclopedia articles.

The members of the Board of Editors are experienced writers who are knowledgeable about social work and social welfare and experienced with editorial processes. They are creative, open to other points of view, patient, hard-working, and responsible. Working individually and in meetings of the Board of Editors, they enjoyed the experience of creating an encyclopedia that reflects both the diversity and common interests and concerns of social work in the 1980s.

Authors

Authors were selected who were experts in areas of concern to social work and who agreed to write articles within the deadlines imposed. They were asked to be as objective as possible, to describe and reflect on their subjects, and to refrain from advocating their own points of view. Obviously, authors' experiences, knowledge, and values guided their selection and presentation of material, but they tried hard to provide an unbiased presentation of their assigned subjects. Almost all the authors are social workers, and those who are in related fields are familiar with social work and its concerns. The commitment of the authors to the social work purpose of improving the quality of life is reflected in their articles.

Staff

This encyclopedia could not have been planned, developed, and published without the experience, hard work, and dedication of the staff of the NASW Publications Department. Jacqueline M. Atkins, Director of Publications, and Kenneth R. Greenhall, Managing Editor of the encyclopedia, worked collaboratively with the Board of Editors in planning and decision making. Their organizational and publication skills, experience, hard work, insights, and hospitality were invaluable. The able staff who worked with them—Editor Susan H. Llewellyn and Editorial Assistant Bradley Frome—dealt with the myriad details and tasks involved in keeping track of work in progress, editing, and production. Senior Administrative Assistant Nancy Larson contributed significantly to the pleasantness and productivity of the meetings of the Board of Editors.

All the members of the Board of Editors are particularly grateful to Managing Editor Kenneth R. Greenhall for his infallible good humor, tact, patience, diligence, fairness, and thoughtfulness.

ANNE MINAHAN
Editor-in-Chief

HOW TO USE THIS ENCYCLOPEDIA

The eighteenth edition of the *Encyclopedia of Social Work* has been specifically designed with the user in mind. In the words of the computer-oriented society of the 1980s, it is meant to be "user-friendly." Although the encyclopedia contains a wealth of information gathered from the top practitioners and scholars of the profession on the scope of social work, its ultimate value lies in the usability of the material. Thus, a basic principle throughout, from choosing topics for development through determining the format, has been how to make the information in the three volumes most accessible.

The new edition differs from previous editions in five major respects. These differences, all of which make it easier for the reader to use the encyclopedia, are as follows:

1. The edition consists of three volumes. The first two volumes are hardcovered and contain 225 articles and 4 appendixes covering the full range of major topics and issues in social work. The third volume, a paperback, is a statistical and demographic supplement made up of tables, graphs, and charts; this volume will be updated periodically to keep the encyclopedia current.

2. An extensive index to the articles now appears in both main hardcover volumes to aid readers in finding information quickly and easily.

3. All biographical entries are contained together in a separate section of Volume 2 of the encyclopedia.

4. Comprehensive free-standing cross-reference boxes, called Reader's Guides, have been added for the following key terms:

Administration
Children and Youth
Clinical Social Work:
  Approaches and
  Perspectives
Clinical Social Work:
  Methods
Community
Community Planning
Corrections System
Education
Family
Health and Mental
  Health
Income Support and
  Poverty
Justice System
Management
Medical Care
Minorities and
  Special Populations
Planning
Poverty and Income
  Support
Practice Approaches
  and Perspectives
Practice Methods
Profession
Research
Social Planning
  and Community
  Work

These guides supply the reader with the titles of all pertinent entries within a given subject area. For example, the box on the subject of Administration contains the following information:

> **Reader's Guide**
>
> ## ADMINISTRATION
>
> The following articles contain information on this general topic:
>
> Administration: Environmental Aspects
> Administration: Interpersonal Aspects
> Administration in Social Welfare
> Financial Management
> Information Systems: Agency
> Information Systems: Client Data
> Information Utilization for Management Decision Making
> Macro Practice: Current Trends and Issues
> Organizations: Impact on Employees and Community
> Personnel Management
> Program Evaluation
> Quality Assurance
> Supervision in Social Work

5. The two main volumes are paged individually rather than consecutively. The index will include a notation of which volume the entry appears in immediately preceding the page number; for example, 1:108, 2:435.

Scope. The 225 general entries in this edition are arranged in alphabetical order under the titles the Board of Editors believe readers will be most likely to consult. The coverage includes articles on areas such as fields of practice, populations, social issues and problems, direct practice, macro practice, social institutions, human development, and research. The biographical section contains 100 articles on deceased individuals who made significant contributions to the profession of social work in the United States. The titles of all these 325 articles are specified in the List of Entries that follows this introduction. The eighteenth edition also contains more than 200 tables, graphs, and charts, most of which appear in Volume 3, but a few of which accompany articles in the first two volumes.

Locating a Specific Article. The reader who is looking for information on a specific topic, such as child abuse, may look in any of three places: (1) in the appropriate alphabetical position among the articles, such as Child Abuse and Neglect; (2) in the List of Entries at the end of this section; or (3) in the index in either Volume 1 or Volume 2, which will list the volume and page number of the article. The index will also include cross-references, as in the following example:

Children
    abuse of. See Child abuse and
    neglect; Child sexual abuse

The order of entry for the articles is alphabetical, letter by letter, up to any punctuation mark in a title. This principle is illustrated by the following sequence of entries:

Family
Family: Contemporary Patterns
Family: Multigenerational
Family and Population Planning

Although the Board of Editors has tried to place each article under the title readers would be most likely to consult, the board recognizes that it is helpful to include subject cross-references (free-standing cross-references with article headings but without text). Among the factors that make cross-references necessary are readers' individual viewpoints and backgrounds, together with changing fashions in terminology. (The reader who looks under the heading "Native Americans" is referred to "American Indians and Alaska Natives"—the terms that most members of those populations found preferable at the time the 18th edition was being prepared.) Thus, numerous subject cross-references

have been included to help readers find the material for their topics. For example:

AIDS. See Homosexuality: Gay Men.

DAY CARE. See Child Care Services; Child Welfare Services.

NATIVE AMERICANS. See American Indians and Alaska Natives; Civil Rights; Ethnic-Sensitive Practice; Intergroup Relations; Minorities of Color.

Locating Several Related Articles. As noted previously, Reader's Guides specify the titles of key articles. After locating a key article, the reader may find a reference to related articles in the cross-references at the end of the entry. Such citations, which precede the article's reference list, are introduced by the phrase "For further information, see . . ." and are shown in capitals and small capitals. The article Juvenile Offenders and Delinquency, for example, contains the following cross-references:

For further information, see Juvenile Courts, Probation, and Parole; Juvenile Justice System; Juvenile Offender Diversion and Community-Based Services; Juvenile Offender Institutions.

Locating Names, Definitions, and Key Topics. The highly detailed, comprehensive index that appears in both main volumes of this encyclopedia is the most convenient source of specific referrals for names of people and organizations, definitions of terms, and so forth. The index also indicates where a wide range of key topics and phrases may be found.

Locating Statistical and Demographic Data. The encyclopedia's third volume, *Face of the Nation*, is the reader's primary source of statistical data. The tabular data are accompanied by brief captions that capture the significance of the information and help the reader in interpreting the material presented. The basic statistical tables are supplemented by graphs and charts that also help make much of the data more accessible. *Face of the Nation* has its own table of contents. Many of the articles in the first two encyclopedia volumes also present statistical data either within the narrative of the text or in accompanying tables.

Locating Bibliographic Data. The integrity of any reference book rests largely on the authors' documentation of the information they present. In this edition of the *Encyclopedia of Social Work*, the sources are indicated parenthetically in the text of an entry by the citation of the source author's surname and the year of publication, as in the following example: (Acosta, Yamamoto, & Evans, 1982; Alexander & Kronfein, 1983). Full bibliographic information is cited alphabetically by authors' surnames at the end of each entry in a list headed "References." The style of the list is a modified version of the American Psychological Association style that is becoming the standard citation form in social science databases and library indexes.

References

Acosta, F. X., Yamamoto, J., & Evans, L. A. (1982). *Effective Psychotherapy For Low Income and Minority Patients.* New York: Plenum Press.
Alexander, J., & Kronfein, M. (1983). "Changes in Family Functioning Amongst Nonconventional Families." *American Journal of Orthopsychiatry, 53*(4), 408–417.

Many entries also include a list headed "For Further Reading," in which the reader may find citations of reference materials that, although not specifically mentioned in the text, contain helpful information on the topic of the entry. The student, teacher, or practitioner who wants to conduct a search of the growing literature of social work will find the new edition's extensive reference lists particularly helpful. For example, the references following the survey article Adolescents, when supplemented by those following the articles on specific related problems, such as Adolescent Pregnancy, Juvenile Offenders and Delinquency, or Runaways, will furnish a comprehensive guide to the literature in this general area.

Conclusion

As indicated in the list of entries that follows, the knowledge base of social work continues to expand and diversify, reflecting the activities and thought of a vigorous, healthy profession. The staff is grateful to the eighteenth edition's Board of Editors and to the contributing authors, who have found time in their busy schedules to hold a mirror up to the profession, allowing a fresh assessment of social work's history as well as its recent accomplishments and trends.

JACQUELINE M. ATKINS
Executive Editor

KENNETH R. GREENHALL
Managing Editor

LIST OF ENTRIES

The following list contains the titles of the articles in this encyclopedia. It shows the precise form of the titles and the order of entries. By consulting this list, the reader may quickly gain an overview of the contents of the new edition.

BIOGRAPHIES

Abbott, Edith
Abbott, Grace
Addams, Jane
Altmeyer, Arthur J.

Barrett, Janie Porter
Barton, Clarissa (Clara) Harlowe
Beers, Clifford Whittingham
Bethune, Mary McLeod
Brace, Charles Loring
Breckinridge, Sophonisba Preston
Brockway, Zebulon Reed
Bruno, Frank John
Buell, Bradley
Burns, Eveline Mabel

Cabot, Richard Clarke
Cannon, Ida Maud
Cannon, Mary Antoinette
Coyle, Grace Longwell

Day, Dorothy
De Forest, Robert Weeks
Devine, Edward Thomas
Dix, Dorothea Lynde
DuBois, William Edward Burghardt
Dunham, Arthur

Eliot, Martha May
Epstein, Abraham

Fauri, Fedele Frederick
Fernandis, Sarah A. Collins
Flexner, Abraham
Follett, Mary Parker
Frankel, Lee Kaufer
Frazier, Edward Franklin

Gallaudet, Edward Miner
Gallaudet, Thomas

Gallaudet, Thomas Hopkins
Garrett, Annette Marie
Gonzalez Molina de la Caro, Dolores
Granger, Lester Blackwell

Hamilton, Gordon
Haynes, Elizabeth Ross
Haynes, George Edmund
Hearn, Gordon
Hoey, Jane M.
Hopkins, Harry Lloyd
Howard, Donald S.
Howe, Samuel Gridley

Jarrett, Mary Cromwell
Johnson, Campbell Carrington

Kelley, Florence
Kellogg, Paul Underwood

Lassalle, Beatriz
Lathrop, Julia Clifford
Lee, Porter Raymond
Lenroot, Katharine Fredrica
Lindeman, Eduard Christian
Lindsay, Inabel Burns
Lodge, Richard
Lowell, Josephine Shaw
Lurie, Harry Lawrence

Manning, Leah Katherine Hicks
Matthews, Victoria Earle

Newstetter, Wilber I.

Pagan de Colon, Petroamerica
Perkins, Frances
Pray, Kenneth

Rapoport, Lydia
Reynolds, Bertha Capen
Richmond, Mary Ellen
Riis, Jacob August
Rivera de Alvarado, Carmen
Robison, Sophie Moses
Rodriguez Pastor, Soledad
Rubinow, Isaac Max
Rush, Benjamin

Schwartz, William
Seton, Elizabeth Ann Bayley (Mother Seton)
Simkhovitch, Mary Kingsbury
Smith, Zilpha Drew
Spellman, Dorothea C.
Switzer, Mary Elizabeth

Taft, Julia Jessie
Taylor, Graham
Terrell, Mary Eliza Church
Thomas, Jesse O.
Titmuss, Richard Morris
Towle, Charlotte
Truth, Sojourner
Tubman, Harriet

Wald, Lillian
Washington, Booker Taliaferro
Washington, Forrester Blanchard
Wells-Barnett, Ida Bell
White, Eartha Mary Magdalene
Wiley, George
Wilkins, Roy
Williams, Anita Rose
Witte, Ernest Frederic

Young, Whitney Moore, Jr.
Youngdahl, Benjamin Emanuel
Younghusband, Dame Eileen

CONTRIBUTORS

The positions and affiliations given are those
held by the contributors at the time they
prepared the articles.

CHAUNCEY A. ALEXANDER, MSW,
ACSW
Chauncey A. Alexander & Associates,
Inc., Huntington Beach, California
HISTORY OF SOCIAL WORK AND SOCIAL
WELFARE: SIGNIFICANT DATES

LESLIE B. ALEXANDER, Ph.D., ACSW
Associate Professor, Graduate School
of Social Work and Social Research,
Bryn Mawr College, Bryn Mawr,
Pennsylvania
UNIONS: SOCIAL WORK

NANCY AMIDEI, MSW
Social policy writer and commentator,
Washington, D.C.
HUNGER AND MALNUTRITION

SANDRA C. ANDERSON, Ph.D., ACSW
Professor, Graduate School of Social
Work, Portland State University,
Portland, Oregon
ALCOHOL USE AND ADDICTION

F. EMERSON ANDREWS (deceased)
President Emeritus, Foundation Center,
New York
FOUNDATIONS AND SOCIAL WELFARE
(with Zeke Kilbride)

STEPHEN ANTLER, DSW
Consultant and Lecturer, Smith College
School for Social Work,
Northampton, Massachusetts
PROFESSIONAL LIABILITY AND
MALPRACTICE

PATRICIA AUSPOS, Ph.D.
Research Associate, Manpower
Demonstration Research Corp., New
York
WORKFARE (with Judith M. Gueron)

DAVID M. AUSTIN, Ph.D., ACSW
Bert Kruger Smith Professor, School of
Social Work, University of Texas at
Austin
SOCIAL PLANNING IN THE PUBLIC
SECTOR

MICHAEL J. AUSTIN, Ph.D., ACSW
Dean, School of Social Work,
University of Pennsylvania,
Philadelphia
PERSONNEL MANAGEMENT (with Peter
J. Pecora)

LAWRENCE NEIL BAILIS, Ph.D.
Senior Research Associate, Center for
Human Resources, Florence Heller
School, Brandeis University,
Waltham, Massachusetts
WORK EXPERIENCE PROGRAMS (with
Joseph Ball)

JOSEPH BALL, Ph.D. (deceased)
Manager of Implementation Studies,
Manpower Demonstration Research
Corp., New York
WORK EXPERIENCE PROGRAMS (with
Lawrence Neil Bailis)

ROBERT L. BARKER, DSW, ACSW
Associate Professor, National Catholic
School of Social Service, Catholic
University of America, Washington,
D.C.
PRIVATE AND PROPRIETARY SERVICES

MARK G. BATTLE, MSSA, ACSW
Executive Director, National
Association of Social Workers, Silver
Spring, Maryland
PROFESSIONAL ASSOCIATIONS:
NATIONAL ASSOCIATION OF SOCIAL
WORKERS

ROSINA M. BECERRA, Ph.D.
Professor, School of Social Welfare,
University of California, Los Angeles
ADOLESCENT PREGNANCY (with Eve P.
Fielder)
VETERANS AND VETERANS' SERVICES
(with Gene Rothman)

R. LARRY BECKETT, MSW
Assistant Commissioner, West Virginia
Department of Human Services,
Charleston
VOCATIONAL REHABILITATION (with
Gordon R. Kent)

RAYMOND M. BERGER, Ph.D., ACSW
Clinician, Counseling Institute of the
Champaign County Mental Health
Center, and Associate Professor,
School of Social Work, University of
Illinois, Urbana
HOMOSEXUALITY: GAY MEN

BARBARA BERKMAN, DSW, ACSW
Professor, MGH Institute of Health
Professions, Massachusetts General
Hospital, Boston
HEALTH CARE SPECIALIZATIONS

L. DIANE BERNARD, Ph.D., ACSW
Interim Executive Director, Council on
Social Work Education, Washington,
D.C.
PROFESSIONAL ASSOCIATIONS:
COUNCIL ON SOCIAL WORK
EDUCATION

DAVID E. BIEGEL, Ph.D., ACSW
Associate Professor, School of Social
Work, University of Pittsburgh,
Pittsburgh, Pennsylvania
NEIGHBORHOODS

ANDREW BILLINGSLEY, Ph.D.
Professor of Sociology and Afro-
American Studies, Affiliate Professor
of Family and Community
Development, University of
Maryland, College Park
FAMILY: CONTEMPORARY PATTERNS

EVELYN LANCE BLANCHARD, MSW
Director, Special Projects, National
Indian Social Workers Association,
Tulsa, Oklahoma
AMERICAN INDIANS AND ALASKA
NATIVES

MARTIN BLOOM, Ph.D.
School of Social Work, Virginia
Commonwealth University,
Richmond
PREVENTION

BETTY J. BLYTHE, Ph.D., ACSW
Assistant Professor, School of Social
Work, University of Michigan, Ann
Arbor
DIRECT PRACTICE EFFECTIVENESS (with
Scott Briar)

NEIL F. BRACHT, MSW, MPH, ACSW
School of Social Work, University of
Minnesota, Minneapolis
PREVENTIVE HEALTH CARE AND
WELLNESS

JUDITH B. BRADFORD, Ph.D.
Research Associate, Survey Research
Laboratory, Virginia Commonwealth
University, Richmond
LITERACY (with Grace E. Harris)

RUTH A. BRANDWEIN, Ph.D.
Dean, School of Social Welfare, State
University of New York, Stony
Brook
WOMEN IN MACRO PRACTICE

DIANE BLAKE BRASHEAR, Ph.D.,
ACSW
Assistant Professor, Department of
Obstetrics and Gynecology, Indiana
University, Indianapolis
SEXUAL DYSFUNCTION

EDWARD A. BRAWLEY, DSW, ACSW
Professor, Department of Sociology,
Pennsylvania State University,
University Park
MASS MEDIA

KATHARINE HOOPER BRIAR, DSW
Assistant Professor, School of Social
Work, University of Washington,
Seattle
UNEMPLOYMENT AND
UNDEREMPLOYMENT

SCOTT BRIAR, DSW, ACSW
Dean and Professor, School of Social
Work, University of Washington,
Seattle
DIRECT PRACTICE EFFECTIVENESS (with
Betty J. Blythe)
DIRECT PRACTICE: TRENDS AND ISSUES

DONALD BRIELAND, Ph.D., ACSW
Dean, Jane Addams College of Social
Work, University of Illinois at
Chicago
HISTORY AND EVOLUTION OF SOCIAL
WORK PRACTICE
LEGAL ISSUES AND LEGAL SERVICES
(with Samuel Z. Goldfarb)

ELAINE M. BRODY, MSW, ACSW
Director, Department of Human
Services, and Associate Director of
Research, Philadelphia Geriatric
Center, Philadelphia, Pennsylvania
AGED: SERVICES (with Stanley J.
Brody)

STANLEY J. BRODY, JD
Professor of Physical Medicine and
Rehabilitation in Psychiatry,

University of Pennsylvania, Medical
School, Philadelphia
AGED: SERVICES (with Elaine M.
Brody)

STEVE BURGHARDT, Ph.D.
Associate Professor, School of Social
Work, Hunter College, New York
COMMUNITY-BASED SOCIAL ACTION
RADICAL SOCIAL WORK (with Michael
Fabricant)

EDMUND M. BURKE, Ph.D.
Director, Center for Corporate
Community Relations, Boston
College, Chestnut Hill,
Massachusetts
CORPORATE SOCIAL RESPONSIBILITY

JAMES W. CALLICUTT, Ph.D.
Professor and Associate Dean,
Graduate School of Social Work,
University of Texas, Arlington
MENTAL HEALTH SERVICES

JOAN CARRERA, MPA, MSW
Senior Program Liaison Specialist, U.S.
Department of Health and Human
Services, Office of Family
Assistance, Washington, D.C.
AID TO FAMILIES WITH DEPENDENT
CHILDREN

GEORGE CASTELLE, JD
Director, Juvenile Advocates, Inc.,
Office of the Public Defender,
Charleston, West Virginia
JUVENILE OFFENDER INSTITUTIONS

CATHERINE S. CHILMAN, Ph.D.
Professor Emeritus, School of Social
Welfare, University of Wisconsin,
Milwaukee
ABORTION

JOAN L. CLEMENT, MSW
Assistant Director, Social Work
Department, Harborview Medical
Center, Seattle, Washington
EMERGENCY HEALTH SERVICES (with
Jacqueline S. Durgin)

RICHARD A. CLOWARD, Ph.D.
Professor, School of Social Work,
Columbia University, New York
VOTER REGISTRATION (with Frances
Fox Piven)

DENISE COBURN, MSW, ACSW
Associate Professor, School of Social

Work, Michigan State University,
East Lansing
TRANSACTIONAL ANALYSIS

ELIZABETH S. COLE, MSW, ACSW
Director, Permanent Families for
Children Unit, Child Welfare League
of America, New York
ADOPTION

ALICE COLLINS, MSW (deceased)
Consultant, Portland, Oregon
NATURAL HELPING NETWORKS (with
Diane L. Pancoast)

SARAH CONNELL, MSW, ACSW
Regional Director, New York State
Office of Mental Health, New York
City Regional Office
HOMELESSNESS

GERALDINE L. CONNER, DSW
Associate Professor, Graduate School
of Social Work, Boston College,
Chestnut Hill, Massachusetts
FAMILY AND POPULATION PLANNING

JON R. CONTE, Ph.D.
Assistant Professor, School of Social
Service Administration, University of
Chicago, Chicago, Illinois
CHILD SEXUAL ABUSE

LYNN B. COOPER, D.Crim.
Professor, Coordinator of Women's
Studies, Department of Social Work,
California State University,
Sacramento
FEMINIST SOCIAL WORK (with Nan Van
Den Bergh)

LELA B. COSTIN, MSW, ACSW
Professor, School of Social Work,
University of Illinois, Urbana-
Champaign
SCHOOL SOCIAL WORK

CLAUDIA J. COULTON, Ph.D., ACSW
Professor, School of Applied Social
Sciences, Case Western Reserve
University, Cleveland, Ohio
QUALITY ASSURANCE

RICHARD T. CROW, Ph.D., ACSW
Professor, School of Social Work,
University of Alabama, University
PLANNING AND MANAGEMENT
PROFESSIONS

ROCCO D'ANGELO, Ph.D.
Professor, College of Social Work,

Ohio State University, Columbus
RUNAWAYS

SHELDON DANZIGER, Ph.D.
Professor of Social Work and Director,
Institute for Research on Poverty,
University of Wisconsin, Madison
POVERTY

NANETTE J. DAVIS, Ph.D.
Professor, Department of Sociology,
Portland State University, Portland,
Oregon
PROSTITUTION

MARY LOU DAVIS-SACKS, Ph.D.
Private organizational consultant, Ann
Arbor, Michigan
ORGANIZATIONS: IMPACT ON
EMPLOYEES AND COMMUNITY (with
Yeheskel Hasenfeld)

DIANE de ANDA, Ph.D.
Associate Professor, School of Social
Welfare, University of California,
Los Angeles
ADOLESCENTS

RONALD B. DEAR, DSW, ACSW
Associate Professor, School of Social
Work, University of Washington,
Seattle
LEGISLATIVE ADVOCACY (with Rino J.
Patti)

MELVIN DELGADO, Ph.D.
Professor, School of Social Work,
Boston University, Boston,
Massachusetts
PUERTO RICANS

WYNETTA DEVORE, Ed.D.
Associate Professor, School of Social
Work, Syracuse University,
Syracuse, New York
ETHNIC-SENSITIVE PRACTICE (with
Elfriede G. Schlesinger)

CARMEN DÍAZ, Ph.D., ACSW
Assistant Professor, School of Social
Work, University of Pittsburgh,
Pittsburgh, Pennsylvania
FAMILY: MULTIGENERATIONAL (with
Leon F. Williams)

MARÍA ELISA DÍAZ, DSW, ACSW
Professor Emeritus, University of
Puerto Rico, Rio Piedras
SOCIAL WORK IN THE U.S.
TERRITORIES AND COMMONWEALTH
(with John F. Longres and E.
Aracelis Francis)

MILAN J. DLUHY, Ph.D.
Associate Professor of Social Work and
Adjunct Associate Professor of
Political Science, University of
Michigan, Ann Arbor
HOUSING

FRED C. DOOLITTLE, Ph.D., JD
Public Affairs Analyst, Woodrow
Wilson School, Princeton,
University, Princeton, New Jersey
SOCIAL WELFARE FINANCING

HOWARD J. DOUECK, Ph.D., ACSW
Assistant Professor, State University of
New York at Buffalo
JUVENILE OFFENDER DIVERSION AND
COMMUNITY-BASED SERVICES (with
J. David Hawkins)

RUTH E. DUNKLE, Ph.D.
Associate Professor, School of Applied
Social Sciences, Case Western
Reserve University, Cleveland, Ohio
PROTECTIVE SERVICES FOR THE AGED

JACQUELINE S. DURGIN, MSW, ACSW
Associate Director, Social Work
Department, Harborview Medical
Center, Seattle, Washington
EMERGENCY HEALTH SERVICES (with
Joan L. Clement)

ROBERT ELKIN, Ph.D., ACSW
Associate Professor, School of Social
Work and Community Planning,
University of Maryland, Baltimore
FINANCIAL MANAGEMENT

ARTHUR C. EMLEN, Ph.D.
Professor of Social Work and Director,
Regional Research Institute for
Human Services, Portland State
University, Portland, Oregon
CHILD CARE SERVICES

KATHLEEN C. ENGEL, AB
Project Director, Women in Prison
Legal Project, Smith College School
for Social Work, Northampton,
Massachusetts
FEMALE OFFENDERS (with Katherine
Gabel)

A. GERALD ERICKSON, AM, ACSW
President, United Charities of Chicago,
Chicago, Illinois
FAMILY SERVICES

LEOBARDO F. ESTRADA, Ph.D.
Associate Professor of Urban Planning,
Graduate School of Architecture and

Urban Planning, University of
California, Los Angeles
HISPANICS

MICHAEL FABRICANT, Ph.D.
Associate Professor of Policy and
Research, School of Social Work,
Hunter College, New York
RADICAL SOCIAL WORK (with Steve
Burghardt)

KATHLEEN COULBORN FALLER,
Ph.D.
Assistant Professor, School of Social
Work, University of Michigan, Ann
Arbor
PROTECTIVE SERVICES FOR CHILDREN

RONALD A. FELDMAN, Ph.D., ACSW
Professor and Associate Dean, School
of Social Work, Columbia
University, New York, and Director,
Center for Adolescent Mental Health,
Washington University, St. Louis,
Missouri
YOUTH SERVICE AGENCIES

EVE P. FIELDER, MPH
Director, Survey Research Center,
Institute for Social Science Research,
University of California, Los Angeles
ADOLESCENT PREGNANCY (with Rosina
M. Becerra)

JOHN P. FLYNN, Ph.D.
Professor, School of Social Work,
Western Michigan University,
Kalamazoo
LICENSING AND REGULATION OF
SOCIAL WORK SERVICES

SUSAN S. FORBES, Ph.D.
Senior Associate, Refugee Policy
Group, Washington, D.C.
REFUGEES

E. ARACELIS FRANCIS, DSW, ACSW
Assistant Professor of Social Work,
University of Maryland, Baltimore
SOCIAL WORK IN THE U.S.
TERRITORIES AND COMMONWEALTH
(with John F. Longres and María
Elisa Díaz)

BARBARA J. FRIESEN, Ph.D., ACSW
Associate Professor, Graduate School
of Social Work, Portland State
University, Portland, Oregon
ADMINISTRATION: INTERPERSONAL
ASPECTS

KATHERINE GABEL, Ph.D., JD, ACSW
President, Pacific Oaks College and
Children's School, Pasadena,
California
FEMALE OFFENDERS (with Kathleen C.
Engel)

EILEEN D. GAMBRILL, Ph.D.
Professor, School of Social Welfare,
University of California, Berkeley
BEHAVIORAL APPROACH

IRWIN GARFINKEL, Ph.D.
Professor, School of Social Work,
University of Wisconsin, Madison
CHILD SUPPORT

CHARLES D. GARVIN, Ph.D., ACSW
Professor, School of Social Work,
University of Michigan, Ann Arbor
GROUP THEORY AND RESEARCH

SHELDON R. GELMAN, Ph.D., ACSW
Professor, Social Work Program,
Pennsylvania State University,
University Park
BOARDS OF DIRECTORS

URSULA C. GERHART, Ed.D., ACSW
Professor, School of Social Work,
Rutgers—The State University of
New Jersey, New Brunswick
PSYCHOTROPIC MEDICATIONS

CAREL B. GERMAIN, DSW, ACSW
Professor, School of Social Work,
University of Connecticut, West
Hartford
ECOLOGICAL PERSPECTIVE (with Alex
Gitterman)

GUADALUPE GIBSON, MSW, ACSW
Professor Emeritus, Worden School of
Social Service, Our Lady of the Lake
University, San Antonio, Texas
MEXICAN AMERICANS

NEIL GILBERT, Ph.D.
Professor, School of Social Welfare,
University of California, Berkeley
SOCIAL PLANNING AND COMMUNITY
ORGANIZATION (with Harry Specht)

DAVID F. GILLESPIE, Ph.D.
Professor, George Warren Brown
School of Social Work, Washington
University, St. Louis, Missouri
ETHICAL ISSUES IN RESEARCH

LEON H. GINSBERG, Ph.D., ACSW
Professor, College of Social Work,

University of South Carolina,
Columbia
ECONOMIC, POLITICAL, AND SOCIAL
CONTEXT

JOSEPH GIORDANO, MSW, ACSW
Director, Center on Ethnicity, Behavior
and Communications, American
Jewish Committee, New York
WHITE ETHNIC GROUPS (with Irving M.
Levine)

JEANNE M. GIOVANNONI, Ph.D.,
ACSW
Professor, School of Social Welfare,
University of California, Los Angeles
CHILDREN

ALEX GITTERMAN, Ed.D., ACSW
Professor, School of Social Work,
Columbia University, New York
ECOLOGICAL PERSPECTIVE (with Carel
B. Germain)

HARVEY L. GOCHROS, DSW, ACSW
Professor, School of Social Work,
University of Hawaii, Honolulu
SEXUALITY

NAOMI GOLAN, Ph.D., ACSW
Professor, School of Social Work,
University of Haifa, Israel
CRISIS INTERVENTION

GALE GOLDBERG, Ed.D.
Professor, Raymond A. Kent School of
Social Work, College of Urban and
Public Affairs, University of
Louisville, Louisville, Kentucky
SOCIAL WORK PRACTICE WITH GROUPS
(with Ruth R. Middleman)

SAMUEL Z. GOLDFARB, JD
Staff Attorney, Legal Aid Bureau,
United Charities of Chicago,
Chicago, Illinois
LEGAL ISSUES AND LEGAL SERVICES
(with Donald Brieland)

EDA G. GOLDSTEIN, DSW, ACSW
Associate Professor and Chairperson,
Practice Area, School of Social
Work, New York University, New
York
MENTAL HEALTH AND ILLNESS

SOL GOTHARD, MSSA, JD, ACSW
Senior Judge, Jefferson Parish Juvenile
Court, Gretna, Louisiana
JUVENILE JUSTICE SYSTEM

NAOMI GOTTLIEB, DSW
Professor, School of Social Work,
University of Washington, Seattle
SEX DISCRIMINATION AND INEQUALITY

JUDITH M. GUERON, Ph.D.
Executive Vice President, Manpower
Demonstration Research
Corporation, New York
WORKFARE (with Patricia Auspos)

GRACE E. HARRIS, Ph.D.
Dean, School of Social Work, Virginia
Commonwealth University,
Richmond
LITERACY (with Judith B. Bradford)

ANN HARTMAN, DSW, ACSW
Dean, Smith College School for Social
Work, Northampton, Massachusetts
FAMILY PRACTICE (with Joan Laird)

YEHESKEL HASENFELD, Ph.D.
Professor and Associate Dean, School
of Social Work, University of
Michigan, Ann Arbor
ORGANIZATIONS: IMPACT ON
EMPLOYEES AND COMMUNITY (with
Mary Lou Davis-Sacks)

J. DAVID HAWKINS, Ph.D.
Director, Center for Social Welfare
Research, School of Social Work,
University of Washington, Seattle
JUVENILE OFFENDER DIVERSION AND
COMMUNITY-BASED SERVICES (with
Howard J. Doueck)

SHIRLEY C. HELLENBRAND, DSW,
ACSW
Associate Professor, School of Social
Work, Columbia University, New
York
TERMINATION IN DIRECT PRACTICE

DEAN H. HEPWORTH, Ph.D., ACSW
Professor, Graduate School of Social
Work, University of Utah, Salt Lake
City
INTERVIEWING (with Jo Ann Larsen)

ROBERT B. HILL, Ph.D.
Senior Research Associate, Bureau of
Social Science Research, Inc.,
Washington, D.C.
INTERGROUP RELATIONS

THOMAS P. HOLLAND, Ph.D., ACSW
Professor, School of Applied Social
Sciences, Case Western Reserve
University, Cleveland, Ohio

ORGANIZATIONS: CONTEXT FOR SOCIAL
SERVICE DELIVERY (with Marcia K.
Petchers)

STEPHEN M. HOLLOWAY, Ph.D.
Professor and Executive Director,
Columbia University Community
Services, Columbia University, New
York
STAFF-INITIATED ORGANIZATIONAL
CHANGE

JUNE GARY HOPPS, Ph.D.
Dean, Graduate School of Social Work,
Boston College, Chestnut Hill,
Massachusetts
MINORITIES OF COLOR
PROFESSION OF SOCIAL WORK:
CONTEMPORARY CHARACTERISTICS
(with Elaine B. Pinderhughes)

WALTER W. HUDSON, Ph.D.
School of Social Work, Arizona State
University, Tempe, and School of
Social Work, Florida State
University, Tallahassee ·
RESEARCH MEASURES AND INDICES
(with Bruce A. Thyer)

DAVID S. HURWITZ, MSW, MPA
Consultant, Educated Retirement
Associates, Silver Spring, Maryland,
and Deputy Associate Commissioner
for Family Assistance, Social
Security Administration, U.S.
Department of Health and Human
Services, Washington, D.C. (retired)
RETIREMENT AND PENSION PROGRAMS

ANDRÉ M. IVANOFF, Ph.D., ACSW
Assistant Professor, School of Social
Welfare, The Nelson A. Rockefeller
College of Public Affairs and Policy,
State University of New York at
Albany
SUICIDE

BARRY IVKER, Ph.D., ACSW
School social worker in private
practice, New Orleans, Louisiana
ADULTHOOD (with William C. Sze)

DORIS S. JACOBSON, Ph.D., ACSW
Professor and Chair, Doctoral Program,
School of Social Welfare, University
of California, Los Angeles
DIVORCE AND SEPARATION

BRUCE S. JANSSON, Ph.D.
Associate Professor, School of Social
Work, University of Southern
California, Los Angeles
FEDERAL SOCIAL LEGISLATION SINCE
1961

SHIRLEY JENKINS, Ph.D.
Professor of Social Research, School of
Social Work, Columbia University,
New York
IMMIGRANTS AND UNDOCUMENTED
ALIENS

RAPHAEL JEWELEWICZ, MD
Associate Professor and Director,
Division of Reproductive
Endocrinology, College of Physicians
and Surgeons, Columbia University,
New York
INFERTILITY SERVICES

HARRIETTE C. JOHNSON, Ph.D.,
ACSW
Associate Professor, School of Social
Work, Adelphi University, Garden
City, New York
HUMAN DEVELOPMENT: BIOLOGICAL
PERSPECTIVE

LINDA E. JONES, Ph.D.
Assistant Professor, School of Social
Work, University of Minnesota,
Minneapolis
WOMEN

LINDA R. WOLF JONES, DSW
Director of Public Policy and
Employment Programs, YMCA of
Greater New York, New York
UNEMPLOYMENT COMPENSATION AND
WORKERS' COMPENSATION
PROGRAMS

ALFRED KADUSHIN, Ph.D., ACSW
Julia C. Lathrop Distinguished
Professor of Social Work, School of
Social Work, University of
Wisconsin, Madison
CHILD WELFARE SERVICES

JILL DONER KAGLE, Ph.D., ACSW
Associate Professor, School of Social
Work, University of Illinois, Urbana
RECORDING IN DIRECT PRACTICE

ALFRED J. KAHN, DSW, ACSW
Professor, Social Policy and Planning,
School of Social Work, Columbia
University, New York
SOCIAL PROBLEMS AND ISSUES:
THEORIES AND DEFINITIONS

SHEILA B. KAMERMAN, DSW, ACSW
Professor, Social Policy and Planning,
School of Social Work, Columbia
University, New York
FAMILY: NUCLEAR

ROSALIE A. KANE, DSW, ACSW
Professor, School of Social Work and
School of Public Health, University
of Minnesota, Minneapolis
LONG-TERM CARE

KATHERINE A. KENDALL, Ph.D.,
ACSW
Honorary President, International
Association of Schools of Social
Work, Vienna, Austria
INTERNATIONAL SOCIAL WORK
EDUCATION

GORDON R. KENT, Ph.D.
Coordinator, Disabled Student Services
and Research Assistant Professor,
Rehabilitation Research and Training
Center, West Virginia University,
Morgantown
VOCATIONAL REHABILITATION (with R.
Larry Beckett)

PAUL KEYS, Ph.D.
Associate Professor, School of Social
Work, Hunter College, New York
SETTLEMENTS AND NEIGHBORHOOD
CENTERS (with Grant Loavenbruck)

S. K. KHINDUKA, Ph.D.
Dean and Professor, George Warren
Brown School of Social Work,
Washington University, St. Louis,
Missouri
SOCIAL WORK AND THE HUMAN
SERVICES

ZEKE KILBRIDE, MLS
Coordinator, Foundation Center
Cooperating Collections, Foundation
Center, New York
FOUNDATIONS AND SOCIAL WELFARE
(with F. Emerson Andrews)

E. MILLING KINARD, Ph.D.
Adjunct Lecturer, Florence Heller
Graduate School for Advanced
Studies in Social Welfare, Brandeis
University, Waltham, Massachusetts
CHILD ABUSE AND NEGLECT

HARRY H. L. KITANO, Ph.D.
Professor of Social Work and

Sociology, University of California,
Los Angeles
ASIAN AMERICANS

DAVID J. KLAASSEN, MA
Archivist, Social Welfare History
Archives, University of Minnesota
Libraries, Minneapolis
ARCHIVES OF SOCIAL WELFARE (with
Susan D. Steinwall)

RUTH I. KNEE, MA, ACSW
Consultant, Long Term/Mental Health
Care, Fairfax, Virginia
PATIENTS' RIGHTS

DONALD F. KRILL, MSW, ACSW
Professor, Graduate School of Social
Work, University of Denver, Denver,
Colorado
EXISTENTIAL APPROACH

PAUL A. KURZMAN, Ph.D., ACSW
Professor and Chair, World of Work
Program, School of Social Work,
Hunter College, New York
INDUSTRIAL SOCIAL WORK

JOAN LAIRD, MS, ACSW
Associate Professor, Department of
Social Work, Eastern Michigan
University, Ypsilanti
FAMILY PRACTICE (with Ann Hartman)

DOROTHY LALLY, DSW, ACSW
Member, International Advisory Board,
International Council on Social
Welfare, Washington, D.C.
INTERNATIONAL SOCIAL WELFARE
ORGANIZATIONS AND SERVICES

PAMELA S. LANDON, Ph.D., ACSW
Professor and Chairperson, Department
of Social Work, Colorado State
University, Fort Collins
GENERALIST PERSPECTIVE (with
Bradford W. Sheafor)

JO ANN LARSEN, DSW
Private practitioner, Salt Lake City,
Utah
INTERVIEWING (with Dean H.
Hepworth)

JAMES LEIBY, Ph.D.
Professor, School of Social Welfare,
University of California, Berkeley
HISTORY OF SOCIAL WELFARE

CARL G. LEUKEFELD, DSW, ACSW
Chief Health Services Officer, U.S.

Public Health Service, and Deputy
Director, Division of Clinical
Research, National Institute on Drug
Abuse, Rockville, Maryland
PUBLIC HEALTH SERVICES

IRVING M. LEVINE
Director of National Affairs and the
Institute for American Pluralism,
American Jewish Committee, New
York
WHITE ETHNIC GROUPS (with Joseph
Giordano)

RISHA W. LEVINSON, DSW, ACSW
Professor, Director of Service
Development, School of Social
Work, Adelphi University, Garden
City, New York
INFORMATION AND REFERRAL
SERVICES

RONA L. LEVY, Ph.D.
School of Social Work, University of
Washington, Seattle
SINGLE SUBJECT RESEARCH DESIGNS

PHILIP LICHTENBERG, Ph.D.
Professor, Graduate School of Social
Work and Social Research, Bryn
Mawr College, Bryn Mawr,
Pennsylvania
MEN

FLORENCE LIEBERMAN, DSW, ACSW
Professor Emeritus, School of Social
Work, Hunter College, New York
MENTAL HEALTH AND ILLNESS IN
CHILDREN

GARY A. LLOYD, Ph.D., ACSW
Private practice, and Adjunct
Professor, School of Social Work,
Tulane University, New Orleans,
Louisiana
GESTALT THERAPY
SOCIAL WORK EDUCATION

GRANT LOAVENBRUCK, DSW
Formerly Associate Executive Director,
United Neighborhood Centers of
America, Inc., New York
SETTLEMENTS AND NEIGHBORHOOD
CENTERS (with Paul Keys)

JOHN F. LONGRES, Ph.D.
Professor, School of Social Work,
University of Wisconsin, Madison
JUVENILE OFFENDERS AND
DELINQUENCY

SOCIAL WORK IN THE U.S.
TERRITORIES AND COMMONWEALTH
(with María Elisa Díaz and
E. Aracelis Francis)

DOMAN LUM, Ph.D., Th.D.
Program Director and Professor,
Division of Social Work, California
State University, Sacramento
HEALTH SERVICE SYSTEM

HARRIETTE PIPES McADOO, Ph.D.
Acting Dean, School of Social Work,
Howard University, Washington,
D.C.
BLACKS

LYNN McDONALD-WIKLER, Ph.D.,
ACSW
Assistant Professor, School of Social
Work, University of Wisconsin,
Madison
DISABILITIES: DEVELOPMENTAL

BRENDA G. McGOWAN, DSW, ACSW
Professor, School of Social Work,
Columbia University, New York
ADVOCACY

EDWARD A. McKINNEY, Ph.D.
Professor and Chairman, Department of
Social Work, Cleveland State
University, Cleveland, Ohio
HEALTH PLANNING

PETER J. McNELIS, Col., DSW, ACSW
Headquarters, U.S. Army Medical
Research and Development
Command, Fort Detrick, Maryland
MILITARY SOCIAL WORK

MARYANN MAHAFFEY, MSW, ACSW
Professor, School of Social Work,
Wayne State University, Detroit, and
Councilmember, Detroit City
Council, Detroit, Michigan
POLITICAL ACTION IN SOCIAL WORK

HENRY W. MAIER, Ph.D., ACSW
Professor Emeritus, School of Social
Work, University of Washington,
Seattle
HUMAN DEVELOPMENT:
PSYCHOLOGICAL PERSPECTIVE

DAVID MALDONADO, Jr., DSW
Associate Professor, Perkins School of
Theology, Southern Methodist
University, Dallas, Texas
AGED

GORDON MANSER, MSW
Formerly Interim Executive Director,
Association of Junior Leagues, New
York
VOLUNTEERS

LEONARD J. MARCUS, Ph.D.
Assistant Professor, MGH Institute of
Health Professions, Social Work in
Health Care Program, Massachusetts
General Hospital, Boston
HEALTH CARE FINANCING

EMILIA E. MARTINEZ-BRAWLEY,
Ed.D., ACSW
Professor of Social Work, Department
of Sociology, The Pennsylvania State
University, University Park
RURAL SOCIAL WORK

THOMAS M. MEENAGHAN, Ph.D.,
ACSW
Professor, School of Social Work,
Loyola University of Chicago,
Chicago, Illinois
MACRO PRACTICE: CURRENT TRENDS
AND ISSUES

HENRY N. MENDELSOHN, MA, MSL
Associate Librarian, Bibliographer and
Reference Librarian, Graduate
Library for Public Affairs and Policy,
State University of New York at
Albany
Appendix 4: GUIDE TO SOURCES OF
INFORMATION ON SOCIAL WELFARE
AGENCIES

CAROL H. MEYER, DSW
Professor, School of Social Work,
Columbia University, New York
DIRECT PRACTICE IN SOCIAL WORK:
OVERVIEW

RUTH R. MIDDLEMAN, Ed.D., ACSW
Professor, Raymond A. Kent School of
Social Work, College of Urban and
Public Affairs, University of
Louisville, Louisville, Kentucky
SOCIAL WORK PRACTICE WITH GROUPS
(with Gale Goldberg)

IRVING MILLER, DSW
Professor, School of Social Work,
Columbia University, New York
SUPERVISION IN SOCIAL WORK

ROSALIND S. MILLER, MS, ACSW
Associate Professor, School of Social

Work, Columbia University, New
York
PRIMARY HEALTH CARE

BRIJ MOHAN, Ph.D.
Professor and Dean, School of Social
Work, Louisiana State University,
Baton Rouge
INTERNATIONAL SOCIAL WELFARE:
COMPARATIVE SYSTEMS

ROBERT M. MORONEY, Ph.D.
Professor of Social Policy and Planning,
School of Social Work, Arizona State
University, Tempe
SOCIAL PLANNING

ROBERT MORRIS, DSW
Kirstein Professor of Social Planning,
Emeritus, Brandeis University,
Waltham, Massachusetts, and
Cardinal Mederios Lecturer,
University of Massachusetts, Boston
SOCIAL WELFARE POLICY: TRENDS
AND ISSUES

ALLISON D. MURDACH, MA, ACSW
Social Worker, Veterans
Administration Medical Center, Palo
Alto, California
RESOURCE MOBILIZATION AND
COORDINATION

ELIZABETH MUTSCHLER, Ph.D.
Associate Professor, School of Social
Work, University of Michigan, Ann
Arbor
COMPUTER UTILIZATION

WARREN NETHERLAND, MSW, ACSW
Assistant Director, Department of
Labor and Industries, State of
Washington, Olympia
CORRECTIONS SYSTEM: ADULT

HELEN NORTHEN, Ph.D.
Professor Emerita, School of Social
Work, University of Southern
California, Los Angeles
ASSESSMENT IN DIRECT PRACTICE

JULIANNE S. OKTAY, Ph.D.
Associate Professor, School of Social
Work and Community Planning,
University of Maryland, Baltimore
FOSTER CARE FOR ADULTS

MARTHA N. OZAWA, Ph.D., ACSW
Bettie Bofinger Brown Professor of
Social Policy, George Warren Brown
School of Social Work, Washington

University, St. Louis, Missouri
SOCIAL SECURITY

DIANE L. PANCOAST, Ph.D.
Research Associate, Regional Research
Institute for Human Services,
Portland State University, Portland,
Oregon
NATURAL HELPING NETWORKS (with
Alice Collins)

T. M. JIM PARHAM, MSSW, ACSW
Professor, School of Social Work,
University of Georgia, Athens
WHITE HOUSE CONFERENCES

RINO J. PATTI, DSW, ACSW
Professor, School of Social Work,
University of Washington, Seattle
LEGISLATIVE ADVOCACY (with Ronald
B. Dear)

PETER J. PECORA, Ph.D.
Assistant Professor, Graduate School of
Social Work, University of Utah,
Salt Lake City
PERSONNEL MANAGEMENT (with
Michael J. Austin)

FELICE DAVIDSON PERLMUTTER,
Ph.D., ACSW
Professor, School of Social
Administration, Temple University,
Philadelphia, Pennsylvania
ADMINISTRATION: ENVIRONMENTAL
ASPECTS

MARCIA K. PETCHERS, Ph.D.
Associate Dean, School of Applied
Social Sciences, Case Western
Reserve University, Cleveland, Ohio
ORGANIZATIONS: CONTEXT FOR SOCIAL
SERVICE DELIVERY (with Thomas P.
Holland)

ELAINE B. PINDERHUGHES, MSW,
ACSW
School of Social Work, Boston College,
Chestnut Hill, Massachusetts
PROFESSION OF SOCIAL WORK:
CONTEMPORARY CHARACTERISTICS
(with June Gary Hopps)

FRANCES FOX PIVEN, Ph.D.
Professor of Political Science, Graduate
School and University Center, City
University of New York, New York
VOTER REGISTRATION (with Richard A.
Cloward)

ROBERT D. PLOTNICK, Ph.D.
Associate Professor of Social Work and
Public Affairs, University of
Washington, Seattle
INCOME DISTRIBUTION

LINDA J. PROFFITT, MSSA, MBA
Vice-President, M. Zunt Associates,
Cleveland, Ohio
HOSPICE

JUAN RAMOS, Ph.D.
Deputy Director for Prevention and
Special Projects, National Institute of
Mental Health, Rockville, Maryland
MIGRANT AND SEASONAL FARM
WORKERS (with Celia Torres)

CHARLES A. RAPP, Ph.D.
Associate Professor and Associate
Dean, School of Social Welfare,
University of Kansas, Lawrence
INFORMATION UTILIZATION FOR
MANAGEMENT DECISION MAKING

ELOISE RATHBONE-McCUAN, Ph.D.
Director, Social Work Program,
University of Vermont, Burlington
DAY CENTERS: ADULT

FREDERIC G. REAMER, Ph.D.
Associate Professor, School of Social
Work, Rhode Island College,
Providence
VALUES AND ETHICS

WILLIAM J. REID, DSW, ACSW
Professor, Nelson A. Rockefeller
College of Public Affairs and Policy,
School of Social Welfare, State
University of New York at Albany
RESEARCH IN SOCIAL WORK
SECTARIAN AGENCIES (with Peter K.
Stimpson)
TASK-CENTERED APPROACH

DONALD P. RILEY, MSW, ACSW
Director, Clinical Service, Family
Service of Greater Boston, Boston,
Massachusetts
FAMILY LIFE EDUCATION

ROGER A. ROFFMAN, DSW, ACSW
Associate Professor, School of Social
Work, University of Washington,
Seattle
DRUG USE AND ABUSE

SHELDON D. ROSE, Ph.D.
Professor, School of Social Work,
University of Wisconsin, Madison

SOCIAL SKILLS TRAINING (with Ronald
Toseland)

SALIE ROSSEN, MSW
Director, Society for Hospital Social
Work Directors, American Hospital
Association, Chicago, Illinois
HOSPITAL SOCIAL WORK

WILLIAM ROTH
Associate Professor, Nelson A.
Rockefeller College of Public Affairs
and Policy, School of Social Welfare,
State University of New York at
Albany
DISABILITIES: PHYSICAL

GENE ROTHMAN, DSW, ACSW
Social Work Researcher, V.A. Medical
Center of West Los Angeles,
Brentwood Division, Los Angeles,
California
VETERANS AND VETERANS' SERVICES
(with Rosina M. Becerra)

JACK ROTHMAN, Ph.D., ACSW
Professor, School of Social Welfare,
University of California, Los Angeles
COMMUNITY THEORY AND RESEARCH

ALLEN RUBIN, Ph.D.
Associate Professor, School of Social
Work, University of Texas, Austin
CASE MANAGEMENT

BETTY SANCIER, MSW, ACSW
Professor, Division of Outreach &
Continuing Education, and School of
Social Welfare, University of
Wisconsin-Milwaukee
CONTINUING EDUCATION

DANIEL S. SANDERS, Ph.D., ACSW
Dean, Professor, and Director of
International Programs, School of
Social Work, University of Hawaii,
Honolulu
SOCIAL WORK IN THE PACIFIC
TERRITORIES

ROSEMARY C. SARRI, Ph.D.
Professor, School of Social Work,
University of Michigan, Ann Arbor
ADMINISTRATION IN SOCIAL WELFARE

ELFRIEDE G. SCHLESINGER, Ph.D.,
ACSW
Professor and Associate Dean, School
of Social Work, Rutgers—The State
University of New Jersey, New
Brunswick

ETHNIC-SENSITIVE PRACTICE (with
Wynetta Devore)

DICK SCHOECH, Ph.D.
School of Social Work, University of
Texas, Arlington
INFORMATION SYSTEMS: AGENCY

RODNEY G. SCHOFIELD, Ed.D., ACSW
Supervisor, Student Support Services,
Colorado Springs School District No.
11, Colorado Springs, Colorado
PARENT TRAINING

OLIVER C. SCHROEDER, Jr., JD
Weatherhead Professor of Law and
Criminal Justice, Director, Law-
Medicine Center, Case Western
Reserve University, Cleveland, Ohio
CIVIL RIGHTS

LEROY G. SCHULTZ, MSW, ACSW
School of Social Work, West Virginia
University, Morgantown
VICTIMIZATION PROGRAMS AND
VICTIMS OF CRIME

BRETT A. SEABURY, DSW, ACSW
School of Social Work, University of
Michigan, Ann Arbor
CONTRACTING AND ENGAGEMENT IN
DIRECT PRACTICE

STEVEN P. SEGAL, Ph.D., ACSW
Professor and Director, Mental Health
and Social Welfare Research Group,
School of Social Welfare, University
of California, Berkeley
DEINSTITUTIONALIZATION

BRADFORD W. SHEAFOR, Ph.D.,
ACSW
Professor and Associate Dean, College
of Professional Studies, Colorado
State University, Fort Collins
GENERALIST PERSPECTIVE (with Pamela
S. Landon)

EDMUND SHERMAN, Ph.D., ACSW
Professor, School of Social Welfare,
State University of New York at
Albany
COGNITIVE THERAPY

LAWRENCE SHULMAN, Ed.D
Professor, School of Social Work,
Boston University, Boston,
Massachusetts
CONSULTATION

KRISTINE A. SIEFERT, Ph.D., ACSW
Associate Professor, School of Social

Work, University of Michigan, Ann
Arbor
NUCLEAR WAR AND DISARMAMENT

PHYLLIS R. SILVERMAN, Ph.D.
Professor, Social Work and Health
Program, MGH Institute of Health
Professions, Massachusetts General
Hospital, Boston
MUTUAL HELP GROUPS

BERTHA G. SIMOS, DSW, ACSW
Licensed Clinical Social Worker,
private practice, Los Angeles,
California
LOSS AND BEREAVEMENT

MAX SIPORIN, DSW, ACSW
Professor Emeritus, School of Social
Welfare, State University of New
York at Albany
DISASTERS AND DISASTER AID
RESOURCE DEVELOPMENT AND
SERVICE PROVISION

BARBARA BRYANT SOLOMON, DSW
Professor, School of Social Work,
University of Southern California,
Los Angeles
HUMAN DEVELOPMENT:
SOCIOCULTURAL PERSPECTIVE

MICHAEL R. SOSIN, Ph.D.
Associate Professor, School of Social
Work and Institute for Research on
Poverty, University of Wisconsin,
Madison
GENERAL AND EMERGENCY
ASSISTANCE

HARRY SPECHT, Ph.D.
Dean, School of Social Welfare,
University of California, Berkeley
SOCIAL PLANNING AND COMMUNITY
ORGANIZATIONS (with Neil Gilbert)

IRVING A. SPERGEL, DSW, ACSW
Professor, School of Social Service
Administration, University of
Chicago, Chicago, Illinois
COMMUNITY DEVELOPMENT

BARBARA STAR, Ph.D., ACSW
Associate Professor, School of Social
Work, University of Southern
California, Los Angeles
DOMESTIC VIOLENCE

SANDRA M. STEHNO, Ph.D.
Assistant to the President,
Kaleidoscope, Inc., Chicago, Illinois

JUVENILE COURTS, PROBATION, AND
PAROLE

THEODORE J. STEIN, Ph.D.
Professor, School of Social Welfare,
State University of New York at
Albany
FOSTER CARE FOR CHILDREN

SUSAN D. STEINWALL, MA
Director, Area Research Center,
University of Wisconsin, River Falls
ARCHIVES OF SOCIAL WELFARE (with
David J. Klaassen)

PETER K. STIMPSON, MSW, ACSW
Reverend, Counseling Service of the
Episcopal Diocese of Albany, Inc.,
Albany, New York
SECTARIAN AGENCIES (with William J.
Reid)

WILLIAM C. SZE, Ph.D., ACSW
Associate Professor of Psychiatry and
Chief, Social Work Section,
Department of Psychiatry, School of
Medicine in New Orleans, Louisiana
State University, New Orleans
ADULTHOOD (with Barry Ivker)

TOSHIO TATARA, Ph.D.
Director, Research and Demonstration
Department, American Public
Welfare Association, Washington,
D.C.
INFORMATION SYSTEMS: CLIENT DATA

PAUL TERRELL, DSW
Adjunct Lecturer and Coordinator of
Academic Programs, School of Social
Welfare, University of California,
Berkeley
PURCHASING SOCIAL SERVICES

EDWIN J. THOMAS, Ph.D., ACSW
Fedele F. Fauri Professor of Social
Work and Professor of Psychology,
School of Social Work, University of
Michigan, Ann Arbor
DEVELOPMENTAL APPROACH TO
RESEARCH

BRUCE A. THYER, Ph.D., ACSW
Associate Professor, School of Social
Work, Florida State University,
Tallahassee
RESEARCH MEASURES AND INDICES IN
DIRECT PRACTICE (with Walter W.
Hudson)

BILLY J. TIDWELL, Ph.D.
Acting Director of Research, National Urban League, Inc., Washington, D.C.
RACIAL DISCRIMINATION AND INEQUALITY

BEVERLY G. TOOMEY, Ph.D.
Associate Professor, College of Social Work, The Ohio State University, Columbus
SEXUAL ASSAULT SERVICES

CELIA TORRES, MSW
Chairperson, National Network of Hispanic Women, Los Angeles, California
MIGRANT AND SEASONAL FARM WORKERS (with Juan Ramos)

RONALD TOSELAND, Ph.D.
Associate Professor, Nelson A. Rockefeller College of Public Affairs and Policy, School of Social Welfare, State University of New York at Albany
SOCIAL SKILLS TRAINING (with Sheldon D. Rose)

HARVEY TREGER, MA, ACSW
Professor, Jane Addams College of Social Work, University of Illinois at Chicago
POLICE SOCIAL WORK

TONY TRIPODI, DSW, ACSW
Professor, School of Social Work, University of Michigan, Ann Arbor
PROGRAM EVALUATION

ELMER J. TROPMAN, MA, ACSW
Director of The Forbes Fund, Supporting Organization of the Pittsburgh Foundation, and Consultant to The Pittsburgh Foundation and the Howard Heinz Endowment, Pittsburgh, Pennsylvania
VOLUNTARY AGENCIES (with John E. Tropman)

JOHN E. TROPMAN, Ph.D.
Professor, School of Social Work, University of Michigan, Ann Arbor
POLICY ANALYSIS: METHODS AND TECHNIQUES
VOLUNTARY AGENCIES (with Elmer J. Tropman)

FRANCIS J. TURNER, DSW
Chairperson, Department of Social Work, York University, Toronto, Ontario, Canada
PSYCHOSOCIAL APPROACH

EDGAR D. VAN CAMP, MSW, ACSW
Inspector General, West Virginia Department of Human Services, Charleston
QUALITY CONTROL IN INCOME MAINTENANCE

NAN VAN DEN BERGH, Ph.D.
Associate Professor, Department of Social Work Education, California State University, Fresno
FEMINIST SOCIAL WORK (with Lynn B. Cooper)

ESTHER WALD, Ph.D., ACSW
Clinical Director, Family Service of South Lake County, Highland Park, Illinois
FAMILY: STEPFAMILIES

ESTHER WATTENBERG, MA, ACSW
Professor and Staff Associate, School of Social Work and Center for Urban and Regional Affairs, University of Minnesota, Minneapolis
FAMILY: ONE PARENT

ANDREW WEISSMAN, DSW, ACSW
Director, Social Work Operations, Mt. Sinai Hospital, and Assistant Professor of Community Medicine, Mt. Sinai School of Medicine, New York
LINKAGE IN DIRECT PRACTICE

ELLEN M. WELLS, MA
Policy Associate, American Public Welfare Association, Washington, D.C.
FOOD STAMP PROGRAM

STANLEY WENOCUR, DSW, ACSW
Associate Professor, School of Social Work and Community Planning, University of Maryland, Baltimore
SOCIAL PLANNING IN THE VOLUNTARY SECTOR

JAMES K. WHITTAKER, Ph.D., ACSW
Professor, School of Social Work, University of Washington, Seattle
GROUP CARE FOR CHILDREN

JANET B. W. WILLIAMS, DSW, ACSW
   Associate Professor of
   Clinical Psychiatric Social Work
   (in Psychiatry), Department of
   Psychiatry, College of Physicians
   and Surgeons, Columbia University,
   New York
   DIAGNOSTIC AND STATISTICAL
   MANUAL (DSM)

LEON F. WILLIAMS, Ph.D.
   Associate Professor, Graduate School
   of Social Work, Boston College,
   Chestnut Hill, Massachusetts
   FAMILY: MULTIGENERATIONAL (with
   Carmen Díaz)
   PROFESSIONAL ASSOCIATIONS: SPECIAL
   INTEREST

PEGGY WIREMAN, Ph.D.
   Chief, Technical Assistance Division,
   Economic Development

Administration, Department of
   Commerce, Washington, D.C.
   CITIZEN PARTICIPATION

NATALIE JANE WOODMAN, MSS,
ACSW
   Associate Professor, School of Social
   Work, Arizona State University,
   Tempe
   HOMOSEXUALITY: LESBIAN WOMEN

NORMAN L. WYERS, DSW, ACSW
   Professor, School of Social Work,
   Portland State University, Portland,
   Oregon
   INCOME MAINTENANCE SYSTEM

JOHN A. YANKEY, Ph.D., ACSW
   Professor, School of Applied Social
   Sciences, Case Western Reserve
   University, Cleveland, Ohio
   PUBLIC SOCIAL SERVICES

CONTENTS

ECONOMIC, POLITICAL, AND SOCIAL CONTEXT

Perhaps more than any other profession, social work is affected by the times in which it is practiced. Each decade of post–World War II America has clearly changed the content and extent of social work services and practice modes. The 1980s, of which this edition of the *Encyclopedia of Social Work* is a product, have been a distinct time in American history. These years—clearly defined by the 1980 presidential election—have had a significant impact on the practice of social work comparable in many ways to the 1930s, in which the modern profession is rooted.

Throughout the encyclopedia are articles on the ways in which social change and sociopolitical circumstances have modified social work. Public philosophies, economic circumstances, and sociopolitical goals have always governed the profession. During the 1950s, for example, strong beliefs about the perfectibility of human beings and the belief that human problems could be solved through public policy and public programs led to the development of the many public welfare and mental health programs that continue today. In the 1960s, powerfully held beliefs about social justice, the rights of minorities, and the necessity to overcome hunger and poverty in the United States led to the programs of the New Frontier, the Great Society, and other governmental solutions to persistent human problems. Eliminating discrimination, hunger, poverty, mental illness, and disease became major goals of the Kennedy and Johnson presidential administrations. The 1970s witnessed continuing efforts to eradicate discrimination and overcome the social difficulties that have persistently concerned social work practice.

From the end of World War II through the late 1970s, federal, local, and state attention to social problems developed and increased. Public aid soon dwarfed the voluntary sector. Whether it took the form of assistance to public and higher education, disease control, or public assistance programs to eradicate poverty, government policy was directed toward solutions.

The 1980s, however, have witnessed changes in public social welfare policy. Of course, the seeds of these changes were found in earlier decades. For example, despite Lyndon B. Johnson's landslide victory in the 1964 presidential election—with his support for the Great Society, for services to secure the rights of minorities, and for efforts to bring world peace through U.S. aid and intervention—a significant minority of the population supported the most conservative presidential candidate since the 1920s, Senator Barry Goldwater of Arizona. In the 1980s, Ronald Reagan, who had become a nationally recognized political figure through his articulate support of Goldwater in 1964, was elected president.

The Reagan presidency, renewed by an overwhelming majority of American voters in 1984, has been marked by a change in federal policy. More than anything else, Reagan has insisted on major shifts in the allocation of federal resources and on changes in the conduct of the federal government. He has called for a return to the federal government's pre-1930s role—to the basic tasks of international relations, defense, and management of the national economy—and for a retreat from its newer roles in social welfare, which are basic to social work.

As in earlier decades, Supreme Court decisions have played a major role in setting the public policy agenda for the 1980s. The members of the Court who have previously concurred in decisions favoring strict separation of church and state, desegregation of schools and other public facilities, liberalization of the right to abortion, and other issues of great consequence in the 1960s are becoming elderly. Observers of the Supreme Court suggest that President Reagan could be expected to alter the composition of the Court in ways that could modify or even reverse these decisions. Nonetheless, throughout the 1980s, the more liberal positions that caused significant social breakthroughs in the 1960s and 1970s have been maintained.

This summary outlines some of the elements in the American context of the 1980s that have affected social work most. These elements have had significant consequences for the development and practice of social work during the time in which this edition of the encyclopedia was developed.

Retreat from Social Welfare

Until the 1980s, American social welfare programs continued to grow. With programs such as social security for the handicapped, the widowed, orphans, and the elderly; cash assistance for low-income families; rehabilitation programs for the disabled; food stamps for the hungry; and community action, education, and social and personal development programs for those who need them, the modern history of the United States has reflected increasing public responsibility for the well-being of individual citizens. Such efforts had become the goal not only of some individual political figures but, until recently, of the federal government as well.

Ronald Reagan was elected and reelected on a platform that called for the removal of most of these programs from American life, particularly from any federal participation in them. This philosophy, supported to a lesser extent by a Republican majority in the U.S. Senate, demands that programs for the disadvantaged be reduced and eventually eliminated. There should be no federal role, the Reagan Administration insists, in services to individuals and families. If local and state governments and private charities want to continue or to expand these services, they can do so with their own funds, leaving the federal government to develop the national economy and manage the money supply, to deal with defense and foreign affairs, and to see to the orderly operation of those functions that are "appropriate" for a national government.

Part of the movement to restructure government included an attempt to modify the tax structure to significantly limit incentives for charitable contributions and deductions for state and local taxes. If fully pursued, these proposed changes—which were only partially adopted in the early 1980s—would have significant negative consequences for privately funded social services agencies and for state and local human services programs.

Although its constitutionality has been challenged, the Balanced Budget and Emergency Deficit Control Act of 1985 (P.L. 99-177)—commonly known as the Gramm-Rudman-Hollings Act—has already resulted in spending reductions in nondefense programs. President Reagan's budget proposal for fiscal 1987 called for an increase in defense spending of $16.4 billion and a cut of $19.7 billion from domestic programs.

As several articles in the encyclopedia confirm, although the Reagan Administration has not been able to carry out its ambition to divest itself of all human services programs, it has been able to slow their growth. Perhaps more important, it has used administrative discretion to reduce or eliminate programs whenever it could. It has also been able to exercise influence over the operation of some programs that have had a significant impact on human services in general. By appointing less-than-militant civil rights advocates to the U.S. Civil Rights Commission, for example, the Administration has reduced the commission's efforts. By taking a hard administrative line on applicants for social security disability payments, it has limited the effectiveness of the social security program. By appointing to many of the social welfare–oriented agencies top administrators who disagree with the past growth in social welfare programs, the federal government has decreased its support for such programs. The Administration's leaders on juvenile justice suggested that the reforms of earlier decades, which social workers had helped bring about, were misguided and ought to be replaced by firm law enforcement approaches to juvenile misconduct.

The Administration has concentrated its efforts on defense programs, which have experienced great funding growth; on the strength of the U.S. economy, which has overcome a long and persistent movement toward high inflation; and on restoring the strength of the U.S. dollar, which—almost immediately upon Reagan's election—began to dominate the world economy after a significant decline compared to other currencies during the Jimmy Carter presidency. (By early 1986, the dollar had declined slightly once again.) Reagan's policies have come as no surprise to observers of the president's career. For two decades prior to his election, he advocated precisely these steps, and the most enthusiastic Republican supporters of his candidacy advocated similar steps.

The policies of the Reagan Administration are not especially new. They reflect traditional conservative American thinking.

Herbert Hoover enunciated similar ideas at the height of the Great Depression in the 1930s and in his campaign for reelection in 1932, and Goldwater's 1964 presidential campaign was based on similar ideas.

Impact on Social Work

What has happened to social work under Reagan's presidency? In some ways, social work professionals have followed the lead of the national government. When the government began moving away from the social activism of the 1960s and 1970s, so did some social workers, although the profession as a whole has—through NASW—continued demanding a strong federal role in social welfare. In practical terms, the increase in employment for social workers fell off in such programs as community development, civil rights, day care, Head Start, and others that had been created and had grown in the preceding decades. Among the other victims of the reduced federal role in human services have been some scholarships and educational support services for social work education. The federal training program under Title XX of the Social Security Act, which had been available to the states with few restrictions for educating social workers, became tightly restricted and has been virtually eliminated. Grants for educating social workers in such fields as mental health, services to veterans, vocational rehabilitation, and child welfare have also been reduced or eliminated. As educational and employment opportunities for professional social workers have dropped, so have applications to and enrollments in schools of social work. The growth in education and practice has been arrested and in some cases reduced in the 1980s, although social work enrollments began increasing in some regions by the middle of the decade.

New opportunities for social workers are more likely to be in such services as social work practice with individuals and families facing personal problems. Although an increase has occurred in psychiatric and medical social work and in private practice, opportunities for employment in planning and development programs and particularly in programs designed to bring about social change have been significantly eroded. Increasing numbers of social workers are being employed in the workplace. Employers, emulating models long established in other na-

tions, have found social workers useful in helping employees and their families overcome problems of substance abuse and in helping them arrange solutions to other needs—such as obtaining day care for their children and resolving marital conflicts—and in obtaining social and health services. Thus, industrial (or occupational) social work, as some call this emerging field of practice, is one of the growing areas of employment for social workers.

The configuration of social work employment and practice has begun to mimic the field as it existed in the 1950s and the early 1960s, before the great growth in social work programs for disadvantaged communities began. Despite Reagan's policies, however, programs such as Aid to Families with Dependent Children (AFDC), public child welfare, food stamps, and services to the disabled—the core of social work efforts—have continued to exist and to serve disadvantaged clients through public social services systems. The continuation of these efforts was guaranteed by a combination of political pressure from the states and an insistence on the maintenance of such programs in Congress.

Funding for these programs has not generally kept up with inflation, however, so the net result has been a reduction in their impact. The Reagan Administration believes that these programs contribute to inflation and has therefore made their reduction part of its overall attack on inflation. The decline in inflation, which probably resulted more from other factors than from reductions in the relatively small human services programs—which comprise only 7 percent of the federal budget—has benefited most Americans, including low-income people.

Conservation and the Environment

The retreat from programs designed to bring about social justice through governmental action has extended beyond social welfare services. Programs designed to protect the environment and to conserve natural resources have also come under attack. The necessity—even the virtue—of preserving the environment, eliminating strip mining, and maintaining virgin public lands was questioned by the secretary of the interior and even by the president himself.

Antipollution regulations have been

softened or shifted from federal to state and local control. Although conservation and environmental protection statutes and regulations have always been in some conflict with the objectives of the American business community, the Reagan Administration—with its high priority on business and economic development—has supported economic development over environmental protection.

War and Peace

As the Reagan Administration has focused its attention on defense rather than on domestic problems, the defense budget has risen, although never to the level proposed by the president. New and increasingly complex weapons systems are being developed. Overt military action was taken in the Caribbean island nation of Grenada, to forestall the possibility of its coming under Cuban and Russian influence. Strong emotional and, in some cases, material alliances have been forged with governments whose philosophies are similar to those of the Reagan Administration, such as the British government of Prime Minister Margaret Thatcher.

Despite—or perhaps because of—this emphasis on a strong defense stance, small but potentially dangerous events have begun to threaten the lives and safety of ordinary citizens as well as top government officials. International violence in the 1980s has more and more become acts of individual terrorism such as assassination and kidnapping. Such acts, little known and only infrequently encountered by Americans until the 1960s, have been a part of the pattern of life in the developing nations for a long time. Where large armies are not possible, small bands of people with a particular concern or ideology try to win their point through kidnapping or assassinating prominent leaders or wealthy businesspeople. In the 1980s, for example, the United States and the rest of the world saw the kidnapping of American embassy officials in Iran, the hijacking of a Trans World Airlines plane in Greece by militants from Lebanon, and the takeover of an Italian cruise ship and the murder of an American passenger by Arab terrorists.

In 1986, the United States bombed Libya in retaliation for actions that nation was assumed to have taken against the United States. President Reagan threatened to retaliate against other nations that harbored anti-American terrorists or that attacked the United States and its citizens.

Assassination has also become an instrument of policy. Prime Minister Indira Gandhi of India and Prime Minister Olof Palme of Sweden have fallen victim to assassination, and Pope John Paul II, Prime Minister Thatcher, and President Reagan himself have been targets of assassination attempts. Leadership has changed hands in Middle Eastern nations through political killings, as well. Bombings, assassinations, and kidnappings have become international means of social change. Although its strong defense posture prevents concerted military action against the United States, acts of terrorism have continued to immobilize the nation at times during the 1980s.

Many citizens of the United States, Europe, and other parts of the world have maintained a constant concern about the possibility of nuclear war and the need for disarmament and an established and permanent peace. The year 1985 was the fortieth anniversary of the only use of atomic weapons in war. That anniversary as well as an active international antinuclear peace movement have been major forces in the 1980s. But nuclear war has not been the only concern. The increasing use of atomic energy in producing electricity has frightened many people, especially after history's worst nuclear accident in Chernobyl, U.S.S.R., in 1986. That catastrophe killed and injured large numbers of people and contaminated the soil, water, and food within a wide radius of Chernobyl's nuclear plant. A much less serious accident at Pennsylvania's Three Mile Island reactor in 1979 left many Americans as wary of the use of atomic energy for nonmilitary purposes as they were of nuclear war.

There has also been resistance to U.S. policies and military involvement in such nations as Nicaragua and El Salvador, where civil conflicts have endangered not only internal stability but world peace. U.S. support for nondemocratic governments has disturbed many Americans. Internal disorders in South Africa have also been of major concern to Americans, who almost universally oppose apartheid.

For some social workers—those serving in the military, for example—the issues of war and violence are personal ones, experienced at firsthand. Their clients, families, and they themselves are real or potential victims, or they may assist in the release and reentry into freedom of hostages. Others have found that anxiety about nuclear war and terrorism causes emotional problems for clients. In addition, defense needs drain funds from possible use in social welfare services. An orderly, safe, and free world remains an objective of social work.

Health and Health Care

In the 1980s, health problems and health care have both taken on new characteristics and qualities. Because so many social workers are employed in health services, these changes have had significant consequence for the profession. Since the middle of the century, health services and their cost have increased in patterns similar to those affecting social welfare programs.

The great strides made in preserving human life through the development of antibiotics during and after World War II gave hope to Western society that most infectious diseases could be eradicated. In fact, in the United States and other developed nations, most health problems are experienced by people in the upper reaches of the life span. Most mortality in these countries now results from diseases of the heart, cancer, and strokes—all of which are closely correlated with aging—instead of from conditions such as dysentery and dehydration, frequent causes of death in the developing world where infant mortality remains high.

However, the good news about general health did not last forever. One piece of bad news was Acquired Immune Deficiency Syndrome (AIDS), which has emerged in the 1980s as a shocking and almost always fatal disease. In the United States, it first struck male homosexuals but, as the disease has spread, it has affected many other groups, particularly those requiring blood transfusions, intravenous drug users, and those who have had heterosexual contacts with partners who have the disease. By the mid-1980s, AIDS had become the most frightening—and potentially the most dangerous—infectious disease known. Although a cure is being sought, there is still only minimal understanding of its characteristics and its transmission.

Nevertheless, longevity continues to increase, causing additional social concerns for the United States. Not only are people living longer, but the growth in the population of the frail elderly has caused great increases in medical and other care costs. As American citizens live longer, as medicine discovers new ways to maintain the lives of people who might have died in earlier times, and as families become less and less able to keep their elderly parents and grandparents at home, nursing homes and other extended care facilities have begun to grow into a major American industry. Federal and state funds are available through Medicaid and Medicare for the care of many citizens who require nursing home services. By the second half of the 1980s, the annual cost for nursing home care is some $20,000 per individual.

Government policies on Medicaid—the health care assistance program for low-income people—requires not only limited income as an eligibility criterion but also the disposition of most personal property, particularly cash and, in some cases, personal homes. These "spend down" policies of Medicaid pose significant hardships for elderly, infirm people and their families.

One of the most important initiatives of the Reagan Administration has been the effort to arrest the growth of expenditures on health care. Although the U.S. government has always avoided "socialized medicine" or national health insurance, throughout the post–World War II era, payment for much health care has become a social responsibility. Medicare, part of the social security program, has become the major system of health care services for people 65 and over as well as for victims of specific diseases, and Medicaid provides a comprehensive health insurance program for public assistance clients and other low-income people through state and federal funding. However, considering that employees of local, state, and federal governments are invariably covered by health insurance paid by taxpayers (about one of every eight working people is employed by government) and that labor contracts increasingly include health insurance benefits for workers, it is clear that more and more of the costs of health care are borne by all the people of the nation. The cost of health insurance for automotive workers, for example, is more than the cost of the steel used in most automobiles. But every purchase an American consumer makes—of food, clothing, housing, and everything else—includes some of the cost of the health insurance for the people who produce, sell, and maintain American products and services.

The social financing of health care has consequences that go beyond the provision of care. Perhaps most significant is the frequent lack of concern that service providers—doctors, hospitals, and others—have for the cost of the health care provided. Defensive medicine, designed to prove that everything has been tried, has become routine. If they are covered by insurance, the feeling persists, why not obtain and use all available services? And the virtually unlimited financing of health care—as costs increase, premiums have simply gone up to match—has led to a great expansion in the development of new equipment and new procedures. Technological and professional developments in the health care industry have both added to the costs and extended the services. In fact, health care services are becoming such a large part of the American economy that they threaten to become the single greatest expenditure of all.

Hence, the Administration has begun to restrict and reduce services and especially payment for services. It has attempted to reduce the federal portion of Medicaid financing. In the Medicare program, it has developed one possible means for holding down health care cost increases, the diagnostic related group (DRG) method for determining payments. Under this system, hospital patients are no longer supported to the full extent of hospital stays and for the full cost of the services they receive if these costs exceed—without careful and reliable justification—the cost customarily associated with the condition being treated. The DRG approach shortens hospital stays, curtails the provision of nursing and other services, and generally begins, if not to decrease the cost of Medicare, at least to reduce the cost of increases in Medicare services.

Because hospitals and other health care providers tend to establish and maintain single standards for providing services, the DRG approach has also reduced the cost of services provided to patients financed through private insurance, Medicaid, and other programs.

Although it is not yet certain how effective health care cost controls will be or what long-term impact they will have on health care services, it is clear that national policy is leading to a reduction in the growth of expenditures for health care in the United States.

These changes have led to intense discussions on their consequences. Will this country begin formally to ration health services? Will kidney transplants, heart bypass operations, and lengthy maintenance of comatose patients on respirators be limited to the wealthy? Will national policies determine, in effect, who will live and who will die and when? These moral and medical issues have become major points of discussion and debate.

Information Dissemination and the Computer

In the 1980s the computer has become a common tool, and automatic data processing has become accessible to a large segment of the population. Although computer programming remains a scientific complexity for most people, computers have become part of the normal procedures of everyday life in the United States. Automobiles have been changed by sophisticated computer hardware, and transportation as a whole has been affected by computerization. Everything from complicated airline fare structures and reservations to local bus routes is now designed and implemented with computer systems. Fast-food restaurants use computers to calculate costs and maintain inventories, as do most large retail stores. Toys with small computers have become the favorite playthings of preschool children, and more complex electronic games have become the fad of the decade for people of all ages.

Of course, computers and the silicon chips that make them possible have significant application in the human services. Computerized record keeping, information on services, planning and evaluating programs, research on public welfare and other kinds of assistance programs, and information dissemination are critical factors in the total practice of social work. Thus, for the 1980s, knowing about and working with computers are essential elements in the operation of social work programs.

Work, Leisure, and the Family

In the 1980s, the structure of American work as it will be for the balance of the century has become more clearly defined. For the most part, it has been an era in which the small number of heavy manufacturing jobs in the United States declined even further, as did other traditional areas of employment such as coal mining and the steel industry. A combination of economic decline, the growth of overseas economies—especially those of Asia—and new methods using fewer people have made American industries less competitive with those in other nations and caused a further shift away from such manufacturing industries. As a result, automobiles, steel, textiles, and other manufactured goods are less and less commonly the sole province of U.S. companies.

The American economy, which had for decades been organized primarily around services, has become even more service oriented. The new jobs in the American service economy vary significantly. Some are low-paying positions in building maintenance, fast-food services, and health care. Others, however, in such fields as accounting, computer science, and business, pay well and have brought increasingly larger numbers of people into middle- and upper-class employment. But unquestionably, many jobs that were traditionally considered major sources of employment in the United States have been "exported" to developing nations or have otherwise become unavailable to American workers.

These job changes and other social forces have had their impact on the American family. Increasingly, married families have two adult wage earners and fewer and fewer women work exclusively in the home, caring for a husband and children. In addition, divorce, births outside marriage, and a longer life span have led to more and more single-person and single-parent households.

These factors have led to smaller families and, in turn, to fewer school-age children—a group that declined by 2.7 million in the early 1980s and that had decreased by 8 million in the 1970s. However, the number of children under age 5 grew by 9 percent in the early 1980s (nearly three times faster than the rest of the population), meaning that the number of school-age children, as a group, would increase before the end of the decade. And, although percentage increases slowed, the population continued to grow. In 1983, the United States had an estimated 234 mil-

lion people, up from the 1980 census count of 226.5 million. The greatest percentage growth was among the elderly, who had increased by 7.2 percent—more than twice as much as the population as a whole. Even more striking was the absolute growth of people of working age (18–64), who had grown by 46 million since 1960 against an overall increase of 55 million. With such an enormous working-age population, it is no wonder that employment and unemployment became the major domestic issues of the 1980s, in some ways displacing education—the major concern of earlier decades when the school-age population was rapidly growing.

Leisure activities are also changing. Television is still the major pastime, and reading continues to decline as a direct result. Television itself has changed with the widespread availability of cable service and video recorders, which allow viewers to see whatever they want whenever they choose. Other activities—particularly jogging, swimming, and other active sports—have become more common ways to spend one's leisure hours.

With the annual addition of thousands of new immigrants from all parts of the world—but increasingly from Third World nations—bringing with them different traditions, pastimes, and interests, family life in the United States is more diverse than it has been in the past. In all, family life has been subject to major modifications in the 1980s. Although the rights of women and minorities have continued to move toward parity with those of white males, female-headed and minority households continue to lag economically behind white two-parent households.

Religion

The 1980s have been an era of some religious resurgence. The growth experienced during the decade has not always been in the mainstream religions of the United States, however. Although traditional Protestant groups such as the Baptist, Methodist, Presbyterian, and other Christian churches have maintained their importance, as has the Roman Catholic church, the major increases in Christian religious participation have come through independent and evangelical churches. There is evidence that Jews, too, are becoming more actively religious. Some are also identifying with fundamentalist groups such as the Hassidim, especially in larger urban areas.

The era has become one of some religious confusion and of unorthodox, experimental behavior. For example, new religious minorities, which some define as cults or sects, have developed large followings. In November 1978, the People's Temple, a religious sect from California that followed the teachings of Jim Jones and that had migrated to Guyana, ended its existence through mass suicide by cyanide poisoning after a visiting U.S. congressman was murdered by its adherents. The Hare Krishna movement, which started in the United States during the 1960s, began developing communities throughout this country. Dedicated chanters and solicitors of financial contributions for the movement are prominent throughout the United States.

It is likely that the nature of all religious observance in the United States has been changing during the 1980s. Traditionally powerful religious institutions with traditionally acceptable approaches to liturgy, worship, and theology are giving way to new (in some ways) and very traditional (in other ways) organizations and movements.

Religious institutions continue to be prominent in the delivery of social work services. Some churches deliver social services directly. Other churches, particularly those that have grown to greater strength in the 1980s, believe that their activities are and ought to be all-encompassing and that all needs—religious, social, cultural, and educational—can be met through the structure of the religious institution. But in almost all religious institutions, various kinds of emergency assistance for the disadvantaged, of counseling on personal problems, and of child development activities have been part of the program. Of course, the values held and promoted by religious organizations affect social welfare programs.

In addition, increasing numbers of religious organizations entered the political arena during the 1970s and 1980s. Religious leaders and members of their congregations attempt to influence foreign policy, domestic policy (particularly as it affects religion), and educational policy through the traditional methods of fundraising, lobbying, and, from time to time, the same kind of political action committees organized by industry and labor to press their points of view. Religion, as the historical source of most social welfare programs, has been and continues to be a factor in social welfare and social work practice.

Education

Closely related to social work practice and social welfare programs have been developments in elementary, secondary, and higher education. The 1980s have been marked by a number of studies, reports, and other highly visible efforts to define and eliminate what some have described as a crisis in education. These reports—such as *A Nation at Risk, High School, Involvement in Learning, What Works*, and various studies by the Carnegie Commission—took as their theme the deterioration of all levels of education in the United States. Evidence included declining scores on standardized tests such as the Scholastic Aptitude Test, illiteracy problems, the delinquency and school dropout rates, and other manifestations of students' difficulties. In 1985, NASW issued a report, *The Human Factor: A Key to Excellence in Education*, which suggests that excellence requires humane schools and educational attitudes.

These studies did not always take into account changes in the demographics of education in the United States. Some critics point out that in recent years, more and more disadvantaged and handicapped young people have not only entered but have also stayed in school. Part of the cost of their doing so has been lower scores on certain tests, but in reality the advantages to the nation of educating more of its young people are overwhelmingly important to its future.

On the other hand, it has been a difficult time for education. Less is known about the practical classroom aspects of learning than ought to be for the successful operation of educational programs. The frustration and imprecision of attempting to teach make education a difficult task, and controlling for factors such as family support for education, student motivation, and communication skills makes it all the more so. Thus, although there may have been no major educational crisis in the 1980s, the turbulent problems of educational enterprises continue to affect all those attempting to teach as well as learn.

Education is, of course, a pivotal factor in the development of a complex society.

Employment without proper education and training is nearly impossible for most people. The employment needs of industry cannot be met without a sound educational enterprise. For many, the difference between disadvantage and economic success is education, and thus, education is not only a factor in a society's quality of life but also a commonly used strategy for serving social work clients. Sound relations with schools are common for social workers in the 1980s and as important as they always have been throughout the history of social work.

Conclusion

The 1980s, like any historical era, have provided a special context for the development and practice of social work. Effective and high-quality social work practice requires a clear understanding of and careful attention to the context in which it takes place. Social work, as a practice-oriented, community-based profession, must always be cognizant of the social and political environment in which it is practiced.

The encyclopedia contains articles that explore in great detail all the subjects discussed here. Understanding the contextual backdrop of the populations, services, programs, and methods described in these articles will help the reader understand the articles themselves as well as the point of view from which each article is written. The 1980s have been an unusual, important time. They have contributed to marked changes in the practice of social work. It is likely that the agendas described here will set the tone of human services for the rest of the twentieth century.

LEON H. GINSBERG

ARTICLES A-I

ABBOTT, EDITH. See biographical section.

ABBOTT, GRACE. See biographical section.

ABORTION

Abortion is the expulsion of the fetus from a woman's body before the fetus is viable—usually within the first 28 weeks of pregnancy. Abortion may occur spontaneously or it may be induced; the latter type of abortion is the subject of this article.

Recent medical advances have made abortion generally safe, with fewer than 1 percent of abortions performed in the United States resulting in medical complications. The safest procedures are those performed before the thirteenth week of pregnancy; methods become more complex at later stages. Most abortions in the early weeks of pregnancy (first trimester) can be performed in a free-standing clinic (Feldman & Chilman, 1983). Fewer than 10 percent of all U.S. abortions in 1980 were performed in the second trimester. Although improved techniques have lowered the death rate from second-trimester abortions markedly in recent years, such abortions are still not recommended (Benditt, 1979).

Significance of Abortion

The moral and legal aspects of abortion have become highly controversial and are bitterly debated. Factors fueling this controversy include the legalization of abortion, provisions for public funding of abortions for poor women, the sharp increase in the numbers of reported abortions, and a general swing toward more conservative attitudes throughout much of the nation since the late 1970s.

Historical Aspects

Abortion was legalized in the United States through a 1973 Supreme Court decision, *Roe v. Wade,* which declared unconstitutional all state laws that prohibited or re-

stricted abortion during the first trimester of pregnancy. The ruling also limited state interventions in second-trimester abortions and left the issue of third-trimester abortions up to each individual state.

Legal abortions are available in many parts of the world today, with many nations having preceded the United States in allowing them. Before antiabortion attitudes and legislation emerged in Western Europe and the United States during the nineteenth century, little official attention had been paid to the matter (David, 1972).

Even after abortion was legalized in the United States, however, a number of states in 1974 and 1975 enacted laws requiring that teenagers be barred from getting abortions unless they obtained parental consent. This legislation was declared unconstitutional by the Supreme Court in a 1976 decision, which stated that a minor should have free access to sex-related health care and that a third party, such as a parent, could not veto a decision made by the physician and the patient to terminate the patient's pregnancy (Rodman, Lewis, & Griffith, 1984).

In another 1976 decision, the Supreme Court invalidated a state law to the effect that parents must be notified in all cases before an abortion is performed on a minor daughter. The Court declared that a "mature minor" had the right to obtain an abortion without parental consent if such a decision, made with her physician, was in her best interests. However, the definition of "mature" was not clarified by the Court, leading to considerable continuing confusion.

According to Rodman, Lewis, and Griffith (1984), these Supreme Court actions had profound significance because they created a new and different view of the age-old issue of parents' vs. children's rights. Although the courts have traditionally upheld the authority of parents over their children in most instances, the area of "reproductive rights" (as they apply to both contraception and abortion) appears to be different, and to entail many thorny complexities far beyond the effective reach of jurisprudence.

The Hyde Amendment, passed by Congress in 1976, struck a blow at the availability of federal funds to defray abortion costs for low-income women. After the 1973 Supreme Court decision, such funding had been available to the states through Title XIX of the Social Security Act (Medicaid).

State policies vary widely. As of January 1985, ten states (Alaska, Colorado, Hawaii, Maryland, Michigan, New York, North Carolina, Oregon, Washington, and West Virginia) and the District of Columbia used their own funds voluntarily for abortions and four states (California, Connecticut, Massachusetts, and Pennsylvania) were required by court interpretation of their constitutions to fund abortions. Five states (Iowa, Maine, Tennessee, Virginia, and Wisconsin) funded abortions for reasons slightly less restrictive than federal policy. The remaining states funded abortions only when the woman's life was in danger.

Despite these restrictions on government reimbursement, the reported incidence of abortion rose throughout the 1970s from about 0.9 million reported abortions in 1974 to over 1.5 million in 1980 (Moore, 1983).

Adolescent Pregnancies: A Special Concern

In general, the birth rate in this country (including the birth rate for adolescents) has been declining since 1958 and, as of 1986, is at an all-time low at less than two children born per couple. This decline appears to be largely the result of increased use of effective contraceptives by the majority of sexually active women of childbearing age. Adolescents, however, are far less likely than older people to use such contraceptives consistently. Although sexually active adolescents, as a group, increased contraceptive use during the 1970s, more of them became sexually active and fewer used the more effective methods (probably as a result of widespread publicity reporting the possibly adverse side effects of oral contraceptives in particular). As a result, teenage pregnancy (though not birth) rates increased markedly throughout most of the 1970s (Zelnik, Kantner, & Ford, 1982). If about half of the pregnant adolescents had not resorted to abortion, their childbearing rates, instead of showing a decline, would have been extremely high.

The high and rising rate of nonmarital pregnancies among teenagers is a matter of considerable concern, with over 80 percent of teenage pregnancies occurring outside of marriage. Young women, especially those who are white, are particularly apt to marry

the putative father or terminate nonmarital pregnancies through abortion. In 1980, 4.5 percent of all white females aged 15–19 and 9.5 percent of all black females in the same age group gave birth. One-third of the births to young white mothers, but 86 percent of the births to young black mothers, were outside of marriage (Moore, 1984).

These high rates of nonmarital births among adolescents contribute to the growing problem of the "feminization of poverty." It is not clear, however, that marriage would solve the economic problems of these adolescent mothers, especially those who are victims of racism, because the unemployment rates for young males are over 20 percent; this figure increases to more than 50 percent for inner-city minority youths of both sexes.

Factors Associated With Electing an Abortion

A number of recent studies have investigated the characteristics of women who reported that they had terminated their pregnancies through abortions. Although further research is needed, present findings include the following factors associated with the choice to abort: not being black or Hispanic; low religiosity; having parents with high levels of education; placing low value on fertility, as well as favoring contraceptives and abortion; having mothers and peers with proabortion attitudes; high personal educational-occupational aspirations; high self-esteem; single status; and seeing aid from family and partner as not available (Zelnik & Kantner, 1980; Smetna & Adler, 1979; Eisen, Zellman, Leibowitz, Chow, & Evans, 1983; Chilman, 1983).

Social and Psychological Effects

Research is especially scanty on the social and psychological costs and benefits of abortion. Particularly scarce are relevant studies of the effects of abortion over the life span; the impact of abortion on putative fathers and members of the extended family; and the effects on all concerned of alternate ways of handling an unwanted pregnancy, such as carrying the pregnancy to term and placing the child for adoption or carrying the pregnancy to term and keeping the child in various living arrangements as a single or married parent.

The few studies that have thus far

attempted to measure the psychological effects of abortion on women suggest that negative reactions occur in about 25 percent of cases. These reactions tend to be associated with the following factors: preexisting personal problems and poor psychological adjustment; religious beliefs that oppose abortion; abortion decision forced by parents or partner; lack of parental or partner support during and after the procedure; strong ambivalence about electing an abortion; low socioeconomic status and background; low educational achievement and low educational-occupational expectations (Osofsky & Osofsky, 1972; Martin, 1973; Evans, Selstad, & Welcher, 1976; Cobliner, Schulman, & Romney, 1973; Chilman, 1983; Eisen & Zellman, in press).

Contemporary Debates

As sketched above, there are sharp debates for and against the legalization of abortion and financial support for abortion services, especially through public funding. An allied debate confronts the issue of whether or not adolescents should have access to abortion without (1) parent notification and (2) parent consent. Following are some of the major prevalent pro and con arguments regarding the legalization and general availability of abortion.

Those who favor the legalization and ready availability of abortion are said to hold a "pro-choice" position. They believe that the human fertilized ovum is not a person, prenatally, and that the pregnant woman has a right to freedom of choice as to whether or not she will terminate an unwanted pregnancy, because a woman has a right to exercise control over her own body. Those who are against abortion are said to maintain a "pro-life" position. They argue that the human fertilized ovum is a human being and therefore has a right to life.

Role of Men. "Pro-choice" advocates remark that if men had to bear children, they would have legalized abortion many years ago. "Pro-life" proponents argue that a woman does not have a sole right to make decisions about the child she is carrying and that the man who impregnated her has equal rights as well as equal responsibilities.

Religion. Some religious doctrines and their adherents hold that because the fertilized ovum is a developing human being, it has a soul and a right to be born and to have access to salvation through religious rituals. "Pro-choice" proponents argue that each person has the right to follow her or his own religion but not to impose religious beliefs on others.

Is Abortion Murder? "Pro-choice" advocates believe that abortion is a technical procedure that deals with a prehuman organism and is not murder. Their opponents state that abortion is murder and that it therefore should be condemned by society and not left up to individual choice.

Unwanted Children? Unwanted pregnancies, "pro-choice" advocates argue, lead to unwanted children whose development is apt to be damaged by parental rejection. "Pro-life" advocates insist that all pregnancies should be brought to term, if possible. A life is sacred. Moreover, they add, many pregnancies that may have been unwanted initially result eventually in children who become a boon to their parents and society.

Pregnancy and Marriage. "Pro-life" advocates believe that unmarried people should not have coitus in the first place; if they do, they should pay the price of their misbehavior. The putative father should be obligated to marry the woman he impregnates and to support the child. "Pro-choice" advocates argue that putative fathers often would not make good husbands, and marriage, therefore, is a poor option in many cases, especially if the father is unemployed. Then, too, they point out, many putative fathers are already married to other women. To this last point, "pro-life" advocates are likely to respond by pointing out that coitus with a person other than one's spouse is adultery, and that women and men who engage in this behavior should pay the price of their sin.

Use of Contraceptives. "Pro-life" proponents, if they are not opposed to the use of contraceptives altogether, argue that people who are not prepared to become parents should always use effective contraceptives when they have intercourse, especially if they are not married; and they must bear the consequences of their own carelessness responsibly if a pregnancy occurs. "Pro-choice" proponents point out, however, that there are no perfect contraceptives. Each kind has its negative aspects, especially for teenagers and others who may not anticipate having intercourse, who may not understand the importance of using contraception, or who may not have access to contraceptives.

Adoption. "Pro-life" proponents argue that if parents have a child that they do not want or cannot care for, they can release the child for adoption. There are many more people eager to adopt a child than there are children available. "Pro-choice" advocates respond by pointing out that adoption is not a simple solution. Many biological parents mourn all their lives for the child they surrendered, and many adoptive children search for their biological parents for years and resent their adoptive status.

Reasons Why Pregnancy Is Unwanted. "Pro-choice" advocates point out that many pregnancies are unwanted because the parents cannot afford to have a child or because they have not finished their education. "Pro-life" advocates feel that parents who think they cannot afford to have a child should examine their priorities. Perhaps they do have the resources if they forego other material goals, which is what they should do, because a human life is of higher value. If they are at the poverty level, they can apply for welfare. If a man's or woman's education is interrupted by parenthood, he or she can go to school at a later date; a new human life is more important.

Public Funding for Abortion. "Pro-choice" advocates hold that public funding for abortion should be available from the federal government for poor women who would otherwise be deprived of health services available to those who are financially more fortunate. This supports the basic democratic principles of our nation. "Pro-life" proponents believe, on the contrary, that public funds, especially *federal* funds, should not support what they considered to be an immoral act. States, they think, should have the privilege of developing their own policies in such a highly sensitive area as abortion.

Population Control. "Pro-choice" pro-

ponents point out that the population of the United States has grown too large and that abortion is one important means of population control. "Pro-life" proponents counter that the birthrate in the United States has declined sharply and is now at less than replacement levels. Moreover, they say, abortion is morally wrong and not an ethical means of population control.

Sexual Abstinence. "Pro-life" advocates argue that the most moral and effective means of population control is abstinence from intercourse. There is no evidence, they say, that such abstinence in itself causes any serious problems. But "pro-choice" advocates think that sexual abstinence is an unrealistic objective for most people. According to them, it may well cause a host of problems, including repression, guilt, conflicted marital relationships, and various forms of deviant behavior.

Nonmarital Adolescent Sexual Activity. "Pro-choice" advocates believe that nonmarital sexual activity is inevitable for teenagers in a technologically advanced, highly mobile mass society, especially when youth unemployment is high and marriages are therefore delayed. But "pro-life" advocates argue that stronger controls within homes, schools, and the larger society should be instituted in order to prevent such high rates of nonmarital adolescent sexual activity.

High Adolescent Birthrate. "Pro-choice" advocates note that pregnancy rates among adolescents have been growing rapidly and that most of these pregnancies are nonmarital. Half of these pregnancies are terminated by abortion. Without abortion, the adolescent birthrate would be very high, with adverse economic, social, and psychological effects for the teenagers, their families, their children, and society. "Pro-life" proponents argue, however, that making abortion available to adolescents compounds their immoral behavior and leads them to further immorality. They should not have nonmarital coitus in the first place and should not marry before age 18. Moreover, parents should have a right to know if their child is pregnant and considering an abortion.

When Pregnancy Threatens the Health of the Mother. "Pro-choice" proponents believe that abortion should be available if continuation of a pregnancy threatens the physical or mental health of the mother. Many "pro-life" advocates would agree; but some would still give priority to the child's "right to life."

Cases of Rape. "Pro-choice" advocates believe that the right to choose an abortion in cases of rape is a matter of simple justice. Some "pro-life" advocates would agree with this point; others would argue that, nevertheless, the child still has a "right to life."

Handicapped Child. Some "pro-life" advocates would hold that even if a child is apt to be born with a serious physical or mental handicap, the right of a mother to choose an abortion would still be against the child's "right to life," and some would also hold that parents of handicapped children often develop a special love for them and grow spiritually through their devotion to the care of such children. Other "pro-life" advocates would agree with the "pro-choice" advocates who claim that the right to choose an abortion in such circumstances would be in the best interests of both the parents and the unborn child. The "pro-choice" advocates might also add that handicapped children are often overburdened with suffering and unhappiness and that the personal growth of parents is more apt to occur through positive, rather than negative, experiences with their children.

Illegal Abortions as the Alternative. If abortions are not legal, "pro-choice" advocates say, people will resort to illegal ones, which are apt to be performed under poor conditions and are therefore extremely hazardous, often resulting in injury or death. "Pro-life" advocates counter that women who have illegal abortions are both breaking the law and violating moral principles. If their own behavior results in injury or death, they are responsible for these misfortunes because they chose this behavior.

Majority View

In a recent nationwide study, Luker (1984) found that the majority of Americans took a moderate view, favoring abortions for such reasons as pregnancies that might result in a deformed child or that posed a threat to the mother's health or were the result of incest or rape. Only a minority took extreme "pro-life" or "pro-choice" positions. Those in the first group were predominantly mothers who were full-time homemakers with limited educational or occupational training or interests; those in the second group were primarily highly educated women who were successful in professional or managerial careers. The first group held a traditional view of the primacy of motherhood as woman's central role; the second held a modernist view that emphasized equality between women and men and rational control over one's life.

Implications for Practice

Clearly, the arguments for and against "free choice" are numerous and complex. Each social worker who is involved as a professional in issues related to abortion will need to think through carefully his or her beliefs and values about this subject and such associated ones as nonmarital coitus, contraception, adolescent sexuality, unwanted pregnancies, forced marriages, and adoption. Social workers who find that they cannot take an objective, informed approach to these topics should probably abstain from both direct and indirect professional practice dealing with problem pregnancies unless they are employed by agencies with clearly stated "pro-life" or "pro-choice" policies with which they personally agree.

Social Policymakers and Planners

Social workers employed as policymakers or program developers in agencies that espouse an objective position concerning problem pregnancies will need to be well informed about providing a full complement of free or low-cost high-quality resources available in their communities. These may include human sexuality education and counseling, contraception and pregnancy diagnostic services, health and welfare services for pregnant women and mothers and fathers, comprehensive problem pregnancy counseling and referral programs (including abortion services), adoption agencies, education and training programs for young parents, and the like (Chilman, 1983). Workers will also need to be well informed about the legal, medical, social, and financial aspects of the many existing or potential resources in their communities.

Ideally, social policymakers and planners in this field will advocate a wide range of viable choices and related resources for persons facing problem pregnancies. They will also advocate *preventive* services that include early individual and family counseling, education on such topics as human sexuality and family planning, and availability of free or low-cost contraceptive services.

In general, it seems desirable that professionals in all areas of social work practice advocate the rights of people, within the limits of the law, to express and act upon their values and beliefs concerning problem pregnancies, how to prevent them, and alternate pathways to their management. To the extent that various groups desire changes in pertinent laws, their rights and responsibilities to work for such changes through peaceable, orderly, legal processes should be protected.

Problem Pregnancy Counseling

Problem pregnancy counseling is characterized by clear time constraints and focuses on making and implementing a specific decision. The decision must be made early if abortion is to be used. Women, especially adolescents, often delay action when they suspect a pregnancy. Thus, the counselor's first concern is to arrange for tests that will confirm or deny that conception has occurred and, if tests are positive, determine when the baby is due. When tests are positive, counseling sessions turn to the examination of options. Abortion is one among several alternatives; other alternatives include having the baby and rearing it alone or with the help of parents or the father, marrying and having the baby, or placing the child for adoption.

Counseling can help expectant parents understand what their options are (Chesler & Davis, 1980; Mace, 1972, Gilchrist & Schinke, 1983). The ultimate decision, however, should be made chiefly by the pregnant woman herself, preferably in consultation with the baby's father and family members. To make the decision that is best for the couple and their child, the pregnant woman— ideally, with the expectant father—needs to view each option in the context of the cou-

ple's present skills, resources, values, goals, emotions, important interpersonal relationships, and future plans. The counselor's role is to support and shape a realistic selection of the most feasible pregnancy resolution alternative.

High levels of knowledge and skills are needed to implement necessarily rapid decision making, if abortion is an option. The counselor must be able to employ an adaptation of crisis intervention techniques that include helping people handle such intense feelings as shock, anxiety, rage, and guilt.

Although a rational decision-making process is the accepted model for abortion counseling, it is often extraordinarily difficult to implement, especially with adolescents. For example, in one study of 40 adolescent women seeking abortions, Cain (1979) found that pregnancy was often the symptomatic expression of a host of chronic problems with parents, peers, and school that preoccupied these young women. A focus solely on the problem pregnancy was found to be a mistake in that it prevented treatment of more fundamental and important difficulties.

Male sexual partners of pregnant women are ignored by most human service professionals in discussions of abortion and pregnancy resolution. A recent questionnaire and interview study of 1,000 men in waiting rooms of abortion clinics revealed that most of them, like the women patients, were torn between feelings of guilt about the abortion and relief that an unwanted pregnancy was being terminated (Shostak, McLouth, & Seng, 1984). These men had difficulty expressing their feelings, but other small studies provide evidence that a partner's abortion can be profoundly disturbing for many males (Rappaport, 1981; Rothstein, 1978).

If the decision to abort is made, counselors should prepare women and, if indicated, their partners and other family members, for the procedure itself. Many people, especially males, know almost nothing about the abortion process. Providing information and reassurance can significantly increase a woman's ability to cope with this potentially unnerving medical procedure.

Follow-up counseling appointments should be scheduled from one to three weeks after the abortion. If the woman's sexual partner and parents were involved in the process, they should be included in the follow-up. Counseling and provision of services for contraception are a very important aspect of this follow-up (Gilchrist & Schinke, 1983).

CATHERINE S. CHILMAN

For further information, see ADOLESCENT PREGNANCY; FAMILY AND POPULATION PLANNING; WOMEN.

References

Benditt, J. (1979). "Second Trimester Abortions." *Family Planning Perspectives, 11*(Nov./Dec.), 357–362.

Cain, L. (1979). "Social Worker's Role in Teenage Abortions." *Social Work, 24*(1), 52–56.

Chesler, J., & Davis, S. (1980). "Problem Pregnancy and Abortion Counseling With Teenagers." *Social Casework: The Journal of Contemporary Social Work, 61*(3), 173–179.

Chilman, C. (1983). *Adolescent Sexuality in a Changing American Society: Social and Psychological Perspectives for the Human Services Professions.* New York: John Wiley & Sons.

Cobliner, G., Schulman, H., & Romney, S. (1973). "The Termination of Adolescent Out-of-Wedlock Pregnancies and the Prospects for Their Primary Prevention." *American Journal of Obstetrics and Gynecology, 115*(3), 422–444.

David, H. (1972). "Abortion in Psychological Perspective." *American Journal of Orthopsychiatry, 42*(1), 61–68.

Eisen, M., & Zellman, G. (in press). "Factors Predicting Pregnancy Resolution Decision and Satisfaction of Unmarried Adolescents." *Journal of Genetic Psychology.*

Eisen, M., Zellman, G., Leibowitz, A., Chow, W., & Evans, J. (1983). "Factors Discriminating Pregnancy Resolution Decisions of Unmarried Adolescents." *Genetic Psychiatric Monograph, 108*(1), 69–95.

Evans, J., Selstad, G., & Welcher, W. (1976). "Teenagers: Fertility Control Behavior and Attitudes Before and After Abortion, Childbearing or Negative Pregnancy Test." *Family Planning Perspectives, 8*(4), 192–200.

Feldman, M., & Chilman, C. (1983). "Contraceptive and Abortion Services for Adolescents." In C. Chilman, *Adolescent Sexuality in a Changing American Society: Social and Psychological Perspectives for the Human Services Professions* (pp. 251–274). New York: John Wiley & Sons.

Gilchrist, L., & Schinke, S. (1983). "Counseling With Adolescents About Their Sexuality." In C. Chilman, *Adolescent Sexuality in a Changing American Society: Social and Psychological Perspectives for the Human Services Professions* (pp. 230–250). New York: John Wiley & Sons.

Luker, K. (1984). *Abortion and the Politics of Motherhood.* Berkeley, Calif.: University of California Press.

Mace, D. (1972). *Abortion: The Agonizing Decision.* Nashville, Tenn.: Abingdon Press.

Martin, C. (1973). "Psychological Problems of Abortion for the Unwed Teenage Girl." *Genetic Psychiatric Monograph, 88*(Aug): 23–110.

Moore, K. (1983). *Teenage Parents and Teenagers at Risk of Pregnancy: Federal Welfare Social Services and Related Programs for These Adolescents.* Washington, D.C.: The Urban Institute.

Moore, K. (1984). *Facts at a Glance.* Washington, D.C.: The Urban Institute.

Osofsky, J., & Osofsky, H. (1972). "The Psychological Reaction of Patients to Legalized Abortions." *American Journal of Orthopsychiatry, 42*(1), 48–60.

Rappaport, B. (1981). "Helping Men Ask for Help." *Public Welfare, 39*(2), 22–27.

Rodman, H., Lewis, S., & Griffith, S. (1984). *The Sexual Rights of Adolescents.* New York: Columbia University Press.

Rothstein, A. A. (1978). "Adolescent Males, Fatherhood, and Abortion." *Journal of Youth and Adolescence, 7*, 203–214.

Shostak, A., McLouth, G., & Seng, L. (1984). *Men and Abortion.* New York: Praeger.

Smetna, J., & Adler, N. (1979). "Decision-Making Regarding Abortion: A Value and Expectancy Analysis." *Journal of Population, 2*, 338–357.

Zelnik, M., & Kantner, J. (1980). "Sexual Activity, Contraceptive Use, and Pregnancy Among Metropolitan Area Teenagers: 1971–1979." *Family Planning Perspectives, 12*, 230–237.

Zelnik, M., Kantner, J., & Ford, K. (1982). *Adolescent Pathways to Pregnancy.* Beverly Hills, Calif.: Sage Publications.

ACCOUNTABILITY. See DIRECT PRACTICE EFFECTIVENESS; FINANCIAL MANAGEMENT; INFORMATION SYSTEMS: AGENCY; QUALITY ASSURANCE; QUALITY CONTROL IN INCOME MAINTENANCE.

ACCOUNTING. See FINANCIAL MANAGEMENT.

ADDAMS, JANE. See biographical section.

ADDICTION. See ALCOHOL USE AND ADDICTION; DRUG USE AND ABUSE.

Reader's Guide

ADMINISTRATION

The following articles contain information on this general topic:

Administration: Environmental Aspects
Administration: Interpersonal Aspects
Administration in Social Welfare
Financial Management
Information Systems: Agency
Information Systems: Client Data
Information Utilization for Management Decision Making
Macro Practice: Current Trends and Issues
Organizations: Impact on Employees and Community
Personnel Management
Program Evaluation
Quality Assurance
Supervision in Social Work

ADMINISTRATION: ENVIRONMENTAL ASPECTS

Organizational leadership is a complex phenomenon that is becoming more so as society becomes more turbulent, as social values are challenged, and as technologies become increasingly sophisticated. In social work there is a real danger that—as greater demands are made on agencies for services while resources decline—the administrative response will be to focus exclusively on organizational maintenance and survival.

This possibility is viewed with alarm because the raison d'être of social agencies is to address unmet needs and to serve popula-

tions at risk, stigmatized groups, and others who cannot cope unaided with life in American society. If survival alone becomes the critical issue, agencies will be increasingly tempted to shift their focus from dependent clients who cannot carry their weight financially to those who have the means to support an agency's services through private fees or third-party payments.

Selznick (1957) addresses this issue in his distinction between "organizational achievement" and "institutional success." Although organizations focus on the achievement of immediate goals and thus have a short time perspective, institutions are "infused with value" and represent fundamental aspirations of various segments of the community. The test of an effective administrator is to recognize and understand the process of institutionalization: "the institutional leader . . . *is primarily an expert in the promotion and protection of values*" (p. 28). It is this concern with the protection of values, moreover, that catapults the administrator into an externally oriented role: values are societally based.

This article examines the impact of an organization's environment on executive performance and the administrator's role in dealing with the environment. The discussion begins with a review of the literature on organizations and their environments. This is followed by a model of organizational development that can serve as a guide for administrative action. The article then presents three external dimensions that influence administrative and organizational behavior: policy and politics, interorganizational relationships, and resource mobilization. The last section of the article discusses the implications of organizational leadership for the practice of social welfare administration.

Organizations and Their Environments

Organization theory serves as a base for the practice of social administration in much the same way that psychology does for clinical practice with individuals. Although several theorists have examined organizational environments and the uncertainties they create (Clark, 1956; Katz & Kahn, 1966; Selznick, 1949; Thompson, 1967), their discussions are directed at the environment as a context for, and an influence on, the organization. The reciprocities and interactions between the organization and external elements have not been adequately addressed.

Pfeffer and Salancik (1978) highlight this gap in the literature and focus attention on "an external perspective on organization." They point out that the environment is usually handled as a special section or an introductory chapter in texts on organizational behavior; that the major concern is with internal processes, such as authority, structures, and personnel; and that problems are solved "by changing elements within the organization without regard to their contextual basis" (p. 8). They present several concepts they hope will bring "coherence" to the work on organizations and environments.

Organizational effectiveness and efficiency are coupled with an internal versus an external perspective. Pfeffer and Salancik suggest that the *effectiveness* of a system is judged *externally* and is a sociopolitical measure; by contrast, *efficiency* is an *internal* measure, derived from "the ratio of resources utilized to output produced" (Pfeffer & Salancik, 1978, p. 11). Of interest here is the focus on the critical nature of external judgments from not only an economic but also an ideological perspective. Given the open-system social welfare enterprise and its dependence on larger systems both for resources and for sanction, the need for executive consideration of the external dimension becomes patently clear.

The environment of a social welfare agency is a complex one. To deal with it administratively, its most important elements must be identified. Hasenfeld and English (1974) provide a useful analytic framework. They differentiate the environment into three subsystems—"ecological, sociocultural, and economic-political" (p. 98)—each of which is linked to the resources the agency must acquire in order to function.

Thus the ecological subsystem, which consists of both geographic and demographic elements, is central because it provides the physical and population resources needed by the agency. The sociocultural subsystem is critical because it sets the ideological framework in which the agency makes its choices regarding the appropriate use of resources. And the economic-political subsystem not only gives sanction to and demands accountability from the agency, but it is also involved

in providing resources, which include "the beneficiaries of the organization's services; suppliers of clients, fiscal resources, staff and equipment; regulating groups that oversee . . . the organization; other organizations offering needed complementary services; and competing organizations" (Hasenfeld & English, 1974, p. 98).

It is important to note that because most social welfare agencies are nonprofit, their dependence on the environment is accentuated, with little countervailing power. Consequently the relationship between the organization and its environment requires the social welfare administrator's priority attention.

The concept of coupling has been suggested as a useful one in understanding this relationship. According to *Webster's Third New International Dictionary* (1961), coupling implies the bringing together of two systems wherein the behavior of one influences the behavior of the other. However, it must be noted that these relationships are usually imperfect and incomplete. Consequently, Hasenfeld and English (1974) suggest that the term "loose-coupling" appropriately depicts the relationship:

> Loose-coupling is an important safety device for organizational survival. If organizational actions were completely determined by every changing event, organizations would constantly confront disaster and need to monitor every change while continually modifying themselves. The fact that environmental impacts are felt only imperfectly provides the organization with some discretion as well as the capability to act across time horizons longer than the time it takes for an environment to change. (p. 13)

Loose-coupling is a useful construct in understanding organizations in the social welfare domain; the capacity of social welfare administrators to read the environment carefully, and to respond appropriately, is critical.

Theoretical Framework

In this exploration of the administrator's role in the control of organizational environments, it is important to understand the unique properties of human service organizations. This requires an appreciation not only of the mission, or purpose, of the system, but also of its developmental requirements, compatible with Selznick's (1957) call for "a historical perspective" in the light of "developmental stages" (pp. 102–112).

The literature on organizational stages of development is sparse but interesting. Bos (1969) focuses on "phases of development" and suggests that "one is able to diagnose more clearly what takes place and consequently one can manage in a more conscious and alert way" (p. 17). His intent is to call attention to the use of a developmental model as a tool for management. Whereas Bos's discussion is generic to all organizations, B. R. Scott (*N.Y. Times*, 1973) focuses on large, production-oriented corporations. Leik and Matthews (1967) explore the concept as it applies to a variety of social phenomena, including "an individual, an interpersonal relationship, a group, an organization, or perhaps a social institution" (p. 62). This notion is also explored by Hage and Aiken (1969) and Katz and Kahn (1966). Perlmutter (1969) and Patti (1983) are specifically concerned with developmental stages in social agencies.

Perlmutter's (1969) evolutionary model of social agency development posits three stages:

Stage I, Self-Interest, is characterized by a concern with establishing an institutional mission, defined as linkage of ideology and values to the social problem that served as the stimulus for the formation of the agency. An *external* orientation, which is dominant in this stage, requires the agency to meet client needs while negotiating its domain in the broader agency network.

Stage II, Professionalism, evolves when the initial social problem has abated and the most urgent needs have been met. Attention is now directed *inward* to a focus on quality and standards, the hallmark of professionalism. Once this "greater coherence and rationality" (Patti, 1983, p. 52) has been achieved, the agency is free to turn its attention again to new societal needs and can move on to the final stage.

Stage III, Social Interest, requires that a new social problem be addressed by the agency, similar to the problem that led to its initial formation. Secure in its professional competence, the agency can now take risks in moving into new areas that may be based on "precarious" values of its earlier stages of development, as opposed to its present "secure" values (Clark, 1956, p. 328).

To negotiate and deal with external elements, administrators must have a clear understanding of the organization's stage of development because the basic mandate is to provide leadership that will allow the organization to fulfill its mission in the institutional sense suggested by Selznick (1957).

A case illustration demonstrates the utility of this model for guiding administrative strategies. Middleton Children's Center, a newly formed agency in the voluntary sector designed to serve vulnerable children of broken homes, abuse, incest, and the like, has addressed some of the critical problems that led to its formation and has moved from the self-interest stage to the initial phase of the professionalism stage. It has been able to attract more qualified staff as a result of hard work in its formative stage, and it is now giving attention to techniques for meeting the complex needs of its diverse clientele.

Middleton's United Way has been impressed with the agency but is facing its own constraints. There has been a drop in local annual giving, and United Way is confronting a new, unserved population of "street people"—adults without shelter as a result of deinstitutionalization or unemployment. United Way requests that Middleton Children's Center begin to serve street people as well as its present population of children and promises to increase appropriations to assist in this new mandate. If the agency cannot provide this additional service, funds for its existing programs will be cut 25 percent because United Way must reallocate moneys in line with its new priorities.

The Children's Center board is confused about the problem, and the executive must provide leadership in determining an appropriate response. The developmental model presented earlier suggests three options: the agency can return to Stage I and, given the budgetary cuts, provide limited services; the agency can continue to develop its professionalism (Stage II) and seek alternative approaches to quality care for the children in its charge; or the agency can move to Stage III and seek a rationale for accepting the street people into its sphere of service.

The model provides a handle for assessment. Remaining at Stage I might be the easiest route, but the negative consequences would be that the quality care that was beginning to develop would have to be sacrificed and services cut. If the executive looked to the new money for the street people as a way to rescue the agency, the strategy would be to move to Stage III and incorporate that population, with the rationale that they, like the agency's primary clientele, were vulnerable and at risk. However, careful study of the model suggests that this decision would also have negative consequences—loss of an opportunity to develop effective approaches for the variety of problems faced by the agency's current clients. Stage II is the time to develop quality services, and a premature leap to Stage III would sacrifice the agency's professional aspect. The choice that would best meet the agency's institutional needs and protect its ideology and mission would be to remain in Stage II. It would, however, necessitate seeking other sources of funds to make possible the careful progression into professionalism. Multiple-source funding would become essential.

Managing External Boundaries

Policy and Politics. These two areas are closely intertwined: policy is defined as program intentions that reflect decisions made on the basis of principles and supporting rationales; politics consists of the actions of interest groups that are trying to affect or are affected by policies. The administrator must be well versed in both activities. Four policy constraints that require sophisticated managerial responses can be identified: competing mandates, conflicting mandates, ambiguous mandates, and incompatible sources of policy (Perlmutter, 1980). Each constraint stems from external sources but is inextricably linked to internal operations.

Competing mandates result when several policies underpinning a program are appropriate in their own terms and are compatible with each other. A problem arises when no clear priorities are set and when resources are inadequate to support both programs. For example, the Mental Retardation and Community Mental Health Construction Act of 1963 mandated both prevention and treatment as part of the program's mission. As a result, from the program's inception there were strains in community mental health centers, involving structural, ideological, professional, and administrative difficulties (Perl-

mutter, 1973; Perlmutter & Silverman, 1972; Perlmutter & Vayda, 1978).

In dealing with competing mandates, the appropriate strategy may be to garner increased resources in order to fulfill the competing mandates simultaneously. If increased resources are not available, ordering priorities and long-range planning may be appropriate. In the case of the Middleton Children's Center, the agency is faced with competing mandates from United Way. In this situation the administrator must not be seduced by the promise of additional resources but rather address the long-term consequences, particularly in light of the agency's current stage of development.

In the case of *conflicting mandates,* the executive usually has few options and must choose to support one or the other. In these circumstances, it becomes necessary to examine the options and to choose the one most appropriate to the organization's developmental stage. For example, agencies funded under the Older Americans Act of 1965 were required to work toward coordination of services at the local level. Yet this requirement from one federal program conflicted with those from other state and federal programs that were also funding services in the same agency. These were "conflicts of domain" (Kutza, 1984). Accordingly, an executive of an agency in Stage III, Social Interest, would maximize the coordination mandate in an attempt to serve the agency's expanded mission. By contrast, an executive of an agency in Stage II, Professionalism, might seek to maximize work with families to improve the quality of care to the agency's clientele, downplaying efforts at coordination.

Ambiguous mandates, in which expectations are unclear, can be used as an opportunity for creative leadership. The executive who is a risk taker can take advantage of the lack of clarity and press for unconventional options and new directions. A less imaginative administrator might press for clarification of the policies and mandates, thus losing an opportunity for leadership. Furthermore, in the press for greater clarity, the executive could precipitate a less satisfactory situation, particularly the reformulation of an ambiguous mandate into a competing or conflicting one.

Because, to an increasing degree, public policy affects not only public but also voluntary agencies, the expectations of federal, state, and local governments create another executive bind. The expectations of each level are often different, and access to each level requires different skills. For executives to function effectively in these policy arenas, they must develop political skills. As Gummer (1984) suggests, such skills should be seen as an integral part of the executive's administrative role:

> The environments of these organizations are evolving in ways that increasingly demand political responses on the part of administrators. Specifically, control of agency resources has spread over several external bodies, while intense interagency conflict over domain ("turf") continues unabated. . . . The organizational environment of the social agency has become dense and more complicated, with the result that the successful social administrator has had to develop the technical and political skills needed for acquiring the information and formulating the negotiating strategies upon which the survival of programs and agencies are increasingly dependent. (p. 25)

Policy is clearly intertwined with politics, and the executive must become adept at differentiating the political skills needed to work effectively not only with bureaucracies at different levels but also with the broad array of interest groups at the several levels. Bevilacqua (1984) provides a detailed approach to working with state government. He notes (as does Lynn, 1980) that the experience and expertise developed during the 1960s and 1970s in relation to the federal level must be broadened and tailored to the new reality of state dominance in social policies and programs. Bevilacqua identifies points of access at the state level and suggests that the challenge for the social administrator is to develop appropriate strategies for getting to them. Human service administrators, he argues, must "enter the governmental political system and compete for [their] share of resources and support" (p. 90).

In the case discussed earlier, the executive of the Middleton Children's Center made the decision to remain at Stage II, Professionalism, so that the agency could develop its services in the most effective manner. The consequence of this decision is that United Way cut the agency's allocation

by 25 percent. The executive must now begin to explore new avenues of funding and become well versed in the public priorities at the county, state, and federal levels. This may be a new arena for an executive in the voluntary sector, but the agency must develop strategies for entry into those domains if it is to serve a broad span of vulnerable children, *compatible with its mission*.

The political aspect of social agency life must also be addressed at the local level. It is here that many of the agency's operations are carried out, and the administrator must be aware of and effective in working not only with county officials but also with other local agencies and advocacy groups. Thus the Middleton executive would be well advised to contact other voluntary agencies and advocacy organizations concerned with children. The potential power of this broader set of interest groups could yield a different set of outcomes, especially in the negotiations with United Way (Perlmutter, 1984).

The importance of the deliberate use of *charismatic leadership* in this political process cannot be overestimated. Thus, for example, a controversial demonstration project in Pennsylvania that integrated all public programs in three counties was made possible, in part, by the charismatic leadership of the administrator, which "helped neutralize opposition and enhance support among local groups, while her ties to the state bureaucracy helped protect from intrusions" (Perlmutter, Richan, & Weirich, 1979, p. 20). In addition, direct involvement of the administrator in the political arena includes standard political activities, such as letter writing, visiting legislators, testifying at hearings, and the like (Armstrong, 1980).

Interorganizational Relationships. Because social agencies depend on one another for the exchange of resources, executives must be adept at working at this level. Levine and White (1961) identified the exchange mechanisms inherent in interorganizational relationships and found that the implication for the administrator is always to examine the quid pro quo in the situation. Aguilar (1967) suggests that "scanning the . . . environment" includes attending to the external relationships in a company's environment and that the very process of identifying the elements assists "top management in its task of charting the company's future course of action" (p. 1).

The scanning function is critical in the 1980s when social agencies, in both the voluntary and public sectors, face shrinking resources and social need that is growing and becoming more complex. The problems created by deinstitutionalization, increasing domestic violence, the needs of single-parent families, a growing aging population, and discharge of hospital patients earlier as a result of diagnostic related groups (DRGs) require more varied and sophisticated professional responses.

Because new administrative strategies must be developed to make viable the array of services currently distributed among many agencies, an underlying assumption is that system redesign is necessary to meet the dramatic realities of the present decade. Among the options available for system redesign are strategic planning, cutback strategies, and coalition formation.

Kahn (1984) suggests that *strategic planning* is a sine qua non to ensure the viability and effectiveness of the voluntary sector. Strategic planning, as opposed to operational planning, requires that an organization engage in a wide-ranging exploration of "all aspects of the agency's operations and particularly such elements as agency purpose, client needs, priorities of programs, and the allocation of resources" (p. 60). This is a time-consuming process that requires the active involvement of the executive. Business as usual and organizational maintenance must give way to this critical examination not only of the individual agency but also of the systems of agencies involved in meeting communal needs:

> The current existence of an institution with all of its subunits is not in itself justification for continuation. In most instances, services being delivered, client needs, effectiveness of programs, and similar factors justify continuity. The changes in governmental funding streams and policies . . . create the need for many agencies to consider their future directions. . . . Parenthetically, a decision not to continue with current services need not mean the automatic termination of an agency. . . . Emphasis on service delivery needs to be the bedrock of the social agency's strategic planning. (p. 61)

Kahn further argues that agencies must be ready to examine an array of service modalities, including mergers, conglomerates, and relationships between profit and not-for-profit organizations. He suggests that "the levels of inter-organizational collaboration developed over the years appear to be far less than what is feasible and warranted under current circumstances" (p. 63).

Cutback strategies are the appropriate next step after the initiation of strategic planning. To ensure compatability with the agency's developmental needs, the executive must tread carefully in selecting possible areas for retrenchment and agencies with which to collaborate.

Weatherley (1984) presents an array of cutback strategies that the administrator can consider and argues that the choices will largely be shaped by whether the administrator assumes the role of "statesman" or functions as a "technician." He presents an interesting scheme for examining cutbacks, identifying three strategies: administrative and labor efficiencies, service reductions, and cost sharing and merger.

Administrative and labor efficiencies include such efforts as the reduction of support services, increased work loads, contracting-out services, and deprofessionalization. The statesman proceeds cautiously with this approach because potentially cost-saving advantages may be offset by severe problems of disaffection by staff. *Service reductions* can be accomplished by eliminating programs, rationing access, or diluting the quality of services. Again, the statesman must proceed cautiously and identify the costs and benefits of this approach.

Cost sharing and mergers are increasingly used in other sectors of society, including business and public education. There is room for much creativity in this arena. The Greater New York Fund/United Way (1981) addresses this matter in a volume entitled *Merger: Another Path Ahead*. The discussion explores the definitions, rationales, procedures, critical issues, and consequences of mergers and provides case examples to help clarify the process. The report emphasizes that although each merger is unique, a knowledge of the common principles and processes involved can help inform the decision on how to proceed. "Merger can be a path ahead, and those pioneers who set out on the path with foreknowledge of possibilities and pitfalls are likely to be best equipped for the journey" (p. 17).

Coalition formation is the final interorganizational strategy to be discussed. Weiner (1984) argues that "while it may not be possible to halt the 'irresistible tide' toward funding cutbacks, executives need not passively sit back and merely wring their hands" (p. 197). He presents a case study in the field of addictions. In the face of dramatic cuts in methadone services, a group of executives banded together and developed a series of strategies in ascending order of risk. The most militant option was to initiate a lawsuit. The existence of a powerful coalition made this high-risk strategy possible after all other approaches were unsuccessful. This use of a broader base of action, including the Hospital Association of Pennsylvania, demonstrates the importance of involving other interested groups in the development of interorganizational strategies in the political arena.

Resource Mobilization. The term "resource mobilization" has come to the fore in the 1980s. Aside from its current popularity, the idea of resource mobilization has always commanded attention in the voluntary sector because agencies struggled with fundraising and fiscal survival for many years before the development of federated fundraising agencies such as United Way. The critical difference is that in earlier years the agencies developed their own sense of mission, with little hope of attracting support from other than their own particular constituents. Until the antipoverty legislation of the 1960s, public and private funds were clearly separate, with little intermixing (Perlmutter, 1971). The radical shift in the federal government's posture toward financial subvention to private agencies (contracts, grants, and purchases of service) changed the nature of both the public and private sectors. New needs were identified, new populations were served, new moneys were available, and new expectations emerged.

This changing external context combined with a changing technology in resource mobilization. Although changes in professional (Sidel, 1971) and information (McFarlan, 1984) technologies have received much attention, little has been paid to the technology of resource mobilization. Bonoma (1984) emphasizes the necessity of

good leadership in the management of marketing, which must include a strong sense of identity and direction, clarity of theme and vision, and a consumer focus. The executive must be involved in resource mobilization from the inception of the activity through monitoring and follow-up. The following discussion of the executive's role in resource mobilization focuses on communications and development.

Communications. It is helpful to think of institutional communications as public relations. Steiner (1983) views public relations as a critical function of management. He argues that the survival of human service organizations is linked to their ability to command resources, which in turn is linked to the stake external bodies have in the agency's survival. Steiner suggests that this is supported by:

> the ability and strength of professional associations and interest groups to state their case to all factions of society; the encouragement of favorable public opinion to provide a supportive base on which administrative and legislative bodies can justify positive funding decisions; the development and instigation of client pressure for increased services and programs . . . ; convincing the public they are well served or benefitted by massive financing of the human services. (p. 152)

Although responsibility for public relations rests with the human service administrator, it must in reality be part of everyone's job. The more people involved, the greater the probability of external contacts.

An effective public relations program requires technical expertise, a subject addressed by Brawley (1983) in an important volume entitled *Mass Media and Human Services.* Brawley discusses the urgency of "reaching the public," identifies some of the priorities to be set in this effort, and provides important technical advice on how to do it. There is little evidence of concern about this process, but the subject merits considerable attention (Goldman, 1960; President's Commission on Mental Health, 1978).

Brawley examines specific areas of consumer need, such as prevention of mental illness and self-help, and suggests that the mass media provide an excellent channel for promulgating these efforts. The various media offer unequaled possibilities, and it is important to understand the special access routes to effective use of newspapers and magazines, radio and television. Thus, for example, Brawley discusses the use of UHF television channels in relation to appropriate strategies (pp. 195–197).

Development. Development is another long-neglected arena for administrative attention. It consists of focused efforts to generate resources, usually through fundraising and marketing. Marketing has become a highly visible and important part of the business and political worlds but is only beginning to be addressed in the human services. Cooper (1983) discusses market strategies for hospitals and suggests that they need to apply such business concepts as "market share, product quality, research and development expenditures, investment intensity, productivity, and diversification" (p. 15). Because human service organizations are investment-intensive, which is negatively correlated with profitability, their expenditures must be carefully made and clearly linked to the system's objectives. In a social agency, a social worker can play a unique and critical role in development. Invaluable in this activity is the social worker's framework of professional values, knowledge about services, understanding of people and their needs, and commitment to advocacy for unpopular programs (Richan, 1980).

K. Kirby (personal communication, September 19, 1984) emphasizes the executive's responsibility for development. In a small agency the executive may actually have to do the work; in larger settings there may be a part-time or full-time development officer who works closely with the executive and has the executive's full trust. The development function is particularly important because the board of directors is constantly and intimately involved in it. The role of the board is vital to this process, almost akin to its policymaking function. It is the board that must sanction the strategy to be pursued and carry out much of the activity. For example, although the development officer is the one to develop a list of foundations whose interests are compatible with those of the agency and to submit the proposal, it is the board member who usually follows up with direct contact.

The board is also part of the development process in other ways. First, it is important that an array of expertise be available, with clout and with access to resources. Second, all board members must be educated to accept responsibility in the resource development arena, either through direct contributions or by helping to raise money for the agency. Kirby (personal communication, September 19, 1984) points out that board involvement in development is not automatic but requires extensive education. The use of external consultants can be an invaluable asset in the process, which can take as much as five years.

The executive must understand the function of development and provide an appropriate structure to carry out its activities. Both the board and the professional staff must be involved. Incentives such as autonomy, salary, and travel money should be used to encourage staff to write development proposals. Staff initiatives and creative ideas must be supported and encouraged by a development-oriented environment.

Development activities most frequently include special events, mail solicitations, corporate and foundation solicitations, and major gifts and deferred giving, or bequests, from individuals. A good development program includes ongoing and systematic evaluation. Although "the bottom line" is certainly one measure of development success, other elements must be included, such as public education, foundation awareness, building political support, and fostering helpful professional contacts.

More resources are becoming available to help the executive with development. These include development journals such as *Profiles in Hospital Marketing* and books, tapes, and other materials from consulting firms. For example, the TAFT group in Washington, D.C., develops material for nonprofit agencies. Their 1984 catalog included such titles as *Philanthropy and Marketing, People in Philanthropy,* and *Prospecting: Searching out the Philanthropic Dollar.*

The potential return for the agency on a well-designed development program cannot be overestimated, and the executive is the one who must set it in motion. Although it is tempting to "go for broke," to try everything and anything in the quest for resources, the model of agency development again helps to set the boundaries for what is desirable. It is important that the executive provide leadership that protects the integrity and the direction of the organization; the mandates of the agency should guide the direction of resource development. The resources sought must be appropriate to the stage of agency development and congruent with its short- and long-range plans.

Implications for the Administrator

Attention to the external environment is an essential part of the executive's role. It comprises various elements, some of which are critical and must be given priority.

1. The environment can no longer be viewed merely as a context or backdrop; it must be viewed as organically linked to the internal system. This approach is necessitated both by the dramatic shift of responsibility for social services from federal to state and local authorities and also by the broader backing away from public responsibility in this area.

2. Negotiating the environment appropriately requires a thorough understanding of the particular organization. An analytical tool, such as the model for agency development, helps the executive to determine what is appropriate given the particular organizational setting.

3. Administrators must be aware of the differences between policy and politics. They must be skilled in dealing with the various constraints imposed by public policy and must also be comfortable in dealing with the numerous actors who are currently or potentially interested in the agency's domain.

4. Any cutback strategies must be carefully planned to ensure the meaningful continuity of a service system that meets clients' needs.

5. Resource mobilization is a complex endeavor that must be designed to maximize the organization's integrity. Special attention must be paid to the communications process that directly links the agency to the broader community.

6. Development work is a complex phenomenon that requires the active involvement of all aspects of the agency. Of particular importance is the role of the board of directors, which must work closely and constantly in this arena. Even if a development officer is involved, the executive must remain in charge of development, setting its direction and providing leadership.

The increasingly complex demands placed on agencies require that administrators acquire a broad array of knowledge and skill in dealing with the environment. Social welfare administrators must maintain an open and flexible posture, must be ready for change, and must recognize the necessity for using experts to ensure high-quality leadership for the organization in managing the external environments.

FELICE DAVIDSON PERLMUTTER

For further information, see ADMINISTRATION: INTERPERSONAL ASPECTS; ADMINISTRATION IN SOCIAL WELFARE; FINANCIAL MANAGEMENT; PERSONNEL MANAGEMENT; RESOURCE DEVELOPMENT AND SERVICE PROVISION; RESOURCE MOBILIZATION AND COORDINATION.

References

Aguilar, F. J. (1967). *Scanning the Business Environment.* New York: Macmillan Publishing Co.

Armstrong, B. (1980). "Psychiatry in the Political Arena." *Hospital and Community Psychiatry, 31* (9), 606–609.

Bevilacqua, J. J. (1984). "State Politics Is the Name of the Game." In F. D. Perlmutter (Ed.), *Human Services at Risk* (pp. 75–91). Lexington, Mass.: Lexington Books.

Bonoma, T. V. (1984). "Making Your Marketing Strategy Work." *Harvard Business Review, 84*(2), 69–76.

Bos, A. H. (1969). "Development Principles of Organizations." *Management International Review, 9*(1), 17–30.

Brawley, E. A. (1983). *Mass Media and Human Services.* Beverly Hills, Calif.: Sage Publications.

Clark, B. R. (1956). "Organizational Adaptation and Precarious Values." *American Sociological Review, 21,* 327–336.

Cooper, R. B. (1983). "Market Strategies for Hospitals in a Competitive Environment." *Hospital and Health Services Administration,* May-June, 9–15.

Goldman, M. W. (1960). "Radio: A Medium for the Presentation of Social Work." *Social Work, 5*(2), 84–90.

Greater New York Fund/United Way. (1981). *Merger: Another Path Ahead,* New York: Author.

Gummer, B. (1984). "The Social Administrator as Politician." In F. D. Perlmutter (Ed.), *Human Services at Risk* (pp. 23–36). Lexington, Mass.: Lexington Books.

Hage, J. & Aiken, M. (1969). *Social Change in Complex Organizations.* New York: Random House.

Hasenfeld, Y., & English, R. A. (1974). *Human Service Organizations.* Ann Arbor, Mich.: University of Michigan Press.

Kahn, E. M. (1984). "The Voluntary Sector Can Remain Alive—and Well." In F. D. Perlmutter (Ed.), *Human Services at Risk* (pp. 57–74). Lexington, Mass.: Lexington Books.

Katz, D. & Kahn, R. L. (1966). *The Social Psychology of Organizations.* New York: John Wiley & Sons.

Kutza, E. A. (1984), "Aging Services and Executive Leadership." In F. D. Perlmutter (Ed.), *Human Services at Risk* (pp. 165–179). Lexington, Mass.: Lexington Books.

Leik, R. K., & Matthews, M. (1967). "A Scale for Developmental Processes." Paper presented at the Pacific Sociological Association Meeting, Long Beach, Calif.

Levine, S., & White, P. (1961). "Exchange As a Conceptual Framework for the Study of Interorganizational Relationships." *Administrative Science Quarterly, 5,* 583–601.

Lynn, L. E., Jr. (1980). *The State and Human Services.* Boston: M.I.T. Press.

McFarlan, F. W. (1984). "Information Technology Changes the Way You Compete." *Harvard Business Review, 84*(3), 98–101.

New York Times, March 11, 1973.

Patti, R. (1983). *Social Welfare Administration: Managing Social Programs in a Developmental Context.* Englewood Cliffs, N.J.: Prentice-Hall.

Perlmutter, F. D. (1969). "A Theoretical Model of Social Agency Development." *Social Casework, 50*(8), 467–473.

Perlmutter, F. D. (1971). "Public Funds and Private Agencies." *Child Welfare, 50*(5), 264–270.

Perlmutter, F. D. (1973). "Prevention and Treatment: A Strategy for Survival." *Community Mental Health Journal, 10*(3), 267–281.

Perlmutter, F. D. (1980). "The Executive Bind." In F. D. Perlmutter & S. Slavin (Eds.), *Leadership in Social Administration* (pp. 53–71). Philadelphia: Temple University Press.

Perlmutter, F. D. (1984). "The Executive in Child Welfare." In F. D. Perlmutter (Ed.), *Human Services at Risk* (pp. 149–163). Lexington, Mass.: Lexington Books.

Perlmutter, F. D., Richan, W. C., & Weirich, T. W. (1979). "Services Integration and Transferability: Implications of the United Services Agency Demonstration Project." *Administration in Social Work, 3*(1), 17–31.

Perlmutter, F. D., & Silverman, H. A. (1972). "The Community Mental Health Center: A Structural Anachronism." *Social Work, 17*(2), 72–85.

Perlmutter, F. D., & Vayda, A. M. (1978). "Barriers to Prevention Programs in Community Mental Health Centers." *Administration in Mental Health, 5*(3), 140–153.

Pfeffer, J., & Salancik, G. (1978). *The External Control of Organizations.* New York: Harper & Row.

President's Commission on Mental Health. (1978). *Report to the President: Vol. 4. Report of the Task Panel on Public Attitudes and Use of the Media for Promotion of Mental Health.* Washington, D.C.: U.S. Government Printing Office.

Richan, W. C. (1980). "The Administrator As Advocate." In F. D. Perlmutter & S. Slavin (Eds.), *Leadership in Social Administration* (pp. 72–85). Philadelphia: Temple University Press.

Selznick, P. (1949). *TVA and the Grass Roots.* Berkeley: University of California Press.

Selznick, P. (1957). *Leadership in Administration.* New York: Harper & Row.

Sidel, V. W. (1971). "New Technologies and the Practice of Medicine." In E. Mendelsohn, J. P. Swazey, & I. Travis (Eds.), *Human Aspects of Biomedical Innovation* (pp. 131–155). Cambridge, Mass.: Harvard University Press.

Steiner, R. (1983). *Managing the Human Service Organization.* Beverly Hills, Calif.: Sage Publications.

Thompson, J. D. (1967). *Organizations in Action.* New York: McGraw-Hill Book Co.

Weatherley, R. (1984). "Approaches to Cutback Management." In F. D. Perlmutter (Ed.), *Human Services at Risk* (pp. 39–56). Lexington, Mass.: Lexington Books.

Webster's Third New International Dictionary. (1961). Springfield, Mass.: G. & C. Merriam Co.

Weiner, H. (1984). "Survival through Coalition: The Case of Addiction Programs." In F. D. Perlmutter (Ed.), *Human Services at Risk* (pp. 197–122). Lexington, Mass.: Lexington Books.

ADMINISTRATION: INTERPERSONAL ASPECTS

The overall goal of social welfare organizations is the provision of high-quality, effective services to the clients and communities they serve. Adequate funding, space, equipment, and community support must be in place, but perhaps the most crucial organizational resource is the people who provide the services. Thus, an important aspect of the social welfare manager's work is the attitudes and behaviors of workers for whom he or she is administratively responsible.

Worker Satisfaction and Performance

Before addressing the skills, behaviors, and strategies that managers employ in their work, it is important to define what is meant by worker satisfaction and performance, since these are two important goals toward which the manager's effort is directed.

Worker satisfaction is the degree to which workers hold positive attitudes and feelings about their work, working conditions, and the employing agency. Considerable research has been conducted to discover the components of worker satisfaction as well as the organizational conditions that promote it. The different definitions of satisfaction that have been used in this research range from an assumption that job satisfaction is a unitary concept ("How satisfied are you with your job?") to definitions that include a number of relatively independent components. One widely used instrument, the Job Descriptive Inventory (JDI), includes five areas: work, pay, opportunities for promotion, supervision, and relationships with coworkers (Smith, Kendall, & Hulin, 1969).

The term "worker performance" also includes a number of concepts. Patti (1983) suggests that performance has four components: productivity, efficiency, quality of service provided, and service effectiveness. Productivity refers to worker output, or quantity of services provided. Efficiency includes two ideas. The first of these—the relationship between resources spent (time and money) and productivity—is often expressed in terms of unit costs, such as the cost of providing one counseling session or an hour of homemaker service. The second involves the relationship between cost and service outcomes, such as the cost of services to help an elderly person live at home rather than in a nursing home (Patti, 1983). Quality of service refers to the competent use of service methods and procedures in accordance with professional or agency standards. Service effectiveness is defined as the degree to which the worker's activities result in the achievement of outcome objectives—for example, improved family functioning as a result of family therapy, or a reduction in psychiatric hospital readmission rates among clients receiving case management services.

Conventional wisdom holds that worker attitudes and behaviors are related— that is, that increased job satisfaction leads to better worker performance. There is evidence, however, that they may be independent: that maximizing one goal may detract from the other. This phenomenon challenges social welfare managers, whose concern is to facilitate both high worker performance and job satisfaction.

Leadership Theory and Research

Leadership is a broad concept encompassing many of the interpersonal aspects of management. Mintzberg (1973), who studied the work of five top-level administrators, identified "leader" as one of ten major roles. He defined leadership as including "virtually all managerial activities involving subordinates" (p. 92). Leadership can also be defined in terms of a manager's social influence—as behavior or characteristics whose aim is directly or indirectly to influence the behavior or attitudes of subordinates.

No commonly accepted theory of leadership exists. Early studies, assuming that leadership consisted of personal traits, examined the physical, social, and psychological characteristics of great historical figures in an attempt to discover the secrets of effective leadership. When the results of these "trait studies" proved inconclusive, research attention turned to defining leader effectiveness in behavioral terms, usually using worker job satisfaction and performance as criteria.

Leader Behavior. During the last 30 years, hundreds of leadership studies have been conducted, many of them designed around the assumption that one set of ideal behaviors constituted effective leadership. Two broad conceptions of leadership received the most extensive attention. The first examines the influence of task-oriented versus relationship-oriented behaviors or combinations of the two. The second—often discussed in terms of "participatory management"—measures the leader's behavior on an autocratic-to-democratic continuum.

Task vs. Relationship. Much of the research examining the extent to which leaders are (or should be) task- or relationship-oriented, or how these two sets of behaviors should be combined, has used a variety of instruments developed at Ohio State University (Halpin & Winer, 1957). These instruments measure two dimensions of behavior labeled "consideration" and "initiation of structure." "Consideration" includes leader behavior indicative of friendship, mutual trust, respect, and warmth (emphasis on relationship). "Initiation of structure" refers to (task-oriented) behavior that organizes and defines roles and establishes organizational patterns, channels of communication, and ways of getting the job done (Yunker & Hunt, 1976).

Many studies were designed to test the proposition that leaders who are both highly task-oriented and considerate toward staff are most likely to promote worker job satisfaction and performance. Generally, the results suggest that leader consideration is positively associated with worker satisfaction but often unrelated to worker performance. One notable exception to this trend is found in the work of Olmstead and Christiansen (1973). They concluded that human service workers who perceived their supervisors as supportive were not only more likely to have higher job satisfaction but also to perform at a higher level. Supervisors' task-oriented behaviors were often associated with higher productivity but also with lower worker job satisfaction. This pattern was particularly apparent when supervisors' task-oriented behaviors were considered as a cluster, not distinguished from one another.

Recent evidence suggests that when task-oriented behaviors are examined separately, different relationships to satisfaction and performance are evident. Schriesheim (1978), for example, distinguishes between behaviors designed to promote role clarity for workers, those that tell workers what work to do, and those that tell workers how to do it. Initial testing suggests that workers respond favorably to role clarification and task assignment but are less satisfied when their supervisors provide a great deal of direction about job content. This suggests that managers should provide the initial structure and clarity that enables workers to understand what their work entails, but that it is possible to oversupervise with regard to how the work is actually done.

Another important body of theory and research is found in the work of McGregor (1960), Agyris (1964), Likert (1967), and Blake and Mouton (1964), who present a "human relations" approach to leadership. Like other theorists, these authors propose a general leadership style thought to be effective in all work situations. They assume that human beings are basically self-directing and self-motivating and that they desire fulfillment and growth. The leadership style that complements this conception of human nature is democratic, supportive, and participatory. The primary function of leadership is to provide workers with freedom to fulfill their own needs and contribute to organizational goals. Likert (1977) summarizes the results of a large number of studies generally supporting the postulate that employees perform better and are more satisfied in organizations that encourage trust, open communication, and worker participation than in those characterized by top-down communication and little worker involvement in decision making. However, because these studies are concerned with organizational properties as well as leader behaviors, their findings are somewhat difficult to translate into specific principles of leadership.

Leadership research has failed to reveal any one best way for leaders to behave under all circumstances. Major reviews of the leadership research—Korman (1966), Kerr et al. (1974), and Bass (1981)—reveal inconclusive results. These reviewers conclude that a major weakness has been the failure to consider other variables (for example, task characteristics or worker personality) that might affect worker response to the leader's behavior.

Some critics have noted the failure to consider other possible influences, such as organizational structure, on worker satisfaction and performance. Still others address the focus of leadership research itself, questioning whether the behavior of the leader is as important as is generally assumed. Katz and Kahn (1978) view leadership as "incremental influence" over and above that exerted by organizational structure and processes. Kerr and Jermier (1978) suggest that such variables as worker skill level, task clarity, and feedback mechanisms may serve as substitutes for leadership under some circumstances. In this view, the concept of leadership substitutes may be particularly applicable to workers in professional organizations because of their high skill levels and professional orientation.

Contingency models have been developed as the complexity of leadership has become more apparent. These models posit the conditions under which relationship- or task-oriented leader behaviors are likely to be the most effective. Widely researched contingency models include Fiedler's (1964) contingency leadership model; path-goal theory, popularized by House (1971); and Hershey and Blanchard's (1977) life-cycle theory of leadership.

Although no single theory or model has been shown to be the most effective in all situations, an important contribution of contingency models is their emphasis on the need for managerial flexibility—that is, for recognition that different work situations may call for different responses. For example, according to Hershey and Blanchard (1977) a worker who is new to the agency or the job may initially need considerable supervision and direction. Path-goal theory suggests that workers whose tasks are routine and clearly specified do not need much direction from the manager and may in fact resent unnecessary supervision. Such workers may need extra support and consideration to compensate for some of the negative reactions to work situations allowing for little worker autonomy and creativity.

Sex-Role Theories. There has been much discussion—and a limited number of studies—of sex-role issues related to managers' task- and relationship-oriented behaviors. Of particular interest is the assertion that male and female managers are likely to behave in terms of sex-role stereotypes; that is, that female managers will be more considerate, warm, and understanding and that male managers are more likely to be task-oriented. This assertion has been used to support the suggestion that women's lack of task orientation may make it more difficult for them to function in managerial roles. Feminist authors (for example, Brandwein, 1981), on the other hand, suggest that management practice would be enhanced by emphasizing behaviors traditionally thought to be female. Most research on the actual behavior of male and female managers has produced mixed results. In the one study reported from the social welfare field, Munson (1979) found that supervisees did not perceive their male and female supervisors as behaving in accordance with sex-role stereotypes.

A second, related theme is that both men and women (but particularly men) prefer male supervisors—that men are more likely to be seen as competent to manage and direct others. Although evidence from research involving hypothetical supervisory situations supports this belief, many studies focusing on actual situations do not provide such support. In Munson's (1979) study, male and female subordinates of female social work supervisors generally reported higher satisfaction with supervision than did those with male supervisors.

A third proposition is that supervisees' satisfaction is related to supervisors' expected sex-role behavior. In other words, women who are managers will be more favorably perceived by subordinates when they are considerate, and men will be evaluated more favorably when they are task-oriented. Although results from a number of studies reviewed by Petty and Odewahn (1983) provided some support for this proposition, their own study of supervision in social welfare agencies did not.

Further study of these complicated issues should help to distinguish myth from reality. Research is needed to understand sex-role phenomena related to current management practice and to develop ways to change counterproductive attitudes and behaviors of workers and managers.

Considerable attention has been given here to issues and research findings pertaining to the mixture of task and relationship behaviors most likely to be effective in facilitating the job satisfaction of people who work in social welfare organizations. Another area that has been the subject of much study and debate is primarily concerned with decision making and examines managerial behavior on an autocratic-to-democratic continuum. These issues are often discussed under the rubric of "participatory management."

Participatory Management. The positive value of a participatory management approach that includes workers in decisions affecting their work "has long been an article of faith," as Patti (1983, p. 168) points out. The general concept of participatory management has been embraced by writers, managers, and practitioners in the social welfare field, but translating it into effective practice is by no means straightforward. To avoid the confusion and controversy that often surround the topic, a clear understanding of the definition and practice of participatory management is necessary.

The concept of participatory management is congruent with the democratic, humanistic values held by many who work in the social welfare field. It can also be argued that because the complex work performed in social welfare organizations is best understood by the staff members who do it, their involvement in decisions will contribute to better problem solving. There is evidence that those who are involved in making a decision are more committed to its implementation, and that worker satisfaction and (in some cases) performance are enhanced by participation in the decision-making process. Such organizational benefits as the control of conflict and enhanced communication have also been demonstrated.

Disagreement about the practice of participatory management relates to two major issues. The first concerns what participatory management is and is not: lack of a common understanding of the concept may produce confusion and conflict among staff in social welfare agencies. The second involves the conditions under which various participatory strategies are appropriate.

In a general sense, the term "participatory management" refers to a management style that encourages and facilitates the involvement of workers in decisions affecting their work. Beyond this general definition, however, lie specific questions: What does participation actually mean? How much influence should staff have? Who makes the final decision?

The most fundamental issue is, of course, the definition of "participation" itself. Somewhere between "autocracy," where the manager makes all the decisions, and "democracy," which suggests that all staff, including the manager, have an equal vote, lies a large area within which the options for staff participation can vary widely. Participation may be defined according to two dimensions: the degree of staff involvement in various issues and the extent to which they actually have influence on what is decided (Vandervelde, 1979).

To illustrate, consider an agency situation where a new intake system is being considered. One manager might meet with staff several times to solicit their opinions about various options but reflect little of their thinking in the final decision. There is some research evidence that in this situation workers are likely to feel that their time has been wasted and resent their lack of influence (Vandervelde, 1979). Another manager might work jointly with a staff task force to design the new system, while a third might give staff a set of principles and budget constraints within which they must operate but turn the actual design of the intake system over to them. In each of these situations, staff involvement would be high, but only in the last two could staff influence how their work would be organized and carried out.

Clearly, participatory management can take many forms, each involving different patterns of staff involvement and various degrees of worker influence. Conflicts arise when the distinction between involvement and influence is not clearly understood and when there are disagreements—usually between management and staff—about the degree of involvement and influence staff members should have.

Another important issue is the degree to which the manager should or can turn over decisions to staff. In the intake example, in no case did the manager abdicate responsibility for the decision, and it would have been improper to do so. Participatory management involves the inclusion of staff in making decisions, but final responsibility for those decisions rests with the manager regardless of the decision-making process.

Enthusiasm for the concept of participatory management has sometimes led its advocates to ignore its limitations or to assert benefits for which there is sparse empirical support. One common assertion is that participation in decision making leads to higher employee job satisfaction and performance. The assertion that participation promotes employee satisfaction is supported by a large number of studies. Worker participation in decisions has been linked to increased satisfaction with supervision and with the employing agency (Hage & Aiken, 1969) and to a positive sense of control and job investment (Ebert & Mitchell, 1975). In a major review of over 100 studies, Locke and Schweiger (1979) found a positive relationship between participation and worker satisfaction in 60 percent of the studies reviewed, a negative relationship in 9 percent, and no relationship between participation and satisfaction in the remaining 30 percent.

Evidence for a link between worker participation and performance is much less solid. Locke and Schweiger (1979) reported that only 13 percent of the studies they reviewed showed a significant positive relationship between participation and worker productivity. There is some evidence that worker participation in decision making in social welfare organizations may contribute to better employee performance in the form of higher quality of services (Holland, 1973; Martin & Segal, 1977). However, the evidence with regard to productivity is largely negative. Glisson and Martin (1980) found that employee productivity was higher in social welfare organizations with a centralized (less participatory) decision-making structure. These results lend some support to the commonly voiced concern that involvement in decision making may reduce productivity and efficiency by diverting time and energy from services to clients.

Questions about the extent of worker involvement often relate to specific decisions. The practice of participatory management therefore involves flexibility and "contingency thinking" on the part of the manager. Different blends of worker involvement and influence will be appropriate depending on the different factors present in a decision situation. These include the nature, scope, and importance of the decision in question; who has the necessary information and expertise; how much staff acceptance is necessary for successful implementation of the decision; and the time frame within which the decision must be made.

Clearly, all staff members cannot be (and probably do not wish to be) included in all decisions. But workers have a very real stake in those issues that affect the way their work is organized and in conditions that facilitate or hinder their ability to provide appropriate services. Although agency staff may not have much say in making the policies that determine what must be done, they can have considerable influence and involvement in decisions about how their work will be structured and carried out.

Ongoing communication provides managers with information about the issues staff members consider important; it also helps to identify workers with particular interests,

knowledge, and expertise relevant to specific decisions. Involving workers in a decision they must implement is likely to improve the quality of the decision and to increase their commitment to its implementation. The decision time frame also determines who can be involved in a particular decision as well as the extent of that involvement. When decisions must be made quickly, an optimal level of participation may not be possible.

A participatory management style can promote worker satisfaction, improve the quality of decisions, facilitate decision implementation, and increase staff members' sense of control and autonomy. But participatory management also involves some costs, such as reduced efficiency and productivity because of the investment of time and energy on the part of workers and managers. Managerial flexibility, commitment, creativity, and efficiency are required to maximize the positive aspects of joint decision making with staff.

Managing Task Groups

Much of the manager's work is done in such settings as staff meetings, task forces, advisory committees, and team meetings, which constitute an important vehicle for accomplishing the goals of the social welfare organization. Meetings can provide an efficient way for staff members to exchange information, give and obtain feedback, distribute tasks, and coordinate their work. Planning and decision-making efforts can benefit from the variety of perspectives, skills, and experience group members can contribute. Unit, or team, meetings also provide an opportunity for mutual support and problem solving focused on specific work-related issues. Meetings can also be boring, frustrating, and unproductive. Without careful planning and skillful leadership, staff groups may drift aimlessly or become immobilized by conflict and indecision. By helping the staff group develop around the goal of high-quality services to clients, the manager or team leader promotes a supportive but task-oriented culture that can contribute to the satisfaction and productivity of team members.

Group Functions: Task and Maintenance. Two major issues, which parallel managerial focus on staff members' productivity and satisfaction, affect every group. The first of these, task accomplishment, focuses on group productivity. It requires that the group be organized to accomplish its purposes, with adequate information, resources, and communication for decision making.

Group maintenance, or preservation of the group as a functioning entity, emphasizes members' satisfaction with the group. This requires attention to their social and emotional needs by creating a cohesive group to which they continue to be attracted. Group maintenance issues include role and status differences, subgroup formation, establishing norms of expected behavior, and the constructive management of conflict.

Effective task groups are organized and conducted in relation to purposes and goals. Members of effective task groups know why they are meeting, what tasks must be accomplished, when they have finished their work, and who has responsibility for carrying out decisions. Without this clear focus, meetings—especially regularly scheduled meetings—may become ends in themselves rather than means for accomplishing the group's tasks.

Maintaining a focus on the task group's purpose requires thought and planning both inside and outside group meetings. Resnick (1982) conceptualizes task group activities as taking place in three related phases: a premeeting, or preparatory, phase; a during-meeting phase; and a follow-up, or postmeeting, phase. The manager's activities in the premeeting phase are at least as important as his or her leadership behavior during the actual meeting. Preparation for the meeting includes establishing its purpose, setting the agenda, and scheduling adequate time. Activities associated with agenda setting are particularly important in helping the group leader and other members prepare for the meeting. Asking members to contribute items to the agenda (and to indicate their relative importance) is a way of increasing staff involvement. This process also provides information about important staff concerns; allowing the group leader to set priorities among topics and plan for any special problems that may arise during the meeting. The agenda should be set far enough in advance to obtain any additional resources (for example, consultants or information) that may be required.

Written reports or proposals should also be provided in advance so that members are prepared to make informed decisions instead of consuming valuable meeting time with efforts to digest large volumes of written material.

Activities during the meeting include agenda building, recording the minutes, conducting the meeting, and providing for review and task assignment (Resnick, 1982). The agenda should be reviewed at the beginning of the meeting to allow for the addition of important items and to establish the order in which items will be addressed and the time allotted to each. The most important items should be scheduled for the middle third of the meeting, when the most members are likely to be present and to be the most attentive (Tropman, 1980).

Responsibility for conducting each meeting should be assumed by a chairperson or facilitator. Major functions of this role include maintaining the integrity of the agenda, ensuring that all members have an opportunity to participate, clarifying and summarizing discussion, and facilitating the decision-making process. The chair or facilitator role can be assumed by the manager or can be rotated among group members. Rotation encourages all members to assume responsibility for the group and promotes the development of leadership skills among group members.

Voting (majority rule) and consensus approaches are probably the most commonly used decision-making procedures in social welfare organizations, and each has advantages and limitations. Voting, while relatively efficient in terms of time, may leave a dissatisfied minority with little investment in the decision. Although consensus decision making has many advantages, it requires time and a high degree of commitment to create a solution acceptable to all members. Attempts at decision making by consensus are often truncated when members become fatigued or unwilling or unable to resolve conflicts. This phenomenon results in "quasi-consensus," a condition of apparent agreement in which unexpressed conflict and dissatisfaction remain.

The postmeeting phase involves following up on decisions and assignments made during the meeting, developing plans for implementing decisions, and gathering additional resources needed to translate decisions into action (Resnick, 1982).

Group Development. Knowledge and skills about how groups develop over time is also essential to promoting effective task groups. Although theoretical models (for example, Tuckman, 1965; Garland, Jones, & Kolodny, 1965) assign different labels to the stages of group development, common concepts can be identified.

Newly formed groups are characterized by dependence on the leader for direction, and by some degree of caution and uncertainty on the part of members. Members are often concerned with creating a favorable impression and with evaluating whether or how the group will meet their individual needs. During this initial phase, the group leader's tasks include helping members to discover common values and interests and promoting the development of group norms, or rules for behavior. Achieving some degree of mutual understanding and agreement about group goals is crucial during this period. As group members begin to be invested in the group, the leader also seeks ways to deemphasize his or her central role, encouraging members to assume more responsibility for group tasks and processes.

Managers holding unit meetings for the first time can promote the development of group goals by encouraging members to express their expectations for the group, and by clearly stating their own. Through discussion and negotiation, common goals can be derived. The manager comes to the group with more authority than the workers in the unit, and because supervisees often expect the manager to be "in charge" and to assume responsibility for the meetings, it may be difficult to encourage them to assume leadership within the group. Rotating the role of facilitator and encouraging staff members to give their opinions first are mechanisms that can help to reduce the manager's central role.

As group members become more invested in and responsible for the direction of the group, conflict commonly develops about goals and ways of accomplishing them. Challenges to group leadership are characteristic of this phase. This phase is troubling to the manager and other group members both because of the unpleasantness involved and feelings that the group effort is floundering.

During this period it is important to acknowledge the conflict, discuss differences openly, and maintain a focus on the overall purpose of the group. Understanding that conflict is "normal" at this stage, and that successfully addressing it will strengthen the group's problem-solving ability and cohesiveness, can help the manager and group members to maintain their investment in the group. Groups without such understanding and investment may be prematurely abandoned because of their inability to manage conflict.

After successfully managing the conflict stage, the group can turn its attention to accomplishing the tasks it has set itself. During this "performing" stage (Tuckman, 1965), the group is goal-directed, tasks are distributed among group members according to ability and preference, and group productivity is high. Problem-solving and communication skills learned during the conflict stage can be applied to new problems, which are more easily handled. As members assume major responsibility for accomplishing the work of the group, the manager can become more of a facilitator or resource person than a leader.

These stages of group development are usually not clear cut or linear. Groups move back and forth from one mode of functioning to another, particularly in response to changes in membership or new demands imposed from outside. Knowledge of group development and processes can help the manager to understand these phenomena and intervene appropriately to promote group effectiveness.

Intervening in Conflict Situations

The management research and practice literature has given scant attention to effective conflict management skills. This is not surprising, because conflict is often seen as an unusual, negative event that is best avoided. Realistically, however, conflict is a normal and unavoidable organizational phenomenon that can arise when resources are scarce, under conditions of change and uncertainty, when there are differences in basic beliefs about desirable goals or means for achieving them, and where there are differences in status and power. Because all these conditions characterize social welfare (and other) organizations, some degree of conflict is thus inevitable and may be read as a sign of the organization's vitality. Katz (1964) has made the suggestion that "organizations without internal conflict are on the way to dissolution" (p. 114).

Unmanaged conflict may result in difficult working relationships. Lack of cooperation, inhibited communication, and other by-products of conflict can lower staff satisfaction and productivity by diverting time, energy, and effort from client service. However, conflict can also serve positive functions, such as identifying important problems and providing an impetus for needed change. Slavin (1978) suggests that conflict can sharpen interest in the issues at stake, clarify alternatives, distinguish divergent points of view, and deepen analysis. Properly managed, conflict can foster the development of better problem-solving skills and stimulate innovative solutions.

Conflict Management. The term "conflict management" is used here rather than "conflict resolution" to describe the ongoing process of dealing constructively with conflict. Some small, discrete issues may be permanently resolved, but because conflict is related to the distribution of power and resources, most "solutions" are effective only until a change occurs. Conflict management involves four basic steps: (1) recognition of conflict or potential conflict, (2) assessment of the conflict situation, (3) selection of an appropriate strategy, and (4) intervention.

Conflict may be overtly expressed in verbal or physical encounters. Because many people tend to avoid such confrontations, however, conflict in organizations is often expressed indirectly. Staff members may avoid working together, treat each other with excessive politeness, use sarcasm or aggressive humor, or complain to others. The manager may also receive complaints, requests to rule on issues, or requests for transfer from the work unit. Direct questioning of those who appear to be involved will often confirm the presence of conflict.

Assessing the conflict situation involves accurate identification of the sources of conflict and the individuals or groups involved. Conflict always involves two or more parties and is thus by definition interpersonal. It may occur between individuals, within teams, among different work units in an organization, or between organizations. Be-

cause it is expressed interpersonally, conflict is often explained as a relationship problem or personality clash. Although such explanations may be accurate, other possibilities should be investigated because different interventions are appropriate depending on the source of the conflict.

Sources of conflict may include personality differences and contrasting beliefs, values, or reference group identities—for example, interracial or intercultural conflict, conflict between the sexes, or conflict between disciplines (Slavin, 1978). Structural problems may also give rise to conflict. Unclear assignment of responsibility for tasks or lack of clear work procedures can lead to disputes over territory, particularly when new work demands or new personnel are added. Agencies or unit structures that promote physical or social isolation or status and salary discrepancies may increase competition and conflict within or between work groups. Zander (1983) emphasizes the importance of careful assessment to distinguish real disagreements from those caused by unclear or incomplete communication.

Once the source of conflict has been identified, strategies can be selected. Structural and interpersonal strategies can be applied separately or in combination. Structural strategies may include reorganizing and clarifying work assignments, developing work procedures, and addressing salary and status inequities. Reducing physical or social isolation may be accomplished by such interventions as moving the office of a staff "outsider" to a more central location or changing part-time staff members' work schedules so that they can attend staff meetings.

If the conflict appears intractable—as in the case of severe value differences—distancing, or separating the parties to a conflict, may be accomplished by transfer or changes in work assignments. Structural strategies that remove conflict-causing conditions may obviate the necessity for direct intervention with the parties to a conflict (Zander, 1983).

When the source of conflict is not amenable to structural intervention, face-to-face strategies may be the methods of choice. Bargaining and negotiation are particularly appropriate when the conflict situation involves scarce material resources that can be divided, scheduled, or distributed among the parties. Satisfactory compromises involving use of space, equipment, or secretarial time, for example, can often be achieved in this way. Problem-solving, or "integrative," strategies are often advanced as the most desirable (Zander, 1983; Slavin, 1978) because they are directed toward achieving a solution to the conflict, and can result in improvement in individual or group functioning. Problem solving involves establishing an accurate and commonly understood description of the problem, identifying possible solutions, agreeing about the most desirable alternative, and implementing the decision. Because problem solving requires a high degree of commitment, time, and energy, it may not be practical in all conflict situations.

Integrative solutions may be the most appropriate in those conflict situations that involve differences in work-related beliefs or values, conflicts over work group goals or methods for achieving them, and other substantive issues that impinge on working relationships. Because conflicts about incompatible values are often impossible to resolve, efforts may be directed toward developing agreements about "peaceful coexistence."

Each step in the problem-solving process may be fraught with difficulties because antagonism and disrupted communication are likely to be present. Zander (1983) suggests several strategies that may increase the effectiveness of problem solving in such situations: (1) have each speaker accurately paraphrase what the opponent has said before stating his or her side of the argument; (2) act out for opponents how they present their cases to increase their understanding of how they are perceived; (3) have parties to the conflict list their similarities and points of agreement; (4) ask opponents to identify the needs of others who may be invested in the outcome of the conflict; (5) seek superordinate goals valued by all, toward which solutions can be directed; (6) agree on values that can be used to evaluate possible solutions; and (7) ask each party to agree explicitly to make concessions to meet the other party's needs.

The effective management of conflict demands creativity, persistence, and at least a small amount of courage from managers. Understanding the conditions that promote conflict can also enable managers to prevent potential conflict situations by structural or interpersonal intervention.

The quality and effectiveness of the services provided by social welfare organizations depend on the attitudes and behaviors of the staff members who deliver them. Awareness of the interpersonal aspects of management can promote worker job satisfaction and performance. A working knowledge of leadership theories, effective task group skills, and conflict management strategies are important tools for the social welfare manager in creating and maintaining a goal-oriented, supportive work situation.

BARBARA J. FRIESEN

For further information, see ADMINISTRATION IN SOCIAL WELFARE; ORGANIZATIONS: IMPACT ON EMPLOYEES AND COMMUNITY; PERSONNEL MANAGEMENT; STAFF-INITIATED ORGANIZATIONAL CHANGE; SUPERVISION IN SOCIAL WORK.

References

Agyris, C. (1964). *Integrating the Individual and the Organization.* New York: John Wiley & Sons.

Bass, B. M. (1981). *Stogdill's Handbook of Leadership.* New York: Free Press.

Blake, R. R., & Mouton, J. J. (1964). *The Managerial Grid.* Houston, Tex.: Gulf Publishing Co.

Brandwein, R. A. (1981). "Toward the Feminization of Community and Organization Practice." *Social Development Issues, 5*(2–3), 180–193.

Ebert, R. J., & Mitchell, T. R. (1975). *Organizational Decision Processes.* New York: Crane, Russak & Company.

Fiedler, F. E. (1964). "A Contingency Model for the Prediction of Leadership Effectiveness." In L. Berkowitz (Ed.), *Advances in Experimental Psychology* (Vol. 1, pp. 150–190). New York: Academic Press.

Garland, J., Jones, H., & Kolodny, R. (1965). "A Model for Stages of Development in Social Work Groups." In S. Bernstein (Ed.), *Explorations in Group Work,* (pp. 12–53). Boston: Boston University School of Social Work.

Glisson, C., & Martin, P. Y. (1980). "Productivity and Efficiency in Human Service Organizations as Related to Structure, Size and Age." *Academy of Management Journal, 23*(1), 21–37.

Hage, J. & Aiken, M. (1969). *Social Change in Complex Organizations.* New York: Random House.

Halpin, A. W., & Winer, B. J. (1957). "A Factorial Study of the Leader Behavior Descriptions."

In R. M. Stogdill & A. E. Coons (Eds.), *Leader Behavior: Its Description and Measurement*. Columbus: Ohio State University, Bureau of Business Research.

Hershey, P., & Blanchard, K. H. (1977). *Management of Organizational Behavior: Utilizing Human Resources* (3rd ed.). Englewood Cliffs, N.J.: Prentice-Hall.

Holland, T. P. (1973). "Organizational Structure and Institutional Care." *Journal of Health and Social Behavior, 14*(3), 241–251.

House, R. J. (1971). "A Path-Goal Theory of Leadership." *Administrative Science Quarterly, 16*(3), 321–338.

Katz, D. (1964). "Approaches to Managing Conflict." In R. L. Kahn & E. Boulding (Eds.), *Power and Conflict in Organizations* (p. 114). New York: Basic Books.

Katz, D., & Kahn, R. L. (1978). *The Social Psychology of Organizations* (2nd ed.). New York: John Wiley & Sons.

Kerr, S., et al. (1974). "Toward a Contingency Theory of Leadership Based upon the Consideration and Initiating Structure Literature." *Organizational Behavior and Human Performance. 12*(1), 62–82.

Kerr, S., & Jermier, J. J. (1978). "Substitutes for Leadership: Their Meaning and Measurement." *Organizational Behavior and Human Performance, 22*(2), 375–403.

Korman, A. K. (1966). " 'Consideration,' 'Initiating Structure,' and Organizational Criteria—A Review." *Personnel Psychology, 19*(4), 349–361.

Likert, R. (1967). *The Human Organization*. New York: McGraw-Hill Book Co.

Likert, R. (1977). *Past and Future Perspectives on System 4*. Ann Arbor, Mich.: Rensis Likert Associates, 1977.

Locke, E. A., & Schweiger, D. M. (1979). "Participation in Decision-Making: One More Look." In B. M. Staw (Ed.), *Research in Organizational Behavior* (pp. 265–339). Greenwich, Conn.: JAI Press.

Martin, P. Y., & Segal, B. (1977). "Bureaucracy, Size, and Staff Expectations for Client Independence in Halfway Houses." *Journal of Health and Social Behavior, 18*(4), 376–390.

McGregor, D. (1960). *The Human Side of Enterprise*. New York: McGraw-Hill Book Co.

Mintzberg, H. (1973). *The Nature of Managerial Work*. New York: Harper & Row.

Munson, C. E. (1979). "Evaluation of Male and Female Supervisors." *Social Work, 24*(2), 104–110.

Olmstead, J. A., & Christiansen, H. E. (1973). *Research Report No. 2: Effects of Agency Work Contexts: An Intensive Field Study* (Vol. 1). Washington, D.C.: Department of Health, Education and Welfare, Social and Rehabilitation Service.

Patti, R. (1983). *Social Welfare Administration*. Englewood Cliffs, N.J.: Prentice-Hall.

Petty, M. M., & C. A. Odewahn (1983). "Supervisory Behavior and Sex Role Stereotypes in Human Service Organizations." *The Clinical Supervisor, 1*(2), 13–20.

Resnick, H. B. (1982). "Facilitating Productive Staff Meetings." In M. J. Austin & W. E. Hershey (Eds.), *Handbook on Mental Health Administration* (pp. 183–199). San Francisco: Jossey-Bass.

Schriesheim, C. A. (1978). "Development, Validation, and Application of New Leadership Behavior and Expectancy Instruments." Doctoral dissertation, Ohio State University.

Slavin, S. (1978). "Concepts of Social Conflict." In S. Slavin (Ed.), *Social Administration* (pp. 521–540). New York: Haworth Press and Council on Social Work Education.

Smith, P. C., Kendall, L. M., & Hulin, C. L. (1969). *The Measurement of Satisfaction in Work and Retirement*. Chicago: Rand McNally & Co.

Tropman, J. E. (1980). *Effective Meetings*. Beverly Hills, Calif.: Sage Publications.

Tuckman, B. W. (1965). "Developmental Sequence in Small Groups." *Psychological Bulletin, 63*(6), 384–399.

Vandervelde, M. (1979). "The Semantics of Participation." *Administration in Social Work, 3*(1), 65–77.

Yunker, G. W., & Hunt, J. G. (1976). "An Empirical Comparison of the Michigan Four-Factor and Ohio State LBDQ Leadership Scales." *Organizational Behavior and Human Performance, 17*(1), 45–65.

Zander, A. (1983). *Making Groups Effective*. San Francisco: Jossey-Bass.

ADMINISTRATION IN SOCIAL WELFARE

Social welfare agencies are confronted with major challenges in the 1980s because of internal and external constraints on organizational behavior. The latter, however, in particular, pose serious dilemmas because these agencies cannot significantly change environmental conditions. Among the major external challenges are (1) the decrease in economic resources for social services relative to other societal priorities; (2) the global distribution of resources, which influences national and industrial planning throughout the world; (3) the development of the information industry and its related technologies; (4) major demographic shifts in the population; and (5) changes in the interrelationships between capitalism, the welfare state, and the American family.

The size and complexity of the social welfare industry continue to grow despite these constraints. In the United States, social welfare is ranked as the tenth largest industry with regard to the personnel employed. However, the vast majority of personnel is not professionally trained in social work, and only a small minority is trained in social work administration. Thus, problems related to performance and accountability arise just when demands in these sectors are viewed as priorities.

The changing roles of men and women and the rapid aging of the population in the postindustrial society also pose special challenges. Given current sociodemographic characteristics, general societal values, and family structures, it is unlikely that the social welfare industry will decline in the foreseeable future, despite the scarcity of resources and the changes in public policy that characterized the early 1980s. However, it is also apparent that, because of external constraints on growth, the industry will not grow as rapidly in the future as it did between 1950 and 1980. In addition, the industry is changing rapidly because of growth in the provision of social services by profit-making institutions. Some argue that the methods and incentives of capitalism have vitiated the industry's essential values of concern for the well-being of everyone.

History

Social administration has long been recognized as the generic method of social work in Western Europe and in Canada. In the United States, however, greater emphasis has been placed on direct-service methods of interpersonal intervention targeted on individuals as the focus of change, rather than on structural or systemic change in social institutions and programs. Moreover, administrative functions were customarily performed by people without professional social work training.

Beginning in 1900 and continuing through World War II, there was partial acknowledgment of public welfare administration as a professional responsibility.

Among others, Abbott (1931), Street (1931), and Atwater (1940) outlined directives for practice in administration and recommended that agency executives be trained in social work. Although courses in social work administration date back to 1914, the social work profession was slow to accept administration as a bona fide professional method (Atwater, 1940). The professional organizations resisted recognizing administration as a method. The Council on Social Work Education (CSWE) further hindered acceptance of administration with its curriculum policy statements and accreditation criteria, rejecting administration as a method equivalent to casework in which students could be fully trained. Instead, there was a preference for either promoting excellent casework practitioners to administrative positions or for selecting trained administrators from other professions to fill these positions.

With the change in CSWE curriculum policy in 1962, professional training in social work administration was approved, and a number of schools developed programs. The National Association of Social Workers (NASW) also encouraged training in administration, and the federal government provided financial support for formal training. The dominant orientation was one that recognized the common elements of administration in all organizations but also emphasized the development of social work administration as a special variant because it required knowledge of social problems, services, and values. Administration was viewed as a cumulative responsibility shared by all organizational members, and its key function was to enable individuals and groups within the social agency to maximize their participation and contribution to the organization voluntaristically (Trecker, 1946).

Social welfare programs, expenditures, and clientele expanded considerably in the 1960s and 1970s. Training in administration was supported by the professional organizations, by the federal government (in the form of specialty training and demonstration grants), and by those states in which opportunities rapidly opened up. However, as Patti (1983) has noted, training programs in social work administration per se grew slowly. During the period of growth in the civil rights and welfare rights movements in the United

States, many people expressed the concern that, because it was associated with maintenance of the status quo, existing administrative practice in social welfare was part of the problem rather than a potential solution. This factor slowed the development of administration within the profession.

Federal spending for all social programs grew from $24 billion in 1960 to $314 billion in 1980, representing an increase of 460 percent in constant 1980 dollars (Meyer, 1984). Overall, that equaled an increase from 28.5 percent to 54.1 percent of all federal budget outlays. State and local governments and the voluntary sector also increased their support of and funding for social programs, although not to the extent of the federal government.

As the social welfare system grew in size and complexity, concern about the control and management of this vast enterprise increased. With the politics of scarcity in the late 1970s and 1980s, greater emphasis was placed on retrenchment and on knowledge of technical management in the planning, implementation, maintenance, and evaluation of programs. The threat that administrators trained in social work would be replaced by individuals trained in business or public administration became increasingly apparent in many states (Gummer, 1979). As external control over resources became more prevalent and as uncertainty increased, the need for administrators who were skilled in the sociopolitical arena became evident. Brannon (1985) points out that agency administrators increasingly find themselves in a squeeze between an anarchic organizational reality and rationalistic demands from the environment. The organizational solution has frequently been to select an administrator who possesses only technical management skills, ignoring substantive and ethical policy issues.

In summary, the administration of social welfare agencies grew substantially in size and complexity between 1970 and 1985, but professionally trained social workers continued to compose only a minority of all administrators in these agencies. Both professional associations and schools of social work were reluctant to give high priority to the training and placement of social workers for management positions in social welfare agencies.

Area of Practice

Administration is accepted as one of the basic methods of social work practice, but it is also more broadly conceived to include responsibility for goal attainment and organizational maintenance activities in social welfare. It shares this responsibility with public, hospital, and educational administration and, even more generally, with the management of a broad sector of private and quasi-public human service organizations. Since 1980, the distinction between administration in the public and private sectors as well as between administration in the human services and the business and industrial sectors has become obscure in the United States. However, this change appears not to have occurred in other countries where public social services are accepted as a core part of the commitment to the welfare state.

In discussions of management, contemporary authors have emphasized structural and behavioral aspects, rational-technical elements, resource and environmental constraints, and political controls. The dramatic changes in social welfare in the United States since 1980 have pointed to administration as an essentially political process that is concerned with when, why, how, and to whom services are allocated. In this context, administration assumes even greater importance as a core social work method (Perlmutter & Slavin, 1980).

Definitions are inevitably culture- and time-bound, reflecting the development of knowledge and of societal values and professional ideologies. Thus, developments in administration in the 1980s are a consequence of modifications in the external environment that center on efficiency, privatization, accountability, cutback management, computerization, and standardization rather than on distributive justice, solutions to major social problems, effective service delivery, and the enhancement of human rights (Richan, 1983).

Any definition of administration is arbitrary and contentious because of the many differences in the conception of its domain and correlates. However, there is substantial consensus for a broad definition of administration in social welfare. Within a single organization, administration is the sum of all the processes involved in:

1. Formulation of policy and its translation into operative goals

2. Program design and implementation
3. Funding and resource allocation
4. Management of internal and interorganizational operations
5. Personnel direction and supervision
6. Organizational representation and public relations
7. Community education
8. Monitoring, evaluation, and innovation to improve organizational productivity.

Some authors have distinguished administration and management as distinct processes, and others have treated them as essentially synonymous concepts. Although the above definition lists management as part of administration, it is accepted that this distinction is more or less arbitrary (Alexander, 1982; Patti, 1983; Slavin, 1981). Mintzberg's (1973) delineation of management roles includes those that are commonly accepted in social work administration. However, in the social work literature, the role of the manager is expanded to include responsibility for resource development, public relations, and community representation. In contrast, the literature in Western Europe often treats management as a broad concept, defining administration as internal organizational responsibility.

In human service organizations, administrative activities are directed toward the achievement of effective services for clients in accordance with the values and laws of society. These activities are emphasized differentially, depending on geography, politics, clients, technologies, and professional ideologies. This does not presume that one individual will perform all these tasks; rather, it is expected that administration will be performed by several individuals at different levels of the organizational structure. A few or many people share administrative responsibilities, depending on the size and structure of the organization.

There is substantial debate as to whether social administration differs from administration in private entrepreneurial businesses and in industrial organizations (Cyert, 1975; Drucker, 1980; Stein, 1981). Undoubtedly, there is a body of knowledge common to business and public and social administration. Yet there is also distinctive knowledge related to the substantive problems and mission of an organization. Stein (1981) argues that human service organiza-

tions do not have distinctive features. However, a substantial body of empirically based knowledge supports the perspective that—because the human qualities of clients provide the raw material and product of the organization—there are substantive differences in goals and objectives and in means that may be employed to attain them.

According to this perspective, administration includes the formulation of policy and the delivery of service, in addition to the management activities of coordination, control, and integration of agency operations. The administrator's responsibility includes the translation of policy into programs as well as policy innovation and change (Richan, 1983; Selznick, 1957). Responsibilities in the area of service delivery include monitoring the quality and responsiveness of the delivery system rather than providing services per se.

Theoretical Foundations

Management principles have been developed from practice-derived, codified empirical generalizations and from theories of organizational behavior. Social administration has borrowed extensively from the disciplines of sociology and political science and from the professions of public, and health, industrial, and business administration. Theories have centered on the nature and structure of the organization and on issues affecting organizational behavior. Most of the contemporary social administration literature is eclectic and is based on several theories of organizational behavior.

During the 1960s and 1970s there was substantial growth in the management literature generally and in social welfare particularly. Although the latter cannot be said to have contributed significantly to organizational theory, the work of Patti (1983) on organizational development, of Vinter (1985) on program design and fiscal management, of Austin (1983) on administrative complexity, and of Gummer (1984) on the impact of reduced resources, loose structures, and managerial ambition has added to knowledge of the political aspects of organizational behavior. Others, including Perrow, Zald, Street, and Hage, have done much of their research in human service organizations.

Classical Scientific Management Theories. Historically, organizational theory has undergone substantial change as organizations have grown in size and complexity. Weber first defined the attributes of bureaucracy and demonstrated that it was both a cause and a consequence of societal change. His early work on rational-legal authority was a major foundation of contemporary administration theory. The scientific management theories of Frederick Taylor, Mary Follett, Lyndall Urwick, and others incorporated Weberian theory but also sought to optimize efficiency and effectiveness through the application of scientifically based principles from industrial engineering and other professions.

The recent emphasis on technology and productivity has created a resurgence of interest in scientific management theory (Cook & Russell, 1980; Elkin & Molitor, 1984). This resurgence is particularly apparent in operations management and systems theory—both concerned with scientifically based management principles for productive transformation of inputs into outputs in an organizational context. (Operations management deals primarily with design, scheduling, operations, and control within a systems framework.)

All scientific management theories assume external sources of goals, uniformity of events, immutability of structural patterns, and precise allocation of authority and responsibility. Informal relations and social organization are largely disregarded. It is expected that people can be taught how to behave productively within the organization, although some systems theorists emphasize ways in which individuals cope with indeterminacy and even anarchy (Brannon, 1985).

Human Relations Theories. A second major influence on administration, human relations theories remain significant today for the human services. These theories are based on four assumptions:

1. Workers are viewed as motivated more by sociopsychological rather than economic rewards.

2. Individual productivity is determined primarily by group norms.

3. Leadership and communication styles critically influence worker behavior.

4. Excessive specialization is dysfunctional.

The literature on these theories, which emphasizes the sociopsychological problems of bureaucracies, includes the work of such authors as Chester Barnard, Rensis Likert, Robert Kahn and Daniel Katz, and Chris Argyris. Research has focused on employee morale and productivity; on satisfaction, motivation, and leadership; and on the dynamics of small-group behavior in organizations. The focus on individual performance assumes that organizational goals and individual interests are compatible. Human relations theories have had a special appeal to administrators of human service organizations because of their compatibility with the predominant interpersonal technologies, with notions about the relative importance of client commitment and motivation, and with the assumption that the quality of interactions among staff critically influences the roles of both staff and clients.

Structuralist Models. Perhaps the largest number of organizational theorists can be broadly classified as structuralists. Most structuralists incorporate both structure and process in their formulations but place more emphasis on one than the other. Herbert Simon (1976), one of the early structuralists, developed the concept of public administration theory but later moved on to more general aspects of organizational behavior. He and his colleagues were responsible for the focus on decision-making theories that addressed nonrational as well as rational aspects of behavior, and to some extent they represent a bridge to the human relations theorists. March and Simon (1958) identified "bounded rationality," "satisficing," and "uncertainty absorption" as critical decisional strategies in organizational problem solving.

The structural functional theories of Hage (1980), Woodward (1965), Thompson (1967), Hall (1982), Drucker (1980), Perrow (1979), Kanter (1977), and Goodsell (1983) direct attention to such variables as goal implementation, environmental relations, power, and centralization and to such characteristics as interdependence, adaptation, informal relations, participation and representation, and unanticipated consequences. These theories assume that bureaucratization is a continuously changing process that arises from the interactions between extra- and intraorganizational phenomena.

The work of Mintzberg (1979) on structure, Kanter (1977) on power and differential participation, and Galbraith (1973) on liaison devices has directed attention to matrix structures and has led to a wider variety of alternative organizational forms. These latter approaches are particularly useful for social welfare agencies, which often have more horizontal structures and multiple interdependencies than do other types of agencies. Structuralists have also called attention to the legitimation and status of the goals of the organization in the larger society as crucial determinants of its behavior.

Contingency theory is an adaptation of structural theory that addresses the structural variations among organizations and calls attention to the importance of planned organizational design. The work of Lawrence and Lorsch (1967) and Hickson et al. (1971) is representative of these theories, which emphasize environmental demands and contingencies and the attributes of technologies as determinants of variable structures.

Political economy theories are exemplified by the work of Hasenfeld (1983) and Zald (1978). Although these authors can be classified as structuralists, they are primarily concerned with political factors in the external and internal environments as critical determinants of behavior. Attention is directed to the processes through which power and legitimation are differentially acquired and distributed; and organizational goals, strategies, and rewards are viewed as deriving from exchanges between contending parties within the organization and the external environment. Behavior that might otherwise appear nonrational is seen as rational within the political decisional context. Effective administrators are viewed as active participants in the political contexts within and between organizations rather than as bureaucratic technicians. Austin (1983) and Gummer (1985) argue that political economy theories are particularly pertinent for social welfare agencies because of the greater administrative complexity of these agencies and because of the effort that must be devoted to dealing with political factors if an agency is to be effective.

One of the more provocative approaches to organizational theory has been the "garbage can" model of March and Olsen (1976), subsequently adapted by Street (1979) in his study of public welfare. This model views organizations as organized anarchies that face high levels of uncertainty, both internally and externally, and that have ambiguous goals and indeterminate technologies. Because of these attributes, it is suggested that four interacting elements are critical foci for administrative decision making: problems, solutions, participants, and choice behavior. Choice behavior refers to situations in which there is potential for the resolution of problems and situations and for definitive decision making, including avoidance and oversight. Conventional notions about rationality in managerial decision making are challenged, and political strategies are often substituted for them.

Systems Theories. These theories represent an attempt to synthesize structuralist and human relations perspectives. They attempt to incorporate other theories in efforts to formulate more general theory. Systems theorists begin with the assumption that a bureaucracy is a social system with several subsystems that are capable of performing various functions such as maintenance, production, boundary maintenance, adaptation, and management (Katz & Kahn, 1978). The organization, regardless of its goals, is viewed as analogous to a biological system— an organic whole of interrelated interdependent parts. Rationality is deemphasized, and consideration is given instead to ways of coping with indeterminacy and inconsistency.

Although they are still in the developmental stage, theories of organizational behavior that address gender similarities and differences are receiving increased attention. Kanter's (1977) study of men and women in a corporation argues that attitudes, beliefs, and behavior are a function of organizational and hierarchical structures. The concepts of power and opportunity and the gender distribution in corporate subunits are viewed as predictors of morale, satisfaction, and productivity. Women and minorities tend to occupy lower positions in the organizational hierarchy and to have less power and less opportunity for promotion. To a considerable extent, their behavior is a consequence of these statuses. Kanter argues further, as does Hage (1980), that power is critical to the effective behavior of people in organizations, because without it most individuals are incapacitated.

Kanter influenced several authors who have studied human service organizations, including Norman and Mancusco (1983) and Perlmutter and Alexander (1978). Norman and Mancusco observed that administration is traditionally defined as rational and task oriented and, therefore, the domain of the male—even in a female-dominated profession. Sarri (1984) observed that among top executives in social welfare agencies, males and females were sharply differentiated with regard to the relative importance placed on meeting the demands of personal, professional, and organizational roles. Males and females also differed in that females placed greater emphasis on interpersonal relations, on participatory decision making, on contingency planning, and on collective leadership. The preference of females for horizontal and matrix rather than vertical structures has been repeatedly observed, as has their emphasis on consensual and participatory decision making (Josefowitz, 1980; Kravetz & Austin, 1984).

This brief and incomplete review of the major organizational theories highlights the multidisciplinary nature of the knowledge base from which the principles of administrative practice can be developed. Although there is no general consensus on the "best" theory, Astley and Van den Ven (1983) point to the value of synthesis among these various theories for application to management. The interest of most theorists in delineating the major dimensions of organizational behavior has provided a basis for interpenetration, as have large-scale comparative studies of a variety of organizations.

Methodological advancements have enhanced the abilities of researchers to handle large sets of data in comparative studies of organizations. The broad approach of systems theory permits analyses of behavior at several different levels, concern about interfaces, and the transformation of units and objects of analysis. Traditional theory has been prematurely concerned with closed-system characteristics and with unidimensional perception of behavior. The greater emphasis today on open-system approaches, on interorganizational exchange, on environmental constraints, on developmental patterns, on evaluation and accountability, and on participatory decision making is expected to aid the development of additional knowledge that has application to administration.

Functions and Roles

Administrative functions are performed through a series of interactive activities that include:

1. Setting and ordering goals
2. Planning the means for goal attainment, including the acquisition of needed material and nonmaterial resources
3. Controlling and coordinating the performance of organizational members
4. Negotiating and problem solving
5. Developing and motivating staff
6. Communicating and managing information
7. Monitoring the quality and quantity of services delivered to clients
8. Assessing future needs of the organization
9. Representing the organization in the external environment.

These activities are performed at the institutional level, where the organization interacts with the environment in setting goals, obtaining resources, communicating, and representing the organization; at the managerial level, where activities involve planning, designing, directing, allocating, coordinating, communicating, monitoring, innovating, and evaluating; and at the technical level, which is concerned with such activities as client intake and processing, the development, maintenance, and integration of technology, staff supervision and development, quality control and assessment, and innovation in services and their delivery. Although each of these sectors has distinct functions, there is overlap among them. Moreover, events and how they are managed at one level influence subsequent behavior at the other levels.

Mintzberg (1973) has identified administrative roles in relation to three sectors: interpersonal (figurehead, leader, liaison, representative), informational (monitor, disseminator, and spokesperson), and decisional (entrepreneur, disturbance handler, resource allocator, and negotiator). Patti's (1983) formulation of organizational development in program administration builds on Mintzberg's formulation. Authors such as

Levinson (1981) and Selznick (1957) emphasize the roles of administrator as leader and innovator. Each of these approaches has disadvantages when viewed separately, but together they provide a more complete understanding of administrative roles.

The Mintzberg approach can be linked to various organizational structures that help in understanding the substantive and technical requirements of the various roles. It also highlights the differential knowledge and skill needed for the performance of each. Levinson emphasizes leadership, pointing out that effective organizations require excellence in the performance of executive roles because leaders provide rewards and expertise in addition to the legitimate and coercive power of formally delegated authority. Social welfare administrators face particular problems because their exercise of formal power is often constrained, although standards for performance and accountability are not lowered. Frequently, the use of alternative types of social power and staff participation in decision making are the only ways in which such dilemmas can be resolved.

Proactive and reactive strategies of administrative behavior are best understood in the context of leadership style and roles. The importance of a proactive style was noted by Derthick (1975), who argued that such behavior was a major factor in the expansions of federal social welfare programs in the 1960s and early 1970s. Since that time, leadership has been reactive to the initiatives of politicians, who have stressed retrenchment and elimination of social welfare programs. Not surprisingly, programs for the poor, minorities, the disabled, and the handicapped have suffered most because they have relatively weak constituencies with which to influence political decision makers.

Patti's studies (1983) indicate that administrators in social service organizations tend to spend more time on organizational maintenance and control functions rather than on activities related to goal attainment, such as planning, directing, procuring resources, innovating, and representing the organization. Cyert (1975) notes that administrators of nonprofit organizations that are faced with resource-related problems tend to rely on retrenchment and maintenance rather than on innovation and proactive behavior to increase resources.

Power is the critical thread of administration, but how it is to be exercised is a point of contention among those who favor centralized, rational decisional structures and those who favor participatory decision making, recognizing that social agencies are loosely coupled organizations that face high levels of uncertainty (Mintzberg, 1983). Still others emphasize the need for matrix and other alternate forms, supporting widespread power sharing among clients, citizens, and staff.

Staffing

Although personnel deployment in social work is analyzed elsewhere in this encyclopedia, there are certain features of the utilization of administrative personnel that deserve consideration here. There was a rapid growth of professionally trained administrators after federal and state governments began to support the training of administrative personnel in the 1960s and 1970s. However, the supply of personnel was never sufficient to meet even a substantial part of the need. Moreover, because much of the available social work training did not address the reality of social welfare administration, preference was given to administrative personnel with training in business and public administration or in law.

Nevertheless, a 1969 survey indicated that just over 50 percent of members of the National Association of Social Workers (NASW) occupied administrative roles—a substantially higher percentage than in earlier surveys (Stamm, 1969). Comparable data for 1985 indicated that only 30 percent of NASW members had primarily administrative roles. Those for whom administrative functions were secondary responsibilities brought the total to 41 percent (National Association of Social Workers, 1985). Thus, it appears that there was a decline in the percentage of social workers in administration in the 1980s. Research to determine whether the characteristics of NASW members changed in that period has yet to be conducted.

The 1985 data also indicated that 55 percent of all members were employed in the private sector, whereas 45 percent worked in the public sector. When secondary employment is also considered, 86 percent of all members held jobs in private for-profit and nonprofit organizations. Although the proportion of social workers employed in private agencies has always been high in some sections of the United States, this domination by the private sector represents a dramatic shift (Gilbert, 1983). Members were found disproportionately in medical settings (15 percent), in mental health settings (29 percent), and in family and children's services (25 percent), with a high level of employment in private agencies. Federal and state governments have strongly encouraged the shift to the private sector, and—as Gilbert (1983) has noted—these data suggest that such policy initiatives have been effective.

The proportion of NASW members who are female or belong to minority groups also shifted between 1975 and 1985. NASW reported that its membership was 63 percent female in 1975. By 1985 that figure had increased to 72 percent, whereas the proportion of nonwhite members declined from 14 to 11 percent (Fanshel, 1976; National Association of Social Workers, 1985). Despite the increase in the proportion of female NASW members, it is unlikely that the proportion of females in administrative roles in social work agencies has increased. Instead, membership characteristics are likely to resemble those of the 1950s.

Although the numbers of schools providing specialized training in administration grew rapidly in the 1970s, the proportion of students trained in administration did not. According to the Council on Social Work Education (1975, 1983), in 1975, 9 percent of all master's-level social work students were being trained specifically for administrative and policymaking positions; that proportion declined to 3 percent by 1983. Increases in the proportion of female students were accompanied by a rapid growth in the numbers of those preparing for direct service practice rather than for administration.

Social work agencies once relied on the promotion of direct service practitioners to recruit administrators. This trend no longer predominates because of employers' stringent demands for administrators with sophisticated knowledge of both organizations and management, as well as skills in information management, budgeting, staff development, negotiation, political leadership, policy formulation, and planning (Neugeboren, 1985). Unless schools of social work and training institutions in social agencies are able to prepare larger numbers of social workers for administrative positions, it is probable that Gummer's (1979) prediction will be realized—namely, that social work professionals will not have primary control of most social agencies.

Major Issues and Trends

Social welfare administrators in the United States confront numerous issues in the 1980s. These issues must be addressed and problems must be solved if the industry is to survive and to meet generally accepted societal needs. The welfare state is under profound attack, particularly in relation to its ability to meet the needs of children, the poor, minorities, the handicapped, and the dislocated. In addition, changes in the workplace—segmentation of the labor market, technological change, decline in unionism, and the restructuring of labor-management relations—also affect the management of human services.

Declining Resources. In the 1980s, administrators of social welfare programs are plagued by serious problems arising from the substantial decline in the amount of resources earmarked for social services in the social welfare budget. The increasing costs of social security and other related nonincome-tested programs has resulted in sharply reduced resources to aid populations at risk or to effect redistribution of income or services to the poor and disadvantaged. Stringent controls on expenditures by legislatures and executive budget offices have hampered administrative flexibility, as has pressure for stringent controls on expenditures, for zero-based budgeting, for reliance on the private sector, and for rigorous program evaluation. Any one of these procedures, if applied properly, might enhance organizational performance. But because such procedures are used only to reduce resources, without respect to need, many service providers show little enthusiasm for them (Perlmutter, 1984).

Although cutback management has become a central administrative concern, much of the literature has addressed the related decision-making dilemmas as if they were "value free" (Vinter & Kish, 1985). Professional ethical codes, such as the NASW Code of Ethics, provide no specific principles to guide the administration of retrenchment

(Levy, 1982). Arguments based on utilitarianism are particularly unsatisfactory because programs aimed at solving the most intractable problems and serving those at highest risk may be the least efficient with respect to so-called objective cost-benefit analysis. Rawls (1973) has suggested that principles of distributive justice should guide social policy initiatives. Curiously, although they are not practiced, these principles are consistent with the stated philosophy of social policy.

The political nature of social work administration becomes apparent in attempts to implement principles of distributive justice. When it is recognized that resources are unlikely to increase in the foreseeable future, critical dilemmas are highlighted by questions of who should be served. Pawlak et al. (1983) offer a series of political strategies for administrators experiencing problems in maintaining existing resources and in obtaining new sources of funding.

Privatization of Social Services. Although private agencies have always been a significant part of social services, private for-profit and private nonprofit social service organizations have grown considerably in the 1980s. (The shift in the deployment of social workers that was noted earlier is just one manifestation.) The federal government strongly advocated this change and provided numerous incentives for its development. Unfortunately, the extent of purchase-of-service contracts between public agencies and private organizations is not fully known (Gilbert, 1983; Salamon & Abramson, 1982). It is probable, however, that more than 50 percent of social service delivery since 1985 has involved private organizations (Willis, 1984), with major industrial and business organizations provide mental health, child welfare, health, correctional, employment training, and substance abuse services.

These shifts are of particular concern to administrators because they often involve shifts in goal priorities, in clients, in requirements for efficiency, and in ideological perspectives on the value of entrepreneurial activity. Although federal and state funds provide more than two thirds of the budgets of these private organizations, it is unclear whether the level of accountability is the same as that ordinarily required of public service administrators. Moreover, as Sala-

mon and Abramson (1982) note, it is clear that the private sector itself is unable to raise sufficient funds to cover even minimal social services. Therefore, the present dual system will continue, despite ideological assertions to the contrary.

Information Management. The utilization of computers has grown rapidly in social welfare agencies and is likely to continue in the future. Information systems designed to facilitate decision making by practitioners and managers have been developed, as have systems to monitor and evaluate programs and to expedite responsive service delivery. By the mid-1980s, microcomputer technology was sufficiently developed to be used on a cost-effective basis for operations as well as for evaluation and research. One benefit of automated information systems that is being increasingly acknowledged by administrators is the new feasibility and efficiency of interagency cooperation and coordination.

Participatory Management. Interest in Japanese management techniques grew rapidly in the 1980s and stimulated innovation and experimentation in participatory management techniques such as quality circles. The term "quality circles" refers to a management-initiated technique widely used in Japan for sharing responsibility with workers in locating and solving problems of productivity and coordination. Although they have spread throughout American industry, their use is still far less than in Japan, where it is estimated that one out of eight workers participates in a quality circle (Cole, 1982). As yet they are used only minimally in human service organizations, and some have expressed concern about the use of this technique as an infringement of workers' autonomy and freedom to associate as they wish. However, because of the growing interest in the use of this technique, it can be expected to spread along with other participatory devices.

The development of matrix and parallel organizations illustrates many of the benefits to be derived from less centralized, more open organizations. Matrix organizations are those in which every employee belongs to two streams of authority and communication—one related to a functional department and the other to a specific service or client group. Parallel organizations, as developed by Kanter (1983), refer to temporary rotating task forces managed by a steering committee of the conventional line organization. They bring together people from many organizational levels to participate in group problem solving related to productivity, morale, and especially to innovation and change. All these alternative structures force individuals to examine the issues of interconnectedness and interdependency (Mintzberg, 1983).

Interest in these alternative models resulted from concern about the negative effects of overly bureaucratized organizations. Kanter (1983), Mintzberg (1983), and Toch and Grant (1982) have proposed several participatory decision-making models that are being applied increasingly in human service organizations. Research suggests that participation in organizational decision making can reduce job dissatisfaction and strain, increasing productivity and morale. These mechanisms have also been used in affirmative action and in grievance management to address problems that have been difficult for management to deal with successfully.

Ethical Issues in Management. Ethical issues pervade every function and position in the social welfare agency, but only recently have administrators taken seriously their full responsibilities in this area (Levy, 1982). Among the functions that require skillful administration are expediting the delivery of effective services to clients and handling staff-client conflict in ways that reduce the likelihood of negative or harmful effects. Studies of human service administrators have indicated that they place more emphasis on accountability to funders than on improving the quality of service, expanding the number of clients served, or improving staff morale and satisfaction (Finch, 1978).

Concern about malpractice has increased, as has concern about social responsibility regarding clients' rights to effective service without negative secondary consequences. Some argue that clients deserve compensation whenever they suffer deprivation as a result of how services are organized and delivered. Lewis (1977) argues that agencies should adopt ethical principles to guide program development, ensuring that the most disadvantaged clients receive needed services in a manner that does not exacerbate their condition.

Affirmative Action and Pay Equity. Despite the lack of enthusiasm of federal authorities for enforcing affirmative action laws and guidelines, the issue remains on the public agenda, accompanied in many states by pressure for pay equity or "comparable worth" legislation to reduce wage and salary differentials between men and women. Minnesota has passed legislation to implement pay equity throughout the state government, and in several other states court actions are in process to determine the legality of class-action comparable worth suits.

Given the predominance of women in the social work profession, the implementation of these directives presents substantial administrative challenges. These issues have also triggered concern about discrimination based on race, on age, on physical handicap, and on seniority and have highlighted the lack of progress in eliminating institutionalized racism. These factors are likely to be of increasing concern as traditional labor-management relations are challenged in both the public and private sectors during the 1980s and 1990s.

Services and Service Delivery. Empirically based practice models developed rapidly in the 1970s and 1980s, but agencies continue to be plagued by problems in the design, implementation, and delivery of effective social services. Knowledge remains embryonic in many areas; moreover, because it is often applied only to limited populations, its generalizability is unknown. All too often organizational correlates of performance do not use service effectiveness as a criterion variable.

Other issues to be resolved include the inaccessibility of services when and where clients need them; the disconnectedness between services that require linkage; fragmentation and gaps in services among various interdependent sectors; the lack of participation of clients and direct service staff in critical decision making linked to other structures of the organization; and the lack of attention to empowerment strategies for serving clients in self-help or mutual assistance settings.

Changing Context of Human Services. Social welfare agencies are being restructured in a variety of ways that affect the role of managers. Lynn (1981) predicts movement toward megaorganizations that encompass small service agencies, increasing efficiency and productivity through resource pooling, coordination, and more effective central management. However, there also appears to be an equally strong countertrend toward small, grass-roots mutual assistance agencies, which are more flexible in adapting to changing environmental conditions and are able to respond quickly to clients' needs as they arise. It is also probable that they can more effectively withstand ideological challenges related to the efficacy and viability of social services.

Conclusion

Dynamic leadership in administration is critical to the survival and enhancement of human service organizations in a hostile social environment. This leadership must be based on empirically derived knowledge of effective administration as well as on subjective judgment. It also involves ethical and moral behavior that is congruent with the basic values of democratic society. As Tead suggested, the administrator is "the custodian of opportunity—opportunity for associated persons to enhance the quality of life by the contributions of their labors" (Tead, 1951). The executives of human service organizations will face challenging opportunities in the remainder of this century, as democratic societies come to terms with some of the problems and dilemmas of the welfare state.

ROSEMARY C. SARRI

For further information, see ADMINISTRATION (READER'S GUIDE).

References

Abbott, E. (1931). *Social Welfare and Professional Education*. Chicago: University of Chicago Press.

Alexander, C. (1982). "An Overview Of Administration, Policy and Planning as Specializations in Social Welfare Practice." *Administration in Social Work, 6*(2–3), 7–18.

Astley, W. G., & Van den Ven, A. H. (1983). "Central Perspectives and Debates in Science Organization Theory." *Administration Science Quarterly, 28*(2), 245–273.

Atwater, P. (1940). *Problems of Administration in Social Work*. Minneapolis: University of Minnesota Press.

Austin, D. (1983). "Administrative Practice in the Human Services: Future Directions for Curriculum Development." *Journal of Applied Behavioral Science, 19*(2), 141–161.

Brannon, D. (1985). "Decision Making in Public Welfare: Scientific Management Meets Organized Anarchy." *Administration in Social Work, 9*(1), 23–33.

Cole, R. (1982). "Diffusion of Participatory Work Structures in Japan, Sweden, and the United States." In P. S. Goodman (Ed.), *Change in Organizations: New Perspectives on Theory, Research, and Practice*. San Francisco: Jossey-Bass.

Cook, T., & Russell, R. (1980). *Contemporary Operations Management*. Englewood Cliffs, N.J.: Prentice-Hall.

Council on Social Work Education. (1975). *Statistics on Social Work Education in the U.S.: 1975*. New York: Author.

Council on Social Work Education. (1983). *Statistics on Social Work Education in the U.S.: 1983*. New York: Author.

Cyert, R. (1975). *Managing the Non-Profit Organization*. Lexington, Mass.: D. C. Heath & Co.

Derthick, M. (1975). *Uncontrollable Spending for Social Service Grants*. Washington, D.C.: The Brookings Institution.

Drucker, P. (1980). *Managing in Turbulent Times*. New York: Harper & Row.

Elkin, R., & Molitor, M. (1984). *Management Indicators in Nonprofit Organizations*. New York: Peat, Marwick, Mitchell & Co.

Fanshel, D. (1976). "Status Differentials: Men and Women in Social Work." *Social Work, 21*(6), 448–454.

Finch, W. (1978). "Administrative Priorities: The Impact of Employee Perception on Agency Functioning and Worker Satisfaction." *Administration in Social Work, 2*(4), 391–400.

Galbraith, J. (1973). *Designing Complex Organizations*. Reading, Mass.: Addison-Wesley Publishing Co.

Gilbert, N. (1983). *Capitalism and the Welfare State*. New Haven, Conn.: Yale University Press.

Goodsell, Charles T. (1983). *The Case for Bureaucracy: A Public Administration Polemnic*. Chatham, N.J.: Chatham House.

Gummer, B. (1979). "Is the Social Worker in Public Welfare an Endangered Species?" *Public Welfare, 37*(4), 12–21.

Gummer, B. (1984). "The Changing Context of Social Administration." *Administration in Social Work, 8*(3), 5–16.

Gummer, B. (1985). "A Social Worker's Guide to Organizational Politics." *Administration in Social Work, 9*(1), 13–22.

Hage, J. (1980). *Theories of Organizations*. New York: John Wiley & Sons.

Hall, R. (1982). *Organization: Structure and Process* (rev. ed.). Englewood Cliffs, N.J.: Prentice-Hall.

Hasenfeld, Y. (1983). *Human Service Organization*. Englewood Cliffs, N.J.: Prentice-Hall.

Hickson, D. J., et al. (1971). "A Strategic Contingencies Theory of Interorganizational Power." *Administration Science Quarterly, 23*, 454–465.

Josefowitz, N. (1980). *Paths to Power*. Reading, Mass.: Addison-Wesley Publishing Co.

Kanter, R. (1977). *Men and Women of the Corporation*. New York: Basic Books.

Kanter, R. (1983). *The Changemaster: Innovations for Productivity in the American Corporation*. New York: Simon & Schuster.

Katz, D., & Kahn, R. (1978). *Social Psychology of Organizations* (rev. ed.). New York: Wiley.

Kravetz, D., & Austin, C. (1984). "Women's Issues in Social Service Administration." *Administration in Social Work, 8*(4), 25–38.

Lawrence, P., & Lorsch, J. (1967). *Organizations and Environment: Managing Differentiation and Integration*. Cambridge, Mass.: Harvard University Press.

Levinson, H. (1981). *The Executive*. Cambridge, Mass.: Harvard University Press.

Levy, C. (1982). *Guide to Ethical Decisions and Actions for Social Service Administrators*. New York: Haworth Press.

Lewis, H. (1977). "The Future Role of the Social Service Administrator." *Social Work, 1*(2), 115–122.

Lynn, L. (1981). *Managing the Public's Business: The Job of the Government Executive*. New York: Basic Books.

March, J. G., & Olsen, G. P. (1976). *Ambiguity and Choice in Organizations*. Bergen, Norway: Universitetsförlaget.

March, J., & Simon, H. (1958). *Organizations*. New York: John Wiley & Sons.

Meyer, J. (1984). "Budget Cuts in the Reagan Administration: A Question of Lawness." In D. L. Bawden (Ed.), *The Social Contract Revisited* (pp. 34–35). Washington, D.C.: Urban Institute.

Mintzberg, H. (1973). *The Nature of Managerial Work*. New York: Harper & Row.

Mintzberg, H. (1979). *The Structuring of Organizations*. Englewood Cliffs, N.J.: Prentice-Hall.

Mintzberg, H. (1983). *Designing Effective Organizations*. Englewood Cliffs, N.J.: Prentice-Hall.

National Association of Social Workers. (1985). *NASW Membership—National Summary Tables. Report No. 1*. Washington, D.C.: Author.

Neugeboren, B. (1985). *Organization, Policy and Practice in Human Services*. New York: Longman.

Norman, R., & Mancusco, A. (1983). *Women's Issues and Social Work Practice*. Itasca, Ill.: F. E. Peacock Publishers.

Patti, R. (1983). *Social Welfare Administration: Managing Programs in a Developing Context*. Englewood Cliffs, N.J.: Prentice-Hall.

Pawlak, E. J., Jeter, S. C., & Fink, R. L. (1983). "The Politics of Cutback Management." *Administration in Social Work, 7*(2), 1–10.

Perlmutter, F. (Ed.). (1984). *Human Services at Risk*. Lexington, Mass: Lexington Books.

Perlmutter, F., & Alexander, L. (1978). "Exposing the Coercive Consensus: Racism and Sexism in Social Work." In R. Sarri & Y. Hasenfeld (Eds.), *The Management of Human Services* (pp. 207–234). New York: Columbia University Press.

Perlmutter, F., & Slavin, S. (1980). *Leadership in Social Administration*. Philadelphia: Temple University Press.

Perrow, C. (1979). *Complex Organizations: A Critical Essay* (2nd ed.). Glenview, Ill.: Scott, Foresman Co.

Rawls, J. (1973). *A Theory of Justice*. Cambridge, Mass.: Harvard University Press.

Richan, W. (1983). "Social Work Administration under Assault." *Administration in Social Work, 7*(3–4), 9–20.

Salamon, L., & Abramson, A. (1982). "The Nonprofit Sector." In J. Palmer & I. Sawhill (Eds.), *The Reagan Experiment* (pp. 219–246) Washington, D.C.: Urban Institute Press.

Sarri, R. (1984). *Executive Leadership in Turbulent Environments*. Launceston, Tasmania: Australian Council on Social Work Education.

Sarri, R., & Hasenfeld, Y. (Eds.). (1978). *The Management of Human Services*. New York: Columbia University Press.

Selznik, P. (1957). *Leadership in Administration*. New York: Harper & Row.

Simon, H. A. (1976). *Administrative Behavior* (3rd ed.). New York: Free Press.

Slavin, S. (1981, November). *Some Conceptual Issues in Social Work Administration*. Paper presented at the National Association of Social Workers Symposium, Philadelphia.

Stamm, A. (1969). "NASW Membership: Characteristics, Deployment, and Salaries." *Personnel Information, 12*(1), 34–45.

Stein, H. (Ed.). (1981). *Organization and the Human Services: Cross-Disciplinary Reflections*. Philadelphia: Temple University Press.

Street, D. (1979). "Social Organization of Public Assistance." In D. Street, G. Martin, & L. Gordon, *Functionaries and Recipients: The Outputs of Urban Public Aid* (pp. 23–46). Beverly Hills, Calif.: Sage Publications.

Street, E. (1931). *Social Work Administration*. New York: Harper & Bros.

Tead, O. (1951). *The Art of Administration.* New York: McGraw-Hill Book Co.

Thompson, J. (1967). *Organizations in Action.* New York: McGraw-Hill Book Co.

Toch, H., & Grant, J. D. (1982). *Reforming Human Services: Change Through Participation.* Beverly Hills, Calif.: Sage Publications.

Trecker, H. (1946). *Group Process in Administration.* New York: Woman's Press.

Vinter, R., & Kish, R. (1985). *Budgeting for Not-for-Profit Organizations.* New York: Free Press.

Willis, C. (1984). "Purchase of Social Services: Another Look." *Social Work, 29*(6), 516–519.

Woodward, J. (1965). *Industrial Organization Theory and Practice.* London, England: Oxford University Press.

Zald, M. (1978). "Political Economy: A Framework for Comparative Analysis." In M. Zald (Ed.), *Power in Organizations* (pp. 221–261). Nashville, Tenn.: Vanderbilt University Press.

ADOLESCENT PREGNANCY

Since the 1960s, adolescent pregnancy has come to be perceived as a major social problem in the United States. The reasons underlying this perception are too complex to be summed up by a simple statement that more adolescents are becoming pregnant today than in the past. In fact, the birthrate for adolescents aged 15–19 has declined during this period, although the number of live births to adolescent mothers has increased. The explanation for this seemingly contradictory data is that the adolescent population to which the rate is applied has increased.

Demographics

After World War II, the birthrate in the United States began to climb, peaking in the late 1950s and decreasing since then. In 1960, there were 7 million adolescent females aged 15–19. In 1970, as the result of the post-World War II baby boom, there were 10 million adolescent females—an increase of 35 percent. Today, the number of adolescent females (roughly 13–19 years of age) is decreasing and thus the birth rate—defined as the number of births per 1,000 females aged 15–19—for adolescents is declining along with the actual number of births (Baldwin, 1981).

Why then has interest in this phenomenon increased? The reasons are several: (1) the birthrate for nonadolescent women has decreased significantly whereas that of adolescents has declined less (see Figure 1), (2) the decline in the adolescent birthrate has been concentrated in older adolescents (ages 18–19) while the birthrate is actually increasing among younger adolescents (ages 15–17), (3) the number of out-of-wedlock pregnancies has risen for adolescents, (4) the greatest increase in adolescent out-of-wedlock pregnancies has been among white adolescents (although the birthrate is higher for blacks, the rise in the adolescent birthrate has been confined to whites, as shown in Figure 2), and (5) public funds for the care of young adolescent mothers and their children have increased (Baldwin, 1981; Moore & Burt, 1982).

Table 1 shows the significant increase—62 percent—in the rate of white unmarried adolescents aged 15–19 giving birth from 1970 to 1982 (the latest available data). This dramatic increase has occurred while adolescents of other ethnic and racial groups have experienced a decline in out-of-wedlock births. The increase among white adolescents has been most dramatic among 15–17-year-olds whose unmarried birthrate (72 percent) is twice that of all white women (36 percent). In addition, the increase in the birthrate among whites aged 15–17 is almost three times that for all adolescents of the same age (25 percent).

Table 2 shows that the unmarried adolescent birthrate has steadily increased and in 1982 (28.9 per 1,000) was almost twice what it was in 1960 (15.3 per 1,000). It also shows a decrease in the overall number of births to adolescent females and an increase in the illegitimate birthrate.

Although little information is available for minority groups other than blacks, recent population data suggest that the birthrate for Hispanics is increasing. In 1982, the birthrate was 17.7 for white non-Hispanics, 87.0 for blacks, and 24.1 for Hispanics. Teenage childbearing is more frequent among Mexican American and Puerto Rican women living in the United States than among white non-Hispanic women. In 1981, 19 percent of Mexican American mothers and 23 percent of Puerto Rican mothers were under age 20, compared with 12 percent of white non-

Fig. 1. Birthrates by Age of Mother: United States 1970–1981

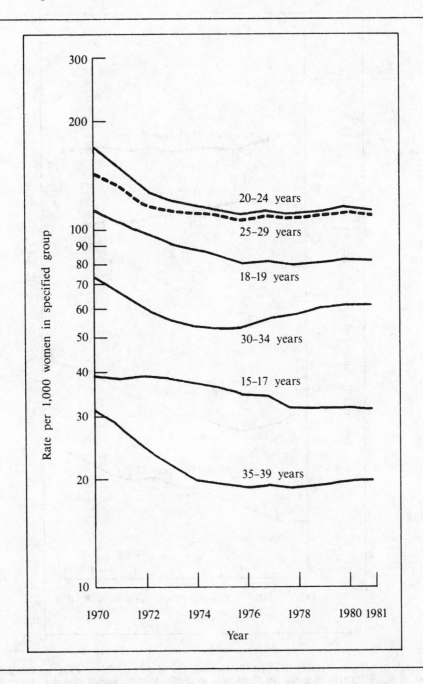

Source: S. J. Ventura, *Trends in Teenage Childbearing, United States, 1970–81: Vital and Health Statistics* (Series 21, No. 41, DHHS Pub. No. [PHS] 84-1919; Rockville, Md.: National Center for Health Statistics, Sept. 1984), p. 3.

Fig. 2. Birthrates for Unmarried Women Aged 15–17 and 18–19 Years by Race of Child: United States 1970–1981

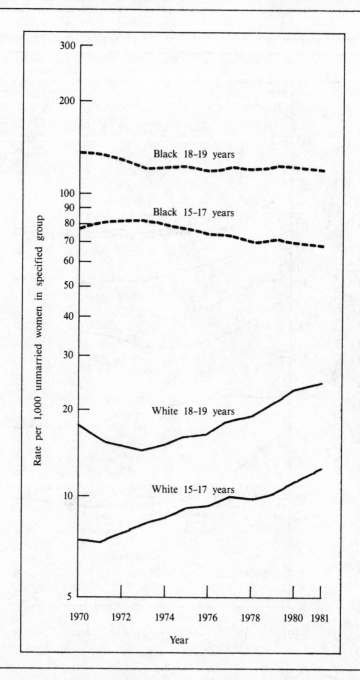

Source: S. J. Ventura, *Trends in Teenage Childbearing, United States, 1970–81: Vital and Health Statistics* (Series 21, No. 41, DHHS Pub. No. [PHS] 84–1919; Rockville, Md.: National Center for Health Statistics, Sept. 1984), p. 7.

Table 1. Birthrates for Unmarried Women by Age and Race of Mother: United States, 1970 and 1982[a]

	1970	1982	Percent Change
All Races			
All ages	28.4	30.0	+13.6
15–17	17.1	21.5	+25.7
18–19	32.9	40.2	+22.1
Under 20	22.4	28.9	+22.5
White			
All ages	13.8	18.8	+36.2
15–17	7.5	12.9	+72.0
18–19	17.6	25.1	+42.6
Under 20	10.9	17.7	+62.4
Black			
All ages	95.5	79.6	−16.6
15–17	77.9	67.6	−13.2
18–19	136.4	115.8	−15.5
Under 20	96.9	87.0	−10.2
All other			
All ages	89.9	73.9	−17.8
15–17	73.3	60.7	−17.2
18–19	126.5	107.0	−15.4
Under 20	90.8	83.0	− 8.6

Source: *Monthly Vital Statistics Report* (Sept. 28, 1984), *33*(6 Supplement), pp. 31, 32.
[a] Birthrates are in terms of live births per 1,000 unmarried women in specified group, estimated as of July 1.

Hispanic and 26 percent of black non-Hispanic mothers (Ventura, 1984).

Black adolescents have the highest birthrate of all adolescents (87 births per 1,000 in 1982 for females under 20). Birthrates for all black teenagers (married and unmarried) fell more sharply than for white teenagers, however, particularly the rates for younger teenagers (ages 15–17) for whom the rate declined by 20 percent for black women and 16 percent for white women between 1970 and 1981. The decline in black adolescent pregnancies is associated with a reduction in nonmarital birthrates for black adolescents. By comparison, birthrates for white adolescents have risen in recent years, reflecting the increase in nonmarital fertility among white teenagers (National Center on Health Statistics [NCHS], 1984).

The rates of first births show a smaller racial differential than do the rates of all births by race. The overall gap in fertility between white and black adolescents is thus partly accounted for by the much higher level of second and subsequent births for black adolescents than for whites (NCHS, 1984).

Correlates of Early Sexual Behavior

The rate of premarital sexual activity has risen for adolescents. This rise in sexual activity has been increasingly found in younger teenagers. Although premarital sex has always occurred, the prevalence and acceptability of such activity, especially among females, have increased in recent years. In the last 2 decades, societal norms and mores that govern sexual attitudes and behavior have liberalized. This sexual revolution has resulted in a sharp increase in the number of women engaging in premarital sex. In a national poll on sexual attitudes and experience, Hunt (1974) found that 81 percent of females aged 18–24 reported having had premarital coitus compared to only 31 percent of females 55 and older. This trend toward premarital sex at a younger age continued through the 1970s. Zelnik and Kantner (1980) report a 20 percent increase in premarital sex among females aged 15–19 living in metropolitan areas. In a 1979 study they found that 50 percent of the women aged 15–19 had engaged in premarital sex, while in their 1977 study, they found that only 30 percent had done so.

From the mid-1960s through the late 1970s, attitudes favoring premarital petting and intercourse became more widespread (Chilman, 1979; Phipps-Yonas, 1980; Sorenson, 1973; Vener & Stewart, 1974). The prevalence of sexual activity also increased during this period for all age groups and, in particular, for white adolescent females (Cvetkovick & Grote, 1976; Zelnik, Kantner, & Ford, 1981).

Age and race are strong predictors of premarital sexual activity for women. The older the adolescent, the more likely she is to have engaged in premarital intercourse. Zelnik, Kantner, and Ford (1981) found that among 15–19-year-olds, 23 percent of white adolescent females had engaged in premarital intercourse and 40 percent of black adolescent females had done so. For 19-year-olds, 67 percent of white females and 84 percent of black females had engaged in premarital sexual intercourse. Zelnik, Kantner, and Ford (1981) showed a continued increase in sexual

**Table 2. Fertility of Women under 20 in the United States:
1960, 1970, 1978, and 1982[a]**

Age	1960	1970	1978	1982
Number of births				
Under 15	7,462	11,752	10,772	9,773
15–17	177,904	223,590	202,661	181,162
18–19	423,775	421,118	340,746	332,596
Under 20	609,141	656,460	554,179	523,531
Number of out-of-wedlock births				
Under 15	4,600	9,500	9,400	8,720
15–17	43,700	96,100	116,500	117,696
18–19	43,400	94,300	123,200	142,930
Under 20	91,700	199,900	249,100	269,346
Illegitimate births per 1,000 unmarried women				
15–19	15.3	22.4	25.4	28.9

Source: W. Baldwin, "Adolescent Pregnancy and Childbearing—An Overview" (January 1981), 5(1); and S. J. Ventura, *Trends in Teenage Childbearing, United States, 1970–81: Vital and Health Statistics* (Series 21, No. 41, DHHS Pub. No. [PHS] 84-1919, Rockville, Md.: National Center for Health Statistics, Sept. 1984), p. 3.
[a] Fertility is defined as number of pregnancies.

experience among females aged 15–19, rising from 43.4 percent in 1976 to 49.8 percent in 1979. White adolescent females showed the highest increase, rising from 38.3 percent to 46.6 percent. The rate of sexual activity for black adolescent females, although higher, remained fairly stable (66.3 to 66.2 percent).

Vener and Stewart (1974) surveyed one community in 1970 and again in 1973, investigating the sexual behavior of boys and girls aged 13–19. The most significant increase in levels of sexual behavior occurred in the younger age groups (14–15), indicating, like Zelnik and Kantner (1980), a trend for sexual intercourse to occur earlier. For every age group, Zelnik and Kantner (1980) and Vener and Stewart (1974) found similar rates of sexual intercourse and an overall rate increase of 30 percent.

The age of menarche, or onset of menstruation, is another indicator of early sexual activity. Women who mature earlier initiate sexual activity earlier (Zelnik, Kantner, & Ford, 1981). The average age for the onset of menstruation has been decreasing. One hundred years ago, the estimated average age was 17. By 1940, it was 13.5, and by the 1960s, it was estimated to be 12.5 (Moore & Burt, 1982). This trend toward an earlier biological maturation serves to lower the age

at which female adolescents are likely to become sexually active and to increase the period of time during which they are at risk of pregnancy (Bolton, 1980; Cutright, 1972; Lipsitz, 1980).

Religious belief has been found to be negatively related to the probability of engaging in sexual intercourse. The more important religion is to an adolescent female and the greater the frequency of church attendance, the less likely she is to engage in premarital intercourse (Chilman, 1979). In Jessor and Jessor's (1975) study, nonvirgins indicated significantly less church attendance and were less likely to view themselves as religious than respondents who were virgins. Zelnik, Kantner, and Ford (1981) measured the church attendance of respondents. Both black and white teenage girls reporting high attendance were less likely to engage in permarital intercourse. Within the whole sample, only those with little religious belief engaged more frequently in sexual intercourse. Zelnik, Kantner, and Ford (1981), however, caution against the temptation to attribute rising sexual activity and declining marriage to the decreasing influence of religion without also examining the effects of family stability and other factors.

An adolescent's future orientation also

plays a role in the likelihood of engaging in premarital sex. Female adolescents with higher educational expectations, career goals, and positive future expectations are less likely to engage in early sexual intercourse (Jessor & Jessor, 1975; Urdy, Bauman, & Morris, 1975). Female adolescents with more highly educated parents are also less likely to engage in premarital sex at an early age because they, too, tend to have stronger future-oriented goal expectations (Zelnik, Kantner, & Ford, 1981).

How the adolescent perceives herself—her sense of self-esteem and self-concept—is also associated with early sexual activity. Again, this may be an indicator embedded in a host of other factors such as goal orientation and family of origin. Nevertheless, the better the adolescent's self-image, the less likely she is to become sexually active at an early age or to experience an out-of-wedlock pregnancy. Another factor relevant to the adolescent's sense of self and future is her involvement in outside activities. The probability of being sexually active is greater for adolescents who are not involved in social groups and recreational activities.

A variety of family factors also appears to correlate with early sexual activity for adolescent females. A poor relationship with the parent or parents and divorced or single-parent households seem to provide the conditions for early sexual activity (Zelnik, Kantner, & Ford, 1981). Adolescents who become pregnant are more likely to have mothers who were themselves teenage parents. Similarly, sexually active adolescent females are more likely to have sisters who were sexually active or pregnant in their teenage years. Finally, the sexually active adolescent is more likely to come from a lower socioeconomic household. For example, Zelnik and Kantner (1978) found an inverse relationship between the socioeconomic status of the respondent's parent-figure and the prevalence of sexual intercourse—the lower the status, the higher the prevalence. Adolescents from unskilled working-class and poverty backgrounds were more likely to have had premarital intercourse, particularly if they had migrated to an urban environment from a rural one (Kantner & Zelnik, 1972).

Moreover, the general emotional climate of family life is considered to be a powerful influence on sexual behavior. Adolescents from homes with poor or inadequate communication patterns with their parents are more likely to have sexual experiences in early adolescence (Abernethy, 1976; Jessor & Jessor, 1975; Kantner & Zelnik, 1972; Sorenson, 1973). Adolescent girls who engage in premarital sexual relations appear to lack affection and support from their parents and may seek to meet these needs by acquiescing in the expectations of their male partners. Although poor relationships with parents have been linked to the incidence of sexual intercourse, no findings indicate that good parent-child relationships inhibit sexual behavior (Jessor & Jessor, 1975; Walters & Walters, 1980).

The mother-daughter relationship is thought to be the strongest family relationship for females, although for the most part the father-daughter relationship has been neglected as a focus of study. Studies of sexually acting-out and pregnant adolescents by Friedman (1971) and Cheetham (1977) offer contradictory descriptions of respondents' fathers. Fathers in the former study were described as weak and passive, and those in the latter study were described as dominating, abusive, and rejecting.

Jessor and Jessor (1975) found respondents with early sexual experiences tended to have mothers who were not very expressive of affection and who failed to provide firm and consistent discipline. A number of researchers have reported a similar pattern of behavior alternating with periods in which the mother encouraged dependency. This "dependency-deprivation syndrome" results in intense feelings of ambivalence in the adolescent regarding the mother-daughter relationship (Abernethy, 1974; Daniels, 1969).

Peer influence is also a major factor in an adolescent's behavior. The attitudes and behaviors of the peer group are typically adopted by the individual. In many instances, the values and norms of the group will prevail over those imparted by the family. This is especially true in the area of sexual attitudes and behaviors. If the adolescent female belongs to a peer group with liberal sexual attitudes and behaviors, she is likely to exhibit the same characteristics. Thus the sexually active adolescent female is usually found among other females who are sexually active. The degree of guilt an adolescent experiences regarding her sexual behavior is determined not only by her own mores but to a significant extent by the values and attitudes of her peer group (Perlman, 1974; Reiss, 1967). Although the adolescent herself may not feel ready for sexual relations, as a member of a group she may feel compelled to conform to the group's mores (Klein, 1978).

Sexual behavior is increasingly regarded as a personal choice, and peers tend to express a high level of social tolerance for premarital intercourse. Reiss, Banwart, and Foreman (1975) contend that abstinence is no longer the behavioral norm within the adolescent population and that permissiveness with affection appears to be the most increasingly accepted standard—that is, engaging in sexual intercourse because an adolescent female is fond of her male partner.

The view of adolescents as promiscuous does not appear to be supported by the research data (Phipps-Yonas, 1980; Sugar, 1980; Zelnik, Kantner, & Ford, 1981). Although white teenage girls are reported to have more sexual partners and engage in sexual intercourse more frequently than black teenage girls, this is true for only 30 percent. The rest follow the pattern of having only one partner. Most sexually active adolescents are involved in stable, intense relationships with only one partner (Akpom, Akpom, & Davis, 1976; Chilman, 1978; Vener & Stewart, 1974).

Consequences of Early Childbearing

The various consequences of early childbearing affect both the young mother and her child. The adolescent who has experienced an early pregnancy is at much greater risk of not completing her high school education or not going on to higher education. This lack of education and the subsequent lack of marketable skills makes the adolescent mother more likely to be either unemployed or employed in low-paying, low-skill work that provides few if any benefits and opportunities. Often, because she is unemployed or working for low wages with an infant to support, the adolescent mother must turn to public assistance. If she does marry, she runs a greater risk of divorce. She is likely to have more pregnancies than average because she has begun her family earlier in her childbearing years than the average mother. The ado-

lescent mother's child is likely to be raised in poverty with a poor outlook for educational attainment, has a greater likelihood of also being an adolescent mother if female, and, as some have suggested, may be abused or neglected physically or emotionally because of the greater probability of the mother's having poor parenting skills.

Adolescent mothers and their babies are also at higher medical risk than older mothers. Young mothers are more likely to experience problems with their pregnancy such as toxemia, anemia, miscarriages, and stillbirths and premature births (Moore & Burt, 1982). Adolescent mothers experience higher rates of infant and maternal mortality (Bolton, 1980; Moore & Burt, 1982) and are more likely to have low-birthweight babies. Low birthweight, with its corresponding low Apgar scores, is a major cause of more serious long-term problems such as mental retardation, cerebral palsy, epilepsy, and other neurological defects (Alan Guttmacher Institute, 1981). Many of these complications can be prevented by good prenatal care and nutrition starting early in pregnancy, although this is less true for mothers 15 and younger. And even with the provision of proper medical care, the poor diet, lack of education, late confirmation of pregnancy, and poor general health care of most teenagers makes positive pregnancy outcomes more difficult to achieve (Baldwin & Cain, 1980).

The education of adolescent mothers also suffers dramatically from a pregnancy. Card and Wise (1978) found that by age 29, 50 percent of the women who had experienced a pregnancy during their school years had acquired a high school diploma, while 96 percent of women who delayed their first birth until age 20 had done so. Adolescent mothers who marry have the highest probability of dropping out of school. Because they are educationally disadvantaged, young mothers without a high school education are nearly twice as likely to live in households receiving public assistance (Moore, Wertheimer, & Holden, 1981).

Pregnancy and Its Resolution

Because of the increasing prevalence of early sexual activity among teenagers, premarital pregnancy rates have continued to rise. In 1978, Tietze projected that among adolescent females who would turn 20 in

1984, one in five would have been pregnant by her eighteenth birthday and one in three would have been pregnant by her twentieth birthday.

The issue of adolescent pregnancy prevention and intervention can be viewed on a continuum. First is the prevention of early premarital sexual activity. Second is the prevention of pregnancy through contraception if the adolescent is sexually active. Third are issues related to pregnancy termination, and fourth is the provision of care for the mother and child before and after birth. The second and third areas will be addressed here.

Contraception. Research findings report low and inconsistent use of contraceptives among adolescents. A 1976 survey by Zelnik, Kantner, and Ford (1981) indicates that 28 percent of the white sample and 43 percent of the black sample of sexually active adolescents aged 15–19 never used contraception and that only about one-fourth of each of these groups used any birth control measures consistently. Similarly, Becerra and de Anda (1984) found that 44 percent of white non-Hispanic adolescents, 52 percent of highly acculturated Mexican American adolescents, and 39 percent of little acculturated Mexican American adolescents rarely or never used contraception. According to Zelnik, Kantner, and Ford (1981), however, 40 percent of teenagers who used any type of contraception during first intercourse used methods requiring no purchase or contact with the medical system, such as withdrawal or rhythm. The next one third relied on condoms or contraceptive jellies, and only 10 percent relied on methods that required contact with the medical establishment, such as birth control pills, diaphragms, or intrauterine devices.

Two major areas examined by researchers concerning the use of contraceptives by adolescents are the extent of knowledge regarding contraception and access to contraceptive services. In general, studies indicate that contraception is either not included or not adequately addressed in sex education classes provided by the schools (Lindemann, 1974; Zelnik & Kantner, 1979). Adolescent females seek out peers as the initial source of information on contraception. This is unreliable, however, as peers often provide inadequate information or mis-

information regarding birth control methods. As a result, adolescents may incorrectly perceive themselves as sufficiently knowledgeable regarding contraception. The reasons given for not using contraceptives included adolescents thinking they could not become pregnant because they had intercourse when it was not a fertile time of the month, they were too young to become pregnant, or they had intercourse too infrequently to become pregnant. Others simply never considered pregnancy a likely possibility. In addition, a number of adolescents believed that contraceptive methods might be dangerous to their health, and feared harmful physical consequences (Ager, Shea, & Agronow, 1979; Reichelt & Werley, 1975; Rogel & Zuehlke, 1982).

Even when knowledge about reproduction and fertility is increased, adolescents do not readily apply it to their own experience. Chilman (1978) concludes that no direct relationship exists between knowledge of contraceptives and consistent contraceptive use, so that although it is important to include contraception in the content of sex education programs, other psychological and social factors must also be taken into account in a pregnancy prevention program. Zelnik and Kantner (1978) point out that if all teenagers had consistently used contraception, 467,000 unintended premarital pregnancies would not have occurred in 1976.

Pregnancy Resolution. Of the 1.14 million pregnancies among women under age 20 in 1978, 49 percent resulted in live births. Of these, 22 percent were out-of-wedlock births, and 27 percent were to women who married just before or just after the birth of the child. In 1978, 38 percent of pregnancies to women under age 20 were terminated by abortions, and 13 percent resulted in miscarriages (Alan Guttmacher Institute, 1981). The type of pregnancy resolution seems to vary by the age, race, and class of the mother. The proportion of births terminated by abortion decreases with age and seems to be related also to race, with black women choosing abortion more often than white women. Miscarriages are highly related to class in that they are associated with inadequate nutrition and prenatal care (Henshaw et al., 1981).

Adoption is more often selected by whites than by blacks. In Kantner and

Zelnik's 1971 study (1972), 2 percent of adolescent blacks bearing an out-of-wedlock child placed the child for adoption, compared to 18 percent of white adolescents. Although recent data on adoption by race are lacking, it appears that more teenagers of all races are keeping their babies as opposed to placing them for adoption. A variety of factors account for this, including greater familial support, paternal acknowledgment, availability of Aid to Families with Dependent Children (AFDC) and other public support programs, and a decrease in the stigma attached to being an unwed adolescent mother.

Prevention and Intervention

Sex Education. Research on the effectiveness of sex education is limited and shows mixed findings. Studies on the impact of sex education on preventing adolescent pregnancy are still at the exploratory stage (Kirby, Alter, & Scales, 1979).

Sex education in schools is an issue of great concern to the public. Sex education is still not universally taught in schools; in 1978 it was found that only 36 percent of all U.S. high schools offered a separate course in sex education (Moore & Burt, 1982). Part of the difficulty is the various definitions of what constitutes a sex education course.

Moreover, the majority of the states leave the decision on whether to offer a sex education course to local school officials and boards. Kenney and Alexander (1980) found that 6 out of the 31 states they surveyed had an explicit sex–family life education policy statement that encouraged but did not require local districts to provide sex education courses. Sex education is also offered through a variety of other groups such as religious organizations, youth centers, local social service centers, family planning clinics, and other organizations.

Even when students report having taken a sex education course, however, considerable doubt remains as to what they have learned. The little information that can be gathered about the content of existing sex education programs shows that (1) most courses last for a total of less than 10 hours; (2) few go beyond providing information on reproductive anatomy, menstruation, venereal disease, and ethical standards, and fewer than 40 percent cover contraception; (3) few

include parental involvement and programs for parents; (4) the majority of the well-planned courses are offered in high schools and colleges; and (5) few junior high schools focus on sexual and emotional feelings toward the opposite sex, and those that do generally do so within other courses or units such as physical education (Kirby, Alter, & Scales, 1979; Shapiro, 1980).

Key issues surrounding sex education as a prevention method are its effectiveness, whether a school-based program is the appropriate place for such programs, the extent to which parents and community groups support such programs, the appropriateness of the content, and the effectiveness of electronic media as educational tools. Some goals of these programs are sexual awareness; decision making, assertiveness, and communication skills; responsible sexual behavior; effective contraception; and prevention of unwanted or unintended pregnancies.

Family Planning. The Family Planning Services and Population Research Act (P.L. 91-572, Title X of the Public Health Service Act) was enacted in 1970 and reauthorized in 1981. The goal was to create a national family planning program to give low-income men and women access to effective contraception. Forest (1980) estimates that 1.5 million adolescents under age 20 obtained contraceptive services from a family planning clinic in 1979, while approximately 1.2 million received contraceptive services from private physicians.

Some reasons why adolescents use family planning clinics include the low cost of obtaining services, the sex education that is often part of the service, greater confidence in confidentiality, more flexible clinic hours, and the subsidized services (Torres, Forrest, & Eisman, 1980). Although the impact of family planning clinic services on the birthrate of adolescents is unclear, a few studies support the hypothesis that the availability of these services is associated with reduced fertility among low-income teenage women (Moore & Caldwell, 1976).

One key issue facing family planning clinics is the question of parental consent and notification of contraceptive services. Various views support both the right of teenagers to privacy and the right of parents to be informed about the actions of their children. Some feel that parents should be notified only in the event of pregnancy, while others feel that parents should be notified if the adolescent seeks any type of contraception (Ooms, 1981; Torres, Forrest, & Eisman, 1980).

Future Orientation. Much has been written about the relationship between adolescent pregnancy and low expectations or lack of future goals. In this regard, one approach has been to work with adolescents to instill the desirability of educational goals as a way of achieving some future occupation or status. A sense of goal orientation for the future may be helpful in delaying the initiation of sexual activity or increasing the practice of contraception (Devaney, 1978). Opportunities for women in the labor force should be explored because they affect the role of women and consequently the decision to bear children early.

Family Relationships. Closely related to future goals is the issue of the structural consequences of family relationships. The communication patterns established in a family may inhibit a daughter's early childbirth. This means that programs could focus on strengthening family relationships as a way of deterring early sexual activity. Families that encourage communication, set high expectations, and provide an environment in which educational and occupational achievement are applauded are less likely to have daughters who experience early premarital pregnancy. More work is needed to design programs to help families develop communication skills that would enable them to educate their children and transmit to their children some of their own hopes and dreams for them.

Programs and Services

Unmarried adolescent mothers are eligible for AFDC. As AFDC recipients, they are also eligible for Medicaid, which covers their medical care. The policies regarding Medicaid coverage vary across states, however, and not all states provide the same coverage for teenage mothers. Idaho, North Carolina, Texas, and Wyoming do not provide full medical coverage if the adolescent is not also an AFDC recipient, for example, while the other states provide pregnancy medical care even if the adolescent is not an AFDC recipient (Moore & Burt, 1982). Poli-

cies also differ with regard to eligibility determination for these state programs. In-kind contributions may be required, for example, or teenage parents' income may be considered in determining need. Some age restrictions may also apply.

According to a 1975 AFDC survey, 56 percent of the mothers receiving AFDC in 1975 were teenagers when their first child was born (Moore, Wertheimer, & Holden, 1981). Expenditures for these households totaled $8.55 billion in 1975, a figure that includes the cost of AFDC, food stamps, and Medicaid. It is these statistics that give rise to the charge that welfare provides an economic incentive for early childbearing. The evidence is mixed, however, and studies in general do not support the idea that welfare programs encourage early childbearing (Moore & Burt, 1982).

Numerous programs exist to assist adolescent mothers. The Department of Health and Human Services identified between 1,000 and 1,500 programs authorized under Title VIII of the Health Services and Centers Amendments of 1978 (P.L. 95-626). Various other federal government and state agencies also provide programs aimed specifically at pregnant adolescents, adolescents who are parents, or adolescents who are sexually active. Many school systems, medical systems, and private delivery systems also provide some form of programming aimed at the adolescent pregnant female or those at greatest risk of pregnancy. However, like many other services aimed at particular target groups, these services are scattered over many delivery sites, and many have been affected by the cutback in funds for social service programs.

Agencies that target adolescent pregnant females include the Department of Health and Human Services for family planning, maternal and child health services, AFDC, Medicaid, and community health centers; the Department of Agriculture for food stamps; and the Department of Labor for job training services. On the state level, departments that sponsor programs focusing on adolescent family life include education, public social services, and health. On the local level, agencies may include health departments, city and county hospitals, and local school districts. Services provided by private philanthropy and nonprofit social service agencies include United Way, the March of Dimes, Planned Parenthood, the YMCA and YWCA, Boys and Girls Clubs of America, and church-affiliated services such as Catholic Charities.

Although service programs are abundant, the need for an integrated and comprehensive service delivery system remains. In response to this need, the Office of Adolescent Pregnancy Programs was created in 1978 under the Department of Health and Human Services and renewed under Title XX of the Social Security Act in 1981 as the Adolescent Family Life Demonstration Projects. The programs funded under this project were designed to deliver comprehensive services including medical, educational, parenting, family planning, and referral and counseling services to help adolescents with problems associated with early pregnancy. In all these programs, social workers have played a significant role as clinicians, administrators, program planners, and policy analysts.

ROSINA M. BECERRA
EVE P. FIELDER

For further information, see ABORTION; ADOLESCENTS; ADOPTION; FAMILY AND POPULATION PLANNING.

References

Abernethy, V. (1974). "Illegitimate Conception among Teenagers." *American Journal of Public Health, 64*(7), 662–665.

Abernethy, V. (1976). "Prevention of Unwanted Pregnancy among Teenagers." *Primary Care, 3*(3), 399–405.

Ager, J. W., Shea, F., & Agronow, S. (1979, September). *Consequences of Teen Contraceptive Program Dropout and of Method Discontinuance.* Paper presented at the 87th Annual Conference of the American Psychological Association, New York.

Akpom, C. A., Akpom, K. L., & Davis, M. (1976). "Prior Sexual Behavior of Teenagers Attending Rap Sessions for the First Time." *Family Planning Perspectives, 8*(4), 203–206.

Baldwin, W. (1981). "Adolescent Pregnancy and Childbearing: An Overview." *Seminars in Perinatology, 5*(1), 1–8.

Baldwin, W., & Cain, V. (1980). "The Children of Teenage Parents." *Family Planning Perspectives, 12*(1), 34–43.

Becerra, R. M., & de Anda, D. (1984). "Pregnancy and Motherhood among Mexican-American Adolescents." *Health and Social Work, 9*(2), 106–123.

Bolton, F. G. (1980). *The Pregnant Adolescent.* Beverly Hills, Calif.: Sage Publications.

Card, J., & Wise, L. (1978). "Teenage Mothers and Teenage Fathers: The Impact of Early Childbearing on the Parents' Personal and Professional Lives." *Family Planning Perspectives, 10*(4), 199–218.

Cheetham, J. (1977). *Unwanted Pregnancy and Counseling.* London, England: Routledge & Kegan Paul.

Chilman, C. S. (1978). *Adolescent Sexuality in a Changing American Society: Social and Psychological Perspectives.* Washington, D.C.: U.S. Government Printing Office.

Chilman, C. S. (1979). "Teenage Pregnancy: A Research Review." *Social Work, 24*(6), 492–498.

Cutright, P. (1972). "The Teenage Sexual Revolution and the Myth of an Abstinent Past." *Family Planning Perspectives, 4*(1), 24–31.

Cvetkovich, G., & Grote, B. (1976, May). *Psychological Factors Associated with Adolescent Premarital Coitus.* Paper presented at the National Institute of Child Health and Human Development, Bethesda, Md.

Daniels, A. M. (1969). "Reaching Unwed Mothers." *American Journal of Nursing, 69*(2), 332–335.

Devaney, B. (1978). *An Analysis of the Determinants of Adolescent Pregnancy and Childbearing.* Washington, D.C.: National Institute of Child Health and Development.

Forest, J. D. (1980). *Exploration of the Effects of Organized Family Planning Programs in the United States on Adolescent Fertility.* Bethesda, Md.: National Institutes of Health.

Friedman, A. A. (1971). *Therapy with Families of Sexually Acting Out Girls.* New York: Springer Publishing Co.

Alan Guttmacher Institute. (1981). *Teenage Pregnancy: The Problem That Hasn't Gone Away.* New York: Author.

Henshaw, S., et al. (1981). "Abortion in the United States, 1978–1979." *Family Planning Perspectives, 13,* 6–18.

Hunt, M. (1974). *Sexual Behavior in the 1970s.* New York: Dell Publishing Co.

Jessor, S., & Jessor, R. (1975). "Transition from Virginity to Non-Virginity among Youth: A Social-Psychological Study Over Time." *Developmental Psychology, 11*(4), 473–484.

Kantner, J., & Zelnik, M. (1972). "Sexual Experience of Young Unmarried Women in the United States." *Family Planning Perspectives, 4*(8), 9–18.

Kenney, A., & Alexander, S. (1980). "Sex/Family Life Education in the Schools: An Analysis of State Policies." *Family Planning/Population Reporter, 9*(3), 44–55.

Kirby, D., Alter, J., & Scales, P. (1979). *An Analysis of U.S. Sex Education Programs and Evaluation Methods*. Washington, D.C.: U.S. Department of Health, Education, & Welfare.

Klein, L. (1978). "Antecedents of Teenage Pregnancy." *Clinical Obstetrics and Gynecology, 21*(4), 1152–1159.

Lindemann, C. (1974). *Birth Control and Unmarried Young Women*. New York: Springer Publishing Co.

Lipsitz, J. S. (1980). "Adolescent Psychosexual Development." In P. B. Smith & D. M. Mumford (Eds.), *Adolescent Pregnancy: Perspectives for the Health Professional* (pp. 1–13). Boston, Mass.: G.K. Hall & Co.

Moore, K. A., & Burt, M. R. (1982). *Private Crisis, Public Cost: Policy Perspectives on Teenage Childbearing*. Washington, D.C.: Urban Institute.

Moore, K. A., & Caldwell, S. B. (1976). "The Effect of Government Policies on Out-of-Wedlock Sex and Pregnancy." *Family Planning Perspectives, 9*(4), 164–169.

Moore, K. A., Wertheimer, R., & Holden, R. (1981). *Teenage Childbearing: Public Sector Costs*. Bethesda, Md.: National Institutes of Health.

National Center for Health Statistics. (1984). *Trends in Teenage Childbearing, United States 1970–81* (Publication No. [PHS] 84-1919). Rockville, Md.: Author.

Ooms, T. (1981). *Teenage Pregnancy in a Family Context: Implications for Policy*. Philadelphia, Pa.: Temple University Press.

Perlman, D. (1974). "Self-Esteem and Sexual Permissiveness." *Journal of Marriage and the Family, 36*(3), 470–473.

Phipps-Yonas, S. (1980). "Teenage Motherhood: A Review of the Literature." *American Journal of Orthopsychiatry, 50*(3), 403–431.

Reichelt, P. A., & Werley, H. H. (1975). "Contraception, Abortion, and V.D." *Family Planning Perspectives, 7*(2), 83–88.

Reiss, I. L. (1967). *The Social Context of Sexual Permissiveness*. New York: Holt, Rinehart & Winston.

Reiss, I. L., Banwart, A., & Foreman, H. (1975). "Premarital Contraceptive Usage: A Study and Some Theoretical Explorations." *Journal of Marriage and the Family, 37*(3), 619–630.

Rogel, M. J., & Zuehlke, M. E. (1982). "Adolescent Contraceptive Behavior: Influences and Implications." In I. R. Stuart & C. F. Wells (Eds.), *Pregnancy in Adolescence* (pp. 194–216). New York: Van Nostrand Reinhold Co.

Shapiro, C. (1980). "Sexual Learning: The Short-Changed Adolescent Male." *Social Work, 25*(6), 489–493.

Sorenson, R. (1973). *Adolescent Sexuality in Contemporary America*. New York: World Publishing Co.

Sugar, M. (1980). "The Epidemic of Adolescent Motherhood." In M. Sugar (Ed.), *Responding to Adolescent Needs*. New York: SP Medical & Scientific Books.

Tietze, C. (1978). "Teenage Pregnancies: Looking Ahead to 1984." *Family Planning Perspectives, 10*(4), 205–207.

Torres, A., Forrest, J., & Eisman, S. (1980). "Family Planning Services in the United States, 1978–1979." *Family Planning Perspectives, 13*(3), 132–141.

Urdy, J., Bauman, K., & Morris, N. (1975). "Changes in Premarital Coital Experience of Recent Decade of Birth Cohorts of Urban America." *Journal of Marriage and the Family, 37*(4), 783–787.

Vener, A., & Stewart, C. (1974). "Adolescent Sexual Behavior in Middle America Revisited: 1970–1973." *Journal of Marriage and the Family, 36*(4), 728–735.

Ventura, S. (1984). *Births of Hispanic Parentage, 1981* (Pub. No. 85-1120). Hyattsville, Md.: U.S. Department of Health and Human Services.

Walters, J., & Walters, L. (1980). "Parent-Child Relationships: A Review, 1970–1979." *Journal of Marriage and the Family, 42*(4), 807–822.

Zelnik, M., & Kantner, J. F. (1978). "First Pregnancies to Women Aged 15–19: 1976–1977." *Family Planning Perspectives, 10*(1), 11–20.

Zelnik, M., & Kantner, J. F. (1979). "Reasons for Non-use of Contraception by Sexually Active Women Aged 15–19." *Family Planning Perspectives, 11*(5), 289–296.

Zelnik, M., & Kantner, J. F. (1980). "Sexual Activity, Contraceptive Use and Pregnancy among Metropolitan Area Teenagers: 1971–1979." *Family Planning Perspectives, 12*(5), 230–237.

Zelnik, M., Kantner, J. F., & Ford, K. (1981). *Sex and Pregnancy in Adolescence*. Beverly Hills, Calif.: Sage Publications.

ADOLESCENTS

The concept of adolescence—a period in the life cycle between childhood and adulthood—was introduced at the beginning of the twentieth century by Hall (1904). Whereas Hall considered adolescence to extend from 12 years to between 22 and 25 years, most researchers and theorists consider the age span to be from 12 to 18 years. Adolescence has also been divided into phases or age groupings, most typically preadolescence,

Table 1. Adolescent Population, by Age, Gender, and Ethnicity, 1980

Age (in years)	Total	Male	Female	White	Black	Spanish Origin
12	3,518,982	1,796,333	1,722,649	2,786,155	517,587	285,634
13	3,643,189	1,856,566	1,786,623	2,889,432	537,569	289,555
14	3,782,784	1,932,778	1,850,006	2,992,789	567,872	297,613
15	4,059,898	2,069,726	1,990,172	3,232,449	595,146	311,277
16	4,180,875	2,135,125	2,045,750	3,343,837	600,439	316,742
17	4,223,848	2,160,114	2,063,734	3,380,772	600,169	324,585
18	4,251,779	2,153,292	2,098,487	3,417,053	589,101	319,622
19	4,451,724	2,237,152	2,214,572	3,587,991	600,008	334,102
Total	32,113,079	16,341,086	15,771,993	25,630,478	4,607,891	2,479,130

Source: U.S. Bureau of the Census. (1984). *1980 Census of the Populaiton: Vol, 1, Characteristics of the Population.* Washington, D.C.: U.S. Government Printing Office.

early adolescence, middle adolescence or adolescence proper, and late adolescence (Blos, 1941, 1979; Dunphy, 1963; Sullivan, 1953).

Although menarche (the onset of menstruation) serves as a fairly clear biological marker for the entry of girls into adolescence, no similar clear-cut criterion exists for boys. Moreover, whereas all cultures formally or informally recognize puberty—"the biological and physiological changes associated with sexual maturation" (Muuss, 1952, p. 5)—adolescence appears to be a phenomenon primarily of postindustrial societies.

The criteria that can indicate the end of adolescence are even less clear. The lack of uniformity in the laws discriminating between the status of minors and the status of adults for activities that range from voting to marriage to alcohol consumption is a pointed example.

Demographic Data

According to the U.S. Bureau of the Census (1984), adolescents aged 12 to 19 years are 14.2 percent of the U.S. population. Their distribution by age, sex, and ethnicity is shown in Table 1.

Indicative of the trend toward lower birthrates during the 1960s is the fact that the size of the population in each age group decreases from the oldest to the youngest cohort. Therefore, 19 year olds constitute 13.86 percent of the adolescent population, whereas 12 year olds are only 10.96 percent.

In every age category, the size of the male cohort is larger than the female cohort.

However, the difference is quite small, ranging from .5 percent among 19 year olds to 2.3 percent among 17 year olds for an average of 11.7 percent in the adolescent population as a whole. White 12 to 19 year olds constitute 79.8 percent of the adolescent population compared to 14.3 percent and 7.7 percent, respectively, for their black and Latino cohorts.

Biological Development

The development of primary and secondary sexual characteristics during adolescence is the result of endocrine changes, which produce changes in hormone levels. Although the growth rate during infancy proceeds at a more accelerated rate, the magnitude and rate of change experienced during puberty is more significant because the adolescent is more cognizant of the changes he or she is experiencing (Tanner, 1972). The sequence of development is considered universal; however, individual timetables for the various stages differ, and the areas of development may not be synchronous (Peterson & Taylor, 1980).

Over the past 100 years (and especially the last 50 years), physical maturation has continued to occur earlier with each successive generation. This "secular trend" is particularly evident in the earlier onset of menarche and in the increases in the rate of growth and full adult stature over the past century. In the United States, the average age of menarche at the beginning of the century was slightly over 14 years; by mid-century, it was less than 13 years (Tanner,

1962). Factors hypothesized to explain these phenomena include improvements in health and nutrition as well as the "hybrid vigor" hypothesis, which attributes the changes to the intermarriage of various groups because of greater social mobility (Muuss, 1970).

Among the most dramatic of the physical changes during adolescence is the height spurt. Girls generally experience their major increase in height at around age 12—about two years earlier than boys. However, there is great individual variation so that the range for girls is 10 1/2 to 14 years, and for boys, it is 12 1/2 to 15 years.

Changes also occur in weight; girls develop increased subcutaneous fatty tissue and boys usually become heavier than girls. Although the hips and shoulders become wider in both boys and girls, the boys' shoulders become wider than their hips, and girls' hips wider than their shoulders. Changes in skin texture and oiliness take place, along with gradual changes in the timbre and pitch of the voices of both boys and girls (Faust, 1977; Peterson & Taylor, 1980; Tanner, 1972).

Clausen's (1975) review of the literature indicated that early physical maturation generally has a positive effect on boys; boys who mature early are rated as more relaxed and poised, less dependent, and more attractive to and popular with their peers than those who mature later (Clausen, 1975; Jones, 1965; Mussen & Jones, 1957; Peskin, 1967). Girls seem to have the opposite experience; early maturation appears to result in negative evaluations, including feelings of isolation, submissive behavior, and less popularity with and leadership of their peers (Clausen, 1975; Jones & Mussen, 1958; Peskin, 1973; Weatherly, 1964). In any case, research indicates that the individual's idiosyncratic rate of physical development and its mesh or lack of sync with cultural norms has an impact on his or her overall development.

Although research in the biological aspects of adolescent development is straightforward, the literature on other aspects of adolescent development is characterized by controversy and conflicting viewpoints. Theorists and researchers agree that adolescence is a period in the life cycle when notable development occurs in a number of areas.

They differ, however, about the following aspects of adolescence:

1. Whether the development is continuous or discontinuous with the preceding and following stages in the life cycle.

2. Whether the period of adolescence is one of turmoil and stress or relatively uneventful.

3. Whether it is critical for adolescents to experience or resolve specific developmental tasks or issues during this time.

4. Whether internal or environmental factors have a more significant influence on the experiences and outcome of adolescent development.

5. Whether there are specific adolescent responses (such as coping or defense mechanisms) to internal and external changes.

For example, Hall (1904), often referred to as the father of the psychology of adolescence, viewed adolescence as a discontinuous experience—a period that is qualitatively and quantitatively different from childhood and from adulthood. The discontinuity, along with the great physical changes that adolescents experience, caused Hall to label the period as one of *sturm und drang*. Hall's biogenetic approach posited that adolescence was a "recapitulation" of one of mankind's stages of evolution—a turbulent time for the species and, therefore, for the individual.

Psychological Development

Psychosexual Theories. Psychoanalytic theorists have posited a different recapitulation theory. Specifically, they see the developmental processes of adolescence as a recapitulation of earlier infantile stages of development through the reexperiencing of either oedipal or preoedipal conflicts (Blos, 1941, 1979; A. Freud, 1948; S. Freud, 1924/1973).

The physiological changes that bring about sexual-reproductive maturation are considered to usher in the genital stage, which disturbs the psychological equilibrium achieved during the latency period (S. Freud, 1924/1973). The sheer "quantity of the instinctual impulses" (A. Freud, 1948, p. 164) is thought of as rekindling a conflict over dominance between the ego and the id, the latter of which has predominated and matured during the latency period. The ego is conceptualized as torn between the impulses and demands of the id and the restrictions of the superego (A. Freud, 1948). Consequently, adolescence is viewed as a period of stress and turmoil and as discontinuous with other phases in the life cycle.

According to the psychosexual theorists, two tasks must be accomplished during this stage if psychological maturity is to be attained: (1) detachment from the opposite sex parent as an incestuous love object and (2) establishment of a nonantagonistic, nondominated relationship with the same sex parent. This process of detachment may result in negativism and hostility toward parents and other authority figures for a time. S. Freud (1924/1973) believed that this process is seldom completed ideally.

Blos (1941, 1979) modified traditional psychoanalytic theory, stressing the importance of "the cultural milieu and social stratum" (Blos, 1941, p. 7) in personality formation and positing a reciprocal influence between the individual and his or her environment. Although he insisted that adolescent development must be considered in the context of a particular culture and the family's "unique version of the culture" (Blos, 1941, p. 260), like his psychoanalytic predecessors, he saw adolescence as a transitional period that involves a recapitulation of earlier familial patterns of interaction. However, he considered this process to be qualitatively different from earlier developmental experiences because of the significant maturation of the ego (ego supremacy and ego differentiation) during the latency period (Blos, 1941). This ego development allows the adolescent in most cases to resolve the oedipal conflicts and the component infantile dependencies (Blos, 1979).

According to Blos (1979), the second individuation process that occurs during adolescence requires a "normative regression in the service of development" (p. 153); that is, only in adolescence is regression an essential and normal process. Though normal, this regression still produces turmoil, volatile behavior, and anxiety that, if it becomes unmanageable, may result in the use of a variety of defense mechanisms such as withdrawal and secrecy, fantasy, temporary compulsive habit formation, compensation, intel-

lectualization, rationalization, projection, and changes in the ego ideal (Blos, 1941).

Chodorow (1974, 1978) has reinterpreted the individuation process, challenging the male sex bias of earlier formulations. According to Chodorow, because the male's first love object—the mother—is of the opposite sex, separation and individuation are critical to male gender identity and development but not to the progress of female identity development.

Psychosocial Theories. Psychosocial theories of adolescence, although based on Freud's psychosexual conceptualization of development, emphasize the impact of the sociocultural context on individual development. Erikson (1963, 1968) viewed development as proceeding through a sequence of stages, each of which is characterized by a specific crisis. Not only are the crises of each stage produced by internal mechanisms, they are the result of the interaction between the individual and his or her social environment, which makes cultural demands in the form of social expectations, norms, and values.

Erikson thought of identity formation as a process that continues throughout one's life; but he believed that identity "has its normative crisis in adolescence" (1968, p. 23). Like the psychosexual theorists, Erikson described adolescence as a time of turmoil and stress. However, he (1968) considered it to be the the the result of an "identity crisis" that typifies this stage, rather than of a conflict between the ego and the id. Furthermore, he viewed adolescence as a necessary and productive period during which the adolescent experiments with and works to consolidate his or her personal, occupational, and ideological identity. This identity is formed through the individual's psychological integration as well as through the social environment, which serves critical functions during this process. In the search for self-definition, conflict arises between the adolescent and his or her parents as a necessary movement toward establishing the adolescent's own view of self, of the world, and of his or her place in that world.

Erikson's conceptualization has been criticized for its sex bias in that he generalized changes in the life cycle from a male model of development (Chodorow, 1974, 1978; Gilligan, 1979). Gilligan (1979, p. 434) noted that individuation and separation from the mother are accepted as critical for the development of gender identity among males, but she proposed the opposite dynamic for females: "Femininity is defined through attachment" to the mother. According to Gilligan (1979, p. 434), "male gender identity will be threatened by intimacy while female gender identity will be threatened by individuation." Erikson viewed separation as a healthy sign of progressive development and attachment as a problem. However, Chodorow (1974, 1978) and Gilligan (1979) proposed that, in the course of female development, intimacy may more appropriately precede separation or at least be fused with identity formation.

Social Learning Theory. Social learning theorists describe adolescence as a period of development that, for the majority of individuals, proceeds from childhood with great continuity in behavior, interpersonal relationships, and self-evaluation (Bandura & Walters, 1963). The behavioral and social learning principles that apply in infancy and childhood remain the same, with the possible expansion of sources of reinforcement in the environment, a greater number and variety of models, and an expanded capacity for self-regulated behavior.

The process of socialization includes the development of behavioral repertoires through differential reinforcement, stimulus and response generalization, higher order conditioning, modeling, and rule learning (Bandura, 1969; Gagne, 1970). Differential reinforcement refers to the process whereby behavior that is reinforced increases in frequency and behavior that is punished or placed on extinction decreases. For example, adolescents shape each other's social behaviors by positively responding to specific mannerisms, dress, and the latest slang terms and by ostracizing or ridiculing behaviors that do not meet the norms of their peers. Response generalization involves the production of behaviors (responses) that have properties similar to the response that has been reinforced. Via stimulus generalization, the adolescent is likely to respond with the same repertoire of responses to other peers he or she perceives as being similar to those from whom he or she received reinforcement. In higher order conditioning, certain individuals, environments,

objects, words, symbols, and the like become positive or negative stimuli for the individual and result in specific responses because they are associated with positive or negative events.

Modeling is a mode of imitative or vicarious learning that involves the observation, coding, and retention of a set of behaviors for their performance at a subsequent time. It is particularly efficient for learning complex behaviors, such as interpersonal skills. Furthermore, modeled behaviors are more readily learned in situations for which the individual has no prior repertoire of responses. Moreover, the adolescent also combines behaviors of various models into novel responses or abstracts a rule that allows him or her to act as the model would act in a novel situation for which specific responses have not been observed (Mehrabian, 1970). Hence, as one moves from childhood into adolescence and is exposed to a greater number and variety of models, one's potential behavioral repertoire increases substantially.

Finally, as an individual progresses through childhood into adolescence and adulthood, one notes an increase in self-regulatory behavior, most notably self-evaluation and self-reinforcement (Bandura, 1969). Self-reinforcement is generally established through modeling as the observer evaluates and reinforces his or her performance via the same criteria as the model. Over time, the responses become independent of the original learning experience and are generalized to other situations. Although self-evaluation and reinforcement can be independent of social norms, they often correspond.

Bandura and Walters (1963) note that empirical research has not borne out the claim that adolescence constitutes a sudden and drastic change from childhood, particularly in parent-child relations. They indicate that the pattern instead appears to be one of gradual socialization toward independence by means of a gradual change in reinforcement conditions.

Cognitive Development

According to Piagetian theory, cognitive development consists of the progression through stages of quantitatively and qualitatively more complex thought processes and structures. Piaget and Inhelder (1958) emphasized the discontinuity between the concrete operational thinking of the child and the qualitatively different formal operations of the adolescent. Piaget (1972) viewed the progression from concrete to formal operations as the product of individual "spontaneous and endogenous factors" (p. 7) and experiences in the environment that stimulate intellectual growth.

Formal operational thought is characterized by hypothetico-deductive reasoning: As the adolescent's thinking is no longer tied to concrete objects, he or she is able to construct possibilities, to manipulate and reflect upon mental constructs, and to assess probabilities. According to Piaget and Inhelder (1958), this new capacity enables the adolescent to "analyze his [or her] own thinking and construct theories" (p. 340). The adolescent's thought is no longer tied to trial and error but can generate hypotheses regarding all the possible relations among the various factors in solving a problem. Moreover, the adolescent systematically tests alternative hypotheses, varying one factor at a time while holding all other factors constant (Piaget & Inhelder, 1958).

Cognitive development also is conceptualized as a process of decentering. Decentering involves the reduction of egocentric thought that thereby allows for the generation and testing of hypotheses. Formal operations progress through transitional stages (generally from ages 11 to 14) in which the operations of formal thought are confounded by the adolescent's egocentrism. Elkind (1967, 1974, 1978) believes this results in the phenomenon he calls "the imaginary audience." That is, the adolescent feels as though his or her actions and appearance are constantly being scrutinized by others. Elkind (1978, p. 387) believed that this egocentrism may explain the feelings of self-consciousness that are prevalent during adolescence and "a good deal of adolescent boorishness, loudness, and faddish dress."

Also demonstrative of cognitive egocentrism is the complementary development of the "personal fable" (Elkind, 1967, 1974, 1978; Inhelder & Piaget, 1978). The personal fable involves viewing one's thoughts and feelings as unique experiences, often ones that should be saved for posterity (via diaries or poetry). Feelings of invulnerability accompany this perception and have been linked to such adolescent problems as the failure to use contraceptives and risk-taking behavior (Elkind, 1967). This cognitive egocentrism also results in projecting one's preoccupation with and plans for the future onto the society as a whole and viewing oneself in a Messianic role (Inhelder & Piaget, 1978). Primarily because of reality testing and the sharing of perceptions and experiences with peers, the egocentrism of early adolescence gives way to full formal operations by age 15 or 16 (Elkind, 1978; Inhelder & Piaget, 1978).

Moral Development

Moral development is incorporated in psychoanalytic theory via the development of a conscience in childhood and such conceptualizations as the "reexternalization" of the superego in adolescence (Settlage, 1972). The latter consists of a conscious appraisal, challenging, and discarding of values and an incorporation into the superego of reappraised ideals and values (which are no longer mirrors of parental values) (Hoffman, 1980). Erikson (1970) described the adolescent in the process of identity development as moving from the specific moral learnings of childhood to the pursuit of a moral ideology that facilitates identity formation.

Piaget (1965) formulated a simple two-stage dichotomous model, moving from moral realism to subjectivism. In the stage of moral realism, the child judges the moral value (rightness or wrongness) of an act by the magnitude of the damage or injury or simple conformity with stated rules, irrespective of intention. In the second or autonomous stage of subjectivism, intention becomes the foremost consideration in judging the moral value of an act. The subjective nature of rules and the concept of rules by mutual consent are recognized.

It is only with the attainment of formal operations in adolescence that the individual has the capacity for developing postconventional morality, recognizing individual and cultural differences as well as universal principles. Although Kohlberg and Gilligan (1975) propose that many adolescents regress to an instrumental level of moral development, Turiel (1974) describes the extreme relativism of the adolescent as a transitional phase. With attainment of formal operations and the recognition of differences in perspectives, the adolescent questions the rigid law-and-order morality of the conventional stage and rejects the imposition of moral codes and values on the individual. The adolescent's extreme relativism results from the rejection of conventional criteria for moral judgment, which leaves the individual for a time with the sense that no basis exists for objectively verifying values.

Hoffman (1980) proposed that the development of empathy and its transformation during cognitive development is the fundamental basis of moral development. As a result of his or her cognitive development, the adolescent begins to conceptualize others not only as distinct but to project the self into another's experiences beyond the immediate concrete situation and, therefore, to respond with empathic distress and "a more reciprocal feeling of concern for the victim" (Hoffman, 1980, p. 311). Moreover, this empathic distress can also be transformed into feelings of guilt if the victim's distress leads to self-blame with respect to one's action or inaction. Finally, one's empathic distress, sense of guilt, and impetus to relieve the distress perceived in another are viewed as the significant motivational components for moral action.

In social learning theory, moral values, judgments, and behaviors are viewed as being dependent on a variety of environmental factors, such as the long- and short-term consequences, the setting, the type of act, and the characteristics of the victim. Moral development involves a process of learning through direct instruction (rule learning), reinforcement contingencies, modeling, and evaluative feedback. By exposure to diverse situations and models, one learns which factors are important to consider in various situations when moral judgments are required (Bandura, 1977; Rosenthal & Zimmerman, 1978).

Social Development

The adolescent's social development is closely related to his or her psychological development, particularly identity formation and the need for intimacy. Sullivan (1953) viewed interpersonal relations as central to one's individual identity. He posited three stages of adolescent development, which are distinguished by different needs and expressions of interpersonal intimacy: preadolescence, early adolescence, and late adolescence. Preadolescence is characterized by the need for intimacy expressed through strong relationships, usually with persons of the same sex as the preadolescent. These relationships differ from those of childhood in their exclusivity and extent of personal intimacy, evidenced by disclosure of one's secret thoughts, feelings, and aspirations.

The stage of early adolescence is ushered in by the physiological changes of puberty with the concomitant appearance of the lust dynamism (Sullivan, 1953). Lust—a psychological rather than a moralistic construct—refers to genital drives that impel the individual toward sexual satisfaction. This new integrating dynamism results in the shift to intimate relations with persons of the opposite sex, patterned, to some degree, after preadolescent same-sex relationships.

According to Sullivan (1953, p. 297), a person enters late adolescence when he or she "discovers what he [she] likes in the way of genital behavior and how to fit it into the rest of life." By late adolescence, Sullivan claimed, the majority of adolescents have established heterosexuality as their preferred mode of sexual relationships and continue to develop and expand their interpersonal skills. Intimacy is the core of what Sullivan (1953, p. 310) described as the mature person; it involves "a very lively sensitivity to the needs of the other and to the interpersonal security or absence of anxiety in the other."

Although little research has been done on sex differences in the development of friendships, Coleman's review of the literature (1980) pointed out that the need for friendships changes and that the greatest need (especially for girls) occurs during middle adolescence. It is during middle adolescence that the dread of rejection and the lack of social confidence take their toll. Moreover, girls experience more feelings of anxiety about friendships than do boys, probably because the socialization of girls places greater emphasis on the fulfillment of emotional needs through relationships. In contrast, boys tend to be socialized to seek relationships that are focused on actions (Douvan & Adelson, 1966).

Bandura (1964) and others indicate that increased peer interaction does not usually result in a simultaneous shifting away from parental relationships and values. A number of studies (Hess & Goldblatt, 1957; Maxwell,

Connor, & Walters, 1961; Bandura & Walters, 1963; Bandura, 1964; Offer, Sabshin, & Marcus, 1965; Meissner, 1965; and Offer, 1967) found adolescents and parents to hold positive views of one another. With increasing age, an adolescent's decisions and values rely less on either parents or peers and reflect his or her own views (Gardner & Thompson, 1963).

Sexual Development

Sexual development is the result of the interaction of intrapsychic, sociocultural, and biological factors. The physiological changes initiated in puberty influence the individual in a social context (Miller & Simon, 1980) and via the personal evaluation of their meaning and significance.

Gender identity and gender role expectations form the foundation of the young adolescent's sexual identity "since the sexual and social scenarios of the society are organized around norms for gender-appropriate behavior" (Miller & Simon, 1980, p. 383). Particularly in early adolescence, motivations for sociosexual behavior may be nonerotic, impelled instead by what are considered gender-appropriate behaviors in the specific social context (Miller & Simon, 1980).

With the onset of puberty, the adolescent must add a sexual dimension to his or her gender identity. According to Miller and Simon (1980, p. 388), the progress of psychosexual development and concomitant sexual behavior depend on two factors and their interaction: (1) "the intrapsychic history and life of the individual" and (2) "the interpersonal requirements of social life"—the social context. The intrapsychic life of the individual refers to idiosyncratic values that result in the eroticizing of events, attributes, relationships, and so forth. Interpersonal "scripts" are less idiosyncratic because they reflect the present social expectations and constraints, which vary with time and the individual's reference group (Miller & Simon, 1980; Gagnon, 1974). Hence, majority and minority adolescent cohorts may have significantly different interpersonal scripts.

When there is congruence between intrapsychic and interpersonal factors, sexual identity formation proceeds smoothly. When these two factors are discordant, the adolescent must choose to risk either alienation from others or a sense of self-betrayal. Particularly vulnerable in this regard are individuals whose intrapsychic content is homoerotic, but who feel constrained by sociocultural norms and demands (Miller & Simon, 1980).

Current Problems and Issues

Pregnancy. The present concern with adolescent sexual activity results primarily from a concern over the growth in adolescent pregnancy. Over one million adolescent girls become pregnant every year; of these, approximately 400,000 are 17 years or younger (Alan Guttmacher Institute, 1981). Although pregnancy rates for black adolescents are still higher than those for white adolescents, the rise in the rates over the last 10 years has been the result of a significant increase in teenage pregnancy in the white population. The birthrate among Latino adolescents is also significant because Latinos have the highest fertility rate in the nation and one in five of these births is to an adolescent (Ventura, 1982; Ventura & Heuser, 1981). Moreover, the rate of unwed 15- to 17-year-old parents has continued to rise; it was 17 per thousand in 1970, 19 per thousand in 1976, and 21 per thousand in 1980 (National Center for Health Statistics, 1982). Concern about adolescent mothers and their children has intensified because nine out of 10 unmarried adolescent mothers decide to rear their children (Alan Guttmacher Institute, 1981).

Runaway and Homeless Youths. Runaway youths are those "under the age of eighteen who are away from home at least overnight without parent or caretaker permission" (U.S. Department of Health & Human Services [USDHHS], 1983). The homeless youths are a subpopulation of this group who have no parent, parent-figure, or institutional caretakers.

In 1975, the National Statistical Survey on Runaway Youth estimated the runaway population to be 733,000. By the 1983 national survey, the estimate had risen to 1.3–1.5 million runaway and homeless youths (USDHHS, 1983). Runaway and homeless youths are particularly at risk for victimization from robbery, assault, drug addiction, and criminal activities, primarily prostitution and pornography (Wooden, 1976).

Only 50 percent of these runaway youths will eventually return home or find an alternative placement; 25 percent will remain on their own as hard-core street kids who earn their living at least partially through criminal activity (Chelimsky, 1982; National Network of Runaway and Youth Services, 1985; USDHHS, 1983). Although a small percentage of runaway youths are attracted to large urban centers that offer anonymity and financial "opportunities," nearly 75 percent remain in their home cities (USDHHS, 1983).

Agencies that have served runaway youths over time describe the most recent cohort as more disturbed and evidencing more complex and multiple problems than did former runaway populations. Only 20 percent are now estimated to leave home because of short-term or relatively minor crises; 80 percent run away from chronic, long-term problems, 36 percent of them from physical and sexual abuse (USDHHS, 1983).

The Runaway and Homeless Youth Act was passed in 1974 to provide grants and technical assistance to agencies to develop and support community-based programs to deal with the immediate needs of runaway youths (including shelter, counseling, and aftercare services) and to encourage a reunion of the youths with their families by working toward the resolution of problems in these families and strengthening familial relationships. The act has resulted in an increase in service to only about 6 percent of the runaway population, and aftercare and outreach services are rare and limited (Chelimsky, 1982). However, it has established linkages among state, regional, and national agencies that have helped reunite families and have provided a means for dealing with status offenders outside the judicial system.

Suicide. Suicide ranks third among the leading causes of death for adolescents, after accidents and homicides (Holinger & Offer, 1982; Peck, 1982), in contrast to its rank of ninth or tenth among the population as a whole (Peck & Litman, 1982). Moreover, the suicide rates for 15–19 year olds doubled between 1961 and 1975 and tripled from 1956 to 1975 (Holinger & Offer, 1982). Between 1970 and 1980, the rates for 15–24 year old males rose nearly 50 percent (National Cen-

ter for Health Statistics, 1982). In 1986, unpublished data from the National Center for Health Statistics showed the following suicide rates per 100,000 for 15–19 year olds: total, 8.7; white males, 15.1; black males, 6.5; white females, 3.5; and black females, 1.7.

These comparative rates parallel those of the population as a whole: significantly more males than females commit suicide and the highest suicide rate is among white males. Furthermore, although some studies indicate that the suicide rate for Latino youths is lower than that of their black cohorts and white cohorts (Peck, 1982), other studies claim that the gap between the white rate and the Latino rate is narrowing in that the rates for whites were 2.2 times higher in 1977 and 1.92 times higher in 1980 (Smith & Warren, 1983). Moreover, these rates are probably underestimated because a percentage of the deaths of youths reported as accidents actually may be suicides.

The available morbidity statistics do not account for the even greater number of attempted, but unsuccessful, suicides. A number of authors claim that suicide attempters are a larger proportion of the youth population than their counterparts in the adult population and that the ratio of suicide attempts to actual suicides may be as high as 50 to 1 (Peck, 1982) or 150 to 1 (Tishler, McKenry, & Morgan, 1981). The gender ratio for suicide attempts is the reverse of that for completed suicides, with females attempting suicide two to three times more often than males (Holinger, 1978; Toolan, 1975; Peck, 1982). One reason for this discrepancy is that males generally select more potentially lethal methods (such as firearms or jumping from buildings) than do females, who usually attempt to overdose on drugs (Finch & Poznanski, 1971; Holinger, 1978).

Youthful suicide attempters have consistently been found to be the products of families with higher rates of divorce, separation, and parental death particularly at an early age (Hawton, 1982). Physical abuse and a family history of suicide also are characteristic of suicide attempters (Green, 1978; Kerfort, 1979; Tishler et al., 1981). A higher incidence of drug abuse has also been noted in this population (McKenry, Tishler, & Kelley, 1983), with drug overdose being the most frequent method of attempted suicide (Hawton, 1982). Most suicide attempts occur

Table 2. Use of Drugs by Youths Ages 12 to 17, (Percentages of Those Surveyed) 1982

Type of Drug	Ever Used	Current User
Marijuana	26.7	11.5
Hallucinogens	5.2	1.4
Cocaine	6.5	1.6
Heroin	(less than .5)	(less than .5)
Analgesics	4.2	2.6
Stimulants	6.7	1.3
Sedatives	5.8	.9
Tranquilizers	4.9	.7

Source: National Institute on Drug Abuse. (1982). *National Survey on Drug Abuse: Main Findings.* Washington, D.C.: Author.

after a "major disruption of a personal relationship," either parental or romantic (Hawton, 1982, p. 501). The prognosis for unsuccessful suicide attempters is generally good, with only 10 percent repeating the suicide attempt (Hawton, 1982), which indicates that many suicide attempts are extreme and atypical responses to a crisis.

A significant third population includes adolescents who have not attempted suicide but experience suicidal ideation. According to Peck (1982), as many as 10 to 20 percent of the youths in this country may contemplate suicide at any one time.

Drug Abuse. Although drug abuse is recognized as a serious problem among a segment of the adolescent population, data conflict on the proportion of the youth population for which this is an issue. Table 2 lists the percentages of 12–17 year olds ($N = 1,581$) who reported drug use in the National Survey on Drug Abuse (National Institute on Drug Abuse (1982).

Other studies using regional populations have found notably higher rates. For example, studies of senior high school students found the marijuana ever-used rate to be over 54 percent in New York State in 1978 (Tessler, 1980), 68.1 percent in San Jose, California, in 1979 (Tessler, 1980); and 47.5 percent in New Jersey in 1981 (Jalai et al., 1981). Jalai et al.'s study (1981) of 2,131 students reported a 21.6 percent rate for frequent (once a week to daily) use of mari-

juana. Rates for other drugs ever used also were higher than the national figures.

Data on the use of inhalants were not available in the national survey, but the regional figures show it to be a problem for a portion of the youth population: 16.1 percent in New York State (Tessler, 1980); 7.1 in San Jose, California (Tessler, 1980); and 10.1 percent in New Jersey (Jalai et al., 1981). Inhalant abuse has been noted by a number of researchers to be particularly high among Latino youths (Barnes, 1979; Dworkin & Stephens, 1980; Medida & Cruz, 1972; Padilla et al., 1979). Padilla et al. (1979) estimated that Latino youths are 14 times more likely to abuse inhalant substances than are their cohorts nationwide.

Gender differences in the use of marijuana appear to be minimal, with rates of 13 percent and 10 percent, respectively, for male and female youths (National Institute on Drug Abuse, 1982). When drug use over the previous year is surveyed, the figures increase dramatically, to 48 percent for females and 50 percent for males. These 1983 figures demonstrate a continued decreasing trend by youths in the use of marijuana, which peaked in 1978 (Johnston, Bachman, & O'Malley, 1984). The rate for combined illicit drugs other than marijuana is slightly higher for females (33 percent) than for males (32 percent). The rates for males are higher, however, if stimulants (which may include "diet" pills) are removed from the data. For example, nearly 14 percent of the male sample used cocaine, compared with fewer than 10 percent of the females (Johnston, Bachman, & O'Malley, 1984).

White and minority rates for the use of marijuana also were similar: 12 percent of all white adolescents and 10 percent of all minority youths (12–17 years) (National Institute on Drug Abuse, 1982). Various drugs appear to be used differentially by different ethnic groups. Most hallucinogenics and barbiturates have been identified as "white" drugs (Jalai et al., 1981), but phencyclidine (PCP) has a particularly high rate of use among black and Latino youths (National Institute on Drug Abuse, 1979). Moreover, adolescents seem to begin using PCP at an earlier age than illicit drugs other than marijuana and alcohol; over half a national sample of PCP users began using PCP prior to high school (Johnston, Bachman, & O'Malley, 1984).

Alcohol Abuse. Alcohol is the drug of choice and the drug most frequently abused by the adolescent population. The National Survey on Drug Abuse (National Institute on Drug Abuse, 1982) ($N = 1,581$) found a slight increase among current users of alcohol, aged 12–17, from 24 percent in 1972 to 26.9 percent in 1982 for both boys and girls. However, the proportion of these adolescents who had used alcohol in the past year was 87.3 percent, and the rate for males was slightly higher.

Whereas most drug abusers are introduced to illicit drugs by peers, family members most often introduce the adolescent to alcohol (Milgram, 1982) and, according to some studies, remain the adolescent's main source (Jalai et al., 1981). Although parents are an important source of alcohol in early adolescence, numerous studies have shown that an adolescent's drinking pattern clearly parallels that of his or her friends (Biddle, Blank, & Marlin, 1980; Globetti, 1972; Kandel et al., 1976; Potvin & Lee, 1980).

Drinking of alcoholic beverages is illegal for adolescents; however, problem drinking involves "frequent drinking to the point of drunkenness or intoxication" or drinking that results in "negative social consequences and that compromises role obligations and interpersonal relations" (Jessor, 1985, p. 75). One-fourth of the male adolescents and one-sixth of the female adolescents who drink seem to be problem drinkers. In 1983, 114,159 youths under age 18 were arrested nationwide for violating a state liquor law and 28,833 were arrested for drunkeness (Federal Bureau of Investigation [FBI], 1985).

Jessor (1985) indicated that adolescents who abuse alcohol appear to engage in a syndrome of deviant behavior that includes delinquent behavior and drug use. However 50 percent of the males and 75 percent of the females who were problem drinkers as adolescents were no longer problem drinkers as young adults (Jessor, 1985).

Crime. Adolescents under age 18 accounted for 16.8 percent of the arrests nationwide in 1983 and 17.2 percent in 1984 (FBI, 1985). Although substantially more adolescent males (1,197,697) than adolescent females (339,991) were arrested, the adolescent females constituted a higher proportion (22.8 percent) of the arrested female population than did the arrested adolescent males (16.1 percent) of the arrested male population. In relation to the ethnic origin of the adolescents who were arrested in 1984, 993,345 (63.3 percent) were white, 354,038 (23.1 percent) were black, and 160,268 (11.9 percent) were Hispanic.

The most frequent offenses were crimes against property, primarily larceny and theft, which represented 34.9 percent of all such crimes for which arrests were made nationwide in 1984. In addition, adolescents, primarily males, committed 16.8 percent of the nation's violent crimes in 1984 (FBI, 1985).

School Leavers. The term "school leavers," rather than the pejorative term "dropout," is being used more frequently to refer to youths who leave school before graduating from high school. According to a nationwide study conducted by the National Center for Education Statistics (Plisko & Stern, 1985), of the high school sophomores who left school in 1980, 14.6 percent were male and 12.6 were female. Minorities had the highest school-leaving rates (Hispanics, 18.7 percent, and blacks, 16.8 percent, compared to the rate for whites of 12.2 percent). Therefore, it is not surprising that the rates for urban youths, particularly for minorities, were notably higher than those for suburban or rural youths. Moreover, a larger percentage of adolescents who left school came from economically disadvantaged families. For whites and Hispanics, there was an inverse relationship between socioeconomic status and school-leaving rates: the lower the socioeconomic status, the higher the school-leaving rate. Regional differences also were noted: the school-leaving rates for white youths were highest in the South and West and those for black youths were highest in the Northeast and North Central areas. A similar pattern was found in relation to test scores, with those scoring the lowest having the highest school-leaving rates across all groups (Plisko & Stern, 1985). Furthermore, it should be pointed out that the rate of high school graduation among the nation's 17 year olds has decreased steadily every year since 1968 (76.7 per 100) to 71.8 per 100 in 1981 (Grant & Snyder, 1983–84).

Unemployment. The problem of unemployment among minority youths continues to be of major social and economic significance, particularly since over one-half the unemployed minority youths come from families whose income is below the poverty level ($10,000 or less) compared to 25 percent of the white unemployed youths (U.S. Commission on Civil Rights, 1980). A number of reasons have been posited for the significant differences in the unemployment rates among 16–19-year-old adolescents in the various ethnic groups, particularly for black youths whose unemployment rate in 1985 was 2 1/2 that of their white cohorts (40.2 percent for blacks, 24.3 percent for Hispanics, and 15.7 percent for whites) (U.S. Bureau of Labor Statistics, 1986). First, employment opportunities for youths in general are limited, the majority being in food handling and retail businesses. Second, most of these establishments are in white suburban locales that are not accessible to most minority youths. For example, transportation was given as the Number One barrier to employment in a national survey of minority youths (U.S. Commission on Civil Rights, 1980). Third, minority youths have no informal network for finding or making jobs available to them.

Interacting with these factors are the direct and indirect effects of discrimination. Discrimination in housing leads to minority youths living in segregated, impoverished areas that have few occupational opportunities and are significantly distant from the white neighborhoods where jobs are available. The poorer educational preparation that often occurs in predominantly minority schools further limits minority youths by disadvantaging them in competition for the few jobs that are available. Finally, discrimination against minorities limits the number of establishments available to this population and the salaries they are given; even when black youths are employed, then tend to work for lower wages ($2.60 per hour) than do their white cohorts ($3.00 per hour) (U.S. Commission on Civil Rights, 1980).

Conclusion

It is important to recognize that the foregoing issues and problems of adolescent populations often do not exist in isolation, but interact with and exacerbate one another. For example, depressed youths have a higher risk for suicide, and drug abuse has been found to be particularly high among those who attempt to commit suicide and those who succeed (Kandel & Davies, 1982). Substance abuse also has been identified as one element of a syndrome of delinquent behaviors (Jessor, 1985). And poverty has been linked to higher school-leaving and youth unemployment rates. However, it also should be pointed out that, according to Offer and Sabshin (1984), only 20 percent of adolescents find adolescence to be a severely stressful period.

Therefore, to address the needs of adolescent populations, social work practitioners and policymakers must take a multipronged approach. Furthermore, they must overlay their analyses of these problems with a keen recognition of developmental processes and how developmental factors interact with environmental and cultural factors to alter or exacerbate the problems.

The blatant absence of significant studies of the development of minority and poor adolescents is a particular problem. Given that these are the populations whom social workers primarily serve, serious questions should be raised about whether existing models of practice can be validly generalized to these populations. Offer and Sabshin (1984), for example, hypothesized that the number of normal adolescent growth patterns would increase if research samples were expanded to include subjects from different cultures and socioeconomic statuses. Given the broader sociocultural context of the mainstream culture with which minority adolescents must deal, it is possible that their experience with adolescence may be particularly conflicted. However, there is evidence that identification with one's primary culture positively enhances the developmental process, particularly with respect to self-esteem (Zimbardo, 1971). The application of theories or principles that address the impact of various sociocultural factors on an individual's behavior, values, and beliefs hold the most promise and are most consonant with the practice of social work, which views the individual within his or her psychosociocultural context. Meanwhile, the deficiencies of the literature on adolescence need to be dealt with so that developmental guidelines that are applicable in a culturally plural society can be established.

DIANE DE ANDA

For further information, see ADOLESCENT PREGNANCY; CHILDREN; DRUG USE AND ABUSE; HUMAN DEVELOPMENT: BIOLOGICAL PERSPECTIVE; HUMAN DEVELOPMENT: PSYCHOLOGICAL PERSPECTIVE; HUMAN DEVELOPMENT: SOCIOCULTURAL PERSPECTIVE; JUVENILE OFFENDERS AND DELINQUENCY; RUNAWAYS.

References

Alan Guttmacher Institute. (1981). *Teenage Pregnancy: The Problem that Hasn't Gone Away.* New York: Author.

Bandura, A. (1964). "The Stormy Decade: Fact or Fiction?" *Psychology in the Schools, 1,* 224–231.

Bandura, A. (1969). *Principles of Behavior Modification.* New York: Holt, Rinehart & Winston.

Bandura, A., & Walters, R. M. (1963). *Social Learning and Personality Development.* New York: Holt, Rinehart & Winston.

Bandura, A. (1977). *Social Learning Theory.* Englewood Cliffs, N.J.: Prentice-Hall.

Barnes, G. (1979). "Solvent Abuse: A Review." *International Journal of Addictions, 14,* 1–26.

Biddle, B. J., Blank, B. J., & Marlin, M. M. (1980). "Social Determinants of Adolescent Drinking." *Journal of Studies on Alcohol, 41*(3), 215–241.

Blos, P. (1941). *The Adolescent Personality.* New York: D. Appleton-Century Co.

Blos, P. (1979). *The Adolescent Passage: Developmental Issues.* New York: International Universities Press.

Chelimsky, E. (1982). *Statement before the Subcommittee on Human Resources on the Runaway and Homeless Youth Program.* U.S. House of Representatives, Committee on Education and Labor. Washington, D.C.: U.S. Government Printing Office.

Chodorow, N. (1974). "Family Structure and Feminine Personality." In M. Rosoldo & L. Lamphere (Eds.), *Women, Culture and Society.* Stanford, Calif.: Stanford University Press.

Chodorow, N. (1978). *The Reproduction of Mothering.* Berkeley: University of California Press.

Clausen, J. A. (1975). "The Social Meaning of Differential Physical and Sexual Maturation." In S. E. Dragastin & G. E. Elder, Jr. (Eds.), *Adolescence in the Life Cycle: Psychological Change and Social Context* (pp. 24–47). New York: John Wiley & Sons.

Coleman, J. C. (1980). "Friendship and the Peer Group in Adolescence." In J. Adelson (Ed.), *Handbook of Adolescent Psychology.* New York: John Wiley & Sons.

Douvan, E., & Adelson, J. (1966). *The Adolescent Experience.* New York: John Wiley & Sons.

Dunphy, D. S. (1963). "The Social Structure of Urban Adolescent Peer Groups." *Sociometry, 26,* 230–246.

Dworkin, A. G., & Stephens, R. C. (1980). "Mexican-American Adolescent Inhalant Abuse." *Youth and Society, 11*(4), 493–506.

Elkind, D. (1967). "Egocentrism in Adolescence," *Child Development, 38,* 1025–1034.

Elkind, D. (1974). *Children and Adolescents: Interpretive Essays on Jean Piaget* (2nd ed.). New York: Oxford University Press.

Elkind, D. (1978). "Egocentrism in Adolescence." In J. K. Gardner (Ed.), *Readings in Developmental Psychology* (2nd ed.). Boston: Little, Brown & Co.

Erikson, E. H. (1963). *Childhood and Society* (2nd ed.). New York: W. W. Norton & Co.

Erikson, E. H. (1968). *Identity, Youth and Crisis.* New York: W. W. Norton & Co.

Erikson, E. H. (1970). "Reflections on the Dissent of Contemporary Youth." *International Journal of Psychoanalysis, 51,* 11–22.

Faust, M. S. (1977). "Somatic Development of Adolescent Girls." In *Monographs of the Society for Research in Child Development, 42*(1).

Federal Bureau of Investigation. (1985). *Uniform Crime Reports for the United States, 1984.* Washington, D.C.: Author.

Finch, S. M., & South, D. R. (1972). "Dilemma of Youth: The Choice of Parents or Peers as a Frame of Reference for Behavior." *Journal of Marriage and the Family, 34,* 627–634.

Freud, A. (1948). *The Ego and the Mechanisms of Defense* (C. Baines, Trans.). New York: International Universities Press.

Freud, S. (1973). *A General Introduction to Psychoanalysis.* New York: Pocket Books. (Original work published 1924.)

Gagne, R. (1970). *The Conditions of Learning.* New York: Holt, Rinehart & Winston.

Gagnon, J. H. (1974). "Scripts and the Coordination of Sexual Conduct." In J. K. Cole & R. Deinstbrier (Eds.), *Nebraska Symposium on Motivation* (Vol. 21). Lincoln: University of Nebraska Press.

Gardner, E. F., & Thompson, G. G. (1963). *Investigation and Measurement of the Social Values Governing Interpersonal Relations Among Adolescent Youth and Their Teachers.* Washington, D.C.: U.S. Government Printing Office.

Gilligan, C. (1979). "Woman's Place in Man's Life Cycle." *Harvard Educational Review, 49*(4), 431–446.

Globetti, G. (1972). "Problem and Non-problem

Drinking Among High School Students in Abstinence Communities." *International Journal of Addictions, 1*(3), 511–523.

Grant, W. V., & Snyder, T. D. (1983–84). *Digest of Educational Statistics, 1983–84.* Washington, D.C.: National Center for Education Statistics.

Green, A. H. (1978). "Self-Destructive Behavior in Battered Children." *American Journal of Psychiatry, 135,* 579–582.

Hall, G. S. (1904). *Adolescence: Its Psychology and Its Relations to Physiology, Anthropology, Sociology, Sex, Crime, Religion, and Education* (Vols. 1 & 2). New York: D. Appleton-Century Co.

Hawton, K. (1982). "Annotation: Suicide in American Children and Adolescents." *Journal of Child Psychiatry, 3*(4), 497–503.

Hess, R. D., & Goldblatt, I. (1957). "The Status of Adolescents in American Society: A Problem in Social Identity." *Child Development, 28,* 459–468.

Hoffman, M. L. (1980). "Moral Development in Adolescence." In J. Adelson (Ed.), *Handbook of Adolescent Psychology* (pp. 295–343). New York: John Wiley & Sons.

Holinger, P. C. (1978). "Adolescent Suicide: An Epidemiological Study of Recent Trends." *American Journal of Psychiatry, 135,* 754–756.

Holinger, P., & Offer, D. (1982). "Prediction of Adolescent Suicide: A Population Model." *American Journal of Psychiatry, 139*(3), 302–307.

Inhelder, B., & Piaget, J. (1978). "Adolescent Thinking." In J. K. Gardner (Ed.), *Readings in Developmental Psychology.* Boston: Little, Brown & Co.

Jalai, B., et al. (1981). "Adolescents and Drug Use: Toward a More Comprehensive Approach." *American Journal of Orthopsychiatry, 51*(1), 119–130.

Jessor, R. (1985). "Adolescent Problem Drinking: Psychosocial Aspects and Developmental Outcomes." *Alcohol, Drugs and Driving, Abstracts and Reviews, 1*(1–2). University of California, Los Angeles.

Jessor, R., & Jessor, S. L. (1977). *Problem Behavior and Psychosocial Development: A Longitudinal Study of Youth.* New York: Academic Press.

Johnston, L. D., Bachman, J. G., & O'Malley, P. M. (1984). *Highlights from Drugs and the Class of '78: Behaviors, Attitudes and Recent National Trends.* Washington, D.C.: Department of Health & Human Services.

Jones, M. C., & Bayley, N. (1950). "Physical Maturing Among Boys as Related to Behavior." *Journal of Educational Psychology, 41,* 129–148.

Jones, M. C. (1965). "Psychological Correlates of

Somatic Development." *Child Development, 36,* 899–911.

Jones, M. C., & Mussen, D. H. (1958). "Self-Conceptions, Motivations, and Interpersonal Attitudes of Early- and Late-Maturing Girls." *Child Development, 29,* 491–501.

Kandel, D. B., et al. (1976). "Adolescent Involvement in Legal and Illegal Drug Use: A Multiple Classification Analysis." *Social Forces, 55,* 438–458.

Kandel, D. B., & Daves, M. (1982). "Epidemiology of Depressive Mood in Adolescents: An Empirical Study." *Archives of General Psychiatry, 39*(October), 1205–1212.

Kerfort, M. (1979). "Self-Poisoning by Children and Adolescents." *Social Work Today, 10,* 9–11.

Kohlberg, L., & Gilligan, E. C. (1975). "The Adolescent as a Philosopher: The Discovery of Self in a Post-Conventional World." In J. Conger (Ed.), *Contemporary Issues in Adolescent Development* (pp. 414–443). New York: Harper & Row.

Maxwell, P. H., Conner, R., & Walters, J. (1961). "Family Members' Perceptions of Parent Role Performance." *Merrill-Palmer Quarterly, 7,* 31–37.

McKenry, P. C., Tishler, C., & Kelley, C. (1983). "The Role of Drugs in Adolescent Suicide Attempts." *Suicide and Life-Threatening Behavior, 13*(3), 166–175.

Medida, M., & Cruz, A. (1972). *A Survey of Paint and Glue Inhalation Among Phoenix Inner City Youth.* Phoenix, Ariz.: Valle del Sol.

Mehrabian, A. (1970). *The Tactics of Social Influence.* Englewood Cliffs, N.J.: Prentice-Hall.

Meissner, W. W. (1965). "Parental Interaction of the Adolescent Boy." *Journal of Genetic Psychology, 107,* 225–233.

Milgram, G. G. (1982). "Youthful Drinking: Past and Present." *Journal of Drug Education, 12*(4), 289–309.

Miller, Y., & Simon, W. (1980). "The Development of Sexuality in Adolescence." In J. Adelson (Ed.), *Handbook of Adolescent Psychology* (pp. 383–407). New York: John Wiley & Sons.

Muuss, E. (1962). *Theories of Adolescent Development.* New York: Random House.

Muuss, R. E. (1970). "Adolescent Development and the Secular Trend." *Adolescence, 5,* 267–286.

Mussen, P. H., & Jones, M. C. (1957). "Self-Conceptions, Motivations, and Interpersonal Attitudes of Late- and Early-Maturing Boys." *Child Development, 28,* 243–256.

National Center for Health Statistics. (1982). *Annual Summary: Morbidity and Mortality Weekly Report.* Rockville, Md.: Author.

National Institute on Drug Abuse. (1982). *National*

Survey on Drug Abuse: Main Findings. Washington, D.C.: Author.

National Network of Runaway and Youth Services. (1985). *To Whom Do They Belong?* Washington, D.C.: Author.

Offer, D. (1967). "Normal Adolescents: Interview Strategy and Selected Results." *Archives of General Psychiatry, 17,* 285–290.

Offer, D., & Sabshin, M. (1984). *Normality and the Life Cycle: A Critical Integration.* New York: Basic Books.

Offer, D., Sabshin, M., & Marcus, I. (1965). "Clinical Evaluation of Normal Adolescents." *American Journal of Psychiatry, 21,* 864–872.

Padilla, E., et al. (1973). "Adolescents as Mothers: An Interdisciplinary Approach to Complex Problems." *Journal of Youth and Adolescence, 2*(3), 233–249.

Peck, M. (1982). "Youth Suicide." *Death Education, 6,* 29–47.

Peck, M., & Litman, M. D. (1982). *Current Trends in Youthful Suicides.* Unpublished manuscript.

Peskin, H. (1967). "Pubertal Onset and Ego Functioning." *Journal of Abnormal Psychology, 72,* 1–15.

Peskin, H. (1973). "Influence of the Developmental Schedule of Puberty on Learning and Ego Development." *Journal of Youth and Adolescence, 2,* 273–290.

Peterson, A. C., & Taylor, B. (1980). "The Biological Approach to Adolescence." In J. Adelson (Ed.), *Handbook of Adolescent Psychology.* New York: John Wiley & Sons.

Piaget, J. (1965). *The Moral Judgment of the Child.* New York: Free Press.

Piaget, J. (1972). "Intellectual Evolution from Adolescence to Adulthood." *Human Development, 15*(1), 1–12.

Piaget, J., & Inhelder, B. (1958). *The Growth of Logical Thinking from Childhood to Adolescence.* (A. Parsons & S. Seagrin, Trans.). New York: Basic Books.

Plisko, V. W., & Stern, J. D. (1985). *The Condition of Education.* Washington, D.C.: National Center for Education Statistics, U.S. Department of Education.

Potvin, P. H., & Lee, C. (1980). "Multistage Path Models of Adolescent Alcohol and Drug Use." *Journal of Studies on Alcohol, 41,* 531–541.

Rosenthal, T. L., & Zimmerman, B. J. (1978). *Social Learning and Congnition.* New York: Academic Press.

Settlage, C. F. (1972). "Cultural Values and the Superego in Late Adolescence." *Psychoanalytic Study of the Child, 27,* 57–73.

Smith, J. C., & Warren, C. W. (1983). *Comparison of Anglo and Hispanic Suicide in Four Southwestern States.* Paper presented at the 11th Annual Meeting of the American Association of Suicidology, Dallas, Tex.

Sullivan, H. S. (1953). *The Interpersonal Theory of Psychiatry.* New York: W. W. Norton & Co.

Tanner, J. M. (1962). *Growth at Adolescence.* Springfield, Ill.: Charles C Thomas, Publisher.

Tanner, J. M. (1972). "Sequence, Tempo, and Individual Variation in Growth and Development of Boys and Girls Aged Twelve to Sixteen." In J. Kagan & R. Coles (Eds.), *Twelve to Sixteen: Early Adolescence.* New York: W. W. Norton & Co.

Tessler, D. J. (1980). *Drugs, Kids, and Schools, Practical Strategies for Educators and Other Concerned Adults.* Santa Monica, Calif.: Goodyear Publishing Co.

Tishler, C. L., McKenry, P. C., & Morgan, K. C. (1981). "Adolescent Suicide Attempts: Some Significant Factors." *Suicide and Life-Threatening Behavior, 11*(2), 86–92.

Toolan, J. M. (1975). "Suicide in Children and Adolescents." *American Journal of Psychotherapy, 29*(3), 339–344.

Turiel, E. (1974). "Conflict and Transition in Adolescent Moral Development." *Child Development, 45,* 14–29.

U.S. Bureau of the Census. (1984). *1980 Census of the Population: Vol. 1, Characteristics of the Population.* Washington, D.C.: U.S. Government Printing Office.

U.S. Bureau of Labor Statistics. (1986, January). *Employment and Earnings.* Washington, D.C.: Author.

U.S. Commission on Civil Rights. (1980, September 18). *Youth Employment.* Presentation to the U.S. Commission on Civil Rights, Washington, D.C.

U.S. Department of Health and Human Services. (1983). *Runaway and Homeless Youth: National Program Inspection.* Washington, D.C.: Author.

Ventura, S. (1982). "Births of Hispanic Parentage, 1979." *Monthly Vital Statistics Report, 32* (Supplement). Hyattsville, Md.: National Center for Health Statistics.

Ventura, S., & Heuser, R. (1981). "Births of Hispanic Parentage, 1978." *Monthly Vital Statistics Report, 29* (Supplement). Hyattsville, Md.: National Center for Health Statistics.

Weatherley, D. (1964). "Self-Perceived Rate of Physical Maturation and Personality in Late Adolescence." *Child Development, 35,* 1197–1210.

Wooden, K. (1976). *Weeping in the Playtime of Others: America's Incarcerated Children.* New York: McGraw-Hill Book Co.

For Further Reading

Agar, M. (1973). *Ripping and Running*: A Formal Ethology of Urban Heroin Addicts. New York: Seminar.

Bacon, L. (1974). "Early Motherhood: Accelerated Role Transition and Social Pathologies." *Social Forces*, 52(3), 333–341.

Baldwin, W. H., & Cain, V. (1980). "The Children of Teenage Parents." *Family Planning Perspectives*, 12(1), 34–43.

Blane, H. T., & Hewitt, L. E. (1977). *Alcohol and Youth: An Analysis of the Literature, 1960-1975*. Rockville, Md.: National Institute on Alcohol Use and Alcoholism.

Bolton, F. G., Jr. (1980). *The Pregnant Adolescent*. Beverly Hills, Calif.: Sage Publications.

Braen, B., & Forbush, J. B. (1975). "School Age Parenthood: A National Overview." *Journal of School Health*, 45(5), 256–262.

Brittain, C. V. (1963). "Adolescent Choices and Parent-Peer Cross-Pressures." *American Sociological Review*, 23, 385–419.

Burden, D. S., & Klerman, L. V. (1984). "Teenage Parenthood: Factors that Lessen Economic Dependence." *Social Welfare*, 29, 11–16.

Conger, J. J. (1977). *Adolescence and Youth: Psychological Development in a Changing World*. New York: Harper & Row.

Dembo, R., et al. (1982). "Supports for, and Consequences of, Early Drug Involvement Among Inner City Junior High School Youths Living in Three Neighborhood Settings." *Journal of Drug Education*, 12(3), 191–210.

Dunford, F. W., & Brennen, T. (1976). "Taxonomy of Runaway Youth." *Social Service Review*, 50(3), 457–470.

Emery, P. E. (1983). "Adolescent Depression and Suicide." *Adolescence*, 18(7), 245–258.

English, C. J. (1973). "Leaving Home: A Typology of Runaways." *Transaction*, 10(5), 22–24.

Federal Railroad Administration. (1980). *On the Run*. Washington, D.C.: U.S. Department of Transportation.

Floyd, H. H., & South, D. R. (1972). "Dilemma of Youth: The Choice of Parents or Peers as a Frame of Reference for Behavior." *Journal of Marriage and the Family*, 34, 627–634.

Halikas, J., & Remmer, J. (1974). "Predictors of Multiple Drug Use." *Archives of General Psychiatry*, 31, 414–418.

Hirano-Nakanishi, M. (n.d.). *Hispanic School Dropouts: The Extent and Relevance of Pre-High School Attrition and Delayed Education*. Los Alamitos, Calif.: National Center for Bilingual Research.

Huba, G. J., & Bentler, P. M. (1980). "The Role of Peer and Adult Models for Drug Taking at Different Stages in Adolescence." *Journal of Youth and Adolescence*, 9(5), 449–465.

Jessor, R., & Jessor, S. L. (1975). "Adolescent Development and the Onset of Drinking." *Journal of Studies on Alcohol*, 36, 27–51.

Johnson, C. (1974). "Adolescent Pregnancy: Intervention into the Poverty Cycle." *Adolescents*, 9, 391–404.

Josselson, R. (1980). "Ego Development in Adolescence." In J. Adelson (Ed.), *Handbook of Adolescent Psychology* (pp. 188–210). New York: John Wiley & Sons.

Kandel, D. (1975). "Some Comments on the Relationship of Selected Criteria Variables to Adolescent Illicit Drug Use." In D. J. Lettieri (Ed.), *Predicting Adolescent Drug Abuse: A Review of Issues, Methods, and Correlates* (pp. 343–361). Washington, D.C.: Department of Health, Education, & Welfare.

Kohlberg, L. (1969). *Stages in the Development of Moral Thought and Action*. New York: Holt, Rinehart & Winston.

Leonard, C. V. (1974). "Depression and Suicidality." *Journal of Counseling and Clinical Pathology*, 42(1), 98–104.

Lettieri, D. J., Sayers, M., & Pearson, H. W. (Eds.). (1980). *Theories on Drug Abuse*. Washington, D.C.: U.S. Department of Health & Human Services.

Levine, S., & Stephens, R. C. (1973). "Types of Narcotic Addicts." In R. Hardy & J. Cull (Eds.), *Drug Dependence and Rehabilitation Approaches* (pp. 55–87). Springfield, Ill.: Charles C Thomas, Publisher.

Moore, K., Hofferth, S., & Wertheimer, R. (1979). "Teenage Motherhood: Its Social and Economic Costs." *Children Today*, 8(5), 12–16.

Naditch, M. (1980). "Ego Mechanism and Marijuana usage." In D. J. Lettieri (Ed.), *Predicting Adolescent Drug Abuse: A Review of Issues, Methods, and Correlates* (pp. 207–222). Washington, D.C.: U.S. Department of Health & Human Services.

National Institute on Drug Abuse. (1979). *California Oriented Data Acquisition Process*. Washington, D.C.: Author.

Norem-Hebeisen, A. A. (1980). "Self Esteem as a Predictor of Adolescent Drug Abuse." In D. J. Lettieri (Ed.), *Predicting Adolescent Drug Abuse: A Review of Issues, Methods, and Correlates* (pp. 195–206). Washington, D.C.: U.S. Department of Health & Human Services.

Osofsky, H., et al. (1973). "Adolescents as Mothers: An Interdisciplinary Approach to Complex Problems." *Journal of Youth and Adolescence*, 2(3), 233–249.

Piaget, J. (1950). *The Psychology of Intelligence* (M. Percy & D. E. Berlyn, Trans.). London, England: Routledge & Kegan Paul.

Sacker, I. M., & Neuhoff, S. D. (1982). "Medical and Psychosocial Risk Factors in the Pregnant Adolescent." In I. R. Stuart & C. F. Wells (Eds.), *Pregnancy in Adolescence:*

Needs, Problems, and Management (pp. 107–139). New York: Van Nostrand Reinhold Co.

Scott, K., Field, T., & Robertson, E. (Eds.). (1981). *Teenage Parents and Their Offspring.* New York: Grune & Stratton.

Steffenhagen, R. A. (1980). "Self-Esteem Theory of Drug Abuse." In D. J. Lettieri, M. Sayers, & H. W. Pearson (Eds.), *Theories on Drug Abuse* (pp. 157–163). Washington, D.C.: U.S. Department of Health & Human Services.

Stephens, R. C. (1982). "The Concept of 'Self' in Adolescent Drug Abuse Theories." *Youth and Society, 14*(2), 213–234.

Teicher, J. D., & Jacobs, J. (1966). "Adolescents Who Attempt Suicide: Preliminary Findings." *American Journal of Psychiatry, 122,* 1248–1257.

Waldorf, D. (1973). *Careers in Dope.* Englewood Cliffs, N.J.: Prentice-Hall.

Walker, W. L. (1980). "Intentional Self-Injury in School-age Children." *Journal of Adolescence, 3,* 217–228.

Weatherly, R. A., et al. (1985). *Patchwork Programs: Comprehensive Services for Pregnant and Parenting Adolescents.* Seattle, Wash.: Center for Social Welfare Research.

Winich, C. (1980). "A Theory of Drug Dependence Based on Role Access to and Attitudes Towards Drugs." In D. J. Lettieri, M. Sayers, & H. W. Pearson (Eds.), *Theories on Drug Abuse* (pp. 225–235). Washington, D.C.: U.S. Department of Health & Human Services.

Wurmser, L. (1978). *The Hidden Dimension: Psychodynamics in Compulsive Drug Use.* New York: Jason Aronson.

Zelnick, M., & Kantner, J. F. (1980). "Sexual Activity, Contraceptive Use and Pregnancy Among Metropolitan-Area Teenagers: 1971–1979." *Family Planning Perspectives, 12*(5), 230–237.

Zelnick, M., Kantner, J. F., & Ford, K. (1981). *Sex and Pregnancy in Adolescence.* Beverly Hills, Calif.: Sage Publications.

Zimbardo, P. G. (1971). "The Social Bases of Behavior." In F. L. Ruch & P. G. Zimbardo (Eds.), *Psychology and Life* (10th ed.). Glenview, Ill.: Scott, Foresman.

ADOPTION

Adoption is both a legal act and a social service. The Child Welfare League of America (CWLA) defines legal adoption as "the method provided by law to establish the legal relationship of parent and child between persons who are not so related by birth" (Child Welfare League of America, 1978). Adoption social services are the necessary array of professional assistance services offered and coordinated by an agency, first, to place a child in an adoptive family, and second, to preserve and strengthen the adoptive family.

Adoption is different from foster care. After an adoption, parents are invested with the same legal rights and responsibilities as biological parents. Foster parents do not have these legal rights, which are either retained by the biological parents or transferred by the courts to a social agency.

History

Legal adoption in the United States did not exist until the mid-nineteenth century. Children who were orphaned or whose parents were unable or unwilling to care for them were provided for in a variety of ways. The earliest methods were indenture and apprenticeship. Although some children were housed in orphan asylums, a more common practice was to have them live in almshouses along with elderly and mentally ill or retarded adults. Mid-nineteenth-century investigations into the conditions at almshouses led to a movement to place children with foster or adoptive parents (Brace, 1859, pp. 13–14).

The first adoption law in the United States was passed in 1850 in Texas. It provided for adoption by deed, which, though a step up from indenture, still signified that the child was property to be exchanged. Adoption had to be created by statute because there was no tradition for it in English common law (Presser, 1972).

In 1851, Massachusetts passed an adoption statute establishing court procedures and guidelines that were to provide a model for other states. This law expressed the novel notion that the child's welfare was to be the primary consideration in adoption. It established that the state, through the court, has an obligation to protect biological parents from an uninformed and coerced decision to relinquish the child, and the adoptive parents from an uninformed and hasty decision to take the child. These principles are the cornerstone of current adoption law.

Twentieth-century adoption practice evolved to serve, fairly exclusively, infant white children born to unmarried parents

(Benet, 1976). During the late 1960s, several factors combined to give attention to older, minority, and handicapped children who needed to be placed for adoption. First, the civil rights movement raised consciousness within the child welfare field about the lack of service to these children. Second, a marked decline began in the number of readily placeable infants surrendered for adoption (National Center for Social Statistics, 1968).

This decrease in the number of available infants continues, not only because of the use of birth control and abortion by some mothers who in the past would have placed children for adoption, but, primarily, because more parents who in the past would have placed their children have chosen to keep and raise them (Moore, Hofferth, & Wertlheimer, 1979). A relaxed moral code has reduced the stigma that was once attached to unmarried parents raising children. The increase in single parents as a result of divorce has created a society in which never-married single parents are not as noticeable as they once were.

As a result of the decline in infants needing placement, adoption agencies began to look at children in foster care to determine their suitability for adoption. In addition, the foster care reforms of the 1970s, including requirements for case plans and foster care review, along with an emphasis on return of children to their parents or termination of parental rights has led to the identification of more minority, older, and handicapped children for adoption placement (Shyne & Schroeder, 1978).

Current standards for adoption services stress that children should not be excluded by virtue of their age, race, or handicaps. This principle is one of several that should underlie the provision of service.

The Child Welfare League of America (1978) has outlined the key assumptions that support adoption services:

1. All children, regardless of age, sex, race, and physical, intellectual, or emotional status, are entitled to a continuous, caring environment.

2. For most children, the biological family, in its broadest definition, provides the best environment.

3. When a child's family of birth is not able or willing to nurture him or her, the child is entitled to a timely placement with a family that is.

4. For most children, adoption provides a new family better than any other form of substitute parenting.

5. Adoption is a means of finding families for children and not of finding children for families. The emphasis is on the child's needs.

Types of Adoption

Not all adoptions are arranged by social agencies. Independent or private adoptions are those in which legal adoption is planned and implemented without the participation of an organized social agency. There are four types of independent adoptions: (1) relative adoptions; (2) direct placements; (3) intermediary placements—not for profit; and (4) intermediary placements—for profit (Cole, 1978).

The largest category of independent adoptions is that of relative adoptions (National Center for Social Statistics, 1975). Most frequently these involve a stepparent who adopts a spouse's child. The second largest category of independent adoptions, that of direct placement, involves an arrangement made by the legal parents to someone known to them.

In the third category of independent adoption, that of intermediary placement—not for profit, the biological parent and prospective adoptive parents are usually strangers. Dealings between them are handled by an intermediary who is not profiting financially from the placement. The arrangement may or may not involve payment of the mother's living and medical expenses. Intermediary placements differ from direct placements in that the biological and prospective adoptive parents are not known to each other and have limited knowledge of each other during and after the adoptive placement.

The fourth category of independent adoption is that of intermediary—for profit, generally known as "black market" adoption. Here the intermediary charges a high fee for arranging the adoption. Black market adoption is against the law in all 50 states and the District of Columbia. Five states—Delaware, Connecticut, Massachusetts, Minnesota, and Michigan—have outlawed all nonrelative forms of independent adoptions. The rest of the states have either eliminated or regulated the role of the nonagency intermediary in adoption while continuing to allow direct placements by biological parents (Meezan, Katz, & Russo, 1978).

Two major studies on independent adoptions that are arranged by intermediaries (Witmer, Herzog, Weinstein, & Sullivan, 1963; Meezan, Katz, & Russo, 1978) have indicated that there are some deficits in privately arranged adoptions, such as the lack of background information given to adoptive parents and poor counseling for the biological parents, especially fathers, who were often not contacted. Neither study, however, showed that serious harm was done to biological parents, children, or adoptive families as a result of independent adoption.

Scope of Adoption Placements

Statistical data on adoption are for the most part nonexistent, outdated, or unreliable. We have few trustworthy sets of data to determine the scope of adoption placements.

The most recent reliable collection of national statistics on children receiving child welfare services (National Center for Social Statistics, 1975) found that, of the total of 104,188 children adopted in 1975, 62 percent were related to the adoptive parent. This continued an upward trend begun in the late 1960s (National Center for Social Statistics, 1968). Stepparent adoptions were the cause of the rise in adoptions in this category—an incline tied to the increase in the divorce and remarriage rates. Significantly, stepparent adoptions probably constitute the largest single category of adoptions.

In 1975, 77 percent of the children placed with unrelated adoptive parents were placed by licensed agencies. Some observers believe that since 1975 there has been a sharp decline in the proportion of adoptions handled by licensed agencies and a rise in those arranged by intermediaries (Meezan, Katz, & Russo, 1978). Unfortunately, no reliable national data exist to test these hypotheses.

The majority of children adopted in 1975 were problem-free, white infants and preschool children. Nearly 9 (8.8) percent of every ten children placed by agencies were under the age of 6. Six of every ten children were under 1 year old. Seven in ten were white.

Although no statistical information existed to support their impressions, adoption practitioners in 1984 reported to the Child Welfare League, as they had before, that (1) there was a continued decline in the number of white infants and preschool children being placed for adoption; (2) despite some increase in the number of older, handicapped, and minority children being placed, children under 6 were still the majority of children being placed for adoption by agencies; (3) there continued to be an increase in the number of parents wishing to adopt infants and young children (Permanent Families for Children, 1982, 1983, 1984).

Who Adopts?

Adoptive applicants may be older than they have been in the past. Census data suggest that married women are postponing pregnancy to work (Bonham, 1977). Consequently more women will be older when they detect a fertility problem and come to an agency. Many agencies have an age cutoff of 35 for prospective parents, making it likely that more applicants will be eliminated from adopting infants or preschool children through an agency.

All these factors make it probable that there will continue to be efforts on the part of prospective adoptive parents to (1) seek intercountry adoptions, (2) adopt independently of agencies, (3) explore taking older children or those with handicaps, and (4) seek new remedies for infertility problems, such as artificial insemination, in vitro fertilization, embryo transport, and surrogate pregnancies.

Intercountry adoptions have steadily increased over the last ten years. In 1973, 4,000 children from other countries were adopted by U.S. citizens. In 1983, this figure had risen to 8,000 (U.S. Immigration and Naturalization Service, 1973, 1983). Most of the children came from Latin America and Asia. There were four times as many children adopted from South Korea as there were from the next highest-ranking country, Colombia. These were followed by India and El Salvador (U.S. Immigration and Naturalization Service, 1983). There are no recorded cases of American children being sent to other countries for adoption by their citizens.

Who Needs to Be Adopted?

At the same time that prospective adopters are seeking infants and preschool children to adopt, there are other children who are free for adoption but not yet placed. These children reside in foster families, group homes, or institutions.

In 1982, a national survey of child welfare agencies collected information on children not yet placed for adoption (Maximus Incorporated, 1983). In 1984, the data were summarized by the U.S. Children's Bureau (Gershenson, 1983, Note 2). The 50,000 children then waiting for adoptive families included minority children; the severely handicapped; boys, slightly more than girls; children over 11; and children who had been in foster care for four or more years.

These data also reflect the different and vexing pattern for black children in the child welfare system. On the whole, black children are not placed as readily as white children. Gershenson (1983, Note 2) points out: "Although black children comprise 14 percent of the child population, they are 24 percent of the foster care population, 33 percent of the children free for adoption who are not yet in adoptive placements." A similar racial disparity can be seen in the number of handicapped children placed: only 17 percent of black handicapped youngsters free for adoption are ever placed, compared to 38 percent of white handicapped children.

This record exists despite statistics showing that black families adopt at a rate 4.5 times greater than that of white or Hispanic families (Gershenson, 1984, Note 3). There are three Hispanic adopted children per 10,000 families, four white adopted children per 10,000 families, and 18 black adopted children per 10,000 families.

These figures have convinced practitioners that certain steps need to be taken to improve the chances for minority children to be placed in permanent families. These steps include: (1) reducing the number of black children who come into foster care by providing more intensive services to their families; (2) intensifying recruitment of adoptive parents; and (3) placing more children across racial lines.

The imbalance between who needs to be placed for adoption and who actually is placed is a major issue for adoption practitioners and advocates. It will be discussed again later in this article.

Adoption Process

The Child. The adoption process begins with the identification of children for whom the service is appropriate. In infant adoptions, the biological parents generally sign legal documents giving the child to the agency or, in the case of an independent adoption, to the prospective adoptive parents. These documents may be known as "surrenders of custody" or "relinquishment forms." In the past, an unmarried mother's relinquishment alone was sufficient to proceed with the placement. In 1972, a footnote to a Supreme Court decision, *Stanley v. Illinois*,[1] mentioned that unmarried (putative) fathers also had the right to be notified that the child was to be placed for adoption. This court decision has created confusion and widely divergent responses. Some commentators believe that all identified fathers should be contacted and asked if they wish to assume the responsibility of parenting the child or consent to the adoption. Others disagree and feel that such rights should be attended only to those who come forward.

Frequently, in the case of an older child in foster care, parental rights may need to be terminated against the parents' desire in order to free the child legally for an adoptive placement. This is generally referred to as an involuntary termination of parental rights. The standard of evidence needed to justify this action is set by state statute and elaborated by case precedent. The standard varies from state to state. Strict standards—for example, those used in criminal cases—are not easy to meet in termination cases, and agencies report great difficulty in obtaining termination in those instances. Some states use the lesser standards of evidence that apply in civil cases. The termination process may take a considerable amount of time, as there are postponements and delays. Freeing children for adoption requires that social workers be proficient in gathering evidence, organizing records, and preparing testimony in a fashion acceptable to courts.

The preparation of an infant for placement entails getting together the complete

---

[1] See Stanley v. Illinois, 645 U.S. 92 J. Ct. 1208 (1972). For more recent decisions: Quilloin v. Walcot, 434 U.S. 246, 98 J. Ct. 594 (1978); Caban v. Mohammad 441 U.S. 380, 99 J. Ct. 2560 (1978).

medical, developmental, and social history of the child to pass on to the adoptive parents. For the older child, much more is necessary in addition. Older children need to be able to understand who they are; why they are in placement; why they cannot be with their biological family; what adoption is; what will happen to them; and what role they themselves will play in finding and choosing their adoptive family. Adoption workers must have skills in dealing with separation and attachment and in interviewing children of all ages (Donley, 1975; Jewett, 1978).

Adoptive Parents. Currently, there is a surplus of applicants for white infants and children under 11 who do not have irremediable handicaps. Agencies rarely need to recruit families for this type of child and can be selective in their choice of adoptive parents. It is common in infant adoptions to find agencies imposing age limits of 35–40 for applicants, requiring evidence of infertility, and not placing a second or third child with a family (Meezan, Katz, & Russo, 1978).

This practice contrasts sharply with the constant need to recruit parents for minority, older, or severely handicapped children, often referred to as "special needs" children. Applicants for special needs children will find that eligibility requirements are relaxed. Although retaining the mandatory requirement that parents must be willing and able to parent, agencies have waived marriage (single people may apply), maximum age, family size, and infertility as preconditions to adoption.

All 50 states and the District of Columbia have initiated programs of financial assistance—known as adoption subsidy—for special needs children. Adoption subsidy makes placement possible with families who may otherwise be deterred by fear of the added financial burden; it is considered to be a critical tool in the placement of special needs children. Ninety percent of subsidized adoptions involve foster parents whom the subsidy has enabled to adopt children with whom they have formed a relationship. Most of these children are minorities or have special needs. Placing a child with subsidy has been estimated to cost, on the average, 37 percent less than maintaining the same child in foster care (Seelig, 1977).

Once parents have applied to adopt a child, the adoption process may involve group or individual sessions with the adoption worker. Couples may be seen individually or together. Current emphasis is less on investigation and more on education. Mutual decision making between the applicants and the agency is stressed in the major choices of whether or not to adopt a child, and, if so, which child.

The final selection of a child is preceded by introductory visits—a phase that takes on added importance for the older child. The placement of a child or children is followed by a period of adjustment during which supportive and educative services continue. This period varies by jurisdiction and from case to case. Generally, nine months to a year later, the adoption is finalized in court.

Previously, agencies rarely offered formal services after the adoption had been legally finalized. In response to requests from adoptive families with minor children, more agencies are and will be offering an organized array of counseling, education, and crisis intervention services. Added to these services are those aimed at assisting adult adoptees who are dealing with their identities and wish to have more information about their biological parents.

Until the late 1970s it was rare for birth parents to be involved in the adoption process once they had given legal permission for the child's adoption or had had their parental rights terminated. This is no longer the case. More birth families have and will continue to have some contact with the adoptive family. This is especially true in the adoption of older children who have emotional ties with birth parents, siblings, and extended family. In most foster parent adoptions, there has generally been contact with the birth family, or, at the very least, the birth family has known the child's whereabouts.

Less experience is available to evaluate these "open adoptions" in the case of infants. It is clear that there is a broad spectrum of possible contact between the birth family and the adoptive family. On the more confidential end of the continuum, neither family may have any knowledge of the other except for an exchange of nonidentifying social and medical information at the time of placement. This is traditionally how agency infant adoptions have been handled. Moving toward more openness, the process now allows for the continuing exchange of nonidentifying but vital social and medical information after the placement, with the agency serving as intermediary. Current practice in many agencies also allows for birth and adoptive parents to decide whether or not they want to be known to each other; whether or not they wish to continue contact after the adoption and what the nature of that contact might be. Some adoptive and birth parents are opting to know one another and have continued contact after the adoption.

There is general acknowledgment of the continuing need for sharing of vital medical and social information after the adoption. There is no professional consensus on the relative value of the fully disclosed or totally open adoption; this is an issue that needs research. It is clear that the controversy will continue into the future, and that variety in the degree of contact allowed will also continue.

Connected to the move to create more open adoption at the time of placement is the effort of adult adoptees to open adoption records that have been sealed to them. For the most part, state adoption laws require that all adoption records be sealed and that the information in them be shared with the primary parties to the adoption (birth and adoptive parents and the adoptee) only by the court or, on its order, by another party (such as a social agency) if the court finds good cause (Harrington, 1984).

Adult adoptees and some adoption professionals have been seeking to have these laws changed so that adoptees might have access to information about their biological parents. Opposition has come from courts, adoptive parents, and some adoption professionals who believe that the confidentiality of the biological parents must be maintained or that the information may prove harmful to the adult adoptee as well as to the adoptive parents (Pierce, 1984).

As a compromise solution, some states are creating registries where birth parents and adult adoptees can signal their wish for contact. Some of the registries take an active role in seeking out the other party to determine their wishes; others do not.

It is important to distinguish between the adoptee's search for more information about his or her origins and a search for the biological parents themselves. Many

adoptees want only the information, not contact with their biological parents. Research is needed on how many adoptees are searching for siblings rather than parents, and whether the contacts, once made, are traumatic or helpful. In any case, the need for information expressed by adult adoptees is now causing agencies to obtain and transmit to the adoptive family far more background information than they used to (Jones, 1976).

Outcomes of Adoption

Studies on the outcomes of adoption for both infants and special needs children show that both families and children are doing well (Hoopes, 1982). Nelson (1985) confirmed the earlier findings of Franklin and Massarik (1969) and Kadushin (1970) that families who adopt special needs children are well adjusted.

Nelson's study also touched on the adoption process and made several recommendations for practice; the study found that children are their own best recruiters and that prospective parents are most often found in the ranks of foster parent applicants, people wishing to adopt infants and preschoolers, and people who already know the child. Nelson also noted that adoptive parents need better information about the child's past and current functioning; many adoptive families have initiated contact with the child's biological family, and this has not presented serious problems.

Issues in Adoption

Independent Adoptions. Aside from relative adoptions, should the law and social policy outlaw independent adoptions? Arguments for this position cite the risks to the child and family involved in such placements and stress the benefits of agency services. Those who oppose the outlawing of independent adoptions claim that studies do not justify total control by agencies of such placements and feel that couples can find children more easily on their own than through agencies. Midway between these two positions is an argument for strict regulation of all independent placements. Such regulation would include agencies, responsibility for counseling birth parents, approving prospective adoptive parents prior to placement, and supervising the adoptive family for a period of time before court approval of the adoption.

Fathers. To what degree should the known or presumed father be involved in adoption planning? Some observers believe that most fathers are unconcerned and that unless the father is assertive about establishing his rights and making plans, he should be disregarded. Dealing with the father takes too much time and delays early placement and bonding with adoptive parents. Others hold that what may appear to be disinterest on the part of the father may in fact be ignorance of his paternity. The lack of rigorous attempts to involve the father in the planning process allows him to escape the moral, financial, and social responsibility that should accompany the act of fathering a child. Moreover, it is as important to know about the father's medical and social background as it is to know about the mother's.

Funding Adoption Services. As the number of readily placeable infants and young children has declined and the number of special needs children who are placed has escalated, the per capita cost of adoption services has increased dramatically. Agencies believe that some biological parents who choose intermediaries rather than agencies for adoption arrangements do so because the intermediaries can provide more costly medical and shelter arrangements than the agencies can afford. Agencies could raise more money to pay these expenses by charging higher fees for services to adoptive parents. The result may be to put adoption out of the reach of prospective families with modest incomes. Other solutions are being examined that might circumvent this situation, such as medical insurance to cover maternity benefits to clients, contracts with physicians to care for pregnant clients from several agencies, as well as health maintenance organization coverage.

Surplus of Black Children Needing Placement. Despite the considerably higher adoption rate among black families, far more black children await placement than white children. Suggested solutions include (1) increased recruitment of black families, enhanced by more flexible eligibility requirements and adoption subsidies; (2) reduction of the number of black children coming into care, by providing more intensive services to preserve their original families; and (3) placement of more children in families of other races.

Transracial adoptions continue to be controversial. Research on the early adjustment of children placed in families of different races shows the youngsters to be faring well (Fanshel, 1972; Grow & Shapiro, 1974; Ladner, 1977; Feigelman & Silverman, 1983). White families continue to appear to be willing to adopt children of other races. Even so, strong opposition to transracial adoptions exists among some professionals, who argue that the child suffers from discrimination and is prone to have problems with identification. They also claim that agencies will not vigorously recruit black families but will turn to white families instead (Day, 1979; Ladner, 1977). The issue is likely to become the subject of increasingly intense debate as the number of black children awaiting adoptive families far outnumbers the number of black families being recruited.

Openness in Adoption. Some adoption practitioners fear that the continued efforts to have contact between birth parents and adoptive parents will reduce adoption to foster care. They also fear that such contact may result in "coparenting," which will present increasing problems for the parents and confusion for the children.

This view is not shared by the proponents of openness, who believe that more birth parents will choose to place their children in adoption if they can continue to have contact with them. Adoptive parents will not become foster parents as long as they have legal status and autonomy in decision making. One cannot assume that all relationships will be problematic. Most families will be able to cope with the problems and the benefits that come with them. Knowledge and acceptance of one another by birth and adoptive parents will outweigh the negatives.

Should sealed adoption records be opened to adult adoptees? Do biological parents have a right to maintain their anonymity? Do adoptees have a paramount right to information about their genetic background? If there should be contact, what is the best way to arrange it? These questions are still debated.

Disruption and Post–Legal Adoption Services. Another factor that raises questions is disruption, which is the situation in which a child who is placed in an adoptive home is returned to the agency before a legal adoption has taken place. What is the true incidence of disruption? What effect does it have on children? What are the implications for practice? Some observers believe that disruptions should be regarded as the prime evaluative indicators of the success or failure of adoption practice. Should this be so? Perhaps, say others, our expectation that certain children will need only one placement is wrong. If we accept disruption as an indicator of inadequate services, we are implying that we possess a scientifically valid measure to predict which families will succeed, when we know that in fact we do not have that kind of standard.

Could disruptions be reduced and problems after legal adoption be prevented if agencies offered an array of services to support families better? Some argue that even if adoptive families need help, this does not mean that adoption agencies should provide that service when the community has other family service and mental health organizations. Are the parenting problems of adoptive parents so unique that they must be dealt with only by an adoption agency?

Conclusion

Adoption is one of the oldest of child welfare services and will always be necessary. Literally millions of children have benefited from it. What is changing and will continue to change are the kinds and numbers of children and parents adoption programs will serve and the different ways in which adoption will be accomplished. Whatever forms adoption may take, the skill and knowledge of the social work professional will continue to be necessary to enhance the process and to safeguard the rights and welfare of children.

ELIZABETH S. COLE

For further information, see CHILDREN; CHILD WELFARE SERVICES; FOSTER CARE FOR CHILDREN; PUBLIC SOCIAL SERVICES; YOUTH SERVICE AGENCIES.

References

National Center for Social Statistics. (1968). *Adoption in 1968*. Washington, D.C.: Social and Rehabilitation Service, U.S. Department of Health, Education and Welfare.

National Center for Social Statistics. (1975). *Adoption in 1975*. Washington, D.C.: Social and Rehabilitation Service, U.S. Department of Health, Education and Welfare.

Benet, M. (1976). *The Politics of Adoption*. New York: Free Press.

Bonham, G. S. (1977). "Who Adopts: The Relationship of Adoption and Social-Demographic Characteristics of Women." *Journal of Marriage and the Family, 39*(2), 295–306.

Brace, C. L. (1859). *The Best Method of Disposing of Pauper and Vagrant Children*. New York: Wyncoop & Hallenbeck.

Child Welfare League of America. (1978). *Standards for Adoption Service* (rev. ed.). New York: Author.

Cole, E. S. (1978). "Adoption Services Today and Tomorrow." In A. Kadushin (Ed.), *Child Welfare Strategies in the Coming Years*. Washington, D.C.: U.S. Department of Health & Human Services, Administration for Children, Youth and Families, Children's Bureau. (OHDS 78–36158)

Day, D. (1979). *The Adoption of Black Children: Counteracting Institutional Discrimination*. Lexington, Mass.: Lexington Books.

Donley, K. (1975). *Opening New Doors*. London, England: Association of British Adoption and Fostering Agencies.

Fanshel, D. (1972). *Far From the Reservation*. Metuchen, N.J.: Scarecrow Press.

Feigelman, W., & Silverman, A. (1983). *Chosen Children: New Patterns in Adoptive Relationships*. New York: Praeger Publishers.

Franklin, D. S., & Massarik, F. (1969). "The Adoption of Children with Medical Conditions: Part III—Conclusions." *Child Welfare, 48*(10), 595–601.

Gershensen, C., Maza, P., & Fucillo, A. (1983–84). *Child Welfare Research Notes*, Nos. 1–6. Washington, D.C.: U.S. Department of Health and Human Services, Administration for Children, Youth and Families, Children's Bureau.

Grow, L., & Shapiro, D. (1974). *Black Children, White Parents: A Study of Transracial Adoption*. New York: Child Welfare League of America.

Harrington, J. (1984). "Adoption and the State Legislatures." *Public Welfare, 42*(2), 35–40.

Hoopes, J. L. (1982). *Prediction in Child Development: A Longitudinal Study of Adoptive and Non-Adoptive Families—The Delaware Family Study*. New York: Child Welfare League of America.

Jewett, C. (1978). *Adopting the Older Child*. Harvard, Mass.: Harvard Common Press.

Jones, M. A. (1976, July). *The Sealed Adoption Record Controversy: A Report of Agency*

Policy, Practice and Opinion. New York: Child Welfare League of America.

Kadushin, A. (1970). *Adopting Older Children.* New York: Columbia University Press.

Ladner, J. (1977). *Mixed Families.* Garden City, N.Y.: Anchor Press.

Maximus Incorporated. (1983). *Child Welfare Indicator Survey* (Contract No. 105-82-C-011). Washington D.C.: U.S. Department of Health and Human Services, Administration for Children, Youth and Families, Children's Bureau.

Meezan, W., Katz, S., & Russo, E. (1978). *Adoptions without Agencies.* New York: Child Welfare League of America.

Moore, K. A., Hofferth, S. L., Wertlheimer, R. (1979). "Teenaged Motherhood: Its Social and Economic Costs." *Children Today, 8*(12), 10–14.

Nelson, C. (1985). *On Adoption's Frontier.* New York: Child Welfare League of America.

Permanent Families for Children. (1982, 1983, 1984). *Minutes of Advisory Committee Meetings.* New York: Child Welfare League of America.

Pierce, W. (1984). "Survey of State Laws and Legislation on Access to Adoption Records." Washington, D.C.: National Committee for Adoption.

Presser, S. B. (1972). "The Historical Background of the American Law of Adoption." *Journal of Family Law, 28*(2), 448–460.

Seelig, G. (1977). "Implementation of Subsidized Adoption Programs: A Preliminary Survey." *Journal of Family Law, 15*(11), 732.

Shyne, A., & Schroeder, A. (1978). *National Study of Social Services to Children and Their Families.* Washington, D.C.: U.S. Department of Health & Human Services.

U.S. Immigration and Naturalization Service. (1973, 1983). *Annual Reports.* Washington, D.C.: U.S. Government Printing Office.

Witmer, H., Herzog, E., Weinstein, E., & Sullivan, M. (1963). *Independent Adoptions.* New York: Russell Sage Foundation.

For Further Reading

Children's Home Society of California. (1984). *The Changing Picture of Adoption.* Los Angeles, Calif.: Author.

Coyne, A., & Brown, M. E. (1980). "The Adoption of Children with Developmental Disabilities: A Study of Public and Private Child Placement Agencies." New York: Child Welfare League of America.

Emlen, A., Lahti, J., Downs, G., McKay, A., & Downs, S. (1977). *Overcoming Barriers to Planning for Children in Foster Care.* Portland, Ore.: Portland State University, Regional Research Institute for Human Services.

Reid, J. (1963). "Principles, Values, and Assump-

tions Underlying Adoption Practice." In E. Smith (Ed.), *Readings in Adoption.* New York: Child Welfare League of America.

Sorosky, A. D., Baron, A., & Pannor, R. (1978). *The Adoption Triangle: The Effects of the Sealed Record on Adoptees, Birth Parents, and Adoptive Parents.* Garden City, N.Y.: Anchor Press.

ADULTHOOD

Adulthood is an age-related concept that has biological, legal, social, and behavioral parameters. From a biological viewpoint, the average person becomes capable of reproduction between the ages of 11 and 14. In traditional societies, puberty signals the onset of adult roles—especially for females. By contrast, in the United States, individuals are not legally recognized as adults until they are between the ages of 16 and 21, depending on which area of law is involved and whether the state or the federal government has jurisdiction. On a behavioral level, adults are expected to be able to function economically, socially, and psychologically apart from their families of origin. Although this functioning may vary by family and socioeconomic group, the general consensus in the United States is that adulthood begins at about the age of 21.

It is difficult to identify when the period of adulthood ends. In the United States, where the average life span extends to the early or middle 70s, the aged can be considered to have problems that are sufficiently distinctive to mark a specific life period, one to be dealt with separately. Physiologically, markers appear only gradually, are highly variable, and are probably not useful in this article. Legally mandatory retirement, the receipt of pensions and of social security benefits, and "senior citizen" status occur in the mid-60s. The 50s, however, represent a pivotal period as far as developmental tasks are concerned and signal a transition from the middle to the later period of adulthood. This discussion focuses on the adult period spanning the years between ages 21 and 54, although it also deals with the years 55 to 60.

Adults between the ages of 21 and 54 represent 44.4 percent of the population of the United States (43.2 percent of the men

Table 1. Marital Status of the Population by Sex and Age: 1982 (Percentage)[a]

	Men				Women			
Age	Single	Married	Widowed	Divorced	Single	Married	Widowed	Divorced
20–24	72.0	26.7	—	1.3	53.4	42.9	0.1	3.5
25–29	36.1	57.9	—	6.0	23.4	67.4	0.5	8.8
30–34	17.3	73.4	0.1	9.2	11.6	75.6	0.7	12.1
35–44	8.8	81.4	0.3	9.4	5.6	79.4	2.4	12.6
45–54	5.4	84.9	1.5	8.2	4.1	78.5	6.8	10.6

Source: U.S. Bureau of the Census, *Statistical Abstract of the United States* (Washington, D.C.: U.S. Government Printing Office, 1984), p. 44.
[a] Because of rounding, totals may not add to precisely 100 percent.

and 43.8 percent of the women) (U.S. Bureau of the Census, 1984, p. 31). Adulthood, a relatively healthy period of life, is seldom affected by degenerative, chronic, or terminal illnesses. Cancer, coronary heart disease, and stroke most often make their initial appearance after age 55 (U.S. Bureau of the Census, 1984, p. 45). Adulthood is also a time of expanding social horizons in which much energy is expended on educational and vocational preparation, work, and family and social obligations. Tamir (1982) calls this period "the apex of life" (p. 48).

Among subgroups in the population, marital status, educational preparation, and vocational achievement are diverse. Table 1 indicates that more than half of all adults over age 24 are married. Women tend to marry earlier than men, and a greater proportion of women than men marry between the ages of 25 and 29. In every age bracket, the incidence of divorce and widowhood is higher for women than for men, and more men than women remain unmarried.

The U.S. Bureau of the Census (1984, p. 45) indicates that from 1970 to 1982, the divorce rate among men and women almost tripled. Among men aged 25 to 34, the divorce rate increased from 3 percent in 1972 to 10 percent in 1982 and from 5 percent to 12.6 percent in the same period for women in this age bracket. The U.S. Bureau of the Census (1984, p. 45) also indicates that the separation rate of black men and women was higher than that of their white counterparts, for example, 2.4 percent for white men and 9.3 percent for black men in 1982 and 3.5 percent and 17.3 percent for black and white women, respectively, in the same year.

Table 2 indicates the educational level completed during the adult years. By age 25, 83.6 percent of white men have completed

Table 2. Education Level by Age, Sex, and Ethnic Group: 1980 (Percentage)

	Men						Women					
	White		Black		Spanish Origin		White		Black		Spanish Origin	
Age	HS[a]	College	HS	College	HS	College	HS	College	HS	College	HS	College
20–24	83.6	9.5	69.8	3.6	58.4	3.4	85.9	10.1	76.7	5.5	61.8	3.8
25–29	87.0	25.8	73.8	10.7	58.4	9.7	87.2	22.0	76.5	12.1	59.2	8.4
30–34	86.9	31.5	72.4	12.5	56.3	12.1	85.9	21.4	73.4	11.5	54.4	7.4
35–39	82.0	27.7	64.4	11.0	49.6	11.0	81.5	17.2	65.6	9.8	47.6	6.3
40–44	77.3	23.6	56.0	9.1	44.8	9.8	77.0	13.6	58.0	8.4	43.1	6.1
45–49	72.7	22.6	47.9	8.4	40.9	9.2	72.6	11.6	50.4	8.3	37.7	5.3

Source: U.S. Bureau of the Census, *1980 Census of Population, Detailed Population Characteristics: United States Summary* (Washington, D.C.: U.S. Government Printing Office, 1980), pp. 43, 45, 51. The figures indicate percent of high school graduates and percent who completed four plus years of college.
[a] HS = high school.

Table 3. Labor Force of Adults by Age, Sex, and Ethnic Group (Percentage)

Age	Men			Women		
	White	Black	Spanish Origin	White	Black	Spanish Origin
20–24	84.3	82.2	83.5	69.5	61.4	59.1
25–29	93.4	85.1	89.8	66.1	70.5	58.1
30–34	95.3	86.5	91.5	62.0	73.0	56.7
35–39	95.6	86.1	92.1	63.6	71.9	57.5
40–44	94.8	83.6	91.4	64.6	70.0	58.2
45–49	93.1	78.3	89.9	61.2	65.1	55.2

Source: U.S. Bureau of the Census, *1980 Census of Population, Detailed Population Characteristics: United States Summary* (Washington, D.C.: U.S. Government Printing Office, 1980), pp. 119–120, 123.

high school, compared with 69.8 percent of black men and 58.4 percent of men of Spanish origin. Women in the three ethnic groups complete high school at a slightly higher rate than do their male counterparts. Across all age groups, the rate of college completion among whites is about three times greater than that among blacks or Hispanics (23.6 percent versus 9.4 and 6.0 percent, respectively). Among women, the rate is 17.2, 9.7, and 6.4 percent respectively. In all three ethnic groups, more women than men complete college in their early 20s; after age 25, more men than women complete college.

Table 3 indicates the participation of adult Americans in the work force. A total of 84.3 percent of whites are gainfully employed, and that percentage steadily increases with age. This increase is slower among Hispanics and nonexistent among blacks. Although the rate of employment decreases among individuals in all these ethnic groups after age 44, the amount of decrease is greater among blacks than among the other two groups. The rate of employment among white women aged 20–24 is 69.5 percent; this figure declines between the ages of 24 and 44 and then declines further. The rate of employment among black women increases from 61.4 to 70.5 percent during the childbearing years. Hispanic women of all ages are less likely to work than either black or white women.

As shown in Table 4, types of employment also vary in relation to ethnic group and gender. About 38 percent of white men are at the managerial level, compared with 22 and 23 percent, respectively, of black and Hispanic men; the figures for women are 22, 18,

and 15 percent, respectively. A greater percentage of women than men hold clerical positions—33 percent of white women, 28 percent of black women, and 34 percent of Hispanic women, compared with 10, 18, and 14 percent, respectively, of the men. Thirty-four percent of black men and 27 percent of Hispanic men hold service-related jobs, such as waiters and janitors, compared with 13 percent of white men. Similarly, a high percentage of black women are employed in the domestic services.

Table 5 indicates that the earning capacity of white men increases steadily with age. In contrast, the incomes of black men and women show a decline of 7 and 17 percent, respectively, after age 45; among their Hispanic counterparts, the income drops 2 and 6 percent, respectively, for the same period.

Among those aged 20 to 24, this employment picture translates into an earning differential of 26 percent between white and black men and of 12 percent between white and Hispanic men; these differentials increase to 41 and 35 percent, respectively, by age 45. These figures, as well as high rates of divorce and separation, may in part be the underlying causes of the entrance of black women into the work force in larger numbers at a time when the number of employed white women has decreased. Compared with white women, the earning capacity of black women changes from a deficit of 24 percent from age 20 to 24 to a deficit of 7 percent from age 25 to 34. Black women aged 35 to 44 earn 3 percent more than do white women; this figure increases to 18 percent after age 45. Hispanic

Table 4. Selective Occupational Categories of Employed Persons by Sex and Ethnic Group: 1980

Category	Total No. of Labor Force	Men			Women		
		White	Black	Spanish Origin	White	Black	Spanish Origin
Managerial and Professional Specialty	22,553,473	12,411,595 (38%)	573,688 (22%)	408,036 (23%)	8,073,437 (22%)	804,433 (18%)	282,284 (15%)
Professional Specialty	12,160,174	5,694,168 (17%)	292,716 (11%)	183,162 (10%)	5,243,393 (15%)	574,629 (13%)	172,106 (9%)
Sales Occupation	10,365,685	4,915,345 (15%)	202,466 (8%)	199,585 (11%)	4,495,264 (12%)	331,009 (7%)	222,016 (12%)
Administrative Support Occupation—including Clerical	17,750,924	3,355,512 (10%)	470,927 (18%)	247,542 (14%)	11,759,115 (33%)	1,291,493 (28%)	627,335 (34%)
Service Occupation	13,801,940	4,320,713 (13%)	893,140 (34%)	473,370 (27%)	6,126,079 (17%)	1,502,133 (33%)	486,505 (26%)
Farming Forestry and Fishing Occupation	3,105,461	2,217,615 (7%)	180,208 (7%)	243,748 (14%)	377,104 (1%)	32,509 (1%)	54,277 (3%)
Total	79,737,657	32,913,948	2,613,145	1,755,443	36,074,392	4,546,206	1,844,523

Source: U.S. Bureau of the Census, *1980 Census of Population, Detailed Population Characteristics: United States Summary* (Washington, D.C.: U.S. Government Printing Office, 1980), pp. 177–179. Age begins at 16 years or over.

Table 5. Median Income in 1979 of Persons by Age, Sex, and Ethnic Group: 1980

	Men			Women		
Age	White	Black	Spanish Origin	White	Black	Spanish Origin
20–24	$ 7,881	$ 5,828	$ 6,922	$ 5,392	$ 3,951	$ 4,706
25–34	14,995	10,162	10,967	7,604	7,068	6,195
35–44	19,590	12,631	13,101	7,265	7,459	6,325
45–54	19,808	11,737	12,852	7,545	6,181	5,939

Source: U.S. Bureau of the Census, *1980 Census of Population, Detailed Population Characteristics: United States Summary* (Washington, D.C.: U.S. Government Printing Office, 1980), pp. 434–435.

women of all ages earn less than both white and black women.

Life Stages and Lifestyles

The literature on adulthood has increased over the past few decades, for example Neugarten (1968a), Sheehy (1974), Sze (1975), Lidz (1976), Levinson et al. (1978), Gould (1978), and Maas (1984). Current interest centers on the idea of human growth and development as a continuum from infancy to old age—an ongoing process of interaction between the internal life of the individual and the sociocultural world (Clark & Anderson, 1967, p. 63). Such a dynamic concept reflects the etymology of the term "adult" (from the Latin *adolescere*, to grow up) and echoes that Oriental concept of maturity, such as that found in Confucianism, as a process of becoming rather than of attainment (Rogers, 1979, p. 7).

Most influential is Erikson's work (1950), which contends that adult life is contingent on the success of the earlier stages of infancy, childhood, and adolescence. Erikson puts a time limit on each stage of development and hypothesizes that, over time, stability in personal development depends on the successful negotiation of essential psychosocial tasks at the appropriate time. Erikson's model of the eight-stage psychosocial development of the individual (1950, pp. 219–234), Levinson's structural conception (Levinson et al., 1978, p. 150), and Erickson and Martin's (1984, p. 165) emphasis on crises or turning points all mark age-specific transitions that transcend individual personality development.

Normative expectations then arise from age stratifications that are seen as regulating the timing and sequencing of various transitions to adult activities (Featherman, Hogan, & Sorensen, 1984, p. 162). The concept of life stages sometimes has the appearance of age-role stereotypes (Rogers, 1979, p. 7) or seems to reflect socially defined timing, which itself is capable of change when norms are rapidly changing (Neugarten, 1979, p. 88). Adult tasks are frequently embedded in traditional or conventional values that may not be evident to much of contemporary society.

In *Adult Development*, Whitbourne and Weinstock describe the "typical" pattern of major life events (1979, p. 126). This pattern identifies (1) tasks of early adulthood (ages 20–30), which are the searching for a mate and the establishment of a family; (2) tasks of middle adulthood I (ages 30–45), which involve child rearing and settling into family life; and (3) tasks of middle adulthood II (ages 45–60), which are anguishing over and finally accepting the empty nest and redefining the marital relationship.

Lifestyles have changed in recent years. An increasing proportion of adults do not marry between the ages of 20 and 30, have the requisite number of children, or remain with the same spouse. Women are increasingly choosing to delay marriage until they are in their 30s and opting not to have children. Men and women are living together without being married. Single-parent marriages, serial marriages, homosexual "marriages," communal living arrangements, and single lifestyles are on the increase. The nuclear family of father, mother, and children is no longer the typical family pattern. In short, there are many "alternate lifestyles" that cannot be dismissed as aberrant merely because they do not fit conveniently into a single schematological model.

Whitbourne and Weinstock (1979, p.

127) acknowledge the lack of information about the variations in life patterns among adults. These variations can be potentially rewarding or devastating, depending on the person or the ethnic or social context in which the person finds himself or herself and chooses to conform or rebel. In the view of Vaillant and Milofsky (1980, p. 1352), adult maturation is open ended. In addition, psychosocial maturity is not a foregone conclusion, nor are landmarks, like occupational and interpersonal competence, clearly fixed chronologically. Neugarten (1979, p. 88) has expressed doubt that any "invariant sequence of stages" in adulthood would correspond to the physiological, cognitive, and emotional stages of infancy and childhood. Rogers (1979, p. 422) similarly rejects the implied precision of some life-stage theories, and Weick (1983, p. 134) believes that adult development is nonlinear and is filled with periods of stagnation, progression, continual adjustment to each task and cross-task, regression, side stepping, and occasional great leaps forward.

Development might be seen as a process of fluctuation as opposed to an age-specific succession of periods of stability and transition (Gould, 1972, p. 531). Variability rather than conformity to a few dominant, socially recognized patterns might be accepted as part of the normal changing pattern, and crisis might then be seen less as an abnormality or as a set of difficulties to be remediated than as an opportunity to refine life strategies and to hone coping skills (Brennan & Weick, 1981, p. 17).

Young Adulthood

Society expects individuals to begin to find themselves, apart from their families of origin, toward the end of adolescence. The extended family has lost much of its stabilizing and determining force. Together, freedom of conscience, existentialist and therapeutic concepts of authenticity and self-actualization, and the relaxation of behavioral standards in the enforcement of the law allow young adults to determine how they wish to conduct their lives, as long as they do not abridge or violate anyone else's rights in the process. Even the predominant therapeutic code of ethics calls less for fitting the nonconformist individual back into the dominant social mold than for accepting whatever

value system the individual espouses as long as it is not destructive to the self or to others; an example is, the changing attitude toward homosexuality in the second and third editions of the *Diagnostic and Statistical Manual of Mental Disorders* (Freedman, Kaplan, & Saddock, 1975, p. 842).

Typically, adolescents experiment with adventurous and sometimes flamboyant lifestyles and choices, often to the consternation of their parents. Early adulthood is the time when these experiments are to be molded into what hopefully will be a stable, productive life pattern. In the face of the many choices of lifestyle and the rapidity of changing fashion, it is not surprising that many young adults experience confusion. Fromm's (1941) *Escape From Freedom* and Toffler's (1972) *Future Shock* both address this fear and confusion in the population at large and in part suggest why some people seek to return to simple answers that are readily understandable and easily arrived at.

Of particular importance is the workplace, which provides an arena for both women and men to apply their energies to developing lifelong goals, such as carving out a place in the world, establishing a sense of identity, leaving a mark, and gaining pride and a sense of accomplishment (DiCori, 1977, p. 283). Today's highly technological society places considerable emphasis on the growth of technically trained and skilled workers. This has led to prognostications of an eventual bifurcation of workers into those who understand how to run computers and computer-controlled machines (the new literate) and those who do not. Increasingly, training is associated with schooling among all individuals, from those with blue-collar ambitions to those with professional aspirations. The former group is required to remain in school until age 16; the latter group must delay entrance into the work force and the achievement of economic independence and security until their professional or graduate education and training is completed—possibly in their late 20s or early 30s. For many, early adulthood represents economic hardship, as well as anticipation of economic improvement on reaching the late 20s or early 30s.

The current challenge faced by urban and rural public education to teach basic skills effectively, let alone the high-technology skills modern industry requires for its expansion and maintenance, further accentuates the split between those who are being prepared for careers and those who will hold jobs—if they are fortunate. People with inadequate training—usually women, minorities, and those in rural areas—often find themselves in low-status, low-paying jobs, with little or no chance for economic or societal advancement, in a job market that itself is relatively unstable because of market conditions.

Women who bear children at a young age, when marriages or relationships fail and financial support from partners and family is inadequate, apply for welfare benefits or face years of struggle for subsistence. With the annual pregnancy rate in the United States at 96 per 1000 among girls aged 15 to 19 (Cancila, 1985, p. 15), many young adults find that their lives have been mortgaged by the events and choices of their adolescent years.

The wives of upwardly mobile men may work to support the family until the husband reaches a higher income level and then drop out of the labor market to raise their children. The stresses of professional training are high and take their toll on a marriage. Increasingly, women are entering professional fields previously dominated by men, and families are learning to cope with overlapping male and female household roles to a degree greater than has been traditional. For some years, popular magazines and professional journals have been focusing on the special stresses of two-career families. One fifth of women delay marriage until the age of 30, and the demand for maternity leave, day care centers, and other social supports are influencing the M-shaped curve that used to characterize the employment of women (O'Rand & Henretta, 1982, p. 62). As mentioned earlier, geographic mobility and changing family patterns frequently force young couples to cope with these new demands without the support of their extended families.

Ironically, stress is also associated with unanticipated, rapid occupational advancement. Some women or minorities, for example, may find themselves in managerial or supervisory positions before they are fully prepared for them. Those in direct human services, like teachers or nurses, frequently find that rapid economic advancement can be attained only by entering administrative posts for which training or motivation may be lacking. Those in the junior ranks in business and the military may have to prove that they are motivated by relocating frequently, resulting in stressful family systems. Professionals may also be overwhelmed by the amount of time required to become successful or to maintain the status they achieve initially.

In summary, early adulthood is characterized by peak levels of physical health and energy that are balanced by the stresses of new life events, such as the struggle for economic security, social recognition, and emotional fulfillment. Statistics reflect the impact of these stresses: an increase in the development of mental disorders between the ages of 25 and 45 (Beiser, 1978, p. 620).

Middle Adulthood

For many writers—for example, Lidz (1976), Levinson (1978), and Tamir (1982)—the decade of the 30s is seen as a transition period between early adulthood and the midlife crisis. Personal income is usually at a high point, although an increase in family size may more than offset such gains. Political involvement increases, with voting participation almost doubling from ages 20 to 24 (28.4 percent) and 35 to 44 (52.2 percent) (U.S. Bureau of the Census, 1984, p. 266).

Voting is also correlated with increases in income. U.S. Census reports indicate that in 1983, the voting record was 34.1 percent for the unemployed, 39.1 percent for blue-collar workers, and 57.8 percent for white-collar workers. In the same year, 27 percent of those aged 25–44 who earned less than $5,000 voted. In the same age group, 35.1 percent of those earning $10,000–14,999 voted; the figure was 60.9 percent among those earning more than $35,000 (U.S. Bureau of the Census, 1983, p. 61). A more conservative political outlook begins to appear in middle adulthood, although this tendency is minimized in some minority groups, such as blacks and Jews (Rothenberg, Licht, & Newport, 1982, p. 1). In the same vein, support for federal spending in social programs generally weakens during this period (Rothenberg, Licht, & Newport, 1982, pp. 47, 50).

Possibly because of this image of settling down, more has been written about the obvious crises of adolescence and middle age than about the middle-adult period. Levinson and his colleagues (1978, p. 151) found that all their subjects went through some structural changes during this period: Almost 55 percent advanced in their careers within a stable life structure and 45 percent experienced serious failures or declines within a stable life structure, attempted a new life structure, advanced but underwent new life structures, or underwent considerable instability of life structure.

Claussen (1976, p. 102) found that men aged 30–40 are more likely to change jobs because of job dissatisfaction than because of limited opportunities for advancement. At age 38, more than half the men sampled expected to advance occupationally, although a decade later only a third believed they had achieved their aspirations. Chiriboga and Dean (1978, pp. 45–55) indicate that although the sheer number of life events begins to drop off in the 30s, the potentially disruptive effect of such events may increase. Alcohol consumption in men, which frequently increases in the early 20s, continues unabated in middle adulthood (Boyd & Weissman, 1981, p. 211) and has a potential impact on both family interaction and job performance. Women who drink heavily often begin to use alcohol and to misuse prescription drugs in their 30s (Boyd & Weissman, 1981, pp. 207–211). In summary, the decade of the 30s represents no relaxation of the manifestations of psychological disturbances. The demands on and options of both men and women during these years make middle adulthood a period worthy of additional research.

Middle-Age Crisis

In the early 40s, the individual "generally operates at his optimal level as he interacts with others, is at his peak earning capacity and executes projects at his greatest level of efficiency" (Tamir, 1982, p. 48). Neugarten (1968b, p. 93) points out that the middle aged are the norm bearers and the decision makers. Even in a youth-oriented society, these individuals are the ones who are largely in control. The middle aged guide the next generation—their children and their proteges (Erikson, 1950, p. 231; Tamir, 1982, p. 51). They should be at the peak of their lives and have a sense of competence, self-confidence, and purpose.

Before the riches of middle age can be enjoyed, however, a period of self-assessment must be traversed. Whitbourne and Weinstock (1979, p. 126) cite five major problem areas: questioning of identity, concern over mortality, discontent with marital relationships, concern about children leaving the home, and dissatisfaction with career accomplishments. The middle-age crisis is marked by a fear of aging and the notion that whatever has been achieved—sometimes far less than what has been envisioned—represents a brief peak to be followed by a gradual, perceptible decline of both physical prowess and mental acuity (Levinson et al., 1978, p. ix). During this time, there is a heightened preoccupation with one's existence and with relationships. Physical signs of aging are more evident and are interpreted in relation to growing deficits in beauty, attractiveness, vigor, and sexual energy, all of which carry implications that are both individually and socially negative. There may also be a growing worry about having to step aside at work for the next generation—freshly trained, energetic, and equipped with new ideas and a willingness to accept, at least initially, substantially lower salaries.

Medley (1980, pp. 198–200) indicates that standard of living and family life are the most powerful predictors of life satisfaction in this age group, with the latter being especially important for women. Chiriboga (1981, p. 14) found that men are most concerned with instrumental activity and their sense of control and confidence and that women tend to lack confidence and are more troubled and dependent. Tamir (1982, p. 49) notes that compared to those with a high-school education or less, college-educated men are more depressed, display more symptoms of psychological immobilization, have more drinking problems, turn more often to drugs to relieve tension, and have a higher level of self-esteem. Claussen (1976, p. 102) found that most of those who change jobs voluntarily after age 40 do so in the hope of advancing rather than of increasing job satisfaction, per se. Kalleberg and Lascocco (1983, p. 82) note a leveling of job satisfaction from age 41 to 55, a phenomenon that is difficult to deal with for the two thirds of those who feel they have not yet achieved their career goals. In cases in which job change is not voluntary because of occupational displacement, extensive retraining may be necessary to maintain social status and standards of living. For women entering the work force for the first time or after an interval of 10 to 20 years, retraining may be an absolute necessity that is particularly difficult for widows and divorced women who are left in financial straits.

Stress is clearly felt in the marital dyad. Couples who tolerated each other for the sake of their children or who overlooked serious problems in their relationships no longer have children on hand to buffer their discord (Friedman, 1981, pp. 103–115). Erikson (1950, p. 231) points to an obsessive need for pseudointimacy, punctuated by moments of mutual repulsion, with a pervading sense of individual stagnation and individual impoverishment. Lowenthal and Weiss (1976, p. 14) point out that both men and women yearn for intimacy at this point as a resource against stress. Sexual intimacy, however, may be dulled by habitude, by the apparent failure of physical prowess, by the first symptoms of debilitating disease, by the onset of menopause, by deep-seated anger toward the partner, and by the occasional, vague feeling of having missed something in life.

The rate of divorce among those married 15 years or longer has gradually increased. In 1975 alone, the number of divorces of middle-aged couples exceeded 350,000 (Berardo, 1982, p. 134). The social and psychological adjustments that must be made by middle-aged divorced people are great. Among these adjustments are coping with a sense of failure after a lengthy period of personal investment, dealing with a loss of identity after being part of a marital dyad, and potentially losing friends and in-laws whose loyalty remains with the estranged partner. In addition, middle-aged divorced people who begin to date after many years find that the rules have changed. Because their self-esteem has decreased and their sense of desperation has increased, these individuals are vulnerable to being used and then discarded.

Men, including custodial fathers, may find it easier to remarry than women, and they sometimes marry significantly younger women. To the degree that a social stigma is still attached to marriages between older women and younger men, women may find the pool of eligible partners relatively small.

In addition, the logistics of socializing and courtship, particularly if there are still children in the house, become difficult. Reconstituted families are faced with challenges such as blending the children of two or more previous marriages, defining the role of step-parents, and dealing with the ongoing influences of previous spouses. If divorce is avoided and the marital dyad is maintained, the problem of dealing with aging and sometimes infirm parents and the prospect of many years of dependence persist at a time when the empty nest might have offered the promises of new-found freedom.

In combination, these stresses result in mental and emotional strain. Innumerable studies have shown that the rate of depression is higher among women than among men—7.0 percent compared with 2.9 percent, respectively, during the middle-age period (Boyd & Weissman, 1981, p. 206). Although the causes of this gap cannot be elucidated, it is true that, in our society, women are given more permission to show their feelings than men and that women experience less social stigma than men when they seek out professional help to deal with emotional problems.

In cases in which help is provided by those without training in counseling techniques, treatment may be offered in the form of prescription drugs for depression, anxiety, sleeping difficulties, and nonspecific pain or malaise. Such treatment may result in drug dependence or in postponement of dealing with problems. Conversely, men may treat their depression with alcohol and may not seek help until their problems are severe enough to require hospitalization. The rate of alcoholism is higher among men than among women. However, alcoholism among women is somewhat more difficult to detect because of the tendency of women to drink alone at home, rather than in public places. When men do seek the help of physicians for depression-related problems, their presenting problems are more likely to be those of sexual impotence, work difficulties, or alcoholism as opposed to a depressed mood (Boyd & Weissman, 1981, p. 211).

Those who suffer from severe depression are at risk of committing suicide. Across all age groups, women attempt suicide more often than do men. However, men are generally more successful in their attempts, and the most successful suicides occur in middle-aged, seemingly successful men (Cath, 1980, p. 55). Men are successful in their attempts three times more often than women. Whereas the risk of depression eases somewhat in women over age 50, the rate of depression and the risk of suicide in men increases steadily with age (Boyd & Weissman, 1981, pp. 211–216).

Late Middle Adulthood

If the midlife crisis is successfully negotiated, there is the promise of a reintegration of personality, a redefinition of the marital bond, and a final effort to achieve career security for the duration of the work life. Beiser (1978, p. 620) notes that individuals aged 45–60 are less vulnerable to the development of psychiatric disorders than are those aged 25–45 or over age 60. In the middle years, there is a high level of job responsibility and of political participation, reflecting a sense of integration with the community. There is also a tendency toward greater political conservatism in an effort to preserve the relatively high standards that may have been achieved through long years of employment and occupational advancement (Seagull, 1971, p. 90).

The middle class has achieved its highest status at this time. Upwardly mobile, working-class people who have improved their economic situation are more giving and sympathetic than are those of middle- and upper-class origins. In contrast, downwardly mobile persons lack control and are withdrawn, self-defeating, preoccupied with psychosomatic complaints, anxious, and concerned with their own adequacy (Claussen, 1976, p. 103). Chiriboga (1981, p. 14) found that men tend to distance themselves gradually from the manipulative and assertive stance of earlier years and to move toward emotional sensitivity and interest in interpersonal relations. Conversely, women frequently move toward greater assertiveness, mastery, and self-confidence. Whitbourne and Weinstock (1979, p. 126) also discuss this increased overlapping of sex roles between the ages of 45 and 60. It should be noted, however, that the impact of the women's movement may, in the past few decades, have initiated the overlap at an earlier period. Medley (1980, p. 200) indicates that, although health considerations have become increasingly important for both sexes, they are a

distant second to family life in the discussions of women regarding their life situations.

The supposition that the anguish of the midlife crisis abates somewhat after age 45 or 50 should not support the notion that this period is without sources of stress. Spouses and aged parents frequently die during this period, and individuals must cope with failing physical health and the prospect of dying in a society that, currently, is not dealing well with the problems of aging and of dying. The threat of suicide, at least in men, increases gradually throughout this period (Boyd & Weissman, 1981, p. 216).

Implications for Social Work Practice

As mentioned earlier, the difficulties of adulthood are complex and often involve a balance of competence, self-sufficiency, and energy with the struggle for economic security, social recognition, and emotional fulfillment. The developmental approach enables social workers to assess the kinds of services needed by people at a given life stage and to view the change process as a normative rather than abnormal event. It enables social workers to identify populations at risk and "to anticipate future consequences for clients if necessary competencies are not mastered at each stage and to plan appropriate interventions" (Streever & Wodarski, 1984, p. 278). In addition, the approach allows workers to evaluate the level of ability of individuals, families, and social groups to deal with crises; the strength of support systems; and the extent of available resources. Thus, the approach facilitates the formation of social policy and gives direction to planning in the human services.

The application of developmental theory to social work practice and program development can be seen in the work of Strean (1972), Pincus and Minahan (1973), Germain and Gitterman (1980), Bloom (1980), and Weick (1983). Strean (1972) traces the roots of the life model social work practice to the "social data-gathering of Richmond, the diagnostic and evaluative orientation of Hamilton, the treatment typologies of Hollis and the 'participation' and 'focus' of Perlman"(p. 53). Pincus and Minahan's (1973) approach, in particular, integrates the knowledge of "life tasks confronting people and the resources and conditions which could facilitate their coping with these tasks, then help them realize their values and aspirations, and alleviate their distress'' (p. 9).

The social worker must evaluate the whole range of psychological forces and social constraints in the client system. As Sze (1975) states:

> The objective of social work is human service, and the means by which this objective is accomplished are rather broad in scope. It is therefore imperative to be well acquainted with as many social constraints and individual determinants affecting the individual's functioning and well-being as possible. Such a broad base of theoretical understanding will lead to better formulation of social policy, more effective service to the people, and more accountability in psychosocial counseling. (p. xi)

As alluded to earlier, developmental theory is not an effective basis for social work practice if it is used to produce stereotypic images of any given life stage and its developmental tasks. Weick (1983, p. 132) contends that physiological changes are more idiosyncratic in adults than in children and that changes over time are more gender related, more unpredictable, more complex, and more tightly linked to sociocultural role expectations at particular ages. Life events that one person perceives as crises may not be considered traumatic or even noteworthy by another individual. Members of certain ethnic groups may be more vulnerable than other groups in situations involving given life tasks and may have a greater need for formal or informal resources or for the development of cohesive responses to social demands or pressures. However, they may develop, for example, alternate coping mechanisms for dealing with being a single parent that may be overlooked by social workers if alternative family structures are considered *ipso facto* pathological or defective. (For further discussion, see Billingsley, 1968, & Thompson, 1974).

The environmental or ecological approach to social work considers people within their social context (in the various systems and subsystems of which they are a part). It focuses on the multifaceted nature of intervention needed in different situations (the therapy, casework, and advocacy skills required in the arenas in which intervention would be most helpful). Germain and Gitterman (1980), for example, treat stress as ''a

psycho-social condition generated by discrepancies between needs and capacities, on the one hand, and environmental qualities on the other. It arises in three interrelated areas of living: life transitions, environmental pressures and interpersonal processes'' (p. 7).

Intervention on the individual level might focus on the inadequate ego adaptability of the client—what traditionally has been labeled ''psychopathology.'' The impact of life-change events may camouflage deeply rooted personality problems. Sze and Lamar (1981, p. 23) found that the most frequently reported cases of child abuse cited by both abusers and investigators involve stress-related life events. However, 76 percent of the primary-cause variables in all cases of child abuse examined by the researchers were found to have been psychopathological in origin.

A cognitive approach can be used to elucidate the sources of problems and of distorted perceptions that lead to irrational behavior among many individuals. It might confront a person's reluctance to share feelings of isolation, confusion, and helplessness with family and friends. In addition, this approach might provide perspective and facilitate adjustment to the crisis situation. At the same time, specific crises might be prevented by family life education geared to nonclinical populations (Rhodes, 1977, p. 302). A recognition of the sources of stress can lead to increased coping capabilities among individuals and their family systems (Dill & Feld, 1982, p. 193). For example, educating a middle-aged couple about human development and necessary life changes might facilitate the granting of greater independence and autonomy to adolescent children, as well as the management of the approaching ''empty nest'' period of life. The role of the social worker in such an intervention is that of teacher, expert, and consultant (Pincus & Minahan, 1973, p. 113). The social worker may also intervene on the social level to help contribute to changes in public perception that are supportive of the stresses and strains of adult life in general and of populations with specific needs and vulnerabilities in particular.

Interpersonal discord frequently arises from maladaptive interpersonal processes, from differences of role perception or expectation, and from inadequate channels of communication. Spiegel (1975, p. 446) suggests that role conflict results when the ego and the alter ego have conflicting or incompatible notions of how to play their reciprocal roles. Relinquishing a social role (for example, employee or parent) without proper substitution frequently involves loss of self-esteem, of goal-directed activity, of productive utilization of time, and of social recognition. The redefinition of roles and of priorities and the establishment of a new set of behaviors—role expectations and modes of role complementarity—are critical to a sense of well-being.

Changes in role and life stage and their impact on the family can be facilitated if there is adequate communication. The return of a woman to a working role may be resented by both her husband and children. Such resentment leads to discouragement and a sense of guilt and anger in the woman. The role of the social worker in short-term counseling would be to facilitate the exchange of information and to stimulate and mediate linkages within and between systems.

The predictability of life events can provide a knowledge base for a preventive social work approach (Brennan & Weick, 1981, p. 19). Bloom's (1980, pp. 4–13) developmental tables illustrate age-specific life events that help social workers deal with vulnerable groups, especially those whose resources for coping with change are limited. Loewenstein (1978, p. 72) introduced life-transition counseling as a time-limited, transition-oriented group intervention method that is based on the theoretical and practical roots of adult education, of problem-focused group therapy, of the self-help movement, and of crisis intervention.

Another approach to the crises inherent in life transitions is crisis consultation. Kadushin (1977, p. 26) views this mode of intervention as a way of providing both direct and indirect service to the client in an attempt to minimize predictable developmental stresses. Providing avenues of care for families, such as those of the demented elderly, might avoid the further breakdown of physically and emotionally exhausted family members and allay feelings of anger and guilt. Such intervention can free family members to resume "relevant psychosocial tasks required for subsequent maturation and growth" (Rapaport, 1970, p. 272).

Weick (1983, p. 135) emphasizes that efforts to create and to support human growth must be seen in the context of patterns of societal values that either support or create barriers to growth. She further notes that work with the individual may imply efforts to weaken or to overturn such barriers. Society may create the illusion that things are the way they should be and that adjustment implies continuity of social norms rather than a possible change of those norms to conform to new perceptions of optimal human growth and development that are responsive to people's rights, goals, and capacities (Weick, 1983, p, 136; Hartmann, 1958, p. 32).

Environmental pressure can stem from social injustice, from cultural biases, and from racial and gender discrimination. As Chestang (1980) points out, the hostility of the American environment "confronts the black person throughout his life and in large measure determines his character development" (p. 41). In general, the discrepancies in educational achievement, in vocational success, and in marital stability between whites and blacks, as reflected in the statistics presented earlier, can be traced both directly and indirectly to environmental constraints and institutional injustice. Dealing with the impact of injustice on the client system without addressing the sources of stress in the environment tends to put the burden of change on the individual. At this point, the social worker should assume an advocacy posture to help the person obtain needed resources or "to obtain a policy change or concession from a disinterested, or unresponsive system" (Pincus & Minahan, 1973, p. 113).

Much of what has been learned about and legislated for blacks and women has gradually been applied to other groups (for example, the physically handicapped, the mentally retarded, and the chronically emotionally disturbed) whose articulation, eloquence, and sociopolitical influence has been less clearly manifested. Public buildings are now constructed with ramps and bathroom facilities to meet the needs of the physically handicapped. The sexual needs of the disabled and the elderly are also being addressed, as are legal and moral questions concerning such issues as the sterilization and housing and voting rights of the mentally retarded. The deinstitutionalization of large numbers of the chronically emotionally disturbed calls into question the adequacy and suitability of the current policies of agencies and the government regarding the allocation of resources to deal with populations that are unable to hold steady jobs or to maintain effective relations with significant others in the community (McCoin, 1983, p. 184).

The pervasiveness across all socioeconomic groups of drug abuse, spouse abuse, elder abuse, and the physical and sexual abuse of children has helped sensitize society to the array of adult stresses. Other areas of concern among adults are the problems arising from society's rapidly developing technology, to which individuals have not yet developed satisfactory ways of relating, as well as the new patterns of unemployment, transplant surgery, refinements in life support systems for the terminally ill and for neonates with extensive physical and mental deficits, and new fertility techniques for genetic manipulation.

At the core of social work practice is the transcendence of the remediation of crisis to (1) coping and the potential for human growth (Rapaport, 1970, p. 272), (2) enhancing a person's effectiveness in the biological, psychological, social, cultural, and political arenas (Germain & Gitterman, 1980, p. 62), and (3) striving for genuinely rewarding lives (Rogers, 1979, p. 169). The common understanding between practitioners and clients is not to usurp the capacity of clients to shape their development (Weick, 1983, p. 137).

Movements such as the Grey Panthers and the Gay Liberation Movement demonstrate the willingness of diverse groups to join together in an effort to achieve common political goals. The burgeoning of the self-help movement—from Alcoholics Anonymous to Mothers Against Drunk Drivers—reflects the discovery that individuals can contribute to the well-being of others experiencing similar life stages, crises, and growth situations, with or without the help of a professional. The vision of a responsive society is integral to the human development model and lies beyond the individual case; dependence; and bureaucratically dictated procedures, perceptions, and programs. The goal of such a society is to develop modes of intervention and advocacy to facilitate the health process and the innate human striving for dignity, self-definition, and self-determination. As Maas (1984) so eloquently states:

The greater the number of contexts with which people can cope, the fewer the situations in which they are overwhelmed by feelings of helplessness and stress. The more often they engage in socially responsive interaction, the more likely they are to help to generate or sustain a caring and sharing society. (p. 3)

WILLIAM C. SZE
BARRY IVKER

For further information, see AGED; ECOLOGICAL PERSPECTIVE; HUMAN DEVELOPMENT: BIOLOGICAL PERSPECTIVE; HUMAN DEVELOPMENT: PSYCHOLOGICAL PERSPECTIVE; HUMAN DEVELOPMENT: SOCIOCULTURAL PERSPECTIVE; MEN; WOMEN.

References

Beiser, M. (1978). "Psychiatric Epidemiology." In A. M. Nicholi, Jr. (Ed.), *The Harvard Guide to Modern Psychiatry*. Cambridge, Mass.: Belknap Press of Harvard University.

Berardo, D. H. (1982). "Divorce and Remarriage at Middle Age and Beyond." *Annals of the American Academy of Political and Social Sciences, 464*, 132–139.

Billingsley, A. (1968). *Black Families in White America*. Englewood Cliffs, N.J.: Prentice-Hall.

Bloom, M. (Ed.). (1980). *Life Span Development*. New York: Macmillan Publishing Co.

Boyd, J. H., & Weissman, M. M. (1981). "The Epidemiology of Psychiatric Disorders of Middle Age: Depression, Alcoholism, and Suicide." In J. G. Howells (Ed.), *Modern Perspective in the Psychiatry of Middle Age* (pp. 201–221). New York: Brunner/Mazel.

Brennan, E. M., & Weick, A. (1981). "Theories of Adult Development: Creating a Context for Practice." *Social Casework, 62*(1), 13–19.

Cancila, C. (1985, March 29). "Teen Pregnancy, Abortion Rates Highest in U.S." *American Medical News*. p. 5.

Cath, S. H. (1980). "Suicide in the Middle Years: Some Reflections on the Annihilation of Self." In W. H. Norman & T. J. Scaramella (Eds.), *Mid-Life: Developmental and Clinical Issues* (pp. 53–72). New York: Brunner/Mazel.

Chestang, L. W. (1980) "Character Development in a Hostile Environment." In M. Bloom (Ed.), *Life Span Development* (pp. 40–50). New York: Macmillan Publishing Co.

Chiriboga, D. A. (1981). "The Developmental Psychology of Middle Age." In J. G. Howells (Ed.), *Modern Perspectives in the Psychiatry of Middle Age* (pp. 3–25). New York: Brunner/Mazel.

Chiriboga, D. A., & Dean, H. (1978). "Dimensions

of Stress." *Journal of Psychosomatic Research, 22*(1), 47–55.

Clark, M. M., & Anderson, B. G. (1967). *Culture and Aging.* Springfield, Ill.: Charles C Thomas, Publisher.

Claussen, J. A. (1976). "Glimpses Into the Social World of Middle Age." *International Journal of Aging and Human Development, 7*(2), 99–106.

DiCori, F. (1977). "Work and Creativity." In R. C. Simons & H. Pardes (Eds.), *Understanding Human Behavior in Health and Illness* (pp. 283–294). Baltimore, Md.: Williams & Wilkins.

Dill D., & Feld, E. (1982). "The Challenge of Coping." In D. Belle (Ed.), *Lives in Stress* (pp. 190–198). Beverly Hills, Calif.: Sage Publications.

Erickson, V. L., & Martin, J. (1984). "The Changing Adult: An Integrated Approach." *Social Casework, 65*(3), 162–171.

Erikson, E. H. (1950). *Childhood and Society.* New York: W. W. Norton & Co.

Featherman, D. L., Hogan, D. P., & Sorensen, S. B. (1984). "Entry into Adulthood: Profiles of Young Men in the 1950's." In P. B. Baltes & G. B. Orville, Jr. (Eds.), *Life: Span Development and Behavior* (Vol. 6, pp. 160–200). New York: Academic Press.

Freedman, A. M., Kaplan, H. I., & Saddock, B. J. (Eds.). (1975). *Comprehensive Textbook of Psychiatry—II* (2nd ed.). Baltimore, Md.: Williams and Wilkins.

Friedman, H. J. (1981). "The Divorced in Middle Age." In J. G. Howells (Ed.), *Modern Perspectives in the Middle Age* (pp. 103–115). New York: Brunner/Mazel.

Fromm, E. (1941). *Escape From Freedom.* New York: Farrar & Rinehart.

Germain, C. B., & Gitterman, A. (1980). *The Life Model of Social Work Practice.* New York: Columbia University Press.

Gould, R. L. (1972). "The Phases of Adult Life: A Study in Developmental Psychology." *American Journal of Psychiatry, 129*(5), 33–43.

Gould, R. L. (1978). *Transformations.* New York: Simon & Schuster.

Hartmann, H. (1958). *Ego Psychology and the Problem of Adaptation.* New York: International Universities Press.

Kadushin, A. (1977). *Consultation in Social Work.* New York: Columbia University Press.

Kalleberg, A. L., & Lascocco, K. A. (1983). "Aging, Values, and Rewards: Explaining Aging Differences in Job Satisfaction." *American Sociological Review, 48*(1), 78–90.

Levinson, D., et al. (1978). *The Seasons of A Man's Life.* New York: Alfred A. Knopf.

Lidz, T. (1976). *The Person* (rev. ed.). New York: Basic Books.

Lowenstein, S. F. (1978). "Preparing Social Work Students for Life-Transition Counseling Within the Human Behavior Sequence." *Journal of Education for Social Work, 14*(2), 66–73.

Lowenthal, M. F., & Weiss, L. (1976). "Intimacy and Crises in Adulthood." *The Counseling Psychologist, 6*(1), 10–15.

Lowenthal, M. F., et al. (1977). *Four Stages of Life.* San Francisco: Jossey-Bass.

Maas, H. S. (1984). *People and Contexts.* Englewood Cliffs, N.J.: Prentice-Hall.

McCoin, J. M. (1983). *Adult Foster Homes.* New York: Human Sciences Press.

Medley, M. L. (1980). "Life Satisfaction Across Four Stages of Adult Life." *International Journal of Aging and Human Development, 11*(3), 193–209.

Neugarten, B. L. (Ed.). (1968a). *Middle Age and Aging.* Chicago: University of Chicago Press.

Neugarten, B. L. (1968b). "The Awareness of Middle Age." In B. L. Neugarten (Ed.), *Middle Age and Aging* (pp. 93–98). Chicago: University of Chicago Press.

Neugarten, B. L. (1979). "Time, Age and the Life Cycle." *American Journal of Psychiatry, 136*(7), 887–894.

O'Rand, A. M., & Henretta, J. C. (1982). "Women at Middle Age: Developmental Transitions." *Annals of the American Academy of Political and Social Sciences, 464,* 57–64.

Pincus, A., & Minahan, A. (1973). *Social Work Practice: Model and Method.* Itasca, Ill.: F. E. Peacock Publishers.

Rapaport, L. (1970). "Crisis Intervention as a Model of Brief Treatment." In R. W. Roberts & R. H. Nee (Eds.), *Theories of Social Casework* (pp. 267–311). Chicago: University of Chicago Press.

Rhodes, S. L. (1977). "A Developmental Approach to the Life Cycle of the Family." *Social Casework, 58*(5), 301–311.

Rogers, D. (1979). *The Adult Years.* Englewood Cliffs, N.J.: Prentice-Hall.

Rothenberg, S., Licht, E., & Newport, F. (1982). *Ethnic Voters and National Issues.* Washington, D.C.: Free Congress Research and Education Foundation.

Seagull, L. M. (1971). "The Youth Vote and Change in American Politics." *Annals of the American Academy of Political and Social Sciences, 397,* 88–96.

Sheehy, G. (1974). *Passages.* New York: E. P. Dutton & Co.

Spiegel, J. P. (1975). "The Resolution of Role Conflict with the Family." In W. C. Sze (Ed.), *Human Life Cycle* (pp. 445–467). New York: Jason Aronson.

Strean, H. S. (1972). "Application of the Life Model to Casework." *Social Casework, 17*(5), 46–53.

Streever, K. L., & Wodarski, J. S. (1984). "Life

Span Developmental Approach: Implications for Practice.'' *Social Casework, 65*(5), 267–278.

Sze, W. (Ed). (1975). *Human Life Cycle*. New York: Jason Aronson.

Sze, W. C., & Lamar, B. (1981). ''Causes of Child Abuse: A Re-examination.'' *Health and Social Work, 6*(4), 19–25.

Tamir, L. M. (1982). ''Men at Middle Age: Developmental Transitions.'' *Annals of the American Academy of Political and Social Sciences 464*, 47–56.

Thompson, D. C. (1974). *Sociology of the Black Experience*. Westport, Conn.: Greenwood Press.

Toffler, A. (1972). *Future Shock*. New York: Bantam Books.

U.S. Bureau of the Census. (1980). *1980 Census of Population, Detailed Population Characteristics: United States Summary*. Washington, D.C.: U.S. Government Printing Office.

U.S. Bureau of the Census. (1983). *Current Population Reports, Voting and Registration in the Election of November, 1982* (Series P-20, No. 383). Washington, D.C.: U.S. Government Printing Office.

U.S. Bureau of the Census. (1984). *Statistical Abstract of the United States*. Washington, D.C.: U.S. Government Printing Office.

Vaillant, G. E., & Milofsky, E. (1980). ''Natural History of Male Psychological Health: IX. Empirical Evidence for Erikson's Model of the Life Cycle.'' *American Journal of Psychiatry, 137*(11), 1348–1359.

Weick, A. (1983). ''A Growth-Task Model of Human Development.'' *Social Casework, 64*(3), 131–137.

Whitbourne, S. K., & Weinstock, C. S. (1979). *Adult Development*. New York: Holt, Rinehart, & Winston.

ADVOCACY

Despite the social work profession's long tradition of social action on behalf of clients, the concept of case advocacy as an integral component of social work practice was not introduced until the mid-1960s. Some of the activities now labeled ''case advocacy'' were carried out earlier under the rubric ''environmental manipulation'' or ''indirect action,'' but casework theorists and practitioners did not give these activities as much attention as they gave direct work with clients. It was Charles Grosser (1965), a community organizer writing about the experience of workers in a New York City neighborhood community development program called Mobilization for Youth, who first recommended that social workers act as advocates for their clients.

Early Views of Case Advocacy

The early writings on advocacy practice (Ad Hoc Committee on Advocacy, 1969; Brager, 1968; Briar, 1967; Grosser, 1965; Terrell, 1967; Wineman & James, 1969) were exhortative and somewhat polemical in nature, reflecting the social ferment of the times and a desire to redefine professional priorities. Social workers were often under attack during this period for their alleged failure to deal with the structural problems of the urban poor. The successes and failures of the civil rights movement and the War on Poverty had highlighted in new ways the strength of the forces arrayed against the interests of various oppressed groups. Social welfare institutions became targets of intervention for welfare rights and legal reform groups attempting to redress various social inequities. These pressures led some within the profession to reexamine long-standing assumptions about the nature of client problems and change processes and to raise hard questions about whose interests were really being served by the agencies by whom they were employed. Thus the concept of case advocacy was first promulgated in what was by definition an adversarial context, and workers were told that they must become partisans in social conflict.

Although many of the activities inherent in the concept of advocacy practice were consonant with the environmental modification efforts traditionally carried out by caseworkers and with the social reform efforts of early group workers, the change in terminology signaled a changing conceptualization of the social worker's role and responsibilities. Deriving from an institutional perspective on social welfare policy, the concept of case advocacy assumes that social services and benefits in the United States today constitute a form of property to which different classes of people have specific rights and entitlements (Reich, 1964). However, because social welfare organizations tend to function in ways that serve their own interests rather than those of their intended beneficiaries, client rights and service entitlements often need to be protected. In this context it was suggested that for the social worker—like the lawyer—the primary responsibility is to the client, not to an employer or to the larger society, and that the social worker must assume a partisan position and do everything possible to protect client interests (Ad Hoc Committee on Advocacy, 1969).

These ideas, now widely accepted in the profession, were seen as quite radical when they were first espoused—which explains much of the "cause" flavor of early writings on case advocacy. Social work practitioners at that time were simply not accustomed to defining themselves as potential adversaries in situations of social conflict or to considering client interests as independent of agency services. The general sense of discomfort and disarray created by the adversarial context in which the concept of advocacy was introduced was accentuated by its initial association with a late-1960s move toward deprofessionalization (Mailick & Ashley, 1981). Moreover, specific concerns were raised (Schwartz, 1969) about the inherent risks of creating a dichotomy between client and agency concerns and of engaging in the political, potentially manipulative tactics that Brager (1968) had identified as essential.

Because of these tensions, few could have anticipated how easily case advocacy would become institutionalized within the profession. However, the idea was promulgated during a period of intense internal turmoil and questioning about the appropriate focus of social work activities and about how to balance the profession's historic concerns about personal and environmental problems. The concept of an advocacy function for direct service practitioners was seen as a way to reduce the traditional tensions between those supporting individual treatment and those supporting social reform. Interest in advocacy practice spread quickly in the decade following Briar's (1967) recommendation that case advocacy be viewed as an integral part of the professional casework role.

The Ad Hoc Committee on Advocacy (1969) established by the National Association of Social Workers (NASW) Task Force on the Urban Crisis and Public Welfare Problems declared that social workers' obligation to engage in advocacy flows directly from the NASW Code of Ethics. At least one school of

social work instituted structural procedures to protect students who engage in advocacy (Wineman & James, 1969). Robert Sunley (1970) introduced the idea of "from case to cause," a model for practice in family service agencies that was later endorsed by Family Service America (formerly Family Service Association of America). And a number of authors (Davidson & Rapp, 1976; Gilbert & Specht, 1976; Levy, 1974; Manser, 1973; McCormick, 1970; McGowan, 1974; Panitch, 1974; Richan, 1973; Riley, 1971) began to discuss the strategic and ethical dilemmas inherent in advocacy practice.

Institutionalization

With few exceptions (Epstein, 1981; Kutchins & Kutchins, 1978; Mailick & Ashley, 1981; McGowan, 1978; Sosin & Caulum, 1983), there has been relatively little conceptual analysis or empirical study of advocacy reported in the social work literature during the past decade. Yet during this period case advocacy came to be almost universally viewed as one of the essential tasks of direct service practitioners. Most of the recent texts on social work practice refer routinely to advocacy as an interventive role or strategy for helping clients (Compton & Galaway, 1984; Germain & Gitterman, 1980; Hollis & Woods, 1981; Northern, 1982; Shulman, 1984; Weissman, Epstein, & Savage, 1983). Students in many schools of social work are now taught systematically when and how to engage in advocacy. Through its Committee on Inquiry, NASW has established specific standards and procedures to ensure that workers are not penalized by their agencies for engaging in advocacy. And advocacy is frequently described as an important component of practice in different social work settings (Berg, 1981; Nulman, 1983; Pearlman & Edwards, 1982; Sancier, 1984; Shanker, 1983; Staudt, 1985).

A number of forces have contributed to the rapid institutionalization of what was initially viewed as a social cause. First, within the profession, expanded knowledge of recent developments in ego psychology, general systems theory, and ecological theory has increased practitioners' awareness of the developmental impact of individual-environmental transactions and of the ways in which environmental change efforts can enhance clients' sense of mastery and competence. It has also stimulated development of a range of integrated practice models that emphasize goals rather than methods of intervention and contributed to an emerging consensus that the purpose of clinical social work is to maintain and enhance psychosocial functioning "by maximizing the availability of needed intrapersonal, interpersonal, and *societal* [emphasis added] resources" (Cohen, 1980, p. 30). These developments have served collectively to legitimize the call for clinicians to engage in case advocacy.

Second, during the past decade, in response to changes in the larger society, the focus among many professionals trained as community organizers has gradually moved away from involvement in social change efforts toward social planning and administration. This shift has reduced the pressure on clinicians to move from case to cause and to engage in advocacy efforts that extend beyond the needs of their particular clients. At the same time, the community organizers who promulgated the importance of advocacy practice in the late 1960s and early 1970s left behind a body of knowledge about organizational intervention and conflict resolution that permits direct service practitioners to advocate more effectively for their clients.

Third, during the 1970s various government agencies began to establish advocacy systems designed primarily to monitor and ensure the quality of services provided to specific client populations (Kutchins & Kutchins, 1978). Although most such programs are currently labeled "case management systems," these initiatives provided public sanction and funding for what were termed "advocacy services," thus broadening the meaning of the concept and further legitimizing social workers' case advocacy function. The fact that advocacy, originally envisioned as a means of challenging the status quo, is now commonly listed as one of the official responsibilities of case managers illustrates the bureaucratization of this professional function.

Definitional Issues

Another factor that may have contributed to widespread endorsement of the advocacy concept is the profession's failure to achieve consensus about what it actually means. As Gilbert and Specht (1976) have noted:

applying the abstract notion of advocacy to the practice of social work has some felicitous results: everyone is free to dream their own dreams and hope their own hopes, most of which are not detrimental to practice. Further, as a symbolic response to the demands that social work become more relevant to the quest for social justice, the call for advocacy has been attractive to the profession. (p. 288)

Yet this lack of specificity has also been dysfunctional in two important ways—preventing careful delineation of the ethical directives and limits inherent in the concept and mediating against the systematic study of contexts and processes of case advocacy necessary to ensure that practitioners carry out this function as effectively as possible.

The dilemmas created by this lack of clarity have been identified repeatedly (Epstein, 1981; Gilbert & Specht, 1976; Kutchins & Kutchins, 1978; Sosin & Caulum, 1983). The early writings on advocacy practice described the advocate both as one who gives primacy to the interests of individual clients and as one who works for a cause assumed to represent the interests of a particular class of people (Ad Hoc Committee on Advocacy, 1969). More recent writings have distinguished carefully between the former, case advocacy, and the latter, class advocacy. However, differences persist whether case advocacy is a professional role (Weissman, Epstein, & Savage, 1983), a function (McGowan, 1978), an activity (Sosin & Caulum, 1983), or a technique (Kutchins & Kutchins, 1978). There also is no agreement whether case advocacy refers only to the use of adversarial strategies (Germain & Gitterman, 1980, p. 154), includes mediating as well as adversarial approaches (Hollis & Woods, 1981, p. 195), or encompasses the full range of potential strategies—adversarial, mediating, and collaborative (McGowan, 1978) or normative (Sosin & Caulum, 1983).

Despite the different definitions of case advocacy in the professional literature, Epstein's (1981) exploratory survey of 105 Michigan social workers (sampled because they considered advocacy a major part of their work) suggests a beginning consensus among practitioners. When asked for their definitions of advocacy, most gave responses related to the notion of intervening or in the client's behalf in problems "in the relationship between the client and an unresponsive 'system'" (p. 8). This idea is implicit in all the recent, more formal discussions of advocacy practice.

Therefore, at its present stage of development, case advocacy can perhaps be most accurately defined as partisan intervention on behalf of an individual client or identified client group with one or more secondary institutions to secure or enhance a needed service, resource, or entitlement. More precise definitional issues, such as the amount of conflict inherent in case advocacy, cannot be resolved until the practice is examined more systematically.

Case Advocacy Process

Case advocacy is a planned, dynamic process involving a number of interacting variables. As with other types of social work interventions, decisions about when and how to implement a particular effort can be made only after the worker and client have engaged in careful problem exploration, assessment, and contracting to determine their objectives and the potential risks and benefits of alternative approaches.

One model for decision making in case advocacy suggests that 10 key variables need to be assessed in designing an intervention.[1]

Problem Definition. Does the problem arise because of a special client need, a maladaptive relationship between the client and the service system, a structural or personnel deficiency in a service agency, an interorganizational difficulty, or a dysfunctional social policy?

Objective. Is the objective to secure or enhance an existing service, resource, or entitlement; to develop a new one; or to prevent or limit client involvement with a dysfunctional service system?

Target System. Is the target of intervention some component in the worker's own organization (internal advocacy) or in another institution (external advocacy)? What is the service rendered by the organization? Is the relationship between advocate and

---

[1] These variables represent a slightly modified version of those identified in an exploratory study of 195 incidents of advocacy reported by 39 direct service practitioners in eight child advocacy programs in different parts of the country (McGowan, 1978).

decision maker one of allies, neutrals, or adversaries (Sosin & Caulum, 1983)?

Sanction. What gives the worker the right or authority to intervene in a system that has not requested help? Does this derive from a client's legal right, an administrative entitlement, a discretionary benefit, or a professional assessment of client need?

Resources. What assets does the advocate possess or have access to that could be utilized in the proposed intervention? Assets might include knowledge of a client's situation, organizational and political dynamics, and community resources; influence with members of the target system or community power sources; communication and mediation skills; and assistance from a client's natural support system, professional colleagues, or agency officials.

Potential Receptivity of Target System. What is the likelihood that the significant decision makers in the target system will be receptive to the advocate's request? Will the advocate's role and request be viewed as legitimate?

Level of Intervention. At what level should the intervention be carried out? Can the objective be achieved by the action of an individual decision maker in the target system or does it require administrative or policy change (Davidson & Rapp, 1976)?

Object of Intervention. With whom should the advocate intervene to secure the change needed? The object of intervention might be a line staff member, supervisor, or administrator in the target system; a policy-making or funding body; a public official; an independent service organization or community group; or an adjudicatory or legislative body.

Strategy and Mode of Intervention. What approach and means should be used to achieve the desired objective? Should the advocate assume a collaborative, mediatory, or adversarial strategy? What actual modes of intervention should be employed: intercession, persuasion, negotiation, pressure, coercion, or indirect action—for example, preparing a client to take independent action, organizing a community or client group, asking an outside party to intervene?

Outcome of Prior Advocacy Efforts. What can be learned from prior efforts to address the identified problem? Were there any unanticipated obstacles or consequences? Have new resources or problems emerged? Is there any need to reassess the problem, renegotiate the client contract, or revise the plan of intervention based on prior experience?

Relatively little is known about how these variables actually interact. Sosin and Caulum (1983) have proposed a typology for advocacy practice based on the concept of social influence. They suggest that interventive decisions on who is responsible for determining what is to be advocated, the appropriate level of intervention, and the strategy and methods to be employed are related to the context of intervention—that is, whether the relationship and level of agreement between the advocate and the potential decision maker reflect an alliance, neutrality, or an adversarial situation. This typology echoes a theme in the community-organizing literature indicating that change strategies can range from consensus to conflict and that selection of specific tactics is largely dependent on the relationship and degree of agreement between the change agent and the target system.

The findings of the only reported study of methods of case advocacy (McGowan, 1974) suggest that in practice (1) choice of strategy is influenced by the nature of the problem, the objective, and the sanction for the intervention as well as the change agent and target system; (2) the primary determinants of outcome are the resources of the change agent and the receptivity of the target system; and (3) the most effective advocates employ a wide range of resources and interventive techniques but emphasize the use of communication and mediation rather than power. These findings support the view that case advocacy is a complex, skilled interventive process shaped by multiple interactive variables. Current knowledge does not permit more precise delineation of the relationships among these variables.

Ethical, Practice, and Policy Dilemmas

Research studies have repeatedly demonstrated that advocacy efforts contribute to service effectiveness and that clients tend to evaluate these activities positively. Yet many practitioners are still reluctant to engage in advocacy practice or to value this activity as highly as direct service to clients. For exam-

ple—based on a comprehensive 20-year review of research about the usefulness of social work in the United States, Great Britain, Australia, and Canada—Rees and Wallace (1982) conclude: "Clients have highly valued negotiation and advocacy on their behalf, or in association with them, but social workers have not considered such roles to be important" (p. 162). One explanation for this discrepancy may be that advocacy practice not only requires some different skills but also forces social workers to address a number of ethical dilemmas not encountered in direct work with clients.

Social workers engaged in case advocacy frequently confront the three inherent dilemmas that were first identified by Richan (1973).

Competing Loyalties. Although the social worker's responsibility to give priority to clients' interests is stated clearly in the NASW Code of Ethics, this precept does not resolve such issues as how to balance the interests of different clients, when to violate the norm of cooperative decision making essential to collaboration in interdisciplinary settings (Mailick & Ashley, 1981), or how severe a problem should be to justify challenging the authority of a publicly sanctioned social institution.

Paternalism. The very concept of advocacy implies acting on behalf of another, yet such action runs the risk of undermining the sense of mastery and autonomy clients gain from acting on their own behalf and limiting their opportunities for self-determination. Under what circumstances are these risks justified?

Redress versus Reform. Case advocacy is essentially a conservative social intervention that assumes problems can be addressed on an individual basis by workers employed in organizations that are part of the established social order. Although it may enhance the lives of individual clients, in the long run, successful case advocacy can serve only to reduce the pressure and conflict necessary to stimulate more widespread social change. The case-to-cause formulation was proposed as one way of resolving this dilemma; however, because individual and group needs are seldom synonymous, social workers who attempt to engage in both case and class advocacy inevitably confront other issues related to competing loyalties and paternalism.

Other obstacles and problems encountered by social work advocates derive from the social context in which advocacy is practiced. As might be expected, 90 percent of the respondents in the exploratory survey reported by Epstein (1981) encountered external obstacles to their work, but over two-thirds (71 percent) of these self-defined advocates said they also met internal obstacles, such as restrictive agency policies and job definitions and lack of hierarchical support. Moreover, 40 percent experienced burnout as a moderate or great problem, and this perception was closely associated with the presence of internal, not external, obstacles to their advocacy. This finding suggests that despite exhortations to social workers to place client needs above agency interests, the decision to do so can result in great personal stress.

Another dilemma, identified by Kutchins and Kutchins (1978), derives from the recent institutionalization of advocacy practice. Although the creation of governmental advocacy systems and official recognition of employees' case advocacy responsibilities can eliminate the stress experienced by workers whose employers do not sanction engaging in advocacy, publicly supported programs and roles often have the same weaknesses as the social institutions they were established to challenge. Moreover, workers functioning as case advocates often influence, disturb, or come into conflict with representatives of the same interests that employed them. This suggests that there may be an inherent contradiction in the concept of a publicly sponsored, institutionalized case advocacy role, which limits the types of problems that can be addressed and the strategies that can be pursued.

Finally, it must be noted that although case advocacy efforts are highly valued by clients and essential to meeting client needs and ensuring individual rights, they can never become a substitute for responsible social policy. Case advocacy can be practiced freely and effectively only in the context of responsive legal, political, and administrative systems.

BRENDA G. McGOWAN

For further information, see Appendix I: NASW CODE OF ETHICS; CASE MANAGEMENT; DIRECT PRACTICE IN SOCIAL WORK; OVERVIEW; LEGISLATIVE ADVOCACY.

References

Ad Hoc Committee on Advocacy. (1969). "The Social Worker as Advocate: Champion of Social Victims." *Social Work, 14*(2), 16–22.

Berg, W. E. (1981). "Working with Physically Handicapped Patients: Advocacy in a Nursing Home." *Health and Social Work, 6*(2), 26–32.

Brager, G. A. (1968). "Advocacy and Political Behavior." *Social Work, 13*(2), 5–15.

Briar, S. (1967). "The Current Crisis in Social Casework" (pp. 19–33). In *Social Work Practice (1967)*. New York: Columbia University Press.

Cohen, J. (1980). "Nature of Clinical Social Work." In P. Ewalt (Ed.), *Toward a Definition of Clinical Social Work* (pp. 23–32). Washington, D.C.: National Association of Social Workers.

Compton, B. R., & Galaway, B. (1984). *Social Work Processes* (3rd ed.) Homewood, Ill.: Dorsey Press.

Davidson, W. S., II, & Rapp, C. A. (1976). "Child Advocacy in the Justice System." *Social Work, 21*(3), 225–232.

Epstein, I. (1981). "Advocates on Advocacy: An Exploratory Study." *Social Work Research and Abstracts, 17*(2), 5–12.

Germain, C. B., & Gitterman, A. (1980). *The Life Model of Social Work Practice*. New York: Columbia University Press.

Gilbert, N., & Specht, H. (1976). "Advocacy and Professional Ethics." *Social Work, 21*(4), 288–293.

Grosser, C. F. (1965). "Community Development Programs Serving the Urban Poor." *Social Work, 10*(3), 15–21.

Hollis, F., & Woods, M. E. (1981). *Casework: A Psychosocial Therapy* (3rd ed.). New York: Random House.

Kutchins, H., & Kutchins, S. (1978). "Advocacy and Social Work." In G. H. Weber & G. J. McCall (Eds.), *Social Scientists as Advocates: Views from the Applied Disciplines* (pp. 13–48). Beverly Hills, Calif.: Sage Publications.

Levy, C. (1974). "Advocacy and the Injustice of Justice." *Social Service Review, 48*(1), 29–50.

Mailick, M. D., & Ashley, A. A. (1981). "Politics of Interprofessional Collaboration: Challenge to Advocacy." *Social Casework, 62*(3), 131–137.

Manser, E. (Ed.). (1973). *Family Advocacy: A Manual for Action*. New York: Family Service Association of America.

McCormick, M. J. (1970). "Social Advocacy: A New Dimension in Social Work." *Social Casework, 51*(1), 3–11.

McGowan, B. G. (1974). "Case Advocacy: A Study of the Interventive Process in Child Advocacy." Doctoral dissertation, Columbia University, New York, N.Y.

McGowan, B. G. (1978). "The Case Advocacy Function in Child Welfare Practice." *Child Welfare, 57*(5), 275–284.

Northern, H. (1982). *Clinical Social Work.* New York: Columbia University Press.

Nulman, E. (1983). "Family Therapy and Advocacy: Directions for the Future." *Social Work, 28*(1), 19–22.

Panitch, A. (1974). "Advocacy in Practice." *Social Work, 19*(3), 326–332.

Pearlman, M. H., & Edwards, M. G. (1982). "Enabling in the Eighties: The Client Advocacy Group." *Social Casework, 63*(9), 532–539.

Rees, S., & Wallace, A. (1982). *Verdicts on Social Work.* London, England: Edward Arnold Ltd.

Reich, C. (1964). "The New Property." *Yale Law Journal, 73*(5), 733–787.

Richan, W. C. (1973). "Dilemmas of the Social Work Advocate." *Child Welfare, 52*(4), 220–226.

Riley, P. V. (1971). "Family Advocacy: Case to Cause and Back to Case." *Child Welfare, 50*(7), 374–383.

Sancier, B. (Ed.). (1984). "A Special Issue: Advocacy." *Practice Digest, 7*(3).

Schwartz, W. (1969). "Private Troubles and Public Issues: One Social Work Job or Two." In *Social Welfare Forum, 1969* (pp. 22–43). New York: Columbia University Press.

Shanker, R. (1983). "Occupational Disease, Worker's Compensation, and the Social Work Advocate." *Social Work, 28*(1), 24–27.

Shulman, L. (1984). *The Skills of Helping Individuals and Groups.* Itasca, Ill.: F. E. Peacock Publishers.

Sosin, M., & Caulum, S. (1983). "Advocacy: A Conceptualization for Social Work Practice." *Social Work, 28*(1), 12–17.

Staudt, M. (1985). "The Social Worker as Advocate in Adult Protective Services." *Social Work, 30*(3), 204–208.

Sunley, R. (1970). "Family Advocacy: From Case to Cause." *Social Casework, 51*(6), 347–357.

Terrell, P. (1967). "The Social Worker as Radical: Roles of Advocacy." *New Perspectives: The Berkeley Journal of Social Welfare, 1*(1), 83–88.

Weissman, H., Epstein, I., & Savage, A. (1983). *Agency-Based Social Work.* Philadelphia: Temple University Press.

Wineman, D., & James, A. (1969). "The Advocacy Challenge to Schools of Social Work." *Social Work, 14*(2), 23–32.

AFFIRMATIVE ACTION. See AMERICAN INDIANS AND ALASKA NATIVES; ASIAN AMERICANS; BLACKS; CIVIL RIGHTS; DISABILITIES: DEVELOPMENTAL; DISABILITIES: PHYSICAL; HISPANICS; MEXICAN AMERICANS; MINORITIES OF COLOR; PERSONNEL MANAGEMENT; PUERTO RICANS; WHITE ETHNIC GROUPS; WOMEN; WOMEN IN MACRO PRACTICE.

AFRO-AMERICANS. See BLACKS; CIVIL RIGHTS; ETHNIC-SENSITIVE PRACTICE; INTERGROUP RELATIONS; MINORITIES OF COLOR.

AGED

The aging of the population has become a dominant demographic characteristic of the twentieth century, a condition that will continue into the twenty-first century as well. Birthrates now are being controlled and even lowered, and changing lifestyles and medical technology are increasing life expectancy. Thus, the population of older persons is projected to increase throughout the world, especially in the developing nations. In some of the more industrialized nations, however, the proportion of older persons has begun to fall from already high levels (Palmore, 1980). The United States is a special case: a highly developed and industrialized nation that is facing a dramatic increase in the number and proportion of older persons.

Since the turn of the century, the American older population has risen steadily. In 1900 those over 65 made up 4 percent of the total U.S. population and numbered some 3.08 million persons. By 1950 this segment had more than quadrupled to over 12.2 million persons and had doubled its proportion to 8.1 percent of the total population. By 1980 the 65 and older group had more than doubled again to over 25 million persons and had grown in proportion to 11.3 percent of the total population. It is projected that by the year 2000 the older population (65 and over) will number more than 35 million and represent 13.1 percent of the nation. As the baby boomers enter old age, a dramatic jump in the figures will occur; by the year 2020 older Americans will number more than 50 million and represent 17.3 percent of the population. By the year 2050 the 65 and older population will represent 21.7 percent of the American people and consist of more than 67 million persons (U.S. Senate, 1984). Dynamics contributing to such an increase probably include lower mortality rates, control of fertility rates, rise of life expectancy, and ongoing immigration (close to half a million per year).

As the older population becomes a significant proportion of the total populace, society is confronted with a variety of issues and challenges. Better understanding of the basic nature of the biological and physiological aspects of the aging process continues to challenge the scientific and medical fields. The problem of allocating national resources to address the needs of this older population is both an economic and a political issue. Communities and families will confront new dilemmas regarding the immediate and long-term needs for care of a population that is living longer and requiring increased support. Human service administrators and providers will continue their quest for more effective methods of assisting the elderly. As human life is lengthened, society and individuals alike will face moral and ethical questions regarding not just the quality of life, but its very meaning and definition.

The question of definition is a matter of debate, especially in regard to public policy (Neugarten, 1982). Aging has been defined and addressed chronologically, sociologically, biologically, physiologically, psychologically and functionally and in other ways. Historically, the age of 65 has been broadly used in the United States as a point of definition. However, the age point is becoming quite blurred as a universal measurement of old age. For example, 65 is no longer the automatic age of retirement; mandatory retirement has been extended to age 70, and early retirement has become quite common. Nonetheless, census information and current understanding suggest that 65 can still be a useful age for measuring the demographic dynamics.

The older population can no longer be treated as a homogeneous segment; rather, it needs to be viewed as an increasingly complex and diverse group. More specifically,

this segment of the general population tends to be subdivided into four groups: (1) the young old (55–64), (2) the old (65–74), (3) the older old (75–84), and (4) the very old (85 and older) (U.S. Senate, 1984). It should be noted, however, that there are those who question such categorizations on the basis of age alone and who propose a more social and functional definition (Neugarten, 1982).

Contributing to the complexity and diversity of the older population is the continuing significance of gender and ethnic classification. Because of key historical (pre–civil rights) experiences, these two variables have a strong influence on how people have aged and the socioeconomic resources that are available to them in old age. Among the current generation of older people, women and ethnic minorities are products of the pre–civil rights era and were greatly affected by the discriminatory and segregationist practices of the 1960s and before (Maldonado, 1982).

It is not surprising that aging has become such a challenging field of study and work. The views are many and the approaches are multiple. In dealing with aging, the various dynamics of society, family, and the individual experience interact. Gerontology and the field of social work gerontological practice have become equally complex and demanding. Multiple sets of knowledge and skills are required—especially the ability to integrate and reconcile such a diversity into a holistic and sensible base of understanding and practice.

Demographic Characteristics

Population Trends. Special attention needs to be given to the variations within the older population, particularly between the age subgroups. Such a focus will be helpful in appreciating the nature of the graying of America today and in the foreseeable future. For example, although the overall 65-and-older population grew by 2.1 percentage points of the total population, and its numbers grew by 154 percent during the last 2 decades, the very old (85 and older) grew by 241 percent numerically. By the year 2000 the very old segment will grow by 229 percent, and the total old population will grow by 137 percent. Thus, although the very old population is probably the fastest growing subgroup in numbers, its proportion to the general population has not changed as dramatically. It is projected that, by the year 2000, the old population (ages 65–74) will number over 17 million and reflect 6.6 percent of the population, the older old (75–84) will number 12 million and represent 4.6 percent, and the very old (85+) will number more than 5 million and represent 1.9 percent of the population. In all, there will be about 35 million people over 65 years of age, and this will reflect 13.1 percent of the total U.S. population. When the generation born in 1985 reaches 65 years of age (in the year 2050), the 85 and over cohort will be 5.2 percent of the total population and those 65 and over will number more than 67 million and be 21.7 percent of all Americans (U.S. Senate, 1984).

Life Expectancy. At the turn of the century a newborn could expect to live 49 years; by the 1980s, life expectancy had increased to almost 74 years. At age 65 a person in 1900 could expect to live 11 to 12 more years; in 1980 the expectancy had increased to 14 to 18 years depending on gender. It is particularly important that gender has emerged as a significant variable in the question of life expectancy. In 1900 life expectancy was, comparatively speaking, quite similar for men and women. Males could expect to survive to the age of 46 and females had a life expectancy of 49 years. However, by 1980 the gender spread had widened. Males now had a life expectancy of 69.85 but females had a 77.53 life expectancy, a spread of nearly 8 years in 1980 compared to 3 years in 1900. In 1980 a 65-year-old female could expect 18.35 more years of life, but the 65-year-old male could only expect 14.08 years (U.S. Senate, 1984).

Race and ethnic characteristics also have significance in the matter of life expectancy. For example, in 1980 blacks could expect 5 years less of life than whites; this is an improvement from 1940, when the difference was 11 years less for blacks. However, once the age of 65 has been reached, the difference between blacks and whites diminishes and in fact reverses after age 75 (U.S. Senate, 1984). In comparing white with nonwhite life expectancy differences, Manton (1982) suggests a number of possible explanations such as socioeconomic differences, different mortality rates at earlier

stages of life, overnumeration of elderly blacks (a census enumeration error), and the possibility of higher robustness among the black elderly.

Gender. As has been noted above, women have a higher life expectancy at birth as well as in old age. In every age category within the older population, women outnumber men. For example, in 1982 older women (65–70) outnumbered older men by almost 3 to 2; for the 75 to 84 age bracket, the ratio was 5 to 3; and among the very old (85 and older) women outnumber men 10 to 4. The significance of these data is not only that men have a lower life expectancy, but that aging becomes an issue of great importance for women. For example, the prospect of widowhood increases more dramatically for women than for men. In comparing men and women in the 75-and-over age category, 68.5 percent of the women but only 21.7 percent of the men were widowed in 1982. As women outlive men, they also confront the more chronic problems of aging, diminishing of resources, and other complexities related to the very old.

Marital Status and Living Arrangements. The marital status and living arrangements of older persons are greatly influenced by gender. Generally the elderly tend to be found in family settings, with a higher proportion of men living in such settings. Also, a large proportion of men are married (75 percent) but only 40 percent of the women are married. Approximately half of the elderly females are widowed, but only one out of eight older males is in a similar situation. Remarriage rates are also significantly (seven times) higher for older men than for women (Taeuber, 1983). According to the U.S. Senate Committee on Aging (1984), the situation among the very old category (85 and older) becomes even more marked: 21.7 percent of the men and 68.5 percent of the women are widowed. In this age category, too, 70.2 percent of the very old men are married and live with their wives, and only 22.4 percent of the very old women are married and live with their spouses.

Data regarding the living arrangements of older persons also reflect a disparity between men and women. For example, in the 65 to 74 age category 11.7 percent of the men live alone, but the rate is three times higher (34.2 percent) for women. In this same age category, 7.8 percent of the men live in households, but a higher percentage (16.2 percent) of the women do not. A review of the very old generation (85 and older) indicates a worsening situation for men and—even more so—for women: only 19 percent of the men live alone, but 45.1 percent of the women live alone. In summary, in 1982 more than 7 million elderly persons lived alone; the majority were women (U.S. Senate, 1984).

Ethnic Classification. Along with gender, ethnic classification has emerged as a key variable in understanding the dynamics of aging. Of special significance is the ethnic minority factor that refers to the status and special experiences of nonwhite populations such as blacks, Hispanics, Asian Americans, and American Indians. Special problems in deciphering the ethnic minority data are the issues of definition and enumeration by the Bureau of the Census, Bureau of Health Statistics, and the other public centers of information. A major concern involves the categorization of nonwhites and whites, and the enumeration of Hispanics. Nonetheless, the data that are available reflect the significant increase in the number of older ethnic minority persons as well as the disparities between minorities and nonminorities.

Although the white elderly population has been increasing at a rapid rate in recent decades, the minority elderly have been growing at an even faster pace. For example, Taeuber (1983) reports that since the mid-1970s the elderly black population grew by about one-third and the elderly white group expanded by one-fourth. Estrada (1984) reports that the elderly Hispanic population has tripled during the last 2 decades. In 1981 the Federal Council on Aging [FCA] (1981) projected that between 1950 and the year 2000 the older black population will grow by 252 percent, but the older white population will expand by only 145 percent. Thus, the proportion of blacks in the elderly population will increase from 8 percent in 1950 to 11 percent in 2000 and to 18 percent in 2050. Interestingly, blacks are projected to outgrow their white counterparts in all four subcategories of older persons (FCA, 1981). In 1980 over 2 million older persons were nonwhite. This number will increase to almost 4 million

in 2000 and to over 12 million by the year 2050.

Geographic Distribution. The 1980 geographic distribution of older persons reflects several significant variations. At the state level, the proportion of older persons varies from a low of 2.9 percent in Alaska to 17.3 percent in Florida. Seven states have more than 1 million older residents; these states are (in decreasing order) California, New York, Florida, Pennsylvania, Texas, Illinois, and Ohio. California had nearly 2.5 million persons 65 and older; at the other extreme, Alaska had the lowest number (12,000). It is interesting to note, however, that—like Florida—several midwestern states tend to have a greater proportion of older residents. From 1970 to 1980 the largest percentage increase occurred in the western and Sunbelt states (U.S. Senate, 1984).

In 1970 more elderly people lived inside the central cities than in the outlying areas; by 1981 over half lived outside the central cities. However, approximately two-thirds lived in metropolitan areas; yet they represent only about 10 percent of the metropolitan population. Ethnic minorities tend to be city dwellers but older whites are more likely to be found in suburbs. In nonmetropolitan areas, old persons represent a slightly higher proportion (12 percent); the largest concentration of these seems to be in the South (Taeuber, 1983).

One example of how ethnic classification may affect geographical distribution is the case of the older Hispanic population. These people tend to live in metropolitan areas; in larger urban areas, older Hispanic persons have begun to move to the suburbs. Only 16.6 percent live in nonmetropolitan areas (Estrada, 1984).

Social Conditions of the Elderly

The social conditions under which older persons live are the result of a complex interaction among the life experiences and resources of the individual, the family, and society. Because of the increasing numbers and proportion of older persons, these life conditions have become matters of public concern and policy. Of special concern are the characteristics that indicate a need for support and assistance from the family and from the public, private, or voluntary sectors. As in the demographic profile, both gender and ethnic status have special significance and account for the variations in life and social conditions of older persons.

Health. Probably no factor is of more immediate concern to older persons than physical health. The U.S. Department of Health and Human Services (1982) reported that health issues were among the greatest concerns for older Americans. The National Council on Aging (1981), in a nationwide survey, reaffirmed the high priority of health issues among the elderly. It was also reported that health issues were of special concern to the black, Hispanic, and poorer elderly.

Self-assessment has been widely used as an indicator of health. Generally, older Americans tend to be positive regarding their health; unfortunately, however, elderly blacks and Hispanics do not share the general optimism. For example, in its national survey, the National Council on Aging (1981) reported that 71 percent of the older population believed they were healthier now than before; nearly half of the older blacks and Hispanics disagreed. The U.S. Senate Special Committee on Aging (1984) reported that, in 1981, eight of ten elderly persons described their health as good or excellent. Among the elderly with incomes of $25,000 or more, 42 percent rated their health as excellent, but among those elderly with incomes of less than $7,000 per year, only 23 percent did so. The elderly poor had the highest proportion of persons (11 percent) rating their health as poor (U.S. Senate, 1984).

Another major indicator of health status is the limitation of activity experienced by older persons. In 1981 the Federal Council on Aging reported that among the 65-and-older population a total of 46 percent experienced some limitation of activity because of a chronic condition; this compares to 7 percent for the under 45 age bracket and 23 percent for the population between 45 and 64 years of age. Data indicated that the older categories of the elderly reflect a higher proportion of persons experiencing limitations. For example, more than 50 percent of the 75-to-84 age group will face some limitation and among those 85 and older the percentage rises to 60 percent. In 1984 the U.S. Senate Special Committee on Aging published comparable information affirming the trend toward greater limitation on activity among the older and very old groups.

The limitation of activities tends to be caused by chronic conditions much more than by acute situations. Although the causes of chronic conditions among the elderly vary widely, several are significant. Specifically, arthritis and hypertensive diseases are the leading chronic conditions among men and women 65 and older. Other leading chronic conditions include hearing impairments, heart conditions, visual impairments, orthopedic impairments, and arteriosclerosis.

In 1980, approximately 10.7 million persons over age 65 experienced some limitation. By the year 2000 this number will increase to 16.3 million and will reach 31.7 million by 2050. Data clearly indicate that limitation of activity caused by chronic conditions will be an expanding phenomenon among the elderly. Of special concern is the need that will be generated for long-term care services and the increase in cost for these services.

Economic Status. Among the elderly the only other concern that could compete with health is the question of economics. The extensive debates at the 1981 White House Conference on Aging with regard to income maintenance have been supported by a national survey (National Council on Aging, 1981). Older persons worry about their economic status. There is great concern regarding recent inflation rates, the high cost of health services, and the increasing challenges to the social security system and its benefits.

Older persons have reason to be concerned. Although the current generation of older Americans is better off than previous generations, the present situation is not very comforting. Generally, the over-65 population has a lower economic status than the rest of the populace. In 1981, some 75 percent of older persons had incomes of less than $10,000, compared to 42 percent of those 25 to 64 years of age. Both men and women over 65 had lower median incomes than their counterparts among the younger generations.

The source of income is an important factor for the elderly. Traditionally, the main source of income for households headed by a person 65 or older has been wages and earnings, but this is changing. Today social security income has taken on a more prominent role. Of the elderly population, 91 percent receive some social security benefits; more than half receive over 50 percent of their income from this public source. Approximately one-fifth depend on social security for 90 percent of their income. For blacks and Hispanics, social security and Supplemental Security Income are especially important (U.S. Senate, 1984).

It is not surprising to find higher levels of poverty among the elderly, especially among ethnic minorities and women. For example, although the older population in general had a slightly lower poverty rate than the younger generation (14.6 to 15 percent), 38 percent of the black elderly were living in poverty and 26.6 percent of the Hispanic elderly were below the poverty line. When the gender factor is introduced, elderly white women are twice as likely to be poor as elderly white men. More than 42 percent of older black women and 31.4 percent of older Hispanic women also live in poverty. The near-poor are another important indicator of economic status. When households are headed by older women, the proportion of the near-poor becomes dramatic. For example, for all races the near-poor (125 percent of poverty level) rate is 40.6 percent. When the single head of a household is a minority female, these levels increase to 65.1 percent for blacks and 59.3 percent for Hispanics (U.S. Senate, 1984).

How the elderly spend their money is another key indicator of economic status. Historically, the largest expenditure for older persons has been for food (excluding health care and housing); in 1972 and 1973 food took up 57.5 percent of their income. In 1980 and 1981 food expenditures had dropped to 49.6 percent. However, this was not because food became less expensive; on the contrary, inflation affected food prices as well. The largest increases have been in fuel costs. Ten years ago the elderly were spending 23 percent on fuel. Today one-third of their income goes to purchase fuel. Apparently fuel costs have been reducing the amount of money available to purchase food for the elderly.

Employment. As recently as 1950 half of the elderly men were employed. The trend, however, is toward a lower labor participation rate. In 1970 one-fourth of the elderly

men worked; by 1980 less than one-fifth were employed. It has been suggested that early retirement programs and a decrease in self-employment accounts for this trend (Taeuber, 1983). The U.S. Senate Special Committee on Aging reports that in 1982 only 17.6 percent of the men and 7.7 percent of the women over age 65 were employed (U.S. Senate, 1984, p. 46).

Part-time employment, on the other hand, has increased among the elderly. Almost half of the elderly men and 60 percent of the women who are employed work on a part-time basis. There has been an increase during the last 2 decades of part-time employment among the elderly. This reflects an important economic resource. The type of work that the elderly do reflects the changing nature of employment in society. Thus there has been an increase in service-related jobs. For example, in 1974 about 45 percent of the elderly men were employed in service-related jobs, but in 1981 some 63 percent were employed in similar work (U.S. Senate, 1984).

It is important to note that labor participation also is influenced by gender and ethnic status. Among elderly women the participation has not changed much since 1950, when approximately 10 percent were employed. In 1981, 9.1 percent of women 65 and older were employed, compared to 16.7 percent of the men. Younger women have entered the work force in recent decades and this will have a great impact on the employment status of older women. For example, in 1950 a little more than one-fourth of the women aged 55 to 64 and older were employed, but in 1982 about 42 percent were working. Black women, however, have a longer history of employment at a higher rate than white women; it is estimated that the rate of employment among white women will eventually equal that among black women (Taeuber, 1983, p. 22).

Housing. Housing is a key factor in determining the social conditions of the elderly. Usually this factor provides the immediate environment for the elderly and can contribute to or limit their quality of life—especially their safety, physical movement, and comfort. Housing represents a major investment for older persons; in 1980 more than 70 percent owned their own homes. A vast majority of the homes owned with no outstanding obligations are the property of older persons. However, the housing of the elderly tends to be older and contain more flaws than that of the younger generation. This raises questions about the adequacy of their housing and the conditions of the houses themselves. Housing certainly has been important to this generation; the high ownership rates reflect that. Ownership, however, does not guarantee adequacy, and old age does not always provide the resources for the upkeep of the structures.

Mental Health. The question of the mental health status of older persons is limited by the scarcity of data and clouded by the various myths that are propagated about their behavior. It is known, however, that dramatic differences exist between older persons living in the community and those in nursing homes. Community-based older persons tend to have better mental health than those based in nursing homes. It has been estimated that 56 percent of nursing home residents suffer from chronic mental conditions of senility and 16 percent have been diagnosed as suffering from a mental disorder; only 5 to 6 percent of community-based older persons have been classified as suffering from senile dementia (FCA, 1981).

The primary mental health problem of the elderly is cognitive impairment. The U.S. Senate Special Committee on Aging (1984) reports that the rate (40 percent for men and women) of mild impairment is higher than severe impairment, which was recorded at 5.6 percent for men and 3 percent for women. It is of interest that older men have a higher rate of mental disorders than women. Alzheimer's disease has recently attracted great attention and much remains to be learned about it. It affects more elderly persons than any other disease involving cognitive impairment. It is known that the rates of impairment are higher for the very old.

Suicide rates are another indication of mental health; the elderly tend to have a higher suicide rate than younger generations. It is interesting to note that, among the elderly, the rate of suicide increases with age but drops off at age 85 (U.S. Senate, 1984, p. 75).

In comparison to the general population, the elderly tend to underutilize mental health services. Older persons use mental health services at less than half the rate of the general population (7 versus 16 admissions per 1,000) in spite of their significant mental health needs. Of special concern is the trend toward moving the elderly out of mental health facilities and into nursing homes and from inpatient to outpatient status; the quality and availability of mental health services may not be sufficient in these new settings— especially in nursing homes.

It must be acknowledged, however, that generally the elderly are active and mentally well-adjusted. Nonetheless, preventive attention needs to be given to common stresses in old age that can affect emotional and mental health. Older persons undergo various life changes and financial adjustments when they retire, they experience the loss of spouses and friends, they may be victimized, and they are subject to health problems and other emotionally difficult experiences (Butler & Lewis, 1982).

Responses of Society

The graying of America has become part of the national consciousness and has brought about a variety of concerns including economic, political, and ethical questions. It has developed into an extensive and at times controversial enterprise (Estes, 1979) that reflects a broad range of professional, voluntary, private, and public interests and perspectives. Society has responded in various ways ranging from local self-help groups to national programs of human services and income maintenance.

Aging, however, is first of all the aging of persons, most of whom are related to a family and a community. In the past, the response to the changes wrought by aging has been the responsibility of individuals and their families. Older persons today tend to be independent and self-reliant, utilizing informal support networks along with occasional assistance from the family. As need increases, the family has played the role of primary caregiver. However, with the massive entry of women into the work force, geographic mobility, and increasing longevity, families are beginning to have difficulty in providing care for their older members. Thus the elderly turn more and more to formal structures and institutions for assistance.

Governmental Responses. Historically, the federal government has played a major role in responding to issues that affect the welfare of a large number of its citizens. As the aged have become a significant segment of the population, numerous federal programs have been established that reflect national concern for older Americans. Kutza (1981) reports that although more than 134 federal programs can be listed, 8 major programs reflect the thrust of the government's response. These are Old Age, Survivors' and Disability Insurance (OASDI), Medicare, the Older Americans Act, Supplemental Security Income (SSI), Medicaid, food stamps, housing subsidies, and taxation policies. In 1983, between 25 and 30 percent of the federal budget was spent on programs that directly helped the elderly. Of this, 57 percent went for OASDI payments, 22 percent for Medicare, 10 percent for retirement programs, 3 percent for Medicaid, 2 percent for housing, 2 percent for veterans' programs, and 1 percent for SSI (U.S. Senate, 1984).

The Social Security Act of 1935 was probably the most important measure that the federal government passed regarding the elderly; today social security is the most visible public program affecting older persons. Under Title II of the Social Security Act, the Old Age Insurance program provides direct cash payments to recipients on the basis of age, insured status, and retirement. The program is financed by employers and employees through a payroll tax and is administered by the Social Security Administration.

The original Social Security Act has been amended many times. Survivors' insurance benefits, added in 1939, provide support for the survivors in the event of the death of an insured worker. Approximately 90 percent of the labor force is covered by social security, which is the major source of income for many retired persons. More than 91 percent of the elderly population receives social security benefits (U.S. Senate, 1984, p. 33).

Medicare is the second largest federal expenditure (22 percent) for older persons. Under Title III of the Social Security Act (1966), this federal program provides health insurance for persons 65 and over and for some other selected groups. It includes the Hospital Insurance Program (Part A) and the Supplemental Medical Insurance Program (Part B). Part A pays for hospital care, extended-care facilities, and home health care. Part B (with voluntary enrollment involving a premium) provides for physicians' and outpatient services. Medicare is administered by the Health Care Finance Administration of the Department of Health and Human Services. Along with OASDI, Medicare covers most of the elderly population. It is considered a major step in social legislation.

Medicaid is a federal-state cooperative program that provides aid to disadvantaged and low-income persons such as the aged, blind, disabled, or families with dependent children. This program is authorized under Title XIX of the Social Security Act, passed in 1965, and is intended for the economically disadvantaged. It provides critically needed services for the elderly poor, especially the black and Hispanic elderly.

SSI was authorized by Title XVI in 1974 and is intended to provide a basic income for disabled or elderly persons. Thus, eligibility is based on age and financial need.

The Older Americans Act of 1965 (P.L. 89-73) established a nationwide network of regional, state, and substate agencies (area agencies on aging) responsible for the planning, coordination, and delivery of a variety of social services, including multipurpose senior centers and nutrition, recreation, transportation, information, and referral services. The Administration on Aging (AOA) headed by the commissioner on aging is responsible for its overall administration. Other key activities sponsored by the legislation include research and training, employment efforts, and special programming for American Indians. Federal programs provide food stamps, tax benefits, and housing subsidies including low rent public housing, loans, and rent supplements.

Part of the federal response has been the creation of governmental structures to address issues on aging. Within the legislative system, Congress has established both the House Select Committee on Aging and the Senate Special Committee on Aging. The executive branch has developed a variety of organizational programs throughout the bureaucracy; these include, in the Department of Health and Human Services, AOA, the National Institute on Aging, and the Center on Aging at the National Institute of Mental Health. The Social Security Administration, of course, is another key government organization.

Voluntary Responses. The voluntary sector has played an important role in making services available to older persons. This sector includes programs sponsored by United Way organizations, national religious institutions (through local congregations and community centers run by such organizations as Catholic Charities, Jewish Welfare Federations, and Wesley Community Centers), and other independent providers of care. Private nonprofit organizations such as foundations also provide urgently needed financial resources. With the trend toward cutbacks in federal funding, voluntary and nonprofit organizations increasingly provide leadership in responding to the needs of older persons. This sector, which normally does not give direct cash assistance, does provide many social services involving nutrition, transportation, and so on.

Private Responses. As the demand for health, residential, recreational, and other services for the elderly increases, and as the ability to pay becomes more common among older persons or their families, a private, for-profit sector has emerged. This sector includes the retirement community industry, nursing homes, and adult day care centers. Professionals have begun to offer their services directly to older persons, especially in their homes; nursing services are one example. Other private businesses catering to the elderly include travel and leisure activities and financial management. In essence, the profit-making industries will provide whatever services the older person is willing to purchase.

Organizational Responses. The interest in aging and concern for the elderly has generated a broad array of professional, consumer, and advocacy organizations. Among the earlier ones are the American Geriatrics Society (1942) and the Gerontological Society (1975). The former publishes the *Journal of the American Geriatrics Society* and the latter offers two publications: *The Gerontologist* and the *Journal of Gerontology*. The Gerontological Society has become a highly respected, multidisciplinary professional organization. The National Council on Aging (1960) has also emerged as a key organization that provides important information and formats in the field of aging. On the national

level, older individuals have organized the American Association of Retired Persons, the National Retired Teachers Association, and the National Council of Senior Citizens. The Gray Panthers are a multigenerational group that addresses social issues extending beyond aging itself. Some organizations have made efforts to combine professionals and older persons in their membership. These include the American Gerontological Society, the Southwest Society on Aging, and other regional organizations. Ethnic minority populations have also developed organizations to address the particular situation of their older persons. These include the National Hispanic Council on Aging, the Asociación Nacional Pro Personas Mayores, the National Center on Black Aged, the National Indian Council on Aging, and the National Pacific/Asian Resource Center on Aging. Other organizations reflect particular professional interests such as the National Association of State Units on Aging. The Long-Term Care Policy Centers have organized as have senior citizen centers and their directors.

In summary, the people of the United States—through their government, churches, business, and voluntary associations—have responded to the aging phenomenon. They have passed legislation, allocated large sums of money, created many organizations, and given a great amount of volunteer time to provide for the well-being of older Americans.

Theoretical Perspectives and Trends

The role of theory is crucial because it guides the interpretation and explanation of experience, information, and observation and it assists in anticipating the future. Theory also requires the recognition of assumptions that are at work. Unfortunately, in the field of aging, theory and theory development have played secondary roles. Although much is known about the condition of the aged and descriptions abound regarding the aging experience, relatively little has been offered in the way of understanding and explaining the aging process. The field of social gerontology, in particular, is in need of sound theoretical frameworks that can assist in making sense of the aging phenomenon. Of special concern is the emergence of perspectives in social gerontology that reflect normative frameworks rather than objective explanations.

One of the first efforts to propose a theory in social gerontology is found in the work of Cummins and Henry (1961). Known as disengagement theory, this framework proposes:

> Aging is an inevitable mutual withdrawal or disengagement, resulting in decreased interaction between the aging person and others in the social systems he belongs to. The process may be initiated by the individual or by others in the situation. . . . When the aging process is complete, the equilibrium that existed in middle life between the individual and his society has given way to a new equilibrium characterized by a greater distance and an altered type of relationship. (Cummins & Henry, 1982, p. 334)

The response to the disengagement theory was quick and challenging and various questions were raised. Was disengagement truly universal and inevitable? Was the new equilibrium established through disengagement natural? Did it in fact result in high morale?

Critics proposed an alternative framework known as activity theory. Although it has been suggested that this is not really a theory but a value judgment (Quadagno, 1980), it has generated much-needed debate at the theoretical level. Activity theory suggests that as people age they continue to have the same needs and desires as the middle aged, and that the elderly, in fact, resist pressures to withdraw from society. The theory also suggests that optimal aging is experienced by the person who stays active and thus enjoys higher morale.

Other theoretical proposals have been made in an effort to understand and explain aging in its social context. For example, minority group theory views the elderly as a minority population (Barron, 1983), suggesting lower socioeconomic status, discrimination, prejudice, and the many other factors that have been part of the minority experience in the United States. Another approach is the use of a "subculture" perspective on aging. Rose (1980) suggests that the elderly share with each other two critical experiences that make up a subculture—that (1) members have a particular affinity toward each other, and (2) members are excluded from interaction with other groups of the general population. Subculture theory proposes that age discrimination and a sense of mutuality have contributed to the potential emergence of an aging subculture. This concept of subculture could be used to explain many current dynamics and trends.

A most helpful framework is that of age stratification (Riley, 1973). This refers to the conceptualization of a society divided by age and social class. Distinct age strata and generations can be defined and compared according to key historical experiences. This approach is helpful in understanding and explaining characteristics and conditions of particular generations, including younger generations. The age stratification framework deemphasizes chronological age but emphasizes the course of life and the historical dimensions shared by age cohorts. This suggests that each generation of cohorts of older persons is unique, reflecting the particular experience of that generation.

The theory-building task continues in other aspects of aging, including the biological, psychological, economic, and political aspects. However, one framework that addresses several of those fields is social exchange theory. Dowd (1975) suggests viewing aging as an exchange. In this perspective, social interaction is maintained because it is found to be rewarding. An essential ingredient is the belief that rewards should exceed the costs of maintaining the interaction; an imbalance or dependency generates the dynamics of power. It is suggested that the relationship between the aged and society can be defined as an imbalance—one in which power is operating economically, politically, and socially. Thus the problems of aging involve lessening power vis-à-vis society.

Professional Practice

Aging affects the whole person and all the various dimensions of life—physical and spiritual, economic and psychological, social and political. The aging process is experienced in the diverse American social and cultural settings and is the concern of all generations. The comprehensiveness and systemic nature of the aging process makes social work a key form of professional practice in this field. Social work—in its value orientations, its holistic approach, and its linkage functions—is ideally suited to serve the aged population.

Historically, two sets of values have formed the normative foundation of the profession. These are "the worth, dignity, and uniqueness of the individual and the right to self-determination by individuals, groups, or constituents in a community" (Lowy, 1979, p. 53). In working with older people, these values are helpful guidelines in resisting negative stereotypes, promoting independence and activity among the elderly, and advocating for the basic rights of older people.

Social work practice also takes a comprehensive approach to understanding the nature of individual, family, and community problems and to appreciating the systemic ramifications of professional intervention. This perspective is appropriate for addressing the personal, familial, and community issues of aging. Social workers understand the interconnections of the psychological, social, economic, physical, and political dynamics; they possess a broad repertoire of skills to use as sensitively as possible. These skills include individual, group, and family counseling; social planning; community organization; and administrative activities.

A major function performed by social work is to link the individual, group, family, or community with those internal or external resources that are necessary to correct, improve, or maintain a particular situation. This requires a broad knowledge of those resources, the ability to assess particular needs, and the skill to make the proper connection and use of those resources. Social workers must understand the aging process. They must be familiar with the vast number of programs and services for the elderly and have the skills needed to communicate with and relate to older persons.

Two areas in need of special attention are social work education and research. The profession depends on well-prepared and sensitive graduates from social work educational programs. Although from its beginnings social work has been serving the elderly, a sense of urgency is now needed. The accelerated pace in the expansion and development of the field of aging has left social work in a kind of catch-up position. Because other professions have taken active roles in producing practitioners to work in this field, social work runs the risk of losing its historical role. The professional curriculum needs to incorporate aging content throughout, as well as to provide special-focus courses. Specialization in aging with a generalist formulation or even with method specialization needs greater attention. Continuing education in aging is of major importance.

The practice of social work with the elderly also relies on credible and useful information. Research on the aging process and on the needs and conditions of the elderly must be conducted from the systemic perspective of social work. Of special need is research on practice modalities: What works and what does not work with an older population and why? Another need is for program evaluation and assessment.

Trends and Future Directions

As the United States confronts the twenty-first century with a dramatically growing older population several significant themes have emerged. These involve long-term care, economic resources, and responsibility. Long-term care goes beyond the traditional concern of nursing homes; the concept today refers to the broad question of developing and maintaining a continuum of care systems that will address the whole spectrum of the needs of older persons. These range from the highly active and healthy elderly who need challenges for personal growth to the chronically ill elderly who require total care, raising such issues as what types of services a diverse older population will require in the year 2000 and in 2050, what the gaps are, and how the system can be made more accessible.

At the bottom line is the question of cost—of how much the individual, the family, and society can afford; of what is a reasonable and just standard of life for everyone, especially the elderly; of what the limits of entitlement are; and of how the aging enterprise will be financed or who will pay. These questions in turn address the issue of responsibility—of the roles of government, religious organizations, and the family and of who is ultimately responsible.

The demographics, conditions, issues of service, and trends discussed above are complex and intertwined. None of them can be confronted in isolation from the others. Indeed, they are one, just as society is one. The basic challenge of the graying of America is to determine the kind of society the United States intends to be and how this society is to be manifested in the lives of its older members.

DAVID MALDONADO, JR.

For further information, see AGED: SERVICES; FEDERAL SOCIAL LEGISLATION SINCE 1961; FOSTER CARE FOR ADULTS; LONG-TERM CARE; PROTECTIVE SERVICES FOR THE AGED; RETIREMENT AND PENSION PROGRAMS; SOCIAL SECURITY.

References

Barron, M. L. (1983). "Minority Group Characteristics of the Aged in American Society." *Journal of Gerontology, 8*, 477–482.
Butler, R. N., & Lewis, M. (1982). *Aging and Mental Health.* St. Louis, Mo.: C. V. Mosby Co.
Cummins, E., & Henry, W. E. (1961). *Growing Old, The Process of Disengagement.* New York: Basic Books.
Cummings, E., & Henry, W. E. (1982). "Two Theories of Aging." In P. McKee (Ed.), *Philosophical Foundations of Gerontology* (pp. 333–342). New York: Human Services Press.
Dowd, J. J. (1980). "Aging as Exchange: A Preface to Theory." In J. S. Quadagno (Ed.), *Aging, The Individual and Society* (pp. 103–121). New York: St. Martin's Press.
Estes, L. C. (1979). *The Aging Enterprise.* San Francisco, Calif.: Jossey-Bass.
Estrada, L. (1983, November). *Social Demography of the Hispanic Elderly: 1970–1980.* Paper presented at the Conference of the American Public Health Association, Dallas, Tex.
Federal Council on Aging. (1981). *The Need for Long Term Care: Information and Issues (A Chartbook).* Washington, D.C.: U.S. Department of Health and Human Services.
Kutza, E. A. (1981). *The Benefits of Old Age.* Chicago, Ill.: University of Chicago Press.
Lowy, L. (1979). *Social Work with the Elderly.* New York: Harper & Row.
Maldonado, D. (1982). "Prevention Among the Minority Elderly." In S. Miller et al. (Eds.), *Primary Prevention Approaches to the Development of Mental Health Services for Ethnic Minorities* (pp. 94–109). New York: Council on Social Work Education.
Manton, K. G. (1982). "Differential Life Expectancy: Possible Explanations During the Later Ages." In R. Manuel (Ed.), *Minority Aging: Sociological and Social Psychological Issues* (pp. 63–68). Westport, Conn.: Greenwood Press.
National Council on Aging. (1981). *Aging in the Eighties: America in Transition.* Washington, D.C.: Author.
Neugarten, B. (1982). *Age or Need? Public Policies for Older People.* Beverly Hills, Calif.: Sage Publications.
Palmore, E. (1980). *International Handbook on Aging.* Westport, Conn.: Greenwood Press.
Quadagno, J. (Ed.). *Aging, the Individual and Society.* New York: St. Martin's Press.
Riley, M. W. (1973). 'Social Gerontology and the Age Stratification of Society." *Gerontologist, 11*(1), 79–87.
Rose, A. M. (1980). 'The Subculture of the Aging: A Framework for Research in Social Gerontology." In J. Quadagno (Ed.), *Aging, the Individual and Society* (pp. 73–86). New York: St. Martin's Press.
Taeuber, C. M. (1983). *America in Transition: An Aging Society* (Current Population Report, Special Studies). Washington, D.C.: U.S. Bureau of the Census.
U. S. Department of Health and Human Services. (1982). *Final Report: The 1981 White House Conference on Aging.* Washington, D.C.: Author.
U. S. Senate. (1984). Special Committee on Aging. *Aging America: Trends and Projection.* Washington, D.C.: American Association of Retired Persons.

AGED: PROTECTIVE SERVICES FOR.

See AGED: SERVICES; PROTECTIVE SERVICES FOR THE AGED.

AGED: SERVICES

The phenomenon of a large aging population is one of the most dramatic and influential developments of the twentieth century. This demographic situation, unique to our time, has profound significance for the planning and delivery of health and social services. Consequently, the past three decades have witnessed much activity directed toward identifying the needs of older people and determining the sources of services required to meet those needs.

The numerical and proportionate increase of people 65 years of age and older is a trend that will continue. In 1900, there were 3 million older people in the United States, representing 4 percent of the total population, but by 1983 there were 26.8 million older people, constituting more than 11 percent of the population. The number will increase to 35 million by the year 2000 and to about 64.3

million, or 21 percent of the population, by the year 2030 (U.S. Bureau of the Census [U.S.B.C.], 1982a).

Disabling chronic illnesses (mental and physical) that result in the need for help are more likely to occur in advanced old age. Therefore, in estimating service needs, the growth in the number of persons 75 years of age and over is even more important than the growth of the total 65-and-over population. People 75 and over are the fastest-growing age group in the United States. This group increased from 1 million in 1900 to 9.5 million in 1980. By the year 2000, there will be more than 17 million and by 2025, more than 25 million. The 85-and-over population, which was about 2.3 million in 1980, will more than triple by the year 2025, reaching over 7 million (Brotman, 1982).

In the new terminology that has emerged, the main needs-meeting service systems have been characterized as the "formal" and "informal" systems. The formal system comprises governmental and voluntary agencies and facilities; the informal system consists of family members, friends, and neighbors. This discussion will deal with the two systems in terms of their overall responses to the basic needs of older people for income support, medical care, and health and social services. Various components of the support systems are discussed elsewhere in this encyclopedia.

Formal System

Public policy in the last 50 years has responded unevenly to the demographic imperatives of an aging society. In the two areas of income maintenance and medical services there has been substantial and, for the most part, effective response. But public policy has faltered in the area of health and social services.

Income Maintenance. Society's response to the economic aspects of the new phenomenon of a large aging population—which was approaching 7 percent of the total population in 1940—was the enactment of a coordinated income maintenance program: Old Age Assistance-Title I (OAA) and Old Age Insurance-Title II (OAI) of the Social Security Act (SSA) of 1935. During the depression years of the 1930s, more than half of the aged were totally dependent economi-

cally on their families and an additional 18 percent depended similarly on welfare programs (Upp, 1982). To offer immediate stable relief and to replace the stopgap Federal Emergency Relief Program, OAA provided an initial income base, although it varied from state to state.

To augment and eventually replace much of the OAA program, social insurance (OAI) was enacted simultaneously. While OAA aimed to provide the older person with subsistence funds immediately, the avowed purposes of the insurance program were (1) to provide a subsistence base, (2) to encourage older workers to leave the work force in order to make room for younger entries, and (3) to replace OAA with a more adequate program that was nationally based.

The program achieved all three of those goals. During the 1950s, the number of OAI beneficiaries surpassed those receiving OAA for the first time, thus initiating the replacement of that program and providing the beginning of a national subsistence base. The percentage of the aged in poverty dropped from about 75 percent in 1936 to 35 percent in 1959 and then to 18.6 percent in 1972 (Social Security Administration, 1982). Paralleling this decrease was a virtual elimination of total economic dependency of the elderly on their adult children, which dropped from 50 percent in 1936 to 1.5 percent in 1982; the proportion of those receiving OAA dropped to 8 percent by 1972 (Upp, 1982). There was a major change in the patterns of work force participation. At the time SSA was enacted, about half of the men 65 years of age or over were in the work force; by 1960 this had dropped to one-third and by 1970, to 27 percent. Men aged 55 to 64 had decreased their participation slightly, with 87 percent working in 1960 and 83 percent in 1970 (U.S.B.C., 1982b, Table 626, p. 377).

One unexpected result of the changing demography and the increase in economic independence of the elderly was the change in demand for institutional facilities. Prior to mid-century, most residential services under public and voluntary auspices were for the nondisabled indigent. OAA and OAI funds enabled older people who were indigent to live independently in the community. At the same time, as life expectancy increased and swelled the numbers of the disabled very old, voluntary and public old age homes were gradually converted to nursing homes catering to the infirm and disabled. Proprietary nursing homes mushroomed.

The objectives of the income maintenance program changed in the late 1960s, and there was increasing congressional testimony that considered replacement of income, rather than minimum subsistence, as a goal. The 1971 White House Conference on Aging issued a call that an "immediate goal for older people is that they should have total cash income in accordance with the 'American Standard of Living.' " President Nixon's message to Congress called for a "comprehensive strategy," the first element of which was "Protecting the Income Position of the Elderly" (U.S. Senate, 1972, p. 3.). It was estimated that maintaining the same income level after retirement required an income equivalent of 60 percent of the gross preretirement income.

In keeping with this agenda, enactment of the 1972 Amendments to SSA increased OAI by 20 percent, introduced an annual automatic cost of living adjustment tied to the consumer price index, and replaced OAA with a national pension program that provided a uniform minimum income floor for the aged. Increases in OAI benefits between 1967 and 1972 amounted to 71.6 percent, virtually doubling the average monthly payments, and a new computation point for the 62-year-old male retiree was introduced (U.S. Senate, 1973).

Augmenting the "*new* Social Security program" was the Employment Retirement Income Security Act (ERISA) passed in 1974 primarily to protect the pension rights of workers and their beneficiaries. ERISA provided for full vesting after ten years' service and for joint and survivor provisions to protect spouses. Approved pension plans were guaranteed by a nonprofit government corporation. In addition, ERISA created Individual Retirement Accounts (IRAs) and extended Keogh plans, both of which allow for tax-deductible contributions for accruing retirement benefits (U.S. Senate, 1973, pp. 141, 143).

This new approach to income maintenance has resulted in substantial progress toward the goal of replacing income for a significant number of retirees. In 1982, the mean income per month of recent retirees was $1,956 for couples and $1,024 for unmarried individuals. Although OAI provides the main component of income for retirees up through the middle income levels, today's retirees commonly receive pension or asset income as well (Maxfield & Reno, 1985). Earnings from continued work, if only part-time, were another source of income for about one-fourth of the new beneficiaries (Trout & Mattson, 1984), and there is evidence that this source is significant for only the first five years of retirement (Fox, 1984). Postretirement earnings represent about one-third of total income in those early years, but the earners are mostly in the higher income groups.

The drop in labor force participation of elderly men and women was accelerated by the 1972 legislation. In 1970, only one-fourth of older men were working or looking for work. By 1981, this proportion had dropped to less than one in eight. Moreover, labor force participation of the 55- to 65-year-olds had decreased precipitously from 83 percent in 1970 to less than 70 percent in 1982 (American Association of Retired Persons, 1984, pp. 46–47). Indeed, age 62 rather than 65 had become the preferred age for retirement (U.S. Senate, 1983, p. 337). However, increasing numbers of retirees were working part-time for the first four years of retirement (Fox, 1984).

While the 1972 social security amendments and ERISA accelerated progress toward new goals of income replacement, the enactment of Title XVI (Supplementary Security Income [SSI]) of these amendments to replace Title I (OAA) provided a new national structure for ensuring a uniform minimum level of subsistence. SSI created a nationally funded and administered program in lieu of state matching and administration under OAA. As a result, there no longer were wide discrepancies among the states as to eligibility and the amount of benefits. The common state restrictions of legally responsible relatives, liens on beneficiaries' homes, and residency requirements were abolished. The original SSI benefit level established for an individual in 1972 represented an amount equal to 78 percent of the government's poverty index. (For couples it was 92 percent.) To protect SSI beneficiaries from inflation, they were covered by cost of living adjustment provisions similar to the OAI provisions. Thus, although the poverty level for an individual escalated from $2,005 in 1972 to $4,630 in 1982, the SSI benefit level held at 71 percent of the poverty level. For couples the poverty index likewise doubled during that time and the SSI benefit level held at 85 percent of the poverty level (Trout & Mattson, 1984). In addition, states were encouraged to supplement the SSI grant to provide special or emergency assistance. Three states actually raised SSI levels above the national poverty index.

Far fewer aged have become eligible for SSI than was originally anticipated. It had been expected that 4 million individuals aged 65 or older would be eligible for SSI. In fact, there never have been more than 2.4 million aged SSI recipients in any given year. Furthermore, there has been a steady decrease in new aged SSI applicants during the period from 1972 to 1982, resulting in only 1.6 million elderly recipients by the end of that time. Of these aged SSI recipients, nearly 70 percent also received OAI benefits, testifying to the complementary relationship of the two programs (Trout & Mattson, 1984).

While the SSI program has succeeded in establishing a national income floor for the aged, it still averages only about 75 percent of the current poverty index. Because 70 percent of the SSI recipients are also eligible for OAI, the burden of poverty often falls disproportionately on those with an employment history of low wages—widowed black women and, to a lesser extent, white widows. Thus, about two-thirds of black women living alone are still mired in poverty (U.S.B.C., 1982b, Table 728, p. 441).

In the 50-year history of SSA, the poverty rate among the aged dropped from 75 percent to 15 percent. The proportion rises to 20 percent when the near-poor are counted (those at 125 percent of the poverty line), including more than two-thirds of elderly black women who live alone.

There are two major support programs that augment the SSI subsistence program. The Food Stamp program was created in 1964 to increase the purchasing power of low-income households. Originally, most households were required to pay cash for their stamps, which had a value greater than the purchase price. The benefit of the program resulted from that difference. Older households, in particular, had difficulty in raising the cash necessary for purchasing the stamps. In 1977, this requirement was eliminated, spurring a one-third gain in the participation of elderly households. About 5 percent of all elderly receive food stamps, but they make up one-third of those aged in poverty. Since 1977, the Food Stamp program has been under continuous review by Congress and the Administration with a view to reducing the cost of the program by restricting eligibility and the growth in benefit rates. While the purchasing power of the elderly was slightly reduced, indexing the benefit levels to reflect food price inflation helped the aged on fixed incomes. The Food Stamp program is one element of an intricate and interrelated network of programs for needy older persons. Many elderly food stamp recipients also benefit from other needs-based programs such as SSI, Medicaid, or assisted housing. Loss of benefits from any one program could trigger other ineligibilities and create serious difficulties for those aged who do not have the physical ability or resources to compensate for any losses.

The Veterans Administration (VA) provides the other major economic support and is becoming a more important resource, since two-thirds of all men over the age of 65 will be eligible for veterans' pensions in the next decade. By Administrative fiat, the VA defines all veterans 65 years and over as disabled and therefore eligible for a veteran's pension if their incomes are below certain levels. These levels are almost 50 percent higher than those for SSI, providing support mandated to meet the national standard of need. This pension program is more generously administered than SSI, and together with disability and survivor benefits, the VA provides all or part of the income of 1.65 million persons age 65 or older.

Currently, the income maintenance elements of OAI and VA are under threat of reduction to balance the federal budget. It is uncertain whether a new goal for the income maintenance will be set.

Medical Services. Provision of publicly supported medical services has evolved from the early 1912 reform period, when state legislatures actively considered State Health Insurance, to the 1965 enactment of the age-categorical National Health Insurance program of Medicare (Title XVIII of SSA). The two parts of Medicare (A and B) along with Medicaid (Title XIX of SSA) made up a kind of "three-level cake." These three elements reflected the various interests whose support was necessary for its enactment. Again, the goals were specific. Hospitals saw the legislation as a means of avoiding collection problems, whereas the American Nurses Association viewed it as a way to improve the substandard wages of nursing. The American Federation of Labor & Congress of Industrial Organizations recognized the economic burden resulting from its worker members paying the medical bills for their aged parents. Overall, the global purpose of Medicare was to make high-quality medical services available to the elderly and to protect them from the catastrophic costs of a bout with acute medical problems.

Part A of Medicare provided for Hospital Insurance for all OAI eligibles, and Part B provided for Supplemental Medical Insurance, which paid for ambulatory care—primarily the costs of outpatient physician visits. To placate the American Medical Association, fee-for-service was ensured and only available to those who paid a monthly subscription rate. Provision was also made for short-term intermittent home health services, short-term nursing home care, and the furnishing of medical appliances. All of these services required physician prescription and were medically oriented as to need. The nursing home, which had consistently been defined legislatively as a medical institution, was now described as an extended care facility and was later (in 1972) called a skilled nursing facility (SNF).

For the indigent patient, Medicaid was enacted as the third layer of the cake. Funding for medical care of the indigent was first initiated as vendor payments under the Federal Emergency Relief Administration of the early depression years and was continued under the categorical assistance programs of SSA. In 1960, those were expanded to include the "medically indigent" under the short-lived Kerr-Mills program until it was replaced by Medicaid. While Medicare was federally administered, Medicaid retained the categorical assistance approach through state administration, matching funding, benefit definition, and eligibility determination. Title XIX did eliminate residency requirements, legally responsible relatives, and liens against

houses from state options and required minimum provisions of hospital inpatient care, outpatient services, and nursing home care. States also could reimburse for these programs at "reasonable" rates (U.S. House of Representatives, 1983).

The goal of making acute catastrophic coverage available was met. The elderly increased their use of short-stay hospitals after the enactment of Medicare. The rate of discharge from acute care hospitals increased by more than half for the 65- to 74-year-old group between 1965 and 1981. Hospital services are the largest personal health expenditure for the aged, representing 44 percent of the total and mostly paid for by Medicare. Those over 65 years of age (11 percent of the population) used almost 40 percent of acute care hospital bed days in 1981. Hospital expenditures represent the single largest component of Medicare, accounting for over 70 percent of the Medicare dollar. Visits to physicians by the elderly are about one-third more frequent than those of younger adults and since the enactment of Medicare have been consistent at 6.3 visits per year. This type of care is not as well covered by Medicare, since the elderly are required to pay about $150 a year (in 1985) to enroll, must absorb the first $75 of charges, and are only reimbursed for 80 percent of "reasonable" charges.

Thus, if catastrophic acute medical care were defined in hospital and physician terms, between 1978 and 1982, Medicare has paid for about 75 percent of hospital care and a little more than half of physician costs. Ninety-seven percent of all the aged are covered by Medicare, Part A (Hospital Insurance), and more than 94 percent have opted for coverage under Part B (Supplemental Medical Insurance). In addition, 70 percent carry private insurance which pays for 6.6 percent of acute costs, primarily through reimbursement of Medicare deductibles and coinsurance charges (U.S. Health Care Financing Administration, 1984).

Although Medicare has paid for an increasing share of the costs of personal health care, the elderly have consistently expended 20 percent of their total income from 1965 to 1981 for health care costs even after Medicare reimbursement. The total personal cost net of Medicare rose from $472 in 1965 to $1,713 in 1981. A significant number of the enrolled aged (over 40 percent) received no Medicare reimbursement at all, and about 7 percent accounted for 70 percent of the Medicare expenditure, attesting to the catastrophic nature of the program's coverage.

In 1984, to control Medicare costs and protect the viability of the Medicare trust fund, Congress discontinued the practice of paying hospitals on a charge basis and, through the Health Care Financing Administration, instituted a system of prospective payment. In most states, this has taken the form of diagnostic related groups (DRGs), in which payment is keyed prospectively to one of 468 primary diagnoses, each of which carries its own reimbursement irrespective of the length of stay or charges incurred during the hospital stay.

Prospective payment has resulted in a sharp drop in the lengths of hospital stays as well as admission rates and has had the effect of providing hospitals with incentives to develop "step-down" services. These services provide what has been called short-term long-term care (STLTC)—that is, less intense levels of service and facilities, which are used for a short period of posthospital time (S. Brody & Magel, 1984). There has been concern that older patients are being discharged inappropriately, and studies are currently under way to determine the validity of such charges. At the same time, evidence suggests that many hospitals are changing their emphasis from providing acute care to being health care centers that offer transitional (STLTC) services to ensure appropriate care. Some measure of this trend is evidenced by the American Hospital Association's adopting the continuum of care services for the aged as a critical concern. Medicare's coverage of these STLTC services includes some minimum skilled nursing facility (SNF) stays (usually less than 30 days), home health services, and rehabilitation care (inpatient, day-hospital, or outpatient, which are exempted from DRGs). Many hospitals are using the excess capacity caused by the drop in utilization for short-term nursing care and rehabilitation beds and are moving into providing home health services directly.

Long-Term Care. Responding to the needs of the chronically disabled and their families is the one area in which public services have not mounted a significant effort. A

consequence of the increase of very old people is an escalation in the incidence and prevalence of age-related chronic disorders such a senile dementia, diabetes, rheumatoid arthritis, osteoporosis, and cardiovascular and cerebrovascular diseases (Butler, 1976). People live longer nowadays after the onset of such ailments—a phenomenon that Gruenberg (1977) called "the failures of success."

In contrast to acute illnesses, chronic ailments cannot be cured and require sustained supportive health and social services as well as ongoing medical and medically related treatment. Moreover, mental and physical ailments are highly correlated and interact strongly, and the symptoms of one ailment often mask and exacerbate others (Goldfarb, 1962; Lowenthal, 1964; Schuckit, 1974).

These chronic ailments of older people have major effects on social functioning. A host of studies have found correlations between health and morale, health and social behavior, and health and leisure activity (Lawton & Cohen, 1974). Emotional factors and stress can precipitate physical illness. Conversely, physical illness can trigger negative psychological and emotional reactions. Chronic physical disability, for example, is strongly implicated in the etiology of depression (Gurland, 1976).

A most important consequence of chronic illness in the aged is that it tends to lead to disability (that is, to limitations in mobility and daily activities) and in turn to dependence on others. To put the matter in perspective, however, it should be emphasized that the stereotype of old age as inevitably associated with disability is incorrect. At any one time, approximately 55 percent of all older Americans have no activity limitations due to chronic conditions and many of those with health problems are able to perform essential tasks. However, as people move through the aging phase of life their chances of needing help increase; very few people reach advanced old age without experiencing some period of dependency.

Based on her national survey, Shanas (1982) estimates that one-fourth of noninstitutionalized older people require home care services, including those who are bedridden or housebound (8 percent) or able to go out but with difficulty (6 to 7 percent). Depending on the nature of services included, others estimate the proportion at one-third (S. J. Brody, 1973), 41 percent (Pfeiffer, 1973), and 30 percent (Gurland, 1976). Some of these people need considerable help. About 10 percent of the noninstitutionalized elderly (more than 2.5 million individuals), for example, are as severely disabled as the 5 percent who live in nursing homes and other institutions. The U.S. National Center for Health Statistics (1982) found that 2.1 percent of noninstitutionalized persons aged 65 and older were confined to bed; 2.6 percent needed help with bathing; 2.6 percent needed help with dressing; 1.4 percent needed help with using the toilet; and 0.8 percent with eating. Over a third of those who are among the most incapacitated are over 80, 9 out of every 10 are women, and 6 out of 10 are married.

The risk of physical disability increases with advancing age. Age 75 is a rough marker for significant increases in the need for help with personal care activities such as grooming, bathing, dressing, and ambulation (Jette & Branch, 1981), and in instrumental activities such as housekeeping chores, shopping, and transportation.

A particularly disabled segment of the elderly population (mentally and physically) live in institutions. About 5 percent of older people (about 1.3 million individuals) are in institutions at any one time. The risk of admission rises with advancing age; rates rise from 2.1 percent of those between the ages of 65 and 74 to 19.3 percent of those 85 and over (National Academy of Sciences, 1977). In comparison with the noninstitutionalized, this group has a much larger number of physical and mental diagnoses. Their poor health is reflected in severe functional disabilities. The majority needs help in all activities of daily living and personal care, and about half are incontinent. Most are in advanced old age, with an average age of almost 83 (about a decade higher than that of the total elderly population).

Such information about the capacities and incapacities of older people is of vital importance not only because the extent of disability determines how they function in their daily lives but also because it determines the need for the provision of health and social services by the family and society. For these reasons, gerontologists have long insisted on functional criteria of health and functional assessment rather than medical diagnosis alone (Lawton, 1972; World Health Organization, 1974). The importance of individual assessment cannot be overstated since it is pivotal in determining the kind of treatment, support, and care required and in the implementation of the plan of care.

The U.S. Health Resources Administration (1977) has established a framework for the services needed by defining long-term care as

> those services designed to provide diagnostic, preventive, therapeutic, rehabilitative, supportive and maintenance services for individuals . . . who have chronic physical and/or mental impairments in a variety of institutional and noninstitutional health care settings, including the home, with the goal of promoting the optimum level of physical, social and psychological functioning. (p. 4)

The major public provision, to date, has been for SNF care under the Medicaid program. The average age of SNF residents is 83 years; more than 75 percent of them are widowed women without available children and with poor functional capacity. About two-thirds of all SNF residents are there for more than 90 days (long-term long-term care [LTLTC]) rather than STLTC (less than 90 days). Between 60 percent and 70 percent of those in LTLTC have cognitive impairments and one-quarter have a functional mental disorder. Their average length of stay is two and a half years. The long-term stays are mostly supported by Medicaid; the proportion of residents on Medicaid rises with the length of stay, in part reflecting the spend-down process (U.S. National Center for Health Statistics, 1979).

While Medicaid provides for about 14 percent of the health costs of the elderly, most of this expenditure is for the small percentage of the elderly (3.5 percent at any one time for LTLTC) using SNF. Of the $20 billion spent for SNF care in 1981, about half was paid by Medicaid. SNF care accounted for 23 percent of all the health care expenditures for the elderly in 1981 (U.S. Senate, 1982, Chap. 13).

The other long-term care public expenditures (1981) are minimal (less than $2 billion) compared to the more than $53 billion spent for medical services, which include SNFs by legislative definition. The provision of nonmedical services—which constitute the major needs of the functionally disabled whether in the home, community, or institutions—has not been recognized as a legitimate public responsibility. Neither Medicare nor Medicaid is permitted to support services other than those that are medically prescribed or health administered. Even under the Medicaid rubric, few states provide adult group care services that have to be supervised by a registered nurse. Personal health care services, for those who are eligible, are minimally provided and do not respond to the major need for personal maintenance services (homemaking, shopping, chores, access, and so on). An exception was made in 1985 for those elderly who would otherwise be institutionalized. These personal maintenance services are provided through Area Agencies on Aging under Title III of the Older Americans Act and, in 1981, were funded for less than $1 billion. The Area Agencies on Aging agenda also includes supporting socially oriented citizen centers. Title XX of SSA (Social Support Services) provides funds under a block grant to states for similar services, which, for the aged, also amount to less than $1 billion.

In addition to these sources of funding, about 150 federal programs purport to serve the aged. The amounts budgeted to them do little more than fund a bureaucracy with few services reaching the elderly. The problems of scarcity and underfunding are compounded by the fragmentation of existing services and entitlements:

> Health services for the aged are multiple, parallel, overlapping, non-continuous and at the very least confusing to the elderly consumer. Rarely do they meet the collective criteria of availability, accessibility, affordability or offer continuity of care in a holistically organized system. Planning for health services for the aged is similarly confused. Parallel systems of service have their own planning mechanisms. As a result, the various planning efforts overlap, contradict and are unrelated one to the other.
>
> Virtually all the services are funded by differing public money streams and have varied administrative arrangements, widely ranging eligibility requirements and different benefits for the same or similar services. (S. Brody, 1979, p. 18)

The professional response to these ser-

vice delivery problems has been to embrace alternatives to nursing home care as one major issue and coordination of care as another.

With the growth in the number of SNF beds (which the Census Bureau predicts will continue exponentially as the population ages) and the quadrupling of their cost from 1965 to 1985, a call for alternatives to nursing homes became the slogan of public officials (U.S.B.C., 1984; S. J. Brody, 1985). In some states, Medicaid, the major public support for SNF care, absorbs between 10 and 15 percent of the state operating budget. In addition, many professionals, claiming that there are many inappropriate SNF placements and in the spirit of "deinstitutionalization," urged community and in-home services as an "alternative" to SNF placement, as with the deinstitutionalization of the mentally ill, states have moved to put barriers to SNF placement under the guise of health planning and the assessing of "appropriate" placement by instituting preadmission assessment screening programs for Medicaid recipients.

The predictions of an inevitable long-term increase in the number of SNF beds are being challenged by data that may indicate the very old—the major users of SNFs—are achieving a longer period of what Katz et al. (1983) have called "active life expectancy" with minimum limitations of mobility and activity. At the same time, there is concern that the real major alternative support resource—daughters and daughters-in-law—may become less available (80 percent of home health care is given by the informal support system). The notion that community services for the severely disabled are less costly than institutional care has been challenged repeatedly (U.S. Comptroller General, 1979).

While endorsing the value of community-based services, the federal government is engaged in a systematic reduction of health and social services (U.S. House of Representatives, 1985). Furthermore, it is virtually eliminating housing subsidies, particularly for congregate residences with services that have been of great significance. States are sharply reducing their programs as well.

The major public effort since 1972 in the social service arena has been the mounting of demonstration projects to rationalize these intermittent efforts and establish a pattern of continuous care. The first such projects, undertaken in 1972, were in the form of Medicaid and Medicare waivers. These were succeeded 10 years later by long-term care "channeling" demonstration projects to test the feasibility of a service concept that integrates health and social services. Ten states are participating in two versions: the basic case management model and a financial control model. The evaluation of these projects will be completed in 1987, although preliminary data indicate that community services do not prevent SNF placement (Weissert, 1985).

Meanwhile, the Medicare Community Care Act of 1981 (enacted as Sec. 2176 of the 1981 Omnibus Budget Reconciliation Act) authorized the Secretary of the Department of Health and Human Services to waive Medicaid requirements to allow states to mount a range of health and personal care services as well as case management. Although the Office of Management and Budget has slowed the approval process, 86 waiver requests from 46 states were approved between 1981 to 1985. Many of these were for small demonstration projects, however.

Demonstrations in which social services are added to the Health Maintenance Organization (HMO) model through a Social Health Maintenance Organization have been mounted in four loci to provide continuity of medical, health, and social service care. This program took 4 years to become operational and the first clients were being served in late 1984.

With the increase in the income of the elderly and the meeting of their catastrophic medical care needs, interest is growing in private insurance funding of the entire range of long-term care services (S. J. Brody & Magel, 1986).

Mental Health. Though the true extent of need among the aged for mental health care has not been fully established (Butler & Lewis, 1973; Schuckit, 1974), Cohen (1980) has concluded that between 18 percent and 25 percent of older people have significant mental health symptoms. He also emphasizes that (1) mental illness is more prevalent among the elderly than among younger adults, (2) psychosis increases significantly after age 65 and is more than twice as common in the over-75 age group than in 25 to 35 year olds, (3) senile

dementia is thought to be the fourth leading cause of death, (4) suicide occurs more frequently among the elderly than in any other age group, and (5) many chronic physical ailments result in significant negative psychological reactions.

Some experiences common to many older people may contribute to or exacerbate their mental health problems. Among these are reduced opportunities for social interaction, reduced income and poverty, loss of role, and multiple interpersonal losses such as deaths of a spouse, other relatives, and peers.

Contributing to the sharp rise in rates of mental impairment with advancing age are ailments associated with the later phase of life—that is, the forms of senile dementia now often referred to as Alzheimer's and related disorders. Again, there is a lack of definitive data, but some surveys estimate that about 5 percent of older people in the community have a significant degree of such impairment and an equal proportion are mildly impaired (see Kay & Bergmann, 1980, for a summary of such estimates). The incidence of senile dementia rises with advancing age so that about 22 percent of those 80 years of age or over are afflicted.

Old people with such cognitive impairments are overrepresented in institutions, undoubtedly because the symptoms make such heavy demands on caregivers and are so socially disruptive. About 50 to 60 percent of all older people in nursing homes and old age homes at any given time have been diagnosed as suffering from senile dementia, and an additional 16,000 such cases reside in psychiatric facilities. The elderly represent about one-fifth of all first admissions to psychiatric hospitals and occupy almost one-fourth of the beds there; the vast majority of these patients have senile dementia or functional psychoses. (For reviews, see Schuckit, 1974; Butler & Lewis, 1973; Kramer, Taube, & Redick, 1973.)

Unfortunately, the mental health needs of older people are inadequately met, and they have limited access to a full spectrum of appropriate services. For example, they are served at less than one-fourth the rate of the 25- to 44-year-old age group (President's Commission on Mental Health, 1978). Moreover, the aged tend to have mental and emotional symptoms for longer periods of time, often years, before receiving help (Eisdorfer & Lawton, 1973). Only 4 percent of community mental health center patients are elderly, and only 2 percent are among those served by private practitioners and clinics. Yet many of the mental disorders of the elderly are treatable and reversible.

The following are among the barriers to mental health care cited by the U.S. Senate Special Committee on Aging (1982) and by others (U.S. General Accounting Office, 1982; Committee on Aging, 1983): (1) reimbursement structures under federal health care programs and other financial barriers, (2) fragmented, disorganized systems of health and social services available to the elderly, (3) the low number of mental health professionals who are interested in and trained to provide care for the elderly, (4) continued ageism, or negative attitudes toward aging and the aged, on the part of mental health and health professionals, (5) fear of the cost of treating the mentally ill in general, (6) the limited availability of transportation services and other problems involving accessibility, and (7) "turf guarding" by agencies seeking to protect their share of reduced resources.

Elderly persons themselves may not seek mental health care, because of a lack of awareness of mental health services, distrust and fear based on stigmas created by attitudes toward mental health that were prevalent a generation ago, low levels of self-esteem resulting from loss of meaningful life roles, and beliefs that senile dementia and other mental conditions are part of normal aging (Hagebak & Hagebak, 1983).

A persistent complaint about Medicare and Medicaid is that they come close to bypassing any real help in the area of mental health. The U.S. Senate Special Committee on Aging (1971) has asserted, for example, that "Medicare discriminates against provision of mental health services for older Americans. Medicaid fails to live up to a legislative mandate that it provide such services" (p. 2).

The inadequacy of the formal medical system in responding to the needs of the mentally ill elderly is consistent with the focus of that system on physical care and on the provision of catastrophic acute medical care. This is reinforced by the failure of the community mental health programs to respond to congressional mandates to provide such services to the elderly.

Informal System

Though the formal system has failed to develop a coherent and complete system of health/social services for the aged, the family did respond to the vastly increased needs. Despite the stubborn and widespread myth that families do not take care of older people as in the "good old days," 30 years of research have produced enough definitive information to the contrary that the matter is no longer at scientific issue.

The theory of the isolated nuclear family, which was thought to be a consequence of increased industrialization, urbanization, and mobility, has been rejected. The elderly are knitted firmly into the fabric of the family and continue to maintain close contacts and viable relationships with family members. The flow of intergenerational services is primarily downward from the old to the young, but that flow changes its direction when older people become disabled (Shanas & Streib, 1965).

It bears repeating that at any given time most older people do not need help, apart from the garden-variety services family members normally exchange on a day-to-day basis and at times of emergency. It is undeniable, however, that demographic developments have resulted both in an exponential increase in the number and proportion of elderly who depend on their families for help and in a dramatic difference in the nature and duration of the help required.

The informal system is, by far, the main source of help for older people, providing at least 80 percent of the health/social services received by the elderly (U.S. General Accounting Office, 1982, 1983). Families provide the vast majority of medically related services, transportation and shopping, household maintenance, and personal care (such as bathing, feeding, dressing, toileting, and supervision) and share their homes when the older person cannot live alone. Family members also provide the expressive support— the affection, emotional support, socialization, and sense of having someone on whom to rely—that is the form of help most wanted by the old.

Caregiving Spouses. When an older person in need of help is married, the spouse is the principal provider of care. Owing to the shorter life expectancy of men and their tendency to marry women younger than they are, elderly men are much more likely than elderly women to have a spouse on whom to rely. Most of the 9 million widowed older people are women. At age 65 and over, most older women (52 percent) are widowed and most older men (77 percent) are married. Rates of widowhood rise sharply with advancing age, and the imbalance in the proportions of women to men increases. Between the ages of 65 and 74, the ratio of women to men is 131:100; between 75 and 84, the ratio is 166:100; and at age 85 and over, there are 224 women to every 100 men (Allan & Brotman, 1981).

Whether they are husbands or wives, older people exert great effort to care for a spouse, but their capacities are limited by their own advanced age, reduced energy and strength, and age-related ailments. Compared with other relatives who provide care, they experience the most stress (Horowitz & Shindelman, 1981). Elderly wives who care for disabled husbands, for example, have been found to suffer from low morale, isolation, loneliness, economic hardship, and "role overload" owing to multiple responsibilities (Fengler & Goodrich, 1979).

Caregiving elderly spouses therefore require close attention to their own needs for temporary respite from caregiving activities, concrete helping services, and emotional support. The physical strain may be accompanied by tremendous anxiety and fear of losing one's partner in a marriage that may have endured half a century or more. Since more couples nowadays survive together into advanced old age, such situations are likely to occur with increasing frequency.

Caregiving Adult Children. An elderly couple's children will assist the "well" spouse in caring for the disabled parent; when an older person is widowed, the bulk of care is given by adult children (Shanas, 1979a; Sussman, 1965; Tobin & Kulys, 1980). The accumulated evidence documents the strength of intergenerational ties, the continuity of responsible filial behavior, the frequency of contacts between generations, the predominance of families rather than professionals in the provision of health and social services, the strenuous efforts of family members to avoid institutional placement of the old, and the central role they play in caring

for dependent noninstitutionalized elderly people (E. Brody, 1978).

Most older people realize their preference to live near, but not with, their children, sharing households primarily when health or economic circumstances make it necessary. About 18 percent of the elderly live with children, and (counting shared households) about 84 percent of those with children live less than an hour away from one of them. Fifty-three percent of elderly respondents in a survey had seen their children within the last 24 hours (Shanas, 1979a).

Daughters, and to some extent daughters-in-law, have been identified as the principal caregivers to dependent parents and parents-in-law. In addition to providing most of the helping services noted earlier, daughters predominate among these who share their homes when the elderly cannot manage on their own (E. Brody, 1978; Horowitz, 1982; Myllyuoma & Soldo, 1980; Shanas, 1979b; Troll, 1971). Sons also sustain bonds of affection, perform certain gender-defined tasks (such as money management), and become the "responsible relatives" for the old who have no daughters or none close by.

Parent care is now a normative experience for individuals and families (E. Brody, 1985a), and responsible filial behavior has persisted despite two broad influential trends that affect the capacity of adult children to provide care. The first trend is the radical increase in the number of older people—particularly the very old, who are vulnerable to dependency—and the resultant sharp growth in the demands for parent care. Many caregiving adult children are grandparents; the four-generation family has become commonplace, with about 40 percent of older people with children being great-grandparents (Shanas, 1980). During the time span in which the number and proportion of older people in the population increased dramatically, the birth rate fell sharply. People now in advanced old age therefore have fewer children to share caregiving responsibilities than used to be the case.

In addition, since parents and children age together, the adult children of the people in advanced old age most often are in middle age, and some are in their 60s and 70s. Between 1900 and 1976, the number of people who experienced the death of a parent before the age of 15 dropped from one in four to one in 20, while the number of middle aged couples with two or more living parents increased from 10 percent to 47 percent (Uhlenberg, 1980). In the early 1960s, about 25 percent of people over the age of 45 had a surviving parent, but only a decade later, 25 percent of people in their late 50s had a surviving parent (Murray, 1973). By 1980, about 40 percent of people in their late 50s had a surviving parent (some had both parents), as did about 20 percent of those in their early 60s, 10 percent of those in their late 60s, and 3 percent of those in their 70s (National Retired Teachers Association–American Association of Retired Persons, 1981). Ten percent of all people now 65 years or older have a child over the age of 65. The need to provide parent care, then, occurs at a time of life when the adult children themselves may be experiencing age-related interpersonal losses, the onset of chronic ailments, lower energy levels, and may be retired or approaching retirement. Their responsibilities often extend both upward to the old and downward to the younger generations.

The second broad trend has been the rapid entry of middle-aged women into the work force. Sixty percent of women between the ages of 45 and 54 work, as do 42 percent of women between the ages of 55 and 64 (U.S. Department of Labor, 1981). Some work because of career commitment, but most because they need the money. Millions of women, therefore, find themselves confronted with multiple and often competing roles: wife, homemaker, mother, paid worker, and helper to an elderly parent as well.

The need to care for the old arises for many women, whether or not they do paid work, at a time when they expect to have "empty nests" but find that those nests are refilled literally or in terms of increased responsibility by impaired older people in need of care (E. Brody, 1978). As women advance from 40 years of age to their early 60s, for example, those who have a surviving parent become more likely to have that parent be dependent on them, to spend more time caring for the parent, to do more difficult caregiving tasks, and to have the parent in their own household (Lang & Brody, 1983). Middle-aged women, then, may not only be experiencing their own age-related problems, but their responsibilities may peak rather than diminish at this stage in their lives. Caregiving to elderly parents is not limited to the middle-aged, of course. As many as one-third of caregiving daughters may be either under 40 or over 60.

Effects of Family Caregiving. The caregiving efforts of families are not without social as well as economic cost to them. Evaluation of the service needs of the elderly therefore must take into account the situations and problems of the families concerned: the unique family constellation, the family's capacities, and family members' anxieties and symptoms of stress. Though different families react differently to caregiving, genuine concern and affection for the older person generally exist. At the same time, however, they are concerned about themselves and the duration and intensity of the caregiving efforts they will need to exert.

Depending on their own personalities and the demands of the situation, family members may feel guilty about not doing enough for the older person. Some are angry at finding themselves in the predicament of needing to do more than they feel capable of, though they may not be aware of their anger or able to express it. Unresolved relationship problems—which most families have at least some vestiges of—may be reactivated so that the older person becomes the focus of exacerbated latent and overt conflicts. These may arise between elderly spouses, among their adult children and their spouses, and between the generations (E. Brody & Spark, 1966). In some families, conflicts erupt over such issues as the fair sharing of caregiving responsibilities or where the older person should live.

Recently, research on the effects of caregiving has accelerated. The studies, which are cited specifically in the following discussion, indicate that in the main, having an elderly parent is gratifying and helpful. Older people are a resource to their children, providing many forms of assistance. Most people help their parents willingly when need be and derive satisfaction from doing so. Some adult children negotiate this stage of life without undue strain and experience personal growth during the process. However, when a parent becomes more dependent on children, the family homeostasis—whether it is precarious or well balanced—must shift accordingly. Such shifts have potential for stress, particularly because they augur increasing dependency in the future.

Some people experience financial hardship and some experience decline in their physical health from the arduous tasks of caring for a disabled parent. Certainly, such problems require attention. However, study after study has identified emotional strains as the most pervasive and severe consequences. A long litany of mental health symptoms such as depression, anxiety, frustration, feelings of helplessness, sleeplessness, lowered morale, and emotional exhaustion are related to restrictions on time and freedom, isolation, the competing demands of various responsibilities, difficulties in setting priorities, and interference with lifestyle and social and recreational activities (Archbold, 1978; Cantor, 1983; Danis, 1978; Frankfather, Smith & Caro, 1981; Gurland et al., 1978; Hoenig & Hamilton, 1966; Horowitz, 1982; Robinson & Thurnher, 1979; Sainsbury & Grad de Alercon, 1970). Such findings are not unique to the United States. Similar information is emerging from other countries (Gibson, 1982; Horl & Rosenmayr, 1982). Caregiving daughters appear to be more vulnerable to such effects than sons. When sons do become principal caregivers, they take on fewer tasks and are often helped by their wives, therefore experiencing less strain (Horowitz, 1985).

The women who are the principal caregivers and who often are under considerable stress from competing responsibilities have been characterized as "women-in-the-middle" (E. Brody, 1981). The pressures they experience put them at high risk for mental and physical health symptoms. Our culture has designated parent care as well as child care to women as gender-appropriate, but a ripple effect involves their husbands, children, and other family members. Among the family strains are lack of privacy, changed routines, and postponement of vacations and other future plans.

Attention has focused on another kind of cost to the family as a consequence of caregiving. Some caregiving wives and daughters are deterred from participation in the labor force (Soldo, 1980). Others leave their jobs or cut back on working hours because of the care needs of elderly husbands and parents, thereby entailing sharp reductions in family income (E. Brody et al., 1984).

While the extent of this pattern in the United States has not yet been determined, a British survey found that among women between the ages of 40 and 59, the need to look after people other than their husbands was second only to ill health as a motivation for giving up work. Nineteen percent of women in their 40s and 14 percent of those in their 50s left the work force for this reason (Hunt, 1978).

Information is just beginning to emerge about the effects on parent care of women's participation in the work force. Scattered findings indicate that working women continue to meet their responsibilities to their families, their elderly parents, and their jobs, but give up their own free time and opportunities for socialization (Cantor, 1983; Horowitz, Sherman & Durmaskin, 1983; Lang & Brody, 1983). One recent study found that the impaired parents of working women and nonworking women received the same amount of care (E. Brody & Schoonover, in press). The two groups of daughters provided equal amounts of emotional support, service arrangement, financial management, help with shopping, and transportation. When the daughters worked, however, outside help was purchased for household maintenance and personal care. There was no increase in the utilization of subsidized services.

Elderly without Close Family. Elderly individuals without family or whose family members are not close at hand and whose illness or disability is severe or likely to be prolonged are at high risk. They therefore require special attention from formal system providers.

A significant minority of older people do not have a close family member on whom to rely, and the proportion rises with advancing age. At age 74 and over, for example, 68 percent of women and 24 percent of men are widowed in addition to the 9 percent of women and 7 percent of men who are divorced or had never married. About 20 percent of the people now 65 or over have never had a child, and an undetermined number have outlived all their children (Allan & Brotman, 1981). Although the vast majority of those with children see them frequently, 11 percent (almost 2 million old people) do not see a child as often as once a month (Shanas, 1979). For most of these, geographic distance prevents a child from providing day-to-day supportive health care; for a minority, little or no help can be expected owing to long-standing alienation. Overall, more than 1 in 20 (5.3 percent) of all people 65 and over are entirely kinless—that is, without spouse, children, or siblings.

While spouse and children are the first to be relied on for care, other family members (such as siblings, grandchildren, nephews, and nieces), neighbors, and friends also play significant roles in helping older people. The assistance friends and neighbors provide to those without close kin is important, but in level or duration, the health-related help they give does not approach that given by family (Cantor, 1979).

Family Relationships of the Institution-alized Aged. Despite the widespread notion that old people are "dumped" into nursing homes by hard-hearted, uncaring families, research has established definitively that such placement is usually made only after families have made prolonged and strenuous efforts to avoid it. The 5 percent of those 65 and over who are in institutions at any one time are outnumbered two to one by equally disabled noninstitutionalized old people being cared for by their families (S. Brody, Poulshock, & Masciocchi, 1978; U.S. Comptroller General, 1977), a proportion that did not change between 1962 and 1975 (Shanas, 1979b). The role of family in providing social support is highlighted by the fact that, in contrast to those who live in the community, the vast majority (88 percent) of the institutionalized aged are not married (widowed, divorced, or never married), about half are childless, and those who have children have fewer children than the noninstitutionalized (E. Brody, 1981).

Though most research on the family relationships of older people has focused on noninstitutionalized older people, existing information refutes the notion that family ties are severed when institutionalization takes place. Families continue to be interested and concerned, to visit their elderly relatives regularly, and to experience strains such as worry and guilt (E. Brody, 1985b; George, 1984).

Formal System Vis-à-Vis Informal System. A major social policy issue concerns the role of the formal system vis-à-vis that of the family. In recent years, as part of an effort to reduce the formal system to save public dollars, there has been an insistent call for the family to increase its efforts to care for the disabled elderly. The rationale for that approach—that the family has repudiated the value that care for the elderly is a family responsibility—is unfounded in fact. Considerable information bears on this issue:

1. The amount of care provided by families dwarfs the efforts of the formal system, and the evidence indicates that family efforts have not diminished. To the contrary, when taken together, various findings suggest that the family nowadays provides more care for more difficult health problems to more elderly people over longer periods of time than ever before in history (E. Brody, 1985a).

2. Nursing home beds are deficient in both number and quality. It is primarily the Medicaid-eligible older person or the one who requires "heavy care" (such as for Alzheimer's disease or a related disorder) who is denied admission (U.S. General Accounting Office, 1983).

3. In-home care for severely disabled older people is not cheaper than institutional care (Fox & Clauser, 1980; U.S. Comptroller General, 1977; Palmer, 1983), nor does it reduce their rates of institutionalization (Grana, 1983).

4. When formal services are provided, they do not substitute for family services; rather, they supplement family services and strengthen the family's caregiving capacities (Horowitz, 1982; Zimmer & Sainer, 1978; Sherwood, Morris, & Morris, 1984; Zawadski, 1983b).

Despite the accumulated knowledge about the role of the family and the resultant call of gerontologists for a family-focused policy, social policy has made virtually no response to the needs of families providing home care. For example, respite care and day care are scarce and not universally or adequately available. There is limited regular public or private funding for their consistent support, and the programs that do exist are episodic, discontinuous, and vary greatly among the states (Meltzer, 1982). Economic supplements to caregiving families (such as attendance allowances or social security credits for caregivers remaining at home) are much more prevalent in other industrialized nations (Gibson, 1984). Community health and social services are limited and disproportionately underfinanced as compared to acute medical care services for the aged (S. Brody, 1979). Enormous inequities exist among the various states in their expenditures for Medicaid services, both for nursing home care and community-based services (see U.S. General Accounting Office, 1983).

Blenkner (1969) pointed out many years ago that the needs of the elderly for help had gone beyond the "self-solution" and the "kinship solution" and required societal solutions. Whether or not policy meets the challenge depends on values. The "alternatives" issue that characterized the decade of the 1970s—that is, the notion that community services are cheaper, better, and could substitute for institutional services—proved to be spurious. Both types of services are required to meet the often changing needs of a heterogeneous population.

The goal, then, is to develop a viable partnership in which the formal system complements, supplements, and supports the efforts of the informal network and substitutes when the latter becomes or is about to become overburdened.

Role of Social Work

The vulnerability of older people and the impact of their problems on the family and society legitimate the aging population as a prime concern of social work in all of its traditional forms: individual and group services, community organization, policy formulation, education, and research. The profession should have a major role in identifying needs and in designing and delivering preventive, supportive, and restorative services.

If social work is to assume a leadership role, it must recognize and respond to the implications of an aging society. New groups of people are constantly entering the aging phase of life. The profession must be proactive and flexible in responding to new needs of those who will have had different life experiences and have been exposed to different socioeconomic conditions. The elderly will have changing values and higher expectations in terms of the quality of services and the quality of their lives. Moreover, new cohorts of older people experience changing policy climates; former needs may have been addressed and new ones emerge.

Research is essential to identify the nature and extent of the needs, to ensure that programs are operated as efficiently and economically as possible without sacrificing quality, and to stimulate the invention of new services. Services must be evaluated to determine whether they reach the people in need, whether they are effective, and how much they cost; this knowledge must then be disseminated. In short, the profession's efforts should be data-based as well as values- and skills-based.

Marketing. Effective programs designed for the elderly must be marketed properly if they are to reach the people for whom they are intended. Study after study has found that services (even income maintenance programs) often are grossly underutilized because the older people do not know of their existence, have difficulty in accessing them, find accessing procedures unpalatable, or are bewildered by the complexities of entitlements and regulations. It is emphasized (because of the tendency to interpret the word "market" incorrectly) that the marketing of programs and services does not imply exploitation or a compromise of values (S. Brody & Persily, 1984). "The societal marketing concept is a consumers' needs orientation backed by integrated marketing aimed at generating consumer satisfaction and *long-run consumer welfare*" (Kolter, 1975, p. 47). By contrast with business marketers, "social marketers typically aim to serve the interests of the target market or society without personal profit" (Kolter, 1975, p. 283). Social work has a responsibility not only to examine the needs and develop appropriate programs, but to market them so that they reach the people who need them. The profession also must be careful not to perpetuate services in which it has an entrenched interest if they no longer are appropriate.

Organizational and Individual Case Management. One of the major roles of social work is in organizational and individual case management. Many elements of the array of services needed are in place in most communities, though they are often uneven regionally, are in short supply, are underdeveloped, lack consistent funding, and are unavailable to many people who need them. Moreover, development of services has been a "shotgun" categorical approach. They exist in parallel and overlapping arrangements called community mental health and retardation, vocational rehabilitation, housing, Area Agencies on Aging, hospitals, nursing homes, in-home services agencies, family service agencies, veterans' services, meals-on-wheels, and so on.

The problem is to organize these varied planning and service-delivery agencies so that they constitute a system in each community. Such a system would articulate the formal and informal medical and social/health services and relate the acute, STLTC, and LTLTC subsystems so they can respond in a coordinated manner to each individual and family in need. Organizational arrangements should respond to the values and resources of each locality; there can be no single, universally applicable prescription for organization and delivery. The underlying objective should be to provide a continuity of appropriate levels of care as the older person's needs vary in kind, level, and intensity.

The problem at the level of organizational systems inevitably is reflected at the level of the individual and family, for whom it is a baffling problem to mobilize and coordinate the needed services. The sheer existence of an array of services is not equivalent to their actual utilization. Among the barriers to obtaining services are the lack of administrative linkages from one to the other. Other barriers include the clients' lack of knowledge about the service, inability to connect with it, unpalatable eligibility criteria or humiliating procedures, the tendency of service agencies to perceive need only in terms of the services they offer, the complexities of entitlements, and bewildering regulations. Interventions designed to deal with such issues are variously called information and referral service, service management, outreach, case management, matrix management, or channeling.

More subtle issues also impede service utilization and speak to the need for counseling, or casework. There are psychological barriers to using needed services. The acceptability of services differs among older people with different socioeconomic and ethnic backgrounds and among individuals and families with diverse personalities and expectations. Therefore, whatever the label given to the process now most commonly referred to as case management, it must include the enabling process called counseling or casework.

Effective case management is a highly skilled, knowledge- and values-based activity. It should not, as often happens, be artificially divided into the mechanical manipulation or arrangement of services on the one hand and the offering of sensitive help with psychosocial issues on the other hand. The blending of these activities cannot be carried out by untrained people, no matter how well-meaning they may be. The task is to utilize all existing sources of services and funding including governmental entitlements and the resources of older people themselves and their families so as to ensure continuity of appropriate levels of care.

Social Work Role as Family Surrogate-Supplement. Recognizing the importance of family leads inevitably to concern about old people who have no family or whose family resources are slender. The increase in the number of couples having only one child or remaining childless makes it unlikely that future generations of old people will have more family members on whom to depend.

Social work should supplement or substitute for the family role of case management—that is, act as a combination of advocate, mediator, and mobilizer to obtain, arrange, and monitor the complex entitlements and services provided by the formal system. It can bring to that task the values and quality that underpin its activities and roles. Though the case management role is usually thought of as a professional role, basically it is enacted by the family. The family, however, needs help in doing so. And where there is no available family, the need is obvious.

Advocacy. Finally, a major part of social work's responsibility lies in the policy arena. The profession must press hard so that government meets *its* responsibilities, mobilizing in an advocacy role to influence the political process.

Advocacy for the elderly means advocacy for the family as well. Apart from ethical considerations, information assembled through research and observation indicates that the well-being of the generations is interlocked and that setting priorities for services and entitlements in terms of age levels is a false and destructive practice. The well-being of the generations is interlocked collectively as well as individually. Because of the economic, social, and psychological linkages between the generations, the situation of an elderly family member has a direct impact on all family members. For example, the economic stress of caring for old people places a burden on adult children that may result in deprivation of the grandchildren. The capacity of the family to function in its role of informal support system for the elderly depends on the health and well-being of the people in the supportive generations.

The ways in which concern for the elderly are expressed by society at this juncture will mold the attitudes of younger generations and therefore have implications for many future generations. As the World Health Organization pointed out, "It is not only for the sake of the aged themselves that we must try to raise their conditions of life to a level of dignity—it is also for the sake of their children" (World Health Organization, 1959, p. 7). The challenge to social work and to society is to close the gaps between knowledge, practice, and policy to give dignity and well-being to the closing years of life.

ELAINE M. BRODY
STANLEY J. BRODY

For further information, see AGED; DAY CENTERS: ADULT; FOOD STAMP PROGRAM; FOSTER CARE FOR ADULTS; HOSPICE; HUNGER AND MALNUTRITION; LONG-TERM CARE; MENTAL HEALTH AND ILLNESS; RETIREMENT AND PENSION PROGRAMS; SOCIAL SECURITY; PROTECTIVE SERVICES FOR THE AGED.

References

Allan, C., & Brotman, H. (1981). *Chartbook on Aging in America*. Compiled for the 1981 White House Conference on Aging, Washington, D.C.

American Association of Retired Persons. (1984). *Aging America, Trends and Projections*. Washington, D.C.: U.S. Senate Special Committee on Aging and Author.

Archbold, P. (1978). *Impact of Caring for an Ill Elderly Parent on the Middle-aged or Elderly Offspring Caregiver*. Paper presented at the 31st Annual Meeting of the Gerontological Society, Dallas, Tex.

Blenkner, M. (1969). "Normal Dependencies of Aging." In R. Kalish (Ed.), *The Dependencies of Old People* (pp. 27–39). Ann Arbor:

University of Michigan Institute of Gerontology.

Brody, E. M. (1978). "The Aging of the Family." *The Annals of the American Academy of Political and Social Science*, 438(July), 13–27.

Brody, E. M. (1981). "The Formal Support Network: Congregate Treatment Settings for Residents with Senescent Brain Dysfunction." In *Clinical Aspects of Alzheimer's Disease and Senile Dementia* (pp. 301–331). New York: Raven Press.

Brody, E. M. (1985a). "Parent Care as a Normative Family Stress." *The Gerontologist*, 25(1), 19–29.

Brody, E. M. (1985b). "The Role of the Family in Nursing Homes: Implications for Research and Public Policy." In M. S. Harper & B. Lebowitz (Eds.), *Mental Illness in Nursing Homes: Agenda for Research*. Washington, D.C.: U.S. Government Printing Office.

Brody, E. M., et al. (1984). *Women Who Help Elderly Mothers: When Work and Parent Care Compete*. Paper presented at the 37th Annual Meeting of The Gerontological Society of America, San Antonio, Texas, November.

Brody, E. M., & Schoonover, C. (in press). "Patterns of Care for the Dependent Elderly: When Daughters Work and When They Do Not." *The Gerontologist*.

Brody, E. M., & Spark, G. (1966). "Institutionalization of the Aged: A Family Crisis." *Family Process*, 5(1), 76–90.

Brody, S. J. (1973). "Comprehensive Health Care for the Elderly: An Analysis." *The Gerontologist*, 13(4), 412–418.

Brody, S. J. (1979). "The Thirty-to-One Paradox: Health Needs and Medical Solutions." *National Journal*, 11(44), 1869–1873.

Brody, S. J. (1985). "Future of Nursing Homes." *Rehabilitation Psychology*, 30(2), 109–120.

Brody, S. J., & Magel, J. S. (1984). "DRG: The Second Revolution in Health Care for the Elderly." *Journal of the American Geriatrics Society*, 32(9), 676–679.

Brody, S. J., & Magel, J. S. (1986). "LTC: The Long and Short of It." In C. Eisdorfer (Ed.), *Long-Term Care*. Baltimore, Md.: Johns Hopkins University.

Brody, S. J., & Persily, N. F. (1984). *Hospitals and the Aged: The New Old Market*. Rockville, Md.: Aspen Publications.

Brody, S. J., Poulshock, S. W., & Masciocchi, C. F. (1978). "The Family Caring Unit: A Major Consideration in the Long Term Support System." *The Gerontologist*, 18(6), 556–561.

Brotman, H. B. (1982). *Every Ninth American*. An Analysis for the Chairman of the Select Committee on Aging, House of Representatives. Washington, D.C.: U.S. Government Printing Office.

Butler, R. N. (1976). *Medicine and Aging: An Assessment of Opportunities and Neglect.* Testimony in Hearings of U.S. Senate Special Committee on Aging (p. 12). Washington, D.C.: U.S. Government Printing Office.

Butler, R. N., & Lewis, M. (1973). *Aging and Mental Health: Positive Psychosocial Approaches.* St. Louis, Mo.: C. V. Mosby Co.

Cantor, M. H. (1979). "Neighbors and Friends: An Overlooked Resource in the Informal Support System." *Research on Aging, 1,* 434–463.

Cantor, M. H. (1983). "Strain among Caregivers: A Study of Experience in the United States." *The Gerontologist, 23*(6), 597–604.

Cohen, G. D. (1980). "Prospects for Mental Health and Aging." In J. E. Birren & R. B. Sloane (Eds.), *Handbook of Mental Health and Aging* (pp. 971–994). Englewood Cliffs, N.J.: Prentice–Hall.

Committee On Aging, Group for the Advancement of Psychiatry. (1983). *Mental Health and Aging: Approaches to Curriculum Development* (Part 1, pp. 1–35). New York: Mental Health Materials Center.

Danis, B. G. (1978). *Stress in Individuals Caring for Ill Elderly Relatives.* Paper presented at 31st Annual Meeting of the Gerontological Society, Dallas, Tex.

Eisdorfer C., & Lawton, M. P. (1973). *The Psychology of Adult Development and Aging.* Washington, D.C.: American Psychological Association.

Fengler, A. P., & Goodrich, N. (1979). "Wives of Elderly Disabled Men: The Hidden Patients." *The Gerontologist, 19*(2), 175–183.

Fox, A. (1984). "Income Changes At and After Social Security Benefit Receipt: Evidence from the Retirement History Study." *Social Security Bulletin, 47*(9), 22.

Fox, P. D., & Clauser, S. B. (1980). "Trends in Nursing Home Expenditures: Implications for Aging Policy." *Health Care Financing Review,* (Fall), 65–70.

Frankfather, D., Smith, M. J., & Caro, F. G. (1981). *Family Care of the Elderly: Public Initiatives and Private Obligations.* Lexington, Mass.: Lexington Books.

George, L. K. (1984, December). *The Dynamics of Caregiver Burden.* Final Report submitted to the American Association of Retired Persons Andrus Foundation, Los Angeles, Calif.

Gibson, M. J. (1982). "An International Update on Family Care of the Ill Elderly." *Ageing International, 9*(1), 11–14.

Gibson, M. J. (1984, October 19). *Women and Aging.* Paper presented at International Symposium on Aging, Georgian Court College, Lakewood, N.J.

Goldfarb, A. I. (1962). "Prevalence of Psychiatric Disorders in Metropolitan Old Age and Nursing Homes." *Journal of American Geriatrics Society, 10*(1), 77–84.

Grana, J. M. (1983). "Disability Allowances for Long-term Care in Western Europe and the United States." *International Social Security Review* (February), 207–221.

Gruenberg, E. M. (1977). "The Failures of Success." *Milbank Memorial Fund Quarterly* (Winter), 3–24.

Gurland, B. (1976). *The Epidemiology of Depression in the Elderly.* Paper presented at Conference on Depression in the Elderly, Philadelphia Geriatric Center, Pennsylvania.

Gurland, B., et al. (1978). "Personal Time Dependency in the Elderly of New York City: Finding from the U.S.-U.K. Cross–national Geriatric Community Study." In *Dependency in the Elderly of New York City* (pp. 9–45). New York: Community Council of Greater New York.

Hagebak, J. E., & Hagebak, B. R. (1983). "Meeting the Mental Health Needs of the Elderly: Issues and Action Steps." *Aging,* (January-February), 26–31.

Hoenig, J., & Hamilton, M. (1966). "Elderly Patients and the Burden on the Household." *Psychiatra et Neurologia* (Basel), *152,* 281–293.

Horl, J., & Rosenmayr, L. (1982). "Assistance to the Elderly as a Common Task of the Family and Social Service Organizations." *Arch. Gerontol. Geriatr., 1,* 75–95.

Horowitz, A. (1982, May). *The Role of Families in Providing Long–term Care to the Frail and Chronically Ill Elderly Living in the Community* (Final report submitted to the Health Care Financing Administration, Department of Health and Human Services). Washington, D.C.: U.S. Government Printing Office.

Horowitz, A. (1985). "Sons and Daughters as Caregivers to Older Parents: Differences in Role Performance and Consequences." *The Gerontologist, 25*(6), 612–617.

Horowitz, A., Sherman, R. H., & Hurmaskin, S. C. (1983, November). *Employment and Daughter Caregivers: A Working Partnership for Older People?* Paper presented at 36th Annual Meeting of the Gerontological Society of America, San Francisco, Calif.

Horowitz, A., & Shindelman, L. W. (1981, November). *Reciprocity and Affection: Past Influences on Current Caregiving.* Paper presented at the 34th Annual Meeting of the Gerontological Society of America, Toronto, Canada.

Hunt, A. (1978). *The Elderly at Home.* London, England: Office of Population Censuses and Surveys, Her Majesty's Stationery Office.

Jette, A. M., & Branch, L. G. (1981). "The Framingham Disability Study: II. Physical

Disability among the Aging." *American Journal of Public Health*, 71(11), 1211–1216.

Katz, S., et al. (1983). "Active Life Expectancy." *The New England Journal of Medicine*, 309(20), 1218–1224.

Kay, D. W. K., & Bergmann, K. (1980). "Epidemiology of Mental Disorders among the Aged in the Community." In J. E. Birren & B. R. Sloane (eds.), *Handbook of Mental Health* (pp. 34–56). Englewood Cliffs, N.J.: Prentice–Hall.

Kolter, P. (1975). *Marketing for Nonprofit Organizations* (2nd ed.). Englewood Cliffs, N.J.: Prentice–Hall.

Kramer, M., Taube, C. A., & Redick, R. W. (1973). "Patterns of Use of Psychiatric Facilities by the Aged: Past, Present, and Future." In C. Eisdorfer & M. P. Lawton (Eds.), *The Psychology of Adult Development and Aging* (pp. 428–528). Washington, D.C.: American Psychological Association.

Lang, A., & Brody, E. M. (1983). "Characteristics of Middle–Aged Daughters and Help to Their Elderly Mothers." *Journal of Marriage and the Family*, 45, 193–202.

Lawton, M. P. (1972). "Assessing the Competence of Older People." In D. P. Kent, R. Kastenbaum, & S. Sherwood (Eds.), *Research, Planning and Action for the Elderly* (pp. 122–143). New York: Behavioral Publications.

Lawton, M. P., & Cohen, J. (1974). "The Generality of Housing Impact in the Well–Being of Older People." *Journal of Gerontology*, 29(2), 194–204.

Lowenthal, M. F. (1964). *Lives in Distress.* New York: Basic Books.

Maxfield, L., & Reno, V. (1985). "Distribution of Income Resources of Recent Retirees: Findings from the Beneficiary Survey." *Social Security Bulletin*, 48(1), 7–13.

Meltzer, J. W. (1982, June). *Respite Care: An Emerging Family Support Service.* Washington, D.C.: Center for the Study of Social Policy.

Murray, J. (1973). "Family Structure in the Preretirement Years." *Social Security Bulletin*, 36(10), 25–45.

Myllyuoma, J., & Soldo, B. J. (1980). *Family Caregivers to the Elderly: Who Are They?* Paper presented at the 33rd Annual Meeting of the Gerontological Society, San Diego, Calif., November.

National Academy of Sciences, Institute of Medicine. (1977). *A Policy Statement: The Elderly and Functional Dependency.* Washington, D.C.: Author.

National Retired Teachers Association–American Association of Retired Persons. (1981). *National Survey of Older Americans.* Washington, D.C.: Author.

Palmer, H. C. (1983). "The Alternatives Question." In R. J. Vogel & H. C. Palmer (Eds.), *Long–Term Care, Perspectives from Research and Demonstrations* (pp. 255–305). Washington, D.C.: Health Care Financing Administration, U.S. Department of Human Services.

Pfeiffer, E. (1973,). *Multidimensional Quantitative Assessment of Three Populations of Elderly.* Paper presented at Annual Meeting of the Gerontological Society, Miami Beach, Fla., November.

President's Commission on Mental Health. (1978). *Report to the President, Vol. 1.* Washington, D.C.: U.S. Government Printing Office.

Robinson, B., & Thurnher, M. (1979). "Taking Care of Aged Parents: A Family Cycle Transition." *The Gerontologist*, 19(6), 586–593.

Sainsbury, P., & Grad de Alercon, J. (1970). "The Effects of Community Care in the Family of the Geriatric Patient." *Journal of Geriatric Psychiatry*, 4(1), 23–41.

Schuckit, M. A. (1974,). *Unrecognized Psychiatric Illness in Elderly Medical-Surgical Patients.* Paper presented at 27th Annual Meeting of the Gerontological Society, Portland, Oregon, November.

Shanas, E. (1979a). "Social Myth as Hypothesis: The Case of the Family Relations of Old People." *The Gerontologist*, 19(1), 3–9.

Shanas, E. (1979b). "The Family as a Social Support System in Old Age." *The Gerontologist*, 19(2), 169–174.

Shanas, E. (1980). "Older People and Their Families: The New Pioneers." *Journal of Marriage and the Family*, 42, 9–15.

Shanas, E. (1982). *National Survey of the Aged* (DHHS Publication No. OHDS83-20425). Washington, D.C.: Office of Human Development Services.

Shanas, E., & Streib, G. F. (Eds.). (1965). *Social Structure and the Family: Generational Relations.* Englewood Cliffs, N.J.: Prentice-Hall.

Sherwood, S., Morris, S., & Morris, N. J. (1984, November). *Relationships between Formal and Informal Service Provision to Frail Elders.* Paper presented at 37th Annual Scientific Meeting of the Gerontological Society of America, San Antonio, Tex.

Social Security Administration. (1982). *Social Security Bulletin, Annual Statistical Supplement, 1982.* Washington, D.C.: U.S. Department of Health and Human Services.

Soldo, B. J. (1980,). *The Dependency Squeeze on Middle-aged Women.* Paper presented at meeting of the Secretary's Advisory Committee on Rights and Responsibilities of Women, Department of Health and Human Services, Washington, D.C.

Sussman, M. B. (1965). "Relationships of Adult Children with Their Parents in the United

States." In E. Shanas & G. F. Streib (Eds.), *Social Structure and the Family: Generational Relations* (pp. 62–92). Englewood Cliffs, N.J.: Prentice-Hall.

Tobin, S., & Kulys, R. (1980). "The Family and Service." In E. Eisdorfer (Ed.), *Annual Review of Gerontology and Geriatrics, Vol. 1* (pp. 370–399). New York: Springer Publishing Co.

Troll, L. E. (1971). "The Family of Later Life: A Decade Review." *Journal of Marriage and the Family, 33,* 263–290.

Trout, J., & Mattson, D. R. (1984). "A Ten-Year Review of the Supplemental Security Income Program." *Social Security Bulletin, 47*(1), 3–24.

Uhlenberg, P. (1980). "Death and the Family." *Journal of Family History, 5,* 313–320.

Upp, M. (1982). "A Look at the Economic Status of the Aged Then and Now." *Social Security Bulletin, 45*(3), 16–20.

U.S. Bureau of the Census. (1982a). *Decennial Censuses of Population, 1900–1980 and Projections of the Population of the United States: 1982 to 2050* (Current Population Reports, Series P-25, No. 922). Washington, D.C.: U.S. Government Printing Office.

U.S. Bureau of the Census. (1982b). *Statistical Abstract of the United States, 1982–83* (103rd ed.). Washington, D. C.: U.S. Government Printing Office.

U.S. Bureau of the Census. (1984). *Developments in Aging: 1983* (Vol. 1, p. 425). Washington, D.C.: U.S. Government Printing Office.

U.S. Comptroller General. (1977). *The Well-Being of Older People in Cleveland, Ohio.* Washington, D.C.: U.S. General Accounting Office.

U.S. Comptroller General. (1979). *Entering a Nursing Home—Costly Implications for Medicaid and the Elderly.* Washington, D.C.: U.S. General Accounting Office.

U.S. Department of Labor, Bureau of Labor Statistics. (1981). "Labor Force by Sex, Age and Race." *Earnings and Employment, 28,* 167.

U.S. General Accounting Office. (1982). *The Elderly Should Benefit from Expanded Home Health Care but Increasing These Services Will Not Insure Cost Reductions* (U.S. GAO 1PE–83–1). Washington, D.C.: Author.

U.S. General Accounting Office. (1982). *The Elderly Remain in Need of Mental Health Services* (Pub. No. HRD 82-112). Washington, D.C.: U.S. Government Printing Office.

U.S. General Accounting Office. (1983). *Medicaid and Nursing Home Care: Cost Increases and the Need for Services are Creating Problems for the States and the Elderly* (U.S. GAO 1PE–84–1). Washington, D.C.: U.S. Government Printing Office.

U.S. Health Care Financing Administration. (1984, December). "Trends." *Medicare Program Statistics, 1982* (HCFA Pub. 03189). Washington, D.C.: U.S. Government Printing Office.

U.S. Health Resources Administration. (1977). *The Future of Long-Term Care in the United States: The Report of the Task Force.* Washington, D.C.: U.S. Government Printing Office.

U.S. House, Select Committee on Aging. (1983). *Crisis in Health Care: An Overview* (H. Prt. 98-389). Washington, D.C.: U.S. Government Printing Office.

U.S. House, Select Committee on Aging. (1985). *The President's 1986 Budget: An Assault on America's Aged and Poor* (H. Prt. 99-481). Washington, D.C.: U.S. Government Printing Office.

U.S. National Center for Health Statistics. (1979). *The National Nursing Home Survey: 1977 Summary for the United States.* Washington, D.C.: U.S. Department of Health, Education and Welfare.

U.S. National Center for Health Statistics. (1982). *Current Estimates from the National Health Interview Survey: United States, 1981* (Vital and Health Statistics, Series 10, No. 141). Washington, D.C.: U.S. Department of Health and Human Services.

U.S. Senate Special Committee on Aging. (1971). *Mental Health Care and the Elderly–Shortcomings in Public Policy.* Washington, D.C.: U.S. Government Printing Office.

U.S. Senate Special Committee on Aging. (1972). *Developments in Aging: 1971, Vol. 1.* Washington, D.C.: U.S. Government Printing Office.

U.S. Senate Special Committee on Aging. (1973). *Developments in Aging: 1972, Vol. 1.* Washington, D.C.: U.S. Government Printing Office.

U.S. Senate Special Committee on Aging. (1982). *Developments in Aging: 1981, Vol. 1.* Washington, D.C.: U.S. Government Printing Office.

U.S. Senate Special Committee on Aging. (1983). *Developments in Aging: 1982, Vol. 1.* Washington, D.C.: U.S. Government Printing Office.

Weissert, W. G. (1985). "Seven Reasons Why It Is So Difficult to Make Community-Based Long Term Care Cost-Effective." *Health Services Research, 20*(4), 423–435.

World Health Organization. (1959). *Mental Health Problems of the Aging and the Aged* (Technical Report Series, No. 171, p. 7). Geneva, Switzerland: Author.

World Health Organization. (1974). *Planning and Organization of Geriatric Services* (Technical Report Series 548). Geneva, Switzerland: Author.

Zawadski, R. T. (Ed.). (1983a). "Community-

Based Systems of Long Term Care" [Special Issue], *Home Health Care Services Quarterly*, 4(3/4).

Zawadski, R. T. (1983b). "Research in the Demonstrations: Findings and Issues." In Zawadski, R. T. (Ed.), Community-Based Systems of Long Term Care [Special Issue], *Home Health Care Services Quarterly*, 4(3/4), 209–228.

Zimmer, A. H., & Sainer, J. S. (1978,). "Strengthening the Family as an Informal Support for Their Aged: Implications for Social Policy and Planning." Paper presented at the 31st Annual Meeting of the Gerontological Society, Dallas, Tex., November.

AGENCY INFORMATION SYSTEMS.

See COMPUTER UTILIZATION; INFORMATION SYSTEMS: AGENCY; INFORMATION SYSTEMS: CLIENT DATA; INFORMATION UTILIZATION FOR MANAGEMENT DECISION MAKING.

AIDS.

See HOMOSEXUALITY: GAY MEN.

AID TO FAMILIES WITH DEPENDENT CHILDREN

The major program in the United States concerned with the welfare of needy children deprived of parental support is the Aid to Families with Dependent Children (AFDC) program. Its stated purpose as expressed in the Social Security Act, the authorizing legislation, is

encouraging the care of dependent children in their own homes or in the homes of relatives by enabling each State to furnish financial assistance and rehabilitation and other services, as far as practicable under the conditions in such State, to needy dependent children and the parents or relatives with whom they are living to help maintain and strengthen family life and to help such parents or relatives to attain capability for the maximum self-support and personal independence con-

sistent with the maintenance of continuing parental care and protection. (U.S. Department of Health and Human Services [USDHHS], 1985, p. 241)

To this end, in 1983, the program served 10,866,000 people in 3,720,000 families. Of those served, over 7 million were children. The cost was approximately $15.4 billion—of which slightly more than half was paid by the federal government from general revenues of the U.S. Treasury (USDHHS, Office of Family Assistance [OFA], 1985).

AFDC, however, does not stand alone in meeting the needs of dependent children. It is usually administered in close coordination with such other federal programs as child welfare, food stamps, Medicaid, social services, and child support and enforcement.

Federal Requirements

AFDC is a grant-in-aid program. This means that Federal Financial Participation (FFP) is available to those states that agree to implement the program as specified in the Social Security Act and in federal regulations.

In 1935, when AFDC was established, grants-in-aid were the primary mechanism for distributing federal funds to states for programs that the federal government did not administer directly. This was some forty years before alternative methods of funding state programs such as general revenue sharing and block grants were conceived.

A grant-in-aid can best be described as "a scheme by which the national government offers to match the states, dollar for dollar, or on some such basis in promoting enterprises which are properly within state jurisdiction but need to be speeded up" (Council of State Governments, 1949, p. 28). A grant-in-aid program, therefore, has certain characteristics that make it unique. In addition to federal legislation authorizing appropriations and a method for apportioning funds among states, there must be conformance to federal statute and requirements, federal approval of state plans, and federal supervision of the state's operation of the program (Council of State Governments, 1949).

Funding for AFDC—except for Guam, Puerto Rico, and the Virgin Islands—is through an open-ended appropriation for grants to recipients and program administration. Because there is no ceiling on expenditures, the federal government will match what the states spend.

The percentage of federal reimbursement to a state for its AFDC grants to recipients is tied to the per capita income of the state: poorer states receive a higher percentage of reimbursement for each dollar spent than wealthier states. The range is from a minimum of 50 percent to a maximum of 77.63 percent under what is called the federal medical assistance percentage. The percentage is subject to change every two years.

The reimbursement of the cost of administering the program is also established by law and ranges from 50 percent for general administration and staff training to 90 percent incentive funding for states developing and implementing approved computer-based information systems meeting federal specifications. Total administrative expenditures for Fiscal Year 1984 were $1.7 billion with the federal government assuming more than half the costs (USDHHS, OFA, 1985a).

The Social Security Act also delineates those conditions a state must meet in order to receive federal funding. The state must develop a document known as the state plan, which in effect becomes the contract between the state and the federal government. The document describes the state's AFDC program, spelling out how the state meets federal requirements. To comply with the law, the AFDC program must (1) be in effect in and mandatory for all political subdivisions of the state, (2) be administered or provide supervision of local agencies by a single state agency, (3) provide state or local financial participation for meeting grants to recipients and administrative costs, (4) implement proper and efficient methods of operation, and (5) have safeguards that restrict the disclosure of certain client information.

Examples of other requirements are providing opportunities for fair hearings to applicants and recipients questioning agency decisions, and submitting required reports to the federal government. In addition, the state plan must show that the program complies with federal eligibility income and resources and work program policies as well as administrative requirements specified in the *Code of Federal Regulations* (Office of the Federal Register, 1984, Vol. 45, CFR Parts 200 et seq.) and manuals that have been designated as having the force and effect of regulations.

The Office of Family Assistance (OFA) in the Social Security Administration of the U.S. Department of Health and Human Services supervises the AFDC program at the federal level. OFA's national office in Washington, D.C., translates the intent of Congress—as expressed in the legislation—into the regulations that form the basis of the state program. OFA also has responsibility for the fiscal management of the program. The day-to-day work with the states is carried out through OFA's 10 regional offices. These regional offices provide interpretation of program and fiscal policies, monitor compliance with federal requirements, audit state expenditures, review each state's quality control findings (to ensure the accuracy of the findings, the correctness of payments to clients, and the percentage of cases found to be ineligible) and provide assistance to states in bringing about overall improvements in the administration of the program.

State Latitude

Although states must adhere to federal requirements, AFDC is essentially a state-run program; each state determines whether it wishes to operate such a program and how it is going to administer it. At present, all states and territories have AFDC programs, although there are great variations in the administration of the program.

Thirty-six states and territories directly administer the program and 18 supervise local entities, usually counties, which in turn administer the program. Some AFDC programs are administered in agencies having limited scope focusing on income maintenance programs; others are in large umbrella agencies that have multiple responsibilities for income maintenance, social services, mental health, and corrections (USDHHS, 1983a).

Other differences pertain to agency organization, staffing, salaries, resources, space, and equipment. These differences result in the wide range of administrative costs: whereas one state may claim about $2 million annually, another claims over $259 million annually.

There are also many options within the program requirements. States may select all, a portion, or none. States also determine their own standards of need and payment (the amount actually paid) usually taking into account such factors as their own financial resources and cost of living. State need standards range from a low of $112 to a high of $673 per month for a family of two with a payment standard for the same size family ranging from $56 to $617 per month (USDHHS, OFA, 1985c). As of 1982, only 19 states paid the full need standard, 4 states paid the full need standard for a smaller size family but limited payments to larger families, and 31 paid a lesser amount than the need standard (USDHHS, 1983a).

States also determine the items covered in the need standard. In some instances the need standard includes all basic needs such as food, clothing, shelter, utilities, and household supplies. Other states give separate shelter allowances; a number make provision for meeting other needs such as special diets, replacement of clothing or furniture destroyed in a disaster, or even for the purpose of establishing a household.

Evolution of the Program, 1935–1984

The recognition that it is better to raise children in their own homes in the care of their mothers rather than in institutions came in the early part of this century. In 1911 Missouri was the first state to enact legislation allowing its counties to provide cash assistance to mothers with dependent children. From there the idea spread, and by 1919, 39 states had some form of legislation. By 1935, all states except South Carolina and Georgia helped dependent children. Most states had also extended the concept of cash assistance—originally for widows with dependent children—to all needy mothers, whether the children were born in wedlock or not and whether their fathers were dead or not (Trattner, 1984).

The Great Depression of the 1930s provided the impetus for action at the national level to provide "some safeguards against misfortunes which cannot be wholly eliminated in this man-made world of ours" (Trattner, p. 271). Franklin D. Roosevelt recognized the need for a system that "would provide at once security against several of the great disturbing factors of life" (Trattner, p. 271). Thus, President Roosevelt established a Committee on Economic Security that in 1935 submitted to Congress a bill that was to become the Social Security Act. The act was, and to this day is, a measure to ensure the economic security of the American people through two lines of defense against want: social insurance and public assistance.

From the time of inception, the purpose of AFDC has remained the same: to be the last line of defense against want for needy children deprived of parental support. It was also conceived to be a temporary measure that would eventually be phased out when the Social Security Insurance System became operational. In 1935, deprivation of parental support was seen primarily as the result of the death of the wage-earner, the father. It was not until after World War II, with the increase in broken families and out-of-wedlock births, that the thrust of the program changed and desertion became the major deprivation factor.

The extent of the program also changed. Between 1935 and 1980 it was considerably broadened. When the program was first established, a dependent child was defined as a child under the age of 16. In 1939, states were given the option to extend the ages to 16 and 17 if the child was regularly attending school and in 1965 to ages 18 through 20 if attending high school, college, or university, or enrolled in a course of vocational or technical training. Another major change occurred in 1950 when the needy relative with whom the child lived could be included as a recipient for federal funding. A needy relative was defined as a father, mother, grandparent, brother, sister, stepparent, stepsister or stepbrother, or uncle or aunt. Then in 1956, the law expanded the eligible relatives to include a first cousin, nephew, or niece. Finally, one of the most extensive changes in concept occurred in 1962 when states were given the option to extend the program to children deprived of support by reason of the unemployment of the father (later to be changed to the unemployment of either parent). In 1962, the name of the program was also changed from Aid to Dependent Children to Aid to Families with Dependent Children.

In addition, the mid-1950s saw AFDC move from mainly a cash assistance program to a program with a social services orientation. The 1956 amendments to the Social Security Act gave recognition to the belief that money alone would not break the dependency cycle and provided federal funding for social services for AFDC families.

The notion that AFDC was not solely a program to provide money payments but rather was a program to prevent further social ills and to rehabilitate AFDC families was embodied in the 1962 amendments that increased funding for social services from 50 percent to 75 percent and gave emphasis to in-service training and graduate education through schools of social work for AFDC staff.

During the 1960s a number of external factors influenced the direction of the program. The problems of the poor were brought to the fore through the works of Harrington (1981) and May (1980). It was the time of the civil rights movement, the War on Poverty, and the emergence of the National Welfare Rights Organization. There was a belief that people receiving AFDC had a right to know the rules and regulations of the program and how decisions affecting them were made, as well as a mechanism to question and appeal decisions. Well beyond that, it was felt that the poor had a right to be involved in the development of public policy and to serve on those boards overseeing the operation of welfare agencies.

During the latter part of the 1960s the federal government gave support to simplification of program requirements, separation of services from income maintenance, and a declaration system. The declaration system was based on the premise that poor people were just as honest as other people and that AFDC should be based on applicants and recipients attesting to the fact that they were eligible. Lengthy investigations documenting need and eligibility would no longer be required. Instead those ineligible would be detected through special audits similar to those used by the Internal Revenue Service.

There were several underlying reasons for the second major change—separation of services from income maintenance. The belief now was that someone who needed cash assistance did not always need social services. Also, individuals have the right to make their own decision as to whether or not they need social services; the two need not be tied together. Another contributing factor for the separation of services from income maintenance was the difficulty of properly tracking expenditures that states were claiming as social services at 75 percent federal funding. In 1974 this resulted in the passage of separate social services provisions, which completely removed social services from the AFDC except for the territories.

Another phenomenon taking place in the 1960s, affecting society as a whole, was that more and more women were returning to the labor force. The consensus was that a mother need no longer remain in the home until her children were grown. This conviction resulted in the passage of the Work Incentive Program (WIN) in 1967 and WIN II in 1971. WIN II stated that to be eligible for AFDC, every individual over the age of 16 had to register for manpower services, training, or employment unless attending school or exempted because of illness, the care of an incapacitated adult, or the care of a child under 6 years of age. This meant that AFDC mothers with children over 6 had to participate in WIN.

The late 1960s saw AFDC expand to a program for the working poor. Federal law allowed states to disregard the earnings of full-time and part-time students and provided a disregard of the first $30 and one-third of the remainder of the monthly income earned by all other family members.

These changes, coupled with the declaration system, resulted in increased caseloads and expenditures. Reviews of state programs showed that a high number of recipients were ineligible, and that states were not effectively combating this.

Although errors due to ineligibility and incorrect payments were of long-standing concern to the federal government, it was not until the 1970s that major emphasis was given to error reduction. In October 1970 the U.S. Department of Health, Education and Welfare introduced new quality control procedures setting specific requirements for states to follow to determine case, payment, and client errors. (For the most part, those procedures are still in place.) The department also set error tolerance levels (3 percent for ineligibility and 5 percent for overpayments and underpayments) that states were not to exceed. Then in 1972 the department published regulations establishing a zero tolerance level and calling for the disallowance of federal funds for all erroneous payments. The department also strengthened its own ability to review state findings.

The entire area of quality control resulted in tension between the states and the federal government. The federal government had to modify its position of the zero tolerance level and revert back to 3 and 5 percent. This still did not satisfy states, which sought remedy through the courts. In 1976 a U.S. District Court judge in the State of Washington found these tolerance levels to be arbitrary and capricious although he upheld the concept of disallowances (Jernigan, undated). Through negotiations with the states a new regulation was promulgated in 1979. Under this regulation, target error rates were established for each state to achieve. The 1979 regulation allowed flexibility and recognized that errors may occur that are outside the state's control. In such cases, a state could request a waiver of disallowance for not meeting the established rate.

As with the prior regulations, no disallowances were taken. States, however, made a concerted effort to reduce errors. The result was that the national error rates declined from 16.5 percent in 1973 to 7.3 percent for the period of October 1981 to March 1982 (USDHHS, 1983b).

Initially, the issue of error rates and sanctions was handled administratively. Then, in 1979, Representative Robert H. Michel (R, Illinois) introduced an amendment that for the first time mandated in statute that the federal government would not match erroneous payments; it set target error rates that states had to achieve decreasing to 4 percent by Fiscal Year 1983. The Michel amendment was later superseded by the Tax Equity and Fiscal Responsibility Act of 1982, which established a 4 percent tolerance for Fiscal Year 1983 and 3 percent for the years thereafter.

Another major change to the Social Security Act in 1974 were provisions to deal with the growing problems of locating absent parents and establishing paternity of a child born out of wedlock. States were required to implement child support and enforcement programs.

The 1970s was also the period of growing caseloads, rising costs, taxpayer revolts, and concerns about waste in government. In 1981, with the passage of the Omnibus Budget Reconciliation Act (OBRA), Congress enacted legislation to deal with these concerns. The AFDC legislative changes were also part of President Reagan's overall plan for economic recovery to curb inflation and restore productivity by limiting eligibility to those most in need, improving program administration, and strengthening work requirements.

Major changes included: (1) reducing the eligibility of working households by setting absolute gross income ceilings limiting eligibility to families whose income was 150 percent below the state's standards of need; (2) setting a standard for work expenses of $75 and allowing child care of no more than $160 per month per child; (3) limiting the $30 and one-third disregard to a four-month period; and (4) reducing the age of dependent children to age 18 or (at state option) to age 19 if the child is completing high school.

In addition, states were required to improve the administration of the program by establishing retrospective budgeting (a more precise way of determining current need) and monthly reporting by clients as a quick means to pick up changes in client circumstances.

OBRA gave emphasis to work programs by stressing the responsibility of employable recipients to seek and accept employment and by giving states more flexibility to develop work programs. States were allowed to use WIN funds to set up special demonstration projects best suited to the individual state's needs. The law also established the Community Work Experience Program (CWEP), which is designed to help recipients learn job skills and acquire work experience to enhance their ability to find regular employment. States could set up CWEP in areas such as health, environmental protection, recreation, and day care. States could require recipients to work a specified number of hours computed by dividing their monthly grant by the minimum wage. In legislation passed in 1982, states could also require applicants and recipients to participate in job search programs. As of June 30, 1985, 23 states had implemented WIN Demonstration Projects, 22 states were operating Community Work Experience Programs, 11 states had set up Job Search Programs, and 12 states had established Works Supplementation/Grants Diversion Programs (USDHHS, OFA, 1985b).

Other legislation, passed in 1982, continued to support efforts to limit eligibility and reduce costs. However, there has been some redirection in focus in the legislation passed by the 98th Congress in the Deficit

Reduction Act of 1984. Although some parts of the congressional action clarified OBRA provisions and continued the support of work programs, others liberalized AFDC eligibility. Changes included raising the gross income ceiling from 150 percent to 185 percent of need and extending the $30 disregard for an additional eight months after the four-month period expired. This meant that individuals whose assistance was being terminated for having received the full amount of the $30 disregard or the $30 and one-third disregard would receive Medicaid coverage for nine months, or up to 15, if the state selects the additional six-month option.

Fundamental Concepts and Issues

Although AFDC has undergone many changes since 1935, a number of basic concepts have remained the same. One is the recognition that government has responsibility for needy dependent children to help maintain them in their own homes. Such aid, however, has always been the last line of defense against want after all other sources of income have been sought—including support from legally responsible relatives—and all such resources exhausted. It also is a temporary measure with benefits based on a means test substantiating financial need and meeting all conditions of eligibility. In addition, the program has remained a grant-in-aid in which the state voluntarily participates and agrees to comply with federal statutes and requirements but has wide latitude in how it operates the program.

There still are fundamental issues that have not been completely resolved. One of the most basic is whether the federal government should be in this business at all or whether such a program as AFDC should be left entirely up to each state to implement (if it wishes) and to administer as it sees best. Related to this is the question of whether the federal government is imposing a regulatory burden upon states. In a sense this reverts back to questions about states' rights.

More broadly, there are values in our society that come into play. Ours is a society founded on the Judeo-Christian belief that one should help the less fortunate when they are unable to help themselves. We are also a nation that strongly believes in the work ethic, which implies that people who want to can take care of themselves. Opportunities are still there. People have to find them, and it is not the place of the government to take care of those who will not take care of themselves.

Taken all together, our differing views of governments, conflicting values and beliefs, personal feelings, and concerns of how government money should be spent, make it difficult to arrive at a consensus on the way in which to meet individual needs without encouraging dependency.

Trends and Issues

President Nixon attempted to bring about a major change in AFDC during his first Administration through the Family Assistance Plan, which was an attempt to nationalize the AFDC program and to provide a minimum-income guarantee of $2,400 for a family of four. There was to be a decrease in the income in proportion to the amount the family earned. Built into the program were work requirements and funding for public service jobs. The House of Representatives and the Senate could not agree and there was opposition from recipient groups and professional organizations, all of whom wanted a higher minimum-income guarantee. Eventually the Family Assistance Plan was dropped, but a Supplemental Security Income Program (SSI) for the aged, blind, and disabled was passed. During the early years of the Carter Administration, efforts to set up a similar national program for the working poor never got beyond the drawing board.

In 1982 the Reagan Administration proposed that AFDC become the financial responsibility of the states with the federal government in turn assuming responsibility for Medicaid. There was also some discussion about making AFDC a block grant, thereby limiting federal funding and giving states broader options for administering the program. There has been considerable state opposition to these suggestions, and it does not seem likely that there will be major overhauls in the way the AFDC program is administered in the near future. There are, however, societal forces at work that may have an impact on the future of the program in the next decade. One unknown is the effect of computerization and high technology on the average wage earner. Another is the fact that the institutions we have today may not be able to provide adequate defenses against want. The single most pressing social problem affecting the future course of AFDC is the continuing feminization of poverty and the continuing increase in households headed by a single female.

The nation will need to address the issue of breaking the dependency cycle by focusing on the millions of children who are the beneficiaries of AFDC. Concrete steps need to be taken to assure that they will develop into productive, healthy adults. Their social, emotional, and economic development depends on their having, during their developmental years, an acceptable standard of living (adequate food, shelter, clothing, and medical care) and good education, training, and employment opportunities. Accomplishing these goals would necessitate a comprehensive approach by government, voluntary agencies, and the private sector. We can only hope that new configurations will arise and that our nation will be better able to utilize its resources to meet the needs of dependent children and their families, helping them to attain maximum levels of self-support and self-sufficiency—the stated purpose of AFDC as expressed in the Social Security Act.

JOAN CARRERA

For further information, see CHILD WELFARE SERVICES; FOOD STAMP PROGRAM; PUBLIC SOCIAL SERVICES; SOCIAL SECURITY.

References

Council of State Governments. (1949). *Federal Grants-in-Aid.* Louisville, Ky.: Author.
Harrington, M. (1981). *The Other America: Poverty in the United States.* New York: Penguin Books. (First published 1962.)
Jernigan, D. (undated). *Controlling AFDC Error Rates.* Unpublished paper, Harvard University, Cambridge, Mass.
May, E. (1980). *The Wasted Americans.* Westport, Conn.: Greenwood Press. (First published 1964.)
Office of the Federal Register. (1984). *Code of Federal Regulations,* Title 45, Pts. 200–499. Washington, D.C.: U.S. Government Printing Office.
Trattner, W. I. (1984). *From Poor Law to Welfare State.* New York: Free Press.
U.S. Department of Health and Human Services. (1983a). *Characteristics of State Plans for Aid to Families with Dependent Children under the Social Security Act, Title IVA.* Washington, D.C.: U.S. Government Printing Office.
U.S. Department of Health and Human Services. (1983b). *Quality Control Findings for Aid to Families with Dependent Children: October 1981–March 1982.* Washington, D.C.: U.S. Government Printing Office.
U.S. Department of Health and Human Services. (1985). *Compilation of the Social Security Laws.* Washington, D.C.: U.S. Government Printing Office.
U.S. Department of Health and Human Services, Office of Family Assistance. (1985). *Fiscal Year 1983 Caseload and Assistance Payments: Preliminary Data.* Unpublished data.
U.S. Department of Health and Human Services, Office of Family Assistance. (1985a). *Administrative Cost per Case for Fiscal Year 1983.* Unpublished data.
U.S. Department of Health and Human Services, Office of Family Assistance. (1985b). *IV-A Work Program Status Report.* Unpublished data.
U.S. Department of Health and Human Services, Office of Family Assistance. (1985c). *Need and Payment Amounts.* Unpublished data.

For Further Reading

Davis, L. F. (1983). *A Study of Goal Displacement.* Ann Arbor, Mich.: University Microfilms International.
Friedlander, W. A., & Apte, R. Z. (1980). *Introduction to Social Welfare.* Englewood Cliffs, N.J.: Prentice-Hall.
Ginsberg, L. H. (1983). *The Practice of Social Work in Public Welfare.* New York: Free Press.
Lurie, I. (Ed.). (1975). *Integrating Income Maintenance Programs.* New York: Academic Press.
U.S. Department of Health and Human Services. (1983). *Annual Statistical Supplement to the Social Security Bulletin.* Washington, D.C.: U.S. Government Printing Office.

ALCOHOLISM: See ALCOHOL USE AND Addiction.

ALCOHOL USE AND ADDICTION

Although the majority of adult Americans drink alcoholic beverages and approximately 10 million of them suffer from alcoholism, there has never been a universally accepted definition of the disease. Given current knowledge, the diagnosis of alcoholism is most appropriately based on physical symptoms of addiction and behavioral symptoms of loss of control. Thus, alcoholism can be defined as the repetitive consumption of alcohol without the ability consistently to control the occasion or the amount of drinking, resulting in physical or psychosocial harm to the drinker (Keller, McCormick, & Efron, 1982).

Epidemiology

A national survey of alcohol consumption conducted in 1982 consisted of personal interviews with over 5,000 randomly selected respondents from the household population of the contiguous United States (Miller & Cisin, 1983). This survey found that for all age groups, the use of alcohol was significantly less prevalent than it had been in 1979. Past-month use of alcohol was reported by 27 percent of youths aged 12–17, 68 percent of young adults aged 18–25, and 57 percent of adults over age 25. Current daily alcohol use was reported by 11 percent of the older adults and 7 percent of the younger adults.

The data on the correlates of heavy drinking provided by the 1979 national survey of adult alcohol consumption (U.S. National Institute on Alcohol Abuse and Alcoholism, (1981) indicated that drinking patterns differed by sex, religious affiliation, education, and income. Twenty percent of male drinkers and 10 percent of female drinkers reported experiencing some symptoms of alcohol dependence in the year prior to the survey. Jews evidenced low-to-moderate rates of alcohol dependence, or addiction, whereas Roman Catholics, Protestants, and those with no religious affiliation indicated relatively high proportions of heavy drinkers (defined in the 1979 survey as those who sometimes drink five or more drinks per occasion *and* who drink on at least ten occasions per month). The proportion of abstainers was high among the fundamentalist Protestant groups, but among those in this category who did drink, the rate of alcohol dependence v 's quite high. The proportion of heavy drinkers increased with education among men, but there was no difference for either sex in alcohol dependence between the lower and higher educational categories. Higher income was related to the amount of drinking only with regard to the number of abstainers, which decreased with income; the survey showed no relationship between heavy drinking and income for either sex.

Some major groups within the alcoholic population are adolescents, the elderly, women, lesbians and gay men, ethnic minorities, and skid row alcoholics.

Adolescents. Although 70 percent of high school seniors consume alcohol at least occasionally, adolescents only rarely evidence physical dependence on alcohol. Thus, it is not appropriate to apply the model of adult alcoholism to adolescents. Among the most significant antecedents of adolescent alcohol use are peer and parental drinking and approval, a predisposition toward nonconformity and independence, poor academic performance, and engaging in minor delinquent acts (Polich, Ellickson, Reuter, & Kahan, 1984). There is a growing consensus that prevention programs offer the most promising method of reducing adolescent alcohol use. Unfortunately, most treatment programs are not adapted to the special needs of adolescents (e.g., developmental issues such as the importance of peers; educational needs; greater prevalence of poly-drug use), and there are few guidelines for providing the best treatment approach for each client.

The Elderly. National survey data indicate that the proportion of heavy drinkers drops significantly for women over age 50 and for men over age 60. Nevertheless, a significant number of the elderly are alcoholic; current estimates range from 2 percent to 10 percent of the general elderly population (Schuckit, Morrissey, & O'Leary, 1978). Much higher rates of alcoholism are found among widowers, those who are single, and those living in skid row areas. Alcoholism in the elderly is generally characterized as a coping response to the stresses of aging ("late onset") or as a lifelong pattern of dependency continued into old age ("early onset"). The treatment prognosis is good for older alcoholics, particularly for those with late onset. Treatment may be more effective when delivered through facilities that utilize a multidisciplinary team to serve the aged. Alcoholism can be a significant complicating factor in the physical and psychosocial problems of the elderly, although it is unfortunately underdiagnosed.

Women. The differences between alcoholic men and alcoholic women are relevant to both diagnosis and treatment. Women generally report a later onset of heavy drinking than men but enter treatment at an earlier age. They are more likely than men to link alcoholism with a specific life crisis and are more likely to develop alcoholism secondary to an affective disorder. They more often report early family disruptions and losses and have more guilt and lower self-esteem than alcoholic men. Women report high rates of sexual and reproductive disorders both before and after the onset of alcoholism.

Little is known about optimal settings and length of treatment for alcoholic women, and data on the effectiveness of specific methods are quite limited. Most research to date has focused on programs serving primarily white, middle-class women. Anderson and Grant (1984) have reviewed the literature in relation to one subgroup that is attracting more attention nationally—pregnant alcoholic women—and have discussed the implications for social work practice.

Lesbians and Gay Men. A number of studies report that homosexuals, particularly lesbians, are more prone to alcoholism than heterosexuals (Ziebold & Mongeon, 1982). It is thought that the stress of living as part of an oppressed minority group greatly increases vulnerability to developing alcohol problems. Overt societal condemnation of homosexuality may result in low self-esteem, depression, and feelings of isolation; alcohol may be used to cope with these emotions. In addition, heavy drinking is a norm in many gay and lesbian communities, and the gay bar is often a central institution of gay life.

Many homosexual alcoholics do not reveal their sexual orientation in nongay alcohol treatment agencies, and some observers believe that only gay-oriented agencies will be able to treat this population effectively. Because it is unlikely, however, that all communities will be able to develop such specialized programs, it is critical that traditional programs begin to hire homosexual staff and provide their nongay staff with opportunities for education and attitudinal change.

Ethnic Minorities. Of all racial groups, American Indians are the most seriously affected by alcohol problems. Alcoholism is implicated in the three leading causes of death among American Indians: cirrhosis of the liver, suicide, and homicide. It should be noted, however, that alcoholism rates vary greatly between regions and between tribes in the same region. Many researchers believe that the breakdown of traditional group customs plays a major role in etiology, and most native-oriented treatment programs emphasize native culture and customs.

Recent surveys suggest that there are few differences between the drinking patterns of black and white men but show that black women are more likely to be heavy drinkers than white women. Harper (1976) reviewed national survey data and concluded that blacks tended to be group drinkers rather than solitary drinkers, suffered more violent consequences of alcohol use, and tended to be younger than white alcoholics. They were less likely to utilize treatment facilities than were whites; but, when admitted to hospitals, blacks showed stronger motivation for treatment. Unfortunately, there are relatively few facilities engaged in outreach and treatment in black communities.

The Hispanic population of the United States comprises a number of subgroups, but most of the alcoholism research has focused on Mexican Americans. The lack of homogeneity among subgroups makes generalization of the findings risky, but research indicates that the prevalence of alcoholism among Hispanic males is greater than among the general population and second only to that among American Indians. Interestingly, a larger proportion of Hispanic women and youths abstain than is true for the general population. Hispanics underutilize available alcoholism services, which often fail to address language and cultural differences.

Asian Americans, like Hispanics, comprise several different subgroups, and relatively little is known about their use of alcohol. It appears that their rates of alcoholism are low at present, but some observers have predicted that rates will increase for this group in the future in response to urbanization, cultural conflict, and changes in family structure (Gomberg, 1982). Asian Americans tend to underutilize mental health services in general, and it is likely that prevention programs are most appropriate for this group.

Westermeyer (1982) reviewed alcoholism services for ethnic populations and concluded that ethnic bias was most evident in the access to treatment; that is, poor minorities were admitted to treatment programs less frequently than was epidemiologically warranted. Although ethnically oriented programs have proven more effective in facilitating entry into treatment, there is at present no evidence that these programs have outcomes superior to those without an ethnic emphasis.

Skid Row. Those residing on skid row constitute only about 5 percent of all alcoholics, but they are the most visible subgroup and perhaps the most resistant to treatment. In general, this group is disaffiliated, unemployed, poor, and homeless males. The female population is growing in numbers but has been largely ignored in terms of services. There is a great need for emergency shelters, transitional housing, and long-term residences for alcoholics on skid row. They tend to revolve through detoxification centers with little overall benefit and rarely receive the long-term rehabilitation needed for recovery.

Physical and Psychosocial Consequences

Approximately 10 percent of adult drinkers will develop alcoholism at some point in their lives, with profound health and psychosocial consequences. The U.S. NIAAA survey (1981) reported that mortality rates for alcoholics were 2.5 times higher than for the general population, and alcoholism ranked only behind heart disease as the leading cause of death. Long-term use of substantial amounts of alcohol can result in heart muscle disease, high blood pressure, hepatitis, cirrhosis, lesions of the stomach, and chronic pancreatitis. Alcoholism results in the loss of brain cells, and studies report brain atrophy in anywhere from 50 percent to 100 percent of alcoholics. Heavy alcohol intake contributes to nutritional deficiency and often results in lowered testosterone in males. Heavy drinking is also related to increased risk of cancer of the mouth, pharynx, larynx, and esophagus. Heavy drinking during pregnancy can result in harm to the fetus ranging from mild physical and behavioral deficits to the fetal alcohol syndrome (FAS). Alcohol is involved in the majority of fatal traffic accidents and deaths from falling, fires, and drowning. The risk of suicide among alcoholics is 30 times greater than in the general population; accidental lethal overdoses frequently occur when alcohol is combined with other drugs.

It is estimated that 25 percent of all families in the United States will be affected by alcoholism at some time. Alcoholism increases the likelihood of family violence, incest, and divorce. More than 12 million children live in alcoholic families, and they are at a greatly increased risk of developing alcoholism themselves, as well as eating disorders and delinquent behavior.

Theories of Etiology

The etiology of alcoholism is unknown, and research efforts have failed to show a definite, single cause of the disease. It is probable, in fact, that there is no single cause and that various factors interact to produce the disorder. The major theories of etiology can be categorized as physiological, psychological, and sociological.

Physiological Theories. Genetic and biophysiological theories of alcoholism rest on the assumption that alcoholics are constitutionally predisposed to develop physical dependence on alcohol. It is well known that much higher rates of alcoholism exist among the relatives of alcoholics than in the general population, and a number of studies of twins and adoptees support the probability of a strong genetic component in alcoholism. For example, Kaij found that the rate of concordance for alcoholism in identical twins was 54 percent whereas the rate for same-sex fraternal twins was 28 percent (cited in Murray & Stabenau, 1982). Children of alcoholics adopted close to birth and raised without knowledge of their biological parents have high rates of alcoholism, whereas sons of nonalcoholics reared by alcoholics have low rates of alcoholism (Goodwin, 1976). The evidence supporting a genetic influence is impressive, but the cause-and-effect relationship remains unclear. It has not been possible so far to distinguish between metabolic effects caused by genetic factors and those resulting from alcohol consumption itself.

Psychological Theories. The major psychological theories of etiology can be categorized as personality, transactional, psychodynamic, and learning theories. As is the case with physiological theories, research in this area has not resolved the issue of cause and effect. Psychological factors can be viewed as the cause or consequence of alcoholism.

Personality Theory. This theory assumes that there are certain personality traits that predispose an individual to alcoholism. The term "alcoholic personality" is often used to describe the client who is immature, dependent, impulsive, and easily frustrated. There is some research support for this description, but these traits can just as easily be attributed to the effects of alcoholism. There is not a prealcoholic personality structure per se, and experimental studies have been unable to distinguish the personality traits of alcoholics consistently from those of the general population.

Transactional Theory. Some theorists, utilizing the concepts of transactional analysis, view alcoholism not as a disease but rather as a "game" with an interpersonal "payoff" (Steiner, 1971). This theory is attractive to family practitioners because it highlights the adaptive consequences of alcoholism and the enabling behaviors of family members. Although it is important to address family transactions that develop in response to alcoholism, there is no empirical support for the notion that these "games" lead to addiction.

Psychodynamic Theory. According to this theory, childhood deprivation or overindulgence leads to excessive unconscious needs for nurturance. When these dependency needs cannot be met by others, the individual becomes anxious and develops compensatory needs for power and control. Alcohol serves to reduce the anxiety and create a false sense of power and grandiosity. When sober, however, the individual is again overwhelmed with feelings of failure and anxiety, which motivate continued drinking. The major shortcoming of this theory is that although early childhood deprivation or overindulgence may increase vulnerability to the development of alcoholism, these experiences are not specific to alcoholism. In fact, they are commonly reported by adults with a variety of psychosocial problems.

Learning Theory. This theory assumes that alcohol ingestion results in a decrease in anxiety or tension and is thus positively reinforced. This learned response to coping with stress continues until physical dependence develops, at which point withdrawal symptoms become the stimuli for drinking. This theory is helpful in treatment planning because it addresses the adaptive consequences of drinking. On the other hand, the simple tension-reduction hypothesis has not been supported empirically; it may be more relevant in treatment to address various types of social reinforcement for excessive drinking.

Sociological Theories. Sociologists generally explain the etiology of alcoholism by applying sociocultural, socialization, and social deviance theories. White (1982) reviewed these theories and proposed a socioenvironmental model of alcoholism attempting to integrate them. According to this model, the individual likely to become an alcoholic experiences a great deal of stress, has learned that alcohol relieves stress and uses it for this purpose, and does not belong to a group that regulates his or her behavior.

As the diverse theoretical hypotheses on the etiology of alcoholism have thus far failed to demonstrate an unequivocal, single cause of the disease, it seems appropriate at this time to view alcoholism as the final product of the interaction of a number of complex variables. In any particular individual, one or more of these etiological variables may predominate.

Development of Alcoholism

All alcoholic beverages contain ethanol, which is a central nervous system depressant. One-half ounce of ethanol is contained in 1 ounce of 100 proof liquor, 12 ounces of beer, or 4 ounces of wine. Various factors influence the onset and intensity of alcohol's effects, and time is the major factor in the removal of alcohol from the body. Continued use of alcohol produces tolerance for its physiological effects; more and more must be consumed to produce the desired result. The increase in dosage over time produces physical dependence, after which withdrawal can be severe or even fatal. When combined with other central nervous system depressants, such as minor tranquilizers, alcohol exhibits synergism—that is, a greater depressant effect is produced than if the two drugs were taken singly and their effects added together.

The development of alcohol addiction

can be briefly summarized as follows. The susceptible individual experiences gratification from alcohol consumption, ingestion becomes more frequent, psychological dependence develops, and ingestion continues to increase until tolerance and physical dependence develop. At this point, withdrawal symptoms act to maintain the alcoholic drinking. Although this is the essence of the addiction process, it should be noted that most alcoholics experience spontaneous periods of abstinence alternating with periods of prolonged drinking.

Diagnosis of Alcoholism

It is estimated that Alcoholics Anonymous (AA) and various treatment agencies reach only about 15 percent of the alcoholic population. A general failure to detect alcoholics is undoubtedly related to lack of knowledge about the disease, negative attitudes toward alcoholics, treatment of alcoholism as a symptom rather than as a disease, and agency barriers to effectively involving the alcoholic in treatment (Googins, 1984). For any number of reasons, alcoholism is frequently underdiagnosed and misdiagnosed by practitioners in social service agencies, resulting in inappropriate and ineffective treatment.

Because most social service agencies have a significant number of alcoholics among their clientele, social workers are in a unique position for prevention and early intervention. It is critical that practitioners learn to detect alcoholism and treat or appropriately refer clients with alcohol-related problems. In making an assessment of any presenting problem, it is important for the worker to ask questions regarding the client's drinking history and problems associated with drinking. An adequate history will include information on alcohol use, current social relationships, and family and developmental issues.

In the area of alcohol use, workers need to explore the physical and psychosocial problems associated with drinking; it is particularly important to assess the extent of tolerance and withdrawal symptomatology accompanying physical dependence. It is also necessary to evaluate the psychosocial antecedents and consequences of drinking, pattern of drinking, history of alcohol use without problems, history of attempts to reduce or stop drinking, and reasons for seeking help at this particular time.

In the area of current social circumstances, information should be gathered about relationships with friends and family, employment and economic status, and relevant sociocultural factors. Finally, one should explore early family relationships and attitudes about drinking, as well as a personal or family history of major depression, mania, or sociopathy. It is also important to assess the drinking patterns, attitudes, and enabling behaviors of significant others. Patterns of handling stress and any crisis event associated with problem drinking should also be evaluated.

Types of Alcoholism

The major types of alcoholism are classified as primary, secondary, and reactive. *Primary alcoholism* appears to be a genetically influenced disease, and there is frequently a family history of alcoholism (Murray & Stabenau, 1982). The onset occurs typically between ages 25 and 35 and is not related to a life crisis. There is no preexisting psychiatric disorder. The primary alcoholic has high tolerance and drinks in response to physiological withdrawal symptoms. He or she has a strong compulsion to drink and puts drinking over almost all other activities. It has been found that 61 percent of female and 73 percent of male inpatients meet the criteria for primary alcoholism (Winokur et al., 1970).

The client with *secondary alcoholism* has a history of a major psychiatric disorder antedating the first significant life problem related to alcohol. The underlying psychiatric problem is most commonly an affective disorder (unipolar or bipolar) or antisocial personality disorder. The client with a primary unipolar affective disorder has no personal or family history of mania but has experienced at least one depressive episode before the onset of alcoholism. The episode typically occurs when the client is in his or her thirties or forties and is seen in approximately 25 percent of alcoholic female and 3 percent of alcoholic male inpatients (Winokur et al., 1970).

The client with a primary bipolar affective disorder usually has a personal or family history of mania, and the onset of symptoms occurs in the twenties or thirties. This disorder is characterized by euphoria, hyperactivity, and sometimes delusions and hallucinations. The manic symptoms often alternate with depressive symptoms in one continuous episode. As in the case of unipolar affective disorder, these symptoms occur before the onset of alcoholism.

Clients with a primary antisocial personality disorder demonstrate antisocial problems with schools, peers, police, and family before age 15 and prior to the first major alcohol problem. Approximately 20 percent of men and 5 percent of women entering alcohol treatment facilities have a preexisting antisocial personality disorder and secondary alcoholism (Schuckit, 1973).

Reactive alcoholism is seen in clients who initiate heavy or excessive drinking shortly after experiencing a severe life crisis. They do not have a preexisting psychiatric disorder and usually have a history of using alcohol without problems. Although excessive drinking may be self-limiting in this case, it can also progress to addiction in some clients.

Implications for Treatment

The purpose of making a diagnosis is not to label but to select the most appropriate treatment for each client. The primary alcoholic should be offered detoxification services followed by outpatient counseling or a brief inpatient stay. With several days to several weeks of abstinence, symptoms of alcohol-induced depression will lift without any medication. The use of minor tranquilizers and sedatives beyond detoxification is always contraindicated in the treatment of the primary alcoholic. Clients with secondary alcoholism should be treated, after detoxification, for their primary disorder. Unlike primary alcoholics, these clients will continue to show symptoms of affective disorder after several weeks of abstinence. With drug treatment for the primary disorder, the secondary alcoholism usually lessens or disappears. Clients with reactive alcoholism should be offered crisis intervention followed by supportive treatment that addresses resolution of the loss accompanying the life crisis.

As soon as the diagnosis is clear, it should be shared with the client. The supporting evidence for the diagnosis and the recommended treatment plan need to be discussed in an objective, nonpunitive manner.

Significant others should be included early in the treatment process; regardless of their role in formal treatment, they should be encouraged to attend Al-Anon or Ala-Teen.

Treatment Models

The most widely used treatment approaches to alcoholism include individual psychodynamic therapy, group therapy, family therapy, drug treatment, Alcoholics Anonymous (AA), and behavior modification. These models reflect the various theories of alcoholism etiology; all can be effective when appropriately applied to the individual needs of clients.

Individual Therapy. Zimberg (1982) is one of the leading advocates of individual psychotherapy for alcoholism. Recognizing that psychoanalytic psychotherapy has been unsuccessful with alcoholics because uncovering techniques frequently lead to anxiety and resumption of drinking, he proposes a modified psychodynamic approach to working with these clients. Treatment consists of several stages, with the stance that all drinking must be terminated if therapy is to be effective. In Stage I, the client is detoxified and encouraged to avoid stressful situations and to attend AA meetings. The alcoholic's predominant defenses of denial, projection, and rationalization are not interpreted or confronted in this stage but are instead redirected toward the achievement of sobriety. In Stage II, control becomes internalized and sobriety continues to be positively reinforced through supportive therapy. Stage III represents conflict resolution and is achieved through insight. Zimberg points out that termination can occur after Stage II and that few alcoholics have the motivation or need to complete Stage III.

Group Therapy. Group therapy is currently the most widely practiced modality of treatment with alcoholics. Groups are frequently utilized for financial reasons, but they are particularly helpful to alcoholic clients who are lonely, moderately anxious, or depressed, and who have a poor self-image. Alcoholics frequently respond more favorably to confrontation by their peers and are better able to learn new patterns of relationships in a group. Anderson (1983) has reviewed the literature on group therapy in alcoholism.

Family Therapy. Most alcoholics continue to live in intact families. The etiology of alcoholism may be physiological, psychological, or social; but once the pattern of addiction develops, the family adapts to it to maintain its equilibrium. There is no single alcoholic family personality, but families coping with alcoholism do manifest some characteristic patterns of functioning. In particular, boundaries, communication, role fulfillment, and ritual life become patterned so as to preserve family homeostasis.

The effective family therapist focuses on both the disease of alcoholism and the family's adaptation to it. Once the drinking behavior has been modified, treatment goals center on improving the functioning of the entire family system. Anderson and Henderson (1983) have reviewed various treatment models and specific techniques utilized in family therapy with alcoholics. Although well-designed studies of family therapy are lacking, there is considerable clinical consensus that this modality reduces the incidence of premature dropouts and promotes structural change (Kaufman, 1981).

Drug Treatment. Zimberg (1982) has summarized the use of Antabuse, minor tranquilizers, sedatives, major tranquilizers, and antidepressants in the treatment of alcoholism. Antabuse is a deterrent drug that produces flushing, nausea, vomiting, and anxiety when alcohol is consumed. It is most effective with the motivated alcoholic as an aid to sobriety during the early stage of treatment. Its use is contraindicated in clients with Organic Brain Syndrome, psychosis, cardiovascular disease, cerebral insufficiency, or liver or kidney failure, and with pregnant women.

Minor tranquilizers (for example, Librium and Valium) and sedatives (such as Dalmane and Doriden) are cross-tolerant with alcohol (that is, the organism tolerant to one of these drugs is tolerant to all), and are contraindicated with alcoholics beyond detoxification. Major tranquilizers (for example, Thorazine, Mellaril, and Haldol) are contraindicated in primary alcoholism but are indicated after abstinence is obtained, when alcoholism is secondary to a psychotic disorder. Tricyclic antidepressants (such as Tofranil and Elavil) are contraindicated in primary alcoholism but are the treatment of choice when alcoholism is secondary to unipolar affective disorder. Lithium is the appropriate treatment when alcoholism is secondary to bipolar affective disorder.

Alcoholics Anonymous. AA is a leaderless self-help group based on the assumption that alcoholism is a disease and recovery involves complete abstinence. The relationship between AA and agency treatment programs is becoming increasingly supportive, and many social workers view AA as an important adjunct to formal treatment. AA's 1980 membership survey indicated that about half its newcomers remain more than three months, and 41 percent with less than one year of sobriety make it through the next year without drinking. Al-Anon and Ala-Teen, which were inspired by but are not part of AA, educate the families of alcoholics about their enabling behaviors that serve to maintain and reinforce the alcoholics' drinking; the goals of these organizations are quite compatible with family systems theory in that they provide support for emotional disengagement from the alcoholic until drinking behavior is modified.

Behavior Modification. The major techniques of this model can be conceptualized as aversive, operant, and cognitive-behavior techniques. Aversive conditioning involves pairing the sight, smell, and taste of alcohol with an unpleasant stimulus, such as an electric shock, a nausea-inducing chemical, or an aversive image. At the present time, aversive conditioning alone has not been shown to be an effective treatment for alcoholism. Of the available techniques, chemical aversion appears to be the most effective.

Operant conditioning (contingency management) attempts to reduce drinking by manipulating its consequences. It has been demonstrated, for example, that alcoholics can voluntarily control their drinking in order to improve their living situation in a structured setting. The ability of the addicted alcoholic to control drinking outside the institution, however, remains questionable.

Perhaps the most effective behavioral approach is the cognitive-behavioral model (Marlatt, 1979). This approach is based on the social-learning model that views alcoholism as a learned behavior that can be modified through various skill-training procedures. These include the teaching of coping skills and responsible drinking skills, and the replacement of drinking with some form of "positive addiction" (for example, jogging or meditation).

Alcoholics are treated in general hospitals, emergency rooms, mental hospitals, alcoholism rehabilitation centers, aversion conditioning hospitals, outpatient clinics, halfway houses, and employment-based programs. Within these settings, they are offered a variety of treatment modalities and techniques. A comprehensive review of the differential effectiveness of various settings and modalities is beyond the scope of the present article; however, there is substantial research evidence of the value of matching subgroups of alcoholics with the most appropriate facilities and methods. Emrick (1982) has comprehensively reviewed the program effectiveness literature and has concluded that outpatient treatment is preferable to inpatient treatment for the socially integrated client; active aftercare is necessary for all clients; and long-term residential, nonhospital treatment should be considered for the socially deteriorated client. No firm conclusions can be drawn about the relative effectiveness of marital or group therapy versus individual therapy.

Social Policy Issues

Social policy in the area of alcohol use has vacillated between harsh regulation (prohibition) and extreme permissiveness; unfortunately, data are lacking on the effectiveness of most social policies pursued to date. Mandell (1982) discussed five models of social control and their implications for social policy. Pattison (1982) noted that social policies have shifted (with societal attitudes) from punitive to therapeutic directions, from policies emphasizing public drinking to those emphasizing treatment of the sick alcoholic. He argued that future social policy must address the alcohol use of the entire society, not just the alcoholic, and that social sanctions against dyssocial drinking behavior should be increased. He noted that overpermissive policy promotes rising consumption, which ultimately increases the number of people at risk for alcohol-related problems.

There is some evidence that social policy is becoming less permissive. For example, some states are enacting laws dealing with host and bartender responsibility, police campaigns against drunk driving have been intensified, and organizations such as Mothers Against Drunk Driving (MADD) and Students Against Drunk Driving (SADD) have become increasingly visible and effective.

Contemporary Debates and Issues

A number of unresolved issues in the alcoholism field have been mentioned here. Perhaps the most debated are the definition of alcoholism, the related issue of controlled drinking, and the relative efficacy of primary prevention versus various treatment approaches.

Controversy continues about the "disease concept" of alcoholism and the relative role of psychological and sociological factors in its etiology. Although there is persuasive evidence that genetic factors play a significant role in primary alcoholism, the mechanism of transmission remains unclear, and psychosocial variables clearly play important roles in the development of secondary and reactive alcoholism and in the maintenance of all types of alcoholism.

The controversy over appropriate treatment goals, that is, controlled drinking versus abstinence, has raged in the alcoholism literature for the past 25 years. The disease concept of alcoholism adopted by AA emphasizes permanent loss of control over drinking and views abstinence as the only ethical treatment goal. Advocates of controlled drinking, on the other hand, do not view all problem drinkers as addicted primary alcoholics who must attain lifelong abstinence. The literature on controlled drinking has been comprehensively reviewed by Miller (1983), who concluded that moderation-oriented approaches are as effective as abstinence-oriented methods in treating less dependent problem drinkers. Controlled-drinking approaches are clearly most effective with younger nonaddicted drinkers and least effective with older clients with symptoms of alcohol addiction. In essence, in spite of the continuing debate, there appears to be agreement in the field that abstinence is the most appropriate goal for addicted primary alcoholics. It is likely that treatment in the future will make better use of differential diagnosis to utilize abstinence and moderation methods in complementary ways.

Finally, public and professional opinion continues to be polarized on the most effective approach to prevention of alcohol-related problems. Some believe that priority should be given to early identification and treatment of alcohol-dependent individuals, while others favor a focus on education and limitation of alcohol availability aimed at the entire citizenry. It seems clear that treatment alone, since it currently addresses only a small percentage of the alcohol-impaired population, is unlikely to have much of an impact on the overall alcohol problem in society. There is a growing demand for more attention to primary prevention approaches in the field. Traditionally, most social work effort has gone into direct intervention with individuals and families, but there is increasing interest in sound policy development as an approach to prevention. It is therefore incumbent upon the profession to prepare not only clinicians but also those capable of beginning the arduous task of developing a comprehensive preventive strategy.

SANDRA C. ANDERSON

For further information, see MUTUAL HELP GROUPS.

References

Alcoholics Anonymous. (1980). *1980 Survey Analysis.* New York: Author.

Anderson, S. C. (1983). "Group Therapy with Alcoholic Clients: A Review." In B. Stimmel (Ed.), *Current Controversies in Alcoholism.* New York: Haworth Press.

Anderson, S. C., & Grant, J. F. (1984). "Pregnant Women and Alcohol: Implications for Social Work." *Social Casework, 65*(1), 3–10.

Anderson, S. C., & Henderson, D. C. (1983). "Family Therapy in the Treatment of Alcoholism." *Social Work in Health Care, 8*(4), 79–94.

Emrick, C. D. (1982). "Evaluation of Alcoholism Psychotherapy Models." In E. M. Pattison & E. Kaufman (Eds.), *Encyclopedic Handbook of Alcoholism.* New York: Gardner Press.

Gomberg, E. (1982). "Special Populations." In E. Gomberg, H. White, & J. Carpenter (Eds.), *Alcohol, Science, and Society Revisited* (pp. 337–354). Ann Arbor: University of Michigan Press.

Goodwin, D. (1976). *Is Alcoholism Hereditary?* New York: Oxford University Press.

Googins, B. (1984). "Avoidance of the Alcoholic Client." *Social Work, 29*(2), 161–166.

Harper, F. (Ed.). (1976). *Alcohol Abuse and Black America.* Alexandria, Va.: Douglass.

Kaufman, E. (1981). "Family Therapy: A Treatment Approach with Substance Abusers." In J. H. Lewinson & P. Ruiz (Eds.), *Substance Abuse: Clinical Problems and Perspectives.* Baltimore: Williams & Wilkins.

Keller, M., McCormick, M., & Efron, V. (1982). *A Dictionary of Words about Alcohol.* New Brunswick, N.J.: Rutgers Center of Alcohol Studies.

Mandell, W. (1982). "Preventing Alcohol-Related Problems and Dependencies through Information and Education Programs." In E. M. Pattison & E. Kaufman (Eds.), *Encyclopedic Handbook of Alcoholism.* New York: Gardner Press.

Marlatt, G. A. (1979). "Alcohol Use and Problem Drinking: A Cognitive-Behavioral Analysis." In P. Kendall & S. Hollon (Eds.), *Cognitive-Behavioral Interventions: Theory, Research, and Procedures.* New York: Academic Press.

Miller, J. D., & Cisin, I. H.(1983). *Highlights from the National Survey on Drug Abuse: 1982.* Rockville, Md.: National Institute on Drug Abuse.

Miller, W. R. (1983). "Controlled Drinking: A History and a Critical Review." *Journal of Studies on Alcohol, 44*(1), 68–83.

Murray, R., & Stabenau, J. (1982). "Genetic Factors in Alcoholism Predisposition." In E. M. Pattison & E. Kaufman (Eds.), *Encyclopedic Handbook of Alcoholism.* New York: Gardner Press.

Pattison, E. M. (1982). "Alcohol Use: Social Policy." In E. M. Pattison & E. Kaufman (Eds.), *Encyclopedic Handbook of Alcoholism.* New York: Gardner Press.

Polich, J. M., et al. (1984). *Strategies for Controlling Adolescent Drug Use.* Santa Monica, Calif.: Rand Corporation.

Schuckit, M. A. (1973). "Alcoholism and Sociopathy—Diagnostic Confusion." *Quarterly Journal of Studies on Alcohol, 34*(1), 157–164.

Schuckit, M., Morrissey, E., & O'Leary, M. (1978). "Alcohol Problems in Elderly Men and Women." *Addictive Diseases: An International Journal, 3*(3), 405–416.

Steiner, C. M. (1971). *Games Alcoholics Play.* New York: Ballantine Books.

U.S. National Institute on Alcohol Abuse and Alcoholism. (1981). *Alcohol and Health: Fourth Special Report to the Congress.* Washington, D.C.: U.S. Government Printing Office.

Westermeyer, J. (1982). "Alcoholism and Services for Ethnic Populations." In E. M. Pattison & E. Kaufman (Eds.), *Encyclopedic Handbook of Alcoholism.* New York: Gardner Press.

White, H. R. (1982). "Sociological Theories of the

Etiology of Alcoholism." In E. L. Gomberg, H. R. White, & J. A. Carpenter (Eds.), *Alcohol, Science and Society Revisited*. Ann Arbor: University of Michigan Press.

Winokur, G., et al. (1970). "Alcoholism III. Diagnosis and Familial Psychiatric Illness in 259 Alcoholic Probands." *Archives of General Psychiatry, 23*(8), 104–111.

Ziebold, T., & Mongeon, J. (Eds.). (1982). *Alcoholism and Homosexuality*. New York: Haworth Press.

Zimberg, S. (1982). *The Clinical Management of Alcoholism*. New York: Brunner/Mazel.

ALIENS. See IMMIGRANTS AND UNDOCUMENTED ALIENS.

ALTERNATIVE FAMILIES. See FAMILY: CONTEMPORARY PATTERNS.

ALTMEYER, ARTHUR J. See biographical section.

AMERICAN INDIANS AND ALASKA NATIVES

What is viewed as the American Indian population is composed of Indians, Eskimos, and Aleuts. Indians include all tribes in the lower 48 states and the Athabascans of eastern Alaska. Athabascans, Eskimos, and Aleuts constitute the Alaska Natives population. These distinctions result from aboriginal differences and the inclusion of Alaska into the Union in 1959.

Population

From 1970 to 1980, the American Indian population increased from 574,000 to 1,366,676—an increase of 72 percent. This large increase was the result of a higher birthrate and a lower infant mortality rate. In addition, as the U.S. Bureau of the Census (1984, p. 2) noted, there were other factors:

. . . improvements in census procedures, including modified enumeration procedures on American Indian reservations . . . the use of self-identification to obtain the race of respondents in all areas of the country [and] a greater frequency in 1980 than in 1970 for individuals, especially those of mixed Indian and non-Indian descent, to report their race as Indian.

The U.S. Bureau of the Census (1984) also reported that in 1980 Alaska Natives constituted 16 percent of the population of Alaska and numbered 64,103. Of that number, 21,869 were American Indians (including Athabascans), 34,144 were Eskimos, and 8,090 Aleuts. The largest number of Alaska Natives (9,247) resided in the Bethel area, followed by those in the Anchorage area (8,953) and in the Nome area (5,174). According to the bureau's report (1984):

Of the 39,301 Alaska Natives living in the 209 Alaska Native villages, Eskimos were the largest group, 26,574, accounting for about 68 percent of the total Alaska population. About one-fifth, or 8,023, were American Indians and approximately 12 percent, or 4,704, were Aleuts. (Table 6, p. 29)

. . . . .

Of the 209 Alaska Native villages, only 3— Barrow, Bethel, and Kotzebue—had more than 1,000 Alaska Natives. Seven villages which had between 500 and 1,000 Alaska Native residents were Dillingham, Emmonak, Hoonah, Hooper Bay, Mountain Village, Selawik, and Unalakleet. (Tables 1 and 6, pp. 14, 29)

In the lower 48 states in 1980, one-fourth of the American Indian population (339,836) lived on 278 federal and state reservations; 49 percent of the people on these reservations were American Indians. As a consequence of the displacement policies of the federal government, including the Dawes Act, large sections of land within the exterior boundaries of various reservations are owned or leased by non-Indians. Among the non-Indian populations resident on reservations are non-Indian spouses, ranchers, farmers, merchants, teachers, health care professionals, and other governmental officials.

Most reservations had fewer than 1,000 American Indians, with the exception of the Navajo reservation, which had more than 100,000 American Indians. The Navajo Nation, which numbers about 150,000, is the largest tribe in the United States. In 1980, the

Navajo reservation in Arizona, New Mexico, and Utah contained 104,978 American Indians; this figure represents 30.9 percent of the total American Indian population on reservations and 21.5 percent of the total American Indian population (U.S. Bureau of the Census, 1984). Numerous tribes number in the several thousands, while the smallest tribes number less than 200.

In 1980, American Indians and Alaska Natives lived in the following areas: reservations, 24 percent; historic areas of Oklahoma (including urbanized areas), 8 percent; Alaska Native villages, 3 percent; tribal trust lands, 2 percent; and the remainder of the United States, 63 percent (Indian Health Service, 1985). The states with 100,000 or more American Indians and Alaska Natives were, in rank order, California, Arizona, New Mexico, and Oklahoma. Nine states had American Indian populations of 50,000 to 99,999: Alaska, Washington, Montana, South Dakota, Minnesota, Wisconsin, Michigan, New York, and North Carolina. Most of the American Indian population on and off the reservations still reside in the West. As of 1980, approximately 330,000 American Indians lived in central cities, 260,000 lived in the urban fringe, and 700,000 lived in rural areas, 26,802 of whom lived on farms.

The median age of American Indians was 24.0 years. The median age of those in the central cities and on farms was 24.8 years; of residents of the urban fringe, 25.1 years; and of the total rural population (including farm residents), 21.9 years.

Labor Force Participation

Of the 1,022,411 American Indians who were 16 years or older in 1980, 598,626 were in the labor force—able to work (14,147 in the armed forces and 584,479 in the civilian labor force) with 507,614 employed and 76,865 unemployed.

Of the 423,785 American Indians who were not in the labor force, 13,877 men and 4,266 women were inmates of institutions. The total number of American Indian women in the labor force was 252,207 (1,299 in the armed forces and 250,908 in the civilian labor force). Of the women in the civilian labor force, 220,927 were employed and 29,981 were unemployed; 272,467 American Indian women were not in the labor force.

Of the 118,162 unmarried women with children under 6 years, 53,474 were in the labor force. Of the 114,383 unmarried women with children 6–17 years, 67,477 were in the labor force. American Indian women over 16 years with a husband present numbered 256,562; 123,505 of them were in the labor force. Of this group, women with children under age 6 numbered 87,293, of whom 38,897 were in the labor force, while 45,582 of the 87,335 women with children 6–17 years were in the labor force. Of the 497,737 American Indian males aged 16 and over in the labor force, 286,687 were employed and 46,864 were unemployed; 151,318 were not in the labor force.

Of the reported 507,614 employed persons 16 years and over, private wage and salary workers numbered 336,463, 4,771 of whom were employees of their own corporations. Individuals employed by the federal government numbered 55,009; by the state governments, 30,794; and by local governments (including tribal governments), 59,121. Self-employed workers numbered 24,241, of whom 3,823 were in agriculture. Of the 1,986 unpaid family members, 509 were in agriculture (U.S. Bureau of the Census, 1980, Table 124). Of all the employed workers in the labor force, approximately 40 percent were in white-collar occupations. The breakdown of occupations is as follows: 81,840, in managerial and professional specialty occupations; 122,676, in technical, sales, and administrative support occupations; 91,813, in service occupations; 18,614, in farming, forestry, and fishing occupations; 76,107, in precision production, craft, and repair; and 116,564, in operator, fabricator, and laborer occupations.

In 1980, the mean income of 442,898 American Indian households was $15,418. Those households that averaged $5,000 or less numbered 91,786, or about 21 percent, while those earning $50,000 or more numbered 9,017, or approximately 2 percent of the population.

Health Problems

The health care problems of American Indians and Alaska Natives are related to their lifestyles and the severely high levels of stress that characterize their communities. The four leading causes of death among Indians and Alaska Natives are heart disease, accidents, cancer, and chronic liver disease and cirrhosis (Indian Health Service, 1985). The incidence of hypertension and diabetes in this population is high. Of all the American Indian and Alaska Native people who died during 1980–82, 37 percent were under 45 years compared to 12 percent of the general population. Alcohol abuse plays a prominent role in Indian deaths. The age-specific death rate from alcoholism in 1980–82 for Indian men in all age groups was higher than that for Indian women. The rate for men aged 35–74 ranged from 95 to 120 deaths per 100,000 people, compared to 53 to 72 deaths per 100,000 people for Indian women in the same age range.

The population is fast growing. The birthrate of Indians for 1981 of 27.9 births per 1,000 population was over 75 percent greater than the 1981 birthrate of 15.8 for the general population. In spite of the severe stresses in these communities, the infant mortality rate dropped from 24.7 infant deaths per 1,000 live births in 1969–71 to 11.9 in 1980–82—a decrease of 52 percent. The rate is currently equal to that of the general population. These rates resulted from a heavy concentration on prenatal services by Indian Health Service and tribal field health workers. Young children and the elderly receive special health care in all tribes. However, services to older children, adolescents, and young adults are poorly developed, and these groups are the most underserved (Indian Health Service, 1985).

Historical Background

Many explanations are advanced about how the Indians got to America but each tribe has its own explanation of how it came to be a people (the Indian names of the tribes invariably translate as "the people"). Indian people view identification from the perspective of origin and one's place in the world. Estimates of the number of Indians who were living in the territory that is now the United States when Columbus arrived in the Caribbean range from 900,000 to 12,000,000 (Dobyns, 1976; Fey & McNickle, 1970; Martin, 1978). Enumerating Indians was difficult in early times, but by 1880, the census reported 250,000 remaining Indians. In 1950, Tax (as cited in Fey & McNickle, 1970, pp. 9–12) estimated a population of 571,824. In 1960, the Bureau of the Census reported a population of 523,591. As Fey and McNickle (1970, p. 12) described:

> In 1910, the Bureau of Indian Affairs estimated that there were 236,000 Indians who . . . resided in and considered themselves part of tribal communities, settlements, or reservations. If this Bureau figure can be accepted as accurate (and probably it is a minimum figure), then in forty years Indians in this category have increased nearly *80 per cent.* Professor Sol Tax concludes: "Thus we cannot even say that while the number of Indians is increasing they are simply whites who still identify as Indians. Indians living in societies of Indians are greatly increasing in numbers" [emphasis added].

The contemporary increase in population of 72 percent and the fact that 63 percent of the current population does not live on reservations or trust lands highlights and illuminates the complexity of the Indian population met by social workers.

The aboriginal population, as is true today, was concentrated most heavily in the West. The greatest concentration was in what is now California with 43.3 inhabitants per 100 sq km and 28.3 inhabitants in the Northwest coast area extending into Alaska. The Southwest ranked third, with 10.7 inhabitants per 100 sq km, while the eastern shore numbered 6.95 for the same area and the Arctic coast 4.02 (Fey & McNickle, 1970).

Today, about 300 tribes remain from an estimated 1,000 at the time of Columbus. They range in size from the 150,000-member Navajo Nation and its large sectional land base to the Shoalwater Bay Tribe in western Washington with less than 200 members and a land base of only 335 acres.

Tribes derive their differences from their origins and the geographic areas in which they emerged as a people. The first people of any tribe brought with them the character and strength of beings from the other world from which they came; these beings played a deciding role in the philosophical interpretations that the people developed about their life and its meaning. In addition, families in tribes elaborated on the primary influences of the tribe and developed a history of their specific family. It is these combined influences or interpretations that were the basis of the specific art and material as well as spiritual culture of the tribes. The ritual costume, the clay pot, and the totem pole are all observable expressions of basic interpretations of the tribe's history. Thus, because of its geography and ecology, a southwestern desert tribe developed a different view of what has been with them through time than did a northwestern tribe whose physical world is filled with abundant vegetation. Although all tribes are intertwined in a philosophical mosaic and adhere to the presence of a Creator, each tribe has its specific belief system developed from tribal and familial history.

Nationhood. The relationship of Indians with the federal government grew out of a complex situation of domination of the new world by France, Spain, England, Holland, and Sweden. In the early days of contact, all these countries entered into agreements or treaties with Indians in the areas that they occupied. It was not until the end of the 18th century that "the settler offspring of the British" who referred to themselves as Americans emerged as the dominant force in the east; Spain maintained dominance in the west.

The domination of the country by the Americans resulted in the annihilation of a vast number of Indian people from disease, warfare, and displacement. Such slogans as, "The only good Indian is a dead Indian" depicted the attitudes and behavior of the dominant society during the 19th century. The vast destruction of Indian life during that period led to its being labeled the "extermination period."

The present situation of tribes developed from their relationship with the federal government and its executive, legislative, and judicial actions. The issues through time have been *nationhood,* which includes the right to maintain territorial boundaries without intrusion, and *self-government,* which recognizes the sovereign right of the people to govern themselves. Although there have been continuous efforts to nullify the right of tribes to self-government, this right was upheld and clarified by the Supreme Court decisions in *Cherokee* v. *Georgia* (1831) and *Worcester* v. *Georgia* (1832). The first case dealt with the nature of Indian land title and concluded that Indians had a possessory right in the land, while the United States, as successor to Great Britain's claims as well as to claims of other European nations, had the

ultimate legal title (Fey & McNickle, 1970). The second decision "examined the question whether an Indian tribe was in fact a foreign state competent to bring action against one of the United States in federal court" (Fey & McNickle, 1970, p. 58). It was determined that tribes did not have this status because they did not not meet the contextual definition of "foreign." The opinion rendered in this case further examined the status of an Indian tribe and held that

> The Indian nations had always been considered as distinct, independent, political communities, retaining their original natural rights . . . the settled doctrine of the law of nations is, that a weaker power does not surrender its independence—its right to self-government— by associating with a stronger, and taking its protection. (Fey & McNickle, 1970, p. 58)

It is from this decision that the denomination of Indian tribes as "domestic dependent nations" was fabricated.

In 1890, 60 years after these decisions were rendered, the last massacre of Indians, at Wounded Knee, South Dakota, occurred. This massacre marked the final removal of Indians from their aboriginal homelands to reservations, which resulted from a federal policy of the early 1800s that sought to contain Indians to allow for greater westward expansion. The dislocation experiences were abrupt; many people were forced to move to distant and ecologically foreign environments where they could no longer visit their shrines and sacred places or gather customary foods and medicines.

In 1887, the General Allotment Act authorized the president of the United States when in his opinion

> . . . any reservation or any part thereof of such Indians is advantageous for agricultural and grazing purposes, to cause said reservation, or any part thereof, to be surveyed, or resurveyed if necessary, and to allot the lands in said reservation in severalty to any Indian located thereon . . . . (Spicer, 1969, p. 200)

This action was designed to promote further western expansion by vesting ownership of tribal lands in the individual who was then free to sell the property and providing for the purchase of surplus lands by the federal government after the individual Indian allotments had been made. The act proved successful: in 1887, approximately 140,000,000 acres remained in Indian ownership but in 1922, 45 years later, only 50,000,000 acres remained in Indian ownership. The Dawes Act, as this legislation is commonly called, emphasized the dislocation of the reservation period but focused it more closely on the individual and family. It has been influential in the migration of Indian people to cities and rural areas from their homelands. The Dawes Act marked the end of the extermination period and the introduction of direct assimilation efforts that continue.

Assimilation. The earliest efforts of the federal government to assimilate a group of Indians through scholastic education occurred in 1803 as a provision of a treaty with the now extinct Kaskaskia tribe. The treaty provided for the payment of $100 annually over a seven-year period toward the support of a priest who would "instruct as many of their children as possible in the rudiments of literature" (Schmeckebier, 1927, pp. 38–39). This treaty provision stimulated a response to the problem of education and civilization of the Indians, which occupied the attention of the fathers of the Republic and their successors. In 1818, the House Committee on Indian Affairs introduced a bill that resulted in a permanent appropriation of $10,000 for the industrial and scholastic education of Indians. Congress saw that the appropriation had the "direct tendency to produce the desirable object (civilization) through the establishment of schools at convenient and safe places among those tribes" that were friendly to the government (Schmeckebier, 1927, p. 39). It also considered the appropriation an inducement to hostile tribes to see that their true interest lay in peace, not war, thus providing protection against their further decline and final extinction by introducing among them the habits and arts of civilization (Schmeckebier, 1927, p. 39).

This appropriation established the foundation for the off-reservation boarding schools that led to more and larger institutions to educate a greater number of Indian children. What began as a benign effort to assimilate was transformed into an assaultive and coercive action to remove Indian children from their families and to establish them in the mainstream of American life. In this instance, the dislocation effort was focused primarily on children, notwithstanding the impact on the family and community. As Powell (1983, p. 123) described:

> In the early years of Western education of Indians, children of very young age were rounded up from their tribes and forced to attend schools established by the government. They were required to discard their language, dress and food. The entire encounter in these educational institutions was with foreignness. . . . They were required to spend eight continuous years away from their families and tribes. By now the socioeconomic systems of Indian people has been permanently disrupted. Survival necessitated the request and acceptance of rations. These rations were withheld from families and tribes who refused to enroll their children in these institutions.
>
> The impact on the family and tribe was considerable. Generations of Indian children were denied the education required to survive in their world. Most were unable to invest themselves in the new experience because the world view was antithetical to what they had previously learned. The handicaps developed from this experience are a major cause for the disruption of Indian family life today.

In the years that followed, criteria for admission to boarding schools were expanded to broad areas of educational and social need. The boarding schools became the primary placement resource for Indian children whom federal and state agents determined were in need of protection or who had educational deficits. Indian people themselves found a use for the schools as a protection for their children during the hard winter months and continuing economic depression in their communities.

In 1952, the Bureau of Indian Affairs instituted a policy of relocation and training for unemployed Indian people in the local labor force. Indian people were settled in urban areas where they could be trained or find employment. Unemployment was extremely high in reservation areas at that time, and the bureau considered this policy as a way of relieving this problem and furthering the assimilation effort of the federal government. The program deeply affected the fiber of the extended family in Indian society. The primary difficulties experienced by relocatees were the foreignness of the urban setting and the absence of a proper support group. The relocatees were a young population without access to elders and other family members for support and guidance. As a consequence, there are now third-generation dependent Indian families in urban areas that have had a lengthy relocation history. Child welfare and protective services have become familiar services delivered to these families.

In 1954, the federal status of the Klamath Tribe of Oregon was terminated; this act signaled the federal government's clear intent to end its status of trustee of all Indian tribes, as provided for in the Constitution. The legislation sought to relinquish federal jurisdiction to the states by abrogating the federal government's treaty obligations with the tribes. From the perspective of the delivery of social services, the termination of federal status meant that tribes were left abruptly without protection from the encroaching needs and values of surrounding communities. House Concurrent Resolution 108 proposed the termination of this status for all tribes in the states of California, Florida, New York, and Texas and further specified the Flathead of Montana, Klamath of Oregon, Menominee of Wisconsin, Potowatamie of Kansas and Nebraska, and members of the Chippewa Tribe on the Turtle Mountain Reservation in North Dakota. Tribal governments rallied in opposition and widespread termination stopped.

However, the intent was carried forward in P.L. 280, enacted by Congress in 1953, whereby the federal government relinquished its responsibility for direct financial assistance and social services to tribes in a number of states. P.L. 280 provided for state jurisdiction over matters of dependence and status violations on these reservations and resulted in the widespread removal of Indian children from their families. In other states where this legislation was not binding, the Bureau of Indian Affairs entered into contracts with the states to provide child welfare services to Indian communities. The primary reimbursements to the states are for the provision of foster care and institutional services to Indian children.

Current Laws

P.L. 280 is still in effect, but the provision for tribes to reassume jurisdiction in matters of Indian child welfare is in the Indian Child Welfare Act. The consequences of governmental action and inaction in services to Indian families caused the passage of the act in 1978. Stimulated by efforts of the Devils Lake Sioux Tribe and other tribes to regain custody of their children, the American Indian Policy Review Commission—an agency of the U.S. Congress—requested that a nationwide statistical survey of Indian child welfare be conducted by the Association on American Indian Affairs. The survey identified Indian children who had been removed from their families and who were either in foster care or adoptive placement. It revealed that one out of every four Indian children were not living with their families and that 85 percent of the children in placement were in non-Indian substitute homes (Task Force Four, 1976). Testimony presented to Congress convinced the Congress that federal intervention was necessary to stop the destruction of Indian families. The 1978 act was the result.

The Indian Child Welfare Act requires that the tribes and Indian parents or custodians be notified when an Indian child is the subject of a child custody hearing and allows the tribes to transfer the matter to their tribal court. The legislation also provides for the establishment of family development programs on reservations and in urban areas for services ranging from emergency care to prevention. The law was passed without an appropriation; therefore, the Bureau of Indian Affairs had to siphon funds from other services to support the programs. In 1980, the first year that family development programs were funded, $5.5 million was made available. Funding rose to $9.7 million, but Congress reduced the amount to $8.7 million in 1984, at which level it has remained. Approximately 400 applicants, including tribes and off-reservation programs, are eligible for family development program grants. The budget that was submitted to Congress in 1980 by the Reagan administration called for the termination of funds to urban programs in 1982 and to tribal programs in 1983 (U.S. Senate, 1984, p. 5).

Outside of the few efforts made possible by War on Poverty programs and P.L. 93-638, the Indian Self-Determination and Education Assistance Act, which provided for tribes to contract to deliver services previously administered by the Bureau of Indian Affairs, the Indian Child Welfare Act was the tribes' first real opportunity to regain extensive control over family and children's services. The act requires that Indian children be placed with their families and tribes and that they can be placed elsewhere only when resources are not available. State and local courts and agencies have resisted implementing the law partly because they are ignorant of the resources of the tribes and partly because of the widely held belief that removal of an Indian child from a substitute parent to whom a psychological attachment has been established will result in irreparable psychological damage and harm to the child. Although the programs required by the act have been successful in maintaining children in their homes, placement abuses by state agencies continue, and it is difficult to retrieve children who have been in the system for a long period and are in the foster care drift. Recent Children's Bureau reports revealed that only 1.1 percent of Indian children in state custody are in placement with relatives and extended family members as required by law (U.S. Senate, 1984). The passage of the Adoption Assistance and Child Welfare Act of 1980 aggravated the situation and in many places has contributed directly to abuses in the implementation of the Indian Child Welfare Act. That is, when a case is reviewed, an attempt is made to integrate provisions of both laws; thus, protection of the tribes' greatest natural resource—children—is pitted against case management practices of permanency planning.

Organizations and Movements

Indians have always responded to inequity by consolidating their strength and sense of purpose. Some 300 years ago, the Pueblos of the Southwest joined together in a revolt against the Spanish government in response to continued destruction and exploitation of the Indian society. In 1908, educated Indian people and their colleagues founded the little-known Society of American Indians and served as influential spokespersons in forums not available to tribes. These individuals, who were among the first of their people to achieve professional status, experienced the conflict of being between two worlds, and their views toward policies of the federal government varied widely. One of the society's founders, Carlos Montezuma, was as fierce an opponent of the Bureau of Indian Affairs as prominent American Indian Movement leaders of today.

The society was the first national Indian rights organization, and much attention was given to the ideas of pan-Indianism during its history; this, in large part, led to its dissolution. The pan-Indianism espoused by the society was greatly influenced by the idea of the melting pot that, following World War I, was overcome by themes of self-determination and cultural pluralism and the view of the United States as a "nation of nations." As Hertzberg (1971, p. 179) noted:

> Another [influence] was the growth of an American nativism which viewed the American past as exclusively an Anglo-Saxon product and foreigners, immigrants, and non-whites as lesser breeds—the domestic counterpart of imperialism. Yet another was the shift of focus from the individual to the group, the growing belief in a rugged American groupism, and the waning strength of the idea of rugged American individualism. . . . All were hostile in varying ways to the old conception of the melting pot as a producer of a new American; as a unifying process to which individuals from many and diverse backgrounds contributed, resulting in an American product which was different and better—than any of its components.

Hertzberg further observed that although the society made statements about self-determination, its statements were not much more than catchwords added to the older ideology of individual assimilation.

> The final effort to make the Society function as a national political pressure organization was doomed to failure, if only because the Indians did not possess the power or willingness to act together as a significant pressure group. A substantial number of Indians lacked the right to vote. Many of those who did have the vote were unwilling to use it for fear of losing their property rights or their special relationship to the tribe. Even if all the Indians had been able to vote in both national and state elections, political action would necessarily have been based largely on reservation Indians who were concerned primarily with local or tribal rather than national issues except as the latter affected them directly (Hertzberg, 1971, p. 199).

Thus the tribal culture emphasis weakened the force of pan-Indianism as viewed by the society. However, the society was successful in its effort to have the Indian Citizenship Bill enacted into law in 1924. The passage of the bill

. . . might also be regarded as the symbolic date of the demise of the Society of American Indians. It was by this time almost completely inactive—but one of the most important goals for which it had fought so long had been won. (Hertzberg, 1971, p. 205)

The National Congress of American Indians, founded in 1944, is credited with being the oldest and most broadly representative national Indian organization in the country. Its primary mandate is to secure the rights and well-being of American Indians and Alaska natives. In the past decade, it has concentrated on issues of government-to-government relations and has taken the position of the political separation of the Indian nations from the United States. This position advocates the right of the Indian nations to determine their external political relations in accordance with their needs and wants, distinct from all other groups in this country. The congress is a forum for the presentation and discussion of concerns and issues that covers the full spectrum of Indian life. Membership in the organization is open to tribes and individual Indians; non-Indians may become associate members.

The National Tribal Chairmen's Association was founded in the 1960s. Its efforts are directed toward the protection of tribal rights. Voting membership is restricted to tribal chairpersons.

The continuing destruction of Indian life was felt most strongly by those Indians who were forced to be separated from their homelands because of a lack of resources. In the urban areas, they found that society believed that all Indians were the responsibility of the federal government and therefore were not entitled to services provided to other citizens. The tribes' resources were restricted, and they were not able to provide services to members who did not reside on the reservation. These populations of Indians lived in the ghetto areas of other minority groups, and basic and individual survival was their primary concern. The expressions of the American Indian Movement in the takeover of the Bureau of Indian Affairs building in Washington, D.C. (1972), and at Wounded Knee (1973) impressed on the public the fragility and the strength of Indian life. Today, the movement's organizational efforts are more frequently community based, and tribal chairpersons are among the movement's leadership.

The National Indian Youth Council, founded in the 1960s, has concentrated on the education of Indian people about law and social policy and the political role they play in the process; it has supported numerous complaints of discrimination by students and employees. The National Indian Social Workers Association, founded in 1970, advocates for the rights of Indians in human services through political and educational activities. The goals and objectives of these organizations focus on amalgamation.

The two agencies that have primary and statutory responsibility for services to American Indians and Alaska Natives are the Bureau of Indian Affairs and the Indian Health Service. Eligibility for services varies but frequently is limited to Indians with one-fourth or more Indian blood who reside on a reservation or who can establish direct, ongoing, and close socioeconomic ties with the reservation, which often is difficult to do. In general, services from these agencies supplement rather than precede services of the state and local governments. The Branch of Social Services in both agencies is the primary entry point for tribes and Indian organizations about information and resources.

Role of Social Work

Social work with American Indians and Alaska Natives is similar to social work with other groups in this country who are deprived of the resources of the broad community partly because of the differences they judiciously and closely maintain but predominantly because the social service system does not respond to their primary concerns. However, the legislative mandate regarding services to Indian families and children is clear: the services must focus on maintaining and strengthening the Indian family. This mandate is buttressed by the Adoption Assistance and Child Welfare Act whose intent is to keep families together. At the practice level, social workers must become students of the Indian community and must direct their efforts to the identification of problems and needs and assistance in the development of community resources. Success as a social worker in an Indian community requires the acceptance of a basic tenet of the field—acceptance of the person.

The contact between Indian and non-Indian social workers has increased greatly through the establishment of family development programs mandated by the Indian Child Welfare Act. The program descriptions of many tribal and nontribal programs require the employment of social workers with master's degrees. Although the number of Indians with master's degrees has increased over the past decade, during which time Indian social work programs have been established in schools of social work throughout the country, the number of Indian social workers is still insufficient to meet the needs. Non-Indian social workers work primarily in supervisory positions and consequently exert tremendous influence over the development and operational efforts of local programs.

Therefore, social work education needs to expand its attention to and increase its depth of understanding of Indian concerns. Interorganizational efforts are necessary to eradicate the ignorance that underlies many problems in the delivery of services and to create a common ground and cause. Information about and support for efforts to secure the rights of American Indians and Alaska Natives need greater exposure in the field.

EVELYN LANCE BLANCHARD

For further information, see CIVIL RIGHTS; ETHNIC-SENSITIVE PRACTICE; INTERGROUP RELATIONS; MINORITIES OF COLOR; RACIAL DISCRIMINATION AND INEQUALITY.

References

Byler, W. (1977). "The Destruction of American Indian Families." In S. Unger (Ed.), *The Destruction of American Indian Families.* New York: Association on American Indian Affairs.

Dobyns, H. F. (1976). *Native American Historical Demography: A Critical Bibliography.* Bloomington: Indiana University Press.

Fey, H. E., & McNickle, D. (1970). *Indians and Other Americans: Two Ways of Life Meet.* New York: Harper & Row.

Hertzberg, H. W. (1971). *The Search for an American Indian Identity: Modern Pan-Indian Movements.* New York: Syracuse University Press.

Indian Health Service. (1985, April). *Chart Series Book.* Washington, D.C.: U.S. Government Printing Office.

Martin, C. (1978). *Keepers of the Game.* Berkeley: University of California Press.

Powell, G. J. (1983). *The Psychosocial Development of Minority Group Children.* New York: Brunner/Mazel.

Schmeckebier, L. F. (1927). *The Office of Indian Affairs: Its History, Activities and Organization.* Baltimore, Md.: Johns Hopkins University Press.

Spicer, E. H. (1969). *A Short History of the Indians of the United States.* New York: Van Nostrand Reinhold Co.

Task Force Four. (1976). *Report on Federal, State, and Tribal Jurisdiction: Final Report to the American Indian Policy Review Commission.* Washington, D.C.: U.S. Government Printing Office.

U.S. Bureau of the Census. (1980). *Characteristics of the Population: General, Social, and Economic Characteristics* (PC 80-1C1). Washington, D.C.: U.S. Government Printing Office.

U.S. Bureau of the Census. (1984). *Supplementary Report: American Indian Areas and Alaska Native Villages: 1980* (PC 80-S1-13). Washington, D.C.: U.S. Government Printing Office.

U.S. Senate. (1975). *Indian Child Welfare Program* (hearings before the Subcommittee on Indian Affairs, April 1974). Washington, D.C.: U.S. Government Printing Office.

U.S. Senate. (1984). *Oversight of the Indian Child Welfare Act of 1978* (hearings before the Select Committee on Indian Affairs, U.S. Senate, April 25, 1984). Washington, D.C.: U.S. Government Printing Office.

ARCHIVES OF SOCIAL WELFARE

The archives of social welfare are among the cumulative by-products of social welfare activities. In the process of planning and delivering services to individuals, families, groups, and communities, individuals, organizations, and agencies create records. Long after these records have served their intended function, they retain a secondary value for persons and purposes other than those for which they were created. Because these records are being used for an unintended purpose, the evidence they offer the historical researcher is, in comparison with other sources of information, unique.

Relatively few of the memoranda, diaries, correspondence, minutes, reports, speeches, financial records, case files, photographs, and other documents that fill social welfare file cabinets were written or saved with an "external" audience in mind. In most cases they are a part of the action they record. Compared with the books and articles that are the basis of traditional library research, they are more spontaneous and less self-conscious. Published works generally represent finished products, whereas archival materials record, and are a part of, the process—the preparations, the negotiations, the rejected alternatives. Compared with the survey and questionnaire data that support much empirical research, archival sources offer evidence that exists independent of the researcher's bias. Researchers who use archives also have the obvious advantage of not having their research topics limited by respondents' availability for survey or interview.

This tell-it-like-it-was integrity has its drawbacks, however. There are no guarantees that the information the researcher needs was ever recorded or, if it was, that it has been preserved and can be located. Archival materials are, by definition, unique or nearly so. Correspondence, memoranda, and other records are often prepared with, at most, only a single duplicate. Even minutes, reports, and conference proceedings that were mimeographed or photocopied for wider distribution are unlikely to have been systematically preserved in many places. It is for precisely this reason that archival records are seldom allowed to circulate. Thus "going to the source" often implies just that. Rarely does a single research library or interlibrary loan facility bring together all the primary source materials needed for a research project.

Sources of Records

The effective exploitation of archival source materials begins with the researcher supposing the existence of a potentially useful source of information—an individual or organization that, as a participant or observer, might have created a useful record—and then setting out to verify its existence and location. When Chambers (1977) analyzed the archives of social welfare, it was still possible to list and describe outstanding collections held in approximately 20 archival repositories and to have confidence that such a bibliographic essay fairly represented the richest available sources. That essay remains a valuable checklist that deserves to be con-

sulted. It is not repeated here because in the intervening time the complexity of the situation has increased, and such a detailed approach is no longer practicable. As social welfare activities continue, new records are created. Equally important, as awareness of the importance of social welfare history expands, archivists and researchers locate additional older records and develop new ways to exploit source materials previously thought to be of little or no value.

To appreciate the diversity of the available sources, it is useful to survey the range of institutions whose activities would have resulted in the creation of records. Organizations with the primary purpose of planning or providing some kind of social service are the obvious starting point. National associations have long provided leadership in specialized areas, often serving a network of affiliated local agencies but sometimes working directly in communities throughout the country. Bondy (1965) offers a helpful discussion of the various types of national voluntary organizations and their relation to their constituencies. Research has relied heavily on the records of these associations because of their relative convenience: the associations' outlook and activity predisposed them toward careful analysis of existing conditions and of appropriate remedial actions. Furthermore, there have been relatively few prominent national associations, and most of them were affiliated with the National Conference on Social Welfare or the National Social Welfare Assembly, which is now the National Assembly of National Voluntary Health and Social Welfare Organizations. This makes the identification and use of their records a manageable proposition.

Records of national associations best document high-level planning and setting of standards. They also often reflect an awareness of conditions and activities in specific locales, but usually only as secondary or summary accounts received from a local affiliate. For a more intimate picture of social work as it was actually practiced and of the condition of client populations, it is often necessary to rely on the records of local agencies. Partly because records of local agencies can be difficult to locate, particularly for more than a case-study approach, social welfare historians have tended to assume that the prescriptive literature of social work journals and conference proceedings provides an accurate description of practice.

Many of the same generalizations can be applied to the records of government agencies. Their value for researchers is shaped by the nature of the agency's or department's responsibilities. Since the advent of social security and New Deal–based welfare programs, federal records have documented the lives of individual citizens to a much greater degree than do records of national organizations in the private sector. For pre-1930s topics, researchers interested in local conditions and activities must rely on records of state and local public relief or welfare programs. Public records at any level present researchers with considerable bulk and complexity.

The list of potential sources does not end with the organizations and agencies most directly involved in the planning and delivery of services. Personal papers of individuals associated with these institutions often reflect the historical legacy of "taking work home" and provide a valuable supplementary source. Records of social work education—of schools of social work, of their organizations, of their students and faculty—are particularly appropriate as evidence of social work's aspirations. In some cases, such as records related to field placement, they also provide a view of patterns of practice.

The field of social welfare is not the exclusive province of the social work profession. Records from the fields of business, labor, religion, and health care provide perspectives of their respective contributions to improving the well-being of individuals, groups, and communities.

A special category of historical source material must be distinguished from the foregoing in that it is a self-conscious effort to recreate or analyze events long after their occurrence. This category includes published and unpublished personal memoirs and oral histories—interviews designed either to fill the gaps in existing written records or to provide an alternative in their absence. The National Association of Social Workers sponsored an oral history project in 1980–1981 to record the recollections of eight social workers who were pivotal figures in the development of the social work profession. The resulting transcripts of interviews with Harriett Bartlett, Arthur Dunham, Arlien John-son, Gisela Konopka, Inabel Lindsay, Helen Harris Perlman, Gladys Ryland, and Gertrude Wilson are available at the University of Minnesota, Columbia University, University of Washington, and the Library of Congress. Additional leading social work figures have been interviewed in other ongoing oral history projects, most notably those at Columbia University and at the Bancroft Library of the University of California at Berkeley. All these interviews provide a type of insight and understanding that written records seldom capture.

Custody of the Records

Surviving archival records fall into two categories: those that have remained in the custody of the institution or individuals that created or accumulated them and those for which responsibility has been transferred to another party. No rational plan governs the overall disposition of records, and the resulting dispersal reflects the free-market approach to the preservation of records. Regardless of custody, the condition in which records are maintained and the policies governing their use by researchers vary greatly.

Public records are the most predictable. State and federal laws establish archival agencies with responsibility for preserving government records of enduring value. For example, all surviving records of the U.S. Department of Health and Human Services and its predecessors are the responsibility of the National Archives and Records Administration, and the records of the Minnesota Department of Public Welfare are a part of the state archives administered by the Minnesota Historical Society. The already noted volume and complexity of government records, particularly those of the post–World War II era, try the resources of the archives. As a result, researchers using these records can expect to find no more than the most rudimentary checklists summarizing records in the condition in which the archives received them. Local government records, in particular, are badly neglected.

Other institutions and organizations support their own archival programs to the extent that their administrative needs and their sense of historical legacy can be squared with budgetary realities. Relatively few social service organizations maintain a full archival program in the sense of systematically selecting, arranging, describing, and preserving their inactive records and providing reference service to researchers. Among the notable exceptions are the Salvation Army, the national board of the Young Women's Christian Association (YWCA), and, at the local level, the Young Men's Christian Association (YMCA) of Greater New York. The typical organization, however, saves inactive records from destruction as much through inertia as through intentional efforts.

In contrast to institutional archives, which exist primarily to satisfy the administrative needs of the parent institution, a variety of manuscript repositories collect unpublished materials to promote the study of a particular area or subject. Most manuscript repositories collect in relation to a specific geographic area. State historical societies have long been the dominant institutions of this type, and some of them serve the dual role of state archives and of collecting in the general area of the state's history. There are growing numbers of city historical societies and regional research centers; the latter are usually housed in university libraries.

A number of manuscript repositories define their collecting policies in terms of a subject. The Social Welfare History Archives at the University of Minnesota is a relevant example. Other related theme collections include the Schlesinger Library on the History of Women, at Radcliffe College; the Sophia Smith Collection, also concentrating on women's history, at Smith College; and the Walter P. Reuther Library of Labor and Urban Affairs, at Wayne State University. Important collecting emphases are also found in more broadly defined repositories. The State Historical Society of Wisconsin has assembled an outstanding collection of materials relating to social action, particularly in the 1960s and 1970s. The Yale University Archives and Manuscripts Division has considerable strength in the area of public health. The Boston University Department of Special Collections includes a collection relating to the history of nursing.

Institutional archives occasionally act as manuscript repositories by collecting materials to supplement the records of the parent institution. The National Archives and Records Administration administers a network of presidential libraries (beginning with Herbert Hoover's), each of which seeks to document the activities of a presidential administration by bringing together the personal papers of the president and the records and papers of various organizations and individuals associated with that administration. Thus, for example, the Dwight D. Eisenhower Library in Abilene, Kansas, holds the papers of Oveta Culp Hobby, the first secretary of health, education, and welfare. Similarly, college and university archives solicit the papers of notable faculty members and administrators and, occasionally, of prominent alumni.

Because areas of collecting interest overlap, sets of archival records can often end up in any of a number of repositories. For example, the papers of prominent social workers might attract the interest of the college archives of their alma maters, the city or state historical societies of the areas in which they live, any of a number of subject collections, or even the Library of Congress Manuscripts Division.

Until about 1960 little collecting was done in the area of social services. Most of what was collected was in the form of personal papers of reformers, particularly such individuals as Frances Perkins, Jane Addams, and Lillian Wald, who were significantly involved in public policy debates. Radcliffe College (specifically its Schlesinger Library), Columbia University, the Library of Congress, the New York Public Library, and the State Historical Society of Wisconsin were among the few repositories to show an early interest in records of social service and social reform.

The rediscovery of poverty in America during the early 1960s and the concomitant expansion of academic historians' interest in social as well as political and economic history created a climate that encouraged the preservation of social welfare records. The Social Welfare History Archives was founded at the University of Minnesota in 1964. This repository concentrates primarily on records of national nongovernmental organizations in the welfare and service fields. Represented in its more than 6,000 linear feet of records are 40 national organizations, 50 local agencies and organizations (most of them from the Minneapolis–St. Paul area), and 60 individuals. The establishment of this archival center was soon followed by the founding of four other university-affiliated urban archives: the Archives of Industrial Society, at the University of Pittsburgh; the Manuscripts Collection of the University of Illinois at Chicago; the Urban Archives Center, at Temple University; and the Baltimore Region Institutional Studies Center, at the University of Baltimore. These repositories attempt to document the whole range of urban life in their respective cities. In each case the records of organized social reformers and social service agencies represent an important segment of the holdings.

Transfers of records by creating organizations to manuscript repositories can occur before or after the organization's demise. Many once ambitious in-house archival programs were badly eroded by the budget cuts of the 1970s. Among the results of this were the acquisition by the Social Welfare History Archives of the records of the Child Welfare League of America, the Council on Social Work Education, and the YMCA of the United States and the acquisition by Columbia University of the records of the Community Service Society of New York.

Locating the Records

Given the variety of institutional settings in which social welfare records may be held, the possibility of their being held by private individuals, and the lack of an overall system to provide for their preservation, it should come as no surprise that there is no single means of locating records. Basically there are three approaches.

Citations by Previous Researchers.
One can follow the tracks of previous researchers by scrutinizing their footnote citations and source notes. This approach produces no previously unused sources but occasionally identifies some that escape notice in other approaches.

Directories and Computerized Data Bases.
One can rely on bibliographic aids that have been devised to inform the research community of available materials. The most comprehensive source is the *National Union Catalog of Manuscript Collections* (*NUCMC*) (Library of Congress, 1959–). Its 1959–1982 editions cumulatively provide brief descriptions of 50,740 collections held in 1,241 repositories, complete with extensive

indexing. *NUCMC's* unquestioned value is limited by its bewildering format and by the fact that it represents only a small fraction of the total holdings of manuscript repositories. For example, it categorically excludes reports of the holdings of institutional archives.

There are other guides and directories to supplement *NUCMC*. The *Directory of Archives and Manuscript Repositories* (National Historical Publications and Records Commission, 1978) provides repository-level information for more than 3,000 repositories. *Women's History Sources: A Guide to Archives and Manuscript Collections in the United States* (Hinding, 1979) contains descriptions of 18,000 collections, including many related to social welfare. A new resource, *The National Inventory of Documentary Sources in the United States* (Chadwyck- Healey, 1984–), uses microfiche reproduction to bring together detailed finding aids that describe the contents of thousands of collections in repositories throughout the United States and to make this information available in major research libraries. Initially, this resource will be most comprehensive in its coverage of federal records (national archives and the presidential libraries) and the holdings of the Library of Congress Manuscripts Division, but its coverage of other repositories should improve over time. In addition to these interinstitutional guides, many archives and manuscript repositories periodically publish guides to their own holdings.

Inadequate resources, variations in practice from one repository to the next, and the complexity of primary sources have combined to limit the effectiveness of existing efforts at information-sharing among repositories. Researchers who rely on existing guides and directories have no grounds for confidence that they have identified all relevant sources. There is reason to expect significant improvement, however. The application of database technology to archival finding aids systems is still in its early stages, but it can only improve the existing system.

Informed Speculation.
In the absence of specific information, one can draw on either of the two previous approaches to provide the basis for informed speculation about where inquiries about a particular collection might best be directed. Staff members

at repositories with significant social welfare holdings are often good sources of information.

Special Problems

Researchers who rely on archival sources to re-create and analyze social welfare history must come to terms with several problems. One of them has to do with the changing nature of modern records, most notably their sheer volume. Records, particularly of government but of other entities as well, accumulate at a nearly unmanageable rate, often exceeding the resources available to institutional archives and leaving manuscript repositories reluctant to accept responsibility for massive collections.

The changes are qualitative as well as quantitative. More complex bureaucratic structures inevitably spawn extensive housekeeping paperwork that offers little of interest to most researchers. Developments in office technology shape the historical record as well. The typewriter and such copy processes as mimeograph and photocopy machines increase the accumulation of paper. Conversely, many important discussions conducted by telephone are never recorded. The transition to the automated office and electronic storage and transmission of data represents another step in this process that will profoundly affect future researchers. The easy manipulation and alteration of machine-readable records offers improved capabilities for long-term storage and use, but only if policies to ensure that files of enduring value are not routinely destroyed are conscientiously implemented.

Data privacy is another critical issue for social welfare researchers. When a field involves as many shared confidences as does social welfare, access to its records by third parties inevitably raises difficult questions. Klaassen (1983) traced the historical development of social workers' attitudes toward the confidentiality of case records, showing how the early, relaxed policies were gradually tightened. Current professional standards permit research use, depending on the informed consent of the client. This does not adequately address the circumstances of historical research in which, years later, scholars rely on information contained in files to reconstruct the circumstances of client populations or the methods of helping professionals. Archivists who administer case records have derived their access policies from experience with other sensitive materials such as census records. The key element is the effect of the passage of time. The assumption is that after sufficient time has elapsed—75 years in the case of census manuscripts—the need to protect individual privacy has diminished and is offset by societal interest in learning from the lessons of history. Social workers, archivists, and historians need to engage in a dialogue that addresses this issue more satisfactorily. Individual researchers need to anticipate the likelihood of encountering sensitive references in all types of social welfare records—not just in case records, but in passing references in correspondence, in committee and board proceedings, and in other administrative documents as well. They also need to acknowledge their personal responsibility to disguise personal identities in any disclosure of such material.

Another issue has to do with the problem of balance in the documentation provided by the archives of social welfare. It is obvious that most of the records discussed in this article are the product of planners and providers of social services. Despite recent commitments to maximum feasible participation and consumer advocacy, it is doubtful that existing records adequately document the consumer's perspective of social welfare. That much of social welfare history is similarly skewed toward an analysis of social welfare institutions and their professionals is, in part, both a cause and an effect of this situation. Researchers intent on studying social welfare consumers must use imaginative methods to overcome a significant difficulty. They can make effective use of case records and files relating to client ombudsmen. They can utilize the records of consumer and self-help organizations. Or they can turn to information contained in sources other than the ones defined here as the archives of social welfare.

Archival source materials mirror the subtleties and ambiguities of the events to which they owe their existence. For precisely that reason, they can be irreplaceably valuable for researchers, and they can be exasperating. In many ways, their complexity is their charm; for much of the fun is in the chase.

DAVID J. KLAASSEN
SUSAN D. STEINWALL

For further information, see RECORDING IN DIRECT PRACTICE; RESEARCH IN SOCIAL WORK.

References

Bondy, R. E. (1965). "National Voluntary Organizations." In *Encyclopedia of Social Work* (15th ed., pp. 526–530). New York: National Association of Social Workers.

Chadwyck-Healey, Inc. (1984–). *National Inventory of Documentary Sources in the United States.* Teaneck, N.J.: Author.

Chambers, C. A. (1977). "Archives of Social Welfare." In *Encyclopedia of Social Work* (17th ed., pp. 80–84). Washington, D.C.: National Association of Social Workers.

Hinding, A. (Ed.). (1979). *Women's History Sources: A Guide to Archives and Manuscript Collections in the United States.* New York: R. R. Bowker.

Klaassen, D. (1983). "The Provenance of Social Work Case Records: Implications for Archival Appraisal and Access." *Provenance: Journal of the Society of Georgia Archivists, 1*(1), 5–30.

Library of Congress. (1959–). *National Union Catalog of Manuscript Collections* (NUCMC). Washington, D.C.: Library of Congress.

National Historical Publications and Records Commission. (1978). *Directory of Archives and Manuscript Repositories in the United States.* Washington, D.C.: National Archives and Records Service.

For Further Reading

Brooks, P. C. (1969). *Research in Archives: The Use of Unpublished Primary Sources.* Chicago: University of Chicago Press.

Jones, H. G. (1980). *Local Government Records: An Introduction to Their Management, Preservation, and Use.* Nashville, Tenn.: American Association for State and Local History.

ARMED SERVICES. See MILITARY SOCIAL WORK.

ASIAN AMERICANS

Asian Americans have been in the United States since the middle of the nineteenth century. However, they are one of the least visible minorities for several reasons: (1) their geographic isolation (the residence of most is on the West Coast and in Hawaii), (2) their small numbers, (3) their adaptive styles, which encouraged them to adopt a "low posture" and to avoid conflict, and (4) their lack of prominent, charismatic leaders. History has also worked against them in that the primary focus of American immigration was on immigrants from Europe, with the Statue of Liberty, Ellis Island, and New York City as symbols.

Yet the immigration of Asians was, in most ways, similar to that of the Europeans. Asian people came to this country for economic betterment, increased educational opportunities, and a brighter future for their children. Many even landed on the West Coast's version of Ellis Island, enticingly named Angel Island, in San Francisco Bay. They came at the same time as several of the waves of European immigrants in the late nineteenth and early twentieth centuries and faced problems that all immigrants endure: an unfamiliar culture, lack of skills or training, hostility, and prejudice. What caused their experience to be different was their membership in a "different" race in the race-conscious West Coast society. By looking different, Asians faced structural barriers that severely limited their participation in American society.

Discrimination

For example, in 1920, Governor Stevens of California wrote to Secretary of State Bainbridge Colby concerning the "Japanese problem." He reminded the secretary that California earlier had awakened the U.S. Congress to the "Chinese problem," which resulted in the Chinese Exclusion Acts of 1882 and 1902; now, he stated, a similar issue had arisen with regard to the Japanese immigrants. Although the governor took pains to deny racism and to affirm his "admiration" of the qualities of the Japanese people, he wrote that he was transmitting the wishes of Californians who wanted to retain the state for their own kind. "They recognize the impossibility of that peace producing assimilability which comes only when races are so closely akin that intermarriage within a generation or two obliterates original lines'' (''Report of the State Board of Control,'' 1920/1978, p. 15). To strengthen his argument about controlling Japanese immigration and to gain wider acceptance for his position, the governor, in a burst of rhetoric, asked how Southerners would react at the thought of wide-scale marriages of blacks and whites.

The basis for the argument about the undesirability of Asians was racism: How could the ''superior'' white race mix with the ''inferior'' yellow race? There also were references to the unassimilability of Asian people, their strange languages, smelly foods, alien religion and cultures, their use of women and children in employment, and their unfair labor practices, as well as the fact that they were willing to work long hours for low wages. Therefore, although the mongrelization of the races was the basic fear, the dominant society also dreaded the cultural differences of and the economic competition from the Asians. It is of interest to note that similar arguments are still heard today.

Although most immigrant groups suffered from nativist sentiments, few were subject to intense discriminatory legislation in such a short period as were the Asians. Such discriminatory actions included these:

1. Restrictions on immigration that culminated in the Immigration Act of 1924, which prohibited the immigration of Asians.

2. Restrictions on citizenship, which placed Asian immigrants in the category of ''aliens ineligible for citizenship.'' Alien land laws completed the nightmare in that ''aliens ineligible for citizenship'' were denied the right to own property.

3. Antimiscegenation laws, which prohibited interracial marriages.

Restrictions based on race covered many other areas of life. Employment and housing opportunities were limited, and the full use of public and private facilities was denied. Structural and social-psychological constraints relegated Asian Americans to a second-class status.

Gains in civil rights and civil liberties occurred only after World War II. The 1952 McCarran-Walter Immigration Bill provided naturalization privileges and the Immigration Act of 1965 eliminated national origin quotas. Antimiscegenation laws were overturned by the U.S. Supreme Court (*Loving v. Virginia*) in 1967.

One important consequence of their unequal treatment has been the internalization by Asians of the ''less than equal'' status. Behaviors such as shyness, hesitance, a low posture, politeness, and a lack of aggression, often attributed to the Asian culture, can just as easily be attributed to being in a dominated, powerless, minority status.

Stereotypes

By looking different and by growing up in cultures that are not familiar to the dominant majority, Asians have acquired a number of unflattering but common stereotypes. The images have also been influenced by American foreign policy; for example, World War II portrayed the Japanese as fanatics, the Korean War pictured the North Koreans and Chinese as Communist hordes, and the Vietnam War projected the North Vietnamese as a ruthless, cunning enemy. Other stereotypes have also been uncomplimentary: the little ''brown brothers'' of the Philippines, the dope fiends of Hong Kong, the wise but eunuchlike Charlie Chan, and the sinister Fu Manchu (Kitano, 1981, p. 126).

Current stereotypes are more positive. Asians are viewed as studious, hard working, and achievement oriented and as placing a high value on education. But even though the stereotypes may have changed, or, as Ogawa (1971) phrased it, ''from Jap to Japanese,'' the problem remains: an entire group of people cannot be understood through a few oversimplified adjectives.

Current Issues

Social workers should be aware of three current problems when dealing with Asian Americans: (1) the error of interchangeability or homogeneity, (2) the assumption that all Asian Americans have intimate ties with the homeland, and (3) the heavy reliance on non-Asian models for social welfare programs and mental health counseling.

Interchangeability. Asian Americans come from over 20 different countries, each with its own history, language, culture, and experiences. Yet they often are presumed to be homogeneous, as typified by the phrase ''they all look alike,'' which also assumes that their cultures are comparable. Therefore, a Chinese is mistaken for a Japanese, who, in turn, may be mistaken for a Korean, who may be perceived as belonging to another Asian group. Many non-Asians think that the differences in nationality among Asian Americans are inconsequential.

For example, a common practice in agencies is to assign Asian clients automatically to Asian workers. Although there is some commonsense wisdom to this practice, such a procedure may not always be the wisest. A Korean immigrant who lived under harsh Japanese rule in Korea for many years may find it difficult to relate to a worker of Japanese ancestry, even though the latter may be American born with little knowledge of the historical problem.

Ties with the Mother Country. Another common practice is to think that all Asian Americans have intimate ties to the mother country. It is assumed that an individual with Asian features knows the language and culture of the country of origin—a premise that rarely is made for individuals of European or African ancestry. Americans are genuinely surprised when a second- or third-generation Asian American does not speak an Asian language or does not know the history and culture of the ancestral homeland. Conversely, third-generation Asian Americans who have lived their entire lives in the United States still hear, "But you speak English so well!"

The presupposed tie between Asians and their ancestral homeland has led to tragic consequences. During World War II, all persons of Japanese ancestry, regardless of citizenship, were placed in concentration camps because it was believed that the Japanese Americans' relationship with Japan was so strong that their loyalty and their Americanization were in question. In 1982, Vincent Chin, of Chinese ancestry, was beaten to death by two whites who thought he was Japanese. The murderers were angered by the high unemployment in the automobile industry because of the competition of Japanese imports (Takaki, 1983).

Non-Asian Models. The final area of concern is the heavy reliance in social welfare policies, mental health programs, counseling, and therapeutic models on European and American philosophies, which often are incongruent with Eastern thought.

Asians have been influenced by Confucianism, Taoism, and Buddhism. Asian cultures are apt to respect hierarchical stratification, the role of authority, and the internalization of problems. The unity of the family may take priority over individual preferences, while duty and obligation may be important bases for behavior. The discussion of innermost feelings and problems, especially with a stranger, may be difficult. It is important to appreciate these differences; Eastern cultures, philosophies, and thought can contribute as much to the American culture as can the European, African, and Latin American systems of thought. The growth of the field of cross-cultural counseling (Marsella & Pedersen, 1981; Pedersen et al., 1981) is one step in recognizing the problems caused by "cultural imperialism."

Interracial Marriage

Intermarriage is a sensitive indicator of intergroup relations. In the two areas where the Asian Americans are the most populous—California and Hawaii—there is a great deal of marital interaction among the various Asian American groups and the majority group. It would be reasonable to expect even higher rates of outmarriage (marriage outside the ethnic group) where Asian Americans are less numerous. For example, in Los Angeles in 1979, the outmarriage rate of the Chinese was 41.2 percent; the Japanese, 60.6 percent; and the Koreans, 27.6 percent. Approximately 10 percent of the outmarriages were to other Asians, so the interracial marriage rates (marriage to non-Asians) of the three groups were approximately 10 percent lower. The outmarriage rates in Hawaii for 1980 were as follows: Korean, 83 percent; Chinese, 76 percent; Filipino, 65 percent; Japanese, 59 percent; Vietnamese, 54 percent; and Samoan, 53 percent.[1] A high proportion of outmarriages was to other Asian groups; rates of marriages to Caucasians were as follows: Koreans, 34 percent; Chinese, 25

---

[1] Although the conventional spelling "Filipino" is used in this article, it should be noted that there is no "f" sound in the Pilipino language and the spelling and pronunciation "Pilipino" is increasingly being used of the people as well as the language.

Table 1. Asian Americans in the United States, 1970 and 1980

Year	Chinese	Guamanian	Japanese	Korean	Filipino	Samoan	Vietnamese
1970	435,062	N.A.[a]	591,290	70,000[b]	343,060	N.A.	N.A.
1980	806,040	32,158	700,974	354,593	774,652	41,948	261,729

SOURCE: U.S. Bureau of the Census, "U.S. Summary," *Characteristics of the Population: 1980* (Washington, D.C.: U.S. Government Printing Office, May 1983), Vol. 1, pp. 1–20.
[a] N.A. = not available.
[b] Estimated.

percent; and Japanese, 22 percent (Kitano et al., 1984).

Population

The population distribution of Asian Americans in 1970 and 1980 is shown in Table 1. In 1970, the most populous Asian American group according to the U.S. Census was the Japanese (591,290), followed by the Chinese (435,062) and the Filipinos (343,060). However, in 1980 the Chinese were the most numerous (806,040), followed by the Filipinos (774,652) and the Japanese (700,974). A fast-growing group are the Koreans, who jumped from an estimated 70,000 in 1970 to 354,593 in 1980—a fivefold increase. Other Asian groups identified by the U.S. Census, but who are not included in Table 1 are the Asian Indians (361,531) and the native Hawaiians (166,814). The rise in the population of these groups is primarily due to the Immigration Act of 1965 and U.S. policy on refugees that resulted from the Vietnamese War.

The Chinese

The Chinese were the first immigrants from Asia to arrive in significant numbers. In 1852, about 25,000 Chinese were in California; by the 1860s, their number had risen to more than 50,000. The Chinese came to this country for better economic opportunities; many found employment laying ties for the railroad. They left behind severe economic problems, as well as political and social discontent (Purcell, 1965).

Primarily men, the Chinese faced more than verbal prejudice; they were robbed, beaten, and murdered, especially if they tried to compete with whites in the mining districts. California justice included the provision that no Chinese person could testify against a white person. Therefore, for safety, the Chinese retreated to the urban "Chinatowns" and entered occupations in

which white men would not engage: house cleaning and working in laundries and restaurants (Daniels & Kitano, 1970).

The anti-Chinese movement was so strong that Chinese immigration was prohibited from 1882 until 1943. In December 1943, during World War II, when China was an ally, the United States, in attempting to reduce the effectiveness of Japanese propaganda about a "race war," repealed Chinese exclusion legislation and assigned the Chinese a token quota of 105. A large number of Chinese did not enter the United States until after the passage of the Immigration Act of 1965, which did away with national-origin quotas.

The Chinese Revolution of 1949 shut off migration from the mainland and changed the pattern of immigration. Lai (1980) noted that the new immigrants who came after 1965 were different in many ways from the original Chinese. The old-timers spoke Cantonese and came from mainland provinces such as Kwangtung and Fukien, whereas the newcomers are from Hong Kong, Taiwan, and Southeast Asia. The old timers were primarily uneducated peasants, unskilled laborers, and men; many of the newcomers are well-educated urbanites who have emigrated in family groups.

Family Patterns. Hsu (1971) described one style of Chinese family—the cohesive, extended (traditional) family in which roles are clearly defined and the father and eldest son rule. In this type of family, emphasis is placed on duty, obligation, ancestor worship, and the family name. Traditional families, which can be found with minor variations in all Asian groups, tend to arrange suitable marriages, to keep women in a subordinate role, to exert a good deal of social control over family members, to have clear definitions of good and bad, and to believe in the submergence of individual desires for family unity. They are affected most by exposure to the American system.

Weiss (1977) and Wong (1976) described two other types of families—the bicultural family and the modern family. Members of bicultural families are usually of the second and third generations. They are the products of both the Chinese and American cultures, and the majority have successfully integrated the two cultures. Members of modern families are cosmopolitan, more American than Chinese. They desire full acculturation. Their language, thinking, and expectations are "American"; only their physiological features are Chinese.

The "mutilated family," as Sung (1967) labeled it, is a family in which the husband and wife, although formally married, were separated for many years. This type of family was common in the early days when Chinese men would leave their families to seek their fortune in the United States. Poverty prevented them from returning to China, and the immigration law did not allow them to bring their families to this country. It was only after the liberalization of the immigration law in 1965 that some of these mutilated families were reunited. The years of living separately in different cultures have created problems for many of these couples. They are asked to restart married life at an advanced age with virtual strangers.

Another phenomenon that resulted from the early migration of single men and the subsequent restrictions on immigration was the large number of lonely Chinese men in America's Chinatowns. After the immigration law was liberalized, a steady stream of bachelors traveled to Hong Kong in search of wives. Most of them preferred Chinese-born women, because they thought that American-born Chinese women, aside from their scarcity, were too "Americanized." Although the discrepancy in age and life experiences could be hypothesized as sources of high strain, marital problems usually were not visible.

Another situation caused by discriminatory legislation was the creation of "artificial fathers." Lai (1980, p. 223) described the "slot system," in which Chinese Americans returning from China would falsely report the birth of children, usually sons, to the authorities, thereby creating slots for future immigrants. Prospective immigrants were then assigned or sold these "slots" so that "paper son" and "paper father" were familiar terms in the Chinese vocabulary.

Problems. A characteristic of Asian American communities is the hidden nature of many problems. That is, families prefer to deny or mask their problems so the problems remain invisible to outsiders. Thus, a mentally ill person may be taken care of at home, and a delinquent child may be handled by the extended family. The important point is that official sources, which are charged with keeping statistics, are not used, except as a last resort.

The Chinatowns, especially in San Francisco, Los Angeles, and New York, are one visible problem. In these areas, one finds inadequate housing, unsanitary conditions, and overcrowding. The people have difficulty speaking English, workers receive low wages and are otherwise exploited, unemployment and underemployment are high, and talent is underutilized. These conditions are compounded by inadequate health and welfare services.

Two other problems are delinquency and mental illness. The influx of young immigrants, who can barely speak English and who have few marketable skills, has been associated with a rise in the number of criminal acts and delinquent behavior. Berk and Hirata (1973), who studied mental illness among the Chinese in California, found that the rate of hospitalization initially was one-quarter of the rate for the general population. However, in recent years, there has been a sharp increase in commitments to mental hospitals, which cannot be attributed solely to the demography of the group (old single men). Rather, Berk and Hirata hypothesized that the rise may be due to a reduction in the cohesion of the ethnic community, the ineffectiveness of the ethnic community and family in coping with problem behavior, and the transfer of social control from the ethnic to the larger community.

Other problems are much more typical of the conflict between acculturated children and their tradition-oriented parents. They include such intergenerational difficulties as disputes about educational and vocational choices, dating and marriage, spending patterns, and overall lifestyles.

Personality. Sue and Kirk (1972) tested differences in personality between Chinese students and students from other backgrounds at the University of California, Berkeley. They found that Chinese students (1) score higher on quantitative sections and lower on verbal abilities, (2) are more interested in the physical sciences, applied technical fields, and business occupations and less interested in the social sciences, esthetic and cultural fields, and verbal and linguistic vocations, (3) prefer more concrete and tangible approaches to life and (4) are more conforming and less socially extroverted than are other students.

Sue and Kirk explained these differences in terms of family structure, dependence, tradition, and a distrust of the outside world. The behavior of Chinese people is controlled through guilt and shame and, for many Chinese students, attending a university may be the first time they have left their family. Also, a high proportion of Chinese students live at home, so that commuting, rather than living on the campus, is common. With minor variations, the generalizations for the Chinese students apply to other Asian groups, especially those whose parents were immigrants.

Personality tests and other standardized instruments can be valuable when used appropriately. However, in most cases, the scores of middle-class white people define normality, so that individuals from cultures whose socialization patterns, values, and experiences are different often are viewed as impaired, abnormal, and dysfunctional (Tong, 1971).

The Japanese

Several features of Japanese immigration were similar to those of the Chinese. Many of the early immigrants were single men with a sojourner's orientation; they were imported for their labor (many came as "contract laborers" for the plantations in Hawaii) and soon became the targets of racial hostility. But, in other ways, the Japanese immigrants were different. They came from a rapidly industrializing nation that was soon to challenge the Western nations for territory and resources; they came from 1890 to 1924, after the Chinese exclusion laws; they looked for support and protection from the Japanese embassy and consular officials; and they

started families. Many used the "picture bride" method of marriage in which a man in this country and a woman in Japan exchanged photographs so that a bride arriving from Japan took up married life with a husband who often was a stranger. (The practice of bringing over brides from Japan was terminated in 1924 when the new immigration restrictions went into effect.) Although there must have been many difficult moments in these marriages, the vast majority have lasted.

Because the Japanese were able to start families in this country, the issue of the acculturation of their American-born children arose much earlier for them than for the Chinese. One consequence has been that the Japanese are more acculturated than the Chinese, even though the Chinese have been in this country for a longer time.

Generations. Because of legal restrictions that cut off Japanese immigration from 1924 to well after World War II, the Japanese have well-defined generational categories based on age and similar experiences. These generations are the *Issei,* the *Nisei,* the *Sansei,* and the *Kibei.*

The Issei. The *Issei,* or first-generation immigrants, came to the United States between 1890 and 1924. They were relatively homogeneous in terms of age (young at the time of immigration), education (four to six years of schooling in Japan), and general background. They faced discrimination in almost all aspects of their lives and internalized the values of the *Meiji* era of Japan (1867–1912), which emphasized duty, obligation, loyalty, and an orientation to the group. Most *Issei* expected little for themselves, thinking of themselves as living for the sake of their children ("*kodomo no tame ni*") (Ogawa, 1978).

Few of this original generation are still alive. Those who are live with their children or grandchildren or with other elderly Japanese people in senior citizens' housing projects in California, Hawaii, and Washington. Factors such as food preferences, friendship patterns, family relationships, language, entertainment, and life experiences have led them to prefer to be with their own kind.

The Nisei. The children of the *Issei* are called *Nisei,* or the "second generation." Most were born between 1910 and World

War II and are now between 50 and 75 years old. Although they were born in this country, they faced an early life of prejudice and discrimination, which culminated in their incarceration in concentration camps during World War II.

The *Nisei* faced problems that are common to children of immigrants: acculturation, identity, and marginality. Some writers have called them the "quiet generation" (Hosokawa, 1969), although the title itself caused a stir in the Japanese community. Much of the energy of the *Nisei,* after the close of the internment camps, was to compensate for their losses while imprisoned. It was not unusual to find the entire family seeking employment—a factor that was reinforced by the more open occupational opportunities after World War II.

Although there was still prejudice and discrimination, the next several decades saw the struggles for civil rights, equal opportunity, and affirmative action. Because of the Japanese family's past emphasis on education, even when such opportunities were slim, college-trained and skilled *Nisei* were able to take advantage of a more racially liberal society. Some have even referred to the Japanese as this country's most successful minority, although Kitano and Sue (1973) questioned the reality of that success and the high price paid for being so achievement oriented.

The Sansei. The *Sansei,* or third generation, are the children of the *Nisei* and make up the current young-adult group. They are American in their values (Iga, 1966) and in almost all aspects of their lives. They have not faced the kind of structural discrimination that was an integral part of the lives of their parents and grandparents. As a consequence, many question the acquiesence of the *Issei* and the *Nisei* to the wartime evacuation and the need for an ethnic community.

Almost all the *Sansei* are integrated in the mainstream society. Schools, workplaces, and residential areas reflect the mobility of this group (Montero, 1980); the "Japan Towns" are primarily for tourists and small businesses.

However, in major areas of Japanese concentration such as Los Angeles, San Francisco–San Jose, and Honolulu, ethnic communities are still lively. There are numerous *Sansei* athletic leagues (basketball and

volleyball are the most popular); ethnic churches, both Protestant and Buddhist, that provide religious and social activities; Asian-American fraternities and sororities; and various Japanese celebrations in Honolulu, Los Angeles, and San Francisco that have *Sansei* queen contests with all the American trimmings. The inclusion of queen candidates of mixed Japanese ancestry has raised a number of interesting questions about the role of ethnicity and "racial purity." One such question is, Should candidates be "pure" Japanese, or can candidates with only one Japanese parent qualify?

The major difference between the *Sansei* and *Nisei* organizations is the issue of voluntarism. The *Nisei* felt forced to rely on pluralistic structures because they faced discriminatory barriers. However, the *Sansei's* preferences vary; some choose all-ethnic organizations, while others have acculturated and have few ethnic ties. Kishiyama (1984) highlighted the results of this difference in an article on the imminent closure of the Japanese Hospital in Los Angeles. The Japanese Hospital was started in 1929 in response to the discriminatory practices of other hospitals that excluded Japanese patients and physicians. However, the *Sansei* no longer support the tradition of or see the need for a Japanese hospital, and the *Nisei* physicians who practiced and referred patients to the Japanese Hospital are now old or retired. Therefore, the hospital will soon be out of business unless there is an unforseen turnabout.

Other Groups. Other groups include the *Kibei* and businessmen and students from Japan. The *Kibei* are *Nisei* who were born in the United States but were sent to Japan at an early age to be socialized by grandparents and other relatives. This practice was most common in the decades that preceded World War II.

Japanese businessmen, who are sent to this country for a few years as representatives of their Japanese companies, return to Japan after their tour of duty. Their number is not insignificant; in a meeting with a group of Japanese businessmen in Los Angeles in 1984, the author was given an estimate of 10,000 (including their families) in Los Angeles and over 20,000 in the New York area. Much of their lives revolves around the business community; their social contact with Japanese Americans is minimal. These businessmen have developed their own community, based on Japanese models, with clubs, organizations, sports activities (golf is common), bars, and places of entertainment that reflect a Japanese rather than an American ambience.

Students and tourists from Japan, who exhibit a wide variety of interests and lifestyles, are two other groups. Some of the students are studious and have clearly defined educational goals; others may be more prone to enjoy the individual freedom of the new experience, while a few may be more interested in finding employment. Japanese tourists often come on a tour that covers as many places as possible in a short period, so their impression of the United States is fleeting. Because they usually are in regimented group tours, they have little opportunity to meet individual Americans.

Problems. A convenient way to analyze the problems of the Japanese is by ethnicity, generation, and social class. The generational terms are related to age and the common experiences, needs, perceptions, lifestyles, and ways of handling and facing problems. For example, the needs and problems of the *Issei* involve aging, health, and housing. The problems of the *Nisei* include planning for retirement, identity, the empty-nest syndrome, redress for their wartime internment, and relationships with aged parents, peers, and children. The *Sansei* face the problems of all young adults—occupation, education, plans for a family and a future—and a bicultural identity. The Japanese businessmen face problems of isolation, cultural conflict, alcoholism (Kitano, 1985), and the future of their family after they return to Japan. Students and temporary workers from Japan face immigration and visa problems. The common denominator that ties all the Japanese together is their physiological features—all are apt to bear the epithet, "Jap," which serves as a reminder that stereotypes and prejudices linger. The term *Nikkei,* which refers to Japanese born in the United States, is beginning to take the place of the generational referents.

Wartime Evacuation. The central event in the lives of the Japanese in the United States was the wartime evacuation

(Bosworth, 1967; Daniels, 1971; Eaton, 1952; Girdner & Loftis, 1969; Grodzins, 1949; Irons, 1983; Kitano, 1976; Leighton, 1945; Myer, 1971; Okubo, 1946; Spicer et al., 1969; Tateishi, 1984; tenBroek, Barnhart, & Matson, 1954; Thomas, Kikuchi, & Sakoda, 1952; Thomas & Nishimoto, 1946).

The long period of anti-Japanese prejudice culminated in the forced removal in 1942 of over 110,000 Japanese, 75 percent of them American citizens, to relocation centers. Japan's attack on Pearl Harbor on December 7, 1941, provided the trigger; the ostensible reasons behind the evacuation included "their own protection" and the fear of sabotage. But it would not be difficult to detect other, more powerful reasons: racism, economic corruption, and the need for scapegoats.

President Roosevelt signed Executive Order 9066 on February 19, 1942, which authorized the removal; by November, the Japanese population was behind barbed wire. The evacuation was quick and efficient; the years of toil by the Japanese to achieve a foothold in this country in the face of discriminatory barriers were quickly erased. Homes and possessions were abandoned, personal property and treasures were sold at a fraction of their worth, farms and gardens were destroyed, and family life disintegrated.

There were riots (Kitano, 1976, p. 34), draft dodging (Daniels, 1971), and acts of resistance, but, in general, most Japanese resigned themselves—(*shikata ga nai*) ("it cannot be helped")—to the power of the U.S. government. Tateishi (1984) wrote of the experiences of a number of evacuees during that period. The stories cover all the human emotions—despair, frustration, anger, and resignation, interspersed with moments of peace, insight, and small pleasures.

Four cases of individuals who resisted the evacuation—Minory Yasui, Fred Korematsu, Gordon Hirabayashi, and Mitsuye Endo—made their way to the U.S. Supreme Court. The Court upheld the doctrine of military necessity; however, on November 11, 1983, the *Los Angeles Times* reported that a federal judge had vacated the conviction of Fred Korematsu, who had attempted to evade internment during World War II. In vacating the conviction, the judge said that the government had relied on unsubstantiated facts, distortions, and the racist views of a military commander to justify the detention. Irons (1983), in investigating the individual cases, found serious flaws in the U.S. government's case, including the alteration and destruction of crucial evidence.

In 1980, the Commission on Wartime Relocation and Internment of Civilians was established by the Congress to review the facts and circumstances of Executive Order 9066, which had forced the evacuation of the Japanese from the West Coast. The commission (1982) concluded, among other things, that detention and exclusion were not militarily necessary. The broad historical causes that shaped the decision to evacuate were racial prejudice, war hysteria, and the failure of political leadership. The commission reported (1982, p. 18) that "a grave injustice was done to American citizens and resident aliens of Japanese ancestry who, without individual review or any probative evidence against them, were excluded, removed and detained by the United States during World War II." Recommendations by the commission included an apology and financial compensation to the evacuees. Congressional action is pending.

Filipinos

The Filipinos, with 774,652 individuals recorded in the 1980 census, are the second largest Asian group in the United States. As with the Koreans and the Chinese, most of the growth in the Filipino population can be attributed to the Immigration Act of 1965, which went into effect in 1968. The growth in this population may be illustrated by the fact that 2,545 Filipinos entered the United States in 1965, compared to 25,417 in 1970. Unstable political and economic conditions in the Philippines and better educational and economic opportunities in this country were the main incentives (Melendy, 1980).

The Philippines became a possession of the United States as a result of the Spanish American War and the Treaty of Paris (1899). A concerted attempt was made to "Americanize" the islands, including the establishment of a network of elementary schools and a curriculum built on American models. American teachers were imported, and English was required in the classrooms, although its influence on rural youngsters was negligible. Melendy (1980) noted that although the schools were popular, American

control over the islands was not so strong that demands for Philippine independence were constant.

Filipinos had the right to enter the United States freely until 1934, when the Tydings-McDuffie Independence Act conferred commonwealth status on the Philippines. Filipinos then became aliens for the purposes of immigration; their immigration quota was 50 per year. In 1946, when President Truman proclaimed Philippine independence, the immigration quota was raised to 100, which remained in effect until the Immigration Act of 1965.

The Philippines are an island nation with numerous ethnic groups and a diversity of languages and dialects. The majority of immigrants to the United States speak Visayan, Tagalog, or Ilocano, and these major language divisions are the basis for identification and community divisions. Melendy (1980) indicated that many services (such as barbershops) are based on language differences, which may be one obstacle to the development of an overall Filipino identity.

The Filipinos may be divided into a number of different groups (Cordova, 1973; Melendy, 1980; Morales, 1974; Munoz, 1971). These groups include the early immigrants, the second generation, and the postwar migrants.

Early Immigrants. The earliest Filipino immigrants were students who were encouraged by the U.S. colonial government to attend colleges and universities in the United States. According to Melendy (1980), some 14,000 students had enrolled in various colleges by 1938. Most of these students returned to the Philippines and eventually assumed prominent roles in the economic and political life. Their success encouraged others to follow in their steps.

However, students were a small minority of the early immigrants. The great majority were young single men of peasant background who came as unskilled laborers. American hostility toward the Chinese and the Japanese led to the recruitment of Filipinos, especially for the plantations in Hawaii and the agricultural fields in California. Language, the lack of education and marketable skills, prejudice, and discrimination kept most of these men out of the American mainstream. Many spent their lives working long hours for low wages in dull jobs without wives and families. Antimiscegenation and immigration laws limited their hopes for a family-oriented future. Thus, they often turned to such leisure-time pursuits as dance halls, gambling, and prostitutes (Melendy, 1980). The absence of a stable ethnic community with lasting social, religious, and political institutions contributed to the transient quality of their lives, and many returned to the Philippines.

The majority of the surviving early pioneers are now retired, living in cheap one-room hotels and apartments in the less desirable areas of a community. Their problems include housing, finances, health care, recreational opportunities, and isolation.

Second Generation. Significant family life for the Filipinos did not begin until after World War II. After independence in 1946, earlier immigrants sought to fill the annual quota of 100 with wives, children, other kin, and Filipino women they could marry. Most of the Filipinos, including the newly arrived, found jobs only in the unskilled and semi-skilled occupations, especially agriculture.

The American-born (second) generation faces problems that are common to second generation Asian Americans. Occupational, educational, and marital choices; relationships with peers and parents; and questions of ethnic identity are ongoing issues. The problem of an ethnic identity is confused by the prevalence of Hispanic surnames.

Postwar Immigrants. The new immigrants started to come to this country in the 1960s, and their migration still continues. The new immigrants include wives and children with clear intentions of permanent settlement. As Melendy (1980) indicated, many of the new immigrants are young professionals, both men and women, aged 20–40, who are looking for better opportunities; some have left the Philippines for political reasons.

A large number of the new immigrants arrived as professional, technical, and kindred workers whose skills were deemed necessary to the United States. Although most of the discriminatory legislation against Asians had fallen in the face of the civil rights movement, the new immigrants face other barriers. Most important are the procedures

required to become licensed physicians, dentists, pharmacists, and nurses.

The new immigrants have settled in such cities as Honolulu, Los Angeles, Chicago, and New York. Their migration is family and kinship oriented, and they have the same problems as all new immigrants—occupation, housing, education, income, and the acculturation of their children. An internal problem is that family and regional-group loyalties make it difficult to organize the community on a broader basis. Filipino organizations are more likely to multiply rather than coalesce, and provincial allegiances and personality choices take precedence over community organization and cohesion (Melendy, 1980).

One other noticeable group is the veterans of World War II, including Filipinos who served as stewards in the U.S. Navy. Most are dependent on retirement pay and have retained their military bearing.

The Koreans

Although early immigrants from Korea faced the same barriers to participation in the American society as the Chinese and Japanese, a number of factors made their migration unique. First, a high proportion of these immigrants were Christians because American missionaries in Korea played a major role in their immigration. Second, their migration was short-lived—from 1903 to 1905—at which time the Japanese took over effective control of their homeland so that significant immigration ceased until after the Immigration Act of 1965 (Kim, 1980). Third, the number of immigrants was small, slightly over 7,000. Therefore, these early immigrants did not develop large self-sufficient communities, such as the Chinatown in San Francisco and Little Tokyo in Los Angeles. As a consequence, descendants of the original group achieved much more rapid upward social and economic mobility than did other Asian groups, especially in Hawaii. As Kim (1980) stated, the second generation stayed in school longer and achieved a higher rate of professional training than did the Chinese and Japanese, mastered English faster, left plantation work earlier, abandoned their native diet and dress, and more quickly exhibited the attitudes of the dominant society. But the group also paid a price for the rapid acculturation in high rates of divorce, mental illness, suicide, and delinquency. The descendants of this early group also had high rates of outmarriage (Kitano et al., 1984).

Much of the energy of the early immigrants was directed toward freeing their homeland from Japanese colonialism. Kim (1980) wrote that although many groups were working for liberation, they did not unite under one banner; rather, they were split into factions, characterized by a variety of ideologies and personal rivalries. The divisions in the community remain to this day. The end of World War II saw the liberation of Korea, and Syngman Rhee, an ex-missionary school student and leader of one of the groups working toward liberation, became the first president of the Republic of Korea in 1948.

New Immigration. Kim (1980) estimated that 90 percent of the Koreans in the United States have been here less than 15 years—since the Immigration Act of 1965 went into effect in 1968. Most of the 20,000 to 30,000 immigrants who arrive in this country annually come for many of the same reasons as all immigrants—for better economic and educational opportunities and to rejoin family members. The new immigrants include a sizable proportion of wives and children and of educated middle-class professionals from urban areas. The majority intend to become naturalized Americans, and their family orientation has spurred them to build communities with goods and services appropriate for family life. Similar experiences, a common culture, and problems with the English language have added impetus to the development and maintenance of ethnic ties. Many Korean-language newspapers serve the community.

Los Angeles, with an estimated 150,000 Korean people, has the largest Korean community in this country. Although the Korean population is not densely concentrated in any single neighborhood, Koreatown is clearly visible, with shops, restaurants, offices, night clubs, and a community building. Many Koreans have opened small businesses, although Kim and Wong (1977) pointed out that these small enterprises can be viewed as symptoms of disguised poverty and the lack of opportunity rather than of material success. There has been a high turnover rate in these businesses, and many of the failures have been caused by insufficient capital,

long-term leases, a lack of information, poor planning, and entrance into high-risk enterprises.

The major problems of these new immigrants are underemployment and low income. Many arrive in the United States with professional skills and training but face an uncertain job market. For example, Kim and Wong (1977) noted that, in the late 1970s, 49 percent of those with professional degrees as physicians, pharmacists, and nurses were working as crafts people or salespeople. The situation was even worse for those trained in the liberal arts; only 7 percent were able to obtain the kind of employment for which they were trained.

Yu (1979) described a typical Korean family as one in which both the father and mother work, often seven days a week. The parents are hard working and high-achievement oriented and have high educational expectations for their children. The children study for long hours and are competitive in school. The major hindrance to their mobility and acceptance is their difficulties with the English language.

Korean families have the same problems as all immigrant families. The father and mother generally retain old-world expectations and values and, because of their age and employment, remain isolated from the mainstream. The children, especially the younger ones, are exposed to the American culture and quickly acquire a facility with the language and lifestyles that often are in conflict with parental norms. Acculturative strains and culture conflict can be expected.

The Korean community needs many services: employment, health care, family counseling, child care, and welfare (Kim & Condon, 1975). But the Korean immigrants face conditions that are much more optimistic than the hostility and structural discrimination experienced by the early Chinese and Japanese immigrants. They have many of the characteristics of the other Asian groups —a high motivation to succeed, high educational aspirations, and a strong family orientation. Many are well trained and highly educated; Sherman (1979) described them as affluent, well educated, aggressive, dynamic, and ruthless in their business dealings. Despite this improved situation, the problem of discrimination is not dead. Yu (1979) observed that the longer a Korean person lives in the United States, the more likely he or she is to report instances of racial discrimination.

The Pacific Islanders

A number of diverse immigrant groups fall under the title Pacific Islanders, all of whom are new immigrants. These groups are the Samoans, Tongans, Guamanians, and a small number from Tahiti and the Fiji Islands. Interisland migration also has taken place between Saipan, Ponape, Yap, Nauru, New Zealand, and Hawaii (Shore, 1980).

Samoans. Significant immigration from Samoa began in 1951 when the U.S. Navy, then the largest employer of Samoans, closed its island base. The Samoans come from a culture that stresses kinship ties and minimizes individuality (Mead, 1961). The chief (*matai*) makes decisions and assumes responsibility for the family members. Family bonding patterns provide for socialization, affection, and identity. The family members are interdependent and problems are handled and social control is exerted through the extended family system (Shu & Satele, 1977). Exposure to the American system and acculturation have placed a strain on the traditional system.

The church, primarily Congregational, Mormon, Methodist, and Catholic, plays an important role in the community. In addition to its religious role, the church helps Samoans find employment and raise funds; it is a vehicle of acculturation as well.

Guamanian immigration was facilitated by the 1950 Organic Act, which conferred American citizenship on inhabitants of the territory of Guam. Tongan migration was aided by contact with the Church of Jesus Christ of Latter-day Saints; because of the Mormon influence, Tongans have settled near Salt Lake City.

Although each of the islands has a different culture, their problems may be summarized as follows:

■ Differences in the cultural, economic, and life styles between the isolated island culture and the industrialized United States (Kitano, 1985).

■ The loss of status, rank, and prestige. Men have been employed in construction and maintenance jobs and as security guards and watchmen. Women find jobs as hotel maids, hospital aides, nursing home aides, and as cannery workers. Few find white-collar or professional employment.

■ Low wages and high expenses. The Pacific Islanders generally have large families and help members of their extended family. Most contribute regularly to the church. Often, both the husband and wife work, and some even hold several jobs.

■ Problems of identity. Identity has been traditionally local and tied to the land, to the islands, and to local kinship groups and villages. Time and distance from the islands weaken the old sources of identity. The new identity encourages individualism based on achievement, occupation, and income.

■ Unrealistic stereotypes. The image of the Pacific Islander is that of a romantic, erotic "native" of the South Seas, as portrayed in popular novels and films, or of an aggressive, heavy-drinking, barroom brawler (Shore, 1980).

The Pacific Islanders are relatively few in number and have no visible strong ethnic community. Their cultural ties, including their native languages, are nonfunctional for trade, education, power, or negotiability; therefore, unless these ties are artificially supported they probably will disappear. It is reasonable to assume that these immigrants would rapidly become acculturated to and integrated in the American society, although their adaptation may be accompanied by high stress and cultural conflict.

Southeast Asians

The Southeast Asians—people from Cambodia, Laos, and Vietnam—came to this country primarily as refugees. For example, prior to the influx of refugees in the 1970s, there were approximately 20,000 Vietnamese in the United States, and the number of Cambodians and Laotians was too small to be counted. However, by 1980, 415,238 Indochinese were in this country, of which 78 percent were from Vietnam, 16 percent were from Cambodia, and 6 percent were from Laos. Although attempts were made to scatter the refugees throughout the country, the majority have resettled in California (135,308), Texas (36,198), and Washington (16,286) (Montero & Dieppa, 1982).

The refugees escaped from civil wars, dictatorships, communist regimes, and natural disasters. Many had held satisfactory and prominent positions in their country of origin and were committed to that country's system. However, because of changed conditions, they faced persecution because of their race, nationality, religion, or political beliefs. They fled out of sheer necessity and gave little thought to the consequences of migration. Many hope that the conditions will change so they can return to their country of origin (Stein, 1983). Grant (1980) noted that, in addition to those who fled crisis conditions, some refugees left their country of origin for reasons common to most immigrants—the hope for a better life in the United States, Australia, or Western Europe.

Cambodia, Laos, and Vietnam were part of the old French colonial empire and were lumped together as French Indochina, even though they were ethnically and culturally diverse. Wright (1980) indicated that the population of Cambodia is primarily ethnic Khmer, and the Cambodian culture was influenced by India, Siam, and Annam; the people of Laos are mainly ethnic Thai, and the Laotian culture was closely related to that of Siam; the people of Vietnam are basically a Mongoloid people, and their culture was heavily influenced by China. The divisions between these groups have deep historical roots, and some carryover of these feelings can be expected in this country, even though they all belong to the same refugee category.

The exodus of Vietnamese refugees began in 1975 when the fall of Saigon seemed imminent. President Ford created a special Interagency Task Force representing 12 federal agencies to coordinate the resettlement of the Vietnamese refugees. Resettlement camps were set up at Camp Pendleton, California, Fort Chafee, Arkansas, Eglin Air Force Base, Florida, and Fort Indiantown, Pennsylvania, to facilitate the assimilation of the refugees into the United States as quickly as possible (Wright, 1980). Efforts were made to find sponsors and employment for the refugees to minimize their dependence on public welfare. Sponsors were responsible for food, clothing, and shelter; for helping to find employment; for enrolling the children in school; for financing medical care; and for giving advice and encouragement.

The 1975 group constituted the first wave of refugees; a second wave was admitted to this country after 1975 and consisted of less well educated people.

Because the resettlement camps were closed after 1975, the second wave of refugees were much more dependent on the voluntary agencies for sponsorship. A common question among those working with the refugees is, Did you come in 1975 or after 1975? No major study has compared the two groups, but the general impression of these workers, which were based on the refugees' previous education and training, was that the after-1975 group would have a more difficult time adjusting to the United States.

Stein (1979) compared the occupational adjustment of Vietnamese refugees with other refugee groups. He found that the Vietnamese refugees were better off than the Cuban refugees and less well off than the 1956 Hungarian refugees and the refugees from Nazi Germany four to eight years after their arrival in this country. He found much downward mobility but believed that this pattern would be ameliorated by time, acculturation, improved facility with the English language, retraining programs, hard work, and determination. Stein (1979) saw the early years as most critical; if some degree of success is not achieved and problems are not solved early, the refugees become discouraged and may become dependent on the public welfare system.

Three factors hinder the adaptation of the refugees from Southeast Asia to American life: (1) the great disparity between their culture and the American society, (2) the lack of an already established ethnic community to help them adjust, and (3) the poor economic conditions in this country at the time of their arrival. Despite these barriers, however, the refugees from Southeast Asia entered the country at a period when structural discrimination was minimal, and the lack of an ethnic community may encourage their rapid acculturation.

Rose (1982b) visited the refugee camps in Southeast Asia and commented on the role of the voluntary agencies and caseworkers in facilitating the movement of refugees to the United States. He observed that the most effective caseworkers were those who spent some time resettling people in the United States before going into the field. Although he found that most of the workers were competent and sympathetic, those who observed the initial struggle of refugees in this country were at a decided advantage over those who did not. Furthermore, he noted, the English and cultural-orientation teachers, for example, were too far removed from the everyday life of the refugees to be effective. Rose (1982b) also mentioned the important role played by the agency workers, especially those who were Indochinese, in the United States in receiving the refugees.

In summary, Rose (1982a) presented the following picture of the Southeast Asian refugees: They were starving people at the border; they were females who had been repeatedly raped by pirates and bandits; they were giggling, full-of-life children once their bellies were full; they were the disoriented priests and former professional people; they were anxious teenagers who had known nothing but the struggle to survive and who were still hustling; they were the families of six crowded into a corner of a small room shared by 25 others; and they were the patient faces lined up for a 4:00 A.M. flight with their few possessions, waiting to go to places they could hardly pronounce, much less understand. Yet, they do make it to this country and, by and large, have started the process that should lead to a successful life.

Conclusion

Asian Americans have needs and face problems and conflicts, as do all groups who live in this competitive, multicultural, industrialized society. Problems such as poverty, overcrowded housing, the formation of juvenile gangs, and mental health issues are a part of urban life. In addition, Asians have been the targets of prejudice, discrimination, segregation, and racism so that life in the United States has been a constant adjustment from positions of lower power.

From a social work perspective, the special problems of Asian Americans include the following:

Immigration. Problems that revolve around immigration include the reunification of families, undocumented aliens, marriages motivated by citizenship, and the issue of refugees.

Acculturation. Problems associated with acculturation include the generation gap between immigrant parents and their American-socialized children; clashes in communication, language, and lifestyles; and differing expectations for and definitions of the meaning of becoming an American.

Cross-Cultural Issues. Cross-cultural problems include different ways of defining and solving such problems as wife beating, child abuse, and mental illness. Solutions may include the use of nonprofessionals.

Care of Dependents. The care of dependents covers problems related to child care and care of the aged. In Asian families, both parents often work, and child care facilities in Asian communities may be inadequate. The elderly face severe adjustment problems in American-style "retirement facilities"; their adult children suffer from feelings of guilt and shame for not taking care of their elderly parents in their own homes.

Identity. It is difficult for Asian Americans to achieve a full American identity in the face of negative stereotypes, physical visibility, and a phenotype that does not fit readily into the American image. Underemployment, especially among the refugees and new immigrants, also has an effect on the identity of individuals.

In spite of their many problems, Asian Americans do not generally turn to social welfare services for assistance. Miranda and Kitano (1976) identified several barriers to such participation in the social welfare system. They include (1) the fragmentation of services, so that clients are referred from one worker to another, (2) the discontinuity between the life of the professional and that of the client, (3) the inaccessibility of services, and (4) the primary focus of the professional on being accountable to fellow professionals rather than to the ethnic community. Appropriate services that take into account the variety of Asian groups and their cultural backgrounds, values, problems, expectations, and goals will no doubt lead to a higher use of social welfare services. (Green & Tong, 1979).

HARRY H. L. KITANO

For further information, see ETHNIC-SENSITIVE PRACTICE; IMMIGRANTS AND UNDOCUMENTED ALIENS; MINORITIES OF COLOR; SOCIAL WORK IN THE PACIFIC TERRITORIES.

References

Berk, B., & Hirata, L. (1973). "Mental Illness among the Chinese: Myth or Reality?" *Journal of Social Issues, 29*(2), 149–166.

Bosworth, A. R. (1967). *America's Concentration Camps.* New York: W. W. Norton & Co.

Commission on Wartime Relocation and Internment of Civilians (1982). *Personal Justice*

Denied. Washington, D.C.: U.S. Government Printing Office.

Cordova, F. (1973). "The Filipino-American: There's Always an Identity Crisis." In S. Sue and N. Wagner (Eds.), *Asian Americans* (pp. 136–139). Palo Alto, Calif.: Science & Behavior Books.

Daniels, R. (1971). *Concentration Camps U.S.A.: Japanese, Americans and World War II*. New York: Holt, Rinehart & Winston.

Daniels, R., & Kitano, H. H. L. (1970). *American Racism: Exploration of the Nature of Prejudice*. Englewood Cliffs, N.J.: Prentice-Hall.

Eaton, A. H. (1952). *Beauty Behind Barbed Wire: The Arts of the Japanese in Our War Relocation Camps*. New York: Harper & Bros.

Girdner, A., & Loftis, A. (1969). *The Great Betrayal*. New York: Macmillan Publishing Co.

Grant, B. (1980). *The Boat People*. New York: Penguin Books.

Green, J. W., & Tong, C. (Eds.). *Cultural Awareness in the Human Services: A Training Manual*. Seattle: University of Washington Center for Social Welfare Research.

Grodzins, M. (1949). *Americans Betrayed*. Chicago: University of Chicago Press.

Hosokowa, W. (1969). *Nisei*. New York: William Morrow & Co.

Hsu, F. (1971). *The Challenge of the American Dream: The Chinese in the United States*. Belmont, Calif.: Wadsworth Publishing Co.

Iga, M. (1966). "Changes in Value Orientation of Japanese Americans." Paper delivered at a meeting of the Western Psychological Association, Long Beach, Calif., April 28, 1966.

Irons, P. (1983). *Justice at War*. New York: Oxford University Press.

Kim, B. L. C., & Condon, M. E. (1975). "A Study of Asian Americans in Chicago: Their Socio-Economic Characteristics, Problems and Service Needs." *Interim Report to the National Institute of Mental Health*. Washington, D.C.: U.S. Department of Health, Education & Welfare.

Kim, D. S., & Wong, C. (1977). "Business Development in Koreatown, Los Angeles." In H. C. Kim (Ed.), *The Korean Diaspora* (pp. 229–245). Santa Barbara, Calif.: Clio Press.

Kim, H. C. (1980). "Koreans." In S. Thernstrom, A. Orlov, & O. Handlin (Eds.), *Harvard Encyclopedia of American Ethnic Groups* (pp. 601–606). Cambridge, Mass.: Harvard University Press.

Kishiyama, D. (1984, August 17). "Financial Ill Health Plagues an Ethnic Hospital," *Los Angeles Times*, Part 2, p. 1.

Kitano, H. H. L. (1976). *Japanese Americans: The Evolution of a Subculture* (2d ed.). Englewood Cliffs, N.J.: Prentice-Hall.

Kitano, H. H. L. (1981, March). "Asian Americans: The Chinese, Japanese, Koreans, Pilipinos, and Southeast Asians." *Annals of the American Academy of Political and Social Science, 454*, 125–138.

Kitano, H. H. L. (1985). *Race Relations* (3d ed.). Englewood Cliffs, N.J.: Prentice-Hall.

Kitano, H. H. L. et al. (1984). "Asian American Interracial Marriage," *Journal of Marriage and the Family, 46*(1), 179–190.

Kitano, H., & Sue, S. (1973). "The Model Minorities," *Journal of Social Issues, 29*(2), 1–10.

Lai, H. M. (1980). "Chinese." In S. Thernstrom, A. Orlov, & O. Handlin (Eds.), *Harvard Encyclopedia of American Ethnic Groups* (pp. 217–234). Cambridge, Mass.: Harvard University Press.

Leighton, A. H. (1945). *The Governing of Men: General Principles and Recommendations Based on Experience at a Japanese Relocation Camp*. Princeton, N.J.: Princeton University Press.

Loving v. Virginia. (1967). *United States Supreme Court Reports, 388*, 1014–1015.

Marsella, A., & Pedersen, P. (Eds.). (1981). *Cross-Cultural Counseling and Psychotherapy*. New York: Pergamon Press.

Mead, M. (1961). *Coming of Age in Samoa*. New York: William Morrow & Co.

Melendy, H. B. (1980). "Filipinos." In S. Thernstrom, A. Orlov, & O. Handlin (Eds.), *Harvard Encyclopedia of American Ethnic Groups* (pp. 354–362). Cambridge, Mass.: Harvard University Press.

Miranda, M., & Kitano, H. H. L. (1976). "Barriers to Mental Health: A Japanese and Mexican Dilemma." In C. Hernandez, N. Wagner, & M. Haug (Eds.), *Chicanos: Social Psychological Perspectives*. St Louis: C. V. Mosby & Co.

Montero, D. (1980). *Japanese Americans: Changing Patterns of Ethnic Affiliation over Three Generations*. Boulder, Colo.: Westview Press.

Montero, D., & Dieppa, I. (1982). "Resettling Vietnamese Refugees: The Service Agency's Role," *Social Work, 27*(1), 74–82.

Morales, R. (1974). *Makibaba*. Los Angeles: Mountain View Publishers.

Munoz, A. (1971). *The Filipinos in the United States*. Los Angeles: Mountain View Publishers.

Myer, D. (1971). *Uprooted Americans*. Tucson: University of Arizona Press.

Ogawa, D. (1971). *From Japs to Japanese*. Berkeley, Calif.: McCutchan Publishing Co.

Ogawa, D. (1978). *Kodomo no Tame Ni*. Honolulu: University of Hawaii Press.

Okubo, M. (1946). *Citizen 13660*. New York: Columbia University Press.

Pedersen, P. et al. (Eds.). (1981). *Counseling Across Cultures*. Honolulu: University of Hawaii Press.

Purcell, V. (1965). *The Chinese in Southeast Asia* (2d ed.). London, England: Oxford University Press.

"Report of the State Board of Control of California to Governor Wm. D. D. Stephens, June 19, 1920." (1978). In *California and the Oriental*. New York: Arno Press.

Rose, P. (1982a, March). "Links in a Chain: Observation of the American Refugee Program in Southeast Asia," *Catholic Mind, 80,* 2–25.

Rose, P. (1982b, April). "Southeast Asia to America: Links in a Chain, Part II." *Catholic Mind, 81,* 11–25.

Sherman, D. (1979, February 25). "Koreatown's Extent, Population Grow Daily," *Los Angeles Times,* Sec. 8, p. 1.

Shore, B. (1980). "Pacific Islanders." In S. Thernstrom, A. Orlov, & O. Handlin (Eds.), *Harvard Encyclopedia of American Ethnic Groups.* (pp. 763–768). Cambridge, Mass.: Harvard University Press.

Shu, R., & Satele A. S. (1977). *The Samoan Community in Southern California.* Chicago: Asian American Mental Health Research Center.

Spicer, E. H. et al. (1969). *Impounded People.* Tuscon: University of Arizona Press.

Stein, B. N. (1979). "Occupational Adjustment of Refugees: the Vietnamese in the United States," *International Migration Review, 13*(1), 25–45.

Stein, B. N. (1983, May). "The Commitment to Refugee Resettlement," *Annals of the American Academy of Political and Social Science, 487,* 187–201.

Sue, D., & Kirk, B. (1972). "Psychological Characteristics of Chinese American College Students," *Journal of Counseling Psychology, 19,* 471–478.

Sung, B. L. (1967). *Mountain of Gold.* New York: Macmillan Co.

Takaki, R. (1983, September 29). "Who Really Killed Vincent Chin," *Asian Week, 5*(6), 7.

Tateishi, J. (1984). *And Justice for All.* New York: Random House.

tenBroek, J., Barnhart, E. N., & Matson, F. W. (1954). *Prejudice, War and the Constitution.* Berkeley: University of California Press.

Thomas, D. S., Kikuchi, C., & Sakoda, J. (1952). *The Salvage.* Berkeley: University of California Press.

Thomas, D. S., & Nishimoto, R. (1946). *The Spoilage.* Berkeley: University of California Press.

Tong, B. (1971). "The Ghetto of the Mind: Notes on the Historical Psychology of Chinese America," *Amerasia Journal, 1*(3), 1–31.

U.S. Bureau of the Census. (1983, May). "U.S. Summary," Characteristics of the Population: 1980 (vol. 1, pp. 1–20). Washington, D.C.: U.S. Government Printing Office.

Weglyn, N. (1976). *Years of Infamy.* New York: William Morrow & Co.

Weiss, M. (1977). "The Research Experience in a Chinese American Community," *Journal of Social Issues, 33*(4), 120–132.

Wong, B. (1976). "Social Stratification, Adaptive Strategies and the Chinese Community in New York," *Urban Life, 5*(1), 33–52.

Wright, M. B. (1980). "Indochinese." In S. Thernstrom, A. Orlov, & O. Handlin (Eds.), *Harvard Encyclopedia of American Ethnic Groups* (pp. 508–513). Cambridge, Mass.: Harvard University Press.

Yu, E. Y. (1979). "Occupation and Work Patterns of Korean Immigrants in Los Angeles." Paper presented at the Korean Community Conference sponsored by Koryo Research Institute, Los Angeles, Calif., March 10, 1979.

ASSERTIVENESS TRAINING. See Social Skills Training.

ASSESSMENT. See Assessment in Direct Practice; Diagnostic and Statistical Manual (DSM); Direct Practice Effectiveness; Research in Social Work; Research Measures and Indices in Direct Practice.

ASSESSMENT IN DIRECT PRACTICE

From the earliest efforts to develop practice theory to the present day, some form of diagnosis or assessment has been described as essential to sound social work practice. The essence of diagnosis, according to Richmond (1917), is to develop a precise and accurate definition of clients and their social situations. Assessment is thus essentially a social diagnosis. Siporin (1975) defined assessment as "a differential, individualized, and accurate identification and evaluation of problems, people, and situations and of their interrelations, to serve as a sound basis for differential helping intervention" (p. 224).

Assessment is thus a process consisting of two parts—the collection of pertinent data about the client system and its environment, and the appraisal of the data as a basis for developing a plan of intervention.

Because of the strong association of "diagnosis" with illness or disability, "assessment" has become the preferred term. Many social workers continue to refer to "diagnosis," however, often using that word interchangeably with "assessment." Unlike diagnosis, assessment goes beyond the identification of a problem or illness and includes an appraisal of the interrelation among biological, psychological, and sociocultural factors and an identification of positive motivations and capacities. To achieve an accurate appraisal of the meaning of the facts that have been secured, the worker makes appropriate use of typologies of needs and problems, sources of information, and criteria for judging the adequacy of the functioning of individuals or groups in their environments.

In recent years, assessment has become part of a continuous process of interaction between the social worker and the individual or group being served. With a few exceptions, it is not a formal phase that precedes treatment. It involves efforts to engage the client system in an exploration for facts and in an analysis and interpretation of the facts as they become evident. In accordance with social work values, the search for understanding is reciprocal between a practitioner and a client system. Clients not only react to the worker's communications, but they actively contribute information and evaluate the worker's tentative ideas about their needs and ways of behaving. Such feedback either corrects or reaffirms the worker's analysis of the situation.

In engaging the client system in the assessment process, practitioners work toward certain goals. They seek to disclose the nature and significance of the need or problem and to identify strengths, motivations, and available resources in the client system or other related social systems. They seek to involve the clients in an orderly process of problem solving, through which clients learn productive means of identifying and working on difficulties. The attainment of these goals makes it possible for practitioners to select the appropriate modality of service

and, within that modality, to develop a plan of action for achieving the outcomes the worker and clients have mutually agreed on. The preliminary assessment is a tentative one, to be elaborated and modified as the worker and clients interact in regard to one or more mutually agreed-on goals. The content and processes need to be in harmony with the values of the profession as those values are translated into principles of practice.

Psychosocial Needs and Problems

The needs and problems clients bring to social agencies or private practitioners are greatly varied. It is the presenting request or complaint that provides a beginning for the process of assessing client needs. Problems are conditions or situations that are perplexing, difficult, or undesirable. They are barriers to the achievement of goals sought by the client or by others in the client's social network. If a person or family decides to apply for a service, the practitioner elicits each person's views of the need or problem. If a client system is referred by someone else, the initial concern is defined by the referral agent. The client reacts to the definition of the problem, either confirming or rejecting the practitioner's idea of the difficulty and the need for help. Even when the service is a developmental or preventive one, there is often a discrepancy between potential and actual achievement or a desire for enhanced opportunities. In exploring the nature and scope of the needs with the clients, the worker seeks their perceptions about who is involved in, or affected by, the problems, when and by whom the problem was first identified, and what feelings and reactions are attached to the problem. The worker seeks to learn how the problem is experienced by the client; the amount of discomfort or stress that accompanies it; the extent to which the steady state or equilibrium is disrupted; what efforts have been made to deal with the situation; and what capacities the client has to deal with the difficulties. As exploration proceeds, the problem as defined may be quite different from the presenting problem, or a constellation of problems may be identified, one or more of which is considered appropriate for social work help.

Typologies of Psychosocial Needs and Problems. Although each individual is unique in many respects, a typology of needs and problems can aid the practitioner in identifying the need and selecting a focus for intervention. The needs and problems addressed by social workers are those that pertain to the social and psychological functioning of individuals or to the social or organizational functioning of larger social systems. The literature, including results of research, indicates that people tend to define their problems in terms of social relationships, social role functioning, and external difficulties (Gurin, Veroff, & Field, 1960; Ripple, Alexander, & Polemis, 1964; Schmidt, 1969).

Several social workers have formulated tentative classifications of clients' needs and problems in a way that accords with the profession's purpose of enhancing the social functioning of individuals, families, and other groups. Perlman (1968), emphasizing that the major problems faced by clients are in the area of role performance, classified such problems as (1) deficiencies or deficits in tangible material means, deficiencies in personal capacity that restrict or thwart role performance, and deficiencies of knowledge and preparation; (2) personality disturbances or mental disorders; and (3) discrepancies found in roles, including discrepancies between several valued roles, between expectations of self and others, or between personality needs and role requirements, or discrepancies that result from ambiguous and contradictory definitions of roles.

A nationwide survey of hospital social work practice by Coulton, Paschall, Foster, Bohnengel, and Slivinske (1979) included a section on the types of needs and problems dealt with by social workers in health settings. This typology of problems and needs was based on an earlier instrument by Berkman and Rehr (1978). Included were 27 categories of problems dealing with the psychosocial functioning of patients, family functioning in relation to patient illness, and environmental needs. Further work is taking place to refine the taxonomy and improve its reliability. Germain and Gitterman (1980) classified people's needs, problems, or predicaments into three categories: life transitions involving developmental changes, status role changes, and crisis events; unresponsiveness of social and physical environments; and communications and relationship difficulties in families and other primary groups.

Building on earlier formulations by Reid and Shyne (1969) and Reid and Epstein (1972), Reid (1978) developed a classification of problems for task-centered social work practice and tested its reliability. The categories are interpersonal conflict, dissatisfaction in social relations, problems with formal organizations, difficulties in role performance, decision problems, reactive emotional distress, inadequate resources, and psychological or behavioral problems not elsewhere classified. Problems are defined as unsatisfied wants. Within these categories, particular problems must be acknowledged by the client. The problem must be explicitly defined and delimited, and it must be one that the client can alleviate through actions performed outside the treatment session.

Reid's classification is consistent with other models of social work practice, even though the requirements for the definition of a particular problem may be different. Northen (1982) accepted Reid's classification of problems, with minor variations, and added categories of loss of relationships, cultural conflicts among persons and between groups, and maladaptive functioning of families and other groups. Problems of groups have been dealt with by Pincus and Minahan (1973), Garvin and Glasser (1969), the Group for the Advancement of Psychiatry (1970), and Scherz (1970). These authors conceptualize a group's problems as dysfunctions in the structure and processes of the group.

These various formulations of the problems with which social workers deal are not contradictory, and it is possible that they can be reconceptualized into a more complete system of classification. The advantages of such a system would be clarity concerning which problems are best addressed by which form of practice and a fairly uniform way of reporting and accounting for the services rendered by social workers.

Medical and Psychiatric Classifications. In medicine, diagnosis is defined as the art and science of identifying a disease or disability. In contrast, social work deals with psychosocial problems. The use of medical and psychiatric diagnoses is an issue for the profession. It is generally agreed that if a physical disease is suspected, a physician makes the diagnosis and is responsible for the medical treatment. Even so, social workers need to be alert to symptoms that suggest an illness, to the symptoms of drug use and the effects drugs have on people, and to the psychosocial aspects of illness and disability. Physical, social, and psychological well-being are intimately interrelated: when medical problems are suspected, it is necessary to rule out the presence of organic conditions through referral to, or consultation with, physicians. Social workers practicing in health settings need considerable knowledge about diseases to make appropriate psychosocial assessments.

The use of diagnoses of mental disorders in social work practice is another matter of controversy in the profession. Regardless of their attitudes toward attaching diagnostic labels to clients, many social workers are now required by insurance companies or funding agencies to classify their clients' difficulties according to the categories in the third edition of the *Diagnostic and Statistical Manual* (DSM III) of the American Psychiatric Association (1980). DSM III conceptualizes each disorder as a clinically significant behavioral or psychological syndrome, which is typically associated with painful symptoms or impairment of functioning. The dysfunction is perceived to reside in the individual, not in the relationship between an individual and other persons or society. In arriving at a diagnosis of mental disorder, the practitioner makes a multiaxial evaluation. The five axes are (1) all mental disorders, except personality and developmental ones, (2) personality and developmental disorders, (3) physical disorders and conditions, (4) severity of psychosocial stressors that are significant in the development or exacerbation of the current disorder, and (5) the highest level of adaptive functioning in the past year. The first three axes comprise the official diagnosis; axes 4 and 5 are supplemental. The classifications do not include consideration of disturbed dyadic, family, or other social relationships or of developmental needs or environmental opportunities and obstacles. For most disorders, the etiology is unknown, and varied theoretical explanations of causation are given.

Use of Classifications

Although many practitioners endorse the use of typologies of mental and behavioral disorders, others have serious questions about their value for social work practice. They refer to the work of social scientists (Hobbs, 1975; Schur, 1971; Toch, 1979; Waxler, 1974) who studied the effects of labeling persons as handicapped, mentally retarded, delinquent, psychotic, or terminally ill. The use of labels is thought to play a crucial role in the development and maintenance of deviant behavior: people tend to behave according to the expectations conveyed by the label. The label also tends to create stereotyped reactions from others. When categories are not adapted to new information, they become perpetuated in their initial form. The label may then become an instrument of social control, as when children with handicaps in the use of English are labeled mentally retarded and progressively denied equal educational opportunities. When people are inappropriately labeled, they are devalued and stigmatized. The diagnosis can become a self-fulfilling prophecy: the way a problem is defined determines its solution (Hobbs, 1975).

Social workers have made similar objections to classifications that label individuals as deviant. Reid (1978), Fischer and Gochros (1975), and Smalley (1967), for example, argue that classifications can do an injustice to the client by providing a worker-oriented rather than a client-focused approach to helping. Classification denies the uniqueness of a person or group and violates the ethical principles of individualization and self-determination. Labels, particularly those used in psychiatry, tend to be unidimensional, whereas people are multidimensional. As Reid (1978) notes, most mental disorders are a product of complex interactions among the client, other persons, and collectivities; diagnoses, particularly of mental disorders, do not account adequately for the sociocultural and environmental aspects of problems. Because categories often lack empirical support, they often give practitioners a false sense of confidence in their understanding of clients. Furthermore, they emphasize problems rather than positive motivations, capacities, and achievements. Reid (1978) noted that "categories of deviance, particularly psychiatric labels, are given more weight than they merit" (p. 77). The diagnostic label may be taken for the totality of a person's functioning. The objections to classifications, then, refer primarily to labeling persons as deviant, as distinct from categories of psychosocial problems that are acknowledged by clients.

In spite of reservations, most scientists argue that some form of categorization is necessary. Allport (1958), for example, notes that categories are essential to orderly thinking and planning. Many social workers agree. Lewis (1982) strongly asserts the need for typologies to serve diagnostic ends:

> A sound assessment scheme should free the worker to consider more carefully the unique aspects of individual requests and to tailor the process of intervention to fit the peculiarities of each instance of a class of cases. (p. 197)

Lewis was not referring to any particular kind of classification scheme, but many social workers favor the use of classifications of mental disorders (Hollis & Woods, 1981; Levy, 1981; Strean, 1978; Turner, 1984). Turner, for example, states that labels have not been used sufficiently and that they are important aids to conscious and deliberate planning and treatment. The many contemporary articles in journals and books that utilize medical classifications attest to their growing popularity in social work. Social workers agree, however, that if diagnoses of mental disorders are used, they must be used in consort with other information of a psychosocial nature. The major problem lies in the misuse of classifications.

Typologies are for use, and the utility of any classification depends in part on how adequately it covers the range of situations with which it deals and in part on how competent the practitioners are in applying the typology to their practice. Principles of practice suggested by Northen (1982) can ensure the proper use of typologies of problems:

1. The problem should be based on facts, not inferences, and it should be defined in operational terms.

2. Classifications are merely tools that alert a practitioner to major combinations of relevant factors. They are thus useful in communicating the central tendency of the condition to colleagues.

3. The classification influences what is perceived and how the perceptions are organized for action. Formulating a useful psychosocial assessment requires knowledge beyond that in the classification. The evaluation is of patterns of behavior or sets of environmental obstacles, not of a person or family.

4. Classification is a means of ascertaining what characteristics a person or family has in common with other individuals or groups in a population. It emphasizes also what is unique in the person or family, that is, how an individual or group differs from others of its type. This is the well-known principle of individualization.

5. Problems are viewed not as existing in the person only, but as a characteristic of the person-situation interaction. Interpersonal, environmental, and intrapersonal processes are all taken into account in defining the problem.

6. In undertaking service with a client identified as having a particular type of problem, the social worker does not permit the label to obscure the client's strengths or the value of intervening in a variety of systems to meet the client's needs.

7. The search for understanding is reciprocal between a practitioner and a client. In line with social work values, clients have a right and a responsibility to participate actively in the process.

Content of Assessment

The content of assessment is essentially psychosocial in nature because that focus is congruent with the purpose of social work. It therefore includes four levels of analysis: the individual, interpersonal systems, the family unit, and the family's interchange with its social network and other environmental or ecological factors (Briar & Miller, 1971; Siporin, 1975; Meyer, 1976; Northen, 1982). Comparative analyses of theoretical approaches to practice tend to conclude that, in spite of some differences, almost all theorists use systems ideas for organizing the data of assessment (Simon, 1970; Meyer, 1976; Northen & Roberts, 1976; Turner, 1974). The trend is toward approaching the issue of assessment with full consideration of the multiple and complex transactions that occur among people in their varied social situations.

Several writers (Compton & Galaway, 1979; Goldstein, 1973; Pincus & Minahan, 1973; Siporin, 1975) have offered detailed outlines of the content deemed essential for making a sound assessment. Practitioners can become overwhelmed by the vast amount of data it is possible to secure unless they have clear guidelines for exploring pertinent data and selecting appropriate means for obtaining the desired information. Questions that are usually appropriate include:

1. Who is the client? What are the client's identifying demographic characteristics and stage of development in the life cycle?

2. What problems are of concern to the client, the worker, and significant other persons in the client's social network?

3. How, when, and to whom did the need or problem become evident, and what were the precipitating factors?

4. What are the core intrapersonal, interpersonal, group, and community stressors that interfere with the client's adequate or optimal functioning and that may contribute to an explanation of the need for service?

5. What feasible goals, acknowledged by the client, might serve as a beginning focus for help?

6. How adequately does the client perform his or her roles in the systems of which he or she is a part?

7. To what extent is the client motivated to use the help of the worker or other resources? What indications are there of positive motivation, and what is the nature of any resistance?

8. What are the strengths and resources in the individual, family, group, and social systems that can be supported and developed further in behalf of the client?

9. In what ways are the problems, the characteristics of the client, the social situation, and the agreed-on goals interconnected?

10. What types of action are apt to best meet the needs of the individual or family?

To understand clients in their situations, it is necessary to understand the fit between the individual and the family and other groups to which the client belongs. This requires an evaluation of the structure, functions, and interactional processes in these systems. Questions used to guide the practitioner in understanding the functioning of families and other groups include:

1. What are the strengths and difficulties in the patterns, quality, and depth of relationships among the members?

2. Are there problems in the membership or composition of the system?

3. How effective or dysfunctional are the patterns of communication, including the extent to which the boundary is open or closed to new inputs?

4. What are the major subsystems and how effective are their structures of formal and informal roles?

5. Who makes what kinds of decisions that affect varied members, what processes are used, and how do these influence the achievement of individual and system goals?

6. What are the major conflicts that occur and what are the means used toward their solution?

7. What values and norms govern the expectations of behavior for the members, and how are these norms enforced?

8. What sociocultural influences and group interactions in the larger community affect the individuals and the system as a whole?

The amount and nature of the data sought vary with the service, particularly with its purpose and structure and the practitioner's theoretical orientation. The understanding of the client-group-situation gestalt cannot encompass all aspects of the individual's or group's functioning, and in accord with the value of the right to privacy, the information sought should be limited to what is essential for achieving agreed-on goals. If a service is one of primary prevention or enhancement of normal development, the data obtained are often limited initially to the descriptive characteristics common to the clients, such as phase of development, common experience or status, and certain potential risks to healthy development. Later, during the process of service, the worker may elicit additional information as it seems relevant or as individuals who exhibit special problems are identified. If the service is therapeutic or rehabilitative, helpful treatment cannot be given unless the worker has an adequate understanding of the nature, causative factors, and course of the problem and of the adequacy of the client's current functioning in particular situations.

Each model of practice describes particular foci for assessment. For example, behavioral models require the practitioner to secure precise information about the observable behaviors to be extinguished, modified, or acquired (Gambrill, 1977; Rose, 1981; Schwartz & Goldiamond, 1975; Thomas, 1970), in addition to information about other aspects of psychosocial functioning. When an individual is in a state of crisis, the information sought centers around the hazardous event, the emotional reactions to it, and the client's use of defenses and adaptive patterns (Golan, 1978; Parad, 1965; Rapoport, 1970). The initial assessment may be limited to what is necessary to make a tentative decision about accepting the applicant for service, with additional data secured as the need for it becomes evident. In most instances, as described by Toseland and Rivas (1984), it is essential to balance the need for detailed information against the need for immediate action.

The primary issues concerning the content of assessment are the extent of the exploration for data before intervention and the extent of the attention given to genetic or historical data. Most models of practice now agree that the worker must obtain sufficient information to ascertain whether, within the function of the service agency, the need or presenting problem calls for social work intervention and to make an initial assignment to a modality of service. Beyond that, the models differ widely: behavior modification models, for example, require obtaining detailed baseline data prior to intervention, and reciprocal (Schwartz, 1976) and functional (Smalley, 1967) models limit data collection to that which turns out to be an integral part of the helping process. Practitioners differ, too, in their opinions about the need for data concerning the client's past experiences, with psychoanalytically oriented therapy (Allan, 1979) at one end of a continuum and the structural approach (Middleman & Goldberg, 1974) at the other extreme. However, comparative analyses of theoretical approaches by Simon (1970), Roberts and Northen (1976), and Turner (1979) indicate that concentration on details of early history and on unconscious components of human behavior is not a principal focus of attention. According to Turner (1979), all approaches, including psychoanalytically oriented practice, have a twofold thrust on person and situation in the present and utilize exploration of the past on a highly selective basis.

Sources of Information

The psychosocial study of the individual-group-situation configuration is accomplished through a variety of means: epidemiology, examination of the relationship between the worker and the client system, interviews with individuals and families, group sessions, and measuring instruments.

Epidemiology. According to Meyer (1976), epidemiology is as essential for a social worker as for a doctor. Knowledge about the characteristics of caseloads and the common needs of people living in an agency's catchment area is important in setting priorities for service. Preventive, developmental, and community action services are based on knowledge of the extent of the problem or condition and the demographic characteristics of persons affected by the condition. Neglect of epidemiological data can distort the reality of people's lives because it encourages treating a person with a problem as an isolated instance of deviance, rather than as one instance of a problem common to many people in similar situations. Although the worker has a responsibility to help the initial client, the incidence of the difficulty also suggests a need for broader programs that offer preventive services to those who share the common condition or for programs that participate in community actions to solve the problem (Middleman & Goldberg, 1974).

Worker-Client System. The relationship between a worker and an individual or group is an important source of information for the assessment. As clients become engaged with a practitioner, they often feel the acceptance and empathy that are conveyed. When this occurs, these feelings encourage trust and openness to new ideas, and clients become more willing to disclose information about their feelings, themselves, and their situations. As practitioners examine their own spontaneous reactions to the individual or to members of the client system, they can learn much about the individual or group. Clients provoke emotional reactions. Some reactions may result from the worker's attitudes, but others derive from elements in the relationship between worker and client. A person or group often elicits similar reactions from other people, and the pattern of interpersonal behavior involved may be destructive to the client. The other side of the interaction is the client's reaction to the worker. Some such reactions are realistic evaluations, but others result from distortions in perception. Understanding this two-way process can make an important contribution to assessment.

Interviews with Individuals. The most frequent source of assessment data is the personal interview in which facts about prospective clients and their situations are elicited. Through direct observation of verbal and nonverbal behavior, the social worker derives clues as to patterns of relationships and perceptions of self in relation to others. Individual interviews are especially useful in understanding and clarifying clients' goals and their reactions to the available services and the conditions under which help is given. Such interviews offer an opportunity to explore feelings and to secure information that is pertinent to the selection of interventions. They are useful in screening individuals, referring them, and preparing them for experiences in groups.

In many instances, interviews with other staff, relatives of the client, or persons in the client's social network contribute to an understanding of the client's needs. This is particularly true in work with children and in interdisciplinary settings, such as schools and hospitals. In addition, the information gained from such interviews is useful in team planning to meet the needs of clients and their relatives.

Joint and Family Sessions. Increasingly, joint or family sessions are used as the major procedure or as supplementary to interviews with individuals. Such interviews have special value to assessment. A nationwide survey of agencies affiliated with the Family Service Association of America (now Family Service America) (Couch, 1969) documented the opportunities such interviews provided for simultaneous observation and evaluation of both partners or the entire family. Family sessions revealed interactions in ways similar to joint interviews, but with increased subtlety and greater illumination of marital relationships and family functioning. The major contributions joint and family interviews make to the assessment of marital problems are as follows: (1) they often reveal

otherwise hidden strengths and positive mutual bonds that may become essential therapeutic aids, (2) they illuminate pathological destructiveness, restrictiveness, and mutual pain in family members' interactions, (3) they provide greater clarity about the life situation of the couple or family, especially when the interviews are conducted during home visits, (4) they improve opportunities for the worker to observe the impact of treatment on the couple and members of the family, and (5) they make possible greater speed and accuracy in assessment.

From a review of the Family Service Association's empirical study and of the literature on the use of such interviews, Couch (1969) concluded that

> the diagnostic microscope has been fitted with a wide-angle lens, with the result that the picture under scrutiny looks different. No longer does the individual loom largest, with marriage, family, workaday world and the wider society seen as background for him. Instead, he is now viewed at one and the same time as a unit and as a functional part of various groups, each of which is in turn part of a larger cluster. (p. 54)

Group Sessions. Similar benefits accrue from meetings with clients in small groups. The literature documents the successful use of assessment sessions with small groups of adoptive parents, children referred to child guidance centers, and patients or their relatives (Churchill, 1965; Redl, 1944; Sundel, Radin, & Churchill, 1974). In addition, group sessions provide insight into the nature and quality of relationships with peers. In children's groups, the relationship with an adult practitioner gives clues concerning strengths and difficulties in relationships with parents and other adults with whom the child has an association. Such groups augment the limited information provided by parents, teachers, or doctors. In one family service center, King (1970) found that groups provided an accurate and vivid vision of the child's level of functioning.

Measuring Instruments. Measuring instruments are increasingly used to obtain and analyze data relevant to assessments of problems and person-situation configurations (Siporin, 1975). Many social workers make little use of formal instruments, preferring to use the unobtrusive methods in which observation and data collection are part of an ongoing process of interaction between the worker and the client system. Social workers often distrust devices that may intrude on the developing professional relationship and the exploratory dialogue between the worker and the client system. Some practitioners have learned, however, that selective use of such tools can improve assessment, further the treatment process, and document the outcomes of the helping endeavor.

Manuals of mental disorders and classifications of psychosocial problems are forms of instruments. Siporin (1975) and Toseland and Rivas (1984) identify others, including self-rating inventories, questionnaires, formal scales, sociograms, and forms of simulation that measure some aspect of social functioning. In behavioral approaches, such means as records of self-observations, formal scales, and direct observations of clients by social workers or other responsible persons in direct interaction with clients provide baseline data. The purpose is to secure adequate measures of the frequency of the behaviors that are the target of change efforts and the precipitants and consequences of those behaviors. Numerous instruments have been developed for measuring the psychological or social problems of individuals and the social interactions, relationships, and cohesiveness of groups. Some of the instruments and descriptions of others can be found in Hudson (1982), Levitt and Reid (1981), and Toseland and Rivas (1984). The tools used need to be clearly related to the goals of service and to the particular needs of the individual, family, or group that is being assessed.

Analysis of the Data

Once the practitioner has obtained the pertinent information, the actual assessment consists of analyzing the individual-group-environment gestalt. The purpose is to identify the most critical factors and to define their interrelationships. The assessment is the worker's professional opinion about the facts and their meaning. Perlman (1970) and Somers (1976) referred to this process as one of problem solving by the worker, done through a process of reflective thinking. Lewis (1982) refers to it as a logical process that also incorporates intuitive insights. Realistic appraisal provides the basis for action that should be guided by facts. What is to be understood is the nature of the need or trouble, the factors that contribute to it, and the participants' motivations and capacities; the practitioner also makes a judgment about what can be changed, supported, or strengthened in the person-group-situation configuration.

Assessment is not completed when a problem or condition has been identified and pertinent data obtained. There remains the need to explain how the situation came to be the way it is. The practitioner draws inferences from the data and relates these judgments to the service that can be given. The behavioral science theory that is used determines largely the inferences that are made.

Use of Norms. Any given culture has norms or expectations that are used to judge the extent to which a person or a group is functioning adequately. Appraisal of a person's functioning on a continuum ranging from very effective to very ineffective clues the worker into both capacities and problems. Although norms are necessary, rapid changes in lifestyles and the conditions of life make it difficult for workers and clients to assess the adequacy of functioning, as do the varied cultural backgrounds of clients. A task for the worker is to ascertain the influence of socioeconomic status, race, and ethnicity on psychosocial functioning. Although there are certain characteristics that differentiate one group from another, efforts to define these characteristics may lead to negative stereotyping. Persons in positions of power, including social workers, come to expect stereotyped behavior and plan and act accordingly (Martinez, 1973). Awareness of one's own norms and culture is essential to prevent stereotyping, as is accurate knowledge about other cultures and lifestyles.

Determining the adequacy of behavior requires such judgments as whether the behavior is appropriate to the client's stage of development; how long it has persisted; whether it is a reaction to a change in circumstances or a devastating crisis; whether it is socially acceptable behavior in the client's sociocultural group; whether the behavior interferes with only one or several roles; the type, severity, and frequency of symptoms; and whether the individual's behavior has changed in ways that are not expected in terms of normal maturation and development.

The social worker understands that all phases of human development overlap, that each person has his or her own rate of maturation and development within what are average expectations, and that there are many variations in a normal pattern of functioning. People's feelings about their assigned roles, the way they interpret them, and their responses to the expectations of others give clues to the fit between persons and their environments. A person may adapt well to one situation and poorly to another. The worker is concerned, therefore, with variations in the effectiveness of functioning in different social systems—whether ineffective functioning in one system is affecting the ability to adapt elsewhere, and if successful functioning in one system can be used as a bridge to more effective functioning in other systems.

Models of Practice. Each model or theoretical approach to practice provides different, often contradictory, explanations. Roberts and Nee (1970), Roberts and Northen (1976), Tolson and Reid (1981), and Turner (1979) have all written comparative studies of the various models.

The theory that is utilized directs the practitioner's attention to certain variables and gives them meaning. A model might derive its explanation of behavior from psychoanalytic theory or ego psychology, for example, but even authors subscribing to the same theory might emphasize different concepts or adapt the theory to psychosocial, problem-solving, or crisis intervention approaches to practice. Psychoanalytic theories are rejected in other models, including the behavioral modification and structural approaches, which explain behavior as learned responses. Several models emphasize current as opposed to historical factors of causation.

No model of social work practice views problems as only individual pathology, but models differ in the emphasis they give to intrapersonal, interpersonal, and ecological influences on the client's situation. All social work models of family and group services utilize theories that explain the structure, processes, and development of small social systems, but they vary greatly in the emphasis they give to individual behavior and environmental influences. The theoretical base influences the definition of problems, the outcome goals, the structure of service, and the choice of interventions.

Alternative Explanations. Lewis (1982) observes that explanations are most useful when they account for all the known facts and suggest others not previously identified. Explanations arrived at through logical thinking apply only to a particular case. For example, not everyone subjected to social injustice develops the same responses. The assessment explains how a particular individual or family was actually victimized and what its responses to this event did or did not bring about. Both strengths and difficulties are located. Because it establishes the unique and the common responses to factors that contribute to a particular condition, such an approach deemphasizes stereotyping of client systems.

Accurate assessment requires consideration of alternative explanations. Making a causative statement requires a choice among alternatives, even though the worker may not yet have identified the full range of available alternatives. Accuracy requires, however, that the selection of alternatives be a conscious one (Pincus & Minahan, 1973). Solomon (1976) gives the example of a girl who is assessed as discriminated against in school or, alternatively, as a child having difficulty adapting to a new school in which she feels isolated and lonely. Determining which alternative is more probable requires careful exploration of one's preferences and of the client's or group's situation.

The need for rapid intervention in urgent situations often limits the worker's decision-making ability. Ultimately, however, skill in rapid assessment requires an extensive and thorough knowledge of human behavior and of possible alternative explanations. Knowing when and how to alter initial assumptions is also essential to the exercise of professional judgment. According to Siporin (1975), the product of the analysis is a formulation that integrates the data, draws conclusions about the interrelated factors contributing to the problem, and leads to decisions about which interventions to implement.

Conclusion

Assessment is an essential means of understanding the needs of clients and thereby providing them with individualized services. There is a considerable body of generic knowledge about the purposes, content, and processes of assessment and about the differential use of that knowledge in varied models and modalities of social work practice with individuals, families, and formed groups. However, further theoretical development and research are necessary on several important issues:

1. How can contributions from existing formulations of psychosocial needs and problems be used to develop a reliable and valid typology of the needs and problems suitable for direct social work services?

2. What effects do diagnoses of mental disorders have on practitioners' attitudes toward and evaluations of clients, on clients' attitudes toward themselves, and on the use clients make of professional services?

3. In working toward particular psychosocial goals, how important is knowledge of earlier life experiences and unconscious motivations compared to knowledge of present experiences and conscious processes?

4. How does the amount of data secured influence the selection of interventions and the outcomes of service?

Answering these questions would refine the knowledge about assessment and help clarify the differential use of such knowledge in providing services. This, in turn, would help the profession achieve important goals related to its purpose of enhancing social functioning.

HELEN NORTHEN

For further information, see DIAGNOSTIC AND STATISTICAL MANUAL (DSM); DIRECT PRACTICE: TRENDS AND ISSUES; DIRECT PRACTICE EFFECTIVENESS; DIRECT PRACTICE IN SOCIAL WORK: OVERVIEW.

References

Allan, E. F. (1979). In F. J. Turner (Ed.), *Social Work Treatment: Interlocking Theoretical Approaches* (pp. 13–32). New York: Free Press.

Allport, G. W. (1958). *The Nature of Prejudice.* New York: Doubleday Anchor.

American Psychiatric Association. (1980). *Diagnostic and Statistical Manual* (3rd ed.). New York: Author.

Berkman, B., & Rehr, H. (1978). "Social Work Undertakes Its Own Audit." *Social Work in Health Care, 3*(1), 273–286.

Briar, S., & Miller, H. (1971). *Problems and Issues in Social Casework.* New York: Columbia University Press.

Churchill, S. R. (1965). "Social Group Work: A Diagnostic Tool in Child Guidance." *American Journal of Orthopsychiatry, 35*(3), 581–588.

Compton, B. R., & Galaway, B. (Eds.). (1979). *Social Work Processes* (2nd ed.). Homewood, Ill.: Dorsey Press.

Couch, E. H., (1969). *Joint and Family Interviews in the Treatment of Marital Problems.* New York: Family Service Association of America.

Coulton, C. J., Paschall, N. C., Foster, D. L., Bohnengel, A., & Slivinske, L. (1979). *Nationwide Survey of Hospital Social Work Practice.* Cleveland, Ohio: School of Applied Social Sciences, Case Western Reserve University.

Fischer, J., & Gochros, H. L. (1975). *Planned Behavior Change: Behavior Modification in Social Work.* New York: Free Press..

Gambrill, E. D. (1977). *Behavior Modification: Handbook of Assessment, Intervention, and Evaluation.* San Francisco: Jossey-Bass.

Garvin, C. D., & Glasser, P. H. (1969). "The Bases of Social Treatment." In *Social Work Practice, 1969* (pp. 149–177). New York: Columbia University Press.

Germain, C. B., & Gitterman, A. (1980). *The Life Model of Social Work Practice.* New York: Columbia University Press.

Golan, N. (1978). *Treatment in Crisis Situations.* New York: Free Press.

Goldstein, H. (1973). *Social Work Practice: A Unitary Approach.* Columbia, S.C.: University of South Carolina Press.

Group for the Advancement of Psychiatry. (1970). *The Field of Family Therapy.* New York: Science House.

Gurin, G., Veroff, J., & Field, S. (1960). *Americans View Their Mental Health.* New York: Basic Books.

Hobbs, N. (1975). *The Futures of Children: Categories, Labels, and Their Consequences.* San Francisco: Jossey-Bass.

Hollis, F., & Woods, M. E. (1981). *Casework: A*

Psychosocial Therapy (3rd ed.). New York: Random House.

Hudson, W. (1982). *The Clinical Measurement Package*. Homewood, Ill.: Dorsey Press.

King, B. L. (1970). "Diagnostic Activity Group for Latency Age Children." In Community Service Society of New York, *Dynamic Approaches to Serving Families* (pp. 55–67). New York: Community Service Society of New York.

Lewis, H. (1982). *The Intellectual Base of Social Work Practice: Tools for Thought in a Helping Profession*. New York: Haworth Press.

Levitt, J. L., & Reid, W. J. (1981). "Rapid Assessment Instruments in Social Work Practice." *Social Work Research and Abstracts, 17*(1), 13–20.

Levy, S. (1981). "Labeling: The Social Worker's Responsibility." *Social Casework, 62*(6), 332–342.

Martinez, C. (1973). "Community Mental Health and the Chicano Movement." *American Journal of Orthopsychiatry, 43*(4), 595–610.

Meyer, C. H. (1976). *Social Work Practice: The Changing Landscape*. New York: Free Press.

Middleman, R. R., & Goldberg, G. (1974). *Social Service Delivery: A Structural Approach to Social Work Practice*. New York: Columbia University Press.

Northen, H. (1982). *Clinical Social Work*. New York: Columbia University Press.

Northen, H., & Roberts, R. W. (1976). "The Status of Theory." In R. W. Roberts & H. Northen (Eds.), *Theories of Social Work With Groups*. New York: Columbia University Press.

Parad, H. J. (ed.). (1965) *Crisis Intervention: Selected Readings*. New York: Family Service Association of America.

Perlman, H. H. (1968). *Persona: Social Role and Personality*. Chicago: University of Chicago Press.

Perlman, H. H. (1970). "The Problem-Solving Model in Social Casework." In R. W. Roberts & R. H. Nee (Eds.), *Theories of Social Casework*. Chicago: University of Chicago Press.

Pincus, A., & Minahan, A. (1973). *Social Work Practice: Model and Method*. Itasca, Ill.: F. E. Peacock Publishers.

Rapoport, L. (1970). "Crisis Intervention As a Mode of Brief Treatment." In R. W. Roberts & R. H. Nee (Eds.), *Theories of Social Casework*. Chicago: University of Chicago Press.

Redl, F. (1944). "Diagnostic Group Work." *American Journal of Orthopsychiatry, 14*(1) 53–67.

Reid, W. J. (1978). *The Task-Centered System*. New York: Columbia University Press.

Reid, W. J., & Epstein, L. (1972). *Task-Centered Casework*. New York: Columbia University Press.

Reid, W. J., & Shyne, A. (1969). *Brief and Extended Casework*. New York: Columbia University Press.

Richmond, M. E. (1917). *Social Diagnosis*. New York: Russell Sage Foundation.

Ripple, L., Alexander, E., & Polemis, B. W. (1964). *Motivation, Capacity and Opportunity*. Chicago: School of Social Service Administration, University of Chicago.

Roberts, R. W., & Nee, R. H. (Eds.). (1970). *Theories of Social Casework*. Chicago: University of Chicago Press.

Roberts, R. W., & Northen, H. (Eds.). (1976). *Theories of Social Work With Groups*. Chicago: University of Chicago Press.

Rose, S. (1981). "Assessment in Groups." *Social Work Research and Abstracts, 17*(1), 29–37.

Scherz, F. (1970). "Family Therapy." In R. W. Roberts & R. H. Nee (Eds.), *Theories of Social Casework*. Chicago: University of Chicago Press.

Schmidt, J. (1969). "The Use of Purpose in Casework Practice." *Social Work, 4*(1), 77–84.

Schur, E. (1971). *Labeling Deviant Behavior: Its Sociological Implications*. New York: Harper & Row.

Schwartz, A., & Goldiamond, I. (1975). *Social Casework: A Behavioral Approach*. New York: Columbia University Press.

Schwartz, W. (1976). "Between Client and System: The Mediating Function." In R. W. Roberts & H. Northen (Eds.), *Theories of Social Work With Groups*. New York: Columbia University Press.

Simon, B. K. (1970). "Social Casework Theory: An Overview." In R. W. Roberts & R. H. Nee (Eds.), *Theories of Social Casework*. Chicago: University of Chicago Press.

Siporin, M. (1975). *Introduction to Social Work Practice*. New York: Macmillan Publishing Co.

Smalley, R. E. (1967). *Theory for Social Work Practice*. New York: Columbia University Press.

Solomon, B. B. (1976). *Black Empowerment: So-*

cial Work in Oppressed Communities. New York: Columbia University Press.

Somers, M. L. (1976). "Problem-Solving in Small Groups." In R. W. Roberts & H. Northen (Eds.), *Theories of Social Work With Groups*. New York: Columbia University Press.

Strean, H. S. (1978). *Clinical Social Work*. New York: Free Press.

Sundel, M., Radin, N., & Churchill, S. R. (1974). "Diagnosis in Group Work." In P. Glasser, R. Sarri, & R. Vinter (Eds.), *Individual Change Through Small Groups*. New York: Free Press.

Thomas, E. (1970). "Behavior Modification and Casework." In R. W. Roberts & R. H. Nee (Eds.), *Theories of Social Casework*. Chicago: University of Chicago Press.

Toch, H. (1970). "The Care and Feeding of Typologies and Labels." *Federal Probation, 34*(3), 15–19.

Tolson, E. R., & Reid, W. J. (1981). *Models of Family Treatment*. New York: Columbia University Press.

Toseland, R. W., & Rivas, R. F. (1984). *An Intro-duction to Group Work Practice*. New York: Macmillan Publishing Co.

Turner, F. J. (Ed.). (1979). *Social Work Treatment: Interlocking Theoretical Approaches* (2d ed.). New York: Free Press.

Turner, F. J. (Ed.). (1984). *Adult Psychotherapy*. New York: Free Press.

Waxler, N. E. (1974). "Culture and Mental Illness: A Social Labeling Perspective." *Journal of Nervous and Mental Disease, 159*(6), 379–395.

ASSOCIATIONS. See PROFESSIONAL ASSOCIATIONS: COUNCIL ON SOCIAL WORK EDUCATION; PROFESSIONAL ASSOCIATIONS: NATIONAL ASSOCIATION OF SOCIAL WORKERS; PROFESSIONAL ASSOCIATIONS: SPECIAL INTEREST.

BARRETT, JANIE PORTER. See biographical section.

BARTON, CLARISSA (CLARA) HARLOWE. See biographical section.

BATTERED WOMEN. See CRISIS INTERVENTION; DOMESTIC VIOLENCE; WOMEN.

BEERS, CLIFFORD WHITTINGHAM. See biographical section.

BEHAVIORAL APPROACH

Behavioral methods were first introduced into social work education in the 1960s by Thomas (1965, 1967) at the University of Michigan. These methods draw on theory and research in psychology and social psychology to inform practice decisions. This literature points to a reciprocal influence process between behavior and environmental events. Attention is given to the contingencies that influence behavior and to the relationships between behavior and what happens before and afterward (Bandura, 1969, 1977). Contingency analysis is an important aspect of assessment within a behavioral perspective. This involves a description of the relationship between behaviors of concern and related antecedents and consequences. Behavior is assumed to consist of different response systems including affective, cognitive, and overt behaviors that may or may not be related to each other, depending on individual learning histories. A distinction is made between the form and function of behavior; that is, the form of a behavior may not indicate its function.

Literature and theory related to behavioral practice have grown substantially since the last review of this approach in the *Encyclopedia of Social Work* (Thomas, 1977b; Thyer, 1983a). There are now over 20 behavioral journals and a number of yearly books containing reviews and articles (*Progress in Behavior Modification, Annual Review of Behavior Therapy, Theory and Research,* and *Behavioral Group Therapy*), as well as hundreds of other articles scattered in journals related to education, social work, medicine, psychology, psychiatry, counseling, business, and rehabilitation.

Characteristics

Although different emphases within the behavioral perspective can be identified (Kazdin, 1978), all share the following characteristics: (1) reliance on empirical findings rather than speculation to inform assessment and intervention, (2) identification of personal and environmental resources that can be drawn on to attain desired outcomes, (3) description of baseline levels of relevant outcomes and skills, (4) clear description of assessment and intervention procedures, (5) close relationship between assessment and intervention, (6) clear description of desired outcomes, and (7) concern with evaluation. A range of theoretical orientations appear within the behavioral perspective. At one end of the spectrum is applied behavior analysis, which eschews unobservable events and focuses on observable behaviors and related environmental factors. Attention is focused on specific behaviors in real-life settings such as the classroom, home, boardroom, or residential setting. This approach emphasizes the importance of conducting functional analysis of behavior in which the environmental factors related to certain behavior are identified through rearrangement of contingencies (altering what happens before and after behavior). Contributors to this approach have taken a leading role in developing and evaluating programs to alter behavior in the classroom, enhance the competencies of developmentally disabled individuals, decrease delinquent behavior, and enhance employment opportunities, to name but a few major areas. The work of B. F. Skinner has been a leading influence in the area of applied behavior analysis.

At the other end of the spectrum is cognitive behavior modification, which focuses on altering thoughts presumed to be related to troublesome reactions. Examples include cognitive behavioral treatment of depression, anger, pain, and anxiety that focuses on altering what people say to themselves (Kendall & Hollon, 1979). Both ends of the spectrum emphasize careful evaluation of results, relying on observable outcomes. If this focus were lost, efforts would fall outside what would be considered a behavioral perspective. Some argue that cognitive behavioral procedures can be conceptualized within the framework of applied behavior analysis—that is, without reliance on unobservable events such as thoughts (Ledwidge, 1978). They contend that cognitive behavioral methods involve the rearrangement of environmental cues and consequences and that it is these changes rather than an alteration of cognitive events that are responsible for change. The key question from a behavioral perspective is whether assumptions are testable. For example, if it is assumed that verbal instructions can change behavior, then this can be tested with an appropriate research design focusing on changes in observed events. Whether cognitive behavioral methods represent something new or represent simply another name for procedures based on social learning theory—is debatable. Many procedures developed early in the history of the use of behavioral procedures, such as systematic desensitization, for example, depend heavily on the alteration of unobservable events such as thoughts and images (Wolpe, 1958). Symbolic processes such as modeling, vicarious learning, and the anticipation of consequences are critical components of social learning theory. Social learning theory is a social systems approach in which attention is given to the social cues and consequences related to behaviors.

Another emphasis within the behavioral perspective focuses on changing emotional reactions through respondent conditioning by altering the relationship between stimulus events (see, for example, articles in *Behavior Research and Therapy*).

Distinguishing Characteristics

Several characteristics distinguish the behavioral approach from other social work frameworks. A behavioral approach constrains social workers to draw on empirical research in selecting assessment and intervention procedures. For example, if research demonstrates that the observation of behavior in the natural environment offers valuable information that can complement and correct impressions given by self-reports concerning the interaction between clients and significant others, then this kind of information would be used if feasible and ethical. If the literature shows that one kind of intervention is more effective than another, then within ethical and practical limits, social workers would use this approach regardless of personal theoretical preferences.

The behavioral approach requires social workers to be familiar with and to draw on empirical research related to their practice. In areas in which research is sparse, the behavioral social worker draws on behavioral theory to fill in the gaps. This approach also requires familiarity with research in related fields. For example, recent work shows the importance of positive school environments in making up for deficiencies in home environments (Rutter et al., 1979). Other research indicates that programs designed to prevent dropping out of school may actually help maintain delinquent behavior (O'Donnell & Tharp, 1982).

The clear identification of desired outcomes and evaluation of progress using relevant, sensitive, and feasible progress indicators are additional hallmarks that distinguish a behavioral approach from other approaches. Practice is often evaluated in other approaches, but it is the requirement to do so—and to do so in an ongoing fashion—that distinguishes the behavioral approach. The extensive literature on behavioral methods shows the wide variety of presenting problems that can be clearly defined and evaluated using multiple indicators of progress. Examples include depression, child abuse and neglect, marital discord, and communication problems between parents and teenagers. Many other outcomes, such as maintenance of full-time employment, can be readily defined.

A behavioral perspective encourages the view that people are doing the best they can at any given moment under current contingencies. This decreases the likelihood of personal blame and criticism and increases the likelihood of exploring how environmental factors limit opportunities for reinforcement. If clients are reluctant to participate in helping efforts, rather than blaming them for a lack of motivation, the social worker should explore how contingencies can be arranged so that participation will be worthwhile for them (Shelton & Levy, 1981). The behavioral perspective is a constructional approach in terms of focusing on personal and environmental assets that can be used to attain desired outcomes (Schwartz & Goldiamond, 1975). This discourages undue attention to pathology, which may limit discovery of promising options for intervention.

Another hallmark of the behavioral approach is concern for maintaining desired changes (Goldstein & Kanfer, 1979; Marlatt & Gordon, 1985; Stokes & Baer, 1977). Procedures that will encourage the durability of desired outcomes are an integral ingredient of behavioral practice with individuals, groups, families, and communities. This concern for durability requires attention in all stages of work with clients. For example, if family members are partially responsible for the troubling behavior of a schizophrenic relative, their involvement in all stages of intervention is more likely to result in the generalization and maintenance of changes. Attention is devoted to the arrangement of cues and incentives to encourage the durability of desired outcomes.

The behavioral perspective requires a firm grounding in basic behavioral principles. Training in contingency analysis permits the informed application of behavioral principles to presenting problems and allows the behavioral practitioner to fill in the gaps in empirical knowledge in a manner that is faithful to a behavioral perspective. This allows practitioners to identify more readily those circumstances in which it is unlikely that any intervention will be of value in achieving a particular outcome.

The importance of social influence variables in working with clients is clearly shown by research in interpersonal helping (Rosenthal, 1980; Wills, 1982). Thus, an understanding of and competence in providing conditions associated with these variables are important skills of the behavioral social worker. For example, enhancing positive expectations, clarifying mutual roles, and offering supportive feedback increase the likelihood of client participation and positive outcome.

Assessment Considerations

One characteristic of assessment within a behavioral approach is the use of multiple sources of information including, when feasible and ethical, the direct observation of clients and significant others in relevant environments. If the observation of behavior in real-life settings is not feasible, an alternative is the observation of behavior in simulated situations designed to be as similar as possible to real-life conditions. The objective is to observe a sample of relevant behaviors and situations. Self-monitoring—in which the client or significant others keep track of behaviors, feelings, thoughts, or outcomes or concern—is another important source of information that can be used with many clients (Bloom & Fischer, 1982). Other sources of information include physiological measures and self-report data, including completion of self-report measures. Making assessment of value to clients by clarifying presenting problems, offering helpful accounts, and identifying available assets is stressed (Stuart, 1980).

The clear description of presenting problems, related events, and desired outcomes is another characteristic of a behavioral approach to assessment. The purpose of assessment is to identify desired outcomes and to discover how contingencies can be altered to achieve them. This requires attention to individual, family, and community concerns and includes attention to distal as well as proximal antecedents. For example, some studies have found that parents are more punitive to their children on days when they have few contacts with friends (Wahler, 1980). A change in parental behavior may therefore require attention to the parent's social networks (a distal antecedent) as well as to the parent-child interaction, in which proximal antecedents and consequences affect behavior.

The products of assessment include (1) specific objectives that must be achieved to address presenting problems, (2) baseline information regarding behaviors or outcomes of concern, (3) intermediate steps related to these, (4) personal and environmental resources that can be drawn upon to achieve objectives, (5) significant others who could be involved and a plan for their involvement, (6) specific intervention methods that are likely to be useful in achieving desired outcomes, (7) progress indicators that will be used to assess outcomes, (8) obstacles that must be overcome and a plan to address them, and (9) clients and significant others who feel optimistic and who are ready to participate in plans to the degree possible.

Intervention Considerations

Assessment and selection of intervention methods are closely related in the behavioral approach; what is found during assessment directly informs selection of intervention methods. Assessment will yield information about the likelihood of attaining desired outcomes as well as information about alternative routes toward these ends. A clear definition of desired outcomes and ongoing monitoring progress offers feedback to clients, significant others, and social workers and permits the appropriate alteration of plans. Rearranging antecedent events (known as stimulus control) is often as important as rearranging the consequences of relevant behaviors, feelings, or thoughts.

Rearranging Antecedents. Desired outcomes can often be attained by rearranging what happens before the behaviors of concern. For example, Shorkey and Taylor (1973) decreased a child's generalized crying that was related to the painful changing of bandages by suggesting that personnel who changed the dressings wear a particular color gown and that all others, including the parents, wear other colors. Crying decreased in the presence of others not involved in this painful procedure. In another example, serving food family style (in bowls) rather than on individual plates increased the conversation of elderly people in a nursing home (Risley, Gottula, & Edwards, 1978). The work of Gambrill (1977) offers other examples of the use of stimulus control.

Rearranging Consequences. Both behavior surfeits (the presence of unwanted behavior) and behavior deficits (the absence of expected behavior) call for the rearrangement of contingencies. A person may continue behavior surfeits such as temper tantrums, lying, drinking, and stealing because of the contingent presentation of positive reinforcers or because of the contingent avoidance or removal of aversive events. Behavior deficits may be related to an absence of required competencies—an individual does not have the skills required to engage in desired reactions—a lack of cues and adequate schedules of reinforcement for be-

haviors, competing contingencies that maintain behavior interfering with desired reactions, a history of punishment, or various kinds of obstacles that decrease opportunities for reinforcement, such as physical limitations. Both antecedents and consequences must be carefully examined in each situation to identify how desired changes could be attained. For example, if staff complain about apathetic residents who just sit around a nursing home all day, skills in contingency analysis could help to identify how prompts and incentives could be rearranged to increase residents' participation in social activities. Enhancement of positive parenting skills often requires alteration of parental instructions and rules as well as the consequences they offer to their children (Dangel & Polster, 1984).

Multifaceted Intervention Programs. Many behavioral programs—especially those involving the communities in which clients reside, such as the job-finding program developed by Azrin and Besalel (1980)—include a variety of intervention methods consistent with the complexity of the circumstances related to a desired outcome. Programs designed to decrease depression often consist of many components including procedures to decrease dysfunctional thoughts, rearrange consequences offered by significant others, enhance social skills, and alter material circumstances related to depression. Weight reduction programs similarly consist of many components, including procedures to increase exercise, alter eating patterns, and gain support from significant others.

Applications

The social work contribution to behavioral practice is many-faceted. One concerns application of existing behavioral methods to new clients, problems, or settings. A second involves the replication of these procedures with similar clients, problems, or settings. A third contribution is the creation and evaluation of new procedures drawing on behavioral research and theory. Since 1975, a marked increase has occurred in attention to the assessment phase of work with clients from a behavioral perspective (Kendall & Hollon, 1981; Nay, 1979). The quantity of material in this area is reflected in the *Dictionary of Behavioral Assessment Methods*

(Hersen & Bellack, 1985). Social workers have contributed to the development of new assessment measures (Hudson, 1982; Stuart & Stuart, 1975) and have used an increasingly rich package of assessment tools. They have been in the forefront of the application of the behavioral perspective in new areas, including work with elderly clients and their significant others, efforts to decrease unwanted pregnancies, and work with groups. Social workers have made contributions to the development and evaluation of programs designed to decrease excessive anxiety (Thyer, 1983b). A cognitive behavioral perspective, which emphasizes altering thoughts related to desired outcomes, has received a warmer welcome in social work than has applied behavior analysis (Berlin, 1983). The emphasis on thoughts is more compatible with the overall Zeitgeist already popular in social work. A brief overview of major areas of application within social work is given in the sections that follow.

Family Settings. Social workers have been especially active in the application of behavioral methods in family settings, drawing on the rich literature in this area (Patterson, 1982). The first major book that reviewed parent training programs was edited by two social workers (Dangel & Polster, 1984), and social work researchers have made major contributions in the area of marital counseling (Stuart, 1980; Thomas, 1977b). The social systems focus inherent in a behavioral perspective requires involvement of family members as well as the identified client—for example, a child, adolescent, or elderly person. Observation of interactions among family members is used as a valuable assessment tool as well.

Child Welfare. Behavioral procedures have been used in working with families in which child maltreatment is a concern both to prevent unnecessary out-of-home placement and to enhance permanency planning for children who have already been removed from the care of their biological parents (Stein, Gambrill, & Wiltse, 1978). Written agreements are used to clarify mutual expectations and to identify the consequences that can be expected if objectives are not met. The variety of behavioral procedures used match the variety of problems associated with child abuse and neglect. These include negotiation training, point programs, problem-solving training, relaxation training, anger management training, programs to decrease substance abuse, marital counseling, and programs designed to enhance positive parenting skills. Supervisory procedures to complement methods used by line staff have also been developed (Gambrill & Stein, 1983). Behavioral training programs have been used with foster parents as well (Rinn, Markle, & Wise, 1981).

Schizophrenics and Their Families. One of the most recent and promising applications of behavioral methods involved in-home behavioral therapy with the families of schizophrenic patients (Fallon, Boyd, & McGill, 1984). Two-year follow-up results showed that involvement of family members during the 9-month intervention was more successful—fewer hospital days, greater decrease in problems of family members, and lower cost—than individualized treatment of schizophrenic patients in the clinic. Assessment involved three levels: (1) identifying the assets and deficits of family members, (2) identifying the assets and deficits of the family group as a whole, and (3) identifying the roles played by specific problem behaviors in the overall functioning of the family. Assessment information was gained from multiple sources, including observation of family interaction in the home and clinic, observational data collected by family members, and semistructured interviews with family members. The possible consequences, both positive and negative, of any change were carefully considered. Information on each family member's assets and deficits suggested their potential in coping with problems. Critical deficits in communication and problem solving were identified that, if improved, would facilitate positive changes. Intervention programs were tailor-made for each family. For example, different patterns of decision making—for example, democratic or autocratic—were considered in the development of more effective problem-solving techniques.

The intervention program included an educational workshop for patients and relatives, communication skills training for families, enhancement of problem-solving skills, strategies for symptom management, rehabilitation, counseling, and attention to medication regimes. The ongoing evaluation of progress was a routine part of the intervention. A behavioral approach to working with schizophrenics and their significant others emphasizes the development of a supportive environment in which family members are included as participants rather than emphasizing a cure. Hudson (1978) and Spiegler and Agigian (1977) provide other discussions of behavioral work with schizophrenic clients in the community.

Elderly Clients and Their Families. Family members are the major caregivers for elderly people, and many behavioral programs focus on these significant others (Pinkston & Linsk, 1984). The aim is to help family members and elderly clients change troublesome interactions and to provide needed material resources. The behavior deficits and excesses of both caregivers and elderly clients are identified, as are factors related to these behaviors, including inadequate or ineffective incentive and cuing systems. Attention is also given to possible physical obstacles to desired behavior and to a lack of material resources. Helping clients to take advantage of available services is a critical component of this program. A seven-step linkage procedure is used that includes problem identification, resource location, exploration of options, and resource selection. A caregiver checklist allows the social worker to review the behavior of caretakers on a number of dimensions such as physical health and frequency of contact with the client. Observation of family interaction is a critical component of assessment. Maintaining desired behaviors is especially important with the elderly.

The behavioral approach focuses on increasing opportunities for the reinforcement of desired behaviors and removing barriers that interfere with desired outcomes. For example, relatives of elderly clients may assume many tasks during a period of illness and not return these to the elderly when they recover. Physicians are also guilty of this: For example, a physician may recommend that an elderly person be confined to bed for fear of falling. Attention is devoted to arranging prompts to encourage desired behavior. Social workers have also explored the utility of behavioral group work and social skills training with the elderly both in community

and residential settings (Gambrill, 1985; Linsk, Howe, & Pinkston, 1975).

Other Client Groups and Their Families. Although many reports describe the use of behavioral procedures with delinquents and their families, few involve social workers. This is also true of work with clients with various kinds of developmental disabilities (Rose, 1974). An extensive behavioral literature in the latter area is promising in terms of effects achieved, yet relatively little use has been made of it by social workers. Involvement of significant others in programs designed to help clients lose weight, decrease substance abuse, or deal with medical problems is common in behavioral programs.

Schools. An extensive literature describes the application of behavioral procedures in schools. Some social workers take advantage of this in their work with clients; others have made contributions by drawing together reports in a specific area, such as the use of "home-based" reinforcement (Barth, 1979; Polster, Lynch, & Pinkston, 1981).

Health Concerns. The field of behavioral medicine has burgeoned over the last few years (Melamed & Siegel, 1980), applying behavioral research and theory to medical concerns. A Society for Behavioral Medicine now exists and the *Journal of Behavioral Medicine* and *Behavioral Medicine Abstracts* publish in this area. Behavioral medicine includes methods designed to prevent medical problems, to ameliorate problems that already exist along with their social and emotional consequences, to decrease discomfort involved in treatment, and to decrease discomfort arising from intractable medical problems. Social workers have contributed to this field in programs designed to decrease smoking and to increase preventive efforts (Levy, Weinstein, & Milgrom, 1977). They have also worked on generic concerns related to such interpersonal helping as enhancing client participation in programs (Shelton & Levy, 1981).

Prevention. Social workers have taken the lead in exploring the utility of behavioral programs designed to decrease, for example, unwanted pregnancies (Blythe, Gilchrist, & Schinke, 1981). Schinke and his colleagues, working with adolescents, have conducted a number of studies designed to decrease behaviors (such as smoking) that may result in future problems (Schinke, 1981). A concern with arranging for maintenance of desired outcomes within a behavioral perspective increases the likelihood that preventive programs will succeed.

Group Settings. Social workers have also made major contributions to the use of behavioral procedures in group settings. Some groups include participants with similar concerns, whereas others include people who desire different outcomes. Lawrence and Sundel (1972), for example, developed a procedure to use with clients with different concerns. Rose (1977, 1980) and his colleagues explored the use of group settings with a variety of desired outcomes and a variety of client groups. Edleson (1984) developed a group program designed to decrease spouse abuse. Schinke (1981) and his colleagues took advantage of group settings to enhance the interpersonal skills of adolescents and to train professionals. Antisocial children were the population of concern to Wodarski, Feldman, and Pedi (1976).

Neglected Areas of Application

Social workers have taken little advantage of other behavioral programs that address especially challenging problems such as unemployment. Azrin and his colleagues designed a job-finding program that was evaluated in 15 cities with over 900 clients with positive results (Azrin & Besalel, 1980; Azrin et al., 1980). Few social workers have used this program to help clients find jobs, however. Similarly, few American social workers have used procedures developed in the Portage Project—a program that involves parents in upgrading the quality of education offered to their handicapped children (Kysela et al., 1979)—and this program is in wider use in Great Britain than it is in the United States, where it was first developed. Few reports of behaviorally designed residential programs appear in the social work literature, even though many studies describe the use of behavioral procedures in both day care and residential care. Many of these programs have been carefully evaluated, and detailed guidelines are available for their implementation (Herbert-Jackson et al., 1977; Risley &

Favell, 1979). Programs that involve two different kinds of participants, such as foster grandparents and severely handicapped persons, to the mutual benefit of both (Fabry & Reid, 1978) have also been neglected, as has the application of behavioral procedures to redesign contingencies available in larger settings such as social work agencies. Procedures developed for one group of clients in one setting are often not used with other groups of similar clients in other settings. For example, little effort has been made to explore the utility of parent training and enhancement of children's skills to prevent the disruption of adoptive home placement, although this has worked well in nonadoptive homes (Edleson, 1981).

Unique Contributions

The behavioral approach offers unique contributions to the field of social work, many of which are compatible with the profession's historical themes such as an interest in basing assessment and intervention on empirical research, attending to environmental as well as individual factors, and "starting where the client is" in terms of attending to and taking advantage of personal and environmental assets. Social learning theory offers a social systems approach that is rich and flexible yet also sufficiently detailed and prescriptive to suggest assessment and intervention procedures for many kinds of presenting problems, including troublesome family interaction, unwanted pregnancies, and burnout among agency staff. It is the only approach that offers evaluated programs that address some perennial problems such as job finding.

A unique characteristic of the behavioral social worker is a blending of the practitioner and researcher roles (Jayaratne & Levy, 1979). Empirical research informs selection of assessment and intervention procedures. The ongoing evaluation of progress provides critical case management information and permits over a number of cases the collection of useful information regarding patterns of effects achieved with certain clients or problems. Research on behavioral methods indicates that this approach compares favorably to alternative approaches for a number of desired outcomes (Rachman & Wilson, 1980). Detailed information on the antecedents and consequences of specific problems collected during assessment with clients with similar presenting concerns offers information about typical patterns in controlling conditions. The emphasis on evaluation encourages attention to the negative as well as the positive side effects of programs. As empirical information on social work practice expands, assumption of this practitioner-researcher role becomes a more clear ethical responsibility.

Many programs in social work require the coordination of services from a variety of sources. Case management requires the planning, coordination, and evaluation of services from a number of different providers in relation to an individual, group, or family. The use of written agreements between service providers has been suggested as one way to clarify mutual expectations and ensure that services offered are complementary rather than conflicting. From a behavioral approach, the emphasis on clear outcomes and progress indicators increases the likelihood that these will be clearly defined in agreements.

Future Prospects

Given the potential utility of behavioral methods in relation to problems of concern within social work, it is to be expected that this approach will be widely used by social workers. There are some indications that such methods have increased in popularity among social workers. For example, one survey found that one-third of a sample of 267 clinical social workers selected behavioral theory as their theoretical orientation (Jayaratne, 1978). An increasing number of social work publications have a behavioral perspective. The Social Work Group in Behavioral Methods holds meetings during the annual Council on Social Work Education Conference and publishes a newsletter. A similar special interest group—the Behavioral Social Work Group—exists in Great Britain. This group holds a yearly conference and publishes the *Behavioral Social Work Review*.

Mistaken assumptions about behavioral methods are also rife, however—for example, that such methods involve a heavy reliance on aversion and that they dehumanize people (Gambrill, 1984). The large number of behavioral articles in social work journals does not necessarily reflect the pop-

ularity or acceptance of this approach in the field. Rather, certain characteristics of a behavioral perspective, such as the emphasis on evaluation, may complement a preference by the editorial boards of certain journals for data on program effectiveness.

The number of books and articles in the behavioral area has increased geometrically. A sense of the quantity of work in the field can be gained from the *International Handbook of Behavior Modification and Behavior Therapy* (Bellack, Hersen, & Kazdin, 1982) and the *Dictionary of Behavioral Methods* (Hersen & Bellack, 1985). One of the implications of this rapid growth for behavioral practitioners is that it will be necessary to specialize. It is no longer possible for any one person to keep up with and develop expertise in empirically based practice procedures related to many different kinds of desired outcomes as well as to keep up with research findings in related areas. A social worker specializing in parent-child relationships, for example, would require a thorough research grounding in child development and behavioral work with children and parents.

A second implication is the need for effective information retrieval skills. More and more, the term "behavioral perspective" fails to convey the broad array of empirical data that is of direct concern to social work practice with individuals, families, groups, and communities. The term "empirically based practice" captures this breadth more fully.

As the history of social work shows, options are not necessarily pursued. The vision that some had in the 1960s of the future role of behavioral methods has not been realized; the majority of social workers do not use behavioral methods in their work with clients and significant others. A number of factors will continue to limit the extent to which social workers make use of such methods, including lack of knowledge about the depth and range of relevant empirical literature; the lack of high-quality training opportunities (for example, most schools of social work do not provide a thorough grounding in basic behavioral principles); inadequate tools, prompts, and incentives favoring use of empirically based methods; and disagreements about the relevance of empirical knowledge for social work practice.

On the other hand, some trends—such

as the increasing concern for accountability on the part of funding sources and service consumers—may encourage greater use of empirically based procedures. This interest will encourage clear description of outcomes, evaluation of progress, and selection of empirically based intervention methods. Recognition of common themes in many practice approaches (Goldfried, 1982) will discourage unproductive and often inaccurate polarization of different practice frameworks, as will a focus on finding out what procedures work best with what clients with what particular concerns. It is generally recognized today (but not usually put into practice) that asking such global questions as, Is approach X more effective than approach Y? is not productive.

EILEEN D. GAMBRILL

For further information, see ASSESSMENT IN DIRECT PRACTICE; CASE MANAGEMENT; ECOLOGICAL PERSPECTIVE.

References

Azrin, N. H., & Besalel, V. A. (1980). *Job Club Counselor's Manual: A Behavioral Approach to Vocational Counseling*. Baltimore, Md.: University Park Press.

Azrin, N. H., et al. (1980). "A Comparative Evaluation of the Job Club Program with Welfare Recipients." *Journal of Vocational Behavior, 16*(2), 133–145.

Bandura, A. (1969). *Principles of Behavior Modification*. New York: Holt, Rinehart & Winston.

Bandura, A. (1977). *Social Learning Theory*. Englewood Cliffs, N.J.: Prentice-Hall.

Barth, R. P. (1979). "Home-Based Reinforcement of School Behavior: A Review and Analysis." *Review of Educational Research, 49*(3), 436–458.

Bellack, A. S., Hersen, M., & Kazdin, A. E. (1982). *International Handbook of Behavior Modification and Therapy*. New York: Plenum Publishing Corp.

Berlin, S. (1983). "Cognitive-Behavioral Approaches." In A. Rosenblatt & D. Waldfogel (Eds.), *Handbook of Clinical Social Work* (pp. 1095–1119). San Francisco: Jossey-Bass.

Bloom, M., & Fischer, J. (1982). *Evaluating Practice: Guidelines for the Accountable Professional*. Englewood Cliffs, N.J.: Prentice-Hall.

Blythe, B., Gilchrist, L., & Schinke, S. (1981). "Pregnancy Prevention Groups for Adolescents." *Social Work, 26*(6), 503–504.

Dangel, R. F., & Polster, R. A. (Eds.). (1984). *Parent Training: Foundations of Research and Practice*. New York: Guilford Press.

Edleson, J. (1981). "Teaching Children to Resolve Conflict." *Social Work, 26*(6), 488–493.

Edleson, J. L. (1984). "Working with Men who Batter." *Social Work, 29*(3), 237–242.

Fabry, P. L., & Reid, D. H. (1978). "Teaching Foster Grandparents to Train Severely Handicapped Persons." *Journal of Applied Behavior Analysis, 11*(1), 111–123.

Falloon, I. R. H., Boyd, J. L., & McGill, C. W. (1984). *Family Care of Schizophrenia*. New York: Guilford Press.

Gambrill, E. D. (1977). *Behavior Modification: Handbook of Assessment, Intervention, and Evaluation Methods*. San Francisco: Jossey-Bass.

Gambrill, E. D. (1984). "Social Worker Attitudes and Knowledge about Behavior Modification: 1972–1982." Unpublished manuscript. Berkeley: University of California.

Gambrill, E. D. (1985). "Social Skills Training with the Elderly." In L. L'Abate & M. Milan (Eds.), *Handbook of Social Skills Training* (pp. 326–357). New York: John Wiley & Sons.

Gambrill, E. D., & Stein, T. J. (1983). *Supervision: A Decision Making Approach*. Beverly Hills, Calif.: Sage Publications.

Goldfried, M. R. (Ed.). 1982. *Converging Themes in Psychotherapy: Trends in Psychodynamic, Humanistic and Behavioral Practice*. New York: Springer Publishing Co.

Goldstein, A. P., & Kanfer, F. H. (1979). *Maximizing Treatment Gains: Transfer Enhancement in Psychotherapy*. New York: Academic Press.

Herbert–Jackson, E., et al. (1977). *The Infant Center—A Complete Guide to Organizing and Managing Infant Day Care*. Baltimore, Md.: University Park Press.

Hersen, M., & Bellack, A. S. (1985). *Dictionary of Behavioral Assessment Techniques and Methods*. New York: Pergamon Press.

Hudson, B. (1978). "Behavioral Social Work with Schizophrenic Patients in the Community." *British Journal of Social Work, 8*(2), 159–170.

Hudson, W. W. (1982). *The Clinical Measurement Package: A Field Manual*. Homewood, Ill.: Dorsey Press.

Jayaratne, S. (1978). "A Study of Clinical Eclecticism." *Social Service Review, 52*(4), 621–631.

Jayaratne, S., & Levy, R. L. (1979). *Empirical Clinical Practice*. New York: Columbia University Press.

Kazdin, A. E. (1978). *History of Behavior Modification: Experimental Foundations of Contemporary Research*. Baltimore, Md.: University Park Press.

Kendall, P. C., & Hollon, S. D. (Eds.). (1979). *Cognitive-Behavioral Interventions: Theory, Research and Procedures*. New York: Academic Press.

Kendall, P. C., & Hollon, S. D. (1981). *Assessment Strategies for Cognitive Behavioral Interventions.* New York: Academic Press.

Kozloff, M. A. (1979). *A Program for Families of Children with Learning and Behavior Problems.* New York: John Wiley & Sons.

Kysela, G. M., et al. (1979). "The Early Education Project." In L. A. Hamerlynck (Ed.), *Behavioral Systems for the Developmentally Disabled: I. School and Family Environments* (pp. 128–171). New York: Brunner/Mazel.

Lawrence, H., & Sundel, M. (1972). "Behavior Modification in Adult Groups." *Social Work, 17*(2), 34–43.

Ledwidge, G. (1978). "Cognitive Behavior Modification: A Step in the Wrong Direction?" *Psychological Bulletin, 85*, 353–375.

Levy, R. L., Weinstein, P., & Milgrom, P. (1977). "Behavioral Guidelines for Plaque Control Programs." *Dental Hygiene, 51*, 13–18.

Linsk, N., Howe, M. W., & Pinkston, E. M. (1975). "Behavioral Group Work in a Home for the Aged." *Social Work, 20*(6), 454–463.

Marlatt, G. A., & Gordon, J. R. (1985). *Relapse Prevention: Maintenance Strategies in the Treatment of Addictive Disorders.* New York: Guilford Press.

Meichenbaum, D. (1977). *Cognitive Behavior Modification: An Integrative Approach.* New York: Plenum Publishing Corp.

Melamed, B. G., & Siegel, L. J. (1980). *Behavioral Medicine: Practical Applications in Health Care.* New York: Springer-Verlag.

Nay, W. F. (1979). *Multimethod Clinical Assessment.* New York: Gardner Press.

O'Donnell, C. R., & Tharp, R. G. (1982). "Community Intervention and the Use of Multidisciplinary Knowledge." In A. S. Bellack, M. Hersen, & A. E. Kazdin (Eds.), *International Handbook of Behavior Modification and Therapy* (pp. 291–318). New York: Plenum Publishing Corp.

Patterson, G. R. (1982). *A Social Learning Approach, Vol. 3: Coercive Family Process.* Eugene, Oreg.: Castalia Publishing Co.

Pinkston, E. M., & Linsk, N. L. (1984). *Care of the Elderly: A Family Approach.* New York: Pergamon Press.

Polster, R. A., Lynch, M. A., & Pinkston, E. M. (1981). "Reaching Underachievers." In S. P Schinke (Ed.), *Behavioral Methods in Social Welfare* (pp. 41–60). New York: Aldine Publishing Co.

Rachman, S. J., & Wilson, G. T. (1980). *The Effects of Psychological Therapy* (2nd ed.). London, England: Pergamon Press.

Rinn, R. C., Markle, A., & Wise, M. J. (1981). "Positive Parent Training for Foster Parents: A One-Year Follow-Up." *Behavioral Counseling Quarterly, 1*(3), 213–220.

Risley, T. R., & Favell, J. (1979). "Constructing a Living Environment in an Institution." In L. A. Hamerlynck (Ed.), *Behavioral Systems for the Developmentally Disabled: II. Institutional, Clinic, and Community Environments* (pp. 3–24). New York: Brunner/Mazel.

Risley, T. R., Gottula, P., & Edwards, K. (1978). *Social Interaction during Family and Institutional Style Meal Service in a Nursing Home Dining Room.* Paper presented at the Nova Behavioral Conference on Aging, Port St. Lucie, Fla.

Rose, S. D. (1974). "Training Parents in Groups as Behavior Modifiers of Their Mentally Retarded Children." *Journal of Behavior Therapy and Experimental Psychiatry, 5*(2), 135–140.

Rose, S. D. (1977). *Group Therapy: A Behavioral Approach.* Englewood Cliffs, N.J.: Prentice-Hall.

Rose, S. (1980). *Casework in Group Therapy: A Cognitive–Behavioral Approach.* Englewood Cliffs, N.J.: Prentice-Hall.

Rosenthal, T. L. (1980). "Social Cueing Process." In M. Hersen, R. M. Eisler, & P. M. Miller (Eds.), *Progress in Behavior Modification* (Vol. 10, pp. 111–146). New York: Academic Press.

Rutter, M., et al. (1979). *Fifteen Thousand Hours: Secondary Schools and Their Effects on Children.* Cambridge, Mass.: Harvard University Press.

Schinke, S. P. (1981). "Social Skills Training with Adolescents." In M. Hersen, R. M. Eisler, & P. M. Miller (Eds.), *Progress in Behavior Modification* (Vol. 11, pp. 66–115). New York: Academic Press.

Schwartz, A., & Goldiamond, I. (1975). *Social Casework: A Behavioral Approach.* New York: Columbia University Press.

Shelton, J. L., & Levy, R. L. (1981). *Behavioral Assignments and Treatment Compliance.* Champaign, Ill.: Research Press.

Shorkey, C. T., & Taylor, J. E. (1973). "Management of Maladaptive Behavior of a Severely Burned Child." *Child Welfare, 52*(8), 543–547.

Spiegler, M. D., & Agigian, H. (1977). *The Community Training Center: An Educational–Behavioral–Social Systems Model for Rehabilitating Psychiatric Patients.* New York: Brunner/Mazel.

Stein, T. J., Gambrill, E. D., & Wiltse, K. T. (1978). *Children in Foster Homes: Achieving Continuity of Care.* New York: Praeger Publishers.

Stokes, T. F., & Baer, D. M. (1977). "An Implicit Technology of Generalization." *Journal of Applied Behavior Analysis, 10*(2), 349–367.

Stuart, R. B. (1980). *Helping Couples Change: A Social Learning Approach to Marital Therapy.* New York: Guilford Press.

Stuart, R. B., & Stuart, F. M. (1975). *Family Counseling Inventory and Guide*. Champaign, Ill.: Research Press.

Thomas, E. J. (Ed.). (1967). *The Socio–Behavioral Approach and Applications to Social Work*. New York: Council on Social Work Education.

Thomas, E. J. (1977a). *Marital Communication and Decision Making*. New York: Free Press.

Thomas, E. J. (1977b). "Social Casework and Social Groupwork: The Behavioral Modification Approach." In *Encyclopedia of Social Work* (17th ed., pp. 1309–1321). Washington, D.C.: National Association of Social Workers.

Thomas, E. J., & Goodman, E. (Eds.). (1965). *Socio–Behavioral Theories and Interpersonal Helping in Social Work—Lectures and Institute Proceedings*. Ann Arbor, Mich.: Campus Publications.

Thyer, B. A. (1983a). "Behavior Modification in Social Work Practice." In M. Hersen, R. M. Eisler, & P. M. Miller (Eds.), *Progress in Behavior Modification* (Vol. 15, pp. 173–216). New York: Academic Press.

Thyer, B. A. (1983b). "Treating Anxiety Disorders with Exposure Therapy." *Social Casework, 64*(2), 77–82.

Wahler, R. G. (1980). "The Insular Mother: Her Problems in Parent Child Treatment." *Journal of Applied Behavior Analysis, 13*(2), 207–219.

Wills, T. A. (Ed.). (1982). *Basic Processes in Helping Relationships*. New York: Academic Press.

Wodarski, J. S., Feldman, R. A., & Pedi, S. J. (1976). "Reduction of Antisocial Behavior in an Open Community Setting Through the Use of Behavior Modification in Groups." *Child Care Quarterly, 5*(3), 198–210.

Wolpe, J. (1958). *Psychotherapy by Reciprocal Inhibition*. Stanford, Calif.: Stanford University Press.

For Further Reading

Fischer, J., & Gochros, H. L. (1975). *Planned Behavior Change: Behavior Modification in Social Work*. New York: Free Press.

Gambrill, E. D. (1977). *Behavior Modification: Handbook of Assessment, Intervention and Evaluation*. San Francisco: Jossey-Bass.

Gambrill, E. D. (1983). *Casework: A Competency Based Approach*. Englewood Cliffs, N.J.: Prentice-Hall.

Martin, G., & Pear, J. (1978). *Behavior Modification: What It Is and How To Do It*. Englewood Cliffs, N.J.: Prentice-Hall. (See also 2nd Edition.)

Pinkston, E. M., et al. (1982). *Effective Social Work Practice: Advanced Techniques for Behavioral Intervention with Individuals, Families, and Institutional Staff*. San Francisco: Jossey-Bass.

Rose, S. D. (1977). *Group Therapy: A Behavioral Approach*. Englewood Cliffs, N.J.: Prentice-Hall.

Sheldon, B. (1982). *Behavioral Modification*. London, England: Tavistock Publications.

Sundel, M., & Sundel, S. S. (1975). *Behavioral Modification in the Human Services: A Systematic Introduction to Concepts and Applications*. New York: John Wiley & Sons.

BEHAVIOR MODIFICATION. See BEHAVIORAL APPROACH.

BETHUNE, MARY MCLEOD. See biographical section.

BIRTH CONTROL See ABORTION; ADOLESCENT PREGNANCY; FAMILY AND POPULATION PLANNING; FAMILY LIFE EDUCATION; PUBLIC HEALTH SERVICES.

BLACKS

Blacks are the largest ethnic group of color in the United States. Although some blacks came to this country from Africa as freemen before the beginning of enslavement and others came as indentured servants who eventually earned freedom, most are descendants of ethnic groups from the western coast of Africa who were enslaved and transported to North America. Their different modes of introduction to this continent, their numerous cultural groups of origin, and their disbursement to many geographic areas in the United States and to plantations that varied in size and format led to the development of diverse lifestyles, family forms, and cultural patterns. Many of these differences still exist.

Because blacks are an oppressed ethnic group of color, their lives have been shaped by denigration for carrying the physical and sometimes cultural evidence of an African heritage (Hopps, 1982). Western societies have consistently preferred groups and cultural patterns that are European in origin over those whose heritage is African, Asian, Native American, or Hispanic. Ever since they arrived on this continent, people of European origin have had a deeply ingrained sense of the superiority of Anglo-Saxons (Chase, 1977; Quarles, 1971).

The increased awareness of the broad patterns of history and of communication among persons of color throughout the world has stimulated a change in the terms used to designate persons of color. Because "minority" and "race" often are used to describe oppressed people of color but "ethnic" is used for people of European origin, which indicates the acceptance of the cultural diversity of more favored groups and a denial of the ethnic and cultural validity of those of color, the tendency has been to reject the term "minority." The term "minority" also is often used for psychological and political control, as in South Africa, where the ruling white group has attempted to separate the 80 percent of the population who are black (the majority) into different ethnic minority groups to dilute their collective political effectiveness and power. By designating ten "minority" groups instead of one major group, supporters of apartheid are able to justify the removal of minorities to their separate "homelands," to keep them oppressed, and to attempt to stifle or slow the formation of national political responses to their oppression.

In the United States, however, one of the characteristics of oppression is to stereotype members of a group by denying their economic, cultural, and historical differences and by treating them as a monolithic whole. Thus, social scientists, among others, continue to refer to "the black family," social programs and policies are still designed without a consideration of the many intragroup differences that have formed over the generations, and problem areas are customarily compared in terms of race.

Because social scientists repeatedly fail to make the appropriate cross-tabulations for both racial and economic differences and hence do not make accurate comparisons, what are often described as racial differences are really social-class differences. For exam-ple, the rate of adolescent pregnancies is much higher for blacks than for whites. However, when the data are controlled by the economic levels of the adolescents' families, racial differences are not as great (Dash, 1986). Furthermore, adolescent pregnancies are a result of poverty and the lack of health care. If preventive health care was available, poor young girls would have an ongoing relationship with medical personnel, who could give them information on the subject of birth control.

Demographic Characteristics

The black population grew twice as fast as the nonblack population from 1980 to 1984 and included 28.6 million people as of July 1, 1984 (Rich, 1985). Blacks—the largest ethnic group—were 11.8 percent of the population in 1980 and 12.1 percent in 1985. The Hispanic population, which totaled 15.4 million people as of April 1982, is the fastest-growing ethnic group; it is composed of blacks and nonblacks and thus is not counted as a separate ethnic *racial* group ("U.S. Hispanic Population," 1986) by the U.S. Bureau of the Census. (The U.S. Bureau of the Census counts blacks, whites, and others as racial groups and then counts Hispanics of all races.) The black population is younger and has a higher fertility rate than the nonblack population. In 1984, the average age of blacks was 26.3 years compared to 32.2 years for whites, and the increase in the black population from 1980 to 1984 was 6.7 percent versus 3.2 percent in the white population. Also in 1985, black children constituted 15.4 percent of all American children (Rich, 1985).

Black women outnumbered black men by 1.4 million in 1984, which means that there were 15 million women to 13.6 million men. This unbalanced sex ratio has made it more difficult for black women to find husbands and to remarry if they get divorced, thus perpetuating the formation of single-parent families (U.S. Bureau of the Census, 1984c).

Familial Structures

Some 50 years ago, Frazier (1939) noted that the social conditions with which black people had to contend throughout their history in this country led them to form three distinct familial structures—two that were patriarchal and one that was matriarchal. Freemen and freedmen in the North and

South had family structures that were puritanical and patriarchal. Those who were craftsmen, farmers, or small businessmen often became financially secure while others lived just above poverty. Owing to their greater stability and financial resources, many freemen and freedmen were able to take greater advantage of the education provided by the Northern missionary schools and colleges. "Screens" of opportunity (Billingsley, 1968, pp. 97–101) were provided to blacks by members of the black community as well as by nonblacks.

Those slaves who were fortunate to live on plantations that allowed long-term monogamous unions or who were bought by persons with smaller farms tended to have traditional husband-wife unions, often with additional nonmarried kin in residence. However, the slaves on the large Southern plantations that were devoted to specific crops, such as cotton, tobacco, or slave breeding, were unable to form stable traditional families. They were forced to live polygamously. The plantation owner was the head of the slave families and often controlled more than one mother-child unit on the plantation—one that was white and others that were black (Peters & McAdoo, 1983). When the importation of slaves was legally ended, slaves were bred as animals (Franklin, 1947) for distribution within the United States, and families often were brutally torn apart when one or more members were sold to other slave owners (Gutman, 1976). At that point, a domestic pattern of mother-child units evolved on the plantation—a pattern that continued during Reconstruction—which was one of the strong functional techniques for survival (Frazier, 1939).

During Reconstruction, former slave owners and politicians worked to eradicate the new freedoms of the former slaves through the Black Codes and activities of the Ku Klux Klan (Fishel & Quarles, 1967; Painter, 1977). Blacks were forced to return to a slave status. The stability that many families had just begun to establish was eroded, and community life was destroyed (DuBois, 1910/1973; Fishel & Quarles, 1967; Painter, 1977). These hardships led to a mass exodus of freedmen from the South to Missouri, Kansas, and farther west, which removed many families from their extended family networks.

The next disruption of black families began in the 1930s, when adult family members migrated to the northern cities in search of jobs during the era of industrialization. Family members were temporarily separated and removed from some of their family and community supports. Many black families benefited from the industrial jobs in the North and were able to move into solid working-class and lower middle-class status. Their children were often helped by the better education in the North and went on to form a core of black professionals—among them teachers and social workers.

Since the mid-1970s, blacks have faced another form of disruption—increased levels of impoverishment and deteriorating social conditions, which have led to further economic and structural changes in their families. From Emancipation until the late 1960s, female-headed families accounted for no more than 25 percent of black families. In the early 1900s, families without husbands were usually composed of widows and their children (Pleck, 1972). By the 1940 census, 72 percent of black families with children under age 18 and 82 percent of all black families had both parents in the home, and most single mothers were widows. From 1940 to 1960, the number of widows decreased, and the number of divorced and separated women increased to the point where divorced and separated women constituted the greatest proportion of single mothers. Out-of-wedlock births began to contribute to the growing proportion of single mothers (Wilson & Neckerman, 1986).

The percentage of female-headed families with no husband present rose from 17.9 percent in 1940 to 21.7 percent in 1960 to 28.3 percent in 1970 to 41.9 percent in 1983 (Wilson & Neckerman, 1986). The percentage of children who lived in female-headed families increased from 23.6 percent in 1960 to 33.7 percent in 1970, to 50.6 percent in 1984 (Children's Defense Fund, 1985). In 1983, 81.1 percent of the black children were living with their parents; 17.1 percent, with their grandparents; and 1.8 percent with nonrelatives (Children's Defense Fund, 1985).

Thus, it can be seen that the reasons for the female-as-head family structure have changed since the beginning of this century. In the early 1900s, widowhood was the main reason; by the mid-1980s, the dissolution of marriage (for 28.4 percent of the children living in a single-mother family) and the nonformation of marriages (for 24.1 percent of the children) were the main reasons.

The debate on the causes and sources of the structures of black families has been wide ranging, particularly in relation to the continuation of aspects of the African culture in American family forms (Dodson, 1981; Pipes, 1951). Some have proposed that the traditional culture and family were destroyed during enslavement (Frazier, 1939, pp. 7–8). They have done so despite Gutman's (1976) clear documentation of the strong familial patterns that existed even on plantations and the fact that 75 percent of the slave families consisted of both parents. Others have maintained that there are many cultural continuities (some of which may have been modified over time) that contributed to differences in the family forms of blacks and nonblacks (Blassingame, 1972; DuBois, 1908/1969; Herskovits, 1941/1958; Nobles, 1974; Park, 1919; Sudarkasa, 1981; Woodson, 1936).

The one structural difference between black families and white families is the higher proportion of mother-child family units among black people. Those who thought that slavery destroyed the black family stated that single-mother families are evidence of that destruction. Those who proposed that remnants of African family forms are represented in the higher proportion of black single-mother units cited the strong matrifocal characteristic of some African families (both one parent and two parent) as the source of this "adaptive" structure. However, Sudarkasa (1981) refuted this contention, pointing out that an unmarried mother-child unit is alien to almost all traditional African cultures and would not be allowed to exist.

Sudarkasa (1981, p. 49)—considered to be the leading American anthropologist on African and American family forms and on the migration of diverse African groups to this continent—has proposed that scholars should move beyond the traditional debate to a greater understanding of the "institutional transformation" of these forms that are the result of the interactions between the African and American culture. Thus, the flexibility of the family structures has enabled families to respond to external environmental and economic stresses; the result has been diverse family structures. The strong extended

"blood-kin" relationships among women and the reciprocal obligations to close kin are strong familial patterns (McAdoo, 1982; Stack, 1974). For example, African children have always been born into a close network of extended family members and would be the responsibility of the entire extended family if the father could not provide for them; they would not be allowed to fall into poverty, as has occurred in this country. Moreover, widows traditionally were married to appropriate male relatives, and errant fathers would be put under severe pressure by the elders, whose role it was to ensure the stability of the entire family. Some of these African cultural patterns are still practiced but modified by the experiences of black people in this country. For example, Afro-American cultural norms stress that children should be kept in the family unless there is no alternative; this norm has resulted in many types of informal adoption (Hill, 1971).

Poverty

From 1979 to 1983, the percentage of people in poverty in the United States steadily increased. Even though the proportion of white families and black families below the poverty level decreased from 12.2 percent to 11.5 percent and from 35.7 percent to 33.8 percent, respectively, in 1984, the poverty rate for all families was still the highest it had been since 1966 (U.S. Bureau of the Census, 1984a, 1985b).

Thus, as an economic unit, the family has lost ground. Children of all races are now the largest group of impoverished persons in the United States. Elderly people are comparatively better off than are children because of the indexing of social security payments. The poverty rate for the elderly declined in 1984 to 12.4 percent, the lowest it had ever been. But children of color are disproportionately poor: in 1984, 46.5 percent of all black children and 39 percent of all Hispanic children were living in poverty, compared to 16.5 percent of all white children (U.S. Bureau of the Census, 1985a).

In 1984, the poverty level for a family of four was $10,609 and for a family of three, $8,277 (U.S. Bureau of the Census, 1985b). The median income of white families was $27,690; of Hispanic families, $18,830; and of black families, $15,430. Between 1983 and 1984, the actual number of black families in poverty decreased only a trace, and the poverty rate in the South—where most blacks live—was the highest of all. In comparison, the number of Hispanic families in poverty did not change, and 1.2 million white families were lifted out of poverty. Therefore, it is obvious that the much-heralded strengthening of the American economy is not trickling down to families of color, especially black families, who are worse off than they ever were before.

Feminization of Poverty

The concept of the feminization of poverty has a different meaning in black families and in white families. Although women of all races who are raising their children without a husband are the most economically vulnerable (Pearce & McAdoo, 1981), white single mothers are vulnerable because traditionally they have not worked when their children were young—a pattern that changed only in the 1970s. The increased divorce rate and the refusal or inability of their husbands to support their children has caused many of them and their children to move from a stable financial situation into poverty. Many mothers who had not worked outside the home before the divorce have been forced to seek employment without previous training or experience in the labor market, have faced sex biases, and have sunk into poverty. Those who did work earned less than their husbands. The loss of approximately two-thirds of the family income after a divorce can be devastating.

In contrast, black families were impoverished *before* the divorce occurred—an event that happens twice as frequently as in other families. Most black women traditionally have been in the labor market since their children were young, but their income has been low because of racial and sex discrimination. Therefore, when black women divorce and their family unit loses the husband's income, they cannot add income by going to work because they already are working.

The percentage of children who live in female-headed families has increased for both whites and blacks. The proportion of white children rose from 6.8 percent in 1960 to 14.3 percent in 1983, whereas the proportion of black children soared from 23.6 percent in 1960 to 50.6 percent in 1984 (Children's De-

fense Fund, 1985). The higher median income and the higher proportion of two-parent families mean that white children are not as vulnerable as are black children to economic stresses.

The changes in the black family structure are not the result of a dependence on welfare, as popularly believed. Rather, they are caused by lower marital fertility, increases in the rates of divorce and separation, the earlier sexual activity of black youths, the reluctance to give children up for adoption outside the familial networks, delays in marriage, the imbalance in the ratio of men to women, and the high unemployment rate of young black men (Hill, 1971; Wilson & Neckerman, 1986).

Furthermore, when a black woman becomes pregnant, in or out of wedlock, the father often is unable to provide sufficient support to her and her child. This situation is worsened by welfare policies that do not reinforce the maintenance of the family unit when support is provided, which, in turn, encourages the father not to contribute whatever he can.

Single parenting by teenagers is a serious problem regardless of race, but this age group bears just 40 percent of the black babies outside marriage. The majority of out-of-wedlock babies are born to women in their twenties (Children's Defense Fund, 1984). Most adolescent mothers are supported by their extended families and are not reflected as separate units in the poverty statistics. However, 100 percent of the black teenage mothers and 98 percent of the white teenage mothers who maintain a separate household live in poverty (Kamerman, 1985). Over 90 percent of all families that receive Aid to Families with Dependent Children (AFDC) are headed by single mothers, according to the Congressional Budget Office, and nearly two-thirds of the AFDC recipients gave birth to their first child when they were teenagers ("Conference Focuses on Teen Pregnancy," 1985).

Although the race and marital status of a single mother are significant predictors of poverty, the age of the children in the household is another important factor. Sixty-four percent of all black single mothers are impoverished, but when their children are under age 6, the percentage rises to over 72 percent. In contrast, 40 percent of all nonblack single mothers and 57 percent of those with children under age 6 are poor.

In addition, the more children there are in a family, the higher the rate of poverty. Thus, with one child in the family, the poverty rate is 50 percent; with two children, 66 percent; with three children, 71 percent; and with four children, 86 percent (Kamerman, 1985). The higher poverty rates for larger families reflect the greater strains of single parenting, the advancing ages of the mothers and their consequent health problems, and the greater difficulty these women have in obtaining job training and employment.

One myth about single mothers who are poor is that they produce babies out of wedlock and deliberately maintain their single status to obtain greater AFDC payments and thus that the availability of transfer payments causes a dependence on welfare. Studies have refuted this myth. They have found that AFDC is not the underlying cause of change to a one-parent familial structure (Ellwood & Bane, 1984) and that welfare is not an economic incentive to have babies outside marriage (Wilson & Neckerman, 1986), for additional children bring the mothers into even greater poverty and do not improve their economic situation (M. R. Cutler, as quoted in Rich, 1986).

Education

The primary and secondary education of blacks is inferior to that of whites. The higher proportion of black children in poverty, learning problems related to poor prenatal medical care, and stressed parents all contribute to the lessened ability of children to profit from the education that is provided. An additional impediment, which has been substantiated by several studies, is the expectation by teachers that poor and black children cannot achieve. Teachers give more positive reinforcement to white, middle-class, and female students. Their lower expectations for black and poor students often are internalized by these students, who then fulfill the prophecy of failure (Rosenthal & Jacobson, 1968). Furthermore, parents who are poor and not well educated have high, sometimes unrealistic, expectations of what their children can achieve but often are intimidated by the school system and do not have the knowledge to push it to work to the advantage of their children.

Test Scores. These factors are reflected in the scores of black children on standardized tests. Standardized tests have been dismissed by some black psychologists, social workers, and educators as culturally biased against poor and nonwhite children because they are designed to reflect the biases of the wider society and of the schools. However, these are the environments through which the children must pass and master if they are to be prepared to function as adults. The results of deprivation are shown most clearly in the scores on the Scholastic Aptitude Test (SAT) reported by the College Board for the 1983–84 school year. Black students have increased their SAT scores faster than have whites, and the gap between the races was smaller in 1985 than it was in 1976 ("Blacks' Scores Continue to Rise," 1985). Because these scores were not partialed out for racial and socioeconomic groups, it is not possible to examine racial differences when social class is controlled. The common error that is made when blacks are compared to whites is that the results of the different socioeconomic classes within races are not obtained before the racial groups are compared. The larger proportion of blacks who are poor should be compared only with whites who also are poor, as should be done for middle-class people. Only when differences in social class are controlled can the actual differences in test scores be found. A partial race-by-class comparison was made by the College Board, when families with incomes of over $50,000 were found to have an average SAT score difference of 120 points. Therefore, the larger proportion of blacks who live in poverty would predispose them to lower scores because of poverty-related conditions. Moreover, the predictive validity of these tests for blacks has been improved when multiple measurements are made (Johnson, 1979).

Once genetic inferiority (Chase, 1977), the barriers of limited resources, and the comparatively poor academic preparation of black children are rejected as explanations of the children's lower level of educational attainment, the students themselves are blamed. One theory of black children's lower achievement is that black students have external loci of control or a sense of powerlessness in the schools (Spencer, 1981). Another theory is that black children are not socialized at home to be as competitive in academics as they are in athletics (Howard & Hammond, 1985). This competitive edge is what would enable black students to overcome earlier deprivation. Comer (1985) and others have stated that the lack of achievement is related to economic class differences between parents and school employees. Middle-class children, but not working- and under-class children, develop skills at home that facilitate their learning in school. Poor parents are intimidated by the school and are not able to exert the pressure on or give the support to school personnel that would enable their children to maximize their abilities.

Elementary and Secondary Education.

It has been found that 75 percent of all the black students in the public schools are concentrated in approximately 2 percent of the nation's school districts, or in 350 out of 16,000 school districts (Moody, 1985). There are 202 school superintendents, 120 black and 82 nonblack, who are responsible for educating more than 50 percent of all the black children from kindergarten to the twelfth grade. Any significant changes in the education of the majority of black children will have to occur in these schools.

One earlier proposed solution to lower achievement was the racial integration of the schools, aimed at exposing black children to the resources that were available to nonblacks. However, the segregated enrollment patterns of 75 percent of the black children reflect the intensification of housing segregation in urban centers that will prevent the racial integration of neighborhoods. The excessive busing required for black children to attend integrated schools and the negative experiences many of these children had with forced busing made busing an impractical solution. It has finally been realized by parents, educators, and researchers alike that high-quality education is possible regardless of the racial mix in classrooms. Although integration efforts are being continued in many communities, the emphasis has shifted to meeting the educational needs of children wherever they may be.

Unfortunately, the resources that could be used to provide remediation, enrichment, and intensive instruction have become more limited because governmental policies no longer favor the elimination of these educational inequities. If the school systems with the largest enrollments of poor and black children could be targeted to receive greater resources and to provide stronger expectations of black children's achievement and closer cooperation with the children's families, many of these deficiencies could be eliminated. The community will have to continue to pressure the schools, and support must be given to families to reinforce the achievement of their children.

College Education.

Despite the increase in the number of black high school graduates from 1975 to 1980, the percentage of high school graduates who enrolled in college decreased. In 1982, only 36 percent of the black high school seniors entered colleges—a decline from the 45 percent in 1981. Blacks tend to enroll in junior colleges and in the first two years of universities; their enrollment in two-year colleges is three times greater than in four-year colleges, and there is a strong pattern of dropping out before graduation ("Minorities Still Underrepresented," 1984).

Blacks, along with other ethnic groups of color except Asians, are underrepresented in higher education. In 1984, they represented 9.2 percent of all postsecondary enrollments, compared to Hispanics, who represented 3.9 percent; Asians, 2.4 percent; and Native Americans, 0.7 percent ("Minorities Still Underrepresented," 1984). Not only have the blacks been underrepresented in enrollments, their enrollment has *decreased* in both the two- and four-year colleges since 1978, while that of Hispanics and Asians has increased. In addition, the absolute number and the percentage of degrees earned by blacks decreased from 1976 to 1981, while those of all other ethnic groups of color increased. Furthermore, fewer blacks are enrolled in medical, dental, and other professional schools—a fact that will accelerate the decline in the number of middle-class black families.

Another theory related to poor achievement is that blacks enter white schools and universities to find that they are in hostile environments (Peters, 1985). This theory has received empirical support. For example, in a study of black students who were enrolled in predominantly white state-supported schools across the nation, Allen (1984) found that the students were highly motivated to achieve, had positive self-concepts, felt they were well prepared for college, and were mostly from middle-class backgrounds and from stable intact families. Despite these positive factors, Allen indicated, the students were ambivalent about their experiences at the white schools and with the white faculty members. They felt isolated from campus life and felt the lack of black role models and peers on campus, which they compensated for by becoming immersed in the activities of black organizations. In addition, 65 percent had experienced primarily subtle forms of racial discrimination. These experiences contribute to the fact that one-half the black college students choose to attend predominantly black institutions. One-third of black medical students are concentrated in only three medical schools, all predominantly black ("Decline Found in Proportion of Blacks in Medical Schools," 1985). The enrollment of blacks in schools of social work is more diverse, but a decline has occurred, mostly because of the elimination of training grants and changes in governmental policies that have restricted student loans.

College Faculty. In the future, black college students will have even greater difficulty finding role models and emotional support, for there has been a decline in the number of doctorates earned by blacks when ethnic groups of color are combined. A greater number of bright black college students are forgoing graduate school degrees that would prepare them for academic careers (Richburg, 1985). The decline of financial support to graduate students, the need to enter careers that have more immediate financial rewards, and the uncertainties of academic careers have led many prospective doctoral candidates into business or legal careers. As of 1984, only 8 percent of the full-time professional employees in higher education were black. Blacks are concentrated in the lower-status positions, with an inordinate proportion in auxiliary services, rather than mainstream faculty jobs that would allow them to rise to higher-status university positions (Wilson, 1984). Furthermore, they are hired on tenure tracks or granted tenure at a rate that is below their retirement and extension rate (Wilson, 1984).

Employment

The unemployment and underemployment of men are two of the most serious problems of blacks. At the end of 1984, the unemployment rate of black male teenagers aged 16–18 was 44 percent—almost three times higher than that of white male teenagers (16 percent). Only 23 percent of the black male teenagers and 35 percent of Hispanic male teenagers were employed, compared to 48 percent of the white male teenagers. The rate of participation in the labor market in 1983 for these two groups of ethnic males was the lowest in history. Educational achievement does not appear to help blacks, for in 1984, the unemployment rate of black youths who completed high school (38 percent) was higher than that of white high school dropouts (24 percent) (U.S. Bureau of Labor Statistics, 1984a). In 1930, the proportion of adult black men who were employed was 80 percent; this proportion declined to 56 percent in 1984 (U.S. Bureau of Labor Statistics, 1984b).

The employment and training programs for youths that were implemented in the 1960s and 1970s produced positive results, as measured by the higher earnings and job placements of those who completed the programs compared to those who did not participate in these programs (U.S. Bureau of Labor Statistics, 1984a). Unfortunately, two of the programs—the Job Corps and the Work Incentive program—have been reduced because the federal government does not want to be responsible for such programs.

Race is still a powerful determinant of who does and who does not get employed. Blacks are underrepresented in well-paying or status jobs. They tend to be employed in low-skilled jobs and insecure positions.

Health

The death rate of poor blacks is still significantly higher than that of whites. Undesirable living conditions are the major factor in the deaths of children—more so than the nonavailability of health services. In Wise's (1985) study of an urban area in New England, race was the major predictor of the deaths of infants, 90 percent of whom were black, when the cause of death was premature births, low birth weight, or poor prenatal care. The death rate for older children and youths was clearly linked to environment, rather than race. The leading cause of death for inner-city youths, regardless of race, was injury or violence.

With regard to life expectancy, in 1979 blacks lived an average of 68.5 years and whites, 74.6 (a difference of 6.10 years). By 1983, both groups had added an average of one year to their lives, with blacks living to 69.6 years and whites to 75.2 years (a difference of 5.60 years) ("Life Expectancy Gap Narrows," 1984).

Health Problems. Blacks have more serious health problems than do whites because their undesirable living conditions, diets, and working conditions expose them to more carcinogens and stress-related diseases. Stress, anger, depression, and low self-esteem are particular problems in black communities. All these problems are the consequences of poverty and discrimination and the fact that blacks (as well as women) are not allowed or encouraged, through a variety of methods, to go beyond them (Gary, 1984). Because they cannot afford to pay for medical care, poor blacks overuse the emergency facilities of hospitals for primary care and do not receive preventive medical care.

Lung cancer is the most frequent disease of black men, followed by prostate tumors. Breast cancer and colon-rectal cancer are on the increase, and hypertension affects one-third of all blacks. Stress, alcohol consumption, cigarette smoking, and diets that are high in fat and salt contribute to these diseases (Gregg, 1984; "Life Expectancy Gap Narrows," 1984). Moreover, blacks tend to be in poorer health and to be fighting more than one major disease at a time, so they tend to have lower survival rates when they do become ill.

Some of the therapies used in fighting debilitating diseases are less effective with blacks than with whites (Gregg, 1984). For example, beta blockers do not work as well as diuretics in fighting hypertension in blacks as in whites. Therefore, physicians must consider the race of their patients in selecting appropriate medical therapies.

Causes of Death. The causes of death are different for black men, black women, white men, and white women. Although heart disease and cancer are the leading causes of death for all four groups, more black men

than any other group die from these diseases. The rate of diabetes in black women is 2.5 times higher than in white women and almost twice as high in black men than in white men. However, black men and black women have significantly lower rates of suicide than do white men and white women; that is, in 1984, the suicide rate of white men was 1.66 percent times higher than that of black men, and the suicide rate of white women was 2.38 times higher than that of black women.

Homicide is the third highest killer of black men, whose rate of death from homicide is over 6.5 times higher than that of white men, 5.25 times higher than that of black women, and 22.47 times higher than that of white women ("Life Expectancy Gap Narrows," 1984). The frustrations, stresses, and anger of black men about their living conditions, unemployment and underemployment, and lessened ability to support their families are acted out through violent attacks on others. Because most violent crimes are directed at those in the immediate environment and most blacks live in ghettos, the victims of violence usually are other blacks.

The pressures that blacks as a group face, because of their devalued status and the fewer economic resources that are available to their families, result in significantly high levels of stress that make it more difficult to maintain their mental health. The coping strategies that have been developed have provided networks of support that help mitigate the external pressures (McAdoo, 1982).

Implications of the Black Situation on American Society

The decline in the educational achievements, health, and employment of blacks has importance beyond the black communities. The lack of educational attainment will become of greater concern to all Americans because by the year 2020, it is predicted, 35 percent of the American population will be ethnic groups of color ("Minorities Still Underrepresented," 1984). This increase in population of the comparatively younger blacks and Hispanics means that a majority of the labor force may be composed of these undereducated groups and women. Their lack of education, skills, and occupational prospects will cause the productivity of this country to decline. The aging white population will be forced to depend more and more on these groups to provide the taxes for social security and other governmental services that will be needed by the growing aged population. Attempts to increase the educational opportunities and attainments of blacks necessitate the immediate resolution of serious governmental policy issues so that the quality of life of the entire nation will not be destroyed. The growth in the number of children and people of color in poverty will eventually lead to "diminished futures" for all Americans (Hechinger, 1985) unless the poverty and poor education of black children are reduced.

Roles of Black Community Institutions

Cooperative groups, social service organizations, and religious institutions traditionally have provided social support and services to members of black communities. After Emancipation, cooperative efforts, often made with great sacrifices, enabled the former enslaved Africans to build schools, churches, and cooperative businesses. When blacks were able to expand their professional involvements beyond the black communities, they continued their self-help efforts while expanding their network of professional and service-related fraternal organizations. The latter newer organizations combined with the traditional service and religious organizations to provide valuable support to individuals and families.

The self-help efforts continued even after governmental programs were instituted because some leaders in the black community believed that the private and governmental programs were not sensitive to the unique pressures faced by black people (Martin & Martin, 1985). Others in the black community thought that nonblack social workers perceived them in a stereotypic manner and that they were being given services that were inferior to those in other communities.

The final impetus for the preservation of the traditional self-help groups has been the changing social policies. Over the generations, blacks have found that local and federal policies shifted support and emphasis periodically and, therefore, that they could not depend on governmental support. The 1980s have proved the validity of this belief and have made these supportive networks more important. The coordinated network of churches, social agencies, and professional and fraternal organizations that helped transform the civil rights movement is now attempting to address the empoverishment of all people of color.

Black Churches. One of the strongest institutions in black communities has been and still is the network of churches, especially those that have been black. In 1978, the churches of the seven historically black Protestant denominations (different, independent denominations that have not been a part of the white Protestant denominations), composed of approximately 20 million persons, incorporated into the Congress of National Black Churches—a nonprofit organization that provides leadership in addressing the social and political ills endured by blacks ("Black Churches Forging Coalitions," 1982). This organization instituted several community-based programs related to the life of black families, economic development, employment and training, child care, and the prevention of teenage pregnancy. It relies more on the interactive structure of several strong organizations than on the efforts of a few leaders, who can be eliminated at will by those who do not support the progress of black people.

Efforts are being made to coordinate the economic resources of the different denominations and their programs to promote the stability of the organizations so they may continue to develop more resources for black communities. Specific programs in parenting skills, educational tutorials, responsible male-female relationships, and economic planning are now being implemented in scores of churches across the country. Although the economic programs are paramount, these churches continue to emphasize the ethical and moral obligation to provide social services to those in need, through such activities as credit unions, insurance programs, central purchasing, and family-centered services.

Role of Social Workers

The role of social workers in black communities must be threefold. The first role is to understand and empathize with how many black people live, the pressures they face, and the stereotypic manner in which they are viewed. The second role is to make use of the skills and resources in the field to alleviate these pressures and to promote better living conditions. The third role is to expand activities in relation to advocacy so that institutional and governmental policies will change and discrimination against blacks will be ameliorated. Too often, social workers internalize the negative perceptions of blacks that are held by those in the wider society, which interferes with their ability to operate on behalf of their clients.

Black social workers have utilized two approaches to improving the profession's understanding of the needs of black individuals and families (National Association of Black Social Workers, 1978). One approach has been the formation of the National Association of Black Social Workers. Another approach has been the attempt to get the professional social work associations to be more responsive to and active in meeting the needs of blacks through educational programs, the support of the professional education of social workers of color, and the development of curricula in schools of social work and practice materials that include information on persons of color, specifically blacks.

The effort to include more black social workers in the professional organizations and the development of practice material have met with some success. However, attempts to integrate information about blacks in the curricula of schools of social work, rather than segregating it in separate courses, as well as to change the attitudes of social workers about black people, have been limited. These areas must receive more attention in the future.

National Association of Black Social Workers. The National Association of Black Social Workers, founded in May 1968, was formed from various groups that were working in the social welfare arena (National Association of Black Social Workers, 1978). These groups presented position statements to two major organizations—the Council on Social Work Education in 1968 and the National Association of Social Workers in 1969—that led these organizations to take steps to include more blacks in the profession. Attention then was paid to the delivery of services in black communities and the analyses of policies that have an impact on blacks. The association has taken positions

on the quality of services delivered to families, transracial adoption, social work practice, professional training, and social service on the international level. Its annual conferences, international study tours, and publications have dealt with issues related to the provision of services to black people.

HARRIETTE PIPES MCADOO

For further information, see CIVIL RIGHTS; ETHNIC-SENSITIVE PRACTICE; INTERGROUP RELATIONS; MINORITIES OF COLOR; RACIAL DISCRIMINATION AND INEQUALITY.

References

Allen, W. (1984). *Undergraduate Survey of Black Undergraduate Students Attending Predominantly White, State-Supported Universities.* Ann Arbor: Center for Afro-American and African Studies, University of Michigan.

Billingsley, A. (1968). *Black Families in White America.* Englewood Cliffs, N.J.: Prentice-Hall.

"Black Churches Forging Coalition to Battle Economic and Social Ills." (1982, December 12). *New York Times*, p. A14.

"Blacks' Scores Continue to Rise, College Board Entrance Results Compiled." (1985, January 10). *Washington Post*, p. A7.

Blassingame, J. (1972). *The Slave Community: Plantation Life in the Antebellum South.* New York: Oxford University Press.

Chase, A. (1977). *The Legacy of Malthus: The Social Costs of the New Scientific Racism.* New York: Alfred A. Knopf.

Children's Defense Fund. (1984). *Children Having Children.* Washington, D.C.: Author.

Children's Defense Fund. (1985). *Black and White Children in America: Key Facts.* Washington, D.C.: Author.

Comer, J. (1985). "Empowering Black Children's Educational Environments." In H. McAdoo & J. McAdoo (Eds.), *Black Children: Social, Educational, and Parental Environments* (pp. 12–138). Beverly Hills, Calif.: Sage Publications.

"Conference Focuses on Teen Pregnancy." (1985, August 23). *This Week in Washington, 6*(23), 1.

Dash, L. (1986, January 26). "At Risk: Chronicles of Teen-Age Pregnancy." *Washington Post*, p. A1.

"Decline Found in Proportion of Blacks in Medical Schools." (1985, October 10). *New York Times*, p. A26.

Dodson, J. (1981). "Conceptualizations of Black Families." In H. McAdoo (Ed.), *Black Families* (pp. 23–36). Beverly Hills, Calif.: Sage Publications.

DuBois, W. E. B. (1969). *The Negro American*

Family. New York: New American Library. (Originally published in 1908)

DuBois, W. E. B. (1973). "The College-bred Community." In H. Aptheker (Ed.), *The Education of Black People: Ten Critiques, 1906–1960* (pp. 33–35). New York: Monthly Review Press. (Originally published in 1910)

Elwood, D., & Bane, M. J. (1984). *The Impact of AFDC on Family Structure and Living Arrangements*. Paper prepared for the U.S. Department of Health & Human Services under Grant No. 92A-82.

Fishel, L., & Quarles, B. (1967). "The Burdens of Reconstruction." In *The Black American: A Documented History* (pp. 258–288). Glenview, Ill.: Scott, Foresman & Co.

Franklin, J. H. (1947). *From Slavery to Freedom: A History of Negro Americans*. New York: Alfred A. Knopf.

Frazier, E. F. (1939). *The Negro Family in the United States*. Chicago: University of Chicago Press.

Gary, L. (1984, September 27). *Mental Health Consequences of Unemployment*. Paper presented at the Health Braintrust Workshop, Congressional Black Caucus, Washington, D.C.

Gregg, S. (1984, December 10). "The Black-White Health Gap: Disparity Widening, Congressional Caucus Is Told." *Washington Post*, p. D6.

Gutman, H. (1976). *The Black Family in Slavery and Freedom: 1750–1925*. New York: Random House.

Hechinger, F. (1985, August 13). "Expert Warns of Need to Teach Poor Children." *New York Times*, p. C7.

Herskovitz, M. (1958). *The Myth of the Negro Past*. Boston: Beacon Press. (Originally published in 1941)

Hill, R. (1971). *The Strengths of Black Families*. New York: Emerson Hall Publishers.

Hopps, J. (1982). "Oppression Based on Color." *Social Work*, 27(1), 3–5.

Howard, J., & Hammond, R. (1985, September 9). "The Rumors of Inferiority." *The New Republic*, pp. 17–21.

Johnson, S. (1979). *Issues in Selection for Professional Schools and Employment: Measurement Mystique*. (Occasional Paper No. 2). Washington, D.C.: Howard University Institute of Educational Policy.

Kamerman, S. (1985). "Young, Poor, and a Mother Alone: Problems and Possible Solutions." In H. P. McAdoo & H. T. J. Parham (Eds.), *Service to Young Families, Program Review and Policy Recommendations*. Washington, D.C.: American Public Welfare Association.

"Life Expectancy Gap Narrows." (1984, March 3). *U.S.A. Today*, p. A1.

McAdoo, H. (Ed.). (1981). *Black Families*. Beverly Hills, Calif.: Sage Publications.

McAdoo, H. (1982). "Levels of Stress and Family Support in Black Families." In H. McCubbin, E. Cauble, & J. Patterson (Eds.), *Family Stress, Coping and Social Support*. Springfield, Ill.: Charles C Thomas, Publisher.

Martin, J., & Martin, E. (1985). *The Helping Tradition in the Black Family and Community*. Silver Spring, Md.: National Association of Social Workers.

"Minorities Still Underrepresented in Higher Education." (1984). *Higher Education & National Affairs*, 33(21), 3, 5.

Moody, C. (1985). "Black Students Concentrated in Two Percent of Nation's Schools." *Black Press Review*, 3(1), 31.

National Association of Black Social Workers. (1978, May 1–6). "National Association of Black Social Workers: History in Progress." In *Silhouettes of Past Promises: Definition of Future Faces* (Anniversary Conference Program, pp. 10–11). San Francisco, Calif.: Author.

Nobles, W. (1974). "Africanity: Its Role in Black Families." *Black Scholar*, 5, 10–17.

Painter, N. (1977). *Exodusters: Black Migration to Kansas after Reconstruction*. New York: Alfred A. Knopf.

Park, R. (1919). "The Conflict and Fusion of Cultures with Special Reference to the Negro." *Journal of Negro History*, 4(2), 118.

Pearce, D., & McAdoo, H. (1981). *Women and Children: Alone and in Poverty*. Washington, D.C.: U.S. Government Printing Office.

Peters, M. (1985). "Racial Socialization of Young Black Children." In H. McAdoo & J. McAdoo (Eds.), *Black Children: Social, Educational, and Parental Environments* (pp. 159–173). Beverly Hills, Calif.: Sage Publications.

Peters, M., & McAdoo, H. (1983). "The Present and Future of Alternative Lifestyles in Ethnic American Cultures." In E. Macklin & R. Rubin (Eds.), *Contemporary Families and Alternative Lifestyles* (pp. 288–307). Beverly Hills, Calif.: Sage Publications.

Pipes, W. H. (1951). *Say Amen, Brother! Old-Time Negro Preaching: A Study in American Frustration*. New York: William-Frederick Press.

Pleck, E. (1972). "The Two-Parent Household: Black Family Structure in Late Nineteenth-Century Boston." *Journal of Social History*, 6, 3–31.

Quarles, B. (1971). "Black History's Diversified Clientele." In L. A. Williams (Ed.), *Africa and the Afro-American Experience*. Washington, D.C.: Howard University Press.

Rich, S. (1985, June 8). "U.S. Black Population Rises 6.7% in 1980s, Growth Rate Is Double that of Whites." *Washington Post*, p. A7.

Rich, S. (1986, April 19). "Child, Poverty Spiral, No Welfare Gain after First Baby." *Washington Post*, A10.

Richburg, K. (1985, December 16). "Blacks Forgoing Academic Life, Many Students Seek More Secure and Remunerative Careers." *Washington Post*, p. A3.

Rosenthal, R., & Jacobson, L. (1968). *Pygmalion in the Classroom*. New York: Holt, Rinehart & Winston.

Spencer, M. (1981). "Racial Variations in Achievement Prediction: The School as a Conduit for Macrostructural Cultural Tension." In H. McAdoo (Ed.), *Black Families* (pp. 85–111). Beverly Hills, Calif.: Sage Publications.

Stack, C. (1974). *All Our Kin*. New York: Harper & Row.

Sudarkasa, N. (1981). "Interpreting the African Heritage in Afro-American Family Organization." In H. McAdoo (Ed.), *Black Families* (pp. 37–53). Beverly Hills, Calif.: Sage Publications.

U.S. Bureau of the Census. (1984a). "Money Income and Poverty Status of Families and Persons in the United States: 1983." In *Current Population Reports* (Series P-60, No. 145). Washington, D.C.: U.S. Government Printing Office.

U.S. Bureau of the Census. (1984b). "Projections of the Population of the United States, by Age, Sex and Race: 1983 to 2080." In *Current Population Reports* (Series P-25, No. 952). Washington, D.C.: U.S. Government Printing Office.

U.S. Bureau of the Census. (1985a). *Estimates of Poverty Including the Value of Noncash Benefits: 1984*. Washington, D.C.: U.S. Government Printing Office.

U.S. Bureau of the Census. (1985b). "Money Income and Poverty Status of Families and Persons in the United States: 1984." In *Current Population Reports* (Series P-60, No. 149). Washington, D.C.: U.S. Government Printing Office.

U.S. Bureau of Labor Statistics. (1984a, January). *Employment and Earnings*. Washington, D.C.: Author.

U.S. Bureau of Labor Statistics. (1984b). *The Youth Employment Situation, December 1984*. New York: Eleanor Roosevelt Institute.

"U.S. Hispanic Population Fastest-Growing Sector." (1986, January 31). *New York Times*, p. A.

Wilson, R. (1984). "Office of Minority Concerns Result of Joint Effort." *Higher Education & National Affairs*, 33(21), 5, 8.

Wilson, W. & Neckerman, R. (1986). "Poverty and Family Structure: The Widening Gap Between Evidence and Public Policy Issues." In S. Danzibar & D. Weinberg (Eds.), *The War on Poverty: Taking Stock of What Worked and What Did Not*. Cambridge, Mass.: Harvard University Press.

Wise, P. (1985, August 23). "Death Rates Much Higher Among Black Infants." *This Week in Washington*, 6(33).

Woodson, C. (1936). *The African Background Outlined*. Washington, D.C.: Associated Publishers.

BOARDS OF DIRECTORS

From the earliest days of organized philanthropy in the United States, interested and committed individuals have served as trustees, overseers, and board members of charities and social service and other nonprofit organizations. Although it is not possible to specify the exact number, the U.S. Bureau of the Census (1984) identified a total of 16,518 such associations in 1982. Of these, 1,160 were categorized as social welfare agencies and 1,582 as health and medical organizations. Each of these is governed by a board of directors.

Years of experience have provided insight into the functioning of organization boards; however, they remain one of the least understood entities in the human service field. According to Zelman (1977) and Gelman (1983), this lack of understanding persists in spite of clear directives for board role and responsibility and despite the application of modern principles of corporate trusts to the nonprofit sector.

Board Functions

Agency charters and bylaws clearly specify the responsibilities and obligations of boards and their individual members. Whereas boards of public agencies are advisory or administrative and therefore do not have as broad powers or responsibilities, boards of directors or trustees of private or voluntary organizations are charged with the general direction and control of those organizations (Mitton, 1974). The board is the policymaking body of the organization, with a legal duty to ensure the achievement of the agency's goals and objectives. Current or past board members were responsible for the creation of the agency and share collective responsibility for the fiscal and programmatic aspects of its performance. The board is responsible to funding sources, to the community, to governmental and private regulating bodies, and to consumers of the agency's services.

Board members of a social service agency thus have a legal and moral obligation to keep themselves fully informed about the agency's operations. Their functions can be classified as follows:

■ General direction and control of the agency—policy development

■ Short- and long-term planning—program development

■ Hiring competent administrative staff—personnel

■ Facilitating access to necessary resources—finance

■ Interpretation of the organization to the community at large—public relations

■ Evaluation—accountability

According to Perlmutter (1969, 1973), boards and their members will relate differently to these functions depending on the agency's stage of evolution and development and its needs at a particular time.

Who Serves and Why?

Individuals agree to serve as members of an agency board for a variety of reasons. Generally, board members are prominent and successful community leaders who donate their time to community service activities. Some are individuals who have a vested personal interest in a particular cause or issue (for example, a handicapped relative). According to Klein (1968), others are motivated because "charitable and related activities are, in our culture, a source of social prestige, and occasionally an auxiliary means of access to the power structure" (p. 194). Although some individuals may be motivated by a quest for prestige or political power or by some other self-interest, Stein (1962) observes that others serve for altruistic reasons. Many individuals serve on boards of charitable or nonprofit agencies as an expression of religious or moral obligation, others because of professional commitment. Past or present consumers of an agency's services often serve as board members or in an advisory capacity to the board. Although consumer presence is mandatory on the boards of most public agencies, it is increasingly found on the boards of private nonprofit organizations

in the health, mental health, and disability fields. The growth of the self-help and self-advocacy movement has contributed to this involvement and has resulted in greater awareness, understanding, and responsiveness by board members to clients' needs and concerns. Regardless of the motivation for serving, acceptance of a board position brings with it an obligation that must be met with care and diligence.

Obligations of Board Members

Serving on a board of directors is more than a social experience or get-together. The directors of charitable, nonprofit corporations, like those of for-profit corporations, are required to exercise reasonable and ordinary care in the performance of their duties, exhibiting honesty and good faith. They must discharge their duties with the degree of care, skill, and diligence any prudent person would exercise under similar circumstances. The initiation, implementation, and operation of a social service agency is thus the "business" of the board and according to Weber (1975), board members are expected to approach their responsibilities as they would approach other "business" transactions.

Hanson and Marmaduke (1972) indicate that the board of directors as a group manages the nonprofit corporation, delegating responsibilities appropriately but retaining ultimate responsibility for the agency's image and performance. The board of directors is legally and morally accountable to the agency's various constituencies for its actions. According to Gelman (1983), "a board which fails in its function of both determining policy and evaluating achievement in support of those policies is negligent in performing its mandated functions" (p. 88).

Pasley (1966) notes that the legal standard of care applied to directors of nonprofit organizations is the same as that applied to directors of for-profit corporations, even though the latter receive compensation for their services. This standard of conduct has replaced the more lenient standard that existed for charitable organizations in many states. The old standard required proof of bad faith, fraudulent breaches of trust, or gross and willful negligence before a director could be held accountable.

According to the *Harvard Law Review* ("The Charitable Corporation," 1951), the modern trend is to apply corporate rather than trust principles in determining board members' liability in nonprofit agencies. As Zelman (1977) points out, the concept of charitable immunity has been rejected in most states. In those jurisdictions, charitable organizations—their governing boards and their employees—are liable for harm resulting from negligent actions. Negligence can occur through acts of omission as well as acts of commission by responsible persons. Board members are expected to attend to the affairs of the agency with the skill and care they would exercise in the conduct of their own personal affairs. Language like the following, taken from Pennsylvania law (Purdon's, 1972), can be found in the statutes pertaining to nonprofit corporations in virtually every state:

> Officers and directors shall be deemed to stand in a fiduciary relation to the corporation, and shall discharge the duties of their respective positions in good faith and with that diligence, care and skill which ordinarily prudent men would exercise under similar circumstances. (p. 120)

Board Composition

In setting up a board, it is crucial to select individuals whose personal commitment, energy, and areas of knowledge are related to the agency's mission and to the specific tasks that need to be performed. Above all, board members must have the time, interest, and willingness to be of service to the agency. As indicated earlier, the business of a board is business; it is not a social activity or get-together. Individuals who are overcommitted or who spend much time away from the community tend to slow down the board in carrying out its mandated responsibilities. Unavailable or irresponsible board members force committed members to assume more responsibility than they can or should. The lack of regular and consistent attendance at board meetings is one indicator of a board member's failure to meet the required standard of care.

The individuals who serve on boards should have the ability to work cooperatively and tactfully with one another. Interpersonal skills are critical because board members interact not only with their peers on the board but also with the agency's director and staff; with community leaders and officials; and

with members of the community at large, who may also be clients of the agency. Members of the board should have legitimacy or standing in the community and be recognized as credible and responsible individuals.

Although the agency's charter may require that the board include bankers, politicians, clergy, and representatives of various professions and designated constituencies, every prospective member should be screened for interest and relevant expertise. It may be advisable to appoint prestigious community leaders as honorary members of the board. This prevents their potential lack of time, interest, or commitment from hindering the board in the conduct of its business.

All board members should fully understand the nature of the organization and their individual and collective responsibilities as board members. Given the possibility of personal liability, all board members should receive explicit and comprehensive orientation. In selecting board members, every effort should be made to identify individuals with the following characteristics: (1) interest in the organization and in its mission, (2) ability to work with others, (3) time and willingness to be of service, (4) specific knowledge or expertise in an area or areas of the agency's overall functioning, and (5) a point of view responsive to both community and agency interests.

The optimal size of the board of directors of a nonprofit organization cannot be specified. Often the size and composition of the board are dictated by the agency's charter or bylaws. Although Weber (1975) suggests that boards be composed of 30 to 36 members, this may be too large to permit the development of effective group process. Boards that are excessively large tend to lack strong feelings of commitment and obligation, resulting in poor or sporadic participation and attendance on the part of members.

As a rule, the board must be workable in terms of size—neither too large nor too small. It must have sufficient members to accomplish its work. Size and composition should therefore be related to the agency's goals and objectives. Sufficient members must regularly be present to ensure a division of labor and that no member or small group has to carry disproportionate responsibility. In this author's experience, a board of 15 to 18 members is sufficient to monitor the six areas of board responsibility previously identified.

Collectively, members of the board must have the expertise to monitor and evaluate the various elements of the agency's operation. Ideally, each member's individual role and unique contribution to the overall effectiveness of the agency should be clear, and the board should develop into a cohesive work group.

Terms of board service should be limited to three years. Reappointment to a second three-year term should be an option for those members who have fulfilled their obligations and functioned effectively. Those who have been unable to meet the expectations set for board members or who can no longer commit themselves to board service should not be recommended for reelection or reappointment. Individuals who fail to meet their obligations should be asked to resign.

Board members should serve on a rotating basis, with one-third of the board's positions replaced each year. Such a format promotes continuity, allows ongoing monitoring of the enterprise, and provides for a regular infusion of new blood and the grooming of new leaders. The systematic addition of new members with identified expertise and commitment and the ongoing training of board members help the agency to become self-evaluating. According to many authors (Austin et al., 1982; Gelman, 1983; Newman & Van Wijk, 1980; Wildavsky, 1972), the development of a capacity for self-evaluation is the only way that an agency can be responsive and accountable to its goals, mission, and constituencies.

Orientation and Training

New board members need orientation and continuing members need ongoing training. Board members should be fully aware of their roles and responsibilities and of what kind of time commitments they are expected to make. All members should be provided with written descriptions of these expectations and obligations. Members of the board should be familiar with the agency, its facilities, programs, services, and personnel. Based on their interests and expertise and on the agency's needs, individual board members should be assigned to committees corresponding to the six functional areas of board responsibility. Staggered membership fosters the development of expertise and familiarity with agency operations. Board members should understand the potential for personal liability inherent in their acceptance of a board position and should receive information on liability insurance for directors and officers.

According to Stein (1962), board members have a social responsibility to be knowledgeable not only about the purpose and operation of their own agency but also about the social welfare context in which the agency exists. Such a perspective enables them to anticipate opportunities for and obstacles to the achievement of agency goals.

Board-Executive Relations

The literature (Blau & Scott, 1962; Robins & Blackburn, 1974; Senor, 1965; Wiehe, 1978) is filled with contradictory statements about board-executive relations and with cautions about duplication and overlap in role and functions. The administrator or executive director is an employee of the board of directors and serves at their pleasure. The board is responsible for evaluating the administrator and the agency's operations at regular intervals. Although the executive director is delegated authority for the day-to-day operations of the agency and for handling the majority of personnel matters, law and charter invest the board with the power and authority to make policy. In other words, the ultimate responsibility for agency functioning and for the performance of the executive and staff resides with the board.

Some authors (Tripodi, 1976; Volunteer Bureau of Pasadena, 1972) suggest that the agency executive must provide leadership for the board in policymaking, but such an arrangement may contradict both the agency's charter and the requirements of law. According to Harris (1977), many formulations that deal with board-executive relations treat the subject as if two separable spheres of activity existed—one occupied by the board and the other by the professional executive. Although the executive may be an ex officio member of the board, Senor (1965) warns that granting the executive the right to vote on policy matters creates a potential conflict of interest. It also grants the executive disproportionate power, based on the control of information the board needs to do its job. The key is thus the degree to which the board retains its mandated role. Although the board can draw on the executive's expertise and knowledge, it cannot allow its legal responsibility to be diluted or co-opted by overdependence. A collegial working relationship is essential between the board and the executive, but the executive—no matter how long employed—remains an employee of the organization.

Board-Staff Relations

According to Trecker (1981), appropriate, effective, and efficient board-staff relations are based on a clear and common understanding of their functions and responsibilities within the organization. As indicated previously, the board is responsible for developing and establishing the policies that guide the organization. Staff are responsible for implementing the policies adopted by the board of directors and transmitted to them through the executive. In implementing and achieving board policy, staff may choose among several alternatives, but the board is ultimately responsible and therefore must hold staff, including the executive, accountable. Although the evaluation of staff should rest with the designated administrator or supervisory staff, the staff's performance reflects on the agency's goal or mission and on the performance of the board.

This analysis may appear unbalanced in the board's favor. However, ongoing interaction between board and staff is essential to the development of a responsive and accountable agency. It is crucial for staff to have regular opportunities to report to the board about their experiences in implementing board policies, about obstacles they encountered, and about unmet needs they identified. In this way the board can adjust or modify its policies based on staff experiences. Staff members should know members of the board examining various programs and feel comfortable with them.

A three-way partnership should thus exist among board, administrator, and staff. Such a partnership is facilitated by clear job descriptions that specify obligations and responsibilities. Personnel standards consistent with those of the National Association of Social Workers (1975) help to clarify the rights, responsibilities, and expectations of employees. Similarly, an understanding of the necessity and desirability of creating a self-evaluating agency and a commitment to this objective by all parties are essential for the achievement of agency goals.

The board of directors is ultimately responsible for the performance of the agency it serves. An effective board is critical not only to the efficient operation of an agency but also to meeting identified needs of the community. Board membership in nonprofit organizations requires more than altruism and interest—it requires time, a commitment to the development of expertise, and an understanding of the potential for personal liability. The development of an accountable agency requires that the board, in partnership with the executive and staff, continuously monitor and evaluate the agency's finances and programs.

SHELDON R. GELMAN

For further information, see ADMINISTRATION in SOCIAL WELFARE; CITIZEN PARTICIPATION.

References

Austin, M. J., et al. (1982). *Evaluating Your Agency's Programs.* Beverly Hills, Calif.: Sage Publications.

Blau, P. M., & Scott, W. R. (1962). *Formal Organizations.* San Francisco: Chandler Publishing Co.

"The Charitable Corporation" [Note]. (1951). *Harvard Law Review, 64*(7), 1168–1181.

Gelman, S. R. (1983). "The Board of Directors and Agency Accountability." *Social Casework, 64*(2), 83–91.

Hanson, P. L., & Marmaduke, C. T. (1972). *The Board Member—Decision Maker for the Non-profit Corporation.* Sacramento, Calif.: HAN/MAR Publications.

Harris, J. E. (1977). "The Internal Organization of Hospitals." *Bell Journal of Economics, 8*(2), 467–482.

Klein, P. (1968). *From Philanthropy to Social Welfare.* San Francisco: Jossey-Bass.

Mitton, D. G. (1974). "Utilizing the Board of Trustees: A Unique Structural Design." *Child Welfare, 53*(6), 345–351.

National Association of Social Workers. (1975). *Standards for Social Work Personnel Practices.* Washington, D.C.: Author.

Newman, H., & Van Wijk, A. (1980). *Self-Evaluation for Human Service Organizations.* New York: Greater New York Fund/United Way.

Pasley, R. S. (1966). "Non-Profit Corporations—Accountability of Directors and Officers." *Business Lawyer, 21*(3), 621–642.

Perlmutter, F. (1969). "A Theoretical Model of

Social Agency Development." *Social Casework, 50*(8), 467–473.

Perlmutter, F. (1973). "Citizen Participation and Professionalism: A Developmental Relationship." *Public Welfare, 31*(3), 25–28.

Purdon's Penna. Stat. Ann. (1972). tit. 15, §7734, 120.

Robins, A. J., & Blackburn, C. (1974). "Governing Boards in Mental Health: Roles and Training Needs." *Administration in Mental Health,* (Summer), 37–45.

Senor, J. M. (1965). "Another Look at the Executive/Board Relationship." In M. N. Zald (Ed.), *Social Welfare Institutions: A Sociological Reader* (pp. 418–427). New York: John Wiley & Sons.

Stein, H. D. (1962). "Board, Executive and Staff." In H. Millman (Ed.), *The Social Welfare Forum* (pp. 215–230). New York: Columbia University Press.

Trecker, H. B. (1981). *Boards of Human Service Agencies: Challenges and Responsibilities in the 80's.* New York: Federation of Protestant Welfare Agencies.

Tripodi, T. (1976). "Social Workers As Community Practitioners, Social Welfare Administrators and Social Policy Developers." In T. Tripodi et al. (Eds.), *Social Workers at Work* (2nd ed., pp. 162–169). Itasca, Ill.: F. E. Peacock Publishers.

U.S. Bureau of the Census. (1984). *National Data Book and Guide to Sources.* Washington, D.C.: Author.

Volunteer Bureau of Pasadena. (1972). *So . . . You Serve on a Board.* Pasadena, Calif.: Author.

Weber, J. (1975). *Managing the Board of Directors.* New York: Greater New York Fund.

Wiehe, V. R. (1978). "Role Expectations among Agency Personnel." *Social Work, 23*(1), 26–30.

Wildavsky, A. (1972). "The Self-Evaluating Organization." *Public Administration Review, 32*(5), 509–520.

Zelman, W. N. (1977). "Liability for Social Agency Boards." *Social Work, 22*(4), 270–274.

For Further Reading

Houle, C. O. (1960). *The Effective Board.* New York: Association Press.

Slavin, S. (1978). *Social Administration: The Management of the Social Services.* New York: Council on Social Work Education.

Swanson, A. (1984). *Building a Better Board: A Guide to Effective Leadership.* Washington, D.C.: Taft Corporation.

BRACE, CHARLES LORING. See biographical section.

BRECKINRIDGE, SOPHONISBA PRESTON. See biographical section.

BROCKWAY, ZEBULON REED. See biographical section.

BRUNO, FRANK JOHN. See biographical section.

BUDGETING. See ADMINISTRATION IN SOCIAL WELFARE; FINANCIAL MANAGEMENT; SOCIAL PLANNING IN THE VOLUNTARY SECTOR.

BUELL, BRADLEY. See biographical section.

BURNS, EVELINE MABEL. See biographical section.

CABOT, RICHARD CLARKE. See biographical section.

CANNON, IDA MAUD. See biographical section.

CANNON, MARY ANTOINETTE. See biographical section.

CASE MANAGEMENT

Case management is an approach to service delivery that attempts to ensure that clients with complex, multiple problems and disabilities receive all the services they need in a timely and appropriate fashion. It is a boundary-spanning approach in that, instead of providing a specific direct service, it utilizes case managers who link the client to the maze of direct service providers. These case managers are expected to assume ultimate responsibility for seeing that the service delivery system is responsive to all the needs of each client. Case management has been used in various fields of practice, especially in mental health with the chronically mentally disabled, in the care of the aging and of those with physical or developmental disabilities, and in child welfare (Bedford & Hybertson, 1975; Fitz, 1978; Beatrice, 1979; Caragonne, 1980, 1981; Steinberg & Carter, 1983).

Although the emphasis in case management is on linkage, case managers in theory do whatever it takes—whether brokerage, advocacy, or resource development—to ensure that all client needs are met; they may even provide a missing service themselves. Holding one worker responsible for the overall fate of the client and for the responsivity of the entire service delivery system is a strategy for overcoming the neglect and fragmentation that are thought to typify the way in which myriad service providers have historically dealt with multiproblem or profoundly impaired clients. In other words, designating one person as the case manager is an attempt to ensure that there is somebody who is accountable and who is helping the client hold the service delivery system accountable, someone who cannot "pass the buck" to another agency or individual when and if services are not delivered quickly and appropriately (Miller, 1983).

Growth and Aims

Little was known about case management before the mid-1970s (Platman, Dorgan, Gerhard, Mallam, & Spiliadis, 1982). Its emergence as a distinct concept was linked to the growth of human service programs during the 1960s. Public funding for those service programs was provided largely through categorical channels, resulting in a network of services deemed "highly complex, fragmented, duplicative and uncoordinated" (Intagliata, 1982, p. 655). As different programs emerged to offer specialized services or to serve narrowly defined target groups, the perception developed that persons with multiple problems and needs were not being served adequately by disconnected programs dealing with narrow aspects of their problems. For example, an elderly client might need cash supports from one source, housing from another, nutritional services from a third, care for physical or mental impairments from a fourth or fifth, social interaction and support from a sixth, and so on.

During the early 1970s, the Department of Health, Education and Welfare funded a series of demonstration projects to test various approaches to improving the coordination of federal service programs at the state and local levels (Mittenthal, 1976; Morrill, 1976). These "service integration" projects featured such techniques as "client-tracking systems, information and referral mechanisms, one-stop service centers, specialized management information systems, interagency planning and service delivery agreements, computerized resource inventories, and management reorganization projects" (Intagliata, 1982, p. 656). Most projects also featured case managers, called "system agents," who were expected to coordinate resources for clients and be accountable for their appropriate passage through the service system.

Another force giving rise to the growth of case management was the deinstitutionalization movement, particularly in the fields of mental health and developmental disabilities.

After the discovery of psychotropic drugs in the mid-1950s mental health systems began moving people from institutional to community settings in the belief that, with the ability of these drugs to inhibit their symptomatology, these clients would benefit from being in the community, which was thought to be less restrictive and more humane than institutions. The expansion of community-based human service programs during this period fostered this belief. However, during the 1970s evidence accumulated indicating that previously institutionalized individuals with profound, multiple needs did not always fare well in the community. They often lived in squalor and were rejected and perhaps victimized by their neighbors. Although aftercare was comprehensive in some localities, in most it was not. In many places human service agencies, even community mental health centers that were established to offset institutionalization, responded inadequately to the plight of the formerly institutionalized (Arnhof, 1975; Kirk & Therrien, 1975; General Accounting Office, 1977; Lamb, 1979a; Mechanic, 1980).

As the literature began to expose these problems, the field began to learn that the mere presence in the community of expanded categorical services did not mean that those services would be utilized. It also learned that community settings would not necessarily be less restrictive or more humane than the protected institutional environment (Bachrach, 1980, 1981), particularly for individuals whose profound impairments and unresponsiveness to conventional treatment approaches favored by professionals but geared to less impaired clientele made them unattractive to some community-based agencies and practitioners (Hogarty, 1971; Lamb, 1976; Rubin & Johnson, 1982). These clients often are unable or unmotivated to negotiate an unresponsive service delivery system themselves (Test, 1979). Research has shown that many of them, even with adequate community-based care, will be in and out of institutions throughout their lives (Talbott, 1978).

Consequently, a service component termed case management was recommended in an effort to accomplish the following objectives: (1) ensure continuity in care across services at any given point or over time (for example, as the individual moves between the institution and community through cycles of relapse and recovery); (2) ensure that services will be responsive to the full range of the person's needs as these needs change over time, perhaps throughout the person's life if necessary; (3) help these individuals gain access to needed services, overcoming obstacles to accessibility associated with eligibility criteria, regulations, policies, and procedures; and (4) ensure that the services that are provided match the client's needs, are provided in a proper and timely fashion, and are not inappropriately duplicative (Intagliata, 1982).

During the late 1970s, the National Institute of Mental Health funded demonstration projects in 19 states to implement and test its services integration concept, which was termed the community support system (CSS) (Turner, 1977; Turner & TenHoor, 1978; Turner & Shiffren, 1979). The CSS concept included the allocation of special coordinating power and authority to a specified agency at the local level. This "core CSS agency" would assess the needs of the chronically mentally ill in its area, negotiate interagency linkages and agreements for providing all needed support services, and develop new service components to connect existing gaps in the service network. A keystone of the CSS approach was the case manager, whose coordination efforts were empowered by the formal set of contracts that were negotiated by the core agency and that bound providers to deliver the specified services to the case manager's clients. During the same period, Congress (P.L. 94-103 and P.L. 95-602) mandated that service integration mechanisms featuring case managers be provided to deinstitutionalized developmentally disabled persons, and the Joint Commission on Accreditation of Hospitals (1979) established the requirement that community mental health services provide case management. By 1984, Johnson (1984) reported that 36 states required case management in their mental health services and that an additional 12 states recommended it.

Core Functions

Although the term "case management" grew in response to recent forces, it is not a new concept. It has antecedents in the knowledge bases of vocational rehabilitation, public health nursing, and social work (Platman et al., 1982; Miller, 1983). In social work the parallels are strongest in theories of generalist social work practice, which emphasize boundary spanning by developing resource systems, linking people to resource systems and making those systems more accessible and responsive to people's needs, and enhancing the coordination of resource systems (Minahan, 1976). Some authors from other disciplines consider case management "a well-established social work technique" (Schwartz, Goldman, & Churgin, 1982, p. 1006). Miller (1983) considers case management "part of the history of the profession of social work" (p. 6).

The range of case management functions varies depending on such contextual factors as the characteristics of the target population, environmental constraints, the type of agency employing the case manager, caseload size, and the nature of the service delivery system (Intagliata, 1982; Intagliata & Baker, 1983). For example, the extent to which case managers become engaged in linking clients to existing services as opposed to creating the needed services may depend on the range of services already available. This variation notwithstanding, four basic functions—assessment, planning, linking, and monitoring—appear in almost every description of case management and are deemed essential regardless of context.

Assessment. Case managers are expected to remain aware of their clients' comprehensive needs as well as their current and potential strengths and weaknesses. They are expected to be familiar with, although not necessarily directly involved in, the initial intake and assessment. They are expected to stay in close regular contact with direct service staff to ensure that their information is comprehensive and up to date. They are also expected to remain in regular contact with their clients so as to observe changes in client capabilities and needs. This includes a recurring evaluation of the amount of support currently and potentially available to the client, such as through natural helping networks and informal support systems. The case manager has been called "the only provider in the system whose responsibility is being aware of the 'whole' client" (Intagliata, 1982, p. 660).

Planning. Case managers may be expected to develop an overall case plan for each client. It should include provision for services the client might need day or night. It should focus on the progression of services to be provided over time and on the linkages among them and between them and the informal support system. In case management, planning is done early. In deinstitutionalization, for example, the case manager does not wait until the client has left the institution and entered the community-based agency to begin assessment and planning. Instead, an awareness of the community resources for a given client is part of the discharge planning process, and the case manager is the one practitioner who assumes responsibility for ensuring that the plan is implemented in a timely fashion and as intended. The assumption of this responsibility has been deemed the core, overarching principle of case management (Intagliata, 1982; Miller, 1983). To enhance their contribution to case planning, case managers maintain a complete roster of service agencies and organizations in the community, know what services each provides and its policies and procedures, supply information to case planners on available resources, and interpret the purpose and function of the case plan to service providers (Gerhard & Dorgan, 1983).

Linking. Case managers are expected to link clients to the services and entitlements that are available to meet their needs. This includes referring or transferring clients to all required services and informal support networks. It also includes helping clients overcome barriers to utilizing the required services or receiving entitlements. Such barriers may include eligibility requirements or restrictive regulations and policies. Some generic agencies, for example, may be reluctant to serve clients with particular disabilities, such as the mentally ill or developmentally disabled. More subtle barriers might include practitioners who informally resist serving the chronically and profoundly disabled, perhaps by delays in followthrough or by a lack of enthusiasm or persistence in working with these less articulate clients who do not respond well to conventional therapies. To overcome these barriers, case managers sometimes have to function as case advocates for their clients, particularly those clients whose profound impairments make them unable to speak for themselves. (Advocacy is often listed as an additional, separate function of case management.)

Case managers therefore establish and maintain contact with service providers and maintain formal and informal relationships with administrative personnel who can facilitate referrals (Gerhard & Dorgan, 1983). However, this does not mean that the case manager always must bear the brunt of advocating directly with external agencies. In more difficult situations (for example, those not responsive to informal interpersonal negotiation), case managers might enlist the support of supervisors or administrators in their own agency or seek the help of legal aid services or of agencies set up to provide advocacy services for specified target populations, such as the National Association for Retarded Citizens. Although the type of advocacy most often undertaken is case advocacy—interceding on behalf of an individual client—this function can also lead to class advocacy in response to documented service deficiencies detected through the accumulation of case advocacy efforts involving numerous clients.

Not all barriers to linkage come from service providers. Sometimes clients resist being served or drop out of service. Some are unable to utilize services unless appropriate supports are provided (Test, 1979). For example, some profoundly impaired clients recently discharged from institutions may need transportation assistance to keep appointments or may forget to take their prescribed medications. To be effective, linkers need to remain aware of these contingencies and ensure that the appropriate emotional or tangible supports are provided to help clients do their part toward implementing the case plan. Nevertheless, the case manager respects a client's right to refuse treatment.

Monitoring. Case managers are expected to monitor continuously the services provided to their clients. This requires ongoing contact with clients and service providers to ensure that appointments are kept and that appropriate and effective services are provided with minimum delay. This contact is often face to face and includes visits with the client while the service is being provided. Firsthand contact is thought to enhance the quality of the feedback and to improve the case manager's relationship with service providers and clients and therefore his or her ability to influence them. Implicit in the monitoring function is an evaluation function in which the case manager systematically rates and records progress toward attaining the objectives each component of the service plan is designed to attain. Information gained from monitoring can lead to reassessment and the development of new plans or linkages.

Other Common Functions. As the link between the client and the service system— the persons ultimately responsible for seeing that the client's needs are met—case managers are often not able to pass the buck. They often function as troubleshooters and are expected to be ready to perform whatever role it takes to ensure that their clients receive appropriate, coordinated, and continuous care despite the inadequacies of the service system (Miller, 1983). As noted earlier, case managers at times deliver a service, secure advocacy services, or become directly involved in creating needed services. This might involve developing natural support systems.

Outreach is another common role. Case managers are often expected to identify eligible clients, and they may have to invest time in finding clients and encouraging them to utilize services. Such outreach often must be persistent and aggressive and include home visits. Case managers cannot remain office-bound or deem their clients "unmotivated" and therefore neglect them when they fail to keep appointments or are hard to locate. This relates to a most critical and controversial issue—the degree to which case managers themselves provide direct services to clients.

To some extent, the direct service function of case management may be inescapable. For example, the case manager may provide the one stable relationship the client can rely on—a relationship that endures and provides continuity as the client moves back and forth across institutional, community, and agency boundaries. This relationship can be rewarding and reassuring to individuals devalued by society, and perhaps by other human service practitioners. It also can give them a sense of stability and hope and enhance the case manager's capacity to motivate clients to utilize services or comply with case plans, for example, by taking their medications.

When other direct service staff are unavailable, the case manager may be responsible for performing some of their functions. This might include training clients in basic living skills, such as those required for personal hygiene, using public transportation, or household management. For example, the case manager might also help clients shop for groceries or might transport them to a needed service if no other arrangements can be made. Case managers may have to provide crisis intervention when unexpected changes in the environment overwhelm clients, particularly those, such as formerly institutionalized psychiatric patients, whose ability to cope is impaired and whose social adjustment is tenuous. Case managers are not necessarily expected to function as therapists or to aid clients directly in resolving crises, but they do need to provide personal support and be on hand to refer and perhaps accompany the client to a crisis intervention service provider. In this connection, case management services are expected to be available around the clock; in some sites case managers are on call 24 hours a day (Intagliata & Baker, 1983, p. 83).

Role Issues and Authority

Case management was conceived as a boundary-spanning function. It was intended primarily to coordinate and monitor the efforts of multiple service providers, not to create another group of specialized direct care staff. Yet case managers are expected to be prepared to depart from their boundary-spanning role to fulfill their ultimate responsibility for ensuring that clients' needs are met in the face of incomplete service delivery systems.

Some find it difficult to envision how case managers can properly and effectively implement their assessment, planning, and linking functions without performing direct care tasks and utilizing specialized direct service knowledge and skills (Lourie, 1978; Lamb, 1980; Intagliata, 1982; Miller, 1983). For example, case managers working with the chronically mentally disabled may need to recognize early signs of decompensation or unmanageable stress and to understand the

likely psychological effects of various enviromental circumstances. They may have to use their relationship with the client to motivate and secure client compliance with the discharge plan. In view of this, Lamb (1980) argues that it is difficult for the case manager to possess the requisite psychological knowledge of the client outside the context of the therapeutic relationship. Lamb therefore believes that the clients' therapists should be their case managers, although he adds the qualification that the type of therapy he envisions is supportive and ecologically oriented, not in-depth psychotherapy.

In view of the breadth of the case management role, Lamb further argues that good case management and good direct service provision are inseparable. If case management functions are part of the normal duties of a conscientious caseworker and if extensive direct service skills and involvement are necessary for a case manager to assess needs adequately and ensure that they are met, then why add another layer (the case manager) to the already complex system of services and communication? Instead, why not simply deal directly with direct service providers who fail to perform case management functions?

Others point out that the foregoing conceptions overlook the authority of case management. The case manager has the ultimate authority for the case. In theory, this authority separates real case management from the referral, linkage, and coordination functions of direct service providers who are part of a professional treatment team. In this view case managers are distinguished by their *empowerment* to negotiate on behalf of consumers (R. E. Dorgan, personal communication, April 19, 1983).

However, the degree of empowerment of case managers has not always been as much as was envisioned in the original community services system concept. The authority case managers have varies widely in different localities and service delivery systems. Ross (1980) and Caragonne (1981) have identified different models of case management, ranging from situations in which case managers or their agencies have minimal authority over provider programs to those in which the authority is more comprehensive.

Some believe that the extent of the case manager's authority is the most critical factor influencing the effectiveness of case management. Various ways have been proposed to enhance the case manager's authority with service providers (Schwartz et al., 1982). One way is to increase the formality and clarity of policies, procedures, and agreements that provide case management authority in and between agencies. Another is through fiscal control, by giving case managers discretion over the funds needed to purchase specific services for individual clients. A third way recognizes the importance of informal authority and informal working relationships and focuses on the case manager's credibility with administrators and clinical service providers. Will they accept the case manager as a peer and perhaps as an ally? Or will they reject the case manager as an intruder, perhaps one who is clinically unsophisticated or otherwise not qualified? One suggestion for enhancing the informal clout of case managers has been to provide them with adequate agency resources, such as office space and secretarial support, so as to signify the importance the agency attaches to their work. Another suggestion calls for locating case managers in clinical service units. Most attention concerning the informal authority of case managers, however, has been focused on their professional status.

Status and Training

Just as programs vary in the scope they assign to the case management role and the amount of autonomy and authority they give case managers, there is variation in the level of education reported for case managers. It ranges from a high school diploma to a doctoral degree and may depend on what a given program expects the case manager to do (Intagliata, 1982). Prior experience may influence education requirements. One system, for example, employs as case managers for the chronically mentally ill either individuals with bachelor's degrees plus extensive experience in working with psychiatric patients in state institutions, or individuals with master's degrees in social work or counseling but without prior contact with these clients (Baker, Jodrey, & Morrell, 1979).

Most programs require case managers to have a bachelor's degree (Intagliata, 1982). However, concern has been expressed as to whether that is sufficient in view of the range of activities case managers may need to per-

form without supervision and the difficulties they may have in establishing credibility with administrators and other professionals, who may denigrate them as "paraprofessionals" (Schwartz et al., 1982; Intagliata, 1982; Johnson & Rubin, 1983; Bagarozzi & Kurtz, 1983). At the same time, doubt exists about the willingness and enthusiasm of more highly educated professionals, MSWs included, when faced with the less prestigious functions case managers frequently perform, such as transporting clients to an appointment or accompanying them on a shopping trip (Schwartz et al., 1982; Intagliata, 1982; Johnson & Rubin, 1983). There is also concern that highly qualified case managers may be prone to burnout more quickly than case managers without advanced degrees, who may not be as likely to perceive the less prestigious duties as beneath them (Intagliata, 1982).

Doubt has been expressed as to whether any level of formal education can adequately prepare a person to perform competently the full range of case management roles. Some wonder whether it is realistic to expect any worker, regardless of prior education and training, to be able and willing to blend diagnostic and therapeutic understanding and skills, political savvy in overcoming bureaucratic rigidity, the ability to develop formal resource systems and informal helping networks, rehabilitation skills, and patience in helping clients achieve minute and simple changes in their basic living skills (Johnson & Rubin, 1983).

In view of the scope of the case management role and the potential for role ambiguity and conflict, orientation and in-service training are deemed essential for case managers, regardless of their professional level (Intagliata, 1982; Bagarozzi & Kurtz, 1983). Orientation sessions could focus on the full range of functions and responsibilities the case management role entails, the rationale for the role, and the values that guide it. Case managers would be helped to understand that their clients often have disabilities that severely limit their ability to progress and that the goal of case management for these clients is to improve the quality of care they receive and enhance the quality of their lives, not to attain any dramatic improvement in their level of functioning. Lamb (1979b) has warned that without a realistic conception of what they can accomplish with their clients, case managers will experience frustration and burnout as a result of their overreaching expectations.

The components of in-service training vary, depending on prior education and experience. They might include information on assessing and understanding client disabilities, common psychotropic medications and their side effects, the range of local services and client entitlements available, legal rights of clients, and record keeping. They might also include skill development in relating to clients, goal setting, problem solving, crisis intervention, and advocacy.

Attention has been given not just to the level of education and training recommended for case managers, but also to the preferred academic disciplines. Conclusive empirical data are lacking as to which disciplines offer the best preparation for case management. Most case managers have been educated in a human services discipline, but there is no clear consensus that any one human services discipline offers the best preparation. The fields most commonly cited as likely to offer good preparation are social work, public health nursing, vocational rehabilitation, and human services generalist practice. Which, if any, level or type of preparation best prepares individuals to perform case management roles skillfully, enthusiastically, and effectively remains a key question for future research. Conceivably, such research might find that the answer varies, depending on the range of functions, expectations, level of autonomy, and organizational supports the case manager has in a given setting.

Caseload and Supervision

The literature identifies a number of additional factors that may influence how case management services are delivered. One factor is caseload size. Research reviewed by Intagliata (1982) found that a large increase in caseload size may impair the quality and effectiveness of case management services by reducing the case managers' contact with clients and predisposing them to respond to crises rather than anticipate problems and help clients plan ahead. It also might predispose them to do things for clients instead of helping clients become more independent.

Likewise, heavy caseloads often diminish the opportunity to build close relationships with clients and increase the propensity to wait for clients to take the initiative to make contact instead of reaching out to them. Estimates of the ideal caseload size vary, depending on client attributes, their geographic proximity to one another, and the case manager's competencies. Suggested estimates for an individual case manager working with chronic psychiatric clients have ranged from a low of 15 to a high of 30. The typical caseload size for these clients appears to range from 25 to 35 (Intagliata & Baker, 1983).

Some have recommended that comprehensive case management responsibilities might be better assigned to a case management team instead of individual case managers (Kirk & Therien, 1975; Test, 1979; Turner & TenHoor, 1978; Intagliata, 1982). The members of the team may all be case managers, or the team might comprise a single case manager along with other professionals, such as a psychiatrist, nurse, psychologist, or social worker. It is argued that a team would increase staff availability to provide continuous coverage, add viewpoints for managing difficult problems, and avoid the isolation that can lead to burnout of the individual case manager.

Another factor affecting case management services is how case managers are supervised. Concern about supervision stems in part from the potential for role ambiguity and role conflict and the consequent need to monitor the activities of case managers, which might depart from what is expected of them. Caragonne (1981), for example, found that many supervisors were not aware that the pattern of activities of the case managers they supervised differed markedly from their prescribed roles. Supervision is also cited as an important source of recognition and support, encouraging case managers to experience a sense of value in their work. Such a sense of value is often difficult for case managers to derive given the limited potential for improvement in the social functioning of many of their clients and the relatively low value that others sometimes attach to the case manager's work. In view of this, adequate supervisory support is deemed essential in sustaining the motivation of case managers and preventing burnout (Caragonne, 1981; Intagliata, 1982; Intagliata & Baker, 1983).

Research and Critical Analyses

Evidence is accumulating on the potential efficacy of case management programs. In a rigorous and often cited experiment, Stein and Test (1980) evaluated a community-based service program that incorporated case management principles as part of a comprehensive approach to respond to the needs of the chronically mentally disabled. The program effectively maintained clients in the community without worse consequences than occur in institutionalization; the consequences measured were client symptomatology, self-esteem, social functioning, quality of life and life satisfaction, burden to family or community, and program cost. King, Muraco, and Wells (1984) reported a quasi-experimental study that also had results favoring the effectiveness of case management services. In addition, three experimental evaluations found case management effective in reducing the costs of caring for those who are aged, physically ill, or disabled (Boone, Coulton, & Keller, 1981; Akabas, Fine, & Yasser, 1982; Davies, Ferlie, & Challis, 1984). Not every study of the impact of case management has had positive results, however. Coulton and Frost (1982), for example, found that the receipt of case management services had no effect on the extent to which the elderly utilized mental health services. Ozarin (1978) and Miller (1983) reviewed the evaluative research on the effectiveness of case management programs.

Caution must be exercised in interpreting the meaning of evaluations of case management programs and generalizing from them. Case management programs evaluated experimentally are often implemented under ideal conditions, perhaps as part of a much broader system of service provision geared exclusively to the unique needs of disabled clients and not compromised by such factors as insufficient support, insufficient empowerment of case managers, or critical gaps in service availability. A stiffer test of the case management concept is not how well it works when accompanied by a comprehensive package of direct service provisions targeted

to the needs of the disabled, but how well it works when it stands alone as a boundary-spanning strategy for dealing with an inadequate service delivery system that contains programs unresponsive to the needs of the target population. Given the limitations in the public funding of social welfare programs, a critical issue is whether the impact of case management on a weak service delivery system is sufficient to justify redirecting scarce funds to it from existing direct care provisions (Morris & Lescohier, 1978). In other words, is there a net improvement in client care by transferring resources from other services into a boundary-spanning function?

In this connection, it is important to realize that not everyone who is called a case manager performs most of the core case management functions. Conversely, not everyone who performs some case management functions is called a case manager. Some programs hire "case managers" merely to assist the primary clinician with routinized, mundane activities or to provide concrete services or linkage without any authority (Intagliata & Baker, 1983). Other programs assume that each client's primary clinician also serves as case manager and therefore call every clinician a case manager and assume that every client has a case manager (Kurtz, Bagarozzi, & Pollane, 1984).

This confusion has prompted some to liken the term "case management" to a Rorschach test on which is projected any image one wishes (Schwartz et al., 1982), or to "question whether case management is simply a new term for social work" (Bagarozzi & Kurtz, 1983, p. 13). Lourie (1978) argues that all human service agencies dealing with individual or family social, physical, or mental disability subscribe to and claim to practice case management. Lamb (1980) claims that good therapy must include case management. In theory at least, generalist social work practitioners, no matter whether they are called case managers or something else, are supposed to be prepared to perform assessment, planning, linkage, brokerage, and advocacy functions in a boundary-spanning context. Bachrach (1983) argues that merely designating staff members as case managers is no guarantee that case management aims will be achieved:

If a system of care is truly responsive to the needs of chronic mental patients, it is prima facie evidence that de facto case management exists, whether or not there are people called case managers. (p. 100)

That serious deficiencies in society's care of its profoundly disabled and unwanted citizens can be overcome through service integration strategies, without a much greater expenditure of public resources, can be a seductive notion to those who resist such expenditures or feel that they will not be forthcoming. It dates back over a hundred years to an era when the Charity Organization Society was viewed as a remedy for deficiencies in the voluntary welfare system. Morris and Lescohier (1978) equate the current popularity of case management with this notion. They cite fiscal incentives as more powerful than the efforts of case managers in motivating agencies to modify their services. They note that greater agency responsivity to the clients of case managers requires taking resources away from other demands on these agencies that they may feel better equipped to meet. Rather than use scarce funds to add case managers to the service delivery system, they argue, would not a greater impact be achieved by reserving these funds as incentives to modify agency practices or to create new services?

Process research on case management programs has shown that "case managers' actual activities are shaped ultimately by the constraints of the environments within which they work, not by their formal job descriptions" (Intagliata, 1982, p. 670). This research has also found that even when case managers strive to implement their role as intended, they may lack the authority needed to accomplish their objectives. Based on his review of this research, Intagliata (1982) recommended more research to evaluate and improve the implementation of case management programs. Additional experimental studies also are needed on the outcomes of alternative case management models in different kinds of service delivery systems. The results of such research may help determine whether case management remains a viable strategy or succumbs to the criticisms that it cannot be implemented properly and that its costs might be better spent in directly filling

gaps in existing services rather than through a boundary-spanning mechanism.

ALLEN RUBIN

For further information, see ASSESSMENT IN DIRECT PRACTICE; DIRECT PRACTICE EFFECTIVENESS; GENERALIST PERSPECTIVE; LINKAGE IN DIRECT PRACTICE.

References

Akabas, S. H., Fine, M., & Yasser, R. (1982). "Putting Secondary Prevention to the Test: A Study of an Early Intervention Strategy With Disabled Workers." *Journal of Primary Prevention, 2*(2), 165–187.

Arnhof, F. M. (1975). "Social Consequences of Policy Towards Mental Illness." *Science, 188*(6), 1277–1281.

Bachrach, L. L. (1980). "Is the Least Restrictive Environment Always the Best? Sociological and Semantic Implications." *Hospital and Community Psychiatry, 31*(2), 97–103.

Bachrach, L. L. (1981). "Continuity of Care for Chronic Mental Patients: A Conceptual Analysis." *American Journal of Psychiatry, 138*(11), 1449–1456.

Bachrach, L. L. (1983). "New Directions in Deinstitutionalization Planning." In L. L. Bachrach (Ed.), *New Directions in Mental Health Services: Deinstitutionalization* (pp. 93–106). San Francisco: Jossey-Bass.

Bagarozzi, D. A., & Kurtz, L. F. (1983). "Administrators' Perspectives on Case Management." *Aretê, 8*(1), 13–21.

Baker, F., Jodrey, D., & Morell, M. (1979). *Evaluation of Case Management Training Program: Final Report.* New York: New York School of Psychiatry.

Beatrice, D. F. (1979). *Case Management: A Policy Option for Long-Term Care.* Washington, D.C.: Health Care Financing Administration, Department of Health, Education & Welfare.

Bedford, L., & Hybertson, L. D. (1975). "Emotionally Disturbed Children: A Program of Alternatives to Residential Treatment." *Child Welfare, 54*(2), 109–115.

Boone, C. R., Coulton, C. J., & Keller, S. M. (1981). "The Impact of Early and Comprehensive Social Work Services on Length of Stay." *Social Work in Health Care, 7*(3), 65–73.

Caragonne, P. (1980). *An Analysis of the Function of the Case Manager in Four Mental Health Social Services Settings.* Austin: University of Texas School of Social Work.

Caragonne, P. (1981). *A Comparative Analysis of Twenty-Two Settings Using Case Manage-*

ment Components. Austin: University of Texas School of Social Work.

Coulton, C., & Frost, A. K. (1982). "Use of Social and Health Services by the Elderly." *Journal of Health and Social Behavior, 23*(12), 330–339.

Davies, B. P., Ferlie, E., & Challis, D. (1984). *A Guide to Efficiency—Improving Innovations in the Social Care of the Frail Elderly.* Canterbury, England: Personal Social Services Research Unit, University of Kent.

Fitz, J. (1978). *Case Management for the Developmentally Disabled: A Feasibility Study Report.* Raleigh: North Carolina University Center for Urban Affairs and Community Services.

General Accounting Office. (1977). *Returning the Mentally Disabled to the Community: Government Needs to Do More* (HRD-76-152). Washington, D.C.: Author.

Gerhard, R. J., & Dorgan, R. E. (1983). "The Case Manager: A Vehicle for Consumer Continuity." Unpublished manuscript.

Hogarty, G. (1971). "The Plight of Schizophrenics in Modern Treatment Programs." *Hospital and Community Psychiatry, 22*(7), 197–203.

Intagliata, J. (1982). "Improving the Quality of Community Care for the Chronically Mentally Disabled: The Role of Case Management." *Schizophrenia Bulletin, 8*(4), 655–674.

Intagliata, J., & Baker, F. (1983). "Factors Affecting Case Management Services for the Chronically Mentally Ill." *Administration in Mental Health, 11*(2), 75–91.

Joint Commission on Accreditation of Hospitals. (1979). *Principles for Accreditation of Community Mental Health Service Programs.* Chicago: Author.

Johnson, P. J. (1984). "A Survey of State-Level Emphasis on Case Management." Manuscript under review for publication, University of North Carolina School of Social Work, Chapel Hill.

Johnson, P. J., & Rubin, A. (1983). "Case Management in Mental Health: A Social Work Domain?" *Social Work, 28*(1), 49–55.

King, J. A., Muraco, W. A., & Wells, J. P. (1984). *Case Management: A Study of Patient Outcomes.* Columbus: Ohio Department of Mental Health, Office of Program Evaluation and Research.

Kirk, S. A., & Therrien, M. E. (1975). "Community Mental Health Myths and the Fate of Former Hospitalized Patients." *Psychiatry, 38*(3), 209–217.

Kurtz, L. F., Bagarozzi, D. A., & Pollane, L. P. (1984). "Case Management in Mental Health." *Health & Social Work, 9*(3), 201–211.

Lamb, H. R. (1976). "Guiding Principles for Community Survival." In H. R. Lamb (Ed.), *Com-*

munity Survival for Long-Term Patients (pp. 1–13). San Francisco: Jossey-Bass.

Lamb, H. R. (1979a). "The New Asylums in the Community." *Archives of General Psychiatry, 36*(2), 129–134.

Lamb, H. R. (1979b). "Staff Burnout in Work With Long-Term Patients." *Hospital and Community Psychiatry, 30*(6), 396–398.

Lamb, H. R. (1980). "Therapist–Case Managers: More Than Brokers of Services." *Hospital and Community Psychiatry, 31*(11), 762–764.

Lourie, N. V. (1978). "Case Management." In J. A. Talbott (Ed.), *The Chronic Mental Patient* (pp. 159–164). Washington, D.C.: American Psychiatric Association.

Mechanic, D. (1980). *Mental Health and Social Policy.* Englewood Cliffs, N.J.: Prentice-Hall.

Miller, G. (1983). "Case Management: The Essential Services." In C. J. Sanborn (Ed.), *Case Management in Mental Health Service* (pp. 3–16). New York: Haworth Press.

Minahan, A. (1976). "Generalists and Specialists in Social Work—Implications for Education and Practice." *Areté, 4*(2), 62.

Mittenthal, S. (1976). "Evaluation Overview: A System Approach to Services Integration." *Evaluation, 3*(1,2), 142–148.

Morrill, W. (1976). "Services Integration and the Department of Health, Education and Welfare." *Evaluation, 3*(1,2), 52–55.

Morris, R., & Lescohier, I. H. (1978). "Service Integration: Real Versus Illusory Solutions to Welfare Dilemmas." In R. C. Farri & Y. Hasenfeld (Eds.), *The Management of Human Services* (pp. 21–50). New York: Columbia University Press.

Ozarin, L. (1978). "The Pros and Cons of Case Management." In J. A. Talbott (Ed.), *The Chronic Mental Patient* (pp. 165–170). Washington, D.C.: American Psychiatric Association.

Platman, S. R., et al. (1982). "Case Management of the Mentally Disabled." *Journal of Public Health Policy, 3*(3), 302–314.

Ross, H. (1980). *Proceedings of the Conference on the Evaluation of Case Management Programs, March 5–6, 1979.* Los Angeles: Volunteers for Services to Older Persons.

Rubin, A., & Johnson, P. J. (1982). "Practitioner Orientations Toward Serving the Chronically Disabled: Prospects for Policy Implementation." *Administration in Mental Health, 10*(3), 2–12.

Schwartz, S. R., Goldman, H. H., & Churgin, S. (1982). "Case Management for the Chronic Mentally Ill: Models and Dimensions." *Hospital and Community Psychiatry, 33*(12), 1006–1009.

Stein, L. I., & Test, M. A. (1980). "Alternative to Mental Hospital Treatment." *Archives of General Psychiatry, 37*(4), 392–397.

Steinberg, R. M., & Carter, G. W. (1983). *Case Management and the Elderly.* Lexington, Mass.: Lexington Books.

Talbott, J. A. (Ed.). (1978). *The Chronic Mental Patient.* Washington, D.C.: American Psychiatric Association.

Test, M. (1979). "Continuity of Care in Community Treatment." In L. Stein (Ed.), *Community Support Systems for the Long-Term Patient* (pp. 15–23). San Francisco: Jossey-Bass.

Turner, J. C. (1977). "Comprehensive Community Support Systems for Severely Disabled Adults." *Psychosocial Rehabilitation Journal, 1*(1), 39–47.

Turner, J., & Shiffren, I. (1979). "Community Support System: How Comprehensive?" In L. Stein (Ed.), *Community Support Systems for the Long-Term Patient* (pp. 1–13). San Francisco: Jossey-Bass.

Turner, J. C., & TenHoor, W. J. (1978). "The NIMH Community Support Program: Pilot Approach to a Needed Social Reform." *Schizophrenia Bulletin, 4*(3), 319–349.

CASEWORK APPROACHES AND PERSPECTIVES.

See Behavioral Approach; Cognitive Therapy; Crisis Intervention; Direct Practice: Trends and Issues; Direct Practice Effectiveness; Direct Practice in Social Work: Overview; Ecological Perspective; Ethnic-Sensitive Practice; Existential Approach; Feminist Social Work; Generalist Perspective; Gestalt Therapy; Psychosocial Approach; Radical Social Work; Task-Centered Approach; Transactional Analysis.

CASEWORK METHODS.

See Advocacy; Assessment in Direct Practice; Case Management; Consultation; Contracting and Engagement in Direct Practice; Direct Practice: Trends and Issues; Direct Practice Effectiveness; Direct Practice in Social Work: Overview; Interviewing; Legislative Advocacy; Linkage in Direct Practice; Recording in Direct Practice; Resource Development and Service Provision;

Resource Mobilization and Coordination; Social Skills Training; Social Work Practice with Groups; Staff-Initiated Organizational Change; Termination in Direct Practice.

CASH PAYMENTS.

See Aged: Services; Aid to Families with Dependent Children; Child Support; Federal Social Legislation Since 1961; General and Emergency Assistance; Hunger and Malnutrition; Income Distribution; Income Maintenance System; Poverty; Quality Control in Income Maintenance; Social Security; Social Welfare Financing; Social Welfare Policy: Trends and Issues; Unemployment Compensation and Workers' Compensation Programs.

CATHOLIC SOCIAL SERVICES.

See Sectarian Agencies.

CERTIFICATION AND LICENSING.

See Licensing and Regulation of Social Work Services; Professional Associations: National Association of Social Workers; Profession of Social Work: Contemporary Characteristics; Quality Assurance.

CETA (COMPREHENSIVE EMPLOYMENT AND TRAINING ACT).

See Federal Social legislation Since 1961; Social Welfare Financing; Unemployment and Underemployment; Work Experience Programs; Workfare.

CHICANOS.

See Civil Rights; Ethnic-Sensitive Practice; Intergroup Relations; Mexican Americans; Minorities of Color.

CHILD ABUSE AND NEGLECT

The dramatic rise during the past 25 years in public and professional concern with child maltreatment suggests that this problem has only recently been discovered. On the contrary, the maltreatment of children has been known throughout recorded history (for historical accounts, see Giovannoni & Becerra, 1979; Radbill, 1980; Williams, 1980). In 1874, the well-publicized case of an abused child named Mary Ellen led to the founding of the Society for Prevention of Cruelty to Children (SPCC). For over half a century thereafter, responsibility for protecting children from maltreatment was the purview of private social agencies such as the SPCC. With the passage of the Social Security Act in 1935, child protection became a mandate of public social service agencies.

The present surge of attention to child maltreatment stems from the rediscovery of child abuse by the medical profession. The development of radiology as a diagnostic tool led to the recognition that seemingly unexplained injuries in children, such as fractures or subdural hematomas, were the result of inflicted trauma (Caffey, 1946; Silverman, 1953, 1980; Woolley & Evans, 1955). In 1962, Kempe and his colleagues coined the term "battered child syndrome" to describe this phenomenon (Kempe, Silverman, Steele, Droegemueller, & Silver, 1962). Their landmark report precipitated the interest and involvement of a variety of professional disciplines and led to increases in the allocation of resources, both financial and manpower, to deal with the problem. By the late 1960s, legislation mandating the reporting of suspected child maltreatment had been enacted in every state. In 1974, the Child Abuse Prevention and Treatment Act was signed into law (Public Law 93-247), establishing the National Center on Child Abuse and Neglect to coordinate the federal response to this complex social problem. Although the reporting statutes extended mandatory reporting and hence responsibility for protecting children to a wide range of professional domains (medicine, psychology, psychiatry, education, law enforcement, and social work), the field of social work has remained a dominant force in the organization and delivery of protective services to maltreated children and their families.

Definitions

Definitions of child maltreatment are plagued by vagueness and imprecision. This is exemplified by the absence of any uniformity in the definitions used in state reporting statutes. Although the criteria for determining the existence of maltreatment have been refined and improved over time, a multiplicity of definitions with varying degrees of utility still abounds in the literature. Most definitions distinguish between abuse and neglect, and a distinction is commonly made between the physical and emotional forms of each of these types of maltreatment.

Some definitions focus on the outcomes of abuse and neglect in terms of the child's physical appearance or injuries; others are concerned with the intentions of the perpetrator. The distinction between abuse and neglect is often seen as the difference between acts of commission and acts of omission. Criteria for determining physical abuse are generally the most explicit because physical abuse is manifested in visible injuries to the child's body. Criteria for recognizing neglect are far less concrete than those for physical abuse, even though reports of maltreatment more often involve neglect than abuse. Criteria for ascertaining emotional abuse or neglect are so vague as to be virtually nonexistent. Hence, reports of emotional maltreatment are rarely made.

Given the ambiguity surrounding statutory definitions of abuse and neglect, the application of these definitions necessarily involves interpretations and judgments based on the values and attitudes of the decision maker. Thus, definitions used by professionals designated as mandated reporters often vary according to the discipline of the reporter, whether social work, medicine, psychiatry, psychology, sociology, law, or education. These professional groups recognize the lack of clarity in criteria for judging maltreatment (Giovannoni & Becerra, 1979; Nagi, 1977). Moreover, confusion about definitions is not limited to professionals, but extends to the general public.

Reports of abuse and neglect are generally directed to the child protection divisions of public social service agencies for investigation. Once reports have been substantiated, plans for intervention can be developed and implemented. Again, the determination of whether abuse or neglect has actually occurred reflects the judgment and values of the protective service worker who conducts the investigation. Thus, social work plays a primary role in the official labeling of a case as abuse or neglect, thereby determining whether the case gains entry into the protective service system.

The potential for bias in the labeling process has become an issue of increasing concern. Researchers commonly rely on officially designated cases of abuse and neglect from protective service agencies, hospitals, or courts as sources of samples for their studies. However, any systematic bias in the reporting of cases or the substantiating of reports results in study populations that are not necessarily representative of the true population of maltreatment cases. Because research findings regarding the incidence and etiology of maltreatment serve as bases for formulating prevention and intervention programs, research definitions are a vital component in assessments of the problem (Besharov, 1981; Gelles, 1980; Giovannoni & Becerra, 1979). Factors that appear to be causally associated with maltreatment may be confounded with factors related to the likelihood of being identified and labeled as maltreatment. Research evidence has identified social class and ethnicity as two elements of bias in the recognition and reporting of maltreatment (Hampton & Newberger, 1984; Herzberger & Tennen, 1984; McPherson & Garcia, 1983; O'Toole, Turbett, & Nalepka, 1983; Wolock, 1982).

The difficulties encountered in defining abuse and neglect affect the comparability and generalizability of research efforts. Differences in findings may result in part from disparities in definitions of maltreatment. Resolving the definitional problems requires continued efforts to refine guidelines for recognizing abuse and neglect and to train child abuse professionals in the application of these guidelines.

Incidence

Determining the incidence of child abuse and neglect is hampered by variations in statutory and research definitions of the problem (Sussman & Cohen, 1975, chap. 4). Estimates of the incidence of abuse and neglect are derived from widely varied sources ranging from projections based on surveys to tabulations of officially reported cases. However, available incidence figures represent at best an underestimate of the true incidence of maltreatment because not every case is reported and not every reported case is confirmed.

Gil's (1970) nationwide study represented a pioneering effort to document the scope and magnitude of the problem of physical abuse. Focusing on cases that met the study definition of physical abuse as intentional acts of commission or omission, Gil's data yielded an incidence of 5,993 cases for 1967 (8.4 per 100,000 children under 18 years of age in the total population) and 6,617 cases for 1968 (9.3 per 100,000 children under 18).

That reported cases underestimate the true incidence of abuse is illustrated by projected estimates reported by Gil (1970). Based on an earlier survey of public opinion and knowledge about physical abuse using a nationally representative sample, these estimates indicated that from 2.5 million to 4 million adults knew families who physically abused their children, for a rate of 13.3 to 21.4 incidents per 1,000 persons. Gil pointed out that these figures were likely to overestimate the incidence of abuse because of overlap in families known to more than one respondent. Based on revised calculations from Gil's survey data, Light (1973) estimated the annual incidence of physical abuse to be between 200,000 and 500,000 cases.

Using reported and confirmed cases of abuse from the ten largest states, Sussman and Cohen (1975) estimated the incidence of such cases nationwide to be 35,267 for 1972 and 38,779 for 1973. Straus, Gelles, and Steinmetz (1980) conducted a household survey of a nationally representative sample of two-parent families with children between 3 and 17 years old. Self-reports on the occurrence of parent-child violence yielded an estimate that 3.8 percent of all children 3 to 17 years old (between 1.5 and 2 million children) were abused by their parents in 1975.

Under the auspices of the National Center on Child Abuse and Neglect (NC-CAN) a study was carried out to determine the national incidence and severity of child abuse and neglect for a one-year period from May 1979 through April 1980 (National Center on Child Abuse and Neglect, 1981). Based on data from a sample of child protective service agencies and other community agencies, such as schools, hospitals, courts, and police, the projected estimate for the annual number of abused and neglected children nationwide was 652,000 (10.5 per 1,000 children under 18). Given the study findings that a substantial proportion (79 percent) of maltreated children known to nonprotective service agencies were not officially reported to protective service agencies, the investigators viewed their incidence estimate as conservative and the actual incidence as more likely to be at least one million. The incidence rates for abuse and neglect were similar: 5.7 per 1,000 children for abuse (including physical assault, sexual abuse, and emotional abuse) and 5.3 per 1,000 children for neglect (including physical, educational, and emotional neglect). Restricting the type of maltreatment to physical assault and physical neglect showed that the rate for abuse (3.4) was twice that for neglect (1.7).

The most comprehensive data base on the incidence of reported cases of maltreatment, particularly with respect to ascertaining trends over time, is the American Humane Association's analysis of yearly nationwide official child abuse and neglect reports. Data for the seven-year period from 1976 to 1982 were compiled and analyzed for trends in the incidence of maltreatment (Russell & Trainor, 1984). Although there was a dramatic increase (123 percent) in the number of reports of all forms of maltreatment from 416,000 in 1976 (10.1 per 1,000 children) to 929,000 in 1982 (20.1 per 1,000 children), the rate of increase declined each year. However, this increase in reported cases does not necessarily signify an increase in the actual incidence of maltreatment, but rather indicates that increased attention to the problem has uncovered more cases through reporting. The proportions of reported cases involving physical abuse or neglect have remained relatively constant over time. Composite figures for the seven-year period showed 25 percent of reported cases involved physical abuse (ranging from 19.4 percent to 27.6 percent) and 64 percent involved neglect (ranging from 59.4 percent to 70.6 percent). Categories of sexual, emotional, and other maltreatment were excluded from these figures.

These figures stand in contrast to those from the National Incidence Study (National Center on Child Abuse and Neglect, 1981), which showed that the rates of incidence for abuse and neglect were approximately equal when each was broadly defined and that abuse cases outnumbered neglect cases when only physical abuse or physical neglect was considered. These differences in findings are likely to result in part from differences in the definitions of abuse and neglect and in part from the inclusion of unreported cases in the data of the National Incidence Study.

Patterns of Maltreatment Cases

Source of Reports. Analysis of official reports of abuse and neglect demonstrated a consistent pattern over time regarding the source of reports for all forms of maltreatment: 47 percent were from professionals and 54 percent from nonprofessionals (Russell & Trainor, 1984). Reports from professionals were about equally distributed across type of profession (medicine, education, social services, and law enforcement). The National Incidence Study found that schools were the source of more than half the cases (56 percent) reported to the study from all sources, although schools reported only 13 percent of their recognized cases to protective service agencies. For both physical abuse and physical neglect, schools were the source of the largest proportion of study cases (46 percent in each category). Hospitals were more likely than any other agency to report recognized cases to protective service agencies, but the proportion they reported (56 percent) was only slightly more than half their cases.

Age of Child. The average age of children in reported cases of all forms of maltreatment over the seven-year period of official reports was 7.4 years, two years younger than the average age of all children in the 1980 census of the United States (Russell & Trainor, 1984). This average age declined slightly over time. The proportion of reported cases experiencing neglect declined with age, although neglect still accounted for the majority of reported cases in each age category. Physical abuse was reported for between 15 and 20 percent of each age group, but the highest proportion was for the oldest group (12 to 17 years).

The National Incidence Study indicated that the incidence rate for maltreatment increased with age, with the highest for adolescents 15 to 17 years (14.2 per 1,000) and the lowest for preschool children from birth to 5 years (6.3 per 1,000). Compared to the general population of children, preschool children were underrepresented among maltreated children (17 percent compared to 29 percent), children age 6 to 11 years were about equally represented among maltreated cases (36 percent compared to 33 percent), and adolescents 12 to 17 years were slightly overrepresented among maltreated cases (47 percent compared to 38 percent). Figures on physical abuse alone showed that the proportion of physical abuse was highest in the adolescent age groups (19 percent of the 12 to 14 year olds and 20 percent of the 15 to 17 year olds). In contrast, physical neglect was highest in the youngest age group (23 percent of the 0 to 2 years olds).

Gender of Child. A consistent pattern of virtually equal representation of males and females was found in the analyses of officially reported cases over time and in the National Incidence Study. The National Incidence Study showed a relationship between gender and age. For males, the incidence of physical abuse peaked in the 3 to 5 age group and declined thereafter; for females, physical abuse generally increased with age. For both males and females, the incidence of physical neglect was highest in the 0 to 2 age group and declined to a relatively constant level thereafter.

Ethnicity. Analyses of official reports over time showed that whites consistently constituted about two-thirds of the total reported cases for all forms of maltreatment and that blacks accounted for about one fifth. However, compared to the general population, whites were underrepresented and blacks overrepresented. Data from the National Incidence Study indicated a nearly identical incidence rate for blacks (11.5 per 1,000) and whites (10.5 per 1,000) for all forms of maltreatment. This difference suggests that blacks are more likely to be reported for maltreatment than whites. Among cases of physical abuse and physical neglect, whites outnumbered blacks by approximately 6 to 1.

Socioeconomic Status. Among officially reported cases, an association between maltreatment and socioeconomic status was shown by the gradual increase over time in the proportion of cases with female heads of household (average of 40.8 percent compared to 17.0 percent in the general population) and by the consistently high proportion of cases receiving public assistance (average of 45.0 percent compared to 11.9 percent in the general population). Similarly, the incidence rate for all forms of maltreatment in the National Incidence Study was highest for cases with annual incomes less than $7,000 (27.3 per 1,000). In comparison, the incidence rate for cases with incomes of $25,000 or more was 2.7. Among cases of physical abuse, 35 percent had incomes under $7,000 and 79 percent under $15,000. More than half the cases of physical neglect (57 percent) had incomes under $7,000; 91 percent had incomes under $15,000.

Relationship of Perpetrator to Child. Analyses of reported cases over time showed that the vast majority of perpetrators were not only parents (94.2 percent) but also natural parents (85.0 percent). Overall, perpetrators were more likely to be female (60.8 percent) than male (39.2 percent). In the National Incidence Study, parents or parent substitutes were involved as perpetrators in the majority of all cases of maltreatment (88 percent), physical abuse (87 percent), and physical neglect (87 percent). Natural mothers were perpetrators in 66 percent of physical abuse cases and 83 percent of physical neglect cases. Natural fathers were perpetrators in 45 percent of physical abuse cases and 46 percent of neglect cases. Overall, natural mothers were involved in all forms of maltreatment nearly twice as often as natural fathers (75 percent compared to 41 percent).

Contemporary Issues

Etiology. Although numerous theories have been developed to explain the occurrence of abuse, no one theory has been universally accepted. Just as definitions of abuse and neglect are affected by the personal and professional values and perspectives of the definer, so theories about the causes of maltreatment reflect the beliefs and professional training of the investigator (for reviews of theoretical models, see Belsky, 1978; Friedrich & Wheeler, 1982; Gelles, 1973, 1980; Keller & Erne, 1983; Maden & Wrench, 1977; Parke & Collmer, 1975;

Spinetta & Rigler, 1972; Sweet & Resick, 1979).

Much of the early work in the field approached abuse and neglect from the perspective of the medical model, subscribing to a psychiatric view of the causes of maltreatment. The psychiatric model attributed maltreatment to the psychopathology of the perpetrator, ranging from severe mental illness to deviant personality traits. Although research has linked maltreatment with a variety of personality traits in abusing parents, no consistent pattern of characteristics has emerged. Furthermore, empirical evidence has not supported psychiatric illness as a major factor in the etiology of abuse and neglect.

In the sociological model, emphasis on the causes of maltreatment shifted from attributes of abusing parents to the social context in which maltreatment occurred (Garbarino, 1977; Gil, 1970). In particular, socioenvironmental factors were seen as major precipitating agents of the stress that leads to maltreatment: socioeconomic status, unemployment, financial difficulties, housing and living conditions, family size, family structure, adolescent parenting, and social isolation. Moreover, societal and cultural norms and attitudes toward violence were also seen as important determinants of maltreatment. Again, numerous investigations have reported associations between socioenvironmental factors and abuse and neglect, but none of these factors have been found to characterize all abusing families. Thus, the sociological model cannot completely explain the occurrence of abuse and neglect.

Another theoretical perspective emphasizes the role of the child in precipitating the maltreatment. Studies have focused on particular characteristics of the child that place stress on parenting and interfere with the development of a positive parent-child relationship: low birth weight, prematurity, physical or mental handicaps or illness, and behavioral characteristics (Friedrich & Boriskin, 1976; Friedrich & Einbender, 1983; Frodi, 1981; Parke & Collmer, 1975; Sameroff & Chandler, 1975). Regardless of whether the child manifests such special characteristics, parental perception of the child as different or difficult may increase the risk of maltreatment. Views of the child as a contributor to the occurrence of abuse have

broadened to consider abuse as a sequence of interactions between parent and child that escalate into abuse (Burgess & Conger, 1978; Kadushin & Martin, 1981). Although the perception of maltreatment as an interactional event is more applicable to abuse than to neglect, the occurrence of neglect may also be influenced by the behavior and characteristics of the child.

As conceptual approaches to the etiology of abuse and neglect evolved over time, the recognition that no single factor can account for the occurrence of maltreatment led to the integration of these various approaches into comprehensive models. This approach views child maltreatment as a multidimensional phenomenon resulting from the interaction of several elements: characteristics of the parent and the child, family interactional processes, family socioenvironmental stresses, and the wider community and societal context. To some extent, even the comprehensive models have emphasized one or another of the elements in the model (Keller & Erne, 1983), but empirical research has yet to establish the relative importance of the various components.

Intervention. The approaches to intervention in cases of maltreatment are as numerous as the approaches to etiology. Treatment approaches generally derive from particular conceptual perspectives (Keller & Erne, 1983). The psychiatric model advocated traditional psychotherapy to change personality characteristics of the abuser. The sociological model directed interventions toward eliminating the socioenvironmental stresses associated with abuse and neglect. Conceptual models recognizing the role of the child in maltreatment pointed to the need to alter the child's behavior. Comprehensive models of maltreatment suggested equally comprehensive multifaceted approaches to intervention and treatment.

Evaluations of various intervention strategies have found only limited success (Cohn, 1980; Daro & Cohn, 1984; Keller & Erne, 1983; Kadushin, 1980; Sudia, 1981). Substantial rates of recurrence for abuse and neglect during or following intervention and treatment suggest that even the minimal objective of protecting the child from further harm is difficult to achieve (Daro & Cohn, 1984; Friedrich & Einbender, 1983; Herrenkohl, Herrenkohl, Egolf, & Seech, 1980; Kadushin, 1980). Although the focus of treatment has generally been the abusing parent, there is increasing recognition that treatment is necessary for the child to overcome the detrimental effects of maltreatment. Numerous studies document negative cognitive, neurological, behavioral, and emotional sequelae of abuse and neglect for children (Friedrich & Einbender, 1983; Kinard, 1980; Martin, 1976). However, maltreated children are not yet routinely assessed to determine their treatment needs.

The use of out-of-home placement as a method of intervention is the subject of ongoing debate (Borgman, 1981; Derdeyn, 1977; Fanshel, 1981; Martin & Beezley, 1976; Noonan, 1983; Runyan, Gould, Trost, & Loda, 1981). Decisions to remove a child from the home involve balancing the family's right to privacy against the child's right to be protected from harm. The absence of operational criteria for determining the need for out-of-home placement has resulted not only in unnecessarily removing children but also in failing to remove children who were subsequently reinjured. Although the reluctance to place children outside the home stems in part from the inadequacies of the foster care system, there is evidence that foster care need not have detrimental consequences for maltreated children (Kent, 1976; Kinard, 1982; Martin & Beezley, 1976). Guidelines are also lacking for decision making with respect to the termination of parental rights and permanent placement of the child.

Prevention. Although intervention and treatment remain vital elements in efforts to combat the problem of child maltreatment, attention is increasingly focused on primary prevention, that is, on preventing maltreatment before it occurs. Proposals for primary prevention include eliminating cultural sanctions for violence and physical punishment, reducing poverty and other environmental stresses, and providing parenting education (Keller & Erne, 1983; Zigler, 1980). The success of these programs has yet to be determined.

One approach to primary prevention is controversial—the use of screening techniques to identify parents at risk for maltreating their children. Screening instruments tested in research have been found to discriminate between abusing and nonabusing parents (Hunter, Kilstrom, Kraybill, & Loda, 1978; Milner & Ayoub, 1980; Schneider, Helfer, & Hoffmeister, 1980; Schneider, Hoffmeister, & Helfer, 1976). However, the widespread use of screening in the general population raises ethical issues, such as false predictions of maltreatment, that have not yet been resolved (Brody & Gaiss, 1976).

Cycle of Abuse. A common theme throughout the child abuse and neglect literature is that abusing and neglecting parents were themselves abused or neglected as children (Keller & Erne, 1983; Parke & Collmer, 1975; Spinetta & Rigler, 1972). However, this maxim has begun to be challenged (Jayaratne, 1977; Miller & Challas, 1981; Potts, Herzberger, & Holland, 1979). Careful examination of the empirical evidence reveals that only a small proportion of abusing parents experienced abuse in childhood. Thus, many abusing parents were not abused as children, and many parents who were abused as children do not abuse their own children. One factor that may contribute to the repetitive cycle of maltreatment is the lack of social support resources (Hunter & Kilstrom, 1979; Miller & Challas, 1981).

Role of Social Work

Although no single profession can claim child abuse and neglect as its prerogative, social work plays a dominant role in the protective service field. Public social service agencies are generally mandated to receive reports of abuse and neglect. Social workers in these agencies are responsible for investigating and verifying reports of maltreatment. Intervention and treatment plans are developed and implemented primarily by social workers in public or private agencies. Even when service plans involve several multidisciplinary sources, social workers are often designated to coordinate these services. Thus, as the primary gatekeepers, social workers are in a unique position to influence policy and practice in protective services.

Given the prominent role of social workers in protective services, their experiences with abusive and neglecting families are an important element in their contributions to the field. However, their knowledge about abuse and neglect may be derived from literature that provides little grounding in theory or research. A content analysis of articles on child abuse and neglect appearing in professional journals oriented to social workers showed that most articles focused on programs or practice issues; few presented theoretical concepts or research findings (Cain & Klerman, 1979). Cain (1983) emphasized the need for social workers not only to use research findings to inform their practice but also to conduct research themselves to determine the extent to which their work with maltreating families is successful.

The traditional casework approach to intervention in cases of abuse and neglect has been broadened to include innovative methods and programs. Although considerable attention is focused on describing and evaluating a variety of treatment approaches (Ebeling & Hill, 1983; Kadushin, 1980; Kempe & Helfer, 1980), there is no consensus on what constitutes effective treatment (Keller & Erne, 1983; Sudia, 1981). Therapeutic services, such as counseling or mental health services, are the most common type of service provided to maltreating families, but there is evidence that these services are the least acceptable to families (Giovannoni & Becerra, 1979; Shapiro, 1979). Given the association of maltreatment with problems of poverty, unemployment, housing, and physical health, services to address these problems should be a priority. However, such services are the least likely to be recommended or provided despite evidence of their need and acceptance by families.

Direct services to the abused or neglected child have not been the primary focus of intervention efforts because of the common belief that services to the parents indirectly benefit the child. However, there is increasing recognition that the deleterious consequences of maltreatment for the child require specific interventions (Holleman, 1983; Kinard, 1980; Martin, 1976).

The multidimensional nature of the problem of abuse and neglect calls for a multidimensional approach to intervention and to prevention. The key to the effectiveness of multiple services lies in the coordination of these services, which is generally the responsibility of the protective service worker. Social workers' primary role in service delivery places them in a position to influence policy and program development in child abuse and neglect.

E. MILLING KINARD

For further information, see CHILD SEXUAL ABUSE; PROTECTIVE SERVICES FOR CHILDREN.

References

Belsky, J. (1978). "Three Theoretical Models of Child Abuse: A Critical Review." *Child Abuse and Neglect, 2*(1), 37–49.

Besharov, D. J. (1981). "Toward Better Research on Child Abuse and Neglect: Making Definitional Issues an Explicit Methodological Concern." *Child Abuse and Neglect, 5*(4), 383–390.

Borgman, R. (1981). "Antecedents and Consequences of Parental Rights Termination for Abused and Neglected Children." *Child Welfare, 60*(6), 381–404.

Brody, H., & Gaiss, B. (1976). "Ethical Issues in Screening for Unusual Child-Rearing Practices." *Pediatric Annuals, 15*(3), 106–112.

Burgess, R. L., & Conger, R. D. (1978). "Family Interaction in Abusive, Neglectful, and Normal Families." *Child Development, 49*(4), 1163–1173.

Caffey, J. (1946). "Multiple Fractures in Long Bones of Infants Suffering from Chronic Subdural Hematoma." *American Journal of Roentgenology, 56*(2), 163–173.

Cain, L. P. (1983). "The Social Worker as Researcher: Adding to the Knowledge Base of Protective Services." In N. B. Ebeling & D. A. Hill (Eds.), *Child Abuse and Neglect: A Guide With Case Studies for Treating the Child and Family* (pp. 259–274). Boston: John Wright–PSG.

Cain, L. P., & Klerman, L. V. (1979). "What Do Social Workers Read About Child Abuse?" *Child Welfare, 58*(1), 13–24.

Cohn, A. H. (1980). "Essential Elements of Successful Child Abuse and Neglect Treatment?" In C. H. Kempe, A. F. Franklin, & C. Cooper (Eds.), *The Abused Child in the Family and in the Community, Vol. 1* (pp. 491–496). New York: Pergamon Press.

Daro, D., & Cohn, A. H. (1984, August). *A Decade of Child Maltreatment Evaluation Efforts: What We Have Learned.* Paper presented at the Family Violence Research Conference, Durham, N.H.

Derdeyn, A. P. (1977). "A Case for Permanent Foster Placement of Dependent, Neglected, and Abused Children." *American Journal of Orthopsychiatry, 47*(4), 604–614.

Ebeling, N. B., & Hill, D. A. (Eds.). (1983). *Child Abuse and Neglect: A Guide With Case Studies for Treating the Child and Family.* Boston: John Wright–PSG.

Fanshel, D. (1981). "Decision Making under Uncertainty: Foster Care for Abused or Neglected Children?" *American Journal of Public Health, 71*(7), 685–686.

Friedrich, W. N., & Boriskin, J. A. (1976). "The Role of the Child in Abuse: A Review of the Literature." *American Journal of Orthopsychiatry, 46*(4), 580–590.

Friedrich, W. N., & Einbender, A. J. (1983). "The Abused Child: A Psychological Review." *Journal of Clinical Child Psychology, 12*(3), 244–256.

Friedrich, W. N., & Wheeler, K. K. (1982). "The Abusing Parent Revisited: A Decade of Psychological Research." *Journal of Nervous and Mental Disease, 170*(10), 577–587.

Frodi, A. M. (1981). "Contribution of Infant Characteristics to Child Abuse." *American Journal of Mental Deficiency, 85*(4), 341–349.

Garbarino, J. (1977). "The Human Ecology of Child Maltreatment: A Conceptual Model for Research." *Journal of Marriage and the Family, 39*(4), 721–735.

Gelles, R. J. (1973). "Child Abuse as Psychopathology: A Sociological Critique and Reformulation." *American Journal of Orthopsychiatry, 43*(4), 611–621.

Gelles, R. J. (1980). "Violence in the Family: A Review of Research in the Seventies." *Journal of Marriage and the Family, 42*(4), 873–885.

Gil, D. G. (1970). *Violence Against Children.* Cambridge, Mass.: Harvard University Press.

Giovannoni, J. M., & Becerra, R. M. (1979). *Defining Child Abuse.* New York: Free Press.

Hampton, R. L., & Newberger, E. H. (1984, August). *Child Abuse Incidence and Reporting by Hospitals: Significance of Severity, Class, and Race.* Paper presented at the Family Violence Research Conference, Durham, N.H.

Herrenkohl, R. C., Herrenkohl, E. C., Egolf, B., & Seech, M. (1980). "The Repetition of Child Abuse: How Frequently Does It Occur?" In C. H. Kempe, A. W. Franklin, & C. Cooper (Eds.), *The Abused Child in the Family and in the Community, Vol. 1* (pp. 67–72). New York: Pergamon Press.

Herzberger, S. D., & Tennen, H. (1984, August). *Applying the Label of Physical Abuse.* Paper presented at the Family Violence Research Conference, Durham, N.H.

Holleman, B. A. (1983). "Treatment of the Child." In N. B. Ebeling & D. A. Hill (Eds.), *Child Abuse and Neglect: A Guide With Case Studies for Treating the Child and Family* (pp. 145–181). Boston: John Wright–PSG.

Hunter, R. S., & Kilstrom, N. (1979). "Breaking the Cycle in Abusive Families." *American Journal of Psychiatry, 136*(10), 1320–1322.

Hunter, R. S., Kilstrom, N., Kraybill, E. N., &

Loda, F. (1978). "Antecedents of Child Abuse and Neglect in Premature Infants: A Prospective Study in a Newborn Intensive Care Unit." *Pediatrics, 61*(4), 629–635.

Jayaratne, S. (1977). "Child Abusers As Parents and Children: A Review." *Social Work, 22*(1), 5–9.

Kadushin, A. (1980). "Protective Services." In A. Kadushin, *Child Welfare Services* (3rd ed., pp. 151–234). New York: Macmillan Publishing Co.

Kadushin, A., & Martin, J. A. (1981). *Child Abuse: An Interactional Event.* New York: Columbia University Press.

Keller, H. R., & Erne, D. (1983). "Child Abuse: Toward a Comprehensive Model." In A. P. Goldstein (Ed.), *Prevention and Control of Aggression* (pp. 1–36). New York: Pergamon Press.

Kempe, C. H., & Helfer, R. E. (Eds.). (1980). *The Battered Child* (3rd ed.). Chicago: University of Chicago Press.

Kempe, C. H., Silverman, F. N., Steele, B. F., Droegemueller, W., & Silver, H. K. (1962). "The Battered Child Syndrome." *Journal of the American Medical Association, 181*(1), 17–24.

Kent, J. T. (1976). "A Follow-up Study of Abused Children." *Journal of Pediatric Psychology, 1*(2), 25–31.

Kinard, E. M. (1980). "Mental Health Needs of Abused Children." *Child Welfare, 59*(8), 451–462.

Kinard, E. M. (1982). "Experiencing Child Abuse: Effects on Emotional Adjustment." *American Journal of Orthopsychiatry, 52*(1), 82–91.

Light, R. J. (1973). "Abused and Neglected Children in America: A Study of Alternative Policies." *Harvard Educational Review, 43*(4), 556–598.

Maden, M. F., & Wrench, D. F. (1977). "Significant Findings in Child Abuse Research." *Victimology, 2*(2), 196–224.

Martin, H. P. (Ed.). (1976). *The Abused Child: A Multidisciplinary Approach to Developmental Issues and Treatment.* Cambridge, Mass.: Ballinger Publishing Co.

Martin, H. P., & Beezley, P. (1976). "Foster Placement: Therapy or Trauma." In H. P. Martin (Ed.), *The Abused Child: A Multidisciplinary Approach to Developmental Issues and Treatment* (pp. 189–199). Cambridge, Mass.: Ballinger Publishing Co.

McPherson, K. S., & Garcia, L. L. (1983). "Effects of Social Class and Familiarity on Pediatricians' Responses to Child Abuse." *Child Welfare, 62*(5), 387–393.

Miller, D., & Challas, G. (1981, July). *Abused Children As Adult Parents: A Twenty-Five Year Longitudinal Study.* Paper presented at the Family Violence Research Conference, Durham, N.H.

Milner, J. S., & Ayoub, C. (1980). "Evaluation of 'At Risk' Parents Using the Child Abuse Potential Inventory." *Journal of Clinical Psychology, 36*(4), 945–948.

Nagi, S. Z. (1977). *Child Maltreatment in the United States.* New York: Columbia University Press.

National Center on Child Abuse and Neglect. (1981). *Study Findings: National Study of the Incidence and Severity of Child Abuse and Neglect* (DHHS No. 81-30325). Washington, D.C.: Department of Health and Human Services.

Noonan, R. A. (1983). "Separation and Placement." In N. B. Ebeling and D. A. Hill (Eds.), *Child Abuse and Neglect: A Guide With Case Studies for Treating the Child and Family* (pp. 207–227). Boston: John Wright–PSG.

O'Toole, R., Turbett, P., & Nalepka, C. (1983). "Theories, Professional Knowledge, and Diagnosis of Child Abuse." In D. Finkelhor, R. J. Gelles, G. T. Hotaling, & M. A. Straus (Eds.), *The Dark Side of Families: Current Family Violence Research* (pp. 349–362). Beverly Hills, Calif.: Sage Publications.

Parke, R. D., & Collmer, C. W. (1975). *Child Abuse: An Interdisciplinary Analysis.* Chicago: University of Chicago Press.

Potts, D., Herzberger, S., & Holland, A. E. (1979, May). *Child Abuse: A Cross-Generational Pattern of Child Rearing?* Paper presented at the meeting of the Midwest Psychological Association, Chicago.

Radbill, S. X. (1980). "Children in a World of Violence." In C. H. Kempe & R. E. Helfer (Eds.), *The Battered Child* (3rd ed., pp. 3–20). Chicago: University of Chicago Press.

Runyan, D. K., Gould, C. L., Trost, D. C., & Loda, F. A. (1981). "Determinants of Foster Care Placement for the Maltreated Child." *American Journal of Public Health, 71*(7), 706–711.

Russell, A. B., & Trainor, C. M. (1984). *Trends in Child Abuse and Neglect: A National Perspective.* Denver, Colo.: American Humane Association.

Sameroff, A. J., & Chandler, M. J. (1975). "Reproductive Risk and the Continuum of Caretaking Casualty." In F. D. Horowitz (Ed.), *Review of Child Development Research, Vol. 4* (pp. 187–244). Chicago: University of Chicago Press.

Schneider, C., Helfer, R. E., & Hoffmeister, J. K. (1980). "Screening for the Potential to Abuse: A Review." In C. H. Kempe & R. E. Helfer (Eds.), *The Battered Child* (3rd ed., pp. 420–430). Chicago: Univerity of Chicago Press.

Schneider, C., Hoffmeister, J. K., & Helfer, R. E.

(1976). "A Predictive Screening Questionnaire for Potential Problems in Mother-Child Interaction." In R. E. Helfer & C. H. Kempe (Eds.), *Child Abuse and Neglect: The Family and the Community* (pp. 420–430). Cambridge, Mass.: Ballinger Publishing Co.

Shapiro, D. (1979). *Parents and Protectors: A Study in Child Abuse and Neglect.* New York: Child Welfare League of America.

Silverman, F. (1953). "The Roentgen Manifestations of Unrecognized Skeletal Trauma in Infants." *American Journal of Roentgenology 69*(3), 413–426.

Silverman, F. N. (1980). "Radiologic and Special Diagnostic Procedures." In C. H. Kempe & R. E. Helfer (Eds.), *The Battered Child* (3rd ed., pp. 215–240). Chicago: University of Chicago Press.

Spinetta, J. J., & Rigler, D. (1972). "The Child-Abusing Parent: A Psychological Review." *Psychological Bulletin, 77*(4), 296–304.

Straus, M. A., Gelles, R. J., & Steinmetz, S. K. (1980). *Behind Closed Doors: Violence in the American Family.* Garden City, N.Y.: Anchor Press.

Sudia, C. E. (1981). "What Services Do Abusive and Neglecting Families Need?" In L. H. Pelton (Ed.), *The Social Context of Child Abuse and Neglect* (pp. 268–290). New York: Human Sciences Press.

Sussman, A., & Cohen, S. J. (1975). *Reporting Child Abuse and Neglect: Guidelines for Legislation.* Cambridge, Mass.: Ballinger Publishing Co.

Sweet, J. J., & Resick, P. A. (1979). "The Maltreatment of Children: A Review of Theories and Research." *Journal of Social Issues, 35*(2), 40–59.

Williams, G. J. (1980). "Cruelty and Kindness to Children: Documentary of a Century, 1874–1974." In G. J. Williams & J. Money (Eds.), *Traumatic Abuse and Neglect of Children at Home* (pp. 68–88). Baltimore: Johns Hopkins University Press.

Wolock, I. (1982). "Community Characteristics and Staff Judgments in Child Abuse and Neglect Cases." *Social Work Research and Abstracts, 18*(2), 9–15.

Woolley, P. V., Jr., & Evans, W. A., Jr. (1955). "Significance of Skeletal Lesions in Infants Resembling Those of Traumatic Origin." *Journal of the American Medical Association, 158*(7), 539–543.

Zigler, E. (1980). "Controlling Child Abuse: Do We Have the Knowledge and/or the Will?" In G. Gerbner, C. J. Ross, & E. Zigler (Eds.), *Child Abuse: An Agenda for Action* (pp. 3–32). New York: Oxford University Press.

CHILD CARE SERVICES

"Day care" and "child care" refer to the arrangements parents make when they go to work or for any reason turn to others to supplement the daily care they themselves can provide their children. The term "day care" has been used primarily to refer to care outside the home either in centers under public or private auspices or in the homes of other families in the neighborhood (known as "family day care"). More recently, the term "child care" has come into common usage to describe the variety of often complex arrangements that families make, including care at home by adult members of the family, having someone come in to care for the children at home, care by an older sibling, or arrangements in which children look after themselves.

Society's response to the child care needs of families has taken many forms. One era enthusiastically developed day care facilities as a way to recruit maternal employment for the war effort. Another confidently promoted child care as a setting for compensatory education that could overcome the disadvantages of poverty. Still another era brought repudiation by government of comprehensive involvement in the provision of day care. Over the decades, mothers—both single and married—increased their participation in the labor force in dramatic proportions. However, despite concern about the protection and development of children, an era of deregulation and service retrenchment shifted attention to corporate initiatives, employee benefits, tax breaks for employee child care, and development of the private child care marketplace. Research played a role in shaping the issues, but values dominated the politics of child care. In a continuing debate over the cost of child care services and who should pay for them, issues of quality of care, resource development, and appropriate regulation competed with questions about fairness and what the balance of family, corporate, government, and community responsibilities should be.

This article reviews the history of society's response to child care needs, the services and programs that have been developed, and the magnitude and mechanisms of financing child care. Persistent policy issues and trends are then identified to show how broad the role of social work has become in community planning for child care.

History

There are two histories of day care. One is the history of legislation and public debate, which resulted in major organized programs to provide licensed day care services for low income families, to subsidize licensed child care, or to develop regulatory standards. The other history, driven by the demographics of maternal employment, is the quiet, often invisible, growth of informal child care arranged by families either at home or in the neighborhood or purchased from centers in an expanding private market. The two histories intertwined as public initiatives eventually tried to deal with the demographics by means of universal subsidies through income tax credits, as private corporations began to respond to child care as an employee benefit, and as attention was given to how employees manage work and home.

Nineteenth Century. Although day care in the nineteenth century addressed many of the concerns that would reappear in the twentieth, it was handled as a charitable service under private auspices. Day nurseries were established in the United States early in the 1800s to serve working wives, widows of seamen, and other "worthy" women (Beer, 1957). The federal government became involved in 1863 during the Civil War, when it sponsored a day nursery in Philadelphia for the children of women who worked in clothing factories and hospitals and, later, for war widows (Beer, 1957). Waves of immigration to American cities from Ireland and Europe led to increased concern about slum conditions, educational needs, and the daily care of the children of the industrial revolution. In 1898, the National Federation of Day Nurseries was founded, based on the belief that children were better off in day nurseries than in crowded tenements and justifying nursery care as preventing institutional placement and preserving the home. However, the group care approach came under increasing criticism from friendly visitors, charity workers, and the emerging social work profession. From settlement houses to charity organizations, the social work view—which lasted into the twentieth century—became established that day care should be part of a family service that addressed the problems of the deserving poor. Supervised foster home day care was added to family services offered by social workers in charitable agencies.

Twentieth Century. In the twentieth century, federal legislation for day care was subject to boom-and-bust cycles, the ebb and flow depending on the crisis of the period. For example, in 1935 Works Progress Administration (WPA) nurseries were set up for the children of unemployed teachers, nurses, and others thrown out of work during the Great Depression. By 1937, 1,900 nurseries cared for 40,000 children. It was the first time that both federal and state public funds were spent for day care (Steinfels, 1973). Then the WPA nurseries were allowed to dwindle. Similarly, with the advent of World War II, the nation faced a crisis that could be eased by maternal employment. The result was a new expansion of day care. In 1942, the Community Facilities Act (also known as the Lanham Act) provided 50 percent matching grants to operate day care centers. More than 1,100 of these day care centers were former WPA nurseries (Steinfels, 1973). The Federal Works Agency channeled day care funds through local school systems, bypassing social work agencies and day nursery and family casework interests, and denying funding eligibility to family day care. By the end of the war, more than 1.5 million children were in day care at a cost of nearly $50 million (Steinfels, 1973). Yet, when the war was over, federal funds were withdrawn and few state programs survived—California's children's centers were a notable exception.

1960s. Not until the 1960s did a new federal expansion of day care take place. The first advance came with the 1962 social security amendments (P.L. 87-64) that authorized federal grants-in-aid to state public welfare agencies for day care services. This program permitted the states to develop standards for day care. It has been reported that 43 percent of the $4 million appropriated for day care in fiscal 1965 was spent on personnel engaged in licensing (Steiner, 1970). There was a further increase in day care funds as more states took advantage of the provisions of Title IV-A of the Social Security Act (as amended in 1967, P.L. 90-248) for 75 percent matching funds. In 1971, nearly a quarter of a billion dollars

were spent for all-day care to serve an estimated 440,000 children (Parker & Knitzer, 1971). The 1967 amendment also authorized the Work Incentive Program (WIN), which offered social services and training for permanent jobs, coupled with child care services for the trainees.

At the same time that day care was used to reduce welfare rolls, day care centers also became settings for compensatory education to remedy the disadvantaging effects of poverty. This War on Poverty, under the Economic Opportunity Act of 1964 (P.L. 88-452), authorized grants for day care within community action programs. The largest and most popular of these programs was Head Start—whose sustained popularity for over 20 years has made it resistant to the cyclical downturns suffered by other programs. Other laws that included support of day care were the Elementary and Secondary Education Act of 1965 (P.L. 89-10), the Vocational Education Act of 1963 (P.L. 88-210), and the Manpower Development and Training Acts of 1962, 1966, and 1968 (P.L. 87-415, P.L. 89-792, P.L. 90-636), among others. More than 200 federal programs affecting children had been established by the end of the decade, including Parent–Child Centers, Assistance for Migrant and Seasonal Farm Workers, Assistance for Handicapped Children, Foster Grandparents, Food Services, Health Service, Child Welfare Services, Aid to Families with Dependent Children (AFDC), and the Concentrated Employment Program, to suggest the range of categorical programs contributing to a focus on child care. By the end of the 1960s, annual expenditures for day care, Head Start, and preschool programs under Title I of the Elementary and Secondary Education Act (P.L. 89-10) had reached more than $500 million and were expanding (Brookings Institution, 1972).

1970s. During the 1970s, the politics of day care reached a standoff between an increasingly articulate day care movement and the beginning of a conservative trend that grew to full force in the 1980s. The women's movement brought with it egalitarian demands for the right to subsidized day care, justified as the key to giving women equal opportunity with men in education and employment (Roby, 1973). The concept of comprehensive day care, meaning that it would be developmental rather than merely custodial, became a plank of liberal platforms. Day care would contain such components as health care, nutrition, education, social services, and parent participation—as in the Head Start program, which in 1969, along with the U.S. Children's Bureau, had become part of the new Office of Child Development under the (then) Department of Health, Education, and Welfare. It was hoped that such services would be made available to all families, not just to the poor and disadvantaged, and that they would be subsidized and supported by a nationwide federal commitment to a system of quality day care services. This philosophy was embodied in the Comprehensive Child Development Act of 1971, which passed both houses of Congress but failed to receive the two-thirds majority needed for an override of President Nixon's veto.

In his veto message, President Nixon refused to commit the "vast moral authority of the National Government to the side of communal approaches to child rearing" (Roby, 1973). Some have argued that the veto reflected a conservative backlash against feminist demands (Grubb & Lazerson, 1982; Steiner, 1981); however, the potential costs of a day care entitlement loomed as an additional barrier to national consensus, and debate continued unresolved over who should pay the cost of day care and who should intervene and how. In 1976 and 1979, further attempts to enact legislation for a comprehensive child care program were defeated (Grubb & Lazerson, 1982, p. 214). The 1970s did, however, sustain modest increases in existing programs. By the end of the decade, Head Start had become a $900 million-a-year program serving 400,000 children. Title XX day care subsidies for nearly 500,000 children totaled $800 million, of which 78 percent was used for care in centers (Rose-Ackerman, 1983). A 1978 survey revealed 18,300 all-day centers caring for 900,000 children (Coelen, Glantz, & Calore, 1978). Approximately 100,000 children were estimated to be cared for in 29,329 federally supported family day care homes (Smith & Segal, 1981). Day care programs accounted for 21.7 percent of Title XX expenditures in 1979 (Smith & Segal, 1981). By the end of the decade, the major federal child care programs—including Title XX, AFDC, Head Start, the Department of Agriculture's Child Care Food Program, fed-

erally supported preschool programs, and work-related income tax deductions—had reached estimated expenditures of $3 billion (Malone, 1981).

A hallmark of the 1970s was concern about the quality of federally supported child care. An immense amount of research and policy analysis was devoted to formulating regulatory standards. First written in 1968 under the Equal Employment Opportunity Act (P.L. 88-352), the Federal Interagency Day Care Requirements (FIDCR) focused on day care centers, establishing a standard of a 1:5 adult-to-child ratio. Believing that this ratio was too restrictive for 4-year-olds but too lax for infants, the newly formed Office of Child Development organized a conference of child development professionals in 1970 to develop new standards. These standards set guidelines for optimum child development and were reflected in the revised FIDCR of 1972 that lowered the adult-child ratio for infants and toddlers to 1:3.

There was political debate over the cost of meeting these requirements, and a series of large national studies were undertaken:

1. A consumer study (Moore, 1982; Unco, 1976) found that only 2 percent of family day care was licensed.

2. A study by Abt Associates measured the costs and effects on children aged 3 to 5 in day care centers of the three major controllable variables (group size, adult-child ratio, and child care training). The findings showed that classroom size had consistent relationships to children's development by determining the kind of adult-child interaction (Ruopp et al., 1979).

3. A major study of family day care among blacks, Hispanics, and whites in three cities compared homes affected by ascending degrees of regulation: unregulated, registered, licensed, and agency-supervised. The findings were mixed, giving little support for regulation of family day care as a policy; in general, the most favorable adult-child ratios were found in unregulated family day care (Fosburg et al., 1981).

Another analysis of the appropriateness of FIDCR was made (U.S. Department of Health, Education, and Welfare, 1978; Nelson, 1981) and new regulations were drawn that reflected study findings. Active enforcement of day care standards never became federal policy, except for Head Start, which had always been designed as a quality program. Control of Title XX day care, however, had not been placed in the Office of Child Development, in which standards would have been a primary issue, but in the Community Services Administration, an agency devoted to issues of economic security and reduction of welfare rolls. Title XX day care was originally supposed to comply with FIDCR, but a moratorium on compliance was ordered after a 1973 Department of Health, Education, and Welfare (HEW) audit found that four-fifths of 552 facilities did not meet basic health and safety requirements (Cohen & Zigler, 1977); after that, state licensing laws became the standard. A series of comparative studies of state licensing showed wide variation in adult-child ratios, little attention to group size, and practices that fell short of the revised FIDCR standards (Collins, 1983; Smith & Segal, 1981), but with passage of the Omnibus Budget Reconciliation Act of 1980 (P.L. 96-499), federal regulation of day care was on its way out. By 1981, day care under the social services block grants would comply only with the standards set by state and local laws. In 1985, a model child care standards act (P.L. 98-473) was passed to assist states with guidance and training.

1980s. As the era of federal deregulation and of budget cuts in the social services came into force, child care in the 1980s reflected this conservative trend. President Reagan sought to shift child care initiatives to the private sector. Sharp increases occurred in employer-supported programs, in the use of federal and state tax credits for child care, in attention to child care as an employee benefit, and in concern for child care, work, and family issues in employee assistance programs. Private, for-profit centers, especially national chains, captured a larger share of the child care market. Information and referral (I & R) programs became increasingly widespread as a way of developing resources for a more accessible child care marketplace.

Financing Child Care

Until the 1980s, the dominant federal approach to child care services involved direct financing of care for low-income families that used licensed facilities and participated in programs providing designated services. These programs, which barely kept up with inflation in the 1970s, now came under budget-cutting pressures from the Reagan Administration. Whether or not these service-based programs are sustained through the 1980s, they may be far surpassed by the magnitude of indirect federal subsidy of child care through income tax credits—a mechanism for financing child care that permits families more freedom to select and purchase licensed or unlicensed child care.

Beginning as a tax deduction under the Revenue Act of 1971 (P.L. 92-178), in 1976 child care became a credit or adjustment to income and was expanded by the Economic Recovery Tax Act (ERTA) of 1981 (P.L. 97-34). The tax credit allowed 30 percent for adjusted gross incomes up to $10,000, sliding 1 percent per $2,000 of income to 20 percent for incomes over $28,000 for child care expenses of up to $2,400 for one child or $4,800 for two or more. The average credit in 1982 was $300, with an average credit of $362 to families earning between $10,000 and $15,000 (Campbell, 1985; Friedman, 1985). Among the total number of tax credit claims, 30 percent were from families with incomes under $20,000, 28 percent from those with incomes of $20,000 to $30,000, and 22 percent from those with incomes of $30,000 to $40,000 (Friedman, 1985).

In 1982, when the sliding scale was introduced, the number of tax returns claiming the credit increased by 9 percent and expenditures increased by 39 percent (Blank, 1985). In 1982, 5 million families claimed the credit at a cost in tax revenues of $1.5 million (Blank, 1985). Five million is one-fifth of the number of families in the United States with children under 18, but is probably at least half of the population of families paying for child care (author's estimate, based on Hayghe, 1986).

In 1983, child care tax credits increased 37 percent to $2.06 million, as 1.4 million additional taxpayers claimed the credit (Campbell, 1985). When the Internal Revenue Service (IRS) introduced the tax credit to the short form in 1983, 39 percent of the increased use was accounted for by taxpayers with incomes under $15,000, compared to a 4 percent increase the previous year (Campbell, 1985).

As increasing numbers of taxpayers

take advantage of this subsidy in what probably will be a steady trend, some uncertainty exists as to how the child care tax credit will fare under tax reform legislation—whether it will be eliminated altogether, whether the sliding scale for low incomes will be expanded and the allowable expenses raised, or whether reimbursement will be allowed to benefit families whose incomes and tax liability are so low that they cannot take advantage of the tax credit. On the other hand, increases are expected in the earned income credit, personal deduction, and standard deduction, all of which will improve how low-income parents are treated by the income tax structure.

Child care is also increasingly becoming an employer-paid employee benefit that can take many forms. Reimbursement of child care expenditures can be an option chosen from a menu of benefits. Flexible benefits were first made possible in 1970 under Section 125 of the IRS Code, but there has been uncertainty as to their tax-free status, and they have become more frequent only since 1982. It is estimated that more than 500 U.S. companies include dependent care in flexible-benefit accounts, but only 25 companies are estimated to have developed comprehensive cafeteria plans with dependent care as an optional benefit (Friedman, 1985). The advantages of flexible-benefit plans include more appropriate selection of benefits by employees to fit family needs at different stages of life; cost containment in the overall benefit package; and equity, or a sense of fairness, when child care becomes a benefit for some employees and not others.

Employees can also finance child care through tax-free dollars from their employers through stand-alone salary reduction plans, which can be used to reimburse child care expenses, and through dependent care assistance plans that allow employers to pay for child care with tax deductible dollars (ERTA, P.L. 97-34). Employers also create savings for employees by negotiating reduced rates for child care purchased at a discount from large vendors of center care such as Kinder-Care, La Petite Academy, and Children's World. Other employers finance on-site centers, pay for vouchers that can be used freely by employees to purchase the care of their choice, or finance information and referral

programs to assist employees in finding child care.

A national study of corporate child care initiatives (Burud, Aschbacher, & Mc-Croskey, 1984) reported a nearly 400 percent increase in company-financed centers in 4 years, from 105 in 1978 to 415 in 1982. In 1984 Friedman (1985) estimated that there were more than 1,000. Of 385 employers providing a child care benefit, 40 percent offered on-site centers, 35 percent financed care in an off-site center, 13 percent contracted for I & R services, and 4 percent reimbursed privately arranged child care (Burud, Aschbacher, & McCroskey, 1984).

The financing of child care is complex. Though the majority of the costs are borne by the families of the children, society shares some of the financing in a variety of ways—governments through programs and services or through federal and state income tax credits; business and labor through employee benefits; churches through their facilities; and United Ways, which spend nearly 5 percent of their resources on child care (Friedman, 1985), community agencies, and charitable foundations. Behind all of these programs are taxpayers and voluntary contributions of time as well as money. Indeed, much of the subsidy of child care never involves the exchange of money for services; rather the parties barter, trade, or exchange services or simply share child care responsibilities as an expression of love, service, and informal understanding.

Description of Child Care Services

In addition to programs to finance child care, three kinds of child care services are provided: (1) the provision of care through centers and family homes; (2) specialized-treatment uses of child care as a family-based mental health or child welfare service; and (3) assistance to employees in making decisions about child care, either through employee assistance programs or through I & R programs that also develop child care resources, assess community needs, and advocate for improved services.

The variety of arrangements that families make in order to work are often even more complex than their financing. The arrangements may be intricate packages, contrived with daily variations of short or long duration and relying heavily on husbands, older brothers and sisters, grandmothers, other kin, and householders to the extent possible, or even on the children themselves (Werner, 1984).

Increasingly, however, families are turning to care outside the home. It is estimated that this was the case by 1980 for about half of all children under 6 (U.S. Bureau of the Census, 1982). Smaller families and increased rates of maternal employment have gone hand in hand, and most families using out-of-home care are purchasing care for one child (Emlen, 1974, 1982; Hayghe, 1984).

Family Day Care. The care of children in a relative's home is less common than it used to be (U.S. Bureau of the Census, 1982). Day care is more likely to be nearby with a neighbor. Family day care is provided by women who are not in the labor force, who have child care responsibilities of their own (usually involving larger families), and whose experience and motivations are suited to providing a child care service, typically involving three or four children—less than the limits imposed by regulation. Family day care is the predominant resource used outside the home for infants and toddlers. It is also a major resource for school-age children. Care in family homes affords flexibility in the ages of children accommodated and in the hours that care is provided. Concern has been raised about the use of family day care in deteriorated neighborhoods, about the isolation of caregivers from social support and training, and about their inaccessibility to regulation or to I & R programs. Family day care persists, however, as a viable system of neighborhood care for several million families (Collins & Watson, 1976; Emlen, 1974; Emlen & Koren, 1984; Fosburg et al., 1981; Werner, 1984).

Center Care. Although nonprofit day care centers continue to provide a significant amount of subsidized care for lower-income families, and although churches extensively make their facilities available for day care, the most dramatic development in center care has been the growth of chains of large centers run by profitable companies. Kinder-Care, the largest chain, has over 950 centers in 40 states and Canada and serves about 100,000 children. Headquartered in Montgomery, Alabama, this corporation increased its revenue

500 percent in 5 years (Kinder-Care, 1983) and has the largest market share of the center care business. The second-largest chain, La Petite Academy, has over 400 programs in 24 states, and Children's World serves more than 20,000 children in 160 centers (Friedman, 1985). These chains have been profitable, in part by achieving efficiencies from large numbers of children per center and minimum labor costs, as well as by marketing their discount programs to employers.

Treatment in Day Care Settings. In any community, child care is recognized as occupying an important, though often neglected, position on a continuum of specialized services to families at risk of dissolution. Whether for mental health or child welfare, child care is one of the least restrictive services that can be supportive of family functioning and of a child's treatment program. Child care services play a part in the "reasonable effort" required as alternatives to placement in foster care or residential treatment facilities (Adoption Assistance and Child Welfare Act of 1980, P.L. 96-272).

Employee Assistance. Of wider scope, however, are two kinds of services to families to help them cope with their child care responsibilities. One is the employee assistance program (EAP), which began as a corporate approach to problems related to alcoholism and has been broadened to address the individualized child care needs of employees. Employee assistance programs have expanded in scope as more attention has been paid to how employees manage child care, how it affects their work, and how company policies, in turn, facilitate or adversely affect the ability of employees to combine working with family responsibilities. The flexibility of policies concerning sick leave, maternity and paternity leave, flexible work hours, and absenteeism are being modified by companies, as companies increasingly allow employees greater job flexibility in accommodating child care needs (Emlen & Koren, 1984; Galinsky, 1986). For example, in two successive surveys of companies in Portland, Oregon, the percentage of companies allowing sick leave when a child or other family member is ill increased to 57 percent in 1985 from 43 percent in 1984 (City Club of Portland, 1985).

Sick-Child Services. A regular child care arrangement is one thing; making arrangements for a sick child is quite another. A Portland, Oregon, survey showed that only 20 percent of employed mothers reported using the regular child care arrangement when a child was sick and the employee went to work (Emlen & Koren, 1984). When employees stayed home, the choices frequently involved leave without pay or the use of vacation time.

When parents cannot stay home, the need for a child care solution has led to the development of services for sick children. Some of these sick-child services dispatch caregivers so the child can remain at home (for example, Rent-a-Mom in Portland, Oregon), and others are sick bays at centers (such as Sneeze and Sniffle, an infirmary in Metairie, Louisiana, or Chicken Soup in downtown Minneapolis) or family day care satellites of center programs such as Berkeley's Wheezles and Sneezles or Grandma's House in Fremont, New York (Clinton, 1985; Fasciano, 1985).

Information and Referral Services. Difficulty in finding child care has been reported by a majority of employees in repeated surveys, with a ripple effect at home and at work (Emlen & Koren, 1984). Thus, information and referral (I & R) services, often also called resource and referral services, are a significant, emerging support system for parents seeking child care. Although many generic, all-purpose referral programs dispense information about child care as part of a broad service on where to turn (American Institutes for Research in the Behavioral Sciences, 1979), the most effective child care referral programs have been those that specialize in child care. They make an effort to improve the community's supply of child care and to be responsive to consumer demand. These I & R programs assist parents in making decisions about the kind of child care they want their children to have and in finding care that is conveniently located (Catalyst, 1983; Emlen et al., 1985; Levine, 1982). Microcomputers have enabled many I & R services to automate their resource files.

I & R programs are financed in a variety of ways by local and state governments, United Ways, and corporations. International Business Machines (IBM) developed a national program, contracting with Work/Family Directions of Boston to purchase I & R Services for IBM employees at the rate of $100 per requested referral. In Portland, Oregon, a program called Community Shares shifted financing for an I & R service from the public sector to corporate contracts with 18 companies (Emlen et al., 1985). Burud, Aschbacher, and McCroskey (1984) reported 36 companies supporting child care I & R.

The most extensive statewide program of this kind operates in California, where state funds have supported community programs of child care referral since 1976. The California Child Care Resource and Referral Network was founded in 1980, and by 1985 it represented 55 member agencies in 46 counties. This broad program documents need, monitors policy, educates consumers, coordinates a statewide referral system, publishes a national quarterly journal, *CC I & R Issues*, coordinates state-funded training and technical assistance, and with support by the BankAmerica Foundation and several corporations is assisting communities to develop new resources for child care.

Trends and Issues

Impact of Demographic Trends. Trends in demand for child care and related services are strongly determined by rates of maternal employment and family composition, which means marital status, ages of children, and number of children. The women who are most likely to be in the labor force are previously married mothers who are the heads of their households and have school-age children from 6 to 17. By 1980, three-quarters of this group were working (U.S. House, 1984). Among married women, labor force participation of mothers of children aged 6 to 17 was 62 percent in 1980, up from 49 percent in 1970. The sharpest increase in labor force participation, however, has been among mothers of young children. In households with children under the age of 6, the percentage of married mothers in the labor force increased to 45 percent in 1980 from 30 percent in 1970 and is projected to be 55 percent by 1990 (U.S. Bureau of the Census, 1982). Labor force participation of other "ever married" mothers was already high, increasing to 59 percent in 1980 from 51 percent in 1970 and is projected to be 63 percent by 1990. The rates for never-married mothers are somewhat lower, since they are younger, have had less education, and may be less employable.

These trends in maternal employment increase demand for child care at the same time that they reduce the available supply of caretakers. Family day care, for example, has depended on mothers who are not in the labor force. The trends toward a shortage in the nonemployed mothers will be exacerbated by an age shift in the population of children. One U.S. Bureau of the Census estimate (1982) projects an increase of 3 million children under 10 in single-parent families between 1980 and 1990, barring reversals in the rates of marriage, divorce, or remarriage. Estimates for the 1980s project a decrease in the cohort of teenagers at a time when the numbers of infants, toddlers, and preschoolers will increase (U.S. House, 1984). Unless latchkey solutions are vastly improved, this may well result in more children being home alone, since the family's use of available in-home resources tends to prevail, regardless of family income (Emlen & Koren, 1984).

Tax Credits versus Direct Provision of Services. The two major federal policies for financing child care—the tax system and direct services—continue to compete for priority, though they have complementary advantages. The tax system is a simple, efficient mechanism for supporting child care in a pluralistic society. It adds no extra overlay of bureaucracy. It separates regulation from funding and allows maximum freedom of choice for consumers of child care, although there may be a continuing need to regulate care and to stimulate and improve available supply through an I & R program. The tax credit approaches universal applicability and incorporates a sliding scale without a means test, but it does not sufficiently meet the needs of the poor. Direct provision of child care through such programs as Head Start and through parent-child services, work incentive programs, or Title XX day care has been directed toward defined target populations that are recognized as needing comprehensive social and health services. It is unlikely that income tax credits will meet the specialized needs for child care services that have been demonstrated by low-income pop-

ulations, especially by families who struggle to survive and whose marginal level of functioning threatens the safety and development of their children.

The increased labor force participation of mothers in two-parent households has sharply increased incomes for many families, diverging widely from the income levels of single-parent households, most of which fall below poverty levels. In 1980 in female-headed households, 65 percent of children under age 6 were in poverty, compared to 12 percent in male-headed households. These two tiers of economic circumstance create a disturbing divergence in the ability to purchase child care services, the inequity being especially disproportionate for blacks and other minorities suffering high rates of unemployment and economic disadvantage (Children's Defense Fund, 1982; National Black Child Development Institute, 1984).

Educational Programs. A trend that is helping to reduce the need for child care is the downward extension of public education through kindergarten and nursery school. Between 1967 and 1980, kindergarten enrollment increased to 85 percent from 65 percent, and nursery school for children aged 3 to 4 reached 39 percent. In addition to children in centers, this brought the total of preschoolers in group care to 54 percent (Kamerman, 1983).

Quality of Care. Since the mid-1960s, quality of care has been a dominating concern, although hardly the winning day care issue in public policy. As discussed earlier, child welfare and child development professionals focused their interest on guidelines that would foster optimum child development and on licensing and minimum requirements for protection against abuse, overcrowding, and unhealthy or unsafe conditions (Class & English, 1985).

As the federal government became a major purchaser of child care for low-income families, public concern focused on the quality and cost of the care into which public expenditures would flow. This concern prompted a major study (Ruopp et al., 1979) of the effects on children and costs of regulatable characteristics of day care centers. Group size, caregiver-child ratio, and caregiver qualification were the three regulatable variables, and a consistent pattern of findings related differences in these variables to indicators of quality of care. For preschool children aged 3 to 5 group size had the greatest impact. In smaller groups, lead teachers engaged more actively with children, and the children showed more cooperation, verbal initiatives, and innovative or reflective behavior, as well as less hostility, conflict, or aimless, uninvolved activity. Children in smaller groups also showed greater gains on developmental tests such as the Preschool Inventory and the Peabody Picture Vocabulary Test. In classes with fewer children per caregiver, lead teachers spent less time commanding and correcting children but more time in interaction with other adults and center-related activities. Staff who had education or training specifically related to children spent more time in social interaction with children, and the children showed more cooperation and sustained involvement in activities.

These findings and others (Jones & Prescott, 1982) made a strong case for limiting the size of groups in child care, but the spirit of deregulation prevailed. In addition to regulation, alternative approaches to improving quality of care have included research and education about standards, education for and accreditation of providers, consumer education, I & R, and other supportive services for parents and caregivers. Families that experience difficulty finding child care are more likely to make unsatisfactory arrangements that adversely affect lives at work, at home, and at child care. Therefore, it has been advocated that communities comprehensively address the quality-of-care issue by increasing and improving the range of child care resources that families want their children to have (Emlen et al., 1985).

Legal Issues. The development of child care services has introduced a host of legal issues concerning licensing requirements, zoning, wages, benefits, working conditions, medical care, custody, insurance, and child abuse reporting (Kotin, Crabtree, & Ridman, 1981). A Child Care Law Center was established in San Francisco to meet demands for legal information. Issues involving liability and insurance risks were made especially prominent by child abuse in day care centers. Family day care providers and I & R programs also have seen sharp increases in their insurance rates. Child care by informal arrangement has been one of society's prime examples of shared responsibility, but the business aspects of child care are creating a crisis about whether the risks and liability of sharing child care responsibilities will be safe to assume.

Role of Social Work

Day care, child care, and early childhood programs do not fit into any one profession or existing institutional framework, be it health, education, or welfare. Along with early childhood education, home economics, and other professions, social work has a tradition of advocating for child care programs. Yet, neither the social agency nor the school has provided a service model that could reach all forms of child care and child rearing in the community or relate to the efforts of all families to manage their child care responsibilities.

Social work's role, while not exclusive or entirely unique, draws especially from its work with families, as well as from its concern for the protection of children. Today's world calls on social work to play a wide-ranging role in developing the policies and services that can assist families better to combine working with child care and family responsibilities. Social workers are called upon to provide employee assistance; to analyze needed improvements in child care benefits for employees; to help families in distress to use child care effectively to stabilize their lives; to develop child care programs such as I & R; to assess child care needs in the community; and to provide leadership in bringing together the sectors of the community that must share responsibility if a well-functioning system of child care services is to be created and brought within reach of all families.

ARTHUR C. EMLEN

For further information, see CHILDREN; CHILD WELFARE SERVICES; FOSTER CARE FOR CHILDREN; GROUP CARE FOR CHILDREN; MENTAL HEALTH AND ILLNESS IN CHILDREN; PROTECTIVE SERVICES FOR CHILDREN.

References

American Institutes for Research in the Behavioral Sciences. (1979). *Project Connections: A Study of Child Care Information and Referral*

Services. Phase I Results. Cambridge, Mass.: Author.

Beer, E. (1957). *Working Mothers and the Day Nursery.* New York: Whiteside.

Blank, H. (1985). *Fact Sheet.* Washington, D.C.: Children's Defense Fund.

Brookings Institution. (1972). *Setting National Priorities: The 1973 Budget.* Washington, D.C.: Author.

Bureau of National Affairs. (1984). *Employers and Child Care: Development of a New Employee Benefit.* Washington, D.C.: Author.

Burud, S., Aschbacher, P., & McCroskey, J. (1984). *Employer-Supported Child Care: Investing in Human Resources.* Dover, Mass.: Auburn House.

Campbell, N. (1985). *Analysis of Internal Revenue Service Data.* Washington, D.C.: National Women's Law Center.

Catalyst. (1983). *Child Care Information Service: An Option for Employer-Support of Child Care.* New York: Author.

Children's Defense Fund. (1982). *Employed Parents and Their Children: A Data Book.* Washington, D.C.: Author.

City Club of Portland. (1985). *Survey of Employee-Sponsored Child Care Options.* Portland, Oregon: Author.

Class, N., & English, J. (1985). "Formulating Valid Standards For Licensing." *Public Welfare, 43* (3), 31–35.

Clinton, L. (1985). "Guess Who Stays Home with a Sick Child?" *Working Mother,* 8(10), 55–61.

Coelen, C., Glantz, F., & Calore, D. (1978). *Day Care Centers in the U.S.: A National Profile, 1976–77.* Cambridge, Mass.: Abt Associates.

Cohen, D., & Zigler, E. (1977). "Federal Day Care Standards: Rationale and Recommendations." *American Journal of Orthopsychiatry, 47*(3), 456–465.

Collins, R. (1983). "Child Care and the States: The Comparative Licensing Study." *Young Children,* 8(5), 3–11.

Collins, R., & Watson, E. (1976). *Family Day Care: A Practical Guide for Parents, Caregivers and Professionals.* Boston: Beacon Press.

Emlen, A. (1974). "Day Care for Whom?" In A. Schorr (ed.), *Children and Decent People* (pp. 88–112). New York: Basic Books.

Emlen, A. (1982). *When Parents Are At Work: A Three-Company Survey of How Employed Parents Arrange Child Care.* Washington, D.C.: Greater Washington Research Center.

Emlen, A., Donoghue, B., & Clarkson, Q. (1974). *The Stability of the Family Day Care Arrangement: A Longitudinal Study.* Corvallis, Oregon: DCE Books.

Emlen, A., & Koren, P. (1984). *Hard to Find and Difficult to Manage: The Effects of Child Care on the Workplace. A Report to Employers.* Portland, Oregon: Portland State University.

Emlen, A., et al. (1985). *Community Shares: Corporate Financing of a Child Care Information Service.* Portland, Oregon: Portland State University.

Fasciano, N. (1985). "From Wheezles and Sneezles to Chicken Soup: Some Pioneering Child Care Programs for Sick Kids." *Working Mother, 8* (10), 62–64.

Fosburg, S., et al. (1981). *Family Day Care in the United States* (Vols. I–VI, DHHS Publication No. [OHDS] 80-30282-6). Washington, D.C.: U.S. Government Printing Office.

Friedman, D. (1983). "Employer-Supported Child Care: How Does It Answer the Needs and Expectations of Workers?" *Vital Issues, 32* (10), 1–6.

Frieman, D. (1985). *Corporate Financial Assistance for Child Care.* New York: Conference Board.

Galinsky, E. (1986). "Family Life and Corporate Policies." In M. Yogman & T. B. Brazelton (Eds.), *Stresses and Supports for Families.* Boston: Harvard University Press.

Grubb, W. N., & Lazerson, M. (1982). "The Frontiers of Public Responsibility: Child Care and Parent Education." In W. N. Grubb & M. Lazerson (Eds.), *Broken Promises: How Americans Fail Their Children* (pp. 208–232). New York: Basic Books.

Hayghe, H. (1984). "Working Mothers Reach Record Number in 1984." *Monthly Labor Review, 107* (12), 31–34.

Hayghe, H. (1986). "Rise in Mother's Labor Force Activity Includes Those with Infants." *Monthly Labor Review, 109* (2), 43–45.

Jones, E., & Prescott, E. (1982). "Day Care: Short- or Long-Term Solution?" *Annals of the American Academy of Political Science, 461* (5), 91–101.

Kamerman, S. (1983). "Child-care Services: A National Picture." *Monthly Labor Review, 106* (12), 35–39.

Kamerman, S., & Kahn, A. (1981). *Child Care, Family Benefits, and Working Parents.* New York: Columbia University Press.

Kinder-Care, Inc. (1983). *Annual Report.* Montgomery, Ala.: Author.

Kotin, L., Crabtree, R., & Ridman, W. (1981). *Legal Handbook for Day Care Centers* (DHHS Publication No. [OHDS] 83-30335). Washington, D.C.: U.S. Government Printing Office.

Levine, J. (1982). "The Prospects and Dilemmas of Child Care Information and Referral." In E. Zigler & E. Gordon (Eds.), *Day Care: Scientific and Social Policy Issues* (pp. 378–399). Boston: Auburn House.

Malone, M. (1981). *Child Day Care: The Federal Role* (Issue Brief No. 1). Washington, D.C.:

Library of Congress, Congressional Research Service.

Moore, J. (1982). "Parents' Choice of Day Care Services." *Annals of the American Academy of Political and Social Science*, 461 (5), 125–134.

National Black Child Development Institute. (1984). *Budget Cuts and Black Children: A Response to the President's Budget for FY 1984*. Washington, D.C.: Author.

Nelson, J. (1981). *The Federal Interagency Day Care Requirements (FIDCR): A Case Study of Federal Regulatory Policymaking*. Washington, D.C.: National Research Council.

Office of Inspector General. (1985). *Preventing Sexual Abuse in Day Care Programs: National Program Inspection*. Seattle, Wash.: Department of Health and Human Services, Region X.

Parker, R., & Knitzer, J. (1971). "Day Care and Preschool Services." In *Government Research on the Problems of Children and Youth*. Washington, D.C.: U.S. Government Printing Office.

Powell, D., & Eisenstadt, J. (1980). *Finding Child Care: A Study of Parents' Search Processes*. Detroit, Mich.: Merrill-Palmer Institute.

Roby, P. (1973). *Child Care—Who Cares?* New York: Basic Books.

Rose-Ackerman, S. (1983). "Unintended Consequences: Regulating the Quality of Subsidized Day Care." *Journal of Policy Analysis and Management*, 3 (1), 14–30.

Ruopp, R., & Travers, J. (1982). "Janus Faces Day Care: Perspectives on Quality and Cost." In E. Zigler & E. Gordon (Eds.), *Day Care: Scientific and Social Policy Issues*. Boston: Auburn House.

Ruopp, R., et al. (1979). *Children at the Center*. Cambridge, Mass.: Abt Associates.

Smith, A., & Segal, A. (1981). *Report to Congress: Summary Report of the Assessment of Current State Practices in Title XX Funded Day Care Programs* (DHHS Publication No. [OHDS] 81-30331). Washington, D.C.: U.S. Department of Health and Human Services.

Steiner, G. (1970). *The State of Welfare*. Washington, D.C.: The Brookings Institution.

Steiner, G. (1976). *The Children's Cause*. Washington, D.C.: The Brookings Institution.

Steiner, G. (1981). *The Futility of Family Policy*. Washington, D.C.: The Brookings Institution.

Steinfels, M. (1973). *Who's Minding the Children? The History and Politics of Day Care in America*. New York: Simon & Schuster.

Unco. (1976). *National Child Care Consumer Study*. Arlington, Va.: Author.

U.S. Bureau of the Census. (1982). "Trends in Child Care Arrangements of Working Mothers." In *Current Population Reports* (Series P-23, No. 117). Washington, D.C.: U.S. Government Printing Office.

U.S. Department of Health, Education, and Welfare. (1978). *The Appropriateness of the Federal Interagency Day Care Requirements*. Washington, D.C.: U.S. Government Printing Office.

U.S. House. Select Committee on Children, Youth, and Families. (1984). *Demographic and Social Trends: Implications of Federal Support of Dependent-Care Services for Children and the Elderly*. Washington, D.C.: U.S. Government Printing Office.

Werner, E. (1984). *Child Care: Kith, Kin, and Hired Hands*. Baltimore, Md.: University Park Press.

Women's Bureau. (1982). *Employers and Child Care: Establishing Services Through the Workplace*. Washington, D.C.: Department of Labor.

CHILD CUSTODY. See CHILD SUPPORT; DIVORCE AND SEPARATION; FAMILY: CONTEMPORARY PATTERNS; FAMILY: ONE PARENT.

CHILDREN

In a strictly biological sense, a child is an immature adult. From the time of conception, human beings, like other species, undergo a series of physical changes until they reach maturity, or adulthood, a stage of completed growth. To define "children" simply in biological terms is inadequate. To understand the term fully, one must ask not simply what is a "child" but rather what is the meaning of childhood. Beyond the biological classification, the meaning of childhood cannot be defined outside the context of particular social and cultural milieus, and it is within those contexts that the parameters of childhood are established. For example, the term "child" had very different connotations in 18th-century America than it does today. "Child" denotes a biological status, but equally important within the context of a given society's meaning of childhood are the attendant social and legal statuses. This article will examine the meaning of childhood first from the developmental perspective of individual children and then from the social and legal perspectives of the varying statuses accorded to children.

Developmental Perspective

As Kadushin has aptly noted (1980), childhood is a phenomenon of the 20th century. Previously, children had largely been seen as miniature adults who could assume adult responsibilities when they were biologically ready—when they were big enough. The idea of childhood as a crucial phase in human development introduced new concepts and attendant social values. The developmental perspective of today is not entirely new, but it has been transmogrified. The impact of the Darwinian concept that life is an evolutionary process hastened the perception that childhood itself was a crucial preparatory period for the evolving adult. This is evident in the work of such pioneers in child development research and theory as Hall (1904), who suggested that individual human beings developed in stages similar to those of the evolution of the species as a whole. Freudian theory, linking adult psychological functioning to early childhood experiences, heightened the interest in the manipulability of children's development and the consequences for adult functioning (Bremner, 1971).

This developmental perspective has been integral to social work theory and practice as it has developed. Even Brace (1880), as enamored as he was of the tenets of Social Darwinism, saw as a rationale for his free foster homes the beneficent effects that a "good" environment might have in freeing the latent genetic potential of immigrant slum children. The pioneering efforts of Edith and Grace Abbott and of Jane Addams centered on providing nurturing childhood experiences and education and eschewing adult responsibilities in the labor market until maturation was fostered and complete. The early child guidance movement, a key influence in the development of social work education, was predicated on understanding the stages and processes of children's personality development. Indeed, a cornerstone of social work curricula from the beginning has been an understanding of human behavior from the standpoint of developmental stages and the interaction of the individual and the environment in accomplishing developmental tasks.

Three tenets were and continue to be crucial to our concept of childhood. The first is that adults are shaped through childhood experiences. An investment in shaping childhood experiences is an investment in the future adults of the society. The second is that children's development occurs in sequential stages, with maturation at a given stage dependent on the success of previous stages. The third concerns the effects of children's environment on their developmental accomplishments. Though a genetic clock may regulate physical growth through these stages, full maturation and realization of developmental potential can be influenced, positively or negatively, by the child's environment.

How have these tenets from developmental theory shaped our conception of childhood and hence the definition of "children"? The idea of childhood has been legitimated by the belief that what happens to children while they are young has an impact on their adult functioning. Developing human beings need a chance to go through the phases necessary to achieving maturity. They are granted a state of dependency free of adult responsibilities. In a democratic society, a necessary corollary is that all children be afforded this opportunity. In America, child labor laws and compulsory universal education acknowledge this. In essence, childhood is a state of suspension from adult responsibilities and a legitimated dependency for both care and economic support. There is a corresponding social responsibility to protect children from incursions into this dependency. A crucial point in this legitimation of childhood is the potentially beneficent impact this prolonged dependency will have on the society through the kinds of adults it will produce.

The second tenet—that children pass through stages of development each dependent on the earlier stages—leads us to a differentiated concept of children. Childhood is not an all-or-none proposition. Rather, children should ideally be provided with developmentally appropriate experiences neither rushed nor retarded. A crucial concept in viewing children from this perspective is that of normalcy. In their development, children should be at certain stages at certain times, albeit within a given range of normalcy. Children who are not where they should be are suffering from developmental lags. The key question then becomes whether or not such lags are reversible, and if reversible, what compensatory mechanisms can restore normal development.

Developmental stages are further subdivided according to physical, cognitive, emotional, social, and moral development. Though these are analytically separate domains, it is becoming increasingly apparent that developmentally these spheres are highly interdependent. Emotional deprivation can stunt physical development, nutritional deprivation can retard cognitive development, and social experience is inextricably entwined with moral development. To further complicate the situation, the conception of "healthy," "normal," and "optimal" development is based essentially on value judgments not really about children but rather about what constitutes a desirable or normal adult. In a pluralistic society such as ours, these judgments are not without controversy.

The idea of stages of development is integrally linked with environmental influences. Children's needs are differentiated by their particular developmental stages and tasks, and environmental supports are predicated as necessary to the achievement of these developmental tasks. The interplay between genetic and biological influences is mediated by the environment, and while there may be inherent limitations on each individual's potential, the environment mediates in the fulfillment of that potential. Hence, normalcy or optimality in childhood can be measured in terms of how the environment contributes to the achievement of optimal potential or, at the least, the maintenance of essentials for normal development within the limits of potential capacities. Although abundant evidence supports the idea that children's development may be enhanced or retarded by environmental experiences, both nurturing and challenging, the information available is imprecise. It is unclear just what experiences are necessary and desirable to ensure maximal or even minimal or normal development. In part, this uncertainty is due to the complexity of the interactions that contribute to healthy development. Children bring their own individual characteristics to any interaction, even the inter-

uterine experience, and hence the effects of their life interactions are partly governed by these child-centered variables. Perhaps it might best be said that our present state of expertise, derived from child development theory and research, is more advanced in measuring effects on child development—that is, outcomes—than in explaining causal and contributing factors.

Given these conceptions of childhood derived from the developmental perspective, children may be defined as human beings who, because of their biological immaturity, are accorded special statuses based on their chronological age. Adult expectations are suspended for them, and dependency for both care and economic support is legitimated. Obligation for their nurturance, protection, and education is placed on their environments. As adult obligations are suspended, so also is the relative autonomy that is accorded to adults.

Social Role and Status of Children

The abstract concept of children's dependence on their environments for their developmental needs leaves open the question of just who or what bears responsibility for fulfilling those needs. Social statuses and the roles assigned to them are defined in terms of the rights and duties of those in reciprocal roles and statuses. In American society, the roles and statuses of children in relation to the broader society are for the most part mediated by the family. Primary responsibility for the development of children is assigned to the family, principally to the parents. Children's access to the rights and rewards of the society are conditioned not by their status but by their parents' status in that society. Indeed, it is virtually impossible to discuss the condition of children in America without reference to the status of their parents. In part, this is because society generally relates to children not as individuals but rather as the offspring of their parents. In a sense, from the perspective of the broader society, the dependence of children is masked by the overwhelming expectations of autonomy and independence placed on families. A fundamental policy question may be whether as a society we should have policies for children independent of those for their families, but in fact we have virtually no universal policies for either children or families. Perhaps with the exception of education, what policies we do have are for the most part predicated on compensations for parental failure to meet socially imposed obligations rather than on the assumption of society's responsibility for children and their development.

Even our knowledge about child development is based almost exclusively on the effects of parent-child interaction, especially mother-child interaction, without reference to the social contexts of the interaction, the child, or the parent. Such an approach to understanding children's development has now come under criticism by those such as Bronfenbrenner (1979) who prescribe an ecological approach to the study of human development—an approach he defines as "the scientific study of the progressive, mutual accommodation between the developing person and the changing properties of the immediate and broader contexts in which the person lives" (p. 12). Failure to account for such contexts has severely limited our understanding of all children's development, but especially of those children whose family status in society is disadvantaged and devalued. And it has severely constricted our notions of normal and optimal development in socioculturally diverse contexts.

It would be wrong to leave the impression that we have no social institutions deeply concerned with the development and enhancement of children's lives. The idealized autonomous family does not rear children without sharing responsibilities with a multiplicity of social institutions. However, in describing the role and status of children in American society, it simply is not possible to cite universal rights accruing to all children. Such rights are determined by the accident of their birth and their parents' capacity to purchase developmental supports, to link them with community resources, and to love and cherish them. By the same token, the intrafamilial experiences of children are reserved to the family enclave, which enjoys a highly valued and legally protected privacy. To be sure, the doctrine of *Parens Patriae,* that the state is the ultimate parent to the child, undergirds social institutions that can invade this privacy and infringe upon family autonomy, but the conditions under which they may do so are only vaguely defined and access to their protective mantle is uncertain.

The role and status of children in American society is at best ambiguous. While the dependence of childhood is sanctioned, it is more tolerated than encouraged. In an individualistic, achievement-oriented society, attention centers on the independent adult, and children are valued for the adults they will become, not as the children that they are. However shortsighted this attitude may be, it seems to be the dominant one.

Legal Definitions of a Child

All states define a minor person by age. Minors are entitled to certain protections of the state, and they are denied most legal rights such as buying and selling property, giving consent, and engaging in legal contracts. However, though each state declares a particular age at which one reaches adulthood, the attendant rights and obligations vary from state to state, so that the definition of a minor really is specific to particular rights and protections. Traditionally, women have been granted adult status at younger ages than men, or at younger ages if they marry. Ages vary as to when children may work, marry, give medical consent, obtain a driver's license, buy alcoholic beverages, incur civil damages, be accused of rape, consent to have sexual intercourse, and assume many other rights and responsibilities. The legal age for these activities may be 12, 16, 18, or 21. Until only recently, males were required to give military service at age 18 and men and women had the right to vote in federal elections at 21 (Mnookin, 1978).

The different ages at which children assume different rights and obligations may reflect an appreciation of differences in their capacities as they develop. To some extent, they also reflect a more general ambivalence toward the concept of childhood. In any case, the upper age bounds of what constitutes childhood for legal purposes is best considered as relative and as dynamic rather than static. While it is common to speak of children's rights, legally it makes sense only to speak of specified rights. Unless specifically granted such rights, minors do not enjoy any legal rights.

Children in the Population

Most children live with their families, but most households do not have children. In 1982, only 37.1 percent of U.S. households had one or more children living in them, representing a decline of 8.2 percent since 1970 (House of Representatives, 1983, p. 5). Unfortunately, there is no reliable data on the relationship to the children of other persons living in these households. It is generally surmised, however, that three-generation households are increasingly on the wane and the oldest and youngest generations are becoming more and more separated. Two thirds of all children live in metropolitan areas, reflecting the urban-centered nature of the rest of the population. There are sharp differences by race, however, in the distribution of children within metropolitan areas. Fifty-five percent of black children live in central cities, but only 21.3 percent of white children (House of Representatives, 1983, p. 7).

In 1982, there were 62.7 million children in the United States. They were relatively evenly distributed across age brackets, with 20.6 million age 5 or under, 19.8 million age 6 to 11, and 22.3 million age 12 to 17. The number of children declined in all age brackets after 1970, with the largest decline among those 6 to 11 years old (from 24.6 to 19.8 million). The ethnic composition of the child population changed somewhat between 1970 and 1982. The number of white children declined from 59.1 to 51.4 million, the number of black children remained constant at 9.5 million, and the number of other nonwhite children increased from 1.1 to 1.8 million[1] (House of Representatives, 1983, p. 2).

The proportion of the population that children constitute fluctuates with the birth rate, with the number of women in childbearing ages, and with the life expectancy of adults. The overall birth rate, or fertility rate, reported by the 1980 census was 68 per 1,000 women aged 15 to 44, a rate lower than that needed for the natural replacement of the population. A number of factors are offered as explanations for the continuing drop in the fertility rate, including changes in women's lifestyles and economic strains. Despite the

consistency of this trend in the birth rate, predictions of the future size of the child population and its proportion of the total population remain somewhat uncertain. This is partly because women's fertility is increasing in the lower and upper age groups, with the greatest decline occurring in the middle child-bearing years. Women who have deferred maternity until their 30s will tend to offset the decrease in the overall rate caused by women in their 20s.

Overall, it is expected that the size of the child population will increase owing simply to the number of women entering child-bearing years, which will offset the decrease in the fertility rate. Between 1970 and 1980, while fertility rates decreased markedly from 88 to 68 live births per 1,000 women of child-bearing years, the actual number of births has shown an increase since 1975. Fertility rates have declined in both the white and nonwhite populations, but the latter maintains a rate about one third higher than that among whites (House of Representatives, 1983, p. 3).

Two steady trends characterize the families that children live with. More and more are headed by women, and increasing numbers of mothers, whether married or not, work outside the home. The most rapid increase in the number of working mothers has occurred among mothers of children under 6. There is significant ethnic variation in these trends.

In 1982, 20 percent of all children lived with their mothers only and 2 percent with their fathers only. Most, however, lived with two parents—63 percent with both biological parents, 10 percent with one biological parent and one step-parent, and 2 percent with adoptive parents. Two percent lived with other relatives, and the remaining 1 percent lived with foster parents or in institutions.

Since 1970, the proportion of children living with just their mothers has risen among both white and black children, but the proportion remains much higher among blacks—47.2 percent as opposed to 15.3 percent of white children. The total number of children living with only their mothers increased by 68 percent, with the largest increases among those whose mothers were divorced or never married. The number of those living with widowed mothers declined by 17 percent (House of Representatives, 1983, pp. 8–9).

---

[1] It is difficult to obtain data on more precise ethnic classifications because available data sources use different age brackets. In 1980, there were 940,000 children of Asian Pacific descent and 675,000 American Indians under 14 and 6,282,000 people of Spanish origin under 20 (Statistical Abstracts, 1984). The term "nonwhite" used in this article is derived from the statistical source usage.

The labor force participation of children's mothers has been steadily increasing for decades. In 1983, 65.8 percent of all mothers of children age 6 to 17 were in the labor force, along with 49.9 percent of all mothers of children under 6. These figures rise with the marital status of the mother and age of the children. The lowest rate of participation in the work force occurred among married mothers with children under 6 (48.7 percent). The rate was 55.2 percent for separated mothers of young children and 67 percent for divorced mothers. Among families with children age 6 to 7, 63.2 percent of the married mothers work, 68.4 percent of the separated mothers, and 83.6 percent of the divorced mothers. Clearly the majority of children, regardless of their age, have a mother who is in the labor force. This trend has risen more rapidly among white than among black families, owing to the longer history of black women's labor force participation. Hispanic mothers have the lowest rate of labor force participation (House of Representatives, 1983, p. 13).

The importance of these trends for children cannot be overstated. The rises in both the proportion of children living with their mothers only and the proportion whose mothers are in the labor force represent dramatic changes in the conditions under which children live. Yet despite these changes, there have been no basic alterations in our national policies toward either children or their families.

It is clear that one cannot accurately describe the conditions under which children are cared for without considering extrafamilial arrangements. One estimate is that 3.5 million children under 13 receive some form of daily care from someone other than their parents. About half of them are thought to be cared for by relatives. More disturbing is the estimate that some 7 million children under 13 daily spend some time without any adult supervision. Among younger children of both working and nonworking mothers, 64 percent of those 3 to 5 years old are in part-time or full-time day nurseries (Children's Defense Fund, 1984, p. 160).

Such care is paid for in a variety of ways, but purchase of service is the principal method. Public subsidy benefits the lowest income brackets and tax credits the higher ones. It cannot be said that we have no policies about child care, but there is certainly nothing comprehensive such as the standards proposed in the Comprehensive Child Development Bill that was vetoed by President Nixon in 1972. At best we have a hodgepodge of funding and regulatory mechanisms, and we rely predominantly on market mechanisms dictating both the amount and variety of types of care available. The goals of child care are unclear. Is it primarily a social service, a means of enhancing child development, or simply an ancillary service for increasing the employability of women? The inadequacy of regulatory mechanisms has been demonstrated by recent scandals involving child care personnel's abuse of their wards. Present national policies do not suggest any change in the way the public sector emphasizes reliance on both nonprofit and proprietary agents in the private sector.

Although child care may represent the most obvious aspect of children's welfare that deserves attention as a result of changes in family structure and patterns, other attendant effects on children's lives are now being considered, including the effects of divorce, separation, and reconstituted families. Unless these changes are abated (and there is no indication that they shall be) traditional ideas about the family unit—the most fundamental element of children's lives—will soon be in need of revision if not largely obsolete.

Economic Circumstances of Children

In one sense, almost all children are poor—in fact they are penniless. Their economic status derives from their parents. The economic circumstances of children directly reflect the relative economic advantages of their parents. The dual disadvantages accruing to female and ethnic minority statuses are revealed in the data about poor children. Children in female-headed households are more likely to be poor, children of ethnic minority status are more likely to be poor, and children in both these circumstances simultaneously are most likely to be poor. In 1982, the proportion of all children under 18 who lived below the poverty level was 21.3 percent. For black children this figure was 47.3 percent, for Hispanics, 38.9 percent, and for whites, 16.5 percent. When the threshold is raised to 125 percent of the poverty level, 56.1 percent of black children, 48.2 percent of Hispanic children, and 22 percent of white children can be considered as living in poverty. Thus, virtually half of black and Hispanic children live in poverty or at the threshold of poverty (House of Representatives, 1983, p. 17).

The relationship between the economic conditions of children and their family structure and ethnicity is clearly revealed in 1979 data on median family incomes of related children under 18. Among all children, the median family income was $19,732. For white two-parent families it was $22,714. At the other extreme, among Hispanic families with mothers only, the median income was $5,934. The median incomes of black and Hispanic families were always less than that of whites, whether two-parent or mother-only families (House of Representatives, 1983, p. 16). Maternal unemployment is a growing contributing factor to children's poverty. More women are in the labor force, but rates of unemployment among them are steadily rising. In 1982, unemployment was particularly high among separated mothers with young children (20.1 percent) and those divorced (14.6 percent) (House of Representatives, 1983, p. 13).

For children whose fathers are absent, child support payments remain an unlikely source of relief. Barely one third of women with children receive payments from absent fathers. White, divorced, college-educated women are the most likely to be awarded child support and to obtain it. The average amounts, both awarded and received, are small among all groups (House of Representatives, 1983, p. 20).

The major program devoted to income maintenance for children is Aid to Families with Dependent Children (AFDC). Because of its selectivity, it is the most influential one for poor children, but some children are aided through Supplemental Security Income and as dependents of parents covered under Old Age Survivors Disability Insurance. Although intended to assist poor children, the AFDC program is administered in such a way that neither their poverty nor their status as children are paramount in the policy impact. The federal government pays for half the benefits, but individual states determine the level of benefit according to each state's needs standards. In 1982, every state's needs standard fell below the federal poverty line and often very far below. Eligibility requirements do not center on children's needs, but rather on a multiplicity of factors reflecting their parents' status. For example, poor children of working parents and of unemployed fathers are likely not to receive aid. Twenty-seven states do not participate in the optional AFDC Unemployed Parent Program, which provides aid to intact families with one or both parents unemployed. Even in states that do participate, many such families still go unaided. The end result of these policies is that while AFDC may be the most important program aiding poor children, it is estimated that it benefits less than half the children in low-income families and does not substantially reduce the poverty of those who are aided. There is every indication that the scope of coverage of AFDC is diminishing through increasing restrictions on eligibility and coverage. The proportion of children receiving AFDC in 1981 declined to 11.3 percent from 11.9 percent in 1975, while the proportion of children living in poverty increased from 16.8 percent to 19.5 percent. AFDC benefit payments vary widely from state to state. In 1982, the average monthly family payment was $310 and the lowest was $92. Nationally, the average payment per recipient was $106. When corrected for inflation, the average payment per recipient in 1982 was barely above the 1965 level (House of Representatives, 1983, p. 52).

The AFDC cash program is not the only public subsidy for meeting poor children's needs. There are three nutritional programs: the Food Stamp program, the School Lunch Program, and the Special Supplementary Feeding Program for Women, Infants and Children (WIC). For all three programs, eligible recipient populations have grown steadily while federal fiscal constraints continue to challenge program viability. The number of children served in the National School Lunch program rose steadily through the 1970s before falling in the 1980s, with 23.6 million lunches served in 1982. In 1982, there were 2.4 million recipients of WIC program benefits (House of Representatives, 1983, pp. 55–56).

The information about health status and educational opportunity shows that poverty among children persists as a serious threat to their well-being and future life chances.

Health

Infant mortality in the United States has demonstrated three persistent trends. First, it is consistently going down. Second, it remains, at least for some groups, higher than that in other countries. And third, the black infant mortality rate remains about twice that of the white rate, though they have both decreased proportionately. Since 1974, infant mortality rates for black and white infants have decreased by about 3.5 percent, but while the black rate in 1982 was 19.6 deaths per 1,000 births, the white rate was only 10.1 (National Center for Health Statistics, 1982).

Several other indices on children's health indicate improvements but again with marked disparities by race and income. Approximately one third of all black children but less than 15 percent of white children have been judged to have some kind of nutritional deficit. Children under 6 in poor families had almost twice as many bed disability days as those in the highest income brackets, and the number of hospital days per child was four times greater for poor children than for those in the highest income category (U.S. Public Health Service, 1981).

One of the greatest improvements in children's health has come about through the control of infectious diseases. Once a leading cause of both death and disability, these diseases have become much less of a threat. However, these gains could be in jeopardy according to a current estimate that inoculation against these diseases is decreasing and that at present almost 60 percent of all preschool children have not been inoculated against these preventable diseases. Largely owing to school requirements, 95 percent of children entering kindergarten have now been immunized (House of Representatives, 1983, p. 35).

Health problems among infants account for most child deaths. By adolescence, accidents and violence replace health problems and disease as primary causes of death. Suicide rates have more than doubled since 1960 among all adolescents except black females. They are highest among males, especially white males. Rates of death by homicide have increased for children over the last two decades. Although homicide deaths are most prevalent among older adolescents, they occur more frequently among very young children than among school-age children. Rates for males are three to five times higher than for females and several times higher for black than for white youths (House of Representatives, 1983, p. 33).

Although data on illness and mortality reveal much about the status of children's health, other information is needed to determine the adequacy of available health care. One important indicator is the number of physician visits. Healthy children need not see a physician, but regular medical examination will help prevent morbidity. It was estimated that in 1981, one in 10 children had not seen a physician in two or more years. Among younger children, 2.7 percent had not had medical attention, and the proportion rose to 13.4 percent for those 6 to 16. Besides children's age, the parents' level of education was another major variable related to children's visits to physicians. As for dental care, one in three had not had a dental examination in over a year. Here, the differential among children was primarily due to family income differences and likely due to the lack of third-party payments for dental care (House of Representatives, 1983, p. 38).

About three fourths of all children have their medical care paid for by parents' private health insurance. Those most likely to have such coverage are from better-educated and two-parent families with higher incomes. About half of black children at any given time and about half of the children with absent fathers have no such coverage. Medicaid is the predominant source of medical care for poorer children. Because Medicaid is a state program, coverage is grossly uneven; benefits and regulations tend to favor care for illness over preventive care. Nonetheless, Medicaid has provided medical care to children who otherwise might not have received it, and it has reduced differentials in health care coverage among children of parents with varying economic means. Children are not, however, the primary beneficiaries of Medicaid. Though children constituted 48 percent of Medicaid recipients, the proportion of total vendor payments expended on children in 1982 was only 13 percent (House of Representatives, 1983, p. 53).

Education

Universal education for children through high school remains our only national policy for children. Since 1970, the number of children enrolled in school has declined with the decrease in the school-age population. The proportion of all children enrolled, however, has remained steady at about 94 percent, but the proportion of young children in preschool has increased from 21 percent to 36 percent. About a half million children are enrolled in the federally funded Headstart program for 4-year-olds. Approximately 90 percent of the children enrolled continue to attend public schools (House of Representatives, 1983, p. 21).

The proportion of children completing high school continues to rise, but high school dropouts remain a significant concern. Between 1971 and 1981, estimates of high school dropout rates among white youths fell by 3 percent to 12.1 percent, and among black youths by 8 percent to 17.9 percent. There are gross regional differences, however, and according to some recent estimates, as much as half the inner-city high school age population may drop out (Grant & Snyder, 1984, p. 71).

The classroom achievements of children in both reading and mathematics show greater improvements for black and Hispanic children than for white children. Reading Achievement Test scores for blacks rose by 10 percent between 1970 and 1980, but only by 3 percent among white children, narrowing the gap to a 10 percent differential favoring the latter. Similarly, in Mathematics Achievement Test scores, black and hispanic children's scores showed an improvement of 6.5 percent; white children's gains were half that, but still exceeded the other absolute scores by about 13 percent (House of Representatives, 1983, pp. 24–25). In the results of the Scholastic Aptitude Test, this pattern was even more pronounced. Black examinees' scores rose by 10 percent between 1976 and 1983; those of whites declined by 7 percent, but still retained a 100 point difference in their favor. Female reading achievement continues to be higher than males', whereas males' math achievement and SAT scores tend to be somewhat higher than females' (House of Representatives, 1983, p. 26).

In some areas of the country with large immigrant populations, bilingual education has become increasingly important, and some controversy has arisen concerning the methods for teaching children whose native language is not English. The federally funded Bilingual Education Program has shown a steady increase in the proportion of children served, but funding levels have not increased accordingly. About $3.5 million are currently budgeted for this program with no anticipated increases, although the number of children enrolled has risen 12 percent (Children's Defense Fund, 1984, p. 138).

Special educational resources for children include those for slow learners, the speech impaired, visually and hearing impaired, developmentally disabled, and emotionally disturbed. The proportion of children with specific handicapping conditions has remained fairly constant, with about 13 percent of children recognized as slow learners, 5 percent as speech impaired or emotionally disturbed, and about 1 percent as having one of the other conditions. However, the proportion of children receiving special school resources has increased in each category by about one third to one half, except for emotionally disturbed children, of whom only an estimated 25 percent are served. The passage of the Education for All Handicapped Children Act in 1975 has significantly affected the availability of resources. Nonetheless, only about half of the children in need of these services have access to them (House of Representatives, 1983, p. 23).

In general, then, education benefits for children are gradually increasing. As with health status and services, there are still large discrepancies between white and nonwhite children, but the latter are making significant gains and the disparities are narrowing.

Children with Special Needs

As indicated in the discussion of the developmental perspective, all children have special needs relative to adults. Nonetheless, we do observe special categories of children; many of these simply echo adult categories of deviance, but some are particular to children's status. Even children whose problems mirror those of adults, such as delinquents and the mentally ill, call for special treatment because of their childhood needs and dependence. Children with special needs are of particular concern to social work, and indeed the profession itself has developed, over the last 100 years, out of the professionalization of services to particular categories of children. Yet though children may be categorized according to particular needs and problems, none of these are mutually exclusive, and often multiple problems appear in the same child. Despite this, social institutional resources remain separated according to problem designations, making it difficult for any given system of service to treat the "whole child." There have been some sporadic efforts to create separate "children's" departments at both the state and local level, but none of these has included services for all children. Continuing dangers of such a disarticulated service delivery system are the shunting of children from one system to another (for example, from mental health to juvenile justice facilities) and the failure to provide any service to children who "fall through the cracks" because they do not fit readily into any given category. Whatever problems children have, they all share some universal needs: a place to live and an education. Children with special needs, however, are at risk of having these fundamental needs eclipsed by a primary focus on their problems.

In serving children with developmental disabilities and physical handicaps, the major guiding policies have been, as with adults, those of deinstitutionalization and of "mainstreaming" them with their peers, whenever possible. These efforts have proved successful, and the number of children in long-term institutional care continues to decline while the proportion in the public education system rises. Children requiring some special living arrangements are now most typically cared for in small institutions or group homes (U.S. Public Health Service, 1981, p. 76).

Mental Health. The mental health status of children is almost impossible even to estimate. Children may receive care in specialty mental health settings (such as psychiatric hospitals, community mental health centers, and residential treatment centers) or in private practice settings. However, the mental health problems of children are just as likely to be cared for in a number of other settings, including family social service agencies, school systems, and the correctional system. The adaptability and availability of services for children in specialty mental health settings remains problematic. There are few specialized child therapists, and inpatient facilities are often ill adapted to

children's needs when they exist at all. Although the community mental health movement has sharply defined the civil rights of adults in relation to mental hospitals, children enjoy no such protection. Overall, the advances made in the treatment of the adult mentally ill have not been paralleled for children (U.S. Public Health Service, 1981, pp. 76–77).

The less severe mental health problems of children, as noted, are apt to be treated in a variety of settings and under a wide array of problem classifications. Thus, while receiving services, many children with mental health problems may go officially undiagnosed. Exact statistics are lacking for the number of children receiving care, the natures and types of their problems, and the types of treatment provided.

A number of diagnostic classifications specific to children have been developed and refined, including childhood autism, hyperkinesis, school phobia, specific learning disorders, and conduct disorders. Perhaps the best that can be said about mental health services for children with problems is that diagnostic knowledge outstrips the availability of services, and this may remain so until children's services are fully separated from those for adults.

Two problems related to children's mental health have gained increasing attention. These are adolescent suicide, discussed previously, and substance abuse. Where the line should be drawn between substance use and abuse is debatable, but data on the use of various drugs by high school students would certainly put a significant number at risk for serious abuse problems. In a 1981 survey, 71 percent of high school seniors reported using alcohol in the previous month, 32 percent marijuana, 16 percent stimulants, 6 percent cocaine, and about 8 percent LDS, PCP, or heroin. The percentages among children not in high school would most likely be even larger. Alcoholism among teenagers and even younger children is now recognized as a growing problem as well. Although special programs for children are now being developed, these problems pose a serious challenge for the future (House of Representatives, 1983, p. 39).

Delinquency. Two trends have characterized the treatment of juvenile offenders over the last decade: The treatment of children accused of serious crimes is becoming harsher, while those accused of offenses that are crimes only for children are receiving more lenient or no treatment at all. These trends stem from two changes in ideology. The adult criminal justice system has been moving away from rehabilitation toward punishment and away from punishment that fits the offender (as the practice of indeterminate sentences was intended to do) toward punishment that fits the crime. In the juvenile sphere, adaptation of this thinking has led to more children who have committed serious crimes being adjudicated in the adult rather than juvenile courts. For children whose offenses are crimes only for children (such as truancy, runaway, and incorrigibility), the trend has been in the opposite direction. In many states, such children can no longer be incarcerated in locked facilities and consequently the number of them adjudicated in court has declined markedly. What is happening to them is not known, but some evidence indicates that some are being admitted to mental hospitals with diagnoses such as "behavior disorder" or coming to the attention of Child Protective Services as "out of control of parents" or "abused children." Overall, the handling of delinquents has been influenced by the deinstitutionalization philosophy. The populations of large state institutions have declined, with preference shown for locality-based facilities and probation.

Teenage Pregnancy and Parenthood. Young women pregnant out of wedlock have been a concern of the social work profession since its very beginning. The focus of concern has changed, however, in relation to adolescence, because the number of births to teenagers has increased and the majority of these young mothers now elect to keep their babies rather than place them for adoption. Hence the concern is now not simply with their pregnancy and childbirth but with their parenthood.

Although birthrates have increased among youths of all ages, the relative rates among different age groups bear mention. For children aged 10 to 14, the rate is 30 times lower than for those aged 15 to 17. It is three times greater among those aged 18 to 19 than for those 15 to 17. For 15- to 17-year-olds, the white rate is a third of that for whites 18 to 19,

but among blacks, it is half the rate of the older age group. Birth rates among young black women in these age brackets are several times higher than for white females, but the rates among the latter are increasing while the rates among the former are decreasing (U.S. Public Health Service, 1981, p. 119).

There is no doubt that teenage pregnancy creates problems for both the children giving birth and the children that they bear. Whether they are bearing children in or out of wedlock, younger women tend less often to have had prenatal care, to have children with lower birth weights, and to have higher infant mortality rates. At the national level, one response to these problems has been the creation of the Office of Teen Age Pregnancy in the U.S. Public Health Service, which has primarily been concerned with research and demonstration project funding. In both the public and private sectors at local levels, numerous other programs have emerged intent on providing supports to these young mothers and particularly on enabling them to complete their education; aborted education is one of the greatest economic hazards of early motherhood.

Resolution of the problem is uncertain. On the one hand, premarital sexual experience among adolescents is increasing. Over 70 percent of 19-year-old females are estimated to be sexually experienced, and 80 percent of males. On the other hand, national controversy over abortion and the providing of contraceptive information and services to teenagers without their parents' consent leaves the essential remedies for teenage pregnancy in doubt. As a nation, we seem not to have come to grips with children's sexuality and the changing mores about it. Not only is the rate of teen pregnancy and childbearing in the United States higher than in any other developed country, it is the only one in which such rates are increasing (House of Representatives, 1983, p. 43).

Dependent Children. Although the term "dependent children" might be reserved for those so adjudicated by a court, it is used here in the traditional sense to designate children in need of child welfare services (protective services, foster care, and adoption), including abused and neglected children. Child abuse has become a nationally recognized problem in the last decade, though it is one that has concerned the profession of social work for over a century. Although the treatment of the problem is an interdisciplinary one involving medical, legal, and mental health professionals as well as social work, the specialized child welfare services or child protective services are the primary social response to child abuse and neglect. Whether actual child abuse is increasing or not is unknown, but reported child abuse has continually risen in the last decade. Although the traditional definition has referred primarily to abuse engendered within the family, concern with sexual abuse of children by unrelated persons has received national attention in the mid-1980s.

In 1980, the Adoption Assistance and Child Welfare Act (Public Law 96–272) enunciated a new philosophy for child welfare services. The law responded to concerns about maintaining family integrity by preventing foster home care and to the problem of children lingering in foster care without permanent parents. The service model prescribed by the law for states requires verification of service efforts to maintain family integrity when possible, to reunite families when children are removed, and if such reunification is not possible, to free children for adoption. States are presently implementing this prescription, and it is too soon to determine the feasibility of attaining these policy goals. Nonetheless, the policy constitutes an essential rethinking of the approach to traditional child welfare services and is bound to have some impact on the shape and nature of the distribution of these services in the future.

Social Work and Children

The predominant focus of professional social work has been with the special needs of children described above, whether in primary social work settings such as child welfare facilities or in secondary settings such as schools and hospitals. This does not mean that the profession is not concerned with all children but rather that direct service intervention has focused on those with special needs (Kadushin, 1980).

In the direct service realm, social work has predominantly been concerned with services that Kahn (1979, p. 30) terms "therapy, help, rehabilitation and social protection" in relation to children with special needs. How-

ever, social work—particularly group social work—has long been involved in services aimed at socialization and development. Through such organizations as Settlement Houses, religiously oriented groups, and youth associations, social workers engage at all levels in providing children with enhanced developmental experiences, not simply corrective ones. For example, social workers in schools have increasingly branched out into preventive programs for all pupils, not simply corrective services for troublesome ones. Yet given our national policy stance toward children—that they are fundamentally the responsibility of their families, not of the society—it is readily understandable why social work's role in the general development of all children has been limited. That it will remain so in the future seems likely, and according to some, it is desirable. Morris (1978), for one, has advocated that social work take an even more predominant role in creating humane environments for dependent populations, including dependent children and those with special needs.

Social work's involvement with children is not limited to the direct service level. Many national organizations—including the Child Welfare League of America, Family Service America, the Children's Division of the American Humane Association, and the National Association of Social Workers—play an active advocacy role for children, along with such organizations as the Children's Defense Fund and the Black Child Development Institute. Legislative advocacy at both the state and federal levels, fact gathering, and advocacy in both the private and public sectors are ongoing activities of these organizations. In the public sector, the U.S. Children's Bureau, as part of the Agency for Children, Youth and Families of the Department of Health and Human Services, continues to play the predominant role in meeting children's needs through the federal government, though its scope has been markedly diminished.

As a profession, social work must continue to play a dual role in relation to children, providing direct service primarily aimed at special needs children and advocating and forming policy to improve the lot of all children. Helping children who have already been hurt becomes vastly more difficult in a national environment devoid of universal supports for families and children. Overall, children are fairly healthy, well educated, and problem free—provided that their parents are. But clearly some children are much better off than others. Poverty continues to be a dominant factor shaping the lives of vast numbers of children, and racism and sexism compound the noxious influence that poverty has on their life chances and their development into the adults of our society. A common slogan has been "Children are our most important resource." It is time for that market-oriented sentiment to be reversed. Children are important because they are children, important for the human beings they are now, not simply as the ones they might become. We should devote our most important resources to them, as a profession and as a nation.

JEANNE M. GIOVANNONI

For further information, see AID TO FAMILIES WITH DEPENDENT CHILDREN; CHILD ABUSE AND NEGLECT; CHILD CARE SERVICES; CHILD SEXUAL ABUSE; CHILD SUPPORT; CHILD WELFARE SERVICES; FAMILY: CONTEMPORARY PATTERNS; FOSTER CARE FOR CHILDREN; GROUP CARE FOR CHILDREN; HUMAN DEVELOPMENT: BIOLOGICAL PERSPECTIVE; HUMAN DEVELOPMENT: PSYCHOLOGICAL PERSPECTIVE; HUMAN DEVELOPMENT: SOCIOCULTURALPERSPECTIVE; MENTAL HEALTH AND ILLNESS IN CHILDREN; PROTECTIVE SERVICES FOR CHILDREN; SCHOOL SOCIAL WORK.

References

Brace, C. L. (1880). *The Dangerous Classes of New York City and Twenty Years' Work among Them* (3rd ed.). New York: Wynkoop & Hallenbeck.

Bremner, R. H. (Ed.). (1971). *Children and Youth in America: A Documentary History: Vol. 2. 1866–1932.* Cambridge, Mass.: Harvard University Press.

Bronfenbrenner, U. (1979). *The Ecology of Human Development: Experiments by Nature and Design.* Cambridge, Mass.: Harvard University Press.

Children's Defense Fund. (1984). *A Children's Defense Budget: An Analysis of the President's FY 1985 Budget and Children.* Washington, D.C.: Children's Defense Fund.

Grant, W. V., & Snyder, T. P. (1984). *Digest of Education Statistics 1983–1984.* Washington, D.C.: National Center for Educational Statistics.

Hall, G. S. (1904). *Adolescence, Its Psychology and Its Relation to Physiology, Anthropology, Sociology, Sex, Crime, Religion, and Education.* New York: D. Appleton & Co.

House of Representatives (1983). *U.S. Children and their Families: Current Conditions and Recent Trends.* New York: Foundation for Child Development (Reprinted).

Kadushin, A. (1980). *Child Welfare.* New York: Macmillan Publishing Co.

Kahn, A. J. (1979). *Social Policy and Social Services.* New York: Random House. (1978).

Mnookin, R. H. (1978). *Child, Family and State: Problems and Materials on Children and the Law.* Boston: Little, Brown & Co.

Morris, R. (1978). "Caring for Vs. Caring About People." *Social Work, 22*(5), 353–359.

National Center for Health Statistics. (1982). "Births, Marriages, Divorces and Deaths for 1982," *Monthly Vital Statistics Report, 31* (2), 16–22.

U. S. Bureau of the Census. (1984). *Statistical Abstract of the United States: 1984–85* (105th ed.) Washington, D.C.: U.S. Government Printing Office.

U.S. Public Health Services. (1981). *Better Health for Our Children: A National Strategy* (Vol. 3). Washington, D.C.: U.S. Government Printing Office.

Reader's Guide

CHILDREN AND YOUTH

The following articles contain information on this general topic:

Adolescent Pregnancy
Adolescents
Adoption
Child Abuse and Neglect
Child Care Services
Children
Child Sexual Abuse
Child Support
Child Welfare Services
Foster Care for Children
Group Care for Children
Juvenile Justice System
Juvenile Offender Diversion and Community-Based Services
Juvenile Offender Institutions
Juvenile Offenders and Delinquency
Protective Services for Children
Runaways
School Social Work
Youth Service Agencies

CHILD SEXUAL ABUSE

Although legal definitions of child sexual abuse vary, there is increasing agreement among social workers and other helping professionals that sexual abuse of children involves coercive or nonconsenting sexual acts (Berliner & Stevens, 1982). The acts children are exposed to include all kinds of "normal" and "deviant" sexuality. The concept of sexual abuse incorporates a number of dimensions, including an age difference between partners, the presence of force or coercion, and the developmental appropriateness of the behavior itself.

An age difference between sexual partners of five years or more is regarded as an abusive situation when one partner is a child or young person. Berliner and Stevens (1982) refer to this form of sexual abuse as sexual exploitation, which involves an inequality between the sexual partners (when, for example, an older person uses superior knowledge, resources, or skills to manipulate the younger person into a sexual relationship).

Force or coercion is almost always present in sexual abuse situations. Although the degree of physical force varies considerably, there is an increasing recognition that sexual abuse of children is not as nonviolent as was previously thought. For instance, in the Seattle sample described by Conte and Berliner (1981), force was threatened or used in 38 percent of the cases. The Washington, D.C., sample described by Rogers and Thomas (1984) reported a higher rate of violence: 50 percent. Even without the presence or the threat of force, sexual abuse of children involves coercion. Much abuse begins at an age when the child does not fully understand the nature of the act taking place and when the child lacks the cognitive, emotional, and physical power to say no to the behavior. Finkelhor (1979a) suggested that because these conditions make it impossible for a child to give informed consent to sexual contact with an adult, all sexual contact with children is abusive.

The extent to which the behavior is developmentally appropriate for the child can also be helpful in determining whether it is sexual abuse. Professional concern for children involved in sexual behavior lies with whether children have the physical, intellectual, and emotional capacity to deal with and understand the behavior. In most cases, there is little reasonable disagreement about whether a specific type of behavior is inappropriate. For example, having a 6-year-old child perform oral sex on an adult is not likely to be regarded as developmentally appropriate by most professionals. Ambiguities arise in other situations, however. For example, is a father who routinely walks around his house naked in front of his young children sexually abusing them? This situation is ambiguous because of the absence of data on normal sexual behavior in families, conflicting clinical theories about the degree to which children are sexually stimulated by visual stimuli, and the lack of sufficient clinical data in this brief vignette to make a judgment. In the vast majority of cases, however, the sexual nature of the behavior makes it clear that the behavior is abusive.

Trends

Professionals have long recognized adult sexual use of children as a problem. In the 1890s, Freud suggested a link between childhood sexual abuse and the development of hysterical illness. Only recently, however, have professionals and the public recognized that large numbers of children are sexually abused. The Sexual Assault Center (1984) at Harborview Medical Center in Seattle indicated that in 1979 sexually abused children comprised about 3 percent of its client population; in 1983, over 65 percent (1,174) of its clients were children. The increase in the number of identified cases is dramatic, and in many communities the number of cases is outstripping the capacity of public and private agencies to investigate and provide services.

National statistics on the incidence of child sexual abuse are difficult to obtain. Most professionals are deeply distrustful of official reports to child protection units of state social service departments, even though there is little clear evidence of biases (such as overestimating cases from lower socioeconomic groups) that they fear may distort the data supplied by such official reporting systems. Most incidence studies are based on special populations, such as college undergraduates, or on one region of the country, such as San Francisco. The greatest problem with figures describing the incidence of sexual abuse is that they are so large that they tend to create disbelief in the public and among many professionals.

In spite of these limitations, such figures can be helpful in obtaining a sense of the magnitude of the problem. In a survey of Boston area college undergraduates, Finkelhor (1979b) found that 20 percent of the females and 9 percent of the males had been sexually abused before turning 18. In a methodologically noteworthy study, Russell (1984) surveyed a random sample of 900 homes in San Francisco and found that 38 percent of the female respondents had been sexually abused before turning 18 (28 percent before they had turned 14). This survey did not address the incidence of male victimization. Clinical estimates place the proportion of males in large samples of victims at around 20 percent.

Because there are virtually no data on trends, it is impossible to describe nationally or regionally what the pattern of abuse cases is and how it is likely to change over time. Many states are reporting dramatic increases in the number of allegations of child sexual abuse. In regions with longer histories of public recognition of the problem and corresponding histories of active reporting, professionals have reached intriguing, although preliminary, tentative conclusions. For example, in Seattle, which has almost a ten-year history of attention to child sexual abuse, the average age of the victims and the duration of their exposure to abuse are both decreasing. This may suggest that public and professional awareness of the problem has the effect of identifying cases earlier.

Although case demographics vary, general patterns are consistent throughout the country. Children are abused by a wide range of adults, the overwhelming majority of whom are either known by or related to the child. Only a minority of the cases involve strangers abusing children. The data that Conte and Berliner (1981) reported on 583 children epitomized the pattern that most centers find: fathers were the abusers in 15 percent of the cases, stepfathers in 15 percent, and other family members, such as brothers or grandparents, in 16 percent, adults not related to but known by the child, such as friends of the family, teachers, or others in authority over the child, accounted for 45 percent of the cases; strangers assaulted the child in 9 percent of the cases.

Virtually no cross-cultural or racial data are available in the United States. A widespread clinical belief is that child sexual abuse occurs in every cultural and racial group; however, data supporting this belief are not available.

Social and Psychological Factors

Clinical Perspective. Until recently, clinicians generally described only two kinds of sexual abuse of children: incest and pedophilia. The incestuous family received the majority of professional social work attention. Although there is no single "family" perspective on incest, the various family-oriented approaches rest on a common set of assumptions (for discussion, see Conte, 1985). Incest is the sexual expression of nonsexual needs, such as the offender's need for personal affirmation through sexual contact with a nonthreatening partner. Traditional family views also held that incestuous men did not act out sexually outside the home, and that every member of the family had a psychological reason to create and maintain the problem.

Traditional views of incest are increasingly being challenged for not conforming to case realities. For example, the notion that sexual abuse of children is the sexual expression of nonsexual needs loses much of its meaning when it is noted that virtually all sexuality contains nonsexual components. More important, physiological assessments of sexual arousal provide evidence that incestuous offenders are sexually aroused by children (see, for example, Quinsey, Chaplin, & Carrigan, 1979). New data also indicate that some incestuous men, at least 44 percent, abuse children outside the home during the time they are having sexual contact with their own children (Abel, 1983).

Evidence also suggests that incestuous and nonincestuous offenders share many characteristics. For example, both groups consist of dependent, inadequate individuals with early family histories characterized by conflict, disruption, abandonment, abuse, and exploitation (see, for example, Swanson, 1968; Groth, Hobson, & Gary 1982; and Panton, 1979), although it is not exactly clear how these characteristics are specifically related to sexual abuse. Other studies present data that are inconclusive or not clearly integrated with other empirical work. For example, some adults who have sex with children were themselves abused as children, but others have no prior history of sexual victimization (see, for example, Groth, 1979). Although incestuous and nonincestuous offenders both show sexual arousal to children generally, incestuous offenders appear to exhibit sexual arousal to their own age peers as well (Quinsey, Chaplin, & Carrigan, 1979).

The evidence from these and other studies thus calls into question the traditional clinical view that sexual abuse of children consists of either incest or pedophilia. It may be more appropriate to perceive a continuum in such abuse: some adults have sex only with their own children, others may have sex only with children to whom they are not related, and others may have sex with either type of child. Most important, it is premature to select any set of social or psychological variables as having a causative role in the development of adult sexual interest in children. Current knowledge simply does not support one model of etiology over others (for discussion, see Finkelhor, 1984).

Impact of Sexual Abuse. The effects of sexual victimization on children are the subject of much public and professional discussion. Social workers in many settings see children who have been referred for an assessment of the impact of sexual abuse and for treatment when appropriate. A large body of research on the effects of sexual abuse is available and has been summarized (see, for example, Browne & Finkelhor, 1984; Conte, 1984a). The studies indicate that not all victims are severely or permanently damaged by sexual abuse and that sexually abused clients may experience a range of effects, including depression, guilt, learning difficulties, sexual acting out, running away, somatic complaints (such as headaches and stomachaches), hysterical seizures, phobias, nightmares, compulsive rituals, self-destructive behaviors, and suicide. Adults victimized as children also reflect problems in living thought to be associated with a history of victimization, including a negative self-image, depression, problems in interpersonal relationships (such as mistrust of men), sexual problems, and alcohol and drug abuse.

A few studies have attempted to identify variables that account for different effects of sexual abuse. Unfortunately, these studies do not completely agree. Finkelhor (1979b) found that abuse involving victims of an older age (especially females), older partners, male abusers (regardless of the sex of the victim), and force in the abuse were associated with a more severe impact. The type of sexual behavior, its duration, and the number of times the abuse occurred were not associated with traumatic reactions. Russell (1984) found that the more serious sexual behavior and the duration and frequency of abuse were associated with negative effects.

The available evidence on the impact of sexual abuse seems to indicate that not all children will be permanently damaged by such abuse. Insufficient data are available to identify the children most likely to suffer the most extreme reactions. Therefore, social workers should continue to make an assessment of impact one of the major tasks during their first meetings with sexually abused children and adults victimized as children.

Contemporary Debates

A number of issues are hotly debated among professionals working with sexual abuse cases or are likely to be so in the near future:

Prosecution versus Treatment. Professionals dealing with sexual abuse devote a great deal of energy to debating the appropriate role of justice system in handling sexual abuse cases. Social workers opposed to the involvement of the justice system tend to regard the handling of these cases by justice system personnel and agencies as inherently insensitive. They tend to equate the actions of the justice system with punishment for a mental health problem, and in many cases they feel personally uncomfortable about working with clients whom they might have to report to the justice system.

Social workers recognizing an appropriate role for the justice system tend to believe that many cases of child sexual abuse need the authority of the justice system to encourage offenders' participation in treatment; they recognize that social work lacks the authority and power to ensure that children will not be pressured to change the story of their victimization or be reabused. As increasing numbers of cases are identified in communities throughout the United States, this is a debate many social workers will have to resolve (Conte, 1984b).

Incest versus Pedophilia. As the preceding section on clinical perspectives suggests, a major debate rages over how best to conceptualize adult sexual use of children. This debate includes disagreement about whether sexual abuse is a mental health problem without sexual dimensions or whether it is at least partly a sexual problem. This debate has significant implications for the kinds of interventions that are offered adults who sexually abuse children and, consequently, for the likelihood that treatment will be successful. Viewing incest as fundamentally different from other paraphilias imposes a premature closure on the debate and deprives many social workers of important information developed in the specialized literature dealing with paraphilia. Most important, it deprives clients of potentially useful therapies (Greer & Stuart, 1983).

Children's Credibility. As increasing numbers of child abuse cases are identified, increasing numbers are also unfounded. It is not clear whether increasing numbers of unfounded cases are due to increased workloads within child protection agencies, more false reporting of child sexual abuse, or some other factor. It is clear that the public and professional communities are faced with highly publicized cases in which children are reported to have lied about their victimization ("The Tragedy of Jordan," 1984). The problem of supposedly false reports is exacerbated because there is no research on the issue of children's false reports of victimization. In addition, cases are occasionally poorly handled by professionals, and consequently evidence validating reports is not collected, or children are pressured to change their stories. Professional mishandling of cases and ongoing disbelief that the problem really is as bad as it appears to be occasionally combine to invalidate what children report. Clinical experience suggests that few children falsely report victimization. Social workers must make it clear to clients and the public that justice system actions that fail to validate child abuse allegations, find offenders not guilty, or decline to bring charges do not mean that the children's reports are false. Rather, these actions mean that judicial criteria for decision making have not been satisfied—that the charges filed have not met judicial requirements. A backlash is forming against believing what children report. Social workers can have an important role in handling this backlash so that it does not result in harm to children.

Standards of Practice. Clinical practice in child sexual abuse is so new that there are virtually no guidelines for it. To date no professional group has identified what areas of knowledge, what treatment skills, or what special qualifications are essential to practice in this area. Clinical work in child sexual abuse cases has much in common with other kinds of clinical work in which violations of the law, risk of violence, and other harms (for example, pressure to recant) are major issues, along with such professional issues as confidentiality and legal liability if vulnerable clients are not protected. Although there has been insufficient conceptual and empirical work in this area of practice to determine what special treatment issues are confronted in providing service to these clients, clinical experience suggests that there are a number of such issues. For example, therapists report that adults victimized as children have particular difficulty in forming trusting therapeutic relationships.

Given the large number of theories on which to base practice and the lack of practice standards identifying the knowledge and training that are essential before individuals provide service to clients, it is likely that some service provided to clients will be misdirected, based on weak theory, or delivered by poorly trained individuals. In time, program evaluation data are likely to identify what programs are successful. However, it is also likely that these data will only partially set standards for practice. Social workers would do well to begin developing standards for practice that protect the clients they see and that also protect the profession from assaults by those (for example, the American Medical Association) who prefer that others control the provision of therapeutic services.

Role of Social Work

Because social workers in virtually every field of practice are likely to come in contact with sexually abused children or with adults victimized as children and because social work has long had as its central perspective the person-situation interaction, social workers are in a unique position to fulfill a vital role in the treatment of this major problem. This role, which describes a time-honored view of what a direct practice worker does, includes the tasks of case identification; initial assessment and crisis intervention; referral to other agencies with a role in treating child sexual abuse, including medical services, law enforcement, social services, and mental health services; advocacy on behalf of individual clients to ensure that they are treated appropriately by these systems and on behalf of all clients to develop procedures and policies to ensure that all systems are operated in the clients' best interests; and direct service. Service needs include a range of social services that make it possible for adults to choose to protect children rather than, for example, live with a breadwinner who sexually abuses children. Such services include emergency shelter and job training programs or state-monitored child care arrangements that ensure that children are placed in environments where they are safe from sexual victimization. Service needs also include mental health interventions for abused children, their families, and adults who sexually abuse children.

Various professional groups have legitimate roles in a coordinated response to childhood sexual victimization, but social work is the only profession with a history of integrating or coordinating services. Although the service broker or case manager role should not be the only one social workers undertake, it is an important one in serving these clients, and it is one that the profession executes well.

The vast explosion in the number of sexual abuse cases currently coming to the attention of social workers in a wide range of practice settings suggests that services to these clients will remain an important part of social work in the future. It also suggests that the profession will serve both its clients' and its own future if it continues to assist in the development of new knowledge about all aspects of childhood sexual victimization.

JON R. CONTE

For further information, see CHILD ABUSE AND NEGLECT; PROTECTIVE SERVICES FOR CHILDREN; SEXUAL ASSAULT SERVICES.

References

Abel, G. (1983, September). "Treatment of the Sexual Offender." Paper presented at Treatment of Sex Offender: Fact or Fiction Conference, Chicago, Illinois.

Berliner, L., & Stevens, D. (1982). "Clinical Issues in Child Sexual Assault." *Journal of Social Work and Human Sexuality, 1*(1/2), 93–108.

Browne, A., & Finkelhor, D. (1984). "The Impact of Sexual Abuse on Children: A Review of Research." Durham: University of New Hampshire, Family Violence Research Program. Unpublished manuscript.

Conte, J. R. (1984a). "The Effects of Sexual Abuse on Children: A Critique and Suggestions for Future Research." Paper presented at the Third International Institute on Victimology, Lisbon, Portugal.

Conte, J. R. (1984b). "The Justice System and Sexual Abuse of Children." *Social Service Review, 58*(10), 556–568.

Conte, J. R. (1985). "Sexual Abuse of Children and the Family: Unraveling the Myths." Unpublished manuscript, University of Chicago.

Conte, J. R., & Berliner, L. (1981). "Sexual Abuse of Children: Implications for Practice." *Social Casework, 62*(10), 601–606.

Finkelhor, D. (1979a). "What's Wrong With Sex Between Adults and Children?" *American Journal of Orthopsychiatry, 49*(4), 692–697.

Finkelhor, D. (1979b). *Sexually Victimized Children.* New York: Free Press.

Finkelhor, D. (1984). *Child Sexual Abuse: New Theories and Research.* New York: Free Press.

Greer, J., & Stuart, I. (Eds.). (1983). *The Sexual Aggressor.* New York: Van Nostrand Reinhold Co.

Groth, N. A. (1979). "Sexual Trauma in the Life Histories of Rapists and Child Molesters." *Victimology, 4*(1), 10–16.

Groth, N. A., Hobson, W. F., & Gary, T. S. (1982). "The Child Molester." *Journal of Social Work and Human Sexuality, 1*(1/2), 129–144.

Panton, J. H. (1979). "MMPI Profile Configurations Associated With Incestuous and Nonincestuous Child Molesters." *Psychological Reports, 45*(1), 335–338.

Quinsey, V. L., Chaplin, T. C., & Carrrigan, W. F. (1979). "Sexual Preferences Among Incestuous and Nonincestuous Child Molesters." *Behavior Therapy, 10*(4), 562–565.

Rogers, C. M., & Thomas, J. N. (1984). "Sexual Victimization in the USA: Patterns and Trends." *Clinical Proceedings, 40*(3/4), 211–221.

Russel, D. E. H. (1984). *Sexual Exploitation: Rape, Child Sexual Abuse and Work Harass-*

ment. Beverly Hills, Calif.: Sage Publications.

Sexual Assault Center. (1984). *Statistics.* Seattle, Wash.: Author.

Swanson, D. W. (1968). "Adult Sexual Abuse of Children." *Diseases of the Nervous System, 29*(10), 677–683.

"The Tragedy of Jordan." (1984, December 16). *Chicago Tribune.*

For Further Reading

Groth, N. A., Hobson, W. F., & Gary, T. S. (1982). "The Child Molester." *Journal of Social Work and Human Sexuality, 1*(1/2), 129–144.

Sgroi, S. (1982). *Handbook of Clinical Interventions in Child Sexual Abuse.* Lexington, Mass.: Lexington Books.

CHILD SUPPORT

Child support is the transfer of income to a child who has a living parent, usually the father, absent from the home. Divorce, separation, and out-of-wedlock birth all create children potentially eligible for child support. Conventionally, child support is paid by the noncustodial parent. Since colonial days, however, governments in the United States also have provided child support, and today, this practice is common.

Social workers should have a vital interest in child support policy because children, along with the aged, the disabled, and the poor make up a disproportionate share of their clients, and the social work profession has played the dominant role in shaping child welfare policy. One fact dramatically attests to the vital importance of child support for the future of this country: nearly one of every two children born today will become eligible for child support before reaching adulthood (Moynihan, 1981).[1]

The first two sections of this article describe the current child-support system and its weaknesses. The third explains how we got to where we are now. The fourth,

[1] The estimate in Moynihan's statistical appendix applies to children living in single-parent families. Because in some of these families the father has died, the percentage of children eligible for child support would be smaller.

fifth, and sixth sections discuss respectively recent developments, the debate in the profession, and implications for direct service workers.

The Child-Support System

The current child-support system has two major parts: the family court and Aid to Families with Dependent Children (AFDC). The former establishes the parent's responsibility to pay support, sets the amount of support to be paid, and enforces the parent's obligation to pay. The latter provides cash and in-kind benefits to poor children and their custodial parents. Because of recent federal initiatives, these two systems are becoming increasingly intertwined.

Family Law. Family law is traditionally a province of the states, most of which have explicit statements in their statutes about the obligation of absent parents to pay child support. However, the amount of support to be paid is determined on a case-by-case basis, and the guidelines are general. For example, the Wisconsin statute instructs courts to apply the following criteria in determining the amount of child support: the financial resources of the child; the financial resources of both parents; the standard of living the child would have enjoyed had the marriage not ended in annulment, divorce, or legal separation; the desirability of the custodial parent remaining at home full time; the cost of day care if the custodial parent works outside the home or the value of custodial services performed by the parent if she or he remains at home; the physical and emotional health needs of the child; the child's educational needs; the tax consequences to each party; and any other factors that the court deems relevant. In short, the courts have tremendous discretion.

In some jurisdictions, judges use a child-support obligation schedule, which is similar to a tax table. Most counties in Michigan, for example, use only two facts to determine child support: the absent parent's income and the number of children who require support. But such schedules are the exception rather than the rule.

In the few states that have been leaders in the field, such as Michigan and Wisconsin, a governmental agency has the authority to initiate legal action when child-support obligations are not met. The Michigan Friend of the Court, founded in 1917, is the oldest such agency. Still, except for AFDC cases, in which the proceeds from child-support collections go to the state rather than to the custodial parent, these governmental agencies usually do not use their authority unless specifically requested to do so by the custodial parent (Cassetty, 1978; Chambers, 1979; Krause, 1981). In most cases, the burden of collecting overdue support falls to the custodial parent.

The most effective tool for enforcing child support is a wage assignment—a legal order to the employer of the absent parent to withhold a specified amount from the employee's wages. Wage assignments are being used more frequently. Wisconsin, for example, now requires that a contingent wage assignment be issued in all cases. The county clerk of courts (to whom all child-support payments are made) has the legal authority to order wage assignments once child-support payments are 10 days delinquent. In practice, however, clerks do not pursue delinquencies in welfare cases for three to four months. Moreover, they take no initiative in nonwelfare cases.

The ultimate sanction for those who do not pay is jail. In Michigan, thousands of absent fathers are jailed each year for failing to comply with child-support orders (Chambers, 1979, p. 316). Although imprisonment appears to be used elsewhere throughout the country, there are no data to indicate how frequently it is utilized.

AFDC. The second part of the child support system—AFDC—is the oldest and most important public welfare program for poor children and their custodial parents. In 1935, when AFDC was created by the Social Security Act, eligible "dependent children" included those who lost the earnings of a parent because of death, disability, or absence. Initially, the program paid benefits only to children, but, in 1950, it was amended to include benefits to the custodial parent. In 1961, states also were first permitted to provide aid to families in which the fathers are unemployed. When AFDC was enacted, most of the children who benefited were orphans. Now, the overwhelming majority of the children's mothers are divorced, separated, or have not been married (in 1983, 47 percent of AFDC children were born out of wedlock). Widows constitute less than 2 percent of the AFDC caseload (U.S. House, 1985, p. 366).

In 1981, AFDC accounted for 17 percent of the total welfare expenditures and paid benefits to 11 million custodial parents and their children, most of whom were potentially eligible for child support (Garfinkel, 1982, p. 12). In addition to cash benefits, most AFDC families also received food stamps and Medicaid. If benefits from these and other welfare programs are included, then approximately half the welfare expenditures are devoted to families who are potentially eligible for child support.

Weaknesses of the Current System

The U.S. child-support system tolerates and therefore fosters parental irresponsibility, is inequitable, impoverishes women and children, and encourages dependence. Only 59 percent of the eligible mothers receive child-support awards. Nearly 90 percent of the unmarried mothers and half those who are separated receive no awards. Although the statistics for divorced mothers are more encouraging, one in five fails to get an award. Moreover, of all the children who were awarded support in 1978, only 47 percent received the full amount due them, and 28 percent received nothing (U.S. Bureau of the Census, 1983, p. 6).

Like nearly all social problems, the failures of this country's child-support system are more serious for the poor and minority groups. Only 40 percent of poor mothers compared to 68 percent of nonpoor mothers have child-support awards; only 34 percent of the black mothers and 44 percent of the Hispanic mothers had child-support awards. Most, but not all, the difference in child-support awards for the racial and ethnic groups is attributable to differences in income and the marital status of the mothers. Blacks, for example, have lower incomes and a much higher proportion of out-of-wedlock births than do whites. Although minority-group mothers are much less likely than white mothers to have child-support awards, black and Hispanic mothers with awards are only slightly less likely than are white mothers to receive support—67 percent and 66 percent versus 73 percent. (U.S. Bureau of the Census, 1983, p. 6).

The inequity of the system stems directly from its toleration of irresponsibility, compounded by capricious enforcement of the law. More absent fathers than not pay no child support. Most who do not pay suffer no consequences. Yet others, albeit a small percentage, are sent to jail. The amount of support an absent parent pays depends not just on the parent's ability to pay, but on the various attitudes of local judges, district attorneys, and welfare officials; the beliefs and attitudes of both parents; the current relationship between the parents; and the skills of their respective lawyers. Nearly every absent parent can find someone who earns more but pays less child support. Nearly every custodial parent knows someone who is receiving more child support although the child's father earns less. This inconsistency and the absence of firm legislative guidelines make child support a major source of continuing tension between many former spouses.

Finally, one of every two children living in a female-headed family is poor (U.S. Bureau of the Census, 1984, p. 21). Because one of every two children born today will live in a female-headed family before reaching adulthood, the implications for the next generation of such pervasive poverty among female-headed families are serious. Yet the welfare system, in relieving poverty, encourages dependence. Almost all the poor female-headed households receive welfare, and, during the months they receive benefits, the overwhelming majority of mothers on welfare do not work. Given the confiscatory tax rates on earnings in the AFDC program, this is not surprising. Because AFDC, like any welfare program, is designed to aid only the poor, benefits are reduced when earnings increase. After four months on a job, a woman on AFDC faces a reduction in benefits of a dollar for every dollar that she earns, in excess of her work expenses. This reduction is equivalent to a 100 percent tax on earnings. Thus, what the government gives with one hand, it takes away with the other hand. Yet because they have little education and experience and would have child care expenses if they worked, most women on AFDC could not earn enough to lift their families from poverty even if they worked full time (Sawhill, 1976). If they also received child support from the children's absent father, some, but not all, of these families would attain an income above the poverty level. Clearly, the only way to alleviate this kind of poverty without creating dependence is to supplement rather than replace the earnings of these custodial parents.

Evolution of the Federal Government's Role

As was noted, in 1935 most single mothers were widows. As AFDC cases began to reflect the demographic trends of divorce, separation, desertion, and out-of-wedlock births, congressional interest in child-support payments grew. In 1950, Congress enacted the first federal child-support legislation, which required state welfare agencies to notify law enforcement officials when a child receiving AFDC benefits had been abandoned. Other legislation, enacted in 1965 and 1967, required states to enforce child support and establish paternity and allowed them to acquire the addresses of absent parents from the Internal Revenue Service (IRS) as well as the Department of Health, Education, and Welfare.

The most significant legislation was enacted in 1975, when Congress added Part D to Title IV of the Social Security Act, thereby establishing the Child Support Enforcement (or IV-D) program. Again, responsibility for running the program rests with the states, which are reimbursed by the federal government for 75 percent of the cost of establishing paternity, locating absent fathers, and collecting child support.

Use of the IRS to collect child support owed to AFDC beneficiaries was authorized by the 1975 law. In 1980, this use was extended to non-AFDC families, and new legislation in 1981 required the IRS to withhold tax refunds when states certified that the individual owed child support that was past due. Because of these national measures, by fiscal year 1983, IV-D collections amounted to $2 billion—more than a threefold increase since 1976 (U.S. Department of Health & Human Services, 1983).

Recent Changes

In 1984, both the House of Representatives and the Senate unanimously passed and the president signed the strongest federal child-support legislation to date. The bill requires all states that receive federal AFDC funds to withhold child support from the wages of absent parents whose payments are delinquent for one month. It also requires the appointment of blue-ribbon commissions to devise statewide standards for child support. Furthermore, for the first time, it created financial incentives for states to collect child support from non-AFDC and out-of-state cases. Finally, it authorized the state of Wisconsin to use federal funds that would otherwise have been spent on AFDC to finance a demonstration of a child-support insurance program.

Under a child-support assurance program, all parents who live apart from their children are obligated to share their income with their children. The sharing rate would be levied on their gross income (Garfinkel & Melli, 1982) and would be proportional, according to the number of children who must be supported. The resulting child-support obligation would be collected through paycheck withholding, as are social security and income taxes. All children with an identified living absent parent would be entitled to benefits equal either to the child support paid by the absent parent or to a socially assured minimum benefit, whichever is higher. Should the absent parent pay less than the assured benefit, the difference would be financed out of general revenues, and the custodial parent would be subject to a small surtax up to the amount of the public subsidy.

The Wisconsin demonstration has already begun. As of mid-1984, 10 counties were withholding child-support obligations from income sources in all new cases. In July 1987, all counties will implement immediate withholding. The state Department of Health and Social Services (DHSS), at the direction of the state legislature, published a percentage-of-income standard that judges may use in determining the child-support obligation. Under the standard, child-support awards are equal to 17 percent of gross income for one child; 25 percent, for two children; 29 percent, for three children; 31 percent, for four children; and 34 percent, for five or more children. Several judges are now using the standard. As of July 1987, judges will be required to use the standard unless they make a written finding that justifies their departure from it. Finally, the Wisconsin DHSS has begun intensive planning for implementing the assured benefit portion of the demonstration, which is scheduled to begin in early 1987.

Debate in the Profession

The fundamental issue in child-support policy is how to share the cost of supporting the children among the custodial parent, the noncustodial parent, and the public. A basic premise of both the 1984 federal child-support legislation and the proposal for child-support insurance is that the government should play a stronger role in enforcing the obligation of noncustodial parents to pay child support. Social workers who are familiar with income maintenance policy in the United States should ask, "Why should the government enforce the responsibility of parents to support their children when public policy has moved in the opposite direction with respect to the responsibility of children to support their parents?" In a conversation with the author in 1981, social economist Eveline Burns had a good answer. Whereas parents choose to bring children into the world, children do not choose to be born. Responsibility follows from choice.

Even if the general case for enforcing private child support is granted, it does not follow that increasing the resources devoted to enforcing child support is a wise public policy. It may be that noncustodial fathers are already contributing an optimal share. It is clear that the incomes of noncustodial fathers of children on AFDC are, on the average, low. The two best studies of the incomes of such fathers in Wisconsin indicated that the mean incomes in 1980 were between $8,800 and $10,800 (McDonald, Moran, & Garfinkel, 1983, p. 18; Oellerich, 1984, p. 77). About half the fathers had new dependents (Oellerich, 1984, p. 107).

How much more child support can this group afford to pay? The answer to this question depends on value judgments about what share of his income a noncustodial father should devote to his children and about whether that share should be reduced if he has new dependents. According to the Wisconsin percentage-of-income standard just described and using the lowest estimate of incomes, absent fathers of AFDC children could afford to pay $115 million in child support—about $3\frac{1}{2}$ times more than they actually paid (Oellerich, 1984, p. 140). According to the child-support guidelines developed by the New York Community Council under contract to the federal Office of Child Support Enforcement, absent fathers would pay no child support if their net incomes were below the lower-level living standard of the Bureau of Labor Statistics: $12,200 in 1980 for a remarried father with two new children. Therefore, according to the New York standard, two-thirds of the fathers of Wisconsin AFDC children could not afford to pay child support. However, the New York standard takes 90 percent of the income in excess of the lower-level living standard for child support. As a consequence, according to the New York standard, the remaining one-third of the fathers of Wisconsin AFDC children should pay $133 million in child support, or over four times the amount they actually paid (Oellerich, 1984, p. 140). In short, although the values underlying these two standards differ dramatically, both suggest that fathers in the poorest segment of the population could pay far more child support than they actually pay. A different set of values, however, could lead to the opposite conclusion.

Those in social work who prefer to increase the share of the cost of children borne by the government argue that a children's allowance—a governmental benefit paid to all children—is preferable to child support (see, for example, Schorr, 1976, 1977). The United States is the only industrialized country in the world without a children's allowance. However, unless the children's allowance is set high enough to pay all the costs of child raising, substituting it for child support amounts to eliminating the share of the costs of the child borne by the noncustodial parent at the expense of the children and custodial parent. Child support and children's allowances, therefore, are best viewed as complements rather than substitutes.

There are other important issues in relation to child support (Garfinkel & Melli, 1982; Garfinkel & Uhr, 1984). Should the child-support obligation be determined on a case-by-case basis or through some formula like the Wisconsin standard or New York guidelines? Is the rough justice produced by the latter preferable to the individualization of the former? Should child-support obligations be withheld from wages and other income in all cases? How much will collections increase? Will automatic withholding entail a large-scale invasion of the privacy of noncustodial parents? What is the burden on employers? Finally, how much will an as-

sured benefit in child-support assurance reduce poverty and the dependence on welfare, and at what cost? These questions, along with the question of the appropriate sharing of the costs, are likely to dominate child-support policy in the next decade or two.

Implications for Direct Service Workers

Child-support issues are likely to be of importance to many social workers who are engaged in the delivery of direct services. The implications for social workers employed by family courts or family service agencies are perhaps the most obvious. Child support is an issue that should be discussed thoroughly with all couples who are contemplating or getting a divorce. But child-support issues will be just as relevant to social workers in numerous other settings. For example, for all those who work with single mothers, an exploration of child-support issues should be an integral part of the process of assessing their needs and problems. Familiarity with federal, state, and local child-support laws and practices will enable workers to advise mothers of their legal rights and realistic options. In some cases, it will be appropriate for social workers to use their professional skills as brokers, mediators, and personal and policy advocates to help women get the benefits due them.

Child-support issues are likely to be equally relevant for those who work with men in any context—men's groups, support services, employment, or corrections. Workers should be prepared to explore the issue of the father's responsibility to support his children and to work toward increasing the father's acceptance of this responsibility. In addition, workers should be prepared to advise fathers on their rights, such as the right to visit their children.

Finally, child support is particularly important, and in some cases may be a particularly difficult issue, for direct service workers in public aid. The AFDC program requires mothers to cooperate in obtaining child support from the noncustodial father. If the well-being of the child or mother is threatened by such cooperation, this requirement may be waived. Otherwise, failure to cooperate results in the elimination of the mother's (although not the child's) benefit. Such threats are rare. In 1982, there were only

7,556 good-cause claims by AFDC mothers to be excused from the cooperation requirement (U.S. Department of Health & Human Services, 1984). Because the overwhelming majority of AFDC mothers will become independent after a few years, the advantages of their obtaining child support are clear: child support will not be curtailed—like AFDC—as the mothers' earnings increase. Workers must help mothers to see these advantages and, in the small minority of relevant cases, to weigh them against potential threats from the noncustodial father.

IRWIN GARFINKEL

For further information, see AID TO FAMILIES WITH DEPENDENT CHILDREN; CHILDREN; CHILD WELFARE SERVICES; DIVORCE AND SEPARATION; FAMILY: CONTEMPORARY PATTERNS.

References

Cassetty, J. (1978). *Child Support and Public Policy.* Lexington, Mass.: Lexington Books.

Chambers, D. L. (1979). *Making Fathers Pay: The Enforcement of Child Support.* Chicago: University of Chicago Press.

Garfinkel, I. (Ed) (1982). *Income-Tested Transfer Programs: The Case For and Against.* New York: Academic Press.

Garfinkel, I., & Melli, M. (1982). *Child Support: Weaknesses of the Old and Features of a Proposed New System* (Vol. 1). Madison: Institute for Research on Poverty, University of Wisconsin.

Garfinkel, I., & Uhr, E. (1984). "A New Approach to Child Support." *The Public Interest,* (75), 111–122.

Krause, H. D. (1981). *Child Support in America: The Legal Perspective.* Charlottesville, Va.: Miche Co.

McDonald, T., Moran, J., & Garfinkel, I. (1983). *Wisconsin Study of Absent Fathers' Ability to Pay Child Support.* Madison: Institute for Research on Poverty, University of Wisconsin.

Moynihan, D. P. (1981). "Welfare Reform's 1971–72 Defeat: A Historic Loss." *Journal of the Institute for Socioeconomic Studies,* 6(1), 1–20.

Oellerich, D. T. (1984). *The Effects of Potential Child Support Transfers on Wisconsin AFDC Costs, Caseloads and Recipient Well-Being.* Madison: Institute for Research on Poverty, University of Wisconsin.

Sawhill, I. B. (1976). "Economic Dimensions of Occupational Segregation: Discrimination and Poverty among Women Who Head Families." *Signs, 1*(3), Part 2, 201–211.

Schorr, A. (1976, October). "Enforcing Child Support." *New York Times,* p. A29.

Schorr, A. (1977). *Jubilee for Our Times.* New York: Columbia University Press.

U.S. Bureau of the Census. (1983). *Child Support and Alimony: 1981* (Special Studies Series, P-23, No. 124). Washington, D.C.: U.S. Government Printing Office.

U.S. Bureau of the Census. (1984). *Money Income and Poverty Status of Families and Persons in the United States: 1983* (Series P-60, No. 145). Washington, D.C.: U.S. Government Printing Office.

U.S. Department of Health and Human Services, Office of Child Support Enforcement. (1983). *Child Support Enforcement, 8th Annual Report to Congress for the Period Ending September 30, 1983.* Washington, D.C.: Author.

U.S. Department of Health and Human Services, Social Security Administration. (1984). *Quarterly Public Assistance Statistics, January-March 1984.* Washington, D.C.: Author.

U.S. House, Committee on Ways and Means. (1985). *Background Material and Data on Programs Within the Jurisdiction of the Committee on Ways and Means* (H. Prt. 99–2). Washington, D.C.: U.S. Government Printing Office.

CHILD WELFARE SERVICES

In its most inclusive sense, the term "child welfare" encompasses all policies, programs, activities, and responsibilities that affect the general well-being of children in any way. Relevant are such disparate activities as sanitation (protecting children from disease) and military defense (protecting children from external aggression). Legislation protecting the general welfare of children encompasses everything from compulsory education, child labor laws, and required immunizations to packaging requirements of toxic substances, auto seat belt regulations, and standards of flammability of children's clothing. However, for the purposes of this article, child welfare will be more strictly defined and considered as a specialized field of social work practice.

Definition

As a specialized field in the social work profession, child welfare is accorded sanctioned responsibility by the community to focus on a particular population needing service in response to a particular set of social problems and situations. In general, the child welfare social work service system undertakes to help in the prevention, amelioration, or maintenance without further deterioration of the social situations affecting children.

Child welfare social work has identified a specialized body of knowledge and skill relevant to the population and problems within its sanctioned area of responsibility. Texts are available that focus on child welfare services as a specific area of social work practice. Schools and departments of social work provide a concentration of courses in the field of child welfare social work. Child welfare agencies, which have been staffed, organized, and funded to deal with relevant problems of particular children, define the domain of this specialized social work field.

Child welfare social workers are sanctioned functionaries charged with performing social work activities in behalf of and with the children who are social agency clients. This view mirrors Kahn's (1977) narrow, technical definition of child welfare as "a specialized form of social work practice adapted to the needs of service programs for children" (p. 100).

Recurrent problems that concern the child welfare social work system arise through a dysfunction in the parent-child role network and have the parent, the child, or the community as their locus.

1. Problems occur when the parental role is uncovered because of death, divorce, desertion, separation, imprisonment, or the out-of-wedlock birth of a child.

2. Problems arise when parental roles are inadequately implemented because of mental illness, physical illness, or substance abuse; because parental roles are rejected, as in the case of abuse and neglect; or because two roles carried simultaneously may conflict (such as the role of parent versus the role of employee).

3. Problems in the parent-child role network arise when certain mental, physical, or emotional characteristics of the child make it difficult to meet normal parental and social expectations.

4. Finally, problems may occur because of deficiencies in the family's social system. Widespread unemployment or housing shortages often make it difficult for parents to adequately implement responsibilities toward the child.

An alternative approach to this definition of child welfare is to categorize the need for specialized services in situations involving

1. "absence"—the unavailability of a parent (because, for instance, of desertion) or the absence of a child (because the child has run away);

2. "condition"—characteristics of a parent that reduce capacity for adequate nurturing or characteristics of a child that prevent the acceptance and/or effective utilization of nurturing; and

3. "conduct"—parental behavior detrimental to a child (such as abuse or neglect) or behavior in a child that disrupts the parent-child role network.

Child welfare agencies have found that the parent is most frequently the locus of such problems (parental adequacy, capacity, and motivation to provide care and protection for children). Problems and deficiencies stemming from the child's behavior rank as the second most frequent locus. Finally, questions of income, housing, or employment often contribute to, but only rarely constitute, the primary locus of a problem. Where a specific allocation has been attempted, primary locus ratios approximate 70 to 80 percent parent, 10 to 15 percent child, and 5 to 10 percent situational problems (Jones, Neuman, & Shyne, 1976; Shyne & Schroeder, 1978).

Child welfare services are classified as residual services. The family is the primary child welfare service agency for children. Child welfare social work services are assigned responsibility for intervention only when the family has somehow failed, or is in danger of failing, to meet the child's basic biopsychosocial needs or when parents or children have difficulty implementing their roles in the parent-child role network.

Considerable controversy surrounds this limited, reactive conception of child welfare social work. Proponents of a more proactive, institutional, universal orientation conceive of child welfare services as social utilities directed to all children in the population. Although such a broader orientation may be eminently desirable, the residual orientation reflects the system as it operates currently, has operated in the past, and is likely to operate in the foreseeable future. The definition of child welfare social work given here is descriptive—an analysis of what is—rather than prescriptive—a statement of what should be.

Legislative enactments that, by and large, sanction child welfare social work offer definitions to support a residual conceptualization. The Social Security Act of 1935, the 1962 social security amendments, and the Adoption Assistance and Child Welfare Act of 1980 (P.L. 96-272) all identify particular subgroups of children and address specific problems affecting children. "Deprived," "homeless," "dependent," and "neglected" children are the groups most consistently cited; "neglect," "deprivation," "abuse," and "exploitation" are most consistently isolated as problems of concern.

When the federal Administration for Children, Youth, and Families proposed its *System of Social Services for Children and Families,* it defined the clientele of such services in residual terms. The design notes that such clients "are the children, youth and their families—for whom the traditional measures of the community, the school, the churches, the extended family have been found to be unavailable, inappropriate or inadequate. Therefore, these children, youth and their families must turn to the children and family social service system for treatment to ameliorate or solve their problems" (U.S. Department of Health, Education, and Welfare [U.S. DHEW], 1978, p. 3).

In effect, then, the child welfare social work system is a parent surrogate system doing for the deprived, disadvantaged, dependent child what the effective family does for the advantaged child.

A residual or minimalist orientation is not only a consequence of the current infeasibility of a more universal approach; it is also the result of ideological constraints. Family privacy and autonomy are important values in the American creed. Even benign programs directed toward the support of families are resisted because they are perceived as intrusive.

To define some defensible parameters of child welfare social work requires acknowledgment that such boundaries are blurred and permeable. Furthermore, the discrete child welfare social work network operates, of necessity, as part of a more comprehensive, interdependent network of systems, each of which gives service to children and their families—the school system, medical system, recreational system, legal system, and so forth.

Social work is the predominant (if not the exclusive) profession sanctioned by the community with responsibility for dealing with core child welfare problems. More than most other social agencies, child welfare agencies are staffed and administered by personnel holding the title of social worker. In an editorial in *Social Work,* Meyer (1984) described child welfare as the "centerpiece of social services" and as the "only field in which social workers are in control of their own programs" (p. 499).

Further, in an analysis of the domain of social work, O'Connor and Waring (1981) list child welfare as one of the few fields "in which social work has historically held a dominant and influential position," a field in which the social work profession "remains a viable and influential force," and a field "to which social work, in fact, directs its energies and resources" (p. 3).

Child welfare is thus identified as one of the strongholds of social work.

Services

Child welfare services are derived from the particular population and specific problems assigned to the specialized network within the social work system.

The Child Welfare League of America (CWLA) represents the community of child welfare social work agencies in the United States. A nationwide organization whose membership consists of both public and voluntary child welfare social work agencies, CWLA publishes *Child Welfare,* the journal most directly concerned with the activities, functions, and responsibilities of child welfare social workers.

CWLA has assumed responsibility for establishing and publishing standards for each of the services it defines as "unique and specific" to child welfare social work. Services so defined by the single most authoritative agency speaking for the child welfare social work community thus gain a considerable degree of legitimacy. In the most recent revision of its standards (Child Welfare League of America, 1984), approved by the board of directors of CWLA, the following nine "specific and unique" component services are delineated: Service for children and families in their own home, day care, homemaker service, foster family care, adoption, group home care, residential center care, protective services for children, and services for unmarried parents (p. 88).

The Occupational Outlook Handbook published by the U.S. Department of Labor (1984) defines child welfare social work in similar service terms:

> Social workers who specialize in child welfare seek to improve the well-being of children and youth. They may advise parents on child care and child rearing, counsel children and youth with social adjustment difficulties and arrange homemaker service during the parent's illness. Social workers may institute legal action to protect neglected or abused children, help unmarried parents and counsel couples about adoption. After proper evaluation and home visits, they may place children for adoption, in foster homes or institutions. (p. 88)

These separate services have been grouped in a number of different ways. A two-way classification separates services to children in their own home from those provided to children outside their own home. Services to children in their own home include casework counseling, day care, and homemaker services. Out-of-home services include adoption, foster family care, group homes, and institutional care. A three-way classification includes supportive services, supplementary services, and substitute care services.

Supportive services, which include casework counseling, family therapy, and family life education, are designed to support and reinforce strengths inherent in the family system. In-home services per se are ambiguous and range from irregularly scheduled, informal casework counseling through regularly scheduled, formal casework counseling to home-based family-centered programs (comprehensive, intensive, supportive interventions with the family in their own home), which are based on small caseloads and constant availability. Voluntary family service agencies and community mental health centers provide support to families experiencing parent-child relationship problems; this primarily in-home service consists of a combination of casework counseling and parent-family life education.

Supplementary services take responsibility for actively implementing some of the parental role functions. Included are day care and homemaker services, which act as a supplementary parent while the child continues in the home. Substitute care services—adoption, foster family care, and group home and institutional care—are designed to replace the biological parent, temporarily or permanently.

Critics claim that by justifying and fixing the traditional boundaries of child welfare social work, these classifications discourage innovation. Moreover, some explanation should perhaps be given for not classifying services that might reasonably be regarded as legitimate concerns of child welfare social work—namely, services to handicapped and delinquent children. One such explanation might be attempted by considering the most recent national survey of child welfare services to children—the 1977 report by Shyne and Schroeder (1978). Their list of child welfare social work services included those cited by CWLA: in-home casework counseling, protective services, day care, homemaker service, foster family care, adoption, group home care, and residential treatment. However, services to "juvenile delinquents and handicapped children" were "specifically excluded" from the survey, since services to these groups "are usually provided by other state agencies" rather than by child welfare agencies (Shyne & Schroeder, 1978, p. 14). These children and their families are the primary responsibility, not of the child welfare system, but of other service systems—in the case of the delinquent, the correctional legal system; in the case of the handicapped, the rehabilitation–medical care system.

The exclusion of another set of programs of great relevance to children should also be addressed: the income maintenance and social insurance programs (AFDC and OASDI), which provide support for millions of deprived children. These are not generally included in the rubric of child welfare social work because social work functionaries are by and large absent from such programs. The income maintenance aspects of AFDC are the responsibility of income maintenance workers, for example, not social workers. The OASDI program operates with practically no social workers. In both programs, determination of income assistance and benefits is largely clerical, a highly standardized routine permitting little of the individual attention characteristic of a social work function.

The AFDC program has a social service component in addition to its income assistance program. This aspect of the program is provided by social workers, and child welfare services offered follow the CWLA classifications listed above.

According to CWLA, child welfare social work agencies have responsibilities beyond direct provision and implementation of such services: they must also assess the needs of children in a community with regard to the availability and accessibility of these services and, equally important, vigorously advocate the planning and development of any programs that are lacking. On a more general level, child welfare social work agencies share responsibility for advocating those types of social changes that might be of help in conserving family life and preventing family breakdown.

Child welfare agencies are further categorized under auspices and source of funding: (1) public agencies under federal, state, or county auspices supported by public tax funds; (2) voluntary nonprofit agencies, generally supported by community-donated funds and further subdivided as either denominational (Catholic, Protestant, Jewish) or nondenominational; (3) private for-profit agencies, which are under proprietary auspices and are supported by client fees; and (4) industrially affiliated agencies, such as on-job-site day care centers and employee assistance programs.

A national study of some 900 child welfare workers conducted in 1981 (Vinokur, 1983) found that 41 percent of the workers covered an integrated child welfare caseload and 47 percent covered a specialized caseload. Among those "whose primary caseload assignment is specialized the most frequently indicated fields are protective services (22 percent), foster care (10 percent), shelter care (6 percent), and adoption (5 percent)" (p. 28). Very few workers were involved in such specialized services as day care or homemaker service. Information on task time allocation indicated once again that protective services and foster family care occupied the greatest proportion of the worker's time and efforts.

Within the group of services to children in their own homes, counseling or casework is offered much more frequently than either day care or homemaker services. Child welfare social work involvement with day care or homemaker services accounts for less than 10 percent of the services offered.

In general, casework counseling is the most frequent service offered clients by child welfare social workers, and the worker-client relationship is cited in every study as the most potent, active factor associated with whatever positive changes are effected in the situation. The effectiveness of the "hard services" made available through the child welfare agency depends to a considerable extent on casework counseling. The client must be helped to recognize the need for, accept, and make use of the service. Specialty casework counseling consists of worker activity related to offering support and reassurance, giving advice and suggestions, and providing clarification and information.

Child welfare services have recently undergone a reallocation of priorities. In theory, in-home services—designated primarily as supportive and supplementary—have always been given priority; the permanency planning movement has given such services priority in practice. Keeping the child in the home, providing the permanence and continuity of a caring relationship, is now more than ever before the sine qua non of child welfare services. Providing permanence through adoption also has high priority. Foster family care, on the other hand, has diminished in priority. The group home option has ascending priority, though it still provides service to only a small segment of children receiving child welfare services. With continued emphasis on deinstitutionalization and "normalization," institutions now have lowest priority among substitute care services.

Some particular problems for which child welfare social work has responsibility—such as child neglect and abuse, with a special emphasis on sexual abuse—have been given high priority in response to growing public concern. In response to these problems, a variety of protective services have become the focus of special funding research, demonstration efforts, and increases in programs and staff.

Services related to extramarital teenage pregnancy and child rearing have been given a similar kind of priority but, as yet, receive only limited investment of child welfare social work effort.

Scope of Services

It is not possible at this time to delineate accurately the number of children and families receiving child welfare system services. There is no central agency with responsibility for collecting the overall statistics. A special survey of public social services provided to children determined that in 1977 some 1.8 million children were receiving such service (Shyne & Schroeder, 1978). The survey was limited to child welfare services offered only by public agencies and is now almost a decade old.

In lieu of an overall set of statistics, this article provides data regarding specific child welfare services and problems. The American Humane Association, under contract from the National Center for Child Abuse and Neglect, collates state statistics on child abuse and neglect: in 1982, 929,000 cases of abuse and neglect were reported to protective services agencies. The American Public Welfare Association, through its Voluntary Cooperative Information System (VCIS), offers statistics on children and families provided substitute care (foster family, adoption, and institutional care services) through state and other public agencies. According to data collected in 1981–1982, "the VCIS national estimate of the total number of children residing in substitute care during the 1981–82 period is 273,000" (Tatara, 1983, p. 13).

In 1982, Family Service America (formerly Family Service Association of America) had a membership of 280 local voluntary nonprofit family service agencies. In that year, they offered service to 1,100,000 families, involving some 3,000,000 people; in many cases help was sought to ameliorate dysfunctional parent-child relationships.

Trends and Problems

The percentage of children in the population has been decreasing steadily since the 1950s baby boom, and only a modest increase is anticipated by the turn of the century. However, although the number of children at possible risk for child welfare services is therefore decreasing, there have been increases in the particular subsets of children at significantly high risk for child welfare services. For example, there has been an increase in the percentage of children living in poverty, an increase in the percentage of children living in single-parent families, an increase in the number of children born out of wedlock to teenage parents, and an increase in the percentage of mothers of young children in the work force; moreover, the minority group population birthrates are higher than the national average. All this would seem to repudiate the contention that a decreasing child population in general implies a decrease in the potential need for child welfare services.

The median age of the child receiving child welfare services has increased gradually. With a greater proportion of children in the system approaching adolescence or of adolescent age, service to this age group has been receiving more focused, specialized attention.

Services to involuntary clients has been a special problem of increasing concern. Compared with other fields of social work practice, child welfare service has a disproportionate percentage of involuntary clients referred by reason of abuse and neglect.

A more determined, more consistent effort is being made to avoid out-of-home placement. This is the primary thrust of permanency planning efforts. Providing a permanent out-of-home care arrangement, if in-home care proves improbable or impossible, is an option of secondary importance. Supportive and supplementary services provided to children in their own homes now have priority over substitute care services. A determined effort is also being made to develop innovative home-based services and to increase their utilization.

Permanency planning reform was assisted by acceptance of psychological parenthood, a concept persuasively advocated by Goldstein, Freud, and Solnit (1973) in their book *Beyond the Best Interests of the Child*; by an increasing appreciation of the rights of children vis-à-vis the rights of parents; and by an extension to children of due process safeguards.

There has been a proliferation of small, specialized agencies that offer, for example, service to substance-addicted adolescents, latch-key children, or sexually abused children; promote an adolescent-pregnancy prevention program; or provide crisis-respite day care. The development of such specialized, single-function agencies has allowed public child welfare organizations to progress from a direct-service to a case-management orientation. Instead of directly offering service, workers "manage" services purchased in the client's behalf from an array of more specialized, often voluntary, agencies. This involves planning what services are needed, locating needed services, making needed services available, coordinating services, and monitoring and evaluating services provided.

A broader orientation now exists regarding the factors included for consideration in understanding and treating problems of concern to child welfare social work. Current discussion of such problems emphasizes and advocates a systems approach, an ecological pattern, and a holistic structure for understanding and intervention. The "whole child" in transactional relationship with the "total environmental configuration" provides the comprehensive framework for consideration.

Although such a broadened orientation has increased the complexity of variables attended to by the child welfare practitioner, it has also initiated a stronger trend toward seeing the family rather than the child as the primary client in child welfare social work. Emphasis is now placed on family-centered services.

Greater and more varied demands are being made on the child welfare social services system. With the "rediscovery" of child abuse in the 1960s and the subsequent passage of state and federal legislation mandating reporting of abuse, protective services caseloads have increased sharply. Further increases resulted from additions to the legislation of the conditions requiring reporting—from physical abuse and neglect, to emotional and sexual abuse, to "Baby Doe" situations (children born with serious congenital anomalies, for whom the use of heroic life maintenance procedures are questioned by their parents and doctors). Deinstitutionalization of status offenders and policies that divert delinquents from legal involvement have allowed responsibility for care and treatment of such youths to shift from the correctional system to the child welfare system.

The child welfare service system has always been responsible for guaranteeing children safety and protection, adequate provision of physical care, and a reasonably good home. Now, in addition to this, the system is being asked to guarantee continuity and stability, if not permanence, in a satisfactory parent-child relationship—and not only for reasonably normal children but also for children who present difficult social, emotional, and physical handicaps.

Increasing attention is being given to groups of children for whom the child welfare social work system has had sanctioned responsibility but whose needs have not been actively addressed. Adoptive and foster family homes for special-needs children are being aggressively recruited. To meet the needs of minority group children, attempts are being made to hire minority staff workers; build ethnically identified child welfare agencies, administered by minorities, in minority communities; and provide training to child welfare personnel in an effort to increase knowledge about and correct attitudes toward minorities. The Indian Child Welfare Act of 1978 (P.L. 95-608), which gives tribal groups more direct control over child welfare decisions regarding Indian children, exemplifies this trend.

Child welfare services are being legalized with increasing frequency; the courts, for example, are now more than ever before reviewing and intervening in child welfare decisions regarding placement. There have also been increases in legal actions against child welfare workers and child welfare agencies. Although the actual numbers are still small, there has been a growing trend toward the criminal and civil prosecution of child welfare social workers. Such instances are infrequent and most claims are dismissed, but this does little to mitigate the anxiety felt by workers about the possibility of such action. Most of these cases have to do with protective services and revolve around (1) liability for inadequately protecting a child or (2) liability for violating parental rights to privacy and confidentiality. There have been a smaller number of actions in substitute care, centering on inadequate foster care services and failure to recruit adoptive homes for children "in limbo" (Besharov, 1984, 1985).

Child welfare workers are called upon more frequently to testify in court. Rules of evidence in data-gathering and data-recording procedures are being strictly interpreted to meet the likelihood of legal challenges. There has been an increase in the number of interested parties who have had various legal rights affirmed. Putative fathers' rights to custody, foster parents' rights regarding the foster child, adoptees' rights to "search"— all illustrate the expansion of legalization of child welfare services.

Recently, other professionals have intruded in areas previously assigned almost exclusively to child welfare social workers. Heightened concern with physical and sexual abuse has resulted in an increase in the number of doctors and nurses involved in protective services. The legal profession has also become more involved in the child welfare system, in such areas as adoption practices, child placement, parental rights, and children's rights.

As child welfare decisions have become subject to greater external control, the authority of the direct service worker has decreased. Although the establishment of precise and detailed legislative directives has contributed to this change in decisional flexibility, periodic court reports or citizen/committee reviews of agency placement decisions are generally responsible.

Child welfare services are facing a certain amount of entrepreneurial commercialization and privatization. More proprietary day care centers and homemaker services are being made available through the marketplace by private companies. The increase in independent adoptions indicates a shift in distribution of adoption services from agency to free-market auspices.

Many group homes and residential treatment centers are under proprietary auspices. The corporate sector has become involved in providing or subsidizing the provision of child welfare services. Information and referral services, on-site day care centers, fringe benefit payments that help defray the cost of adoptions, and maternity leave entitlements following adoption are evidence of such corporate involvement.

Child welfare social workers are encouraging a diffusion of responsibility for problems previously under their primary, if not exclusive, jurisdiction. A large number of self-help groups have developed, representing foster parents, the biological parents of children in foster care, adoptive parents, adoptive children, parents of abused and neglected children, and so forth. Almost all the significant clusters of people involved in the child welfare situation are being represented by some organized self-help group. The development of these organizations is fostered and often initiated by child welfare social workers, who provide resources and consultation. Nevertheless, some of these organizations actively implement functions that parallel those more formally provided by the child welfare services system. Many of the self-help groups have developed their own publications; organized conferences; undertaken advocacy activity; offered advice, counsel, and education to members; and provided help in referrals.

During the 1950s and 1960s child welfare as a specialization was clearly identified administratively and conceptually in large public welfare agencies. It enjoyed a special recognition and status as a highly professional sector of social work. Recently, however, child welfare has lost some of its elite status. As units were divided, reallocated, and merged almost into nonexistence, child welfare was no longer able to maintain its unique identity and clearly defined, specialized visibility in public agencies.

Along with all other human services programs, child welfare has been affected by the public policy counterrevolution as initiated and sustained by the Reagan Administration. The steady growth of the welfare state—of initiation, proliferation, and increased funding of federally supported social service programs—that had characterized Roosevelt's New Deal, Truman's Fair Deal, Kennedy's New Frontier, and Johnson's Great Society—has been halted and reversed. Now, human services programs in general receive limited government involvement and support; in many cases staff has been cut back and programming reduced. Child welfare agencies are being asked to do more with less, to work "smarter" rather than "harder," by computerizing operations, standardizing procedures, and routinizing activities in order to increase efficiency.

The federal government has shifted much of its support of child welfare services away from categorical programs and toward block grants and has made states and local communities, rather than federal authorities, responsible for such programs. As a result, a number of specific child welfare programs are in danger of losing their protected funding status.

Redistributing control to the states has reduced the rule-making authority of federal government agencies in child welfare services. In addition, auditing and compliance-monitoring activities of such services by the federal government have declined. Previously, federal government control of program funding and operations created a minimum standardization and uniformity in child welfare programs. However, now that federal participation in regulating and evaluating child welfare programs has lessened, the heterogeneity of such programs has increased.

Despite general and warranted concern about the "counterrevolution" regarding social services, child welfare has continued to receive modest congressional support. Actual funding levels for most programs, however, fall below fiscal authorization levels.

The Gramm-Rudman Deficit Reduction Act (P.L. 99-177), adopted in December 1985 to reduce the federal deficit, specifically exempted from automatic reduction many programs directly affecting children, including AFDC, Medicaid, food stamps, and the women's and children's nutrition program. However, the future status of federal funds directly allocated for child welfare services was open to question at the time the legislation was passed. Because they are not specifically protected, child welfare service programs may be subject to automatic reductions dictated by the legislation. (In 1986, efforts were under way to have the act declared unconstitutional in the courts.)

There is, however, some cause for optimism. Although federal support of social welfare programs has been eroding, there have also been repeated indications that Congress is concerned about children. The Adoption Assistance and Child Welfare Act, passed in 1980, gives clear support for programs assuring greater permanence for children. In 1982, a special congressional committee, the Special Committee on Children, Youth, and Families, was created to give greater visibility to the special needs of children and youth; in addition, Congress supports the objectives of the Child Abuse Pre-

vention and Treatment Act (P.L. 93-247) by continued approval and funding.

Child welfare services are not declining, but the industry is growing more slowly than in the immediate past. Commitment to program objectives has been maintained. Consensual acknowledgment of the need for the programs—as of their legitimacy and social work's responsibility for them—is unquestioned.

Child Welfare Social Work Personnel

Child welfare is a field of practice employing a large percentage of social work personnel. Data from the National Association of Social Workers' 1982 membership survey ("NASW Data Bank," 1985) show that child welfare provided employment for 15.5 percent of NASW membership. Only mental health and medical social work provided more jobs. However, if the group employed by services to children and youth (15.5 percent) were combined with the group employed by family service agencies (11.2 percent), the resulting field of practice providing services to children and their families would employ the largest number of social workers ("NASW Data Bank," 1985, pp. 6–7). A subsequent survey of 9,313 baccalaureate social workers indicated that the single largest group (35.8 percent) were employed in child and family welfare (NASW, 1985).

There has been a decrease in employment opportunities for child welfare workers in general and an increase in the percentage of workers without previous training in social work. Civil service positions have in many cases been reclassified to delete the requirements of educational credentials for access to entry-level positions. In implementing the 1980 Adoption Assistance and Child Welfare Act, federal government regulations recommended, but did not require, the BSW as the minimum qualification for line workers and the MSW for first-line supervisory positions. Few states have in fact set up such requirements.

The 1978–1979 edition of the *Occupational Outlook Handbook* published by the U.S. Department of Labor optimistically noted that "employment of social workers is expected to increase *faster* than the average for all occupation through 1980" (p. 565). The 1984–1985 edition of the handbook notes, however, that "employment of social workers is expected to increase *about as fast* as the average for all occupations through the mid 1990s—the need to replace social workers who leave the occupation or stop working is expected to be the principal source of jobs" (p. 90; italics added).

A 1977 national survey of welfare services to children (Shyne & Schroeder, 1978) found that only 25 percent of public agency child welfare social workers had any formal training in social work—16 percent at the bachelor's degree level, 9 percent at the master's degree level. Thus, three out of every four public child welfare workers came to the position without any social work training (p. 77). According to CWLA studies, a larger percentage of voluntary child welfare agency workers have social work training, and 65 percent have a master's degree in social work (Jones & Moore, 1983, p. 20). Furthermore, child welfare workers are predominantly female, white, young, and with limited experience (Vinokur, 1983, p. 21).

In 1979, the Administration for Children, Youth, and Families responded to the need for training child welfare workers by funding both national and regional child welfare training centers to develop and disseminate training materials and to provide technical assistance in the use of such materials. In addition, special grants were awarded to develop child welfare training curricula for protective service workers, adoption workers, home-based service workers, residential treatment workers, and for those working with minority group clients.

The 1970s "discovery" of burnout in human service workers led to a more explicit examination of stress in child welfare social workers. Admittedly, child welfare social work makes a number of egregious demands on the emotional life of its practitioners. Handling intractable situations with limited resources, in contact with demanding, often unwilling, clients, and having responsibility for significant aspects of children's lives can erode the idealism, conviction, and enthusiasm of many workers. Protective service workers in particular experience stress related to role ambiguity and role conflict. Despite these factors—and even with such adverse conditions as comparatively low pay, high caseloads, and turbulent organizational environments—child welfare workers reported a high level of overall job satisfaction

(Jayaratne & Chess, 1984). Not unexpectedly, however, studies of training needs identified by child welfare workers gave high priority to training in stress management techniques (Vinokur, 1983).

Conclusion

The need for the child welfare services system is unquestionable. Child welfare social workers perform functions indispensable to the amelioration of problems encountered by significantly large numbers of children and families, and it is clear that the public supports such services and programs. The question, however, is whether such occupational activities as a professional function can continue to be assigned to, and controlled by, the profession. To a great extent, this will depend on the ability of the profession to establish convincingly that professional knowledge, skill, and expertise, acquired by social workers as a consequence of professional training, are clearly superior to service provided by nonprofessionals. As yet, the profession has failed to provide clear evidence that such is the case.

ALFRED KADUSHIN

For further information, see ADOPTION; CHILD CARE SERVICES; FOSTER CARE FOR CHILDREN; JUVENILE OFFENDER DIVERSION AND COMMUNITY-BASED SERVICES; PROFESSIONAL LIABILITY AND MALPRACTICE.

References

Besharov, D. J. (1984). *Criminal and Civil Liability in Child Welfare Work: The Growing Trend.* Washington, D.C.: National Legal Resource Center for Child Advocacy and Protection, American Bar Association.

Besharov, D. J. (1985). *The Vulnerable Social Worker.* Silver Spring, Md.: National Association of Social Workers.

Child Welfare League of America. (1984). *Standards for Organization and Administration for All Child Welfare Services.* New York: Author.

Goldstein, J., Freud, A., & Solnit, A. J. (1973). *Beyond the Best Interests of the Child.* New York: Free Press.

Jayaratne, S., & Chess, W. A. (1984). "Job Satisfaction, Burnout and Turnover: A National Study." *Social Work, 29*(5), 448–453.

Jones, M., & Moore, A. (1983). *Annual Salary Study and Survey of Selected Personnel Issues.* New York: Child Welfare League of America.

Jones, M. A., Neuman, R., & Shyne, A. (1976). *A Second Chance for Families.* New York: Child Welfare League of America.

Kahn, A. (1977). "Child Welfare." In *Encyclope-*

dia of Social Work (17th ed., pp. 100–114). Washington, D.C.: National Association of Social Workers.

Meyer, C. (1984). "Can Foster Care Be Saved?" *Social Work, 29*(6), 499.

"NASW Data Bank Releases Latest Analysis." (1985, May). *NASW News*, p. 10, Table D).

National Association of Social Workers. *Baccalaureate in Social Work—B.S.W. Report*. Silver Spring, Md.: Author.

O'Connor, G. G., & Waring, M. L. (1981). "Toward Identifying the Domain of Social Work." *Arete, 6*(4), 1–12.

Shyne, A. W., & Schroeder, A. G. (1978). *National Study of Social Services to Children and Their Families*. Rockville, Md.: Westat, Inc.

Tatara, T. (1983). *Characteristics of Children in Substitute and Adoptive Care—A Statistical Summary of the UCIS Natural Child Welfare Data Base*. Washington, D.C.: American Public Welfare Association.

U.S. Department of Health, Education, and Welfare. (1978). *System of Social Services for Children and Families—Detailed Design*. Washington, D.C.: U.S. Government Printing Office.

U.S. Department of Labor, Bureau of Labor Statistics. (1978). *Occupational Outlook Handbook, 1978–79 Edition*. Washington, D.C.: U.S. Government Printing Office.

U.S. Department of Labor, Bureau of Labor Statistics. (1984). *Occupational Outlook Handbook, 1984–85 Edition*. Washington, D.C.: U.S. Government Printing Office.

Vinokur, D. K. (1983). *The View from the Agency—Supervisors and Workers Look at In-Service Training for Child Welfare*. Ann Arbor: National Child Welfare Training Center, University of Michigan School of Social Work.

CITIZEN PARTICIPATION

The belief that citizens should be involved directly in the organizations that affect them is part of the American democratic tradition. It has been demonstrated in various ways throughout U.S. history. The term "citizen participation" came into widespread use following the enactment of the Economic Opportunity Act of 1964 (P.L. 88-452), which marked the beginning of the War on Poverty. The act required that programs be developed with "maximum feasible participation" of those affected.

Definitions, Goals, and Benefits

Definitions vary, but most authors view citizen participation as a way of making representative government work better and especially as a means of making government bureaucracies more responsive to citizens' preferences. In the 1960s this generally involved a regular, structured interaction between local groups of citizens and branches of government that operated specific programs (Cahn & Passett, 1971; Spiegel, 1974; Wireman, 1977).

Citizen participation in human service programs serves three purposes: It provides those affected by the programs with an opportunity (1) to influence policy decisions and the allocation of resources; (2) to share in the design, implementation, and monitoring of specific programs; and (3) to ensure that the benefits of a program go to the specific neighborhood or group it was designed to serve. Generally, citizen participation for the purpose of implementing programs requires a collaborative approach with agencies, but participation that aims at influencing policy and the allocation of resources more often involves conflict, confrontation, and adversary relationships (Wireman, 1977).

The benefits of citizen participation for individuals and groups range from aiding personal growth to achieving modest social reforms. Benefits may include reducing feelings of alienation toward a specific program, increasing networks and cooperative relationships within a neighborhood and among different ethnic or class groups, and improving specific programs. Potential benefits to the agencies themselves range from mobilizing citizen support for programs and budgets to assisting in the development of policies, programs, and procedures (Wireman, 1984).

Growth in the 1960s and 1970s

During the early days of the War on Poverty, much of the rhetoric of citizen participation dealt with empowerment and citizen control. The newly created federal Community Action Agency required that local programs be run by boards of directors, the majority of whose members represented the poor. Soon, however, local politicians, bureaucrats, and Congress reacted and made it clear that citizen participation was to be only advisory. Some observers concluded that any meaningful involvement of the poor was over, and that continued efforts were only manipulative in nature (Arnstein, 1969; Kershaw, 1970; Levitan, 1969; Moynihan, 1969; U.S. Congress, 1964).

Critics noted that participants were often the least poor in the neighborhood and that low-income board members frequently deferred to other members who had more education or experience. In many cases, however, initially diffident members learned skills and confidence and assumed positions of leadership. In addition, some research indicates that even though community representatives did not greatly influence the community action boards, the boards still represented the interests of their constituents (Levitan & Taggert, 1976).

The citizen participation emphasis of the Community Action Agency spread to other programs. For example, in 1968 the Department of Housing and Urban Development (HUD) issued regulations for citizen participation in urban renewal. The regulations lacked a congressional mandate and were criticized for being weak. Nevertheless, during the first Nixon Administration, some citizen groups were receiving more than a million dollars a year to organize community participation in their local urban renewal programs. The extent of citizen participation requirements in federal government programs increased most markedly—from 16 federal programs in 1969 to 87 by 1975—during the Nixon years (Advisory Commission on Intergovernmental Relations [ACIR], 1979; Wireman, 1984).

Conditions Conducive to Success

For citizen participation to be successful, the following conditions are helpful:

1. The group's mandate for participation must be clear, preferably based on congressional legislation.

2. The group must have sufficient organizational power to command the right to participate.

3. The group must be acknowledged as legitimate spokespersons for the area or for the people affected by the program.

4. The group must have ongoing access to information and to decision makers while they are still considering options.

5. The group's staff must have access to technical experts who are accountable to the group.

6. The group must have sufficient operating funds so that all its energies are not absorbed by fundraising.

7. Group members must be able to function well together and understand the administrative and technical requirements of the program with which they are dealing.

8. The group must have effective input into the program's budget process.

9. The group must be able to turn to the federal government or the courts if local officials deny it the right to participate (Wireman, 1977, 1984).

Unfortunately, there has been little systematic research on the factors that influence the effect of citizen participation. One study of 51 cases in 17 states found that the more influential groups had an elected membership, their own staff, and the power both to investigate grievances and to influence the budget decisions of organizations that provided services to their area. Another study of municipal services found that control over staff was the key to control over services (ACIR, 1979).

Impact in the 1960s and 1970s

The impact of citizen participation in the 1960s and 1970s has been widely debated. Part of the disagreement arises from the lack of systematic comparative research. Another part is based on differences in interpretation of the goals of participation. (For example, if neighborhood residents learned how to contact city hall for the first time and came to know and respect their neighbors of a different race but did not obtain the program changes they wanted, was their participation a failure?) There were also differences in the extent to which programs encouraged citizen participation, ranging from vague suggestions in an agency policy paper to detailed requirements, funds allocated to assist groups to participate, and regular monitoring by federal officials to ensure that citizen participation was occurring properly (ACIR, 1979).

Even within the same program, various federal and local officials interpreted the regulations differently. During the early part of the 1970s, for example, citizen groups in areas administered through the Philadelphia Regional Office of HUD were receiving grants of up to a million dollars for a variety of citizen-directed activities ranging from operating social service programs to planning an urban renewal project. No group in the administrative jurisdiction of the Atlanta or Dallas regional offices, however, had control of operating funds. The effectiveness of citizen participation also depended on the leadership abilities, organizational skills, and political savvy of the local groups and on the local political-administrative environment.

Given this varied national picture, what general conclusions can be drawn? The few systematic studies that exist indicate that citizen participation was not especially effective in making major program changes or in reforming the agencies that were delivering services. In some cases, however, important changes were made. For example, in a study of citizen participation in 62 cities, the Brookings Institution found that such participation had a major influence in 42 percent of the cases and had some influence in an additional 29 percent (ACIR, 1979).

Often the rewards of citizen participation for the individual participant and for the neighborhood are indirect spillover effects—getting to know more people in the neighborhood, especially those of different racial, ethnic, or income backgrounds; learning about resources available in the neighborhood or city; or gaining increased feelings of belonging to the neighborhood. Such effects may have been particularly valuable during the early days of citizen participation just after the civil rights movement, when few Americans had experience in interracial living and housing discrimination had just become illegal.

The potential value of citizen participation for neighborhood relationships has been documented by a number of researchers. Hunter (1974) found that in 75 Chicago neighborhoods, people who belonged to a local organization were more likely than those who did not to evaluate their neighborhood positively and to express feelings of attachment to it. Fischer's (1982) study of northern California communities found that, in listing members of their personal networks, people named as many fellow members of local organizations as they named neighbors or co-workers. Moreover, local organization members were more likely to be named as friends than were neighbors, co-workers, or even kin.

Another spillover effect of citizen participation has been the training of minorities and women. During the 1960s and 1970s citizen participation, and especially employment in programs that involved them, offered women and minority members one of the few available opportunities to develop leadership abilities and gain administrative experience. In 1975, for example, most of the black congressmen and congresswomen were former leaders of citizen participation efforts (Wireman, 1977). Even today, many minority members and women in positions of mid-to-upper management in government gained their first leadership opportunities and training in the citizen participation efforts that began in the 1960s.

Citizen Participation in the 1980s

The atmosphere in the 1980s is quite different from the past. There is less concern with disadvantaged groups, greater distrust of the federal government, and more concern with reducing government spending at all levels. Three trends have greatly reduced citizen participation.

A number of specific programs in which traditions of, requirements for, or support for citizen involvement were high have been eliminated altogether or merged with other programs into block grants. These include the Community Action Program; the Comprehensive Employment and Training Act (CETA, P.L. 93-203), which provided workers for many community-controlled social service programs; and Title XX (P.L. 97-35), which included a number of social service programs. Urban renewal and model cities were merged into the Community Development Block Grant (CDBG) program in the 1970s. CDBG requirements are weaker than those of its predecessor programs, and HUD's concern and monitoring have become increasingly ineffective.

The other programs have weak citizen participation requirements that are not designed to involve those affected directly by the programs or those who live in a particular neighborhood. Furthermore, merging programs meant that groups that were involved in one program, such as child care services, would have to compete for influence with people involved in totally different types of programs, such as those for the elderly or handicapped. For example, a mother who started a play group for 2-year-olds, which over several years developed into a child care center with branches in two neighborhoods, can effectively participate in city decisions about child care—but not about meals-on-wheels or the need for buses equipped for wheelchairs. In addition, the new type of citizen participation tends to cover larger geographic areas and to be more formally structured; it may, for example, involve an annual statewide public hearing on an overall budget as opposed to neighborhood mothers getting together to talk to the child care director at the community center every month. Low-income mothers were generally effective talking to the child care director but lacked the time, transportation, experience, and education to participate effectively at the state budget hearings.

Finally, funds for all programs have been drastically cut. In some cases, groups have concluded that the effort needed to try to obtain these reduced funds is simply not worth their time and energy (M. Bennett & L. Perez, personal communication, March 1985).

A study of citizen participation requirements in four programs covering employment training, social services, special educational services, and community development concluded that in most cases it was ineffective or consisted of participation by the agencies providing services or by middle-income participants handpicked by the participating agencies. Exceptions to this occurred when there was a well-organized local advocacy group for a particular service, such as child care, or in the CDBG program, which had the strongest regulations. Participation in that program also benefited from a legacy of participation in previous HUD programs and from the entire neighborhood organizational movement (M. Bennett & L. Perez, personal communication, March 1985).

Current Trends

What, then, is the current situation? Has the legacy of the activism of the 1960s and 1970s died, returning citizen involvement to the blue-ribbon committees of much earlier times? Not necessarily. Many of the groups that came into existence in response to, or received support from, federal citizen participation efforts moved into other activities long ago. A number of community-based groups that originally concentrated on citizen participation began operating social service programs and then started housing and economic development activities. Before the federal funding cutbacks, one study identified more than 500 neighborhood development organizations undertaking energy, economic development, and housing projects (Mayer & Blake, 1981; Shabecoff, 1979). Some of these have been able to survive with local or state funds or have obtained private or foundation funds in addition to profits from their economic activities. In several cases, federal support continues through CDBG or other programs. The Department of Commerce's Economic Development Administration, for example, funded a number of national organizations with ties to community-based groups to provide training and technical assistance in neighborhood economic development activities.

An alternative route for citizen participation activities has involved accepting institutionalization as a normal part of the city planning process. Some 44 cities have neighborhood councils that are officially recognized as part of the regular planning process. These councils cover the entire city and deal with a range of issues. Another 120 cities use neighborhood councils to comment on only a few programs. Still other cities encourage neighborhood participation, even though they have not institutionalized such activities (Rohe & Gates, 1981; R. Rich, personal communication July, 1983).

A different direction for citizen participation has been the formation of partnerships between citizen groups and private industry. One of the most successful is the Neighborhood Reinvestment Corporation's Neighborhood Housing Services, which promotes housing rehabilitation. (The Neighborhood Reinvestment Corporation is a quasi-government corporation that operates programs with local partnerships between neighborhood members, cities, and the private sector.) In those neighborhoods where the program operates, local residents make up a majority of the board of directors, which also includes representatives of the city and its lending institutions. The staff helps residents rehabilitate their housing, supported by access to improvement loans and city assistance in the form of housing inspections, code enforcement, and public improvements (Hallman, 1984).

New Concepts and Problems

One of the most interesting new concepts of neighborhood resident participation is that of coproduction—in effect, that the amount of service actually obtained by residents is a combination of their efforts (both positive and negative) and those of the government. If there is a litter problem, for example, improvements could be made by increasing government expenditures for street sweeping, by neighborhood cleanups, or by reducing carelessness with trash. One of the advantages of neighborhood organizations is that they can mobilize joint action, and some groups have actually contracted with local governments for management of certain services (Rich, 1980; Wireman, 1984).

Neighborhood provision of services (as opposed to participation in influencing the decisions of service providers) ties in with another current concept—that of networks. There is considerable evidence that varied and strong networks are important in providing emotional and other supports to individuals and families and in fostering strong neighborhoods. A number of projects have successfully used natural networks to assist in mental health programs and to provide support for the elderly and for single or isolated mothers (Wireman, 1984).

The overall reduction in citizen participation requirements may well reduce the responsiveness of human services to those in need. Although some cities and states are substituting their own requirements, this is not a universal situation. Moreover, state legislatures are likely to be most responsive to the majority of their constituents, rather than to the housebound elderly or single parents (unless these groups are articulate and well organized, which takes knowledge, time, and money).

The trend toward reliance on the private sector to make up for the cutbacks and withdrawals of federal funds and programs could introduce new ideas and creativity into service provision. To date, however, the private sector has not matched the federal funds. Furthermore, private sector participation is not free; it is supported indirectly by the taxpayer because it is considered a tax-deductible business expense. Private sector interest in social service provision often must be related to at least indirect benefits for the firm—for example, through publicity. Concerns have been expressed that, in some cases, private sector control of the new participation structures for employment and training funds has resulted in conflicts of interest between the needs of the participating private employer and those of the people eligible for the program (L. Perez, personal communication, March 1984). Indeed, private sector funding has rarely supported controversial efforts that threaten existing power structures or established ways of solving social problems. Yet in a dynamic, changing country, such efforts—like the civil rights and women's movements—make major contributions to peaceful social change.

The new emphasis on the use of volunteers and networks to provide local services supports many traditional values of social workers, including the strength of the family. This is not, however, a substitute for appropriate policies and adequately funded programs. Most of the health care for the elderly, for example, is provided by daughters or daughters-in-law. This has become an increasing burden as more women are employed and as the elderly population grows older and needs more constant and demanding types of care. Some caretakers may depend on their jobs for their own support; others are themselves over 65 and not in good health (Brody, 1979). Although there is strong support for the use of neighborhoods, networks, and families in providing human services, to do so without proper thought and funding is unrealistic and will eventually overburden and destroy these volunteer systems. (An example of what not to do was the deinstitutionalization of the mentally ill, which led to the deterioration of the neighborhoods into which they drifted and to the current crisis of homeless persons living on the streets.) Proper joint family-neighborhood-agency programs must be well designed, with clear and appropriate roles for all participants.

Role of Social Workers

Today many of the avenues for citizen participation are indirect, through work on committees and agencies, and are less accessible because they are geographically discrete and occur in complex organizational structures. Social workers need to become actively involved in whatever participation structures are available. They should also advocate for more direct forms of client involvement and assist clients to learn the skills necessary for effective participation.

Social workers should make sure that the involvement of families, neighborhoods, and networks in the provision of human services is structured in a manner that does not overburden those groups or violate confidentiality. In this age of computers, care must be taken to protect the privacy of the individuals, groups, and neighborhood residents involved (Wireman, 1984). Social workers should also help to educate individuals in the private sector as to the extent and complexity of service needs and the necessity of trying innovative new approaches, especially those suggested by or directed by clients.

PEGGY WIREMAN

For further information, see COMMUNITY-BASED SOCIAL ACTION; LEGISLATIVE ADVOCACY; NATURAL HELPING NETWORKS; NEIGHBORHOODS; POLITICAL ACTION IN SOCIAL WORK; VOLUNTEERS.

References

Advisory Commission on Intergovernmental Relations. (1979). *Citizen Participation in the American Federal System.* Washington, D.C.: U.S. Government Printing Office.

Arnstein, S. R. (1969). "A Ladder of Citizen Participation." *Journal of American Institute of Planners, 35,* 216–224.

Bennett, M., & Perez, L. (1986). *A Look at the States' Administration of Block Grants Four Years Later: Implications for the Future.* Washington, D.C.: Coalition on Human Needs.

Brody, E. M. (1979). "Women's Changing Roles and Care of the Aging Family." In J. Pineau (Ed.), *Aging: Agenda for the Eighties* (pp. 11–16). Washington, D.C.: Government Research Corp.

Cahn, E. S., & Passett, B. A. (Eds.). (1971). *Citizen Participation: Effecting Community Change.* New York: Praeger Publishers.

Fisher, C. S. (1982). *To Swell among Friends: Personal Networks in Town and City.* Chicago: University of Chicago Press.

Hallman, H. W. (1984). *Neighborhoods: Their Place in Urban Life.* Beverly Hills, Calif.: Sage Publications.

Hunter, A. (1974). *Symbolic Communities: The Persistence and Change of Chicago's Local Communities.* Chicago: University of Chicago Press.

Kershaw, J. A. (1970). *Government Against Poverty.* Washington, D.C.: Brookings Institution.

Levitan, S. A. (1969). *The Great Society's Poor Law: A New Approach to Poverty.* Baltimore, Md.: Johns Hopkins University Press.

Levitan, S. A., & Taggert, R. (1976). *The Promise of Greatness.* Cambridge, Mass.: Harvard University Press.

Mayer, N. S., & Blake, J. L. (1981). *Keys to the Growth of Neighborhood Development Organizations.* Washington, D.C.: Urban Institute.

Moynihan, D. P. (1969). *Maximum Feasible Misunderstanding.* New York: Free Press.

Rich, R. (1980). "The Dynamics of Leadership in Neighborhood Organizations." *Social Science Quarterly, 60,* 570–587.

Rohe, W., & Gates, L. B. (1981). "Neighborhood Planning: Promise and Product." *Urban Social Change Review, 14,* 27.

Shabecoff, A. (Ed.). (1979). *Neighborhoods: A Self-Help Sampler.* Washington, D.C.: U.S. Department of Housing and Urban Development.

Spiegel, H. (1974). *Decentralization: Citizen Participation in Urban Development* (Vol. 3). Fairfax, Va.: Learning Resources Corp.

U.S. Congress, 1st Session. (1964). *Statutes at Large, Vol. 78: Economic Opportunity Act of 1964* (Section 202[a][3], 516). Washington, D.C.: U.S. Government Printing Office.

Wireman, P. (1977). "Citizen Participation." In J. B. Turner (Ed.), *Encyclopedia of Social Work* (17th ed., pp. 175–180). Washington, D.C.: National Association of Social Workers.

Wireman, P. (1984). *Urban Neighborhoods, Networks, and Families: New Forms for Old Values.* Lexington, Mass.: Lexington Books.

CIVIL RIGHTS

Civil rights and civil liberties protect the individual from arbitrary, discriminatory, and oppressive actions of the state or of fellow citizens. With their roots in English law, civil rights and liberties have achieved a high level of development in the United States.

Civil rights are a shield to defend the citizen from the state. They require that government deal fairly, justly, and equitably with the individual. Civil liberties are a sword with which the citizen can probe, fashion, and alter government and the conditions of society. Both are essential to maintain a proper relationship between citizen and state and between citizen and citizen. They provide peace and order for society with freedom and dignity for the individual.

Origins

English civil rights were established by Magna Charta on June 15, 1215, when King John agreed under threat of force to grant certain legal rights to the nobility. Among these civil rights were the following:

> No freeman shall be taken or imprisoned or disseised [dispossessed] or exiled or in any way destroyed, nor will we go upon nor send upon him, except by the lawful judgment of his peers or by the law of the land. . . . To no one will we sell, to no one will we refuse or delay, rights or justice.

These principles still live in the English and American legal systems, forming the foundations of human liberty and democratic society.

In the 1600s a movement toward civil liberties began to emerge in England. The Declaration of Rights and Liberties was adopted by Parliament in 1689. It extended legal rights to protect the individual—excessive fines and cruel or unusual punishment were prohibited, the right to a jury trial by impartial jurors was guaranteed, the accused could no longer be subjected to fine or forfeiture unless convicted, the liberties of petitioning the king without restriction and speaking freely were granted, and the king was denied the power to suspend or levy taxes without the approval of Parliament. In 1694, Chief Justice John Holt ruled that the rights and liberties granted to the king's subjects in England also applied to subjects in the colonies. This ruling paved the way for the development of civil rights and liberties in colonial America.

The American Revolution was based on the concept that an individual had certain inalienable rights and liberties derived from Divine Providence, not from any sovereign, and that the king was thus obligated to protect them. The 1776 American Declaration of Independence reflected the 1689 Parliamentary Declaration of Rights and Liberties with one important addition: the king was eliminated as the supreme legal authority, and the American people became the ultimate power in government. The Declaration of Independence also indicted the king for "depriving us, in many cases, of the benefits of trial by jury," "transporting us beyond the seas to be tried for pretended offenses," obstructing "the administration of justice," and making "judges dependent on his will alone."

The supreme achievement of the Declaration of Independence was its espousal of the concept that the individual should be protected by the state. This philosophy included the following tenets: all people are created equal; each is endowed by the Creator, rather than by the state, with the rights of life, liberty, and the pursuit of happiness; and government does not give, but secures, these basic freedoms. Such beliefs fused civil rights and civil liberties into a common concept, making paramount the personal integrity of individuals in their relationships with the state and with other individuals. Underlying this concept is the assertion that government receives its just powers from the consent of the people governed and that the people retain the right to alter or abolish the government and to institute a new government to attain individual safety and happiness.

Although the Declaration of Independence proclaimed national goals in terms of rights and liberties, it did not specify the means for achieving these ends. In 1787, the U.S. Constitution and, in 1791, the Bill of Rights met that need.

Civil Rights in the United States

In a country with a vast wilderness frontier, rights and liberties are not easily denied. Thus, during the frontier period in the United States, dissidents, activists, and nonconformists who were deprived of rights and liberties could resettle in the West. Nevertheless, the legal system established certain important restrictions on civil rights. Females, for example, were held legally inferior to males, and blacks, under slavery, were treated as property rather than as human beings. The Constitution designated that five blacks were equal to three whites in determining population size, which affected the makeup of the House of Representatives and the imposition of direct taxes on the people. American Indians were also denied civil rights protection under the Constitution. They were not citizens but wards of the federal government and were excluded from the population count on which membership in the House of Representatives was based.

The slavery provisions of the Constitution were the result of bargaining between the slave states and the free states. Without such compromises, the federal constitution could not have been adopted. The Northwest Territory Ordinance, however—which applied to the area that now includes Ohio, Indiana, Michigan, Illinois, and Wisconsin—was enacted by the Continental Congress in 1787 and contained an absolute prohibition against slavery.

Attempts to resolve the slavery issue in Congress from 1800 to the 1850s were not successful. During this time an important development took place in the legal process. Under the judicial statesmanship of Chief Justice John Marshall, the Supreme Court firmly established itself as the final arbiter of constitutional questions, including civil rights and liberties, taking precedence over Congress, the president, and state and local governments as the guardian of the citizen.

In 1857, the Supreme Court made a momentous civil rights decision. It ruled that Dred Scott, a black slave, could not become a freeman even though he had moved to a free state. The Court argued that blacks could not acquire civil rights as free citizens because they were designated as unequal to whites in the Constitution. Only by formal Constitutional amendment could blacks be made citizens. Despite the abolitionist movement to free the slaves and the congressional compromises of 1820 and 1850, which admitted free and slave states into the Union in equal numbers, it was politically impossible to achieve such an amendment. The *Dred Scott* decision helped bring about the Civil War and the civil rights revolution that followed.

During the Civil War, President Abraham Lincoln issued the Emanicipation Proclamation (1863) giving blacks in Confederate territory their freedom. Three significant constitutional amendments were passed after the Union victory—the Thirteenth Amendment (1865), prohibiting slavery; the Fourteenth Amendment (1868) securing life, liberty, property, and equal protection of the law for all; and the Fifteenth Amendment (1870), establishing the right of black men to vote.

With new constitutional mandates, the federal judiciary was given many opportunities to interpret and enforce civil rights in both national and state jurisdictions. The federal legislature also exercised its authority to enact national civil rights laws applicable to all states. The Civil Rights Act of 1866 was the first federal statute to provide broad protection of individuals' civil rights. The Civil Rights Act of 1875 completed congressional action on this subject in the immediate post–Civil War period. These acts, which are still widely applied, established both civil and criminal authority for protection of civil rights by the federal government. Private citizens were also given access to the federal judiciary to enforce these rights. Although the laws were designed primarily to assure blacks their civil rights, the statutory language also protected individuals from discrimination because of national origin, religion, or political beliefs. However, these acts did not protect individuals whose rights were denied because of sex or age.

Thus, the legal requirements for comprehensive security of individual civil rights were established by 1875. However, the prevailing social and cultural beliefs made the laws practically unenforceable.

Twentieth Century

In 1920, the Nineteenth Amendment granted women the right to vote—an important early step in women's struggle to achieve equality with men.

Not until 1923 did the Supreme Court use its authority over the interpretation of the Constitution to enforce the civil rights amendment and statutes passed after the Civil War. It began recasting the legal, economic, and social relationships, between blacks and whites with its decision in *Moore* v. *Dempsey* (1923). This case involved black sharecroppers in Phillips County, Arkansas, who sought to improve their economic condition by organizing. Frightened white citizens reacted violently, and more than 200 people were killed.

At the trial of the many blacks who were accused of murder, blacks were excluded from the jury, black witnesses were forced to testify against the defendants, and a white mob threatened lynchings if there were no convictions. Court-appointed defense counsel failed to ask for a change of venue and did not call witnesses or put defendants on the stand. The trial lasted less than an hour. With 5 minutes' deliberation, the all-white jury convicted 12 blacks of first-degree murder. The death sentence was imposed.

The National Association for the Advancement of Colored People, the most powerful ally of black citizens at the time, took up the cause of the convicted blacks. Eventually all defendants were freed on a federal writ of habeas corpus on the grounds that their civil right to a fair trial had been violated.

With this decision, the Supreme Court began an era in which de facto realities were to be more important than *de jure* laws in considering civil rights cases. This point became important in the 1950s and 1960s in cases involving the treatment of blacks in such areas as education, housing, and employment.

World War II. With the advent of World War II, the executive branch of the federal government assumed the initiative in civil rights. Using his authority as commander in chief, President Franklin D. Roosevelt issued Executive Order 8802 on June 25, 1941. Under this order, the denial of employment in defense industries because of race, color, creed, or national origin was forbidden. Additional executive orders (9001, 9346) required the armed forces to eliminate discrimination based on race, color, creed, or national origin.

Two significant advances took place in the late 1940s. President Harry S Truman created the President's Committee on Civil Rights. It studied the nation's civil rights experiences and proposed major new goals in its final report, *To Secure These Rights* (1947). Then the United Nations promulgated the Universal Declaration of Human Rights. Produced in 1948 by the U.N. Human Rights Commission, with Eleanor Roosevelt as chairperson, this document was evidence of worldwide concern for the protection of civil rights.

1950s. By 1950, many legal actions were under way in the area of civil rights. Issues included the peacetime draft, reformation of the court-martial system to improve due process of law for members of the armed services, the right of international war criminals to appeal to the U.S. Supreme Court, preferential treatment for veterans on civil service tests, the president's amnesty board and the status of conscientious objectors, the authority of the military to deprive people of their liberty outside United States territory, and whether control of nuclear weapons should rest with the armed forces or the civilian Atomic Energy Commission.

The rights of communists under the Constitution also produced legal controversies. Considerations included the investigative powers of Congress, loyalty oath requirements, the designation of certain organizations as subversive without specification or hearings, and the requirement that labor union officers file affidavits that they were not communists. Additional legal actions were brought under the First Amendment guaranteeing freedom of speech, the press, religion, and assembly. These addressed labor cases involving picketing rights and the closed shop, a municipality's authority to license the use of public address systems in parks, vague state legislation restricting the publication of stories about crime and violence, and attempts by Jehovah's Witnesses to proselytize their religious beliefs in public parks and private residences.

Persons charged with crimes also asserted their civil rights. Double jeopardy, methods of obtaining confessions, unreasonable search and seizure, self-incrimination, and a defendant's right to counsel in noncapital cases became judicial issues. The civil rights of aliens in deportation, expatriation, and citizenship cases were also considered.

In education, the exclusion of blacks from a state university, the granting of public funds to an exclusively white private school, and salary inequalities between black and white teachers were the subjects of trials. State prohibitions of miscegenation and the denial of commercial fishing rights to aliens ineligible for citizenship were also argued in the courts.

Of the many events that occurred to advance the cause of civil rights, two had particularly far-reaching effects. In *Shelly* v. *Kraemer* (1948), the Supreme Court held that private arrangements to maintain racial segregation in housing patterns could not be legally recognized. In *Brown* v. *Board of Education* (1954) the "separate but equal" doctrine, which had been valid since 1896, was overruled. Segregation of schoolchildren on the basis of race was held to be unconstitutional even if the facilities were of equal quality. Following this decision, racial segregation was eventually eliminated in the public areas of transportation, hotel and restaurant accommodation, theaters and auditoriums, parks and recreational areas, and barbershops. It was only after years of effort, however, including some violence, that the full implications of the *Brown* decision could be applied to American life. In the period from 1955 to 1970, blacks organized into action groups to secure their civil rights. This phase of self-help produced such outstanding leaders as the Reverend Dr. Martin Luther King, Jr.

In 1956, President Dwight D. Eisenhower recommended to Congress a program for the enforcement of civil rights. The Civil Rights Act of 1957 (P.L. 85-315) was the result. The first such act since 1875, it established the Commission on Civil Rights and strengthened federal enforcement powers.

1960s. In 1964, more significant civil rights legislation was enacted. A change in public attitude had been brought about by black self-help activities such as sit-ins and boycotts; by the assassination of President John F. Kennedy, who was fully committed to civil rights programs; and by the civil rights conversion of President Lyndon B. Johnson. A political climate favorable to the acceptance of advanced civil rights legislation now existed.

The 1964 Civil Rights Act (P.L. 88-352) strengthened voting rights. Injunctive relief (the power of a court to order certain acts to be done) was made available to victims of discrimination on the basis of race, color, religion, or national origin in cases that involved interstate commerce. The U.S. Department of Justice was authorized to desegregate public education. The Civil Rights Commission was given expanded investigative power. Any program receiving federal funding was forbidden to discriminate on the basis of race, color, religion, or national origin. The act required that equal employment opportunities be provided in any enterprise affecting commerce among the states. The Equal Employment Opportunity Commission was created to oversee this effort. A Community Relations Service was established in the Department of Commerce to help communities resolve problems involving discrimination. Five months after the 1964 act became law, its most potent feature—injunctive relief against discrimination in private places providing public accommodation—was held constitutional by the Supreme Court. A powerful legal weapon to assure civil rights protection became available to all citizens.

Other federal civil rights acts were subsequently enacted in the areas of voting, housing, and employment. Furthermore, for the first time, American Indians and women were provided federal civil rights protection. The former obtained legal recognition of tribal sovereignty over tribal lands and economic development to improve economic and social conditions. Through the Equal Employment Opportunity Act of 1963 (P.L. 88-38), women were given a legal process to ensure equal pay for equal work and the opening of employment opportunities in practically every occupation. The Supreme Court generated intense political discussion and frequent public violence when it ordered public school busing to achieve racial desegregation (Keyes, 1973).

Another Supreme Court civil rights effort provided protection for all who became involved in federal, state, or local criminal proceedings. Law enforcement personnel were required to protect citizens' rights in arrest, search and seizure, detention, and bail.

1976–1985. The past decade has produced a continuing expansion of civil rights in the criminal justice area. Since the Supreme Court decision in *Mapp* v. *Ohio* (1961), evidence unreasonably seized by a government agent cannot be used against an accused person. Invasion of one's home by the police without a search warrant is generally forbidden. But when the police make a lawful vehicle stop, the entire care (including closed containers) can be searched without a judicially issued search warrant. Also, when police are investigating a suspected crime, no warrant is needed to search a mobile home. (The "unreasonable service" rule of *Mapp* does not apply to a search made by a private person.) Since *Gideon* v. *Wainwright* (1963), the indigent accused have had the right to secure appointment of legal defense at the government's expense.

In 1985, the "unreasonable seizure" rule was applied to strike down a Tennessee statute that authorized the police to shoot a fleeing suspected felon to obtain an arrest. Now, police cannot legally shoot an unarmed, nondangerous fleeing felon. Only when the police or other citizens are threatened with injury by the felon may the police as a last resort shoot to arrest.

The Fifth Amendment privilege against self-incrimination since *Miranda* v. *Arizona* (1966) requires the police to inform a person taken into custody of the right to remain silent and the right to legal counsel. Any confession, admission, or other evidence obtained without this warning cannot be used against the accused. A routine traffic stop by the police does not require the warning, however, because the citizen is not taken into custody. The Supreme Court has also begun to grant exceptions to this rigid *Miranda* rule: no warning need be given when the police officer's recitation might deter a suspect from answering questions that are necessary to prevent an immediate threat to the public safety.

Equal rights in education and employment have generated many new legal decisions. When California created a quota for blacks to be admitted to the university's medical school, a white applicant with higher academic credentials than some admitted black candidates was denied admission. The white student sought legal redress for this "reverse discrimination." In *Regents of University of California* v. *Bakke* (1978), the Supreme Court held that no applicant could be excluded a place in the entering class solely because of race on a quota system. Race, however, could be one factor in the admission decision process if it is used to secure a diverse student body.

Affirmative action programs based on quotas are also suspect in the employment area. When the Memphis, Tennessee, fire department laid off senior white firemen before junior black firemen based solely on a quota for racial employment, it was held illegal (Firefighters, 1984).

Section 1983 of the federal Civil Rights Act of 1871 (ch. 99) has recently been reinterpreted. Now a municipality cannot deny an employee a federally protected civil right. New York City was held liable for denying two female employees their constitutional right of equal protection under the city's maternal health leave policy (Monell, 1978). The Supreme Court has also expanded the civil remedies under the federal Civil Rights Act to include punitive damages for acts that manifest a reckless and callous indifference when denying a person's civil rights. Victims may now be compensated for the value of losses actually incurred and also receive exemplary damages as punishment awards against the violators.

The civil right to vote is paramount. It provides each person, equally, the right to control the government. At one time the Supreme Court required evidence of actual intent to discriminate against a person to prove denial of this right. In 1982, the federal Voting Rights Act (P.L. 97-205) changed this requirement; only evidence of a discriminatory result need be proved.

Groups of people with common characteristics continue to exercise civil rights and civil liberties. Intentional segregation of Hispanic students is illegal. Many men and women seek to pass an Equal Rights Amendment to the Constitution to give men and women equal protection in all constitutional rights and liberties. Women have been more successful in the public employment area. Washington State has recognized the "comparable worth" theory of employment remuneration. Equal pay for equal work is already a women's right. Now a goal is equal pay for work not necessarily equal but comparable in the skills and qualifications needed to perform one's duties. This theory portends major change in employment rights for women.

The "right to life" movement seeks to protect the human fetus from abortion by postulating for the fetus a civil right to life. Three legal pathways are open: constitutional amendment, a Supreme Court decision overruling the female's right of choice in the first trimester of pregnancy established in *Roe* v. *Wade* (1973), or judicial interpretation of the federal Civil Rights Act to define the fetus as a person whose rights are to be protected. The physically handicapped and mentally retarded have also asserted their rights to equal protection under the law. For the physically handicapped, access by ramps to public buildings, public streets, and public transportation is actively pursued. The mentally retarded pressure public schools to provide "mainstream" education or treatment as equal as possible to that of the average pupil.

Homosexuals have recently organized in pursuit of civil rights and liberties. The Supreme Court, by an equally divided vote, 4 to 4, upheld a federal Court of Appeals decision that held invalid an Oklahoma statute providing for dismissal or suspension of teachers who advocated, encouraged, or promoted public or private homosexual activity (National Gay Task Force, 1985). This provision was held to be too sweeping and to deny the free speech rights of homosexual teachers outside school activity. The state's interests in regulating a teacher's speech were recognized, but it was held that—to outweigh the teacher's right of free speech—the teacher's words must result in material or substantial interference or disruption in normal school activities.

Two powerful undercurrents were affecting civil rights and civil liberties in the mid-1980s. One was the concern of many individuals that the "rights industry"—with public interest lawyers, legal activists, judges' clerks, and law professors in the forefront—has generated a national preoccupation with rights to the detriment of the need to recognize citizens' responsibilities and duties. The other was the political intent of President Ronald Reagan's Administration to withdraw, withhold, or decrease the power of the federal executive office in enforcing the civil rights of citizens. The reorganization of the federal Civil Rights Commission with black and white, male and female members sympathetic to this reduction of executive concern is symbolic of the new conservative political philosophy.

Another profound problem for the United States is the emerging immigration issue, which recognizes on the one hand the need to keep open the traditional doors of America as a safe haven for the politically oppressed and on the other, the need to bar entrance to those who allegedly seek economic, not political, sanctuary. Religious groups and churches providing sanctuary for these illegal aliens are reminiscent of the abolitionist movement prior to 1860, when the Underground Railroad of Northern whites helped runaway black slaves from the South seek freedom in Canada or in Northern cities.

Civil rights and civil liberties continue to be forged through reason and experience in American society as it advances toward A.D. 2000. Public debate continues over such issues as the separation of church and state, mandatory busing of public school students, reverse discrimination by affirmative action programs, reducing the power of law enforcement officials to arrest and prosecute criminals, distorting legal authority as it seeks to prevent violence and terrorism in the community, defending both individuals and institutions in the private sector from complete domination by government, and corrupting constitutional rights and liberties through complicated legal technicalities and prolonged legal procedures.

Social Work and Civil Rights

Before the industrial revolution, paramount civil rights issues were the legal right to fair criminal procedures and just civil processes together with the right to speak, write, and petition the government freely. The legal profession was heavily involved in these historic struggles. Social work emerged with the development of an industrial, technological, and communications society and the urbanization and bureaucratization of human life after 1900. Today, aided by a scientific knowledge of human behavior and social problems—especially the complex problems of the young and the old, the sick and the well, the citizen and the illegal alien—social workers must deal with conflicts between individual rights and government regulations.

In the 1930s, minimum standards for personal health, welfare, and opportunity were recognized as the economic and social rights of all citizens. Since World War II, high standards have been attained in the areas of health, education, recreation, and welfare. Whether social workers are involved in casework, group work, community organization, national programs, or research, the challenge of protecting civil rights in contemporary economic and social matters has the highest significance. The professional social worker has become an important adjunct to the lawyer in maintaining individual rights and liberties. Although lawyers have effectively defended the legal and political rights expressed in the Constitution, social workers have helped define and secure modern economic and social rights.

As the United States proceeds into its third century, government must continue to protect individual rights and liberties. A system has been established that affirms the dignity and worth of each human being. Citizens are protected from the repressive tendencies of the state and have the means to fashion for themselves a responsive and responsible government.

The American experience has added a new dimension to the concept of civil rights because of the many heterogeneous groups that constitute the nation. Groups seeking to secure rights include blacks, women, American Indians, unemployed workers, religious minorities, the physically handicapped, prisoners, homosexuals, the mentally disabled, retarded children, those working on behalf of the fetus, and patients subjected to medical experimentation. The individual's right to privacy and confidentiality in dealings with other individuals and with the government continues to be examined. Once rights and liberties became a written expression of the American dream in the Declaration of Independence and the Constitution, it was inevitable that these ideals would be tested by the diverse and changing conditions of American society.

The United States flourishes today because the rights and liberties of its citizens flourish. These rights and liberties have survived because they have been continually fashioned and refashioned in the process of a free people adapting and altering to meet the new demands of each decade.

OLIVER C. SCHROEDER, JR.

For further information, see DISABILITIES: DEVELOPMENTAL; DISABILITIES: PHYSICAL; INTERGROUP RELATIONS; MINORITIES OF COLOR; RACIAL DISCRIMINATION AND INEQUALITY; SEX DISCRIMINATION AND INEQUALITY; VALUES AND ETHICS.

References
Brown v. Board of Education of Topeka, Kansas. (1954). 74 S. Ct. 686
Firefighters Local Union No. 1784 v. Stotts. (1984). 104 S. Ct. 2576.
Gideon v. Wainwright. (1963). 83 S. Ct. 792.
Keyes v. School District. (1973). 93 S. Ct. 2686.
Mapp v. Ohio. (1961). 81 S. Ct. 1684.
Monell v. Department of Social Services of City of New York. (1978). 98 S. Ct. 2018.
Moore v. Dempsey. (1923). 43 S. Ct. 265.
National Gay Task Force v. Board of Education of the City of Oklahoma City. (1985). 105 S. Ct. 1858.
Regents of University of California v. Bakke. (1978). 98 S. Ct. 2733.
Roe v. Wade. (1973). 93 S. Ct. 705.
Shelly v. Kraemer. (1948). 68 S. Ct. 836.
President's Committee on Civil Rights. (1947). *To Secure These Rights* (PR 33.2:R449). Washington, D.C.: U.S. Government Printing Office.

For Further Reading
Abernathy, M. G. (1985). *Civil Liberties under the Constitution* (4th ed.). Columbia: University of South Carolina.
Dorsen, N., Bender, P., & Neuborne, B. (1976). *Political and Civil Rights in the U.S.* (4th ed.). Boston: Little, Brown & Co.
Eisenberg, T. (1984). *Civil Rights Legislation.* Charlottesville, Va.: Michie Co.
Morgan, R. E. (1984). *Disabling America: The "Rights Industry" in Our Time.* New York: Basic Books.
Newman, E. S. (1976). *Civil Liberties and Civil Rights* (4th ed.). Dobbs Ferry, N.Y.: Oceana Publications.
Pollack, H., & Smith, A. (1978). *Civil Liberties and Civil Rights in the United States.* St. Paul, Minn.: West Publishing.

CLASSIFICATION. See PERSONNEL MANAGEMENT; PROFESSION OF SOCIAL WORK: CONTEMPORARY CHARACTERISTICS.

CLIENT DATA INFORMATION SYSTEMS. See INFORMATION SYSTEMS: CLIENT DATA; RECORDING IN DIRECT PRACTICE.

Reader's Guide

CLINICAL SOCIAL WORK: APPROACHES AND PERSPECTIVES

The following articles contain information on this general topic:

Appendix 3: NASW Standards for the Practice of Clinical Social Work (includes definition)
Behavioral Approach
Cognitive Therapy
Crisis Intervention
Direct Practice: Trends and Issues
Direct Practice Effectiveness
Direct Practice in Social Work: Overview
Ecological Perspective
Ethnic-Sensitive Practice
Existential Approach
Feminist Social Work
Generalist Perspective
Gestalt Therapy
Professional Associations: National Association of Social Workers
Psychosocial Approach
Radical Social Work
Task-Centered Approach
Transactional Analysis
(See also Reader's Guide: Clinical Social Work Methods on p. 288.)

COGNITIVE THERAPY

The central tenet in cognitive therapy is that most human emotions and behaviors, whether rational or irrational, functional or dysfunctional, are largely the result of what people think, imagine, or believe—in short, the result of their cognitive processes. Therefore, it is not simply the specific events, interactions, or circumstances people encounter that lead to emotional and behavioral problems; rather, it is what people think or believe about these events, interactions, or circumstances that leads to such problems. The essence of cognitive therapy, then, is to help clients change their cognitive processes in a way that enables them to overcome their emotional and behavioral problems.

Origins

Given this central tenet, it could be said that the origins of cognitive therapy date back to the time of the ancient Greeks, when the philosopher Epictetus observed, around 100 A.D., that people are not disturbed by things but by their perceptions of things. However, it was not until the early 1960s that the modern version of this tenet was systematically tested for purposes of treatment.

Since then the cognitive approach has grown rapidly and may be well on its way to becoming a "third force" between the dominant psychoanalytic and behavioristic orientations to casework and psychotherapy (Werner, 1982). Ellis's (1962) initial formulation of rational-emotive therapy and then Beck's (1976) formulation of cognitive therapy were among the most notable and influential works in this rapid expansion and dissemination of the cognitive approach. Werner's *A Rational Approach to Social Casework* (1965) was the first work to bring an explicit cognitive orientation to social work practice. Since the 1960s there has been a profusion of social work literature on cognitive practice (Fischer, 1978; Fleming, 1981; Goldstein, 1981; Lantz, 1978; Sherman, 1979; Werner, 1979; Werner, 1982).

Theoretical Foundations

Stated in its simplest and boldest form, cognitive theory holds that "thinking shapes behavior" (Werner, 1982). This should not be taken to mean, however, that cognition is "just thinking" in the restricted sense of intellectual functioning that is reflected in I.Q. tests. Cognition includes imagery, memory, sentience, and other subjective forms of consciousness, as well as the intellectual and analytic functions of consciousness. Therefore, cognition is not a purely cerebral function; it is inseparably related to emotion. That is why the cognitive therapist believes it is possible to change dysfunctional emotions by changing dysfunctional cognitive processes through cognitive therapy.

The theory that forms the foundation of cognitive therapy incorporates but is broader than the theory that underlies cognitive-behavioral procedures. That theory restricts its definition and use of cognition to the status of a mediating variable. Goldstein (1982) made an important distinction between the mediational model and the more comprehensive model of cognitive therapy, which he termed phenomenological. The mediational model takes an objective-reactive position in which cognition is defined as an intervening variable that processes the input of outer stimuli and, in turn, affects the emotional and behavioral output. The phenomenological model adds to this by taking into account cognition's intentional, selective, and interpretive qualities, which enable it to determine not only what is outside, but also what that outside *means*. Therefore, the client is seen as a person who cognitively construes or constructs his or her own reality in a highly active, personal, and intentional way. It should be emphasized that cognitive therapy utilizes both models, depending on the assessment and needs of a particular case.

Assessment and Intervention Methods

The essence of cognitive therapy has probably been most simply and directly stated by Ellis (1962, 1974) in his "ABC theory of emotions" in which A is the *activating* event or situation, B is the *belief* or thoughts about the event or situation, and C is the emotional *consequence* of the thoughts or belief. Thus, B is the pivotal factor in the A→B→C experiential process. If B is an irrational belief (iB) or interpretation of A, then it will lead to irrational emotional consequences (iC), and the client will experience A as extremely stressful, upsetting, or even catastrophic. Another person who encounters the same kind of event or situation might believe or perceive it to be a challenge rather than a catastrophe, in which case there would be no dysfunctional emotional consequences requiring intervention.

In the cognitive approach, the client is taught how to explore the implicit thoughts or self-talk associated with the explicit, disproportionate, dysfunctional emotions or behaviors. In this process the client identifies the irrational or unsubstantiated elements in the implicit thoughts and, with the guidance of the therapist, learns how to dispute them and replace them with rational beliefs (rB). This *disputation* (D) represents the core activity of the treatment process, which should lead to a new *evaluation* (E) of the problem situation and the activating event (A). Therefore, there is an A→B→C→D→E sequence involved in the total assessment and treatment process. Beck (1976) uses essentially the same approach as Ellis in that he asks clients to monitor the whole process by identifying automatic thoughts or beliefs and the associated emotions on a form called the "Daily Record of Dysfunctional Thoughts."

The assessment process is largely devoted to identifying and explicating the automatic thoughts and beliefs intervening between the problematic situation and the dysfunctional emotions and behaviors. In addition to this mutual exploration by client and worker, it is sometimes helpful to use self-report assessment instruments that shed light on how the client cognitively construes significant events, persons, and objects related to the problem (Merluzzi, Glass, & Genest, 1981; Sherman, 1981, 1984).

The basic intervention strategy of cognitive therapy has been called cognitive review (Raimy, 1975). It includes the whole process of identifying (assessment) and changing (treatment) dysfunctional thoughts, beliefs, and perceptions. The core of the treatment process is to have the client restructure (repattern) cognitions by continuous use of procedures like the daily analysis of dysfunctional thoughts, together with other cognitive and behavioral techniques. The term "cognitive restructuring" is the generic term for a number of specific cognitive and cognitive-behavioral techniques. Among the more widely used of these techniques are cognitive rehearsal (Beck, 1976), rational imagery (Lazarus, 1971), and vicariation or cognitive modeling (Raimy, 1975). These are often combined with behavioral techniques in a form of cognitive-behavioral modification involving coping skills and problem solving (Meichenbaum, 1977). These techniques are proliferating rapidly and making their way into mainstream social work practice (Berlin, 1982; Fischer, 1978).

Cognitive therapy is insight oriented because clients are often not aware of certain dysfunctional thoughts, beliefs, and behaviors that affect their adjustment but that are accessible to consciousness in order to be worked on and changed (Beck, 1976). Therefore, many of the techniques traditionally used by social workers, such as clarification, explanation, confrontation, and interpretation, are also used in cognitive therapy.

Range of Application

Cognitive therapy is well suited for a number of emotional problems encountered in casework practice, particularly those marked by depression (Beck, Rush, Shaw, & Emery, 1979; Combs, 1980; Beck & Emery, 1979). Because people's cognitive functioning usually remains strong despite the physical decline of old age, cognitive therapy can contribute a great deal to gerontological practice (Emery, 1981). This author has found the approach to be particularly helpful with respect to the two most prevalent emotional problems of old age—depression and anxiety (Sherman, 1979, 1981, 1984). However, cognitive decision-making, problem-solving, and coping techniques (Janis, 1982; Meichenbaum, 1977) can be helpful in treating many of the socioenvironmental and interpersonal problems commonly encountered in social work practice.

Cognitive-behavioral approaches based on the mediational model of cognitive therapy are particularly well suited to brief, time-limited work with clearly specified problems related to assertiveness, situational anxiety, and so on. The phenomenological model of cognitive therapy is probably more appropriate in treating chronic and pervasive problems of living and behavior (Goldstein, 1982; Sherman, 1984). These problems are apt to reflect deeper and more pervasive cognitive distortions than the automatic thoughts, self-talk, and coping statements addressed by the mediational and cognitive-behavioral approaches, and to require a more thorough exploration of the client's subjective experience.

Some of the simpler cognitive-behavioral techniques have been used with children (DiGiuseppe, 1981) and with mildly to moderately retarded adults (Berlin, 1982). Cognitive approaches have also been developed for alcohol dependency (Emery & Fox, 1981; Snyder, 1975). However, it seems unlikely that the effective application of these techniques would extend to persons with severe organic brain disorders or with severe thought disorders, as in schizophrenia.

Group and Family Adaptations

Only minor modifications from individual cognitive therapy or casework are required to conduct groups dealing with adjustment problems of adolescence, adulthood, and old age (Werner, 1982; Sherman, 1981). The group worker discusses the main elements of the cognitive review process with the group in the same manner as with an individual client. The simulated practice situations that can be set up in groups substantially enhance cognitive rehearsal and other techniques used to prepare the individual for real-life situations. An individual's cognitive distortions can often be more effectively identified and validated in a group than in individual treatment. Family therapy with a cognitive approach is less well developed. Werner (1982) described an approach that is not distinguishable from the family systems model based on communication theory (Weakland, 1976). Ellis (1978) proposed an approach that is more distinctly cognitive, but its effectiveness is yet to be tested.

Research

Considerable empirical evidence indicates the effectiveness of cognitive therapy for various kinds of depression (Rush, Beck, Kovacs, & Holon, 1977; Shaw, 1977). There is also some empirical evidence concerning the treatment of anxiety (Glogower, Fremouw, & McCroskey, 1978; Hussian & Lawrence, 1978). Fischer (1978) noted that a number of controlled studies of individual forms of cognitive restructuring reported positive findings. However, he identified a need to study "whole packages" of cognitive intervention processes. In the meantime, the indications of effectiveness are "promising" rather than "proved."

EDMUND SHERMAN

For further information, see BEHAVIORAL APPROACH.

References

Beck, A. T. (1976). *Cognitive Therapy and the Emotional Disorders*. New York: International Universities Press.

Beck, A. T., & Emery, G. (1979). *Cognitive Therapy of Anxiety and Phobic Disorders*. Philadelphia: Center for Cognitive Therapy.

Beck, A. T., Rush, A. J., Shaw, B. F., & Emery, G. (1979). *Cognitive Therapy of Depression*. New York: Guilford Press.

Berlin, S. (1982). "Cognitive-Behavioral Interventions for Social Work Practice." *Social Work,* 27(3), 218–226.

Combs, T. D. (1980). "A Cognitive Therapy for Depression: Theory, Techniques, and Issues." *Social Casework,* 61(6), 361–366.

DiGiuseppe, R. A. (1981). "Cognitive Therapy with Children." In G. Emery, S. D. Holon, & R. C. Bedrosian (Eds.), *New Directions in Cognitive Therapy.* New York: Guilford Press.

Ellis, A. (1962). *Reason and Emotion in Psychotherapy.* Secaucus, N. J.: Citadel Press.

Ellis, A. (1974). *Humanistic Psychotherapy: The Rational-Emotive Approach.* New York: McGraw-Hill.

Ellis, A. (1978). "Family Therapy: A Phenomenological and Active Directive Approach." *Journal of Marriage and Family Counseling,* 4(2), 43–50.

Emery, G. (1981). "Cognitive Therapy with the Elderly." In G. Emery, S. D. Holon, & R. C. Bedrosian (Eds.), *New Directions in Cognitive Therapy.* New York: Guilford Press.

Emery, G., & Fox, J. (1981). "Cognitive Therapy of Alcohol Dependency." In G. Emery, S. D. Holon, & R. C. Bedrosian (Eds.), *New Directions in Cognitive Therapy.* New York: Guilford Press.

Fischer, J. (1978). *Effective Casework Practice: An Eclectic Approach.* New York: McGraw-Hill.

Fleming, R. (1981). "Cognition and Social Work Practice: Some Implications of Attribution and Concept Attainment Theories." In A. Maluccio (Ed.), *Promoting Competence in Clients.* New York: Free Press.

Glogower, F. D., Fremouw, W. J., & McCroskey, J. C. (1978). "A Component Analysis of Cognitive Restructuring." *Cognitive Therapy and Research,* 2(3), 209–223.

Goldstein, H. (1981). *Social Learning and Change: A Cognitive Approach to Human Services.* Columbia: University of South Carolina Press.

Goldstein, H. (1982). "Cognitive Approaches to Direct Practice." *Social Service Review,* 56(4), 539–555.

Hussian, R. A., & Lawrence, P. S. (1978). "The Reduction of Test, State, and Trait Anxiety by Test-Specific and Generalized Stress Inoculation Training." *Cognitive Therapy and Research,* 2(1), 25–37.

Janis, I. (Ed.). (1982). *Counseling on Personal Decisions.* New Haven, Conn.: Yale University Press.

Lantz, J. E. (1978). "Cognitive Theory and Social Casework." *Social Work,* 23(5), 361–366.

Lazarus, A. A. (1971). *Behavior Therapy and Beyond.* New York: McGraw-Hill.

Meichenbaum, D. (1977). *Cognitive-Behavior Modification: An Integrative Approach.* New York: Plenum Press.

Merluzzi, T. V., Glass, C. R., & Genest, M.

(Eds.). (1981). *Cognitive Assessment.* New York: Guilford Press.

Raimy, V. (1975). *Misunderstandings of the Self.* San Francisco: Jossey-Bass.

Rush, A. J., Beck, A. T., Kovacs, M., & Holon, S. D. (1977). "Comparative Efficacy of Cognitive Therapy and Imipramine in the Treatment of Depressed Outpatients." *Cognitive Therapy and Research,* 1(1), 17–37.

Shaw, B. F. (1977). "Comparison of Cognitive Therapy and Behavior Therapy in the Treatment of Depression." *Journal of Consulting and Clinical Psychology,* 45(4), 543–555.

Sherman, E. (1979). "A Cognitive Approach to Direct Practice with the Aging." *Journal of Gerontological Social Work,* 2(1), 43–53.

Sherman, E. (1981). *Counseling the Aging: An Integrative Approach.* New York: Free Press.

Sherman, E. (1984). *Working With Older Persons: Cognitive and Phenomenological Methods.* Boston: Kluwer-Nijhoff.

Snyder, V. (1975). "Cognitive Approaches in the Treatment of Alcoholism." *Social Casework,* 56(8), 481–485.

Weakland, J. (1976). "Communication Theory and Clinical Change." In P. J. Guerin (Ed.), *Family Therapy: Theory and Practice.* New York: Gardner Press.

Werner, H. D. (1965). *A Rational Approach to Social Casework.* New York: Association Press.

Werner, H. D. (1979). "Cognitive Theory." In F. J. Turner (Ed.), *Social Work Treatment.* New York: Free Press.

Werner, H. D. (1982). *Cognitive Therapy: A Humanistic Approach.* New York: Free Press.

Reader's Guide

COMMUNITY

The following articles contain information on this general topic:

Citizen Participation
Community-Based Social Action
Community Development
Community Theory and Research
Health Planning
Macro Practice: Current Trends and Issues
Planning and Management Professions
Policy Analysis: Methods and Techniques
Social Planning
Social Planning and Community Organization
Social Planning in the Public Sector
Social Planning in the Voluntary Sector

COMMUNITY-BASED SOCIAL ACTION

Community-based social action in social work is a distinctive form of community organization practice that draws on two long-standing traditions of reform. One derives from the Progressive Era, which lies at the heart of social work professionalism, and is tied to the field's ongoing commitment to client and community advocacy (R. Fisher, 1984; Trattner, 1974). The other tradition, more sharply ideological in substance and in its critique of American society, has evolved from the combative, class-based struggles of the 1930s. This tradition received further refining in the 1960s, especially from the civil rights movement and the New Left (Piven & Cloward, 1971).

Distinguishing Characteristics

Before turning to a discussion of how these two traditions have merged in current forms of social action, it is important to note what distinguishes community-based social action from community development and social planning (R. Fisher, 1984; Rothman, 1979). Although similar to community development in its interest in education and information, community-based social action is not necessarily consensus oriented or concerned primarily with educational goals of interest to the entire community. There is an expectation of disagreement that may not be resolved amicably, an assumption community development does not share (Biddle & Biddle, 1965; Piven & Cloward, 1977). Also, although thoughtful community-based social action uses planned and well-documented materials as part of any strategy, it does not limit its participation and scope of activity to technically trained professionals in a delimited area of expertise. Professionals with varying levels of training and from many disciplines, as well as community members, may be part of today's community-based social action (Rothman, 1979).

Finally, agencies and groups that engage in social action are different from what many people assume "social action" agencies to be. Although both the ideology and the interest in social change are still part of many community-based social actions

(Burghardt, 1982a; Schechter, 1982), few social work groups function solely in this manner. Instead, community-based social action is undertaken by agencies, professionals, and community members in three often overlapping arenas:

1. *Community-based advocacy around specific issues and populations such as food and hunger and the homeless.* Such activities call for expertise in specific issues and usually result in participants forming coalitions with like-minded community organizations, agencies, and departments concerned with the same issue (Boyte, 1981; Fabricant & Epstein, 1984).

2. *Local and national electoral work, with specific emphasis on technically nonpartisan but nevertheless contentious voter registration drives and the endorsement and support of candidates viewed as sympathetic to social welfare.* This is a significant shift from the past (Piven & Cloward, 1983; Staples, 1984).

3. *Ongoing networking and solidarity groups of professionals and community members who join together for both personal support and ideological commitments* (Burghardt, 1982b; Ecklein, 1984). Unlike the previous two arenas of community-based social action, this work is more likely to be sponsored by individuals rather than agencies. A number of social work feminist alliances, some rank-and-file trade union groups, and social workers concerned with disarmament and other international issues are most representative of this trend.

Therefore two distinctive hallmarks characterize today's community-based social action. First, mainstream agencies and professional associations have taken openly political stands in coalition against other community and economic interests. Second, a developing emphasis is being placed on both issue networks among agencies and ideological and personal support networks by an array of community-based activists. In the 1960s, social action organizers rarely aligned with mainstream organizations on any specific issues; similarly, few openly partisan stands were taken by the profession. Each group has now moved closer to the other. How groups whose traditions were once perceived as so distant from each other can now come together can only be understood by looking at a brief history of each.

Progressive Era and Call to Advocacy

The turn of the twentieth century was a time of great economic transformation and intense ferment for social change (R. Fisher, 1984). Buttressed by the continuation of an expanding industrial economy that itself was rapidly consolidating and yet aware of the ravages that modern industrialization had wrought on working people, activists from the newly formed middle class were fired with hopes of substantial reform. What distinguished these activists from their precursors in the charity movements of the 1870s and 1880s were their new ideas about advocacy and the form of social action. Although similar in class background, they were no longer concerned with documenting dependency. Instead they were enraged by poverty and its effects on poor families and on the neighborhoods in which the poor lived (Trattner, 1974).

Many activists came to see the settlement house as the ideal locus from which to advocate. Located in the poorest neighborhoods, settlement houses gave activists direct access to the conditions, problems, and people touched by poverty. They organized day care, nutrition programs, and literary workshops with twin goals in mind: to learn about people through direct service in the neighborhood and to take this understanding to legislatures, commissions, and the press to make changes. This classical form of advocacy achieved notable success on a number of significant issues, especially in child labor laws, child welfare, and some areas of housing code regulation.

The clearest forms of this advocacy lasted until World War I, when the conservative and prointerventionist fervor of the nation swept aside the far more liberal and often pacifist-socialist sentiments of settlement house leaders like Jane Addams and Lillian Wald. But the tradition of advocacy was established and has lived on, including an emphasis on documented and observed facts about conditions affecting the poor, a reliance on personal care studies drawn from professional practice to supplement these facts, and a self-defined role as spokespersons for the poor, not with them. Similarly, advocacy alliances were based not on class or social standing but on general agreement with the issues. Thus, champions of the Children's

Bureau worked with upper-class supporters and other professionals much more often than directly with poor people. No strategic emphasis was placed on either antagonisms toward a particular group like the ruling class or a desire to mobilize working people on any permanent basis. Advocacy was for the poor, done by professionals and others sympathetic to the cause.

The professional advocacy skills learned in this period continue to be of great value in the field today. They include:

Data Collection and Research Skills. The early reformers did not simply have morality on their side; they had facts. These facts—such as levels of child morbidity, or hours of labor demanded of children in factories—were carefully documented and used in their advocacy for child labor laws. Likewise, their plans for future advocacy campaigns were carefully explored and reflected a knowledge of existing rules and regulations. Professional advocates continue to use such formal expertise as much as possible.

Effective Public Relations and Media Skills. Advocacy translates facts by means of reports and position papers that will attract attention. Developed before electronic media, public relations skills—learning how to present material in a dramatic style, coupled with learning how to work with the press—are important. Skills include writing good press releases, running dramatic news conferences, and maintaining good relations with specific journalists and reporters.

Knowledge of the Legislative Process. Professional advocacy is designed to put pressure on legislatures, city councils, and other public bodies to change and reform laws. Professional social advocates must know how these forums work, which subcommittees are important, and where informal as well as formal decisions are made in a legislative body if they are to be effective advocates.

Ideological, Class-Based Action of the 1930s

An equally distinctive form of social action engaging many social workers emerged during the Great Depression of the 1930s. The catastrophic collapse of the economy was joined by a correspondingly intense outbreak of militant, often ideologically influenced labor struggles throughout the country

(R. Fisher, 1984; Trattner, 1974). It was a time when the Communist Party, still basking in the light cast by the Bolshevik Revolution in 1917 and not yet tarnished by the darkening shadows of Stalinism already on its horizon, was a major influence throughout the working class and among many young, underemployed professionals (J. Fisher, 1980). Although hard to imagine today, at that time everyday discussions, debates, and questions about change almost always included issues of class conflict, ideology, and the nature of reform versus revolution.

The preeminent leadership for change in the 1930s came from the labor movement, especially John L. Lewis's Committee for Industrial Organization (CIO), in which Socialist and Communist activists were influential (R. Fisher, 1984). Unlike the craft- and ethnic-based unionism in the past, CIO struggles were class based throughout industries like steel, auto, and rubber. Class-based organizing took a broader social perspective in its goals—which ranged from radical industrial reforms to actual social revolution—and held a hostile stance toward groups it perceived as having opposing interests. In the 1930s, this type of organizing, including work done by social workers, was broadly defined as "workers" against "the bosses" (J. Fisher, 1980). (In the 1960s, social movements and civil rights organizations refined this perspective to include a racial or gender edge, such as the "black community" versus the "white, male establishment.") Such work emphasized crossoccupational solidarity, multiracialism, and hostility to the ruling group's interests.

The influence of the CIO inevitably touched and directed actions within communities, neighborhoods, and social work itself (Alinsky, 1946; Reynolds, 1951). Just as the CIO pressed for federal relief, so did the newly formed Unemployed Councils, among whom were found many social workers. Just as labor organizers demanded industrywide changes in union rights, so did the Rank and File Clubs inside social work (J. Fisher, 1980). Just as communists and socialists vied for influence and direction inside the CIO, so did the likes of Jacob Fisher, Bertha Reynolds, and Mary Van Kleeck influence new trends inside the American Association of Social Workers.

Unlike settlement house advocacy, so-cial action in communities was clearly class based and openly ideological in its demands for social security, relief, and other welfare-state issues. For example, sectors of the CIO joined on racial issues that cut across union lines, and the Unemployed Councils demanded a multiracial membership. The emphasis was not on middle-class advocacy for those less fortunate, however, but on a united working class advocating for itself.

Social workers committed to social action saw their success in terms of widescale activity by as many people as possible. Only in large numbers lay the power to change conditions in society. Expertise was a tool, but only a minor tool in the larger battle. The point was to get people believing that they could change things, not just a few professionals. This also meant that neighborhood and community social action, although dealing with local needs, often connected local interests to broader national and even international concerns. Activists and community groups worked for better housing conditions like Progressive Era advocates, but joined such demands to the national call for federal relief and, later, for jobs. Local activities were thus not ends in themselves but educational vehicles to larger concerns that united classwide actions and ideas into an ideological whole. Because the system itself needed to be changed, demands for change could not end without at least a clear delineation of the political connections that tied local issues to national trends.

The more traditional Progressive Era advocacy continued to have influence inside traditional professional agencies. Desperate economic and social conditions were so widespread that all professional groups focused most of their attention on federal responsibilities. However, by the mid-1940s, a combination of forces joined to undermine this form of social action. First, President Roosevelt, given the support of the left in the 1936 elections, muted much labor and community unrest with the passage of New Deal legislation. Second, the unity created by World War II forced a significant retrenchment in openly expressed class antagonisms. These brakes on militant social action were further intensified by the Cold War hostility of the late 1940s and 1950s that branded all progressive forms of activism as Communist-inspired or Communist-led movements. When joined by an unprecedented post–World War II economic expansion, these forces diverted energy and attention away from most forms of social action and advocacy.

Civil Rights Movement and Anti-Welfare State Action: 1960–1974

The 1960s saw an eruption of protest led by the civil rights movement. First led by blacks in the South who had honed their tactics during the late fifties and who had then begun work in the North, this movement made their primary objective demands for enfranchisement and an expansion of more equitable welfare state benefits. Throughout this time, the strategic emphases of advocacy and social action more closely overlapped than at any previous time. While a contentious movement fought racial injustice in the South, Harrington's *The Other America* (1962) activated scores of professionals to advocate new forms of social welfare intervention to end inequality. Later, calls of Black Power, Student Power, and participatory democracy emphasized community control of local institutions. At the same time, welfare professionals used their skills and knowledge to pressure for greater and more universal entitlements.

The advocacy was different from the past, however. Progressive Era activists often waged broad campaigns on children's issues, whereas 1960s advocates had to work on specific entitlements because the size and complexity of the welfare state demanded it. Likewise, the militant forms of social action were as contentious as in the 1930s but, reflecting both Alinsky's (1946, 1969) influence and vestiges of Cold War fears over expressed ideology, such action was often less ideologically clear and rarely class based.

Equally important, the tremendous expansion of the welfare state under President Johnson's Community Action Programs led to an extraordinary new funding arrangement. Community organizations, often directly funded through monies available out of so-called block grants, came into existence with the sole purpose of further mobilizing pressure against federal, state, and local governments. Although the funds were never great enough to provide these organizations with significant power, they nevertheless provided activists with enough funds to further

specific, often militant attacks against the welfare state. Using Alinsky's conflict tactics and purposely avoiding electoral activity, groups like the National Welfare Rights Organization and the National Tenants Organization emphasized widespread client mobilization with community members in active opposition to a welfare state seen as an agent of social control (Kramer, 1969; Piven & Cloward, 1971, 1977).

Advocacy was also influenced by the more militant tones of the 1960s. Professionals often undertook advocacy in behalf of groups of clients, not individuals. Joining the activism found in other professions like law and medicine, social work advocates put their expertise behind classwide issues involving consumer rights. Such work emphasized entitlement advocacy—working to expand welfare state benefits into universal categories—such as increasing Medicaid and Medicare coverage and unemployment insurance benefits. In many ways, this work joined professional advocates in a class-based organizing approach. The professionals defined themselves as movement activists rather than as members of a profession. Often they were as hostile to professionalization as were some community activists.

This period of intense social advocacy and militant social action is today looked back upon in terms that still provoke debate and disagreement. Some see it as a time of great promise and energy that opened up new economic and social opportunities for previously disenfranchised people. Others remember programmatic confusion and unsettling trends toward antiintellectualism and antiprofessionalism. Regardless of these different perceptions, however, the strategic orientation emphasized conflict over consensus, direct attacks on the welfare state itself, and a belief in community members, clients, and committed professionals joining together to create change.

The particular skills of this period (and of the 1930s) were refined enough to warrant specific mention. They include:

Skills in Intra-Group Processes. Grassroots social action is people oriented. Activists hold meetings and more meetings, some with old groups, some with new. Learning to work in large, collective settings with multiple agendas while still maintaining democratic procedures is demanding work that is the sine qua non of this form of social action (Burghardt, 1982b; Staples, 1984).

Political Skills in Coalition Work. Whatever a worker's political orientation, coalition work demands an awareness of his or her own and others' political beliefs and political agendas such as goals and immediate objectives. Often these agendas are stated subtly— will a particular person work with someone to get things done? Is he or she consistently hostile to a particular political group? Analyzing issues in terms of political ideas and strategies has become essential to social action work.

Understanding Political and Power Structures. Social activists in the 1930s and 1960s learned to be aware of political structures and the way in which power was distributed, within both society and various institutions. This awareness is still important, especially if one's position takes a critical stance toward different political actors. It is also important because community members' sense of injustice may often be right and yet fuel unrealistic demands given available resources (Staples, 1984).

Confronting Sexism and Racism. The social movements of the 1960s created a tremendous awareness of sexism and racism. To engage in social action now requires exploring one's own attitudes toward race, sex, sexual preference, age, and class. Such self-examination is an important part of intragroup processes that will need continuous refining.

Fund-Raising. Small grass-roots organizations will never get rich, but they cannot survive without some money. Knowing how to write grant proposals, learning how to approach funding agents, and undertaking effective promotional efforts are important skills for any social action group.

Economic Retrenchment and Political Regrouping: 1973–1984

The strategic approaches of the 1960s also contained one other, unspoken assumption: that the post–World War II economic expansion would continue unabated. This assumption crashed against the painful effects of the 1973 oil crisis, increasing American debt and general U.S. economic underproduction as well as leaving American cities helpless in the face of continuing urban decay. Politicians and economic leaders faced these crises with the decision to cut services and entitlement programs drastically and lower living standards generally for working Americans (Tabb, 1983; Silk, L., & Silk, M., 1981). Beginning with the New York City fiscal crisis of 1974–75 and continuing through the 1980s on all levels of political and economic life, the conservative backlash against entitlement benefits led to a major rethinking of how social activists could approach organizing.

A number of overlapping issues began to merge in this context. First, activists wanted to carry on their struggle for greater social justice and equality, but they recognized that funding from the welfare state would not be available as a resource. This has meant that a number of community organizations dedicated to social action no longer exist.

This alteration in the base of material support has led to two distinct directions in community-based social action. The first, most popularly known as neo-Alinskyism (R. Fisher, 1984; Kahn, 1982), still emphasizes social action but does so through membership organizations based on community support. Still unafraid of conflict and, like Alinsky, still uninterested in clear, ideological political positions, this community action tradition has tried to correct some of the mistakes of its original mentor. Unlike Alinsky's groups, national organizations such as ACORN (Association of Community Organizations for Reform Now) and regional associations such as Massachusetts's Mass. Fair Share pay more attention to leadership development and combating racism and sexism in their organizations (Staples, 1984). They recognized that too many groups of Alinsky's making ignored problems like racism that over the years came to discredit their image as a progressive force for change. Likewise, these new organizers saw the need for not only new but also more community leaders, and their careful door-to-door approach, planned meetings, and follow-up with individual members have underscored their commitment.

In keeping with the increasing complexity of the welfare state first noted in the 1960s, the campaigns of these organizations tend to rely on a specific issue, often discussed in terms of consumers' rights, such as high and unfair utility rates, rental issues, and unfair banking practices like redlining. Although their literature states a preference for multiissue campaigns, they tend to focus on one issue at a time. Thus, unlike many groups in the 1930s and 1960s, few organizations work with issues that create an overarching political framework for educational purposes. Political pragmatism is far more important to these new organizations than a specific political program.

This step toward pragmatism was one factor in the coalescence of much of today's community-based social action. Another was the involvement in mainstream social welfare organizations of activists from the 1960s who could no longer afford to organize from their own independent organizations. When funding sources in both the public sector and private foundations dried up, many activists sought work as caseworkers, group workers, and low-level administrators in hospitals, drug programs, and senior centers. Still with visions of social justice, these activists have channeled their efforts into increasing their expertise and advocacy on specific issues that social work has always been known for. Such issues as the plight of the homeless, the abuse of children, and the increasing malnourishment of the poor owe their visibility to single-issue advocacy by many social workers and other activists. By providing well-documented information to their agencies—often gleaned from direct services—they serve as informed members of coalitions that lobby for greater awareness of emerging social problems. Although fiscal constraints continue to hamper the success of such advocacy efforts, the increased use of coalitions, complete with multiagency approval and support, show a breadth of commitment throughout the many sectors of the field.

Finally, social work organizations themselves, once consciously opposed to overt political action, by 1980 started to sense a new urgency in political activism. The widespread cuts in social service budgets, first at the local level and by 1980 from state and federal offices as well, forced traditional agencies and the social work profession to rethink their approach to social action. Although disinterested in militancy per se, the alliances formed in various states across the nation calling for the restoration of service-budget cuts naturally moved from the legislative to the electoral arena. Service leaders,

agency activists, and grass-roots consumer advocates had all reached the same conclusion at the same time: the only way to achieve legislative reform was to put the right elected officials in office. This meant entry into the political electoral process, first locally and then at all levels of government. In 1982, for example, the National Association of Social Workers' Political Action for Candidate Election (PACE) allocated $130,000 to candidates nationwide. By the national election of 1984, the figure had more than doubled.

These new forays into electoral politics led to widespread support for the voter registration drive of Human Serve, an organizing effort led by Piven and Cloward to register social welfare clients to vote (Cloward & Piven, 1983). Originally designed to create pressure inside welfare-state institutions so that new power could be unleashed inside the Democratic Party, Human Serve found a quick and engaged response from major social welfare organizations, schools of social work, and settlement houses. The major tactic was to register people when they applied for or received entitlement benefits, using welfare-state organizations as places in which to find unregistered voters.

The above shifts in activism since the mid-1970s suggest why once distinct traditions now seem to have so much in common. Pitted against an economic and fiscal conservatism, the combination of pragmatic grass-roots organizing, single-issue advocacy by people in coalition, and large alliances against service cuts formed by social welfare agency representatives has come to represent the dominant direction of community-based social action today. Agencies now see political coalitions as an instrument for financial survival. Similarly, grass-roots organizations like ACORN find common cause in pushing consumer legislation. Such activity would have been impossible in the 1960s. This combination of effort has created coalitional and electoral work for groups from distinct traditions that will last throughout the 1980s and perhaps beyond.

Dilemmas

This is not to say that these efforts are without possible problems. A number of activists, especially those who identify themselves with socialist-feminist, black liberation, and rank-and-file trade union traditions, have raised questions worthy of consideration in the years ahead (R. Fisher, 1984; Marable, 1981; Schechter, 1982). Some of these are:

1. Can the strategic emphasis on elections and on single-issue consumer campaigns allow for an adequate political education that is usually associated with developing leadership? Elections and voter registration drives are so fast paced and have such short-term objectives that little time can be given to the slower process of education and skills development, especially of new activists. Similarly, some think single-issue advocacy is too focused to make the necessary educational bridge between immediate consumer needs and the long-term economic problems associated with reindustrialization. Equally important, intense but subtle forms of racism and sexism in organizations may be glossed over in the heat of battles that are perceived as always immediate.

2. Analysts of the welfare state (Gough, 1981) have also raised the question whether all members of the welfare state have similar interests. The new directions in social action make clear that most people no longer view the welfare state as simply an agent of social control. However, many rank-and-file trade union activists in social work agencies wonder if the short-term electoral coalitions around economic survival are clouding another issue—that the leaders of social welfare institutions and their workers have distinct differences related to power and control inside their own organizations. How much this concern is real and how much has changed since the onslaught of the economic crisis and the rightward drift of many political officials will have to be assessed in the coming years.

3. A final question concerns the balance between relying on politicians to push for social change and building more independent, mobilized social movements. Some readings of history suggest that the dynamics of electoralism and movement building is a complex and interrelated phenomenon; other readings suggest that without distinct, independent movements there is little likelihood of substantial social change. This debate is also likely to continue in the coming years.

When discussed as dilemmas, however, such problems take on an abstract quality that is quite different from the ongoing reality of developing strategies. Beneath all these issues is the strategic theme of self-determination; that is, the collective struggle of oppressed people acting in their own behalf to improve conditions affecting their lives. This process has always been as fundamental to social action and political life as any other. How much work can be done in one's own behalf and how much one can improve conditions without the help and support of others have led to major ruptures in progressive political life for over a century. Whether discussed in terms of party and class (the classic political argument over the relationship of the revolutionary party to the working class) or professional and client (the classic social work discussion over the relationship of the skilled clinician to the client), these debates have created raging disagreement.

The above questions are therefore of great importance as social workers and community activists undertake community-based social action today. If activists are too strident in opposing alliances with highly institutionalized forces, for example, they run the risk of isolation and impotence if other activists ignore the rest of their political analysis. On the other hand, many hard lessons were learned by activists in the 1960s, suggesting that complete political pragmatism and an overreliance on official leadership undermine widespread membership development and education. No activist today can make immediate tactical choices with the overconfidence that Eternal Truth is on his or her side or with the naive assumption that "it will all work out." Future social movements will assess each new approach with the same intensity as in the past.

Regardless of one's own strategic choices in these and other matters, the widespread activity of the past few years, although often defensive, can nevertheless be expected to continue in its present direction. Activists in neighborhood groups and others serving as agency representatives will continue to form coalitions. The increasing shortage of funds will continue to intensify the use of professional advocacy around new and more complex social problems. Community-based social action will continue to evolve, learning new lessons, refining old tactics, and taking up new strategies as the fight for more and better social services continues toward the beginning of the twenty-first century.

STEVE BURGHARDT

For further information, see CITIZEN PARTICIPATION; COMMUNITY DEVELOPMENT; FEDERAL SOCIAL LEGISLATION SINCE 1961; LEGISLATIVE ADVOCACY; NEIGHBORHOODS; RADICAL SOCIAL WORK.

References

Alinsky, S. (1946). *Reveille for Radicals*. New York: Vintage Books.

Alinsky, S. (1969). *Rules for Radicals*. New York: Vintage Books.

Biddle, W. & Biddle, L. (1965). *The Community Development Process*. New York: Holt, Rinehart, & Winston.

Boyte, H. (1981). *The Backyard Revolution*. Philadelphia: Temple University Press.

Burghardt, S. (1982a). *Organizing for Community Action*. Beverly Hills, Calif.: Sage Publications.

Burghardt, S. (1982b). *The Other Side of Organizing*. Cambridge, Mass.: Schenkman Publishing Co.

Cloward, R., & Piven, F. F. (1975). *The Politics of Turmoil*. New York: Vintage Books.

Cloward, R., & Piven, F. F. (1983). "Toward a Class-Based Realignment of American Politics: A Movement Strategy." *Social Policy, 13*(3), 3–14.

Ecklein, J. (1984). *Community Organizing*. New York: Free Press.

Fabricant, M., & Epstein, I. (1984). "Legal and Welfare Rights Advocacy: Complementary Approaches in Organizing on Behalf of the Homeless." *Urban and Social Change Review, 17*(1), 15–20.

Fisher, R. (1980). *The Rank and File Movement in Social Work*. Cambridge, Mass.: Schenkman Publishing Co.

Fisher, J. (1984). *Let the People Decide*. Boston: Twayne Publishers.

Gough, J. (1981). *The Political Economy of Social Welfare*. New York: Macmillan Publishing Co.

Harrington, M. (1962). *The Other America*. New York: Macmillan Publishing Co.

Kahn, S. (1982). *Organizing*. New York: McGraw-Hill Book Co.

Kramer, R. (1969). *Participation of the Poor*. New York: Prentice-Hall.

Marable, M. (1981). *From the Grass Roots*. Boston: South End Press.

Piven, F. F., & Cloward, R. (1971). *Regulating the Poor*. New York: Vintage Books.

Piven, F. F., & Cloward, R. (1977). *Poor People's Movements: How They Succeed, Why They Fail*. New York: Pantheon Books.

Reynolds, B. (1951). *Social Work and Social Living*. Secaucus, N.J.: Citadel Press.

Rothman, J. (1979). "Three Models of Community Organization." In F. Cox, J. Erlich, J. Rothman, & J. Tropman (Eds.), *Strategies of Community Organization*, (pp. 25–45). Itasca, Ill.: F. E. Peacock Publishers.

Schechter, S. (1982). *Women and Male Violence*. Boston: South End Press.

Silk, L., & Silk, M. (1981). *The American Establishment*. New York: Avon Books.

Staples, L. (1984). *Roots to Power*. New York: Praeger Publishers.

Tabb, W. (1983). *The Long Default*. New York: Monthly Review Press.

Trattner, W. (1974). *From Poor Law to Welfare State*. New York: Free Press.

COMMUNITY CENTERS. See COMMUNITY-BASED SOCIAL ACTION; COMMUNITY DEVELOPMENT; NEIGHBORHOODS; SETTLEMENTS AND NEIGHBORHOOD CENTERS.

COMMUNITY DEVELOPMENT

Community development has a variety of interrelated meanings for different groups, disciplines, and professions and for public, voluntary, and sectarian agencies. The term is related to such concepts as community organization, community problem solving, community work, grass-roots organizing, neighborhood organizing, mutual aid, self-help, community control, community action, social action, and social movement. It is also related to social, political, or mass education; to physical, economic, social, national, regional, or local planning; and to rural, urban, institutional, cultural, economic, social, and historical development. The term is not new but has come into popular usage since World War II, particularly in reference to international, multinational, governmental, church, and foundation programs to deal at a local level with social, economic, cultural, educational, political, and technical problems of developing (or underdeveloped) countries and in developed countries. Community development has had a long history in the

United States (Fisher & Romanofsky, 1981; Hallman, 1984). In recent years, it has been used in connection with self-help movements focusing on health, mental health, various diseases, energy, and the environment and in such areas as consumers', women's, and homosexuals' problems and interests.

Community development practice suggests a purpose, function, structure, process, and, especially, a strategy and set of activities. It is most often used to describe the social objectives and processes of a community, group, or organization seeking to improve the quality of life or the productivity of residents in a delimited geographic area or of members of an interest group or coalition concerned with a particular social condition or problem. Yet community development efforts are usually not bound to a locality but occur in a framework of internal and external community relationships, resources, interests, and policies.

From the perspective of social work, community development may be regarded as a process of deliberate intervention into the social network or structure of relations among people and organizations in a local area or interest community to facilitate social problem solving and improve patterns of service delivery and sociopolitical functioning. Emphasis is on sociopolitical education, organizational development, and the creation of structures to exercise community influence. Unlike social planning, social policy formulation, and social agency administration, community development usually involves a grass-roots membership or a "bottom-up" rather than a professional, bureaucratic, or "top-down" approach to social problems. Community solidarity is an underlying factor in the mobilization of citizen motives and resources and in the expected consequences of program efforts. Community development also operates in a larger structure of national and international commitment to the social and economic development of socially disadvantaged sectors of the population (Estes, 1984).

Scope

In the past two decades, there has been a remarkable proliferation of community organization and neighborhood groups in this and other countries, developed and developing. "As the groups have matured, many

have evolved from single-issue to multi-issue, from reactive to active, from protest to program (including both service delivery and economic development), from neighborhood to nationwide in scope" (Perlman, 1979, p. 16). The U.S. National Commission of Neighborhoods compiled a list of over 8,000 groups, and the Department of Housing and Urban Development's (HUD's) Neighborhood Development Office started a clearinghouse with 4,000 entries of relevant local organizations (Perlman, 1979). One estimate projected 700 community-based economic development organizations in the United States by the end of the 1970s (Hallman, 1984, pp. 223–224). Another indicated that the number of nonprofit organizations grew from 500,000 in 1975 to nearly 900,000 in 1980, the majority of which were community based (Harris, 1984, p. 27). The President's Commission on Mental Health reported (1978) more than 500,000 self-help programs, noting that Alcoholics Anonymous had a worldwide membership in excess of 750,000 and that the National Association for Retarded Citizens had more than 1,300 local units with a membership of more than 130,000. Ten thousand block clubs were said to be active in New York City alone in the late 1970s (Reissman, 1979, p. 2). Fisher (1984, pp. 126–127) speculated that more than 20 million Americans were active in hundreds of thousands of neighborhood groups throughout the nation. Some of these groups were small; others had units in several states. He reported that the Association of Community Organizations for Reform Now (ACORN) claimed in 1980 that after ten years of operation it had 25,000 dues-paying members in 19 states. The proliferation of local community, self-help, and interest groups through which community development activities were carried out also included tenant, home owner, church social action, business, professional, and neighborhood improvement groups; community watch patrols; rape crisis and battered women's groups; utility boards; and a range of legislatively mandated community advisory groups.

The self-help and community movements may be a response to the growth and consolidation of government and corporate power; the widening influence of the mass media and the consumer culture; the massive shifts of capital away from localities across state, regional, and national boundaries; the uncontrolled economic boom and bust in large areas of the country; the mass migrations of Americans; and groups of newcomers uprooted from traditional family, ethnic, and employment patterns and from community support structures. The recent "citizen action" movement have been an "intuitive attempt" to address these massive structural changes by creating new forms of interpersonal defense from the external environment and new means of influencing that environment (Boyte, 1983, pp. 11–12).

Many types of organization—public, voluntary, sectarian, even profit making—are engaged in various forms of community development. Community development is carried out not only at the local grass-roots level but also at interorganizational, city, state, and regional levels, in limited or broad areas of citizen concern. Each such development effort requires a commitment to communal participation of residents, members, clients, and consumers, or their representatives. To the extent that such participation is attenuated and decision making is exercised mainly by professionals on a strictly rational basis, or under local public sponsorship, the process may be termed planning, whether centralized or decentralized. Both community development and planning contribute to policy analysis and policy formation, legislative action, and program development. Further, in a complex democratic society, both may be complementary or competitive; they are certainly interactive.

Community development is essential to the executive, administrative, and boundary-spanning functions of most organizations. Almost every agency is concerned to some extent with its community relations and at least nominally with enhancing the social environment in which its program must operate. When an organization involves members, clients, consumers, area residents, other citizens, and other organizations in the creation or implementation of its policy or program, key staff, almost by definition, must have at least a secondary community development purpose.

A large number of organizations whose primary or specialized commitment is to community development employ full- and part-time social workers but possibly more non–social work personnel. These include neighborhood organizations; city or state-wide associations; welfare or community councils and funds; civil rights associations; consumer organizations; special coordinating agencies; political education and advocacy groups; economic or business development organizations; health and child welfare services; and alcoholism, drug addiction, and delinquency prevention organizations.

Function

Community development emphasizes self-help and voluntary cooperation among members or residents of disadvantaged communities or sectors of society. It requires the support, or at least the tolerance, of established centers of public and private authority and power, even when those power centers are targets of protest or social change. Working on behalf of disadvantaged citizens, community development strives to further the acquisition or redistribution of resources. It is also an educational process whose purpose is to increase social and political awareness of the causes of problems and to develop the capacities of community leaders to address those problems. Community development is important to the larger processes of social and economic change in a democratic society.

There are limits to the value and function of community development. Problems related to social and racial justice, reindustrialization, and technological development are not amenable to intervention efforts originating solely or primarily from the local community level (Peterson, 1985). Nevertheless, by emphasizing the value of locality and the creation of local mechanisms of service delivery, economic production, and political development, community development strategies have proved useful in managing and partializing a variety of larger societal and institutional problems. A new politics and economy of the local community are manifested in such recent policies as deinstitutionalization, decentralization, neighborhood development, and service accountability. These concepts have become an integral part of government's response to contemporary social problems and popular discontent. A variety of neighborhood councils, community organizations, and decentralized political and administrative structures have become major instruments of public policy for dealing with larger structural problems (Hallman, 1984).

This may be exemplified in recent coalitional efforts of local community groups, agencies, and advocacy organizations to deal at city and state levels with such problems as economic development, unemployment, hunger, homelessness, school dropouts, and youth gangs. These are associations of local groups or organizations, each seeking to attract more attention and funds, often from community development block grants, to address specific neighborhood problems, often through limited and residual or remedial programs, although the genesis of these problems may lie at the larger economic or social structural levels. City and state government representatives also seem to support and encourage these ad hoc community-centered efforts for purposes of political crisis management and functional social control (Harris, 1984).

Although this massive development of local civic action processes may be regarded as a response to social discontent, it does not necessarily suggest an emergent class consciousness or the development of a radical politics in American society, at least not yet. It appears to have arisen out of traditional community concerns for mutual support, recognition, protection, and the control of decisions, services, and facilities vital to the improvement or maintenance of important qualities of a local community's social life. In this respect, community development activities, including student protest, may be viewed not only as a limited and manageable threat to the social and political fabric but as a revitalization of traditional political norms and values. It can lead to some democratization of decision making, opening up some institutional opportunities to deprived groups and facilitating some new and more inclusive forms of participation and tolerance in an increasingly diverse and pluralist society.

Community

The idea of community is central to the nature and purpose of community development. It is an old concept, predating the idea of nation-state. It is based on relationships among family, kin, and friends. The strongest ties, or sense of communality, arise from the juncture of kinship and territory, particularly the neighborhood. The types of community that historically have been extremely potent include those based on ties of religion, status, craft, academy, revolution, and mutual aid (Tönnies, 1940; Nisbet, 1953).

A recent view perceives a loss or attenuation of the bonds of community, at least geographic community, in modern industrial society. People are no longer closely bound to relatives, neighbors, and friends located in the same geographic area. High rates of mobility, the separation of work and residence, and the development of a complex culture have made for communities of limited liability (Janowitz, 1952). There has been a shift from horizontal or local community relationships among people and organizations to more vertical, extracommunity, bureaucratic kinds of relationship (Warren, 1978). The weakness of traditional community, or the partialization of community, especially the separation of work and residential relationships and identities, may also contribute to Americans' failure to develop class consciousness (Katznelson, 1982).

Evidence of lost community is not clear. The bonds of community in traditional rural or peasant societies may not have been as cohesive, valued, or socially constructive as imagined (Dore & Mars, 1981). Further, the idea of social networks has sought to capture the reality of new social support or communal systems that are not tied to territory, kin, or intimate friendships (Collins & Pancoast, 1976; Biegel & Naparstek, 1982). Wireman (1984) proposed that the idea of intimate secondary or limited relations is meaningful for self-help and community development purposes.

Community may also be conceived in political terms. Problems of community may arise when residents and local organizations lack power or control of resources; such conditions impede effective relationships with powerful, established interests. Central authorities, whether public or private, represent political, ethnic, or economic interests of a dominant class and may exercise an extraordinary influence over communities, especially those of low-income and socially or politically disadvantaged persons (Kornhauser, 1959; Janowitz, 1978; Kotler, 1969). The invigoration or reconstruction of a community depends on redistributing resources through a more equitable sharing of political power and improved control of local services and programs. This requires the joining of responsibility with rights and privileges. Community control, consumer, self-help, and civil rights movements are exemplars of the struggle for more equitable and politically responsible communities. From this perspective, the strong community is the good community: it has the will and the capacity to compete effectively with other communities and authorities, and it does so in ways that are socially responsible and attentive to local interests. Furthermore, the good community is not the consensual or equilibrated community but the community in tension and conflict with other organizations, communities, and central authorities.

Strategies of Intervention

Two major strategies of community development are social support and political action. There is some confusion in the literature that suggests these strategies are substantially separable. These two approaches are interrelated, although a community organization may emphasize one or the other at different times. For example, an Alinsky-type organization is often prone to emphasize a militant political action strategy, but it does not completely neglect a social support and community cohesion strategy during its initial period of organizational development (Fish, 1973). A further confusion arises over many analysts' failure to distinguish between strategies and tactics. Protest or conflict tactics are not completely coordinate with a radical action approach and may be used with social maintenance and defensive strategies. Furthermore, tactics of conferencing and negotiation may be used at opportune moments in both political action and social support strategies. Basic objectives of both strategies are the identification of a community problem, the organization of a community group, the use of available resources to attack community problems, and the development of citizen leadership and community cohesion (Ross, 1955; Alinsky, 1946).

Neither a social support nor a political action strategy requires the rigid preservation of community stability or the stimulation of radical structural change. In a democratic society, both strategies operate in a framework of competing interests and a market economy, within the rule of law and human justice. Each assumes sufficient slack in the political system and sufficient availability of resources that minimal social needs of the community can be met. Nevertheless, this formulation may not be relevant when a community group takes extreme positions. Community organizations of homeowners and established residents committed to a social support or community protection strategy may campaign violently against racial integration and school busing. Community organizations comprising the unemployed and students and their local sympathizers may conduct illegal plant sit-ins or destroy property to prevent owners from moving a factory to another city or country.

In general, the social support strategy emphasizes the promotion and maintenance of mutual support networks at interpersonal, interorganizational, and community levels. It is also committed to distributive and redistributive objectives—to the acquisition of resources for a variety of general community services as well as resources that specifically benefit the disadvantaged. Community organization develops from a base or network of friendships and from ethnic, religious, and resident concerns and interests (Thomas, 1983). Dealing with problems requires the collaboration of local persons and organizations, but to the extent that a group concerns itself only with the mutual interests and needs of group members, it is not a community organization, but possibly a self-help group (Spiegel, 1982). The principal purpose of the community development group must be to develop or change some institutional or community condition that affects the community as a whole or a significant sector of it. This is not to deny that many organizations have both self-help or mutual aid and community development purposes in respect to a particular social, physical, or mental health problem.

The political action strategy is ordinarily not applicable to class conflict or radical ideologies. Community action strategies, including those of Alinsky, are often dismissed by Marxists as counterrevolutionary, as "bleeding-heart liberalism," as parochial "emotional tourism," and as offering no critique of the political and economic system (Jacobs, 1984, p. 218). The political action approach may involve radical rhetoric, but more as a tactic or device than as a strategy. This approach emphasizes the development and use of community or organizational power to bring about social change in specific institutions or programs. It also focuses on grass-roots decision making, the aggregation of mass influence by local inhabitants and community groups, and the development of broad coalitions of like-minded citizens with similar organizational interests (Finks, 1984; McKnight & Kretzmann, 1984). Social support activities to meet individual needs are also important; the successful issue-oriented organization has a substantial commitment to, if not a base in, mutual aid or social support activity (Rose, 1981, p. 155).

Operational Structures and Processes

Community organizations vary along a number of dimensions: the nature and extent of individual and group participation, the characteristics of staff, the definition of constituencies, the kind and range of issues addressed, funding sources, program tactics, and activities (Boyte, 1981, p. 231). Organizational structures range from block clubs and mothers' groups to multimillion-dollar, complex networks of community organization, from groups that have only limited memberships or voluntary sources of funds to those with extensive public, voluntary, religious, and even profit-making sources. The structures may be autonomous and limited to a particular neighborhood or affiliated across cities and states. They may be public and voluntary agency-related organizations, with decentralized political or administrative authority. Local community units, whether neighborhood councils or local city halls, may be established or contracted by central public authorities to perform various organizational and service functions. City charters sometimes assign advice and planning responsibilities to local community groups (Hallman, 1984). Kotler (1979, p. 42) suggested that neighborhood government be regarded as an extension of a community's responsibility and right to raise certain taxes and to deal with a limited number of local services and problems.

The range and complexity of program structures established by local community organizations are remarkable. For example, the Southeast Community Organization (SECO) of Baltimore established a Neighborhood Housing Service as a community corporation and placed bankers and neighbor-

hood residents on its board of directors. It created Southeast Development Incorporated, a partnership with government, businesses, and other institutions, to provide jobs and business opportunities for neighborhood residents. It developed a community-controlled company to market the crafts of elderly and handicapped residents. It set up a Neighborhood and Family Service Task Force to help develop natural helping networks. It established a primary health care facility serving 3,000 patients a month (Fisher, 1984, p. 146; Hallman, 1984, p. 194).

At the heart of community development is the face-to-face group, which is based on felt needs and which focuses on issues that community people and community organization staff want to work on. Community group members are expected to do things on a voluntary basis and on behalf of the wider community, utilizing their own resources to the extent possible. The group is expected to provide a variety of satisfying experiences and rewards to its participants—for example, extending their knowledge and skill, improving their self-image, heightening their sense of personal capacity and power, and helping them develop their capacity for leadership. The community development group does all this while providing program solutions to specific community problems that may also directly affect group participants. The community group experience provides simultaneous social education, political development, and even therapeutic values. The specific tactics and activities of the community development organization include conferences, services, studies, expert testimony, grant applications, media support, negotiation, bargaining, program monitoring, strikes, boycotts, sit-ins, public hearings, rallies, civil disobedience, and legislative and court action.

Participation

Participation is an underlying purpose, function, and activity of community development. Participation by individuals, groups, and organizations has psychological, social, administrative, and political value. The nature of this participation often determines the success or failure of a community development organization in its various enterprises. Federal and state legislation mandates citizen participation at the community level in a great many public service areas. The patterns and functions of participation are diverse, ranging from measures to encourage the pro forma participation of residents to provisions that involve community residents in program administration and policymaking. Community organizations and agencies may utilize selected community members for a variety of limited organizational or special interest purposes, to defend against community participation in agency or program affairs. They also involve community members for purposes of genuine sharing and even control of policy development (Wandersman, 1981, pp. 44–45).

Why people participate is a source of considerable practice importance and a focus of continuing research inquiry. Olson (1965) challenged interest group and Marxist theories of why people participate in community activity or social movements. He insisted that the "logic of collective action" inclines people to resist appeals to join community organizations in support of "public goods" or gains. He argued that individuals participate on the basis of calculated individual rather than group or collective interests. Other analysts have argued that people participate for a variety of reasons, including the influence of a friendship network; attitudinal factors, such as discontent with social conditions; and altruism. Such factors as race, income, education, marital status, age, and home ownership are still regarded as important factors predicting participation (Walsh & Warland, 1983). Furthermore, these factors receive different weights, depending on the level, purpose, and degree of community organization required. For example, occasional involvement in block activities based on strategies of social support requires a different set of motivations, interests, and talents than participation in a complex community organization activity involving legal action or even social protest (Kramer & Specht, 1983; Rich & Wandersman, 1983).

Research suggests that some of the values of participation include increased satisfaction with the physical environment; more positive attitudes toward government; increased feelings of control over the social and political environment; decreased alienation; and increases in positive behavior, such as positive neighboring relationships, less vandalism, and fewer housing vacancies (Wandersman, 1981, p. 47). Most such research has focused on social and psychological effects, although there is some evidence that community participation contributes also to community economic and political changes (Hallman, 1984; Fish, 1973). Few researchers have examined the nature and effect of types of interorganizational participation for purposes of community social action. Coalitions that combine community groups with unions to deal with local problems have not been successful (Kaplan, 1983), but statewide coalitions of community groups concerned with lowering utility rates or protecting the environment have proved successful (Creamer, 1983).

Community Development Workers

Community development workers play multiple roles. They are catalysts who initiate groups. They are facilitators or enablers of the group process, helping it to identify problems, objectives, and tasks and to maintain group operations. They are consultants, planners, coordinators, and grantsmen. They are active leaders or laid-back advisors, depending on the situation (King & Meyers, 1981). They are probably more directive than most other human service workers. They are primarily concerned with social injustice, but they still exhibit sensitivity in interpersonal relations. They have the capacity to be cooperative and nonexploitive, and they have faith in the ability of community members to solve problems on their own terms.

The community development philosophy holds that members of a community can and need to organize collectively to identify community needs, set priorities of action, and utilize their own resources to carry out programs to benefit their community (Ross, 1955; Thomas, 1983). The role of the worker is to facilitate a community sociopolitical learning and program development or institution-building process consistent with this philosophy. This is not to deny the importance of outside resources or technical and professional assistance. The community development worker also does not essentially work in or on behalf of the community group but with it in some feasible, limited partnership arrangement (Froland, 1982, p. 265). The role of the professional worker is not that of a fellow member of the community, however.

The community development worker

requires the knowledge and skill of a political operative, organizational developer, and group worker; these skills combined with the sensitivity of a caseworker give the worker the ability to deal interdependently with community organization, group, and individual needs or problems (Burghardt, 1981, pp. 24–25). Above all, community development workers require restraint and self-discipline in the exercise of their strong commitments, and they require technical skills in the development of the competence of various members of the community organization. The community idea essentially designates people as members, not clients, recipients, victims, or any other category that delimits or impugns the capacity of citizens to participate in and make decisions affecting their collective social being. In due course, community workers must withdraw from their activist, general community development roles and assume other roles—advisors, consultants, program administrators, or specialists. They may even be members of the community, possibly leaders.

There are inherent problems when the professional social worker assumes the role of a community developer. Social workers generally operate in the confines of social agencies that are established to achieve particular organizational interests and goals, albeit in social welfare terms. Social work training and practice are still largely developed in a highly individualized or clinical and, to some extent, administrative or policy framework, rather than in a community or interorganizational framework of knowledge, values, and skills. Most important, many people, including trained and experienced social workers and other human service workers who seek to function as community developers, must first resolve a fundamental value question and an interest group dilemma—whether they are to continue to be in a superordinate position primarily responsible for defining problems and presumed solutions to them, or whether deviants or former deviants, such as the poor, the mentally ill, the delinquent, the aged, and perhaps members of minority groups as well, will fairly rapidly progress to the point where, once defined as citizens, they are responsible for institutional or community decisions affecting their own social welfare.

The profession of social work has not clearly defined or adequately prepared its personnel to be coworkers, albeit with specialized knowledge and skill, along with community residents and representatives, to carry out community development tasks. The issue may be one of strategic relationship to the community. The community worker does not necessarily need to be of the community but must be able to share with the community the responsibilities of problem definition, analysis, and implementation of solutions. Further, the worker must reach out to the community and accept it on its own terms. At the same time, the community must penetrate the worker's professional and interpersonal domain, so that a full and equitable relationship is developed. The worker must grow and develop as the community changes and develops.

Schools of social work can perhaps better prepare students to become community organizers or developers through a more personally and politically interactive relationship or experience with, as well as continued analytic or cognitive understanding of, so-called deviant and conventional grass-roots groups, political organizations, and community agencies. Representatives of these various elements of community must be regarded as possessing the capacity to join with students and faculty in a common educative as well as problem-solving process. The current pattern of preparation of social workers as specialized helpers, substantially committed to the interests and needs of particular agencies or entrepreneurships, is not adequate for the role of community development worker and indeed may be contradictory to it.

At the present time, career lines in community development are probably less clearly defined than in other human service areas. There are not many full-time, well-paying positions open for grass-roots organizers or local community developers. This may account for the relatively small number of trained social workers acting as community developers or community organizers in nonplanning or administrative positions.

Future prospects may not be bleak, however. There is a current flowering of local community organization in the United States, although many organizations are weak, transitory, and without adequate resources. The increasing diversity, specialization, polarization, and fragmentation of American society compel a response: the building and rebuilding of community life in new and creative ways. The defects of national policy in recent years have brought a greater concern at various levels of government and private funding sources with the need to strengthen local community groups. Consequently, we may anticipate somewhat greater job opportunity for social workers and greater interest by schools of social work in preparing students for professional community development positions. It is likely that community development roles will continue to supplement and complement treatment, policy, and planning roles in order for social work to deal coherently with current and future social problems.

However, social work practitioners in many service areas will undoubtedly need to acquire greater community development knowledge and skill in their response to an increasing variety of problems related to community breakdown and community building. Such problems would affect not only clients but the domains of administration, planning, program development, and policy (Taylor & Roberts, 1985).

IRVING A. SPERGEL

For further information, see COMMUNITY-BASED SOCIAL ACTION; MUTUAL HELP GROUPS; NEIGHBORHOODS; SOCIAL PLANNING AND COMMUNITY ORGANIZATION.

References

Alinsky, S. A. (1946). *Reveille for Radicals*. Chicago: University of Chicago Press.

Biegel, D. E., & Naparstek, A. J. (Eds). (1982). *Community Support Systems and Mental Health: Practice, Policy, and Research*. New York: Springer Publishing Co.

Boyte, H. C. (1981). "Community Organizing in the 1970s: Seeds of Democratic Revolt." In R. Fisher & P. Romanofsky (Eds.), *Community Organization for Urban Social Change: A Historical Perspective*. (pp. 217–238). Westport, Conn.: Greenwood Press.

Boyte, H. C. (1983). "Beyond 1984." *Social Policy, 14*(3), 10–14.

Burghardt, S. (1981). "Leadership Development for the 80s: Resolving the Contradictions." *Social Development Issues, 5*(2–3), 18–32.

Collins, A. H., & Pancoast, D. L. (1976). *Natural Helping Networks*. Washington, D.C.: National Association of Social Workers.

Creamer, B. (1983). "Illinois Public Action Council." *Social Policy, 13*(4), 23–25.

Dore, R., & Mars, Z. (1981). *Community Development: Comparative Case Studies*. London, England: Croom Helm.

Estes, R. J. (1984). *The Social Progress of Nations*. New York: Praeger Publishers.

Finks, P. D. (1984). *The Radical Vision of Saul Alinsky*. Ramsey, N.J.: Paulist Press.

Fish, J. H. (1973). *Black Power/White Control*. Princeton, N.J.: Princeton University Press.

Fisher, R. (1984). *Let the People Decide: Neighborhood Organizing in America*. Boston: Twayne Publishers.

Fisher, R., & Romanofsky, P. (Eds.). (1981). *Community Organization for Urban Social Change: A Historical Perspective*. Westport, Conn.: Greenwood Press.

Froland, C. (1982). "Community Support Systems: All Things to All People." In D. E. Biegel & A. J. Naparstek (Eds.), *Community Support Systems and Mental Health: Practice, Policy, and Research* (pp. 253–266). New York: Springer Publishing Co.

Hallman, H. W. (1984). *Neighborhoods: Their Place in Urban Life*. Beverly Hills, Calif.: Sage Publications.

Harris, I. M. (1984). "The Citizens Coalition in Milwaukee." *Social Policy, 15*(1), 27–31.

Jacobs, S. (1984). "Community Action and the Building of Socialism From Below: A Defence of the Non-Directive Approach." *Community Development Journal, 19*(4), 217–224.

Janowitz, M. (1952). *The Community Press in an Urban Setting*. Glencoe, Ill.: Free Press.

Janowitz, M. (1978). *The Last Half Century*. Chicago: University of Chicago Press.

Kaplan, C. (1983). "Class and Coalition in New York City." *Social Policy, 13*(4), 45–48.

Katznelson, I. (1982). *City Trenches: Urban Politics and the Patterning of Class in the United States*. Chicago: University of Chicago Press.

King, S. W., & Meyers, R. S. (1981). "Developing Self-Help Groups: Integrating Group Work and Community Organization Strategies." *Social Development Issues, 5*(2–3), 33–46.

Kornhauser, W. (1959). *The Politics of Mass Society*. Glencoe, Ill.: Free Press.

Kotler, M. (1969). *Neighborhood Government: The Local Foundation of Political Life*. Indianapolis, Ind.: Bobbs-Merrill Co.

Kotler, M. (1979). "A Public Policy for Neighborhood and Community Organizations." *Social Policy, 10*(2), 37–43.

Kramer, R. M., & Specht, H. (Eds.). (1983). *Readings in Community Organization Practice* (3rd ed.). Englewood Cliffs, N.J.: Prentice-Hall.

McKnight, J., & Kretzmann, J. (1984). "Community Organizing in the 80s: Toward a Post-Alinsky Agenda." *Social Policy, 14*(3), 15–17.

Nisbet, R. A. (1953). *The Quest for Community*. New York: Oxford University Press.

Olson, M. (1965). *The Logic of Collective Action:*

Public Goods and the Theory of Groups. New York: Schocken Books.

Perlman, J. (1979). "Grass-Roots Empowerment and Government Response." *Social Policy, 10*(2), 16–21.

Peterson, P. E. (Ed.). (1985). *The New Urban Reality.* Washington, D.C.: The Brookings Institution.

President's Commission on Mental Health. (1978). *Report to the President* (Vols. 2–4). Washington, D.C.: U.S. Government Printing Office.

Reissman, F. (1979). "A New Politics via the Neighborhood." *Social Policy, 10*(2), 2.

Rich, R. C., & Wandersman, A. (1983). "Participation in Block Organizations." *Social Policy, 14*(1), 45–47.

Rose, S. M. (1981). "Reflection on Community Organization Theory." *Social Development Issues, 5*(2–3), 151–156.

Ross, M. G. (1955). *Community Organization, Theory and Principles.* New York: Harper & Row.

Spiegel, D. (1982). "Self-Help and Mutual Support Groups: A Synthesis of the Recent Literature." In D. E. Biegel & A. J. Naparstek (Eds.), *Community Support Systems and Mental Health: Practice, Policy, and Research* (pp. 98–117). New York: Springer Publishing Co.

Taylor, S.H., & Roberts, R.W. (Eds.). (1985). *Theory and Practice of Community Social Work.* New York: Columbia University Press.

Thomas, D. N. (1983). *The Making of Community Work.* London, England: Allen & Unwin.

Tönnies, F. (1940). *Fundamental Concepts of Sociology.* New York: American Book Co.

Walsh, E. J., & Warland, R. H. (1983). "Social Movement Involvement in the Wake of a Nuclear Accident: Activists and Free Riders in the TMI Area." *American Sociological Review, 48*(6), 764–780.

Wandersman, A. (1981). "A Framework of Participation in Community Organization." *Journal of Applied Behavioral Science, 17*(1), 27–58.

Warren, R. (1978). *The Community in America* (3rd ed.). Chicago: Rand McNally College Publications.

Wireman, P. (1984). *Urban Neighborhoods, Networks, and Families.* Lexington, Mass.: Lexington Books.

COMMUNITY MENTAL HEALTH. See

DEINSTITUTIONALIZATION; MENTAL HEALTH AND ILLNESS; MENTAL HEALTH AND ILLNESS IN CHILDREN; MENTAL HEALTH SERVICES; PSYCHOTROPIC MEDICATIONS.

COMMUNITY ORGANIZATION. See

Reader's Guides: COMMUNITY; COMMUNITY PLANNING.

━━━━━━   Reader's Guide   ━━━━━━

COMMUNITY PLANNING

The following articles contain information on this general topic:

Citizen Participation
Community-Based Social Action
Community Development
Community Theory and Research
Health Planning
Macro Practice: Current Trends and Issues
Planning and Management Professions
Policy Analysis: Methods and Techniques
Social Planning
Social Planning and Community Organization
Social Planning in the Public Sector
Social Planning in the Voluntary Sector

COMMUNITY THEORY AND RESEARCH

In the recent past, several attempts have been made to review the theoretical foundations of community and organizational intervention in social work (Kahn, 1960; Spiro, 1979; Warren, 1967). This task has become increasingly difficult as the boundaries of the social sciences have expanded dramatically, further broadening the theoretical and conceptual tools available to the social work profession. In addition, social scientists have become increasingly interested in research and theory building in social work contexts, and social work scholars have in turn given greater attention to the implications of social science research and its applications to social work.

This article describes several areas of social science theory that serve as foundations for social planning and community organization. As suggested above, the review cannot be exhaustive, although community theory would probably head everyone's list as the major theory underpinning work in planning and community organization.

Community Theory

One of the difficulties inhibiting theoretical work in community organization is that the notion of community itself has been conceptualized in many different ways by scholars in the field. The problem stems in part from the fact that community does not exist as a clear-cut entity in nature in the way that a person or a boulder exists. Communities do not possess inherent or natural boundaries or uniformly agreed-on characteristics. Rather, "community" is a mental construct—a definition imposed on some social aggregation by an observer or analyst—and the construct implies the parameters and phenomena to be considered. For example, is a community those individuals residing in a given municipality or should the surrounding suburbs also be included in understanding community behavior? Or would it be better to extend the definition to the nearby rural areas that produce agricultural products for the municipality and that may have an intimate interrelationship with it? On the other hand, might it not be desirable to see the community as a set of neighborhoods and ethnic enclaves that occupy contiguous territory and interact with one another for particular purposes? These questions have no established answers; the truth is in the eye of the analyst.

A brief description of some typical ways in which community has been viewed by scholars in the field follows. The discussion has benefited from Warren's (1972) cogent analysis in *The Community in America*.

Writers have approached the subject of community from different vantage points. These may be categorized in five broad areas: structural, social-psychological, people and territory, functional and action process, and social system. These categories are by no means mutually exclusive, but they do offer a rough organizing scheme for discussion.

Structural. Looking at community from a structural point of view suggests several subcategories. The political-legal perspective is perhaps the most common view of community in the eyes of the general public. "Polit-

ical-legal" refers to the official units designated as "municipality," "township," "county," and so forth. This concept implies roles, responsibilities, and benefits in terms of voting, paying taxes, and receiving public services. Political scientists use this formulation extensively in their analyses.

The geographic-spatial perspective is also a common way to look at community, and in some ways it is a simplistic one. It is concerned with a territorial space within which people are physically clustered. The concentration of individuals within this space provides the basis for defining a community. The designation of Standard Metropolitan Areas as entities by the Census Bureau conveys the use of this concept.

Social stratification and power structure are two additional, somewhat similar structural approaches to the concept of community. Both imply an uneven distribution of influence, economic resources, status, or decision-making prerogatives within the community. In this formulation, the study of community becomes the examination of power or class position, including who rules, by what means, and how positions of dominance and subordination change over time.

Social-Psychological. Several versions of the social-psychological approach to community exist. One involves perceived community of interest—the sense among a group of people that they are bound together by a common interest. They have a feeling of mutual belonging, of connectedness based on shared goals, needs, values, or activities. These bonds of common feeling constitute community.

Personal-psychological community is anchored in the individual. This view projects community as perceived by a single person in terms of the other members, the boundaries, and whether it is friendly, hostile, safe, stable, and so forth. The field of environmental or ecological psychology uses this definition. Work in this field has shown that children tend to perceive community within narrower boundaries than adults, as do lower-class individuals compared to those in the middle and upper classes.

The cultural-anthropological view sees community as a form of social living involving attitudes, norms, customs, and behavior. Wirth (1938), for example, has explored urbanism as a way of life. Other scholars have taken an even broader perspective, viewing community as a local society with a comprehensive web of relationships and behavior patterns, as in the Middletown and Plainville studies (Lynd & Lynd, 1929; West, 1945).

People and Territory. This approach to community is demographic or ecological in nature. Demography is the statistical study of populations—birthrates, morbidity, mobility, growth patterns, and changes of various population traits over time. In this view, community consists of people and their aggregate characteristics.

The ecological approach to community involves the study of people in interaction with their environment. It considers the effects of the environment on human life and social organization. The spatial distribution of individuals and institutions is an important aspect. Typifying this approach to community is the pioneering work of such Chicago sociologists as Park, Burgess, and McKenzie (1925) on land use, concentric zones in urban development, and the invasion and succession of populations in urban areas.

Functional and Action Process. The functional and action process approaches are grouped together because they both have relevance as community concepts. The functional approach defines a community in terms of some purpose, function, or problem that needs to be acted on. It is a concept that originates from professional practice literature. Ross (1967) was one of the first to articulate the concept, defining a functional community as one that "includes groups of people who share a common interest or function, such as welfare, agriculture, education, or religion" (p. 42).

An action process perspective on community involves the study of episodes of community action and community development rather than of general community structures and processes. This approach may be thought of as taking a micro rather than a macro orientation to community studies. A frequently cited example of this approach is the work of Kaufman (1959), in which he posits a set of dimensions for differentiating community actions, including the comprehensiveness of the interests pursued, local

identification of the action, the degree of local participation, and the extent of organization.

Social System. A social system approach to community is informed by general systems theory. Two social system formulations that have particular following are those of Warren (1972) and Sanders (1966).

Warren's *The Community in America* (1972) is the more comprehensive and well formulated. He provides a useful perspective in viewing the community through two frames of reference: the horizontal system, by which units are linked at the local level, and the vertical system, by which they are functionally connected with extracommunity units at the state and national levels. He also describes a number of functions of local organization, including production, distribution and consumption, socialization, social control, social participation, and mutual support. Warren argues that community is essentially the organization of social relations to provide people with opportunities to take part in activities necessary for their survival and growth. These activities are embodied in the functions identified above. These functions are the essence of community in that, to all intents and purposes, community is "the combination of social units and systems which perform the major social functions having locality relevance" (p. 6).

Sanders's (1966) social system conceptualization is a more detailed formulation and thus more difficult to summarize briefly. Its critical feature includes the notions of components and operations. Components are the units of a system and their interactive patterns—people, social groupings, and major systems such as the family, economy, religion, government, and the like. Components engage in operations that keep the system viable, such as recruitment of new members, socialization, allocation of goods and services, social control, and social integration.

Planners and community organizers draw on different concepts of community for different purposes. A social actionist concerned with inequality and power relationships has an interest in social stratification and the power structure. Health planners use demographic data. Community development workers and practice theorists rely on an action process perspective. The lack of one theoretical framework may lead to frustration and what appears to be analytic muddling, although a diversity of theoretical outlooks serves the multiplicity of practice objectives and contexts characteristic of the field of community organization and social planning.

Community theory is the broadest and perhaps the most abstract social science construct for social planning and community organization. A number of more delineated areas are also relevant to planning and community organization. In this short review only a few will be described. These include citizen participation, power structure, and social network analysis. Space precludes treatment of several other areas relevant to community organization—ethnic group studies, studies of values, the structure of planning organizations, and the characteristics of welfare agencies as a distinct subsystem.

Citizen Participation

Voluntary associations have had a central place in community organization over the years. Until recently, community organization practice was closely identified with the voluntary or private sector. Citizen participation in planning and action has been a key concept in the field, and the voluntary association was viewed as a vehicle through which such participation might be facilitated—the association serving as a means of linking the individual to larger forces and entities in society. However, voluntary citizen participation is also common in the government sector through advisory boards, appointed and elected commissions, and special task forces. Kramer (1976, 1981) has studied voluntary associations both comparatively and from a social work perspective. Social scientists have tried to specify the functions of voluntary associations, have traced patterns of evolution and transformation of goals in associations, have examined the behavior of specifically welfare-oriented agencies such as the Community Chest, have studied patterns of participation in associations by various population groups, and have differentiated the mutual roles and role conflicts of participants and professionals in the governance of associations (Rothman, 1974). All this information has potential usefulness for the practitioner engaged in fostering citizen participation.

Citizen participation has to a large extent been associated with two theoretical constructs in the literature—"relative deprivation" and "status inconsistency." Researchers and theorists believe that subjective feelings of deprivation and disadvantage have a greater effect on mobilizing people to better their conditions than do the objective circumstances of their lives. According to Matza (1966), subjective feelings of deprivation depend on how one's experiences compare to the experiences of intimate others, on what an individual has been accustomed to previously, or on what is anticipated. Thus, profound degradation in an absolute sense may be tolerated or ignored if those close at hand are doing no better or if an individual never expected to do any better. Several investigations support this hypothesis.

Morrison and Steeves (1967) describe an investigation based on thirteen studies done in eight Midwestern states (the core of the National Farmers' Organization [NFO] membership) that allowed comparisons of NFO members with similar farmers who were not members of the organization. NFO members were found to be in relatively better economic circumstances, but they expressed more dissatisfaction and were more oriented toward changing institutions perceived as detrimental to them. NFO members tended to have higher economic aspirations than nonmembers and to show greater belief in the structural sources of their difficulties.

Initial participants in social action-oriented movements, then, come ordinarily not from the most deprived, but from those who have risen to a somewhat higher economic level. Emphasizing and documenting the relative deprivation of potential participants would likely be a useful organizing tool.

The concept of status inconsistency (and its counterpart, status crystallization) has also been associated with citizen participation. The degree to which the various statuses that define a person's position in society are consistent or inconsistent are viewed as affecting the individual's outlook and predisposition to action (Geschwender, 1968).

Political participation has been an area of particular interest in recent years, and it has been shown to be positively related to the degree of influence or policymaking roles of different groups (Milbrath & Goel, 1981). Long-term analysis has shown that participation is also associated with socioeconomic status, and higher socioeconomic status correlates with more conservative voting behavior. Recent trends include increased political participation by women (Braungart, 1978), a decline in class politics (Abramson, 1977), and reduced support by some Roman Catholics for the Democrats (Nie, Verba, & Petrocik, 1976). Some theoretical work of note includes Lipset's (1981) thesis of working-class authoritarianism and Verba and Nie's (1972) mobilization model predicting increased political participation in larger, more complex communities. Because political participation affects policy, which influences social work clientele, knowledge of this area of study is of special relevance to macrolevel social workers.

Power Structure

Since the publication of Hunter's *Community Power Structure* (1953), numerous studies have appeared on this subject by sociologists, political scientists, anthropologists, journalists, and others. The question of who holds the power and who calls the shots has been a source of fascination for a wide range of people. Hunter's contention that a small elite, made up largely of business interests, predominates has been questioned by such investigators as Dahl (1961) and Banfield (1961), who found a pluralistic pattern of competing elites rather than a monolithic pattern of power in American communities. Sociologists using reputational techniques whereby opinions of informed observers are sought, have generally uncovered monolithic patterns of influence, whereas political scientists using techniques that record who makes decisions in specific instances have discovered pluralistic patterns of influence, with governmental officials having major influence.

As the debate continued, new theoretical perspectives entered the picture, adding to the power elite–pluralistic positions a Marxist view of social class domination (Whitt, 1979; Greer, 1979). The interaction of local community and national centers of power have been highlighted; in Hunter's (1980) revisitation of Atlanta and Domhoff's (1978) restudy of Dahl's New Haven, the influence of national power was underlined.

Some scholars have moved beyond the national level to an understanding of transnational power and its intersection with local situations. Thus, multinational corpora-

tions and their actions and effects have been intensively studied (Barnet, 1980; Kourvetaris & Dobratz, 1980).

At the local level, methodological advances have been made in examining community power through studies that cut across multiple settings. Clark (1973), for example, conducted large comparative studies using common variables in an aggregated fashion.

An understanding of the nature of power at the community level is an important consideration for community practitioners. It enables them to determine possible allies or adversaries in relation to given courses of action, and it facilitates the design of strategies stressing either consensus or conflict in regard to a given goal. It provides ongoing guidance in the general process of community appraisal.

As yet, however, power structure studies have not proved highly fruitful for social work practice. Methodologies of investigation have varied so that results are often conflicting and confusing. Passionate ideological and methodological combat has often substituted for detached analysis.

Still, some findings may be practical, and some methodological approaches may be useful. In the absence of definitive conclusions as to whether reputational, class, positional, or event research approaches for studying community power are appropriate, or appropriate differentially for different purposes, practitioners can make experimental use of all of them, making the best possible analytic judgments until more work is completed in this area. These studies have explicated important conceptual dimensions of power, however, including monolithic versus pluralistic power; overt or symbolic versus covert leadership; variations in influence among institutional areas; interaction of local and extracommunity factors; and differential roles of influence among elites, groups, and variable community structures associated with different power configurations.

Social Network Analysis

In recent years, considerable interest has emerged in the social sciences with regard to the formation and operation of social networks. Two aspects of social networks have been studied that are of particular interest to community organizers—informal helping groups and relationships among formal organizations.

Informal Helping Groups. Mutual assistance or self-help groups have increased in number since the 1970s in response to such social trends as the reduction of funds for professional services, the diminished credibility of professional helpers resulting from the complexity and rapidly changing character of social problems, and a growing ideology favorable to indigenous initiatives. Interest on the part of sociologists and others in theories of social networking have paralleled these developments. Some theoretical areas of study include close-knit interlocking networks, helping social networks per se, loose-knit or radial social networks, and weak social ties. (The discussion that follows is adapted from Warren & Rothman [1981].)

As described by Bott (1957) and Laumann (1973), close-knit networks possess several attributes of intimate primary groups. Consisting of reciprocal friendship and kinship linkages, close-knit networks frequently provide critical social support to individuals. This form of social network is typified in Liebow's classic analysis of a low-income black neighborhood (1967).

In helping social networks, mutual aid is given or received for a specific problem confronted in daily life. Not all components or "members" of the network are found in a single setting, so that their mobilization as a network depends on their activation by one member in a particular location. What sharply separates this form of network from a close-knit one is specialization of concern, otherwise heterogeneous composition, and the general absence of other common values.

Because these problem-anchored helping networks are heterogeneous in composition, they can readily expand outward to other networks. An individual may therefore belong to several helping networks simultaneously. Thus, these networks are bound together only by the common link of that one individual and are not cohesive in any other way. Structurally, however, such networks are "always there" even if a given individual does not use them. Collins and Pancoast (1974) discuss the utility of "natural helping networks" generally as well as specifically for facilitating day care services.

Loose-knit networks consist of hetero-geneous sets of individuals who share superficial interactions but lack either a self-perceived common bond or a shared social status. Such social networks may be highly transient and rootless. They function largely in work settings and neighborhoods or as transitional forms of group life. Although they are impermanent and nonintimate, over time they may spawn significant social groupings approaching the traditional primary group. Laumann (1973) implies that although loose-knit or radial networks are less intimate than close-knit ones, they can be significant in contemporary urban society. They are highly flexible and thus adaptive to the demands of geographic and social mobility.

This review suggests the varied ways in which the social network concept is viewed by different researchers and scholars, but many community organizers are also recognizing the importance of local self-help networks. A number of programs throughout the United States in the fields of health, social services, planning, crime control, and neighborhood redevelopment have attempted to link up with informal helping groups. Some programs have developed their own terminology (for example, "capacity building") to describe their efforts, and others use general terms that are likely to cover a variety of activities (for example, "outreach").

As researchers and practitioners learn more about the positive functions of informal social support systems in helping people cope with stress and other concerns, the importance of ensuring that public and private agencies do not discourage natural support systems becomes increasingly clear. Some functions that are currently performed by formal services may devolve to informal systems because of rising costs. Hospital stays, for example, are growing shorter, placing a greater burden on informal systems to provide convalescent care. Communities are also being asked to care for chronically disabled persons who were previously institutionalized.

Natural support systems have weaknesses, however. They may be too selective, excluding many people who could benefit from them. Undoubtedly, in many urban neighborhoods the residents feel isolated and cannot rely on a neighborhood-based helping system. Thus, formal professional services need to be maintained even as they work with informal helping systems.

Interorganizational Relationships.

The issue of interorganizational relationships is important to the study of social services because the health and welfare field does not function as a well-integrated system. Given the level of autonomy, specialization, and voluntarism in social work agencies, a great need exists for coordination and coalition-building to increase the efficiency of what would otherwise be a largely inchoate organizational structure. Starting with work in the early 1960s by researchers such as Litwak and Hylton (1962) and Levine and White (1961), a school of scholarly inquiry has developed concerning organizational interaction at the community level.

According to Laumann, Galaskiewicz, and Marsden (1978), two lines of inquiry have come into being concerning interorganizational linkages. One is concerned with the transfer of resources and examines how agencies coordinate to attain an overarching goal. These studies usually use exchange theory, which focuses on interchange of resources, as an organizing framework, citing the following types of resource transfers: funds, personnel, referrals of clients, power and influence, value commitments, information, and moral support. (Different researchers emphasize different types of exchanges.)

The other direction of study is based on the interpenetration of organizational boundaries. These studies often view networks as arenas of conflict among organizational interest groups. Most of these studies have examined shared memberships, including those at the board level (Zald, 1969). Other types of interpenetration studies have examined joint programs (Aiken & Hage, 1968).

The qualitative nature of linkages has also been studied, including their intensity; their degrees of interdependence, formalization, standardization, and symmetry; and whether relationships are in a context of cooperation or conflict. The process of forming networks has also been examined (Benson, 1975), often using a resource-dependency theory that analyzes interorganizational relationships in terms of seeking material and other support from organizations in the environment.

Research and Application

In an extensive study of the literature on community and organizational research, Rothman (1974) attempted to formulate empirically based principles of action. He summarized and applied findings in such areas as organizational behavior, citizen participation, political and legislative behavior, diffusion of innovations, and the roles of change-agents.

Two precautions are in order in discussing the application of such research. One has to do with the limitations of social science. Few theoretical issues are resolved in a definitive way. Social phenomena are of such complexity, and the power and scope of current methodology so limited, that much that goes under the name of social science knowledge must be viewed in a highly tentative, skeptical light. Unrealistically high expectations for research or overoptimism may impede the use of social science findings. The other precaution concerns the manner in which social science concepts are carried over to practice. Certain theories may be appropriate only for specific practice issues under limited conditions. A system for refinement must exist if theory and social work practice are to be integrated. Otherwise, as Kadushin (quoted in Rothman & Epstein, 1977) pointed out, "The borrowed material will remain an undigested lump in the body politic of social work, interesting but unintegrated and unused" (p. 1443).

A primary means of achieving integration might be through the efforts of specialized linking agents from either social work or the social science disciplines or with training in both to translate and transmit knowledge from one sphere to the other. This role (and its institutionalization) requires increased recognition and support if it is to make an impact. However, to the extent that social science knowledge is introduced into master's degree programs in social work, future generations of social workers will make increasingly sophisticated demands on social scientists working in areas related to social work practice. Nonetheless, institutions that essentially transmit information (such as consultation agencies) need to be developed to ensure a comprehensive exchange of pertinent material. The Center for Research on Utilization of Scientific Knowledge at the University of Michigan and the national Educational Resources Information Centers (ERIC) program are examples of such institutions.

JACK ROTHMAN

For further information, see CITIZEN PARTICIPATION; COMMUNITY-BASED SOCIAL ACTION; COMMUNITY DEVELOPMENT; MUTUAL HELP GROUPS; NATURAL HELPING NETWORKS; NEIGHBORHOODS; SOCIAL PLANNING; SOCIAL PLANNING AND COMMUNITY ORGANIZATION.

References

Abramson, P. R. (1977). *The Political Socialization of Black Americans*. New York: Free Press.

Aiken, M., & Hage, J. (1968). "Organizational Interdependence and Interorganizational Structure." *American Sociological Review*, *33*(6), 912–933.

Banfield, E. C. (1961). *Political Influence*. Glencoe, Ill.: Free Press.

Barnet, R. J. (1980). *The Lean Years*. New York: Simon & Schuster.

Benson, J. K. (1975). "The Interorganizational Network as a Political Economy." *Administrative Science Quarterly*, *20*(2), 229–249.

Bott, E. (1957). *Family and Social Network*. Glencoe, Ill.: Free Press.

Braungart, R. G. R. (1978). "Changing Electoral Politics in America." *Journal of Political and Military Sociology*, *6*(2), 261–269.

Clark, T. N. (1973). "Citizen Values, Power and Policy Outputs: A Model of Community Decision Making." *Journal of Comparative Administration*, *4*(4), 385–472.

Collins, A. H., & Pancoast, D. I. (1974). *Natural Helping Networks: A Strategy for Prevention*. New York: National Association of Social Workers.

Dahl, R. C. (1961). *Who Governs?* New Haven, Conn.: Yale University Press.

Domhoff, G. W. (1978). *Who Really Rules?* Santa Monica, Calif.: Goodyear Publishing Co.

Geschwender, J. A. (1968). "Status Inconsistency, Social Isolation, and Individual Unrest." *Social Forces*, *46*(4), 477–484.

Green, J. W. & Mayo, S. C. (1953). "A Framework for Research in the Actions of Community Groups." *Social Forces*, *31*(4), 321.

Greer, E. (1979). *Big Steel*. New York: Monthly Review Press.

Hunter, F. (1953). *Community Power Structure: A Study of Decision Makers*. Chapel Hill: University of North Carolina Press.

Hunter, F. (1980). *Community Power Succession: Atlanta's Policy Makers Revisited*. Chapel Hill: University of North Carolina Press.

Kahn, A. J. (1960). "Social Science and the Conceptual Framework for Community Organization Research." In L. S. Kogan (Ed.), *Social Science Theory and Research* (pp. 64–79). New York: National Association of Social Workers.

Kaufman, H. F. (1959). "Toward an Interactional Conception of Community." *Social Forces*, *38*(1).

Kourvetaris, G. A., & Dobratz, B. A. (1980). *Society and Politics: An Overview and Reappraisal of Political Sociology*. Dubuque, Iowa: Kendall/Hall.

Kramer, R. (1976). *The Voluntary Service Agency in Israel*. Berkeley: University of California, Institute of International Studies.

Kramer, R. (1981). *Voluntary Agencies in the Welfare State*. Berkeley: University of California Press.

Laumann, E. O. (1973). *Bonds of Pluralism*. New York: John Wiley & Sons.

Laumann, E. O., Galaskiewicz, J., & Marsden, P. V. (1978). "Community Structure as Interorganizational Linkages." In *Annual Review of Sociology: Vol. 4* (pp. 455–484). Palo Alto, Calif.: Annual Reviews.

Levine, S., & White, P. E. (1962). "Exchange as a Conceptual Framework for the Study of Interorganizational Relationships." *Administrative Science Quarterly*, *5*(4), 583–601.

Liebow, E. (1967). *Tally's Corner*. Boston: Little, Brown & Co.

Lipser, S. (1981). *Political Man*. Baltimore, Md.: Johns Hopkins University Press.

Litwak, E., & Hylton, L. F. (1962). "Interorganizational Analysis: A Hypothesis on Coordinating Agencies." *Administrative Science Quarterly*, (4), 397–420.

Lynd, R. S. & Lynd, H. M. (1929). *Middletown: A Study in Contemporary American Culture*. New York: Harcourt Brace.

Matza, D. (1966). "Poverty and Dispute." In R. K. Merton & R. A. Nisbet (Eds.), *Contemporary Social Problems* (pp. 619–699). New York: Harcourt, Brace & World.

Milbrath, L. W., & Goel, M. I. (1981). *Political Participation: How and Why*. Chicago: Rand McNally & Co.

Morrison, D. E., & Steeves, A. D. (1967). "Deprivation, Discontent and Social Movement Participation: Evidence on a Contemporary Farmers' Movement, the NFO." *Rural Sociology*, *32*(4), 414–434.

Nie, N. H., Verba, S., & Petrocik, J. R. (1976). *The Changing American Voter*. Cambridge, Mass.: Harvard University Press.

Park, R. E., Burgess, E. W., & McKenzie, R. D. (1925). *The City*. Chicago: University of Chicago Press.

Ross, M. G. (1967). *Community Organization: Theory, Principles and Practice* (2nd ed.). New York: Harper & Row.

Rothman, J. (1974). *Planning and Organizing for*

Social Change: Action Principles from Social Science Research. New York: Columbia University Press.

Rothman, J., & Epstein, I. (1977). "Social Planning and Community Organization: Social Science Foundations." In *Encyclopedia of Social Work* (17th ed., pp. 1433–1443). Washington, D.C.: National Association of Social Workers.

Sanders, I. T. (1966). *The Community: An Introduction to a Social System* (2nd ed.). New York: Ronald Press Co.

Spiro, S. (1979). "The Knowledge Base of Community Organization Practice." In F. M. Cox et al. (Eds.), *Strategies of Community Organization* (3rd ed., pp. 79–84). Itasca, Ill.: F. E. Peacock Publishers.

Verba, S., & Nie, N. (1972). *Participation in America*. New York: Harper & Row.

Warren, D. I., & Rothman, J. (1981). "Community Networks." In M. E. Olsen & M. Micklin (Eds.), *Handbook of Applied Sociology*. New York: Praeger Publishers.

Warren, R. L. (1967). "Application of Social Science Knowledge to the Community Organization Field." *Journal of Education for Social Work*, *3*(1), 60–72.

Warren, R. L. (1972). *The Community in America* (2nd ed.). Chicago: Rand McNally & Co.

West, J. (1945). *Plainville, U.S.A.* New York: Columbia University Press.

Whitt, J. A. (1979). "Towards a Class-Dialectical Model of Power." *American Sociological Review*, *44*(1), 81–100.

Wirth, L. (1938). "Urbanism as a Way of Life." *American Journal of Sociology*, *44*(1), 1–24.

Zald, M. (1969). "The Power and Function of Boards of Directors: A Theoretical Synthesis." *American Journal of Sociology*, *75*(1), 97–111.

COMPUTER UTILIZATION

The special advantages of computers lie in their vast storage capacity and the speed, accuracy, and economy with which they process large sets of data. The use of computers as efficient data and word processors has grown at a rapidly accelerating rate since the late 1970s. Advances in computer technology and imaginative work in computer-assisted knowledge applications have begun to affect human service agencies and their clients in dramatic and substantive ways.

This article provides a general orientation to the many uses of computer systems in social service agencies, with particular emphasis on applications in direct practice. Current applications range from data management to computerized client interviews and recently developing decision support systems for practitioners. New trends and emerging research promise to expand even further computer utilization in human services. Computer technologies not only have the potential for providing greater efficiency in routine tasks but also can serve as powerful tools for professional decision making. However, they require practitioners and researchers to become innovators and architects of change if they are to keep the emerging information technology responsive to the needs of social work practice.

Historical Overview

Computer applications in social service organizations began during the 1960s and 1970s when federal programs providing reimbursement for the costs of human services required documentation of who was doing what for whom, when, where, at what cost, and with what results. Other federal and state regulations required studies of program effectiveness, quality control, and mandated participation in professional standards review organizations. These heavy demands on human service organizations for specific information led to the development and use of the management information system (MIS). This management tool systematically collects information through input documents, accumulates these data in organized data files, and processes and summarizes various aspects of the data in periodic or special reports (Hedlund & Wurster, 1982). MISs initially used in human service agencies were not designed as comprehensive data systems but were tailored to relatively specific, well-defined purposes. They usually focused on administrative tasks, such as accounting and fiscal management, inventory, personnel matters, and property management. More recently, client-oriented MISs were developed, which include the demographic characteristics of clients, types of problems, and the amount and types of services provided. By the end of the 1970s, more than three-fourths of all community mental health centers in the United States were utilizing some form of computerized MIS (Gorodezky & Hedlund,

1982). In the 1980s, the development and expansion of online computing, better programming languages, and micro-based network systems are facilitating innovative applications of computers in increasing numbers of human service agencies.

Current Applications of Information Technology

Integrated Database Management Systems. A database management system consists of sets of logically related data files, or databases, and an associated grouping of software (programs) necessary to store, manage, and retrieve data from the database. The artificial boundary lines in many early computer applications separating administrative, direct practice, and research databases are beginning to disappear. Work is under way to create integrated database management systems that can serve such multiple functions as billing, accounting, personnel record keeping, planning, monitoring, and evaluating service delivery (Mutschler & Hasenfeld, in press). Easy-to-use software for integrated database management systems has become available with the advent of smaller, less expensive, but more powerful interactive computers. So-called "general application packages" permit non–computer specialists and nonprogrammers (with relatively small amounts of training) to create and use a sophisticated computerized database (Hedlund, Vieweg, & Dong, 1985).

Newkham and Bawcom (1981) describe an integrated clinical and financial database management system in a community mental health center in Texas. The center provides a wide variety of services through 15 service locations in a six-county region. Annually, 50,000 people are screened and 2,700 people are served in one or more of the programs. A key management principle in the successful development of this system was to compile available data in ways that were meaningful to staff members and could communicate information necessary for their day-to-day tasks. The system's objectives were (1) to document the flow of clients and the provision of services, (2) to give immediate feedback to direct service providers and keep records current, (3) to meet internal and external reporting needs for data on clients and services, (4) to meet financial reporting

requirements for funding sources and provide an audit "trial" for fiscal review, (5) to provide summary information for client and system management, and (6) to allow cost outcome analysis.

One requirement of this computerized database management system was the conversion of the previously used nonstandardized recording system to a problem-oriented record system. A problem-oriented record committee, including direct service practitioners, designed a direct service record form that captured specific client data at each major juncture of treatment. On a single sheet, the direct service record provides a preprinted visual array of data, including the client's case objectives and status, and individual treatment modalities (medication, initial and current level of functioning, and future service plan). Following each service contact, the practitioner records the services provided, the time involved, and billing information. Scales indicating the client's level of functioning are completed at intake, at subsequent intervals of 90 days, at major treatment junctures, and at discharge.

For the fiscal management part of the system, programs were developed to provide (1) integrated flexibility in comparing client-staff service data with the cost of providing that service, (2) timely and regular revenue-expenditure reports, and (3) detailed documentation for audit trails. All levels of staff participated in designing the required internal and external reports to ensure their usefulness and relevance. Newkham and Bawcom (1981) reported that after a 3-year implementation phase, this integrated database management system improved clinical and fiscal accountability and became an indispensable tool for supporting the quality of care provided by the staff of this community mental health center.

What characteristics distinguish this successful database management system from the many partly implemented or failed systems reported (Greist & Klein, 1981; Mutschler & Cnaan, 1985)? A major factor, to be discussed in more detail later, is the acceptance of the system by administrators and practitioners for their day-to-day tasks. Bleich et al. (1985), who developed and implemented a widely used database management system in a medical setting, list the following requirements for a successful system (p. 757):

1. Information should be captured, not on pieces of paper, but directly at computer terminals located at the point of each transaction. The computer in turn should provide immediate benefit to the person who enters this information.
2. Information captured at a terminal anywhere in the system should be immediately available, if needed, at any other terminal. Rather than printed reports which become progressively out of date from the moment they are produced, terminals that provide immediate access to the most-to-date information should be the principal means of retrieval.
3. The response time of the computer should be rapid; for the busy professional, delays that can be measured in seconds are often unacceptable.
4. The computer should be reliable; in the event of a failure, the defect should be corrected within minutes, and users should never lose data.
5. Confidentiality should be protected; only authorized persons should have access to the data.
6. The computed programs should be friendly to the user. There should be no need for user's manuals. It should be easier for the user to obtain a figure or report from a computer terminal than through a telephone call.
7. Finally, there should be a common registry for all patients. For each patient there should be one and only one set of identifying information in the computer, available at all times to authorized users and preserved, if possible in perpetuity.

These criteria are intended to make the database management system responsive to the daily tasks of the practitioner. Bleich et al. (1985) conclude that if the computer is not helpful, if nothing worthwhile happens when the keys are pressed, the terminals will gather dust. If, on the other hand, the system is programmed to help the decision maker, results demonstrate that the system will be heavily used.

Some of the most modern database management systems have at their core an integrated database that permits clinicians, administrators, researchers, and educators to track patients and their progress, follow a course of treatment, keep a service history, analyze staff or trainees' activities, record fees, monitor costs, and keep inventories. The most sophisticated of these systems incorporate a dictionary-driven concept in which the computer is programmed to ask a series of questions about the data that, once answered, establish a "dictionary." The dictionary drives all other programs; it can enter new data, edit existing data, search for the characteristics of patient groups, and generate periodic reports and statistics. Whenever new data are added to one of these subsets, the dictionary automatically makes any required changes in all other subsets of the data system (Greist et al., 1982). Such a constantly updated, comprehensive database management system reduces the need for manually operated client files, and it provides online information for the planning and decision making of administrators, clinicians, and researchers. The outcomes of experiments with comprehensive database management systems will be of considerable importance to social service agencies interested in a common data approach.

Computerized Client Interviews. The application of computers in direct practice has lagged behind fiscal and administrative uses. A number of factors have delayed the development and implementation of clinical applications: (1) early programs were too time consuming to prepare and often operated only in the batch (as opposed to the online) mode; (2) the standardization of treatment processes necessary for computerization was hard to achieve because of the differences in the way different practitioners assess, treat, and evaluate clients with similar problems; and (3) initially too many problems arose at the person-machine interface (that is, when clients or practitioners interacted with the computer).

Direct client interviewing by computer was among the earliest applications of computing in clinical practice. Greist et al. (1982), Slack et al. (1966), and their colleagues clearly recognized the revolutionary prospects of client-computer interviewing and the potential effects of computer applications on clinicians. Their early work addresses fundamental issues surrounding direct client interviewing by computer: client acceptance of the technology (Slack & VanCura, 1968) and client characteristics that interfere with its use (Cole, Johnson, & Williams, 1976); reliability and validity of data (Slack & Slack, 1977); confidentiality (Laska & Bank, 1975); and acceptance by clinicians (Erdman et al., 1981).

Subsequent work on computer interviews has consistently confirmed and extended early findings. Most clients find the interviewing process enjoyable and the interview content relevant to their problems. Several studies have suggested that as subject matter becomes more sensitive—involving alcohol and drug abuse or sexual counseling, for example—respondents appreciate the nonhuman interviewer even more (Greist, Klein, & VanCura, 1973; Slack & Slack, 1977). Many markedly disturbed clients can be interviewed by computer. To date, clinicians have found that 85 percent or more of psychiatric inpatients can be interviewed by computer at the time of admission (Erdman et al., 1981). Clients give data that are at least as reliable and valid and far more complete than those obtained by clinicians (Lucas et al., 1977; Greist, Klein, & VanCura, 1973). Confidentiality can be carefully protected by controlling access to stored computer interviews. Some programs permit clients to decide after giving their information what uses will be made of it. Thus, a client may decide to allow use for clinical purposes but not for research or might choose to delete the interview altogether. Greist et al. (1982) report that clinician acceptance of computer interviews has been slower than expected, attributing this to problems associated with making changes in a conservative profession.

One computer interview used in clinical practice is the Social Adjustment Interview (Greist & Klein, 1980), which collects psychiatric and social history and helps evaluate current role performance. Branching logic built into the interview eliminates irrelevant questions and obtains necessary detail. The entire interview consists of more than 650 questions, but the average respondent is likely to be presented with about 150 questions depending on problem areas. Initial questions gather the following demographic data: (1) educational status and history; (2) current employment or employment seeking; (3) marital history, status, and children; (4) living arrangement and use of leisure time; (5) current and future stress; and (6) changes in roles or lifestyle. After these introductory questions, the client is asked to choose "two

areas that are most involved in your problems right now." Detailed questions follow in the two chosen areas and are organized according to (1) role performance, productivity, and effectiveness; (2) feelings and satisfactions; (3) interpersonal friction and difficulties; and (4) situational stress. Multiple-choice questions are supplemented by open-ended and free-text questions to provide detail.

This example (Greist & Klein, 1980, pp. 165–166) shows a patient's interchange with the computer about her relationship with her boyfriend:

Computer: "How have you and your partner been getting along in the last two months?"

Patient's Answer: "4. Marked friction." (Chosen from five multiple choice answers ranging from "1. Smooth, warm relationship" to "5. Constant friction."

Computer: (Following up on the friction) "When you are angry or irritated with your partner, do you express it?"

Patient's Answer: "3. Sometimes." (Multiple choice ranging from "1. All the time" to "5. Never.")

Computer: "How many arguments, fights, or disagreements do you and your partner have in a month?"

Patient's Answer: "2. Several times a month." (From multiple choice ranging from "1. Once a day" to "5. Never.")

The information obtained in this interview is available immediately to the clinician in a narrative summary format. All responses remain in the computer system and can be scored, summarized, and searched for use in research.

A second computerized interview that clinicians can also use for outcome evaluation is the Symptom Checklist-90 (SCL-90) (Derogatis et al., 1974). The interview begins with instructions for terminal use and questions to confirm informed consent, followed by a series of questions designated to elicit the client's free-text description of up to three target complaints. Ratings of frequency and intensity provide standardization. Branching options permit direct continuation to the SCL-90 items if there are fewer than three target problems. The interview concludes with a brief section assessing client reactions.

The SCL-90 interview is programmed so that it can be repeated over time to evaluate change during therapy, at termination, and during the follow-up period. Repeat interviews present target symptom definitions verbatim for rerating and allow for redefinition and elaboration. The program scores and summarizes the interview immediately. SCL-90 scores include total number of items checked, total weighted symptom intensity, intensity of positive symptoms, and the average rating of each cluster. The interviews were found reliable, accurate, and highly acceptable to most clients (Erdman et al., 1981; Greist & Klein, 1980).

Computer interviews may not be the method of choice for some assessment interviews, such as intensive insight-oriented psychotherapy assessments. As Erdman et al. (1981) caution, intuitive processes that are hard or impossible for a human to describe are even harder to program. The computer's strength lies in its vast and reliable memory and consistency in processing large amounts of information. However, given the current pretechnological stage of the human services field, marked by a lack of standardization and minimal number of tools (Siegel & Alexander, 1985), it is not likely that comprehensive computerized assessment systems will be routinely used in the near future. A more feasible strategy for introducing computerized interviews into direct practice is to train and involve individual clinicians who are willing to participate in the design, use, and evaluation of computerized assessment tools. As separate instruments become successful in discrete areas, they can be merged into a more comprehensive information and assessment system. Because at this stage assessment and treatment approaches vary enormously from one clinician to another and across client populations, routine use of comprehensive computer interviews must await a better fundamental understanding and documentation of the domain of client problems, assessment, and intervention procedures.

Decision Support Systems. A variety of computerized decision support, expert, or consultation systems are being developed, whose primary intent is to assist in decision making (Hayes-Roth, Waterman & Lenat, 1984; Schoech & Schkade, 1980; Siegel & Alexander, 1985). These systems go beyond collecting and retrieving large amounts of client or agency data. Decision support or expert systems consist of a predefined set of facts (a knowledge base) used in conjuction with decision rules that are triggered by the decision maker's input of data. Decision support systems (DSSs) can be categorized in terms of the types of knowledge they utilize. DSSs include models based on numerical data analysis, expert knowledge, scientific-theoretical knowledge, or any of these domains of knowledge combined with an inferential method (Siegel & Alexander, 1984). Early applications of DSSs were diagnostic consultation systems in medical settings. One frequently cited and advanced expert system is MYCIN, an infectious disease treatment consultation system developed at Stanford University. The interactive system consists of 500 rules leading to recommendations for the diagnosis and treatment of specific infectious diseases (Buchanan & Shortcliffe, 1984). Classification tasks such as diagnosis are well suited to expert systems if they can draw on a distinct body of factual information to which decision rules apply.

The human services field is still in the early stages of developing and testing applications of decision support systems. PLACECON is an experimental consulting program for facilitating placement decisions in child welfare. The program is written in the computer language called LISP and can be run on microcomputers. PLACECON prompts the worker to enter facts about the child to be placed and its family, such as the type and severity of abuse, medical evidence, and the availability of a foster or adoptive home. Using these facts and a set of rules, the program recommends the possible types of placement or services indicated in each case. The program can also document how the decision was made by listing the facts and accompanying probabilities of the case that the worker had entered and the rules on which each decision was based. Thus, the worker can examine the decision process and decide whether to concur with or reject the recommendation (Schuerman, 1985).

Another DSS in child welfare, the Enhanced Case Planning and Assessment System, uses an extensive longitudinal database. The database includes client data for all cases served by the agency during the past 9 years. Workers can then examine the history of any current case in their caseload regarding length of stay in various types of care facilities since the initial case opening; they can use a series of predictive models to determine how long a given child is likely to stay in a planned placement as compared with similar placements made by the agency in the past. Special alerts built into the system signal placement turnovers (three in any 3-month period or five in any single year), recidivism, and runaways. The project is now exploring the feasibility of developing an automated child and family assessment instrument, using models from rule-based expert systems as a guide. This DSS still in its experimental phase, has the potential to assist direct service workers in monitoring case progress and making predictions about service outcomes that are a major concern to child welfare agencies: foster placement turnovers, client recidivism, and extended stays in placements outside the natural home (Vogel, 1984).

Humans are limited in their ability to process information and subject to overload and inconsistency, especially under clinical conditions of pressure and peak information load. The computer can support decision tasks through its inexhaustible capacity for routine information processing, its vast memory banks, and its rapid, accurate, and consistent data retrieval capabilities. But the judgment and inferential ability of the computer is completely limited by the rule base used in the DSS, and the computer is rigid in its adherence to these rules. So far, the number of human service areas in which DSSs can be used remains small, not because of technological limitations, but because the human services field still lacks the standardization and extensive codified knowledge necessary for computerization. Confronted with the promise of technology and the limits of human services knowledge, Vogel (1985) suggests a number of issues that need to be addressed before the productive application of sophisticated DSSs is likely to occur. Two of these issues concern the understanding of decision structures and decision-making processes, and the assumption that more data will automatically improve decision making. There is as yet too little information describing decision-making processes and insufficient knowledge about the "rules" human-service decision makers use in arriving at their decisions. But Vogel (1985) also warns

that, in human services, decisions are often based on experience, intuitive judgments, attitudes, and predispositions rather than on data. More data may be perceived as information overload and may not necessarily improve the decision-making process.

The development of DSSs represents a promising field for the joint interests of clinicians and direct practice researchers. Since the mid-1960s, for example, applications of experimental single subject evaluation and evaluation research were frequently hampered by the lack of outcome specifications and limited proceduralization of interventions (Bloom & Fischer, 1981; Fanshel, 1980; Mutschler, 1979; Thomas, 1984). Current efforts to develop the required knowledge base for DSSs, called "knowledge engineering," can support and benefit from evaluation and direct practice research. During the coming decade, joint efforts by human service professionals, practice researchers, and knowledge engineers are needed to develop, implement, evaluate, and diffuse decision support innovations in human services.

Future Trends and Emerging Research

Computers are being used successfully for information processing, interviewing, and beginning decision support in human service agencies. But there are other issues and future trends related to the use of information technology that must be considered by those proposing and opposing computer applications in human services.

Direct Client-Computer Interactions. Currently, computer applications in the human services have at least three constituencies: (1) administrators, case managers, and supervisors can use computers for the efficient production of required reports and to help in their planning and decision making; (2) direct practitioners can use computerized interviews and gather data directly from the client to facilitate case management assessment, planning, and monitoring of services; and (3) clients can increasingly obtain information, even treatment, through direct interaction with a computer. Cuts in federal funding force clinicians to see more clients in less time. Increased attention is therefore given to the third constituency and the potential of direct client-computer interactions. Computer programs are already in use to provide information to clients about entitlement for which they are qualified, to give female teenagers information about birth control, and to help the elderly find available housing (LaMendola, 1985). A computerized lithium library at the University of Wisconsin, containing more than 9,000 citations, is being made available to patients in treatment for depression or related mental health problems. (Jefferson, Greist & Marcetick, 1979).

Computer-assisted treatment programs are less common. However, a number of attempts have been made to develop computer-administered treatment aids and treatment programs, and recent studies compare the benefits from automated approaches with those from human therapists (Hedlund, Vieweg, & Dong, 1985; Schwartz, 1984). One of the most complex and ambitious intervention applications has been a research project by Selmi et al. (1982) based on cognitive behavior principles for the treatment of depression. This six-session computerized treatment program interacts directly with mildly to moderately depressed clients. It was evaluated by randomly assigning homogeneous samples of depressed individuals to one of three groups: computer therapist, human therapist, or treatment-on-demand (the control group). Careful pre- and posttreatment measures of depression showed that both treatment groups improved more than the control group and that the computer program did at least as well as the human therapist.

There has been considerable criticism of the use of computers in human services in general and of computer-assisted treatment programs in particular. Yet critics make assumptions on behalf of a client constituency without directly consulting it. As Greist et al. (1982) have demonstrated, whenever clients have evaluated client-computer interactions, the reaction has been positive, often to the point of preferring the computer. Aided by technological advances, such as videodiscs and voice or visual "recognition" of the user by the computer, direct client-computer interactions might advance faster in the near future than computer use by practitioners. This prediction is at least partly supported by the findings described earlier that more barriers to acceptance are encountered among practitioners than among clients.

Barriers to Acceptance. Managerial computer applications, especially in billing, personnel, and report generation, are now widely accepted in human service agencies. However, when the computer functions as more than an efficient typewriter and fast adding machine and attempts to contribute to the practitioner's decision making, user acceptance diminishes rapidly. This happens although diagnostic interview schedules, consultation, and decision support systems have been demonstrated to increase diagnostic accuracy and to enhance understanding of decision processes (Greist et al., 1982; Hedlund, Vieweg, & Dong, 1985; Slack et al., 1966). As early as 1977, the discrepancy between potential applications and actual use by practitioners in medical settings was noted by Friedman and Gustafson (1977). They sent a questionnaire to 32 principal authors who had written about computer applications during a 5-year period in four major medical journals. The responses showed that 51 percent of the projects had been either abandoned or temporarily stalled. Despite the fact that 63 percent of the authors felt that their programs had lived up to their initial expectations, only 19 percent of the programs were in routine use. Although this survey has not been replicated with applications designed specifically for human service agencies, the results would probably not be much more encouraging.

Earlier concerns of practitioners, related to privacy and confidentiality of information, can now be satisfactorily addressed by computers. Passwords, identification codes, and garbling of sensitive material can protect data stored in computers. Small, stand-alone information systems not accessed by telephone are relatively safe; violating them would require physical access to their location and knowledge of their operation and would be more troublesome for would-be data thieves than rifling a filing cabinet (Erdman et al., 1981). Because the concern about confidentiality does not sufficiently account for the slow dissemination of computers into the day-to-day practice of human service professionals, Mathisen (1985) suggests that this is a complex issue and offers three possible explanations. First, the limited portability of software poses a problem; programs developed for one hardware-software configuration are frequently not compatible with others. Second, slow acceptance, especially among direct practitioners, might arise out of fear of being replaced by a computer or at least of being reduced to playing the role of a technician. Third, practitioners will not accept a new technology until there is reason to expect that it will have a significant impact on direct work with clients. In the past, practitioners frequently bore the heaviest burden in generating the input for new information systems, but only infrequently have they reaped significant benefits from these data. A fourth concern, raised earlier, is whether the knowledge base of human service intervention can be codified sufficiently to reflect acceptable practice.

Responses to these concerns may vary in different environments. It is clear from this brief review of some barriers to acceptance that unless such concerns can be addressed, use of computers in the practitioner's decision-making process is not likely to become routine soon. One positive response has been in the field of education. Undergraduate and graduate programs are now introducing human service professionals to the potential of information technology and training them in at least the basics of computer literacy.

Information Age and Human Service Research. The development and application of information technology is a technological as well as a social problem. But human service research is only beginning to address the implications of the information revolution of recent years. A number of potential research areas are of concern to human service professionals.

Innovations in Service Delivery. In the United States, trends in social behavior since the 1960s show that society has increasingly adopted new perceptions, behaviors, and lifestyles to ensure good health and to prevent or cope with illness. The 1979 annual report of the U.S. surgeon general (cited in Snyder, 1984), for example, presents research examining the causes for statistical variance in the average American life expectancy. Only 10 percent of that variance is due to medical intervention, 20 percent is linked to genetic factors, 20 percent to the physical environment, and 50 percent to life-style.

Given the availability of electronic information networks in a society that has already demonstrated an insatiable desire for information about altering lifestyles and consumption patterns in pursuit of better health, an increasing demand for computer programs that can provide personalized health monitoring, feedback, and diagnostics is likely. Also, in light of the skyrocketing cost of institutional care, home-based care and monitoring of the elderly or chronically ill through online microcomputers will receive more public acceptance. Unless human service practitioners, researchers, and educators participate in defining the role of information technology in the delivery of future health and human services, others will do it for them.

Implications. The widespread public and private use of computers has farreaching implications for social behavior, communication, learning, family structure, and the workplace. In contrast to their colleagues in the United States, European researchers and human service practitioners seem to place more emphasis on studying such potential long-range effects (Brauns & Kramer, 1983; Volpert, 1983). For example, information technology allows the decentralization of work and education activities. With the assistance of home-based, online computers, individuals can structure their work or study time according to their particular needs. Work and workplace lose their central focus of social organization and communication (Rudolph, 1984). A large expansion of the workplace at home via online computer and an increase in computer-based "cottage industries" can transcend the boundary between home and work; it would save individuals transportation time and cost; it could also have significant effects on city traffic, social communication, and the geographic location of private homes. Although some see in the home-based workplace a chance to combine work and family activities in a meaningful way (Rudolph, 1984), other researchers find that it can foster isolation and create additional stress on traditional family structures (Nowotny, 1981).

Creation of New Marginal Subpopulations. With the advance of computers into more and more segments of society, computer literacy will most likely become another basic cultural skill, similar to reading and writing. As a consequence, computer illiteracy could come to characterize new marginal groups in society (Brauns & Kramer, 1983). The acquisition of basic skills should be accessible to all members of society because their mastery will affect income and social status. Unlike reading and writing, however, the use of computers is still too expensive for many individuals. Research is necessary to examine whether increasing use of information technology creates barriers for specific groups. Turkle (1984) has raised a related issue concerning women's access to information technology skills. If information technology becomes a key industry of the future, what will the consequences be if many primary and secondary schools with computer labs teach girls how to use word processing programs and boys how to use programming languages? Human service researchers would be likely to have a particular interest in exploring the potential implications of new technologies for minorities and women.

Such research activities are required in order to understand, anticipate, and deal with the far-reaching social consequences of moving into the information age. The practice activities, values, interests, and knowledge of the human service field are eminently suited to contribute to this task.

Conclusion

This review of the current state of human service computer applications demonstrates that computer support has been most successful with structured decision tasks. Such tasks are generally repetitive and routine, encompassing well-explicated decision procedures. As a consequence, computer use for budgeting and fiscal management, clerical tasks, and efficient report generation has become widespread. Unstructured decisions—such as the planning, implementation, and evaluation of treatment—tend to be confronted anew each time they arise owing to their complexity or the elusive nature of the tasks they require. Work is now under way to achieve a gradual explication of clinical decision-making processes ranging from assessment to evaluation, thus facilitating the acceptability as well as the utilization of computerized decision support systems among practitioners.

The potential for computer applications in human service agencies remains enormous. The hurdles lie not in the power and quality of existing computer technology but in the need for a generation of human service

professionals "who will take the powerful tools presently available and apply them with care, ingenuity, diligence, and patience to difficult mental health problems which will gradually yield to our steady efforts. Over time, this basically conservative approach can produce radically beneficial changes in our professions and in patient outcomes" (Greist, 1982).

ELIZABETH MUTSCHLER

For further information, see ASSESSMENT IN DIRECT PRACTICE; DIRECT PRACTICE: TRENDS AND ISSUES; INFORMATION SYSTEMS: AGENCY; INFORMATION SYSTEMS: CLIENT DATA; INFORMATION UTILIZATION FOR MANAGEMENT DECISION MAKING.

References

Bleich, H. L., et al. (1985). "Clinical Computing in a Teaching Hospital." *New England Journal of Medicine, 312*, 756–764.

Bloom, M., & Fischer, J. (1981). *Evaluating Practice: A Guide for Helping Professionals.* Englewood Cliffs, N.J.: Prentice-Hall.

Brauns, H. J., & Kramer, D. (1983). "Informationstechnologien—neue Aufgaben in der Sozialarbeit?" *Blaetter der Wohlfahrtspflege, 130*(8), 30–50.

Buchanan, B. G., & Shortcliffe, E. H. (1984). *Rule-Based Expert Systems: The MYCIN Experiments of the Stanford Heuristic Programming Project.* Reading, Mass.: Addison-Wesley Publishing Co.

Cole, E. B., Johnson, J. H., & Williams, T. A. (1976). "When Psychiatric Patients Interact with On-Line Computer Terminals: Problems and Solutions." *Behavior Research Methods Instrumentation, 8*, 92–94.

Derogatis, L. R., et al. (1974). "The Hopkins Symptom Checklist (HSCL): A Self-Report Symptom Inventory." *Behavioral Science, 19*, 1–15.

Erdman, H. P., et al. (1981). "The Computer Psychiatrist: How Far Have We Come? Where Are We Heading? How Far Dare We Go?" *Behavior Research Methods and Instrumentation, 13*, 393–398.

Fanshel, D. (Ed.). (1980). *Future of Social Work Research.* Washington, D.C.: National Association of Social Workers.

Friedman, R. B., & Gustafson, D. H. (1977). "Computers in Clinical Medicine: A Critical Review." *Computers and Biomedical Research, 10*, 199–204.

Gorodezky, N. J., & Hedlund, J. L. (1982). "The Developing Role of Computers in Community Mental Health Centers: Past Experience and Future Trends." *Journal of Operational Psychiatry, 13*(2), 94–99.

Greist, J. H. (1982). "Conservative Radicalism." *Computers in Psychiatry/Psychology*, 4(3), 3.

Greist, J. H., & Klein, M. H. (1980). "Computer Programs for Patients, Clinicians, and Researchers in Psychiatry." In J. B. Sidowski, J. H. Johnson, & T. A. Williams (Eds.), *Technology in Mental Health Care Delivery Systems* (pp. 165–166). Norwood, N.J.: Ablex Publishing Co.

Greist, J. H., & Klein, M. H. (1981). "Computers in Psychiatry." In S. Arieti & H. K. H. Brodie (Eds.), *American Handbook of Psychiatry* (pp. 750–777). New York: Basic Books.

Greist, J. H., Klein, M. H., & VanCura, L. J. (1973). "A Computer Interview for Psychiatric Patient Target Symptoms." *Archives of General Psychiatry*, 29, 247–253.

Greist, J. H., et al. (1982). "Clinical Computer Applications in Mental Health." In B. L. Blum (Ed.), *Proceedings: The Sixth Annual Symposium on Computer Applications in Medical Care* (pp. 356–365). Washington, D.C.: Institute of Electrical and Electronics Engineers.

Hayes-Roth, F., Waterman, D. A., & Lenat, D. B. (1984). *Building Expert Systems*. Reading, Mass.: Addison-Wesley Press.

Hedlund, J. L., Vieweg, B. V., & Dong, W. C. (1985). "Mental Health Computing in the 1980s: General Information Systems and Clinical Documentation." *Computers in Human Services*, 1, 3–33.

Hedlund, J. L., & Wurster, C. R. (1982). "Computer Applications in Mental Health Management." In B. L. Blum (Ed.), *Proceedings: The Sixth Annual Symposium on Computer Applications in Medical Care* (pp. 366–370). Washington, D.C.: Institute of Electrical and Electronics Engineers.

Jefferson, J. W., Greist, J. H., & Marcetick, J. R. (1979). "The Lithium Information Center." In T. Cooper et al. (Eds.), *Lithium: Controversies and Unresolved Issues* (pp. 958–963). Amsterdam: Exerpta Medica.

LaMendola, W. (1985). "Introducing Computers into the Mainstream of the Human Services." *Computer Use in Social Services Network*, 5, 6.

Laska, E. M., & Bank, R. (1975). *Safeguarding Psychiatric Privacy: Computer Systems and Their Uses*. New York: John Wiley & Sons.

Lucas, R. W., et al. (1977). "Psychiatrists and a Computer as Interrogator of Patients with Alcohol-Related Illnesses: A Comparison." *British Journal of Psychiatry*, 131, 160–167.

Mathisen, K. S. (1985, June). *Issues in Research on Clinical Computer Applications for Mental Health*. Paper presented at National Institute of Mental Health conference, Research on

Mental Health Computer Applications, Madison, Wis.

Mutschler, E. (1979). "Using Single-Case Evaluation Procedures in a Family and Children's Agency Integration of Practice and Research." *Journal of Social Service Research*, 3(1), 115–134.

Mutschler, E., & Cnaan, R. A. (1985). "Success and Failure of Computerized Information Systems: Two Case Studies in Human Service Agencies." *Administration in Social Work*, 9, 67–79.

Mutschler, E., & Hasenfeld, Y. (1986). "Computer Assisted Decision Making in Social Service Agencies." *Social Work*, 31(5).

Newkham, J., & Bawcom, L. (1981). "Computerizing an Integrated Clinical and Financial Record System in a CMHC: A Pilot Project." *Administration in Social Work*, 5, 97–111.

Nowotny, H. (1981). *The Information Society: Its Impact on the Home, Local Community and Marginal Groups*. Vienna, Austria.

Rudolph, H. (1984). "Die Einuehrung der neuen elektronischen Technologie—Auswirkungen auf die Berufsstruktur von Frauen." *Mitteilungsblatt des Deutschen Akademikerinnenbundes e.V.*, 65, 28–42.

Schoech, D., & Schkade, L. L. (1980). "Computers Helping Caseworkers: Decision Support Systems." *Child Welfare*, 59, 566–575.

Schuerman, J. R. (1985). *PLACECON*. Unpublished manuscript, School of Social Service Administration, University of Chicago, Chicago, Ill.

Schwartz, M. D. (1984). *Using Computers in Clinical Practice: Psychotherapy and Mental Health Applications*. New York: Haworth Press.

Selmi, P. M., et al. (1982) "An Investigation of Computer-Assisted Cognitive-Behavioral Therapy in the Treatment of Depression." *Behavior Research Methods and Instrumentation*, 14(2), 181–185.

Siegel, C., & Alexdaner, M. J. (1984). "Acceptance and Impact of the Computer on Clinical Decisions." *Hospital and Community Psychiatry*, 35(8), 773–775.

Siegel, C., & Alexander, M. J. (1985, June). *Research Activities and Their Methodologies in Mental Health Computing*, Paper presented at National Institute of Mental Health conference; Research on Mental Health Computer Applications, Madison, Wisc.

Slack, W. V., & Slack, C. W. (1977). "Talking to a Computer About Emotional Problems: A Comparative Study." *Psychotherapy: Theory, Research and Practice*, 14, 156–164.

Slack, W. V., & VanCura, L. J. (1968). "Patient Reaction to Computer Based Medical Interviewing." *Computers and Biomedical Research*, 1, 527–531.

Slack, W. V., et al. (1966). "A Computer Based Medical History System." *New England Journal of Medicine, 274,* 194–198.

Snyder, D. P. (1984, October). *The Decade Ahead: The Outlook for Medicine and Healthcare in the Information Age.* Paper presented at the Eighth Annual Symposium on Computer Applications in Medical Care, Washington, D. C.

Thomas, E. (1984). *Designing Interventions for the Helping Professions.* Beverly Hills, Calif.: Sage Publications.

Turkle, S. (1984). *The Second Self: Computers and the Human Spirit.* New York: Simon & Schuster.

Vogel, L. H. (1984). "Enhanced Planning and Assessment System." *Computer Use in Social Services Network, 4*(4), 4.

Vogel, L. H. (1985). "Decision Support Systems in the Human Services: Discovering Limits to a Promising Technology." *Computers in Human Services, 1*(1), 67–80.

Volpert, W. (1983). "Denkmaschinen und Maschinendenken; Computer programmieren Menschen." *Psychosozial, 6*(18), 10–29.

CONSULTATION

Consultation in social work has been described as a problem-solving process with a social work component. The early literature viewed the social worker as the receiver of consultation from other helping professionals. Garrett (1956), for example, described several of the problems and processes involved as social workers attempted to make use of psychiatric consultation to strengthen their practice. She argued that, rather than be "enthralled" by psychiatry, social workers should distinguish their casework practices as unique and use such consultation as professional equals rather than supervisees.

As the profession's self-image strengthened, social workers came to view consultation from other experts as a necessary resource in the performance of their jobs. For example, a social worker in child welfare was not expected to be an expert in law and could understandably make use of a lawyer's special competence when faced with a legal proceeding (Bell, 1985). Lawyers could be helpful in interpreting and clarifying legislation in relation to agency programs, statutes, policies, regulations, and practices. They could be used to represent the agency in

court, review legal documents and procedures, and train service staff in legal issues and courtroom skills.

In recent years, as social work has gained greater recognition for its unique contributions in a wide range of settings, the literature has increasingly focused on the social worker as the provider of consultation. The two types of social work consultation most frequently described are case consultation provided to other professionals and program consultation provided to agencies or other organizations. Case consultation usually involves a social work consultant working with line staff to assist them in providing direct services to clients. Program or organizational consultation usually involves work with administrative staff and, in some instances, may focus on agency policies, programs, and procedures designed to enhance direct practice services.

An interesting third form of consultation is an important synthesis of the two traditional ones. This approach uses the discussion of specific cases as a starting point for the analysis of program and organizational issues. This article discusses each of the three types of consultation, analyzing the role of the social worker, the processes involved, the related current issues, and the impact of variant elements introduced by the field of practice in which the consultation takes place.

Definitions

A simple definition describes consultation as an interaction between two or more people in which the consultant's special competence in a particular area is used to help the consultee with a current work problem (Caplan, 1970). Kadushin (1977) defined social work consultation as a problem-solving process with a social work component. He elaborated on the role of the consultant and on the outcomes of the process, noting that the consultant

> acts as a catalyst, facilitator, motivator, role model; clarifies consequences of different alternatives; helps the consultee to think more systematically and objectively about the problem he faces so as to increase his behavioral options; provides both new knowledge not previously available to the consultee or frees up old knowledge. (p. 152)

In case consultation, the focus is on the

specific client, whether individual, family, group or community. The consultant is involved in helping others who are working directly with the client and is not directly involved in that relationship. For example, in one hospital a doctor sought the aid of the social work consultant on the resources available for a newborn hydrocephalic (Siegel, 1954). In addition to providing the specific information requested, the consultant inquired as to the parents' reactions to the child. Further discussion revealed that a grandparent, the doctor's patient, had initiated the request without fully discussing it with the child's parents. The consultant used her knowledge and experience with families such as this to expand the discussion with the consultee and to promote assistance for the family in handling the grief associated with the birth of such a child. In another example of case consultation (Austin & Kosberg, 1978), the consultant, on request, provided assistance to nursing home staff in handling problems related to specific clients. The social work consultant discussed and interpreted acting-out behavior and developed strategies for coping with patients.

Although the consultant can often provide information that will help the consultee view a problem in a new way, understanding the client or the problem differently may not be enough. The consultee often requires direct help in translating that knowledge into action, focusing the insights on the specifics of interaction with the troublesome client. For example, a child care worker requesting consultation on how to deal with an acting-out teenager in a residential setting needs more than insight into the client's family situation, socioeconomic background, or stage of development. In most cases, the consultant may have to discuss the conversation that takes place when the worker tries to cope with the client, provide an understanding of the feelings invoked in the worker by the acting-out behavior, and even involve the worker in role-playing to break a vicious cycle in the relationship.

Watkins, Holland, and Ritvo (1976) define program consultation as follows:

a mutual problem-solving process by which the consultant helps an agency or consultee to analyze the needs of a community or population group and to develop or improve the organization and delivery of services to that group. It focuses upon the agency's planning, development, organization and administration of services rather than upon the specific problems in serving an individual client. (p. 45)

Rosenberg and Nitzberg (1980) described an example of program consultation. A social work consultant working with staff of a day care center on problems in the relationship between staff and parents focused on changes in the structures for involving parents in constructive roles in the center. Another example of program consultation involved helping staff in a nursing home to develop a group work program for residents (Austin & Kosberg, 1978). In both examples, the focus of the discussion with staff was not on the individual client but rather on a group of clients and the structures, policies, or programs of the agency that affect its services.

Another variation on program consultation involves the social work consultant focusing attention on organizational dynamics. In this case, the process is akin to organizational development. For example, an organization may report underlying administrative problems, difficulty in interpersonal communications among staff, and poor morale. Using approaches such as the problem profile technique (Williams, 1971), the consultant engages the staff in exercises designed to diagnose and deal with the problems. Although helpful in many situations, this approach can create difficulties when the ongoing problems that have not been dealt with through the normal administrative and supervisory channels persist after the exercises designed to reveal them are complete. Administrators who are unable to develop a feeling of safety and openness in communications with their staff members are likely to lack the skills required to make the essential system changes when the consultants leave the agency. It is not uncommon for even greater stress to develop following a consultant's intervention. This use of social work consultation remains a controversial issue.

The third form of consultation, which synthesizes the case and program approaches, deserves mention because of its unique relationship to social work history and theory. A social worker using this approach starts with case consultation, assisting staff members in relation to particular clients. As the consulting relationship proceeds and as patterns emerge, the consultant makes use of these data to focus on program or structural issues related to a particular class of clients. Thus, every individual case consultation becomes a potential opening for dealing with program issues, and program consultation stays closely connected to the day-to-day experiences with individual clients. This integrated approach reflects the traditional concern of the social work profession with both the individual and the social components of practice. Peterson (1976–1977) began her work with a community care facility by providing psychiatric consultation for the administrator regarding specific problem patients. This soon led her to develop a therapeutic community group, which in turn led to major changes in the residents' involvement in the decision-making process of the institution.

Consulting Process

Although there may be consensus on the general definitions of case and program consultation, Rapoport's (1977) observation on this in the previous edition of the *Encyclopedia of Social Work* still holds true: "Despite increasing attempts at description and conceptualization, . . . no one model has emerged clearly" (p. 193). There is, however, some agreement on a number of basic principles. First, consultation must have a purpose, a problem, and a process. Second, the consultee is usually free to reject the help so that the effectiveness of the consultation depends on the value of the ideas, not on the status of the expert. Third, relationship is at the core of the process, and an effective consultant needs to be both knowledgeable in the substantive area of the consultation (for example, child welfare legislation) and skillful in the processes of consultation (for example, in contracting and dealing with resistance). In addition, as described by Watkins, Holland, and Ritvo (1976, p. 45), there is some consensus on the steps leading to an effective consultation process:

1. Determination of the need for consultation.
2. Initiation of the request for consultation.
3. Organizational assessment and problem formulation.

4. Negotiation of the contract.
5. Mutual setting of consultation objectives.
6. Determination of strategies for action.
7. Implementation of plan of action.
8. Measuring and reporting outcomes.

Despite general agreement on these steps, the research of Watkins, Holland, and Ritvo (1976) indicated that the process does not always go smoothly. They studied the practice of 55 social work consultants working in public health programs in regional offices of the federal government, in state and local health departments, and in teaching hospitals and educational institutions. They found that consultants experienced considerable difficulty with mutual contracting, setting objectives, and measuring the results of consultation (p. 47). This is one of the few research reports in the area of consultation that suggests the need for further investigation into the consultation processes.

Impact of Setting

Although the definition and processes described thus far help to identify the generic, or common, elements of consultation, it is important to recognize that the setting or field of practice in which social work consultation takes place can introduce a number of variant elements. These elements may affect the social work consultant's role and introduce unique issues and processes.

Social work consultation in schools provides an example. In many school systems, social workers are employed by the school board or work for an outside agency contracted to provide social work services. Many of these workers soon find themselves overwhelmed by case-by-case demands for their services (Stringer, 1961). As a result, many move into the role of providing consultation to school principals and teachers; they do this in addition to or in place of providing direct services to clients. As Stringer points out, "No one, apparently, will object to being called a consultant" (p. 85). However, social workers are at times put into this role without appropriate training or ongoing support. An understandable response in such a situation is for the consultant to accept the role of expert and to feel responsible for providing solutions. Because most of the problems are too complex for easy answers, the consultation is often doomed to failure.

In the absence of direct contact with students or their families, the consultant may provide advice based on insufficient data. For example, acting-out behavior in the classroom may be in part a result of a child's personal difficulties, or—as is more likely—it may be a result of the interaction between personal stresses and the classroom dynamics, in which the teacher plays a part. Another danger arising from lack of clarity in the school consultation role is that the worker may assume that the teacher is incompetent and inappropriately attempt to train the teacher. As Carter (1975) points out, the consultee is not a client but rather a collaborator, and the focus of the consultation should be clear—on assistance with work-related problems. Carter points out that teachers often experience strong feelings of failure and self-incrimination with difficult children, and the consultant's major task may be to help reduce these. Thus, the role of the social work consultant in schools is more complex and subtle than that of the expert who dispenses advice.

Another example of the impact of field of practice is consultation in a mental health setting. Roberts (1968) described some of the serious entry problems he encountered in beginning a relationship with agencies offering services to clients in poverty areas. He faced barriers relating to his middle-class status, his identity as a professional social worker, and his race. Some of the agencies he consulted with had been established by indigenous people who felt both abandoned and threatened by professionals. Organizers of struggling new programs often experience ambivalence toward professional consultants. They need help but at the same time fear being exposed as inadequate, with a resulting loss of funding. As a consultant to the agencies serving hard-to-reach clients, Roberts found that the agencies themselves were also elusive and difficult to reach. When he recognized he was dealing with new organizations attempting to survive, he changed from a psychodynamic approach to a systems approach in his consultation. Again, a parallel with the client population is possible. In discussing consultation in rural mental health settings, Perlmutter (1979) cited both sources of resistance similar to those described by Roberts and problems unique to the provision of mental health services in a rural catchment area, such as teachers who felt that mental health services did not belong in the school.

Consultation in a hospital combines issues common to all settings with those unique to working in an acute care situation. Geist (1977) described the social work consultant's role in a hospital as "the single connecting link among patients, medical staff, and nonmedical staff on the ward" (p. 432). Line staff often experience severe stress arising from the size of their work loads and from having to deal with patients' problems resulting from hospitalization. This can have a powerful impact on their ability to function, and the task of creating and supporting an empathic climate for staff can be one of the consultant's most important contributions. For example, in small hospitals that lack the resources for a social work staff, consultation may use training and ongoing support to strengthen the line staff's sensitivity and responsiveness to patients (Wenston, 1982).

In recent years, long-term care facilities have become major users of social work consultation services. This movement may have stemmed mostly from federal and state licensing regulations that mandate social work services. One study of such consultation in Arkansas (Mercer & Garner, 1981) raised a number of issues associated with the rapid expansion of this area of consultation. For example, although most of the 49 consultants included in the study were experienced social workers, they were not experienced consultants; 40 percent had 2 years or less of consulting experience. The study also revealed that none of the consultants had tried to develop professional social services in the facility. The questions the study raised but left unanswered were whether the consultants' job description included the development of such services and whether their failure to do so represented self-interest. The study also indicated that the three functions most performed by the consultants were also the three most preferred: teaching casework techniques, performing such clinical tasks as reviewing case records, and planning and assisting with residents' care. The three least preferred functions tended to consume the least amount of the consultants' time: teaching administrative skills, dealing with morale problems, and coordinating the consultee's efforts with those of other staff.

Unger (1978) makes the crucial distinction that social work consultation to long-term care facilities is not comparable to reviews that inspect, judge, and license a facility on the basis of guidelines and standards. Although it may be seductive for the social worker to try to integrate the two roles, Unger believes that in the long run the authority of the reviewer creates more problems than it solves. A study of conflicts between the supervision and consultation roles in day care licensing supports this belief (Lounsbury & Hall, 1976). Unger also highlights the distinction between consultation and direct services to patients, pointing out the danger of creating the illusion that such consultation substitutes for direct, on-site social work services.

The impact of setting on the consultation role can also be seen in child welfare, where mental health consultants are often used to advise courts on such issues as visitation and custody. Because visitation is often used as a weapon in marital disputes, the consultant is often faced with a dilemma when asked for advice. Hoorwitz (1983) points out that the literature available is often unclear on the pros and cons of forced visitation by a noncustodial parent. In such cases, he emphasizes the importance of paying attention to the process involved in making the decision on visitation, ideally helping the parents to render the issue noncontentious. In addition, if forced visitation is to take place, the consultant may perform an educational function, engaging the custodial parent in measures to minimize the negative impact of such contacts. In implementing the consultation role in such disputes, Derdeyn (1975) indicates that it is important for professionals to view their role as consultants to the court instead of consultants to one of the contending adults.

This article highlights the changes that have taken place in social work consultation during the past decade. The period has been marked by an important shift away from consuming and toward providing consultation. Social workers have expanded their roles in providing case and organizational consultation and have made a significant contribution in highlighting the interaction between the two.

Although no one theory of consultation has dominated practice, general agreement has emerged on the processes and skills in-volved. As social work consultants have expanded their work into various fields of practice, they have shaped the general practice model of consultation to fit the specific needs of various settings and populations. This evolutionary process is likely to continue as the unique skills and knowledge of the social work professional become increasingly valued in the health, education, and welfare fields.

LAWRENCE SHULMAN

For further information, see CASE MANAGEMENT; DIRECT PRACTICE: TRENDS AND ISSUES; PLANNING AND MANAGEMENT PROFESSIONS; PROFESSION OF SOCIAL WORK: CONTEMPORARY CHARACTERISTICS.

References

Austin, M. J., & Kosberg, J. I. (1978). "Social Work Consultation to Nursing Homes: A Study." *Health and Social Work, 3*(1), 61–78.

Bell, C. (1975). "Legal Consultation for Child Welfare Workers." *Public Welfare, 33*(3), 33–40.

Caplan, G. (1970). *The Theory and Practice of Mental Health Consultation.* New York: Basic Books.

Carter, B. (1975). "School Mental Health Consultation: A Clinical Social Work Interventive Technique." *Clinical Social Work Journal, 3*(3), 201–210.

Derdeyn, A. P. (1975). "Child Custody Consultation." *American Journal of Orthopsychiatry, 45*(5), 791–801.

Garrett, A. (1956). "The Use of the Consultant." *American Journal of Orthopsychiatry, 26*(2), 234–252.

Geist, R. A. (1977). "Consultation on a Pediatric Surgical Ward: Creating an Empathic Climate." *American Journal of Orthopsychiatry, 47*(3), 432–444.

Hoorwitz, N. A. (1983). "The Visitation Dilemma in Court Consultation." *Social Casework, 64*(4), 231–237.

Kadushin, A. (1977). *Consultation in Social Work.* New York: Columbia University Press.

Lounsbury, J. W., & Hall, D. Q. (1976). "Supervision and Consultation Conflicts in the Day Care Licensing Role." *Social Service Review, 50*(3), 515–523.

Mercer, S. O., & Garner, J. D. (1981). "Social Work Consultation in Long-Term Care Facilities." *Health and Social Work, 6*(2), 5–13.

Perlmutter, F. D. (1979). "Consultation and Education in Rural Community Health Centers." *Community Mental Health Journal, 15*(1), 58–68.

Peterson, C. L. (1976–1977). "Consultation with

Community Care Facilities." *Social Work in Health Care, 2*(2), 181–191.

Rapoport, L. (1977). "Consultation in Social Work." In J. Turner (Ed.), *Encyclopedia of Social Work* (17th ed., pp. 193–197). Washington, D.C.: National Association of Social Workers.

Roberts, R. W. (1968). "Some Impressions of Mental Health Consultation." *Social Casework, 49*(6), 339–345.

Rosenberg, E. B., & Nitzberg, H. (1980). "The Clinical Social Worker Becomes a Consultant." *Social Work in Health Care, 5*(3), 305–312.

Siegel, D. (1954). "Consultation: Some Guiding Principles." In *Administration, Supervision and Consultation: Papers from the 1954 Social Welfare Forum* (pp. 98–114). New York: National Conference on Social Welfare.

Stringer, L. A. (1961). "Consultation: Some Expectations, Principles and Skills." *Social Work, 6*(3), 85–90.

Unger, J. M. (1978). "Consultation: Capitalizing on Hospital Social Work Resources." *Social Work in Health Care, 4*(1), 31–41.

Watkins, E. L., Holland, T. P., & Ritvo, R. A. (1976). "Improving the Effectiveness of Program Consultation." *Social Work in Health Care, 2*(1), 43–54.

Wenston, S. R. (1982). "Social Work Consultation for Small Hospitals." *Social Work in Health Care, 8*(1), 15–26.

Williams, M. (1971). "The Problem Profile Technique in Consultation." *Social Work, 16*(3), 52–59.

CONTINUING EDUCATION

The task of educational preparation for entry into any profession is to equip the neophyte with enough basic skills, concepts, knowledge, and socialization to begin practice in the chosen field. Education for competent practice has become increasingly complex. Professions must strive to keep pace with the constant development of new knowledge; the refinement and reformulation of existing knowledge; technological improvements and inventions that affect practice in the profession; the entry into professional purview of new groups of consumers, clients, or patients; and changing laws and regulations that impinge on professional practice.

By tradition, a person who completes a prescribed curriculum leading to a degree is allowed to participate in and practice the chosen occupation fully at the appropriate level. Thus, students who receive a BSW or MSW from an accredited school of social work are entitled to call themselves professional social workers and to practice their calling. In the minds of educators, students, and the general public, a distinct ending, or break, occurs with the acquisition of a diploma.

Definitions

Beyond initial formal education, an array of educational activities is offered by universities and by many other organizations, groups, and individuals. Collectively, these activities are known as continuing education. Continuing professional education in its broadest conceptualization is "participation in educational activities deemed relevant to a social worker in carrying out a job or following a career in the social services, and undertaken beyond the point of formal educational preparation for entry to the currently held job" (Koch & Brenner, 1976, p. 71). Such educational activities may include credit courses, noncredit offerings, in-service training, and independent professional activities.

Both the National Association of Social Workers [NASW] (1982) and the Council on Social Work Education [CSWE] (1980) endorse broad definitions of continuing education, and the trend among continuing educators is to take an inclusive approach to defining the field (Green & Edwards, 1982; Lauffer, 1977; Webster, 1971). A less widely espoused view is that there are clear differences between continuing education and staff development in regard to content, goals, objectives, and methods. These differences, it is claimed, should be recognized and preserved in order to be of optimum benefit to learners and employers and to maintain the proper boundaries between schools of social work and social agencies (Gibelman & Humphreys, 1982). The idea of facilitating innovations within and by social service organizations is often articulated but has been studied minimally as an additional purpose of continuing education (Lauffer, 1977; Loavenbruck, 1981; Zimmerman, 1978).

The provision of educational opportunities beyond entry-level preparation is universally acknowledged as vital to the health of the profession, to the competence of its practitioners, and to the protection of its consumers. Yet within the profession of social work, the place and role of continuing professional education has been neither fully articulated nor incorporated into a total spectrum of professionalizing activities that occur throughout a practitioner's career. Continuing education, despite a surge of expansion in the past 15 years, remains a relatively undefined and underdeveloped component of social work education. Conflicting trends have become more apparent as the profession faces funding crises, decreasing enrollments in schools, and the loss of public confidence. On the one hand, the contraction of finances and students in social work education as a whole is leading some schools to concentrate resources and attention more heavily than in the past on degree-oriented programs. On the other hand, the contemporary milieu in which professions function makes urgent the need to recognize an integral, broadly defined role for continuing education.

Education of Adults

The principles of the education of adults have been widely espoused as fundamental to continuing professional education in social work, as in other professions. Knowles (1970) has been instrumental in alerting social work continuing educators to the ways in which adult learners differ from children. He has coined the term "andragogy" for the process of educating adults (as opposed to "pedagogy," which he applies to the education of children). The design and presentation of continuing education activities have been significantly influenced by these ideas, which are especially compatible with the social work values of self-determination and professional responsibility.

The first tenet of andragogy puts the primary responsibility for learning on the learner. The adult professional learner is seen as a voluntary consumer of education, unlike the student who follows a required course of study under the guidance of educational experts. Accordingly, in following the principles of adult education, there is a shift or redistribution in the roles, responsibilities, and assumptions of learners and educators. The voluntary professional learner who enters educational programs after completing preservice education is already equipped with certain skills, knowledge, and experi-

ence. Further education must build on, refine, or deepen what has already been learned and put into practice. Alternatively, new skills may be sought as career directions change. Voluntary learners are assumed to have valid ideas about what, where, how, when, and under what conditions they choose to continue their learning.

Second, an andragogical approach assumes that only learners can learn. That is to say, an expert or teacher does not pour information into a passively receptive learner. A personal or professional need motivated the learner to want to learn. But if that motivation is to be satisfied, the instructor or educator must be in touch with the learner's needs and must contrive to meet those needs in a way that the learner perceives as meaningful. In other words, those who teach in continuing education programs often must be prepared to modify classroom techniques and to alter their methods of presentation as the teaching-learning transaction becomes one of mutuality.

The learner brings past learning, past experiences, and an awareness of the skills he or she lacks, whereas the educator is prepared to present and share knowledge in a readily accessible way for immediate application. It is a truism among continuing educators that the voluntary learner desperate for a problem solution on Monday morning will not return on Tuesday night for content that has been deemed irrelevant. This more active role for learners requires involving them in educational needs assessments and soliciting their participation in planning processes for the design and presentation of continuing education programs.

Along with placing responsibility for learning on learners themselves, an andragogical approach encourages many forms of continued learning. The most familiar forms, including formal classroom courses, other organized programs, and participation in professional conferences and symposia, are also the most frequent. But informal activities such as professional reading, peer consultation, and presentations at staff meetings, may be equally recognized and rewarded under approved circumstances.

Some of the means devised to foster the involvement of learners are mail surveys, joint planning committees, face-to-face conferences, and evaluation instruments, all of which may be used to obtain ideas for improved and new programs. When approached seriously and thoughtfully by learners and providers, and when sufficient time is allowed for a frequently lengthy process, such undertakings can contribute significantly to the quality and pertinence of programs offered and can increase the commitment of both parties to a successful outcome. These processes of involvement are being used to design programs for individual learners and to develop educational models on a broader scale for specialty groups, functional organizations, and agencies (Koch & Sancier, 1985).

The altered conditions under which adult continuing education is offered require that new sets of recognitions and rewards be developed and legitimized. The reward for the traditional student is a diploma and, it is hoped, a job. Different, multiple rewards are appropriate for adult learners who have achieved professional status by completing preservice education. These rewards include mastery of new knowledge and skills leading to improved job performance, promotions, raises, new job possibilities, and opportunities for personal growth. As noted previously, an andragogical educational philosophy is congenial with social work values. Continuing educators in social work have adapted the principles of adult education to their offerings and have sought to provide both general and specialized programs to enhance the level of social work services.

At the same time, certain tensions and misunderstandings have arisen between educators who concentrate on the preservice portion of social work education and those who specialize in lifelong education for professional practice, on either a university- or agency-based level. Professional schools generate new knowledge, transmit knowledge to students, and induct students into professional practice. Programs of continuing education offer new or advanced knowledge to enhance the competence of those who are already in professional practice. They are also in a good position to feed back to the schools vital information about practice, with the understanding that different parts of the educational spectrum perform equally valid educational functions.

It is sometimes erroneously assumed that a course that is offered to students in a classroom on a campus transmits a higher order of knowledge than the same course presented by the same instructor to practitioners in weekend sessions at a Holiday Inn. Questions of standards, rigor, and quality are often raised in relation to continuing professional education. Such questions are always appropriate in relation to any educational undertaking. However, it is important that instructors maintain the flexibility, responsiveness, and relevance that are essential to an andragogical approach to continuing professional education. These characteristics should be viewed as demonstrating alternative methods of presenting material, not as a watering down of quality.

Preservice Education and Continuing Education

The foremost thinkers in the field of continuing professional education have highlighted the necessity of reformulating the meaning of professional education to meet contemporary demands (Houle, 1972, 1980; Knowles, 1970; Knox, 1977). Educating for the postindustrial knowledge explosion, anticipating changes throughout the professional career, and satisfying the demands of sophisticated consumers and funders of services for accountability place considerable responsibilities on all professions. It has long been recognized that a preparatory program of education aimed at inducting persons into the profession cannot accomplish all of these goals for all time. Translating that recognition into educational reform has proved to be difficult.

It is proposed that formal educational preparation be designated as preservice education; that education beyond the entry level become as systematic, sequential, and progressive as degree education; and that an organic relationship be forged between preservice education and continuing education. Although no profession has carried this conception to its logical conclusion, the professions of medicine, nursing, law, and pharmacy have made more progress in this direction than has social work.

Implied in the establishment of an integrated social work education system is a continuum that would include continuing education. Important pioneers in social work education, such as Reynolds (1942) and Towle (1954), foreshadowed this concept by insisting that formal education be the stimulus to learning throughout professional life. Modern writers, too, refer to the continuum. Koch and Brenner (1976) discuss methods of including in the continuum continuing education opportunities for bachelor's-level workers. Boehm (1972) proposed a possible schema for implementing a continuum that includes continuing education from associate level to doctoral level. To date, these suggestions have not stimulated widespread discussion of or experimentation with a continuum that embraces all levels and forms of education in social work.

The identification of formal educational preparation for entry into social work as preservice education would have several advantages. It would speed up the efforts, already well begun, to clarify the various levels of induction education. As agreement is reached on the educational basics to be transmitted in the various degree programs, these programs would be freed from pressures to add more and more required courses to accommodate new knowledge. Continuing education would become the vital link in an integrated social work education system that would make the continuum a reality (Robins, 1974). The professional associations and the agencies, in cooperation with the schools, could begin to make systematic plans to address postgraduate needs at all strategic points. Students socialized to such expectations would become more discerning consumers of lifelong professionally oriented education.

Mandatory Continuing Education

There have been few studies of social workers as consumers of continuing education and there is little validation that improved competence or job performance results from participation in continuing professional education programs (Apps, 1981). Despite this, the idea of mandatory continuing education has attracted a number of adherents. Mandated continuing education is frequently advanced as a way of guaranteeing continued competence in the arguments that are made for relicensing and other forms of recertification.

By 1984, 33 states, Puerto Rico, and the Virgin Islands had enacted some form of legal regulation of social work practice. Twenty-two of the statutes either referred to

or set requirements for continuing education as a condition of license renewal. The provisions ranged from an ambiguous regulation allowing renewal applications to contain a questionnaire on continuing education to a requirement for completion of 14 classroom hours at a board-approved accredited school or program (NASW, 1984).

There is growing concern, however, about whether ongoing professional competence can be assured by participation in continuing education programs alone. Continuing education is beginning to be seen as but one means, albeit a crucial one, of achieving competence (Edwards & Green, 1983). Moreover, the rate of participation in programs of continuing education does not seem to be the major issue, for there is some evidence that up to 75 percent of social workers engage in formal and informal activities of an educational nature.

New measures of competence are now being proposed. These include the use of periodic reexaminations, self-assessments, and simulation experiences, along with participation in continuing education. The development of meaningful systems of recognition and reward would provide further motivation to maintain and improve competence (Neugroschel, 1979).

Competence-based measures in bachelor's and master's preservice programs of education are being tested in many schools of social work. The results of these efforts should be useful in devising measures for assessing ongoing competence during lifelong practice. A complex of different kinds of testing and measuring devices, including evidence of participation in continued professional learning, would seem to hold more promise than relying solely on the completion of an arbitrary number of mandated hours in continuing education programs.

Recognition: Credit, Noncredit, CEUs

An unresolved issue in continuing education is how to legitimize and provide recognition for participation in lifelong professional learning. Credit hours are the means by which progress toward achieving an academic degree is measured. Credit has been associated with rigor, quality, and rewards in the minds of many continuing learners, and requests for nondegree credit are frequent. The Continuing Education Unit (CEU) was invented to bridge the gap between traditional classroom course hours and the myriad forms that continuing education programs take. One CEU equals 10 hours of participation in an approved, organized program with qualified instruction. Universities, agencies, professional associations, and private providers may grant CEUs under certain conditions. Hours are recorded and transcripts made available for permanent recordkeeping (Council on the Continuing Education Unit, 1979). Although there have been occasional attempts to work on ways to convert CEUs to academic credits, this effort has been resisted by degree-granting programs. Many employers have accepted the CEU as a credible measure for purposes of promotions and raises.

A related issue is what proportion of social workers with BSWs and other bachelor's degrees actually pursue an MSW. If the overwhelming majority of social workers with undergraduate degrees enroll in advanced-degree programs, the argument for credit is strengthened: Continuing education in schools of social work would be seen largely as feeder education for the MSW program (Feldstein, 1972). Administering the part-time MSW program has, in fact, become a function of the continuing education program in some schools.

Available data, though sparse, cast serious doubt on the assumption that most holders of bachelor's degrees seek additional degrees in social work. A 1973 study of learners (Koch & Brenner, 1976), not since replicated, reported that only 6 percent of employed respondents intended to complete a program to gain an additional degree. The recent "BSW Report" (NASW, 1985) found that 18 percent of a sample of 1978 and 1979 BSWs planned to enroll in an MSW program within one year, 6.5 percent were currently enrolled either full-time or part-time, and 14 percent had already gone on to obtain an MSW. Clearly, it is not possible to reach firm conclusions or to make sound predictions without more information and research.

For personal and other reasons, large numbers of social workers cannot or will not pursue an additional degree. Nevertheless, most of them, whether post-BSW, post-MSW, or holders of non-social work degrees who are employed as social workers, need and want continuing education opportunities to improve skills, qualify for promotions and raises, change career directions, and the like. Forms of legitimation other than academic credit seem more suited to their needs. Agencies, schools of social work, and professional organizations will best meet their collective responsibilities for maintaining standards and for improving competence by experimenting with a variety of models. Such models include not only credit programs but also certification, noncredit programs, advanced standing, CEUs, and forms of recognition that have yet to be developed.

Providers

Agencies, universities, and professional associations provide 95 percent of the continuing professional education in social work. Agencies provide 50 percent of the programs; universities, 25 percent; and professional and functional associations, 20 percent. The remaining 5 percent is offered through private and specialized organizations of various sorts.

Agencies. Social welfare agencies may designate personnel to carry out staff development or in-service training activities for their own employees or for wider audiences, including other human service professionals, clients, and volunteers. An agency may create a separate department consisting of several specialists or may assign part-time training duties to one person. Contract arrangements between public agencies and universities were especially popular prior to 1980, when generous federal training grants were readily available.

Agencies typically offer, as a minimum, orientation sessions for new employees and periodic training to keep workers up to date on rules, regulations, and policies. These narrow activities, which concentrate solely on internal procedural matters, are generally not classified as continuing professional education. However, many agencies have gone far beyond such housekeeping programs. They have supported (1) workshops that attempt to develop basic and advanced skills, (2) attendance at graduate-credit courses, (3) topical programs in their own specialties, and (4) programs that focus on personal growth.

Continuing education that is sponsored and funded by public agencies has diminished drastically with the disappearance of most federal training grants. Extensive training programs in child welfare, aging, family services, and preventive services have been terminated virtually overnight. At the same time, opportunities for workers to participate in other programs, even at their own expense, have also been reduced by agencies' increasingly stringent policies on releasing employees for continuing education programs. The likelihood that eliminating educational opportunities available to staff will have a negative effect on the quality of services delivered to clients must be a matter of concern both to the profession and to policymakers.

Universities. Continuing education that is provided as part of a school of social work or continuing education unit of a university has been the focus of attention more often than has continuing education that is provided by either agencies or professional associations. By 1980, some 100 graduate and undergraduate social work education programs offered organized continuing education activities that were planned and presented by one or more faculty members who were permanently assigned such responsibilities. The decade of the 1970s was one of explosive growth and optimism, with budgets rising to over a million dollars in a few programs with large contracts. Although they have relied heavily on outside funds, university budgets have usually supported at least the position of director of continuing education. For the most part, programs have been expected to be self-sustaining by obtaining grants, fees, and other subsidies (Howery, 1974). Some sponsoring institutions expect continuing education programs to return a profit.

During the period of expansion, a cornucopia of offerings flowed from universities in every corner of the country. Seekers of knowledge could choose, on any given day or evening, presentations ranging from a two-hour sensitivity training session to lengthy, rigorous, formal certificate programs of advanced study. Continuing education programs were on the cutting edge of social significance, preceding degree programs in offering content on minorities, women, homosexuals, poverty, energy-related issues, and rural service delivery, among a number of other topics.

In 1980, directors of university-sponsored continuing education programs formed their own organization under the aegis of CSWE, which had appointed a Continuing Education Project Advisory Committee. For a number of years, CSWE and NASW, through a joint committee, worked on developing standards and guidelines that both organizations were expected to endorse. This was not accomplished, despite some promising beginnings in efforts at collaboration among universities, NASW, and CSWE. The project advisory committee (CSWE, 1980) formulated a set of guidelines for continuing education, but these were never formally adopted by the CSWE board of directors, nor were they written into accreditation standards. Overall, little fundamental change took place in the relationship between the degree-oriented programs of preservice education and the continuing education programs. The hope of continuing educators that programmatic successes would stimulate changes in educational philosophy, gradually leading to an integrated concept of an educational continuum, have not been realized. Continuing education has languished in many schools of social work. Those programs that are available are, by and large, treated as add-ons that are peripheral to the concerns of preservice education.

Professional Associations. Professional and functional associations constitute the third major set of providers of continuing education to social work professionals. The purpose of viewing continuing education as an essential activity is to ensure quality social services for clients and to meet the provisions of the professional Code of Ethics (NASW, 1982). As the largest single provider of continuing education programs, NASW offers a comprehensive array of activities. National conferences and symposia keep general practitioners and those with specialty interests abreast of new developments and the state of the art. An extensive publications program oversees the production of journals, books, monographs, and conference proceedings and maintains a database of published research and literature. Direct programs have been offered collaboratively with state chapters through the Practice Improvement Project and Special Programs in Continuing Education. NASW published a *Chapter Action Guide on Continuing Education*

(Johnson, 1979) to assist the association's chapters in establishing continuing education committees. These committees work within NASW and in collaboration with other professions, educational institutions, and private providers to identify and meet their constituents' educational needs. In states with limited educational resources, NASW chapters have become the primary providers of continuing education. A few states have taken steps to establish guidelines for member participation and provider certification in continuing education. CSWE, Family Service America, the American Public Welfare Association, and the Child Welfare League of America are among the other associations that sponsor important conferences on and programs of continuing education.

NASW has a further role in the development of continuing professional education through bringing to the educational establishment information about educational needs from the perspective of its 100,000-member base. Formal relations with CSWE promote this role on a national level. State chapters have yet to develop to any great extent their potential for establishing an ongoing dialogue at the local level for the purpose of contributing to the educational mission of schools of social work.

Other Providers. The proportion of programs offered under various private auspices, now estimated at 5 percent, may be growing. However, the range of sponsorship, content, and quality is exceedingly variable in these programs, which range from workshops led by a self-styled professional expert, to private psychotherapy consulting groups and large, national continuing education corporations. Although many are reputable and well-qualified, others are of questionable or no value. In the absence of a proven track record or provider certification system, the watchword must be "buyer beware." The entrepreneurial base of such offerings generally makes it less feasible for them than for other providers to follow andragogical principles, such as conducting needs assessments and involving learners in the design of programs.

There are no indications that the pattern of provision of continuing education is about to change drastically in the foreseeable future. It is likely that agencies, universities, and professional associations will continue—in approximately the same proportions as at present—to be the major providers of continuing education. However, competition for the scarce commodities of participants' time and dollars may increase in what is essentially a consumer-oriented, laissez-faire market. Although a free-choice system has many attractions, reservations are increasingly being expressed about wasteful duplication, the inability to demonstrate higher competence as a result of participation, the lack of mechanisms for identifying gaps in programs, and the need to demonstrate accountability to a sometimes skeptical clientele. If the promises of continuing professional education are to be fulfilled, it will be incumbent upon the major providers to heed and overcome these perceived deficiencies in the delivery of high-quality continuing education programs.

Trends and Prospects

Social workers will continue to be learners. Their professional ethos, their desire to enhance competence, and their motivation to improve service have been demonstrated, if not always supported. The future form and direction of continuing education in social work is less certain. Although a consensus about the place of continuing education in a continuum of social work education may emerge over time, the development of a somewhat untidy mix of patterns is a distinct possibility.

As noted previously, the present triad of providers—agencies, universities, and professional-functional associations—will probably continue to offer the bulk of continuing education programs to social workers, with some expansion in the role of private and commercial groups. The shape of continuing education could be altered by a significant shift in the importance of one or the other of the major providers, because each approaches continuing education from a different perspective. Some of these implications may be suggested by looking at each provider-group.

Agency-Centered Providers. Programs that are sponsored and funded by agencies, particularly contracted ones, may again become a dominant mode of continuing education offerings. Social policy initiatives tend to support training efforts that are aimed at ameliorating one or another human service problem, and these initiatives tend to change periodically. Such programs present specific content to targeted employees. They are politically responsive, reflect shifting priorities, and are likely to be time limited. Thus, child protective services workers might be the targeted training group during one funding period, to be superseded by workers in adult protective services. Participation depends on work assignment, and rewards are built into the employment setting.

University-Centered Providers. A future expansion of continuing education in schools of social work could be expected to follow a traditional academic model, with campus-based coursework more emphasized than less formal types of content organization. Programs that offer certificates or nondegree credit for advanced skills and methods would appeal to those wishing to invest in an academic-type program. Recognition or acceptance of the credential would be the option of the employing system.

Professional-Functional Providers. The major professional associations and their specialty subgroups are charged with setting standards for the profession. They also provide continuing education opportunities for their constituents, who make up the membership of the profession. These factors suggest that elevating the function of continuing professional education in professional organizations would be an appropriate direction for these providers to take. The present concerns of professional associations could logically evolve into a focus on lifelong professional career development. Members themselves are the learners whose needs for overcoming deficits, learning new skills, and mastering advanced knowledge may be readily ascertained and met through a variety of directly sponsored or brokered offerings. Associations would have the credibility to negotiate rewards and recognitions for groups of participants who completed approved programs.

Private-Commercial Providers. If the present self-choice, laissez-faire pattern of involvement in postdegree educational activities continues, professionals can anticipate a wide range of choices and auspices from commercial providers. Subject areas will be offered nonsystematically and nonsequentially; decisions about participation will be ad hoc; involvement will be periodic and idiosyncratic; and decisions concerning the factors of time, cost, location, relevance, convenience, and attractiveness will be made by individuals, as will negotiations for rewards and recognition. Without quality-assurance mechanisms, standards will continue to vary from program to program and from provider to provider.

Some futurists project visions of an approaching time when computers will screen clients, conduct therapy, keep records, send out bills—and provide education to practitioners (NASW, 1983). Other electronic media are also becoming important in educational spheres. Video and audio cassettes (the latter convenient for learning while commuting), public-access cable and educational television, and satellite transmissions are among the nonprint, nonparticipatory forms of educational activity undergoing expansion. All of the major providers will avail themselves of these new techniques. How rapidly and to what extent electronically delivered continuing education will become important is speculative. That it will become a factor is, however, sure. Cost and cost-effectiveness are unknowns at this time. The prospect of instant access to national and international expertise is exciting, but the loss of personal interaction and stimulation is a potential drawback. Computers and other media must be recognized as technologies that will inevitably affect continuing education.

It is unlikely that any of these phases of development will be realized in their pure form. However, the ongoing deliberations among continuing learners and educational institutions, professional associations, employing agencies, and other providers should be informed by the implications of many models, as the profession comes to terms with the vital issue of continuing professional education for social workers.

BETTY SANCIER

For further information, see PROFESSIONAL ASSOCIATIONS: COUNCIL ON SOCIAL WORK EDUCATION; PROFESSIONAL ASSOCIATIONS: NATIONAL ASSOCIATION OF SOCIAL WORKERS; SOCIAL WORK EDUCATION.

References

Apps, J. W. (1981). "Continuing Education Trends and Human Service Training." *Journal of Continuing Social Work Education, 1*(4), 3–6, 25–26.

Boehm, W. W. (1972). "Continuum in Education for Social Work." In E. J. Mullen et al., *Evaluation of Social Intervention* (pp. 210–239). San Francisco: Jossey-Bass.

Council on the Continuing Education Unit. (1979). *Criteria and Guidelines for the Use of the Continuing Education Unit.* Silver Spring, Md.: Author.

Council on Social Work Education. (1980). *Manual of Proposed Standards and Guidelines for Social Work Continuing Education Programs.* New York: Author.

Edwards, R. L., & Green, R. K. (1983). "Mandatory Education: Time for Reevaluation." *Social Work, 28*(1), 43–48.

Feldstein, D. L. (1972). "Heliocentric Perspective on Social Work Education." In E. J. Mullen et al. (Eds.), *Evaluation of Social Intervention* (pp. 240–250). San Francisco: Jossey-Bass.

Gibelman, M., & Humphreys, N. A. (1982). "Contracting for Educational Services: The Impact on Schools of Social Work." *Journal of Continuing Social Work Education, 2*(1), 3–6, 32.

Green, R. K., & Edwards, R. L. (1982). "Contracting between Schools of Social Work and Social Welfare Agencies: A Controversial Issue." *Journal of Continuing Social Work Education, 2*(1), 7–10, 33–35.

Houle, C. O. (1972). *The Design of Education.* San Francisco: Jossey-Bass.

Houle, C. O. (1980). *Continuing Learning in the Professions.* San Francisco: Jossey-Bass.

Howery, V. I. (1974). "Continuing Education: Program Development, Administration and Financing." *Journal of Education for Social Work, 10*(1), 34–41.

Johnson, B. [Sancier]. (1979). *Chapter Action Guide—Continuing Education.* Washington, D.C.: National Association of Social Workers.

Knowles, M. S. (1970). *The Modern Practice of Adult Education.* New York: Association Press.

Knox, A. B. (1977). *Adult Development and Learning.* San Francisco: Jossey-Bass.

Koch, W. H., & Brenner, M. N. (1976). "Continuing Education for Social Service: Implications from a Study of Learners." *Journal of Education for Social Work, 12*(1), 71–77.

Koch, W. H., & Sancier, B. (1985, February). "Continuing Education for School Social Workers: A Learner-Friendly Model." Paper presented at NASW National School Social Work Conference, New Orleans, La.

Lauffer, A. (1977). *The Practice of Continuing Education in the Human Services.* New York: McGraw-Hill Book Co.

Loavenbruck, G. (1981). *Continuing Social Work Education Provision: Trends and Future Developments.* New York: Council on Social Work Education.

National Association of Social Workers. (1982). *NASW Standards for Continuing Professional Education.* Silver Spring, Md.: Author.

National Association of Social Workers. (1983). "Computers for Social Work Practice." *Practice Digest, 6*(3), 5, 8, 10.

National Association of Social Workers. (1984). *State Comparison of Laws Regulating Social Work.* Silver Spring, Md.: Author.

National Association of Social Workers. (1985). *BSW Report.* Silver Spring, Md.: Author.

Neugroschel, W. J. (1979). "Policy Analysis on Continuing Education for Social Work Mental Health Practitioners." Unpublished manuscript.

Reynolds, B. C. (1942). *Learning and Teaching in the Practice of Social Work.* Washington, D.C.: National Association of Social Workers.

Robins, A. J. (1974). "Institutional Linkages of Continuing Education." In *Approaches to Innovation in Social Work Education* (pp. 51–61). New York: Council on Social Work Education.

Towle, C. (1954). *The Learner in Education for the Professions.* Chicago: University of Chicago Press.

Webster, T. G. (1971). "Definitions of Continuing Education." In Webster, T. G., Hollman, M. E., & Lamson, W. C. (Eds.), *Continuing Education: Agent of Change* (pp. 195–198). Rockville, Md.: National Institute of Mental Health, Public Health Service Publication No. 2167. Appendix A.

Zimmerman, S. L. (1978). "Continuing Social Work Education: Why Do Social Workers Participate in Continuing Education Programs?" *Journal of Education for Social Work, 14*(2), 111–116.

CONTRACTING AND ENGAGEMENT IN DIRECT PRACTICE

This article discusses the beginning phases of service in direct practice and points out the important tasks that social workers accomplish when they help potential users move from being applicants to being clients (Alcabes & Jones, 1985; Perlman, 1960). It presents the steps to engaging an applicant, to clarifying the services of the agency, and to negotiating a service contract with the client.

Journey to the Agency

Even before potential clients reach an agency's doorstep, they may already have made a long journey in search of help (Golan, 1980). They may have tried to resolve their problem on their own or turned to family and friends for advice and support. If these efforts brought no relief, they may have reached out beyond their intimate networks to a specific indigenous healing system. For example, Hispanic individuals may seek help from a local healer such as a *curandero* or spiritist (Delgado & Humm-Delgado, 1982), American Indians may consult with a local shaman or tribal elder, a black person from a rural area may consult a root doctor, and a white middle-class professional may consult a psychic or ask for advice at a local health food store. When these efforts to solve their distress bring no relief, then they might turn to the formally organized agencies that make up the human service delivery system: hospitals, social service agencies, public welfare departments, mental health agencies, and the like (Garvin & Seabury, 1984). Even though such applicants may come to the agency with some ambivalence about asking for help, they tend to be viewed as *voluntary clients* because they have arrived with some willingness and motivation to seek help with problems they have recognized. (Technically, the term "voluntary client" is redundant; a more accurate term would be voluntary "applicant" because the individual has not yet been offered service or accepted that offer.)

Other individuals may make a different journey to the agency. They may be mandated by a court order to apply for services at a particular agency. For example, a parent who has been accused of abusing or neglecting a child may be required to undergo counseling as one condition for the return of the child or a person on probation may be required to undergo drug counseling. Other individuals are the captives of the service delivery system by virtue of incarceration. In a prison or inpatient psychiatric hospital, therapeutic services may be forced on inmates or patients as part of their rehabilitation. When services are mandated or forced on people who do not think they need such services, such individuals are considered *involuntary clients*, although a more accurate term would be "target system" because these persons are the unit to be changed but they do not agree to be changed. (For a discussion of the differences between clients and target systems, see Garvin & Seabury, 1984, pp. 42–46.)

Some individuals come to an agency at the urging of significant others in their intimate networks. Such persons may not want help or think they need it, but they come to an agency because the significant other has the influence to get them there. For example, a parent may bring a child to an agency because he or she is concerned about the child's behavior, or a wife may convince her husband to get help for a drinking problem. In these situations, the individuals are considered *nonvoluntary clients*, although it would again be more accurate to consider them nonvoluntary applicants.

In some situations, an agency may go into a given community and look for business. By reaching out and "case finding," the agency is trying to attract or influence unsuspecting applicants to take advantage of its services. It may send out fliers or posters and advertize in a local newspaper to describe a support group it is starting for individuals who may be facing a difficult life transition (such as the death of a family member, divorce or separation, or a debilitating medical condition). The Family Union in New York City (Bush, 1977) has successfully used this approach by targeting low-income ethnic neighborhoods, entering the buildings on a block, and contacting each family to offer them help in identifying their needs and getting connected to unutilized community resources.

How an applicant enters an agency's service—whether he or she is coerced by a mandate, influenced by a loved one, motivated by the desire to get help, or attracted by an agency's pitch about the benefits of its services—will influence the engagement process and help determine if the applicant will be able to move into the role of client and become the recipient of an agency's services. The achievement of the status of a client in an agency is not guaranteed for any applicant, nor is it immediately granted to the individuals that arrive at the agency's doorstep.

Service Delivery Issues

Agencies routinely screen applicants before offering them services. Screening is necessary because agencies tend to specialize or focus their services on a particular problem or group of clients. Some agencies, such as child guidance clinics or pediatric services, may focus on children's problems, whereas other agencies may concentrate on particular problems of adults, such as substance abuse or suicide. Agencies are not expected to duplicate each other's services and compete for clients because such duplication is expensive and a waste of scarce resources. In an "ideal" service delivery system, agencies would provide a comprehensive network of services to meet all the potential needs of their community. If there were few gaps in such a network, most of the needs of individual applicants would be addressed. Unfortunately, under Reaganomics and the cutback in funds for social programs, the "safety net" of the service delivery system is full of rips. The ideal of comprehensiveness of services has been replaced by the reality of scarcity of services (Coulton, Rosenberg, & Yankey, 1981).

Because the service delivery system is complex even in this time of shrinking resources, an applicant cannot be expected to know which agency is most appropriately organized to serve his or her problems or needs. Even when a service delivery system has an agency that specializes in referral and information, other agencies must screen applicants to get them to the most appropriate service. Studies of this entrance process have revealed that only about half the applicants who seek help actually are offered services (Kirk & Greenley, 1974). Some clients are rejected and not helped to find alternative services, others are sent to other agencies but do not appear for screening, and others do not accept the agency's offer of service.

A number of service delivery problems keep applicants from entering services. One such problem is "creaming"—taking only those applicants who have the best chance of succeeding or completing the service and avoiding those applicants with the most difficult or undesirable characteristics or problems (Coulton, Rosenberg, & Yankey, 1981;

Kahn, 1969). A scarcity of services may produce long waiting lists and encourage clients to talk about those problems that best fit the agency's mission if they want help. Financial retrenchment may prompt agencies to seek or accept only those applicants who are able to pay full fees for their services. All these problems bear directly on the intake process and dramatically shape the applicants' experience when they enter an agency. Poor, oppressed applicants with complex, entrenched problems may have a difficult time getting through the screening procedures. Instead, they may be passed from agency to agency in a "referral fatigue" runaround (Lantz & Lenahan, 1976).

Agencies are organized to respond not to an applicant's uniqueness but to a common characteristic, such as a problem or need. Some applicants may fit closely with the agency's common perspective, but other applicants may have all kinds of variations or blends. For example, an applicant with a number of different, interconnected problems, such as alcoholism, marital conflict, and mental illness, may approach an agency that is designed to deal only with one type of problem. What happens to the applicant? Is the applicant denied service at the first agency because of his or her other problems and sent to another agency only to be denied service again because he or she has problems the next agency is not designed to handle? Such a Catch-22 situation may result in the applicant's receiving no services at all.

The social worker who performs intake in an agency must be sensitive to all these issues because they will have significantly influenced the applicant's experiences (often in negative ways) in getting to the agency. An intake worker should realize that the applicant's resistance or negative feelings about getting help may be more a product of how the service delivery system processes applicants (Gitterman, 1983; Lindenberg, 1958) than of some underlying disturbance in personality. Intake workers also should recognize their responsibility to help applicants negotiate the complex service delivery system. Just sending an applicant to a more appropriate agency is not good service. A successful referral requires the worker to help the applicant get accepted at the next agency and to follow up all applicants who are referred elsewhere (Weissman, 1976). Because of their service ethic, social workers must be as much concerned about those who do not get help as those who do.

Screening Applicants

During the screening process, then, the social worker is responsible for the applicant, whether the applicant is offered service and becomes a client or is helped and encouraged to seek services at another agency. The global strategy of the worker at this stage is "individualizing" (Meyer, 1976). Individualizing is the process of matching the applicant's individual needs and problems to the service delivery system's resources and services. The worker should help the applicant understand what he or she is seeking and how particular wants, needs, or problems can best be addressed by existing services. Because the fit between the individual and the agency is often imperfect, the worker may coach the applicant about the best way to present himself or herself for services while trying to influence the agency's screening procedures (or that of other agencies) to be less restrictive and more responsive to the individual needs of the applicant. During retrenchment, agencies may strongly resist these individualizing tactics, and workers may have to engage in strategies to help applicants locate services for their individual needs. For example, a worker may have to trick an intake worker in another agency by suppressing information that does not fit the agency's screening criteria.

During screening, the worker should understand and explore the applicant's journey to the agency. Was the applicant mandated to appear or shuffled from one agency to another? Is this the individual's final attempt to resolve a problem that has been unsuccessfully served by many different helpers, both indigenous and professional? The applicant should be encouraged to express his or her feelings about this help-seeking journey so the worker will have some sense of the applicant's frustrations and motivations to continue seeking help.

The worker may then help the applicant express the problem or concern that brought him or her to the agency. "Starting where the client is" is an important well-known ethic of social work practice that involves encouraging the applicant to express the problem from his or her perspective and

facilitating the applicant's expression of feelings about seeking help for the problem. Because of the applicant's previous experiences in seeking help and what the applicant views as a problem, the applicant may have difficulty expressing problems or concerns. For example, when services are scarce or the applicant has been rejected by another agency, he or she may try to present problems that the agency is likely to accept to avoid being rejected. In this situation, the agency is subtly inducing the client to define the problem in a certain way. Or the applicant may be so overwhelmed by a number of troubles that he or she does not know how or where to start.

When an applicant is able to share his or her problems and experiences in seeking help, then the worker can explain how the agency functions and which agency services and resources may be of value to the applicant or that the applicant should seek the services of another agency. In some agencies, this step may be accomplished with groups of applicants as a prescreening procedure; thus, the applicants know what the agency has to offer before they go through the intake process. In other agencies, a computer terminal in the waiting area may help applicants gain information about services before they meet with an intake worker.

It is not necessary or desirable for the worker to complete an extensive assessment of the client at this point or to explain in detail all the agency's services and resources. The task facing the worker and the applicant is to decide whether the agency has services that the applicant can utilize to solve the problem or problems that have been identified. The worker may want to explain to the applicant the next steps that will be involved in moving into the role of client. For example, the worker might describe some of the assessment procedures (such as psychological tests and physical examinations) that a client would go through next or explain that the applicant's name would be placed on a waiting list and how this queuing device works.

At this point, the applicant and the worker should agree on a preliminary contract—a tentative agreement either to continue exploring the applicant's situation or to try some of the agency's service. The worker and applicant also may agree that the applicant's problems and the agency's services do not match and that the applicant should seek services elsewhere. In any event, the applicant is not dropped; it is the worker's professional responsibility to help the applicant locate alternative services. If an applicant is violent and potentially suicidal or dangerous to others, the worker may have to mobilize resources to protect the applicant and prevent him or her from acting on these violent impulses.

Clarifying Roles

When the applicant agrees to continue exploring his or her situation or accepts the offer to become a recipient of services, the applicant has made the transition to clienthood. Then it is the worker's task to clarify the client's and the worker's roles, as well as those of other professionals and laypersons, such as psychiatrists, psychologists, nurses, the clergy, and foster parents, who may be involved in the helping process. Studies have demonstrated that clients' expectations of services often are confused, inaccurate, or inconsistent with the worker's expectations of service (Maluccio, 1979; Mayer & Timms, 1969). This disparity in expectations can lead to negative feelings about services, hidden agendas, and discontinuance (Garfield & Wolpin, 1963; Heine & Trosman, 1960; Lennard & Bernstein, 1960; Mayer & Timms, 1970; Overall & Aronson, 1963; Perlman, 1968; Shapiro & Budman, 1973; Silverman, 1970).

The task of the worker, then, is to clarify the client's expectations of his or her responsibilities and the client's expectations of the worker's (and other service providers') responsibilities. The worker also should share his or her expectations of the client, the worker, and other service providers. This clarification procedure will uncover conflicts between the worker's and client's expectations that can be discussed and resolved (or at least recognized, negotiated, and compromised). The case example that follows demonstrates the confusion and conflict that may exist:

A mother brought her 14-year-old daughter to a family agency for "behavior problems." The mother expected the social worker to discipline the daughter and then report back to her each month about how these disciplinary sessions were going. The mother did not think she needed to be otherwise involved in the service process. The worker's expectations were different. Her MSW training had not taught her how to punish children, nor did she think that punishment was part of her professional role. The worker believed that the mother should be involved in the treatment process and be seen each week with her daughter. When these disparities were shared and discussed, the mother agreed to "try" the worker's plan. Together the daughter and mother improved their relationship.

Service Contract

The service contract is an important practice principle in social work (Maluccio & Marlow, 1974; Seabury, 1976), and considerable research has been conducted on procedures for establishing and maintaining a contract (Estes & Henry, 1976; Hosch, 1973; Knapp, 1980; Rhodes, 1977; Stein & Gambrill, 1977). The contract is a working agreement that usually is negotiated by the client, the worker, and other service personnel who will be involved in the service process. Many different terms may be negotiated in a social work contract. For example, the client and worker may agree on the purpose of their work (why they should interact), the target problem or problems they hope to resolve, the goals of service (what they hope to accomplish), the time limits (how long they expect to work together), the various procedures or special modalities that may be used (such as individual, group, or family-focused interventions), and any special requirements of the agency, such as fees, the hours of operation, the personnel who may be involved, reporting procedures to courts or other agencies, and so forth. The service contract may be in writing and signed by all parties involved, or the parties involved may just agree orally about the terms. The purpose of the service contract is to clarify the various aspects of the service so all parties understand what will transpire.

A service contract is not a legal contract. A legal contract is binding and difficult to change (often requiring court action to be renegotiated or modified), whereas a service contract is more tentative and flexible. With a service contract, the parties can be expected to renegotiate or change their minds about agreements as the service unfolds. For example, the worker and client may identify a number of different target problems or other goals before the service is complete, or time limits may be revised and modalities changed as the case progresses.

In some social work settings, the social worker works in close association with the courts or legal system and has to be careful to differentiate those aspects of the service contract that are court mandated and cannot easily be renegotiated or changed by the client from those aspects that are more flexible. Such a "dual contract" approach can help involuntary clients make use of mandated services (Fusco, 1983; Seabury, 1979).

Another important aspect of the service contract is that the worker encourages and expects the client to be actively involved in developing the terms. The worker does not bully the client into accepting the worker's or the agency's perspective on a given term. Instead, the worker expects the client to be as equal a partner as possible in deciding on the plan for service. This ideal can be operationalized by allowing clients to present their views first on a given issue or decision, by avoiding professional jargon (especially in written contracts), and by putting the terms of the contract in the client's words. Parity is essential to the service contract because it is one way in which the important practice ethic of the self-determination of clients can be realized.

Contracting is an important practice principle in direct work with individuals, families, and groups, but it is not always easy to operationalize it in practice. With some clients and in some practice situations, contracting is difficult and agreements are hard to reach. For example, sometimes a client or a worker may negotiate a contract with a hidden agenda (an issue that has not been discussed) but that one party hopes will somehow be resolved by the service process. This kind of corrupt contract does not usually succeed because the other party is being deceived. Other kinds of corrupt contracts may involve the deliberate efforts of one party to sabotage the agreement when he or she has not been actively involved in the decision process or his or her input has been ignored in whatever final agreement was made. In some situations, both the client and the worker may have problems achieving honest, realistic agreements and even more trouble following through on them.

It is the worker's task, then, to be skilled in how to negotiate contracts in the sensitive areas of a client's life, how to facilitate the participation of clients in reaching agreements, and how to encourage clients and service providers to follow through on the agreements they have made. When the client and worker have agreed to a service plan that takes into account the individual wants and needs of the client as well as the particular constraints and limitations of the agency's resources, together they have established a strong basis for a successful outcome to the service.

BRETT A. SEABURY

For further information, see CASE MANAGEMENT; DIRECT PRACTICE IN SOCIAL WORK: OVERVIEW; LINKAGE IN DIRECT PRACTICE.

References

Alcabes, A., & Jones, J. (1985). "Structural Determinants of 'Clienthood.' " *Social Work, 30*(1), 49–53.

Bush, S. (1977, May). "A Family-Help Program That Really Works." *Psychology Today,* pp. 48–50, 84–88.

Coulton, C. J., Rosenberg, M. L., & Yankey, J. A. (1981). "Scarcity and Rationing of Services." *Public Welfare, 39*(3), 15–21.

Delgado, M., & Humm-Delgado, D. (1982). "Natural Support Systems." *Social Work, 27*(1), 83–90.

Estes, R., & Henry, S. (1976). "The Therapeutic Contract in Work with Groups: A Formal Analysis." *Social Service Review, 50*(4), 611–622.

Fusco, L. J. (1983). "Control, Conflict, and Contracting." *Public Welfare,* 41(1), 35–39.

Garfield, S., & Wolpin, M. (1963). "Expectations Regarding Psychotherapy." *Journal of Nervous & Mental Disease, 137,* 353–362.

Garvin, C., & Seabury, B. (1984). *Interpersonal Practice in Social Work: Process and Procedures.* Englewood Cliffs, N.J.: Prentice-Hall.

Gitterman, A. (1983). "Uses of Resistance: A Transactional View." *Social Work, 28*(2), 127–131.

Golan, N. (1980). "Intervention in Times of Transition: Sources and Forms of Help." *Social Casework, 61*(5), 259–266.

Heine, R., & Trosman, H. (1960). "Initial Expectations of the Doctor-Patient Interaction as a Factor in Continuance in Psychotherapy." *Psychiatry, 23,* 275–278.

Hosch, D. (1973). *Use of the Contract Approach in Public Social Services.* Los Angeles: Regional Research Institute in Social Welfare, University of Southern California.

Kahn, A. J. (1969). *Theory and Practice of Social*

Planning. New York: Russell Sage Foundation.

Kirk, S., & Greenley, J. (1974). "Denying or Delivering Services." *Social Work, 19*(7), 439–447.

Knapp, C. (1980). *Service Contract Use in Preventing and Reducing Foster Care: Final Evaluation Report*. Hampton, Va.: Hampton Department of Social Services.

Lantz, J. E., & Lenahan, B. (1976). "Referral Fatigue Therapy." *Social Work, 21*(3), 239–240.

Lennard, H. L., & Bernstein, A. (1960). *The Anatomy of Psychotherapy*. New York: Columbia University Press.

Levinger, G. (1960). "Continuance in Casework and Other Helping Relationships: A Review of Current Research." *Social Work, 5*(3), 40–51.

Lindenberg, R. E. (1958). "Hard to Reach: Client or Casework Agency." *Social Work, 3*(4), 23–29.

Maluccio, A. (1979). *Learning From Clients: Interpersonal Helping as Viewed by Clients and Social Workers*. New York: Free Press.

Maluccio, A., & Marlow, W. (1974). "The Case for Contract." *Social Work, 19*(1), 28–35.

Mayer, J., & Timms, N. (1969). "Clash in Perspective Between Worker and Client."*Social Casework, 50*(1), 32–40.

Mayer, J., & Timms, N. (1970). *The Client Speaks: Working Class Impressions of Casework*. Boston: Routledge & Kegan Paul.

Meyer, C. (1976). *Social Work Practice: The Changing Landscape* (2d ed.). New York: Free Press.

Overall, B., & Aronson, H. (1963). "Expectations of Psychotherapy in Patients of Lower Socioeconomic Class." *American Journal of Orthopsychiatry, 33*(2) 421–430.

Perlman, H. H. (1960). "Intake and Some Role Considerations." *Social Casework, 41*(4), 171–177.

Perlman, H. H. (1968). *Persona: Social Role and Personality*. Chicago: University of Chicago Press.

Rhodes, S. (1977). "Contract Negotiation in the Initial Stage of Casework Service." *Social Service Review, 51*(1), 125–140.

Seabury, B. A. (1976). "The Contract: Uses, Abuses, and Limitations." *Social Work, 21*(1), 16–21.

Seabury, B. A. (1979). "Negotiating Sound Contracts with Clients." *Public Welfare, 37*(2), 33–38.

Shapiro, R., & Budman, S. (1973). "Defection, Termination, and Continuation in Family and Individual Therapy." *Family Process, 12*, 55–68.

Silverman, P. (1970). "A Reexamination of the Intake Procedure." *Social Casework, 51*, 625–634.

Stein, H., & Gambrill, E. (1977). "Facilitating Decision Making in Foster Care: the Alameda Project." *Social Service Review, 51*(3), 502–513.

Weissman, A. (1976). "Industrial Social Services: Linkage Technology." *Social Casework, 57*(1), 50–54.

CONTRACTING FOR SERVICES.

See PUBLIC SOCIAL SERVICES.

CORPORATE SOCIAL RESPONSIBILITY

The concept of corporate responsibility—that in pursuing its policies a corporation must take into account the objectives and values of society—has a long history in America, according to some business writers. Drucker (1984), for example, has traced it to such early industrialists as Andrew Carnegie and Henry Ford. In truth, however, the modern concept of corporate social responsibility is a more recent phenomenon. The first major work on the subject was written some 3 decades ago by Bowen (1953). Part of a larger study of Christian ethics and economic life, the book was sponsored by the Federal Council of Churches, predecessor to the present National Council of Churches. Bowen found an emerging interest in corporate social responsibility among the corporate representatives he interviewed, but it was not widespread. Much of what corporations viewed as social responsibility at the time was merely public relations. Contributions to the local United Way, or what was then called the United Fund or Community Chest, were the major manifestation of corporate social responsibility.

Phases of Corporate Social Responsibility

Since Bowen's study, corporate social responsibility has gone through a number of phases. In the late 1960s, for example, urban riots in cities such as Detroit, Washington, D.C., Newark, New Jersey, and Los Angeles prompted corporations to focus new attention on issues of social responsibility. Both fear and a concern about the conditions faced by the urban poor motivated major corporations to invest money and human resources to improve conditions in the inner cities. The J. L. Dayton Corporation, General Motors, and Ford, for example, contributed $100,000 each to rebuilding parts of downtown Detroit. In response to the riots in the 1960s, the business-sponsored Urban Coalition was initiated to bring mayors, trade union presidents, civil rights leaders, and corporate executives together to address urban problems. The Urban Coalition was an attempt to rally support from all segments of society to address the problems of the poor and to halt the continuing deterioration of American cities (Urban America, Inc., 1967).

The next flurry of socially responsible corporate activity emerged from the disaffection between business and society in the early 1970s. A survey conducted by the Yankelovitch Organization in 1971 revealed that society's approval rating of business had declined from a high of 58 percent in 1969 to a low of 29 percent in 1970. Yankelovitch further reported that 7 out of 10 adults supported the consumer protection movement, increased government regulation of business, and severe penalties if business failed to meet new pollution standards (Bernays, 1975).

During this period, activist groups such as the Project on Corporate Responsibility, the Environmental Defense Fund, and the National Affiliation of Concerned Business Students increased pressure on corporations to practice greater social responsibility (Bernays, 1975).

Fear of prospective laws regulating businesses and of picketing at stockholder meetings prompted some action. Corporate contributions to philanthropy, which had risen from $785 million in 1965 to only $797 million in 1970, increased dramatically in the 5 years from 1970 to 1975 to $1.2 billion—a 34 percent increase (Chemical Bank, n.d.). Op-ed articles written by corporate executives began to appear in major newspapers covering such subjects as corporate support of the arts and education and other corporate-sponsored programs.

Recent Initiatives. The most recent phase of activity began in the 1980s. Spurred in part by the actions of the Reagan Administration and the reduction in federal aid to community programs, community groups began to search for new sources of support and financial assistance. As a result, corporations in the early 1980s were besieged with requests for funds, the loaning of staff, and donations of equipment. Requests came not just from voluntary agencies but also from governmental agencies faced with large-scale budget reductions. Moreover, President Reagan urged corporate leaders to assume some of the costs of supporting community groups. In 1981, in a speech to the National Alliance of Business, he challenged the business community to become involved in alleviating social problems. He formed a 44-member task force headed by C. William Verity, chairman of Armco, Inc., to stimulate corporate involvement in solving community problems. He also asked corporations to double their philanthropic contributions (Verity, 1982).

Corporations responded. Between 1979 and 1984, corporate contributions increased by $1.3 billion. Significantly, contributions to philanthropy did not decline in 1980, a year in which there was an absolute decline in corporate profits. In the past, contributions to philanthropy had been affected by corporate profits (Chemical Bank, n.d.). But however significant the increases, they did not in any way equal the Reagan decreases in funding of human and social service programs. The Reagan budgets were estimated to reduce federal programs by $33 billion. Richard Neblett, corporate contributions manager of Exxon Corporation, commented, "It's important to remember that if you're going to cut $35 billion out of a budget, it's not going to be replaced by $3 billion from corporations" (quoted in Lewin, 1985, pp. A1, A20).

Traditionally, the arts and higher education have been the principal beneficiaries of contributions from corporations, and contributions to human service programs have been low. In a 1981 study of all charitable contributions, the Chemical Bank predicted a dismal future for contributions to social welfare organizations, anticipating very little growth in voluntary funding for social welfare agencies between 1980 and 1984. The study estimated that the annual growth rate in contributions to social welfare agencies would decrease from 9.6 percent in 1979 to 6.2 percent in 1984 (Chemical Bank, n.d.). This prediction might, however, have been overly pessimistic. A more recent study conducted by the Conference Board, an independent, nonprofit-business research organization, found that corporate contributions increased 26 percent in 1984. More interesting is that the biggest increase—68 percent—was in support of housing, job training, and other projects that aid the poor (Lueck, 1985).

Community Involvement. Another new trend in the 1980s, and one that might have great significance for human service programs, has been the growing involvement of corporations in a wide variety of community programs. Either through the contribution of staff members' time or through financial contributions, corporations now support such programs as foster care (Honeywell) community planning and problem solving (American Express), remedial reading (Time, Inc.), neighborhood youth centers (Clorox), community food banks (H. J. Heinz Company), social service information and referral programs (Mississippi Power Company), fingerprinting programs for children (Southwestern Bell), bilingual education (Dayton Hudson), community schools (Citibank), and job training for the unemployed (IBM). This new interest in community programs and community relations has brought about an increase in corporate staffs to manage these endeavors. In fact, community relations is the fastest-growing segment of corporate social responsibility programming. The trend, moreover, is not likely to diminish, according to the Public Affairs Council, a national organization of corporate social responsibility professionals ("More and More Firms," 1983).

The Reagan initiatives have merely highlighted a development that had been persistently expanding throughout the 1970s. A Conference Board study conducted in the late 1970s reported that 9 out of 10 companies it surveyed had been involved in some kind of voluntary efforts to assist local communities (Winter, 1981). The notion of public-private partnerships urged by President Reagan was suported by the Business Roundtable as early as 1978. Also, President Carter had involved a number of major corporations in working with state human service administrators in improving their planning and management practices (Walter, 1980).

Increasing Corporate Social Responsibility

Three significant changes in society, government, and business have provided the major impetus to the increase in corporate social responsibility in the 1980s: (1) Americans now believe that decisions affecting their communities cannot be made arbitrarily and without their participation; (2) government plays an increasing role as a regulator of business and industry; and (3) the strategic management orientation of the modern corporation requires managers to recognize the impact of the external environment on corporate decision making.

The shift in public attitude had its origins in the citizen participation activities of the 1960s. The civil rights struggle and then later the antipoverty activities in local communities proved that individuals can join together to become a powerful force for change. Governmental agencies learned to be responsive to community groups in the 1960s. In the 1970s and 1980s, corporations began to hear from community groups. For example, the Codex Corporation, a subsidiary of Motorola, spent 7 years fighting with environmental groups to build its corporate headquarters on a 55-acre site adjacent to Route 128 outside Boston. Although it did get permission to build, the environmental groups (all voluntary) wrung from the company concessions on how the site could be developed. In Cambridge, Massachusetts, the Arthur D. Little Company, an internationally known research organization, has fought with community groups over its right to conduct germ warfare research. In response to neighborhood organizations, a half-dozen major corporations in Hartford, Connecticut, have renovated apartment buildings for poor inner-city residents. The companies have also funded job training programs for the unemployed in Hartford (Lueck, 1985). Thus, activist organizations and community groups have brought about a change in corporate management.

Government regulation has become a way of life for today's business. Certain industries, banks, and utilities face more regulation than others, but all are in some ways affected. As a former president of DuPont (Shapiro, 1984) explained:

> At DuPont, for instance, we can expect government to continue to tell us whether we can build a plant at a chosen location. General Motors and Ford can expect the government to continue to help them design cars. All business people can expect government to continue to tell us what fuel to burn in the furnace, what sort of affirmative action we should take in hiring and promotion, and how many pounds, if not tons, of reports we shall submit.
>   Without suggesting for a minute that the private sector ought to take all this lying down, I must admit that some of the government's involvement is desirable and another piece of it is probably inevitable, at least over the short term. (pp. 47–52)

Most modern corporations accept the consequences of a regulatory environment. They are responding, however, by assigning professionals and managers to work with the regulators. They are also trying to forestall increasing regulations by engaging in activities that prevent the need for further regulations, often instituting community programs that benefit both local communities and businesses.

The development of strategic planning in corporations has had a profound influence on almost every aspect of management from marketing to production to human resources. It is not surprising, therefore, that its influence should spread to issues of corporate social responsibility—particularly to the rapidly developing community relations function.

Strategic planning has encouraged corporate social responsibility in two ways. It has caused managers to become sensitive to society and the impact of society on the long-term future of the business. Company survival often depends upon the ability of managers to analyze and cope with an uncertain and turbulent environment. What happens in society and in local communities—sometimes to the embarrassment of managers—has an impact on the firm. Some firms, consequently, have begun to factor community analysis into their strategic plans. Coladzin (1981), former vice president of Champion International, comments:

> A corporation's strategic plan that does not deal with (community) affairs is incomplete.

Our thesis is simple. We believe that "public affairs" is as susceptible to strategic planning as any other function of our business, that it can be just as useful, and that it should be annually included in the process. (p. 3)

A second lesson of strategic planning is that the successful positioning of a company requires intervention in the external environment to bring about change. For example, a company can attempt to modify attitudes toward itself and its products or to influence the development of governmental regulations. Consequently, businesses are intervening in community activities in order to influence and shape those activities in the best interests of the firm. Secondary education is a good illustration. Companies participate in educational programs to ensure that they will have an educated and technically competent work force in the future. Speaking before the American Federation of Teachers, John Creedon, president of the Metropolitan Life Insurance Company (quoted in Maeroff, 1984, p. A19), said, "Business is beginning to act on the recognition that it wants well educated employees, customers, and voters." Emphasizing the strategic perspective of corporate involvement, he added that business "must participate in formulating and advocating the public policy measures." Health promotion is another illustration. Life insurance companies are promoting nonsmoking campaigns in the workplace. This reduces health care costs for society and can lead to increased profits for insurance companies.

Arguments Against Corporate Social Responsibility

Corporate social responsibility is not without its critics and opponents. For example, Friedman (1962)—the widely known economist from the University of Chicago—argues in the tradition of classical economic theory that

> . . . there is is one and only one social responsibility of business—to use its resources and engage in activities designed to increase its profits so long as it stays within the rules of the game, which is to say, engages in open and free competition, without deception or fraud. . . . Few trends could so thoroughly undermine the very foundations of our free society as the acceptance by corporate officials of a social responsibility other than to

make as much money for their stockholders as possible. This is a fundamentally subversive doctrine. (p. 133)

Davis and Frederick (1984, pp. 39–41) outline other arguments against corporate social responsibility, saying (1) that it increases costs, which will be passed on to the consumer without the consumer's knowledge, and (2) that there is no way to hold corporations accountable for their social involvement; permitting corporations to engage in activities, however well meaning, for which they have no accountability is dangerous and can lead to paternalism.

Arguments for Corporate Social Responsibility

Proponents of corporate social responsibility advance three fundamental reasons why corporations should assume a responsibility to society. The first is that business and society have mutual needs. Like any other member of society, business has a responsibility to act in a way likely to maintain the moral system and preserve the interests of other members of society (Davis & Frederick, 1984). The Business Roundtable (1981), a group of 200 corporate leaders, published a statement on corporate social responsibility emphasizing this point of view, saying, "Business and society have a symbiotic relationship. The long-term viability of the corporation depends upon its responsibility to the society of which it is a part" (p. 1). Another business leader quoted in an article on corporate executives as community volunteers (Fenn, 1984) has said, "Businessmen who do not serve on voluntary boards are doing society and the community a grave disservice. The businessman should return to the community that which he has gained in the form of services" (p. 372).

The other two arguments are more pragmatic and doubtless the most compelling from a business perspective. One is that long-range interests and profits of a corporation are enhanced when corporations promote programs that improve society. Life insurance companies that promote safety programs in schools, for example, can expect to receive fewer claims for accidents. Industries involved in programs to reduce health care costs discover that benefit costs for employees are reduced significantly. The second pragmatic argument, touched on earlier, is that responding to social issues is not a matter of choice but a matter of necessity for today's corporations. Today's social issues become tomorrow's regulations. Environmental pollution laws are good examples. The first national standards regarding environmental pollution appeared in the Clean Air Act (P.L. 88-206) in 1963. Four years later, the Air Quality Act (P.L. 90-148) strengthened these provisions. In 1975, nationwide ambient air standards (applying to the measurable mixture of known pollutants in the atmosphere) were established. During the many years when federal legislation was evolving, corporations engaged in activities affecting air quality could choose whether or not to alter them (Ackerman, 1973).

Corporations have begun to learn that business survival necessitates intervening in community affairs. In the 1980s, therefore, arguments against corporate social responsibility appear academic. Corporate involvement in community affairs is likely to persist, becoming a normal function of modern corporate management.

Trends

There are three discernible trends in corporate social responsibility. One is the decentralization of the community relations function. Major corporations, such as IBM and Honeywell, are insisting that line or plant managers begin to assume responsibility for community relations. These managers are the personal presence of the company in the community and can therefore best understand the community and its needs and are best able to respond to emerging community and social issues.

Corporations are consequently encouraging local managers to become involved in community organizations and groups both to improve the community's opinion of the company and to learn more about the community and its organizations. This participation enables the company to discern the important issues in a community and to prepare, if necessary, ways for the company to respond (Useem, 1985).

A second trend is the increasing emphasis on the community relations function of corporate social responsibility. This is a consequence of the growing decentralization of government. As state and local governments begin to assume many of the activities and regulatory functions of the federal government, corporations need to relate less to federal government programs than to state and local programs and regulations. As a result, corporations are expanding and formalizing their community relations functions ("More and More Firms," 1985). According to one study (Post, 1982), 85 percent of 400 companies surveyed by the Boston University School of Management rated community relations as a key function in public affairs.

A third trend is toward developing assessment measures for corporate social responsibility in the form of independent social audits, which were initially proposed to ensure accountability (Bauer & Fenn, 1973). More recently, there has been an attempt to view the actions of a corporation as incurring a social cost. The concept of social cost, or the undesirable consequences of business operations, comes from economists. The objective is to recognize that there are social costs in the operation of a business and that these should be offset through corporate social responsibility to achieve a "social balance"—the point at which society gains at least as much as it loses as a result of a firm's operation (Sawyer, 1985).

Role of Social Work

Social work has two roles to play in the new environment of increasing corporate social responsibility. The first is to provide corporations with trained staff. As businesses begin to expand their community relations interests, they will need people who have the following community work skills: (1) ability to locate and work with community leaders, (2) knowledge of community organizations and their function in communities, (3) ability to evaluate and analyze budgets and requests for contributions of community groups and organizations, and (4) ability to conduct a community needs assessment. In short, the skills needed are those of the traditional community organization worker trained in social work—the skills that social workers employed by United Ways use in their daily activities. (Employment or fieldwork experi-

ence in a United Way would constitute excellent preparation for a career in corporate community relations.)

A second role of social work is to influence and educate the corporate community about human services and human service needs. As corporations begin to expand their contributions to local communities of both money and human resources, they will need advice and guidance. Social workers can provide this advice through community agencies and associations such as chapters of the National Association of Social Workers.

Social work schools can also provide institutes and workshops for corporate executives in community relations. These executives, who are eager to learn about communities and community organizations (Center for Corporate Community Relations, 1985) can also thus become educated about social work and its goals. This in turn can lead to expanding the constituency base for social work.

EDMUND M. BURKE

For further information, see COMMUNITY-BASED SOCIAL ACTION; COMMUNITY DEVELOPMENT; ORGANIZATIONS: IMPACT ON EMPLOYEES AND COMMUNITY.

References

Ackerman, R. W. (1973). "How Companies Respond to Social Demands." *Harvard Business Review, 51*(4), 88–98.

Bauer, R. A., & Fenn, D. H., Jr. (1973). "What is a Corporate Social Audit?" *Harvard Business Review, 51*(1), 37–48.

Bernays, E. L. (1975). "Social Responsibility of Business." *Public Relations Review, 1*(3), 5–16.

Bowen, H. R. (1953). *Social Responsibilities of the Businessman.* New York: Harper & Bros.

Business Roundtable. (1981). *Statement on Corporate Social Responsibility.* New York: Author.

Center for Corporate Community Relations. (1985). [Untitled.] Brochure published by Center for Corporate Community Relations, Boston College, Chestnut Hill, Mass.

Chemical Bank. (n.d.). *Giving and Getting: A Chemical Bank Study of Charitable Contributions Through 1984.* New York: Author.

Coladzin, R. S. (1981, November 18). *Redefining the Role of the Corporation in the Commu-*

nity. Speech by Robert S. Coladzin to Public Affairs Council, Washington, D.C.

Davis, K., & Frederick, W. C. (1984). *Business and Society* (5th ed.). New York: McGraw-Hill Book Co.

Drucker, P. F. (1984). "Doing Good to Do Well: The New Opportunities for Business Enterprise." In H. Brooks, L. Liebman, & C. S. Schelling (eds.), *Public-Private Partnerships: New Opportunities for Meeting Social Needs* (pp. 285–302). Cambridge, Mass.: Ballinger Publishing Co.

Fenn, D. H., Jr. (1984). "Executives as Community Volunteers." In D. N. Dickson (Ed.), *Business and Its Publics* (pp. 369–387). New York: John Wiley & Sons.

Friedman, M. (1962). *Capitalism and Freedom*. Chicago: University of Chicago Press.

Lewin, T. (1985, February 15). "Corporate Giving Fails to Offset Cuts by U.S." *The New York Times*, pp. A1, A20.

Lueck, T. J. (1985, November 25). "Companies Giving a Hand to Hartford's Poor." *The New York Times*, pp. B1, B4.

Maeroff, G. I. (1984, August 23). "Teachers Listen to Business Chief." *The New York Times*, p. A19.

"More and More Firms Formalizing Community Relations Function." (January 1983). *Impact*, pp. 1, 5.

Post, J. E. (1982). *Public Affairs Function*. Boston: Boston University School of Management.

Sawyer, G. C. (1985). *Business and Its Environment: Managing Social Impacts*. Englewood Cliffs, N.J.:Prentice-Hall.

Shapiro, I. (1979). "The Process." In D. N. Dickson, *Business and Its Public* (pp. 47–52). New York: John Wiley & Sons.

Urban America, Inc. (1969). "Urban Coalition: Turning the Country Around." In A. Shank (Ed.), *Political Power and the Urban Crisis* (pp. 466–474). Boston: Holbrook Press.

Useem, M. (1985). "The Rise of the Political Manager." *Sloan Management Review*, 27(1), 15–26.

Verity, C. W., Jr., (1982). "Preface and Acknowledgments." In P. A. Berger et al. (Eds.), *Investing in America: Initiatives for Community and Economic Development* (p. 5). Washington, D.C.: President's Task Force on Private Sector Initiatives.

Walter, S. (Ed.). (1980). *Proceedings of the White House Conference on Strategic Planning*. Washington, D.C.: Council of State Planning Agencies.

Winter, L. (1981). "Business and the Cities: Programs and Practices." *Information Bulletin* (No. 87). New York: Conference Board, Inc.

Reader's Guide

CORRECTIONS SYSTEM

The following articles contain information on this general topic:

Child Welfare Services
Corrections System: Adult
Female Offenders
Juvenile Courts, Probation, and Parole
Juvenile Justice System
Juvenile Offender Diversion and Community-Based Services
Juvenile Offender Institutions
Juvenile Offenders and Delinquency
Legal Issues and Legal Services
Victimization Programs and Victims of Crime

CORRECTIONS SYSTEM: ADULT

If New York has many more times the armed robberies of London, if Philadelphia has two score the criminal homicides of Vienna, if Chicago has more burglary than all of Japan, if Los Angeles has more drug addiction than Western Europe, then must we not concentrate on the social and economic ills of New York, Philadelphia, Chicago, Los Angeles, America? That has not been our approach. We concentrate on locking up the offender while we ignore the underlying causes. (Nagel, 1973, p. 151)

The corrections system in the United States is amorphous, difficult to understand, and costly. It appears to be a fluid, flexible system that is constantly changing, but it is rigid and intractable, a system that has not significantly changed since its inception. This article examines corrections in the United States—its impacts both in cost and on human life; its conflicting philosophies; the results of its various programs; and the role of treatment, specifically social work, in this field. The article concludes with recommendations for the future.

The three major components of the criminal justice system are law enforcement, the courts, and corrections. In 1977 there were approximately 650,000 employees in the law enforcement field, 150,000 in the courts, and 250,000 in corrections. During that year there were an estimated 40.3 million crimes. It is believed that no more than 30 percent of all crimes are reported to law enforcement. Studies that have tracked criminals through the criminal justice system have found that only a few are served by the third component, corrections (Bowker, 1982). The criminal justice system can thus be seen as an ever-narrowing funnel with corrections at the narrow end.

In 1980 approximately 19 percent of all reported index crimes (murder, forcible rape, robbery, aggravated assault, burglary, larceny-theft, and motor vehicle theft) resulted in arrests. Only two crimes had greater than a 50 percent arrest rate, murder and aggravated assault. The system continues to filter out at each step. A study of four states found that 52 percent of those arrested were not prosecuted, of those prosecuted 31 percent were convicted, of those convicted 12 percent were imprisoned, of those imprisoned 5 percent were imprisoned for more than one year (U.S. Department of Justice, 1983).

In 1979, the last year for which data were available, the operating costs of the criminal justice system were $26 billion. In 1981 the direct economic loss to victims was $10.9 billion (U.S. Department of Justice, 1983).

Victimization rates vary dramatically based on age, sex, race, and other factors. Those most likely to be victims of crime are young, low-income males living in urban areas. This is particularly true for violent offenses. Victims and offenders are of the same race in three out of four violent crimes. Despite myths to the contrary, young offenders, those under 21, do not victimize the elderly in a greater percentage than other populations (U.S. Department of Justice, 1983). During 1980 there were approximately 23,000 individuals murdered and an additional 2 million injured as a result of violent crimes.

Situation in the 1980s

In 1983 there were 438,830 individuals in prison, an increase of 5.9 percent from the previous year. The increase in 1983 was approximately half the rate of growth for each of the two previous years. The rates of increase were the greatest in the West (12.6 percent) and the lowest in the South (3 per-

cent). However, the rate of incarceration per hundred thousand population is highest in the South (U.S. Department of Justice, 1983).

Fifteen states reported that they released over 21,000 prisoners early because of overcrowded prison conditions. On average, the state and federal prison systems operate at 110 percent of capacity (U.S. Department of Justice, 1983; Sherman & Hawkins, 1981). Approximately 10 percent of all inmates are held in prisons that were built before 1875, 23 percent in prisons built between 1875 and 1924, 20 percent in facilities built between 1925 and 1949, and the remainder in prisons built after 1950 (U.S. Department of Justice, 1983; Sherman & Hawkins, 1981).

Both the number of individuals incarcerated and the rate of incarceration are at an all-time high in the United States. Compared to other countries, the rates in the United States are shocking. In 1977 and 1978, the highest state incarceration rate was 416 per hundred thousand population, and the average for the country was 245. At that same time, Holland had a rate of 27, Spain 28, Ireland 48, Switzerland 59; no Western European country had a rate even half the United States' average (Bowker, 1982). The problems confronting the prison system in the United States today are so severe that seven states are operating all their facilities under court order, 25 states have one or more facilities under court order or have entered into consent decrees before a final court decree, and nine states have litigation pending (U.S. Department of Justice, 1983). These steps have been taken by the courts to remedy deplorable conditions that were frequently found to be "cruel and unusual punishment."

The prison population of today has a number of salient characteristics. Approximately one-third of all inmates have said they drank heavily just before they committed the offense for which they were convicted, and 20 percent have said they drank heavily every day of the entire year before they entered prison. When the drinking habits of the U.S. population age 18 and over were compared to those of state prison inmates, the findings were dramatic. The general population had 14 percent drinking one or more ounces of alcohol a day, and the inmate population had 47 percent drinking at this level. Drinking was particularly prevalent among the chronic offenders. More than two-fifths of these career offenders drank heavily during the year prior to their offense, compared to approximately one-fourth of those with no prior convictions. Over 80 percent of the drinking inmates, those who drank every day during the year prior to prison, had never been in an alcohol treatment program (U.S. Department of Justice, 1983).

The findings in regard to the abuse of other drugs are similarly disturbing. Approximately one-third of all state prisoners in 1979 were under the influence of an illegal drug when they committed the crime for which they were incarcerated, more than half had taken drugs during the month just prior to their crime, and more than three-fourths had used drugs at some time during their lives. Approximately 78 percent of the inmates had some drug usage, compared to 40 percent of the general population. Heroin was used by 30 percent of the inmates, compared to 2 percent of the general population.

As with alcohol abuse, the more convictions inmates had, the more likely they were to have taken drugs. Three-fifths of all inmates with five or more prior convictions had used drugs during the month prior to their crimes. The use of heroin was particularly significant. The proportion of inmates with five or more prior convictions who had used heroin in the month before their offense was three times greater than among those with no prior convictions. Only one-fourth of these drug abusers had ever been involved in a drug treatment program (U.S. Department of Justice, 1983). Although both drug and alcohol abuse are prevalent among the inmate population and seem to have direct correlations with the patterns of the chronic offender, little meaningful drug and alcohol treatment takes place in most correctional facilities or is provided as part of aftercare.

Racial disparity is of particular interest and concern. All studies based on official data sources, such as Department of Justice and Census Bureau reports, indicate that blacks and certain other minority groups are overrepresented in arrests, convictions, and prisons. They are overrepresented as victims as well. However, studies in which individuals report their own crimes confidentially to researchers indicate that there is little or no relationship between race and crime.

Although blacks represent 12 percent of the national population, they represent approximately 48 percent of all people arrested and imprisoned. Fifty-one percent of the black males living in large urban areas are arrested at least once during their lives for an index crime, compared with only 14 percent of the white males in these areas.

The incarceration figures are even more dramatic. Eighteen percent of black males serve time in an institution either as juveniles or as adults, and only 3 percent of white males are ever incarcerated. Between 1973 and 1979, the white incarceration rate increased from 46.3 per hundred thousand to 65.1 per hundred thousand, and the black incarceration rate rose from 368 to 544 per hundred thousand. Incarceration rates for blacks vary dramatically from state to state. In 1979 they ranged from 50 per hundred thousand in North Dakota to 13,042 in the state of Washington. In 1978 black males accounted for 5.4 percent of the general population but represented 45.7 percent of the prison population (Fehr, 1982; Christianson, 1981). Murder is the leading cause of death for young black males and is also disproportionately high for black females (Fehr, 1982; Christianson, 1981; Petersilia, 1983).

Hispanics are also overrepresented throughout the criminal justice system. Hispanics make up approximately 6 percent of the U.S. population but account for 12 percent of all arrests for violent crimes and 10 percent of the property crimes. Ten percent of the male prison population and 11 percent of the male jail population are Hispanic (U.S. Department of Justice, 1983).

The usual explanation of the statistics showing disproportionate incarceration rates among the races is that more blacks are sent to prison because they commit more crimes than whites, their crimes are more serious, and they have heavier prior records. However, studies indicate that racial discrimination in the criminal justice process itself is a significant factor in determining the racially disproportionate rates of incarceration and lengths of stay. A Rand Corporation study showed that, controlling for age, crime, and prior record, minority status accounted for one to seven months of additional court-imposed sentence time and two to eight months of additional time actually served. The same study also indicated that minorities were not overarrested in proportion to the kind and number of crimes that they committed (Petersilia, 1983). As summarized by Reid in 1979:

> Minorities face discrimination in the system of criminal justice beginning with arrest and following through all of the stages. They are more likely to be arrested and to be the victims of police brutality, less likely to have an attorney immediately, more likely to have appointed rather than retained counsel and less likely to make bail. They are more likely to be convicted. After conviction they are less likely to be placed on probation and after sentencing less likely to be paroled. (p. 356)

Other studies have not been as quick as Reid's to assume discrimination. Pope (1979) concludes that "the ambiguous results of research on the relation between race and crime indicate that categorical statements regarding the extent of overt discrimination in criminal proceedings may be unwarranted" (p. 356). Whether or not there are discriminatory practices taking place in the criminal justice system, the facts are irrefutable; blacks are dealt with at all points in the criminal justice system in disproportionately high percentages. If the system itself is not discriminatory, then other social systems in our society are failing, resulting in these high rates. In either case, there are major social issues that need to be addressed to remedy this problem.

Philosophies in Corrections

Most criminal justice or correctional systems draw from a mixture of the philosophies that follow. Research on them is inadequate and does not support any of these philosophies as being successful in reducing the crime rate. Many factors besides correctional philosophy influence all outcomes in this field.

Retribution. This is the eye-for-an-eye, tooth-for-a-tooth philosophy. It assumes that criminal acts are inherently wrong and therefore must be punished. The punishment serves no other purpose. Under this philosophy, incarceration serves no utilitarian goals; it does not claim to reduce crime, protect society, or rehabilitate.

Restitution. According to this view, offenders should reimburse their victims. They should return them to a whole state, returning what has been taken and providing the victim repayment for any loss, whether it is physical injury, property, or even death.

General Deterrence. The core of this philosophy is that the sanction for crime affects those who are not being punished, that examples made of individuals who commit crimes prevent those who see their suffering from committing like crimes.

Special Deterrence. This philosophy focuses on the effect the punishment has on the individual criminal. It expects that the criminal will learn from the punishment and avoid the behavior that led to that punishment.

Treatment. The theorists of this philosophy contend that the behavior of individuals can be changed by involving them in a variety of programs even if it is against their will. Treatment programs generally focus on rehabilitation, reeducation, and reintegration. It was the treatment model that led to the need for indeterminate sentences.

Incapacitation. Incapacitation is predicated on the probability of recidivism: if society incarcerates those who are most likely to commit future crimes, it affects the crime rate by preventing this high-risk population from being free. The major difficulties of this theory are that many who would not repeat their criminal behavior are incarcerated; the high cost; issues of fairness; the perception that punishment is for future behavior and not past; and the extremely small overall crime reductions that occur with this approach, in relation to its high cost.

Just Desserts. Also known as the justice model, this is basically an attempt to develop a form of the retribution model that can be defended and accomplished. It seeks determinate sentences that are clear and uniform and proportionate to the individual crime or to the individual crime and the extent of the person's criminal history. It greatly reduces the discretionary powers of judges and other criminal justice authorities and allows both offenders and the public to have a better understanding of the outcomes of criminal behavior.

Probation and Parole

The conflicting philosophies of corrections are particularly apparent in probation and parole. In most jurisdictions the probation and parole officer not only performs supervision, surveillance, and counseling roles, but also has the authority to arrest, search, and seize property and otherwise to restrict clients' freedoms.

The objectives of parole are often vague and unrealistic and may have a variety of legal mandates. Probation and parole staff conduct investigations both for parole boards, to determine whether to grant parole, and for courts, to determine what sanctions are appropriate.

In 1981 three-fourths of all adult offenders under correctional supervision were supervised in the community through probation and parole. In that year there were 1.22 million probationers and another 224,000 parolees (U.S. Department of Justice, 1983).

Although insufficient to determine the effectiveness of probation and parole, research has generally found that these approaches are at least as effective as incarceration. With the increased focus on the justice model and on ensuring due process rights, the whole parole system is under severe criticism. A number of states have abolished the power of parole boards, and others have eliminated parole altogether (U.S. Department of Justice, 1983; Gross & von Hirsch, 1981; Krajick, 1983).

Most criticism of both probation and parole focuses on the indeterminacy of the length of stay and the abuse of discretion by probation and parole officers. In most states it is relatively easy to return someone to an incarceration status from either probation or parole. Although Supreme Court decisions since 1970 have limited that ability and ensured due process rights, parole and probation authorities still retain a great deal of discretion in limiting an individual's freedoms, and discriminatory practices and other abuses remain possible in exercising this discretion. Another problem in this area is that liability issues arise when violent offenders released prior to the end of their terms commit additional serious crimes.

Capital Punishment

During the early history of the United States, capital punishment was imposed for many crimes, and the death penalty continued to be a relatively common practice up until the 1960s. In 1960, 44 of the country's 53 jurisdictions authorized the death penalty. In the last four decades, however, the death penalty has been used infrequently. Of the thousands convicted in 1960 of murder, rape, and other capital offenses, only 113 persons were sentenced to death, and approximately half that number were executed. The decrease was dramatic from 1960 to 1967, when legal challenges resulted in a ten-year moratorium on executions.

Between 1930 and 1980, 3,860 persons were executed for eight different crimes. Eighty-six percent of those executed had committed murder, 12 percent rape, and the rest armed robbery, kidnapping, burglary, sabotage, aggravated assault, or espionage. Between 1930 and 1980, 54 percent of all individuals executed were nonwhite. Eighty-nine percent of the persons executed for rape were nonwhite. Only 32 women, 12 of them nonwhite, were executed (U.S. Department of Justice, 1983).

Although executions reached their peak in the 1930s, the number of individuals sentenced to death reached a peak in the 1970s. At present, more than 1,300 persons await execution. With changes in death penalty laws in the early 1980s, the practice of execution resumed. There were a number of executions during 1984, for example.

Justification of the death penalty is based on a number of principles. Many defenders of this practice rest their position on the principle of retribution—basically that convicted offenders deserve to be punished and that a suitable punishment is, like the crime itself, some form of harsh treatment. If the severity of punishment is to be proportional to the gravity of the offense, then the death penalty is the appropriate sanction for murder and other serious crimes.

Incapacitation is a frequent argument because the death penalty is foolproof in this respect: the individual who is executed will never commit another crime. The dispute arises, though, as to whether the person executed would have committed further capital or other offenses and whether others who are not executed will commit such crimes when they are released.

The most common argument in support of the death penalty is general deterrence, that the severe sanction of the death penalty prevents people from committing serious crimes. Research does not substantiate this claim, and one study found just the opposite—that instead of deterring potential murderers, it excites them (Bowers & Pierce,

1980). Some argue for capital punishment based strictly on cost: it is much cheaper to kill someone than to pay for years of incarceration.

The issue of the death penalty is an emotional one, and it is unlikely that decisions to retain or repeal the death penalty will be made on the basis of research to determine its effect on crime. Decisions will be made on the basis of politics and emotion.

Alternatives to Incarceration

A wide variety of programs have been used in the United States as alternatives to incarceration. The most common and formalized are probation and parole, which have widespread use. Fines are also used, alone or in connection with other sanctions, such as probation. Restitution is becoming more common, and several states now require that consideration be given to restitution in all cases.

Partial confinement has gained in popularity in recent years. These half-in-and-half-out arrangements typically involve work release, educational release, and similar programs. Frequently, these partial confinement programs include special treatment programs, such as drug and alcohol treatment, mental health treatment, and sexual offender treatment.

Many community service programs have been developed throughout the United States. Under such programs, sentences consist of performing work projects for governmental or nonprofit agencies.

The most ambitious efforts in developing alternatives to incarceration are the probation subsidy and community corrections programs. These programs attempt to shift responsibility for providing services to offenders away from the state and to the local community (Nagel, 1973).

High-technology industry has entered the correctional field with a bracelet called the GOSSlink. This electronic transmitter is strapped to the ankle or wrist of an individual sentenced to home curfew or house arrest, and a receiver in the individual's home detects the presence or absence of the transmitter signal and automatically transmits information to a central computer. This program is used in Albuquerque, New Mexico, where it has been approved by the state's supreme court as a pilot project.

Research has shown that the expectations of alternatives to incarceration are generally not met, that these programs are no more effective than incarceration. Most of the research in this area is methodologically flawed, however, and it is difficult to draw any definite conclusions. Certainly, compared to most incarceration programs, the alternatives to incarceration are more humane (Austin & Krisberg, 1982; Lipton, 1975; Wilks & Martinson, 1976).

Treatment

The earliest corrections programs in the United States provided religious counseling, as do the majority of programs today. Frequently the religious programs provided are rigid and stereotyped, and only recently have a variety of religious programs been made available, including ones provided by Muslims, American Indians, and other special groups. These programs have shown that when religious programs are individualized and directed toward special populations, there is a much higher level of participation.

Work and vocational training programs have gained popularity as a major treatment approach. Most prison systems have some form of vocational training or work program. However, a large number of these focus more on prison maintenance and operation than on providing useful job skills. Many vocational training programs either use outdated equipment or provide outdated skills for inmates. Both remedial and higher education are becoming an important part of treatment programs, but education programs, like many other prison programs, have difficulty attracting skilled, qualified staff who can develop the special programs to keep inmates motivated. For example, many of the remedial programs use the materials typically used in grade schools rather than develop special materials more appropriate for adults.

Medical and dental treatment programs are usually far from adequate to meet inmates' needs. Salaries are usually low, the working conditions are poor, and there are few benefits to attract the skilled staff needed in this area.

Custody or correctional officers constitute by far the largest staff component in any correctional facility. Few individuals make this field their first career choice. Two-thirds of all correctional officers are male and three-fourths white. One-fifth of all correctional officers are not high school graduates. Only one out of 20 has a college degree.

Correctional officers generally receive short, on-the-job training that focuses on custody issues, such as security, using weapons, and riot control. Few correctional training programs involve any theory or humanistic training (Bowker, 1982). There is frequently a subculture and behavior code among custody staff that emphasizes maintaining security and control, keeping a social distance from prisoners, being tough and dominating prisoners, and not listening to social workers.

Social Work in Corrections

Although over the years there has been considerable controversy over the role of social work in corrections and whether social workers contribute positively to treatment efforts, it is generally accepted that social workers can and do play an important role in the rehabilitation or treatment of correctional clients. The tasks that social workers typically perform in correctional settings include intake and screening, diagnosis and classification, supervision and treatment, and release planning.

Unique Skills. In a 1975 article, Handler pointed out the value of certain unique social work skills in corrections work. Important among these is that social workers are trained to see clients as part of a total social system that contributes to both the problem and the solution. Social workers thus emphasize contacts with employers, teachers, family members, and significant others to identify problems and seek solutions. Handler also noted that social workers have always emphasized case coordination. This is particularly important in the correctional field, where multiple disciplines are brought together and clients are usually multiproblem individuals requiring a multiplicity of services. Social workers' skills in using community resources and making appropriate referrals are also valuable in corrections, as are their treatment techniques, which uniquely qualify them to work with the variety of clients involved in the correctional field.

The general casework and groupwork skills taught to social workers can be appropriately applied in working with correctional clients. Giving feedback, clarifying, questioning, summarizing, confronting, resolving conflicts, interpreting, intervening in crises, referring, formulating goals, interviewing, setting limits, and predicting behavior are all useful in working with correctional clients.

Objectives in Prison Work. As change agents, social workers play a key role in assisting the corrections client to identify the need to change. This requires establishing a helping, meaningful relationship with the client and making some form of diagnosis. Although it is not possible to diagnose clearly the cause of any individual's criminal behavior, the social worker can help inmates identify their maladaptive behaviors and their needs (Hatcher, 1978).

Social workers assist correctional inmates with behavioral changes, particularly with the ones necessary to cope with the many day-to-day prison problems: a great deal of violence; sexual and nonsexual assaults; economic victimization through theft, gambling, and protection rackets; psychological and sociological victimization both by inmates and by some staff; homosexuality; racial conflicts; and drug and alcohol abuse. All these are areas in which social workers can assist their clients.

Social workers can also help inmates develop learning skills and methods of problem solving that can be transferred to other areas of life. In addition, all correctional clients have difficulty in making responsible decisions, and social workers are uniquely qualified to help them look at alternatives and make better choices. These are among the behaviors and learning skills offenders need to cope with the many problems that will confront them upon release, such as their lack of jobs, housing, food, clothing, and transportation and their deficiencies in relating to people.

Social workers also play a key role in working with the total family, helping family members deal with the psychological, social, and economic impacts of a family member's being in prison. Also, they assist the inmate and family in the adjustment involved in the inmate's returning to the family and the impacts of this event on family roles.

Many of the problems and issues prisoners face upon release cannot be solved by talk; they require action and immediate relief by the social worker. In these situations, the social worker's referral and brokerage skills are of paramount importance. Social workers need to work with the individual and the community to develop the best possible support system, providing and directing a network of services for the client after release.

Recognizing Limitations. When working in the correctional field, it is important to be realistic about what can and cannot be done. Treatment programs are frequently oversold or misappropriately sold. There is little that is done with an individual client or groups of clients that will affect crime or offer any real protection to the community. Therefore, the focus should be on individuals and their needs (Hatcher, 1978; Mangrum, 1976). The social worker must also recognize that there are limitations in working with individual correctional clients. Resistance to change is normal, and some offenders do not change. Clearly defined limits are necessary: there must be a recognition that even the corrections client has the right to self-determination and that change cannot be forced. Authority must be used by plan and appropriately.

Over the years a wide variety of treatment techniques have been tried in corrections. Many corrections facilities rely heavily on group counseling programs. Reality therapies, milieu therapies, a variety of individual approaches, and combinations of therapies have also been tried. Because the research shows mixed reviews for any particular type of treatment, and most research has methodological flaws, no firm conclusions can be drawn as to what works best (Lipton, 1975; Wilks & Martinson, 1976).

One danger for social work practice in the correctional field is the pressure to emphasize labeling. Labeling is frequently critical to security classifications, institutional placements, and releases. As much as possible, the focus in the social worker's diagnostic and labeling process should remain on behavioral descriptions rather than on conclusions. Most important, the worker must observe social work practices and ethics.

The Future

At present, the criminal justice system in the United States is an incomprehensible, inefficient, unproductive, multilevel, administrative maze. The prison environment is violent, depressing, regimented, boring, and dehumanizing. Most prisons are located miles away from needed resources and the population they serve. Prisons are outdated, overcrowded, and far too large. Activities are duplicated, programs fragmented, and resources wasted.

In this society, the major emphasis is placed on the back end of the criminal justice system, the prison, which neither corrects offenders nor protects society. To make the criminal justice system successful, resources need to be placed at the front end in the form of prevention strategies. If the correctional system is to move significantly from the jailhouse approach of centuries past, major shifts need to be made, beginning with the following recognitions:

1. That prisons neither prevent crime nor protect society to any significant degree.

2. That prisons are for punishment.

3. That prisons are costly resources and therefore should be reserved for those most needing that type of punishment.

4. That prisons should be located near the communities from which their clients come.

5. That prisons should provide only the level of security needed.

6. That prisons should be limited in size.

7. That prisons need an array of services to address the special needs of the offender population, including drug and alcohol programs, mental health programs, and remedial education programs.

8. That resources and programs should address the causes of crime and explore methods of prevention.

9. That the criminal justice system should be used only for those clients who are dangerous to others and that public drunkenness, abnormal sexual behaviors, and various victimless crimes should be handled by other social institutions and not the criminal justice system.

10. That crime is a local problem that must be addressed by the development of local resources.

11. That alternatives to incarceration need to be developed, tried, and used.

12. That good research must be developed to evaluate the effect of all programs.

Social workers have a variety of roles to play in the future of corrections. In the overall treatment of the offender, they have a multiplicity of roles—preincarceration, during incarceration, and after release. Social workers should also play a key role in creating a public awareness of the problems in the criminal justice field and in initiating changes in the way society deals with this population.

A developing role for social work in the criminal justice system is in victim and witness programs. Far too often in the past, victims were provided no treatment or support and were the forgotten component of the criminal justice system. More and more this group is recognized as one with needs that must be addressed. The social work profession's unique combination of skills is also valuable in aiding this population.

A statement Winston Churchill made in 1910 provides some guidance in looking at corrections: "The mood and temper of the public with regard to the treatment of crime and criminals is one of the unfailing tests of the civilization of any country." (Carney, 1980, p. 19). A look at the present mood and temper in the United States in regard to the treatment of crime and criminals certainly raises serious questions as to just how civilized a people we are.

WARREN NETHERLAND

For further information, see FEMALE OFFENDERS; JUVENILE JUSTICE SYSTEM; JUVENILE OFFENDER INSTITUTIONS.

References

Austin, J., & Krisberg, B. (1982). "The Unmet Promise of Alternatives to Incarceration." *Crime and Delinquency, 28*(3), 374–409.

Bowers, W., & Pierce, G. (1980). "Arbitrariness and Discrimination Under Post-Furman Capital Statutes." *Crime and Delinquency, 26*(4), 453–484.

Bowker, L. H. (1982). *Corrections: The Science and the Art.* New York: Macmillan.

Carney, L. P. (1980). *Corrections: Treatment and Philosophy.* Englewood Cliffs, N.J.: Prentice-Hall.

Christianson, S. (1981). "Our Black Prisons." *Crime and Delinquency, 27*(3), 364–375.

Fehr, L. (1982). *The Disproportionate Representation of Racial Minorities in the Criminal Justice System of Washington State.* Seattle, Wash.: Washington Council on Crime and Delinquency.

Gross, H., & von Hirsch, A. (1981). *Sentencing.* New York: Oxford University Press.

Handler, E. (1975). "Social Work and Corrections: Comments on an Uneasy Partnership." *Criminology, 13*(2), 240–254.

Hatcher, H. A. (1978). *Correctional Casework and Counseling.* Englewood Cliffs, N.J.: Prentice-Hall.

Krajick, K. (1983, June). "Abolishing Parole: An Idea Whose Time Has Passed." *Corrections Magazine, 9,* 32–40.

Lipton, D. (1975). *The Effectiveness of Correctional Treatment: A Survey of Treatment Evaluation Studies.* New York: Praeger Publishers.

Mangrum, C. T. (1976). "Corrections' Tarnished Halo." *Federal Probation, 40*(1), 9–14.

Nagel, W. G. (1973). *The New Red Barn: A Critical Look at the Modern American Prison.* New York: Walker/American Foundation Institute of Corrections.

Petersilia, J. (1983). *Racial Disparities in the Criminal Justice System.* Santa Monica, Calif.: The Rand Corporation.

Petersilia, J., & Greenwood, P. W. (1978). "Mandatory Prison Sentences: Their Projected Effects on Crime and Prison Populations." *Journal of Criminal Law and Criminology, 69*(4), 604–615.

Pope, C. E. (1979). "Race and Crime Revisited." *Crime and Delinquency, 25*(3), 347–357.

Reid, S. T. (1979). *Crime and Delinquency* (2nd ed.). New York: Holt, Rinehart and Winston.

Sherman, M. E., & Hawkins, G. E. (1981). *Imprisonment in America: Choosing the Future.* Chicago: University of Chicago Press.

U.S. Department of Justice. (1983, October). *Report to the Nation on Crime and Justice* (NCO-87068). Washington, D.C.: U.S. Government Printing Office.

Wilks, J., & Martinson, R. (1976). "Is the Treatment of Criminal Offenders Really Necessary?" *Federal Probation, 40*(1), 3–9.

For Further Reading

Austin, M. J., Kelleher, E., & Smith, P. (1972). *The Field Consortium: Manpower Development and Training in Social Welfare and Corrections.* Tallahassee, Fla.: State University System of Florida.

Bailey, W. C. (1966). "Correctional Outcome: An Evaluation of 100 Reports." *Journal of Criminal Law, Criminology and Police Science, 57*(2), 153–157.

Baker, L. (1983). *Miranda: Crime, Law, and Politics.* New York: Atheneum Publishers.

Berkowitz, M., et al. (1975). *An Evaluation of Policy-Related Rehabilitation Research.* New York: Praeger Publishers.

Blumstein, A., et al. (1983). *Research on Sentencing: The Search for Reform* (Vols. 1 and 2). Washington, D.C.: National Academy Press.

Blumstein, A., Cohen, J., & Nagin, D. (1978). *Deterrence and Incapacitation: Estimating* the *Effects of Criminal Sanctions on Crime Rates*. Washington, D.C.: National Academy of Science.

Blumstein, A., & Moitra, S. (1979). "An Analysis of the Time Series of the Imprisonment Rate in the States of the United States: A Further Test of the Stability of Punishment Hypothesis." *Journal of Criminal Law and Criminology, 70*(3), 376–390.

Brake, M., & Bailey, R. (1980). *Radical Social Work and Practice*. Beverly Hills, Calif.: Sage Publications.

Fehr, L. (1983). *Rethinking Imprisonment in Washington State: Critical Public Policy Choices*. Seattle, Wash.: Washington Council on Crime and Delinquency.

Gibbons, D. C. (1961). "Some Notes on Treatment Theory in Corrections." *Social Service Review, 36*, 295.

Glaser, D. (1964). *The Effectiveness of a Prison and Parole System*. Indianapolis, Ind.: Bobbs-Merrill Co.

Greenberg, D. F., Kessler, R. C., & Logan, C. H. (1979). "A Panel Model of Crime Rates and Arrest Rates." *American Sociological Review, 44*(5), 843–850.

Hall, J., Williams, M., & Tomaino, L. (1966). "The Challenge of Correctional Change: The Interface of Conformity and Commitment." *Journal of Criminal Law, Criminology and Police Science, 57*(4), 493–503.

Herrington, L. H., et al. (1982). *Report of President's Task Force on Victims of Crime*. Washington, D.C.: U.S. Government Printing Office.

Hudson, J., & Galaway, B. (1975). *Restitution in Criminal Justice: A Critical Assessment of Sanctions*. Lexington, Mass.: Lexington Books.

Hylton, J. H. (1982). "Rhetoric and Reality: A Critical Appraisal of Community Correctional Programs." *Crime and Delinquency, 28*(3), 341–373.

Inbau, F. E., et al. (1966). *Criminal Law, Criminology and Police Science, 57*(4), 377–538.

Messinger, S. L., & Bittner, E. (1980). *Criminology Review Yearbook* (Vol. 1). Beverly Hills, Calif.: Sage Publications.

Morris, N., & Hawkins, G. (1970). *The Honest Politician's Guide to Crime Control*. Chicago: University of Chicago Press.

Morris, R. (1974). "The Place of Social Work in the Human Services." *Social Work, 19*(5), 519–531.

National Institute of Justice. (1981). *American Prisons and Jails* (Vols. 1–5). Washington, D.C.: U.S. Department of Justice.

Newman, C. L. (1961). "Concepts of Treatment in Probation and Parole Supervision." *Federal Probation, 25*(1), 11–18.

Smith, R. L., & Breed, A. F. (1982). "Of Compel-

ling National Interest." *Corrections Today, 44*(4), 14–89.

Stastny, C., & Tyrnauer, G. (1982). *Who Rules the Joint?* Lexington, Mass.: D.C. Heath & Co.

Toch, H. (1970). "The Care and Feeding of Typologies and Labels." *Federal Probation, 34*(3), 15–19.

Waldron, R. J. (1976). *The Criminal Justice System: An Introduction*. Boston: Houghton Mifflin Co.

Weisman, I. (1967). "Offender Status, Role Behavior, and Treatment Considerations." *Social Casework: The Journal of Contemporary Social Work, 48*(7), 422–425.

COUNCIL ON SOCIAL WORK EDUCATION (CSWE). See HISTORY AND EVOLUTION OF SOCIAL WORK PRACTICE; PROFESSIONAL ASSOCIATIONS: COUNCIL ON SOCIAL WORK EDUCATION; SOCIAL WORK EDUCATION.

COYLE, GRACE LONGWELL. See biographical section.

CRISIS INTERVENTION

Today, crisis intervention is a recognized and accepted form of social work practice in direct work with individuals, families, and groups in a wide range of primary and secondary settings. After years of struggle, during which its adherents often made exaggerated claims of universal applicability and its opponents scornfully dismissed it as ineffectual treatment, it has come to be accepted as a valid form of first-line intervention with clients in stress.

Stressful situations that may lead to crisis states are usually divided into acute situational crises, developmental and transitional changes, and natural or man-made community disasters. Because the last category is considered separately in this encyclopedia, the discussion will be limited to the first two areas.

Origins

Historically, crisis theory and its application to practice is rooted in a number of developments that have occurred over the past forty years in psychology, sociology, and psychiatry as well as in social work itself. Certain significant trends have become intermingled to establish the foundation for practice in crisis situations.

Psychology. In the field of psychodynamic theory, second-generation theoreticians such as Heinz Hartmann, E. Rudolf Loewenstein, Ives Hendrick, Abraham Kardiner, David Rapaport, Franz Alexander, and Abraham Maslow began to interest themselves in the autonomous, conflict-free areas of ego development, producing a far more optimistic view of personality growth and the individual's ability to change throughout the life cycle than had theretofore been presented (for a recent, comprehensive examination of this topic, see Noam, Higgins, & Goethals, 1982).

Erikson (1959), working independently, developed his eight-stage epigenetic approach to the life cycle, during which the person's ability to work on the key psychosocial crises posed by each developmental stage is tested. At the same time, White (1959) posited his theories of how effectance and competence are developed as independent ego energies. In the field of child psychology, Piaget (1963) meticulously built his theory of intellectual and motor processes by which children expand their capacities to organize and incorporate new experiences and to solve problems, while Murphy (1962) investigated their coping and mastery patterns.

Meanwhile, experimental psychologists such as Selye (1956) began to examine individuals' reactions to stressful conditions, using concepts of homeostasis and systemic equilibrium. His breakdown of the stress-induced process into three stages—alarm reaction, which includes shock and countershock; resistance, during which maximal adaptation is attempted; and finally, exhaustion, when adaptive mechanisms collapse—became the prototype on which later stress configurations were based.

Reactions under both naturally stressful conditions such as prison camps and isolation and induced laboratory conditions were examined exhaustively. Of particular interest is the work of Lazarus (1966) on cognitive factors underlying stress, which emphasizes the importance of appraising both the external threat and the individual's potential for solution and mastery. Janis (1958) started to examine patients' response to surgery and other threatening situations, while Moos (1977) and his colleagues examined how people coped with various types of physical illness and disability.

Both learning theorists and behavior modification exponents viewed people in crisis as experiencing some form of physical or psychological overload in their ability to master stressful situations. Emphasis was placed on the cognitive aspects of experience, on the unlearning of old, unsuccessful, or damaging patterns of interaction and the learning of new, constructive ones. They focused on shaping behavior in more socially acceptable, less painful ways to deal with stressful situations (Taplin, 1971).

In the unfolding field of life-span development, theoreticians such as Havighurst (1953) postulated a series of stage-related tasks that the individual must master if he or she is to mature successfully and gain life satisfaction. Riegel (1975) noted two contrasting approaches to the developmental process, one that sees the life cycle as a process of ongoing development and evolution in which sudden, unexpected crises are seen as unpredictable disruptions that do not play a significant role in the individual's development and the other that views the life course progressing through discrete, qualitatively different stages with crises and catastrophes as necessary steps in the process.

Neugarten (1969) pointed out that salient issues of adulthood change at different stages in the life cycle as the individual struggles to master contingencies brought about by various changes in his or her life situation. Although adults carry a sense of the normal, expectable life cycle in their minds, major stresses that are caused by traumatic, unanticipated events upset the sequence and rhythm of the life cycle. She sees timing as the key issue.

Sociology. Starting in the 1930s and 1940s, family sociologists began to look at the impact of stressful events on family structure and interaction. Eliot (1955) classified family crises into those of dismemberment, accession, demoralization, and aggrievement. Hill (1958) found three interacting elements that seemed to determine whether a particular event would produce a family crisis: the external hardship or precipitating event (the stressor), the internal organization of the family, and the family's definition of the precipitating event as stress inducing.

A long series of research projects investigated the impact of various development and transitional crises on families. Typical of these are the work of Rhona Rapoport (1963) on marriage, LeMasters (1957) on parenthood, and Lieberman (1975) on old age. A number of researchers tried to adapt the "social readjustment rating scale" developed by Holmes and Rahe (1967) to measure quantitatively the subjective effect of stressful life events on individuals (see Dohrenwend & Dohrenwend, 1974), although the results have on the whole proved disappointing.

Cumming and Cumming (1962), a sociologist-psychiatrist team, suggested three broad types of crises: those that are biologically tinged and thus inevitable, such as adolescence and menopause; those that are environmentally tinged and to some extent avoidable, such as migration and bereavement; and those that are adventitious, purely chance events, such as accidents and disasters. They saw ego growth as a series of disequilibrations and subsequent reequilibrations between the person and his or her environment, with crisis resolution prompting ego growth by increasing the individual's coping repertoire and ego sets.

Psychiatry. Since the mid-1940s, military psychiatrists have tried to predict the performance of soldiers who might break under field pressures. It was found that persistent dysfunction could be reduced by treating men as close to the front line as possible, focusing on the immediate situational crisis, and returning them to combat within a short time to reduce regression and restore self-confidence. During and after the Vietnam war, the plight of families of prisoners of war and servicemen missing in action began to receive particular attention. Counseling services to discuss stressful problems arising out of the reunion with long-separated husbands and fathers expanded (McCubbin et al., 1974).

Work with bereaved families dates back to the initial work of Lindemann (1944) on grief reactions to the Cocoanut Grove nightclub fire in Boston in 1943, in which hundreds of servicemen and others died. He found that the duration and severity of the bereavement process depended on the extent to which each survivor or relative could carry out his or her grief work successfully—the degree to which people were able to emancipate themselves from their bondage to the deceased, to readjust to an environment in which the deceased was missing, and to form new relationships over time.

Lindemann (1944) concluded that certain inevitable events in the life cycle generate emotional strain and stress that can lead either to mastery of the new situation or failure with impairment of functioning. Although some situations may be stressful to all people, they become crises for people who tend to be particularly vulnerable because of personality factors or the undue pressure on emotional resources. In 1948 Lindemann established the Wellesley Human Relations Service, a community-based project aimed at preventive work in typical hazardous family situations (Klein & Lindemann, 1961).

Closely interwoven with Lindemann's work was that of Caplan (1951), whose interest in crisis grew out of his early work with immigrant mothers and children in Israel after World War II. During the 1950s and 1960s, while at the Harvard School of Public Health, he began to develop an approach based on the public health model of primary, secondary, and tertiary levels of intervention. A series of research studies was carried out under his direction at the Family Guidance Center and elsewhere in the Boston area on various types of situational and maturational crises such as the premature birth of a child (Caplan, Mason, & Kaplan, 1965) and adjustment to marriage (Rapoport, 1963).

Out of these studies, Caplan (1964) developed his core theory on crisis intervention. He defined a crisis as occurring when a person faces an obstacle to important life goals that is, for a time, insurmountable through customary methods of problem solving. He identified two types of crisis situations, those precipitated by changes in the normal life course such as school entry and retirement and those brought on by accidental hazardous events such as acute illnesses, accidents, or family dislocation. During the 1970s, at the Harvard Department of Psychiatry's Laboratory of Community Psychiatry, Caplan (1974) turned his interest to the natural and mutual support systems in the community that can be used to prevent or ameliorate the destructive aspects of crisis situations.

Meanwhile, on the West Coast, Jacobson and his colleagues (1965), using Caplan's approach, opened the Benjamin Rush Center for Problems of Living. They offered brief, immediate crisis intervention for a wide range of social and emotional problems. As their contribution to crisis theory, they differentiated between two approaches—the generic approach, which emphasizes classes of situational and maturational crises that can happen to significant population groups without regard to individual psychodynamics and can be dealt with by paraprofessionals and volunteers, and the individual approach, which stresses and requires more intensive treatment by professionals (Jacobson, Strickler, & Morley, 1968). The crisis approach to mental health spread rapidly across the country during the 1960s and early 1970s.

Suicide Prevention. Suicide prevention services, one of the most active of community mental health programs, developed its own independent frame of reference during the 1950s and 1960s. Much of the early work was carried out by Dublin (1963) and Farberow and Schneidman (1961) at the Los Angeles Suicide Prevention Center. Specific features included the use of a 24-hour telephone service, immediate mobilization of community resources, incorporation of volunteers into the core staff, and an approach that featured the use of authority, extensive activity, and the involvement of significant others.

As the suicide prevention movement spread, the Center for Studies of Suicide Prevention was set up in 1966 to concentrate activities and exchange information. By 1972, almost 200 suicide prevention programs had been established throughout the United States, frequently outside of established community mental health facilities (McGee, 1974). However, as the financial retrenchment of mental health programs demanded the elimination of duplication, many of these centers broadened their scope or merged with other types of community health programs to cover various types of crisis and emergency situations such as alcohol and drug addiction, psychiatric difficulties, spouse and child abuse, and community disasters.

Social Work Developments

Part of the attraction of crisis intervention theory for social workers lies in its compatability with their own approach that historically has been grounded in work with individuals and families in high-stress situations. Ever since Smith College offered its first summer program in psychiatric social work in 1918 to "contribute to the war effort by training workers for the rehabilitation of shell-shocked soldiers" (Reynolds, 1963, pp. 54–55), practitioners have become sensitive to the particular needs of people in acute distress.

The widespread economic and social disruption wrought by the Great Depression of the 1930s forced many previously self-reliant individuals and families to ask for help from public and private social agencies. Caseworkers from private agencies who were recruited to work in public welfare services found themselves at first bewildered and overwhelmed by staggering caseloads but soon learned to combine mass assistance with "reasonable individualization" (Hamilton, 1940, p. 124).

Characteristic of early services developed to meet these unfamiliar needs was the Travelers Aid Society, which usually operated in railway and bus terminals. It developed a unique approach to deal with frightened, upset, disheartened clients by trying to resolve a newly developed crisis, often within one or two interviews, setting up limited goals and starting treatment immediately. During World War II, family agencies undertook to help mothers find jobs in defense industries and to develop child care services for their children, as well as to assist men rejected for service for physical and emotional reasons. Families who were breaking up as the aftermath of separation, war tensions, and hasty war marriages called for quick, skilled services (Rich, 1956).

By the 1950s, social agencies had become concerned with the widening gap between the number of requests for help and the length of time before services could be started. They felt acute pressure from lengthening waiting lists and severe staff shortages on the one hand and frequent dropouts while waiting for services on the other. Perlman (1963) pointed out that the client coming for help was under a double strain: the problem itself was felt as a threat and the individual's inability to cope with it increased the tension. Thus the chance to provide help at the strategic time was lost if the client was asked to wait for help.

Although agency policies were geared to providing long-term treatment, a long series of research studies revealed that one of three cases did not return after the first interview and four of five discontinued by the fifth (Beck, 1962; Ripple, 1964; Shyne, 1957). In a comprehensive survey of family service agencies and psychiatric clinics, Parad and Parad (1968a, 1968b) discovered considerable experimentation in the use of short-term treatment, often within the frame of the crisis intervention format. At the same time, a carefully documented research study at the Community Service Society of New York comparing brief- and long-term treatment definitively established that, along many dimensions, the former was as effective as the latter and, in other ways, even more effective (Reid & Shyne, 1969).

In mental health settings, social workers had been active since the 1950s in early experimentation based on the crisis intervention approach. In some instances, working in such settings as the Longley-Porter Neuropsychiatric Institute in San Francisco, the Benjamin Rush Center in Los Angeles, the Emergency Psychiatric Service of Massachusetts General Hospital in Boston, and the Madeline Borg Child Guidance Institute in New York, social workers became the primary executors of innovative crisis-oriented programs. Social workers such as Howard Parad, David Kaplan, and Lydia Rapoport, working with Gerald Caplan at the Harvard School of Public Health in the late 1950s and early 1960s, began to develop much of the basic social work framework for the crisis intervention approach (Parad, 1961; Kaplan, 1962; Rapoport, 1962). Since then it has been tested in a wide range of primary and secondary settings. Throughout the 1960s and 1970s, reports of its use started to appear in professional journals, and agencies began to hold seminars and workshops to update their staff members' practice skills and to establish spe-

cial units, often with other community resources, to provide immediate, focused help during periods of acute stress.

Theoretical Framework

The basic tenets on which the crisis intervention approach to direct practice rests can be summarized in a series of statements (Golan, 1979) drawn from the initial work by Lindemann and Caplan and expanded and amplified by Parad, Kaplan, Rapoport, Jacobson, and others.

1. An individual (or family, group, or community) is subjected to periods of increased internal and external stress throughout the normal lifespan that disturb his or her customary state of equilibrium with the surrounding environment. Such episodes are usually initiated by some *hazardous event*, which may be a finite external blow or a less-bounded internal pressure that has built up over time. The event may be a single catastrophic occurrence or a series of lesser mishaps that have a cumulative effect.

2. The impact of the hazardous event disturbs the person's homeostatic balance and puts him or her into a *vulnerable state*, marked by heightened tension and anxiety. To attempt to regain equilibrium, he or she proceeds through a series of steps: first, there is an attempt to use one's customary repertoire of problem-solving mechanisms to deal with the situation. If this does not work and the upset increases, an attempt is made to mobilize heretofore untried emergency methods of coping. However, if the problem persists and can not be resolved, avoided, or redefined, tension continues to rise to a peak.

3. At this point, a *precipitating factor* can act as a turning point to push the individual into a state of *active crisis*, marked by disequilibrium, disorganization, and immobility. This is followed by a period of gradual *reintegration* until a new state of equilibrium is reached. These five elements identify the crisis situation.

4. As the crisis situation develops, the individual may perceive the initial and subsequent hazardous events primarily as a *threat*, either to his or her instinctual needs or to his or her sense of autonomy and well-being; as a *loss* of a person, an attribute (role or status), or a capacity; or as a *challenge* to survival, growth, or mastery.

5. Each of these perceptions calls forth

a characteristic emotional reaction that reflects the subjective meaning of that event to the individual. Threat elicits heightened level of anxiety; loss brings forth primarily feelings of depression, deprivation, and mourning; whereas challenge stimulates a moderate increase in anxiety plus a kindling of hope and expectation, releasing new energy for problem-solving.

6. Although a crisis situation is neither an illness nor a pathological experience and reflects a realistic struggle to deal with the individual's current stressful life situation, it may become linked to earlier unresolved or only partially resolved conflicts, resulting in inappropriate or exaggerated responses. Intervention in such situations may provide a multiple opportunity to resolve the present difficulty, to rework the previous conflict, or to break the linkage between them.

7. The total length of time between the initial blow and the final resolution of the crisis situation varies widely, depending on the severity of the hazardous event, the characteristic reaction of the person involved, the nature and complexity of the tasks that have to be accomplished, and the situational supports available. The actual state of active disequilibrium, however, is time-limited, usually lasting up to four to six weeks, until some form of adaptive or maladaptive solution is found.

8. Each particular kind of crisis situation (such as the death of a loved one or the experience of being raped) seems to follow a specific sequence of stages, which can be predicted and mapped out. Emotional reactions and behavioral responses at each phase can often be anticipated. Fixation and disequilibrium at a particular point along the way to reequilibrium may provide the clue as to where the person is "stuck" and what lies behind his or her inability to master the situation.

9. During the unraveling of the crisis situation, the individual tends to be particularly amenable to help. Customary defense mechanisms have weakened, usual coping patterns have proved inadequate, and the ego has become more open to outside influence and change. A minimal effort at such a time can often produce a maximal effect; a small amount of help, appropriately focused, can prove to be considerably more effective than

more extensive help at periods of less emotional accessibility.

10. During the reintegration phase, new ego sets may emerge and new adaptive styles may evolve to enable the person to cope more effectively with the same or similar situations in the future. However, if appropriate help is not available during this critical phase, inadequate or maladaptive coping styles may be adopted which can result in weakened ability to function appropriately and adequately in the future.

It should be kept in mind that, according to the preceding formulation, the crisis intervention approach operates not only on a normality-abnormality continuum, but also on the belief that all people become subjected to various internal and external pressures that can be episodic or related to developmental or transitional life stages. Although people's repertoire of coping patterns and problem-solving techniques may be sufficient for the usual flux in such pressures, a sudden sharp increase in pressures or a decrease in the ability to handle pressures can result in a failure of customary homeostatic mechanisms.

Two different processes can precipitate a crisis situation (Korner, 1973). In the shock crisis, a sudden, cataclysmic change in the social environment—the unexpected death of a mate or a rape—can produce an overwhelming emotional reaction that swamps the individual or family's available coping mechanisms. Because the person has had no forewarning or time to prepare for the tremendous impact, he or she goes into emotional shock and "falls apart." In the exhaustion crisis, the person or family may have coped effectively with a series of diverse or associated stressful conditions, one after the other. But eventually, coping abilities weaken and the person may reach the point where he or she no longer has enough strength or resources—internal and external—to deal with the cumulative effects of these successive blows. A state of active crisis ensues.

Recent Reformulations

As the crisis intervention approach becomes increasingly integrated into social work practice, it has been recognized that the term "crisis" is used ambiguously to apply to both sudden, unanticipated events such as rape or the death of a child and to developmental and transitional events such as divorce and retirement. Part of the difficulty can be attributed to Erikson's idiosyncratic use of the term "psychosocial crisis" to refer to long-term developmental changes and conflicts that often take years to be resolved and are far removed from Caplan's tight description of a crisis situation in which reequilibrium must be achieved in up to six weeks.

Practitioners began to point out their frustration that developmental and transitional uncertainties, which often come to the attention of professionals through acute situational crises that erupt as part of the broader, deeper process, can only be dealt with in a limited, immediate fashion by using the crisis intervention approach. Unless they operate in a special setting such as the Rush Center, where time limits are arbitrarily set in advance, professionals often feel a need to continue beyond the immediate acute situation to help the client deal with the underlying issues uncovered.

Theoreticians have attempted to resolve this ambiguity in recent years. Thus, Jacobson (1980) speaks of a "crisis matrix" of life events that may last for extended periods of time and are not, in and of themselves, crises although a number of specific, separate crises, each lasting from four to six weeks, may be triggered during this process.

Kaplan (1982) has proposed the concept of "disorders of change" as an elaboration of crisis theory. It refers to the problem-solving struggles of individuals to adapt to psychological and social phenomena. Successful outcomes are linked to the resolution of specific coping tasks that take place within the social context of family and community.

Golan (1980) attempted to untangle the relationship between acute, situational events and the developmental and transitional processes by pointing out that the pseudoequilibrium that often follows brief, time-limited treatment often masks more basic disruptions. She (1981) proposed broadening the theoretical frame of reference by which transitional and developmental changes occur by viewing them within the context of adult life-span theory that draws heavily on the work of Neugarten (1976), Duvall (1977), and Rhodes (1977) and on research studies such as those carried out by

Levinson et al. (1978), Vaillant (1977), and Lowenthal et al. (1975).

Although many social work practitioners today find crisis intervention an important, productive approach to clients in acute distress, they also find it helpful in many situations to enlarge their field of vision to include the developmental and transitional changes that may or may not reach crisis proportions.

Application to Practice

As the theoretical formulation of crisis developed, it has been applied and tested in a variety of helping situations. Its current use ranges from incorporation into the treatment program for stressed clients and patients in established social services and mental and physical health settings (Getzel, 1982) to the development of special interdisciplinary centers to provide emergency help to high-risk victims of rape (Vera, 1981), battering (Everstine & Everstine, 1983), and AIDS (Lopez & Getzel, 1984). It has become an integral part of emergency services in hospitals (Bergman, 1976) and has resulted in the mobilization of interdisciplinary teams to go out into the community to intervene (Foxman, 1976) and to provide the impetus to start round-the-clock services to children in need (Franz, 1980). Today, the selection of crisis intervention as the treatment of choice in a stressful situation varies considerably, depending on the nature and philosophy of the setting, the orientation of the practitioner, and the availability of resources, both within the agency and in the community.

Goals of Treatment. According to Parad (1977), the goals in crisis intervention are primarily to cushion the impact of the stressful event by offering immediate emotional first aid and by strengthening the client's coping and integrative struggles through on-the-spot therapeutic clarification and guidance.

More specifically, Rapoport (1970) sees two levels of goals. At minimum, she suggests (1) relief of symptoms, (2) restoration to the precrisis level of functioning, (3) understanding the relevant precipitating events that led up to the state of disequilibrium, and (4) identification of remedial measures that the client or family can take or that are available through community resources.

In addition, notes Rapoport, where the individual's personality and the social situation are favorable and the opportunity presents itself or can be created, two additional goals may be sought: (5) recognition of the connection between the current stress and past life experiences and conflicts, and (6) initiation of new models of perceiving, thinking, and feeling and the development of new adaptive and coping responses that can be useful beyond the period of the immediate crisis situation.

A number of models for crisis intervention have been developed over the past 15 years. Of particular interest to social workers is the "patterned approach" presented by Parad, Selby, and Quinlan (1976), which involves four basic steps: (1) the search for the precipitating event and its meaning to the client, (2) the search for the coping means used by the client, (3) the search for alternate ways of coping that might better fit the current situation, and (4) the review and support of the client's efforts to cope in new ways and an evaluation of results.

Golan (1978) offers a detailed, basic model that can be used flexibly and differentially by practitioners in a large number of primary and secondary settings. It is rooted in the problem-solving theory of casework and is a variation of the short-term, task-centered approach to practice (Reid & Epstein, 1972). It can be divided into three phases:

■ The beginning phase aims at formulation and assessment of the current situation: establishing contact, finding out what is going on, determining whether a state of active crisis (or disequilibrium) actually exists, and setting up a working contract for future activity. Keeping in mind the five elements of the total crisis situation, the practitioner focuses at the start on the precipitating factor, the event or incident that prompted the client's request for help at this time. From this, the practitioner tries to find out the original objective hazardous event that started the stress-producing process and the client's reactions to it, that is, the vulnerable state that would include subjective reactions to the event and earlier attempts to cope with the situation. The practitioner also assesses the present state of active crisis and the extent of the client's inability to function. Finally, the practitioner makes a "running diagnosis" of the current situation and determines the most pressing aspect on which to concentrate. The practitioner presents his or her formulation to the client and they work out a tentative agreement (or contract) on their further activity, including specific goals, tasks, and a detailed working plan for the immediate future, including the number, time, and place of further contacts.

■ The middle phase concentrates on implementation: identifying and carrying out tasks designed to solve specific aspects of the crisis situation. The client is helped to modify previous inadequate or inappropriate ways of functioning and encouraged to try out new coping patterns. As he or she becomes more active in carrying out the tasks set up (and thus regaining the feeling of being in control) the practitioner becomes more passive, acting mainly as a sounding board and supporter. Particular attention is paid to building new relationships and developing or finding support systems in the community with others who have similar problems or are in similar situations.

■ The ending phase deals with termination. It involves reviewing the progress of the case since the client was first seen and recalling key themes that were uncovered, tasks that were carried out, and changes in behavior that were made. Future activity is projected for when the case is closed, leaving the client with the feeling of hope and the expectation that his or her situation can be further improved.

Strategies and Techniques. The overall strategy in crisis intervention is to increase the client's remobilization and return to the previous level of functioning or to an even higher level. Where lasting deficit has occurred, such as in the loss of a meaningful relationship or of part of the body, then effort is made to help the client achieve optimal functioning, despite the limitation. This means the practitioner must pay equal attention to both "material-arrangemental" tasks including the provision of concrete assistance and the working out of service arrangements such as child care and psychosocial tasks dealing with the client's feelings, doubts, ambivalence, anxieties, and despair that hamper efforts to regain control of his or her life.

Treatment techniques vary with the

worker's practice style and the stage of treatment. During the beginning phase, sustainment techniques (Hollis & Woods, 1981), designed to lower anxiety and provide emotional support, are frequently used, along with exploration and ventilation. During the middle phase, techniques of direct influence, geared to promote specific kinds of behavioral change, tend to predominate. Reflective discussion of the person-in-situation configuration is also used, both in the middle and ending phases.

Some practitioners prefer to use behavioral modification techniques (Fischer & Gochros, 1975; Schinke, 1981), particularly those of positive and negative reinforcement, shaping, modeling, coaching, and prompting. Others may use a gestalt or transactional analysis approach to promote active involvement and interaction between worker and client. Over time, most professionals using crisis intervention develop their own eclectic combination of methods and techniques that have proved most effective in their particular practice (Puryear, 1979).

Appropriate Clients. As crisis intervention has developed as a practice approach, a shift has occurred in its application. Although once it was recommended for the very strong or the very weak, it is now used much more flexibly because crises, both anticipated and unexpected, can—and do—affect all kinds of clients.

Social workers who have incorporated the crisis approach into their treatment repertoire often find it useful as a first line of treatment in a broad range of new and ongoing case situations in which recent disruption and change have occurred and the client's customary level of functioning has become seriously impaired. Three key indicators for its use are evidence of a clear-cut hazardous event that has direct bearing on the client's current state of disequilibrium: a high level of anxiety, discomfort, or pain coupled with demonstrated motivation and potential capacity for change; and evidence of a breakdown in problem-solving in the recent past.

Use with Families, Groups, and Communities. Although this discussion has focused primarily on individuals, the crisis approach implies direct work with families as well because most crisis situations develop within a family context. Much of the early theory by Caplan and Lindemann and those who followed was developed out of work with families (Glasser & Glasser, 1970; Langsley & Kaplan, 1968). In recent years, effort has been made to develop models that are particularly appropriate for work with families as a whole (Bonnefil, 1980).

In general, whether a family is considered to be in a state of collective crisis because of the role disruption of one of its members or whether one member's state of crisis acts as the hazardous event that disrupts the rest of the family system, interventive efforts should include evaluation of the family's strengths and weaknesses, of their capacities and motivation for change, and of the resources at their disposal, no matter who the designated client may be. Out of this, the family often becomes involved in a family-therapy program designed to improve communication patterns between members and resolve long-standing issues that have surfaced during the crisis situation (Janzen & Harris, 1980).

The crisis intervention approach has also been used with natural and formed small groups. Ever since the Benjamin Rush Center first started to use open-ended crisis groups as part of their treatment services (Strickler & Allgeyer, 1967), groups have become both targets for intervention and strategies in treatment. Crisis-oriented groups are frequently used as support systems to avoid hospitalization or institutionalization, to deal with potentially hazardous crises such as impending surgery and dislocation, to resolve parent-child or marital conflicts, and to mitigate acute eruptions among members of chronically disordered families or groups (Parad, Selby, & Quinlan, 1976).

On the community level, use of the crisis intervention approach in disasters and emergencies has become commonplace (Parad, Resnik, & Parad, 1976). Professional intervention at this level is often linked with programs for primary prevention or early intervention. At times, the practitioner becomes a consultant to set up new crisis services for community agencies (Webb, 1981). One vital aspect of this form of consultation is the ripple effect, in which the consultation's effect spreads from the direct interchange with the agency to unseen populations tangentially affected.

Current Research Efforts. For the most part, current research on the nature and effectiveness of crisis intervention has been limited to evaluative studies of existing programs. These have ranged from surveys of a large number of services such as one recent study that investigated the role of medical social workers in the delivery of emergency medical care in southern California (Parad, 1984) to the examination of one specific aspect of the treatment paradigm such as clinician-client interaction (Madonia, 1984).

In the Parad study, a major finding of particular interest was that clinical social workers in emergency medical services consider crisis counseling of families and patients regarding impending death, life crises, and serious illness to be a crucial part of their activities, but they experience lower job satisfaction and greater complications in the areas of burnout and stress management than other hospital social workers. Madonia found that workers operating autonomously in both clinical and community crisis programs focused their interventive efforts on helping clients understand the connections between their immediate precrisis situation, the precipitating factors, and the atmosphere of crisis in which they found themselves.

Other studies have produced evaluative descriptions of particular aspects of crisis services, such as the experiences of hotline counselors in responding to callers (Walfish, 1983) or how service is delivered in suicide prevention centers (Lester, 1979). Still others have examined clients' evaluation of services (Rudolph & Eng, 1981) and even community awareness of crisis centers (Snell & Broussard, 1978).

With all this, little systematic investigation of the outcome of crisis intervention as a method of treatment has been carried out. Two studies that did attempt to examine experimentally the outcome in crisis programs reported essentially negative results. Gottschalk, Fox, and Bates (1973) assigned applicants randomly to either a crisis treatment or waiting list group but found virtually no difference in pre-post measures of improvement. Williams, Lee, and Polak (1976) investigated the effects of crisis intervention on family survivors in sudden death situations and reported ambiguous outcomes. When measured six months after the death, they found that short-term crisis treatment seemed to have had no major impact on the families' postbereavement adjustment, although they appeared more capable of making decisions than those in the control group.

Discussing why a comparative study carried out at the Benjamin Rush Center ran into methodological difficulties, Jacobson (1980) pointed out the complexities in measuring outcome. The researchers did find, however, that both the experimental groups receiving crisis intervention and the control groups receiving brief visits and placebo medication were considered to have improved significantly. The experimental groups were also judged to have less need for further treatment, to have developed a better understanding of their life situation, to have developed new coping abilities, and to be less dependent than the control groups.

It may be that future empirical research on crisis intervention will have to await the development of more effective research instruments for measuring and comparing interventive techniques and outcomes that satisfy the validity requirements of both researchers and clinicians. The rapid pace, unpredictable direction, and intense involvement of staff members in crisis treatment programs tend to run counter to the meticulous planning and rigorous controls required by researchers. Although this has been a stumbling block in practice research generally, it becomes particularly evident in crisis intervention. Considerable work remains to be done in this area.

NAOMI GOLAN

For further information, see DIRECT PRACTICE IN SOCIAL WORK: OVERVIEW; DISASTERS AND DISASTER AID; ECOLOGICAL PERSPECTIVE; PSYCHOSOCIAL APPROACH.

References

Beck, D. (1962). *Patterns in Use of Family Agency Service*. New York: Family Service Association of America.

Bergman, A. (1976). "Emergency Room: A Role for Social Workers." *Health and Social Work, 1*(1), 32–44.

Bonnefil, M. C. (1980). "Crisis Intervention with Children and Families." In G. F. Jacobson (Ed.), *Crisis Intervention in the 1980's* (pp. 23–44). San Francisco, Calif.: Jossey-Bass.

Caplan, G. (1951). "A Public Health Approach to Child Psychiatry." *Mental Health, 35*, 235–249.

Caplan, G. (1964). *Principles of Preventive Psychiatry*. New York: Basic Books.

Caplan, G. (1974). *Support Systems and Community Mental Health*. New York: Basic Books.

Caplan, G., Mason, E. A., & Kaplan, D. M. (1965). "Four Studies of Crisis in Parents of Prematures." *Community Mental Health Journal*, 2(2), 150–159.

Cumming, J., & Cumming, E. (1962). *Ego and Milieu*. New York: Atherton Press.

Dohrenwend, B. S., & Dohrenwend, B. P. (Eds.). (1974). *Stressful Life Events: Their Nature and Effects*. New York: Wiley-Interscience.

Dublin, L. I. (1963). *Suicide: A Sociological and Statistical Study*. New York: Ronald Press.

Duvall, E. (1977). *Marriage and Family Development* (5th ed.). Philadelphia, Pa.: J. B. Lippincott Co.

Eliot, T. D. (1955). "Handling Family Strains and Shocks." In H. Becker & R. Hill (Eds.), *Family, Marriage, and Parenthood*. Boston, Mass.: D. C. Heath & Co.

Erikson, E. H. (1959). *Identity and the Life Cycle*. New York: International Universities Press.

Everstine, D. S., & Everstine, L. (1983). *People in Crisis: Strategic Therapeutic Interventions*. New York: Brunner/Mazel.

Farberow, N. L., & Schneidman, E. L. (1961). *The Cry for Help*. New York: McGraw-Hill Book Co.

Fischer, J., & Gochros, H. L. (1975). *Planned Behavioral Change: Behavioral Modification in Social Work*. New York: Free Press.

Foxman, J. (1976). "The Mobile Psychiatric Emergency Team." In H. J. Parad, H. L. P. Resnik, & L. G. Parad, *Emergency and Disaster Management* (pp. 35–44). Bowie, Md.: Charles Press.

Franz, J. (1980). "Being There: A 24-hour Emergency Crisis Care Center." *Children Today*, 9(1), 7–10.

Getzel, G. S. (1982). "Helping Elderly Couples in Crisis." *Social Casework*, 63(9), 515–521.

Glasser, P. H., & Glasser, L. N. (Eds.). (1970). *Families in Crisis*. New York: Harper & Row.

Golan, N. (1978). *Treatment in Crisis Situations*. New York: Free Press.

Golan, N. (1979). "Crisis Theory." In F. J. Turner (Ed.), *Social Work Treatment: Interlocking Theoretical Approaches* (2nd ed., pp. 499–533). New York: Free Press.

Golan, N. (1980). "Using Situational Crises to Ease Transitions in the Life Cycle." *American Journal of Orthopsychiatry*, 50(3), 542–550.

Golan, N. (1981). *Passing through Transitions: A Guide for Practitioners*. New York: Free Press.

Gottschalk, L. A., Fox, R. A., & Bates, D. E. (1973). "A Study of Prediction and Outcome in a Mental Health Crisis Clinic." *American Journal of Psychiatry*, 130, 1107–1111.

Hamilton, G. (1940). *Theory and Practice of Social Casework*. New York: Columbia University Press.

Havighurst, R. J. (1953). *Human Development and Education*. London, England: Longmans, Green & Co.

Hill, R. (1958). "Generic Features of Families under Stress." *Social Casework*, 39(1), 139–150.

Hollis, F., & Woods, M. E. (1981). *Casework: A Psychosocial Therapy* (3rd ed.). New York: Random House.

Holmes, T. H., & Rahe, R. H. (1967). "The Social Readjustment Rating Scale." *Journal of Psychosomatic Research*, 11, 213–218.

Jacobson, G. F. (Ed.). (1980). *Crisis Intervention in the 1980's*. San Francisco, Calif.: Jossey-Bass.

Jacobson, G., et al. (1965). "The Scope and Practice of an Early Access Brief Treatment Psychiatric Center." *American Journal of Psychiatry*, 121, 1176–1182.

Jacobson, G., Strickler, M., & Morley, W. E. (1968). "Generic and Individual Approaches to Crisis Intervention." *American Journal of Public Health*, 58, 338–343.

Janis, I. (1958). *Psychological Stress*. New York: John Wiley & Sons.

Kaplan, D. M. (1962). "A Concept of Acute Situational Disorders." *Social Work*, 7(4), 15–23.

Kaplan, D. M. (1982). "Intervention for Disorders of Change." *Social Work*, 27(5), 404–410.

Klein, D. C., & Lindemann, E. (1961). "Preventive Intervention in Individual and Family Crisis Situations." In G. Caplan (Ed.), *Prevention of Mental Disorders in Children* (pp. 283–305). New York: Basic Books.

Korner, I. N. (1973). "Crisis Reduction and the Psychological Consultant." In G. A. Specter & W. Claiborn (Eds.), *Crisis Intervention* (pp. 30–45). New York: Behavioral Publications.

Langsley, D. G., & Kaplan, D. M. (1968). *Treatment of Families in Crisis*. New York: Grune & Stratton.

Lazarus, R. S. (1966). *Psychological Stress and the Coping Process*. New York: McGraw-Hill Book Co.

LeMasters, E. E. (1957). "Parenthood as Crisis." *Marriage and Family Living*, 19(4), 352–355.

Lester, D. (1979). "The Evaluation of Suicide Prevention Centers." *Crisis Intervention*, 10(4), 144–160.

Levinson, D. J., et al. (1978). *The Seasons of a Man's Life*. New York: Alfred A. Knopf.

Lieberman, M. A. (1975). "Adaptive Processes in Late Life." In N. Datan & L. H. Ginsberg (Eds.), *Normative Life Crises* (pp. 139–159). New York: Academic Press.

Lindemann, E. (1944). "Symptomatology and

Management of Acute Grief.'' *American Journal of Psychiatry, 101*(2), 7–21.

Lopez, D. J., & Getzel, G. S. (1984). ''Helping Gay AIDS Patients in Crisis.'' *Social Casework, 65*(7), 387–394.

Lowenthal, M. F., Thurnher, M., & Chiriboga, D. (1975). *Four Stages of Life.* San Francisco, Calif.: Jossey-Bass.

Madonia, J. F. (1984). ''Clinical and Supervisory Aspects of Crisis Intervention.'' *Social Casework, 65*(6), 364–368.

McCubbin, I., et al. (Eds.). (1974). *Family Separation and Reunion.* San Diego, Calif.: Center for Prisoners of War Studies, Naval Research Center.

McGee, R. (1974). *Crisis Intervention in the Community.* Baltimore, Md.: University Park Press.

Moos, R. H. (Ed.). (1977). *Coping With Physical Illness.* New York: Plenum Press.

Murphy, L. B. (1962). *The Widening World of Childhood.* New York: Basic Books.

Neugarten, B. L. (1969). ''Continuities and Discontinuities of Psychological Issues into Adult Life.'' *Human Development, 12,* 121–122.

Neugarten, B. L. (1976). ''Adaptation and the Life Cycle.'' *Counseling Psychologist, 6*(1), 16–20.

Noam, G. C., Higgins, R. O., & Goethals, G. W. (1982). ''Psychoanalytic Approaches to Development Psychology.'' In B. W. Wolman (Ed.), *Handbook of Developmental Psychology* (pp. 23–43). Englewood Cliffs, N.J.: Prentice-Hall.

Parad, H. J. (1961). ''Preventive Casework: Problems and Implications.'' In *Social Welfare Forum* (pp. 178–193). New York: Columbia University Press.

Parad, H. J. (1977). ''Crisis Intervention.'' In *Encyclopedia of Social Work* (17th ed., pp. 228–237). Washington, D.C.: National Association of Social Workers.

Parad, H. J. (1984). *Role of the Social Worker in Emergency Medical Care.* Unpublished recommendations of the summary report of the project findings, University of Southern California, Los Angeles.

Parad, H. J., & Parad, L. G. (1968a). ''A Study of Crisis-Oriented Short-Term Treatment'' (Part 1). *Social Casework, 49*(6), 346–355.

Parad, H. J., & Parad, L. G. (1968b). ''A Study of Crisis-Oriented Short-Term Treatment'' (Part 2). *Social Casework, 49*(7), 418–426.

Parad, H. J., Resnik, H. L. P., & Parad, L. G. (Eds.). (1976). *Disaster Management.* Bowie, Md.: Charles Press.

Parad, H. J., Selby, L., & Quinlan, J. (1976). ''Crisis Intervention with Families and Groups.'' In R. W. Roberts & H. Northen (Eds.), *Theories of Social Work with Groups*

(pp. 304–330). New York: Columbia University Press.

Perlman, H. H. (1963). ''Some Notes on the Waiting List.'' *Social Casework, 44*(4), 200–205.

Piaget, J. (1963). *The Origins of Intelligence in Children.* New York: W. W. Norton & Co.

Puryear, D. A. (1979). *Helping People in Crisis.* San Francisco, Calif.: Jossey-Bass.

Rapoport, L. (1962). ''The State of Crisis: Some Theoretical Considerations.'' *Social Service Review, 36*(2), 211–217.

Rapoport, L. (1970). ''Crisis Intervention as a Model of Brief Treatment.'' In R. W. Roberts & R. H. Nee (Eds.), *Theories of Social Casework* (pp. 267–311). Chicago: University of Chicago Press.

Rapoport, R. (1963). ''Normal Crisis, Family Structure, and Mental Health.'' *Family Process, 2,* 68–80.

Reid, W. J., & Epstein, L. (1972). *Task-Centered Casework.* New York: Columbia University Press.

Reid, W. J., & Shyne, A. W. (1969). *Brief and Extended Casework.* New York: Columbia University Press.

Reynolds, B. C. (1963). *An Uncharted Journey.* New York: Citadel Press.

Rich, M. E. (1956). *A Belief in People.* New York: Family Service Association of America.

Riegel, K. R. (1975). ''Adult Life Crises: A Dialectic Interpretation of Development.'' In N. Datan & L. H. Ginsberg (Eds.), *Life-Span Developmental Psychology: Normative Life Crises* (pp. 99–128). New York: Academic Press.

Rhodes, S. L. (1977). ''A Developmental Approach to the Life Cycle of the Family.'' *Social Casework, 58,* 301–311.

Ripple, L. (1964). *Motivation, Capacity, and Opportunity.* Chicago: University of Chicago Press.

Rudolph, B. A., & Eng, A. M. (1981). ''Client Evaluation of Short-Term Stress Response Psychotherapy in a Community Mental Health Center.'' *Crisis Intervention, 12*(1), 2–12.

Schinke, P. S. (Ed.). (1981). *Behavioral Methods in Social Welfare.* New York: Aldine Publishing Co.

Selye, H. (1956). *The Stress of Life.* New York: McGraw-Hill Book Co.

Shyne, A. (1957). ''What Research Tells Us About Short-Term Cases in Family Agencies.'' *Social Casework, 38*(3), 223–231.

Snell, L., & Broussard, N. T. (1978). ''An Assessment of Community Awareness of Crisis Intervention Centers.'' *Crisis Intervention, 9*(4), 134–138.

Strickler, M., & Allgeyer, J. (1967). ''The Crisis Groups: A New Application of Crisis Theory.'' *Social Work, 12*(2), 28–32.

Taplin, J. R. (1971). "Crisis Theory: Critique and Reformation." *Community Mental Health Journal, 7*(1), 13–23.

Vaillant, G. E. (1977). *Adaptation to Life*. Boston, Mass.: Little, Brown & Co.

Vera, M. I. (1981). "Rape Crisis Intervention in the Emergency Room: A New Challenge for Social Work." *Social Work in Health Care, 6*(3), 1–11.

Walfish, S. (1983). "Crisis Telephone Counselors' Views of Clinical Interaction Situations." *Community Mental Health Journal, 19*(3), 219–226.

Webb, N. B. (1981). "Crisis Consultation: Preventive Implications." *Social Casework: The Journal of Contemporary Social Work, 62*(8), 465–471.

White, R. W. (1959). "Motivation Reconsidered: The Concept of Competence." *Psychological Review, 66*(3), 297–333.

Williams, W., Lee, J. L., & Polak, P. R. (1976). "Crisis Intervention: Effects of Crisis Intervention on Family Survivors in Sudden Death Situations." *Community Mental Health Journal, 12*(2), 128–136.

For Further Reading

Burgess, A. W., & Baldwin, B. A. (1981). *Crisis Intervention Theory and Practice: A Clinical Handbook*. Englewood Cliffs, N.J.: Prentice-Hall.

Duggan, H. A. (1984). *Crisis Intervention: Helping Individuals at Risk*. Lexington, Mass.: D. C. Heath & Co.

Hodges, W. F., et al. (1984). "The Cumulative Effect of Stress on Preschool Children of Divorced and Intact Families." *Journal of Marriage and The Family, 46*(3), 611–617.

Morley, E. (1980). "Crisis Intervention with Adults." In G. F. Jacobson (Ed.), *Crisis Intervention in the 1980's* (pp. 11–21). San Francisco, Calif.: Jossey-Bass.

Umana, R. F., Gross, S. J., & McConville, M. T. (1980). *Crisis in the Family: Three Approaches*. New York: Gardner Press.

CURRICULUM. See Appendix 2: CSWE CURRICULUM POLICY STATEMENT; CONTINUING EDUCATION; SOCIAL WORK EDUCATION; PROFESSIONAL ASSOCIATIONS: COUNCIL ON SOCIAL WORK EDUCATION.

DAY, DOROTHY. See biographical section.

DAY CARE. See CHILD CARE SERVICES; CHILD WELFARE SERVICES.

DAY CENTERS: ADULT

The cost of health services for the elderly has reached a point of national fiscal crisis that is forcing the federal government to reexamine and even reverse the direction of some health and social service policies in order to reduce expenditure. Growth of the elderly population, especially of the chronically impaired 85 years of age and older; expansion of services reimbursed by Medicaid, Medicare, and Title XX or covered by Title III; and inflationary costs of service provision have been evident since the early 1970s.

During the same period, adult day care programs for the aged, including day centers and day hospitals, were introduced by the federal government through a series of research and demonstration grants authorized by Congress. The rationale for experimenting with this service concept was based on the intention of developing therapeutic alternatives that were less costly than nursing home care. Some of the specific questions to be answered through funded day care research and demonstration were: (1) How many days of institutional care can day care centers and hospitals prevent, and at what cost savings? (2) How many and what types of persons can return to or continue in independent living as a result of services? (3) What particular services are most effective in reducing or eliminating institutionalization? (4) What are the characteristics of the elderly who benefit most from services? (5) What is the impact of the services on families who care for the aged at home (Weiler & Rathbone-McCuan, 1978)?

In Great Britain, where day care services were first introduced in the 1960s, the concept was conceived with great flexibility, and the anticipated outcomes were not related primarily to assurance of lower costs.

Research and demonstration projects were somewhat secondary in British service expansion, and health and social service providers began to make psychogeriatric day hospitals, geriatric day hospitals, and day care centers available within the community (Brocklehurst, 1970; Farndale, 1961). Brocklehurst (1976) estimated that by the mid-seventies 150,000 to 250,000 British elderly were being served in different types of day programs. In 1980, there were an estimated 617 adult day care centers serving an average of about 13,500 old persons per day (Billings, 1982).

U.S. Approach

The introduction of day care concepts into the United States, although originally stimulated by the British model, has been different because of the overall variations in health, long-term policy, and the structures of long-term care continuums in the two countries. The approach in the United States has been to separate the medical and social components of long-term care and to create different legislative policies to deal with them.

A general definition of adult day care that is applicable to many American programs was established by Congress in 1980:

> Services provided on a regular basis, but less than 24 hours per day, to an individual in a multi-purpose senior center, intermediate care facility or agency for the handicapped or other facility licensed by the state, which are provided because such individual is unable to be left alone during the day time hours but does not require institutionalization. Such services may include (but are not limited to) provision of meals, personal care, recreational and educational activities, physical and vocational rehabilitation, and health care services. (U.S. Senate, 1980)

The evolution of the definition of day care centers—whom they serve, what services they provide, and how costs are handled—has been among the points of professional and public policy debate. First, the concept of day care is broad and applicable to diverse subpopulations of the elderly. Second, definitions developed for third-party reimbursement attempt to limit the scope of services, whereas service professionals have tended to be expansive, pushing for a broad scope of services. The National Institute on

Adult Day Care, operated by the National Council on Aging, recommends that a more general definition be applied to ensure the continuation of innovative health and social service programming.

Robins (1981) proposed that day care programs be clustered according to the primary functions of restoration, maintenance, and social services. Her approach suggested a breakdown of programs based on service patterns and client needs. The issue of definition has been especially relevant in view of third-party reimbursement. In order to obtain third-party reimbursement and continue operation, many programs have had to drop certain service components, especially social and recreational ones. Over the years, this has promoted a medicalization of day care.

Padula (1983) as well as Weiler and Rathbone-McCuan (1978) have presented profiles of services provided in day care centers. Programs emphasizing restoration have invested resources to assure the availability of overall health care combined with such alternative services as physical, speech, and occupational therapy. Many of these programs accept only clients with clear potential for rehabilitation. Maintenance programs may offer some of the same services, but there is less emphasis on regaining functional levels because rehabilitation is not the predominant criterion of participation. Maintenance programs tend to balance health and social services through a team approach directed by social workers and nurses. These programs often apply to elderly people who have already achieved maximum gains and need support to maintain them. Socially oriented centers continue to utilize a range of individual and group services that deal with isolation, socialization, and behavioral management goals. Many clients suffer from depression or cognitive impairment but have no prior history of mental institutionalization.

Under the auspices of the National Council on Aging, Isaacs (1981) completed a comprehensive survey of 34 states that maintained state-level standards and of the definitions that had been applied in setting those standards. At that point, the majority of states with reimbursement for day care centers used either Title XX or Title III funding. Medicare was (and remains) the least applicable source of third-party reimbursement, because it predominantly covers acute hos-

pital and skilled nursing home care, physicians' services, and limited home health care. Typically, only rehabilitative day hospitals connected to medical facilities can expect Medicare payment. However, new discharge policies encouraging early hospital departures by impaired elderly patients may force reconsideration of the posthospital treatment potential of day care programs.

Reimbursement Issues

From the onset, day care financing has been entangled with Medicaid reimbursement issues. Under federal guidelines, states are now permitted to include in their Medicaid reimbursement plans adult day health care comprising medical and social services. In 1983 the Health Care Coordination Act amended Title XIX of the Social Security Act (Medicaid) to authorize any state—subject to approval of a waiver of Medicaid requirements by the Department of Health and Human Services (DHHS)—to establish long-term care as part of its state plan. States applying the waiver option must report in detail at least once a year to the Secretary of Health and Human Services because the waivers may be renewable for additional three-year periods (U.S. Senate, 1983). Many states, such as New York, limit the application of waivers for day care services. Nationally, waivers tend to be applied to the medical models of day care services.

The past decade of activity aimed at obtaining a secure reimbursement base, increasing the number of day care centers, and interconnecting them to the community care network has been both facilitated and thwarted by research. The historical progression of day care research has moved from studies that compared general day care service to nursing home or home health care to studies that include day care as part of large-scale research to evaluate cost benefits in long-term care systems. Challenges to the cost-benefit data on day care services, to programs' ability to equalize nursing home care at lower cost, or actually to prevent institutionalization were presented in the research by Weissert (1976, 1977, 1978) and by Weissert, Wan, and Livieratos (1979). However, other evaluators (Weiler, 1980; Shinn, 1980; Clauser, 1980; Tufts & Hall, 1980; Zawadski, 1980; Klapfish, 1980; Baker, 1980) have produced alternative interpretations, showing that the methodological limitations of Weissert's information precluded much substantiation of his findings about the lack of day care cost-benefit effectiveness.

It is the author's assessment that the first phase of research and demonstration projects served to introduce the concept of day care into the American system, to develop some working models of day care, and to stimulate health practitioners and administrators to continue their efforts to ensure some level of day care access for the elderly. Later research served to reinforce an ongoing underutilization of Title XVIII and XIX coverage. It enabled Title XX coverage, in the form of social services block grants, to be realized in many states, placing day care in the continuum of services some states finance through the Older Americans Act.

Future Questions

As the federal government moves toward a better understanding of what it means to develop a backup system of formal services for the informal caregivers of the elderly, there may be a renewal of interest in day care centers. McAuley and Arling (1984) note that the question for the future is how to mix formal and informal care in home, community, and institutional settings. Day care centers have demonstrated their value for supporting family care. Sands and Suzuki (1983) have noted the value of day care programs for Alzheimer's patients and their families, and Bernard (1984) has suggested a range of possibilities for combining voluntary services through limited day care access for the mentally impaired elderly and their relatives.

Reinterpretation of the day care concept, stressing its dual value for both the severely impaired elderly and those caring for them, may be an underplayed point. To the extent that day care helps to bring elderly people and their families out of the isolation of homebound care, it may make an even more valuable contribution. If, through cost-containment policies, care of the aged becomes an enforced family function, day care centers could become the most effective and desirable respite resource in the long-term care system.

ELOISE RATHBONE-McCUAN

For further information, see AGED: SERVICES; DE-INSTITUTIONALIZATION; LONG-TERM CARE; PROTECTIVE SERVICES FOR THE AGED.

References

Baker, J. A. (1980). "Critique of the Weissert Study." *Home Health Care Services Quarterly*, 1(3), 114–121.
Bernard, M. (1984). "Voluntary Care for the Elder Mentally Infirm and Their Relatives: A British Example." *Gerontologist*, 24(2), 116–119.
Billings, G. (1982). "Alternative to Nursing Home Care: An Update." *Aging*, 325–326, 2–11.
Brocklehurst, J. C. (1970). *The Geriatric Day Hospital*. London: King Edward's Hospital.
Brocklehurst, J. C. (1976). "The British Experience with Day Care and Day Hospital." In E. Pfeiffer (Ed.), *Day Care For Older Adults* (pp. 52–57). Durham, N.C.: Duke University Center for the Study of Aging and Human Development.
Clauser, S. B. (1980). "Comments on the 222 Adult Day Care and Homemaker Service Experiments." *Home Health Care Services Quarterly*, 1(3), 103–106.
Farndale, J. (1961). *The Day Hospital Movement in Great Britain*. London: Pergamon Press.
Isaacs, B. (1981). *A Description and Analysis of Adult Day Care Standards in the United States*. Unpublished manuscript, National Council on Aging, Washington, D.C.
Klapfish, A. (1980). "Problems with the Weissert Report's Conclusion About Day Health Services." *Home Health Care Services Quarterly*, 1(3), 112–114.
McAuley, W. J., & Arling, P. (1984). "Use of In-Home Care by Very Old People," *Journal of Health and Social Behavior*, 25(1), 55–63.
Padula, H. (1983). *Developing Adult Day Care: An Approach to Maintaining Independence for Impaired Older Persons* (Monograph). Washington: D.C.: National Council on Aging.
Robins, E. G. (1981). "Adult Day Care: Growing Fast but Still for Lucky Few." *Generations*, 6(2), 22–23.
Sands, D., & Suzuki, T. (1983). "Adult Day Care For Alzheimer's Patients and Their Families." *Gerontologist*, 23(4), 330–339.
Shinn, E. (1980). "Critique of the Section 222 Day Care and Homemaker Experimental Study." *Home Health Care Services Quarterly*, 1(3), 99–103.
Tufts, J., & Hall, H. D. (1980). "Reaction to Weissert Report." *Home Health Care Services Quarterly*, 1(3), 106–107.
U.S. Senate. (1980). 96th Congress, 2nd Session. S. Bill 2809. *Comprehensive Community Based Non-Institutional Long-Term Care Services for the Elderly and Disabled* (p. 4).
U.S. Senate. (1983). 98th Congress, 2nd Session.

S. Bill 1614. *Developments in Aging: 1983* (Vol. 1, pp. 440–441).

Weiler, P. G. (1980). "Response to the Study Effects and Costs of Day Care and Homemaker Services for the Chronically Ill: A Randomized Experiment." *Home Health Care Services Quarterly, 1*(3), 97–99.

Weiler, P. G., & Rathbone-McCuan, E. (1978). *Adult Day Care: Community Work with the Elderly.* New York: Springer Publishing Co.

Weissert, W. (1976). "Two Models of Geriatric Day Care: Findings from a Comparative Model." *Gerontologist, 16*(3), 420–427.

Weissert, W. (1977). "Adult Day Care Programs in the United States: Current Research Projects and a Survey of 10 Centers," *Public Health Reports, 92*(1), 49–56.

Weissert, W. (1978). "Costs of Adult Day Care: A Comparison to Nursing Homes." *Inquiry, 15*(1), 10–19.

Weissert, W., Wan, T., & Livieratos, B. (1979). *Effects and Costs of Day Care and Homemaker Services for the Chronically Ill: A Randomized Experiment* (DHEW Publication No. PHS 79-3250). Hyattsville, Md., National Center for Health Services Research.

Zawadski, R. T. (1980). "Methodological Constraints on the Medicare 222 Day Care/Homemaker Demonstration Project," *Home Health Care Services Quarterly, 1*(3), 109–112.

DEATH AND DYING. See HOSPICE; LOSS AND BEREAVEMENT.

DE FOREST, ROBERT WEEKS. See biographical section.

DEINSTITUTIONALIZATION

Since the early 1900s, national policy has gradually come to reflect the search for an alternative to institutional care and control as the preferred solution to social problems. Deinstitutionalization, as the policy has become known, developed along different lines among populations that were traditionally subject to care and control in large institutions—for example, the aged, children, the mentally ill, the developmentally disabled, and criminal offenders. As it pertains to each of these groups, "deinstitutionalization" is best defined by a 1977 U.S. General Accounting Office (GAO) report:

> the process of (1) preventing both unnecessary admission to and retention in institutions; (2) finding and developing appropriate alternatives in the community for housing, treatment, training, education, and rehabilitation of [persons] who do not need to be in institutions, and (3) improving conditions, care, and treatment for those who need to have institutional care. This approach is based on the principle that . . . persons are entitled to live in the least restrictive environment necessary and lead lives as normally and independently as they can. (p. 1)

Although this definition reflects the broad aims of the policy of deinstitutionalization, the most discernible consequence of the policy has been the reduction of the average daily census of large institutions that deal with problem populations. This article will first discuss some of the reasons why the deinstitutionalization movement took hold. Then the consequences that deinstitutionalization produces for various populations will be considered.

Origins of Deinstitutionalization

Deinstitutionalization did not come about for any single reason. The following influences combined to make deinstitutionalization seem attractive and feasible: (1) the negative effects of institutionalization documented by journalists and social scientists; (2) the growing costs of institutional care relative to its alternatives; (3) advances in social, psychological, and medical sciences that were thought to make the confinement and isolation functions of the institution obsolete; (4) the development of the civil rights movement, which emphasized the protection of individuals' due process rights and the necessity to approach care and treatment in the least restrictive manner; and (5) the development of an extensive system of public aid that allowed the maintenance function of institutions (in-kind room and board) to be replaced by a system of cash grants to clients. This last development, in particular, created a state-subsidized market for the local provision of care by the private sector.

All these trends were supported and created by a unique coalition that spanned the political spectrum. Conservatives viewed the reduction of institutional censuses as a means of saving money, and liberals supported the standards of professional groups who saw in deinstitutionalization the most humane and effective approach to the organization of care. There was little political opposition to deinstitutionalization, other than that of groups such as the California State Employees' Association, which was interested primarily in maintaining its members' jobs in state institutions. Without organized political opposition, and with many groups in the political community viewing deinstitutionalization as a means to an end, the policy gained momentum.

The GAO definition of deinstitutionalization, especially of its three main components, provides a structure that can be used to review the progress of deinstitutionalization as it affects the populations to which it is addressed. A reordering of these components can aid in understanding the general process of deinstitutionalization. Consideration will be given to (1) the goal of improving the care and treatment of those who need institutional care; (2) the need for preventing both unnecessary admission to and retention in institutions; and (3) the process of finding and developing appropriate alternatives in the community for housing, treating, training, educating, and rehabilitating those who do not need institutionalization.

In general, efforts to improve institutional conditions have been linked with an increase in the cost of institutional care. In various right-to-treatment decisions in the mental health, child welfare, and developmental disability fields, the courts have specified the types of treatment to which involuntarily detained patients have a right and the types of treatment they may refuse. The courts have also specified patient-to-staff ratios and have defined parameters of overcrowding (*Donaldson v. O'Connor,* 1974; *Wyatt v. Stickney,* 1972; *Bartley v. Kremens,* 1975).

The expense of carrying out these orders has often prompted institutional officials to reduce patient or inmate loads rather than increase staff or construct new facilities. In California, for example, the majority of correctional institutions are about 100 years old.

The cost of constructing new cells ranges from \$20,000 to \$30,000 per cell. In addition, it may cost up to \$20,000 a year to maintain a single offender in a correctional institution (Carney, 1977). Although the large institution has become both costly and obsolete, its demise may not occur in the near future.

It is estimated that 20 to 50 percent of homeless people in the United States come from the ranks of the deinstitutionalized. This has led to public condemnation of the policy and—coupled with the lack of a viable alternative—to an ambivalent reinvestment in rapidly deteriorating institutional facilities. The total increase of \$36 million in California's 1984 mental health budget has gone toward remodeling the state's hospital facilities. In some instances, this effort is fiscally motivated—for example, hospitals' desire for reaccreditation in order to qualify for federal Medicaid funds. In others, the goal is to save hospital beds in an institutional system whose population cannot be further reduced without bringing about inhumane consequences.

Deinstitutionalizing Five Populations

The major effort of the deinstitutionalization movement has been to prevent unnecessary admissions to institutions and to reduce both the rate and length of retention of individuals in institutions. The relationship between these efforts and the development of appropriate community-based alternatives will be explored with respect to five populations: the mentally ill, the developmentally disabled, criminal offenders, children, and the aged.

Mentally Ill. In 1950, the most prevalent form of institutionalization was admission to a mental hospital. These institutions have been most affected by the deinstitutionalization movement. The census of state and county mental hospitals plummeted by 77 percent from a high of 558,922 in 1955 to a low of 126,359 in 1981. Unpublished estimates indicate that the population continues to decrease. At the end of 1982, the estimated number of resident patients in 277 state and county mental hospitals was 125,000; this figure decreased to 120,000 at the end of 1983 (Mandersheid, 1985).

Although the resident population fell drastically, admissions to state and county mental hospitals increased between 1950 and 1970, finally leveling off after 1970. In 1950, in state and county mental hospitals, there were 152,286 admissions and 512,501 residents—a ratio of .297 admissions for every resident. In contrast, by 1970 there were 348,511 admissions and 337,619 residents—a ratio of 1.4 admissions for every resident. This ratio increased to 1.74 in 1974 (Kramer, 1977), and in 1981 it was 2.83 (358,087 admissions and 126,359 residents) (National Institute of Mental Health, 1985). Thus, in the mental health field, a "revolving door" process of brief hospitalization had led to increasingly high admission rates and short periods of retention.

Justification for this activity came from several points of view. Studies that compared short- and long-term treatment in mental institutions were unable to demonstrate the effectiveness of the latter. In fact, studies that compared hospital treatment to community treatment combined with psychoactive medications supported the community-based approach. The first major clinical trials were used to convince the public that psychoactive medications were a solution to the control of mental health symptomology, thus serving as a justification for trusting patients outside the confines of mental institutions. Patients were to use the hospital merely to have their medication adjusted over a period of time.

Perhaps the major factor in the reduction of the patient population of state mental hospitals was the 1962 decision of the then U.S. Department of Health, Education, and Welfare (HEW) to revise its policies to allow federal matching funds to be used by state public assistance programs for the support of individuals released from mental hospitals. The HEW reinterpretation made categorical aid available to former mental patients through the Aid to the Totally Disabled program (now the Supplemental Security program of the Social Security Act). This action provided support for the maintenance of mental patients in local communities, substituting cash assistance for institutional confinement and simultaneously providing an economic stimulus for the development of community-based residential care.

Ultimately, the civil rights movement put an end to long-term hospitalization. With elimination of indefinite commitment to state mental hospitals and restriction of involun- tary detention to brief periods of time, long-term residence in mental hospitals effectively ceased.

The political coalition that engineered the demise of state mental institutions did not survive to foster the development of alternative care for those who required supportive living arrangements. Most individuals were returned to the community to live either on their own or with their families. A significant proportion—between 10 and 30 percent— went to live in alternative institutions or in sheltered living arrangements, the latter including foster or family care homes, board and care homes, supervised hotels, and halfway houses (Segal & Aviram, 1978). In many respects, a large proportion of these supervised living arrangements were similar to large mental institutions in character and institutional environment. However, they functioned as smaller administrative entities within local communities.

Developmentally Disabled. The deinstitutionalization of the developmentally disabled resulted in large part from the fact that they were maintained in the same institutions as the mentally ill. In 1950, state and county mental hospitals housed 48,000 developmentally disabled residents—27 percent of all developmentally disabled residents in public institutions. By 1981, the number had decreased to 7,831—only 6 percent of developmentally disabled residents in such institutions. Thus, there was an 84 percent decline in the developmentally disabled population of state and county mental institutions. However, during this period there was also an increase in the number of residents of facilities specializing in services to the developmentally disabled. Between 1950 and 1967, this population rose from 176,000 to 193,000, where it peaked. It has declined steadily to 152,000 in 1979; 124,165 in 1981; and 117,850 in 1982 (Lerman, 1982; Rotegard & Bruininks, 1983).

As with the deinstitutionalization of the mentally ill, the deinstitutionalization of the developmentally disabled was prodded by landmark decisions such as *Wyatt v. Stickney* (1972), which dealt with the right to treatment, and decisions related to housing individuals in the least restrictive environments. The movement of the developmentally disabled into the community has also been fostered by the increasing costs of improving institutions, combined with the advent of new technologies, communications, and the concept of normalization (that is, the treatment of people in an environment most closely approximating a normal situation).

Also, as with the mentally ill, most developmentally disabled individuals go on to live with their families or on their own. However, a significant proportion are housed in smaller community-based facilities, foster homes, board and care homes, and some large group homes that begin to approximate the formal character that is typical of many large institutions.

Criminal Offenders. On December 31, 1983, nearly 1.4 percent (or 1,410 per 100,000) of the adult population was either on probation or parole or in prison or jail. The scale of community programs for offenders is now greater than at any other time in history. In 1983, there were 1,502,247 adults on probation in the United States. This figure represents an increase of 38 percent in the probation population since 1979 (Bureau of Justice Statistics, 1984b). By 1977, at least 28 States offered some form of community residential programming for adult felons. At the federal level, the United States Bureau of Prisons established 14 such programs between 1965 and 1973. In 1977, 42 states were operating furlough programs. In the United states, as many as 40,000 offenders enter halfway houses annually (Hylton, 1981).

Although the use of community programming designed to reduce the potential population of prisons has come to characterize the criminal justice system in the United States, the national prison census has continued to grow, spawning controversial measures to finance the construction of new county jails and state prisons. The number of individuals under the jurisdiction of state and federal prisons rose from 307,276 in 1978 to 438,380 in 1983, an increase of 43 percent. Similarly, the population of county jails grew from 158,394 to 223,551 in the same time period, an increase of 41 percent (Bureau of Justice Statistics, 1984a, 1984c).

The implementation of stronger penalties for some crimes notwithstanding, this trend is in part a result of the maturation of the baby boom generation—that is, the coming of age of a huge birth cohort now passing through the young adult period, in which the highest arrest rate traditionally prevails. Thus, while alternatives to institutionalization have proliferated, the pressure on the correctional system to confine large numbers of people has increased dramatically.

Children. The shift to community-based foster home care for dependent and neglected youths dates back to the early part of the twentieth century and represents the first departure from the principle of institutional care. The shift from institutional care to foster care is now being followed by a national drive to find permanent homes for foster children. The U.S. Department of Health and Human Services (HHS) notes that the number of children in foster care dropped from 500,000 in 1977 to 243,000 in 1982 and that the average time spent in care went from 47 months in 1977 to 35 in 1982. Further, the number of children in foster care who were available for adoption dropped from 102,000 in 1977 to 50,000 in 1982 ("A Place," 1984).

For the population of youths under 18, the rate of use of child welfare institutions between 1933 and 1973 decreased by 48 percent (Lerman, 1982). In 1980, the U.S. Bureau of the Census reported that there were 167,306 institutional residents under 18. In children's institutions, the overall capacity for residential care (that is, the number of beds) remained approximately the same between 1966 (171,222) and 1981 (172,939). More important, child welfare institutions now focus primarily on children with special problems rather than on the more general functions of the children's home.

Trends in institutional care may be further delineated by distinguishing—according to the primary type of children and youths they serve—five specialized streams of group residential facilities: child welfare (facilities for dependent, neglected, and abused children); juvenile justice; mental health; substance abuse; and facilities that provide care for pregnant adolescents. Between 1965 and 1981, the number of facilities in the child welfare stream—1,424 and 1,770, respectively—remained about the same; juvenile justice facilities tripled from 647 to 1,642, and mental health facilities increased almost fourfold, from 315 to 1,204. Drug abuse treatment facilities—a category that was not even identified in 1966—numbered 85 in 1981. Only those facilities that served pregnant adolescents declined in number, from 212 in 1965 to 115 in 1981.

These figures indicate a redistribution of function within a relatively stable system—that is, no large increases in bed capacity. Further, they illustrate the shift away from the larger congregate facilities to smaller group residences. Facilities with 7 to 12 residents increased in number by 898 percent between 1965 and 1981. However, they still accounted for only 11 percent of the total bed capacity, compared to 12 percent in facilities with the capacity to serve more than 300 children (Dore, Young, & Pappenfort, 1984).

Some institutions have engaged merely in relabeling processes that are often spurred by the availability of categorical payments—for example, children's institutions have become treatment centers for emotionally disturbed children. Although national data for 1970, 1971, and 1973 indicate a 10 percent reduction in the number of dependent and neglected children living in child welfare institutions, they also show a similar increase in the number of children classified as emotionally disturbed (Lerman, 1982). Recent trends in the deinstitutionalization of juvenile status offenders in California show a similar tendency toward relabeling and confinement in specialized child welfare institutions or mental health facilities (Van Dusen, 1981).

Aged. From the early 1900s to the present, there has been a steady growth in the institutionalization of the aged in the United States. The population of the elderly residing in group quarters of one type or another increased 267 percent between 1910 and 1970. In 1940, census data showed that the institutionalized aged constituted 4.1 percent of the total aged population: 40.5 percent were in noninstitutional group quarters (hotels, boarding houses, and the like); 33 percent, in homes for the aged, infirm, and needy (nursing homes and personal care and residential homes); and 23 percent, in mental institutions (Estes & Harrington, 1981).

Between 1960 and 1980, however, there was a 71 percent decrease in the proportion of the aged living in mental institutions, a 13 percent decrease in the proportion of aged residents of noninstitutional group quarters, and a 318 percent increase in the proportion of the aged living in homes for the aged (nursing homes and personal care and residential care homes). By 1980, 1,340,242 elderly people lived in institutions. Of those, 92 percent resided in homes for the aged; 4 percent, in other institutional group quarters; and 4 percent, in mental institutions. In 1980, the total proportion of the elderly living in institutions had risen to 5.3 percent (U.S. Bureau of the Census, 1980). This increase is largely explained by the growth of the nursing home industry. In 1982, a Senate special committee projected that the population of nursing homes will grow to 1,952,000 by the year 2000 and to 2,952,000 by the year 2030 (U.S. Senate, 1984).

Three major federal programs have had a direct impact on the private nursing home and residential care industry: the Social Security Act of 1935, Medicare, and Medicaid. The Social Security Act provided funds to retired elderly people to live by themselves and to purchase boarding home care. By the late 1950s, shortages of beds in general hospitals created pressure to move chronic patients into nursing homes to make room for acute cases. Medicare and Medicaid legislation passed in 1965 had the most dramatic impact on institutional care for the aged. From its inception, Medicare has been oriented toward acute care services, providing 74 percent of its funds to hospitals and only 1 percent to nursing homes in 1979. For those with long-term chronic illness requiring nursing home care, services are primarily available through the federal and state Medicaid programs designed for the indigent. In 1979, federal and state programs paid for 57 percent of all nursing home care, thus functioning as a major resource for the private nursing home industry (Estes & Harrington, 1981; Gibson, 1980).

The aged population is unique in that deinstitutionalization has affected only one sector—that is, those who were confined to mental hospitals. Often, however, they were moved directly out of hospitals into nursing homes. In many cases, in fact, they were not moved at all; the building names were changed and most of the population stayed in place. It is currently estimated that 80 percent of those 65 and older who live in nursing and personal care homes have some degree of mental impairment (U.S. Senate, 1982).

Given the large scale and institutional character of today's nursing homes, emphasis is being placed on the need for the deinstitutionalization of nursing home residents and the provision of more home-based care. This emphasis is primarily a product of extensive costs of the Medicare and Medicaid systems.

Evaluating Deinstitutionalization Trends

At its best, deinstitutionalization has succeeded in promoting community care that is more humane and effective than care provided in large institutions. At its worst, deinstitutionalization has resulted in both the forced homelessness of former residents of state institutions and an accumulation of individuals in community-based facilities that are no better than their antecedents.

For the most part, the problems of deinstitutionalization derive not from the concept itself but from its naive implementation. The array of community-based services necessary to the support of community care is costly, and as inflation became a severe problem in the 1970s, the bipartisan political coalition that had forged the deinstitutionalization movement fell apart. The fiscal retrenchment of government has left community care ominously incomplete, and the fate of a noble idea may hinge on a poorly designed experiment that is woefully short of resources.

As a result, many residential community care facilities have abandoned the "small is beautiful" philosophy that provided a marked contrast to the operations of large institutions. Capitalizing on economies of scale, many nursing homes, group homes, and the like that cater to various populations have come to resemble community-based versions of the institutions they were intended to replace. The term "transinstitutionalism" has been coined to describe this lateral movement of individuals from one dominant institutional form to another.

There is ample evidence that deinstitutionalization can work. However, insofar as it demands both the improvement of necessary large institutions and the provision of community-based care, deinstitutionalization remains the expensive creation of a frugal era.

STEVEN P. SEGAL

For further information, see AGED: SERVICES; HOMELESSNESS; LONG-TERM CARE; MENTAL HEALTH SERVICES.

References

"A Place for Foster Children." (1984, June 27). *The New York Times,* p. C15.

Bartley v. Kremens. (1975). 402 F. Supp. 1039 (E.D. Pa.).

Bureau of Justice Statistics (1984a). *Prisoners in 1983.* Washington, D.C.: U.S. Department of Justice.

Bureau of Justice Statistics (1984b). *Probation and Parole 1983.* Washington, D.C.: U.S. Department of Justice.

Bureau of Justice Statistics (1984c). *1983 Jail Census.* Washington, D.C.: U.S. Department of Justice.

Carney, L. P. (1977). *Corrections and the Community.* Englewood Cliffs, N.J.: Prentice-Hall.

Donaldson v. O'Connor. (1974). 493 F. 2d 507 (5th Cir.).

Dore, M., Young, T., & Pappenfort, D. (1984). "Comparison of Basic Data for the National Survey of Residential Group Care Facilities: 1966–1982." *Child Welfare, 63*(6), 485–495.

Estes, C., & Harrington, C. (1981). "Fiscal Crisis, Deinstitutionalization and the Elderly." *American Behavioral Scientist, 24*(6), 811–826.

Gibson, R. M. (1980). "National Health Expenditures, 1979." *Health Care Financing Review, 2*(1), 1–36.

Hylton, J. (1981). *Reintegrating the Offender.* Washington, D.C.: University Press of America.

Kramer, M. (1977). *Psychiatric Services and the Changing Institutional Scene, 1950–1985.* Analytical and Special Study Reports, National Institute of Mental Health Series B, No. 12. Washington, D.C.: U.S. Government Printing Office.

Lerman, P. (1982). *Deinstitutionalization.* New Brunswick, N.J.: Rutgers University Press.

Mandersheid, R. (1985). National Institute of Mental Health, [Estimates of Patients in State and County Mental Hospitals as of January 21, 1985]. Unpublished data, National Institute of Mental Health, Rockville, Md.

National Institute of Mental Health. (January, 1985). *Patients in State and County Mental Hospitals.* Rockville, Md.: Author.

Rotegard, L., & Bruininks, R. H. (1983). *Mentally Retarded People in State Operated Residential Facilities.* Minneapolis: University of Minnesota.

Segal, S. P., & Aviram, U. (1978). *The Mentally Ill in Community-Based Sheltered Care.* New York: John Wiley & Sons.

U.S. Bureau of the Census. (1980). *United States Census of the Population 1980: Vol. 1, Char-*

acteristics of the Population: Part 1, Detailed Population Characteristics, United States Summary. Washington, D.C.: U.S. Government Printing Office.

United States General Accounting Office, (January 1977). *Returning the Mentally Disabled to the Community: Government Needs to Do More.* Washington, D.C.: General Accounting Office.

U.S. Senate. (1982). Special Committee on Aging, *Developments in Aging, 1981* (S. Rpt. 97–314). Washington, D.C.: U.S. Government Printing Office.

Van Dusen, K. T. (1981). "Net Widening and Relabeling." *American Behavioral Scientist, 24*(6), 801–810.

Wyatt v. Stickney. (1972). 493 F. Supp. 521, 522.

DELINQUENCY AND JUVENILE OFFENDERS. See CHILD WELFARE SERVICES; JUVENILE COURTS, PROBATION, AND PAROLE; JUVENILE JUSTICE SYSTEM; JUVENILE OFFENDER DIVERSION AND COMMUNITY-BASED SERVICES; JUVENILE OFFENDER INSTITUTIONS; JUVENILE OFFENDERS AND DELINQUENCY.

DEVELOPMENTAL APPROACH TO RESEARCH

Interest is increasing in new approaches to research that generate innovations in services and service delivery. These approaches have a variety of names—for example, social research and development (social R&D), programmatic research, problem-solving research, experimental social innovation, developmental research, technique-building research, model-building research, and evaluation research—but all place emphasis on one or more of the means by which human service interventions may be developed (Azrin, 1977; Benn, 1981; Bloom & Fischer, 1982; Briar, 1980; Briar, Weissman, & Rubin, 1981; Epstein & Tripodi, 1977; Fairweather, 1967; Fischer, 1978; Grinnell, 1981; Gottman & Markman, 1978; Havelock, 1973; Jayaratne & Levy, 1979; Mullen, 1978; Paine,

Bellamy, & Wilcox, 1984; Reid, 1979, 1980; Risley, 1982; Rothman, 1974, 1980; Thomas, 1978a, 1978b, 1980, 1984; Tripodi, 1983; Tripodi, Fellin, & Epstein, 1978; Tripodi, Fellin, & Meyer, 1983; Wortman, 1983). As yet, these approaches have no single established name or model. Because most of them depart significantly from the conventional social science model of research, in which the objective is to make contributions to the knowledge of human behavior, and because all involve some particular aspect of the process of innovation development, they are identified here as examples or aspects of developmental research.

Working Definition

A working definition of developmental research is that it is inquiry directed toward the analysis, design, development, and evaluation of human service innovations (Thomas, 1978a). These innovations consist of human service technology that is the technical means by which social work objectives are achieved. Social work, of course, consists of much more than service or social technology, and it is guided by important values and humane commitments. Nevertheless, human service work is done with social technology. Developmental research is concerned precisely with this technology, and new technology is the product of such inquiry. Further details concerning the need for developmental research and how this approach differs from conventional social science and social work research are discussed in Thomas (1978a, 1978b, 1984).

There are many types of social technology in social work. Thomas (1978a) distinguishes several general types. Among the more familiar ones are assessment methods (for example, interviewing guidelines for practitioners), intervention methods (for example, contingency contracting), service programs (for example, an agency adoption service), organizational structures (for example, decentralized offices), service systems (for example, community mental health agencies), and social and welfare policy (for example, the welfare policy of a particular presidential administration). Less often thought of in this context, although equally relevant, are physical frameworks (for example, the architecture of a residential facility for the aged), electrical or mechanical devices (for example, closed circuit television), and information systems (for example, computer-assisted record keeping).

Model of Developmental Research

A model of developmental research should ideally be applicable to all the various efforts in the development of human service technology. The analysis should come before the design and development phases, and the evaluation phase should follow the development phase, with the diffusion and adoption phases coming thereafter. The first four phases—analysis, design, development, and evaluation—are distinguished here as developmental research. The evaluation phase corresponds to what is generally called evaluation research and is one component of developmental research. The other two phases—diffusion and adoption—are mainly concerned with using the innovation and are called utilization research. Thus, developmental research consists of the early, essential phases that come before the phases involving utilization. The full sequence of phases, with their constituent steps and conditions, is called developmental research and utilization (DR&U). The framework for this model is presented in Figure 1.

In addition to the phases, operational steps pertain to the important components of each phase and embrace a set of specific activities to be carried out. Of the many operational steps of the DR&U model, most relate directly to developmental research. The model also distinguishes a number of material conditions or real, objective phenomena associated with the phases and the consequences of carrying out the operational steps. Most of these material conditions are the real-world outcomes of DR&U activity. Figure 1 shows how all these are related in the process of development and utilization. The developmental effort of any particular individual or team may pertain to only one limited aspect of this process, may embrace several related phases or steps, or, in unusual cases, may embrace all phases, progressing sequentially from one to the next from beginning to end.

Analysis Phase. Analysis, the first phase, embraces the activities that precede the developmental effort itself. Before any developmental activity occurs, some human problem must exist. The existence of such a condition, however, does not necessarily indicate that there is a basis for developing human service technology. To start with, there must be some professional or public recognition that the problem merits attention, that it presents an opportunity to carry out problem analysis and identification—Step 1 in the series of operational steps. Thus, although child abuse has been around for a long time, such abuse—particularly child battering—emerged as a social issue of great importance only through the efforts of a small group of concerned physicians. Radiologists had reported multiple bone breaks in very young children in the 1940s and the 1950s, but it was not until 1961, when investigators at the Denver Medical Center in Colorado coined the emotionally charged diagnostic term "battered child syndrome," that professional and public interest in child abuse began to develop (Antler, 1978). Other tasks in the analysis phase consist of determining whether relevant interventions exist and, if so, whether the development of further interventions is merited (Step 2, State-of-the-Art Review) and of discerning the practicality of the proposed development (Step 3, Feasibility Study). Successful completion of the analysis phase should culminate in a statement of feasibility.

Design Phase. To fashion some aspect of human service technology is central to innovation. As used here, "design" means "the planful and systematic application of relevant scientific, technical, and practical information to the creation and assembly of innovations appropriate in human service intervention" (Thomas, 1984, p. 151).

To qualify as an innovation, the change need not be entirely new, as many writers on innovation have indicated (Pelz & Munson, 1982; Rice & Rogers, 1980). The innovation may range from an invention of novel technology (for example, a new assessment instrument); through adaptation by altering existing technology (for example, modifying an assessment instrument for adults for use with children) and novel application of existing technology, often called technological transfer (for example, using a research instrument for clinical assessment); to the adoption of existing technology by a different user group (Thomas, 1984).

Fig. 1.   Developmental Research and Utilization (DR&U)

Phase	Material Condition	Activities and Steps
I. ANALYSIS	A. Problematic Human Condition B. State of Existing Interventions C. Relevant Information and Resources D. Statement of Feasibility	1. Problem Identification and Analysis 2. State-of-the-Art Review 3. Feasibility Study
II. DESIGN	E. Statement of Objectives and Design Problems F. Relevant Data G. Symbolic Representation of the Innovation H. Interventional Innovation I. Innovation Procedures	4. Determination of Innovation Objective 5. Identification of Innovation Requirements 6. Identification of Design Problems 7. Selection of Information Sources 8. Gathering and Processing Information 9. Generation and Selection of Solution Alternatives 10. Assembly 11. Real-world Representation 12. Proceduralization
III. DEVELOPMENT	J. Development Plan K. Trial Implementation L. Trial Use Data M. Tested Interventional Innovations	13. Formulation of the Development Plan 14. Operational Preparation 15. Trial Use and Developmental Testing
IV. EVALUATION	N. Evaluation Plan O. Evaluation Data	16. Formulation of the Evaluation Plan 17. Carrying Out Evaluation
V. DIFFUSION	P. Diffusion Media	18. Preparation of Dissemination and Diffusion Media
VI. ADOPTION	Q. Broad Use	19. Diffusion of Innovation to Potential Users 20. Implementation by Users

Source: E. J. Thomas, Figure 10.1 in *Designing Interventions for the Helping Professions* by Edwin J. Thomas. Copyright © 1984 by Edwin J. Thomas. Reprinted by permission of Sage Publications, Inc.

Although design is partly an art, inasmuch as it involves the discovery of the untried and new, the design phase also consists of identifying a series of design problems that are capable of being analyzed and solved in a systematic and orderly fashion. Many constituent activities are involved in design, each of which may be viewed as a step to be carried out in the design process (Thomas, 1984). These activities include determining the objective of the innovation, identifying the requirements of the innovation, identifying design problems, selecting information sources, gathering and processing information, generating and selecting alternative solutions, assembling design components, developing real-world representation of the innovation, and implementing proceduralization, or describing how the innovation may be used (Steps 4–12 in Figure 1). Successful completion of each of these steps increases the likelihood that the resulting innovation will have design validity, which is the extent to which the innovation is appropriate for the human service task for which it was designed (Thomas, 1985).

Development Phase. Whereas the innovation is brought into being in the design phase, development is the process by which the innovation is implemented and used on a trial basis, tested for its adequacy, and refined and redesigned as necessary (Thomas, 1984). Trial use involves the implementation of the innovation in practice with the clientele for whom the innovation was intended. Developmental testing is the process in trial use by which an innovation is systematically tested, revised, or redesigned. Developmental testing is similar to performance testing in industrial and scientific research and development, inasmuch as the focus is on the reliability of the innovation, the conditions under which it works, and whether it functions as it was intended. If innovations are not used adequately on a trial basis and have not been tested developmentally, they will not possess developmental validity (Thomas, 1985). Innovations that lack developmental validity have a greater likelihood of not meeting the service needs for which they were developed and of requiring subsequent revision to meet these needs.

The main activities of development consist of formulating the development plan, in which it is necessary to determine the scope of development and a sample relevant to development; operational preparation; and trial use and developmental testing (Thomas, 1984). The completion of these steps (Steps 13–15 in Figure 1) should result in the development of tested innovations.

Evaluation Phase. Evaluation in design and development is empirical inquiry to determine the effects of the innovation. Evaluation methods in developmental research include much of the already established methodology of social science and evaluation research. These basic methods are discussed in other sources (Barlow, Hayes, & Nelson, 1984; Bloom & Fischer, 1982; Grinnell, 1981, 1984; Jayaratne & Levy, 1979; Tripodi, Fellin, & Epstein, 1971, 1978; Tripodi, Fellin, & Meyer, 1983). It is important to emphasize, however, that although the methods of evaluation research are relatively well established, their use in the evaluation phase of developmental research is less to provide program appraisal for practice purposes than to yield outcome information of more general relevance. Such information is an integral part of a research-innovation process in which evaluation follows development, contributes to further design and development as necessary, and ultimately provides a basis for the diffusion and adoption of the innovation.

The main activities of evaluation consist of formulating the evaluation plan and carrying out the evaluation (Steps 16–17 in Figure 1). Areas of evaluation include effectiveness, efficiency, cost, consumer satisfaction, and, in later stages, field testing to determine whether the results of the innovation are satisfactory under normal operating conditions (Thomas, 1984). If the results of the evaluation are not favorable, further design and development are generally required. In general, however, if the evaluation phase ends with favorable results and these can be replicated, the research should yield a user-ready innovation.

Diffusion and Adoption Phases. After the innovation has been evaluated and found to be worthy of use, the diffusion and adoption phases follow. The relevant activities in these phases are preparing dissemination and diffusion materials, diffusing the innovation to potential users, and implementation by users (Steps 18–20 in Figure 1). These activities should result in diffusion materials and, if successful, eventually in the broad use of the innovation.

Sources of Information. Developmental research derives its resources for technological development from many areas. These include basic research and applied research, which are customary sources in social research and development and in literature-retrieval models of development (Mullen, 1978; Rothman, 1974, 1980), as well as scientific technology, allied technology, legal policy, indigenous innovation, practice, personal experience, and professional experience (Thomas, 1978a, 1984).

One or more sources may be relevant to any design task, although often one source is primary with possible supplementary sources. Because the information from a source cannot generally be used in its raw form in design, it must somehow be transformed so that it may be incorporated directly in the design process. Transformations of this type may be thought of as generation processes, which involve the application of legal policy, professional or personal experience, or knowledge such as research findings and the transfer and adoption of already developed technology (Thomas, 1980, 1984).

Techniques. In addition to the methods involved in the phases and steps described above and outlined in Figure 1, many tools and techniques have diverse and specialized application in developmental research. For example, task analysis is a technique that may be used to analyze complex behavioral repertoires to isolate the constituent behavioral components required to accomplish given objectives (Resnick & Ford, 1978; Zemke & Kramlinger, 1982). Among other tools are the critical incident technique, needs assessment, flowcharting, latticing, decision tables, information retrieval and review, and selected practice techniques. Thomas (1984) describes these in detail.

An Illustration. Research conducted by the present author and his colleagues at the Marital Treatment Project of the University of Michigan School of Social Work illustrates the development of new treatment to reach the uncooperative alcohol abuser. The approach that was evolved was called unilateral family therapy for alcohol abuse (UF-T), in which assistance is given to enable cooperative non-alcohol-abusing spouses to function as a positive rehabilitative influence with marital partners who drink excessively and refuse treatment. Spanning a period of some 5 years, the efforts involve systematic progression through the phases of analysis, design, development, and the early portions of evaluation. Although the activities and steps of each phase up to the point at which developmental effort stopped were carried out largely in the order described above, only selected activities for each phase can be highlighted here.

In the analysis phase carried out before the project was funded (under Grant 1 RO1 AA04163-03 of the National Institute on Alcohol Abuse and Alcoholism) the problem of how to reach the uncooperative alcohol abuser through a cooperative spouse was selected and analyzed. In determining the state of the art, the research and practice literature relating to spouse involvement in treatment was reviewed and interviews were conducted with alcohol counselors to determine needs for new treatment techniques and what the current practices were in spouse treatment. In the feasibility inquiry, it was learned that although there was no systematic unilateral approach in any existing treatment, many developments made it timely and technically feasible to evolve a UF-T for alcohol abuse.

An early product of the design phase was the formulation of a working conception of UF-T for alcohol abuse that served as a framework for further development (Thomas & Santa, 1982). Design and development were conducted more or less concurrently. A cohort of some 25 cooperative spouses of uncooperative alcohol abusers was selected according to eligibility criteria that ensured that the clients would be sampled in a way that met the criterion of developmental relevance. Treatment was provided by a team of practitioner-researchers in which practice with the spouse was conducted developmentally to refine and extend UF-T through systematic trial use and developmental testing of the innovations. Further details concerning the concepts of sampling for developmental relevance, developmental practice, and trial use and developmental testing are found in Thomas (1984, 1985).

The treatment program that was evolved consisted of six principal areas: treatment orientation, clinical assessment, spouse-role induction (for example, marital relationship enhancement, disenabling, neutralization of the old influence system), abuser-directed interventions mediated by the spouse (for example, programmed confrontation of the abuser, programmed request, and spouse-mediated sobriety facilitation), spouse-directed interventions (for example, spouse disengagement), and maintenance (for example, relapse prevention training) (Thomas et al., in press).

In keeping with the developmental objectives, the design for evaluation was chosen to allow for clinical and developmental flexibility while also providing results on outcomes. One spouse in each successive pair was assigned at random to receive UF-T for 4 to 6 months and the other to a condition of delayed treatment. Some 20 assessment instruments were administered before and after treatment and at 6- and 12-month follow-ups. The results, in brief, were that UF-T resulted in significantly reduced drinking or entry into treatment for alcohol abuse for two-thirds of the abusers of the treated spouses. In addition to other positive gains, there were no negative changes associated with UF-T. The results of the evaluation confirmed the promise of the unilateral approach and highlighted the importance of conducting systematic experimental evaluation in subsequent research. Although UF-T has considerable potential as a mode of family therapy, more work needs to be done before taking it into the diffusion and adoption phases. (Illustrations of dissemination, diffusion, and adoption may be found in Paine, Bellamy, and Wilcox, 1984.)

Implications

Social work achieves its objectives through human service technology. Developmental research provides a framework for an evolving methodology by which the field can systematically generate this technology, which is so vital to its professional accomplishments. The developmental approach provides the field with a promising new methodology to supplement conventional research methods. However, the promise of developmental research will not be fullfilled without certain changes in research and practice and in the education of social work professionals.

Research must be guided by the perspective and methodology of the developmental approach. Efforts should also be made to conduct developmental practice, which is service having developmental objectives in which selected methods of developmental research are also used (Thomas, 1984). Developmental research should be the main research methodology taught in social work schools (Thomas, 1978b). Research projects and dissertations should be oriented toward developing new models of intervention and human service (Reid, 1979). Finally, high priority should be given to strengthening and extending the methodology of developmental research to accelerate its development.

EDWIN J. THOMAS

For further information, see PROGRAM EVALUATION; RESEARCH IN SOCIAL WORK; RESEARCH MEASURES AND INDICES IN DIRECT PRACTICE; SINGLE SUBJECT RESEARCH DESIGNS.

References

Antler, S. (1978). "Child Abuse: An Emerging Priority." *Social Work*, 23(1), 58–62.

Azrin, N. H. (1977). "A Strategy for Applied Research: Learning Based but Outcome Oriented." *American Psychologist*, 32(2), 140–149.

Barlow, D. H., Hayes, S. C., & Nelson, R. O. (1984). *The Scientist Practitioner: Research and Accountability in Clinical and Educational Settings*. Elmsford, N.Y.: Pergamon Press.

Benn, C. (1981). *Attacking Poverty through Participation*. Melbourne, Australia: Preston Institute of Technology Press.

Bloom, M., & Fischer, J. (1982). *Evaluating Practice: Guidelines for the Accountable Professional*. Englewood Cliffs, N.J.: Prentice-Hall.

Briar, S., (1980). "Toward the Integration of Practice and Research." In D. Fanshel (Ed.), *Future of Social Work Research* (pp. 31–38). Washington, D.C.: National Association of Social Workers.

Briar, S., Weissman, H., & Rubin, A. (Eds.). (1981). *Research Utilization in Social Work Education*. New York: Council on Social Work Education.

Epstein, I., & Tripodi, T. (1977). *Research Techniques for Program Planning, Monitoring and Evaluation.* New York: Columbia University Press.

Fairweather, G. (1967). *Methods for Experimental Social Innovation.* New York: John Wiley & Sons.

Fischer, J. (1978). *Effective Casework Practice: An Eclectic Approach.* New York: McGraw-Hill Book Co.

Grinnell, R. M., Jr. (Ed.). (1981). *Social Work Research and Evaluation.* Itasca, Ill.: F. E. Peacock Publishers.

Grinnell, R. M., Jr. (Ed.). (1984). *Social Work Research and Evaluation* (2nd rev. ed.). Itasca, Ill.: F. E. Peacock Publishers.

Gottman, J.M., & Markman, H.J. (1978). "Experimental Designs in Psychotherapy Research." In S.L. Garfield & A.E. Bergin (Eds.), *Handbook of Psychotherapy and Behavior Change* (2nd ed., pp. 23–63). New York: John Wiley & Sons.

Havelock, R.G. (1973). *Planning for Innovations through Dissemination and Utilization of Knowledge.* Ann Arbor: University of Michigan, Institute for Social Research.

Jayaratne, S., & Levy, R. (1979). *Empirical Clinical Practice.* New York: Columbia University Press.

Mullen, E. J. (1978). "The Construction of Personal Models for Effective Practice: A Method for Utilizing Research Findings to Guide Social Interventions." *Journal of Social Service Research, 2* (1), 45–65.

Paine, S. C., Bellamy, G. T., & Wilcox, B. (Eds.). (1984). *Human Services That Work: From Innovation to Standard Practice.* Baltimore, Md.: Paul H. Brookes Publishing Co.

Pelz, D. C., & Munson, F. C. (1982). "Originality Level and the Innovating Process in Organizations." *Human Systems Management, 3* (3), 173–187.

Reid, W. J. (1979). "Evaluation Research in Social Work." *Evaluation and Program Planning, 2* (3), 209–217.

Reid, W. J. (1980). "The Model Development Dissertation." *Journal of Social Service Research, 3*(2), 215–225.

Resnick, L. B., & Ford, W. W. (1978). "The Analysis of Tasks for Instruction: An Information-Processing Approach." In A. C. Catania & T. A. Brigham (Eds.), *Handbook of Applied Behavioral Analysis: Social and Instructional Processes* (pp. 378–410). New York: Irvington Publishers.

Rice, R. E., & Rogers, E. M. (1980). "Reinvention in the Innovation Process." *Knowledge: Creation, Diffusion, Utilization, 1*(4) 449–515.

Risley, T. (1982, May). *Behavioral Design for Residential Programs.* Paper presented at the annual convention of the Australian Behavior Modification Association, Surfers Paradise, Australia.

Rothman, J. (1974). *Planning and Organizing for Social Change: Action Principles from Social Science Research.* New York: Columbia University Press.

Rothman, J. (1980). *Social R and D: Research and Development in the Human Services.* Englewood Cliffs, N.J.: Prentice-Hall.

Thomas, E. J. (1978a). "Generating Innovation in Social Work: The Paradigm of Developmental Research." *Journal of Social Service Research, 2*(1), 95–116.

Thomas, E. J. (1978b). "Mousetraps, Developmental Research, and Social Work Education." *Social Service Review, 52*(3), 468–483.

Thomas, E. J. (1980). "Beyond Knowledge Utilization in Generating Human Service Technology." In D. Fanshel (Ed.), *Future of Social Work Research* (pp. 91–104). Washington, D.C.: National Association of Social Workers.

Thomas, E. J. (1984). *Designing Interventions for the Helping Professions.* Beverly Hills, Calif.: Sage Publications.

Thomas, E. J. (1985). "Design and Development Validity and Related Concepts in Developmental Research." *Social Work Research and Abstracts, 21*(2), 50–55.

Thomas, E. J., & Santa, C. (1982). "Unilateral Family Therapy for Alcohol Abuse." *American Journal of Family Therapy, 10*(3), 49–58.

Thomas, E. J., et al. (in press). "Unilateral Family Therapy with the Spouses of Alcoholics." *Journal of Social Service Research.*

Tripodi, T. (1983). *Evaluative Research for Social Workers.* Englewood Cliffs, N.J.: Prentice-Hall.

Tripodi, T., Fellin, P., & Epstein, I. (1971). *Social Program Evaluation: Guidelines for Health, Education, and Welfare Administrators.* Itasca, Ill.: F. E. Peacock Publishers.

Tripodi, T., Fellin, P., & Epstein, I. (1978). *Differential Social Program Evaluation.* Itasca, Ill.: F. E. Peacock Publishers.

Tripodi, T., Fellin, P., & Meyer, H. J. (1983). *The Assessment of Social Research* (2nd ed.). Itasca, Ill.: F. E. Peacock Publishers.

Wortman, P. M. (1983). "Evaluation Research: A Methodological Perspective." In M. R. Rosenzweig & L. W. Porter (Eds.), *Annual Review of Psychology* (Vol. 34, pp. 223–260). Palo Alto, Calif.: Annual Reviews, Inc.

Zemke, R., & Kramlinger, T. (1982). *Figuring Things Out: A Trainer's Guide to Needs and Task Analysis.* Reading, Mass.: Addison-Wesley Publishing Co.

DEVELOPMENTALLY DISABLED. See DISABILITIES: DEVELOPMENTAL.

DEVINE, EDWARD THOMAS. See biographical section.

DIAGNOSTIC AND STATISTICAL MANUAL (DSM)

DSM-III is the informal name of the third edition of the *Diagnostic and Statistical Manual of Mental Disorders* of the American Psychiatric Association (1980). It represents the first time an official diagnostic manual has been widely adopted by mental health professionals in the United States, and for that reason the volume has had a major impact on the field of mental health. This edition differs considerably from the two earlier editions published in 1952 and 1968 (Spitzer, Williams, & Skodol, 1980).

The DSM-III manual contains a classification that lists all of the mental disorders as well as certain conditions (called "V code conditions") that are not mental disorders but are nevertheless a focus of attention or treatment. In addition, there is a detailed description of each diagnostic category and specified diagnostic criteria for each mental disorder. Their purpose is to assist clinicians in making reliable diagnoses. The specific diagnostic categories are grouped into the sixteen major diagnostic classes listed in Table 1. Each category is assigned a five-digit code number that can be recorded for statistical and record-keeping purposes.

Multiaxial System

An important and unique feature of DSM-III that is of special interest to social workers is its inclusion of a multiaxial system for evaluation (Williams, 1981, 1985a, 1985b; Williams & Spitzer, 1982). With this system, psychological, biological, and social aspects of an individual's functioning are evaluated, and the results are recorded on different axes. The system includes the five axes listed in Table 2; each axis requires evaluation of a

Table 1. The Major Diagnostic Classes of DSM-III

Disorders usually first evident in infancy, childhood, or adolescence
Organic mental disorders
Substance use disorders
Schizophrenic disorders
Paranoid disorders
Psychotic disorders not elsewhere classified
Affective disorders
Anxiety disorders
Somatoform disorders
Dissociative disorders
Psychosexual disorders
Factitious disorders
Disorders of impulse control not elsewhere classified
Adjustment disorder
Psychological factors affecting physical condition
Personality disorders

different class of information. Axes I and II contain all of the mental disorders, and Axis III is for listing physical disorders and conditions. Axes IV and V provide rating scales that allow clinicians to note the severity of psychosocial stressors that contributed to the development or maintenance of the mental disorder (Axis IV) and the highest level of adaptive functioning that the individual has been able to maintain for at least a few months during the prior year (Axis V).

The rationale for having different axes has been discussed at length elsewhere (Williams, 1981). Briefly, each axis serves as a reminder to clinicians to pay attention to a

Table 2. The Five Axes of DSM-III

AXIS I:	Clinical syndromes
	Conditions not attributable to a mental disorder that are a focus of attention or treatment
	Additional codes
AXIS II:	Personality disorders
	Specific developmental disorders
AXIS III:	Physical disorders and conditions
AXIS IV:	Severity of psychosocial stressors
AXIS V:	Highest level of adaptive functioning in past year

particular aspect of functioning so that none of these important areas is overlooked in an evaluation. Personality disorders and specific developmental disorders are listed on an axis separate from the other mental disorders because they tend to be overlooked owing to their generally chronic and mild symptomatology relative to the Axis I disorders.

Since the advent of DSM-III, initial diagnostic interviews have become more focused as the clinician attempts to make a differential diagnosis of the specifically defined Axis I and II mental disorders, as well as assess the information needed to complete the other axes (Spitzer & Williams, 1984a, 1984b). The fictional character Sherlock Holmes can be used to illustrate the results of a complete multiaxial evaluation, which might look like this:

Axis I:	305.62	Cocaine abuse, episodic
Axis II:	301.40	Compulsive personality disorder
	301.81	Narcissistic personality disorder
Axis III:		Gunshot wound
Axis IV:		4—Moderate (case lost; victim kidnapped)
Axis V:		2—Very good

DSM-III's multiaxial system thus emphasizes areas of information that have traditionally been considered highly important in social work evaluations: stressful life events and adaptive functioning. Such a system encourages a more comprehensive evaluation of an individual than did the previous DSM manuals, which were limited to brief descriptions of the mental disorders and did not include multiaxial systems. Another advantage of the DSM-III system is that it encourages evaluation of an individual's strengths (Axis V) rather than limiting the focus of evaluation to psychological and physical pathology.

Other Important Features

DSM-III differs in other important ways from its predecessors. First, it takes a generally atheoretical approach to the classification of the mental disorders. It attempts to describe the manifestations of the various mental disorders and only rarely attempts to account for the causes of the disturbances, unless the mechanism is included in the definition of the disorder (as in the organic mental disorders). This approach permits clinicians of varying theoretical orientations to use the specified criteria to make diagnoses while still retaining their theories about the causes of the various disorders.

Second, the inclusion in DSM-III of specified diagnostic criteria as guides for making each diagnosis has greatly enhanced the reliability with which these diagnoses can be made. Clinicians are better able to agree about diagnoses when they evaluate patients or clients (even though they may disagree about the etiology of the disorders). However, although diagnostic reliability is essential for effective communication among mental health professionals, it should be noted that high reliability does not necessarily indicate high validity, or accuracy of the diagnostic definitions.

For most mental disorders, the diagnostic criteria are based on clinical judgment and therefore have only what is called "face validity" (Spitzer & Williams, 1980). This validity indicates the extent to which, "on the face of it," the description of a category seems to depict the characteristic features of individuals who have the disorder. (It has been said that the degree of face validity of a category is directly proportional to the number of approving faces and the wisdom of the people behind those faces.) However, most of the categories in DSM-III have not yet been fully validated in studies of such important correlates as clinical course, outcome, family history, and treatment response.

Care was taken in the text and criteria of DSM-III to avoid the use of such phrases as "a schizophrenic" or "an alcoholic," because what are being classified and described are mental disorders that individuals have rather than the individuals themselves (Spitzer & Williams, 1979). Therefore, the text may refer to the more accurate, but admittedly more wordy, "an individual with schizophrenia" or "an individual with alcohol dependence."

In addition, in DSM-III the individuals evaluated are not referred to as "patients." It was recognized that the use of this word might limit the use of DSM-III by mental health professionals who prefer not to refer to their clientele as patients. Finally, in a further attempt to facilitate the use of DSM-III by the various mental health professions, the terms "physician" and "psychiatrist" are not used in the manual. Instead, users are referred to as "clinicians" and "mental health professionals."

It is important to note that although DSM-III is often referred to as a textbook, it does not contain information about treatment of the various disorders. Since the publication of DSM-III, at least two books have become available that deal with this topic, although neither represents an official statement of the psychiatric community (Greist, Jefferson, & Spitzer, 1982; Reid, 1983).

Importance to Social Workers

It is important for psychiatric social workers to become familiar with DSM-III because of its contribution to communication among mental health professionals, its contribution to effective evaluation and treatment planning, its usefulness for teaching psychopathology, and its potential as a basis for research (Spitzer & Williams, 1980). Social workers must be able to communicate with their medical colleagues and with the other members of the interdisciplinary mental health team. In most psychiatric treatment facilities, the language of DSM-III is the standard terminology used in diagnostic case discussions. Familiarity with DSM-III often becomes required for participation in such discussions.

Without doubt, the most significant contribution of DSM-III is its enhancement of the comprehensiveness of diagnostic evaluations and the effectiveness of treatment planning by the inclusion of specified diagnostic criteria and a multiaxial system. The increased reliability and validity with which the various mental disorders are defined by the diagnostic criteria in DSM-III should result in more effective treatment planning, because they have promoted the establishment of a clearer relationship between diagnosis and treatment for many of the categories (Spitzer & Forman, 1979; Spitzer, Forman, & Nee, 1979).

One noteworthy example of this is the splitting of the DSM-II category of anxiety neurosis into two categories in DSM-III: panic disorder and generalized anxiety disorder. Panic disorder is defined as a syndrome in which the individual experiences recurrent panic attacks that are acute episodes of anxiety or discomfort accompanied by various physical and psychological symptoms (such as heart palpitations, sweating, dizziness, and fear of losing control during the attack). In contrast, generalized anxiety disorder is a syndrome in which there is persistent nervousness or worry accompanied by such symptoms as trembling or shakiness, sweating, and irritability or impatience. This division was based on relatively new knowledge about the specificity of the symptoms of panic attacks.

There now exist extremely effective treatments (certain antidepressant medications) for use when the manifestation of anxiety is discrete panic attacks rather than more generalized and persistent anxiety. In addition—although this is as yet unsubstantiated by research—the anxiety present in cases of generalized anxiety disorder may be mediated by psychological factors to a greater extent than the panic attacks of panic disorder. This would obviously have substantial treatment implications. Before DSM-III, both of these conditions would have been given the same diagnosis and presumably, therefore, similar treatments.

A word of caution: As noted in the introduction to DSM-III, it is necessary to obtain much more information beyond a DSM-III diagnosis before an adequate treatment plan can be formulated for any individual. A DSM-III diagnosis represents only the initial step in a comprehensive evaluation leading to a treatment plan. The additional information necessary will, of course, be determined by the theoretical orientation of the clinician and may emphasize psychological, biological, or social aspects of the functioning of the individual being evaluated.

Certain features of DSM-III contribute to its usefulness as an educational tool in teaching students about basic psychopathology (Skodol, Spitzer, & Williams, 1981). A beginning chapter of DSM-III, "Use of This Manual," provides an overview of the multiaxial system, diagnostic criteria, and terms and conventions used. The text for each specific mental disorder includes information under each of the following headings: essential features, associated features, age at onset, course, impairment, complications, predisposing factors, prevalence, sex ratio, familial pattern, and differential diagnosis.

The manual also contains several appendixes that are useful in teaching: "decision trees" for differential diagnosis to aid clinicians in understanding the organization and hierarchic structure of the classification, a glossary of technical terms used in the manual, and an annotated and referenced comparative listing of the DSM-II and DSM-III classifications for clinicians making the transition from the previous system and who are interested in the reasons for many of the changes in the classification. Published with DSM-III is the "Mini-D," a pocket-size quick reference guide containing only the diagnostic criteria and a listing of the differential diagnostic conditions. In addition to DSM-III itself, two case books are available that present various case vignettes, each with a discussion of the DSM-III differential diagnosis (Spitzer et al., 1981, 1983).

Finally, the specificity of the diagnostic criteria in DSM-III and the consequent increase in reliability of diagnoses have made it possible for researchers to select groups of subjects that are more homogeneous diagnostically. Because many social variables are influenced by and have influence on psychopathology, it is important for researchers in the social sciences to pay attention to the diagnostic variable.

DSM-III is seen as a major contribution to the science of mental health and to its practice worldwide (Spitzer, Williams, & Skodol, 1983). The manual has been translated into many languages and is being used routinely by teachers and researchers in other countries. Input from research with individuals from various social and cultural backgrounds will undoubtedly provide a significant body of information that will be useful for future revisions of the DSM.

DSM-III is seen as "only one still frame in the ongoing process of attempting to better understand mental disorders" (American Psychiatric Association, 1980, p. 12). Its specificity has encouraged research that can already provide the basis for improvements in the classification and disorder definitions. A revision of DSM-III (DSM-III-R) has been published (American Psychiatric Association, 1986).

JANET B. W. WILLIAMS

For further information, see ASSESSMENT IN DIRECT PRACTICE; DIRECT PRACTICE EFFECTIVENESS; DIRECT PRACTICE: TRENDS AND ISSUES; MENTAL HEALTH AND ILLNESS.

References

American Psychiatric Association. (1980). *Diagnostic and Statistical Manual of Mental Disorders* (3rd ed.). Washington, D.C.: Author.

American Psychiatric Association. (1986). *Diagnostic and Statistical Manual of Mental Disorders* (3rd. ed., rev.). Washington, D.C.: Author.

Greist, J. H., Jefferson, J. W., & Spitzer, R. L. (Eds.). (1982). *Treatment of Mental Disorders*. New York: Oxford University Press.

Reid, W. H. (1983). *Treatment of the DSM-III Psychiatric Disorders*. New York: Brunner/Mazel.

Skodol, A. E., Spitzer, R. L., & Williams, J.B.W. (1981). "Teaching and Learning DSM-III." *American Journal of Psychiatry*, *138*(12), 1581–1586.

Spitzer, R. L., & Forman, J. B. W. (1979). "DSM-III Field Trials: II. Initial Experience with the Multiaxial System." *American Journal of Psychiatry*, *136*(6), 818–820.

Spitzer, R. L., Forman, J. B. W., & Nee, J. (1979). "DSM-III Field Trials: II. Initial Interrater Diagnostic Reliability." *American Journal of Psychiatry*, *136*(6), 815–817.

Spitzer, R. L., et al. (1981). *DSM-III Case Book*. Washington, D.C.: American Psychiatric Association.

Spitzer, R. L., et al. (1983). *Psychopathology: A Case Book*. New York: McGraw-Hill.

Spitzer, R. L., & Williams, J. B. W. (1979). "Dehumanizing Descriptors?" [Letter to the Editor]. *American Journal of Psychiatry*, *136*(11), 1481.

Spitzer, R. L., & Williams, J. B. W. (1984a). "The Initial Interview: Evaluation Strategies for DSM-III Diagnosis." New York: BMA Audio Cassette Publications.

Spitzer, R. L., & Williams, J. B. W. (1984b). *Structured Clinical Interview for DSM-III (SCID)*. New York: Biometrics Research Department, New York State Psychiatric Institute.

Spitzer, R. L., & Williams, J. B. W. (1985). "Classification of Mental Disorders." In H. Kaplan & B. Sadock (Eds.), *Comprehensive Textbook of Psychiatry* (4th ed., Vol. 1, pp. 591–613). Baltimore, Md.: Williams & Wilkins.

Spitzer, R. L., Williams, J. B. W., & Skodol, A. E. (1980). "DSM-III: The Major Achievements and an Overview." *American Journal of Psychiatry*, *137*(2), 151–164.

Spitzer, R. L., Williams, J.B.W., & Skodol, A. E. (Eds.). (1983). *International Perspectives on DSM-III*. Washington, D.C.: American Psychiatric Press.

Williams, J. B. W. (1981). "DSM–III: A Comprehensive Approach to Diagnosis.'' *Social Work*, *26*(2), 101–106.

Williams, J. B. W. (1985a). ''The Multiaxial System of DSM-III: Where Did it Come From and Where Should it Go? I. Its Origins and Critiques.'' *Archives of General Psychiatry*, *42*(2), 175–180.

Williams, J. B. W. (1985b). ''The Multiaxial System of DSM-III: Where Did it Come From and Where Should it Go? II. Empirical Studies, Innovations, and Recommendations.'' *Archives of General Psychiatry*, *42*(2), 181–186.

Williams, J. B. W., & Spitzer, R. L. (1982). ''DSM-III Forum: Focusing on DSM-III's Multiaxial System.'' *Hospital & Community Psychiatry*, *33*(11), 891–892.

DIRECT PRACTICE: TRENDS AND ISSUES

An expanding diversity characterizes many aspects of social work practice today. This is evident, for example, in the variety of fields of practice, the wide array of theoretical orientations and intervention approaches, and the increasing range of research tools to advance the knowledge base for practice. These changes are the primary focus of the following review of current trends in social work practice.

Before describing these trends, it should be noted that social workers seek to improve the quality of life for all persons by providing rehabilitative and preventive services and social supports to individuals, families, groups, organizations, and communities and by working to bring about needed changes in the society. Although less than perfect as a statement on the nature of social work practice, this definition is sufficiently broad to encompass the variety and diversity of the social work profession, while placing some boundaries on a field that often seems diffuse to observers who do not have detailed knowledge of it.

The practice of most social workers consists of providing services directly to individuals, families, and groups, and this review reflects the prevalence of this form of practice—often called direct practice. It is important to recognize, however, that many social workers perform other practice roles, including community organization, consultation, social action, policy practice, administration and management, research, and professional education. These roles, often but misleadingly categorized as indirect practice, are described in detail elsewhere in this encyclopedia. It should also be noted that these latter ''indirect'' practice roles are often performed by social workers engaged primarily in direct practice.

Changing Conceptual Perspectives

From the 1920s until relatively recently, the practice of social work with individuals and families, and to some extent indirect practice as well, was informed predominantly by psychodynamic perspectives derived from Freudian and neo-Freudian theories of human behavior and society. Even the theoretical controversies within social work during that period—such as the diagnostic-functional debate between Freudian practitioners and adherents to the neo-Freudian theories of Otto Rank that was an issue for decades—were disputes over issues within a single overall perspective, not over fundamentally different theoretical orientations. Thus, most social workers were strongly influenced in their training by derivatives of Freudian theory, such as the developmental theories of Erik Erikson and the ego psychology of Anna Freud.

This dominance of Freudian and neo-Freudian perspectives was eroded and eventually displaced by four key developments. One was the reintroduction into social work, beginning in the late 1940s and 1950s, of systematic social and cultural perspectives, primarily from sociology, social psychology, and anthropology. A second development was a rising chorus of challenges from many sources to the validity of the psychoanalytic perspective, including the criticism from within social work that the psychoanalytic perspective was inadequate to encompass the essential psychosocial orientation needed in social work. Third was the appearance of a number of studies questioning the effectiveness of psychoanalytically oriented treatment, including the evaluation studies in social work that subsequently were summarized by Fischer (1973) and others. The fourth development was the reemergence and rapid growth of professional social work education at the undergraduate level, with an exclusive emphasis on preparing entry-level generic practitioners. This required the formulation of generic models of social work practice that depart from the essentially psychotherapeutic models that had characterized much social work education at the graduate level.

The displacement of psychoanalytic theory as the dominant theoretical orientation was perhaps the single most important factor in the proliferation of new conceptual perspectives and intervention approaches for direct practice. The mainstream of practice formulations moved in two principal directions: clinical social work and the ecological systems perspective, also associated with the generalist model. In addition, new models also emerged, including the behavioral perspective, the task-centered approach, and the empirical practice model.

Clinical Social Work

Although clinical social work is more a movement than a particular orientation to practice, it is a direct descendant of the psychoanalytic perspective that is still used by many social workers identified with this movement. Its origins can be traced at least to the 1960s and the emergence of clinical social work societies throughout the United States. Its significance was recognized by the National Association of Social Workers (NASW) when it established in 1978 a Task Force on Clinical Social Work. This led to NASW's convening of a National Invitational Forum on Clinical Social Work in Denver, Colorado, in June 1979 and to its sponsorship of the first national symposium on clinical social work in 1982. One purpose of the 1979 Denver forum was "to further the definition of clinical social work as a contribution to the profession as a whole" (Ewalt, 1980a, p. iii). Indeed, the search for definition permeates the sizable body of literature that has accompanied the clinical social work movement.

In 1984, the NASW Board of Directors moved toward establishing a definitive description of clinical social work when it accepted a definition developed by the association's Provisional Council on Clinical Social Work. (That definition appears in Appendix 3 of this encyclopedia.) Discussion of the nature of clinical practice continues, however. One leader in the field suggests that clinical social work arose, in part at least, as a

backlash against 1960s criticisms of direct practice—then called social casework—as irrelevant and uncommitted to social change (Meyer, 1983). Other social workers regard clinical social work as a "term of convenience" to refer to the practices previously called casework and group work.

If allowances are made for terms such as "ecology," which were not widely used by social workers 20 years ago, many of the definitions of clinical social work that have been generated at conferences or offered in the literature bear striking similarities to earlier definitions of traditional social casework. In fact, the "remarkable degree of consensus" (Ewalt, 1980b, p. 88), reported to have emerged at the 1979 national forum in Denver focused on the process of clinical social work, whose components again resemble definitions of the casework process that were formulated 2 to 3 decades earlier. What is new, then, in the clinical social work movement?

The continuity with the past is not surprising in view of NASW's organized efforts to address the interests and needs of social workers identified with this movement. As the clinical social work movement developed, it included a number of social workers who were critical of the rest of the profession, especially of NASW, and some of these disaffected social workers advocated that clinical social work should become a separate profession or at least should establish an independent professional organization. In an attempt to heal this division within the profession, NASW encouraged a consensus that would recognize the identity of clinical social workers and, at the same time, clearly identify clinical social work as an integral component of social work. NASW thus appealed to general concepts that are grounded in traditions familiar to the various constituencies involved. Whether NASW's objective will be achieved is a political question that can only be answered in the future. Thus far, it appears that many clinical social workers have responded positively to NASW's initiatives.

A close look at the specifics of clinical social work suggests that the consensus Ewalt (1980) reported from the Denver forum will need to be sturdy to overcome the equally remarkable diversity described in the ambitious *Handbook of Clinical Social Work* (Rosenblatt & Waldfogel, 1983). The *Hand-*

book presents a wide variety of perspectives and practice models, theoretical orientations to practice, and points of view about key issues in clinical social work. Of course, the *Handbook* had no specific political objective, did not seek to achieve a consensus, and included authors not identified with the clinical social work movement.

It is difficult to see how the diversity of perspectives in the *Handbook* could be combined in one practice model, unless it were one so general as to be of little practical use. It is also difficult to envision the achievement of consensus about these perspectives, unless it were a different kind of consensus than the one reached in Denver—namely, a new consensus that, among other things, would celebrate diversity and take an empirical approach to the resolution of controversy. Historically, the social work profession has not always tolerated difference and division easily and comfortably. Perhaps clinical social work will become an arena in which social workers find a way not only to tolerate but to welcome the excitement and clarity that can be generated by professional controversy.

The Ecological Systems Perspective

Following the displacement of the psychoanalytic model, the second principal direction in practice formulations is the ecological systems perspective that was introduced into social work in recent years (Germain & Gitterman, 1980). This perspective draws heavily on the language of ecologists and focuses primarily on relations between persons and their environments. It bears a striking resemblance to the psychosocial perspective, which also focuses on person-environment interactions and which has been an integral part, to varying degrees, of most models of social work practice since the beginnings of the profession. What the ecological perspective seeks to bring to the traditional focus on person-environment interactions is an increased capacity to conceptualize these interactions. To accomplish this, social work theorists developing the ecological perspective tend to rely on the concepts of general systems theory.

One of the limitations of the ecological perspective, thus far at least, is that its concepts and principles tend to be abstract and even vague, making it difficult to derive from them specific guides that can be applied by

practitioners. This limitation, which is acknowledged by a number of advocates of the ecological perspective, results in part from the reliance on general systems theory, which is essentially a heuristic orientation and a framework, not a theory. The systems approach generally has not been capable of producing testable hypotheses or practice prescriptions. A few ecological theorists have made use of the behavioral approach which focuses on person-environment interactions, is compatible with a systems orientation, and is capable of precise specification of interventions and hypotheses (Whittaker, 1974).

The ecological systems perspective also informs most models of generalist practice used in the education of social workers at the undergraduate level (Pincus & Minahan, 1973). The undergraduate generalist practice model encompasses preparation to perform a range of direct and indirect practice roles at an entry level. Some graduate level programs, which prepare specialists for advanced practice, offer a specialization in advanced generalist practice. The search for more useful and effective ways of implementing social work's focus on person-environment interactions continues—a search common to all the orientations discussed here. It is a search worthy of the profession's best efforts because this perspective focuses on a significant dimension of the human experience that no other profession has taken as one of its central contributions.

Other New Approaches and Perspectives

The behavioral approach, introduced into social work in the 1960s, is now in widespread use in the profession, and its applications have been extended to practice with groups (Rose, 1980), administration (Miller, 1978), and social change (Burgess & Bushell, 1969). It has been extended to include the cognitive-behavioral perspective, which gives increased emphasis to cognitive variables in intervention (Berlin, 1983). Because the behavioral approach emphasizes explicit, measurable outcome objectives and interventions, it is readily amenable to research on its effectiveness. Partly for this reason, despite its recent introduction, the behavioral approach has already generated more extensive systematic research than other practice perspectives. This has contributed significantly to the increasing recognition that structured intervention approaches are more effective than unstructured ones (Reid & Hanrahan, 1982).

In the early 1970s, Reid and Epstein introduced the task-centered casework model, which has been widely used by social work practitioners and educators. Although not explicitly identified with it (Reid & Epstein, 1972), task-centered casework is essentially a variation of the behavioral approach. Both emphasize the importance of formulating specific, measurable outcome objectives and explicit intervention techniques. Both have produced research showing that the use of specific, focused outcome objectives is associated with intervention effectiveness (Reid & Hanrahan, 1982).

More recently, another perspective, called the empirical model of practice, has been introduced (Blythe & Briar, 1985; Jayaratne & Levy, 1979). In this model, methods for empirically assessing effectiveness are integrated into the practice process so that feedback about effectiveness can guide the practitioner's interventions (Schinke, 1983). It has been noted that this approach runs counter to the traditional, deductive approach to practice formulations in social work (Ben-Sira, 1986). That is, most previous practice models begin with a general theory (for example, ego psychology, systems theory, learning theory) and attempt to deduce from that theory specific implications and prescriptions for practice. The empirical model, on the other hand, seeks to generate practice propositions or theory by induction from observed empirical relationships. An example of the latter is the previously noted relationship between formulation of specific outcome objectives and practice effectiveness, induced from empirical patterns reported in a number of research studies.

The debate over alternative practice perspectives can be expected to continue, perhaps becoming more usefully focused by the growing body of research on the bedrock question of what does or does not contribute to practice effectiveness.

Practice Research

In 1973 Fischer published his conclusion, based on a review of the accumulated research at that time, that casework, or the direct practice of social work, was not effective (Fischer, 1973). That summary statement cast a pall on the profession and provided support to its critics. Almost a decade later, Reid and Hanrahan (1982) published a review of the research on practice effectiveness conducted after Fischer's review. They found that social workers were effective in over 80 percent of the studies reviewed.

Why such a striking difference in ten years? Whereas most of the studies reviewed by Fischer compared interventions by social workers to nonintervention or intervention by untrained workers, most of the studies reviewed by Reid and Hanrahan compared a specific intervention strategy to a different, usually less specific intervention approach. In other words, the research reviewed by Reid and Hanrahan indicated that how social workers intervened made a difference—that is, certain interventions are more effective than others. This conclusion departed from an assumption implicit in many of the earlier studies reviewed by Fischer, namely that what social workers do is essentially similar and comparable.

The research reviewed by Reid and Hanrahan indicated that if social workers use empirically effective intervention methods, their practice is effective; they are less effective if they use empirically ineffective methods. Further, the more effective methods tend to be structured, focused, and specific. Thus, it is important for practitioners to know which methods are most effective and how to use them in practice.

The methodology of clinical research is receiving increased attention in schools of social work, in practice as well as in research courses, and there appears to be growing interest in clinical research among practitioners. This interest may be strengthened by the development of practitioner-oriented computerized information systems that support a variety of research activities by practitioners. This may well be the most important current trend in the field because of the influence that research and the resultant advances in practice knowledge can be expected to have on the future development of the profession.

Specialization

The trend toward specialization continues in social work, although efforts to formulate a coherent framework for specialization within the profession have been less than successful. Moreover, a countertrend has emerged, represented by the advanced generalist specialization that has appeared in a number of graduate programs.

Specializations continue to be defined according to (1) the population served, as in the cases of child welfare and aging; (2) the focal problem, such as substance abuse; (3) the practice setting, as in corrections or health; or (4) some combination of the above. Conceptual confusion about the most appropriate basis for specialization may not be a serious problem, but lack of clarity about how much difference justifies establishing a specialization is an important issue.

A prominent specialization that has emerged in recent years is industrial social work, sometimes called occupational social work or occupational social welfare. To a considerable extent, this specialization consists of introducing social work services into a new setting—new, at least, in the recent history of social work in the United States— the workplace. Some social workers in this specialization are advocating a broader perspective that would take the workplace itself as the object of intervention. (Developments in this specialization are discussed elsewhere in this encyclopedia.)

Health care continues to be a fertile source of subspecialities, probably because of the extent of specialization in the other health professions. The movement of social workers into subspecialty health areas—such as renal dialysis, oncology, pediatric pulmonary care, and pain control, to name a few— has often led to the formulation of an association of social workers in that area and, to that extent at least, the formation of a subspeciality in the profession of social work.

How to avoid the problems that can follow from excessive specialization remains an issue for social work.

Prevention

Prevention is not a new concept in social work. The need for prevention has been asserted, periodically, throughout much of the profession's history. For the most part, however, the call for prevention has been rhetorical because the knowledge base to support primary and secondary prevention was lacking and because of strained attempts to represent as prevention the treatment of problems after they have appeared.

What is different about the current emphasis on prevention in social work and in related disciplines is that research-generated knowledge to identify effective preventive interventions is being developed. The expanding empirical knowledge base about the relative effectiveness of alternative preventive approaches will make it possible to design preventive interventions with greater confidence than was possible when the only guidelines available were theoretical speculations (Gilchrist, Schinke, & Blythe, 1979). This is an important step forward because one of the major objections to funding prevention programs is uncertainty about their effectiveness. If research efforts continue to expand and if they continue to produce positive results, they can be expected to provide a powerful impetus for practitioners to increase their prevention activities and for agencies to give greater emphasis to prevention in their programs.

Political and Social Action

There are indications that political and social action among social workers, including direct service practitioners, have increased in recent years. These activities are discussed elsewhere in this encyclopedia, and this topic is mentioned here only to indicate that it is an important trend and to call attention to efforts to draw a closer connection between direct practice and policy formulation.

Many clinical practitioners have been drawn into political and social action by their interest in obtaining or protecting licensing legislation and in securing third-party vendor status for reimbursement of social work services. Such efforts often entail participation in coalitions with other groups and therefore broader involvement in and support for other social issues.

Increased participation in social and political action by practitioners, as part of their practice, is increasingly supported by perspectives that link direct practice to policy development and that view individual cases as members of classes of cases with similar problems that can best be addressed through advocacy and system change rather than through individual treatment (Briar & Briar, 1982).

Prospects

This brief review of current trends in direct practice omits a number of important trends that are discussed extensively elsewhere in this encyclopedia, such as those related to ethnic minorities, women, homosexuals, the disabled, and other special groups.

Taken together, the trends described here indicate that social work practice is in a period of active and significant change. Some of these changes appear to be directed internally, to the profession and its practices, which is hardly surprising in a period when the political climate is not supportive of social programs. Most promising, perhaps, many of the trends are affirmative efforts to strengthen the foundations and methodology of practice through conceptual clarification and especially research. If these efforts produce demonstrably successful results—and recent reviews indicate that successful results are feasible—the strength, vitality, and social utility of social work services may increase markedly over the next decade.

SCOTT BRIAR

For further information, see the major survey articles DIRECT PRACTICE IN SOCIAL WORK: OVERVIEW and HISTORY AND EVOLUTION OF SOCIAL WORK PRACTICE; articles on practice specializations, such as INDUSTRIAL SOCIAL WORK (OCCUPATIONAL SOCIAL WORK) and SCHOOL SOCIAL WORK; practice approaches and perspectives, such as ECOLOGICAL PERSPECTIVE and TASK-CENTERED APPROACH; practice methods, such as CASE MANAGEMENT and SOCIAL WORK PRACTICE WITH GROUPS; and APPENDIX 3: NASW STANDARDS FOR THE PRACTICE OF CLINICAL SOCIAL WORK.

References

Ben-Sira, Z. (1986). *A Structured Multivariate Approach to Social Work Practice.* Unpublished manuscript.

Berlin, S. (1983). "Cognitive-Behavioral Approaches." In A. Rosenblatt & D. Waldfogel (Eds.), *Handbook of Clinical Social Work* (pp. 1095–1119). San Francisco: Jossey-Bass.

Blythe, B. J., & Briar, S. (1985). "Developing Empirically Based Models of Practice." *Social Work, 30*(6), 483–488.

Briar, K. H., & Briar, S. (1982). "Clinical Social Work and Public Policies." In M. Mahaffey &

J. W. Hanks (Eds.), *Practical Politics: Social Work and Political Responsibility* (pp. 45–65). Silver Spring, Md.: National Association of Social Workers.

Burgess, R. L., & Bushell, D., Jr. (1969). *Behavioral Sociology: The Experimental Analysis of Social Process.* New York: Columbia University Press.

Ewalt, P. L. (1980a). "Preface." In P. L. Ewalt (Ed.), *Toward a Definition of Clinical Social Work* (p. iii). Washington, D.C.: National Association of Social Workers.

Ewalt, P. L. (1980b). "Social Work Process as an Organizing Concept." In P. L. Ewalt (Ed.), *Toward a Definition of Clinical Social Work* (pp. 87–91). Washington, D.C.: National Association of Social Workers.

Fischer, J. (1973). "Is Casework Effective? A Review." *Social Work, 18*(1), 5–20.

Germain, C. B., & Gitterman, A. (1980). *The Life Model of Social Work Practice.* New York: Columbia University Press.

Gilchrist, L., Schinke, S., & Blythe, B. (1979). "Primary Prevention Services for Children and Youth." *Children and Youth Services Review, 1,* 379–391.

Jayaratne, S., & Levy, R. L. (1979). *Empirical Clinical Practice.* New York: Columbia University Press.

Meyer, C. H. (1983). "Selecting Appropriate Practice Models." In A. Rosenblatt & D. Waldfogel (Eds.), *Handbook of Clinical Social Work* (pp. 736–737). San Francisco: Jossey-Bass.

Miller, L. M. (1978). *Behavior Management: The New Science of Managing People at Work.* New York: Wiley Interscience.

Pincus, A., & Minahan, A. (1973). *Social Work Practice: Model and Method.* Itasca, Ill.: F. E. Peacock Publishing Co.

Reid, W., & Epstein, L. (1972). *Task Centered Casework.* New York: Columbia University Press.

Reid, W., & Hanrahan, P. (1982). "Recent Evaluations of Social Work: Grounds for Optimism." *Social Work, 27*(4), 328–340.

Rose, S. D. (1980). *A Casebook in Group Therapy: A Behavioral-Cognitive Approach.* Englewood Cliffs, N.J.: Prentice-Hall.

Rosenblatt, A., & Waldfogel, D. (Eds.) (1983). *Handbook of Clinical Social Work.* San Francisco: Jossey-Bass.

Schinke, S. P. (1983). "Data-Based Practice." In A. Rosenblatt & D. Waldfogel (Eds.), *Handbook of Clinical Social Work* (pp. 1077–1094). San Francisco: Jossey-Bass.

Whittaker, J. K. (1974). *Social Treatment: An Approach to Interpersonal Helping.* Chicago: Aldine Publishing Co.

DIRECT PRACTICE EFFECTIVENESS

As a profession, social work has long questioned the value of its work with clients. As early as 1931, a presidential address given by Richard C. Cabot to the National Conference on Social Work exhorted social workers to examine the effectiveness of their interventions (Mullen, Dumpson, & Associates, 1972). Since that time, other groups have also urged the profession to conduct such investigations, including governmental units, third-party payers, and clients (Briar & Blythe, 1985; Kisch & Kroll, 1980). Numerous evaluations of social work programs and interventions have resulted. This article summarizes the major reviews of research on practice effectiveness in social work, examines emerging methods of assessing practice effectiveness, and suggests ways of improving and expanding research in this area.

Reviews of Effectiveness Studies

Although they discuss research spanning a longer period, all the major reviews of practice effectiveness were published between 1972 and 1982. Segal published one of the first reviews in 1972. As shall become apparent, each reviewer followed different guidelines for identifying studies to be evaluated. Excluded from Segal's critique, for example, are studies of casework in institutional settings and with clients suffering from psychotic disorders. Segal included studies in which the intervention was delivered by professionals other than social workers as long as social work was a significant part of the interventive program. Segal described the findings of these effectiveness studies as equivocal with trends in the negative direction. Like most reviewers, Segal also suggested means for improving effectiveness research. He argued that involving social scientists would improve the research because they tend to use more sophisticated designs and better measures of outcome.

Also in 1972, Edward Mullen and James Dumpson edited a book that reviewed several studies of social work practice (Mullen, Dumpson, & Associates, 1972). They identified 13 studies meeting their criteria, which called for each study to be a "relevant and major evaluation of the effects of social work intervention" (p. vii), to employ an experimental design, and to suggest innovations for social work programs and education. In a detailed examination of these 13 studies included in the book, Geismar (1972) concluded that 4 projects found almost no significant differences between the experimental and control groups on the major dependent measures, 2 found very limited gains for the experimental group, and the remaining 7 studies reported modest success. Among the suggestions made by the reviewers were the application of more sophisticated research technology and more clearly stated social work goals (Jones & Borgatta, 1972) and grounding the social programs in a theoretical framework (Breedlove, 1972). Finally, Mullen and Dumpson suggested that such broad social problems as poverty and racism must be addressed at macro- and mezzosystem levels, rather than simply through interventions directed toward individuals.

Fischer (1973) wrote one of the best known reviews of effectiveness studies, which he described as the first comprehensive examination of casework effectiveness, in 1973. Before commencing the review, he noted that casework and effectiveness were not well-defined terms. He limited his critique to studies that had some form of control group, were conducted after 1930 within the United States, and involved services in which professional caseworkers constituted more than a minority of the treatment team. Fischer found 11 studies meeting these criteria. Of the 11 studies, 6 compared an experimental group to a no-treatment control group and dealt with children and adolescents. None of these studies found a significant effect for the experimental clients compared to the controls. The remaining 5 studies compared a particular form of professional casework to some other form of treatment. In this category, Fischer cited 3 studies that found little or no significant differences and 2 that had inconclusive results because of methodological problems. He concluded that professional casework was without demonstrated proof of its effectiveness.

Fischer's review caused considerable turmoil in the field. Many of those who responded to Fischer's work argued that the findings were negative because the research methodology of the 11 studies was inadequate to detect client improvement. In particular, many writers stressed that research questions about effectiveness should be stated in specific rather than global terms to address adequately the issue of casework effectiveness (Cohen, 1976; Hudson, 1976). The studies also were criticized for providing insufficient control over the service components of the program and for lacking clear definitions of the interventions. Some blamed the lack of observed success on the researchers' greater attention to measuring long-term rather than short-term goals. Finally, the assessment of outcome was criticized for being "crude and insensitive" (Reid & Hanrahan, 1982, p. 328).

The next major review of effectiveness studies was published by Wood in 1978. Because her criteria for selecting studies for review were slightly different than Fischer's, Wood examined some studies not considered by Fischer. Specifically, she considered evaluations of direct practice that were conducted under social work auspices or had social work as a major component of the intervention, that were carried out in the continental United States, and that included a control, comparison, or contrast group in the research design. Rather than ask questions of general effectiveness, Wood argued that the 22 outcome studies she evaluated should be examined for their potential contributions to knowledge about direct practice. Here too, however, the effectiveness studies were fairly disappointing. The majority of the studies failed to specify sufficiently the treatment programs, the client problems, and the conditions under which the problems operated. Because the interventions were poor in her judgment, Wood was not surprised that the findings suggested that social work was not effective. She was able to extract six principles of quality practice from the studies reporting positive outcomes, however. According to Wood, practitioners should develop an accurate definition of the problem, thoroughly analyze the problem including the factors that create or maintain it and that can help to resolve it, assess with the client how amenable the problem is to change, and set goals, negotiate a contract with the client, plan an interventive strategy, and evaluate client progress.

Although he did not review specific studies, Mullen (1983) made some general

statements about social work's effectiveness at the National Association of Social Workers' (NASW) Professional Symposium held in 1981. He identified four factors that have made it difficult for social workers to demonstrate their effectiveness. The first of these is the difficulty of specifying treatment goals. Accordingly, Mullen advised that social workers should give a high priority to developing the ability to identify treatment goals that can be evaluated. The second factor relates to the complexity of the problems dealt with by social work. When the effectiveness of psychotherapy is examined across the disciplines, Mullen noted that there is more support for interventions addressing circumscribed problems such as anxiety. Yet social workers tend to focus on more complicated client problems that may require intervention at multiple levels. The changing priorities of funding bodies is a third factor that limits effectiveness research in social work. Research topics are frequently dictated by the availability of funds, rather than by a logical progression of inquiry into a complex area. Finally, Mullen argued that social work must devote additional resources to developing expertise in conducting practice effectiveness research.

Mullen suggested that a critical finding from the past 20 years of research, albeit based on indirect generalization from studies of treatment failures, is that multilevel interventions are more effective with certain disadvantaged clients such as the elderly and the poor. He believes that an important item on the social work agenda involves defining and evaluating such multilevel interventions with various client populations. Mullen discussed the findings of research, largely conducted in other professions, that speak to the relationship between outcome and worker characteristics, agency variables, relationship variables, client characteristics, and intervention techniques. The extent to which these findings can be applied to social workers and their clients, however, remains unanswered. Along with several other colleagues, Mullen called for an end to the dichotomy between practice and research and identified education as an important vehicle for ending this dichotomy.

Most recently, Reid and Hanrahan (1982) asked the question of effectiveness, but this time they came up with a more pleasing answer. Noting that doubts about the effectiveness of social work interventions could lead to reduced support for social work by policymakers, funding bodies, community groups, clients, potential social work students, and other professionals, Reid and Hanrahan set out to review effectiveness studies published between 1973 and 1979. Their criteria for including a study in the review were that the study was published; was conducted in the United States predominantly by social workers; used an adequate, unbiased form of measurement; and had random assignment to experimental and control or comparison groups. A literature search uncovered 22 studies meeting these criteria. When these were compared to 16 equivalent studies published prior to 1973, some striking differences emerged. Most significant was the finding that the outcomes in all but two or three of the studies conducted after 1973 were positive, while less than a third of the pre-1973 studies had positive outcomes. For the first time, a major review of social work outcome research suggested that social work was effective. Further, the post-1973 studies that failed to demonstrate success were comparing two forms of treatment, not comparing treatment to an absence of treatment.

Aside from the issue of effectiveness, the most striking differences uncovered by these reviewers occurred in the area of interventions. The newer studies tended to examine structured forms of practice that involved well-explicated procedures aimed at achieving highly specific goals. Intervention components were influenced by client-centered counseling and task-centered methods as well as by learning theory. In contrast, most pre-1973 studies involved "casework," which might cover any of a wide range of methods. When more structured approaches were followed in the later studies, workers and clients had greater agreement on goals than they did in the earlier studies. Moreover, the interventions in all but one of the newer studies were planned and implemented by the researchers. This may have occurred in response to the criticisms of the earlier studies in which researchers acted more like program evaluators, whose ability to select appropriate outcome measures was hampered by their insufficient knowledge of the goals of the interventions. Another difference between the earlier and the later studies

relates to choice of outcome measures. In studies conducted prior to 1973, interviews with clients and standardized questionnaires assessed client change. The later studies more frequently relied on more objective measures, such as observation of actual client performance. Reid and Hanrahan noted that these measures may be of somewhat less practical significance, given that they tend to be circumscribed and often involve performance in analogue situations rather than in real life. They also caution that the brief follow-up periods in the later studies do not establish that client change was durable.

Recent Developments

The primary means of examining practice effectiveness in social work has been to collect all the relevant research and then use the "narrative integration" or "box-score" approach to evaluate it (Berzens, 1984). The research examined using these approaches tends to be experimental or quasiexperimental group design studies. Narrative integration involves reading the studies and writing an evaluative appraisal of them. In the box-score approach, the reviewer determines the number of studies in which some form of social work practice was found to be statistically superior to no treatment or to some alternative form of treatment. Recently, however, researchers have proposed and applied other means of assessing practice effectiveness. These include meta-analysis, evaluation of clinical significance, and single-subject methodology.

Meta-Analysis. Proponents of meta-analysis have expressed concern about the box-score and narrative integration approaches (Smith, Glass, & Miller, 1980). They charge that statistical significance is the sole, *dichotomous* standard for determining effectiveness with the box-score method and that this standard is influenced by sample size. Hence, studies with larger samples can bias the conclusions of a box-score or narrative integration review by achieving statistical significance with relatively weak results. Both approaches have been criticized on the grounds that the reliability of one's conclusions decreases as the number of studies reviewed increases (Cooper & Rosenthal, 1980) and that criteria for selecting studies to review tend to be arbitrary (Berzens, 1984).

In contrast to the traditional literature reviews relying on box-score or narrative integration strategies, meta-analysis involves a systematic survey to identify appropriate research studies and then examines the "effect size" rather than statistical significance. Typically, effect size is determined by calculating the difference between the mean for the treatment group and the mean for the control group on the outcome measure and dividing this difference by the standard deviation of the control group (Smith & Glass, 1977). Effect sizes are then averaged across studies. The control group may be a no-treatment group or any form of comparison group such as an alternative treatment group.

Social work has been slower than other professions to apply meta-analysis strategies (Nurius, 1984). However, a major effort employing meta-analysis procedures was begun in 1983, under the auspices of the Harriett M. Bartlett Practice Effectiveness Project, directed by Lynn Videka-Sherman and funded by NASW. The project's efforts to retrieve research on social work practice were thorough and included searching ten online databases; reviewing *Social Work Research & Abstracts;* scanning literature reviews in social work; surveying agencies, social work research centers, researchers, and schools of social work; examining conference proceedings and government publications; and posting press releases in the *NASW News.* The project attempted to uncover unpublished studies as well as published ones. These attempts to mount a broad-based, extensive search for studies will help the project avoid criticisms of selectivity that have been lodged against previous reviews of effectiveness (Cook & Leviton, 1980).

All in all, the search identified 63 dissertations and 617 research reports related to social work practice effectiveness. Because so many studies were found, it was decided to work with subsets of the studies to make the task more manageable and to make it easier to interpret the findings. In 1985, the studies related to mental health were being submitted to a variation of the meta-analysis procedures developed by Smith and Glass (1977). Rather than simply ask if social work practice is effective, Videka-Sherman and her colleagues intended to pursue a number of specific questions regarding the effects of client, practitioner, treatment, and research

methodology variables in explaining the variation in findings across the studies. Meta-analysis procedures were to be supplemented with other techniques aimed at analyzing the most effective practice methods by identifying the client or intervention characteristics that are associated with the strongest outcomes (Klitgaard, 1978).

The Bartlett project published findings that outlined a number of implications for practice and research. The report concluded with the following statement: "The empirical knowledge base of social work practice in mental health is much broader, and probably of better quality, than most social workers (researchers and clinicians alike) have realized" (Videka-Sherman, 1985, p. 60).

It is important to note, however, that meta-analysis procedures in general have been criticized (Glass & Kliegl, 1983; Nurius, 1984; Wilson & Rachman, 1983). Only the most commonly lodged complaints will be mentioned here. A frequent objection to meta-analysis is that the procedure lumps treatment techniques into gross categories and fails to distinguish adequately among various client problems (Rachman & Wilson, 1980). Smith and her colleagues contend that this is not a problem because meta-analysis provides an overview of psychotherapy effectiveness (Smith, Glass, & Miller, 1980). Perhaps a more serious criticism is that the results of meta-analysis are only as good as the original studies on which they are based (Eysenck, 1978; Kazdin & Wilson, 1978). Disagreement exists on whether effect size is positively or negatively associated with quality of study (Berzens, 1984; Smith, Glass, & Miller, 1980; Wortman, 1981). This criticism is especially apropros in social work since the profession's methodological sophistication is in a developmental state, and the nature of the client population and target problems frequently limits methodological rigor (Azar, 1984). To exclude studies of questionable quality again raises the problem of selectivity in choice of research, while assuming, perhaps prematurely, that relatively objective criteria for judging quality can be developed. Others have suggested that studies be sorted according to their level of rigor and evaluated separately to test for differences across study quality (Strube & Hartmann, 1982). This too requires objective criteria for judging the quality of the studies. In any event, it will be interesting to see the results of meta-analysis applied to practice effectiveness studies in social work and to compare these results to those of the box-score analyses.

Evaluation of Clinical Significance. Practitioners and researchers alike have voiced concern that statistical significance does not necessarily indicate that clients have made clinically (or practically) significant improvement (Reid & Hanrahan, 1982). The problem is that statistically significant differences may be observed when the actual difference in group means is quite small. Further, client improvement may be statistically significant but, in reality, represent movement of only one or two points on a seven-point scale; posttreatment scores may even remain in the pathological range for the experimental group. Some contend that this discrepancy between statistical and clinical significance contributes to practitioners' limited interest in research on practice effectiveness (Barlow, 1980). To address these concerns, social workers and others have suggested that determinations of clinical significance should augment studies of statistical significance (Bloom & Fischer, 1982; Blythe & Briar, in press; Kazdin, 1980; Reid & Smith, 1981).

Unfortunately, clinical significance is not well defined. In general, it means that the observed change holds some practical importance for the client. Methods of evaluating clinical significance have been proposed, but agreement, or even discussion, about the tradeoffs of these various methods is lacking. Kazdin and Wilson (1978), for instance, suggested reporting the proportion of clients who improved significantly, relying on clear-cut clinical criteria of improvement. What these clear-cut criteria are remains to be determined by researchers and practitioners.

Judging clients against certain normative standards has also been suggested. Kazdin (1977) proposed a social comparison method in which posttreatment improvement is judged against a standard supplied by a "nondeviant" peer group. For example, the parenting skills of abusive mothers might be compared with those of nonabusive mothers, after matching for relevant variables such as socioeconomic status, education level, and number of children. Obviously, the selection of a normative group must be done with care

and may be especially difficult for certain client groups (for example, handicapped individuals or schizophrenics). Another approach discussed by Kazdin (1977) is subjective evaluation, which prescribes assessing how others view the client. In this approach, significant others are interviewed to determine if they have observed specific gains in the target areas or more global improvement. As an example, social work researchers have solicited global impressions of the effects of pregnancy-prevention groups on adolescents from their teachers and parents (Schinke, Blythe, & Gilchrist, 1981). Similarly, teachers and parents were queried about the study habits of underachieving students at the conclusion of the intervention (Polster, Lynch, & Pinkston, 1981).

Noting that it remains a poorly defined concept, Jacobson, Follette, and Revenstorf (1984) offered a two-step method for determining clinical significance. First, they proposed that clinically significant improvement be identified as movement from the dysfunctional to the functional area during the course of intervention on the variable selected to assess client change. The functional area is defined by normative data. The change in each client in a treatment group is examined to determine if it meets this criterion for clinical significance. This information is entered into an equation that produces a statistic describing the proportion of clients whose posttest scores connote clinically significant improvement. Note that this step is simply a more objective version of Kazdin's recommendation that normative standards be applied. It is open to the same criticisms as Kazdin's suggestions, namely, that normative functioning may not be an appropriate treatment goal and that it may be difficult, if not impossible, to define an appropriate normative group. If norms are not available, however, the researchers suggest a means of calculating a descriptive statistic with data from the experimental and control groups under study.

The second step in establishing clinical significance proposed by Jacobson and his colleagues involves documenting that the observed change is statistically reliable or, stated another way, that it exceeds the margin of measurement error. In particular, statistical unreliability should be a concern when the functional and dysfunctional distributions overlap. In other words, a client may be in the dysfunctional range before intervention and in the functional range after intervention, but the apparent change may be due to imprecise measurement. To rule out measurement error, Jacobson and his colleagues proposed a reliable change index (RC), which is calculated by subtracting a client's pretest score from his or her posttest score and dividing the difference by the standard error of measurement. If RC is larger than ± 1.96, the client's posttest score can be considered an indication of real change rather than measurement error (P .05).

The authors recommended that future practice effectiveness research routinely report clinical significance determinations following these two steps or alternative methods of making such determinations as they are developed. Their suggestions may sound complex, but they actually require applications of simple formulas. Jacobson and his associates pointed out several limitations accompanying their methods, however. Most notable is the caution that determinations resulting from these methods must be moderated by considering the sophistication of the measurement instrument, along with the caveat that multiple measures may produce conflicting determinations. Finally, they indicated that their suggestions are conservative and may lead to interventions appearing to be less effective than currently is the case. Although still untested, these suggestions are the most objective means proposed thus far for determining clinical significance. Researchers who are planning to examine practice effectiveness in social work should explore these new options.

Single-Subject Methodology. For over a decade, authors have urged practitioners to apply single-subject methodology to evaluate the effectiveness of their work with clients. Proponents of single-subject methodology maintain that the methodology is in some ways superior to methodology based on group designs in evaluating practice effectiveness (Jayaratne, 1977; Levy, 1983; Levy & Olson, 1979).

A frequent criticism of group-design studies is that they obscure important information about specific clients and their individual responses to treatment. By aggregating data across several clients, group-design studies describe only average outcomes for the sample as a whole. Thus, some clients may get better while others get worse, but these varied responses to treatment cannot be discerned. In addition to averaging information about outcomes, group-design studies generally collect this information at only two points in time, before and after treatment. The concern is that simple information about change from pretreatment to posttreatment may not tell the whole story. For example, an intervention may have an immediately positive effect but that effect may diminish over time; such information cannot be detected in a pretest-posttest design. Also lost in group-design studies is information about particular relationships between treatment outcomes and client characteristics such as age, problem onset and severity, and motivation to change.

Single-case evaluations, on the other hand, track specific clients' responses to interventions over time. Outcomes can be associated with client variables that may affect treatment progress. In some ways, single-subject methodology addresses certain concerns outlined in earlier reviews of practice effectiveness research. For example, in single-case studies, research questions are stated in highly explicit, not global, terms. Intervention and measurement are more likely to be well defined and clearly related to each other because the practitioner, rather than an outside evaluator, controls the specification of both independent and dependent variables. In addition, practitioners are more likely to assess circumscribed, short-term (and more attainable) goals than more general, long-term goals.

Another potential advantage of single-subject methodology lies in the area of generalization. Recent studies of practice effectiveness tend to consider the efficacy of a treatment innovation being delivered under highly controlled research conditions. The extent to which favorable outcomes obtained in these controlled settings can be generalized to typical practice settings is questionable. Single-subject methodology allows an examination of the effectiveness of social work practice as it commonly occurs.

Although much of the early work in defining single-subject methodology as a research tool was carried out by behaviorally oriented psychologists and psychiatrists

(Barlow & Hersen, 1984; Kratochwill, 1978) and by agriculture researchers before them (Fisher, 1921), social work has taken the lead in applying this methodology to practice effectiveness. Social work professionals have advanced the application of this methodology in practice through articles describing its importance (Howe, 1974; Levy & Olson, 1979), texts delineating how to use it (Bloom & Fischer, 1982; Jayaratne & Levy, 1979; Tripodi & Epstein, 1980; Wodarski, 1981), and curriculum innovations preparing social workers to evaluate practice with it (Briar, 1973; Gottlieb & Richey, 1980; Siegel, 1984). Besides promulgating this methodology to assess practice effectiveness, the profession has suggested adapting the methodology to fit clinical practice. For instance, social workers recognized that simple designs, such as the AB design, are more appropriate for most clinical applications than are designs requiring withdrawal or reversal of treatment (Gottlieb & Richey, 1980). As another example, social workers have identified the ability of single-case methodology to evaluate intermediate treatment goals, such as a client's expression of feelings, as well as the ultimate treatment outcome (Nelsen, 1984). Social workers also realized the value of collecting retrospective baseline data to facilitate the application of single-case methodology in practice and investigated the accuracy of data collected in this manner (Green & Wright, 1979).

While these advances are being made, other problems are surfacing that must be addressed to make the methodology more compatible with practice. High priority should be given to the issue of measurement. Practitioners often state that measures that fit their client problems are not readily available (Briar & Conte, 1978), which prevents them from carrying out single-case evaluations. Work on rapid-assessment, standardized instruments is helpful in this regard (Edleson, in press; Levitt & Reid, 1981), but other measurement options must be examined. For example, self-anchored scales, in which the client rates the intensity of his or her own thoughts or feelings, can be constructed to assess most client problems and are highly client-specific (Bloom & Fischer, 1982), but means of increasing their reliability and validity must be explored. Although single-case methodology is said to be theory-free, the

fact remains that it more readily fits more structured forms of practice. Some initial efforts have been put forth to define how single-subject research can be conducted by social workers using less structured treatment methods (Nelsen, 1981), but methodologists should extend greater assistance to these practitioners. Similarly, more effort must be devoted to adapting the methodology to work with families and in short-term treatment settings such as crisis centers and hospitals.

Published examples of single-case evaluations can serve as models for other practitioners who wish to examine their effectiveness. Although some social work examples exist (Berlin, 1983; Broxmeyer, 1978; LeCroy, Koeplin-LeCroy, & Long, 1982; Tolson, 1977), the literature should have many more such reports. To assess practice effectiveness more broadly, appropriate methods for aggregating single-subject findings must also be developed. Similar to group-design studies, the box-score approach is most commonly used for aggregating such data. Meta-analysis strategies for single-case data have also been proposed, but they await field testing (Corcoran, 1985; Gingerich, 1984). Finally, certain technical problems in carrying out single-case evaluations demand attention. Practitioners need guidance in handling such matters as a client's noncompliance with data collection, the concern that data are "fudged," and discussing negative data with clients.

Expanding Practice Effectiveness Research

Although the development of meta-analysis strategies and methods for determining clinical significance and the application of single-subject methodology to assess practice effectiveness represent promising improvements in social work's ability to examine practice effectiveness, there is always room for more work. Although any list of suggested future directions is seemingly endless, only recommendations of highest priority will be addressed here.

Based on the review of effectiveness studies by Reid and Hanrahan (1982) and social work's increasingly sophisticated research methodology, it seems time to put to rest the general question of whether social casework is effective. Following Thomlison's

(1984) suggestion, attention should be turned to investigating particular forms of social work intervention with various client groups under a range of conditions and settings. In other words, more specific questions about social work's effectiveness need to be addressed at this time. In particular, work is needed in the areas of family treatment and process variables mediating outcome.

Family Therapy. What was true when Briar and Conte reviewed the literature in 1978 and when Wells did the same in 1981, remains true today—social work has made relatively few contributions to the research on the effectiveness of family therapy. Hence, social workers examining family therapy research must rely heavily on treatment methods developed by psychologists, psychiatrists, or other human service professionals outside of social work. The most recent reviewer, Wells (1981), concluded that family therapy practitioners who want to use empirically based methods must use behavioral techniques in their work with families, particularly when working with aggressive children and delinquent adolescents. He further noted that certain forms of nonbehavioral family therapy have had fair success with particular psychosomatic disorders and with family crisis problems. Unfortunately, these findings may have limited generalizability to social work, as Wells observed, in that few studies have dealt with low-socioeconomic or multiproblem families, who are typical social work clients.

It is clear that social work research resources should be devoted to the central question regarding the effectiveness of family therapy with social work's typical client populations. In this regard, the definition of family therapy needs to reflect current demographic trends. Research on family therapy should not be limited to traditional nuclear families, but should include work with other family compositions including blended, intergenerational, single-parent, and shared custody families. Further, methodologists need to develop means of dealing with problems such as multiple targets of intervention and inadequate control with multiproblem clients (Azar, 1984). Rabin (1981) has suggested that single-subject methodology can be adapted to explore practice effectiveness

with families, but additional methodological solutions need to be found.

Process Variables. Another area receiving relatively limited attention in social work research is the contribution of process variables to client outcome. Process variables can include practitioners' characteristics such as technical interviewing skills, gender, ethnicity, assertiveness, and empathy. They can also refer to clients' characteristics or workers' perceptions of clients such as attractiveness, motivation to change, and assertiveness. Other process variables include characteristics related to the setting such as the worker's office, the waiting room, and the location of the agency. Several investigators have examined how clients are perceived by social workers (Borgatta, Fanshel, & Meyer, 1960; Chalfant & Kurtz, 1972; Jayaratne & Irey, 1981; Pratt, 1970; Rubenstein & Bloch, 1978; Segal, 1970). This research needs to be updated and extended from simply describing social workers' perceptions to studying the effect of these variables on client outcome and dropout. From research conducted in other helping professions, it appears that similarity positively affects outcome (Luborsky et al., 1971; Smith & Glass, 1977). Moreover, the areas of similarity known to be important are social class, interests and values, and orientation to interpersonal relations. In that social workers and their clients often are dissimilar in some of these areas, it is especially important that research examine if these same relationships hold up in the social work profession. To increase the likelihood that findings will be applied, research on process variables should focus on those variables that can be controlled by individual social workers or by agencies (through assignment of clients to workers), rather than on variables that cannot be manipulated.

Conclusion

Although research on practice effectiveness has not yet generated a comprehensive array of interventive techniques, important strides have been made. Recent studies demonstrate the efficacy of social work. Promising methodological developments make it likely that research on practice will yield findings of increasing significance for practitioners. Further, as the volume of research increases and as it extends to areas currently understudied, social work services will improve.

BETTY J. BLYTHE
SCOTT BRIAR

For further information, see DIRECT PRACTICE: TRENDS AND ISSUES; PROFESSION OF SOCIAL WORK: CONTEMPORARY CHARACTERISTICS; PROGRAM EVALUATION; QUALITY ASSURANCE; RESEARCH IN SOCIAL WORK; SINGLE SUBJECT RESEARCH DESIGNS.

References

Azar, S. T. (1984, August). *Methodological Considerations in Treatment Outcome Research in Child Maltreatment.* Paper presented at the National Conference on Family Violence Research, Durham, N.H.

Barlow, D. H. (1980). "Behavior Therapy: The Next Decade." *Behavior Therapy, 11*(3), 315–328.

Barlow, D. H., & Hersen, M. (1984). *Single-Case Experimental Designs: Strategies for Studying Behavior Change* (2nd ed.). New York: Pergamon Press.

Berlin, S. B. (1983). "Single-Case Evaluation: Another Version." *Social Work Research and Abstracts, 19*(1), 3–11.

Berzens, J. I. (1984). "Psychotherapy." In A. S. Bellack & M. Hersen (Eds.), *Research Methods in Clinical Psychology* (pp. 208–232). New York: Pergamon Press.

Blythe, B. J., & Briar, S. (1985). "Developing Empirically Based Models of Practice." *Social Work, 30*(6), 483–488.

Bloom, M., & Fischer, J. (1982). *Evaluating Practice: Guidelines for the Accountable Professional.* San Francisco: Jossey-Bass.

Borgatta, E. F., Fanshel, D., & Meyer, H. J. (1960). *Social Workers' Perceptions of Clients: A Study of the Caseload of a Social Agency.* New York: Russell Sage Foundation.

Breedlove, J. L. (1972). "Theory Development as a Task for the Evaluator." In E. J. Mullen, J. R. Dumpson, & Associates (Eds.), *Evaluation of Social Intervention* (pp. 55–70). San Francisco: Jossey-Bass.

Briar, S. (1973). "Effective Social Work Intervention in Direct Practice: Implications for Education." In *Facing the Challenge* (pp. 17–30). New York: Council on Social Work Education.

Briar, S., & Blythe, B. J. (1985). "Agency Support for Evaluating the Outcomes of Social Work Services." *Administration in Social Work, 9*(2), 25–36.

Briar, S., & Conte, J. R. (1978). "Families." In H. S. Maas (Ed.), *Social Service Research: Reviews of Studies* (pp. 9–38). Washington, D.C.: National Association of Social Workers.

Broxmeyer, N. (1978). "Practitioner-Research in Treating a Borderline Child." *Social Work Research & Abstracts, 14*(4), 5–10.

Chalfant, H. P., & Kurtz, R. A. (1972). "Factors Affecting Social Workers' Judgments of Alcoholics." *Journal of Health and Social Behavior, 13*(4), 331–336.

Cohen, J. (1976). "A Brief Comment: Evaluating the Effectiveness of an Unspecified 'Casework' Treatment in Producing Change." In J. Fischer (Ed.), *The Effectiveness of Social Casework* (pp. 176–189). Springfield, Ill.: Charles C Thomas, Publisher.

Cook, T. D., & Leviton, L. C. (1980). "Reviewing the Literature: A Comparison of Traditional Methods with Meta-Analysis." *Journal of Personality, 48*(4), 449–472.

Cooper, H. M., & Rosenthal, R. (1980). "Statistical versus Traditional Procedures for Summarizing Research Findings." *Psychological Bulletin, 87,* 442–449.

Corcoran, K. J. (1985). "Aggregating Idiographic Data: A Meta-Analytic Statistic for Single-Subject Research." *Social Work Research & Abstracts, 21*(2), 9–11.

Edleson, J. L. (in press). "Rapid-Assessment Instruments for Evaluating Practice with Children and Youth." *Journal of Social Service Research.*

Eysenck, H. J. (1978). "An Exercise in Mega-Silliness." *American Psychologist, 33*(5), 517.

Fischer, J. (1973). "Is Casework Effective? A Review." *Social Work, 18*(1), 5–20.

Fisher, R. A. (1921). "Studies in Crop Variation." *Journal of Agricultural Science,* Part II, *11,* 8–35.

Geismar, L. L. (1972). "Thirteen Evaluative Studies." In E. J. Mullen, J. R. Dumpson, & Associates (Eds.), *Evaluation of Social Intervention* (pp. 15–38). San Francisco: Jossey-Bass.

Gingerich, W. J. (1984). "Meta-Analysis of Applied Time-Series Data." *The Journal of Applied Behavioral Science, 20*(1), 71–79.

Glass, G. V., & Kliegl, R. M. (1983). "An Apology for Research Integration in the Study of Psychotherapy." *Journal of Consulting and Clinical Psychology, 51*(1), 28–41.

Gottlieb, N., & Richey, C. (1980). "Education of Human Services Practitioners for Clinical Evaluation." In R. W. Weinbach & A. Rubin (Eds.), *Teaching Social Work Research: Alternative Programs and Strategies* (pp. 3–12). New York: Council on Social Work Education.

Green, Jr., G. R., & Wright, J. E. (1979). "The Retrospective Approach to Collecting Baseline Data." *Social Work Research & Abstracts, 15*(3), 25–30.

Howe, M. W. (1974). "Casework Self-Evaluation: A Single-Subject Approach." *Social Service Review, 48*(1), 1–23.

Hudson, W. (1976). "Special Problems in the Assessment of Growth and Deterioration." In J. Fischer (Ed.), *The Effectiveness of Social Casework* (pp. 197–224). Springfield, Ill.: Charles C Thomas, Publisher.

Jacobson, N. S., Follette, W. C., & Revenstorf, D. (1984). "Psychotherapy Outcome Research: Methods for Reporting Variability and Evaluating Clinical Significance." *Behavior Therapy, 15*(4), 336–352.

Jayaratne, S. (1977). "Single-Subject and Group Designs in Treatment Evaluation." *Social Work Research & Abstracts, 13*(3), 35–42.

Jayaratne, S., & Irey, K. V. (1981). "Gender Differences in the Perceptions of Social Workers." *Social Casework, 62*(7), 405–412.

Jayaratne, S., & Levy, R. L. (1979). *Empirical Clinical Practice.* New York: Columbia University Press.

Jones, W. C., & Borgatta, E. F. (1972). "Methodology of Evaluation." In E. J. Mullen, J. R. Dumpson, & Associates (Eds.), *Evaluation of Social Intervention* (pp. 39–54). San Francisco: Jossey-Bass.

Kazdin, A. E. (1977). "Assessing the Clinical or Applied Importance of Behavior Change Through Social Validation." *Behavior Modification, 1*(4), 427–452.

Kazdin, A. E. (1980). *Research Design in Clinical Psychology.* New York: Harper & Row.

Kazdin, A. E., & Wilson, G. T. (1978). *Evaluation of Behavior Therapy: Issues, Evidence, and Research Strategies.* Cambridge, Mass.: Ballinger Publishing Co.

Kisch, J., & Kroll, J. (1980). "Meaningfulness versus Effectiveness: Paradoxical Implications in the Evaluation of Psychotherapy." *Psychotherapy: Theory, Research and Practice, 17*(4), 401–413.

Klitgaard, R. (1978). "Identifying Exceptional Performers." *Policy Analysis, 4*(4), 529–547.

Kratochwill, T. R. (Ed.). (1978). *Single Subject Research: Strategies for Evaluating Change.* New York: Academic Press.

LeCroy, C. W., Koeplin-LeCroy, M. T., & Long, J. (1982). "Preventive Intervention through Parent-Training Programs." *Social Work in Education, 4*(2), 53–62.

Levitt, J. L., & Reid, W. J. (1981). "Rapid-Assessment Instruments for Practice." *Social Work Research & Abstracts, 17*(1), 13–19.

Levy, R. L. (1983). "Overview of Single-Case Experiments." In A. Rosenblatt & D. Waldfogel (Eds.), *Handbook of Clinical Social Work* (pp. 583–602). San Francisco: Jossey-Bass.

Levy, R. L., & Olson, D. G. (1979). "The Single-Subject Methodology in Clinical Practice: An Overview." *Journal of Social Service Research, 3*(1), 25–49.

Luborsky, L., et al. (1971). "Factors Influencing the Outcome of Psychotherapy: A Review of Quantitative Research." *Psychological Bulletin, 75*(3), 145–185.

Mullen, E. J. (1983). "Evaluating Social Work's Effectiveness." In M. Dinerman (Ed.), *Social Work in a Turbulent World* (pp. 63–75). Silver Spring, Md.: National Association of Social Workers.

Mullen, E. J., Dumpson, J. R., & Associates (Eds.). (1972). *Evaluation of Social Intervention.* San Francisco: Jossey-Bass.

Nelsen, J. C. (1981). "Issues in Single-Subject Research for Nonbehaviorists." *Social Work Research & Abstracts, 17*(2), 31–37.

Nurius, P. S. (1984). "Utility of Data Synthesis for Social Work." *Social Work Research & Abstracts, 20*(3), 23–32.

Polster, R. A., Lynch, M. A., & Pinkston, E. M. (1981). "Reaching Underachievers." In S. P. Schinke (Ed.). *Behavioral Methods in Social Welfare* (pp. 41–60). Hawthorn, N.Y.: Aldine Publishing Co.

Pratt, L. (1970). "Optimism-Pessimism about Helping the Poor with Health Problems." *Social Work, 15*(2), 29–83.

Rabin, C. (1981). "The Single-Case Design in Family Therapy Evaluation Research." *Family Process, 20,* 351–366.

Rachman, S., & Wilson, G. T. (1980). *The Effects of Psychological Therapy.* New York: Pergamon Press.

Reid, W. J., & Hanrahan, P. (1982). "Recent Evaluations of Social Work: Grounds for Optimism." *Social Work, 27*(4), 328–340.

Reid, W. J., & Smith, A. D. (1981). *Research in Social Work.* New York: Columbia University Press.

Rubenstein, H., & Bloch, M. H. (1978). "Helping Clients Who Are Poor: Worker and Client Perceptions of Problems, Activities, and Outcomes." *Social Service Review, 52*(1), 69–84.

Schinke, S. P., Blythe, B. J., & Gilchrist, L. D. (1981). "Cognitive-Behavioral Prevention of Adolescent Pregnancy." *Journal of Counseling Psychology, 28*(5), 451–454.

Segal, A. (1970). "Workers' Perceptions of Mentally Disabled Clients: Effect on Service Delivery." *Social Work, 15*(3), 39–46.

Segal, S. P. (1972). "Research on the Outcome of Social Work Therapeutic Interventions: A Review of the Literature." *Journal of Health and Social Behavior, 13*(1), 3–17.

Siegel, D. H. (1984). "Defining Empirically Based Practice." *Social Work, 29*(4), 325–331.

Smith, M. L., & Glass, G. V. (1977). "Meta-

Analysis of Psychotherapy Outcome Studies." *American Psychologist, 32*(9), 752–760.

Smith, M. L., Glass, G. V., & Miller, T. I. (1980). *The Benefits of Psychotherapy.* Baltimore, Md.: Johns Hopkins University Press.

Strube, M. J., & Hartmann, D. P. (1982). "A Critical Appraisal of Meta-Analysis." *British Journal of Clinical Psychology, 21*(2), 129–140.

Thomlison, R. J. (1984). "Something Works: Evidence from Practice Effectiveness Studies." *Social Work, 29*(1), 51–56.

Tolson, E. R. (1977). "Alleviating Marital Communication Problems." In W. J. Reid & R. L. Epstein (Eds.), *Task-Centered Practice* (pp. 100–112). New York: Columbia University Press.

Tripodi, T., & Epstein, I. (1980). *Research Techniques for Clinical Social Workers.* New York: Columbia University Press.

Videka-Sherman, L. (1985). *Harriet M. Bartlett Practice Effectiveness Project Progress Report to NASW Board of Directors.* Silver Spring, Md.: National Association of Social Workers.

Wells, R. A. (1981). "The Empirical Base of Family Therapy: Practice Implications." In E. R. Tolson & W. J. Reid (Eds.), *Models of Family Treatment* (pp. 248–305). New York: Columbia University Press.

Wilson, G. T., & Rachman, S. J. (1983). "Meta-Analysis and the Evaluation of Psychotherapy Outcome: Limitations and Liabilities." *Journal of Consulting and Clinical Psychology, 51*(1), 54–64.

Wodarski, J. S. (1981). *The Role of Research in Clinical Practice: A Practical Approach for the Human Services.* Baltimore, Md.: University Park Press.

Wood, K. M. (1978). "Casework Effectiveness: A New Look at the Research Evidence." *Social Work, 23*(6), 437–458.

Wortman, P. M. (1981). "Consensus Development." In P. M. Wortman (Ed.), *Methods for Evaluating Health Services.* Beverly Hills, Calif.: Sage Publications.

DIRECT PRACTICE IN SOCIAL WORK: OVERVIEW

Direct practice in social work is a mosaic of methods and skills based upon many kinds of knowledge and guided by multiple theories. It is carried out by social workers from three levels of professional education, with populations of every age and of all economic classes and ethnic groups in American society. Direct practice takes place wherever people go for help with troubling situations and problems in their lives: in social agencies; clinics and hospitals; the workplace; therapeutic, residential, correctional, and rehabilitative institutions; private offices; and communities.

Given this complexity, it is well to ask what weaves all of these threads together. What are the boundaries of direct social work practice? What makes it distinctive from other helping disciplines? How can one recognize the work of a practitioner in social work? Since 1917, the search for cohesion and unity has been a feature of professional social work's development; and the process of definition in each generation since then has contributed to greater clarity. Yet the task is not done and perhaps, in a field of professional endeavor that is always reflective of its times, should never be done. Each era raises new social issues, even as old ones get resolved; each decade demands new responses to evolving social problems. As social workers learn more and become more visible in society's public and private institutions, they shift the boundaries of their work, move into new arenas, and begin to reshape their traditional practices.

Commonalities in Social Work Practice

Some things remain constant and serve as permanent guideposts that allow social workers to remain anchored to some professional certainties even while they continually make the necessary adaptations to change. The central purpose of social work practice is to effect the best possible adaptation among individuals, families, and groups and their environments. This psychosocial, or person-in-environment, focus of social work practice has evolved over the last 70 years to direct the explorations, assessments, and interventions of practitioners—no matter what their different theoretical orientations and specializations and regardless of where or with what client group they practice.

Social work's values, like its purpose, guide practitioners and often help to distinguish social workers from members of other disciplines. Evident in the National Association of Social Workers (NASW) Code of Ethics and in every social work text are values having to do with clients' rights to self-determination and choice, to participation in his or her own decision making, and to confidentiality, fairness, and justice. Commitment to these and other humane social values contributes to the integrity of social work practice no matter how much diversity there is in the functions actually carried out by social workers.

The history of social work practice is the third thing held in common by all social workers. Practitioners carry out a wide variety of roles and functions, often in different ways, but just as they are bound together by their purpose and values, they are joined through their history. They are what they are because they have shared a common past; and although mostly they do not dwell on that history, it has to be understood in order to rationalize the differences in the way social workers practice currently.

History of Social Work Practice

The practice of offering humane services to those in need can be dated to biblical times, but the use of the term "social work practice" is relatively new, going back to 1970 (Bartlett, 1970; Meyer, 1970). Prior to that, practice was defined in various ways: by methodologies, such as casework, group work, and community organization; by settings, with designations such as child welfare, family service, medical social work, psychiatric social work, or corrections; or by populations, or problem groups, such as the poor, the physically or mentally ill or mentally retarded, neglected children, or alcoholics. Gradually, these narrow and specialized views of practice were transformed into the current broad and general orientation to be discussed later.

The evolution of the term "social work practice," connoting a comprehensive professional role, parallels the development of the profession in the shift from an apprenticeship system to the emerging autonomy of the social worker, the response to changing times, and the impact of new knowledge. But the changes did not come easily; there were the inevitable jurisdictional disputes that occur whenever traditional ways of doing things are challenged, and there were the uncertainties involved in having to exchange the known for the unknown. In current social work practice one can discern all of the

previously delineated threads of methodology, setting, and population groups; but today they are woven into a tapestry of practice and do not simply exist side by side.

Social work practice is the activity carried out by social workers in varied institutional settings, communities, and private practice. These workers address a full range of human problems involving individuals, families, and groups. Given its long history and the necessity to bring together so many strands of professional, practical, and theoretical commitments, the process of defining social work practice was both political and rational—and it is not yet over. It is necessary to cite the many interests involved in the process of building a unified concept of practice in social work, if only to recognize the past in the present and the struggle in the profession to find central concepts that would be acceptable to all of its constituents. The NASW conceptual frameworks conferences reflected this professional struggle (National Association of Social Workers [NASW], 1977, 1981).

Dominance of the Casework Method

Although social work itself can be traced back to the late nineteenth century and the Progressive Era—when its role in social reform was carried out from the base of settlement houses—codified practice was initiated by Richmond (1917) in her book *Social Diagnosis*. The training of "friendly visitors" was made possible by Richmond's development of a general helping approach and was the beginning of social casework, the social work method that proved to be dominant for 50 years (Germain & Hartman, 1980). At least two major themes from Richmond's work have persisted: the need to individualize people (thus, the term "casework"), and the need to understand, or diagnose, their situations. Because of the rising influence of the medical profession at the time of Richmond's early work, the term "diagnosis" suggested to many that cases were to be viewed as sick or well, within a medical framework. About twenty years later, Hamilton (1940) disclaimed the medical-disease metaphor and developed the psychosocial concept, which was intended to be more fully descriptive of all social work cases. Study, diagnosis, and treatment were defined as the methodology of this diagnostic school of thought.

Coincidental with the influence of the later work of Richmond (1922), Freudian theory was finding a highly receptive audience among social workers (Hellenbrand, 1965). It might have been expected that a coherent theory of personality would be attractive to the emerging professional caseworkers, for Richmond was not able to offer a supporting theoretical underpinning to her methodology. She did little to explain the behavior of clients, although she wrote with significant fervor about the conditions of poverty under which they lived. Casework in the 1920s reflected the turning inward of the larger society, and until the Great Depression in the 1930s, attention was given to learning psychoanalytic theory in the search for a supporting knowledge for practice.

During the Depression, the refinement of social casework continued, even while many social workers contributed the work necessary to help people survive the economic disaster. By the end of the 1920s, the publication of *A Changing Pyschology In Social Case Work* by Robinson (1930) introduced a radical ideological shift in thinking among some practitioners and an equally strong opposition to this shift among others. This ideological conflict began as a regional dispute between schools of social work in New York and Pennsylvania, but it turned out to be a long-lived conflict between two schools of thought as well. Robinson and her colleague Jessie Taft, influenced by the psychoanalyst Otto Rank, viewed social casework as a process that mediated between the client's need for service and the agency's function (Smalley, 1965).

The conflict between the two schools was termed the functional-diagnostic conflict, and it centered as much on the differences between Rank and Freud as it did on the practices inherent in each casework method. The functional school emphasized processes of help, particularly through the worker-client relationship. It used the structures of agency function, and among the givens in its methodology were time (as beginning, middle, and end) and fees. Agency function, time, and fees were the structures within which the casework process took place. The diagnostic school was committed to understanding the differential nature of clients' problems and made differential use of agency function, time, and fees.

Whereas the functional school emphasized processes of help, the diagnostic school emphasized the content of cases. The Freudian and Rankian views of personality development—and the methodology derived from each—were so distinct that they evoked distinct views of the world (Hamilton, 1941; Taft, 1937). Even though World War II intervened, the conflict persisted until the last actors in the drama died. Careful analysis of some current practice approaches suggests that functional (existential) and diagnostic (psychodynamic) disparities still exist, although the major conflicts were absorbed by the profession as it turned to other matters.

Perlman (1957) made an effort to bring together the divergent ideas of the diagnostic and functional schools in *Casework: A Problem-Solving Process,* which became a widely accepted primer of casework practice. She created the framework of person, place, problem, and process to incorporate the central ideas of each school. Thomas (1967) and others introduced what was to become the fourth major theoretical stream in casework practice, sociobehavioral approaches, which would have a definitive impact.

The four casework orientations discussed in the previous section—the traditional psychosocial, functional, problem-solving, and sociobehavioral—have been in the mainstream and have affected social workers' methodology the most either because they have had a continuous impact or because aspects of the original contributions can be identified in newer approaches. But there were other movements in casework practice that expressed particular concern with the environmental aspect of the person-in-environment or psyochosocial equation. The work done in this area was no more readily applied to practice approaches than were the theories of the early social reform movement. Reynolds, an outstanding casework figure in professional social activism, spent most of her career in the 1930s and 1940s trying to integrate the new psychoanalytic theory with social reform (Reynolds, 1951; Friedberg, 1984).

In the 1950s there was an emphasis on developing methods of crisis intervention. This approach, introduced by Parad (1965), Rapoport (1970), and others, described practice principles in work with clients in a situational context—that of a defined crisis. This model has evolved into what is currently a highly significant approach in social work practice (Panzer, 1983). Finally in 1965, Hollis wrote *Casework: A Psychosocial Therapy,* which influenced a generation of caseworkers in practicing a refined methodology emphasizing the person-in-environment, or psychosocial, equation. This practice approach might be viewed as the springboard for the clinical social work movement.

Until 1970, casework practice dominated the field of social work. An important feature of all of the approaches mentioned, and one that will help to explain the later shift to social work practice, is that they were all linear in their perspectives and thus were confined to viewing phenomena on a single plane. The person-situation construct has governed all of practice since Richmond produced *Social Diagnosis* in 1917, but the practice approaches all emphasized direct work with persons. Perhaps any such approach to practice, valid though it might have been for specific purposes, could not be "stretched" sufficiently to carry out the accepted mandate of direct work with both the person's situation and the person himself or herself.

Group Work

The methods of group work were introduced in social work in the 1930s (Williamson, 1929; Coyle 1937), although work had been carried on with groups in neighborhoods and settlement houses since the Progressive Era at the end of the nineteenth century (Wilson, 1976). The social reform movement, as expressed concretely in the settlement house movement, included programs of socialization, education, and recreation that were carried out by lay volunteers. Professional social work had not yet been introduced into American society, and group work theory had not been developed.

After World War II, Wilson and Ryland (1949), Konopka (1949), Coyle (1947), and others began to develop their group-work experiences into theory. In 1949, the American Association of Group Workers adopted a definition of group work, and soon it became a standard part of the practice curricula in schools of social work and a recognized methodology in the field of social work. From settlement houses and neighborhoods, it moved into hospitals and other settings in which caseworkers practiced. By 1970, group work had become a significant methodological commitment for many social workers. By that time, social workers identified themselves as caseworkers or group workers, and only occasionally were practitioners able to transfer their knowledge and skills from one method to another.

Reflecting the theoretical developments in casework were the different schools of thought in group work. Most approaches derived from theories supporting existing casework models, supplemented by selected concepts from the behavioral sciences (Roberts & Northen, 1976). Among the major theorists were Glasser, Sarri, and Vinter (1967); Hartford (1972); (Schwartz & Zalba, 1971); Northen (1969); Phillips (1974); and Tropp (1971). The psychosocial (Northen and Hartford), developmental (Tropp), organizational (Glasser, Sarri, & Vinter), functional (Phillips), and mediating (Schwartz & Zalba) models of group work practice were identified with particular authors. Through the 1970s there was heightened intellectual and professional activity in the development of group work methodology.

Family Treatment

In the mid-1950s social workers, along with professionals in other disciplines—and later with the independent discipline of family therapy—became interested in the practice of family treatment. Scherz (1970) was a pioneer among social workers in the development of this practice. In the 1960s, family treatment became an identifiable field in itself, drawing its theoretical structure first from psychiatry and then from systems theory. Its integration into social work practice was effected by Ackerman (Ackerman, Beatman, & Sherman, 1961), Minuchin (1974), Hartman and Laird (1984), and others. Different from traditional casework and group work approaches, family treatment utilizes a nonlinear, systemic orientation to cases and comes closer to addressing a situational context than does casework. Currently, family therapy as a practice modality enjoys popularity among social work practitioners, although it must be emphasized that all direct work with families is not carried out as family treatment. Most of social work practice is family centered, and family members are worked with as individuals, dyads, and triads as well as with the family as a whole system.

Turning Point

In the 1960s and 1970s, when social unrest contributed to serious and effective challenges to all social institutions, professional social work was not excluded from criticism. By that time, the methods of both casework and group work were in their prime. That is, they had been refined so that their techniques were being codified, their interest in certain types of clients and problems was being particularized, and their focus was becoming narrower. In effect, direct practitioners were relatively isolated from the social changes that were brewing in the country.

It became apparent that broadly defined social services could not be delivered through therapeutically oriented casework and group work methods. Despite the many practice models developing at the time, there appeared to be a structural obstacle to their capacity to enter the situational environments that were the targets of social change during the War on Poverty. Population groups—including blacks, Hispanics, and the poor—were newly identified as clients whose problems reached into their environments and whose social and economic resources were limited. They required help that was not as narrowly defined as in existing casework and group work methods. The social dimension of the psychosocial purpose of social work appeared not to have been achieved in the evolution of these two methods. The era of their dominance came into question by the end of the 1970s.

Search for the Common Base

Gordon (1965) and Bartlett (1970) changed the perspective of social work practice. Through the formulation of a framework for social work practice (comprising purpose, values, sanction, knowledge, and skills), they emphasized the common base for all social work practice. They located methods and skills appropriately as merely one spoke of the wheel rather than as the wheel itself. This formulation allowed the practitioner to "step back" and be released from an a priori commitment to a methodology. In so doing, the practitioner would be better able to employ a holistic view of case phenomena and to understand that case-related tasks could be accomplished through a variety of means. Thus, instead of approaching cases with a predetermined method in mind, the social work practitioner would draw upon a common knowledge base and select from a repertoire of skills appropriate to the assessment of the case. Nelsen (1975) explicated this idea further and suggested that the focus on assessment frees the practitioner to choose among interventive approaches.

Following Bartlett, social work theoreticians began to write about social work practice from a perspective in which purpose, values, sanction, knowledge, and skills were in the foreground, giving shape and direction to the use of methods. Among the early writers in this group were Meyer (1970, 1976), Goldstein (1973), Pincus and Minahan (1973), Middleman and Goldberg (1974), and Siporin (1975). By not using a methods model, they were in a sense freed of its constraints and could view case phenomena through more holistic lenses. They took into account the environments of people as aspects of cases that called for intervention. There were different emphases used: Some approaches were centered more on the person and others more on the environment, but all strived to achieve a "situational" or "transactional" perspective that would give social work practitioners the language and skills necessary to become effective using the person-in-environment as the unit of attention.

Subsequent to the development of these social work practice approaches, a newer orientation to practice evolved: that of empirically based models. Fischer (1978) and Reid and Epstein (1972, 1977) eschewed the existing theoretical frameworks. These authors developed pragmatic approaches based on feedback from client to practitioner. This approach emphasized research in the immediate life of the case rather than practice wisdom or coherent theories not drawn from empirical evidence. Research-based practice became yet another stream of practice existing alongside the methods of traditional casework, group work, and family treatment.

Subsequently, as the social work practice orientation became integrated into the profession, other generic practice models not associated with particular methods began to be developed. They included communications theory (Nelsen, 1980) and the life model (Germain & Gitterman, 1980). Because the conception of social work practice as an open system is supported by the current holistic orientation to case phenomena, it is likely that the future will bring forth increasing numbers of newer practice approaches to deal with selected aspects of cases.

Finally, it should be mentioned that some practitioners apply personality, behavioral, or cognitive theories directly without reference to the social work framework of purpose, values, and sanction. In these instances, knowledge and skills derived from the body of theory, as well as those borrowed undiluted from psychiatry and psychology, serve as the practitioner's guidelines. Strictly speaking, these are not social work practice approaches, and they cannot be distinguished in their purpose, values, or sanction from the approaches of other disciplines. However, they are mentioned here because they can be identified in the repertoire of practice approaches used by social workers. Some examples are gestalt therapy, existentialist therapy, est, transactional therapy, behavior modification, cognitive therapy, and psychoanalytic psychotherapy.

Search for a Unifying Perspective

As can be discerned from the preceding review of the history of the development of practice in social work, the variety of approaches to and conceptualizations of practice offers the practitioner a bewildering choice. The situation is made more complicated because social workers often become committed to practice with either individuals, families, or groups, while also becoming invested in one theoretical interpretation of human personality and behavior and one practice model. More often than not, practitioners make these commitments as students and learn to value one modality or theory over another. There is no empirical evidence that one or another approach is necessarily more effective than the others, and the research is yet to be done on matching particular constellations of client needs with appropriate practice approaches. Thus, today's beginning practitioners make more or less personal or arbitrary choices as to what kind of social workers they will become (and will probably remain).

This is the state of the art. In the absence of certainty, with the awareness that new knowledge will develop, that research will clarify the options, and that social change will create still newer requirements of social workers, it is important to find a unifying perspective that will provide greater cohesiveness to social work practice. Such a perspective would have to reflect the person-in-environment focus that has become central to the purpose of social work practice. Furthermore, to capture the multiple strands of practice, it should not espouse any particular approach or theory; ideally, it should allow for an eclectic approach to case phenomena. Finally, such a perspective would have to address the complexity that characterizes the case situations dealt with in social work practice. The purpose of a perspective on practice is to bind together social workers who are all doing different things to carry out the same purposes.

The eco-systems perspective (Meyer, 1983) is but one such perspective. Bartlett (1970), Goldstein (1973), Pincus and Minahan (1973), and Siporin (1975) have sought such a unifying perspective in their practice theories. They deal with different emphases and somewhat different terminology, but they all emphasize transactional, situational, or social functioning ideas as applied to the person-in-situation approach. The eco-systems perspective was developed collegially in the late 1970s and began to find a degree of receptivity in the profession in the early 1980s. It offers a lens for viewing case phenomena; it is an orientation to practice, but it does not provide practice principles to guide intervention.

Through the use of ecological concepts, it identifies adaptive possibilities between persons and their environments. Using general systems theory, it highlights the way the actors and their situational variables are connected. It attempts to examine the environmental context in which people live, thereby addressing the essential focus of social work practice, that of the person in the environment. In the interests of organizing complexity and placing appropriate boundaries around practice situations, it favors a systemic or circular construct as contrasted with a linear view. The perspective simply offers a way of noticing; of using professional vision to encompass the client's complex reality.

Out of this awareness, this cognitive exploration of the scene, the core professional task is to assess the relationships among the case variables. The practitioner must determine what is salient or prominent and in need of intervention, what is relevant and therefore appropriate to do, and what balance or imbalance must be maintained or introduced. Thereafter, the selection of interventions can be drawn from the repertoire of approaches described above. When, how, and where to intervene will depend on the client's need and desires, the practitioner's skills, the available resources, professional and agency sanctions, and—of course—the methodology used. What the practitioner can derive from professional acceptance of the eco-systems, or some other perspective, is professional identity. Social work has grown unevenly and in many directions, and even though diversity is highly regarded in the profession, it is vital that practitioners be able to present themselves to one another and to the public with a unified perspective. As mentioned earlier, there is commonality in purpose, values, and social work practice history. A unifying perspective would help to strengthen intraprofessional communication and practitioners' identity as social workers.

Clinical-Generalist Issue

A common perspective could contribute to a resolution of the current professional tensions that have grown out of the many approaches to social work practice, especially the issue of clinical versus generalist practice. Although there is some confusion in the use of both of these terms, a generalist is usually defined as one who practices with individuals, families, and groups, and across the specialization lines of fields of practice, population groups, and problems. The generalist is not a specialist, but the definitions of the term "clinical" engender some ambiguity as to whether or not a generalist practitioner might be a clinician when working directly with individuals, families, or groups.

The term "clinician" has several meanings, depending on the issue being addressed (Ewalt, 1980; Caroff, 1982). When distinguishing social workers who do direct practice from those who do policy analysis, administration, or research, it is helpful to describe the direct practitioner as a clinician. Some practitioners choose a narrow definition of the term "clinical," applying it only to practitioners who do psychotherapy. Others find the term useful when working with clinicians in other disciplines; still others find it helpful when defining themselves as private practitioners of social work.

A common perspective of the type suggested previously would allow clinicians and generalists, whether broadly or narrowly defined, to apply their knowledge and skills within their preferred practice approach. The case assessment would determine the interventive need, and the appropriate mode of practice would then be called upon to deal with those persons requiring clinical or other social services. It is the framework of social work purpose, values, sanction, knowledge, and skills that always defines the case as a social work case, not whether the practitioner is a clinician or a generalist. Recalling social work practice that was historically characterized by methods, practitioners in the 1980s began to address case situations substantively as the "what" they are about. It is no longer as realistically descriptive of professional practice to define it by the roles and functions of the practitioner.

The Expanding Knowledge Base

As the perspectives on practice have broadened, and as practice roles have multiplied, it is obvious that the social work knowledge base has had to be expanded (Kadushin, 1959; Kamerman et al., 1973; National Association of Social Workers, 1977). As Compton and Galaway (1984) have stated:

> When one speaks of the knowledge base of social work, one usually is speaking of social work theory which is constructed partially of empirically tested knowledge and partially of assumptive knowledge which has not yet been empirically investigated but can be subjected to such investigation. All this is in contrast to values, which are statements of what is preferred. Principles of action rest upon both its values and theories. (p. 37)

Caseworkers who concentrate their attention on individual treatment rest their knowledge in the areas of personality development and ego theory and in behavioral or cognitive theory. Group workers, in a parallel way, find their supporting knowledge in the area of group processes, as family therapists have sought theirs in family processes. Keeping in mind the primary focus of social work practice, the person-in-environment construct, practitioners who work with any unit of attention (individuals, families, or groups) have sought continually to find useful knowledge about environmental processes to support the person-in-environment focus.

This knowledge has not been readily available, and practitioners have not found it easy to work with environmental dynamics that are vaguely defined. Consequently, social workers have tended to view the environment as the context in which individual, family, or group cases live and from where they draw sustenance or suffer deprivation. Where the environment is thus perceived, the decision to intervene as an integral part of direct practice has more or less remained with the individual practitioner and his or her predilections. The knowledge to support environmental interventions is not available in such a way that it can be easily integrated with existing theories about individuals, families, and groups. This tendency to concentrate on the clinical features of cases has a long history in social work practice. Nevertheless, it has been of concern that despite the professional commitment to the person-in-environment focus, relatively little progress has been made in developing theories to guide intervention in clients' environments.

It is hoped that a systemic perspective on cases will ease this perennial problem. Viewing individuals, families, and groups as intricately involved with particular features of their environments will help to dispel the "either-or" idea that intervention is more effective—and thus more valued—when it addresses the person instead of the environment. When these elements are recognized to be systemically interrelated, practitioners might then see the environmental features of cases as having the same dynamic interest as clinical features. As environment has come to be identified and studied, new knowledge is beginning to contribute to the practitioner's repertoire.

Germain (1976; 1978) has written about time and physical space as ecological or environmental variables that can be worked with in behalf of clients. Social network theory (Caplan, 1974; Caplan & Killilea, 1976; Collins & Pancoast, 1976) is accumulating and is having an impact on practice. Because the bulk of social work practice is carried out in social agencies and other institutions, the organizational environment has been specified in organizational theory (Brager & Holloway, 1978; Hage, 1980; Patti, 1974). Stress theory (Dohrenwend & Dohrenwend, 1974) has potential for identifying areas in which interventions would be useful.

The breakthrough in the development of environmental knowledge and theory was probably made possible by the specification and partialization of the concept of environment. As is true of personality, behavioral, and cognitive theories, environmental theories only become useful when they can be identified, studied, and made applicable to actual practice situations. In fact, it might become less useful in the future to talk about environments than to consider the specific features external to the person. These external features include, for example, other people, physical space, social and political forces, economic conditions, and social systems. In this way, practitioners will be better able to connect the client with his or her particular environmental stress or supports.

In addition to noting the expanding knowledge base about individuals, families, and groups and their environments, direct practitioners have come to recognize that their work with these units of attention is always addressed as well to the conditions of life and problems that have brought clients and social workers together. Thus, the parameters of knowledge can reach into the full range of human situations, from transitional events such as a child's attending school for the first time, to depression, out-of-wedlock pregnancy, hospitalization, child placement, and family violence. Thus, depending on the population groups, problem, or setting with which social workers are associated in practice, the potential areas of knowledge are wide. This fact of practice offers direct practitioners opportunities for continual research.

Finally, beyond knowledge of persons and of their life situations, there is yet a third area of knowledge needed by social work practitioners, which is about social work processes that include the hows of practice: how one explores, assesses, and intervenes in case situations and how one evaluates practice outcomes.

Recapitulation

The preceding discussion has examined the commonalities among social work practitioners; the purposes, values, and history that define the profession's unique character. The varied methodologies that are utilized and the expanding knowledge base on which social workers must draw could lead to a fragmented crazy quilt of professional activity if there were not a commonly held perspective that could join all of the parts and yet allow for necessary diversity. The functions and roles currently carried out by social work practitioners is nothing if not diverse. Social workers have gone down a twisting path in this century. Having begun as apprentices to social agencies, they early carried out the functions defined by the settings in which they worked. The development of professional education and the subsequent freeing of practitioners to carry out professionally defined, not agency-based, tasks has enabled social workers to enter the rich complexity of American society.

Where and with Whom Social Workers Practice

There is almost no location, from ghetto neighborhoods to banks, where social workers do not practice. Poor people are the ones most likely to use social agencies and clinics, and thus are most likely to be clients of social workers who are employed in those settings. Today, however, social workers in industry practice with working-class people. In private practice, they are apt to work with upper-middle-class people. In day care and in therapeutic and rehabilitative institutions, and in facilities for the aged, as well as in hospitals, mental health facilities, and family service agencies, they work with a cross section of the population. Clearly, social workers practice with every age group, ethnic group, and economic class, as well as with persons of either gender and every sexual orientation.

Specialization

All professions in their maturity recognize that the more they do and the more they know, the less likely it is that individual practitioners can do it all and know it all. Every profession specializes in accordance with its definition of expertise; thus, physicians specialize in such categories as diseases, parts of the body, age groups, and practice skills, but leave room for the "specialist" in general medicine: the family practitioner. Lawyers specialize along the lines of legislative categories, skills, and the locations in which they practice.

Social workers also face the necessity of drawing some boundaries around their definition of area of expertise. In social work education, master's-degree graduates are expected to concentrate in at least one of four areas: fields of practice, population groups, problem areas and practice roles (Council on Social Work Education, 1983). Although the field of social work is not at present tightly organized into specializations, there is an informal recognition of the necessity of a de facto specialization in some areas and an awareness that specialization will be a requirement in the near future. It is helpful, as a way of organizing one's thinking about where and with whom social workers practice, to use the existing formulations.

Fields of Practice

Although the boundaries could change and do in fact overlap, currently identified fields of practice are: family and children's services, health, mental health, occupational social work, aging, education, and corrections (Compton, 1983). This is the broadest way of organizing specializations, and it requires that the practitioner in a field be knowledgeable about the populations that typically use the agencies in that field, the range of problems worked with, the agencies and other resources specific to the concerns of the field, the governing legislation, the funding sources, the work of other disciplines engaged in that field, and the services that are typically provided. The practitioner must also be aware of the research relevant to significant aspects of the field. The social work practitioner who has expertise in a field of practice applies his or her skills directly with individuals, families, and groups; but there must also be a strong orientation to the context in which the help is being provided.

For example, in hospital-based health care, a direct practitioner must be continually alert to the restrictions placed on his or her practice by Medicare legislation and funding, by stringent discharge policies, and by federal budget requirements. The opportunities for intervention and practice research in this field can be rich in the potential for innovation and social service delivery. A busy urban hospital would be a likely place for planned short-term treatment methods and crisis intervention; it would offer fertile ground for family and group treatment and ample opportunity for displaying skill in using social resources.

In a field that is not highly structured and is undergoing radical changes in philosophy like family and children's services, the legislation and funding and consequent policies that govern practice could encourage the direct practitioner to undertake research into new programming or staffing arrangements. The use of an eclectic practice repertoire is necessary in such a field, which contains activities ranging from preventive and protective services to placement.

Each field of practice generates its own specialized, endemic conditions, which the direct practitioner can exploit to develop services for his or her clients, patients, or consumers. The conceptualization of field of practice is broad and thus demands a broad range and depth of knowledge and skill from the direct practitioner; but it also has advantages over more narrowly defined specializations. It allows for flexible play of the practitioner's skills and interests and also reflects most closely the professional social worker's concerns with the connectedness of practice, policy, and research.

Populations

Specialization according to populations means that the direct practitioner becomes expert in knowledge and skill about groups of people, variously defined according to age, class, ethnicity, or gender. This approach is useful when services are organized around particular situations like migration, poverty, racial discrimination, or oppressed groups. However, more likely than not, a direct practitioner in social work would get to know these populations through being attached to some institutional setting or some problem category.

In a free-standing context, populations classified in this way would probably be known to social workers acting in the role of community organizers. Categories such as children, youths, families, or the aged, are helpful organizing devices, but in the case of age groups, intergenerational overlapping of-

ten occurs. A practitioner would find it difficult to specialize in children, for example, and not be as expert in working with their parents.

Problem Areas

Problem areas such as alcoholism, substance abuse, child abuse, marital conflict, depression, mental illness, physical illness, homelessness, social isolation, school dropouts, and runaways are the most familiar categories to social workers. These and other problems define the work that practitioners do, although some problems appear more typically in some fields than in others. There are obvious advantages to specializing in problem areas: They provide for a convenient classification system, they define clearly and narrowly what the practitioner must know and do in cases, and they make the scope of necessary knowledge and skills more readily encompassable.

The disadvantages lie in the attention given to the problem category itself and the common tendency to place less emphasis upon prevention once problems themselves are in the forefront. Also, it is known that identifiable problem categories often turn out to be symptoms of other dysfunctions. At the least, they are connected to other forces, persons, or conditions in the client's environment. Finally, just because they are problems and defined as such, it is likely that they will appear in various settings that constitute the fields of practice. Then the question posed is: Can direct practitioners in social work carry out their functions with clients having defined problems without addressing the organizational, research, interdisciplinary, and policy considerations involved? The fact is, in social work practice there are almost no cases that can be understood or worked with in a social or institutional vacuum.

Practice Roles

Specialization in social work according to practice roles involves the panoply of professional roles, including direct practitioner, supervisor, administrator, consultant, policy analyst, and researcher. This discussion will consider only the role of the direct practitioner as a specialization. Just as the term "clinical social worker" was noted as being useful in distinguishing a social worker in direct practice from social workers in other roles, so the role of direct practitioner is useful as a specialization, to make the same distinction. However, denoting a single role as a specialization restricts the practitioner's options to mix that role with others (researcher or supervisor, for example).

Further, this definition of expertise reverts to the pre-1970 period when methods were dominant. At that time, substantive knowledge about the person in the environment, organizations, policies, and social services were secondary, and methods and skills were in the foreground. The questions for the profession now as in 1917 are: Which shall be the master and which the servant? Will social workers continue to rely on their skills for self-definition, or will they seek identity through becoming expert in some substantive fashion, about fields of practice, population groups, or problem areas?

Practice roles and functions are integral to the definition of social workers; in fact, there would be no social work without professional practitioners who are knowledgeable and skillful. The issue is not whether there should be practice roles, for their existence is a generic requirement. The issue is only whether practice roles are sufficiently descriptive and substantive to qualify as a specialization. It is well to recall that in all other practicing professions in health, education, and welfare (that is, in medicine, psychiatry, psychoanalysis, psychology, nursing, and teaching), all practitioners use helping or clinical skills of one kind or another. That is what defines all professional practice in service fields. The question of what differentiates social work helping from other helping cannot be resolved on the grounds of skills alone; one professional practice is not sufficiently distinguishable from another. The uniqueness of social work practice will probably derive as much from the "what" to which it attends, as to how it functions.

It is as yet uncertain how social work practice will come to define its specializations. The diversity in the field is such that it may have to have more than one organizing framework. But the purpose of specialization is to develop specialized expertise in one or more areas that can be defined in consonance with the purposes and values of the profession itself. Social work will not organize itself into anatomically defined specializations, because practice does not normally attend to parts of the body as units of attention. There is as yet insufficient consensus as to how it will define that to which it does attend.

What Do Social Work Practitioners Do?

What are the outcomes of this description of practice? What does it all mean in action? In keeping with the broad contexts in which social workers practice, it is obvious that they must carry out multiple roles and functions. Defining problem situations, engaging in purposeful helping relationships, and developing their repertoire of interventive skills, practitioners may treat, educate, advocate, and mediate. Depending on whom they are working with, the sanctions under which they function, and the characteristics of the case at hand, practitioners may participate in bringing people into health and mental health institutions through case finding and intake procedures, and they may effect discharge plans from those same institutions.

In a field of practice like family and children's services, practitioners may place children or aged people in substitute family situations or institutional settings; or they may find it possible to help those same people to remain in their own communities with their families or social networks. In the field of education, practitioners may help a child cope with school or the school cope with the child. In occupational social work, practitioners may help workers to deal with stress on the job, adaptation to retirement, or problems of substance abuse. Permeating all fields of practice is the theme of interpersonal relationships among people, particularly family members and other intimates. Historically, social workers have always given major attention to practice with people and their relationships. Practice methodology is transferable, field to field, population group to population group, and problem to problem.

Yet it is evident that the nature of the setting in any field of practice will determine the typical problems confronted by social work practitioners. The particular constellation of problems brought by a client with a unique personality and set of desires and needs will determine the level and direction of the intervention plan. The resources available in the case situation and the motivation and capacity of the client, along with the knowledge and skills of the practitioner, will shape the processes and outcomes of practice. Clearly, one cannot describe a catalog of practice roles and functions without reference to the contexts in which they take place.

The Future

Direct practice in social work is a rich mosaic. It is made up of many components, and it is applicable to the many forms of the human condition. It is often an expression of society's concern with people; it is designed to help people in the most difficult situations. Despite its long history and energetic theory building, it remains far short of resolving its central concerns.

How scientific can practice be? Can a renewed professional interest in research resolve issues of practice effectiveness, of the relationship of cause and effect, of whether some methods work better than others with particular client groups? Is there sufficient professional self-confidence to tap the knowledge derived from practice experience? Or will social workers continue to pursue knowledge built in laboratories and academies (Rein & White, 1981)?

The future of direct practice will depend, of course, on the future of social work. It will also depend upon the characteristics of practitioner social workers. In a field that is "unfinished" and always at the mercy of society's ambiguities, practitioners will have to be autonomous, thinking, sensitive to people's needs, active in their behalf, knowledgeable, and skillful. In the end, social work purposes and values will be the important controlling factors, because practitioners will need those anchors as they face unending change. The story of direct practice in social work is one of diversity and adaptability. These qualities could serve to guarantee a future.

CAROL H. MEYER

For further information, see Appendix 3: NASW STANDARDS FOR THE PRACTICE OF CLINICAL SOCIAL WORK; ASSESSMENT IN DIRECT PRACTICE; CONTRACTING AND ENGAGEMENT IN DIRECT PRACTICE; DIAGNOSTIC AND STATISTICAL MANUAL (DSM); DIRECT PRACTICE EFFECTIVENESS; DIRECT PRACTICE: TRENDS AND ISSUES; LINKAGE IN DIRECT PRACTICE; PROFESSIONAL LIABILITY AND MALPRACTICE; RECORDING IN DIRECT PRACTICE; SOCIAL WORK PRACTICE WITH GROUPS; TERMINATION IN DIRECT PRACTICE; and articles on specific approaches and perspectives, such as BEHAVIORAL APPROACH or GENERALIST PERSPECTIVE.

References

Ackerman, N., et al. (1961). *Exploring the Base of Family Therapy.* New York: Family Service Association of America.

Bartlett, H. M. (1970). *The Common Base of Social Work Practice.* Washington, D.C.: National Association of Social Workers.

Brager, G., & Holloway, S. (1978). *Changing Human Service Organizations: Politics and Practice.* New York: Free Press.

Caplan, G. (1974). *Support Systems and Mental Health.* New York: Behavioral Publications.

Caplan, G., & Killilea, M. (1976). *Support Systems and Mutual Help: Multidisciplinary Exploration.* New York: Grune & Stratton.

Caroff, P., (Ed.). (1982). *Treatment Formulations and Clinical Social Work.* Silver Spring, Md.: National Association of Social Workers.

Collins, A. H., & Pancoast, D. L. (1976). *Natural Helping Networks: A Strategy for Prevention.* Washington, D.C.: National Association of Social Workers.

Compton, B. (1983). "Traditional Fields of Practice." In A. Rosenblatt & D. Waldfogel (Eds.) *Handbook of Clinical Social Work.* San Francisco: Jossey-Bass Publishers.

Compton, B., & Galaway, B. (1984). *Social Work Processes* (3rd ed.). Homewood, Ill.: Dorsey Press.

Council on Social Work Education. (1983). *Curriculum Policy Statement.* New York: Author.

Coyle, G. L., (Ed.). (1937). *Studies in Group Behavior.* New York: Harper.

Coyle, G. L. (1947). *Group Experience and Democratic Values.* New York: Women's Press.

Dohrenwend, B., & Dohrenwend, B. (1974). *Stressful Life-Events: Their Nature and Effects.* New York: Wiley.

Ewalt, P. L. (Ed.). (1980). *Toward a Definition of Clinical Social Work.* Washington, D.C.: National Association of Social Workers.

Fischer, J. (1978). *Effectiveness Practice: An Eclectic Approach.* New York: McGraw-Hill.

Friedberg, S. (1984). "Bertha Capen Reynolds: A Woman Struggling in Her Times." Unpublished doctoral dissertation. Columbia University School of Social Work, New York, N.Y.

Germain, C. (1976). "Time, an Ecological Variable in Social Work Practice." *Social Casework,* 57(7), 419–426.

Germain, C. (1978). "Space, an Ecological Variable in Social Work Practice." *Social Casework,* 59(9), 515–522.

Germain, C. B., & Gitterman, A. (1980). *The Life*

Model of Social Work Practice. New York: Columbia University Press.

Germain, C. B., & Hartman, A. (1980). "People and Ideas in the History of Social Work." *Social Casework, 61*(6), 323–331.

Glasser, P., Sarri, R. & Vinter, R. (1967). *Individual Change Through Small Groups.* New York: Free Press.

Goldstein, H. (1973). *Social Work Practice: A Unitary Approach.* Columbia: University of South Carolina Press.

Gordon, W. E. (1965). "Toward a Social Work Frame of Reference." *Journal of Education for Social Work, 1*(2), 19–26.

Hage, J. (1980). *Theories of Organization: Form, Process, and Transformation.* New York: Wiley.

Hamilton, G. (1940). *Theory and Practice of Social Casework.* New York: Columbia University Press.

Hamilton, G. (1941). "The Underlying Philosophy of Social Casework Today." In *Proceedings of the National Conference of Social Work* (pp. 237–253). New York: Columbia University Press.

Hartford, M. E. (1972). *Groups in Social Work.* New York: Columbia University Press.

Hartman, A., & Laird, J. (1984). *Family Centered Social Work Practice.* New York: Free Press.

Hellenbrand, S. C. (1965). "Main Currents in Social Casework." Unpublished doctoral dissertation. Columbia University School of Social Work. New York, N.Y.

Hollis, F. M. (1965; 2nd ed, 1972; 3rd ed., 1981). *Casework: A Psychosocial Therapy.* New York: Random House.

Kadushin, A. (1959). "The Knowledge Base of Social Work." In A. J. Kahn (Ed.), *Issues in American Social Work.* New York: Columbia University Press.

Kamerman, S. B., et al. (1973). "Knowledge for Practice: Social Science in Social Work." In A. J. Kahn (Ed.), *Shaping the New Social Work.* New York: Columbia University Press.

Konopka, G. (1949). *Therapeutic Group Work with Children.* Minneapolis: University of Minnesota Press.

Meyer, C. H. (1970). *Social Work Practice: A Response to the Urban Crisis.* New York: Free Press.

Meyer, C. H. (1976). *Social Work Practice: The Changing Landscape.* New York: Free Press.

Meyer, C. H. (Ed.). (1983). *Clinical Social Work in an Eco-Systems Perspective.* New York: Columbia University Press.

Middleman, R., & Goldberg, G. (1974). *Social Service Delivery: A Structural Approach to Social Work Practice.* New York: Columbia University Press.

Minuchin, S. (1974). *Families and Family Therapy.* Cambridge, Mass.: Harvard University Press.

National Association of Social Workers. (1964). *Building Social Work Knowledge.* New York: Author.

National Association of Social Workers. (1977). "Conceptual Frameworks I" (Special Issue). *Social Work, 22*(5).

National Association of Social Workers. (1981). "Conceptual Frameworks II" (Special Issue). *Social Work, 26*(5).

Nelsen, J. C. (1975). "Social Work Fields of Practice, Methods and Models: The Choice to Act." *Social Service Review, 49*(2) 264–270.

Nelsen, J. C. (1980). *Communication Theory and Social Work Practice.* Chicago: University of Chicago Press.

Northen, H. (1969). *Social Work With Groups.* New York: Columbia University Press.

Panzer, B. (1983). "Crisis Intervention." In C. H. Meyer (Ed.), *Clinical Social Work in an Eco-Systems Perspective.* New York: Columbia University Press.

Parad, H. (Ed.). (1965). *Crisis Intervention.* New York: Family Service Association of America.

Patti, R. J. (1974). "Organizational Resistance and Change: The View from Below." *Social Service Review, 48*(3) 367–383.

Perlman, H. H. (1957). *Casework: A Problem-Solving Process.* Chicago: University of Chicago Press.

Phillips, H. U. (1974). *The Essentials of Group Work Skill.* Folcroft, Pa.: Folcroft Press.

Pincus, A., & Minahan, A. (1973). *Social Work Practice: Method and Model.* Itasca, Ill.: Peacock Publishers.

Rapoport, L. (1970). "Crisis Intervention as a Mode of Brief Treatment." In R. Roberts & R. Nee (Eds.), *Theories of Social Casework.* Chicago: University of Chicago Press.

Reid, W., & Epstein, L. (1972). *Task-Centered Casework.* New York: Columbia University Press.

Reid, W., & Epstein, L. (Eds.). (1977). *Task-Centered Practice.* New York: Columbia University Press.

Rein, M., & White, S. (1981). "Knowledge for Practice." *Social Service Review, 55*(1). 1–41.

Reynolds, B. C. (1951). *Social Work and Social Living.* New York: Citadel.

Richmond, M. E. (1917). *Social Diagnosis.* New York: Russell Sage Foundation.

Richmond, M. E. (1922). *What is Social Casework?* New York: Russell Sage Foundation.

Roberts, R. W., & Northen, H. (Eds.). (1976). *Theories of Social Work with Groups.* New York: Columbia University Press.

Robinson, V. (1930). *A Changing Psychology in Social Case Work.* Chapel Hill: University of North Carolina Press.

Scherz, F. (1970). "Theory and Practice of Family Therapy." In R. Roberts & R. Nee (Eds.), *Theories of Social Casework*. Chicago: University of Chicago Press.

Schwartz, W., & Zalba, S. R. (Eds.). (1971). *Social Work with Groups*. New York: Columbia University Press.

Siporin, M. (1975). *Introduction to Social Work Practice*. New York: Macmillan.

Smalley, R. (1965). *Theory for Social Work*. New York: Columbia University Press.

Taft, J. (1937). "The Relation of Function to Process in Social Case Work." *Journal of Social Work Process, 1*(1) 1–18.

Thomas, E. J. (Ed.). (1967). *The Socio-Behavioral Approach and Applications to Social Work*. New York: Council on Social Work Education.

Tropp, E. (1971). *A Humanistic Foundation for Group Work Practice* (2nd. ed.). New York: Selected Academic Reading.

Williamson, M. (1929). *The Social Worker in the Group*. New York: Harper.

Wilson, G. (1976). "From Practice to Theory: A Personalized History." In R. Roberts & H. Northen (Eds.), *Theories of Work with Groups*. New York: Columbia University Press.

Wilson, G., & Ryland, G. (1949). *Social Group Work Practice*. Boston: Houghton Mifflin Co.

DIRECT PRACTICE RESEARCH. See Direct Practice Effectiveness; Program Evaluation; Research In Social Work; Research Measures and Indices in Direct Practice; Single Subject Research Designs.

DISABILITIES: DEVELOPMENTAL

The President's Committee on Mental Retardation (1976) estimated that in 1974 there were 8 million mentally retarded people in the United States and projected that this figure would jump to 12 million by the year 2000. In contrast, a 1981 U.S. Administration on Developmental Disabilities (ADD) report using 1980 state developmental disabilities plans, projected the total number of people with developmental disabilities to be 3,907,000, or 1.72 percent of the nation's 1980 population of 227 million (U.S. Department of Health and Human Services, 1981). The latter estimates, although using a seemingly more inclusive categorical definition, would seem to indicate a drop from 8 million to 4 million.

Has the scope of the problem changed in just a few years? Have prevention programs successfully reduced the social problem of developmental delays in cognitive and adaptive functioning?

The answer is that there have been no dramatic cures. Instead, a new nondiagnostic term has emerged—"developmental disability"—whose definition categorizes eligibility for federally funded programs written into federal law. In particular, the Developmental Disabilities and Bill of Rights Act of 1975 (P.L. 94-103) and the Rehabilitation Comprehensive Services and Developmental Disabilities Amendment of 1978 (P.L. 95-602) have defined developmental disabilities using a functional, noncategorical perspective. The Developmental Disabilities Act, for example, which was revised in 1984, reads as follows:

> The term "developmental disability" means a severe, chronic disability of a person which—
> (A) is attributable to a mental or physical impairment or combination of mental and physical impairments;
> (B) is manifested before the person attains age twenty-two;
> (C) is likely to continue indefinitely;
> (D) results in substantial functional limitations in three or more of the following areas of major life activity; (i) self-care, (ii) receptive and expressive language, (iii) learning, (iv) mobility, (v) self-direction, (vi) capacity for independent living, and (vii) economic self-sufficiency; and
> (E) reflects the person's need for a combination and sequence of special, interdisciplinary, or generic care, treatment, or other services which are of lifelong or extended duration and are individually planned and coordinated.

Substantial functional limitation in each of the seven major life activity areas noted above can be described more specifically:

"Self-care" refers to a long-term condition that requires significant assistance to an individual in feeding, hygiene, and appearance.

"Receptive and expressive language" refers to a long-term condition that prevents a person from effectively communicating directly with another person without the aid of (1) a third person, (2) a person with special skill, or (3) by means of a mechanical device. It also refers to a long-term condition that prevents an individual from articulating thoughts.

"Learning" refers to a long-term condition that seriously interferes with a person's cognition, visual or aural communication, or use of hands to the extent that special intervention or special programs are required to aid that person in learning.

"Mobility" refers to a long-term condition that impairs a person's ability to use fine or gross motor skills to the extent that assistance of another person or a mechanical device is needed in order for the individual to move from place to place.

"Self-direction" refers to a long-term condition that results in a person's needing assistance in order to make decisions concerning social and individual activities, handle personal finances, or protect self-interest.

"Capacity for independent living" refers to a long-term condition that limits a person in performing normal societal roles or makes it unsafe for a person to live alone to the extent that assistance, supervision, or the presence of a second person is required more than half the time.

"Economic self-sufficiency" refers to a long-term condition that prevents a person from working in regular employment or limits productive capacity to such an extent that it is insufficient for self-support.

The current functional definition of developmental disability focuses on the most severely handicapped people and as a consequence excludes a disproportionately high number of the mildly disabled, many of whom come from poor families. The positive relationship between poverty and disability has been amply documented (Hurley, 1969), yet often the poor families have the fewest services made available to them. That societal problems such as poverty interact with the field of cognitive impairment is not a new concept. For example, the American Association of Mental Deficiency (AAMD) decided that Adaptive Behavior Tests should become

a part of the diagnostic criteria for mental retardation (Grossman, 1984). The effects of this decision were shown in Mercer's study (1973) to reduce the percentage of mentally retarded children in Mexican families in California from 14.9 percent to 6 percent.

Several criticisms have emerged from the practice of using intelligence tests as the sole criterion for assigning such an intensely stigmatizing label. It was argued that these tests (such as the Stanford-Binet and the Wechsler) were developed using a middle-class white reference group and were therefore insensitive to cultural differences. As a result, a disproportionately high percentage of people from minority cultures were being diagnosed as mentally retarded and were populating special education classes. Again, Mercer's (1973) classic work showed that by using culturally adjusted IQ tests, the percentage of children from Mexican American families labeled mentally retarded dropped from 6 to 1.53 percent.

On the other hand, the increased prevalence of people with chronically disabling conditions who are raised in poverty is not a matter simply of biased tests or categorical distinctions. The President's Committee on Mental Retardation (1976) asserts that up to 70 percent of mentally handicapping conditions have poverty as their root cause. This association is attributed to such factors as malnutrition or the use of tobacco, alcohol, and other drugs during pregnancy; the high number of teenage pregnancies; the lack of early screening programs; lead poisoning; child abuse; nutritional deprivation in the early, vulnerable years of development; lack of stimulation in early interactions; and so on (Begab, Haywood, & Garber, 1981). It is the mildly handicapped (with IQs ranging from 50 to 70) who seem most affected by early deprivation, infection, and physical trauma. The moderately, severely, and profoundly mentally retarded are distributed randomly across social classes.

All these factors, which are so related to poverty, fall squarely within the domain of social work practice. The skills, values, and knowledge base of social workers (for example, advocacy, linkage to resources, prevention activities, belief in the dignity of each individual, knowledge of the structural causes of poverty, and so on) are all pertinent in addressing the issues of poverty-related disability. The eight most frequent diagnostic categories applied to those who are termed developmentally disabled are described briefly below.

Mental Retardation. A mentally retarded child is one who has trouble learning and applying what is learned to everyday living. The AAMD defines mental retardation as "sub-average general intellectual functioning which originated during the developmental period and is associated with impairment in adaptive behavior" (Grossman, 1984).

The AAMD provides a medical etiological classification system (Grossman, 1984) that includes infections and intoxications, trauma or physical agent, metabolism or nutrition, gross brain disease, unknown prenatal influence, chromosomal abnormality, gestational disorders, psychiatric disorders, environmental influences such as psychosocial disadvantage and sensory deprivation, and other conditions.

Both cognitive and adaptive impairment are relative to expectations for normal development and thus vary according to chronological age (as well as cultural context). Adaptive impairment in preschoolers refers primarily to a lag in motor activities, such as crawling, sitting, walking, eating, and communication skills. In school-age children, adaptive behavior refers mostly to learning; impairments are reflected in difficulties with respect to learning in school and using academic skills. In adults, adaptive behavior refers to adjustment within the community; impairments are reflected in problems of independent living, such as being unable to meet the community's requirements in work, marriage, and parenthood. Mental retardation classifications include mild (IQ 50–70), moderate (IQ 35–50), severe (IQ 20–35), and profound (IQ 0–20).

Cerebral Palsy. Cerebral palsy is a condition caused by damage to the brain either before birth or at birth. It is characterized by lack of control over the muscles of the body. There are three types of cerebral palsy: (1) spastic, in which the person moves stiffly and with difficulty; (2) athetoid, in which the person has involuntary and uncontrolled movements; and (3) ataxic, in which the person's sense of balance and depth perception are disturbed. In general, cerebral palsy is the result of problems with the muscle control centers of the brain. Depending on the location and extent of the brain damage, results can include lack of balance, tremors, spasms, seizures, difficulty in walking, poor speech, poor control of face muscles, problems in seeing and hearing, and mental retardation. The degree of cerebral palsy can range from mild to severe (Tobel & Lambert, 1981).

Autism. Autism refers to a cluster of unusual symptoms that manifest themselves in several areas of functioning before 3 years of age. There is, for example, a distortion in cognitive functioning; the child may seem to progress normally and then regress, and there may be an unevenness across domains of intellectual competence. Motor development is usually normal for chronological age, but often the child engages in repetitive stereotypic motions. Sensory perceptions are usually distorted; for example, pain may not be reported by the child who shrinks from being touched. Although children are often initially referred for diagnosis for hearing problems, it is soon determined that they are listening selectively to nonmeaningful sounds or are endlessly fascinated by watching flickering lights. Language may be nonexistent or seriously delayed; often the quality of speech is echolalic, meaning that the children echo back what they hear. Finally, affect is inappropriate; there is no attachment to people in the caregiving environment. The children are described as being in a world of their own, hence the term "autistic." Although rare, autism is such a pervasive disability, occurring so early in life and having so few interactive rewards, that such children are at severe risk for being placed outside the home.

Orthopedic Problems. Orthopedic problems are physical conditions that interfere with the functioning of the bones, muscles, or joints. An orthopedic problem constitutes a developmental disability only if the condition has been present from birth and impairs a child's ability to function in three of the major life activities. An orthopedic problem can vary from flat feet to the inability to use arms, legs, or body. Orthopedic problems include spina bifida, congenital hip dislocations, bone diseases or deformities, missing arms or legs, and extra fingers and toes (Tobel & Lambert, 1981).

Hearing Problems. A hearing loss is considered a major developmental problem because of the effect on the development of language and speech. Hearing loss can vary from mild to profound (deafness) and may be either conductive, affecting the transmission of sound from the outside world through the outer and middle ear, or sensorineural, affecting the inner ear or auditory nerves (Tobel & Lambert, 1981).

Epilepsy. Epilepsy is a disorder of the brain. Epilepsy results from an excessive discharge of electrical energy in the brain. There are two types of these abnormal energy discharges, generally called seizures: grand mal and petit mal. Grand mal seizures, which are the most common, are known as convulsions and are usually characterized by violent shaking of the entire body that lasts for a few minutes; unconsciousness or a deep sleep usually follows. Petit mal seizures are often hard to detect and may seem to be nothing more than staring spells or daydreaming; in reality, petit mals are slight lapses of consciousness that last only a few seconds but may occur many times a day (Tobel & Lambert, 1981).

Specific Learning Disabilities. Children who have a disorder in one or more of the basic psychological processes involved in understanding or using language have a specific learning disability, which may manifest itself in an imperfect ability to listen, think, speak, read, write, spell, or do mathematical calculations. Disorders include visual-perceptual or visual-motor handicaps, minimal brain dysfunction, and dyslexia. Not included are learning problems that are primarily the result of visual, hearing, or motor handicaps, mental retardation, emotional disturbances, or environmental disadvantages (Tobel & Lambert, 1981).

Co-occurrence of Disabilities. A child may receive more than one diagnosis. Severe cognitive impairments resulting from damage to the brain can sometimes cause multiple disabilities. A person with mental retardation, for example, may also be epileptic and have cerebral palsy. In a study of the frequency of co-occurrence of developmental disabilities, 73 percent of cases had one reported condition, 23 percent had two conditions, 4 percent had three conditions, and 1 percent had four conditions [totals more than 100 percent because of rounding] (Jacobson & Janicki, 1984).

Developmental disabilities may also be viewed in terms of the circumstances that predispose a child to being handicapped. These etiological factors, which increase the risk of developmental problems, can be divided into three major categories: (1) prenatal factors, (2) perinatal and neonatal factors, and (3) postnatal and environmental factors. The nature of the factors and examples illustrating the particular relevance of each factor to the concept "at risk" are summarized in Table 1.

Historical Trends

At the turn of the century, the mental health and social work professions were interested in people with mental retardation, both clinically and with respect to teaching and research activities. However, this active involvement changed rapidly in the next 20 years with two major shifts in professional and societal perspectives. First, the concept of IQ was established in 1913, and with it came the idea of IQ constancy, which reigned almost unchallenged until the 1930s and 1940s (Clarke & Clarke, 1974). At that point, the quantification offered by psychometric intelligence testing began to overshadow the in-depth, individualized case study process. Second, and related, was a dramatic upsurge in emphasis on and belief in fixed genetic causes of mental retardation, seen as interrelated with culture or instruction. These beliefs, in turn, led to false characterizations about people with mental retardation as having many other related social problems (Menolascino & McCann, 1983). An article describing social work practices with the mentally retarded (Branick, 1918) states:

The subject of feeble-mindedness is now recognized as one of the most important educational and social problems of the day because of its relation to other social problems. Various researchers have shown that it complicates practically every one of our social questions, poverty and dependence, delinquency, vice and crime, inebriety, vagrancy, unemployment and industrial inefficiency. . . . An educational campaign has been directed by numerous organizations throughout the country interested in eugenics and mental hygiene, and a special committee, national in scope, was organized in 1915 with objectives to disseminate knowledge concerning the extent and menance of feeble-mindedness and to suggest and initiate methods for its control and ultimate eradication from the American people.

Table 1.   High-Risk Factors for Developmental Disabilities

Prenatal (conception to birth)	Perinatal (around time of birth)	Postnatal (approximately 1 to 12 months)
Genetic Factors Chromosomal abnormalities Down's syndrome Sickle-cell anemia Turner's syndrome Congenital (acquired in uterus) infection in the mother influenza rubella syphilis toxoplasmosis	*Before Labor* Maternal anemia Hemorrhage Twisted umbilical cord *Birth Complications* Fetal position Breech delivery with delay in delivery of the head Face-up presentation Shoulder-, arm-, or leg-first presentation	*Trauma* Skull fractures Concussions Severe burns Brain tumors *Infections and Viruses* Meningitis Encephalitis Measles *Exposure to or Ingestion of Toxins* Lead poisoning Household cleaning agents Poisonous plants
Illnesses in the Mother Kidney disease High blood pressure	Prematurity Respiratory distress syndrome Small infant who was not premature by dates	*Poor Nutrition* Protein deficiency Failure to thrive Malabsorption syndrome
Metabolic Disorders in the Mother Diabetes		
Irradiation Exposure to X-rays especially early in pregnancy *RH Incompatibility*	*Poor Professional Services* Incorrect use of forceps Doctor not arriving Holding back the baby's head Overmedication of mother Precipitating delivery Delaying a cesarean delivery	*Child Abuse Resulting in Brain Damage*
Maternal Age Younger than 15 Older than 35	*Drug-Related Withdrawal Syndromes* Fetal alcohol syndrome Narcotics withdrawal syndrome	
Poor Maternal Nutrition Too much vitamin D Poor diet	*Neonatal Complications* Infant resuscitation Inadequate nursery care Infection of the navel Poor feeding techniques	
Ingestion of Drugs Alcohol Narcotic or addictive drugs Medicine Smoking		

Source: Adapted from H. V. Tobel & M. P. Janicki, *Introduction to Developmental Disabilities: Characteristics and Psychosocial Needs, Vol. 1* (University of Kentucky, Human Development Program, 1981), pp. 18–22.

State legislatures began to act upon these "genetic scare" assumptions by, for example, passing laws enforcing involuntary sterilization of people with low IQs. Simultaneously, there was a documented retreat of professional interest in the person with mental retardation; a trend that stretched over the next several decades. Large rural custodial institutions predominated as the primary caretaking mode. These restricted and isolated settings provided meager (if any) interventions. People in institutional living conditions appeared more incapacitated than they actually were, which reinforced the pervasive professional stance that little could be done to help such people. Emphasis on the assessment of IQ and the belief in IQ constancy remained strong as psychoanalytic schools of therapy appeared. Psychoanalysis was considered to be impossible to conduct, and therefore ineffective as a tool, with a person who was mentally retarded.

This bleak period in the history of services to people with developmental disabilities ended abruptly (1) in 1950 with the formation of the Association for Retarded Citizens (ARC)—an extremely influential group of parents of the mentally retarded whose membership now numbers over 200,000—and (2) in the early 1960s with two programs initiated by President Kennedy. First was the National Institute of Child Health and Human Development (NICHD), established in 1962 with the specification that it focus on the delivery of services for the mentally retarded and those with other developmental disabilities. Also launched was the President's Panel on Mental Retardation (now the President's Committee on Mental Retardation), which, in October of that year, produced a comprehensive report (1962) with over 90 recommendations in broad areas of research, prevention, clinical and medical services, education, and legal issues at local state, and federal levels, all pertaining to mental retardation. In a message to Congress, President Kennedy advocated a comprehensive program aimed at prevention, treatment, and rehabilitation of mental retardation.

In October of 1963, Congress enacted Public Law 88-156, authorizing grants to states for mental retardation planning and grants for maternal and child health aimed at improving prenatal care. That year also marked the enactment of the Mental Retardation and Community Mental Health Facilities Construction Act of 1963 (P.L. 88-164), which authorized funds for the construction of facilities for the diagnosis, treatment, training, and care of the mentally retarded. These facilities, known today as University Affiliated Facilities (UAFs), offer exemplary services to clients and specialized training to professionals. They have enormously enhanced the training and interest of social workers in this social problem.

International cooperation and communication at this time had a significant influence on U.S. federal and state policies affecting people with mental retardation. Through the work of Rosemary and Gunnar Dybwad with the International League of Societies for the Mentally Handicapped (ILSMH), the innovations, in-service design, and delivery that had been advanced in Scandinavia captured the interest of the scientific community. A seminal monograph was published (Kugel & Wolfensberger, 1969) proposing the revolutionary philosophies of normalization and deinstitutionalization as conceptualized by Bengt Nirje.

This national commitment of moneys and philosophy brought renewed visions of hope about the impact of social, psychological, and educational interventions in promoting the competence of people with mental retardation and developmental disabilities. This shift coincided with an upsurge of behaviorism in the field of psychology, which offered effective systematic and empirically based interventions founded on learning theory. In institutional settings, aversive therapies were used to eliminate self-destructive behaviors. Although many of their uses were beneficial, abuses were reported that caused controversy, and behaviorial-ethical monitoring boards had to be established. Positive reinforcement schedules were used to teach mentally retarded adults to walk, talk, acquire self-help skills, and develop social skills. Creative observational studies identified affective ties between severely mentally retarded people, and adaptive behaviors began to be recognized as better predictors than IQ alone of eventual social and economic independence. Pictorial and written exposes of conditions of severe neglect within institutions were shared with the public, and professionals were held responsible for these conditions (Blatt, 1969). Pivotal cases were fought in state and federal courts asserting the right of the person with developmental disabilities to live in the least restrictive environment.

The legislative changes were summarized by the commissioner of ADD (Elder, 1985):

■ The first Developmental Disabilities Services and Facilities Construction Act (P.L. 91-517) was passed in 1970. This act defined developmental disabilities both functionally and categorically. The 1975 amendments (P.L. 94-103) established the requirement that each state operate a system to protect and advocate for the rights of persons with developmental disabilities. This legal mandate supported many court cases affirming the rights of people with developmental disabilities to function in humane living environments and to obtain appropriate treatment. (The act included a section entitled "Rights of the Developmentally Disabled.") In 1975 the Education for All Handicapped Children Act (P.L. 94-142) was passed, giving every child, regardless of level of functioning, the right to a public education. This act supported the mainstreaming of special-needs children into the public school system. In 1978 the Developmentally Disabled Assistance and Bill of Rights Act (P.L. 95-602) was enacted; its functional definition of developmental disabilities eliminated all categorical references and operationalized the specific need for services. In addition, case management services were emphasized as vital for administering to changing needs over time.

■ The Developmental Disabilities Act of 1984 (P.L. 98-527) strove to highlight realistic goals of increased independence, productivity, and community integration. The bill has since been amended to include a new priority service area: employment-related activities. By 1987, each state must provide services that will increase the independence, productivity, or integration of persons with developmental disabilities in work settings.

While these legislative changes have taken place, the judicial branch of the government has also significantly improved the circumstances of people with developmental disabilities. Major court decisions have established a constitutionally protected right to treatment, set up conditions for confinement, required the preparation of individualized

treatment plans, set staffing ratios, and mandated that care and treatment be provided in the least restrictive manner.

In *Wyatt* v. *Stickney* (1971), a constitutional right to treatment in the least restrictive setting was recognized, and a series of standards for adequate habilitation was ordered. In New York, *ARC and Parisis* v. *Carey* (1972), or the Willowbrook Developmental Center case, resulted from a campaign by physicians and social workers who helped to expose unacceptable conditions that existed in the institution. The courts acted to shift the population to community-based settings. Again, in *Halderman* v. *Pennhurst* (1977), the institution was challenged as an appropriate placement, and the residents were ordered to be relocated to appropriate community settings.

In the spring of 1985, the U.S. Supreme Court heard the case of a social worker in *City of Cleburne, Texas* v. *Cleburne Living Center* followed by arguments of attorneys on both sides. The suit focused on zoning ordinances being manipulated to exclude a group home for mentally retarded adults. An amicus brief was filed, which argued that people with mental retardation have been discriminated against and should be given extra protection in their "quasi-suspect" status.

Policies and Program Expenditures

Programs in the field of developmental disabilities are substantially defined by policies. The pattern of monetary expenditures for programs results from these policies. This section discusses the current allocation of funds and draws implications based on a report from the Department of Health and Human Services (DHHS) (Kusserow, 1984).

Combined federal and state expenditures for services to the developmentally disabled were estimated to be $14.33 billion in 1984, of which 48 percent were federal moneys and 52 percent were state moneys.

Federal. Most of the federal money (95 percent) is administered to programs through DHHS. The remaining 5 percent (total $310 million) is administered through the Department of Education (DE). DE supports school programs for children with developmental disabilities and vocational rehabilitation services programs for adults with developmental disabilities.

DHHS expenditures are distributed through four separate administrations: the Health Care Financing Administration (HCFA), the Social Security Administration (SSA), the Office of Human Development Services (OHDS), and the Public Health Service (PHS). Each of these administrations has separate programs that service people with developmental disabilities. Fifty-two percent of all federal developmentally disabled costs, the largest portion of this budget, comes through HCFA.

Health Care Financing Administration. HCFA administered $3.63 billion in 1984. Institutional costs for developmentally disabled clients constitued 40 percent of all federal developmentally disabled costs, although such institutions serviced only 6 percent of the developmentally disabled population. Average costs across states for intermediate-care facilities for the mentally retarded (ICF/MR) ranged from $24 to $167 per day, or $8,760 to $60,955 per year.

SSA. SSA administered $2.3 billion in 1984. Income maintenance programs, including Supplemental Security Income (SSI) and Social Security Disability Insurance (SSDI), amounted to 33 percent of federal developmentally disabled costs. SSI and SSDI, coupled with Medicaid, food stamps, Title XX, and state programmatic funds, provided the basic means of support for developmentally disabled clients living at home, independently, in adult foster care, group homes, and other noninstitutional environments. In a state with a well-developed service system, the total cost ranged from $22 to $40 per day, or $8,030 to $14,600 per year. Roughly 30 percent of the developmentally disabled population received SSI/SSDI.

OHDS. OHDS administered $619 million—9 percent of federal developmentally disabled costs—in 1984. OHDS programs provided for the development and maintenance of community-based services, including Title XX ($500 million), ADD ($62 million), AFDC/Foster Care ($50 million), and Head Start for developmentally disabled children ($7 million). States used Title XX and developmentally disabled funds, along with state contributions, to support day activities, case management, respite care, planning, advocacy, and other services. Current practice

emphasizes the maintenance of developmentally disabled children in family settings, whether their own or those of foster parents.

PHS. PHS administered $67 million—1 percent of federal developmentally disabled costs—in 1984. Programs supported by these moneys included PKU screening, lead content screening, and crippled children services under the Maternal and Child Health Services Block Grant.

As is evident from this summary description of program expenditures, most federal money remains tied up in the institutional care of a small percentage of people with developmental disabilities. The population of the public institutions reached its zenith of 190,000 in 1970. Since then there has been a reduction because of the deinstitutionalization movement, but as of 1982, 125,000 people still resided in institutions.

Controversy continues over whether or not institutions should be maintained at all for any person, regardless of the level of impairment. The amount of money involved—several billion dollars—contributes to the intensity of the debate. A number of judicial decisions have ruled in favor of community-based care and least restrictive environments. Several legislative mandates have supported deinstitutionalization and the development of community-based alternatives. Numerous systematic research studies have demonstrated significant global improvements of people who have moved back into a normal community environment, and the issue has engendered moral arguments and ethical debates, including refutations of all arguments in support of institutionalizing anybody because of mental retardation.

All these separate yet interconnected movements reached a critical juncture in terms of policy and programs in the mid-1980s. The goal was to reallocate federal HCFA moneys and seriously enforce community-based care. A Senate bill (S. 873) submitted in April 1985, known as the Community and Family Living Amendments to the Medicaid Program, calls for two essential requirements:

1. After October 1985, the state Medicaid plan must offer severely disabled individuals who reside in a family home or community living facility an array of community and family support services that will assist in providing for the health, safety, and effective

habilitation of the individual. At a minimum, the state must provide case-management services, individual and family support services, and protective intervention services;

2. By October 2000, the total amount of Medicaid funding available to a state for services provided to severely disabled individuals in facilities having more than 15 beds will be limited to 15 percent of the amount paid for ICF/MR services for any one year prior to 1985. This reduction in funding will take place systematically at the rate of 1 percent per quarter for 10 years, or a 40 percent reduction in the federal match over 10 years.

The combined impact of federal policy and program expenditures directly affects the quality of lives of individuals with developmental disabilities and their families. Social workers should be aware of the policies that affect their clients as well as the mechanisms by which policies are developed.

State. In recent years a related movement to develop family support programs on a state level has emerged, which reflects the collaborative efforts of those who support community-based treatment for the developmentally disabled and those who wish to reduce expenditures allocated for this target population. In 1986, 19 state legislatures had either passed formal family support legislation or are plotting such programs in order to secure the maintenance of the developmentally disabled person in the family home, thereby avoiding the emotional and financial cost of placing the person in an alternative living environment. Support is typically provided through cash subsidies or vouchers given directly to the family for the purchase of individually relevant support services. Services commonly include respite care, transportation, and counseling. Although the number of families directly affected by these programs is now small, the notion of promoting family integrity in this direct fashion is consonant with basic social work principles (Slater et al., in press).

Standards for Programs that Serve Individuals with Developmental Disabilities

Representatives from the National Association of Social Workers (NASW) have had an active role in shaping the philosophy, basic principles, and standards and procedures used for accrediting programs that serve people with developmental disabilities. The National Accreditation Council (also known as ACMRDD, or the Accreditation Council for Services for the Mentally Retarded and other Developmentally Disabled Persons) published its first standards in 1973 and has since conducted voluntary accreditation reviews for programs across the nation, setting current views on the features of exemplary programs. These are constantly being revised, however, as the field shifts its goals. A current major revision is under way, and the following discussion is based on excerpts from drafts of the 1986 standards (M. Cerreto, chief executive officer of ACMRDD, personal communication, May 2, 1986).

The philosophy of ACMRDD is to enhance the development and well-being of individuals with developmental disabilities while maximizing their achievement of self-determination and autonomy. The council does not organize its standards by program components (such as clinic, residence, workshop, and so on), but rather by processes and methods. These processes of habilitation, education, health, social, and employment-related services are applicable to many settings; similarly, standards for the physical and social environment stress normalization and promotion of individual liberty, compatible with necessary requirements for sanitation and safety, in many different settings. The stated agency philosophy must attend to the achievement and protection of the rights of the individual and to the principles of normalization and least restricting environment. It should be designed to recognize and maintain the natural support networks (the connections with family, neighbors, and friends) of people with developmental disabilities.

Each agency is evaluated as part of the service delivery system that must function as a mediator between the developmentally disabled individual and the cultural environment. It must work against and compensate for the abnormalizing effects of disability. The system performs this function by improving the individual's ability to act independently and by modifying the environment to bridge gaps between personal capacity or resources and the normal means of fulfilling needs. To be an effective mediator, the service delivery system should be so organized that services are readily accessible and available to persons with developmental disabilities when they need them. Consequently, the delivery of services must be systematically coordinated both within each agency and among all agencies in the system. This is operationalized by standards on coordination, community education, and involvement, on class and systems advocacy, on prevention, personnel development, program evaluation, research and research utilization, on resource information and data documentation services, information and referral, case finding, entry into the system, and enrollment, admissions, discharge, and follow-along.

The council looks at the array of program components from the perspective of the individual's needs. A program plan unique to each individual must be developed and implemented by an interdisciplinary team in which all principal providers participate. The individual habilitation plan must be based on a relevant assessment of the individual's developmental needs; must reflect the participation of the individual and, as appropriate, the individual's family; must provide for the coordination of the individual's total program across agency settings; and must incorporate a continuous and self-correcting process for reviewing the individual's progress and revising the plan accordingly.

Social Work Role

There have been rapid, important changes in the field of developmental disabilities over the last decade, several of which were described above. These have been matched by NASW efforts to activate interest in the profession about developmental disabilities. Recent activities have included the development, publication, and dissemination of professional standards in developmental disabilities for social workers who practice within health-care settings (NASW, 1984), as well as the copublishing with AAMD of a book of readings delineating current social work practice in the field of developmental disabilities (Wikler & Keenan, 1983). In addition, there has been energetic participation in the International Year of the Disabled (1981), central representation on the National Board of the Accreditation Council for Standards for Programs Serving the Developmen-

tally Disabled, and extensive cooperation between NASW and AAMD to promote the visibility of this social problem area.

Finally, there have been increases in training opportunities for graduate students of social work at universities specializing in developmental disabilities as well as enhanced in-service training for social workers. Each of these developments will be summarized below, followed by an overall perspective on the unique potential contributions of the social work profession to this field of practice.

NASW Professional Standards in Developmental Disabilities. The following paragraphs are excerpts from NASW standards for professional social work practice in developmental disabilities (NASW, 1982):

The Social Work Role
The social work profession strives to use social science data and theory to promote a mutual adjustment between people and their social environment. People can be seen as individuals, families, small or large groups, or large populations. Social work especially attends to socially vulnerable populations. The developmentally disabled are vulnerable not only because of the social consequences of a disability, but also because they are more likely to be poor. That is, the disabled are more likely to live on meager incomes, and economically disadvantaged families are more likely to have developmentally disabled children as one of the sequelae of poverty.

The roles of social work in the field of developmental disabilities have greatly expanded in the past decade. As developmentally disabled clients receive more services in the community, social workers' involvement has become more critical. Along with their generic knowledge and skills, social workers often receive specialized training in developmental disabilities through graduate and continuing education or in-service training. With such preparation they are well equipped to function in a variety of roles.

Social workers offer individual and group social services, engage in supportive counselling with families, and advocate for the needs of clients. Social workers provide case management, linking clients with the variety of services necessary to meet the person's multiple needs. In this role, they also function as interdisciplinary team members. They engage in intake and discharge planning and social skills development, especially in their efforts to facilitate community placements for clients. They also serve as planners, researchers, policy makers, administrators, and program evaluators.

Social workers in developmental disabilities are found in a wide range of settings, as well as at all levels of organizations. For example, they work in institutions, community-based living arrangements, state departments of health and human services, local direct-service agencies, medical settings, and in primary and secondary schools. They may also be found in correctional facilities and nursing homes. In addition, they often teach specialty courses at universities and university-affiliated programs, and they coordinate field instruction for students of social work.

The AAMD [American Association on Mental Deficiency] Social Work Division and NASW have collaborated on these standards because of a shared professional commitment to establishing a level of competence expected of all social workers employed in settings serving the developmentally disabled person. They can be used in various ways, including responses to licensing and certification requirements and regulations. They represent a consensus of current social work opinion across the country on social work practice in developmental disabilities. (pp. 16–20)

Standard 1. All social workers working with developmentally disabled clients shall possess or acquire and develop knowledge about developmental disabilities.

Standard 2. All social workers shall subscribe to a set of principles regarding developmental disabilities which should underlie their practice.

Standard 3. Social work practice and research shall seek to prevent or reduce the incidence of developmental disabilities.

Standard 4. All social workers shall participate in an interdisciplinary approach to serving the needs of developmentally disabled people.

Standard 5. The functions of the social work program shall include specific services to the client population and the community.

Background knowledge (Standard 1) would include a familiarity with the etiology of developmental disabilities and theories of growth and development, an understanding of family dynamics and of cultural norms, an acknowledgment of the kinds of support that may be necessary to enhance the client's functioning, and a grasp of information about resources available to the developmentally disabled in the community. Basic principles that underlie social work practice with the

developmentally disabled client (Standard 2) include concern for providing support over the life span of the client, maximizing the client's potential, the principle of normalization, and maintaining the least restrictive environment for the client. Practice and research aimed at the prevention of developmental disabilities (Standard 3) focus on the social work role in primary, secondary, and tertiary prevention. The interdisciplinary team (Standard 4) is seen as critical for best responding to the practice needs of the person with developmental disabilities. The functions and services of the social worker (Standard 5) include discharge planning, outreach, advocacy, community liaison efforts, and the identification of individuals at risk (Keenan, 1983, pp. 41–44).

Training of Social Workers in Developmental Disabilities. A major impetus in the availability of specialized university training of professional social workers has been federal support provided through university-affiliated facilities (UAFs), which are funded both by the Maternal and Child Health Services Block Grants and ADD. These initially stipended positions drew students into the field and significantly expanded the number of specialist social workers in developmental disabilities. The number of graduate schools providing at least one course on developmental disabilities tripled during the 1970s (Wikler, 1981), a development greatly influenced by the existence of UAFs on those campuses. Several graduate schools now offer concentrations in developmental disabilities, which include several courses in developmental disabilities and an integrated field experience. They have developed a standard curriculum for field placement and have also taken on responsibility for providing in-service training materials and workshops for social workers in the community. Title XX funds were committed to develop innovative, nationally disseminated training materials and training projects on developmental disabilities for social workers in generic agencies (Tobel & Lambert, 1981).

Summary
Community-based support for normalized living is now the treatment philosophy espoused by professionals in the field of developmental disabilities. Major legislation,

pivotal court cases, and dramatic shifts in program functions are enabling the person with disabilities to function in the least restrictive environment. Current definitions of developmental disabilities are similar to traditional conceptualizations of social work intervention, in that both underscore the reciprocal relationship between the individual and the environment (Horejsi, 1979). Social work has always maintained a dual focus on persons and their context advocating and working to maximize the fit between them.

Conceptually, the social worker should be guided by the vision of interlocking social systems that affect the treatment of people who are developmentally disabled. The social work role should integrate information about each of these systems—features of the family, the groups, the culture, the community, and the society in which the developmentally disabled person functions. Although one single level of intervention may ultimately be the treatment of choice, to bring about a better fit of the person in context, the most appropriate level of intervention is not predetermined for the social work practitioner in this field. Instead, an initial assessment of the problem should be sufficiently broad and inclusive as to enable the social worker either to advocate for change in legislative forums or to build social skills in one individual. This flexibility and range of expertise distinguishes the training of social workers from other professionals in the field.

Lynn McDonald-Wikler

For further information, see Deinstitutionalization; Disabilities: Physical; Federal Social Legislation Since 1961; Health Care Services.

References

Begab, M. Haywood, C., & Garber, H. (1981). *Psychosocial Aspects of Mental Retardation Theory, Vol. 1*. Baltimore Md.: University Park Press.

Blatt, B. (1969). "Purgatory." In R. Kugel & W. Wolfensberger (Eds.), *Changing Patterns in Residential Services for the Mentally Retarded*. Washington, D.C.: U.S. Government Printing Office.

Branick, C. (1918). "Principles of Casework with the Feebleminded." *Annals of the American Academy of Political and Social Science, 78*, 60–70.

Clarke, A. S. D., & Clarke, A. M. (1974). "The Changing Concept of Intelligence: A Selective Historical Review." In A. M. Clarke & A. D. B. Clarke (Eds.), *Mental Deficiency* (3rd ed., pp. 142–163). New York: Free Press.

Elder, J. (1985). *The Life Cycle of a Service System: Past, Present and Future*. Paper presented at the World Congress of the International Association for the Scientific Study of Mental Deficiency, New Delhi, India.

Grossman, H. (1984). *Manual on Terminology and Classification in Mental Retardation*. Washington, D.C.: American Association on Mental Deficiency.

Horejsi, C. R. (1979). "Developmental Disabilities: Opportunities for Social Workers." *Social Work, 24*(1), 40–43.

Hurley, R. (1969). *Poverty and Mental Retardation: A Causal Relationship*. New York: Vintage Books.

Jacobsen, J. W., & Janicki, M. P. (1984). "Observed Prevalence of Multiple Developmental Disabilities." *Mental Retardation, 21*(3), 87–94.

Keenan, M. P. (1983). "Standards for Social Workers in Developmental Disabilities." In L. Wikler & M. P. Keenan (Eds.), *Developmental Disabilities: No Longer a Private Tragedy* (pp. 41–44). Silver Spring, Md.: National Association of Social Workers.

Kugel, R., & Wolfensberger, W. (Eds.). (1969). *Changing Patterns in Residential Services for the Mentally Retarded*. Washington, D.C.: U.S. Government Printing Office.

Kusserow, R. P. (1984). *A Program Inspection on Transition of Developmentally Disabled Young Adults from School to Adult Services*. Washington, D.C.: U.S. Department of Health and Human Services.

Menolascino, F., & McCann, B. (1983). *Mental Health and Mental Retardation: Bridging the Gap*. Baltimore, Md.: University Park Press.

Mercer, J. R. (1973). *Labelling the Mentally Retarded*. Berkeley: University of California Press.

National Association of Social Workers. (1982). "Standards for Social Work in Developmental Disabilities." In *NASW Standards for Social Work in Health Care Settings* (pp. 15–21). Silver Spring, Md.: Author.

President's Committee on Mental Retardation. (1976). *Report to the President*. Washington, D.C.: U.S. Government Printing Office.

President's Panel on Mental Retardation. (1962). *Report to the President*. Washington, D.C.: U.S. Government Printing Office.

Slater, M., et al. (in press). "Survey: Statewide Support Programs." *Journal of Applied Research in Mental Retardation*.

Tobel, H. V., & Lambert, L. (1981). *Introduction to Developmental Disabilities: Characteristics and Psychosocial Needs, Vol. 1*. Lexington: University of Kentucky, Human Development Program.

U.S. Department of Health and Human Services. (1981). *Special Report on the Impact of the Change of Developmental Disabilities.* Washingtion, D.C.: U.S. Government Printing Office.

Wikler, L. (1981). "Social Work Education and Developmental Disabilities." In J. A. Browne, B. A. Kirlin, & S. Watt (Eds.), *Rehabilitation Services and the Social Work Role: Challenge for Change* (pp. 285–295). Baltimore, Md.: Williams & Wilkins.

Wikler, L., & Keenan, M. P. (Eds.). (1983). *Developmental Disabilities: No Longer a Private Tragedy: Readings in Social Work.* Silver Spring, Md.: National Association of Social Workers and American Association on Mental Deficiency.

For Further Reading

Adams, M. (1971). *Mental Retardation and Its Social Dimensions.* New York: Columbia University Press.

Dickerson, M. (1981). *Social Work Practice with the Mentally Retarded.* New York: Free Press.

Schreiber, M. (Ed.). (1970). *Social Work and Mental Retardation.* New York: John Day.

DISABILITIES: PHYSICAL

The situation of physically disabled people in the United States is pervasive, serious, and poorly defined. It is pervasive if only because of the vast number of people who are disabled, serious because of the general poverty of disabled people, and poorly defined because disability is defined in a variety of ways.

Definitional Problems of Disability

Although most people think they know a disabled person when they see one, defining disability is difficult. The first definition is medical, and it sees disability as chronic disease leading to various courses of treatment. Subcategories include postpolio, cerebral palsy, epilepsy, and so forth.

The medical definition of disability still has an overwhelming impact on disability and the disabled, if not on social work. Social work's contact with medicine, its location in the hospital, its relationship with psychiatry, and its movement toward a more holistic psychosocial perspective are features of the history of the profession.

Other definitions derive from the medical definition. For example, under the one used in many surveys and as the basis for many income transfer programs—including most conspicuously Social Security Disability Insurance—disabled people are seen as unable to work or unable to work as much and in the same range of jobs as able-bodied people. Thus, disabled people are seen as inherently less productive than able-bodied people—as economically sick.

Another definition attempts to define disability by what the disabled person cannot do. This functional limitation model sees disability as the inability to perform various functions frequently expected in an able-bodied environment. The functional limitation, economic, and medical models all define disability by what a person is not—the medical model as not healthy, the economic model as not productive, the functional limitation model as not capable (Gliedman & Roth, 1980; Hahn, 1984).

More recently, a different model of disability has entered the literature. In the psychosocial model, disability is related to society. It is not taken for granted that medical illness, economic definition, or functional limitation by themselves say what is significant about disability. Rather, what is significant can be revealed only by the ecological framework in which the disabled person exists, by the interactions through which society engages a disability, by the attitudes that others hold, and by the architecture, means of transportation, and social organization constructed by the able-bodied (Gliedman & Roth, 1980; Hahn, 1984).

According to this definition, disabled people constitute a minority. If a disabled person is poor, the cause of poverty is less in the disabled person than in a society that discriminates, ostracizes, and stigmatizes. In a move familiar to social workers, this new definition of disability locates the problem in the interaction between the person and various segments of the social system. Adjustment is not unilaterally up to the person. Rather, frequently it is society that ought to adjust.

This conception of disability has been recognized in public policy by Section 504 of the Rehabilitation Act of 1973 (P.L. 93-112), commonly considered a civil rights act for disabled people, and is a feature of the Education for All Handicapped Children's Act of 1975 (P.L. 94-142), in part a law about better services and in part a law about receiving services in an integrated or mainstreamed way.

Disability is increasingly seen as a situation arising from the broad constellation of the individual's interactions with society. It has become sensible to talk about the effects of disability as one would talk about sex and race, in a manner familiar to social workers. Thus, although men cannot give birth to children and most women do not have the upper body strength of most men, these and other physical differences are trivial compared to the sexism they trigger. Blacks and whites are physically different in even more trivial ways. The tightness of the hair curl and the amount of melanin in the skin are far less likely to distress blacks than the racism triggered by such differences.

Sexism and racism do not reside in women or blacks as products of physical differences. Rather, they are social constructions amenable to social, political, and psychological change, and social policy thus has a role in their amelioration.

Disabled people are physically different from able-bodied people. The physical differences may be more profound than those between women and men and blacks and whites. Yet here, too, it is the social construction of disability that is pernicious, debilitating, and unjust.

Thus, for example, disabled people have worse jobs—if they have jobs at all—not because they are less willing to work or less productive, but because of a social structure that discriminates against them in attitude, architecture, and organization. Similarly, the goal in interaction with disabled people cannot be simply to help them adjust to society. This would be like helping women adjust to their sex or blacks adjust to their race.

Demography

Although surveys of disabled people are at least partially flawed by a lack of consensus about an appropriate definition of disability, results suggest coherent demographic patterns. Not surprisingly, disability is more frequent among older people, poor people, blacks, and blue-collar workers. Although race is causally related to disability, it is difficult to say whether poverty causes or is caused by disability. Indeed, causality runs both ways. Disabled people earn less than able-bodied people—sufficiently less so that they all fall below official poverty levels more frequently. They are more likely to be underemployed or unemployed, and if they are employed, their earnings are likely to be less than those of able-bodied people. Perhaps less obviously, disability rates are higher in rural areas (Haber, 1985).

There are many disabled people. The exact number is hard to determine because of the definitional problems and methodological considerations discussed previously, but surveys have consistently revealed that disabled people constitute from 8.5 to 17 percent of the population (Haber, 1985). Further, disabled people occur more frequently among the populations served by social work. Disability is a prime factor in unemployment, early retirement, working poverty, black poverty, poverty among the old, poverty among the poorly educated, and poverty among the unskilled. Because disability is an important characteristic signaling a vulnerability to poverty, it is of interest to social work.

It is possible to break down disability figures into various subcategories related to the definition of disability. Thus, for example, if functional impairment were used, it would be possible to classify the number of people incapable of performing certain functions. Similarly, if work disability were used, it would be evident how many people were able to work, how many people were restricted from certain kinds of work, and how many people could not work. If the medical definition were used, it would be clear how many people were postpolio, how many had cerebral palsy, how many were deaf, how many blind, and so forth.

But the precise breakdown according to disability—assuming it is clear what is meant by a disability and by its particular subcategories—is usually less important than the fact of disability itself. Disabled people share far more in the way of stigmatization, discrimination, stereotyping, and oppression than divides them by way of individual disability. In general, specific breakdowns of disability are conceptually misleading because they disguise the central fact of disability, which is a vulnerability to social definition and attitude.

History

The conflict between the new social definition of disability and the older medical or quasimedical definitions has profound consequences for the social work role in the field. It is to be expected that as the new definition of disability gains acceptance, social work will find itself in easy empathy with a range of situations that may have seemed unfamiliar before. Defining disabled people socially has naturally led to a conception of disabled people as a minority group, for example. Social work is distinguished by its concern for minorities; indeed, its code of ethics takes particular account of the problems facing minorities.

The opportunities opened to social work by this new definition of disability have not as yet been realized for a variety of reasons, partly historical. Kirlin and Lusk (1981) record a significant part of this history:

> The 1960's was a period . . . during which the rehabilitation field was adding a new dimension as the public vocational rehabilitation services were broadened beyond their traditional employment orientation. The response of the social work profession to the call for a holistic rehabilitation approach was influenced considerably by a number of issues within the profession at the time in addition to the generic curriculum trend, e.g., the profession's concern about identity, its leanings toward treatment-oriented casework in medical settings, the reluctance of many to see social workers involved in the public social welfare settings, and resistance to categorical federal grants. . . . Largely as a result of these issues, social work did not become an integral part of federal-state rehabilitation services, and today still participates in rehabilitation largely in the context of hospitals and medically-oriented rehabilitation centers. (p. 231)

Today the disability service system is in flux. Medicine delivers more, more frequently, and one consequence is that what once might have led to death may now lead to disability. But the federal-state rehabilitation system sees its future partially in terms of a decreasing growth in resources, lack of strong leadership, fragmentation and alteration of power, and a changing consensus about social justice—a set of concerns similar to those affecting the overall social welfare system.

Stone (1985) argues that the ultimate economic issue is receipt of resources for work (on the market) or on the basis of need (public assistance). Exactly what makes a person disabled and, more broadly, excusable from work for any reason is a basic issue not only for disability, claims Stone, but for the welfare state in general and, one might add, for social work in particular.

Policies

A wide variety of federal, state, and local policies affect disabled people. Further, disabled people are frequently affected differentially by programs and policies that do not even mention disability. But some policies are directly related to disability and represent substantial outlays of money.

State laws providing for workers' compensation in the event of job-related injury were introduced largely to prevent litigation over job-related conditions. In 1980 about 88 percent of the U.S. workforce was eligible for medical benefits and cash for any job-related disability, as were the relatives of deceased workers (Berkowitz, 1986).

Social Security Disability Income (SSDI) is a program for those who have paid FICA taxes and are thus eligible for compensation in the event of disability. (Many disabled people who are working are eligible for SSDI if their disability eventually makes them incapable of work.) About 3,790,000 workers and dependents received benefits in 1984, totaling $17.6 billion (Berkowitz, n.d.).

Supplemental Security Income (SSI), that part of President Nixon's Family Assistance Plan that survived, is means-tested and does not require prior contributions for eligibility. In 1984, SSI payments totaled $6.51 million (Berkowitz, 1986).

These three income transfer programs take money from one set of people and give it to another. The attribute that triggers payment is to be work disabled—that is, in general recipients are not able to work in the same way or as much as able-bodied people. Obviously, by this definition of disability, disabled people inherently work less than able-bodied people. This definition of disability reflects how government perceives disability, administers its remedies, and sometimes can even be said to create it.

Social Work Role

Income transfer programs are not the only programs concerned with disabled people. Social workers are involved in many other programs delivering services.

The Education for All Handicapped Children's Act of 1975 assures disabled children of their right to the education traditionally provided to other children in this country. The act provides this education in an integrated or mainstreamed fashion where possible, assures that disabled children are not rejected, and provides individual educational plans for each child. The provisions of this law are far reaching and complex. At times the services mandated are subject to interpretation. It is hardly surprising that social workers are frequently called on to integrate services and to contribute other special talents.

Social workers also contribute to a wide variety of vocational rehabilitation programs that exist in the United States. Such programs, originally designed to rehabilitate disabled veterans, are not extensive, however. At least logically, social workers have a role in rehabilitation, recreation, cultural life, psychological services, and integration. Although this role is underrealized, its demands nonetheless far exceed the education given to social workers in disability at the bachelor's and at the master's levels (Browne, Kirlin, & Watt, 1981).

Ironically, as little as social work may be enamored of the medical model, social workers are likely to work with disabled people in medical settings. Many disabled people enter hospitals, and many able-bodied people leave hospitals disabled. Social workers have a defined role in hospitals, exercised no less vigorously for disabled people than for able-bodied people. Indeed, the opposite is to be expected. Insofar as a disability may signal problems to be encountered in the postdischarge setting, a case can be made for the vigorous intervention of social workers in formulating discharge plans, securing optimal situations in the community, and acting as advocates for disabled people.

Disabled people are likely to be poor and qualified for social services in other ways more frequently than their able-bodied peers. Some private programs exist, as well as programs sponsored by not-for-profit institutions. In addition, there is virtually the whole range of public social services, although only a few government programs explicitly relate to disability. This means that no matter what the setting, social workers are likely to encounter disabled people in it. Social work education must attend to the social worker's capacities to deal with disabled clients, as well as to the worker's attitudes. In fact, given that disabled people are more likely to be in the populations served by social workers than in the rest of the population, disability should be a prime source of concern and a consistent field of study in social work training. The relationship between physical disability and social work should be intimate, whereas it is often distant and confused.

Social workers should be interested in the psychosocial aspects of disabled people from an ecological perspective. They should see disability as a construction of an able-bodied society that is as needlessly painful to the disabled as racism is to blacks, as sexism is to women, and as other species of prejudice are to other human beings.

WILLIAM ROTH

For further information, see FEDERAL SOCIAL LEGISLATION SINCE 1961; SOCIAL SECURITY; UNEMPLOYMENT COMPENSATION AND WORKERS' COMPENSATION PROGRAMS; VETERANS AND VETERANS' SERVICES; VOCATIONAL REHABILITATION.

References

Berkowitz, E. (1986). (n.d.). *Generations of Disability*. Manuscript submitted for publication.

Browne, J. A., Kirlin, B. A., & Watt, S. (1981). *Rehabilitation Services and the Social Work Role: Challenge for Change*. Baltimore, Md.: Williams & Wilkins.

Gliedman, J., & Roth, W. (1980). *The Unexpected Minority*. New York: Harcourt Brace Jovanovich.

Haber, L. D. (1985). "Trends and Demographic Studies on Programs for Disabled Persons." In L. G. Perlman & G. Austin (Eds.), *A Report of the Ninth Annual Mary E. Switzer Memorial Seminar* (pp. 27–40). Alexandria, Va.: National Rehabilitation Association.

Hahn, H. (1984). *The Issue of Equality: European Perceptions of Employment for Disabled Persons* (No. 29). New York: World Rehabilitation Fund.

Kirlin, B. A., & Lusk, M. W. (1981). "Educating Social Workers for Practice in Rehabilitation Services." In J. A. Browne, B. A. Kirlin, & S. Watt (Eds.), *Rehabilitation Services and the Social Work Role: Challenge for Change* (pp. 216–233). Baltimore, Md.: Williams & Wilkins.

Stone, K. (1985). *The Disabled State*. Philadelphia: Temple University Press.

DISASTERS AND DISASTER AID

Whether they affect us directly or indirectly, disasters are facts of our daily lives. The drought and resulting famines that killed many thousands of people in Ethiopia and other African nations during and after 1983 stirred the conscience and generosity of the American people. The devastating deaths and destruction from the earthquakes in Mexico and the volcanic eruption in Colombia in 1985 evoked a similar response. Unlike other countries, which could neither prepare for nor cope with such enormous calamities, the United States has institutionalized disaster aid; it is widely accepted as a governmental and communal social welfare function and as an essential social utility. This responsibility for helping with disasters also applies internationally, particularly to the poor and developing nations that receive substantial American aid each year. As Cuny (1983) has observed:

> No other country responds more fully to disasters than the U.S. It responds to some extent in all phases of a disaster and is extensively involved in predisaster planning, mitigation, and preparedness. The U.S. is one of the largest sources of funds for disaster relief and operates throughout the Third World. (p. 115)

The disaster aid system is a complex, comprehensive set of policies and provisions. It includes traditional, informal, communal arrangements for mutual aid by families and neighbors and by formal public welfare provisions in local, state, and federal programs. These policies and provisions within the social welfare system cover a wide range of financial and social services and benefits in the areas of disaster preparedness and prevention, emergency relief, and long-term rehabilitation. Such benefits are available to individuals, families, and communities and to public and private corporate units (municipalities, other government agencies, and businesses) that are potential or actual disaster victims.

In recent years, increasing attention has focused on disaster prevention and preparedness programs and on efforts to improve program effectiveness. This shift away from emphasis on relief programs is a response to the problems that have been recognized concerning their equity, efficiency, and effectiveness. In addition, there is increasing public recognition of the greater frequency of disasters, the greater vulnerability of people living in disaster-risk areas, and the accelerating social and economic costs of damage and losses and relief and reconstruction. Thus, in the 1970s as compared to the 1960s, there was a 50 percent increase in major worldwide natural disasters to an average of 75 per year; the estimated deaths increased fivefold to 114,000 per year and an estimated 44 million people were injured or suffered other effects (Eckholm, 1984). The incidence, damages, and costs of major disasters have risen even more in the 1980s.

The increasing public recognition that disasters contribute significantly to unemployment, poverty, and other social problems has led to progressive developments in social legislation, policies, and service provisions. Although disaster aid is now a major social welfare area, it nevertheless requires renewal and further evolution in order to develop more effective preventive, preparedness, and service programs.

Nature of Disasters

"Disaster" is a term that may be broadly or narrowly defined; according to Fritz (1961), it is

> an event, concentrated in time and space, in which a society, or a relatively self-sufficient subdivision of a society, undergoes severe danger and incurs such losses to its members and physical appurtenances that the social structure is disrupted and the fulfillment of all or some of the essential functions of the society is prevented. (p. 655)

The term "disaster" has also been used to refer to the effects of severe stress on individuals. Stress effects that comprise substantial loss of life and property constitute a disaster. Efforts have been made to arrive at definitions that refer to some minimum amount of damage or loss, such as 100 deaths or $1 million, but they have proved unsatisfactory because the passage of time renders minimum damage questionable. Moreover, the societal context of a disaster in large part determines its meaning and consequences; an affluent community may be prepared for and easily recover from a severe hurricane but a poor community may be unprepared and unable to recover at all. In most disasters, it is the poor and disadvantaged minorities who are most hurt.

Individual and collective stress may be precipitated by external, natural events, such as hurricanes, tornadoes, earthquakes, floods, tidal waves, lightning, windstorms, frosts, snow- and hailstorms, landslides, avalanches, volcanic eruptions, forest fires, or droughts. Stress may also result from internal, human-made agents such as economic depression or inflation, wars, terrorist attacks, riots, strikes, famines, train and plane crashes, major power outages, explosions, arson, and pollution of the earth and atmosphere by toxic and nuclear wastes.

Wijkman and Timberlake (1984); Tinker (1984); Burton, Kates, and White (1978); and others argue persuasively that many "natural" disasters result from human mismanagement and exploitation. Overpopulation, deforestation, overfarming, and soil erosion, for example, turn a drought into a deadly famine. In our urban, highly industrialized, and densely populated society, everyday hazardous "accidents" are more and more common and escalate into major disasters, as Perrow (1981) well documents. In December 1984, a gas leak in a Union Carbide chemical plant in Bhopal, India, resulted in 2,000 deaths and 200,000 injuries.

An understanding that many aspects of disasters are subject to human control is important so that they can be better prevented and prepared for and their damages mitigated.

Disaster agents or hazards threaten or damage the possessions, identities, and values of individuals and families as well as the structure and functioning of social systems. The extreme social crisis engendered by a disaster may be limited or catastrophic in its effects. Routine coping patterns and available resources of individuals and their social systems are often inadequate, and they become disequilibrated and dysfunctional. There is disruption and disorganization of a community's basic patterns of living, of its status and role relationships, and of its cultural system of values, meanings, and motivation.

When groups of people are exposed to common threats, they have common as well as uniquely personal reactions. Unlike ordinary troubles, disasters involve hardships and losses that are public rather than private, so that a consensual, integrated community of victims and of mutual aid comes into being. Disasters thus open people and social systems to change, creating opportunities for positive individual and social restructuring and for higher levels of individual and group consciousness.

Whether of internal or external origin, a disaster resembles other crisis situations in that it results from the interaction of several basic variables. Hill (1958) identified these basic factors as (1) the characteristics of the hazardous event or the disaster agent, particularly its suddenness, scope, frequency, duration, and controllability; (2) its attendant objective hardships and destructive consequences; (3) the internal and external resources available, including the length and credibility of warning, an individual's locus of control and objective accuracy of perception, prior disaster preparations and experience, and current group supports; and (4) the objective, cultural, and subjective meanings of the disaster-producing event.

The meanings of a disaster to its victims, particularly their causal attributions, are of crucial importance. A natural disaster, such as a typhoon, may be interpreted by individuals and groups as an act of God, as punishment for their sins, or as an exciting challenge. An external causal attribution and positive attitudes about adjusting to the losses and damages involved usually lead to more positive corrective responses in mutual aid and communal self-help. Internal causal attributions may lead to feelings of rage, guilt, and blame; rejection of responsibility for corrective action; and ineffective or self-destructive behavior. Attitudes of blame and guilt following a human-induced disaster, such as a terrorist attack or ghetto riot, often result in scapegoating, repression, outcasting, and exacerbated intergroup conflict (Frederick, 1980).

A disaster also has a history—a sequence of phases in which there is disorganization and reintegration and in which there is also a problem-solving process with either adaptive or maladaptive consequences. First there is the preimpact period of warning and preparation for the impending danger and then the period of impact, with concomitant death, injury, and destruction. These are followed by the immediate postimpact phase of disorganization, demoralization, and the inventory of damage; and by the relief-rescue phase of evacuation and first aid for survivors. Then there is the rehabilitation phase of rebuilding supplies of food, shelter, clothing, and money; rehousing people; and restoring the community's economy, services, social order, and morale. Lastly, there is the reconstruction phase of reorganization and restoration of stability at some optimal level of personal, family, and community life, which may be lower or higher than in the predisaster period.

The following discussion of individual, family, and community reactions to disasters deals for the most part with the effects of natural disasters. It summarizes the recent research on these subjects, and it is based on material given in Bard and Sangrey (1980); Burton, Kates, and White (1978); Cohen and Ahearn (1980); Cuny (1983); Mileti (1980); Parad, Resnik, and Parad (1976); Quarantelli (1978); Rossi et al. (1983); and Wijkman and Timberlake (1984).

Individual Behavior

A disaster presents a set of difficult coping tasks, whose accomplishment is facilitated if people have clearly defined social responsibilities and roles in family, group, organizational, and community associations. Prevention and preparedness programs provide or utilize such membership roles and responsibilities (Foster, 1980). They may provide flood-control systems, storm cellars, and a tracking-warning communications network as well as rehearsal and instruction, group solidarity, and subcultural values and norms for altruistic behavior. All of these increase the likelihood of adaptive and efficient responses to a disaster.

As a result—and contrary to usual stereotyped conceptions of disasters, as Dynes and Quarantelli (1976) point out—in most disaster situations

> individual disorganization is somewhat minimal [and] individuals are able to exhibit

situationally adaptive behavior. . . . [T]he trauma which is inherent in such situations is probably handled more effectively and has fewer long-term consequences than does "normal" trauma. (p. 232)

Some people do, however, develop traumatic neuroses or a "disaster syndrome" of shock, apathy, or euphoria, with severe reactions of grief, guilt, hostility, anxiety, depression, personal isolation, and interpersonal dissension. Most people recover quickly from this state, but some victims develop severe traumatic feelings that have long-term effects and may become chronic. Despite this, the short-term effects of disasters can be beneficial. Mental hospital admissions and suicide, homicide, and crime rates usually decline during the disaster period.

The degree and rate of disorganization and of recovery from mental upsets are influenced by the nature, extent, and severity of the damage and loss; the victim's proximity to death and destruction; personality factors, such as locus of control and religious faith; and social supports. Older single people, members of poor minority groups, mothers with dependent children, and children separated from their families are particularly vulnerable to mental upsets. In recent years, there seems to be a greater incidence of more severe mental upsets in disasters, with a greater need for mental health services; this is discussed further in a later section.

An individual's recovery is significantly influenced by membership in family and other primary groups, which provide valued roles, material resources, and social supports. Being part of a community of sufferers also enables individuals to evaluate losses and damage in terms of relative deprivation. Continued residence in the home territory is another important factor, as are the victim's sense of social responsibility and occupational skills. Thus, skilled male heads of households, with homes and dependents, behave more rationally and are less prone to develop posttraumatic mental symptoms than are other men. Some skilled individuals, however, experience role conflicts when both family and occupational loyalties are expected of them.

Survivors of disasters frequently exhibit altruistic and self-sacrificial behavior. Injured individuals tend to help others rather than focus on themselves, and those who are skilled offer their services to others. Altruistic behavior may be a defense against anxiety; it may provide relief from guilt, reduce feelings of deprivation, and compensate for the traumatic and conflicting feelings evoked by disaster experiences. Yet it is also situationally adaptive in a constructive way, and it is responsive to traditional community norms and values. Thus it strengthens humanitarian motives, fosters a positive self-image, and increases self-esteem.

Family Behavior

A disaster precipitates a family crisis and brings out the best and worst in families, as it does in individuals. A family's ability to cope with a disaster depends on its capacity for integration and adaptation; its patterns of decision making, communication, and mutual support; its life-cycle state and prior experience with disasters; the effectiveness of family role performances; and access to needed community resources. Also crucial is the family's definition of the disaster as an occasion for self-blame or for cohesive response to an externally caused threat.

During the immediate postimpact period, disaster victims give and seek aid within the family first, then turning to close friends, neighbors, and others. The family's behavior is determined to a large extent by information on the condition and safety of its members and by its degree of disruption and separation. Whether families evacuate or stay put, they tend to do so as units. When this is not possible, separated members are more prone to develop mental disorders during the recovery process. The crisis associated with a disaster may result in increased cohesiveness and strength or it may deplete a family's resources, resulting in desertion, separation, or divorce and a subsequent dependence on public welfare.

The extended family, which can offer financial aid, service, and status maintenance, is a preferred source of recovery assistance; it constitutes a primary circle of defense and support in society. Families of low socioeconomic status or with ethnic-minority membership tend to have an external locus of control and different response patterns than do those of higher status and majority group membership (Perry & Mushkatel, 1984). Broken families and poor families with many children or with aged members are more likely to lack relatives and neighbors who can provide helping resources; they therefore tend to need much external aid.

Community Behavior

Community behavior in a disaster is a collective problem-solving response to the disruption and disorganization of the community system. Emergency helping systems are established, synthesized, and then decline when their work is done. This community problem-solving process is carried out on a largely informal basis by existing and ad hoc leaders, groups, and organizations. Its effectiveness depends a good deal not only on the competence of these groups and leaders, but also on the competence of the community as a system.

A major prerequisite of a competent community is the presence of a "disaster culture," described by Moor (1958, pp. 179–180) as having important functions in a successful disaster response. It provides anticipatory experience; preparatory motivation and role definitions; family, organizational, and interorganizational planning; shelter, clothing, and cooking facilities; and communication and coordination systems. It strengthens community cohesiveness; calls on trained professionalism, volunteerism, and indigenous leadership; and offers positive meanings and motives for warning, rescue, and relief operations.

After the impact of a disaster agent, the surviving competent community mobilizes itself for mutual aid, and an emergency welfare system will emerge. Individuals, informal groups, and formal organizations mount a mass assault, with a mobilization and outpouring of energies to cope with the consequences of the disaster. Democratic primary-group relationships and collective patterns of spontaneous behavior come to the fore, and the situation and work tasks are consensually defined. Norms of authority, property rights, and contracts are modified so that existing resources can be procured and allocated according to community needs. Community decision-making and coordinating processes oriented to the requirements of immediate tasks are adopted to provide search, rescue, first-aid, and other emergency services. Survivors experience a major expansion of the citizen role, committing themselves to relief and rehabilitative obligations (Dynes, 1970, pp. 96–97).

There also is a well-intentioned, spontaneous mass convergence of people and supplies from the outside. The greater the damage, the greater the need for external aid. Federal and state disaster agencies and the American Red Cross and other national voluntary agencies, with their mix of national and local staffs and volunteers, make available emergency and long-term rehabilitative services. Often, however, more clothing, food, and other supplies are contributed than are needed, adding to the burden of relief tasks. As Wijkman and Timberlake (1984) and Cuny (1983) emphasize, such relief efforts often become counterproductive; they stimulate and reinforce individual and communal overdependency on external aid.

The altruistic therapeutic community that emerges in the postimpact period has been described as a utopia (Barton, 1969; Siporin, 1976). It is a gemeinschaft of primary relationships, with a strong community identity and cohesiveness based on common dangers and losses, shared objectives, and cooperative self-help experiences. Altruistic, collectivist, volunteerist, egalitarian values, norms, and behavior become prominent in this sociocultural system, along with common feelings of pride, euphoria, grief, and guilt. Such a therapeutic community makes for a responsive and supportive healing experience for disaster victims. In addition, it bolsters their resilience and recuperative powers and, as Fritz (1961, p. 692) observed, may have an "amplified rebound effect" in carrying a community beyond prior levels of integration and functioning.

This altruistic community, however, is short-lived. It declines with the passing of the emergency and with increasing pressures on individuals and organizations for the resumption of normal roles and institutional patterns. It also declines with the development of competition among the survivors for rehabilitation resources and among helping organizations for status and credit. Bureaucratic perspectives and standardized policies and procedures then often become dominant, particularly as a shift in emphasis from emergency mass care to rehabilitation and recovery tasks takes place. The decline of the emergency aid system may in part be related to discrepancies between the victims' conceptions of need and those of the relief organizations. This disparity leads to a degree of resentment, sometimes directed toward the bureaucratic procedures of the federal and state agencies involved. For the most part, however, disasters have long-term positive effects.

Another type of communal response to disaster lies at the opposite pole from the positive, effective one of the competent community just described. This occurs when a vulnerable community suffers major loss of life and property and is unable to cope effectively, and its disaster responses take a downhill course from which it recovers poorly. A dramatic example of this negative kind of process is the Buffalo Creek disaster, which took place in the Appalachian coal-mining area of southern West Virginia in 1972. Three dams suddenly broke and the floodwaters quickly and totally destroyed four communities as well as severely damaging several others. One hundred eighteen people died, 4,000 were left homeless, and there was $50 million in property damage.

The Buffalo Creek communities did not recover for a long time, and many individuals never did so. Almost all the survivors were severely traumatized and most suffered what Lifton and Olson (1976) call a "survivor syndrome," manifested by death imprint, death anxiety, survivor guilt, psychic numbing, impaired human relationships, and a search for significance. Also prominent were feelings of alienation, helplessness, hopelessness, and embitterment about a morally unjust universe in which the responsible coal company went unpunished. These reactions became chronic in many of the survivors.

Erikson (1976) emphasizes the loss of "communality," a culture of shared understandings and altruistic attitudes that cushions pain, provides a context for intimacy, and represents morality and traditions. He points out that this culture had been much weakened before the disaster by the social isolation, chronic economic depression, and welfare dependency of the people in the Buffalo Creek area. As a result, they were particularly vulnerable and lacked the resources with which to cope with the traumas of the disaster.

It is important to note that, in general, such negative effects are largely short-term in nature, and most communities recover quickly and well from disasters (Dacy & Kunreuther, 1969). In their survey of disaster losses in the United States for the decade 1960–1970, Rossi et al. (1981, p. 18) did not find any discernible alteration in national population and housing growth trends as an effect of disasters. This may well be related to the steady and rapid growth of the American population and to the fact that new people move into stricken communities and help in the recovery process. Rossi et al. (1983, p. 181) also found that most communities recovered in a relatively short time and did so largely as a result of aid from external resources.

Welfare Needs and Public Policy

Accounts of the destructive effects of disasters indicate the consequent vast needs of individuals, families, and communities for social services and for economic and vocational assistance. The disability of family members, particularly providers, the loss of jobs and income, and the destruction of and damage to homes and personal possessions create grave social and financial hardships. Poor people in particular, many of whom are uninsured, are required to depend on the relief provided by disaster aid programs and to seek public welfare assistance.

The economic costs of disasters have continued to climb. Hurricane Agnes in 1972 set a record for the costliness of a single disaster in the United States. It resulted in 122 deaths, damaged or destroyed 115,000 homes, hurt 126,250 families, and damaged property worth $3.5 billion (Harriman, 1972). In response, of the billions provided in aid, the American Red Cross spent $23,326,329 and the federal government provided $2.33 billion. Yearly expenditures for disaster aid have been substantial. During fiscal 1982, the federal government spent over $373.7 million; and in fiscal 1983, over $1.9 billion (B. McAda, Office of Public Affairs, Federal Emergency Management Agency. personal communication, 1985). In fiscal 1984, however, the expenditures decreased to under $507.3 million. The American Red Cross spent $36.5 million in fiscal 1979, $63,154,000 in 1983, and $69,629,000 in 1984 (R. D. Vessey, Director of Disaster Operations, American National Red Cross, personal communication, 1985). In fiscal 1984, the American Red Cross responded to 52,738 disaster situations and provided emergency assistance to 742,957 individuals and 60,834 families. In addition, many other voluntary and state and local governmental organizations contributed funds, material, and personnel that added appreciably to the total costs of disaster aid programs.

Many individuals and families suffer great income and property losses in the wake of a disaster. Thus, an American Red Cross survey of the 1969 Hurricane Camille victims in Virginia found that the average family lost $5,200 more than its annual income, and the recovery rate through financial aid from various sources, including insurance payments, was only about 50 percent. (This recovery rate still obtained in 1985.) Rossi et al. (1983, p. 173) found that one-fourth of the disaster victims had a resulting major debt burden. Haas, Kates, and Bowden (1977, p. 180) found that although many families were better off following a disaster, "the loss and destruction of family possessions have continuing negative effects on family happiness" because of their own negative evaluations of their situations. It is increasingly accepted that such effects require compensatory and rehabilitative responses within the disaster aid system.

Disaster aid is the system of organized social welfare policies, benefits, and services that helps individuals, families, organizations, communities, and other collectivities to prevent and resolve the social and economic problems caused by disasters. It is an extensive complex of private, voluntary, and governmental arrangements, providing a vast number of programs that help a great many people. It expresses the development on national, state, and local governmental levels of public policies directly responsive to the increasingly publicized suffering caused by major disasters since World War II.

Public policy decisions in regard to disasters are aimed at preventing destruction and dysfunction and at enhancing the integrity and normal functioning of the environment and of society. This is accomplished through programs designed to (1) modify the hazard to lessen its effects, as in cloud-seeding; (2) decrease vulnerability and increase resources, as in the building of dams and the setting up of detection and warning systems, the enactment of land-use regulations, and the establishment of preparedness programs for high-risk populations; (3) mitigate suffering and lessen social disruption attendant on disasters, for example through emergency relief; and (4) distribute the losses and costs of disasters through insurance, taxation, and rehabilitative services (White & Haas, 1975, p. 57). Such adjustments are interdependent and have dynamic positive or negative results. For example, the building of dams encourages people to move into flood-risk areas. In contrast, building regulations in Japan and California require new structures to be earthquake resistant and have helped save many lives.

Berren, Beigel, and Barker (1982) suggest that interventive programs be based on dimensions of disaster characteristics—the degree of personal impact, the type of disaster and its potential for occurrence or recurrence, control over future impact, and the duration of the disaster. Programs could emphasize responsive approaches in terms of psychotherapeutic versus educational, individual versus systems, prevention versus treatment, and direct versus indirect categories.

Disaster aid policies embody a delicate balance of institutional and residual conceptions of social welfare. In the residual view, disaster aid is primarily the responsibility of individuals, families, and communities, and voluntary and governmental efforts are aimed at supplementing the normal private, voluntary arrangements on the basis of unmet need. In contrast, the institutional conception of disaster aid views the major responsibility for the provision and administration of disaster aid programs as belonging to the government. It was from such an orientation that the federal government established an extensive disaster aid system.

In recent years, however, the federal government and the disaster agencies have shifted public policies and programs away from an institutional toward a more residual orientation. Federal governmental policy now emphasizes individual and family responsibility for coping with disasters and potential losses, particularly through insurance protection. Property insurance coverage is required for individuals and governmental agencies to qualify for federal assistance. As a result, many low-income people are disadvantaged in recovering from the losses they sustain in disasters. Federal policy also emphasizes local governmental and voluntary organizational contributions to disaster relief. Continuing priority is given to immediate disaster relief programs rather than to community development provisions. This is in opposition to Cuny's (1983) observation that because outside intervention aid during the postimpact and emergency periods has disincentive and dependency-reinforcing effects, it is most effective in predisaster and reconstruction periods.

According to a survey by Freudenheim (1979, p. 229) of national and international programs, political problems in disaster aid are both prevalent and obstructive. Such problems may include unwillingness to acknowledge the existence of a disaster, political decisions by donors, and corruption and interference with the relief or rehabilitation processes. Such problems were evident in the efforts to provide relief for the African famine victims.

In their studies of disaster policy development, Wright and Rossi (1981) found that federal and local officials often hold different and discrepant views of the seriousness of disasters. Also, local officials and communities often find national disaster policies to be burdensome, inefficient, and irrational. Yet, according to White and Haas (1975, p. 105) and Cuny (1983, p. 258), both federal and local officials prefer to encourage the use of technological solutions, such as the building of levees, rather than those that require developmental changes in local community ways of living.

These policy considerations apply to the international scene as well. A recent development in disaster policy is the multinational concern with disasters and the growth of multinational relief and rehabilitation programs. This has been stimulated by the understanding that many natural disasters are international in scope, involving economic and social disruption, loss of life and property, mass starvation, and diseases that affect many countries.

The United Nations Disaster Relief Office was established in 1971 to coordinate the distribution of funds and the relief and rehabilitation efforts of United Nations agencies, as well as to stimulate national and international prevention and preparedness programs. Active in such work are the Common Market (European Economic Community), the World Bank, the International League of Red Cross Societies, international religious organizations, and such international voluntary organizations as Oxfam. One trend in this movement is a call for international law to establish rights and responsibilities in regard to disasters. In addition, there are efforts to redefine disaster aid as part of the basic rights guaranteed under the United Nations Universal Declaration of Human Rights (Cuny, 1983, p. 250).

Private and Voluntary Programs

Partly in response to governmental encouragement and partly in response to public altruistic impulses, there has been an extensive expansion of voluntary programs for disaster aid. This is an expression of the religious and secular traditions of charity and neighborly service in the United States. Private voluntary disaster aid comes from many sources: relatives, friends, local religious and other community groups, and the general public. Disaster victims prefer such nonofficial, informal types of assistance to public ones. Private voluntary aid involves expectations and obligations of reciprocity, mostly takes the form of mutual aid and self-help services, and is often offered rather than requested.

The American National Red Cross is the largest voluntary organization providing disaster services in the United States. Founded in 1881 and chartered by Congress to provide emergency relief in disasters, it has remained a voluntary agency financed by voluntary funds and utilizing large forces of community volunteers. Its wide range of programs includes public health, first aid, service to the military, recreation, and blood donations. These programs make possible the mobilization of large cadres of volunteers in disaster work. The Red Cross has provided leadership in preventive, preparatory, mass care, and rehabilitation programs and in the application of professional social work methods and principles.

Many of the voluntary agencies, particularly the Red Cross, have been flexible and responsive to the social changes relating to disaster aid. For example, the Red Cross, the Salvation Army, and others have extended their services to cover needs arising from civil disorders and relocation programs necessitated by dioxin and other pollution di-

sasters. The bureaucratic difficulties associated with governmental programs have meant that the voluntary agencies must help victims deal with program regulations and the red tape involved in obtaining assistance. The Red Cross has increased its information, referral, advocacy, and ombudsman services. New forms of collaboration and cooperation between voluntary and governmental agencies in the formulation of policies and procedures have also been necessary to help resolve problems, especially the inefficiencies and confusions that plague emergency relief programs.

The great toll in mental disorders suffered by many disaster victims in recent years has been increasingly evident as a major area of unmet need. This may be a reaction to the eagerness of mental health professionals and agencies to provide mental health services. It has stimulated the growth of extensive crisis intervention and other mental health services as part of the basic relief and rehabilitation programs offered by the voluntary and the public mental health agencies. The National Institute of Mental Health has been active in supporting this development and in encouraging joint planning and service programs between public and voluntary organizations. (See Cohen & Ahearn, 1980; Fraser & Spicka, 1981; Parad, Resnik, & Parad, 1976; Tierney & Baisden, 1979). It is noteworthy that the $13 million out-of-court settlement made between Pittstown Coal and the survivors of the Buffalo Creek disaster included awards for psychic, socioemotional damages.

But there are increasing difficulties as ever more costly disasters make for ever more costly services. Many of the voluntary agencies, however, do not apply for federal and other governmental subsidies out of their desire to avoid the constraints involved and to maintain their autonomy and private identity. In major disasters, the Red Cross and other voluntary agencies use the services of many volunteer social workers and other helping professionals, large numbers of whom are contributed by their employing social agencies. Although these contributions have been freely acknowledged, professional volunteer help has been harder to come by because many social agencies have had their own resources depleted.

Severe cutbacks in federal funds have

further exacerbated this situation by shifting more demands for direct services to the private sector. One form of response has been the formation and expansion of a national umbrella organization, the National Voluntary Organizations Active in Disaster. In addition, the voluntary organizations have cooperated in pooling their resources and services to help meet the needs of individuals and families who have suffered major losses in disasters, especially where public provisions are inadequate.

Governmental Programs

The disaster aid system developed by the United States government is of fairly recent origin. The assumption of federal responsibility for an ongoing disaster aid program began in 1950 with the passage of the Disaster Act (P.L. 81-875). The series of acts that followed culminated in the landmark Federal Disaster Relief Act of 1974 (P.L. 93-288). This law established two levels of assistance—for major disasters and for emergencies; presidential declarations of either type authorize federal agencies to provide loans and grants, facilities, supplies, and services to supplement the efforts and resources of state and local governments and of voluntary relief organizations. Responsibility for administering the national disaster aid programs and for coordinating varied federal, state, local, and voluntary agency responses was delegated to the Federal Disaster Assistance Administration; this became the Federal Emergency Management Agency in 1979.

As a result of the Federal Disaster Relief Act, the federal government has become the primary source of funds for preparedness, emergency relief, and recovery efforts as well as for research training and technical information concerning disasters and how to cope with them. A summary of such authorized programs is given by the Federal Emergency Management Agency (1983) in its *Program Guide*. In a major disaster, the act provides for grants to states and local governments, including funds for long-range economic recovery activities. Assistance is also offered to individuals and families on a loan or grant basis. This aid includes the provision of food stamps and disaster unemployment compensation; funds for temporary housing, rental payments, and home repair; and relocation assistance, legal

services, and crisis counseling. Assistance in obtaining loans and with tax and insurance problems, including the provision of low interest rates, is also provided to disaster victims and to farm and business organizations. Many of these direct services are made available in one-stop disaster assistance centers established in strategic locations and in mobile units.

Various kinds of restrictions and limitations govern these federal programs, however. For example, by using federal and state matching provisions, state and local social services departments are able to grant up to $5,000 to individuals and families who are disaster victims. But this is a very inadequate sum in major disasters. It is a need-based program that requires state applications and a degree of state funding, and it is subject to inordinate bureaucratic delays in the actual delivery of such funds to people in acute need. The flood insurance program requires prior individual or community insurance coverage and that certain zoning ordinances be in effect.

The issue of equity remains an important problem with governmental disaster programs. People who have insurance or savings are discriminated against by disaster aid programs that give more to the poor or those who live on credit and lack savings. Yet, because poor people are less able than others to cope with application forms and eligibility requirements of disaster programs, they may appear to be treated unfairly. Another point of view, however, asserts that those who have saved to cope with contingencies, including thrifty poor people, should not be penalized for doing so.

There is a related controversy concerning the redistributive aspect of the disaster aid programs. It is manifestly difficult to provide assistance on the justice principle associated with Rawls (1972), which is taken to mean that the most assistance should go to the neediest and most disadvantaged. Such a principle has limited acceptance in a democratic and capitalistic society, where balances are sought between the claims of justice, individual welfare, and reward for merit and productivity.

Another issue concerns the efficiency and effectiveness of the state and national disaster aid programs in the United States. The disaster aid structures in many states still have more of a civil defense than a financial and social services orientation. The states carry out the individual and family grant programs with varying degrees of adequacy and efficiency, with marked discrepancies between states in what they accomplish, and under varying amounts of control by the federal government.

Federal aid programs have long been criticized for allocating insufficient funds for administration and implementation, which severely restricts their abilities to meet demonstrated needs. There has been growing criticism of their serious procedural inefficiencies—overlapping agency domains, duplication of programs and benefits, poor interagency communication, comparatively high administrative costs, inordinate delays in providing benefits because of red tape—and increasing public misunderstandings about available benefits and services. Beginning in 1983, the Federal Emergency Management Agency initiated a major project, Delta, to remedy these deficits and to computerize information and procedures to facilitate this. Also, as part of its preventive "hazard mitigation" program, a computerized national data base is being developed through which information about many types of disasters can be collected and made generally available.

Despite these problems related to governmental programs, there has been a steady improvement in the disaster aid system as a whole. One promising trend is the growing collaboration between governmental and voluntary organizations in preventive as well as relief work, with the voluntary agencies, for example, supplementing the assistance provided by the public welfare departments. The problems with disaster policy and service delivery programs have been and can be further alleviated by contributions from the profession of social work.

Disaster Aid and Social Work

From its beginning as a profession, social work has played an important role in disaster aid. Emergency relief in disasters was a major function of early social work practice. Devine (1904) gives interesting accounts of the work of the Chicago Relief and Aid Society following the great Chicago fire of 1871 and of charity work in other major disasters. At the time of the San Francisco

earthquake and fire of 1906, Devine was general secretary of the New York Charity Organization Society and director of the New York School of Philanthropy (now the Columbia University School of Social Work). In his autobiography, Devine (1939, pp. 134–148) relates how he administered the major relief effort by the American National Red Cross, in association with many social workers from across the country.

It has long been a tradition for professional social workers to volunteer or be assigned by their agencies to assist disaster victims and to participate in the disaster work of the American Red Cross. This tradition continues today, particularly in the southern states, where natural disasters frequently occur. The magnitude and history of such self-effacing, altruistic behavior by the social work profession has not been recognized by the public and often not even within the profession itself.

Social workers provide much more than front-line case and administrative services in disaster relief programs. In addition, they contribute significantly to disaster research, policy planning, and program development and implementation. They are also active in initiating legislative provisions and reforms to improve the procedural operations of the disaster aid system.

Social work contributions are particularly needed to help advance preventive and preparedness programs on the local, state, and national levels. Greater efforts are necessary in the areas of disaster planning and research. The development of disaster cultures through educational programs in vulnerable communities also merits social work attention and research-demonstration efforts, as do means of fostering greater organizational effectiveness and interorganizational coordination in community emergency and rehabilitative operations. Social workers have expert knowledge to contribute in all these areas.

The crisis intervention model of disaster aid work is gradually being complemented by a greater emphasis on longer-term community development activities. The provision of information, referral, outreach, counseling, and advocacy services; of financial and other practical aid; and of supports for informal, neighborhood-based helping networks need to be placed in a community development context. Social workers can assist in the needed integration of informal helping and social support networks with public and voluntary relief organizations, thus permitting the operations, norms, and values of the altruistic community to be continued beyond the postimpact period of disasters. As Barton (1969, pp. 305–306) suggests, the altruistic community can be institutionalized and "mutual aid can be bureaucratized, routinized, and made reliable in spite of the ups and downs of mass emotion." Such an institutionalization of supportive communal networks, welfare provisions, and hazard-mitigating programs will strengthen the forms of altruistic, synergistic behavior and will create badly needed integrative community bonds.

Conclusions

This review of disasters and of how people cope with them emphasizes that disasters provide an opportunity for individual and social change and that, though they have destructive effects for a number of people, they generally produce positive social change. As Fritz (1961) declares, man is

> a highly adaptive social animal, when he is confronted with direct threats to his continued existence. Human societies have survived nearly every conceivable form of danger and horror in the past, and . . . probably will continue to do so in the future. (pp. 682–683)

As part of its adaptive problem-solving processes to help individuals, families, and communities stricken by disasters, society has evolved a highly elaborate, multifarious aid structure. In the United States, the present structure of disaster aid is a basic component of the social welfare system. Recent federal and state legislation reflects improved responses to the ever-increasing vulnerability, needs, and costs of disasters. Disaster relief is and will continue to be subject to the inevitable chaos and confusion that follow disasters. It is heartening, though, that disaster prevention is gaining greater priority in voluntary and government programs.

A great deal more needs to be done, however, to develop and strengthen a comprehensive, rational, and equitable system of disaster aid on the national, state, and local levels, involving public and private voluntary agencies. Despite the valuable advances

made, continuing research into the nature of disasters is needed—into their short- and long-term ecological and socioeconomic effects. There is also a need for better understanding of individual and social behavior in disasters, particularly of the self-help and mutual aid processes that arise in the postdisaster altruistic community and how these may be facilitated and strengthened.

The international disaster scene also warrants American attention and efforts. As Tinker (1984, p. 25) states, many parts of the Third World are "on the verge of ecological collapse. [This] is not just an environmental disaster. It also is a direct threat to the self-interest and security of all of us in the rich, industrialized nations." The public media, in graphically calling attention to disasters in countries around the world, have facilitated an increasing recognition that, in relation to disasters, common vulnerabilities and interests are global in scope.

In developing its contributions of policy planning, administration, and direct services, whether in the United States or internationally, the social work profession can help make disaster aid an exemplary part of the social welfare institution, vital to competent communities and to a just society.

MAX SIPORIN

For further information, see ADMINISTRATION: ENVIRONMENTAL ASPECTS; CRISIS INTERVENTION; MUTUAL HELP GROUPS.

References

Bard, M., & Sangrey, D. (1980). "Things Fall Apart: Victims in Crisis." *Evaluation and Change* (special issue), 28–35.

Barton, A. H. (1969). *Communities in Disaster*. Garden City, N.Y.: Doubleday & Co.

Berren, M. R., Beigel, A., & Barker, G. (1982). "A Typology for the Classification of Disasters: Implications for Intervention." *Community Mental Health Journal, 18*(2), 120–134.

Burton, I., Kates, R. W., & White, G. F. (1978). *The Environment as Hazard*. New York: Oxford University Press.

Cohen, R. E., & Ahearn, F. L. (1980). *Handbook for Mental Health Care of Disaster Victims*. Baltimore, Md.: Johns Hopkins University Press.

Cuny, F. C. (1983). *Disasters and Development*. New York: Oxford University Press.

Dacy, D. C., & Kunreuther, H. (1969). *The Economics of Natural Disasters*. New York: Free Press.

Devine, E. T. (1904). *The Principles of Relief*. New York: Macmillan Publishing Co.

Devine, E. T. (1939). *When Social Work Was Young*. New York: Macmillan Publishing Co.

Dynes, R. R. (1970). *Organized Behavior in Disaster*. Lexington, Mass.: D. C. Heath & Co.

Dynes, R. R., & Quarantelli, E. L. (1976). "The Family and Community Context of Individual Reactions to Disaster." In H. Parad, H. L. P. Resnik, & L. G. Parad (Eds.), *Emergency and Disaster Management* (pp. 231–244). Bowie, Md.: Charles Press.

Eckholm, E. (1984, July 31). "Fatal Disasters on the Rise." *The New York Times*, pp. C1–2.

Erikson, K. T. (1976). *Everything in Its Path*. New York: Simon & Schuster.

Federal Emergency Management Agency. (1983). *Program Guide—Disaster Assistance Programs* (DR & R18). Washington, D.C.: U. S. Government Printing Office.

Foster, H. D. (1980). *Disaster Planning*. New York: Fischer-Verlag.

Fraser, J. R. P., & Spicka, D. A. (1981). "Handling the Emotional Response to Disaster: the Case for American Red Cross/Community Mental Health Collaboration." *Community Mental Health Journal, 17*(4), 255–264.

Frederick, C. (1980). "Effects of Natural vs. Human-Induced Violence." *Evaluation and Change* (special issue), 71–75.

Freudenheim, E. (1979). "Politics in International Disasters." In L. H. Stephens & S. J. Green (Eds.), *Disaster Assistance* (pp. 225–244). New York: New York University Press.

Fritz, C. E. (1961). "Disaster." In R. K. Merton & R. A. Nisbet (Eds.), *Contemporary Social Problems* (pp. 651–694). New York: Harcourt, Brace & World.

Haas, J. E., Kates, R. W., & Bowden, M. J. (1977). *Reconstruction Following Disaster*. Cambridge, Mass.: M.I.T. Press.

Harriman, E. R. (1972), *Agnes* (ARC 2246). Washington, D.C.: American National Red Cross.

Hill, R. (1958). "Generic Features of Families Under Stress." *Social Casework, 39*(2–3), pp. 139–150.

Lifton, R. J., & Olson, E. (1976). "The Human Meaning of Total Disaster: the Buffalo Creek Experience." *Psychiatry, 39*(1), 1–18.

Mileti, D. S. (1980). "Human Adjustment to the Risk of Environmental Extremes." *Sociology & Social Research, 64*(3), 327–333.

Moore, H. E. (1958). *Tornadoes Over Texas*. Austin: University of Texas Press.

Parad, H., Resnik, H. L. P., & Parad, L. G. (Eds.). (1976). *Emergency and Disaster Management*. Bowie, Md.: Charles Press.

Perrow, C. (1981). *Normal Accidents*. New York: Basic Books.

Perry, R. W., & Mushkatel, A. H. (1984). *Disaster Management*. Westport, Conn.: Quorum Books.

Quarantelli, E. L. (Ed.). (1978). *Disasters: Theory and Research*. Beverly Hills, Calif.: Sage Publications.

Rawls, J. (1971). *A Theory of Justice*. Cambridge, Mass.: Harvard University Press.

Rossi, P. H., et al. (1981). "Are There Long-Term Effects of Natural Disasters?" In J. D. Wright & P. H. Rossi (Eds.), *Social Science & Natural Hazards* (pp. 3–23). Cambridge, Mass.: ABT Books.

Rossi, P. H., et al. (1983). *Victims of the Environment*. New York: Plenum Press.

Siporin, M. (1976). "Altruism, Disaster, and Crisis Intervention." In H. Parad, H. L. P. Resnik, & L. G. Parad (Eds.), *Emergency and Disaster Management* (pp. 213–229). Bowie, Md.: Charles Press.

Tierney, K., & Baisden, B. (1979). *Crisis Intervention Programs for Disaster Victims*. Washington, D.C.: U.S. Department of Health, Education, and Welfare, Alcohol, Drug Abuse and Mental Health Administration.

Tinker, J. (1984). "Are Natural Disasters Natural?" *Socialist Review, 14*(78), 7–25.

White, G., & Haas, J. E. (1975). *Assessment of Research on Natural Hazards*. Cambridge, Mass.: M.I.T. Press.

Wijkman, A., & Timberlake, W. (1984). *Disasters—Acts of God, Acts of Man*? Washington, D.C.: Earthscan. International Institute for Environment and Development.

Wright, J. D., & Rossi, P. H. (1981). "The Politics of Natural Disaster: State and Local Elites." In J. D. Wright & P. H. Rossi (Eds.), *Social Science & Natural Hazards* (pp. 45–67). New York: ABT Books.

DIVORCE AND SEPARATION

Whether the United States is experiencing the demise of the family is an issue that has been widely discussed in professional journals and the public media alike. The terms used imply that the only family arrangement of importance—the only unit that can appropriately be defined as a family—is the permanently married couple and their biological children. This is a myth, and myths die hard, especially when they concern the family. What is emerging in the contemporary American social structure is a multiplicity of arrangements, strongly influenced by the current high rate of divorce, including the one-parent household and the remarried family. These changes make it crucial for social workers and other helping professionals to understand the extent of marital separation and divorce and its impact on adults and children. (Although separation and divorce are separate events, much of the literature does not differentiate between them, and throughout this article the terms "marital separation," "divorce," and "dissolution" will sometimes be used interchangeably.) The following material includes sections on demographic information, marital status and emotional well-being, factors associated with emotional adjustment, separation and loss, social issues, and implications for policy, practice, and research.

Demographic Information

A few statistics indicate the extent of divorce in recent times and its impact on the family experience. With small fluctuations, except for a temporary rise after World War II, the divorce rate increased only gradually from 1860 to the 1960s (Thornton, 1982). Between 1960 and 1980, however, the rate more than doubled. By the end of the 1970s, more than 2 percent of all existing marriages were terminated by divorce each year. These rates dropped in 1982, but they still remain high. The actual number of divorces climbed to an all-time high of 1.21 million in 1981 (National Center for Health Statistics [NCHS], 1983). The divorce rate was not only high in the 1960s and 1970s, but it was also pervasive, affecting all races and age groups. Divorce differentials observed in the 1950s, however, which included fewer divorces among whites than blacks and fewer among older than younger groups, persisted through the 1970s. In an article on the changing American family, Thornton and Freedman (1983) reported that differences over time can be seen in the following statistics: 29 percent of all couples married in 1952 were divorced by their twenty-fifth wedding anniversary, 29 percent of couples married in 1957 were divorced by their twentieth anniversary, the same percentage of those married in 1962 were divorced in 15 years, and among couples married in 1967, 28 percent were divorced after 10 years of marriage. If current rates continue, almost half of those married in 1973 will divorce at some time compared to 5 percent of couples married in the 1860s.

(The rates are higher for black Americans [Weed, 1980].)

More refined demographic information has limitations. Reports differ on sources of information, how recent it is, the years for which they are reporting, the cohorts on which the data are based, and the methods by which rates have been estimated. The following is based on these diverse reports.

Ethnicity, income, and education appear to be related to separation and divorce. In regard to ethnicity and race, more information is available on black Americans than other groups. The chances of being separated or divorced are greater for blacks than whites. In June 1971, the percentage of black women born between 1930 and 1934 known to have been divorced was 24.3; for the corresponding group of white women, it was 16.7 (Carter & Glick, 1976). The relationship between divorce and educational level is complex. High school dropouts have the greatest likelihood of divorcing; the rate decreases for high school graduates, rises again for college dropouts, and falls again for college graduates. For women, but not for men, and most clearly for black women, the rate rises again for those who have one or more years of postgraduate education. In general, the highest rate of divorce is for those who did not complete high school. Carter and Glick (1976) link these findings to personality characteristics and life experiences that influence people to complete a particular level of education.

Regarding income and divorce, for white men aged 25 to 44, the likelihood of divorcing becomes smaller at each higher level of income. For white women, the opposite is true. The higher the income, the greater the likelihood a woman will divorce. Income patterns also differ between blacks and whites. A tendency to divorce more often is seen among affluent black men and poor black women compared to whites of similar incomes. The highest divorce rate of all was for white women earning high incomes, and the lowest rate was for women earning little or no income (Carter & Glick, 1976; G. F. Jacobson, 1983).

Over a million children are affected by divorce each year in the United States. The 1.2 million children whose parents divorced in 1979 represent nearly 2 percent of all children under the age of 18. The experience of marital disruption and variations in child custody for children is not a recent phenomenon. What is new is that the main reason for marital disruption has shifted from the death of a parent to parental divorce. Dissolution rates in the 1970s suggest that about 1 of every 3 white children and 2 of every 3 black children born after marriage will experience a parental divorce before 16. Most children of divorce are in the custody of their mother; the majority will experience living in a one-parent household for at least 5 years. The experience of divorce is not necessarily ended when a mother remarries. Approximately one-third of white children and one-half of black children whose mothers remarry will experience a second parental dissolution (Bane, 1976; Bumpass, 1983; NCHS, 1982; Thornton, 1983). So children may be on a moving equilibrium as they experience an intact household, a one-parent custodial household, and the remarriage and subsequent divorce of a custodial parent. The magnitude of the change in children's experiences is indicated by the following: whereas 73 percent of children under 18 were part of a traditional family in 1960, the figure dropped to 63 percent in 1978, and if present trends continue, it is projected that 56 percent of all children will live in a traditional household in 1990. A high percentage of those not living with both biological parents are children of divorce living in a one-parent household or in a remarried family (Glick, 1979). Children in the custody of a single parent are the fastest-growing group and are projected to include 26.5 percent of all children in 1990 (Glick, 1984).

Family Status and Emotional Well-Being

A considerable number of studies report differences between separated and divorced persons and persons of other marital status. These include psychiatric, epidemiological surveys (Ilfeld, 1978; Leaf et al., 1983; Mellinger et al., 1978), comparisons between the separated, divorced, and married or widowed in regard to their physical and mental health (Briscoe & Smith, 1975; Gove, 1973; Hetherington, Cox, & Cox, 1978), and descriptions of disturbances in the divorced (Chester, 1971). According to all reports, the mental and physical health of the divorced is lower than the health of those in other marital status groups. These differences are variously ascribed to either biological, sociological/economic, or psychological factors or some combination of these. There is evidence in the literature that married people are better off in terms of psychological well-being, followed by the widowed, divorced, and separated. However, Mellinger et al. (1978) found the lowest distress in unmarried women.

As suggested above, a sizable number of factors have been reported as potentially mediating relationships. For example, socioeconomic status, income level, and other economic factors have been linked to outcome (Brown et al., 1980; Chiriboga, Roberts, & Stein, 1978; Goode, 1956; Pearlin & Johnson, 1977; Raschke, 1975; Spanier & Fleer, 1979). More problems have been reported when a separation is recent, when there is greater attachment between former spouses, and when there is greater hostility between them (Brown et al., 1980; Chiriboga & Cutler, 1977; Goode, 1956; Hetherington, Cox, & Cox, 1979; G. F. Jacobson, 1983; Kitson, 1982; Weiss, 1975). There is some evidence of a relationship between outcome and length of marriage (Kurdek & Blisks, 1983) and some that social supports are linked to better outcome (Kitson & Raschke, 1981).

Preexisting psychiatric disturbance has been thought by some to explain both the divorce and the disturbance (Bergler, 1970; Briscoe & Smith, 1975). Nontraditional sex roles (Kurdek & Blisk, 1983) and greater self-esteem (Kitson & Raschke, 1981) have been linked to better outcome. The interdependence of the above variables over time is important to investigate.

Those who report that married people are better off psychologically have sometimes related this to the protection from psychological stress that marriage may provide, at least for men. In regard to the fact that more problems have been reported when a separation is recent, much of the literature on psychological well-being and divorce relates to the short run—the time period around the event. In these studies, the most commonly reported psychological problems are aspects of depression such as depressed mood, loneliness, low work efficiency, trouble sleeping, somatic concerns, and feelings of incompetence. Suicidal and homicidal ideation may be present, but attempts are infrequent

(Chester, 1971; Goode, 1956; G. F. Jacobson, 1983; Kitson, Graham, & Schmidt, in press; Weiss, 1975).

One possible explanation for short-run disturbance derives from crisis theory, which states that any change in equilibrium can cause a temporary disorganization that can end spontaneously with a new equilibrium that is higher, lower, or at the same level as before. G. F. Jacobson's (1980) view is that the divorce experience is not necessarily a single crisis around a single event, but crises or multiple crises referred to as a crisis matrix and that there are peaks of disturbance not only around the time of separation but during the long-term adjustment to divorce as well.

Understanding the relationship of parental divorce to the well-being of children is complicated in that many studies have grouped all children from all single-parent custodial households together (Kitson & Raschke, 1981). Also, there are serious methodological problems in the studies that exist in this and in other areas, including small samples, a concentration on white middle-class populations, and diverse methods of measurement. When those studies that exist concerning children of divorce are examined, there is consensus that children are considerably distressed within the first 2 years of parental separation (Fulton, 1978; Hetherington, Cox, & Cox, 1978; D. S. Jacobson, 1978a, 1978b; McDermott, 1968; Wallerstein & Kelly, 1980; Zill, 1978). There is evidence that most experience considerable distress when parents separate but little knowledge about whether or under what conditions such distress leads to later psychological and behavioral difficulties. Zill (1978) reported that children of divorce were found to be at twice the risk of receiving psychiatric attention as children from intact families (13.5 percent compared to 5.5 percent). A number of factors have been reported in the literature as important to the well-being of children after divorce. These include parent-child interaction with specific emphasis on loss, parental conflict, emotional well-being of parents, and age-related responses of children (Hess & Camara, 1979; Hetherington, Cox, & Cox, 1978; D. S. Jacobson, 1978a, 1978b; Mednick & McNeil, 1968; Wallerstein & Kelly, 1980). Other factors identified include social supports for parents and children, economic changes, the stability of the living situation,

and the impact of other life events (Clingempeel, 1982; Emery, 1982; Kurdek & Blisk, 1983; Stolberg & Langner, 1983).

These factors are complicated, however. Discord between parents may be more important in influencing adjustment than the divorce, for example. Children from intact conflict-ridden households have been found to have more problems than children from separated and divorced households where less parental conflict occurred (Emery, 1982; Hetherington, Cox, & Cox, 1978; McCord, McCord, & Thurber, 1962; Nye, 1957; Rutter, 1979). By the same token, children exposed to continued conflict after divorce are reported to have more problems (Anthony, 1974; D. S. Jacobson, 1978b; Westman, Cline, & Kramer, 1970).

Another area related to the well-being of children is the psychological well-being of parents (Mednick, 1968). Also, a high number of household moves has been reported to affect children of divorced parents adversely (Kurdek, 1983; Stolberg & Langner, 1983).

As with adults, most studies of children of divorce have focused on the first year or two after the event. Studies have found evidence of distress during this period for almost all children, most frequently expressed in the form of behavior problems including increased acting out, antisocial and aggressive behavior (especially in boys), and feelings of sadness, anger, and guilt (Fulton, 1978; Hess & Camara, 1979; D. S. Jacobson, 1978a, 1978b; McDermott, 1968; Wallerstein & Kelly, 1980; Weiss, 1975). Hetherington, Cox, & Cox (1978) reported that a reduction of tension appears to occur at the end of 1 to 2 years. As with adults, crisis theory predicts a peak of disturbance in children early in the process.

When academic status was examined, little difference in academic performance was found between chidren in one- and two-parent households (Hetherington, Camara, & Featherman, 1981). Relatively few children in one-parent homes tended to suffer serious or long-term intellectual consequences. However, children in one-parent homes tended to achieve somewhat lower grade point averages and receive lower teacher evaluations. A number of interpretations are proposed for this. One is that some teachers find children from one-parent households more disruptive and less likely to attend school regularly;

teachers may rate children who do not conform to school routine more negatively. Boys were more likely to be adversely affected in this area than girls—a finding that might be considered in light of the fact that most boys live with mothers; comparable data on girls living with fathers is not available.

Little information is available on divorce and black families. Kinship ties may be an important area to investigate. Some authors (Hill, 1972; Martin & Martin, 1980) report that kinship ties are generally strong in black families. McAdoo (1980) suggests that upward and downward mobility due to marriage and divorce does not affect the availability of family supports or the structure of family ties, thereby possibly making the transition of divorced people in black families different and possibly smoother than that of comparable white families. However, increased rates of divorce could have the effect of depleting extended family support if too many persons are drawing on members of an extended family at one time. In her work with black families and their child care arrangements, Hill-Scott (1984) indicates that crisis and financial support tend to be more readily available from extended family members than day-by-day support. Huddleston-Bryant (1983), in a study of the post-divorce adjustment of black middle-class women, reported on the importance of the church as a form of social support for this group.

Factors Associated with Emotional Adjustment

Adults. Not all adults and children are equally affected by the experience of separation or divorce. A number of factors are associated with the emotional distress of adults. There is no conclusive evidence as to the order of their importance. Most studies have dealt with the early divorce period. In the view of the present author, evidence from research findings and clinical observations points to the importance of the relationship between divorcing adults. This has already been mentioned in a previous section, and will be discussed in somewhat more depth below, specifically in regard to attachment and hostility.

Attachment to a former spouse may take a number of forms including longing and yearning for the former spouse, wishing for reconciliation, and seeking ways to interact with the former spouse. Attachment can take place whether or not there is actual contact. Feelings of attachment and anger are not mutually exclusive. Attachment has been operationalized for research purposes by Kitson (1982), Brown et al. (1980), and G. F. Jacobson (1983). In their studies, moderate to high degrees of attachment were found in 40-50 percent of recently separated or divorced persons. All three researchers showed that greater degrees of attachment were associated with more distress.

In regard to hostility, feelings of anger between separating spouses are common. Anger was present in 7 out of 10 respondents of one study (G. F. Jacobson, 1983), and in 90 percent of these situations it was associated with the separation. Greater anger was associated with more anxiety, depression, and somatic disturbances. Of importance is the extent to which anger is manifested in overt hostility, which can occur only if there is contact. Although there is considerable agreement in the literature about the importance of conflict in divorce, no consensus exists on how to measure it. Emery (1982) suggests that three aspects be included: the process by which the conflict is expressed (hitting, arguing, avoiding), the content of the conflict (sex, money, child rearing), and the length of time it lasts. G. F. Jacobson (1983) has classified hostility in four ways: verbal hostility such as putting down the former partner; divorce-related hostility, such as hostility over finances or custody; death-related hostility, such as wishing the former spouse gone or dead; and finally physical hostility. Several of these types of hostility were related to emotional well-being. In most instances, more hostility was associated with more disturbance. Overall findings suggest that the extent of aspects of overt hostility shown between divorcing adults increases disturbance.

Another aspect of the relationship between former spouses associated with emotional distress is ambiguity. This is seen in a spouse who is not clear or consistent in behavior toward the former spouse, including frequent vacillation about the separation and unrealistic assessments of the probability of a reconciliation. Ambiguity was associated with increases in disturbance.

Factors that contribute to the long-term

adjustment to divorce are still poorly understood. Continued attachment to and hostility
toward former partners may be a factor. As
time goes by, even when new relationships
are formed, the way in which the relationship
between former spouses is worked out may
be a factor in emotional well-being. Other
factors may also play a role in long-term
adjustment, such as finances, both in absolute terms and in relation to the predivorce
situation. This is especially important for
women with custody of children who may not
be able to support their families. Another
important area of concern for long-term adjustment about which little is known is how
predivorce disturbance relates to long-term
adjustment. New crises can also arise in the
relationships between former spouses that
exacerbate difficulty and reactive feelings of
attachment or hostility around such events as
the remarriage of a former spouse or the
marriage of children.

Children. Children of divorce are at
increased risk of disturbance. Most studies
have been carried out within the first 2 years
after a parental separation. Although there
are serious methodological problems in existing studies (small samples, concentration on
the white middle class, different methods of
measurement), four areas stand out in association with children's well-being during this
period: parent-child interaction, interparent
conflict, the emotional status of parents, and
the ages of the children. Other factors identified in the literature include the preexisting
emotional difficulties of children, social supports for parents and children, economic
changes, the stability of the living situation,
and the impact of other life events.

Regarding parent-child interaction,
some evidence exists that children's adjustment to separation is associated with their
relationship with both parents (Hess &
Camara, 1979; Hetherington, Cox, & Cox,
1978; Wallerstein & Kelly, 1980). Hess and
Camara studied white middle-class families
with children aged 9 to 11 of whom the
mother had custody and a matched group of
intact families: children who had positive
relationships with both parents experienced
less stress, showed less aggression, and had
better work and peer relationships. Findings
are contradictory about the relationship between the frequency of interaction with the

noncustodial parent and children's adjustment. Some found a positive effect except in
situations of high conflict between the parents or in which the visited parent was emotionally disturbed (Hetherington, Cox, &
Cox, 1979; D. S. Jacobson, 1978a; Wallerstein & Kelly, 1980; Zill, 1978). D. S.
Jacobson (1978a) found a significant relationship between a child's adjustment and the
difference in the number of hours the child
lost in "time spent" with the noncustodial
parent before and after a parental separation.
The study, carried out in the first year after
separation, found that the more time that was
lost, the poorer the child's adjustment. Other
studies have found that frequency of visitation is not related to postseparation adjustment (Kurdek, Blisk, & Siesky, 1981), and in
a recently completed National Institute of
Mental Health (NIMH) project on stepfamily
interaction and child adjustment, D. S.
Jacobson (1983, 1984) found no relationship
between a child's adjustment an average of
6.5 years after a parental separation and the
amount of time typically spent with the
noncustodial parent. In this study, at least
one parent had remarried, and one child who
had seen the noncustodial parent at least
once in the year prior to the interview was
included in the study. Findings may have
been affected by the research design, which
excluded the extremes of contact—that is,
situations in which a parent had deserted the
family and those in which there was joint
custody. In general, the literature suggests
that children of all ages want continued contact with the noncustodial parent (Nolan,
1977; Rosen, 1977; Wallerstein & Kelly,
1980).

Regarding interparent conflict, the idea
that such conflict affects the well-being of
children in intact families has been much
discussed in the clinical literature. In a review of research on parent-child conflict and
children of discord and divorce, Emery
(1982) concluded that a relationship exists
between interparent conflict and children's
problems, with greater effect on boys. Several studies have reported that children from
conflict-ridden intact households are more
likely to have problems than those from divorced families with little conflict (Hetherington, Cox, & Cox, 1979; McCord, McCord, &
Thurber, 1962; Rutter, 1979). Zill (1978) reported that children of divorce are at signifi-

cantly greater risk of developing mental health problems than children from intact homes in which parents report happy marriages. Children from families reported to be "not too happy" do not differ from children of divorce. In their report of a 2-year longitudinal study, Hetherington, Cox, and Cox, (1978) examined the impact of interparent conflict on the development of children from divorced and nondivorced families. Two years after a parental divorce, the high conflict divorced group exhibited the most adjustment problems.

Parental conflict does not necessarily terminate with the end of the marriage, of course. Children may be exposed to ongoing conflict through the divorce and later. It seems reasonable to assume that not only the presence of conflict but also the type and duration of conflict are important. A high level of conflict can affect the positive effect of visiting a noncustodial parent. It can lead to an intensification of conflicting loyalties for the child and interfere with the child's positive relationship with one or both parents. In her recent NIMH report on stepfamily interaction and child adjustment, D. S. Jacobson (1984) found considerable conflict between many parents 6.5 years after separation. Areas of conflict reported by most parents concerned child support and visiting, situations around which continued need exists for communication between parents in the two households a child relates to after a divorce. Jacobson conceptualized these two households as linked, with the child viewed as the link influencing and being influenced by the people in the two households and their interaction with each other. Few other studies give attention to both households (Ahrons, 1981). Interparent conflict can also affect the child indirectly by influencing the emotional state of the parents. Conflict can interfere with the noncustodial parent's ability to support the custodial parent in child-rearing tasks, which can adversely affect child-rearing practices such as consistent discipline. This illustrates how the relationship between parents can affect the child. The child can also affect the parents' relationship to each other. Children can manipulate one or both parents in the interest of their own needs and wishes. As yet no research has been done on the extent to which a parent can separate a conflictual relationship with a former spouse from the relationship with a child. This is an important question in considering under what circumstances, for example, joint custody can work out.

Regarding the emotional status of parents, it is well documented in the literature that children from families in which a parent has a psychological disturbance are at increased risk of behavior problems (Mednick & McNeil, 1968). There is no reason to believe that this is less true for children of divorce. As noted previously, divorced people show greater disturbance and distress in many areas than do married ones, especially immediately after separation or divorce. If either or both parents are highly distressed, depressed, or tense, they may be overwhelmed by parenting responsibilities, which can in turn affect the child (Zill, 1978).

Regarding the age-related responses of children, a major contribution has been made by Wallerstein and Kelly (1980). Their seminal study is based on in-depth clinical observation; they present important descriptive findings and generate many hypotheses for further research. Theirs is the only longitudinal study to date that has examined the age-related responses of children to parental separation. They found that children experience sadness, depression, loneliness, and anger; many have fantasies of parental reconciliation. In the preschool group, children's reactions include depression, irritability, increased anxiety (especially separation anxiety), increased aggressive behavior (especially in boys), and some regression. The most lasting feeling was one of pervasive neediness. Some experienced fears of abandonment. Preschool children have limited cognitive abilities with which to understand the reasons for separation. Unlike older children, they cannot seek out the noncustodial parent or other supports.

The initial reaction of latency or school-age children was pervasive sadness, intense strain, and immobilization. For the older latency age group, the strongest feature was anger, which was more clearly organized and object-directed than in the younger group; their ability to articulate anger was good. It was expressed in the form of temper tantrums and demandingness. One year later, some of the difficulties had subsided; however, the anger persisted longer than other responses (Wallerstein & Kelly, 1976).

School-age children have the cognitive ability to be sympathetic as well as angry. Many had loyalty conflicts and allied themselves with one parent as a way of dealing with or avoiding conflict. For some the separation involved disruption of school achievement and increased behavior problems in school and with peers. For others school became a source of support and renewed effort was put into academic accomplishment.

Most adolescents experienced considerable distress and anger when their parents separated. Their reactions included sadness and feelings of betrayal. They were more successful than younger children, after the initial trauma, in understanding their parents' views, in assigning responsibilities for difficulties, and in avoiding conflict. They sometimes used withdrawal as a way of dealing with the situation. Some stopped idealizing one or both parents; some reacted with increased awareness of their parents' sexuality. Adolescents have the cognitive ability to deal with both the practical and the emotional aspects of the situation, which is helped by the fact that this age group is independently mobile and can seek out extrafamilial relations, including peers, as sources of support.

Separation and Loss

Considerable attention has been given to the importance of understanding the patterns of and reactions to separation and loss in the experience of marital dissolution. Therefore, some theoretical perspectives and descriptive literature will be reviewed.

When divorce takes place, both parents and children experience specific losses in varying degrees. Both also experience the universal loss of being part of an intact family. Part of what needs to be mourned is the partner or parent as a permanent part of one's life in a particular family arrangement. Although the losses of a spouse or parent by divorce and death have been compared, there are differences characteristic of the divorce experience about which much remains to be learned. Death is a specific event that occurs at a precise moment in time. Divorce is a process; the loss takes place over time and is not always immediately complete or permanent. Reconciliations can and do take place; continued contact can and does take place, especially if children are involved. One study reported that three-fourths of recently sepa-

rated spouses who participated had had contact with each other in the 2 weeks prior to the interview; the same was true for one-half the long-term separated spouses (G. F. Jacobson, 1983).

Reactions to loss have been conceptualized by Freud (1971), Bowlby (1973), and Parkes (1972). Both the Freud and Bowlby models have been applied to reactions to loss through divorce (G. F. Jacobson, 1983; Weiss, 1975). Freud (1971) wrote of the difficulty of giving up attachments that provide what he referred to as libidinal satisfaction. Bowlby (1973) proposed that the attachment of a child to a mother is fundamental to all attachments throughout life and forms the basis for reactions to separations from important people in later life. He described anxiety as an expected response to separation. Weiss (1975), who applied Bowlby's concept to divorce, saw the loss of a marital partner as analogous to the loss of a mother for a young child and described separation anxiety as focusing attention on the person "lost"along with much discomfort.

Parkes (1972) described the stages of mourning and bereavement in ways that are relevant to divorcing adults. His stages are shock and denial, yearning for the lost person, and anger and protest. Shock and denial occur especially if the separation is unanticipated. Relief and euphoria may also be a first reaction, although distress may follow (Hunt & Hunt, 1977; Weiss, 1975). Pining and yearning for the lost person can occur, particularly for the spouse who did not seek or want the divorce and who may feel abandoned (Hunt & Hunt, 1977). This may be temporarily relieved by contact with the former spouse. There are risks in much continued contact, however. It can bring back the ambivalent feelings and conflicts that led to the original rift, and frequent contact may make working through the separation more difficult. Parkes's final phase of bereavement is anger and protest. Hostility is common among separating spouses and is often overt.

Although children experience some loss when a parent leaves the custodial household, they do not necessarily experience the complete loss of a major attachment figure. One study of the impact of divorce on children aged 3 to 13 within the first year after a parental separation found that the time spent with the noncustodial parent can either increase, decrease, or remain the same (D. S. Jacobson, 1978a). In the study on stepfamily interaction and child adjustment funded by NIMH, findings indicated that some children whose parents divorced an average of 6.5 years prior to interview typically spent 27 hours during a 2-week period with the noncustodial parent (D. S. Jacobson, 1984).

According to Bowlby (1973), to the extent that children lose a parent after separation or divorce, they can expect to experience acute upset followed by apathy, depression, and loss of interest in parents. Although most children are upset at parental separation, the intensity of their reaction may be related to the degree of loss and to its abruptness. Children who have been exposed to quarrels and physical fighting may sometimes experience relief. Others, even under these circumstances, may be shocked; shock is more likely if they have been protected from parental difficulties. Although there is always some time lost in the presence of the noncustodial parent who has lived in the same household with the child (sleeping time for example), the shock is minimal for some and major for others. However, much of the existing research regarding parental loss focuses on children who experience the total loss of their mothers, especially young children (Ainsworth, 1973; Bowlby, 1966; Klein, 1948), although there is some work on brief separations (Prugh et al., 1953; Robertson, 1953). Because most children do not experience total loss, however, the total loss model illustrated by desertion is not applicable to many situations. The noncustodial parent may not only be alive and well but may live close by.

Current literature indicates that almost all children want to minimize their loss and maintain a relationship with both parents (Wallerstein & Kelly, 1980). But the extent to which this can happen for small children is determined not by their behavior but by that of their parents. Children can become preoccupied with fantasies of bringing their parents together again and with trying to manipulate this occurrence. Some children may experience guilt about the separation, believing they are responsible for it, and hope they can "fix" it by bringing their parents together again.

In addition to the loss of the noncustodial parent, a child may experience loss of time and attention with the custodial parent—usually the mother—who is preoccupied with her own distress concerning the separation. This can intensify children's concern about who will care for them and give rise to a fear of abandonment. Many parents find it difficult to discuss the separation in advance in ways that might minimize children's concerns (D. S. Jacobson, 1978c; Wallerstein & Kelly, 1980).

Social Issues

The reasons for the increase in divorce rates in the 1960s and 1970s and the decrease in 1982 and 1983 are not known. The increase in rates has been attributed to changing attitudes—more people are accepting divorce as a solution to marital difficulties, which has led to more liberal divorce laws. On the other hand, the existence of more liberal divorce laws has made divorce more accessible, which may have contributed to the increased rate. The first no-fault divorce legislation was passed in 1969 in California. By 1980, all states but Illinois and South Dakota had some kind of no-fault divorce legislation.

Divorce litigation, however, remains high, a considerable proportion of which concerns finances and child custody (Thornton & Freedman, 1983). Finances can include issues of spousal maintenance (formerly referred to as alimony), community property, and child support. Spousal maintenance is now awarded primarily to help a former wife temporarily until she can train for or obtain work. Judicial rulings on community property have become somewhat more equitable for women. In the past, property was usually awarded to the person whose name appeared on the title, usually the husband. The definition of what constitutes community property is still being worked out in many areas. Pension rights are now also included. Still in litigation is whether the value of having contributed to the attainment of a professional degree for a spouse during a marriage can be used in the financial settlement after a divorce.

In 1982, child support payments were awarded to 69 percent of white women and 34 percent of black women with minor children (U.S. Bureau of the Census, 1983a). Such awards are not always large and are not always paid in full: 75 percent of allocated child support payments were paid in 1981 and about 50 percent were paid in full. The payment rate is lower for marriages terminated a number of years ago. Federal and state governments now have programs to enforce child support provisions; how successful they have been is not as yet known, however (U.S. Bureau of the Census, 1981).

Judicial decisions in regard to child custody have changed over time. Until the nineteenth century, children were automatically awarded to fathers (Roth, 1976–77). As economic and social conditions changed, laws were revised to award custody to mothers as "nurturers of children during the tender years." Mothers currently receive custody in 9 out of 10 situations, although fathers are now seeking custody more often (Roman & Haddad, 1978). Judges make an effort to consider the best interests of the child, although they are hampered by the fact that there is not necessarily agreement between parents, or among professionals, about what a child's best interests are (Rice, 1982). Research in this area is young. Much has yet to be learned about what conditions and what arrangements are optimal for children and parents. Joint custody—various arrangements in which both parents have a substantial responsibility for raising a child—is now legal in 28 states. As of January 1980, the state of California enacted an amendment to its child custody statutes (Cal. Civ. Code, §4600) making it the public policy of the state to assure minor children frequent and continuing contact with both parents after divorce and to encourage parents to share child rearing. The code states that custody should be preferentially awarded to both parents. If an order for custody is made to one parent, the court should consider, among other factors, which parent is more likely to allow the child continuing contact with the noncustodial parent. Litigation regarding custody and visitation has increased, and with this has emerged a group of professionals who, sometimes in association with the court, offer mediation in these areas (Wooley, 1979).

Since the late 1970s, divorce mediation has emerged as an important professional activity for social workers. Traditionally, each divorcing partner is represented by a separate attorney who is responsible for advocating the best interests of the client. Conflicts between the divorcing partners that cannot be resolved by this procedure are brought before the court, and a judge determines what constitutes a fair decision. It is an adversarial process. In divorce mediation, an adjunct but not necessarily a replacement for this procedure, the divorcing spouses meet with each other and an impartial third party and, through negotiation, attempt to arrive at their own agreement, which the court subsequently formalizes. Advocates of this process see it as a way of reducing antagonism between divorcing spouses, which they believe is fostered by the adversarial process (Irving, 1982; McIsaacs, 1983). Mediation services are provided by social workers and other professionals in an increasing number of services attached to courts. They are also provided in the private sector by social workers, mental health professionals, and others who work alone or in teams with lawyers to help divorcing couples negotiate agreements concerning division of property and assets and child custody and visitation rights. In some states, mediation is now written into the law. In California in 1981, mediation was made mandatory in cases of contested custody and visitation rights (California Civ. Proc. Code, §1731).

Limited research exists about the effectiveness of the mediation process (Irving, 1981; Kessler, 1978; Pearson & Theoeness, 1981, 1982; Pearson & Varderkooi, 1983). In the report of one project, Pearson and Theoeness (1981) state that about half of those referred for mediation rejected the offer. Of those who went to mediation, 58 percent reached an agreement, and those who did so were more likely to report good relationships with former spouses over time. Clients reported satisfaction with having made the effort, regardless of whether they viewed the mediation process as successful. Pearson and Varderkooi (1983) further reported that factors in successful mediation appeared to be an experienced mediator, partners who had some interest in communicating with each other, couples whose conflicts were not intense, and couples whose disputes did not include extended family or other third parties. The researchers stated that more definitive answers regarding who agrees to go to mediation and who has the most success with this method require further research. Little work has been carried out on whether mediation influences the individual adjustment of divorced partners as measured, for example, by the persistence of attachment to the former spouse (Crowe, Mayfield, & Stanton, 1984).

Although the increase of women in the job market and the decline of family size have made it easier for women to consider divorce, it can have serious financial consequences for women. As previously mentioned, financial assets for spousal maintenance and child support are not always awarded; even if they are, they are frequently modest. Child support payments are not paid at all or in full in a substantial number of situations. Women, especially those without special training or who have been out of the job market for some time, are likely to have difficulty in finding a job that pays well enough to support themselves and their children, as well as cover child care. Divorce has become a major route to poverty for women. Mothers who head one-parent households made up 19 percent of all family households with children in 1982, but they accounted for 55 percent of all family households with children that reported income below the poverty line. A high proportion of these households are women and children of divorce (U.S. Bureau of the Census, 1983b). Financial problems also intensify the struggle to find adequate time for child rearing, a task that divorced women with custody must carry out without another adult in the household to share responsibilities.

Role of the Social Worker

The increasing number of adults and children experiencing divorce forms an important body of people needing the services of social workers. Individuals undergoing marital dissolution often experience stress, anxiety, and rage. For many, the difficult period is limited by time, unless there is a previous history of marital difficulty. The first goal of the practitioner is to help with the immediate upset. It is important that the practitioner be aware that intense disturbance is usually characteristic of the situation and that it may involve unexpectedly strong and alternating feelings of attachment and anger to the former partner. For the recently divorced, it is not, in the view of the present author, helpful to focus on what went wrong in the marriage or on characterological problems. This can add to the distress of those who are already overwhelmed by emotion.

Over time, the practitioner's goal is to support adaptive functioning. This involves helping the client to separate emotionally from the former spouse, to accept the end of the marital relationship, to maintain appropriate contact with the former spouse when necessary (for example, in parenting), and to move into new relationships. Some former spouses can establish comfortable working relationships with each other, others have relationships characterized by continued attachment or conflict over years; many fall somewhere in between. Working out visiting arrangements in which it is necessary for the two parents to see each other regularly can be emotionally difficult and a source of continuing discomfort. Often specific life events can upset whatever equilibrium has been achieved and reactivate the intense feelings that existed around the time of the separation. This can happen when increased contact with a former spouse is brought on, for example, by the graduation or marriage of a child. Adults need to understand their contribution to any stressful interaction for their own well-being and to reduce the impact of conflict and ambiguities on the child. Another life event found to be stressful is the remarriage of a former spouse, even when this occurs many years later.

Many parents have a difficult time paying serious attention to their children around the time of a separation because of the intensity of their own discomfort. Although education regarding the needs of the child is important, too much attention by a practitioner to the child without attention to the parents can increase the guilt of distressed adults who may first need help with their own feelings. In one situation that came to the present author's attention, the custodial mother did not follow through on the referral she had requested for her acutely upset preschool child until she had participated in several weeks of group counseling during which her own problems were the focus of discussion.

In regard to children, some issues parallel those of adults. Children who are experiencing parental separation may challenge parents through behavior problems as they express their own depression and anger about the losses and transitions in their lives. Their wish that parents reconcile can place stress on everyone. For children, however, it is likely that the turmoil will be limited unless there is a history of preceding difficulty or continued intense conflict between the parents. Immediate goals for intervention would be to deal with the acute situation to avoid the risk of problems at home or school that may have long-range negative consequences. Goals could include helping the child deal with feelings about separation, loyalty conflicts, and parental relationships and conflict. It is important to give attention to a child's precise concerns and to elicit carefully the child's view of what went on. Children and young people may react more strongly if at the time of the separation there are additional losses such as those of extended family, neighborhood, or peer-group support. In the view of the present author, it is usually more appropriate to see the child alone or with one parent rather than with both parents. For the child to see both parents together can recreate reconciliation fantasies and create cognitive confusion about reality. Life events such as the remarriage of a parent or the birth of a child to a remarried parent can also create stress or reactivate separation issues for the child. Intervention needs to take into consideration the child's age, including an appreciation of the child's cognitive capacity and ability to express feelings. Group sessions with children who have had similar experiences can provide an atmosphere in which some young people can discuss mutual problems more easily.

Early intervention programs targeting adults and children who have recently experienced separation or divorce meet the criteria of preventive services proposed by Goldston (1977) and Bloom (1981) for those at risk for developing later difficulties. Such intervention would address the factors mentioned previously as most likely to constitute stress for parents and children during this period. Such programs can help adults with their own discomfort and reduce the potential impact of the divorce on children. Model programs have been proposed that focus attention on counseling, education, self-help, or some combination of all these (U.S. Department of Health and Human Services, 1980). Overall, the literature suggests that the nature of individual and family crises associated with separation and divorce demand coping abilities that can extend beyond those of individual family members at the time.

Attention during the early period may help in the short run and may prevent the development of long-standing problems for both adults and children.

Implications for Policy and Research

More than one-third of American children will spend some part of their childhood in a household formed after a parental divorce. Adults and children in these families experience some strains that do not affect those in so-called intact families. The nature and amount of support that society should offer these families (and when) needs to be determined. Such support includes attention to the law, finances, child custody, child care facilities, health, and social work and mental health services. The matter is especially relevant for ethnic minorities, the poor, and women, for whom the stresses of marital breakup and of discrimination and poverty may compound each other. These groups are of particular concern to social workers.

Although research in separation and divorce has increased in the last decade, it is still in its early stages. Kitson et al. (1982b) have critiqued a number of studies with regard to sample selection. Another criticism is that a disproportionately large number of studies have dealt with middle-class white subjects only. Studies are needed of adults and children that draw on national samples or samples from defined groups such as specific geographical areas or school systems. Instruments must be developed and refined for variables pertaining to the divorce process for adults and children to measure adjustment, emotional well-being, and other outcome criteria so that findings can be compared and replicated.

In summary, a considerable number of adults and children are now experiencing divorce and separation, and many of them seek help. Thus, social workers need to be increasingly cognizant of the common variations of reactions and responses to divorce and of their implications for practice. There are important implications, too, for policy—for example, in the role of the courts in family affairs—and a great deal remains to be learned from research that can contribute to the refinement of understanding for those involved in these areas.

DORIS S. JACOBSON

For further information, see CHILD SUPPORT; FAMILY: ONE PARENT; FAMILY: STEPFAMILIES.

References

Ahrons, C. (1981). "Continuing Coparental Relationships between Divorced Spouses." *American Journal of Orthopsychiatry, 51,* 315–328.

Ainsworth, M. D. S. (1973). "The Development of Infant-Mother Attachment." In B. M. Caldwell & H. N. Ricciuti (Eds.), *Review of Child Development Research, Vol 3.* Chicago: University of Chicago Press.

Anthony, E. J. (1974). "Children at Risk of Divorce." In E. J. Anthony & C. W. Koupernick (Eds.), *The Child in His Family, III.* New York: John Wiley & Sons.

Bane, M. J. (1976). "Marital Disruption and the Lives of Children." *Journal of Social Issues, 32*(1), 103–76.

Bergler, E. (1970). *Divorce Won't Help.* New York: Harper Brothers.

Bloom, B. L. (1981). "The Logic and Urgency of Primary Prevention." *Hospital and Community Psychiatry, 32,* 839–843.

Bowlby, J. A. (1966). *Maternal Care and Maternal Health.* New York: Schocken Books.

Bowlby, J. A. (1973). *Attachment and Loss, II: Separation.* New York: Basic Books.

Briscoe, C. W., & Smith, J. B. (1975). "Depression in the Bereaved and Divorced, Relationship to Primary Depressive Illness." *Archives of General Psychiatry, 32,* 439–443.

Brown, P., et al. (1980). "Attachment and Distress Following Marital Separation." *Journal of Divorce, 3*(4), 303–316.

Bumpass, L. (1983, January). *Children of Marital Disruption: A Replication and Update* (Center for Demography and Ecology Working Paper No. 82-57). University of Wisconsin, Madison.

Carter, H. & Glick, P. C. (1976). *Marriage and Divorce: A Social and Economic Study.* Cambridge, Mass.: Harvard University Press.

Chester, R. (1971). "Health and Marriage Breakdown: Experience of a Sample of Divorced Women." *British Journal of Preventive and Social Medicine, 25,* 231–35.

Chiriboga, P. A. & Cutler, L. (1977). "Stress Responses among Separating Men and Women." *Journal of Divorce, 1,* 95–106.

Chiriboga, P. A., Roberts, J. & Stein, J. A. (1978). "Psychological Well-Being during Marital Separation." *Journal of Divorce, 2,* 21–36.

Clingempeel, W. G. (1982). "Joint Custody after Divorce: Major Issues and Goals for Research." *Psychological Bulletin, 91*(1), 102–127.

Crowe, T, Mayfield, J. & Stanton, L. (1984). *The Influence of Mediation on Women's Postdivorce Adjustment.* Unpublished master's degree project, School of Social Welfare, University of California, Los Angeles.

Emery, R. E. (1982). "Interpersonal Conflict and Children of Discord and Divorce." *Psychological Bulletin, 92*(2), 310–30.

Freud, S. (1971). "Mourning and Melancholia." In *Collected Papers* (Vol. 4). London, England: Hogarth Press.

Fulton, J. A. (1978, February). *Factors Related to Parental Assessment of the Effect of Divorce on Children: A Research Report.* Paper presented at the National Institute of Mental Health Conference, Washington, D.C.

Glick, P. C. (1979). "Children of Divorced Parents in Demographic Perspective." *Journal of Social Issues, 35*(4), 171.

Glick, P. C. (1984). "Divorce and Living Arrangements." *Journal of Family Issues, 5*(1), 7–26.

Goldston, S. E. (1977). "Defining Primary Prevention." In G. W. Albee & J. M. Joffee (Eds.), *Primary Prevention of Psychopathology.* Hanover, N.H.: University Press of New England.

Goode, W. J. (1956). *After Divorce.* Glencoe, Ill.: Free Press.

Gove, W. R. (1973). "Sex, Marital Status, and Mortality." *American Journal of Sociology, 79,* 45–67.

Hess, R. D. & Camara, K. A. (1979). "Post Divorce Family Relationships as Mediating Factors in the Consequences of Divorce for Children." *Journal of Social Issues, 35*(4), 79–96.

Hetherington, E. M., Cox, M., & Cox, R. (1978). "The Aftermath of Divorce." In J. H. Stevens, Jr., & M. Mathews (Eds.), *Mother-Child, Father-Child Relations.* Washington, D.C.: National Association for the Education of Young Children.

Hetherington, E. M., Cox, M. & Cox, R. (1979). "Family Interaction and Social, Emotional and Cognitive Development in Children Following Divorce." In V. Vaughn & T. Brazelton (Eds.), *The Family: Setting Priorities.* New York: Science and Medicine.

Hetherington, E. M., Camara, K., & Featherman, D. (1981). *Cognitive Performance, School Behavior and Achievement of Children from One-Parent Households.* Report prepared for the Family as Educators Team of the National Institute of Education, Washington, D.C.

Hill, R. B. (1972). *The Strength of Black Families.* New York: Emerson Hall Publishers.

Hill-Scott, K. (1984). *Making Ends Meet: Black Families and Their Child Care.* Unpublished manuscript.

Huddleston-Bryant, B. (1983). *Post Divorce Adjustment of Middle Class Black Women.* Unpublished doctoral dissertation. University of California, Los Angeles.

Hunt, M., & Hunt, B. (1977). *The Divorce Experience.* New York: McGraw-Hill Book Co.

Ilfeld, F. W. (1978). "Psychiatric Status of Community Residents among Major Demographic Dimensions." *Archives of General Psychiatry, 35*, 716–724.

Irving, H. (1981). *Divorce Mediation a Rational Alternative to the Adversary System.* New York: Universe Books.

Jacobson, D. S. (1978a). "The Impact of Marital Separation/Divorce on Children: I. Parent-Child Separation and Child Adjustment." *Journal of Divorce, 1*(4), 341–360.

Jacobson, D. S. (1978b). "The Impact of Marital Separation/Divorce on Children: II. Interparent Hostility and Child Adjustment." *Journal of Divorce, 2*(1), 3–19.

Jacobson, D. S. (1978c). "The Impact of Marital Separation/Divorce on Children: III. Parent-Child Communication and Child Adjustment." *Journal of Divorce, 2*(2), 175–94.

Jacobson, D. S. (1983). *Visiting and Child Adjustment in the Stepfamily: A Linked Family System.* Paper presented at the meeting of the American Orthopsychiatric Association, San Francisco, Calif.

Jacobson, D. S. (1984). *Final Report of NIMH Funded Study on Stepfamily Interaction and Child Adjustment.* (grant no. MH 33908) unpublished.

Jacobson, G. F. (Ed.). (1980). *New Directions for Mental Health Services: No. 6, Crisis Intervention in the 1980s.* San Francisco: Jossey-Bass.

Jacobson, G. F. (1983). *The Multiple Crises of Marital Separation and Divorce.* New York: Grune & Stratton.

Kessler, S. (1978). *Creative Conflict Resolution: Mediation.* Fountain, Calif.: National Institute of Professional Training.

Kitson, G. C. & Raschke, H. J. (1981). "Divorce Research: What Do We Know, What Do We Need to Know." *Journal of Divorce, 4*(3), 1–37.

Kitson, G. C. (1982a). "Attachment to the Spouse in Divorce: A Scale and Its Application." *Journal of Marriage and the Family,* 375–392.

Kitson, G. C., et al. (1982b). "Sampling Issues in Family Research." *Journal of Marriage and the Family,* 965–981.

Kitson, G. C., Graham, A. V. & Schmidt, D. D. (in press). "Troubled Marriages and Divorce: A Prospective Suburban Study." *Journal of Family Practice.*

Klein, M. A. (1948). "Contribution to the Theory of Anxiety and Guilt." *International Journal of Psychoanalysis, 29*, 114–123.

Kurdek, L. A., Blisk, D. & Siesky, A. E. (1981). "Correlates of Children's Long Term Adjustment to Their Parents' Divorce." *Developmental Psychology, 17*, 568–579.

Kurdek, L. A., & Blisk, D. (1983). "Dimensions

and Correlates of Mothers' Divorce Experience." *Journal of Divorce, 6*(4), 1–24.

Leaf, P. J., et al. (1983). *Social Risk Factors for Psychiatric Disorders: The Yale Epidemiological Catchment Area Study.* Unpublished doctoral dissertation, Yale University, New Haven, Conn.

Martin, B. & Martin, C. (1980). *Black Extended Families.* Chicago: University of Chicago Press.

McAdoo, H. (1980). "Factors Related to Stability in Upwardly Mobile Black Families." *Journal of Marriage and the Family, 40*, 762–778.

McCord, J., McCord, W., & Thurber, E. (1962). "Some Effects of Paternal Absence on Young Children." *Journal of Abnormal Social Psychology, 64*, 361–369.

McDermott, J. F. (1968). "Parental Divorce in Early Childhood." *American Journal of Psychiatry, 124*, 1424–1432.

McIsaacs, H. (1983). "Court-Connected Mediation." *Conciliation Court Review, 21*(2).

Mednick, S. A., & McNeil, T. F. (1968). "Current Methodology in Research in the Etiology of Schizophrenia: Serious Difficulties Which Suggest the Use of the High Risk Group Method." *Psychological Bulletin, 70*, 681–693.

Mellinger, G. D., et al. (1978). "Psychic Distress, Life Crises, and the Use of Psychotropic Medication." *Archives of General Psychiatry, 35*, 1048–1052.

National Center for Health Statistics. (1982). "Advanced Report of Final Divorce Statistics 1979." *Monthly Vital Statistics Report, 30*(4), 5.

National Center for Health Statistics. (1983). "Births, Marriages, Divorces and Deaths for 1982." *Monthly Vital Statistics Report, 31*(12), 3.

Nolan, J. F. (1977). "The Impact of Divorce on Children." *Consultation Courts Review, 15*, 25–29.

Nye, F. I. (1957). "Child Adjustment in Broken and Unhappy Broken Homes." *Marriage and Family Living, 19*, 356–360.

Parkes, C. M. (1972). *Bereavement: Studies of Grief in Adult Life.* New York: International Universities Press.

Pearlin, L. I., & Johnson, J. S. (1977). "Marital Status, Life Strains and Depression." *American Sociological Review, 42*, 704–715.

Pearson, J. & Theoeness, N. (1981). "The Decision to Mediate: Profiles of Individuals Who Accept and Reject the Opportunity to Mediate Contested Child Custody and Visitation Disputes." *Journal of Divorce, 1*(3), 17–33.

Pearson, J., & Theoeness, N. (1982). "Divorce Mediation: Strengths and Weaknesses." *Conciliation Court Review, 20*(1), 6–19.

Pearson, J., & Varderkooi, L. (1983). "Mediating

Divorce Disputes, Mediator Behavior, Styles, Roles." *Family Relations, 32.*

Prugh, D., et al. (1953). "A Study of the Emotional Reaction of Children and Families to Hospitalization and Illness." *American Journal of Orthopsychiatry, 23,* 70–106.

Raschke, H. J. (1975). "Social and Biological Factors in Voluntary Marital Dissolution Adjustment." *Dissertation Abstracts International,* 5594a.

Rice, S. (1982). *Joint Custody.* Unpublished paper.

Roman, M., & Haddad, W. (1978). *The Disposable Parent: The Case for Joint Custody.* New York: Holt, Rinehart & Winston.

Rosen, R. (1977). "Children of Divorce: What They Feel about Access and Other Aspects of the Divorce Experience." *Journal of Clinical Child Psychology, 6,* 24–26.

Roth, A. (1976–77). "The Tender Years Presumption in Child Custody Disputes." *Journal of Family Law, 15*(3), 423–462.

Rutter, M. (1979). "Protective Factors in Children's Responses to Stress and Disadvantage." In M. W. Kent & J. E. Rolf (Eds.), *Primary Prevention in Psychopathology: Vol. 3, Promoting Social Competence and Coping in Children.* Hanover, N.H.: University Press of New England.

Spanier, G. B., & Fleer, S. (1979). "Factors Sustaining Marriage, Factors in Adjusting to Divorce." In Corfman (Ed.), *Families Today: A Research Sampler on Families and Children* (pp. 205–231). Washington, D.C.: U.S. Department of Health, Education and Welfare.

Stolberg, A., & Langner, J. (1983). "Cognitive and Behavioral Changes in Children Resulting from Parental Divorce and Consequent Environmental Change." *Journal of Divorce, 7*(2), 23–41.

Thornton, A. (1982). "Divorce American Style." *American Demographics, 4*(3), 13–17.

Thornton, A., & Freedman, D. (1983). "The Changing American Family." *Population Bulletin, 38*(4), 1–44.

U.S. Bureau of the Census. (1981). *Child Support and Alimony, Current Population Reports* (Series P-23, No. 123). Washington, D.C.: U.S. Government Printing Office.

U.S. Bureau of the Census. (1983a). *Child Support and Alimony, Current Population Reports* (Series P-23, No. 124). Washington, D.C.: U.S. Government Printing Office.

U.S. Bureau of the Census. (1983b). *Characteristics of the Population Below the Poverty Level: 1981,* (Series P-60, No. 138). Washington, D.C.: U.S. Government Printing Office.

U.S. Department of Health and Human Services, Office of Human Development Services. (1980). *Helping Youth and Families of Separation, Divorce and Remarriage: A Program Manual* (Publication No. (OHDS) 80-32010).

Washington, D.C.: U.S. Government Printing Office.

Wallerstein, J. S., & Kelly, J. B. (1976). "The Effect of Parental Divorce: Experiences of the Child in Later Latency." *American Journal of Orthopsychiatry, 46,* 256–269.

Wallerstein, J. S., & Kelly, J. B. (1980). *Surviving the Breakup: How Children and Parents Cope with Divorce.* New York: Basic Books.

Weed, J. (1980). "National Estimate of Marital Dissolution and Survivorship." *United States Vital and Health Statistics, 3*(19).

Weiss, R. S. (1975). *Marital Separation.* New York: Basic Books.

Westman, J. C., Cline, D. W., & Kramer, D. A. (1970). "The Role of Child Psychiatry in Divorce." *Archives of General Psychiatry, 23,* 415–20.

Wooley, P. (1979). *The Custody Handbook.* New York: Summit Books.

Zill, N. (1978, February). *Divorce, Mental Happiness and the Mental Health of Children: Findings from the FCD National Survey of Children.* Paper prepared for the National Institute of Mental Health Workshop on Divorce and Children, Bethesda, Md.

DIX, DOROTHEA LYNDE. See biographical section.

DOMESTIC VIOLENCE

Violence is an American way of life, an integral part of the nation's social fabric. Every 24 seconds a violent crime occurs somewhere in the United States (U. S. Dept. of Justice, 1981); excluding countries at war, the United States leads all other Western nations in the number of murders and other violent crimes committed each year. Unfortunately, a large percentage of these crimes occur within the confines of the home and are perpetrated by one family member on another. Each year approximately 20 percent of all homicides involve victims and offenders who are related. A national survey of police reports found that during a four-year period 1.2 million violent incidents occurred in which offenders were related to the victims

(U.S. Dept. of Justice, 1980). But these figures do not accurately portray the incidence of family violence, because the same study found that 55 out of 100 such incidents go unreported to law enforcement officials. So pervasive is violence in the home that the National Commission on the Causes and Prevention of Violence contended, "Contrary to common fears of 'violence in the street' committed by strangers, there is a strong likelihood that when homicides and assaults occur they will be between relatives, friends, or acquaintances" (Mulvihill & Tumin, 1969, p. xxviii).

Violence in the family is certainly not a new phenomenon. Its existence has been reported as far back as the biblical story of Cain and Abel. And in the United States, physical abuse of children was a matter of social concern in the nineteenth century. However, most people believed that reports of violence in the family were isolated incidents involving a small segment of the population. It was only in the 1970s that Americans became aware of the broader scope of family violence beyond child abuse—physical abuse of adults in the form of spousal violence, physical assaults on parents by their adolescent and adult children, and abuse of elderly relatives. Today there is recognition that domestic violence occurs among families in every social, ethnic, and economic group and that no age group or kinship tie is immune from the physical and emotional pain inflicted on thousands of people each year by members of their families.

Domestic violence constitutes a complex social issue of major proportions. However, efforts to understand and ameliorate the problem have been hindered by the lack of standardized definitions, the lack of comprehensive information about the extent and causes of domestic violence, and the lack of federal legislation providing guidelines for the protection of adult victims. This article provides an overview of the current knowledge base about adult domestic violence in the two forms that have received the most attention to date—spouse violence and violence against elderly relatives. It identifies some of the problems and issues that need resolution before effective prevention and intervention can be implemented.

Definitions

Demonstrating the existence of violence in the family has proved easier than reaching a consensus about its meaning. Until the 1970s the term "domestic violence" meant civil unrest and urban riots (Tierney, 1982). Then it was applied as a broad-based concept of violence between spouses—especially battered wives—and the even broader term "family violence" was used to designate the general phenomenon of violence in the family, regardless of the victim-abuser relationship. Today the words domestic violence and family violence tend to be used interchangeably to indicate any form of violence in the family.

Myriad labels have been applied to the phenomenon of adult domestic violence, including "wife battering," "spouse abuse," "conjugal violence," "battered elderly," and "elder abuse." Although these labels are useful for drawing attention to adult maltreatment, their value often lies more in the dramatic impact of the visions they conjure up than in their definitional precision. There has been a tendency to use such words as "violence," "abuse," and "battering" synonymously even though they are not conceptually equivalent (Gelles, 1980). "Violence" refers to all acts of physical aggression, whereas "abuse" can pertain to both physical and nonphysical acts that may cause personal harm. "Battering" connotes the heavy pounding of physical assault, although in the literature it is also used to indicate repeated emotional or psychological abuse. When the word "syndrome"—as in "battered wife syndrome" or "battered elderly syndrome"—is added, it indicates repeated, severe abuse that produces visible injury.

What actions, then, constitute domestic violence? Although for the sake of clarity and precision some writers seek to limit the concept to the use of physical force (Star, 1980; Straus, 1974), most prefer a broader meaning, one that encompasses the full range of abuses occurring between people who are related or who live together in the same household. Consequently, many would subscribe to the definition of domestic violence adopted by the National Association of Social Workers (1983): "Domestic violence refers to emotional, physical, and/or sexual abuse knowingly, purposefully, or recklessly perpetrated on a family member or household member(s)'' (p. 10.1).

The problem becomes more complicated when elder abuse is considered. In addition to direct physical assaults and psychological abuse, most researchers include lack of medical care, malnutrition, isolation, and theft or misuse of money or property in their operational definitions of elder abuse. As a result, domestic violence to the elderly may involve almost anything that can endanger the life of an elderly family member (Rathbone-McCuan & Voyles, 1982). To date there has been no research that exclusively studies the phenomenon of physical violence toward elderly relatives.

A problem in elder abuse thus concerns the intent of the abusive action. Most violent incidents are acts of commission—that is, they are intended to inflict or to threaten harm. However, many forms of family violence, especially those perpetrated on the elderly, involve acts of omission—such as isolation or improper personal or nutritional care—that more accurately fall into the category of neglect. Some writers contend that the crux of the problem is not so much the range of categories considered abusive as the tendency of researchers to include within them the physical consequences produced by neglect as well as intentionally inflicted trauma (Douglass & Hickey, 1983).

Further muddying the definitional waters are such factors as the victim's age and the relationship between the victim and the abuser. The relationship factor clearly reflects the issue of family membership or structure. For example, should cases that involve an abuser and victim who are not legally married still be labeled "spouse abuse"? What if the relationship is a homosexual rather than a heterosexual one? A similar problem occurs with violence against the elderly. As originally conceived, the battered victims were elderly parents who resided with and were abused by their adult, middle-aged children (Steinmetz, 1978), but the literature also includes cases of older men and women abused by their spouses, grandchildren, or other relatives and caretakers. In general, there has been no attempt to limit the concept of family relationship or structure, and the preference has been to include all persons who perform the roles and functions of a spouse or other family member.

The age factor was not even an issue in adult domestic violence until researchers began to study the phenomenon of elder abuse. It was then that the question was raised: At what point in the aging process does an older relative qualify as elderly? For some it is 60 years of age (Chen et al., 1981) and for others it is 65 (Gioglio, 1982). A few studies even differentiate between the young-old—those under 75—and the old-old—those 75 and older. Because these baseline age limits are arbitrarily drawn, they have added to the confusion surrounding the definition and incidence of elder abuse, and they have made comparison of research findings more difficult.

Some writers contend that domestic violence and elder abuse have become political-journalistic notions that are quickly becoming useless as scientific concepts (Pedrick-Cornell & Gelles, 1982; Straus, 1978). Therefore, because legislative policies, program designs, and service delivery procedures are often based on definitions of domestic or family violence and their subcategories, a major first step in prevention and intervention is the development of a clear and consistent definition.

History and Trends

The contemporary study of domestic violence began in the 1960s with a focus on child abuse, and for more than a decade this remained the only form of family violence that received serious attention. Before the 1970s, the prevailing attitude was that family violence occurred only rarely and was the product of some type of psychological disorder (Gelles, 1980). The main barriers to the discovery of the full range of family violence, especially against adult victims, lay in the ingrained social norms and public attitudes regarding the family, the nature of victimization, and the use of violence.

By tradition, the family is the most private of all our social institutions (Straus, Gelles, & Steinmetz, 1980). Family activity takes place behind closed doors and intrusion is considered an invasion of privacy; consequently, family behavior is least subject to mechanisms of social control. Even law enforcement officials, who are charged with the protection of all persons in a community, are frequently reluctant to intervene in domestic disputes. Unless a family member comes forward to dispel the myth that the family is a safe haven for its members, the detection of family violence can be—and often is—hidden for years.

The social perception of victimization also influences attitudes toward domestic violence. In general, the more helpless the victims, the more sympathy they elicit. Infants and young children generate considerable sympathy because they clearly cannot protect themselves. Adult victims of family violence, on the other hand, have options and alternatives that, in the public eye, make them less vulnerable than children to continued victimization. Therefore, many victims of spouse and elder abuse, with the exception of the frail elderly, receive less sympathy and support because the option to leave the abusive situation is seen as more readily available to them. In addition, social approval is more often conferred on victims who physically resist—even though such resistance increases the likelihood of more serious physical injury to the victim—than on those who submit (Bard & Sangrey, 1979). Society casts blame on victims who comply with the abuser or who choose to remain in the violent setting, perceiving them as playing a role in their own victimization.

Social convention legitimizes many forms of violence in the family. Spanking is a widely accepted means of child discipline. A Harris poll reported that 93 percent of 1,500 respondents had been spanked as children and more than 80 percent had themselves spanked a child (Mulvihill & Tumin, 1969). To take another example, in 1824 Mississippi was the first of several states to grant husbands immunity from assault and battery charges for moderately physically punishing their wives in cases of "great emergency" (Eisenberg & Micklow, 1974). Although the laws were repealed, the attitude was not. And even the elderly are not exempt from socially approved violence. The senile elderly may be tied to chairs, strapped to their beds, or overmedicated to make them more manageable (Steinmetz, 1978).

How, then, did spouse and elder abuse become social issues? A major contemporary trend that began with the work of sociologist Murray Straus in the early 1970s has been to examine the whole phenomenon of family violence rather than study only its discrete forms, such as child abuse and wife battering.

This reconceptualization of the problem provided a broader perspective from which inquiries could be made about the extent and patterns of family violence.

However, many earlier events set the stage for the discovery of adult domestic violence. In the case of spouse abuse, one factor was a gradually mounting trend in Western society toward sexual equality in marriage and work (Flanzer, 1982). Efforts to enhance the status of women—seen first in the essays of John Stuart Mill in the mid-1800s and the woman suffrage movement in the early 1900s—were more recently reflected in attempts to pass the Equal Rights Amendment to the U.S. Constitution. But the most instrumental factor was the development of the women's movement and its focus on feminist issues, which provided a forum for women to share and discuss problems they faced in everyday living. It was in this context that the issue of spouse assault began to emerge. Tracing the history of the battered women problem, Tierney (1982) notes that wife beating received public attention not because it had become more widespread or because of greater public concern, but because members of social organizations—many of them at the local, grass-roots level—brought it to public awareness by effectively mobilizing resources to aid battered women. Books by Pizzey (1974) in England and Martin (1976) in the United States and a task force developed by the National Organization of Women helped raise public consciousness and spotlight the need for shelters. These efforts were followed by local and national conferences, legislative hearings, and widespread media coverage of spouse abuse. As a result, "in less than ten years, wife beating has been transformed from a subject of public shame and misery to an object of public concern" (Tierney, 1982, p. 210). Thus, the interest in spouse abuse began with a focus on battered women and, to a large extent, has remained there. Although some researchers have also written about husband battering (Steinmetz, 1977–1978), the concept of spouse abuse is still equated mainly with wife abuse.

To some degree, recognition of the issue of elder abuse was a natural outgrowth of the expanded view of family violence (Pedrick-Cornell & Gelles, 1982). However, the problem has its roots in the major demographic changes that have taken place in the United States during the past 85 years. Medical advances and improvements in the quality of life have extended the life expectancy of the average person by nearly 50 percent (Pedrick-Cornell & Gelles, 1982), and between 1970 and 1976 the population of those 85 and older increased by 40 percent (Steinmetz, 1983). The number of people over the age of 65 has increased steadily since the turn of the century: in 1900 they accounted for 4 percent of the total population; in 1982, 11.6 percent; and by the year 2030 it is anticipated that 20 percent of the population will be over the age of 65 (U. S. Bureau of the Census, 1984). The aging of the population has produced a problem never before encountered by American families—the need for adult children to provide emotional, physical, and financial assistance to their elderly parents for long periods of time. The burden this created for families led to the increase in elder abuse.

Unlike the issue of spouse abuse, which emerged from grass-roots origins, elder abuse (or parent battering, as it was originally called) was discovered through the more traditional methods of case findings by agency personnel who had contact with the elderly. Instances of violence against the elderly were mentioned during congressional hearings that dealt with the general issue of domestic violence. From 1979 through 1981, six congressional hearings that focused exclusively on the physical and psychological abuse of older family members were held throughout the country (U. S. Congress, 1980, 1981). Although two attempts were made to pass federal legislation designed to provide financial assistance for programs that dealt with the prevention, identification, and treatment of elder abuse (Oaker & Miller, 1983), they were unsuccessful, and community resources for the abused elderly remain limited.

Incidence and Demographics

Despite the increasing amount of research in the field of domestic violence, the true incidence of spouse and elder abuse is unknown because victims are reluctant to come forward and mandatory reporting mechanisms have not been established for adult victims of violence as they have for victims of child abuse. Consequently, our knowledge of the extent of adult domestic violence is derived largely from regional and local sources that provide statistical fragments rather than a unitary whole. In addition to the fragmentary nature of the current statistical base, demographic data usually reflect the client base served by the agencies or localities from which information is drawn. These resources are often available to, or used most heavily by, some segments of a community rather than others and, as a result, information about victims and abusers is heavily biased.

Spouse Abuse. Mounting evidence suggests that violence between husbands and wives occurs even more often than does child abuse. Homicide statistics reveal that one-half of all murders among family members involve spouse killing spouse (U. S. Dept. of Justice, 1980). One study estimated that as many as one out of four couples might engage in at least one violent episode during the course of a marriage (Straus, 1977). Considering the tendency to underreport instances of domestic violence, the true incidence rate of spouse abuse may involve 50 to 60 percent of all couples (Straus, 1978). A study of spouse abuse in Texas projected that no fewer than 11.2 percent (483,000) of women and no fewer than 2.2 percent (88,000) of men had been abused by their spouses at some point during their marriages. The study concluded that no fewer than 87,000 persons were subject to spouse abuse on at least a weekly basis (Stachura & Teske, 1979). A Harris poll sponsored by the Kentucky Commission on Women (Schulman, 1979) surveyed a representative sample of 1,793 women who were married or living with a male partner. They estimated that 10 percent (or 80,000 Kentucky women) had experienced some degree of spouse violence within the preceding year and that 21 percent (or more than 169,000 women) had experienced at least one incident of spouse violence at some time. A nationwide study of more than 2,100 intact families estimated that 1.8 million women and 2 million men were battered by their spouses each year (Straus, Gelles, & Steinmetz, 1980).

With the exception of homicide, in which both males and females are almost equally victimized by their spouses, women tend to suffer the most serious injuries in cases of spouse abuse. According to the information provided by the Straus, Gelles, and Steinmetz study (1980), incidents of spouse abuse were found at all socioeconomic and educational levels and in all ethnic and occupational groups; however, it was not present to the same extent in each category. They discovered that spouse abuse was more prevalent among couples in their 20s and 30s; in lower-income families; among blue-collar families; among black, Hispanic, and other minority families; and—to their surprise—among couples who had some high school education. They also found that rates of family violence tend to be evenly distributed throughout all geographic regions of the United States. Smaller studies conducted mostly in shelters confirm some but not all of these findings. A major discrepancy concerns ethnicity. Most studies of shelter populations report a higher incidence of wife battering among Caucasians than among minorities (Fagan, Friedman, & Wexler, 1984; Hofeller, 1982; Star et al., 1979). However, this may be a reflection of the people who use shelters rather than a true indication of the proportion of abuse among ethnic groups.

Elder Abuse. More is known about the incidence and demographics of spouse abuse than about elder abuse because more research has been done in that area. Unfortunately, no nationwide study of elder abuse has yet been conducted, and accurate statistics about its incidence and prevalence are not available. Consequently, there is no way to verify assertions that elder abuse is as prevalent as child abuse (Block & Sinnott, 1979) or that between 500,000 and 2,500,000 elderly persons are abused by family members annually (U. S. Congress, 1980).

Our knowledge of elder abuse comes not from the victims themselves but largely from police, medical, and social service personnel who have had either direct or indirect contact with elderly victims. Although these sources provide only limited information, they have helped to confirm the existence of elder abuse. For instance, during an eight-month period, the state of Connecticut received more than 600 reports of elder abuse, and during a one-year period the Baltimore, Maryland, police reported 149 assaults against people over the age of 60, of which close to 63 percent were committed by relatives other than spouses (U.S. Congress, 1980). The Chronic Illness Center in Cleveland, Ohio, surveyed the records of all patients over the age of 60 within a one-year period and discovered that approximately 9.6 percent of the 404 patients had suffered some type of abuse, usually from a relative (Lau & Kosberg, 1979). Several surveys have been conducted among professional service providers to the elderly (Block & Sinnott, 1979; Hickey & Douglass, 1981; O'Malley et al., 1979). From these it was learned that between 4 and 60 percent of respondents indicated that they had encountered at least one case of elder abuse or neglect.

Although two researchers have interviewed or surveyed elderly people directly, the number of elder abuse cases documented using this approach is small, accounting for less than 7 percent of the population questioned (Block & Sinnott, 1979; Gioglio, 1982). One reason that this problem has been so difficult to document is that older persons tend to deny that abuse has taken place. Refusal to report incidents of abuse to authorities may stem from fear of retaliation, the shame of admitting to such treatment by their own children, the lack of acceptable alternative living arrangements, or the fear of being removed from the family setting (U. S. Congress, 1980).

Despite the limited data, the demographics that have emerged are surprisingly similar and may prove useful in the subsequent identification of older family members who are at risk as victims of abuse. The studies indicate that the majority of victims are widowed women who live with the abuser. Most have physical or mental disabilities that make them dependent on family members to meet their nutritional, medical, personal hygiene, or ambulatory needs. Especially at risk are widows over the age of 75 who are bedridden or who have two or more disabilities that impair their ability to care for themselves. The victims are most likely to be Caucasians—although black and Hispanic families are also represented among the samples—who live in middle-class or poverty neighborhoods. Information about the abusers is less consistent. Some studies report that the abusers are women in their 40s or 50s, related to the victim by blood or marriage, who provide the primary caretaking responsibility (Lau & Kosberg, 1977). Other studies report that the abusers are more likely to be male relatives between the ages of 40 and 60, of low socioeconomic status, possessing less than a high school education, and holding blue-collar jobs (Chen et al., 1981). The studies also reveal that in general, psychological abuse, financial abuse, and physical neglect are much more common than direct physical abuse.

Characteristics of Domestic Violence

From the current literature it is possible to identify the characteristics of domestic violence. For example, all forms of family violence involve some abuse of power (Finkelhor, 1983). The most common pattern in family violence is for the most powerful to abuse the least powerful. The power differential may be one of physical size and strength or of status. Both types of power differential operate in cases of adult domestic violence. In most cases, neither battered women nor the battered elderly possess the physical strength to combat or resist their abusers, and both women and the elderly occupy a second-class status in society.

Not all abuse is of the same severity; it may occur at several points along a continuum ranging from mild to fatal (Scott, 1977; Star, 1980). Although milder forms of abuse, such as shoving or pushing, may serve more to intimidate than to maim, even mild abuse can cause major problems among the elderly, who have fewer recuperative powers and are less resilient than younger people.

Abuse rarely occurs only once; it is usually repeated several times over the course of the relationship. Once the violence barrier is broken, abuse becomes part of the repertoire of family interactions. Not only does it take less provocation to trigger subsequent abusive episodes, but the frequency and severity of the abuse is likely to increase over time (Hofeller, 1982; Star, 1982). There is also no guarantee that the original target of family violence will remain the only person who is abused. There is a high degree of overlap between spouse abuse and child abuse.

Most domestic violence occurs in the context of psychological abuse and exploitation (Finkelhor, 1983). Verbal abuse in the form of swearing or put-downs often precedes or accompanies physical abuse. Victims are made to feel worthless, incompetent, unlovable, insignificant, or less than human (Star, 1982). Psychological abuse can distort the way victims view reality, lower their self-image, and cause them to assume the blame for their own victimization (Finkelhor, 1983).

Victims wrestle with feelings of fear, shame, anger, and guilt yet often maintain a strong degree of loyalty to the abuser (Finkelhor, 1983; Star, 1982). They face inner conflicts not experienced by those attacked by strangers and find themselves "torn between the desire to shield and help a loved one and their responsibility toward their own safety or others in the household" (Hart et al., 1984, p. iii).

Anyone who lives in a violent home experiences an essential loss of security. Domestic violence has an impact on all members of the family, whether they are directly victimized or not (Star, 1981), and acts as a disruptive, intrusive element in family life to which all members must accommodate. Some of the consequences of violence include fear, mistrust, emotional and physical distance, and the stifling of open communication, especially disagreements.

Social and Psychological Factors

Among the social and psychological factors most often identified with domestic violence, the four that apply to both spouse abuse and elder abuse are stress, social isolation, alcohol use, and early exposure to violence (Carlson, 1977; Gelles, 1980; Giordano & Giordano, 1984; Hofeller, 1982; Rosenbaum & O'Leary, 1981).

Violence is highly correlated with social stress in families. Child-rearing issues, sex, pregnancy, financial pressures, unemployment, and long-term medical care are among the many problems that can raise tension levels and lead to abuse. Straus, Gelles, and Steinmetz (1980) discovered that the type and source of stress was less important than the amount of stress encountered. According to their findings, the greater the number of stressful problems a family faces, the higher the rate of serious abuse.

Being homebound, not participating in community activities, and having a limited social support system increases the risk of abuse. Isolation is often imposed on battered women whose spouses control their contact with family and friends or prevent them from going to school or taking a job. The physically impaired elderly who, because of family interference, have no access to friends also remain hidden from public view.

Although substance abuse need not be a factor in domestic violence, the likelihood of severe injuries increases when it is present. Alcohol, especially, has been linked with spouse battering, seen by some as a disinhibitor of impulse control and by others as a rationale to justify the abuse. Many cases of elder abuse also occur in conjunction with an attempt by a relative to obtain the money to support a drug or alcohol habit.

Experiencing or witnessing physical abuse in the family of origin is a common theme in the histories of violent adults and is considered a major contributory factor in spouse abuse. In elder abuse, some case studies indicate that the abusing adult had been an abused child and was retaliating for earlier physical and emotional injuries; this factor has not been confirmed, however.

An additional factor associated with wife abuse concerns the education and occupational status of the victim. Women who are better educated than their husbands or hold a higher occupational status than their husbands are more at risk for abuse (Hornung, McCullough, & Sugimoto, 1981).

Among the elderly two factors have emerged as important. One is lack of knowledge by the abuser of the needs of older relatives; the other is economic, related to financial gain for the abuser (Rathbone-McCuan, 1980; Steuer & Austin, 1980). Case studies reveal that some abusers drain the financial resources of elderly victims by forcing them to sign over property, bank accounts, and social security checks. In other cases relatives refuse to place the elderly in appropriate nursing care facilities because it would mean the loss of income from pension or public welfare sources.

Psychological factors present in both the abused and the abuser have been the subject of extensive research (Hartik, 1982; Hofeller, 1982; Star, 1983; Steinmetz, 1983). Depression, dominance, possessiveness, and pathological jealousy have been reported among spouse abusers. Studies of battered women have mentioned psychological factors of dependency, low self-esteem, and traditional attitudes toward male and female behavior. Among cases of elder abuse the role

reversal created by parental dependency on adult children is seen as a major contributory factor. However, certain victim characteristics, such as demanding or complaining behavior, may also precipitate violence.

Causes of Domestic Violence

Conflict and its resolution are inevitable parts of family living. The resolution of family conflict can take place in a number of ways, only one of which is violence. Violence is a sign that more constructive ways of resolving conflicts have broken down. Some believe that family members resort to physical coercion when they have power over family decision making but have few sources that legitimize their position—for example, a chronically unemployed husband (Straus, Gelles, & Steinmetz, 1980).

At present there is little consensus about the primary cause of domestic violence. A variety of micro and macro theories have been proposed, ranging from organic brain disturbances to sociocultural values and organization. However, the main debate has been between those who subscribe to psychological theories and those who believe in social causation. Psychological theorists emphasize the importance of such intrapsychic phenomena as poor impulse control, frustration-aggression, alcohol, and psychopathology or of learned interpersonal behavior that has reinforced violence through role modeling. Social theorists focus on cultural norms that encourage violence and on a patriarchal social structure that fosters male dominance (Dobash & Dobash, 1979).

Gelles and Straus (1979) identified 15 theories or partial theories that could explain the underlying causes of family violence and demonstrated that no one theory could by itself fully account for all of them. Considering the complexities of human nature, social interaction, and social structure, a more productive approach might be that offered by Steinmetz and Straus (1974), who diagramed a systems model of intrafamily violence. Their model includes family variables, individual characteristics of family members, and societal variables that combine to produce violence. It emphasizes the mutual influences and interactions that act as both antecedents and consequences of family violence. Within this framework it is possible to see how these elements feed into each other without denying that, in any given case, one set of elements may be more heavily weighted than others.

Feminist and Ethnic Issues

Because most victims of serious adult domestic violence are women, feminist issues assume central importance. In fact, some theorists contend that the real issue is violence against women and that such terms as "domestic violence" or "family violence" only serve to misdirect public attention (Pagelow, 1981; Schechter, 1982). From a feminist stance, all violence is a reflection of a social system that sanctions male violence and creates unequal power relationships between the sexes.

Traditional sex role stereotypes perpetuate the portrayal of women as second-class citizens who are manipulative, dependent, and hysterical. People who advance the feminist perspective object to the earlier psychological formulations of battered women as hostile, aggressive, or masochistic. They prefer, instead, a reformulation of the problem as one of women possessing very little power to control their own destinies and being kept from improved status by economic, political, and social factors that reinforce the more traditional views of their role.

The sexist economic and occupational structure of society affords victims of domestic violence few alternatives. Divorce usually means a lower standard of living, and the jobs open are often low both in status and pay. Pfouts (1978) found that abused women base their decisions to leave or to remain in an abusive relationship on their assessment of whether the economic, social, and psychological benefits of remaining in the relationship outweigh the costs.

Physicians and counselors who work with victims of domestic violence often operate from theoretical orientations that unwittingly reinforce traditional marital and sex role stereotypes, either blaming the victim or keeping women at risk for further abuse (Bogard, 1984; Pratt, Koval, & Lloyd, 1983; Stark, 1981; Walker, 1981). Psychoanalytic treatment approaches that focus more on intrapsychic forces than social factors and family systems approaches that attribute the causes of battering to an underlying family system dysfunction are perceived as being particularly biased against women. Advocates of nontraditional therapies favor approaches that focus on the social and psychological power issues of the battering relationship and attempt to eliminate or reduce the inequalities that exist.

Although few studies have examined the role of ethnicity in domestic violence, the factor of ethnic background has been linked with high family violence (Cazenave, 1983; Straus, Gelles, & Steinmetz, 1980). Ethnic norms that permit severe punishment, that equate physical aggression with manliness, or that sanction the head of the household treating other family members as personal possessions frequently foster the use of domestic violence (Carroll, 1980; Fleming, 1979).

A higher percentage of ethnic minorities than Caucasians live in low-income communities and must contend with the stresses produced by poverty. Those who live in low-income communities have fewer opportunities for educational and career advancement and must cope with more unemployment, less money, poorer housing conditions, higher crime rates, higher levels of drug and alcohol abuse, and less adequate health care. It has been found that income has a dramatic effect in determining the rates of marital violence among blacks (Cazenave & Straus, 1979). Moreover, even when compared with Caucasians who live in poverty conditions, older ethnic minority people are more likely to report health problems and physical impairments.

Minority women, especially, are exposed to double discrimination, experiencing the dual effects of sexism and racism in terms of oppression, powerlessness, and subjugation (Kim, cited in U. S. Commission on Civil Rights [CCR], 1978). Many Mexican and Asian women are isolated from the dominant culture by language, customs, and socialization. They are taught to accept a subservient role toward men, and they often have little knowledge of their legal or economic rights and have difficulty in finding adequate social services. These problems reduce their options when faced with domestic violence.

Policies and Programs

The increasing media attention accorded the problem of adult domestic violence stirred considerable federal activity in the late 1970s and early 1980s. An Office of Domestic Violence was established under the

Carter Administration, several bills designed to reduce the incidence of adult domestic violence were introduced in Congress, and federal agencies such as the Office of Juvenile Justice and Delinquency Prevention and the Law Enforcement Assistance Administration funded a variety of research and demonstration projects. At one point 19 different federal agencies were diverting a portion of their resources toward domestic violence programs (USCCR, 1982b). Unfortunately, none of the federally sponsored legislation was passed. The Office of Domestic Violence was dismantled early in the Reagan Administration, and most of the federally funded demonstration projects were discontinued after their grants had expired.

With no national legislation or mandatory reporting laws, the states and local communities have had to devise their own mechanisms for dealing with the problems of adult domestic violence. According to a 1983 survey of state legislation, 43 states and the District of Columbia had enacted legislation that allows battered women to obtain some type of civil protection—usually in the form of temporary restraining orders—from the courts (Lerman & Livingston, 1983). Several states permit the police to make warrantless arrests on the basis of reasonable suspicion rather than requiring that they actually witness the assaultive incident. Some states, however, have chosen not to deal with the problem at all and only 10 have made domestic violence a separate criminal offense.

The elderly have fared about as well. As of 1981 only 16 states had mandatory reporting laws for elder abuse (Salend et al., 1984), and approximately 25 had some type of adult protective services law (U. S. Congress, 1980). The purpose, scope, requirements, and implementation of these laws varies from state to state.

Until more formalized programs were developed, police intervention was the primary source of community help for abuse victims. Because handling domestic violence cases constituted only a small part of total police training, many training programs began to provide more extensive instruction on the causes of and intervention in family violence. Some communities experimented with domestic intervention teams that combined both police officers and civilian counselors who appeared together at the scene of the domestic disturbance. If an arrest was not warranted, the counselors remained at the scene, providing both immediate crisis counseling and referrals to local counseling agencies.

By far the most extensive resources developed for battered women were hot lines and shelters (or safe houses, as many were called). Almost every major city has a hot line that provides crisis counseling for victims and referrals for medical, legal, and shelter assistance. According to K. Lobel, a spokeswoman for the Southern California Coalition for Battered Women (personal communication, January, 1985), there were 700 shelters for battered women throughout the country in 1985. In addition to their function of providing a safe refuge for victims of spouse abuse, many shelters help women find economic, housing, and legal resources (U.S. Dept. of Health and Human Services [HHS], 1979). Several shelters also offer support group counseling services to current or former victims of abuse.

As an adjunct to the criminal justice system, some communities established victim-witness programs for victims of domestic violence and other forms of crime. These programs provide assistance and moral support for victims and encourage them to appear in court. Many shelters also provide victims' advocates who accompany women throughout the criminal justice process.

Within the past five years, a wide range of programs for abusers has been developed by counseling agencies, shelters, and community organizations. Many of these are open to batterers who seek help voluntarily and to those who are referred as part of court-sponsored diversion programs (Star, 1983).

Resources specifically for victims of elder abuse are all but nonexistent. Most cases are dealt with by adult protective services and health professionals. Although some counseling agencies provide support and educational group services to help caregivers cope with the stresses produced by caring for an elderly relative, there are no formal shelters and few programs expressly designed for either victims or abusers. One study found that counselors tend to work with less severe cases of domestic violence to the elderly, referring the more serious cases to other community resources such as the criminal justice system (Pratt, Koval, & Lloyd, 1983).

Evaluation of Policies and Programs. Most of the evaluation in this field has focused on the services provided by law enforcement and criminal justice agencies that deal with adult domestic violence. Even if a state does not have legislation pertaining directly to spouse or elder abuse, every state does have assault and battery laws designed to protect all its citizens, regardless of victim-offender relationship, from physical abuse. However, many studies indicate that the legal system treats violence between strangers more stringently than it does violence against intimates (Parnas, 1967; Taub, 1983). A study undertaken by the U. S. CCR (1982) revealed that "at each stage of the criminal justice system a significant number of abused wives are turned away, with the result that few ever obtain relief. Police officers, prosecutors, and judges often fail to take appropriate action, treating spouse abuse not as a crime against society, but as a private family matter" (p. ii). Although some recent studies indicate more positive changes in the attitudes of police and prosecutors toward the victims of domestic violence (Bowker, 1983; Brown, 1984), the U. S. Attorney General's Office found that many inconsistencies still exist and emphasized that legal responses to family violence should be guided primarily by the nature of the abusive act and not by the relationship between the abuser and the victim (Hart et al., 1984).

A survey of shelter programs for victims (U. S. HHS, 1979) and programs for abusers (Star, 1983) found that most programs did not establish evaluation criteria that permitted a comparison of the services offered and the expected outcomes. One major study discovered that shelter services, counseling, and children's services had their greatest impact not on preventing further abuse but on improving the life circumstances of younger, better-educated victims who had shorter histories of spouse violence (Fagan, Friedman, & Wexler, 1984). There is no comprehensive research comparing the effectiveness of the various treatment approaches. However, many writers note that traditional, insight-oriented interventions are less effective than more active interventions that provide structure for the client and focus on behavioral changes.

The most consistent research findings point to the need for strong support by the legislature and criminal justice system in order to decrease the incidence of violence (Fagan, Friedman, & Wexler, 1984; Jolin, 1983; Sherman & Berk, 1984). Some projects have shown that counseling and referral services in conjunction with police intervention successfully reduce repeat calls to police departments. An active arrest policy and prosecution proved to be the most effective deterrents to further violence, especially in more severe cases. Even diversion programs for abusers are more effective when they are located in prosecutorial agencies.

Role of Social Work

Despite the amount of public attention given the issue of adult domestic violence, the lack of federal legislation, financial support, and services for victims and abusers limits efforts to eliminate the problem. Active lobbying and advocacy efforts, not only by social workers but by all professions that deal with the aftermath of family violence, are required to overcome this limitation. The major issues are the improvement of the quality of family life and the adequate protection of all citizens. Only a national mandate, firmly rooted in public policy and federal legislation, can establish a new baseline below which acceptable family behavior must not be allowed to fall. Such a policy would place as much emphasis on the alleviation of pain and suffering as it currently does on the democratic ideals of individual freedom and individual liberty that permit some people to assert their rights at the expense of others (Sarver, 1982). Without those guidelines, the federal government participates in the benign neglect that has characterized so much of society's response to family violence and thus gives its tacit approval to the continuation of the social and attitudinal conditions that produced the problem.

At the agency level, several preventive and interventive steps are possible in dealing with domestic violence (Bass & Rice, 1979; Bogard, 1984; Costantino, 1981; Giordano & Giordano, 1984; McEvoy, Brookings, & Brown, 1983; Pratt, Koval, & Lloyd, 1983). In addition to supporting state and local legislation, social work agencies can upgrade professional staff's knowledge base and skills regarding the dynamics of and intervention in family violence through in-service training; establishing a legal aide position to keep staff apprised of court rulings and clients aware of their legal rights; offering support groups and family life education programs to clients; and maintaining positive relationships with community agencies to ensure timely and coordinated referrals. However, many writers emphasize that only a multidisciplinary approach that links social work agencies with legal, medical, religious, and shelter organizations can provide the comprehensiveness, continuity, and coordination of services and interventions necessary to reduce the incidence of domestic violence.

At an even more fundamental level, social work intervention, education, and policy have shared with other counseling disciplines the tendency to sanctify and encourage the preservation of the nuclear family (Costantino, 1981). The underlying values reflected by this orientation frequently conflict with actions that are in the best interests of the client. Moreover, when such an orientation combines with a professional inclination to view domestic violence as a symptom of other family problems rather than an important problem in and of itself (Bass & Rice, 1979), the result can be devastating for both the victims of domestic violence and the social work profession—increasing the risk of further injury to victims, removing the responsibility for violence control from abusers, and perpetuating the image of social workers as instruments of social control. The pattern can be broken by becoming more sensitive to the power and opportunity inequities that exist between men and women, using conjoint therapy more appropriately, providing more programs for abusers, and increasing the knowledge of community resources.

The reduction of violence in the family is well within the realm of possibility. Unfortunately, the media and the general public have a short attention span; they search for quick solutions and then move on to something new. Because there are no immediate solutions to a problem that is so deeply ingrained in our society, it remains for professions such as social work to maintain the commitment to reducing domestic violence even when it no longer holds the spotlight of public attention as a social issue.

BARBARA STAR

For further information, see AGED; AGED: SERVICES; CHILD ABUSE AND NEGLECT; CHILD SEXUAL ABUSE; CHILD WELFARE SERVICES; CRISIS INTERVENTION; FAMILY: CONTEMPORARY PATTERNS; PROTECTIVE SERVICES FOR THE AGED; PROTECTIVE SERVICES FOR CHILDREN; VICTIMIZATION PROGRAMS AND VICTIMS OF CRIME; WOMEN.

References

Bard, M., & Sangrey, D. (1979). *The Crime Victim's Book*. New York: Basic Books.

Bass, D., & Rice, J. (1979). "Agency Responses to the Abused Wife." *Social Casework, 60*(6), 338–342.

Block, M., & Sinnott, J. (1979). *The Battered Elderly Syndrome*. College Park, Md.: University of Maryland Center on Aging.

Bogard, M. (1984). "Family Systems Approaches to Wife Battering: A Feminist Critique." *American Journal of Orthopsychiatry, 54*(4), 558–568.

Bowker, L. (1983). "Battered Wives, Lawyers, and District Attorneys: An Examination of Law in Action." *Journal of Criminal Justice, 11*(5), 403–412.

Brown, S. (1984). "Police Response to Wife Beating: Neglect of a Crime of Violence." *Journal of Criminal Justice, 12*(3), 277–288.

Carlson, B. (1977). "Battered Women and Their Assailants." *Social Work, 22*(6), 455–460.

Carroll, J. (1980). "A Cultural-Consistency Theory of Family Violence in Mexican-American and Jewish Ethnic Groups." In M. Straus & G. Hotaling (Eds.), *The Social Causes of Husband-Wife Violence* (pp. 68–81). Minneapolis: University of Minnesota Press.

Cazenave, N. (1983). "Elder Abuse and Black Americans: Incidence, Correlates, Treatment, and Prevention." In Kosberg, J. (Ed.), *Abuse and Maltreatment of the Elderly* (pp. 187–203). Boston: John Wright-PSG.

Cazenave, N., & Straus, M. (1979). "Race, Class, Network Embeddedness and Family Violence: A Search for Potent Support Systems." *Journal of Comparative Family Studies, 10*(3), 281–300.

Chen, P., et al. (1981). "Elder Abuse in Domestic Settings: A Pilot Study." *Journal of Gerontological Social Work, 4*(1), 3–17.

Costantino, C. (1981). "Intervention with Battered Women: The Lawyer-Social Worker Team." *Social Work, 26*(6), 456–460.

Dobash, R. E., & Dobash, R. (1979). *Violence Against Wives*. New York: Free Press.

Douglass, R., & Hickey, T. (1983). "Domestic

Neglect and Abuse of the Elderly: Research Findings and a Systems Perspective for Service Delivery." In J. Kosberg (Ed.), *Abuse and Maltreatment of the Elderly* (pp. 115–133). Boston: John Wright-PSG.

Eisenberg & Micklow (1974). *The Assaulted Wife: 'Catch-22' Revisited.* Unpublished LL.B. thesis, University of Michigan, Ann Arbor.

Fagan, J., Friedman, E., & Wexler, S. (1984). *National Evaluation of the LEAA Family Violence Demonstration Program: Summary of Major Findings.* San Francisco: URSA Institute.

Finkelhor, D. (1983). "Common Features of Family Violence." In D. Finkelhor et al. (Eds.), *The Dark Side of the Family* (pp. 17–28). Beverly Hills, Calif.: Sage Publications.

Flanzer, J. (1982). "Introduction." In J. Flanzer (Ed.), *The Many Faces of Family Violence* (pp. 3–13). Springfield, Ill.: Charles C Thomas, Publisher.

Fleming, J. B. (1979). *Stopping Wife Abuse.* Garden City, N.Y.: Doubleday & Co.

Gelles, R. (1980), "Violence in the Family: A Review of Research in the Seventies." *Journal of Marriage and the Family, 42*(4), 873–885.

Gelles, R., & Straus, M. (1979). "Determinants of Violence in the Family: Toward a Theoretical Integration" (pp. 549–581). In W. Burr et al. (Eds.), *Contemporary Theories About the Family.* New York: Free Press.

Gioglio, G. (1982). *Elder Abuse in New Jersey: The Knowledge and Experience of Abuse Among Older New Jerseyans.* Bureau of Research, New Jersey Department of Human Services.

Giordano, N., & Giordano, J. (1984). "Elder Abuse: A Review of the Literature." *Social Work, 4*(3), 232–236.

Hart, W., et al. (1984). *Attorney General's Task Force on Family Violence.* Washington, D.C.: U.S. Government Printing Office.

Hartik, L. (1982). *Identification of Personality Characteristics and Self-Concept Factors of Battered Wives.* Palo Alto, Calif.: R & E Research Associates.

Hickey, T., & Douglass, R. (1981). "Neglect and Abuse of Older Family Members: Professionals' Perspectives and Case Experiences." *Gerontologist, 21*(2), 171–176.

Hofeller, K. (1982). *Social, Psychological and Situational Factors in Wife Abuse.* Palo Alto, Calif.: R & E Research Associates.

Hornung, C., McCullough, B. C., & Sugimoto, T. (1981). "Status Relationships in Marriage: Risk Factors in Spouse Abuse." *Journal of Marriage and the Family, 43*(3), 675–692.

Jolin, A. (1983). "Domestic Violence Legislation: An Impact Assessment." *Journal of Police Science and Administration, 11*(4), 451–456.

Lau, E., & Kosberg, J. (1979). "Abuse of the Elderly by Informal Care Providers." *Aging,* Nos. 299–300, 10–15.

Lerman, L., & Livingston, F. (1983). "State Legislation on Domestic Violence." *Response, 6*(5), 1–28.

Martin, D. (1976). *Battered Wives.* San Francisco: Glide Books.

McEvoy, A., Brookings, J., & Brown, C. (1983). "Responses to Battered Women: Problems and Strategies." *Social Casework, 64*(2), 92–96.

Mulvihill, D., & Tumin, M. (1969). *Crimes of Violence, Vol. 11.* Washington, D.C.: U. S. Government Printing Office.

National Association of Social Workers. (1985). *Compilation of Public Social Policy Statements.* Silver Spring, Md.: Author.

Oaker, M., & Miller, C. (1983). "Federal Legislation to Protect the Elderly." In J. Kosberg (Ed.), *Abuse and Maltreatment of the Elderly,* (pp. 422–435). Boston: John Wright-PSG.

O'Malley, H., et al. (1979). *Elder Abuse in Massachusetts: A Survey of Professionals and Paraprofessionals.* Boston: Legal Research and Services for the Elderly.

Pagelow, M. (1981). *Woman-Battering: Victims and Their Experiences.* Beverly Hills, Calif.: Sage Publications.

Parnas, R. I. (1967). "The Police Response to the Domestic Disturbance." *Wisconsin Law Review, 1967*(4), 914–960.

Pedrick-Cornell, C., & Gelles, R. (1982). "Elder Abuse: The Status of Current Knowledge." *Family Relations, 31*(3), 457–465.

Pfouts, J. (1978). "Violent Families: Coping Responses of Abused Wives." *Child Welfare, 57*(2), 101–111.

Pizzey, E. (1974). *Scream Quietly or the Neighbors Will Hear.* New York: Penguin Books.

Pratt, C., Koval, J., & Lloyd, S. (1983); "Social Workers' Responses to Abuse of the Elderly." *Social Casework, 64*(3), 147–153.

Rathbone-McCuan, E. (1980). "Elderly Victims of Family Violence and Neglect." *Social Casework, 64*(5), 296–304.

Rathbone-McCuan, E., & Voyles, B. (1982). "Case Detection of Abused Elderly Parents." *American Journal of Psychiatry, 139*(2), 189–192.

Rosenbaum, A., & O'Leary, K. D. (1981). "Marital Violence: Characteristics of Abusive Couples." *Journal of Consulting and Clinical Psychology, 49*(1), 63–71.

Salend, E., et al. (1984). "Elder Abuse Reporting: Limitations of Statutes." *Gerontologist, 24*(1), 61–69.

Sarver, R. (1982). "The Remedies: Rhetoric or Reality?" In J. Flanzer (Ed.), *The Many*

Faces of Family Violence (pp. 87–97). Springfield, Ill.: Charles C Thomas, Publisher.

Schechter, S. (1982). *Women and Male Violence.* Boston: South End Press.

Schulman, M. (1979). *A Survey of Spousal Violence Against Women in Kentucky.* New York: Louis Harris and Associates.

Scott, P. (1977). "Battered Wives." *British Journal of Psychiatry, 125,* 433–441.

Sherman, L., & Berk, R. (1984). "The Specific Deterrent Effects of Arrest for Domestic Assault." *American Sociological Review, 49*(2), 261–272.

Stachura, J., & Teske, R. (1979). *A Special Report on Spouse Abuse in Texas.* Huntsville, Tex.: Sam Houston State University, Criminal Justice Center.

Star, B. (1980). "Patterns in Family Violence." *Social Casework, 61*(6), 339–346.

Star, B. (1981). "The Impact of Violence on Families." *Conciliation Courts Review, 19*(2), 33–40.

Star, B. (1982). "Characteristics of Family Violence." In J. Flanzer (Ed.), *The Many Faces of Family Violence* (pp. 14–23). Springfield, Ill.: Charles C Thomas, Publisher.

Star, B. (1983). *Helping the Abuser.* New York: Family Service Association of America.

Star, B., et al. (1979). "Psychosocial Aspects of Wife Battering." *Social Casework, 60*(8), 479–487.

Stark, E. (1981). "Psychiatric Perspectives on the Abuse of Women: A Critical Approach." In A. Lurie & E. Quitkin (Eds.), *Identification and Treatment of Spouse Abuse* (pp. 9–34). Washington, D. C.: National Clearing House on Domestic Violence.

Steinmetz, S. (1977–1978). "The Battered Husband Syndrome." *Victimology: An International Journal, 2*(3–4), 499–509.

Steinmetz, S. (1978). "Battered Parents." *Society, 15*(5); 54–55.

Steinmetz, S. (1983). "Dependency, Stress, and Violence Between Middle-Aged Caregivers and Their Elderly Parents." In J. Kosberg (Ed.), *Abuse and Maltreatment of the Elderly* (pp. 134–149). Boston: John Wright-PSG.

Steinmetz, S., & Straus, M. (Eds.). (1974). *Violence in the Family.* New York: Harper & Row.

Steurer, J., & Austin, E. (1980). "Family Abuse of the Elderly." *Journal of the American Geriatrics Society, 28*(8), 372–376.

Straus, M. (1974). "Cultural and Social Organizational Influences on Violence Between Family Members." In R. Prince & D. Barrier (Eds.), *Configurations: Biological and Cultural Factors in Sexuality and Family Life* (pp. 53–69). Lexington, Mass.: D.C. Heath & Co.

Straus, M. (1977). *Normative and Behavioral Aspects of Violence Between Spouses: Prelimi-*

nary Data on a Nationally Representative USA Sample. Unpublished Manuscript.

Straus, M. (1978). "Wife-Beating: How Common and Why?" *Victimology: An International Journal, 2*(3–4), 443–458.

Straus, M., Gelles, R., & Steinmetz, S. (1980). *Behind Closed Doors.* Garden City, N.Y.: Doubleday & Co.

Taub, N. (1983). "Adult Domestic Violence: The Law's Response." *Victimology: An International Journal, 8*(1–2), 152–171.

Tierney, K. (1982). "The Battered Women Movement and the Creation of the Wife Beating Problem." *Social Problems, 29*(3), 207–220.

U. S. Bureau of the Census. (1984). *Statistical Abstract of the United States.* Washington, D.C.: U. S. Government Printing Office.

U. S. Commission on Civil Rights. (1978). *Battered Women: Issues of Public Policy* (pp. 440–444). Washington, D.C.: U. S. Government Printing Office.

U. S. Commission on Civil Rights. (1982a). *Under the Rule of Thumb.* Washington, D.C.: U.S. Government Printing Office.

U. S. Commission on Civil Rights. (1982b). *The Federal Response to Domestic Violence.* Washington, D.C.: U. S. Government Printing Office.

U. S. Congress. (1980). Joint Special Committee on Aging. *Elder Abuse* (Hearing) Washington, D.C.: U. S. Government Printing Office.

U. S. Congress. (1981). House of Representatives Select Committee on Aging. *Elder Abuse: An Examination of a Hidden Problem.* Washington, D.C.: U. S. Government Printing Office.

U. S. Department of Health and Human Services (n.d.). Office of Human Development Services. *A Monograph on Services to Battered Women.* Washington, D.C.: U. S. Government Printing Office.

U. S. Department of Justice. (1980). *Intimate Victims: A Study of Violence Among Friends and Relatives.* Washington, D.C.: U. S. Government Printing Office.

U. S. Department of Justice. (1981). *Crime in the United States.* Washington, D.C.: U. S. Government Printing Office.

Walker, L. (1981). "Battered Women: Sex Roles and Clinical Issues." *Professional Psychology, 12*(1), 81–91.

DRGs. See AGED: SERVICES; HEALTH CARE FINANCING; HEALTH SERVICE SYSTEM; HOSPITAL SOCIAL WORK; SOCIAL WELFARE FINANCING.

DRUG USE AND ABUSE

Obtaining clear definitions of some terms pertaining to drug use can be a perplexing task. Even the word "drug" is defined and used in widely differing ways, depending on the context. The pharmacologist might offer the following basic definition of a drug: Any substance, other than food, whose chemical or physical nature alters structure or function in the living organism (Ray, 1983). Those concerned with the social problem of "drug abuse," however, are likely to seek a narrower definition for the term "drug." Such a definition would highlight the psychoactive properties of certain drugs and the motivation of the user to attain a "high" that characterizes drug-taking behavior in nonmedical contexts.

There are some substances—such as the analgesic Dilaudid—that appear to qualify as a "drug" when used illegally for the purpose of getting high and as a "medicine" when prescribed by a doctor for the treatment of pain. THC, the principal mood-changing chemical in marijuana, is illegal when smoked in marijuana joints to control nausea, but is legal when prescribed in capsule form by a medical doctor for the same purpose. Should alcohol, which can be used to get high in nonmedical contexts, be considered a drug? Or should it be considered a medicine, as it was in the "Old West"? Can caffeine and nicotine, which are both mood-changing substances, also be classified as drugs?

The definition of the term "drug" is a product of social custom and law, both of which change over time (Smith, 1970). Societies throughout the world differ considerably in regard to the rules they follow to classify specific substances, such as drugs, poisons, foods, beverages (including coffee and tea), medicines, herbs, and spiritual or religious symbols. In speculating about how these social customs may shift 20 or 100 years from now, a number of questions arise. Will alcohol and tobacco come to be seen as drugs and, consequently, be made illegal? Will marijuana eventually be legalized and treated as alcohol is today? Will legalization extend to heroin, which is illegal in the United States but permissible as a pain killer in some countries? If humans eventually become capable of regulating at will the opioid peptides that

naturally exist in the brain, will a new category of drug abuse ("endorphin abuse") emerge?

The term "drug abuse" is also subject to definitional confusion. In its most general sense, drug abuse is the continued use of a psychoactive drug despite the occurrence of major problems associated with its use, for example, health, vocational, scholastic, legal, social, or economic difficulties. According to this definition, abuse occurs when the user's functioning is deleteriously affected in one or more respects. This approach to distinguishing between use and abuse is borrowed from the vocabulary of the alcohol abuse field. However, there are many who would argue—and indeed the criminal law proclaims—that *any* use of illegal drugs—such as marijuana, heroin, or LSD—constitutes abuse, regardless of the presence or absence of adverse effects. A similar stance is taken in relation to the nonmedical use of drugs, whether legal or illegal, by children and adolescents. It would appear then that the use-abuse distinction, as applied to the nonmedical use of either illegal drugs or prescription drugs, is less acceptable to the general public than is this same distinction as applied to alcohol.

Earlier in the twentieth century, the term "drug addiction" was used to refer to illicit drug use; little regard was given to either the patterns or consequences of such use. Later, drug addiction came to be defined more narrowly, with the World Health Organization (WHO) in 1957 distinguishing between drug addiction (a physical state) and drug habituation (a psychological state).

Today, professionals in the field prefer the term "dependence," which WHO (1974) defined in 1965 as:

> a state, psychic and sometimes also physical, resulting from the interaction between a living organism and a drug, characterized by behavioural and other responses that always include a compulsion to take the drug on a continuous or periodic basis in order to experience its psychic effects, and sometimes to avoid the discomfort of its absence. Tolerance may or may not be present. A person may be dependent on more than one drug. (p. 14)

Distinctions are made between psychological and physical dependence. Those who are psychologically dependent are motivated by a psychic drive that requires periodic or continuous administration of a drug to avoid discomfort or to produce a desired effect, such as a feeling of satisfaction. Physical dependence is said to occur when tolerance has developed (repeated doses of the same amount of a drug become less effective and progressively larger doses are required to achieve the desired effect) and when an abstinence syndrome (characteristic symptoms) results if drug use abruptly ceases.

Drug Classifications

Mood-changing drugs can be classified in a variety of ways. The chemist, the pharmacologist, the police officer, the physician, and the user each are likely to group drugs together in alternate ways, depending on specific issues—for example, chemical similarities, the tendency to cause similar behavioral outcomes, activity at identical sites in the brain, or classification in the same schedule under federal and state law. When drugs are categorized on the basis of their tendency to cause similar behavioral outcomes, the following classifications are commonly used: (1) narcotic analgesics; (2) central nervous system depressants; (3) central nervous system stimulants; (4) cannabis; (5) hallucinogens; and (6) inhalants.

Narcotic Analgesics. Drugs in this group are used by doctors to treat pain, cough, and diarrhea. Some are naturally occurring, such as morphine and codeine—two of the chemicals found in the opium plant (Papaver somniferum). Others are either semisynthetic (heroin) or totally synthetic (methadone). Because these drugs are depressants that produce analgesia and sedation, they are called narcotics.

It is estimated that 500,000 Americans are dependent on heroin. The State Department reports that as much as 1,573 metric tons of opium poppies were produced in 1984 (U.S. Department of State, 1985), and the Select Committee on Narcotics Abuse and Control (U.S. House, 1985) estimates that 4.1 tons of heroin were imported in 1983. Burma is the world's largest producer of the drug. Approximately 1,000 individuals die each year in the United States as a result of heroin overdose. In 1984, the price tag for U.S. heroin sales was estimated at $4 billion.

Central Nervous System (CNS) Depressants. Drugs in this class are used medically in the induction of anesthesia, in the treatment of epilepsy, in the reduction of excitability and anxiety (sedation), and in the summoning of sleep (hypnosis). Often referred to as sedative-hypnotics, these compounds can be used interchangeably, with adjustments in both dosages and routes of administration. When used nonmedically, the CNS depressants produce an alcohol-like state of intoxication.

The barbiturates, of which more than 2,500 formulations have been produced, follow alcohol as the second most commonly used drugs in this category. The benzodiazepines (Librium, Valium, and the like), another group of CNS depressants, are preferred over the barbiturates because the risk of becoming dependent on them is lower.

Central Nervous System Stimulants. The drugs in this family can be divided into three broad groups: the xanthines (among which caffeine is the most common), cocaine, and a third cluster, of which the amphetamines are the prototype. All these substances have the capacity to increase alertness and wakefulness, to bolster strength and endurance, to decrease appetite, and to enhance one's sense of well-being. It is estimated that 6 million Americans use prescription stimulants and depressants illicitly.

Before the Food and Drug Administration (FDA) limited the use of amphetamines to narcolepsy, hyperkinesis, and short-term weight reduction in 1970, these drugs were more widely used. Researchers discovered that people who used amphetamines for the purpose of weight control quickly developed a tolerance to the drugs' appetite-suppressant properties and tended to increase their dosages to a degree that placed them at risk of incurring serious adverse consequences.

Cocaine is extracted from South America's coca plant. Some 4 million people chew the coca leaf for its energy-boosting effects. The plant was an important part of the Incan culture, serving as a religious symbol and as money. Cocaine is now used as a local anesthetic and vasoconstrictor.

In 1984, approximately 20 million Americans spent an estimated $18 billion on cocaine, most of which came from Peru, Bolivia, Colombia, and Ecuador. "Crack," a highly potent yet inexpensive form of cocaine that is smoked in glass pipes, began to appear in the United States in 1985 and rapidly became a national phenomenon. Its low price meant that many new users were adolescents. Despite efforts by the United States to reduce the worldwide supply of illicit drugs, the State Department reports that the production of coca increased by one-third from 1983 to 1984. The Select Committee on Narcotics Abuse and Control (U.S. House, 1985) estimates that 85 tons of cocaine were imported in 1984.

Cannabis. Marijuana and hashish are products of the cannabis plant. THC, the principal psychoactive component of cannabis, was approved as a prescription medicine in 1985 by the FDA for the control of nausea and vomiting in cancer chemotherapy patients. Other potential but unapproved medical uses are in the treatment of glaucoma, muscle spasm associated with multiple sclerosis, and asthma (Roffman, 1983).

Americans spent an estimated $44 billion for marijuana in 1984. The State Department reports that more than half of the U.S. supply of the drug originates in Colombia; Mexico, Jamaica, and Belize also export marijuana. It is believed that between 30,000 and 60,000 tons of marijuana were imported in 1984, augmented by about 4,000 tons that were produced domestically (U.S. House, 1985). As many as 25 million Americans may be regular marijuana users, with another 40 million using the drug occasionally.

Hallucinogens. With a history of more than 5,000 years of use, the many naturally occurring and synthetic substances in this category have in common the capacity to produce mood, sensory, and perceptual changes, including illusions and hallucinations. Among the most widely used hallucinogens are (1) LSD, a semisynthetic compound derived from the alkaloid lysergic acid that is found in ergot; (2) mescaline, the principal alkaloid in the peyote cactus; (3) DOM, a synthetic compound with actions of both a hallucinogenic and stimulant nature; and (4) psilocybin, the psychoactive ingredient in the psilocybin mushroom. It is estimated that approximately 1 million Americans are regular users of hallucinogens. Researchers have explored the therapeutic

potential of LSD and other hallucinogens in the field of psychiatry. As of yet, none of these drugs have been approved for use outside the research context.

Inhalants. Nitrous oxide, ether, and chloroform are all anesthetic gases that are classified as inhalants. Also in this category are volatile hydrocarbons (gasoline, kerosene, benzene, and other chemicals) that are used commercially as aerosols and solvents. Many common household products—for example, cleaning solutions, glues, cements, paint thinners, and lacquers—contain organic solvents comprising psychoactive chemicals, such as toluene and acetone. The amyl and butyl nitrites have had some popularity, presumably as enhancers of sexual performance.

Trends in Drug Use

The American experience with drug abuse began long before the turbulent Vietnam era of the late 1960s. For example, at the turn of the century, as much as 1 percent of the population may have been dependent on the opiates that were widely available in patent medicines (Kebler, 1910). In addition, the smoking of marijuana to get high was introduced in the U.S. in the late 1800s and became the focus of public concern in the early decades of this century (Abel, 1980).

Although this social problem is not new, today there is more information available concerning patterns of and trends in illicit drug use. A number of conclusions can be drawn from periodic national surveys (Johnston, Bachman, & O'Malley, in press; Miller et al., 1983) and from data collected from hospital emergency rooms in urban areas (National Institute on Drug Abuse, 1985):

1. A gradual decline in illicit drug use began in the late 1970s and has continued through the mid-1980s.

2. Among high school seniors in 1984, the lifetime, annual, and monthly rates at which the most popular drugs were used were: marijuana (54.9, 40, and 25.2 percent), stimulants (27.9, 17.7, and 8.3 percent), cocaine (16.1, 11.6, and 5.8 percent), inhalants (19.0, 7.9, and 2.7 percent), hallucinogens (13.3, 7.9, and 3.6 percent), and sedatives other than tranquilizers (13.3, 6.6, and 2.3 percent).

3. Nearly two-thirds of young people

use at least one illicit drug before they complete high school.

4. At least 1 in 20 high school seniors smokes marijuana on a daily or near-daily basis.

5. In 1984, 29 percent of high school seniors used at least one illicit drug.

6. From July 1980 to June 1983, heroin- and cocaine-related visits to emergency rooms increased in most cities. In recent years, this trend has leveled off.

7. In the United States, drug abuse peaked in 1969 as well as from 1974 to 1976. Between 1969 and 1974, and again between 1976 and 1982, drug-related deaths and medical emergencies declined. In New York, however, a dramatic increase in deaths resulting from heroin overdose occurred between 1980 and 1981.

Correlates and Antecedents

What are the psychological, social, and demographic correlates of illicit drug use? Is there a typical sequence of involvement with drugs? Are there measurable antecedents of the initiation of drug use? The answers to these questions are influenced by the point in time at which data are collected.

Illicit drug taking was a more deviant act in the 1960s (and is becoming so again in the mid-1980s) than it was in the middle and late 1970s. Consequently those who engaged in illicit drug use when such behavior was unusual among others in similar social circumstances were likely to differ from the norm along a number of dimensions. These dimensions included involvement in conventional, organized activities, such as religion and attitudes, as well as quality of parent-child relationships, personality measures, general conformity, and antisocial behavior. In contrast, in the mid-1970s, those between the ages of 18 and 25 who had never used an illicit drug were clearly atypical.

In the 1970s, patterns of drug use among white adolescents tended to involve a progression that began with beer and wine and subsequently moved to hard liquor and the smoking of cigarettes before the initial use of marijuana. The use of other illicit drugs occurred in the following sequence: pills (stimulants and depressants), hallucinogens, cocaine, and heroin. Obviously, the further the progression, the fewer the number of users. Among blacks, the order was somewhat different, with marijuana preceding cocaine, followed by heroin, depressants, stimulants, and hallucinogens (Kandel & Faust, 1975). In the 1980s, the initial use of cocaine occurred earlier among whites as well as blacks (Ray, 1983).

The initiation of marijuana use by young people is heavily influenced by the values and modeling of peers. However, a deep involvement in drug-taking behavior is believed to be shaped by intrapersonal factors (Kandel et al., 1976). Furthermore, when an individual's pattern of drug use is substantially different from that of others who share his or her social background and cultural norms, there is a greater likelihood that the person is seriously mentally ill (Kaufman, 1976).

Specialists in the area of prevention view the onset of marijuana use as significantly related to the overall course of adolescent development, and they seek to postpone as much as possible the initiation of such use. When successful, preventive efforts enhance the likelihood of the adolescent avoiding a deviance-prone behavioral pattern (Brunswick & Boyle, 1979; Fleming et al., 1982; Kandel, 1982).

Adverse Consequences

When used abusively, mind-altering drugs can have many adverse effects. The risks include injury or illness caused by nonsterile needles or adulterants, reduced capacity caused by memory deficits or an instability of temperament, and impaired functioning within family, social, or occupational domains.

As of 1980, the annual cost incurred by the United States as a result of drug abuse was estimated at $46.9 billion (Harwood et al., 1984). Reduced economic productivity ($28 billion) accounted for a large share of this estimate. The costs associated with treatment services for drug abusers ($1.4 billion), with the criminal justice system ($5.9 billion), and with drug trafficking and other offenses motivated by drug abuse ($8.7 billion) were additional components of the annual estimate.

In part because of the availability of the Breathalyzer test, more is known about the relationship between alcohol consumption and automobile accidents than is the case with other drugs. Nevertheless, there is evidence that operating a motor vehicle after using marijuana increases the risk of having an accident (Klonoff, 1974). The CNS depressants (sedatives, hypnotics, and antianxiety agents) are also likely to affect driving skills adversely by slowing down response time and the integration of information.

The connection between drugs and crime has been researched fairly extensively (Anglin, Kaplan, & Sells, 1983). Considerable evidence has emerged that supports the association between the initiation of illicit drug use and profit-producing criminal activity (Weissman et al., 1976). Although some narcotic addicts begin to get involved in criminal activities after becoming dependent, the majority are engaged in such activities before the onset of dependence.

The evidence linking drug-taking behavior with violence and aggression is strongest with reference to the use of high doses of CNS stimulants, which is likely to cause increased suspiciousness, paranoia, hyperactivity, and lability of mood. An association has also been found between the excessive use of CNS depressants and increased violence, an anticipated finding in that these drugs produce an alcohol-like intoxication.

Theories of Etiology

Many theoretical approaches have been used to explain the initiation of illicit drug use, progressive involvement with drugs, drug use that persists despite adverse consequences for the user, drug dependence, and the cession of use (Lettieri et al., 1980). Economic models consider monetary forces that shape the behavior of suppliers and consumers under a variety of market conditions, such as potential drug-related risks and their probability. Biological theories seek to explain behavior based on physiological factors that either precede, or occur as a consequence of, drug use. Sociological theories consider the influence of societal conditions, such as unemployment and the functioning of important cultural institutions.

Because illicit drug-taking behavior generally begins during adolescence, considerable effort has been expended in identifying predictors and correlates of substance abuse among adolescents. Research thus far has focused on the following factors that may predispose individuals to drug addiction: (1) negative conduct, such as antisocial behavior

early in life; (2) the quality and consistency of family management, family communication, and parental role modeling; (3) social and academic adjustment in the early school years and the individual's degree of commitment to education; (4) involvement with peers whose behaviors and attitudes support drug use; (5) personality factors such as rebelliousness, nonconformity to traditional values, a high tolerance for deviance, resistance to traditional authority, and a strong need for independence; and (6) measures of personal competence and social responsibility (Hawkins et al., in press).

Many theories have been put forth in an attempt to integrate the evidence concerning predictive factors in an explanatory model. However, there is a need for additional work in this area. Moreover, the turbulent and rapidly changing history of drug abuse challenges the theoretician to account for behaviors that are likely to be shaped by vastly different kinds of influence over time.

Special Populations

The prevalence of drug abuse, the potential for adverse consequences, and the likelihood of receiving effective treatment vary by virtue of gender, race, age, sexual preference, and socioeconomic status. Although less is known about drug abuse in populations other than those consisting of white middle-class males, it is generally assumed that racism, sexism, ageism, homophobia, and society's biased responses to the poor contribute to both the unique causes of drug abuse and the barriers to treatment for special populations, such as those made up of minority groups.

One risk factor unique to women is the potential harm to the fetus when drugs are used during pregnancy and to the infant when drugs are used during breast feeding. In addition, women with child-care responsibilities are impeded from entering treatment unless they can make child-care arrangements. Moreover, the likelihood of women experiencing low self-esteem associated with becoming drug dependent requires special consideration in treatment with respect to both therapeutic focus and the gender of the staff delivering the services. Women are more likely than men to use legal psychoactive drugs, in part because women are more likely to visit physicians and, subsequently, to be issued prescriptions. They are less likely than men to use alcohol as an alternative means of coping with emotional stress (Beschner et al., 1981).

Living at or below the poverty line, gender, race, and other characteristics of special populations may serve as powerful determinants of drug abuse, of the risk of attendant problems, and of barriers to treatment. Regardless of their potential negative consequences, psychoactive drugs are used excessively precisely because they are effective, if only temporarily, in reducing pain—including the pain of being poor.

The belief that treatment resources can help drug abusers is likely to be influenced by (1) norms within one's subculture; (2) the ease of geographic access to an agency; (3) the fee for service; (4) the composition of the staff; (5) the degree to which the service technology is culturally appropriate and pertinent; and (6) the absence of language barriers. Homosexuals and lesbians may resist treatment because of the fear that their sexuality will be misunderstood and targeted for change. Elderly people are more likely to be issued multiple prescriptions and to be undetected as drug abusers because they are usually unemployed. They may never visit an agency if those who might encourage them to seek help instead assume that there is little but intoxication to look forward to in old age. Drug abuse, as is the case with other social problems, is likely to be associated with greater harm and more obstacles to change in populations that are already burdened with the effects of bias.

Policies and Programs

Among the most important international treaties concerning illicit drugs is the Single Convention on Narcotic Drugs of 1961, which obligates signatories to (1) license and restrict the legal production, manufacture, and distribution of narcotic drugs to medical and scientific purposes; (2) eradicate all unlicensed cultivation; (3) suppress illicit manufacture and traffic; and (4) cooperate with each other in achieving the aims of the convention. In response to the pressure it has placed on various countries to combat and eliminate the production of drugs, the United States is often criticized for permitting to exist a demand for drugs that supports an estimated $110 billion "incentive" (U.S.

House, 1985) for those who profit from continued production. Perhaps in part as a response to this criticism, in 1984 the Reagan Administration issued a strategy document—the *National Strategy for Prevention of Drug Abuse and Drug Trafficking*—that signaled a movement toward support of prevention and education.

The major federal law governing illicit drugs in the United States is the Comprehensive Drug Abuse Prevention and Control Act of 1970. This law provides for the classifying of all controlled psychoactive drugs (excluding alcohol) in one of five schedules, based on the medical utility and abuse potential of each substance. Penalties are assigned for illicit manufacturing, distribution, and possession. The National Institute on Drug Abuse (NIDA), established in 1973, is an agency of the U.S. Department of Health and Human Services. NIDA provides leadership in the allocation of funds for basic and applied research, including demonstration treatment and prevention programs.

Before the 1970s, most treatment efforts for opiate dependence involved hospitalization, with a minimum of aftercare services. During this period, readdiction rates were quite high (O'Donnell, 1968). In the 1970s, methadone began to play a prominent role in treatment programs for opiate addicts. Developed in Germany during World War II as a morphine substitute, methadone was researched by Dole and Nyswander (1968) as an agent that would prevent withdrawal symptoms, reduce cravings, and block the pleasurable effects of opiates. By the early 1980s, there were about 90,000 clients in such programs. In recent years, methadone maintenance has been criticized by the general public, which tends to view this modality as the substitution of one addictive drug for another, and by clients themselves, who complain of overly bureaucratized programs, excessively rigid requirements, and uncaring staffs.

Another treatment modality is the therapeutic community (TC), a residential self-help program that is typically modeled, in part, on the structure of Synanon, an organization founded in 1958 by a recovering alcoholic. The milieu of TC is intense, and participants are repeatedly confronted by their peers when they demonstrate nonconformist behaviors. The newcomer advances in the program's status hierarchy by demonstrating pro-social values and by actively participating in the therapeutic process. Unlike Synanon, which encourages its members to remain, most TCs request that addicts remain in treatment from one to two years before returning to the community.

In general, studies that have compared the efficacy of these two modalities indicate that clients are more likely to leave TCs early than to discontinue methadone maintenance prematurely. However, the long-term outcome is somewhat better for those who remain in TCs for longer periods (Bale et al., 1980). Many addicts resist entering treatment, and there is generally a lag time of four to five years between the initiation of heroin use and the initial admission to a treatment program (Eagan and Robinson, 1979). Two out of three individuals who enter treatment leave in less than six months (Simpson, 1978).

In addition to the use of methadone as an aid in opiate withdrawal, both acupuncture (Patterson, 1975) and the antihypertensive drug, clonidine, (Gold, 1980) have been shown to be effective. LAAM (levo-alpha-acetyl-methadol), a long-acting methadonelike drug (Jaffe et al., 1970), is effective in maintenance programs when administered every third day. Recently, the use of naltrexone, a narcotic antagonist, has been approved as a tool in helping addicts to abstain from using drugs. Although it does not reduce the craving for heroin, when taken orally on a daily basis, naltrexone blocks the effects of the drug (Willette & Barnett, 1981), thereby reducing the reinforcement of drug taking. Finally, buprenorphine is being tested for its capacity to prevent opiate withdrawal and to antagonize the effects of other injected opiates (Mello, Bree, & Mendelson, 1982).

Most current data concerning methadone maintenance, residential, and outpatient treatment indicate substantial improvements in clients' social functioning and employment, as well as reductions in their drug use and involvement in criminal activities following treatment (Simpson & Sells, 1982; Rachal et al., 1983; Lorei et al., 1978). Opiate addicts who are also exposed to self-help modalities (McAuliffe, 1983) or to short-term family therapy (Stanton and Todd, 1981) may demonstrate more marked improvement.

The limited amount of research that has examined the nature and effectiveness of nonopiate drug abuse programs indicates that only moderate success is attained when the nonopiate abuser is treated in traditional drug treatment programs (Brown, 1982). Improved clinical assessment and better research with this population may be facilitated with the development of diagnostic tools, such as the Addiction Severity Index (McLellan et al., 1980).

There are several types of prevention approaches. Deterrence strategies include reducing drug supplies and increasing penalties for legal infractions. A study conducted by the Rand Corporation suggested, on the basis of an examination of the economics of drug distribution, that increased law enforcement would not substantially change either the availability or the price of drugs (Polich et al., 1984).

Another approach, that of drug education, focuses on informing potential users and abusers about adverse effects. The evidence thus far is that these efforts by themselves are ineffective in preventing either initial use or abuse (Schaps et al., 1981).

The teaching of either general living skills or specific skills, such as how to resist peer pressure to use drugs, is another type of prevention strategy. Numerous variations in skills training have been researched, with promising indications that early exposure to programs that strengthen individual social competence may subsequently prevent drug abuse.

A developmentally focused prevention model that emphasizes bonding to family, school, and peer groups is currently being studied (Hawkins, Lishner, & Catalano 1985). This approach uses specific strategies to improve the opportunity and reward structures in the family during early childhood, in the elementary school classroom, and in relationships with pro-social peers as young people approach adolescence. In essence, the interventions seek to increase opportunities for achieving success, for improving skills, and for receiving greater and more consistent reinforcement of positive performance in each of these three domains.

A significant aspect of drug abuse prevention in the 1980s is the parents' movement. Local, statewide, regional, and national self-help parents' organizations are producing written educational materials for parents; influencing legislation, such as the laws pertaining to the sale of drug paraphernalia; organizing workshops; and, in general, seeking to reduce societal tolerance for drug-taking by young people.

Social Workers and Drug Abuse

Aside from therapeutic communities that are often staffed by formerly drug-dependent individuals, social workers are commonly employed as practitioners in drug abuse treatment settings. In addition to focusing on general counseling issues, the social worker's role emphasizes intervention with the client's family and with the occupational, health, criminal justice, employment, and social systems in order to facilitate both short- and long-term opportunities for change and improvement in functioning. Graduate-level social workers also function as program or agency administrators, as analysts with local or state governmental bureaus responsible for drug abuse services, and as aides to legislative committees. According to NIDA's national survey of treatment utilization, as of 1982 there were 999 full-time social work positions in drug treatment agencies in the United States. This figure represented 6.8 percent of the 14,793 individuals employed in the area of drug abuse treatment (National Institute on Alcohol Abuse and Alcoholism & NIDA, 1983).

ROGER A. ROFFMAN

For further information, see ALCOHOL USE AND ADDICTION; PSYCHOTROPIC MEDICATIONS.

References

Abel, E. L. (1980). *Marihuana: The First Twelve Thousand Years.* New York: Plenum Press.

Anglin, M. D., Kaplan, J., & Sells, S. B. "Drugs and Crime." In *Encyclopedia of Crime and Justice* (Vol. 2, pp. 636–663). New York: Free Press.

Bale, R. N., et al. (1980). "Therapeutic Communities vs. Methadone Maintenance." *Archives of General Psychiatry, 37*(2), 179.

Beschner, G. M., Reed, B. G., & Mondanaro, J. (1981). *Treatment Services for Drug Dependent Women* (Publication No. ADM 81-1177). Washington, D.C.: U.S. Government Printing Office.

Brown, B. (1982). *Treatment of Non-Opiate De-pendency: Issues and Outcomes.* Washington, D.C.: National Institute on Drug Abuse.

Brunswick, A. F., & Boyle, J. M. (1979). "Patterns of Drug Involvement: Developmental and Secular Influences on Age At Initiation." *Youth & Society, 2*(2), 139–162.

Dole, V. P., Nyswander, M. E., & Warner, A. (1968). "Successful Treatment of 750 Criminal Addicts." *Journal of the American Medical Association, 206*(12), 2708–2714.

Eagen, D. J., & Robinson, D. O. (1979). "Models of a Heroin Epidemic." *American Journal of Psychiatry, 136*(9), 1162–1167.

Fleming, J. P., et al. (1982). "Early Predictors of Age At First Use of Alcohol, Marijuana, and Cigarettes." *Drug and Alcohol Dependence, 9*(4), 285–303.

Gold, M. S., et al. (1980). "Opiate Withdrawal Using Clonidine." *Journal of the American Medical Association, 243*(4), 343.

Harwood, H. J., et al. (1984). *Economic Costs to Society of Alcohol and Drug Abuse and Mental Illness: 1980.* Research Triangle Park, N.C.: Research Triangle Institute (mimeo-graphed).

Hawkins, J. D., Lishner, D. M., & Catalano, R. F. (1985). "Childhood Predictors and the Prevention of Adolescent Substance Abuse." In C. L. Jones & R. J. Battjes (Eds.), *The Etiology of Drug Abuse: Implications for Prevention* (pp. 75–126). Washington, D.C.: U.S. Government Printing Office.

Jaffe, J. H., et al. (1970). "Comparison of Acetylmethadol and Methadone in the Treatment of Long-Term Heroin Users. A Pilot Study." *Journal of the American Medical Association, 211*(11), 1834–1836.

Johnston, L. D., Bachman, J. G., & O'Malley, P. M. (in press). *Student Drug Use, Attitudes, and Beliefs: National Trends 1975–1985.* Washington, D.C.: U.S. Government Printing Office.

Kandel, D. B. (1982). "Epidemiological and Psychosocial Perspectives on Adolescent Drug Use." *Journal of American Academy of Clinical Psychiatry, 21*(4), 328–347.

Kandel, D., et al. (1976). "Adolescent Involvement in Legal and Illegal Drug Use: A Multiple Classification Analysis." *Social Forces, 55*(2), 438–458.

Kandel, D., & Faust, R. (1975). "Sequence and Stages in Patterns of Adolescent Drug Use." *Archives of General Psychiatry, 32*(7), 923–932.

Kaufman, E. (1976). "The Abuse of Multiple Drugs: II. Psychological Hypotheses, Treatment Considerations." *American Journal of Drug and Alcohol Abuse, 3*(2), 293–301.

Kebler, L. F. (1910). "The Present Status of Drug Addicts in the United States." In *Transactions of the American Therapeutic Society XI* (pp. 105–119). Philadelphia, Pa.: F. A. Davis Co.

Klonoff, H. (1974). "Marijuana and Driving in Real-Life Situations." *Science, 186,* 317–324.

Lettieri, D. J., Sayers, M., & Pearson, J. W. (Eds.). (1980). *Theories on Drug Abuse: Selected Contemporary Perspectives.* Washington, D.C.: U.S. Government Printing Office.

Lorei, T. W., Francke, G., & Harger, P. (1978). "Evaluation of Drug Treatment in VA Hospitals." *American Journal of Public Health, 68*(1), 39–43.

McAuliffe, W. (1983). *Exploratory Study of Self-Help for Treated Addicts.* Paper presented at the Self-Help Seminar, National Institute on Drug Abuse, Rockville, Md.

McLellan, A. T., et al. (1980). "An Improved Diagnostic Evaluation Instrument for Substance Abuse Patients: The Addiction Severity Index." *Journal of Nervous and Mental Diseases, 168*(1), 26–33.

Mello, N., Bree, & Mendelson, J. (1982). "Comparison of the Effects of Buprenorphine and Methadone." In L. S. Harris (Ed.), *Problems of Drug Dependence 1981* (Publication No. 82-600540, pp. 67–73). Washington, D.C.: U.S. Government Printing Office.

Miller, J. D., et al. (1983). *National Survey on Drug Abuse: Main Findings 1982* (Publication No. [ADM] 83-1263). Washington, D.C.: U.S. Government Printing Office.

National Drug and Alcoholism Treatment Utilization Survey. (1982). Rockville, Md.: National Institute on Drug Abuse, Division of Epidemiology and Statistical Analysis.

National Institute on Alcohol Abuse and Alcoholism & NIDA. (1983). *National Drug and Alcoholism Treatment Utilization Survey.* Rockville, Md.: Alcohol, Drug Abuse, and Mental Health Administration.

National Institute on Drug Abuse. (1985). *Drug Abuse Warning Network: Semiannual Report* (Series G, No. 14, Publication No. [ADM] 85-1377). Washington, D.C.: U.S. Government Printing Office.

O'Donnell, J. A. (1968). "The Relapse Rate in Narcotic Addiction: A Critique of Follow-up Studies." *New York State Narcotic Addiction Control Commission Reprints, 2*(1), 1–21.

Patterson, M. A. (1975). "Acupuncture and Neuro-Electric Therapy in the Treatment of Drug and Alcohol Addiction." *Australian Journal of Alcoholism and Drug Dependence, 2*(3), 90–95.

Polich, J. M., et al. (1984). *Strategies for Controlling Adolescent Drug Use.* Santa Monica, Calif.: Rand Corp.

Rachal, J. V., et al. (1983). *Treatment Outcome Prospective Study (TOPS).* Washington, D.C.: National Institute on Drug Abuse.

Ray, O. (1983). *Drugs, Society, and Human Behavior.* St. Louis, Mo.: C. V. Mosby Co.

Roffman, R. A. (1983). *Marijuana as Medicine.* Seattle, Wash.: Madrona Publishers.

Schaps, E., et al. (1981). *An Evaluation of An Innovative Drug Education Program: First Year Results.* Napa, Calif.: Pacific Institute for Research and Evaluation.

Simpson, D. D. (1978). "The Relation of Time Spent in Drug Abuse Treatment to Post-Treatment Outcome." *American Journal of Psychiatry, 136*(11), 1449–1453.

Simpson, D. D., & Sells, S. B. (1982). *Evaluation of Drug Abuse Treatment Effectiveness.* (Publication No. 82-1194). Washington, D.C.: U.S. Government Printing Office.

Smith, J. P. (1970). "Society and Drugs: A Short Sketch." In P. H. Blachly (Ed.), *Drug Abuse: Data and Debate,* pp. 169–175. Springfield, Ill.: Charles C Thomas, Publisher

Stanton, M. D., & Todd, T. C. (1981). *The Family Therapy of Drug Addiction.* New York: Guilford.

U.S. Department of State, Bureau of International Narcotics Matters. (1985, February 14). *The International Narcotics Control Strategy Report.* Washington, D.C.: U.S. Government Printing Office.

U.S. House, Select Committee on Narcotics Abuse and Control. (1985). *Annual Report for the Year 1984.* Washington, D.C.: U.S. Government Printing Office.

Weissman, J. C., et al. (1976). "Addiction and Criminal Behavior: A Continuing Examination of Criminal Addicts." *Journal of Drug Issues, 6*(2), 153–165.

World Health Organization Expert Committee on Drug Dependence. (1974). *Twentieth Report* (Technical Report Series No. 551). Geneva, Switzerland: Author.

Willette, R. E., & Barnett, G. (Eds.). (1981). "Narcotic Antagonists: Naltrexone Pharmacochemistry and Sustained-Release Preparations." Washington, D.C.: U.S. Government Printing Office.

For Further Reading

Books

Blum, K. (1984). *Handbook of Abusable Drugs.* New York: Gardner Press.

Department of Health and Human Services. (1984). *Drug Abuse and Drug Abuse Research.* (Publication No. [ADM] 85-1372). Washington, D.C.: U.S. Government Printing Office.

Johnston, L. D., O'Malley, P. M., & Bachman, J. G. (1985). *Use of Licit and Illicit Drugs By America's High School Students 1975–1984.* (Publication No. [ADM] 85-1394). Washington, D.C.: U.S. Government Printing Office.

Miller, J. D. (1983). *National Survey on Drug Abuse: Main Findings 1982.* (Publication No. [ADM] 83-1263). Washington, D.C.: U.S. Government Printing Office.

O'Brien, R., & Cohen, S. (1984). *The Encyclopedia of Drug Abuse.* New York: Facts on File.

Journals and Newsletters

Addiction Intervention with the Disabled Bulletin (Dept. of Sociology, Kent State University, Kent, Ohio 44242).

Addictive Behaviors (Pergamon Press, Maxwell House, Fairview Park, Elmsford, N.Y. 10523).

Advances in Alcohol and Substance Abuse (Haworth Press, 75 Griswold St., Binghamton, N.Y. 13904).

Advances in Substance Abuse; Behavioral and Biological Research (JAI Press, 165 W. Putnam Avenue, Greenwich, Conn. 06830).

Alcohol and Drug Research (Pergamon Press, Fairview Park, Elmsford, N.Y. 10523).

Alcohol, Drug Abuse, and Mental Health News (Alcohol, Drug Abuse and Mental Health Administration, Communications and Public Affairs, Rm. 12C-15, 5600 Fishers La., Rockville, Md. 20857).

American Journal of Drug and Alcohol Abuse (Marcel Dekker, P.O. Box 11305, Church Street Station, New York, N.Y. 10249).

Bibliographic Series/Addiction Research Foundation (Addiction Research Foundation of Ontario, 33 Russell St., Toronto, Ontario, CANADA M5S 2S1).

British Journal of Addiction (E and S Livingstone, Longman Group, Fourth Ave., Harlow, Essex, CM19 5AA, ENGLAND).

Bulletin of the Society of Psychologists in Addictive Behaviors (Society of Psychologists in Addictive Behaviors, c/o Curtis Barret, University of Louisville Medical School, P.O. Box 35070, Norton Psychiatric Clinic, Louisville, Ky. 40232).

Bulletin on Narcotics (United Nations Division of Narcotic Drugs, Sales Section, New York, N.Y. 10017).

Chemical Dependencies (Spectrum Publications, 175-20 Wexford Terrace, Jamaica, N.Y. 11432).

Contemporary Drug Problems (Federal Legal Publications, 157 Chambers St., New York, N.Y. 10007).

Drug Abuse and Alcoholism Newsletter (Vista Hill Foundation, 778 Starling Dr., San Diego, Calif.).

Drugs and Drug Abuse Education Newsletter (Editorial Resources, Subscription Dept., P.O. Box 21133, Washington, D.C. 20009).

Exerpta Medica. Section 30: Pharmacology & Toxicology (Elsevier Science Division, Exerpta Medica, Inc., P.O. Box 3085, Princeton, N.J. 08540).

Exerpta Medica. Section 40: Drug Dependence (Elsevier Science Publishers, P.O. Box 3085, Princeton, N.J. 08540).

Focus on Families and Chemical Dependency (U.S. Journal of Drug and Alcohol Dependence, 1721 Blount Rd., Suite #1, Pompano Beach, Fla. 33069).

Food and Drug Administration Drug Bulletin (Department of Health and Human Services, Food and Drug Administration, Rockville, Md. 20857).

International Journal of the Addictions (Marcel Dekker, P.O. Box 11305, Church Street Station, New York, N.Y. 10249).

Journal-Addiction Research Foundation (Addiction Research Foundation, Department KM, 33 Russell St., Toronto, Ontario, CANADA M5S 2S1).

Journal of Alcohol and Drug Education (Allen B. Rice II, 1120 E. Oakland, P.O. Box 10212, Lansing, Mich. 48901).

Journal of Drug Education (Baywood Publishing

Co., 120 Marine St., Farmingdale, N.Y. 11735).

Journal of Drug Issues (Box 4021, Tallahassee, Fla. 32303).

Journal of Psychoactive Drugs (Haight-Ashbury Publications in association with the Haight-Ashbury Free Medical Clinic, 409 Clayton St., San Francisco, Calif. 94117).

Journal of Substance Abuse Treatment (Pergamon Press, Fairview Park, Elmsford, N.Y. 10523).

National Institute on Drug Abuse-Research Issues (National Institute on Drug Abuse, National Clearinghouse for Drug Abuse Information, Box 416, Kensington, Md. 20795).

National Institute on Drug Abuse Research Monograph Series (National Institute on Drug Abuse, National Clearinghouse for Drug Abuse Information, Box 416, Kensington, Md. 20795).

Neurobehavioral Toxicology and Teratology (Ankho International, 7374 Highbridge Terrace, P.O. Box 426, Fayetteville, N.Y. 13066).

Pharmacology, Biochemistry and Behavior (Ankho International, 7374 Highbridge Terrace, P.O. Box 426, Fayetteville, N.Y. 13066).

Psychopharmacology (Springer-Verlag N.Y., Inc., 175 Fifth Avenue, New York, N.Y. 10017).

Research Advances in Alcohol and Drug Problems (Plenum Press, 233 Spring St., New York, N.Y. 10013).

Research Communications in Substances of Abuse (PJD Publications, Box 966, Westbury, N.Y. 11590).

U.S. Journal of Drug and Alcohol Dependence (1721 Blount Rd., Suite 1, Pompano Beach, Fla. 33069).

DSM. See DIAGNOSTIC AND STATISTICAL MANUAL (DSM).

DUAL-CAREER FAMILIES. See FAMILY: CONTEMPORARY PATTERNS.

DUBOIS, WILLIAM EDWARD BURGHARDT. See biographical section.

DUNHAM, ARTHUR. See biographical section.

ECOLOGICAL PERSPECTIVE

A continuing thread in the historical development of social work has been its dual concern for person and situation, and its attempt to consider the relationship between the two in a way that would give equal attention to both. Yet the complementary nature of the relationship was often obscured by the influence of either external (environmental) or internal (psychological) determinism. Professional shifts from one determinism to the other occurred in response to new knowledge and ideologies, to occupational and educational rewards and sanctions, and to events and processes in the larger society. In social casework, in particular, a treatment emphasis on personality change was sometimes uppermost, causing a tendency to view the environment as a static setting in which people lived out their lives dominated by internal forces.

Origins

A historical analysis carried out in the mid-1960s revealed some of the factors that influenced this acceptance by social casework of a disease metaphor, fostering dichotomies in perspective that became increasingly dysfunctional in the face of changing human needs and environments. The study exposed the need to consider a substitute metaphor (Germain, 1968, 1971, 1973) by reviewing twentieth-century changes in the world views of the physical and life sciences. These new directions involved a move away from Newtonian, mechanistic emphases on universal laws and certainties governing physical and biological phenomena toward emphases on patterns, processes, and flows of energy and information among system elements in field of forces. They also included a shift from certainties to probabilities. The study concluded that, by reflecting these changes, an ecological metaphor might have conceptual advantages over the nineteenth-century disease metaphor rooted in simple, linear etiology. By supporting the dual commitment of social work, the new metaphor might lead to different practice principles more consonant with new conditions and new knowledge.

Ecological ideas had come to the fore in a number of areas out of growing concern about environments and quality-of-life issues—a movement underscored by the observance of Earth Day in 1965. An ecological perspective of people and environments, derived from the new world view, would be holistic and transactional as opposed to analytic (in the sense of a focus on parts rather than on the whole) and linear. Such a metaphor or perspective could be expected to capture conceptually the duality and complementarity intended by the person-situation conception of social work. Because ecologists were among the first systems thinkers, the perspective would be systemic; yet it would avoid the seemingly dehumanizing language of general systems theory. Coming out of the life sciences rather than the physical sciences, it would be less abstract and closer to human phenomena. Therefore, the study selected an ecological metaphor over a systems metaphor.

Then, Gordon (1969) published an elaboration of his and Bartlett's joint work on a definition of social work, begun in the 1950s for the National Association of Social Workers (NASW). The 1969 statement became an important additional influence in the continuing effort to develop an ecological perspective for social work. Gordon had proposed that the professional objective of social work is to bring about person-environment transactions that will promote growth, health, and social functioning and improve environments for those who function within them. Transactional phenomena were said to occur at the interface where people and environments interpenetrate. In Gordon's view, the transactions between a person's coping patterns and qualities of the impinging environment constitute the person-situation duality and hence become the social worker's unit of attention. He suggested that a dual simultaneous focus is the professional responsibility of all social workers.

In somewhat modified form, these ideas about social work's purpose were incorporated into the 1983 curriculum policy statement for social work educational programs (Council on Social Work Education, 1983), in the work on conceptual frameworks by NASW (1977, 1981), and in the definition of clinical social work approved by NASW (1983). This does not mean, however, that the formulation is universally accepted, only that for many social workers it offers a promising avenue for reaching consensus on the distinguishing feature of the profession—at least at the more abstract level of its mission or function in society.

Because Gordon's formulation fits the definition of ecology as the study of relations between organisms and environments, it is an ecological statement. The central concept in ecology is goodness of fit with the environment, or state of adaptedness, achieved over evolutionary time in the case of species and over the life span in the case of individuals. As a metaphor developed for social work, the ecological perspective focuses on the degree of person : environment fit and on the reciprocal exchanges (transactions) between people and environments, which either support or inhibit the striving for adaptedness.

The perspective's concern for the degree of fit between people's rights, needs, capacities, and goals on the one hand and the quality and properties of social and physical environments on the other—all within a particular culture or subculture and in a particular time period—has expanded Gordon's original formulation beyond the notions of coping patterns and impinging environments. It has also been expanded by the use of new concepts in social work and other disciplines. In the ecological perspective, the equation denoting people:environment relationships substitutes a colon for the hyphen to underscore their transactional nature and to signify repair of the former discrete person-situation relationship.

Theoretical Foundations

To begin with, transactions must be understood as continuous reciprocal exchanges in the unitary person:environment system, through which each shapes, changes, or otherwise influences the other over time. Thus transaction is different from the more familiar concept of interaction—a form of linear causality (Lazarus, 1980) in which one entity affects one or more others in a particular episode without itself being changed in the process. Transactions also differ from the one-directional linear causality of the stimulus-response arc in classical behavioral theory. Such differences arise from the fact that transactions are actually circular feedback processes taking place in the person : environment interface and giving rise to reciprocal causality. In such instances, cause can become effect and effect can become

cause all around the circular loop (Maruyama, 1968; Powers, 1973). Although linear causality can explain simple situations, it is less useful than reciprocal causality in explaining complex situations such as those in the social work domain.

Another consequence of reciprocal causality is that people's needs and predicaments are viewed as outcomes of people:environment exchanges, not as the products of personality or environment alone. (There is a notable exception, however, in that certain plights may be created by environmental—societal—processes alone, affecting segments of a population or an entire population.) As important as personality is, so too is the environment and so too are their exchanges. Hence the ecological perspective, with its focus on all three sets of forces, demands greater knowledge and skill of the practitioner than did the older metaphor.

When transactions are adaptive, people's growth, development, and physical and emotional well-being are promoted or supported by significant others, social organizations, and political and economic structures and policies and by the temporal, spatial, and other dimensions of physical settings. When transactions are maladaptive, people's emotional, biological, cognitive, and social development and functioning may be impaired and environments may be damaged. Such untoward outcomes increase people's adaptive burdens and tasks.

The term "adaptedness" is therefore transactional in nature; it expresses a particular person:environment relationship, not merely the attributes of either alone. In common parlance, "adaptedness" and "adaptations" are sometimes confused with passive or conservative adjustments to the status quo. But in their technical usage, both are action-oriented. Biological, cognitive, emotional, and social adaptations are active efforts either to effect personal change in order to meet environmental demands and take advantage of environmental opportunities or to effect environmental change so that social and physical environments will be more responsive to people's needs, rights, and goals (Dubos, 1968; Hartmann, 1958). (An apparent exception is the active decision to remain passive for protection or survival in an extreme situation.)

The next two ecological concepts are

also transactional in nature. First, the concept of life stress refers either to a positive or a negative person:environment relationship (Lazarus, 1980). It is positive when an environmental demand, process, or event is experienced as a challenge and is therefore associated with positive feelings, a favorable level of self-esteem, and anticipation of mastery. It can be a negative relationship when actual or perceived environmental demands, harms, losses, or conflicts (or the future threat of any of these) exceed the actual or perceived capacity for dealing with them (Cox, 1978). This kind of life stress is associated with a sense of being in jeopardy, and it arouses such negative, often disabling feelings as anxiety, guilt, rage, helplessness, despair, and lowered self-esteem. Life stress and challenge express person:environment relationships because they encompass both the external demand and the accompanying subjective experience of physiological or emotional stress.

Second, the concept of coping refers to the special adaptations evoked by the internal experience of stress. Two major and interdependent functions of coping are problem solving and managing negative feelings. Each requires both personal and environmental resources (Lazarus, 1980), therefore "coping" also expresses a particular person : environment relationship. When coping efforts are effective, the demand that generated the stress may be eliminated, ameliorated, or its effects mastered. But if coping activity (cognitive, behavioral, or defensive) is unsuccessful and severe stress persists or intensifies, physical dysfunction, emotional disturbance, or disruption in social functioning may result (Dubos, 1968). These in turn can lead to further stress in a downward spiral that becomes harder and harder to interrupt. Because stress and coping are both transactional, they help the practitioner to sustain a dual focus on people and environments.

Two additional concepts from ecology are useful in work with communities. They are niche and habitat. "Niche" refers to the statuses that are occupied by members of the community:

> To survive, grow and reproduce their kind, all organisms must locate and fit into an environmental niche—as species and as individuals. What constitutes a salutary human niche is

defined differently in different societies and in different historical eras. We don't know for sure what elements of a niche release different human potentialities. "In our own society one dimension of a good niche has long been considered to be a set of rights, including the right to equal opportunity (DeLone, 1979)." (Germain, 1985, p. 45)

However, in urban and rural communities across the nation, color, ethnicity, gender, age, sexual preference, disability, poverty, or other personal or cultural characteristics devalued by society force millions of people to occupy niches that are incongruent with human needs.

In ecology, "habitat" refers to the places where an organism is found:

> In the case of human beings, the physical and social settings within a cultural context are the habitat. Physical settings such as dwellings, buildings, rural villages and urban layouts must support the social settings of family life, social life, work life, religious life, and so on, in ways that fit with life styles, age, gender, and culture. Habitats that do not support the health and social functioning of individuals and families are likely to produce or to contribute to feelings of isolation, disorientation, and despair. Such stressful feelings may interfere further with the basic functions of family and community life. (Germain, 1985, p. 41)

Again, many impoverished rural and urban communities across the nation lack the attributes of habitats that support human well-being.

In addition to these concepts, in the ecological perspective as in others, attention is drawn to various bodies of thought concerning individuals' biological, emotional, cognitive, and social development and functioning and to the dynamic processes involved in dyads, families, groups, networks, communities, neighborhoods, and organizations. But in the ecological perspective, the development and functioning of individuals and collectivities are always viewed as transactional outcomes—in the context of cultural and environmental diversity and of the diverse genetic potentialities that are released by nutritive environments or inhibited by nonnutritive ones (Dobzhansky, 1976). Hence the ecological view gives particular emphasis to four additional concepts—relatedness, competence, self-direction, and self-esteem-identity—whose transactional nature also helps the practitioner to focus on persons, environments, and the exchanges between them.

The concept of relatedness, based on attachment theory (Bowlby, 1973), is different from the concept of object relations, which is rooted in drive theory. Relatedness also incorporates ideas about emotional and social loneliness and isolation (Weiss, 1973; Will, 1959). The difference between attachment and dependency underscores the significance of informal support systems across the life span. A large body of research demonstrates the influence of supportive networks of relatives, friends, neighbors, workmates, and animal companions in protecting people from painful life stress. When stress does befall the individual or collectivity, the presence of informal support is a critical environmental resource for coping with it. People facing stress have been found to suffer less physical, emotional, or social dysfunctioning if they are embedded in supportive social networks than their counterparts who do not have such affiliations (Cobb, 1976). It is thought that the power of these informal systems derives from their communicating to afflicted members that they are valued, esteemed, and even loved participants in a mutual aid system, thereby strengthening and sustaining their self-esteem.

The distinction between attachment and dependency also aids in understanding the role of emotional or social isolation or both in the pervasiveness of loneliness in modern life. Emotional isolation arises from the loss of a primary attachment; the profound loneliness engendered by the loss can only be assuaged by the formation of another primary attachment after the grief has been resolved. Social isolation arises from the absence of a social network or informal support system. Thus the loneliness engendered by uprooting, long institutionalization, and the like can be assuaged only by connecting with a new network or reconnecting with a former one (Weiss, 1973). This suggests the need for differential assessment and intervention in matters of loneliness and isolation.

As an aspect of relatedness, loneliness, too, encompasses a person:environment relationship. Indeed, the ability to control the nature of exchanges to attain the desired degree of privacy or solitude or the desired degree of social interaction rests on both personal resources (verbal, nonverbal, spatial, and temporal behaviors) and on such environmental properties as fences, locks, doors, signs, and the like (Altman, 1975). This aspect of the ecological perspective suggests additional entry points for social workers to help people work out adaptive social arrangements in family, group, community, and institutional life.

"Relatedness" also refers to human beings' relationships to nature in the evolutionary sense of the unity of nature and human nature. For example, with receptive children, youth, and adults, experiences with plants and animals and interpersonal experiences in natural settings such as therapeutic camping, wilderness therapy, and the like can be used to assuage various painful and anxiety-laden states and to bring about enhanced self-realization, deepened awareness of internal and external reality, and increased appreciation and acceptance of others (Searles, 1960).

Relatedness is interdependent with competence, self-direction, and self-esteem–identity. Competence begins in infancy and continues across the life span. When human infants experience repeated success in influencing their caregivers to respond promptly and ungrudgingly to their signals of need, they begin to develop efficacy—the sense of having an effect on their environment. The accumulation of such experiences leads to the sense of competence (White, 1959). For this development to continue, the social and physical environments must provide diverse stimuli and learning opportunities and support for age-appropriate exploration and self-direction in all periods from toddlerhood, childhood, youth, and adulthood to old age.

Without the accumulation of successful experiences in the environment, the sense of competence may not develop fully or it may be stifled by later experiences in harsh environments or in bland, stereotyped institutional environments. But because the basic motivation to be effective in the environment is believed to be innate, then presumably it can be reawakened, mobilized, and supported. Professional knowledge and skill in this area are still limited but are developing in some mother-infant programs and in some services for the institutionalized, deinstitutionalized, the frail elderly, and other groups.

Relatedness and competence influence the development of self-direction. This concept is similar to what is referred to in classical ego psychology as the ego's relative autonomy from internal and external demands and pressures. Such autonomy is gained and maintained through the ego's active efforts to manage internal and external demands while remaining attuned to both internal needs and external processes. Without such active management, the ego would be at the mercy of tyrannical forces in either the internal or external worlds or both (Rapaport, 1958). This again underscores the action orientation of adaptation and the importance of decision making and action. But the notion of self-direction also takes into account issues of power, of one's location in the social structure, and of the nature of societal forces that affect options and opportunities to influence one's environment.

Two more practice concepts, related to the concept of dominance in ecology itself, help to clarify the issues in self-direction. They express negative person:environment relationships that arise from the misuse of power and impair growth, health, and social functioning in those affected. The two concepts are oppression (the withholding of power by dominant groups) based on age, gender, sexual preference, race and ethnicity, religion, social class, and physical or mental disability; and pollution (the abuse of power by dominant groups), including social pollution such as poverty, unemployment, the nuclear arms race, inadequate systems of housing, health care, education, and income distribution; technological pollution of air, water, and food; toxic materials in workplaces, schools, and dwellings; and hazardous wastes in communities. These two major sources of life stress are created by society and so require societal rather than individual or group solutions. They therefore form the base for encouraging the practitioner to participate in efforts to effect changes in public policy, attitudes, and values.

In addition to complex, dynamic personal (internal) processes, the ecological perspective underscores the complex and dynamic nature of the environment. The environment comprises social and physical settings in continuous transaction with each other and with the culture, shaping and changing each other over time. Individuals internalize the culture as knowledge and belief systems, language, symbolic meanings, and norms and values that operate at both conscious and unconscious levels. The culture patterns social life and responses to and uses made of physical settings.

The term "social settings" refers to the human environment, or other people in the life space of the individual or collectivity being served. It is recognized that this idea lacks conceptual clarity inasmuch as, in some instances, dyads, families, groups, networks, communities, and organizations constitute the social environment and in others they are the actual entities served. The social environment also includes larger societal contexts, such as economic, statutory, and political structures and policies at the federal, state, and local levels; health care systems; educational systems; housing systems; justice and correctional systems; occupational structures and workplaces; religious structures; and the like. Some aspects of the social setting, especially the perceptions and expectations of significant others, are—like culture—internalized as part of the self.

Aspects of the physical environment are differentially relevant to the social worker. They may include geographic location (rural-urban differences, terrain, climate), plants and animals, design of space and arrangements of objects in it, and scheduling of time as these reflect personality, cultural patterns, and social structures. They may also include such human creations as the media, computers, and robots and their influences for good and for ill; biomedical technologies that create new ethical dilemmas and moral conflicts; transportation systems that may be present, absent, or inaccessible; and architectural and neighborhood arrangements that support or inhibit relationships or that may or may not be accessible to the disabled. Such physical features may be important to consider in any given situation because of their influence on development and functioning and because they are often (1) sources of life stress (for example, sociogeographic isolation; technological or structural unemployment), (2) objectives of change (for example, temporal and spatial arrangements in family or institutional life and agency structures; media representation of women), or (3) instruments of help (for example, plants and animal companions; use of the media for public education about social needs and social work). In addition, one's place of origin is often part of one's sense of identity, and attachment to place—as well as to others—can be part of the loss experienced in uprooting.

In summary, then, the ecological perspective in social work rests on the assumption that transactional concepts permit the repair of the formerly severed person-situation formulation and actually facilitates the social worker's dual simultaneous focus on both. In relying on transactional ideas, the ecological perspective suggests that neither the people served nor their environments can be fully understood except in relationship to each other. Although the complexity involved may seem overwhelming, it is present and operating whether recognized or not, and the ecological perspective helps organize it for clients and practitioners.

The perspective also requires social workers to serve people as they experience their needs—as individuals and as members of collectivities—rather than differentiating need on the basis of method preference. It supports the variety of practice roles and tasks required by the dual focus. Moreover, it can serve as a base for internal, external, and legislative advocacy; policy and planning; program development, including primary prevention activities; research; and administration. However, only face-to-face practice is considered in this article.

Range of Application

Applications of the ecological perspective to fields of practice include child welfare (Brown et al., 1982; Hartman, 1979b; Laird, 1979; Maluccio & Sinanoglu, 1981); health care (Germain, 1984b); mental health (Goldstein, 1979, 1983; Libassi & Maluccio, 1982); aging (Germain, 1984a; Miller & Solomon, 1979); occupational social work (Akabas, Germain, & Silverman, 1983); school social work (Aponte, 1976; Gitterman, 1971; Winters & Easton, 1983); work with the terminally ill (Fisher, 1979; Goldstein, 1976), delinquent and disturbed youth (Cataldo, 1979,

1983); families (Aponte, 1979; Hartman, 1979a; Janchill, 1979), social support networks (Wells & Singer, 1981, 1985; Whittaker & Garbarino, 1983); groups (Balgopal & Vassil, 1983); empowerment (Pinderhughes, 1983); black language (Draper, 1979), and transient women (Breton, 1984). With two exceptions (Cataldo, 1983; Maluccio, 1979a), ecologically oriented social work research has not undertaken effectiveness studies. Instead, it has so far engaged in knowledge-building studies of person:environment fit (Coulton, 1979) and natural helpers, such as informal support systems of relatives, friends, and neighbors (Patterson, 1984; Swenson, 1983). Not explicitly ecological studies and analysis of person:environment fit include Wetzel (1978), Ewalt and Honeyfield (1981), and Weick (1981).

It is important to note that Meyer (1983) has described an "eco-systems perspective" that rests on concepts from general systems theory and is applicable to any practice approach in clinical social work. Also, three new practice approaches have emerged from the ecological perspective. These are the family-centered approach (Hartman & Laird, 1983), the life model approach (Germain & Gitterman, 1980), and the competence approach (Maluccio, 1979b, 1981). Their distinctiveness lies in their attempt to operationalize the ecological concepts described in this article. However, as would be expected, some differences exist between them. For example, family-centered social work applies the ecological perspective to practice with families; the competence approach focuses on fostering client competence as a desired outcome of people: environment transactions; and the life model approach applies the perspective to an integrated method of social work practice with individuals and collectivities. Many social workers have contributed to the continued development of the life model approach, which will be described in the next section.

Assessment and Intervention

The life model provides practice principles modeled on processes of living rather than on processes found within the idioms of disease, deviance, and the like. The term itself was first used by Bandler (1963), a Boston psychoanalyst, in his discussion of ego-supportive casework. He suggested that the frame of reference for such work should be "life itself, the natural processes of growth, development, and decline, its methods of problem-solving and need-satisfaction" (p. 41). He also observed that although the progressive forces in people may sometimes suffer interference and arrest, they are nevertheless stronger than regressive trends. The task of practice, then, is to help remove obstructions and to mobilize and ally ourselves with the progressive forces.

Bandler's ideas provided the means for deriving a practice approach that would operationalize the ecological perspective (Germain, 1968). This led first to adapting Lewin's (1964) notion of life space (his "psychological environment," impinging environment, and the larger, external environment, or "foreign hull") to a practice concept denoting the social worker's unit of attention and, second, to dividing the life space into three interdependent realms—life transitions, interpersonal processes, and environmental properties.

Life transitions encompass developmental changes such as puberty and aging; desired, imposed, or stigmatized status and role changes; and loss and other crisis events faced by individuals and collectivities. Interpersonal processes include patterns of relationship and communication in dyads, families, groups, social networks, communities or neighborhoods, and organizations. Environmental properties include the aspects of social and physical settings—their formal and informal resources and deficits as described in this article—as they affect individuals and collectivities.

Because these three realms are the contexts in which human growth, development, and social functioning take place and in which challenge is met, welcomed, or even sought for mastery, growth, and zestful living, they are important foci for social work services and programs designed to promote health and well-being for all interested populations—for example, support groups for single fathers, children of divorce, newcomers, and the like. They are also settings for primary prevention activities to obviate potentially negative outcomes for individuals and groups in at-risk situations—for example, psychoeducational programs for teenage parents and their infants, support groups for

mastectomy patients, and the like (Bloom, 1979; Germain, 1982).

However, painful and destructive life stress may be confronted by individuals and collectivities within these same realms. Thus, after "life space," the second practice concept developed for the life model approach was "problems in living," to denote those human predicaments in which stressful demands, harms, losses, and future threats in one or more realms of the life space have led to maladaptive person:environment exchanges. Such life stress may arise in the environmental realm—for example, in the workplace (which in other instances may be the context for growth and mental health). If job stress or unemployment is not coped with successfully, it may spill over into one or both of the other realms—into interpersonal family processes (leading, for example, to marital conflict) or into life transitions (leading, for example, to developmental difficulties for the family's school-age child). Life stress may also arise in either the life transitional or interpersonal realms and then spread to one or both of the others. For example, difficult developmental or role tasks or problem-filled family processes may affect job performance, creating additional stress at the workplace.

Stress may operate in similar ways within the three realms of the community's life space. For example, lack of needed environmental services (shopping, banking, medical care, and so on) after working hours may create stress at the workplace. Transitions in the community as one population moves out, leaving its elderly people, and another moves in may lead to conflict in intergroup relationships and communication patterns and consequent stress for families and elderly residents. Lack of recreational facilities may create stress in connection with the developmental tasks of teenagers, and so on. Housing problems, school problems, violence, and the like—all of which create stress for community members—must often be handled at the neighborhood or community level rather than at the individual or primary group level.

Although they may not define their plights in such terms, it is notable that most, if not all, people applying for or being referred to social work services are experiencing stressful demands that exceed their personal and environmental coping resources.

Even those populations to whom services are offered are usually believed to be in at-risk situations—that is, they are at risk of stressful demands, harms, or losses that will place them in jeopardy.

Assessment seeks to identify the stressors giving rise to the presenting need and to locate the realm or realms of the life space in which they lie. The effects of job stress, for example, may be wrongly assessed as a problem in family relationships if insufficient attention is accorded the environment. Therefore, both parts of the person:environment equation and their transactions require dynamic exploration, engagement, and biopsychosocial assessment by clients and workers—always in the context of personal, environmental, and cultural diversity.

Based on the assessment, action (intervention) is directed to improving people:environment relationships by facilitating self-management of the internal world of feelings, perceptions, thoughts, values, motivations, and attitudes and helping people to increase the responsiveness of the external world where necessary (Gitterman, 1971)—intervening directly and indirectly to modify maladaptive transactions.

More specifically, interventions are oriented toward mobilizing and enhancing personal and environmental resources needed to motivate coping with the life stress, providing support to elevate self-esteem and to help manage and regulate negative feelings aroused by the life stress, and—with client consent—engaging the support of informal and formal helping systems. Interventions also focus on teaching coping and other adaptive skills relevant to internal and external issues and, where needed, on influencing social and physical environments to provide the time and space required for developing and trying out new skills—utilizing or creating opportunities for clients' decision making and action in important areas and influencing environments to provide such opportunities. But—whatever the presenting predicament and whatever the specific goals clients and social workers agree upon—intervention is shaped to enable those being served to rediscover to the greatest degree possible their own capacities for enhanced relatedness, self-direction, competence, self-esteem, and sense of personal identity.

A salient feature of the life model approach is its emphasis on an integrated method of social work practice with individuals and collectivities. The approach recognizes that the development, dynamic processes, and functioning of individuals differs from those of collectivities and that knowledge of both must be part of the practitioner's continuing professional education. It also assumes, however, that the interpersonal, empathic, observational, assessment, problem-solving, communication, and other skills involved are the same whether people are encountered as individuals or as members of collectivities. These skills are conceptualized as worker functions, roles, and tasks (Germain, 1984b), and the techniques used are viewed as reflecting the practitioner's individuality, style, and creativity. The life model approach rests on the same professional values and ethics that underlie all practice approaches.

In respect to work with families and groups, the practice principles and skills of assessment and intervention are easily applied. They have also been readily applied to practice with neighborhoods and communities—either as clients or as environments—in enhancing (1) community relatedness, including social networks and mutual aid systems; (2) community competence in meeting the needs and interests of community members; (3) community self-direction in the development and management of resources within the community or obtained from outside; and (4) a sense of community identity and pride (Germain, 1985). The ecological ideas of niche and habitat are useful foci in mobilizing community members for action to change physical and social settings within the community or neighborhood.

In the case of organizations and societal forces as environmental elements, additional practice principles and skills have been developed to carry out such tasks as (1) internal advocacy to increase, where necessary, the agency responsiveness to clients' (and staff's) needs and external advocacy to help clients obtain needed resources from other organizations (Brager & Holloway, 1978; Gitterman & Germain, 1981; Resnick & Patti, 1980); and (2) legislative advocacy (Mahaffey & Hanks, 1982) to increase the responsiveness of social policy to human needs, enhance the quality and equity of distribution of societal resources, and increase access to them.

The life model approach views the professional relationship as a transactional arena in which all participants enhance their capacity for relatedness as they learn and grow together. Emphasis is placed on the worker's honesty, openness, and authenticity, serving also to reduce social distance and to dilute the influence of transference and its regressive phenomena. The relationship is considered to be a partnership or joint effort, to which each participant brings unique knowledge and experience, thereby implementing the value of mutuality. The focus is on strengths, not deficits, and on the potential for continued growth and needed social change.

Self-direction is linked to issues of power, opportunity, access to options, and action in areas of life that are important in a given culture or subculture. These connections define the terms for programmatic arrangements and practice skills, which are then guided by the principle of empowerment (Grosser & Mondros, 1985; Pinderhughes, 1983; Shapiro, 1983; Solomon, 1976; Weick, 1982). Empowerment begins with the establishment of the client-worker relationship as described above. It continues in the mutual search for and creation of maximal opportunities for choice, decision making, and action consonant with age, physical and emotional states, capacities, and cultural patterns. As a practice principle, it implements the social work value of self-determination.

Empowerment emphasizes efforts—jointly with clients where possible—to remove environmental obstacles and stressors and to increase the environment's responsiveness to clients' needs, rights, and goals, particularly for excluded or vulnerable groups. Under certain circumstances and with certain groups, it may include consciousness raising as a means of shifting from an unrealistic sense of personal inadequacy to a recognition of the sociostructural determinants in a stressful situation. In other instances, it may involve shifting a misperceived locus of control over life events from impersonal societal forces to individual or collective responsibility.

The life model approach has been applied to supervision (Gitterman & Miller,

1977); resistance (Gitterman, 1983); assessment (Peterson, 1979); groups (Lee, 1982; Shulman & Gitterman, 1985); health care (Gitterman, 1982; Kirschner, 1982, 1979); child welfare (Lee & Park, 1978); and work with homeless women (Lee, 1985), the elderly (Lee, 1981; Tonti & Kosberg, 1983); and natural helpers (Patterson & Brennan, 1983; Patterson et al., 1983; Swenson, 1979; Lee & Swenson, 1978). And the life model, but not the practice approach, has been applied to change processes (Oxley, 1971). The competence approach has been applied to practice issues and to work with different population groups by a number of practitioners (Maluccio, 1981).

Because they are newly developed, the life model, family-centered, and competence approaches have not yet undertaken effectiveness studies. Research is needed into the effectiveness of the approaches with different populations experiencing different stressors and functioning in different environments. At a more informal level, however, clients and workers together evaluate effectiveness at the end of the contact through client satisfaction studies (Maluccio, 1979a), single-case designs (Bloom & Block, 1977), problems-oriented recording (Martens & Holmstrup, 1974), or comparative examination of before-and-after eco-maps (Hartman & Laird, 1983).

The ecological perspective—resting on an evolutionary, adaptational base—is itself an evolving system of ideas. As such, it remains open to newly developed theory and knowledge that further illuminate any of the elements of the transacting person: environment system. Presumably, the continuing incorporation of new theory and knowledge will also produce additions to and modifications of the life model of practice for as long as it remains a viable model derived from the ecological perspective.

CAREL B. GERMAIN
ALEX GITTERMAN

For further information, see DIRECT PRACTICE IN SOCIAL WORK: OVERVIEW; DIRECT PRACTICE: TRENDS AND ISSUES.

References

Akabas, S. H., Germain, C. B., & Silverman, B. (1983, March). *What's in the Work?* [Mimeo.] Revision of a paper prepared for the Wingspread Conference on Work and Mental

Health: Clinical Issues for the Professions, Racine, Wis.

Altman, I. (1975). *The Environment and Social Behavior*. Monterey, Calif.: Brooks/Cole Publishing Co.

Aponte, H. J. (1976). "The Family-School Interview: An Eco-Structural Approach." *Family Process, 15*(3), 303–312.

Aponte, H. J. (1979). "Diagnosis in Family Therapy." In C. B. Germain (Ed.), *Social Work Practice: People and Environments* (pp. 107–149). New York: Columbia University Press.

Balgopal, P. R., & Vassil, T. V. (1983) *Groups in Social Work: An Ecological Perspective*. New York: Macmillan Publishing Co.

Bandler, B. (1963). "The Concept of Ego-Supportive Psychotherapy." In H. J. Parad & R. R. Miller (Eds.), *Ego-Oriented Casework* (pp. 27–44). New York: Family Service Association of America.

Bloom, M. (1979). "Social Prevention: An Ecological Approach." In C. B. Germain (Ed.), *Social Work Practice: People and Environments* (pp. 326–345). New York: Columbia University Press.

Bloom, M., & Block, S. R. (1977). "Evaluating One's Own Effectiveness and Efficiency." *Social Work, 22*(2), 130–136.

Bowlby, J. (1973). "Affectional Bonds: Their Nature and Origin." In R. S. Weiss (Ed.), *Loneliness: The Experience of Emotional and Social Isolation* (pp. 38–52). Cambridge, Mass.: MIT Press.

Brager, G., & Holloway, S. (1978). *Changing Human Service Organizations: Politics and Practice*. New York: Free Press.

Breton, M. (1984). "A Drop-In Program for Transient Women." *Social Work, 29*(6), 542–546.

Brown, J., et al. (1982). *Child-Family-Neighborhood: A Master Plan for Social Service Delivery*. New York: Child Welfare League of America.

Cataldo, D. J. (1979). "Wilderness Therapy: Modern Day Shamanism." In C. B. Germain (Ed.), *Social Work Practice: People and Environments* (pp. 46–73). New York: Columbia University Press.

Cataldo, D. J. (1983). "Wilderness Bound Experience: Testing Competence in a Survival Setting." Unpublished doctoral dissertation, Columbia University School of Social Work.

Cobb, S. (1976). "Social Support as a Moderator of Life Stress." *Psychosomatic Medicine, 38*(5), 300–314.

Coulton, C. J. (1979). "Developing an Instrument to Measure Person-Environment Fit." *Journal of Social Service Research, 3*(2), 159–173.

Council on Social Work Education. (1983). *Curriculum Policy for the Master's Degree & Baccalaureate Degree Programs in Social Work Education (1982)*. New York: Author.

Cox, T. (1978). *Stress*. Baltimore, Md.: University Park Press.

DeLone, R. (1979). *Small Futures: Children, Inequality, and the Limits of Liberal Reform*. New York: Harcourt Brace Jovanovich.

Dobzhansky, T. (1976). "The Myths of Genetic Predestination and Tabula Rasa." *Perspectives in Biology and Medicine, 19*(2), 156–170.

Draper, B. (1979). "Black Language as an Adaptive Response to a Hostile Environment." In C. B. Germain (Ed.), *Social Work Practice: People and Environments* (pp. 267–281). New York: Columbia University Press.

Dubos, R. (1968). *So Human an Animal*. New York: Charles Scribner's Sons.

Ewalt, P. L., & Honeyfield, R. M. (1981). "Needs of Persons in Long-Term Care." *Social Work, 26*(3), 223–232.

Fisher, D. (1979). "The Hospitalized Terminally Ill Patient: An Ecological Perspective." In C. B. Germain (Ed.), *Social Work Practice: People and Environments* (pp. 25–45). New York: Columbia University Press.

Germain, C. B. (1968). "Social Study: Past and Future." *Social Casework, 49*(7), 403–409.

Germain, C. B. (1971). *Casework and Science: A Study in the Sociology of Knowledge*. Unpublished dissertation, Columbia University School of Social Work, New York.

Germain, C. B. (1973). "An Ecological Perspective in Casework Practice." *Social Casework, 54*(6), 323–330.

Germain, C. B. (1982). "Teaching Primary Prevention in Social Work: An Ecological Perspective." *Journal of Education for Social Work, 18*(1), 20–28.

Germain, C. B. (1984a). "The Elderly and the Ecology of Death: Issues of Time and Space." In M. Tallmer et al. (Eds.), *The Life-Threatened Elderly* (pp. 195–207). New York: Columbia University Press.

Germain, C. B. (1984b). *Social Work Practice in Health Care*. New York: Free Press.

Germain, C. B. (1985). "The Place of Community Work within an Ecological Approach to Social Work Practice." In S. H. Taylor & R. W. Roberts (Eds.), *Theories and Practice of Community Social Work* (pp. 30–55). New York: Columbia University Press.

Germain, C. B., & Gitterman, A. (1980). *The Life Model of Social Work Practice*. New York: Columbia University Press.

Gitterman, A. (1971). "Group Work in the Public Schools." In W. Schwartz & S. Zalba (Eds.), *The Practice of Group Work* (pp. 45–72). New York: Columbia University Press.

Gitterman, A. (1982). "The Use of Groups in Health Settings." In A. Lurie, G. Rosenberg, & S. Pinsky (Eds.), *Social Work With Groups in Health Settings* (pp. 6–24). New York: Prodist.

Gitterman, A. (1983). "Uses of Resistance: A Transactional View." *Social Work, 28*(2), 127–131.

Gitterman, A., & Germain, C. B. (1981). "Education for Practice: Teaching about the Environment." *Journal of Education for Social Work, 17*(3), 44–51.

Gitterman, A., & Miller, I. (1977). "Supervisors as Educators." In F. W. Kaslow (Ed.), *Supervision, Consultation, and Staff Training in the Helping Professions* (pp. 100–114). San Francisco: Jossey-Bass.

Goldstein, E. (1976). "Social Casework and the Dying Person." *Social Casework, 54*(10), 601–608.

Goldstein, E. (1979). "Mothers of Psychiatric Patients Revisited." In C. B. Germain (Ed.), *Social Work Practice: People and Environments* (pp. 150–173). New York: Columbia University Press.

Goldstein, E. (1983). "Clinical and Ecological Approaches to the Borderline Client." *Social Casework, 64*(6), 353–362.

Gordon, W. E. (1969). "Basic Constructs for an Integrative and Generative Conception of Social Work." In G. Hearn (Ed.), *The General Systems Approach: Contributions Toward an Holistic Conception of Social Work* (pp. 5–11). New York: Council on Social Work Education.

Grosser, C., & Mondros, J. (1985). "Pluralism and Participation: The Political Action Approach." In S. H. Taylor & R. W. Roberts (Eds.), *Theories and Practice of Community Social Work* (pp. 154–178). New York: Columbia University Press.

Hartman, A. (1979a). "The Extended Family as a Resource for Change." In C. B. Germain (Ed.), *Social Work Practice: People and Environments* (pp. 239–266). New York: Columbia University Press.

Hartman, A. (1979b). *Finding Families: An Ecological Approach to Family Assessment in Adoption.* Beverly Hills, Calif.: Sage Publications.

Hartman, A., & Laird, J. (1983). *Family-Centered Social Work Practice.* New York: Free Press.

Hartmann, H. (1958). *Ego Psychology and the Problem of Adaption.* New York: International Universities Press.

Janchill, M. P. (1979). "People Cannot Go It Alone." In C. B. Germain (Ed.), *Social Work Practice: People and Environments* (pp. 346–362). New York: Columbia University Press.

Kirschner, C. (1979). "The Aging Family in Crisis: A Problem in Living." *Social Casework, 60*(4), 209–216.

Kirschner, C., & Rosengarten, L. (1982). "The Skilled Social Work Role in Home Health Care." *Social Casework, 27*(9), 527–530.

Laird, J. (1979). "An Ecological Approach to Child Welfare: Issues of Family Identity and Continuity." In C. B. Germain (Ed.), *Social Work Practice: People and Environments* (pp. 174–212). New York: Columbia University Press.

Lazarus, R. S. (1980). "The Stress and Coping Paradigm." In L. A. Bond & J. C. Rosen (Eds.), *Competence and Coping During Adulthood* (pp. 28–74). Hanover, N.H.: University Press of New England.

Lee, J. A. B. (1981). "Human Relatedness and the Mentally Impaired Older Person." *Journal of Gerontological Social Work, 4*(2), 5–15.

Lee, J. A. B. (1982). "The Group: A Chance at Human Connectedness for the Mentally Impaired Older Person." *Social Work and Groups, 5*(2), 43–55.

Lee, J. A. B. (in press). "No Place To Belong." In A. Gitterman & L. Shulman (Eds.), *Mutual Aid and the Life Cycle.* Itasca, Ill.: F. E. Peacock Publishers.

Lee, J. A. B., & Park, D. N. (1978). "A Group Approach to Depressed Adolescent Girls in Foster Care." *American Journal of Orthopsychiatry, 48*(3), 528–538.

Lee, J. A. B., & Swenson, C. R. (1978). "Theory in Action: A Community Service Agency." *Social Casework, 59*(6), 359–370.

Lewin, K. (1964). *Field Theory in Social Science.* New York: Harper & Row.

Libassi, M. F., & Maluccio, A. N. (1982). "Teaching the Use of the Ecological Perspective in Community Mental Health." *Journal of Education for Social Work, 18*(3), 94–100.

Mahaffey, M., & Hanks, J. W. (Eds.). (1982). *Practical Politics: Social Work and Political Responsibility.* Silver Spring, Md.: National Association of Social Workers.

Maluccio, A. N. (1979a). *Learning from Clients: Interpersonal Helping as Viewed by Clients and Social Workers.* New York: Free Press.

Maluccio, A. N. (1979b). "Promoting Competence Through Life Experiences." In C. B. Germain, (Ed.), *Social Work Practice: People and Environments* (pp. 280–302). New York: Columbia University Press.

Maluccio, A. N. (1981). *Promoting Competence in Clients. A New/Old Approach to Social Work Practice.* New York: Free Press.

Maluccio, A. N., & Sinanoglu, P. A. (Eds.). (1981). *The Challenge of Partnership—Working with Parents of Children in Foster Care.* New York: Child Welfare League of America.

Martens, W. M., & Holmstrup, E. (1974). "Problem-Oriented Recording." *Social Casework, 55*(9), 554–561.

Maruyama, M. (1968). "The Second Cybernetics: Deviation–Amplifying Mutual Causal Processes." In W. Buckley (Ed.), *Modern Systems Research for the Behavioral Scientist* (pp. 304–313). Chicago: Aldine Publishing Co.

Meyer, C. H. (Ed.). (1983). *Clinical Social Work in the Eco-Systems Perspective*. New York: Columbia University Press.

Miller, I., & Solomon, R. (1979). "The Development of Group Services for the Elderly." In C. B. Germain (Ed.), *Social Work Practice: People and Environments* (pp. 74–106). New York: Columbia University Press.

National Association of Social Workers. (1977). "Conceptual Frameworks I" [Special issue]. *Social Work, 22*(4).

National Association of Social Workers. (1981). "Conceptual Frameworks II" [Special issue]. *Social Work, 26*(1).

National Association of Social Workers. (1984). *NASW Standards for the Practice of Clinical Social Work*. Silver Spring, Md.: Author.

Oxley, G. (1971). "A Life-Model Approach to Change." *Social Casework, 52*(10), 46–53.

Patterson, S. L. (1984). *The Characteristics and Helping Patterns of Older Rural Natural Helpers in the Midwest and New England.* Unpublished doctoral dissertation, University of Wisconsin, Madison.

Patterson, S. L., & Brennan, E. (1983). "Matching Helping Roles With the Characteristics of Older Natural Helpers." *Journal of Gerontological Social Work, 5*(4), 55–66.

Patterson, S. L., et al. (1983). *How Effective are Rural Natural Helpers?* Unpublished paper, University of Kansas, School of Social Welfare, Lawrence.

Peterson, K. J. (1979). "Assessment in the Life Model: A Historical Perspective." *Social Casework, 60*(10), 586–596.

Pinderhughes, E. (1983). "Empowerment for Our Clients and for Ourselves." *Social Casework, 64*(6), 331–338.

Powers, W. (1973). "Feedback: Beyond Behaviorism." *Science, 179*(4069), 351–356.

Rapaport, D. (1958). "The Theory of Ego Autonomy: A Generalization." *Bulletin of the Menninger Clinic, 22*(1), 13–34.

Resnick, H., & Patti, R. J. (Eds.). (1980). *Change From Within: Humanizing Social Welfare Organizations*. Philadelphia: Temple University Press.

Searles, H. F. (1960). *The Nonhuman Environment*. New York: International Universities Press.

Shapiro, J. (1983). "Commitment to Disenfranchised Clients." In A. Rosenblatt & D. Waldfogel (Eds.), *Handbook of Clinical Social Work* (pp. 888–903). San Francisco: Jossey-Bass.

Shulman, L., & Gitterman, A. (in press). "The Life Model, Mutual Aid and the Mediating Function." In A. Gitterman & L. Shulman (Eds.), *Mutual Aid Groups and the Life Cycle*. Itasca, Ill.: F. E. Peacock Publishers.

Solomon, B. (1976). *Black Empowerment: Social Work in Minority Communities*. New York: Columbia University Press.

Swenson, C. R. (1979). "Social Networks, Mutual Aid, and the Life Model of Practice." In C. Germain (Ed.), *Social Work Practice: People and Environments* (pp. 213–238). New York: Columbia University Press.

Swenson, C. R. (1983). *Natural Helping Processes*. Unpublished doctoral dissertation, Columbia University School of Social Work, New York.

Tonti, M., & Kosberg, J. I. (1983). "A Transactional Model for Work With the Frail Elderly." In M. Dinerman (Ed.), *Social Work in a Turbulent World* (pp. 156–166). Silver Spring, Md.: National Association of Social Workers.

Weick, A. (1981). "Reframing the Person-in-Environment Perspective." *Social Work, 26*(2), 134–145.

Weick, A. (1982). "Issues of Power in Social Work Practice." In A. Weick & S. Vandiver (Eds.), *Women, Power, and Change* (pp. 173–185). Washington, D.C.: National Association of Social Workers.

Weiss, R. S. (Ed.). (1973). *Loneliness: The Experience of Emotional and Social Isolation*. Cambridge, Mass.: MIT Press.

Wells, L. M., & Singer, C. (1981). "The Impact of Student Visits on Services and Structural Change in Homes for the Aged." *Canadian Journal of Social Work Education, 7*(3), 11–27.

Wells, L. M., & Singer, C. (1985). "A Model for Linking Networks in Social Work Practice with the Institutionalized Elderly." *Social Work, 30*(4), 318–322.

Wetzel, J. (1978). "Depression and Dependence Upon Unsustaining Environments." *Clinical Social Work Journal, 6*(2), 75–89.

White, R. W. (1959). "Motivation Reconsidered: The Concept of Competence." *Psychological Review, 66*(5), 297–333.

Whittaker, J. K., & Garbarino, J. (1983). *Social Support Networks: Informal Helping in the Human Services*. New York: Aldine Publishing Co.

Will, O. (1959). "Human Relatedness and the Schizophenic Reaction." *Psychiatry, 22*(3), 205–223.

Winters, W., & Easton, F. (1983). *The Practice of Social Work in the Schools: An Ecological Perspective*. New York: Free Press.

ELIOT, MARTHA MAY. See biographical
section.

EMERGENCY HEALTH SERVICES

There were more than 85 million visits to
hospital emergency rooms in 1980, a steady
increase in business since the early 1950s.
The emergency room serves as the primary
physician as well as the acute and emergency
treatment facility for the mobile, poor, and
multiple-problem patient (Clement &
Klingbeil, 1981). Thus, the range of patients
in the emergency room at any given time may
include patients with severe trauma or a sore
throat, patients who are intoxicated or psychotic, transients looking for a warm place to
stay, and elderly people who are merely
confused. Particularly during nights and
weekends, when traditional social agencies
are closed, the emergency room is seen as the
only social agency in town for patients in
crisis (Soskis, 1980). These factors have led

to a need for social workers in the emergency
room.

Roles and Functions of Emergency Room Social Work

The role of the emergency room social
worker has developed over the past 20 years.
It is a new and nontraditional specialty that
involves working odd hours and with an
interdisciplinary team that has traditionally
been more attuned to illness and trauma than
to patients' social needs. Initially, social workers provided resource knowledge and referral
and crisis intervention and then expanded
their role to many other areas. Important in
an emergency room setting is the ability to be
flexible, to do what is needed, and to work
with multiple situations simultaneously. Assertiveness and active intervention skills are
qualities necessary to playing a wide range of
roles.

Most cases of trauma and illnesses
have psychosocial problems and consequences, and social workers provide crisis
intervention to help alleviate the stress of the
immediate situation. Crisis intervention in an
emergency room environment has been well
defined as "the active entering into the life
situation of an individual, family or group to:
(a) cushion the impact of a stress that throws
the person (or persons) off balance; and (b)
help mobilize the resources of those affected
directly by the stress" (Resnick, Ruben, &
Ruben, 1975, p. 5).

Social workers interpret the interaction
of the cause of the stress with the strengths
and weaknesses of the patient. They construct a support system and consult with
physicians and nurses to develop realistic
plans for patients. They help the patient to
understand the implications of his or her
illness, bolster social support systems, and
refer the patient on to further appropriate
services.

Social work intervention in an emergency room is concerned with adequate assessment of the patient. The goal is to identify the primary diagnosis, not just the
presenting symptom. "This means that a
woman's broken arm may need to be explored as a case of domestic abuse, that a
seizure or pancreatitis may indicate an exploration of the patient's alcohol use, or that a
straight wrist laceration might require explo-

ration as a suicide attempt" (Clement & Klingbeil, 1981, p. 855). Identifying alcoholism, substance abuse, domestic violence, child abuse, elder abuse, sexual assault, and other high-risk situations and referring the patient to appropriate followup is imperative if the total patient is to be treated. Other staff in the emergency room, from admitting clerks to physicians and nurses, need to be educated to recognize domestic violence, substance abuse, and other psychosocial problems so that such problems will not be missed or denied.

The social worker in an emergency setting must know community resources and must network with a wide variety of community agencies and treatment programs to provide good patient care. Many patients will need followup with agencies ranging from mental health centers to visiting nurse associations to child protective services. In addition, specific services needed by emergency room patients include everything from simple transportation home, to the placing of children in foster care when a parent is hospitalized, to nursing home placement and other discharge planning with the patient and physician. Often assessment and discharge planning result in awareness of gaps in the community social service structure. Advocacy for new services in the community and with other agencies is challenging and important work for the social worker.

The Chronically Mentally Ill. As the chronically mentally ill are being deinstitutionalized and returned to the community, they are increasingly utilizing hospital emergency rooms for treatment. These patients use emergency rooms repeatedly and become "revolving door" patients; those who repeat most often are the most disturbed psychologically, socially, economically, and medically (Munves, Trimboli, & North, 1983). Social workers provide psychosocial evaluations, diagnosis, and referral for this population. Services include arranging acute psychiatric hospitalization, emergency housing, or mental health followup (Lipton, Sabatini, & Katz, 1983).

Working With Families. Emergency room social workers provide intervention and care for families of patients who are critically injured or who have died in the emergency room. The social worker gives the family information, clarifies the treatment process, and acts as a liaison between the medical staff and the family while the medical staff is involved in the patient's care. The social worker, working with families overwhelmed with grief, helps them throughout the hospital emergency room experience. Immediate intervention helps the patient and support system mobilize resources and prepares them for the role changes imposed by the patient's injury or illness. The worker assists the family with the emotional aspects of the immediate crisis and helps them begin to make practical decisions, such as contacting other relatives, organ donation, and funeral arrangements (Holland & Rogich, 1980).

Family counseling is a social work specialty that is used with a wide variety of cases in the emergency room. Families with drug-intoxicated or acting-out adolescents often present themselves for the first time in an emergency room setting and need crisis intervention and referral for ongoing counseling. The family must be included in planning for discharge so that they will have realistic expectations of how the patient will function and what care will be required. Often the spouse or family of a sexual assault victim or accident victim benefit greatly from having an opportunity to discuss their feelings and get information. They are thus enabled to provide realistic support for the discharge plan and to accept their own reactions and those of the patient brought on by the precipitating event.

Teaching and Consultation. Social workers in an emergency room perform an invaluable function by being available to the staff for formal presentations and informal consultations. For example, social workers give general in-service workshops on resources or specific presentations on such diagnostic categories as alcoholism. Informal consultation ranges from how to arrange to get a wheelchair for a patient to discussing staff reactions to a patient's death. Assisting staff to process their reactions to patients increases the team's functioning and helps prevent burnout.

Trends and Issues

The emergency room presents a unique opportunity for social work intervention with victims of domestic violence; but there must be a consistent social work program to identify a wide range of victims, from children to the elderly. Many of these patients are not admitted to the hospital and do not seek help in traditional social agencies. The capacity to identify, educate, and refer this patient population for help may prevent many more serious injuries and possible death in the future. Domestic violence is a major societal problem and has incalculable costs in the lives of many families (Klingbeil & Boyd, 1981). An assertive social work program helps victims deal with the psychological and social results of violence and assists them in obtaining legal and treatment services.

Such disenfranchised and disorganized patients as the chronic alcoholic, the confused elderly, and the chronically mentally ill increasingly utilize the emergency room as a revolving door mental health facility. These patients are making the only effort they can to be part of an increasingly fragmented and inaccessible treatment system. Service delivery and advocacy for this population are special historical missions for social workers, who continue to provide both leadership and treatment to ensure continuity of care. This involves establishing a network of flexible outreach services for patients who are not able to benefit from traditional agencies and who do not respond easily to scheduled appointments.

As cost containment measures continue to be the major thrust of organized health care, the role of social work at the entry point to the hospital is increasingly important. Patients without adequate social or other support systems must be identified as they are admitted. It is important to prevent inappropriate hospital admissions through the provision of such necessary outpatient community resources as nursing home placement and home health care. Appropriate provisions aid both the hospital's fiscal needs and the patient's health care needs. Advocacy for the patient will be needed when there are no appropriate community resources and hospitalization is the only recourse.

The emergency room provides an excellent opportunity to identify emerging community problems and unmet needs for treatment. In the past, research and clinical observation in the emergency setting have facilitated identification of such problems as drugs being currently abused in the community and the prevalence of teenage alcohol abuse.

Summary

Social work practice in a hospital emergency room will reflect the community that the hospital serves. As emergency rooms have increasingly become providers of primary medical care to the disenfranchised patient with multiple psychosocial problems, the emergency room social worker plays an increasingly important role in the interdisciplinary team. Individual and community problems will be focused on in the worker's practice. In response, the social worker must have a variety of skills in his or her practice repertoire, including rapid assessment, crisis intervention treatment, advocacy, knowledge of disease and trauma etiology, resource identification, referral, management, staff education, and consultation. Nothing less will permit the social worker to meet the clinical challenges and the needs of patients in the emergency setting.

JOAN L. CLEMENT
JACQUELINE S. DURGIN

For further information, see HOSPITAL SOCIAL WORK.

References

Clement, J., & Klingbeil, K. (1981). "The Emergency Room." *Health and Social Work, 6*(4), 835–905.

Holland, L., & Rogich, L. E. (1980). "Dealing With Grief in the Emergency Room." *Health and Social Work, 5*(2), 12–17.

Klingbeil, K., & Boyd, S. (1981). "Emergency Room Intervention: Detection, Assessment and Treatment." In A. Roberts (Ed.), *Battered Women and Their Families: Intervention Strategies and Treatment Programs.* New York: Springer Publishing Co.

Lipton, F. R., Sabatini, A., & Katz, S. E. (1983). "Down and Out in the City: The Homeless Mentally Ill." *Hospital and Community Psychiatry, 34*(9), 817–821.

Munves, P. I., Trimboli, F., & North, A. J. (1983). "A Study of Repeat Visits to a Psychiatric Emergency Room." *Hospital and Community Psychiatry, 34*(7), 634–638.

Resnick, H. L., Ruben, H. L., & Ruben, D. D. (1975). *Emergency Psychiatric Care: The Management of Mental Health Crisis.* Bowie, Md.: Charles Press Publishers.

Soskis, C. W. (1980). "Emergency Room on

Weekends: The Only Game in Town." *Health and Social Work*, 5(3), 37–43.

For Further Reading
Bergman, A. S. (1976). "Emergency Room: A Role for Social Workers." *Health and Social Work*, 1(1), 32–44.

EMPLOYEE ASSISTANCE PROGRAMS. See INDUSTRIAL SOCIAL WORK (OCCUPATIONAL SOCIAL WORK).

EMPLOYMENT. See UNEMPLOYMENT AND UNDEREMPLOYMENT; UNEMPLOYMENT COMPENSATION AND WORKERS' COMPENSATION PROGRAMS; WORK EXPERIENCE PROGRAMS; WORKFARE.

EPSTEIN, ABRAHAM. See biographical section.

ETHICAL ISSUES IN RESEARCH

Ethical issues in research are grounded in conflicts among values. These conflicts are expressed in many ways: the individual's right to privacy versus society's need to know, a need to rely on professional expertise versus an individual's desire to control his or her life, the virtue of behavioral change versus the undesirability of manipulation, openness and replication versus confidentiality, future welfare versus immediate relief, and more. Each decision made in research involves a potential compromise of one value for another. Researchers must develop procedures that minimize the risks to participants, colleagues, and society while maximizing the quality of information produced.

Research ethics are guidelines or codes that help reconcile values that are in conflict. Although ethical codes provide direction, the decisions made in research must be reached through the specific alternatives available to the researcher, who makes choices in each case by weighing the potential contribution of the research against the potential risks to the participants. Weighing these alternatives is mostly subjective, entails matters of degree rather than kind, and compares the experiences required in the research to those expected in everyday life.

Ethical codes stipulate responsibilities. The areas of responsibility reflect relationships in research. There are relationships with participants (subjects, clients, respondents), relationships with other colleagues and professional associations, and relationships to sponsoring agencies, the public at large, or the society. More discussion has been devoted to ethical issues involving participants than to the others. The amount of attention given to participants probably derives from the history of biomedical experimentation—from studies in which subjects have been exposed to serious risks and irremediable harm. The emphasis on participants in ethical codes and governmental regulations has been extended to all varieties of research. It has led to some misunderstandings and debates because it blurs the distinctions between biomedical experimentation on human subjects and social science research.

Social work researchers and other social scientists, partly because of developments in the medical sciences, have begun to address the particular ethical issues that arise in their work. Debates have taken place in relation to particular studies that illustrate alternative ethical resolutions of moral dilemmas. Key studies such as Milgram's (1963) research on obedience to authority, Humphreys's (1970) research on homosexuals, and Project Camelot, which involved a study whose aim was to prevent revolutions (Horowitz, 1967), have helped clarify the issues and suggest resolutions.

Risks Encountered in Research

There are three kinds of risks in social research. First, participants may be harmed as a result of their involvement; they may be killed, become stressed, feel guilty, experience a decrease in their self-respect or self-esteem, be treated unfairly, have benefits withheld, or experience minor discomfort. Second, professional relationships and the knowledge base may be damaged through the falsification of data, plagiarism, the abuse of confidentiality, and the deliberate violation of regulations. Third, problems for the community or society may arise because of the effect of cultural values and beliefs on the information that is attained and the impact of that information on the society. Ethical issues will be discussed for each of the three kinds of risk.

Potential Harm to Participants. Although documented cases of death in social research are rare, they have occurred (Appell, 1974; Warwick, 1982). Cases of physical abuse or injury also are rare; however, Zimbardo et al.'s (1973) simulation of a prison environment was prematurely stopped because volunteer prisoners suffered physical and psychological abuse at the hands of participants who were playing the role of guards.

Psychological harm is more frequently found. In a study of obedience to authority, Milgram (1963, p. 375) reported that "subjects were observed to sweat, tremble, stutter, bite their lips, groan, and dig their fingernails into their flesh. These were characteristic rather than exceptional responses to the experiment." Anxiety, depression, and other emotional disturbances have been reported. Humphreys's (1970) study of homosexuals in public restrooms revealed apprehensions about being identified.

Another kind of psychological harm involves feelings of guilt. Studies with the potential to create guilt include those that have participants administer electric shocks to fellow participants, beat prisoners while playing the role of guards, fail to help those in obvious need, steal money from a charity box, or participate in illegal acts brought on by experimental entrapment. Murray's (1980, p. 12) study of helping behavior reported that "virtually every subject who had not responded showed some anxiety to the experimental condition of watching the experimenter drop to the floor after receiving an apparently severe electrical shock."

In addition, social research has the potential to reduce self-esteem or self-respect. Walster (1965) manipulated female participants' feelings of self-worth by giving them a personality test with predesigned results to examine the effects on romantic liking. Although the women were debriefed after the study, Diener and Crandall (1978)

suggested that the participants who received the negative personality reports probably felt bad and those who received the positive reports may have been angry or embarrassed at having been fooled and perhaps disappointed that the report was not genuine. The dating ruse they used may have been even more harmful because college counseling centers report that college students frequently mention dating anxiety and low self-esteem because of a lack of dates as problems (Jaremko, 1984, pp. 422–423).

Relationships with others also may become damaged through research. For example, experimental team-building efforts in organizations can disrupt subsequent relationships on the job. When superiors, peers, and subordinates exchange open feelings and opinions about one another, resentments may fester and come back later to haunt participants. Similarly, individuals who volunteer to participate in sex research may find their morality called into question. Persons serving as informants in studies that become controversial may be subject to sanctions and even ostracized.

Participants in research may suffer career liabilities and other kinds of economic harm. Economic harm occurs when participants earn less money or pay more for things as a result of their involvement. The income maintenance experiments have been criticized for providing participants with short-term income that could encourage them to drop out of the labor force; thus, when the experiments came to an end, these individuals would be without jobs and ineligible for welfare.

Legal sanctions represent another kind of potential harm to participants in research. It is not unusual for information about illegal behavior to be collected in research. Except for special legal protection from subpoena, which can be obtained in certain cases by petition, social research is not protected by the law; because leaks can occur despite safeguards, there is a real potential for harm to some participants. Prosecution was a distinct possibility in the New Jersey–Pennsylvania income maintenance experiment when a prosecuting attorney who was interested in exposing welfare cheaters requested data about individual participants. Knowledge about illegal behavior also carries the potential for blackmail.

Minor feelings of irritation, frustration, or discomfort may be considered a form of psychological harm. Respondents can become irritated when an interviewer is abrasive. Frustration or annoyance may set in when questionnaires ask too many questions or irrelevant questions. Experiments sometimes involve minor physical discomfort, and subjects may be treated in a demeaning or mildly insulting manner.

Potential Damage to Professional Relationships. Damage to professional relationships occurs when the standards of professional behavior are violated. Violations include the falsification of data, plagiarism, the abuse of confidentiality, and the deliberate violation of regulations. Knowledge development depends on the accurate and careful collection of data, thorough analyses, and unbiased reports. The falsification of data ranges from fabrication through selective reporting; in clinical research, it can be directly harmful to individuals.

Burt (1937, 1940, 1966) claimed to have measured the I.Q.s of more than 50 sets of identical twins who were separated early in life. A high correlation between the separated twins' I.Q.s suggested a genetic basis for intelligence. After Burt's death, evidence of faked data was revealed. Coauthors were fictional characters, data were supplied for some of the twins who were never tested, and one set of results was used for more than one publication so there was perfect consistency among the publications. Eysenck (1977) and Jensen (1977) offered some defense for Burt, suggesting that the falsification of data may have been accomplished by research assistants rather than directly by Burt.

There is evidence that at least mild levels of falsification often occur. Azrin et al. (1961) stated that 15 out of 16 graduate students indicated they had successfully completed a study that was designed to be impossible to complete. Sometimes good intentions simply become misguided by boredom or the tedious nature of observation. For example, Hyman et al. (1954) reported a study in which one-fourth of the interviewers fabricated most of the data they collected and all the interviewers "fudged" some of the data. Smith, Wheeler, & Diener (1975) noted that research assistants view the alteration of data as similar to cheating on classroom tests—a common practice.

A study showing that the elderly are not poor and do not need Medicare failed to include minority groups, those on welfare, those in institutions, and those living in apartments (Diener & Crandall, 1978). In laboratory studies and field surveys, researchers can distort findings by the way they give instructions or ask questions. By emphasizing particular words or through body language, an interviewer may bias the information collected. As the case of "Clever Hans"—the Austrian horse apparently able to add numbers—exemplifies, even animal subjects can learn to read subtle body cues to alter their responses.

Research may be carried out with objectivity only to have the findings misreported or "adjusted" to fit the researchers' expectations. Several studies may be completed but only the one supporting a preferred theory may be submitted for publication. McNemar (1960) noted that findings are sometimes discarded as "bad data" when they fail to support hypotheses. A widespread practice is the calculation of numerous statistical tests but the reporting only of those that achieve significance. When Wolins (1962) requested original data from 37 studies, the researchers of 21 of the studies replied that the data had been misplaced or destroyed. Out of the seven published studies that Wolins reanalyzed, three revealed errors large enough to alter the conclusions drawn from the original data analysis.

Plagiarism is rare because it is usually readily apparent in the more actively pursued areas of research. Inadequate citation and the failure to give credit to the work of others are more pervasive problems. The pressure on academics to publish causes some academics to demand that their names be included on manuscripts written by their graduate students or to omit the names of graduate student co-workers from authorship. Fields (1984, p. 7) reported that an increasing number of complaints and inquiries have been received by the APA Ethics Committee from students who believe "they are being exploited in the process of grinding out publications for academic psychologists."

Taking advantage of privileged information or the violation of confidentiality are difficult to detect. Researchers openly discuss their ideas and share them through proposals. Proposals are reviewed by colleagues, university committees and administrators, and any number of outside researchers and practitioners serving on review panels. Articles prepared for professional journals also are subjected to a review process prior to publication. Hence, there are many opportunities for confidentiality to be abused.

Potential for Societal Harm. The designs and procedures used, the topics studied, and the results produced in research can harm as well as benefit the society. It seems a curious inconsistency that researchers list the potential benefits of their study to the society while limiting the potential harm only to individual participants. The use of deception in research undermines trust by undercutting the expectation that what another person says will be true. Similarly, the willingness of one person to help another in times of need or distress is compromised by studies that use deception to learn about helping behavior. The ethical balance of knowledge gained versus the potential for harm to society from deception has only recently shifted in favor of greater restrictions on the use of deception. Studies have been conducted in which stooges fall and release fake blood to test peoples' reactions to medical emergencies (Piliavin & Piliavin, 1972). Reviews of published research in psychology have indicated that 19–44 percent of the research reported included direct lying to participants (Menges, 1973). Gay (1973) wrote that a number of students did nothing when they saw a student shoot someone because they thought it was a psychology experiment.

Social research can raise questions about the legitimacy of institutions. Vaughan (1967, p. 6) reported on federal hearings held over the Wichita jury study in which Senator Eastland stated to one of the researchers: "Now, do you not realize that to snoop on a jury, and record what they say, does violence to every reason for which we have secret deliberations of a jury?" Similar issues have been raised about the harmful results of biased public opinion polls on the legitimacy of political elections. These polls are designed to provide support for a particular candidate or position. The net effect may undermine the legitimacy of the election process and the trustworthiness of the people running for office.

Research may harm special populations such as religious groups, racial or ethnic minorities, and individuals who are considered deviant. A focus on a category of people as "deviant" or "disadvantaged" highlights the problems of these people, and data may create or reinforce the conditions of victimization or scapegoating. For example, Moynihan (1965) wrote that the Negro family suffered from instability, a propensity to produce illegitimate children, and a matriarchal structure that had harmful effects on the children, especially boys. Ryan (1967, p. 463) disagreed with Moynihan's interpretation, stating that

> . . . it draws dangerously inexact conclusions from weak and insufficient data, encourages a new form of subtle racism that might be termed 'savage discovery', and seduces the reader into believing that it is not racism and discrimination, but the weaknesses and defects of the negro himself that accounts for the present status of inequality between negro and white.

The assumptions underlying the interpretations of and the conclusions drawn in research become fastened to concrete descriptions about who is responsible for certain conditions. The creation of stereotyped images is easy to find in research. Catholics have been portrayed as being less hard working than Protestants, as being at a disadvantage because of their conformity to an authoritarian church, and as having too many children, which makes it difficult for them to provide their children with the higher education necessary to compete effectively in contemporary society (Lenski, 1963, p. 344). Groups may protest a stereotype, as did Lopreato (1967) and others, of the image of Italians constructed by Banfield (1958). But the weaker the group, the less likely they are to protest or even be aware that there is something to protest.

Research may provide information to the more powerful groups in a society that helps to maintain their advantage. For example, Project Camelot was criticized because it was believed that the project, designed to prevent revolutions, would have undermined the political sovereignty of the Latin American countries studied. Some thought that the data produced would be fed to the Central Intelligence Agency to control certain affairs in those countries. Others drew less pernicious scenarios but still thought that the information would favor the United States in its relationship with the countries. It is important to note that Project Camelot was canceled because of its politically threatening nature rather than its lack of scientific merit, which provides another illustration of how research may be used at the discretion of those in power. Of course it is equally important to note that research has benefited the poor as well (Lampman, 1985; Macdonald & Sawhill, 1978; Wolf, 1984).

Minimizing Risks

Individual researchers, professional associations, and the government have taken steps to minimize the risks encountered in research. Most of their efforts focus on protecting participants. The ratio of risks to benefits is assessed, informed consent is required, research designs and procedures are built to minimize the potential for risks to occur, participants are screened, diagnostic studies are conducted, procedures are designed to assess and deal with potential harm, and proposals are reviewed by others. Each of these precautions minimizes the risk and, taken together, the prospects are good for only occasional injury.

Protecting Participants. Constructing a risk-benefit ratio for a proposed study is one way to assess its ethical soundness. If the expected benefits exceed the expected risks, the study is presumed ethical. The risk-benefit precaution is a modern version of the utilitarian notion that the end justifies the means. Its most direct application is when those who are exposed to the risks also receive the benefits. That is, a study designed to benefit the participants directly would be justified if the expected harm was outweighed by the expected benefits to the participants. The ratio is more difficult to justify when the participants are subjected to potential harm while the benefits are directed to other individuals or the society.

Risk-benefit ratios have several shortcomings. First, it is impossible to predict the benefits and risks of a particular study before its execution; studies are done because the outcome is unknown. Second, the possible risks and benefits are relative, subjectively assessed, and difficult to measure. Debates about the worth of findings illustrate the problem of quantifying and standardizing benefits. Third, calculating the ratio is complicated when society benefits to the detriment of individual participants. When there are no direct benefits to the participants, it is imperative that the participants fully understand and accept whatever risks there may be. Fourth, there is a conflict of interest in that the risk-benefit ratio is constructed by the researcher who, undoubtedly, believes the research is worth doing. It is reasonable to expect that the researcher would emphasize the importance of the study and play down its potential harm. Even though risk-benefit ratios are insufficient to determine ethical soundness, they provide a useful first step. It may be impossible for a risk-benefit ratio to justify a study, but it can provide enough information to warrant canceling a study.

A second precaution in conducting research is the use of informed consent. Informed consent refers to an individual's willingness to participate freely in a study after being fully informed about and thoroughly understanding what she or he will be asked to do and what the potential risks will be from participation. Thus, individuals who give informed consent have been made aware of the design and procedures with enough detail to exercise a rational decision to participate. The giving of informed consent also includes the knowledge that participation is voluntary and that one has the option of withdrawing from the study at any time. The more dangerous the study, of course, the more important it is to obtain informed consent. Informed consent is essential when participants are to be exposed to serious risks or required to suspend their individual rights, as in research on hypnosis or on the use of drugs. Although informed consent is often desirable and sometimes essential, it is not sufficient by itself to justify a study as ethical.

Another precaution involves constructing research designs and procedures in such a way as to achieve minimal goals while maximizing the protection of participants. The tasks involved include estimating the likelihood and the severity of injury, the probable duration of harmful effects and the extent to which they can be reversed, the probability of the early detection of injury, and the correspondence between potential harm from participation in the study versus the risks of everyday life. Studies are more ethically justified when the probability of harm is low, when only a minor or short-term injury is expected, when the expected harm can be reversed, when measures for the early detection of injury are in place, and when the risks are no greater than one could expect in the normal affairs of one's life. When the achievement of the study's goals entail risks that cannot be avoided, researchers can turn to natural field studies so the research itself does not promote the risks. For example, social work researchers who wish to study the effects of malnutrition could work in those areas of poverty where children are experiencing malnutrition (Klein, Habicht, & Yarbrough, 1973).

Screening individuals to participate in a study provides investigators with an opportunity to choose only those who show a high tolerance for the potential risks. For instance, Zimbardo et al. (1973) administered personality tests to volunteers and selected only those who scored within the normal range. This precaution, the researchers believed, would reduce the risks involved with the role-playing requirements of the study. Researchers who are interested in studying self-esteem might avoid using adolescents or persons with mental health problems. In excluding individuals from a study, it is important not to convey an impression of deviance, abnormality, or unacceptableness.

When the potential harm is uncertain, a useful precaution is a pilot study with follow-up diagnostic interviews in which the effects are assessed and advice is requested from the participants. A pilot study typically increases both the scientific rigor of the study and the protection of the participants. The inclusion of procedures to detect and deal with injury is an important precaution in any study in which the potential for harm can be imagined. Many studies, especially experiments, routinely debrief participants to assess and deal with any negative effects. In experiments using treatments that may have possible side effects, arrangements often are made with a clinical practitioner to accept referrals.

There is little evidence to suggest long-term harm from participation in social re-

search. Neither Milgram (1964) nor Ring, Wallston, & Corey (1970) found any long-term harmful effects from their shock-obedience studies; instead, the subjects they interviewed considered participation to have been a valuable experience. Zimbardo (1973, p. 243) also found no subsequent negative effects, even though one study (Zimbardo et al., 1973) was terminated prematurely because "volunteer prisoners suffered physical and psychological abuse hour after hour for days, while volunteer guards were exposed to the new self-knowledge that they enjoyed being powerful and had abused this power to make other human beings suffer." Clark and Word (1974) found, through a debriefing following their study on altruism, that one participant out of 68 continued to be upset but, that, after six months, no one reported negative aftereffects. Campbell, Sanderson, & Laverty (1964) found it difficult to reverse a conditioned fear, but the evidence leans strongly toward few, if any, long-term negative effects for carefully and ethically constructed studies.

Requesting others to review research proposals is a helpful precaution in minimizing risks. Different people with various positions and perspectives may identify potential injuries and perceive safeguards that were overlooked or could not have been known to the researcher. Of course, for many years, it has been required that proposals for funded research have to be reviewed by institutional review boards. Barber (1967) recommended that all research be reviewed by committees that have representatives from outside a particular profession.

Professional Codes. Two characteristics of professional codes help to clarify how such codes minimize risks in research. First, professional codes have been developed inductively from the research experiences of professionals. Because professionals have a wide variety of work experiences and reasonable people differ in the solutions they offer for particular problems, the standards reflected in ethical codes of professional associations tend to be abstract and related to particular circumstances. Second, professional codes strongly emphasize the responsibility of individual professionals for their research. These two characteristics distinguish professional codes from laws and governmental regulations as a means of protecting individuals and society from unnecessary harm.

The two characteristic features of professional codes—abstract relativity and the responsibility of researchers—are illustrated in the Code of Ethics of the National Association of Social Workers (NASW) (NASW, 1980, Part I, Section E, p. 4):

> Scholarship and Research—The social worker engaged in study and research should be guided by the conventions of scholarly inquiry.
> 1. The social worker engaged in research should consider carefully its possible consequences for human beings.
> 2. The social worker engaged in research should ascertain that the consent of participants is voluntary and informed, without any implied deprivation or penalty for refusal to participate, and with due regard for participants' privacy and dignity.
> 3. The social worker engaged in research should protect participants from unwarranted physical or mental discomfort, distress, harm, danger, or deprivation.
> 4. The social worker who engages in the evaluation of services or cases should discuss them only for professional purposes and only with persons directly and professionally concerned with them.
> 5. Information obtained about participants in research should be treated as confidential.
> 6. The social worker should take credit only for work actually done in connection with scholarly and research endeavors and credit contributions made by others.

Professional codes tend not to specify penalties for the violation of principles. The major penalty is expulsion from the professional association whose code was violated. One-half the 24 codes reviewed by Reynolds (1975, pp. 563–611) included a reference to expulsion. What is interesting is that none of the codes reviewed by Reynolds specified any benefits for those who complied with the codes. The low level of penalties and rewards suggests that professional codes may not be taken too seriously—that the threat of expulsion may carry little weight.

It is possible, for example, to achieve a respectable career without being a member of NASW or any other professional association. Professional codes seem to be a necessary but not sufficient condition of professional self-regulation.

Governmental Regulation. Governmental regulations, like state and federal laws, are designed to protect or advance the interests of society and its individuals. Researchers who do not take certain required precautions are prevented from certain activities on the grounds that failure to follow the law or regulations increases the risk of harm to an individual or to the society. Governmental regulations tend to be absolute in their requirements and are characterized by what Fletcher (1966) called "legalism." According to Fletcher (1966, p. 18) the principles of governmental regulations, "codified in rules, are not merely guidelines or maximums to illuminate the situation; they are *directives* to be followed."

Regulations must be written in language that is specific enough to allow accurate judgments of compliance or noncompliance with their requirements. They do not invite an evaluation of their moral correctness; they are written to be obeyed. Moreover, obeying a law or regulation does not require individuals to consider the underlying ethical issues or moral principles. It is assumed that moral principles were evaluated by those who wrote the law or regulation and that observing the law will result in ethically acceptable behavior.

However, legalism recognizes that laws or regulations can be fallible. Therefore, although obeying the law does not require a consideration of ethical issues, neither does it prevent one from considering them. The important difference between regulations and professional codes is captured in the response made to a law that appears to require an ethical violation. The professional who adheres to the code may violate the law and pay the price, while the legalist must obey the law and try to change it. Principle 3.d of the American Psychological Association's Ethical Principles (1953, p.14) states that "when . . . laws, regulations, or practices are in conflict with Association standards and guidelines, psychologists make known their commitment to Association standards and guidelines and whenever possible work toward a resolution of the conflict." The term "resolution" is not defined, which implies that, under certain circumstances, it might be reasonable to go to jail for contempt of court rather than to release confidential data on participants in a research project. Cases involving scholars whose data were subpoenaed are discussed by Carroll and Knerr (1976).

McCarthy (1981) and Gray (1982) described the development of federal regulations on the welfare of human subjects in research and the controversies surrounding the regulations. Most of the controversy stemmed from the extension of policies or rulings that were generated from abuses in biomedical research to social research or from specifically funded research projects to all projects under the auspices of institutions receiving federal funding. The debates ensued over 15 years, from 1966 to 1981, when the current regulations of the Department of Health and Human Services (DHHS) were adopted. These regulations, carved out of the controversy and written with the benefit of extensive input from researchers were intended to end the controversy while not compromising the protection of human subjects.

The regulations apply only to research conducted or funded by DHHS. But researchers who receive funds from DHHS must provide a statement showing how the institution they work for protects the rights and welfare of human subjects, irrespective of their source of funding. The regulations do not require prior approval by an institutional review board for research not funded by DHHS. Institutions are urged, however, to use institutional review boards and other appropriate procedures to protect human subjects in all research conducted under their auspices. Institutional review boards are given wide latitude for the research they review. The regulations specify particular categories of research as being exempt: research that is conducted in established or commonly accepted educational settings; research that involves the anonymous use of educational tests; research that includes anonymous survey or interview procedures except when there is a risk of criminal or civil liability or the research deals with sensitive behavior, such as illegal conduct, drug use, or sexual behavior; research in which public behavior is observed, with the same exceptions noted under survey and interview studies; and research that involves the anonymous collection or study of publicly available data, documents, records, pathological specimens, or diagnostic specimens (*Federal Reg*

ister, January 26, 1981). The exemptions have been expanded to cover research and demonstration projects involving social security programs (*Federal Register*, March 4, 1983).

The current regulations appear to clarify earlier points of confusion and contention. They indicate that no research involving human subjects should be exempt from federal regulation solely because it belongs to a particular discipline. The regulations acknowledge that much, if not most, social research involves no more risk than what ordinarily is encountered in daily life and that the requirements of participation are sufficiently understood by the public to reduce the need for federal regulations. As a result, research that falls in the exempt categories is not required to be reviewed and approved by an institutional review board.

Many federal and state departments have policies regarding the protection of human subjects. The National Commission for the Protection of Human Subjects of Biomedical and Behavioral Research summarized the policies of federal agencies in a report written in 1978. It noted that most governmental regulations are modeled after those issued by DHHS and that agency rulings, principally those of DHHS, have been the predominant form of governmental regulation. Furthermore, laws passed to govern social research are neither restrictive nor specific. Professionals resist control by laws because laws tend to blur particular circumstances in specific cases. They fear that the resolution of ethical issues through legal statutes will compromise the quality of knowledge developed by exaggerating the potential for risk in social research.

Governmental regulation ought to remain stable for a number of years. It is possible that the revolutionary changes in information technology will inspire renewed attempts to promote legalism in governmental regulation. But today's researchers have learned much from the issues and debates of the late 1960s and 1970s, and it is likely that their responsive and sensitive awareness of ethical issues will work to maintain a balance between self-imposed constraints, guidance from professional associations, and governmental regulations.

DAVID F. GILLESPIE

For further information, see Appendix 1: NASW
CODE OF ETHICS; LEGAL ISSUES AND LEGAL
SERVICES; PROFESSIONAL LIABILITY AND
MALPRACTICE; RESEARCH IN SOCIAL WORK;
VALUES AND ETHICS.

References

American Psychological Association. (1953). *Ethical Standards of Psychologists*. Washington, D.C.: Author.

American Psychological Association. (1973). *Ethical Principles in the Conduct of Research with Human Participants*. Washington, D.C.: Author.

Appell, G. N. (1974). "Basic Issues in the Dilemmas and Ethical Conflicts in Anthropological Inquiry." *Module*, *19*(1), 1–28.

Azrin, N. H., et al. (1961). "The Control of the Content of Conversation Through Reinforcement." *Journal of Experimental Analysis of Behavior*, *4*(1), 25–30.

Banfield, E. (1958). *The Moral Basis of a Backward Society*. New York: Free Press.

Barber, B. (1967). "Experimenting With Humans." *The Public Interest*, *6*(1), 91–102.

Burt, C. L. (1937). *The Backward Child*. New York: Appleton-Century-Crofts.

Burt, C. L. (1940). *The Factors of the Mind*. London, England: University of London Press.

Burt, C. L. (1966). "The Genetic Determination of Differences in Intelligence: A Study of Monozygotic Twins Reared Together and Apart." *British Journal of Psychology*, *57*(1), 137–153.

Campbell, D., Sanderson, R. E., & Laverty, S. G. (1964). "Characteristics of a Conditioned Response in Human Subjects During Extinction Trials Following a Single Traumatic Conditioning Trial." *Journal of Abnormal & Social Psychology*, *68*(6), 627–639.

Carroll, J. D., & Knerr, C. R. (1976, Fall). "The APSA Confidentiality in Social Science Research Project: A Final Report." *P.S.*, 416–419.

Clark, R. D., & Word, L. E. (1974). "Where is the Apathetic Bystander? Situational Characteristics of the Emergency." *Journal of Personality & Social Psychology*, *29*(3), 279–287.

Diener, E., & Crandall, R. (1978). *Ethics in Social and Behavioral Research*. Chicago: University of Chicago Press.

Eysenck, H. (1977). "The Case of Sir Cyril Burt: On Fraud and Prejudice in a Scientific Controversy." *Encounter*, *48*(1), 19–24.

Federal Register. (1981, January 26). *46*(16), Section 46. 101–46. 124, pp. 8386–8392.

Federal Register. (1983, March 14). *48*(9), Section 46. 101(a), pp. 9269–9270.

Fields, C. M. (1984). "Professors' Demands for Credit as Co-authors of Students' Research Projects May be Rising." *Chronicle of Higher Education*.

Fletcher, J. (1966). *Situation Ethics*. Philadelphia: Westminster Press.

Gay, C. (1973, November 30). "A Man Collapsed Outside a UW Building. Others Ignore Him. What Would You Do?" *University of Washington Daily*, pp. 14–15.

Gray, B. H. (1982). "The Regulatory Context of Social and Behavioral Research." In T. L. Beauchamp et al. (Eds.), *Ethical Issues in Social Science Research*. Baltimore, Md.: Johns Hopkins University Press.

Horowitz, I. L. (Ed.). (1967). *The Rise and Fall of Project Camelot*. Cambridge, Mass.: M.I.T. Press.

Humphreys, L. (1970). *Tearoom Trade: Impersonal Sex in Public Places*. Chicago: Aldine Publishing Co.

Hyman, H. H., et al. (1954). *Interviewing in Social Research*. Chicago: University of Chicago Press.

Jaremko, M. E. (1984). "Stress Inoculation Training for Social Anxiety. With Emphasis on Dating Anxiety." In D. Meichenbaum & M. E. Jaremko (Eds.), *Stress Reduction and Prevention* (pp. 419–450). New York: Plenum Press.

Jensen, A. R. (1977). "Did Sir Cyril Burt Fake His Research on Heritability of Intelligence?" *Phi Delta Kappan*, *58*(6), 471–492.

Klein, R. E., Habicht, J. P., & Yarbrough, C. (1973). "Some Methodological Problems in Field Studies on Nutrition and Intelligence." In D. J. Kallen (Ed.), *Nutrition, Development and Social Behavior*. Washington, D.C.: U.S. Government Printing Office.

Lampman, R. J. (1985). *Social Welfare Spending: Accounting for Changes from 1950–1978*. New York: Academic Press.

Lenski, G. (1963). *The Religious Factor: A Sociologist's Inquiry*. Garden City, N.Y.: Doubleday & Co.

Lopreato, J. (1967). *Peasants Know More*. San Francisco: Chandler Publishing Co.

Macdonald, M., & Sawhill, I. V. (1978). "Welfare Policy and the Family." *Public Policy*, *26*(1), 89–119.

McCarthy, C. R. (1981). "The Development of Federal Regulations for Social Science Research." In A. J. Kimmel (Ed.), *Ethics of Human Subject Research* (pp. 31–39). San Francisco: Jossey-Bass.

McNemar, Q. (1960). "At Random: Sense and Nonsense." *American Psychologist*, *15*, 195–300.

Menges, R. J. (1973). "Openness and Honesty Versus Coercion and Deception in Psychological Research." *American Psychologist*, *28*(12), 1030–1034.

Milgram, S. (1963). "Behavioral Study of Obedience." *Journal of Abnormal & Social Psychology, 67*, 371–378.

Milgram, S. (1964). "Issues in the Study of Obedience: A Reply to Baumrind." *American Psychologist, 19*(10), 848–852.

Milgram, S. (1974). *Obedience to Authority.* New York: Harper & Row.

Moynihan, D. P. (1965). *The Negro Family: The Case for National Action.* Washington, D.C.: Office of Planning and Research, U.S. Department of Labor.

Murray, T. (1980, April). "Learning to Deceive." *Hastings Center Report, 10*(2), 1–16.

National Association of Social Workers. (1980). *Code of Ethics.* Silver Spring, Md.: Author.

National Commission for the Protection of Human Subjects of Biomedical and Behavioral Research (1978). *Special Study: Implications of Advances in Biomedical and Behavioral Research.* Washington, D.C.: U.S. Government Printing Office.

Piliavin, J. A., & Piliavin, I. M. (1972). "Effect of Blood on Reactions to a Victim." *Journal of Personality & Social Psychology, 23*(3), 353–361.

Reynolds, P. D. (1975). "Ethics and Status: Value Dilemmas in the Professional Conduct of Social Science." *International Social Science Journal, 27*(4), 563–611.

Ring, K., Wallston, K., & Corey, M. (1970). "Mode of Debriefing as a Factor Affecting Subjective Reaction to a Milgram-Type Obedience Experiment and Ethical Inquiry." *Representative Research in Social Psychology, 1*(1), 67–88.

Ryan, W. (1967). "Savage Discovery: The Moynihan Report." In L. Rainwater & W. L. Yancey (Eds.), *The Moynihan Report and the Politics of Controversy* (pp. 453–478). Cambridge, Mass.: M.I.T. Press.

Smith, R. E., Wheeler, G., & Diener, E. (1975). "Faith Without Works: Jesus People, Resistance to Temptation, and Altruism." *Journal of Applied Social Psychology, 5*(4), 320–330.

Vaughan, T. R. (1967). "Governmental Intervention in Social Research: Political and Ethical Dimensions in the Wichita Jury Recordings." In G. Sjoberg (Ed.), *Ethics, Politics, and Social Research* (pp. 50–77). Cambridge, Mass.: Schenkman Publishing Co.

Walster, E. (1965). "The Effect of Self-Esteem on Romantic Liking." *Journal of Experimental Social Psychology, 1*(2), 184–197.

Warwick, D. P. (1982). "Types of Harm in Social Research." In T. L. Beauchamp et al. (Eds.), *Ethical Issues in Social Science Research*, (pp. 101–124). Baltimore, Md.: Johns Hopkins University Press.

Wolf, D. A. (1984). "Changes in Household Size and Composition Due to Financial Incentives." *Journal of Human Resources, 19*(1), 87–101.

Wolins, L. (1962). "Responsibility for Raw Data." *American Psychologist, 17*(9), 657–658.

Zimbardo, P. G. (1973). "On the Ethics of Intervention in Human Psychological Research: With Special Reference to the Stanford Prison Study." *Cognition, 2*(2), 243–256.

Zimbardo, P. G., et al. (1973, April). "The Mind is a Formidable Jailer: The Pirandellian Prison." *New York Times Magazine, 122*, (Sec. 6), pp. 38–60.

ETHICS. See Appendix 1: NASW Code of Ethics; ETHICAL ISSUES IN RESEARCH; SOCIAL PROBLEMS AND ISSUES: THEORIES AND DEFINITIONS; VALUES AND ETHICS.

ETHNIC-SENSITIVE PRACTICE

The effort to incorporate understanding of the lifestyles and needs of diverse ethnic groups into the theories and principles that guide social work practice has been long standing and persistent.

In *Social Diagnosis*, Richmond (1917) called upon caseworkers who were dealing with recent immigrants to be careful not to think of them as "members of a colony or of a nationality having . . . fixed characteristics" (p. 382). To ignore national and racial characteristics and attempt to apply those of the larger population would be an error, she cautioned.

Prior to World War II, social workers, along with the rest of American society, were concerned with the process of absorbing immigrants of diverse cultural backgrounds. Much attention was paid to the cultures of immigrants, although the prevailing "melting pot" ideology presumed that cultural differences were of a transient nature. This emphasis on differences persisted until the 1954 Supreme Court school desegregation decision, which tended to deemphasize cultural uniqueness and to encourage the integration of diverse groups into the mainstream (Schlesinger & Devore, 1979).

Furthermore, egalitarian motives led many social workers to conclude that attention to lifestyle differences related to ethnicity and social class was somehow incongruent with the profession's commitment to equality and the uniqueness of each individual. Not until the 1960s, following the emerging militancy of segments of the black community, was there an extensive effort to deal with these issues. In 1973, the Council on Social Work Education mandated that instruction concerning the lifestyles of diverse ethnic groups become an integral part of social work education (CSWE, 1973). The Council's 1984 Curriculum Policy Statement reiterated and expanded on this position (CSWE, 1984). Since the mid-seventies, greater attention has been paid to ethnic issues, and efforts to develop practice-related theory and principles have accelerated.

Defining Ethnic-Sensitive Practice

Ethnic-sensitive practice is based on the view that practice must be attuned to values and dispositions related to ethnic group membership and position in the social stratification system (Devore & Schlesinger, 1981). Green (1982) contends that efforts at problem resolution must be attuned to ethnically distinctive values and community practices.

Ethnic-sensitive practice involves the concept of the "dual perspective"—a "conscious and systematic process of perceiving, understanding, and comparing simultaneously the values, attitudes, and behavior of the larger societal system with those of the client's immediate family and community system" (Norton, 1978, p. 3). The concept derives from the view that all clients are a part of two systems: (1) the dominant system, referred to as the sustaining system, which is the source of power and economic resources, and (2) the nurturing system, composed of the physical and social environment of family and community. Devore and Schlesinger (1981) point out that as various groups

> send their children to school, become ill, encounter marital difficulties, and generally live their lives, they bring with them a unique ethnic and class tradition. . . . As they confront "helpers" or "caretakers" they expect . . . that these aspects of their being . . . will be understood [whether or not they are aware

that] some of their strengths and tensions are related to this aspect of their lives.

> Those charged with the responsibility of . . . helping have the obligation to be sensitive to that possibility. (p. 32)

Ethnic Groups and Ethnicity

Most analysts agree that an ethnic group consists of those people who share a unique social and cultural heritage and a historical past (Gordon, 1964). A number of factors are thought to contribute to ethnicity—the associated sense of peoplehood and identification with the group. These include national origin, religion, a common language, and race.

Minorities of Color and Ethnic Groups.

The meaning of the term "minority" has been subject to considerable scrutiny. In this discussion, it is identified with those people who tend to be located "at the lowest end of the spectrum of power and advantage" (Hopps, 1983, p. 77). Those who currently occupy this position are in large measure set apart by the combination of racism and poverty. Included are many blacks, American Indians, Native Alaskans, Mexican Americans, and Puerto Ricans. Some analysts also include Asian Americans in this group. Hopps (1982, 1983) has suggested that these groups, identified in the past as "racial minorities," be referred to as "people of color," or "minorities of color." Minorities of color also share the characteristics identified as those of ethnic groups in general.

Ethnic-sensitive social workers must be attuned to the special dispositions of all ethnic groups and have a particular responsibility to be aware of the oppression experienced by minorities of color.

Relationship Between Social Class and Ethnicity.

Seeking to account for differences in behavior and feeling evidenced by people who occupy the same social class level but who are members of different ethnic groups, Gordon (1964) proposed that the point at which social class and ethnic group membership intersect be characterized as "ethclass." This point of convergence of social class and ethnic group membership generates identifiable dispositions and behaviors. Devore and Schlesinger (1981) have described these dispositions as the *ethnic reality*. It is characterized by deeply ingrained feelings and actions on such matters as appropriate child-rearing practices or proper care for the aged, or dispositions that derive from oppression.

Ethnic-Sensitive Social Work Practice

Ethnic-sensitive practice builds on (1) social work values; (2) awareness of the ethnic reality; (3) components of a professional perspective conceptualized as the "layers of understanding" for social work practice; and (4) current social work practice. A series of assumptions, practice principles, and interventive strategies is involved. The model introduces no new practice principles or strategies; rather it involves the adaptation of prevailing social work principles and skills to take account of the ethnic reality.

Layers of Understanding. It is characterized by deeply ingrained feelings and actions on such matters as appropriate child-rearing practices or proper care for the aged. Included are attitudes such as whether children are to be handled in an authoritative or permissive manner or whether responsibility for the elderly rests at all cost with the family or local community.

The following three layers of understanding, integral components of all practice, must be consciously understood and internalized by the ethnic-sensitive social worker.

1. Knowledge of Human Behavior. Familiarity with the range of theories presented to explain individual, institutional, community, and organizational behavior is essential if workers are to take account of the unique ways in which diverse ethnic groups, including minorities of color, encounter various systems and problems.

2 Self-Awareness. The disciplined and aware self remains one of the profession's major tools. Involved is the process of discovering "*Me*—not always nice, sometimes judgmental, prejudiced and non-caring" (Devore & Schlesinger, 1981, p. 83) and making use of such insight to further empathic skills. In ethnic-sensitive practice the process is expanded to include the question, "Who am I in the ethnic sense?" Thinking through and feeling the impact of one's own ethnicity on one's perception of self and others enhances the capacity to "tune in " to the ethnic reality.

3. Impact of the Ethnic Reality on Daily Life. The ethnic reality seeps into the substance of psychological and social being in myriad ways. Ingrained views about the capacity to master nature or to succumb to uncontrollable forces may manifest themselves in divergent responses to family crises, to illness, and to death. The professional helper may be viewed as one who is appropriately called upon to aid in problem solving, or as an intruder who has no business interfering with intimate matters that had better remain within the family. Members of those ethnic groups that are particular victims of racism and poverty experience persistent barriers as they struggle to achieve minimal standards of living and to enlarge the range of opportunities open to them. Whatever their level of oppression or opportunity, individuals draw on the sustenance and comfort of shared traditions exemplified by the psychic bonds of a common language, history, and sharing of important rituals and celebrations.

Assumptions of Ethnic-Sensitive Practice. The following assumptions are drawn from an examination of the ways in which an ethnic group's history, values, and perspectives affect individuals and the group as a whole. They are: (1) individual and collective history have a bearing on the generation and solution of problems; (2) the present is most important; (3) nonconscious phenomena affect individual functioning; and (4) ethnicity is a source of cohesion, identity, and strength, as well as a source of strain, discordance, and strife.

Each ethnic group and its members have an ethnic history with roots in the past that may affect perceptions of current problems. For example, in the absence of expected intergenerational support, the Slavic elderly may feel ill at ease or, in extreme cases, devastated. The individual and collective history of many blacks leads to the expectation that family resources will be available in times of trouble; yet the movement of the younger generation into the middle class may inhibit its capacity to act in terms of a powerful tradition.

The present, however, is most important. It is in response to present pressures that some Irish people and some American Indians resort to excessive use of alcohol. Some American Indian and black youths respond to current oppression by committing suicide and homicide. Many Mexican American and Puerto Rican women feel tension as they attempt to move beyond traditionally defined sex roles into the mainstream as students and paid employees.

Practice Principles

The Route to the Social Worker. The paths to social work services have been conceptualized by Devore & Schlesinger (1981) on a continuum ranging from totally coercive to totally voluntary. Members of oppressed ethnic groups are most likely to encounter social workers via coercive routes, being directed by the schools, the courts, or other authoritative institutions. Those with greater resources are more likely to be voluntary clients.

Simultaneous Attention to Individual and Systemic Concerns. Ethnic and class history and traditions highlight institutional sources of oppression. Out of this emerges the principle that social work is a problem-solving endeavor that must pay simultaneous attention to individual systemic concerns.

The models most consonant with the principles of ethnic-sensitive practice are the following (with references to representative examples): the problem-solving models (Perlman, 1957); the systems models (Pincus & Minahan, 1973); the structural models (Middleman & Goldberg, 1974); select segments of task-centered practice (Reid & Epstein, 1972; Reid, 1978); and institutional change models (Rothman, 1979).

Cognitive, Affective, and Behavioral Skills. Ethnic-sensitive practice involves the capacity to adapt the cognitive, affective, and behavioral skills of social work in keeping with an understanding of clients' ethnic reality.

Cognitive Areas. At a cognitive level, ethnic-sensitive practice involves knowledge of the rationale behind the stages of the helping process characteristic of most models of practice. The preparatory work involved in identifying the characteristics of the community, the agency context, and the nature of the ethnic populations that tend to be served is crucial. Social workers should make efforts to know something about indigenous helping networks, the use of formally organized helping systems, and the ways in which various ethnic groups are likely to define and cope with problems.

Also essential is attention to such matters as whether there are ethnic-based traditions about discussing intimate concerns with a stranger (albeit a professional) or about avoiding eye contact with strangers. Also involved is knowledge of how to adapt strategies such as "launching the interaction process," "stage setting," "tuning in," and displays of warmth, empathy, and genuineness in keeping with clients' ethnic reality.

Affective Areas. Workers should continually seek to enhance their emotional appreciation of matters such as ethnic-based dispositions and fears associated with seeking or receiving help. The fact that so many clients—especially minorities of color—have not sought services voluntarily calls for ongoing effort to tune in to the affective component. Sharpening ethnic self-awareness and developing the capacity to respond to others' sense of self are ongoing processes.

Behavioral Areas. In the final analysis, ethnic-sensitive practice is manifested at the level of daily practice behavior. It represents the capacity to draw on assumptions and facts about diverse ethnic groups in problem solving. Social workers should demonstrate the capacity to move with each client at a pace and in a direction determined by the client's perception of the problem, with an understanding that that perception is likely to be affected by the client's ethnicity. In some situations, the process may involve the worker's giving up cherished notions about the value of verbal exression of tension-laden emotions, or about the superiority of modern psychiatry over the ministrations of the folk healer. The worker must learn to respect the view of many American Indians, Asian Americans, eastern Europeans, and others that to express one's negative feelings may be more painful than the trauma that evoked those feelings. The folk healer's capacity to smooth troubled family situations or to alleviate symptoms that do not respond to conventional medical treatment may never cease to surprise. Finally, ethnic-sensitive practice means vigilant attention to systemic sources of oppression that would deny minorities and others access to the goods, services, work, and esteem that are consonant with professional social work values.

Ethnic Competence in the Human Services

There is a substantial congruence between the model of ethnic-sensitive practice described here and the view that services should be provided in a culturally acceptable manner that enhances the "sense of ethnic group participation and power" (Green, 1982, p. 4). Human services systems and policies, according to Green, are obliged to meet the client "not only in terms of the specific problem presented but in terms of the client's cultural and community background" (p. 4). Green presents a model of "help-seeking behavior" that adapts insights and procedures developed by medical anthropologists. The model includes: (1) focus on culturally based criteria of problem definition; (2) recognition of group-specific linguistic categories involved in labeling problems; and (3) incorporation of lay strategies into problem resolution.

Critical to ethnic-sensitive practice is a "performance-level response of cultural awareness [that] represents a depth of comprehension of others that surpasses the usual injunction about patience, genuineness and honesty in client-worker relationships" (Green, 1982, p. 52). This capability is termed ethnic competence, which is the ability "to conduct one's professional work in a way that is congruent with the behavior and expectations that members of distinctive culture recognize as appropriate among themselves" (p. 52). Ethnic competence requires the social worker to be aware of his or her own cultural limitations, to be open to cultural differences, to possess a client-oriented systematic learning style, to utilize the client's cultural resources, and to acknowledge the client's cultural integrity. Suggested ways of achieving ethnic competence include background preparation, use of cultural guides, and participant observation in diverse communities.

If social workers are to be responsive to the special needs and dispositions that derive from ethnic group membership and minority status, prevailing social work knowledge and skill must be adapted to take account of a group's history, its particular coping styles, and its stance on using professional services.

Wynetta Devore
Elfriede G. Schlesinger

For further information, see INTERGROUP RELATIONS; MINORITIES OF COLOR; RACIAL DISCRIMINATION AND INEQUALITY; WHITE ETHNIC GROUPS.

References

Council on Social Work Education. (1973). *Handbook of Accreditation Standards and Procedures*. New York: Author.

Council on Social Work Education. (1984). *Handbook of Accreditation Standards and Procedures* (rev. ed.). New York: Author.

Devore, W., & Schlesinger, E. G. (1981). *Ethnic-Sensitive Social Work Practice*. St. Louis, Mo.: C. V. Mosby Co.

Gordon, M. M. (1964). *Assimilation in American Life*. New York: Oxford University Press.

Green, J. W. (1982). *Cultural Awareness in the Human Services*. Englewood Cliffs, N.J.: Prentice-Hall.

Hopps, J. G. (1982). "Oppression Based on Color." *Social Work, 27*(1), 3–5.

Hopps, J. G. (1983). "Minorities: People of Color." In *1983–84 Supplement to the Encyclopedia of Social Work* (17th ed., pp. 76–83). Silver Spring, Md.: National Association of Social Workers.

Middleman, R., & Goldberg, G. (1974). *Social Service Delivery: A Structural Approach to Practice*. New York: Columbia University Press.

Norton, D. G. (1978). *The Dual Perspective: Inclusion of Ethnic Minority Content in the Social Work Curriculum*. New York: Council on Social Work Education.

Perlman, H. H. (1957). *Social Casework*. Chicago: University of Chicago Press.

Pincus, A., & Minahan, A. (1973). *Social Work Practice: Model and Method*. Itasca, Ill.: F. E. Peacock Publishers.

Reid, W. J. (1978). *The Task-Centered System*. New York: Columbia University Press.

Reid, W. J., & Epstein, L. (1972). *Task-Centered Casework*. New York: Columbia University Press.

Richmond, M. E. (1917). *Social Diagnosis*. Glencoe, Ill.: Free Press.

Rothman, J. (1979). "Three Models of Community Organization Practice, Their Mixing and Phasing." In Cox et al., *Strategies of Community Organization* (3d ed.). Itasca, Ill.: F. E. Peacock Publishers.

Schlesinger, E. G., & Devore, W. (1979). "Social Workers View Ethnic Minority Teaching." *Journal of Education for Social Work, 15*(3), 20–27.

EXISTENTIAL APPROACH

After World War II, existentialism emerged as a major philosophical perspective in both Europe and America. The fascination with such concepts as the absurd, dread, and despair was related to disappointment and disillusionment with rationalism and pragmatism and their cohorts—technology, industrialism, and mechanization. Hopes for happiness, security, and an enlightened society were shattered by the recurring terrors of the modern age.

Since Kierkegaard and Nietzsche in the 19th century, existentialists have been saying that human dignity and personal meaning and destiny lie in freedom of choice and the assumption of responsibility for one's actions. Personal truth is a matter of subjectivity, an awareness that the individual alone finally decides the meaning of any situation. It is by living in the world and by engaging oneself with it—especially with other people—that one comes to know oneself. This differs from cognitive models that view human beings as objects that can be comprehended analytically in terms of instincts, behaviors, roles, and so on. The existentialists have reintroduced the human spirit into the modern age.

Alienation results from a flight from dread, or existential anxiety. This stems from a refusal to accept and live out of the finite human condition. According to Reinhold Niebuhr (1949), human beings hide from their finite nature in two ways. They can deny reality, claiming to be infinite rather than finite, independent rather than dependent, powerful rather than weak. This renders absolute what is relative and contingent in the world and in essence makes each individual his or her own god. Such is the way of pride and pretension. The second form of flight is sensuality, which can include not only the abuse of sexuality but a total immersion in the processes, activities, and interests of the world. Here awareness is both restricted and dulled, and a pseudosecurity is maintained for a time.

The helping professions can fall victim to anomie, or alienation. They can also contribute to alienation among the people they serve. The existential truth and mission of social work were clear to the "friendly visitor" of yesteryear. Social work was the profession helping the widest variety of troubled people—the chronic misfits and the poor, lost, condemned, and institutionalized. The profession looked for ways to normalize their fears and inspire hope in their troubled lives, yet it often had to settle for conveying compassionate understanding and affirmation. Social workers knew they operated from schemes of human knowledge that were limited and often erroneous for the situation. With few time-tested, valid methods of helping, their best tools were their human sensitivity and caring.

Contrast this image with that of today's social work clinical sophisticates. They work mostly with middle-class people like themselves. They embrace and defend theories of practice on the basis of elitist tradition or bandwagon popularity, despite current research that questions the validity of such theories. They often play the role of guru-expert (maturity guide), although their personal lives are seldom happier or more enlightened than those of their clients (Krill, 1986).

Existential social work presents neither a new theoretical model nor a system of "existential interventions." Rather, it is a perspective that acts as a gadfly to awaken and prod the profession toward correction.

Theory

Existential themes were developed in the writings of such psychotherapists as Rollo May, Viktor Frankl, Abraham Maslow, Gordon Allport, and William Offman. Social work writers on this subject included Kirk Bradford, Andrew Curry, Gerald Rubin, Robert Sinsheimer, John Stretch, David Weiss, and this author. For social workers, perhaps the most pertinent writing in recent years has been that of Ernest Becker, an anthropologist. His book *The Denial of Death* (1973) is a reevaluation of Freudian thinking from an existential viewpoint, drawing from the writings of Otto Rank and Søren Kierkegaard. Because both the functional and dynamic perspectives of social work theory incorporated Rank and Freud, Becker's integration of the two is especially pertinent.

The present author conceptualized five themes of special significance for social work from this literature: (1) aiding the process of disillusionment and self-deception, (2) discovering the necessity and potential meaning

of suffering, (3) recognizing freedom of
choice and its accompanying responsibility,
(4) seeing the centrality of dialogue—the interplay of personal identity and growth with
the quality of one's personal relationships—
and (5) understanding the importance of personal commitment and its relation to integrity
(Krill, 1969).

The existential perspective of social
work can be described in relation to nondoing
and doing activities. Nondoing activities emphasize the worker's nondiagnostic, nonprog-
nostic, nonmodel, nontechnician, nonguru,
and nonrescuing orientation. In contrast to
the sophisticated medical model, this orientation implies a more humble sense of not
knowing what is best for clients. In contrast
to social engineering, which seeks to maneu-
ver toward a "sane society," it emphasizes
the individual's use of family, significant others, neighborhood, and community to specify
problems and potential solutions. This
nondoing stance reflects the existentialist's
scorn for systems, categories, and prescriptions when it comes to understanding human
beings.

In view of these nondoing activities,
the doing ones become clearer. The existentialist agrees that social work assessment
should focus on the interrelationship between
person, problem, and situation. The existentialist emphasizes, however, how these three
areas of knowledge interrelate in a given
client's unique and specific situation. To put
it simply, a client's symptoms or problems
can be seen as obvious, understandable expressions of a basic life style. Human beings
are responsible for conceptualizing and ordering their lives, and there are no problem-
free life stances. Because symptoms express
these stances, they are commonly seen as
means of denying responsibility for some
aspect of one's lifestyle.

Psychological and social theories, then,
are of secondary, not primary, importance in
assessment. This is in contrast to traditional
preoccupations with generalizations and
classifications of symptoms, behaviors, and
"pathological developmental issues." Knowledge derived from any of the theories may
help to sensitize social workers to possible
meanings in a given person-problem-situation
configuration, but no particular theory is idol-
ized as "the truth." Exploration and understanding of a client's problem are mutual

activities involving the worker, the client,
and often the client's significant others; they
do not result from theory imposition.

Practice

Far more important than formalized
conceptual knowledge is human sensitivity
and the use of intuition and imagination.
Social workers develop their capacities for
compassion and spontaneity through experiences with varied client situations. A compatible heightening of self-awareness is also required. The existentialist emphasizes the
social worker's authenticity, vitality, and
personal uniqueness because the sensitized
worker is far better able to normalize clients'
problems while inspiring hope for change.

Techniques aim at engaging clients'
spontaneity and creative efforts in relation to
their problems. In addition to expressing
compassion and inspiring hope, social workers are engaged in activating choice. Here the
existentialist generally shares the behaviorist's preference for techniques that research
has shown to be useful (Fischer, 1978).

Such knowledge is not seen as objecti-
fied and finalized in any sense, but rather as
providing a direction that can help counter
the biases and theoretical myths that commonly color practice. Problems usually reveal clients' values and the complexities of
their lifestyles. Although social workers
refuse the role of guru, they nonetheless use
the counseling arena to identify value issues
that appear to relate to the client's problems.
These usually reflect the five existentialist
themes whose significance for social work
was cited earlier. Clients may deceive themselves and others about the nature of their
needs and failures and about the sources of
their real guilt and anxiety. Clients may doubt
their ability to choose and fear accepting
responsibility for the choices they make. Clients often believe that pain and suffering
indicate immaturity or failure; therefore they
prefer to avoid rather than confront their
pain. Clients too often assume that identity is
a matter of self-understanding and self-
actualization; thus they fail to appreciate the
importance of high-quality relationships in
their lives. Clients imagine that meaningful
living results from conformity to and fulfillment of social roles and expectations posited
by others. They may have no understanding

of the interrelationship of integrity, commitment, and a sense of personal destiny.

Existential dialogue is a creative interchange between people. Social workers stimulate dialogue by being sensitive to spontaneity and vitality, both in themselves and in clients' responses. The most critical form of therapeutic dialogue has to do with managing motivations, especially fear and hope, and with sidestepping clients' control maneuvers. To release creative reflection and exploration, the relationship must move beyond manipulation, games, and role posturing.

It is preferable that such dialogue occur between clients and their natural significant others rather than in the artificial confines of the counseling situation. High priorities of treatment, therefore, are the affirmation, restoration, and repair of clients' key relationships or assistance in building new ones. This interpersonal emphasis differentiates existential social work from existential psychology.

The interpersonal emphasis also affects the selection of a treatment modality. Family or marital therapies have top priority. When exceptions must be made, group therapy is the choice. Individual therapy comes third, and even then, emphasis remains on the client's relationship with others in daily life. Within individual or group therapies, the primary concern is that clients' therapeutic gains are demonstrated in their daily relationships (Krill, 1978).

The existentialists' belief in the mutuality of growth through dialogue is reflected in the kinds of clients they are likely to work with. Although they are comfortable with middle-class clients, their creative preference is for clients quite different from themselves—social work's chronic, at-risk population. They reject the dehumanizing methods so often used in "helping" such groups and utilize research to upgrade the quality of service to these people.

DONALD F. KRILL

References

Becker, E. (1973). *The Denial of Death*. New York: Free Press.

Fischer, J. (1978). *Effective Casework Practice*. New York: McGraw-Hill Book Co.

Krill, D. F. (1969). "Existential Psychotherapy and the Problem of Anomie." *Social Work, 14*(2), 33–49.

Krill, D. F. (1978). *Existential Social Work*. New York: Free Press.

Krill, D. F. (1986). *The Beat Worker*. Washington, D.C.: University Press of America.

Niebuhr, R. (1949). *The Nature and Destiny of Man*. New York: Charles Scribner's Sons.

For Further Reading

Bradford, K. (1969). *Existentialism and Casework*. Jericho, N.Y.: Exposition Press.

Frankl, V. (1967). *Psychotherapy and Existentialism: Selected Papers on Logotherapy*. New York: Simon & Schuster.

Maslow, A. (1962). *Toward a Psychology of Being*. New York: Van Nostrand Reinhold Co.

May, T. (1967). *Psychology and the Human Dilemma*. New York: Van Nostrand Reinhold Co.

Sinsheimer, R. (1969). "The Existential Casework Relationship." *Social Casework, 50*(2), 67–73.

Weiss, D. (1975). *Existential Human Relations*. Montreal, Canada: Dawson College Press.

FAMILY: CONTEMPORARY PATTERNS

Since the 1970s, both the structure and the functioning of American families have continued to undergo rapid and far-reaching changes that were set in motion some three decades ago. These changes have been occurring to some degree in all the major Western industrialized countries. They are reflected in changing norms and values about the family, increased levels of divorce, later marriages, decreased fertility, increased longevity, increasing remarriage, increased alternatives to marriage, increasing adult singlehood, and a wide variety of family structures. Through all these changes, however, family life continues to be a central unit of social organization in all strata of American society.

In *Marriage and Family: Coping with Change*, Cargan (1985) observed:

> An examination of textbooks in introductory sociology would reveal that society consists of various institutions designed to meet its basic needs. The major ones are economics, education, the family, politics and religion. The most pervasive of these is considered to be the family because all persons are born into some form of family. Through its role of socializer of the young, the family transmits society's norms and values and thus becomes society's "traditional culture-bearer."

> This outcome of family function makes it difficult to accept and adjust to social changes that are, in turn, affecting family relations. Thus, controversies abound in regard to gender roles, sexual behavior, alternatives to traditional marriage, family roles, childbearing, living with children, and even the future of the family. (p. xi)

This article provides an overview of the American family, reflecting the major dimensions of these changes and controversies. It addresses three questions: What are the major trends and social forces shaping family life in America? What are the major trends among families in reaction to these forces? What are the consequences of the changing nature of family life for family members and for society?

Social Forces Affecting Family Life

As Cargan indicated, the family is only one of the major institutions of contemporary society, all of which are being affected by similar basic forces, although not always in the same ways. Certainly the response patterns of different institutions vary enormously. Nevertheless, in all industrial societies to some degree, the family institution is affected by changes in the basic structure of society brought on by changing technology and expanding knowledge and exchange of information.

The sociologist Bell (1973) described modern society as "post-industrial society" and set forth the major characteristics of this era that set it apart from past eras. In a similar vein, Toffler (1980) described the major changes in society as three waves of civilization ushered in respectively by the Agricultural Revolution 10,000 years ago, the Industrial Revolution 300 years ago, and the present "third wave" civilization ushered in by the new era of technology beginning about 30 years ago. For Toffler, each of these eras had profound and different effects in shaping different types of institutional structures to meet the changing functions assigned to them:

> A powerful tide is surging across much of the world today, creating a new, often bizarre environment in which to work, play, marry, raise children, or retire. In this bewildering context, businessmen swim against highly erratic economic currents; politicians see their ratings bob wildly up and down; universities,

hospitals, and other institutions battle desperately against inflation. Value systems splinter and crash, while the life boats of family, church, and state are hurled madly about.

Looking at those violent changes, we can regard them as isolated evidences of instability, breakdown, and disaster. Yet, if we stand back for a longer view, several things become apparent that otherwise go unnoticed. To begin with, many of today's changes are not independent of one another. Nor are they random. For example, the crack-up of the nuclear family, the global energy crisis, the spread of cults and cable television, the rise of flex-time and new fringe benefits packages, the emergence of separatist movements from Quebec to Corsica, may all seem like isolated events. Yet precisely the reverse is true. These and many other seemingly unrelated events and trends are interconnected. They are, in fact, parts of a larger phenomenon: the death of industrialism and the rise of a new civilization. (pp. 1–2)

But unlike some other futurists, and unlike many commentators on the American family, Toffler holds that these cataclysmic changes need not be thought of as simply destructive of established institutions; although mandating changes in those institutions, these forces may indeed enhance their functioning if the changes are properly perceived and adjusted to. "Many of the very same conditions that produce today's greatest perils also open fascinating new potentials." It is Toffler's view that "in the very midst of destruction and decay, we can now find striking evidences of birth and life." In a seminal statement of his own beliefs, Toffler holds that "with intelligence and a modicum of luck—the emergent civilization can be made more sane, sensible, and sustainable, more decent and more democratic than any we have ever known" (p. 3).

For institutions such as the family, however, and for individuals caught up in the changes they are undergoing, it is sometimes difficult to see the forest of Toffler's vision for the trees of daily events. This is in part because social change takes a long time to perceive and to understand and even longer to learn how to manage.

Naisbitt has made an effort to synthesize the major changes taking place in society and to state them as ten major trends. In his book *Megatrends* (1984, p. xvii), he sets forth the following major trends that are affecting

all aspects of contemporary life. These trends are:

- from industrial society to information society
- from forced technology to high tech–high touch
- from national economy to global economy
- from short term to long term
- from centralization to decentralization
- from institutional help to self-help
- from representative democracy to participatory democracy
- from hierarchies to networking
- from north to south
- from either-or to multiple option.

By far the most profound trend according to Naisbitt is the transition from an industrial society to an information society. He observes:

It always surprises me that so many people passionately resist the notion of an economy built on information and despite a wealth of evidence, deny that the industrial era is over. (p. 1)

Dating the onset of the new information era at about 1956, Naisbitt continues:

Outwardly, the United States appeared to be a thriving industrial economy, yet a little noticed symbolic milestone heralded the end of an era: in 1956, for the first time in American history, white-collar workers in technical, managerial, and clerical positions outnumbered blue-collar workers. Industrial America was giving way to a new society, where, for the first time in history, most of us worked with information rather than producing goods. . . . The next year came Sputnik, and the age of global communication was upon us. (p. 2)

According to Naisbitt, Toffler, Bell, and others, the nature of these technological changes meant that the American family would never be the same.

How then do these massive technological changes affect the structure and function of American families? Toffler (1980) suggested that agricultural society demanded large extended families, whereas industrial society demanded small nuclear families. He suggests that the new society requires still different family constellations.

As industrial society began to replace

agricultural society, Toffler holds, families felt the stress of change. "Within each household, the collision of wave fronts took the form of conflict, attacks on patriarchal authority, altered relationships between children and parents" (p. 28).

As economic production shifted from the field to the factory, the family no longer worked together as a unit. To free workers for factory labor, key functions of the family were parceled out to new, specialized institutions. Education of children was turned over to schools; care of the aged was turned over to poorhouses, old age homes, or nursing homes. Above all, the new society required mobility. It needed workers to follow jobs from place to place. Toffler continues:

> Burdened with elderly relatives, the sick, the handicapped and a large brood of children, the extended family was anything but mobile. Gradually and painfully, therefore, the family structure began to change. Torn apart by the migration to the cities, battered by economic storms, families stripped themselves of unwanted relatives, grew smaller, more mobile, and more suited to the needs of the new techno-sphere. . . . The so-called nuclear family—father, mother and a few children with no encumbering relatives—became the standard, socially approved modern model in all industrial societies, whether capitalist or socialist. (p. 28)

If this analysis of the origin and function of the nuclear family, which is supported by a wide range of social scientists and historians, is correct, it can be seen that the nuclear family form, which has come to be worshiped in America, may not have been made in heaven after all. It may not have been the original form of family life and may not be the last. Even more important, it may not be the most functional for a given people, for a given time, or a given era.

Yet what is also clear from this analysis is that elements of eras linger on even after their dominance has passed. Moreover, elements of a new era appear long before it becomes dominant. Thus the theory of cultural lag, propounded by Ogburn (1964), helps to explain how mixed family forms may exist at the same time in different parts of a particular country and among different people in a particular country. While the industrial North in the United States was moving rapidly in step with the Industrial Revolution prior to the Civil War, for example, large sectors of the agrarian South were still enmeshed in the agricultural era. Later, while the more privileged sectors of the dominant white society, even in the South, were experiencing the effects of the industrial era, large sectors of the subjugated black community were still bound up in the remnants of the agricultural era. Similarly, different structures of family life adapt to the technological forces of society to best meet the functions required of them by their members and by society. If these adaptations are seen to be in keeping with the basic survival needs of a particular people at a particular time, it will not be surprising that different structures may predominate among different people in the same place at the same time. The operative question is not what forces are affecting the total society, but rather how they affect a given people in society at a given time.

Studies of black families in the United States, for example, have shown how families are influenced in both structure and functioning by the systems and forces of contemporary society as much as by their particular history and cultural values. Black families are shaped not by how these forces affect other families or all families, but by how these forces affect black families, given such intervening forces as race, region, religion, and social class. It is not surprising or mystical, therefore, that even the three basic family structures identified in the black community—nuclear, extended, and augmented—are not so much reflections of the radical identity of black families as they are manifestations of the place these families occupy in the wider social system (Billingsley, 1968). The same is true for families of other ethnic, racial, religious, and cultural backgrounds.

This line of reasoning suggests that black families have clung to the extended family form longer than white families in part because of the conditions of life that particularly affect them. It further suggests that white families have clung to the nuclear family form longer than other families in part because of the conditions of life they faced. It suggests as well that all families will abandon the nuclear and extended family forms for what are called "augmented" and "attenuated" family forms—and other forms as well—when and if they are affected in reality by the influences of the postindustrial, third wave, high technology, communication, professional, and service-oriented society.

Finally, this reasoning suggests that the wide variety of family structures among different people and among the same people at different times may be both normal and normative to the extent that these structures reflect the forces of technology, social pressures, and opportunities that affect particular people at particular times. Hence, rather than searching for the pathology of different family forms or collective handwringing over the passing of others, it is more constructive to seek better understanding of how various technological and social forces require different family forms and how various family forms function to meet the needs of family members and the basic requirements of the given society.

Technological and social forces affect groups that are differently situated in the social structure in different ways. Although this is most obvious in different ethnic, racial, religious, and regional groupings, it should be noted that different generations within the same ethnic group, for example, also constitute different cultural groups. Thus the family forms that meet the needs of one generation may not meet those of another, even if the two generations share the same house. In a time of rapid transition, this is indeed a hard lesson for families to learn. Yet, as Masnick and Bane (1980) have pointed out, major insights may be gained from understanding that three different generations now exist side by side in the United States, separated by a narrow age gap but with different world views, social perspectives, and social needs. They describe this mixture of generations as "explosive":

By 1980, in a fashion similar to the alignment of the sun, earth, and moon during a solar eclipse, three very different generations of adult Americans are exerting their forces simultaneously to pull and tug at the very foundations of traditional family and household structure. The older generation, born 1920 or before, and age sixty or over in 1980, survived the Great Depression. Most had been through two world wars, many were immigrants or sons and daughters of immigrants, and all had been born at a time when over half of the U.S. population was rural. They married late and had small families. Today, many live alone.

The middle generation, born between 1920 and 1940—ages forty to fifty-nine in 1980—entered adulthood during a period of optimism and affluence. And, as if to avenge the injuries history bestowed on the preceding generation, its members married early, bought large cars and houses, gave witness to civil rights and had babies. Many in this generation are now in the empty-nest stage of their lives, and many are divorced.

The younger generation is made up of the babies born during the "boom" years that began in World War II. Although many in this group of today's under 40-year-olds have only just begun their adult lives, they have already had a profound influence on American family life by virtue of their numbers and life-styles. They have begun to settle down in the central cities and in small towns, two areas abandoned by their parents. More of the women have put their independence and work before marriage and childbearing. Both the men and women are better educated than earlier generations. In these and other ways, this younger group of adults stands in sharp contrast to its parents and grandparents. (p. 11)

Against this background, then, the second question addressed in this article arises—namely, What are the major trends and patterns manifested by contemporary American families as they seek to adapt to current technological and social forces? In this light, the breakdown of the nuclear family should not be viewed as a breakdown in the family per se and certainly not as the disappearance of the family, but rather as a transition in the family structure of a given people at a given time in response to the conditions of life as they attempt to meet the needs of their members and the requirements of their society.

Major Trends in Family Structures

Students of the family in social work and the social sciences are generally agreed that family structure follows family function and not the other way around. Sussman (1977) defined family functions and then laid out a typology of contemporary and emerging family structures:

The family functions as a facilitating, mediating, and confronting system for its members who have different aspirations, capabilities, and potential. Families adapt to urban or industrial life and simultaneously influence the development, structure, and activities of contemporary social institutions and organizations. Largely because of variations in family structure and the life cycle, families differ in how well they adapt to the complexities of modern life, their efforts to mitigate the demands of nonfamily groups, and their ability to influence the behavior of outside organizations such as the school, welfare agency, or factory. Consequently, the main tasks of families are to develop their capacities to socialize children, to enhance and facilitate the competence of their members to cope with the demands of other organizations in which they must function, to use these organizations for the benefits they provide, and to provide for their members' satisfactions and a mentally and physically healthy environment that is intrinsic to the well-being of the family. (p. 357)

To meet these functions, a variety of structures have evolved. Sussman delineated six traditional forms of family structure and the approximate percentage of the population they comprised in 1976 (p. 359): nuclear intact family (37 percent), nuclear dyad (11 percent), nuclear remarried family (11 percent), single-parent family (12 percent), kin network (4 percent), and single and related families (19 percent). Sussman also listed four "emerging experimental forms" of family structure that accounted for 6 percent of the population in 1976 (p. 359): monogamous commune families, group-marriage commune families, unmarried parent and child families, unmarried couple and child families, and cohabitating dyads.

Sussman concluded:

> Individuals move in and out of all these experimental forms and may eventually opt for a traditional nuclear form. The innovations in communication, relating, role modeling, and parenting developed in these families have influenced the ideology and practice of traditional forms. This author views this as a positive catalytic process that enables the traditional nuclear family to adapt to the changes in the values and life-styles of the 1970s. (p. 363)

An insightful projection of changes in American family structures between the years 1960 and 1990, designed by Masnick and Bane (1980), is presented in Table 1. The table shows among other changes that the proportion of families headed by married couples will sustain a 20 percent decline over the 30-year period, falling from roughly 75 percent of all American families in 1960 to 55 percent in 1990. All other family structures are projected to show substantial increases. A striking finding is that among all types of family structures, the proportion of families with children under 15 years of age will show a dramatic decline.

Consequences for Family Functioning

What, then, are the consequences for family functioning of these vast changes in basic technology and family structure? An overview has been provided by Kirkendal and Gravatt (1984), who asked a variety of family specialists to speculate on the dimensions of family life by the year 2020. Clanton (1984) observed the following, writing from the year 2020:

> Family life today is diverse, and most people are relatively tolerant of those whose values and behavior are different from their own. There is very little conflict about these matters because sex, love, marriage, and family are viewed as private matters. On this nearly all Americans now agree. After failing to ban abortion by constitutional amendment, many persons with traditional values have agreed that sexual and family issues should be viewed as private matters. Feminists softened their attack on marriage and the family and agreed that privacy is the best policy in such matters once their first effort to win ratification on the Equal Rights Amendment ended in defeat.
>
> Leaders of the gay and lesbian community agreed that privacy in sexual matters is the best policy when they were unable to get laws passed that would guarantee homosexual rights. The majority of Americans simply grew tired of topics such as abortion, sexual preference, and orgasm count; these topics largely dropped out of casual conversation. Today most people discuss these matters primarily with family and close friends. Rather than demand that sex be denied, hidden or persecuted as did some late Victorians, or that sexual style be publicly celebrated (as did some gays and swingers in the 1960's and 1970's), most Americans today treat sexuality as a private matter. As a result, public controversy about abortion and homosexuality has diminished in the last thirty years. (p. 38)

Considering the wave of violence unleashed against abortion clinics in 1985 and the intensified assault on homosexual conduct by the so-called Moral Majority, also in 1985, it may be that Clanton's assessment—

Table 1. Types of Households in 1960 and 1975 and Projected for 1990 (Percentages)

Household Type	1960		1975		1990	
Married Couples (total)	74.8		65.4		54.9	
No children under 15 present	33.3		34.0		27.2	
Children under 15 present	41.5		31.4		27.7	
Other Male Head (total)	8.1		10.9		16.0	
Never married	3.2		4.7		6.8	
Previously married	4.9		6.2		9.2	
No children under 15 present		4.4		5.6		8.3
Children under 15 present		0.5		0.6		0.9
Other Female Head (total)	17.2		23.6		29.0	
Never married	2.8		4.4		6.3	
No children under 15 present		2.6		3.7		5.0
Children under 15 present		0.2		0.7		1.3
Divorced/Separated	4.7		8.2		10.8	
No children under 15 present		2.6		4.2		5.8
Children under 15 present		2.1		4.0		5.0
Widowed	9.7		11.0		11.9	
No children under 15 present		8.6		10.2		11.2
Children under 15 present		1.1		0.8		0.7

Source: Adapted from G. Masnick and M.J. Bane, *The Nation's Families: 1960–1990* (Cambridge: Joint Center for Urban Studies of Massachusetts Institute of Technology and Harvard University, 1980), p. 57. Used with permission.

looking back from just 35 years in the future—is overoptimistic.

Still, a wide variety of functional and adaptive patterns characterize family life in the 1980s. Two-career families, commuter families, the empty nest syndrome and the reverse empty nest syndrome, remarried families, and stepfamilies have all become common, and many of these adaptive patterns have produced new national organizations such as the Stepfamily Association of America.

Two-Career Families. One of the most profound trends among American families in the 1980s has been the increase in two-career families. It was estimated that by 1984, 25 million American families had husbands and wives working, and that in nearly 5 million of these families, the wife was seriously committed to her career ("Focus on Families," 1985, p. 4).

Commuter Families. Gerstel and Gross (1983) described the relatively new phenomenon of "commuter marriage," in which one or both partners are experiencing opposing pulls from commitment to individual career development on the one hand and commitment to family on the other. What is it that holds commuter families together? Gerstel and Gross (p. 180) find three factors to be characteristic of these marriages: an equal commitment on the part of both partners to their individual and separate careers, limited local career opportunities that force one of the partners to live away from home, and a strong attachment and preference for living together.

Empty Nest Syndrome. The empty nest syndrome continues to be a trend in the 1980s, with children growing up and leaving home at earlier ages than previously. But a newly observed phenomenon among American families is the "empty nest syndrome in reverse," with older children coming back to live with their parents. This occurs primarily because of divorce and separation among young couples, the economic pressures brought on by the housing shortage, and unemployment. Experts predict that this reverse syndrome is a growing phenomenon with important potential for both harmony and conflict.

Clifford Swenson ("Focus on Families," 1985, p. 7), a psychologist at Purdue University, urges parents to limit the amount of time an adult son or daughter may stay with them and suggests that during that time, the returning family member should be a fully contributing member of the family economically and socially. Moreover, other experts see an essential need for ample space and open communication to make this family form endurable ("Focus on Families," 1985, p. 7).

Remarriage. Goetting (1985, pp. 323–340) describes what she has found to be the six "stations" of remarriage. They are (1) emotional remarriage, "the often slow process by which a divorced person reestablishes a bond of attraction, commitment, and trust with a member of the opposite sex," (p. 323) (2) psychic remarriage, whereby a person begins to change conjugal identity from a single individual to a couple, (3) community remarriage, whereby a couple establishes relationships with people outside the marriage, (4) parental remarriage, which involves the acceptance and incorporation of the children of the other spouse, (5) economic remarriage, whereby the couple agrees to patterns of earning, sharing of productivity, and consumption, and (6) legal remarriage, which involves settlement of financial and other responsibilities toward children and former spouses. The problems associated with each station are often distinct, but just as often they overlap from one station to another. Stations do not follow in any particular order, but most remarried couples experience most of them at some time during their remarriage.

Stepfamilies. One of the many consequences of the high rate of remarriage has been the evolution of stepfamilies. More than 30 million adults are part of stepfamilies and nearly 20 percent of all American children live in such families. This family type was increasing in early 1985 at a rate of 1,800 people per day ("Focus on Families," 1985, p. 5).

Elizabeth Einstein of the Stepfamily Association of America observed that it takes between 4 and 7 years for new stepfamilies to adjust to their new identity. She has also identified five myths that make it difficult and must be overcome to make the transition successfully. These are the myths (1) that

making a stepfamily is simple and instantaneous, (2) that stepfamilies operate in the same way as simple nuclear families, (3) that members of stepfamilies love each other instantly, (4) that part-time stepfamily living is easier than full time, and (5) that stepfamilies form more easily after a death than a divorce ("Focus on Families," 1985, p. 6).

In the July 1984 issue of *Family Relations*, Pepernow summarized the seven stages of stepfamily development. These are (1) fantasy, during which one member of the adult pair fantasizes rescuing children from the excesses of the other or fantasizes about the inadequacies of the former spouse and other matters, (2) assimilation, during which stepfamily members attempt to carry out the above fantasies, (3) awareness, by which stepfamily members come to a realization of their new situation, (4) mobilization, in which energies are focused on solving joint problems, (5) action, by which couples begin to be able to work together effectively, (6) contact, which involves increasing intimacy among members, and (7) resolution, a final stage at which the stepfamily feels solid and reliable.

Family Violence

Some aspects of contemporary family life have been reflected in increased public awareness of family violence. The attention given in early 1985 to a high-level government official who was accused of and later admitted to beating his wife over 18 years of their marriage dramatized the presence of family violence among high-income white American families. Media accounts of family violence had already called attention to the widespread incidence of this phenomenon. Levy (1984) published a book designed to teach young people even before they get married that family violence is widespread, serious, and prevalent among people of all socioeconomic backgrounds.

American families have increasingly become centers of violent behavior. Three types of intrafamily violence have come to public attention since the 1970s. These are violence and abuse directed toward young children by their parents and caretakers, toward one spouse by another, and toward elderly relatives in the home by their offspring. Straus, Gelles, and Steinmetz (1980) reveal the appalling statistics gathered by a research program on family violence at the

University of New Hampshire. On an annual basis, more children under age 5 were killed by family violence than by tuberculosis, polio, whooping cough, measles, diabetes, rheumatic fever, and appendicitis put together. Moreover, they point out that at least 2 million married people have threatened their spouses at least once with a handgun, and more than a third of all children in the nation have been severely attacked or injured by a sibling. The cause of this violence is still obscure, but it occurs in all socioeconomic classes and racial and ethnic groups.

Future of the American Family

By mid-decade, the 1980s had seen dramatic and, no doubt, long-term changes in both the structure and functioning of American families in all sectors and strata of society. These changes resulted from the changing technological, economic, and demographic forces in society. The struggle for permanence seemed clearly to be losing ground under these strains, and yet the family, in one form or another, continued to provide a goal toward which most Americans aspired, often again and again and again. Moreover, happiness had not completely vanished as a consequence of changes in family life. Stinnett et al. (1981) of the University of Nebraska found that five characteristics and qualities distinguished happy families from others: (1) spending substantial amounts of time together, (2) insisting on continuing communication among all members, (3) showing appreciation for each other, (4) dealing with crises positively, and (5) maintaining an intellectual, emotional, social, and financial commitment to family life as a form of social organization (pp. 33–42).

In his provocative study "The Myth of the Declining Family," Caplow (1985) concluded:

The Middletown family is in exceptionally good condition. Tracing the changes from the 1920's to the 1970's, we discovered increased family solidarity, a smaller generation gap, closer marital communication, more religion, and less mobility. With respect to the major features of family life, the trend of the past two generations has run in the opposite direction from the trend that nearly everyone perceives and talks about. . . . We have noted the likelihood that the trend for the entire country is similar. These conclusions obviously are contrary to the prevailing belief that the family has been declining for a long time, that its survival past the present generation is in doubt, and that massive intervention is required to save it. (p. 15)

Perhaps a less rosy but more balanced view of the future of the American family is presented by Orthner and Boyd (1984) in "Beyond the Melting Pot: Nationalism, Militarism and the Family." They describe the social context of the changing forces that affect contemporary family life and the death of the melting pot concept, which insisted on the simple nuclear family as the form to which all people should aspire, arguing that it has been replaced by a more pluralistic conception of family life.

The melting pot as a version of equality and cultural homogeneity has been replaced in the twenty-first century by an emphasis on distinctiveness and an appreciation of cultural heterogeneity. Factors influencing the demise of the melting pot dream were changing immigration patterns, the shifting balance of control over the world's resources, declining supplies of energy and natural resources, and finally a decline in the world's image of America as exclusive in providing a superior quality of life. American families of the twenty-first century are experiencing the effects of the changing way in which Americans view themselves and are viewed by the world community. Acceptance of diversity in life-styles, in cultural and racial heritage, in values, in language, and in family forms is now the norm. (p. 270)

Orthner and Boyd identify national, political, military, and economic changes as helping to shape these new values and patterns of family life.

Alan's (1984) article titled "2020 and Beyond" contains the following observations:

The formal tie called marriage has been largely dispensed with. People move freely between different kinds of relationships. Most spend a portion of their lives in a group relationship, but the major share is spent with single primary partners. The attraction of a committed intimate relationship is most powerful. There seems to be no substitute for the security and satisfaction of having a reciprocal caring relationship with one primary individual. Even with all the flexibility available and essential in a space-age society, the most common form of intimate relationship remains monogamy. We expect this trend to continue well beyond 2020. (p. 293)

Family Policy

One recent trend in American family life has been the increasing attention paid to families at all levels of government. This attention has been uneven, however. The present author's work has been allied with efforts to generate a national family policy, partly reflected in a series of hearings in 1973 before Senator Walter Mondale's Subcommittee on Children and Youth of the Senate Committee on Labor and Public Welfare. A recent, cogent analysis of the trends in public policies affecting American families has been produced by Zigler et al. (1983). They conclude that for family policy to develop more effectively, a greater collaboration is necessary between social scientists who are students of the family and who have pertinent data and analyses and elected and appointed public officials who have the power to translate these into legislation.

But the idea that the national government would provide some significant leadership in the enhancement of family life through a coordinated family policy—an idea that seemed filled with promise during the 1970s—had all but faded in the 1980s. This may be a dramatic illustration that the American family has fallen to the megatrends outlined by Naisbitt (1984). Still, a number of family watchers had not given up hope. In "Social Forces and the Changing Family," Clanton (1984) predicted the following for 2020:

Because of the full employment economy and the National Health Insurance System, very few American children today are without adequate food, shelter and medical care. As the number of children in orphanages and reform schools declined, these formerly dismal institutions underwent a renewal. (p. 41)

Once again the futurists run the risk of minimizing the retrogression in public school policy ushered in during the late 1970s and early 1980s, some of which will surely be felt for decades to come. Still, one can hope for a turnaround in the latter part of the 1980s and the decades beyond. If Clanton is correct in his predictions, however, public policy in the United States will reflect a philosophical commitment to the enhancement of national family life for the first time in 2 centuries—a

commitment calling for a strong social work involvement.

ANDREW BILLINGSLEY

For further information, see AGED; CHILDREN; FAMILY LIFE EDUCATION; FAMILY: MULTI-GENERATIONAL; FAMILY: NUCLEAR; FAMILY: ONE PARENT; FAMILY: STEPFAMILIES.

References

Alan, S. E. (1984). "2020 and Beyond." In L. A. Kirkendal & A. E. Gravatt (Eds.), *Marriage and the Family in the Year 2020*. Buffalo, N.Y.: Prometheus Books.

Bell, D. (1973). *The Coming of Post-Industrial Society: A Venture in Social Forecasting*. New York: Basic Books.

Billingsley, A. (1968). *Black Families in White America*. Englewood Cliffs, N.J.: Prentice-Hall.

Caplow, T. (1985). "The Myth of the Declining Family." In L. Cargan (Ed.), *Marriage and Family: Coping with Change*. Belmont, Calif.: Wadsworth Publishing Co.

Cargan, L. (Ed.). (1985). *Marriage and Family: Coping with Change*. Belmont, Calif.: Wadsworth Publishing Co.

Clanton, G. (1984). "Social Forces and the Changing Family." In L. A. Kirkendal & A. E. Gravatt (Eds.), *Marriage and the Family in the Year 2020*. Buffalo, N.Y.: Prometheus Books.

"Focus on Families." (1985, January). *Health and Fitness, 6*(6), 3–7.

Gerstel, N., & Gross, H. (1983). "Commuter Marriage: Couples Who Live Apart." In E. Macklin & R. H. Rubin (Eds.), *Contemporary Families and Alternate Lifestyles*. Beverly Hills, Calif.: Sage Publications.

Goetting, A. (1985). "The Six Stations of Remarriage: Developmental Tasks of Remarriage and Divorce." In L. Cargan (Ed.), *Marriage and Family: Coping with Change*. Belmont, Calif.: Wadsworth Publishing Co.

Kirkendal, L. A., & Gravatt, A. E. (Eds.). (1984). *Marriage and the Family in the Year 2020*. Buffalo, N.Y.: Prometheus Books.

Levy, B. (1984). "When Family Anger Turns to Violence." In O. Pocs & R. Walsh (Eds.), *Marriage and Family 1984/85* (pp. 171–174). Guilford, Conn.: Dushkin Publishing Group.

Masnick, G., & Bane, M. J. (1980). *The Nation's Families: 1960–1990*. Cambridge: Joint Center for Urban Studies of Massachusetts Institute of Technology and Harvard University.

Naisbitt, J. (1984). *Megatrends*. New York: Warner Books.

Ogburn, W. F. (1964). *On Culture and Social Change: Selected Papers*. Chicago: University of Chicago Press.

Orthner, D. K., & Boyd, J. C. (1984). "Beyond the Melting Pot: Nationalism, Militarism and the Family." In L. A. Kirkendal & A. E. Gravatt (Eds.), *Marriage and the Family in the Year 2020* (pp. 248–283). Buffalo, N.Y.: Prometheus Books.

Pepernow, P. (1984). "The Seven Stages of Step-Family Development." *Family Relations.*

Stinnett, N., et al. (1981). *Family Strengths Three: Roots of Well-Being.* Lincoln: University of Nebraska Press.

Straus, M. A., Gelles, R. J., & Steinmetz, S. (1980). *Behind Closed Doors: Violence in the American Family.* New York: Doubleday & Co.

Sussman, M. B. (1977). "Family." In *Encyclopedia of Social Work* (17th ed., pp. 357–368). Washington, D.C.: National Association of Social Workers.

Toffler, A. (1980). *The Third Wave.* New York: Bantam Books.

Zigler, E., et al. (1983). *Children, Families, and Government: Perspectives on American Social Policy.* New York: Cambridge University Press.

FAMILY: MULTIGENERATIONAL

Since the 1970s there has been a renewed interest in the family owing to its centrality in providing support and care for its vulnerable members, particularly dependent children and the elderly, who are also the most vulnerable groups in society. Among the various circumstances that prompted this resurgence of interest, the most critical have been the growth of single-parent households, the effects of the increased longevity of the elderly, and new political and social philosophies that espouse a decreased role for the government in the provision of social services—a domain that the proponents of these philosophies would return to the family. As the family received greater attention, many scholars discovered that there was no unique family form but a proliferation of alternative family forms that gave rise to a multiplicity of definitions and descriptions of the family. As Sussman (1985) noted, scholars, practitioners, researchers, administrators, and others who define the family do so from personal or organizational predilection; that is, they perceive, conceptualize, and describe families according to their ideology, professional needs, or relationship with their own families. For example, human service professionals, who are mandated to provide various services to "eligible" families, describe the families on that basis. Although such a definition is not always the most realistic, it meets the utilitarian needs of the professionals and their employing organizations for establishing eligibility for services.

The incidence of single-parent families alone has triggered a major review and analysis of the family in its idealized form. Since at least the 1930s, social policies in this country have been predicated on the conception of a nuclear family that consists of a pair, legally married, with legally sanctioned children (see Sussman, 1985). In 1970, this type of family unit constituted 87.1 percent of all the families in the United States, but, by 1984, the proportion of such families had dropped to 74.3 percent while the proportion of families headed by single parents had risen to 25.7 percent, according to the U.S. Bureau of the Census (cited in "Population Profile of the United States," 1984). The tone of most reports of the increase in single-parent households has been negative; the reports have viewed the incidence of such households as being a social problem of potential harm to the pyschological development of children, a threat to economic stability, a factor in the growth of poverty among women, and ultimately a threat to the stability of the nation. Giovannoni and Billingsley (1977) cited the work of Pollack (1964) and Perlman (1964) as critical to the social-problem view of the single-parent family and concluded (p. 397) that

> categorization of the one-parent family as a social problem rests on three factors: (1) the vulnerability of such families to economic dependency, especially when the lone parent is a woman, (2) the potential deleterious effects on the psychological development of the children, (3) the threat to the stability of a social and economic structure that is predicated on the tradition of the two-parent family as the basic social unit.

Assistant Secretary of the Department of Health and Human Services Dorcas Hardy provided an example of the prevailing attitude of policymakers toward single parents in her statement that "two parent families are still the integral units of our society, and . . .

we have a responsibility to our children to try to break the cycle of family dissolution" (cited in "Single Parents," p. 42). With regard to the well-being of children in single-parent units, the evidence suggests they are at no greater risk than are children in other types of families. Zimmerman and Bernstein (1983) studied the effects of working mothers on the cognitive, emotional, and social development of children in nuclear families, in single-mother families, in living-together situations, and in communal relationships and found no evidence of a negative effect. What was most important was that children from single-mother units were not distinguishable from children in other types of families.

This general attitude toward alternative family arrangements is predicated on the idealized view that the nuclear family is the normative family—the model of how families ought to be. Ganter and Yeakle (1980, p. 233) argued that those who continue to view the idealized family as the keystone of American life fail to grasp the implications such ideals have for troubled relationships:

> The notions that the American family is endangered, that it is eroding, and that we are losing the very underpinnings of the society, are frequently informed simply by the expectation that the traditional nuclear family is the only model for family life.

Ganter and Yeakle (1980) noted that the family is evolving in response to environmental demands and that it is being redefined in direct response to sweeping changes in contemporary society that have forced women into the workplace, have encouraged smaller family units, and have demanded new modes of family adaptation. The past generation of Americans seems to have experienced considerable alterations in the traditional pattern of intimacy provided by the family and to have experimented with new family forms (London, 1978). Yet, the nuclear family model persists as a symbol of "family and kin," which, however defined, will continue to be those primary groups who will respond in service and in kind (food, clothing, and the like) when members ask for help or are in need (Sussman, 1985).

What appears to have changed most for families is the social context of family life. That is, the family is being called on more and more to provide essential services to groups

at risk, particularly the aged and children, which has added to the stress of family life and forced alterations in the structure of the family and in the patterns of relationships.

The task of analyzing the family is similar to that of appraising a jewel: one must view it from all sides because different facets are revealed according to one's angle of perception. It is clear that the classical nuclear family of legend does not encompass the current situation of most families. However, there is a relative scarcity of literature on the nature and structure of families composed of several generations—the multigenerational family. In the analyses of the family that have been done, this characteristic (multigenerationality) has been implicit, and Americans tend to think of family life in terms of more than one generation: children, parents, and grandparents.

This article discusses the multigenerational aspects of families as a basis for broadening the understanding of the family as a natural but dynamic unit of social support and cohesion that has both vertical (involving family relationships within two generations) and longitudinal (involving intergenerational family relationships) dimensions. It presents a theoretical framework that provides an additional perspective on the family—its issues, problems, and adaptations—as it strives to care for its members from infancy to old age and into the future.

Definitions

At the broadest level of conceptualization, the multigenerational family appears to be a natural mode of family intimacy involving more than one generation of family members at a single point in time. It has its roots in the classical conjugal or consanguineous basis for family organization and consists of spouses and their offspring surrounded by a fringe of relatives (Linton, 1936; Sussman, 1985). Most definitions of the family agree that it is founded on putative blood ties (consanguinity) among members. Its structure includes more than one generation of blood relatives; these blood relationships constitute biological bonds between the primary unit of procreation (the mother and father) and subsequent units produced by the offspring. The central figures who bind members to the kinship system are the parents, who are the children of parents, who are, in turn, the children of parents.

Thus, the multigenerational family varies from other family types by virtue of biological lineage and intergenerationality, or time. These factors confront the family with the task of survival in the present and in the future, coincident with the history and life span of regions, nations, and societies. In Middle Eastern, Asian, African, and, to a degree, Western societies, this task is played out in the vestigial practices that accord boys greater respect as persons who carry out the family line (boys retain the family name on marriage whereas girls do not). The concept of a line or lineage also invokes an additional function for the family—that of maintaining intergenerational solidarity (see Sussman, 1985).

It can be argued, theoretically, that the more natural state of family living is within the multigenerational structure. Couples wed generally to produce children, and most do. Thus, the multigenerational family unit is the basic unit of family organization and serves as the context or measure of all other variations or alternatives. In social systems terms, the boundaries of such a family fall at the upper limit of reciprocity—the point at which members of the linear family (in the sense of a linear progression, two persons with children who will have children of their own) cease to feel obligated to engage in acts of mutual aid based on perceived filiative ties.[1] As with all families, the boundaries of the multigenerational family are behavioral and are evidenced by the intensity and frequency of interaction among the components of this type of family (Anderson & Carter, 1976).

The most obvious instance of a multigenerational family is one in which three generations of the same family occupy a single household, from the children to the maternal or paternal grandparents. However, propinquity or physical proximity is not a

valid indicator of the filiative ties between family members. In highly mobile industrial societies, adult children and their spouses generally establish separate households and may migrate from their home community for economic or personal reasons (see Cantor & Little, 1985). Despite geographic or spatial separation, the literature reports a high degree of interaction among family members (Shanas, 1979; Sussman, 1985). The emerging pattern of family life today is one of separate households for all but the very old or sick and the maintenance of a complex pattern of viable and supportive family relationships (Butler & Lewis, 1982). Sussman (1965) referred to this pattern as a "modified extended family"—one that is highly integrated within a network of social relationships and mutual assistance and operates along bilateral kinship lines and vertically over several generations. The core of this type of family is the primary unit of procreation, the original parents, who must elicit a sense of family unity, filiate responsibility, and intergenerational solidarity among the members over time.

The actual prevalence of multigenerational families must be gleaned from data on family patterns and from general population statistics, particularly those having to do with the aged and children, because reliable nationwide statistics are not available on the number of households considered to be multigenerational. Brody (1985), for example, reported that having a dependent elderly parent is now a normative experience for individuals and families. She observed that between 1900 and 1976, the number of people who experienced the death of a parent before age 15 dropped from 1 in 4 to 1 in 20, while the number of middle-aged couples with two or more living relatives increased from 10 percent to 47 percent. By 1963, about 25 percent of the people over age 45 had a surviving parent, but, by the early 1970s, 25 percent of the people in their late fifties had a surviving parent, as did 20 percent of those in their early sixties, 10 percent of those in their late sixties, and 3 percent of those in their seventies. Furthermore, 10 percent of all people aged 65 or older had a child over age 65 (Brody, 1985). The consequences are that people who are now 25 years old or younger will feel a "kin squeeze." That is, many of them have had few or no brothers and sisters and will have no more than one or two

---

[1] The term used in the literature to convey the attitude of personal responsibility toward family members is "filial responsibility"—responsibility to one's parents. The author prefers the term "filiation," meaning a line of descent or being the child of a certain parent, because it conveys a sense of mutual family responsibility, from parent to child, from child to parent, over the generations (See Hanson et al., 1983).

children; yet, they are likely to have parents, grandparents, and even great grandparents in their immediate family. The kin family is shrinking relatively in each generation, but it is stretching out for the first time over four and even five generations (Butler & Lewis, 1982).

Another pattern is the return of an adult child to the home after a personal setback. In numerous families, one suspects that many adult children delay their departure because of the dramatic rise in the cost of living and the cost of college. In 1984, according to the U.S. Bureau of the Census (cited in "Population Profile of the United States," 1985) about 16 percent of the men and 8 percent of the women aged 25 to 29 were living with at least one of their parents, compared to 10.9 percent of the men and 5.2 percent of the women in 1970.

In summary, the multigenerational family is a ubiquitous social unit, consisting of blood relatives of more than one generation who share a common allegiance to the family as an intergenerational entity. The characteristics of such a family include biological lineage and feelings of unity, solidarity, and kinship derived from an allegiance to the core unit. As Sussman (1985) described, multigenerationality is a state of existence—a form—wherein family members may either reside together or at a distance and maintain their identity with and loyalty to the family. The goals of such a unit are the intergenerational survival and prosperity of its members, accomplished through acts of filiation that nurture and sustain the primary kinship system.

Cultural Variations

Many writers have observed that various ethnic and racial groups in this country have different orientations to the family that manifest themselves in unique forms of family organization (Antonucci, 1985; Hill, 1972; McAdoo, 1981; Shanas, 1979; Sussman, 1985). Billingsley (1968) first put forth this cultural relativistic theory of family organization when he proposed that groups that are under duress from racial discrimination, oppression, and poverty evolve unique family structures as a defensive strategy. This theory has been refined by such writers as Nobles (1974) and Sedarka (1981). Sedarka's (1981) position is that various subcultures in

this country have retained some aspects of the family structures of their countries of origin. Sedarka noted that because the organization of families in Africa was different from that of Western Europe, the structure of the black family in the United States is unlike that of the majority. That is, since the Middle Ages, by dint of historical and economic circumstances, the organization of families in Anglo-European societies has been dominated by the principle of conjugality—affinal kinship that was created and rooted in law. In contrast, African families have been organized around consanguineous cores of blood relationships. She concluded that these forms of family organization were carried over to this country.

The traditions of families whose origin was in Western Europe also appear to differ from those of families whose origins were in Asia, Latin America, the Pacific Islands, and Eastern Europe. Asians, Pacific Islanders, Hispanics, Jews, Poles, Greeks, and Italians, among others, tend toward the extended family model of organization (Harbert & Ginsberg, 1978). Thus, one can conclude, in theory, that family structure constitutes a functional adaptation to the environment.

The multigenerational family structure can be a focal form or rendered subordinate to other family forms. Anglo-European families chose to organize in "couple units" or nuclear families (rather than extended families), which apparently met their needs under conditions of rapid industrial expansion and entrepreneurial opportunities. However, modern economic and political realities have brought increased pressure to bear on this type of unit and exposed some of its weaknesses. Ganter and Yeakle (1980) observed that the idealized nuclear family is dysfunctional over time; they cited Birdwhistell (1970, p. 196)—an early proponent of the view that the idealized nuclear family is a pathological unit—who noted:

If the only legitimate personal relationships must come from within the unit [nuclear] and if the young, as they mature, must leave the unit to set up another such unit, such an organization is, by necessity, short-lived and self-destructive, and the elderly are left lonely and isolated, and the maturing young are guilty of destroying the unit by the act of maturation.

There is some question about whether the

idealized nuclear family exists in any context; certainly, it does not exist to the degree envisioned by Birdwhistell. However, it is known that beliefs and expectations about family life have made it difficult for members of many families to perceive themselves as worthwhile (Ganter & Yeakle, 1980).

Hispanic American Families. The traditions and patterns of living among Hispanic Americans, for example, stand in direct contrast to the idealized view of nuclear family life. Hispanic American families, which are multigenerational, emphasize the preservation of family unity, respect, and loyalty. They stress helpfulness and the maintenance and nuturance of extended family ties. As Acosta, Yamamoto, and Evans (1982) demonstrated, the family connections and the frequency of contact among members of Hispanic American families are greater than those among Anglo-American families. They observed that Hispanic extended families often include lifelong friends and fictive kin as well as members of the immediate family and other relatives. Fictive kin are created through a Catholic custom whereby the child acquires a godmother (*madrina*) and godfather (*padrino*), both of whom share responsibility for the child's welfare as coparents (*comadre and compadre*). The creation of fictive kin or lifelong family friends, who come to be considered as relatives and who take on obligations and instrumental and affectional ties similar to those of conventional kin (Sussman, 1985), is also typical of black families, who often call these quasi-relatives "uncle" and "aunt." Aschenbrenner (1973) noted that it was not uncommon for unrelated older individuals in the South to be given the surname of "Aunt" and "Uncle." Other fictive kinship relations were referred to as "play mother" or "play father" or "play brother" or "play sister."

Japanese and Chinese Families. This pattern of extended family relationships is also characteristic of other ethnic groups, most of whom have strong ties to the family as a system of blood relationships and a tradition of filial piety. This tradition is notable in Asian American families whose younger members show considerable respect for the elderly (Harrison, Serafica, & McAdoo, 1985). Harrison, Serafica, and McAdoo (1985) observed that Japanese and Chinese families, in particular, have similar types of family orientation that involve a singular loyalty to the family. They noted that the two cultures share the common characteristics of filial piety, in-group cohesion, a sense of collectivity or group consciousness, loyalty to the hierarchical structure of the family, dependence, respect, and a sense of duty or obligation to one's family. The Japanese instill early the values of total dependence on *ie* (the household), with each member assuming the benevolence (*amae*) of all other members.

What generally distinguishes the two cultures is their orientation to the extended family. The Japanese encourage loyalty to *ie* while the Chinese emphasize dependence on the clan—a complex multigenerational family structure based on consanguineous relationships that have endured over centuries (Harrison, Serafica, & McAdoo, 1985). Kitano (1980) observed that relatives are essential to the Chinese family system and to the members' individual and collective identities. The widespread combining of Chinese families can be seen in the relatively small number of surnames (400–500) that constitute the bulk of Chinese names (Kitano, 1980). Many of the features found in Japanese and Chinese families are common to other Asian American families as well.

American Indian Families. In contrast, American Indian families may be bifurcated, which means that the mother's and father's sides of the family are divided into separate lineages and that relatives of the same sex and generation are grouped together in helping clusters. Although there are variations from tribe to tribe, the mother's sister is generally close to her and her child and behaves toward the child as would the mother (Lum, 1986). Grandparents retain official and symbolic leadership in family communities. In this context, grandparents have a voice in child rearing, and parents seldom overrule the corrective measures of their elders. Younger people seek social acceptance from an older member of the community and, as a consequence, elders establish the norms for the family. Nonrelative leaders are incorporated into the family as fictive kin, and the functional and flexible roles of "grandparents," "aunts," and "uncles" establish an important structure of family support and assistance (Red Horse et al., 1978).

Effects of Oppression. As can be seen, the extended family seems to be essential for families of color and other minorities whose experience in this country is beset by race-based discrimination, oppression, and poverty (Hopps, 1982). The critical function of these family traditions for oppressed minorities or persons of color is the collective and mutual survival of their families under adverse conditions of racial prejudice. And, as Sussman (1985) noted, the functionality of this family system is so extensive among blacks that its existence is necessary for the survival of the individual as well as the black culture.

It seems reasonable, given their history, that groups that have been affected by racism would have different forms of family organization with different functions than would those who have not faced pervasive discrimination because their family orientation would be a major vehicle of survival and eventual social integration. It can be argued that only groups with the strongest orientation to family solidarity and to intergenerational mobility and with the highest affinity and filiative ties would increase their chances for survival, individually and collectively, under the harsh circumstances of racial prejudice. There would be no particular advantage, at least in the short run, for these groups to adopt the family norms of the dominant group. A family structure that promotes family solidarity seems to be the most viable alternative.

However, this thesis has received little or mixed support in the research literature. Few large-scale studies have compared the family functioning of different ethnic groups, and the findings of those that have been conducted have been less than sanguine about the influence of race and ethnicity on family orientation and structure. Unfortunately, most studies begin with the assumption of preexisting racial and ethnic differences among families; as a result, information about any real differences comes as a byproduct of other interests. For example, Hanson et al. (1983) deliberately set out to study the differences between black and white families in terms of their expression of willingness to care for elderly parents (filial

responsibility). They found that the white families were stronger than the black families (but not significantly so) in their support of filial responsibility and that the younger respondents of both races were stronger than the older respondents in support of these norms. In an extensive cross-cultural study conducted in New York City, Cantor (1975) compared the lifestyles of black, Hispanic, and white elderly persons and found (1) that ethnicity was a predictor of family assistance and family solidarity only for Hispanic families, who generally had larger families, saw their families more often, and received more help from their offspring and (2) that the blacks and Hispanics were similar in the help they gave to their children, providing greater financial assistance than did the whites. Cantor saw the second finding as being indicative of a subcultural adaptation to the effects of poverty. In Bengston et al.'s (1981) study of black, Mexican American, and white families in Los Angeles County, Mexican Americans were found to demonstrate the highest degree of family solidarity, while whites and blacks evidence less solidarity. The authors concluded that race is not uniformly predictive of family patterns and the allocation of responsibility for meeting the needs of the aged.

It seems evident that the support given by family members is dependent on how much income they have and hence that class and ethnic factors are not independent of one another. Clearly, ethnic minorities and persons of color have less income than do whites, which is reflected in the amount of care they provide or desire. As a consequence, research that uses income as an indicator of family support does not tell the full story of family relationships, which may involve less-tangible exchanges.

It seems that research has not tapped the salient features of race and ethnicity. Most theoreticians agree that there are qualitative as well as quantitative differences in the extent of filiation in families of various ethnic backgrounds but appear to disagree on how much importance to attribute to these factors. Thus, although there seem to be ethnic differences in the provision of social support, the nature of these differences is influenced by both demographic factors, including age, income, education, and geographic location, and structural factors, such as the size and composition of families and of support networks (Antonucci, 1985).

White Ethnic Groups. Studies on ethnicity have been hampered by sampling limitations and a tendency to regard ethnicity as a minority issue of whites and others. The tendency is to minimize subcultural variations among groups of European extraction, with the result that all whites are treated as one (Cantor & Little, 1985). When whites have been contrasted with blacks or Hispanics, for example, the true differences between groups are suppressed because the white group contains Italians, Jews, Greeks, Poles, and the like—groups that have strong family ties and whose family life is more similar than dissimilar to that of blacks and Hispanics. Most researchers (largely white) are unconscious of the lifestyles and cultural variations of different ethnic and racial groups; they have brought to their studies a strong subjective bias toward Anglo-European behavior as the norm and assimilation as the preferred mode of adaptation for ethnic and racial groups. This bias has hindered the collection of adequate, comprehensive, and valid data on ethnic families and persons of color (Harris, Serafica, & McAdoo, 1985). When the rich history of and literature about these groups are considered, it is apparent that social scientists' knowledge of ethnic and cultural variations in family orientations is sorely deficient.

Developmental Perspectives

Duvall (1971) posited eight stages in the development of the traditional nuclear family, ranging from the establishment of the original core unit, through the birth of children, to the retirement or death of a spouse, and covering a period of about 55–60 years. This view of the nuclear family with a limited life span in which one family ceases to exist while another comes into being is in contradiction to emerging theories that consider the family to be of longer duration and in dynamic interchange with other families, with extended family members and relatives, with fictive kin, with its various generational components and other elements that constitute its expanded environment. Given the previous discussion, this section describes the stages of family development that include the developmental life tasks confronting the multi-generational family in all its complexity and throughout its existence.

Stage 1. The formation of the initial family, or the original unit of reproduction, is the beginning of the life cycle of all families and represents, for the multigenerational family, a point of disassociation from prior family networks. This stage of family development was and is often accompanied by the experience of migration, which puts family members at a distance from parents, siblings, relatives, and friends, loosening the bonds of affinity to the old world and old ways. European ethnics migrated to the United States, Southern blacks to the North, and Puerto Ricans to the mainland, to name but a few instances.

Stage 2. The second stage is initiated by the birth of children and the forging of new networks. Its characteristics include the establishment and extension of the family network and the management of childbearing and child rearing in a two-generation unit.

Stage 3. In the third stage, the nuclear family unit expands to three generations when the children leave or remain at home as adults, beginning or postponing their own families. The original parents have to adapt to potential or actual grandparenting roles, become repositories of family wisdom and lore, and relinquish some aspects of the authoritarian parental role. The young adults remain quasi-dependent; they may visit frequently, ask for advice, and need financial and emotional support, thus cementing the family as a three-generation unit. The parents must also come to grips with their adult children's in-laws, lovers, and friends, who may become fictive kin, joining the family as "wives" or "husbands" of the original household.

This stage of development also pits the core multigenerational unit against other units, represented by the presence of sons-in-law and daughters-in-law, which threatens the unity of the core unit. Research is needed on the conflict between families and how it is resolved: which families expand by adding members and which families contract by losing members and the reasons for the changes that occur. One can assume that family status and the degree of cohesion among family members are two factors involved in the process. In sum, what the multigenerational family confronts in this stage is its potential dissolution or expansion and the task of coping with the loss or addition of significant members.

Stage 4. The fourth stage can be considered a period of autonomy and equilibrium in intergenerational family relations. The children are successfully established in separate households, and the parents, 50–65 years old, are at the peak of their careers and are preparing for retirement. During this period, family solidarity is forged, the family structure is at an optimum, all generations are present, and most members experience some degree of autonomy, self-sufficiency, and respect. The adult members of the family also achieve a measure of "filial maturity," which is demonstrated by their competence in undertaking supportive and, if necessary, caretaking roles with their parents. Sussman (1985) observed that with the increasing economic and psychological independence of the young married couples, some hiatus is induced in generational relationships until the retirement of the parents, which is perceived as old age—the period of decreasing vigor and health.

Stage 5. The fifth stage can be called the "caregiver" stage. As was indicated earlier, the structure of the multigenerational family becomes more complex, and the family stretches out over more generations. There are more persons to be cared for and a higher potential for frailty and illness among older members who are living longer than previous generations. However, the declining birthrate has resulted in a marked decrease in the number of potential caregivers for the increasing population of older people who need care (Brody, 1985). Therefore, it becomes more and more probable that the average family will have to take care of its older members.

Caregiving thus appears to be a distinct stage in the developmental life of the multigenerational family that now encompasses infants to great grandparents. Shanas (1980) detailed some of the complexities of this stage, noting that some middle-aged children are in key "orchestrating" positions for multiple activities and functions within generationally linked kin networks. They may be providing a home for an aged parent or looking after a divorced daughter and her child; supporting their children through college; providing guidance and sometimes a home for relatives who migrate to their area for jobs, school, or marriage; running a boardinghouse for the families of children who never seem to leave home; and caring for the children of their adult children who are working or looking for work. These exacting roles are unappreciated and unresearched, according to Shanas. This is the typical "sandwich generation"—a term that has been used to characterize this middle generation that is caught between the demands of youth and old age (Moroney, 1980).

The care of aging or frail parents is the focal task of this stage and the source of a significant amount of stress and strain on the family. In addition, the unity of the family is threatened by the disability or death of the original parents. The family has to confront and cope with the developmental life tasks of reversed roles, mourning, grief, and loss while managing an orderly transfer of leadership from the aging core unit to the next generation.

Stage 6. The sixth stage is the final period in the family life cycle and is termed "reconstructed." The complexity of roles is reduced as a new head of the family emerges and the immediate members of that family become the representatives of the reconstructed multigenerational family. This reconstructed unit is the second generation in the life cycle of the family—not a new family. Continuity with the original unit is sustained through family legends and through rites and rituals that hark back to customs unique to the family over the years.

Social Policies

The social policies that affect the nuclear family also affect the multigenerational family. However, few policies acknowledge changes in the family beyond the life cycle of the nuclear family; most policies operate on the assumption that the family ends with the death of the original parents. To have a positive impact on the multigenerational family, social policies would have to be intergenerational in scope and oriented to the quality of life of individuals as well as their families.

They would have to acknowledge the critical role of families as vehicles of social support that have a dual purpose in society: (1) to nurture, socialize, and support their individual members and (2) to manage their own development and continuity over time, from one generation to another, beyond the 65-year span.

A prime example of the failure of social policies to recognize the multigenerational family is the social security system, which is financed through payroll tax deductions. The cost of social security benefits continues to rise, owing to built-in cost-of-living adjustments, a growing population of retirees, and a shrinking labor force. The rising cost has polarized workers and retirees and led to intergenerational conflict (Clark & Baumer, 1985; Kingson & Hirshorn, 1985). A generation of workers is coming to see aging parents and grandparents as adversaries.

Intergenerational Equity vs. Cooperation.
Thus, the critical issue in most current social policies is that of "intergenerational equity" versus "intergenerational cooperation" (Kingson & Hirshorn, 1985). Intergenerational equity is a position that stresses conflict between the generations over scarce resources. This emphasis results in and encourages age-group, class, racial, and intergenerational competition; parents are pitted against children, children against the aged, the poor against the working class, and workers against retirees. Intergenerational cooperation stresses the common stake that all generations have in social policies that respond to the needs of individuals and families in all stages of the life cycle.

To benefit multigenerational families, social policies must, at a minimum, be based on the values of intra- and intergenerational cooperation and well-being. Policies that affect the young inevitably affect the old in the short run and, in the long run, significantly affect the well-being of the family as an instrument of social cohesion.

Elderly People vs. Young People.
Two such examples are immediately apparent: social policy with regard to the elderly and policies affecting the employment opportunities of young people, particularly Hispanic and black youths. As was noted, current social policies are being shaped in an atmosphere of competition, characterized by re-

duced governmental spending for social programs. As a result, policies that benefit one age group have the effect of reducing benefits to another. As the society grapples with the specific interests and needs of the elderly, programs designed for hard-core unemployed black youths aged 16–24 have been severely curtailed (Moss, 1982). These programs were instituted under the Manpower Development and Training Act of 1962 that culminated in the Comprehensive Employment and Training Act of 1973.

Moss (1982) and Glasgow (1980) are among those who noted the establishment of a permanent underclass made up of these youths. Virtually an entire second generation of ghetto (and *barrio*) youths will never enter the labor force (Moss, 1982). As a result, the society has indirectly condemned a generation or more of workers of all ages to "social insecurity" in their retirement years because social security is financed out of current wages. Hodgkinson (as quoted in Curwood, 1985, p. 4) pointed out that, by the year 2020, the majority of workers (real and potential) will be black and Hispanic:

> The poorer their education, the lower will be their income and resulting contribution in social security taxes. The white middle class can only accomplish its goal of a secure retirement if the minority youths now surging into the work force can make enough salary to finance white retirement.

Further, it can be surmised that chronic unemployment and poor education among minority youths is threatening the prosperity of the nation, representing a diminished resource in taxes, labor, and productivity.

Black and other minority families are beset by the problems of caring for age groups made increasingly at risk by current policies. These risks are compounded by problems of discrimination and poverty. Minority families are under inordinate pressure to survive. The present plight of the black family, for example, is directly traceable, among other things, to economic and employment policies that adversely affect black men (Gary & Leashore, 1982; Glasgow, 1980). Because of their low economic status, black men experience difficulties in fulfilling their roles as providers and protectors of their families. Gary and Leashore (1982) pointed up a number of negative effects for the black family, including divorce, desertion, incarceration of male members, and drug abuse, noting that the economic survival of the black family in the absence of the black man continues to be marginal.

What is obvious is the tremendous social assault on such families created by age-based policy interests. Such families are confronted with diminished chances throughout the life cycle. If the intergenerational perspective is valid, then succeeding generations of a family must experience upward social mobility. Although black families have been resilient and upwardly mobile for the past 50 years, the trend has been reversed since the end of the civil rights movement. The United States is now witnessing the downward mobility of a generation of black youths, particularly in educational achievement (McAdoo, 1981). Hence, the major threat to ethnic minority families (and all families) is not their survival in a single generation but over the long term—a survival that is not being abetted by current policies. Will the families that emerge from the failed and conflict-ridden policies of the 1980s be able to make a contribution to the family kin networks of a cohesive society in 2024, or will that society continue to experience the difficulties of wasted human resources, fragmentation of effort, and intergenerational conflict and competition to the detriment of family continuity and resulting in an expanding underclass—unemployed, unemployable, alienated, and marginal?

Implications for Practice

The following observations summarize the implications of the theory of the multigenerational family for the field of family practice.

New modes of family practice must be developed that are more comprehensive than current practice theories, which are designed for intervention into the nuclear family as an atomistic unit, isolated from all but its most intimate members. Although theories that take a systems or network view of the family are emerging, the author still finds them biased toward the intragenerational family of two and three generations rather than the multigenerational family structure (see Allen & Pasick, 1983; Carter & McGoldrick, 1980).

These theories have not been widely adopted by the profession, however.

Models must be devised that deal with more than the psychological (intrapersonal) aspects of family functioning. Previous models have ignored both the complexities of interactions among members of the multigenerational family and the social-structural and historical influences on family functioning. Interventions that view the family as a microsystem that deteriorates with the death or institutionalization of a member underestimate the resilience of the family throughout its life cycle.

A generation of family practitioners is being trained without knowledge of the diversity of cultures and lifestyles among ethnic minority groups and the techniques necessary to engage in advocacy and methods of intervention in the larger social institutions in behalf of such beleaguered families.

The objectives of family practice must keep pace with trends in the evolution of the family. Since the early 1970s, the traditional nuclear family has constituted a declining percentage of all households. More and more families are either nontraditional, such as dual-career families, single-parent families, or stepfamilies, or units that are experimental, involving communal and affiliated families and group and open marriages (Alexander & Kronfein, 1983; Cogswell, 1970). White middle-class nuclear units are on the decline, and practice must be sensitive to emerging and even nontraditional family patterns, the prototypes of which are to be found in social experiments being conducted among divorced and single parents, among persons of color, and among the elderly.

LEON F. WILLIAMS
CARMEN DÍAZ

For further information, see FAMILY: CONTEMPORARY PATTERNS; FAMILY PRACTICE.

References

Acosta, F. X., Yamamoto, J., & Evans, L. A. (1982). *Effective Psychotherapy For Low Income and Minority Patients*. New York: Plenum Press.

Alexander, J., & Kronfein, M. (1983). "Changes in Family Functioning Amongst Nonconventional Families." *American Journal of Orthopsychiatry, 53*(4), 408–417.

Allen, J. A., & Pasick, R. (1983, June). "A Multigenerational Family Therapy Approach to Retirement." Paper presented at the American Family Therapy Association Conference, New York.

Anderson, R. E., & Carter, I. E. (1976). *Human Behavior in the Social Environment: A Social Systems Approach*. Chicago: Aldine Publishing Co.

Antonucci, T. C. (1985). "Personal Characteristics, Social Support, and Social Behavior." In R. H. Binstock & E. Shanas (Eds.), *Handbook of Aging and Social Services* (2nd ed., pp. 94–218). New York: Van Nostrand Reinhold Co.

Aschenbrenner, J. (1973). "Extended Families Among Black Americans." *Journal of Comparative Family Studies*, *4*, 257–268.

Bengston, V. L., et al. (1985). "Generations, Cohorts, and Relations Between Age Groups." In R. H. Binstock & E. Shanas (Eds.), *Handbook of Aging and Social Services* (2nd ed., pp. 304–338). New York: Van Nostrand Reinhold Co.

Billingsley, A. (1968). *Black Families In White America*. Englewood Cliffs, N.J.: Prentice-Hall.

Birdwhistell, R. L. (1970). "Idealized Model of the American Family." *Social Casework*, *51*(4), 195–198.

Brody, E. M. (1985). "Parent Care as a Normative Family Stress." *The Gerontologist*, *25*(6), 627–631.

Butler, R. N., & Lewis, M. I. (1982). *Aging and Mental Health: Positive Psychosocial and Biomedical Approaches*. St. Louis, Mo.: C. V. Mosby Co.

Cantor, M. (1980). "The Informal Support System: Its Relevance in the Lives of the Elderly." In E. Borgotta & N. McCluskey (Eds.), *Aging and Society* (pp. 111–146). Beverly Hills, Calif.: Sage Publications.

Cantor, M., & Little, V. (1985). "Aging and Social Care." In R. H. Binstock & E. Shanas (Eds.), *Handbook of Aging and Social Services* (2nd ed., pp. 745–781). New York: Van Nostrand Reinhold Co.

Carter, E., & McGoldrick, M. (1980). *The Family Life Cycle: A Framework for Family Therapy*. New York: Gardner Press.

Clark, R. L., & Baumer, D. L. (1985), "Income Maintenance Policies." In R. H. Binstock & E. Shanas (Eds.), *Handbook of Aging and Social Services* (2nd ed., pp. 666–695). New York: Van Nostrand Reinhold Co.

Cogswell, B., & Sussman, M. (1970), "Changing Family and Marriage Forms. In Sussman (Ed.), *Non-traditional Family Forms In the 1970's* (pp. 137–148). Minneapolis, Minn.: National Council on Family Relations.

Curwood, S. (1985, July 22). "Warning Issued on Minority Education." *Boston Globe*, p. 4.

Duval, E. (1971). *Family Development*. Philadelphia: J. B. Lippincott Co.

Ganter, G., & Yeakle, M. (1980). *Human Behavior and the Social Environment*. New York: Columbia University Press.

Gary, L. E., & Leashore, B. R. (1982). "High-risk Status of Black Men." *Social Work*, *27*(1), 54–58.

Giovannoni, J., & Billingsley, A. (1977). "Family, One-Parent." In *Encyclopedia of Social Work* (17th ed., Vol. 1, pp. 397–408). Washington, D.C.: National Association of Social Workers.

Glasgow, D. G. (1980). *The Black Underclass: Poverty, Unemployment, and Entrapment of Ghetto Youth*. San Francisco: Jossey-Bass.

Hanson, S. L., et al. (1983). "Racial and Cohort Variations in Filial Responsibility Norms." *The Gerontologist*, *25*(6), 627–631.

Harbert, A. S., & Ginsberg, L. H. (1979). *Human Services for Older Adults: Concepts and Skills*. Belmont, Calif.: Wadsworth Publishing Co.

Harrison, A., Serafica, F., & McAdoo, H. (1985). "Ethnic Families of Color." In E. Parke (Ed.), *The Family* (Vol. 7 of *Review of Child Development Research*, pp. 329–371). Chicago: University of Chicago Press.

Hopps, J. G.(1982). "Oppression Based on Color." *Social Work*, *27*(1), 3–5.

Kingson, E. R., & Hirshorn, B. (1985). "The Common Stake: The Interdependence of Generations in an Aging Society." Unpublished manuscript, Washington, D.C.; Gerontological Society of America.

Kitano, H. L. (1980). *Race Relations* (2nd ed.). Englewood Cliffs, N.J.: Prentice-Hall.

Linton, R. (1936). *The Study of Man*. New York: Appleton-Century-Crofts.

Lum, D. (1986). *Social Work Practice and People of Color: A Process Stage Approach*. Monterey, Calif.: Brooks/Cole Publishing Co.

London, P. (1978). "The Intimacy Gap." *Psychology Today*, *12*(11), 40.

McAdoo, H. P. (1981). "Patterns of Upward Mobility in Black Families." In McAdoo (Ed.), *Black Families* (pp. 155–169). Beverly Hills, Calif.: Sage Publications.

Moroney, R. M. (1980). *Families, Social Services and Social Policy: The Issue of Shared Responsibility*. Washington, D.C.: U.S. Department of Health & Human Services.

Moss, J. A. (1982). "Unemployment among Black Youths: A Policy Dilemma," *Social Work*, *27*(1), 47–52.

Perlman, H. H. (1964). "Unmarried Mothers." In N. E. Cohen (Ed.), *Social Work and Social Problems* (pp. 270–320). New York: National Association of Social Workers.

Pollack, O. (1964). "The Broken Family." In N. E. Cohen (Ed.), *Social Work and Social Prob-*

lems (pp. 321–339). New York: National Association of Social Workers.

"Population Profile of the United States." (1985, November 8). *The Boston Globe*, p. 11.

Red Horse, J., et al. (1978). "Family Behavior of Urban American Indians." *Social Casework*, 59(2), 67–72.

Sedarka, N. (1981). "Interpreting the African Heritage in Afro-American Family Organization." In H. P. McAdoo (Ed.), *Black Families* (pp. 37–53). Beverly Hills, Calif.: Sage Publications.

"Single Parents." (1985, July 15). *Newsweek*, pp. 42–50.

Sussman, M. B. (1985). "The Family Life of Old People." In R. H. Binstock & E. Shanas (Eds.), *Handbook of Aging and Social Services* (2nd ed., pp. 415–449). New York: Van Nostrand Reinhold Co.

Sussman, M. B. (1965). "Relationship of Adult Children with Their Parents in the United States." In E. Shanas and G. Streib (Eds.), *Social Structure and the Family: Generational Relations.* Englewood Cliffs, N.J.: Prentice-Hall.

Zimmerman, I. L., & Bernstein, M. (1983). "Parenthood and Work Patterns in Alternative Families." *American Journal of Orthopsychiatry*, 53(3), 418–425.

FAMILY: NUCLEAR

The U.S. Bureau of the Census and most national and international statistics define a family in similar terms: two or more people related by blood, marriage, or adoption and living together. In other words, the family as it is thought of today in the United States is a nuclear family. Moreover, in contrast to conventional wisdom, families in the United States have been nuclear in structure since colonial days (Demos, 1970). The same is true of families in Great Britain and in western Europe generally (Laslett, 1972; Mitterauer & Sieder, 1982; Shorter, 1975).

Emergence of the Modern Family

At one time, it was commonly supposed that a major consequence of the industrial revolution was to destroy an older family type characterized by an extended family household that included many children, adult siblings and their children, as well as grandparents—all living under one roof. It was believed that today's nuclear family, consisting of a small conjugal unit with one or two parents, a few children, and only limited ties with any but immediate kin, was the result of industrialization and had emerged, in fact, as an adaptive replacement for the extended family.

According to the leading authorities on the history of the Western family, writing since the late 1960s as part of the new school of family history, the reality was very different (Degler, 1980; Demos, 1970; Hareven, 1971; Laslett, 1972; Mitterauer & Sieder, 1982; Shorter, 1975). Indeed, in *structure,* the family of 300 or even 400 years ago did not differ substantially from the family of today. Wrigley (1977), a leading family historian, writes:

> The co-resident family group from Elizabethan times onward normally consisted only of the basic reproductive unit of husband, wife, and children, or of a remnant of the same, supplemented by servants in the households of the more prosperous. (p. 77)

Only in *some* parts of eastern Europe did large, complex households exist, with many children and multiple generations living together. But for the most part, the pattern throughout central and western Europe was one in which the nuclear family dominated (Mitterauer & Sieder, 1982). Marriage was often late and there were relatively few children. The typical family size in urban areas was between three and five members. Marriage almost always involved setting up a new household under a separate roof, and only occasionally was a grandparent present.

If the nuclear family was the preindustrial norm and not the consequence of industrialization, and if family structure in much of the Western world has remained relatively stable since then, what, if anything, happened to the family in the intervening years? Certainly, the family did change during that period.

Part of the confusion in the discussion of extended and nuclear families is that the presence of the nuclear family does not preclude the importance of kinship networks in many subgroups in society. These networks have been important historically, and still are.

It is the *functions* of the family rather than its structure that changed significantly with the industrial revolution. Social change stripped the family of its traditional functions, and as a result, the history of the modernization of the family can be described as "a story of the loss of its functions as a school, a church, a correctional institution, a hospital, and a workshop"—and of a growing substitution of formal, bureaucratic service organizations to carry out these functions in its place (Hareven, 1971, p. 221).

Education as a Function Relinquished by the Family.

One interesting and important illustration of this reallocation of functions between the family and a new social institution was the removal of the responsibility for children's education from the family and the home to the schools, and the subsequent development of public, compulsory education. Historians ascribe the growth of public education in nineteenth-century America and Great Britain to changes in the role of the family in relation to economic production as well as to changes in the nature of the economy (Smelser & Halpern, 1978). The separation of home and workplace that occurred as a consequence of industrialization began the erosion of parental authority over youth. In addition to the physical separation of parents and children, new technologies, new patterns of labor recruitment, and changes in the organization of work made it possible for young people themselves to obtain employment, thus giving them economic independence from their parents as well as physical distance. Further technological advances, however, soon made the labor of unskilled youth less attractive to factory owners, with the result that many young people lost their jobs.

In the mid-nineteenth century, youth became viewed increasingly as a social problem and as a danger to the social order. Parents no longer had the economic power over their children that they had possessed in earlier years. Young people were both out of work and on their own, and often on the streets.

The search for a new instrument for the social control of youth—in addition to a strong emphasis on the value of self-improvement, the desire for a trained labor force, and the conviction that mass education would lead to a more responsible electorate— was a very important aspect of the development of compulsory, public education in the nineteenth century in the United States. As Smelser and Halpern (1978) point out, "schools proliferated at a time when older patterns of family and community control over youth had proved ineffectual" (p. 298). However, they add: "By assuming tasks that the family no longer could accomplish, educational institutions often constituted an augmentation of parental influence" (p. 298).

Thus, when families relinquished to the schools their function of educating children, it was not because schools usurped parental control. Rather, schools became more important after both parents and community had revealed their inability to exercise control over youth. As the schools emerged as a new social institution for educating children, they emerged also as an ally of the family and the community in socializing youth. Instead of undermining family ties, the schools strengthened these ties by supplementing the family's role and offering an important additional societal source of socialization. It was in this context that reformers successfully pressed for more schools and more government support for schools.

The Continuing Process.

Some historians have suggested that much of the uproar in recent years about the "death" of the family has occurred not out of fear of what will happen to families, but out of society's failure or lack of readiness to adapt to these changes (Mitterauer & Sieder, 1982, p. 90). Thus, many of the trends that have been discerned regarding the contemporary family are merely part of an ongoing process. Among these are the continued importance of the nuclear family and the continued decline in fertility and birth rates. Even the current pattern of marriage at a later age is not unique; this too was the pattern in earlier eras, and has varied over time from earlier to later marriage.

In assessing what has happened to the family, and what is still happening to this basic social institution, it is especially important *not* to use the 1950s as the baseline for comparison. The post-World War II generation, in part the cohort that married and had children in the 1950s, was in many ways a deviant generation (Cherlin, 1981). Women married at an earlier age than at any other time in the twentieth century and the rate of childbearing also was unusually high by twentieth-century standards. Much of the experience of the 1970s with regard to the timing of marriage, childbearing, and family size seems less unusual if this decade is viewed in the context of the first half of the century, and the decade of the 1950s is viewed as the anomaly it was. There are other trends and developments that are unusual, however, and some that are dramatic. These are discussed in the following section.

Demography of the American Family

Changes in Structure and Composition. Out of a total U.S. population of 233 million in 1983, 229 million lived in households (U.S. Bureau of the Census, 1984a, 1983a). Of those, 73 percent were family households, compared with 81 percent in 1970, but they included 88 percent of the population. Clearly, the vast majority of the population lives in family households, even though nonfamily households are increasing at a rapid pace.

The number of families in the United States has increased by about 20 percent since 1970; the number of families with children, however, has increased by only 8 percent (U.S. Bureau of the Census, 1984a). Although the number of families continues to grow, the proportion with children has declined steadily—from 56 percent in 1970 to 49 percent in 1983. In effect, less than half of all families in the United States today have children under age 18 present in the household, even though for most people the word "family" implies children.

The proportion of families with children is higher among minorities—black or Hispanic—than among whites. Almost 11 percent of *all* families are black and 6 percent are Hispanic; however, when it comes to families with children, almost 13 percent are black and 8 percent Hispanic. Thus, more than one-fifth of all families with children are racial and ethnic minorities.

Two-parent families are still the most important type in numerical terms, but they have declined significantly as a proportion of all families with children from 88.6 percent in 1970 to 78.2 percent in 1983. It is also important that, among these families, the "traditional" American family of a breadwinner husband, an at-home wife, and several chil-

dren has declined even more during these years. This family type constitutes only 31 percent of families with children (and 16 percent of all families) in 1983 as compared with 54 percent of families with children (and 30 percent of all families) in 1970. The average family with children has two (a statistical 1.87). This family with just *two* children, a father in the labor force, and an at-home mother, constitutes only 9 percent of families with children (Hayghe, 1984). Ten percent of all children (6.2 million children) lived with one biological parent and one stepparent in 1982 (U.S. Congress, 1983).

One of the most dramatic changes in household and family composition over the past decade has been the increase in one-parent families (U.S. Bureau of the Census, 1984a). Between 1970 and 1983 the number of two-parent households declined by 5 percent, but the number of one-parent households more than doubled. Because families headed by women constitute 90 percent of all one-parent households, the fact that mother-only families increased by more than 107 percent and now constitute almost 20 percent of all families with children (49 percent of black, 33 percent of Hispanic, and 15 percent of white) is an indication of how important this family type has become. Of this increase, 84 percent is attributable to women who are either divorced or have never married.

Even more dramatic than the high percentage of families with children now headed by women alone is the probability of women experiencing this status (Kamerman, 1985; Norton & Glick, in press). Current estimates are that between 15 and 20 percent of young women approaching childbearing age will eventually give birth to at least one child before marriage.[1] About 35 to 40 percent of all young women are likely to become single mothers for a significant period of time. It is estimated that about 60 percent of all children born since 1983 are likely to live in a single-

---

[1] This and the following estimates were provided by Arthur J. Norton, Assistant Chief, Population Division, U.S. Bureau of the Census, and by Martin O'Connell and Carolyn Rogers, also of the Population Division, in letters and personal communication, 1984. See Kamerman, S. B. (1985). "Young, Poor and a Mother Alone." In McAdoo, H., & Parham, T. J. (Eds.), *Services to Young Families*. Washington, D.C.: American Public Welfare Association.

parent family for at least several months before they are 18—and some estimates are even higher (Hofferth, 1985).

Since 1970 a similarly dramatic change has occurred in the living arrangements of children (U.S. Bureau of the Census, 1985a). The number of children under 18 declined by 10 percent, and the number of those living with two parents declined by 21 percent, but those living only with their mother *increased* by 70 percent. In 1984, some 20 percent of all children under 18 were living with their mothers only (50 percent of black, 25 percent of Hispanic, and 15 percent of white children); another 2 percent lived with their father. The number of children living with divorced mothers has increased by 138 percent since 1970 and the number living with never-married mothers has more than quintupled. Of the children living with single mothers in 1984, 41 percent lived with divorced mothers, 25 percent with never-married mothers, 27 percent with separated mothers, and 7 percent with widowed mothers. Increased incidence of separation and divorce is the major factor leading to the growth in the numbers of white mother-only families; both a decrease in marriage and increased childbearing among never-married women are the factors leading to the even larger increase among black female-headed families (Bane & Ellwood, 1984).

Not all single-mother families are alike (Kamerman, 1985b). Some are at higher risk of poverty than others; some constitute a larger group than others; and some seem more accessible to policy interventions than others. For example, widows with children are a small and declining group among the single mothers, and they are far less vulnerable to poverty than others (U.S. Bureau of the Census, 1984a). In contrast, another small group of single mothers—the very young, teenage, or school age mothers—now are viewed as having an especially complicated amalgam of problems. These mothers require extensive and comprehensive aid from policies and programs if they are to become successful in their parenting, labor force, and economic roles (Furstenberg, 1976; McGee, 1982; Moore & Burt, 1982).

Single motherhood is now a well-established phenomenon and is likely to remain significant even if, and when, the rate of growth slows. These families are at the high-est risk of poverty; almost half were poor in 1983 (41 percent of white and 63 percent of black mother-only families). Divorced, separated, or never married families are at particularly high risk. Black families are clearly worse off, by far, than white families. Women with children under age 6 are more likely to be poor than women with older children. Young mothers—those under age 30—are at higher risk of poverty than older mothers.

Social Change and the American Family

Changes in Gender Roles: Women. The most significant change that has occurred to U.S. families is the change in adult gender roles as women, especially married women with children, entered the labor force in record numbers in the 1970s (Department of Labor, 1983; Hayghe, 1984). In 1970 the labor force participation rate of all women with children under age 18 was 42 percent; in 1984 it was 61 percent, an astonishing 45 percent increase in less than 15 years. The rate for married women increased even more: from 40 to 59 percent during those same years, a 48 percent increase. The most dramatic change has been the increase in labor force participation by married women with children under age 6: from 30 percent in 1970 to 48 percent in 1984, a startling 60 percent increase. In contrast, the rate for women heading families, although higher than that of married women, increased very modestly during those years— from 59 to 67 percent.

Black married women with children continue to have a higher rate of labor force participation than white women, and both white and black wives are more likely to be in the work force than Hispanics. However, this black–white difference has decreased sharply since 1970. In that year, 56 percent of black married mothers were in the labor force in contrast to only 38 percent of whites. By 1984, the rates were 69 and 56 percent, respectively; the rate for Hispanic women was substantially lower (47 percent) even in 1984. It is of interest that black married mothers not only continue to have higher labor force participation rates than white or Hispanic mothers, but there is no appreciable difference in the rates by the age of the youngest child, as shown in Table 1 for 1983. In contrast, the labor force participation rate of

Table 1. Mothers' Rates of Participation in the Labor Force by Age of Youngest Child, 1983

Age of Child	Mothers' Rates of Participation		
	White	Black	Hispanic
Under 18	56.2	68.5	46.8
6 to 17	63.4	69.1	53.5
Under 6	48.2	67.8	41.9

Source: Hayghe, H. (1983). "Married Couples: Work and Income Patterns." *Monthly Labor Review, 106*(12).

white women heading families is significantly higher than for blacks or Hispanics. These rates are 70 percent for white mothers, 60 percent for blacks, and 48 percent for Hispanics.

One of the major changes occurring as a result of the growth in labor force participation rates of married women is that many of the differences that were previously correlated with the age of youngest child have become blurred or disappeared entirely (Waldman, 1983). Half of the women with children ages 2 and younger and more than 60 percent of all mothers of children ages 3 and older were in the labor force in 1985 ("Labor Force Activity of Mothers," 1985); the 2- to 3-year age bracket seems to be the only significant demarcation point in contrast to 1970, when there were several points at which children's ages affected the labor force activity of their mothers.

About 33.5 million children, well over half of all children under age 18, had a mother in the labor force in 1985 ("Labor Force Activities of Mothers," 1985). Almost 10 million of these children were under age 6, and 15 million were ages 6 to 13—age groups that require either full- or part-day (before and after school) care. Whatever their ages, a smaller proportion of white than black children in married-couple families had working mothers, whereas in mother-only families the opposite prevailed.

This change in women's labor force activity is central to the economic well-being of women, children, and their families. The poverty rate of mother-only families declined from 49 percent to 29 percent for those who worked at some time during the year, and the rate declined to 10 percent for women who

worked full time all year. Although the poverty rate for husband and wife families was 9 percent in 1983, the rate for families in which the wife worked was under 6 percent, but it was almost 18 percent for families in which the wife remained at home. Median family income in 1983 was $32,000 for husband and wife families in which the wife was in the labor force, but only $22,000 when she was not.

Changes in Gender Roles: Men. Most of the public attention to changes in gender roles has been on the significance of these changes for women. Inevitably, however, when women's roles change, so do men's roles. Any effort to equalize the status of women cannot ignore the implications and consequences for the roles and responsibilities of men. The process, although slow, is reciprocal (Lamb & Sagi, 1983; Lewis & Pleck, 1979).

Father-only families have begun to be identified as a "new" family type. In 1984 they constituted only 2.4 percent of all families with children, and 11 percent of all single-parent families with children. These families have more than doubled in number and as a proportion of families with children since 1970 (U.S. Bureau of the Census, 1984a). Although still few in number, men are increasingly seeking and obtaining custody of their children after divorce, or finding themselves left alone to rear children when their wives leave home.

Despite the growth in the proportion of wives entering the labor force, husbands continue to spend little time in family work. Research findings on the amount of time fathers spend in basic child care tasks (such as feeding and diapering) are remarkably similar regardless of the method employed to measure time use. Typically, fathers spend about 2 hours per week on child care tasks; their wives spend between 9 and 18 hours per week on these tasks (Russell & Radin, 1983). It is of interest, however, that employed men with working wives are estimated to spend 2.7 hours per week *more* on child care than men with at-home wives (Pleck, 1979, p. 487).

Research continues to document the importance of the parenting role for fathers, and there seems to be a modest increase in the participation of some men (Pleck, 1985).

Women, however, continue to carry the primary responsibility for child care and child rearing.

Acknowledging the importance of effecting intrafamilial role change if there is to be any significant impact on male roles, several countries have begun to try to legislate gender equity in the family. One device has been to establish parenting policies, rather than maternity policies, in relation to childbirth and child rearing. Sweden is the prototypical country in this regard, with a parent insurance benefit available to natural and adoptive parents. Parents are entitled to up to a year of fully protected job leave at the time of childbirth, paid at 90 percent of wages (up to the maximum wage covered under social insurance) for 9 months and a minimum flat rate for the last 3 months. Either parent can take the leave or they can share it. Since 1974, when the Parent Insurance Law was first passed, the proportion of fathers claiming some portion of the leave has increased from 2 percent in 1974 to 25 percent in 1983—a significant increase even if not nearly equal to women's use of the leave. Sweden also permits working parents paid time off to care for a sick child at home. Men make almost as much use of this benefit as do women. The other Nordic countries (Finland, Denmark, and Norway) all now permit fathers some use of the post-childbirth leave. These countries, as well as West Germany, also make it possible for fathers to take care of a sick child by mandating some paid leave—at least a few days—for all working parents. No such policies exist in the United States.

Although the process of role change for men to increase activity in the family so as to parallel women's increased activity in the labor force is slow, it has begun. For more to occur and for the pace to accelerate, there must be legislation and policy initiatives to encourage these developments, and changes in the culture and policies at the workplace that would make them possible.

Family Policy Agenda

Despite the continuity of the nuclear family from preindustrial times, and the continuity of certain trends from the eighteenth and nineteenth centuries, some aspects of the family have changed dramatically. Families are smaller; the typical family has fewer than two children. There are more mother-only

families in which the father is still alive but living separately; these families continue to be at high risk of poverty. Children are more likely to experience divorce and to be reared by only one parent, overwhelmingly, their mother. There is a growing group of unwed, adolescent mothers who are likely to have multiple problems in addition to being at high risk of poverty and long-term welfare dependency. Women, as well as men, are likely to be in the labor force. Becoming a mother no longer means leaving one's job, although it is likely to mean a higher rate of unemployment as women cope with the multiple burdens of home, family, child rearing, and child care at the same time as they cope with their jobs. Men are beginning to do more at home, but women still have the major responsibility for child care.

The following are among the most important policies affecting families at present (Kamerman, 1984; Kamerman & Kahn, 1981):

1. Training, job opportunities, and employment policies will become an increasingly important social policy arena for families, now that male *and* female employment has become central to the economic well-being of families.

2. Both cash and in-kind income transfers remain important, with Aid to Families with Dependent Children (AFDC) and food stamps critical to maintain the level of living for low-income, mother-only families if women are not working. Tax reform may stimulate some attention to family-related benefits.

3. Unlike 67 other countries, the United States still does not have any child or family allowance. With the proportionate decline in the child population in this country and the decline in birth and fertility rates, some attention may be paid to this policy gap, either for pronatalist or human capital investment purposes.

4. Assuring private as well as public income transfers related to child support, when the father is absent from the household, will continue to be important as the rate of single parenthood remains high, even if it does not rise so rapidly in the future.

5. Health insurance—Medicaid as well as other approaches—to cover all low- and moderate-income families with children who do not have adequate coverage from their

jobs will become an increasingly important issue.

6. As the homeless population grows and includes more families with children, housing allowances and related policies will become far more important than ever before in the United States.

7. Child care services, both for preschoolers and for primary school aged children, will become increasingly critical if, as more women enter the labor force, their children are to be reared well.

8. Parenting policies, permiting men as well as women to take time off when a new baby arrives, without financial or career penalties, are essential if men are to become more involved fathers and if men and women are to be given the opportunity to be responsible and responsive parents.

9. Family support systems, such as providing information; long- and short-term counseling on marital, family, parent-child, and individual problems; family life and parenting education; help with elderly and handicapped members; and home help services will all get more attention and will be provided in both public and private sectors. These are central to social work.

Life Course Perspective

To understand the experience of families, it is essential to have knowledge about the families' particular stage of development, as well as knowledge of the families' location in history. Historians and sociologists refer to this as the life course perspective on the history of the family (Elder, 1978a, 1978b; Hareven, 1978). Some adults are just becoming parents, some are parents of adolescents, and some are entering the "empty nest" stage; each stage is a very different experience for the family unit and for family members. Similarly, becoming a parent for the first time may be a very different experience in wartime or peace, or in a period of economic growth or severe recession. Being a young child or an adolescent is also a very different experience depending on what is occurring in the world. For example, the "baby boom" cohort has had a unique "life course"; it is important to remember that every cohort has some unique experiences that will mark them in special ways, depending on the stage they were in when they experienced the event. The rebellious youth

of the late 1960s are now rearing their own children. How will their youthful experiences affect their parenting roles? For the children of today's divorced couples, the experience of growing up in a one-parent family may differ drastically from the experience of children in such a family as recently as 20, or even 10, years ago. The same is true of the children of today's working mothers.

Thus, to assess the experience of family members and of the family unit, and to intervene effectively in their problems requires a knowledge of what is normative for the family today. It also requires knowledge of the history of the era in which family members live (and lived), as well as of the lives of the individual and the family, the developmental stage they have reached, and the problems they are currently facing. The nuclear family, resilient as it is and has been, is experiencing significant changes in composition and adult roles; certain functions will never be regained. Yet in child rearing and child socialization, in caregiving and nurturing of elderly and handicapped family members, and—most importantly—in reproducing the future citizenry, the family will continue to be the primary unit. The normal family today is a stressed family. The role of social work is to understand the person and his or her family in the context of individual development, and also in the context of the society in which they live and the times in which they have grown up.

SHEILA B. KAMERMAN

For further information, see CHILDREN; FAMILY: CONTEMPORARY PATTERNS; FAMILY: ONE PARENT; FAMILY: STEPFAMILIES; MEN; WOMEN.

References

Bane, M. J., & Ellwood, D. (1984). "Single Mothers and Their Living Arrangements." Harvard University. Unpublished.

Cherlin, A. J. (1981). *Marriage, Divorce and Remarriage*, Cambridge, Mass.: Harvard University Press.

Degler, C. (1980). *At Odds: Women and the Family in America from the Revolution to the Present*. New York: Oxford University Press.

Demos, J. (1970). *A Little Commonwealth: Family Life in Plymouth Colony*. New York: Oxford University Press.

Department of Labor, Bureau of Labor Statistics. (1983). "Families at Work: The Jobs and the

Pay." [Special Issue]. *Monthly Labor Review, 106*(12).

Elder, G. H. Jr. (1978a). "Approaches to Social Change and the Family." In J. Demos & S. S. Boocock (Eds.), *Turning Points: Historical Sociological Essays on the Family* (pp. S1–S38). Chicago: University of Chicago Press.

Elder, G. H. Jr. (1978b). "Family History and the Life Course." In T. K. Hareven (Ed.), *Transitions: The Family and the Life Course in Historical Perspective* (pp. 17–64). New York: Academic Press.

Furstenberg, F. (1976). *Unplanned Parenthood: The Social Consequences of Teenage Childbearing*. New York: Free Press.

Hareven, T. K. (1971). "The History of the Family as an Interdisciplinary Field." In K. Rabb & R. I. Rotberg (Eds.), *The Family in History: Interdisciplinary Essays* (pp. 211–226). New York: Harper & Row.

Hareven, T. K. (1978). "The Historical Study of the Life Course." In T. K. Hareven (Ed.), *Transitions: The Family and the Life Course in Historical Perspective*. New York: Academic Press.

Hayghe, H. (1983). "Married Couples: Work and Income Patterns." *Monthly Labor Review, 106*(12), 26–29.

Hayghe, H. (1984). "Working Mothers Reach Record Numbers in 1984." *Monthly Labor Review, 107*(12), 34–35.

Hofferth, S. (1985). "Updating Children's Life Course." *Journal of Marriage and the Family, 47*(1), 93–115.

Kamerman, S. B. (1984). "Women, Children and Poverty in Industrialized Countries." *Signs, 10*(2), 249–271.

Kamerman, S. B. (1985). "Young, Poor and a Mother Alone." In H. McAdoo & T. J. Parham (Eds.), *Services to Young Families*. Washington, D.C.: American Public Welfare Association.

"Labor Force Activity of Mothers of Young Children Continues at Record Pace." (1985, September 19). *Bureau of Labor Statistics News*.

Lamb, M. E., & Sagi, A. (1983). *Fatherhood and Family Policy*. Hillsdale, N.J.: Lawrence Erlbaum Associates.

Laslett, P. (Ed.). (1972). *Household and Family in Past Time*. Cambridge, England: Cambridge University Press.

Lewis, R. A., & Pleck, J. H. (Eds.). (1979). "Men's Roles in the Family." [Special Issue]. *The Family Coordinator, 28*(4).

McGee, E. A. (1982). *Too Little, Too Late: Services for Teenage Parents*. New York: Ford Foundation.

Mitterauer, M., & Sieder, R. (1982). *The European Family*. Oxford, England: Basil Blackwell.

Moore, K. A., & Burt, M. R. (1982). *Private Crisis,* *Public Cost*. Washington, D.C.: Urban Institute.

Norton, A. J., & Glick, P. C. (in press). "One-Parent Families: A Social and Economic Profile." *Journal of Family Relations*.

Pleck, J. H. (1979). "Men's Family Work: Three Perspectives and Some New Data." *Family Coordinator, 28*(4),

Pleck, J. H. (1985). *Working Wives/Working Husbands*. Beverly Hills, Calif.: Sage Publications.

Russell, G., & Radin, N. (1983). "Increased Paternal Participation: The Father's Perspective." In M. E. Lamb & A. Sagi, *Fatherhood and Family Policy* (pp. 139–165). Hillsdale, N.J.: Lawrence Erlbaum Associates.

Scheirer, M. A. (1983). "Household Structure Among Welfare Families: Correlates and Consequences." *Journal of Marriage and the Family, 45*(4), 761–771.

Shorter, E. (1975). *The Making of the Modern Family*. New York: Basic Books.

Smelser, N. J., & Halpern, S. (1978). "The Historical Triangulation of Family, Economy and Education." In J. Demos & S. S. Boocock (Eds.), *Turning Points: Historical and Sociological Essays on the Family* (pp. S288–S315). Chicago: University of Chicago Press.

U.S. Bureau of the Census. (1983a). *Population Profile of the United States: 1982*. (Series P-23, No. 130). Washington, D.C.: U.S. Government Printing Office.

U.S. Bureau of the Census. (1984a). *Household and Family Characteristics: March 1983*. (Series P-20, No. 388). Washington, D.C.: U.S. Government Printing Office.

U.S. Bureau of the Census. (1985a). *Marital Status and Living Arrangements: March 1984*. (Series P-20, No. 399). Washington, D.C.: U.S. Government Printing Office.

U.S. Bureau of the Census (1985b). *Characteristics of the Population Below the Poverty Level: 1983*. (Series P-60, No. 147). Washington, D.C.: U.S. Government Printing Office.

U.S. Congress, House of Representatives, Select Committee on Children, Youth, and Families. (1983). *U.S. Children and Their Families: Current Conditions and Recent Trends*. Washington, D.C.: U.S. Government Printing Office.

Waldman, E. (1983). "Labor Force Statistics from a Family Perspective." *Monthly Labor Review, 106*(12), 16–20.

Wrigley, E. A. (1977). "Reflections on the History of the Family." *Daedalus, 106*(2), 71–85.

For Further Reading

Goode, W. J. (1964). *The Family*. Englewood Cliffs, N.J.: Prentice-Hall.

Kamerman, S. B., & Kahn, A. J. (1981). *Child*

Care, Family Benefits, and Working Parents. New York: Columbia University Press.

Kamerman, S.B., & Kahn, A. J. (1978). *Family Policy: Government and Families in Fourteen Countries.* New York: Columbia University Press.

FAMILY: ONE PARENT

The most profound change in family formations since the 1950s has been the emergence of the one-parent family. This phenomenon is so pervasive that the U.S. Commission on Civil Rights (1983) predicts that by 1990, half of all American children will spend part of their childhood living with one parent only.

Single parenthood is chiefly a phenomenon of women alone, heading families with dependent children. Despite some gender role changes over the past 2 decades, only a small proportion of men (2.8 percent, with only slight variation over the past 20 years) are single parents of dependent children (U.S. Bureau of the Census, 1984e). (Single fathers have received a degree of media coverage out of proportion to their numerical strength.) Unless otherwise noted, all data presented here refer to female-headed families with dependent children.

"One-parent family" is a collective term embracing a variety of family types and responsibilities. Marital status is the criterion commonly used to mark the differences in the various categories of one-parent families. Disruption of marriage may come about through separation, divorce, or prolonged absence or death of the spouse. These marital events may convert the mother into a lone head of household with dependent children, the common definition of a one-parent family. Increasingly, however, no marriage may have occurred. When a child is born out of wedlock, the mother is statistically referred to as "never married." It is interesting to note that men become custodial parents principally as a result of separation and divorce—rarely as unwed fathers—and that black men are more likely to be custodial parents than are white men.

Although one-parent families accounted for 26 percent of all families in 1984, compared with 22 percent in 1980 and 13 percent in 1970 (U. S. Bureau of the Census, 1984e), the diversity of one-parent families is considerable. This is illustrated in Figure 1.

A multitude of government publications, large-scale studies, and diverse reports from concerned organizations throughout the country have addressed the phenomenon of the rise in one-parent families since the early 1970s. These include, from the U.S. Bureau of the Census, "Marital Status and Living Arrangements: March 1981" (1982) and subsequent years (1983c, 1984d, 1985a), "Household and Family Characteristics, 1982" (1983b) and subsequent years (1984c, 1984e), and *"Statistical Abstract of the United States, 1984* (1984f), as well as works by Bane (1976), Ross and Sawhill (1975), Johnson (1975), Kamerman (1982), and Wattenberg and Reinhardt (1979).

Significant Changes in Demographic Data

The following data confirm the profound changes that have occurred in both the social and economic lives of one-parent families (unless otherwise noted, derived from U.S. Bureau of the Census, 1984b):

1. The number of one-parent families with children under 18 more than doubled from 1970 to 1984. These were chiefly families headed by women.

2. In 1960, there were about 25.7 million families with one or more children under 18 years of age. Of these, about 1.89 million (7.4 percent) were headed by women. By 1970, there were about 28.8 million families, of which about 2.8 million (10.2 percent) were headed by women. In 1982, there were about 31 million families, of which about 5.9 million (18.9 percent) were headed by women (U.S. Bureau of the Census, 1984f).

3. As of March 1984, almost 23 percent of families with dependent children were maintained by women—that is, one-fifth of all American families.

4. Significantly, the highest proportion of these female-headed families had only one child under 18, but a noteworthy number—almost 10 percent—had more than three children, although this percentage dropped between 1980 and 1984. The steep decline of large families as a proportion of all families among single parents sharpens the picture of changes in family size. Inasmuch as family

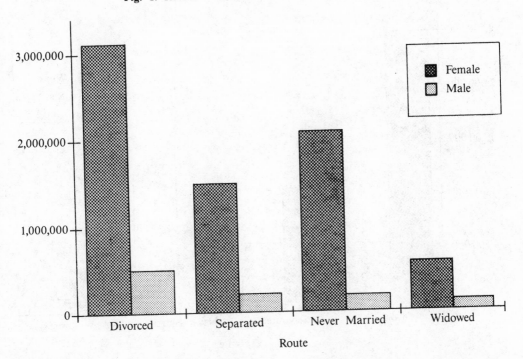

Fig. 1. Routes to One-Parent Family by Sex, 1984

Source: U.S. Bureau of the Census, "Household and Family Characteristics: March 1984," in *Current Population Reports,* Series P–20, No. 398 (Washington, D.C.: U.S. Government Printing Office, 1984).

size generally predicts the level of economic viability, this is an optimistic trend.

The most telling social commentary is revealed in the following data, which reflect the factor of race (unless otherwise noted, derived from U.S. Bureau of the Census, 1984e, Table D):

1. The growth of single-parent families in the black community has been steady and dramatic. This family type now outnumbers two-parent families and comprises a larger portion of all black families with children under 18 than any other family type. Having grown from 33 percent of all black families in 1970 to over 59 percent in 1983, this trend is unmistakable.

2. The proportion of families headed by a single parent in the white community is approximately one in five. The ratio for black families is one in two. Female-headed fami-

lies are three times as prevalent among black families as among white families.

The racial factor is also significant in examining the various routes to single parenthood, as shown in Figure 2:

1. For white women, single parenthood chiefly denotes a change in marital status—namely divorce. For black women, single parenthood most frequently occurs without marriage, through the birth of a child out of wedlock.

2. More than half the white female-headed families are maintained by women who are divorced. Just over 25 percent of black female-headed families originate in divorce. For both groups, the divorce rate has risen steadily over a period of 13 years. The data from 1980 to 1984, however, appear to show some slowing in the rate of increase in American divorces.

Fig. 2. Routes to One-Parent Family by Race, 1984

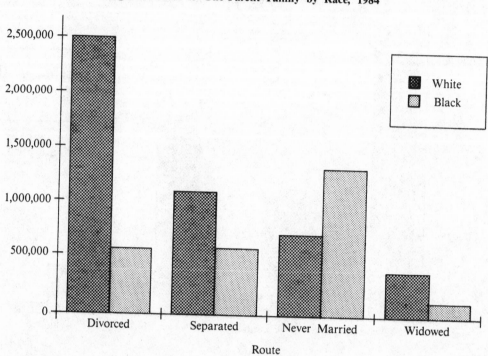

Source: U.S. Bureau of the Census, "Household and Family Characteristics: March 1984," in *Current Population Reports,* Series P-20, No. 398 (Washington, D.C.: U.S. Government Printing Office, 1984).

3. The "separated" category, which is subsumed statistically under the "spouse absent" category, represents about one-fifth of the families with children maintained by women. This family formation, typically a stage preceding divorce, is declining for black families and rising for white families.

4. The number of widowed spouses with minor children is a small proportion of all families—under 10 percent—and has dwindled slowly but steadily over 13 years for both black and white families.

The fastest-growing portion of female-headed families overall is in the "never-married" category. Here, too, racial differences appear:

1. From 1970 to 1983, the number of never-married mothers grew by over 259 percent.

2. Of all never-married mothers, more than half are black, highly disproportionate to their numbers in the population. Of all black women heading families in 1984, over half had never married, a dramatic increase from 1970 when they made up 18 percent of the single parent population. Their numbers had doubled (see Figure 3). In white single-parent families, the increase is even more startling: 3.3 percent of mothers of single-parent families in 1970 had never married, compared to 11.1 percent in 1984. Their numbers had tripled. However, as formidable as this increase is, the sheer number of never-married women heading white families (729,000), although substantial, points to the significance of the number of never-married women heading black families (1,332,000).

The pervasive changes in the demographic data reflect the social and economic changes in the role of women in the family,

Fig. 3. Never-Married Route to One-Parent Family for Women by Race, 1970–1984

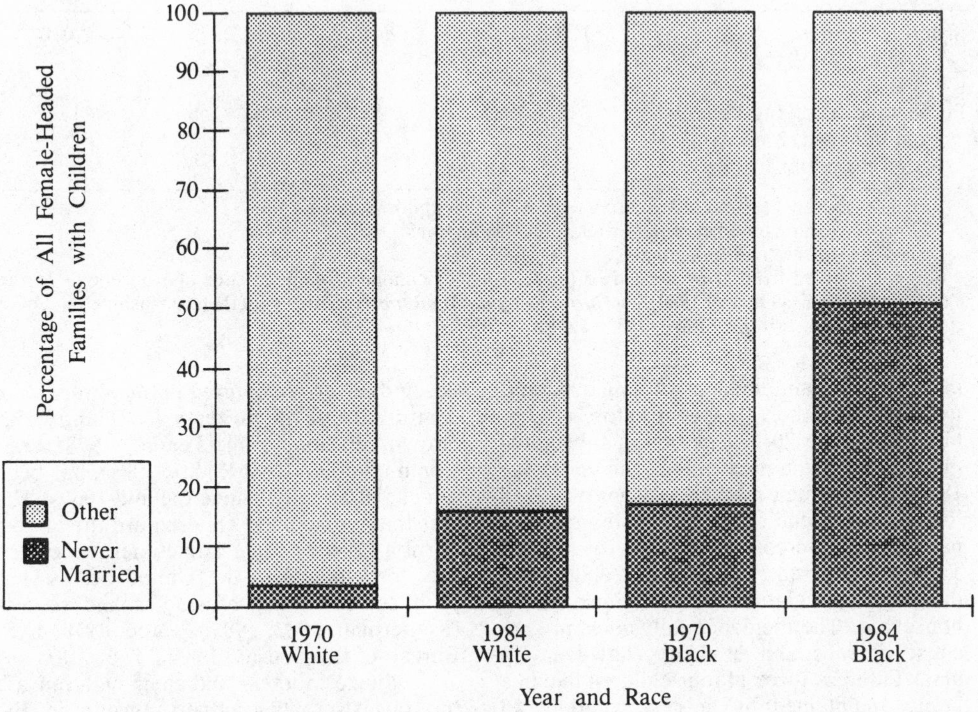

Source: U.S. Bureau of the Census, "Household and Family Characteristics: March 1984," in *Current Population Reports,* Series P-20, No. 398 (Washington, D.C.: U.S. Government Printing Office, 1984).

labor market, and society; the advent of small families; and changes in attitudes and values surrounding the institution of marriage. For black families, the disproportionate rates of unemployment, underemployment, and discouraged workers borne by black men sharply reduce the availability of men as viable marriage partners (Center for the Study of Social Policy, 1984). The interactive nature of these factors has produced an era marked by marital instability and nonmarital families. As discussed previously, the paths to one-parent family status are various. What the demographic data do not reveal is the dynamic movement in and out of one-parent family status through remarriage, stable cohabitation relationships, and varying periods of single-parent status.

Although one of two marriages ends in divorce, remarriage occurs with striking regularity. The incidence is uneven between men and women, however. In every age group, a significantly higher proportion of women than men remain unmarried following divorce. From 1970 to 1980, the remarriage rate for women dropped by 30 percent. The rate of remarriage for black women particularly declined (U.S. Bureau of the Census, 1984f, Table 70).

Children's Living Arrangements

The diversity of circumstances leading up to one-parent families sheds light on the changing nature of the family structures in which American children are being reared. A higher proportion of children are now living

Table 1. Average Monthly Cash Income of Households in the United States

	All Households	Female-Headed[a] Households	Married Couples	Householder 65 and Over
Monthly median income (in dollars)[b]	1,768	841	2,335	1,010
Percentage receiving benefits from noncash, means-tested programs[c]	14.7	53	8.8	17.7

[a] Female householder, no husband present, with own children under 18.
[b] Monthly cash income before taxes and other deductions.
[c] Chiefly Medicaid and food stamps.
Source: Derived from U.S. Bureau of the Census, "Economic Characteristics of Households in the United States: Third Quarter 1984," in *Current Population Reports*, Series P-70, No. 6 (Washington, D.C.: U.S. Government Printing Office, 1985, Tables 5, 6).

in a family maintained by a single parent, usually the mother, than ever before in U.S. history. Over a 20-year period, a substantial increase in the number of children under age 18 living with their mother only has occurred for all groups studied: black, white, and Hispanic (U.S. Bureau of the Census, 1984f, Table 69). Currently, one in five children in the general population lives in a single-parent household. The incidence falls unevenly because of race and ethnicity, however. In black families, three of four children live in a family maintained by only one parent. In Hispanic families, this is true for one of four children, and in white families, for one of seven children (U.S. Bureau of the Census, 1983c, 1984f, Table 70).

The family structures in which children are being reared is also diverse. Children living with divorced mothers increased by 122 percent since 1970, and the number living with never-married women more than quadrupled. The incidence of black children living with never-married mothers rose steadily from 1970 to 1982, but the rate for Hispanic and white children during this period increased even faster (U.S. Bureau of the Census, 1984f, Table 70).

Economic and Social Circumstances

One-parent families, with the implied disruption and discontinuity, claim major attention from the social work profession. The economic problems of such families and their social and emotional resources are continuing concerns.

The link between female-headed families and poverty, captured in the phrase "the feminization of poverty" (Brandwein, Brown, & Fox, 1974; Pearce, 1978; U.S. Commission on Civil Rights, 1983), has been a focus of attention since the mid-1960s. The fact that women and children are the largest portion of poor people, sometimes designated the "new poor" in the United States, has produced a variety of studies and reports (Kamerman, 1982, 1985; Pearce, 1978; U.S. Bureau of the Census, 1984a, Table 18).

Single mothers and their children are the fastest-growing poverty group in the United States (U.S. Bureau of the Census, 1984f, Table 779). Of significance is the disproportionate number of black families maintained by women who are poor (63.7 percent), compared to white families who are poor (39.3 percent). (The presence of more than one child makes for a higher incidence of poverty for all families, black as well as white.)

The sharp disparity in average monthly income of young female-headed families, compared to other types of families, is revealed in Table 1. Female-headed households must sustain themselves on half the median income of all U.S. households, and on almost two-thirds less than married couples. To augment their slender resources, more than half rely on Medicaid and food stamps, compared to less than 10 percent of married couples.

Five years after a divorce, however, only the lower one-third in income categories must rely on Aid to Families with Dependent Children (AFDC) or food stamps for their survival. Poor women are impoverished before and after divorce, 50 to 70 percent of them requiring public assistance to augment their slender earnings and intermittent child support payments. Time appears to treat middle- and upper-income single-parent families with a kinder economic fate, although even in these income groups, the descent into poverty immediately after divorce is so sharp that one in seven needs public assistance. However, by the end of the fifth year following a divorce, through remarriage or earnings, these families are often economically self-sufficient (Weiss, n.d.).

The difficulties in replacing the father's contribution to family income may be noted in the sharp reversal of economic roles that occurs in many divorced families. In predivorce families, fathers typically contribute almost 80 percent of the family income, with 50 percent of families also relying on mothers' earnings that, on average, constitute 20 percent of family income. These proportions are reversed 5 years after divorce. (Weiss, n.d.).

The capacity of women as lone parents to assemble different kinds of income to meet family needs is highly variable. Commonly, income includes wages from working outside the home, public assistance, a combination of work and public assistance, child support, and noncash items such as food stamps, housing subsidies, Medicaid, and child care subsidies. Control over these resources is of primary importance.

The route to economic independence through earnings has dismal promise for low-income women. Only one-third of those who left AFDC were able to do so by relying on their earnings only (Bane & Ellwood, 1983; Johnson & Waldman, 1983). Further, unemployment—frequently associated with other employment problems such as low hourly earnings, part-year employment, and involuntary part-time employment—falls more heavily on single parents than on other groups of women workers (Ryscavage, 1982).

Resorting to AFDC for support remains the only viable option for 10.4 million people. Of these, 70 percent were children; the rest were chiefly mothers. A report on characteristics of women receiving AFDC in the last decade discloses that they have become younger, better educated, and have fewer children. One in four were either working or seeking employment (U.S. Department

of Health, Education, & Welfare, 1978, 1979). A dwindling number report that they are needed at home for child care (Duvall, Goudreau, & Marsh 1982).

Whether one-parent families succumb to the serious and long-term consequences of poverty depends on the age of the custodial parent, race, number of children, labor market attachment, and social strata. Inasmuch as women aged 20 to 29 are now among the largest number of mothers on AFDC, they should be acknowledged as a particular target group for income and social service strategies.

Of all one-parent families, however, the never-married category is the most economically disadvantaged. Only one in ten never-married mothers receives child support, and the awards are only half as large as those received by divorced women (U.S. Bureau of the Census, 1983a). Long-term poverty is almost assured if the mother is a high school dropout, has no labor market experience, and has three or more children in the family. If these factors are compounded by race—with its inherent discriminatory consequences—young, black, never-married mothers face long-term welfare dependency (Bane & Ellwood, 1983).

Social Work's Response

A major issue for social work concerns paternity adjudication to protect the rights of children. This issue will be a focus of attention into the 1990s (Wattenberg, 1984). Furthermore, a concerted effort to involve unwed fathers in the life of unwed families is now emerging (Barrett & Robinson, 1982; Winger, 1984). This will probably absorb social work in outreach efforts for some time to come.

Social work's interest in social policies to ameliorate the poverty status of one-parent families has focused on strategies for augmenting the income of these vulnerable families. Areas of attention include employment, housing, health care, child care, food stamps, AFDC, and child support.

Social work has also been concerned with both the short- and long-term social and emotional consequences of one-parent families. Whether these families are created by nonmarital relationships and the birth of out-of-wedlock children, death, separation, desertion, or divorce, the process of becoming a sole parent may be traumatic, especially if the custodial parent was unprepared or had no choice in the matter (Bloom, White, & Asher, 1978; Wallerstein & Kelly, 1980).

However, no absolute consequences for either the custodial parent or the children have been determined. Just as the literature on the causes of marital instability reflect ambiguity and contradictions (Espenshade, 1979; Wattenberg & Reinhardt, 1979), the effects on children of living in a one-parent family are complex. A variety of intervening factors come into play. Situations in which family members experience social rejection, acute loneliness, and uncertainty aggravated by unstable and meager incomes are familiar to every social worker in family and children's agencies. On the other hand, studies report that leaving a stressful relationship (such as through divorce) contributes a degree of relief that provides an environment for the healthy development of children (Kulka & Weingarten, 1979; McCubbin et al., 1982).

Social work's position has generally been that single-parent families are a necessary adaptation to a postindustrial society that created rising expectations of living with dignity and self-determination. The preservation of marriage at any cost is considered too high a price to pay for harm inflicted on parents and children in injurious situations. The decision to separate from damaging relationships may be seen as a strong, independent, self-renewing choice. Although social work has been absorbed in the prevention of marital breakup through counseling and making available resources for family survival, it has also been concerned with policies to promote ways of dissolving marriages beyond repair that minimize penalties for both partners and children. Social work's concern is to create more equitable responsibilities through joint custody and child support enforcement and to retain, if possible, the child's access to both parents with visitation procedures that provide the best environment for the child.

The complex interplay between single parents and their environments is not easily understood. Although society has made some limited change in socially prescribed roles and provided wider options for families to live without fear and injury, these changes do not always coincide with perceived needs. Access to economic and social support systems for single-parent families is a persistent concern of social work. Identifying barriers and overcoming problems remain high on the research agenda. At least the language has changed, however—single-parent families are no longer thought to be living in "broken homes."

ESTHER WATTENBERG

For further information, see AID TO FAMILIES WITH DEPENDENT CHILDREN; CHILD SUPPORT; DIVORCE AND SEPARATION; FAMILY: CONTEMPORARY PATTERNS; FAMILY PRACTICE; FAMILY SERVICES; INCOME MAINTENANCE SYSTEM.

References

Bane, M. J. (1976). *Here to Stay: American Families in the Twentieth Century*. New York: Basic Books.

Bane, M. J., & Ellwod, D. T. (1983). *The Dynamics of Dependency: The Routes To Self Sufficiency*. Report prepared by Urban Systems Research and Engineering, Harvard University, Cambridge, Mass.

Barrett, R. L., & Robinson, B. E. (1982). "Teenage Fathers: Neglected Too Long." *Social Work, 27* (6), 484–488.

Bloom, B. L., White, S. W., & Asher, S. J. (1978). "Marital Disruption As A Stressor—A Review." *Psychological Bulletin, 85*(4), 867–894.

Brandwein, R. A., Brown, C. A., & Fox, E. M. (1974). "Women and Children Last: The Social Situation of Divorced Mothers and Their Families." *Journal of Marriage and the Family, 36*(3), 498–514.

Center for the Study of Social Policy. (1984). *The "Flip Side" of Black Families Headed by Women: The Economic Status of Black Men*. Washington, D.C.: Author.

Duvall, H. J., Goudreau, K. W., & Marsh, R. E. (1982). "Aid to Families with Dependent Children: Characteristics of Recipients in 1979." *Social Security Bulletin, 45*(4), 3–9.

Espenshade, T. J. (1979). "The Economic Consequences of Divorce." *Journal of Marriage and the Family, 41*(3), 615–625.

Johnson, B., & Waldman, E. (1983). "Most Women Who Maintain Families Receive Poor Labor Market Returns." *Monthly Labor Review, 106*(12), 30–34.

Johnson, S. B. (1975). "The Impact of Women's Liberation on Marriage, Divorce and Family Life Styles." In C. B. Lloyd (Ed.), *Sex, Discrimination and Division of Labor* (pp 401–424). New York: Columbia University Press.

Kamerman, S. B. (1982). *Families that Work:*

Children in a Changing World. Washington, D.C.: National Academy Press.

Kamerman, S. (1985). "Young, Poor and a Mother Alone." In H. McAdoo & T. M. J. Parham (Eds.), *Services to Young Families: Program Review and Policy Implications* (pp. 1–38). Washington, D.C.: American Public Welfare Association.

Kulka, R. A., & Weingarten, H. (1979). "The Long-Term Effects of Parental Divorce in Childhood on Adult Adjustment." *Journal of Social Issues, 35*(4), 50–78.

McCubbin, H. I., et al. (1982). "Family Stress and Coping: Decade Review." *Journal of Marriage and the Family, 42*(4), 885.

Pearce, D. (1978). "The Feminization of Poverty: Women, Work and Welfare." *Urban and Social Change Review, 11*(1,2), 28–36.

Ross, H. K., & Sawhill, I. V. (1975). *Time of Transition.* Washington, D.C.: Urban Institute.

Ryscavage, P. M. (1982). "Employment Problems and Poverty: Examining the Linkages." *Monthly Labor Review, 105*(6), 55.

U.S. Bureau of the Census. (1982). "Marital Status and Living Arrangements: March 1981." In *Current Population Reports* (Series P-20, No. 372). Washington, D.C.: U.S. Government Printing Office.

U.S. Bureau of the Census. (1983a). "Child Support and Alimony: 1981." (Advance Report, Special Studies, Series P-23, No. 124). Washington, D.C.: U.S. Government Printing Office.

U.S. Bureau of the Census (1983b). "Household and Family Characteristics: March 1982." In *Current Population Reports* (Series P-20, No. 381, Table A). Washington, D.C.: U.S. Government Printing Office.

U.S. Bureau of the Census. (1983c). "Marital Status and Living Arrangements: March 1982." In *Current Population Reports* (Series P-20, No. 380, Tables 1, 2). Washington, D.C.: U.S. Government Printing Office.

U.S. Bureau of the Census. (1984a). "Characteristics of the Population in Poverty: March 1982." In *Current Population Reports* (Series P-60, No. 144, Table 18). Washington, D.C.: U.S. Government Printing Office.

U.S. Bureau of the Census. (1984c). "Household and Family Characteristics: March 1983." In *Current Population Reports* (Series P-20, No. 388, Table E). Washington, D.C.: U.S. Government Printing Office.

U.S. Bureau of the Census. (1984d). "Marital Status and Living Arrangments: March 1983." In *Current Population Reports* (Series P-20, No. 389). Washington, D.C.: U.S. Government Printing Office.

U.S. Bureau of the Census. (1984e). "Household and Family Characteristics: March 1984." In *Current Population Reports* (Series P-20, No. 398, Table D). Washington, D.C.: U.S. Government Printing Office.

U.S. Bureau of the Census. (1984f). *Statistical Abstract of the United States, 1984.* Washington, D.C.: U.S. Government Printing Office.

U.S. Bureau of the Census. (1985). "Marital Status and Living Arrangements: March 1984." In *Current Population Reports* (Series P-20, No. 399). Washington, D.C.: U.S. Government Printing Office.

U.S. Commission on Civil Rights. (1983). *A Growing Crisis: Disadvantaged Women and Their Children* (Clearinghouse Publication No. 78). Washington, D.C.: U.S. Government Printing Office.

U.S. Department of Health, Education and Welfare. (1978). *AFDC: A Chart Book* (Publication No. SSA78-11721). Washington, D.C.: U.S. Government Printing Office.

U.S. Department of Health and Human Services. (1979). *AFDC: 1979 Recipient Characteristics Study* (Table 31, p. 50). Washington, D.C.: U.S. Government Printing Office.

Wallerstein, J. S., & Kelly, J. B. (1980). "Effects of Divorce on the Visiting Father-Child Relationship." *American Journal of Psychiatry, 137*(12), 1534–1539.

Wattenberg, E. (Ed.). (1984). *The Project on Paternity Adjudication and Child Support Obligations of Teenage Parents.* Report to the Ford Foundation, Center for Urban and Regional Affairs, Minneapolis, Minn.

Wattenberg, E., & Reinhardt, H. (1979). "Female-Headed Families: Trends and Implications." *Social Work, 24*(6), 460–467.

Weiss, R. S. (n.d.). *Impact on Single Parents of Post-Marital Income Loss.* Washington, D.C.: U.S. Department of Health and Human Services.

Winger, R. (1984). "Review of Literature on Unwed Fathers." In E. Wattenberg (Ed.), *The Project on Paternity Adjudication and Child Support Obligations of Teenage Parents.* Report to the Ford Foundation, Center for Urban and Regional Affairs, Minneapolis, Minn.

FAMILY: STEPFAMILIES

The hallmark of the contemporary American family is its diversity. Included in its many configurations is the stepfamily. The increased visibility of stepfamilies in the general population and as social agency clients suggests the changing patterns of marriage, divorce, and remarriage in the United States.

Social change and family change thus reflect changes in individual values and goals, and yet the trend toward remarriage suggests that close relationships in a family context continue to be an enduring goal for individuals in this society.

Although social trends indicate that the stepfamily is an important segment of the family population, a significant paradox is that the literature on this particular family configuration has been sparse and contradictory. Social work practitioners have observed a similar dearth of clinical literature to guide intervention at clinical, educational, and social policy levels. Stepfamily clients have commented on their frustration because the professional community has been insufficiently sensitive to the unique issues and realities of their situation. Indeed, the stepfamily is considered by many to be the same as the traditional nuclear family, despite the differences between the two.

Definitions

Both nuclear families and stepfamilies are two-parent, two-generation structures. They differ in kinship and legal arrangements, however, as well as in family development stages and cultural identity. The typical nuclear family—the idealized and baseline family unit against which all others are measured—comprises a legally married husband and wife who are biological or adoptive parents of mutual children who live with them until they are old enough to live on their own. In contrast, the typical stepfamily comprises a legally married husband and wife, one or both of whom has children from a prior relationship or marriage. These children may reside with the remarried couple or live elsewhere. Other children may also be born to the remarried couple, so a nuclear family may coexist within the stepfamily.

Variations in stepfamilies occur when an unmarried parent adopts or has a biological child and later marries for the first time. In this situation, the parent's spouse becomes the child's stepparent. Another variant occurs when a cohabiting man and woman have children from prior relationships living with them. Such families have been described as "socially remarried" because they meet some but not all of the criteria of the stepfamily defined above.

In addition to its differences from the nuclear family, the stepfamily presents variations in parent-child structure. Thus, only the husband may have children from a prior marriage, or only the wife, or both may have children from prior marriages. These variations have significant implications for family dynamics and the nature of the stress the family experiences.

Stepfamilies are described by many other terms, including "reconstituted" or "reconstructed families" (used by sociologists) and "blended," "combined," or "remarried families" (used by social workers). All these terms describe families in which at least some of the children belong to one spouse and not the other. This key characteristic sets up the step situation that has significance for many of the normal, nonpathological issues these families encounter.

Social Trends and Demographics

The stepfamily is as old as the human family. References to this family structure are found in the Bible and in folk and classical literature. Early on, stepfamily formation represented the effort of a parent who had lost a spouse through death to repair the loss through remarriage.

The word "step" is derived from Old English and Old High German terms that were tied to the experience of bereavement and defined as "to deprive of children or parents" (Webster's Third New International Dictionary, 1961, p. 2237). Later, the term was broadened to include the "replacement" parent, whether male or female. Ultimately, the term also came to include stepsibling relationships if a stepparent had children from a prior marriage.

Over time the term "step" acquired a negative connotation. This is reflected in such fairy tales as "Cinderella," "Hansel and Gretel," and "Snow White." The persistent theme is that of children whose mother has died. When the father remarries, the stepmother victimizes the stepchild and the father is either absent or helpless to intervene. This fairy-tale motif is present in cultures all over the world; for example, the theme of Hansel and Gretel has been identified in African cultures, and the Cinderella theme has been identified in ninth-century Chinese culture. The continuing appeal of these stories is evident in current anthologies that depict the wicked stepmother as unnaturally cruel to her stepchildren. Stepfamily relationships are also used to reflect mistreatment or neglect, as in "our department is treated like a stepchild." The current belief is "step is less" (Wald, 1981, pp. 47–57).

Although the initial use of the prefix "step-" referred to the death of a spouseparent, the term today also includes any relatives acquired when a biological or adoptive parent remarries after divorce. Whatever the antecedent negative connotations still surround the term, and the families still experience marital dissolution for spouses and the loss of a parent for children. The stepfamily has been further burdened by its lack of institutionalization, reflected in the lack of reference in textbooks to the stepfamily as a unique family structure, the lack of clarity about appropriate role expectations for stepparents, and the failure of many social agencies to differentiate between nuclear families and stepfamilies for statistical or clinical purposes. The U.S. Bureau of the Census also has no specific category for stepfamilies or stepchildren. Figures on the incidence of these families and children in the general population are thus inferred from related questions and government documents. These estimates do not reflect a direct census count (P. C. Glick, Senior Demographer, U.S. Bureau of the Census, personal communication, August 1980; S. Laue, U.S. Bureau of the Census, personal communication, January 1986).

Although not institutionalized as a unique family structure, remarriage has been common in the United States since early colonial days, when death rates were high and most people who were widowed remarried. Because divorce was rare until the end of the nineteenth century, few remarriages were preceded by divorce. After the turn of the century, however, divorce rates climbed steadily. They sharply accelerated after World War II and in the counterculture years of the 1960s. By the mid-1960s, the primary antecedent to remarriage had changed from death to divorce, and remarriage rates tended to parallel divorce rates. By 1978, 12 percent of those who remarried had been widowed, and 88 percent had been divorced (Cherlin, 1981, p. 29). The current divorce rate has increased from one of every three marriages in the 1970s to one of every two marriages in the 1980s. Reasons given for the increased divorce rate have included changing attitudes toward the sanctity of the nuclear family and a philosophy of self-actualization that includes the right to be happy in a marriage.

Sixty percent of those who divorce have minor children and thus become part of the single-parent family pool from which stepfamilies are formed. The single-parent stage is transitional, however; 75 to 80 percent of these parents remarry within 2 to 5 years and reestablish a two-parent, twogeneration family structure. Of the 62 million families in the United States, 39 percent are two-parent, two-generation families comprising a husband, wife, and one or more children (U.S. Bureau of the Census, 1984a). As indicated earlier, there is no direct count of stepfamilies. However, estimates are that in one out of five households one or both spouses were formerly divorced and are currently remarried (Cherlin & McCarthy, 1985, p. 25). Most remarriages include children from previous marriages (Cherlin & McCarthy, 1985, p. 26), so it can be estimated that 20 percent of the two-parent, twogeneration families in the United States are stepfamilies. (Not included in this number are the live-in or cohabiting stepfamilies defined earlier.) Census figures also indicate that from 1973 to 1983 the number of unmarried couples who live together and have children from prior marriages has grown, thus further increasing the number of people who live in stepfamily situations (Glick & Norton, 1977; U.S. Bureau of the Census, 1984b, p. 7).

The number of stepchildren who live with a natural parent and a stepparent has also grown. In 1960, the Bureau of the Census estimated that one of ten minor children was a stepchild residing with a biological parent and a stepparent (Glick, 1979, pp. 170–175). By 1978, estimates were that one of eight children under 18 was a stepchild living in a stepfamily. Projections were that if no modifications occurred in existing trends, 45 percent of the children born in 1977 would live for some period of time in a single-parent family, with the potential of becoming stepchildren (U.S. Bureau of the Census, 1980). Assuming that divorce and remarriage rates would remain approximately the same, estimates were that one of four children born in 1977 would live for some period of time as a stepchild in a stepfamily (Glick, 1979, p. 176).

These estimates did not include children with the potential of becoming stepchildren when a widowed parent remarried or when an unmarried single parent later married for the first time. Other children not included in these estimates were those living with a cohabiting parent in a social remarriage or who continued to live with a single parent but had contact with a noncustodial remarried parent and his or her spouse. Thus, the numbers of children and the variety of ways in which they experience the step situation are dramatic.

Information on those who divorce a second time is sparse and tentative. However, what evidence is available indicates that the redivorce rate is 54 percent, with an average duration of 6 to 7 years in the remarriage, compared to 47 percent for first marriages with an average duration of 7 years (Cherlin, 1981, p. 30). This shows that although the increase in divorce rates between first and subsequent marriages is modest, the hoped-for goal of reestablishing an enduring family is achieved by fewer than half who try. Beyond the statistical significance of this number is the human drama of further loss and trauma for many parents and children.

Strengths and Strains

The strengths and strains typically experienced by the stepfamily are intricately related to the characteristics that differentiate it from the two-parent, two-generation family structure—the nuclear family. The framework for this analysis includes kinship and legal structures as well as family life-cycle developmental stages and cultural identity.

Unlike the nuclear family, the stepfamily has one partner who is a biological and legal parent to children from a prior marriage and another who has no kinship or legal ties. Unless a stepparent legally adopts a stepchild, no legal obligations inhere in the relationship except as designated by a limited number of states for welfare eligibility (Kargman, 1983, pp. 231–238). By adopting a stepchild, a stepparent becomes an adoptive parent and is no longer a stepparent. In contrast, in the nuclear family both partners have mutual kinship or biological ties to their children, because by definition the nuclear family has no children from a prior marriage. As indicated earlier, if mutual children are born

to a remarried couple, a nuclear family is created within the stepfamily structure.

The stepfamily experiences three unique developmental stages: a process of family dissolution, a period of time as a single-parent family, and a process of reconstitution as a two-parent, two-generation stepfamily. The duration of the first two stages varies: the first stage averages 7 years after the first marriage, and the second stage usually lasts between 2 and 5 years. The dissolution stage introduces great loss—the loss of the original nuclear family, the loss of a parent and frequently the loss related to a change in neighborhood, school, and significant friendships or support systems. The third stage involves the integration of at least one and often many more family members of the acquired spouse-stepparent. Each stage has accompanying developmental tasks—for both the family and individuals—that are not known to the nuclear family. Thus the dissolution stage requires the resolution of ambivalence over whether spouses should divorce or not divorce, and the single-parent stage requires reorganization and adaptation to new routines and lifestyles. The major developmental task of the reconstitution stage is to achieve a balance between old and new relationships.

An examination of cultural identity reveals that the cultural perceptions of society attribute lesser status to stepfamilies than to nuclear families. This perception contributes to negative self-images among stepfamily members. This is reinforced by laws that do not accord stepparents the rights and duties that facilitate positive family functioning. For example, a stepparent does not have the right to make medical decisions for a stepchild unless some accord on this has been reached through power of attorney with the biological parents. Nor does a stepchild automatically become an heir to a stepparent's estate unless this is clearly specified in a will. The differences between nuclear parents and stepparents introduce barriers to the formation of close bonds between stepparent and stepchild in addition to the barriers created by the fact that husband and wife do not share the same biological and legal ties to the same children and the additional developmental stages in the life of the stepfamily (Wald, 1985, chap. 2).

Despite these barriers, stepfamilies

typically bring to their new family a high level of motivation to succeed, to avoid a repetition of early mistakes in the nuclear family and to encourage the growth and development of all family members. These strengths have enabled many stepfamilies to cope successfully with the problems these barriers generate.

Some problems in stepfamily functioning reflect interpersonal stress in the family itself. Stepmothers, in particular, may feel excluded by stepchildren and may have few guidelines for the appropriate discipline of stepchildren. Husbands cite difficulties in arriving at common goals and priorities within the family unit. They emphasize the need to develop a lifestyle congruent with the new stepfamily rather than continue a divided lifestyle in which the values of a former single parent may be pitted against those of the other. On the other hand, children tend to emphasize their feelings of loss for the absent parent, whether deceased or divorced. When divorce has occurred, children may ask for easier access to the noncustodial parent and cooperation between their biological parents to ease the split loyalties they experience (Wald, 1985, pp. 127–129).

Additional problems concern insufficient space and time as well as insufficient money to meet all of the demands of the stepfamily. Another area of stress involves renegotiation of child custody, child support, and visitation rights engendered by changing from a single-parent family to a stepfamily. Social agencies are often involved in these negotiations as the courts increasingly rely on them to deal with the social and psychological consequences of these revisions. In response, social agencies often work with clients' attorneys in the hope of avoiding costly and unnecessary litigation over these issues.

Central to all stepfamilies is the essential task of clarifying ambiguous role relationships and establishing appropriate role expectations. Integral to this task is the process of secondary bond formation. The developmental processes of the nuclear family that facilitate early attachment and bond formation are not available to the stepfamily. Although a family by definition, the stepfamily in many ways resembles a group struggling with issues of approach-avoidance and power and control. During this process feelings of exclusion emerge, of stepchild for stepparent and

of stepparent for stepchild. This may result in marital problems if the spouse-parent attempts to force feelings that have not had time to develop.

Variations in the kinship and legal structure of the stepfamily may contribute to further family stress. Evidence indicates that when children of both partners are in the stepfamily, there is a tendency for greater interfamily stress (Wald, 1985, p. 185). This is understandable because of the greater number of people in the family, the conflicting pulls of kinship ties, and the added number of relationships with noncustodial parents. Families with children of only the husband or only the wife typically experience fewer problems (Wald, 1981, pp. 67–77). Because the presence of custodial fathers is relatively recent, however, families often experience greater difficulties integrating the stepmother into the family than the stepfather. The literature reflects that, in general, stepmothers have more difficulty with stepchildren than do stepfathers (Bernard, 1971, pp. 224–226; Duberman, 1973, pp. 190–224). Stepmothers mention a negative self-image and a tendency to compare themselves to the wicked stepmothers of the fairy tales (Pflegler, 1957, pp. 125–126; Wald, 1981, pp. 70–71; 1985, pp. 93, 111–112).

Implications for Social Work

The unique characteristics of the stepfamily as well as the nature of the stresses they generate have implications for social work practice. Appropriate attention must be given to the inherent differences between nuclear families and stepfamilies along with recognition that these differences introduce normal transitional, nonpathological issues. With this in mind, practitioners can begin to develop clinical, educational, and social policy programs to institutionalize the stepfamily as a legitimate family structure.

The mission of social work—to serve distressed populations and develop programs that enhance their functioning—suggests that social agencies should become involved in programs of intervention that are relevant to the unique characteristics of stepfamilies. Because the literature on the stepfamily has been historically sparse and contradictory, there is a tendency for practitioners to draw from the literature on the nuclear family. This has often resulted in stepfamily members complaining that the complexity of their family situation was not understood by the professionals to whom they turned for help.

It is essential for practitioners to understand that the characteristics inherent in the stepfamily do not reflect pathological dynamics but rather normal and transitional adjustments to a new situation. When practitioners can convey this to the stepfamily they are often better able to cope with their difficulties. Practitioners must also perceive the stepfamily as capable of growing and of forming appropriate role definitions and secondary bonds. This confidence is essential because many stepfamily members seek professional help when these goals appear unattainable. Findings indicate that the most stressful adjustment period is the first 3 years, which gives hope to families that they too will master these strains (Wald, 1981, p. 131; 1985, p. 79).

Practitioners who work with stepfamilies must also intervene with individuals concerning personal issues of loss and negative self-concept and with the whole family concerning appropriate rules, routines, and roles. Involvement of the noncustodial parent often arises in discussions of changing custodial, visitation, or child support arrangements.

Working out balances among family members about shared time, space, and money is often the focus of work with spouses. In addition, couples often need to identify the factors that interfere with their ability to develop attachments to stepchildren. Crisis intervention may be appropriate, and short- and long-term approaches as well as interventions with the whole family, the marital subsystem, parent-child subsystems, and individuals may be used. Practitioners will find that various theoretical orientations are appropriate. Although no definitive models exist for family therapy, some clinicians may find that a psychodynamic approach is more effective, whereas others may prefer a structural or behavioral approach.

At the preventive level, social agencies should develop educational programs to alert single parents to the complexities of remarriage so that they are better prepared to deal with normal transitional adjustments. Difficulties can be anticipated and families can develop strategies for coping before they become rigid and less amenable to change. Stepparents often mention how helpful it would have been to have such knowledge before they remarried (Messinger, 1976).

The media can also be helpful in changing negative stereotypes of the stepfamily by articulating some of the problems these families experience. Social agencies can alert the media to the timeliness of this subject as part of a widespread educational campaign. Evidence of the growing interest of the media and the public in this area is apparent in the appearances of social work practitioners on talk shows to discuss these issues. On a social policy level, practitioners can show the courts and legislatures that stepfamilies experience difficulties because legal codes inhibit approved social goals of family cohesion and compatability.

Modification of custodial arrangements is an issue that social work practitioners frequently confront in their work with stepfamilies, and they need to develop a body of knowledge about the circumstances under which these requests are made. This can be combined with an understanding of the development of the child and his or her family as well as with the legal rights and obligations of the biological parents. Frequent requests for changes in custody because children do not seem able to adjust in the home of either parent require careful evaluation so that changes are not made routinely. Issues of child visitation must also be carefully assessed so that legal requirements are consistent with the child's developmental stage while observing the rights of the noncustodial parent. Finally, issues of child support often intrude on the process of role definition and the formation of secondary bonds. These, too, must be addressed by social agencies and the legal community to take advantage of the expertise of both professions (Brinn et al., 1984, pp. 29–32).

The greater incidence of divorce and the tendency of divorced people to remarry has given rise to an increasing number of stepfamilies. But higher rates of redivorce suggest that the stepfamily is a family at risk. Social agencies that work with these families must understand the factors that contribute to redivorce so that they can help these families achieve the enduring relationships that stimulated the remarriage. The differences between the nuclear family and the stepfamily, the many kinship and custodial variations among stepfamilies, and the problems stepfamilies experience must be understood as inherent in the stepfamily situation. This nonpathological approach normalizes the stepfamily and facilitates relevant interventions. Education can help single parents who are planning to marry or remarry to anticipate these normal, nonpathological stresses. Social agencies must also develop family life education programs for stepfamilies themselves to interrupt negative family patterns before they become too rigid to change. Closer work with the courts and legislators is needed to integrate the goals of family cohesion and stability with legal codes that currently thwart these goals. Finally, to reduce the negative stereotypes that are now common, further education must help society understand the unique strengths and strains that stepfamilies experience. A new sensibility must emerge—a sensibility that "step is not less; it is just different."

ESTHER WALD

For further information, see CHILD SUPPORT; DIVORCE AND SEPARATION; FAMILY: CONTEMPORARY PATTERNS; FAMILY: ONE PARENT; FAMILY LIFE EDUCATION; LEGAL ISSUES AND LEGAL SERVICES; MASS MEDIA.

References

Bernard, J. (1971). *Remarriage: A Study of Marriage* (rev. ed.). New York: Russell and Russell.

Brinn, R., et al. (1984). "Divorce Mediation— Social Work and the Law." *Practice Digest,* 7(2), 29–32.

Cherlin, A. (1981). *Marriage, Divorce and Remarriage: Social Trends in the United States.* Cambridge, Mass.: Harvard University Press.

Cherlin, A., & McCarthy, J. (1985). "Remarried Couple Households: Data from the 1980 Current Population Survey." *Journal of Marriage and the Family, 47*(1), pp. 25–26.

Duberman, L. (1973). *On Becoming a Family.* Unpublished doctoral dissertation. Case Western Reserve University.

Glick, P. C. (1979). "Children of Divorced Parents in Demographic Perspective." *Journal of Social Issues, 35*(4), 170–175.

Glick, P. C., & Norton, A. J. (1977). "Marrying, Divorcing and Living Together in the United States Today." *Population Bulletin, 32*(5), 4–8. Washington, D.C.: Population Reference Bureau, Inc.

Kargman, M. W. (1983). "Stepchild Support Obligations of Stepparents." *Family Relations,* 32(2).

Messinger, L. (1976). "Remarriage Between Divorced People and Children from Previous Marriages: A Proposal for Preparation for Remarriage." *Journal of Marriage and Family Counselling, 2,* 193–200.

Pflegler, J. (1957). "The Wicked Stepmother in Child Guidance Clinics." *Smith College Studies in Social Work, 17,* 125–126.

U.S. Bureau of the Census. (1984a). "Household and Family Characteristics, March 1984." *Current Population Reports* (Series P-20, no. 398). Washington, D.C.: U.S. Government Printing Office.

U.S. Bureau of the Census. (1984b). "Marital Status and Living Arrangements, March 1984." *Current Population Reports* (Series P-20, no. 399). Washington, D.C.: U.S. Government Printing Office.

Wald, E. (1981). *The Remarried Family: Challenge and Promise.* New York: Family Service Association of America.

Wald, E. (1985). *The Remarried Family: A Special Case of Family.* Unpublished doctoral dissertation. University of Chicago.

Webster's Third New International Dictionary. (1961). Springfield, Mass.: G. & C. Merriam Co.

FAMILY AND POPULATION PLANNING

Population growth and distribution and their social, political, and human consequences have long been subjects of interest and concern. As early as the fourth century B.C., Aristotle warned that no entities, including states, retained their natural powers when they were either too large or too small (cited in Young, 1968, p. 112). Some 600 years later, the Roman theologian Tertullian complained that areas of high population density were "burdensome to the world" (cited in Brown, 1954). In modern times, Malthus (1816/1973) warned that increasing numbers of people could outstrip the food supply because population, unchecked, increased geometrically whereas subsistence increased only arithmetically. Following Malthus, the nineteenth-century German scientist Justus von Liebig stated his "law of the minimum," which hypothesized that not only subsistence resources, but whatever requisite of life was in shortest supply, would limit the life of an individual or a population (Ehrlich & Ehrlich, 1972, p. 59).

Despite these early observations, it was not until the 1950s that generalized and persistent concern was voiced about the "population explosion" in the underdeveloped and developing countries. With this came increasing recognition of the need to combine centralized social and economic development planning with family-level fertility planning to facilitate the transition from a natural to a controlled fertility pattern in these countries.

A brief history of the population issue follows, together with a survey of organizational and family responses to population expansion. The current and projected consequences for quality of life, related to the rapidly increasing numbers of people who occupy our planet, are also examined.

Population Growth

It took approximately 2 million years for the earth to acquire its first billion people (1830), 100 years for the second (1930), 30 years for the third (1960), 15 years for the fourth (1975), and about 11 years for the fifth (1986) (Brown, 1974). By the year 2000, it is anticipated that 6 billion people will live on earth. By the year 2050, that figure could double. Of the projected 6 billion people, probably 5 billion will live in the developing countries (Hepworth, 1984).

Despite this rapid acceleration, in much of the developing world fertility rates are declining, some by as much as 10 to 35 percent since 1960 (International Planned Parenthood Federation [IPPF], 1983). Although rates may continue to fall within the next 20 years, only a precipitous decline below replacement levels will avoid dramatic increases in the number of people who need to be supported by the world's resources (Hepworth, 1984). Currently, no evidence exists of such a decline, and at the extreme, it is estimated that none of the 36 less developed countries will achieve a net reproduction rate[1] of one before the year 2005. At that time China is expected to attain this goal,

with the majority needing another 15 to 40 years to do so (*World Development Report*, 1981).

Two countries may be used as examples of the possible consequences. Taking Ethiopia, where a stationary population is not anticipated before the year 2140, as a "worst case," the population will increase from its 1980 base of 31 million to a projected 53 million by the year 2000 and to 162 million by the year 2140. The "best case" example is Sri Lanka, which expects to reach a stationary population by the year 2065. Its 1980 population was estimated at 4 million; the projected population for the year 2000 is 9 million and for the year 2065 is 17 million (*World Development Report*, 1981).

At the vortex of the population issue lies the challenge of assisting people in developing countries to make the transition from high to low fertility rates that occurred in most of the developed Western nations by the middle of the eighteenth century. In developed countries, the movement toward population stability was concomitant with industrialization, urbanization, and other factors related to modernization. It proceeded through three stages: the first was characterized by equally high birth- and death rates; the second was marked by high birthrates but a sharp decline in death rates caused by improved sanitation and control of infectious diseases; and the final phase was marked by a corresponding drop in birthrates.

The current population explosion in Third World countries has been attributed to a situation in which "death control caught on more rapidly than did birth control" (Rogers, 1973, p. 1). Some evidence suggests, however, that this demographic transition may be occurring more rapidly in some developing countries than it did previously in developed countries (*World Development Report*, 1981). Although birthrates fell only an average of 0.3 per thousand per year in the last stage of the transition in developed countries, Chile, Sri Lanka, Malaysia, and others have had reduced rates of 0.5 to 1.0 per thousand per year since 1960 (*World Development Report*, 1981). A recent note documents even more rapid declines in five provinces in China ("Population Growth Rates," 1981). By and large, countries experiencing these declines are those that have instituted vigorous family planning programs along with social and eco-

---

[1] "Net reproduction rate" refers to the number of daughters a newborn female will bear during her lifetime, given fixed fertility and mortality rates.

nomic planning efforts associated with modernization. Thus, growing empirical evidence indicates that both family planning and development efforts contribute to fertility decline and that the two have a "synergistic effect" that gives impetus to short-term changes in individual and national fertility patterns. (IPPF, 1983; Mauldin, 1983; *World Development Report*, 1981).

Family Planning

Efforts to control fertility to limit family or population size are as old as recorded history (Ehrlich & Ehrlich, 1972); however, family planning programs designed to alter human fertility behavior are "newer than nuclear fission" (Rogers, 1973, p. 5). The family planning movement began not as an effort to control population—birthrates were already on the decline in Europe and in the United States—but was promoted as a way to enhance the economic, social, and physical well-being of women, children, and families, particularly the working poor. The movement was born in England in 1822, during the Industrial Revolution, when Francis Place began distributing tracts to laborers that informed them of birth control methods and urged them to limit family size as a step toward improving their own social and economic well-being.

Over the years that followed, opposition to this movement abounded in the form of legislative and religious prohibitions. Although the first birth control clinic was not established in the United States until 1912 through the efforts of Margaret Sanger, by the 1940s—through the cooperative and concerted efforts of women such as Sanger in the United States, Dr. Aletta Jacobs in Holland, Dr. Marie Stopes in England, Mrs. Elise Ottesen-Jensen in Sweden, and Lady Dhanvanthis Rama Rau in India—birth control clinics and related maternal and child health services had been established around the world (Ehrlich & Ehrlich, 1972). Only recently has government opposition diminished in the predominantly Roman Catholic countries, however. Not until 1975 did France include contraceptive advice and services in its social security programs, and it was 1976 before Portugal provided these services in its public health centers. In 1978, Spain repealed legislation that had prohibited the advertising, distribution, and practice of contraception. The Roman Catholic Church continues to oppose other than natural family planning methods (IPPF, 1983).

As of 1981, family planning services in the United States were provided through both government and private facilities. About 2,500 separate agencies operated about 5,000 clinics. Of these clinics, health departments served 40 percent of the patients, Planned Parenthood affiliates served 27 percent, and neighborhood health clinics served 33 percent. These family planning clinics continue to serve primarily low-income women. In 1981, they served about 58 percent of the 9.5 million low-income women known to be at risk of unintended pregnancies (Torres & Forrest, 1983). Federally funded programs provide a range of family planning services including sterilization, but not abortion (IPPF, 1983). Overall, survey data support the estimate that "almost all married couples, regardless of income, use some form of contraception" (IPPF, 1983, p. 38). Specific estimates place this proportion at about 79 percent of all married women of reproductive age (Torres & Forrest, 1983).

Family planning programs designed to alter fertility patterns in the interests of limiting population began initially in Japan and India in 1952. By 1960, only three Third World countries had population planning policies, only one government was actually offering family planning services, and no international development agency was working in the field of family planning (Berelson, 1969). By 1972, "twenty-eight countries in Asia, Africa, and Latin American nations, representing about 73 percent of the population of these continents, had official family planning policies *and* programs" (Rogers, 1973, pp. 6–7). By 1983, 35 countries had such programs, encompassing about 80 percent of the population of the developing world (Mauldin, 1983).

Over this time an international population assistance network has emerged, with funding estimated to be about $500 million per year for the promotion and support of population programs. Activities supported by these moneys include research, public information and education, program development and construction of facilities, training of personnel, and family planning services, the latter receiving approximately 75 percent of the total moneys available. The largest single governmental contributor was the United States in 1980. Multilateral organizations included the United Nations Fund for Population Activity (UNFPA), the World Health Organization (WHO), the World Bank, the United Nations, UNICEF, and UNESCO. Private organization contributors included the International Planned Parenthood Federation (IPPF), Family Planning International Assistance, the Population Council, and the Ford, Rockefeller, Mellon, and Hewlett foundations. About 50 percent of the funding is derived from the governments of nine developed countries, about 40 percent from multinational organizations, and the remainder from private agencies (Mauldin, 1983).

Family Planning Methods

Varied methods of fertility control have been used throughout human history. The two most common forms used in preindustrialized society were infanticide and abortion. Some evidence suggests that infanticide was practiced as early as the Upper Paleolithic era (Carr-Saunders, 1922) and that it may have been the most widely used method of population control throughout human history (Harris, 1977). The Old Testament contains references to the practice of coitus interruptus; the Egyptians used barrier methods; the Greeks used social constraints, such as discouraging heterosexual marriages; and many other early cultures used a wide variety of herbs, chemicals, and rituals to prevent unwanted births (Ehrlich & Ehrlich, 1972). The methods believed to be associated with the demographic transition were coitus interruptus, use of the condom, the rhythm method, and abortion.

Current evidence suggests that infanticide is still practiced. A study of 112 small societies indicated that 36 percent made common use of infanticide with an additional 15 percent making occasional use of it (Divale & Harris, 1976). Forms of infanticide range from deliberate killing to placing the child in a dangerous position, abandonment, "accidents," excessive physical punishment, or less-than-required biological or psychological support. Scrimshaw (1983) noted that in "today's world, both developed and developing, such unconscious underinvestment is more prevalent than the deliberate killing of a child" (p. 247). For obvious reasons, the incidence of infanticide is difficult to quantify; however, Scrimshaw notes that

> current data on differential infant and young child mortality by sex strongly indicate behavioral differences in the care of male and female children in some cultures under some circumstances. . . . [For example,] the money that must be set aside for a dowry can make a female child less attractive to her parents. (pp. 251, 255)

As with infanticide, the data base for estimating the incidence of abortion is inadequate. This can be attributed to such factors as legal, religious, and cultural constraints and to problems in the definition of what constitutes abortion. A recent review found that abortion is legal in only 32 of 144 countries reported. It remains illegal in most of the populous countries of Asia, in all of Latin America except Cuba, in all of sub-Saharan Africa, and in all the Muslim countries of the Middle East and North Africa except Tunisia and Kuwait (David, 1983). Even where it is legal, it is frequently exceedingly difficult to obtain because of local regulatory requirements. Despite this, abortion is believed to be the most common form of birth control in the world today (Ehrlich & Ehrlich, 1972). At the beginning of the 1980s, abortion ratios were estimated to range from 207 to 450 per 1,000 live births, based on estimates of from 13.5 (Rochat et al., 1980) to 55 million (IPPF, 1983, based on 1978 observations) abortions performed worldwide.

Approximately 1.55 million abortions were performed in the United States in 1980. It was estimated in that year that about three percent of the 53 million women of reproductive age obtained an abortion, and one-fourth of pregnancies—a little less than half of all that were unintended—were terminated by abortion (Henshaw et al., 1982, p. 4).

Since the 1960s, a significant change in contraceptive technology has occurred. All methods have been surpassed by the pill, intrauterine devices (IUDs), simplified female sterilization, and simplified abortion (Ross, 1983). Innovations such as vaccines, once-a-month pills, injectables, and the biological suppression of sperm are also being tested. In 1983, it was estimated that approximately 270 million couples used some form of contraception. About two-thirds of these live in developed and one-third live in developing countries. Of these, approximately a third have been sterilized, 20 percent use the pill, 15 percent use an IUD, and 10 percent use condoms. The remaining 20 percent use other available methods such as contraceptive injections, some form of natural family planning (the calendar, temperature, symptothermal, or cervical mucus methods), coitus interruptus, or reliance on breastfeeding to inhibit a woman's ovulation. This is in addition to the millions of women who rely on induced abortion for fertility control (IPPF, 1983).

Family Planning Outcomes

As noted earlier, the change from natural to controlled fertility patterns and the rate at which that change takes place hinge not only on the success of modernization efforts within a country, but also on the success with which family planning programs can engage and support an individual's or a family's efforts to practice deliberate fertility control. The family planning program outcome evidence is discouraging. Over time, rates of program discontinuation among acceptors have remained uniformly high in relation to all methods. A 1973 comprehensive review (Hellman) noted 20 percent discontinuation of birth control methods in 12 months and 40 to 50 percent by 18 months to 2 years, depending on the method used. In 1981, a similar survey noted discontinuance of natural family planning methods by 33 to 66 percent, of the IUD by 20 to 30 percent, and of oral contraceptives by 30 to 50 percent after a year (Liskin). It is currently estimated that the average period of use in most developing countries is 2 years (Mauldin, 1983). Evidence suggests that this pattern of use may well account for the more rapid lowering of birthrates in developing countries that have comprehensive family planning (Xenos, 1977) and, conversely, that it may account for the projected inability of these countries to reach population stability in the near future.

Research in Fertility

On a more positive note, there has recently been a growing effort to develop and test models, at both the macro and micro levels, to explain fertility behavior. At the macro level is the challenge of isolating causal factors related to the shift from high to low fertility during the process of moderniza-

tion across the world (Easterlin, 1983). At the micro level is the ongoing effort to determine the factors responsible for the "back door loss," through discontinuation, of individuals from family planning programs (Rogers, 1973). The convergence of macro- and micro-research efforts is clear in that (1) a shared subset of factors in macro and micro equations relate to the costs of regulation, attitudes, and demographic characteristics, (2) 60 percent of all people using contraceptive methods do so under the guidance of some family planning programs, and (3) a strong empirical correlation has been demonstrated between contraceptive use and fertility control. Thus, research that attempts to explain why people use contraceptive services may provide direction for family planning agencies and field workers in assisting women or couples to engage in planned fertility control in the present as well as the future.

Two systematic reviews summarize a voluminous literature on factors and models generated to explain service utilization. McKinlay (1972) identified several research approaches used to explain why individuals seek and use health and social services. The approaches fell within six broad categories of variables: economic, sociodemographic, geographic, sociopsychological, sociocultural, and organizational or service delivery variables. Of these, sociocultural factors (such as lifestyle, subgroup membership, family structure, and networking patterns) and sociopsychological factors (such as perceptions of the problem and its consequences and beliefs about health and the effectiveness of action) appeared to hold the most promise in developing predictors of services use and outcome.

More recently, Cummings, Becker, and Maile (1980) analyzed fourteen services utilization models that had been generated and extensively tested between 1950 and 1980 to determine structural similarities in an effort to take a first step toward the development of a unified theory. The modelers included Anderson (1968), Anderson and Barthus (1973), Antonovsky and Kats (1970), Fabrega (1973, 1974), Green (1975), Hochbaum (1958), Kar (1977, 1978), Kasl and Cobb (1966), Kosa and Robertson (1975), Langlie (1977), Mechanic (1968), Rosenstock (1966), and Suchman (1966). In the analysis, six groupings of factors were found, including those related to accessibility of services, attitudes toward care, threat of illness or poor outcome, knowledge about disease, selected demographic characteristics, and social interaction, social norms, and social structures.

An example of the utility of these variable structures in guiding research for program development and service delivery is evident in a program survey and evaluation of a natural family planning program in the island nation of Mauritius, in the Indian Ocean (Conner & Veeder, 1980, 1984). Variables derived from the services utilization models were used to identify predictors of continuation or discontinuation in two probability samples of acceptors using the program. The predictors found were considered amenable to intervention at the program or service level. Specifically, four of the factors found to predict discontinuation were related to the accessibility of services. They included the previous acceptance of and then discontinuation from a family planning program, fewer visits or contacts with the educator or field worker during the preregistration period than were found among those who continued in the program, the educator's difficulty in teaching the method in the acceptor's home, and a significantly lower likelihood that potential discontinuers would discuss child-rearing, marital, or home management problems with the educator. Two factors were related to attitudes toward care. These were the wish to use a planning method to space rather than deter future pregnancies and low motivation and interest in using the particular method chosen. Factors related to social interaction, social norms, and social structure were low interest expressed by the husband together with a lack of support from other family members for taking the planning action. The two categories of variables that did not distinguish continuers from discontinuers were those related to the threat of pregnancy and selected demographic variables—the latter probably reflecting the relative homogeneity of the population.

Other research involving Third World samples lends support to some of these variables and brings into focus the potential explanatory power of others. Studies of natural family planning programs also found discontinuation related to prior unsuccessful use of a method (Weeks, 1982), lack of inter-

est (Ghosh, 1976), and desire to space rather than prevent pregnancy (Klaus, 1982). Personal instruction and home follow-up were found to be particularly important in promoting continuation of use by supporting a couple's motivation (Billings, 1970; Hilgers, 1980; Johnston et al., 1978; Kippley & Kippley, 1979; Klaus, 1982; Liskin, 1981; McKay, 1978). A couple's cooperation was also found to influence continuation (Billings & Westmore, 1980; Curry, 1979; Elder, 1978; Madigan, 1972; Liskin, 1981; Tolar et al., 1975).

Education may well act as an intervening variable in relation to understanding instructions and to the ability to communicate with the educator, partners, and family members as well as in relation to knowledge about resources and options (Dorairaj, 1981; Marshall, 1975; Wade et al., 1980; World Health Organization, 1978). It was also found that when the concerns of the husband or partner were addressed as well as those of the acceptor, continuation rates improved (Phillips, 1978).

These research findings are only a small sample of findings to date on factors associated with or predictive of family planning program continuation. Voluminous literature also exists on fertility determinants, or those factors determining additional fertility. The methods used in these investigations show considerable variation in approach and level of competence. Sufficient coalescing of findings in the areas of partner dynamics and interaction, attitudes, and family and community networking, however, has enabled policymakers, social planners, and service deliverers to begin to focus Third World family planning programs and action efforts more deftly than they have in the recent past.

Projections and Long-Range Concerns

The developed and developing worlds are in sharp contrast. Although it is estimated that less than 20 percent of the world's population lives in developed countries, this segment of the population has a per capita gross national product of about $9,400 per year, compared to an average of $230 per year in the low-income developing countries (*World Development Report*, 1981). This population also accrues 60 percent of the world product as opposed to 18 percent in developing countries (Jacobson & Sidjanski, 1982). Although many countries in the developed world are concerned about the steady decline in their populations and are taking steps to encourage increases in the birthrate (IPPF, 1983), many of the developing countries are trying to decrease birthrates by pursuing vigorous family planning and other types of incentive and disincentive programs.

These differences in numbers and dollars have profound consequences for the quality of life of people in the developing world. In 1980, it was estimated that 780 million people in the Third World (excluding China and other centrally planned economies) lived in absolute poverty, although the proportion of people living in poverty had decreased between 1970 and 1980. Half of them lived in South Asia, mainly in India and Bangladesh; a sixth lived in East and Southeast Asia, mainly in Indonesia; another sixth lived in sub-Saharan Africa; and the remaining sixth lived in Latin America, North Africa, and the Middle East (*World Development Report*, 1980, p. 35). In some low-income countries such as Ethiopia, only 6 percent of the population had access to safe water (p. 152); 31 of the 36 low-income countries failed to meet the minimum daily caloric intake requirements for their populations (p. 152). Many of the middle-income countries fared little better (pp. 152–153).

Across the developing world, about 600 million people are illiterate and only two-fifths of the children complete 3 years of primary school (*World Development Report*, 1980, p. 33). In 1978, 550 million people lived in countries where the life expectancy at birth was less than 50 years (p. 33), and 400 million lived in countries where the average annual death rate of children aged 1 to 4 was more than 20 times that in developed industrialized countries (*World Development Report*, 1980, pp. 33, 35). This means that "of every 10 children born to poor parents, two die within a year; another dies before the age of five; and only five survive to the age of 40" (*World Development Report*, 1980, p. 33). Despite this high mortality rate, about 25 percent of the population in developing countries is in the infant and primary school group and, in some African countries, this number exceeds 40 percent.

Research has confirmed that high fertility is associated with a variety of poverty-related social ills. As early as 1967, the President's Science Advisory Council in the United States noted that malnutrition across the developing world resulted in observable physical, social, and mental retardation problems (Heilbroner, 1975). A 1971 review of research related this to conditions of family stress, dissolution of marriage, deterioration in family economic and emotional support patterns, and a downward spiral in social and economic development opportunities (Meier, 1971). The unprecedented flight of people from rural to urban areas in recent years appears to be associated with a search for employment and opportunity. This trend in Africa, Asia, and Latin America has resulted in a potential doubling of the population in 8 to 10 years in some municipalities such as Mexico City (Wagner, 1983), which only serves further to entrap the poor and to impair the family's ability to serve as a nurturing unit. Studies about the effects of population density on behavior in the family and society have found that crowding causes family members to display more violent behavior toward each other (Russell & Russell, 1979) and countries to be involved more frequently in wars and civil strife.

A recent survey of social and economic problems observed by national social welfare councils (Hepworth, 1984) projected several major areas in which worldwide crises would occur, which interlock with issues related to family and population planning. These crises include environmental deterioration and a decline in environmental resources; erosion of human rights, particularly related to children, women, minorities, the disabled, and the aged; threats to the survival of the family as an institution in the face of crowding, increasing unemployment, civil strife, discrimination, and segregation; and the unprecedented population movement from one geopolitical area to another to escape war, hunger, persecution, and oppression. It is estimated that 200 million people have fled their countries during this century (Brandt Commission, 1980).

Some 20 years ago, Brown (1967) observed that few developing countries were capable of economic growth rates rapid enough to improve visibly the average person's economic and social well-being during a single lifetime. Certainly, current quality-of-life indicators only update the validity of that statement. It appears that two types of challenges must be met if family and population planning efforts are to be accelerated. The first is the need for increased economic development of sufficient strength to raise the aspirations of people and trigger action to control fertility (Davis, 1963). The second is the development of family planning and other social development programs to diffuse information and services and to support individual and family aspirations. The latter falls within the scope, techniques, and personnel currently available in the human services community.

Traditionally, volunteers constitute the largest single personnel category for the delivery of family planning services to people in both the developed and developing worlds, followed by medical specialists and nurse-practitioners. In 1981, the 700 Planned Parenthood–affiliated clinics in the United States were staffed by a total of 20,000 people. Almost every clinic had a trained family planning nurse-practitioner. In total, there were 700 nurse practitioners, 1,300 physicians, and 17,000 volunteers and other paid staff. A survey that same year of the National Abortion Federation (three-fourths of which facilities are free-standing nonhospital facilities operated for profit) revealed that only 1.1 percent of its counselors with advanced degrees were other than physicians or nurses (Landy & Lewit, 1982). Among these were social workers and other professionals specially trained to provide counseling or various supportive services to clients.

In the developing world, volunteers specifically trained in family planning methodologies are used almost exclusively to provide in-person instruction and counseling services in clinic and field situations. Nurses and other health services personnel usually assume administrative responsibilities. Recruitment and selection of volunteers are frequently made from among persons who have successfully used family planning services as former clients of the particular organization or who are indigenous leaders drawn from the particular communities and social, economic, and cultural groups for whom they volunteer. In clinics using predominantly natural family planning methods, almost all volunteers, trainers, and administrators are drawn from the successful-user group (Conner & Veeder, 1986).

A review of the recent periodical literature failed to reveal family planning per se as a major social work practice field in the United States. Social work's contributions to the literature in this area are more frequently in research and training than in direct practice. It must be assumed, however, that social workers have a profound impact on family life, family structure, and family planning, including fertility planning, through their wide-ranging family-oriented approach to practice in family services and health and school settings. Social workers have extensive involvement in the related areas of marital counseling, unintended teenage pregnancies, foster care and adoption, feminist counseling related to women's health and rights issues, and genetic and postabortion counseling. They are involved in providing information and referral services to family planning facilities and are involved in the entire range of counseling related to individual and family quality-of-life issues.

Currently, family planning clinics are expanding their services to include outreach to involve men in the planning process, educational services to help parents become more competent in their roles as parents and sexuality educators, and services for teenagers and the handicapped (IPPF, 1983; "Digest," 1983). With this expansion, it is anticipated that additional social work personnel will be incorporated into these programs to provide the quality of individual and family care required to serve these special groups and situations.

GERALDINE L. CONNER

For further information, see ABORTION.

References
Anderson, J. C., & Barthus, D. E. (1973). "Choice of Medical Care: A Behavioral Model of Health and Illness Behavior." *Journal of Health and Social Behavior, 14*, 348–362.
Anderson, R. (1968). *A Behavioral Model of Families' Use of Health Services.* Chicago: University of Chicago, Center for Health Administration Studies.
Antonovsky, A., & Kats, R. (1970). "The Model Dental Patient: An Empirical Study of Preventive Health Behavior." *Social Science Medicine, 4*, 367–379.
Berelson, B. (1969). "Family-Planning Programs and Population Control." In B. Berelson (Ed.), *Family Planning Programs: An International Study.* New York: Basic Books.

Billings, J. J. (1970). *The Ovulation Method.* Melbourne, Australia: Advocate Press.

Billings, E., & Westmore, A. (1980). *The Billings Method: Controlling Fertility Without Drugs or Devices.* New York: Random House.

Brandt Commission. (1980). *North-South: A Programme for Survival, The Report of the Independent Commission on International Development Issues Under the Chairmanship of Willy Brandt.* Cambridge, Mass.: M.I.T. Press.

Brown, H. (1954). *The Challenge of Man's Future.* New York: Viking Press.

Brown, H. (1967, June 24). "The Combustability of Humans." *The Saturday Review.*

Brown, L. (1974). *In the Human Interest.* New York: W. W. Norton & Co.

Carr-Saunders, A. M. (1922). *The Population Problem: A Study in Human Evolution.* London, England: Clarendon Press.

Conner, G. L., & Veeder, N. W. (1980). *Report: Program Review and Evaluation, Action Familiale, Rose Hall, Mauritius, Indian Ocean* (Xerox). Boston: Boston College.

Conner, G. L., & Veeder, N. W. (1984). "Natural Family Planning in Mauritius, Indian Ocean: Utilization Patterns and Continuance Predictors." *Journal of Social Service Research.* 8(1), 29–48.

Conner, G. L., & Veeder, N. W. (1986, January). "A Program Evaluation of Natural Family Planning in Mauritius, Indian Ocean: Services Delivery and Volunteer Training Implications." *International Journal of Social Work,* 29, 59–72.

Cummings, K. M., Becker, M. H., & Maile, C. M. (1980). "Bringing the Models Together: An Empirical Approach to Combining Variables Used to Explain Health Actions." *Journal of Behavioral Medicine,* 3(2), 123–145.

Curry, M. T. (1979). "Counseling Clients in Natural Methods of Family Planning." *Maryland Nurse.* 2, 26–29.

David, H. P. (1983). "Abortion: Its Prevalance, Correlates, and Costs." In R. Bulateo & R. D. Lee (Eds.), *Determinants of Fertility in Developing Countries. Fertility Regulation and Institutional Influences* (Vol. 2, pp. 193–244). New York: Academic Press.

Davis, K. (1963, September). "Population." *Scientific American,* pp. 62–71.

"Digest." (1982). *Family Planning Perspectives.* 14(5), 274–276.

Divale, W. T., & Harris, M. (1976). "Population, Warfare, and the Male Supremacist Complex." *The American Anthropologist,* 78, 521–538.

Dorairaj, K. (1981). *Fertility Control in India: Natural Family Planning as an Alternative Strategy.* New Delhi, India: Indian Social Institute.

Easterlin, R. A. (1983). "Modernization and Fertility: A Critical Essay." In R. Bulateo & R. D. Lee (Eds.), *Determinants of Fertility in Developing Countries. Fertility Regulation and Institutional Influences* (Vol. 2, pp. 562–586). New York: Academic Press.

Ehrlich, P. R., & Ehrlich, A. H. (1972). *Population, Resources, Environment: Issues in Human Ecology.* San Francisco: W. H. Freeman & Co.

Elder, N. (1978). "Natural Family Planning: The Ovulation Method." *Journal of Nurse Midwifery.* 23, 25–30.

Fabrega, H. (1973). "Toward a Model of Illness Behavior." *Medical Care, 11,* 470–484.

Fabrega, H. (1974). *Disease and Social Behavior. An Interdisciplinary Perspective.* Cambridge: Massachusetts Institute of Technology.

Ghosh, A. K. (1976). "Natural Family Planning by Symptothermic Control." *Journal of Indian Medical Association,* 66(11), 286–288.

Green, L. W. (1975). "Diffusion and Adoption of Innovations Related to Cardiovascular Risk Behavior in the Public." In A. J. Enclow and J. B. Henderson (Eds.), *Applying Behavioral Science to Cardiovascular Risk: Proceedings of a Conference.* Washington, D.C.: American Heart Association.

Harris, M. (1977). *Cannibals and Kings: The Origins of Cultures.* New York: Random House.

Heilbroner, R. L. (1975). *An Inquiry into the Human Prospect.* New York: W. W. Norton & Co.

Hellman, M. (1973). "Discussion." In W. A. Urichio (Ed.), *Natural Family Planning.* Washington, D.C.: Human Life Foundation.

Henshaw, S. K., et al. (1982). "Abortion Services in the United States, 1979 and 1980." *Family Planning Perspectives, 14*(1).

Hepworth, H. P. (1984, August). *Social Welfare in a World in Crisis: Perceptions and Responsibilities.* Paper prepared for the International Conference on Social Welfare, Montreal, Canada.

Hermalin, A. E. (1983). "Fertility Regulation and Its Costs: A Critical Essay." In R. Bulateo & R. D. Lee (Eds.), *Determinants of Fertility in Developing Countries. Fertility Regulation and Institutional Influences.* (Vol. 2, pp. 1–53). New York: Academic Press.

Hilgers, T. W. (1980). "Two Methods of Natural Family Planning." *American Journal of Obstetrics and Gynecology, 136*(5), 696–697.

Hochbaum, G. M. (1958). *Public Participation in Medical Screening Programs. A Socio-Psychological Study.* Washington, D.C.: U. S. Government Printing Office.

International Planned Parenthood Federation. (1978). "Unmet Needs." *People, 5,* 25–32.

International Planned Parenthood Federation. (1983). *Family Planning in Five Continents.* London, England: Author.

Jacobson, H. K., & Sidjanski, D. (1982). *The Emerging International Economic Order.* Beverly Hills, Calif.: Sage Publications.

Johnston, J. A., et al. (1978). "NFP Services and Methods in Australia: A Survey Evaluation." *International Review of Natural Family Planning, 2*(3).

Kar, S. B. (1977). "Community Interventions in Health and Family Planning Programmes: A Conceptual Framework." *International Journal of Health Education, 20*(1), supplement.

Kar, S. B. (1978). "Consistency Between Fertility Attitudes and Behavior: A Conceptual Model." *Population Studies, 12.*

Kasl, S. V., & Cobb, S. (1966). "Health Behavior, Illness Behavior, and Sick Role Behavior." *Archives of Environmental Health, 12.*

Kippley, J., & Kippley S. (1979). *The Art of Natural Family Planning.* Cincinnati, Ohio: Couple to Couple League International.

Klaus, H. (1982). "Natural Family Planning: A Review." *Obstetric and Gynecology Survey, 37*(2), 128–150.

Kosa, J., & Robertson, L. S. (1975). "The Social Aspects of Health and Illness." In J. Kosa & I. Zola (Eds.), *Poverty and Health: A Sociological Analysis.* Cambridge, Mass.: Harvard University Press.

Landy, U., & Lewit, S. (1982). "Administrative, Counselling and Medical Practices of National Abortion Federation Facilities." *Family Planning Perspectives, 14*(5).

Langlie, J. K. (1977). "Social Networks, Health Beliefs, and Preventive Health Behavior." *Journal of Health and Social Behavior, 18.*

Liskin, L. S. (1981). "Periodic Abstinence: How Well Do New Approaches Work?" *Population Report Series, 1*(13), 1–71.

Madigan, F. C. (1972). "The Philippine Program." In W. A. Uricchio & J. K. Williams (Eds.), *Natural Family Planning* (pp. 249–255). Washington, D.C.: Human Life Foundation.

Malthus, T. R. (1973). *Essay on the Principle of Population* (7th ed.). London, England: J. M. Dent and Sons. (Original work published 1816)

Marshall, J. (1975). "The Prevalence of Mucous Discharge as a Symptom of Ovulation." *Journal of Biosocial Science, 7*(1), 49–55.

Mauldin, W. P. (1983). "Population Programs and Fertility Regulation." In R. Bulateo & R. D. Lee (Eds.), *Determinants of Fertility in Developing Countries. Fertility Regulation and Institutional Influences* (Vol. 2, pp. 267–294). New York: Academic Press.

McKay, M. (1978). "The Ovulation Method and Planned Parenthood." *Planned Parenthood News, 1*(3), 4.

McKinlay, J. B. (1972). "Some Approaches and Problems in the Study of the Use of Services:

An Overview." *Journal of Health and Social Behavior, 13*(2), 115–152.

Mechanic, D. (1968). *Medical Sociology: A Selective View.* New York: Free Press.

Meier, G. (1971). "Research and Action Programs in Human Fertility Control: A Review of the Literature." In F. Haselkorn (Ed.), *Family Planning* (pp. 227–244). New York: Council on Social Work Education.

Phillips, J. F. (1978). "Continued Use of Contraception among Philippine Family Planning Acceptors: A Multivariate Analysis." *Studies in Family Planning, 7,* 182–192.

"Population Growth Rates Decline in Five Provinces." (1981). *Asian and Pacific Census Forum, 10*(3), 16.

Rochat, R. W., et al. (1980). "Induced Abortion and Health Problems in Developing Countries." *Lancet, 2,* 1027–1028.

Rogers, E. M. (1973). *Communication Strategies for Family Planning.* New York: Free Press.

Rosenstock, J. M. (1966). "Why People Use Health Services." *Milbank Memorial Fund Quarterly, 44*(3).

Ross, J. A. (1983). "Birth Control Methods and Their Effect on Fertility." In R. Bulateo & R. D. Lee (Eds.), *Determinants of Fertility in Developing Countries. Fertility Regulation and Institutional Influences* (Vol. 2, pp. 54–88). New York: Academic Press.

Russell, C., & Russell W. (1979). "The Natural History of Violence." *Journal of Medical Ethics, 5*(3).

Scrimshaw, S. C. M. (1983). "Infanticide as Deliberate Fertility Regulation." In R. Bulateo & R. D. Lee (Eds.), *Determinants of Fertility in Developing Countries. Fertility Regulation and Institutional Influences* (Vol. 2, pp. 245–266). New York: Academic Press.

Suchman, E. A. (1966). "Health Orientation and Medical Care." *American Journal of Public Health, 56*(1).

Tolar, A., et al. (1975). "Personality Patterns of Couples Practicing the Temperature-Rhythm Method of Birth Control." *Journal of Sex Research, 11*(2), 119–133.

Torres, A., & Forrest, J. D. (1983). "Family Planning Clinic Services in the United States, 1981." *Family Planning Perspectives, 15*(6).

Wade, M. E., et al. (1980). "Reply to Dr. Billings" [Letter to the editor] and "Reply to Dr. Hilger" [Letter to the editor]. *American Journal of Obstetrics and Gynecology, 136*(5), 698.

Wagner, D. A. (Ed.). (1983). *Child Development and International Development: Research and Policy Interfaces.* San Francisco: Jossey-Bass.

Weeks, J. R. (1982). "An Evaluation of the Use-Effectiveness of Fertility Awareness Methods of Family Planning.'' *Journal of Biosocial Science*, *14*(1), 25–32.

World Development Report. (1980). New York: World Bank.

World Development Report. (1981). New York: World Bank.

World Health Organization. (1978). *Special Programme of Research Development and Research Training in Human Reproduction*. Geneva, Switzerland: Author.

Xenos, C. (1977). *Fertility Change in Mauritius and the Impact of the Family Planning Program*. Port Louis, Mauritius: Ministry of Health.

Young, L. (1968). *Population in Perspective*. New York: Oxford University Press.

FAMILY LIFE EDUCATION

Before the turn of the century, parents began forming groups to increase their knowledge of child development and gain other knowledge or skills that would help them to become better parents. The most prominent of the early organizations specializing in parent education was the Child Study Association of America. Their early programs, which started in the 1880s, began with parents meeting informally to learn about children, using books as their guides. Didactic lectures were added because parents wanted to find out more about children and their own role in child development. Lectures became lecture-discussions, with parents responding to the lectures by asking questions. These formats were later supplanted by parent discussion groups in which parents were encouraged to express their thoughts and feelings about common parental concerns (Auerbach & Goller, 1953).

Family Service America (FSA) (formerly Family Service Association of America [FSAA]), has been the other major national organization involved in family life education (FLE) programs. Its involvement began in the 1930s, and in 1943 FSAA set up its Committee on Current and Future Planning. The committee's report, submitted in June 1946 (cited in Nichols, 1952), included the following statements:

> There is a pressing need for it [the family agency] to move into the field of generalized family life education. . . . Adult education,

through discussion meetings with groups of young couples, Mothers' Clubs and Parent Teachers Associations can become one of the effective media through which the family agency can disseminate useful information concerning the essential ingredients of healthy family life. (p. 2)

FLE practice remained essentially the same between 1940 and 1970. It consisted of three distinct types of programs: single speeches to large groups, followed by questions and answers; half-hour speeches to small- or medium-size groups, with the rest of the time for group discussion; and leader-led discussion groups on subjects of mutual interest, with one and a half to two hours allotted for each meeting and 6 to 12 meetings in a series. The primary focus of practice was parenting, and the audience was mainly women, although the literature cites fine examples of FLE with delinquent boys in Boston and Cincinnati and with groups that prepared men to become fathers (Nichols, 1952). The early FLE leaders of the Child Study Association were mainly college-educated volunteers; the leaders in the Family Service Association's FLE programs were primarily social workers who were trained as caseworkers.

Overview

Family life education is a leader-directed group-learning service that is appropriate for most of the population. It builds knowledge, develops skills, and examines attitudes to help people adjust, cope, and grow as they experience normal, predictable life transitions. It is also useful for people experiencing unpredictable events, such as time-limited crises and acute medical conditions (Fallon et al., 1982), and for those dealing with chronic conditions.

FLE groups are usually small, with 6 to 12 participants. In some situations, up to 100 people may participate. Typically groups meet once a week, and their sessions run from one and a half to two hours. A FLE series most often consists of six to eight sessions. Single-session groups and long-term or open-ended groups are also common. They are usually led by a professional with a master's degree in social work and specialized training in curriculum design, educational group process, and experiential-learning methods. Participants come from varied social class, religious, and educational backgrounds. They share a particular life situation, such as parents of newborns, recently separated or divorced individuals, relatives of Alzheimer's victims, or people who need to be more assertive.

Family life education groups differ from most therapeutic groups. A primary goal of therapy groups is to identify early-life causative factors of present maladaptive behavior and to have corrective emotional experiences through the group interaction. In addition, group therapy patients usually have a problem that is causing them considerable distress and pain. The goal for most FLE groups is knowledge enhancement, skill development, or personal growth for a current life transition or one that has yet to take place. FLE can help people prepare for such transitions or can help them understand those they are already experiencing. Even in FLE crisis and life adjustment groups, the primary intervention is educational.

There are common elements in therapeutic and FLE groups. Sharing of experiences is one such element, although in FLE groups intense emotional sharing is not encouraged and participants who need to do this are referred for psychotherapeutic services. Learning is a primary goal in FLE, but it is common to both methods and may evolve as part of an emotional process in group therapy. Emotional support is important to the development of group cohesion, and it facilitates learning. In therapy, support is the major method for developing group cohesion so that patients can have corrective emotional experiences.

Types of Programs

Because they address various developmental stages of the life cycle, FLE services are appropriate for all people, of all ages. The services are based on the premise that all individuals experience periodic transitions in their lives that can be handled with greater ease if they have information about what to expect during that transition. FLE groups can be broken down into four categories: normal development, crisis, personal growth, and life adjustment groups.

Normal development groups are designed for the general population and provide information and skills to help individuals negotiate predictable life transitions. Examples of groups in this category are parenting groups (newborn, preschool, adolescents), groups preparing for marriage, "empty nest" groups, and retirement groups.

Crisis groups are designed for populations that have undergone severe experiences that were unexpected or that could not have been predicted. The individuals have little information about the normal range of expected behavior, the duration of their reaction, or the adaptive skills needed to cope with the experience and resume a normal living pattern. The groups in this category include people who have been recently separated or divorced, widows and widowers, and the unemployed. Besides utilizing adult education techniques to help participants gain a better understanding of the phenomena, leaders of these groups also provide emotional support to participants and strongly encourage group support. The majority of participants in these groups resolve their crises and resume normal patterns of living.

Personal growth groups provide educational services to people who—although they may not be going through a particular life transition or experiencing a crisis—need to change their attitudes and develop skills that will enhance how they think about themselves and their interaction with others. They want to improve the quality of their lives. These needs are sometimes met in individual or group therapy sessions. Personal growth FLE groups do not look for historical causes, for explanations of why the participants did or did not develop specific behaviors; rather, they build on a desire to change through the use of an educational method. Examples of personal growth FLE groups are those that provide assertiveness training, self-esteem enhancement, stress management, and communications skills.

Life adjustment FLE groups are for people who are experiencing, or are living with someone else who is experiencing, a chronic condition—usually a medical or developmental disability—that is not likely to improve. This category differs from the other types of groups in that it is not a transition, crisis, or growth period but rather an extended adjustment to a chronic condition. Life adjustment groups rely heavily on leader and group support, and the educational component includes specific information relating to medical conditions and considerable content on personal growth and life enrichment.

Life adjustment FLE groups include those for parents of handicapped children and relatives of Alzheimer's victims.

Current Trends

It is possible to identify specific trends in FLE practice, which has changed considerably since the early 1970s. Family life education is provided by many different disciplines in a vast array of settings. As FLE practice evolved from a small service in some family agencies to a major service component in most, it expanded from being primarily a mothers' group to concentrations on areas and issues of other family members and the total family (Carder, 1982). Curricula for FLE series have changed dramatically to include adult education theories and techniques. In addition, practice has moved out of the agency and local community into industry, schools, and government settings.

With the increase in mental health clinics in FSA agencies since 1975, a tendency developed to view these agencies as just another type of mental health clinic. The growth of FLE programs and practice helped to counteract that perception. Family agencies with the strong educational component provided by FLE are broader in scope and mission than most mental health clinics. FLE services have also been integrated as a strong component in the family service movement— evidence of FSA's commitment to preventive services (FSAA, 1977).

A significant trend has been the shift toward developing programs for all family members. Parenting groups in the past involved mostly mothers. Present practice in parenting is geared to both parents, and the participation of fathers has increased significantly. This reflects the FSA philosophy that parenting is truly the responsibility of both parents and that both can benefit from educational programs. As stated previously, the FLE philosophy is that all people can use educational services to help them cope, adapt, and grow. This ideal has been implemented through the development of programs for all family members, particularly programs that address the later stages of the life cycle. Men are attending FLE groups on fathers' issues, stress management, self-esteem enhancement, and other areas of interest to them. FLE groups for children are increasing; they include groups on communications skills, assertiveness training, the transition to adolescence and junior high school, and preparation for marriage.

Early FLE groups were oriented to developmental stages or themes and followed a question-and-answer format. These groups provided an important service in helping participants gain knowledge. A trend that began in the mid-1970s broadened the goal of FLE not only to increase knowledge but also to develop skills and examine attitudes. With the broadening of goals came a change in methodology. Incorporating adult education theories and techniques meant a shift to greater reliance on the participants' capacity to learn, develop skills, and examine attitudes. Knowles (1973, 1975) was especially influential in his adult education theories and their application. Along with this change came the development of published curricula on many different types of life transitions. This provided FLE leaders with a suggested resource to adapt to the needs of their group members. Standard components of most FLE groups are specific lectures, experiential learning exercises, and the processing of educational materials. The series on family life education curriculum published by FSA has had a profound impact on changing practice, enabling group leaders to be more ambitious in their educational goals. Because it was made available to other groups and professionals, the series has also had an influence on family life education services outside FSA agencies.

A strong trend in FLE has been toward new sites for service delivery. Whereas the primary sites were once agencies and such community settings as libraries, housing projects, and community centers, FLE groups are now conducted in industrial, school, and governmental settings. Stress management, assertiveness training, balancing work and family life, the working couple are popular topics among industrial FLE groups. FLE services have also become a primary service component of many employee assistance programs, which have grown in popularity. The strong need for FLE services in industry led to the development and publishing of FLE curricula for that audience (Apgar et al., 1982). Schools have been interested in marriage preparation groups for high school students and in self-esteem, assertiveness-training, and friendship-building groups for all students. Local governments have been interested in employee programs that address all phases of life transitions. Some areas of government and industry have had a special interest in retirement planning. Groups in these new sites are most often run during work or school time or as lunchtime seminars in industry.

FLE services were initially seen and practiced as separate, independent entities from other services offered by family service agencies. This was especially true of counseling and psychotherapy services. Gradually, some counseling clients were offered the opportunity to join FLE groups for adjunctive services. Now a trend is developing to integrate FLE into initial treatment plans. At intake, clients are assessed not only for psychosocial needs but also for life education needs. The treatment plan then includes both educational and treatment goals. Mini- and full series on communication, assertiveness, and self-esteem are often included in the service plan. This trend is expected to strengthen and to become an accepted model of social work practice.

A recent focus of FLE practice is to provide services to groups that may be outside the mainstream of society or that are shunned by many service providers. For example, FLE programs are now available to prostitutes on parenting issues; to prisoners on parenting, communication, and self-esteem issues; and to mothers regarding regaining custody of their children. FLE services are also available to new immigrants to help them learn about their new country and adjust to its culture, expectations, and norms. This is especially evident in services to Southeast Asian and Russian immigrants.

Issues

Funding is a major issue affecting FLE. Prevention services are not usually popular with funding sources or agency boards of directors. Such services also generate less income than other services and are not covered by third-party insurers. The immediate future offers little hope that this will change. Without a strong funding base, a service is prone to cuts in size and scope, especially in difficult financial times. For family life education to maintain its momentum and to grow, it is crucial to develop and sustain community, board of trustee, and United Way support for FLE programs. Industrial programs will become an even more important FLE component because income derived from these groups can be used for partial support of groups that produce less income.

Training social workers as FLE leaders is another important issue. Agencies will continue to train leaders, using their own expertise and newly developed training manuals. Efforts to train bachelor's and master's degree social work students have met with minimal success. The integration of FLE concepts into social work is important for the expansion of the service and for the continued development of new models of practice that utilize both therapeutic and educational methods. It has met with little success, however, because schools have chosen to highlight clinical training rather than introduce adult learning.

There has been little research on FLE practice. If this service is to maintain its integrity, more FLE research must be developed. Outcome measures often influence the decisions of funding services. The effectiveness of FLE groups whose goal is primary prevention is difficult to research because the time needed after the intervention is long and because the tendency of scientific analysis is to attribute change to other variables. Research should be encouraged on FLE groups of a secondary or tertiary nature because these services are more accessible to better research methodology and the results should be more widely accepted.

Historically, social work has taken an important role in FLE services. From FLE's beginnings in settlement house education for immigrants, to the mothers' group-discussion phase, to the present phase involving comprehensive models of the life cycle, social work agencies and practitioners have exercised leadership in this field of practice. Now, as the FLE curriculum develops, it is also being taught by other professionals, such as industrial trainers, psychologists, nurses, physicians, and teachers. It is being integrated into the various health and human service professions. From the inception of FLE, its impact and importance have been widely recognized, and this crucial educational service is now witnessing enormous growth and popularity.

Donald P. Riley

For further information, see FAMILY: CONTEMPO-RARY PATTERNS; FAMILY PRACTICE; FAMILY SERVICES; MUTUAL HELP GROUPS.

References

Apgar, K., et al. (1982). *Life Education in the Work Place*. New York: Family Service Association of America.

Auerbach, A., & Goller, G. (1953). "The Contribution of the Professionally Trained Leader of Parent Discussion Groups." *Marriage and Family Living, 15*(3), 265–269.

Carder, J. (1982). "New Dimensions to Family Agency from Family Life Education." *Social Casework, 53*(6), 355–360.

Fallon, B., et al. (Eds.). (1982). *Training Leaders for Family Life Education*. New York: Family Service Association of America.

Family Service Association of America. (1977). *Task Force Report on Family Life Education*. New York: Author.

Knowles, M. (1973). *Self-Directed Learning*. Chicago: Association Press.

Knowles, M. (1975). *The Modern Practice of Adult Education*. New York: Association Press.

Nichols, M. S. (1952, May). *The Contribution of the Family Service Agency to Family Life Education*. Paper presented at the National Conference of Social Work, Chicago, Ill.

FAMILY PRACTICE

Social work has vigorously renewed an old commitment to a focus on the family, a commitment that lapsed for several decades. This shift, congruent with social work's person-in-environment emphasis, has been accomplished in an intellectual context that has included major changes in the epistemological or paradigmatic foundations for family theory and some 30 years of theoretical and practice innovations in the family therapy field. There is now an extensive body of social science and clinical family research available to social workers for model building. If, with few exceptions, such as Virginia Satir, social workers were inconspicuous during the pioneering years of the family therapy movement, they have made significant and creative contributions to family theory and practice in the movement's second and third generations. Family therapy theory and practice have deeply infiltrated the traditional mental health disciplines as well as other counseling disciplines.

Social work's renewed concern with the family has occurred during a time of growing interest in the family in the social sciences, the political world, the arts, and among average citizens. In the social sciences, an avalanche of publications, new journals, and research projects attest to scholarly interest in the family, providing a rich source of resources for better understanding this ancient and fascinating human system. Findings, however, on the state of the family differ. High rates of divorce and changing marital roles have led some to predict the coming demise of the family, but others report that the family is demonstrating its strength and vitality by adapting and creatively transforming itself in the face of the rapid social changes in the postindustrial world. Politicians from the right and the left continue to debate the nature of the state's relationship with the family and the family's place in social policy and programs.

The American public's fascination with the family is demonstrated by the enthusiastic consumption of television programs, movies, and literary works tracing family fortunes; *Dallas, Dynasty, Falcon Crest,* and *Knots Landing,* all modern variations of *The Forsyte Saga,* are extremely popular, as are family-issue movies such as *Kramer vs. Kramer* and *Ordinary People.* The study of family genealogy, once the hobby of an occasional aging relative, has become common to numerous Americans who, following Alex Haley's example, seek to trace their roots. Many families are energetically planning family reunions. These phenomena may, perhaps, be interpreted as responses to the isolating and disruptive results of the increasing dispersion and geographic distance among family members in our urban, technologically differentiated world.

The first step in this overview will be to provide some key definitions and draw boundaries around this vast and complex topic. Then, the social work-family relationship in its historical context will be briefly reviewed, followed by a discussion of the epistemological developments that provide a context for the state of family theory and practice today. Common themes, concepts, or perspectives in the family therapy movement will be examined, with emphasis on the way in which family theory and practice concepts may be integrated into social work models and applied to the various fields in the profession. Finally, there will be a discussion of unresolved issues and future directions.

What Is Family-Centered Practice?

There is no general agreement on a definition of family-centered practice. Some equate it with family therapy and even further limit it to a specific method in which all or several members of a family are seen together. In the broader view of family-centered practice, however, it is defined not in terms of method but in terms of perspective.

Family-centered practice may be described as a way of thinking about human beings in relation to their intimate and larger environments, translated into approaches to helping. Such a perspective locates the family in the center of the field of action, affirming the family as the "unit of interest." This does not mean that the person must be subordinated; it does not even necessarily imply that the social worker must work with the entire family. It means, rather, that human beings can be understood and helped only in the context of the intimate and powerful human systems of which they are a part. The most important of these systems usually is the family.

This definition of family practice places it squarely within social work's traditional domain: the person-in-environment. The domain of family practice is restricted neither to families and their members nor to those larger environmental systems that affect the nature of family life. It implies a concern with and a focus on those transactions among person, family, and environment that affect individuals, families, and even the larger social forces and systems in which families are enmeshed. Thus it assumes a "generalist" practice character.

The family practitioner may perform a wide variety of roles and work with different size systems. The social policy analyst, the agency administrator, or the program developer may be family-centered practitioners. This presentation, however, will focus primarily on direct service to individuals, families, and groups. Family practice may also take place across a range of settings and in the various fields of social work, including health, mental health, child welfare, gerontology, the justice system, the world of work, and, of course, the family agency.

What Is a Family?

How the family is defined has momentous implications for policy, program, and practice. Most human beings have at least two families—the here-and-now family and the family of origin. The definition of the here-and-now family was the issue, more than any other, that split the 1980 White House Conference on Families. If the current family is narrowly defined as a married couple with children, then policy, program, and practice designed to support such families push toward conformity of family structure and constrain life style choices. Support for such definitions led to the Reagan-supported Family Protection Act. If, on the other hand, the family is broadly defined, policy, program, and practice can protect and nurture a range of intimate living forms defined by the people themselves as "family."

Although such a broad definition raises difficult conceptual and policy questions, family-centered practice, in the authors' view, should be based on an inclusive, self-determining, or phenomenological definition of the family. A family, then, is created when two or more people construct an intimate environment that they define as a family, an environment in which they generally will share a living space, commitment, and a variety of the roles and functions usually considered part of family life.

The second family, common to all human beings and psychologically important whether or not close ties have been maintained, is the family of origin—that family of blood or bloodlike ties, both vertical (intergenerational) and horizontal (kinship), living and dead, close and distant, known and unknown. The term "bloodlike" is used because different families and various ethnic groups draw boundaries around the family in different ways. In some instances, a person may have more than one family of origin, as in situations involving adoption or remarriage. As present-day family structures change and become more complex, so do kinship networks and intergenerational family systems.

Historical Context

Family practice in social work has been created by the joining of two quite separate historical streams: (1) the long and ambivalent relationship between the social work profession and the family and (2) the interdisciplinary family therapy movement. To understand the complexity, the inconsistencies, and the strengths of family-centered practice in social work today, it is helpful to consider it in the context of its historical antecedents.

Direct practice, or casework, began in the Charity Organization Societies, later named the family service associations. Mary Richmond, a master builder of the profession, defined the family as the unit of attention. In her monumental work and the first major casework text, *Social Diagnosis,* Richmond (1917) clearly specified the family as the unit to be assessed and strengthened. "The family itself," she wrote, "continues to be the pivotal institution around which our destinies revolve" (p. 134). Richmond (1930) later warned that positive results in individual treatment would crumble away if caseworkers failed to take account of the family (p. 262).

The first professional journal was named *The Family* (now *Social Casework*). Social workers, as experts in the social environment, were called on in mental hospitals, in health care services, in schools, and in the child guidance movement, to work with the client's family as a central part of that social environment. Historians of the family therapy movement generally fail to acknowledge social work's early focus on the family. They speculate, for example, on which family therapy pioneer was the first to see family members together, without mentioning that more than 50 years before those momentous "firsts," social workers regularly met with families in their homes to help resolve social and emotional difficulties.

If social work was founded with the family as the unit of service, how was that special approach lost, not to be regained until the 1960s and beyond? *Social Diagnosis* was published in 1917, at the dawn of the mental hygiene movement—a movement that brought the concepts of psychiatry and, eventually, of psychoanalysis into social work, and made *Social Diagnosis* out of date almost before the ink was dry. The mental hygiene movement shifted the emphasis in diagnosis and in treatment from social to psychological aspects, and the focus or definition of the "case" from the family to the individual. E.E. Southard, a psychiatrist and leader in mental hygiene, spoke out at the 1918 National Conference of Social Welfare. Attacking Richmond's conceptualization, he wanted to "demolish what seems to be an erroneous pet view of social workers . . . . I want to replace the family as the unit of social inquiry with the individual" (Southard, 1919, p. 337). The repudiation of the social and familial emphasis was continued at the next year's conference by Mary Jarrett (1920), a founder of the Smith College School for Social Work, who said: "The adaptation of the individual to the environment, in the last analysis, depends upon mental make-up" (p. 587).

Southard, Jarrett, and the so-called psychiatric deluge won the day. Focus on the family largely was submerged for the following 40 years. Even in the family agency, where the enhancement of the welfare of the family continued to be the major mission, this goal was to be achieved through individual counseling of various family members (Scherz, 1954, p. 343). The notion of seeing family members together had been lost because of the psychoanalytic concern with the protection of the transference and its use in treatment. Thus, in the child guidance field, parents were only seen to obtain the family history or to report on the child's progress. Thus, the therapist-child relationship remained protected. Even in the early 1960s, a nationwide report of family agency practice refers to joint marital interviewing as an "experimental treatment approach" (Family Service Association of America, 1963).

Besides the impact of powerful psychological theories, other developments eclipsed interest in the family. First, the family as a potential unit of attention generally was disregarded in the historical split between "inner" and "outer" focus and in the pendulum swings between psychological and social explanatory systems and approaches to change. The family seemed to fall into the chasm between psychotherapy and social change.

Further, the traditional organization of practice around methods characterized by size of the client system created no place for the family. Caseworkers saw the family as a small, primary group whereas group workers, although contributing to the growing knowledge base, viewed the family as casework's domain. Finally, the historical development of family services as a field of practice may also have limited the growth of family practice in other fields, as the assumption was made that expertise on the family was lodged in a specific group of agencies rather than being an essential part of practice in all fields. The profession is still struggling with this issue. Both the Council on Social Work Education (CSWE, 1982) and the National Association of Social Workers (NASW-CSWE, 1979) have defined "family, children, and primary groups" as a field of practice. Yet the family can also be viewed as a unit of central concern in the other identified fields—health and mental health, education, justice, and the world of work.

Ideological, organizational, and conceptual characteristics of the profession militated against the continued development of a practice focused on the family. In the 1960s and 1970s, instead of developing knowledge and practice in their own profession and drawing on its long tradition of interest in the family, social workers turned to the family therapy movement and to leaders from other disciplines to learn about the family and its treatment. However, their background, values, and person-in-situation orientation made them apt and creative students. Today social workers represent the largest core of trained and practicing family therapists and have assumed leadership positions in this interdisciplinary movement.

Family Therapy Movement

Current family-centered social work practice cannot be understood apart from the central themes and theoretical advances in family therapy and other related fields, from the work of the family therapy pioneers, or from the various practice approaches that have developed over time in the family therapy field. Although a detailed recital of these developments is beyond the scope of this presentation, the major figures will be introduced and the major trends sketched in broad strokes.

Some favor "great leader" theories of history; others tend to explain the origin and development of major theoretical advances in terms of the ripeness of time. Family therapy developed out of recursive interactions between creative charismatic leaders and hospitable and exciting developments in the intellectual and social environment. It is evident that what may yet amount to a full-scale paradigmatic revolution in Kuhn's (1962) sense has been brewing for several decades, and accompanied the birth of family systems thinking. If one theme relevant to the discussion here can be identified from this revolution, it is a shift from interest in "things," "entities," or "truths" to an emphasis on form, structure, pattern, and most of all on relationships between and among entities. In individual or family terms the central questions are no longer these: "Why has this come about?" "What is wrong according to our preconceived categories of health?" Rather, these are becoming the main questions: "What is this family's view of themselves and the world, its patterns of meanings, values, and relationships?" "What are the forces for stability and change in this family and how does the identified problem help the family maintain itself or cope with its environment?" Theoretical developments that might be placed in this growing tradition include general systems theory, cybernetic theory, gestalt theory, various communication theories, and ecological theories. These theoretical developments have either been stimulated by, or grown parallel with, epistemological shifts in physics and biology, philosophy, linguistics, anthropology, and sociology—indeed, in almost every field of knowledge. "Relativity" has become the hallmark of modern science. It is reflected in the family therapy movement and in social work, as the search for ways to understand human behavior in terms of relationships rather than in terms of intrinsic essences has become the critical theoretical challenge.

Furthermore, in the human and social sciences, it was becoming increasingly evident that people were "open systems," shaping others and being shaped throughout life in mutual and circular interactions with their social and physical environments. It is in the context of this emerging world view that family therapy began to develop in the early 1950s quite spontaneously and separately in different parts of the country among researchers and practitioners.

On the West Coast, in Palo Alto, California, anthropologist Gregory Bateson, whose work continues to light a beacon for contemporary thinkers, led a research team in the study of communication, particularly of families which included a schizophrenic member. The findings of this research were published by Bateson with Don Jackson and other associates (1956) in the landmark paper titled "Toward a Theory of Schizophrenia," which introduced the concept of the double bind and suggested that schizophrenia could be understood as an adaptive response to paradoxical communication patterns in families. Before long, these findings began to be translated into treatment approaches focused on family communication patterns. Satir, one of the few social workers to take leadership in the first years of the family therapy movement, was brought by Don Jackson to the Mental Research Institute in Palo Alto, Calif., in 1959.

Concurrently, family approaches were developing on the East Coast. The first practitioner thought to have actually treated a whole family together for a series of sessions was John Bell, psychologist at Clark University in Worcester, Massachusetts (see Silverman & Silverman, 1962). Nathan Ackerman, the other early pioneer on the East Coast, came to family work via psychoanalysis, child psychiatry, and child guidance. Translating psychoanalytic concepts into direct work with the family, and in close association with social workers, in 1957 he established the family mental health clinic at Jewish Family Services in New York City. Ackerman organized the first session on family diagnosis at the American Orthopsychiatric Association meetings in 1955 and, with Don Jackson, in 1961, founded *Family Process*, the first journal devoted entirely to family therapy theory and practice. In 1958 he published the first volume on family therapy, *The Psychodynamics of Family Life*.

Between the two coasts, Murray Bowen, out of his research interest in symbiosis, began observing and studying family relationships at the Menninger Clinic in the mid-1950s. He moved to the National Institute of Mental Health (NIMH) in Washington, D.C., launching his famous research project that involved moving whole families with disturbed children into the hospital and working with them in multiple family therapy

groups (Bowen, 1978). Although Bowen, at NIMH and later at Georgetown University, continued his major interest in the nature of what he came to call "fusion" and its opposite "differentiation," he began to focus on the multigenerational family system and to work individually with adults, constructing a model of family systems therapy that identifies family-of-origin relationships as the arena for change. Ivan Boszormenyi-Nagy, Norman Paul, James Framo, and Carl Whitaker should also be counted among those early leaders who were interested in intergenerational issues and developed creative practice approaches to working with families.

Although Salvador Minuchin began to work with families almost a decade later than the pioneers, his innovations and wide influence dictate that he be considered among the founders. Minuchin began his family work at the Wiltwyk School in a program for delinquent children. Out of this experience came structural family therapy and the influential study *Families of the Slums* (Minuchin et al., 1967). Minuchin subsequently assumed leadership of the Philadelphia Child Guidance Clinic where he, along with, at various times, Jay Haley, Marianne Walters, Harry Aponte, Braulio Montalvo, and others developed one of the largest and most extensive centers for family treatment, training, and research. Working frequently with disorganized families caught in destructive and depriving environmental situations, Minuchin and his colleagues emphasized the family's relationship with its ecological environment as well as the structure and organization of the family itself.

In the past decade, many social workers have made major contributions to the field in the form of writing, research, and training. Lynn Hoffman, Peggy Papp, Monica McGoldrick, Elizabeth Carter, Olga Silverstein, Harry Aponte, Froma Walsh, and Marianne Walters are among those who should be noted particularly. Furthermore, social workers constitute a large percentage of the members of the American Family Therapy Association, a small organization that limits its membership to those with extensive experience in teaching, research, and writing in the field of family therapy, as well as of the much larger American Association for Marriage and Family Therapy (AAMFT). However, many of these leaders have identified themselves, or have been identified by others, not as social workers but as family therapists; they have not taken central positions at social work conferences and have not published to any extent in the social work literature. This state of affairs was lamented by Walters (1983) in a major speech at the AAMFT conference, in which she articulated the sexist and elitist implications. The social work education and practice establishments, however, have not always provided welcoming or fertile environments for renewed interest in the family or the emerging innovations in family theory and practice.

The course of the development of family therapy has not only had political implications but also, and even more pervasive, it has had ideological and practice implications. Building on the differing emphases, approaches, and views of the founders, family therapy began to be organized around different and sometimes competing schools of thought. Although a focus on the family binds the field together and there are a number of widely understood and shared concepts that lend considerable coherence, there is no unified body of theory or practice technology. This is undoubtedly a healthy situation, a phase of development in which younger thinkers are questioning, differentiating from, and deepening the ideas of the pioneers. The literature is marked by lively debate as the body of theory, research, and practice technology available for integration into social work practice grows.

Common Themes in Family Therapy

Several authors have attempted to compare or classify family therapy theories and practice approaches, presenting a collage of different perspectives on this lively field (see, for example, Beels & Ferber, 1969; Foley, 1974; Guerin, 1976; Laird & Allen, 1983; Madanes & Haley, 1977; Nichols, 1984; and Ritterman, 1977). The following is a summary of a few of the common themes.

First, and most important, family theorists share, at least to some degree, a view that human behavior is not exclusively a product of the personality, influenced by events of the past. Rather, it is greatly affected by circular or recursive patterns of interaction between individuals and their environments. A particularly salient part of that environment is the family. Family therapists differ in the extent to which they emphasize past or present, that is, individual behavior in the context of family history or current interactions.

Second, the family has been conceptualized by many theorists as a self-regulating, homeostatic (or rule-governed) cybernetic system with fairly consistent patterns, processes, structures, and prescriptions that have developed over time. Even Ackerman (1971), who initially conceptualized family interactions in psychoanalytic terms, began to use systems language and concepts in his article "The Growing Edge of Family Therapy." Within the overarching view of the family as a system, however, there are significant differences as to what aspects of that system should be considered central in assessment and intervention, such as family structure (Minuchin, 1974; Minuchin & Fishman, 1981), communication (Watzlawick, Beavin, & Jackson, 1967; Watzlawick, Weakland, & Fisch, 1974), organization (Haley, 1976; 1980), rule-governing processes (Papp, 1980; Selvini-Palazzoli et al., 1978), ecological or network relationships (Auerswald, 1968; 1971; Rueveni, 1979; Speck & Attneave, 1973), or intergenerational patterns (Boszormenyi-Nagy & Spark, 1973; Bowen, 1978).[1] Problematic behaviors or individual symptoms usually are seen in one of three ways: (1) as the result of faulty structure, organization, or communication, or of inadequate or stressful ecological relationships; (2) as serving some important function in maintaining the coherence of the family system; or (3) as outmoded and maladaptive behaviors being inadvertently reinforced by the family's responses. Many family therapists have come to question the homeostatic emphasis, arguing that change or perpetual motion may be more characteristic of families than stasis and that families do not regulate themselves in such a way as to return to a fixed, normative structure or organization (see, for example, Speer, 1970; Wertheim, 1973). Keeney and Ross (1985) conceptualize the family as a cybernetic or communication system in which problems or symptoms are seen as part of an encompassing systemic pattern of organization. The family is characterized by a

---

[1] These references are merely representative; many others have also made significant contributions in these areas.

moving, steady state that includes elements of stability and change.

Third, treatment approaches and strategies are marked by some significant differences, but they also share some common characteristics. The family system as a whole and various interactions among family members are addressed rather than individual characteristics. The practitioner may act as catalyst, enabler, director, or provider of a context. He or she may teach, challenge, reframe, sculpt, direct, or coach. The resources for change lie in the powerful system of family relationships and in the newly created ecosystem that includes family and therapist. The practitioner does not "change" individuals or the family. Rather, he or she helps to create a context in which the family can choose to change by participating in a new construction of reality. Keeney and Ross (1985) describe the process as one in which the therapist introduces "meaningful noise" or new communications around which the family can reorganize its patterns of complementary change and stability.

In the early years, many family therapy leaders, influenced by psychoanalytic thinking, made use of the transference in the change process. Most now attempt to avoid or minimize the development of transference, believing that significant change is promoted better by mobilizing the family's own power for change. Family therapists recognize, however, that they become part of and are changed themselves by the ecosystem that includes family and therapist (Keeney, 1979). Family therapists are likely to be open, active, and sharing of themselves. This stance tends to mimimize the development of transference since the therapist is a "real person." In most if not all models, life experience is considered the major resource for change. In family sessions, using circular interviewing, enactments, structural movements, communication exercises, family sculpture, the performance of specific tasks, or messages from behind the one-way mirror, or simply talking together in a manner that encourages new levels of awareness, families experience themselves in new ways and encounter the possibilities of change.

Most family therapists plan experiences that are designed to extend to daily life the changes catalyzed in the session, through the use of assignments, directives, tasks, or of paradoxical injunctions that remain unprocessed and uncommented upon and thus active until the next session. The traditional counseling pattern of weekly interviews has been altered; frequently, families are seen biweekly or even less often as time is allowed for the task to be completed or the injunction to take effect.

Family therapists are more likely to attend to structure and process within the relationship system rather than to the actual content of family communications. *What* the family talks about is less important than *how* it talks together. Actions and interactions—what various members *do* in response to others—are tracked, rather than feelings. Thus, such dimensions as the family's repetitive patterns of interaction (sometimes called the family "dance"), its positioning of members in relation to one another, its monitoring of space and time, its nonverbal communication as well as its special metaphors and stories, all become considerations in family therapy.

The boundaries of family work tend to be open and inclusive rather than closed and exclusive. Often extended family members and other important actors in their world may be included in the treatment system or participate in family sessions. The outer limits of this have been demonstrated by network therapists who include a minimum of 40 members of the family's network in therapy sessions (Speck & Attneave, 1973). The boundaries may also extend back in time as the development and transmission of family themes and patterns are examined over several generations.

Finally, the openness of the boundaries around the family–therapist constellation also has implications for models of cotherapy, consultation, and training. Cotherapists, for example, have been widely used to keep family therapists from becoming too absorbed by the family system. Increasingly, however, cotherapists, consultants, or "team" members participate from behind the one-way mirror. This process allows cotherapists to stay out of the system and to observe patterns and connections that might otherwise be missed. It also keeps the treatment system from being further complicated by the addition of another person in direct interaction with the family and the first therapist. Live supervision, with the supervisors observing from behind the mirror, is also common among family therapists, and training programs make extensive use of observation and videotaping to help learners capture the complexity and patterned interactions of the family system and to monitor the process of change.

The preceding discussion suggested some of the common themes that tend to characterize family therapy theory and practice. There is considerable diversity in conceptualization and technique among practitioners and among groups of individuals organized around various training centers; some represent particular "schools" of family therapy and others are eclectic. Differences exist, for example, in how the individual and his or her relationship with the family is viewed; in notions about what aspect of the family system should be placed at the center of the lens; in ideas about the origin of a problem or symptom; in goals of intervention, such as symptom relief or broad family and individual change; in preferred length of treatment; in ideas about who should be included in the meeting; in how resistance should be understood and handled; and so on. The family therapy field seems to have room for differing views and for practitioners from a range of divergent intellectual and professional backgrounds. The field has been characterized by rapid growth, flexibility, tremendous vitality, and continued differentiation of points of view. The growing number of family therapy journals and annual conferences are providing considerable opportunities for discussion, networking, and debate. The next section examines the linkages between the family therapy movement and the field of social work.

Family-Centered Social Work Practice

In family-centered social work practice, the worker, although attending to the total person-in-environment complex, considers the family or intimate social network as central in the assessment-intervention process. As has been suggested, family therapists vary in terms of which aspects to focus on in the individual–family–environment complex. The view taken here is that social workers, at this stage at least, should not adhere to a specific "school" or single approach, and that all of the aspects identified

must be considered to be potentially useful in building family-centered models of practice. In any one family, ecological, structural, communication, rule-governing, historical, and even mythical processes are occurring simultaneously; the practitioner may, based on a number of criteria, choose to emphasize different aspects in different cases or move from one emphasis to another throughout the course of work with a family. However, the worker should develop criteria for the use of varying emphases, striving to maintain coherence.

The first focus for assessment and intervention is the family-environment interface, as worker and family examine the fit or lack of fit between the family and its "surround." Grounded in an ecological perspective and drawing on practice conceptualizations developed in family therapy by Auerswald (1968; 1971) and others, and in social work by Germain (1973; 1979), Hartman (1978), Meyer (1970), and others, this approach attempts to capture a composite view of family-environment transactions. Assessment may be aided with the use of an eco-map (Hartman, 1978). Mutually arrived-at goals may emphasize enhancing the goodness of fit between family and environment by helping the family meet their needs for material goods, services, stimulation, and social involvement, and by developing new experiences of participation, competence, and effectiveness on the part of family members. Interventive strategies include those primarily focused on altering the environment, such as resource development and discovery, brokering, and advocacy, and those that may help the family and its members to make better use of that environment. Powerlessness, in particular, has been identified in recent years as a major issue in the lives of many of the families served by social workers (Pinderhughes, 1985; Solomon, 1976). A major goal in ecological family work may be altering the family–environment relationship so that family members have more power and control over important areas of their lives and their world.

For example, underorganized families often live in contexts that are similarly underorganized in terms of both space and time. The family practitioner, recognizing that a recursive relationship exists between the family and its environment, may help the family influence the systems around it by (1) uncovering discriminatory or unresponsive practices, (2) negotiating for goods and services, (3) strengthening weak or inadequate ties with potentially nourishing personal and social resources, (4) helping the family take better advantage of community and personal resources through, for example, planned use of time and space, or (5) helping to strengthen family identity and coherence through the development of rituals. Such restructuring may alter aspects of the environment as well as the internal organization of the family. (For an extended case example illustrating an ecological emphasis in family-centered practice, see Hartman & Laird, 1983, especially chaps. 8 and 9.)

A second major focus for change is the intergenerational family system. Based on the conviction that human beings and their current families are shaped in major ways by powerful intergenerational forces, a study of these influences sheds light on current family patterns of relationship and action. Furthermore, these forces may be mobilized for change. An assessment tool useful in gathering data for the intergenerational system is the genogram, an intergenerational family map on which the life history of the family may be traced and organized so that principal themes, patterns, and relationships among events may be perceived.

The genogram is constructed in and augmented by an interviewing mode that taps intergenerational family systems of meaning and belief, the family's world view, its paradigm for living. Akin to the methods of ethnographic study, interviewing strategies are designed to encourage the family to share and explore their "culture" in a way that reveals how they experience and interpret themselves and their world. Such interviewing may include the careful exploration of family myths, rituals, and stories, categories of symbolic action that are packed with family meanings, as well as the patterns for belief and experience which serve as the family's prior texts and its code or explanatory system for communication and action (Laird, 1984). Although these areas for exploration are useful in work with any family, they have special promise in identifying and elucidating cultural differences and in helping the social worker to become more aware of and sensi-

tive to values, lifestyles, and world view differences.

Some family therapists insist that the focus remain on the present, believing that the impact of the past is available in the present; others work almost exclusively in an intergenerational frame. However, most family therapists gather at least some history in order to understand the family's historical context. Similarly, family-centered social workers, depending on the context and on case goals, may choose to place more or less emphasis on intergenerational patterns and relationships.

In some situations, family-of-origin relationships may be the primary focus of change. Working mainly with adults, in individual, marital or other dyadic, family, or group sessions, the worker guides and coaches clients as they become explorers of and, later, experts on their family histories, examining secrets, demystifying mysteries, exposing distortions, and traversing forbidden territories of family communication. Eventually, based on their studies, clients working in this mode are coached to take specific steps to refashion their relationships with key members of the family of origin. The worker as coach helps clients explore the possibilities, suggests potential strategies for altering their own actions with family members, provides support, and helps monitor the results. The outcome of such work is the enhancement of an individual's differentiation in the family of origin and, consequently, in other important relationships. Even when such intensive study is not practical, some familiarity with family history and experience with family-of-origin techniques can be useful in work with families in crisis or short-term situations and in many fields of practice.

The third dimension for attention is the current family system. Depending on a number of variables, the practitioner must choose the aspects of the family on which to focus. Some of the variables that help to determine the focus are client need, the practice setting, the training and theoretical bias of the worker, the referring network, presentation of the problem, urgency of resolution, the family's culture and style, their prior experiences with therapeutic or other social service resources, and the rigidity of the family structure and interaction patterns. Alterations in family structure may be indicated if the family is (1) underorganized, (2) has insufficient or opaque boundaries between itself and the world or among individual family members, or between the sexes or the generations, (3) has experienced a breakdown of hierarchy, or (4) has formed perverse triangles or alliances—for example, if a child replaces one of the adults in the spouse system. Many families and marital pairs may be helped by focusing on the family's communication processes. In rigid families or those in which one member's behavior is extreme or symptoms are severe, more dramatic, paradoxical interventions may be needed to help create a context for change.

The structural, communication, and organizational aspects of the family system are assessed by means of observation, family sculpture, and spontaneous enactments that take place in the session. Family-centered practitioners tend to be active and personal in their dealings with clients and in their attempts to influence the family's transactional patterns in office sessions or home visits. The worker tries to create a context in which the family has a different experience of itself and its world. Through new "punctuations" of the family's descriptions of its concerns, the family begins to view itself and its problems differently.

Through the interviewing process itself, new communications emerge that challenge the family's constructions. Circular or systemic interviewing techniques shift the understanding of the problem from one of individual symptomatology to one that reveals the ways in which family members move in relation to each other, highlighting the ways in which the family maintains coherence. The problem is reframed as one of the movements in the family's complex system of relationships. Interviewing techniques include joining, tracking sequences of interaction in the family, reframing, and positively connoting the family's view of the problem. The worker may, for example, encourage the family to "enact" scenes that occur at home using "family sculpture" or role playing, thus having the family experience its own emotional system. Or, the family may enact its relationship system in response to circular interviewing questions. The worker may also have the family perform various tasks in the sessions or in homework assignments, usually to throw into relief and/or shift some

aspect of the family's structural and organizational arrangements.

In some situations, the identified problem may be linked tightly to the processes essential for the maintenance of the system, serving an important function in preserving the family (Selvini-Palazzoli et al., 1978). Because the problem serves the system's survival, direct efforts to alleviate it can be experienced by the family as extremely threatening. In working with such frightened and rigid families, it is often effective to draw upon positive connotation and other paradoxical communication techniques in stimulating the forces for change. Positive connotation, used by many family therapists but developed into a fine art by Selvini-Palazzoli and her associates, communicates to the family an acceptance of the system as it is and an understanding of the importance of the problem to the family's stability. Through positive connotation, the family's resistance is joined and disarmed.

Paradoxical intervention is used in many ways but, generally, it is more accurately a counterparadox (Selvini-Palazzoli et al., 1978). That is, the family itself has approached the therapist with a paradoxical request: "Change the symptom but don't change our family!" As these are two contrary commands, the family therapist is placed in a paradoxical situation and responds by presenting the family with the hypothesis that indicates how the symptom is helping the family maintain itself, positively connoting it, and cautioning the family concerning the possible outcomes of change. The family is thus left with the counterparadox and must accept either the inevitability of the symptom or the risk of change. The third option, as in any double-binding situation, is to invalidate the therapist; a variety of management strategies have been developed to circumvent this option.

Life cycle transitions have been of particular interest in understanding and working with family systems. Transitions disrupt family organization and require change. It is frequently because of the inability to complete transitions, to go through the necessary transformations, that symptoms develop as a way to stabilize a shaky family equilibrium. Haley (1980), for example, applies his approach to families in which the young adult has been unable to "leave home," and Carter and McGoldrick (1980) have made a major contribution with their work on the family life cycle.

Applications Across Fields of Practice

Many social workers in mental health settings, family agencies, and in private or group practices, have embraced family systems concepts and techniques for work with individuals, couples, and families. It is here that the influence of the family therapy movement can most easily be seen. However, social workers in all or most fields of practice and across methods have been shifting to a family focus in the delivery of services. They are adopting assessment and intervention approaches from family therapy to their own settings and purposes. A few are noted here.

Child welfare, for example, has become increasingly family-centered, both in policy and in program as it is recognized that the fortunes of children are largely dependent on those of the families in which they live (Laird & Hartman, 1985). Protective and preventive services, services aimed at the reunification of families and children, foster care, adoption, and residential and institutional services increasingly have focused on the family as the unit of attention. Ecological and structural theories and practice techniques have proven particularly useful. Family systems assessment techniques have been used in constructing a model for the adoptive home study as well as for services to families after adoption (Hartman, 1979; 1984). Heightened understanding of the power of kinship ties has led to an increased respect for intergenerational family issues, seen in the widespread use of the genogram and "life books" in the child welfare field.

In health care and in gerontology a similar emphasis is developing as patients and the elderly live within the family unit. Families provide a major portion of the care to both groups and it has become increasingly apparent that the needs and welfare of the family system must be included as part of the planning in the delivery of health care and services to the aging (Moroney, 1980). Ecological, communication, and structural techniques may be particularly helpful, and the knowledge of intergenerational family systems as well as the use of the genogram have

been central in life review with the aging population.

The unit of attention for the school social worker has broadened to include school–family relationships (Aponte, 1976). Similarly, social workers in industry or in employee assistance programs are increasingly taking account of the family. It is, in fact, difficult to conceive of any field of practice in which knowledge of family theories and techniques will not be relevant. Social workers bring a wealth of historical experience, particularly in their commitment to family–environment relationships, that can enrich and expand the more narrowly treatment-focused perspectives predominant in the family therapy field.

The recent recommendations for specialization in social work practice and education identified family and children's services as an area of specialization (CSWE, 1982; NASW-CSWE, 1979). It is hoped that this identification will not obscure the possibility that if social workers remain faithful to their traditional person-in-situation orientation, then a family focus is generic to practice in any setting since families are a salient part of most people's situations.

Current Issues

Family therapy is a vital social and intellectual movement that has had tremendous influence on social work practice. It has grown rapidly and has blazed several divergent trails, some of which have led at times to considerable confusion. Some areas have been developed quite fully, whereas other important territories remain largely unexplored.

Today's family-centered practitioners have been enriched by, but also must struggle with, the legacy of the creative pioneers. Several of these pioneers, although united by a family systems orientation, developed approaches to the family that focused on only one dimension. Many therapists believe that the task now facing this growing and changing field is one of integration. Clearly, all of the dimensions described above are an important part of the life of every family. Exclusive attention to one approach for every family seems unnecessarily limiting, but a tested scheme for the differential use of various approaches in specific family situations has not been devised. Furthermore, procedures and guidelines for moving from one focus to another in the course of working with a particular family must also grow from the ingenuity and creativity of individual practitioners. Although there are those who are wedded to particular approaches, most social workers seem to be drawing from a range of different orientations in the family field.

Another issue involves future directions in family therapy research. Both family therapy process and outcome research studies, as well as summaries and reviews of such studies, proliferate. However, in attesting to the relative success of family approaches compared with other therapeutic approaches, the profession is at a stage where it needs to review the reviews and, more importantly, to review the epistemological groundings for current research paradigms. Most research models have been extended from those used in behavioral and other therapies grounded in nonsystemic epistemologies. In general, research in the family therapy field has been less creative than family theory and practice models; there is a gap between the epistemologies informing practice and traditional research methods (Simon, 1983). A crucial task for the next period will be that of seeking new models for research on practice with families.

One of the relatively neglected areas in family systems theory and practice involves women's issues, feminism, and the relationships between women and the family. The roots of the family therapy movement reach back into the 1950s, a time of sharp gender role differentiation when a woman's place was in the home. The Parsonian vision of the normative family in which women played expressive roles and men instrumental roles influenced views of the healthy family. The political structure of the movement itself was hierarchically sexist in the early years. Male physicians occupied the podiums, and large numbers of women, from professions with less status, filled the audiences. The radical feminist view of the family as a major instrument in the oppression of women in a sexist society served to make conflict between feminists and family therapists inevitable. Recent scholarship on women's moral and psychological development also has raised questions of whether family therapists have adopted gender-biased views of emotional and mental health (Gilligan, 1982). For example, Bow-

en's (1978) concept of "differentiation" or Minuchin's (1974) concept of "enmeshment" carry definitions of normative behavior and mental health that speak in clearly male voices. Recently, some women and men in the field have begun to address sexism in family therapy and to struggle with the task of developing a gender-sensitive family-centered approach.

The family therapy movement has been similarly myopic on the subject of ethnic and cultural differences in family norms and processes. It is necessary to adapt family approaches so that they will be more congruent with and supportive of the needs, values, and lifestyles of different ethnic groups. Social scientists and family therapists are beginning to work in this important area and some valuable materials are now available to practitioners (McGoldrick, Pearce, & Giordano, 1982).

Another intriguing challenge that some students of the field believe must be faced involves the integration of individual psychological theories and practice models and family systems approaches. Individually oriented psychological theories do not provide enlightenment about family systems approaches and, conversely, family systems theories (although they have much to say about individual actions) do not tell much about inner psychological processes. To slip from one level to the other often leads to reductionism. For example, role is a concept widely used in family theory and practice to characterize the interactive situation and behaviors of the individual. Although Thomas à Becket's famous statement, "Make me archbishop and I will be archbishop," resounds with truth, role theory and family theory do not describe the parellel psychological processes operating in the inner worlds of people carrying specific roles.

Relations between individual and family-oriented practitioners have sometimes been competitive and acrimonious. Individual practitioners have criticized family approaches as superficial or manipulative, and dismissed them as a fad. Family therapists have directly challenged many of the fundamental theories of individual work and accused such practitioners of being myopic, reactionary, and, worst of all, "linear" in their thinking. Such attacks and counterattacks, although understandable in a period of rapid change, polarize positions and provide a context that is antithetical to the development of collaborative efforts to explore common themes or reach toward integration.

Some psychologists have turned their attention to families and family therapy and have sought to discover concepts that link familial and psychological events (see Boszormenyi-Nagy & Spark, 1973; Skynner, 1976; and Stierlin et al., 1980). Similarly, some family therapists are turning to psychology. For example, analysts and family therapists have drawn on object relations theory for linking concepts. In therapies grounded in object relations theory, the origin of interpersonal relationships in the unconscious, internalized remnants of one's early familial relationships are explored. However, the development of a practice model for treating troubled families that integrates object relations and family systems theories or, in fact, any other individual psychology has yet to be achieved.

The discovery of the connections between different systems levels is, perhaps, the exciting and challenging intellectual task of the 1980s and 1990s. The discovery of such connections was a major concern of Gregory Bateson, considered by most to be the intellectual parent of family therapy. A recent conference in his honor brought together physicists, biologists, artists, theologians, family therapists, social workers, and others to explore connections among systems of thought. The task of connecting psychological and family theories is part of that larger task that many agree is a major priority in study and research.

Continuing to rely heavily on psychology and sociology for a knowledge base has not moved the field very far toward integration, since each discipline has its own language, its prevailing research paradigms, and its carefully bounded territory. The ecological metaphor has helped to expand social work's person-in-environment conception. But because its origins are in biology, it influences practitioners to construct images that exclude meaning and value, memory and imagination, fantasy, spirituality, and aesthetics—all important dimensions of human life.

Innovative thinkers in many fields, including family studies and family therapy, in the search for connections, are crossing boundaries not only between the physical and social sciences, but also between these sciences and the arts. They are discovering science in art, art in science, and social theory in all human activity and creativity.

In the family field, some are turning to the use of aesthetic genres that can capture human experience in multidimensional ways. For example, family rituals, stories, myths, metaphors, and analogies express the patterns that connect past and present, different realms of human experience, and human beings with each other. These forms provide sources of meaning and integration not readily accessible in other ways of knowing people and their worlds.

ANN HARTMAN
JOAN LAIRD

For further information, see DIRECT PRACTICE IN SOCIAL WORK: OVERVIEW; FAMILY LIFE EDUCATION; FAMILY SERVICES; SOCIAL WORK PRACTICE WITH GROUPS.

References

Ackerman, N. (1958). *The Psychodynamics of Family Life*. New York: Basic Books.

Ackerman, N. (1971). "The Growing Edge of Family Therapy." *Family Process, 10*(2), 143–156.

Aponte, H. (1976). "The Family-School Interview: An Ecological Approach." *Family Process, 15*(3), 303–311.

Auerswald, E. (1968). "Interdisciplinary vs. Ecological Approach." *Family Process, 7,* 202–215.

Auerswald, E. (1971). "Families, Change and the Ecological Perspective." *Family Process, 10*(3), 263–280.

Bateson, G., et al. (1956). "Toward a Theory of Schizophrenia." *Behavioral Science, 1*(4), 251–264.

Beels, C., & Ferber, A. (1969). "Family Therapy: A View." *Family Process, 8*(3), 280–318.

Boszormenyi-Nagy, I., & Spark, G. (1973). *Invisible Loyalties: Reciprocity in Intergenerational Family Therapy*. New York: Harper & Row.

Bowen, M. (1978). *Family Therapy in Clinical Practice*. New York: Jason Aronson.

Carter, E., & McGoldrick, M. (Eds.). (1980). *The Family Life Cycle: A Framework for Family Therapy*. New York: Gardner Press.

Council on Social Work Education. (1982). *Curriculum Policy for the Master's Degree and Baccalaureate Degree Programs in Social Work Education*. New York: Author.

Family Service Association of America. (1963). *Range and Emphasis of a Family Service Program*. New York: Author.

Foley, V. D. (1974). *An Introduction to Family Therapy*. New York: Grune & Stratton.

Germain, C. (1973). "An Ecological Perspective in Casework Practice." *Social Casework, 54*(6), 323–330.

Germain, C. (1979). *Social Work Practice: People and Environments*. New York: Columbia University Press.

Guerin, P. (1976). "Family Therapy: The First Twenty-Five Years." In P. Guerin (Ed.), *Family Therapy: Theory and Practice* (pp. 2–22). New York: Gardner Press.

Gilligan, C. (1982). *In a Different Voice*. Cambridge, Mass.: Harvard University Press.

Haley, Jay. (1976). *Problem-Solving Therapy*. San Francisco: Jossey-Bass.

Haley, J. (1980). *Leaving Home*. New York: McGraw-Hill Book Co.

Hartman, A. (1978). "Diagrammatic Assessment of Family Relationships." *Social Casework, 59*(8), 465–476.

Hartman, A. (1979). *Finding Families: An Ecological Approach to Family Assessment in Adoption*. Beverly Hills, Calif.: Sage Publications.

Hartman, A. (1984). *Working with Adoptive Families Beyond Placement*. New York: Child Welfare League of America.

Hartman, A., & Laird, J. (1983). *Family-Centered Social Work Practice*. New York: Free Press.

Jarrett, M. (1920). "The Psychiatric Thread Running Through All Social Case Work." In *Proceedings* (pp. 587–593). Chicago: National Conference on Social Welfare.

Keeney, B. (1979). "Ecosystemic Epistemology: An Alternate Paradigm for Diagnosis." *Family Process, 18*(2), 117–129.

Keeney, B., & Ross, J. (1985). *Mind in Therapy*. New York: Basic Books.

Kuhn, T. (1962). *The Structure of Scientific Revolutions*. Chicago: University of Chicago Press.

Laird, J. (1984). "Sorcerers, Shamans, and Social Workers: The Use of Ritual in Family-Centered Practice." *Social Work, 29*(2), 123–129.

Laird, J., & Allen, J. (1983). "Family Theory and Practice." In A. Rosenblatt & D. Waldfogel (Eds.), *Handbook of Clinical Social Work* (pp. 176–201). San Francisco: Jossey-Bass.

Laird, J., & Hartman, A. (Eds.). (1985). *A Handbook of Child Welfare*. New York: Free Press.

McGoldrick, M., Pearce, J., & Giordano, J. (Eds.). (1982). *Ethnicity and Family Therapy*. New York: Guilford Press.

Madanes, C., & Haley, J. (1977). "Dimensions of Family Therapy." *Journal of Nervous and Mental Disease, 165*, 88–98.

Meyer, C. (1970). *Social Work Practice: A Response to the Urban Crisis*. New York: Free Press.

Minuchin, S. (1974). *Families and Family Therapy*. Boston, Mass.: Harvard University Press.

Minuchin, S., & Fishman, H. (1981). *Family Therapy Techniques*. Cambridge, Mass.: Harvard University Press.

Minuchin, S., et al. (1967). *Families of the Slums*. New York: Basic Books.

Moroney, R. (1980). *Families, Social Services, and Social Policy: The Issue of Shared Responsibility*. Rockville, Md.: National Institute of Mental Health.

NASW-CSWE Task Force on Specialization. (1979). "Specialization in the Social Work Profession." *NASW News, 24*(20), 31.

Nichols, M. (1984). *Family Therapy: Concepts and Methods*. New York: Gardner Press.

Papp, P. (1980). "The Greek Chorus and Other Techniques of Family Therapy." *Family Process, 19*(1), 45–58.

Pinderhughes, E. (1985). "Power, Powerlessness, and Practice." In S. Grey, A. Hartman, & E. Saalberg (Eds.), *Empowering the Black Family* (pp. 29–39). Ann Arbor: National Child Welfare Training Center, University of Michigan School of Social Work.

Richmond, M. (1917). *Social Diagnosis*. New York: Russell Sage Foundation.

Richmond, M. (1930). *The Long View*. New York: Russell Sage Foundation.

Ritterman, M. K. (1977). "Paradigmatic Classification of Family Therapy Theories." *Family Process, 16*(1), 29–46.

Rueveni, U. (1979). *Networking Families in Crisis*. New York: Human Sciences Press.

Scherz, F. (1954). "What Is Family Centered Casework?" *Social Casework, 34*(8), 343–348.

Selvini-Palazzoli, M., et al. (1978). *Paradox and Counterparadox* (English translation). New York: Jason Aronson.

Silverman, M., & Silverman, M. (1962). "Psychiatry Inside the Family Circle." *Saturday Evening Post*, Nov. issue, 46–51. Quoted in C. B. Broderick & S. S. Schrader (1981). "The History of Professional Marriage and Family Therapy." In A. Gurman & D. Kniskern (Eds.), *Handbook of Family Therapy* (pp. 5–38). New York: Brunner/Mazel.

Simon, R. (Ed.). (1983). "Research: Why Bother?" [Special issue]. *Family Therapy Networker, 7*(4).

Skynner, A. (1976). *Systems of Family and Marital Psychotherapy*. New York: Brunner/Mazel.

Solomon, B. (1976). *Black Empowerment: Social Work in Oppressed Communities*. New York: Columbia University Press.

Southard, E. E. (1919). "The Kingdom of Evil: Advantages of an Orderly Approach in Social Case Analysis." In *Proceedings* (pp. 334–340). Chicago: National Conference on Social Welfare.

Speck, R., & Attneave, C. (1973). *Family Networks*. New York: Vintage Books.

Speer, D. (1970). "Family Systems: Morphostasis and Morphogenesis, or 'Is Homeostasis Enough?'" *Family Process, 9*(3), 259–278.

Stierlin, H., et al. (1980). *The First Interview with the Family*. New York: Brunner/Mazel.

Walters, M. (1983, October 8). *Coming of Age: Reflections on the Journey*. Speech given at the Annual Conference of the American Association for Marriage and Family Therapy, Washington, D.C.

Watzlawick, P., Weakland, J., & Fisch, R. (1974). *Change: Principles of Problem Formation and Problem Resolution*. New York: W. W. Norton & Co.

Watzlawick, P., Beavin, J., & Jackson, D. (1967). *Pragmatics of Human Communication*. New York: W. W. Norton & Co.

Wertheim, E. S. (1973). "Family Unit Therapy. The Science and Typology of Family Systems." *Family Process, 12*(4), 361–376.

FAMILY SERVICES

The term "family service" encompasses a wide range of social services. Generally, these services are provided by social agencies that emphasize a concern for families in their mission or statement of purpose. These agencies are often called "family service agencies."

Family service programs may be remedial in nature, as in counseling services, or educational in focus, addressing issues of personal and family growth and development. Most family service programs focus on individual, family, or small-group situations. Some family service agencies also include in their range of services programs that seek to effect social change for the betterment of large groups of people in the society.

Because there is no clear and universally accepted definition of what constitutes a family service agency, it is difficult to determine how many such agencies exist. In 1984, Family Service America (FSA), which was called Family Service Association of America until 1983, had 268 member agencies and 16 affiliate members, and 110 agencies were affiliated with the Association of Jewish Family and Children's Agencies. In addition, there are family service divisions of the Salvation Army and the American Red Cross, and an unknown number of family service programs provided by the hundreds of church-related social agencies. In 1977, Ambrosino estimated that there were about 1,000 voluntary family service agencies in the United States. Although this estimate still seems reasonable, it may be understated, given the proliferation of small neighborhood-based agencies providing "family services" that have been established since then.

In any event, the number of family service agencies is dependent on the definition used. The most clearly defined agencies are the members of FSA that have in common certain criteria for governance, administration, programs, funding, and facilities. All FSA member agencies are expected to have programs in family counseling, family life education, and family advocacy and may have a range of other programs. Despite the diversity of programs, the members of FSA are relatively homogeneous in purpose, organizational structure, staffing, and programs. Because they are organized into a national organization, these agencies also are the source of the most reliable data in that they supply statistical information on an annual basis to FSA.

History

The Charity Organization Societies of the late 1800s often are considered to be the forerunners of today's family service agencies. Actually, the roots to many family service agencies go back to the Relief and Aid Societies of the early 1800s. Two such agencies are the Child and Family Services of Hartford (175 years) and Family Service Association of Indianapolis (150 years).

The Relief and Aid Societies of the early 1800s were organized in various communities by affluent volunteers who distributed relief, usually in kind, via home visits. These societies were active in aiding the poor sporadically when economic panics swept across the nation and unemployment skyrocketed. The needs were great because the government took only limited responsibility for such aid and there were no organized programs in the private sector. The Charity Organization Society began in London, England, in 1869 as an attempt to coordinate the efforts of various organizations in aiding the poor. Buffalo, New York, was the first U.S.

city to form a Charity Organization Society. According to Rich (1956, p. 5), the purpose was to "organize all existing charitable relief agencies into a working whole for the better division of labor and more effective aggregation of effort."

The Charity Organization Societies, in spite of their name, considered large-scale relief giving to be injurious and they tried to eliminate poverty by discovering and removing its causes. They were convinced that scientific methods could be used to cure the "illness" of poverty. Along with an emphasis on factual knowledge and methods based on theory, these societies were characterized by a strong sense of fairness and a belief that life should not be so bleak and barren for the working class and the poor. Furthermore, they recognized the need for self-fulfillment, for human dignity, for recreation, and for planning for old age.

Although the original intent of the Charity Organization Societies was to coordinate and systematize relief giving to individuals and families, the societies also adopted a strong orientation toward social reform. They became advocates for improved working conditions, more adequate pay, and better housing and health practices. They established what eventually became Social Service Exchanges, in which all "cases" in a community were centrally registered so that services could be coordinated, the duplication of services could be prevented, and data could be gathered to support efforts toward reform.

Volunteer "friendly visitors" were the primary "staff" of direct service agencies. Paid professionals appeared as "agents" or "secretaries" of these societies before the turn of the century. Friendly visitors reported to case committees that reviewed the cases and decided courses of action, including the amount of relief to be given.

Case committees became an important vehicle for training friendly visitors. In their meetings, information on methods was exchanged and analyzed by what became a mixture of paid staff and volunteers. Eventually, training in some agencies was organized into formal courses. As knowledge accumulated, supervisors began to appear. Concurrently, information and experiences were exchanged and articles and books were published as the foundation of professional

literature in social work was put into place. Richmond's *Friendly Visiting Among the Poor: A Handbook for Charity Workers* (1899) became a basic text for both volunteers and professionals. As knowledge and experience became broader, training programs in agencies expanded; these programs eventually led to the establishment of professional schools of social work.

After Charity Organization Societies were established in a number of cities, the societies began to come together to exchange information and ideas in a Charity Organization Committee of the National Conference of Social Work. By the 1890s, the need for a national organization of Charity Organization Societies was being discussed. The political aspects surrounding the organization of a national association were intense. For example, in a letter to John M. Glenn, one of the volunteer founders, Mary Richmond stated her agreement with Zilpha Smith, associate director of the Boston Charity Organization Society and Richmond's first tutor, that "we must not undertake to include the Relief Societies or any agencies not responsible for the Organization of Charity in their particular community" (as quoted in Ormsby, 1969, p. 42). The New York Association for the Improvement of the Conditions of the Poor applied informally for membership in 1906 and was denied.

Richmond and Francis H. McLean, a leader in the Charity Organization Societies movement who had served in many cities including Montreal, Chicago, and New York, obtained financial support from the Russell Sage Foundation to establish the National Association of Societies for Organizing Charity in 1911. McLean was the first general secretary. The name of the national organization changed three times by 1919, in 1930, in 1946 when it became the Family Service Association of America, and in 1983 when it became Family Service America.

Role of the Government

No history of family service agencies would be complete without a recognition of the role of the government. In the early years, city, state, and local governments made sporadic attempts to address the needs of the poor. However, the role of the government in family services became more firmly established only with the passage of the Social Security Act in 1935, which provided for a pattern of shared federal-state responsibility for public assistance. Amendments to the act have expanded coverage for families and for categorically defined others, including the aged, the blind, and the disabled.

Title XX, the social service amendments of 1974, marked a significant change in the Social Security Act. This title brought major funding from the national level for social services. Often the services were provided in a collaborative effort between governmental and family service agencies. The expansion of direct financial benefits as well as funding for services continued unabated until 1980 when federal policies changed and funding for social service programs was frozen or reduced.

This sharp shift in policies came after 20 years of increased funding for family service agencies, particularly from the federal government. For example, from 1961 to 1981, the proportion of the income of family service agencies from federal and state governmental sources rose from 17 percent to 79 percent, and funds from local governments decreased from 83 percent to 21 percent (FSA, 1982). In 1981, the overall growth of family service agencies was the lowest in 15 years, the result of increased costs because of high inflation and the cutbacks in governmental funds to support programs. Many of the federal programs from which the agencies received income, such as Title XX, the Comprehensive Education and Training Act, and a variety of mental health programs, showed particularly large decreases.

Trends

Programs. The programs of voluntary family service agencies have always been shaped by the needs of communities and by the resources that were available to meet those needs. When the government assumed increasing responsibility for financial support of the poor following the Great Depression, counseling became the core service of family agency programs. As skills in counseling were developed and refined, programs that addressed problems on only a remedial basis were seen as too limited. Hence, preventive services were developed that were geared toward early intervention to prevent problems and to facilitate normal growth and development. By the late 1960s, in response to the inability of the various systems to meet the needs of clients, the emphasis on social action programs was renewed in family service agencies. In the late 1960s, the national board of the then-named Family Service Association of America gave impetus to social action by encouraging its member agencies to implement the concept of family advocacy as a basic strategy.

The 1970s brought refinements in counseling programs and new developments in educational programs and family advocacy as family agencies moved ahead with this tripartite program. The inflation of the late 1970s had a major impact on the poor because governmental revenues became more limited and only entitlement programs received increased funding.

Social problems were exacerbated in the early 1980s as the result of high inflation, high unemployment, new policies of more limited resources and, for the first time since the passage of the Social Security Act, a national administration that espoused less governmental responsibility. To respond to these changing social conditions and the changing needs of families, family service agencies altered their programs to increase the provision of financial assistance, reminiscent of the early days in the history of family social agencies.

Sources of Revenue. As governmental funding diminished, so did private funding through the United Way of America. In 1981, member agencies of FSA received less income from United Way agencies and sectarian federations than in 1980. Many family service agencies looked for new sources of revenues.

Some agencies increased their fees; others explored new opportunities for the reimbursement of counseling costs through third-party insurance payments. Some agencies were concerned that increased fees from whatever source would skew the mission of agencies to serve economically disadvantaged clients. Some of these agencies developed programs to raise funds via personal contributions to supplement other sources of revenue. But the limitations in revenue had their effect. After many years of exceptional growth, FSA member agencies reported decreases in the number of professional staff employed in 1982 and in 1983 (FSA, 1984).

Family service agencies found a new source of revenue in the provision of services to business and industry, often under programs known as employee assistance programs. The proportion of FSA agencies that provided such services rose from 10 percent in 1975 to 60 percent in 1982 (FSA, 1982). The major impetus for the proliferation of these services was a contract between FSA and the Xerox Corporation to provide an employee assistance program to Xerox employees throughout the country via the network of FSA member agencies. In 1984, FSA signed a multimillion dollar contract with General Motors to provide alcohol and drug abuse services to General Motors employees, their dependents, and retirees.

Empowering Clients. In another playback to their roots, family service agencies of the 1980s developed a renewed interest in the importance of empowering families to manage their lives. Pearlman and Edwards (1982) described the beginnings of this trend in a project called ENABLE, which was carried out in the late 1960s. Pinderhughes (1983) noted that the lack of power is the critical issue in people's lives.

Helping people to help themselves through the provision of services and resources has always been a part of the programs that undergird the family service movement. The new emphasis is on personal assertiveness to empower families to seek changes in systems and institutions that affect their daily lives. Individuals and families are encouraged to seek resources, appeal decisions, and join groups and coalitions to change policies and procedures that negatively affect them and their existence. Such efforts help people to build a positive self-image and to alleviate their feelings of isolation and depression because they develop a sense of their own competence and power and are actively involved in coping with the reality of their lives rather than passively accepting whatever befalls them.

Role of the Social Worker. The role of the social worker in a family service agency in the 1980s is partly dependent on how a particular agency defines its mission and program. A common underpinning of the social

work role in any agency, however, is an understanding of human behavior and a professional discipline used to effect change. The skills used may be administrative, clinical, educational, or of a research or advocacy nature. No matter what skills are used, they are performed in a context in which human behavior is understood and the goal is to effect change in individuals, families, or social systems.

Council on Accreditation. In recent years, the effectiveness of family services and other social services has come under increasing question. Since its founding, FSA had seen its role as providing national leadership for the family service movement by setting standards for family services. Until 1978, FSA was the accreditation body of local family service agencies. However, on July 1, 1978, that function was assumed by the Council on Accreditation of Services for Families and Children (COA). COA was established jointly by FSA and the Child Welfare League of America to ensure that accreditation would be independent of any membership organization and hence free from possible conflicts of interest. The goal is work for the accreditation and accompanying upgrading of standards of a wider range of agencies.

Conclusion

In certain ways, the 1980s have brought family service agencies back to some of their roots. The renewed concern with the daily problems of family living necessitated by the increasing number of families who are struggling with survival issues has created more of a balance in programming between problems of daily living and intrapsychic issues. Financial assistance on an emergency basis has become commonplace although there is no expectation that private voluntary agencies can replace the government in the ongoing financial support of dependent citizens. The renewed interest in social action or family advocacy, along with the empowerment of clients, also is embedded in the history of the Charity Organization Society movement.

FSA's first *The State of Families* report, published in 1984, indicated that family service agencies are a reliable barometer of family problems. The report stated that a 1983 FSA survey of 280 family service agencies in the United States and Canada found that the major concerns of families are unemployment, single-parenthood, increased family violence, incest, blurred sex roles, depression and loneliness, and alcohol and drug abuse. The report concluded that the current prospects are bleak for families near and at the bottom of the economic scale. Families in multiproblem situations often feel helpless. Family structures are besieged and weakened by unemployment, poor schools, loss of family support systems, family violence, drug and alcohol abuse, and depression, and new classes of the poor are emerging.

Family service agencies encompass a wide variety of programs and services, including family, individual, and group counseling; educational programs; financial assistance programs; employee assistance programs; and programs geared toward effecting social or institutional change. Undergirding these programs are social workers with an impressive array of skills that place family service agencies in a strong position to help families meet the challenges they face in today's society.

A. GERALD ERICKSON

For further information, see BEHAVIORAL APPROACH; CASE MANAGEMENT; DIRECT PRACTICE IN SOCIAL WORK: OVERVIEW; FAMILY LIFE EDUCATION; FAMILY PRACTICE; FEDERAL SOCIAL LEGISLATION SINCE 1961; SOCIAL WORK PRACTICE WITH GROUPS.

References

Ambrosino, S. (1977). "Family Service: Family Service Agencies." *Encyclopedia of Social Work* (17th ed., pp. 429–435). Washington, D.C.: National Association of Social Workers.
Family Service America. (1982). *Family Service Profiles: Expenditures and Income.* New York: Author.
Family Service America. (1984) *Family Service Profiles: Agency Staffing and Coverage.* New York: Author.
Family Service America. (1985). *The State of Families: 1984–85.* New York: Author.
Ormsby, R. (1969). *A Man of Vision.* New York: Family Service Association of America.
Pearlman, M. H., & Edwards, M. (1982). "Enabling in the Eighties: The Client Advocacy Group." *Social Casework, 63*(9), 532–539.
Pinderhughes, E. B. (1983). "Empowerment for Our Clients and for Ourselves." *Social Casework, 64*(6), 331–338.

Rich, M. E. (1956). *A Belief in People.* New York: Family Service Association of America.
Richmond, M. E. (1899). *Friendly Visiting Among the Poor: Handbook for Charity Workers.* New York: Macmillan Co.

For Further Reading

Germain, C. B. (Ed.). (1979). *Social Work Practice: People and Environments, An Ecological Perspective.* New York: Columbia University Press.
Manser, E. (1973). *Family Advocacy: A Manual for Action.* New York: Family Service Association of America.
Riley, P. V. (1981). "Family Services." In N. Gilbert & H. Specht (Eds.). *Handbook of the Social Services* (pp. 82–101). Englewood Cliffs, N.J.: Prentice-Hall.
Sunley, R. (1970). "Family Advocacy: From Case to Cause." *Social Casework, 51*(6), 347–357.
Sunley, R. (1983). *Advocating Today: A Human Service Practitioner's Handbook.* New York: Family Service Association of America.
Weick, A. (1981). "Reframing the Person-in-Environment Perspective." *Social Work, 26*(2), 140–143.

FAMILY TREATMENT. See DIRECT PRACTICE IN SOCIAL WORK: OVERVIEW; FAMILY LIFE EDUCATION; FAMILY PRACTICE; FAMILY SERVICES.

FAMILY VIOLENCE. See CHILD ABUSE AND NEGLECT; CHILD SEXUAL ABUSE; DOMESTIC VIOLENCE; WOMEN.

FAURI, FEDELE FREDERICK. See biographical section.

FEDERAL SOCIAL LEGISLATION SINCE 1961

From 1960 through 1968, Americans gave the national government a major role in the areas of mental health, health, children and families, and gerontology. New legislation pertaining to economic security was also enacted. The social welfare reforms passed during this period were so broad that it can be termed "the second New Deal." This liberal trend was followed by a conservative reaction that persisted into the mid-1980s. Although some major social reforms were enacted in the 1970s, the focus in the 1980s was directed exclusively in the area of cuts in social programs.

Context of Reforms in the 1960s

A number of factors account for the passage of reforms in the 1960s (Bornet, 1983; Matusow, 1984; Sundquist, 1968). A coalition of unions, workers, ethnic minorities, blacks, and liberals was drawn together during the 1960 presidential campaign of John Kennedy. By force of personality and vision Kennedy was able to put forth reform ideas that appealed to the Democratic coalition and the broader public, but he was unable to obtain legislative passage of most of his proposals, partly because of opposition from a conservative coalition of Republicans and Southern Democrats. He nonetheless secured passage of the Manpower Development and Training Act of 1961, which funded job training for low-income adults; the Juvenile Delinquency Control Act of 1962, which provided funds for pilot projects in many cities; and the Community Mental Health Act of 1963, which provided funds for a national network of mental health facilities offering a range of community-based services (Matusow, 1984).

It was left to President Lyndon Johnson, in the several years following Kennedy's assassination in November 1963, to obtain major legislative success. He was aided by an electoral landslide in the 1964 presidential election, which gave the Democrats large majorities in both houses of Congress, but he was also skilled in parliamentary maneuvering (Bornet, 1983; Meranto, 1967). Major social reforms came with dizzying rapidity before the Great Society lost political momentum.

Great Society Reforms

Reforms Passed in 1964. The War on Poverty, under the Office of Economic Opportunity (OEO), was multifaceted legislation designed to address the needs of inner-city and rural victims of poverty. It contained two major components (Matusow, 1984; Moynihan, 1973a). First, Title II provided funds for development of community action agencies (CAAs) that were to plan and coordinate services for the poor in specific geographic areas. A number of service programs were also funded by Title II, including the popular Head Start program, which provided a variety of services to low-income preschool children. Second, a number of specific service programs were provided under various other titles of the legislation, including the Job Corps, the Neighborhood Youth Corps, legal aid services, job training for welfare recipients, and health clinics in low-income areas. The War on Poverty provided important services to low-income populations, but many CAAs became controversial when they sought to implement a clause in the legislation that required "maximum feasible participation" of the poor on their boards, a policy that precipitated social action against local officials. Critics note as well that War on Poverty programs often lacked sufficient funding and administrative direction to accomplish their objectives (Bornet, 1983; Matusow, 1984).

The Food Stamp program was initiated by Democrats to address widely documented problems of malnutrition among the poor (Steiner, 1971). For a relatively nominal sum, certified families purchased food stamps to use at participating markets to buy items worth considerably more than the purchase price of the stamps. Localities were given the option to participate in the program; the Department of Agriculture paid the entire cost with no local funds required.

Families on welfare were automatically eligible. Some localities chose not to participate in the program or set extremely restrictive eligibility standards. The 1970s, however, saw marked expansion of the program, including reforms such as setting national eligibility standards in 1971, requiring localities to participate in the program in 1973, and developing new procedures in 1978 that allowed people to receive food stamps without having to advance cash payments (Levitan & Taggart, 1976).

Attention was riveted on the South in 1963 when Martin Luther King, Jr., and other civil rights activists demonstrated for black access to public facilities. Massive lobbying by civil rights groups and skillful legislative maneuvering by President Johnson led to the passage of the historic Civil Rights Act of 1964. This act established the Equal Employment Opportunity Commission (EEOC) to investigate reports of racial or gender-based discrimination in employment, outlawed discrimination in public accommodations such as hotels and restaurants, and outlawed intentional segregation of schools by local officials (Bornet, 1983; Sundquist, 1968).

Reforms Passed in 1965. Additional civil rights legislation was needed to eliminate procedures used in the South to disqualify blacks from voting. The Civil Rights Act of 1965 not only prohibited literacy tests and other devices for disqualifying blacks but also provided for federal registration of voters when necessary (Bornet, 1983; Sundquist, 1968).

Landmark health legislation was enacted in 1965 through additions of legislative titles to the Social Security Act. Medicare (Title XVIII) provides selected medical benefits to the elderly. Participation in Part A is mandatory, financed from payroll contributions of the nonelderly, and provides coverage for hospital costs not exceeding 60 days. Participation in Part B is voluntary, financed by a combination of premiums from elderly participants and contributions from the general revenues, and provides coverage for selected services from physicians (Marmor, 1970; Starr, 1982). Medicaid (Title XIX) was enacted to address the needs of low-income individuals who could not afford medical services. Under this legislation, the federal government shares the cost of medical care with the states on condition that the latter agree to cover specified services. The states were empowered to devise eligibility policies, but in 1967, because of soaring costs, Congress decided that states could not set eligibility ceilings higher than 125 percent of the prevailing standard for Aid to Families with Dependent Children (AFDC) (Stevens & Stevens, 1974).

The Older Americans Act created a national network of agencies to plan and coordinate services for the elderly in specific jurisdictions; required states to set up a state office on aging to plan and coordinate programs for the elderly; and funded a variety of service programs, such as the Title III nutritional programs (Gelfand & Olsen, 1980).

Reforms were also enacted in the housing and community development sector. The Housing and Urban Development Act, enacted in 1965, greatly expanded housing programs by providing rent subsidies and subsidies for moderate-income housing and scattered-site public housing (Sundquist, 1968). (Under the Model Cities legislation to be passed in 1967, the Department of Housing and Urban Development would provide funds for the planning and implementation of community development projects that pooled a variety of housing and service programs.) The Appalachian Regional Commission, also established in 1965, was authorized to develop strategies to coordinate economic and service programs in rural areas (Sundquist, 1969).

Congress had wrestled for years with issues of public assistance to local school districts but had never been able to resolve constitutional questions pertaining to separation of church and state. The Elementary and Secondary Education Act of 1965 provides federal assistance to local public schools based on the number of low-income children enrolled in them; it also allows public school districts to share curriculum materials with private schools (Meranto, 1967).

Additional Great Society Reforms. There was mounting concern in the early 1960s about the rapidly increasing numbers of women and children who received benefits under AFDC. A "services strategy" developed in 1962 addressed the problem by increasing the federal share of the cost of social services provided to AFDC families from 50 to 75 percent. Because welfare rolls soared even more dramatically after 1962, however, Congress enacted a work requirement provision in 1967 that required women to seek employment as a condition of receiving benefits (Steiner, 1971). Congress also provided work incentives that enabled many AFDC recipients to remain on the rolls even after they had obtained employment, a policy that had the unanticipated effect of further increasing the size and cost of the AFDC program (Levitan & Taggart 1976).

Analysis of Great Society Reforms. Social reforms of the 1960s vastly expanded the role of the federal government in social welfare; brought major advances in civil rights;

and allowed low-income people to obtain medical and nutritional benefits and job training (Levitan & Taggart, 1976). Some critics contend, however, that legislation on Medicaid, community mental health, older Americans, and job training often provided only vague guidelines to local authorities (Lowi, 1969). Traditional reluctance to expand social welfare programs was manifest in disparities between lofty intentions and the funds allocated to achieve them (Bornet, 1983). The War on Poverty, the most publicized program of the Great Society, never received more than $2 billion in a year, Model Cities did not receive more than $1 billion a year, and only a fraction of the originally planned community mental health centers were in operation by 1970. When Medicaid grew beyond the initial intentions for the program, Congress hurriedly enacted drastic restrictions on eligibility.

Beginning of Conservatism: The 1970s

When Richard Nixon defeated Vice President Hubert Humphrey in 1968, an era of policy conservatism ensued. Words like "scarcity," "prioritizing," "fiscal conservatism," and "retrenchment" replaced the social reform language of the preceding decade (Levitan & Taggart, 1976; Reichley, 1981; Steinfels, 1979). It is useful to distinguish the 1970s from the 1980s, however, because a number of new programs were established in the former decade, whereas in the mid-1980s the focus was exclusively on retrenchment.

Many factors contributed to the conservatism of the 1970s, including deficits in the federal budget, runaway inflation, conservative presidents, electoral gains by Republicans and moderates in the Congress, grass-roots movements suspicious of social welfare, and increasing skepticism about the effectiveness of Great Society reforms (White, 1982). The reform-oriented presidencies of Kennedy and Johnson were succeeded by the more conservative presidencies of Richard Nixon, Gerald Ford, and Jimmy Carter (Leuchtenburg, 1983; Siegel, 1984). Although Nixon and Ford initiated some pieces of reform legislation, they vetoed numerous others and criticized the programs of the Great Society (Reichley, 1981). The Carter presidency, which was a curious blend of Democratic reform rhetoric and con-

servatism, emphasized the value of reducing social welfare expenditures (Califano, 1981; Shoup, 1980).

Despite the conservatism of the 1970s, however, most social programs were not substantially cut. Indeed, federal spending for social programs increased dramatically in the 1970s, and a number of liberal policy reforms were proposed that were not enacted.

New Federalism. Many reforms of the 1970s can be placed under the rubric of the "new federalism," a movement to give local government unrestricted funds and enhanced policy roles (Magill, 1979). General revenue sharing was established by passage of the State and Local Fiscal Assistance Act of 1972, which provided funds to finance municipal improvements as well as ongoing costs of government. Legislation in 1972 also established "special" revenue sharing, under which federal funds were given to local governmental units to meet community development, manpower training, transportation, education, and law enforcement needs.

Social Services and Title XX. New grant-in-aid programs included, in 1975, Title XX of the Social Security Act. The AFDC program had been funded under Title IV of the Social Security Act, with a policy whereby, beginning in 1962, federal authorities financed 75 percent of the states' expenditures for services to recipients. When costs rose sharply in the early 1970s as many states began to apply for these funds, Congress became alarmed. Federal audits revealed that some states had even used the funds for road construction (Derthick, 1975). To establish more control, Congress consolidated funding for services to existing and potential welfare recipients under the new Title XX and placed a $2.5 billion ceiling on federal expenditures for these services. Funds were dispersed through state agencies to local public and private agencies, for day care, counseling, foster care, and a host of other programs.

Economic Security Reforms. The Comprehensive Employment and Training Act (CETA) for 1973 provided training and public service employment in public and nonprofit agencies (Levitan, 1980). Like the public employment programs of the 1930s, CETA encountered criticism on the grounds that it subsidized make-work jobs and that many trainees could have found employment in the private sector.

A major restructuring of welfare programs occurred in 1972 when the Aid to the Blind, Aid to the Disabled, and Old Age Assistance programs were consolidated into the Supplementary Security Income (SSI) program. Wholly financed by federal authorities, SSI has a nationally prescribed eligibility standard and is administered by the Social Security Administration (Levitan, 1980).

Changes in the Social Security, Food Stamp, and unemployment insurance programs dramatically increased federal funding of social programs. Legislation in 1974 required social security benefits to be adjusted upward annually to keep pace with inflation; this indexing required large increases in pensions when the nation experienced high inflation during the ensuing decade. The Food Stamp program was federalized in 1970 and its benefits liberalized. Congress enacted emergency legislation in 1974 authorizing the use of federal funds to extend unemployment benefits, a policy that was used in subsequent recessions.

Unsuccessful Reform Proposals. Presidents Nixon and Carter advanced several major proposals that—although not enacted—exposed important policy issues. With the assistance of advisor Daniel Moynihan, President Nixon introduced a reform package in 1969 to merge general assistance and AFDC programs; to establish a national eligibility and benefit schedule; to increase federal funding; and to provide job training, employment, and day care programs (Moynihan, 1973b). The proposal was defeated as a result of opposition from liberals, who wanted higher national standards for payments, and from conservatives, who wanted tougher work requirements. President Carter presented but did not vigorously support a similar welfare proposal (Califano, 1981).

National health insurance reforms were proposed by Presidents Nixon and Carter and supplemented by alternative plans developed by Senator Edward Kennedy as well as other legislators (Davis, 1975). Under the Nixon and Carter proposals, the federal government would have required employers to provide basic and minimum health benefits to their employees and would have continued federally funded programs for the poor and the elderly. Neither president was able to overcome the opposition of physicians and conservatives who argued that the legislation would be too costly or would give federal authorities an excessive policy-making role. Senator Edward Kennedy proposed a national health insurance plan that would have placed all Americans under a single federal health program, but it lacked a wide base of legislative support (Davis, 1975).

Assessment of Social Programs. Economic security reforms, including SSI, social security indexing, CETA, food stamps, and expansion of the unemployment insurance program, substantially reduced the percentage of the population falling beneath official poverty lines (Haveman, 1977; Levitan & Taggart, 1976). Court decisions and actions of the Equal Employment Opportunity Commission led to reforms in hiring and promotion policies that assisted women and minorities. But funding of service programs in the mental and general health sectors lagged in the 1970s, as reflected by the budget problems of many community mental health centers and neighborhood health programs.

Policies After 1980

During Ronald Reagan's first term as president, a variety of social programs were frontally attacked, the federal government's roles in policy were markedly reduced, and tax policies were enacted that made the federal tax system significantly more regressive. A number of factors facilitated the passage of these kinds of policies (Barrett, 1983; Cannon, 1982; Evans & Novak, 1981). Reagan won a substantial victory in an election that gave Republicans control of the Senate. He was able to obtain support from a large number of Democrats, including many Southerners whose constituencies favored conservative policies. The Democrats were in disarray and lacked leadership that could resist conservative policies. By exempting from cuts certain politically popular programs, such as social security and Medicare, the president obtained further support for his policies.

Reagan achieved major social policy successes in his first year in office, including regulatory, budget, and tax reforms. Vice

President George Bush chaired a cabinet-level Task Force on Regulatory Relief that recommended elimination of many federal regulations—recommendations that were often implemented by the large number of high-level officials in the Executive Branch who shared an antipathy to governmental regulations (Barrett, 1983; Cannon, 1982).

On the budget and tax fronts, Reagan decided early in his administration not to dilute his policies through compromises, for example, with the leadership of the Democratic Party. By enlisting conservative Democrats, he obtained a wide base of legislative support for two major budget measures. The Budget Resolution of May 1981 set general ceilings for the budget recommendations of each congressional committee, and the Omnibus Budget Reconciliation Act of June 1981 established a series of block grants that included funds for social services; community services; alcohol and drug abuse and mental health; preventive health; maternal and child health; community development; and primary health care (Barrett, 1983). Although this legislation simplified federal programs by eliminating 57 specific categorical programs and pooling their funds into these various block grants, funding reductions of almost $1.2 billion were made in the process.

Sweeping tax reductions were obtained through the Tax Equity and Fiscal Responsibility Act of July 1981. These reductions fulfilled the hopes of many supply-side economists who believed that economic growth could occur only as businesses and affluent individuals obtained more resources. Critics, however lamented the fact that poor and middle-income individuals received considerably fewer benefits from the measure (Lekachman, 1982).

The initial budget cuts of 1981 were followed in succeeding years by many more cuts in individual programs. A massive increase in military spending, coupled with tax cuts and a recession, led to unprecedented and mounting deficits in the federal budget, which increased legislative pressure to make further cuts in domestic spending (Dallek, 1984). Reagan nonetheless encountered increasing opposition to his policies after 1981. Some of his proposed reductions in specific programs were defeated, as were initial efforts to cut Social Security and Medicare benefits. Little support existed for an ambi-

tious scheme to transfer to the states total responsibility for AFDC and Food Stamp programs. Critics focused attention on the magnitude of defense spending as well as the lack of equity in many budget and tax policies of the Reagan Administration. They also feared that the states would not continue to fund many of the categorical programs that had been consolidated into block grants. Democrats slowed Reagan's policy momentum when they made gains in the 1982 congressional elections.

When Reagan won a landslide victory in the 1984 Presidential elections, many liberals feared that he would continue to cut social programs, including Social Security and Medicare, which had emerged relatively unscathed from his first term, particulary since he insisted that the massive federal deficit should be decreased by slashing non-military federal expenditures.

But his victory was more a personal mandate than a policy mandate to cut social programs. A political stalemate developed in the early portion of his second term; while Reagan insisted that cuts in social programs should continue to receive priority, many legislators placed more emphasis on tax increases and sharp reductions in defense spending. The stalemated politics of 1985 contrasted sharply with the policy successes that Reagan had experienced in 1981.

In the wake of Reagan's cuts in social programs, many Americans paused to reconsider the merits of governmental roles in social welfare. A number of theorists continued to argue that social programs increased dependency or to contend that Reagan had been too timid in cutting programs (Murray, 1984; Glazer, 1984). Other theorists countered that substantial evidence existed that many Great Society programs, as well as some social reforms of the 1970's, had proven effective (Levitan & Johnson, 1984). Some theorists argued that Americans had become so concerned with individual goals that social commitment was itself endangered (Bellah et al., 1985). Further, there was growing recognition that Reagan's spending cuts had focused disproportionately on social programs that benefit the poor, leaving programs assisting the middle and upper classes relatively untouched (Meyer, 1984).

Reagan's conservative policies, then, had triggered a far-reaching reassessment of

American social policy (Bawden, 1984; Hulten & Sawhill, 1984; Palmer & Sawhill, 1984; Salamon & Lund, 1985). Future elections would determine whether the policy pendulum would again swing in a liberal direction.

BRUCE S. JANSSON

For further information, see AID TO FAMILIES WITH DEPENDENT CHILDREN; FOOD STAMP PROGRAM; HISTORY OF SOCIAL WORK AND SOCIAL WELFARE: SIGNIFICANT DATES; SOCIAL PLANNING IN THE PUBLIC SECTOR; SOCIAL WELFARE FINANCING; SOCIAL WELFARE POLICY: TRENDS AND ISSUES.

References

Barrett, L. I. (1983). *Gambling with History: Reagan in the White House*. New York: Penguin Books.

Bawden, D. (1984). *The Social Contract Revisited: Aims and Outcomes of President Reagan's Social Welfare Strategy*. Washinton, D.C.: Urban Institute Press.

Bellah, R. N., et al. (1985). *Habits of the Heart: Individualism and Commitment in American Life*. Berkeley, Calif.: University of California Press.

Bornet, V. D. (1983). *The Presidency of Lyndon B. Johnson*. Lawrence: University of Kansas.

Califano, J. A. (1981). *Governing America*. New York: Simon & Schuster.

Cannon, L. (1982). *Reagan*. New York: G. P. Putnam's Sons.

Dallek, R. (1984). *Ronald Reagan: The Politics of Symbolism*. Cambridge, Mass.: Harvard University Press.

Davis, K. (1975). *National Health Insurance*. Washington, D.C.: The Brookings Institution.

Derthick, M. (1975). *Uncontrollable Spending for Social Services*. Washinton, D.C.: The Brookings Institution.

Evans, R., & Novak, R. (1981). *The Reagan Revolution*. New York: E. P. Dutton & Co.

Gelfand, D. E., & Olsen, J. K. (1980). *The Aging Network: Programs and Services*. New York: Springer Publishing Co.

Glazer, N. (1984). "The Social Policy of the Reagan Administration." In D. Bawden (Ed.), *The Social Contract Revisited* (pp. 221–240). Washington, D.C.: Urban Institute Press.

Haveman, R. H. (1977). *A Decade of Federal Antipoverty Programs*. New York: Academic Press.

Hulten, C. R., & Sawhill, I. V. (Eds.). (1984). *The Legacy of Reaganomics*. Washington, D.C.: Urban Institute Press.

Levitan, S. A. (1980). *Programs in Aid of the Poor for the 1980's*. Baltimore, Md.: Johns Hopkins University Press.

Levitan, S. A., & Johnson, C.M. (1984). *Beyond the Safety Net: Reviving the Promise of Opportunity in America*. Cambridge, Mass.: Ballinger Publishing Co.

Levitan, S. A., & Taggart, R. (1976). *Promise of Greatness*. Cambridge, Mass.: Harvard University Press.

Lekachman, R. (1982). *Greed Is Not Enough: Reaganomics*. New York: Pantheon Books.

Leuchtenburg, W. E. (1983). *In the Shadow of FDR: From Harry Truman to Ronald Reagan*. Ithaca, N.Y.: Cornell University Press.

Lowi, T. (1969). *The End of Liberalism*. New York: W. W. Norton & Co.

Magill, R. S. (1979). *Community Decision Making for Social Welfare*. New York: Human Sciences Press.

Marmor, T. R. (1970). *Politics of Medicare*. London: Routledge & Kegan Paul.

Matusow, A. J. (1984). *The Unraveling of America: A History of Liberalism in the 1960's*. New York: Harper & Row.

Meranto, P. (1967). *The Politics of Federal Aid to Education in 1965*. Syracuse, N.Y.: Syracuse University.

Meyer, J. A. (1984). "Budget Cuts in the Reagan Administration: A Question of Fairness." In D. Bawden (Ed.), *The Social Contact Revisited* (pp. 33–64). Washington, D.C.: Urban Institute Press.

Moynihan, D. P. (1973a). *Maximum Feasible Misunderstanding*. New York: Random House.

Moynihan, D. P. (1973b). *Politics of a Guaranteed Income*. New York: Random House.

Murray, C. (1984). *Losing Ground: American Social Policy, 1950–1980*. New York: Basic Books.

Palmer, J. L., & Sawhill, I. V. (1984). *The Reagan Record: An Assessment of Amercia's Changing Domestic Priorities*. Washington, D.C.: Urban Institute Press.

Reichley, A. J. (1981). *Conservatives in an Age of Change*. Washington, D.C.: The Brookings Institution.

Salamon, L. M., & Lund, M. S. (1985). *The Reagan Presidency and the Governing of America*. Washington, D.C.: Urban Institute Press.

Shoup, L. H. (1980). *The Carter Presidency and Beyond*. Palo Alto, Calif.: Ramparts Press.

Siegel, F. F. (1984). *Troubled Journey: From Pearl Harbor to Ronald Reagan*. New York: Hill & Wang.

Starr, P. (1982). *The Social Transformation of American Medicine*. New York: Basic Books.

Steiner, G. Y. (1971). *State of Welfare*. Washington, D.C.: The Brookings Institution.

Steinfels, P. (1979). *The Neoconservatives*. New York: Simon & Schuster.

Stevens, R., & Stevens, R. B. (1974). *Welfare Medicine in America: A Case Study of Medicaid*. New York: Free Press.

Sundquist, J. L. (1968). *Politics and Policy: The Eisenhower, Kennedy, and Johnson Years*. Washington, D.C.: The Brookings Institution.

Sundquist, J. L. (1969). *Making Federalism Work*. Washington, D.C.: The Brookings Institution.

White, T. H. (1982). *America in Search of Itself*. New York: Harper & Row.

FEMALE OFFENDERS

Over 1.7 million women are arrested each year (United States Department of Justice, Federal Bureau of Investigation [USDOJ, FBI], 1983, p.186). The majority of these women are arrested for crimes of an economic nature. After their convictions, many women are sentenced to prison. These women are disproportionately poor, uneducated, and black. When they go to prison they rarely gain skills that might help them escape from poverty or from crime. Many are incarcerated far from their homes and their children. Female offenders are a neglected population, lost within the courts and correctional systems and, because of their small numbers, ignored in research.

Women and Crime

Criminologists have attempted to explain changes in the crime rate by looking at the changing status of women in society. Some (Chapman, 1979; Chesney-Lind, 1980; Crites, 1976; Steffensmeier, 1980) argue that as the increase in the number of female heads of household has resulted in higher rates of poverty among women, there has been a corresponding increase in economic crime among women. Adler (1975), by contrast, attributes changes in the crime rate to the women's movement, which, she claims, has led to more "male-like" criminal behavior among women. Still another explanation is that women's increased participation in the workforce has led to an increase in female white-collar crime (Simon, 1975).

Crime is a difficult phenomenon to measure. In fact, no crime statistics can be considered definitive. Each state has different methods of classifying and reporting crime. Many crimes go unreported. Some crimes are easier to detect than others, which makes it seem that these crimes occur more frequently. In some cases, reporting agencies adjust figures based on their own political priorities. In addition, the population census undercounts ethnic minority groups, which serves to inflate the actual percentage of the total minority population that is involved in crime. However, existing crime data support the hypothesis that relates poverty to female crime, but they offer little evidence to support the arguments made by Adler (1975) or Simon (1975).

In the following brief review of summary statistical data on women and crime, Table 1 compares trends in male and female arrests between 1974 and 1983 and Table 2 lists total arrests by sex in 1983. It is not possible to compare changes in total arrests between 1974 and 1983 because not all agencies reported arrest data in both years. Rather, data for those agencies that did submit reports in 1974 and 1983 have been compared and this information is compiled as arrest trends. Table 3 summarizes the composition of female arrests by offense, and Table 4 outlines the composition of crime by sex and offense.

Table 1 shows that the female crime rate, which increased 19.8 percent from 1974 to 1983, rose more quickly than the crime rate for both sexes, which rose 14.3 percent. Despite this relative growth in female arrests since 1974, Table 2 shows that women represented only 16.6 percent of those arrested in 1983, a small increase from 1974 when they comprised 16.1 percent of all those arrested (USDOJ, FBI, 1974, p. 189). Table 3 indicates that women are most likely to commit crimes of an economic or behavioral nature and that there has been an increase in economic crime and a corresponding decrease in behavioral crime since 1974. Table 4 shows that female arrests as a percentage of total arrests are most often for economic crimes and that this figure is on the rise.

The "feminization of poverty" hypothesis, which is based on the fact that women are disproportionately represented among those living below the poverty level, suggests that there would be an increase in the number of economic crimes committed by women.

Table 1. Arrest Trends by Sex, 1974–1983 (Including Juveniles)[a]

	Women			Men		
	1974	1983	Percent Change	1974	1983	Percent Change
Index crimes[b]						
Murder/nonnegligent manslaughter	2,033	1,713	−15.7	12,021	11,188	−6.9
Forcible rape	144	201	+39.6	17,258	20,649	+19.6
Robbery	7,238	7,280	+.6	99,041	91,751	−7.4
Aggravated assault	20,258	23,483	+15.9	129,831	147,404	+13.5
Burglary	17,783	18,815	+5.8	312,580	260,714	−16.6
Larceny-theft	217,114	247,272	+13.9	489,163	580,606	+18.7
Motor vehicle theft	6,648	6,976	+4.9	95,770	69,262	−27.7
Arson	1,085	1,423	+31.2	9,250	10,083	+9.0
Nonindex crimes						
Other assaults	38,436	51,027	+32.8	236,313	297,963	+26.1
Forgery/counterfeiting	11,211	16,930	+51.0	28,668	32,715	+14.1
Fraud	33,443	61,586	+84.2	65,599	101,604	+54.9
Embezzlement	1,520	1,414	−7.0	4,474	3,020	−32.5
Stolen property	7,780	9,035	+16.1	66,553	70,015	+5.2
Vandalism	11,294	14,884	+31.8	129,455	141,648	+9.4
Weapons	9,469	8,732	−7.8	105,325	104,193	−1.1
Prostitution	38,507	60,180	+56.3	13,017	28,111	+116.0
Sex offenses	3,266	4,255	+30.3	38,448	49,036	+27.5
Drugs	64,788	59,943	−7.5	391,661	372,376	−4.9
Gambling	4,146	3,154	−23.9	45,566	25,955	−43.0
Offenses against family/children	4,938	3,303	−33.1	35,646	21,637	−39.3
Driving under the influence	53,677	116,076	+116.2	617,533	882,051	+42.8
Liquor laws	27,608	48,128	+74.3	154,463	237,402	+53.7
Drunkenness	68,019	56,233	−17.3	884,607	575,624	−34.9
Disorderly conduct	110,075	85,252	−22.6	412,223	444,506	+7.8
Vagrancy	4,236	2,338	−44.8	29,490	22,723	−22.9
All other offenses	122,142	217,478	+78.1	636,302	1,204,194	+89.2
Curfew/loitering	15,745	8,758	−44.4	51,753	24,505	−52.7
Runaways	83,526	45,924	−45.0	63,588	32,909	−48.2
Total	986,129	1,181,793	+19.8	5,175,598	5,863,844	+13.3

[a] Arrest trend data do not reflect annual totals because some agencies reported in only one of the two years.
[b] Index crimes are those offenses that are classified as the most serious.
Source: U.S. Department of Justice, Federal Bureau of Investigation, *Uniform Crime Report for the United States* (Washington, D.C.: U.S. Government Printing Office, 1983), p. 174.

The data on arrest trends in Table 1 do show significant increases in women's participation in economic crime—namely in forgery and counterfeiting, fraud, larceny-theft, vandalism, and prostitution. Furthermore, it is evident from Table 3 that economic crime constituted the largest category of female arrests in 1974 and 1983. Table 2 shows that the only crimes (other than status offenses) for which women constituted more than 20 percent of those arrested were economic crimes. Table 4, in which crimes are grouped into categories, indicates that economic crimes among women increased in the years 1974–1983 in about the same proportion as they decreased among men.

On the surface, these data might appear to support Simon's (1975) argument that as more women have entered the work force, there has been an increase in female white-collar crime. However, a close examination actually calls Simon's hypothesis into ques-

Table 2. Total Arrests by Sex, 1983 (Including Juveniles)

	Women		Men	
	Total Arrests	Percent of Total	Total Arrests	Percent of Total
Index crimes				
Murder/nonnegligent manslaughter	2,411	13.3	15,653	86.7
Forcible rape	300	1.0	29,883	99.0
Robbery	9,859	7.4	124,159	92.6
Aggravated assault	35,333	13.5	226,088	86.5
Burglary	28,147	6.8	387,504	93.2
Larceny-theft	345,249	29.5	823,817	70.5
Motor vehicle theft	9,406	8.9	96,108	91.1
Arson	2,104	12.2	15,099	87.8
Nonindex crimes				
Other assaults	70,644	14.7	410,971	85.3
Forgery/counterfeiting	24,920	33.4	49,588	66.6
Fraud	105,333	40.2	156,511	59.8
Embezzlement	2,463	32.4	5,141	67.6
Stolen property	12,844	11.4	99,580	88.6
Vandalism	20,455	9.6	192,174	90.4
Weapons	12,532	7.8	148,002	92.2
Prostitution	83,777	70.2	35,485	29.8
Sex Offenses	5,750	7.5	71,369	92.5
Drugs	86,259	14.0	530,677	86.0
Gambling	4,194	10.9	34,209	89.1
Offenses against family/children	5,112	11.1	40,999	88.9
Driving under the influence	181,030	11.2	1,432,154	88.8
Liquor laws	69,892	16.4	357,338	83.6
Drunkenness	85,282	8.7	892,642	91.3
Disorderly conduct	109,848	16.2	569,069	83.8
Vagrancy	3,181	10.2	28,081	89.8
All other offenses	306,192	15.3	1,699,605	84.7
Curfew/loitering	16,049	23.6	52,099	76.4
Runaways	65,122	57.9	47,354	42.1
Total	1,703,688	16.6	8,571,359	83.4

Source: U.S. Department of Justice, Federal Bureau of Investigation, *Uniform Crime Report for the United States* (Washington, D.C.: U.S. Government Printing Office, 1983), p. 186.

tion. Simon predicted that there would be increases in embezzlement and fraud, yet embezzlement actually declined during the period when the number of working women increased. Furthermore, the majority of fraud arrests were for welfare fraud and passing bad checks—offenses that are more closely linked to poverty than to white-collar crime (Chapman, 1975).

Like Simon, Adler (1975) believed that the women's movement would change the nature of female crime and that women would begin to engage in criminal activities that had previously been associated with men. Specifically, she predicted a dramatic increase in violent crimes committed by women. Table 1 indicates that female arrests for forcible rape, aggravated assault, and other assaults were on the rise and that arrests for murder declined. For the first of these crimes—forcible rape—an increase of 57 arrests accounted for a 39.6 percent increase. The combined increase in aggravated assault and other assaults accounted for only 8 percent of the

Table 3. Composition of Crime by Female Arrests, 1974–1983

	1974		1983	
	Total Arrests	Percent of Total Arrests	Total Arrests	Percent of Total Arrests
Violent	67,967	8.9	118,547	9.0
Economic	355,750	46.5	635,775	48.4
Behavioral	341,336	44.6	559,899	42.6

Source: U.S. Department of Justice, Federal Bureau of Investigation, *Uniform Crime Report for the United States* (Washington, D.C.: U.S. Government Printing Office, 1974), p. 189; and (1983), p. 186.

total increase in female crime. Furthermore, Table 3 shows that when the data are aggregated into categories, violent crime remained fairly constant at 9 percent of total female arrests. Table 4 indicates that, of all people arrested for crimes of violence, women represented 12 percent in 1974 and 12.8 percent in 1983. These statistics do provide evidence that violent crime among women increased; however, the increase was small, particularly compared to the increase in economic crime and the overall increase in female crime. In sum, these data provide little support for Adler's hypothesis.

Many factors other than an actual increase in criminal activity may have affected the changes in female crime rates. Crimes that were misdemeanors in the past have been changed to felonies in recent years. Larceny, which used to be limited to items over $50, now includes thefts of the smallest amounts. As a result, petty shoplifters are charged with larceny. Since the mid-1970s,

there has been increased concern with crime control. Police departments have been expanded. Businesses and the police have improved their detection systems; coupled with better reporting techniques, these contribute to easier prosecution. In addition, stores are more likely to prosecute than they were in the past, and the police—who were traditionally more lenient toward female offenders and might give warnings rather than file charges—seem to have abandoned this paternalistic attitude. Lastly, states have become stricter in prosecuting welfare fraud. All these factors have certainly contributed to increases in the women's crime rate, but it is impossible to know whether, or by how much, women's actual participation in criminal activities has increased (Crites, 1976; Potter, 1978; Steffensmeier, 1980).

Demographic statistics on women who are arrested would be useful in understanding more about female criminality; however, with the exception of data on age, the FBI—

Table 4. Composition of Crime by Sex and Offense, 1974–1983[a]

	1974		1983	
	Women	Men	Women	Men
Violent	67,967	498,519	118,547	806,754
	(12.0%)	(88.0%)	(12.8%)	(87.2%)
Economic	355,750	1,267,957	635,775	1,873,989
	(21.9%)	(78.1%)	(25.3%)	(74.7%)
Behavioral	341,336	2,621,898	559,899	4,076,459
	(11.5%)	(88.5%)	(12.1%)	(87.9%)

[a] Numbers in parentheses indicate percent of total arrests in each category.
Source: U.S. Department of Justice, Federal Bureau of Investigation, *Uniform Crime Report for the United States* (Washington, D.C.: U.S. Government Printing Office, 1974), p. 189 and (1983), p. 186.
[a] Numbers in parentheses indicate percent of total arrests in each category.

Table 5. Females Arrested for Index Crimes by Age, 1983 (Total Arrests)

Age	Violent Crime	Percent Distribution	Property Crime	Percent Distribution
Under 18	7,970	16.6	115,268	29.9
18	2,017	4.2	19,428	5.0
19	2,245	4.7	18,014	4.7
20	2,272	4.7	16,801	4.4
21	2,281	4.8	15,257	4.0
22	2,322	4.8	14,790	3.8
23	2,282	4.8	13,624	3.5
24	2,165	4.5	12,953	3.4
25–29	9,193	19.2	53,361	13.9
30–34	5,854	12.2	34,732	9.0
35–39	3,607	7.5	21,091	5.5
40 and over	5,695	11.9	49,587	12.9

Source: U.S. Department of Justice, Federal Bureau of Investigation, *Uniform Crime Report for the United States* (Washington, D.C.: U.S. Government Printing Office, 1983), pp. 183–184.

the only source for national arrest data—does not separate sociodemographic characteristics by sex when it compiles crime statistics. As a result, comprehensive statistics on the race, marital status, and income levels of arrested women are not available. It is known, however, that poor and black women are disproportionately represented in prison (Glick & Neto, 1977), and it can be inferred from this that there is a similar trend among women who are arrested. The FBI statistics in Table 5 also indicate that age is a significant factor in female crime. In 1983, over 50 percent of all women arrested for violent or index crimes were found to be between the ages of 18 and 29.

Women and Sentencing

After arrest, women are either detained while they await trial or freed on bail or personal recognizance. In some cases, the courts will not set bail because they believe that the defendant is dangerous or that she

will not appear at her trial if released beforehand. Although information on bail decisions is limited, a study based on 1962 data found that women were more likely than men to be released on bail. This apparent leniency toward women was true only for white women, however (Nagel & Weitzman, 1971).

Not all women who are arrested are convicted. Some cases are dropped because of faulty or insufficient evidence. On occasion, cases will be continued without a finding only to be reopened if the defendant has further problems with the law or does not comply with certain conditions of the continuance. Many are found innocent of the charges filed against them. There are, of course, those who are found guilty and penalized through a prison sentence, probation, fine, community service, alternative sentence, or a combination of these sanctions. But, even for those who are penalized, judges

Table 6. State and Federal Prisons, 1978

	Federal	State
Women's prisons	2	40
Men's prisons	31	460
Coed prisons	5	21

Source: U.S. Department of Justice, *Bureau of Justice Statistics* (October 1983), p. 79.

Table 7. Women in State and Federal Prisons, 1975–1983

Year	Number	Percent Change
1975	9,667	
1979	12,995	+34.4
1983	19,019	+46.4

Source: U.S. Department of Justice, *Bureau of Justice Statistics* (April 1984), p. 5.

Table 8. Race and Ethnicity of Female Prisoners, 1981[a]

Race	Number	Percent of Total
White	7,301	47.3
Black	7,687	49.8
American Indian/ Alaskan Native	191	1.2
Asian/Pacific Islander	46	<1.0
Not known	212	1.4
Ethnicity		
Hispanic	876	5.7

[a] Ethnic data is computed separately from racial data.

Source: U.S. Department of Justice, *Bureau of Justice Statistics* (March 1983), pp. 20–22.

will sometimes suspend prison or jail sentences and place the defendant on probation.

However, dramatic increases in the female prison population have led criminologists to suspect that judges are treating women more harshly than they have in the past. There are various explanations (Crites, 1978) as to why judges may have become stricter with women. There are more women on the bench, which may mean less paternalistic judicial attitudes. In many states, sentencing has become more standardized and judges have less discretion in determining an offender's sentence, making judges who were lenient with women in the past less able to be so now. There is indirect evidence to support this hypothesis. Between 1974 and 1983, the female crime rate, based on arrest trends, rose by 19.8 percent. Because there was little change over this period in the type of crimes for which women were arrested, one would expect the incarceration rate for women to have risen by a similar amount—that is, approximately 20 percent. However, between 1975 and 1983, the number of women in prison increased by 96.7 percent (USDOJ, FBI, 1983, p.174; USDOJ, Bureau of Justice Statistics [BJS], April 1984, p.5). The implication of these findings is that judges are sentencing women to prison for crimes that would not have been so punished in the past or by handing down longer sentences for the same crimes.

Nationwide data on sentencing and court dispositions do not specify the sex of the defendants. This makes it impossible to examine court dispositions on a large scale. Nagel and Weitzman (1971), who had the largest sample, found that in cases of grand larceny, men were more likely to be convicted and also to be sentenced to prison than women. However, among those charged with felonious assault, there was less discrepancy in convictions and women were more likely to be sentenced to prison. The study also found that women received shorter sentences than men for violent crimes, but longer sentences for larceny. These findings are somewhat dated and have also been criticized because the researchers did not control for such important variables as prior record and criminal status.

More thorough work (Bernstein et al., 1977; Pope, 1975; Pope, 1976) that did control for these variables has shown that paternalism in the judiciary is not as strong as was initially thought, though in these more recent studies, certain aspects of gender have still been found to affect sentencing dispositions. One study (Bernstein, Cardascia, & Ross, 1977) refuted Nagel and Weitzman's findings with evidence that women who committed crimes that were considered "nonfeminine" were often given harsher sentences than their male counterparts. Pope (1976) found that white women were more likely than men and black women to be placed on probation as an alternative to prison. Another finding (Bernstein, Cardascia, & Ross, 1977) was that married women were less likely to be imprisoned than unmarried women. Marital status was not found to have a significant effect on sentences for men. Further work by Kruttschnitt (1980–1981) found that welfare recipients and unemployed women were given stricter sentences than working women. It was also found that black women received stricter sentences than white women. Lastly, delinquent girls are often confined on lesser charges and serve longer sentences than do boys with the same charges (Haft, 1974). In sum, while there is evidence that judges have, at least in the past, treated women somewhat chivalrously, there is also evidence that poor women, black women, unmarried women, and juvenile female offenders actually receive harsher treatment.

Department of Justice statistics (USDOJ, BJS, September 1984), which do not control for sex, indicate that probation as a disposition is increasing at approximately the same rate as incarceration. It is impossible to know, however, if this trend holds true for women. Parole has not increased at the same pace as incarceration or probation. This is in part because of changes in sentencing guidelines and limitations that have been placed on parole board discretion (USDOJ, BJS, September 1984). The only national statistics (USDOJ, BJS, 1983) that are broken down by sex show that on December 31, 1983, there were 144,290 women on probation (31 states reporting) and 14,835 women on parole (45 states reporting).

Women's Prisons

Women are incarcerated in a variety of prisons from coed rural jails to large, single-sex federal prisons, depending on their sentences and the given region or state and jurisdiction. Jails generally house women who are awaiting trial or serving relatively short sentences, whereas prisons almost always house sentenced women, most of whom are serving sentences longer than a year. Seventy-five percent of the states have separate prisons for women. The remainder have coed prisons, except New Hampshire, which has no women's prison and sends its women prisoners to institutions in neighboring states (Potter, 1978, p.15). In addition to prisons, most states have halfway houses that enable inmates to reenter the community gradually. Only a few of these halfway houses are for women. Table 6 shows the total number of state and federal prisons for men and women in 1978. As the figures indicate, there were fewer women's prisons than men's prisons. In fact, most states still have only one prison for female offenders. For many women, this means serving their sentences hundreds of miles from home. The problems that they encounter as a result are exacerbated by the fact that women's prisons tend to be located in isolated areas. This makes it difficult for them to participate in work-release and other community programs. It also limits their ability to maintain direct contact with their children and other family members, friends, and attorneys. Men need not share this isolation because there are numerous male prisons in every state, which makes it possible for them to serve their sentences closer to their

homes. In addition, men's prisons are generally built in urban areas (Ramstad, 1975).

Male offenders are incarcerated in minimum, medium, or maximum security institutions depending on the offender's security classification. The less restrictive the classification, the more access male offenders have to programs and privileges. Because there are so few prisons for women, female inmates of various security levels are housed in the same institution. All the women are subject to the same rules, and those rules must meet the security requirements of the highest-risk inmates. In addition, men can be transferred to prisons close to their homes as they near their release dates, which helps them to reestablish family and community ties and to look for work (United States General Accounting Office [USGAO], 1980). Corrections officials are reluctant to extend the same programs and classification systems to women because of the expense of providing a range of programs or separate institutions for a small population. Thus, the fact that women participate less than men in criminal activities becomes a liability once they go to prison.

The cost of providing adequate resources and programs at women's prisons has led some states to adopt coed prisons. Although this movement generated considerable excitement at first, recent evidence has shown that women have not benefited from this sytem. Most states merely began sentencing men to their women's prisons, and the situation for women did not change. They still lacked adequate programs and were restricted by the fact that they were not divided according to their security classification. One study (Smykla, 1980) found that in coed institutions, women held more menial jobs and were paid less than male inmates. Women worked as clerks, typists, and laundry workers, which qualified them for low-paying jobs. Men worked as cabinetmakers, electricians, painters, and plumbers, which prepared them for well-paid jobs that could support a family. It appears that more emphasis is put on male inmates' need for skills, even though most female inmates are single heads of households.

Security presents added problems in coed prisons. Standards often require men and women to be segregated. Because there are usually fewer women than men, corrections departments exclude women from classes that men attend. Men have more regular access to recreational facilities, and women are often denied certain jobs or access to training programs because administrators do not want to mix the sexes (USGAO, 1980).

Most women who are being held until their trials (and some women who are serving short sentences) are housed in a section of a men's jail. The men have access to various activities to relieve the boredom of prison, yet the women are often denied exercise areas and dayrooms and, in many jails, they must take their meals in their cells. In other areas, men are able to serve their jail sentences at work camps, but women cannot. When there are only a few sentenced women in a jail, they are often housed with pretrial detainees. This is a particularly questionable practice because the pretrial women, who are presumed innocent until found guilty, must abide by the same rules as those governing women who have already been found guilty. Rural jails produce even greater problems since they often lack lavatory facilities for female inmates, making it easy for male guards to exploit the women (Chesney-Lind, 1978).

Female Prisoners

Federal and state prisons in the United States had a total female population of 19,019 as of December 31, 1983, compared with a male prison population of 419,811. In 1982, 13,852 women and 195,730 men were incarcerated in jails (USDOJ, BJS, February 1983, p.1; USDOJ, BJS, April 1984, p.2). These numbers represent a dramatic increase in the number of women in prison since the mid-1970s, also reflected in Table 7.

The number of women in prison doubled between 1975 and 1983; during the same period, the total U.S. prison population increased by 75 percent. From 1975 to 1983, when the women's prison population increased by approximately 10,000 inmates, the men's prison population increased by 175,000 inmates (USDOJ, BJS, April 1984, p.1). In 1975, women accounted for 3.8 percent of the U.S. prison population, and by 1983, this figure rose to 4.3 percent (USDOJ, BJS, April 1984, p.5). Despite the increase in the female incarceration rate, women still comprise a small percentage of the total prisoner population. Figures based on 1983 data indicate that 14 women per 100,000 population and 352 men per 100,000 population were in prison (USDOJ, BJS, April 1984, p.2).

Racial and ethnic breakdowns of women in prison generally show an equal proportion to black and white women, with small proportions of American Indian, Asian, and Hispanic women. Table 8 summarizes 1981 data on the race and ethnicity of women inmates.

Although black women comprised 11 percent of the women in the United States, they represented close to 50 percent of the total female prison population (Wyrick & Owens, 1978, p.85). In all likelihood, the disproportionately high number of black female inmates reflected their lower socioeconomic status. Most black women offenders were young and uneducated. Even more important, they were usually poor and often single mothers (Wyrick & Owens, 1978). This overrepresentation of black women, however, did not hold true for other racial minorities. Hispanics, who comprised 6 percent of females in the United States, represented 5.7 percent of women in prison (USDOJ, BJS, March 1983, p. 22; USDOJ, BJS, October 1983, p.36). This suggests that there may be factors, such as racism, in addition to socioeconomic status that explain the overrepresentation of blacks among the female prison population.

A nationwide study (Glick & Neto, 1977, pp.108–140) of female inmates at 14 prisons found that at least 90 percent of the inmates sampled had held jobs at some point during their adult lives, but the majority had worked for low wages at semiskilled and unskilled jobs. More than 50 percent of the women had been on welfare at some point and between 60 and 80 percent had dependent children. Twenty percent of the women were married and the remainder were either single, separated, divorced, or widowed. Two-thirds of the sample were under 30 with a median age of 27. Lastly, most (85 percent) of the women had completed elementary school, and 41 percent of the total sample had finished high school or better.

Problems Facing Women in Prison

Women face an array of problems in prison. Most never learn a useful skill, all are separated from their children (some lose custody), and many have health problems. There is a pressing need for lawyers and social workers to respond to these problems.

On the whole, male inmates have greater access than female inmates to training programs that teach them a skill. Women in prison have minimal opportunities for marketable vocational training and are rarely able to participate in work-release programs (USGAO, 1980). On average, 10.2 training programs are available per prison for men, and only 2.7 such programs in women's prisons (Klein & Kress, 1976, p.44). Most educational programs in women's prisons are limited to remedial courses, GED (general education diploma) preparation, and occasional junior college classes. There are even fewer programs in jails (Glick & Neto, 1977).

Women in prison do not have necessary health care facilities. Gynecological services are provided infrequently and sometimes not at all. Because the most common medical problems among women in prison are gynecological, this lack of adequate care means that many women's health care problems are neglected (Resnik & Shaw, 1980). Women prisoners are usually poor and have never had proper health care. They often come to prison with medical problems and, once there, further problems frequently arise. Contagious diseases spread quickly in the close quarters of prison. Internal pelvic searches, usually done on arrival at the prison and often before and after visiting periods, increase the likelihood of vaginal and cervical infections, which can be particularly dangerous for pregnant women (Resnik & Shaw, 1980).

Women who are pregnant face additional difficulties in prison. Although it is not known exactly how many women prisoners are pregnant, estimates range around 1,000 per year. Women who are in their first trimester and therefore able to elect to have an abortion often face bureaucratic procedures that cause delays, which may make it impossible for them to have abortions within the medically prescribed time limit. In other cases, prisoners are forced or coerced to abort their children. Pregnant women often do not get the necessary prenatal care. The failure of prisons to provide medical help is especially tragic for women who have complications of pregnancy. Most women's prisons do not have delivery rooms and are located in isolated areas far from hospitals.

After giving birth, women who have been hospitalized are sent back to prison as soon as possible and may be subjected to vaginal searches on their return (Holt, 1981–82).

Women who give birth while serving a prison sentence almost always have their children taken away from them in the delivery room, and they frequently do not see them again until they are released from prison. The only exception is New York's Bedford Hills Prison, where women can keep their newborn children with them for up to a year. Women are often urged to give up custody of their children at birth and, for those who do, there is little chance that they will ever be reunited with their offspring. The act of separating the mother from her child at birth critically interrupts the essential bonding process that occurs at the beginning of a child's life. Increasingly, psychologists point to such separation as seriously dangerous to the emotional and psychological growth of the children involved (Sametz, 1980).

Role of Social Work

The social work profession has a history of working in the courts and prisons, counseling inmates and helping with problems that arise after release. Although this participation has been important in improving the situation of women in prison, crucial needs still go unmet. Useful services that social workers can provide for incarcerated women include (1) courses on birth control, parenting, substance abuse, self-esteem and empowerment, and spouse abuse; (2) programs that help inmates' families by arranging for children to visit and by holding workshops and individual sessions for the families on how to cope during their separation and after the mother's release; (3) helping women to gain skills through identifying resources and encouraging corrections departments to provide valuable training programs; and (4) working with the courts to design alternative sentences for women that rely on community resources rather than incarceration. Once women leave prison, they face such added problems as finding work and housing. In helping released prisoners, as well as women in the courts, it is important to remember that many of the women are repeat offenders who need to break from poverty as well as from crime. Community-based prison facilities would enable women to look for housing and work and to have family contact. Social workers, serving as advocates, can urge states and localities to provide such facilities and they can also assist inmates as they begin their reintegration process (Hoffman, 1983).

KATHLEEN C. ENGEL
KATHERINE GABEL

For further information, see CORRECTIONS SYSTEM: ADULT; WOMEN.

References

Adler, F. (1975). *Sisters in Crime*. New York: McGraw–Hill Book Co.

Bernstein, I., Cardascia, J., & Ross, C. (1977, September). *Institutional Sexism: The Case in Criminal Court*. Paper presented at the meeting of the American Sociological Association.

Bernstein, I., et al. (1977). "Charge Reduction: An Intermediary State in the Process of Labelling Criminal Defendants." *Social Forces, 56*, 362–384.

Chapman, J. R. (1979). *Summary Report: Criminal Justice Programs for Women Offenders*. Washington, D.C.: Center for Women Policy Studies.

Chesney-Lind, M. (1978). "Chivalry Reexamined: Women and the Criminal Justice System." In L. H. Bowker & M. Chesney-Lind (Eds.), *Women, Crime and the Criminal Justice System* (pp. 197–223). Lexington, Mass.: Lexington Books.

Chesney-Lind, M. (1980). "Re-Discovering the Lilith: Misogyny and the 'New' Female Criminal." In C. T. Griffiths & M. Nance (Eds.), *The Female Offender* (pp. 1–35). Burnaby, B. C., Canada: Simon Fraser University, Criminology Research Center.

Crites, L. (1976). "Women Offenders: Myth vs. Reality." In L. Crites (Ed.), *The Female Offender* (pp. 33–44). Lexington, Mass.: Lexington Books.

Crites, L. (1978). "Women in the Criminal Court." In W. L. Hepperle & L. Crites (Eds.), *Women in the Courts* (pp. 160–175). Williamsburg, Va: National Center for State Courts.

Glick, R. M., & Neto, V. V. (1977). *National Study of Women's Correctional Programs* (Stock No. 027-000-00524-1). Washington, D.C.: National Institute of Law Enforcement and Criminal Justice.

Haft, M. (1974). "Women in Prison: Discriminatory Practices and Some Legal Solutions." *Clearinghouse Review, 1*, 1–6.

Hoffman, K. S. (1983). "Women Offenders and Social Work Practice." In A. R. Roberts (Ed.), *Social Work in Juvenile and Criminal Justice Settings*. Springfield, Ill.: Charles C Thomas, Publisher.

Holt, K. E. (1981–82). "Nine Months to Life—The Law and the Pregnant Inmate." *Journal of Family Law, 20*, 523–543.

Klein, D., & Kress, J. (1976). "Any Woman's Blues: A Critical Overview of Women, Crime and the Criminal Justice System." *Crime and Social Justice, 5*, 34–49.

Kruttschnitt, C. (1980–1981). "Social Status and Sentences of Female Offenders." *Law and Society Review, 15*, 247–265.

Nagel, S., & Weitzman, L. (1971). "Women as Litigants." *Hastings Law Review, 23*, 171–181.

Pope, C. E. (1975). *Sentencing of California Felony Offenders*. Washington, D.C.: Criminal Justice Research Center.

Pope, C. E. (1976). "The Influence of Social and Legal Factors on Sentence Dispositions: A Preliminary Analysis of Offender–Based Transaction Statistics." *Journal of Criminal Justice, 4*, 203–221.

Potter, J. (1978). "In Prison, Women are Different." *Corrections Magazine*, pp. 14–24.

Ramstad, S. A. (1975). "Female Offenders: A Challenge to the Courts and the Legislature." *North Dakota Law Review, 51*, 827–853.

Resnik, J., & Shaw, N. (1980). "Prisoners of Their Sex: Health Problems of Incarcerated Women." In I. Robbins (Ed.), *Prisoners' Rights Sourcebook* (pp. 319–413). New York: Clark Boardman.

Sametz, L. (1980). "Children of Incarcerated Women." *Social Work, 25*, 298–303.

Simon, R. (1975). *Women and Crime*. Lexington, Mass.: Lexington Books.

Smykla, J. O. (1980, November). *The Sexual Oppression of Women in Coed Prison: Notes on the Myth of Equal Treatment*. Paper presented at the meeting of the American Society of Criminology.

Steffensmeier, D. J. (1980). "Assessing the Impact of the Women's Movement on Sex–Based Differences in the Handling of Adult Criminal Defendants." *Crime and Delinquency, 26*, 344–357.

U.S. Department of Justice, Bureau of Justice Statistics. (1983). Unpublished data on probation and parole. Rockville, Md.: National Criminal Justice Reference Service.

U.S. Department of Justice, Bureau of Justice Statistics. (1983, February). *Jail Inmates 1982* (NCJ-87161). Rockville, Md.: National Criminal Justice Reference Service.

U.S. Department of Justice, Bureau of Justice Statistics. (1983, March). *Prisoners in State and Federal Institutions on December 31, 1981* (NCJ-86485). Rockville, Md.: National Criminal Justice Reference Service.

U.S. Department of Justice, Bureau of Justice Statistics. (1983, October). *Report to the Nation on Crime and Justice* (NCJ-87068).

Rockville, Md.: National Criminal Justice Reference Service.

U.S. Department of Justice, Bureau of Justice Statistics. (1984, April). *Prisoners in 1983* (NCJ-92949). Rockville, Md.: National Criminal Justice Reference Service.

U.S. Department of Justice, Bureau of Justice Statistics. (1984, September). *Probation and Parole 1983* (NCJ-94776). Rockville, Md.: National Criminal Justice Reference Service.

U.S. Department of Justice, Federal Bureau of Investigation. (1974). *Uniform Crime Report for the United States.* Washington, D.C.: U.S. Government Printing Office.

U.S. Department of Justice, Federal Bureau of Investigation. (1983). *Uniform Crime Report for the United States.* Washington, D.C.: U.S. Government Printing Office.

U.S. General Accounting Office. (1980, December). *Women in Prison: Inequitable Treatment Requires Action* (GGD-81-6). Gaithersburg, Md.: Author.

Wyrick, E. S., & Owens, O. H. (1978). "Black Women: Income and Incarceration." In C. E. Owens & J. Bell (Eds.), *Blacks and Criminal Justice* (pp. 85–92). Lexington, Mass.: Lexington Books.

For Further Reading

Adler, F., & Simon, R. J. (1979). *The Criminology of Deviant Women.* Boston: Houghton Mifflin Co.

Anderson, E. A. (1976). "The 'Chivalrous' Treatment of the Female Offender in the Arms of the Criminal Justice System: A Review of the Literature." *Social Problems, 23*, 350–357.

Armstrong, G. (1977). "Females Under the Law—Protected but Unequal." *Crime and Delinquency, 23*, 109–135.

Bowker, L. H., & Chesney-Lind, M. (1978). *Women, Crime and the Criminal Justice System.* Lexington, Mass.: Lexington Books.

Crites, L. (1976). *The Female Offender.* Lexington, Mass.: Lexington Books.

Fabian, S. (1979). "Towards the Best Interests of Women Prisoners: Is the System Working?" *New England Journal on Prison Law, 1*, 1–60.

Feinman, C. (1979). "Sex Role Stereotypes and Justice for Women." *Crime and Delinquency, 24*, 87–94.

Feinman, C. (1980). *Women in the Criminal Justice System.* New York: Praeger Publishers.

French, L. (1978). "The Incarcerated Black Female: The Case of Social Double Jeopardy." *Journal of Black Studies, 8*, 321–335.

Gabel, K., et al. (1982). *Legal Issues of Female Inmates.* Northampton, Mass.: Smith College School for Social Work.

Griffiths, C. T., & Nance, M. (1980). *The Female Offender.* Burnaby, B. C., Canada: Simon Fraser University, Criminology Research Center.

Hepperle, W. L., & Crites, L. (1978). *Women in the Courts.* Williamsburg, Va.: National Center for State Courts.

Hoffman-Bustamante, D. (1973). "The Nature of Female Criminality." *Issues in Criminology 8*, 117–136.

Krause, K. (1974). "Denial of Work Release Programs to Women: A Violation of Equal Protection." *Southern California Law Review, 47*, 1453–1490.

Mann, C. R. (1984). *Female Crime and Delinquency.* University: University of Alabama Press.

McHugh, G. A. (1980). "Protection of the Rights of Pregnant Women in Prisons and Detention Facilities." *New England Journal on Prison Law, 6*, 231–263.

Pollak, O. (1950). *The Criminality of Women.* Philadelphia: University of Pennsylvania Press.

Price, B. R. (1982). *The Criminal Justice System and Women.* New York: Clark Boardman.

Rafter, N. H., & Stanko, E. A. (1982). *Judge, Lawyer, Victim, Thief.* Boston, Mass.: Northeastern University Press.

Simon, R. (1975). *The Contemporary Woman and Crime.* Washington, D.C.: U.S. Government Printing Office.

Singer, L. R. (1973). "Women and the Correctional Process." *American Criminal Law Review, 11*, 295–308.

Smart, C. (1976). *Women, Crime and Criminology: A Feminist Perspective.* London, England: Routledge & Kegan Paul.

Stanton, A. M. (1980). *When Mothers Go to Jail.* Lexington, Mass.: Lexington Books.

Sutherland, E. H., & Cressey, D. R. (1978). *Criminology* (10th ed.). Philadelphia: J. B. Lippincott Co.

Temin, C. E. (1973). "Discriminatory Sentencing of Women Offenders: The Argument for ERA in a Nutshell." *American Criminal Law Review, 11*, 355–372.

Terry, R. M. (1979). "Trends in Female Crime: A Comparison of Adler, Simon and Steffensmeier." *California Sociologist, 2*, 200–212.

U.S. Department of Justice, Bureau of Justice Statistics. (1983). *Sourcebook of Criminal Justice Statistics—1982* (NCJ-86483). Rockville, Md.: National Criminal Justice Reference Service.

FEMINIST SOCIAL WORK

Feminism is a vision, a practice, and an ideology. It is a call for transforming the world from competitive, hierarchical, and authoritarian relationships to a world based on gender and racial equality. It is "a commitment to altering the processes and the manner in which private and public lives are organized and conducted. . . . Basically, feminism is concerned with ending domination and resisting oppression" (Van Den Bergh & Cooper, 1986, pp. 1–2).

Historical Foundations

Feminism is not an invention of the 1960s. It has a long, rich history dating to the 1800s when many women challenged slavery and demanded rights for women as well as actively supported and provided myriad social services to women and families (Withorn, 1984, p. 32).

In the late 1800s and early 1900s, organizations such as the Women's Christian Temperance Union, the Women's Trade Union League, and the National Consumers League provided a wide range of both indirect and direct services to women, including lobbying for legislation, referral and advocacy for clients, nursery schools, and family aides (Withorn, 1984, pp. 32–35). Although these services did not fundamentally challenge the conditions of women's lives nor their social and economic domination within society, these services did accomplish the important goal of linking together "efforts to change women's daily lives and to transform the broader society. . . . Important ideological connections were made between the problems of a male-dominated society and the troubles faced in their lives" (Withorn, 1984, p. 34).

These connections became a fundamental part of the second wave of the women's movement in the 1960s. Women in the United States began to reassert a commitment to altering the specific conditions of women's lives and challenging the allocation of power, resources, and privileges throughout American society. Abortion counseling, women's health clinics, assistance to victims of rape and battering, and so forth were important components of the movement, as were marches, demonstrations, and similar direct political activities.

In the 1960s, the commitment of feminism to "the personal is political" meant that all areas of oppression—in the home, in the workplace, at the doctor's office, in the classroom—were to be scrutinized, challenged, and altered. The "personal is political" viewpoint stresses the fact that individual realities are reflections of political, social, and economic forces. What one experiences on a personal level is a statement concerning the status quo.

Challenging current ideological and structural realities is not an easy task. No readily available models or programs exist from which to work. However, the impetus to restructure institutions emanates from an underlying commitment to democratic decision making as well as to egalitarian sharing and a concern for learning from each other's experiences.

Principles of Feminist Social Work

In studying the feminist movement, Withorn (1984) notes that in spite of the many difficulties faced in the movement itself—racism, homophobia, classism—it was and continues to be making a significant impact on the development of a feminist social work practice. Withorn writes:

> It is this practice that required new goals, new methods, new values—that holds equalitarianism between service provider and service consumer as a foundation for work and change—that has a vision of society where it is no shame to acknowledge one's needs . . . [to] admit interdependency, and develop radically different, humane, and responsible ways to care for each other. (p. 227)

Feminist social work practice is a radical alternative to traditional social work, although it has a theoretical similarity with established social work practice. Both express a fundamental concern with the "relationship between individual and community, between individually and socially defined needs, as well as concern with human dignity and rights of self-determination" (Van Den Bergh & Cooper, 1986, p. 3). Most important, feminist social work practice differs from the historical trends in social work that stress adjusting to rather than challenging existing conditions. Feminist social work is actively committed to making alterations in the relationships, processes, and institutions in American society.

Feminist social work practice is built on five fundamental principles:

> eliminating false dichotomies and artificial separations, reconceptualizing power, valuing processes as equally important as product,

validating renaming and believing that the personal is political. (Van Den Bergh & Cooper, 1986, p. 4)

Eliminating False Dichotomies. Feminist analysis emphasizes the interrelatedness of all phenomena. It is only from a holistic, integrated, and ecological perspective that lasting changes for individuals, families, and communities can be made. False dichotomies serve to reinforce dangerous and ultimately unhealthy patterns of action and behavior through which people and communities are isolated and separated. As Eisenstein writes, "Making separations out of unities and dividing a whole into conflicting components is the quintessence of patriarchal processes which isolate, separate and divide, and is the model for hierarchical organization and order" (1976, p. 16).

Reconceptualizing Power. A fundamental component of feminism is challenging the traditional definitions and uses of power.

Power is viewed as property, analogous to money, involving control and domination of subordinates to make them subservient. Accordingly, those who control power manage the environment and determine goals, information is withheld and rules are created to censure behavior. (Hooyman, 1980, p. 6)

Feminists believe that patriarchal concepts of power must be altered. Power is not accepted as a finite commodity to be controlled by a few. Instead, power is redefined

as infinite, a widely distributed energy of influence, strength, effectiveness and responsibility. Power is viewed as facilitative; empowerment to action occurs rather than domination. Empowerment, or claiming personal power, is a political act because it allows people control over their own lives and the ability to make decisions for themselves. (Van Den Bergh & Cooper, 1986, p. 6)

Valuing Process Equally with Product. How a goal is achieved is as important as the goal itself. A feminist vision of process and outcome is based on an assumption that the merit of a goal is directly related to the way in which it is pursued. Goals achieved with coercive, inequitable, or otherwise oppressive processes must always be mistrusted. Consequently, how one pursues an objective becomes a goal in and of itself. The processes used to make decisions are as important as the final determinations. For example, estab-

lishing a work requirement for mothers receiving welfare but not providing adequate child care or appropriate job training is inherently troublesome. The overall goal of reducing welfare dependence is rarely achieved by current workforce programs.

Renaming. The right to name one's own experience has been an important goal of the civil rights movement as well as the women's movement. Renaming includes four processes—using new words or labels for people; altering meanings by changing the configuration of language, places, or things; remembering ancient definitions; and expanding existing definitions (Van Den Bergh, 1982). Each process involves challenging the power and authority of the dominant culture's language to discredit and control the unique experiences of oppressed people. Having the right to rename one's experience becomes an action of self-determination.

The Personal is Political. "The personal is political" serves as an all-encompassing component of feminism. It has developed out of an understanding that "the values and beliefs a person harbors, the goals that one sets and the type of life style one chooses to pursue can be considered a political statement" (Van Den Bergh & Cooper, 1986, p. 9). This feminist principle binds individual behavior and actions to the social structure. Social movements affect personal behavior, and personal actions when collectively pursued can engender social movements. There is a dialectical relationship between how individuals and their communities exist and interact.

Each of these feminist principles requires both a vision and a process which reorders current social work priorities; they question the notion of business as usual. Each principle challenges the power, prestige, and dynamics of many social work practices, policies, and programs. These feminist principles are evolving, expanding, and growing. They can be used to both critique and inform social work practice.

Feminist and Traditional Direct Practice

Feminist therapy has risen out of discontent with conventional clinical approaches that include sexist assumptions about male and female gender roles as well as encouragement to adapt to rather than challenge the status quo (Gilbert, 1980, p. 246). Feminist clinical services are based on the assumption that "ideology, social structure and behavior are inextricably woven" (Brodsky & Hare-Mustin, 1980, p. 242). For example, a feminist therapist believes that a client's symptoms are the logical outcome of oversubscription to traditional sex role assumptions. Women have been taught to be passive, dependent, and reactive rather than assertive, independent, and proactive. The basis of feminist therapy includes (1) an awareness of the effects on human behavior of sexist values and patriarchal structures, (2) working for the development of autonomous, self-actualized individuals, and (3) developing social structures based upon egalitarian principles (Mander & Rush, 1974; Marecek & Kravetz, 1977; Rawlings & Carter, 1977).

Although feminist principles allow for variation, the literature on this practice approach notes several common denominators used in treatment. A synopsis of guidelines, follows culled from a variety of sources, (Berlin, 1976; Bricker-Jenkins & Hooyman, 1984; Israel, 1984; Kaschak, 1981; Lowenstein, 1983; Marecek & Kravetz, 1977; Radov, Masnik, & Hauser, 1977; Rawlings & Carter, 1977):

1. A client's problems are interpreted within a sociopolitical framework. This underscores the notion of "the personal is political." By using this proposition, a therapist can help a client ascertain the extent to which his or her current problems may be an inevitable outcome of male-female inequality.

2. Automatic submission to traditional sex roles is questioned, yet support is provided for pursuing a free choice of lifestyle. However, clients are encouraged to develop an androgynous sex role repertoire whereby they have the ability to manifest both instrumental and expressive behaviors.

3. Treatment is focused on articulating and augmenting clients' strengths rather than centered on pathologies. Therapy seeks to be an empowering process whereby clients increase their ability to control environments to get what they need.

4. Encouragement is given to the development of an independent identity that is not defined by one's relationships with others. Women tend to be overresponsible for maintaining relationships and frequently defer their own interests to care for others.

Through a feminist approach, clients are aided in developing individual strengths and pursuing personal mastery in their chosen endeavors.

5. Reassessment of women's relationships with other women is encouraged so that bonding between women is valued as highly as developing relationships with men. Based on sex role stereotypes, women tend to undervalue themselves; consequently, they may view each other in a derogatory or competitive fashion. In a feminist approach, women are valued.

6. Emphasis is placed on developing a balance between work and interpersonal relationships. Both men and women are encouraged to be nurturers as well as economic providers.

7. Whenever possible, the personal power between therapist and client approaches equality. This means that feminist therapists do not view themselves as experts on clients' problems; rather, they act as catalysts for helping clients empower themselves. This reconceptualization of the therapeutic relationship is based on the feminist concern with eliminating dominant-submissive relationships.

To what extent do these feminist therapy principles challenge traditional social work practices? Feminist treatment does not entail developing a clinical approach separate from extant modalities. Rather, it is an orientation that can modify conventional therapy models (Marecek & Kravetz, 1977). Holroyd (1976) considers feminist treatment to be a radical philosophy with humanistic therapy techniques, as it uses a political analysis to understand the etiology of a client's problem. A feminist therapist brings society into the treatment context and advocates political, social, and economic equality between the sexes. Although a clinician may not have the ability to alter the reality of a client's world, he or she can help the client understand the impact of environmental realities upon his or her distress. Such awareness encourages a plan of action that can potentially affect others or alter adverse environmental conditions (Mander & Rush, 1974; Marecek & Kravetz, 1977; Rawlings & Carter, 1977; Gluckstern, 1977).

A feminist approach is inconsistent with treatment models—such as traditional psychoanalysis—that focus almost exclusively on altering a client's intrapsychic processes (Sherman, 1977). Although the psychosocial approach looks at the relationship between person and environment, it lacks an analysis of the potential deleterious outcomes of gender inequality on individuals. Because no clear indication exists about how sex, race, class, or ethnicity converge to affect individuals and engender problems (DeVore & Schlesinger, 1981, p. 104), the psychosocial model exemplifies "benign neglect." It fails to address the outcome of sexism and other institutionalized inequalities on clients.

On the other hand, problem-solving approaches including task-centered casework (Epstein, 1977; Perlman, 1957; Reid & Epstein, 1972) are consistent with a feminist approach. They emphasize developing clients' problem-solving skills to secure needed resources. These approaches analyze the systemic inequalities that underlie clients' difficulties as well as advocate for reform. The resolution of problems experienced by families with special hardships, for example, are seen by Epstein as dependent "upon development of social policies to mitigate the oppressive restraints of racial, ethnic and sex discrimination; poverty; unavailability of quality education, daycare and the like" (cited in DeVore & Schlesinger, 1981, p. 114). What differentiates a feminist approach from problem-solving approaches is the latter's failure to see that patriarchal domination-subordination processes underlie the pervasive inequities experienced by all oppressed groups.

Structural approaches (Middleman & Goldberg, 1974) and systems approaches (Pincus & Minahan, 1973) to social work practice are also compatible with a feminist perspective. The former model's underlying assumptions that individual problems are the outcome of social disorganization and that all social workers have an ongoing responsibility to pursue social change are consistent with feminist ideology. A systems perspective specifically seeks to eliminate prevalent dichotomies such as those between clinical practice and social action and is similar to a core feminist premise. In addition, a systems approach focuses on the gaps between people and institutional resources that prevent individuals from improving their lives. Although both practice modes share principles with feminist ideology, however, as was true with

the problem-solving approaches, they lack an analysis that shows the etiology of most systemic inequity to be based on patriarchal domination-subordination politics.

In summary, a feminist approach to direct services examines the interrelationship between personal distress and inequitable social structures. Practice approaches are humanistic, which is consistent with many prevalent social work modalities, except for those focusing exclusively on intrapsychic dynamics. What differentiates a feminist-based direct practice, however, is its analysis of patriarchy as a cause of much unilateral human suffering and its imperative to eliminate the outcomes of gender inequality.

Other Practice

Indirect Practice. Incorporating feminist principles in indirect practice means delivering services in a more holistic fashion, with attention on the interconnected nature of past, present, and future policies. Applying this principle to planning for juvenile delinquents, for example, would move treatment away from isolation and segregation. Placing youngsters in institutions away from their home communities does nothing to enhance their community responsibilities. Similarly, it does not help localities effectively deal with drugs, high unemployment, and poor education, which tend to be prevalent in high crime areas. When interconnectedness is a basis for social work practice, policies and plans reflect the relationships that exist among the agencies providing services and the residents of the community. In addition, the manner in which services are organized and implemented must not contradict program goals. A service designed to facilitate community participation cannot be based on an elitist and isolating process, for example. Similarly, a program providing multiple services for a specified population must include consumer participation in the development and implementation stages to determine precisely what services should be offered. Consumer participation must be solicited, listened to, and respected. Programs using segregating processes create insecurities, alienation, and underutilization. Integrating processes engender a sense of security and connectedness, while facilitating greater utilization. Having influence also empowers consumers.

The reconceptualization of power in indirect practice requires that information and skills be shared. In the workplace, feminist principles require that flexibility be the norm when establishing employee-employer relationship policies. For example, processes such as quality circles, whereby different ranks of employees come together to solve problems, are consistent with feminist practice. Activities that facilitate cooperation in establishing working conditions and employee benefits or that allow for the creation of job-sharing and flexitime scheduling are likely to enhance employee morale and agency operations. The use of peer accountability, team sharing and multiskill development, also feminist in orientation, enhance agency goals.

A feminist approach also reflects the importance of valuing process and product equally. The different experiences and perspectives of workers are as important as an individual worker's needs. Valuing multidimensionality reflects a process orientation and the assumption that multiple means can be pursued to achieve a desired end. The reward of a process orientation is enhanced effectiveness in achieving goals because participants are more motivated to comply with tasks.

Generalist versus Specialist Practice. A feminist social work practice questions the increasing use of specializations such as clinical social worker, community practitioner, and administrator. The emphasis on specialization creates artificial separations within the profession, rather than underscoring the interconnected purpose of social work to alleviate individual and social difficulties. Feminist social work practice requires the integration of clinical and organizing skills, treatment and administration, and service development and delivery.

Feminist practice inherently follows a generalist model of social work in that it seeks to eliminate false dichotomies within the profession. This does not mean that practitioners should be without specific expertise. Practitioners would want to develop specialized competence in certain areas. However, the overall model for education and practice would be generalist, stressing an integrated

approach to personal as well as social problems. Consequently, feminist "social work practice would be more holistic, ecological, and preventive. Practitioners would be as committed to working for social change as to ameliorating individual client problems" (Van Den Bergh & Cooper, 1986, p. 13).

Practice with Oppressed Groups. The feminist principle of renaming one's experience holds special implications for working with oppressed groups. By supporting individual clients' choices and life experiences, feminist social workers validate and strengthen the cultural heritage of ethnic clients. Individuals become empowered by specifying their own interpretation of cultural events and frame of reference.

Renaming also validates ethnic-sensitive as well as gender-centered services. Providing funding for programs serving a particular ethnic clientele are encouraged, as are rape crisis services, battered women's shelters, and policies requiring ethnic children to be placed in foster or adoptive care with a family of similar ethnicity.

The "personal is political" premise of feminist practice is manifested by social workers demonstrating personal activism in challenging discriminatory ideologies, policies, and programs. This includes a willingness to challenge the racism and sexism within and outside service delivery systems. Social workers demonstrating against apartheid in South Africa, for example, or in support of reproductive freedom model "the personal is political" for both clients and practitioners.

Research as Practice. Feminist principles decry the false dichotomy between research and practice by seeing research as a type of social work practice. However, a feminist model does suggest certain alternatives to traditional positivist approaches to scientific inquiry.

For example, there would be no artificial separation between the development of a research proposal, the research itself, and the evaluation of results. Research topics would be developed in line with the specific needs of underserved or oppressed populations.

An extraordinary amount of social science knowledge has been formulated from studies done by and on white males and generalized to the experience of all persons. Feminist researchers see a need to engage in research with an activist perspective in order to engender social change. (Van Den Bergh & Cooper, 1986, p. 14)

Research must also operate from the principle of client empowerment. Instead of being invasive and oppressive, research should be designed to meet individual and community needs. Studies should guarantee "informants are not excluded from important aspects of the research process, such as determining the study questions, deciding on methodology, analyzing findings and providing interpretation analysis" (Van Den Bergh & Cooper, 1986, p. 17).

The feminist premise of renaming also affects research. Because feminists value multidimensional thinking, feminist research would use both right and left functions of the brain, or analytic and intuitive processes. Consequently, data would be considered equally valid from qualitative and quantitative sources of knowledge. This feminist premise also suggests the need for individuals from oppressed groups to research themselves. Examples of this have recently appeared in publications from the National Association of Social Workers (NASW) concerning research on people of color and feminist and gay and lesbian issues (Hopps & Tripodi, 1983; Weick & Vandiver, 1982; Hildalgo, Peterson, & Woodman, 1984).

Where is Feminist Social Work Practiced?

Feminist social work is practiced by people who identify themselves as feminists in all types of social work settings. Many feminists believe that skill, expertise, and commitment to feminist philosophy are more important credentials than formal degrees and titles. Therefore, having a professional degree is not sufficient qualification, nor is merely believing that women and men should be equal. Commitment to the principles of feminism in both one's personal and professional life is requisite (Rawlings & Carter, 1977).

Men can be feminist in their social work approach, although this has been renamed "profeminist." The label implies support for the principles of feminism but acknowledges that a male cannot know the personal experience of sexist discrimination as a woman knows it (Tolman, Mowry, Jones, & Brekke, 1986, p. 3).

Some consensus exists among feminists that male practitioners should not treat women in certain situations. Rawlings and Carter (1980, p. 71) cite the following types of clients as being inappropriate for treatment by men: (1) all-female groups, which may reinforce stereotypic dependencies or set up competition for male attention; (2) women who are hostile to men unless they work as a cotherapist in the therapeutic process; (3) women who relate to male therapists primarily in a seductive manner; (4) extremely dependent, inhibited women who equate femaleness with passivity and docility; (5) women who are in the midst of a divorce crisis and who may, as the result of intense transference feelings, see the male therapist as a surrogate spouse.

Profeminist male social workers have been active in designing and providing treatment for male perpetrators of domestic violence (Tolman et al., 1985). In addition, some profeminist men have begun to articulate the liabilities, for men, of oversubscription to patriarchal values concerning dominance, competition, achievement, and aggression. All male social workers should examine the extent to which they have succumbed to patriarchal values and actively purge them from their personal and work lives.

Some social work educators and practitioners have undertaken to develop and support task forces and commissions in existing social work professional organizations such as NASW and the Council on Social Work Education (CSWE) to promote feminist principles. NASW has the National Committee on Women's Issues (NCOWI) and CSWE has the Commission on the Status of Women. NCOWI recently funded a project to substantiate empirically the parameters of feminist social work practice (Bricker-Jenkins & Hooyman, 1984). In addition, an umbrella organization of practitioners, educators, and students concerned with feminist issues was formed in 1984—the Association for Women in Social Work. A journal concerned with feminist issues, *Affilia: Women and Social Work*, has also recently been established.

In short, feminist social work can be practiced by any individual who subscribes to the ideology of feminism and who practices feminist beliefs in his or her personal work and life.

Summary and Implications

Feminist social work practice is not carved in stone. It is an evolving process that not only incorporates change and fluidity, but encourages taking risks and moving out of the relative safety of traditional and acceptable ways of doing things.

Its concern with eliminating false dichotomies and encouraging wholeness requires that social workers be generalist in their approach. Advocating for environmental and structural change is as important as aiding individual clients. Feminist practice suggests the need to rename social workers as active agents for social change rather than as do-gooders. This may significantly modify public understanding of the potential for social work and social workers to challenge exploitation and oppression. Feminist practice suggests that "the personal is political" becomes the guiding principle by which everyone should live and work. Personal and work relationships should not be separated and isolated, but rather should reflect a unity of commitment to changing the world. Professional knowledge and skills should be shared with the ultimate goal of working together to build communities based on sharing and caring rather than on exploitation and oppression.

Feminist social work practice is a broad and inclusive perspective. It is not a woman's practice or a women's issue. It offers a different way of operating as a social worker. It is a model of activism and sensitivity, of growth and change, of challenge and risk. A feminist social work practice is a viable way to accomplish the unique mission of social work, to improve the quality of life by facilitating social change.

NAN VAN DEN BERGH
LYNN B. COOPER

For further information, see WOMEN; WOMEN IN MACRO PRACTICE.

References

Berlin, S. (1976). "Better Work with Women Clients." *Social Work, 21*(6), 492–497.

Bricker-Jenkins, M., & Hooyman, N. (1984, March). *Not For Women Only: Teaching for Feminist Practice in the 1980s.* Paper presented at the annual program meeting of the Council on Social Work Education, Detroit, Mich.

Brodsky, A., & Hare-Mustin, R. (Eds.). (1980). *Women and Psychotherapy.* New York: Guilford Press.

DeVore, W., & Schlesinger, E. (1981). *Ethnic-Sensitive Social Work Practice.* St. Louis, Mo.: C. V. Mosby Co.

Eisenstein, Z. (Ed.). (1976). *Capitalist Patriarchy and the Case For Socialist Feminism.* New York: Monthly Review Press.

Epstein, L. (1977). *How to Provide Social Services with Task-Centered Methods: Report of the Task-Centered Service Project (Vol. 1).* Chicago: University of Chicago, School of Social Service Administration.

Gilbert, L. (1980). "Feminist Therapy." In A. Brodsky & R. Hare-Mustin (Eds.), *Women and Psychotherapy* (pp. 245–265). New York: Guilford Press.

Gluckstern, N. (1977). "Beyond Therapy: Personal and Institutional Change." In E. Rawlings & D. Carter (Eds.), *Psychotherapy For Women* (pp. 429–444). Springfield, Ill.: Charles C Thomas, Publisher.

Hildalgo, H., Peterson, T., & Woodman, N. (Eds.). (1984). *Lesbian and Gay Issues: A Resource Manual for Social Workers.* Washington, D.C.: National Association of Social Workers.

Holroyd, J. (1976). "Psychotherapy and Women's Liberation." *Counseling Psychologist, 6*(6), 22–28.

Hooyman, N. (1980, September). *Toward a Feminist Administered Style.* Paper presented at the National Association of Social Workers First National Conference on Social Work Practice in a Sexist Society, Washington, D.C.

Hopps, J., & Tripodi, T. (Eds.). (1984). "Research on People of Color" [Entire research section]. *Social Work Research and Abstracts, 19*(4), 1–45.

Israel, J. (1984). "Feminist Therapy." *Women and Therapy, 2*(2&3), 157–161.

Kaschak, E. (1981). "Feminist Psychotherapy: The First Decade." In S. Cox (Ed.), *Female Psychology: The Emerging Self* (pp. 387–407). New York: St. Martin's Press.

Lowenstein, S. (1983). "A Feminist Perspective." In A. Rosenblatt & D. Waldfogel (Eds.), *Handbook of Clinical Social Work* (pp. 518–548). San Francisco: Jossey-Bass.

Mander A., & Rush, A. (1974). *Feminism as Therapy.* New York: Random House.

Marecek, J., & Kravetz, D. (1977). "Women and Mental Health: A Review of Feminist Change Efforts." *Psychiatry, 40*(4), 323–329.

Middleman, R., & Goldberg, G. (1974). *Social Service Delivery: A Structural Approach to*

Practice. New York: Columbia University Press.

Perlman, H. (1957). *Social Casework.* Chicago: University of Chicago Press.

Pincus, A., & Minahan, A. (1973). *Social Work Practice: Model Method.* Itasca, Ill.: F. E. Peacock Publishers.

Radov, C., Masnick, B., & Hauser, B. B. (1977). "Issues in Feminist Therapy: The Work of a Women's Studies Group." *Social Work,* 22(6), 507–511.

Rawlings, E., & Carter, D. (1977). "Psychotherapy for Social Change." In Rawlings & Carter (Eds.), *Psychotherapy For Women* (pp. 447–463). Springfield, Ill.: Charles C Thomas, Publisher.

Reid, W., & Epstein, L. (1972). *Task-Centered Casework.* New York: Columbia University Press.

Sherman, J. (1977). *Freud's Theory and Feminism: A Reply to Juliet Mitchell.* Paper presented at the annual meeting of the American Psychological Association, San Francisco, Calif.

Tolman, R., Mowry, D., Jones, L., & Brekke, J. (1986). "Developing a Profeminist Commitment among Men in Social Work." In N. Van Den Bergh & L. B. Cooper (Eds.), *Feminist Visions for Social Work* (pp. 61–79). Washington, D.C.: National Association of Social Workers.

Van Den Bergh, N. (1986). "Renaming: Vehicle for Empowerment." In J. Penfield (Ed.), *Women and Language in Transition.* Albany, N.Y.: State University of New York Press.

Van Den Bergh, N., & Cooper, L. B. (Eds.). (1986). *Feminist Visions for Social Work.* Washington, D.C.: National Association of Social Workers.

Weick, D., & Vandiver, S. (Eds.). (1982). *Women, Power and Change.* Washington, D.C.: National Association of Social Workers.

Withorn, A. (1984). *Serving the People: Social Services and Social Change.* New York: Columbia University Press.

FERNANDIS, SARAH A. COLLINS.

See biographical section.

FINANCIAL MANAGEMENT

Financial management is one of three major components, along with personnel management and information management, required to manage any kind of organization, whether profit or nonprofit. All three components are integral parts of the manager's role. Because most social welfare organizations are nonprofit, operating under either governmental or voluntary auspices, they draw on a broad range of financial management technologies from business and public administration as well as from those especially developed for their unique requirements.

This article defines financial management in the governmental and voluntary parts of the nonprofit sector, presents the range of financial management activities that are typically performed, and makes an assessment of the general state of the art in financial management.

Definition

What is financial management? Certainly, it starts with budgeting and accounting. Some authors define financial management in a way that limits it to managing money (Harper, McLaughlin, & Bartley, 1981). They focus on the techniques of recording financial information in the accounting system, on meeting external requirements for reporting financial information to resource providers and regulators, and on meeting internal management needs for determining costs, developing budgets, controlling expenditures, and safeguarding the assets of an organization.

Other authors merge their thinking about financial management into a broader concept of management control (Anthony & Herzlinger, 1980; Ramanathan, 1982.) They focus on the level of control between strategic planning, which establishes the overall goals and strategies of the organization, and the detailed operating decisions that are the focus of operational control. This perspective defines management control as the process by which management ensures that the organization carries out its strategies effectively and efficiently.

This article integrates these varying concepts of financial and general management as they are practiced in governmental and voluntary nonprofit social welfare organizations. This approach has much in common with a definition offered by Lohmann (1980):

> In the human services, financial management has generally to do with the control and

planned use of money and other scarce resources in a manner designed to further organizational goals, and be consistent with the law, professional ethics, and community standards. (p. 7)

Lohmann points out that financial management, when viewed as a system of ends, is a narrow, technical, and subsidiary matter concerned with budgets, grant applications, payrolls, tax forms, and journal entries. At the same time, as a system of means, financial management in social welfare has a broad effect on the attainment of program goals.

Financial management is presented in this article as a process composed of six components:

- Planning or predicting financial requirements and sources of funds
- Resource development
- Allocating resources
- Recording financial and program transactions
- Controlling expenditures and managing resources
- Reporting and interpreting.

Although the article discusses each of these six components separately, they are best viewed as integral parts of an overall financial management process. In practice there is considerable interaction among the components, and they tend to occur concurrently. In addition, the management of each year's funds often extends over many years, starting 18 to 24 months before the fiscal period with the planning component and ending after the fiscal year with audits and reports. The technologies and logic of the process are typically implemented in a political environment in which judgment plays a large role in decision making (Wildavsky, 1979).

Planning

When advocacy for an organization is recognized as an essential part of the social adminstrator's role, integrating planning into the financial management process gains importance (Richan, 1980). It is through the planning process that the general aspirations of an organization are refined into specific program proposals. This integration of planning and the budget process is typically realized during the annual budget cycle. For example, a state department of human resources begins planning a budget in January of year A for a fiscal period starting 18

months later in July of year B. In the spring of year A, the director requests program proposals from staff, or the request may be initiated by local or state-level staff. A similar, although not so formal, procedure may be followed in a voluntary agency participating in a United Way.

Lee and Johnson (1977) report that this phase is the most difficult to describe because it has been subjected to the most reform. Responsibility for the preparation and submission of budgets varies greatly among governmental jurisdictions. Although a majority of the states' governors have this responsibility, some share it with other elected officers, civil service appointees, or legislative leaders. For the most part, however, planning initiatives come from the agencies rather than from elected officials or the legislature. The same pattern holds for voluntary organizations in the relationships they establish with resource providers.

This initial phase may consist only of projecting into the next year the program statistics and dollars for current client populations, staff, and nonpersonnel expenses. Sometimes these projections are required by a United Way, a legislature, or a governor to estimate what it would cost to maintain the same level of operations the next year. In addition, proposals may be made for new programs or for expansion of current programs, or they may be necessary to meet a new legislative or court-ordered requirement.

As indicated earlier, this year-by-year planning focus directed toward specific budget proposals is the typical orientation in both governmental and voluntary social agencies. In these settings, budgeting is the process of translating plans into specific resources, such as personnel, supplies, payments to clients, and equipment, and stating these resources for a specific time frame and in specific dollars.

Strategic planning is another level of planning. It is the process of deciding on the goals of the organization and on the broad strategies to be used in attaining these goals. These decisions are made only occasionally and at the highest levels in an organization. All views of strategic planning emphasize the importance of the process by which key actors in an organization participate to develop these long-range goals and strategies (Lorange & Vancil, 1976). In social welfare

organizations, "long range" can be interpreted as five years but is typically seen as
not longer than three years (Community
Council of Greater Dallas, 1980). The steps in
a typical strategic-planning system represent
an orderly, gradual process of commitment to
certain strategic alternatives.

Since the mid-1960s, both the public
administration and voluntary social welfare
sectors have attempted to bring planning and
budgeting together in more formal ways
(Schick, 1971; United Way of America, 1975;
Wildavsky, 1979). To structure financial and
program planning into a single process, a
series of budget innovations such as Planning
Programming Budgeting (PPB), Zero-Based
Budgeting (ZBB), and "Planned Budgeting"
have been promulgated with varying levels of
success.

Resource Development

In the 1980s, cutbacks in government
funding and important shifts in the way that
government and voluntary social welfare
agencies are funded emphasized the key role
of resource development in financial management (Demone & Gibelman, 1984; Urban
Institute, 1983; Greenstein, Adams, &
Bickerman, 1984). The rationale is pointed: if
there are no funds, there will be no services!

In a major study of funding for voluntary agencies, the Urban Institute (1983)
found that for fiscal year 1982, the first full
year of the Reagan budget cuts, government
at all levels still provided a relatively high
level of support—39 percent of the revenues
for voluntary agencies, with 58 percent receiving some level of public support. For
those agencies receiving government funding, almost two-thirds of their income came
from this source, with some variations for
regional differences. As noted in Table 1,
government support was the major funding
source for voluntary agencies. In support of
the Rosenbaum and Smith (in press) study,
the Urban Institute found that the second
most important source was earned income
from operations, 29 percent.

In the voluntary sector, developing
needed resources has always been a major
issue for most agencies. Table 1 illustrates
the variety of funding sources that are currently used. Each of these sources has a
different agenda and usually a different timetable and format for providing resources.

Table 1. Sources of Support for Voluntary Agencies, Fiscal Year 1982, in Rank Order

Source	Percent-age
Government (grants, con-tracts, third-party pay-ments, etc.)	39
Dues, fees, and charges	29
Federated giving (including sectarian)	7
Individual giving	6
Endowment and investment income	5
Corporate grants	3
Foundation grants	3
Other	8

Source: Urban Institute (1983, September). *Serv-
ing Community Needs: The Nonprofit Sector in an
Era of Government Retrenchment.* Washington,
D.C.: Author.

Thus, skills are needed to tap these resources
in such varying areas as contracting for services, billing for third-party payments, and
developing grant proposals. In addition, the
need to bring in more money from operations
requires skills in setting client charges and in
training staff to implement those charges.
Dealing with federated funding organizations
involves a year-long relationship usually focused on annual budget proposals and negotiation. Campaigns for individual contributions call for another set of fund-raising skills.
Dealing with endowment and investment income requires access to information and
business acumen to maximize interest and
dividend revenue while limiting the risk of
losing the value of the investment capital.
Investing temporarily surplus funds for brief
periods requires knowledge of the investment
market and the ability to analyze the cash
flow needs of the organization. In addition,
some agencies view developing profit-making
subsidiaries as an attractive new opportunity.
This is an area that should be approached
with caution, however, because of the potential for losing money as well as earning a
profit (Williams, 1982).

For governmental agencies, developing
resources principally means dealing with government itself. Thus, a department of human
services, after developing its initial proposed

budget, typically finds itself involved in a series of negotiations and special studies. Negotiations usually start with the bureau of administration or with a budget proposal to the legislature. Once these negotiations have been completed and the governor's budget is developed, the department is responsible for making formal presentations to the legislature in support of the budget and for conducting impact and other studies on demand. Informally, the department also needs to deal with its constituencies, who may have political clout, and with individual legislators. In addition, the agency needs skills in grantsmanship to secure special government or foundation funding (Lauffer, 1984).

Allocating Resources

When the amount of money that will be available for a fiscal period becomes known, the organization must allocate these funds and other resources to competing requirements. If the organization secures all the funds it originally requested and its original formal proposal was realistic in terms of client demands and organizational aspirations, the task of allocating resources is relatively simple—the proposed budget becomes the actual budget. However, even in times of expanding funding, this is hardly ever the case. In times of decreasing funds, the allocation of available resources can be a major effort with potentially serious effects on many parts of an organization (Hirschhorn & Associates, 1983). Organizational strategies that were successful in times of growth often fail when exposed to the rigors of cutbacks. When a growing agency plans, it can afford to make errors in allocating resources because today's errors can be corrected with tomorrow's new resources. Conditions of decline leave an agency little margin for error.

The discussion that follows presents two ways of viewing an organization's allocation process. The process can be viewed in the context of the organization's program structure or in terms of the interpersonal and decision-making implications of the allocations.

Program Structure. A social welfare agency's program structure is the way in which it organizes its program services. An agency's principal programs are its major services, which are also its major objectives.

The definition of program services, or indeed of social welfare itself, presents a continuing quandary for the field. There are two major obstacles to uniformity. First, each agency defines its services somewhat differently, presumably as a result of the specialized needs of its clients and differences in its professional commitments and financial resources. In states with locally administered public welfare departments, for example, the local agencies typically vary widely in the scope and intensity of their program services. Second, program structures differ according to agencies' differing historical bases. For example, a child welfare agency typically forms most of its services around a setting in which children live, such as institutional care, whereas family agencies form their services around a process, counseling. Other services are formed around objectives (adoption, rehabilitation), a mode of service (homemakers), or a condition (mental health) (Elkin, 1967).

This confusion in the nomenclature and classification of services presents serious problems for anyone attempting to evaluate or compare such things as costs or productivity among agencies—information that could help in making allocation decisions (Elkin, 1980). For example, the federal government was frustrated in getting valid reports from the states on expenditures for Title XX social services. The Standards of Accounting and Financial Reporting for Voluntary Health and Welfare Organizations (National Health Council et al., 1975) requires a financial statement of functional expenses that discloses expenses for program services separately from those for management, general, and fund-raising expenses.

Of the many attempts to clarify the definitions of program services, the most successful is the United Way of America's services identification system (UWASIS) (United Way of America, 1976). This system describes programs in the framework of fundamental goals in the field of human services. *UWASIS II* (United Way of America, 1976) outlines the basic social goals, the service systems that promote these goals, the specific services in these systems, the programs that perform such services, some elements of these programs, and the suggested program products in terms of the types of persons served and efforts expended on their behalf.

Interpersonal and Decision-Making Implications. The interpersonal and decision-making implications of resource allocation go to the heart of the task of managing an organization, especially in times of cutbacks. When considering allocations, the first condition a manager must clarify is the validity of the original budget proposal in the light of the current client and community situation. Because of the politics of budgeting (Wildavsky, 1979), the agency may have requested more than it expected to receive in order to have a fallback position during negotiations. On the other hand, especially in situations where budget proposals must be made 18 months or longer before the fiscal year starts, inadequate funds may have been requested to meet increasing client demands. This is a special problem in governmental agencies that are mandated to serve a particular population.

Fiscal stress may be either long term or short term, and the optimal approach to dealing with it differs according to the factors that underlie the situation and the options available. Levine (1980) suggests several questions as useful guides for organizing the tough decisions and for designing innovative solutions.

Although rational decison-making techniques help determine the alternatives, no algorithm or formula ever produces the best solution. Hirschhorn and Associates (1983) concluded that although managers always base their decisions on subjective information and on their relationship with personnel both in the organization and outside it, retrenchment poses particularly difficult demands on managers and staff. They found that patterns of denial, anxiety, and the balance between optimism and pessimism all shape the framework for rational decision making. The emotions and uncertainty of these situations must be confronted realistically, they found, to make sound decisions for an organization as it faces long-term changes in its environment. In some instances, the technological, legislative, and financial climate changes so drastically that many agencies seek new missions. These conditions call for broader concepts of working conjointly with other organizations.

Recording Transactions

As services are provided and funds expended, these transactions must be re-corded as a basis for both internal and external reports. Recording both service and financial information in a planned way is necessary for functional accounting and budgeting, cost analysis, evaluating costs of different ways of providing services, and reporting to resource providers, regulators, and constituents. As noted earlier, defining services is a major unresolved issue in social welfare. However, each organization must come to grips with the issue and carefully and specifically define its services so that information can be aggregated in the same framework from three systems—accounting, personnel, and services.

The section on control discusses recording information for internal management. This section discusses the impact external accountability requirements have on record keeping.

Historically, the concept of accountability of government and voluntary nonprofit organizations developed around concerns for how these organizations spent funds entrusted to them. In a democratic society, responsibility entails holding elected officials answerable to their constituents (Lee & Johnson, 1977). The concept of stewardship of funds is central to accounting principles as they have evolved in both the government and voluntary sectors. Although there are pressures to shift to measures of effectiveness—a nonfinancial measurement—the demands for financial accountability continue and require the informed attention of the managers of nonprofit organizations.

Accountability in the Voluntary Sector. Following a first effort in the mid-1960s, three national social welfare organizations in 1975 published a revised set of standards for accounting and financial reporting (National Health Council et al., 1975). These standards are compatible with a guide published by the American Institute of Certified Public Accountants, *Audits of Voluntary Health and Welfare Organizations* (1974), which describes generally accepted accounting principles applicable to voluntary health and welfare organizations. In 1974 the United Way of America published a guide for United Ways and not-for-profit human service organizations that was compatible with the other two publications. The compatibility of these three guides provides a significant base for the communication of financial information from service providers to their diverse audiences.

Accountability in Government. In the government sector, almost all funds come from government itself, through tax revenues at federal, state, and local levels. Although each level of government is accountable to its legislative body and through it to the taxpayers, a major flow of resources also occurs downward from federal to state and local levels and from state to local levels. At each level, the resource providers exercise their accountability responsibilities and options by imposing reporting requirements. Because of the magnitude of federal funds and the accompanying regulations and reporting requirements, the federal attitude toward accountability strongly influences the entire chain of accountability for governmental funds as they flow to different levels of government and to the voluntary sector through grants and purchase-of-service contracts (Comptroller General of the United States, 1981).

Accounting practices vary widely in the different branches and units of government. Many organizations have encouraged local governments to adopt a standard accounting system to allow a greater exchange of information among these governmental units. However, state governments and the federal government do not have standardized accounting systems. Each agency may have one or more systems. At the federal level, there are approximately 160 systems in civilian agencies and 125 systems in the Department of Defense. The comptroller general of the General Accounting Office is responsible for approving first the principles and standards of each system and then the system design (Lee & Johnson, 1977).

Against this background of variations in government accounting practices, many federal agencies have developed specialized requirements for organizations that receive federal funds. These reporting requirements are designed to fit in with the unique accounting systems of the various departments, with differing concepts of reporting content and format, and with differing regulations and guidelines for many critical aspects of reporting, such as the allocation of indirect costs and measuring performance.

Controlling Expenditures and Managing Resources

Control is a fundamental management responsibility and is an integral part of the financial management process. It is based on the broad economic concept that all resources are scarce and therefore must be used wisely. Specifically, management control is defined as the process by which management ensures that the organization carries out its strategies effectively and efficiently (Anthony & Herzlinger, 1980). Lohman (1980) emphasized the concept of "break even" for nonprofit managers in which the *financial* goal is to end a fiscal period with neither a surplus nor a deficit. In the multigoal environment of nonprofit organizations, a general *program* goal is to provide the maximum amount of service for the clients of the organization. If an organization ends up with a surplus, questions may be raised as to whether the manager might have overstressed the financial goal to the detriment of the program goals.

Controlling Expenditures. Exerting control over expenditures requires a method of monitoring financial and program transactions and then taking corrective action. It also requires comparing actual experience against some criterion or standard to detect any deviation from a plan or objective. The budget is the major criterion against which actual experience is monitored. It is based on projections of levels of program services and personnel and provides an annual plan stated in dollars for both revenues and expenditures. To serve as an instrument of control, an annual budget must estimate the high and low months in the organization's cycles of expenditures and revenues. Then, actual expenditures and revenues for each month—and the cumulative figures to date—are compared with the plan. When significant variance occurs in any line item or in the overall budget, corrective action is called for. Corrective action requires judgment on where savings can be made in expenditures. It may include cutbacks in the items overexpended, or it may mean cuts in other items that have less priority, are more controllable, or can be deferred. Accordingly, an overexpenditure in payments for foster family care because of an unexpected increase in the rates for foster families may be met by cuts in out-of-town travel or conferences, two line items not related directly to foster care.

There are several implications of this brief example. The first is that financial controls are best exercised when the accounting system is on an accrual or semiaccrual basis. Compared with accounting on a strict cash basis, which records only cash transactions, accrual keeps track of accounts receivable and accounts payable, and certain other transactions, and adjusts the accounting records to recognize these transactions in the period in which they were earned or committed. This adjustment means that accounting records that produce accrued information present a more complete and accurate picture for a specific period, such as a month or a year. Although, in contrast, strict cash accounting provides limited information, in some instances organizations may need to develop cash flow analyses to ensure that they have adequate cash to meet their ongoing obligations and to invest surplus cash.

A second implication of the foster care example is that the line-item budget is most powerful when applied to control activities— its primary purpose. Although line-item budgets are often maligned because of their concentration on objects of expenditure rather than on program purposes, this type of budget is universally used in governmental and voluntary social welfare organizations and serves an important control function.

A third implication is the importance of relating program considerations to budgetary controls. In the example of the foster care overexpenditures, the decision to cut another line item was based on a program commitment to continue the same level of service to foster children. The control problem for management was how to deal with an unplanned increase in rates that resulted in a deficit for this line item. The decision to make up the line-item deficit from another line item is typical of the kinds of decisions that social welfare managers make continuously in balancing financial and program goals.

Management Indicators. One of the dynamic innovations of the 1980s in social welfare is the increasing use of management indicators to help managers to monitor all aspects of an organization. Management indicators identify *limited* numbers of areas designated by top management as *critical* to

the continuing successful functioning of the organization and *monitor* these indicators on a regular basis. An indicator is made up of a ratio of operational statistics and includes a criterion or standard against which it may be compared. For example, an indicator of nursing home capacity utilization would show the ratio of average number of patients in residence compared to total number of licensed beds. This ratio would be compared to some standard of utilization known to represent efficiency.

Indicators are generally analyzed as trends over time and lend themselves to display in graphic form (Elkin & Molitor, 1984). Management indicators generally are directed toward program as well as administrative and financial concerns. One approach identifies three major management concerns as the basis of a conceptual framework for indicators—effectiveness, efficiency, and adequacy of finances (Elkin & Molitor, 1984).

Interest is increasing in applying management indicators to specialized areas. Sorensen, Zelman, Hanbery, and Kusic (1984) developed management indicators for community mental health services; Bowers, Aravanis, and Ficke (1984) developed and demonstrated a methodology to be used by state agencies for the aging; Benton and Neves (1984) are developing indicators for local departments of public welfare. All these efforts recognize that individual managers must select their own indicators to reflect their understanding of the pressures, goals, and constraints the organization faces, but they also seek a core of indicators that would be meaningful in a grouping of organizations. Sorensen and his associates (1984) successfully identified such a core of indicators in a group of community mental health centers. These indicators are summarized in four major areas of concern: revenue, clients, staff, and services. The resulting data provide a significant base for management control and for comparing the experience of all the centers in the study.

Managing Resources. Control may be viewed as one aspect of a broader concern for managing the resources of an organization. Resources thus include all the assets of an organization, including its cash, investments, buildings, furniture, supplies, prepaid expenses, and accounts receivable. Managing this broad array of resources requires an accounting system that meets the criteria of generally accepted accounting principles suitable for this type of agency. Systems must also be in place for collecting program, financial, and administrative data in the framework of an organization's defined services and its responsibilities for reporting to sources of funds. Managing these resources further requires an ongoing cycle of activities, as follows:

■ On a day-to-day basis, procedures must be established for handling cash, checks, and credit cards; for maintaining internal controls; and for recording transactions.

■ On a monthly basis, appropriate steps must be taken to adjust the accounting books and to monitor for variances from budgeted income and expenses and from program and administrative objectives. Corrective action must be taken promptly when indicated.

■ Annually, a budget must be established by those authorized to do so. As indicated earlier, the budget is the primary financial criterion against which expenditures are monitored. At the end of each year, an external audit should be made by a certified public accountant using standards of accounting appropriate to the type of organization. The auditor should express an opinion on the fairness with which the financial statements present the financial position of the organization and provide a management letter assessing the internal controls and systems and recommending any necessary corrective actions. The executive and representatives of the board or the supervising governmental agency should examine the auditor's reports and the staff's plans to correct deficiencies noted in the management letter. Annual reports are made to resource providers and constituencies, in addition to any monthly or periodic reports that may be made.

■ On an ongoing basis, an organization's financial management should include the following: investing surplus cash, taking or giving loans, insurance coverage, maintenance and replacement of fixed assets, monitoring the costs of programs, establishing and reviewing purchase-of-service contracts, control and reduction of costs, and imaginative ways to increase revenue for the agency.

Reporting and Interpreting

Although social welfare services may be provided under proprietary auspices (Born, 1983), in nonprofit organizations most are provided under either governmental or voluntary auspices. Nonprofit organizations typically depend for a portion of their revenues on providers other than the clients who directly receive the services. These resource providers represent a wide variety of organizations: federal, state, and local governments; federations for fund raising; foundations; and corporations.

Because of pressures on them to be accountable, the resource providers require social welfare agencies to report on both financial and nonfinancial aspects of their service delivery operations. The very multiplicity of funding sources that social welfare organizations have creatively developed presents a problem for them because different resource providers have different reporting requirements. These differences are based on varying concepts of accountability, different historical patterns, and different relationships between resource and service providers. In addition, other constituencies and organizations demand information about the performance of nonprofit organizations. These include better business bureaus, chambers of commerce, charities' regulatory agencies, and contributor information bodies (Elkin, 1985).

Therefore, managers of social welfare organizations have a wide array of external groups to which they must report. Each of these bodies may have life-or-death power over the organization or some part of its program. In addition, experience suggests that the larger the portion of an organization's resources that comes from a single source, the greater the control that resource provider can wield. Moving toward multiple sources of funds may mean that new services must be developed or that current service delivery patterns have to be altered. Such an action may require marketing skills to define new target populations and new service packages. Obtaining funding from additional resource providers also adds to the diversity of the accountability requirements.

In a study for the Financial Accounting Standards Board, Brace, Elkin, Robinson, and Steinberg (1980) explored the issue of whether financial accounting for what they refer to as "nonbusiness" organizations should broaden its scope to consider service efforts and accomplishments. They found that a wide group of these organizations, including human service organizations, reported service efforts and accomplishments. However, they reported that information on efforts (inputs and processes) was found more readily than was information on accomplishments (outputs and outcomes). Information on efficiency was more prevalent than information on effectiveness. Both trend information and quantified data were lacking. Most reporting of the service efforts and accomplishments appeared in reports other than the general purpose financial reports. After concluding that information about service efforts and accomplishments is well suited to communicating organizational performance in nonbusiness organizations, the study also reported that the state of the art concerning *results* is minimal and that its inclusion in financial reporting at this time may detract from, rather than enhance, the usefulness of financial reporting. With the caveat that further research is needed, Brace and his associates suggested that information on efficiency and service efforts can be successfully combined with financial data to strengthen the reports of nonbusiness organizations. In another work, Rapp (1984) proposed a model for improving management's use of existing information systems. The combination of financial and nonfinancial information in the reports of social welfare organizations is of considerable interest also to the researchers who are working on management indicators because indicators may also be powerful sources of reporting information to external sources.

As management indicators and other methods of objectifying or quantifying social welfare agency reports are considered more seriously by resource providers, one of the critical issues that must be resolved is that of *criteria*. What criteria should be used in forming judgments about the information reported? The following are possible criteria.

Benchmarks. Empirical data that simply report some phenomenon or describe some existing situation are known as benchmarks. The simplest benchmark is the preceding year's experience. It could also be the experience of a group of similar organizations or the average experience of that group of

organizations. In their outstanding work on management indicators, Sorensen and his associates (1984) presented benchmarks for community mental health centers.

Industry Standards. Empirical data adjusted to indicate the program or management goals of an industry provide industry standards. Such standards usually represent the consensus of a group of people who have worked together to clarify their concept of what the standards should be. In the nonprofit sector, standards for program management or financial experience are typically set in two ways: (1) by legislation, following considerable study or public hearings, or (2) by national organizations that secure the consensus of a group of informed individuals brought together for the purpose. Among the many issues involved in applying standards to the nonprofit sector are those of identifying comparable institutions and defining services.

Standard Costs. Primarily used in business, standard costs are similar to industry standards except that they are built on a foundation of conventional cost accounting. The classification of cost elements into those that vary with volume and those that do not has facilitated the analysis of many business problems (Anthony & Herzlinger, 1980).

Unit Costs. The *average* cost of producing something, unit costs provide a single measure that uniformly quantifies a level of effort and the resources expended. The application of unit costs is particularly important because it normalizes or standardizes the gross dollars expended (Elkin, 1980). Although unit costs have the advantage of being empirically based, they have the disadvantage of representing a midpoint of experience without the knowledge of range and distribution. In addition, they do not distinguish between fixed and variable costs.

Ratio Analysis. This is an analytical technique that uses summary indicators to facilitate and enhance the user's understanding of complex data. A ratio is, of course, simply the relationship between two numbers. The trend of a ratio is the direction or tendency indicated by the changes in the ratio over several periods, usually years. Financial ratios are used extensively in the nonprofit sector (Peat, Marwick, Mitchell & Co., undated) and are applied to nonfinancial data in management indicators.

All these approaches and others are available to assist social welfare organizations in making their reports more meaningful. This goal will be met by reducing the volume of narrative, descriptive data now reported and replacing it with carefully selected information that has been made more objective and interpreted by using consistent criteria, such as those just illustrated.

Future Trends

Cutbacks in the financing of social welfare organizations will strongly influence all aspects of financial management for the 1980s and 1990s and perhaps beyond. In addition to developing new management techniques for dealing with cutbacks, social welfare organizations will also be searching for new means of funding their operations. As less government funds become available, pressure will mount to increase revenues from the operations themselves—through fees paid by clients, by insurers and other third parties, and by industry through employee assistance programs. Voluntary agencies will increasingly diversify their fund-raising activities and begin operating profit-making subsidiaries.

Improved skills in financial management will include not only traditional skills in planning and controlling expenditures but also management indicators, financial ratios, graphics, and other developments. The computer's impact on financial management in social welfare will increase through automated spread sheets to support analysis and reporting and through increasingly sophisticated accounting and statistical software packages. An increasing number of social workers will receive training in financial management in schools of social work, many of which have already established such training programs.

ROBERT ELKIN

For further information, see ADMINISTRATION IN SOCIAL WELFARE; INFORMATION UTILIZATION FOR MANAGEMENT DECISION MAKING; PERSONNEL MANAGEMENT; PLANNING AND MANAGEMENT PROFESSIONS; SOCIAL WELFARE FINANCING.

References

American Institute of Certified Public Accountants. (1974). *Audits of Voluntary Health and Welfare Organizations*. New York: Author.

Anthony, R. N., & Herzlinger, R. E. (1980). *Management Control in Nonprofit Organizations*. Homewood, Ill.: Richard D. Irwin.

Benton, B. B., & Neves, C. M. P. (1984, October). "The Base of Management Indicators in Improving Organizational Performance." Paper presented to the Joint Meeting of the Evaluation Research Society and the Evaluation Network, San Francisco, Calif.

Born, C. E. (1983). "Proprietary Firms and Child Welfare Services: Patterns and Implications." *Child Welfare*, 62(2), 109–118.

Bowers, G. E., Aravanis, S., & Ficke, R. (1984). *A Procedure for Developing Management Indicators for State Units on Aging*. Washington, D.C.: National Association of State Units on Aging.

Brace, P. K., Elkin, R., Robinson, D., & Steinberg, H. I. (1980). *Reporting of Service Efforts and Accomplishments*. Stanford, Conn.: Financial Accounting Standards Board.

Comptroller General of the United States. (1981). *Standards for Audit of Governmental Organizations, Programs, Activities, and Functions* (GAO Publication No. 020-000-00205-1). Washington, D.C.: U.S. Government Printing Office.

Community Council of Greater Dallas. (1980). *Corporate Long-Range Planning*. Dallas, Tex.: Author.

Demone, H. W., Jr., & Gibelman, M. (1984). "Reaganomics: Its Impact on the Voluntary Not-for-Profit Sector." *Social Work*, 29(5), 421–427.

Elkin, R. (1980). *A Human Service Manager's Guide to Developing Unit Costs*. Falls Church, Va.: Institute for Information Studies.

Elkin, R. (1967). *Conceptual Base for Defining Health and Welfare Services*. New York: Family Service Association of America, Child Welfare League of America, National Traveler's Aid Society.

Elkin, R. (1985). "Paying the Piper and Calling the Tune." In S. Slavin (Ed.), *Social Administration*. New York: Haworth Press.

Elkin, R., & Molitor, M. (1984). *Management Indicators in Nonprofit Organizations: Guidelines to Selection and Implementation*. New York: Peat, Marwick, Mitchell & Co.

Greenstein, R., Adams, G., & Bickerman, J. (1984). *End Results: The Impact of Federal Policies Since 1980 on Low-Income Americans*. Washington, D.C.: Interfaith Action for Economic Justice, Center on Budget and Policy Priorities.

Harper, C. L., McLaughlin, C. P., & Bartley, J. W. (1981). *Financial Systems for Community Health Organizations*. Belmont, Calif.: Lifetime Learning Publications.

Hirschhorn & Associates. (1983). *Cutting Back, Retrenchment and Redevelopment in Human and Community Services.* San Francisco, Calif.: Jossey-Bass.

Lauffer, A. (1984). *Strategic Marketing for Not-for-Profit Organzations.* New York: Free Press.

Lee, R. D., Jr., & Johnson, R. W. (1977). *Public Budgeting Systems.* Baltimore, Md.: University Park Press.

Levine, C. (Ed.). (1980). *Managing Fiscal Stress: The Crisis in the Public Sector.* Chatham, N.J.: Chatham House Publishers.

Lohmann, R. A. (1980). *Breaking Even: Financial Management in Human Service Organizations.* Philadelphia: Temple University Press.

Lohmann, R. A. (1980). "Financial Management and Social Administration." In F. D. Perlmutter & S. Slavin (Eds.), *Leadership in Social Administration.* Philadelphia: Temple University Press.

Lorange, P., & Vancil, R. (1976). "How to Design a Strategic Planning System." *Harvard Business Review, 54*(5), 75–81.

National Health Council, National Assembly of National Voluntary Health and Social Welfare Organizations, and United Way of America. (1974). *Standards of Accounting and Financial Reporting for Voluntary Health and Welfare Organizations.* New York: Author.

Peat, Marwick, Mitchell & Co. (Undated.). *Ratio Analysis in Voluntary Health and Welfare Organizations.* New York: Author.

Ramanathan, K. V. (1982). *Management Control in Nonprofit Organizations.* New York: John Wiley & Sons.

Rapp, C. A. (1984). "Information, Performance, and the Human Service Manager of the 1980s: Beyond 'Housekeeping'." *Administration in Social Work, 8*(2), 69–80.

Richan, W. (1980). "The Administrator As Advocate." In F. D. Perlmutter & S. Slavin (Eds.), *Leadership in Social Adminstration.* Philadelphia: Temple University Press.

Rosenbaum, N., & Smith, L. R. (in press). *The State of the Voluntary Sector.* Washington, D.C.: C. R. G. Press.

Sorensen, J. E., Zelman, W., Hanbery, G. W., & Kusic, R. (1984). *Key Performance Indicators for Community Mental Health Organizations: Demonstration Findings.* Denver, Colo.: University of Denver.

Schick, A. (1971). *Budget Innovation in the States.* Washington, D.C.: The Brookings Institution.

United Way of America. (1974). *Accounting and Financial Reporting: A Guide for United Ways and Not-For-Profit Human Service Organizations.* Alexandria, Va.: Author.

United Way of America. (1975). *Budgeting: A Guide for United Ways and Not-For-Profit Human Service Organizations.* Alexandria, Va.: Author.

United Way of America. (1976). *UWASIS II: A Taxonomy of Social Goals and Human Service Programs.* Alexandria, Va.: Author.

Urban Institute. (1983, September). *Serving Community Needs: The Nonprofit Sector in an Era of Government Retrenchment.* Washington, D.C.: Author.

Vinter, R., & Kish, R. (1984). *Budgeting for Not-For-Profit Organizations.* New York: Free Press.

Wildavsky, A. (1979). *The Politics of the Budgetary Process* (3rd ed.). Boston: Little, Brown & Company.

Williams, R. M. (1982, January-February). "Why Don't We Set Up a Profit-Making Subsidiary?" *Grantsmanship Center News,* pp. 15–23.

FLEXNER, ABRAHAM. See biographical section.

FOLLETT, MARY PARKER. See biographical section.

FOOD STAMP PROGRAM

The Food Stamp program, which was created to supplement the food-buying power of low-income people, is the nation's chief response to its hunger problem. Monthly benefits in the form of coupons used to purchase food are entirely federally financed. States are responsible for administration of the program and divide the cost of operation equally with the federal government. In fiscal 1983, over 21 million people received benefits at a cost of $11.8 billion to the federal government (U.S. Department of Agriculture [USDA], 1984b, p. 27). Eligibility for the program is restricted to households that meet income, resource, and work requirements prescribed by law. Unlike that for other assistance programs, food stamp eligibility is based solely on income and resources. Intact families and single adults not eligible for cash assistance such as Aid to Families with Dependent Children (AFDC) may receive benefits under the Food Stamp program.

Almost from its inception, the Food Stamp program has been subject to continuing criticism and political debate. This program has more beneficiaries than any other program specifically geared to aid low-income people. Ironically, as the program has grown (suggesting fulfillment of program goals), its very size has become a matter of concern leading to attempts to control or reduce growth. In fact, Congress has substantially amended the program no less than seven times since 1977. Despite the often heated controversy surrounding food stamps, there has been a reluctance to replace the program with direct cash assistance for fear that the money will not necessarily be used for food.

Food Stamp Recipients

Surveys by the U.S. Department of Agriculture (USDA) (1984a; 1984b) draw the following portrait of food-stamp recipients. First, there is diversity among the recipients. According to the department's most recent survey of program participants in 1981, the average household size is 2.7 persons. Forty-five percent of all households are white and 36.8 percent are black. Close examination of actual household composition indicates certain trends, most notably the feminization of poverty—more women living in poverty than men. Recipients fall into several basic categories, including children (47 percent), the elderly (9 percent), and the disabled (3 percent). Female-headed households predominate, constituting 70 percent of the caseload. Households containing children age 17 or under make up 56.4 percent of the caseload, and 40 percent of these receive AFDC. Male-headed households with children are only 13 percent of the total. Recipient households with children tend to be larger than the norm, averaging 3.6 persons. As a result, monthly benefits are greater among households with children.

The elderly make up over half of the single-member households and, again, women predominate in this group. Owing to smaller household size—1 to 2 people—and relatively larger income, benefits to elderly households are smaller than for any other group. The chief income source for 88 per-

cent of elderly households is social security or supplemental security income (SSI).

Households with earners—the working poor—make up 20 percent of the caseload, and most of the breadwinners in this group have full-time jobs. More than half of the earners report no income other than their salaries. The remainder receive private retirement income, alimony, AFDC, social security, or SSI. Among working households, women as household heads constitute the largest segment of earners (8.8 percent).

Despite the large number of people receiving food stamps, there is growing concern about nonparticipation by potentially eligible households. A precise measure of nonparticipation among low-income households is not available; however, it is estimated that only 60 to 65 percent of those potentially eligible actually receive benefits (Physicians' Task Force on Hunger in America, 1985). Ignorance about eligibility requirements seems to keep many from applying for assistance. Another likely reason for nonparticipation is the stigma associated with food stamp use. In planning for future nutrition assistance needs, the reasons for nonparticipation and characteristics of nonparticipants are likely to become increasingly important.

Program History

Although the Food Stamp program is now an integral part of the safety net for the poor, this was not always the case. Food assistance has evolved from commodity distribution in 1933 into a program that seeks to ensure adequate diets for poor people. Prior to the 1960s, federal programs for food assistance were chiefly directed at supporting farm prices by removing excess food supplies from the market through food distribution to the needy. The roots of the Food Stamp program are found in the 1933 Agricultural Adjustment Act (P.L. 73-10) and the 1935 amendments to that act (P.L. 74-320), which was specifically aimed at eliminating surplus food and stabilizing the farm economy during the Depression.

In 1961, the Kennedy Administration established a pilot program to provide food to welfare recipients. The principal objective remained the elimination of surplus food, but for the first time, nutritional improvement became an explicit goal. Then, in 1964, Congress authorized the first Food Stamp Act

(P.L. 88-525). The stated purpose of the program was to use the nation's food abundance to "raise the levels of nutrition among low-income families" (p. 1).

Responsibility for setting eligibility standards and overseeing the day-to-day operations was left to the states. The 1964 act eliminated the receipt of public assistance as the basis for eligibility, thus making benefits available to all households that satisfied state-determined income and resource standards. The law also required a national, uniform benefit structure in which benefit levels and purchase prices were determined by USDA.

In response to the mandate for uniform benefits, USDA nutritionists devised the Economy Food Plan (EFP), whose goal was to provide a nutritionally adequate, low-cost diet for households of varying sizes. Monthly benefits were based on EFP until 1976, when a new diet—the Thrifty Food Plan (TFP)—was developed. In addition, the 1964 act provided for full federal funding of benefit costs and of a portion of state administrative costs. Food stamps were not issued free of charge to eligible households. The food stamp purchase price set by USDA was based on the amount of money households of different sizes and income would spend on food according to consumption surveys for "normal" food expenditures. To determine household allotments, states relied on federally prepared issuance tables. The tables—one for states in the North and West and one for states in the South—included income groupings and household sizes corresponding to purchase prices and benefit levels. Benefits received by households were based on the cost of purchasing the EFP and included a federally provided "bonus," which was the difference between the price paid for the coupons by the recipient and the true value of the coupons.

The impetus for the current Food Stamp program was provided by a report documenting the existence of severe hunger in many parts of the country. A group of physicians toured economically depressed areas in 1967. The study, *Hunger, U.S.A.* (Citizens' Board of Inquiry, 1968), sponsored by the Field Foundation, uncovered hunger and malnutrition related to poverty. The federal response to this problem ushered in a period of major program reform and expansion during the early 1970s. Amendments to the 1964

act in 1971 (P.L. 91-671) emphasized nutritional improvement objectives. Recipients were to have an "opportunity to obtain a nutritionally adequate diet" (p. 1). A household was expected to contribute no more than 30 percent of its income for the coupons. Prior to this change, the purchase price ranged from 10 percent to over 30 percent of net income.

The 30 percent ceiling on the purchase price represented the intent of Congress that households be charged according to what would be a "reasonable investment" rather than normal expenditures for food. Consequently, the purchase price was reduced for some households and increased for others. The 1971 amendments were also important for introducing national income and resources eligibility standards to replace the various state-established criteria. Equally important, they introduced special deductions from household income, meant to recognize the income-reducing effects of work costs, medical bills, shelter expenses, and the like. The first work registration requirements also were part of the 1971 law: able-bodied people were required to register for and accept suitable employment.

Passage of the 1973 amendments (P.L. 93-86) mandated nationwide implementation of the Food Stamp program. Before this change, food assistance in many areas of the country remained limited to commodity distribution. Congress now signaled a national commitment to provide nutrition assistance chiefly through food stamps.

In 1977, through the Food Stamp Act of 1977 (P.L. 95-113), Congress removed a significant barrier to program participation by eliminating the purchase requirement under which a household was required to pay for a portion of its benefits allotment. Roughly 2.9 million people were added to program rolls within the first year of eliminating this requirement (U.S. House, 1980). It has been estimated that prior to this change, 50 percent of all eligible households simply could not afford food stamps.

In addition to increasing participation, elimination of the purchase requirement made income supplementation a part of the program's focus. Although food stamps were still a means of providing nutrition assistance, dropping the purchase requirement meant that recipients would now receive, in a sense, cash income transfers (that is, the bonus value of the coupons) without having to spend money on stamps. Household income that had been used to purchase program benefits would be freed for other purposes. However, Congress also required that benefits issued would be reduced by an amount equal to 30 percent of all net income. This benefit reduction represented the congressional estimate of the portion of household income that would reasonably be invested in food purchases. As a result, household allotments based on the Thrifty Food Plan were reduced by thirty cents for every dollar of countable (net) income.

The 1977 Food Stamp Act also was significant for provisions intended to tighten eligibility criteria. The act restricted eligibility to households with net incomes below the official poverty line established by the Office of Management and Budget. Congress also streamlined the method for determining income available for buying food. For determining net income, it mandated a standard deduction available to all households, replacing a host of itemized deductions for various living expenses; a combined shelter deduction, available when actual housing and utility costs exceed 50 percent of gross income; and a dependent care deduction for the care of a child or other dependent person. In place of deductions for work-related expenses (transportation, union dues, clothing, and so on), an earnings disregard was instituted. In some instances, these changes reduced household benefits or resulted in terminations, and it is estimated that from 500,000 to 700,000 persons became ineligible and were removed from the program owing to those changes (U.S. House, 1977).

Congress sought to control escalating program costs by imposing a ceiling, or cap, on expenditures, thus ending the true entitlement nature of the program. (An entitlement program provides benefits to people who meet eligibility requirements.) As a result, the Food Stamp program—unlike AFDC or Medicare—receives a yearly appropriation instead of an unlimited grant through budget authority. Therefore, in any fiscal year, spending may not exceed the authorized ceiling without a change in law.

As the program has expanded both in size and cost, it has come under closer scrutiny by elected officials and the general public. Since 1977, reforms have generally been an attempt to better manage an expanding program. Recent legislative changes have further tightened eligibility criteria, stiffened penalties for fraud and abuse, and sought to eliminate waste and inefficiency in program administration (P.L. 97-35, P.L. 97-98, P.L. 97-253, and P.L. 98-204). In 1981 and again in 1983, Congress acted at the urging of the Reagan Administration to make benefits available only to individuals meeting strict income eligibility criteria—net income may not exceed the federal poverty line, and gross income may not exceed 130 percent of that line. To prevent people from receiving more benefits than they are entitled to by falsely claiming not to share food with the people they live with, parents, children, and adult siblings are required to apply as single households. In addition, prison sentences, program disqualification periods, and fines are specified for recipients who misrepresent factors affecting eligibility and benefits.

Amendments to the act in 1981 (P.L. 97-98) established a system to sanction states for errors in issuing benefits. The first error rate liability provisions were part of the 1980 amendments (P.L. 96-249). State performance was measured against a weighted mean that represented the national payment standard error rate. The 1981 amendments required each state to reduce errors to 5 percent by fiscal year 1985 or suffer the withholding of a percentage of the federal payment toward administrative costs. The error rate and sanction system is intended to encourage better state program management and thus reduce overall costs to the federal government.

Another major change occurred in 1981 concerning the Food Stamp program in Puerto Rico. Reacting to the size and expense of the program in Puerto Rico and to charges of mismanagement, Congress replaced food stamps with a nutrition assistance block grant. The block grant funds all food assistance and 50 percent of related administrative costs.

Program Effectiveness

The growth of the Food Stamp program as the nation's primary means of providing nutrition assistance can be viewed in part as testimony to its demonstrated effectiveness. Moreover, the development of the program from commodity distribution to a nutrition and income supplement was shaped by social and cultural factors as much as by political and economic concerns. The Food Stamp program provides aid for the working poor, the unemployed, and the underemployed. It is responsive to changes in household income, because benefits increase as income falls.

In 1977, the Field Foundation sponsored another group of physicians to retrace the steps of their colleagues in 1967. The study 10 years earlier had revealed significant hunger in America. The new study showed that federal food programs, particularly food stamps, had substantially improved the diet and health of poor people. The improvement, according to the investigators, resulted from increased availability of food and not from any improvement in living standards (Kotz, 1979).

Another indication of the program's effectiveness centers on its interaction with other programs designed to meet health and general welfare needs. The Food Stamp program acts as a cushion or equalizer by minimizing the effect of disparities among states in program benefits such as AFDC. For example, food stamp allotments, which vary according to household size and income, are greater in states with low AFDC grants. Food stamps are intended to work in conjunction with other programs to make it possible for low-income families to maintain a standard of living that at least provides for basic needs. There is concern, however, that for most recipients, food stamp benefits—even when combined with AFDC or SSI—are still inadequate.

Since January 1976, food stamp allotments have been based on TFP, which replaced EFP. In *Rodway v. USDA* (1975), the Court found that EFP failed to provide the nutritionally adequate diet mandated by statute. TFP is the least costly diet devised by USDA for a low-income family of four persons (adjusted for households of different sizes). It includes greater quantities of meat, poultry, and fish than EFP and fewer eggs, potatoes, and dried beans. TFP suggests an assortment of foods from 15 food groups that may be used to develop economical and nutritious meals. Critics of TFP claim the plan deviates from normal eating patterns to keep costs within minimum expenditure goals (U.S. Senate, 1985).

A further indication of program effectiveness is the impact on the economy. Food retailers are generally strong supporters of the program. Food stamps make it possible for poor people to buy food even during periods of economic recession. The nearly 22 million people receiving food stamps are a vital part of the retail market and in turn contribute to the health of the agricultural economy. The link between the retail and farming sectors is reflected in the rural-urban coalition in Congress that has traditionally found common ground in the program and worked to help it expand.

Program effectiveness can also be judged by the opportunities it offers for intervention by social workers. Helping a family or individual obtain food assistance frequently presents the social worker with a means of relieving some of the stress caused by economic hardship. Applying for food stamps can be a traumatic and embarrassing experience. Moreover, the stigma associated with food stamps keeps many people from applying until long after the need for assistance is acute. The demise in 1981 of outreach activities, through which states informed low-income households of program benefits and eligibility requirements, may have made this aspect of the social worker's job more difficult.

Future Directions

The future of the Food Stamp program depends largely on the political and economic forces shaping policy decisions. Early in the development of the program, a coalition of rural and urban congressional leaders cast aside their differences in order to enlarge the program. This meant a shift in focus from commodity distribution—a prime concern of the farming industry—to nutrition. The focus on improved nutrition for greater numbers of people served the interests of food producers and retailers. Elected officials, however, are now grappling with shrinking resources and the need to reduce or control rising program costs. In response to a growing federal budget deficit, food stamps must compete with other social welfare programs for scarce resources. As a consequence, the traditional rural-urban coalition for food stamps has been weakened by conflicting demands for benefit enrichment and cost containment. Moreover, considerable negative publicity has arisen from reports of fraud and abuse in the program. Together, the program's bad public image and relatively high cost will figure prominently in the future direction of food assistance policy.

Renewed concerns about hunger in America began to emerge in 1981. These stemmed from the economic recession and high unemployment then current, which worsened the condition of the existing poor and also gave rise to new poor—formerly employed, middle-class households experiencing joblessness for the first time. By the summer of 1983, significant public concern had been aroused by reports indicating an alarming increase in demand for public and private food assistance (Center on Budget, 1983, U.S. Conference of Mayors, 1983). Among the groups investigating allegations of resurging hunger was a task force on food assistance commissioned by President Reagan in August 1983.

The President's task force found no statistical evidence of hunger or malnutrition; however, its report did indicate that hunger exists to the extent that some people do not have enough to eat. The recommendations offered by the task force reflected the difficulty of extending aid in an environment of cost consciousness and suspicion of the potential for fraud, even when a moral obligation to help the poor is felt (President's Task Force, 1984).

The task force's chief proposal was the creation of a food assistance block grant that would allow states to receive a single appropriation, or fixed funding, each year for food assistance. Funding would be based on forecasts of economic conditions, including food prices. States would have the authority to establish eligibility criteria and benefits, thereby replacing national program standards. Critics of the block grant approach, including the states themselves, contend that under a fixed funding scheme, states would be financially unable to respond promptly to increased need. In addition, a block grant would remove current program safeguards designed to meet minimum nutrition needs regardless of state of residence.

A less dramatic alternative would maintain the Food Stamp program structure but make revisions designed to simplify administration and reduce costs through fewer errors. One frequently heard proposal for fine-tuning the program is to make AFDC and food stamps more compatible administratively. Currently, these two programs share a significant caseload but have dissimilar program rules and procedures. Bringing them closer together would involve resolving differences in program definitions (such as what constitutes household income). Once such issues are resolved, proponents of consolidation believe errors could be reduced, leading to more efficient use of staff time through computerization of eligibility determinations and benefit calculations.

Increased attention may also be paid to alternative forms of issuance in order to eliminate as much as possible the opportunity for fraud and theft. Electronic transfer of benefits could eliminate over-the-counter and mail issuance. Under this arrangement, recipients could simply insert magnetic cards into a machine, key in their personal identification numbers, and receive all or a portion of their benefits for the month. To eliminate coupons, use of the "smart card" is an option under consideration. A magnetic card would be inserted into a computer terminal at the grocery checkout and the recipient's benefit account would be reduced by the purchase amount.

Some support exists for eliminating the cap on program expenditures, thus making food stamps a true entitlement. The actual cost of the program in any year is tied to prevailing economic conditions. The cap for a particular year is set in the authorizing legislation, based on projections of funding needs supplied by USDA. However, although Congress imposed the cap as a means of controlling program costs, in reality the cap is effective only to the extent that Congress appropriates less money than the authorized ceiling. All too often, the initial appropriation is insufficient; then, as in 1982, 1983, and 1984, Congress must approve a supplemental appropriation in order to avoid a funding shortfall that would result in a benefit reduction before the end of the fiscal year. Moreover, the supplemental request and approval process is often fraught with delays, creating confusion for clients and administrators. Legislative change may be sought to remove the statutory condition making the program subject to the availability of appropriated funds.

As a way of focusing on the income supplement aspect of food stamps and making the program more like other forms of public assistance, there may be efforts in the future to provide cash instead of coupons. Under a "cash out" approach to food assistance, benefits could be based on national eligibility and allotment formulas. For the recipient, the stigma of using food stamps would be replaced by freedom of choice regarding the best use of household income. Cash out would also simplify program administration by eliminating federal regulations. In addition, it would eliminate the cost of printing and storing food stamps.

In the final analysis, the Food Stamp program has proved generally successful in meeting its stated objective of nutrition supplementation and the unstated goal of income transfer. Future proposals to change the way food assistance is provided will be measured against the current program in terms of nutritional impact, effect on the economy, and benefit equity among recipients. In the long term, such issues will probably overshadow concerns about reducing administrative complexity and cost. After 20 years, the notion that hunger should be alleviated even though its root cause—poverty—remains is an integral part of U.S. social policy.

ELLEN M. WELLS

For further information, see AID TO FAMILIES WITH DEPENDENT CHILDREN; FEDERAL SOCIAL LEGISLATION SINCE 1961; HUNGER AND MALNUTRITION; POVERTY; SOCIAL WELFARE FINANCING; SOCIAL WELFARE POLICY: TRENDS AND ISSUES.

References

Center on Budget and Policy Priorities. (1983). *Soup Lines and Food Baskets: A Survey of Increased Participation in Emergency Food Programs.*

Citizens' Board of Inquiry into Hunger and Malnutrition in the United States. (1968). *Hunger U.S.A.* Washington, D.C.: New Community Press.

Kotz, N. (1979). *Hunger in America: The Federal Response.* New York: Field Foundation.

Physicians' Task Force on Hunger in America. (1985). *Hunger in America--the Growing Epidemic.* Cambridge, Mass.: Harvard University School of Public Health.

President's Task Force on Food Assistance. (1984). *Report.* Washington, D.C.: U.S. Government Printing Office.

Rodway v. USDA. (1975). 514 F. 2d (D.C.).

U.S. Conference of Mayors. (1983). *Hunger in American Cities: Eight Case Studies.* Washington, D.C.: Author.

U.S. Department of Agriculture Food and Nutrition Service. (1984a). *Characteristics of Food Stamp Households: August 1981.* Alexandria, Va.: Author.

U.S. Department of Agriculture Food and Nutrition Service. (1984b). *The Food Stamp Program.* Alexandria, Va.: Author.

U.S. House. (1977). *Food Stamp Act of 1977: Report on H.R. 7940* (H. Rpt. 95-464). Washington, D.C.: U.S. Government Printing Office.

U.S. House. (1980). *Food Stamp Act of 1980: Report on S. 1309* (H. Rpt. 96-788). Washington, D.C.: U.S. Government Printing Office.

U.S. Senate Committee on Agriculture, Nutrition, and Forestry. (1985). *The Food Stamp Program: History, Description, Issues, and Options* (S. Rpt. 99-32). Washington, D.C.: U.S. Government Printing Office.

FOSTER CARE FOR ADULTS

Community care, personal care homes, board and care homes, and family care homes are among the many foster care programs for adults. However, although there is no single definition of adult foster care, most definitions have some components in common.

1. Care is provided in a private home in which the primary caregiver (a nonrelative) resides.

2. In exchange for financial remuneration, the caregiver provides room and board, also providing supervision, assisting with the tasks of daily living, administering medications or treatment, and acting as patient advocate.

3. The home is small enough to create a familylike environment.

4. Some supervision and monitoring is provided by the professional staff of the agency that administers the program.

There is a wide variation in the definition of all components of care but the first. For example, the number of residents in each home varies. Some programs include homes that serve only one resident, others serve from 2 to 4 residents and still others include homes with 10 or even 20 residents.

The nature of the caregivers' responsibility is rarely specified. Many programs provide no training for caregivers, and others train caregivers to provide skilled nursing care. The frequency of staff monitoring is equally variable. In some programs, staff members visit homes on a weekly basis, but monthly visits are more commonly required. In a 1-year period, about half the caregivers in a New York State program were visited by staff members fewer than three times a year (Sherman & Newman, 1979).

Steinhauer (1982) suggests that in a prototype adult foster care program, the core services of all programs should include recruiting and inspecting homes, matching, monitoring and supervision, and coordinating medical and social services as well as respite care services and mechanisms for the emergency placement of clients. Beyond these core services, foster home programs for adults should coordinate with existing agencies to provide transportation, meals, home health care, day care, counseling, and physical therapy.

Adult foster homes serve primarily three populations: the mentally ill, many of whom are placed following institutionalization; the mentally retarded; and the frail elderly. Although programs for the mentally ill are the oldest and the most predominant, programs for the frail elderly can be expected to expand rapidly as this population mushrooms in the coming decades.

Adult foster homes lie on a continuum between institutional care and in-home care. They are especially suited to those who cannot live independently and who lack family resources. Certain individuals such as those who require extensive care, those who exhibit violent or abusive behavior, and those who need more than one caregiver (for example, the obese bedbound), are not good candidates for foster care.

Adults in foster care benefit primarily from the small, familylike atmosphere of the foster home. Such an atmosphere—unlike that of an institution—creates a more normal living environment, allows for individualized care, fosters individuality and self-esteem, enables integration into the neighborhood and the community, and provides easy access to existing family members. Another benefit of foster care is that its cost is probably lower than that of institutional care. Finally, foster

homes have been easily accepted by neighbors, which has not always been the case with other community-based alternatives to institutionalization.

The number of people living in adult foster homes can only be estimated. "Official" statistics generally underestimate the total because they exclude unknown members of this population who have informal care arrangements with neighbors, landlords, friends, or boarding home operators. McCoin (1983) estimates that there are about 50,000 adults in state and local foster care programs and an additional 12,000 to 15,000 in the Veterans Administration (VA) program. Of those in state and local programs, more than 50 percent are mentally ill, only 10 percent are mentally retarded, and about 20 percent are dependent elderly people. Other adults in foster care cannot be easily classified because they fall into multiple categories—for example, mentally ill and elderly. Although the number of adult foster care programs has tripled since 1960, they remain relatively unknown, and they are unavailable in many parts of the United States.

History

The idea of the adult foster home is said to have originated in Gheel, Belgium, where the mentally ill have historically been placed in homes in the community. In this rural area, the residents contribute to the foster family by helping out with farm chores.

In the United States, early foster home programs for mental patients were started after Dorothea Dix returned from a visit to Scotland, where mental hospitals placed some of their patients with families in surrounding communities. Massachusetts first placed mental patients in private homes in 1882. Another early program was that initiated in 1916 by the Springfield State Hospital in Maryland.

However, not until the depression years did states begin to establish foster home programs for adults on a large scale. New York created a program in 1935, and by 1959, 17 states had programs. This number had grown to 23 by 1965, and it was estimated that there were 17,292 residents in foster homes by 1963 (Morrissey, 1967). The size of the programs varied widely by state. In 1965, seven states housed 83 percent of foster home residents. Since the 1960s, foster care for the mentally ill and the mentally retarded has expanded rapidly in response to the de-institutionalization movement.

Foster care for the aged is a relatively new development. In 1967, a demonstration program was authorized by the Department of Health, Education, and Welfare under Section 1115 of Title XI of the Social Security Act (Fenske & Roecker, 1971). This program sponsored foster homes for the aged in three cities in Washington State: Pasco, Seattle, and Tacoma. Since that time, many public welfare departments have developed foster home programs for the aged. In addition, several hospitals have recently developed foster home programs as an alternative to nursing home care for elderly patients who are discharged from the acute setting. In contrast to programs for the mentally ill and retarded, programs for the elderly attempt to prevent or postpone institutionalization rather than serve as a stepping-stone from institution to independent living.

The VA has the only national adult foster care program. It began placing mental patients in foster homes in 1951, opening foster homes to medical and surgical patients in 1962. Between 12,000 and 15,000 people are in VA-operated adult foster homes at any given time. Of these, 7,000 are estimated to be elderly.

Caregivers

One question frequently asked by those not familiar with adult foster care is: "Who would become a caregiver?" Most caregivers are middle-aged women, many of whom are married. The majority are high school graduates who have had previous experience in a caregiving role, such as that of nurse or nurse's aide. Most caregivers indicate that their primary reasons for becoming caregivers are altruistic, although family-related reasons also appear to be important. Some caregivers want to continue playing a nurturing role after their children are grown; others—especially widows—use the program to combat loneliness.

Well-established programs report that the best caregivers are those who are flexible and tolerant. Those who are too rigid, or authoritarian, and those who are motivated primarily by financial remuneration are likely to fail as caregivers.

Standards and Licensing

There are no uniform licensing criteria for adult foster homes. Adult foster home programs are administered by a variety of federal, state, and private agencies, each of which sets its own standards. Even within a single agency, standards often vary by locality. The VA, for example, has no uniform national policy. Other agencies that administer adult foster home programs include state departments of mental hygiene, state departments of mental retardation, and state and local departments of social services. Smaller programs are administered by private social agencies and, in recent years, by hospitals.

The setting of standards in programs that serve primarily recipients of Supplemental Security Income (SSI) was encouraged by the passage in 1976 of the Keyes Amendment (P.L. 94-566, Section 505d). This legislation grew out of concern that the SSI program was being used to fund substandard living facilities. It required states or local authorities to establish standards for community residences in which a number of SSI recipients resided. These standards were to be made a part of the State's Title XX plan. However, no federal role was established to review standards or to enforce the legislation.

In general, all programs set standards for food, sanitation, and for the basic safety and civil rights of residents. Licensed programs may set additional standards, such as those for medication control, record keeping, training of caregivers, and regular physical examinations for residents.

Ideally, authorities should be able to set standards for homes, to inspect homes for the purpose of licensing, to monitor homes, and to enforce standards in the face of violations. However, few agencies incorporate all these steps: some have inspection but no monitoring, and others have monitoring but no enforcement. Progress in this area has been slow partly because of the concern that adult foster home programs may become overregulated. Overregulation could stymie the development of programs by proving costly and limiting the number of eligible caregivers. The issue of how much regulation should be built in poses a dilemma for those eager to expand adult foster care. If adequate regulation is not built in, agencies and funders worry about liability, abuse, and scandal. However, when more regulation is imposed, caregivers object to strangers inspecting their homes and requiring, for example, safety devices that make homes appear more like institutions.

Financing

There is no single funding source for adult foster care. In general, the caregiver is paid directly out of resident's personal resources—often SSI benefits or, in the case of VA programs, veterans' pensions. The cost of care for residents with inadequate incomes is often supplemented by the sponsoring agency, which also covers administrative expenses, such as staff salaries. A few programs are limited to those residents who can pay a monthly fee that covers the caregiver's remuneration and administrative costs.

The amount paid to the caregiver varies from program to program. In general, it ranges from about $200 to $700 a month for each resident. Some programs pay more for residents with intensive caregiving needs. Most foster home programs allow the resident to keep between $25 and $75 a month for personal expenses. Although little has been published about the staffing and administrative costs of these programs, a rough estimate can be obtained by doubling the monthly payments a caregiver receives from each resident. Thus, a program in which a caregiver's monthly payment averages $300 might cost a total of $600 a month to operate.

In recent years, hospital-based programs in Boston, Baltimore, and Honolulu have received payments from Medicaid to cover caregivers' fees, staff salaries, residents' personal care, and housekeeping and case management services for residents who are Medicaid recipients.

Trends and Issues

One important trend has been the continued expansion of adult foster care programs to serve varied populations. Programs that once served only the mentally ill have expanded to include the mentally retarded and the frail elderly. Other developments include the establishment of hospital-based programs to serve those in need of skilled nursing care, as well as the creation of programs for those who do not fit the narrow confines of categorical eligibility. Privately funded programs are available in some areas, so that programs are not limited to the elderly

poor. Although foster homes were once used to care for those who were able to move out of institutions, they are now instrumental in preventing or postponing institutionalization.

There is also a trend toward higher standards in adult foster home programs. The level of payment is rising, and caregivers are beginning to see themselves as part of the treatment team rather than people doing volunteer work—a view fostered by increasing levels of caregiver training. Perhaps in the future organizations of foster home caregivers will develop, which will push to professionalize their members' role.

As the concept of level of care moves from long-term care into the broader health and social service systems, adult foster care programs will have to address several critical issues. For example, should homes (or programs) be certified for a certain level of care, necessitating a different type of patient, a different caregiver with different training, and a different payment structure? Should homes (and programs) be mixed, providing the opportunity for stability in the home even if the patient's condition deteriorates or improves? Another question, already coming up in relation to programs run by state social services departments, is whether residents with different disabilities should be housed together.

Research Findings

There has been surprisingly little research on adult foster care. Considering the numbers of people placed in care and the number of years the programs have been in existence, even the most basic descriptive information—how many are in care and data on their age, sex, and functional level—is sketchy at best. The absence of central administration makes such research difficult to carry out. For example, what steps should be taken in developing a sampling frame? Lack of funding earmarked for research has also been a significant factor.

Descriptive Studies. Only one national survey of adult foster care has been completed in the last decade (McCoin, 1983), but several descriptive surveys of programs based primarily in New York State have been conducted (Mor, Gutkin, & Seltzer, 1980; Sherman & Newman, 1977, 1979; Willer & Intagliata, 1984). Most studies have found that foster care residents are well integrated into their families, neighborhoods, and communities (Mor, Gutkin, & Seltzer, 1980; Sherman & Newman, 1977; Willer & Intagliata, 1984). Some studies revealed low levels of supervision and training for caregivers (Sherman & Newman, 1977, 1979), and others reported that programs failed when residents found family life too confining or experienced rejection after caregivers left the program and when caregivers experienced burnout (McCoin, 1983). Research has also pointed to social isolation among residents in rural areas or areas with limited community resources—for example, lack of transportation (Oktay & Volland, 1981; Sherman & Newman, 1977; Willer & Intagliata, 1984).

Evaluative Research. Linn et al. (1977) used an experimental design to compare foster home care and continued hospital-based care in a population of 572 VA psychiatric patients. Patients were randomly assigned to one of the two care settings and were tested on several measures before placement, at placement, and 4 months after placement. Findings revealed that 73 percent of the patients were still in foster care homes after 4 months. The patients in foster homes did better on scales of social functioning and adjustment than did the hospitalized patients; the two groups showed no significant differences in mood. A follow-up study (Linn, Klett, & Caffey, 1980) analyzed the characteristics of foster homes associated with more positive outcomes. The results indicated that those in small homes, in homes with few residents, and in homes with children improved most in social functioning.

In Honolulu and Baltimore, programs for the frail elderly who are placed in foster homes following hospitalization have found that these patients do as well as those in nursing homes in activities of daily living and mental status; however, the findings are contradictory with respect to the effect on attitude or morale.

Role of Social Work

Social work agencies and departments have been instrumental in the initiation of many adult foster care programs. It is social workers who perform the key services of selecting homes, organizing training programs, matching residents and caregivers, monitoring the homes, providing for respite care, coordinating community services, arranging finances, and handling emergencies. Social work skills in assessment, family counseling, home visiting, coordination of services, case management, advocacy, and administration are all well suited to foster home programs. The conceptual model of person-environment fit is extremely helpful in adult foster care because the key to a program's success is its ability to achieve a good fit between the needs of residents and the environments of foster homes.

JULIANNE S. OTKAY

For further information, see AGED; AGED: SERVICES; DEINSTITUTIONALIZATION; PROTECTIVE SERVICES FOR THE AGED.

References

Fenske, V., & Roecker, M. (1971). "Finding Foster Homes for Adults." *Public Welfare, 29*(4), 404–410.

Linn, M. W., et al. (1977). "Hospital vs. Community (Foster) Care for Psychiatric Patients." *Archives of General Psychiatry, 34*(1), 78–83.

Linn, M. W., Klett, C. J., & Caffey, E. M., Jr. (1980). "Foster Home Characteristics and Psychiatric Patient Outcome." *Archives of General Psychiatry, 37*(2), 129–132.

McCoin, J. M. (1983). *Adult Foster Homes: Their Managers and Residents*. New York: Human Sciences Press.

Miller, M. C. (1977). "A Program for Adult Foster Care." *Social Work, 22*(4), 275–279.

Mor, V., Gutkin, C., & Seltzer, M. (1980, October). *Integration of the Dependent Aged into the Family Life of Personal Care Homes*. Paper presented at the thirty-third annual scientific meeting of the Gerontological Society of America, San Diego, Calif.

Morrissey, J. R. (1967). *The Case of Family Care for the Mentally Ill*. New York: Behavioral Publications.

Oktay, J. S., & Volland, P. J. (1981). "Community Care Program for the Elderly." *Health and Social Work, 6*(2), 41–47.

Sherman, S. R., & Newman, E. S. (1977). "Foster-Family Care for the Elderly in New York State." *The Gerontologist, 17*(6), 513–520.

Sherman, S. R., & Newman, E. S. (1979). "Role of the Caseworker in Adult Foster Care." *Social Work, 24*(4), 324–328.

Steinhauer, M. (1982). "Geriatric Foster Care—A Prototype: Design and Implementation Issues." *The Gerontologist, 22*(3), 293–300.

Willer, B., & Intagliata, J. (1984). *Promises and Realities for Mentally Retarded Citizens*. Baltimore, Md.: University Park Press.

FOSTER CARE FOR CHILDREN

Foster care refers to full-time, substitute care of children outside their own homes. All states operate foster care programs as one type of child welfare service. Substitute care may be provided directly by the state's public welfare agency, purchased by the state from a voluntary agency's foster care program, or both. Foster caretakers may be related or unrelated adults other than a child's biological parents. Foster care of children occurs in family homes, group homes, and institutions. The focus of this article is on foster family care.

History

Societies have evolved ways of caring for children whose families would not or could not provide for them. Methods of providing care have ranged from the ancient Jewish practice of placing orphaned children in family homes to the development, after the century, of institutional care; they have included the practice of binding out children under indenture contracts and placement in free foster care in family homes.

The early American colonies adopted the English practice of indenture, or the binding out of orphaned, destitute, or neglected children. Indenture contracts required that children serve as apprentices and servants during their minority. The family was obliged to provide the basic necessities of life and to teach a craft or trade to the child. Indenture provided the young person with a family identity and a skill, the family obtained needed labor, and the practice took the poor off the town rolls. Institutional care was used only when Indian massacres, natural disasters, or epidemics created homeless orphans in large numbers (Bremner et al., 1970, p. 29).

As a result of a diminished need for the labor of very young people, the late 18th and early 19th centuries saw changes in the methods of caring for dependent children. Although binding out was still preferred, the age at which children were indentured began to increase. The early practice of binding out infants was extended, and children came to be maintained as public charges until the age of 8 to 12. At the same time, the practice of outdoor relief (noninstitutional care) came under severe criticism as conviction grew

that it increased pauperism. In the 19th century, in the face of increased use of nonsegregated almshouses for children and adults, separate institutions and private orphans' asylums for children were established. This followed investigative reports that detailed the deplorable conditions under which children were living in almshouses.

In the mid-1850s, a new and significant pattern of caring for dependent children began when Charles Loring Brace of the New York Children's Aid Society pioneered the development of free foster homes. Brace, like others before him, believed in the importance of removing children from the evil influences found in cities. Unlike his contemporaries, he did not see merit in placing children in institutions and favored instead a method of sending children West to be placed with farm families. Like the indenture system that preceded it, Brace's system was based on economic considerations: the child's labor was exchanged for their care. There was no indenture contract, however, and custody was retained by the New York Children's Aid Society, theoretically permitting the removal of the child.

There was opposition to Brace's system. Charity workers rejected Brace's approach, citing the lack of supervision of children and noting that the youngsters were overworked, uneducated, and poorly fed and clothed. The Catholic Church charged that Protestant organizations were drawing children away from their religious heritage. Opposition also came from poor families who did not want their children taken away and from the Western states, which began to resist the practice of "scattering thousands of needy children within their borders" (Trattner, 1974, p. 104).

Whatever the problems in Brace's system, he firmly established the principle of free foster care and the preference for placement in a family setting. His work led to the practice of free foster care and of placing youngsters in family homes in their own states. By the turn of the century, free foster home care and institutional placement were firmly established as the principal methods of providing care for dependent children.

Children and Their Families

Since 1977 a number of reports have described the population served by agencies providing foster care. The data differ from one report to another as a result of varying definitions of the foster care population and different sampling techniques (for a review, see Tatara & Pettiford, 1983). The description of the children in foster care and their families that is presented here follows the most recent data gathered by the American Public Welfare Association (APWA) (Tatara & Pettiford, 1985, pp. 23–76). In a national survey, the APWA asked public child care agencies to describe all children in their care in 1983, regardless of whether the children were receiving services directly or through purchase of service agreements from voluntary agencies. Where appropriate, the following discussion compares these data with information gathered by APWA describing children in care in 1981–82 as well as with data gathered in 1977 [Shyne & Schroeder, 1978].

Use of Foster Care. There were about 251,000 children living in substitute care arrangements in 1983.[1] The national prevalence rate is approximately 3.7 children in care for every 1,000 children under 20 years of age. Thirty-eight states provided detailed information about the living arrangements of children in substitute care. Almost 70 percent were in foster family homes or "nonfinalized" adoptive homes; 5.1 percent were receiving postplacement services in their own homes; 8.9 percent were in group homes; 1.5 percent in emergency shelters; 10.3 percent in child care facilities such as residential treatment settings; 0.9 percent in independent living situations; and 3.8 percent in unspecified living arrangements.

The number of children living in substitute care has decreased significantly from the 1977 figure of 500,000. This is probably a result of the emphasis on providing services to children in their own homes and the imperative that permanent homes be found for

children in substitute care. The rate of decrease was greatest in the years 1977–79, when about 40 percent of the total decrease occurred. The rate slowed down to 10 percent between 1979 and 1982. In 1983, 184,000 children entered care and 178,000 were discharged, resulting in a net increase of 2.3 percent.[2] In all, 447,000 children were served in the substitute care system in 1983.

The age of children in substitute care is increasing. The median age in 1977 was 10.8 years compared to 12.6 years in 1983. In 1983, 3.3 percent of children were less than 1 year of age (compared to 2 percent in 1977), 20.2 percent were between the ages of 1 and 5, and 27.9 percent were aged 6 to 12. (Different categories were used in 1977, precluding direct comparisons. In 1977, 32 percent of children were aged 1 to 6 and 22 percent were between 7 and 10 years of age.) In 1983, 45.3 percent of children were aged 13 to 18. Forty-three percent of the 1977 sample were between the ages of 11 and 17. Three percent of children were more than 19 in 1983. Age was unknown in 0.2 percent of cases. These data must be qualified because they were provided by only 30 states, accounting for 61.8 percent of the population of children in care.

Females represent 47 percent of the foster care population and males 53 percent, which is a similar ratio to that found in 1977. In 1983, 52.7 percent of the children were white (down from a 1977 figure of 62 percent), 33.9 percent were black (an increase from 1977, when black children constituted 28 percent of the foster care population), 7.3 percent were Hispanic (similar to 1977 figures), and about 4.8 percent of children were categorized as "other." Race or ethnicity was unknown for 1.3 percent of the children.

Legal Custody of Children in Care. Twenty-six states provided data on children's legal custody, accounting for about 40 percent of the children in care in 1983. Seventy-nine percent of these children had court-

---

[1] Two-thirds of the states reporting included children in nonfinalized adoptive homes as part of the substitute care population, but the number of children involved was not reported. An additional 12,000 children who were receiving in-home postplacement services were included as part of the substitute care population by 15 states. When the latter population is included, the total number of children in substitute care increases to 263,000.

[2] Approximately 75 percent of the children entering care were new entrants, defined as not having been placed in the preceding 12 months. The remaining 25 percent reentered care within a year of discharge. These data must be viewed with caution because most of the 10 states with the highest substitute care populations did not report this information.

ordered placement without termination of parental rights, and an additional 11.2 percent were placed under court order with parental rights terminated. For 5.8 percent of children, custody remained with parents or other authorized persons (these children had been placed on a voluntary basis), and 1 percent had been placed voluntarily with parental rights terminated. Custody arrangements were described as "other" for 2.3 percent and as unknown for 0.5 percent.

Children's Disabilities. Twenty-four states, accounting for 52.8 percent of children, reported data describing children's disabilities. Most children (75.6 percent) had no known disabilities, 22.3 percent were reported as having one or more disabling conditions, and for 2.1 percent this information was unknown or unreported.

Number of Placements. Only 18 states, accounting for 39.3 percent of the children in care in 1983 reported the number of placements. For slightly less than half of the children (45.8 percent), their current placement was their only placement. A total of 53.1 percent had been in multiple placements, 20.1 percent having been placed two times, 24.2 percent three to five times, and 8.8 percent six or more times. This information was not available for 1.1 percent of the children. The percentage of children experiencing multiple placements increased from 1982 (when approximately 43 percent experienced changes in care facility) and from 1977 (when 47 percent of children had more than one placement).

Length of Time in Care. Twenty-seven states accounting for 57.9 percent of the population of children in care provided data on this subject. The median length of time in continuous substitute care (approximately 18 months) was less than the 1977 median of 29 months. Twenty-two percent of children were in care 6 months or less, 15.2 percent 6 months to 1 year, 19.5 percent 1 to 2 years, 22 percent 2 to 5 years, and 18.2 percent were in continuous care 5 years or more. In 1977, 20 percent of children had been in care from 25 to 48 months, 11 percent from 49 to 72 months, and 23 percent for 73 months or more. Length of time in placement was not

known for 2.4 percent of the children on whom data was reported to APWA.

Entry into Foster Care. Children may be placed in foster care voluntarily through a contract between a parent and child care agency either under a voluntary contract that is ratified by the court or involuntarily by court order. A 1983 study that compared the use of voluntary and court-ordered placements (Yoshikami & Emlen, 1983) reported the following: Nationally, 73.5 percent of children are in care under court order, 25.5 percent on a voluntary basis. Children placed voluntarily tend to be younger than those placed under court order (under 6 years of age as opposed to over 12). Family conflicts or family conditions such as parental absence, financial hardship, illness, disability, or substance abuse of a parent or child occasion most voluntary placements. Involuntary placements are most often caused by child abuse or neglect.

Although voluntary and court-ordered placements differ in their legal authority, they are not different in the "degree to which they reflect parental choice" (Yoshikami & Emlen, p. xiv). Many voluntary placements are coerced or strongly influenced whereas many placements arranged through the court are initiated by members of the child's family who support such placements. Regardless of the voluntary or involuntary nature of the placement, most tend to occur in a state of emergency. Placement was the service sought by many parents and the service offered by the agency. As such, preplacement services were not in heavy demand and were not even a practical possibility in many instances when the child was already out of the home by the time the agency became involved.

Services were routinely provided subsequent to placement, and parents were pleased with the services they received— which were oriented toward achievement of permanency goals. There was no difference in the level of effort directed toward family reunification on the basis of whether the placement was voluntary or court ordered.

Reason for Entry into Care. Twenty-four states, accounting for 51 percent of the substitute care population provided data on this subject. About 56 percent of children were in care for protective service reasons, 7.9 percent were status offenders, 2.6 percent were placed because of disabilities or handicaps, 21.5 percent because of parental condition or absence, 2 percent were placed following relinquishment of parental rights, and 5.7 percent for other state-defined reasons. For 4.6 percent of children, the reason for placement was not known.

For several reasons, it is difficult to make comparisons across studies concerning the reason for entry into care. First, the lack of commonly accepted typologies for problem classification is of major concern. For example, the response categories reported by APWA for 1981–82 included only conduct or condition of the child's caretaker and conduct or condition of the child. In 1977, Shyne and Schroeder reported categories of abandonment, unwillingness to care for children, and conflict in parent-child relationships—none of which are cited as reasons for placement in the APWA report.

A second problem is that there are no rules for classifying problems in any given way even when common typologies are used. Thus, one cannot assume that problems classified as neglect in one study are comparable to those in other studies using the same classification. Also, some classification schemes do not distinguish between cause and effect. For example, there are data showing that voluntary placements are occasioned by financial hardship, illness, disability, or substance abuse, whereas abuse and neglect are cited as leading to court-ordered placements. The situations or conditions cited as reasons for voluntary placement are often reported as causes of abuse and neglect. The question is, What are the conditions under which the reason for placement would be cited as mental illness rather than abuse or vice versa?

Whether children enter placement voluntarily or under court order might explain some of the differences in categories. Because the law gives the courts jurisdiction over neglected and abused children, and because these categories are vague and subject to broad interpretation, it may be easier to have a petition for placement sustained when the reasons are general. For charges such as mental illness, confirming evidence may be difficult to obtain. The use of different theoretical frameworks by persons conducting assessment may further clarify differences in problem classification.

Permanency Plans. In 1977, case plans existed for 69 percent of the children in care. APWA reports that 31 states, representing 67.9 percent of the substitute care population, reported that there were plans for 89.9 percent of the children. In descending order of frequency, the plans reported were: return to parents, relatives, or other caretakers (46.6 percent), long-term foster care (18.4 percent), adoption (14.7 percent), and independent living or emancipation (10.2 percent). No goal other than care and protection was reported for 5.6 percent of children. For 4.5 percent, the planning goal was unknown.

The Policy Framework

Federal policy has a significant effect on state actions on behalf of dependent, neglected, and abused children. The Adoption Assistance and Child Welfare Act of 1980 (P.L. 96-272) is the major federal policy affecting children in substitute care. This section of the article begins with a brief description of the policies replaced or modified by P.L. 96-272 and identifies the problems in the child welfare system that gave rise to passage of the new law. It then reviews the provisions of the new law as they affect children in substitute care.

The AFDC Foster Care Program. In 1961, Title IV-A of the Social Security Act authorized the Aid to Families with Dependent Children (AFDC) program to provide federal funds for the care of children in out-of-home placement. To prevent the arbitrary removal of children from the care of their biological families, AFDC funds could be used for placement only in the event of a judicial determination that remaining at home was counter to the child's welfare. In the late 1970s, just prior to passage of P.L. 96-272, 100,000 children (20 percent of the 500,000 estimated to be in care) were supported by AFDC–Foster Care monies (Knitzer, Allen, & McGowan, 1978). States that were heavily dependent on these funds had no incentive to move children out of foster care because funding was lost each time a child was discharged from placement.

The Child Welfare Services Program.

Initially authorized in 1935 under Title V of the Social Security Act, the Child Welfare Services Program had its authorization changed to Title IV-B in 1967. The program's original emphasis was to facilitate the development of child welfare services in rural areas. This was changed and the scope of the program was broadened in 1962 when funds were made available for any social service necessary to promote the well-being of all children, not just services for homeless, dependent, and neglected children.

Title IV-B has always been underfunded, precluding fulfillment of its promise of making child welfare services available to all families regardless of income. In 1982, Title IV-B funds accounted for only 5 percent of the states' funds for child welfare services (other sources of funding were Title XX [30 percent]; Title IV-E/A [9 percent]; state, local, and private sources [53 percent]; and other [3 percent]) (Koshel & Kimmich, 1983).

The Problem.

The assumption underpinning the AFDC foster care program was that out-of-home placement was a temporary arrangement. Plans were to be developed to ensure that each child received proper care and that services were provided to improve the conditions in the child's home or to make possible placing the child in the home of a relative. The foster care system was not serving children in this manner.

In 1959, Maas and Engler published their seminal study "Children in Need of Parents," which described the status of children in out-of-home placement. The findings from their investigation were reinforced by a series of studies conducted over the next two decades (for review, see Stein, Gambrill, & Wiltse, 1978). In summary, those studies showed that many children entered foster care easily, with little consideration to provision of services that might have permitted them to remain in their own homes. Foster care, rather than a temporary arrangement, was long term for a majority of the children— 29 percent were in care for up to one year, 36 percent for one to four years; and 34 percent for 4 years or more (Shyne & Schroeder, 1978). Although federal law required case plans for each child, planning was the exception. In various states, the percentage of children with no plans ranged from a low of

13 percent to a high of 77 percent. Moreover, services to biological parents that might have facilitated the child's return home and that were necessary for alternative forms of planning such as adoption were not being provided. Parental visiting of children in care was not encouraged.

The identified problems went beyond matters related to the provision of direct services to embrace the child-caring system in all its facets. Many states did not know how many children they had in care nor where the children were placed. Regularly scheduled case review was the exception, and when it did occur, it often consisted of little more than a rubber-stamping procedure. State laws made termination of parental rights difficult if not impossible. As already noted, the fiscal arrangements between the federal government and the states provided funds only so long as children remained in care and thus offered no incentive to the states to take action to return children to their families of origin or to make alternative permanent plans.

In the early 1970s, several research and demonstration projects were undertaken whose goal it was to identify and remove barriers to adoption (Emlen et al., 1977), to develop methods for involving biological parents in case planning (Stein, Gambrill, & Wiltse, 1978), and to offer intensive services to prevent placement and to facilitate early reunification (Jones, Neuman, & Shyne, 1976; Stein, Gambrill, & Wiltse, 1978). These projects, which collectively came to be known as permanency-planning projects, showed that the provision of intensive services to a child's birth parents and the development of goal-oriented, written case plans and assertive casework could facilitate family reunification and other forms of permanent planning for children. The procedures developed in these projects influenced the content of federal and state policies and child welfare practice. There has been extensive dissemination to the field through the publication of training manuals and through in-service training programs (for review, see Downs et al., 1981; United States Children's Bureau, 1979).

The Adoption Assistance and Child Welfare Act.

Signed into law in June 1980, this legislation (P.L. 96-272) addresses matters that pertain to both the entry and exit of children from care. It includes measures to stop the drift that characterized the tenure of many children in placement. The law requires that states know what is happening to children in their care, and it redefines the relationship between federal and state government with respect to children at risk of placement and those already in care. This is accomplished mainly through a fiscal restructuring that offers states incentives to accomplish the goals of the act. P.L. 96-272 replaces the AFDC–Foster Care program, formerly authorized under Title IV-A of the Social Security Act, with a new Title IV-E. Title IV-B Child Welfare Services was amended.

Federal Payments for Adoption Assistance and Foster Care. Title IV-E funds are available to the states for foster care for AFDC eligible children and for adoption subsidies for AFDC and SSI eligible children who have special needs. Children who receive federally reimbursed subsidies are automatically eligible for Medicaid. For the first time, federal funds are available for preventive services. States must make reasonable efforts to prevent placement and to provide reunification services as a condition for Title IV-E funding. If children enter care through a court proceeding, the court must determine whether reasonable efforts to prevent placement have been made. State plans for foster care and adoption assistance must be approved by the Department of Health and Human Services.

Title IV-B. Although authorized for general child welfare services, Title IV-B funds have been used mainly to pay for the cost of maintaining children in care. Seventy-five percent of the states' Title IV-B funds had been used for this purpose (Calhoun, 1980). To constrain this practice, P.L. 96-272 limits the amount of IV-B monies that states can use for foster care room and board to each state's specified share of the $56.5 million appropriated by Congress in 1979. The new law stipulates that any increase in funds over the $56.5 million must be used for preventive and reunification services. Eligibility for increased IV-B funding was made contingent on the development and implementation of programs directed toward permanency.

The new law creates linkages between

IV-E and IV-B funding. States are allowed to transfer unused maintenance funds provided under IV-E to IV-B service programs if they cap their federal foster care program and if they implement the IV-B protections required by law. The capping provision was intended to reduce agency investment in foster care maintenance and to promote the development of prevention, reunification, and other permanency services. The ceiling on IV-E funds, however, could be imposed only if the states were provided the means for developing their service delivery capacity through sufficient funding of the IV-B program. Once the appropriation level for IV-B reached $266 million for two consecutive years, states were required to cap their foster care program and to implement a preventive service program to help children remain with their families in order to receive in excess of their share of $56.5 million. Appropriations reached the required level in 1981. Specific elements of the new law require:

1. *Written case plans* that must describe the type and appropriateness of the placement and services to be provided and the plan for achieving permanence for each child. Placement, moreover, must be in the least restrictive, most familylike setting in close proximity to the home of biological parents.

2. *Case review* must occur every 6 months. Review may be under court auspices, or it may be an administrative review. If agencies chose the latter, the review panel must contain at least one person who is not responsible for the case management of, or the delivery of services to, the child or parents. Review hearings must be open to the participation of the child's parents. There must be a dispositional review no later than 18 months subsequent to the child's placement and periodically thereafter.

3. *A one-time inventory* of all children in care for 6 months or more must be conducted. States must establish statewide information systems that contain data describing the demographic characteristics of the children, their status, and their permanent plans.

4. *Fair hearings* must be available to appeal the denial of the benefits or services offered under the act.

5. *Reunification, prevention, and adoption subsidy programs* must be in place.

6. *Voluntary placements* will be eligible

for reimbursement for the first time, permitting federal funds to be used for services to families without a court order for placement.

Services in Foster Care Programs

The goals of foster care programs are realized through the provision of services to children and to their biological and foster families. Services may focus mainly on the child whose special needs require interventions by physicians, social workers, and educators; on a biological parent or parents who require professional assistance to solve problems; or on the family unit, as is the case when family counseling is required to resolve parent-child problems. Some services, such as therapeutic day care, offer parents respite from ongoing child care, allowing them time off to work on personal problems while the service provides treatment for their children. Services to foster parents may include training in child management, direct intervention in the foster home to resolve difficulties that emerge between the foster caretaker and the child, and adoption-related services for those foster parents who adopt the children for whom they have provided care.

In keeping with the family reunification focus of foster care programs, the bulk of services should be directed toward the child and biological family to help them resolve the difficulties that necessitated placement. The brief review that follows is concerned with the services that may be offered to resolve the problems of a child's birth family. Before beginning the review, two caveats are in order. First, the reader should bear in mind that foster care, in addition to being a program, is also a service. This is illustrated by its use to provide temporary child care when a single parent, who has no personal resources for child care, must enter the hospital for surgery. Second, hard services such as cash, medical assistance, and housing assistance are significant to a majority of families served by public agencies. These programs are not included in this review because, unlike services such as homemakers or counseling, which may be used for multiple purposes and whose use may require a complex decision-making process, the reasons for offering hard services are straightforward and their value to clients is more generally known than is the case with the "softer" services.

Case Management Services. Most families receiving child welfare services have diverse problems whose resolution requires assistance from multiple providers. Attorneys, medical personnel, psychologists, psychiatrists, and child welfare workers may share responsibility for assisting families with problems. Some providers move in and out of a client's life as need dictates. A public health nurse, for instance, may assist a parent in acquiring basic child care skills, terminating services once the client demonstrates the acquisition of new skills. The nurse may reenter the case if, as the child grows older, new learning experiences are required by the parent.

To ensure that clients receive needed services in an efficient manner, one person must arrange for a thorough evaluation of the family. The case manager must know the services available and their eligibility requirements and must be able to link clients with needed services. The services must be coordinated to ensure that all providers are working toward mutually accepted goals under established schedules, and the case manager must see that the information needed for case review is gathered and summarized for reporting in a timely manner. Case management services are important in all child welfare cases.

Parent Education. Deficiencies in parents' knowledge and skills may be antecedents to acts of maltreatment and to the placement of a child. Parent education provides instruction in such areas as basic child care skills, money management, and noncorporal methods of disciplining children. Parent education may take place in the client's home or in formal, classroom settings. Instructional methods include small-group discussion, in vivo training, role playing and modeling, and programmed self-instruction.

Respite Services. Stress resulting from a family crisis or from uninterrupted child care responsibilities may cause the placement of children. Respite services provide time out from ongoing child care responsibilities. Their use may help reduce stress and hence the risk that a child will have to enter out-of-home care.

Respite may be provided in a variety of ways. Children may be enrolled in day care; a homemaker who is helping a parent acquire new child care skills may also afford a parent time out by assuming responsibility for child care several hours each week. The services of a "foster grandparent" may be enlisted specifically for the purpose of providing respite. One of the original purposes of foster care was to provide relief from continual child care responsibilities during family illness or other crises.

Self-Help Groups. Self-help groups are organizations developed by and for persons whose lives are directly affected by social, physical, or emotional problems. Members may be offered educational services and emotional support. Networks of parents living in close geographical proximity to each other may develop support groups.

Self-help groups are often initiated by professionals who maintain distinct roles as trainers or consultants to the group. If self-help groups are to play a viable role in helping clients attain their goals for themselves and their children, they must be a part of the service network; hence there must be a liaison between these groups and professional service providers.

Counseling. The terms "counseling" and "therapy" are often used synonymously. The methods counselors or therapists use to effect change include techniques developed from psychoanalysis, behavior modification, ego psychology, and communications theory, to mention just a few. Some counselors adhere to a single school of thought; others are eclectic, using whatever techniques seem most appropriate in relation to client problems. Therapy may be offered on a one-to-one basis or in groups whose focus may be the individual or the family.

Counseling may be seen as the major way in which family problems will be resolved, or it may be one of several services offered by child welfare workers. Counseling is apt to be emphasized if it is assumed that the reasons children enter placement are intrapsychic—that they lie totally in the individual's emotional/psychological makeup, as opposed to being the result of both personal and environmental problems, such as inadequate income, the lack of social supports, and skill and knowledge deficits.

Role of the Social Worker

Two trends that affect the role of professional social workers in providing foster care services are the declassification of social work positions and the emerging legal framework around social work practice. The term "declassification" refers to a reduction in standards, whether educational or work related, for social service positions. Declassification has assured that the number of professionally trained staff in public welfare settings will remain low. A 1975 survey by the National Association of Social Workers showed that, with the exception of positions requiring workers with the title of psychiatric social worker, state personnel practices deemphasized the master's in social work (MSW) degree. In 33 of 50 states, a college degree was the main requirement for "general" social workers. Twenty states included the bachelor's in social work (BSW) as one of several possible degrees; only six required this degree. Thus, an undifferentiated bachelor's degree is the academic requirement for social work in county-level public welfare agencies.

Data reported by Shyne and Schroeder (1978) illustrate the practical effects of declassification. Ninety-six percent of the children who receive social services are served through the public sector, either directly or through purchase agreements with voluntary agencies or proprietary organizations. MSW social workers are a small percentage of the personnel providing direct services in public settings. Only 9 percent of the children on whom Shyne and Schroeder (1978, p. 78) report data were assigned to workers with an MSW or doctoral degree in social work, 16 percent to persons holding a BSW degree. When professionally trained social workers serve children in substitute care, they are most likely to do so under purchase agreements between the public sector and voluntary organizations, where most MSWs are employed. Public agency standards and requirements in federal and state law affect the professional autonomy of staff who serve children under purchase-of-service contracts.

Factors that contributed to declassification included the paucity of social work personnel available in relation to the number of social service positions, an increase in the use of paraprofessionals, a willingness to accept experience as a substitute for professional training, and questions regarding the effectiveness of social work practice. Unions and agency administrators further questioned the need for high entrance requirements for social service positions on the grounds that it was not clear that the knowledge and skills acquired in an MSW program were valid predictors of job success. It is questionable whether schools of social work prepare students for practice in public settings. Professional training tends to focus on developing skills for clinical practice, for which there is little demand in public agencies. Growing competition from related disciplines, such as counseling, educational psychology, and vocational rehabilitation, contribute to the declining role of professional social work in providing child welfare services (for review, see Seaberg, 1982; Stein, 1982).

Legal Issues. There has been a significant amount of litigation against child-caring agencies in recent years, and court decisions have been equivocal. The tendency has been to recognize that each of the parties with an interest in foster care placement—the children, their birth parents, and their foster caretakers—have rights, and the exercise of these rights reduces worker and agency autonomy by supporting an imperative toward shared decision making. The courts have established mechanisms to closely monitor workers' decisions (National Council of Juvenile and Family Court Judges, 1981). The courts have ruled that the doctrine in loco parentis, under which agencies have been immune from lawsuits for actions taken on behalf of children in their care, cannot be used to overcome a child's constitutional rights (for review, see Rose, 1978). Almost all states provide for counsel for biological parents and guardians ad litem for children in dependency proceedings. Some courts have acknowledged the validity of the concept of psychological parenthood, recognizing foster parents' rights to have a say in the plans made for children for whom they have provided care. Courts have acknowledged the right of foster parents to file petitions to terminate parental rights and to request the suspension of a natural parent's right to visit.

These rulings point to the ways in which worker autonomy to make decisions is restricted. Staff must balance the interests of all clients, and this requires substantial client involvement in the decision-making process. Moreover, the current legal situation has substantially changed workers' interactions with attorneys who represent clients at various stages of court and case-planning processes. Attorneys sometimes play pivotal roles in the development of plans for services, and they can advocate with the agency for services, help in the formulation of agreements between the agency and the parents, and facilitate the parents' fulfillment of their part of an agreement.

The review requirements in P.L. 96-272 provide a mechanism for ensuring that worker behavior conforms to the expectations set out in policy regarding case plans and the involvement of biological parents. Biological parents may participate in semiannual reviews, and at dispositional hearings they must have due process rights, including the rights to counsel, to written advance notice of a hearing, and to participate in the hearing.

The effects of the emerging legal framework go beyond the need to negotiate with clients and their attorneys. Whereas in the past worker decisions frequently prevailed unchallenged, today practitioners have to support their arguments with factual information showing why any one position is more sound than another. Defending one's choices in the context of legally enforceable rights necessitates that workers modify their typically inferential approaches to gathering and reporting information. To determine what to look for during assessment and treatment, workers will have to learn legal rules for evidence. "Uncorroborated admissions, hearsay testimony and untested social investigations [will no longer be acceptable] as the basis for adjudication" (Bell & Mylniec, 1974, p. 27). Information will have to be recorded in a descriptive manner, informing a third party of what a worker observed and was told.

It makes little difference whether the court is initially involved in a case. The critical issue for practitioners is that it may end there. Workers may decide to petition the court if parents fail to participate in case-planning activities, or court action may be initiated by clients. The current trend toward increased litigation indicates that workers must act as if cases will go to court by recording all information with court standards in mind.

Future Issues

Declassification is likely to continue, and the emerging legal framework is apt to grow. Admonishing agencies to hire professionally trained social workers is not likely to change hiring practices. Schools of social work must identify the skills required by public agency practice, and they must teach those skills or yield control over the "only field in which social workers were in control of their own programs" (Meyer, 1984, p. 499). As noted earlier, court decisions have been equivocal regarding the exact rights of each party with a vested interest in the outcomes of foster care. From the standpoint of professional social work, the likelihood that court decisions will continue to prescribe and limit practice is more significant than whether the courts will delineate the exact conditions under which the rights of any one party supersede those of other parties.

The emphasis on permanency planning will continue. This is ensured by revised federal and state statutes, coupled with changes in agency practice. However, there are a number of issues regarding the implementation of permanency planning that require attention. Poor implementation may result in inappropriately reuniting children with their biological parents, in children's reentry into foster care, or in moving toward the termination of parental rights when a rigorous assessment of family problems and carefully monitored interventions might have resulted in family reunification. There have been few systematic evaluations of how permanency planning has been implemented, but there is evidence to suggest that there are problems. Despite the emphasis on providing services to birth parents, families often receive few, if any, community services while their children are in care or subsequent to reunification (Turner, 1984). The reintegration of children to their biological homes is a difficult process, and reentry to care occurs at a fairly high rate—32 percent reentry for children returned to biological families compared to 2 percent for children adopted (for review, see Maluccio & Fein, 1985). The source of these difficulties is not known. Rigorous evaluation of how permanency

planning is being implemented is warranted so that refinements can be made.

The emphasis on offering services to maintain children in their own homes may be undermined by budget cuts. One of the ways in which the states are coping with their fiscal problems is to prioritize services in favor of crisis programs, including foster home placement, and to deemphasize prevention (Kimmich, 1985). Thus, the demand for foster care services may increase.

Of additional concern are the data showing that the population of children entering care is changing. Because placement reduction efforts may be screening out inappropriate cases, it is possible that the cohort of children currently entering care has more severe personal or family problems than in the past. Moreover, the average age of children in care is increasing. This may result, in part, from efforts to divert status offenders to the foster care system as a way of dealing with the federal requirement that these young people not be placed in institutional settings with youngsters adjudicated as delinquent (Shyne & Schroeder, 1978). This makes family reunification or adoption more difficult to attain and makes it necessary for professionals in the field to learn more about emancipation planning.

Conclusion

In recent years, significant efforts have been made to change the foster care system. Federal policy has been rewritten to reflect the importance of maintaining children in their own homes and to support efforts toward permanency planning for youngsters in care. The methods developed and tested in permanency projects have been disseminated to the field of practice. The 45 percent reduction in the number of youngsters in substitute care points to the effects of these changes. However, there can be little confidence that the trend reflected in these data will continue or that the changes that have occurred are easily interpreted.

Data gathered before permanency planning became an accepted aspect of practice suggested that many of the children in placement should not have been there. Although there has been a rapid reduction in the foster care population, the number of children leaving care has been decreasing and in 1983 began being offset by the growing numbers who are entering placement. These young people represent an older population whose problems may be more difficult to resolve. It is not clear that the foster care system, accustomed to dealing with younger children, is equipped to deal with an older, perhaps more troubled population of youngsters. Procedures for realizing goals such as emancipation and independent living, which may be more relevant alternatives for this age group, are less well developed than are methods for facilitating family reunification and adoption. Moreover, youngsters who enter care in their teens, who will not be reunited with their families of origin, and for whom adoption is not a realistic alternative may remain wards of the state for long periods of time.

Although its meaning is difficult to determine in the absence of historical data, the recidivism rate appears high and generates concern that some youngsters may be reunited inappropriately. It also points to the importance of follow-up services that are not routinely provided. Budget cuts and the suggestion that crisis services are being funded at the expense of preventive services may undermine the entire permanency planning effort, producing a situation like the one that existed before permanency planning became a normative aspect of practice. The failure to monitor the implementation of permanency planning is unfortunate because it limits professionals' ability to make suggestions for change.

Other changes described in this article include the emerging legal framework surrounding child welfare practice and the continued trend to declassification of social service positions. To date, there is little evidence to suggest that social work educators have taken seriously the admonition to train for practice in public settings, and this has created a risk that the link between professional social work and the provision of substitute care services will be eliminated.

THEODORE J. STEIN

For further information, see ADOPTION; CASE MANAGEMENT; CHILD CARE SERVICES; CHILDREN; CHILD WELFARE SERVICES.

References

Bell, C., & Mylniec, W. J. (1974). "Preparing for a Neglect Proceeding: A Guide for the Social Worker." *Public Welfare, 32*(4), 26–37.

Bremner, R. H., et al. (Eds.). (1970). *Children and Youth in America: A Documentary History* (Vol. I). Cambridge, Mass.: Harvard University Press.

Calhoun, J. A. (1980). "The 1980 Child Welfare Act: A Turning Point for Children and Troubled Families." *Children Today, 9*(5), 2–4.

Downs, S. W., et al. (1981). *Foster Care Reform in the 70s: Final Report of the Permanency Planning Dissemination Project.* Portland, Oreg.: Portland State University, School of Social Work, Regional Research Institute for Human Services.

Emlen, A., et al. (1975). *Overcoming Barriers to Planning for Children in Foster Care.* Portland, Oreg.: Portland State University, Regional Research Institute for Human Services.

Jones, M. A., Neuman, R., & Shyne, A. W. (1976). *A Second Chance for Families: Evaluation of a Program to Reduce Foster Care.* New York: Child Welfare League of America.

Kimmich, M. H. (1985). *America's Children: Who Cares.* Washington, D.C.: Urban Institute.

Knitzer, J., Allen, M. L., & McGowan, B. (1978). *Children without Homes: An Examination of Public Responsibility to Children in Out-of-Home Care.* Washington, D.C.: Children's Defense Fund.

Koshel, J. J., & Kimmich, M. H. (1983). *Summary Report on the Implementation of P.L. 96-272.* Washington, D.C.: Urban Institute.

Maas, H., & Engler, R. (1959). *Children in Need of Parents.* New York: Columbia University Press.

Maluccio, A. N., & Fein, E. (1985). "Growing Up in Foster Care." *Children and Youth Services Review, 7*(2/3), 123–134.

Meyer, C. H. (1984). "Can Foster Care Be Saved?" *Social Work, 29*(6), 499.

National Council of Juvenile and Family Court Judges. (1981). *Judicial Review of Children in Placement Deskbook.* Reno, Nev.: National Council of Juvenile and Family Court Judges.

Rose, C. M. (1978). *Some Emerging Issues in Legal Liability of Children's Agencies.* New York: Child Welfare League of America.

Seaberg, J. R. (1982). "Getting There from Here: Revitalizing Child Welfare Training." *Social Work, 27*(5), 441–448.

Shyne, A. W., & Schroeder, A. G. (1978). *A National Study of Social Services to Children and Their Families* (Publication No. [OHDS] 78-30150, pp. 109–123). Washington, D.C.: United States Children's Bureau.

Stein, T. J. (1982). "Child Welfare: New Directions in the Field and Their Implications for Education." In E. S. Saalberg (Ed.), *A Dialogue on the Challenge for Education and Training: Child Welfare Issues in the 80s* (pp. 57–76). Ann Arbor, Mich.: National Child

Welfare Training Center, University of Michigan, School of Social Work.

Stein, T. J., Gambrill, E. D. & Wiltse, K. T. (1978). *Children in Foster Homes: Achieving Continuity in Care.* New York: Praeger Publishers.

Tatara, T., & Pettiford, E. K. (1983, 1985). *Characteristics of Children in Substitute and Adoptive Care.* Washington, D.C.: Voluntary Cooperative Information System, American Public Welfare Association.

Trattner, W. I. (1974). *From Poor Law to Welfare State: A History of Social Welfare in America.* New York: Free Press.

Turner, J. (1984). "Reuniting Children in Foster Care with Their Biological Parents." *Social Work, 29*(6), 501–505.

United States Children's Bureau. (1979). *Catalogue of Training Materials for Child Welfare Services* (DHEW Contract No. 105-78-1105). Washington, D.C.: Department of Health, Education & Welfare.

Yoshikami, R. T., & Emlen, A. C. (1983). *A Comparison of Voluntary and Court-Ordered Foster Care: Decisions, Services, and Parental Choice.* Portland, Oreg.: Regional Research Institute for Human Services, Portland State University.

For Further Reading

Allen, M. L., & Golubock, C. (1985). "An Emerging Legal Framework for Permanency Planning." *Children and Youth Services Review, 7*(2/3), 135–160.

Allen, M. L., & Knitzer, J. (1983). "Child Welfare: Examining the Policy Framework." In B. McGowan & W. Meezan (Eds.), *Child Welfare: Current Dilemmas-Future Directions* (pp. 93–142). Itasca, Ill.: F. E. Peacock Publishers.

United States Children's Bureau. (1978). *Child Welfare Strategy in the Coming Years* (Publication No. [OHDS] 78-30158). Washington, D.C.: Author.

Fanshel, D., & Shinn, E. G. (1978). *Children in Foster Care: A Longitudinal Investigation.* New York: Columbia University Press.

Hardin, M. (1983). *Foster Children in the Courts.* Boston, Mass.: Butterworth Legal Publishers.

FOUNDATIONS AND SOCIAL WELFARE

The foundation in its broadest sense is a nonprofit organization that distributes private wealth for the public good. It is private in that it is nongovernmental and funded by private donors. It is public in that it devotes its resources exclusively to educational, social, charitable, religious, or other public purposes. Foundations are usually set up under state laws as corporations or trusts.

There are essentially four types of foundations. Independent foundations, which comprise the largest segment of foundations, are grant-making organizations whose funds are generally derived from an individual, a family, or a group of individuals. Grant funds are usually generated from endowment income and may be supplemented by annual contributions by the donors. Operating foundations are similarly funded but make few if any grants; they plan and carry through programs managed by their own staffs. Community foundations derive their principal funds from the gifts and bequests of many donors, generally make grants only in their own communities, and are governed by boards broadly representative of their communities. Company-sponsored or corporate foundations derive their funds from profit-making companies but are legally independent. Most do not have large principal assets but carry on their programs through year-to-year receipts and disbursements.

The ability of private foundations to sustain programs of charitable giving is affected by market conditions influencing the value of assets, by investment income, and by the level of gifts received. In addition, a number of government regulations imposed on foundations affect their charitable giving. A detailed discussion of government regulation of foundations follows.

History

The present-day philanthropic foundation is primarily an American invention and a product of the twentieth century. However, it had its early counterparts. For example, groups of individuals in some ancient civilizations provided recurring sacrificial feasts that benefited priesthoods, travelers, and the poor. In Egypt, the pharaohs set up perpetuities for religious purposes, and the ancient Greeks and Romans established endowments. Before his death in 347 B.C., Plato directed that the natural income of his fields should be used for the perpetual support of his school. The school survived nearly 900 years. In England under the Tudors and later, thousands of ecclesiastical and charitable trusts were instituted.

A few trusts were set up in the United States as early as the eighteenth century. A typical example was the William Carter Fund (1739), which was intended for the relief of poor people in the city of Philadelphia. Such trusts were small, narrow in purpose, and usually served a limited locality. Two funds were set up in Boston and Philadelphia in 1791 under the will of Benjamin Franklin to provide loans to young artisans.

In the nineteenth century, foundations concentrated on direct relief to indigent individuals, such as children, widows, or the aged. For example, the Peabody Education Fund, established in 1867, was set up to aid the war-devastated South.

At the beginning of the twentieth century the basic concept of foundations was well established, but significant differences from nineteenth-century methods and goals were developing. Endowments were set up, often in perpetuity, but with a new, wider latitude of purpose. The Rockefeller Foundation charter, for example, declared an intention to promote the well-being of peoples throughout the world. Special purpose funds were also set up, but they characteristically had great freedom of application. Trustees spent less time in conserving money than in exploring ways of spending it. The newer doctrines asserted that some of the assets of foundations should be treated as venture capital for enterprises requiring risk and foresight but that were not likely to be supported by the government or private individuals. The primary purpose of foundations was no longer relief or even cure; it was research, prevention, and discovery.

Many notable foundations were established early in the twentieth century. In 1902, Andrew Carnegie set up his first important foundation, the Carnegie Institution of Washington, with the broad purposes of applying knowledge to improve humanity. In the same year, the General Education Board was organized; this was a Rockefeller benefaction of which Carnegie was an active trustee.

Also founded in this era were the Milbank Memorial Fund and the Carnegie Foundation for the Advancement of Teaching (1905); the Russell Sage Foundation (1907); the New York Foundation (1909); the

Carnegie Endowment for International Peace (1910); the Carnegie Corporation of New York, the largest and most general of the Carnegie benefactions (1911); the Rockefeller Foundation, the giant of the major early foundations (1913); and the Cleveland Foundation, the first of the community foundations (1914).

The depression decade of the 1930s was scarcely a favorable period for foundations, and some were dissolved or found their funds depleted. However, some major foundations were founded in this decade, including the Ford Foundation, the Robert Wood Johnson Foundation, and the Lilly Endowment, each with current assets exceeding $1 billion.

By the mid-1940s a new period of foundation growth had begun, induced in part by high levels of taxation resulting from World War II. Many of these were family foundations that were set up by living individuals and funded and controlled by family groups. Another category consisted of foundations established by business corporations to receive substantial contributions in years when profits or taxes were high. The funds were disbursed through good years and bad in the customary patterns of corporate giving.

Since the 1950s, there has been a gradual decline in the number of new foundations established—a fact that might be attributed to increased regulation and taxation of foundations, questions about the favorability of corporate charitable programs over company-sponsored foundations, and changes in the overall economy. Table 1 shows the period of establishment by asset categories for foundations listed in *The Foundation Directory*. This directory's financial criteria for inclusion are that the foundation have assets of $1 million or more or total grants of $100,000 or more.

Patterns of Giving

Foundations have made many important contributions to the solution of problems and the advancement of medicine, science, and the arts. Activities that have benefited from foundation support include the founding of free public libraries, the development of public television as a cultural resource and a teaching tool, the control of yellow fever, the cracking of the "genetic code," pilot experiments in combating poverty, the National

Table 1. Period of Establishment for *Directory* Foundations by Asset Categories

Decade Established	Total Foundations		$100 million or more		$25 million–under $100 million		$10 million–under $25 million		$5 million–under $10 million		$1 million–under $5 million		Under $1 million	
	No.	%	No.	%	No.	%	No.	%	No.	%	No.	%	No.	%
Before 1900	38	0.9	0	—	0	—	1	0.2	6	1.0	31	1.3	0	—
1900–1909	20	0.5	0	—	6	2.3	1	0.2	3	0.5	10	0.4	0	—
1910–1919	68	1.5	8	8.3	14	5.3	9	2.0	11	1.9	25	1.2	1	0.1
1920–1929	141	3.2	7	7.3	19	7.2	16	3.5	27	4.6	69	2.9	3	0.4
1930–1939	183	4.2	19	19.8	19	7.2	39	8.6	30	5.1	67	2.9	9	1.3
1940–1949	678	15.4	28	29.2	61	23.0	103	23.0	95	15.1	327	14.1	64	9.4
1950–1959	1,510	34.3	21	21.9	77	29.0	149	33.0	195	33.1	816	35.2	252	37.0
1960–1969	973	22.1	5	5.2	39	14.7	72	16.0	139	24.5	530	22.9	188	27.6
1970–1979	516	11.7	5	5.2	24	9.0	43	9.5	59	10.0	283	12.2	102	15.0
1980–1984	169	3.8	2	2.1	6	2.3	14	3.1	16	2.7	88	3.8	43	6.3
Data not available	106	2.4	1	1.0	0	—	4	0.9	9	1.5	72	3.1	20	2.9
Total	4,402	100.0	96	100.0	265	100.0	451	100.0	590	100.0	2,318	100.0	682	100.0

Source: *The Foundation Directory* (10th ed.; New York: The Foundation Center, 1985).

Table 2. General Foundation Funding Trends, 1981–1984

Category	1981		1982		1983		1984	
	Amount	Percent	Amount	Percent	Amount	Percent	Amount	Percent
Cultural activities	$ 192,559,945	15.3	$ 208,717,410	14.0	$ 277,306,737	15.4	$ 229,020,327	14.0
Education	265,851,305	21.1	355,630,604	23.9	286,005,941	16.0	285,587,060	17.4
Health	282,531,602	22.5	312,068,761	20.9	389,520,571	21.7	390,445,485	23.7
Religion	24,678,672	2.0	27,907,365	1.9	37,503,575	2.1	38,350,986	2.3
Science	86,727,544	6.9	96,280,905	6.5	160,917,379	9.0	122,880,071	7.5
Social science	75,431,276	6.0	102,362,933	6.9	132,062,310	7.4	126,325,557	7.6
Welfare	329,275,755	26.2	387,278,277	25.9	509,202,800	28.4	454,101,191	27.5
Total	1,257,056,099	100.0	1,490,246,255	100.0	1,792,519,313	100.0	1,646,710,677	100.0

Source: *The Foundation Directory* (10th ed.; New York: The Foundation Center, 1985).

Table 3. Largest Foundations by Assets

Name	Assets	Total Giving	Fiscal Date
Ford Foundation	$3,497,800,000	$122,083,061	9/30/84
J. Paul Getty Trust	2,684,185,155	45,948,959	9/30/84
John D. and Catherine T. MacArthur Foundation	1,920,260,560	38,197,518	12/31/83
W. K. Kellogg Foundation	1,291,843,298	60,835,879	8/31/84
Robert Wood Johnson Foundation	1,173,836,335	57,742,282	12/31/84
Pew Memorial Trust	1,171,419,665	45,617,847	12/31/83
Rockefeller Foundation	1,101,856,013	37,889,957	12/31/84
Andrew W. Mellon Foundation	1,016,625,922	61,066,230	12/31/84
Lilly Endowment	889,437,000	24,271,000	12/31/84
Kresge Foundation	813,648,263	43,145,000	12/31/84

Source: *The Foundation Directory* (10th ed.; New York: The Foundation Center, 1985).

Merit Scholarship program, the advancement of scientific agriculture, and legal aid and defense for the poor.

Programs supported by foundations are extremely varied, but there is an evident concentration in certain fields. Early in this century grants went chiefly to health and education, with social welfare a close third. Then grants to education mounted so that in the 1970s the largest proportion of foundation funds went directly to educational institutions for such activities as research or studies in international affairs. In the 1980s, giving to education has declined as a proportion of total foundation giving. In 1984, education grants accounted for only 17 percent of the total foundation dollars reported, with the largest drop occurring in the area of general higher education. This downward trend is somewhat alleviated by substantial increases in funding for research and education in the sciences and social sciences.

In the 1980s, foundations have put their strongest emphasis on funding in the general welfare category. Giving to health programs has remained fairly constant in the early 1980s, accounting for between 21 and 23 percent of the foundation dollars reported. Cultural activities accounted for about 14 percent of foundation dollars through the early 1980s.

Complete data on all grants are not available, but for many years the Foundation Center, a source of public information about foundations, has collected substantial data based on samplings of grants of $5,000 or

Table 4. Largest Foundations by Total Giving

Name	Total Giving	Assets	Fiscal Date
Ford Foundation	$122,083,061	$3,497,800,000	9/30/84
Andrew W. Mellon Foundation	61,066,230	1,016,625,922	12/31/84
W. K. Kellogg Foundation	60,835,879	1,291,843,298	8/31/84
Robert Wood Johnson Foundation	57,742,282	1,173,836,335	12/31/84
J. Paul Getty Trust	45,948,959	2,684,185,155	9/30/84
Pew Memorial Trust	45,617,847	1,171,419,665	12/31/83
Kresge Foundation	43,145,000	813,648,263	12/31/84
John D. and Catherine T. MacArthur Foundation	38,197,518	1,920,260,560	12/31/83
Rockefeller Foundation	37,889,957	1,101,856,013	12/31/84
San Francisco Foundation	37,753,057	461,040,287	6/30/84

Source: *The Foundation Directory* (10th ed.; New York: The Foundation Center, 1985).

more paid out by over 400 foundations. See
Table 2.

Government Regulation

The growth and activities of foundations have been challenged. In the 1950s,
charges were made of Communist penetration and subversion, but two successive congressional investigations failed to substantiate the charges. In the 1960s, the disclosure
of irregular fiscal and administrative practices
led to the passage of new tax law provisions.
In the 1970s, critics mainly outside Congress
raised questions about foundation decision
making, the composition of boards, and accountability to the public, citing the need for
social responsibility and change. In the
1980s, there have been congressional hearings concerning foundations' business holdings, their public information reporting, and,
in response to charges that they are neglecting ethnic, community, and grass-roots
causes, their funding priorities.

Tax Reform Act of 1969. The Tax Reform Act of 1969 dealt extensively with foundations. Among the act's principal provisions
were an annual excise tax on net investment
income, marking the first time in American
history that philanthropies had been taxed;
strict prohibitions on self-dealing, which refers to the use of foundations for personal
advantage and gain rather than for charitable
purposes; minimum payout requirement in
grants or other qualifying distributions; a
requirement that a foundation's investments
not jeopardize the carrying out of its exempt
purposes; limitations on the ownership of any
single company by a foundation to prevent
control; a requirement that annual information returns to the Internal Revenue Service,
including data on grants, administrative expenses, income, capital, and investments, be
open to public inspection; and a requirement
that grants to individuals meet government-
approved standards. The restrictions and
complications in this act have resulted in the
dissolution of some foundations and have
slowed the creation of new ones.

Later Tax Reforms. Later tax legislation
modified some of the restrictions and complications of the Tax Reform Act of 1969. Under
the Tax Reform Act of 1984, the annual
excise tax on net investment income can be

reduced to 1 percent; foundations are required to spend 5 percent of the fair market
value of assets but only .65 percent of assets
can be counted toward grant administrative
expenses; the amount of deductibility for
gifts of cash to private foundations has been
increased from 20 percent to 30 percent. The
deductibility limit for gifts to public charities
is 50 percent. The main distinction between
the status of a private foundation and a public
charity is the amount of private financing
received from a single source. Congress assumed that although publicly supported organizations are subject to the discipline of public opinion, institutions drawing their funds
from private sources are not subject to this
corrective influence and should be regulated
differently. Therefore, special rules exist for
private foundations.

Current Information

In 1983, foundations held assets of an
estimated $64.5 billion and awarded annual
grants of about $4.8 billion. Of the approxi-
mately 24,000 active grant-making foundations, only 4,402 held assets of $1 million or
more in 1983. This relatively small number of
foundations accounted for over 97 percent of
the total foundation assets and 85 percent of
the total foundation grants awarded in that
fiscal year. (See Tables 3 and 4.)

Foundations are not the vast reservoir
of unlimited wealth that has sometimes been
pictured. But because they have had long
experience in giving and must disburse their
funds with care, they have built an enviable
record of accomplishment. The Foundation
Center in New York City and the Council on
Foundations in Washington, D.C., provide
current information on private foundations.

ZEKE KILBRIDE
F. EMERSON ANDREWS

For further information, see CORPORATE SOCIAL
RESPONSIBILITY; SOCIAL WELFARE FINANC-
ING.

For Further Reading
Abramson, A. J., & Salamon, L. M. (1982). *The
Federal Budget and the Nonprofit Sector.*
Baltimore, Md.: Urban Institute.
Andrews, F. E. (1973). *Foundation Watcher.*
Lancaster, Pa.: Franklin and Marshall Col-
lege.
Commission on Foundations and Private Philan-
thropy. (1970). *Foundations, Private Giving*

and Public Policy. Chicago: University of Chicago Press.

Cuninggim, M. (1972). *Private Money and Public Service: The Role of Foundations in American Society*. New York: McGraw-Hill Book Co.

Foundation Center. *Foundation Directory* (biennial). New York: Author.

Council on Foundations. *Foundation News*. Washington, D.C.: Author.

Foundation Center. *Foundations Today*. New York: Author.

Freeman, D. F. (1981). *Handbook on Private Foundations*. Washington, D.C.: Council on Foundations.

Fremont-Smith, M. R. (1965). *Foundations and Government: State and Federal Law and Supervision*. New York: Russell Sage Foundation.

American Association of Fund Raising Counsel. *Giving USA*. New York: Author.

Hodgkinson, V. A., & Weitzman, M. S. (1984). *Dimensions of the Independent Sector*. Washington, D.C.: Independent Sector.

Foundation Center. *National Data Book*. New York: Author.

Nielsen, W. A. (1972). *The Big Foundations. A Twentieth Century Fund Study*. New York: Columbia University Press.

Richman, S. (1973). *Public Information Handbook for Foundations*. Washington, D.C.: Council on Foundations.

U.S. General Accounting Office. (1984). *Statistical Analysis of the Operations and Activities of Private Foundations*. Washington, D.C.: Author.

Weaver, W. (1967). *U.S. Philanthropic Foundations: Their History, Structure, Management, and Record*. New York: Harper & Row.

Zurcher, A. J. (1972). *Management of American Foundations: Administration, Policies, and Social Role*. New York: New York University Press.

Rockefeller Foundation. (1915). *Annual Report, 1913–14*. New York: Author.

FRANKEL, LEE KAUFER. See biographical section.

FRAZIER, EDWARD FRANKLIN. See biographical section.

FUNDRAISING. See ADMINISTRATION: ENVIRONMENTAL ASPECTS; FINANCIAL MANAGEMENT; FOUNDATIONS AND SOCIAL WELFARE; RESEARCH MOBILIZATION AND COORDINATION; RESOURCE DEVELOPMENT AND SERVICE PROVISION; SOCIAL PLANNING IN THE VOLUNTARY SECTOR; SOCIAL WELFARE FINANCING.

GALLAUDET, EDWARD MINER.
See biographical section.

GALLAUDET, THOMAS. See biographical section.

GALLAUDET, THOMAS HOPKINS.
See biographical section.

GARRETT, ANNETTE MARIE. See biographical section.

GENERAL AND EMERGENCY ASSISTANCE

Since the enactment of the Social Security Act of 1935, the federal government has come to play the dominant financial role in the provision of income supports in the United States. However, federal financial participation is generally limited to categorical benefit programs, such as Aid to Families with Dependent Children (AFDC) or Supplemental Security Income (SSI), that serve only certain groups of the needy. In addition, these programs emphasize cash grants designed to meet only specified, basic needs; out-of-the-ordinary expenses are not always covered.

General assistance (sometimes called general relief), emergency assistance, and special needs programs meet needs that are not covered by the basic income maintenance components of the federally funded categorical programs. General assistance programs are efforts by state or local governments to provide for the basic needs of those individuals or families who are not eligible for a federal categorical program. Groups served may include single individuals or couples without children, married couples with children who live in states that do not participate in the unemployed parent component of the Aid to Families with Dependent Children (AFDC) program, individuals or families who do not meet specific procedural requirements

of a federal program, poor individuals or families whose income or assets are somewhat above the limits allowed by the federal programs, or those awaiting certification for a federally funded categorical grant.

In contrast, emergency assistance and special needs programs meet types of needs that are not covered by the basic income maintenance grants. The supplemented grants may be federally supported or locally supported, and the federal government may or may not be involved in supplementation. Needs may arise from such causes as a natural disaster, the breakdown of a major appliance, a lost or stolen check, a medical situation that requires a special diet, or even an occasional shortage of cash to meet normal expenses. It should be noted that, despite the conceptual distinction, some states or localities use the terms "general assistance" and "emergency assistance" interchangeably.

General Assistance

History. Because the federal role in income maintenance was extremely limited before 1935, virtually all public income support dispensed before then can be considered as general assistance (Leiby, 1978; Trattner, 1984). In colonial times public income maintenance grants were modeled after the English Poor Law. Most of the colonies had a Poor Law provision, and the responsibility for administering it and providing support was delegated to local areas.

The Poor Law was administered by local overseers, who normally had great discretion and could grant or refuse aid nearly at will. The overseer might refuse to grant aid on the basis of moral criteria, such as the perception that the individual or family was responsible for the economic need. The level and type of aid were also discretionary. Support could be granted directly to an individual or family, a member of the community might bid for a grant to support those in need, indentured servitude could be used, or the needy might be placed in an almshouse or workhouse.

Even though they continued to vary by local area and state, general assistance programs generally changed with the times. The first three decades of the nineteenth century witnessed increased utilization of workhouses and almshouses. Toward the middle of the nineteenth century, cash and in-kind benefits were used more frequently, and overseers were generally replaced by conventional local civil servants. Toward the end of the century, nearly half of the country's urban areas closed their general assistance offices and ceded authority to private charities. Many general assistance programs were reinstituted, however, during the early part of the twentieth century.

As federal participation in income maintenance programs expanded in the period of the New Deal, general assistance programs came to provide for a smaller proportion of the needy. Nevertheless, the programs retained much of their traditional, local, discretionary flavor. Even today, programs vary widely by state and local area, and workers are allowed considerable discretion. In addition, it appears that the earlier moral concern about recipients remains strong in many localities and results in strict rules and low benefits. Because many potential recipients are of working age, some members of the public believe that most could work if they desired to do so; other members of the public are simply not very interested in ensuring the economic support of a group that contains many healthy adults. In addition, the programs often rely on the property tax for funds, thus placing strong pressure on local officials to keep costs low.

Trends in Caseloads and Expenditures. Not coming under as much national scrutiny as federally funded programs, general assistance programs tend to be rarely studied, and even when they are, the information may be somewhat questionable. For example, although the best available data on general assistance costs and caseloads stem from a federal survey of states that has been conducted each year since 1936 (for example, Social Security Administration, 1976, 1982, 1983), not all the states report general assistance information. Further, given the local control of programs in some states, it is unclear whether the reports are accurate. Indeed, in recent years the federal statistics include caseloads and not costs.

The federal data indicate considerable year-by-year fluctuation in caseloads. The total number of recipients appears to decrease when federal programs are expanding and thus reducing the proportion of the needy

who must rely on the state and local programs. Caseloads appear to increase in years in which unemployment increases. The number of recipients also appears to vary with trends in the willingness of states and localities to provide support.

For example, during 1936 about 4.5 million general assistance recipients in an average month were reported. The average monthly caseload dropped to about 0.5 million by 1945, after the Social Security Act had been implemented and the depression-level unemployment rate had been reduced. The average monthly caseload increased to nearly 0.9 million by 1950, and has ranged from about 0.7 to 1.0 million since that time. There was a drop of about 0.1 million recipients per month between 1950 and 1955, a period in which the federally funded Aid to the Permanently and Totally Disabled program was instituted. The reported monthly caseload expanded after 1955, then declined by about 0.4 million between 1961 and 1967, a period of economic growth in which many states instituted the unemployed parent component of AFDC. During the 1970s, as the population grew, benefit levels increased, and unemployment rates rose, the monthly caseload swelled by about 0.4 million. There were approximately 1.08 million recipients in December 1983.

The average cost per recipient rose throughout this period. Monthly grants per recipient averaged $8.00 in 1936 and rose to $127.18 in 1981. Over 60 percent of the reported increase occurred during the 1970s. Total program costs for the nation were about $1.4 billion in 1981.

The Current Programs. General assistance programs vary widely across the nation. States and localities, operating under varying economic conditions and with distinct philosophies, develop programs that apparently reflect local views of who deserves support. General assistance may be viewed as a "program of last resort" available to all who fall below a certain income limit and who do not receive federally supported categorical benefits. Alternatively, programs may be limited to a small group, like the disabled. Indeed, according to a 1982 survey that included Washington, D.C., as a "state" and used information from large counties in localized programs (Urban Systems Research & Engineering, 1983), 23 of the 42 states for which there was information supported most of those who fell below a given financial limit and did not receive a categorical grant in a general assistance program. All of those in need except for employable adults are covered in ten states. One state covers only families. Eight states have general assistance only for the "disabled" or "unemployable," although the latter category may include healthy older adults.

The benefit package also varies in structure. Of the 41 states for which there are data, 33 have programs that provide benefits that may be received for an indefinite period, although some of these programs may discourage a lengthy recipient status through the recertification process. Four state programs provide only short-term benefits, and two provide only emergency assistance under the general assistance program. Two states allow the disabled to obtain benefits indefinitely and limit the term of support for the employable. In addition, some form of medical assistance exists in 33 states and in some localities in 11 others; county hospitals may be available in the remaining jurisdictions.

Another important set of differences involves the role of the states; local control is still evident in some jurisdictions. Twenty-five states administer a centralized program that usually has standard benefit levels and eligibility rules. A general assistance program is mandated by the state but administered locally in 13 states, and the local areas may have widely different rules, procedures, or even benefit levels. Assistance is a local option in the remaining states and may not exist in some localities of these states. In keeping with this variation, 22 programs are financed entirely by states, ten are funded jointly by states and localities, and the remainder are locally funded.

The lack of trust in general assistance recipients referred to previously is evident in the various procedural rules. For example, although federal categorical basic grant programs normally provide for cash aid, only 21 programs require that general assistance benefits be provided in cash form. In other states, in-kind benefits (vouchers, vendor payments, or even tangible goods) are mandated, or local variation is allowed. Similarly, although categorical grants are normally relatively standard across recipients in similar situations within a state, only 20 states have a specific grant standard or one that varies only by geography for general assistance; in 20 others, grants are dispensed "as needed" up to a maximum. Other states allow for local variation in the type of grant or have a system that standardizes some components of the grant and allows discretion in other components. Discretion seems to allow officials to determine the degree to which each applicant "deserves" assistance.

It is no surprise that general assistance grants vary significantly both among states and within them. According to the 1982 survey, maximum grants varied from $27 a month to $297 a month in states with specific state payment standards; variations within states that do not have standards are often nearly as great. Grants tend to be lower than those for AFDC or Supplemental Security Income (SSI), particularly when the programs serve the able bodied. Recipients may be expected to work for their grants; compulsory work programs for certain recipients are mandated in all localities in nine states and in some localities in 14 others.

Contemporary Pressures. In the mid-1980s, general assistance programs are under pressure in most states and localities. As a result of a high level of long-term unemployment and a recent narrowing of federal programs, a large number of individuals and families are turning to local and state programs. In addition, growing divorce rates are increasing demands for service on the part of "displaced homemakers" who have particular difficulties in obtaining employment. Many of the chronically mentally ill who were deinstitutionalized in the 1970s may not obtain SSI benefits; they also add to the demands. Perhaps as a result of the lack of coverage of some groups, there are currently between 250,000 (a federal estimate) and 2.5 million (an estimate from a private source) homeless individuals, and there are pressures to serve this group. As yet, however, few general assistance programs give aid to those who have no address or are residing in temporary shelters.

States and localities are also facing serious financial pressures. The tendency to reduce benefits or add conditions to the receipt of general assistance dominated the early 1980s. For example, between 1981 and

1983 at least three states added mandatory work programs to general assistance. One state dropped the entire general assistance income maintenance program, and 11 others either reduced benefit levels or limited the scope of eligibility in a new way. The scope of eligibility increased in only one state during this period. Some counties are beginning to contemplate a return to the use of institutions, such as workhouses, and Sacramento, California, has instituted a workhouse for employable recipients of general assistance.

Emergency Assistance and Special Needs Programs

Emergency assistance programs normally provide temporary benefits for situations that are not covered by basic income maintenance grants, and special needs programs cover out-of-the-ordinary needs. In the everyday operation of programs, however, the distinction may break down. Some emergency programs may provide aid over an extended period of time, and some special needs programs may meet one-time-only expenses.

Historically, the roles of emergency assistance and special needs assistance have changed. Until the early 1970s most income maintenance grants were dispensed in a highly discretionary manner (Handler & Hollingsworth, 1971). Workers often could adjust the budget to an individual's or family's actual need. Specialized emergency assistance or special needs programs might not be needed because the basic grant could be delivered in a flexible manner. At most, because basic grants might have a ceiling or might specify the items whose cost could be calculated in the basic grant, emergency and special needs programs might have existed in a poorly differentiated manner.

Since the early 1970s, many of the basic grant programs have reduced the extent to which discretion is allowed in calculations of benefits. State and federal grants have thus become more "flat," with fewer individualized circumstances available for coverage within the grant structure. Without individualization, the need for separate emergency and special needs programs has become more apparent. Indeed, in recent times there has been an expansion of emergency assistance programs in particular. One such program is AFDC–Emergency Assistance (AFDC–EA),

which is available to states on a 50 percent cost-sharing basis with the federal government. The program became an allowable state option in 1967, and most states that implemented AFDC–EA did so about the time their state AFDC grant became flat, between 1973 and 1975 (Sosin, 1982).

According to a 1983 survey, a typical county with a population of at least 25,000 had 5.5 specialized programs (Handler & Sosin, 1983), which may have included AFDC–EA, AFDC–Special Needs, a state or local emergency program, a supplement to general assistance, the federal Low Income Energy Assistance program, an SSI special needs program, or the use of social services to meet emergency needs. In theory, each county should have the federally mandated expedited Food Stamp program, which provides for quicker service when food stamp applicants have no income.

Despite the wide range of potentially available programs, surveyed administrators viewed specialized assistance as inadequate in particular ways. Roughly one third of the respondents claimed that SSI recipients and those who did not receive a continuing basic grant were not able to obtain sufficient specialized aid. Half or more of the officials reported that there was no coverage at all for sudden one-time expenses, special needs, or the inability to meet basic needs on the normal assistance grant. A lack of coverage may occur because specialized programs may meet only a subset of need and may cover only some groups of clients. For example, many AFDC–EA programs provide aid for only one set of circumstances, ranging from natural disasters to threatened utility cutoffs. The programs are also limited to families with children.

There are no national statistics combining the costs and caseloads of all emergency and special needs programs. However, statistics are kept for AFDC–EA. For example, monthly figures indicate that about 22,500 families were served in December 1983. The average grant was $296.46.

Survey data including a limited sample of programs indicate that AFDC–Special Needs programs are approximately the same size as AFDC–EA programs in many states and counties (Handler & Sosin, 1983). Like AFDC–EA, the special needs program has been instituted in about half of the counties in the nation. In addition, special needs programs that are attached to SSI benefits exist in only about a dozen states; however, these programs are often relatively comprehensive where they do exist. In 1983, an amount slightly less than $2 billion was allocated for the federal Low Income Energy Assistance program, another emergency program.

Like general assistance, emergency assistance and special needs programs tend to be administered at a lower level than basic, categorical grants. States often delegate much responsibility for the programs to counties, and counties often allow workers to maintain flexibility in deciding whether a specific case demands specialized aid. Some distrust of recipients is indicated by a high use of vouchers or payments directly to vendors, the systems of choice in roughly 70 percent of the counties.

The specialized programs are subject to cross-pressures similar to those faced by general assistance programs. As basic grants lose ground to inflation and as the caseloads of categorical programs are limited by program changes, additional pressure is placed on the specialized programs to meet needs. However, because state and local tax money may be involved, there are also pressures to cut costs. According to the 1983 survey data, attempts to ration existing aid or even reduce coverage in emergency and special needs programs were more common than attempts to increase the scope of the programs (Handler & Sosin, 1983).[1]

MICHAEL R. SOSIN

For further information, see AID TO FAMILIES WITH DEPENDENT CHILDREN; FOOD STAMP PROGRAM; HOMELESSNESS; SOCIAL SECURITY; WORKFARE.

---

[1] When public emergency and special needs programs are deemed to be insufficient, a local community might expect private social service agencies to supplement them. Private agencies indeed occasionally maintain food pantries, hot meal programs, clothing dispensaries, general purpose material assistance programs (dispensing cash, housing or food vouchers, appliances, and so forth), and other, similar service programs. However, this private effort is generally smaller than the public emergency and special needs system; furthermore, existing research suggests that it is only minimally sensitive to the extent to which public programs leave needs unmet (Sosin, in press).

References

Handler, J. F., & Hollingsworth, E. J. (1971). *The "Deserving Poor": A Study of Welfare Administration*. Chicago: Markham Publishing Co.

Handler, J. F., & Sosin, M. (1983). *Last Resorts: Emergency Assistance and Special Needs Programs in Public Welfare*. New York: Academic Press.

Leiby, J. (1978). *A History of Social Welfare and Social Work in the United States*. New York: Columbia University Press.

Social Security Administration. (1976). *Annual Statistical Supplement to the Social Security Bulletin*. Washington, D.C.: U.S. Department of Health, Education & Welfare.

Social Security Administration. (1982). *Annual Statistical Supplement to the Social Security Bulletin*. Washington, D.C.: U.S. Department of Health & Human Services.

Social Security Administration. (1983). *Social Security Bulletin, 46*(11), 34.

Sosin, M. (1982). "Emergency and Special Needs Programs in the AFDC System." *Social Service Review, 56*(2), 196–210.

Sosin, M. (in press). *Private Benefits: Material Assistance in the Private Sector*. New York: Academic Press.

Trattner, W. (1984). *From Poor Law to Welfare State* (3rd ed.). New York: Free Press.

Urban Systems Research & Engineering, Inc. (1983). *Characteristics of General Assistance Programs, 1982*. Cambridge, Mass.: Author.

GENERALIST PERSPECTIVE

Social work practice is inherently generalist. The profession defines itself as focusing on the person and environment in interaction, and social work practitioners attend to factors ranging from individual needs to broad social policies. The generalist perspective provides a conceptual framework that allows the social worker the versatility necessary to engage in practice of such broad scope.

Although this perspective has been a part of social work from its beginnings, only in recent years has the concept of generalist practice clearly emerged in the social work literature. Despite the fact that it is an accepted feature of accreditation standards in social work education at both the baccalaureate and master's levels, "generalist practice" has become a catch-phrase—like many emerging concepts—lacking clear definition or common understanding among social workers. Therefore, the following overview traces the emergence of this practice perspective, clarifies the generalist concept, specifies its relationship to the generic foundation of all social work practice, and identifies its key components.

Emergence of the Generalist Perspective

A review of the development of social work in the United States quickly reveals that it emerged as a discipline with a mission to serve vulnerable populations long before it developed practice approaches to support that mission. During most of its first century of development, social work was a profession in search of a practice approach. That search was guided by the view that the social worker must be concerned with the whole person and must be able to understand the person's complex set of social interactions. The social worker must simultaneously pay attention to the impact of the person on the environment and that of the environment on the person.

Social work thus began with the provision of services and, based on that practical experience, sought to build its practice framework. A historical analysis of the practice agencies from which social work evolved reveals that the elements of the generalist perspective have always been present. The Charity Organization Societies in the late 1800s and early 1900s were an important root of social work. From them evolved the first caseworkers, called friendly visitors, and their role in coordinating agencies was a forerunner of community organization. The Charity Organization Societies were not just concerned with conditions of poverty; they also addressed other social problems faced by those who lacked the skills required for success in a rapidly urbanizing and industrializing society. The focus was on the whole person and on the person's interaction with family, employer, neighborhood, and community (Pumphrey & Pumphrey, 1961, pp. 168–191).

Similarly, the settlement house workers—the root from which the group work and the social action aspects of social work emerged—focused on enabling people to meet their needs and develop their full potential. The practice activities of these workers ranged from teaching immigrants English to helping them develop the necessary skills for employment in an industrial society. In addition, as they sought to eliminate social injustices—particularly as they affected women and children—these social workers served as change agents for both the individual and the community (Pumphrey & Pumphrey, 1961, pp. 192–201). In this activity, the social workers in the settlement house movement showed characteristics of a generalist perspective.

The capstone of the early search for a practice theory was the publication of Mary Richmond's *Social Diagnosis*. In the preface to that classic book, Richmond (1917) spoke about her discovery of the common features in social work practice:

> Fifteen years ago, I began to take notes, gather illustrations, and even draft a few chapters for a book on Social Work in Families. In it I hoped to pass on to the younger people coming into the charity organization field an explanation of the methods that their seniors had found useful. It soon became apparent, however, that no methods or aims were peculiarly and solely adapted to the treatment of the families that found their way to a charity organization society; that, in essentials, the methods and aims of social case work were or should be the same in every type of service, whether the subject was a homeless paralytic, the neglected boy of drunken parents, or the widowed mother of small children. Some procedures, of course, were peculiar to one group of cases and some to another, according to the special social disability under treatment. But the things that most needed to be said about case work were the things that were common to all. (p. 5)

Recognizing these common features in various applications of work with individuals and families, Edith Abbott later noted that Richmond became concerned about the narrow focus of social work practice that had evolved. Reflecting Richmond's generalist orientation, Abbott (1919) reported:

> The good social worker, says Miss Richmond, doesn't go on helping people out of a ditch. Pretty soon she begins to find out what ought to be done to get rid of the ditch. (p. 313)

The culmination of these years of searching for a practice perspective occurred in a series of meetings key agency executives held over a several-year period in the 1920s under the auspices of the American Association of Social Workers (AASW). This group engaged in a careful examination of the similarities and differences found in social casework in varied settings. Their conclusion, as stated in *A Report of the Milford Conference* (AASW, 1929/1974), was that there existed a common or generic social casework practice that superseded any of the specializations based on a particular social problem or practice setting. However, this recognition of a common base for practice did not provide a conceptual framework to guide the development of social work in the United States.

Barriers to the Generalist Perspective. The search for a practice perspective sufficiently broad to incorporate the range of social work activities continued. The generalist perspective, which showed promise of meeting this objective, competed with two forces that directed social work toward more narrowly conceptualized specializations: political and economic fluctuations, and social work's intense desire for professional recognition.

Because of social work's emphasis on helping people improve their transactions with their environment, factors that have an impact on the environment have an impact on social work. The changing political and economic climate during the twentieth century has been no exception. When the U.S. economy has been weak—as in the pre–World War I era, the Great Depression, and the 1960s and 1970s—social problems have affected large numbers of people, and the demand for human services has consequently increased. The generalist perspective was prominent during these periods; it served social workers well in their efforts to address a broad array of human problems. However, in times of a stronger economy, conservative political climates emerged, public services were reduced, and social workers moved toward private practice and the voluntary agencies, which have a narrower service orientation. With funding shifted to the private sector, the leading edge of practice and practice innovations was in the voluntary agencies. Conservative periods thus fostered the development of specialized practice approaches, particularly in regard to clinical practice (Johnson, 1983, pp. 25–29).

Social work's drive to become a recog-

nized profession has also had a substantial impact on the nature of its development (Morales & Sheafor, 1983, pp. 39–55) and, consequently, on its practice ideology. Abraham Flexner's (1915) address to the National Conference on Charities and Corrections detailed a concept of the profession based on the models of the medical and legal professions. Flexner's criteria for a recognized profession required that social work possess, among other things, "an educationally communicable technique" (p. 580). Lacking any well-developed practice framework at that time, social work began searching for a suitable and accepted practice approach. Periodically, theoretical discoveries in the social sciences were combined with emerging service activities to yield new practice frameworks. For example, psychoanalytic and social learning theory influenced social casework, group dynamics theory influenced group work, and planning theory became an important part of community organization practice. At times these approaches served aspects of social work well, but they also distracted social workers from their unique focus on the person-environment interaction and diverted the profession from its search for a unifying practice orientation. Until the post–World War II era, practice methods (for example, casework, group work, and community organization) and practice settings (for example, psychiatric, medical, or community) defined the perspective of the social worker. In reality, "social work" was an umbrella term for several professions that maintained unique practice perspectives.

Unification of the Profession. The 1950s emerged as a time of ferment as social work sought to identify the common elements that could bind a wide range of practitioners into a single profession. A milestone in this effort was the publication of the "Working Definition of Social Work Practice" (Bartlett, 1958; Gordon, 1962), whose conceptualization of social work was broad enough to encompass the range of methods, settings, and problems addressed by social workers.

During the same period, the profession merged its specialized professional practice associations and the American Association of Social Workers into the National Association of Social Workers (NASW). Further, the two social work education organizations merged into the Council on Social Work Education (CSWE). That thrust to establish a single profession was accompanied by a renewed search for a common practice approach. The Hollis-Taylor (1951) report on the status of social work education resulted in the recognition of graduate programs as the only professional level of social work education and stressed the use of a *multimethod* approach to practice in which the social worker was expected to have at least a familiarity with the three primary methods—casework, group work, and community organization—and a general understanding of the secondary methods of research and administration. Although it added to the sense of unity in the profession, the multimethod approach did not address the commonality in social work practice and thus failed to produce a common practice perspective.

The emergence of social systems theory provided a conceptual tool for developing a framework or perspective that could support the breadth of social work practice. Hearn (1969), Bartlett (1970), Goldstein (1973), Pincus and Minahan (1973), Siporin (1975), and others brought these diverse threads together in a "holistic," "unitary," or "generalist" perspective of social work practice. This perspective focused on the commonalities in social work practice and conceptualized the generalist as a *utility worker* who could understand and intervene in a wide range of client situations. Some social workers resisted this development, which seemed to detract from the more popular and status-conferring specialized practice approaches, but most found that the generalist perspective placed their practice in a context that reflected social work's unique contribution among the helping professions. Further, the generalist perspective was supported by the "Working Definition of Social Work Practice," which was gaining general acceptance (Bartlett, 1958).

Institutionalizing the Generalist Perspective. Social work education, particularly at the undergraduate level, played a key role in institutionalizing the generalist perspective. The theoretical framework that Bisno (1969) developed for teaching social work methods and skills to undergraduate students reinforced this perspective. In 1971, the Southern Regional Education Board (SREB) published a report that spelled out in some detail the roles commonly performed by social workers and the skills required to carry them out. Although these generalist roles could be applied differentially at varying practice levels, they were primarily developed for inclusion in the baccalaureate curriculum (McPheeters & Ryan, 1971).

Prior to the full implementation of baccalaureate-level accreditation in 1974, curriculum guidelines for undergraduate programs seeking approval from the Council on Social Work Education also reflected the intent to adopt the generalist perspective. These guidelines (CSWE, 1971) stated:

> A generalized approach to social work intervention is recommended rather than separate courses in the traditional social work methods, such as casework, groupwork, and community organization. Learning experiences in the generalized practice approach should provide content in the use of differential concepts and principles that are applicable to a broad range of situations requiring social work intervention. (p. 17)

The 1974 accreditation standards for undergraduate programs again required that schools prepare graduates for generalist social work practice, but they failed to delineate further the nature of that practice or to present a clear statement of that perspective (CSWE, 1974). In 1975, the Social and Rehabilitation Service of the U.S. Department of Health, Education and Welfare funded a three-year project to clarify the generalist concept and help translate it into undergraduate curricula (Baer & Federico, 1978–1979). Known as the West Virginia Project, this effort helped to delineate and standardize the generalist perspective in social work education.

On July 1, 1984, after several years of discussion and several draft documents, the Council on Social Work Education implemented a new set of accreditation standards and the related Curriculum Policy Statement. The Curriculum Policy Statement (CSWE, 1984, Appendix 1, p. 5) identified baccalaureate-level education as the point of entry for professional social work and required that the curricula of undergraduate programs "include the knowledge, values, processes, and skills that have proved essential for the practice of social work, which is hereafter re-

ferred to as the professional foundation."
That foundation includes the generic elements of social work practice organized into
five curriculum areas: human behavior and
the social environment, social welfare policy
and services, social work practice, research,
and the field practicum. In summary, the
professional, or *generic,* foundation provides
the knowledge, value, and skill base necessary for generalist practice.

Although the Curriculum Policy Statement fails to define a perception of generalist
practice, it implies the utility worker conception and requires that each baccalaureate program prepare students to practice within that
framework (CSWE, 1984, Appendix 1, p. 5):

> Students who receive a baccalaureate degree
> from an accredited social work program
> should possess the professional judgment and
> proficiency to apply differentially, with super-
> vision, the common professional foundation
> to service systems of various sizes and types.
> There should be special emphasis on direct
> services to clients, which includes organiza-
> tion and provision of resources on clients'
> behalf. Each program shall explicate the ways
> in which students are being prepared for gen-
> eralist practice.

The Curriculum Policy Statement
(CSWE, 1984, Appendix 1, p. 6) goes on to
assert that "BSW and MSW programs hold in
common their integral relationship to social
work purposes and to the fundamental values, knowledge, and skills of social work."
In short, the generic foundation that supports
the generalist perception is the common bond
between the two levels of entry into the
profession. In addition, the Curriculum Policy Statement (CSWE, 1984, Appendix 1, p.
9) identifies "advanced generalist" practice
as a permissible concentration for an advanced (MSW) curriculum. Thus, the generalist perspective is currently well accepted as
a central orientation of social work education
at both the baccalaureate and master's levels.
Because education influences the practice
activities of its graduates for a number of
years after they enter the employment market, it can also be expected that the generalist
perspective will continue to be a dominant
one in practice.

Generalist Concept

Generalist practice requires that the
social worker examine the various facets of a
situation that needs intervention and apply
the knowledge, values, and skills either to
initiate service or to secure appropriate specialized expertise. Thus, generalist practice
involves both the capacity to take a wide
view of the practice situation and the necessary abilities to intervene at multiple levels
and in a range of situations.

As the generalist perspective has
evolved, at least two distinct practice orientations have been so labeled. One conception, a view that has gradually lost favor in
social work, is that of the *multimethod
worker* (Ripple, 1974) who has mastered several distinct practice methods or treatment
modalities and so is able to "operate on
several levels utilizing an intricate combination of intervention levels" (p. 28). The
other, the dominant generalist conception in
recent years and the conception used in the
remainder of this article, is that of the more
versatile *utility worker* (Ripple, 1974) who has
a general "understanding of people, situations, resources, etc., and who has basic
skills of observation, communication, problem solving, etc." (p. 28). The fit of the utility
worker concept of generalist practice with
the nature of social work is clearly identified
in Balinsky's (1982) statement that "the complexity of human problems necessitates a
broadly oriented practitioner with a versatile
repertoire of methods and skills capable of
interacting in any one of a number of systems" (p. 47).

Although the generalist framework
serves as a valid practice orientation in itself,
it is also a foundation for specialization. One
form of specialization involves gaining considerable depth or detail in narrow dimensions of social work practice. Typically, this
type of specialization is based on practice
method or approach, social problem, client
characteristics, practice setting, or some
combination of these dimensions. The rationale for this in-depth approach to specialization was the subject of an NASW study
(Thiemann & Battle, 1974) that concluded:

> The continuing explosion of knowledge, the
> emergence of new practice areas, the devel-
> opment of new technology and the increasing
> practice collaboration with related profes-
> sional disciplines . . . pointed to the pressing
> need, possibly the overriding need, for defin-
> itive development of social work specializa-
> tion. (p. 2)

Clearly, some social workers in some practice settings are required to have this more detailed background for practice. Most master's degree programs provide students with a choice of at least one in-depth specialization.

A second form of specialization reflects a broader and more in-depth form of generalist practice—the advanced generalist. To date it has not been determined how to differentiate clearly between the generalist and advanced generalist levels. Andrew (1976) offers an initial point of clarification by predicting that as social work evolves greater specification about these two levels, "practice at beginning levels will be defined by concepts in simplest form [and that] more advanced practice will incorporate initially learned concepts into more complex concepts and principles" (p. 5). Furthermore, whereas the beginning generalist is largely prepared for the provision of direct services to individuals, families, and groups, the scope of the advanced generalist typically expands into such indirect service areas as administration, research, and policy development. Thus the advanced generalist has both greater depth and expanded breadth.

Generic Foundation

The generalist social worker must command the generic foundation common to all social workers. Although the terms "generic" and "generalist" have, at times, been used interchangeably in the social work literature, increasingly the perception has grown that there is a common, or *generic*, foundation that underlies all social work practice, whether generalist or specialized.

What is this generic foundation? At one level, the generic foundation can be described as those universal elements that differentiate social work from other professions (Leighninger, 1980). At another level, Anderson (1981, pp. 9–19) argues that a social worker's purpose, function, focus, and objectives are constant whatever the setting or service. In addition, particular beliefs or values about people and about society's role in enhancing the quality of life are held in common by social workers. All social workers are also required to have fundamental knowledge concerning the growth and development of people (individually and in interaction with others and the society), an understanding of the scientific process, and recognition of the range of human diversity. The generic foundation also includes a commitment to the professional responsibility of the social worker to clients, employers, the social work profession, and society (NASW 1980).

From this generic foundation, from the knowledge base of the profession, and from the practice wisdom that has emerged from the experience of providing social work services, a group of practice principles has evolved. These incorporate many of the values of the profession and reflect a transition between the more abstract content of the generic foundation and the concrete knowledge and skills required for practice. The discussion of these practice principles takes various forms in the social work literature, as exemplified by Anderson (1981), Biestek (1957), Middleman & Goldberg (1974), and Siporin (1975). One list of practice principles (Sheafor, Horejsi, & Horejsi, in press) suggests that the social worker should:

1. Practice within social work's purpose, objectives, and sanctions.
2. Engage in conscious use of self.
3. Maintain professional objectivity.
4. Respect human diversity.
5. Seek personal and professional growth.
6. Engage in conscious knowledge- and value-guided practice.
7. Be concerned with the whole person.
8. Treat the client(s) with dignity.
9. Individualize the client(s).
10. Lend vision to the client(s).
11. Build on client strengths.
12. Maximize client participation.
13. Maximize client self-determination.
14. Maximize use of conventional resources.
15. Protect client confidentiality.
16. Continuously evaluate progress of the change process.
17. Be accountable to client, agency, community, and the social work profession.

These practice principles, in combination with the generic foundation, are prerequisite to both generalist and specialist practice.

Components of Generalist Practice

Generalist practice is both a perspective about practice and an approach to providing service consistent with that perspective. According to Schutz and Gordon (1977):

A true social work generalist is a specialist in knowing very well the most universally held and hence most widely applicable social work concepts, generalizations, principles and professional values. The generalist, like the biological 'genus,' covers a much wider range than any of the species or specialists that make it up. As a consequence, the generalist would know less about that which is special to more limited situations which, although necessary and highly desirable to intensive practice in those limited situations, is not readily generalizable to other . . . situations. (p. 1)

Three basic assumptions may be inferred from such a broad definition of generalist practice. First, it is assumed that the social worker has an eclectic theoretical base for practice and is grounded in a systems framework suitable for assessing multiple points for potential intervention. Second, the social worker perceives that productive intervention occurs at every practice level (individual to community) and that frequently the most effective and beneficial changes occur through multilevel interventions. Third, a central responsibility of social work practice is the guidance of the planned change or problem-solving process; this consists of exploration and assessment, goal formulation and planning, contract implementation, as well as the stabilization and termination of the process.

Perspective. Generalist practice first establishes the perspective from which the social worker approaches a practice situation. This perspective directs the social worker to assess all aspects of a situation, with special attention given to the client system—"people who sanction or ask for the change agent's services, who are the expected beneficiaries of service, and who have a working agreement or contract with the change agent" (Pincus & Minahan, 1973, p. 63)—and the various internal and external factors affecting them. As Nelsen (1975) indicates, the generalist is trained to see the widest possibilities for intervention.

Further, the generalist perspective allows the social worker to approach practice unencumbered by any particular practice approach into which the client might be expected to fit. Teisiger (1983) suggests that, for the generalist social worker:

The appropriate starting point for interventions must be determined by an examination of the entire situation and not be framed by what is initially presented. The problem . . .

selected for intervention will determine the methodology of choice rather than the methodological bias or expertise of the worker being used to define the problem. (p. 80)

Requirements. The generalist concept of practice requires that certain knowledge and skills be included in the social worker's repertoire. Although practice is differentially expressed in work related to various social problems (poverty, spouse abuse), system size (individual, group, community), or location of practice (hospital, school, rural community), common elements of generalist practice are transferable to all aspects of social work practice. Among these components of generalist practice are an eclectic knowledge base, mastery of the change process, as well as a particular set of helping skills.

The *knowledge base* for generalist practice reflects a combination of several theoretical frameworks. Currently there is no agreed-on theory of generalist practice, but at least four identifiable theoretical approaches are central to informing the actions of the generalist social worker:

Systems Framework. This framework provides a basis for assessing client situations from a holistic perspective and enables the social worker to focus on linkage between people and their formal and informal resource systems. This framework stresses work with people as they relate to complex multilevel systems and avoids the traditional dichotomies—micro versus macro practice and treatment versus social action. According to this framework, the task of the social worker is to target the appropriate client system for intervention, identify the relevant associated systems for change, and engage those systems in the change process. The systems framework directs the social worker to the functions of linkage and networking.

Structural Framework. This approach reflects the basic perspective that to aid the micro client system, it is essential to effect changes in the various structures that either support or constrain opportunity for self-actualization. Bartlett (1970) presaged the structural model when she observed:

Social workers characteristically begin by trying to understand a situation from the viewpoint of the people involved in it . . . [and are] also concerned with the welfare of others in the immediate environment. [Yet they] must give consideration to the problems of all persons suffering from the same difficulties, . . . the planning groups involved in any situation, and the interests of the whole community. (p. 178)

Middleman and Goldberg (1974) and, more recently, Anderson (1981) operationalize Bartlett's initial insight by specifying particular arenas for a systems change. These include (1) direct work with individuals experiencing difficult situations, (2) work with groups of individuals experiencing similar problems, (3) influencing natural and institutional systems affecting individuals, and (4) influencing natural and institutional systems affecting all persons suffering from a particular situation. This model establishes principles to be followed in effecting change in structures impinging on each problem area and prescribes a hierarchy of social work roles to be taken in making such change.

Ecological Framework. This model centers on the Gordon and Schutz (1977) proposition that "problems arise when the coping capacities of individuals are not sufficiently well matched with the nature of their impinging environments to produce transactions resulting in growth for them and improvement of the environment." Thus, according to this approach, social work practice is carried out at the interface between systems, and the worker's primary function is that of mediation.

Social Learning Framework. This model is based on the acquisition of the knowledge and skills required to resolve social problems through the process of human interaction. In this approach, the social worker is primarily concerned with defining the tasks to be accomplished and helping clients learn how to complete them. The principal function of the social worker, therefore, becomes one of education.

From these and other frameworks, the generalist social worker selects the most pertinent knowledge and intervention skills for each practice situation. By selecting that which is most useful from the various practice frameworks, the generalist social worker adopts an *eclectic theoretical position*. Siporin (1975) argues persuasively that eclecticism is not an excuse for "wild" or irresponsible practice. Rather, to select the best parts from various doctrines is quite appro-

priate so long as it is "consistent with other elements of social work's body of values and knowledge" (p. 153).

Planned Change Process. Having command of multiple theoretical frameworks for making eclectic practice decisions, the generalist social worker then must guide the client system through the planned change process. Satir (1964) correctly indicated that the social worker—not the clients—should direct the process. It is important to note that although each phase of the process should be carefully completed, the terms that describe the phases reflect points at which particular matters should be given primary attention. Unlike infancy and adolescence, they are not stages through which one passes never to return; rather, these phases are often overlapping and circular in nature. The social work literature describes the phases of this change process in several different forms, of which the following is just one conception:

Intake and Engagement. In this phase, the social worker devotes primary attention to preparing to initiate the helping activity, defining the matters to be addressed, determining if service can be provided or if the client system should be referred elsewhere for service, initiating a helping relationship, and engaging the client system in the process of change.

Assessment. The assessment phase emphasizes collecting and analyzing factual and impressionistic data concerning the client system's situation and the various other systems affected.

Planning and Contracting. In this phase, the client system and worker consider the range of solutions available and the implications of using various means to achieve them, select the most viable approaches to the necessary change, and develop a formal or informal contract that clarifies the responsibilities of all parties concerned and the timetable for action.

Intervention. During this phase the action to achieve the planned change occurs, and the various affected systems, including the social worker, carry out the responsibilities they accepted in the previous phase.

Monitoring and Evaluation. Although monitoring and evaluation occur to some degree throughout the change process, special attention must be paid to the success of the planned interventions to determine their degree of success and the advisability of revising the plan to attempt other means of achieving the desired change.

Termination. In this final phase, the social worker must help the client system to (1) determine when it is appropriate to discontinue the provision of this service and (2) build continuing support systems or select other sources of helping that can satisfy unmet needs.

Essential Activities. To carry out the planned change process, the generalist social worker must be skilled in at least five basic activities (Landon & Fiet, in press).

Preparing for each encounter with clients and related systems is the initial activity that must be undertaken. This involves a review of what is known about the system itself, relevant knowledge regarding the situation, anticipated ethical and value issues, and possible personal reactions and difficulties in order to sensitize oneself to potential trouble spots.

Throughout the planned change process, the social worker must be skilled in *communicating*. This is the primary process and tool of social work and consists of verbal, nonverbal, and written transactions through which workers arrive at and implement the client system's goals for planned change. Interviewing and recording are important subsets of this skill.

The principal cognitive skill is *analyzing*. A substantial part of the considerable person-to-person communication that social work requires involves sorting and thinking through the various factors that have an impact on the client system and selecting the appropriate intervention approach.

Contracting is the process by which the social worker and the client system arrive at a plan to work together toward specific goals with the resources, timetable, tasks, and evaluation points established.

Generalist practice involves the social worker in *role-taking*. The goals that are identified, the demands of the client system, and the requirements of other systems targeted for change determine which roles the social worker selects. Roles typically performed by the generalist social worker include conferee, enabler, educator, manager, broker, mediator, and advocate.

The generalist practitioner must also have *stabilizing* skills. Stabilization in the planned change process involves both process and summative actions. It involves monitoring with the client what is going in at each stage in order to support and solidify change and to make necessary changes in the analysis, contract, or intervention strategy. It also involves a final summation of what has been attempted, identification of successful change and work still to be done, and positive disengagement from the professional relationship (Landon & Fiet, in press).

Future of the Generalist Perspective

The emergence of the generalist perspective gives the social worker both a theoretical outlook and a means of approaching practice that are compatible with the broad range of social work practice. The next steps in the development of the generalist perspective should be its refinement into a solid conceptual framework and further clarification of the appropriate breadth and depth for each level of generalist practice.

Bradford W. Sheafor
Pamela S. Landon

For further information, see Appendix 2: CSWE Curriculum Policy Statement; Direct Practice: Trends and Issues; Ecological Perspective.

References

Abbott, E. (1919). "The Social Caseworker and the Enforcement of Industrial Legislation." In *Proceedings of the National Conference on Social Work, 1918* (pp. 310–317). Chicago: Rogers & Hall.

American Association of Social Workers. (1974). *Social Casework: Generic and Specific, A Report of the Milford Conference.* New York: National Association of Social Workers. (Original work published 1929)

Anderson, J. (1981). *Social Work Methods and Processes.* Belmont, Calif.: Wadsworth.

Andrew, G. (1976). "Doing Concepts: Thoughts Toward Resolution of the Continuum Dilemma." *Journal of Education for Social Work, 12*(1), 3–10.

Baer, B. L., & Federico, R. (Eds.). (1978–1979). *Educating the Baccalaureate Social Worker* (Vols. 1–2). Cambridge, Mass.: Ballinger.

Balinsky, R. (1982). "Generic Practice in Graduate Social Work Curricula: A Study of Educators' Experiences and Attitudes." *Journal of Education for Social Work, 18*(3), 46–54.

Bartlett, H. M. (1958). "Toward Clarification and

Improvement of Social Work Practice." *Social Work, 3*(3), 3–9.

Bartlett, H. M. (1970). *The Common Base of Social Work Practice.* New York: National Association of Social Workers.

Biestek, F. (1957). *The Casework Relationship.* Chicago: Loyola University Press.

Bisno, H. (1969). "A Theoretical Framework for Teaching Social Work Methods and Skills, With Particular Reference to Undergraduate Social Welfare Education." *Journal of Education for Social Work, 5*(1), 5–17.

Council on Social Work Education. (1971). *Undergraduate Programs in Social Work: Guidelines to Curriculum Content, Field Instruction, and Organization.* New York: Author.

Council on Social Work Education. (1974). *Standards for the Accreditation of Baccalaureate Degree Programs in Social Work.* New York: Author.

Council on Social Work Education. (1984). *Handbook of Accreditation Standards and Procedures* (rev. ed.). New York: Author.

Flexner, A. (1915). "Is Social Work a Profession?" In *Proceedings of the National Conference on Charities and Corrections, 1915* (pp. 576–590). New York: National Conference on Charities and Corrections.

Goldstein, H. (1973). *Social Work Practice: A Unitary Approach.* Columbia, S.C.: University of South Carolina Press.

Gordon, W. E. (1962). "A Critique of the Working Definition." *Social Work, 7*(5), 3–13.

Gordon, W. E., & Schutz, M. L. (1977). "A Natural Basis for Social Work Specializations." *Social Work, 22*(5), 422–426.

Hearn, G. (Ed.). (1969). *A General Systems Approach: Contributions Toward an Holistic Conception of Social Work.* New York: Council on Social Work Education.

Hollis, E. V., & Taylor, A. L. (1951). *Social Work Education in the United States.* New York: Columbia University Press.

Johnson, L. C. (1983). *Social Work Practice: A Generalist Approach.* Boston: Allyn & Bacon.

Landon, P. S., & Fiet, M. (in press). *The Realities of Generalist Practice.* St. Paul, Minn.: West Publishing.

Leighninger, L. (1980). "The Generalist-Specialist Debate in Social Work." *Social Service Review, 54*(1), 1–12.

McPheeters, H. L., & Ryan, R. M. (1971). *A Core of Competence for Baccalaureate Social Welfare.* Atlanta, Ga.: Southern Regional Education Board.

Middleman, R. R., & Goldberg, G. (1974). *Social Service Delivery: A Structural Approach to Social Work Practice.* New York: Columbia University Press.

Morales, A., & Sheafor, B. W. (1983). *Social Work: A Profession of Many Faces* (3rd ed.). Boston: Allyn & Bacon.

National Association of Social Workers. (1980). *NASW Code of Ethics.* Silver Spring, Md.: Author.

Nelsen, J. C. (1975). "Social Work's Fields of Practice, Methods, and Models: The Choice to Act." *Social Service Review, 49*(2), 264–270.

Pincus, A., & Minahan, A. (1973). *Social Work Practice: Model and Method.* Itasca, Ill.: F. E. Peacock Publishers.

Pumphrey, R. E., & Pumphrey, M. W. (1961). *The Heritage of American Social Work.* New York: Columbia University Press.

Richmond, M. E. (1917). *Social Diagnosis.* New York: Russell Sage Foundation.

Ripple, L. (1974). *Report to the Task Force on Structure and Quality in Social Work Education.* New York: Council on Social Work Education.

Satir, V. (1964). *Conjoint Family Therapy.* Palo Alto, Calif.: Science & Behavior Books.

Schutz, M. L., & Gordon, W. E. (1977). "The Social Work Generalist as a Specialist." Paper presented at the Annual Program Meeting, Council on Social Work Education, Phoenix, Ariz.

Sheafor, B. W., Horejsi, C., & Horejsi, G. (in press). *Techniques for Social Work Practice.* Boston: Allyn & Bacon.

Siporin, M. (1975). *Introduction to Social Work Practice.* New York: Macmillan Publishing Co.

Thiemann, B., & Battle, M. (1974). *Specialization in Social Work Profession.* Washington, D.C.: National Association of Social Workers.

Teisiger, K. S. (1983). "Evaluation of Education for Generalist Practice." *Journal of Education for Social Work, 19*(1), 79–85.

GESTALT THERAPY

Gestalt therapy takes its name from the German word *Gestalt*, which denotes "whole" or "configuration." It was developed as an alternative to Freudian explanations of behavior and therapy by the psychoanalyst Frederick S. (Fritz) Perls. Perls's ideas were first published in his *Ego, Hunger and Aggression: A Revision of Freud's Theory and Method* (Perls, 1947). Information on the origins of and early theoretical developments in gestalt therapy is found in the works of

Perls (see especially 1969a,b) and Perls, Hefferline, and Goodman (1951). Further details on theoretical and practice dimensions of gestalt therapy may be found in the works of Polster and Polster (1973) and Zinker (1977). *The Handbook of Gestalt Therapy* (Hatcher & Himmelstein, 1976) is a useful compendium. Most recent trends, issues, and research in gestalt therapy are regularly reviewed in the *Gestalt Journal,* published semiannually.

Basic Concepts

Basic concepts of gestalt therapy include figure/ground, contact, awareness, wholeness, self-regulation, and the here-and-now. Gestalt therapy is ahistorical in approach—existential and phenomenological. In the gestalt view, "talking about" a feeling or problem is insufficient. Therapy involves the whole organism; no dichotomies are drawn between mind and body, thought and action. The connection between thoughts, feelings, and bodily expression is a critical task. As Polster and Polster (1973, p. 7) noted:

> Some of the most pervasive of the new perspectives which are the foundations of gestalt therapy . . . are the following: 1) power is in the present; 2) experience counts most; 3) the therapist is his own instrument; and 4) therapy is too good to be limited to the sick.

Awareness is a key concept and therapeutic tool in gestalt therapy. It refers to an organism's degree of contact with the environment and its internal feelings and processes. Awareness also refers to the ability to describe and experience sensations and perceptions that flow into the organism from the social and physical environment and from memories, thoughts, and past experiences that are stored in the mind. As Polster and Polster (1973, p. 211) defined it, awareness is "a continuous means for keeping up-to-date with one's self." The gestalt therapist works with a client not only to keep up to date but to expand awareness.

Contact with other people and with one's self—connections to internal and external environments—is essential to awareness. *Self-support* is the result of risking exchanges across contact boundaries and the full utilization of "contact functions" or the senses. Gestalt therapists believe that human beings begin life with the capability for awareness, excitement, and growth but are quickly taught that some behaviors (and therefore even some thoughts) are bad and intolerable. Such messages may stifle a person's sense of being able to cope with the world. If introjected or incorporated, such (usually parental) messages create conflict with the person's sense of self, often being experienced as compelling and repetitive yet somehow foreign. Therefore, gestalt therapists work toward expanding the range and scope of contact so the early repertoire of coping behaviors and attitudes may be reclaimed. Chronic modes of deflecting or diminishing contact (stereotyped mannerisms, for example, or chattering) are brought into "figure," that is, into awareness out of the "ground" (background) of habit or neglected experiences. New ways of expression and expressiveness are experimented with and explored.

Because of the here-and-now and contact principles of gestalt therapy, social workers may have to learn new ways of looking at, understanding, explaining, and experiencing the world. In this ahistorical, present-oriented approach, some typical concerns of social workers are not addressed. "Why" questions, whose intent is to get at the causes of behavior, for example, are not of interest to gestalt therapists. The ways in which an individual fails to use resources in the environment, deflects or diminishes excitement, or uses rigid boundaries to reduce contact are of greater interest. Feelings attached to a past event may be recaptured and dealt with according gestalt therapists, but a search for causes can be draining and itself be used as a deflection of awareness. Because gestalt is both a world view and a therapeutic approach, social workers who wish to use gestalt principles will find it necessary to rethink traditional notions of the uses of the past. Gestalt therapy always returns to the realities and potentialities of present awareness, to experience, to expression and action, and to considerations of choices.

Although it is ahistorical, gestalt therapy does not deny the reality and the weight of the past in present experience. Rather than talking about the past, the gestalt therapist and the client use experiments so that past sensations can be experienced in a fresh way, fragments of the past can be drawn into a new "figure," and "unfinished" business can be finished. *Unfinished business* refers to the events and emotions of the past which, for whatever reason, were not brought to closure. The gestalt experiment is the theater (and distinctive method) of gestalt therapy, in which the client can try out new roles or play old roles with new variations, or express emotions in a safe environment. Past events are spoken of in the present tense and acted out so that their impact on the current outlook or circumstances of the client can be heightened and immediately felt. Experiments involve both physical and verbal expression. The gestalt therapist helps the client to get at the impact of past experiences on present behavior by assisting him or her to focus on what happened, to feel again the emotions attached to events and people, and to acknowledge or claim (rather than deflect or deny) his or her feelings in the present.

Purpose

The purpose of gestalt therapy is to produce or sustain change in the direction of a heightened sense of self-support and self-responsibility. Because it is an existential therapy, practitioners give careful attention to process (Zinker, 1977). Content is not ignored, but processes that evolve and will keep evolving are of higher interest. Recognition is given to life as a process and to the fact that as life unfolds, "problems" arise and new obstacles to awareness and contact appear. Gestalt therapists, therefore, are unwilling to discuss character reconstruction or abreaction in any way that would imply a "cure" or that the life process is anything other than ongoing and dynamic. The client may experience closure in a given therapeutic episode or situation, but his or her own process of maintaining freshness, awareness, and openness to change and new experiences is the focus. That gestalt point of view is related to, and extends, the problem-solving approach in social work.

Although gestalt therapists do not focus on resistance to change in the same way as do those of a psychodynamic persuasion, they are aware that the prospect of change may be unsettling; movement toward change, hesitant; and the heightening of responsibility and responsiveness, difficult. Gestalt therapists agree with psychodynamic therapists that people adopt and repetitively use certain

mechanisms of protection or defense. They do not believe, however, that those mechanisms are necessarily explained by theoretical constructs about contending structures (such as ego, id, and superego) in the unconscious. Instead, gestalt therapists pay careful attention to the ways in which individuals protect themselves from the excitement of experience and awareness through such resistances as introjection, projection, retroflection, deflection, and confluence (Polster & Polster, 1973, pp. 70–92). Resistance to conflict is of more interest to gestalt therapists than is unconscious resistance.

Gestalt therapists are skeptical of technique *qua* technique. A preoccupation with technique can diminish the therapist's ability to use himself or herself fully, to stay in the present, and to remain open to surprises in the therapeutic encounter. The gestalt therapist's major therapeutic tool is his or her own openness to arousal and experience and willingness to attend closely to another person. Techniques such as the exaggeration of nonverbal expression, directed fantasy, and the therapist's use of his or her experience in the moment are useful but must be highly individualized. Experiments, by definition, emerge from the interplay of client-issue-therapist and are created for specific therapeutic purposes in the present.

Gestalt Therapy and Social Work

The gestalt therapist does not begin work with clients in the ways prescribed by prevailing modes of direct practice in social work. That is, the gestalt therapist does not work from a history, does not formulate treatment plans based on a diagnosis, and does not expect that some goal (predetermined or otherwise) will be attained. The therapist may bring to the situation excitement about what *may* happen but not expectation that something *has to* happen. That point of view about goals is linked to the principle of self-support and self-responsibility. The perspective on treatment plans and diagnoses follows from assumptions about the validity of present experience and the need to work with experience as it occurs.

Many of the assumptions and approaches of gestalt therapy are compatible with many of the common elements of social casework or direct methods of social work intervention, whether taken from a psychosocial or problem-solving perspective. Both gestalt therapists and social workers call attention to the person-in-situation, take whole systems into account, prize self-awareness, and value the stimulation of clients toward self-support. Gestalt principles may not have had a broader influence on social workers because the ahistorical perspective is in conceptual and ideological conflict with the prevailing psychodynamic theoretical and practice formulations.

Gestalt and social work perspectives can be contrasted on a number of points. Both "begin where the client is" and focus on the person-in-environment. Whereas social workers tend to work within a goal-oriented, "helping" relationship, gestalt therapists emphasize a process-oriented, existential relationship. Social work treatment is often based on a study of the client's history, while gestalt therapy uses the experiments that arise in the therapeutic situation. For the social worker, history is causation, but for the gestalt therapist, history is ground. The purpose of social work intervention is usually to solve problems or to attain goals; the purpose of gestalt therapy is to look for enhanced awareness and the capacity for contact. The "why" perspective of social work stands in contrast to the "what and how" perspective of gestalt therapy, which also emphasizes such purposes as revelation, integration, and the development of the self, rather than "reconstruction." Resistance to awareness attracts the interest of the gestalt therapist, while the social worker might find unconscious defenses more important. Whereas the social worker might focus on content, the gestalt therapist will focus on process. The social worker might tend to stress a professional worker/client relationship, but the gestalt therapist will look for a relationship characterized by mutuality and reciprocity.

Both as a world view and a therapeutic approach, gestalt therapy can be a useful adjunct to the principles and practice wisdom of the direct practice methods of social work. Accommodation must be made for gestalt therapy's orientation to the present, which cannot be introduced idly into the traditional methods. Because the gestalt experiment is often dramatic, neophytes may be tempted to use experiments as a "gestalt technique." However, an experiment can be of value only when it arises both from an understanding of the gestalt philosophy and the context of a particular therapeutic encounter. Therefore, social workers who wish to use gestalt therapy in their practice need training in this form of therapy in addition to their professional social work education. Training programs are located throughout the country; among the oldest are those located in New York City; Cleveland, Ohio; Los Angeles, California; and La Jolla, California.

GARY A. LLOYD

References

Hatcher, C., & Himelstein, P. (1976). *Handbook of Gestalt Therapy*. New York: Jason Aronson.

Perls, F. S. (1947). *Ego, Hunger and Aggression*. London, England: Allen & Unwin.

Perls, F. S. (1969a). *Gestalt Therapy Verbatim*. Moab, Utah: Real People Press.

Perls, F. S. (1969b). *In and Out of the Garbage Pail*. Moab, Utah: Real People Press.

Perls, F. S., Hefferline, R. F., & Goodman, P. (1951). *Gestalt Therapy*. New York: Julian Press.

Polster, E., & Polster, M. (1973). *Gestalt Therapy Integrated: Contours of Theory and Practice*. New York: Brunner/Mazel.

Zinker, J. (1977). *Creative Process in Gestalt Therapy*. New York: Vintage Books.

GONZALEZ MOLINA DE LA CARO, DOLORES. See biographical section.

GRANGER, LESTER BLACKWELL. See biographical section.

GRIEF. See LOSS AND BEREAVEMENT.

GROUP CARE FOR CHILDREN

The Child Welfare League of America (CWLA) defines residential group care services for children as

a child welfare service that provides 24-hour care for a child in a residential facility designed as a therapeutic environment. Within this setting are integrated treatment services, educational services and group living on the basis of an individual plan for each child who cannot be effectively helped in his or her own home, with a substitute family or in a less intensive group setting. . . . (CWLA, 1982, p. 15)

The goal of residential centers is for every child to return to life in the community with improved ability to cope and succeed, whether with his or her own family or a substitute family, in another type of group care (for example, a group home), or, for older youths, through independent living. Residential services should be planned with a foreseeable termination. Prolonged or indefinite periods of residential care are not acceptable practice (CWLA, 1982, p. 15).

Several types of group care settings exist for children who are dependent or have behavioral or emotional difficulties. These include residential treatment centers, group homes, crisis and shelter care facilities, children's psychiatric facilities, respite care programs, training schools, and residential drug and alcohol programs. Group care services are provided through all the major sectors of care: child welfare, developmental disabilities, juvenile corrections, and mental health. Although residential group care settings vary in treatment philosophy and organization, virtually all involve the use of the 24-hour living environment as a vehicle for altering maladaptive behavior. Often such environmentally oriented treatment is referred to as "milieu treatment," defined as

> a specifically designed environment in which the events of daily living are used as formats for teaching competence in basic life skills. The living environment becomes both a means and a context for growth and change, informed by a culture that stresses learning through living. (Whittaker, 1979, p. 36)

Teaching formats include rule structures, token economies, daily routines, and play and other activities as well as specialized education, counseling, and treatment for children and families. Great variation exists in group care services with respect to intensity and duration of treatment, locus of treatment (for example, campus-based cottages or community group homes), and staffing patterns. Typically, direct care responsibilities (and sometimes major treatment and educational responsibilities) are given to staff referred to

as child or youth care workers, house parents, teaching parents, group care counselors, and the like. Complementary and supportive areas often include social work, special education, recreation and occupational therapy, psychiatry, and clinical psychology (Hobbs, 1982; Phillips et al., 1974; Whittaker, 1979).

In many types of residential group care, social workers perform a variety of key tasks including provision of treatment services to children and families, service coordination and case management, community consultation, and advocacy. In certain sectors of care—for example, child welfare—social workers and social work agencies play a dominant role in delivering group care services.

In general, one must be wary of attempts to explain group care services as a single entity. Rather, they include a range of different kinds of residential placements that overlap considerably in terms of definition, purpose, and population served. Nor is the implied impression that the most severely disturbed children are served in more sophisticated and more restrictive residential treatment centers empirically borne out in existing programs. Severely disturbed children are being treated in less restrictive, more family-oriented settings (Cherry, 1976; Dimock, 1977; Rubenstein et al., 1978). Moreover, Maluccio and Marlow's (1972) observation regarding the process of placement in institutional care is still largely correct:

> The decision to place a child in residential treatment is presently a highly-individualized matter based on a complex set of idiosyncratic factors defying categorization. The literature does not indicate agreement on consistent criteria or universal guidelines and it is not certain whether institutions diverse in origin, philosophy, policy, and clientele can agree on a basic set of premises. (p. 239)

Recent reform in public child welfare policy, notably the passage of the Adoption Assistance and Child Welfare Act of 1980 (P.L. 96-272), mandates that any out-of-home placement be undertaken only after "reasonable efforts" have been made to prevent family breakup. This intent is consistent with the statement made by CWLA (1982) on the undesirability of "prolonged or indefinite periods of residential care" (p. 15). The presumption of most recent reform efforts in child and youth services has been that substitute care alternatives have been overused (in lieu of home-based alternatives), have been improperly monitored, and have led, in some instances, to institutional abuse and neglect. Most professionals would agree that to the extent these presumptions are valid as well as for reasons having to do with the extreme cost of 24-hour-a-day care, a more judicious, parsimonious use of residential group care services is warranted. Attitudes toward group care have always been strong and have occasioned much debate within the profession of social work.

Historical Legacy

The century-old debate between residential group care and foster family care detailed by Wolins and Piliavin (1964) in the early 1960s continues today. From its inception, this debate has engendered controversy, criticism, and countercriticism, much of it finding its most articulate and passionate expression in leaders of the institutional and foster care field itself. In 1925, for example, Reeder argued: "As a permanent home for the early years of dependent children, the orphan asylum should go out of business" (p. 286). Langer (1925) replied: "The foster home is not a panacea for social ills and should not be advertised as the 'Soothing Syrup' of social work" (p. 624). The following constitute some of the more important milestones in the historical development of residential group care services in the United States:

■ The establishment of an orphanage by the Ursuline nuns of New Orleans in 1729 to care for children orphaned by an Indian massacre at Natchez—the first children's institution in the present boundaries of the United States (Bremner, 1970, pp. 60–61; Whittaker, 1971a).

■ House of Refuge, first institution for juvenile delinquents, founded in New York in 1825. Similar institutions founded in Boston (1826) and Philadelphia (1828) (Bremner, 1970, p. 820).

■ Lyman School, first state reform school for boys, founded in Westborough, Massachusetts, in 1847 on the model of the German agricultural reformatory. It is not without irony that Lyman School was also the first state training school to close in the

now famous "Massachusetts experiment" with deinstitutionalization in the early 1970s (Bremner, 1970, pp. 697–711; 1974, pp. 1084–1086; Coates, Miller, & Ohlin, 1978).

■ New York Children's Aid Society sends its first band of children to the West in 1855. What Charles Loring Brace and others saw as saving children from the evil influences of the city and congregate institutions, others—notably, the Irish Catholic community in New York whose children were most affected—saw as a nativist plot to separate their children from their culture, family, and religion. One direct outgrowth of the "placing out" movement was the growth of Roman Catholic and other denominational institutions to care for dependent and neglected children (Bremner, 1970, pp. 669–670, 747–750).

■ The move in the late nineteenth century from congregate to cottage-style institutions in an attempt to achieve a more "familylike" atmosphere (Rothman, 1980, pp. 265–283).

■ The inception and growth of the mental hygiene movement in the first quarter of the twentieth century, beginning with the work of Healy in Chicago, with its emphasis on classification of childhood disorders and on differential diagnoses and treatment (Bremner, 1970, pp. 536–538; Whittaker, 1971b).

■ The slow transition of many children's institutions in the 1930s, 1940s, and 1950s from care of essentially "dependent" children to "residential treatment" of "emotionally disturbed" children (Bettelheim & Sylvester, 1948; Bremner, 1974, pp. 637–643; Mayer & Blum, 1971; Redl & Wineman, 1957).

■ Recent "discoveries" of abuse and neglect in residential institutions for disturbed and delinquent youths coupled with and, in part, responsible for efforts to deinstitutionalize service programs in mental health, juvenile correction, child welfare, and mental retardation (Coates, Ohlin, & Miller, 1978; National Commission on Children in Need of Parents, 1979; Taylor, 1981; Wolfensberger, 1972; Wooden, 1976).

These events in the history of group care for children cluster in four phases:

1. The period of physical separation sought to extricate dependent, delinquent, and "defective" children from indiscriminate

mixing in almshouses, workhouses, jails, and the like and provide a separate set of institutions specifically for their use (Whittaker, 1971a).

2. The move from congregate to cottage-style care, begun in the late nineteenth century, sought to replace older barracks-style institutions with smaller, family-style units staffed by house parents. Although the intent of this movement was clear, the resulting "cottage" was often quite large by today's standards, although it maintained at least the overlay of a familylike atmosphere.

3. The psychological phase begun in the early part of the twentieth century sought to apply organizational and treatment concepts from the emerging child guidance movement to the institutional field (Whittaker, 1971b). These included the use of psychological tests, the psychiatric team concept, and the delineation of child care and child treatment functions. Later, the pioneering work of Herschel Alt, Bruno Bettelheim, Fritz Redl, and others in the late 1940s and early 1950s developed various psychoanalytically grounded expressions of the "therapeutic" milieu with more attention to factors like group dynamics and greater focus on line staff as primary agents of treatment.

4. Finally, what might be called the ecological or environmental phase was stimulated by outcome evaluations that showed differences in treatment outcome related more to factors like presence or absence of postplacement community supports than to factors like caseworker judgment, degree of success achieved in program, treatment model, or severity of presenting problems (Whittaker & Pecora, 1984). Such findings, as well as broader policy trends toward deinstitutionalization and service normalization, forced the attention of residential programs from an almost total preoccupation with what went on inside the institution to such external factors as community linkages, family work, and aftercare.

Thus, the history of residential group care for children suggests that rather than passing from the scene completely, it is once again in the process of transformation. This transformation is readily apparent in the changing demography of the group care population and the changing structure of group care agencies.

Demography of Group Child Care

The most recent systematic and comprehensive census of children and youths in group care was completed by Pappenfort and his colleagues at the University of Chicago's School of Social Service Administration.[1] This survey, for the year 1981 (Dore, Young, & Pappenfort, 1984; Pappenfort & Young, 1983), updates an earlier survey conducted by Pappenfort in 1965 (Pappenfort, Kilpatrick, & Roberts, 1973). The recent survey included residential facilities in virtually all sectors of care—mental health, juvenile corrections, and child welfare, for example—and identified the following trends:

■ Although the number of residential group care facilities has increased markedly since 1966, the number of children and youths in care has declined.

■ Growth in the number of facilities has been concentrated in juvenile justice facilities for children and youths considered delinquent or status offenders and in mental health facilities.

■ Facilities in all categories have declined in size over the past 16 years. In 1966, less than 50 percent of the facilities surveyed had fewer than 26 children and youths in residence. The majority of all facilities surveyed in 1982 were of this size.

■ In 1982, the number of children were almost evenly divided between public and private facilities. Slightly more than one third of all children were in juvenile justice facilities, one fourth were in mental health facilities, and about one fifth were in child welfare facilities. The remainder of children were in short-term care facilities (Pappenfort & Young, 1983).

In all, more than 125,000 children were in group care in more than 3,900 facilities in 1981, down from 155,000 children in 2,300 facilities in 1965. The drop in placement figures reflects both a decline in actual placements and a decline in the rate of group care placement: from 19.9 per 10,000 youths in

---

[1] The California Association of Services for Children has also conducted a comprehensive survey of several thousand children in its member group care agencies. This survey documents the multiplicity and seriousness of problems presented by children and parents and illustrates the diverse uses of placement across different sectors of care (Fitzharris, 1985).

Table 1. U.S. Family Environment

	Children under 18	
Child Living With:	Number (in millions)	Percentage
Both biological parents	39.3	63
Mother only	12.5	20
Father only	1.2	2
One biological parent and one stepparent	6.2	10
Two adoptive parents	1.2	2
Grandparents or other relatives	1.6	2
Foster parents, other nonrelatives, or in institution	0.4	1
Total	62.4	100

Source: *Select Committee on Children, Youth, and Families: A Report.* (1983). Washington, D.C.: U.S. Government Printing Office.

1965 to 17.3 per 10,000 youths in 1981 (Pappenfort & Young, 1983; Dore, Young & Pappenfort, 1984).

In certain sectors of care, nongovernmental services play a major role. For example, 92 percent of children and youths in group care services for the emotionally disturbed received that care from voluntary and proprietary agencies. Proprietary vendorship is apparently on the rise and currently includes 4.5 percent of all children in group care and 8.5 percent of all children in nongovernmental group care (Pappenfort & Young, 1983).

Dore, Young, & Pappenfort (1984) conclude from these data that, at least with respect to the downward trend in facility size, there is some evidence for the success of previously identified major policy initiatives in normalization, deinstitutionalization, and the right to treatment (Dore & Kennedy, 1981). Analyses in progress by Pappenfort and his colleagues are attempting to determine whether the other goals of these initiatives—such as increased family involvement, shorter lengths of stay, greater interaction between community and facility, and rights of residents to have regularly scheduled case reviews—are also evident from the survey data.

Some analysts are concerned with what appears to be a shift of youngsters—as a result of the removal of status offenders from the juvenile justice system, for example—from more traditional sectors of care to private drug rehabilitation and psychiatric residential settings that are often proprietary

(Schwartz, Jackson-Beelk, & Anderson, 1983). Similarly, several investigative accounts in recent years have documented abuses in voluntary placements in group care services sponsored by religious institutions, which often avoid both public funding and public licensing (Taylor, 1981; Wooden, 1976). Other investigations have pursued the occurrence of abuse and neglect in residential settings, which many experts view as a growing problem (National Center on Child Abuse and Neglect, 1978). These two categories of group care—private psychiatric placements, often funded directly by third-party payments, and private, voluntary placements in religious institutions—constitute what some have called the "hidden sector" of group care.

A central factor influencing present policy for all out-of-home services for children and youths is that, in the aggregate, across all kinds of substitute care service, children receiving such services represent less than 1 percent of the nation's population 0–17 years (Select Committee on Children, Youth, and Families, 1983). This explains, in part, why foster family care and group care for children and youths have not ranked higher on the national policy agenda. The overwhelming majority of American children reside with one or both biological parents or in adoptive homes, as is shown in Table 1.

In contrast, developmental disabilities involve approximately 10 percent of the nation's general population. Such relative lack of visibility for group care and foster care may be either the cause or a consequence of the situation described by Steiner (1981) in the *Futility of Family Policy*:

> Foster care has been no First Lady's "principal interest," nor has a secretary of HEW taken it on as a personal crusade. Consequently, it did not receive the high-level attention in the late 1970s that was briefly accorded mental health policy and the dangers of cigarette smoking. Because foster care neither makes a substantial difference in the federal budget nor involves millions of people, it does not automatically command attention. Scandal does provide occasional visibility, but it is scandal usually limited to childrearing practices in a particular setting rather than intolerable scandal entailing fraud in benefit claims or other continuing misuse of public money (p. 144).

Whether foster care and group care will become a "first lady's interest" remains to be seen. What is clear is that for reasons of survival, group care agencies for children and youths will increasingly need to relate their mission to developments in foster family care (such as foster family–based treatment) and intensive, in-home services.

Given the relatively small proportion of children in care, it is noteworthy that reform of out-of-home care did surface on the national political agenda, culminating in the passage of the previously cited Adoption Assistance and Child Welfare Act of 1980.[2] The intent of this act is to provide permanent homes for children cast adrift in the foster care system, either by returning them to their biological parents or putting them up for adoption. For those children at risk of "disruption," the act mandates that "reasonable efforts" at prevention of placement be carried out prior to placement and compels a judicial review to occur before such placement is made. Various other provisions include conducting an inventory of all children in the foster care system (including residential care) and providing special subsidies for the adoption of "special needs" children. The means for achieving these objectives include development of statewide information systems, case review procedures, judicial review of placements, preventive family-

oriented services, and development of statewide plans for child welfare services. In general, the implementation of various components is tied to continuance of federal funding for foster care payments, although the present administration has given the states considerably more latitude in determining compliance than was the case with the original regulations from the Department of Health and Human Services.

Although it is still too early to assess the overall impact of the legislation, the U.S. Children's Bureau recently estimated that both the total number of children in foster care and group child care and the mean length of stay have declined markedly since a national estimate was conducted in 1977 (Shyne & Schroeder, 1978). Other findings from several studies conducted after the passage of the legislation were as follows:

- There are approximately equal numbers of males and females in foster care [includes group care].
- The percentage of the foster care population that is minority appears to be about 40–45%.
- About 70% of children in foster care reside in foster family homes, 30% in group residential settings.
- Return to parents and relatives is the placement goal for 40% of the children in substitute care, while 49% actually do return home.
- Three-fourths of the children entered foster care because of family-related reasons and over three-fourths of these were for abuse and neglect (U.S. Children's Bureau, 1983).

These findings and the general policy direction of the 1980 act suggest that the case for placement—of any sort—will be more difficult to make and will rest on the presumption that reasonable efforts have been made to keep the child and family together. For social work agencies engaged primarily in the delivery of group care services for children—and in certain sectors of care, the overwhelming proportion of children receive care from voluntary social service agencies (Dore et al., 1984)—the question increasingly becomes: What are the consequences of limiting the agency's mission to a population that, at most, represents a declining fraction of less than 1 percent of the nation's children and youths? In addition to these demographic

---

[2] A brief overview of this legislation—its antecedents and consequences—will be offered here. For further detail, see the excellent review of issues leading up to the reform provided by Maluccio (1977) and McGowan and Meezan (1983).

data, a growing body of research on the effectiveness of group care services now exists that will doubtless influence the future direction of group care services.

Implications of Outcome Research

The following is a brief summary of what outcome research says about the effectiveness of group care services (Whittaker & Pecora, 1984; Kadushin, 1980; Durkin & Durkin, 1975). Basically, such effectiveness depends on how one reads the data, when one reads the data, and how confident one is in the methodology of the various investigators. To take the last first, methodological problems involving internal and external validity and reliability abound in studies of residential group care. Typically, these involve the absence of control or contrast groups, the absence of random assignment, vaguely defined service units, narrow or inappropriate selection of outcome criteria, and sample selection bias or observer/rater bias (Whittaker & Pecora, 1984). On the remaining questions of how and when one reads the data, certain generalizations appear to be borne out across many studies. First, if one limits analysis to hard indicators of adjustment such as school behavior, court contacts, and the like, group care fares poorly. On more subjective indicators such as a therapist's judgment of progress or various forms of consumer evaluation, group care appears effective. Second, if one samples behavior during residential treatment or immediately at discharge in relation to the treatment environment, group care looks reasonably effective. If one samples behavior at increasing intervals in such environments as school, community, and family, the decay of treatment effects appears pronounced.

Given the potential weaknesses in research design and the difficulty in interpreting results, the outcome research in residential group care still yields several general findings. First, the postdischarge environment appears to be a powerful factor in determining successful adjustment, irrespective of gains made while in the program. Studies by Allerhand, Weber, and Haug (1966); Taylor and Alpert (1973); Cavior, Schmidt, and Karacki (1972); and others all support this general finding. The Allerhand et al. (1966) study, which involved the extensive follow-up of 50 graduates of a sophisticated residential treatment agency located in Ohio (Bellefaire), summarizes its major findings as follows:

> Perhaps the most striking finding of the study is that none of the measurements of within-Bellefaire performance at discharge, either in casework or in cottage and school roles, were useful in themselves in predicting postdischarge adaptability and adaptation. Only when the situation to which the child returned was taken into account were performances at Bellefaire related to postdischarge adequacies. In a stressful community situation, strengths nurtured within the institution tended to break down, whereas in a supportive situation, these strengths tended to be reinforced. (p. 140)

The importance of the postplacement environment was underscored in later research by Taylor and Alpert (1973), which indicated that contact with biological parents while the child was in placement was positively correlated with postdischarge adjustment. The researchers conclude that neither the child's presenting symptoms nor any specific treatment variables were strongly associated with postdischarge adjustment: it "is not possible to predict a child's postdischarge adaptation on the basis of a given set of preadmission characteristics" (p. 35). Similar findings with respect to specific treatment variables and outcome were identified in studies conducted by Davids, Ryan, & Salvatore (1968). They conclude that "treatment variables, especially conventional psychotherapy, seem to bear little relationship to subsequent adjustment" (p. 474; Davids and Salvatore, 1976). This lack of demonstrated effect may partly stem from still primitive attempts to conceptualize and measure the key treatment variables in a complex intervention like residential treatment. Nelson, Singer, and Johnsen (1978) found that children and youths leaving residential treatment with supportive community ties to family, friends, neighbors, schools, and the like were more likely to maintain their treatment gains than those who left without such ties. Those with support maintained over 70 percent of their gains, while those without support maintained only 50 percent. Although the sample size was small (22), this study is notable in that it measured behavior at four points in time beginning with a pretreatment baseline of community ties. Similar results were obtained by Lewis (1982) in a followup of a RE-ED program, although again, the small sample size limits generalization.

These and similar findings are not surprising to anyone involved in either service delivery or program evaluation in child and youth services. The maintenance and generalization of treatment effects as well as, ultimately, the replication of program models remain paramount issues for those involved in planning residential services for children. Jones, Weinrott, and Howard (1981), in their national evaluation of the Teaching Family Model (TFM) of group home treatment, widely hailed in the field as an exemplary program, state the concern as follows:

> TFM . . . has demonstrated its capability for modifying a wide range of in-program behavior . . . [but] recall that our self-report data suggested little non-maturational change in either deviant or drug behavior across pre, during, and postprogram phases. The message is simple, a program could be an apparent success if the criterion is modification of target behavior during the program experiences. The same program may be seen as far less successful if the criterion is the postprogram adjustment and reintegration of youth. (p. 134)

Although the full meaning of these findings remains open to question, at the very least they serve to temper the enthusiasm that accompanied earlier evaluations which reached the conclusion that the Teaching Family Model "works better [than comparison programs] and costs less" (Stumphauzer, 1979, p. 119; Kirigin et al., 1979). Jones, Weinrott, and Howard's analysis of national data supports no such conclusion.

Trends and Issues in Group Care Services

Ecological Factors. As the outcome research clearly indicates, success in residential care, however defined, is largely a function of the supports available in the post-treatment community environment and has much less to do with either presenting problems or type of treatment offered. Consequently, what has come to be known as the ecological perspective has profound implications for residential children's services (Whittaker, 1979). It views the residential environment as the complex interplay of many different elements both within and outside the formal service context. Notable is the quality of the linkages between the residential program and the family, the neighborhood, the peer group, the world of work, and other potential sources of support in the community. The Massachusetts experiment in deinstitutionalization highlighted the importance of these community linkages as they interact with the formal service program (Coates et al., 1978). One potential implication of this trend for professionals in residential care is that they will be spending less time in direct treatment of children and more time working with and through the environment, particularly in creating or maintaining social support networks for children and their families (Whittaker, 1979; Whittaker et al., 1983). Specifically, this will mean factoring the environment more prominently into the youth service equation—whether that service occurs in a residential treatment center, specialized foster home, or the youth's own home. Specifically, such tasks would include: (1) teaching children and families practical skills to cope effectively with their environment; (2) working to enhance naturally occurring support networks where they exist and helping to create them where they do not (Dumas & Wahler, 1983); (3) recognizing that "environmental helping" is not synonymous with "aftercare"—it begins prior to placement, continues during placement, and lasts as long after placement as it is needed.

Parents as Partners in Substitute Care. If the residential treatment center is to be seen as a temporary support for families in crisis, rather than as a substitute for families that have failed, it must engage families as full and equal partners in the helping process. Traditionally, and for a variety of reasons, parents have been kept at arm's length from the process of treatment in institutional settings. In *The Challenge of Partnership*, Maluccio and Sinanoglu (1981) document a variety of ways in which parents of children in foster and residential care can assume a meaningful role. Such activities include parenting education, family support groups, family participation in the life-space of the residential institution, and family therapy (Whittaker, 1981). As in adoption and foster family care, the enormous potential helping power of parents has only barely been touched. Maluccio and Whittaker (in press) suggest a variety of means for involving biological parents, foster parents, and other professionals in meaningful partnerships. Without a strong family work component, it is doubtful that any model of residential treatment (or foster family–based treatment) can improve on the meager results emerging from outcome studies with respect to ultimate community reintegration.

Continuum of Care. Finally, as an intervention, group care is best viewed as part of an overall continuum of care that includes home-based, family-centered programs designed to prevent unnecessary out-of-home placement; services designed to reunify separated children and families; specialized adoption services; family support and education programs; and specialized areas of foster care. Such services are best viewed as complementary, although the precise relationship between these services with respect to things like criteria for intake are anything but clear at this time. In all areas of youth services, only primitive technologies of change exist, and even more primitive methodologies for measuring their effects. Perhaps the greatest single lesson to be learned from the recent history of residential group care is to guard against premature enthusiasm and the premature tendency to generalize or overinterpret from less than complete evaluations. Issues like maintenance and generalization and community reintegration will be around for years to come, and they ought not to define the entire set of variables against which individual programs are measured. As a case in point, the frequently cited Teaching Family Model, although disappointing in its lack of distinctive effects in distal environments, has taught us a great deal about the environment of the treatment setting—what its component parts are, how these processes can be tracked and evaluated, and how staff can most effectively be trained to carry out their various program objectives.

Social Work Involvement

As in the past, social workers will continue to play an important role in the design, implementation, and evaluation of group care services for children. A renewed focus on the family, for example, will require knowledge and skill in areas such as family treatment, family life education, and parent support. Concern with the maintenance and generalization of treatment gains will lead to a renewed emphasis on aftercare services, including community liaison work and consultation with informal helping networks. As the boundaries become more permeable, social workers in foster care services, adoptions, and home-based services will look for ways to creatively combine service strategies—for example, in the preparation of children in group care settings for adoption (Donley & Haimes, 1984; Powers, 1982). Within group care agencies, many possibilities exist for creating partnership with child and youth care workers, for example, in the provision of family work services. Finally, in the area of research, social workers will, as they have in the past, take the lead in developing specific components of group care services as well as in carrying out outcome evaluations of children and youths in existing group care programs. In this last area, creative programmatic research in the area of aftercare services holds considerable promise for both improving the efficacy of group care services and providing new service techniques for use in preventive programs (Hawkins & Catalano, 1985; Cahill & Meier, 1984).

JAMES K. WHITTAKER

For further information, see CHILD CARE SERVICES; CHILDREN; FAMILY PRACTICE; FOSTER CARE FOR CHILDREN; MENTAL HEALTH AND ILLNESS IN CHILDREN; PROTECTIVE SERVICES FOR CHILDREN.

References

Allerhand, M. E., Weber, R., & Haug, M. (1966). *Adaptation and Adaptability: The Bellefaire Follow-up Study*. New York: Child Welfare League of America.

Bettelheim, B., & Sylvester, E. (1948). "A Therapeutic Milieu." *American Journal of Orthopsychiatry, 18*(2), 191–206.

Bremner, R. H. (1970, 1974). *Children and Youth in America: A Documentary History* (Vols. 1 & 3). Cambridge, Mass.: Harvard University Press.

Cahill, B., & Meier, J. (1984). *Secondary Prevention of Child Assault: Provision of Specialized Foster-adoptive Placements and Reunification Aftercare to Prevent Drift and Recidivism*. Unpublished manuscript. Woodland Hills, Calif.: Childhelp USA.

Cavior, E. C., Schmidt, A., & Karacki, L. (1972).

An Evaluation of the Kennedy Youth Center Differential Treatment Program. Washington, D.C.: U.S. Bureau of Prisons.

Cherry, T. (1976). "The Oregon Child Study and Treatment Centers." *Child Care Quarterly,* 5(2), 146–155.

Child Welfare League of America. (1982). *CWLA and Standards for Residential Centers for Children.* New York: Author.

Child Welfare League of America. (1984). *Directory of Member Agencies.* New York: Author.

Coates, R. B., Miller, A. D., & Ohlin, L. E. (1978). *Diversity in a Youth Correctional System.* Cambridge, Mass.: Ballinger Publishing Co.

Davids, A., Ryan, R., & Salvatore, P. (1968). "Effectiveness of Residential Treatment." *American Journal of Orthopsychiatry, 38*(3), 469–475.

Davids, A., & Salvatore, P. (1976). "Residential Treatment of Disturbed Children and Adequacy of Their Subsequent Adjustment." *American Journal of Orthopsychiatry, 46*(1), 62–73.

Dimock, E. T. (1977). "Youth Crisis Services: Short-term Community-based Residential Treatment." *Child Welfare, 56*(3), 187–196.

Donley, K., & Haimes, R. (1984). "New Dimensions in Child Placement: Residential Group Care/Adoption Collaboration." Unpublished manuscript.

Dore, M. M., & Kennedy, K. E. (1981). "Two Decades of Turmoil: Child Welfare Services 1960–1980." *Child Welfare, 60*(6), 371–383.

Dore, M. M., Young, T. M., & Pappenfort, D. M. (1984). "Comparison of Basic Data for the National Survey of Residential Group Care Facilities: 1966–1982." *Child Welfare, 63*(6), 485–497.

Dumas, J. E., & Wahler, R. G. (1983). "Predictions of Treatment Outcome in Parent Training: Mother Insularity and Socioeconomic Disadvantage." *Behavioral Assessment, 5,* 301–313.

Durkin, R. P., & Durkin, A. B. (1975). "Evaluating Residential Treatment Programs for Disturbed Children." In M. Guttentag & E. L. Struening (Eds.), *Handbook of Evaluation Research* (Vol. 2). Beverly Hills, Calif.: Sage Publications.

Fitzharris, T. L. (1985). *The Foster Children of California.* Sacramento: Children's Services Foundation & the California Association of Services for Children.

Hawkins, J. D., & Catalano, R. (1985). *Project Adapt.* Seattle: University of Washington, Center for Social Welfare Research.

Herrera, E. G., et al. (1974). "A 10-year Follow-up Study of 55 Hospitalized Adolescents." *Journal of Psychiatry, 131*(7), 769–774.

Hobbs, N. (1982). *The Troubled and Troubling Child.* San Francisco: Jossey-Bass.

Johnson, H. L., et al. (1976). "Program Evaluation in Residential Treatment." *Child Welfare, 55*(4), 279–291.

Jones, R. R., Weinrott, M. R., & Howard, J. R. (1981). *Impact of the Teaching Family Model on Troublesome Youth: Findings from the National Evaluation.* Rockville, Md.: National Institute of Mental Health. (NTIS No. PB82-224353)

Kadushin, A. (1980). *Child Welfare Services* (3rd ed.). New York: Macmillan Publishing Co.

Kane, R. P., & Chambers, G. S. (1961). "Seven-year Follow-up of Children Hospitalized and Discharged from a Residential Setting." *American Journal of Psychiatry, 117*(5), 1023–1027.

Kirigin, K. A., Wolf, M. M., Braukmann, C. J., Fixsen, D. L., & Phillips, E. L. (1979). "Achievement Place: A Preliminary Outcome Evaluation." In J. S. Stumphauzer (Ed.), *Progress in Behavior Therapy with Delinquents* (pp. 118–155). Springfield, Ill.: Charles C Thomas, Publisher.

Langer, S. (1925). "Reply." *Survey, 54*(5), 624.

Lewis, W. W. (1982). "Ecological Factors in Successful Residential Treatment." *Behavioral Disorders, 7*(3), 149–156.

Maluccio, A. N. (1977). "Community-based Child Placement Services: Current Issues and Trends." *Child and Youth Services, 1*(6), 2–12.

Maluccio, A. N., & Marlow, W. D. (1972). "Residential Treatment of Emotionally Disturbed Children: A Review of the Literature." *Social Service Review, 46*(2), 230–251.

Maluccio, A. N., & Sinanoglu, P. A. (1981). *The Challenge of Partnership: Working with Children of Parents in Foster Care.* New York: Child Welfare League of America.

Maluccio, A. N., & Whittaker, J. K. (in press). "Foster Family-based Treatment: Implications for Parental Involvement." In R. Hawkins & J. Breiling (Eds.), *Issues in Implementing Foster Family-based Treatment.* Rockville, Md.: National Institute of Mental Health.

Mayer, M. F., & Blum, A. (Eds.). (1971). *Healing through Living: A Symposium on Residential Treatment.* Springfield, Ill.: Charles C Thomas, Publisher.

McGowan, B., & Meezan, W. (1983). *Child Welfare.* Itasca, Ill.: F. E. Peacock Publishers.

National Center on Child Abuse and Neglect. (1978). *Child Abuse and Neglect in Residential Institutions.* (DHEW Publication No. OHDS 78-30160). Washington, D.C.: U.S. Government Printing Office.

Nelson, R. H., Singer, M. J., & Johnsen, L. O. (1978). "The Application of a Residential

Treatment Evaluation Model." *Child Care Quarterly, 7*(2), 164–175.

Pappenfort, D. M., Kilpatrick, D. M., & Roberts, R. W. (Eds.). (1973). *Child Caring: Social Policy and the Institution.* Chicago: Aldine Publishing Co.

Pappenfort, D. M., & Young, T. M. (1983). *Children and Youth in Residential Group Care: 1981.* Unpublished manuscript, University of Chicago, School of Social Service Administration.

Phillips, E. L., Phillips, E. A., Fixsen, D. L., & Wolf, M. M. (1974). *The Teaching Family Handbook.* Lawrence: University of Kansas, Bureau of Child Research.

Piliavin, I. (1963). "Conflict between Cottage Parents and Caseworkers." *Social Service Review, 37*(1), 17–25.

Powers, D. (1984). *Adoption for Troubled Children.* New York: Haworth Press.

Redl, F., & Wineman, D. (1957). *The Aggressive Child.* Glencoe, Ill.: Free Press.

Reeder, R. R. (1925). "Our Orphaned Asylums." *Survey, 54,* 283–287.

Rothman, D. J. (1980). *Conscience and Convenience: The Asylum and its Alternatives in Progressive America.* Boston: Little, Brown & Co.

Rubenstein, J. S., et al. (1978). "The Parent Therapist Program: Alternative Care for Emotionally Disturbed Children." *American Journal of Orthopsychiatry, 48*(4), 654–662.

Schwartz, I. M., Jackson-Beelk, M., & Anderson, R. (1983). *Minnesota's "Hidden" Juvenile Control System: Inpatient Psychiatric and Chemical Dependency Treatment.* Unpublished manuscript, University of Minnesota, Hubert H. Humphrey Institute of Public Affairs.

Select Committee on Children, Youth, and Families: A Report. (1983). Washington, D.C.: U.S. Government Printing Office.

Shyne, A. W., & Schroeder, A. G. (1978). *National Study of Social Services to Children and their Families.* Washington, D.C.: National Center for Child Advocacy.

Steiner, G. (1981). *The Futility of Family Policy.* Washington, D.C.: The Brookings Institution.

Stumphauzer, J. S. (1979). "Editorial Comments." In J. S. Stumphauzer (Ed.), *Progress in Behavior Therapy with Delinquents* (pp. 118–119). Springfield, Ill.: Charles C Thomas, Publisher.

Taylor, D. A., & Alpert, S. W. (1973). *Continuity and Support following Residential Treatment.* New York: Child Welfare League of America.

Taylor, R. B. (1981). *The Kid Business.* Boston: Houghton Mifflin & Co.

Whittaker, J. K. (1971a). "Colonial Child Care Institutions: Our Heritage of Care." *Child Welfare, 50*(7), 396–400.

Whittaker, J. K. (1971b). "Mental Hygiene Influences in Children's Institutions: Organization and Technology for Treatment." *Mental Hygiene, 55*(4), 444–450.

Whittaker, J. K. (1979). *Caring for Troubled Children: Residential Treatment in a Community Context.* San Francisco: Jossey-Bass.

Whittaker, J. K. (1981). "Family Involvement in Residential Child Care: A Support System for Biological Parents." In A. N. Maluccio & P. Sinanoglu (Eds.), *The Challenge of Partnership: Working with Parents in Foster Care* (pp. 67–89). New York: Child Welfare League of America.

Whittaker, J. K., Garbarino, J., & Associates. (1983). *Social Support Networks: Informal Helping in the Human Services.* New York: Aldine Publishing Co.

Whittaker, J. K., & Pecora, P. (1984). "A Research Agenda for Residential Care." In T. Philpot (Ed.), *Group Care Practice: The Challenge of the Next Decade* (pp. 71–87). Surrey, England: Business Press International.

Wolfensberger, W. (1972). *Normalization.* New York: National Institute on Mental Retardation.

Wolins, M., & Piliavin, I. (1964). *Institution and Foster Family: A Century of Debate.* New York: Child Welfare League of America.

Wooden, K. (1976). *Weeping in the Playtime of Others.* New York: McGraw-Hill Book Co.

GROUP THEORY AND RESEARCH

From the earliest period of social work literature to the present day, social work writers have recognized that it is essential for practitioners to study small-group phenomena to understand human behavior and how it may be changed. Richmond, a leader in establishing a theoretical base for the profession, wrote about "the new tendency to view our clients from the angle of what might be termed *small-group psychology*" (Richmond, 1920, p. 256). Writing much later, Northen (1982) presented the point of view of virtually all contemporary theorists when she stated that, "The most influential system to which most people belong is the family" (p. 40). She then quickly added that the family is a group and that

people belong to many other types of groups during their life spans. Early in his [or her] development, a child participates in many informal play and fellowship dyads and larger groups; these affiliations change as he [or she] grows older and assumes new roles. People spend many years of their lives in formal or informal educational groups. Many join groups of a supportive, self-help, developmental, or therapeutic nature. Many adults are members of committees and organizations that further their interests or make contributions to the community. (pp. 40–41)

Although the concept of the group is a familiar one, the use of the term can be ambiguous. This essay discusses the small group, defining it as Hartford (1971) does:

. . . at least two people—but usually more—gathered with common purposes or like interests in a cognitive, affective, and social interchange in single or repeated encounters sufficient for the participants to form impressions of one another, creating a set of norms for their functioning together, developing goals for their collective activity, evolving a sense of cohesion so that they think of themselves and are thought of by others as an entity distinct from all other collectivities. (p. 26)

This definition separates the small group from collectivities that may exist with little interaction among individuals, such as an audience, and also from very large groups and organizations in which individuals rarely encounter all other individuals in the system in such a way as to set in motion the processes listed by Hartford. These larger aggregates are likely, moreover, to accomplish their purposes by subdividing into small groups to work on tasks.

The significance of small groups in our lives can be examined at several levels. The first is the *individual level*. The group meets important individual needs for intimacy and support, especially if the two-person situation is included as the limiting case of the small group. People also seek to meet these needs in small groups of family members, peers, co-workers, and so forth. Such groups help persons to define their reality and norms and to learn socially appropriate behaviors. Society utilizes such groups to fulfill the social function of socializing its citizens.

Social workers make use of this knowledge in several ways. They seek to help people affiliate with groups to meet their individual needs (Garvin, 1981; Toseland & Rivas, 1984). They establish a variety of

community institutions to provide opportunities for individuals to gather together with others for a great variety of purposes. They create groups to help individuals who require professional assistance in coping with social situations. They work directly with families, friendship groups, and other so-called natural groups that temporarily require professional assistance to enhance their functioning. They consult with a variety of institutions, such as schools and workplaces, to help them establish the group conditions required for successful individual functioning.

Social work has always had a major investment in strengthening family life. Practice with families draws on many different sets of theories, including small-group theory. The family is a small group, although its functions and characteristics differ in some ways from other small groups. Family workers, therefore, can and do profit from small-group studies (Bell, 1961).

Small groups can also be examined at the *organizational level*. All organizations such as schools and workplaces are primarily structured along group lines. In the school, this is represented by the classroom; in the workplace, by work units. Hierarchical levels in organizations also lead to the formation of groups, such as supervisory or executive groups. The "informal system" is a term used by organizational theorists to refer to the informal interactions among small numbers of employees that are not part of the formal structure of the organization. These interactions create groups that at times enhance the functioning of the organization and at other times impede it.

Social workers use their knowledge of the functioning of groups in organizations in several ways (Resnick & Patti, 1980). In working with individuals who are having trouble in organizations, the social worker may help them to become more competent members of organizational groups. In this role of organizational development consultants, social workers consult with teachers in schools and supervisors in the workplace to assess and enhance the quality of their group life.

The third level at which small groups can be examined is the *community level*. Early group workers were heavily influenced by the works of Follett (1918) and Lindeman (1924), who saw the health of the community and the society as based on the quality of small-group associations. In their view, the very existence of democracy depends on the ability of people to gather together to make their influence felt. Political associations, religiously based groups, block clubs, and many types of social action organizations are among the groups that accomplish such purposes. It is no accident that totalitarian regimes seek to restrain people from gathering together in informal associations.

Social workers engaged in community organization and social action make considerable use of the knowledge of small groups in their practice (Burghardt, 1982). They create groups and help them to identify and carry out their tasks and to have an impact on the environment in the process. These groups usually take the form of committees, task forces, or commissions. A literature has been emerging that makes use of the latest developments in small-group theory to enhance practice in the area of community organization (Tropman, 1979).

History

Social scientists initiated the study of the small group in the early part of this century. Social workers contributed to this effort almost from the beginning and worked with social scientists to create an understanding of how small groups function in natural settings.

LeBon was among the first social scientists to deal with small group phenomena. In *The Crowd* (1895) he described the contagion effects that arise in group situations. McDougall (1920) was another pioneer in seeking ways to analyze group-level events. Simmel (1950), a sociologist who wrote early in the twentieth century, was highly original in his studies of the effect of the size of the group. He noted that participants in a two-person group develop a responsibility to each other not found in larger groups; he also analyzed the changes in the interaction when a third person is added and predicted that one of the three will often be viewed as an intruder. Simmel also noted that small groups require more participation than larger ones. Freud (1922) also contributed to these early efforts to understand groups, analyzing the emotional reactions to group leaders and how these affect the interaction among members.

An important contribution to these

early efforts was made by Cooley (1909), who developed the term "primary group," which he defined as follows:

> By primary groups I mean those characterized by intimate face-to-face association and cooperation. They are primary in several senses, but chiefly in that they are fundamental in forming the social nature and ideals of the individual. The result of intimate association, psychologically, is a certain fusion of individualities in a common whole, so that one's very self, for many purposes at least, is the common life and purpose of the group. Perhaps the simplest way of describing this wholeness is by saying that it is a "we"; it involves the sort of sympathy and mutual identification for which "we" is the natural expression. (p. 23)

Cooley described the small group's functions both in the socialization of the individual and in the creation and stabilization of behavior.

In her comprehensive summary of the development of small-group theory and of social workers' role in this endeavor, Hartford (1971) points out that the early leaders of the adult education movement, such as Harrison Elliott, Alfred Sheffield, and Eduard Lindeman, contributed substantially to the discovery of small-group forces. Their major interest in doing this was their belief that democracy depended on small-group associations. Other writers concerned with this issue were MacIver (1924), a sociologist, and Follett (1918, 1924), a political scientist.

The 1930s saw important developments in the study of how small groups relate to social issues. Ronald Lippitt, a social psychologist, and Kurt Lewin, a Gestalt psychologist, engaged in classic experiments on leadership styles (Lewin, Lippitt, & White, 1939). At the Massachusetts Institute of Technology in 1946, Lewin and his associates created the Research Center for Group Dynamics. After Lewin died in 1947, the center was moved to the University of Michigan. Throughout its history, the center has sponsored highly influential research on the small group.

Another important type of investigation was carried on during the 1930s by J. L. Moreno and his associates. Moreno, a psychiatrist, referred to his approach as "sociometry." He saw the patterns of interpersonal relationships in the group as the key to understanding other group phenomena. His book *Who Shall Survive?* (Moreno, 1934) and another book, *Leadership and Isolation* by his associate Helen Hall Jennings (1950) are influential contributions from this perspective. Moreno also founded the journal *Sociometry*, now called *Social Psychology*, and that publication through the years has published outstanding research on the small group.

Although some of these investigators focused on laboratory experiments, others were interested in examining small groups that occur naturally. Among the most influential investigations of natural groups were those by Thrasher (1927) of the delinquent gang, Whyte (1943) of natural youth aggregates in the community, and Newcomb (1943) of youth affiliations on the college campus and the impact such groupings have on the individual's attitudes. Muzafer Sherif conducted investigations in both natural and laboratory settings. Under laboratory conditions, he investigated how the perceptions of others affect the individual's judgments (Sherif, 1936); he also studied group processes under such natural conditions as youth gangs (Sherif & Cantril, 1947) and children's camps (Sherif & Sherif, 1953).

Several social workers were involved in this type of research because of their interest in establishing a scientific basis for social work with groups. One of the most influential of these was Grace Coyle, whose doctoral dissertation, *Social Process in Organized Groups*, was published in 1930. To test her ideas, Coyle drew on her experiences with women in industry and YWCA programs, with children in settlement house groups, and with discussion groups in the adult education movement. She contributed substantially to an understanding of group formation, membership, goals, structure, process, and cohesiveness.

W. I. Newstetter, another social worker, also worked to create knowledge for group-oriented practice. He began his investigations while he was the head worker at a Cleveland settlement house, and he urged the School of Applied Social Sciences at Western Reserve University to develop training for work with groups. In 1926 he became chair of the group program at that school. In the same year, he established an experimental camp known by the fictionalized name "Wawokiye," where he developed an elaborate experimental design to study such phenomena

as group leadership and group process. The results of this study were published under the title *Group Adjustment* (Newstetter, Feldstein, & Newcomb, 1938). In the 1930s, Newstetter also established University Settlement in Cleveland as a place to engage in training and research related to groups.

All these efforts led in the 1950s and 1960s to an outpouring of reports of small-group research and to theoretical work related to groups. Important developments during this period were reported by Homans (1950), who analyzed the research of others on five types of groups in an effort to create a unified approach; by Bales (1950), who developed a widely used typology to classify the actions of group members; and by Cartwright and Zander (1968), who continued the theoretical developments begun by Lewin.

A review of the literature on social group work that appeared throughout the 1950s and 1960s demonstrates that social workers sought to use small-group research and theory as a foundation for principles of group practice. Important examples of this were Vinter's "Small Group Theory and Research: Implications for Group Work Practice Theory and Research" (1960) and Schwartz's "Small Group Science and Group Work Practice" (1963).

Approaches to Theory and Research

As is apparent from the discussion thus far, the small group is a complex social phenomenon. To date, no unified theoretical approach to the small group has emerged, although there have been several useful efforts to create such a system. Instead, several distinct perspectives dominate theory and research in this area. These perspectives are usually characterized as the field theory, the social exchange theory, and the social systems theory. A number of practice ideas have also been derived from psychoanalytic views of the meaning of groups to participants.

Field Theory. The central feature of the field theory approach, which Lewin and his colleagues and students were most influential in developing, is its view of the group as an entity in motion toward goals. This movement of the group is toward regions with "positive valences" (those positively valued) and away from regions with "negative valences" (those negatively valued). Forces both within and outside the group affect the direction of this movement and enhance or hinder it. According to this theory, group cohesiveness is "the resultant of all forces acting on members to remain in the group" (Festinger, 1968, p. 187).

As noted by Nixon (1979), Olmsted (1959) pinpointed major weaknesses of the field theory approach:

> In sum, the achievements of Group Dynamics (or field theory) include its concern for carefully formulated hypotheses, the large amount of interest it has aroused in group behavior, and its findings which spell out in detail some relationships which we might otherwise only have suspected. Its limitations . . . lie in the inadequacy and probable inappropriateness of its working-level concepts (including *locomotion, valence, vector, power field,* and *group forces*) and in its failure to pay attention to what non-Lewinian thinking might have to suggest as to major problems or variables in group life—especially with reference to the dimensions of role differentiation. (pp. 116–117)

Dunphy (1972) noted the main value of field theory:

1. stress on some variables of tested value, particularly variables of a . . . holistic kind, such as cohesiveness;
2. stress on the importance of examining the relationship of the group to its environment; and
3. emphasis on two central facets of all group life, namely goal orientation and group integration. (p. 31)

Social Exchange Theory. Exchange theory places many of the processes that are the subjects of behavioral psychology in a social perspective. As Nixon (1979) points out, "The field perspective is rich in the imagery of physics, in suggesting a picture of groups struggling to stick together while contending with various positive and negative forces in their environment that could affect their progress toward goal attainment" and "The social exchange perspective is rich in imagery derived mainly from animal psychology and elementary economics" (p. 31). For example, in behavioral psychology the terms "reinforcement" and "punishment" both describe processes related to the notion that behavior is determined by its consequences: when the likelihood that a behavior will recur is established, the consequence is described

as reinforcement, and when the likelihood that a behavior will not recur is established, the consequence is described as punishment. Viewed from a group perspective, people in groups maintain interaction and become interdependent as they pursue rewarding experiences and avoid painful ones. Exchange theorists introduce this important social perspective, examining the group processes that determine what is pleasurable and painful.

A leading exchange theorist who applied these concepts to small groups was Homans (1961). He postulated that people enter into social interactions with the expectation of rewards. Because each person in the interaction has the same motivation, it logically follows that each must offer something of value to the other in the exchange. This simple proposition is considered to be the basic premise of social interaction; hence the characterization of this approach as "exchange theory."

What an individual offers another in an exchange—whether energy, time, or resources—is referred to as a "cost." Exchange theorists see a variety of group-level conditions as governing these transactions, including notions of justice and other group norms that maintain functional exchanges.

Thibaut and Kelley (1959) contributed to the development of exchange theory in different ways than Homans. They emphasized dyadic interactions, and their behavioral emphasis can be seen in their definition of interaction as occurring when individuals "emit behavior in each other's presence," "create products for each other," or "communicate with each other." They conclude, "In every case that we would identify as an instance of interaction there is at least the possibility that the actions of each person affect the other" (p. 10).

For Thibaut and Kelley, the important unit of analysis is the behavioral sequence (a series of interactive behaviors leading to a "payoff" for each actor). Like Homans, they analyze outcomes of interactions in terms of costs and rewards. To analyze a group event—two individuals in interaction, for example—they use a behavioral matrix to define the value of the outcome for each individual of each different interaction in a sequence of interactions. This presents a logical model for analyzing interactions, but it is difficult in practice to measure the value of outcomes for different individuals in a comparable manner. Nevertheless, useful principles have emerged from this framework, such as the notion that people enter into and remain in interactions when the outcomes are likely to be greater than those expected from alternative interactions. Thibaut and Kelley use the terms "comparison level" to refer to a person's internal measure of the value of an outcome and "comparison level of alternatives" to refer to the measure the person uses to decide whether to remain in an interaction or to leave it.

Those who look to exchange theory as a guide to understanding group behavior do so because it helps to explain much of the data derived from small-group experiments; it also is useful in suggesting how practitioners might encourage members to enter and remain in groups by helping them to evaluate the costs and benefits of one group experience as compared to others. In assessing Homan's work, Buckley (1967) stated the limitations of this theory:

> He agrees that pigeons do not use symbols and men do, but he seems not to want to go the rest of the way to agree that men, and not pigeons, have selves and self-awareness, and will thereby suffer for long periods all kinds of deprivation, negative reinforcements, and even death for mere symbols and self-esteem. (p. 112)

However, recent developments in so-called cognitive behavior modification appear to provide tools for incorporating such distinctly human thoughts and feelings into exchange frameworks (Berlin, 1983).

Social Systems Theory. In a sense, all small-group theories may be thought of as systems oriented inasmuch as they portray the small group as an organic entity with boundaries, purposes, and mechanisms for attaining change while maintaining stability. Another important feature of a systems perspective is the notion that whatever happens to one component of the system has a direct or indirect effect on the others. A social systems perspective on the small group seeks to explain these various aspects of the group in a unified manner and draws parallels between the small group and other types of social systems.

In noting the key components of a systems approach to the small group, Nixon (1979) states:

> What are these "other features of social behavior" to which social-system models draw our attention? Beyond equilibrium, there are things such as functional needs, structural differentiation, patterns of interpersonal sentiment, conformity, leadership, and status relations. (p. 40)

Various writers, including Bales and Homans, have contributed to this perspective on groups. Homans made his contribution in *The Human Group* (1950), which was written before his exposition of the social exchange perspective in *Social Behavior: Its Elementary Forms* (1961). Bales drew heavily on his work with Parsons (Parsons, Bales, & Shils, 1953) to create his highly influential perspective. These theorists see social systems as developing mechanisms to resolve the following issues: (1) integration, or how the parts of a system are to relate to one another; (2) pattern maintenance, or how the traditions and processes of a system are to be adhered to; (3) goal attainment, or how the activities of a system are to be oriented toward a desired outcome; and (4) adaptation, or how a system adjusts to its environment.

Bales sees groups as functioning to maintain an equilibrium between task actions (goal attainment and adaptation) and social-emotional actions (integration and pattern maintenance). Task actions include asking for or giving information, evaluation, or suggestions. Social-emotional actions are classified as positive when they operate to reduce tensions, increase agreement, or show solidarity and as negative when they operate in the opposite manner. Bales's classic work, *Interaction Process Analysis* (1950), describes these variables in detail and provides means for measuring them. In 1979 Bales and Cohen created an empirical approach to diagramming the relationships among members of a group in an even more complex manner.

Homans (1950) approached his systemic analysis of groups in a different manner. He identified group phenomena as related to activities, interactions, sentiments, and norms. Activities are the things people do with each other in the group, interactions are exchanges with others, sentiments are internal states of members, and norms are ideas about how individuals in the group should act with each other.

Homans offered a number of propositions about the relationships that may be found among these dimensions. He also generated the concept of the internal and external systems of the group. The internal system consists of activities, interactions, sentiments, and norms as these relate to the adaptation of the members to each other; the external system consists of these variables as they relate to the way the group adapts to its environment.

Others have drawn on general systems theory for ways of examining group conditions and means of changing them. To generate useful propositions about how group conditions are maintained or altered, Durkin (1981) analyzed phenomena present in all systems related to boundary maintenance, relationships among system levels, and forces that promote both stability and change.

Psychoanalytic Theory. Although psychoanalytic theory is usually thought of as providing a basis for understanding the individual, it has also been used as a basis for examining group phenomena. This use is often traced to Freud's influential work *Group Psychology and Analysis of the Ego* (1922). Psychoanalytically oriented group theorists draw attention to the emotional responses of group members to each other and the leader, to the distorted perceptions members may have of each other and of group events because of forces in the personality, and to the ways in which group interactions may recapitulate family dynamics.

Bion (1959) did much to further the understanding of these forces from the psychoanalytic perspective. He was particularly interested in how the emotional responses of group members interacted with their accomplishing the work of the group. These responses constitute an emotional regression to states of dependency on the leader, fight or flight from the leader, or pairing with other members in ways that defeat the attainment of group purposes.

Importance to Practice

Certain conditions that occur in groups are often important to practitioners, including environmental effects on groups, group size

and composition, group structure, group process, group climate and group contagion, group development, group culture, and the effects of gender and ethnicity. This section discusses each of these conditions in sequence.

Environmental Effects. Some who write about groups come close to presenting a group as a closed system in which events are solely determined by conditions present within the group. This defies the reality that all groups of human beings constitute open systems in that they exchange information and resources with their environments in ways that affect both the group and the environmental systems involved. Social workers who facilitate groups of any type must recognize this. According to Wilson (1978, pp. 159–218), major ways that environments such as an agency or community influence groups that they encompass or with which they interact include the following:

■ The types of resources provided by the environment, such as money or consultants, affect the activities carried out by the group.

■ The environment sometimes imposes purposes on the group, often as a condition for receiving resources.

■ The environment may provide the group with information.

■ The environment may impose penalties on the group, such as by withdrawing resources.

■ Other groups in the environment may interact with the group, competitively, collaboratively, or in other ways.

■ The environment may impose a cultural or belief system on a group or it may help a group maintain its systems. For example, a Hispanic group in a Hispanic community may be used to sustain aspects of the larger culture, such as its language and customs; or a Hispanic group might receive negative sanctions from the larger, non-Hispanic community when it manifests aspects of the ethnic culture.

■ The environment may interact with members of the group differently from the way it interacts with the group as an entity. Thus, the other systems in the environment may seek to prevent a member from remaining in the group, may interact with a member as a way of influencing the group, or may award high or low status to members because of their group membership.

The physical environment of the group also has an impact on conditions in the group. Shaw (1981, pp. 161–166) offers a number of propositions about this dimension that have considerable empirical support. His propositions include the following: light and noise have effects on the group, but these effects vary depending on whether they are seen as within the control of the group and on how they affect specific group activities; groups develop a proprietary orientation toward certain geographical areas; under certain conditions, the close proximity of members to each other negatively affects group performance; and communication patterns are affected by the seating arrangements in the group.

Group Size and Composition. Important distinctions can be made among two-person, three-person, and larger groups (Thomas & Fink, 1963). Because a dyad can be destroyed by the withdrawal of a single member, groups of this size tend to focus on social-emotional issues to a greater degree than larger ones. Triads tend to divide into a dyad and an isolate, although in some triads the composition of the dyad may shift from time to time.

In his review of the research on group size, Nixon (1979, p. 12) states that members of five-person discussion groups indicate the highest level of satisfaction. The advantages of this size group are that a high level of participation is possible, the odd number of members prevents a deadlock, and there are enough members for any one member to be able to withdraw from an untenable position.

As groups become larger, the pressure on each member to participate decreases. This may be desirable or undesirable depending on the group's purpose. Larger groups tend to polarize into talkers and nontalkers, with the former directing most of their communications to each other. It is possible to counteract this tendency by rewarding nontalkers and limiting talkers, but some such intervention is necessary to create group norms that are conducive to more equal participation.

With reference to composition, a frequently researched question is the effect the gender composition of the group has on group process. Martin and Shanahan (1983) present a comprehensive review of the research on this topic. Some of their conclusions are the following:

- Females are negatively evaluated in groups in which they are tokens.
- Women talk less and are talked to less in mixed male-female groups than in all-female groups.
- Females are perceived of less positively than males even when they are equally influential to male group members.
- All-female groups will outperform all-male groups on a task that requires cooperation and unanimity.
- Females in an all-female group experience more positive growth than in a mixed group but subjectively evaluate the experience as less interesting.
- Men in mixed groups are more likely to deal with personal issues than men in all-male groups.
- Three-person groups composed of two males and a female are less productive than other types of three-person groups because competition arises between the men.

Davis (1979) has added considerably to our understanding of racial factors in group composition. In addition to pointing out the problems of the token member, Davis uses the concept of psychological majority and minority to explain findings from his research on this subject. Black members, for example, experience positive attitudes toward a group in which they constitute at least half of the membership. Whites begin to feel uncomfortable when black membership in a group exceeds the proportion of blacks in the larger environment.

Shaw (1981, pp. 256–261) summarizes many of the findings on another major topic related to composition, namely the degree of homogeneity and heterogeneity among group members with references to personal characteristics such as age, race, gender, and personality characteristics. People with similar attitudes are likely to be attracted to one another, and this leads to higher group cohesiveness. Nevertheless, groups are more likely to be productive when members have differing abilities and personalities. There is little research related to group composition in social work groups, but practitioners tend to compose groups so that one member is not isolated from others by virtue of being unique with respect to too many of the characteristics deemed important by other group members.

Group Structure. Shaw (1981) defined group structure as "the pattern of relationships among the differentiated parts of the group" (p. 263). As such, the group's structure may be likened to a snapshot of the group from which inferences can be drawn about relationships in the group at a given moment in time. Because of the forces that maintain stability in the group, this pattern may remain stable for substantial periods.

Because a group's structure can represent a highly complex picture that is difficult to visualize, investigators usually refer to one or another of its aspects, which Garvin (1983) identified as:

1. *Sociometric or affectional*: This refers to the pattern of attraction and rejection among group members and is manifested in the existence of *subgroups* (two or more individuals in the group who are attracted to each other and interact more with each other than with persons not in the subgroup) and *isolates* (persons who have few interactions with other group members).
2. *Communications*: This refers to the pattern of who communicates, verbally and nonverbally, with whom, and about what in the group.
3. *Roles*: This refers to the statuses that are created in the group and how persons fulfill them. These statuses include both formal roles (chairperson, secretary) as well as roles that grow out of group interactions (mediator, clown, scapegoat). Leadership roles are an important component of the role structure.
4. *Division of Labor*: This refers to how tasks are allocated among group members.
5. *Power*: This refers to the patterns of influence that exist within the group. (p. 161)

With regard to both group structure and process, the practitioner first identifies a group-level problem or a desired group state. The practitioner then seeks to modify or help the group members to modify an aspect of structure or process that will lead to a reduction of the problem or the attainment of the desired state.

Group Process. Group process, continuing the analogy used earlier, can be likened to a motion picture of the group in

Table 1. Categorization of Group Processes

	Goal-Oriented Activities	Quality of Interaction
Overt	Goal determination Goal pursuit	Role differentiation Communication-interaction Conflict resolution and behavior control
Covert	Values and norms	Emotions

which a *sequence of events* is examined. It refers, therefore, to changes in group conditions over time. Like group structure, group process is a complex phenomenon that is difficult to visualize. For this reason, it is useful to conceptualize the sequence of events in terms of two main components: the enactment of the group's *activity* or the *interactions* among the members.

Some aspects of the group's process may be observed in terms of the overt behaviors of group members; others are covert and often must be either inferred from overt behaviors or extracted from information provided by members about their thoughts and feelings. The aspects of group process described in the literature on small groups can be categorized as related to activities or interactions and to overt or covert phenomena, as is shown in Table 1. *Goal determination* includes all the activities members engage in to decide on group goals. *Goal pursuit* includes all the activities members engage in to attain these goals. A group's covert goal-oriented activity is the way members' *values* evolve as they interact with the group's goals and ways of pursuing those goals.

Much of a group's time and energy go into the pursuit of its goals. Social psychologists use the term "group tasks" to refer to the activities in which the group engages to attain its goals. Practitioners often refer to this as the group's "program." Important theoretical developments have led to a new classification of the tasks in which groups engage and provided an understanding of the conditions that impede or enhance those activities and of the phenomena that occur as different types of tasks are undertaken.

McGrath (1984, p. 61) identifies four types of tasks—activities that generate, execute, negotiate, or choose. Generative tasks include those in which members create new ideas or new plans. Execution tasks include performing psychomotor activities or engaging in contests or "battles." Negotiation tasks involve resolving either conflicts among cognitions or conflicts among interests. Choosing tasks are those in which members must solve problems that may or may not have correct answers.

McGrath's typology sheds light on conflict in groups. Because of differences in members' aspirations and needs and limitations in the group's resources, nearly all group experiences generate conflict, but some tasks are more likely to do so—tasks in which members' cognitions of the situation conflict, tasks in which members' interests conflict, and tasks that are intrinsically competitive.

McGrath has described successful approaches for resolving these types of group conflict situations. Techniques derived from social judgment theory help resolve cognitive conflicts. These techniques involve helping members to communicate such things as their mental organizing principles and the weights they assign to various types of information in making a decision. Negotiation techniques are used to resolve conflicts of interest. Successful negotiation usually requires members to give some consideration to each other's interests.

The research literature regarding competitive situations focuses on the effects such situations have on individual and group outcomes. For example, intergroup competition often increases attraction within the group. Group members in a competitive situation are also more likely to evaluate the experience based on whether they won or lost than on how well they performed.

Referring again to Table 1 and to group processes related to the quality of interactions, *role differentiation* refers to the evolution of the group's role structure. *Communication-interaction* refers to the messages members send to one another as they define and enact their roles. *Conflict resolution* and *behavior control* refer to the interactions that occur among members as they seek to maintain the group through constraining tension-inducing or group-threatening behavior. Co-

vert interactions consist of changes in the members' *emotions*, both caring and hostile emotions.

Garvin (in press) explains how the practitioner can identify, understand, and change all the aspects of group process described in Table 1. The task of practitioners is to link an understanding of process to actions they and members can take to produce group conditions conducive to attaining group goals.

Group Climate and Group Contagion. In a sense, a group consists only of the individuals who constitute its membership. Nevertheless, because of the systemic properties it assumes, a group can be spoken of as an entity, as more than the sum of its parts. One of the ways that it assumes these properties is that some member's ideas, attitudes, and feelings may become those of others by the process of association. This phenomenon deserves comment.

One type of association, that of feelings, leads to the creation of the group's climate. Upon entering a group, one can usually detect whether the members are largely depressed, angry, or elated. Some practitioners even assert that they can "smell" the group's climate. As Luft (1984) states:

> The social-emotional *climate* may be crucial to enabling group members to be more open with one another. The climate consists of degrees of tension and harmony (Lieberman, Yalom, & Miles, 1973) that determine the psychological safety felt within the group. A supportive climate is one in which participants might be more willing to risk self-disclosure. In other words, sanctions, criticism, or other punishments by the group, its leader, or individual members will not be imposed for expressing feelings. (p. 127)

Redl and his co-workers (Redl, Polansky, & Lippitt, 1950) were among the earliest writers to examine contagion effects in groups. They discovered through their experiments that low-status members were more subject to contagion from high-status members and that this was one of the forms of power possessed by the latter.

Whitaker and Lieberman (1964) utilize their understanding of contagion effects in groups to describe a model of group process referred to as the focal conflict model. This model is a basis for their approach to group therapy. They explain that members' wishes become linked associatively so as to constitute a "disturbing motive" and that fears regarding these wishes also become linked and constitute a "reactive motive." The group members reach a "solution" to this conflict between the disturbing and reactive motives often without being aware of it; that solution may or may not facilitate satisfaction of the wish.

Group Development. All students of small-group phenomena have noted that small groups tend to proceed through phases of development (Garland, Jones, & Kolodny, 1973; Sarri & Galinsky, 1974; Tuckman, 1965; Hartford, 1971). The remarkable thing is that, although using differing terms, these investigators describe group development in similar ways. Knowledge of groups' phases of development enables practitioners to understand many group events, even troubling ones, as necessary to the evolution of the group. Such events can also be anticipated so that the practitioner can devise, or help the group to devise, means of coping with them.

Hartford's (1971, p. 67) conceptualization of groups' phases integrates several of the most useful frameworks, as follows:

I. Pregroup Phases
   A. Private Pregroup Phase
   B. Public Pregroup Phase
   C. Convening Phase
II. Group Formation Phase
III. Integration, Disintegration, and Conflict Reintegration or Reorganization Synthesis Phase
IV. Group Functioning and Maintenance Phase
V. Termination Phases
   A. Pretermination Phase
   B. Termination
   C. Posttermination Phase

Hartford's conception of pregroup phases recognizes that much of consequence to the future of the group occurs before the members actually gather together. The people who will form the group select members, inform them about the group, and engage in planning for the group. Following the convening of the members, additional processes occur before the group members engage themselves fully in working together to attain their individual and joint objectives. These processes include seeking to agree on the purposes of the group, overcoming ambivalence about being in the group, developing relationships with other members, choosing courses of action, obtaining resources, and developing a tentative group structure.

After the group has accomplished the tasks of formation, it frequently enters into a period of conflict. This tension is created by the likelihood that the kind of leaders who were useful in getting the group started may not be the kind who will be useful for the accomplishment of subsequent group tasks and that differences of opinion will arise about how the group may best pursue its objectives. This period is marked by some decline in group cohesiveness until a reorganization of the group or a synthesis of opposing views takes place.

After one or more such conflict phases, the members are usually ready to invest their energies in task accomplishment. In therapy groups, this later phase may be divided into subphases in which members at first only appear to be facilitating each other's problem solving and only later attain an optimal degree of intimacy and self-disclosure.

Hartford is again insightful in her awareness of several phases in the termination process. Members must first decide on termination plans and then must go through the actual process of ending the group. Afterwards, members may contact each other and even hold reunions as part of a posttermination phase.

Some groups do not proceed through all the phases just described. Short-term groups, open-ended groups (groups in which members enter and leave at different times), and even one-session groups may accomplish their purposes without proceeding beyond formation activities. Groups that meet for a few sessions may accelerate their development, and long-term groups may spend much time deciding on their purposes and the means to accomplish them.

Group Culture. Members bring to the group an assortment of beliefs, traditions, and values that they have acquired from experiences throughout their lives. As they interact with other people in the group, they are likely to develop beliefs, traditions, and values that are in some ways unique to the group. As Hartford (1971) has pointed out:

This culture not only develops within the group but also is influenced by the surroundings of the group, the prevailing customs and norms of the community, and also the nature of the world and general customs of the time. Normative behavior develops out of the cultural expectations of a particular group at a specific time. (p. 270)

The observer of a group will see derivatives of the group's culture manifested in the group's customs, language, and rules and even in whether members come on time and how they dress. It is well known that the more attracted members are to the group, the more likely they are to conform to the group's cultural expectations. Because the group's culture may be taken for granted by its members, they may not be aware of it and how it affects their lives. Practitioners who have cultural views that differ from those of the members of a group may also fail to perceive their own cultural expectations, thus creating a source of conflict between them and the group.

Effects of Gender and Ethnicity. An earlier section of this article described how a group is affected by the proportion of men and women among its members. Gender issues affect groups in many other ways as well. One of these is whether the leaders, including the practitioners with the group, are male or female. Reed (1983) points out that issues are posed for women leaders because of "status incongruence." This phenomenon occurs because maleness is often the more valued state in the society outside of the group. As Reed (1983) notes:

Thus, a woman occupying a leadership role is not only role-incongruent; she is also status-incongruent. She simultaneously occupies (at least) two roles; female, which is the lower status of gender, and leader, which is a higher status position than member. . . . Similar to role incongruence, status incongruence leads to conflicting expectations and confusion about how to interact with the person whose status characteristics are inconsistent. It is often stressful both for the woman in the position and for those who must interact with her. . . . They are likely to discount a woman's leadership. . . . They may also act as if someone else is the leader, try to take over the leadership themselves, or behave as if the group has no leader. If these strategies are unsuccessful because her leadership is

inescapable or because she is clearly a competent leader, they may try to ignore her gender. If that too fails, then members have to adjust their perceptions. . . . (pp. 37–38)

Gender issues also have a considerable impact on the group's purposes and activities. Practitioners often seek to engage in "consciousness raising" by helping group members to examine their stereotypes regarding gender and how these impair the optimal growth of themselves and others. Members may fear selecting group purposes that do not conform to gender stereotypes, such as to enhance the assertiveness of women or the expression of feelings among men. Members often require help in separating role issues (how men and women behave as men and women) from issues of sexual preference (the choice of a sexual partner).

The ethnic backgrounds of the group's members also have an impact on their reactions to the group experience. One of the ways this occurs relates to the views that prevail in the members' culture as to the acceptable use of groups. In some Asian-American communities, for example, individuals are not expected to discuss family matters with nonfamily members, but in some Native-American communities, the tribal meeting is the place deemed proper to discuss personal and family matters.

The status accorded certain individuals in the ethnic community may also affect group processes. For example, if a culture pays honor to older people, this type of recognition carries over into groups formed by social workers. Practitioners, therefore, should become familiar with the group members' culture and the status it accords people based on their age, gender, occupation, role in the community's religious institutions, and other such factors.

Another example of how ethnicity affects group experience is in the culture's behavioral norms. In some cultures, emotional expression is proscribed; in others, it is encouraged. In some cultures, people are expected to remain silent until they have something relevant to say; in others, silence is a mark of disrespect. All such norms have an impact on the group's processes.

Contemporary Issues

A major question that has troubled practitioners is whether findings from research on groups conducted under laboratory conditions apply to groups meeting for real purposes in the community. In his comparison of research conducted in laboratory and natural settings, Shaw (1981) states that

> it can be shown that investigations of similar problems often lead to similar conclusions, whether the subjects be college students or members of the larger population and whether the groups are ad hoc laboratory groups or natural groups functioning in the "real world." (p. 430)

Nevertheless, insufficient attention has been paid to testing this conclusion with reference to the many kinds of groups with which social workers interact, and this remains an important gap in the knowledge base.

Another issue of concern to practitioners is the potential harm to individuals that can come from some group experiences. This harm can occur if group pressures stimulate members to express emotions, provide personal information, or engage in other behaviors with highly stressful consequences. Additional research must be conducted to determine what group processes lead to these consequences and what causes some people to be vulnerable to harm from groups.

This article has discussed some of the ways that gender and ethnicity affect groups, but much more research must be done on this topic. Also, there is virtually no research on how gender and ethnicity interact. A preliminary investigation of this subject suggests, for example, that small groups see black women as powerful leaders to the same degree as white men but that this does not hold true for white women and black men (Brower, Garvin, Hobson, Reed, & Reed, 1984).

The entire field of small-group research has been quiet in recent decades. A consequence is that research approaches to the small group have not kept pace with those in other fields. Researchers need less obtrusive ways of studying small-group phenomena so that the research is less likely to confound the variables under investigation.

A major theoretical and research topic is the most effective means of promoting change in groups. Because many forces interact to determine group outcomes, the effects of an intervention are often offset by the group reactions that result from it. Various pieces of research demonstrate that groups can be changed by changes in the behavior of one group member who possesses power; by changes in subgroup interactions; by changes in such group conditions as composition, structure, and process; and by changes in the way the environment intrudes on the group. Nevertheless, much remains to be learned about the most effective means of bringing about change in groups, with the least harmful side effects and with appropriate attention to social work ethics and values.

The list of the kinds of research required to advance social work practice with groups is long. The following are a few priority areas:

1. The ways in which gender, age, ethnicity, social class, and other cultural variables affect groups encountered in social work practice.

2. The most effective and efficient means of creating group conditions that facilitate the attainment of social work objectives.

3. The comparative effectiveness of nonverbal activities (art, dance, and so forth) and verbal activities (such as discussion) in the attainment of social work objectives.

4. The ways that groups affect and are affected by their environments in social work settings.

5. The relationships that exist between changes in group conditions and the social, intellectual, and emotional growth of group members.

CHARLES D. GARVIN

For further information, see SOCIAL WORK PRACTICE WITH GROUPS.

References

Bales, R. F. (1950). *Interaction Process Analysis: A Method for the Study of Small Groups.* Cambridge, Mass.: Addison-Wesley Press.

Bales, R. F., & Cohen, S. P. (1979). *Symlog.* New York: Free Press.

Bell, J. E. (1961). *Family Group Therapy* (Public Health Monograph No. 64). Washington, D.C.: U.S. Government Printing Office.

Berlin, S. (1983). "Cognitive-Behavioral Approaches," In A. Rosenblatt & D. Waldfogel (Eds.), *Handbook of Clinical Social Work* (pp. 1095–1119). San Francisco: Jossey-Bass.

Bion, W. (1959). *Experiences in Groups.* New York: Basic Books.

Brower, A., Garvin, C. D., Hobson, J., Reed, B., & Reed, H. (1984, October). "The Impact of the Gender and the Race of the Leader on the

Group.'' Paper Presented at the Sixth Annual Symposium of the Committee on the Advancement of Social Work with Groups, Chicago, Ill.

Buckley, W. (1967). *Sociology and Modern Systems Theory*. Englewood Cliffs, N.J.: Prentice-Hall.

Burghardt, S. (1982). *Organizing for Community Action*. Beverly Hills, Calif.: Sage Publications.

Cartwright, D., & Zander, A. (1968). *Group Dynamics: Research and Theory* (3rd ed.). New York: Harper & Row.

Cooley, C. H. (1909). *Social Organization: A Study of the Larger Mind*. New York: Charles Scribner's Sons.

Coyle, G. (1930). *Social Process in Organized Groups*. New York: Richard R. Smith.

Davis, L. (1979). ''Racial Composition in Groups.'' *Social Work*, 24(3), 208–213.

Dunphy, D. (1972). *The Primary Group: A Handbook for Analysis and Field Research*. New York: Appleton-Century-Crofts.

Durkin, J. E., (Ed.). (1981). *Living Groups: Group Psychotherapy and General System Theory*. New York: Brunner/Mazel.

Festinger, L. (1968). ''Informal Social Communication.'' In D. Cartwright & A. Zander (Eds.), *Group Dynamics: Theory and Research* (3rd ed., pp. 182–191). New York: Harper & Row.

Follett, M. P. (1918). *The New State*. New York: Longmans, Green & Co.

Follett, M. P. (1924). *Creative Experience*. New York: Longmans, Green & Co.

Freud, S. (1922). *Group Psychology and the Analysis of the Ego* (J. Strachey, Trans.). London: International Psychoanalytic Press.

Garland, J., Jones, H., & Kolodny, R. (1973). ''A Model for Stages in the Development of Social Work Groups.'' In S. Bernstein (Ed.), *Explorations in Group Work* (pp. 17–71). Boston: Milford House.

Garvin, C. D. (1981). *Contemporary Group Work*. Englewood Cliffs, N.J.: Prentice-Hall.

Garvin, C. D. (1983). ''Theory of Group Approaches.'' In A. Rosenblatt & D. Waldfogel (Eds.), *Handbook of Clinical Social Work* (pp. 155–175). San Francisco: Jossey-Bass.

Garvin, C. D. (in press). ''Group Process: Usage and Uses in Social Work Practice.'' In P. Glasser, M. Sundel, R. Sarri, & R. Vinter (Eds.), *Individual Change Through Small Groups* (2nd ed.). New York: Free Press.

Hartford, M. (1971). *Groups in Social Work: Applications of Small Group Theory and Research to Social Work Practice*. New York: Columbia University Press.

Homans, G. C. (1950). *The Human Group*. New York: Harcourt Brace Jovanovich.

Homans, G. C. (1961). *Social Behavior: Its Ele-*

mentary Forms. New York: Harcourt Brace Jovanovich.

Jennings, H. H. (1950). *Leadership and Isolation*. New York: Longmans, Green & Co.

LeBon, G. (1895). *The Crowd* (T. Fisher, Trans.). London: Alan Unwin.

Lewin, K., Lippitt, R., & White, R. (1939). ''Patterns of Aggressive Behavior in Experimentally Created 'Social Climates'.'' *Journal of Social Psychology*, 10(2), 271–299.

Lieberman, M., Yalom, I. D., & Miles, M. (1973). *Encounter Groups: First Facts*. New York: Basic Books.

Lindeman, E. (1924). *Social Discovery*. New York: Republic Press.

Luft, J. (1984). *Group Processes: An Introduction to Group Dynamics* (3rd ed.). Palo Alto, Calif.: Mayfield Publishing Co.

MacIver, R. (1924). *Community*. New York: Macmillan Publishing Co.

Martin, P. Y., & Shanahan, K. A. (1983). ''Transcending the Effects of Sex Composition in Small Groups.'' *Social Work with Groups*, 6(3/4), 19–32.

McDougall, W. (1920). *The Group Mind*. New York: G. P. Putnam's Sons.

McGrath, J. (1984). *Groups: Interaction and Performance*. Englewood Cliffs, N.J.: Prentice-Hall.

Moreno, J. L. (1934). *Who Shall Survive?* Washington, D.C.: Nervous and Mental Disease Publishing Co.

Newcomb, T. (1943). *Personality and Social Change*. New York: Dryden.

Newstetter, W. I., Feldstein, M. C., & Newcomb, T. (1938). *Group Adjustment*. Cleveland, Ohio: School of Applied Social Sciences, Western Reserve University.

Nixon, H. L. (1979). *The Small Group*. Englewood Cliffs, N. J.: Prentice-Hall.

Northen, H. (1982). *Clinical Social Work*. New York: Columbia University Press.

Olmsted, M. S. (1959). *The Small Group*. New York: Random House.

Parsons, T., Bales, R. F., & Shils, E. A. (Eds.). (1953). *Working Papers in the Theory of Action*. New York: Free Press.

Redl, F., Polansky, N., & Lippitt, R. (1950). ''An Investigation of Behavioral Contagion in Groups.'' *Human Relations*. 3(4), 319–348.

Reed, B. G. (1983), ''Women Leaders in Small Groups: Social-Psychological Perspectives and Strategies.'' *Social Work with Groups*. 6(3/4), 35–42.

Resnick, H., & Patti, R. J. (Eds.). (1980). *Change From Within: Humanizing Social Welfare Organizations*. Philadelphia: Temple University Press.

Richmond, M. (1920). ''Some Next Steps in Social Treatment.'' In *Proceedings of the National*

Conference of Social Work. Chicago: University of Chicago Press.

Sarri, R., & Galinsky, M. (1974). "A Conceptual Framework for Group Development." In P. Glasser, R. Sarri, & R. Vinter (Eds.), *Individual Change through Small Groups* (pp. 71–88). New York: Free Press.

Schwartz, W. (1963). "Small Group Science and Group Work Practice." *Social Work, 8*(4), 39–46.

Shaw, M. (1981). *Group Dynamics* (3rd ed.). New York: McGraw-Hill Book Co.

Sherif, M. (1936). *The Psychology of Social Norms*. New York: Harper & Row.

Sherif, M., & Cantril, H. (1947). *The Psychology of Ego Involvements*. New York: John Wiley & Sons.

Sherif, M., & Sherif, C. (1953). *Groups in Harmony and Tension*. New York: Harper & Row.

Simmel, G. (1950). *The Sociology of George Simmel* (K. H. Wolff, Trans. and Ed.). New York: Free Press.

Thibaut, J. W., & Kelley, H. (1959). *The Social Psychology of Groups*. New York: John Wiley & Sons.

Thomas, E., & Fink, C. (1963). "Effects of Group Size." *Psychological Bulletin, 60*(4), 371–384.

Thrasher, F. M. (1927). *The Gang*. Chicago: University of Chicago Press.

Toseland, R., & Rivas, R. (1984). *An Introduction to Group Work Practice*. New York: Macmillan Publishing Co.

Tropman, J. (1979). *Effective Meetings*. Beverly Hills, Calif.: Sage Publications.

Tuckman, B. W. (1965). "Developmental Sequence in Small Groups." *Psychological Bulletin, 63*(6), 384–399.

Vinter, R. (1960). "Small Group Theory and Research: Implications for Group Work Practice Theory and Research." In L. Kogan (Ed.), *Social Science Theory and Social Work Research*. New York: National Association of Social Workers.

Whitaker, D. S., & Lieberman, M. (1964). *Psychotherapy through the Group Process*. New York: Atherton Press.

Whyte, W. F. (1943). *Street Corner Society*. Chicago: University of Chicago Press.

Wilson, S. (1978). *Informal Groups: An Introduction*. Englewood Cliffs, N. J.: Prentice-Hall.

GROUP WORK. See DIRECT PRACTICE: TRENDS AND ISSUES; DIRECT PRACTICE EFFECTIVENESS; GROUP THEORY AND RESEARCH; SOCIAL WORK PRACTICE WITH GROUPS.

HAMILTON, GORDON. See biographical section.

HANDICAPPED. See DISABILITIES: DEVELOPMENTAL; DISABILITIES: PHYSICAL.

HAYNES, ELIZABETH ROSS. See biographical section.

HAYNES, GEORGE EDMUND. See biographical section.

Reader's Guide

HEALTH AND MENTAL HEALTH

The following articles contain information on this general topic:

Emergency Health Services
Health Care Financing
Health Care Specialization
Health Planning
Health Service System
Hospice
Hospital Social Work
Mental Health and Illness
Mental Health and Illness in Children
Mental Health Services
Preventive Health Care and Wellness
Primary Health Care
Psychotropic Medications
Public Health Services

HEALTH CARE FINANCING

Health care services are financed through a combination of governmental programs, private insurers, and direct payments by consumers themselves. Unlike other consumer service industries, the field of health care has unique qualities that color the consideration of costs, payments, and choices. First, health care decisions are technologically sophisticated, often requiring the patient to rely on the provider of services for information and direction. Second, since service decisions frequently involve life/death, wellness/illness implications for the patient, cultural predilections virtually mandate the spending of unlimited resources when it is technologically feasible either to save a life or significantly improve its quality. Third, much of the health care bill is paid by the public or corporate sector, and not by the user of services. Consequently, questions about the level of spending have become major public policy issues.

Perhaps the greatest issue facing the health care system in recent years has been the increase in the cost of providing health care services. Although previous periods were dominated by the growth and expansion of health benefits, the current period is characterized by efforts to limit the scope and availability of services.

During the 1940s and 1950s, the federally financed Hill-Burton Act spurred the building of numerous acute care hospitals. Private insurance plans also were greatly expanded at this time. But these insurance plans, often provided as an employee benefit, did not extend to the poor and aged. The 1960s and early 1970s saw the introduction of major government entitlement programs that assured health benefits to these underserved populations. By the late 1970s and early 1980s, efforts were shifted to limit the expansion of health care expenditures by introducing a variety of mechanisms to monitor, limit, and ultimately control costs.

In 1984, the United States spent a total of $387.4 billion on health care, or $1,580 for each man, woman, and child in the country. This figure represents 10.6 percent of the Gross National Product (GNP), as compared with 5.3 percent of GNP for health expenditures in 1960 (Table 1). The 1984 health care bill was 9.1 percent higher than the previous year, a decrease in the rate of growth, from 10.3 percent in 1983 and 15.3 percent in 1980 (U.S. Department of Health and Human Services [USDHHS], 1985d). It is this rate of growth that is the focus of policy concern, and the target of efforts to curtail costs.

A number of factors have contributed to the increase in health care spending, which has outpaced the growth in the economy as a

Table 1. U.S. Aggregate and Per Capita National Health Expenditures, by Source of Funds and Percent of Gross National Product: Selected Calendar Years, 1929–1984

Item	1984	1983	1982	1981	1980	1970	1965	1960	1950	1940	1929
National health expenditures in billions	$387.4	$355.4	$322.3	$285.8	$248.0	$75.0	$41.9	$26.9	$12.7	$4.0	$3.6
Percent of the Gross National Product	10.6	10.8	10.5	9.7	9.4	7.6	6.1	5.3	4.4	4.0	3.5
Source of funds in billions											
Private expenditures	227.1	206.6	186.5	164.2	142.2	47.2	30.9	20.3	9.2	3.2	$3.2
Public expenditures	160.3	148.8	135.8	121.7	105.8	27.8	11.0	6.6	3.4	.8	.5
Federal expenditures	111.9	102.7	93.3	83.5	71.1	17.7	5.5	3.0	1.6	NA	NA
State and local expenditures	48.3	46.1	42.6	38.1	34.8	10.1	5.5	3.6	1.8	NA	NA
Per capita expenditures[a]	$1,580	$1,459	$1,337	$1,197	$1,049	$350	$207	$146	$82	$30	$29
Private expenditures	926	848	774	688	601	221	152	110	60	24	25
Public expenditures	654	611	564	510	448	130	54	36	22	6	4
Federal expenditures	457	422	387	350	301	83	27	16	10	NA	NA
State and local expenditures	197	189	177	160	147	47	27	20	12	NA	NA
Percent distribution of funds	100.0	100.0	100.0	100.0	100.0	100.0	100.0	100.0	100.0	100.0	100.0
Private funds	58.6	58.1	57.9	57.4	57.3	63.0	73.8	75.3	72.8	79.7	86.4
Public funds	41.4	41.9	42.1	42.6	42.7	37.0	26.2	24.7	27.2	20.3	13.6
Federal funds	28.9	28.9	28.9	29.3	28.7	23.5	13.2	11.2	12.8	NA	NA
State and local funds	12.5	13.0	13.2	13.3	14.0	13.5	13.0	13.5	14.4	NA	NA
Addenda											
Gross national product (billions)	$3,662.8	$3,304.8	$3,069.2	$2,957.8	$2,631.7	$992.7	$691.0	$506.5	$286.5	$100.0	$103.4
Population in millions	245.2	243.6	241.1	238.7	236.4	214.0	203.0	183.38	154.7	134.6	123.7
Annual percent changes											
National health expenditures	9.1	10.3	12.8	15.2	15.3	14.2	9.3	8.7	12.2	.8	NA
Private expenditures	9.7	10.8	13.6	15.5	14.5	16.0	8.8	9.0	11.2	.1	NA
Public expenditures	8.2	9.5	11.7	15.0	16.5	11.3	10.6	7.8	15.5	4.6	NA
Federal expenditures	9.0	10.1	11.7	17.5	16.5	9.8	12.9	8.5	.0	NA	NA
State and local expenditures	6.5	8.2	11.6	9.7	16.5	14.0	8.5	7.2	8.4	NA	NA
Gross national product	10.8	7.7	3.8	12.4	8.8	5.2	6.4	4.8	11.1	-.3	NA
Population	.9	1.1	1.0	1.0	1.1	1.1	2.0	1.8	1.4	.8	NA

[a] Based on July 1 social security area population estimates.
NA = Data not available.
Source: Office of Financial and Actuarial Analysis. Bureau of Data Management and Strategy, U.S. Health Care Financing Administration.

whole (Gibson et al., 1984). First, as an economy grows, consumers generally expect that an increasing proportion of overall spending will be devoted to such services as travel, dining, and health care. Second, health care is labor intensive and productivity growth is low, despite recent advances in technology. Economists theorize that industries with slower-growing productivity, such as health care, may experience a more rapid price inflation than industries with faster-growing productivity. Third, the rapid development of technology has expanded the scope and breadth of available treatments, resulting in a higher per capita consumption of health care services. As providers compete to offer the latest technology, the market can become oversaturated, thereby raising costs. Fourth, there is a growing aged population demanding expensive health care services. In 1960, 9.1 percent of the population was 65 and over, while in 1983, 11.5 percent of the population fell in that age group, a 20 percent increase (Arnett & Trapnell, 1984). Older people are also living longer. In 1977, a 65-year old had a life expectancy of 16.4 years, while in 1982 life expectancy was up to 16.8 years. The median age of the aged population was 71.6 in 1977, and 71.9 in 1983, reflecting a declining death rate for people 85 years of age and over (Waldo & Lazenby, 1984).

Another major reason for the growth of health care spending relative to GNP is the nature of third-party payments. The intention of health care insurance has been to remove the cost factor from decisions about health care services for both consumers and providers (Aaron & Schwartz, 1984). For consumers, insurance serves as a protection from large financial obligations for catastrophic or other expensive illnesses. For providers, the insurance coverage of patients assures payment for services rendered and is payable regardless of the outcome of treatment.

When a third party pays for services, the acts of consumption and payment are separated, and the consumer's interest in the true cost of service is lessened. Since the perceived cost of service is lower than the actual cost, consumers and providers may use more services. In addition, payment for these services is often cost based, or retrospective, which means that the insurance company pays the bills based on the cost of services that have been provided. This is yet another disincentive for consumers or providers to eliminate procedures, tests, or activities that may not be an essential part of treatment. Finally, employer contributions are excluded from employees' taxable income and from earnings subject to payroll tax. The tax-exempt status of health insurance has encouraged employers, and has not discouraged employees, from substituting more comprehensive health insurance coverage for higher money wages.

Sources of Health Care Funds

The three primary sources of health care funds are government agencies, insurance companies, and patients themselves (Table 2). In 1984, $160.3 billion, or 41 percent of all health spending, was financed through various levels of government: two-thirds from the federal level and the remainder from state and local sources (USDHHS, 1985d). Insurance companies, such as Blue Cross and Blue Shield, covered $120.5 billion, or 31 percent of the total cost. Consumers paid directly for $95.4 billion in health services and supplies, or 25 percent of the amount spent on health care. The remaining 3 percent of the total was derived from philanthropic organizations, industrial in-plant health service sources, and privately financed construction.

The source of funding varies according to specific type of service, with governmental sources and insurance companies covering large, institution-based expenses, and consumers tending to pay a greater proportion of small, periodic charges. For example, although consumers directly pay for only 8 percent of total hospital costs, they cover 28 percent of all physicians' fees. The government pays for 53 percent of hospital costs, but only 28 percent of physicians' fees. Private insurance companies financed 37 percent of the total hospital bill ($71.9 billion) and 44 percent of physicians' service fees ($54.5 billion).

Public Expenditures. The government has several major programs that provide funding for health care services. Each of these programs is designed to provide insurance for those who would not otherwise be covered by other arrangements, such as employment benefits.

Table 2. National U.S. Health Expenditures in 1984, by Type of Expenditure and Source of Funds (Amount in Billions)

	All Sources of Funds	Private					Public		
		All Private Funds	Total	Consumer		Other^a	All Public Funds	Federal	State and Local
				Direct	Insurance				
Total	$387.4	$227.1	$215.9	$95.4	$120.5	$11.2	$160.3	$111.9	$48.3
Health services and supplies	371.6	220.3	215.9	95.4	120.5	4.4	151.2	105.4	45.9
Personal health care	341.8	206.5	202.5	95.4	107.2	3.9	135.4	101.1	34.3
Hospital care	157.9	73.5	71.9	13.7	58.2	1.6	84.3	65.6	18.7
Physicians' services	75.4	54.5	54.4	21.0	33.5	—	20.9	16.9	4.0
Dentists' services	25.1	24.5	24.5	16.3	8.3	—	.5	.3	.3
Other professional services	8.8	6.0	5.9	3.5	2.4	.1	2.8	2.2	.6
Drugs and medical sundries	25.8	23.5	23.5	19.7	3.8	—	2.4	1.2	1.2
Eyeglasses and appliances	7.4	6.3	6.3	5.5	.8	—	1.2	1.1	.1
Nursing home care	32.0	16.3	16.1	15.8	.3	.2	15.7	8.8	6.9
Other personal health care	9.4	2.0	—	—	—	2.0	7.5	5.1	2.4
Program administration and net cost of health insurance	19.1	13.9	13.4	—	13.4	.5	5.2	2.9	2.3
Government public health activities	10.7	—	—	—	—	—	10.7	1.4	9.3
Research and construction of medical facilities	15.8	6.7	—	—	—	6.7	9.0	6.6	2.5
Noncommercial research^b	6.8	.4	—	—	—	.4	6.4	5.8	.6
Construction	9.0	6.4	—	—	—	6.4	2.6	.7	1.9

^a Spending by philanthropic organizations, industrial inplant health services, and privately financed construction.
^b Research and development expenditures of drug companies and other manufacturers and providers of medical equipment and supplies are excluded from "research expenditures," but they are included in the expenditure class in which the product falls.
Source: Office of the Actuary, U.S. Health Care Financing Administration.

Medicare. The Medicare program was initiated on July 1, 1966 as a federal insurance program intended to cover the high health care costs of the elderly. In 1973, the program was extended to include persons with end-stage renal disease, as well as permanently disabled workers and their dependents eligible for old age, survivors, and disability insurance (OASDI) benefits. Medicare does not provide care directly, but reimburses private providers for services received by enrollees (Gibson et al., 1984).

Medicare has two benefit programs, each with its own trust fund. Hospital Insurance, or Part A, pays for hospital services, posthospital skilled nursing services, and home health services. In October 1983, hospice care was added as a benefit. Part B is voluntary supplementary medical insurance (SMI) that covers physicians' services, home health services, outpatient hospital services and therapy, in addition to a number of other services.

Unlike other federal health programs, Medicare is not financed solely by general revenues. In 1983, 84 percent of all funding for the Hospital Insurance Trust Fund, Part A, was derived from a 1.3 percent payroll tax levied on employers and employees for the first $35,700 in wages. Only 10 percent was taken from general revenues. SMI, however, received 22 percent of its funding from enrollee premiums, and the largest share, 74 percent ($14.2 billion), from general revenues, an increase from a 50 percent share of general revenues in 1971. In 1985, premiums for SMI beneficiaries totaled $15.50 per month (USDHHS, 1985a).

In 1967, during its first full year of operation, Medicare expenditures amounted to $4.7 billion. By 1983, expenditures had risen to $58.8 billion, an average annual rate of Medicare increases of 17 percent, as compared to a general rate of increase of 13 percent for all health care costs. Of the over 30 million people enrolled in Medicare in 1983, two-thirds required services, at an average cost of $2,900 per person. Nearly one-half of all government spending on personal health care was derived from Medicare. This amounts to 18.3 percent of all spending on personal health care. Because such a sizable portion of health spending is devoted to this single program, major cost-cutting efforts, such as prospective payment, have specifically targeted the Medicare reimbursement system.

Medicaid. The Medicaid program provides medical assistance to certain categories of low income people, including the blind, aged, disabled, and members of families with dependent children. Medicaid, like Medicare, was established in 1966 as part of the Social Security Act. It is administered and, to a large extent, funded at the state level, but receives matching funds from the federal government. In 1983, 54 percent was funded by the federal government, with the remainder funded by the states (Gibson et al., 1984).

Medicaid is in many ways a blanket label for the different programs offered on a state by state basis (McCarthy, 1981). Federal law, however, requires that states participating in Medicaid provide certain services to recipients. These include: inpatient and outpatient hospital care; laboratory and x-ray services; skilled nursing home care; home health care for those 21 and older; early and periodic screening for those under 21; family planning services; and rural health clinic services. Medicaid, to a greater extent than Medicare, finances long-term, nonacute care in nursing facilities, psychiatric hospitals, and home health agencies. These expenditures totaled almost half of all 1983 Medicaid spending (Gibson et al., 1984).

In 1983, combined federal and state expenditures for Medicaid were $35.6 billion. Ten years earlier, $5.5 billion was spent on Medicaid, an average annual rate of increase of 13 percent per year. A total of 21.5 million persons received Medicaid benefits in 1983, up from 10 million in 1967. On average, 1983 per capita spending for Medicaid recipients was $1,500. Two-thirds of the recipients qualify as members of families with dependent children. The aged and disabled, who make up 28 percent of the recipients, account for 70 percent of all Medicaid expenditures (Gibson et al., 1984).

Other Government Programs. A number of other federal, state, and local programs provide both direct services and funding for a variety of health services on a much smaller scale than Medicare and Medicaid (Gibson et al., 1984). The Veterans Administration (VA) provides medical care for veterans of military service, as well as compensation and pensions for veterans and their survivors. Although not all veterans apply, 28.2 million people are eligible for VA medical care. Hospitalization and other medical care amounted to $7.7 billion, or 31 percent of the total VA budget. Most of those expenses were incurred in the 172 VA medical centers and other hospitals.

The federal government also provides health care services to active and retired military personnel, along with their survivors and dependents. In 1983, $6.5 billion was spent in 168 hospitals and for health care compensated by the Civilian Health and Medical Program of the Uniformed Services (CHAMPUS).

The federal Indian Health Service provides personal health care and public health services to 888,000 American Indians and Alaska natives in a network of hospitals and clinics. The total cost for these services in 1983 was $517 million, or $582 per capita.

Federal health block grants, introduced in 1982, make monies available for maternal and child health, preventive health, and alcohol, drug abuse, and mental health. In fiscal year 1982, $887 million was appropriated to these programs, an 18 percent decrease from the $1.1 billion that had been appropriated for these activities during the previous year. This funding approach reduces both the federal budgetary obligations and regulatory control of the programs, and transfers them to state and local levels.

Although the largest proportion of public health care funding is derived from the federal level, a number of programs and services are financed directly by state and local government. For example, state-administered income maintenance programs provide benefits for work related disability and death. In 1980, approximately 29 percent of the benefits paid by these programs was for medical services. In 1983, a total of $5 billion was spent on health and medical benefits for disabled workers.

State and local governments also contributed $7.9 billion for the operation of hospitals and other health care services for their communities. The introduction of Medicare and Medicaid greatly altered the financial picture of these state and local hospitals. Many patients, who otherwise would have been provided uncompensated care, are now covered by some public insurance program. As a result, the net cost of care for state and local governments has declined from 61 per-

cent in 1965 to 25 percent in 1977, and has remained at approximately that level ever since. In addition, states also provide care for the poor who are not covered by Medicaid, and who do not qualify as part of federal matching fund programs. These services totaled $1.8 billion in 1983. Temporary disability insurance, school health, and vocational rehabilitation programs received another $.9 billion in 1983.

Private Health Insurance. There are three major categories of private health insurance: Blue Cross and Blue Shield; commercial insurance companies; and prepaid and self-insured plans. In 1983, private health insurers paid $100 billion in medical benefits, 31.9 percent of all spending on personal health care (Gibson et al., 1984). This figure represents a 10.2 percent increase over the amount spent in 1982. Insurance companies received $110 billion in premiums, which resulted in a $10.5 billion net cost for insurance services. The net cost for insurance in 1982 was $8.6 billion, representing a 22 percent increase in a 1-year period (Gibson et al., 1984).

The strength and growth of the private insurance industry stems from a number of factors (McCarthy, 1981). First, health care providers have had an interest in assuring a stable source of payments for services offered. Blue Cross, for example, evolved out of the nonprofit payment programs developed in the early 1930s by hospitals seeking to build a secure source of financing. The American Hospital Association (AHA) supported the growth of these plans, and special insurance legislation mandated the establishment of Blue Cross plans in each state. The close partnership between providers and insurers was established, and continued until 1972, when the Blue Cross and AHA formally separated. Blue Shield also evolved out of a provider interest in assuring funding, in this case, the physicians and state medical societies.

Second, the cost of health care services, particularly in the case of a severe or prolonged illness, is a prohibitive out-of-pocket expense for the vast majority of the American population. Consumers enroll in a health insurance program to assure that decisions regarding health care services during a time of illness will not depend on the availability of personal financial resources (Aaron & Schwartz, 1984). In 1983, 75 percent of the civilian noninstitutional population in the United States had some private health insurance coverage for hospital services, surgical physician care, outpatient X-ray and laboratory examinations, prescribed drugs and/or nursing services (Health Insurance Association of America, 1985). In 1940 only 10 percent of the population had some form of private health insurance (Freund & Jellinek, 1983).

Third, health care insurance has emerged as an expected employee benefit, often covering both employees and their dependents. During the 1940s, Congress circumvented a wartime control on wages by declaring that health insurance benefits would not be considered as a salary increase. For the first time, the portion of the health insurance premium paid for by employers was treated as a tax-exempt business expense. As a result, health insurance emerged as an attractive benefit in the collective bargaining process.

Finally, as noted, government provided important encouragement to the growth of the private, voluntary health insurance industry. Through both legislative mandates for health coverage and favorable tax treatment, opportunities were created for an industry that was outside of the public domain (Anderson, 1985). Once created, this industry itself emerged as an important player in policy development and implementation regarding health finance. For example, Blue Cross and Blue Shield serve as the primary fiscal intermediary between federal and state government in the administration of Medicare and Medicaid (McCarthy, 1981).

In 1983, commercial insurance companies, such as Aetna and Metropolitan Life, financed $48 billion of health care benefits, representing 48 percent of the market. Blue Cross and Blue Shield paid for $35.2 billion in health benefits in 1983, 35 percent of the private market share. This percentage has decreased from the 45.2 percent share that Blue Cross and Blue Shield enjoyed in 1965. That portion of the market was lost to independent plans, consisting of all private health insurers, including Health Maintenance Organizations ($6.1 billion in 1983), self-insured employer plans, and union plans (Table 3).

Direct Patient Payments. Consumers paid directly for $85.2 billion in health services during 1983, or 24 percent of all health expenditures. Consumer financing paid primarily for physicians' services ($19.6 billion), drugs and medical supplies ($18.4 billion), and dental services ($13.9 billion). The percentage of consumer financing has decreased dramatically over time. In 1929, consumers paid directly for 88 percent of all health care spending. In 1970, following the introduction of Medicare and Medicaid, consumer spending dropped to 41 percent; it had dropped to 29 percent by 1980 (Gibson et al., 1984). As health care became a more expensive service, with new technologies and potential, and as it came to be seen as a universal right, regardless of ability to pay, the need for funding resources that could supplement consumer payment became more important. The increases came through the development of public and private third-party funding sources. Consequently, from 1960 to 1983, third-party payments increased over three times the rate of consumer payments.

Approximately 15 percent of the population is without any form of health insurance, either public or private. Because 61 percent of the population is covered by a health insurance plan related to the current employment of a family member (U.S. Bureau of the Census, 1983), the problems of the uninsured are particularly sensitive to changes in the rate of unemployment. As unemployment rises, access to health care services is restricted for those who are unemployed but are ineligible for public assistance. Hospitals have become less willing to provide services to uninsured patients, because both public and private third-party payers have become reluctant to subsidize the losses incurred through "uncompensated care." As a result, uninsured people in need of health services have sometimes been shunted from one hospital to another, or have been denied health care altogether.

Spending of Health Care Funds

National health expenditure figures include all spending on health care for individuals, nonprofit and government program administrative costs, the net cost to enrollees of private health insurance, government expenditures on public health programs, noncommercial health research, and construction of

Table 3. Private Health Insurance Benefits and Percent Distribution by Type of Insurer: United States, Selected Years 1965–83 (Amount in Billions)

Year	Total Private Health Insurance[a]		Insurance Companies[b]		Blue Cross and Blue Shield		Self-Insured Plans[c]		Prepaid Plans[d]	
	Amount	%	Amount	%	Amount	%	Amount	%	Amount	%
1965	$8.7	100.0	$4.2	48.4	$3.9	45.2	$.3	3.9	$.2	2.6
1970	15.3	100.0	7.1	46.4	7.0	46.1	.7	4.3	.5	3.2
1975	31.2	100.0	12.8	41.1	14.2	45.5	3.0	9.6	1.2	3.8
1976	37.6	100.0	15.0	39.8	16.2	43.2	4.9	13.2	1.5	3.9
1977	43.0	100.0	16.4	38.3	17.8	41.5	6.8	15.9	1.9	4.3
1978	49.1	100.0	19.1	38.8	19.5	39.7	8.3	16.9	2.3	4.6
1979	56.9	100.0	21.8	38.4	21.7	38.2	10.5	18.5	2.8	5.0
1980	67.3	100.0	25.6	38.0	25.5	37.8	12.7	18.8	4.4	5.6
1981	78.8	100.0	30.6	38.8	29.2	37.1	14.5	18.5	4.4	5.6
1982	90.8	100.0	37.1	40.9	32.1	35.4	16.2	17.8	5.3	5.9
1983	100.0	100.0	41.3	41.3	35.2	35.2	17.4	17.4	6.1	6.1

[a] Detail may not add to totals because of rounding.
[b] Includes minimum premium plans (MPP).
[c] Includes administrative service only (ASO) plans.
[d] Includes health maintenance organizations and other prepaid plans such as dental and vision.
Source: Office of Financial and Actuarial Analysis, Bureau of Data Management and Strategy. U.S. Health Care Financing Administration.

medical facilities. Spending on environmental improvement and subsidies and grants for health professionals' education are excluded from the definition of national health expenditures (Gibson et al., 1984)

There are two primary categories of health spending: those that refer to *current* health, and those that refer to *future* health. Current health includes health services and supplies, personal health care, program administration, and public health activities. Future health concerns the construction of medical facilities and research.

In 1984, 96 percent of all health spending, or $371.6 billion, was for health services and supplies (Table 4). Of that amount, the vast majority was spent on personal health care, and only 3 percent was devoted to public health activities. The largest share of the personal health care expenditure—46 percent—was for hospital care. Physicians' services comprised 22 percent of spending, and nursing home care 9 percent.

The proportion of spending on hospital care has grown steadily over the years. In 1929, hospital care accounted for only 22 percent of the spending on personal health care. By 1950, it had increased to 36 percent, and by 1970, it had jumped to 43 percent. These increases reflect the changing function of the hospital in the health care system, and the financial resources demanded by changing methods of service delivery. Before World War II, health care was typically obtained from one's neighborhood general practitioner, who offered for a direct fee a wide range of primary care services. Hospital services were limited and rudimentary by today's standards. As medical knowledge and technology expanded, medical care became more specialized and sophisticated (Freund & Jellinek, 1983). The required information and instrumentation can best be offered in a centralized hospital setting, which also provides a more antiseptic environment for treatment and rehabilitation. Demographic changes, particularly in regard to the ability of family members to care for their ill at home, also contributed to the trend toward institutional provision of health care. Hospital care is an expensive service because it is labor intensive and technologically sophisticated, and because it must include room and board as a part of health care services. The average 1983 per diem costs in a community hospital were

$369.49 compared to $81.01 in 1970, and $32.23 in 1960 (Health Insurance Association of America, 1985).

Although physicians' services account for only 22 percent of personal health care expenditures, their influence on spending is pervasive. It is primarily the physician who determines who will be hospitalized, what type and quantity of services patients will receive, and what prescription drugs will be purchased. By some estimates, physicians influence 70 to 80 percent of health care spending (Gibson et al., 1984). While the actual amount of money spent on physician services has steadily increased, the proportionate share has decreased over time. In 1929, physician services constituted 31 percent of spending on personal health. By 1960, the share had decreased to 24 percent. This trend reflects several developments: the changing function of direct physician contact in patient care, which was complemented by greater use of other less trained personnel; the availability of new medications; and the larger proportional share of institutional expenses.

Expenditures on nursing home care have undergone among the most significant changes of all major spending categories. From 1950 to 1960, nursing home care remained at about 2 percent of overall spending on personal health care. By 1965, its proportional share had risen to 5.8 percent, and the expansion continued with the introduction of Medicare. By 1970, the share had grown to 7.2 percent, and by 1975, to 8.6 percent. This trend reflects a growing aging population who lived longer but who needed more and more intensive care for longer periods of time; demographic changes, in particular a larger proportion of middle-aged, working women who were unavailable to care for their aging parents; and the availability of monies for nursing home care, which stimulated the growth of a new industry that by its very presence offered a health care alternative that encouraged demand.

Another important and relatively recent development in health care spending has been the increased utilization of Alternative Delivery Systems (ADS). These include Health Maintenance Organizations (HMOs), Individual Practice Associations (IPAs), Primary Care Networks, Health Care Alliances, and Preferred Provider Organizations

Table 4. National Health Expenditures, by Type of Expenditure: United States, Selected Years, 1929–84 (Amount in Billions)

Type of expenditure	1984	1983	1982	1981	1980	1970	1965	1960	1950	1940	1929
Total	$387.4	$355.4	$322.3	$285.8	$248.0	$75.0	$41.9	$26.9	$12.7	$4.0	$3.6
Health services and supplies	371.6	340.1	308.1	272.7	236.1	69.6	38.4	25.2	11.7	3.9	3.4
Personal health care	341.8	313.3	284.7	253.4	219.1	65.4	35.9	23.7	10.9	3.5	3.2
Hospital care	157.9	147.2	134.9	117.9	101.3	28.0	14.0	9.1	3.9	1.0	.7
Physicians' services	75.4	69.0	61.8	54.8	46.8	14.3	8.5	5.7	2.7	1.0	1.0
Dentists' services	25.1	21.8	19.5	17.3	15.4	4.7	2.8	2.0	1.0	.4	.5
Other professional services	8.8	8.0	7.1	6.4	5.6	1.6	1.0	.9	.4	.2	.3
Drugs and medical sundries	25.8	23.7	21.8	20.5	18.5	8.0	5.2	3.7	1.7	.6	.6
Eyeglasses and appliances	7.4	6.2	5.5	5.6	5.1	1.9	1.2	.8	.5	.2	.1
Nursing home care	32.0	28.8	26.5	23.9	20.4	4.7	2.1	.5	.2	.0	.0
Other health services	9.4	8.5	7.6	7.0	5.9	2.1	1.1	1.1	.5	.1	.1
Expenses for prepayment and administration	19.1	15.6	13.4	10.6	9.2	2.8	1.7	1.1	.5	.2	.1
Government public health activities	10.7	11.2	10.0	8.6	7.7	1.4	.8	.4	.4	.2	.1
Research and construction of medical facilities	15.8	15.3	14.2	13.2	11.9	5.4	3.5	1.7	1.0	.1	.2
Research[a]	6.8	6.2	5.9	5.6	5.4	2.0	1.5	.7	.1	.0	.0
Construction	9.0	9.1	8.3	7.6	6.5	3.4	2.0	1.0	.8	.1	.2

[a] Research and development expenditures of drug companies and other manufacturers and providers of medical equipment and supplies are excluded from "research expenditures," but they are included in the expenditure class in which the product falls.

Source: Office of Financial and Actuarial Analysis, Bureau of Data Management and Strategy, Health Care Financing Administration.

(PPOs). Traditionally, the financing of health care and the provision of services have been handled separately. Health services are then offered by providers who are not employed by the insurer. It has been argued that this arrangement encourages excessive health care utilization, since the patient only minimally supplements insurance payments, and providers are given no incentive to be cost efficient. Alternative delivery systems, on the other hand, consolidate the *financing* and the *provision* of care into one entity (Freund & Jellinek, 1983).

In an ADS arrangement, the purchaser of an insurance plan pays a fixed premium in advance and, in return, receives services at no charge, or for a nominal fee. It is in the consumer's interest to select the most efficient plan, which offers the greatest number of services for the least cost. This creates a direct incentive for the providers of care to minimize the cost of providing that care.

While ADS began in the 1920s, and expanded with the establishment of the Kaiser plan in California during the 1940s, it was not until the late 1960s and 1970s that their popularity significantly increased. This was due in large part to funding incentives offered by the federal government. Enrollment has grown steadily, increasing from 5.3 million persons in 1974, to 14 million in 1983. Spending increased from $0.5 billion in 1970, to $6.1 billion in 1983. From 1970 to 1983, such prepaid health plans doubled their proportion of the market share, from 3 percent to 6 percent.

Patterns of spending for home health care and hospice care have also changed significantly in recent years. Both of these services can be less expensive than hospital care, and are, for many patients, a preferable form of treatment. Medicare spending for home health services has increased at an average annual rate of 24 percent, rising from $60 million in 1968 to $1.5 billion in 1983. The growth stems in part from the elimination of the prior hospitalization requirement for coverage, as well as removal of the 100-visit limit. The importance of home health treatment is likely to increase, as hospital stays are shortened, and sicker patients are discharged. Starting in October 1983, Medicare expanded insurance benefits to include hospice care for terminally ill patients. Approximately $148 million was spent on hospice care in 1984.

Efforts to Control Health Care Expenditures

Current efforts to control health care costs are not aimed at decreasing real spending, but rather are intended to limit the rate of growth of health care expenditures. Short of a revolution in health care financing, health care expenditures inevitably will grow. A number of factors, not all of them directly health related, contribute to this trend: general economic factors, such as inflation and changes in GNP; demographic factors, such as a growing population, and in particular, a growing and longer living older population who need expensive services for a longer period of time (Freeland & Schendler, 1984); and technological developments, which offer new and often expensive treatment (such as kidney dialysis or heart transplants) for diseases that previously may have been untreatable but are now demanded by a large segment of the population. The problem with efforts to curtail the growth of costs is typical of any attempt to change or limit the availability of services: what criteria or mechanisms can be utilized that simultaneously assure cost efficiency as well as accessible, quality care?

Restricting the rate of growth of health care expenditures requires modifications in the behavior, attitudes, and expectations of both providers and consumers. There are two primary approaches being used to effect cost containment: regulatory and competitive strategies (Freund & Jellinek, 1983). Both approaches seek to reduce costs by encouraging greater efficiency in the production and consumption of health care services, although the mechanisms utilized to accomplish these aims are somewhat different.

Regulatory Approaches. The federal government spent $111.9 billion on health care in 1984, 29 percent of the total bill. By 1990, it is projected that the federal share of health spending will increase to 32 percent (Arnett et al., 1984). Therefore, both the federal and state governments have the incentive and the authority to limit the rate of growth of health care expenditures. There are several methods of cost containment: prospective payment, utilization and quality review, certificate of need, and rate review.

Prospective Payment. This system shifts the responsibility for absorbing costs from the third party to the provider of services. The rate of reimbursement is set in advance, in accordance with a formula that delineates the payment schedule for all patients who fall into a certain diagnostic category. If more than the prescribed rate is spent in providing care, the provider must absorb the cost. However, if less than the prescribed rate is spent, the provider is able to keep the full reimbursement. In October 1983, the Department of Health and Human Services introduced the diagnostic related group (DRG) system for reimbursing hospitals providing acute-care services for Medicare patients. Predetermined reimbursement rates were established for over 400 different diagnostic categorizations (USDHHS, 1985a). Although prospective payment had previously been used in several states, the national mandate for implementation provided a jolt to the health care system (Dolenc & Dougherty, 1985; Ross et al., 1985). Because the major cost savings could be realized by reducing the length of stay, new emphasis was placed on efficient discharge planning and patient transfer.

According to the Health Care Financing Administration, the average length of stay decreased from ten days in 1983 to nine days in 1984, a one-day decline (USDHHS, 1985c). Average length of stay in those few states exempted from the DRG system declined only .6 days, while in those states using the DRG system, there was a decline of 1.1 days.

Although private insurance companies have not adopted prospective payment on a national scale, they are known to be considering some form of prospective payment as a means of establishing control over their own health care expenditures.

Utilization and Quality Review. The Peer Review Improvement Act of 1982 established utilization and quality control Peer Review Organizations (PRO). These organizations review services funded under Title XVIII of the Medicare Act to determine whether services are "reasonable, medically necessary, furnished in the appropriate setting and are of a quality which meets professionally recognized standards" (USDHHS, 1985b). It is the responsibility of these organizations, which range in size from small

local groups to large statewide organizations, to review a range of patient care questions, including the accuracy of diagnostic classification, the appropriateness of length of stay, and the treatment plan.

Certificate of Need. The purpose of the Certificate of Need (CON) legislation is to control the capital expansion of hospitals by controlling the number and distribution of hospital beds and expensive equipment. The rationale for this legislation is that once beds or equipment are in place, there will be an incentive to use them fully, thereby inflating costs. The National Hospital Planning and Resources Act of 1974 provided support for the establishment of a national network of Health Systems Agencies (HSA) that must approve all large capital expenditures.

Rate Review. Rate review is a generic designation for a wide range of rate-setting and revenue negotiations imposed upon providers by regulators on all levels of government. For example, hospital and physician fees can be set in advance of service provision. Regulators in some jurisdictions have outlawed the practice of "balanced billing," in which providers accept third-party payment, but also expect a supplemental fee from the patient. Some states have also imposed a cap on overall hospital revenues and expenditures, as a way to curtail the rate of growth in expenditures.

Competitive Approaches. A number of factors have combined to increase the competitive environment among health care providers. The growth of for-profit health care conglomerates, ADS, and outpatient "surgi-center" type clinics have increased the choices available to consumers. Employers concerned about the spiraling cost of providing health insurance benefits, and employees concerned about the large portion of their compensation that is siphoned off to pay health insurance premiums, have joined forces to bargain for lower health costs. As the purchasers and consumers of health care have become more conscious about making cost-effective choices regarding health insurance plans and services, providers are being induced to deliver care with greater efficiency. In a competitive system, providers will increase their income by offering the most efficient care, thereby attracting patients from inefficient providers.

Insurance companies and ADS have used a number of strategies to cut the cost of providing care to patients. An increased emphasis has been placed on outpatient care, even for procedures traditionally provided in a more expensive inpatient setting. HMOs have stressed the cost-cutting potential of preventive care and outpatient treatment. Insurance companies are increasingly willing to pay for a second opinion before patients undergo surgery to encourage the consideration of less expensive and less intrusive options.

The increased competitive environment and decreased per capita costs have raised questions regarding the quality of care. Are providers reducing costs by improving efficiency (Dolenc & Dougherty, 1985)? Or, are they lowering costs by compromising quality of care? Are insurers and providers lowering their costs by selecting a healthier patient population through eligibility requirements for insurance policies, or by locating hospitals in suburbs with healthier populations than those in inner-city areas? The very nature of health care complicates the resolution of these issues, because the patient is often a relatively uninformed consumer of services, and also because the determination of appropriate quality is difficult to define. Critics of the competitive approach contend that health care services do not lend themselves to a competitive marketplace. It is argued that an overemphasis on competition and cost cutting will ultimately return health care services to the preinsurance period, when finances and ability to pay were the major criteria for decisions regarding a patient's care and treatment.

LEONARD J. MARCUS

For further information, see AGED: SERVICES; HEALTH PLANNING; HEALTH SERVICE SYSTEM; HOSPICE; HOSPITAL SOCIAL WORK; LONG-TERM CARE; SOCIAL SECURITY.

References

Aaron, H., & Schwartz, W. B. (1984). *The Painful Prescription: Rationing Hospital Care*. Washington, D.C.: Brookings Institution.

Anderson, O. (1985). *Health Services in the United States*. Ann Arbor, Mich.: Health Administration Press.

Arnett, R., III, & Trapnell, G. (1984). "Private Health Insurance: New Measures of a Complex and Changing Industry." *Health Care Financing Review*, 6(2), 31–42.

Dolenc, D., & Dougherty, C. (1985). "DRG's: The Counter-Revolution in Financing Health Care." *Hastings Center Report*, 15(3), 19–29.

Freeland, M., & Schendler, C. E. (1984). "Health Spending in the 1980's: Integration of Clinical Practice Patterns with Management." *Health Care Financing Review*, 5(3), 1–68.

Freund, D., & Jellinek, P. S. (1983). "Financing and Cost Containment for Personal Health Services." In S. C. Jaine & J. E. Paul (Eds.), *Policy Issues in Personal Health Services* (pp. 43–64). Rockville, Md.: Aspen Systems Corp.

Gibson, R. M., et al. (1984). "National Health Expenditures 1983." *Health Care Financing Review*, 6(2), 1–29.

Health Insurance Association of America. (1985). *Source Book of Health Insurance Data 1984–1985*. Washington, D.C.: Author.

McCarthy, C. (1981). "Financing for Health Care." In S. Jones (Ed.), *Health Care Delivery in the United States* (2nd ed., pp. 272–312). New York: Springer Publishing Co.

Ross, H., III (1985). "Health Spending Trends in the 1980's: Adjusting to Financial Incentives." *Health Care Financing Review*, 6(3), 1–26.

U.S. Bureau of the Census. (1983). *Economic Characteristics of Households in the United States: Fourth Quarter 1983* (Household Economic Studies, P70-83-4). Washington, D.C.: U.S. Government Printing Office.

U.S. Department of Health and Human Services. (1984). *HCFA Statistics* (Publication No. 03197). Washington, D.C.: U.S. Government Printing Office.

U.S. Department of Health and Human Services. (1985a). "Medicare Programs; Changes to the Inpatient Hospital Prospective Payment System and Fiscal Year 1986 Rates." *Federal Register*, 50(111), 24365–24445.

U.S. Department of Health and Human Services. (1985b). "Medicare and Medicaid Programs; Peer Review Organizations; Final Rules." *Federal Register*, 50(74).

U.S. Department of Health and Human Services. (1985c). *Health Care Spending Bulletin*, No. 85-02.

U.S. Department of Health and Human Services. (1985d, July 31). *HHS News*, p. 1.

Waldo, D., & Lazenby, H. C. (1984). "Demographic Characteristics and Health Care Use and Expenditures by the Aged in the United States: 1977–1984." *Health Care Financing Review*, 6(1), 1–29.

HEALTH CARE SPECIALIZATIONS

In 1898 a social work agency, the New York Charity Organization Society, established the first formal program in social work education. By 1919, 15 schools of social work had been established, some as independent schools similar to the one begun by the Charity Organization Society and others sponsored by institutions of higher learning (Bernard, 1977). In addition, from 1918 to 1948, seven professional social work associations were established. Many of these associations, such as the American Association of Medical Social Workers, set standards for the curriculum components designed to prepare students for practice in the field represented by the association.

By 1935 it had become mandatory that all accredited schools of social work be affiliates of colleges or universities, and although many association members continued to influence curriculum design in their practice area (Stites, 1955), the shift to university-based education significantly diminished the pattern of agency involvement in curriculum and teaching.

By the 1960s the influence of specific fields of practice on curriculum further diminished as the profession sought to identify and define a common base for social work practice. In the search for professional unity, differences among practice settings were downplayed. This resulted in a reduction in emphasis on health-specific education in social work. Although early programs of social work education were closely identified with specialized practice areas, such as medical social work or psychiatric social work, a generic conceptualization of practice dominated social work education until the mid-1970s when a combination of factors led to a resurgence of interest in specialization, health care being one such field of practice.

Trends

The number of social workers employed in health care in the United States has more than doubled since the 1960s, with estimates now at approximately 45,000. In 1982, 45 percent of the membership of the National Association of Social Workers (NASW) practiced in health or mental health programs ("Membership Survey Shows Practice Shifts," 1983). Passage of Title XVIII (Medicare) and Title XIX (Medicaid) of the Social Security Act stimulated this increase in health care social workers. The increased need for social work services in health care was a product of the highly complex social and economic problems surrounding illness and the increasing numbers of patients and families who needed help in coping with the impact of illness, hospitalization, and posthospital care. With continued population growth—an estimate of 268 million people in the United States by the year 2000 (*1983–84 Supplement to the Encyclopedia of Social Work*, 1983, p. 187)—social work services will undoubtedly continue to grow as a vital component in the delivery of health care.

Further developments have influenced the current interest in health-specific education. In 1975 the Society for Hospital Social Work Directors (SHSWD) of the American Hospital Association and the Council on Social Work Education (1975) recommended that social work education for health care practice include a stronger knowledge base and that the curriculum be strengthened in biological and physiological content and in other practice skills specific to health care. In 1978, SHSWD commissioned a paper to identify the knowledge base and program needs for health care social work practice (Berkman, 1978). In 1980, in cooperation with the Council on Social Work Education (CSWE), the society sponsored a national conference to address further the problem of education for social work in the health field (Berkman, 1980).

This combination of increasing numbers of social workers practicing in health settings and professional action in support of health-specific education brought widespread recognition of the need for contemporary practice standards. The American Association of Medical Social Workers and the American Hospital Association had begun work on such standards in the 1920s (Stites, 1955). Contemporary social work practice standards for health care were developed by the National Association of Social Workers (1977; 1981).

Health care is now recognized as a specialization in social work. For medicine, nursing, and other health care professions, such as physical therapy and dietetics, health care is a general concept that subsumes many subspecialties such as ophthalmology, oncology, and renal disease. Many of these subspecialties developed as a direct result of earmarked funding and sophisticated specialized technology. Similarly, in social work in health care, subspecialties are beginning to emerge ("Specialization and Specialty Interests," 1981). In 1982, specialized standards for social workers in the areas of developmental disability and end-stage renal disease were added to the *NASW Standards for Social Work in Health Care Settings* (National Association of Social Workers, 1981). Moreover, many social workers identified with subspecialties such as perinatal practice, oncology practice, or nephrology have joined groups affiliated with national health specialty organizations such as the American Cancer Society.

With these societal and professional factors as motivating forces, increasing numbers of health care concentrations or specializations are being developed in schools of social work. In the academic year 1972–73, 65 of 85 schools accredited by CSWE responded to a survey on whether they were preparing students for practice in health care. Although half of these schools offered health content, only seven had a definite health specialization (Perretz, 1976).

By 1982, 42 schools reported having a health concentration in some stage of development (Caroff & Mailick, 1984). This increase in the number of schools of social work interested in education for health care practice reflects the growing demand from health professionals that social work graduates be adequately prepared to enter specialized practice as well as students' growing interest in specializing in health care. In the 1982 survey, the responding schools reported that 27 percent of all their students chose to receive some of their education in a health concentration (Caroff & Mailick, 1984).

The challenge facing social work faculties, therefore, is to develop curricula to meet the specialized needs of practice in health care. These curricula must be based on the goals and objectives of social work in health care and offer the knowledge necessary for competent practice.

Goals and Objectives

The goals of social work in health care are generally described on a global level of abstraction, with the level of specificity to health depending on the generic or specific orientation of the author. From Bartlett's (1961) work to Phillips's (1971), Kahn's (1972), and Carlton's (1984), the concept of enhancing or improving social functioning dominates the conceptualization of social work goals to health.

The professional literature reveals widespread agreement about the objectives to achieve these goals in health care. The primary objective of all professionals in health care is the care of the patient's physical and mental health. The objectives for social work can be categorized in eight areas:

1. To assess the psychosocial and environmental stresses that physically ill persons and their families may encounter and to provide direct therapeutic help.

2. To help patients and families make optimal use of social health care programs.

3. To make appropriate social health care programs, including preventive programs, available and accessible to all patients in need.

4. To socialize and humanize the institutional program in the interest of patients' needs.

5. To contribute to the comprehensive treatment of the patient in collaboration with the physician and other personnel.

6. To contribute to the analysis and improvement of social policy and to program development.

7. To provide leadership in areas of consumer participation and education.

8. To administer and evaluate social health care delivery through the assumption of a research responsibility.

To support the social functioning of the individual, family, and community, social work offers a comprehensive, holistic approach to humanity and society. Whereas in the past social work education emphasized the psychological and interpersonal elements of this approach, the curricula now emphasize social, cultural, environmental, and physical dimensions of social functioning (Carlton, 1984).

Knowledge Base

The middle of the 1980s finds a significant move in social work education to develop health care curricula. Although there seems to be agreement that the complexities of the health care field necessitate specialized education, a review of the literature reveals great diversity among the curricula that have been designed to supply this specialized training. However, certain basic premises underlie these curricula.

The social worker brings the same generic knowledge and practice to health care as to any other area. However, in the health setting, the services offered by the social worker are inevitably affected by the structure and program in which they are offered, and it requires adaptation and specification of the social worker's skills to meet the goals and objectives of the health setting and to address the complex organizational structure of health care.

To understand the needs of the patient in the health care system, the social worker must comprehend the nature of illness and consider a multitude of pyschological, social, and physiological factors relevant to the causation of the disease and the patient's care. Etiological factors are not always simple or clear, and the social worker must appreciate that adaptation to illness is not only a matter of an individual's personality; while examining the interaction between physical and pyschological development, the health professional must also address the family system, ethnic and cultural backgrounds, and socioeconomic status. The attitudes and values of the patient's helping network and support system also affect how he or she copes.

The health care social worker is necessarily involved in a multidisciplinary approach to patient care, collaborating with doctors, nurses, and many other health service workers and sharing expertise and knowledge. Social workers in health settings must be familiar with the vocabulary of modern health care.

The complex systems of organization that offer health care services are influenced by a multitude of forces, which interact in a manner that produces policies and procedures. To understand the complex workings of these systems, the social worker needs a conceptual approach to organizations and a set of intervention techniques to provide support and advocacy for the patient. Students planning social work careers in health care thus require in-depth knowledge of health care policies, programs, and services and

special skills in negotiating the complex system of health care resources. They also need a solid understanding of the effects changes in broad social policies have on the provision and delivery of health care services.

Therefore, social workers in the health care system must consider the individual, the family, and the social system and its organizations. The worker's treatment repertoire should include individual, family, and group counseling; advocacy; and social policy interpretation. The hospital-based worker in particular must be prepared to provide a broad range of services, most of which will directly involve discharge planning because this is the key to the patient's posthospital recovery. The most appropriate focus of intervention may be facilitating adaptation to social systems and negotiating resources. In many cases, the social worker's emphasis is on supporting the patient's family or friends— the natural support system—as it adjusts to a changing set of needs.

Educational Issues

Although the goals, objectives, and knowledge base required for social work practice in health care are now well documented in the literature, significant issues remain. In developing specialized education for social work in health care, can the profession agree on the educational content necessary for a beginning social worker to practice in a health setting? How should such training be organized? What should be the relationship between the field practicum and the academic program in the school of social work? Where in the educational continuum should such specialization occur? How much of this health care content can be appropriately integrated into the two-year master's program? How much should be assumed by the field practicum, by apprenticeship training, and by continuing education? As new technologies further increase the complexity of health care delivery, where in the educational continuum should the profession offer the knowledge and skills necessary to serve the specific needs of health care subspecialties and the special populations they create?

Answers to these questions will emerge as faculties adapt curricula to meet the expectations of the most recent curriculum policy statement adopted by the Council on Social Work Education (1982). This policy supports the preparation of social work students for specialized practice and specifies that such preparation occurs at the graduate level.

Schools of social work are developing creative educational innovations that hold promise as structural means to improve education for practice in health care. In addition to traditional efforts to develop health courses that can be integrated with practicum content, some schools are preparing to offer joint degree programs or to incorporate into the social work program courses available from other health programs at the university. In addition, school-agency consortiums or partnerships are being established so that teams of educators and clinicians can jointly teach classes in the clinical setting. Similar efforts to bring field and classroom together are evident in models whereby the field instructor is part of the health care institution, that is, the faculty person and the fieldwork instructor are one and the same. This effort toward coordinating the field and the classroom is enhanced by practitioner participation in the development of the goals, objectives, and curriculum content, which allows for changes in curriculum in response to contemporary health care practice.

There is a consensus that even a well-developed concentration or specialization at the master's level does not fully equip a student with the competence required as a specialist in a field of practice (Caroff & Mailick, 1984). Therefore, continuing education is a necessary concern of both field and school, and a third-year internship to further support specialized education for practice has been suggested.

The social work profession is now undergoing a revival in its commitment to excellence in practice in health care. The collaborative efforts by academic and field faculty to design new curricula and restructure programs are aimed at a better integration of education and practice.

BARBARA BERKMAN

For further information, see DISABILITIES: DEVELOPMENTAL; DISABILITIES: PHYSICAL; EMERGENCY HEALTH SERVICES; HEALTH SERVICE SYSTEM; HOSPITAL SOCIAL WORK; MENTAL HEALTH SERVICES.

References

Bartlett, H. (1961). *Social Work Practice in the Health Field*. New York: National Association of Social Workers.

Berkman, B. (1975). *Preparation for Practice of Social Work in the Health Field*. Chicago: Society for Hospital Social Work Directors of the American Hospital Association.

Berkman, B. (1978). *Knowledge Base and Program Needs for Effective Social Work Practice in Health: A Review of the Literature*. Chicago: Society for Hospital Social Work Directors of the American Hospital Association.

Berkman, B. (1980). *Educating for Social Work Practice in Health: Dilemmas for School and Agency*. Paper presented at a joint national conference of the Society of Hospital Social Work Directors of the American Hospital Association and the Council on Social Work Education, Albuquerque, N.M.

Bernard, L. D. (1977). "Education for Social Work." *Encyclopedia of Social Work* (17th ed., pp. 290–300). Washington, D.C.: National Association of Social Workers.

Carlton, T. (1984). *Clinical Social Work in Health Settings*. New York: Springer Publishing Co.

Caroff, P., & Mailick, M. (1984). "Health Concentrations in Graduate Schools of Social Work: The State of the Art." *Health and Social Work, 10*(1), 5–14.

Council on Social Work Education. (1982). *Curriculum Policy for the Master's Degree and Baccalaureate Degree Programs in Social Work*. New York: Author.

Kahn, E. (1972, March). *Social Work Services in Health Settings*. Cockeysville, Md.: Society for Hospital Social Work Directors.

"Membership Survey Shows Practice Shifts." (1983). *NASW News, 28*(10), 6–7.

National Association of Social Workers. (1977). *NASW Standards for Hospital Social Services*. Washington, D.C.: Author.

National Association of Social Workers. (1981). *NASW Standards for Social Work in Health Care Settings*. Washington, D.C.: Author.

1983–84 Supplement to the Encyclopedia of Social Work (17th ed.). (1983). Silver Spring, Md.: National Association of Social Workers.

Phillips, B. (1971). "Social Workers in Health Services." *Encyclopedia of Social Work* (16th ed., pp. 615–625). New York: National Association of Social Workers.

Perretz, E. A. (1976). "Social Work Education for the Field of Health: A Report of Findings from a Survey of Curriculum." *Social Work in Health Care, 1*(3), 357–365.

"Specialization and Specialty Interests." (1981). *Health and Social Work, 6*(4) (Suppl.).

Stites, M. A. (1955). *History of the American*

Association of Medical Social Workers.
Washington, D.C.: American Association of
Medical Social Workers.

For Further Reading

Bassoff, B. Z. (1976–77). "Interdisciplinary Education for Health Professionals." *Social Work in Health Care, 2*(2), 219–228.

Bracht, N. (1978). *Social Work in Health Care.* New York: Haworth Press.

Bracht, N. (1975). "Health Maintenance: Legislative and Training Implications." *Journal of Education for Social Work, 11*(1), 36–44.

Bracht, N., & Anderson, I. (1975). "Community Fieldwork Collaboration Between Medical and Social Work Students." *Social Work in Health Care, 1*(1), 7–17.

Caroff, P. (1977). "A Study of School-Agency Collaboration in Social Work in Health Curriculum Building." *Social Work in Health Care, 2*(3), 329–339.

Dalgleish, K., Kane, R., & McNamara, J. (1976). "Rotating Social Work Students Within a Medical Center" *Health and Social Work, 1*(2), 166–171.

Dana, B. (1965). "Implications of Social Change for Social Work Education." In *Proceedings of a Conference for Social Workers in the Health Field, USPHS.* Pittsburgh, Pa.: University of Pittsburgh and Montefiore Hospital Association of Western Pennsylvania.

Garber, R. (1970). "Required Changes in Social Work Curricula to Prepare Social Workers for New Responsibilities As Members of Interdisciplinary Health Teams." In *The Preparation of Social Workers for Comprehensive Health Programs* (pp. 80–96). Syracuse, N.Y.: School of Social Work, Syracuse University.

Grossman, L. (1975). "Social Work Education for Microlevel Practice in Health Delivery: Some Selected Aspects." In *Proceedings of the 10th Annual Meeting of the Society for Hospital Social Work Directors.* Kansas City, Mo.: Society for Hospital Social Work Directors.

Harris, J., Saunders, D., & Zasorin-Connors, J. (1978). "A Training Program for Interprofessional Health Care Teams." *Health and Social Work, 3*(2), 35–53.

Hooky, P. (1976). "Education for Social Work in Health Care Organizations." *Social Work in Health Care, 1*(3), 337–345.

Kane, R. (1976). "Interprofessional Education and Social Work: A Survey." *Social Work in Health Care, 2*(2), 229–238.

Lurie, A., & Pinsky, S. (1977, March). "Social Work Education for Health Care." Paper presented at the Annual Meeting of the Council on Social Work Education, Phoenix, Ariz.

Quartaro, E., & Hutchison, R. (1976). "Interdisciplinary Education for Community Health: The Case for Nursing and Social Work Collaboration." *Social Work in Health Care, 1*(3), 347–356.

Raymond, F. (1977). "Social Work Education for Health Care Practice." *Social Work in Health Care, 2*(4), 429–438.

Regensburg, J. (1978). *Toward Education for Health Professions.* New York: Harper & Row.

Rehr, H., & Rosenberg, G. (1977). "Today's Education for Today's Health Care Social Work Practice." *Clinical Social Work Journal, 5*(4), 342–350.

Shulman, L. (1977). "Social Work Education for Health Care Practice: Response to Professor Raymond." *Social Work in Health Care, 2*(4), 439–444.

Snyder, G., Kane, R., & Conover, C. G. (1978). "Block Placements in Rural Veterans Administration Hospitals: A Consortium Approach." *Social Work in Health Care, 3*(3), 331–341.

Wittman, M. (1977). "Application of Knowledge About Prevention in Social Work Education and Practice." *Social Work in Health Care, 3*(1), 37–48.

HEALTH MAINTENANCE ORGANIZATIONS. See HEALTH CARE FINANCING; HEALTH SERVICE SYSTEM.

HEALTH PLANNING

For many years, the United States has recognized the need for health planning to assure an equitable distribution of health resources, including facilities, equipment, technology, and health care providers. In more recent years, the astronomical rise in the cost of medical services, especially in the hospital sector, has made health planning even more imperative. Several significant studies and presidential commissions over the years have helped to highlight this need. The first attempt at health provision planning came as a result of a study of medical education in the United States (Flexner, 1910). This study, which identified major deficiencies in the education and training of physicians, had a significant influence on establishing standards for their education, training, and entry into the profession. A major report (Committee on the Cost of Medical Care, 1933) financed by such foundations as Carnegie, Macy, Rosenwald, and Sage clearly identified the inequities in the area of personal health services. A study by Lee and Jones (1933) was considered a landmark in the planning for an efficient use of hospital beds and personnel within the health care system. A commission on heart disease, cancer, and stroke was appointed by President Kennedy to study ways of reducing the increasing incidence of these diseases and to recommend a mechanism that would disseminate the knowledge and technology that were already available to the country as a whole (Stebbins & Williams, 1972).

Health planning has been defined as "the process of developing and redirecting health resources to meet the population's present and future health needs" (Chavkin & Runner, 1980, p. 832). The process usually involves (1) taking an inventory of all the health resources in a geographically defined area, such as a city, region, community, or neighborhood; (2) assessing current and future community health needs; (3) developing a health plan to bring health resources into line with assessed health needs; and finally (4) implementing the plan.

Early History of Health Planning

Some form of health planning has always existed in the United States. Prior to government intervention and voluntary efforts by individuals and organizations to work together cooperatively, health care providers did their own planning in isolation from each other and other outside influences. The providers themselves determined the location of their practices and size of their fees. Community leadership decided whether or not a hospital was needed.

The first organized or cooperative efforts in health planning were carried out by volunteers, primarily on a local level. These voluntary efforts emerged out of the councils of social agencies that had been formed in the 1920s by wealthy or philanthropic donors in response to overwhelming requests from social organizations for financial contributions. They joined together not only for joint

fundraising efforts but also to plan for human needs in the community (Tannen, 1980).

It was out of these councils that the first organized attempts at health care planning emerged. The councils, bombarded with requests for capital for hospital construction, concluded that a separate body with an emphasis on hospital planning and construction was needed; thus, hospital-planning councils began to develop. The first such council was the Hospital Council of Greater New York, established in 1937 (Tannen, 1980).

As hospital councils emerged in cities such as Rochester, New York; Pittsburgh, Pennsylvania; and Cleveland, Ohio, other voluntary health planning efforts were under way. These efforts have been described as health–disease-oriented or categorical approaches (Stebbins & Williams, 1972). One example in the early 1900s was the work of the National Association of Tuberculosis. During this time, an organized network of voluntary health workers, reaching across the country, dramatized the problems of TB and encouraged the development of both public and private programs toward prevention and treatment. The National Health Council was created in 1963 in response to a need for bringing some form of organization and coordination to all the voluntary efforts taking place.

Voluntary efforts in health planning have been more prominent in the United States than in other countries. Three factors have contributed to this phenomenon: (1) the ready availability of technical assistance from professional organizations and individuals, (2) an American tradition of distrusting government, especially "big government," and (3) the flexibility of voluntary associations (Breslow, 1968).

Federal Government Intervention

With the increasing complexities of the health system—the rising cost of services, advanced technology, population growth and distribution, and the overall problem of limited client access owing to cost and distribution problems—it became necessary for the federal government to become more involved.

Hill-Burton Act. Although categorical because of its primary focus on facilities, the Hill-Burton Act (P.L. 79-725) became a significant piece of health planning legislation. Before the Great Depression, there were some 6,852 hospitals in the United States with approximately 1 million poorly distributed beds (Greenberg, 1976).

The major provision of the Hill-Burton Act dealt with assistance to states for taking an inventory of hospital facilities, developing a comprehensive plan for hospital construction, and constructing public and nonprofit facilities. In order to qualify for assistance, the states were required to establish a single state agency for implementing the law. The U.S. surgeon general had the responsibility for establishing criteria for bed needs, construction, and priority classification. Several significant amendments followed the original act: grants were established in 1954 for chronic disease and rehabilitation centers, nursing homes, and diagnostic and treatment centers (P.L. 83-482); in 1964, for the creation of areawide hospital planning agencies, commonly referred to as "318" agencies (P.L. 88-443); and in 1970, for the modernization of hospitals, especially in urban areas (P.L. 91-296).

The act provided an excellent mechanism for financing hospital and health-related construction and for establishing areawide hospital planning agencies. However, several criticisms have been directed at this significant and early government involvement in health planning. First, it included a "separate but equal" facility clause that allowed for the exclusion of black patients from white hospitals; not until 1963 did the courts rule that such a clause was unconstitutional. Another criticism was that the act "became little more than a conduit for funds used to finance primarily private facility expansion" (Chavkin & Runner, 1980, p. 832). Leadership supporting the act was too slow in recognizing the need for nursing home facilities and chronic and rehabilitative centers, as well as for instituting or improving facilities in urban areas. Finally, the areawide hospital planning councils, although viewed as an innovative creation, provided little leadership in preventing overbedding or the duplication of facilities and equipment. For example, in 1975, 30 years after passage of the Hill-Burton Act, there were approximately 67,000 excess beds (mostly financed by federal money through the act) costing approxi-

mately $1 to $2 billion dollars annually (Kane, 1969; Greenberg, 1976).

Regional Medical Programs Act. A major commitment to health planning on the part of the federal government came with the passage in 1965 of the Regional Medical Programs (RMP) Act (P.L. 89-239). This legislation became known as the war against heart disease, cancer, and stroke. The act provided grants to establish regional cooperative arrangements among medical schools, research institutions, and hospitals for research and training and for related demonstrations of patient care in the fields of heart disease, cancer, and stroke (Willard, 1968). The hope was that the new scientific knowledge and technology resulting from the highly sophisticated research being conducted would be made available to practicing physicians throughout the country, especially in isolated areas.

The RPM Act had several unique features. First was the concept of regionalization, a process of dividing a large geographical area into smaller units. A region, for example, could consist of several counties within a state or within two states in close proximity working together cooperatively. Second was the formation of regional advisory councils with the participation of medical institutions, health agencies, and professionals and public and private groups. Third was the dual-funding scheme, by which—for the first time—the federal government would provide funding for both planning and operational purposes.

There were some concerns about the new legislation. Because of the pluralistic nature of the health system, which included medical schools, practicing physicians, hospitals, and voluntary health agencies, there was doubt that all its components could work cooperatively together. The organized medical community questioned whether the RMP Act was the beginning of some master plan by the federal government to control eventually all medical care in the United States. Medical schools feared that they would be pushed into service commitments they could not handle (Willard, 1968).

The RMP represented a major governmental commitment to bring some order to a fragmented health system, especially in the areas of heart disease, cancer, and stroke.

Comprehensive Health Planning Act.

In 1966, a year after the passage of the RMP Act, President Johnson signed into law the Comprehensive Health Planning (CHP) Act (P.L. 89-749). This act provided funds to states for establishing state health planning agencies, referred to as A agencies. State-wide advisory councils were established according to the law. The state planning agencies, including the advisory councils, had the primary responsibility of developing state health plans for all health planning activities, including family planning, environmental health, health education, and so on.

The act called for authorizing funds to locally based public and private groups within a state, designated B agencies. The state agencies had the responsibility of approving all applications from areawide agencies for funding as B agencies. Once designated as such by the Department of Health, Education, and Welfare on the recommendation of the state agencies, the B agencies were responsible for developing a program to determine the health needs and goals of the area.

Two amendments followed the passage of the CHP Act: (1) In 1967, local government representatives were placed on the boards of B agencies (P.L. 90-174); (2) in 1970, these boards were altered to include representatives from hospitals and other health care facilities as well as physicians, and health planning councils were created for each area with the requirement that membership on such councils represent a consumer majority. The CHP legislation was history making because it recognized consumers as an important or significant part of the planning process (P.L. 91-515).

Several differences existed between the RMP Act and the CHP Act: (1) CHP provided a wider framework for planning under state auspices, whereas RMP was more professionally oriented; (2) CHP was a comprehensive program, whereas RMP was categorical; and (3) CHP was inherently a planning program, whereas RMP was more or less an operational program that included a planning phase. The passage of CHP was an attempt to introduce a comprehensive approach to the development and allocation of health resources in the United States.

Certificate of Need.

During the era of the comprehensive health planning legisla-tion, the United States witnessed a proliferation of certificate of need (CON) programs at the state level. The concept first appeared in 1962, when a study team from the University of Michigan strongly urged state government involvement in regulating health facility development to try to prevent duplication of facilities, equipment, and services (McNerney, 1962). This concept became a topic of debate, and in 1965, New York State adopted the first CON legislation. It mandated that no construction of a public or private hospital could be carried out in the state without the approval of the State Commission of Health. The law included a section relating to expansion, alterations, or conversions (N.Y. Soc. Serv. Law, 1965).

The American Hospital Association endorsed this concept in 1968 and by 1969, following New York's example, 17 other states either had such a measure on the books or had introduced one into their legislatures. States moved toward the enactment of CON laws for several reasons. First, congressional leaders were increasingly concerned about the astronomical rise in the cost of medical care, especially in the hospital sector. Second, states were encouraged to move toward the adoption of CON legislation by the threat of increased federal regulations. As a prod to states to adopt CON legislation, Congress added Section 1122 of P.L. 93-603 to the social security amendments of 1972. This move gave states the option of identifying and designating a particular state agency (such as a health department) to approve all health facility capital investments. "Two years after the passage of the 1122 amendments, 37 states had opted to establish a state-designated agency for the purpose of implementing the federal law" (Hyman, 1977, p. 7). By the time the Health Resources and Development Act (P.L. 93-641) was passed in 1974, approximately half the states had CON laws or programs.

Health Resources and Development Act.

The federal government's next major intervention in support of health planning was the passage in 1974 of the Health Resources and Development (HRD) Act (P.L. 93-641). This legislation was enacted to deal with the identifiable weaknesses that had made CHP programs ineffective—too few resources to support implementation, insufficient staffing and volunteer training, little or no regulatory powers, and competition with other federally supported programs, such as the areawide hospital planning agencies of the Hill-Burton Act (Ardell, 1974).

The HRD Act, including its subsequent amendments, had four major components. First, the secretary of Health, Education, and Welfare was made responsible for issuing guidelines for comprehensive health planning. The act also called for the establishment of the National Council on Health Planning and Development (20 voting members with a minimum of 8 nonproviders) to advise the secretary. Second, a network of health system agencies (HSAs) responsible for health planning was established across the country. Third, assistance was provided to state governments for the development of state health planning and development agencies (SHPDAs) and state health coordinating councils (SHCCs). The SHPDAs would have the responsibility for the entire state, whereas the HSAs would have responsibility for a specified geographical region of the state. Overall, the SHPDAs decided whether or not to approve all the actions of the HSAs within a state. Fourth, procedures and criteria for implementation were established (Chavkin, 1980).

One of the most controversial sections of the HRD Act concerned its relationship to the state CON laws. The major regulatory tool assigned by the new legislation to the state governments was through their CON programs. CON became "a mandated activity of state government if it chose to establish a SHPDA." The legislation threatened to cut off state funds if CON functions were not implemented by state governments before September 30, 1980. Another very significant section required the new HSAs to play an advisory role in state care programs (Sieverts, 1977, p. 79).

The HRD Act was distinguishable from the previous CHP legislation in several ways. First, the HRD Act provided for strong regulatory powers that were not in the CHP legislation. It gave the state and local agencies the power to review all health facilities to determine their appropriateness and the authority to oversee CON programs in each state. Second, under CHP, it was necessary to raise funds on a local level; HRD provided increased funding for staffing and other planning activities. Third, HRD called for one-third of each board to be made up of direct providers—a departure from the consumer majority called for in the CHP legislation. Finally, the HRD Act was less comprehensive in scope than the CHP Act. The focus of HRD was on the health care system, not on involvement in such activities as family planning and environmental health (Lively, 1978; Sieverts, 1977). The HRD Act represented a major step for the government in the area of health planning, especially in regard to regulatory powers.

Omnibus Budget Reconciliation Act. In 1981, the Omnibus Budget Reconciliation Act (P.L. 97-35) gave governors the option of eliminating all HSAs within their states. The act seriously weakens the reviewing process for such issues as appropriateness, proposed use of federal funding, and CON, and it hinders the dissemination of hospital charges.

Social Work in Health Planning

Historically, social work has been involved in health planning in various ways. This is especially true for those social workers who were employed by the Community Chests and councils of social agencies in the 1920s. Early attempts at voluntary focused planning emerged from these councils of social agencies. The leadership of the councils at that time consisted, for the most part, of professional social workers.

Social work became more directly involved in the planning aspects of health care as voluntary effort decreased and the role of government increased, especially after enactment of the CHP Act. At the peak of planning under CHP, social workers were very visible. They provided leadership not only as directors and deputy directors of CHP agencies but also in key staff roles. One study (Finney, Pessin, & Matheis, 1976) of health planning agencies under CHP demonstrated the wide range of activities in which social workers were involved. In the 196 agencies studied, social workers held 9 percent of the executive director positions and 7 percent of the deputy positions. Of the 165 social workers in the agencies under study, 117 (71 percent) held master's degrees, and 48 (20 percent) had bachelor's degrees in social work. Seventy-four percent were working in the area of plan development and implementation and 26 percent in project review. Also, "179 social workers were spread out among 50% of all the agency boards, and 25% of the 196 agencies had two or more social work members" (Finney, Pessin, & Matheis, 1976, p. 18).

At the time of this study, CHP agencies were preparing for the transition from CHP to the requirements of the HRD Act of 1974. The study pointed out that 48 percent of all CHP agencies had social workers involved in the transition process leading to the establishment of the new HSAs. This strongly indicated that social workers would continue their involvement as staff and executives as well as board members of the health planning agencies being created by the HRD Act (Finney, Pessin, & Matheis, 1976).

Future of Health Planning

There is much uncertainty concerning the future of health planning, especially the role of the federal government in the process. The Reagan Administration "is opposed to health planning on the grounds that it interferes with competition in the health care sector" (Tierney & Waters, 1983, p. 95).

An address by the Assistant Secretary of Health and Human Services before a convention of the American Medical Association summarizes the Reagan Administration's stance on the subject:

> We propose to phase out over the next two years all federal support for state and local health planning. This is not to be interpreted as a dismissal of planning as a useful tool for health administrators. Rather, it reflects the strong belief . . . that we must 'return government to those closest to the people affected.' . . . This administration is not convinced that a national health planning standard is either fair or effective. (Brandt, 1982, p. 95)

The Reagan Administration has not proposed any funding for health planning activities. The limited federal spending support currently enjoyed by health planning agencies is the result of congressional compromises that have weakened the regulatory powers of the HRD Act. A compromise proposal—the Health Planning Block Grant of 1982—"required states to revise but continue their certificate of need programs" and continued limited funding for the HSAs or local planning agencies (Tierney & Waters, 1983, p. 95).

Although the future of health planning looks bleak, especially in regard to federal support, communities across the country have recognized the need for such efforts and will look for and find ways to keep the process going, if on a limited basis. The immediate future of health planning will depend to some extent on private funding, voluntary cooperation among local groups, and funding from state and local governments. Although the Reagan Administration did not propose any funding for health planning activities in its first term, some legislators have been able to maintain a limited amount of funding within the federal budget. This is an indication that health planning is not dead. Furthermore, with the continuous concern over the cost of health care—especially in the hospital sector—politicians, leaders in the health care field, and community advocates will keep the issue of health planning before the American people.

EDWARD A. McKINNEY

For further information, see FEDERAL SOCIAL LEGISLATION SINCE 1961; HEALTH SERVICE SYSTEM; PUBLIC HEALTH SERVICES; SOCIAL PLANNING IN THE PUBLIC SECTOR; SOCIAL PLANNING IN THE VOLUNTARY SECTOR.

References

Ardell, D. B. (1974). "The Demise of CHP and the Future of Planning," *Inquiry, 11*(3), 233–235.

Brandt, E. N., Jr. (1982). "Health Planning of the Reagan Administration," *Journal of Connecticut Medicine, 46*(2), 94–96.

Breslow, L. (1968). "Political Jurisdictions, Voluntarism, and Health Planning" *American Journal of Public Health, 58*(7), 1147–1154.

Chavkin, D. F., & Runner, M. W. (1980). "An Advocate's Guide to Health Planning," *Clearing House Review, 13*(11), 831–847.

Committee on the Cost of Medical Care. (1933). *Final Report No. 28.* Chicago: University of Chicago Press.

Finney, R., Pessin, R., & Matheis, L. (1976). "Prospects for Social Workers in Health Planning." *Health and Social Work, 1*(3), 8–25.

Flexner, A. (1910). *Medical Education in the United States and Canada.* New York: The Carnegie Foundation for the Advancement of Teaching.

Greenberg, R. B. (1976). "Federal Health Planning, Part I: Legislative Background." *American Journal of Hospital Pharmacy, 33*(10), 1049–1051.

Hyman, H. H. (1977). "Introduction to Key Issues

in Regulation of Health Facilities and Services." In H. H. Hyman (Ed.), *Health Regulation CON and 1122* (pp. 1–25). Rockville, Md.: Aspen Systems Corporation.

Kane, D. A. (1969). "Comprehensive Health Planning: A Study in Creative Federalism," *American Journal of Public Health, 59*(9), 1706–1712.

Lee, R. I., & Jones, L. W. (1933). *The Fundamentals of Good Medical Care.* Chicago: University of Chicago Press.

Lively, C. A. (1978). "PL 93-641: A Recipe for Action." *Hospitals, 52*(12), 65–68, 124.

McNerney, W. (1962). *Hospitals and Medical Economics.* Chicago: Hospital Research and Educational Trust.

N. Y. Soc. Serv. Law. (1965). Ch. 795, Art. 28, § 2802.

Reinke, W. (1972). *Health Planning: Qualitative Aspects and Quantitative Techniques.* Baltimore, Md.: Johns Hopkins University Press.

Sieverts, S. (1977)."Certificate of Need." In S. Sieverts (Ed.), *Health Planning Issues and P.L. 93-641* (pp. 95–98). Chicago: American Hospital Association.

Stebbins, E. L., & Williams, K. N. (1972). "History and Background of Health Planning in the United States." In W. A. Reinke (Ed.), *Health Planning: Qualitative Aspects and Quantitative Techniques.* Baltimore, Md.: Johns Hopkins University Press.

Tannen, L. (1980). "Health Planning as a Regulatory Strategy: A Discussion of its History and Current Uses," *International Journal of Health Services, 10*(1), 119–123.

Tierney, J., & Waters, W. (1983). "The Evolution of Health Planning." *New England Journal of Medicine, 308*(2), 95–98.

Willard, W. R. (1968). "Diverse Factors in Regional Medical Planning," *American Journal of Public Health, 58*(6), 1026–1028.

HEALTH SERVICE SYSTEM

The health care delivery system in the United States has evolved from a free enterprise cottage industry of practitioners working alone or in small groups. Since the mid-1960s, there has been an increase of group practice, ambulatory care centers in hospitals, and centralized primary care. The health system consists of a provider-facility organization interacting with federal and state government, third-party reimbursement institutions, and the patient-consumer.

Overview of Delivery Systems

The provider-facility organization focuses on the primary care physician and subspecialists who practice in individual or group practice or hospital settings. Primary care is first-contact family health care, whereas secondary and tertiary care occur on referral to specialists or subspecialists. Primary care is usually for an acute condition. In many settings, the nurse-practitioner or physician-assistant are involved in the primary care treatment of patients and are under the supervision of the physician. There is a trend toward group practice in which three or more physicians provide medical care while sharing equipment, personnel, records, and management structure. The Kaiser-Permanente Health Plan, the Health Insurance Plan of Greater New York, and the Group Health Cooperative of Puget Sound are examples of three large prepaid group practices. Cost-effective measures (such as emphasis on outpatient care and a 20 percent reduction in hospitalization compared to fee-for-service plans) characterize this alternative health care system.

The hospital system in the United States comprises general medical and surgical community hospitals, university teaching hospitals, federal and state hospitals, and proprietary hospitals. The majority are short-term-care hospitals with an average general capacity of 450 beds. Specialty hospitals are long-term-care facilities for psychiatric illness, chronic disease, tuberculosis, and other disorders. Hospitals are owned by state and federal governments, private proprietary (for-profit) organizations, and nonprofit (voluntary) corporations. In order for a hospital to incorporate on a nonprofit basis, it must reinvest all profits back into the facility and not distribute any to the owners. Hospitals generally offer inpatient and outpatient care. The ideal occupancy rate for an acute care community hospital is approximately 85 percent of total capacity. The current average occupancy rate in the United States of below 75 percent implies that hospitals are overbedded and underutilized high-cost facilities. Hospital outpatient care consists of outpatient, emergency, and ancillary diagnostic departments. Attached to hospitals or affiliated satellite facilities may be special emergency clinics and clinics for weight reduction and obesity, longevity related to diabetes and heart disease, acupuncture, and birthing. Long-term care encompasses a variety of health facilities dealing with mental disability, chronic-degenerative disability, geriatrics, and slow-acting contagious diseases. The average length of stay in a long-term-care facility is 30 days or more (Mackintosh, 1978).

Since the mid-1960s, the supply of health practitioners has increased greatly both in numbers and in proportion to the population. The proportion of women in health professional schools rose significantly by 1980, when women accounted for 23 percent of the graduates in medicine, 14 percent of those in dentistry, and 41 percent of those in pharmacy. Blacks rose from 2.7 percent of first-year medical students in 1968 to 7.5 percent in 1974 and declined slightly to 6.5 percent in 1979. The number of active registered nurses increased from 335,000 in 1950 to 1.3 million in 1980, while the proportion of those working part-time increased from 11 to 32 percent during the same period. Public general hospitals accounted for nearly one-third of all short-term general nonfederal hospitals in 1977. Particularly in metropolitan areas, public hospitals treated more minority patients (20 percent), Medicaid patients (15 percent), and uninsured patients (12 percent) than voluntary hospitals in the same vicinity. Both urban and rural public hospitals had higher death rates among newborns and a greater incidence of low birthweight in infants owing to patient composition (V. S. Department of Health and Human Services, 1983).

The present structure of the health care system makes it unresponsive to providing appropriate incentives for the efficient use of resources. Hornbrook (1983) points out at least three liabilities: (1) extensive first-dollar health insurance coverage, which isolates consumers from the true cost of services; (2) the nonprofit status of most hospitals that have the cost-reimbursement mechanism and lack of effective price competition; and (3) fee-for-service physicians able to prescribe services according to their professional objectives.

Key Legislation

Present health policy stems from legislative programs passed during the mid-1960s and early 1970s and 1980s. Medicaid and Medicare, landmark health coverage programs for the poor and elderly, were part of Titles XVIII and XIX of the 1965 Social Security Amendments (P.L. 89-97). They were prototype programs for universal health coverage that was proposed and debated without being enacted during the 1970s. As a result of spiraling health costs from federal Medicaid and Medicare budgets, legislation was subsequently passed to curb rising health expenditures. Regional medical programs and comprehensive health planning centers were established in 1966 to foster regional examination of the quality of care and to coordinate institutional expansion. Health maintenance organizations (HMOs) were funded in 1973 to offer a prepaid-group-practice alternative to a fee-for-service system. The 1974 National Health Planning and Resources Development Act (P.L. 93-64) strengthened the 1966 Comprehensive Health Planning Act (P.L. 89-749) by authorizing health system agencies to examine health facility expansion through a certificate-of-need approach.

The Carter Administration proposed to cap hospital costs at an annual growth maximum. However, the hospital industry argued against such external regulation and volunteered to impose an annual growth limit on itself. Owing to economic inflation, lack of political consensus, and medical-hospital lobbying, national health insurance was a dead issue by the end of the 1970s. However, the Reagan Administration was instrumental in the passage of the 1982 Tax Equity and Fiscal Responsibility Act (P.L. 97-248), which set prescriptive reimbursement (a prospective payment system for diagnosis-related groups) for Medicare and Medicaid recipients who are in hospitals.

Medicare and Medicaid. Congress established Medicare and Medicaid in 1965. Medicare is a federal entitlement program that guarantees uniform benefits to the elderly (persons over age 64) and the long-term disabled. In the 1986 federal budget, Medicare provided health insurance coverage for 28 million elderly persons and 3 million persons who were disabled or suffering from end-stage renal disease. Since 1980, Medicare has increased at an annual rate of 13.2 percent so that the Medicare budget is projected to reach $87.5 billion by 1988. In 1985, Medicare was separated from the federal health budget and placed with Social Security. Together, both programs for elderly and disabled Americans accounted for more than a quarter of federal outlays for 1986 (Executive Office of the President, 1985).

Medicare consists of two parts: Part A is hospital insurance financed by Social Security payroll taxes covering hospital care, skilled nursing facilities, home health agencies, and hospices; Part B is supplementary medical insurance, which is voluntary, including outpatient and inpatient physician services, hospital outpatient and laboratory services, durable medical equipment, treatment for end-stage renal disease, and medical supplies. From 1966 to 1973, Part B was financed through a 50 percent beneficiary premium, with the remaining 50 percent funded through federal general revenues. However, from 1974 to 1982, the Part B premium was adjusted according to the rate of the Social Security cost-of-living adjustment. As a result, premiums made up less than 25 percent of Part B program costs in 1982, with the difference financed by the federal government (Executive Office of the President, 1985).

To keep down the cost of hospital inpatient services under Medicare, a prospective payment system was introduced in 1984, which fixed the rates for specific classes of diagnostic illness. This has given hospitals an incentive to control costs and cut unnecessary expenditures. The 1986 federal budget for Medicare freezes at the 1985 level all Part A Medicare reimbursement for hospital inpatient services, skilled nursing facilities, home health agencies, payment to physicians, payment for clinical laboratory tests, durable medical equipment, and other supplies. Part B program premium costs are projected to increase from 25 percent in 1985 to 35 percent by 1990. Premiums for 1986 cover 27 percent of the program cost and would increase 2 percent annually until 1990. In 1987, the Part B deductible would increase annually from its current annual deductible of $75 based on price changes (Executive Office of the President, 1985).

The 1986 Medicaid program budget consisted of $23.7 billion in federal and $19.3 billion in state funds to finance the health care needs of 22.5 million Americans in poverty. The Omnibus Budget Reconciliation Act of 1981 (P.L. 97-35) significantly reduced the extent of services and tightened eligibility standards for Medicaid. As a result, the annual rate of increase for Medicaid dropped from 15.3 percent (1979 to 1981) to 9 percent (1981 to 1983). However, these reforms expired in 1984.

For 1986, the Reagan Administration proposed to limit Medicaid cost growth to the increase in prices in the medical care sector. States would be given more control of cost through increased flexibility to target services, alternatives to costly services, and improved third-party liability efforts. It also proposed terminating open-ended state entitlement for federal Medicaid funds to cover administrative expenses, replacing this funding with new federal grants. Medicaid funds for 1986 were frozen at the 1985 level, and future payments to states would be limited to the growth in the implicit price deflator for the gross national product. This would mean the elimination of federal and state matching requirements, detailed cost allocation plans, and federal expenditure reviews. In return, states would have the flexibility to use federal grants, and they could transfer up to 10 percent of the grants to other state-administered public assistance programs. However, states would suffer significant loss of federal Medicaid matching funds and would be forced to make up the financial difference, reduce the service coverage level, or introduce stringent eligibility standards to exclude potential Medicaid recipients (Executive Office of the President, 1985).

Health Maintenance Organizations. The Health Maintenance Organization (HMO) Act of 1973 (P.L. 93-222) represents a major federal government attempt to foster an alternative to the fee-for-service delivery structure. An HMO delivers comprehensive health services to its enrolled members for a prepaid fixed fee (capitation payment) covering a specified period of time. HMO members represent, on the whole, middle-class working professional families who are basically healthy. There is a tendency toward more ambulatory and preventive services with primary care physicians, less hospitalization (20 percent less than in fee-for-service plans), and centralization of facilities, records, and staff. An HMO can predetermine its income revenue based on fixed monthly or quarterly capitation payments and offer its staff a profit margin incentive based on maintaining the health of the membership.

The primary purpose of the HMO Act was to encourage the growth and development of this cost-saving system through grants for feasibility studies and loan guarantees for planning, initial development, and operating costs. The original 1973 legislation was amended in 1976 (P.L. 94-460) to reduce the mandatory comprehensive service coverage (for example, dental care was dropped and open enrollment modified) so the program could remain competitive with other health insurance. However, there are basic and supplementary services: physician, outpatient and inpatient, emergency, mental health, family planning, physical examination, immunization, and a variety of other services. Consumers must make up at least 50 percent of the board of an HMO. There must be grievance procedures for resolving consumer complaints. Health education, nutrition, and social services should be available. No more than 75 percent of the membership can come from a medically underserved area, and only 50 percent may be from Medicaid and Medicare federal programs. The intent is to have a balanced and mixed socioeconomic membership. HMO services are subject to a quality assurance program (which includes peer review and outcome studies) under monitoring from the Department of Health and Human Services.

Coulton (1982) identifies four assumptions concerning HMOs: (1) they rely on fewer days of hospitalization than traditional organizations, lowering health care costs; (2) they use more ambulatory and preventive services, providing better access to primary care; (3) quality is higher and there is less unnecessary surgery and greater continuity; and (4) they make effective use of ancillary health professionals.

Feldstein (1983) has proposed that HMOs, prepaid group practices, or prepaid health plans become the primary model for launching a competitive system of health care. They have a number of structural features that lend themselves to cost-effective competition: incentives for hospital efficiency, less duplication of facilities, minimization of medical treatment cost, increased physician productivity and greater use of auxiliary medical personnel, incentives for

preventive care and health education, use of generic drugs, and unique diagnostic, management, and health service delivery methods. Feldstein (1983) believes that HMOs will have an effect on fee-for-service providers:

> For market competition to have desirable consequences, fee-for-service providers and insurers should respond to HMO competition by attempting to minimize their enrollees' health care costs and to increase consumer satisfaction. Thus, in addition to benefiting their own enrollees, HMOs, through their competition, should benefit all consumers in the area. (p. 347)

The net effect of HMOs has been to underscore the need for a cost-effective structural system for health care providers. However, Coulton (1982) points out that HMOs have grown slowly because of the range of mandated services, initial development, and client recruitment. Increasingly, HMOs are recognized as health delivery treatment structures that will be cost-effective in marketplace competition.

Health Planning. The National Health Planning and Resources Development (NHPRD) Act of 1974 (P.L. 93-641) consolidated and replaced three previous legislative programs dealing with health facility construction and planning: Hill-Burton, Comprehensive Health Planning, and Regional Medical Programs. The deregulation of certain government programs by the Reagan Administration and Congress now appears to be phasing out the NHPRD program and health systems agencies. State health planning divisions are beginning to monitor regional health facility growth. Health planning has been criticized as ineffective. However, much of the problem has been in the limitation imposed on the 1974 legislation. Harrington (1982) poses a number of questions: (1) Should health planning change its emphasis from improving the health delivery system to improving the health status of the population through economic, social, and environmental changes? (2) Should present health planning legislation be criticized for its limited scope and its restriction of authority by omitting provisions for controlling reimbursement, regulating physicians, and authorizing the closure of unnecessary services and facilities? (3) Did inadequate funding of health systems agencies create organizational and operational problems and limit their capability to implement regulatory activities?

The original goals of the NHPRD Act were to improve the health of residents of a health service area; increase the accessibility, acceptability, continuity, and quality of health services; restrain increases in the cost of health services; and prevent unnecessary duplication of health resources. In order to bring about these objectives, an organizational structure was formed among four groups: (1) health systems agencies, which encompassed health service areas between 500,000 and 3 million in population, were required to develop long-range health plans for communities and had advisory authority over certificate-of-need decisions concerning health facility development; (2) state health planning and development agencies were required to develop state health plans, state medical facilities plans, and related health plans based on health systems agency actions, documents, and recommendations; (3) statewide health coordinating councils served as advisory bodies to state health planning and development agencies and reviewed health systems agency plans, applications for planning grants, state plans and applications for federal funds and health systems agency annual budgets and funding applications; and (4) the United States Department of Health and Human Services, which administered the NHPRD program, established health planning goals and health planning operational regulations and monitored the performance standards of the other three groups.

Unique to the NHPRD program was the involvement of health consumers and providers with various planning boards in health systems agencies and the statewide health coordinating councils. This provided an opportunity to educate a body of consumer volunteers in planning issues (such as facility expansion, service review, health care cost, and regulatory decision making) within the context of support from the health services agencies' professional staff and interaction with regional health providers.

Unresolved Legislation. With the launching of Medicare and Medicaid in 1965, the political atmosphere was ripe for renewed interest in national health insurance and cost containment measures. A national health in-

surance clause was not included in the 1935 Social Security Act because President Roosevelt feared that doing so would jeopardize the major provision of old age insurance and unemployment compensation. During the late 1930s, the 1940s, and the 1950s, a succession of national health insurance bills was introduced in Congress but failed to pass. Major opposition came from the medical profession and the private insurance industry. However, Medicare and Medicaid signaled universal coverage to two needy populations: the elderly and the poor. The political strategy was to demonstrate the viability of national health insurance to two groups and to follow up with a national health insurance program for the rest of the American population.

In 1970, Senator Edward Kennedy introduced the Health Security Bill (S. 92-3, H.R. 92-22), which stimulated the introduction of a wide range of national health insurance proposals. There was disagreement on such major issues as population coverage, scope of benefits, funding modality, extent of regulation, and program delivery pattern. Eventually, the Carter Administration proposed 10 principles of national health insurance with phases contingent on the state of the economy. President Carter and Senator Kennedy could not agree on an appropriate compromise. As a result, the enactment of national health insurance legislation was no longer a political possibility by the end of the 1970s.

Meanwhile, with the rising cost of medical care services, the Carter Administration focused on legislation that would impose a direct cap on the annual rate of hospital cost increase in the event that the hospital industry could not maintain its voluntarily self-imposed limit over a period of 2 years. However, the 96th Congress enacted no meaningful cost containment legislation. The hospital industry set a voluntary goal of an 11.6 percent annual rate increase for 1979. Nevertheless, hospital costs increased 12.5 percent and reached an annual rate of 17 percent in 1981. With the election of President Reagan, cost containment took the form of fixed rates of reimbursement for specific disease categories, in the belief that individual hospitals would regulate and monitor their operations in a cost-effective manner.

Fixed Reimbursement. Since the passage of Medicare and Medicaid, cost reimbursement has increased significantly, particularly for hospital expenditures. For both programs, but particularly for Medicare, this increase resulted from a growth in the number of beneficiary categories, an expansion of the over-65 population, increased utilization, and the rising cost of a hospital day.

The Tax Equity and Fiscal Responsibility Act of 1982 (TEFRA, P.L. 97-248), allowed states to charge all Medicaid beneficiaries nominal copayments for certain mandatory and optional services. However, states cannot impose copayments on categorically needy children under 18; patients needing emergency care, family planning services, or services related to pregnancy; or categorically needy patients in skilled nursing or intermediate care facilities or enrolled in HMOs. The copayment policy provision was estimated to decrease Medicaid expenditures by $45 million in 1983, $50 million in 1984, and $56 million in 1985 (Gibson, 1983). Accordingly, federal matching rates for Medicaid to states were reduced by 3 percent in 1982, 4 percent in 1983, and 4.5 percent in 1984. In addition, there were incentives for federal support. A state could receive a 1 percent increase in federal payment if it had a qualified hospital cost review program, an unemployment rate 50 percent higher than the national average, or recoveries from fraud and abuse greater than or equal to 1 percent of the quarterly federal payments to states. A state could also receive relief from the 3 percent federal reduction by keeping federal Medicaid reimbursement in fiscal 1982 from growing more than 9 percent over federal 1981 levels. If federal reimbursement growth was less than 9 percent, a state qualified for a dollar-for-dollar offset of the difference between actual federal spending and the 9 percent target growth rate (Gibson, 1983). As a result, state Medicaid programs limited the scope of services and restricted eligibility as a means of controlling Medicaid budgets.

TEFRA shifted the reimbursement from a retrospective implicit per diem system to a prospective explicit per case system. The case-mix formular was incorporated into the payment system and a limit was placed on the rate of allowable increase in costs per case. The payment level for each diagnostic related group (DRG) should be established on a national basis by 1987 but will vary by hospital location (urban/rural), area wage levels, and teaching level. For example, the Medicare cost per case of urban hospitals is approximately 20 percent higher in the east-north-central region than in the east-south-central region, and teaching hospitals receive higher reimbursement than community hospitals because of the indirect costs associated with teaching and the greater severity and complexity of patient disorders (Lave, 1984).

DRGs are central to hospital reimbursement formulas established in the 1982 TEFRA legislation and refined in the 1983 amendments to the Social Security Act (P.L. 98-21). They are the basis for a classification system to determine federal reimbursement. The variables include the patient's medical diagnosis, prescribed treatments, length of stay, and adjustment margins on a per case basis. The 467 DRG categories are grouped into 23 Major Diagnostic Categories of body system and disease etiology. Clinical and medical criteria (principal diagnosis, secondary diagnosis, and surgical procedure) are applied in combination with patient characteristics (age, sex, and discharge status). A predetermined reimbursement rate provides a built-in incentive for the hospital to regulate itself and become cost-effective. Because the hospital receives a fixed reimbursement for a particular DRG category, it is motivated to treat and discharge the patient within a prescribed time frame. If the patient is effectively cared for before the end of the prescribed time period, the hospital can retain some of the difference and makes a profit. However, if the length of the patient's stay exceeds the set time limit, the hospital must absorb the financial loss. As a result, particular hospitals have carefully scrutinized their services, treatment procedures, patient-staff ratios, and administrative–financial management policies. Moreover, the hospital's budgetary restraints make physicians and hospital administrators mutually interdependent partners (Caputi & Heiss, 1984).

In evaluating the DRG system, Levine and Abdellah (1984) observe, "Paying hospitals an amount fixed in advance is viewed as a potent mechanism for encouraging efficiency and containing costs of hospital care" p. 105). Yet they warn that the tendency to reduce nursing staff or substitute aides and practical nurses may have an adverse effect on the quality of care. A longitudinal study of the effects of the TEFRA legislation and DRG prescriptive reimbursement is the next step in determining whether this method maintains both cost effectiveness and quality of care. A pilot study (Grimaldi & Micheletti, 1982) conducted in New Jersey focused on Relative Intensity Measures. The 23 Major Diagnostic Categories were grouped in 13 nursing resource clusters. Estimates were made of the average amounts of nursing care (measured in minutes) received by patients in the different categories. These estimates were used to determine the allocation of nursing costs to patients in the DRG classifications.

Trends and Issues

New trends are emerging in the second half of the 1980s. Berki (1983) succinctly summarizes them:

> Increased reliance on private markets, on competition among organized groups, on prospective rather than retroactive payment, and on altering the incentives facing consumers by shifting to them a higher share of the costs of care are the suggested remedies for the ills of the health care system. (p. 10)

There seems to be movement away from the federal regulation of the 1970s, which attempted to curb rising costs with professional standards review organizations, health systems agencies, and certificate-of-need laws. As a result, some states (New York, Massachusetts, Maryland, Washington, Michigan, and Colorado) have utilized rate-setting of Medicaid programs, which has stabilized hospital payments and budgets. HMOs have contributed to cost savings. During the 1980s, a major trend has begun toward prospective reimbursement (Brown, 1983). Meyer (1983) observes, "The principal problem in health care today is the need for a workable mechanism to achieve a proper balance between acceptable cost and an ensured level of quality" (p. 1). Increasingly, cost management strategies seek to isolate waste, deny payment for unnecessary care, encourage efficient provider services, and induce consumers to seek cost-effective care. Various issues surrounding cost escalation, cost containment, quality of care, and accessibility are paramount in the 1980s.

Cost. The average annual rate of increase in national health expenditures from 1960 to 1965 was 9.2 percent; this figure rose to 12.4 percent during the period from 1965 to 1970, with the rise of Medicare and Medicaid. There was also a significant increase in public sources of funds from 10.4 percent (1960 to 1965) to 20.8 percent (1965 to 1970). The annual rate of increase in expenditure reached a peak of 15.8 percent (1979 to 1980) but leveled off to 12.5 percent (1981 to 1982). In the 17-year period from 1965 to 1982, public and private expenditures went from $41.7 billion to $322.4 billion. Of particular concern has been a rise in the average annual rate at which hospital expenses increase; from 13.4 percent for 1971 and 1972, it rose to a high of 17.6 percent for 1974 and 1975, with only a slight decrease to 16.4 percent for 1980 and 1981. In 1982, 71.3 percent of all Medicare expenditures were for hospital care, while nursing home care accounted for 40.7 percent and hospital care for 36.4 percent of Medicaid expenditures (U. S. Department of Health and Human Services, 1983). Berki (1983) estimates that the total national health expenditures exceed $290 billion annually, absorb over 10 percent of the gross national product, and grow faster than expenditures in any other sector of the economy.

Free-Market Competition. The free-market competition model has been proposed by Enthoven (1980), among others. It is based on the notion that government regulation of health care cost has met only limited success. The alternative is to rely on free-market mechanisms to yield solutions to health care problems related to service coverage, accessibility, quality of care, and cost containment (Hornbrook, 1983). Ideally, a sound market should meet certain universal structural requirements: a sufficient number of competitors, a price mechanism felt by both consumers and producers, freedom for competitors to enter and leave the market, no collusion or cartel behavior among competitors, and adequate information for consumers about their choices. McClure (1983) argues that serious violation of one or more of these structural requirements causes the market to fail and the desired incentives to disappear. The competition model proposes increased deductibles and coinsurance to raise consumer cost-consciousness under fee-for-service reimbursement, increased HMO market penetration to provide more competition with fee-for-service providers, and prospective reimbursement of hospitals on a diagnostic-specific basis to provide institutional incentives for minimizing cost (Hornbrook, 1983).

By March 1982, the free-market competition model was abandoned politically because of opposition from many groups. Labor opposed the competitive scheme fearing that it would disrupt traditional collective bargaining prerogatives and that competition would have a negative impact on the poor. Employers expressed concern about the more highly regulated and uniform health insurance system that would arise. Insurance companies wondered about changes in the federal tax code and federalization of health insurance regulation. Physicians recognized the potential shift in regulations and financial reimbursement. Hospitals became anxious over the potential for lower payments and cost shifts accompanying competition. The elderly felt that competitive vouchers and copayments meant reduced Medicare requirements and higher out-of-pocket costs.

Weisbrod (1983) raises questions regarding competition: "increased numbers of competitors would not necessarily bring increased price competition; moreover, increased price competition would have uncertain effects" (p. 65). Similarly, Ginzberg (1983) points out reasons for caution: selling and administrative costs could skyrocket, the consumer is in a poor position to judge the complex coverage for health services, ensuring against adverse selection could make coverage expensive for those most in need, and eliminating regulations governing new hospital expansion and construction could result in neighborhoods and communities being cut off from facilities. Pauly and Langwell (1983) argue that we have virtually no knowledge of the extent or impact of cross-firm competition in the hospital market or of how competition among hospitals works now. Finally, Kinzer (1984) concludes that the competitive strategy is a mad scramble for a larger share of the private market, has limited relevance to cost control, and has little congressional support since increasing numbers of citizens are unable to pay for their health services.

Quality of Care. It is important to define, operationalize, and maintain a standard of care responsive to the medical needs of health services consumers as well as to ensure medical excellence among health care practitioners. Donabedian (1980) has defined high-quality medical care as "the management that is expected to achieve the best balance of health benefits and risks" (p. 13). He further points out that contrary to popular belief, quality is not defined in terms of the consequences of care but in terms of the attributes of the providers and of their behavior. Major quality-of-care studies stress interpersonal management more than the technical aspects. Nevertheless, criteria for assessing the quality of care in a health system are important. Among these criteria are (1) health status outcomes (mortality, morbidity, life expectancies, capacity for functioning), (2) estimated quality of service (study of hospital services through patients' records and visual observation), (3) quality of services provided (ambulatory medical services, hospitalizations, prescribed drugs, dental services, number of patients per physician hour), (4) attitudes of recipients (survey of patients receiving the service, quantity of grievances, rate of malpractice suits), and (5) resources made available (personnel and physical resources: range of general practitioners and specialists, range of equipment, and scope of services offered in hospitals and health centers).

Accessibility. Economic and organizational factors may present barriers to health care. An individual's level of income and health insurance coverage dictate the extent of medical services available. The belief in access to health care as a basic human right has given way to restricted eligibility requirements for Medicaid and the lack of indigent medical services in cost-conscious community hospitals. At the same time, access may be limited by distant locations of health facilities, the inconvenience of transportation, long waiting periods, and the unavailability of primary care providers in certain geographical areas. Socioeconomic barriers to health care access affect the range of available treatment and continuity of care; furthermore, deductibles and coinsurance discriminate against the poor and the elderly on tight fixed incomes.

Aday and Andersen (1974) link access to the availability of financial and health system resources in an area. They identify a number of factors that affect access, including health policy objectives, the characteristics of the health care delivery systems and populations at risk, and the utilization of health care services and consumer satisfaction. Financing, education, manpower, and health care reorganization programs affect the political context of accessibility. The health delivery system, consisting of labor and capital resources, and the coordination and control of the medical service organization affect access and the treatment process. The populations at risk determine the degree of utilization of health care. Age, sex, race, religion, values, income, insurance coverage, and community location are major factors related to the patient population. Kinds of providers, services, medical care site, purpose of visits, and lengths of visits are external indicators of service utilization. Finally, consumer satisfaction is determined by convenience of care, coordination and cost, provider courtesy, information given about the illness, and patient judgment on the quality of care.

Minority Issues and Health Care. There are still disparities in health services for racial and ethnic minorities and handicapped people. Trevino and Moss (1983) report that a significant percentage of minorities are uninsured for medical expenditures (30 percent of Mexican Americans and 20 percent of black, Cuban, and Puerto Rican Americans). The inability of Mexican Americans to pay for health insurance and the failure of their employers to provide health insurance benefits were cited as the major reasons for their lack of health insurance coverage. These working poor were caught in the middle between Medicaid ineligibility and insufficient income to obtain their own health care plan.

In a report by the Institute of Medicine (1981), the Committee for a Study of the Health Care of Racial/Ethnic Minorities and Handicapped Persons found that (1) minority patients who were seriously ill, badly injured, or in active labor were turned away from hospitals, transferred to other public hospitals, or subjected to long delays before care; (2) racial/ethnic minorities who needed more medical care than whites did not receive more hospitalization or physician visits; (3)

racial separation or segregation exists in American health care facilities, with blacks having less access to private physicians or specialists than whites; (4) less qualified health professionals provide care to some minority groups; and (5) data limitations prevent an adequate description of differences in health care provision for racial/ethnic minorities and an adequate analysis of possible causes. This same committee concluded that (1) health care patterns for racial/ethnic minorities deserve serious research and statistical study; (2) there is a need to focus on racial segregation in health care facilities and on related discrepancies in quality of care; and (3) there should be a study of factors contributing to the striking racial patterns regarding dental care.

Furthermore, Harwood (1981) advocated (1) that health services be modified to accommodate ethnic epidemiological patterns and behavioral styles; (2) that more ethnic professionals be hired in health care institutions; (3) that information concerning the cultural, social, and psychological-phenomenological background of problems be obtained from patients or their families, relatives, or associates to supplement the strictly biological data on their illnesses; (4) that health care workers familiarize themselves with sociocultural information on various ethnic groups to guide health care, to anticipate culture shock and cognitive discrepancies, and to suggest different ethnic milieu resources for supporting the individual or family with a health problem; and (5) that clinicians and health planners obtain specific knowledge of lay treatment practices (self-medication and health maintenance) and lay caretakers (healers, herbalists, curanderos, spiritualists, acupuncturists). Harwood (1981) also established specific guidelines for culturally appropriate health care, recognizing intraethnic variations, ethnic concepts of disease and illness, patient evaluations of symptoms, and ethnic-cultural means of coping with illness and related issues.

Computers and Health Care. A growing body of literature deals with computer application for patient care. Bronzino (1982) observes that during the 1980s, computer systems will perform a host of health care diagnostic and treatment functions: automating clinical chemistry laboratories, storing patient medical records, monitoring critically ill patients, developing diagnostic support systems (such as ECG interpretation), and performing computerized tomography, diagnostic ultrasound, and the techniques of nuclear medicine. Presently, computers are used extensively to collect, retrieve, and present patient-related information and records; in clinical laboratories to store, retrieve, route, sort, and verify the flow of laboratory information, providing an efficient and cost-effective means of handling patient data; in computerized multiphasic health testing, which employs digital processing techniques to gather patient data for physician review; and in other health care information systems.

Role of Social Work

NASW Health Policy Statement. The National Association of Social Workers (*NASW News*, 1980) set forth a comprehensive public policy statement on national health for the 1980s. This document reflected an understanding of the fundamental interaction among health care, social services, education, and income maintenance, all of which affect the health status of Americans. A national health policy must take into account its own relationship to other social and economic policies. It must affirm the individual rights of Americans to a minimum standard of healthful living, educational opportunities, and social self-fulfillment; equitable access to education, training, employment, housing, transportation, and all public services without regard to race, religion, sex, age, or ethnic status; adequate education and social services resources to support good health and well-being; and protection from unhealthy commercial promotions.

Social work is also aware of rising health costs, which divert resources from other human services and can threaten a family with economic catastrophe. Moreover, health costs promote socioeconomic and geographic lack of access to adequate treatment.

The NASW statement addresses the entire resident population, ensures uniform services for all groups, and provides equal access without separate categories, arrangements, and services. The primary emphasis is on preventing illness and dysfunction and promoting health. Health services must be

seen in terms of medical, psychological, and social components. There must be allowance for decentralized community planning and management and consumer involvement and participation. Delivery systems should take into account local variations in need, continuity and linkage in levels of care, opportunity for consumers to choose plans, input by professional providers (including qualified social workers) into planning and service delivery, and individual and family service needs. The federal government must establish organizational and fiscal standards and assure accountability at the national, state, and local levels. A national health care program must be publicly funded through progressive taxation for long-term stability. There must be fair and equitable income payment for professional personnel based on cost-funding methods and standards. The payment mechanism should provide incentives for illness prevention programs, cost containment, negotiable rates of reimbursement, and cost-saving health systems such as HMOs.

Standards for professional competence must be set by the professions with consumer and peer review. Health personnel must receive education, training, licensure, and certification. Emphasis should be on the development of primary care providers, the recruitment of minorities and women in health care professions, and uniform national licensure and certification standards.

Health research is outlined in terms of basic biomedical, psychosocial, and clinical technology; human behavior exploration integrating healthy physical, psychological, and social adaptation; epidemiological research to identify populations at risk; and health management, organization, and technology. Health planning should strive for an adequate, integrated, and efficient health care system, a health-sustaining society and healthy personal lifestyles, coordination of services, and distribution of resources and manpower to underserved areas and minority groups.

Finally, policy must protect products, services, and human environments and develop appropriate education, social support, and lifestyles promoting and maintaining optimum health.

Social Workers in Health Care. Of the 45,000 social workers employed in health care, the majority are in acute and long-term hospitals—16,500 administering various aspects of the Medicare program in hospitals, 2,700 in extended care facilities, and 2,600 in the Veterans Administration Hospital system. Social work practice in hospitals includes (1) early patient case finding to identify stress situations and problems; (2) interpreting the meaning of shared information with patients and their families for decision making; (3) mediating and coordinating medical care projections with the patient and the practitioner; (4) working for social-environmental changes to safeguard the continuation of services to the patient; (5) early and appropriate discharge planning; and (6) adhering to the utilization requirements for reimbursement (Miller & Rehr, 1983).

Berkman (1984) believes that in light of the movement toward DRGs, hospital social work services need to reestablish their claim to expertise in discharge planning. Coulton (1984) has devised a resource utilization system attuned to prospective payment for hospital social work departments. It includes a method of tracking and recording costs for units of service, average total costs of care, cost-payment ratios, productivity, and service utilization patterns. Berkman (1984) reports that clients received more help from social workers in seven areas of concrete need: transportation services, visiting nurses' services, aids such as prostheses or equipment, financial assistance, home help, health education, and letters and reports. Black (1984) believes that social work must address community health and lifestyles, taking into account (1) community-based care for chronic illness and disability and self-care among chronically ill individuals (such as coping strategies and social supports for problems in daily living); (2) assaults on environmental problems associated with community health, such as automobile accidents, bronchial ailments connected to poor housing and nutrition, and dog bites from wild dog packs roaming the neighborhood; (3) the design of public health protocols to help communities handle environmental health catastrophes, the provision of clinical services addressing environmental stresses, and community organization to mobilize health professionals and the public for political action to prevent health hazards; and (4) the attitude toward health maintenance expressed in the

Surgeon General's report (U.S. Surgeon General's Office, 1979), how behavior and lifestyle affect health, and how cultural, political, and economic elements of the environment interrelate with one another.

Social Worker–Client Interaction in Health Care. Underlying social work skills is the proactive stance toward the patient-client. Rehr (1983) delineates various consumer and provider dynamics in care (choosing care, access to care, guaranteed access and case finding, individual motivation and compliance, and the relationship between caregiver and receiver), health consumerism (patients' rights, patient advocacy and ombudsman programs, and consumer advisory groups), and health promotion (self-help, patient groups, and consumer health education). The objective is to develop the relationship between the professional and client as full partners in direct care. Likewise, Rosenberg (1983) regards social work health care practice as the clinical process of care. Referral is the basis for entry into the social work system of care. With new clients, social workers must be able to perform preparatory screening and review as well as exploratory interviewing and problem definition. Assessment involves selection of information, data collection, and early intervention interpretation. Collaborative practice is based on networking with physicians and other team members in a biopsychosocial approach. Contracting consists of an agreement between the client and the worker, who must have the ability to conceptualize a problem in terms of a solution. Intervention is based on the preceding steps and involves formulating an intervention strategy, selecting specific intervention procedures, and developing a method of evaluating the program impact. Termination occurs when the task is accomplished and the problem resolved. Discharge planning is the culmination of the social work process in health care.

Summary

This article has sought to give an overview of the health delivery system, along with a history of key legislation that has shaped health services in the United States since the mid-1960s. Trends and issues were discussed in terms of the crisis of rising health care costs and varied cost containment strategies. Amid these developments stands social work in health care, which has a responsibility to influence health policy, planning, legislation, and client practice.

DOMAN LUM

For further information, see EMERGENCY HEALTH SERVICES; FEDERAL SOCIAL LEGISLATION SINCE 1961; HEALTH CARE FINANCING; HEALTH PLANNING; HOSPITAL SOCIAL WORK; PREVENTIVE HEALTH CARE AND WELLNESS; PRIMARY HEALTH CARE; PUBLIC HEALTH SERVICES.

References

Aday, L. A., & Andersen, R. (1974). "A Framework for the Study of Access to Medical Care." *Health Services Research, 9*(3), 208–220.

Berki, S. E. (1983). "Preface." *Annals of the American Academy of Political and Social Science, 468*, 9–11.

Berkman, B. (1984). "Editorial: Social Work and the Challenge of DRGs." *Health and Social Work, 9*(1), 2–3.

Black, R. B. (1984). "Looking Ahead: Social Work as a Core Health Profession." *Health and Social Work, 9*(2), 85–95.

Bronzino, J. D. (1982). *Computer Applications for Patient Care.* Reading, Mass.: Addison-Wesley Publishing Co.

Brown, L. D. (1983). "Competition and Health Care Policy: Experience and Expectations." *Annals of the American Academy of Political and Social Science, 468*, 48–59.

Caputi, M. A., & Heiss, W. A. (1984). "The DRG Revolution." *Health and Social Work, 9*(1), 5–12.

Coulton, C. J. (1982). "Health Maintenance Organizations." In D. Lum (Ed.), *Social Work and Health Care Policy* (pp. 75–89). Totowa, N.J.: Allanheld, Osmun.

Coulton, C. J. (1984). "Confronting Prospective Payment: Requirement for an Information System." *Health and Social Work, 9*(1), 13–24.

Donabedian, A. (1980). *The Definition of Quality and Approaches to Its Assessment.* Ann Arbor, Mich: Health Administration Press.

Enthoven, A. C. (1980). *Health Plan.* Reading, Mass.: Addison-Wesley Publishing Co.

Executive Office of the President, Office of Management and Budget. (1985). *Budget of the United States Government, Fiscal Year 1986.* Washington, D. C.: U.S. Government Printing Office.

Feldstein, P. J. (1983). *Health Care Economics.* New York: John Wiley & Sons.

Gibson, R. (1983). "Quiet Revolutions in Medi-
caid." In J. A. Meyer (Ed.), *Market Reforms in Health Care: Current Issues, New Directions, Strategic Decisions* (pp. 75–101). Washington, D. C.: American Enterprise Institute for Public Policy Research.

Ginzberg, E. (1983). "The Delivery of Health Care: What Lies Ahead." *Inquiry, 20*(3), 201–217.

Grimaldi, P. L., & Micheletti, J. H. (1982). "RIMs and the Cost of Nursing Care." *Nursing Management, 13*(12), 12–27.

Harrington, C. (1982). "National Health Planning and Resources Development." In D. Lum (Ed.), *Social Work and Health Care Policy* (pp. 90–108). Totowa, N.J.: Allanheld, Osmun.

Harwood, A. (1981). "Introduction: Guidelines for Culturally Appropriate Health Care." In A. Harwood (Ed.), *Ethnicity and Medical Care* (pp. 1–36, 482–507). Cambridge, Mass.: Harvard University Press.

Hornbrook, M. C. (1983). "Allocative Medicine: Efficiency, Disease Severity, and the Payment Mechanism." *Annals of the American Academy of Political and Social Science, 468*, 12–29.

Institute of Medicine. (1981). *Health Care in a Context of Civil Rights.* Washington, D. C.: National Academy Press.

Kinzer, D. M. (1984). "Care of the Poor Revisited." *Inquiry, 21*(1), 5–16.

Lave, J. R. (1984). "Hospital Reimbursement under Medicare." *Milbank Memorial Fund Quarterly, 62*(2), 251–268.

Levine, E., & Abdellah, F. G. (1984). "DRGs: A Recent Refinement to an Old Method." *Inquiry, 21*(2), 105–112.

Mackintosh, D. R. (1978). *Systems of Health Care.* Boulder, Colo.: Westview Press.

McClure, W. (1983). "The Competition Strategy for Medical Care." *Annals of the American Academy of Political and Social Science, 468*, 30–47.

Meyer, J. A. (1983). "Introduction." In J. A. Meyer (Ed.), *Market Reforms in Health Care: Current Issues, New Directions, Strategic Decisions* (pp. 1–11). Washington, D. C.: American Enterprise Institute for Public Policy Research.

Miller, R. S., & Rehr, H. (1983). "Health Settings and Health Providers." In R. S. Miller & H. Rehr (Eds.), *Social Work Issues in Health Care* (pp. 1–19). Englewood Cliffs, N.J.: Prentice-Hall.

NASW News. (1980). [Health policy statement]. *25*(1), 18–19.

Pauly, M. V., & Langwell, K. M. (1983). "Research on Competition in the Market for Health Services: Problems and Prospects." *Inquiry, 20*(2), 142–161.

Rehr, H. (1983). "The Consumer and Consumerism." In R. S. Miller & H. Rehr (Eds.), *Social Work Issues in Health Care* (pp. 20–73). Englewood Cliffs, N.J.: Prentice-Hall.

Rosenberg, G. (1983). "Practice Roles and Functions of the Health Social Worker." In R. S. Miller & H. Rehr (Eds.), *Social Work Issues in Health Care* (pp. 121–180). Englewood Cliffs, N.J.: Prentice-Hall.

Trevino, F. M., & Moss, A. J. (1983). "Health Insurance Coverage and Physician Visits among Hispanic and Non-Hispanic People." In *Health, United States 1983 and Prevention Profile*. Hyattsville, Md.: U. S. Department of Health and Human Services.

U. S. Department of Health and Human Services. (1983). *Health, United States 1983 and Prevention Profile*. Hyattsville, Maryland: Author.

U. S. Surgeon General's Office. (1979). *Healthy People: The Surgeon General's Report on Health Promotion and Disease Prevention*. Rockville, Md.: U. S. Public Health Service.

Weisbrod, B. A. (1983). "Competition in Health Care: A Cautionary View." In J. A. Meyer (Ed.), *Market Reforms in Health Care: Current Issues, New Directions, Strategic Decisions* (pp. 61–71). Washington, D. C.: American Enterprise Institute for Public Policy Research.

HEARN, GORDON. See biographical section.

HISPANICS

The Hispanic population of the United States has grown dramatically, leading to the prediction that if present trends continue, this group will someday replace blacks as the nation's largest minority group (Daris, Haub, & Willette, 1983). The growth of the Hispanic population has serious implications for service providers. Census statistics offer a comprehensive portrait of the Hispanic population and can function as useful tools for service providers.

Dramatic Growth of Hispanics

The growth of the Hispanic population that took place in the United States in the 1970s was an impressive demographic development. It occurred at a time when the trends of the general population were characterized by a decrease in growth and lower fertility rates resulting from the postponement of marriage and childbirth, as well as from a proportion of unmarried women over age 25.

As reflected in Tables 1 and 2, a comparison of the 1970 and 1980 census figures indicate that during the 1970s (1) the population of the United States grew by approximately 23 million, (2) minority groups constituted 20 percent, or one out of every five citizens, but collectively they accounted for 52 percent of the difference between the 1970 and 1980 figures; (3) Hispanics represented 6.4 percent of the population but accounted for 23 percent—or 5.5 million out of 23 million—of its growth during this period.

Explaining the Growth of the Hispanic Population

Women of childbearing age are responsible for reproducing the next generation. Because the frequency of birth is highest among women aged 20 to 34, this age group is referred to as the high-childbearing years. The younger the age structure of a population, the higher its proportion of women who are in the high childbearing years and the greater its proportion of adolescent females who are entering the childbearing years. The older the age structure of a population, the lower its proportion of women who are in the high-childbearing years and the greater its proportion of women who are beyond the childbearing years (age 45 and older). When two populations have similar fertility rates, the population with the youngest age structure contains more children because of the large number of women within it who are in their childbearing years.

The upward trajectory of growth of the Hispanic population contrasts sharply with the flatter growth curve of the rest of the population of the United States. Why are the growth trends among Hispanics and non-Hispanics so divergent? Addressing this question requires an understanding of the differences between the two populations in relation to age structure and the process and trends of immigration. The Hispanic population has a younger age structure and a faster rate of growth than the general population

Table 1. Comparison of 1970 and 1980 Population Growth by Race and Ethnicity (numbers in millions)

	1970	1980	1970–1980 Difference	Percentage of Change
U.S. total	203,212	226,505	23,293	11.5
Spanish origin	9,073	14,606	5,533	61.0
Black	22,580	26,488	3,908	17.3
Asian and Pacific Islander	1,539	3,501	1,962	127.5
American Indian, Eskimo, and Aleutian	827	1,418	591	71.5
Total minority	34,018	46,012	11,994	52[a]
Remainder (nonminority)	169,194	180,493	11,299	48[a]

[a] Percentage of population growth.
Source: U.S. Department of Commerce, "1980 Census Population Totals for Racial and Spanish Origin Groups Announced by Census Bureau" (Washington, D.C.: *U.S. Department of Commerce News*, 1981, February 23), Table 1.

and can be expected to continue to grow quickly in the near future.

The impact on society of the different age structures of the two populations is apparent in the enrollment figures of elementary schools, which indicate that enrollment among Hispanics is greater than among the general population. In time, this trend is likely to be reflected at the high school and college levels as well. It is expected that minority children will outnumber nonminority children in the public school systems of the major cities in the United States until early in the next century (U. S. Department of Education, 1977).

Although social service planning must take into account the patterns of the general population, these patterns can mask the cross-current trends of large subgroups of the pop-

ulation. Therefore, it is important to look beneath the surface for distinctions between population groups before arriving at conclusions based on the assumption that the characteristics of the general population are representative of the subgroups that make up the whole.

Although fertility in the United States is falling steadily among all groups, including Hispanics, the current fertility rate of Hispanic women is about 65 percent higher than that of non-Hispanic women. Factors that have accelerated the decline in Hispanic fertility include (1) a high rate of divorce; (2) a slight increase in the number of childless couples; and (3) an increase in the use of contraception. If the birthrate of Hispanics does not decline as quickly as expected, it will probably be because Hispanic women

Table 2. Changes in Proportional Representation of Racial and Ethnic Groups from 1970 to 1980 (numbers in millions)

	1970	1980	Percentage of Difference
U.S. total	203,212	226,505	—
Spanish Origin	4.5	6.4	+1.9
Black	11.1	11.7	+ .6
Asian and Pacific Islander	0.8	1.5	+ .7
American Indian	0.4	0.6	+ .2

Source: U.S. Department of Commerce, "1980 Census Population Totals for Racial and Spanish Origin Groups Announced by Census Bureau" (Washington, D.C.: *U.S. Department of Commerce News*, 1981, February 23), Table 2.

usually marry earlier than non-Hispanic women and because the fertility rate of immigrant Hispanic women is 100 percent higher than that of non-Hispanic women. Even as fertility among Hispanics declines, it is unlikely that this population will stabilize because of the influx of Hispanic immigrants into the United States.

Continued Hispanic Immigration

The continued replenishment of the population through immigration cannot be ignored because it not only adds to the number of Hispanics in the United States but also reinforces the use of the Spanish language and the traditions and customs of Hispanic culture. From 1961 to 1980, approximately 2.3 million legal immigrants from Latin America and Mexico entered the United States. Some chose to return to their native countries, but the majority are now permanent residents in the United States (Bean et al., 1984). Although there is no reliable method to estimate the number of undocumented immigrants in the United States, there is agreement that the majority are from Mexico and from Latin America (Passel & Woodrow, 1984). These additions to the population through immigration further fuel the growth of the Hispanic population.

Use of the Spanish Language

Because of the magnitude of Hispanic immigration, Spanish is the most frequently spoken non-English language in the United States. According to the U.S. Bureau of the Census (1981), 5 percent of all people over age 5 speak Spanish. Although this percentage may appear small, it represents more than 12 million individuals—an increase of more than 2 million since 1970. Two thirds of those who speak Spanish report that they speak English "well" or "very well," which is indicative of the bilingual nature of the majority of Hispanics who live in the United States.

It is significant that the vast majority of Hispanics are bilingual. Yet it should be acknowledged that some of the more vulnerable segments of the Hispanic population, such as the elderly and new immigrants, are likely to speak only Spanish and, therefore, to have the most need of bilingual services.

Geographic and Regional Concentration

In 1980, Hispanics constituted only 6.4 percent of the total population of the United States (U.S. Bureau of the Census, 1981). If they were evenly dispersed throughout the 50 states, Hispanics would be likely to receive little attention. Its geographic concentration is what gives the small precentage visibility. As Table 3 indicates (1) just over 60 percent of the 14.6 million Hispanics in the United States reside in just three states: California, Texas, and New York; (2) Hispanics represent 10 percent or more of the total population in five states: New Mexico (37 percent), Texas (21 percent), California (19 percent), Arizona (16 percent), and Colorado (12 percent); and (3) 85 percent of all Hispanics in the United States live in nine states.

Although Hispanics reside in all 50 states, they predominate and are particularly visible in four areas. The southwestern states—including Arizona, California, Colorado, New Mexico, and Texas—account for 60 percent of all Hispanics, most of whom are Mexican. Fifteen percent of all Hispanics, primarily Puerto Ricans but also people of Caribbean and Latin American origin, live in New York and in New Jersey. The Cuban population is concentrated in Florida, in which 6 percent of all Hispanics live. Finally, there are many Hispanics in Illinois, especially in the Chicago metropolitan area, which contains 4.5 percent of all Hispanics.

Within each of these four areas, the extent of concentration is greatest in metropolitan areas. Table 4 indicates that 55 percent of the Hispanic population resides in 15 metropolitan areas, six of which are located in California, five in Texas, and one each in New York, Florida, Illinois, and Arizona.

Eightly-eight percent of Hispanics reside in urban areas; this percentage is second only to the Asian population (91 percent) and is 13 points higher than the national figure (75 percent) representing all urban residents. Seventy-one percent of blacks reside in inner cities, as do 58 percent of Hispanics. The latter percentage is 18 points higher than the national figure of 40 percent (U.S. Bureau of the Census, 1981).

Given these geographic concentrations, individuals who wish to target services to Hispanics will find it a relatively simple task. However, there are indications that

Table 3. Persons of Spanish Origin by State: 1980

Area	Persons of Spanish Origin	Percentage of Total Population in Each Area	Percentage of Total Spanish Population
United States	14,608,673	6.4	100.0
California	4,544,331	19.2	31.0
Texas	2,985,824	21.0	20.4
New York	1,659,300	9.5	11.4
Florida	858,158	8.8	5.9
Illinois	635,602	5.6	4.4
New Jersey	491,883	6.7	3.4
New Mexico	477,222	36.6	3.3
Arizona	440,701	16.2	3.0
Colorado	339,717	11.7	2.3
Michigan	162,440	1.8	1.1
Pennsylvania	153,961	1.3	1.1
Massachusetts	141,043	2.5	1.0
Connecticut	124,499	4.0	0.9
Washington	120,016	2.9	0.8
Ohio	119,883	1.1	0.8
Louisiana	99,134	2.4	0.7
Indiana	87,047	1.6	0.6
Virginia	79,868	1.5	0.5
Hawaii	71,263	7.4	0.5
Oregon	65,847	2.5	0.5
Maryland	64,746	1.5	0.4
Kansas	63,339	2.7	0.4
Wisconsin	62,972	1.3	0.4
Georgia	61,260	1.1	0.4
Utah	60,302	4.1	0.4
Oklahoma	57,419	1.9	0.4
North Carolina	56,667	1.0	0.4
Nevada	53,879	6.7	0.4
Missouri	51,653	1.1	0.4
Idaho	36,615	3.9	0.3
Tennessee	34,077	0.7	0.2
South Carolina	33,426	1.1	0.2
Alabama	33,299	0.9	0.2
Minnesota	32,123	0.8	0.2
Nebraska	28,025	1.8	0.2
Kentucky	27,406	0.7	0.2
Iowa	25,536	0.9	0.2
Mississippi	24,731	1.0	0.2
Wyoming	24,499	5.2	0.2
Rhode Island	19,707	2.1	0.1
Arkansas	17,904	0.8	0.1
District of Columbia	17,679	2.8	0.1
West Virginia	12,707	0.7	0.1
Montana	9,974	1.3	0.1
Delaware	9,661	1.6	0.1
Alaska	9,507	2.4	0.1
New Hampshire	5,587	0.6	—
Maine	5,005	0.4	—
South Dakota	4,023	0.6	—
North Dakota	3,902	0.6	—
Vermont	3,304	0.6	—

Source: U.S. Bureau of the Census, *State and Metropolitan Area Data Book, 1982* (Washington, D.C.: U.S. Government Printing Office), p. 451.

Table 4. The 15 Standard Metropolitan Statistical Areas with the Largest Spanish Origin Population, 1980

Los Angeles–Long Beach, California	2,065,727
New York–New Jersey	1,493,081
Miami, Florida	581,030
Chicago, Illinois	580,592
San Antonio, Texas	481,511
Houston, Texas	424,901
San Francisco–Oakland, California	351,915
El Paso, Texas	297,001
Riverside–San Bernardino, California	289,791
Anaheim–Santa Ana–Garden Grove, California	286,331
San Diego, California	275,176
Dallas–Fort Worth, Texas	249,613
McAllen–Pharr–Edinburgh, Texas	230,212
San Jose, California	226,611
Phoenix, Arizona	198,999

Source: U.S. Bureau of the Census, *1980 Census of Population Supplementary Reports PC-80-S1-5—Standard Metropolitan Statistical Areas and Standard Consolidated Areas* (Washington, D.C.: U.S. Government Printing Office, 1981), p. 9.

Hispanics are relocating to the suburbs at an increasing rate (Estrada, 1981). Suburbanization among Hispanics is distinctive. Unlike prior outward movement that was associated with social mobility ("moving out is moving up"), the current movement of Hispanics is toward areas that are mere extensions of low-socioeconomic barrio communities. Thus, the poor will continue to reside to a large extent in the inner city, and other pockets of poor and needy Hispanics will be found in suburban areas.

Overlap with Other Minority Groups

On a national level, the black population is larger than the Hispanic population. However, with the exception of Chicago, New York, and Miami there is a comparatively small proportion of blacks in cities that contain both blacks and Latinos (U.S. Bureau of the Census, 1981). Several cities in the Southwest are predominantly black, for example, Compton and Inglewood in California. In general, however, Hispanics make up the largest minority in all but 9 of the 42 metropolitan areas in the western part of the United States. In addition, there are several cities east of the Mississippi River in which Hispanics make up the largest minority group. These cities are Allentown, Bethlehem, Easton, Lancaster, and Reading,

Pennsylvania; Lawrence-Haverhill, in Massachusetts and New Hampshire; Lowell and Worcester, Massachusetts; Miami, Florida; and Patterson, Clifton, and Passaic, New Jersey. In contrast, much overlap exists between Hispanics and the Asian and Pacific populations, the majority of whom reside in California and New York, and between Hispanics and American Indians, who reside largely in the western states.

Overlap among Hispanic Subgroups

Approximately 85 percent of all individuals of Mexican origin reside in the five southwestern states (Arizona, California, Colorado, New Mexico, and Texas), at least 80 percent of all Puerto Ricans live in New York and New Jersey, and about 80 percent of all Cubans inhabit South Florida (U.S. Bureau of the Census, 1981). Thus, each of the three major Hispanic subgroups has a distinct geographic domain that allows it to develop its own particular social and cultural institutions. The major disadvantage of this geographical separation is the limited nature of the first-hand knowledge that members of each subgroup have of each other.

In several cities, especially those in the Midwest (for example, Milwaukee, Wisconsin; Detroit, Michigan; and, Chicago, Illinois), the mix of subgroups allows observers

Table 5. Selected Socioeconomic Characteristics of Racial and Ethnic Groups in the U.S., 1980 (Percentages)

Characteristics	White	Black	Asian and Pacific Islanders	Spanish Origin
Family Type				
Families with children under 18 years	49.4	61.0	61.5	67.8
Female-headed households; no husband present	11.1	37.3	10.9	19.8
Female-headed households with children under 18 years	56.1	68.8	56.5	72.6
Education				
Persons 25 years or older with less than high school degree	31.3	49.4	25.8	56.7
Persons 25 years or older with at least a college degree	17.2	8.4	32.5	7.6
Employment				
Persons 16 years or older in labor force	62.2	59.2	66.3	63.4
Unemployed persons 16 years or older	5.8	11.7	4.8	9.1
Females 16 years or older in labor force	41.5	48.4	45.0	39.1
Income				
Median income	$20,840	$12,618	$22,075	$14,711
Persons living below poverty level in 1979	9.4	30.2	13.9	23.8
Persons who own homes	67.8	44.4	51.5	43.5

Source: U.S. Bureau of the Census, *1980 Census Population Supplementary Reports PHC 80-S1-1—Provisional Estimates of Social, Economic, and Housing Characteristics: States and Selected Standard Metropolitan Statistical Areas* (Washington, D.C: U.S. Government Printing Office, 1982), pp. 47, 100.

to focus on the special inter- and intragroup dynamics of Hispanic environments. Although their interactions heighten the differences between them, the subgroups usually coalesce for political and social purposes.

The sociohistorical background of each Hispanic group is distinct, and this geographical separation often leads to misconceptions that are based on a lack of knowledge about the various groups. It should not be assumed that all Hispanics are alike, nor that a member of one subgroup will necessarily know or understand the particular nuances of another. Service providers should not expect that each of the subgroups will react similarly to programmatic thrusts or to the same messages. However, a common ground exists among the subgroups that can be built on by those with an understanding of the history and culture of at least one of the groups.

Socioeconomic Characteristics

The brief information provided in Table 5 is presented as a descriptive review of the differences between Hispanics and other groups. It is not intended as a detailed analysis of the socioeconomic status of Hispanics, which would require a sophisticated study aimed at separating long-term Hispanic residents of the United States from recent arrivals, small families from large extended families, dual-earner families from single-earner families, and other such statistical controls.

Hispanic families are more likely than either black or white families to have children under age 18. One out of every five Hispanic households is headed by a female whose spouse is not present. Hispanic households that are headed by women are more likely to include children than are those headed by black and white women.

The educational levels of Hispanics, who make up the largest proportion of people without a high school degree and the smallest proportion of those with at least a college degree, remain among the lowest in the nation. However, recent data indicate that Hispanics have made substantial progress in educational achievement (U.S. Bureau of the Census, 1981).

Despite comparatively high unemployment rates, a relatively large proportion of Latinos are part of the labor force. Because of the high percentage of Hispanic children, women are less likely to be employed outside the home than men.

The median income of Hispanic households is $6,000 below the national average. However, it is higher than might be expected for a population characterized by a low level of educational attainment and a high level of unemployment. Because the proportion of individuals living in poverty is high and homeownership rates are low, it can be surmised that income levels of Hispanics reflect the urban nature of their jobs, which pay a higher wage than those in rural areas. The median income of Hispanics is higher than expected and is offset by the high cost of living in the metropolitan areas in which they live, as well as by their large family size, which demands that income be stretched.

The descriptive portrait drawn here is no different from that of the 1970s, when Hispanics had the lowest level of educational attainment and the highest rate of unemployment. Although data indicate that Hispanics have clearly made gains in education during this period, they continue to earn 70 percent of the income earned by non-Hispanics (Davis, Haub, & Willette, 1983).

National data hide regional economic effects that are significant in view of the geographic concentration noted earlier. To provide insight into these effects, four regions will be briefly described. The first, South Florida, experienced phenomenal growth in the 1970s. Cubans have been at the forefront in establishing Miami as an international business center for Latin America. Equally important is the entrepreneurship that is reflected in small, Cuban-owned businesses and that has created a solid economic base for the local Cuban community.

The New York metropolitan area, the second region, has experienced economic decline since the mid-1970s. In an area in which housing and transportation are among the costliest in the nation, such a decline undoubtedly spurs the movement of Puerto Ricans, Dominicans, and other Hispanics to neighboring states or to Puerto Rico.

The third region, the Midwest, has also undergone economic decline. Despite an upturn in the automobile-related industries during the early 1980s, it is likely that trained industrial workers will continue to return to the East Coast and to the Southwest.

The Southwest, the fourth region, has expanded economically as a result of the westward shift of the national economy. Hispanics in the Southwest will make up a significant proportion of the working-age population (James et al., 1984). However, low educational attainment will probably prevent Mexicans, who are predominant in this region, from taking advantage of the expanding job market, which is concentrated in high-tech industries that require skilled and trained labor. All these regional differences are important in regard to positive and negative changes that could affect economic opportunities for Hispanics.

Conclusion

The Hispanic population of the United States cannot be overlooked in examinations of those issues that are likely to confront service providers in the future. It is a growing population whose characteristics distinguish it as being "at risk." The frequency with which the Spainsh language is spoken and the continued immigration to the United States of Mexicans and Latin Americans further complicate the plight of this population. Although Mexican Americans have resided in the United States for more than 4 centuries and some immigrants from El Salvador arrived only yesterday, both groups are regarded as parts of the same whole. Because the people who constitute this population are so distinct, generalizations about Hispanics are by their very nature misleading.

In a period in which the general population has begun to focus on the problems of adults and the elderly, the Hispanic population is youthful and is focused on early marriage and child-related issues. For the most part, the large baby boom cohort, which consists of those born from the late 1940s to the early 1960s, is no longer a part of the educational system and is now approaching middle age. The size of this cohort has affected the focus of social policy in this country. Like the rest of the cohort, Hispanics must confront the problems of finding adequate prenatal care and affordable preschool training, child care, and quality bilingual education programs. They must also deal with school truancy, an extrordinarily high dropout rate among high school students, delinquency, youth violence, and pregnancy among adolescents. Finally, they must secure adequate job training. Although these issues are considered important, attention is now being given to concerns that are more closely related to an adult population. These concerns include inflation, high interest rates, second careers, private pension plans, retirement, and the value of housing.

It is not the intent of this article to imply that no overlap exists between the concerns of Hispanics and non-Hispanics, but rather to draw attention to the shift from youthful to adult issues that has accompanied the aging of the general population. As the nation concerns itself with these issues, it should remember that youthful Hispanics continue to focus on concerns that receive comparatively little attention from the general population.

Although the national data presented in this article can be useful, they are superficial owing to their general scope. Other available data should be used to shed light on the individual circumstances of each Hispanic community. Decisions that will influence intervention strategies, efforts at program outreach, and programmatic objectives should be based on local-level information, and national statistics should be used for purposes of comparison.

Because the Hispanic population is so heterogeneous, the area in which a service provider is located will determine which of several diverse approaches best meets the needs of the Hispanic subgroup or subgroups in question. In addition to data on a particular community, the practitioner should draw on face-to-face interaction with potential clients in the community as a major source of information about trends and changes in the local population. Census data become obsolete with time, unlike the information gathered by field personnel, who continuously monitor their respective communities in an effort transmit valuable collective knowledge.

LEOBARDO F. ESTRADA

For further information, see CIVIL RIGHTS; ETHNIC-SENSITIVE PRACTICE; INTERGROUP RELATIONS; IMMIGRANTS AND UNDOCUMENTED ALIENS; MEXICAN AMERICANS; MINORITIES OF COLOR; PUERTO RICANS; RACIAL DISCRIMINATION AND INEQUALITY.

References

Bean, F., et al. (1984). "Generational Differences in Fertility Among Mexican Americans." *Social Sciences Quarterly, 65*(2), 573–582.

Davis, C., Haub, C., & Willette, J. (1983). *U. S. Hispanics: Changing the Face of America.* Washington, D.C.: Population Reference Bureau.

Estrada, L. F. (1981). *Dynamic Growth and Dispersion of the Latino Population.* Unpublished manuscript.

James, F., et al. (1984). *Minorities in the Sunbelt.* New Brunswick, N. J.: Center for Urban Policy Research, Rutgers—The State University.

Passel, J. S., & Woodrow, K. A. (1984). "Geographic Distribution of Undocumented Immigrants: Estimates of Undocumented Aliens Counted in the 1980 Census by State." *International Migration Review, 18*, 642–671.

U.S. Bureau of the Census. (1981). *General Social and Economic Characteristics: U.S. Summary* (P.C. 80-1-cl). Washington, D.C.: U.S. Government Printing Office.

U.S. Department of Education (1977). *The Condition of Education* (Vol. 3, Tables 4, 7–9). Washington, D.C.: U.S. Government Printing Office.

HISTORY AND EVOLUTION OF SOCIAL WORK PRACTICE

Three topics provide a framework for considering the history of social work practice: the shift from apprenticeship to formal methods, the movement toward a common framework of practice, and specializations on a generalist base. Also included in this history will be a discussion of the political and economic developments and other influences that have affected practice.

From Apprenticeship to Formal Methods

Friendly Visitors and Charity Organization Societies. The almshouse or poor farm was the major helping resource in colonial America. In the 1800s, friendly visiting by volunteers, intended to establish a personal link with the needy, became a major model for dealing with the urban poor. In its first annual report in 1818, the New York Society for the Prevention of Pauperism proposed this approach to friendly visiting:

> . . . to divide the city into very small districts, and to appoint, from the members of the Society, two or three visitors for each district, whose duty it shall be to become acquainted with the inhabitants of the district, to visit frequently the families of those who are in indigent circumstances, to advise them with respect to their business, the education of their children, the economy of their houses, to administer encouragement or admonition, as they may find occasion. . . . (Pumphrey & Pumphrey, 1961, p. 59)

The society also sought a plan

> by which all the spontaneous charities of the town may flow into one channel, to be distributed in conformity to a well-regulated system, by which deception may be prevented, and other indirect evils arising from numerous independent associations, be fairly obviated. (p. 62)

Associations for Improving the Conditions of the Poor were formed in the 1840s to provide relief for the needy. These associations—as their name implies—concentrated on the conditions that created poverty rather than on assuring donors that moneys were spent on worthy recipients. Ninety-two charity organizations modeled on the London Society for Organizing Charitable Relief and Repressing Mendicancy were established in the major cities of the United States and Canada between 1877 and 1892. These Charity Organization Societies (COSs) are regarded as the forerunners of modern casework. The societies considered friendly visiting a substitute for alms, using investigation, registration, cooperation, and coordination in the determination of what should constitute adequate relief.

Zilpha D. Smith (1892), a leader in the Boston Charity Organization Society, described the education of friendly visitors:

> Life itself will still be the chief schoolmaster of the friendly visitor; and the part of the society with which he works must be to bring him into relation with new aspects of life, and to help him by contact and conferences with other workers to see them rightly, and to use to the best advantage his opportunities for doing good. (p. 445)

Smith believed that friendly visitors needed conference meetings to learn about the work of others and to give each other suggestions. Manuals were written to familiarize the visitors with the basic rules. Sympathetic counsel to rekindle hope became the preferred treatment. Relief was provided only reluctantly and in the form least subject to abuse—the poor were not to be given money. Necessities were provided in small amounts—just enough to meet immediate needs. Supporting the poor in their homes (so-called outdoor relief) was considered both wasteful and injurious to their morals.

Was friendly visiting really friendly?

> The relation between visitor and client may have been personal, but it was not "friendly" in the sense of the informal, natural cohesiveness of peers sharing similar social and cultural backgrounds. Consequently, the visitor saw in her client less an equal or potential equal than an object of character reformation whose unfortunate and lowly condition resulted from ignorance or deviations from middle-class values and patterns of life-organization: temperance, industriousness, family cohesiveness, frugality, foresight, moral restraint. (Lubove, 1965, p. 16)

The charity organization movement was based on the conviction that it provided the means to save cities from the evils of pauperism, reduce the cost of charity, and deal with antagonism created by social class differences. In its *Fifth Annual Report* the Charity Organization Society of New York (1888) warned:

> Honest employment, the work that God means every man to do, is the truest basis of relief for every person with physical ability to work. The help which needlessly releases the poor from the necessity of providing for themselves is in violation of divine law and incurs the penalties which follow any infraction of that law. (p. 29)

COSs stressed religious values based on love (Leiby, 1984). A major goal was to save "the miserable from the sin of poverty" (DeSchweinitz & DeSchweinitz, 1948, p. 109). COSs sought to obtain "a thorough understanding of the background of each case of dependency combined with a series of preconceived moral judgments and presuppositions about the character of the poor and about human nature" (Lubove, 1965, p. 7). They developed employment services and legal aid as well as counseling services that were later to be offered by family agencies.

Paid staff replaced most friendly visitors by the turn of the century. Moral superiority had not provided the basis for a satisfactory relationship between middle-class volunteers and dependent citizens.

Settlement Movement. The philosophy of the settlement movement, the forerunner of social group work, stands in contrast to that of COSs. Rather than provide charity, the settlements sought to help immigrants with all the problems they faced in their geographic area. Staff were linked to the community because they lived there. Many were young idealistic college graduates with a broad liberal education. Hull House, the best known settlement house, was established in 1889 in Chicago by Jane Addams and Ellen Gates Starr. It served 19 nationalities with a working girls' home, a day nursery, a labor museum, a boys' club, and a little theater. Males participated in social activities and females in group education; citizenship training was provided principally to adult males. Settlement workers used persuasion to get local politicians to provide basic services, including garbage collection and sanitation, to the areas they served. Working conditions, especially for women and children, were major targets for social reform. Settlements used group work, community organization, and advocacy.

Addams (1902) contrasted relief given by the charity visitor with that given by one neighbor to another:

Let us take a neighborhood of poor people, and test their ethical standards by those of the charity visitor, who comes with the best desire in the world to help them out of their distress. A most striking incongruity, at once apparent, is the difference between the emotional kindness with which relief is given by

one poor neighbor to another poor neighbor, and the guarded care with which relief is given by a charity visitor to a charity recipient. The neighborhood mind is at once confronted not only by the difference of method, but by an absolute clashing of two ethical standards.

A very little familiarity with the poor districts of any city is sufficient to show how primitive and genuine are the neighborly relations. There is the greatest willingness to lend or borrow anything, and all the residents of the given tenement know the most intimate family affairs of all the others. The fact that the economic condition of all alike is on a most precarious level makes the ready outflow of sympathy and material assistance the most natural thing in the world. There are numberless instances of self-sacrifice quite unknown in the circles where greater economic advantages make that kind of intimate knowledge of one's neighbors impossible. (pp. 19–20)

Addams (1899) described the attitudes of people served by COSs: "When they see the delay and caution with which relief is given, these do not appear to them conscientious scruples, but the cold and calculating action of the selfish man" (p. 165).

The charity organization movement and the settlement movement required different knowledge bases. COSs dealt with investigation of applicants for relief and also with housing and school attendance. The settlements directed their attention more to working conditions and economic reform. In spite of their differences, however, the two did cooperate. Settlement staff often served as friendly visitors in COS programs, and some visitors lived in settlements where they served as volunteers.

Social Casework. COS leaders were instrumental in the development of social casework. The major contribution came from Mary Richmond, who joined the Baltimore COS, became the general secretary of the Philadelphia COS in 1900, and later joined the staff of the Russell Sage Foundation.

Richmond's first book, *Social Diagnosis* (1917), provided techniques for assessing the situation of the poor. *What is Social Case Work?* (1922) defined the casework method: "Social case work consists of those processes which develop personality through adjustments consciously effected, individual by individual, between men and their social environment" (pp. 98–99). She presented six examples of casework that resulted in "genuine growth in personality" from "strengthened and better adjusted social relations" (pp. 99–100). Richmond's concept of casework treatment involved the use of resources to facilitate the individual's adjustment to social living, to assist clients to understand their needs and possibilities, and to help them to work out their own programs.

COSs, not psychiatric social work, inaugurated the model of long-term service. In Richmond's book on casework, each family portrayed was seen over several years. Zilpha D. Smith was a friendly visitor with the same family for 47 years.

Richmond (1898) made a compelling plea for a training school in applied philanthropy at the National Conference on Charities and Corrections in 1897. The next year the first training school, the New York School of Philanthropy (now the Columbia University School of Social Work) was started. Richmond was to be one of its key part-time faculty members. The program began as a 6-week summer school, soon expanded to a full academic year, and in 1910 was increased to a 2-year program. By 1919, there were 17 schools of social work in the United States; by 1923, 13 of them were affiliated with universities.

Social work degree programs enrolled part-time students and the curricula included special tracks for various fields of practice. Family casework and child welfare came out of the COS tradition and were soon influenced by the growth of psychiatry. Medical and school social work developed in host settings and received the support of physicians and educators.

Family Casework. In the development of family casework, the family came to be seen as the nuclear social institution through which the community transmitted its moral, cultural, and spiritual heritage. Training sought to achieve skill in differential diagnosis. The concern with the worthy and unworthy poor was no longer as relevant, and financial aid for those who were dependent became an acceptable element in the treatment process.

The insights of differential diagnosis also affected the practice of child welfare. Personal considerations, as well as the environment, became important. Differentiation based both on the characteristics of the home and the unique needs of the child was required in the selection of foster homes. The Boston Children's Aid Society provided a 2-year training program for new staff members, restricting each worker to about 40 cases. The society cooperated with the Judge Baker Foundation, which focussed on diagnosis and treatment of children, including those appearing in the newly established juvenile court.

Medical Social Work. Dr. Richard C. Cabot introduced medical social services at Boston's Massachusetts General Hospital in 1905 to contribute to the development of preventive medicine. Ida M. Cannon was hired as the first social worker. The service began in the outpatient department and was not offered to ward patients until 1919. Although the original nucleus of medical social workers was drawn from nursing, medical social workers did not wish to assume the subordinate status of nurses. Social work provided "an enlarged understanding of any psychic or social conditions which may cause the patient distress of mind or body" (Cannon, 1923, p. 98). The fields of study and activity for medical social workers were character, human relationships, and community life. To Cannon, the most precious asset of casework was the capacity to put oneself in another's place and still see the situation objectively.

By 1912, based on the program at Massachusetts General Hospital, the Boston School of Social Work offered a 1-year course in medical social work. The New York and Philadelphia Schools of Social Work soon developed similar courses.

School Social Work. What is now known as school social work emerged from cooperative projects of some settlement houses in New York that provided visiting teachers for three school districts. The visiting teachers were to help adjust conditions in the lives of individual children to promote their school programs.

The visiting teacher dealt with those for whom neither the attendance officer, school nurse, nor classroom teacher was equipped. The teacher or principal referred children whose educational experience was obstructed by deficient scholarship, demoralizing home conditions, misconduct, physical defect, and similar handicaps. After an examination into the background and personality of each child, the visiting teacher used whatever personal influence or social adjustments were necessary to insure efficient performance. She relied upon casework as her major technical resource. (Lubove, 1965, p. 39)

Psychiatric Social Work Social work was expanding to include various fields of practice; at the same time, the relationship between psychiatry and casework was developing. Both psychiatrists and caseworkers came to see the individual as a product of the environment rather than as an independent agent to be judged by fixed moral norms. Under the leadership of Adolf Meyer, psychiatry extended itself from the mental hospital to the community. After 1910, the mental hygiene movement directed attention to environmental factors in the prevention and treatment of mental illness. Clinics established in conjunction with the juvenile courts soon became general child guidance resources; research was conducted on delinquency, criminality, and mental deficiency, as well as on general behavior problems. Casework was no longer an approach for use only with the poor but a helpful technique for everyone's serious problems.

The psychiatrist had to reach into the community, and the role of the psychiatric social worker was to reach into the home and supervise the activity of the patient in relation to the family and the community. Social psychiatry involved casework based on patients' social environment as well as their mental and physical condition. Behavior was dynamic because it adapted to the pressures and tensions of the environment.

The first formal psychiatric material was offered in 1908 at the Chicago School of Civics and Philanthropy by Dr. William Healy. Before World War I a training course was offered at the Boston Psychopathic Hospital and was later moved to Smith College. Similar instruction became available at the New York and Philadelphia schools. The war helped psychiatry become accepted because its skills were used to select and treat servicemen.

The 1920s were characterized by the use of Freudian concepts and the growing conviction that insight into emotions and psychic life provided a key to skilled casework. Clinics began to deal with universal problems of mental health and emotional adjustment rather than with the narrower problems of economic dependence and relief. The child guidance clinics supported by grants from the *Commonwealth Fund* provided experience for psychiatric social workers who soon became consultants to family and child welfare agencies. Freudian psychology had made casework attractive to middle-class people as a source of support and insight. To serve this clientele, social work in private practice—analogous to medical care from a private physician—appeared as a logical next step.

Training and Education. Social work training and education in the 1920s still depended heavily on informal agency-based training for staff, but dissatisfaction with these casual efforts led to undergraduate and graduate programs in which students could enroll part-time. Most graduate programs required the equivalent of one academic year in full-time study.

The principal fields of social work practice constituted separate educational tracks, which made it difficult to move from one field of practice to another. Caseworkers needed a unified educational model.

The Milford Conference, which held its initial session in 1923 and completed its report in 1928, involved social work leaders who dealt with the problems presented by the several fields of practice in an attempt to develop generic casework. The conference report (American Association of Social Workers, 1931, p. 15) identified eight generic aspects of casework:

1. Knowledge of typical deviations from accepted standards of social life.
2. The use of norms of human life and human relationships.
3. The significance of social history as the basis of particularizing the human being in need.
4. Established methods of study and treatment of human beings in need.
5. The use of established community resources in social treatment.
6. The adaptation of scientific knowledge and formulations of experience to the requirements of social case work.
7. The consciousness of a philosophy which determines the purposes, ethics, and obligations of social case work.
8. The blending of the foregoing into social treatment.

The conference report defined the distinguishing concern of social casework as the capacity of individuals to structure their social activities within a given environment, a departure from Richmond's emphasis on the reciprocal relationship between "men and their social environment" (1922, p. 99). Social casework, it held, could make the most significant contribution to society by dealing with the human being's capacity for self-maintenance when it has become impaired by deviations from accepted standards of normal social life. The Milford report provided a formulation relevant to all fields of practice that would help unite practitioners and provide the conceptual basis for a professional education program in casework.

Cause and Function. The relationship between social change and social service was also a consistent theme in defining the parameters of social work practice. The issue of cause and function was highlighted at about the same time as participants in the Milford Conference sought a generic casework model. Porter R. Lee, chairman of the report committee of the Milford Conference and director of the New York School of Social Work, chose "Cause and Function" as the topic of his presidential address at the 1929 National Conference on Social Work. The paper (Lee, 1930) became a classic in casework literature.

Lee held that causes involve the elimination of evil, but function makes permanent the good that has been achieved:

Charity in its origin and in its finest expression represents a cause. The organized administration of relief, under whatever auspices, has become a function. The campaigns to obtain widows' pensions and workmen's compensation have many of the aspects of the cause. The administration of these benefits has become a function of organized community life in most American states. The settlement movement began as a cause, and the activities of many of its representatives still give it that character. In general, however, it has developed as a function of community life. The abolition of child labor has been, and still is, a cause. As the result of its success as a cause, it again has become a well-established function in many American states. (p. 4)

Zeal is perhaps the most conspicuous trait in adherents to the cause, while intelligence is perhaps most essential in those who adminis-

ter a function. The emblazoned banner and the shibboleth for the cause, the program and the manual for the function; devoted sacrifice and the flaming spirit for the cause, fidelity, standards, and methods for the function; an embattled host for the cause, an efficient personnel for the function. (p. 5)

A cause involves a personal motivation to help, but those who support a function are motivated to provide a service. Social work's functional responsibility requires that problems be accurately measured and that the need for facilities be accurately estimated. Too great an insistence on measuring the results of social work, however, may blind the functionally minded social worker to its great mission as a cause. Lee went on, "In the capacity of the social worker to administer a routine functional responsibility in the spirit of a servant in a cause lies the explanation of the great service of social work" (p. 20). Concern with cause and function is reflected in the literature on social group work and community work, as well as on casework.

Public Programs. Jane Addams and her colleagues were identified with the new Progressive Party under Theodore Roosevelt and with the peace movement during World War I. According to Leiby (1978), the 1920s were the seed time for New Deal reforms. But while caseworkers were developing services for the middle class, they missed an opportunity to take leadership in new public agency programs for the poor occasioned by the depression of the 1930s, which led to the passage of the Social Security Act. One of the principal architects of the act was a social worker, Harry L. Hopkins. Social workers were too few to meet the crisis, however, and many of them were no longer involved with the poor. Public assistance programs employed some social workers as administrators, and social workers were recruited especially for direct service to children. As in the COS era, cost control became a major issue. Most state officials considered people outside social work to be more efficient managers of large relief programs. Public agencies have never placed the same emphasis on hiring professional social workers as voluntary agencies have.

Social Group Work. Most pioneer group workers in the settlement movement did not have systematic training. Jane Addams, for example, the head of Hull House, did not emphasize social work principles. She set the philosophy and chose the activities to meet the interests and needs of neighborhood residents as she saw them.

The Salvation Army, the settlement houses, and the youth-serving agencies emphasized character building. The latter brought group work to the middle class so that contributors' families benefited directly from such programs as the YMCA, the YWCA, and scouting.

Grace L. Coyle provided leadership in the development of the group work method. She advocated John Dewey's ideas of progressive education and his definition of structure:

> The structure of organized groups consists of the agreed upon instruments through which the group puts its purpose into action. They take the form sometimes of written constitutions and established precedents; sometimes of unwritten or even unspoken assumptions, commonly accepted by the organization as a permanent part of the group life. Their apparent stability is in fact, an illusion produced by the more swiftly moving processes that go on by and through them. They too change and shift as the group creates, uses and modifies them for its purposes. (1930, p. 79)

By the mid-1930s, group work placed more emphasis on the interaction of members than on direct leadership and more on cooperative projects than on competition. Group workers were influenced by the research of Kurt Lewin and his colleagues, indicating that democratic leadership made group activities more self-sustaining (Lewin, Lippitt, & White, 1939).

Clubs, classes, and committees encompassed the activities of the group worker. Group records were developed in the 1920s—about the time instruction in that method was inaugurated by the School of Applied Social Science at Western Reserve University in Cleveland, Ohio. The term "group work," as a parallel to casework, was first used in 1927 at Western Reserve. By 1937, 13 institutions—10 of them schools of social work—were offering group work courses.

Wilson (1976) described the social reform goals of group workers, which were developed over half a century:

Workers engaged in these activities in the early part of the century ferreted out large social problems such as poverty, low wages, long working hours, poor housing and exploitation by landlords, inadequate sanitation, political corruption, and caste-class treatment of people. They provided direct service to feed the hungry and care for the sick, and created opportunities for cultural and recreational activities. They carried on programs of social action to alleviate or eliminate identified social problems through engaging the privileged and the oppressed in informational activities and by making bridges to local, state, and federal officials to secure social legislation and enforcement. (p. 7)

Wilson also summarized requisite knowledge for group workers:

> When a worker undertook the responsibility of serving a group, the prime requisite was that he have knowledge about and as much understanding as possible of the dynamics of three constructs: (1) groups, (2) human beings, and (3) social situations. He had to be familiar with the range of behavior implied in all three cases. He had to be aware that all groups are different because all human beings are different, as are all social situations. He had to know that the purposes of every group differ, even if the activities are similar. (p. 16)

The group work section of the National Conference on Social Work was formed in 1935, and the National Association for the Study of Group Work was started the next year. The name was changed to the American Association of Group Workers in 1946.

Although the American Association of Social Workers began in 1921, group workers were not admitted until 1937. Many caseworkers regarded them as people who "play with children," "do dances," "go camping," or "teach arts and crafts."

Group workers gained recognition for their professional knowledge and skill when clinics and hospitals added group work services. Neva Boyd recounted the first use of group work with the mentally ill at the National Conference in 1935. She described a program of exercise, games, and dance at the Chicago State Hospital—valuable activities used with both excitable and apathetic patients (Reid, 1981). Similar projects had been carried on under Boyd's leadership in correctional schools and facilities for the retarded. She reported that retarded patients who were provided group work services quarreled less, worked more willingly, had more respect for property, and attempted fewer escapes.

Psychiatric group work in the 1940s grew out of the need for psychotherapy for veterans who had served in the armed forces in World War II. Clients whose assessment for individual therapy revealed similar problems were assigned to a group. Groups began to be used in child guidance as well. After 1945, groups developed rapidly in mental hospitals, with leadership coming from the Veterans Administration and the Menninger Clinic in Topeka, Kansas, as well as from state hospitals. By the 1950s, one-quarter of recent graduates in group work were working in such specialized settings.

Caseworkers began to work with family members in groups in the 1960s to develop social skills, improve communication and decision making, and provide treatment. To serve the family as a small group required techniques already well known to group workers.

The following purposes were attributed to social group work by the Practice Committee of the National Association of Social Workers (NASW) in the 1960s:

> Social group work maintains or improves the personal and social functioning of group members within a range of purposes. Groups may be used for corrective purposes when the problem involves the behavior of the group member; for prevention when there is the potential danger of dysfunction; for normal growth, particularly at critical growth periods; for enhancement of the person; and for the purpose of education and citizen participation. A group may be used for any one or all of these purposes simultaneously and may change as the particular needs of the client change. (Reid, 1981, p. 185)

A six-part typology helps clarify the diversity of group work and provides a hierarchy involving the increasing professional skill of leaders (Euster, 1980). In a recreation group, the leader provides facilities and equipment. In recreation-skill activities, the role of teacher or coach is added. Education groups usually involve more complex skills including group discussion. Socialization groups depend on a leader for program activities and mediation leading to gains in social skills. In patient-governance groups, the group worker facilitates communication and decision making on issues of group living and

may act as an advocate with the treatment facility. Finally, therapeutic groups involve the assessment of individual needs, selection of members to facilitate achieving group goals, and the use of program activities as treatment techniques. The first three types of groups do not require social work education and training. The last three may be used in conjunction with individual casework.

A decisive step that brought casework and group work together was taken when practitioners began to work with a client both individually and in a group setting. Courses and workshops were developed on casework for group workers, group work for caseworkers, and eventually on combined individual and small-group methods that were to constitute micro practice. Adopting a treatment focus had finally made group work a key social work method.

Community Work. The terms "community organization" and "community work" have come to be used interchangeably to refer to planning and activity on behalf of organizations or neighborhood groups. "Community work" fits better with "casework" and "group work" and sometimes has broader implications than "community organization." Charity Organization Societies and settlement houses both engaged in community work. COSs emphasized rational order in welfare activities, including the requirement that programs share information about recipients. The social reformers in the settlements based their programs on political action and social legislation to relieve distress among the working classes. In this tradition were efforts to obtain workers' compensation, child labor laws, and New Deal programs.

Community work took a new direction after 1908 when local councils of social agencies provided planning and coordination and set standards for the voluntary field. As a result, community work came principally to involve the maintenance of the voluntary welfare system. The Community Chest as a mechanism for federated funding was created out of a need for funds for relief during World War I. "One gift for all" was especially attractive to businessmen and later to labor groups. Community Chests developed membership criteria for agencies that promoted both fiscal responsibility and conservative program goals.

Along with the growth of public agencies and the labor movement, the Depression of the 1930s raised many public policy issues. Stimulated by the New Deal, attention was directed to poverty, dependence, ghettos, discrimination, and unemployment. Some people found it difficult to perceive of community work as part of a direct service profession, but Dunham (1949) highlighted the need in social work for direct service as well as for community planning, administration, and coordination.

The Association for the Study of Community Organization was formed in 1946. Like its counterpart in group work 10 years before, the organization grew out of a section of the National Conference on Social Work. The new association had no educational requirements for membership but soon cast its lot with social work. By 1953, 80 percent of the members were also members of the American Association of Social Workers. Sixteen schools of social work offered at least one basic course in community organization by 1950.

Ross (1967, p. 40) identified the elements in community organization—identification of needs, ordering of needs, finding the resources to meet needs, and taking action through cooperative and collaborative efforts. This process results in an increased capacity to undertake other cooperative projects.

Community planning in the 1960s began to include community residents—the consumers of services. New models of involvement were developed by Mobilization for Youth. The federal antipoverty program dealt directly with the major cities to establish neighborhood advocacy and service programs funded under the Model Cities Program. Consumer participation, however, was often controlled by sophisticated bureaucrats and politicians who used the power of the establishment.

Community work since the 1960s has accommodated both protest and advocacy, causing discomfort to some social workers. The civil rights movement was spurred on by grass-roots organizations that sought to empower minorities. Social workers, more as individuals than as agency workers, supported freedom marches, rent strikes, protests against nuclear war, and demonstrations at nuclear power plants.

Currently, community work under social work auspices is typified more by systems maintenance and planning than by activism. Some of the major community organization concepts have become a part of the curriculum for direct service students who take courses in administration and planning that promote service networks and client advocacy.

Toward a Common Framework

The 1950s were a decade of consolidation for organizations concerned with social work practice and education. Seven social work membership organizations for practitioners came together to form NASW in 1955. Four had been long established: the American Association of Medical Social Workers (1918), the National Association of School Social Workers (1919), the American Association of Social Workers (1921), and the American Association of Psychiatric Social Workers (1926). The other three were less than 10 years old: the American Association of Group Workers and the Association for the Study of Community Organization (both founded in 1946) and the Social Work Research Group (1949).

All members of these groups were grandfathered into NASW. New members were required to have a graduate degree from an accredited school of social work. Membership was extended to holders of accredited bachelor's degrees in 1969. NASW also established the Academy of Certified Social Workers for those who had 2 years of supervised experience beyond the master of social work (MSW) degree. Membership in the academy now requires passing a written examination. among other stipulations.

NASW originally created sections to represent special practice interests, but the sections were discontinued after a 1963 reorganization. NASW facilitated the development of standards and guidelines for social work practice through various commissions. It developed personnel standards, recommended salary levels, and promoted legislation for the legal regulation of practice, protecting the social worker title and licensing. The NASW Code of Ethics served to make social work values explicit. Over its history, NASW has expended more of its resources on refining and promoting social work practice than on social action and social change. One of the association's persistent concerns has been to get clearer agreement on what constitutes social work.

Education. Social work education was eventually unified by a single association. The Association of Training Schools for Professional Social Work (1919) became the American Association of Schools of Social Work. The National Association of Schools of Social Administration, representing undergraduate schools, was formed in 1942, largely to preserve undergraduate social work education. Most undergraduate programs had developed in the Midwest and prepared social workers for the public sector. The National Council on Social Work Education (1948) was charged with resolving conflicts between the competing associations. Finally, in 1952, the Council on Social Work Education (CSWE) superseded the rival groups.

Gradually academic requirements were standardized and increased. In 1932, the minimum required curriculum included classroom and field work in casework, supported by medical and psychiatric information and courses in research and social legislation or the legal aspects of social work. By 1933, member schools were required to offer 1 year of graduate study. By 1935, schools had to be associated with universities, and 4 years later a 2-year master's degree was mandated. Curriculum requirements were expanded to the "basic eight" in 1944—casework, group work, community organization, public welfare, social administration, social research, medical information, and psychiatric information.

The National Council on Social Work Education asked Hollis and Taylor to devise an improved pattern for education. Their report (1951) recommended a single professional organization for social work education and recognition of only graduate education as professional preparation. It saw social work education as a 4-year program—the last 2 undergraduate years and 2 years of graduate study.

CSWE dealt with practice concepts when it published its first curriculum policy statement (Council on Social Work Education, 1952) along with accreditation standards. The curriculum was to include classes,

field work, and research covering social services, human behavior, and social work practice. The policy statement specified that a curriculum should

> provide a framework of classroom and field courses and research within which the student may test and use theoretical knowledge, acquire professional skill, achieve a professional self-discipline, and develop a social philosophy rooted in an appreciation of the essential dignity of man. (p. 1)

With organizational consolidation came increasing interest in the commonalities of the three principal social work methods—casework, group work, and community work. CSWE sponsored a curriculum study under the direction of Boehm (1959). The curriculum was seen as an integrated whole, and schools were expected to develop interrelationships among their components. Social work was to have a single goal, the enhancement of social functioning. Social functioning involved the activities that individuals must carry out in the performance of their various roles as members of social groups. Social work theory was derived from the sciences and the social sciences, and research was the means to test this body of theory.

The study indicated that students need an education broad enough to apply to all settings and yet explicit in each of the three methods of social work. The study emphasized two other methods, administration and research, that never gained the same attention as the basic three. Ethics and values were also a central concern for the classroom and the field. Faculty and field instructors were to serve as role models.

The study recommended that the major part of a student's education in social, biological, and psychological theory would come in the last 2 years of baccalaureate liberal arts education. The first graduate year would concentrate on social work methods, research, and concurrent field work as well as professional values. By this time, the student should have knowledge of all methods and beginning skill in one. The last graduate year would include a block field placement and integrating seminars to provide the knowledge and skill base for competent professional practice. At that time, however, the profession did not adopt the undergraduate emphasis and the block placement.

The 1959 curriculum study strongly influenced CSWE's 1962 Curriculum Policy Statement. As Dinerman and Geismar (1984) observed, the policy statement begins with the basic concept from the curriculum study:

Social work as a profession is concerned with the restoration, maintenance and enhancement of social functioning. It contributes, with other professions and disciplines, to the prevention, treatment and control of problems in social functioning of individuals, groups and communities. (p. 11)

Consensus. The need for unity was still important, however. For 25 years, social workers had primary loyalties to the many social work organizations already mentioned and to others as well. Conceptualizing generic social work, not just generic casework, was one means to develop unity.

Two books were especially important in the search for unity. Towle's *Common Human Needs* (1945) was intended to reflect human needs of concern in public assistance, but it presented needs that affected everyone. Bartlett's *The Common Base of Social Work Practice* (1970) explicated the "Working Definition of Social Work Practice" (1958) developed by the NASW Commission on Practice, which she chaired:

The social work method is the responsible, conscious, disciplined use of self in a relationship with an individual or group. Through this relationship the practitioner facilitates interaction between the individual and his social environment with a continuing awareness of the reciprocal effects of one upon the other. It facilitates change: (1) within the individual in relation to his social environment; (2) of the social environment in its effect upon the individual; (3) of both the individual and the social environment in their interaction.

Social work method includes systematic observation and assessment of the individual or group in a situation and the formulation of an appropriate plan of action. Implicit in this is a continuing evaluation regarding the nature of the relationship between worker and client or group, and its effect on both the participant individual or group and on the worker himself. This evaluation provides the basis for the professional judgment which the worker must constantly make and which determines the direction of his activities. The method is used predominantly in interviews, group sessions, and conferences. ("Working Definition," p. 7)

In *The Common Base,* Bartlett commented on the use of models that could be tested against the base:

Some social workers are fearful that models are too controlling. Actually, perspectives and frames of reference are positive devices for more effective thinking. They give professions their distinctiveness; they identify what is characteristic and thus give the practitioner security; they describe what is common so that thinking can converge; they are essential for effective communication, which requires that people be in the same universe of discourse; they are essential for cumulative thinking and theory-building. (p. 206)

In the 1960s a consensus seemed to be emerging on a generalist model of graduate social work education built on a base of undergraduate social science knowledge and the active discouragement of undergraduate professional education. The term "untrained" signified the attitude toward the caseworker not holding an MSW.

Consensus, however, did not last long. Federal studies predicted the need for many more social workers in the 1970s, colleges were developing undergraduate vocational and professional programs to place their graduates, and tuition costs were going up. These trends influenced NASW and CSWE to sanction a professional bachelor of social work (BSW) degree, raising the issue of redundancy and reopening the question of specialization.

To encourage the development of a conceptual framework for social work, NASW held two conferences, sponsored by the NASW Publications Committee, that led to special issues of the NASW journal *Social Work* in 1977 and 1981. The first ("Conceptual Frameworks," 1977) included commissioned papers, each addressing six topics: the mission of social work, its objectives, activities of social workers, sanctions, available knowledge and skills, and the implications for the profession. The papers were circulated, discussed at the conference, and published with reactions from other conferees. The second conference looked at specific fields of practice including the family, community mental health, health, schools, industry, and aging ("Conceptual Frameworks II," 1981). A paper on corrections was commissioned but not finished.

The outcome from the second conference of most interest to the profession was a working statement on the purpose and objectives of social work that represented progress toward the sought-after common framework (see Table 1).

Five issues were identified in "Conceptual Frameworks II":

1. Critical service needs vs. universal services.

2. A network concept of support within a system vs. attention to individual problem areas.

3. Case management (that is, the social worker acting as a coordinator of a variety of services, most of which he or she would not directly provide) vs. provision of limited specific services.

4. The relative importance of improving general conditions of life vs. recognizing organizational realities.

5. Changing people vs. changing society. (Brieland, 1981, p. 79)

According to Briar (1981), who summarized the conference, person-environment interaction and the status accorded to social work values were the major commonalities. Briar still felt the need for a clearer definition of what social workers do in terms the general public can understand. Most of the conferees and other members who prepared critiques accepted the general statement of purpose but, in trying to apply it, revealed many differences.

Why is obtaining a consensus on the nature of social work so difficult? The three (or perhaps five) social work methods do not lend themselves well to a single unified concept. The different theoretical approaches include diverse views of both humanity and the individual that have produced bitter debates and discouraged eclecticism. A growing array of specializations within the profession detract from unitary constructs. Nonetheless, social work does involve common values and process.

In spite of the large number of different methods, theoretical approaches, and specialized fields of practice, six steps in the social work process applicable to all methods, approaches, and fields can be distilled from the vast literature.

1. Intake and establishing contact.

2. Assessment, diagnosis, and problem identification.

3. Goal identification, service planning, and basis for contract.

4. Service, treatment, and intervention.

5. The evaluation of outcomes through group and single-system techniques. (The term "single-system" [Bloom & Fischer, 1982] rather than "single-subject" accommodates community work as well as casework and group work.)

6. Feedback and application of results in future practice.

Specializations on a Generalist Base

The current approach is a generalist-specialist hybrid. Although in the earlier years it seemed that education was defining practice, with the acceptance of specializations, practice now tends to define education. Agencies support specializations in social work education because graduates have more usable skills and experience than if they had been trained as generalists. A task force from NASW/CSWE (1979) endorsed a specialization concept based on several criteria—a population with a common condition to be altered, competence and skill within social work to serve the population, and conditions complex enough to involve a substantial body of knowledge translatable into effective interventions.

NASW gave more recognition to specializations in 1985 when it announced the creation of five practice commissions to respond to the diverse practice interests of its members: physical and mental health, family and primary associations, education, employment/economic support, and justice. This move is consistent with developments in social work education. The task force that recommended the commissions felt that "membership self-identification was the key to the whole thing" (National Association of Social Workers, 1985, p. 1). A database will be derived from the membership that chooses to affiliate with each commission.

The current educational model described in CSWE's 1983 Curriculum Policy Statement and CSWE's 1984 accrediting standards requires that faculty members who teach practice or coordinate field instruction hold an MSW. It established a professional foundation that begins with a liberal arts base that puts particular emphasis on the social sciences. Generalist preparation is provided in the BSW or the first year of the MSW program. BSW graduates get advanced standing as second-year MSW students. The

Table 1. Working Statement on the Purpose of Social Work

The purpose of social work is to promote or restore a mutually beneficial interaction between individuals and society in order to impove the quality of life for everyone. Social workers hold the following beliefs:

—The environment (social, physical, organizational) should provide the opportunity and resources for the maximum realization of the potential and aspirations of all individuals, and should provide for their common human needs and for the alleviation of distress and suffering.

—Individuals should contribute as effectively as they can to their own well-being and to the social welfare of others in their immediate environment as well as to the collective society.

—Transactions between individuals and others in their environment should enhance the dignity, individuality, and self-determination of everyone. People should be treated humanely and with justice.

Clients of social workers may be an individual, a family, a group, a community, or an organization.

OBJECTIVES

Social workers focus on person-and-environment *in interaction*. To carry out their purpose, they work with people to achieve the following objectives:

—Help people enlarge their competence and increase their problem-solving and coping abilities.

—Help people obtain resources.

—Make organizations responsive to people.

—Facilitate interaction between individuals and others in their environment.

—Influence interactions between organizations and institutions.

—Influence social and environmental policy.

To achieve these objectives, social workers work with other people. At different times, the target of change varies—it may be the client, others in the environment, or both.

Source: "Conceptual Frameworks II—Special Issue." (1981). *Social Work, 26*(1), p. 6.

second year of the MSW involves advanced practice and includes experience with a concentration—that is, usually a specialization by field of practice. The second year of the MSW also has a substantial field work component. More days are generally spent in the field than in the classroom.

A generalist program gives attention not only to all social work methods but also to advocacy and research, including evaluation of one's own practice. Truly generalist field placements are not easy to find. Many placements still emphasize casework almost exclusively. A combination of primary direct service and case management using a network of agencies may best meet the requirement of generalist training.

Both generalist and advanced practice offer a wide range of theoretical options. Psychodynamic, behavioral, ecological, or systems approaches are widely followed singly or in combination. Presentations by those who espouse the major theoretical approaches are now available for each of the traditional social work methods. Roberts collaborated with Nee in editing a volume on casework (1970), with Northen on group work (1976), and with Taylor on community work (1985).

Field Instruction. Given its roots in apprenticeship, social work practice has used field experience as a central element in professional education. Lee and Kenworthy (1929) saw field instruction as the means to help the aspiring social worker experience and test the professional self (p. 238). Students needed as much help as clients because they had to adjust to a new professional role incompatible with their past experience.

Students employed in agencies who went to school part-time were automatically getting social work experience concurrently with their classroom learning. With the increase in the number of full-time students, however, came the need to standardize the field component. The following provisions are generally accepted for field work and are reinforced by accrediting standards (Council on Social Work Education, 1984):

1. Field instruction should involve a minimum number of hours (900 hours for master of social work students in 1985) that total about 50 percent of the student's effort.

2. A social worker with a professional degree and experience should serve as supervisor. If this requirement cannot be met, a faculty member or other qualified professional will provide supplementary supervision.

3. New field instructors will receive instruction in that role.

4. The educational institution should provide liaison personnel for field instructors and students to deal with assignments to field placements and any learning problems that are encountered.

5. A manual setting forth the objectives of field instruction and the basis for student evaluation should be devised jointly by the schools and field instructors.

6. A specific learning contract should be developed and signed by the student, field instructor, and faculty field liaison.

7. Paid placements are neither advocated nor prohibited.

8. If the student is to receive field instruction in the agency of employment, the job assignment should be different from the student's regular position and should involve a different supervisor.

9. Schools are free to choose concurrent or block placements.

10. The curriculum should provide an educationally focused review of field experiences, usually in the form of a practice seminar.

Although many schools of social work prefer that full-time faculty members serve as field instructors, without grant support this model tends to be too expensive. It has virtually disappeared as federal funds for training have been curtailed. In addition, practices differ widely concerning field instructors' formal faculty status, autonomy in grading students, and role in planning educational programs.

Organizational Affiliations. The variety of organizations helps fragment approaches to social work practice. NASW alone does not speak for social work. Some professional workers have primary loyalty to the National Association of Black Social Workers, to the National Federation of Societies for Clinical Social Work, or to some other national group. Specialized associations that set standards in child welfare and family social work seek individual members and sponsor educational activities for practitioners. Some educators choose to belong only to CSWE.

Some social workers give their energy to state associations that represent their own specialty. Both public and private agency staff members may be active in unions. The diversity of interests is shown in testimony on licensing bills when public agencies find educational requirements too stringent and clinical associations find them too lax. Social workers may also choose to take no part in organizations and thereby have no easy access to the literature that should be a resource for continuing education.

Education Continuum. Several other influences serve to divide social workers and retard unified concepts of practice. In spite of being part of an educational continuum, the BSW has not achieved its promise. Some BSW educational programs are small, located in isolated areas, and deprived of adequate resources. Some professionals still reject people with BSWs as professional colleagues. Further, BSW jobs have not developed according to predictions and many BSWs have no professional affiliation. Out of 98,000 NASW members, only an estimated 5 percent hold the BSW as their highest professional degree.

Most public agencies make no distinction between a social work major and other fields at the bachelor's degree level. To make matters worse, agencies have often declassified MSW jobs so experience may be substituted for professional education.

Paraprofessional personnel tend to affiliate with labor unions rather than social work organizations, but an increasing number are becoming candidates for graduate degrees in part-time social work programs. Obtaining their advanced degree may have a significant effect on their outlook about professionalism.

Host Settings. Social service was a principal activity of COSs and the settlement houses. Contemporary social workers, however, are not likely to work in a social work setting unless they serve in a family or children's agency or perhaps a neighborhood center or a community mental health clinic. Host settings, or settings controlled by other professions, provide a variety of jobs, and opportunities for social workers have increased. Hospital social work and occupational social work (in employee assistance programs) have been areas of significant growth.

Host settings tend to fragment the social work profession, however. They may constrain social work roles and impose their own certification requirements, as is the case for school social work. Social workers also have less job security in host settings and less influence. Current modes of mental hospital care result in short stays for patients, for example, meaning that social workers can provide only the briefest crisis services.

Further, school social workers have been in demand to meet federal mandates by negotiating individual educational agreements with parents of handicapped children, but funds for nonteacher personnel have been curtailed in most school districts. Police social work developed with special grants but has been discontinued as grants have ex-

pired, and social work in corrections has been adversely affected by the increased use of fixed sentences and the deemphasis on rehabilitation and parole.

Public Policy and Social Action. Finally, recent federal public policy has reduced the resources available to social work professionals as well as lowered their prestige. The Reagan Administration's initiatives during its first term of office resulted in dire predictions for social work. Federal concern, federal funding, and federal control have been reduced, but the effects were not as serious as might have been predicted. Social work is still very much alive. It was clear that volunteers and self-help groups could not assume the major roles of professional practitioners. Nevertheless, although Congress blocked some of the Reagan proposals, dealing with the federal deficit under the terms of the Gramm-Rudman legislation will no doubt lead to further cuts.

Social workers will need to continue their functions and choose their causes carefully. Nevertheless, the social work profession will continue to seek both unity and diversity in its mission, in its knowledge base and principles of practice, and in its social action programs.

DONALD BRIELAND

For further information, see BIOGRAPHICAL SECTION; DIRECT PRACTICE IN SOCIAL WORK: OVERVIEW; HISTORY OF SOCIAL WORK AND SOCIAL WELFARE: SIGNIFICANT DATES; HISTORY OF SOCIAL WELFARE; PROFESSIONAL ASSOCIATIONS: COUNCIL ON SOCIAL WORK EDUCATION; PROFESSIONAL ASSOCIATIONS: NATIONAL ASSOCIATION OF SOCIAL WORKERS; SOCIAL WORK EDUCATION.

References

Addams, J. (1899). "The Subtle Problems of Charity." *Atlantic Monthly, 83,* 163–168.

Addams, J. (1902). *Democracy and Social Ethics.* New York: Macmillan Publishing Co.

American Association of Social Workers. (1931). *Social Case Work–Generic and Specific: A Report of the Milford Conference.* New York: Author.

Bartlett, H. M. (1958). "Toward Clarification and Improvement of Social Work Practice." *Social Work, 3*(2), 3–9.

Bartlett, H. M. (1970). *The Common Base of Social Work Practice.* Washington, D.C.: National Association of Social Workers.

Bloom, M., & Fischer, J. (1982). *Evaluating Practice: Guidelines for the Accountable Professional*. Englewood Cliffs, N.J.: Prentice-Hall.

Boehm, W. W. (1959). *Objectives of the Social Work Curriculum of the Future*. New York: Council on Social Work Education.

Briar, S. (1981). "Needed: A Simple Definition of Social Work." *Social Work 26*(1), 83–84.

Brieland, D. (1981). "Definition, Specialization, and Domain in Social Work." *Social Work 26*(1), 79–82.

Cannon, I. M. (1923). *Social Work in Hospitals*. New York: Russell Sage Foundation.

Charity Organization Society of New York. (1888). *Fifth Annual Report*. New York: Author.

"Conceptual Frameworks, Special Issue." (1977). *Social Work. 22*(5), 338–444.

"Conceptual Frameworks II—Special Issue." (1981). *Social Work. 26*(1), 5–96.

Council on Social Work Education. (1952). *Curriculum Policy for the Master's Degree in Social Work Education*. New York: Author.

Council on Social Work Education. (1962). *Curriculum Policy for the Master's Degree in Graduate Schools of Social Work*. New York: Author.

Council on Social Work Education. (1983). *Curriculum Policy for the Master's Degree and Baccalaureate Degree Programs in Social Work Education*. New York: Author.

Council on Social Work Education, Commission on Accreditation. (1984). *Handbook of Accreditation Standards and Procedures*. New York: Author.

Coyle, G. L. (1930). *Social Process in Organized Groups*. New York: Richard R. Smith.

DeSchweinitz, E., & DeSchweinitz, K. (1948). "The Contribution of Social Work to the Administration of Public Assistance." *Social Work Journal. 29*(4), 153–162, 177.

Dinerman, M., & Geismar, L. L. (1984). *A Quarter Century of Social Work Education*. Washington, D.C.: National Association of Social Workers.

Euster, G. L. (1980). "Services to Groups." In D. Brieland, L. B. Costin, & C. K. Atherton (Eds.), *Contemporary Social Work* (2nd edition, pp. 102–106). New York: McGraw-Hill Book Co.

Hollis, E. V., & Taylor, A. L. (1951). *Social Work Education in the United States*. New York: Columbia University Press.

Lee, P. R. (1930). "Cause and Function." In *National Conference on Social Work, Proceedings: 1929* (pp. 3–20). Chicago: University of Chicago Press.

Lee, P., & Kenworthy, M. (1929). *Mental Hygiene and Social Work*. New York: Commonwealth Fund.

Leiby, J. (1978). *A History of Social Welfare and Social Work in the United States*. New York: Columbia University Press.

Leiby, J. (1984). "Charity Organization Reconsidered." *Social Service Review, 58*(4), 522–538.

Lewin, K., Lippitt, R., & White, R. K. (1939). "Patterns of Aggressive Behavior in Experimentally Created Social Climates." *Journal of Social Psychology, 10*(2).

Lubove, R. (1965). *The Professional Altruist*. Cambridge, Mass.: Harvard University Press.

National Association of Social Workers. (1985, May). "Practice Commissions Adopted by Directors." *NASW News*, pp. 1, 16.

National Association of Social Workers, Council on Social Work Education Task Force on Specialization. (1979, April). "Specialization in the Social Work Profession." *NASW News*, p. 20.

Pumphrey, R. E., & Pumphrey, M. W. (1961). *The Heritage of American Social Work*. New York: Columbia University Press.

Reid, K. E. (1981). *From Character Building to Social Treatment*. Westport, Conn.: Greenwood Press.

Richmond, M. E. (1898). "The Need of a Training School in Applied Philanthropy." In *National Conference on Charities and Corrections, Proceedings: 1897*. Boston: George H. Ellis.

Richmond, M. E. (1917). *Social Diagnosis*. New York: Russell Sage Foundation.

Richmond, M. E. (1922). *What is Social Case Work?* New York: Russell Sage Foundation.

Roberts, R. W., & Nee, R. (Eds.). (1970). *Theories of Social Casework*. Chicago: University of Chicago Press.

Roberts, R. W., & Northen, H. (Eds.). (1976). *Theories of Social Work with Groups*. New York: Columbia University Press.

Ross, M. G. (1967). *Community Organization*. New York: Harper & Row.

Smith, Z. D. (1892). "The Education of the Friendly Visitor." In *National Conference on Charities and Corrections: Proceedings*. Boston: George H. Ellis.

Taylor, S. H., & Roberts, R. W. (Eds.). (1985). *Theory and Practice of Community Social Work*. New York: Columbia University Press.

Towle, C. (1945). *Common Human Needs*. Washington, D.C.: Federal Security Agency.

Wilson, G. (1976). "From Practice to Theory: A Personalized History." In R. W. Roberts & H. Northen (Eds.), *Theories of Social Work in Groups* (pp. 1–44). New York: Columbia University Press.

"Working Definition of Social Work Practice." (1958). *Social Work. 3*(2), 5–8.

HISTORY OF SOCIAL WELFARE

This article considers the general course of development of social welfare and social work in the United States. It outlines the ideas and institutions brought by European colonists, the relation between 19th century charities and correction and 20th century social welfare, the changing scope of social welfare, and the origin and growth of professional social work.

Textbooks on social welfare and social work usually define those phenomena by their functions regarded from the perspective of sociology. In a historical perspective, it makes more sense to ask when and how ideas and institutions came into use and changed. Although international conditions and influences were significant, the main continuity of decisions and history was in the modern nation-state; therefore, this article focuses on ideas and events in the United States.

The terms "social welfare" and "social work" came into use in this country between 1900 and 1910, superseding the earlier terms "charities and correction" and "charity work." They were never clearly defined, but they denoted the interests and ideas that were drawn together in the National Conference of Charities and Correction in 1874, which was renamed the National Conference of Social Work in 1917 and the National Conference on Social Welfare in 1947. Many state conferences and state and local administrative agencies that represented these interests and ideas also changed their names in this way.

There is, therefore, a definite historical continuity between present-day social welfare and the activities during the years 1870–1900. In pondering the records of that earlier generation, it is easy to see foreshadowings and beginnings of situations and issues that later became large and complicated. However, the records show that, at that time, people viewed their understanding and efforts as a culmination rather than as a beginning. They looked forward to more progress, but they did not envision the specific policies and programs that we now think of (still not clearly) as the welfare state and the profession of social work. In thinking of how their experience relates to ours, it is important to reconstruct their impression of their situation and heritage.

Such a reconstruction is difficult because although particular ideas and facts are not recondite, their relationships are ramified and confused. Thus, it is easy to find evidence for a plausible reconstruction that ignores or bypasses other kinds of relevant evidence.

Monographs about problems and responses may be well reasoned but nevertheless misleading because they have no reference to larger contexts. The problem, which is common in historical scholarship, is especially perplexing in studies of the history of social welfare because the various lines of development—the parts of the field that specialists need to comprehend—are usually dependent on developments in the broadest patterns of social change in economic, social, intellectual, and political history.

Religion and Charity

How did people who were active in charities and correction in the generation before 1900 conceive of their heritage and the broad context of their work? Almost all believed that epochal changes were under way and that their efforts were somehow part of those changes. Almost all thought that the changes were from a social order that was relatively simple and stable to one that was complex and changing. Beyond those points, they disagreed about the nature, causes, and direction of the changes and about the place of charities and correction in personal and social life.

Traditional Religious Doctrine. There is no way to quantify beliefs or world views or to measure their intensity, but it appears that most people were satisfied with traditional religious doctrine. That is, they believed the Biblical account of creation and human nature and destiny. They believed that a divine Revelation defined right and wrong and pointed the way to Heaven or Hell. Charity, or love, was, in this view, the greatest commandment, and its practice manifested the spirit of God. To obey this commandment was a responsibility of individuals and of communities. Most people accepted the principle and its authority, but they differed about the specifics of its application. Even good people believed they were sinful (thinking themselves sinless was the worst sin); they were relieved to know that God loved and forgave sinners. But God also said that they should punish sin and correct (reform) sinners. How could they manage that, beginning, presumably, with themselves? God did not decree a specific political or social organization, it seemed. Although Heaven was described as a monarchy and patriarchy, in earthly communities the critical condition was a pious and righteous spirit rather than a given social arrangement. Nevertheless, God called the community to correct and reform itself, and pious people differed greatly about how to apply that principle. God's Revelation lent itself to different opinions about sin and salvation, the relation of the individual to the community of the faithful (the church), and the relation of the church to the unchurched and to the secular political authorities. These differences took the form of sectarian or denominational antagonisms that were the scandal of Christendom.

Scientific Naturalism. Meanwhile, there were always questions about how literally a believer should take the Biblical text. Most believers made room for some continuing revelation or inspiration, and many religious philosophers (theologians) recognized the need to reconcile Revelation with the insights of profane philosophers, as St. Augustine did with Plato; St. Thomas, with Aristotle; and those of the modern era, with Bacon, Descartes, Hobbes, and Locke who propounded philosophies based on scientific naturalism. This type of thinking was risky because although pious theologians and scientists might find a reconciliation, an increasing number of laymen would simply reject the authority of Revelation and perceive religion to be obscurantist and superstitious, if not politically reactionary—an opiate of the masses. Scientific naturalists might honor the ethical teaching of Jesus (along with many other ethical seers), yet they preferred to put ethical and social philosophy on a rationalist basis (ignoring the dogmas of Revelation); they might even reject the ethic of love and unselfishness along with the theology of Creation, Sin, and Salvation. Scientific naturalism was always the enthusiasm of a small educated class, but its proponents increased rapidly in number, confidence, and influence in the 18th and 19th centuries, along with epochal advances of a technology based on

science and, in the generation before 1900, with the Darwinian theory of evolution.

By 1900, historians in Europe and the United States had divided the past into ancient, medieval, and modern periods. They defined the modern period as beginning around 1500 and distinguished by the rediscovery of pre-Christian culture (the Renaissance), the Protestant Reformation, the organization of nation-states, the improvement of natural science and its influence on technology and social thought, and the opening of America to European commerce and settlement. They often thought of "revolutions"—a word that originally meant a cycle, as in the turning of a wheel, but which came to mean a fundamental change—as the overthrow of the *ancien regime* in France. (The term "Industrial Revolution" was coined in 1884 by Arnold Toynbee, a historian at Oxford after whom the first settlement house, Toynbee Hall, was named.) Well-educated citizens of the United States—business and professional people and their families, for the most part, a small but influential proportion of the population—understood this doctrine about "modern history," and most of them affirmed the optimistic doctrine of "progress" that many thinkers drew from it.

The factors of modernity operated in the United States with exceptional freedom and scope. In European nations, there were restraints on innovation: the older traditions of a paternalistic sovereign and aristocracy, an authoritative and established church, an academic and artistic high culture, and a network of family and community ties. In the United States, there were fragments, shadows, and echoes of these phenomena, but they had only such authority as their particular supporters chose to afford them.

Influence of Religious Groups. The institutional forms of charity in the United States were patterned largely after those in England. However, American forms manifested especially the ideas and practices of Protestant denominations that had refused to conform to the ways of the Church of England—Baptists, Congregationalists, Presbyterians, Quakers, and Methodists. These sects emphasized a personal, emotional religious experience, focused on the conversion of individuals and the awakening or revival of a Christian spirit in communities that were unreached or congregations that had fallen into complacency. They thought of charity as a work of the awakened spirit—as part of their life together in a religious fellowship or of their evangelical and missionary work with those who were not yet saved. Insofar as they had a general social goal, it was the "Kingdom of God" on earth, but they supposed that personal piety was the foundation of the Kingdom.

Although these evangelical Protestant sects advocated legislation and social action to eliminate temptation and to support pious observances, they did not have much interest in the political or social reforms advocated by those with worldly interests and arguments. Presumably, most of their charitable activity was informal and ad hoc, neighborly and mutual. When they invested their time and money in formal organized charity, it was likely to be in sectarian orphanages for children, almshouses for the elderly, hospitals for the sick and travelers, charity schools where poor children could learn to read the Bible (with proper sectarian interpretation), or organizations to bring Bibles and religious tracts or missionaries to the unchurched. They often supported the "city missions," which attempted to reach the friendless and demoralized in big-city slums. Perhaps their most notable achievement in formal organized charity in the nineteenth century was the Young Men's Christian Association (YMCA), which began in the 1850s and became a well-funded, well-organized resource for country boys who came to seek their fortune in the big city.

Alongside these dissenting evangelical Protestant groups were congregations that could recall the social responsibility of an established church. Preeminent among them was the Episcopal (Anglican) Church, which strongly appealed to wealthy families who thirsted for gentility. Others were the Roman Catholic Church, especially in Baltimore, St. Louis, and New Orleans, where it served many elite families; and, to a lesser degree, various churches that had once been dominant, such as the Congregationalists and Presbyterians in New England, the Dutch Reformed Church in New York and New Jersey, and, in a way, the Quakers around Philadelphia. The common denominator among these congregations was a genteel spirit of service (noblesse oblige), supported by ample means, as the rich got richer, and stimulated by the way the society pages of local newspapers celebrated their charity balls, bazaars, and benefits, for their lavish charities raised these worthies above the common lot and put the community in debt to them. These people often were genuinely pious, public spirited, able, and well informed, and they figure largely in the history of social work and social welfare. They were likely to be more interested in the ethical, social, and practical side of charity than in its sectarian mission and to support ecumenical or even secular public philanthropies.

A third group of religious congregations served immigrants who came to the United States after 1845 in an extraordinary mass migration from Europe, usually (with large exceptions) to the big cities of the industrial Northeast. Roman Catholics were by far the most numerous (at first Irish or Germans and later Italians, Poles, and French Canadians). There also were large groups of Lutherans from Germany and Scandinavia, Jews from Russia, and congregations of Greeks, Russians, Armenians, and Turks.

In their religious life, the immigrant churches were likely to be traditional and fearful of the latitudinarianism and secularism of American religion, and their charitable activities were likely to be strongly sectarian, intended to help hold the group together and retain its ethnic and religious integrity.

To summarize, people in the late 19th century were aware of large and cumulative changes in their lives, and their ideas about charity and correction appeared in the context of their ideas about social change. For most people, ideas about human nature, society, change, and destiny were religious— the heritage of a common Bible and the social organizations of Christian Europe. However, even in the centuries that were called medieval, when European leaders aspired to a universal (or catholic) authority in religion and a universal empire (like that of Rome), the common heritage had fatal divisions of idea and interest. In the centuries after 1500, the factors of modernity exacerbated these divisions: religious dissenters (Protestants) fostered a variety of theologies and organizations, often at odds among themselves, and the impressive insights of scientists into the natural order and of historians into social development offered a rationalistic and naturalistic basis of intellectual, moral, and political authority. In the United States, organized groups affirmed a wide spectrum of these inherited opinions: some espoused the most traditional and orthodox types of Judaism, Greek Orthodoxy, Roman Catholicism, or Lutheranism or followed the strictest Calvinists or the most fervid antinomians; others supported leaders who were less traditional and more "liberal" in the language of Protestant theology (meaning opposed to a belief in strict predestination and the inerrancy of Scripture). Religious leaders differed in how and how much they went beyond the Bible and the tradition of their denomination to incorporate rationalist, naturalistic scientific thought, and a growing number of conscientious and well-educated people could not accept traditional dogmas and beliefs, however qualified.

Charitable attitudes and acts were central to all traditional religions, but charitable practice differed according to denominations and circumstances. In traditional churches, the practice was decidedly sectarian and missionary. Other congregations, usually those that were affluent and "liberal," might take a more ecumenical and practical view of the charities, the problems they addressed, and the community they served.

Church, State, and Charity

In the Christian and medieval tradition, politics and charity were separate. Charity was given by families, friends, neighbors, or members of a community who helped each other in a spirit of brotherly love. Politics involved powerful people, families, and groups who negotiated to define and protect their common interests. Charity was helping the needy or helpless. Politics was an alternative to fighting among the powerful. The typical medieval political structure was a military aristocracy: a hierarchy of warlords acting according to a feudal and ideally a Christian code of honor. The main civil business of the aristocrats was to enforce custom or law among their retainers; enforcing customary or legal claims and duties was the practical meaning of "justice." Kings were mighty warlords, with many mighty retainers (dukes and so forth). In theory, their authority came from God and hence they ruled by "divine right." They assisted the hierarchy of the church in establishing a pious and dutiful community (for example, stamping out dissenters or fighting the Muslims).

Transition to Nationhood. In the change to the modern nation-state, kings lost the hedge of divinity. They became executives of a ruling class, which included not only warlords but wealthy merchants and manufacturers who could buy and sell warlords. A nation also included more popular elements: a large lower middle class and an even larger body of people who rallied around an ethnic identity that was usually based on common language and religion. The active support of these larger bodies of people became more important as the technology of war and industry changed. The basis of authority in the modern nation-state was the consent of the governed, meaning, ordinarily, the members of the ruling class or those defined as "citizens" and excluding others, even though they might be a large majority.

Political leaders in the nation-state learned to look far beyond the enforcement of local justice toward a "policy" that would promote the interests of the nation. They would decide on a "foreign policy" to guide their relations with other nations and various "domestic policies" that would strengthen the nation. Domestic policies addressed the problem of political representation and the form of consent, taxes, or the relation between church and state when religious congregations divided into hostile factions. Domestic policy also responded to economic interests, encouraging and directing production and commerce.

Countries on the western border of the medieval Holy Roman Empire, particularly England, France, and the Netherlands, first made the transition to nationhood. As they worked out domestic policies, the traditional concerns of charity came under their purview. For example, in England in the 16th century, after the bishops separated themselves from the Pope and became subject to the king, the king and parliament passed a series of laws intended to help the parishes of the church do their traditional job of relieving the poor. This legislation culminated in the famous Elizabethan Poor Law of 1601, which was later recognized as the foundation of public welfare in England and its American colonies.

Elizabethan Poor Law. The Poor Law defined the duty of the parish to relieve the poor, established overseers to perform it, and gave them power to raise funds and administer relief. Parish poor relief was a last resort when the ordinary informal help of family, neighbors, and friends was not available or not sufficient. It provided for helpless people whose needs were large and likely to be prolonged—orphans, the handicapped, the chronically ill, and the feeble aged. Ordinarily, the overseers engaged a family to board and care for these unfortunates. The overseers might indenture children who were able to work, much as the children's own parents might do. They were empowered to assess and collect a tax to pay all costs.

When the king and parliament moved to strengthen the parishes' administration of poor relief, they faced a problem that had always confused religious organizations for charitable relief. Children and handicapped people might be capable of partial self-support, and it was good for them and the community that they pay their way, if possible. More important, there was a class of sturdy beggars who lived a vagrant life and who were pitiful but troublesome—a nuisance and a threat to the peace. It seemed important that the administrators of poor relief should prevent these beggars from abusing the law (as they had under the former strictly religious administration) and that the parishes that were responsible for these misfits should take care of them. This view was fine in theory, but in practice it was often more trouble than it was worth to distinguish and discipline potential abusers. In the 17th century, as merchants organized a trade in American tobacco, fish, and furs, it occurred to the government that it might send sturdy beggars to the New World where they could be useful.

Meanwhile, in 1601 the king and Parliament enacted the Statute of Charitable Trusts and Uses, which clarified and strengthened the power of citizens and associations to endow or support helping agencies without going through the machinery of government. They conceived the law to help rich people make large benefactions, usually in the form of land, to establish an almshouse, hospital, or school. Previously, the wealthy could have given the money to the church, which presumably would follow their wishes and administer the agency in perpetuity. The new statute made it possible for them to enter into a legal contract with a specific group of trustees and its successors. It stimulated voluntary philanthropy.

Origins of American Public Welfare. When the American colonies became independent, the state legislators acknowledged freedom of religion and eliminated established churches (except in New England, where tax support continued until the 1830s). The First Amendment to the federal Constitution, ratified in 1789, declared that "Congress shall make no law respecting an establishment of religion or prohibiting the free exercise thereof"; this freedom of religion was an important early form of the concept of equality. Religious sects were permitted to establish charitable agencies, and such agencies and their property were free of taxation. Sectarian and other voluntary agencies—ethnic or local—became the ordinary vehicles through which people responded to problems of the group or place.

In constitutional theory, the state governments succeeded the British Parliament, except for certain powers that they delegated to the federal government: to conduct foreign relations and defense, to regulate interstate commerce, to manage and sell public lands owned by the nation, and to define and mint money (legal tender). Ordinary domestic policy regarding conditions of labor, family, health, crime, education, and local transportation and services was the business of the states. Thus, the enactment of legislation regarding charity and correction was the province of the states, but the states usually required local governments—the counties, townships, or municipalities—to fund and administer it. This was the case with the poor law, in its several state incarnations, as well as with law enforcement and jails and with the public schools that came into being after 1830.

Public welfare in the United States began, therefore, as agencies mandated by state law but established, financed, and managed by officials of local governments. Ordinarily, a committee in charge of poor relief (composed perhaps of elected county supervisors) gave the needy what was necessary to maintain themselves ("home relief" or "outdoor relief") or arranged for their board and care with a local family or, if the number of needy people was large enough, opened a "poor farm" (poorhouse or almshouse, "indoor relief") for their care. Those whose behavior was a nuisance or dangerous ("lunatics," the "feebleminded," or vagrants) might go to the local jail along with those charged with a crime; in such a case, a part-time constabulary and justices of the peace took charge.

Early Problems. As rural settlements became cities and the number of transients, strangers, and misfits increased, outdoor relief, the almshouse, and the jail often became large and employed a sizable full-time staff. This growth brought about two problems: the expenditures were "spoils" over which rival politicians fought, and the spoilsmen on the staff were not likely to have much technical knowledge of or interest in helping. Often conditions in these local receptacles were scandalous. Consequently, one main line of improvement in mid-19th century charities and correction was to persuade the state government to open specialized institutions that would take various kinds of problem people and provide these people with a program of care, education, or discipline that would really help them and, moreover, to set up these state agencies in a way that would minimize partisan politics and put the agencies under technically qualified career specialists. This argument led state legislators to create state prisons, lunatic asylums, schools for the feebleminded, reform schools or reformatories for juvenile or first offenders, hospitals for the tuberculous, orphanages, almshouses for veterans, and other institutions. Some of these state institutions had a stable administration, relatively free from politics (the Association of Medical Superintendents of American Institutions for the Insane [1844], which later became the American Psychiatric Association [1921], was the first national professional association). However, most institutions suffered from political interference and, at best, their programs failed to realize the hopes of their founders.

To summarize, toward the end of the 19th century, the institutional pattern of charities and correction was based on a much-honored religious commandment to love others as one loves God. Ordinarily, this charity manifested itself in mutual respect and kindness among family members, neighbors, and friends. But often it was provided by formal institutions that helped people whose needs were extraordinary or who were more or less strangers and for whom some collective (social) responsibility seemed appropriate. These formally organized charities usually gave form to a sense of belonging to a religious fellowship or an ethnic group or sometimes simply to a local community. People supported them by voluntary gifts of money or time; sometimes, wealthy people gave such organizations an endowment for their work. Alongside the voluntary or "private" charities was "public charity"—the poor law administration and various specialized state institutions that were established by legislation, paid for by taxes, and managed by public officials. Sometimes the county supervisors or the state legislators would award a subsidy to a private charity rather than establish or expand a public agency or they might take a private agency into the local or state system. The big picture was a scatter of agencies that represented many local influences and contingencies. Patrons and workers followed European traditions and models, but they had little of the sense of a common situation and destiny that might animate the traditional hierarchies of church and state in Europe. Their efforts were, as everyone observed, disorganized.

Federal Policies

Federal officials did not feel any responsibility for charity and correction as ordinarily conceived in the 19th century, but they did act in ways that bore on local problems. For example, they regulated international commerce; the main source of their funds was the tariff, which they collected in federal custom houses in ports of entry. Such ports were the largest cities of the time, awash in human flotsam—transients and sick and distressed people. Town fathers thought that the federal government, which forbade them from taxing the stream of commerce and collected the tariff for federal purposes, should at least pay for the care of sick seamen who were strangers. The federal government agreed; and, in 1798, the federal Treasury Department, which collected the tariff, established maritime hospitals that in time grew into the U.S. Public Health Service.

American Indians and Slaves. Federal officials also took responsibility for dealing with American Indians who were organized under tribal leadership and lived on Western lands administered as territories of the federal government. Although Christian missionaries had been active in proselyting and "civilizing" the Indians, the federal officials dealt with them in the spirit of diplomacy and war, not religious charity. When Congress decided to establish reservations, it put the reservations in charge of the Indian Bureau of the Department of the Interior—the agency that managed public lands. The bureau's initiatives for health, education, police, and vocational training did not usually appear in contemporary discussions of charity and correction.

The federal government had a peripheral interest in the problems associated with slavery and emancipation. The Constitution provided that the African slave trade should end in 1808, and the Navy enforced that embargo. As for emancipation, leaders of the antislavery movement had been concerned more with the immorality of the institution than with practical plans for helping ex-slaves. When the Emancipation Proclamation (1862) and the 13th amendment (1865) abolished slavery, the federal army of occupation tried various ways of helping the ex-slaves to reestablish themselves, and Congress authorized the Freedmen's Bureau to work with the reconstructed state governments in helping the ex-slaves adapt to the new situation. Like most governmental ventures of that time, the policy was better than the execution. In any case, the federal government returned the problem to the local authorities in a few years. These policies did not appear in contemporary discussions of charities and correction.

Immigrants. At about the time that the federal government left the problem of helping the ex-slaves to the governments of the states in which they lived, public-spirited people began to demand that it limit immigration. Even before the Civil War, a large wave of immigrants from Ireland and Germany had stirred anxiety and hostility among the citizenry, resulting in the nativist "American" ("Know Nothing") parties of the 1850s. When the European immigration of a large number of Italians, Poles, Jews, Slavs, and Greeks reached flood tide between 1865 and 1914, doubt and hostility increased. The foreigners became a very large part of the unskilled labor force in transportation, mining, and manufacturing; labor leaders viewed them as degrading the proud status of the craftsmen that had earlier symbolized labor. These foreigners were conspicuous in the human flotsam in commercial and industrial cities. They filled hospitals, jails, and almshouses. They gathered in slums that obviously threatened the health, safety, and morals of the community. Above all, it was hard to imagine that they had the right stuff to enter the vanguard of progress that was led by the Founding Fathers of the Republic and their progeny (or, in more cosmopolitan pronouncements, by the Anglo-Americans, or the Anglo-Normans, or the Nordics, or the Teutonic peoples, or simply people of Northwestern Europe, including the Celts, of course).

The effort to get Congress to close the gates to these backward infamous hordes had some success against the "Yellow Peril"—the Chinese and Japanese who were coming to California—but it encountered much resistance. Businessmen in shipping and railroad companies opposed it, as did land speculators and the mill owners and mine owners who employed the immigrants. The immigrants soon found a voice in their religious leaders and in the bosses of the notorious urban political machines that played a rapidly increasing role in decisions of state and national political parties and officials. Not until the xenophobia of the first World War did Congress sharply limit immigration, in 1921 and 1924.

Meanwhile, the plight and problems of immigrant families and communities were important concerns of experts in charities and correction. In the 1880s, the experts succeeded in getting Congress to turn away individuals who were convicts, lunatics, or likely to be paupers or those who had certain illnesses. Leaders of established Catholic and Jewish charities were usually (not always) disposed to help the newcomers, as were many Protestant city missions and nonsectarian or "community" agencies. Immigrant charitable leaders appeared in conferences and organizations of philanthropists, and immigrant political leaders learned to look beyond the spoils of public welfare. Immigrant communities and problems interested professional social workers, especially in Chicago. It was in Chicago that Grace Abbott, who was later to be a national leader in child welfare, made a reputation as executive of the Immigrants' Protective League and her sister Edith, dean of the School of Social Service Administration at the University of Chicago, published authoritative scholarship on the subject.

The social settlement movement, taking form in the 1880s, often opened its houses in immigrant neighborhoods and furnished many opportunities for the neighbors to get together for mutual aid, service, recreation, and even political action. Settlement house leaders like Jane Addams and Lillian Wald were influential interpreters of immigrant cultures and values, and settlement workers led the "Americanization" programs that were intended to help the foreign born and their children adapt to prevailing ways of life.

In general, the federal government became involved in charity and correction in the 19th century incidentally to its functions of regulating commerce (the slave trade and immigration) and military government (in the territories and in the states of the defeated Confederacy). It allowed free immigration (with a few exceptions) and easy access to citizenship (naturalization). Its public land policy stimulated settlement of the territories. In the 1840s, reformers led by Dorothea Dix tried to get Congress to set aside public land to finance the care of the mentally ill, but that effort was defeated by veto of President Franklin Pierce (1854) and never revived, even when, after 1862, the federal government gave large land grants to states to support state colleges to train specialists in agriculture and mechanical industry.

Scientific Charity

The National Conference of Charities and Correction (1874) brought together the precursors of professional social work and gave a practical foundation to the later concept of social welfare. The groups that joined it emerged as leaders in particular lines of work who tried to put their efforts in a larger perspective.

State Boards of Charities and Correction.
The initiators of the conference were members of "Boards of Charities and Correc-

tion" (state boards) that several states had established, beginning with Massachusetts in 1863. State boards differed in their names, composition, and duties, but, in general, their mission was to advise the state legislature and the governor about the administration of the state's institutions. State boards were needed because state government was rudimentary. State officials in those days were typically elected for two-year terms and served part time. In its term, the legislature met in regular sessions once, or perhaps twice, for a few weeks. The governor and other executives could carry out their duties in a few hours a week, in the weeks when they were actually at the state capital and on the job.

The state institutions were the largest part of the state government (except for the state militia). They were usually in charge of an institutional "board of managers" that appointed and advised the institution's executive. The boards of managers were appointed for long overlapping terms, usually because they had some reputation as philanthropists or experts. They were not paid, and they were supposed to protect the institution from the spoils system and to win public confidence for it. Sometimes they succeeded, but generally they became advocates among the legislators for their institution, playing politics in their own way. The state board was supposed to look past particular institutions and their boards to the big picture—the general state interest. Because the state institutions were usually a backup for the local almshouse and jail, taking especially difficult or hopeless cases the local agencies could not help or did not want to help, the state boards often got into questions of state-local relations and finance, as well as technical questions about what sorts of institutions and programs the legislature should support.

Board members from different states first encountered each other at the organization of the American Social Science Association (1866), in later years the forebear of national associations of economists, historians, sociologists, and political scientists. State board members separated themselves because the parent organization was too theoretical and too inclusive to respond to their immediate practical interests.

Charity Organization Societies.
In the 1880s, the state boards were joined in the

National Conference of Charities and Correction by leaders of the Charity Organization Societies that had appeared in forward-looking cities, beginning with Buffalo, New York, in 1877. These leaders were typically active in local voluntary charities, avatars of noblesse oblige, who looked beyond their own pet charities to envision more methodical, systematic, efficient, constructive ways of helping in the scores or even hundreds of local private agencies in a city. They were often acquainted with the members of boards of managers of state institutions and state boards, who were drawn from their ranks. Because they were based in cities, they outnumbered the people who were related to state institutions.

Settlement Houses. Finally, the leaders of settlement house work began to appear in the conferences in the 1890s. The first American settlement house was Neighborhood Guild, started in New York in 1886; by 1896, there were 44 settlements and by 1911, almost 400. The settlement house programs developed in an empirical and incremental way, similar to those of the YMCA, except that the settlements did not proselyte; instead, they offered to help the neighbors organize clubs or services that they wanted. The settlement houses were the forerunners of the community centers; they were more interested in informal education and recreation than in providing charity and correction, but, in their never-ending informal neighborly services, their workers got many valuable insights into problems and services and advocated improvements in agencies and policies.

The business of the conference was an annual meeting to share experiences and forward-looking ideas; its objective was to help the helpers and thus encourage them and the communities that sponsored their efforts. Members of the conference were more practical than speculative; they did not feel a need to define the boundaries of their common interests. Looking back, a historian of social welfare might formulate their assumptions about boundaries as including agencies and programs that were (1) formally organized, (2) socially sponsored, and (3) intended to be helpful in a familiar tradition of "charity" and "correction." Each of these assumptions meant more then than it does now. The idea

of *formally organized* helping, for example, emerged in contrast to helping that was informal and not organized—the spontaneous help of family, neighbors, and friends. The idea of *social sponsorship* referred to the fact that these agencies and programs were set up by groups of people, associated perhaps through affiliation in a particular church or simply by a common purpose or in a common government. Socially sponsored helping was distinguished from service or goods that one bought in the marketplace. The idea of a *tradition of helpfulness* appeared in the words "charity" and "correction," which had, at the time, distinctively religious connotations.

Religious Ideas. The dominance of secular social thought in the twentieth century has erased the religious connotation that "charity" and "correction" had before 1900. "Charity" meant "love," but not the personally gratifying attachment of lovers or of parents and children; it referred to the notion, well established in Pauline theology, of a spirit that held a Christian community together. The spirit was manifest, for example, in the familiar phenomena of the conversion or rebirth of sinners who felt their sinfulness and the redeeming love of God and in the revival meeting, which awakened complacent congregations to God's love. The symbol of profane love was the shapely Venus; the symbol of sacred love was the Cross, sometimes with the sacrificial Lamb bleeding on it. "Charity," in this religious connotation, involved loving people as a way of loving God—serving mankind as a way of serving God. "Correction" referred then (as now) to the "correctional" (distinct from "penal") institutions in the 19th century. "Correction" involved the religious notion of "reform" (as in the Protestant Reformation); correctional institutions were called "reform schools" or "reformatories." Like conversion and revival, "correction" involved the notion of an inner change, a renewal of the spirit, that made an offender responsible and dutiful.

Arising from these notions of charity and correction was a religious ideal of a community, suggested by Hebrew prophecy and by Jesus' parables of the Kingdom of God ("Thy will be done on earth as it is in Heaven," in the words of the Lord's Prayer). The ideal of a Godly community was central to the religious utopian or communitarian societies that flourished in mid-century America, such as the Shakers, the Rappites, Brook Farm, or Oneida. Perhaps the best 20th century translation of 19th century "charity" would be "solidarity"—a sense of all for one and one for all—or team spirit (note the word "spirit") or reciprocal feelings of "social responsibility" and "personal responsibility."

Liberalism. People who gathered at the National Conference of Charities and Correction were mostly pious (many were clergymen), but they also had secular ideas. The political philosophy of the United States, as set forth in the Declaration of Independence and the federal and state constitutions, is called "liberalism." It depended not on a revelation of God in the Bible, but on a secular notion of natural law, such as Roman Stoics and other non-Christians might affirm, or, in its modern English form, on the rationalistic utilitarianism of Jeremy Bentham, John Stuart Mill, and Herbert Spencer. English political and ethical liberalism also included the doctrine of political economy (or economics, as it came to be called) associated with Adam Smith and his followers, which was a model of social science. In one late 19th century form, liberalism took the extremely individualistic character later called "social Darwinism." Meanwhile, liberalism evoked various other "scientific" doctrines of political economy, for example, Marxist "scientific socialism," the national socialism of German academics such as Gustav Schmoller and Adolph Wagner (which rationalized Bismarck's economic and social legislation), Christian socialism, and, in the United States, many odd popular panaceas such as Henry George's single tax, the Greenback and Free Silver movements, and Edward Bellamy's Nationalism.

It might seem that the people who attended the conference would offer a forum to those who wanted to debate the grand issues of individualism and collectivism, capitalism and socialism. They did not. In general, they held to the dominant tradition of liberalism, but, like Adam Smith, they believed that laissez-faire economic policy should be tempered by the moral attitudes of personal and social responsibility in the religious tradition of charity. They began with

the tradition and practice of charity and the ideal of a caring, sharing community (to use a later term). Their starting point was not that a better political economy might solve social problems, but that the practice of helping was often mistaken and self-defeating. Their name for their cause was "scientific charity" or "scientific philanthropy." Their notion of "scientific" was naive by later standards; they meant that helpers should base their efforts on the facts of the situation (they were busy fact collectors) and that helping should be rational, with a clear idea of means and ends.

Scientific Charity. The import of "scientific charity" emerged in the way they contrasted it with charity that was sentimental, undiscriminating, or perfunctory. Their notorious example of perfunctory charity was local public relief under the poor law: outdoor relief without any rational standard or plan or indoor relief that was custodial and minimal—in either case, relief that was subject to abuse in the pervasive spoils system of American government. State institutions and their boards were supposed to be more rational and helpful than local public relief as it was practiced. The charity organization societies, for their part, pointed to the foolishness of the casual almsgiving that was so common in the impersonal relations of cities and to the ease with which mendicants or charitable promoters exploited the good will of cheerful givers. They also criticized the perfunctory administration of established charities in which helping seemed to be as important for gratifying the giver as for improving the lot of the recipient. Adopting ideas set out by Thomas Chalmers and his followers in England, charity organizers worked out a method of investigation and planned helping, case by case, that would build on and strengthen the informal or natural "fountains of charity" and not displace or weaken them. The settlement house workers, who were often young people linked to colleges, thought of science in terms of academic sociology in its then-current form of "applied ethics" or "Christian sociology."

These notions of scientific charity were, in a way, obvious, but they found support primarily among members of the urban business and professional class, especially those who were associated with theologically liberal religious congregations—the forerunners of the social gospel. Scientific charity found little support among farmers and rural townspeople, who were likely to regard the plight of the urban poor as punishment for sin, rum, and Roman Catholicism; among the big-city poor themselves, who were likely to affirm traditional and sentimental charity as a sign of good will; among shopkeepers and skilled workers, who were likely to look to politics or unions as a solution to their problems; or, indeed, among the majority of the urban business and professional class, which was likely to be complacent or, if concerned, to support doctrinaire social Darwinists or socialists, who seemed to get at the roots of problems.

To summarize, professional social work had its origin in the late-19th-century advocates of "scientific charity" or "scientific philanthropy." These people took a critical view of policy and administration in the variety of organizations and programs then called "charities and correction," meaning the local public and private agencies and the state institutions of the time. Many advocates of scientific charity were intelligent and conscientious agency executives, set off by their career interests from the superannuated clergymen, feckless clerks, and political spoilsmen who were the bane of charitable administration. Many more were weighty volunteers in the work, often clergymen or society ladies who had the will and insight to become leaders, who called attention to responsibilities that had been too much neglected. They thought "scientific" meant "rational" and "practical"—a critical insight into ends and means. They liked to focus on agency problems—problems of method. They eschewed efforts to relate services to the theological disputation that separated religious denominations and to the theoretical disputation of schools of political economy or social theory. They thought theology and social theory were likely to distract people from simply doing good works in better ways. As a general goal, they were satisfied with a vague conception of the ever-coming Kingdom of God on Earth in which Christian charity would harmonize personal responsibility and social responsibility. They were vulnerable to the charge of being snobs, not really charitable and not really scientific, and when, around 1900, they began to arrange a professional education similar to that of clergy, physicians, engineers, and teachers, it was not hard to see elements of confusion and pretense in their aspiration.

The Progressive Years: 1900–1930

When the term "social welfare" came into currency, it contrasted with "individual welfare" in the debate over individualism and collectivism; in a more specific sense it was a euphemism for "charity" or "charitable agencies." Meanwhile, the 19th century terms "charity work" and "philanthropist" (in the sense of someone who did good deeds, not someone who endowed philanthropies) gave way to the term "social work." In time, "social welfare" came to refer to agencies and programs and "social work" to an occupation in such agencies. Other terms were sometimes used; "social service," for example, referred to a class of agencies and a type of occupation.

Whatever the vagaries of usage, it was clear that the term "charity" had become unpopular. It had the connotation of the well-to-do patronizing the poor (it persisted on the society pages of newspapers, where society ladies fussed over their charity balls and bazaars). The terms "social welfare" and "social work" also reflected the rapidly increasing importance of nonsectarian private agencies and publicly sponsored agencies that required a secular rationale. It is helpful to analyze this general trend in three periods: 1900–1930, when the action was at the level of local and state governments and local private agencies organized under the Community Chest; 1930–1968, when the federal government took important initiatives; and, since 1968, when the progress of the "welfare state" has seemed to stop if not turn back.

The expansion and improvement of state and local agencies between 1900 and 1930 was influenced by the progressive movement in political history. Political progressivism had various sources and directions. At the level of theory, it was a modification of 19th-century liberalism, especially the individualistic form associated with Herbert Spencer and social Darwinism. The modification was to approve more limitations on individual liberty and laissez-faire policy in pursuit of collective interests and goals. The areas of limitation—the objects of government intervention and control ("social control," as it was then called)—were the conditions of labor, public education, public health, and the conservation of resources. Legislation along these lines ("social legislation") was early and persistently challenged in the courts and often defeated. When it succeeded, it was justified by an expansion of the police power of the government, as judges called the power of government to act to protect the health, safety, and morals of the people. Social welfare legislation now fell under this legal doctrine: child labor laws, for example, and preventive policies of all sorts. The police power was ordinarily thought of as a power of state governments; it certainly was not among the enumerated powers of the federal government.

Concept of Poverty. The police power might provide a constitutional justification for legislation, but it did not say why particular legislation was desirable. Much of the argument for progressive social welfare legislation stemmed from a refinement of the concept of poverty. In the 19th century, poverty often had been conflated with indigence, pauperism, or dependence. Pauperism was viewed as extreme deprivation—the point at which a person who had no resources and no relatives, neighbors, or friends who could or would provide sustenance had to come to private or public charities for help. In the 1880s, Charles Booth clarified the idea of poverty in the course of an epochal survey of *The Life and Labor of the People of London* in which he defined a standard or norm of adequacy and observed how many families were above it or below it. His concept of poverty as *deprivation related to a norm of adequacy* brought out the fact that paupers who were dependent on charity were few compared with a much larger number who were deprived but not dependent. Booth's purpose in making the survey was to get an empirical measure of how workers were doing under a policy of laissez-faire, but the long-run effect of his survey was to turn attention *from* paupers *to* a much larger and more hopeful class that was vulnerable and on the verge of pauperism. It was possible to generalize about the risks that reduced poor people to pauperism—sickness, accident, fire, for example—and to imagine policies and programs to reduce those risks.

Political Progressivism and the Social Gospel. This line of thought gave new force to ongoing efforts to improve health and safety in residential neighborhoods and in the workplace. It fostered more and better laws about housing, the water supply, sewage disposal, food supply (the pasteurization and refrigeration of milk, for example), and about conditions of labor. The well-being of mothers and children took on new importance (in Europe the wish for healthy, competent soldiers was an important stimulus for such legislation, and military interests supported many kinds of economic and social planning).

In the prolonged uphill struggle for social legislation, state by state, progressives could rally some people from the business and professional class, some union leaders, some bosses of urban political machines, even some leaders of the rural population (an important variant of progressivism appeared in the agricultural states of the South and West). However, these elements were hard to unite and confused by enthusiasts for other popular causes. For example, many foes of strong drink believed that Prohibition would go far to solve social problems. Other people wanted to restrict immigration to keep out nationalities that seemed to be troublesome. Still others thought that women's suffrage would bring a new vision to politics. Everyone had high hopes for education.

An important contemporary religious movement, the social gospel, gave inspiration and support to many partisans of progressive politics. Its theologians accepted the so-called higher criticism of the Bible and thus separated themselves from the doctrine of "inerrancy of scripture" that continued to be held by Fundamentalist sects. They looked beyond personal sin, righteousness, and salvation—the individualism of the so-called Protestant ethic—toward social legislation intended to "Christianize the social order." They emphasized social service rather than sectarian rivalry.

Political progressivism and the social gospel created a favorable climate for the development of social agencies and of a professional spirit in them. The original idea of scientific charity—its emphasis on means and ends in helping and its deference to social science—helped experts to look beyond immediate relief to see a process that suggested causes and cures and prevention and rehabilitation. Members of state boards, Charity Organization Societies, and settlement houses were conspicuous among advocates of social legislation in the rise and flowering of progressivism. Experts who believed in scientific charity could also imagine an educational curriculum that would teach career-minded people about the history and policy of contemporary agencies and about the best methods (or means) of work. There was a demand for the service of career-minded people as executives of or skilled workers in social agencies to work alongside and to supervise the volunteer or untrained workers, much as a trained musician, athlete, or craftsman might lead a group of amateurs. Many people saw an opportunity to fill that demand, moving into a social work career from business, the clergy, teaching, journalism, or the law. Women especially found it promising, compared with the opportunities as salesladies, secretaries, schoolmarms, nurses, librarians, journalists, or home economists that were also opening for them at that time.

Beginning of the Profession. Professional social work was only one of many professions that were then taking form in which some academic training and certification were the basis of a claim to special knowledge and skills. Clergymen, physicians, military officers, and lawyers had been in the vanguard of this movement, followed by graduates of the engineering and agricultural colleges of the late 19th century and then by adepts trained in schools for dentists, pharmacists, nurses, teachers, secretaries, businessmen, librarians, journalists, architects, sanitary engineers, and public administrators, among others.

It was easy to think of a professional social worker as a certified career-minded expert doing what volunteers or amateurs did but doing it better, but the experts soon faced more difficult questions about their professional identity. It happened that many career social workers found employment in medical and educational bureaucracies in which technical specialization was relatively advanced. Because it seemed that social work overlapped with what nurses, physicians, and teachers did, the question then arose, Where, precisely, was the line between them? Moreover, there was, in schools of medicine and

education, much thought about a knowledge base and its relation to practice skills, about the level of professional education (whether it should follow high school or college), and about generic training and advanced specializations. In 1915, the National Conference of Charities and Correction invited Abraham Flexner, a leading authority on professional education, to speak on whether social work was a profession. (Flexner's momentous report on medical education, *Medical Education in the United States and Canada,* published in 1910, had, in effect, closed two-thirds of the medical schools and upgraded most of the rest.) Flexner said that, by his criteria, social work was not a profession. His words did not affect the market for career social workers or applications to the professional schools, but they were a stimulus to a more rational and formalized curriculum.

Distinctive Competence. What was the distinctive competence of a professional social worker? The 19th-century founders—members of state boards, institutional executives, leaders in charity organization, and head workers in settlement houses—were concerned mostly with questions that would later be considered policy and administration. They themselves had learned by experience; insofar as they had an academic association, it was with a general "social science." When that social science divided into academic specializations—economics, sociology, history, political science, anthropology—their association was mostly with economics, particularly a subspecialty called, around 1910, "social economics." Edward T. Devine, for example, was a rural schoolmaster who studied economics in Germany and then received a Ph.D. in economics from the University of Pennsylvania. He was engaged in adult education when he became general secretary of the New York Charity Organization Society in 1896. In 1898, he helped organize the society's School of Philanthropy and directed it; in 1905, he became professor of social economics at Columbia University, with which the school later merged. Professional social work might have focused on policy and administration as it did, to some extent, in England, and as professionals did in business administration, public health, and public administration. The leaders of the University of Chicago School of Social Service Administration, who were in close touch with the growing public bureaucracies involved in child welfare and with legislation about child labor, education, health, and the juvenile courts, were determined that professional social workers should be prepared to advise legislators and executives and to implement their decisions in a knowledgable and circumspect way.

However, the legislators and executives were not inclined to look to professional social workers for advice about their decisions and how to implement them at the top of the bureaucracy. The market for professional social workers, early and late, was agency boards or executives who wanted people who could do casework in a knowledgable and expert way and supervise untrained people on the job. Some of this demand was in public agencies: schools, hospitals, probation and parole offices, institutions for the mentally ill and mentally retarded, child welfare departments, and even local public relief. But employment in public agencies depended largely on politicians getting the vision of a properly qualified civil service—a distant vision for them to get.

More promising was the demand from private agencies, local and regional or national. The sponsors of these agencies were mostly business and professional people who thought in terms of technical solutions and technical competence. These sponsors were mobilized and guided by the spread of federated fundraising through the Community Chest, much stimulated in the 1920s by the success of the fundraising drives during World War I for the Red Cross and war bonds. The leaders of local charity, including the wives and daughters of the businessmen and professionals, looked to professional social workers for advice and executive leadership; they furnished the market for the managerial competence that became identified in the 1920s as the social work method of community organization. But the agencies themselves mostly wanted caseworkers.

Casework Casework began as a way to individualize helping to suit particular people and situations. It was an alternative to the bread line or soup kitchen—the impersonal casual handout. Charity organizers had divided the job into three parts. First, a district secretary of the society would receive requests for help and make inquiries about them. Second, the district secretary would summon a "case conference" of members of the Charity Organization Society and others who might have some special knowledge of the circumstances. The case conference would try to consider all sides of the situation and arrive at a plan of help that would take them into account. The plan might involve relatives, friends, neighbors, the landlord, the employer, the teacher, the pastor, and representatives of local charitable agencies. Third, a "friendly visitor" would try to establish a personal relationship—a sort of follow-up to the plan although the relationship was supposed to bring a benefit to the helper as well as to the helped. Of course, district secretaries, case conferences, and friendly visitors fell short of the need and the ideal. Agency boards and executives felt the need to recruit and train volunteers who would be reliable or to hire people they could count on. There was much interest in better training and better work. Just when Abraham Flexner was expressing doubt about whether social work had a knowledge base and skills that could be communicated, Mary Richmond was preparing to summarize her extensive experience and the studies she had made under the aegis of *The Survey* magazine and the Russell Sage Foundation, which she published in 1917 as *Social Diagnosis*.

Richmond's discussion of method drew largely on the rhetoric of law; she spoke of collecting and sifting "evidence" about "cases" and helping "clients," for example. (Leaders at the University of Chicago School of Social Service Administration also looked to law schools as a model, although they were more interested in legislative policy than in preparing cases.)

Mental Hygiene Movement. Meanwhile, the idea of "mental hygiene" came to play an increasing part in professional education. Mental hygiene followed from the understanding that people who were mentally ill often had a long history of tell-tale signs and problems; if someone could recognize the signs and problems at an early stage, it might be possible somehow to correct or control them. This thought was relevant to the progressive interest in child welfare and juvenile courts and to the widespread use of intelligence tests and the idea that mental retardation explained a good deal about people who were dependent and delinquent (the "feebleminded" had always been among the "defective'' class counted in the census). The first mental hygiene clinics appeared at juvenile courts, and they established the team of psychiatrist, psychologist (mental tester), and social worker that became the model in the rapid expansion of mental hygiene clinics or child guidance clinics in the 1920s. From a professional point of view, work in one of these clinics was thought to be especially challenging and rewarding.

Psychology, in the sense of the analysis of mental states and motivation, had always been part of helping, but the academic discipline of psychology had never been related to social work. It had its roots in epistemology and physiology, not indoor and outdoor relief or even psychiatry. The discovery of the conditioned reflex and the theory of behaviorism that Ivan Pavlov and John Watson built on it suggested a theory of learning that became important in teachers' colleges, as did the IQ test. Another, newer, line of psychological investigation—developmental psychology—was more relevant to social work because it fit in with mental hygiene and the interest of psychiatrists and social workers in dealing with psychopathology. The peculiar theories of Sigmund Freud about psychological development and pathology, which got short shrift before 1930 in psychiatry and academic psychology but which had a vogue in avant-garde intellectual and artistic circles, won a warm response among social workers. Virginia Robinson's dissertation, *A Changing Psychology of Social Case Work* (1930) elucidated an unmistakable trend toward a knowledge base and practice skills that were akin to psychoanalysis, in addition to or in place of the older notion of social diagnosis.

In summary, after 1900, agencies for charity and correction were supplemented by various programs aimed at prevention and rehabilitation and established by legislation of state and local governments. The constitutional justification of the legislation was the police power. The general rationale was to protect common or public interests against the activities of employers, landlords, businessmen, or others who put their individual advantage above the well-being of society (the social welfare). In political rhetoric, the campaigns for social legislation were often described as campaigns for social justice; they elaborated aspirations for equality and

fraternity that politicians of the Jacksonian era had once proclaimed.

The main support for the improvement of charitable and correctional agencies came from the business and professional class, especially those elements that were impressed by social science and encouraged by the social gospel. In these circles, the notion of professional social work found a warm reception, especially among women. There were questions about its knowledge base and technical competence, but experts could point to more critical ideas about methods—casework, community organization, and a foreshadowing of group work—as examples of professional progress. When the hopes for social legislation diminished in the politics of the 1920s, the hopes for professional development continued to shine.

Federal Initiatives: 1930–1968

In 1930, the system of social agencies was as confused as ever. From the first, social workers had aspired, as part of their professional mission, to look at the whole system and to organize it. This effort faltered because agencies and their personnel and programs and supporters continually changed. At best, the supporters and personnel were nodes of self-consciousness forming and reforming amid the much larger currents of national life that they could hardly perceive or understand.

In retrospect, it seems that the main continuity of the next 40 years in social welfare was the increasing importance of the federal government. At the time, it seemed that the federal government had to take leadership to meet national emergencies—the Great Depression (1929–1941) and World War II (1941–1945)—and then a long sequel of managing the economy and waging the cold war. These political events had sources in a more general and less obvious trend: the development and spread of a more homogeneous national society and culture (sometimes identified by sociologists as a "mass society"). The federal government acted in many ways that bore on social welfare. Some were related to providing for the dependent, defective, and delinquent classes, in the old phrase, and prevention and rehabilitation, in the progressive spirit. However, others were newer and broader—managing the business cycle and employment, for example, and advancing civil rights in new ways.

Social Insurance and Public Assistance. With regard to the earlier range of social welfare, the most important innovation was federal sponsorship of social insurance and certain categories of public assistance and federal laws governing the conditions of labor (such as wages and hours) and labor-management relations (supporting collective bargaining and unions). The income maintenance programs (as social workers came to call social insurance and public assistance) carried on two pre-1930 themes. Social insurance was originally proposed as a substitute for charity—a form of prevention, as it were, by which workers (with the assistance of employers and the government) would join together to share and rationalize the risks of loss of income among wage and salary earners. Social insurance was supposed to be better than old-fashioned charity because it enhanced the dignity of the beneficiary; working people provided in advance for their needs (much as business and professional people took out private insurance) and made a rightful claim for help rather than going cap in hand to a charitable agency.

Social workers had been advocates of social insurance, following the lead of experts in "labor economics." They also supported a modern form of outdoor poor relief called "public assistance," which was written into the Social Security Act of 1935 in the form of federal grants-in-aid for state-sponsored special (or "categorical") programs for the aged, the blind, and dependent children. Social workers had little to do with the new bureaucracies that were created to administer social insurance, but they played a part in the state and county welfare departments that administered the new public assistance. As executives, supervisors, and interested observers, they tried to encourage a professional constructive spirit in the determination of eligibility, the notion of rules and rights in administration, and adequacy of the aid. On the one hand, social workers were a precious few in those huge makeshift bureaucracies, and their professional training, such as it was, hardly prepared them for the task. On the other hand, the bureaucracies were civil service, often willing to respect professional doctrine that dignified their work and related

it to the proper goals of democratic society, as Charlotte Towle did, for example, in her influential book, *Common Human Needs,* published by the Social Security Administration in 1945.

Local Voluntary Services. The new public assistance and social insurance programs relieved local private charities of the task of giving material relief, except in emergency and residual cases, and left those agencies to concentrate on services. The Community Chests, which supported local services, survived the depression, during which they presented themselves as a community response to a common emergency. They later flourished during World War II, alongside the wartime United Service Organization, when they joined the mobilization for the war effort. The federal government took part in local services by way of grants under the Social Security Act for the strategic services of child welfare and public health. These federally supported activities and the wartime Red Cross and other services helped to spread professional notions of social service to rural areas from the cities where they had first taken hold.

Mental Health Services. While the government at all levels steadily increased its support of social services and the Community Chests and philanthropies maintained their activities, in intellectual circles the advance of academic psychology and sociology, as well as economics and political science, and the exciting improvements in medicine that followed the success of the antibiotic drugs during the war, gave credibility to the cause of a scientifically based helping profession. Insofar as this scientific enthusiasm had a practical application, it focused on two subjects in which social work was heavily involved: mental health and the family.

The pre-1930 insight that mental hygiene might forestall delinquency, mental illness, and the antisocial tendencies of the mentally retarded developed into a thorough appreciation of the importance of one's emotions and self-image for all sides of one's life and of the influence of family life on mental health. In the depression, the social worker Harry Hopkins had proposed the huge work relief programs partly because of their psychological benefit compared with the dole.

During World War II, mental health was a central idea in innovative practices in military psychiatry and penology (after the war, the military services and the Veterans Administration hospitals became the largest employers of professional social workers). In the religious revival of the postwar years, middle-class churches presented religion as a form of good mental health or necessary to it, and pastoral counseling took on a decided psychotherapeutic spirit.

In 1949, the federal government brought a number of grants for mental health services to a culmination in the National Institute for Mental Health (NIMH), one of the National Institutes of Health. The leaders of NIMH proved to be much interested in the public health side of mental health care—in "secondary prevention" (early treatment in the community) and even in "primary prevention" (efforts to foster positive mental health). Their interest in community-based services for the mentally ill corresponded to that of state mental health authorities, who were facing an enormous expansion of their facilities, at staggering expense, and who were learning from sociologists and others why care in traditional mental hospitals was not likely to be therapeutic. The prospect for community-based treatment seemed more hopeful, especially after the advent of the mood-altering drugs in 1954. In the excitement about "community mental health," social workers stood to gain as the largest professional group in the work force—far more numerous than psychiatrists or psychologists (whose role was still mostly to conduct and interpret tests).

The Family. While social work responded to the many-sided interest in mental health in the 1940s and 1950s, it also responded to concern about the family. At a time when family "togetherness" was much praised, the divorce rate rose. As states relaxed eligibility standards for Aid to Families with Dependent Children (AFDC) (to take advantage of federal subsidies), the program reached many mothers who were not widows, not even divorced or deserted, but unmarried. Scientific research reaffirmed one of the early insights of scientific charity—that individuals in trouble meant families in trouble and that family troubles were likely to be complicated. The new name for this insight

was the "multiproblem family," and the new vision pointed, as the old one had, to more services and better coordination of services. In 1956, Congress authorized more services in relation to public assistance, especially AFDC; in the "services amendments" of 1962, it offered a generous matching grant (three federal dollars for every state-local dollar) for services. Increasing attention to the problems of the aged, youths (especially delinquents, as the baby boomers reached adolescence), and the mentally retarded supported the market for trained social workers. In helping every target group, mental health seemed important.

The Welfare State. Meanwhile, in 1948, the social legislation of the Progressive years and the New Deal got a new name: the "welfare state." The term came into currency in the American presidential election of that year, introduced by Republican opponents of the New Deal who used it to label the program that the Labour Party had enacted in Great Britain in 1946. The Republicans meant it to be pejorative, but they lost the election and the term caught on, here and elsewhere, as a national policy that was between doctrinaire liberal laissez-faire and doctrinaire socialist planning. The policy, as set out in the Beveridge Plan (named after Lord William Beveridge, the English economist), which inspired much of the British legislation, was that the state should guarantee every citizen a minimum of economic security as a right. It much enlarged the earlier notion of civil and political rights, of the sort that Americans had put in their federal and state bills of rights.

The idea of a right to welfare did not suit American constitutional theory. (The poor laws were state, not federal, and were rationalized at first as a responsibility of the community—not a right of the needy—and later as an exercise of the police power.) In any case, the term "welfare state" was ordinarily used for description rather than analysis. Arguments about the welfare state were mostly about the tendency of the social legislation so labeled. Deep thinkers had not expected such a compromise, and they continued to doubt its soundness. Traditional liberals regarded it as a road to serfdom, traditional socialists as an unstable precursor of socialism. In the United States, the term was useful because politicians came to accept the labor (and other economic) legislation of the New Deal and the Social Security Act, which was consonant with the Keynesian economics that was becoming dominant. In an international view, it suggested an alternative to the "totalitarian" governments that made people skeptical about political collectivism.

Whatever people thought of the welfare state, domestic politics in the United States in the 1950s rested on an impressive degree of prosperity and social stability. Significant books in the decade celebrated *The American Century* and criticized *The Affluent Society*. Amid much complacency, public and private service bureaucracies went about their business, improving rules here and practices there as seemed proper and feasible in a technical and professional spirit.

In 1961, President John F. Kennedy brought a more active spirit to the federal administration, different from the caution of President Dwight D. Eisenhower's domestic policy and a balance to the coalition of Republicans and southern Democrats that had for many years dominated Congress. From economists who advised him on managing the economy, Kennedy learned how a number of groups were left out of the general affluence. Liberals thought that the federal government should take more forceful initiatives to eliminate such "pockets of poverty." Policies that began cautiously in 1962 culminated, under President Lyndon B. Johnson, in the War on Poverty and the extraordinary burst of legislation in 1965–1966.

War on Poverty. The War on Poverty had many precedents; at the time, it seemed to be unfinished business rather than a new departure. In retrospect, it appears to have altered the concept of social welfare and the rationale of social sponsorship. The New Deal of the 1930s had been a response to the depression; leaders had understood the depression in economic terms as a problem of the business cycle, which (as it turned out) the national government might resolve by countercyclical economic measures. The War on Poverty of the 1960s involved an understanding that poor people faced sociological and psychological problems as well as an economic problem. Many sympathetic observers believed that the disadvantaged lived

in a culture of poverty that alienated and discouraged them, especially when poverty was complicated by racial prejudice and by a move from rural to urban areas (for example, southern blacks or Puerto Ricans to cities of the Northeast or Mexicans into cities of the Southwest). Prejudice not only frustrated the newcomers' search for jobs and homes, it rendered unresponsive the public services for education, health, and welfare. These poor people needed more than to adapt their ways to new circumstances; they needed important changes in the social order that received them. So the War on Poverty initiatives looked past employment and labor market policies, past the labor legislation and the policies that helped the organization of unions in the 1930s, to a different kind of group and individual (psychological and sociological) empowerment.

The War on Poverty is puzzling because it did not have widespread strongly organized political support or incur strong opposition. The strongest support came from the civil rights movement. The civil rights movement had a long history and enjoyed many successes in the 1950s. Its core at that time was well-established black congregations; its leadership, their clergy. Around these people gathered many others, including many conscientious whites and their clergy, union leaders, and other liberals. Its main line of advance had been legal tests of segregation laws ("separate but equal"), but in the 1950s, it began to move against de facto segregation by direct action (sit-ins, boycotts, or picketing). These activities helped to mobilize a broader base of support, especially among young blacks, urban blacks, and sympathetic whites. Civil rights leaders had always looked to the federal government for help against state and local officials who were reluctant, if not antagonistic. Blacks were gaining political influence because they were becoming better organized in the big cities that dominated state governments in the Northeast; they sometimes held a balance of power between parties or factions of parties in those cities.

When civil rights leaders turned from legal contests against segregation to the poverty and disadvantages of so many of their constituents, they saw the strategic importance of the social services. Whereas professionals in health, education, and welfare, not to mention police, fire, and other city services, wanted to improve services from the top down, with attention to professional and bureaucratic concerns, the civil rights leaders and their friends took the client's view. They saw that service bureaucracies might afford jobs and power as well as services. Black leaders were, therefore, ambivalent about social services and social work. On the one hand, they wanted more and better services and could appreciate that professional social workers were more disposed to accommodate and help than were many authorities with whom they dealt. On the other hand, they were critical of many policies and much administration, dubious about many professional concerns, and eager to open up jobs and influence decisions.

On balance, black militance (and similar efforts among other "minority groups") supported the War on Poverty, the demand for social services, and the relevance of professional social work (which recruited many candidates from these groups). It also brought a new emphasis on "rights" as a rationale for service. These rights were procedural rather than substantial; that is, they were based on the 14th amendment's prescription of "equal treatment under the law." If legislators passed a law providing assistance or service, it had to be fairly administered. In supervising public assistance, federal officials had long used this principle to effect far-reaching improvements in state and local administration, although they could not compel states to make their assistance more adequate. Other interests also advanced this conception of rights: the Association for Retarded Children (now the Association for Retarded Citizens) insisted that public schools provide the same services to retarded children as to "normal" children, and the physically handicapped began to protest that they were unfairly passed by. In time, the federal Civil Rights Commission and like-minded groups would seek out patterns of discrimination against women and the elderly as well as ethnic groups and the physically handicapped. Meanwhile, the War on Poverty stimulated legal aid for the poor, furnishing them with more and more aggressive lawyers than they had earlier.

The Scope of Social Welfare. After 1930, the federal government took initiatives that expanded the scope of social welfare. During the depression, it established forms of social insurance and public assistance that, with regard to expenditures, caseload, and staff, dwarfed the earlier programs and agencies. In historical perspective, these elaborated the social provision for the "dependent classes," mostly by the poor law, but, because they were so large and important, they came to dominate thinking about the welfare state. The idea of income maintenance (replacing part of the loss of wages or income when the loss was due to certain contingencies, such as unemployment, disability, retirement, or the death of the breadwinner) merged with general questions of political economy about management of the economy, the distribution of income, work incentives, and economic development and beyond that into questions of social equality, individual liberty, and social justice.

Federal initiatives also stimulated efforts to help the "defective and delinquent" classes, in the 19th-century term. These efforts were termed "direct services" by social workers, to distinguish them from income maintenance, and "human services" by people in public administration and political science, to differentiate them from the maintenance and construction of public works or support of general administration. Traditionally, they were organized by state and local governments and especially by local private agencies funded by the Community Chest. The federal government operated many high-quality institutions (its corrections system was a model for the states, as were the Veterans Administration's mental hospitals). However, it stimulated these services primarily by offering conditional grants-in-aid to states and imposing professional supervision of the states' conformity with its conditions, especially in the administration of public assistance, of social services in relation to the money grant, and of certain activities in public child welfare and public health.

In constitutional theory, those federal initiatives (and analogous programs in other fields, such as highway construction) were labeled "cooperative federalism." Before 1930, it was said, the federal government was inhibited by a constitutional doctrine of "dual federalism," which held that federal and state governments had different responsibilities and powers and that it was wrong to confuse them. The emergencies of the depression and World War II seemed to require federal leadership, which came in the form not of a takeover but of a conditional grant-in-aid. That is, the federal government would offer the states support if the states undertook some work that Congress thought desirable. The form of federalism was preserved because the states did not have to accept the support; if they did, they had to meet the federal conditions, but they still had much authority and discretion.

The War on Poverty was entirely a federal initiative (there were no precedents in state policy). National leaders saw a problem—a complex of problems—and boldly utilized the devices of cooperative federalism to confront it. The antipoverty legislation included measures to improve both income maintenance and direct services, as well as important measures for health, education, the labor market, economic development, and civil rights.

In the direct services for children and families, youths, the aged, the mentally ill, the mentally retarded, the physically handicapped, and offenders with which professional social workers were especially concerned, the main effects of the federal initiatives were to stimulate the development of "community-based services" (distinguished from care in institutions, and sometimes called "deinstitutionalization" or "community care") and better planning by local and state authorities. To get the grant, authorities had to propose a plan that involved the assessment of need, decisions about priorities, and stipulations about accountability. A new twist, typical of antipoverty legislation, was that representatives of users and community groups would participate in planning, determining priorities, and monitoring the services.

Professional Social Work. The immediate consequence of the expansion in the 1960s was a large increase in the demand for social workers. Many programs included grants for training personnel. In 1962, 56 schools of social work enrolled 6,039 students in MSW programs; in 1973, 79 enrolled 16,099. In 1970, the Council on Social Work Education began to accredit undergraduate professional curricula (a policy that had been rejected in the 1940s). In the 1960s, the hand-

ful of doctoral programs expanded, and most professional schools offered advanced work, mainly in research and the preparation of teachers. The National Association of Social Workers, established in 1955 by seven specialized professional associations, which aspired to speak for the profession as a whole, grew apace.

Professional identity, as represented in the curricula of MSW programs, was formalized in 1939 around the methods of social casework, group work, and community organization plus social administration, public welfare, social research, medical information, and psychiatric information. A major review in 1959 emphasized a more general and academic knowledge base for the methods of practice. In the 1960s, the methods were sometimes reclassified as "direct services" (casework, group work, and the grassroots sort of community organization) and "indirect services" (policy analysis, planning, administration, and research—skills helpful to decision makers and managers).

Disenchantment and Reconsideration: Since 1968

Presidents Richard M. Nixon (1969–1973), Gerald R. Ford (1973–1977), and Ronald Reagan (1981—) were self-conscious conservatives, doubtful about or hostile to the policies of the 1960s. They did not control Congress or the federal courts and their advisers often disagreed, but events seemed to enhance conservative views. The prosperity of the 1950s and 1960s foundered and raised doubts about the Keynesian economic theories that had rationalized it. Advantages in labor costs, productivity, and quality diverted investment in manufacturing to foreign lands. High taxes, the result of federal and state grants-in-aid that increased expenditures and taxes cumulatively, stimulated increased resistance and then a "tax revolt." Social security taxes rose inexorably to pay for new and higher benefits, while the falling birthrate and increased longevity threatened the long-run solvency of the system.

Evaluations of the hopeful initiatives of the 1960s were disappointing. The civil rights movement advanced from the strong moral ground of equality of opportunity to the controversial policy of equality of results and affirmative action. Growing recognition of dangers to the environment, toxic wastes, and health hazards on the job fostered federal programs in the 1970s that regulated life and restrained economic development. Organized labor lost membership among the blue-collar workers that had been its strength; the largest unions of service workers were governmental employees, subject to doubts about public bureaucrats. The Vietnam War, Watergate, and other problems reduced the confidence of citizens in the government. As the baby-boom generation reached voting age, the collective memory of the depression and World War II faded. Foes of "permissiveness" in sex and family relations, education, and criminal justice found a large audience.

These events are so recent that it is difficult to measure their tendency or judge their long-term significance. It seems certain that the confidence of the 1960s is gone, spending for "social programs" no longer increases and in many programs goes down, and intellectual proponents of "conservatism" are on the offensive. The policy of cooperative federalism that rationalized the enormous expansion of the grant-in-aid and regulatory apparatus is being dismantled along the lines of the "New Federalism" first proposed by President Nixon. The federal government continues to make large grants on domestic programs, but states get them with no restrictions (revenue sharing) or few restrictions (block grants). Something similar is happening between the state and local governments. The intention is to increase discretion and authority at the local or community level. Local authorities increasingly contract with service providers rather than establish public services.

How far will this devolution of social services go? How responsive, efficient, effective, adequate, and accountable will it be? What political interests will it generate, and how will they connect with other currents and forces in national life, such as those that have historically encouraged and inhibited better social services? No one can say now, as no one could have predicted the future in 1860, 1900, 1930, or 1968.

As for professional social work, it has historically been closely related to social agencies. When the scope of these agencies changed, with the progressive social legislation and the interest in mental hygiene after 1900 or the advent of the great income-maintenance bureaucracies in the 1930s or the antipoverty and community-based agencies of the 1960s, the social work profession stretched to meet new demands. It was never a large proportion of the labor force in these agencies, except perhaps in family and child welfare and in mental health. The great expansion in public support and programs in the 1960s increased the division among social work specialties and attracted people from other fields. Pastoral counseling became more professional, as did educational counseling, vocational rehabilitation, and correctional counseling. Psychologists turned from testing to therapy, often based on behaviorist principles. Gerontology was a specialty, as was child development, marriage and family counseling, work with drug abusers and alcoholics, and sex therapy. Policy analysis, planning, and administration found many academic homes and many career lines; social administration did not seem significantly different from public administration, and policy analysis might rest on economics, political science, or sociology. The historic effort to define professional social work in terms of a particular technical competence—a method and a knowledge base—was difficult to maintain. The relation between social work specializations seemed more like that between economist or sociologist and social scientist than between family lawyer or criminal lawyer and lawyer.

Yet, the social services have always been a scatter of agencies, the workers in them a scatter of vocations, and the common cause always hard to define. When experts first delineated a profession, they began with (and almost took for granted) values—not the values of a physician with a patient or a lawyer with a client, but the values of organizations that were set up to realize the moral demand of personal responsibility for others and the social responsibility of a community for its members. They thought of this moral demand as religious but not sectarian, and they had no use for political panaceas. Perhaps they were mistaken in their affirmations that a spirit of sympathy and helpfulness were the essence of our historical religious values, that the spirit required an active sense of personal responsibility and social responsibility, and that social science was a means to make those moral values more rational and efficacious. Perhaps their hopes for charity and science were illusory or superficial. But those hopes were the matrix in which the profession of social work took form.

Bibliographical Note

The bibliography of the history of social welfare and social work in the United States is, like the subject, ramified and unfocused. Two surveys by professional historians cite extensive references: Walter I. Trattner, *From Poor Law to Welfare State: A History of Social Welfare in America* (3d rev. ed.; New York: Free Press, 1984) and James Leiby, *A History of Social Welfare and Social Work in the United States* (New York: Columbia University Press, 1978). They differ widely in their interpretation and in the sources they draw on; Trattner has chapter-by-chapter lists of titles, Leiby a review essay. Trattner and W. Andrew Achenbaum, eds., *Social Welfare in America: An Annotated Bibliography* (Westport, Conn.: Greenwood Press, 1983) is fuller than either of the two; it has 1,410 entries with annotations (many titles appear in more than one context). Its editors might have included many more: note their principles of selection (pp. xxiv–xxvii) and their general comments on the literature.

To go beyond these published bibliographies, which one must do for materials published after 1982 and one may well do for earlier periods, see *America: History and Life* (1964–), which indexes and abstracts journals in history and social science; its index to book reviews is a guide to recent books. Frank Freidel, ed., *Harvard Guide to American History* (rev. ed., 2 vols; Cambridge, Mass.: Harvard University Press, 1974) is a general bibliography. *The Public Affairs Information Service Bulletin* (published bimonthly since 1915) is the most useful guide to current governmental documents and occasional publications of private organizations and study groups, as well as to a wide selection of articles and books. The subject headings in these general guides do not correspond to professional jargon, so one must be patient in sifting through them. *Social Work Research and Abstracts* (published quarterly since 1965) abstracts over 150 professional journals in social work and related fields. Years 1977 to present are accessible through SWAB, an online database. Since 1975, the journal has included abstracts of

doctoral dissertations in social work in its fall issue each year; from 1954 to 1974, these dissertations were abstracted in the September issue of the *Social Service Review*.

Practitioners and students interested in particular fields of practice, policies, and technical considerations are likely to find the historical literature disappointing. Fortunately, they may find what they want in readily available primary sources. Previous editions of the *Encyclopedia of Social Work,* for example, have brief authoritative articles in which one can trace changes in perception, knowledge, insight, and organization related to fields and methods of practice. The encyclopedia began as the *Social Work Yearbook* in 1929, appeared biennially until 1951, and then in 1954, 1957, and 1960. The present expanded version appeared in 1965, 1971, and 1977, with a supplement in 1983. Articles are signed and include contemporary bibliographies. Academic and large public libraries are likely to have full sets. Another serial that is readily available and comprehensive in scope is the proceedings of the annual National Conference on Social Welfare, which began in 1874; indexes were published in the 1906, 1933, and 1964 volumes, but they are not detailed. Frank Bruno, *Trends in Social Work, 1874–1956* (rev. ed.; New York: Columbia University Press, 1957) is based on this series and is a useful guide to it (Bruno had a good personal knowledge of the last three decades he wrote about). The editions of Amos Warner, *American Charities: A Study in Philanthropy and Economics* (New York: Thomas Y. Crowell & Co., 1894; rev. 1908, 1917, and 1930), the first survey of the field and widely used, depict changing interests and views and carry contemporary bibliographies. The 1930 edition, much revised by Stuart A. Queen and Ernest B. Harper, who both were presidents of the American Sociological Association and deans of schools of social work, is a useful overview of the situation when the Great Depression began. Stuart Queen's *Social Work in the Light of History* (Philadelphia: Lippincott, 1922), the first American version of a history of the profession, is omitted from the historical bibliographies already mentioned.

There are also some published collections of historical documents: Sophonisba Breckinridge, *Public Welfare Administration* (rev. ed.; Chicago: University of Chicago Press, 1938); Grace Abbott, *The Child and the State* (2 vols.; Chicago: University of Chicago Press, 1938); Edith Abbott, *Public Assistance* (Chicago: University of Chicago Press, 1940); Ralph Pumphrey and Muriel Pumphrey, *The Heritage of American Social Work* (New York: Columbia University Press, 1961); Robert Bremner et al., *Children and Youth in America: A Documentary History* (3 vols. in 5; Cambridge, Mass.: Harvard University Press, 1970–74). These all have good editorial comments and bibliographies.

Many reference books have historical information that is easy to find and use. A valuable annotated guide is James H. Conrad, *Reference Sources in Social Work: An Annotated Bibliography* (Metuchen, N.J.: Scarecrow Press, 1982), which should be available in professional school and academic libraries. Other examples include Peter Romanofsky, ed., *Social Service Organizations* (2 vols.; Westport, Conn.: Greenwood Press, 1978), which presents well-researched short histories and a bibliography; Edward T. James, ed., *Notable American Women, 1607–1950, A Biographical Dictionary* (Cambridge, Mass.; Harvard University Press, 1971), with a supplement (1980), the most helpful of several biographical dictionaries because it pays attention to many women who were active in social welfare; and E. R. A. Seligman, ed., *Encyclopedia of the Social Sciences* (15 vols.; New York: Macmillan, 1930–35), a comprehensive and authoritative account of the state of knowledge at the time that gives more attention to professional social work than its successor, David L. Sills, ed., *International Encyclopedia of the Social Sciences* (17 vols., New York: Macmillan and Free Press, 1968). (When such encyclopedias lose their value as current references, they become valuable for students of history.)

JAMES LEIBY

For further information, see ARCHIVES OF SOCIAL WELFARE; FEDERAL SOCIAL LEGISLATION SINCE 1961; HISTORY AND EVOLUTION OF SOCIAL WORK PRACTICE; HISTORY OF SOCIAL WORK AND SOCIAL WELFARE: SIGNIFICANT DATES; and individual biographies in biographical section.

HISTORY OF SOCIAL WORK AND SOCIAL WELFARE: SIGNIFICANT DATES

Seventeenth Century

1601
Elizabethan Poor Law, enacted by the English Parliament, established three categories of people eligible for relief: the able-bodied poor, the unemployable, and dependent children.

1647
First colonial Poor Law enacted by Rhode Island.

1657
Scots' Charitable Society, first American "friendly society," founded in Boston.

1662
Settlement Act (Law of Settlement and Removal) passed by English Parliament to prevent movement of indigent groups from parish to parish in search of relief.

1697
Workhouse Test Act passed by English Parliament as means of forcing unemployed to work for their relief.

Eighteenth Century

1729
Private home established for mothers and children by the Ursuline Sisters in New Orleans to care for survivors of Indian massacres and a smallpox epidemic.

1773
First public mental hospital established in Williamsburg, Virginia.

1777
John Howard completed study of English prison life and inhumane treatment of prisoners; this influenced reform efforts in the United States.

1790
First state public orphanage founded in Charleston, South Carolina.

1797
Massachusetts enacted first law regarding the insane as a special group of dependents.

1798
U.S. Public Health Service established after diseases brought in by increased shipping caused severe epidemics in Eastern Seaboard cities.

Nineteenth Century

1812

Medical Inquiries and Observations Upon the Diseases of the Mind, by Dr. Benjamin Rush, published—the first American textbook on psychiatry.

1813

First labor legislation enacted by Connecticut requiring mill owners to have children in factories taught the three R's.

1817

First free U.S. school for the deaf founded— the Gallaudet School located in Hartford, Connecticut.

1818

New York, Baltimore, and Philadelphia Societies for the Prevention of Pauperism established to help victims of the depression following the War of 1812.

1819

Bill passed by U.S. House of Representatives granting the Connecticut Asylum for the Deaf and Dumb six sections of public land.

1822

First state institution for the deaf established in Kentucky.

1824

House of Refuge, first state-funded institution for juvenile delinquents, founded in New York.

1829

New England Asylum for the Blind (later the Perkins Institution) founded—the first such private institution.

1834

Poor Law Reform Act of 1834, the first major poor law legislation in England since the Elizabethan Poor Law of 1601, influenced American social welfare with its emphasis on complete assumption by the able-bodied of responsibility for their own economic security.

1836

First restrictive child labor law enacted in Massachusetts; at the time, two-fifths of all employees in New England factories were aged 7 to 16.

1837

First state institution for the blind established in Ohio.

1841

Investigation into the care of the insane begun by Dorothea Dix—ultimately responsible for establishment of 41 state hospitals and the federal St. Elizabeth's Hospital in Washington, D.C.

1843

New York Association for Improving the Condition of the Poor organized by Robert Hartley and associates; later merged with Charity Organization Society of New York to form what is at present Community Service Society.

1846

John Augustus, a shoemaker in Boston, gave up his work to devote himself to taking persons on probation from the courts; from 1841 to 1858, Augustus took 1,152 men and 794 women on probation.

1848

Pennsylvania established first minimum wage law in the United States.

Communist Manifesto published by Karl Marx and Friedrich Engels, influencing worker demands in the United States for social welfare reforms.

1850

First school for "idiotic and feebleminded" youths incorporated in Massachusetts.

1853

Children's Aid Society of New York—first child placement agency separate from an institutional program—founded by Charles Loring Brace.

1854

A bill, initiated by Dorothea Dix and passed unanimously by Congress, authorizing grants of public land for the establishment of hospitals for the insane, was vetoed by President Pierce; the rationale for the veto was that the U.S. Constitution's general welfare clause reserved such care to the states, not to the federal government—an interpretation that established federal policy until the Social Security Act of 1935.

First day nursery in the United States opened in New York City.

1855

First Young Men's Hebrew Association organized in Baltimore.

Young Men's Christian Association (YMCA) organized in Boston by retired sea captain, Thomas C. Sullivan; originally organized 1844 in London by drapery clerk, George Williams.

1859

Origin of Species published by Charles Darwin, setting forth the theory of evolution and providing a scientific approach to the understanding of human development.

1861

U.S. Sanitary Commission organized—forerunner of the American Red Cross.

1862

Freedmen's Aid Societies established in the North to send teachers and relief supplies to former slaves.

1863

New York Catholic Protectory established, eventually becoming the largest single institution for children in the United States.

First State Board of Charities established in Massachusetts to supervise administration of the state's charitable, medical, and penal institutions.

1865

Freedmen's Bureau (Bureau of Refugees, Freedmen, and Abandoned Lands) founded—the first federal welfare agency and a joint effort of federal government with private and philanthropic organizations providing food, clothing, and shelter for freedmen and refugees and responsible for the administration of justice in order to protect rights of black men, protection from physical violence and fraud, and education.

1866

Young Women's Christian Association (YWCA) founded in Boston.

First municipal Board of Health created by the New York Metropolitan Health Law.

1867

County homes for children authorized by state of Ohio.

1868

Payments begun by Massachusetts Board of State Charities for orphans to board in private family homes.

1869

First permanent State Board of Health and Vital Statistics founded in Massachusetts.

1870

First "agent" appointed by Massachusetts Board of State Charities to visit children in foster homes.

National Prison Association (now American Correctional Association) founded in Cincinnati.

Home for Aged and Infirm Hebrews of New York City opened—first Jewish institutional home in United States.

1871

The Descent of Man published by Charles Darwin, applying the theory of evolution to the human species; broke the authority of theologians in the life sciences and provided basis for scientific approach to humans and their social relationships.

1872

American Public Health Association organized.

The Dangerous Classes of New York, by Charles Loring Brace, helped initiate the adoption movement in the United States.

1874

Conference of Boards of Public Charities, within the American Social Science Association, organized May 20, 1874, by representatives of the State Boards of Charities of Massachusetts, Connecticut, New York, and Wisconsin; an annual conference, in 1879 it became the National Conference of Charities and Corrections—precursor to the National Conference on Social Welfare.

1875

New York State granted per capita subsidies to the New York Catholic Protectory for the care of children who would otherwise be public charges.

New York Society for the Prevention of Cruelty to Children incorporated.

1876

New York State Reformatory at Elmira founded—a model penal institution for children; Zebulon R. Brockway, noted corrections reformer and founder of the National Prisons Association, appointed first warden.

1877

First Charity Organization Society founded in December in Buffalo, New York, by Rev. S. H. Gurteen, operating on four principles: (1) detailed investigation of applicants, (2) a central system of registration to avoid duplication, (3) cooperation between the various relief agencies, and (4) extensive use of the volunteers in the role of "friendly visitors."

1879

Franklin B. Sanborn, chairman of the Massachusetts State Board of Charities, advocated use of foster homes for delinquent and dependent children.

Conference of Boards of Public Charities, later renamed National Conference of

Charities and Correction in first session independent of American Social Science Association (founded in 1865).

1881

American Association of the Red Cross organized by Clara Barton.

Tuskegee Normal and Industrial Institute founded by Booker T. Washington; a leading black educational institution, it emphasized industrial training as a means to self-respect and economic independence for black people.

1883

Federal Civil Service Commission established.

1884

Germany, under Bismarck, inaugurated accident, sickness, and old age insurance for workers, influencing U.S. worker demands for social welfare measures.

Toynbee Hall, first social settlement, opened in East London by Samuel A. Barnett, vicar of St. Jude's Parish; visited by many Americans, it served as model for American settlement houses.

1885

First course on social reform initiated by Dr. Francis G. Peabody at Harvard University; Philosophy II was described as "The Ethics of Social Reform. The questions of Charity, Divorce, the Indians, Labor, Prisons, Temperance, etc., as problems of practical ethics—Lectures, essays and practical observations."

1886

First settlement house in the United States, the Neighborhood Guild (now University Settlement), founded on New York City's Lower East Side.

1887

The only nineteenth-century National Conferences of Charities and Corrections "dealing with Indians and Negroes" organized in 1887 and 1892 by Phillip C. Garrett; he stated that society had a special responsibility toward ['] [']the Indian because of being displaced and toward the Negro because of being here through no wish of their own."

1889

Hull House, the most famous settlement house, opened September 14 by Jane Addams on Chicago's West Side.

1890

How The Other Half Lives, by Jacob A. Riis, published—a documentary and photographic account of housing conditions in the slums of New York City, it helped initiate the public housing movement in the United States.

1893

Nurses Settlement founded by Lillian Wald in September—a private nonsectarian home nursing service, it moved in 1895 to become the famous Henry Street Settlement.

1894

American Charities, by Amos G. Warner, published—a social work classic, it was the first systematic attempt to describe the field of charities in the United States and to formulate the principles of relief.

1895

First federation of Jewish charities established in Boston.

1896

First special class for the mentally deficient in an American public school established in Providence, Rhode Island.

1897

First state hospital for crippled children founded in Minnesota.

1898

First social work training school established as an annual summer course for agency workers by the New York Charity Organization Society.

National Federation of Day Nurseries (NFDN) organized (later merged into Child Welfare League of America).

1899

First juvenile court in the United States established in June as part of Circuit Court of Chicago.

National Consumers League organized by Florence Kelley (who initiated fact-finding as a basic approach to social action) in New York City—a combination of several local leagues, the earliest of which was formed in New York by Josephine Shaw Lowell to campaign against sweatshops and to obtain limits on hours of work for girls.

National Conference of Jewish Charities established in New York to coordinate developing network of private Jewish social services.

Twentieth Century

1902

Maryland enacted first workmen's compensation law in the United States; declared unconstitutional in 1904.

1903

Chicago School of Civics and Philanthropy (now the University of Chicago School of Social Service Administration) founded by Graham Taylor.

1904

National Child Labor Committee organized by combination of New York and Chicago settlement groups, primarily responsible for 1909 White House Conference on Care of Dependent Children.

New York School of Philanthropy (now Columbia University School of Social Work) founded, with one-year educational program.

National Association for the Study and Prevention of Tuberculosis (now American Lung Association) founded.

Poverty, the classic work by Robert Hunter, published; it stated that at least 10 million Americans, or one out of every eight, were poor.

1905

Medical social work initiated with employment of Garnet I. Pelton by Richard C. Cabot, MD, at Massachusetts General Hospital in Boston.

1906

National Recreation Association organized; became National Recreation and Park Association following 1965 merger of American Institute of Park Executives, American Recreation Society, National Conference on State Parks, and National Recreation Association.

Boys Clubs of America founded in Boston.

First school social workers' programs introduced in Boston, Hartford, and New York under private agencies.

1907

Russell Sage Foundation incorporated "to improve the social and living conditions in the United States"; it later financed publication of *Social Work Year Books* (now *Encyclopedia of Social Work*).

Psychiatric social work initiated with the employment of Edith Burleigh and Mary Antoinette Cannon by James J. Putnam, MD, to work with mental patients in the neurological clinic of Massachusetts General Hospital.

1908

First community welfare council organized in Pittsburgh, Pennsylvania, as Pittsburgh Associated Charities.

A Mind That Found Itself, by Clifford Beers, published; an exposé of the inadequacies of mental hospitals, it initiated the mental health movement.

Federal Council of Churches of Christ in America started to coordinate its network of social services.

Workmen's Compensation enacted by the federal government—earliest form of social insurance in the United States.

1909

National Committee for Mental Hygiene (now National Mental Health Association) founded by Clifford Beers.

Jane Addams elected first woman president of the National Conference of Charities and Correction (now National Conference on Social Welfare).

England's Royal Poor Law Commission majority report sought to modify the Poor Law, "the principle of 1834," defining the relationship of private, voluntary welfare organizations to the public assistance system; the minority recommended breaking up the Poor Law and the transferring responsibility to divisions of local government, implying the creation of universal services and anticipating features of the twentieth-century welfare state.

Juvenile Psychopathic Institute established in Chicago by Dr. William Healy, on initiative of Julia Lathrop, to study offenders brought to juvenile court; initiated delinquency research and examination of children by a professional team.

First White House Conference on Children (concerned with care of dependent children) initiated under sponsorship of President Theodore Roosevelt.

Pittsburgh Survey begun—the first exhaustive description and analysis of a substantial modern city.

National Association for the Advancement of Colored People formed.

1911

National League on Urban Conditions Among Negroes (now National Urban League) organized October 16 by Dr. George E. Haynes and Eugene Kinckle

Jones through a union of the Committee for Improving the Industrial Conditions of Negroes in New York (1907), the National League for the Protection of Colored Women (1906), and the Committee on Urban Conditions Among Negroes (October 1910).

First Mother's Aid Law enacted in Illinois.

First state workmen's compensation law not later declared unconstitutional enacted by state of Washington.

National Association of Societies for Organized Charities (now Family Service Association of America) federated from 62 relief and charitable societies.

Social workers placed on payrolls of New York's mental hospitals; aftercare work became an integral part of the services of such institutions throughout the United States.

National Federation of Settlements founded.

1912

Children's Bureau Act (c.73, 37 Stat. 79) passed April 9—established U.S. Children's Bureau as a separate governmental agency, an idea initiated by Florence Kelley and Lillian Wald; Julia C. Lathrop appointed first chief.

Girl Scouts of the United States of America founded.

1913

Social Insurance, by I. M. Rubinow, advocated a comprehensive social insurance system to provide financial protection for industrial accidents, sickness, old age, invalidism, death, and unemployment.

Modern Community Chest movement begun with organization of Cleveland Federation for Charity and Philanthropy as an experiment in federated financing, after first trial in Denver in 1888.

1914

National Negro Health Week—the first health program for blacks inaugurated by a black—begun by Booker T. Washington.

1915

Bureau for the Exchange of Information Among Child-Helping Organizations (later merged into Child Welfare League of America) organized.

Abraham Flexner, addressing National Conference of Charities and Correction on "Is Social Work a Profession?", stated it did not qualify as a bona fide profession; this initiated continuing definition efforts.

1916

National health insurance advocated by I. M. Rubinow, executive secretary of the American Medical Association's Social Insurance Commission.

First birth control clinic opened by Margaret Sanger in Brooklyn, New York.

Child Labor Act (c. 676, 520 Stat. 1060) passed by Congress June 25, forbidding interstate commerce in goods manufactured by child labor; declared unconstitutional by Supreme Court in 1918.

1917

Social Diagnosis, by Mary Richmond, published—first textbook on social casework—marking the development of a body of social work knowledge and skills.

First state department of public welfare established in Illinois.

National Conference of Charities and Correction became National Conference of Social Work (now National Conference on Social Welfare).

National Social Workers' Exchange (American Association of Social Workers from 1919, merged into NASW 1955) organized—"the only social work organization with specific concern for matters of personnel [and] additional functions pertaining to professional standards."

National Jewish Welfare Board established.

1918

American Association of Hospital Social Workers (later American Association of Medical Social Workers; subsequently merged into NASW) organized.

First formal training program for psychiatric social workers instituted at Smith College, Northampton, Massachusetts.

Vocational Rehabilitation Act of 1918 (c. 107, 40 Stat. 617) passed June 27—first national program providing physically handicapped veterans with occupational training and prostheses; extended in 1920 for rehabilitation into civilian life.

1919

National Association of Visiting Teachers (later National Association of School Social Workers; subsequently merged into NASW) formed.

Association of Training Schools for Professional Social Work (forerunner of American Association of Schools of Social Work, now Council on Social Work Education) formed by leaders of 15 schools of social work—the first organization concerned exclusively with social work education.

1920

Chicago School of Civics and Philanthropy became the Graduate School of Social Service Administration, University of Chicago.

Atlanta School of Social Service (now Atlanta School of Social Work) opened in September, originating from 1919–1920 Institutes of Social Service sponsored by Neighborhood Union of Morehouse College; complete professionalization came under directorship of E. Franklin Frazier in 1922; incorporated and chartered March 22, 1924.

National Conference of Catholic Charities founded to coordinate network of sectarian social services.

Boy Scouts of America founded.

Camp Fire Girls founded.

1921

National Social Workers' Exchange became American Association of Social Workers (later merged into NASW), first national professional association of social workers.

Maternity and Infancy Hygiene Act (Shepard-Towner Bill) (c. 135, 42 Stat. 224) passed by Congress November 23—first national maternal and child health program.

Commonwealth Fund established demonstration child guidance clinics, initiating child guidance clinic movement and establishing essential role of social workers.

1923

First organized homemaker service established by Jewish Welfare Society of Philadelphia.

First course in group work in a school of social work introduced at Western Reserve University, Cleveland, Ohio.

Education and Training for Social Work published—the first major study of social work education, conducted by Professor James H. Tufts, University of Chicago.

1926

American Association of Psychiatric Social Workers (later merged into NASW) organized.

1927

First school of social work professionally certified by American Association of Schools of Social Work.

American Association for Old Age Security

organized to further national interest in legislation for the aged; Abraham Epstein appointed director.

1928

Generic social casework defined in committee report accepted by Milford Conference, November 9–10, 1928.

1929

Social Work Year Book (now *Encyclopedia of Social Work*) initiated under auspices of Russell Sage Foundation.

Social Case Work: Generic & Specific, result of 1928 Milford Conference, published by American Association of Social Workers in June.

1930

American Public Welfare Association founded.

1931

Nobel Peace Prize awarded to renowned social worker Jane Addams.

Temporary Emergency Relief Administration established in New York State by Governor Franklin Delano Roosevelt—prototype of federal public relief to the unemployed.

1932

President Herbert Hoover signed Emergency Relief and Construction Act (c. 520, 47 Stat. 709) into law July 21; a provision of the act enabled Reconstruction Finance Corporation to lend money to states for relief purposes, moving federal government into field of public relief.

Formal accreditation initiated by American Association of Schools of Social Work with development of a minimum curriculum requiring at least one academic year of professional education encompassing both classroom and field instruction.

1933

Civilian Conservation Corps Act (c. 17, 48 Stat. 22) passed by Congress on March 31—established to meet part of need caused by Great Depression to provide work and education programs for unemployed, unmarried young men in the age group 17 to 23.

Federal Emergency Relief Act (c. 30, 48 Stat. 55) passed May 12; created Federal Emergency Relief Administration (FERA), providing 25 percent matching and direct grants to states for public distribution for relief; social worker Harry Hopkins became director on May 22; FERA superseded April 8, 1935, by Works Progress

Administration (WPA) and phased out in 1936.

1934

First licensing law for social workers passed in Puerto Rico—precursor to later state laws.

National Housing Act of 1934 (c. 847, 48 Stat. 1246) enacted by Congress June 27—first law in U.S. history designed to promote housing construction.

National Foundation for Infantile Paralysis initiated by President Franklin D. Roosevelt to raise funds for Warm Springs, Georgia, treatment center; became successful Annual March of Dimes under Basil O'Connor.

1935

Health, Education and Welfare Act (Social Security Act; c. 531, 49 Stat. 620) passed by Congress August 14, providing old-age assistance benefits, a social security board, and grants to states for unemployment compensation administration, aid to dependent children, maternal and child welfare, public health work, and aid to blind; social worker Jane M. Hoey appointed first director of Federal Bureau of Public Assistance, which administered federal-state aid to the aged, the blind, and dependent children under provisions of the act.

In its program reorganization, National Conference on Social Work recognized group work as a major function of social work along with social casework, community organization, and social action.

Works Progress Administration created by presidential executive order May 6, on termination of Federal Emergency Relief Administration, committing federal government to provide work "for able-bodied but destitute workers."

1936

American Association for the Study of Group Work organized; (became American Association of Group Workers in 1946; later merged into NASW).

1937

State-administered program in North Carolina pioneered development of family planning as part of maternal and child health services.

Housing Act (c. 896, 50 Stat. 885) passed by Congress September 1 to provide subsidies and credit to states and local governments—first attempt to finance residential

accommodations for tenants not exclusively federal employees.

1938

Works Progress Administration Act (c. 554, 52 Stat. 809) passed by Congress June 21.

National Association of Day Nurseries (formerly National Federation of Day Nurseries, 1854) founded; merged in 1943 with Child Welfare League of America.

1939

Food Stamp Plan to dispose of agricultural commodities began in Rochester, New York.

1941

United Service Organization (USO) incorporated in February to coordinate services provided to armed forces and defense workers by six voluntary agencies: National Jewish Welfare Board, National Catholic Community Service, National Travelers Aid Association, Salvation Army, Young Men's Christian Association, and Young Women's Christian Association.

1942

First U.S. responsibility to provide day care for children of working mothers initiated through the Lanham Act (c. 260, 55 Stat. 361); provided 50 percent matching grants to local communities for use in the operation of day care centers and family day care homes.

United Seamen's Service established in September to provide medical, social work, and other services to merchant seamen; Bertha C. Reynolds named director.

National Association of Schools of Social Administration (now Council on Social Work Education) formed through consolidation of 34 land-grant college undergraduate social work programs.

1943

United Nations Relief and Rehabilitation Administration (UNRRA) established by 44 nations for postwar relief and refugee resettlement.

American Council of Voluntary Agencies for Foreign Service established "to promote joint program planning and coordination of national voluntary agency activities on foreign relief and rehabilitation."

1945

National Social Welfare Assembly (formerly National Social Work Council, 1923) organized; now National Assembly of National

Voluntary Health and Social Welfare Organizations.

United Nations chartered in April, including Economic and Social Council to provide "international machinery for the promotion and social advancement of all peoples" and coordinate agencies dealing with social welfare problems, such as World Health Organization (WHO), United Nations International Children's Emergency Fund (UNICEF), International Labor Office (ILO), and International Refugee Organization (IRO).

Common Human Needs, by Charlotte Towle, published by American Association of Social Workers; reaffirmed the principle of public assistance services as a right and the need for public assistance staffs to understand psychological needs and forces and their relationship to social forces and experiences.

1946

Hospital Survey and Construction Act (c. 958, 60 Stat. 1040) (Hill-Burton Act) passed by Congress August 13, initiating massive construction and expansion of inpatient hospital facilities.

National Mental Health Act (c. 538, 60 Stat. 421) passed July 3, recognizing mental illness as a national public health problem.

Association for the Study of Community Organization (ASCO) formed (later merged into NASW).

Full Employment Act of 1946 (c. 33, 60 Stat. 23) passed by Congress February 20; established policy of federal responsibility for employment; not yet implemented.

1949

Social Work Research Group (SWRG) organized (later merged into NASW).

1950

Social Workers in 1950 published by Bureau of Labor Statistics—first survey of 75,000 social workers, with 50,000 replies.

Social Security Act Amendments of 1950 (c. 809, 64 Stat. 477) passed August 28; established program of aid to permanently and totally disabled, broadened Aid to Dependent Children to include relative with whom child is living (becoming Aid to Families with Dependent Children, AFDC), extended old age and survivors' insurance, and liberalized other programs.

1951

Social Work Education in the United States, by Ernest V. Hollis and Alice L. Taylor, published—a comprehensive study of social work education "in relation to the responsibility of social work in the broad field of social welfare."

1952

U.S. Children's Bureau granted funds for special projects to develop and coordinate statewide programs for medical and social services to unwed mothers.

Council on Social Work Education (CSWE) created from temporary study and coordinating body—National Council on Social Work Education (formed in 1946)—to unite school accrediting responsibility of National Association of Schools of Social Administration and American Association of Schools of Social Work; included schools, faculty, agencies, and the public in educational policy and decisions.

1953

U.S. Department of Health, Education, and Welfare established April 11.

1954

Rutland Corner House, Brookline, Massachusetts, established—first urban transitional residence (halfway house) for mental patients.

1955

National Association of Social Workers (NASW) formed July by merger of five professional membership associations and two study groups: American Association of Group Workers, American Association of Medical Social Workers, American Association of Psychiatric Social Workers, American Association of Social Workers, Association for the Study of Community Organization, National Association of School Social Workers, and Social Work Research Group.

1957

Civil Rights Act of 1957 (P.L. 85-315, 71 Stat. 634) passed by Congress September 9—the first such act since 1875; established the Commission on Civil Rights and strengthened federal enforcement powers.

1958

A Working Definition of Social Work Practice, developed by the NASW National Commission on Practice, published by NASW; established the basic constellation of elements of social work practice.

1959

Social Work Curriculum Study, by Werner Boehm, a 13-volume "milestone in the development of effective educational programs for professions," published by CSWE.

1960

National Committee for Day Care established to promote day care as an essential part of child welfare services and to develop standards of care.

Newburgh, New York, established restrictive work requirements for welfare recipients provoking nationwide retrogression in public welfare.

1961

Juvenile Delinquency and Youth Offenses Control Act of 1961 (P.L. 87-274, 75 Stat. 572), recognizing economic and social factors leading to crime, passed by Congress; authorized grant funds for demonstration projects for comprehensive delinquency programs in ghettos.

1962

The Other America, by Michael Harrington, published, alerting the United States to the problem of poverty.

1963

Mental Retardation Facilities and Community Mental Health Centers Construction Act of 1963 (P.L. 88-164, 77 Stat. 282) passed October 31, authorizing appropriations to states; initiated significant development of community health and retardation services with single state agency administration and advisory committees with consumer representation.

Peak of the coalition civil rights movement reached with the March on Washington.

1964

Civil Rights Act of 1964 (P.L. 88-352, 78 Stat. 241) passed by Congress July 2, resulting in significant changes for minorities in institutional health care programs and procedures to assure equal treatment, in policies to eliminate discrimination in employment and preemployment, and in policies to open entry opportunities in particular occupations.

Food Stamp Act (P.L. 88-525, 785 Stat. 703) passed August 31, providing cooperative federal-state food assistance programs for improved levels of nutrition in low-income households.

Economic Opportunity Act (P.L. 88-452, 78 Stat. 508) passed by Congress August 20, establishing the Office of Economic Opportunity and calling for the creation of VISTA, Job Corps, Upward Bound, Neighborhood Youth Corps, Operation Head Start, and community action programs.

1965

Older Americans Act (P.L. 89-73, 79 Stat. 218) passed by Congress July 14, creating the Administration on Aging, the first central body within the federal government dealing with the aged.

Medicare Act (P.L. 89-97, 79 Stat. 286) enacted July 30 as Title XVIII of Social Security Act; provided federal health insurance program for hospital and related care for the aged and disabled and voluntary supplemental insurance for physicians' fees.

Medicaid enacted July 30 as Title XIX of Social Security Act; provided federal grants to match state programs of hospital and medical services for welfare recipients and medically indigent.

Elementary and Secondary Education Act of 1965 (P.L. 89-10, 79 Stat. 27) passed April 11, initiating first major infusion of federal funds into U.S. educational system; provided aid to economically disadvantaged children, counseling and guidance services, community education, and planning.

Academy of Certified Social Workers (ACSW) established by NASW as the national standard-setting organization for social work practice.

1966

Narcotic Addict Rehabilitation Act of 1966 (P.L. 89-793, 80 Stat. 1438) passed by Congress November 8, emphasizing total treatment and aftercare rather than criminal prosecution and fragmented efforts.

Comprehensive Health Planning and Public Health Services Amendments of 1966 (P.L. 89-749, 80 Stat. 1180) passed by Congress November 3, authorizing grants to support comprehensive state planning for health service personnel and facilities.

1967

In re Gault decision in May by U.S. Supreme Court ruled that timely notice of all charges against a juvenile must be given, that the child has a right to be represented by legal counsel and the right to confront and cross-examine complainants, and that the child has the right to protection against self-incrimination in juvenile deliquency proceedings.

Child Health Act of 1967 (P.L. 90-248, 81 Stat. 821) passed by Congress January 2, adding three new types of medical care project grants (infant care, family planning, and dental care) to social security.

1969

Family Assistance Plan proposed by President Richard M. Nixon in historic message to Congress; asserted failure of welfare system and recommended a federal welfare system with virtually a guaranteed annual income; never voted out of Congressional committee.

1971

ACTION agency formed through President Nixon's reorganization plan, centralizing direction of volunteer agencies, including VISTA, Peace Corps, and others.

Comprehensive Child Development Act passed by Congress to provide comprehensive, high-quality day care and support services to all children; vetoed by Nixon.

Education-Legislative Action Network (ELAN) initiated by NASW as formal legislative structure, committing social work profession to legislative advocacy as a professional responsibility.

1972

Community-based work and education programs for juvenile delinquents established by Massachusetts Youth Services Department to abolish juvenile reformatories.

Supplemental Security Income (SSI) (P.L. 92-603, 86 Stat. 1329) established in social security amendments of 1972, passed October 30, effective January 1, 1974. Principle of "right to treatment" established in *Wyatt v. Stickney* by Frank M. Johnson, Jr., chief judge of U.S. Middle District Court in Montgomery, Alabama; ruling set forth minimal constitutional standards of care, treatment, and habilitation for patients involuntarily confined to public mental hospitals in Alabama.

National Institute on Drug Abuse established March 21 by Drug Abuse Office and Treatment Act of 1972 (P.L. 92-255, 86 Stat. 65) to provide leadership, policies, and goals for the total federal effort to prevent, control, and treat narcotic addiction and drug abuse.

Professional Standards Review Organizations (PRSO) initiated October 30 as part of social security amendments of 1972 (P.L. 92-603, 86 Stat. 1329)—a national program of local and state organizations to establish service standards and review quality and costs of health services provided to beneficiaries of Medicare, Medicaid, and Maternal and Child Health programs; through NASW intervention, included social workers in all phases.

1973

Health Maintenance Organization Act of 1973 (P.L. 93-222, 87 Stat. 914) enacted December 29, authorizing federal aid to support and stimulate group medical practice; through NASW intervention, included social service components and standards.

1974

Child Abuse Prevention and Treatment Act (P.L. 93-247, 88 Stat. 4) passed by Congress January 31, initiating financial assistance for demonstration programs for prevention, identification, and treatment of child abuse and neglect and establishing National Center on Child Abuse and Neglect.

1975

National Health Planning and Resources Development Act of 1974 (P.L. 93-641, 88 Stat. 2225) enacted January 4, combining Regional Medical Programs, Comprehensive Health Planning, and Hill-Burton programs to establish an integrated system of national, state, and area planning agencies with consumer majorities on policy bodies.

Social Service Amendments of 1974 (P.L. 93-647, 88 Stat. 2337) enacted January 4 as Title XX of the Social Security Act, initiating comprehensive social service programs directed toward achieving economic self-support and preventing dependence; five levels of services, meeting federal standards, were implemented by states with 75 percent federal subsidy; initiated and planned through NASW intervention.

Education of All Handicapped Children Act of 1975 (P.L. 94-142, 89 Stat. 773) enacted November 29, extending national public education policy to mandate free public education for all handicapped and (through NASW intervention) providing for social work services in the schools by 1978.

Political Action for Candidate Election (PACE) initiated under Federal Campaign Elections Act as political action committee of NASW, committing social work profession to political action as a professional responsibility.

1976

In a class action suit, Judge Frank M. Johnson, Jr., U.S. Middle District Court, Montgomery, Alabama, ruled on January 13 that conditions of confinement in the Alabama penal system constituted cruel and unusual punishment when they bore no reasonable relationship to legitimate institutional goals.

Health Professional Educational Assistance Act of 1976 (P.L. 94-484, 90 Stat. 2243) enacted October 12, applying to all health professions; authorized funding to train social workers in health care, including administration, policy analysis, and social work; first mention of schools of social work to make an appearance in national health legislation.

1978

Child Abuse Prevention and Treatment and Adoption Reform Act of 1978 (P.L. 95-266, 92 Stat. 205) passed April 24, extending the 1974 act and initiating new programs to encourage and improve adoptions.

Full Employment and Balanced Growth Act of 1978 (P.L. 95-523, 68 Stat. 590) passed by Congress October 27 through the tenacity of Representative Augustus Hawkins of California; reaffirmed right of all Americans to employment and asserted federal government's responsibility to promote full employment, production, real income, balanced growth, and better economic policy planning and coordination.

1981

Omnibus Budget Reconciliation Act of 1981 (P.L. 97-35, 95 Stat. 357) passed by Congress August 13, initiating federal policy reversal on "general welfare" responsibility for human services, dismantling federal programs (including food stamps, child nutrition, comprehensive employment and training, community development) by means of block grants under the guise of decentralization to states.

Social Service Block Grant Act (P.L. 97-35, 95 Stat. 357) passed August 13; part of Omnibus Budget Reconciliation Act of 1981, it amended Title XX of Social Security Act to consolidate social service programs and decentralize responsibility to the states.

1982

Tax Equity and Fiscal Responsibility Act of 1982 (P.L. 97-248, 96 Stat. 324) passed by Congress September 3, initiating severe cutbacks in service provisions of Medicare, Medicaid, Utilization and Quality Control Peer Review, AFDC, child support enforcement, Supplemental Security Income and unemployment compensation; also provided "largest tax increase ever recommended in a single piece of legislation."

1983

Social Security Amendments of 1983 (P.L. 98-81, 97 Stat. 65) passed April 20, securing the program and providing mandatory coverage of federal employees and employees of nonprofit organizations; withdrew and reduced benefits such as cost-of-living delay to calendar year, increased retirement age, and reduced initial benefits.

1985

Balanced Budget and Emergency Deficit Control Act (Gramm-Rudman-Hollings Act, P.L. 99-177) passed by Congress; although challenged in the courts, it resulted in anticipatory budget cuts from domestic programs.

CHAUNCEY A. ALEXANDER

For further information, see biographical section; HISTORY AND EVOLUTION OF SOCIAL WORK PRACTICE; HISTORY OF SOCIAL WELFARE.

HMOs SEE HEALTH CARE FINANCING; HEALTH SERVICE SYSTEM; PRIMARY HEALTH CARE

HOEY, JANE M. See biographical section.

HOME HEALTH CARE. See LONG-TERM CARE.

HOMELESSNESS

Every day, in all parts of the country, but particularly in urban centers, more single adults, families, and youths join the ranks of the homeless. No level of government or concerned group can agree on the magnitude of the problem. According to Bassuk (1984), the National Coalition for the Homeless estimated that there were 2.5 million homeless persons in 1983 and that this probably increased to 3 million in 1984. The U.S. Department of Housing and Urban Development (HUD) estimates that there were 250,000 to 350,000 homeless persons in 1984 (Bassuk, 1984). It is likely that the HUD estimate was too low and that the Coalition's estimate was too high.

The severity of the homeless problem varies noticeably by region and city size. The West has the highest share of the nation's homeless. Almost one third of all homeless people in metropolitan areas are in the West, although only 19 percent of the country's population lives there. The greater concentration of homeless persons in the West probably reflects the attractiveness of its climate and perceived employment opportunities. It should be noted that this area generally lacks old, low-cost housing such as single room occupancy (SRO) hotels (U.S. Department of Housing and Urban Development [HUD], 1984).

No census of homeless persons has been conducted in America because one can count only those homeless persons who use emergency shelters. A significant group of homeless persons do not use the emergency shelter system, however, and cannot be counted reliably. No study can describe their condition, and their needs can only be guessed (Perales, 1984). Whatever their number and wherever their location, homeless persons are visible, their numbers appear to be increasing, and they present an array of problems without easy solutions.

The homeless person has been defined as a person with no fixed abode (Lamb, 1984) or a person without a settled way of living (Baasler et al., 1983). Homelessness is not a modern phenomenon. It can be traced as far back as the ancient cities of Greece (Bahr, 1973). It is, however, a phenomenon not found among tribal societies. Homelessness is most prevalent during periods of social

change and natural disasters such as war, the industrial revolution, famine, flood, or earthquake. Today, significant numbers of homeless persons are found in both developed and underdeveloped countries.

Until the 1970s, a homeless person was generally viewed as a white male alcoholic who had broken all ties with his family and refused help from social agencies. He lived in a distinctive area known as "Skid Row." Skid Row was easy to recognize by its cheap hotels, bars and restaurants, rescue missions, parks, day labor offices, burlesque theaters, all-night movies, liquor stores, and blood banks (Blumberg, 1978).

Skid Row was an American invention. In 1872, Jerry McAuley opened the Water Street Mission in New York City, followed one year later by the Rev. John Dooley, who opened the first cheap Bowery lodging house. With the appearance of the gospel mission and the lodging house, Skid Row was born (Bahr, 1973). Homelessness, powerlessness, poverty, addiction, and alienation make up the lifestyle of a person on Skid Row. By the 1970s Skid Row was viewed as a human condition and not just a residential location (Blumberg, 1978). The unifying element underlying the diversity of definitions of Skid Row was a " 'detachment from society characterized by the absence or attenuation of the affiliative bonds that link settled persons to a network of interconnected social structures,' or, in a word, disaffiliation" (Bahr & Garrett, 1976, p. 13).

In 1973 Bahr wrote

> The general trend toward a gradual disappearance of Skid Rows will probably continue. Among the concomitants of the decline . . . will be an increase in the number of multiple-problem persons, higher rates of mental illness, alcoholism, violent crime. . . . The clients who remain will have more severe problems, or a wider variety of problems, and the chances of successful treatment . . . can be expected to decline. (p. 37)

One of the most dominant responses to Skid Row people is fear, and avoidance prompted by fear. This is especially true with regard to Skid Row men. The homeless man is seen as dirty, defective, and morally inferior. He is diseased, hopeless, and nonredeemable. He tends to be treated by agents of society with intolerance and disrespect, fear, disgust, and apprehension. Even representatives of helping professions or charitable organizations are more apt to refer homeless men elsewhere, to "where they belong," than to treat them as people with solvable problems (Bahr, 1973). Although Skid Rows have generally disappeared, these attitudes persist.

Causes of Homelessness

Except for persons who are victims of war or natural disasters, no single, simple reason exists for an individual's becoming homeless, although there is agreement about the general causes of homelessness in America today. These include:

■ The recession—unemployment reached a peak of 10.7 percent in November 1982, the highest level since the Great Depression.

■ A dearth of low-cost housing.

■ The impact of long-term changes in national policy regarding the mentally ill.

■ The deliberate attempt by the federal government to decrease the number of people receiving Social Security Disability Insurance (Bassuk, 1984, pp. 40–45).

Unemployment. The social and psychological effects of unemployment are often devastating. Unemployment creates internal distress, disrupts personal support networks, and causes social dislocation (Baxter et al., 1981). The impact of the recession on many people who were barely surviving has not been fully appreciated. These people lost not only jobs but also health insurance and the ability to pay for housing (Jones, 1983).

Dearth of Low-Cost Housing. An absolute shortage of affordable, low-cost housing exists today in the United States. In 1982 the Bureau of the Census's annual survey of housing found that the number of households with two or more related families sharing space jumped from 1.2 million units to 1.9 million units—an increase of 58 percent. This was the first such significant increase since 1950 (Cuomo, 1983).

Nationally, the number of new housing starts in 1982 was the lowest since the Bureau of the Census began reporting such data in 1959. Of great concern is the loss of SRO units in urban areas, which have always been inexpensive and which single persons and disabled people have always used for refuge (Perales, 1984). In New York City from 1978 to 1982, SRO units declined from 50,500 to 18,000. The gentrification of inner-city neighborhoods replaced old low-cost housing with fewer units at higher costs. As many as 2.5 million people may be involuntarily displaced from their homes each year—people who are casualties of "revitalization projects, evictions, economic development schemes, and rent inflation," while at the same time, half a million units of low-rent dwellings are lost each year through the combined forces of conversion, abandonment, inflation, arson, and demolition (Cuomo, 1983).

More and more often, people sleeping in emergency shelters include parents and children whose primary reason for homelessness is their poverty. They have arrived in shelters not from the streets, but from some dwelling (typically not their own) where they were no longer welcome or where they could no longer afford to stay. Across New York State in 1983, for example, more than 143,000 poor families were "doubled up" in the homes of other people. At least 4,000 such families were "tripled up" (Perales, 1984). Rural areas were also affected. The Mortgage Bankers Association reports that in 1982, 130,000 Americans lost their homes as a result of foreclosure. Press and media coverage of farm foreclosures—often with tragic human consequences—is becoming increasingly common.

Deinstitutionalization. A report by Goldman (1983) observed that the deinstitutionalization of mental patients has been widely assumed to be a major reason for the increase in the homeless population. Nationally, the same report observed, the number of mental patients declined from 505,000 in 1973 to 125,000 in 1981. But most of the decline in the population of state hospitals resulted from deaths of elderly patients (20 to 40 percent) and from transfers to nursing homes (85,000).

The relationship between homelessness and mental illness is to be found in the changing admission policies of state hospitals, which have resulted in a shift in the locus of care from the state hospital to the local mental health clinic (Goldman, 1983). The chronically mentally ill, who in the past would have been cared for as long-term patients of state mental hospitals, are now treated on a short-term basis in local general hospitals or clinics. It is this group, along with those who have never received any psychiatric care, who constitute a significant proportion of the homeless (Goldman, 1983). The estimates range from 20 to 60 percent, although confusion exists as to whether these figures refer to the number of persons who were ever in a psychiatric hospital or the number who now show psychotic symptoms. Whatever the number, and it is probably more like 25 percent, the majority of the homeless poor are not seriously mentally disabled (Cuomo, 1983). Nevertheless, those who are mentally disabled are highly visible and require a range of services that does not presently exist.

Because of this high visibility, the governor of New York State (Cuomo, 1983) observed, the link with chronic mental disability was the least understood aspect of homelessness today. If all the homeless mentally ill persons in America were committed to institutions, a "homeless" problem in America would still exist. Chronically mentally ill persons did not create the homeless problem. They are among the victims, for in addition to their chronic mental illness they also have no place to live.

Federal Support Programs. In March 1981, the federal government implemented an attempt to find ineligible recipients of Social Security Disability Insurance. Between March 1981 and April 1984, when the administration halted its review of the beneficiary rolls, from 150,000 to 200,000 people lost their benefits. It is not unreasonable to infer that the loss of disability benefits left some people without the means to pay for their housing (Bassuk, 1984). During this same period the numbers of persons seeking shelter continued to increase.

Who Are the Homeless?

On an average night in 1983, 20,210 people in New York State spent the night in emergency accommodations provided by government, churches, synagogues, or private charities. Of these, more than 11,000 were members of homeless families and 9,000 were single individuals (Perales, 1984). The number of homeless people who will not

accept shelter care and are on the streets cannot be estimated.

The homeless of today are extremely heterogeneous. No longer do they fit the traditional stereotype—a single, middle-aged, white alcoholic male. They are men, women, runaway youths, and families. Some have chronic disabilities—mental illness, alcoholism, and other forms of substance abuse. They are persons who are experiencing severe personal crisis and who have suffered from adverse economic conditions (HUD, 1984).

Homeless Men. Single homeless persons are predominantly men who reflect the ethnic composition of the area in which they are sheltered. They have limited skills and no support network. Few have been married. They are relatively young and either without any resources or chronically dependent on public welfare. About one-third have histories of psychiatric hospitalization and about one-half are substance abusers (Hoffman et al., 1982).

Homeless Women. Homeless women as a group are widely thought to be increasing. In New York City, for instance, no separate facility for homeless women existed until 1950, and then on a relatively small scale. From 1978 to 1984, however, women, both in numbers and as a percentage of total shelter users, have made increasing use of city shelter services. The New York City January–August shelter census shows an increase from 46 women (versus 2,074 men) in 1978 to 736 women (versus 5,374 men) in 1984 (New York City Human Resources Administration, 1984).

Demographic information for 1983 indicates a high proportion of minorities, although fewer Hispanics are found among homeless women than among homeless men—54 percent black, 26 percent white, 8 percent Hispanic. Of the women, 30 percent were ages 21–29, with 66 percent under 40. Most women fall into the "personal crisis" category of homelessness (HUD, 1984).

Homeless Families. Homeless families appear to be the fastest growing segment of the homeless population, as well as the group most clearly homeless because of economic distress. According to New York City's Human Resources Administration (quoted in Rimer, 1984), the October 1984 figure of 3,179 homeless families known to the city represents an increase of 1,000 families from 1983.

A 1984 HUD report concludes that homeless families are not for the most part the middle-class stereotype—that is, people who had steady jobs and owned houses but who became victims of the 1982–1983 recession. Rather, they were families who were already in a marginal situation, such as single-parent welfare households unable to afford the rent. According to the HUD report, family members make up 21 percent of the total homeless population.

Homeless Youths. It is estimated that between 242,000 and 500,000 youngsters are homeless in the United States. Although there are 1–2 million runaways nationally, about one quarter (500,000) are homeless. A runaway youth is different from a homeless youth, however.

A runaway episode is usually the result of impulsive acting-out behavior. The youngster knows that his or her behavior will not permanently sever family ties and that the family will contact local authorities to bring the youth back and achieve a reconciliation. Runaway youngsters generally want to return home.

In contrast, a youngster usually becomes homeless in response to an overall family situation. It is not an impulsive response to a specific family problem. Usually deep family pathology is present and the entire family is in trouble. For a long time the young person may have been living under intolerable conditions such as physical or sexual abuse or verbal attacks (U.S. Senate, 1980).

Characteristics of homeless youths include the following: the average age for males is 17–18 and for females, 15–16; slightly more males are homeless than females; the ethnicity of homeless youths reflects the geographic locale in which they are found; educational achievement ranges from the third to eighth grade; the majority have had some type of counseling; many have medical problems; and a majority come from recombined families that include an original parent and one other adult. The increased number of youths who are homeless appears to reflect the decreased ability or willingness of parents to

invest time and energy to help their children grow to adulthood. Abused adolescents make up one quarter of all reported abuse cases (U.S. Senate, 1980), and from 20–30 percent of runaways report a foster care background. Many youths are neglected, abused, or forced out by their families. The incidence of physical abuse by parents is high among homeless youth, about 84 percent; sexual abuse is not as prevalent. A significant correlation appears to exist between child neglect or abuse and alcoholism. Many youngsters who have been forced to leave home experienced sexual and physical abuse by parents who were alcohol abusers (U.S. Senate, 1980).

Homeless Mentally Ill. The characteristics of the homeless mentally ill are similar in many respects to the general homeless population. They tend to be young, predominantly male, and reflective of the local ethnicity. Many have been in psychiatric hospitals at some time in their lives, and they tend to reject institutional solutions to their problems. A complicating factor is that many homeless mentally ill are known to be alcoholics and substance abusers, and a significant number have been in jail or prison.

Based on a sample study of men who use New York City emergency shelters, it is estimated that approximately 22 percent of the homeless adults were found to be in need of some level of mental health care and 3 percent of these needed psychiatric hospitalization (Hoffman, 1982, pp. 13, 14). In addition, the street people who live in the streets, parks, subways, and bus and rail terminals are difficult to reach, difficult to count, and resistant to contact. They do not use shelters. It is estimated that 50 percent of the street people need some level of patient care (Bachrach, 1984).

Who Serves the Homeless?

Homelessness reflects the failure of various federal and state policies. The controversy about its origins has been used to avoid confronting the more basic question—will society provide adequate housing for its citizens and will society care for its most disabled individuals? No single programmatic initiative exists at any level of government to solve the problem of homelessness. Rather, there has been a scattered response by all levels of government and charitable groups to meet the emergency needs of homeless people by developing emergency shelters. Emergency shelters are necessary, but there is little beyond emergency shelters to address the homeless problem on a permanent basis.

Federal Government. In 1983, public laws P.L. 98-8 and P.L. 98-181 were enacted. P.L. 98-8 provides emergency food and shelter. A program was to be administered by the Federal Emergency Management Agency (FEMA), for which $100 million was appropriated—half for use by a national board consisting of voluntary agencies and chaired by FEMA. The remaining $50 million was to be distributed among the states to support local programs. P.L. 98-181 authorized $60 million to HUD to make grants to states, localities, and non-profit agencies to operate programs for the homeless.

A federal Interagency Task Force on Food and Shelter was also organized. It is chaired by the Secretary of the Department of Health and Human Services who acts as a "broker" between the federal government and the private sector when the latter wants to initiate a food or shelter project (HUD, 1984).

Governments. States have provided services to the homeless by "passing through" to local governments monies from federal sources such as FEMA, Community Service Block Grants, and Social Services Block Grants. In addition, many states have appropriated additional funds for new or expanded programs; for example, California allocated $2.5 million, Massachusetts $4 million for emergency shelters, and New York $50 million over four years for sheltering the homeless.

Not-for-Profit Sector. Nationally, the not-for-profit sector operates most of the homeless shelters, provides almost two-thirds of the financing for shelters, volunteers a large amount of labor, and makes in-kind donations of food and supplies. It is the major direct provider of shelters with the possible exception of New York City (HUD, 1984).

Shelter. In October 1979, six homeless men filed a class-action suit against the State and City of New York challenging the sufficiency and quality of shelters for homeless men in New York City—*Callahan v. Carey*. In August 1981, the City of New York signed a consent decree in which it agreed to provide shelter and board to each homeless man who applies provided that (1) the man meets the eligibility standard to qualify for the general relief program established in New York State, or (2) the man by reason of physical, mental, or social dysfunction is in need of temporary shelter. The consent decree recognized the right to shelter and established guidelines for the provision of public shelter care. Although not part of the formal decree, these provisions were extended to women also.

Nationwide, an estimated 111,000 persons can be housed on any given night in emergency shelters. Of this number, 12,000 are beds for runaway youths and 8,000 for battered or abused women. The remaining 91,000 beds serve all other homeless persons—single men, single women, and families. By the federal government's minimum estimate of 250,000 homeless people nationwide, this figure is 139,000 beds short of the need. By the National Coalition for the Homeless's estimate of 3 million, this figure is 2,889,000 beds short of the need. In either case, it is obvious that on any given night, a significant number of Americans do not have a place to sleep.

Solutions

Homeless persons are a heterogeneous group but they have one common need—permanent, affordable housing. Housing is a fundamental problem for the homeless (HUD, 1984). In addition, some subgroups among the homeless such as homeless youths and the chronically mentally ill need special services.

Based on a knowledge of homeless youths and their families, special services would include the early identification of such families and intervention of supportive services. A large majority of homeless young people have had some kind of prior counseling under the aegis of the school, public assistance, juvenile justice, mental health, or child welfare system (U.S. Senate, 1980). Helping professions need to review and evaluate the significance and appropriateness of this counseling. Homeless youths have very pessimistic expectations. They see few viable options for themselves. Experts believe that these youngsters will probably repeat their own histories, abuse their own children, and eventually throw their children out to become homeless themselves. Unless some means can be found to break the cycle, the pattern of homelessness will be perpetuated by the current youth population on the next generation (U.S. Senate, 1980).

Chronic mental illness does not by itself cause homelessness (Bassuk, 1984). The majority of chronically mentally ill persons live with their families or in sheltered living situations. A minority of the total population of chronically mentally ill are homeless (Lamb, 1984). Deinstitutionalization did not cause homelessness. It did change the way society treats patients, however, including where society treats them, and it resulted in mentally ill people becoming more visible in all communities.

Deinstitutionalization was a well-intentioned and enlightened reform but it did not proceed according to plan. The first step was accomplished—fewer patients now reside in state hospitals. But the second step, the development of a continuum of care in the community that includes supervised homes, has not occurred to the degree necessary. The promise of the 1963 Community Mental Health Center Act was also never fulfilled. The promised federal aid to build and operate community mental health centers never occurred in the magnitude required (Bassuk, 1984). One solution to the problems of the chronically mentally ill is to carry out the aborted plans of the 1963 act by providing a spectrum of housing options and related health care and social services to this needy population. In addition, one must recognize the limitations of psychiatry. Some people cannot be rehabilitated, and for these persons the goal should be a safe and humane asylum (Bassuk, 1984).

The energies being consumed in blaming deinstitutionalization for the plight of the chronically mentally ill and homeless are of no help to the chronically mentally ill. The sole purpose of the continuing argument is to divert and postpone the responsibility that must be assumed by the states and federal government for the care of our chronically mentally ill citizens.

As long as people are homeless, society must provide emergency shelter care, including food, beds, and bathing facilities. But emergency shelter care is no solution to homelessness. Individuals and families should not live in emergency shelters. This country needs a national housing program for low-income individuals and families, a program that will fund the construction of permanent housing and a rent subsidy program (Cuomo, 1983). For those people who cannot work because of physical or mental disability, society must provide income assistance sufficient to allow for decent, stable housing (Cuomo, 1983).

The solution to the problem of homelessness is neither complicated nor profound. It is true that the solutions must be targeted to different populations, but common to all the solutions is the commitment of government to provide decent, safe housing for those who cannot do so on their own.

Social workers have a role in every aspect of the problem of homelessness—as counselors, case managers, advocates, and agents of change. Schools of social work need to train their students to work with the most disadvantaged groups and to develop techniques that are responsive to the needs of these people. Two good programs have been undertaken by the Columbia University School of Social Work and the New York University School of Social Work, who have developed case management services in several New York City shelters.

SARAH CONNELL

For further information, see DEINSTITUTIONALIZATION; GENERAL AND EMERGENCY ASSISTANCE; MENTAL HEALTH AND ILLNESS; RUNAWAYS.

References

Baasler, T. et al. (1983). "On Vagrancy and Psychosis." *Community Mental Health Journal, 19*(1), 27–40.

Bachrach, L. L. (1984). "Research on Services for the Homeless Mentally Ill." *Hospital and Community Psychiatry, 35*(9), 910–913.

Bahr, H. M. (1973). *Skid Row: An Introduction to Disaffiliation.* New York: Oxford University Press.

Bahr, H. M., & Garrett, G. R. (1976). *Women Alone: The Disaffiliation of Urban Females.* Lexington, Mass.: D.C. Heath & Co.

Bassuk, E. (1984). "The Homelessness Problem." *Scientific American, 251*(1), 40–45.

Baxter, E., et al. (1981). *Private Lives/Public*

Spaces. New York: Community Service Society.

Blumberg, L. U. et al. (1978). *Skid Row as a Human Condition*. New Brunswick, N.J.: Rutgers Center of Alcohol Studies.

Cuomo, M. (1983, August). *1933/1983—Never Again*. Report to the National Governor's Association Task Force on the Homeless, Portland, Maine.

Goldman, H., et al. (1983). "Deinstitutionalization: The Data Demythologized." *Hospital and Community Psychiatry*, *34*(2), 129–134.

Hoffman, S., et al. (1982, May). *Who are the Homeless*? Study prepared by New York State Office of Mental Health, New York City.

Jones, R. E. (1983). "Street People and Psychiatry." *Hospital and Community Psychiatry*, *34*(9), 807–811.

Lamb, R. H. (1984). "Deinstitutionalization and the Homeless Mentally Ill." *Hospital and Community Psychiatry*, *35*(9), 899–907.

New York City Human Resources Administration. (1984, April). *New York City Plan for Homeless Adults*. Report prepared for Administration of Mayor Edward I. Koch, New York City.

Perales, C. A. (1984). *Homeless in New York State*. Albany: New York State Department of Social Services.

Rimer, S. (1984, November 19). "Homeless Spend Nights in City Welfare Office." *New York Times*, p. A1.

U.S. Department of Housing and Urban Development. (1984). *A Report to the Secretary on the Homeless and Emergency Shelters*. Washington, D.C.: U.S. Government Printing Office.

U.S. Senate. Subcommittee on the Constitution of the Committee on the Judiciary. (1980). *Homeless Youth: The Saga of "Pushouts" and "Throwaways" in America* (S. Prt. 96-80). Washington D.C.: U.S. Government Printing Office.

HOMOSEXUALITY: GAY MEN

That this is the first inclusion of a specific entry on "Gay Men" in the *Encyclopedia of Social Work* is a measure of recent changes in the public's perceptions of homosexuality. Prior to the 1970s, public discussion of this phenomenon was minimal. What little research existed generally assumed that homosexuality was an illness or antisocial behavior, or the research limited itself to the study of disturbed homosexuals who had sought treatment (Bieber et al., 1962). Even among gay and lesbian people, there was little sense of community and few opportunities for meeting others for social support and increased self-awareness (Berger, 1982a, pp. 187–188).

In the last 15 years a revolution has taken place in gay people's perception of themselves. Gay people began to discredit the notion of homosexuality as an individual illness and replace it with a political definition: "homosexual" is a socially constructed category used by oppressive societies to control behavior (Wittman, 1972). To be gay is to be a member of an oppressed minority, similar in many ways to racial and ethnic minority groups (Hacker, 1971; Paul, 1982). Following models provided by earlier civil rights groups, gays organized support groups, political action organizations, and specialized social services, all directed at alleviating oppression and changing social views to accommodate the new view of gays as oppressed people deserving of civil rights.

The underlying theme has been one of legitimization. "Gay is Good" was adopted as the slogan of a movement that is now international in scope, and the emphasis has been on a newly found self-pride. Even the vocabulary has changed. Gay people rejected the term "homosexual," which they saw as imposed by a medically oriented heterosexual perspective, and substituted the term "gay." Their success in achieving public recognition of their new status is reflected in the widespread public acceptance of the word "gay." Despite its inaccurate connotation of flightiness or joy, the new term is one that gay people have used for centuries to describe themselves (Boswell, 1980, p. 43). Its current use signals a new stance: gay people will no longer allow the heterosexual majority to define their status. (Because the term "gay" is often assumed to refer to men, however, many homosexual women prefer to call themselves "lesbians.")

What Is a Gay Person?

Confusion and misconceptions have characterized public understanding of gayness. Prior to the 1960s, both in the professional literature and in the popular media, the absence of information about homosexuality allowed inaccurate public perceptions to thrive. Since then, many popular presentations—books, plays, television programs—have perpetuated inaccuracies, and professionals have sometimes joined in.

A good way to begin correcting the inaccuracies is by establishing a definition of homosexuality and describing its incidence. It is also necessary to challenge a number of common misconceptions about gay men.

Moses & Hawkins (1982, pp. 43–44) argue that to understand homosexuality it is necessary to distinguish among three components of sexual identity. Each component is independent of the others. *Gender identity* is the individual's perception of himself or herself as male or female and is established early in life. Research indicates that gender identity is firmly fixed and highly resistant to change by the age of 3 or 4 (Money & Ehrhardt, 1972, pp. 176–179).

Gender role refers to the set of role behaviors generally expected of males and females; that is, women are expected to be "feminine"—unaggressive, emotional, and reliant on others—and men are expected to embody "masculine" attributes that are the opposite of feminine ones. Although these gender role distinctions have been attacked by feminists, gay men, and others, they still play a major role in defining socially appropriate male and female behavior.

Sexual orientation concerns the individual's preference for partners of the same sex, opposite sex, or both sexes for sexual and affectional relations. Although many people believe that sexual attraction is the only determinant of sexual orientation, the desire to share affection or become life partners also plays a role. A gay man, then, is one who is attracted primarily to other men to satisfy sexual and affectional needs.

This model is useful in clarifying misconceptions that have arisen as a result of confusing the three components of sexual identity. Men with a gay sexual orientation perceive themselves as men and want to remain that way (gender identity); they almost universally act in ways that are socially perceived as masculine (gender role).

But homosexuality is too complex to be understood by this model alone. Beginning with the pioneering work of Kinsey and his associates, researchers have come to recognize that sexual orientation in human populations occurs on a continuum from those who are exclusively homosexual to those who are exclusively heterosexual (Kinsey, Pomeroy, & Martin, 1948, pp. 636–641). Most individuals fall somewhere in between. As Kinsey argued,

> Males do not represent two discrete populations, heterosexual and homosexual. . . . The living world is a continuum in each and every one of its aspects. The sooner we learn this concerning human sexual behavior, the sooner we shall reach a sound understanding of the realities of sex. (Kinsey, Pomeroy, & Martin, 1948, p. 639)

In addition, sexual orientation may change over time. A man who is primarily homosexual in early adulthood may become more heterosexual in later life. Or, as discovered by Berger (1984) in his study of older gay men, it is not uncommon for a man with a primarily heterosexual orientation in early adulthood to develop primarily homosexual interests in middle age.

To understand the complexities of sexual orientation, it is necessary to view homosexuality as an *identity formation process* that occurs over time. In an identity formation model proposed by Berger (1983b), a homosexual identity results when the individual completes three independent tasks. The most important features of the model are that these tasks operate independently, that they occur over time, and that homosexuality is a personal and social identity that is the result of intrapsychic and social events.

One task in the homosexual identity formation model is *sexual encounter,* that is, physical contact of a sexual nature with a member of the same sex. *Social reaction,* or the labeling of the individual by others as homosexual, is another task. A number of subtasks are subsumed under the *identity* task, in which the individual experiences identity confusion, a state of discomfort triggered by an incongruence, for example, between an overt same-sex experience and a self-image as heterosexual.

Over time the individual begins to label himself or herself as a "gay person," and confronts the question of how to manage this new identity. Should the new or emerging self-identity be shared with others and, if so, under what circumstances? The individual generally resolves these and other identity issues with the help of peer association, developing a network of other self-identified homosexuals. For some gays a period of militancy results from their recognition of the oppression of gay people and sets the stage for eventual self-acceptance. Continuing involvement with gay peers exposes the individual to norms that counter prevalent hostile social attitudes and provides support for the view that being gay is a legitimate identity. This is a crucial factor in gay self-acceptance.

Viewing homosexuality as the result of an identity formation process that requires the completion of independent tasks helps to clarify definitions of homosexuality. Several important implications follow from this model.

Individuals do not necessarily become gay because they have had sexual experiences with persons of the same sex, even if these experiences have occurred repeatedly. Reiss (1967), for instance, described a group of adolescent boys who repeatedly had sex with older men but never identified themselves as gay. This phenomenon is also common in prisons and in some male-dominant cultures in which restrictions on the type of sexual activity (for example, inserter role only) or the circumstances of the activity allow men to engage in same-sex behavior without developing a gay identity. This phenomenon also explains why the incidence of homosexual behavior that Kinsey discovered among men is greater than the number of men who identify themselves as gay.

It is also true that others may label an individual as gay without altering the individual's self-perception as heterosexual. The media have reported individuals who viewed themselves as heterosexual but were nevertheless subjected to discrimination because others labeled them as gay (Berger & Kelly, 1981; Freiberg, 1984).

The model also implies that the social worker's identification of a client as gay may be too simplistic. The client may be anywhere along the identity formation path from identity confusion to self-acceptance. The worker can help the client to work through tasks such as dealing with the initial conflict of self-labeling as gay, problem solving around identity management issues (for example, "Should I tell my parents?"), and locating and becoming involved with gay peers.

These complexities in defining homo-

sexuality suggest the difficulties in estimating the incidence of homosexuality in the general population. How many gay men are there? The survey research Kinsey, Pomeroy, and Martin (1948) conducted on male sexual behavior shortly after World War II still provides the best estimates. Based on this work, many authors have used 10 percent as the best estimate of the proportion of men who are gay. Perhaps a more detailed picture of the incidence of male homosexuality is revealed by looking at figures reported by Kinsey, Pomeroy, and Martin (pp. 650–651):

■ Thirteen percent of males had predominantly homosexual orientations for at least three years between the ages of 16 and 55.

■ Twenty-five percent of males had more than incidental homosexual experience or reactions for at least three years between the ages of 16 and 55.

■ Thirty-seven percent of males had at least some overt homosexual experience to the point of orgasm between adolescence and old age.

Virtually everyone, whether self-identified as homosexual or heterosexual, has a close relationship with a gay man. This becomes clear in considering the typical size of an individual's network of family members, friends, work associates, and others. One of every ten males is likely to be gay.

In political terms, this means that gay people, although a minority, are a large minority. Proportionately somewhat smaller than the black minority, they are nevertheless larger than many well-recognized ethnic minority groups. Recognition of this fact set the stage for the enormous growth in gay and lesbian political clout during the 1970s and 1980s. Today gay political organizations are active on both local and national levels, and candidates for public office often openly court the newly touted "gay vote." The 1984 presidential election was the first time that gays succeeded in implementing a gay civil rights plank in the platform of the Democratic party. All this occurred in the face of a conservative political climate, suggesting that the visibility and influence of the gay minority will continue to grow.

Misconceptions and Reality

Few minority groups have been maligned as seriously and inaccurately as gay men. The invisibility of gay men, even in their own families, perpetuated misconceptions. As a result, laypersons, professionals, and even gay men themselves often have distortions in their views of male homosexuality. It is appropriate, then, to examine some of the most prevalent misconceptions.

Male homosexuality is caused by a fear of women. Gay men are also said to be repulsed by women or to be misogynists. Tripp (1975, pp. 78–79), among others, noted that the idea of the gay man as antifemale probably originated from psychoanalytic writings that stressed the role of a pathological mother in producing a gay child. According to this formulation, the son is driven away from women by the aversive role model provided by his mother.

Gay activists have pointed out that these views originated from the heterosexual bias of mental health professionals who could not understand from their perspective why a man would choose to relate intimately with another man. What these professionals failed to understand is that male homosexuality represents a proactive rather than a reactive stance—gay men act in response to their positive feelings toward men, rather than any feelings they may have toward women. Few gay men report fears of women or revulsion toward them.

Psychoanalytic explanations of male homosexuality as a fear reaction to women are sometimes humorously illogical. For example, Tripp (1975) criticized the castration-complex theories that psychoanalysts frequently used to explain male homosexuals' purported fear of heterosexuality. These theories explain homosexuality by positing that gay men fear women because they fear loss of their penis through heterosexual contact. According to one such theory, which Tripp (1975, p. 79) ridicules, "A man can become homosexual because he unconsciously imagines there are teeth in the vagina, and so, unaccountably, he chooses to place his penis in a cavity where there are real teeth."

As Tripp noted, these theories gained wide acceptance not only among psychoanalysts but also among the public. This has had unfortunate consequences. It has led to ineffective treatment programs that assume that gay men can be "converted" to heterosexuals simply by having sexual experiences with women. Some of these programs encourage promiscuity (heterosexual), teach male clients to treat women as sexual objects, and lead to disillusioned clients. Many gay men have made the unfortunate assumption that heterosexual marriage would eliminate their homosexual desires, an error that has led to many unhappy marriages (Ross, 1983).

This simplistic view of male homosexuality as a fear of women is also contradicted by the large proportion of gay men who have related sexually to women. The Kinsey data certainly indicate that most predominantly homosexual men also have significant heterosexual experiences or fantasies, and recent research indicates that 10 to 20 percent of gay men have at some time been heterosexually married (Ross, 1983). Many men function sexually with both men and women.

Gay men are compulsively sexual. In the public mind, the sexual component of homosexuality has been exaggerated. Kinsey, Pomeroy, and Martin (1948, pp. 631–632) found lower levels of sexual activity among their predominantly homosexual respondents (as measured by the frequency of orgasms), although post–Gay Liberation lifestyles may have changed this. Recent research by the Kinsey Institute and others indicates that gay men are likely to have a greater number of sexual partners than heterosexuals and that nonmonogamy is certainly more acceptable in gay partnerships than in heterosexual ones (Bell & Weinberg, 1978; Moses & Hawkins, 1982, p. 158). The Kinsey Institute's estimates of gay sexual activity are probably overstated because the institute recruited respondents only from the San Francisco area where gay lifestyles are more open than in other areas of the country. Compulsive sexuality—repeated sexual encounters that the individual finds difficult to control and uses as a means of dealing with depression or low self-esteem—is a problem that occurs among both homosexuals and heterosexuals, men and women. Like heterosexual men, most gay men spend most of their time doing things other than looking for sex or having it.

Since 1982, there have been changes in the sexual practices of gay men because of increasing public awareness of the Acquired Immune Deficiency Syndrone (AIDS) epidemic. AIDS is a viral illness that destroys the body's immune system and is nearly always fatal. About three-quarters of its victims are gay men. The discovery that the AIDS virus is sexually transmitted, together with its rapid spread through the gay male population, have led many gay community groups to advocate a new standard of sexual responsibility. Dramatic drops in the incidence of non-AIDS sexually transmitted diseases among gay men show that these appeals have worked.

Gay men sexually molest children. Some do, but statistics show consistently that the great majority of adults who sexually molest children are men whose victims are minor females and that the incidence of homosexual molesters is proportionate to their numbers in the population (National Center on Child Abuse and Neglect, 1975; Task Force on Sexual Preference, 1977). Many child molesters molest both male and female children, suggesting that this phenomenon is often independent of sexual orientation.

A related myth is that gay men "recruit" children into their ranks by sexually molesting them. There is no evidence that childhood homosexual experience causes adult homosexuality (Bell, Weinberg, & Hammersmith, 1981). Most adult homosexuals do not report a childhood homosexual experience with an adult, and many men who do report such an experience become adult heterosexuals. In any case, it is hard to understand how an experience that children perceive as traumatic can lead them to choose similar experiences as adults. Furthermore, gay men have no need to recruit because a significant proportion of men in every historical period is gay.

Most gay men today flaunt their homosexuality. In fact, most gay men conceal their sexual orientation at least some of the time. Given the high likelihood of social ostracism, the threat of difficulties in employment and housing, and the prevalence of violence against openly gay men and women, it is not surprising that concealment is a way of life for many gay people (Weinberg & Williams, 1974, Chap. 13; Bell & Weinberg, 1978, pp. 62–65; Moses & Hawkins, 1982, p. 80). Because gay men are generally indistinguishable from other men, public attitudes about gay men are formed on the basis of those who are most open about their sexual orientation. The popular media, in particular, tend to highlight the most extreme forms of public behavior, and, in the absence of more complete information about gay men, the public forms a biased view of male homosexuality.

Heterosexuals who have not confronted their homophobia may not recognize the double standard they apply to same-sex and opposite-sex behavior. Public behaviors that are taken for granted between a man and a woman are labeled flaunting when they occur between two men. Heterosexuals who complain about flaunting seem to insist that gay men conceal their sexual orientation in every situation.

However, gay men are becoming increasingly vocal with their families, friends, and work associates, and this often confuses heterosexuals who see sexual orientation as a private matter. Gay men who refuse to "pass" as heterosexual do so precisely because being gay is a public matter. Their openness is a reaction to societal oppression. Concealment means isolation from other gays, and that isolation leads to vulnerability to discrimination. Gays who refuse to pass often do so out of a desire to be part of a political process in which vulnerable members can no longer be picked off one by one; gay people who are open are free to oppose discrimination and organize to fight for redress.

Many gay men reveal their sexual orientation to others for personal reasons. They are no longer able or willing to endure the tensions that result from passing in a homophobic society—tolerating antigay remarks; living with the fear of losing a job, home, or family; and having to act out a heterosexual role to avoid rejection. An increasing number of gay men are choosing the alternative of being themselves.

Gay men are "obvious" in their dress, behavior, and mannerisms. Many people believe that all gay men are effeminate or flamboyant or that they embody characteristics typical of women. This heterosexual perspective arises because most gay men are indistinguishable from other men and are thus able to pass effectively. The statistics on the incidence of male homosexuality belie the contention that gay men can be easily differentiated. Despite its concerted efforts and its use of trained psychiatrists, the U.S. Army prior to the original Kinsey study believed that only 0.1 percent of its male inductees were homosexual; the true incidence is 100 times greater (Kinsey, Pomeroy, & Martin, 1948).

Furthermore, gay men exist in substantial numbers in every occupation, social class, and geographic region. Although Kinsey first discovered this fact in his post–World War II survey, only in the last 15 years has it become more obvious to the public, as gay men of every ilk have "come out," that is, declared their homosexuality publicly. Gay men are even in occupations formerly thought to be impervious to them. Athletes (Garner & Smith, 1977), police officers, physicians, engineers, public officials, and many others have come out, and these as well as most other occupations have organized support groups of gay colleagues. (For example, Gay Officers Action League [GOAL] represents police officers in the New York City area and, in 1984, had 74 members [*Advocate,* 1984, November 13]).

Gay men have chosen to be gay. There is a great deal of confusion about the role personal volition plays in the formation of a gay identity. Some gay men claim to have consciously chosen to be gay. As described earlier, the process of homosexual identity formation is characterized in part by individual choices. That is, an individual man may choose to apply a label to himself, he may choose to associate with others who are self-identified as gay, and he may choose how to manage others' accessibility to information about his sexual orientation.

Perhaps to emphasize the idea of choice, some gay men prefer to use the term "sexual preference." An unfortunate result of this usage, however, has been to overstate the extent to which a man may choose to be gay. This notion of choice has made it difficult for the gay community to argue that it is a minority group analogous to racial and ethnic minorities, who have no choice about their differences from the majority. Opponents of gay rights stress that gay men have chosen their status and are therefore not deserving of rights that accrue to racial and ethnic minorities. Nevertheless, the relationship between personal choice and civil rights is not a simple one. According to the U.S. Constitution, an individual may choose to practice a given religion, and the right to do so must, within limits, be protected.

Do some men become gay because they choose to do so? Most gay men admit that they had no choice about their feelings of attraction to men. However, they did choose how to react to those feelings, and their reactions may range from repression to the development of an openly gay lifestyle. It is only in that sense that gay men make a choice. Still, it is a highly constrained choice in that the repression of gay feelings in a homophobic culture can lead to a loss of self-esteem, with its attendant alienation; it also consigns the individual to the strain of living a concealed life. Berger's (1984) research on older gay men and Weinberg and Williams's (1974) survey of gay men of all ages both suggest that concealment is associated with psychological problems.

Turn-of-the-century theorists of homosexuality stressed its predetermined biological basis. One prevalent theory was that gay men represented a "third sex," a constitutionally ordained cross between the two sexes (Lauritsen & Thorstad, 1974, pp. 46–51). With the ascendancy of psychoanalytic theories in the twentieth century, professionals and the public came to believe that gays were made, not born—made as the result of faulty experiences in early childhood (Bieber, 1965). Such "nurture" theories predominate today.

It is ironic that the scientific community is today returning to biology to explain the origins of homosexuality. In a recent and exhaustive study of the practices and life histories of almost 1,500 homosexual and heterosexual men and women, Bell, Weinberg, and Hammersmith (1981) could find few factors in the individual's early life history that predicted adult homosexuality. One factor that did differentiate between homosexuals and heterosexuals was gender nonconformity—homosexuals were less likely to conform during their youth. One of these researchers, Bell (1982), suggested that adult homosexuality may be determined primarily by biology, particularly in-utero hormonal events, and modified by early childhood experiences. After many biologists failed to discover hormonal differences between heterosexuals and homosexuals, some researchers claimed to have isolated such differences by using newer and more accurate technology. As of this writing, their work remains controversial (Bohn, 1982).

Gay men are a threat to family life. There is little question that the nuclear family is today experiencing severe stress and change. Geographic mobility, changing sex roles, and intergenerational value conflicts are reshaping the family. It is unlikely that the new openness about gay lifestyles can be blamed for these changes. The increasing willingness of people to "come out," along with factors such as changes in women's career values and increases in single-person and single-parent lifestyles, are helping to change society's definition of the family.

Gay people are part of families, too. They usually have heterosexual parents and siblings and have grown up in families. Many gay men (one fifth to one third) marry heterosexually, and many of these men raise children (Ross, 1983). Other gays form nontraditional families by coupling with another same-sex individual, and some are choosing today to have children through nontraditional means such as blending, in which partners bring children from a previous marriage into a same-sex relationship; foster and adoptive parenting; and artificial insemination by donor, which is used by some lesbian families. Others become involved in family life in other ways. There is the phenomenon of the "gay uncle"—a gay relative or friend of a heterosexual couple who helps to care for that couple's children and provides an adult role model for them (Giteck, 1984). As an older gay man said to the author, "Gay people have a right to belong to the families of the world."

All religions teach that homosexuality is wrong. Although religious groups are often in the forefront of organized opposition to gay people, it is not true that all religions are opposed to gay people. Interpretations of biblical views of homosexuality vary widely, with advocates on both sides of the issue able to find biblical justification for their respective views. In any case, many people do not follow Judeo-Christian biblical teachings.

In recent years a number of religious groups have publicly stated their support for gay rights ("Support from Religious Leaders," 1984), but recognition of the sanctity of gay couples and of the rights of gays to be ordained as ministers is less widespread. Progress toward recognizing the legitimate spiritual needs of gays in their churches has been steady but uneven. In 1984, for example, the large and influential United Methodist Church General Conference forbade the ordination of openly gay men or women (Nush, 1984). At about the same time, the Unitarian Universalist Association became the first major religious denomination to approve the religious union of same-sex couples (Jones, 1984).

In response to the inhospitality of some religious groups, gays have organized alternative churches. The largest and best known is the Metropolitan Community Church (MCC), a nondenominational group begun by an openly gay minister in the late 1960s. Today MCC has over 100 member churches. Gay people of other denominations have organized religious institutions along the same lines, including Dignity (Catholic) and Integrity (Episcopalian) and the Metropolitan Community Synagogue (Jewish). These groups also have local churches and synagogues in major cities across the country.

Homosexuality is a mental illness. Szasz (1979), a radical psychiatrist, described the ways in which personal and social issues were once seen as the province of Christian theology but today have become the domain of medicine and psychiatry. Homosexuality is a prominent example in his arguments. Whereas gay men were once seen as sinners, they came to be seen as victims of a "mental illness" (Szasz, 1979, p. 5). Szasz's point is that the "medicalization" of disapproved behaviors such as homosexuality had more to do with the need of the medical and helping professions to increase their hegemony than with the behaviors themselves.

The politicization of the diagnostic process was beautifully illustrated by Bayer (1981) in a book that described the intense factionalization and in-fighting that accompanied the decision in 1973 by the American Psychiatric Association (APA) to remove homosexuality from its official list of mental disorders. For years, the inclusion of homosexuality in the APA's *Diagnostic and Statistical Manual* was cited as proof that homosexuals were mentally ill. Its removal, which was preceded by intense lobbying by gay activists, has had a profound effect on public policy and popular views. Today there is little support for the position that homosexuality is a mental illness.

Becker (1963), Gagnon and Simon (1967), and other proponents of the societal reaction theory have argued that homosexuality is not a fixed attribute intrinsic to the individual in the same way that an illness is. Rather, homosexuality is more accurately viewed as a social construct, a definition supplied by others who apply the label of homosexual or deviant to the individual. The model of homosexual identity formation presented earlier is based on this perspective.

That homosexuality is not a mental illness is buttressed by numerous studies that compared homosexuals to heterosexuals on the basis of a variety of standardized psychological tests. In the 1950s Hooker (1957, 1958), a pioneer in this area, showed that trained clinicians were unable to differentiate nonclinical samples of homosexuals from heterosexuals, based on responses of both groups to Rorschach tests, and that the two groups did not differ in their level of psychological adjustment as measured by a battery of personality tests. In the 1960s and 1970s, researchers continued to compare homosexuals and heterosexuals, using reliable, valid, and well-established measures of psychological health. In his review of these studies, Gonsiorek (1982, p. 79) stated his conclusion unambiguously: "These studies overwhelmingly suggest that homosexuality per se is not related to psychopathology or psychological adjustment."

Gay men are more sensitive and artistic than heterosexual men. Despite the popularity of this belief, it has never been subjected to empirical testing. Because all gay people at some time experience the need to hide their identities, they are probably more sensitive to the socially constructed nature of roles in contemporary society. This has been used to explain the attraction that some gay men have to the theatrical arts. Nevertheless, the research evidence indicates that gay men are found in all occupational groups.

A likely explanation for the widespread belief that gays predominate in the "artistic" professions such as interior design and theater is that, traditionally, gay men have been able to be more open about their sexual orientation in these professions. Although an openly gay police officer is likely to experience much opposition from his peers and possibly from the public, the gay lifestyle of an interior designer is socially accepted. Because being homosexual is a highly stigmatized status in American culture, gay men may also be sensitive to the experiences of oppression that they share with other minorities and with women.

Special Needs

In most ways, gay men are not special. Like other groups, they sometimes need the help of social workers. The young transient, the elderly client in need of protection, the welfare client, the chronically mentally ill client, the single parent, the depressed student, the hospital patient, the alcoholic, the acting-out adolescent, the wheelchair-bound client—any of these clients may be a gay man. In most cases the sexual orientation of the client should not be an issue. However, the gay community has many special needs that make it important for the social worker to have specialized knowledge about the ways in which sexual orientation interacts with the needs of clients.

Because of recent publicity about the epidemic of AIDS in the gay male community, the unique health care needs of gay men have received much attention (Berger, 1983a). Until recently, the most important medical needs of gay men concerned the high rates of syphilis and the problem of gonorrheal infection in atypical sites, which were often left unscreened because of the ignorance of health care professionals (Berger, 1977).

Today, additional sexually transmitted diseases pose serious threats to the health of gay men. These include a high incidence of hepatitis-B and previously rare enteric infections. AIDS is the most dramatic of these diseases, with 73 percent of its victims gay and bisexual men, according to the Centers for Disease Control (1986). Because of its association with homosexuality and often unfounded concerns about its contagious potential, AIDS is an illness that creates many secondary problems. In addition to a medical crisis, patients often experience the loss of support from friends or family, who may not be accepting of the patient's homosexuality; the loss of housing and employment as a result of the irrational fears and prejudices of landlords and employers; and poor care from hospital and clinic personnel who seek to avoid the patient. Social workers can play an important role in helping patients and families to deal with concerns about death and can serve as advocates for the civil and medical rights of AIDS patients (Dunkel & Hatfield, 1986).

Some gay men are disabled. These men may be doubly isolated: they are not part of mainstream heterosexual society, and their access to other gay people may be severely limited because of physical barriers. Given the emphasis among gay men on "good looks," a disabled gay may not find easy acceptance into a gay support network. Service providers, who often ignore the sexual needs of the disabled heterosexual, may be unprepared to deal with the disabled gay. In large cities, there are self-help groups for gays with particular disabilities.

Some writers (Weathers, 1976; Mongeon & Ziebold, 1980) believe that substance abuse is particularly high among gay men and lesbians. There are two reasons why this may be true. First, drugs and alcohol are often used to relieve the pressures of living in a homophobic society, especially by individuals who face the burden of hiding their sexual identity from family, friends, or employers. Second, in many communities gay life centers around a bar, in which the consumption of alcohol is almost a social necessity.

In treating substance abuse among gay clients, social workers need to avoid the traditional pattern of attempting to change the client's sexual orientation (Berger, 1983a, pp. 66–67). Rather, they need to restore the client to a level of self-esteem and ability to cope with stress that will make it possible for him or her to abandon the use of alcohol and drugs. Workers also need to include lovers and other members of the gay client's social network in their treatment plans.

The very young and the very old are special populations within the gay community. Although most gay men realize that they are gay between the ages of 9 and 15 (Jay & Young, 1979, p. 105), problems often arise because social workers refuse to believe that a child can be gay. Gay young people are a particularly vulnerable population because of the emotional and financial dependence of youngsters on often rejecting families and because of the absence of safe and legal outlets for gay youth to meet their peers. An excellent collection of case histories of gay adolescents may be found in Heron (1983).

Gay men do not disappear when they grow older; the incidence of homosexuality is just as great among the elderly. Recent research has shown that most older gays adjust well to aging and that in some ways being gay facilitates that adjustment (Berger, 1982; 1984). Still, old people—especially the very old—often require supportive services, and

these services should not assume that all old persons are heterosexual.

Gay men are also members of minority racial and ethnic groups. Black and Chicano gays may fail to find acceptance either among majority group gays or in their own minority communities. Majority gay institutions are at times racist, or they lack responsiveness to the concerns of racial and ethnic minorities. Minority communities may be homophobic because of a traditional cultural emphasis on machismo and because being gay is seen as capitulating to white oppression.

Heterosexually married gays and gay parents are often overlooked groups. Many gay men choose to marry, sometimes before they have realized the full extent of their homosexual orientation (Ross, 1983). This situation may generate marital problems that come to the attention of social workers. Many gay men are parents. They may have children from a marriage that ended after they realized their sexual orientation, or they may have fathered or adopted children as openly gay men. Although social workers should not assume that gay parenthood is always filled with problems, they should be aware of the phenomenon of gay fatherhood.

Conclusion

Conflicting and inaccurate definitions of homosexuality and the perpetuation of myths have often impeded services to gay men. Today, accurate information is available as a result of the proliferation of research on nonclinical samples of gays. The increased visibility of gay people has also increased the availability of accurate information about gays, as have such professional groups as the Commission on Lesbian and Gay Issues of the Council on Social Work Education (CSWE) and the National Committee on Lesbian and Gay Issues of the National Association of Social Workers (NASW).

In the past, social workers joined other helping professionals in suppressing homosexuality by defining it as an illness and subjecting gays to "treatment" to convert them into heterosexuals (see, for example, Wasserman, 1976). Although social work was a relative latecomer to more progressive views (DeCrescenzo, 1984), the profession has now taken a strongly affirmative stance, as reflected in NASW's "Policy on Gay Issues" (1977):

NASW views discrimination and prejudice directed against any minority as inimical to the mental health not only of the affected minority, but of the society as a whole. The association deplores and will work to combat archaic laws, discriminatory employer practices, and other forms of discrimination which serve to impose something less than equal status upon the homosexually oriented members of the human family.

RAYMOND M. BERGER

For further information, see HOMOSEXUALITY: LESBIAN WOMEN; SEXUALITY.

References

Bayer, R. (1981). *Homosexuality and American Psychiatry: The Politics of Diagnosis*. New York: Basic Books.

Becker, H. S. (1963). *Outsiders: Studies in the Sociology of Deviance*. New York: Free Press.

Bell, A. P. (1982, November). "Sexual Preference: A Postscript." *SIECUS Report, 11*(2), pp. 1–3.

Bell, A. P., & Weinberg, M. S. (1978). *Homosexualities: A Study of Diversity Among Men and Women*. New York: Simon & Schuster.

Bell, A. P., Weinberg, M. S., & Hammersmith, S. K. (1981). *Sexual Preference: Its Development in Men and Women*. Bloomington: University of Indiana Press.

Berger, R. M. (1977). "Report on a Community-Based Venereal Disease Clinic for Homosexual Men." *Journal of Sex Research, 13*(1), 54–62.

Berger, R. M. (1982). "The Unseen Minority: Older Gays and Lesbians." *Social Work, 27*(3), 236–242.

Berger, R. M. (1983a). "Health Care for Lesbians and Gays: What Social Workers Should Know." *Journal of Social Work and Human Sexuality, 1*(3), 59–73.

Berger, R. M. (1983b). "What Is a Homosexual?: A Definitional Model." *Social Work, 28*(2), 132–135.

Berger, R. M. (1984). *Gay and Gray: The Older Homosexual Man*. Boston: Alyson Press.

Berger, R. M., & Kelly, J. J. (1981). "Do Social Work Agencies Discriminate Against Homosexual Job Applicants?" *Social Work, 26*(3), 193–198.

Bieber, I. (1965). "Clinical Aspects of Male Homosexuality." In J. Marmor (Ed.), *Sexual Inversion: The Multiple Roots of Homosexuality* (pp. 248–267). New York: Basic Books.

Bieber, I., et al. (1962). *Homosexuality: A Psychoanalytic Study of Male Homosexuals*. New York: Basic Books.

Bohn, T. (1982, November 17). "The Politics of Research on Homosexuality." *Long Island Connection*, p. 12–14, 25.

Boswell, J. (1980). *Christianity, Social Tolerance, and Homosexuality*. Chicago: University of Chicago Press.

Centers for Disease Control. (1986, May). *Weekly Surveillance Report*.

DeCrescenzo, T. A. (1984). "Homophobia: A Study of the Attitudes of Mental Health Professionals Toward Homosexuality." In R. Schoenberg, R. S. Goldberg, & D. A. Shore (Eds.), *Homosexuality and Social Work*. New York: Haworth Press.

Dunkel, J., & Hatfield, S. (1986). "Countertransference Issues in Working with Persons with AIDS." *Social Work, 31*(2), 114–117.

Freiberg, P. (1984, October 2). "Gay Teachers: Lesbians Battle Prejudice in the Blackboard Jungle." *Advocate*, pp. 21–23.

Gagnon, J. H., & Simon, W. (Eds.). (1967). *Sexual Deviance*. New York: Harper & Row.

Garner, B., & Smith, R. W. (1977). "Are There Really Any Gay Male Athletes? An Empirical Survey." *Journal of Sex Research, 13*(1), 22–34.

Giteck, L. (1984, October 2) "Family by Design: The Gay Theory of Relativity." *Advocate*, pp. 28, 33, and 56.

Gonsiorek, J. C. (1982). "Results of Psychological Testing on Homosexual Populations." In W. Paul, J. D. Weinrich, J. C. Gonsiorek, & M. E. Hotvedt (Eds.), *Homosexuality: Social, Psychological, and Biological Issues* (pp. 71–80). Beverly Hills, Calif.: Sage Publications.

Hacker, H. M. (1971). "Homosexuals: Deviant or Minority Group?" In E. Sagarin (Ed.), *The Other Minorities* (pp. 65–92). Waltham, Mass.: Xerox.

Heron, A. (1983). *One Teenager in Ten*. Boston: Alyson Press.

Hooker, E. (1957). "The Adjustment of the Male Overt Homosexual." *Journal of Projective Techniques, 21*(1) 18–31.

Hooker, E. (1958). "Male Homosexuality in the Rorschach." *Journal of Projective Techniques, 22*(1), 33–54.

Jay, K., & Young, A. (1979). *The Gay Report*. New York: Summit Books.

Jones, J. E., Jr. (1984, August 7). "The Unitarian Universalist Association Has Become the First Major Religious Denomination to Approve Ceremonies Celebrating the Union of Gay and Lesbian Couples." *Advocate*, p. 13.

Kinsey, A. C., Pomeroy, W. B., & Martin, C. E. (1948). *Sexual Behavior in the Human Male*. Philadelphia: W. B. Saunders Co.

Lauritsen, J., & Thorstad, D. (1974). *The Early*

Homosexual Rights Movement. New York: Times Change Press.

Money, J., & Ehrhardt, A. A. (1972). *Man and Woman, Boy and Girl.* Baltimore, Md.: Johns Hopkins University Press.

Mongeon, J. E., & Ziebold, T. O. (1980, May). *Preventing Alcohol Abuse in the Gay Community: Towards a Theory and Model.* Paper presented at the National Council on Alcoholism Forum, Seattle, Wash.

Moses, A. E., & Hawkins, R. O., Jr. (1982). *Counseling Lesbian Women and Gay Men: A Life-Issues Approach.* St. Louis, Mo.: C. V. Mosby Co.

Nash, P. (1984, August 7). "Methodist Faction Aims to Defrock Gay Minister." *Advocate,* p. 13.

National Center on Child Abuse and Neglect. (1975). *Child Abuse and Neglect: The Problem and Its Management* (DHEW Publication No. OHD 75-30073). Washington, D.C.: U.S. Dept. of Health, Education and Welfare.

"N. Y. Police Reach Out to Gay Recruits." (1984, November 13). *Advocate,* p. 13.

Paul, W. (1982). "Minority Status for Gay People: Majority Reaction and Social Context." In W. Paul, J. D. Weinrich, J. C. Gonsiorek, & M. E. Hotvedt (Eds.), *Homosexuality: Social, Psychological, and Biological Issues* (pp. 351–369). Beverly Hills, Calif.: Sage Publications.

"Policy on Gay Issues." (1977, July). *NASW News, 22*(7), 31–32.

Reiss, A. J., Jr. (1967). "The Social Integration of Queers and Peers." In J. H. Gagnon & W. Simon (Eds.), *Sexual Deviance* (pp. 197–228). New York: Harper & Row.

Ross, M. W. (1983). *The Married Homosexual Man: A Psychological Study.* London, England: Routledge & Kegan Paul.

"Support from Religious Leaders." (1984, June 26). *Advocate,* p. 45.

Szasz, T. S. (1979). *Ideology and Insanity: Essays on the Psychiatric Dehumanization of Man.* Garden City, N.Y.: Anchor Press.

Task Force on Sexual Preference. (1977). *Report of the Task Force on Sexual Preference.* Portland, Oreg.: Oregon State Department of Human Resources.

Tripp, C. A. (1975). *The Homosexual Matrix.* New York: McGraw-Hill Book Co.

Wasserman, S. (1976). "Casework Treatment of a Homosexual Acting-Out Adolescent in a Treatment Center." In F. J. Turner (Ed.), *Differential Diagnosis and Treatment in Social Work* (2nd ed., pp. 250–262). New York: Free Press.

Weathers, B. (1976, June). "Alcoholism and the Lesbian Community." Unpublished manuscript, Alcoholism Center for Women, Los Angeles.

Weinberg, M. S., & Williams, C. J. (1974). *Male Homosexuals: Their Problems and Adaptations.* New York: Oxford University Press.

Wittman, C. (1972). "A Gay Manifesto." In K. Jay & A. Young (Eds.), *Out of the Closets: Voices of Gay Liberation* (pp. 330–342). New York: Douglas/Links.

HOMOSEXUALITY: LESBIAN WOMEN

Webster's *Third New International Dictionary* (1961) defines "lesbian" as "a female homosexual" (p. 1296) and then proceeds to relate homosexuality to "manifestation of sexual desire. . . erotic activity. . . libidinal gratification" (p. 1085). Lesbianism as an identity or orientation encompasses more than sexual behavior, however, and may not include sexuality. Clark's definition (1977), although applied primarily to males, is more comprehensive in that it includes the multilevel involvement of emotional, sexual, spiritual, and intellectual dimensions of self (p. 73). In general, identifying oneself as lesbian relates to primary affiliations with similarly identified women. This may be actualized because of intense sexual, affectional, and social attractions that have been reciprocated. In such instances, women may choose to enter committed, ongoing relationships. An alternative is to ascertain one's orientation yet not feel the need for a specific partner. Some women choose not to act sexually on this self-acknowledged identity. However, they consciously, politically, or socially consider themselves to be a part of the lesbian community. To paraphrase Berger (1983), there are many definitions, roles, and issues involved with being lesbian.

Identity

The process of defining oneself as lesbian may come as a result of self-awareness arising from the physical, emotional, or social attraction to women; may be accepted when imposed by others; may be rejected as a label; or can be denied to others as a possible identification of self. At the physiological level, biological factors often result in less emphasis on genital responsiveness than usually occurs with boys and men. Also, the socialization of women generally focuses more attention on the relational aspects of interactions than on sexual responsiveness per se. As a result, self-identification as lesbian often comes at a later age for women than does self-identification as gay for men—in the late teenage or adult years rather than in childhood or the early teens (de Monteflores & Schultz, 1978; Stanley & Wolfe, 1980). Socialization also results in pressure to marry for many females who may be more attracted to women yet who feel unable or unwilling to act on these feelings. As described by Lewis (1984),

> Many women who would fall in the mid-range of Kinsey's scale (0 as exclusively heterosexual and 6 as exclusively homosexual) do not have a sense of being different as strongly as those closer to the exclusively homosexual end. Because of strong socialization to become heterosexual, a woman in the mid-range may fit fairly easily into a heterosexual lifestyle. She may marry and have children, yet feel something is missing. At some point, her feelings of attraction or her political beliefs may lead her to exploring same-sex attractions. If feminism becomes central to her life, she may use political values such as having an egalitarian relationship and personal independence as an ideological framework for her explorations. . . . Changes in the social environment and the increasing emphasis on liberation and personal growth provided these women a less hostile and frightening atmosphere in which to try new kinds of relationships. (p. 465)

It is not uncommon for women to reject being labeled lesbian, either by themselves or others, because of a rejection of the concept of labeling in itself, a lack of identification with the historical or political connotations associated with the term, a need to protect themselves from real or perceived oppression, or continuing denial. The concept "lesbian" itself is considered by some women to be a reflection of society's need to limit human behavior rather than a descriptive noun associated with sexual-affectional lifestyles. Cross-generationally, some women still consider the generic use of "gay" as more acceptable and less value laden politically and historically.

In addition, women as a group encounter very real oppression in a sexist society,

which is doubled for women who are lesbians in a homophobic environment and trebled for Third World lesbians in a racist environment (Goodman, 1979; Hidalgo, 1985a). The loss of jobs or occupational opportunities, the loss of significant support systems, or an inability to access traditional resources are often real obstacles in an oppressive society. A knowledge of the deprivations and struggles encountered by other lesbians can result in perceiving hazards to oneself that may or may not become reality (Simpson, 1976). Again, historical perspectives are relevant in the self-identification process.

Finally, some homosexually identified women see their intimate or dyadic relationships as distinct from the larger political arena and current community activities. Lesbians are perceived as "them" and are frequently seen in stereotyped images so that the individual may protect herself from unacceptable feelings that would be generated by association with the term "lesbian." Continuing isolation from self-identified lesbian individuals or groups usually feeds negative stereotyping, however, which continues to make the term unacceptable for oneself.

The cross-generational use of "butch" or "femme" appellations is also present, usually based on behavior or physiological characteristics that fit masculine or feminine stereotypes. "Dyke" may be an alternative to "butch" or may be used as an assertive political term. One may hear women identify themselves as a "fifties butch," an "eighties baby dyke," or a "politically radical bull dyke."

Social workers should be aware that lesbian identity is related to sexual affectional orientation. This identity should be viewed in the context of a client's intimate relationships, social milieu, political stresses, and activism, as well as intrapersonally. The terms that women choose to use about themselves may vary and are equally valid, particularly given the history of the individuals involved.

Demographics

It is currently estimated that 10 percent of the population is homosexual (Bell & Weinberg, 1978). This proportion can be generalized to women and could be even greater. Women are often vulnerable economically or in relation to child care and custody. They may therefore remain isolated in dyads, small groups, or socioeconomically or culturally segregated cliques. This has resulted in less than accurate demographics. The closeted lifestyle of many lesbians makes them unavailable to researchers, much less to census takers. However, using word of mouth, person-to-person contacts, social support groups (including lesbian bars), contacts with noncloseted lesbians, and other networking techniques, it has been ascertained that lesbians are represented in all socioeconomic strata, all ethnic groups, and all ages (Brooks, 1981). Current biographies, autobiographies, and fiction written about and by women of all ages, ethnic groups, and lifestyles attest to their diversity and to the hidden lives of many. The annotated bibliography from the Council on Social Work Education (1983) includes a wide representation of such works.

It is important for social workers to recognize the breadth of lifestyles and the number of subpopulations among lesbians. To some degree, overlapping occurs, and subgroups usually find a need to affiliate with those who share their special concerns or unique problems. Communities often have social networks for women of varying ages. For example, youths, middle-aged women, and elders have different historical roots, interests, and problems.

Class differences can also divide lesbian communities. Classism is definitely present and is reflected in social gatherings. It is not uncommon for economically deprived women or women who are financially pressed because of dependents to feel excluded from activities sponsored by more affluent lesbians who expect financial contributions.

Third World lesbians have ongoing encounters with racism, not only in society at large, but also with other lesbians (Hidalgo, 1985a). Third World lesbians may also be split by the many demands on their time (by ethnicity, as women, as lesbians, as employees, and as partners in relationships) or be isolated from one or more significant groups.

Finally, role and status differences exist among lesbians. Mothers frequently feel that nonparents do not understand their special problems and do not provide support systems. The need for support may arise at particularly stressful periods or may be ongoing, such as wanting child care to be available for times of social relaxation. Also, self-disclosure as a lesbian or networking to find other mothers and children is more difficult for fear or risk of losing child custody. To combat this, some communities have established confidential mother-child social and problem-solving groups with great success.

Other subgroups include professional lesbian associations that act as financial, vocational, and social networks and educational resources. Women in committed couples may be reluctant to associate with women who live a single lifestyle or who have open relationships. These latter groups may in turn form subgroups. Lesbians who are physically challenged (yet another subgroup) usually have not received the attention or support they need (Wohlander & Petal, 1985).

In summary, many communities and lifestyles exist within the lesbian community, all with particular interests, needs, and problems. Social workers should know a client's overall affiliations and not make the assumption that lesbianism per se is a client's only social affiliation.

"Etiology"

As various authors (Brooks, 1981; Woodman & Lenna, 1980) have indicated, the attempt to identify etiological factors for homosexuality and lesbianism has involved research and reflection by social groups, individuals, and scientists for centuries. The root of this concern has been a need to explain differences in societal groups. "Causes" have ranged from possession by the devil to endowment with special powers, from criminality to excessively positive talents and creativity, from madness to better than average personal adjustment (Katz, 1978). Until 1973, homosexuality was considered by the psychiatric and, ipso facto, the social work professions to be a form of mental illness. New knowledge and trends have reversed such opinions (American Psychiatric Association, 1974). For social workers engaged in in-service training on lesbian and gay issues, the questions "why" and "how" are almost always first on a group's agenda and can be dealt with if there is an understanding of the historical and social contexts for such inquiries.

Women personally define lesbianism in many ways, and self-identification occurs at varying ages. No one cause can be pinpointed. Bell, Weinberg, and Hammersmith

(1981), after thorough statistical analyses of a breadth of factors, concluded that no specific genetic, intrapsychic, or interpersonal etiological factors could be generalized to the lesbian population at large. Brooks (1981) considers that the recognition of a loss of personal individuality and egalitarianism in traditional heterosexual relationships may be a primary factor in some women's identifying themselves as lesbian. Sexual orientation for some women may be set as early as age 3 or 4 and, therefore, might be attributed to biophysiological factors. However, women also identify themselves as lesbian after 20 or more years of only intimate heterosexual relationships. Furthermore, many in this latter group report no prior interest in a lesbian sexual-affectional orientation. Given the generally good social and interpersonal adjustment of lesbians (Brooks, 1981; Chafetz et al., 1974; Siegelman, 1972), it is not reasonable to ascribe denial or repression as a universal explanation for this later acceptance.

The current state of research findings in this area indicates that no generalities lead to or significantly predict lesbianism. Since lesbianism is considered neither a physiological nor a mental illness, consideration of causation is pertinent for social work intervention only insofar as the anxiety of those who need to know "why" becomes a factor in problem solving with particular individuals.

Homophobia

Homophobia as a social phenomenon is both personalized and institutionalized. As with racism and sexism, it perpetuates oppression of a group that is different from those in the dominant social structure. By definition, homophobia refers to the irrational fear of homosexuality and to the negative attitudes and behavior toward lesbian women and gay men that result (Freedman, 1976). It is necessary for social workers to be sensitive to the existence of the fears, attitudes, and behaviors that affect lesbians both intra- and interpersonally.

On the intrapersonal level, lesbians frequently internalize negative stereotypes and either repress their identification as lesbian or isolate themselves from lesbian support systems. Institutionalized homophobia supports a socialization process that pictures lesbianism as sick, bad, crazy, or stupid. Because this portrayal does not usually fit a woman's self-image, the idea of her own lesbian identity or association with other lesbians is rejected. Women are often socialized to be affectionate, and they may enjoy childhood or adolescent sexualized encounters with female peers. However, adult strictures and external forces frequently support a perception that such feelings and activities are "only a phase" to be outgrown as a woman attains "mature genitality." The fear of losing significant others (parents, extended family, children, close friends) can be very real, leading to hiding one's sexual-affectional orientation within oneself or from others in daily interactions. The cost may be significant unless counterbalanced by meaningful alternative support systems.

On the interpersonal level, institutionalized homophobia has deemed it acceptable (and sometimes mandatory) for societal structures to discriminate against lesbian women and gay men. Inasmuch as women collectively are already oppressed by sexism, lesbians are even more vulnerable. This contributes to a realistic fear of dealing openly with clergy, employers, the court system, and helping professionals.

Many traditional religious bodies still consider homosexuality to be a sickness, at best, but more usually to be sinful. Some changes are occurring, however, as noted in the section on resources. Employers are not required to include sexual orientation as one of the areas for nondiscrimination (unlike race, ethnicity, sex, or age). The armed forces and most top security positions provide clear examples of a double bind for lesbians. That is, if a lesbian discloses this dimension of her identity, she either is not hired or is employed and subsequently fired. The homophobic rationalization is that she is at risk because of potential blackmail. However, if the lesbian conceals her orientation, she is in jeopardy if discovered and exposed and, therefore, has been made vulnerable to blackmail. The judicial system as it relates to custody, in particular, has been particularly homophobic toward lesbian mothers despite evidence that lesbianism and motherhood are not incompatible (Goodman, 1977, 1980; Kirkpatrick, Smith, & Roy, 1981; Riddle & de Lourdes Arguelles, 1981). Part of this oppression relates to the continued criminal or felony status of homosexuals (including lesbians) in many states, thereby leading the court system to view lesbian mothers as unfit.

The helping professions, including social work, have also had a history of homophobic attitudes derived from a view of lesbianism as psychopathological stemming from "arrested development." As a result, many women are hesitant to reveal their lesbianism to a counselor or a physician or will not seek help from traditional sources. It is the lack of access to nonhomophobic institutional supports that increases stress for lesbians and their significant others.

Support for homophobia derives from a continuing perpetuation of myths about homosexuality. A woman interviewed in the film *Pink Triangles* (Cambridge Documentary Films, 1982) describes, as fact, the myth that "they" are out to recruit young children—except that she isn't positive about lesbians because she never read about them pursuing little girls. Other myths include that lesbians are emotionally unstable, are diseased, hate men, need a good heterosexual experience, or are doomed to a life of sadness and lonely old age. Such myths have been perpetuated in the media, by homophobic persons and institutions, and in subtle jokes, offhand remarks, and condescension. The National Association of Social Workers (NASW) *Code of Ethics* (1980) mandates the elimination of homophobia. One step in the process is for social workers to become knowledgeable about the facts and research that refute the distortions, misinformation, myths, and stereotypes on which this oppression is built.

Legislation and Discriminatory Policies

By 1975, 7 states had decriminalized consensual adult homosexuality with no adverse effects (Geis et al., 1976). By 1984, 26 states had implemented decriminalization. Further, in Wisconsin it has become illegal to discriminate against people on the basis of sexual orientation. Seven other states prohibit discrimination in public employment, and some form of protection is provided by 51 municipalities and 12 counties through the United States (National Gay Task Force, 1984). However, in 24 states women still risk prosecution for being in a lesbian relationship. This has significant implications for child custody hearings, employment (for example, for teachers or other public employ-

ees), or access to social welfare services. With the exception of Wisconsin, most government systems and private sector organizations continue to reserve the right to deny lesbians equal rights in education, employment, lending, housing, and medical settings. These realities must be considered by lesbians deciding whether to be open about their lifestyle.

Legal services and handbooks to counteract discriminatory legislation, policies, and procedures have increased in number as shown in the Council on Social Work Education annotated bibliography (1983), particularly on pages 35–37. It is important for social workers to be involved in the process to end discrimination on at least three levels. First, professionals should be aware of the realities in their city and state. Second, social workers should identify specific areas of oppression and work with their NASW chapter to enable lesbian clients to have equal status under the law. Third, social workers should have a sound knowledge of current legislation, policies, procedures, and alternative strategies for changing oppressive systems. Social workers can engage in educative counseling (including sharing readings), advocacy, and brokering with clients and those who would impede clients' ability to gain access to needed resources. This includes combating discriminatory practices in social service settings. In this area, a social worker–lawyer team can be invaluable, not only in dealing with crises but in gathering evidence and preparing legal documents (Bernstein, 1977; Lesbian Rights Project, 1979).

Resources

Many traditional religions currently have groups for lesbian women and gay men. These include Dignity for Roman Catholics and Integrity for Episcopalians. Affirmation is the name of both the Methodist group for lesbians and gay men and for gay and lesbian members of the Church of Jesus Christ of Latter-day Saints. Other associations are Mishpachat Am for Jewish gays and Lutherans Concerned for Lutherans. Metropolitan Community Churches are nondenominational Christian groups located in most large cities. These organizations exist to address the spiritual needs of the homosexual community and to provide support systems.

Colleges and universities frequently

have lesbian and gay caucuses or clubs that enable students and faculty to address issues of mutual concern while meeting a need for social activities. Some high schools also have lesbian and gay clubs for youths.

In the political arena, state chapters of the National Gay Task Force supplement the work of the National Gay Task Force. Primary goals are to work toward nondiscriminatory legislation to secure institutional benefits such as health care services for lesbians and gays. Participation in the election process also is a focus.

Professional associations such as NASW, the American Psychological Association, and the National Association for Librarians have lesbian and gay committees or task forces. Educational activities for colleagues include in-service training, political action, and service to the homosexual community, as well as peer support. Other associations may be developed around particular needs or areas such as Alcoholics Anonymous groups for lesbians, parenting, music, sports, or other recreational or avocational interests.

For formal organizations, *Lesbian and Gay Issues* (Hidalgo, Peterson, & Woodman, 1985), the NASW resource manual, has a helpful listing of contact persons and addresses. Lesbian and gay task forces or committees of NASW state chapters, where they exist, can usually provide information about local resources, as can information and referral agencies or lesbian and gay hot lines. Before referring clients to resources, social workers should be sure that contact persons, telephone numbers, and organizational activities will meet client needs.

Social Work Roles and Practice

The social work roles of educative counselor, advocate, and broker have been discussed. Also described has been the role of facilitator in networking for particular populations to establish support systems and self-help groups. Social workers must bring a commitment to social justice in their work with homophobic organizations and communities (Balint, 1985; Goodman, 1985; Hidalgo, 1985b).

Another major activity in social work practice with lesbians and their significant others is problem solving during crises or stress. Although lesbianism per se is not a

mental illness, it is reasonable to expect that the generalized one of every four persons needing professional help would include lesbians and their parents, heterosexual spouses, or children. Stress from homophobic institutions combined with isolation from support groups may also trigger a need for intervention. A question frequently raised by helping professionals is, "How are the problems of lesbians different from those of other people and what is different about intervention strategies?" Similarities exist in the presenting problems of lesbians and other women, but there are also significant differences that require additional knowledge. A familiarity with alternative lifestyles, oppression and its effects, resources (including the literature, local organizations, and some community contacts), and the concepts and terminology used in the lesbian community is crucial. Furthermore, it is important for social workers to be sensitive to their own attitudes toward sexuality and sexual orientation.

One area in which individuals seek help is the coming out process (Moses & Hawkins, 1981; Woodman & Lenna, 1980). Women frequently identify themselves as lesbian in adulthood, after having been in committed heterosexual relationships (with and without children). The process of dealing with divorce, the loss of a prior relationship, and establishing new parental roles is similar to the process of grieving in general but is complicated by the need to redefine oneself. Social workers in such situations must be able to accept homosexuality and not be biased by homophobic attitudes. They then can proceed to engage in problem solving, bringing to the intervention a knowledge of the coming out process and its implications for interpersonal relationships (Wirth, 1978).

Life-stage crises also present unique demands for lesbians. Moses and Hawkins (1981) address issues such as establishing and maintaining relationships, parenting, and aging. For lesbians in relationships, problems common to any couple may exist in communication, money or financial matters, sexuality, values, and time and household management. Unique differences occur in that lesbians often do not have other same-sex couples as role models for dealing with conflicts or relationship tasks, however. Their families of origin may not be seen as available for help. Furthermore, such family members may be a source of stress if they reject the homosexual lifestyle. Only limited support may be available for stress management, and a couple's isolation may exacerbate day-to-day problems. Social workers must not discount the importance of these additional factors when counseling lesbians.

Parenting also presents special concerns for lesbians. Although comparisons may be drawn to the problems of heterosexual stepfamilies, the impact of homophobia on parents and children requires special attention. If only one partner is a parent, the other partner may have problems in role definition when joining the family. Therefore, an understanding and knowledge of lesbianism in general and lesbian mothers in particular is obviously crucial if the helping process is to be effective (Goodman, 1977; Steinhorn, 1985).

Although growing older presents few problems for the majority of lesbians, some women encounter unique stresses that may require social work intervention (Laner, 1977). Among these are financial pressures, problems in dealing with medical and legal services, and dwindling lesbian-identified support systems.

A specific understanding of lesbianism is important for other problem areas and special populations. These include stresses in adolescence, substance abuse, health issues, and loss of partners. Other than those previously mentioned, special populations include lesbians in rural communities, the parents of lesbians, and military personnel. Social work with these and other groups and issues is addressed in *Lesbian and Gay Issues: A Resource Manual for Social Workers* (Hidalgo, Peterson, & Woodman, 1985).

Summary

This article has discussed lesbianism as a dimension of personality with many facets, definitions, subgroups, and communities. Differentiation between lesbian women and gay men, particularly in self-identification and expression of that identity, has been addressed. Homophobia, coupled with sexism, has been described as a primary factor affecting the lives of lesbian women relative to self-identity, access to informal support systems, and traditional social institutions. Resources and strategies to combat this op-

pression have been cited. The particular needs of lesbian women who seek social work services have been identified, along with the requirement for a total professional commitment to address the needs of this population. Finally, it should be stressed that lesbian women have contributed significantly to social work and other professions and to the community at large. An ever-growing body of literature attests to the viability of this dynamic and increasingly visible group in our society.

NATALIE JANE WOODMAN

For further information, see HOMOSEXUALITY: GAY MEN; SEXUALITY; WOMEN.

References

American Psychiatric Association. (1974). *Diagnostic and Statistical Manual of Mental Disorders* (2nd ed.). Washington, D.C.: Author.

Balint, R. (1985). "Changing the Traditional Human Service Agency on Behalf of Lesbian and Gay Clients." In H. Hidalgo, T. Peterson, & N. J. Woodman (Eds.), *Lesbian and Gay Issues: A Resource Manual for Social Workers* (pp. 119–122). Silver Spring, Md.: National Association of Social Workers.

Bell, A. P., & Weinberg, M. S. (1978). *Homosexualities. A Study of Diversity among Men and Women.* New York: Simon & Schuster.

Bell, A. P., Weinberg, M. S., & Hammersmith, S. K. (1981). *Sexual Preference.* Indianapolis: Indiana University Press.

Bernstein, B. E. (1977). "Legal and Social Interface in Counseling Homosexual Clients." *Social Casework, 58*(1), 36–40.

Berger, R. M. (1983). "What is a Homosexual: A Definitional Model." *Social Work, 28*(5), 132–135.

Brooks, V. (1981). *Minority Stress and Lesbian Women.* Lexington, Mass.: D. C. Heath & Co.

Cambridge Documentary Films (Producer) & Pink Triangles Group (Director). (1982). *Pink Triangles* [Film]. Cambridge, Mass.: Cambridge Documentary Films.

Chafetz, J. S., et al. (1974). "A Study of Homosexual Women." *Social Work, 19*(6), 714–723.

Clark, D. (1977). *Loving Someone Gay: A Gay Therapist's Guidance for Gays and People Who Care about Them.* Millbrae, Calif.: Celestial Arts.

Council on Social Work Education. (1983). *An Annotated Bibliography of Lesbian and Gay Readings* (1st ed.). Washington, D.C.: Author.

De Monteflores, C., & Schultz, S. J. (1978). "Coming Out: Similarities and Differences for Lesbians and Gay Men." *Journal of Social Issues, 34*(3), 58–72.

Freedman, M. (1976, April). "Homophobia." *Blueboy*, 24–27.

Geis, G., et al. (1976). "Reported Consequences of Decriminalization of Consensual Adult Homosexuality in Seven American States." *Journal of Homosexuality, 1*(4), 419–427.

Goodman, B. (1977). *The Lesbian: A Celebration of Difference.* New York: Out and Out Books.

Goodman, B. (1979). *Confronting Homophobia.* New York: National Gay Health Coalition Educational Foundation.

Goodman, B. (Ed.). (1980). *Where Will You Be? The Professional Oppression of Gay People: A Lesbian/Feminist Perspective.* W. Hempstead, N.Y.: Womanmade Products.

Goodman, B. (1985). "Model for Institutional Change." In H. Hidalgo, T. Peterson, & N. J. Woodman (Eds.). *Lesbian and Gay Issues: A Resource Manual for Social Workers* (pp. 114–118). Silver Spring, Md.: National Association of Social Workers.

Hidalgo, H. (1985a). "Third World." In H. Hidalgo, T. Peterson, & N. J. Woodman (Eds.). *Lesbian and Gay Issues: A Resource Manual for Social Workers* (pp. 14–16). Silver Spring, Md.: National Association of Social Workers.

Hidalgo, H. (1985b). "Administrative, Personnel, and Professional Policies of Social Work Agencies and Institutions: Lesbian and Gay Issues." In H. Hidalgo, T. Peterson, & N. J. Woodman (Eds.). *Lesbian and Gay Issues: A Resource Manual for Social Workers* (pp. 126–129). Silver Spring, Md.: National Association of Social Workers.

Hidalgo, H., Peterson, T., & Woodman, N. J. (Eds.). (1985). *Lesbian and Gay Issues: A Resource Manual for Social Workers.* Silver Spring, Md.: National Association of Social Workers.

Katz, J. (1978). *Gay American History.* New York: Avon Books.

Kirkpatrick, M., Smith, C., & Roy, R. (1981). "Lesbian Mothers and Their Children: A Comparative Survey." *American Journal of Orthopsychiatry, 51*(3), 545–551.

Laner, M. R. (1977). "Growing Older Female: Heterosexual and Homosexual." *Journal of Homosexuality, 4*(3), 267–276.

Lesbian Rights Project. (1979). *Lesbian Rights Handbook.* San Francisco: Author.

Lewis, L. A. (1984). "The Coming Out Process for Lesbians: Integrating a Stable Identity." *Social Work, 29*(5), 464–469.

Moses, A., & Hawkins, R. (1981). *Counseling Lesbian Women and Gay Men: A Life-Issues Approach.* St. Louis, Mo.: C. V. Mosby Co.

National Association of Social Workers. (1980). *Code of Ethics.* Silver Spring, Md.: Author.

National Gay Task Force. (1984). *Updated Report on State, County and Municipal Statutes, Executive Orders and Rulings Relative to Civil Rights.* New York: Author.

Riddle, D., & de Lourdes Arguelles, M. (1981). "Children of Gay Parents: Homophobia's Victims." In I. R. Stuart, & L. E. Abt (Eds.). *Children of Separation and Divorce.* New York: Van Nostrand Reinhold Co.

Siegelman, M. (1972). "Adjustment of Homosexual and Heterosexual Women." *British Journal of Psychiatry, 120*(558), 477–481.

Simpson, R. (1976). *From the Closet to the Courts.* New York: Penguin Books.

Stanley, J. P., & Wolfe, S. (Eds.). (1980). *The Coming Out Stories.* Watertown, Mass.: Persephone Press.

Steinhorn, A. I. (1985). "Lesbian Mothers." In H. Hidalgo, T. Peterson, & N. J. Woodman (Eds.). *Lesbian and Gay Issues: A Resource Manual for Social Workers* (pp. 33–37). Silver Spring, Md.: National Association of Social Workers.

Webster's Third New International Dictionary. (1961). Springfield, Mass.: G. C. Merriam & Co.

Wirth, S. (1978). "Coming Out Close To Home: Principles for Psychotherapy with Families of Lesbians and Gay Men." *Catalyst, 1*(3), 237–246.

Wohlander, K., & Petal, M. (1985). "People Who Are Gay or Lesbian and Disabled." In H. Hidalgo, T. Peterson, & N. J. Woodman (Eds.). *Lesbian and Gay Issues: A Resource Manual for Social Workers* (pp. 38–42). Silver Spring, Md.: National Association of Social Workers.

Woodman, N. J., & Lenna, H. (1980). *Counseling with Gay Men and Women: A Guide to Facilitating Positive Life Styles.* San Francisco: Jossey-Bass.

HOPKINS, HARRY LLOYD. See biographical section.

HOSPICE

Hospice, or hospice care, is a multidisciplinary program that provides an array of services to assist terminally ill persons during the last months of life. The goal of hospice care is to provide comfort to the patient and a supportive environment to the family. Hospice care is appropriate when the physician, patient, and family determine that no further curative treatment will be effective. Palliation then becomes the intervention of choice, with a concomitant focus on quality of life rather than duration. Hospice recognizes that death is part of the human life cycle and seeks to make this phase as enriching an experience as possible for the patient as well as for family members.

The Hospice Philosophy

According to the National Hospice Organization (1979), hospice care is guided by seven major principles:

1. The focus of care encompasses the family as well as the patient. Since loss through death affects the entire family, services must be provided to all family members to enable them to cope with the patient's illness and to prepare themselves for their impending loss.

2. Hospice care is palliative rather than curative in nature. Controlling pain and other symptoms is the treatment of choice, rather than surgery and other curative procedures. This medical care requires sophisticated knowledge about control of symptoms and attention to details. It is only after symptoms such as nausea, vomiting, and pain are controlled that the patient is in a condition to benefit from social, psychological, and spiritual support.

3. Hospice care is provided by a multidisciplinary professional team of physicians, nurses, home health aides, social workers, therapists, clergy, and volunteers. The team is coordinated by one member, frequently the nurse or social worker. A licensed physician must be responsible for the medical direction of the program. The patient's primary physician is encouraged to continue care during the hospice period in order to provide continuity and support to the family. The hospice medical director acts as a consultant to the primary physician.

4. Hospice care is differentiated from standard home, hospital, and nursing home care in its extensive use of volunteers. To enhance the quality of life, a volunteer who is not assigned a specific task can be flexible and meet many needs that may arise within the family, such as the need for legal guidance, music or poetry therapy, or just friendly visiting.

5. The services of the hospice program are available 24 hours a day, seven days a week. Even though families may never actually call for help at night, they are reassured to know that a nurse or social worker is available to discuss new problems and will come to their home to provide any necessary support. This service enables families to keep the patient at home when they might otherwise think it necessary to admit him or her to the hospital or a nursing home.

6. Hospice is a comprehensive program that provides care whether the patient is in the hospital, in a nursing home, or at home. Patients are not simply discharged from one setting to another; rather, the hospice program bridges the settings and is in charge wherever the patient is, thereby ensuring continuity of care.

7. Care is provided to the family even after the patient dies. Anticipatory grief counseling begins before death to prepare family members. Bereavement support after the patient dies helps them deal with their loss.

History of Hospice Care

The hospice movement is rooted in the Middle Ages, when facilities to care for travelers were called hospices, later hostels. These facilities (which eventually evolved into hospitals) offered shelter to any traveler, whether sick or well, and to the orphaned, the needy, and the dying. Generally, they were run by religious orders.

In the early 1800s, Sister Mary Aikenhead founded a home in Dublin, Ireland, specifically to care for the dying. In 1906, the Sisters of Charity established St. Joseph's Hospice in London, England; the success of this venture in pain management spurred the opening of St. Christopher's Hospice, also in London. Here Dame Cicely Saunders began her historic work on the management of pain in cancer patients. That work led directly to the modern hospice movement.

In America, the Dominican Sisters are credited with first caring for the dying who had nowhere else to turn. Their facilities, patterned after England's in-patient models, were established in the late 1800s. They are still in operation today. However, most American hospice programs did not evolve from the in-patient model. Rather, families of the terminally ill wanted the opportunity to provide care for them at home as they had done before modern medical technology became involved. What came to be known in the early 1970s as the American Hospice Movement was home-based. It stressed care provided by the family and death at home made possible with support from the hospice team (Koff, 1980).

By mid-1984, over a thousand hospice programs were in operation across the United States. (National Hospice Organization, 1984). Some were run completely by volunteers, but most were operated by a combination of paid and volunteer staff. Most early American hospices provided only one component—home care. These programs lost control of the patient's care when in-patient (hospital or nursing-home) treatment became necessary, with little if any continuity of care. In 1982, federal legislation was passed providing reimbursement for hospice care for the elderly. Congress mandated that the home, in-patient, and bereavement components of the hospice program all be managed by the hospice. As a result, hospice care in America became a comprehensive service from the time of referral through the bereavement period.

Hospice Services

A comprehensive hospice program consists of three primary services: home care, in-patient care, and bereavement care. After confirmation that the patient is terminally ill, an initial assessment of the needs of the patient and family is made by a nurse or social worker. A plan of care is then established, with the family agreeing that members of the hospice team will provide appropriate services. Initially the family is taught how to manage the patient's physical symptoms. Once these have been addressed, other team members can then focus on the patient's psychosocial, spiritual, financial, and other needs. Weekly hospice team meetings are held to reassess each patient and to adjust the plan as necessary. Throughout the program, the family has access to the team 24 hours a day, seven days a week. As a result, families are often prepared to share the time of death without a team member present.

In-patient care is utilized for two purposes: symptom control and respite care. When the patient's symptoms cannot be controlled at home or the family needs a rest from the demands of 24-hour care, in-patient services may be provided in a hospital, a nursing home, or a facility used exclusively for hospice care. Usually in-patient stays are short, from seven to ten days at most. Whenever possible the patient returns home, in keeping with the hospice philosophy that an in-patient care setting is only a service alternative, not a place to go to die.

The goal of the third component, bereavement care, is to ensure that the spouse and other bereaved family members are expressing their grief and coping with their loss. Otherwise, repressed grief may be exhibited in destructive physical or emotional ways. Bereavement care takes several forms. Individual counseling may be provided in the home. Group sessions, which are therapeutic as well as social in nature, may be held. Often memorial services are sponsored by the hospice program to provide an opportunity for the family as well as staff and volunteers to remember the loved one and express their loss. Bereavement support is provided over a one-year period or until the family members are coping well.

Role of Social Work

The need for hospice care in America is rooted in the basic social work philosophy that the dignity of every human being must be preserved and that an individual should have control over his or her own destiny. The popularity of hospice programs grew in response to rapid technological advances in medicine in the mid-1900s that emphasized accurate diagnoses but tended to acknowledge only the bodily functions, while ignoring the whole person. At the moment of death, families were customarily removed to a waiting room and prevented from being with their loved one. This sterile medical approach often had a bad effect on the quality of the patient's remaining life and on the family's ability to cope after death. To counter these effects, social workers joined with concerned members of the medical profession to develop an alternative way to care for the dying patient.

Social workers play a significant role on a hospice team, providing both direct services to the hospice patient and family and indirect services through administrative support. The psychosocial family assessment is completed by the social worker and presented at team conferences. The social worker's primary responsibility consists of counseling the patient, as well as counseling family members both before and after the patient's death. In addition, the social worker coordinates numerous community resources and may be responsible for group bereavement services. Often, the social worker acts as a consultant to other team members as they work with a specific patient or family member.

The social worker may also administer the volunteer program, often supervising the volunteers as their relationship with hospice families becomes intense. Finally, the social worker is often called upon to provide support to the entire team or to individual team members who need help in coping with their own grief at the repeated losses they experience in the hospice program.

Reimbursement and Funding

In its early development hospice care was provided primarily by volunteers. As the demand for care increased, such full-time professionals as registered nurses and trained social workers were required. To meet this demand, demonstration projects began to be funded through local insurance plans along with community foundations. An ongoing funding base was finally solidified in 1982 with passage of the federal Tax Equity and Fiscal Responsibility Act. It included a hospice reimbursement benefit for Medicare-eligible recipients. This benefit was a historic milestone for hospice for two reasons: (1) it provided a reimbursement base for approximately 70 percent of all hospice patients; and (2) it established the prepaid per capita reimbursement system, replacing the previous fee-for-service system. As a result, hospices are paid on a per diem basis, with the level of reimbursement based on the level of care required for the patient for that particular day. The routine home care rate is reimbursed if the patient is not receiving either continuous care (at least eight hours of care in the home), respite care, or acute in-patient care.

By the end of 1984, a significant number of insurers included hospice as a benefit. A study completed by the Hospice Council for Northern Ohio (Brooks & Smyth-Staruch, 1983) demonstrated the cost effectiveness of hospice care in addition to its psychosocial benefits. The cost of care for hospice patients was compared to the cost of care for a similar group of terminally ill cancer patients not receiving hospice care; the study showed savings of approximately 25 percent for patients receiving hospice care. This and other studies spurred the health care insurance industry to include hospice as a routine benefit. At present, however, there is little consistency among the various reimbursement groups as to what services are to be covered, the level of reimbursement, and incentives to ensure that quality of care remains the focus.

Current Trends and Issues

Two major issues emerged during the first ten years of hospice development in the United States. The first issue centers around admission criteria that eliminate many patients from the option of receiving hospice care. Second, although it is beneficial that hospice funding is now stabilized, the new reimbursement mechanisms encourage cost effectiveness regardless of the quality of care.

Most American hospices mandate that the potential hospice patient have a primary caregiver (usually a close family member) as a condition of acceptance in the program. This is a logical outgrowth of a program emphasizing home care: because the hospice team cannot be in the home 24 hours a day, seven days a week, every hospice patient needs someone to take primary responsibility for the caregiving. Although this requirement is a rational one and appropriate for individuals who have strong family units, it eliminates from hospice care single elderly people, widows and widowers, and individuals whose spouse must work in order to maintain the home. Medicare restrictions require that at least 80 percent of all hospice care be provided in the home, thus excluding people who do not have a primary caregiver and who would need to receive all of their hospice care in the in-patient setting. This is an unfair situation, considering that these single individuals may have the greatest need for hospice care of anyone. The effort to keep the program cost effective (with home rather than in-patient care) has actually excluded many potential clients from the program.

The delivery of quality hospice care is also being challenged by a reimbursement system that is new not only to hospice but also to the entire American health care system. Since per diem rates were established in 1982, the hospice program has been faced with deciding which services to provide within a limited fixed fee. Thus if a patient requires intense medical care, the service priority will more than likely focus in that direction. If sufficient funds are not available to provide counseling, spiritual care, and volunteer services that enhance the quality of life, the hospice program may deteriorate to being no more than a standard home care program for the terminally ill. Unless the whole person is served, the entire philosophy and value of hospice care will have been lost. The challenge, then, to professionals, including social workers, who provide nonmedical services will be to demonstrate not only the value of those services compared to medical care but also their cost effectiveness.

The way in which these two issues are addressed will determine whether or not hospice care survives and flourishes in America in the future. Hospice workers must challenge the system to be flexible, to meet the needs of all potential users, and to provide a quality of life beyond medical care for every terminally ill person it serves.

LINDA J. PROFFITT

For further information, see HOSPITAL SOCIAL WORK; LONG-TERM CARE; LOSS AND BEREAVEMENT.

References

Brooks, C. H., & Smyth-Staruch, K. (1983). "Cost Savings of Hospice Home Care to Third-Party Insurers." Cleveland, Ohio: Case Western Reserve University School of Medicine, Department of Epidemiology and Community Health.

Koff, T. H. (1980). *Hospice: A Caring Community.* Cambridge, Mass.: Winthrop Publishers.

National Hospice Organization. (1979, February). *Standards for a Hospice Program of Care* (6th rev. ed.). Washington, D.C.: Author.

National Hospice Organization. (1984). *Hospice News*, 2(9), 1.

HOSPITAL SOCIAL WORK

The first hospital social work department was established in 1905 at Massachusetts General Hospital (MGH) in Boston. Ida M. Cannon directed this effort for the primary purpose of helping patients to make a smooth transition from the hospital to the community. The goal of hospital social work was then and remains today to ensure that gains made in the acute-care setting are maintained in the patient's home and community environments. The purpose of hospital social work, like the broad goals of the profession itself, is to improve person-environment fit in a way that maximizes independent functioning.

When Richard Cabot, the physician who directed MGH in 1905, assigned Cannon to initiate a social work department, he recognized the importance of comprehensive care that included psychosocial aspects. He also recognized the importance of continuity of care. Both concepts constitute the primary directives of hospital social work as it exists today.

With the establishment of Medicare in 1966, hospital social work expanded tremendously. Although hospitals were not required to provide social work services as a condition of participation in Medicare, the legislation stipulated that any such services were to be organized under the direction of a professional social worker with a master's degree in social work. As hospital Medicare caseloads increased, so did the number of hospital social workers. In particular, social workers were critical in meeting the needs of elderly patients and their families. Most people over 65 suffer from one or more chronic conditions. Chronic illness generally requires some measure of change in lifestyle or long-term adjustment.

Another historic event for hospital social work occurred in 1966, when the American Hospital Association established the Society for Hospital Social Work Directors. This national organization gave hospital social workers a voice in the hospital industry and contributed to the credibility of the social work department as an integral hospital function. It also established standards through joint efforts with the National Association of Social Workers. In 1973 a chapter on the subject of social work services was added to the Hospital Accreditation Program of the Joint Commission on Accreditation of Hospitals (JCAH).

In 1972, Congress passed legislation (P.L. 92-603) that called for the creation of professional standards review organizations (PSROs). Among the multiple components of this law was a provision to set up peer review mechanisms and to participate in the quality assurance program of the hospital. The social work profession accepted this provision and participated in hospital efforts to establish professional accountability programs. This enhanced the profession's credibility and strengthened its recognized function.

In 1978 Congress amended the Social Security Act (Titles II and XVIII, P.L. 95-292) to provide expanded benefits for patients with end-stage renal disease. To qualify for funding under this program, hospitals were required to employ MSW social workers in the treatment of these patients. This was the first federally sponsored health program to require participation by master's-level social workers and thus contributed significantly to legitimizing hospital social work. Other important advances for hospital social work were the licensing and certification laws enacted by about half the states. In addition, various third-party payers granted vendor status to social work, enabling hospital social workers to be paid on a fee-for-service basis in certain specified circumstances.

Another development with important implications for hospital social work was the passage in March 1983 of the Deficit Reduction Act, which established a prospective pricing system for Medicare. This system created the diagnostic related group (DRG) as the unit for determining the amount Medicare would pay for a hospitalization, regardless of the actual cost. It is too soon to determine precisely what effects this new system will have on social work in hospitals, but it is already having a revolutionary effect on hospitals. Anecdotal information indicates that because the DRG system emphasizes outcome, the hospital social work function will grow in direct relation to its ability to help hospitals achieve their goals of shorter stays and an improved continuum of care.

Clinical Components

Clinical social work practice in an acute-care hospital setting deals with human issues not unlike those that social work faces elsewhere. The components that are different, and that require specialized training and knowledge, are the short-term setting, the interdisciplinary collaboration, and the physical or medical components.

A typical client could be an elderly female, 74 years old, living alone in a fourth-floor walkup apartment and having social security as her only income. She might come to the hospital because she fell and fractured her hip. Medical treatment would require surgery, physical therapy, and approximately 10 days in the hospital, followed by continuing care at home. The social worker would know about the case because the social work department has a system for identifying high-risk individuals who are likely to be in need of social work services. The intervention would include the following types of social work activities:

- Helping the patient understand the prognosis and its implications for activities of daily living.
- Helping the patient cope with her emotional reactions to this threat to her lifestyle and her independence.
- Helping the patient adjust to her new and sudden dependence on family, friends, and other caregivers.
- Helping the patient overcome her natural anger, anxiety, and fear about her current predicament.
- Helping the patient decide about the appropriate services for continuing care.
- Helping the patient evaluate her eligibility for the needed services and arranging for adequate coverage.
- Supporting the patient's decision.
- Facilitating communication among members of the hospital team to ensure comprehensive care that includes the psychosocial aspects.

Another typical case might be a patient suffering from a terminal illness who is likely to die while hospitalized. In such cases—in which the social work role is often complicated by the patient's receiving conflicting information from the family and different members of the health care team—the social worker must support the patient's and family's processes of inquiry and coping and yet be honest about the prognosis as stated by the physician. This includes facilitating open communication among the patient, family, and members of the health care team. The worker must also be prepared to provide practical information and services in case they are needed.

The emphasis of clinical social work intervention varies with each individual case.

The components of the intervention, however, are generic:

■ Coping with the potentially life-threatening changes precipitated by illness and hospitalization.

■ Facilitating communication among the patient, family, and health care team.

■ Counseling patients to help them adjust to their illness.

■ Providing patients with information and referrals and helping them determine their eligibility for coverage.

■ Arranging practical and concrete services.

■ Helping the patient and family to establish a discharge plan for continuing care.

Much of this clinical work is characterized by crisis intervention. This is so because hospitalization in half the cases is sudden and requires major personal adjustments and because the outcome of treatment is uncertain. Hospital social work generally includes arranging for the concrete services the patient will need after discharge from the hospital. Work with families is often a major part of the social work intervention.

In many hospitals, social workers have organized groups of patients facing similar problems. Sometimes this leads to the creation of self-help groups around virtually unlimited lists of issues and patient and family concerns. Hospital social workers frequently organize advocacy groups with the goal of creating new services or expanding clients' eligibility.

With the government and other payers pressing for shorter lengths of stay, it becomes increasingly difficult for hospital professionals to make significant contributions to patients' health. For social work this means a high level of training and experience are required to ensure that the goals of treatment can be achieved despite the severe constraints of time. Unlike social work in any other setting, hospital social work usually has only five to nine days to accomplish its goals. Often it cannot follow clients after discharge because new clients are coming in.

Settings

Hospital social work is practiced in a wide variety of hospital-affiliated settings, including the following:

■ General and specialized acute-care hospitals and medical centers

■ Psychiatric hospitals, both long and short term

■ Rehabilitation centers

■ Long-term care facilities, such as nursing homes, hospices, and adult day care programs

■ Primary care settings, such as health maintenance organizations (HMOs) and physicians' offices

■ Ambulatory clinics

■ Home health care programs

Moreover, social workers employed in hospitals provide services in every area of patient service, including medical-surgical, pediatric, psychiatric, obstetric-gynecologic, intensive care, rehabilitation, and emergency services.

Characteristics

The hospital environment is dramatically different from that of any other social work setting. First, hospitals provide 24 hours of service; they never close. They do not directly control whom they serve, and they routinely admit emergency cases. For these reasons, hospital social work has developed seven-day-a-week and 24-hour on-call systems.

Second, hospitals are centers of multidisciplinary practice. People come to hospitals because they believe they need medical care. That idea is changing, however—sometimes a patient may require a primary intervention that is not medical at all. Self-care may be the issue, or it may be physical mobility, family relationships, stress, pain, or inadequate alternative services. Adequate services frequently require the involvement of several disciplines. In hospitals, no practitioner can function without support and involvement by the interdisciplinary team. Therefore, interdisciplinary collaboration characterizes successful hospital social work.

Another characteristic of hospitals is confusion over functions, or "role blurring." Especially in these times of rapid change, few roles in hospitals are exclusive and totally prescribed. What often results is a fair amount of energy being devoted to defining roles. For example, social workers and nurses often have overlapping roles in discharge planning. Social workers and psychiatrists, psychologists, nurse clinicians, clergy, and patient representatives are often in conflict over counseling functions. In addition, the differential roles of master's-level and bachelor's-level social workers typically require ongoing definition.

Roles

Continuity of care with a strong emphasis on the psychosocial needs of patients and their families remains the central focus of hospital social work. This focus is reflected in many of the roles hospital social workers perform. The central role of hospital social work is discharge planning, which the American Hospital Association (1985) defined as

> any activity or set of activities which facilitates the transition of the patient from one environment to another. The complexity of discharge plans varies and may be described by four levels of outcome. These are 1) patient and family understanding of the diagnosis, anticipated level of functioning, discharge medications, and anticipated medical follow-up, 2) specialized instruction or training so that the patient or family can provide post-hospital care, 3) coordination of community support systems which enable the patient to return home, and 4) relocation of the patient and coordination of support systems or transfer to another health care facility. (p. 2)

Social work's concern with the person-environment fit makes the profession particularly qualified to be effective in hospital discharge planning. Coordination of discharge planning for patients with psychosocial complications—adjustment to illness, major changes of lifestyle, multiple follow-up services, and so forth—is commonly done by the hospital social work department.

Hospital social workers usually have a role in aiding victims of domestic violence, including victims of rape, child abuse, spouse abuse, and elder abuse. The specific roles of social workers are in clinical assessment and treatment, in the development of hospital protocols, and in collaboration with community agencies. Social workers trained in crisis intervention play a major role in crisis situations, which are routinely found in hospitals.

Much hospital social work involves other health-related agencies in the community, such as home health programs, nursing homes, or home-delivered meals. Frequently it involves such social services as child welfare, ethnic organizations, or geriatric centers. Thus hospital social workers are often the hospital's ambassadors to the commu-

nity. This diplomatic function is gaining importance as competition and consumerism become factors in the hospital industry.

In addition to their patient care roles, hospital social workers increasingly serve on hospital committees involving biomedical ethics, utilization review, DRG coordination, quality assurance, and risk management. In teaching hospitals, social workers participate in educating other health care practitioners and in collaborative research. In teaching and community hospitals, social workers conduct their own research on the psychosocial aspects of patient care.

Social workers often lead hospitals into new social health programs. Their leadership in developing and directing employee assistance programs and various self-help groups is widely recognized. In addition, social workers are almost always involved in comprehensive hospital programs to serve the elderly, and often they direct such programs. These programs frequently include home health care, hospice services, nursing homes, and other long-term care provisions.

Issues and Trends

The most notable characteristic of the hospital industry in the 1980s is change. The forces of change also exert powerful effects on hospital social work.

With the increase in the number of elderly people in America and the tremendous advances in medical technology, the cost of health care has skyrocketed. With costs at unprecedented levels, society is no longer willing to pay for the bulk of health care. In a growing number of communities, private businesses are forming coalitions to restrict the health care services they subsidize. Such actions have forced the experimental restructuring of payment mechanisms and changes in the way health care is provided and obtained. They have also raised ethical issues concerning access to and payment for advanced medical technology.

Consumerism is another major force for change in the health care field. Patients commonly seek second opinions, ask for hospital and physician fee schedules, and question hospital bills even though they are paid by third-party payers.

To remain viable, hospitals have had to become competitive. They have attempted to be more cost conscious and become more sensitive to the consumer. On finding their growth impeded in one area of the market—acute hospital care, for example—hospitals increasingly expand their products and services to capture other markets, offset losses, and ensure continued growth. Thus, many hospitals undertake vertical diversification into such areas as home care, nursing homes, rehabilitation, and the supply of durable medical equipment.

Cost containment has been achieved by forming multihospital systems (horizontal integration) and centralizing control, which allow hospitals to purchase in larger volume and command lower unit prices. These approaches also facilitate comparisons between institutions and result in the establishment of efficiency standards.

An important and tangible measure of efficiency is length of stay. Because many of the costs of hospital care are expressed as part of the daily rate, length of stay is in many ways a good indicator of the cost of care. Because inpatient care is the most costly, hospitals are moving more and more services to ambulatory care centers and are rapidly developing alternative delivery models. Many policymakers believe the best way to control costs is to offer health care at the most appropriate level under one per capita system in which the provider assumes all the risk. This one-system delivery model is called the health maintenance organization (HMO) and, along with issues of cost control, is growing in popularity.

Managed care, like that in an HMO, is an issue that has led to a great deal of experimentation. Case management provides another means to manage the care of a given population at the most cost-efficient level. It is also intended to ensure greater continuity of care. One experimental model for case management includes a federally funded project to test social HMOs for the elderly. Primarily concerned with cost efficiency, this project is based on the belief that many of the health problems of the elderly could be avoided if appropriate social programs such as counseling, chore services, and transportation were available. These experimental models have shown the ability to improve continuity of care. However, the goal of payers, politicians, and policymakers is cost efficiency, and they fear any expansion of obligations to cover unmet (and unknown)

social needs. The great debate of the 1980s and possibly the 1990s will be whether continuity of care can enhance the quality of life while reducing the overall cost of services. The debate will become more heated as the elderly population increases and the viability of the Medicare Trust Fund is threatened. These challenges present a tremendous opportunity for hospital social workers, who are in a position to demonstrate the viability of managed care.

The future of hospital social work appears to be both powerful and weak, expanded and diminished. Many social work directors have been so successful at managing and organizing various functions that they have been given additional responsibility and status. Social workers in hospitals today serve in the highest administrative roles. Some have management responsibility for such programs as mental health, aging, wellness, community outreach, rehabilitation, substance abuse, and long-term care. Hospital social workers have responded to the challenge of competition by leading in the development of these and other programs and also by becoming entrepreneurs and developing fee-for-service practice models. They have contracted to provide social work counseling and rehabilitation services to industry, thus providing hospitals with additional sources of revenue.

Nonetheless, at the same time as these and many other creative social work initiatives are occurring, the traditional roles of many hospital social workers are being challenged, especially in the area of discharge planning. Reductions in social work staff have sometimes resulted.

The key to the future of social work in hospitals is the profession's ability to articulate its role in the context of change. Once this articulation process is accomplished, mechanisms for measuring and demonstrating professional accountability to both consumers and payers will be critical to the continued support and expansion of hospital social work.

SALIE ROSSEN

For further information, see EMERGENCY HEALTH SERVICES; HEALTH CARE FINANCING; HEALTH PLANNING.

Reference

American Hospital Association. (1985). *The Role of the Social Worker in Planning*. Chicago: Author.

For Further Reading

American Hospital Association. (1984). *Guidelines on Discharge Planning*. Chicago: Author.

Bartlett, H. M. (1975). "Ida M. Cannon: Pioneer in Medical Social Work." *Social Service Review, 49*(2).

Berkman, B., & Henley, B. (1981). "Medical and Surgical Services in Acute Care Hospitals." *Health and Social Work, 6*(4).

Berkman, B., Rehr, H., & Rosenberg, G. (1980). "A Social Work Department Develops and Tests a Screening Mechanism to Identify High Social Risk Situations." *Social Work in Health Care, 5*(4).

Boone, C. R., Coulton, C. J., & Keller, S. M. (1981). "The Impact of Early and Comprehensive Social Work Services on Length of Stay." *Social Work in Health Care, 7*(1).

Bracht, N. F. (1978). *Social Work in Health Care: A Guide to Professional Practice*. New York: Haworth Press.

Carlton, T. (1984). *Clinical Social Work in Health Settings: A Guide to Professional Practice with Exemplars*. New York: Springer Publishing Co.

Dockhorn, J. (1982). *Essentials of Social Work Programs in Hospitals*. Chicago: American Hospital Association.

Doremus, B. (1976). "The Four Rs: Social Diagnosis in Health Care." *Health and Social Work, 1*(4), 120–139.

Lister, L., & Shore, D. (Eds.). (1984). *Human Sexuality in Medical Social Work*. New York: Haworth Press.

Lurie, A., & Rosenberg, G. (1984). *Social Work Administration in Health Care*. New York: Haworth Press.

Miller, R., & Rehr, H. (Eds.). (1983). *Social Work Issues in Health Care*. Englewood Cliffs, N.J.: Prentice-Hall.

Munson, C. (Ed.). (1983). *An Introduction to Clinical Social Work Supervision*. New York: Haworth Press.

Munson, C. (Ed.). (1984). *Supervising Student Internships in Human Services*. New York: Haworth Press.

Regensburg, J. (1978). *Toward Education for Health Professions*. New York: Harper & Row.

Wax, J. (1968). "Developing Social Work Power in a Medical Organization." *Social Work, 13*(4).

HOUSING

In the 1970s and early 1980s, housing continued to be an important component of the well-being of this society. Americans still aspired to home ownership and, when asked in what type of dwelling they would prefer to live, 75 percent indicated a strong desire for a single-family detached home (U.S. Department of Housing & Urban Development, 1978b). Owning one's home was still a central part of the American Dream. People usually think of changing the type of household in which they live when the life cycle of their family changes. In the past, those Americans who could afford to, bought a home as soon as they had the money for a down payment.

During the 1970s, owning a home became a mandatory strategy for coping in an inflationary milieu. Only the truly affluent could afford to ignore that home ownership was the major investment most families made in a lifetime, that it was one of the best hedges against rapid inflation, that it provided an excellent tax shelter, and that, over time and with appreciation, it built equity for many families. In this context, housing was seen more as an investment. The U.S. Bureau of the Census (1983b, p. 758) indicated that, in the late 1970s and early 1980s, the average age of first-time buyers of homes was 28.3 years. As the needs of households changed, many families sold their homes and then bought others that were of greater value. Eventually, as children left the household and other changes took place, these families then sold their homes for other types of dwellings. Throughout this cycle, for most people, the home was a protected investment that rarely depreciated in value. However, many people in this society have been unable to own a home. They may not have had enough money for a down payment, their income may have been too low to support home ownership, or they may not have had access to financing. This group was confined largely to the rental market, and they viewed housing more as shelter than as an investment. What was of concern to them was whether they would be required to spend an excessive amount of their income on rent and thus have fewer resources for other basic needs.

Table 1. Selected Characteristics of Housing Units, 1960–81

Characteristic	1960	1970	1980	1981
Median number of rooms	4.9	5.0	5.1	5.1
Median persons per unit (owner occupied)	3.1	3.0	2.6	2.6
Median persons per unit (renter occupied)	2.6	2.3	2.0	2.0
Percentage of units lacking some or all plumbing facilities	13.2	6.5	2.7	2.7
Percentage of units with 1.01 persons or more per room	12.0	8.0	N.A.[a]	4.0
Percentage of units that were dilapidated or in need of major repairs	6.9	4.6	N.A.[a]	N.A.[a]

Source: U.S. Bureau of the Census, *Statistical Abstract of the United States: 1984* (Washington, D.C.: U.S. Government Printing Office, 1983), p. 748; and U.S. Bureau of the Census, *Annual Housing Survey: 1981* (Washington, D.C.: U.S. Government Printing Office, 1983), Table A-1, p. 4.
[a] N.A. = not available.

Challenge of the 1980s

In the early 1980s, the fundamental challenge has become whether, after a decade of rapid inflation and escalating housing costs, a large portion of people in this society can fulfill the American Dream of owning a home and whether this society can continue to make progress in ameliorating the impact of inflation on the poor and those who cannot take advantage of home ownership. In years past, the poor benefited from the overall improvements in the quality of housing in this country as better-quality housing trickled down to them. Today, the critical issue for both the poor and the middle class is the *affordability* of housing. Can both groups continue to improve their housing situation without having to shift more of their resources into the consumption of this housing?

Since World War II, the general standard of housing in this country has steadily improved (U.S. Department of Housing & Urban Development, 1982a). Tables 1 and 2 provide some of the evidence of that continuing improvement. Table 1 shows a steady decrease in the crowding of dwellings and significant strides in the elimination of the worst housing stock. The U.S. Department of Housing and Urban Development (1982a) estimated that only about 4 percent of the nation's housing stock is seriously inadequate and that an additional 6 percent is moderately inadequate. Table 2 demonstrates the dramatic decrease in the size of households since World War II, and future projections indicate this continued reduction for at least another decade. However, as the qual-

ity of housing improved, the ability to afford housing declined. As will be shown, both renters and first-time home buyers in the 1980s were faced either with spending a higher proportion of their income on housing or with reducing the quality of their housing.

Table 2. Average Size of Households, 1940–90

Year	Average Size of Households
1940	3.67
1950	3.37
1955	3.33
1960	3.33
1965	3.29
1970	3.14
1971	3.11
1972	3.06
1973	3.01
1974	2.97
1975	2.94
1976	2.89
1977	2.86
1978	2.81
1980[a]	2.75
1990[a]	2.41

Source: U.S. Bureau of the Census, "Population Characteristics," *Current Population Reports*, Series P-20, No. 313 (September 1977), p. 4, and No. 327 (August 1978), p. 3.
[a] Estimated, as reported in U.S. Department of Housing and Urban Development, *The President's National Urban Policy Report: 1982* (Washington, D.C.: U.S. Government Printing Office, 1982), p. 33.

Table 3 shows the historical shift of American society toward home ownership. Although all races have made progress toward home ownership since 1920, whites are still more likely to own a home than are blacks. Projections of housing consumption for the next 25 years suggest at least a modest increase in home ownership through the turn of the century. If home ownership is to remain an American Dream, then the costs of a home must remain within the reach of Americans or society must invest more resources in housing than it did in the past. However, as Sternlieb and Hughes (1981) cautioned, an overinvestment in housing may inhibit the resurgence of industrialization and take much-needed resources from other areas of high priority. It may not be possible in this economic environment to make the goal of home ownership a reality for an increasing number of families unless Americans are willing to sacrifice other goals. If, in the future, more families are forced to rent because of the high costs of home ownership, then an equally important concern would be to assure that the quality of their housing is maintained (or increased) without these households being forced to spend higher proportions of their income on rent.

Sociodemographic Aspects

Housing can be seen as shelter and as an investment, but it can also provide families with access to many other things they value, including employment, good schools, a package of public services, or a high-quality neighborhood (Meeks, 1980; Roske, 1983). The choice of where to live involves many considerations beyond the cost and the physical quality of the dwelling.

Choice of Where to Live. When the U.S. Department of Housing and Urban Development (1978b) commissioned a survey of the housing preferences of Americans, it found that, as was already mentioned, 75 percent of the American adult population preferred a single-family detached home. The survey also found that the respondents varied in their choice of location as follows: 48 percent preferred a rural area, small city, town, or village (not a suburb); 28 percent, small or medium-sized suburbs; 16 percent, a city of over 250,000 people; and 8 percent, a

Table 3. Home Ownership by Race: 1920–2000 (percentage)

Year	Owner Occupied, All Races	Owner Occupied, White	Owner Occupied, Black and Other
1920	45.6	48.2	23.9
1930	47.8	50.2	25.2
1940	43.6	45.7	23.6
1950	55.0	57.0	34.9
1960	61.9	64.4	38.4
1970	62.9	65.4	42.1
1980	64.4	67.8	44.2
1981	65.3	68.6	43.7
1985[a]	65.1	N.A.[b]	N.A.[b]
1990[a]	65.7	N.A.[b]	N.A.[b]
2000[a]	68.3	N.A.[b]	N.A.[b]

Source: U.S. Bureau of the Census, *Statistical Abstract of the United States: 1984* (Washington, D.C.: U.S. Government Printing Office, 1983), p. 753.

[a] Estimated, as reported in U.S. Department of Housing & Urban Development, *Projections of Housing Consumption in the U.S., 1980 to 2000, by a Cohort Method* (Washington, D.C.: U.S. Government Printing Office, 1980), pp. 71–73.

[b] N.A. = not available.

medium-sized city of 50,000–250,000 people (not a suburb).

These figures show a clear preference for living in less-dense and less-stressful living environments. Over 75 percent of the population preferred other than medium- or big-size city living. These kinds of subjective preferences may help explain why population figures indicate that nonmetropolitan areas, especially those on the fringe of metropolitan areas, continue to have a higher net in-migration of households than do any other geographic areas (U.S. Department of Housing & Urban Development, 1979b). Of particular interest is that 30 percent of the respondents, or roughly one out of every three Americans in the survey, anticipated a move in the next two years. On the one hand, people who were living in medium- and large-sized cities and who anticipated moving indicated about an equal preference for relocating within their current city (47 percent) or for moving to a suburb or a small town (45 percent). On the other hand, potential movers who were living in the suburbs showed a strong preference for continued suburban liv-

Table 4. Types of Households, 1960 and 1975 and Projected for 1990 (percentages)

Household Type	1960	1975	1990
Married Couples	74.8	65.4	54.9
No children present	33.3	34.0	27.2
Children under age 15	41.5	31.4	27.7
Other Male Head	8.1	10.9	16.0
Never married	3.2	4.7	6.8
Previously married	4.9	6.2	9.2
Other Female Head	17.2	23.6	29.0
Never married	2.8	4.4	6.3
Divorced or separated	4.7	8.2	10.8
Widowed	9.7	11.0	11.9

Source: G. Masnick & M. J. Bane, *The Nation's Families: 1960–1990* (Cambridge, Mass.: Joint Center for Urban Studies of M.I.T. & Harvard University, 1980), p. 57.

ing (80 percent), and only 13 percent were interested in moving to a city. Finally, 87 percent of the potential movers in rural areas and small towns anticipated moving within or to another similar type of community, while only 11 percent anticipated moving to a city. Net in-migration figures taken from the Annual Housing Survey of 1981 (U.S. Bureau of the Census, 1983a) reinforce these subjective preferences in that the urban-fringe areas, the suburbs, and medium-sized cities, in that order, have been the net gainers in households, while large central cities have continued to lose population.

Regardless of accounts of the revitalization and gentrification of cities, home buyers in revitalizing neighborhoods appear to be people who have moved from rented apartments to homes in the same city (James, 1980). Those who live outside the city do not seem to be returning in any great numbers to the city; rather, urban dwellers who are forming families and who cannot afford the high costs of housing in the suburbs or urban-fringe areas are turning to older homes that they can afford (Goetz, 1983). Thus, the costs of new housing may largely shape the revitalization of many of the larger central cities. If affordable suburban and urban-fringe housing

becomes available to families who reach the age of household formation, further revitalization may slow down considerably. Alternatively, as many analysts argue (Goetz, 1983; James, 1980; Sternlieb & Hughes, 1981), if the cost of new housing continues to escalate, especially in suburban and fringe areas, the revitalization of large central cities may flourish further because of the relative price differentials between new and older housing. This prospect for revitalization assumes a continued and strong preference for home ownership among new households.

Demographic Patterns. Two demographic patterns also are important in understanding the housing situation. They are the "baby-boom" generation and the changing composition of households.

Baby-Boom Generation. This cohort, born from 1947 to 1957, reached the age of household formation in the late 1970s and will peak some time in the 1990s, depending on the age of marriage and childbearing (U.S. Department of Housing & Urban Development, 1980). Because of lower fertility rates, when the next cohort forms households, it will place fewer demands on the housing system. The pressure for new housing units or rehabilitated units therefore will be considerable until the early 1990s after which it will decline. What is of particular significance is the type and location of housing that this group prefers. As was indicated earlier, the forces for fixup and revitalization of the city appear strong for the group who now live in cities, but this situation could change if new housing becomes more affordable in other locations. A critical issue, then, is whether larger central cities can continue to retain the baby-boom generation or whether this cohort will abandon the cities.

The Changing Composition of Households. Table 4 reveals the extraordinary changes in household composition occurring in this society. The number of households with married couples (with or without children) is definitely decreasing, while female-headed households (with or without children) are expected almost to double by 1990. Further, the Department of Housing and Urban Development (1982a) estimated that, of the households that will be formed in the 1980s, 51 percent will be composed of single persons and unrelated individuals, 22 percent will be of single-parent families, and only 27 percent will contain married couples (with or without children). The implications of these figures are significant because another study by the U.S. Department of Housing and Urban Development (1979b) indicated that higher-income married households are much more likely than are lower-income nonmarried households to change from renters to buyers in any type of area. In addition, this research found that never-married, separated, divorced, and widowed households have a high probability of shifting from home ownership to rental units. In short, the changing composition of households may presage the demand for specific types of housing. Households with relatively high incomes, in which one or both of the marital partners are working will continue to have the option of home ownership as an investment. However, other types of households, particularly the income-deficient, female-headed, and one-parent families, will increasingly be confined to the rental market and will choose housing as shelter—not as an investment (Sternlieb & Hughes, 1981).

Thus, the key to the future of housing in this country in the 1980s and beyond is best understood by examining the connections between housing preferences, the size of the cohort-forming households, and the nature and composition of these households. Because of insufficient income and escalating housing costs, the dream of home ownership at an early age will be available only to a shrinking number of households in the future unless economic circumstances change dramatically in the next decade.

Economics of Housing

Since 1970, the major influences on the housing situation in this country have been economic (Colton, 1981; Montgomery & Marshall, 1979; Smith, 1983). The heart of the economic problem has been continued inflation, especially double-digit inflation for much of this period. The main effects of inflation were to make the affordability of housing a central problem for both the middle class and the poor, to facilitate a movement to deregulate the housing finance system, and to help shift housing policy from a production-oriented approach to a more consumer-oriented one. When the dust settled in 1982, a different housing system was in place. A

housing system that had been protected since the depression from many private-market forces was now subject to periodic fluctuations in the supply and demand for housing.

Housing Starts. Table 5 serves as background for the discussion of the economic trends to follow. As can be seen, from 1960 to 1982, housing starts (the number of new units under construction) were predominantly single-family homes. With the exception of 1969–1973, single-family housing starts were well above 60 percent each year—a percentage that reinforces the earlier discussion of this country's commitment to home ownership. For the entire period (1960–1982), publicly owned housing accounted only for a tiny fraction of the new starts. Thus, private-market single-family units accounted for the overwhelming majority of new units. This commitment to single-family units meant that, by the early 1980s, a little over six out of every ten households were classified as single-family owner-occupied units (see Table 3). The housing starts for this period also illustrate the cyclical nature of the housing market. From 1960 to 1982, housing starts increased for a few years and then decreased somewhat only to increase again. This up-and-down phenomenon is related to the larger economy, the availability of financing at reasonable interest rates, and the demand for housing by consumers. If anything, the ups and downs of the 1970s were more severe than in the 1960s, as evidenced by the magnitude of annual percentage increases or decreases represented in Table 5.

Impact of Inflation. The volatility of housing starts reveals only a small part of the broader economic picture. Table 6 more dramatically shows the impact of inflation in the 1970s on housing prices. Although there are many ways of portraying this impact, the main thrust is that the purchase of a home slowly became more difficult as the price of houses rose at a faster rate than the general price index and median family income. Table 7 indicates that, from 1970 to 1982, the median sale price of new housing almost tripled, while the median family income only doubled. The major increase in sale prices occurred between 1973 and 1979 when new housing prices increased by 87.7 percent (see Table 6). Since 1980, price increases have

Table 5. New Housing Starts 1960–82 (in thousands of units)

Year	Total Housing Starts (number)	Increase or Decrease from Previous Year (percentage)	Publicly Owned Starts (number)[a]	New Privately Owned Units Started (number)	One-Family Homes as a Percentage of New, Privately Owned Units Started
1960	1,296		44	1,252	79.5
1961	1,365	+ 5.3	52	1,313	74.2
1962	1,492	+ 9.3	30	1,463	67.7
1963	1,635	+ 9.6	32	1,603	63.1
1964	1,561	− 4.5	32	1,529	63.4
1965	1,510	− 3.3	37	1,473	65.4
1966	1,196	−20.8	31	1,165	66.9
1967	1,322	+10.5	30	1,292	65.3
1968	1,545	+16.9	38	1,508	59.6
1969	1,500	− 2.9	33	1,467	55.3
1970	1,469	− 2.1	35	1,434	56.7
1971	2,085	+49.1	32	2,052	56.1
1972	2,379	+14.1	22	2,357	55.5
1973	2,057	−13.5	12	2,045	55.4
1974	1,353	−34.2	15	1,338	66.4
1975	1,171	−13.5	11	1,160	76.9
1976	1,548	+32.2	10	1,538	75.5
1977	2,002	+29.3	15	1,987	73.0
1978	2,036	+ 1.7	16	2,020	70.9
1979	1,760	−13.6	15	1,745	68.4
1980	1,313	−25.4	20	1,292	65.9
1981	1,100	−16.2	16	1,084	65.0
1982	1,072	− 2.5	10	1,062	62.4

Source: U.S. Bureau of the Census, *Statistical Abstract of the United States: 1984* (Washington, D.C.: U.S. Government Printing Office, 1983), p. 743.

[a] Publicly owned housing includes housing units for which construction contracts were awarded by federal, state, or local governments.

begun to moderate. Table 7 shows more sharply what happened. The ratio of sale price to income went from 2.37 to 3.44 in just 12 years.

The issue of affordability comes directly into focus in Table 8. Using an assumption about the percentage of down payment required on a new home, Tuccillo and Goodman (1983) calculated the percentage of families that were able to afford new houses in the 1970s, given all housing costs and a constant amount of income available for housing. As is evident in Table 8, there is no doubt that a decreasing proportion of families have been able to afford new housing since 1970. Unless families are willing to take on larger mortgage payments and spend a significantly higher percentage of their monthly income on housing, new housing may become even less affordable to many families.

Table 9 shows the differences between the sale price of new homes and of existing homes. These differences were minor in 1970 and 1971, but they steadily increased in magnitude from 1972 to 1979, when they began to decrease again. As was just noted, one interpretation of these differences in the prices of new and existing homes is that older homes in many cities became a bargain for those families who wanted to move from rental to home-owner status. Therefore, urban revitalization occurs partly because existing homes are a better bargain than are new homes during a period of rapid inflation. By the early 1980s, the affordability of housing had become a serious problem for the middle class.

The picture for renters was comparable to that for home owners. Rent burden is the amount of rent paid monthly as a percentage of the household income. For many years,

Table 6. Median Sale Price of New Privately Owned One-Family Houses: 1967–82

Year	Median Sale Price	Increase from Previous Year (percentage)
1965	$20,000	—
1966	$21,400	7.0
1967	$22,700	6.1
1968	$24,700	8.8
1969	$25,600	3.6
1970	$23,400	−8.6
1971	$25,200	7.7
1972	$27,600	9.5
1973	$32,500	17.8
1974	$35,900	10.5
1975	$39,300	9.5
1976	$44,200	12.5
1977	$48,800	10.4
1978	$55,700	14.1
1979	$62,900	12.9
1980	$64,600	2.7
1981	$68,900	6.7
1982	$69,300	1.5

Source: U.S. Bureau of the Census, *Statistical Abstract of the United States: 1984* (Washington, D.C.: U.S. Government Printing Office, 1983), p. 745.

the U.S. Department of Housing and Urban Development (1982a) considered any figure in excess of 25 percent to be an indication of problems in the affordability of housing. Since 1981, this figure was raised to 30 percent. By the earlier standard of 25 percent, one-person households, couples over age 65, male-headed households, and all forms of female-headed households had an excessive rent burden. Table 10 shows the increase in the average rent burden, by the type of household, in 1973, 1976, and 1979. It also indicates that the rent burden got worse during that period for all categories of households except one-person households, in which the average rent burden was about the same. Of special note is the average rent burden of female-headed households (under age 65), which jumped from 26.6 percent to 38.3 percent in just six years. The U.S. Department of Housing and Urban Development (1982a) also estimated, using its Annual Housing Surveys, that one-third of all renters and three-quarters of renters in the lowest

Table 7. Median Sale Price of New One-Family Houses and Median Family Income, United States: 1960–82 (selected years)

Year	Median Sale Price	Median Family Income	Ratio of Sale Price to Income
1960	$15,200	$ 5,417	2.81
1965	$20,000	$ 6,957	2.87
1970	$23,400	$ 9,867	2.37
1975	$39,300	$13,719	2.86
1982	$69,300	$20,171	3.44

Source: U.S. Bureau of the Census, *Statistical Abstract of the United States: 1984* (Washington, D.C.: U.S. Government Printing Office, 1983), pp. 460, 745.

income quartile paid more than 35 percent of their incomes for rent. By any standard, certain households have become more disadvantaged by excessive rent burdens.

Reform of Housing Finance System. In the 1970s, historically high rates of inflation drove up interest rates and put extreme pressure on the housing finance system. The need for reform in housing finance led to the pas-

Table 8. Families in the United States that Were Able to Afford New Houses: 1967–78 (percentage)[a]

Year	Able to Afford New Houses (percentage)
1967	41.2
1968	37.6
1969	38.3
1970	45.2
1971	44.0
1972	42.8
1973	36.8
1974	31.4
1975	31.5
1976	27.2
1977	34.4
1978	29.1

Source: J. Tuccillo & J. Goodman, *Housing Finance: A Changing System in the Reagan Era* (Washington, D.C.: The Urban Institute, 1983), p. 25.

[a] This table is based on the assumption of a 25 percent down payment.

Table 9. Difference Between the Median Sale Price of New Privately Owned One-Family Houses and the Median Sale Price of Existing One-Family Houses: 1970–82

Year	New Median Sale Price Minus Existing Sale Price of One-Family Houses
1970	$ 400
1971	$ 400
1972	$ 900
1973	$3,600
1974	$3,900
1975	$4,000
1976	$6,100
1977	$5,900
1978	$7,000
1979	$7,200
1980	$2,400
1981	$2,500
1982	$1,500

Source: U.S. Bureau of the Census, *Statistical Abstract of the United States: 1984* (Washington, D.C.: U.S. Government Printing Office, 1983), pp. 745–746. Calculations were made from the tables on these pages.

sage of the Depository Institutions Deregulation and Monetary Control Act of 1980 (Tuccillo & Goodman, 1983). This bill broadened the power of mortgage-lending institutions and brought them in line with their more lightly regulated competitors. Further, the act provided for the gradual removal of interest ceilings on all classes of deposits. During the late 1970s, other federal agencies also relaxed their rules and authorized the use of alternatives to the standard 30-year fixed-rate mortgage, so that savings and loan associations and banks could more successfully compete with other financial institutions like money-market mutual funds. As a result, a variety of mortgage instruments became available to lenders. Such instruments as adjustable-rate mortgages, renegotiated-rate mortgages, and shared-appreciation mortgages were introduced to allow more flexibility in mortgage financing.

Along with other changes made by the Reagan administration in the early 1980s, the trend toward deregulation of the housing finance system was continued (Struyk, Mayer, & Tuccillo, 1983). In the near future, the

Reagan administration visualizes a housing finance system in which the providers of mortgage credit will be indistinguishable from the providers of credit to any other segment of the economy (President's Commission on Housing, 1981). Deregulation will no doubt lead to a better match between interest rates and the general economy because housing will no longer receive the preferential treatment it historically enjoyed. But it also means that mortgage interest rates will be higher than before deregulation because these rates will move up and down in relation to other types of borrowing. However, a return to the high inflation rates of the mid-1970s could again drive up interest rates and severely hamper the ability of families to obtain affordable housing credit.

The Reagan administration also proposes to move the federally related secondary mortgage-market firms, the Federal National Mortgage Association and the Federal Home Loan Mortgage Corporation, into the private sector and to phase out of existence the Government National Mortgage Association (Tuccillo & Goodman, 1983). Removal of

Table 10. Median Rent of Renter Households as a Percentage of the Median Income: 1973, 1976, 1979

Household Composition by Age of Head	1973	1976	1979
Two-or-more-person households	19.6	22.6	24.1
One-person households	30.7	31.0	30.2
Male Head, Wife Present	18.2	18.9	20.0
Under 25 years	19.8	20.3	21.3
25–29 years	17.4	18.3	19.0
30–34 years	17.0	17.8	18.6
35–44 years	17.1	17.7	19.0
45–64 years	16.4	17.5	19.1
65 years and over	29.6	29.6	27.8
Other Male Head	21.0	26.3	28.3
Under 25 years	20.7	26.2	28.1
65 years and over	28.0	28.8	31.0
Female Head	26.9	35.8	37.2
Under 65 years	26.6	35.4	38.3
65 years and over	31.1	33.2	32.4

Source: U.S. Bureau of the Census, *Current Housing Reports*, Series 150–79; and U.S. Bureau of the Census, *Annual Housing Survey: 1979* (Washington, D.C.: U.S. Government Printing Office, 1981), Parts A and C.

these secondary banking institutions that buy and sell mortgages would further reduce the presence of the federal government in the housing sector. In sum, high rates of inflation in the 1970s put a strain on the housing finance system and eventually contributed to its deregulation. However, throughout this period, the affordability of housing for the middle class and the poor was the critical issue.

Public Policy and Housing

The results of the Experimental Housing Allowance Program, which began in 1973 and was finally evaluated in 1982 at a cost to the government of $200 million, set the stage for policy changes (Friedman & Weinberg, 1983). Along with other evaluations done by the U.S. Department of Housing and Urban Development (1978a; 1979c; 1979d; 1982b) during the past ten years, a body of evidence supporting a more consumer-oriented approach to housing policy developed. The central finding of most of these studies and experiments was that a housing allowance paid directly to a low-income renter was by far the least costly and most equitable way of assisting low-income households. Other programs used by the federal government were more production oriented in that they subsidized landlords, developers, or lending institutions as long as they agreed to serve income-eligible families (Weicher, 1980). These programs included subsidizing the building of a public housing project in a community or

the interest on a loan to a sponsor of low-to-moderate-income housing or executing a lease with a landlord to provide below-market rent to a low-income renter. Such indirect approaches were far more costly than the consumer-oriented approaches, which did not rely on any middlemen to deliver program benefits.

It was argued that a simple housing allowance issued directly to a low-income household to make up the differences between 30 percent of the household's income and a predetermined market value for the rent on the apartment would be the most efficient way of serving low-income households (Struyk & Bendick, 1981). In addition, such a housing allowance would give the low-income household freedom of choice because it would not be tied to a particular housing unit or project through a lease or long-term mortgage.

According to the *Budget of the U.S. Government* (1984, Part 5, p. 116), the federal government's commitment to helping low-income persons with housing, through a variety of federal programs, rose from assistance to 3.3 million households in 1980, to 3.6 million households in 1982, to an estimated 4.1 million households in 1984. Table 11 gives a breakdown of these federal programs and the number of occupied units covered by each program in 1982. Of particular interest is that, using 1982 figures, there were 91,561,000 housing units in this country (U.S. Bureau of the Census, 1983a), but only 3.3

Table 11. Type of Housing Assistance Activity, by Category, for Fiscal Year 1982

Housing Category	Number of Occupied Units	Percentage of Total Units
Section 8 (rental housing)	1,319,000	37
Existing leases	844,000	
New construction and rehabilitation	475,000	
Public Housing (rental housing)	1,200,000	34
Section 236 (rental housing)	537,000	15
Section 235 (home ownership)	241,000	7
Rent supplement (rental housing)	158,000	4
Section 202 for the elderly or handicapped (rental housing)	97,000	3
Total units	3,552,000	100

Source: *Budget Summary, U.S. Department of Housing and Urban Development, Fiscal Year 1983* (Washington, D.C.: U.S. Government Printing Office, 1982).

Table 12. Summary of Changing Federal Housing Activities, Fiscal Year 1981 to Fiscal Year 1987 (in millions of dollars)

Activities	1981	1982	1983	1984[a]	1985[a]	1986[a]	1987[a]
Housing Assistance							
Outlays, U.S. Department of Housing and Urban Development	5,747	6,726	7,352	7,831	8,401	8,867	9,205
Community Development[b]							
CDBG	3,695	3,456	3,456	3,456	3,456	3,456	3,456
Urban Development grants	675	440	440	440	440	440	440
Enterprise zones	—	—	—	310	620	930	930
Other[c]	2,100	189	23	118	116	—	—
Housing Credit							
Direct Loan Guarantees[d]	3,901	4,110	1,456	1,451	1,474	1,466	1,456
Guar. Loan Comm.[e]	65,785	76,609	73,400	—	—	—	—
House. Tax Exp.[f]	32,645	37,695	42,755	46,640	51,935	59,905	69,095

Source: *Budget of the United States Government, Fiscal Years 1984 and 1983* (Washington, D.C.: U.S. Government Printing Office, 1984 and 1983, respectively), Parts 5–8; and R. Struyk et al., *The Reagan Experiment* (Washington, D.C.: The Urban Institute, 1982), p. 415.

[a] Estimated.

[b] Budget authority.

[c] Includes Section 312, neighborhoods self-help, housing counseling, public housing modernization, and so forth.

[d] Includes Farmer's Home Administration and Federal Housing Administration.

[e] Includes the Federal Housing Administration's and Government National Mortgage Association's mortgage-backed securities. The Reagan administration gives no figures after 1984.

[f] Includes mortgage interest on owner-occupied homes, property-tax deductions on owner-occupied homes, deferral and exclusions of capital gains, exclusion of interest on state and local housing bonds, and investor deductions.

million of them were assisted in some way by governmental programs. The number of units assisted by governmental programs represents about 3.9 percent of all the housing units in this country, which puts into perspective the degree of assistance provided directly to low-income households. Khadduri and Struyk (1982) estimated that 9 million households in the United States need housing assistance. These households, according to their definition, include renters whose incomes fall below 50 percent of the median family income in their respective geographic areas. Even using the 1984 estimated figure of 4.1 million assisted units just cited, the households covered by the foregoing definition would still represent program coverage of only 45.5 percent of the estimated need. Other budgetary information (*Budget of the U.S. Government* (1984) suggests that, in the near future, the Reagan administration does not anticipate going beyond the number of assisted units anticipated for 1984. The opportunity to serve all eligible low-income households with a housing allowance or some

other form of subsidy appears to have stalled for the moment.

Table 12 gives a more balanced view of federal activity in the housing sector. The figures on outlays for housing assistance represent commitments to serve low-income households in a variety of programs. Community development covers programs that help communities preserve and upgrade neighborhoods, while the housing credit category includes a combination of direct-loan and loan-guarantee programs that help underwrite the private sector's risk in lending mortgage money to many families and nonprofit sponsors of group housing. Housing tax expenditures include all those deductions claimed by home owners on their federal income taxes, as well as those deductions afforded investors in rental housing.

Table 12 indicates the balance and priorities represented in federal policy. For example, in fiscal year 1982, $10.8 billion were allocated to all housing assistance and community development programs, while $37.6 billion in tax breaks went to home owners and owners of rental property. Since these tax breaks are skewed toward higher-income households, it is reasonable to conclude that the federal government subsidizes home owners 3½ times more than it does lower-income households. (This statement assumes that community development dollars benefit just low-income households, which they do not.) The ratio of housing assistance and community development to housing tax expenditures increased to 3.8 in 1983 and to an estimated 4.0 in 1985, 4.4 in 1986, and 4.9 in 1987. If one looks carefully at the figures in Table 12, one will see a slight projected increase over time in housing assistance, no growth in the community development part of the budget, and more than a doubling of tax expenditures across these seven years. Tax breaks for home owners appear to be one of the more hidden parts of the federal budget that primarily benefit middle- and upper-income households.

In sum, federal policy has moved toward a more consumer-oriented housing assistance approach for low-income households, even though there appears to be no movement toward assisting a larger percentage of these households. For the moment, community development programs are being maintained, but they are not growing in relation to inflation, and tax breaks for home owners are scheduled to grow at a rapid pace in the future. In the previous section, it was pointed out that the Reagan administration had made progress in deregulating the housing finance industry and that it was proposing to withdraw the federal government further from the housing credit system. Taken together, public policy appears to be moving away from protecting the housing finance system, maintaining modest support for low-income households, slipping in its support of community development programs, and continuing the heavy subsidy of home owners. If the critical problem in the late 1980s still is the affordability of housing, on balance, middle- and upper-income households should have more reason for optimism than should low-income households. Ironically, federal tax policy, by default, has become the dominant strand of national housing policy. Without other initiatives, it appears that the Reagan administration hopes that macroeconomic policy, which fosters economic growth and lower interest rates, will eventu-

ally pay off in a more privatized housing market in which credit is more readily available for middle- and upper-class home owners. The lower class, given this view, will benefit primarily from filtering and, when necessary, housing assistance in the form of vouchers.[1]

Special Issues in Housing

The general issue of the affordability of housing cuts across a broad range of households in this country. However, a number of more specialized issues are of particular concern to the social work profession. One of the values of social work has long been to help the disadvantaged, which, in this context, means those who cannot function without assistance in a privatized housing market system. A first priority should be to identify these key target groups and then to intervene on their behalf. What follows is a list of target groups in need of assistance, along with a brief rationale for why they need help.

The Homeless. Lamb (1984) estimated that the homeless population in the United States ranges from 250,000 to 3 million. He further estimated that from one-fourth to one-half of these homeless people suffer from such mental illnesses as schizophrenia and manic-depression. Homelessness accelerated rapidly when state hospitals began to release mental patients in response to the availability of mood-altering drugs, the increase in fiscal pressures, and the upsurge in the patients' rights legal movement. Most communities need well-run and, wherever possible, rehabilitative shelters. Shelters usually provide a temporary answer, but more creative alternatives are needed if rehabilitation is to be emphasized (Sloss, 1984).

Resistance to Group Homes. The deinstitutionalization of the mentally ill, developmentally disabled, physically handicapped, and both young and adult criminal offenders places tremendous pressures on communities

---

[1] Filtering refers to the phenomenon whereby the upper and middle classes pass their housing on to the lower class when they move into newer and more expensive housing. Thus, when a middle-class family purchases a new home at a higher price than its existing home, the existing home is then passed on to a lower-class family. The lower-class family therefore gets a better-quality house at about the same cost as its current house.

to provide mental health and other residential services in a noninstitutional setting. Many communities across the country have resisted group homes, despite the attempts of states to supersede local zoning ordinances. These ordinances have been the major instrument for resisting group homes. Today, careful thought must be given to the process of gaining community acceptance if group homes are to be used (Stickney, 1977). The goal is to balance the interests of clients for the least restrictive environment with the neighborhood's fear of lowered property values and disruptive behavior by the residents of group homes.

Renovation of Public Housing. The U.S. Department of Housing and Urban Development (1979c) identified 700 public housing projects containing 180,000 units as "troubled." These projects, which are some of the oldest in the United States, are located primarily in urban areas and are situated in crime-ridden neighborhoods. They are troubled because they have a combination of financial, physical, managerial, and social problems. They represent 15 percent of all the public housing units in this country. Given the lack of affordable housing for a large number of low-income households, these projects need to be modernized and then properly managed so they can continue to be utilized by low-income households or families who would otherwise pay excessive rent. Adaptive reuse would be preferable to destruction of these units (Struyk, 1980). Community involvement is especially needed to guarantee their renovation.

Displacement. In previous years, urban renewal and highway projects displaced many low-income households. Today, the issues are gentrification and the conversion of rental apartments to cooperatives and condominiums. Gentrification and the accelerating conversion of rental housing into condominiums or cooperatives are forcing mostly low-income households from their areas of residence to other parts of the city. Although Nenno and Brophy (1982) reported that state and local governments have begun to react with regulatory laws and ordinances, only about half the states have legislated protection for tenants in converted buildings and fewer than one in five of the cities that are experiencing such conversions have passed regulatory ordinances. The predominant ap-

proach appears to be prior notification of and hearings for the displaced, rather than helping these persons with resettlement (Henig, 1981).

Rent Control. As of 1976, eight states and the District of Columbia have enacted legislation and two states (New Jersey and New York) have statewide rent control involving 97 and 110 jurisdictions, respectively (Nenno & Brophy, 1982). The principal argument against rent control is that it keeps a lid on rent increases but discourages proper maintenance and further improvements of the property unless such improvements are heavily subsidized (Goetz, 1983). Given the earlier discussion, the development of a more realistic housing allowance tagged to fair-market rents might be a better solution to the problem. Other changes in the tax code might facilitate reinvestment in older rental property without decreasing the supply of adequate housing for low-income households (Seidel, 1978).

Growth of Female-Headed Households. Table 10 showed that female-headed households have the highest rent burden, and, over time, the lack of affordable housing is likely to affect them more than any other type of household. Female-headed households in all age groups are likely to have significantly lower incomes than two-parent or father-only families (U.S. Department of Housing & Urban Development, 1979b). Low income dictates the worst location and poorest quality of housing in most communities. Much needs to be done through the public welfare system to ameliorate the plight of female-headed households because the shelter portion of the income-maintenance grant goes to housing. Creative joint programs of welfare departments and landlords could help, but, ultimately, public welfare grants and housing-assistance payments need to be coordinated or merged to increase efficiency (U.S. Department of Housing and Urban Development, 1979a).

Elderly People Who Are Living Alone. Almost half (44 percent) the elderly households are occupied by people living alone (U.S. Bureau of the Census, 1981). With age and impaired health, these isolated elderly people need a wider range of services to remain at home and out of costly institutions (Lammers, 1983). Home health care, homemaker and chore services, and transportation are essential and can be organized as cost-efficient solutions to institutional care.

Racial and Ethnic Minorities. Of special concern are those households that include racial and ethnic minorities. Because minorities generally are (1) overrepresented in public housing; (2) more subject to displacement because of gentrification, the conversion of rental apartments to condominiums and cooperatives, reindustrialization (the closing of manufacturing plants and the opening of high-technology industry in the same geographic area), and other public redevelopment projects; and (3) disproportionately members of low-income households, they are more likely to be subject to many of the problems just identified. For many minority groups, these problems are commonplace and a reminder of how these groups must constantly adapt to their surrounding environment. For minority groups, inadequate shelter is a constant problem and a continuing source of concern, rather than just an infrequent inconvenience (Bingham & Kirkpatrick, 1975).

Role of Social Work

First and foremost, social work must support public policies that improve the plight of low-income households. With the shift to market solutions, social workers must be careful to monitor housing policy, especially tax policy, to make sure that low-income households get their fair share of resources and that the problems of affordable housing do not become more serious. As a start, social work should support the coverage of the approximately 5 million low-income households that do not receive housing assistance. Second, the profession should continue its traditional roles in managing public housing and attendant services, organizing neighborhood self-help groups of all kinds, and facilitating the construction of group homes for the elderly, handicapped, and disabled. Third, emerging roles present a challenge to social work. There seems to be a considerable revival of housing assistance bureaus and the development of new bureaus that counsel and place the homeless, those in emergency situations, the displaced, those interested in home sharing, and elderly people who need barrier-free housing with congregate facilities. Because housing markets vary so much across the country (Struyk, 1977), much care is needed to link the supply

with the demand. A consumer-oriented housing allowance of a sufficient amount may provide many households with the opportunity to choose alternative housing that is of a better quality and located in a more desirable area (Frieden, 1980). But without proper counseling and assistance in relation to housing, many households may not be able to realize this opportunity.

Another emerging role is home care for the elderly. This type of care can take a variety of forms, including visiting or reassurance services, home-health aid, homemaker and chore services, or transportation. With the projected growth of the old-old group (over age 80), the future will see many more elderly persons remaining in their homes who will need services to remain independent (Lammers, 1983).

Overcoming resistance to group homes is a challenge of the 1980s. The deinstitutionalization of populations now currently served by social work means that community-oriented professionals are needed to plan, develop, and manage acceptable group homes in many more neighborhoods. Although they are more closely tied to the mental health system, community planners could just as easily be located in a variety of nonprofit settings in which community placement is just one of many services provided by an agency. In the end, housing is both shelter and an investment. Social work must attend to the basic needs of shelter. And, as Egan (1981) stressed, housing assistance should not be provided by bureaucratized organizations that alienate people, but by mediating structures that provide accessible and responsive services. These mediating structures would empower local residents and provide an alternative setting for service delivery.

In sum, social work is faced with a dual role. On the one hand, it must initiate and support public and private efforts aimed at solving problems of groups with special needs like the homeless, the displaced, female-headed households, racial and ethnic minorities, and elderly people who live alone. In a clear-cut way, the profession needs to continue to be a political advocate for disadvantaged groups. On the other hand, the profession must continue to carve out professional practice roles for itself in the housing field, as it did in the past. However, in the future, these practice roles must move beyond political advocacy. With the profession's broader emphasis on service delivery and intervention on behalf of clients, it could provide the type of personnel that the housing field now needs: people with specialized skills in information and referral; counseling and relocation assistance; tenant-landlord relations; housing management, including planning for social services; and social planning to help neighborhoods, communities, and cities develop realistic housing-assistance plans. The professional social worker can and should be a testimony to the old adage that we ought to plan with people, not for people. Many career opportunities in the housing field will be open to those social workers who develop the necessary specialized skills.

MILAN J. DLUHY

For further information, see COMMUNITY DEVELOPMENT; HOMELESSNESS; NEIGHBORHOODS; SOCIAL PLANNING; SOCIAL PLANNING AND COMMUNITY ORGANIZATION.

References

Bingham, R., & Kirkpatrick, S. A. (1975). "Providing Social Services for the Urban Poor: An Analysis of Public Housing Authorities." *Social Service Review, 49,* 64–78.

Budget of the U.S. Government, Fiscal Year 1985. (1984). Washington, D.C.: U.S. Government Printing Office.

Colton, K. W. (1981). "Housing Finance in the 1980s: Economic Factors Indicate Future Directions." *Journal of Housing, 38,* 15–20.

Egan, J. J. (1981). *Housing and Public Policy: A Role for Mediating Structures.* Cambridge, Mass.: Ballinger Publishing Co.

Frieden, B. (1980, Spring). "Housing Allowances: An Experiment That Worked." *Public Interest, 59,* 15–35.

Friedman, J., & Weinberg, D. (Eds.). (1983). *The Great Housing Experiment.* Beverly Hills, Calif.: Sage Publications.

Goetz, R. (1983). *Rescuing the American Dream: Public Policies and the Crisis in Housing.* New York: Holmes & Meier.

Henig, J. (1981). "Gentrification and Displacement of the Elderly." *Gerontologist, 26*(1) 67–75.

James, F. (1980). "The Revitalization of Older Urban Housing and Neighborhoods." Reprinted in A. P. Solomon (Ed.), *The Prospective City* (pp. 130–160). Cambridge, Mass.: M.I.T. Press.

Khadduri, J., & Struyk, R. J. (1982). "Housing Vouchers for the Poor." *Journal of Policy Analysis and Management, 1*(2), 196–208.

Lamb, R. (Ed.). (1984). *The Homeless Mentally Ill.*

Washington, D.C.: American Psychiatric Association.

Lammers, W. (1983). *Public Policy and the Aging.* Washington, D.C.: Congressional Quarterly.

Masnick, G., & Bane, M. J. (1980). *The Nation's Families: 1960–1990.* Cambridge, Mass.: Joint Center for Urban Studies of M.I.T. and Harvard University.

Meeks, C. (1980). *Housing.* Englewood Cliffs, N.J.: Prentice-Hall.

Montgomery, R., & Marshall, D. R. (1979). "Symposium on Housing Policy." *Policy Studies Journal* (entire issue), 8(2).

Nenno, M. K., & Brophy, P. (1982). *Housing and Local Government.* Washington, D.C.: International City Management Association.

President's Commission on Housing: Interim Report. (1981, October). Washington, D.C.: U.S. Government Printing Office.

Roske, M. D. (1983). *Housing in Transition.* New York: Holt, Rinehart & Winston.

Seidel, S. R. (1978). *Housing Costs and Government Regulations.* New Brunswick, N.J.: Center for Urban Policy Research.

Sloss, M. (1984). "The Crisis of Homelessness: Its Dimensions and Solutions." *Urban and Social Change Review, 17,* 18–20.

Smith, W. R. (1983, January). "Housing America." *Annals of the American Academy of Political & Social Science, 465,* 9–149.

Sternlieb, G., & Hughes, J. (1981). *The Future of Rental Housing.* Piscataway, N.J.: Center for Urban Policy Research.

Stickney, P. (1977). *Gaining Community Acceptance: A Handbook for Community Residence Planners.* White Plains, N.Y.: Westchester Community Services Council.

Struyk, R. J. (1977). "The Need for Local Flexibility in U.S. Housing Policy." *Policy Analysis, 3,* 471–484.

Struyk, R. J. (1980). *A New System for Public Housing: Salvaging a National Resource.* Washington, D.C.: The Urban Institute.

Struyk, R. J., & Bendick, M. (1981). *Housing Vouchers for the Poor.* Washington, D.C.: The Urban Institute Press.

Struyk, R. J., Tuccillo, J., & Zais, J. (1982). "Housing and Community Development." Reprinted in J. L. Palmer and I. V. Sawhill (Eds.), *The Reagan Experiment* (pp. 393–417). Washington, D.C.: The Urban Institute Press.

Struyk, R. J., Mayer, N., & Tuccillo, J. (1983). *Federal Housing Policy at President Reagan's Midterm.* Washington, D.C.: The Urban Institute Press.

Tuccillo, J., & Goodman, J. (1983). *Housing Finance: A Changing System in the Reagan Era.* Washington, D.C.: The Urban Institute Press.

U.S. Bureau of the Census. (1981). *Annual Hous-*

ing Survey: 1979, Part A. Washington, D.C.: U.S. Government Printing Office.

U.S. Bureau of the Census. (1983a). *Annual Housing Survey: 1981*. Washington, D.C.: U.S. Government Printing Office.

U.S. Bureau of the Census. (1983b). *Statistical Abstract of the United States: 1984*. Washington, D.C.: U.S. Government Printing Office.

U.S. Department of Housing & Urban Development. (1978a). *Lower Income Housing Assistance Program (Section 8): Nationwide Evaluation of the Existing Housing Program*. Washington, D.C.: U.S. Government Printing Office.

U.S. Department of Housing & Urban Development. (1978b). *The 1978 HUD Survey on the Quality of Community Life*. Washington, D.C.: U.S. Government Printing Office.

U.S. Department of Housing & Urban Development. (1979a). *The Housing Needs of Non-Traditional Households*. Washington, D.C.: U.S. Government Printing Office.

U.S. Department of Housing & Urban Development. (1979b). *Population Redistribution and Changes in Housing Tenure Status in the United States*. Washington, D.C.: U.S. Government Printing Office.

U.S. Department of Housing & Urban Development. (1979c, January). *Problems Affecting Low Rent Public Housing Projects*. Washington, D.C.: U.S. Government Printing Office.

U.S. Department of Housing & Urban Development. (1979d, September). *Housing for the Elderly and Handicapped: The Experience of the Section 202 Program*. Washington, D.C.: U.S. Government Printing Office.

U.S. Department of Housing & Urban Development. (1980). *Projections of Housing Consumption in the U.S., 1980 to 2000, by a Cohort Method*. Washington, D.C.: U.S. Government Printing Office.

U.S. Department of Housing & Urban Development. (1982a). *The President's National Urban Policy Report*. Washington, D.C.: U.S. Government Printing Office.

U.S. Department of Housing & Urban Development. (1982b, May). *The Costs of HUD Multifamily Housing Programs*. Washington, D.C.: U.S. Government Printing Office.

Weicher, J. C. (1980). *Housing: Federal Policies and Programs*. Washington, D.C.: American Enterprise Institute for Public Policy Research.

HOWARD, DONALD S. See biographical section.

HOWE, SAMUEL GRIDLEY. See biographical section.

HUMAN DEVELOPMENT: BIOLOGICAL PERSPECTIVE

For many years, social work has embraced the so-called "biopsychosocial" paradigm of human development and behavior. The biopsychosocial model is consistent with general systems theory. It represents an attempt to understand behavior as the overt manifestation of complex interactions between biological, psychological, and environmental factors that impinge on, and are generated by, individuals.

The importance of knowledge about biological factors that affect emotions and behavior has been demonstrated dramatically in two recent studies of undiagnosed medical illness in psychiatric patients (Hall et al., 1981; Koranyi, 1979). Among 2,090 patients screened at a psychiatric clinic, 43 percent were found to be suffering from a major physical illness (Koranyi, 1979). Nonpsychiatric physicians had missed major illness in one-third of the patients they referred, psychiatrists had missed major illness in one-half of the patients they referred, and social agencies and individual social workers had not had even a suspicion of major illness in 83 percent of the cases they referred! Social workers were no more knowledgeable than self-referred patients. Further, researchers judged that 69 percent of these major physical illnesses contributed significantly to the psychiatric state of the patients (Koranyi, 1979). In another study, 46 of 100 patients admitted to a state psychiatric hospital were found to have previously undiagnosed physical illnesses that had either caused or exacerbated their psychiatric illnesses (Hall et al. 1981). Twenty-eight of the 46 patients showed rapid and dramatic diminution of psychiatric symptoms when the underlying physical illnesses were treated. The failure of social workers as well as physicians to recognize the possibility that physical conditions may be factors in psychiatric disturbance led in the cases studied by Koranyi to delays in beginning effective treatment as well as to the inappropriate and stigmatizing labeling of patients.

Diseases most frequently implicated in psychiatric pathology in the Hall et al. and Koranyi studies were endocrine dysfunction, metabolic disturbances (diabetes, hypoglycemia), nutritional deficiencies, and circulatory and digestive disorders. The studies provided clinical evidence that the centers of the brain regulating the emotions are profoundly affected by the endocrine system, by processes related to carbohydrate metabolism, by deficiencies in certain vitamins and minerals, and by other bodily factors. Failure to recognize the physical bases of psychiatric conditions has resulted in several recent lawsuits against psychiatrists (Taylor, cited in Hall, 1981) and social workers (Besharov, 1985).

A major purpose of this article is to alert practitioners to information about biological factors that can be used to help avoid preventable disorders and more effectively respond to problems and conditions once they occur. These factors may be inherent or may occur at any time in the life cycle. This article emphasizes disorders. The reader who seeks information on normal development is referred to the work of Miller (1978) and Specht and Craig (1982).

Biological Problems in Birth and Aging

Pregnancy. Two major types of factors affect fetal development: genetic or chromosomal factors, and environmental factors occurring after conception. About 250,000 defective babies are born each year in the United States. Although it is often difficult to determine the cause of the baby's defect, some researchers have estimated that as few as 30 percent of these anomalies are due solely to hereditary factors; more than 50 percent are thought to be preventable (Schuster & Ashburn, 1980, p. 84).

Substances known to cause congenital malformation are known as teratogens, which can alter the structure of chromosomes, prevent transfer of nutrients to vital areas, or cause arrest in the cellular division or growth of the fetus (Schuster & Ashburn, 1980, p. 85). Most teratogens have an immediate effect on the fetus by causing retarded growth or organ deformity (see Table 1). Some effects do not appear until years later, how-

ever, and are dose related, causing harm only at certain dosage levels. Fetuses also differ in their sensitivity to teratogens.

Drugs have often been implicated in congenital anomaly. The effect of the drug on the infant depends on the kind of medication and the dose, the gestational stage of the fetus, and the sensitivity of particular organs. Mothers should take no drug during pregnancy unless it is reported safe in the *Physicians' Desk Reference* (Baker, 1982) and the insert in the drug package. Physicians do not always review this information carefully when prescribing; consumers should be advised to do so routinely themselves. Exposure to x-ray also is associated with chromosomal change, so women should avoid all exposure to radiation before and during pregnancy, especially during the first trimester (Schuster & Ashburn, 1980, p. 84).

LSD (lysergic acid diethylamide) is known to cause chromosomal defects, and marijuana is also under suspicion. Alcohol consumption is a well-documented cause of congenital anomaly. One study of 633 mothers showed that 17 percent of infants born to mothers who consumed alcohol at any point during pregnancy experienced congenital anomalies (Ouellette et al., 1977). The severity and frequency of the anomalies correlated with the frequency and amount of alcohol consumed.

Other factors affecting the fetus are the mother's nutrition, maternal disease, and level of maternal stress (Schuster & Ashburn, 1980, pp. 86–88). The fetus grows rapidly between 26 and 32 weeks of gestation. Inadequate protein and calorie intake at this time can permanently reduce the number of brain cells by as much as 40 percent (Winick, 1971, p. 969). Chronic maternal disease, especially diabetes, cardiac disease, and anemia, increase risks to the fetus. Severe maternal stress may also cause biochemical responses that can change the electrical activity of the brain of the fetus, which may correlate with low Apgar scores (explained in the following section), neonatal problems, and neurological abnormalities (Brazelton et al., 1976).

Birth. Most hazards arising from birth relate to oxygen deprivation. Lack of oxygen is a frequent cause of minimal brain damage, which may not show up until the child is a few years old in the form of hyperactivity,

Table 1. Teratogenic Agents and Their Effects on the Fetus

Agent	Effect on Fetus
Drugs	
Alcohol	Neonatal addiction, IGR[a], anomalies, microcephaly, postnatal growth retardation, cognitive deficiencies, fine motor dysfunction, increased fetal and perinatal death rate
Antihistamines[b]	Fetal death, anomalies
Aspirin	Neonatal bleeding
Barbiturates	Neonatal addiction, neonatal bleeding, neurological impairments
Cigarette smoke	Prematurity, IGR
Corticosteroids	Anomalies, cleft lip, IGR
DES (diethylstilbestrol)	Cancer of reproductive system 20 years later in female reproductive system, anomalies in male
Ergot	Fetal death
Hormones	Masculinization of female infant, feminization of male infant
Insulin	Fetal death through shock
LSD (lysergic acid diethylamide)	Chromosomal damage, anomalies
Lead	Fetal death, anemia, hemorrhage
Marijuana[b]	Chromosomal damage
Morphine	Neonatal addiction, anomalies
Smallpox vaccination	Fetal vaccinia, fetal death
Streptomycin	Damage to 8th cranial nerve
Sulfa drugs	Jaundice
Tetracycline	Discoloration of permanent teeth, inhibited bone growth
Thalidomide	Fetal death, abnormal extremities, hearing loss, cardiac anomalies
Radiation	Anomalies, microcephaly, chromosomal damage, leukemia
Maternal Diseases	
Cytomegalic inclusion disease	Jaundice, blood dyscrasis, microcephaly, IGR
Diabetes	Large birth weight, stillborn baby, anomalies
Gonorrhea	Neonatal blindness
Hepatitis	Neonatal hepatitis
Herpes virus	Neonatal infection/death, microcephaly, retinal dysplasia
Influenza	Abortion, cardiac defects
Syphilis	Fetal death, anomalies, congenital syphilis, prematurity
Toxoplasmosis (carried by cat feces)	Blindness, mental retardation, fetal death, cardiac anomalies
Rubella	Abortion, cardiac defects, deafness, blindness, mental retardation, IGR

[a] IGR = intrauterine growth retardation.
[b] Evidence strong but not conclusive.
SOURCE: Adapted from Clara Shaw Schuster and Shirley Smith Ashburn, *The Process of Human Development: A Holistic Approach*, p. 86. Copyright © 1980 by Little, Brown and Company (Inc.). Reprinted with permission.

poor attention span, and aggressive outbursts, or as severe handicapping such as retardation or cerebral palsy. Oxygen deprivation may occur because of an irregular blood supply to the fetus during labor, cord compression, breech delivery, premature separation of the placenta from the uterine wall, implantation of the placenta near or over the cervix, medications given to the mother during labor, failure of the infant's respiratory system to activate immediately after birth, and loss of body heat after birth.

The infant's adaptation to extrauterine life is measured one minute and again five minutes after birth by the Apgar newborn scoring system (Apgar et al., 1958). Infant death as well as subsequent neurological defects are correlated with low Apgar scores. Factors evaluated include the infant's color, heart rate, reflex irritability, muscle tone, and respiratory effort.

Medications given to the mother may slow down the activation of the infant's respiratory system, risking oxygen deprivation. Loss of body heat by the newborn results in an inability to produce surfactant, a thin film that coats the lining of the lungs. The lungs then do not expand adequately, and the infant obtains insufficient oxygen.

Prematurity. Babies born at a gestational age under 37 weeks or weighing less than 2,500 grams (roughly 5.5 pounds) are classified as premature. They constitute 8 percent of all births in the United States (Schuster & Ashburn, 1980, p. 107). Respiratory distress is common among premature infants. Infection is also a danger, especially in the second week of life. Premature babies have a higher incidence of mental retardation, cerebral palsy, convulsive disorders, and later hyperactivity than full-term children. Although early developmental milestones such as smiling, sitting, and walking are likely to be delayed, normal premature children usually catch up with full-term babies by age 2 or 3 (Schuster & Ashburn, 1980).

Childhood. One of the most common health problems among American children is allergic disease. The U.S. National Health Survey reported that nearly 33 percent of children under age 17 have allergies (Schiffer & Hunt, 1963). Some observers believe that the importance of allergies in causing a wide spectrum of other disorders has been underestimated (Schuster & Ashburn, 1980, p. 353). Agents that cause allergic reaction include inhalants (pollens, dust, mold, spores, animal dander), ingestants (foods, drugs), contactants (plant oils, cosmetics, clothes, detergents), injectants (drugs, foreign sera), and infectants (bacteria, viruses). In addition to a wide variety of physical symptoms, allergic reactions can be manifested as fatigue, hyperactivity, mental apathy and dullness, confusion, poor attention span, mood changes, insomnia, irritability, and restlessness (Schuster & Ashburn, 1980, pp. 356–357).

Aging. The hallmark of aging is the decline of various functions at varying times in the aging process (Schuster & Ashburn, 1980). Of relevance here is information on possible biological factors that practitioners should be aware of because they are often overlooked, even by physicians. Forty-two percent of the elderly have some limitation on their activity because of chronic conditions (Galton, 1979, p. 3). Symptoms of mental disturbance or confusion are common in old age and are often referred to as senility. A large number of diverse factors, many of them remediable, can produce senile dementia. Symptoms may be due to treatable physical conditions, drug reactions, or nutritional deficiencies (Galton, 1979, p. 3).

Various treatable physical conditions include narrowing of the blood vessels to the brain, which can be dilated biochemically; coagulation and clotting of blood cells due to a slower blood flow through narrowed vessels, which can be treated with anticoagulants; congestive heart failure that reduces the flow of blood to the brain; anemia, which can be treated with diet and nutritional supplements; and high blood pressure, thyroid and parathyroid dysfunction, and adrenal insufficiency or overproduction, all of which can be treated with drugs.

The drugs prescribed for many illnesses in the elderly, however, can also cause mental and emotional symptoms. A certain proportion of users of various drugs experience negative reactions due to a particular sensitivity to the drug, incorrect dosage, interaction of the drug with other drugs being taken concurrently, or interaction of the drug with certain foods. Galton (1979, pp. 126–132) lists the possible mental side effects of almost eighty medications commonly prescribed for many conditions including high blood pressure, thyroid malfunction, peptic ulcer, angina pectoris, infections, insomnia, anxiety, depression, allergies, and arthritis. Galton enumerates ways in which these drugs can produce mental symptoms, either alone or in combination with other drugs or certain foods.

In addition to physical illness and the effects of drugs, nutritional deficiencies have been demonstrated to cause deterioration in mental functioning in elderly people. Nutritional deficiencies can be caused not only by the inadequate intake of certain nutrients, but also by an inability to absorb nutrients properly (even when present in the diet) or interference with the body's utilization of the nutrient (even though absorbed). Aged people have frequently been found to be deficient in thiamine (vitamin B1), riboflavin (vitamin B2), niacin (vitamin B3), pyridoxine (vitamin B6), cobalamin (vitamin B12), folic acid, potassium, magnesium, and zinc (Galton, 1979, pp. 145–154). Inadequacies in these substances can result in confusion, memory impairment, irritability, difficulty in concentration, depression, hallucinations, insomnia, apathy, and disorientation.

Because physicians sometimes neglect to perform exhaustive investigations for possible nutritional deficiencies, drug reactions, drug-diet interactions, or disorders in absorption, practitioners working with the elderly need to become familiar with the wide range of possible causes of senile dementia. Familiarity with these possible causes should enable the worker to raise questions pertinent to the care and treatment of their clients. It should enable them to assess whether sufficiently comprehensive evaluations have been carried out before cases of senile mental deterioration are dismissed as inevitable and untreatable.

Disabilities in Children

About one in every seven families has a child with a defect (Schuster & Ashburn, 1980, p. 728), ranging from minor physical anomalies such as a facial birthmark to impairments in circumscribed areas of functioning such as specific learning disabilities (dyslexia, dyscalculia), from major disabilities

such as blindness, deafness, mental retardation, orthopedic handicaps, and neurological impairment to limitations arising from chronic or debilitating illness such as asthma or muscular dystrophy to severe or fatal illnesses such as leukemia.

There is widespread agreement on the organic etiology of most of the disabling conditions of childhood. Some notable exceptions are autism (pervasive developmental disorder), childhood schizophrenia, specific learning disabilities (specific developmental disorders), and attention deficit disorder with and without hyperactivity (American Psychiatric Association [APA], 1980). Psychogenic theories of etiology such as those propounded by Bettelheim (1967), Mahler (1949), and others are contradicted by an ever-increasing body of research that is unequivocal in support of physiological causation for autism, childhood schizophrenia, and specific learning disabilities. The evidence for physiological etiology in cases of attention deficit disorder that are of long-standing duration and early onset is also impressive (Johnson, 1980).

When the disability is gross and appears at birth, it may interfere with the process of parental bonding with the child. If the disability is identified after an extended period of time, however, strong ties between parent and child may already have been established. Parental bonding is essential for parents to make the emotional investment and provide the ongoing nurturance that children require.

The severity of the disability or deformity may intensify parental response to the child, but no direct relationship has been found between the degree of severity of a child's defect and the disturbed feelings of the parent. To some parents, even a facial birthmark may be experienced as a significant trauma. Orthopedic anomalies and blindness appear to create significant barriers to maternal bonding because of the marked degree of disparity from normality, the expectation that the child will remain physically dependent or helpless for an indefinite period, or the inability to establish eye contact with the mother, which is a powerful reinforcer for maternal caretaking (Baum, 1962; Fraiberg, 1974).

Financial burdens arising from the special needs of some disabled children may be crushing. Medical bills not covered by insurance, the need for the mother to stay home rather than work and for the father to find a second job, or the need to move to a different location where more appropriate medical or educational facilities are available may impose severe financial as well as emotional hardship on families.

Caring for a disabled child is often physically and emotionally draining. Schuster and Ashburn (1980) observed:

> Hoping against the odds and facing the uncertainty of the future are emotionally exhausting. Caring for a child who requires special care or exercises or who is frequently in pain will exact its toll even from exceptionally stable and mature parents. It is frequently the mother who must absorb the pressures of day-to-day care of the severely disabled child. (p. 736).

In view of the multiple stresses that beset these parents, it should not be surprising that parents of disabled children have an increased incidence of marital problems, divorce, suicide, and alcoholism (Bloch, 1978).

Practitioner's Role. Social workers are often in the position of having to discuss a child's condition with the parents. A trap that professionals sometimes fall into is to engage the parents in discussions of what more they can do and how better they can help the child. This represents an unwitting complicity by the professional in Social Darwinist attitudes that are pervasive in American culture. Family members are expected to make it on their own no matter what extraordinary burdens they bear. The failure of society to provide financial relief, services, alternative living arrangements, and respite care is often overlooked by the professional, who intensifies the burden on families already strained emotionally, physically, and financially. Although it is necessary for professionals to supply information to parents about methods and techniques for improving care, at the same time they should avoid contributing additional pressure to the situation. A powerful statement about the needs of parents has been written by Harvey and Connie Lapin (1976), parents of an autistic child. Much of it applies to parents of children with a variety of handicaps.

Workers should encourage parents to express grief and anger at what has happened to them, but only when the parents give some indication of a need to express such feelings. The worker should always be honest and direct. It is often necessary to repeat explanations several times because parents' grief or anxiety may prevent them from fully absorbing information the first or second time it is offered. It is crucial to interpret the situation in terms of realistic hope. Positive qualities in the disabled child should be identified. It is not helpful to give negative predictions for the future, because reliable prediction is seldom possible. Parents should be apprised of realistic alternatives and helped to examine all the options open to them for the child's care, upbringing, and education. The future should be considered in relation to maximizing the child's potential, rather than attempting to "normalize" the child. Striving for normality may simply result in frustration, disappointment, and further feelings of failure and inadequacy. Families should be helped to recognize the normal as well as the exceptional needs of the child and to respond to the normal needs. In an exhausting and frustrating situation, it is always desirable to help parents to take one day at a time. To contemplate the future is overwhelming. Feelings of competence and hope are developed as parents learn to cope on a day-to-day basis.

Parents should be offered information about peer support groups for families with a similar problem. The help of others who have been experiencing the same stress and heartbreak is likely to be comforting. Participation in advocacy actions in behalf of the group suffering from the child's disability helps overcome feelings of helplessness and breaks down the crushing sense of isolation that families of the disabled often experience.

Disability in Adults

The onset of disability in young or older adults arises from a wide spectrum of illnesses and accidents. The list of possible causes of adult disability is too long to include here. Medical and nursing texts as well as the literature published by advocacy groups contain information about particular conditions.

Becoming disabled in adulthood brings with it a host of physical, social, and environmental problems in addition to emotional distress. The practitioner's sensitivity to the gamut of stresses to which the disabled are subject is crucial to the ability to be helpful. In addition, workers must deal with their own feelings of repugnance if a physical anomaly is involved or their attitudes of pity, discomfort with the painful feelings of the disabled person, or other negative feelings that can lead them to avoid the disabled person. The following section on disability in adults has been adapted from Johnson and Hart (1984).[1]

Disabilities entail loss of physical or mental functioning or both. As frustrating and frightening as the loss of physical abilities is, observers tend to agree that the prospect of losing mental faculties—of becoming "crazy"—is more devastating. Also, in progressive diseases, the pain of the disability today is made immeasurably worse by the prospect that tomorrow (or next year, or 10 years from now), impairment will be more severe than it already is.

Reactions to Loss of Physical Functions. Patients with cancer, parkinsonism, multiple sclerosis, Huntington's disease, muscular dystrophy, and other diseases face progressive worsening of symptoms ranging from pain, nausea, and bowel problems to tremors, unsteady gait, difficulty in self-feeding and dressing, drooling, inability to swallow, and fear of choking, falling, and bumping into things. Slowness in perceiving, responding, and moving are also characteristic of some diseases. Loss of the capacity to speak, even when the intellect remains completely intact, is an enormous source of frustration.

People suffering with chronic nonprogressive conditions (such as cerebral palsy or traumatic brain injury) may experience any of the symptoms that patients with progressive disorders experience. The chief difference is that in nonprogressive disorders, the patient does not have to fear continual worsening of an already bad situation. Adjustments that individuals have made to their condition can be expected to continue to be appropriate. In progressive diseases, new adjustments are continually required.

It is sometimes difficult for patients to

[1] Adapted with permission of The Free Press, a Division of Macmillan, Inc. from *Adult Psychopathology*, edited by Francis J. Turner. Copyright © 1984 by The Free Press.

cope with physical symptoms both because they often have very low energy levels and because they lack control of their muscles. A well spouse or friend must often assume a parental role with the patient in relation to physical care. Breakage and spillage often result from lack of manual dexterity. Simple activities like making a cup of instant coffee or smoking a cigarette pose hazards of spilling boiling water or setting a home on fire.

Embarrassment or Humiliation. Some diseases, particularly neurological conditions, subject sufferers to behavior that ranges from mildly embarrassing to repulsive. These include tremors, jerky movements, bladder and bowel incontinence, speech impairment, bodily distortions, and other symptoms. Feelings of shame, embarrassment, and humiliation are common among patients who have outwardly visible manifestations of this nature. Individuals who have epilepsy are frequently mortified by having grand mal seizures in public. Family members are also embarrassed by the patient's symptoms.

Stages of Reaction to Diagnosis. Psychological reactions to the diagnosis of a progressive disease have been conceptualized in terms of stage theory, for which the Kübler-Ross (1969) model of stages in the acceptance of impending death serves as a prototype. The Kübler-Ross progression—denial, anger, bargaining, depression, and acceptance—is applicable to conditions expected to result in death in the near future. Models applicable to chronic disability also have been proposed (Falek, 1979). The Falek model includes denial and shock, anxiety, anger or guilt, depression, and psychological homeostasis. In general, the patient's frustration leads to a period of anger. Patients may show resentment, anger, or envy toward well relatives or acquaintances and hostility toward even the people who care most about them.

Depression. Depression occurs over the loss of one's former capacities, unfulfilled hopes and desires, increasing need to be physically dependent on other people, loss of control over one's life, and deprivation of formerly enjoyable activities that have become painful or embarrassing. Depression is a salient feature accompanying most disabling illnesses and accidents.

Uncertainty. Difficulty in diagnosis and the uncertainty about the progression of a disease even when the diagnosis is unambiguous causes patients and families to be apprehensive and often to fear the worst.

Fear of Fatal Attack. Patients as well as family members may live in constant fear of a fatal attack, both when the condition is clearly life threatening (as in a heart attack or stroke) and when ramifications of the disease (such as falling, choking, losing consciousness) may result in severe physical harm or even death. Fears of the latter kind are common in epilepsy, Huntington's disease, and other disorders that disrupt motor function.

Marginality. Another issue related to physical disability is what has been called marginality, or the borderline phenomenon. These terms refer to people whose disability is minimal and who must live on the borderline between health and sickness. Patients are often fatigued, weak, or uncomfortable but do not as yet have outward signs of illness. They may feel ambivalent about this situation, wishing both to maintain an appearance of normality and to surrender to the fatigue or other distressing symptoms. Family expectations of the patient remain the same as they were before the onset of illness, as do expectations of people outside the family. These expectations can create added stress for the patient (Hartings et al., 1976).

Redefinition of Lifelong Social Norms. Adaptation to chronic disease with physical disability requires that patients redefine their daily experiences and unlearn social norms that have been internalized since childhood (Hastings et al., 1976). An obvious example relates to the loss of bladder control. Patients may have to wear diapers. The stark physical reality of a condition may occur long before the individual has made the cognitive and emotional shifts that alleviate the sense of humiliation and failure that accompanies the physical problem.

Adaptation to Physical Dependence. Asking for help in situations in which the request is entirely appropriate may represent weakness and defeat to the patient. Family members must walk a tightrope between reinforcing the patient's feelings of inadequacy by doing too much and giving help when it is really needed.

Expressions of Aggression. Expressions of aggression take on new meaning in families with a disabled member. It is not considered acceptable to be angry at ill people. Sick and disabled people themselves may fear to express irritation or anger because they feel they are burdens to spouses, children, or other relatives. To vent anger might risk abandonment or loss of affection by the already taxed relative on whom the patient is dependent.

Sexuality. Difficulty in sexual function is a highly charged issue. It is often helpful for patients to discuss their problems and concerns about sex in individual or group counseling. Some, however, may find the subject too traumatic to talk about.

Competence. The patient's competence is also an area of great vulnerability. Doubts about patients' mental competence, whether based in reality or not, often lead family members, physicians, and other professionals to treat patients as nonpeople by withholding information, offering "reassuring" lies, preventing patients from participating in the process of making decisions about their own lives, or talking about them in their presence as if they were not there. Such behavior is demeaning and often frightening to patients. It reinforces their worst fears about the seriousness of their condition and the loss of their mental functions.

Distress in Family Members. In families with a physically disabled member, other members experience certain common concerns and emotions. Initially, denial is common. Spouses may feel extremely burdened by the constant physical care necessitated by the patient's illness; round-the-clock care can become extraordinarily wearing even for healthy, energetic, and devoted relatives. When the signs of the disorder are socially embarrassing, the trauma of going out with the patient may lead the family to stay home. Entertaining in the home may become difficult or uncomfortable. Spouses may have to assume new and unaccustomed responsibilities: breadwinning, childrearing, bathing, feeding, diapering, lifting adult patients, managing financial affairs, and a plethora of household chores. Anger is an appropriate reaction to excessive burdens, combined with decreased pleasure and enjoyment in life. Depression is also common among spouses and other family members. The spouse (or child or parent) may lose companionship, affection, and nurturing as the disability causes the ill person to become more and more self-engrossed.

Loss of Mental Functions. In some diseases, deterioration of mental functions occurs. Patients may become disoriented or forgetful. They may have difficulty following conversations. They may become depressed, withdrawn and secretive, or suspicious and hostile. They may have marked fluctuations in mood, with inappropriate crying or laughing. Hypochondriacal preoccupations may occur. Occasionally, overt psychosis may appear, with hallucinations or delusions. Violent or aggressive outbursts are characteristic of certain conditions such as Huntington's chorea. In Tourette's disorder and presenile dementias, sufferers may call out obscenities. Brain-injured people may display changes in their character ranging from mild to severe.

Brain-injured patients tend to have an impaired capacity for social perceptiveness. They may be self-centered, impulsive, impatient, or irritable and may lack empathy and the ability to be self-reflective. They may be disorganized and unable to plan or execute activities. They may verbalize intentions that they do not carry out. They may exhibit dependence on others, overreaction to stimuli, need for immediate gratification, silliness, or greatly increased or decreased interest in sex. Patients are frequently unable to learn from experience although their intellectual ability to absorb information appears intact. These changes bewilder family members who remember the patient as he or she was and may leave family members feeling cheated, angry, and probably guilty about harboring such feelings toward a disabled person.

Family members may wonder what they are doing wrong and believe—sometimes with professional reinforcement—that their behavior toward the patient is causing the behavioral changes. When the patient is recovering from a sudden-onset brain condition, such as stroke or head injury, family members are likely to be initially solicitous and supportive. "Delight at [a patient's] survival, however, can turn into impatience, exasperation, and ultimately anger as discrete capabilities improve but an increasingly irritable, demanding, and dissatisfied patient makes little or no effort to resume his ordinary responsibilities" (Trethowan, 1970, p. 594). Considerable time is often needed for families to realize that their loved one is not the same person he or she was prior to the disability. Neither counseling nor trying to

reason or plead with the patient tends to improve the situation (Lezak, 1978).

Environmental Sources of Stress. In addition to the sources of stress arising from loss of physical and mental functions, economic and social factors place a burden on patients and families. An almost universal problem is financial hardship. Income maintenance programs for the disabled provide no more than poverty-level subsistence for most. Loss of earning capacity by the patient, enormous medical bills, and the need for expensive supportive services all contribute to making financial problems a major component of disability for both patient and family.

To qualify for Medicaid, families must often spend their life savings on medical services for the patient before they become eligible for assistance. This means, in effect, that many families lose everything they have worked for during a lifetime because of the misfortune of having an ill family member.

The shortage or absence of necessary services such as home health care, transportation, socialization opportunities for the patient, and, above all, respite services for the family immeasurably adds to the grief and anguish that patients and families experience. The inadequacy of treatment and care options is particularly striking in the area of part-time alternatives to home or institutional care. The all-or-nothing nature of the decision to institutionalize, with the anguish it brings to both patient and family, is a sad commentary on the dearth in our society of alternative residential and care arrangements for chronically ill and incapacitated people (Counts, 1978).

Total home care limits the patient's opportunity for socialization with others with similar problems who might constitute an invaluable source of emotional support and companionship. It intensifies the patient's feelings of being a burden on loved ones, and it generates hostility between patient and family members from the high level of stress inherent in the situation.

Full-time hospitalization or other institutionalization, on the other hand, deprives patients of family life, separates them from any community other than the institution, dehumanizes them, and frequently amounts to de facto incarceration. Patients often feel that families have deserted them. Families, too, are burdened with guilt at having "abandoned" their family member.

Part-time out-of-home care, used creatively in combination with home care, could do much to alleviate the adverse effects of the full-time care alternatives. Day, night, weekday, weekend, or other part-time hospitalization or inpatient nursing homes, group homes, foster family care, and supervised apartment living for less severely disabled persons are urgently needed. Development of such resources is a challenge to communities. It requires concerted effort by patients, families, and professionals to demonstrate need, lobby for funding, and ensure competent implementation.

Biological Factors in Minority Issues

In recent years, a few central questions have emerged in consideration of minority issues. Two major issues have been racial inferiority and superiority and the origins of sexual preference.

Racial Inferiority. In the 1960s and early 1970s, publication of research by Jensen (1969), Shockley (1972), Burt (1972), and others about levels of intelligence among minority groups touched off heated controversy. Jensen and Shockley concluded, on the basis of data from 122 pairs of identical twins separated soon after birth, that heredity is responsible for about 80 percent of measured intelligence. That is, heredity is four times as important as environment in determining intellectual ability. Because their research also indicated that blacks tested on average about 15 IQ points lower than whites, the inference was clear: blacks were genetically inferior to whites in native intelligence.

Rapid response to these findings was geared to discrediting the conclusions. The study of the twins was criticized on the basis that separate environments were not necessarily different environments. Just because identical twins were raised in separate homes was no indication that the level of intellectual stimulation and nurturance was necessarily different. Both homes might have provided equivalent intellectual environments, thus accounting for similar scores between the two twins by environment rather than genetics. Second, IQ tests were found to have cultural biases that favored children brought up in a white middle-class milieu over children from a minority poverty environment. Alternative tests have since been developed using information with which minority children are more familiar than white children. One such test is BITCH (Black Intelligence Test for Cultural Homogeneity), on which black children are reported to have scored higher than white children. At this writing, no IQ tests that satisfy most critics as culture free have been developed.

Third, methodological weaknesses were identified in the Jensen and Shockley studies. They failed to account for differences in factors such as nutritional levels and quality of schooling. Fourth, because many blacks are racially mixed, no way exists to distinguish the effects of "pure" race.

Reynolds and Jensen (1983) have since identified differences in performance levels on subtests of the revised WISC between white and black children matched for IQ. Because the two groups of children had equivalent IQs, difference in overall intelligence was not at issue, but differences in particular components of intelligence were. No differences were found on verbal subtests, but whites scored better on performance tests, largely spatial visualization, while blacks scored better on memory tests. The degree to which criticisms directed to earlier studies also applies to the more recent work that attempts to discriminate levels of ability by race is not clear.

Sexual Preference. The ascendancy of psychoanalytic thought until recent years contributed to the widespread belief among social workers that homosexuality was a psychopathological condition. Recently, however, the American Psychiatric Association revised its classification to make its view of homosexuality consistent with the prevailing view that homosexuality is a lifestyle preference rather than an illness (APA, 1980). The reasons for its occurrence, however, are still obscure.

The role of biological factors in the etiology of male and female homosexuality, particularly the effects of differences in hormonal balances during pregnancy on the developing brain of the fetus, have been studied by various researchers. In a review of 45 studies, MacCulloch and Waddington (1981) found heterogeneity in the group of people displaying homosexual behavior. It appears that biological and psychological factors make different contributions to the development of homosexuality in different individuals. Lack of exposure to androgens (male hormones) in a critical period of intrauterine life may account for some incidence of male homosexuality, and exposure to abnormally high levels of androgens may predispose to homosexuality in the female.

On the other hand, identical twins, who share the same genes, reared together, have been found to have opposite sexual preferences and behavior, suggesting that in some instances the discordance must be explained in other than genetic terms (MacCulloch & Waddington, 1980, p. 341). The current level of research suggests that both biological and social factors contribute to the development of a homosexual lifestyle, with one or the other predominating in a given instance.

Physical Origins of Psychological Problems

A major area of ambiguity for the practicing social worker is the diagnosis of mental health problems. Social workers in a myriad of settings ranging from mental health facilities to child care institutions, schools, and hospitals as well as gerontological services engage in mental health assessment and counseling daily. The prevalence of misdiagnosis is dramatized by the Koranyi study (1979) cited previously in which social workers failed to recognize underlying physical conditions in 83 percent of the cases they referred to an outpatient psychiatric clinic.

Some case examples illustrate the variety of problems in which apparently psychological problems arise from physical causes:

A six-year-old boy was referred to a child psychiatric facility because of constant trouble at school, at home, and in the neighborhood. He had changeable moods, was sometimes wild and violent, punched and poked other children, knocked them down, and took their toys. He often provoked his father, who would then fly into violent rages himself and beat the boy quite mercilessly. It would have been natural to ascribe all the child's difficulties to the chaotic and punitive environment at home.

EEG abnormalities were identified and the boy was treated with methsuximide (an anticonvulsant) and amphetamine and placed in a special class for brain dysfunctioned children. His behavior improved markedly. Within eight months his arithmetic and spelling performance had increased by three grade levels and his reading by four grade levels. The atmosphere at home improved considerably as the father responded to the improvement in the child. When the amphetamine was discontinued for a few days, the boy reverted to hyperactive and hyperaggressive behavior. (Gross & Wilson, 1974, pp. 113–115)

A married mother of three in her forties was subject to severe depression. She was treated unsuccessfully with psychotherapy and finally hospitalized at the nearby state hospital, where she remained for two years. Her husband spoke with the social worker about getting a divorce, although, he said, they had been happy together before her illness. When an in-depth physical examination revealed the presence of hypoglycemia, treatment with diet was instituted. Within a few months, she was home with her family, fully recovered. Her husband appeared surprised when the worker alluded to his earlier plans for divorce, stating that the family was very happy and that separation was totally out of the question. (Johnson, 1980, p. 18)

A 72-year-old woman was hospitalized because of severe memory loss and chronic confusion. For several years, she had become increasingly unable to perform household tasks, cope with small sums of money, remember a short shopping list, find her way about . . . or recall events. She had lost all regard for the feelings of others, was given to purposeless outbursts of activity and marked emotional ups and downs, with a tendency to sexual misdemeanor. . . . The results of (extensive) physical examination were normal.

She had been taking 400 milligrams of quinidine sulfate and 50 milligrams of hydrochlorothiazide daily (for a heart condition). . . . Finally, her physicians decided to discontinue the quinidine. . . . Within forty-eight hours she was well oriented for time and place and could be discharged from the hospital. A month later her memory had greatly improved, her power of concentration was markedly increased, and her personality had reverted to what it had been before she became ill. (Galton, 1979, pp. 115–116)

In each of the above examples, the problem was alleviated by a physiological intervention (institution of medication, a change of diet, or removal of medication). In none of the examples could counseling have solved the problem because the origin of the

Table 2. Physical Factors That Affect Emotional and Cognitive Functions

HISTORY and **DIAGNOSIS** often give clues about possible physical causes for emotional, behavioral, or cognitive disorders.

A. HISTORY
  1. **Developmental:**
      Problems during pregnancy of mother:
        Was she ill?
        During pregnancy or at time of birth, did she have rubella, diabetes, cytomegalovirus, or herpes?
        Did she take any medications?
        Did she use alcohol or drugs?
        Did she smoke heavily?
      Perinatal events (events at time of birth):
        premature delivery
        cesarean section
        forceps delivery
        breech birth
        placental detachment
        mother given oxygen during birth
      Head injury:
        infancy
        childhood
        adolescence
        adulthood
  2. **Medical:** Is there a history of illness or condition in which mental or emotional problems sometimes occur secondary to the underlying medical condition?[a]

CEREBRAL HYPOXIA
  Anemia
  Apgar score low at birth
  Lowered cardiac output
  Pulmonary insufficiency
  Toxic (carbon monoxide)
DRUGS, MEDICATIONS, AND POISON
  Alcohol
  Amphetamine
  Anticholinergic agents
  Antipsychotics
  Barbiturates
  Bromides
  Caffeine
  Carbon disulfide
  Carbon monoxide
  Cocaine
  Cycloserine (Seromycin)
  Digitalis
  Disulfiram (Antabuse)
  Hallucinogens
  Isoniazid (INH and others)
  Marijuana
  Methyldopa
  L-Dopa
  Lead or other heavy metal (mercury, cadmium, copper, bismuth)

  Opiates
  Oral contraceptives
  Other sedatives
  Propanolol (Inderal and others)
  Reserpine
  Steroids (hormonal compounds)
NUTRITIONAL DEFICIENCIES
  B_{12}
  Inadequate absorption of nutrients in elderly
  Macrominerals (calcium, phosphorus, magnesium, potassium, sulfur, sodium, chlorine)
  Niacin
  Thiamine
  Zinc and other trace elements (iron, manganese, iodine, selenium, molybdenum, vanadium, chromium, tin, cobalt, fluorine, nickel, aluminum, copper)
  Protein
SENSITIVITY/ALLERGIC REACTION
  Additives
  Inhalants
  Sugar
  Wheat gluten

(*Continued on next page*)

[a] Glossary of terms available from Harriette C. Johnson.

Table 2. (Continued)

VASCULAR DISORDERS
  Aneurysm (aneurism)
  Collagen vascular disease
  Hypertensive encephalopathy
  Intracranial hemorrhage
  Lacunar state
EFFECTS OF TUMORS
  Cancer of the bowel
  Cancer of the pancreas
  Cerebral tumor
  Metastases
  Oat cell carcinoma
INFECTIOUS DISEASES
  Brucellosis
  Encephalitis (viral)
  Hepatitis
  Influenza
  Malaria
  Meningitis
  Mononucleosis
  Postencephalitic state
  Subacute bacterial endocarditis
  Syphilis
  Toxoplasmosis
  Tuberculosis
  Typhoid
  Viral pneumonia

METABOLIC AND ENDOCRINE
DISORDERS
  Addison's disease
  Cushing's disease
  Diabetes mellitus
  Electrolyte imbalance
  Hepatic disease (liver disease)
  Hyperparathyroidism
  Hyperthyroidism
  Hypocalcemia (low calcium)
  Hypoglycemia (low blood sugar)
  Hypokalemia (low potassium)
  Hyponatremia (low sodium)
  Pellagra
  Pernicious anemia
  Pituitary insufficiency
  Porphyria
  Thyroid disease (thyrotoxicosis and myx-
    edema)
  Uremia
  Wernicke-Korsakoff's syndrome
  Wilson's disease
MISCELLANEOUS DISORDERS
  Chronic pyelonephritis
  Lupus erythematosus
  Pancreatitis
  Peptic ulcer
  Postpartum state
  Rheumatoid arthritis

B. DIAGNOSIS. *Psychiatric* and *neurological* diagnoses that indicate likely influence of
physiological factors on emotional, behavioral, or cognitive states.[b]

PSYCHIATRIC
  Attention deficit disorder
  Episodic dyscontrol
  Major depression
  Manic depressive disorder
  Pervasive developmental disorder
    (autism)
  Schizophrenia
  Severe alcoholism
  Some kinds of antisocial behavior
  Specific developmental disorder (learning
    disability)

NEUROLOGICAL
  Alzheimer's disease
  Amyotrophic lateral sclerosis (ALS)
  Brain abscess
  Brain or spinal cord injury
  Cerebral palsy
  Cerebrovascular disease
  Epilepsy
  Huntington's chorea
  La Tourette's syndrome
  Metastatic cerebral tumor
  Multiple sclerosis
  Neurofibromatosis
  Parkinson's disease
  Postconcussion syndrome
  Postencephalitic syndrome
  Primary cerebral tumor
  Spina bifida
  Subdural hematoma
  Normal pressure hydrocephalus

[b] For information relating to these diagnoses, see current texts on psychiatry and neurology.
Source: Adapted with permission of The Free Press, a Division of Macmillan, Inc., from *Adult Psychopathology*, edited by Francis J. Turner. Copyright © by The Free Press.

problem was physiological. For a social work practitioner to be effective in any of these situations it would be necessary to know that subtle neurological dysfunction can cause aggressive behavior, that hypoglycemia can cause emotional disturbance, and that prescribed medication can cause disorientation and personality change. Without this knowledge, the worker would be likely to focus almost exclusively on interpersonal transactions, which might be *effects* rather than *causes*. Only when an in-depth evaluation indicates that *nothing can be done about the causes themselves* should attention be directed exclusively to effects. In the absence of such an evaluation, attention to interpersonal effects may simply impede the identification of causes.

Psychiatric disorders known to be caused or strongly determined by biological factors include attention deficit disorder, episodic dyscontrol, major depression, manic depressive disorder, pervasive developmental disorder (autism), schizophrenia, severe alcoholism, some kinds of antisocial behavior, and specific developmental disorder (learning disability). Biological factors are also implicated in almost every other DSM-III diagnosis. The list continues to expand in the wake of new discoveries in neurobiological research.

The list of known contributors to emotional and cognitive disorders includes an extensive inventory of metabolic, infectious, vascular, endocrine, neurological, and neoplastic diseases, toxic substances, head trauma, and nutritional deficiencies. The practitioner is advised to consult Table 2 when attempting to formulate a biopsychosocial diagnosis.

Social Work Functions

The preceding discussion of the role of biological factors in many aspects of child and adult functioning suggests the need for a wide variety of social work functions.

Case Management. The fragmentation of services, staff turnover, poor communication between agencies, and other obstacles often impede the use of services. During the course of a protracted illness or chronic disability, the social worker is the logical professional to assume the role of monitoring the combination of services received by indi-

viduals and families, to stay in contact with service providers to assure maximum accountability, and to serve as a coordinator of information.

Linkage and Advocacy Functions. Throughout the course of an illness or chronic disability, a variety of referrals may be needed to income support resources; health care services; lawyers or financial counselors for such matters as guardianship, wills, and financial concerns; educational and vocational counseling, especially for wives who may have to prepare to become breadwinners; and to daycare, sheltered workshops, homemaker services, and respite care. When the social worker encounters obstacles that interfere with the obtaining of benefits or services, the advocacy role becomes paramount.

Family Counseling. Counseling with families can be enhanced by attention to the common problems families face. Lezak (1978) outlined issues that frequently confront families of patients with brain injuries, many of which also pertain to the care of physically disabled people. When families do not raise these issues, the social worker should. The worker should emphasize that anger and frustration as well as grief are natural emotions for close relatives. It is difficult enough to feel chronically annoyed or tied down by a once-beloved person; these feelings become harder to endure when complicated by guilt. After months of caring for an unhappy, ungrateful, difficult patient with no end in sight, close kin are apt to be frightened or upset by their irrepressible wish for the patient's early death (Lezak, 1978, p. 595).

Placing a patient in an institution when home management becomes too difficult is an enormously traumatic step for all concerned. In many situations, however, it may be the only realistic alternative. The social worker's sensitivity to the needs and feelings of the patient and the family at the time such a decision is being considered may play a crucial role in their adjustment—or lack of adjustment—to institutionalization. Alleviation of the family's guilt is a major task at this stage.

Issues of discrimination, shame, and embarrassment pertaining to the minority status of an individual or family are often best handled in peer group situations.

Peer Groups, Self-Help Groups, and Advocacy Organizations. Peer support groups have been widely used for individuals with disabilities and their families. In cases of disability, peer groups are used at the stage of initial diagnosis and during the course of disabling conditions. Major purposes of these groups are to educate patients and relatives about the condition, to mobilize the kind of support that comes only from others who are suffering a similar problem, to break down the social isolation that many of these illnesses generate, to disseminate information about resources, to expose participants to a range of coping strategies being used by their peers, to enhance self-image, and to help patients redefine their lives in relation to changed abilities and opportunities.

Engaging in political action to obtain changes in the law or enforcement of existing laws is often a useful and effective way for victims of discrimination to deal with their problems.

Peers may be more effective in helping an individual with a specific problem than professionals. However, professional skills are often helpful in planning and convening groups, in providing structure and direction when needed, in facilitating communication, and in resolving conflict or alleviating disruption when it occurs. Self-help and advocacy groups cannot be overstressed as a resource for both individuals and families. (Information on such resources can be obtained from the National Self-Help Clearing House, City University of New York, New York City.)

Natural Helping Systems. In addition to the chief natural helping system of the peer group, the use or enhancement of natural helping networks is potentially of great importance. For example, a neighbor who may feel isolated or unimportant might be engaged to help care for the patient on a short-term basis to allow the caretaker to go out.

Conclusion

In conclusion, biological factors are of major significance not only in the physical but also in the mental functioning of people of every age. This review supplies information about biological factors in development and suggests social work interventions appropriate to a variety of problems of biological origin.

HARRIETTE C. JOHNSON

For further information, see ADOLESCENTS; ADULTHOOD; CHILDREN; DISABILITIES: DEVELOPMENTAL; DISABILITIES: PHYSICAL; HUMAN DEVELOPMENT: PSYCHOLOGICAL PERSPECTIVE; HUMAN DEVELOPMENT: SOCIOCULTURAL PERSPECTIVE; MEN; WOMEN.

References

American Psychiatric Association. (1980). *Diagnostic and Statistical Manual* (3rd ed.). Washington, D.C.: Author.

Apgar, V., et al. (1958). "Evaluation of the Newborn Infant—Second Report." *Journal of the American Medical Association, 168*,1985.

Baker, C. E. (Ed.). (1982). *Physician's Desk Reference.* Oradell, N.J.: Medical Economics Books.

Baum, M. H. (1962). "Some Dynamic Factors Affecting Family Adjustment to the Handicapped Child." *Exceptional Children, 28*, 387.

Besharov, D. J. (1986). *The Vulnerable Social Worker.* Silver Spring, Md.: National Association of Social Workers.

Bettelheim, B. (1967). *The Empty Fortress.* New York: Free Press.

Bloch, J. (1978). "Impaired Children." *Children Today, 7*(6), 2–6.

Brazelton, T. B., Parker, W. B., & Zuckerman, B. (1976). "Importance of Behavioral Assessment of the Neonate." *Current Problems in Pediatrics, 7*(2), 1–82.

Burt, C. (1972). "Inheritance of General Intelligence." *American Psychologist, 27*(3), 175–190.

Counts, R. (1978). *Independent Living Rehabilitation for Severely Handicapped People: A Preliminary Appraisal.* Washington, D.C.: Urban Institute.

Falek, A. (1979). "Observations on Patient and Family Coping with Huntington's Disease." *Omega, 10*, 35–42.

Fraiberg, S. (1974). "Blind Infants and Their Mothers." In M. Lewis & L. A. Rosenbert (Eds)., *The Effect of the Infant on Its Caregiver* (pp. 215–232). New York: John Wiley & Sons.

Galton, L. (1979). *The Truth About Senility—And How to Prevent It.* New York: Thomas Y. Crowell Co.

Gross, M., & Wilson, W. (1974). *Minimal Brain Dysfunction.* New York: Brunner/Mazel.

Hall, R. C. W., et al. (1981). "Unrecognized Physical Illness Prompting Psychiatric Admission: A Prospective Study." *American Journal of Psychiatry, 138*(5), 629–635.

Hartings, M. F., et al. (1976). "Group Counseling of MS Patients in a Program of Comprehensive Care." *Journal of Chronic Disease, 29*(2), 65–73.

Jensen, A. R. (1969). "How Much Can We Boost IQ and Scholastic Achievement?" *Harvard Educational Review, 39,* 1–123.

Johnson, H. C. (1980). *Human Behavior and Social Environment: New Perspectives, Vol. 1. Behavior, Psychopathology, and the Brain.* New York: Curriculum Concepts.

Johnson, H. C., & Hart, E. J. (1984). "Neurological Disorders." In F. J. Turner (Ed.), *Adult Psychopathology: A Social Work Perspective* (pp. 73–118). New York: Free Press.

Koranyi, E. K. (1979). "Morbidity and Rate of Undiagnosed Physical Illness in a Psychiatric Clinic Population." *Archives of General Psychiatry, 36*(4), 414–419.

Kübler-Ross, E. (1969). *On Death and Dying.* New York: Macmillan Publishing Co.

Lapin, H., & Lapin, C. (1976). "The Plight of Parents in Obtaining Help for Their Autistic Child and the Role of the National Society for Autistic Children." In E. R. Ritvo et al. (Eds.), *Autism: Diagnosis, Current Research, and Management* (pp. 287–290). New York: Spectrum Books.

Lezak, M. D. (1978). "Living with the Characterologically Altered Brain Injured Person." *Journal of Clinical Psychiatry, 39*(7), 592–598.

MacCulloch, M. J., & Waddington, J. L. (1981). "Neuroendocrine Mechanisms and the Aetiology of Male and Female Homosexuality." *British Journal of Psychiatry, 139*(10), 341–345.

Mahler, M. (1949). "On Childhood Psychosis and Schizophrenia, Autistic and Symbiotic Infantile Psychosis." *Psychoanalytic Study of the Child, 7,* 286–305.

Miller, J. G. (1978). *Living Systems.* New York: McGraw Hill Book Co.

Ouellette, E., et al. (1977). "Adverse Effects on Offspring of Maternal Alcohol Abuse During Pregnancy." *New England Journal of Medicine, 297*(10), 528.

Reynolds, C. R., & Jensen, A. R. (1983). "WISC–R Subscale Patterns of Abilities of Blacks and Whites Matches on Full Scale IQ." *Journal of Educational Psychology, 75*(2), 207–214.

Schiffer, C. G. & Hunt, E. P. (1963). *Illness among Children* (U.S. Children's Bureau Publication No. 405). Washington, D.C.: U.S. Government Printing Office.

Schuster, C. S., & Ashburn, S. S. (1980). *The Process of Human Development: A Holistic Approach.* Boston: Little, Brown & Co.

Shockley, W. (1972). "Dysgenics, Geneticity, Raceology: A Challenge to the Intellectual Responsibility of Educators." *Phi Delta Kappan, 53,* 297–307.

Specht, R., & Craig, G. J. (1982). *Human Development: A Social Work Perspective.* Englewood Cliffs, N.J.: Prentice-Hall.

Trethowan, W. H. (1970). "Rehabilitation of the Brain Injured: The Psychiatric Angle." *Proceedings of Social Medicine, 63,* 32–36.

Winick, N. (1971). "Cellular Growth During Early Malnutrition." *Pediatrics, 47*(6), 969.

HUMAN DEVELOPMENT: PSYCHOLOGICAL PERSPECTIVE

The *psychological* facet of human development has always been at the forefront of the teaching and practice of social work. Nevertheless, the emphasis on the psychological aspect of human development has had a checkered history and still is a pertinent but debatable issue. In the past 50 years, psychological components have been understood as being synonymous with cognitive, perceptual, affective, attitudinal, temperamental, or behavioral operations. Psychological functioning can be conceived as intra- or interpersonal processes that are applicable to people in general or as an ever-changing phenomenon throughout an individual's life span. Psychological components may be influenced by an interplay of personal development, primary and secondary life experiences, and cultural, societal, and other contextual factors. In short, in social work practice and education, human development has various psychological bases, depending on the practitioner's perspective.

Regardless of a practitioner's leanings, psychological determinants are ever-present and basic ingredients in all social work services. Psychological processes are manifested in such activities as organizational planning, negotiating, and decision making on the macro level. In direct (micro) practice, helping professionals rely heavily on psychological processes while trying to mesh human and societal requirements. Moreover, social work prides itself in meeting human and societal requirements on the basis of the client's particular life situation. To this end, a *developmental* perspective (the understanding of human beings for their progressive change in their particular societal contexts), is particularly useful to set up relevant services or to deliver them appropriately (Germain & Gitterman, 1980, p. 7).

Psychological Development

Whether it is viewed as part of a progressive process in the life cycle (Erikson, 1982) or as a progression of experiences throughout a person's life (Bloom, 1984; Datan & Ginsberg, 1975; Maas, 1984; Specht & Craig, 1982), human development gives credence either way to the idea that people can be effectively studied and worked with for their developmental status and potential. Furthermore, what formerly were viewed as pathological or deviant behaviors are now conceived and approached in a contemporary developmental perspective as ordinary but inopportune and untimely developmental occurrences (Kegan, 1982, p. 298).

The term "development" refers to orderly and sequential changes in all areas of human functioning. Changes may occur in any one or several of the areas, as well as in their relationship to each other. Most important, developmental changes are empirically predictable and can be charted. Although they occur over time, few occur as a result simply of the passage of time; rather, they require relevant experiences. Development signifies that human beings are in a constant state of change and that their situations change as they do. The realization of a continuum of change with discernible and expectable developmental and societal phases throughout the life span has resulted in psychological formulations by Sigmund Freud (1856–1939) and Erik H. Erikson (1902–), Jean Piaget (1896–1980), and, to a lesser degree, in works by Kohlberg (1976) and Levinson (1978), and texts (Bloom, 1984; Datan and Ginsberg, 1975; Maas, 1984; Maier, 1978; Smart and Smart, 1982) with a phasal or stage orientation that are particularly utilitarian for social work. Life is different in each stage, and each sphere of life produces different experiences, depending on whether the individual is an adult or a child, a newcomer or an old timer, in a moment of crisis or in a stable period (Maas, 1984).

Psychological development may encompass *biological* or *genetic* development with a focus on anatomical structures and capabilities, especially body growth and maturation (basic resource: Smart & Smart,

1982; best-known representative psychological scientist is: Arnold L. Gesell, 1880–1961).

Social work practice and training of professionals have always recognized biological human requirements, but this sphere of knowledge has never been central to dealing with clients' psychological or life complexities. However, cognitive, behavioral, and affective development and functioning have assumed a place of importance in the education and practice of social work.

Cognitive Development. Human development also may be interpreted as being essentially cognitive development. This interpretation considers the processes of comprehension and reasoning to be the determinants of human behavior. Piaget, Leo Vygotsky (1896–1934), and Jerome Bruner (1915–) are the leading scientists who have dealt with this dimension of development, and Brainerd (1976) is one of the many basic textbooks. Although developmental cognitive knowledge, particularly Piaget's rich studies (Brainerd, 1976; Maier, 1978, chap. 1), found a full audience in the academic circles of psychology, education, and child development, it had a limited impact on social work.

Social work turned decisively to cognitive psychology as a personality theory rather than to the vast knowledge accumulated by developmental psychologists. Cognitive personality theory expands the notion that human emotions are a function of a person's thinking (Ellis, 1962). In the past 10 years, behavioral social work practice frequently incorporated this cognitive dimension. The cognitive approach builds on the idea that the way an individual conceives (thinks about and understands) a situation is the way the person will feel and act on it. As Lantz (1978, p. 361) described:

> When people's thoughts and beliefs are rational, they feel emotions that are functional. When their thoughts and beliefs are irrational, people begin to develop dysfunctional emotions, various psychiatric symptoms, and dysfunctional behavior patterns. It [then becomes the social worker's] . . . responsibility to help clients change irrational ideas and beliefs that create such dysfunctional emotional states.

This cognitive or behavioral-cognitive approach (see later sections) is essentially a linear, corrective perspective that views dysfunctional human emotions and behaviors as the consequences of incorrect understanding and ideation that people hold about themselves or about their life situation. It is the correction of these misconceptions, which frequently are beyond the awareness of the owner, that requires a social worker's intervention (Lantz, 1978).

Behavioral Development. Human development also can be viewed in relation to behavioral learning. Behavioral learning can be viewed according to an operant conditioning stance to a more eclectic learning theory base. B. F. Skinner (1904–) is the key theoretician of the operant conditioning approach, and Albert Bandura (1925–) is a leading scholar of the learning theory approach (Bandura, 1977; Hepworth, 1985).

Regardless of behavioral orientation, all behavioral formulations build on the idea that people's behavior decides the course of their life, that is, what persons *do* determines other people's image of them, as well as their image of themselves. Consequently, in social work practice, the focus is on achieving behavioral changes—in assisting clients with their behavioral competence. The attainment of behavioral competence is extended to a behavioral-cognitive effort in which clients' behavioral repertoires and conceptions of their situation are tuned to the demands of reality for which they sought help.

A behavioral (as well as a behavioral-cognitive) basis of social work practice builds on a linear conception of human life and intervention. Moreover, this form of social work is inherently linked with additional features of the social sciences, namely, a solid adherence to empirical procedures, a high commitment to research, and an unshakeable belief in the rationality of human beings.

Affective Development. Human development also has been described for its affective (emotional) dimension, in which affective energies are considered to be the primary factors that determine a person's life experiences. Decades ago, the psychoanalytic formulations were seen as most important, especially the ones by Freud and Erikson's subsequent psychosocial theory (Maier, 1978, chap. 2). More recently, the interactional research and concepts on attachment and connectiveness by Ainsworth (1972), Kegan (1982), and Sroufe (1978) have gained prominence.

Psychoanalytic thinking not only penetrated social workers' views of human beings, it also reached into every aspect of Western thought—child rearing and human relations, education and commerce, the arts and literature, and the activities of helping professionals. Today, although its influence has since waned, it still has an impact. Contemporary social workers who intend to focus on the centrality of affect to human functioning depend in part on the concepts of ego psychology (Datan & Ginsberg, 1975; Maas, 1984). However, they are more apt to search for alternates or additions from a wide array of concepts that deal with the irrational, affective side of human functioning. Such concepts include existential, experimental, and sensitivity-encounter formulations, as well as more empirically grounded ideas concerning a person's connectedness and communal anchorage (Kegan, 1982; Maas, 1984; Sroufe, 1978). The equation of emotion with the degree of personal social anchorage moves this dimension of affect from purely a personality theory into the realm of developmental theory, embracing a nonlinear (contextual) framework. Regardless of the social worker's preoccupation with one or the other direction of affect theory, as long as affect is hypothesized as being the predominant factor in life, it is assumed that affect determines the nature of an individual's behavior and understanding of his or her life situation. It is then further assumed that once a person's affect is altered, the individual can understand and manage more effectively the social demands at hand (Maier, 1976, p. 65).

What once was conceived as being solely within the realm of affective processes is currently viewed and researched as part of the physiological (Hofer, 1981) and neurological (Gottlieb, 1982) makeup of people. Emotional energy is closely intertwined with a person's body biochemistry and the electronic apparatus of the nervous system. Chemicals (drugs) have proved to be powerful agents for fomenting emotional imbalance as well as fostering emotional stability. Another sphere of psychosomatic knowledge is in the making; it will either be added to the spectrum of psychological knowledge or introduced as a new discipline of "physiological behavioral sciences" that is parallel to the psychological.

Other psychological conceptions of human development, such as Maslow's (1962) self-actualization and Roger's (1961) view of humans as autonomous beings, also present a challenge. However, they lack specificity in comprehending individual development and seldom have been useful to social work practitioners and educators.

Ecological Perspective. A substantially different perspective of human development has emerged in the 1980s. It is an ecological perspective, which builds on the idea that people are multidimensional and that their affective, behavioral, cognitive, and physiological processes are in constant transaction with their relevant environments. This perspective postulates that to understand human development to the fullest, a person's context must be recognized. The person's transactions with others—his or her family life, organizational associations, community experiences, and enmeshment in the manifold systems of everyday encounters—are all relevant forces (Bronfenbrenner, 1979). The ecological approach has its roots in Kurt Lewin's (1890–1947) field theory and general systems theory. Ecological theorems introduce an interactional mode of thinking for research and work with people, including new terms such as "microsystems," "mesosystems," and "macrosystems" (Bronfenbrenner, 1979; Garbarino, 1982). This mode of thinking no longer emphasizes the individual; rather, it focuses on the individual in context (Garbarino, 1982) or on the individual in his or her situation (Meyer, 1976). Such a perspective requires that social workers understand individuals and their respective interfacing environments. Social work is challenged to accept a nonlinear format of thinking and action. Both clients and the environment must be influenced by efforts to improve human conditions (Germain & Gitterman, 1980). A multidimensional, ecological, or contextual perspective on human development also opens up solid opportunities for dealing with gender, as well as all cultural and racial pluralism as fundamental issues of human development (Maas, 1984; Specht & Craig, 1982).

Historical Review

Before World War II, especially during the years of the Great Depression, social work, along with the field of developmental psychology, held essentially to a psychological orientation that focused on the maturation of human capabilities. After World War II, the psychoanalytic perspective found little acceptance in the circles of developmental psychology; however, it was ardently absorbed by the helping professions, especially by clinical practitioners in psychiatry and social work. In the 1950s and 1960s, the teachings of Sigmund Freud, Anna Freud (1895–1982), Otto Rank (1884–1939), and Erik H. Erikson formed the basic theoretical backdrop for understanding people as psychological beings. Social work was readily attracted to psychoanalytic thought because of its individual orientation, its presumedly nonjudgmental view, and, above all, for its promise of a developmental theory that would span the course of human life and contain an inherent interventive methodology. During the post–World War II years, this aspect of the curriculum—the human behavior–social-environment (HBSE) content—was taught in schools of social work as "psychiatric information" by instructors from departments of psychiatry; social work instructors would then attempt to "translate" those teachings into content that was applicable to practice (Butler, 1959). The difficulties of adapting such psychiatric concepts to social work practice and the recommendation of the 1959 *Curriculum Report* of the Council on Social Work Education that schools of social work should develop HBSE courses or course sequences to be taught by social work faculty in master's degree programs helped such applicable content to materialize in a few years (Butler, 1959).

CSWE's accreditation standards of the 1960s (Marks, 1965, p. 281) and Standards 7.8 and 7.9 of the 1980s (CSWE, 1984) required coverage of the known information about the development of individuals over the life span and the interrelationship of individuals with their family, community, and cultural and societal groupings. CSWE has never recommended a minimum level or core of knowledge to be mastered for any social work degree (Dinerman, 1981, pp. 38–43). In general, social work education tends to favor a "multidisciplinary potpourri" with a heavier emphasis on individual behavior and development (HB) than on social environmental factors (SE) (Gibbs, 1984).

Nevertheless, in the 1960s, CSWE took notice of the awakening interest in issues related to the aged and in the desirability of racial and cultural diversity as well as changes in the roles of women and possibilities for various forms of partnership arrangements and gender commitments. These developments led to specific standards (1971 and 1973) that required schools of social work to add an array of discrete content to combat sexism and racism and to offer a perspective of ethnic pluralism. Social work practice had to incorporate knowingly a new conception of aging, sexuality, cultural differentiation, and ethnic pluralism. Emerging societal perspectives challenged social work practitioners and educators to review their practice stances and frames of reference; simultaneously, social workers responded to the challenge to advocate contemporary progressive societal points of view. There also was a shift to empirical rather than primarily theoretical data, overcoming an earlier inclination to rely too readily on psychological hypotheses rather than on substantiated findings.

Throughout the 1970s and early 1980s, psychodynamic psychology (it can be assumed in the absence of reliable data), continued to be the single primary orientation in social work practice. Today, however, no one psychological basis is primary. Behavioral, cognitive, interactional, psychodynamic, and ecological psychologies, individually or more frequently in some sort of combination, are identified as the primary modality by various types of social work practitioners. Schools of social work also vary greatly and generally are unclear which psychological basis is theirs.

Critical Analysis

As a group of service providers and as a training system that endeavors to alleviate human and organizational stresses, the profession is in trouble as long as it has no common commitment to what knowledge of human behavior and of the relevant social environment should be offered. It is equally unclear how a beginning professional needs to master and subsequently apply his or her learning. The permissiveness of CSWE toward the wide diversity of HB and SE content seems to imply a limited commitment to any of these areas of potentially basic knowledge. Furthermore, social work education had difficulties in pursuing its own studies such as the Hollis study (Hollis, 1951) and the *Curriculum Study* of 1959 (Butler, 1959, p. 52), which attempted to devise a psychosocial formulation of "social functioning" (the formulation used was still based on the medical model).

In the two decades after World War II, social work education and practice, with their pervasive commitment to a closed psychoanalytic-system formulation, made it difficult to link psychoanalytic knowledge with other relevant informational systems about people and their environments. Social workers' psychological knowledge, consequently, was not only scattered but parochial. In the two post-World War II decades, the psychological research and teachings of such behavioral scientists as Kurt Lewin (1890–1947), Robert R. Sears (1908–), Rogers, and especially Piaget, in the neighboring departments of psychology, had a minimal impact on what was taught under the rubric of HBSE.

In time, social work practitioners and educators became prepared to adopt the notion of "the person-in-the-situation" (Meyer, 1976) and to shift their paradigm to one that modeled intergenerational connectiveness and diversity in ethnicity, race, sexual orientation, and culture in a pluralistic society. Social workers and their educators became ready to embrace a wide range of psychological formulations (Gibbs, 1984). Social work was quickly in the market to adopt unabashedly new psychological references in its practice. As a counterreaction to psychoanalytic theories, behavioral reasoning, with its stress on accountability and what is verifiable, was readily adopted by a good number of educators and social workers. With its acceptance, emotions, once the cornerstone of social workers' psychoanalytic base, apparently became an extinct variable for social work practice.

Social work education and practice are now in a relatively uncommitted psychological position, still dealing with people as primarily behavioral, cognitive, or affective beings who are assessed essentially apart from their total life situation. In the years to come, the challenge remains whether social work can conceive "person and environment as inseparable; one without the other distorts both, directing attention away from the dual foci of special turf" (Lewin, 1981, p. 75). Such a conception represents the logical corollary of dealing with people as multifunctional beings. It accepts that individuals are intimately enmeshed with their social situation; not only are they a part of their situation but they are the agent to define it. Simultaneously, the very circumstances of each person's social context determine the individual's developmental possibilities.

Trends and Issues

The impact of systems thinking, combined with an intensified concern with and an increased ability for empirical explorations, including use of the computer, links the psychological basis of human development with energy management. Hence, psychological issues become attributes of both thermodynamic laws and psychological hypotheses. The idea of human action, thought, and emotion being energy laden empowers the developmental aspects of human interactions. In the future, psychologists and social workers will be more and more concerned with the full life span. They will no longer envisage early childhood behavior as the exclusive formative agent. Rather, they will see that subsequent and adult life experiences as well as the developing individuals' degree of receptiveness also determine the relevance of current and later experiences (Kagan, 1984).

Social work education and practice currently face a triple challenge. The first challenge is whether they can move beyond previous preferences for single linear formulations such as analytic, behavioral, or cognitive theorems and can proceed on a nonlinear (contextual) developmental basis (Garbarino, 1982). The second challenge is to accept the reality that the life span is a continuum. Acceptance of this idea would be demonstrated by studying and working with people for their ongoing developmental, contextual, and personal circumstances. For instance, an adult is as dependent as a child on the environment, although the adult's environmental requirements may continuously have altered forms and seats of authority. The third challenge is for social work to diversify its recently gained focal interests: knowledge and practice competencies with regard to issues of gender or sexuality, as well as the delivery of special services in relation to aging, death and dying, and so forth. These recent competencies need to become a regular and universal component of social work practice. Knowledge of moral development—the details of the progressive developmental components of value judgments (Kohlberg, 1973)—has gained added importance with Gilligan's (1983) generative view of female and male gender-role behaviors. These emerging conceptual perspectives, combined with Bandura's "self-efficacy" (Bandura, 1977; Hepworth, 1985), typify the view that human beings are complex but knowable and continuously changing. Consequently, changes brought about by intervention have to verify, build on, and enhance developmental change.

Among the many contemporary trends and manifold scientific breakthroughs, probably none will stir social work so much as the contemporary "rediscovery" of emotions (affect). Social scientists are taking "a hard look at how emotions are or are not incorporated in existing models of cognition and behavior. . ." (Social Science Research Council, 1984, p. 99). This ferment of the 1980s is reflected in the growing empirical research on the relationship between affect, cognition, and behavior (Higgins, Hartup, & Ruble, 1983). Social workers, along with psychologists and other professional colleagues, may well be able, with this integrative approach, to deal with clients as multifunctioning persons.

Social workers' efforts currently encompass primary-group associations of family, peers, work, and neighborhood and immediate secondary, organizational, and cultural involvements. Ultimately, social work planning and activities that are anchored by a contextual, ecological (or person-in-the-situation) psychological base may be achieved.

HENRY W. MAIER

For further information, see DIRECT PRACTICE: TRENDS AND ISSUES; HUMAN DEVELOPMENT: BIOLOGICAL PERSPECTIVE; HUMAN DEVELOPMENT: SOCIOCULTURAL PERSPECTIVE.

References

Ainsworth, M. D. (1972). "Attachment and Dependency: A Comparison." In J. S. Gerwitz (Ed.), *Attachment and Dependency* (pp.

97–136). Washington, D.C.: H. Winston & Sons.

Bandura, A. (1977). "Self–Efficacy: Toward a Unifying Theory of Behavioral Change." *Psychological Review, 84*(2), 191–215.

Bloom, M. (1984). *Configurations of Human Behavior: Life Span Development in Social Environments.* New York: Macmillan Publishing Co.

Brainerd, C. J. (1976). *Piaget's Theory of Intelligence.* Englewood Cliffs, N.J.: Prentice-Hall.

Bronfenbrenner, U. (1979). *The Ecology of Human Development.* Cambridge, Mass.: Harvard University Press.

Butler, R. M. (1959). *An Orientation to Knowledge of Human Growth and Behavior in Social Work Education.* New York: Council on Social Work Education.

Council on Social Work Education, Commission on Accreditation. (1984). *Handbook of Accreditation on Standards and Procedures.* New York: Author.

Datan, N., & Ginsberg, L. H. (1975). *Life-Span Developmental Psychology.* New York: Academic Press.

Dinerman, M. (1981). *Social Work Curriculum at the Baccalaureate and Master's Levels.* New York: Lois & Samuel Silberman Fund.

Ellis, A. (1962). *Reason and Emotion.* New York: Lyle Stuart.

Erikson, E. H. (1982). *The Life Cycle Completed: A Review.* New York: W. W. Norton & Co.

Garbarino, J. (1982). *Children and Families in the Social Environment.* Chicago: Aldine Publishing Co.

Germain, G., & Gitterman, A. (1980). *The Life Model of Social Work Practice.* New York: Columbia University Press.

Gibbs, P. (1984). "HBSE in the Undergraduate Curriculum." Morgantown: West Virginia University.

Gilligan, C. (1983). *In a Different Voice.* Cambridge, Mass.: Harvard University Press.

Gottlieb, G. (1982). *Studies of the Development of Behavior and the Nervous System.* New York: Academic Press.

Hepworth, D. H. (in press). "Enhancing Students' Self-Efficacy and Competency in Practice," *Journal of Social Work Education.*

Higgins, E. T., Hartup, W. W., & Ruble, D. N. (Eds.). (1983). *Social Cognition and Social Development.* New York: Cambridge University Press.

Hofer, J. (1981). *The Roots of Human Behavior.* San Francisco: Freeman Press.

Hollis, E. (1951). *Social Work Education in the United States.* New York: Columbia University Press.

Kagan, J. (1984). *The Nature of the Child.* New York: Basic Books.

Kegan, R. (1982). *The Evolving Self.* Cambridge, Mass.: Harvard University Press.

Kohlberg, L. (1976). *Collected Papers on Moral Development and Moral Education.* Cambridge, Mass.: Center for Moral Education.

Lantz, J. E. (1978). "Cognitive Theory and Social Casework." *Social Work, 23*(5), 361–367.

Levinson, D. (1978). *The Seasons of a Man's Life.* New York: Alfred A. Knopf.

Lewin, H. (1981). "Are the Traditional Curriculum Areas Relevant?" *Journal of Education for Social Work, 17*(1), 73–80.

Maas, H. S. (1984). *People and Contexts.* Englewood Cliffs, N.J.: Prentice-Hall.

Maier, H. W. (1976). "Human Functioning as an Interpersonal Whole: The Dimensions of Affect, Behavior, and Cognition." In *Teaching for Competence in the Delivery of Direct Services* (pp. 60–71). New York: Council on Social Work Education.

Maier, H. W. (1978). *Three Theories of Child Development* (3rd ed.). New York: Longman.

Marks, R. B. (1965). "Education for Social Work." In *Encyclopedia of Social Work* (pp. 277–283). New York: National Association of Social Workers.

Maslow, A. H. (1962). *Toward a Psychology of Being.* New York: Van Nostrand Reinhold Co.

Meyer, C. (1976). *Social Practice: The Changing Landscape.* New York: Free Press.

Rogers, C. R. (1961). *On Becoming a Person.* Boston: Houghton Mifflin Co.

Smart, M. S., & Smart, R. C. (1982). *Children: Development and Relationships* (4th ed.). New York: Macmillan Publishing Co.

Social Science Research Council. (1984). "Essay Review of a Publication on Emotions, Cognition, and Behavior." *Items, 38*(4), 99–100.

Specht, R., & Craig, G. J. (1982). *Human Development.* Englewood Cliffs, N.J.: Prentice-Hall.

Sroufe, L. A. (1978). "Attachment and the Roots of Competence." *Human Nature, 1*(10), 50–57.

HUMAN DEVELOPMENT: SOCIOCULTURAL PERSPECTIVE

Becoming human involves not only the maturation of biological systems that permit the individual to grow and function as an organism, but also the development of cognitive operations and personality as well as learning how to get along with and behave like others in a cultural group. The latter is what transforms an organism into a person. Clients of the social work profession include persons of diverse cultural backgrounds, physical conditions, levels of emotional functioning, ages, social classes, and geographical communities. Despite their common humanity, no one theoretical system is able to explain why they all behave as they do and how their behavior is determined.

Theories of Human Development

The social work profession has been accused of retreating to a narrow focus on the individual and on psychological determinants of behavior in response to the overwhelming number of variables that appear to define the human condition (Briar, 1968; Gronjberg, Street, & Suttles, 1978; Toren, 1972). As clinical practice has focused its attention more squarely on the interaction of person and environment, however, its knowledge base has become more eclectic, with greater emphasis on sociocultural factors in human development (Grinnell, 1973; Hollis, 1980; Meyer, 1979).

Critics of the human development model incorporated in psychoanalytic theory point to its message that the personality is set in the first 5 years of life (Evans, 1967, pp. 11–12). More recent theories have adopted a life-span approach, which assumes that developmental changes occur throughout the life cycle (Erikson, 1963; Havighurst, 1979; Peck, 1968). Developmental theorists have demarcated the life cycle into critical periods or age-stages. The editors of *The Futurist,* for example, have constructed a life calendar of events for seven age-stages: infancy and early childhood (0–5), late childhood (5–12), adolescence (12–18), young adulthood (19–25), adulthood (25–40), middle age (40–65), and retirement years (64 and over) (Selim et al., 1979). That these age-stages are culture bound is suggested by the fact that the last stage may have little meaning for some cultural groups in which retirement rarely occurs (for the Amish in Pennsylvania, for example, who are predominantly rural; or for American Indians, who have low life expectancies).

Developmental theorists have also used the concept of the developmental task, which is defined as

a task which arises at or about a certain period in the life of the individual, successful achievement of which leads to his happiness and success with later tasks, while failure leads to unhappiness in the individual, disapproval by the society, and difficulty with later tasks. (Havighurst, 1972, p. 2)

Whereas Piaget (1952) and Freud (1953) described developmental stages—cognitive and personality, respectively—that end long before adulthood, Erikson (1963) and Havighurst (1972) identified developmental tasks that extend into later life. Others have criticized age-stage models and developmental tasks on the basis that individuals tend to change with a changing society. That is, tasks or goals will vary with generations and with life cycles (Kaluger & Kaluger, 1984, p. 30; Lacy & Hendricks, 1980). This perspective suggests that different cultural groups have different norms and expectations for people at different stages of the life cycle and furthermore, that these norms and expectations may change over the generations.

Sociocultural factors may also affect biological development. For example, studies have shown that an impoverished environment with inadequate food and shelter may increase the likelihood of low-birthweight infants who have more limited potential for physical and cognitive development (Birch, 1972). Similarly, in some cultural groups, rigid sex role norms may generate a higher incidence of dependent personalities among females and aggressive personalities among males (Mussen et al., 1979). However, it is in the individual's development of culturally approved values, beliefs, attitudes, and behaviors that sociocultural factors have their strongest influence, and these factors can be viewed most clearly through the lens of the cultural group.

U.S. Cultural Groups

Race or ethnicity has been the most powerful force in the creation of subgroups in American society. The validity of race as the sole explanatory variable of an individual's behavior has been effectively challenged, however. Overwhelming evidence exists of at least as much difference within racial groups as between them (Dobzhansky, 1973; Montagu, 1963), which points to the importance of cultural groups in American society.

The racial minorities in the United

States are a legacy of the eighteenth and nineteenth centuries when European colonials migrated to Africa, Asia, and the Americas and subordinated indigenous populations for economic exploitation. The key element in the subordination was alleged genetic inferiority. Subordinated populations include groups in American society "who have a long history of being subjected to discrimination and deprivation" (Makielski, 1973, p. 4). Blacks, American Indians, Puerto Ricans, and Chicanos as well as various Asian groups have all been identified at some time or another as racial minorities.

In regard to human development, the question has been posed, To what extent does race define human potential? The most controversial debate on this issue has focused on the relationship between race and intelligence. Some researchers argue that significant differences between blacks and whites on intelligence tests remain after controlling for environmental variables and thus can be attributed only to genetic differences (Jensen, 1969). Others argue even more strongly that the research data do not provide an adequate basis for such generalizations (Goldsby, 1971, pp. 117–123; Jencks, 1972).

A different question is, To what extent does race determine one's cultural group? It can be easily demonstrated that not all blacks share a common culture. Blacks from Africa, the United States, and the Caribbean have different values, lifestyles, and beliefs. Ethnic group members, on the other hand, share a common culture and a common history. Therefore, "ethnic group" is a broader concept than "cultural group." "Ethnic group" has been defined as a collectivity with "a distinctive identity which is rooted in some kind of a distinctive sense of its history" (Parsons, 1975, p. 56). Blauner (1972, p. 129) suggests that society's characterization of Jews, Italians, or Greeks as ethnic groups as well as blacks, Puerto Ricans, or American Indians is based on locating ethnicity in certain distinctive values, orientations to life and experience, and shared memories that exist within the framework of the dominant American culture. Admittedly, this is a broader conceptualization of ethnicity than the classic anthropological or holistic view that requires ethnic groups to possess a distinctive language, a unique religion, and a national homeland (Brotz, 1964). Perhaps the most

widely accepted view of ethnic groups in social work is the subjective one, which defines ethnic groups by their members' sense of shared past, perception of distinctive cultural traditions, and heightened sense of identity when in contact with other groups (Green, 1982; Vigilante, 1972).

Evidence exists that ethnic identity develops differently for minority and nonminority children. Six-year-old white children are unaware of the ethnic identification of the children with whom they play and choose their playmates more on qualities of age and size than sex and color (Williams & Morland, 1976). Four-year-old black children barely understand racial differences; however, 7- or 8-year-old blacks not only understand but react with hostility if they feel rejected because of their ethnicity (Lessing, 1977). The minority child's ethnic awareness is often increased by membership in a homogeneous neighborhood peer group. This makes adjustment easier during middle childhood, as it tends both to improve self-esteem and to increase in-group solidarity and out-group hostility. However, sometimes the norms of the neighborhood peer group conflict with the norms of the larger community (Rainwater, 1966).

The significance of ethnicity in the development of adult behavior has been documented for most of the minority ethnic populations in the United States. The largest minority group—blacks—has been the subject of intensive study. Blacks are considered an important subculture of American society, different in many ways from whites but possessing a value system, patterns of behavior, and institutions that can be described, understood, and appreciated for their own strengths and characteristics (Peters, 1981, p. 221). The theories that seek to explain these differences can be placed in two major schools of thought: the cultural ethnocentric school and the cultural relativity school (Dodson, 1981).

The cultural ethnocentric school assumes that the United States is culturally homogeneous, that there are universal norms for American cultural behavior to which all groups must conform, and therefore that it is necessary to explain why blacks are deviant in regard to these norms (Bernard, 1966; Frazier, 1949; Gilder, 1981). In contrast, the cultural relativity school assumes that the

United States is a multicultural society that possesses a cultural integrity neither related to nor modeled on white American norms. These differences between black and white culture are largely accounted for by variation in both the historical and contemporary life experiences of American blacks and whites (Billingsley, 1968; Nobles, 1978; Stack, 1974; Staples, 1971).

The research literature includes a large number of works that document cultural variation among black American families. Myers (1982) has reviewed this literature in regard to (1) the structure, functioning, and stability of black American families, (2) the effect of low-income, single parenting on achievement and sex role socialization, (3) parental roles and power, and (4) kinship networks and support systems. He concludes that a great diversity exists in this ethnic group and the conceptual synthesis of its fundamental biculturalism is the major task facing researchers.

A burgeoning literature on various Asian American populations presents research data on the significance of their ethnicity. Some focus on Chinese Americans (Fong, 1973; Hsu, 1971), Japanese Americans (Kiefer, 1974; Kitano, 1969), Filipino Americans (Bulatao, 1962; Cordova, 1973), and Southeast Asian refugee populations (Kelly, 1977; Montero, 1979). Although child-rearing practices and family functioning are the primary focus of this literature, attention has also been given to such issues as health practices (Ling, King, & Leung, 1975) and aging (Cheng, 1978; Ishikawa, 1978; Peterson, 1978).

The Hispanic population in the United States is the most rapidly growing (Rackley, 1980). However, not always recognized is that this population incorporates a number of different cultural groups such as Chicanos and Puerto Ricans as well as various Central American groups. These groups differ in the three subjective characteristics of ethnic groups: a shared history, self-identification, and a heightened sense of separateness when in contact with other groups. However, as with other immigrant groups, it is not the common language or even the shared discrimination by the white majority that most significantly influences the course of human development. It is more likely to be the values that have roots in their traditional cultures. These values have been described in regard to Chicanos (Gibson, 1980; Sena-Rivera, 1979) and Puerto Ricans (Ghali, 1977; Longres, 1974; Montalvo, 1974). Puerto Ricans, in addition to differences in cultural values, must also deal with a largely mixed-race population that has meant intragroup divisiveness, particularly on the mainland, based on the degree of an individual's blackness or whiteness. In that sense, the mixed-race Puerto Rican child may have to struggle with discrimination based on society's attitudes toward blacks as well as toward Puerto Ricans and other Hispanics (Mizio, 1974).

American Indian culture represents the clearest example of how ethnocentric notions of human development in general and child rearing in particular may be. According to Blanchard and Barsh (1980), for example, among the Pueblos of New Mexico, the child's first bed or crib is provided by an uncle because he will take a major role in the child's development, including major responsibility for discipline and for certain areas of the child's instruction. Nowhere in the planning of child welfare services or educational programs for American Indians is this acknowledged, however. More often, social workers have perceived giving responsibility for the child to the extended family as neglect by the nuclear parents and as grounds for termination of parental rights (Miller, Hoffman, & Turner, 1980). It has been well documented (Dlugokinski & Kramer, 1974; Unger, 1977) that American Indian children have been disproportionately removed from their families and placed in out-of-home settings, particularly before the passage of the Indian Child Welfare Act (P.L. 95-608) in 1978.

As a consequence of the strident but often successful struggles of racial and ethnic minorities over the past 2 decades to obtain relief from discrimination and oppressive social policies, other groups with similar grievances have emerged. These include groups of people who do not have a sense of a shared past or cultural traditions but do have a sense of shared discrimination because of some physical or behavioral characteristic such as physical disability, religion, poverty, sexual orientation, or age. Because attitudes toward these groups are culturally determined, however, they represent significant sources of variation within cultural groups in regard to the supports available to members in their efforts to resolve developmental tasks.

Intragroup Variation

Socialization is a key process of human development. Sociologists concerned with the social structure view socialization as the process whereby people are equipped with the beliefs, values, motives, and skills that characterize their cultural group. Socialization is measured by the extent to which a person is able to perform effectively for self and society in valued social roles (Brim, 1966; Inkeles, 1966; Linton, 1936). Socialization is also perceived as the process through which personality and self-concept emerge in the course of role taking. From this perspective, the emphasis is on interpersonal rather than structural concepts in the tradition of symbolic interactionist theory (Blumer, 1969; Mead, 1934). In either case, the developmental aspect of socialization relates to the characteristic roles an individual must learn to perform at different stages of the life cycle. The norms for role performance may reflect considerable variation within a cultural group, however. The major intervening variables that at times modify the relationship between the cultural group and observed behavior, values, attitudes, and so forth are social class, sex, age, and the nature of the physical and social environment.

Social Class. There is general although not complete agreement that social class involves in some way the three components of occupation, education, and economic assets. Furthermore, social class groupings vary in regard to lifestyles, values, and beliefs (Jeffries, 1980). At the same time, there is increasing recognition that both the manner in which social class is defined and its association with specific behavior may vary from cultural group to cultural group (Billingsley, 1968, pp. 122–146; Green, 1982, p. 8). The literature documents a continuing controversy over the issue of which has greater significance, social class or ethnicity (Palmore & Manton, 1973; Solomon, 1976b; Wilson, 1978). A more relevant question concerns how social class and ethnicity interact to influence human development. Evidence suggests that the answer will vary according to the particular ethnic group. For example, some research indicates that lower-class par-

ents differ from middle-class parents in their child-rearing practices in ways that are not consistent across racial or ethnic groups (Kohn, 1977; Scanzoni, 1971). Other research indicates that differences exist between black parenting and white parenting regardless of social class (Alvy, 1981). Similarly, differences exist between white parenting and parenting in other minority populations, again regardless of social class (Ho, 1976; Red Horse, 1980).

At one time, significant support existed for the concept of a "culture of poverty" (Lewis, 1966 p. xxiv), which refers to a way of life, transmitted across generations. The behavior of the poor was thought to be governed by a system of values largely different from those of the middle class, self-perpetuating and transcending racial, regional, and even national differences. Currently, however, this concept has been effectively disputed (Valentine, 1968). The most cogent criticism is that behavior is not always a consequence of people's beliefs or values. Criticism of the "culture of poverty" concept does not obscure the fact that poor people share common threats to effective socialization in the dominant culture, however. They are more likely to have beliefs, attitudes, and behaviors that are functional in their own culture but dysfunctional in the dominant culture (Glasgow, 1980; McNeil, 1969, pp. 115–116).

Sex. The women's movement gave considerable impetus to research concerning the relative contribution of genetic inheritance and cultural conditioning in producing "typical" masculine or feminine behavior. A distinction should be made between "sex"—that is, the biologically given attribute of the individual's reproductive system—and "gender"—the psychological orientation of the individual with respect to feelings of masculinity or femininity. Although sex and gender are similar for most people, this is not true for all people. Further distinction needs to be made between gender identity and choice of love object. Lowenstein (1980) has pointed out that

> although various degrees of gender inversion (trans-sexuality) may indeed coexist with a homosexual love-object orientation, the two are separate characteristics. . . .In fact, it is the feminine style that is valued in the lesbian

subculture, that stresses mutual supportiveness, open communication, and emotional expressiveness as behavioral ideas. (p. 30)

From the perspective of human development, socialization is directed toward establishing sex role norms, achieving congruence between sex and gender, and choosing a culturally acceptable love object. When this does not occur, either because of genetic predisposition or inadequate or ineffective socialization, society's response is usually punitive. As a consequence, subgroups have developed based on a shared sense of victimization (Humm, 1980; Lopata, 1971). It may well be that these subgroups represent a future expansion of the concept of cultural group to include even those without a shared past or cultural traditions.

Aside from anatomical differences, other differences between males and females appear to derive from biological inheritance: males are spontaneously aborted more often in the fetal stage, develop more slowly after birth, are more active, are slightly larger than female babies, and have heavier musculature. Females tend to talk, walk, and cut teeth earlier (Specht & Craig, 1982; Wesley & Sullivan, 1980). Throughout their lives, the sexes produce different hormones in different amounts. Despite the number of distinct anatomical, hormonal, and other physiological differences between the sexes, however, it is generally not known if and to what degree such differences influence the behavior, attitudes, and feelings of females and males. It is known that sex role identity is established in early childhood (Hochschild, 1973; Mischel, 1973) and that many aspects of sex role behavior are learned (Angrist, 1969; Block, 1973; McNeil, 1969).

The content of sex role learning for females most often emphasizes marriage, home, and children; the "feminine" qualities of nurturance, sympathy, and compassion; physical attractiveness; and bans direct assertion, aggression, and striving for power. In contrast, males are taught to be forceful, self-confident, realistic, assertive, and emotionally reserved in preparation for leadership roles in the family and in the world of work (Bem, 1974; Williams, Bennett, & Best, 1975). However, indications are that strict adherence to these rigid expectations for sex role behavior is changing in society (Specht

& Craig, 1982; p. 135). Evidence also suggests, however, that this change is not occurring to the same extent in all cultural subgroups, especially those in which traditional values have supported even more differentiation in male and female roles (Werner, 1979). On the other hand, among blacks, sex role behavior has traditionally been less highly differentiated (Jackson, 1972; Mack, 1974). Therefore, in this instance at least, it might be suggested that the dominant group is moving more in the direction of a subculture's normative pattern than vice versa.

Age. The inclusion of age as a factor in human development and its intragroup variations is a consequence of two relatively new phenomena. The first is the rapid social change that has fostered large differences in attitudes, beliefs, lifestyles, and even values between one generation and the next. For example, the social consequences of being homosexual 30 years ago were quite different from what they are now. In a single cultural group, traditional values may be upheld by the older generation but rejected by the younger generation. The power of the parent generation to socialize its children has been considerably weakened by changes parents have experienced in their own lives, which make them less certain that their beliefs, values, and behavior are appropriate for their children. The school and the media may, in fact, be more powerful socializing agents than parents for new generations of children.

The other factor in the increasing significance of age as an intervening variable in the relationship between culture and human development is the recent emphasis on the life-span view of development. When development occurs at every age of the life cycle, developmental issues will be experienced by individuals of different ages in the same family at the same time. In a family that has just experienced the death of the mother, for example, the development not only of her school-age children will be affected but also of her middle-aged husband and her parents, all of whose reactions will in turn affect each other. A multiple developmental perspective must be considered when addressing the issue of culture and human development.

Environment. Both physical and social environments are perceived as influencing human development. The physical environment refers to the natural world consisting of elements such as space, climate, and geography as well as human-made structures and modifications of the natural world. The social environment refers to an individual's network of social relationships. Both environments influence and are influenced by cultural norms, knowledge, and beliefs (Germain, 1979).

The early social work literature that considered the effects of the physical and social environment (except for the family environment) on human development tended to be descriptive and atheoretical (Addams, 1930; Richmond, 1922). The settlement movement was particularly concerned with the environment as the source of most urban problems. From approximately 1890 until World War I, settlement house workers pushed for the more systematic use of social science data to understand environmental influences on the etiology of human distress. This effort declined after World War I, however, when caseworkers perceived environmental issues only in relation to the provision of concrete services or to working with clients' problem situations.

Recently, ecological theorists in social work have systematically attempted to develop theoretical models of the relationship between environment and human growth, development, and change (Germain, 1979; Germain & Gitterman, 1980; Maluccio, 1981). Bartlett (1970) first identified the need for this approach in a monograph in which she sought to clarify the nature of the social work profession. She wrote:

> The manner in which the social environment operates to bring pressures upon people needs to be better understood. This is not the same thing as obtaining general knowledge about social conditions or social problems. . . .This knowledge must analyze and clarify the impact of the social environment on people, whether as individuals, groups, or communities. (p. 105)

From this theoretical perspective, two concepts emerge that are closely related to developmental issues: environmental stress and environmental support.

A "supportive environment" could be defined as one in which a balance exists between environmental demands and an individual's capacity to meet them. Thus environmental stress might be defined as "that condition in which perceived demands exceed previous adaptation" (Keefe, 1984, p. 265). Stressful conditions in the environment range from concrete experiences such as unemployment, illness, or divorce to more generalized experiences such as institutionalized discrimination or oppression. From the perspective of human development, questions have been raised about the relative importance of environmental stress and the consequences of experiencing such stress at various stages of the life cycle—for example, the effects of racial discrimination (Powell, 1982), the loss of a love object (Albrecht, 1980; Jenkins & Norman, 1972), and unemployment (Keefe, 1984).

With increasing emphasis on the social work role of finding a good fit between people and environments, the importance of identifying supports in an individual's environment is crucial. The literature on environmental or social supports is voluminous. It includes findings from empirical research that document the strong relationship between the level of social support received by an individual and the achievement of developmental tasks (Bretherton, 1980; Gottlieb, 1981).

Other supports that influence total development include personal possessions and available artifacts; the relative ease of obtaining food, clothing, and shelter; the degree of physical isolation in the environment; and the cohesiveness and mutual support provided by the neighborhood, community, or social unit (Kaluger & Kaluger, 1984, p. 65). It is exactly their relative disadvantage in relation to these variables that characterizes racial minorities in this country. Fortunately, evidence suggests that the effects of the environment on social and physical functioning are not irreversible (Malcolm X, 1965).

Implications for Education and Practice

In summary, American society can best be described as an ethnosystem that is multicultural in nature (Solomon, 1976a). A dominant ethnic group, by virtue of its historical control over economic resources, has been able to wield political and psychological power over other ethnic groups and thereby to achieve a dominant position for its own cultural values and norms. Countervailing forces within other ethnic groups have resisted this cultural domination to varying degrees, however.

The psychosocial factors that influence human development are largely a function of the values, beliefs, attitudes, communication styles, and behavioral norms of the socializing agents—in other words, functions of culture—and their effect on human development can best be perceived through the lens of the cultural group. A knowledge of this group is required whenever a practitioner must assess the etiology of an individual or family problem in social functioning. Does the problem stem from inadequate socialization or from socialization to values and behavioral norms that conflict with those outside the cultural group? To provide effective treatment, the practitioner must have adequate knowledge of social systems and their cultural dynamics.

Human behavior and social environment courses in schools of social work traditionally provide the knowledge base from which skills in assessing individuals, families, groups, and communities are derived, particularly skills in assessing so-called normal versus deviant behavior. The individual is only one of several systems that must be addressed when considering human development.

Several textbooks published recently seek to incorporate a sociocultural perspective using a life-span approach (Ganter & Yeakel, 1980; Specht & Craig, 1982), a systems approach (Anderson & Carter, 1978), or a mixture of the two (Berger & Frederico, 1982; Bloom, 1984). Although a sociocultural perspective can be identified in these works, few objective measures assess the relative importance of the myriad sociocultural variables in the lives of specific individuals and families, some of which may be influenced by more than one cultural group. This reflects a major need in social work practice and research—how to develop assessment models for determining whether generalizations made about collectivities can or cannot be made about individual members.

BARBARA BRYANT SOLOMON

For further information, see ECOLOGICAL PERSPECTIVE; HUMAN DEVELOPMENT: BIOLOGICAL PERSPECTIVE; HUMAN DEVELOPMENT: PSYCHOLOGICAL PERSPECTIVE; MEN; WOMEN.

References

Addams, J. (1930). *The Second Twenty Years at Hull House*. New York: Macmillan Publishing Co.

Albrecht, S. L. (1980). "Reactions and Adjustments to Divorce: Differences in the Experiences of Males and Females." *Family Relations, 29*(1), 59–68.

Alvy, K. (1981). *Effective Black Parenting*. Studio City, Calif.: Center for Improvement of Child Caring.

Anderson, R. E., & Carter, I. (1978). *Human Behavior and the Social Environment: A Social Systems Approach* (2nd ed.). Chicago: Aldine Publishing Co.

Angrist, S. (1969). "The Study of Sex Roles." *Journal of Social Issues, 25*(1), 215–232.

Bartlett, H. (1970). *The Common Base of Social Work Practice*. Washington, D.C.: National Association of Social Workers.

Bem, S. L. (1974). "The Measurement of Psychological Androgyny." *Journal of Consulting and Clinical Psychology, 42*(2), 155–162.

Berger, R., & Federico, R. (1982). *Human Behavior: A Social Work Perspective*. New York: Longman.

Bernard, J. (1966). *Marriage and Family among Negroes*. Englewood Cliffs, N.J.: Prentice-Hall.

Billingsley, A. (1968). *Black Families in White America*. Englewood Cliffs, N.J.: Prentice-Hall.

Birch, H. G. (1972). "Malnutrition, Learning and Intelligence." *American Journal of Public Health, 62*(6), 773–784.

Blanchard, E. L., & Barsh, R. L. (1980). "What Is Best for Tribal Children? A Response to Fischler." *Social Work, 25*(5), 350–357.

Blauner, R. (1972). *Racial Oppression in America*. New York: Harper & Row.

Block, J. (1973). "Conceptions of Sex Roles: Some Cross-Cultural and Longitudinal Perspectives." *American Psychologist, 28.*

Bloom, M. (1984). *Configurations of Human Behavior: Life Span Development in Social Environments*. New York: Macmillan Publishing Co.

Blumer, H. (1969). *Symbolic Interactionism: Perspective and Method*. Englewood Cliffs, N.J.: Prentice-Hall.

Bretherton, I. (1980). "Young Children in Stressful Situations: The Supporting Role of Attachment Figures and Unfamiliar Caregivers." In G. V. Coelho & P. I. Ahmed (Eds.), *Uprooting and Development* (pp. 179–210). New York: Plenum Publishing Corp.

Briar, S. (1968). "The Casework Predicament." *Social Work, 13*(1), 5–11.

Brim, O. G., Jr. (1966). "Socialization through the Life Cycle." In O. G. Brim, Jr., & S. Wheeler

(Eds.), *Socialization after Childhood: Two Essays* (pp. 3–49). New York: John Wiley & Sons.

Brotz, H. (1964). *The Black Jews of Harlem.* New York: Free Press.

Bulatao, J. C. (1962). "Philippine Values: The Manilenos Mainsprings." *Philippine Studies, 10*(1), 51–86.

Cheng, E. (1978). *The Elder Chinese.* San Diego, Calif.: San Diego State University, Center on Aging.

Cordova, F. (1973). "The Filipino-American: There's Always an Identity Crisis." In S. Sue & N. Wagner (Eds.), *Asian-Americans: Psychological Perspectives* (pp. 136–139). Palo Alto, Calif.: Science and Behavior Books.

Dlugokinski, E., & Kramer, L. (1974). "A System of Neglect: Indian Boarding Schools." *American Journal of Psychiatry, 131*(6), 670–673.

Dobzhansky, T. (1973). *Genetic Diversity and Human Equality.* New York: Basic Books.

Dodson, J. (1981). "Conceptualizations of Black Families." In H. P. McAdoo (Ed.), *Black Families* (pp. 23–36). Beverly Hills, Calif.: Sage Publications.

Erikson, E. H. (1963). *Childhood and Society* (2nd ed.). New York: W. W. Norton & Co.

Evans, R. D. (1967). *Dialogue with Erik Erikson.* New York: Harper & Row.

Fong, S. L. M. (1973). "Assimilation and Changing Social Roles of Chinese Americans." *Journal of Social Issues, 29*(2), 115–127.

Frazier, E. F. (1949). *The Negro in the United States.* New York: Macmillan Publishing Co.

Freud, S. (1953). *A General Introduction to Psychoanalysis.* New York: Permabooks.

Ganter, G., & Yeakel, M. (1980). *Human Behavior and the Social Environment: A Perspective For Social Work Practice.* New York: Columbia University Press.

Germain, C. B. (1979). "Introduction: Ecology and Social Work." In C. B. Germain (Ed.), *Social Work Practice: People and Environments.* New York: Columbia University Press.

Germain, C. B., & Gitterman A. (1980). *The Life Model of Social Work Practice.* New York: Columbia University Press.

Ghali, S. B. (1977). "Cultural Sensitivity and the Puerto-Rican Client." *Social Casework, 58*(8), 459–468.

Gibson, G. (1980). "Chicanos and Their Support Systems in Interaction with Social Institutions." In M. Bloom (Ed.), *Life Span Development: Bases for Prevention and Interventive Helping* (pp. 456–459). New York: Macmillan Publishing Co.

Gilder, G. (1981). *Wealth and Poverty.* New York: Basic Books.

Glasgow, D. (1980). *The Black Underclass.* San Francisco: Jossey-Bass.

Gottlieb, B. H. (1981). "Preventing Interventions Involving Social Networks and Social Support." In B. H. Gottlieb (Ed.), *Social Networks and Social Supports.* Beverly Hills, Calif.: Sage Publications.

Green, J. W. (1982). *Cultural Awareness in the Human Services.* Englewood Cliffs, N.J.: Prentice-Hall.

Grinnell, R. M., Jr. (1973). "Environmental Modification: Casework's Concern or Casework's Neglect?" *Social Service Review, 47*(2), 208–220.

Gronjberg, K., Street, D., & Suttles, G. D. (1978). *Poverty and Social Change.* Chicago: University of Chicago Press.

Havighurst, R. J. (1972). *Human Development* (2nd ed.). New York: David McKay.

Havighurst, R. J. (1979). *Developmental Tasks and Education* (4th ed.). New York: David McKay.

Ho, M. K. (1976). "Social Casework with Asian Americans." *Social Casework, 57*(3), 196–201.

Hochschild, A. R. (1973). "A Review of Sex-Role Research." In J. Huber (Ed.), *Changing Women in a Changing Society* (pp. 249–267). Chicago: University of Chicago Press.

Hollis, F. (1980). "On Revisiting Social Work." *Social Casework, 61*(1), 3–10.

Hsu, F. L. K. (1971). *The Challenge of the American Dream: The Chinese in the United States.* Belmont, Calif.: Wadsworth Publishing Co.

Humm, A. (1980). "The Personal Politics of Lesbian and Gay Liberation." *Social Policy, 11*(2), 40–45.

Inkeles, A. (1966). "Social Structure and the Socialization of Competence." *Harvard Educational Review, 36*(3), 265–283.

Ishikawa, W. H. (1978). *The Elder Guamanian.* San Diego, Calif.: San Diego State University, Center on Aging.

Jackson, J. J. (1972). "Black Women in a Racist Society." In C. Willie, B. Kramer, & B. Brown (Eds.), *Racism and Mental Health* (pp. 185–268). Pittsburgh, Pa.: University of Pittsburgh Press.

Jeffries, V. (1980). "Class Stratification in the United States: Methods and Empirical Studies." In V. Jeffries & H. E. Ransford (Eds.), *Social Stratification: A Multiple Hierarchy Approach* (pp. 104–136). Boston: Allyn & Bacon.

Jencks, C. (1972). *Inequality: A Reassessment of the Effect of Family and Schooling in America.* New York: Basic Books.

Jenkins, S., & Norman, E. (1972). *Filial Deprivation and Foster Care.* New York: Columbia University Press.

Jensen, A. R. (1969). "How Much Can We Boost I.Q. and Scholastic Achievement?" *Harvard Educational Review, 39*(1), 1–123.

Kaluger, G., & Kaluger, M. F. (1984). *Human Development: The Span of Life* (3rd ed.). St. Louis, Mo.: Times Mirror/Mosby.

Keefe, T. (1984). "The Stresses of Unemployment." *Social Work, 29*(3), 264–268.

Kelly, G. P. (1977). *From Vietnam to America: A Chronicle of Vietnamese Immigration to the United States.* Boulder, Colo.: Westview.

Kiefer, C. W. (1974). *Changing Cultures, Changing Lives.* San Francisco, Calif.: Jossey-Bass.

Kitano, H. L. (1969). *Japanese Americans: The Evolution of a Subculture.* Englewood Cliffs, N.J.: Prentice-Hall.

Kohn, M. L. (1977). *Class and Conformity: A Study in Values* (2nd ed.). Chicago: University of Chicago Press.

Lacy, W. B., & Hendricks, J. (1980). "Developmental Models of Adult Life: Myth or Reality?" *International Journal of Aging and Human Development, 11*(2), 89–110.

Lessing, E. E. (1977). "Racial Prejudice: Doing What Comes Naturally?" *Contemporary Psychology, 22*(3), 680–682.

Lewis, O. (1961). *The Children of Sanchez.* New York: Random House.

Ling, S., King, J., & Leung, V. (1975). "Diet, Growth and Cultural Food Habits in Chinese-American Infants." *American Journal of Chinese Medicine, 3*(2), 125–132.

Linton, R. (1936). *The Study of Man.* New York: Appleton-Century-Crofts.

Longres, J. F. (1974). "Racism and Its Effects on Puerto Rican Continentals." *Social Casework, 55*(2), 67–75.

Lopata, H. Z. (1971). "Widows as a Minority Group." *The Gerontologist, (11)*(1), 67–77.

Lowenstein, S. F. (1980). "Understanding Lesbian Women." *Social Casework, 61*(1), 29–38.

McNeil, E. B. (1969). *Human Socialization.* Belmont, Calif.: Brooks/Cole Publishing Co.

Mack, D. (1974). "The Power Relationship in Black Families and White Families." In R. Staples (Ed.), *The Black Family: Essays and Studies* (pp. 144–149). Belmont, Calif.: Wadsworth Publishing Co.

Makielski, S. J., Jr. (1973). *Beleaguered Minorities: Cultural Politics in America.* San Francisco: W. J. Freeman & Co.

Malcolm X. (1965). *The Autobiography of Malcolm X.* New York: Grove Press.

Maluccio, A. N. (Ed.). (1981). *Promoting Competence in Clients.* New York: Free Press.

Mead, G. H. (1934). *Mind, Self and Society.* Chicago: University of Chicago Press.

Meyer, C. H. (1979). "What Directions for Direct Practice?" *Social Work, 24*(4), 267–272.

Miller, D. L., Hoffman, F., & Turner, D. (1980). "A Perspective on the Indian Child Welfare Act." *Social Casework, 61*(8), 468–471.

Mischel, W. (1970). "Sex Typing and Socialization." In P. H. Mussen (Ed.), *Carmichael's Manual of Child Psychology* (3rd ed., vol. 2, pp. 3–72). New York: John Wiley & Sons.

Mizio, E. (1974). "Impact of External Systems on the Puerto Rican Family." *Social Casework, 55*(2), 76–83.

Montagu, A. (1963). *Race, Science and Humanity.* New York: Van Nostrand Reinhold Co.

Montalvo, B. (1974). "Home-school Conflict and the Puerto Rican Child." *Social Casework, 55*(2), 100–110.

Montero, D. (1979). "Vietnamese Refugees in America: Toward a Theory of Spontaneous International Migration." *International Migration Review, 13*(4), 624–648.

Mussen, P. H., et al. (1979). *Psychological Development: A Life-Span Approach.* New York: Harper & Row.

Myers, H. (1982). "Research on the Afro-American Family: A Critical Review." In B. B. Bass, G. E. Wyatt, & G. J. Powell (Eds.), *The Assessment of Afro-American Families* (pp. 35–68). New York: Grune & Stratton.

Nobles, W. W. (1978). "Toward an Empirical and Theoretical Framework for Defining Black Families." *Journal of Marriage and the Family, 40*(4), 674–688.

Palmore, E. P., & Manton, K. (1973). "Ageism Compared to Racism and Sexism." *Journal of Gerontology, 28*(3), 363–369.

Parsons, T. (1975). "Some Theoretical Considerations on the Nature and Trends of Change of Ethnicity." In N. G. Glazer & D. P. Moynihan (Eds.), *Ethnicity: Theory and Experience* (pp. 53–83). Cambridge, Mass.: Harvard University Press.

Peck, R. C. (1968). "Psychological Development in the Second Half of Life." In B. L. Neugarten (Ed.), *Middle Age and Aging* (pp. 88–92). Chicago: University of Chicago Press.

Peters, M. F. (1981). "Parenting in Black Families with Young Children: A Historical Perspective." In H. P. McAdoo (Ed.), *Black Families* (pp. 211–224). Beverly Hills, Calif.: Sage Publications.

Peterson, R. (1978). *The Elder Filipino.* San Diego, Calif.: San Diego State University, Center on Aging.

Piaget, J. (1952). *The Origins of Intelligence in Children.* New York: International Universities Press.

Powell, G. J. (1982). "Coping with Adversity: The Psychologic Development of the Afro-American Child." In G. J. Powell, A. Moreales, & J. Yamamoto (Eds.), *The Psycho-Social Development of the Minority Group Child* (pp. 49–76). New York: Brunner/Mazel.

Rackley, R. (1980). *Facts and Trends about Children, Youth and Families.* Washington, D.C.: U.S. Department of Health and Human Services, Administration of Children, Youth and Families.

Rainwater, L. (1966). "Crucible of Identity: The Negro Lower Class Family." *Daedalus, 95*(1), 172–316.

Red Horse, J. G. (1980). "Family Structure and Value Orientation in American Indians." *Social Casework, 61*(8), 462–467.

Richmond, M. (1922). *What Is Social Casework?* New York: Russell Sage Foundation.

Scanzoni, J. H. (1971). *The Black Family in Modern Society.* Boston: Allyn & Bacon.

Selim, R., et al. (1979). "The Stages of Life: A Life Cycle Calendar." *The Futurist, 13*(1), 60–61.

Sena-Rivera, J. (1979). "Extended Kinship in the United States: Competing Models and the Case of La Familia Chicana." *Journal of Marriage and the Family, 41*(1), 121–129.

Solomon, B. B. (1976a). *Black Empowerment: Social Work in Oppressed Communities.* New York: Columbia University Press.

Solomon, B. B. (1976b). "Is it Sex, Race, or Class?" *Social Work, 21*(6), 420.

Specht, R., & Craig, G. J. (1982). *Human Development: A Social Work Perspective.* Englewood Cliffs, N.J.: Prentice-Hall.

Stack, C. B. (1974). *All Our Kin: Strategies for Survival in a Black Community.* New York: Harper & Row.

Staples, R. E. (1971). "Towards a Sociology of the Black Family: A Theoretical and Methodological Assessment." *Journal of Marriage and the Family, 33*(1), 119–138.

Toren, N. (1972). *Social Work: The Case of a Semi-Profession.* Beverly Hills, Calif.: Sage Publications.

Unger, S. (Ed.). (1977). *The Destruction of American Indian Families.* New York: Association of American Indian Affairs.

Valentine, C. A. (1968). *Culture and Poverty: Critique and Counterproposals.* Chicago: University of Chicago Press.

Vigilante, J. (1972). "Ethnic Affirmation, or Kiss Me, I'm Italian." *Social Work, 17*(3), 10–21.

Werner, E. (1979). *Cross-cultural Child Development.* Monterey, Calif.: Brooks/Cole.

Wesley, F., & Sullivan, E. (1980). *Human Growth and Development: A Psychological Approach.* New York: Human Sciences Press.

Williams, J. E., Bennett, S. M., & Best, D. (1975). "Awareness and Expression of Sex Stereotypes in Young Children." *Developmental Psychology, 5*(2), 635–642.

Williams, J. E., & Morland, J. K. (1976). *Race, Color and the Young Child.* Chapel Hill: University of North Carolina Press.

Wilson, W. J. (1978). *The Declining Significance of Race: Blacks and Changing American Institutions.* Chicago: Univ. of Chicago Press

HUNGER AND MALNUTRITION

As a human issue, hunger is a constant in the lives of poor Americans. In bad economic times, it becomes more visible and is more likely to be recognized as a national issue. During good economic times, there is a tendency to ignore the problem of hunger, even for those poor who are most vulnerable because of age (the very young and the very old) or ill health. But in good times or bad, poverty puts people at risk of hunger and malnutrition, and even in good times, there is poverty in America.

The term "hunger" refers to the sensation—involving both physical and psychological elements—caused by not having enough food. If hunger is prolonged, it can affect health, growth, behavior, mental attitudes, and even the likelihood of survival. It is because hunger means not having enough food that it is so closely related to poverty.

"Malnutrition," on the other hand, is a clinical term. Malnutrition occurs when the body so lacks the raw materials provided by food that it cannot function properly. Those most vulnerable because of age or stage of growth are the first to experience the harmful effects of malnutrition: infants, children, pregnant and nursing women, and the elderly. But for people of all ages, malnutrition has been described as a disease caused by long-term deficiency, excess, or imbalance of calories or nutrients available to the body. Thus hunger and malnutrition, although not the same, are related.

As a public policy issue, however, hunger in the United States is not a question of particular nutrient deficiencies (though they exist) or even of clinical evidence of malnutrition (though that is available). Hunger in a country where food supplies are abundant is rather a political question—manifesting the sad failure of wage, employment, and income maintenance policies that leave millions with too little money for even minimally adequate diets and no reasonable substitute in the form of public or private food assistance. Hunger is not a new problem, moreover, and as a public policy issue it has had several distinct and occasionally well-documented phases.

Early Governmental Response

The federal government has been involved in food assistance and domestic hunger relief since the depression of the 1930s. At that time, Congress was troubled by the plight of the farmers. The farm economy was in ruins and farm communities across the nation were devastated. At the same time, millions of Americans were out of work and unable to buy the food that farmers so desperately needed to sell. Whether producers or consumers, people needed help to feed their families.

In 1933 Congress responded by creating the Federal Surplus Relief Corporation, with authority to buy up and distribute to needy families food commodities that were being produced but that people could not afford. This gave way in 1935 to the Federal Surplus Commodities Corporation, under which food commodities were distributed through state and local relief agencies and given to schools as well as other social institutions.

In 1939, with many Americans still out of work and much of the farm economy still in financial distress, the Department of Agriculture instituted a food stamp plan to enable needy people—usually those receiving public assistance—to purchase food. The program provided blue stamps for foods named on an official monthly list as being in surplus and orange stamps for foods the families would ordinarily buy.

That original food stamp program operated until about 1943, when the combination of a wartime economy and an end to the dustbowl conditions of the depression changed everything. Americans were back at work and able once again to buy what the revitalized farm economy produced.

Perhaps the most notable legacy of the public policy response to hunger in the 1930s has been the dual purpose of food assistance legislation—to help the food producers and at the same time to help hungry families. That dual purpose is reflected in all the congressional debates over food assistance legislation since the 1930s.

The immediate post–World War II period was significant for the 1946 enactment of the National School Lunch Act. In 1945, during congressional hearings on the operation of the national draft, Congress and the public had been shocked by testimony from the Surgeon General, who revealed that "70% of the boys who had poor nutrition 10 to 12 years ago were rejected by the draft" (U.S. Senate, 1945, p. 9).

To prevent recurrences of this situation, Congress passed the National School Lunch Act of 1946, with authority to use federal funds to aid state-run efforts to provide meals at school. The opening lines of the 1946 act read:

> It is . . . declared to be the policy of Congress, as a measure of national security, to protect the health and well-being of the Nation's children and to encourage the consumption of nutritious agricultural commodities . . . by . . . the establishment . . . of nonprofit school lunch programs. (p. 1)

Just as in the previous decade, Congress combined the goal of protecting the interests of the nation's food producers with that of addressing the nutritional needs of some of the nation's hungry—its children. (The National School Lunch Act also made unique reference to a third goal, national security.)

The decade that followed saw no significant food assistance legislation, despite the fact that poverty and the concomitant risks of hunger and malnutrition had not been eliminated from national life. In the 1950s—although the poverty line had not yet been established and estimates of the number of poor Americans would not be comparable to the statistics maintained by the *Current Population Reports* of the Bureau of the Census since 1959—poverty was a fact of life for millions. Especially vulnerable in those days were racial minorities and other population groups not yet covered by cash welfare or social security.

To the degree that Congress responded to the plight of the poor in the 1950s, it did so by expanding welfare and social insurance mechanisms (adding mothers to Aid to Dependent Children; providing federal welfare aid to state programs for the elderly, blind, and disabled; and creating the Disability Insurance Program). Professionals in the social welfare field and politicians alike regarded in-kind aid as a less satisfactory, second choice.

At the same time, many states were unwilling to provide any type of assistance to poor and needy minorities, and many of the working poor were not yet included under the protections established by the Social Security

Act. Poverty may not have been well documented during the 1950s, but—along with the risk of hunger—it was a fact of low-income life, as social welfare professionals knew better than most.

Turning Point—the 1960s

The 1960s represented a dramatic contrast with the decades just before and marked the beginning of the shift to providing aid through in-kind benefits rather than through expansion of cash mechanisms. At the same time, events focused a spotlight on hunger in ways that helped create the political base for a more aggressive public policy response.

By all accounts, a pivotal event for presidential candidate John F. Kennedy was receiving an advance copy of Michael Harrington's *The Other America* (1962). He is said to have been genuinely moved to learn that there were millions of Americans unnoticed by most, who lived in an America of want, anxiety, and marginal existence. Then, as he campaigned in West Virginia, he met the people of that "other America" in those towns of played-out mines and unemployment. Kennedy vowed that if he won the election, his first act would be to bring food relief to the hungry people he'd met.

On January 23, 1961, Kennedy signed two executive orders. The first expanded the number and kind of food commodities that could be purchased and distributed to needy Americans (under the authority established by Congress in the early 1930s), and the second revived the Food Stamp program (under the same authority relied on by Congress in 1939)—this time as a pilot demonstration program in eight counties, including McDowell County, West Virginia.

Thanks to the presence of Detroit Congressman Philip Hart among Kennedy's advisers, Wayne County, Michigan (which includes Detroit) was one of those pilot counties. Hart argued that if all the counties in the experiment were rural, it would be impossible to convince Congress that the same approach could be used in urban areas. Hart's action ensured that the growing ranks of urban poor were not left out of the equation.

Other forces were at work, beyond a president's willingness to sign two executive orders. The civil rights movement had awakened many Americans to the facts of poverty

and discrimination in the lives of minorities, and a sense of urgency brought to the surface a whole range of social issues that had been gaining momentum for many years. After President Kennedy was assassinated, the politically masterful Lyndon B. Johnson was able to capitalize on these forces to forge a political consensus for major social reforms: for Medicaid, for Medicare, for economic opportunity, for aid to schools with large concentrations of poor children, and for civil rights.

By 1964, too, several hundred counties had won permission to participate in the Food Stamp program, which had proved very successful. Early tests had shown that the stamps were an efficient way to increase the food-purchasing power of low-income households; that they were not burdensome to grocery stores; and that shoppers used them to purchase wholesome foods (such as dairy products, inexpensive meats, and fruits and vegetables). Moreover, the stamps were found to be a marked improvement over surplus commodity food distribution. Congress gave the program its modern legislative base in 1964.

The cause of hunger got another piece of statutory authority when Kentucky Congressman Carl Perkins became concerned over reports that poor children in his rural district often came to school without breakfast. Perkins obtained authorization for a federally financed school breakfast program.

Then, in 1967, a team of nationally prominent pediatricians went to the rural South for the New York–based Field Foundation and examined several thousand poor children. In their report (U.S. Senate, 1968), based on examinations of the children, material from published studies, and their combined experience as physicians, they provided a detailed summary of their clinical findings and then concluded:

> We don't want to quibble over words, but "malnutrition" is not quite what we found. The boys and girls we saw were sick, in pain, weak. They are suffering from hunger and disease and directly or indirectly they are dying from them, which is exactly what starvation means. (p. 44)

That testimony set off a chain reaction, in time leading to establishment of the Senate

Select Committee on Nutrition and Human Needs; a congressionally mandated national nutrition survey that examined over 47,000 Americans in 10 states and New York City; a series of hearings throughout the country; a comprehensive review of all the legislative authorities then available for alleviating hunger and malnutrition; and a White House Conference on Food, Nutrition, and Health called by President Richard M. Nixon.

The early congressional investigations were augmented by the reports of health and social welfare professionals, with the reviews undertaken by both public and private groups coming to similar conclusions about the help then available for the hungry. Their findings can be summed up in two words: not much. At that time, federal food assistance efforts were fragmentary and inadequate. Many programs now taken for granted did not even exist—the Women's, Infants', and Children's Supplementary Food Program (WIC) and the elderly nutrition programs among them. Some (like school breakfasts) had legislative authority but no funding, and still others (like food stamps, school lunches, and even the oldest—surplus commodities) were available but only on a limited basis.

The same proved true of private food assistance. Most Americans did not even think of hunger as a problem here at home. To the degree that churches or charitable groups were doing anything, for the most part they were aiding food relief efforts overseas. Hunger was thought to be a problem in Africa, Asia, and South America—but not at home.

Although the Salvation Army, the Catholic Worker, and other organizations maintained soup kitchens in the "skid row" areas of the bigger cities, otherwise there were virtually no soup kitchens, food pantries, or food banks. Soup lines were just something remembered from the depression.

Consequently, when the public food programs were improved and expanded—in response to studies, reports, evaluations, and the testimony of health and social welfare professionals and of poor people themselves—they did not "drive out" private, charitable efforts: there were almost no private efforts under way to supplant. So much work was needed just to document conditions, raise public awareness, and develop the public programs that the charitable im-

pulses and energies of that period were channeled into efforts of various congressional and federal investigators to build a base of information and support for changes in the public food assistance programs.

During the 1970s, as the medical and statistical evidence of widespread hunger and its consequences became generally available and as public pressure kept hunger on the national agenda, Congress responded. By 1974 the inadequacies of surplus food distribution had been so amply documented that Congress mandated Food Stamp programs for every county (a circumstance that later caused some who were unfamiliar with the program's history to cite the sudden increase in participation as evidence that the program had grown out of control). A variety of programs targeting especially vulnerable groups were put in place in the 1970s, and school meal programs became universally available.

By the late 1970s two apparently contradictory things had happened. First, evidence showed that hunger and malnutrition were no longer major problems, chiefly because of the public policies adopted since the doctors' testimony a decade earlier. From May to September 1977, six teams of health professionals had gone back to the rural South and to the urban North and other areas of the country as well. Some of the original group of doctors took part, and this time their report to Congress was very different:

> Our first and overwhelming impression is that there are far fewer grossly malnourished people in this country today than there were ten years ago. . . . The Food Stamp . . . Head Start, school lunch and breakfast . . . and . . . Women-Infant-Children (WIC) feeding programs have made the difference. (U.S. Senate, 1977)

In social policy terms, the physicians were taking note of something quite remarkable (corroborated by other studies, reports, program evaluations, and academic reviews). It is rare to go from identifying a major national social problem to putting a response in place to having evidence of the effectiveness of that response and to have it all happen in less than a decade. But in the case of hunger and federal policy response, that is just what happened. All of the experts now agree: by the late 1970s, hunger and malnutrition were no longer serious problems in

America, and the federal food assistance programs had played a pivotal role in that achievement.

Nonetheless, despite their record of proven effectiveness, the federal food assistance programs got caught in the growing hostility to social programs shown by the public and policymakers alike. Among the causes for this change in public attitudes was the cost involved. Public money is never willingly devoted to poor people even in the best of times; in recessionary periods like the decade of the 1970s, public support for social welfare spending commonly declines. Reflecting this, Congress and the president began to cut back, and by 1978, the proportion of social program spending to all federal spending was already beginning to decrease.

Turning Back the Clock—the 1980s

The recession that began in 1978 and extended into the mid-1980s brought with it sharp increases in poverty (to a level not seen in the United States since the early 1960s) and unusually high rates of long term under- and unemployment. Hardest hit were children. Not only did the poverty rate among children begin to climb again, but it rose even in two-parent families with a full-time worker. The progress that had been made in reducing poverty among families with children in the 1960s was quickly erased in the 1980s. The one group for whom progress appeared to be sustained was the elderly, but otherwise, the groups most likely to be at risk of hunger and malnutrition by virtue of low income were similiar to those so identified by the U.S. Public Health Service in the late 1960s and early 1970s: infants, children, women, and minorities. Children living in households headed by a minority woman proved to be in greatest jeopardy.

One factor had changed, however. The food assistance programs that had been built up over the previous two decades and that had proved so successful in preventing and alleviating hunger were not expanded to meet the growing need; instead, they were cut substantially.

When President Reagan launched his attack on nonmilitary government spending in 1981, his chief targets (and those of Congress) were programs serving the politically most vulnerable: poor people, including the working poor. Seventy percent of the budget

cuts between 1981 and 1984 came from programs that help poor people; programs helping those with incomes over $80,000 were cut by only 1 percent. Overall, during the period from 1982 to 1985, poor people's programs accounted for 30 percent of all the federal spending cuts, although by then such programs represented only about 7.5 percent of all federal spending. Food programs were among those most severely affected.

Thus an otherwise generous nation, which had responded effectively to accounts of hunger less than 20 years earlier, embarked on a path certain to make hunger and malnutrition serious problems once again. During the same period that poverty and unemployment were high and rising, public food assistance efforts were cut by amounts so great ($13 billion over a 3-year period) that no combination of religious and private charities could possibly replace them.

Through it all, the private charitable impulse that had been so important in getting public food assistance in place during the 1970s was available to turn in other directions. Over the course of the recession, the most obvious remaining gap—the area of private food aid—became the focus for religious, student, social service, and other groups concerned about hunger in their communities.

Like their predecessors in the 1960s, determined to respond, these people collectively produced an emergency food phenomenon. It began in the industrial Midwest, where whole industries and entire local economies were collapsing, and eventually it spread to cities and towns of every size. Across the country emergency food centers were opened and staffed by volunteers and low-paid staff, becoming part of the long tradition of community social service (in this instance dependent on donations of food and cash) and reaching out to people in need. By 1984, a survey carried out by the Urban Institute (Salamon & Teitelbaum, 1984) found that 46 percent of religious congregations were involved in providing emergency food (though less than 10 percent were operating some form of meal program or shelter). Nevertheless, at a time when 47,000,000 Americans were living in low-income households and nearly 10,000,000 workers were unemployed, collecting canned goods for an occasional three-day supply of groceries or staffing a soup kitchen for a few meals a week proved not to be enough.

By the mid-1980s evidence of hunger and malnutrition was plentiful once again. Week by week the evidence mounted—from hospital-based studies and the careful reviews of state health departments, from the Harvard-based Physicians' Task Force on Hunger in America, from the reports of commissions appointed by Republican and Democratic governors and the special committees created by state legislatures, from the reports of the U.S. Conference of Mayors and representatives of the National Governors' Conference, and from religious and advocacy groups across the nation. The reports documented unacceptably high levels of stunted growth, anemia, and other conditions in children—the fastest-growing group among the poor—of American infants hospitalized with Third World conditions like water intoxication and kwashiorkor; and even of "walking bedsores" in dehydrated, malnourished elderly. Longitudinal studies documented an increase in the number of adults who go without solid food, sometimes for days at a time.

The evidence of hunger in the mid-1980s far exceeded anything available to Congress in the late 1960s. Moreover, economic analyses made clear that the recession—which had ended for some sectors of the economy in the fall of 1983—wasn't over for poor people. In fact, it had been so deep and so long that, even with sustained economic growth above 3 percent, it would take a decade or more just to return to the poverty levels of 1979. Without decisive, adequate intervention, poverty, hunger, and malnutrition would be serious problems for years to come.

And yet, even though the evidence mounted, the political response did not. By 1985 only five states had chosen to supplement the WIC program for nutritionally vulnerable pregnant women and young children, no state had voted to replace lost federal food stamp funds, and just a few states and localities had acted to replace even a small part of the nearly one-third lost from school meal programs. For press and politicians alike, hunger in the 1980s was yesterday's issue, although for its victims, it was—as always—immediate. And for the United States, the price to be paid for the consequences of national neglect has yet to be fully calculated.

NANCY AMIDEI

For further information, see AID TO FAMILIES WITH DEPENDENT CHILDREN; FEDERAL SOCIAL LEGISLATION SINCE 1961; FOOD STAMP PROGRAM; POVERTY.

References

Citizens' Board of Inquiry into Hunger and Malnutrition in the United States. (1968). *Hunger, U.S.A.* Washington, D.C.: New Community Press.

Harrington, M. (1962). *The Other America.* New York: Macmillan Publishing Co.

National School Lunch Act of 1946 (P.L. 80-396).

Salamon, L. M., & Teitelbaum, F. (1984). "Religious Congregations as Social Service Agencies: How Extensive Are They?" *Foundation News, 25*(5), 62–65.

U.S. Senate. (1946). Committee on Agriculture and Forestry. *Providing Assistance to the States in the Establishment, Maintenance, and Expansion of School Lunch Programs* (S. Rpt. 553). Washington, D.C.: U.S. Government Printing Office.

U.S. Senate. (1968). Committee on Labor and Public Welfare. *Hunger in America: Chronology and Selected Background Materials.* Washington, D.C.: U.S. Government Printing Office.

U.S. Senate. (1977). Select Committee on Nutrition and Human Needs. *Final Report.* Washington, D.C.: U.S. Government Printing Office.

For Further Reading

Food Research and Action Center. (1984). *Hunger in the Eighties: A Primer.* Washington, D.C.: Author.

Kotz, N. (1970). *Let Them Eat Promises: The Politics of Hunger in America.* Englewood Cliffs, N.J.: Prentice-Hall.

Kotz, N. (1979). *Hunger in America: The Federal Response.* New York: The Field Foundation.

Palmer, J., & Sawhill, I. (1984). *The Reagan Record.* Cambridge, Mass.: Ballinger Publishing Co.

Physicians' Task Force on Hunger in America. (1985). *Hunger in America—The Growing Epidemic.* Middletown, Conn.: Wesleyan University Press.

U.S. House. (1985). Committee on Ways and Means. *Children in Poverty.* (H. Rpt. 99-8). Washington, D.C.: U.S. Government Printing Office.

IMMIGRANTS AND UNDOCUMENTED ALIENS

Immigration, or the movement of people across national boundaries for the purpose of resettlement, is by definition an international phenomenon and best understood in the context of international political and economic issues. People have always been on the move and, except in cases of forced transport (as slaves and prisoners of war), have responded to the pushes and pulls of both the homeland and the new society. Several main factors affect current trends: the wide disparity in living standards between highly industrialized nations and Third World countries; the availability of air transport; the existence of an international labor market served by the temporary movement of "guest workers"; and the aftermath of war and political change, with attendant use of refugee policy as an arm of foreign policy, as well as an expression of humanitarian feelings.

Immigration policy, then, is the national response to the international movement of people, and it seeks to rationalize national interests and control national boundaries. This is not to say that the national interest is unidimensional. The United States, in fact, has for a century been ambivalent in its immigration policy and has vacillated between acceptance and exclusion, depending on the strength of various interest groups.

The most recent major immigration law, established in 1965, diversified the national origins of immigrants, thus reversing earlier racist patterns. The current national debate on immigration policy is different from that of earlier times. It does not focus on size of quotas but rather on enforcement of existing legislation, on penalties for employment of undocumented aliens, and on amnesty for longtime illegal residents.

History of Legislation

The peopling of the present United States territory is closely linked with the history of immigration policy, supplemented by territorial acquisition. From the beginning of settlement, five main periods have been identified (Bernard, 1980): colonial times (1609–1775); the unrestricted, or Open Door, period (1776–1881); the period of regulation

(1882–1916); the years of restricted immigration (1917–1964); and the period of liberalization (after 1965).

Colonial Period. In the colonial years, immigration policies of the British Crown and the local governments shared two goals—to people the colonies and to make available a substantial source of labor for agriculture and skilled occupations. Local governments had jurisdiction over entry, and different patterns emerged in the various colonies. There was substantial advertising abroad, offers of land grants, and promises of religious tolerance. There were also shipments of convicts and an active policy of indentured servitude, under which poor individuals were bound to serve for from 4 to 7 years in return for passage, housing, and a share of their produce. At the end of the time of indenture, they became free and could hold title to land. In addition to adult settlers, records show the arrival of boatloads of children of the poor, taken from cities in Europe, who served in families under a similar system of indenture (Bremner, 1970).

The absolute number of immigrants from settlement to just after statehood (1630–1790) was estimated at under 1 million, fewer than in subsequent years. A classification of surnames in the 1790 census shows that virtually all white immigrants were from northwestern Europe, mostly from the British Isles (78.9 percent). Thus, as far back as colonial times the ethnic die was cast, and the earliest colonists set the mold for a national Anglo-Saxon image.

Open Door Period. In its first 100 years, the United States encouraged the free entry of settlers from abroad, with a view to populating the continent and increasing the labor force. The first federal laws on naturalization of aliens were passed by Congress in 1790, and these provided that any free white person residing for 2 years in the United States or under its jurisdiction could become a citizen. Review of such applications was left to the common law courts in the states. Except for the short-lived Alien Act of 1798 (in effect for only 2 years), which was designed to harass political opponents of the party in power, there were no serious legal impediments to immigration. The first count of immigrants by the U.S. Immigration and

Naturalization Service was taken in 1820. From 1820 to 1880 over 10 million people immigrated to the United States, of whom an estimated 95 percent were from northern and western Europe. It should also be noted that although the slave trade was prohibited by Congress in 1808, it did not actually end until the Civil War. By 1860, an estimated 9.5 million Africans had been brought to the Americas, over 6 percent to the United States specifically (Fogel & Engerman, 1974).

In spite of the open legislative door for immigrants, domestic forces of nativism and restrictionist policy were gathering support. Keely (1979) describes nativism as strong opposition to an internal group on the grounds that it has foreign connections. Nativist feelings arose in response to the large influx of Irish and German immigrants, whose arrival coincided with critical economic and political conditions in Europe. Nativism was often expressed in an anti-Catholic context.

Era of Regulation. Early attempts at regulation took one of three forms: establishment of federal control, emphasis on "undesirable" categories, and exclusionary legislation on racial grounds. In 1891, Congress transferred jurisdiction over immigration to the federal government and established the Treasury Department as the administrative authority. A series of criteria that offered grounds for exclusion were subsequently developed and enforced. Specific problems, as well as a series of personal, political, and moral issues, could result in refusal of entry. This led ultimately to the Chinese Exclusion Act of 1882 (ch. 126, 22 Stat. 58), which was aimed at an entire nation and later extended to almost all Asians.

In spite of the growing negative attitude toward newcomers, immigration burgeoned. In the 3 decades from 1881 to 1910 about 17.7 million people entered the United States; in 1907, the peak year, 1,285,349 persons were admitted (U.S. Immigration and Naturalization Service [U.S. INS], 1983). There was a change in national origins, however; the "old" immigration from northwestern Europe gave way to the "new" immigration from southern and eastern Europe. The restrictionist movement developed racist theories that presumed the inferiority of these newcomers, and in 1911 a Joint Commission on Immigration, led by Senator William P. Dillingham, issued a report that supported this position. This thrust coincided with organized labor's concern that immigrant workers would take away jobs and lower wages.

Years of Restriction. This era was marked by the Immigration Act of 1917 (ch. 29, 39 Stat. 874) and the establishment of a literacy test for immigrants over 16. Further restrictions were placed on laborers from other Asian countries, including India, Indochina, and Afghanistan. But the major feature of this period was the introduction of national quotas, first in 1921 and then more rigorously with the Immigration Act of 1924 (ch. 190, 43 Stat. 153). The latter reduced the annual national quota of immigrants to 165,000 and set quotas at 2 percent of the foreign born of that nationality recorded in the 1890 census (later revised to relate to the 1920 census). The system favored northern and western Europeans, who comprised about 82 percent of the total quota. Aliens ineligible for citizenship (such as nonwhites, particularly Chinese) were not allowed to enter. The requirement that visas be obtained in the home country allowed U.S. consular officials overseas considerable authority to screen applicants on various criteria. Furthermore, the new legislation did not distinguish between refugees and immigrants; annual quotas thus limited the entry of those fleeing Nazi extermination.

World War II and its aftermath forced certain changes in immigration policy. The Chinese Exclusion Act was repealed in 1943, and a token quota of 105 was set up for Chinese immigrants. The War Brides Acts of 1945 and 1947 (ch. 591, 59 Stat. 659; ch. 289, 61 Stat. 401) allowed admission outside the quotas of about 120,000 spouses and children of American servicemen.

The Displaced Persons Act of 1948 (ch. 647, 62 Stat. 1009) granted about 220,000 persons admission, but the legislation was very restrictive; sponsors were required to guarantee support, and applicants were not given nonquota status. The act was liberalized in 1950, and in 1953, 205,000 were allowed nonquota status. The principle of distinguishing between immigrants and refugees was thus established.

The Immigration and Nationality Act of 1952 (McCarran-Walter Act; ch. 477, 66

Table 1. Numerically Limited Immigrants (270,000)

Preference	Percentage Limit
First: Unmarried adult children of U.S. citizens and their children	20
Second: Spouses and unmarried sons and daughters of permanent resident aliens	26
Third: Professionals, scientists, and artists of exceptional ability and their spouses and children	10
Fourth: Married children of U.S. citizens and their spouses and children	10
Fifth: Brothers and sisters of adult U.S. citizens and their spouses and children	24
Sixth: Skilled and unskilled workers in occupations where labor is needed in the United States, their spouses and children	10
Nonpreference: Other qualified applicants	Unused quotas

Source: U.S. Immigration and Naturalization Service, *1983 Statistical Yearbook of the Immigration and Naturalization Service* (Washington, D.C.: U.S. Government Printing Office, 1983), p. viii.

Stat. 163) codified previous legislation and tightened national quotas. By setting separate quotas for colonies, black immigrants from the British West Indies were removed from the substantial British quota. Token quotas were given to Asians, and their exclusion from eligibility for naturalization was ended. This act was the last major legislation of the restrictive era, because global politics were altering the direction of American foreign policy.

Liberalization. The relationship among immigration policy, domestic policy, and foreign policy was illustrated in the Immigration and Nationality Act Amendments of 1965 (P.L. 89-236) and later modifications, the legislative base of current United States policy. In response to a more pluralistic internal society and some redistribution of power among nations, the 1965 immigration legislation abolished national quotas and put an end to the discriminatory Asian restrictions. An overall ceiling of 290,000 visas was determined; only 120,000 were reserved for the Eastern hemisphere, however, and these were limited to 20,000 per country, to be distributed primarily to designated family members and persons with specific skills. In 1976, the differences between the Western and Eastern hemispheres were abolished, and both became subject to the same system of preferential treatment. With the passage of the Refugee Act (P.L. 96-212) in 1980, the overall ceiling was reduced to 270,000, but a substantial number of refugees gained en-

trance outside the immigrant quotas after processing by the international refugee organizations.

Current Law, Numerical Limits, and Preferences

Legislation in effect in 1985 allowed for three major streams of entry for permanent residence in the United States. The first category, which was exempt from numerical restrictions, comprised immediate relatives of United States citizens, such as spouses, unmarried minor children, and parents of adult citizens. Also exempt were specific categories of immigrants: certain ministers of religion, certain former employees of the United States government abroad, and certain former United States citizens.

The second category included immigrants who entered under the allowed overall quota of 270,000 (every foreign country was limited to an annual ceiling of 20,000 visas; dependent areas and colonies were limited to 600, charged against the mother country). There were six preference classifications for entry visas in this category, four based on family ties and two on occupation; each preference had a specified percentage allocation, as shown in Table 1.

The third category consisted of refugees, whose numbers were determined annually by the president after consultation with Congress. This flexibility was built into the legislation: the refugee program was designed not to establish a stable population policy but to respond to special needs. After being in the

United States 1 year, refugees could acquire legal permanent resident status. A special category, "entrants," was established to meet the emergency situation faced by the arrival, directly from their homelands, of large numbers of Cubans and Haitians who were not accorded refugee status. Another category, "asylees," was created to protect aliens in the United States or at a port of entry who faced persecution if they returned to their home country. Asylees were allowed to apply for permanent status after 1 year, but not more than 5,000 per year could have their status adjusted.

For an understanding of the size of the newcomer population, it is important to note that refugees, entrants, and asylees were outside established immigrant quotas, as were immediate relatives who did not come in under numerical restrictions.

In addition to immigrants and refugees, there were large numbers of temporary admissions to this country, such as students, tourists, foreign officials, and businesspersons. Immigration legislation stipulated both the conditions of their admission and whether or not they could work. Legislation also specified grounds for exclusion and deportation, although these particular laws were wide open to interpretation and application (as evidenced by the sporadic invoking of reasons for denial of entry visas on both political and personal grounds).

Firm data are difficult to come by, in part because of a lack of systematic records and in part because of different statuses and jurisdictions. A recent report of the National Research Council was titled *Immigration Statistics, A Story of Neglect* (Levine, Hill, & Warren, 1985). Data from the U.S. Immigration and Naturalization Service (U.S. INS) (1983) show that in fiscal 1983, 559,763 immigrant aliens were admitted. Of these, 336,799 were new arrivals, and the rest—222,964—were aliens who were adjusted to permanent resident status in the United States. About 34 percent of new arrivals and 78 percent of adjusted status cases were exempt from numerical restriction. A total of 57,064 refugees and 2,914 asylees were granted permanent resident status, and approximately 9.8 million people entered the country as temporary admissions—mainly visitors, businesspeople, airline and ships' crews, and temporary workers.

Undocumented Aliens

The term "undocumented aliens" applies to those who enter the country without permission and those who enter legally but violate the terms of their entry by overstaying their visas. It is difficult to formulate policy on immigrants in this category, in part because of a lack of knowledge as to their actual numbers in the United States. The total number of undocumented aliens has been estimated at anywhere from under 1 million to over 12 million. In addition to political motivation to under- or overstate the numbers, Bos (1984) points out the many real difficulties regarding whom to count as illegal—for example, whether to include people awaiting adjustment of status or seasonal or commuter workers? Another problem in arriving at a count is that most estimates are based only on entry; mortality figures and data on emigration or return to home country are rarely estimated. Unfortunately, the statistic is the net immigration, not the total number of entries.

The most careful current estimation uses a residual technique, subtracting legal aliens known to the Immigration and Naturalization Service from the total number of resident aliens reported in the 1980 census (with modifications to account for data deficiencies). The final estimate indicates approximately 2.06 million undocumented aliens included in the 1980 census, almost 55 percent of whom are Mexicans (Passel & Woodrow, 1984).

Of major concern to policymakers is the impact of undocumented workers on the economy (North & LeBel, 1978). Most studies conclude that the undocumented take jobs North Americans do not want and thus are not in direct competition with native workers. In periods of unemployment and underemployment, however, the undocumented may reduce job opportunities and depress wages for the unskilled domestic worker. These are only hypotheses, however.

A second concern with undocumented aliens is the extent to which they drain social service resources. Not often recognized is the fact that those who are regularly employed have social security and income tax deductions. Small sample studies have shown that illegal aliens generally make below-average use of income transfer programs, in part because they are a young working population and in part because they fear exposure and are therefore reluctant to use their entitlements. They also use the educational system less than their numbers would indicate, although their children do have entitlements to attend. They tend to use public hospitals for health care, and if they are not covered by any insurance program, the cost must be borne by the local community. North (1983), who reviewed a series of studies, concludes that refugees have above-average, immigrants average, and undocumented aliens below-average take-up of social service benefits and entitlements.

Immigration Debate

The national debate on immigration legislation continued in the mid-1980s, focusing on such issues as enforcement, penalties, and amnesty. In all cases the major concerns related to the undocumented, primarily Hispanics. For 3 years, 1982, 1983, and 1984, attention focused on the Simpson-Mazzoli Bill, which had as its two main elements employer sanctions and amnesty, or legalization of longtime residents who were undocumented aliens.

The proposed legislation, which was hotly debated, passed the House and Senate in different versions, and failed to get House-Senate consensus. It had proposed employer sanctions with both civil and criminal penalties for knowingly employing undocumented workers. There was concern in some quarters that this would lead to employer discrimination against all Hispanics and to an invasion of civil liberties if it became necessary to introduce a national identity system that would require workers to prove their legality.

The amnesty proposal of the bill differed in its House and Senate versions, but both required applicants to prove previous residence in the United States and denied eligibility for public benefits for several years after declaration. There was a proposal to boost the overall immigrant ceiling to 425,000 and to increase the use of temporary foreign workers, with attendant limitations on their entitlements.

In spite of what appeared to be strong support, the bill never became law, victim of a coalition of diverse critics. Opposition came from Hispanic groups charging discrimination, from civil liberties opponents of identity cards, from government officials who felt

that amnesty legislation would be expensive and not viable, and from labor opposition to the temporary worker program. In 1984 the bill was dead, but not the issues that prompted it.

In 1985 Senator Simpson introduced another version of immigration legislation. This bill included penalties against anyone who knowingly hired unauthorized aliens, and it provided civil and criminal procedures for employer offenses, funding for enforcement of restrictions, continuation of the transitional labor program—with 350,000 foreign workers allowed to work at one time in the perishable crop industry—and establishment by the president of a legalization commission that was to determine if illegal immigration had been curtailed. Amnesty for illegal aliens was to be delayed for 3 years or until certification of reductions in illegal immigration was made. When allowed, amnesty was to apply to illegal aliens continuously resident since January 1, 1980. No newly legalized aliens were to receive federally funded public assistance for 6 years, and such entitlements were to be earned. This bill was passed by the Senate, and the Rodino-Mazzoli Bill was introduced in the House. Different in some respects from the Senate bill, by mid-1986 it had not yet passed the House.

Although there is general concern for more effective control of borders and for regularizing the situation of long-term undocumented alien residents, serious questions remain about the efficacy of sanctions and the inability to determine adequately either the number of undocumented aliens in the United States or their impact on the job market. It is questionable whether the population movement from Latin America, given its proximity and extensive land border, can be effectively controlled by a single legislative act.

Characteristics of Newcomers

In general, the literature distinguishes between the "old" immigrants, primarily English, Irish, and German, who came in the first half of the nineteenth century, and the "new" immigrants from southern and eastern Europe, including Italians and Russians, who came at the end of the nineteenth and beginning of the twentieth centuries. But in response to changed world politics, the 1965 immigration legislation and the Refugee Act

Table 2. Percentage Distribution of Foreign-Born Population in the United States by Area of Birth 1970 and 1980

	1970	1980
Total population (in thousands)	203,210	226,505
Foreign born	9,619	14,080
Percentage of foreign born	4.7	6.2
Percentage distribution of foreign born	100.0	100.0
Europe	54.6	33.7
USSR	4.8	2.9
Asia	8.6	18.0
North and Central America[a]	24.5	33.1
South America	2.7	4.0
Africa	0.6	1.4
All other countries	0.9	0.6
Country not reported	3.3	6.3

[a] Includes Canada, Mexico, and West Indies.

Source: *U.S. Census of Population: 1970* (Table 68); and *U.S. Census of Population: 1980* (Table 79) (Washington, D.C.: U.S. Government Printing Office, 1970, 1980).

of 1980 both accelerated and altered the flow of the newest ethnic immigration.

During the last 2 census decades, from 1970 to 1980, the United States population grew by 11.5 percent, and the foreign-born population increased from 4.7 to 6.2 percent. Table 2 shows that the Asian influx more than doubled.

These figures show foreign born in relation to the entire population. As Tobier points out (1982, p. 163), when immigration figures alone are cited for the 15 years before and after the 1965 legislation, the shift in sources of entry as a result of the legislation is even more apparent. Total immigration for 1951–1965 was 3,965,700; in 1966–1979, it rose to 5,834,000. European and Canadian immigration declined considerably. Cuban, Caribbean, and Asian immigration rose substantially, the latter moving from 6.5 to 29.7 percent.

In addition to the geographical shifts, there were other demographic changes. The immigrant group is young, which is usually the case for newcomers. But what is unusual is that there tends to be a small majority of women, reflecting both an emphasis on family reunion and the opening of job markets to women workers. There are fewer newcomers with skills and advanced professional training, which may reflect the increasing immigration from developing countries.

Two broad categories emerge in the most recent immigrant waves that are of major significance to the future demographic composition of the United States.

Asians. After a century of virtually total exclusion, Asians are now the fastest-growing minority in the United States. By 1981, over 40 percent of refugees and immigrants were Asian, as compared with 6 percent in 1965. Furthermore, data indicate emigration primarily from populous areas, and projections estimate that by 2050 Asians will be as large a minority as Hispanics in the United States (Bouvier & Agresta, 1985).

Although there is a geographic area known as the Asia-Pacific triangle, Asians in fact emigrate from at least a dozen different countries, speak different languages, and have different cultural and political backgrounds. In addition, they come from a range of economic classes and fall into categories anywhere from self-supporting immigrants to dependent refugees.

There are shifts in the relative numbers of Asian peoples in the United States. The Japanese predominated from 1910 to 1970; by 1980 the Chinese were the most numerous; by 1990, the Filipinos will probably outnumber the Chinese. The Koreans are on their way to becoming the third largest group. Also growing in numbers are immigrants from the Indian subcontinent, many of whom are seeking to enter business, industry, and the professions. Augmenting Asian immigrants are the Indochinese refugees, originally from Vietnam, Cambodia, and Laos. Their future numbers are difficult to predict because at issue is American policy on numbers of refugees to be admitted. Thousands await that decision in refugee camps in Thailand.

Although adaptation needs differ according to social class, educational level, and prior existence of the specific immigrant group, all Asians except the Indians have difficult language problems, and all without exception experience social and cultural distance from their new communities.

Hispanics. The situation of Hispanics among the new immigrants also deserves special attention, because of the large numbers involved, the relationship to earlier resident groups, and the historical background of the Hispanic population in the United States. Large numbers of Hispanic people became citizens as a result of territorial acquisition (Mexico) and wartime gains (Puerto Rico). Thus, large numbers of Hispanics did not immigrate to the United States but were incorporated into it. Subsequent immigrants, both legal and illegal, could identify with these resident Hispanics, who had maintained their language and culture. A second distinguishing feature is the proximity of the Latin countries; these particular Hispanic immigrants, who were able simply to walk across a border, became known as "feet" people. Whereas Mexican newcomers are heavily concentrated in California and the Southwest, those entering from the Caribbean tend to settle in Florida and the northeastern states. In 1980, it was estimated that the non–Puerto Rican Hispanic population in New York City alone ranged from 900,000 to 1 million (Tobier, 1982, p. 187), with Dominicans, Cubans, and Colombians predominating (these numbers included immigrants, refugee entrants, and undocumented aliens).

Problems of Immigration

Immigration problems arise for immigrants, for national policy, and for the role of social work. Immigrants have all the social problems of citizens, exacerbated by their experiences of dislocation, readjustment, and adaptation. Refugee populations often suffer a severe residue of wartime deprivation, persecution, and time in camps. Undocumented

aliens face apprehension and uncertainty about the future. All groups struggle with cultural differences that can invalidate Western concepts of health and mental health and therefore frustrate the treatment methods themselves. Newcomers need social services that recognize the unique cultural and social patterns of each group and their traditional methods of coping with problems.

National social policy issues in relation to immigrants may be roughly grouped in four categories: issues of nationhood and civic unity, labor market issues, welfare issues, and humanitarian and civil liberties concerns.

All sovereign nations seek control of their own borders and enforcement of their laws. Both are violated by the substantial number of illegal entries, and many voices express concern. One related issue is civic unity, a conception of population size and ethnic composition with accompanying homogeneity of language and custom. For a nation with a long history of immigration, however, this concept is hardly persuasive. Less ephemeral is the labor market issue, which argues that new immigrants, in particular the undocumented, are likely to take jobs from unemployed Americans. Evidence on this is not conclusive. Many newcomers work at jobs not considered desirable by native workers, and many work in ethnic enterprises (such as restaurants). On the other hand, the resurgence in the garment industry of sweatshops using immigrant labor supports the labor market argument: the availability of a new cheap labor supply can depress wages and lower standards for the marginal and minority worker. Unions have since taken it upon themselves to bring the newcomers up to approved standards, which appears to be a recurring pattern for immigrant groups.

Another critical problem facing labor is the demand of domestic agricultural interests for an expansion of the temporary worker program to handle seasonal produce, on the basis that enforcement of borders will diminish the number of undocumented aliens used for such work. Without severe policing and surveillance, contract workers may become the new pool of undocumented aliens, however, and these two phases of immigration reform could cancel each other out.

Extension of amnesty to the longtime undocumented, based on evidence of residence, would help that group to regularize its status, as would opening opportunities for citizenship. Hispanic spokespersons and civic liberties leaders, however, have claimed that the price of employer sanctions, border patrols, and possible national identity cards is too high. Some groups express concern that employers, fearing sanctions, might discriminate against all Hispanics, including citizens.

Another policy question is the issue of the welfare dependency of newcomers. In reality, new immigrants are not a special burden on the welfare system; the selection process itself leads to a motivated, younger, family-related, self-supporting group. The welfare dependency of refugees is higher for certain populations, particularly those from rural areas without education or skills. Since refugee policy is linked to foreign policy aftermath, however, self-support training for these groups remains a lingering cost of national overseas involvement.

Finally, civil liberties and humanitarian issues arise in relation to immigration policy. The concept of refuge and sanctuary is strong in the United States, particularly with regard to those fleeing political persecution. More complicated are the rights of those fleeing economic deprivation. The uneven treatment of newcomers based on country of origin, race, and political ideology is an issue that has been raised, for example, with regard to Cuban and Haitian entrants.

Social Work Role

Historically, immigrants depended for help primarily on earlier arrivals of their own group, self-help ethnic associations, sectarian charities, and a few specialized nonsectarian social agencies. With the large influx of refugees before and after World War II, work with newcomers accelerated. More recently, specialized agencies have been concerned with the international adoption of children. But despite these specific and vigorous efforts, social work with immigrants was not integrated into the mainstream of social work training and practice.

The development of large-scale refugee programs under the Refugee Act of 1980 activated a new system that gave the public sector a stronger role in service delivery. The U.S. Department of State has initial responsibility for negotiating refugee contracts on a case-by-case basis with the voluntary reset-

tlement agencies (VOLAGS), who then assume responsibility for 90 days. The VOLAGS include the American Council for Nationalities Services, the Church World Service, the Hebrew Immigration Aid Society (HIAS), the International Rescue Committee, the Lutheran Immigration and Refugee Service, the United Catholic Conference, the World Relief Refugee Service, the Presiding Bishop's Fund for World Relief, the Tolstoy Foundation, and one agency for Czech and one for Polish refugees. Following this initial effort, responsibility at the federal level shifts to the U.S. Department of Health and Human Services, which, through its regional offices, undertakes a series of activities in relation to refugees in the various states. Such activities include arranging a program for assistance, which depends on matching funds, and contracting with both public and voluntary agencies, including mutual assistance associations (MAAs), to serve as providers in relation to specific social services. Although targeted to refugees, this delivery option has also served to support the numerous ethnic groups that provide services directly to their own members, thus establishing a model for ethnic organization.

A number of ethnic associations now exist for immigrants as well as for refugees, and those that are able to offer services may ultimately effect the establishment of a new delivery system with a particular capacity to recognize ethnic needs and relate to cultural differences (Jenkins, Sauber, & Friedlander, 1985). Whether these new groups will be integrated into the established social welfare system and, if they do, whether they will retain their particular identity are major questions. Current operations, however, indicate that the effort to bring social work services to new immigrants can now move simultaneously in two directions: encouragement for social work in all sectors to develop an ethnic-sensitive practice, and recognition of the validity of the ethnic association and the ethnic agency as appropriate segments of the service delivery system.

SHIRLEY JENKINS

For further information, see ETHNIC-SENSITIVE PRACTICE; MIGRANT AND SEASONAL FARM WORKERS; MUTUAL HELP GROUPS; REFUGEES.

References

Bernard, W. S. (1980). "Immigration: History of U.S. Policy." In S. Thernstrom (Ed.), *Harvard Encyclopedia of Ethnic Groups* (pp. 486–495). Cambridge, Mass.: Harvard University Press.

Bremner, R. H. (Ed.). (1970). *Children and Youth in America, A Documentary History.* Cambridge, Mass.: Harvard University Press.

Bos, E. (1984). "Estimates of the Numbers of Illegal Aliens: An Analysis of the Sources of Disagreement." *Population Research and Policy Review, 3*(3), 239–254.

Bouvier, L. F., & Agresta, A. J. (1985). "The Fastest Growing Minority." *American Demographics, 7*(5), 32.

Fogel, R. W., & Engerman, S. L. (1974). *Time on the Cross: Evidence and Methods—A Supplement.* Boston, Mass.: Little, Brown & Co.

Jenkins, S., Sauber, M., & Friedlander, E. (1985). *Ethnic Associations and Services to New Immigrants.* New York: Community Council of Greater New York.

Keely, C. B. (1979). *U.S. Immigration: A Policy Analysis.* New York: Population Council.

Levine, D. B., Hill, K., & Warren, R. (Eds). (1985). *Immigration Statistics: A Story of Neglect.* Washington, D.C.: National Research Council.

North, D. S. (1983). "Impact of Legal, Illegal, and Refugee Migrations on Social Service Programs." In M. M. Kritz, *U.S. Immigration and Refugee Policy* (pp. 269–285). Lexington, Mass.: Lexington Books.

North, D. S., & LeBel, A. (1978, February). *Manpower and Immigration Policies in the United States.* Special Report of the National Commission for Manpower Policy (Special Report No. 20), Washington, D.C.

Passel, J., & Woodrow, K. (1984). "Geographic Distribution of Undocumented Immigrants: Estimates of Undocumented Aliens Counted in the 1980 Census by State." *International Migration Review, 18*(3), 642–675.

Tobier, E. (1982). "Foreign Immigration." In C. Brecher & R. D. Horton (Eds.), *Setting Municipal Priorities* (pp. 154–201). New York: Russell Sage Foundation.

U.S. Immigration and Naturalization Service. (1983). *1983 Statistical Yearbook of the Immigration and Naturalization Service.* Washington, D.C.: U.S. Government Printing Office.

INCEST. See CHILD SEXUAL ABUSE; PROTECTIVE SERVICES FOR CHILDREN.

INCOME DISTRIBUTION

The term "income distribution" refers both to the process that determines individual and family incomes and to the outcome of that process. In Western economies, interactions among markets and government policies dominate the process. Individuals have labor market skills and some also own capital or land. These inputs to the production process have prices—wage rates, interest rates, and land rental rates—that are established in markets by supply and demand. A family's market income is determined by the prices of its members' inputs and the amounts of each they are willing and able to sell. In addition, some income arises from the profits of entrepreneurs who successfully create and organize business opportunities. Many government policies—such as minimum wage laws or regulations that restrict business competition—influence wage rates, other input prices, and profits. Taxes and government income transfers directly redistribute market incomes to produce the final income of a family, which it can use to buy goods and services.

To ascertain the "income distribution" or the "size distribution of income," incomes are divided into income classes and the number of families in each class is determined. The income distribution is often viewed as a rough indicator of the distribution of material well-being in a society. Thus, there is wide interest in the extent and causes of inequality in income distribution.

Definition and Measurement Issues

Inequality in income distribution may be defined as "simply differences in income, without regard to their desirability as a system of reward or undesirability as a scheme running counter to some ideal of equality" (Kuznets, 1953, p. xxvii). Measurement of inequality is a descriptive exercise that does not by itself provide a basis for judging whether the income distribution process and outcome are equitable. It describes differences in income during a specified time period (usually 1 year) but does not show whether individuals or families move up or down in the distribution over time. That is, the extent of inequality reveals nothing about the degree of income mobility. Income inequality issues should also be distinguished from those of poverty, which focus only on the lower portion of the income distribution. Questions of income inequality generally deal with the population as a whole.

Any analysis of income distribution and inequality must begin by (1) defining income, (2) defining the income unit, (3) determining the accounting period over which income will be measured, and (4) establishing measures of inequality. Because these determinations may significantly influence an assessment of the degree of inequality and because different analyses often use different determinations, anyone planning to use or compare income distribution data should be familiar with these issues (Atkinson, 1983; Blinder, 1980; Osberg, 1984).

Income. Income is the flow of purchasing power during a fixed time period. The U.S. Bureau of the Census' Current Population Survey (CPS), which provides the only reasonably consistent, long-term record of income distributions, defines income as all cash receipts from labor market earnings, dividends, interest, rent, public and private transfers and pensions, and miscellaneous sources (U.S. Bureau of the Census, 1985). This definition omits many significant sources of income, including capital gains, fringe benefits and perquisites, noncash public transfers such as food stamps, the value of housework and other products produced at home, and the imputed rental value of owner-occupied housing. The Census Bureau is developing methods of incorporating noncash transfers into its income distribution statistics and has already done so on an exploratory basis for poverty statistics. CPS data do not subtract income and payroll taxes, do not adjust for regional cost-of-living differences, and are plagued by underreporting of most sources of cash income. Some analysts argue that the value of leisure time should be included in a complete income measure, but this suggestion is controversial and methods to implement it remain uncertain.

To assess differences in the abilities of living units to consume economic resources requires as comprehensive an income measure as possible. If, on the other hand, interest centers on understanding how the market process rewards persons or families for their overall economic contributions, the appropriate measure would be market income—private labor and property incomes before adjusting for taxes and public transfers. To analyze the distribution of labor market rewards requires only data on pretax cash earnings and, if available, data on fringe benefits.

Income Unit. The Census Bureau reports separate income distributions for families, unrelated individuals, and households. A family consists of "two persons or more related by birth, marriage, or adoption and residing together" (U.S. Bureau of the Census, 1985, p. 210). Unrelated individuals are "persons 15 years old and over (other than inmates of institutions) who are not living with any relatives" (U.S. Bureau of the Census, 1985, p. 211). "A household consists of all the persons who occupy a housing unit" (U.S. Bureau of the Census, 1985, p. 210).

In principle, the appropriate living unit for analyzing differences in economic well-being is the income sharing unit. If income is pooled within a household, then households are suitable units. If income is typically not shared among unrelated cohabiting individuals and families, then families and unrelated persons are more appropriate. If interest centers on the distribution of labor earnings, the proper units of analysis are persons, regardless of their household relationships.

Separating income distributions for families and unrelated persons adjusts crudely for differences in needs across units. A less crude adjustment would treat all members of a living unit as having the same needs and calculate income per person. This does not recognize that needs may vary by age or may not rise in strict proportion to the unit's size. "Adult equivalent scales" allow finer adjustments of incomes for differences in unit size and composition and have been constructed using a number of sophisticated statistical methods.

Accounting Period. CPS and most other sources of income distribution data measure income on an annual basis. Using a longer accounting period would smooth out year-to-year income fluctuations, making income distribution look less unequal. Moreover, some of the inequality among incomes in any one year arises because people are at different stages in their lives and incomes vary systematically with age. Among people

Fig. 1. Lorenz Curve

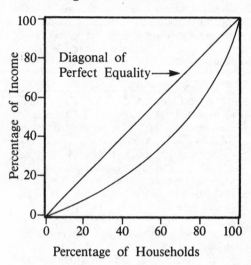

Percentage of Households

of equal age, annual income differences may exaggerate lifetime differences. For example, a person who attends school has far less income than a full-time worker but may later enjoy a higher income. For these reasons, some analysts think that the distribution of lifetime incomes would give a better picture of true economic inequality, though it is rarely possible to gather enough data to chart such a distribution (Osberg, 1984). Analyses of income over multiyear periods find 4 to 20 percent less inequality than 1-year analyses, depending on the choices of income concept and measure of inequality.

Measuring Inequality. A simple method for measuring inequality is to examine shares of total income received by specific income groups such as the poorest 20 percent or the richest 5 percent of the population. Constructing a Lorenz curve and computing summary indexes are alternative methods.

To construct a Lorenz curve (see Fig. 1), plot the cumulative percentage of living units, starting with the poorest, on the horizontal axis. Plot the corresponding cumulative percentage share of income received by those units along the vertical axis. The line connecting the income shares is the Lorenz curve. If incomes were equally distributed, the poorest 10 percent would have 10 percent

of total income, the poorest 20 percent would have 20 percent, and so on. The Lorenz curve would be a diagonal line showing perfect equality. In any real economy, the Lorenz curve will lie below the diagonal, since the poorest 10 percent must receive less than 10 percent of all income; the poorest 20 percent, less than 20 percent, and so on; until 100 percent of the population—which of course receives 100 percent of all income—has been accounted for. The closer a curve is to the diagonal, the less inequality it represents.

The Gini coefficient is the most popular numerical index of inequality. It equals the ratio of the area between a Lorenz curve and the diagonal of perfect equality (Area A in Fig. 1) to the total area under the diagonal (Area A plus Area B). This ratio can range between 0 and 1. Larger values indicate greater inequality. Another common index is the coefficient of variation, which equals the standard deviation of an income distribution divided by its mean. Again, larger values indicate greater inequality. Economists have developed many other indexes as well (Cowell, 1977).

If the inequality of two distributions is compared by constructing Lorenz curves and

Table 1. Distribution of Money Income Among All Families, 1984

Total Money Income[a]	Families (percentage)[b]
$2,499 and under	2.0
2,500–4,999	3.0
5,000–9,999	9.4
10,000–14,999	10.8
15,000–19,999	10.8
20,000–24,999	10.7
25,000–29,999	10.2
30,000–34,999	8.8
35,000–49,999	18.4
50,000–74,999	11.1
75,000 and over	4.7

[a] Median income = $26,433; mean income = $31,052.
[b] Number of families = 62.706 million.
Source: U.S. Bureau of the Census, "Money Income and Poverty Status of Families and Persons in the United States: 1984." In *Current Population Reports* (Washington, D.C.: U.S. Government Printing Office, 1985, Series P-60, No. 149).

Table 2. Trends in Inequality of the Distribution of Money Income among Families, 1947–1984

Year	Percentage Share of Income						Gini Coefficient
	Lowest Fifth	Second Fifth	Third Fifth	Fourth Fifth	Top Fifth	Top 5%	
1947	5.0	11.9	17.0	23.1	43.0	17.5	.376
1950	4.5	12.0	17.4	23.4	42.7	17.3	.379
1955	4.8	12.3	17.8	23.7	41.3	16.4	.363
1960	4.8	12.2	17.8	24.0	41.3	15.9	.364
1965	5.2	12.2	17.8	23.9	40.9	15.5	.356
1967	5.5	12.4	17.9	23.9	40.4	15.2	.348
1970	5.4	12.2	17.6	23.8	40.9	15.6	.354
1975	5.4	11.8	17.6	24.1	41.1	15.5	.358
1980	5.1	11.6	17.5	24.3	41.6	15.3	.365
1982	4.7	11.2	17.1	24.3	42.7	16.0	.381
1984	4.7	11.0	17.0	24.4	42.9	16.0	N.A.[a]

[a] N.A. = not available.

Source: U.S. Bureau of the Census, "Money Income of Households, Families and Persons in the United States: 1983." In *Current Population Reports* (Washington, D.C.: U.S. Government Printing Office, 1985, Series P-60, No. 146); and U.S. Bureau of the Census, "Money Income and Poverty Status of Families and Persons in the United States: 1984." In *Current Population Reports* (Washington, D.C.: U.S. Government Printing Office, 1985, Series P-60, No. 149).

the curves do not cross, a wide class of indexes, including the Gini ratio and the coefficient of variation, will all indicate that the distribution closer to the diagonal is less unequal. If the two curves do cross, however, different indexes may yield conflicting conclusions. This can occur because all indexes embody implicit value judgments about the weight given to income differences at each part of the overall distribution. The choice of a summary measure, then, is never "value free" or a purely statistical operation (Atkinson, 1983).

Current and Past Income Distributions

Table 1 displays the 1984 income distribution for all families as determined by the CPS. The distribution clusters around the median, which was $26,433. It exhibits significant upper and lower tails and is skewed to the right (the mean is $31,052). About 30 percent of families had incomes between $20,00 and $35,000. Over 14 percent had less than $10,000, 11.1 percent had between $50,000 and $75,000, and 4.7 percent had $75,000 or more. The poorest fifth received 4.7 percent of all income, the middle fifth got 17.0 percent, and the top fifth got 42.9 percent (see Table 2).

Fragmentary evidence suggests that U.S. income inequality rose sharply from 1820 to 1860, continued upward more slowly until the U.S. entered World War I, declined sharply but briefly, and then returned to a high level by 1929 (Williamson & Lindert, 1980). Inequality declined significantly during the years of the depression and World War II. The Gini coefficient for the pooled distribution of family and unrelated individual incomes dropped from .49 in 1929 to .40 in 1947 (Budd, 1967). After 1947, no long-term trend is evident; the Gini coefficients for 1947 and 1983 differ by only 1.3%. Table 2 shows that inequality in CPS family incomes declined between 1947 and the late 1960s, then reversed direction. Inequality has increased most rapidly since 1980. The absence of a long-term trend over the past 35 or 40 years reflects a rough balance between disequalizing social and economic factors (notably a substantial increase in the relative numbers of the elderly, the young, single-parent families, and other lower-income living units) and equalizing factors (particularly the rapid growth of public income transfers) (Blinder, 1980).

Table 3. Income Mobility: Percentages of Persons in Various Combinations of 1971 and 1978 Family Income Fifths

Family Income Fifth in 1971	Family Income Fifth in 1978					
	Lowest	Second	Third	Fourth	Top	All
Lowest	11.1	4.4	1.9	1.4	1.2	20.0
Second	4.3	6.9	4.3	2.7	1.8	20.0
Third	2.7	4.7	6.1	3.7	2.8	20.0
Fourth	1.2	3.0	5.1	6.3	4.4	20.0
Top	0.7	0.9	2.8	5.9	9.7	20.0
All	20.0	19.9	20.2	20.0	19.9	100.0

Source: G. J. Duncan, *Years of Poverty, Years of Plenty: The Changing Economic Fortunes of American Workers and Families* (Ann Arbor, Mich.: Institute for Social Research, 1984).

Market income is distributed much more unequally than CPS income, which is market income plus public transfers. In 1978, for example, the Gini coefficient for household market income was .489, while the corresponding value for CPS income was .418. Market income has become more unequal since 1965, when its Gini coefficient was .441.

Inequality in the earnings distribution among men increased between 1959 and 1978 (Dooley & Gottschalk, 1982; Henle & Ryscavage, 1980) and has probably continued upward since then. Inequality in the earnings distribution among women appears to have stayed fairly constant over this period (Henle & Ryscavage, 1980).

A nearly constant level of inequality over many years indicates either an income distribution process in which families' relative income positions stayed nearly fixed or one with a great deal of income mobility. Substantial inequality in any one year is more likely to be tolerated socially if the chances for mobility are perceived as reasonable. The data suggest considerable mobility in U.S. income and earnings distributions (Duncan, 1984; Schiller, 1977). Table 3 illustrates this. The first row of figures, for example, shows that among the 20 percent of the U.S. population living in the poorest families in 1971, only 11.1 percent fell into the same category in 1978. The other 8.9 percent had moved upward. Overall, 59.9 percent of the population moved up or down at least one fifth, while 23.1 percent moved at least two fifths in 7 years.

Wealth is the quantity of tangible and financial assets owned at a given time. Because wealth generates dividends, interest, and rental incomes, wealth inequality partly determines income inequality. Moreover, if people possess wealth that can be liquidated or used as collateral for loans, their command over goods and services extends beyond their current incomes. For these reasons, data on the distribution of wealth usefully supplement data on income distribution.

There is no regular, comprehensive survey of assets and liabilities in the United States. The scanty data that exist show wealth inequality far exceeding income inequality. In 1969, the top 5 percent of households owned 49.2 percent of the country's net worth (Wolff, 1982). In contrast, for household CPS income, the share of the top 5 percent was 16.8 percent. Wealth inequality declined during the depression and World War II but remained constant from the late 1940s to 1969 (Smith & Franklin, 1974). Preliminary data for 1983 suggest little change since 1969 (Avery, Elliehausen, & Canner, 1984).

Socioeconomic Sources of Income Differences

Analyses of factors determining income differences generally focus on labor earnings, which account for about 75 percent of all cash income. Their distribution fundamentally influences the distribution of total income.

Some differences in earnings arise from individual choices. Others reflect innate personal characteristics, such as race and sex, which affect market rewards. Still others arise from institutional features of labor markets, such as trade unions. Substantial controversy exists about the interpretation and relative importance of these sources. A significant portion of the variation in earnings cannot be explained by contemporary theory, methods, and data and derives from a combination of chance events and the effects of unmeasured variables.

Work Time. Differences in the amounts of time devoted to paid work and in the intensity of the work account for a significant degree of earnings inequality. Some differences are involuntary; greater unemployment leads to greater inequality because the income losses fall disproportionately on low earners. Other differences are not, such as those brought on by decisions to seek part-time or temporary jobs, to accept overtime, to be self-employed, or to work at jobs that permit self-pacing.

Compensating Differentials. Some jobs are more difficult, more unpleasant, or more dangerous than others. Controlling for level of skill, such jobs must pay higher wages to induce people to fill them. There is good evidence that riskier jobs command a wage premium, but with the exception of compensation for more education, compensating differentials do not explain much of the observed earnings inequality.

Education and Experience. A strong association between years of schooling and earnings level has been well established. However, theoretical interpretation of this relationship generates debate. Human capital theory (Becker, 1964; Mincer, 1974) argues that jobs requiring more education must pay more to attract enough workers because people generally expect a financial return—a compensating differential—for their decision to defer working and invest in themselves. This theory assumes that greater schooling creates greater productive skills that are valued by employers. According to screening theory (Spencer, 1974; Stiglitz, 1975), formal education teaches little that is directly applicable to future work. Instead, because more able students tend to attain more education, educational systems sort people by ability. Employers value ability and, therefore, seek better-educated individuals and reward them more highly. Neo-Marxist theorists (Bowles & Gintis, 1976) argue that eduation sorts people according to their social class, not their ability. They also suggest that longer schooling promotes better discipline and socializes future workers to accept capitalist

institutions. For these reasons, businesses prefer more educated workers and reward them more highly.

Controlling for education, there is a strong relationship between years of work experience and earnings. According to the human capital interpretation, experience is generally accompanied by on-the-job training. Thus, greater earnings for more experience represent a reward for the increased productivity resulting from such training. The observed relationship is also consistent with customary pay differentials for seniority independent of productivity.

Ability. Although people with more ability, as measured by intelligence tests, tend to receive more education, ability also has a direct effect on earnings. What kinds of ability are most closely related to making money remains a matter of intense debate. Empirical studies using IQ or similar tests to measure ability tend to find positive but relatively small effects of ability on earnings after controlling for the impact of education (Jencks et al., 1979).

Family Background. Family financial circumstances limit some individuals' access to educational opportunities, thereby indirectly affecting their earnings. Parental ability to motivate and assist their children in school, to maintain their health, and to help them secure admission to apprenticeship programs or high-quality colleges may also have important indirect effects on earnings by influencing educational achievement. Family background and socioeconomic status may directly affect earnings through parental job contacts or if family socialization tends to transmit and reproduce a class structure across generations. An empirical analysis (Jencks et al., 1979) suggests that family background variables have a major influence on educational attainment. Their direct influence on earnings, controlling for their impact on education, is uncertain but probably not large.

Race and Sex. Women and minorities earn substantially less than white men, even when such other factors as education or experience remain constant. Most analysts interpret the differences as evidence of labor market discrimination (Corcoran and Duncan [1979] are representative of this view). Others, such as Mincer and Polacheck (1974), believe that labor markets are sufficiently competitive that equally productive workers cannot long receive unequal wages, and they conclude that unmeasured, perhaps subtle, differences in motivation, the quality of schooling, or other factors are responsible for the observed differences.

Trade Unions. Unions raise the wages of their members relative to similarly productive nonunion workers through the exercise of bargaining power. The union wage differential usually falls in the 10 to 20 percent range. Whereas unions increase earnings inequality across industries, their bargaining practices reduce inequality among their members and narrow production worker–nonproduction worker differences within firms. The net effect of unions is to reduce male earnings inequality (Freeman, 1980).

Internal and Secondary Labor Markets. Earnings differences may arise from company and industry job structures. A firm's internal labor market is characterized by a ladder of jobs offering stable employment. Workers usually enter the ladder near the bottom. They progress with experience because the better jobs are filled by promotion rather than by hiring people on the open labor market. As a result, internal labor markets are partly insulated from market pressures, and relative wages within them depend heavily on custom, job status, and workers' notions of equity. Employers select workers for jobs in internal labor markets on the basis of education, race, sex, and other characteristics thought to be related to job-training costs. Those denied access to internal labor markets are thrown into the economy's "secondary labor markets," where wages, working conditions, job stability, and chances for training and advancement are poor. Emphasis on the duality between internal and secondary labor markets (or in some variations, multisegmented labor markets) as a major determinant of differences in earnings (Doeringer & Piore, 1971) clashes with human capital theory's emphasis on individual choice and open competitive labor markets. Debate is vigorous over which perspective is more accurate.

Other Factors. In addition to these sources of earnings inequality, several other socioeconomic factors directly affect the distribution of family and household income. Changes in the relative size of demographic groups that have different mean incomes and degrees of income inequality will affect inequality in overall income distribution. Demographic changes in the United States since 1947 have had disequalizing impacts. The joint distribution of husbands' and wives' earnings affects the distribution of total family income. Wives' earnings add relatively more to the income of families in which the husbands have low earnings and, thus, tend to equalize the family income distribution. Blank and Blinder (1986) show that inflation has had no effect on inequality, despite common assertions to the contrary. Inequality of wealth generates unequal property incomes. Because property income is a small proportion of total income, its inequality is much less important than earnings inequality in producing the observed inequality of total income.

Cash and noncash transfers mostly go to living units in the lower part of the income distribution. They reduce the Gini coefficient by 19 percent and raise the share of the poorest fifth from less than 1 percent of market income to about 7 percent of total income (Danziger, Haveman, & Plotnick, 1981). In contrast, the tax system has a negligible impact on inequality. Transfers and taxes indirectly influence inequality through their effects on work effort, savings behavior, decisions about living arrangements, and other factors that help determine the distribution of market income.

Policy Debates Related to Income Distribution

The fundamental policy question of how extensively government should interfere with market forces has broad implications for income distribution. In the United States, an underlying acceptance of free market forces, which create inequality, has produced minimal public pressure to lessen inequality of income and wealth. Although many policies influence income distribution, achieving some specified level of inequality has never been an explicit American policy objective. Instead, debates over distributional issues tend to focus more narrowly on reducing income differences across geographic regions and race, sex, age, industry, and occupational groups.

Broader support exists for altering the process of income distribution to reduce inequality of opportunity. Antidiscrimination laws, federal college loans, preschool Head

Start programs, and other policies support this goal and indirectly affect inequality of result. Yet a strategy of equalizing opportunity by restricting large inheritances or otherwise restraining wealthy families has never been seriously pursued.

Tax and social welfare policies were instituted and are supported for the purposes of reducing insecurity with respect to income loss from old age, unemployment, disability, or loss of a family breadwinner; helping people pay for essentials such as food, housing, or health care; reducing poverty; and fairly sharing tax burdens (Lampman, 1984). Because of the huge sums involved, such programs have major side effects on the overall distribution of income.

Most political factions agree that income taxes should be progressive: as income rises, the proportion of income paid in taxes should also increase. The appropriate degree of progressivity remains in dispute. Debate exists on the effect of tax rates on incentives to work, save, invest, and take business risks. Also keenly debated is the worth of many "tax expenditures" (such as tax exemptions on most fringe benefits, lower taxation of capital gains, and deductions for mortgage interest), which allow large amounts of income to escape taxation, mainly benefit more affluent taxpayers, and create different tax liabilities for persons with similar gross incomes. Tax reforms during the first Reagan Administration reduced the equalizing effect of the federal income tax, which was already small.

Mean-tested benefits, provided mainly by Aid to Families with Dependent Children, Supplemental Security Income, food stamps, and Medicaid, play an important role in alleviating poverty and reducing inequality. These income assistance programs perennially generate controversy, and reforms to clean up the "welfare mess" are always being sought. Presidents Nixon and Carter proposed sweeping welfare reforms that would have reduced the number of separate programs, broadened eligibility categories, and placed a federal floor under state benefits. Carter's plan also called for a massive public jobs program for welfare recipients classified as expected to work but unable to find a job. These proposals failed as divisive debate swirled around their potential costs, administrative problems, the generosity of

the minimum benefit, and possible adverse effects on work and family stability.

Since the late 1970s, comprehensive welfare reform has lain dormant. Policy debates instead have centered on whether and how to scale back social programs without injuring the "truly needy." The retrenchment of mean-tested programs under President Reagan has pared welfare rolls, altered work incentives for Aid to Families with Dependent Children, reduced the incomes of many poor and near-poor families, and helped increase income inequality.

If social workers wish to reduce inequality, they should continue supporting stronger antipoverty and income maintenance policies, knowing that success in achieving these goals will promote less income inequality as well. The precise equilizing impact of such policies will depend on their specific eligibility and benefit rules. Working to defend and expand equal opportunity policies can simultaneously help make the process of income distribution more equitable.

ROBERT D. PLOTNICK

For further information, see FEDERAL SOCIAL LEGISLATION SINCE 1961; INCOME MAINTENANCE SYSTEM; SOCIAL PLANNING IN THE PUBLIC SECTOR; SOCIAL WELFARE POLICY: TRENDS AND ISSUES.

References

Atkinson, A. B. (1983). *The Economics of Inequality*. New York: Oxford University Press.

Avery, R., Elliehausen, G., & Canner, G. (September 1984). "Survey of Consumer Finances, 1983: A Second Report." *Federal Reserve Bulletin, 70*(9), 857–868.

Becker, G. (1964). *Human Capital*. New York: Columbia University Press.

Blank, R., & Blinder, A. (1986). "Macroeconomics, Income Distribution and Poverty." In S. Danziger & D. Weinberg (Eds.), *Fighting Poverty: What Works and What Doesn't*. Cambridge, Mass.: Harvard University Press.

Blinder, A. S. (1980). "The Level and Distribution of Economic Well-Being." In M. Feldstein (Ed.), *The American Economy in Transition*, (pp. 415–479). Chicago: University of Chicago Press.

Bowles, S., & Gintis, H. (1976). *Schooling in Capitalist America*. New York: Basic Books.

Budd, E. (1967). "Introduction." In E. Budd (Ed.), *Poverty and Inequality*. New York: W. W. Norton & Co.

Corcoran, M., & Duncan, G. (1979). "Work History, Labor Force Attachment, and Earnings

Differences Between the Races and Sexes."
Journal of Human Resources, 14(1), 3–20.

Cowell, F. (1977). *Measuring Inequality.* Oxford, England: Philip Alan Publishers.

Danziger, S., Haveman, R., & Plotnick, R. (1981). "How Income Transfer Programs Affect Work, Savings, and the Income Distribution: A Critical Review." *Journal of Economic Literature, 19*(4), 975–1028.

Doeringer, P., & Piore, M. (1971). *Internal Labor Markets and Manpower Analysis.* Lexington, Mass.: D.C. Heath & Co.

Dooley, M., & Gottschalk, P. (1982). "Does a Younger Male Labor Force Mean Greater Earnings Inequality?" *Monthly Labor Review, 105*(11), 42–45.

Duncan, G. J. (1984). *Years of Poverty, Years of Plenty: The Changing Economic Fortunes of American Workers and Families.* Ann Arbor, Mich.: Institute for Social Research.

Freeman, R. (1980). "Unionism and the Dispersion of Wages." *Industrial and Labor Relations Review, 34*(1), 3–23.

Henle, P., & Ryscavage, P. (1980). "The Distribution of Earned Income among Men and Women, 1958–1977." *Monthly Labor Review, 103*(4), 3–10.

Jencks, C., et al. (1979). *Who Gets Ahead? The Determinants of Economic Success in America.* New York: Basic Books.

Kuznets, S. (1952). *Share of Upper Income Groups in Income and Savings.* New York: National Bureau of Economic Research.

Lampman, R. (1984). *Social Welfare Spending: Accounting for Changes from 1950 to 1978.* New York: Academic Press.

Mincer, J. (1974). *Schooling, Experience, and Earnings.* New York: Columbia University Press.

Mincer, J., & Polachek, S. (1974). "Family Investments in Human Capital: Earnings of Women." *Journal of Politial Economy, 82*(2), S76–S111.

Osberg, L. (1984). *Economic Inequality in the United States.* Armonk, N.Y.: M. E. Sharpe, Inc.

Schiller, B. (1977). "Relative Earnings Mobility in the United States." *American Economic Review, 67*(5), 926–941.

Smith, J., & Franklin, S. (1974). "The Concentration of Personal Wealth 1922–1969." *American Economic Review, 64*(2), 162–167.

Spence, M. (1974). *Market Signalling.* Cambridge, Mass.: Harvard University Press.

Stiglitz, J. (1975). "The Theory of 'Screening,' Education and the Distribution of Income." *American Economic Review, 65*(3), 283–300.

U.S. Bureau of the Census. (1985). "Money Income of Households, Families and Persons in the United States: 1983." In *Current Popula-*

tion Reports (Series P-60, No. 146). Washington, D.C.: U.S. Government Printing Office.

Williamson, J., & Lindert, P. (1980). *American Inequality: A Macroeconomic History.* New York: Academic Press.

Wolff, E. (1982). "The Size Distribution of Household Disposable Wealth in the United States." *Review of Income and Wealth, 28*(2), 125–146.

INCOME MAINTENANCE SYSTEM

Although at least three of every ten citizens of the United States receive income maintenance, the term has only recently been popularized, and it has multiple definitions. Fiscally, income maintenance is a field or sector in social welfare that provides income assistance to eligible individuals and families. Functionally, income maintenance is a social service, along with housing, health, education, employment and training, and personal services. Programmatically, income maintenance is a system or network of related programs, not necessarily well integrated, that are designed to ameliorate certain social problems and economic conditions, including poverty, retirement, survivorship, disability, and unemployment.

For the purposes of this article, "income maintenance" is broadly defined as the provision of local, state, or federal financial assistance, in the form of cash or voucher, to individuals and families during periods of income interruption or reduction, either temporarily or on a long-term basis. Income maintenance is usually provided when people are not employed, either because they are not employable or because they have been excused from employment, and need financial assistance to meet their basic survival needs or when people are otherwise eligible to receive income maintenance benefits.

According to this definition, individuals and families are "maintained," through the provision of income, either because of emergency conditions or because long-term economic aid is indicated. Such a definition places income maintenance in the domain of social welfare, identifies it as a social service, and implies multiple jurisdictional levels and program designs, suggesting an income maintenance "system." Not included are tax transfers and occupational fringe benefits received by many who are employed or who earn profits from personal or other financial activities. Such benefits have been described as fiscal welfare and occupational welfare. They are outside the domain of income maintenance (Titmuss, 1969).

Overview in the United States

In 1973, there were at least 100 income maintenance programs in existence in the United States (Storey, Townsend, & Cox, 1973). These programs differed from one another in scope, criteria of eligibility, sources of funding, and intent. They were and are administered by the federal government, by state and local governments, or by some combination of these political jurisdictions. Since 1973, several of the programs have been consolidated, some have been terminated, and additional ones have been added. Although it is difficult to ascertain exactly how many programs are in existence, the estimate of 100 remains reasonable.

Most income maintenance programs are under the aegis of five federal departments (Health and Human Services, Agriculture, Labor, Housing and Urban Development, and Interior), the Office of Economic Opportunity, the Veterans Administration, the Railroad Retirement Board, and the Civil Service Commission. The income maintenance programs administered by state and local governments fall under the umbrella of an even greater number of state and local governmental organizations.

Although the total number of income maintenance programs is large, many of the specific programs are small and do not receive much public attention. The large programs, however, are under constant scrutiny and are subject to ceaseless political uncertainty. These programs include Old Age, Survivors, and Disability Insurance (OASDI, commonly referred to as social security); Unemployment Compensation; Aid to Families with Dependent Children (AFDC); General Assistance; Food Stamps; Workers' Compensation; and Supplemental Security Income (SSI).

A Brief History. The antecedents of income maintenance in the United States are in the British Elizabethan Poor Laws of 1597 to 1601. These laws were brought to colonial America by English settlers. Each colonial government enacted its own set of laws modeled after the British prototype. The colonial Poor Laws, harsh and punitive by today's standards, remained intact until the Civil War era. In 1865, after the emancipation of multitudes of impoverished slaves who could not have survived without assistance, the federal government created the Bureau of Refugees, Freedmen, and Abandoned Lands (commonly referred to as the Freedmen's Bureau). By so doing, the federal government assumed responsibility for the first time for providing financial and other assistance to destitute citizens, both black and white (Trattner, 1974). Earlier, in 1862, the federal government had assumed limited responsibility for assisting another category of citizens, war veterans. Although the original legislation covered only disabled Union soldiers and the wives, children, and dependent family members of those who were killed, by 1900 federal and state responsibility was established for disabled as well as needy veterans and their families (Axinn & Levin, 1975).

Another modification in the provision of financial aid to poor people occurred in the 1870s. This was the temporary shift in emphasis from statutory (state and local) to voluntary (private) responsibility for setting standards of poor relief. The shift was related to the establishment and proliferation of the Charity Organization Societies (COSs). These societies were based on the philosophy of "scientific charity," or relief based on scientific study and observation. Their guiding principle was relief coordination: only the deserving were to be assisted. So successful were they in this regard that one 1887 study of 28,000 COS cases (Warner, 1894) discovered that 63.3 percent of the applicants for relief were denied because they were deemed either to need work rather than relief or to be unworthy of relief.

The historical evolution of income maintenance in the nineteenth century must be viewed in the context of that era. The social values of that century were affected enormously by rugged individualism, social Darwinism, and a powerful Protestant Ethic, which stressed the salvation of work. The policies and principles of early income maintenance programs were based on such a value structure.

The Progressive Era (1900–1914) was a time of partial reform of social and economic policy in the United States. One important change in the field of income maintenance was the advent of pensions for mothers of dependent children. These pensions were funded under public auspices and arose out of concern for child welfare and the high value placed on the stability of the family. Forty states had mothers' or widows' pensions by 1921 (Leiby, 1978). A second reform was the development of Workmen's (Workers') Compensation programs. Between 1909 and 1920, 43 states enacted legislation protecting workers against some of the hazards of the workplace (Coll, 1969). Although these early laws excluded many hazards and many workers, they were an improvement over no protection at all.

In 1929, the most severe depression the nation had ever experienced catapulted millions of individuals and families into poverty or placed them in serious economic jeopardy. The extant income maintenance programs were unable to meet the resultant economic need. Reluctantly, the federal government created income maintenance programs to assist certain categories of those most adversely affected. This historic action culminated in the passage of the Social Security Act of 1935, the foundation of contemporary income maintenance policy.

Current Programs. Today's income maintenance programs have many shortcomings. They do not make up a balanced, well-designed, well-integrated system. The various programs were created during different historical times, serve a range of objectives, have extremely divergent eligibility criteria, and are administered by a variety of governmental jurisdictions and bureaucracies. According to Lurie (1975), the system of income maintenance programs is discontinuous and enormously complex. The various programs overlap in coverage, yet exclude many who are in need and often work in opposing ways. Rodgers (1982) criticized the lack of integration of the various income maintenance programs and the impact on recipients of the categorical nature of many of these programs.

Other analysts (Barth, Carcagno, & Palmer, 1974) concluded that the lack of integration of the programs resulted in two unplanned or unintended effects: (1) undesirable effects on recipients and (2) benefit levels and ranges of coverage that are inadequate and inefficient in terms of their impact on lessening poverty. Although Bell (1983) saw many accomplishments of the various income programs, she also criticized the same programs because of gaps in their coverage of many people who are in need, the inequity and inadequacy of benefit structures, and the weakness of several of the specific programs, particularly unemployment compensation, disability programs, and public aid. Stein (1980) maintained that the system inadvertently affects individual and family behavior negatively. Divorce, separation, and desertion are behaviors that may result from individuals and families striving to become eligible for financial aid or continuing to utilize benefits that they might otherwise lose. Some (Piven & Cloward, 1971) have argued that public aid programs serve a latent social control function that is more congruent with the profiteering motives of capitalism than with the economic needs of poor people.

There are also many positive aspects to the income maintenance programs. They transfer needed income to millions of Americans, just as they provide social and economic stability in the society. Their importance should not be overlooked or denigrated; they contribute to the economic livelihood of both individuals and the society. Their shortcomings and imperfections must be noted, however, if the programs are to be reformed. A long-term reform objective is a more just distribution of the national income (Schorr, 1977).

Dominant Programs

Reference has already been made to the multiplicity of income maintenance programs in the United States. Several of them dominate by virtue of their overall importance to recipients and the concern they raise with politicians and society in general. The following several programs are those generally so designated. Although the distinctions between them are not always clear, the programs are characterized as being either social insurance or public aid.

Social Insurance Programs. These are programs under which the beneficiary must make a financial contribution before he or she can establish eligibility. This contribution is in the form of a special tax and is paid by the future beneficiary, by his or her employer, or by both. Benefits are viewed more as rights than as privileges. There is little, if any, social stigma attached to their receipt. OASDI benefits are received by retired workers, their survivors, and the disabled. There is no relationship between receipt of social security benefits and income level (except income earned through employment). A greater proportion of all social security benefits is received by the nonpoor than the poor. OASDI is the largest of the social insurance programs. The other major social insurance programs in the United States are Unemployment Compensation and Workers' Compensation.

Public Aid Programs. These programs are means-tested; that is, the applicant must show evidence of need and be without an alternate source of meeting that need. Further, these programs generally do not expect the recipient to have made a contribution prior to receipt of benefits. The funding source of public aid programs is the general fund, not special taxes earmarked for relief. Public aid is generally viewed as a privilege because it is based on the charitable approach to relieving poverty. The imposition of a stigma frequently accompanies the receipt of public aid. Public aid programs are categorical in that, generally, only certain categories of individuals and families are eligible to receive benefits. These programs are frequently described as "safety net" programs, and they usually exclude childless couples and the working poor. The major public aid programs are AFDC, SSI, General Assistance, and Food Stamps.

The scope, diversity, and costs associated with the major income maintenance programs are enormous. Table 1 highlights these dimensions.

Eligibility for one of the income maintenance programs listed in Table 1 does not necessarily preclude eligibility for another. Therefore, the unduplicated number of total recipients is difficult to determine. Because the majority of those receiving benefits under income maintenance programs utilize more than one such program (Storey et al., 1973), it is reasonable to assume that as many as 60

million individuals in the United States utilize at least one income maintenance program. Total annual benefits allocated amount to $233 billion, not including administrative costs. Obviously, income maintenance constitutes a major function of government in the United States, playing a necessary part in the lives of millions of citizens, both poor and nonpoor.

Recent Trends

Until the 1960s, the major income maintenance programs grew slowly. This slow growth was related to the gradual maturing and specific policies of the programs and to general economic prosperity. In 1955, as an example, the total federal and state expenditures for social insurance and public assistance programs represented only 3.2 percent of the Gross National Product (GNP).

By 1980, that percentage had risen to 11.5 (*Social Security Bulletin: Annual Statistical Supplement, 1982*, 1982). During the same period, overall expenditures in the field of social welfare as a percentage of government expenditures rose from 32.7 to 57.4 percent ("Public Social Welfare Expenditures, Fiscal Years 1981 and 1982," 1984).

During the 1960s and most of the 1970s, growth in the major income maintenance programs was phenomenal. The growth was a function of changing national demographics, of millions of new recipients claiming benefits, and of increases in benefit levels. It was also a function of program expansion, which affected the pool of eligible persons. The three biggest expansions were the 1973 and 1977 expansions of the Food Stamp program that broadened the categories of eligible persons and eliminated the Food Stamp purchase requirement; the 1973 amendments to OASDI, which indexed benefit levels, beginning in 1975, to rise automatically when inflation rose above 3 percent during one year; and the creation in 1974 of SSI, which currently guarantees up to $314 per month to eligible single individuals and $465 per month to eligible couples. Possible state supplementation is not included in these federally guaranteed levels. Table 2 documents the dramatic growth of the income maintenance programs during this period.

The accelerated growth of the income maintenance programs was curbed by the late

Table 1. Number of Beneficiaries, Total Benefits Distributed, and Average Benefit Levels: Major Federal and State Income Maintenance Programs, 1983

Beneficiaries (millions)	Total Benefits Distributed (billions)	Average Benefit Amount
Old Age, Survivors, and Disability Income (OASDI)		
25.0 (Old Age)		$441/month
7.3 (Survivors)		$393/month
3.8 (Disability)		$456/month
36.1	$167.0	
Unemployment Compensation		
2.0[a]	$18.9	$123/week[b]
Workers' Compensation		
N.A.[c]	$12.5	$223/week[d]
Aid to Families with Dependent Children (AFDC)		
10.3[e]	$13.0[f]	$305/family/week[g]
Supplemental Security Income (SSI)		
3.9[h]	$ 9.5	$189/month[i]
		$ 95/month[j]
Food Stamps[k]		
21.7	$10.2	$ 39/person/month
General Assistance[l]		
1.0[m]	$ 1.4	$130/person/month

[a] Average weekly number, October.
[b] October.
[c] Not available.
[d] 1980.
[e] September 1982.
[f] 1981.
[g] July–September 1982.
[h] December.
[i] Federal payments, December.
[j] State supplementation, December.
[k] 1982.
[l] 1980.
[m] September 1982.

Sources: *Social Security Bulletin: Annual Statistical Supplement, 1982* (Washington, D.C.: U.S. Government Printing Office, 1982); "Current Operating Statistics" (1984), in *Social Security Bulletin, 47*(6), 25–60, and (1984), *47*(7), 28–64; and D. P. Price (1984), "Workers' Compensation: 1976–80 Benchmark Revisions," in *Social Security Bulletin, 47*(7), 3–23.

1970s. A troubled national economy, escalating inflation, unemployment, and a potent conservative mood all influenced the movement toward cutbacks and program restrictions. The culmination of this activity was the passage in 1981 of the Omnibus Budget Reconciliation Act (OBRA). This Act was in-

tended to trim OASDI, SSI, AFDC, and the Food Stamp program. Not since the Social Security Act was passed in 1935 was such a conservative political philosophy superimposed on income maintenance programs (Ginsberg, 1983). AFDC recipients, particularly those who were employed, were espe-

Table 2.　Changes in Federal and State Benefit Expenditures and in Numbers of Beneficiaries: Major Federal and State Income Maintenance Programs, 1960–1980

Program and Year	Expenditures (billions)	Beneficiaries (millions)
Old Age, Survivors, and Disability Income (OASDI)		
1960	$ 11.2	14.8
1965	18.3	21.0
1970	31.9	26.2
1975	67.0	32.1
1980	121.0	35.6
Unemployment Compensation		
1960	$ 2.9	1.7
1965	2.3	1.2
1970	4.2	1.6
1975	18.2	3.5
1980	18.8	2.8
Workers' Compensation		
1960	.9	N.A.[a]
1965	1.2	N.A.
1970	2.0	N.A.
1975	4.6	N.A.
1980	9.6	N.A.
Aid to Families with Dependent Children (AFDC)		
1960	$ 1.0	3.0
1965	1.7	4.3
1970	4.9	8.5
1975	9.2	11.3
1980	12.5	10.8
Supplemental Security Income (SSI)		
1960	—	—
1965	—	—
1970	—	—
1975	$ 5.9	4.4[b]
1980	7.9	4.2[b]
Food Stamps		
1960	—	—
1965	$ .3	.4
1970	.6	4.3
1975	4.4	17.1
1980	8.7	21.1
General Assistance		
1960	$ .3	1.1
1965	.3	.7
1970	.6	1.0
1975	1.1	1.0
1980	1.4	1.0

[a] Not available.
[b] December.
Sources: *Social Security Bulletin: Annual Statistical Supplement, 1982* (Washington, D.C.: U.S. Government Printing Office, 1982); and D. P. Price (1984), "Workers' Compensation: 1976–80 Benchmark Revision," in *Social Security Bulletin, 47*(7), 3–23.

cially hard hit by OBRA (Ginsberg, Mesni-koff, & Kulis, 1984).

If the 1960s and 1970s can be characterized as a time of phenomenal growth in the income maintenance programs, followed by a leveling off or retardation of that growth, they can also be characterized as a time of attempted reform and change. This was the case particularly with OASDI, AFDC, and Food Stamps.

The period of attempted reform began in the early 1960s in conjunction with the 1964 War on Poverty. During those years, a national debate was held about the efficacy and feasibility of the reform of public aid programs. Juxtaposed with discussions about how to modify them was advocacy for the children's allowance and the negative income tax. Before he left office, President Johnson appointed a national commission to study and recommend changes in the public aid programs. The commission, which reported early in the Nixon Administration, recommended a negative income tax, to be administered by the federal government. The income base recommended was $2,400 for a family of four, with supplementation to cease at $4,800 (*President's Commission on Income Maintenance Programs*, 1969). The commission's recommendations were rejected by the Nixon Administration.

The proposed Family Assistance Plan of 1969 and its 1971 descendant, H.R. 1, both also attempted to reform AFDC by federalizing benefit levels and including the working poor, although under circumstances different from those that obtained during the War on Poverty. Neither passed the Senate Finance Committee, but out of the attempt at reform came SSI, implemented in 1974. SSI combined the less controversial categories of public assistance recipients into a new federal program, established a guaranteed benefit level, and transferred the administration of these categories of poor people to the Social Security Administration. The 1977 Better Jobs and Income Act also attempted to reform AFDC and also failed to secure passage.

OASDI was also a focus of concern during these two decades. Rising levels of expenditures and the threatened depletion of the OASDI trust funds prompted the appointment by both Democratic and Republican administrations of national commissions to study the OASDI situation ("Reports of the 1979 Advisory Council on Social Security," 1980; "Report of the National Commission on Social Security Reform," 1983). Although the perception of the seriousness of the problems faced by OASDI and the proposed solutions to these problems fell partially along political lines, basic revisions were introduced in 1983. They eliminated deficits in OASDI funding, mandated the inclusion of new federal civilian employees and employees of nonprofit organizations, began the taxation of OASDI benefits above certain income levels, delayed the cost-of-living adjustment, changed the OASDI tax schedule, and advanced the age at which full benefits can be received (Ginsberg, 1983; Stein, 1980; Svahn & Ross, 1983).

Issues

The field of income maintenance is laden with difficult, divisive issues that inhibit both the reform of existing programs and the creation of new ones. These issues include but are not limited to: (1) whether benefits should be provided in the form of cash, in-kind services, or vouchers; (2) how to achieve both vertical and horizontal equity in income maintenance programs; (3) whether to base eligibility on categorical or noncategorical definitions; (4) whether program design should stress cost effectiveness or social effectiveness; and (5) whether policy determination and implementation should be federal, state, or local. These issues have perplexed policymakers for the past several decades; they pose questions that have been politically impossible to solve. The following three questions are representative.

1. What is the relationship between work and the receipt of income maintenance? In other words, should recipients work, and under what circumstances? Although research has verified the strength of the work ethic of the poor (Goodwin, 1972), the suspicion has existed for centuries that income maintenance assistance robs recipients of their incentive to work. Since 1977, clear work requirements have been attached to most income maintenance programs that assist the poor. The society has tended to excuse from work children, certain of their mothers, the blind and handicapped, and the elderly. It expects that most able-bodied recipients will work or be denied assistance.

So basic is this expectation and so

important is information about the impact of income maintenance on recipients that a series of income maintenance experiments were conducted between 1972 and 1976. The incomes of participating recipient families were supplemented at several levels, and the impact of this supplementation on their work effort over time was scrutinized. Analysis showed that the loss of work effort as measured by fewer hours worked by husbands in intact families was about 6 percent on the average. Their wives experienced a 20 percent loss in work effort on the average, and females who headed their own families experienced a loss in work effort averaging between 5 and 12 percent. These minimal losses in work effort, which were less than anticipated (Bell, Lines, & Linn, 1979; Kershaw & Fair, 1976), contradict the conventional wisdom about the negative impact of income assistance on work motivation.

The problematic relationship between work and receipt of benefits is also manifest in policy decisions about the rate at which earnings are taxed. If there is to be an incentive to work, recipients must keep a significant amount of their earnings, necessitating a relatively low marginal tax rate on those earnings. If the pools of eligibles and recipients are to be kept at a politically tenable level, marginal tax rates on earnings must be relatively high. Also, if individuals receive benefits from more than one program and if benefit levels are conditioned by income, the cumulative rate of taxation may provide a work disincentive.

2. Should benefit levels be based on the principle of equity or adequacy? That is, should benefit levels bear a direct relationship to the amount of contribution already made, or should benefit levels disproportionately favor those at the lower level of the economic ladder by moving them to a predetermined level of income adequate for them to meet their basic needs? OASDI has been plagued with this issue since its inception (*Social Security and the Changing Roles of Men and Women,* 1979), and changes in OASDI policies have generally favored the adequacy side of the equation. As adequacy is addressed, however, those who have made greater financial contributions to OASDI during their years of work are penalized. This issue has been cited recently by those who

favor the elimination of the mandatory nature of the OASDI contribution. Only in recent years, however, have OASDI benefit levels been sufficient to raise large numbers of recipients to or above the poverty level. Food Stamps, AFDC, Unemployment Compensation, and many other programs remain unable to raise many recipients to that level, suggesting that benefit levels in those programs are inadequate. Some of the appeal of reforming the income maintenance system by creating a negative income tax or a children's allowance is that such programs would address the adequacy of benefits for working people or children.

3. Should income maintenance programs be universal or selective? Asked differently, should all members of the society be eligible for income maintenance benefits, or should benefits be allocated only to people in need? OASDI and Unemployment Compensation are examples of programs that approach universality. Food Stamps, SSI, and AFDC are selective because benefits are distributed only to those in economic need.

Universal programs are more expensive in the short run and frequently benefit the middle and upper classes more than the lower. They are also unpopular with those who do not understand them because they distribute benefits to millions who are not in economic need. Selective programs appear to be more reasonable and to have greater "target efficiency." Because selective programs are means-tested, however, their potential for imposing a social stigma on recipients is higher than it is for universal programs. Although little is known empirically about the actual stigmatizing effect of selective programs, the probability of its presence must be assumed (Pinker, 1971). However, to oppose all selective programs because of their stigma potential would be to retard policy change. As Loewenberg (1981) has pointed out, an effective mix of universal and selective programs is indicated because a major realignment to universal programs is unlikely at this time in history.

Also thought to be related to selectivity and its potential impact is the nonparticipation of many who may be eligible. If a stigma is associated with programs that are selective or if programs are administered in a way that demeans recipients when they apply for or receive benefits, some who are eligible may not apply. The extent of nonparticipation is not a major policy issue or concern in the United States, but the research conducted on nonparticipation has found that, on the average, only 46 percent of those eligible participate in the common public aid and related programs (Bendick, 1980).

Barriers to participation are difficult to isolate, and it is clear that additional study is necessary before policies to improve participation rates can be formulated. Stigma and lack of information have been cited as barriers to participation, but there is evidence to support the contention that, for the most financially needy individuals, the inaccessibility caused by bureaucratic barriers is the most significant reason for lack of participation (Bendick, 1980).

Income Maintenance and Social Work

One strand of the history of social work is intertwined with the development of income maintenance in the United States. The "friendly visitors" of the COS are frequently identified as the first social workers. Although the activities of the friendly visitors and those of today's professional social workers are distinctly different, there is a relationship between the COS volunteers, the subsequent development of social casework, and the quest for professionalization.

In the early decades of the twentieth century, many of the pioneers of professional social work, including Mary Richmond and Jane Addams, argued for mothers' pensions and other reforms. During that era, the administration of many relief agencies was in the hands of social workers. Social workers also contributed to the design and development of the 1935 Social Security Act. So close was the relationship between social work and the determination of eligibility and provision of services to recipients of public assistance that the public continues to equate "welfare work" with social work.

Beginning in 1972, the provision of social services under AFDC and other public aid programs was separated from the provision of income maintenance. Before separation, these functions had been conducted by the same person or within the same organization. Separation mandated a division of both front-line and organizational activities. Whether this separation of social services

from income maintenance has met the intended objectives of enhanced choice and diminution of negative sanctions being imposed on those who did not elect to use social services is largely untested (Benton, 1980). One study (McDonald & Piliavin, 1981) showed that separation tended to reduce social service utilization in the host public welfare agency but to enhance social service utilization in other agencies. The usefulness of these alternate services in solving the problems the recipients faced is unknown.

Since separation, professional social work has maintained a strong presence in social service delivery organizations but not in the income maintenance delivery organizations (Wyers, 1983). This is true in both service delivery and program administration. Historically, the presence of social work in the other income maintenance programs has been weak. However, its presence need not remain weak in the future (Briar, 1983; Wyers, 1980).

During the past decade, a call has been made for the reconceptualization of the income maintenance worker's function and for improvement in service delivery. Originally, it was maintained that income maintenance work would be highly standardized, similar to the role of clerk, and that only limited service delivery skills would be required. That position has been challenged (Greene, 1979), and efforts to redefine income maintenance work have begun. The most impressive contribution to date is the model proposed by the U.S. Department of Health and Human Services (*Income Maintenance Worker Study: A Two-Way Taxonomy and Analysis,* 1981). Based on empirical observation of what income maintenance work consists of throughout the United States, the model identifies eight job activities, eight practice skills, performance standards, and hiring standards for income maintenance workers. The activities and skills are far more complex than originally conceptualized.

Income maintenance workers have also begun efforts to professionalize their work. The newly established National Eligibility Workers Association (NEW) is leading that professionalization. Although NEW members are primarily employees of AFDC and Food Stamp Programs, they identify their role as that of income maintenance eligibility workers, implying a possible role in other income maintenance programs. NEW is not affiliated with the National Association of Social Workers (NASW); NEW members do not identify themselves as social workers. Further evidence of the professionalization of income maintenance work is the emergence in the past several years of income maintenance work curricula, especially at the associate degree level. The curricula in schools of social work do not seriously address income maintenance as a field of practice for their graduates at either the baccalaureate or master's degree levels.

Research has shown that additional training of income maintenance workers is cost effective. One study (*Improving Interviewing in the AFDC Programs,* 1979) found that improved interviewing on the part of income maintenance workers would lead to a reduction in their errors. Bendick, Lavine, and Campbell (1978) concluded that a 50 percent increase in training expenditures for income maintenance workers could result in a decrease in the national case error rate of about 1.3 percent and a decrease in the national payment error rate of about 1.0 percent. Such training, which is closely related to the impetus to professionalize income maintenance work, would likely have other positive results as well, including improved morale among both workers and recipients.

Summary

The evolution of income maintenance in the United States is usually viewed as a function of enhanced humanitarianism and a part of the liberal tradition, even though income maintenance programs are less well developed in the United States than in other Western nations. Millions of individuals and families receive financial assistance from them. Their development has been slow and uneven, but it is likely that their growth will continue. If social work is to play a role in the further development of income maintenance programs, it must educate itself to the issues of income maintenance and become actively involved in pushing for change. It is in social work's best interests, as well as the best interests of millions of recipients, that the profession reach affirmative decisions on both these endeavors.

NORMAN L. WYERS

For further information, see AID TO FAMILIES WITH DEPENDENT CHILDREN; FOOD STAMP PROGRAM; GENERAL AND EMERGENCY ASSISTANCE; POVERTY; SOCIAL SECURITY; WORK EXPERIENCE PROGRAMS; WORKFARE.

References

Axinn, J., & Levin, H. (1975). *Social Welfare: A History of the American Response to Need.* New York: Dodd, Mead & Co.

Barth, M. C., Carcagno, G. J., & Palmer, J. L. (1974). *Toward an Effective Income Support System: Problems, Prospects, and Choices.* Madison: University of Wisconsin Institute for Research on Poverty.

Bell, W. (1983). *Contemporary Social Welfare.* New York: Macmillan Publishing Co.

Bell, J. G., Lines, P. M., & Linn, M. (Eds.). (1979). *Proceedings of the 1978 Conference on the Seattle and Denver Income Maintenance Experiments.* Olympia: State of Washington Department of Social & Health Services.

Bendick, M., Jr. (1980). "Failure to Enroll in Public Assistance Programs." *Social Work, 25*(4), 268–274.

Bendick, M., Jr., Lavine, A., & Campbell, T. H. (1978). *The Anatomy of AFDC Errors.* Washington, D.C.: Urban Institute.

Benton, B. B., Jr. (1980). "Separation Revisited." *Public Welfare, 38*(2), 15–21.

Briar, K. H. (1983). "Unemployment: Toward a Social Work Agenda." *Social Work, 28*(3), 211–216.

Coll, B. D. (1969). *Perspectives in Public Welfare: A History.* Washington, D.C.: U.S. Government Printing Office.

"Current Operating Statistics." (1984). *Social Security Bulletin, 47*(6), 25–60.

"Current Operating Statistics." (1984). *Social Security Bulletin, 47*(7), 28–64.

Ginsberg, L. H. (1983). "Federal Social Welfare Programs: Recent Trends." In *1983–84 Supplement to the Encyclopedia of Social Work* (17th ed., pp. 31–44). Silver Spring, Md.: National Association of Social Workers.

Ginsberg, M. I., Mesnikoff, A. M., & Kulis, S. (1984). *Work, Welfare, and the Family: The Consequences of AFDC Losses for New York City Working Mothers and Their Families.* New York: Columbia University School of Social Work.

Goodwin, L. (1972). *Do the Poor Want to Work?* Washington, D.C.: Brookings Institution.

Greene, E. L. (1979). *The Hidden Agenda: Content and Nature of the Income Maintenance (IM) Worker's Job.* Washington, D.C.: Office of Family Assistance, Social Security Administration.

Improving Interviewing in the AFDC Programs. (1979). Washington, D.C.: Office of Research and Statistics, Social Security Administration.

Income Maintenance Worker Study: A Two-Way Taxonomy and Analysis. (1981). Washington, D.C.: Office of Research and Statistics, Social Security Administration.

Kershaw, D., & Fair, J. (1976). *The New Jersey Income-Maintenance Experiment.* New York: Academic Press.

Leiby, J. (1978). *A History of Social Welfare and Social Work in the United States.* New York: Columbia University Press.

Loewenberg, F. M. (1981). "The Destigmatization of Public Dependency." *Social Service Review, 55*(3), 434–452.

Lurie, I. (1975). "Integrating Income Maintenance Programs: Problems and Solutions." In I. Lurie (Ed.), *Integrating Income Maintenance Programs* (pp. 1–38). New York: Academic Press.

McDonald, T. P., & Piliavin, I. (1981). "Impact of Separation on Community Social Service Utilization." *Social Service Review, 55*(4), 628–635.

Pinker, R. (1971). *Social Theory and Social Policy.* London, England: Heinemann Educational Books.

Piven, F. F., & Cloward, R. A. (1971). *Regulating the Poor: The Functions of Public Welfare.* New York: Pantheon Books.

President's Commission on Income Maintenance Programs. (1969). *Poverty Amid Plenty: The American Paradox.* Washington, D.C.: U.S. Government Printing Office.

Price, D. P. (1984). "Workers' Compensation: 1976–80 Benchmark Revisions." *Social Security Bulletin, 47*(7), 3–23.

"Public Social Welfare Expenditures, Fiscal Years 1981 and 1982." (1984). *Research and Statistics Note* (Report No. 1). Washington, D.C.: Office of Research, Statistics, and International Policy, Social Security Administration.

"Report of the National Commission of Social Security Reform." (1983). *Social Security Bulletin, 46*(2), 3–38.

"Reports of the 1979 Advisory Council on Social Security." (1980). *Social Security Bulletin, 43*(2), 3–15.

Rodgers, H. R., Jr. (1982). *The Cost of Human Neglect: America's Welfare Failure.* Armonk, N.Y.: M. E. Sharpe.

Schorr, A. L. (1977). "Fair Shares." In A. L. Schorr (Ed.), *Jubilee for Our Times: A Practical Program for Income Equality* (pp. 1–24). New York: Columbia University Press.

Social Security and the Changing Roles of Men and Women. (1979). Washington, D.C.: U.S. Government Printing Office.

Social Security Bulletin: Annual Statistical Supplement, 1982. (1982). Washington, D.C.: U.S. Government Printing Office.

Stein, B. (1980). *Social Security and Pensions in Transition: Understanding the American Retirement System.* New York: Free Press.

Storey, J. R., Townsend, A. A., & Cox, I. (1973). "How Public Welfare Benefits Are Distributed in Low-Income Areas." *Studies in Public Welfare Policy* (Paper No. 6). Washington, D.C.: U.S. Congress, Joint Economic Committee, Subcommittee on Fiscal Policy.

Svahn, J. A., & Ross, M. (1983) "Social Security Amendments of 1983: Legislative History and Summary of Provisions." *Social Security Bulletin, 46*(7), 3–48.

Titmuss, R. M. (1969). "The Social Division of Welfare: Some Reflections on the Search for Equity." In *Essays on the Welfare State* (pp. 34–55). Boston: Beacon Press.

Trattner, W. I. (1974). *From Poor Law to Welfare State: A History of Social Welfare in America.* New York: Free Press.

Warner, A. G. (1894). *American Charities: A Study in Philanthropy and Economics.* New York: Thomas Y. Crowell Co.

Wyers, N. L. (1980). "Whatever Happened to the Income Maintenance Line Worker?" *Social Work, 25*(4), 259–263.

Wyers, N. L. (1983). "Income Maintenance and Social Work: A Broken Tie." *Social Work, 28*(4), 261–268.

INDUSTRIAL SOCIAL WORK (OCCUPATIONAL SOCIAL WORK)

In the United States, industrial (or occupational) social work generally is defined as programs and services, under the auspices of labor or management, that utilize professional social workers to serve members or employees and the legitimate social welfare needs of the labor or industrial organization. It also includes the use, by a voluntary or proprietary social agency, of trained social workers to provide social welfare services or consultation to a trade union or employing organization under a specific contractual agreement. The employing organizations are not only labor unions and corporations, but often government agencies and not-for-profit organizations.

The Department of Economic and Social Affairs of the United Nations (1971, p. 3) defines industrial social welfare as "the range of programs, operations and activities carried out at any level or by any group which promotes or preserves the welfare of the worker and protects him and his family from the social costs of the work process and work setting." The three major differences between the international definition provided by the United Nations and the definition commonly accepted in the United States are instructive. First, the United Nations offers a somewhat broader conception of what actually constitutes industrial social welfare activities; second, professional social workers are not emphasized in their guidelines as the principal providers of services; and third, the international definition places little emphasis on the *auspices* of programs and services, which is a central focus of the American definition.[1]

As frequently conceptualized in the United States, industrial social work is a concentration or specialization within the broad conceptual framework of the "world of work." Professional practice in world-of-work settings also includes addressing, for example, the need for youth-employment training, personnel and guidance services, sheltered workshops for the disabled, and programs of vocational rehabilitation. Although the broader world-of-work rubric is helpful in identifying a conceptually important larger perspective, which includes a general emphasis on the social welfare needs of workers and work organizations, industrial social work per se is narrower and more specific in focus.

The concept of industrial social welfare flows from Titmuss's notion of a third, or occupational, welfare system over and above the social and fiscal welfare systems that have been more commonly understood. Titmuss (1968) referred to the occupational system of benefits and services as one in which individuals participate as a result of their employment status. Weiner et al. (1971, p. 6) further defined this occupational social welfare system in the United States as composed of

> benefits and services, above and beyond wages, directed at social and health needs, provision for which is not legislatively mandated. Entitlement to these benefits and services results from affiliation with a job in a particular company, or membership in a particular union, or a dependent relationship to an entitlee.

The conceptualization of an occupational social welfare system and the social work profession's entry into this arena as a site for program development and service delivery are important, given current fiscal trends. Public welfare expenditures, which now total some $400 billion yearly, have been declining for some time. However, the private, occupational welfare system, which also spends about $400 billion annually in the form of employee benefits and services, has been expanding rapidly. In 1980, employers were financing health and welfare benefits to employees and their families at the rate of 32.3 percent of regular pay (Friedman & Hausman, 1982). The social work profession's willingness to play a role in the development and administration of such benefits and services becomes increasingly important,

---

[1] Although a discussion of international industrial social welfare programs is beyond the scope of this article, it should be noted that industrial social work practice has existed on a large scale abroad for many years as a permanent and frequently government-supported field of practice. Such countries as Belgium, Brazil, France, Germany, Holland, India, Peru, Poland, and Zambia have well-established industrial social welfare programs and services.

therefore, as the occupational system takes on an ever greater role in financing services to the more than 100 million Americans in the work force and their families.

Furthermore, industrial social work provides easy access to a population in its natural life space and offers the profession an opportunity to develop a universal service delivery system unencumbered by the usual eligibility and categorical requirements of the public sector. Service here is an earned entitlement, universally available to all participants in the work force without cost and in a familiar environment—the world of work. In Kahn's sense (1973), these are not stigmatized "case services." Rather, these programs and services represent social utilities of the workplace—on tap, as needed, for all work-force participants and their families. Like the social worker in the school system or the settlement house worker in the neighborhood, an industrial social worker serves clients from within the functional community of work.

In industrial and other employing organizations, employee assistance or employee-counseling programs are perhaps the best known and most rapidly developing social work services. Usually located in a medical or personnel office, these programs employ the largest number of individual social workers today and represent the fastest growing social work service under the auspices of the major institutional arrangements in the world of work: employers and trade unions. Social workers, however, also serve in company training units, affirmative action offices, corporate social responsibility departments, and human resources divisions. Typical titles might include employee counselor, affirmative action officer, community relations consultant, substance abuse services coordinator, employee resources manager, corporate relocation officer, human resources policy adviser, career planning and development counselor, training consultant, charitable allocations analyst, urban affairs adviser, or coordinator of corporate health and wellness programs.

The majority of social workers employed by organized labor provide services through union counseling and advocacy programs, frequently called personal or membership service units. Such union programs are a major source of employment for industrial social workers, especially in the Northeast. The International Ladies' Garment Workers' Union, for example, employs 18 master's-level social workers in its Member Assistance Program alone—more social workers than are currently employed in any corporate-sponsored setting in the country.

Professional social workers have assumed responsibility in a variety of individual programs sponsored by union locals and district councils and in the headquarters of international unions and the American Federation of Labor and Congress of Industrial Organizations (AFL-CIO), which oversees and coordinates the work of the labor union movement as a whole. Typical titles for social workers employed in these organizations include personal services worker, education program director, occupational safety and health officer, health and security plan manager, membership services coordinator, career training and upgrading adviser, preretirement services worker, day care consultant, legislative analyst, benefit plan administrator, community services coordinator, alcoholism program supervisor, and director of retiree services.

A job description for the prototypical industrial social welfare specialist might list some of the following duties:

■ Counseling and other activities with troubled employees or members in jeopardy of losing their job to assist them with their personal problems and to help them achieve and maintain a high level of performance.

■ Advising on the use of community services to meet the needs of clients and establishing linkages with such programs.

■ Training front-line personnel (union representatives, foremen, line supervisors) to enable them to determine when changes in an employee's job performance warrant referral to a social service unit and carrying out an appropriate approach to the employee that will result in a referral.

■ Developing and overseeing the operations of a union or management information system, which will record information on services and provide data for analyzing the unit's program.

■ Conceiving a plan for the future direction of the program that is based on the identification of unmet needs and current demographic trends.

■ Offering consultation to labor or

management decisionmakers concerning the development of a human resource policy.

■ Helping to initiate welfare, community health, recreational, or educational programs for active and retired employees or members.

■ Assisting in the administration of the benefit and health care structure and helping plan for new initiatives.

■ Consulting on the development and administration of an appropriate affirmative action plan for women, minorities, and the disabled.

■ Advising on corporate giving or labor coalition building and on organizational positions in relation to pending social welfare legislation (Akabas & Kurzman, 1982, pp. 201–202).

Historical Background

The relationship between social welfare and industry can be traced to the Middle Ages. In the medieval guilds, funds were set aside to ensure workers' economic security in case of accident, poverty, old age, or death, and money for loans to young workers was obtained by assessments levied on guild members. Laws soon replaced guild levies, but the guild continued to maintain schools and almshouses and was, along with the church, the central social welfare institution for guild workers and their families throughout the Middle Ages and until the advent of the Poor Laws of 1601. In the early 1800s in England and Scotland, leading factory owners began to provide similar benefits; by the late 1800s, many German companies and labor unions began to follow suit (Carter, 1975).

The historical roots of this field in the United States can be found in what has been termed "welfare capitalism"—those benefits and services provided voluntarily by employers in the late 19th and early 20th centuries in an effort to socialize, retain, and control a raw, unskilled, and badly needed labor force at a time of rapid industrialization (Brandes, 1976). Paternalistic in nature, inconsistent and inadequate in provision, directed at fostering dependence and loyalty in employees, these programs were more an instrument of management than a service to workers. Companies hired staff, usually called welfare secretaries, to administer the programs and services, which might include improving san-

itation, providing housing, supervising safety, and offering classes.

The welfare secretaries, as the handmaidens of management, increasingly were perceived as policing an immigrant work force to prevent malingering and to discourage workers' identification with a growing trade union movement. Their covert responsibility to investigate employees and to see that labor unions did not gain a foothold in industry ensured the enmity of AFL President Samuel Gompers and a distrust by workers of employers' motives for providing such programs.

Although initially these welfare secretaries had no formal training, this situation gradually began to change after World War I. The idea of welfare secretaries received considerable attention from two national organizations whose goals prominently included industrial social welfare services—the National Civic Federation and the American Institute for Social Service. Popple (1981) noted that this stimulus was important and that by 1920 more graduates of the New York School for Social Work were taking jobs in industry than in any other setting. Social workers often served in the role of social welfare secretaries, although not always with that title.

Distrust of the emerging social work profession by working Americans was widespread and understandable, given the welfare secretaries' role as messengers of management and the increasingly narrow psychoanalytic approach that had become popular in the profession. This feeling was reinforced by leaders of the growing labor union movement who saw the welfare secretary as inhibiting their organizational drives and confirming their theory that social workers were not only antistrike, but essentially antiunion. During the 1920s, welfare secretaries began dying out, and by 1935 they had largely disappeared, with some of their functions being assumed by personnel officers and some by industrial nurses.

Industrially based social work reemerged during World War II when new groups of employees entered the labor force to respond to the wartime shortage in the work force. These new workers, many of them women and minorities, needed help in becoming acculturated to the experience of full-time employment in industry and often in balancing the complex roles of employee and single parent. The major employers of industrial social workers were the airplane and munitions industries and the unions representing the shipping industry and merchant seamen. Bertha Reynolds, a prominent social work theoretician and practitioner, was hired to direct the joint labor-management program of the United Seamen's Service, which served members of the National Maritime Union (NMU).

Social workers were accepted in this situation because they were members of the social service union and handled themselves not as therapists, but as advocates for the members. Moreover, the social work profession had established a rapprochement with the trade union movement in the 1930s through active support of CIO organizing drives and through their caring service to unemployed workers during the height of the Great Depression. Reynolds's (1975) superb work at the NMU during World War II further strengthened these bonds of trust between organized labor and social work and demonstrated the viability of an alternative model for serving the more than 20 million Americans who in 1980 were members of organized labor.

Often overlooked as a model for promoting the growth of industrial social work was the participation of social workers in the armed forces during World War II. With its numbers swelled by a war effort on two fronts, the military became the major national employer. This work force, moreover, had to adapt to new job specifications in an alien environment under hostile and anxiety-producing working conditions. Social workers took on major direct service roles in helping to meet the needs of soldiers and their families and thereby established an ongoing role for the profession in the military for the postwar period. In 1946, the office of the Surgeon General established a permanent army commissioned officer corps of social workers, which grew and expanded to the other branches of military service in succeeding years (Bevilacqua & Darnauer, 1977). The professional social workers in the Medical Service Corps of the three branches of the armed forces may be conceptualized as industrial social workers insofar as they work for an employing organization to serve the health and welfare needs of its work force.

Although industry in Europe and South America employed growing numbers of social workers, there was relatively little such activity in the United States during the two decades following World War II. Industry reabsorbed its prewar work force, and the country entered a period of economic and social laissez-faire. The social work profession once again became psychoanalytic in focus, mirroring the inactivity of the nation as a whole with respect to issues of social innovation and organizational change. A few social workers were employed at Kaiser Industries and the J. L. Hudson Department Store in Detroit at this time, but they were the exception.

As Wilensky and Lebeaux (1965, p. 163) correctly noted in 1965,

> Industrial social work in the European tradition of social workers offering family and other services from outposts in the plant. . . hailed for the past twenty years as a "new frontier in social work," simply has not materialized in America.

The 1965 edition of the *Encyclopedia of Social Work* accurately reflected the times by making no general reference to union or management programs. Skeels's (1965) entry in that edition, entitled "Social Welfare Programs of Labor and Industry," did not mention industrial social work practice or the kinds of programs and services under labor and industrial auspices that are so common today.

Modern industrial social welfare practice can be dated from the mid-1960s, when two important events occurred. Management at Polaroid in Boston decided that their innovative employee counseling program was meeting a definite need of this growing corporation and should become a permanent part of the organization ("Counseling and Consultation," 1978). Directed by an experienced social worker, the counseling department had proved its value to the workers and to management both through the direct service function and through its role as human resource consultant to the decisionmakers of the corporation. At the same time, Weiner, Akabas, and Sommer (1973) in New York were establishing a labor-based mental health and rehabilitation program at the Sidney Hillman Health Center of the Amalgamated Clothing Workers of America. With labor and management support and governmental funding, the model brought to workers in the men's clothing industry a service that was sensitive to their cultural style and unmet needs. These two innovations of the late 1960s continued into the early 1970s and set the stage for the growth and development of the field.

If one were to apply Rostow's (1971) paradigm for analyzing the growth of an economy to the growth of a social welfare sector in industry, one might say that the "traditional" period for industrial social welfare was up through the end of World War II. The postwar period, up until the mid-1970s, saw a "development of preconditions" and was followed by a period of "take off" from 1975 to the present. There are signs now that the field may be close to entering the early stages of its "drive to maturity," although it is too early to predict whether Rostow's final phase of "high mass consumption" is realistic in the foreseeable future.

Evolution of Practice

As was just noted, there has been a marked growth and expansion of industrial social work practice since the mid-1970s. This growth was not accidental. It reflected a concerted effort and a concentration of human and fiscal resources; leaders in the educational and practice sectors of social work responded to an idea whose time had come. By the mid-1970s, employers were coming to the realization that they had to deal with a changing work force and new social legislation. The Hughes Act, the Vocational Rehabilitation Act, the Occupational Safety and Health Act, the Employee Retirement Income Security Act, the Age Discrimination in Employment Act, and Title VII of the Civil Rights Act were among the new work-related laws to which industry had to become responsive. Women, minorities, and the disabled were entering the work force in great numbers and with new needs. In the movement-oriented spirit of the day, they were voicing their needs for day care, nondiscriminatory assignments, flextime, barrier-free work sites, career-training and upgrading programs, and concessions on some "quality of life" issues.

The permanent attachment of women to the world of work reminded industry of what social workers already knew—that work and family were not separate worlds and that what occurs in one inevitably affects what happens in the other. Therefore, employers needed to understand that linkages to the family, the neighborhood, and the community at large were outcomes not merely of the new mandates of social legislation but of the changing complexion both of the American work force and of the communities in which they manufactured their goods and marketed their goods and services. Employers needed help from a profession that would offer generalists who were capable of bringing both clinical and organizational sophistication to bear on industry's new human service agendas.

The trade union movement had to deal with the effects of its own success. As Akabas (1977, p. 743) noted:

> When the benefits of labor organization are available to all workers, either through collective bargaining or through employers' unilateral efforts to avoid organization, some new enticement must be offered to achieve union membership growth and loyalty.

Responding to this situation, unions began to develop a system of direct services to members; these services were in addition to the occupational social welfare benefits that were essentially fiscal. Organized labor, having won significant financial gains at the bargaining table, now needed to bring in new services to maintain the loyalty of members to the union and its leaders.

Thus, the human service agenda, in the broadest sense, became markedly greater in size and scope for labor and industry. Although management's concern for productivity and profit did not disappear, new quality-of-life issues emerged on which managers believed they did not have the requisite expertise. Similarly, although wages and working conditions remained labor's primary agenda, members' concern for "bread and roses" emerged once they had achieved some measure of job security and economic reward. The social work profession's readiness to help labor and management with these issues and its academic and practice preparation to do so created mutually fortuitous conditions for initiating joint ventures.

Federal agencies, responding to these conditions and to the various mandates of the new social legislation, began to support social work education and training programs in this arena. Foremost in this effort was the National Institute on Alcohol Abuse and Alcoholism, which began to realize that alcoholism in industry was an issue of growing concern that required federal support for training and for introducing programs at the work site. The National Institute of Mental Health, the Rehabilitation Services Administration, and the Manpower Administration of the U.S. Department of Labor also showed their interest and support for social work initiatives at the workplace. Several philanthropic foundations, especially the Lois and Samuel Silberman Fund and the Johnson Foundation, demonstrated their interest in fostering the systematic development of curriculum and practice models for this growing field of practice.

The National Association of Social Workers (NASW) underwrote a two-year joint project with the Council on Social Work Education (CSWE) to promote the preparation of professional social workers for industrial social work practice. The association later provided special program advancement funds to several of its state chapters to further their development of models and standards for industrial practice.

As not-for-profit family service agencies and community mental health centers developed expertise in serving workers and their families, they began offering contractual social service programs to industries in their community. They were joined by Human Affairs, Inc., Personal Performance Consultants, and other social work-directed proprietary firms that began to market industrial social services to leading corporations.

Several graduate schools of social work provided leadership in conceptualizing industrial practice and in refining models for this field. The first among the landmark events in this area was the establishment of an Industrial Social Welfare Center at the Columbia University School of Social Work in 1970. This event was followed by the initiation of industrial social work programs in 1974 at the schools of social work at Boston College, Hunter College, and the University of Utah. Then, in 1978, Columbia University and Hunter College, along with CSWE, sponsored the First National Conference on Social Work Practice in Labor and Industrial Settings. This conference brought industrial

social work practitioners together for the first time so that, from the vantage point of practice, they might begin to define both the generic and the specific (Akabas, Kurzman & Kolben, 1979). Generous support from NASW and the Lois and Samuel Silberman Fund from 1977 to 1980 permitted the education community to take strides toward (1) refining and then sharing models for teaching and practice, (2) developing sites for the placement and employment of students, and (3) building a literature to interpret industrial social work to the profession and to labor and industrial organizations.

The importance of the educational community's undertaking to develop a cohesive conceptual literature for the field cannot be overestimated; it provided a foundation for the steady growth and maturation of industrial social work practice. Models were constructed on the basis of sound social work theory and then tested in the field through graduate practicum arrangements and pilot labor and industrial programs. On the basis of historical understanding and on an appreciation of what the social work profession had to offer, the opportunities, dilemmas, advantages, and risks of industrial practice were explored.

The academic leaders were committed to the systematic development of models of policy and practice, rather than merely seizing an opportunity to gain a foothold in a new field of practice. They harnessed resources from government, foundations, universities, and professional organizations to initiate a developmental process. Simultaneously, they obtained sanction from the gatekeeping professional associations, social agencies, and major labor and industrial organizations.

The early leaders recognized the need for a reconceptualization of the area. This recognition ensured that the emerging literature would be not just descriptive but conceptual and would view the emerging field in all its richness and complexity. A relatively sophisticated harnessing of diverse public and private institutional resources occurred, along with the development of the organizational sanction and support of NASW and CSWE. The resulting proliferation of articles in professional journals (Brooks, 1975; Kurzman & Akabas, 1981; McBroom et al., eds., 1984; Ozawa, 1980; "Social Work and the Workplace," 1982; Yasser & Sommer, 1975), newspapers (Dullea, 1982; Leven, 1980; Lovenheim, 1979; Tyson, 1980), business magazines (Akabas & Akabas, 1982; Cook, 1981; "Hiring Outside Help," 1975; Kerpen, 1983), monographs (Akabas, Kurzman, & Kolben, 1979; McGowan, 1984; *Meeting Human Service Needs,* 1980; Vinet & Jones, 1981), research studies (Erfurt & Foote, 1977; Glasser et al., 1975; Leavitt, 1983; Spiegel, 1974), doctoral dissertations (Carter, 1975; Googins, 1979; Green, 1983; Jorgensen, 1979), course outlines and bibliographies (Aronson, Stone, & Rauch, 1976; *Educational Resource Material,* 1979; Torjman, 1978; Weiner et al., 1971), books (Akabas & Kurzman, 1982; Feinstein & Brown, 1982; Masi, 1984; Thomlison, ed., 1983; Weiner, Akabas, & Sommer, 1973), and interpretive brochures (*Human Resource Workshops,* 1983; *U.S.C. Industrial Social Work Program,* 1982; *We Are Now "At Work,"* 1981) placed the profession in a good position to enter the competitive labor and industrial arena as a knowledgeable contributor to the needs of workers and work organizations.

Education for Practice

The results of this concentration of attention and resources were remarkable. In 1977, only 26 graduate schools of social work had even one industrial social work field placement, and only four had an industrial social work concentration or specialization. Five years later 50 schools had such field placements, 17 had established formal industrial social work specializations, and 22 additional graduate schools were planning to develop an industrial social work concentration in the near future (*Final Report,* 1980, Appendix 3; Gould, 1984, p. 37).

In general, most graduate schools started slowly, first with one or two field placements and then with an elective course offering. This step typically preceded an administrative decision to support a specialization, which would move the school toward hiring a faculty member to provide leadership in conceptualizing and developing the program. A subsequent expansion of required and elective course offerings and the development of a range of practicum opportunities generally marks the advent of a recognized concentration.

With the program firmly in place, a school then typically moves toward conducting occupationally based research, developing new program thrusts, offering human resource consultation to selected labor and industrial organizations, and initiating continuing education courses for experienced practitioners who are interested in moving into the field. Evidence to date shows that the designation of faculty who will have a primary commitment to developing the new program and building appropriate class and field opportunities is essential to the successful initiation of an industrial social work training program.

Educational preparation for the field has been limited to graduate social work programs. This focus is appropriate because industrial social work is an area of specialization and CSWE has stipulated that specialization is a graduate-level educational responsibility. Many graduate schools also are assigning a priority to developing continuing education offerings to prepare experienced practitioners to deal with the unique policy and practice issues in the labor and industrial arena.

Current Issues

Like any new venture, industrial social work is not without its issues and controversies. If one accepts the proposition that the existence of such tension is essentially healthy in an open system, then the profession's willingness to acknowledge such disagreement in its ranks can be conceived of as a normal and even useful occurrence. Industrial social work teachers and practitioners need not agree on all issues, any more than they would in such established fields as family treatment or child welfare. Especially at this early juncture, industrial social workers recognize that some internal disagreement is a sign of the vigor of the field and is likely to lead to more thoughtful and broadly acceptable resolutions as the field matures.

Focus on Alcoholism. An early issue concerned whether direct service programs should focus primarily on substance abuse, particularly alcoholism, or whether the service should be more broadly conceptualized, offering services to workers or members with any personal or emotional problem. Because the early funding for the labor and industrial service programs came largely from the National Institute on Alcohol Abuse and Alcoholism and the early affiliation of industrial social workers was primarily with the Association of Labor-Management Administrators and Consultants on Alcoholism (ALMACA), the focus on substance abuse prevailed. Leadership was provided by such organizations as ALMACA and the Hazelden Foundation, with little activity from NASW, CSWE, or the schools and agencies of the social work profession.

Today this situation has changed, partly in response to leadership from social work, but also in reaction to the needs of the field. Practice experience has taught social workers that alcoholism is not the only, or even the primary, problem of most clients who come for help at the workplace. Most clients need help with a variety of personal, emotional, family-oriented and community-centered problems. A broad model of service, customarily offered in industry under the auspices of an employee assistance or employee counseling program or, in unions, under a personal services or member assistance program, has become the prevailing model. The focus is direct service, but, as Akabas, Kurzman, and Kolben (1979, p. 5) noted,

> direct service in these settings is an all-encompassing term. It includes counseling, organization of support groups, concrete services, consumer advocacy, linking an individual to community services, training and staff development for union representatives and management personnel, and consultation to union and industrial decision makers.

Confidentiality. Another issue has been whether confidentiality is truly possible in these settings, especially in management-sponsored programs. The placement of such programs generally under the personnel or medical department, both of which have manifest or latent monitoring functions, makes the issue more serious. Because a breach of confidentiality could mean the loss of a worker's job or a stigma that could affect the worker's advancement in a job, the issue of confidentiality takes on special importance in this setting. Because the corporate world is not oriented to human services, the social worker must always be prepared to question managers' understanding of the nature and boundaries of confidentiality and their willingness to respect workers' rights.

Although this issue remains central to all industrial social work practice, instances of actual abuse are rare. Practitioners, however, must acknowledge and respect workers' apprehensions. Under the circumstances, these concerns are appropriate, and the extent to which they are allayed conditions the worker's willingness to use the service. The profession's guidelines for confidentiality, embodied in NASW's Code of Ethics, must be scrupulously observed, and information should be shared only with the voluntary and informed consent of the client (Akabas & Kurzman, 1982, pp. 221–226; Erfurt & Foote, 1977, pp. 45–46; Kurzman & Akabas, 1981, pp. 55–56).

A Question of Motives. Some have questioned the motives of the social work profession in embracing the industrial arena as a new setting for practice, especially at a time when corporations dominate the allocation of national resources. They ask whether the profession is motivated to move into the area primarily to demonstrate its capacity for entrepreneurship and to maximize practitioners' income and prestige. Does the trend toward industrial social work mean that social work is or will become less committed to serving the poor, who often are not members of the work force? Given the national trend toward "privatization" of the economy in general and of the human services in particular, is industrial social work another step in this direction by a profession historically committed to the public and voluntary sectors? In view of the recent growth of private entrepreneurship in such service sectors as child care, nursing homes, and home health care and the parallel growth of private clinical practice, will industrial social work become still a further move toward modeling the profession on the profit-making sector?

Although the profession has begun to address some of these ethical issues (Akabas, 1983; Bakalinsky, 1980; Kurzman, 1983; NASW Code of Ethics, 1980), the answers to these questions are not yet clear and must await the further evolution and maturation of this field of practice. However, there are several promising signs. First, is the willingness of leaders in the profession to discuss these issues openly, partly to increase awareness of potential problems and to ensure that the fundamental issues will be addressed both by individual social workers and by gatekeepers in professional agencies and organizations. Second, the recent growth of industrial social work in trade union and not-for-profit settings has created a balance in this emerging field that gives promise of a measured and varied perspective in the field. Third, leaders in the development of industrial social work have suggested a broader world-of-work perspective as the arena for specialization, and this perspective has generally been supported by NASW and CSWE. This view of the field casts the net for service more broadly than merely over those with an active and relatively permanent attachment to the labor force and includes the newly employed, the unemployed who are looking for work, and the disadvantaged and disabled.

Agents of Social Change. The final issue is related to the question of "privatization" and is perhaps the most fundamental of all. Briefly stated, it is whether social workers' participation in the world of work will be exclusively, or even largely, as providers of service or whether social workers also will act as agents of social change. This issue is an old and honored one and embraces Richmond's (1917) focus on the tension between "retail" and "wholesale," Schwartz's (1969) discussion of "private troubles" and "public issues," Wilensky and Lebeaux's (1958) concern with the "residual" and "institutional," and the Milford Conference's (1929) attention to "cause" as well as "function."

Inseparably related to this question is the issue of social control and whether industrial social workers' professional use of self will be primarily in service to the individual or to the employing organization. As Bakalinsky (1980, p. 472) wrote:

> Concern for the well-being of people, individually and collectively, historically has been social work's trademark. Industry, on the other hand, places its primary value on production and profits. Its people are viewed as a commodity having only instrumental value for the industry's central purpose.

Walden (1978) questioned whether industrial social workers will serve only the individual needs of workers or will move organizationally to address collective issues, such as hazardous working conditions, the dehumanization of workers, and violations of affirmative action.

The willingness of colleagues to raise these questions is helpful. There is a danger that industrial social workers will become more concerned with questions of social service than with issues of social change. The resulting displacement of goals, whereby practitioners could become as much agents of social control as providers of social service, is a risk that must be acknowledged and discussed if it is to be avoided.

Ultimately, however, the question cannot be answered easily or absolutely. Social workers have had to deal with these same dilemmas in such settings as public welfare, corrections, school social work, addiction services, and child welfare. The fundamental question that social workers must ask is, Whose agent are we? Clarity about role and function means that people are the central focus of attention and yet that social workers develop the organizational sophistication necessary to mediate between individuals and their environment. In industrial social work, no less than in other fields of practice that appear to constrain options, practitioners must hold fast to their dual commitment to being providers of social services and agents of social change. This is a historical mandate of the profession.

Trends and Projections

The growth and development of industrial social work has been rapid and promises to continue at this rate. A marked increase in the number of practitioners in this field is predictable, and with it will come an increase in their identification of themselves as social workers, informed for their practice by the knowledge, values, skills, and standards of their profession. This change will come in part from the profession's recognition of the field and thereby of its practitioners. However, it also should emanate from the fact that, in 10 years, most industrial social workers will have been trained for the specialization, either during their graduate social work education or through a social work continuing education program.

Although training for industrial social work is now at the master's degree level, educational efforts should begin to spread shortly to doctoral education. Tasks for holders of the bachelor's degree in social work can also be envisioned, although baccalaureate programs would not train for specialization. The number of accredited schools of social work formally recognizing the world of work and, in turn, industrial social work as a specialization will expand. Factors in this development will include the success of schools with current programs, the profession's interest in pursuing new markets for its graduates, and CSWE's new curriculum standards, which emphasize the need for specialization at the graduate level and suggest the world of work as an appropriate area.

Labor and industry will continue to expand their human service programs. Increasingly, they will select social work as a profession of choice for designing and operating these programs. Both in-house and contractual models of service should grow, and there is likely to be a marked increase in the employment of industrial social workers in the public and not-for-profit sectors. Federal agencies, with encouragement and funding from the U.S. Department of Health and Human Services, will be joined by more and more departments of state, county, and municipal governments in sponsoring employee assistance programs for their work forces. In addition, the number of public and voluntary hospitals and universities moving to establish such programs will continue to increase, and they will turn to their social service departments and schools of social work, respectively, to help establish and staff their programs.

With formal recognition of the field and its importance to the social work profession as a whole will come the formation within CSWE, NASW, and other national organizations of permanent constituency structures for industrial social work. The development of regular regional and national conferences, the launching of a professional specialty journal, and the formal establishment of educational and practice standards for industrial social work will be components of maturation over the next five years. Clearly, the future of industrial social work is secure.

PAUL A. KURZMAN

For further information, see CORPORATE SOCIAL RESPONSIBILITY; ORGANIZATIONS: IMPACT ON EMPLOYEES AND COMMUNITY.

References

Akabas, S. H. (1977). "Labor: Social Policy and Human Services." In *Encyclopedia of Social Work* (17th ed., pp. 738–744). Washington, D.C.: National Association of Social Workers.

Akabas, S. H. (1983). "Industrial Social Work: Influencing the System at the Workplace." In M. Dinerman (Ed.), *Social Work in a Turbulent World* (pp. 131–141). Silver Spring, Md.: National Association of Social Workers.

Akabas, S. H. & Akabas, S. A. (1982). "Social Services at the Workplace: New Resources for Management." *Management Review, 71*(5), 15–20.

Akabas, S. H., & Kurzman, P. A. (Eds.). (1982). *Work, Workers and Work Organizations: A View From Social Work*. Englewood Cliffs, N.J.: Prentice-Hall.

Akabas, S. H., Kurzman, P. A., & Kolben, N. S. (Eds.). (1979). *Labor and Industrial Settings: Sites for Social Work Practice*. New York: Columbia University, Hunter College, & Council on Social Work Education.

Aronson, M., Stone, J., & Rauch, C. T. (1976). *Behavior Dynamics in Industry: An Employee Assistance Program*. Washington, D.C.: Community Mental Health Institute.

Bakalinsy, R. (1980). "People vs. Profits: Social Work in Industry." *Social Work, 25*(6), 471–475.

Bevilacqua, J. J., & Darnauer, P. F. (1977). "Military Social Work." In *Encyclopedia of Social Work* (17th ed., pp. 927–931). Washington, D.C.: National Association of Social Workers.

Brandes, S. D. (1976). *American Welfare Capitalism: 1880–1940*. Chicago: University of Chicago Press.

Brooks, P. R. (1975). "Industry-Agency Program for Employee Counseling," *Social Casework, 56*(7), 404–410.

Carter, I. E. (1975). "Industrial Social Welfare: Historical Parallels in Five Western Countries." Unpublished doctoral dissertation, University of Iowa.

Cook, D. D. (1981, September 21). "Companies Put Social Workers on the Payroll." *Industry Week*, pp. 73–79.

"Counseling and Consultation at Polaroid." (1978). *Practice Digest, 1*(1), 6–7.

Department of Economic and Social Affairs. (1971). *Industrial Social Welfare*. New York: United Nations.

Dullea, G. (1982, February 15). "Solving Problems on the Job." *New York Times*, p. C-18.

Educational Resource Material for Social Work Practice in Labor and Industrial Settings. (1979). New York: Council on Social Work Education.

Erfurt, J., & Foote, A. (1977). *Occupational Employee Assistance Programs for Substance Abuse and Mental Health Problems*. Ann Arbor: University of Michigan & Wayne State University.

Feinstein, B. B., & Brown, E. G. (1982). *The New Partnership: Human Services, Business and Industry*. Cambridge, Mass.: Schenkman Publishing Co.

Final Report of the CSWE and NASW Project on Social Work in Industrial Settings. (1980). New York: Council on Social Work Education.

Friedman, B., & Hausman, L. (1982, January 5). "Welfare: Public and Private." *New York Times*, p. 15.

Glasser, M. A., et al. (1975). "Obstacles to Utilization of Prepaid Mental Health Care." *American Journal of Psychiatry, 132*(7), 710–715.

Googins, B. (1979). "The Use and Implementation of Occupational Alcoholism Programs by Supervisors." Unpublished doctoral dissertation, Brandeis University.

Gould, G. M. (1984). "Developing Industrial Social Work Field Placements." *Journal of Education for Social Work, 20*(2), 35–42.

Green, R. R. (1983). "Social Work Consultation to Employee Assistance Program Personnel: An Exploratory Study." Unpublished doctoral dissertation, Institute for Clinical Social Work, Berkeley, California.

"Hiring Outside Help to Solve People Problems." (1975, January 20). *Business Week*, pp. 30–31.

Human Resource Workshops: A Service of Employee Counseling Programs. (1983). New York: Jewish Board of Family and Children's Services.

Jorgensen, L. B. (1979). "Social Work in Business and Industry." Unpublished doctoral dissertation, University of Utah.

Kahn, A. J. (1973). *Social Policy and Social Services* (chap. 3). New York: Random House.

Kerpen, K. S. (1983). "Industrial Counseling Benefits Everyone." *Connektions: Business Network Magazine, 1*(1), 22,23,39.

Kurzman, P. A. (1983). "Ethical Issues in Industrial Social Work Practice." *Social Casework, 64*(2), 105–111.

Kurzman, P. A., & Akabas, S. H. (1981). "Industrial Social Work as an Arena for Practice." *Social Work, 26*(1), 52–60.

Leavitt, R. L. (1983). *Employee Assistance and Counselling Programs: Findings From Recent Research on Employer-Sponsored Human Services*. New York: Community Council of Greater New York.

Leven, P. S. (1980, October 5). "A New Service From a Seattle Bank: Social Work." *Seattle Post–Intelligencer*, pp. 1–2.

Lovenheim, B. (1979, April 1). "More Care Given to Employees' Psyches." *New York Times*, sec. 3, pp. 3,5.

Masi, D. (1984). *Designing Employee Assistance Programs*. New York: American Management Association Publications.

McBroom, E., et al. (Eds). (1984). "Industrial Social Work." *Social Work Papers* (Los Angeles: University of Southern California School of Social Work), *18*(1, entire issue).

McGowan, B. G. (1984). *Trends in Employee Counselling*. Elmsford, N.Y.: Pergamon Press.

Meeting Human Service Needs in the Workplace. A Role for Social Work. (1980). New York: Columbia University, Hunter College, & Council on Social Work Education.

NASW Code of Ethics. (1980). Washington, D.C.: National Association of Social Workers.

Ozawa, M. N. (1980). "Development of Social Services in Industry." *Social Work, 25*(6), 464–470.

Popple, P. R. (1981). "Social Work Practice in Business and Industry: 1875–1930." *Social Service Review, 55*(2), 257–269.

Reynolds, B. C. (1975). *Social Work and Social Living* (Classics Reprint Series). Washington, D.C.: National Association of Social Workers.

Richmond, M. E. (1917). *Social Diagnosis*. New York: Russell Sage Foundation.

Rostow, W. W. (1971). *Stages of Economic Growth* (2d ed.). Cambridge, England: Cambridge University Press.

Schwartz, W. (1969). "Private Troubles and Public Issues: One Social Work Job or Two?" *Social Welfare Forum, 1969* (pp. 22–43). New York: Columbia University Press.

Skeels, J. W. (1965). "Social Welfare Programs of Labor and Industry." In *Encyclopedia of Social Work* (15th ed., pp. 735–741). New York: National Association of Social Workers.

Social Case Work: Generic and Specific—A Report of the Milford Conference. (1929 and 1974). Classics Series reprint of 1929 edition. Washington, D.C.: National Association of Social Workers.

"Social Work and the Workplace." (1982). *Practice Digest, 5*(2, entire issue).

Spiegel, H. (1974). *Not For Work Alone: Services at the Workplace*. New York: Urban Research Center, Hunter College.

Thomlison, R. J. (Ed.). (1983). *Perspectives on Industrial Social Work Practice*. Ottawa: Family Service Canada Publications.

The U.S.C. Industrial Social Work Program. (1982). Los Angeles: University of Southern California.

Titmuss, R. M. (1968). *Commitment to Welfare*. New York: Pantheon Books.

Torjman, S. R. (1978). *Mental Health in the Work-*

place: *Annotated Bibliography*. Ottawa: Canadian Mental Health Association.

Tyson, D. O. (1980, October 16). "Social Workers in Three Trust Departments Look After Confined Beneficiaries." *American Banker, 145* (204), 7.

Vinet, M., & Jones, C. (1981). *Social Services and Work: Initiation of Social Workers into Labor and Industry Settings*. Seattle: Washington State Chapter, National Association of Social Workers.

Walden, T. (1978). "Industrial Social Work. A Conflict in Definitions." *NASW News, 23*(5), 3.

We Are Now "At Work" to Help You Safeguard Your Most Valuable Resource: People. (1981). New York: Columbia University, Hunter College, & Council on Social Work Education.

Weiner, H. J., et al. (1971). *The World of Work and Social Welfare Policy*. New York: Columbia University School of Social Work.

Weiner, H. J., Akabas, S. H., & Sommer, J. J. (1973). *Mental Health Care in the World of Work*. New York: Association Press.

Wilensky, H. L., & Lebeaux, C. N. (1965). *Industrial Society and Social Welfare*. New York: Free Press.

Yasser, R., & Sommer, J. J. (1975). "One Union's Social Service Program." *Social Welfare Forum, 1974* (pp. 112–120). New York: Columbia University Press.

For Further Reading

Akabas, S. H., & Kurzman, P. A. (1982). "The Industrial Social Welfare Specialist: What's So Special?" In Akabas & Kurzman (Eds.), *Work, Workers and Work Organizations: A View From Social Work* (chap. 9). Englewood Cliffs, N.J.: Prentice-Hall.

Briar, K. H. (1983). "Unemployment: Toward a Social Work Agenda." *Social Work, 28*(3), 211–216.

Efthim, A. (1976). "Serving the U.S. Work Force: A New Constituency for Schools of Social Work." *Journal of Education for Social Work, 12*(3), 29–36.

Filipowicz, C. A. (1979). "The Troubled Employee: Whose Responsibility?" *Personnel Administrator, 24*(6), 17–22.

Fine, M., et al. (1982). "Cultures of Drinking: A Workplace Perspective." *Social Work, 27*(5), 436–440.

Gullotta, T. P., & Donohue, K. C. (1981). "Corporate Families: Implications for Preventive Intervention." *Social Casework, 62*(2), 109–114.

Lanier, D. (1981). "Industrial Social Work: Into the Computer Age." *EAP Digest, 1*(2), 19–31.

Maypole, D. E., & Skaine, R. (1983). "Sexual

Harassment in the Workplace." *Social Work, 28*(5), 385–390.

Molloy, D. J., et al. (1980). "A Union Alcoholism Program Working With Many Employers." *NCA Labor-Management Alcoholism Journal 9*(6), 234–245.

Moss, J. A. (1982). "Unemployment Among Black Youths: A Policy Dilemma." *Social Work, 27*(1), 47–52.

Perlis, L. (1977). "The Human Contract in the Organized Workplace." *Social Thought, 3*(1), 29–35.

Pertzoff, L. (1979). "An Alcoholism Program in an Industrial Setting." *Smith College Studies in Social Work, 49*(3), 209–228.

Roman, P. M. (1981). "From Employee Alcoholism to Employee Assistance." *Journal of Studies on Alcohol, 42*(3), 244–271.

Vigilante, F. W. (1982). "Use of Work in the Assessment and Intervention Process." *Social Casework, 63*(5), 296–300.

Wrich, J. T. (1980). *The Employee Assistance Program* (rev. ed.). Center City, Minn.: Hazelden Foundation.

INFERTILITY SERVICES

Infertility is one of the more common medical problems affecting couples of childbearing age. It is estimated that 10 to 15 percent of couples in the United States are infertile, as defined by failure to achieve conception during one or more years of intercourse without the use of any contraception. Management of the infertile couple requires in-depth knowledge of reproductive biology and endocrinology, an understanding of the emotional aspects of reproduction, and special surgical skills. At present in the United States, a growing number of physicians specialize in this discipline—reproductive endocrinology. Because of the emotional and social problems involved in infertility, psychiatrists, psychologists, and social workers are increasingly involved in its management.

Causes of Infertility

Infertility may be caused by a number of factors affecting the male or female. When the infertile couple is considered as a unit, the cause of infertility in 40 percent of cases is in the male. Failure to ovulate accounts for 10 to 15 percent, tubal pathology or anatomical abnormalities for 20 to 30 percent, and cervical factors for 5 percent. There is no discernible cause for the infertility of the remaining 10 to 20 percent of couples, and it is probable that psychological or emotional factors play a major role in this last group.

In order for conception to occur, the female must ovulate and release an ovum, which must be picked up by the fringelike fimbriae of one Fallopian tube. Spermatozoa must be produced in the testes and deposited in the vicinity of the mouth of the cervix, or cervical os. They must be transported through the cervix, uterine cavity, and Fallopian tubes and meet and fertilize the ovum near the fimbriated end of the tube. Once the ovum is fertilized, it must be able to pass down the tube and into the uterine cavity. The endometrium, or mucous membrane lining the uterine cavity, must provide a proper hormonal milieu for the implantation and development of the young embryo.

The most common areas of interference with this chain of events are:

- Production and delivery of sperm— male factor
- Survival of sperm in the cervical canal—cervical factor
- Transport of sperm or conceptus through the Fallopian tube—tubal factor
- Release of an ovum and production of normal ovarian hormones—endocrine factor.

Evaluation of an infertile couple entails assessment of all of these factors.

Basic Evaluation

The couple is evaluated as a unit, and each of the areas outlined is investigated prior to initiating therapy. The workup includes a detailed history and examination of the couple, with assessment of the normalcy of the female genital tract and ovulation and of semen and sperm survival. The evaluation usually takes from 8 to 12 weeks and can be completed in five to six office visits. This type of screening will reveal the cause of infertility in 85 to 90 percent of cases that can be treated adequately in the office.

Diagnostic Procedures

Basal Body Temperature (BBT). Early in the 20th century, Van de Velde reported that the normal basal body temperature during the menstrual cycle is biphasic. Since then, BBT has been widely used in the assessment of ovulation. (Basal temperature is taken orally or rectally with a regular thermometer, immediately on awakening and before undertaking any activity. Basal body temperature is lower than the usual 98.6° F (37°C)—in most cases around 97–97.6°F (36.11–36.44°C). After ovulation the basal body temperature increases 0.5–1.0°F (.28–.56°C), generally to over 98° F (36.67°C). When BBT is charted for a month, a biphasic (two-part) curve should be found, with a nadir at the time of ovulation. The luteal phase—the second half of the menstrual cycle, named for the corpus luteum that develops in the ovary after ovulation—normally lasts 14 ± 1.5 days. If it is considerably shorter, the luteal phase may be inadequate. Coital exposure should be indicated on the BBT chart so that the time of ovulation can be correlated with intercourse. In this way it can be determined whether infertility is related to anovulation (absence of ovulation), improper coital timing, or neither.

Postcoital Test (PCT or Sims-Huhner Test). This test is performed around the expected time of ovulation as determined by the BBT chart. Patients are advised to have intercourse 10 to 16 hours before the test is performed. In the office, a small amount of cervical mucus is removed, placed on a slide, and examined microscopically for the presence of live sperm. The presence of large numbers of actively motile sperm indicates satisfactory insemination, adequate semen, and normal cervical mucus. There is generally a good correlation between a positive PCT and fertility.

Test for Tubal Patency. The standard procedure used at present to determine that the Fallopian tubes are not obstructed is hysterosalpingography. In this procedure radiopaque dye is injected through the cervix and several X rays are taken. This technique allows the physician to visualize the uterine cavity and Fallopian tubes and to assess their anatomical normality. Hysterosalpingography will reveal congenital anomalies of the genital tract, distortion of the uterine cavity by fibroid tumors or other adhesions, and anomalies of the Fallopian tubes.

Test for Adequacy of the Endometrium. A study of the premenstrual endometrium gives presumptive evidence of ovulation and information about implantation sites for the fertilized ovum. Tissue for an endometrial biopsy can be obtained in the office in a relatively short and simple procedure. Using the BBT chart as a guide, the biopsy should be timed as close as possible to the onset of menses but before the actual flow has started. The tissue is then fixed and a histological evaluation is done (its structures and composition are analyzed). Normally the histological data should coincide with the BBT. Abnormal endometrial development may indicate ovulatory dysfunction or corpus luteum failure. Endometrial biopsy occasionally reveals the presence of chronic infection.

Laparoscopy. When infertility investigation has failed to demonstrate any etiologic factor (disease or other abnormality) and no pregnancy has resulted within one year of the complete workup, a laparoscopy is indicated.

Laparoscopy is a surgical procedure that allows direct visualization, inspection, and assessment of the pelvic organs. Because general anesthesia is required, the patient is admitted to the hospital for one day. The procedure involves insufflation (blowing up) of the abdominal cavity with three to four liters of CO_2 in order to displace the bowel upward and out of the pelvic area. An instrument with a lens and light source is then inserted through the navel for direct inspection of the pelvic area, manipulation of the pelvic organs, and perfusion of the Fallopian tubes—in which a fluid is passed through the tubes to assess their patency. In about 20 percent of patients, some previously unsuspected pelvic pathology can be seen, most often pelvic adhesions, fibroids, or endometriosis (the presence elsewhere in the pelvic cavity of tissue resembling the endometrium). In about 80 percent of cases, laparoscopy discloses no abnormalities.

Treatment

Treatment depends on the cause of infertility. When there are anatomical abnormalities in the genital tract, treatment is surgical. Tubal occlusion (obstruction) may be the result of adhesions from pelvic inflammatory disease due to gonorrhea, tuberculosis, or postabortal or postpartum infections, or it may result from a previous tubal ligation—surgical tying off of the Fallopian tubes for

sterilization. Adhesions causing tubal occlusion or immobility may be due to endometriosis or extrapelvic inflammatory processes such as a ruptured appendix. The degree of success of tubal surgery depends both on the site and cause of the obstruction and on the extent of disease. Generally, the more extensive the damage, the poorer the outcome of surgery. The success rate—as measured by live births—varies from 10 to 65 percent. The best results are obtained in women whose tubes are intrinsically normal but who have adhesions that hinder mobility. Lysis (dissolution) of adhesions offers a 40 to 65 percent success rate.

When the tube itself has been damaged, the eventual pregnancy rate is considerably lower. The results have improved somewhat in the past decade with the introduction of microsurgical techniques, particularly in previously sterilized women whose tubes are essentially normal. However, the overall rate of ectopic pregnancies—in which implantation and gestation occur in a Fallopian tube or other nonuterine site—following tubal surgery is approximately 12 percent, which is much higher than in the normal population.

In the majority of cases in which the uterine cavity is distorted by fibroids, they can be surgically removed. The operation which is called a myomectomy, has about a 50 percent success rate. Congenital uterine anomalies account for a small fraction of cases of infertility. They can be corrected surgically with satisfactory results in many cases.

In 1978 the first live human offspring resulting from in vitro fertilization and embryo transfer (IVF-ET) was born in England, where much of the pioneering work in the field had been done by Patrick Steptoe and Robert Edwards. Since then, IVF programs have been established in many countries. Initially, the procedure was designed to bypass the Fallopian tubes, but current indications for IVF-ET include all causes of longstanding infertility. The procedure is quite simple. The woman is pretreated with ovulation-inducing drugs in order to achieve multiple ovulation. At the time of ovulation, a laparoscopy is performed and the ova recovered. The ova are fertilized with the husband's sperm and incubated for 36 to 48 hours until a two-to-eight-cell embryo develops. The embryo is then transferred back to the uterus. The general success rate, as measured by live births, is 10 to 20 percent.

Anovulation is one of the most successfully treated causes of infertility. Due to our increased understanding of the normal and abnormal physiology of the menstrual cycle and to the development of sophisticated diagnostic techniques, anomalies in the cycle can be diagnosed accurately and treated with "fertility drugs" that induce ovulation.

Clomiphene citrate (Clomid) stimulates the body to release gonadotropins (female sex hormones) and promotes ovulation in women whose hypothalamic-pituitary-ovarian axis is intact. Among properly selected patients, the pregnancy rate following clomiphene treatment is around 40 percent, with a multiple-pregnancy rate of about 7 percent. Side effects and complications are minimal.

Human menopausal gonadotropins (Pergonal) contain luteinizing hormone and follicle-stimulating hormone, involved in the formation of the corpus luteum in the ovaries. They are very effective in inducing ovulation and pregnancy in hypogonadotropic women (those deficient in female sex hormones) and patients who fail to respond to clomiphene. The overall pregnancy rate is approximately 65 percent, with a multiple-pregnancy rate of around 20 percent. Complications are quite rare but can be serious.

Gonadotropin-releasing hormone (GnRH), given as a long-term pulsatile intravenous infusion by means of a small continuous-infusion pump, is the latest method of treatment for anovulatory patients. GnRH stimulates the patient's gonadotropins. The pregnancy rate is lower than with Pergonal, but multiple-pregnancy and complication rates are also considerably lower.

Bromocriptine (Parlodel) is a dopamine agonist effective in reducing prolactin (a hormone that stimulates lactation) to normal levels in women who produce too much and in those who are anovulatory. (It is believed that dopamine is actually the prolactin-inhibiting factor in the brain. Dopamine agonists are substances that have a dopaminelike action.) Treatment restores normal ovulatory cycles in 80 percent of such patients, and 80 percent of those who ovulate conceive. Side effects are minimal and the multiple-pregnancy rate is the same as in the normal population.

In cases where the male is sterile, artificial insemination using donor sperm is an acceptable and successful way of treatment.

Last but not least, emotional factors play a role in infertility. It is difficult to know the relative incidence of emotional factors as a significant cause of infertility, but it appears to be high. The mechanisms by which emotional stress can affect ovulatory function are only beginning to be unraveled. For example, the endogenous opioids—a group of peptides recently isolated from the brain and other organs—play a significant role in the control of endocrine function. They are affected by emotional and environmental changes, and they are significant in the sensation of pain and other behavioral phenomena. The social worker counseling infertile clients should be alert and sympathetic to their problems and provide adequate support. Social workers as well as physicians should also be able to recognize individuals who need help with emotional problems and refer them to a specialist.

RAPHAEL JEWELEWICZ

For further information, see SEXUAL DYS-FUNCTION.

For Further Reading

Behrman, S. J., & Kistner, R. W. (Eds.). (1968). *Progress in Infertility*, (2nd ed.). Boston: Little, Brown & Co.

Buttran, Jr., V. C., Reiter, R. C. (1985). *Surgical Treatment of the Infertile Female*. Baltimore, Md.: Williams & Wilkins.

Edwards, R. G. (1980). *Conception in the Human Female*. New York: Academic Press.

Gold, J. J., & Josinowich, J. B. (Eds.). (1980). *Gynecologic Endocrinology* (3rd ed.). New York: Harper & Row.

Speroff, L., Glass, R. H., & Kase, N. G. (1983). *Clinical Gynecologic Endocrinology and Infertility* (3rd ed.). Baltimore, Md.: Williams & Wilkins

Van de Velde, T. (1904). *On the Connection Between Ovarian Activity, Cyclical Periodicity and the Menstrual Flow*. Haarlem, the Netherlands: F. Bohm's Successors.

Wallach, E. E., & Kemper, R. D. (Eds.). (1982). *Modern Trends in Infertility and Conception Control* (Vol. 2). New York: Harper & Row.

Yen, S. S. C., & Jaffe, R. B. (1978). *Reproductive Endocrinology*. Philadelphia: W. B. Saunders Co.

INFORMATION AND REFERRAL SERVICES

Little consideration has been given to assuring fair access to available resources in the complex and highly bureaucratized health and social welfare systems in the United States. Although there has been a steady proliferation of public social services since the mid-1930s, knowledge of these resources is often nonexistent, and many impediments to access persist, especially among the sick, the poor, and the elderly. Among these are restrictive eligibility requirements, discriminatory practices, the high cost of services, and the lack of needed resources.

Even when there is knowledge of services, asking for help may bear the stigma of "welfare," and qualifying for benefits and entitlements can be confusing, overwhelming, and even demeaning. Budget slashes and curtailments of essential services have further limited the public's access to needed services, as social problems tend to mount in the face of dwindling government support and diminishing resources. Moreover, many who seek help are subjected to a succession of referrals and shunted from one agency to another in a "Ping-Pong process" that leads to frustration and and a sense of futility.

One innovative organizational response to the need for access to information and services has been the development of information and referral (I&R) services. The rapid expansion of I&R in the United States over the past 25 years may be viewed as a reaction to the changing conditions and human needs of a postindustrial society, in which the unprecedented proliferation of services has led to the pressing need for additional organized access services (Zimmerman, 1979).

I&R Defined

It is generally agreed that I&R is essentially a human service system that is universally available, free of charge, and designed to link the inquirer with needed resources. This is accomplished by means of an organized, up-to-date information retrieval system, either manually operated or automated. In response to telephone, walk-in, or written inquiries—and with due regard for the individual's need for privacy and confidentiality—trained staff provide information, advice, appropriate referrals to existing resources, and follow-up. Varying levels of counseling and advocacy are offered in accordance with the user's needs and the mission of the I&R organization. Transportation, escort services, legal assistance, and a variety of support services may also be supplied.

Public relations programs and organized outreach to potential clients are indispensable in promoting utilization of I&R services (Levinson, 1981). Indirect services, using organized data obtained from I&R operating programs, are also offered. Such data may be marshaled for purposes of policymaking, social planning, class advocacy, and research.

I&R Systems

The basic underpinning concept of I&R is the system. As a service system, I&R represents a continuum of functional elements ranging from information assistance and advice giving to referral and follow-up. Whether, by means of "steering," the client is able to follow through independently with minimal assistance or whether the client requires more intensive follow-up, counseling and advocacy are generally determined by the organizational mission and by the professional judgment of the I&R agent.

As an organizational system, I&R may function as an independent, free-standing agency that is primarily responsible for the delivery of I&R services. An I&R program may also operate within a unit or department of a host agency, such as a social services department or a local library. In large service organizations, such as medical centers or multiservice centers, an I&R service may also be conducted as an intraagency system. A variety of I&R hot lines, and such prerecorded caller services as Tel-Med for health and medical information and Tel-Law for legal information, may also become built-in structural components of I&R organizations.

Operationally, I&R is viewed as an interagency system or network that interacts with multiple service systems within its organizational environment. For purposes of analysis, an I&R system may be viewed as either a centralized or decentralized system. As the hub of multiple I&R systems, a centralized system may function as a major generic system (or suprasystem) within a given service area. Examples of centralized services are the countywide Info-Line system in Akron, Ohio, and the statewide Info-Line system in Connecticut, both of which serve as generic I&R providers in their respective county and state service areas. Member I&R agencies within a centralized system may collectively share a standardized resource file, collaborate in educational and training programs, contribute to joint funding plans, and engage in social policy and planning programs based on centrally reported data.

The I&R system can be regarded as primarily decentralized in service areas in which two or more independent I&R providers operate autonomously at varying levels of development, without the presence of a single generic I&R provider. For example, the Mile High I&R system is one of twelve I&R programs operating in the Denver, Colorado, metropolitan service area. Another example of a decentralized system is the I&R program that operates in two rural counties of northern California, each of which has developed its own approach to the delivery of I&R services. A decentralized system may actually be preferred by local communities because specific agencies can engage hard-to-reach people and respond to certain citizen groups more effectively than a single generic I&R. In practice, I&R systems generally reflect aspects of both centralized and decentralized systems.

The parameters of I&R systems vary widely in scope and range of services, in sources of funding, and in levels of operation, depending on their geographic size, demography, political supports, and developmental history (Shanahan, Gargan, & Apple, 1983). For example, the I&R Federation in Los Angeles, California, serves a multitude of specialized agencies that cater to a metropolitan population of 7.5 million. It operates on a $1.6 million budget financed by public and voluntary funding. In contrast, the I&R system that operates in two rural counties in northern California serves fewer than 150,000 people on a budget of less than $64,000, is supported by the official Area Agency on Aging, and is designed specifically for elderly residents.

The statewide I&R system in Connecticut operates through regional offices, and South Dakota's State Tie Line provides a statewide toll-free telephone I&R service,

centrally located in the governor's office. In Memphis, Tennessee, the citywide, library-based I&R system known as LINC was created through an unanticipated release of county general revenue funds. The regional Hampton Roads Information Center (HRIC) in southeastern Virginia began as a health-specific I&R and, through state funding, developed into a generic I&R system. The Mile High United Way I&R System in Denver, Colorado, evolved as an informal grass-roots system supported almost exclusively by voluntary funds. The wide diversities and unique adaptations of I&R systems, as reflected in the examples above, are also reflected in the history of I&R.

Historical Development

I&R services can be traced to the Social Service Exchanges that were operated by the Charity Organization Societies of the 1870s. To avoid duplication of relief, these exchanges maintained centralized files on reported clients, which were shared by social agencies in order to restrict rather than facilitate access to services (Long, 1973).

Community health and welfare councils began to evolve in the early 1920s under the national leadership of the United Community Funds and Councils of America (renamed United Way of America in 1970). During this period, community councils began to shift away from the maintenance of client inventories toward the use of organized files and published directories of community resources. By the early 1940s, a new transformation occurred as Social Service Exchanges were abandoned and information and referral programs began to take shape within growing numbers of community councils in the United States and Canada.

A notable antecedent of American I&R services is the network of British Citizens Advice Bureaus (CABs), initially organized in 1939 to meet the emergency conditions that prevailed during World War II. After the end of the war, CABs remained in operation as community information centers, staffed primarily by trained volunteers and designed to provide information, advice, and advocacy to all inquirers (Brasnett, 1964). Local CABs are affiliated with the National Association of Citizens Advice Bureaus, a regulatory standard-setting body that provides a uniform resource file to all local bureaus, conducts mandatory training programs, and supplies up-to-date information on policies, procedures, and legislative issues. In 1984, over 900 CABs were in operation in England, Wales, Scotland, and Northern Ireland.

Paralleling the British experience, but with significant variations, was America's response to the aftermath of World War II—the creation of Veterans Information Centers in 1946. The restrictive policy of serving only veterans may have contributed to the closing of these centers by 1949. A study of British CABs (Kahn et al., 1966) concluded that although the CAB model is an exemplary access system, the United States needed to create its own organized access system through experience and experimentation.

Emergence of I&R Services

Identifiable I&R services did not emerge until the 1960s. To reduce hospitalization and to promote utilization of community resources, particularly among the chronically ill and the elderly, the United States Public Health Service authorized funds to establish I&R programs in selected communities under the Community Health Services and Affiliates Act of 1961. Under Title III of the Older Americans Act of 1965, the Administration on Aging (AOA) sponsored projects to better link the elderly with community-based services. These projects included a series of large-scale research studies carried out under Title IV of the same act. AOA has continued to sponsor major studies in I&R practice, program development, and evaluative research. Other federal agencies that recognized I&R as an important program component were the Social Security Administration, the Department of Housing and Urban Development, the Office of Economic Opportunity, and the then-emerging Comprehensive Mental Health Centers (Holmes & Holmes, 1979).

Concurrent with the development of I&R programs in the public sector was the emergence of I&R programs among the affiliates of national voluntary health organizations, such as the National Easter Seal Society for Crippled Children and Adults and the American Red Cross. On the local level, volunteer groups organized I&R services to deal with the special problems of substance abuse and single-parent families as well as women's issues and various other com-

munitywide concerns. Hot lines to provide peer counseling, especially for youths involved in crisis situations, appeared to spring up overnight. Newspapers and radio and television programs also created I&R-related services, such as the popular "Call for Action" programs.

The first extensive national survey of I&R services, conducted in 1967 under the joint sponsorship of Brandeis University and the United States Department of Public Health, documented a preponderance of specialized I&R services in the fields of aging, health, and mental health (Bloksberg & Caso, 1967).

Expansion of I&R Organizations

By the early 1970s specialized services for target populations were superseded by the rapid growth of broader, more generic I&R programs in established social agencies, as well as in nontraditional settings such as public libraries (Jones, 1978), shopping malls, banks, train stations, bus depots, and other places where people congregate. I&R services at the workplace were provided through union counseling activities, employment assistance programs, and referral agent programs in industry sponsored by the United Way of America (UWA) (United Way of America, 1978). Mobile I&R services and toll-free telephone services gained popularity as means of surmounting problems of distance and inaccessibility.

Title XX of the Social Security Act of 1974, which designated I&R as a universal service for all citizens, spurred the rapid expansion of I&R programs. It adopted a flexible approach and permitted I&R programs to be administered by state social services departments or to be provided under contract with nongovernmental agencies. Another important catalyst in the expansion of I&R was the deinstitutionalization movement, which attested to the unavailability and inaccessibility of community services for discharged mental patients. The consumer rights movement also became more vocal, demanding access to personal data and insisting on confidentiality under the Federal Privacy Act of 1974 (P.L. 93–579).

Advances in information technology promoted the centralization of information services, as computer operated programs produced more efficient and cost-effective information systems, making automation more affordable (Gunderson, 1983). Centralized information bases provided up-to-date resource inventories, systems for tracking nursing home vacancies, and access to other data sources, including census data and vital statistics. By the mid-1970s the impact of information technology made possible the transformation of manually operated I&R programs into automated information systems whose ability to classify, compile, store, and retrieve information increased through the use of microcomputers and terminals connected to centralized data systems (Garrett, 1984).

The leadership role of AOA expanded under the 1973 amendments to the Older Americans Act, which mandated the development of networks of coordinated I&R systems at local, state, and regional levels. The Interdepartmental Task Force, organized by AOA by means of working agreements with 15 federal agencies in 1975, was reorganized in 1983 as an I&R consortium. There was now representation from the voluntary and private business sectors, including the American Association of Retired Persons (AARP) and the International Telephone and Telegraph Corporation (Administration on Aging, 1984).

After more than 50 years of promoting I&R, UWA produced the first set of I&R standards in 1973. That same year, UWA published the first comprehensive service identification system, known as UWASIS. This system, modified in 1976 as UWASIS II (United Way of America, 1976), has been adopted by many I&R agencies throughout the country. The directors of I&R programs implemented by UWA convened annual meetings of the National Conference on Social Welfare until 1973. By this time I&R had expanded to the point where it was desirable to launch a new independent national organization—the Alliance of Information and Referral Services (AIRS), renamed the National Alliance of Information and Referral Systems in 1983.

In 1978, a study carried out by the Office of Management and Budget documented the lack of planning and fragmentation that characterized proliferating I&R programs. The study concluded that I&R is "a complex system that needs improvement" and recommended setting up federal centralized bases for I&R operations. A trenchant and insightful observation was the comment that "those who provide I&R have themselves become part of the same maze to which they were supposed to offer guidance" (U.S. General Accounting Office, 1978). What was implied was the need for an I&R on I&R.

Networking I&R

In the 1980s, diminished public funding and cutbacks in social services ushered in a new era of austerity that called for increased collaboration and expanded networking. Competition for scarce resources increased, particularly as block grants for social services replaced the earlier Title XX allocations for I&R. Support for I&R programs, notably those in the areas of employment assistance and child day care, increased in the private sector and among private corporations (Sallee & Berg, 1983). Private corporations and foundations provided grants to various I&R systems, contributing to the implementation and expansion of automated I&R systems (Garrett, 1984).

The set of national standards jointly produced in 1983 by UWA and AIRS pointed to several new directions for "shared functions" in I&R operations. The Report on Model Information and Referral Systems, conducted by AIRS and funded by AOA, analyzed exemplary I&R systems based on the viability and capacity of I&R networks to operate interagency linkages (Shanahan, Gargan, & Apple, 1983). According to Austin (1980), I&R represented "the new glue" to promote "facilitative networks" for social welfare agencies (p. 38).

Because there is no central reporting agency that functions as a regulatory body for I&R activities, it is difficult to ascertain the volume of I&R services. However, there may be as many as 10,000 I&R programs in operation, considering the large number of unreported, informal, and diversified programs in the public, voluntary, and private sectors in the United States. A bibliography on I&R listed 289 entries (Bolch, Long, & Dewey, 1972); the *Directory of Information and Referral Services* reported 598 I&R programs in the United States and 41 in Canada (Alliance of Information and Referral Systems, 1984); and 330 I&R programs were operated by UWA affiliates in 1984.

Staffing and Training

To date there is no prescribed or ideal model for the staffing of I&R programs, nor are the tasks of staff members universally delineated or clearly defined. Some I&R services, such as the Info-Line system in Connecticut, are operated exclusively by a professional staff. Many locally based I&R agencies are staffed by paraprofessionals, for whom I&R provides a full-time career or a way of qualifying as human service professionals. Volunteers constitute the core staff of many I&R organizations, and they play a pivotal role in the local delivery of I&R services provided by special interest groups, hot lines, and self-help groups for the elderly.

No one profession plays a dominant role in I&R operations. Although social workers occupied most of the managerial positions in I&R programs during the 1960s, since that time other helping professionals have become involved in the administration and delivery of I&R programs, including nurses, teachers, librarians, psychologists, and computer specialists (Levinson, in press).

The momentum of the rapidly expanding I&R movement has pointed to new directions for interprofessional collaboration to promote service delivery and reduce competitiveness and specialization. For example, the complementary roles of the librarian as information expert and the social worker as human relations and community organization expert have suggested the mutual benefit of a professional partnership. This would combine the librarian's technical capabilities with the social worker's interpersonal skills in interviewing, delineating problems counseling, outreach, and advocacy.

In many I&R service training programs, staff and volunteers generally focus on the specific policies and procedures of the particular agency (Mathews & Fawcett, 1981). Some schools of social work and library science have initiated educational programs in I&R practice and program development (Braverman & Martin, 1978; Durrance, 1984). The Adelphi University School of Social Work has conducted I&R field internships and continuing education programs since 1975. Under a 1984 federal grant from AOA, the school established a joint training program that paired social work and library student interns with older volunteers in library-based I&R programs.

International Perspectives

Viewed from an international perspective, the British and American I&R models have influenced the development of access systems in various developed and developing countries. Because of Canada's proximity to the United States and because of funding supplied by UWA, access services in various parts of Canada closely resemble the American I&R model. Countries that have had an association with Great Britain—for example, Australia, India, Israel, and South Africa—have patterned their access systems after the British model. Some unique and innovative features of planned access systems have been reported by Cyprus, Japan, and Poland. Reports of access systems from many countries have magnified the role of the volunteer as the direct service agent and have emphasized the capabilities of organized access systems to contribute to social planning, policy formulation, and social reform (Levinson & Haynes, 1984). Whether international I&R systems can adequately serve the crisis conditions and transient needs of mobile population groups on a cross-national basis remains to be explored.

Trends, Issues, and Projections

Serious question has been raised concerning whether a separate I&R access system will diminish access services that are offered as a marginal function of many social agencies. Will I&R services further fragment and complicate an already disjointed human service system? To what extent do issues of organizational autonomy and jurisdiction limit the creation of coordinated I&R networks? A logical caveat is that I&R must guard against developing the rigid bureaucracies it seeks to overcome.

Although the concept of I&R often tends to be restricted to direct contact with clients, its significance as a planning, policy, and research mechanism has broad implications. Many groups of constituents draw on the capabilities of I&R, including legislators, planners, policymakers, and community workers. Clearly, I&R cannot solve the societal problems of poverty, discrimination, and unemployment. It can, however, spot trends, indicate needs, and identify gaps, inadequacies, and insufficiencies in existing services.

Traditionally, I&R has been a reactive service designed to respond to consumers' requests and users' demands. But in an effort to be responsive to current priorities and changing needs, I&R leaders are assuming a more proactive stance through outreach and advocacy programs that involve community action and political support. However, I&R must guard against becoming a "cause agency," a position that could limit universal, nonpartisan access to services.

The critical issue in I&R involves determining who the beneficiaries of an information society are. Being "information poor" is a handicap in obtaining services; being "information rich" enables one to reap the benefits of a service society. Because the possession of information denotes power, debate focuses on how "information equity" can be established and on who shall control the sources and distribution of information, with due regard for confidentiality.

The roles of the professional, the paraprofessional, and the volunteer require sharper delineation in order to optimize staff capabilities in the delivery of I&R services. The multifaceted tasks of the I&R professional combine expertise in direct services to clients with competence in policymaking, planning, consultation, and administration. The result is the blended role of the "professional synergist," who is capable of delivering quality service and who is effective in creating service linkages within organizational networks.

Interprofessional collaboration and interdisciplinary training in I&R practice and program development can pool and tap the specialized skills and expertise of professionals. The expanded role of trained volunteers and the availability of competent instructors to provide staff training will be indispensable to the comprehensive and effective delivery of I&R services. The implications for professional education and for curriculum enrichment in I&R content and practice present new educational challenges.

Although I&R services are usually available without cost, provision of services is not free. In fact, the expense of staffing, providing efficient resource files, and overseeing operational maintenance may be high.

As restricted funding and retrenchment of services require the maximization of available resources, it is anticipated that I&R programs will continue to expand. With diminishing government funds in the public and voluntary sectors, it seems likely that the private sector—particularly the corporate community—will assume a more active role in I&R programs as a management function and an employee benefit. To facilitate access at the nearest point of consumption, the delivery of I&R services at the local level will remain a primary focus. Contrary to the frequently cited ideal of a single central point of access for I&R services, experience indicates the advisability and practicability of multiple service entries for I&R systems, which can offer a range of choices to meet consumer preferences. The major impetus for the development of I&R—the federal government—will shift to the state, regional, and local levels as broader networks continue to develop across jurisdictional and geographic boundaries.

The extent to which I&R can influence the total social welfare system will essentially depend on dynamic leadership and on the political support that I&R can gain in acquiring adequate resources to operate viable and responsive systems. I&R may be the precursor of more rational and coherent human services networks than have yet been developed.

RISHA W. LEVINSON

For further information, see LINKAGE IN DIRECT PRACTICE.

References

Administration on Aging, Office of Human Development Services, Department of Health and Human Services. (1984). *Report of the Consortium on Information and Referral Services.* Washington, D.C.: U.S. Government Printing Office.

Alliance of Information and Referral Systems. (1984). *Directory of Information and Referral Services in the United States and Canada.* Indianapolis, Ind.: Author.

Austin, D. M. (1980). "I&R: The New Glue for the Social Services." *Public Welfare, 38*(4), 38–43.

Bloksberg, L. M., & Caso, E. K. (1967). *Survey of Information and Referral Services Existing Within the United States: Final Report.* Waltham, Mass.: Brandeis University, Florence Heller Graduate School for Advanced Studies in Social Welfare.

Bolch, E., Long, N., & Dewey, J. (1972). *Information and Referral: An Annotated Bibliography*. Minneapolis, Minn.: Institute for Interdisciplinary Studies of the American Rehabilitation Foundation.

Brasnett, M. E. (1964). *The Study of the Citizens Advice Bureaux*. London, England: The National Council of Social Service, Inc.

Braverman, M., & Martin, M. (1978). "The Education of Information and Referral Librarians and Implications for the Future." In C. Jones (Ed.), *Public Library Information and Referral Service* (pp. 139–153). Hamden, Conn.: Shoe String Press.

Durrance, J. C. (1984). "Community Information Services—An Innovation at the Beginning of Its Second Decade." In *Advances in Librarianship* (Vol. 13, pp. 100–123). New York: Academic Press.

Garrett, W. (1984). "Technological Advances in I&R: An American Report." In R. W. Levinson & K. S. Haynes (Eds.), *Accessing Human Services: International Perspectives* (pp. 171–198). Beverly Hills, Calif.: Sage Publications.

Gunderson, R. (1983). "Is Computerization Right for My Agency?" *Information and Referral, 5*(1), 1–11.

Holmes, B., & Holmes, D. (1979). *Handbook of Human Services for Older Persons*. New York: Human Sciences Press.

Jones, C. S. (Ed.). (1978). *Public Library Information and Referral Services*. Syracuse, N.Y.: Gaylord Brothers.

Kahn, A. J., et al. (1966). *Neighborhood Information Centers: A Study and Some Proposals*. New York: Columbia University School of Social Work.

Levinson, R. W. (1981). "Information and Referral Services." In N. Gilbert & H. Specht (Eds.), *Handbook of the Social Services* (pp. 13–34). Englewood Cliffs, N.J.: Prentice-Hall.

Levinson, R. W. (in press). *Doorways to Human Services: Information and Referral*. New York: Springer Publishing Co.

Levinson, R. W., & Haynes, K. S. (Eds.). (1984). *Accessing Human Services: International Perspectives*. Beverly Hills, Calif.: Sage Publications.

Long, N. (1973). "Information and Referral Services: A Short History and Some Recommendations." *The Social Service Review, 47*(1), 49–62.

Mathews, M. R., & Fawcett, S. B. (1981). *Matching Clients and Services, I&R*. Beverly Hills, Calif.: Sage Publications.

Sallee, A. L., & Berg, B. (1983). "Day Care I&R As a Corporate Child Care Option." *AIRS Journal, 5*(2), 1–18.

Shanahan, J. L., Apple, N., & Gargan, J. J. (1983). *Model Information and Referral Systems: A Bridge to the Future*. Akron, Ohio: Alliance of Information and Referral Systems, Inc.

United States General Accounting Office. (1978). *Information and Referral for People Needing Human Services—A Complex System That Should Be Improved* (H. Doc. 77-134). Washington, D.C.: U.S. Government Printing Office.

United Way of America. (1976). *UWASIS II: A Taxonomy of Social Goals and Human Service Programs* (2nd ed.). Alexandria, Va.: Author.

United Way of America. (1978). *Information and Referral: Challenge to United Way*. Alexandria, Va.: Author.

United Way of America. (1983). *National Standards for Information and Referral*. Alexandria, Va.: Author.

Zimmerman, S. L. (1979). "I&R Services: A Manifestation and Response to Post Industrial Society." *Information and Referral, 1*(3), 33–48.

INFORMATION SYSTEMS. See COMPUTER UTILIZATION; INFORMATION AND REFERRAL SERVICES; INFORMATION SYSTEMS: AGENCY; INFORMATION SYSTEMS: CLIENT DATA; INFORMATION UTILIZATION FOR MANAGEMENT DECISION MAKING; RECORDING IN DIRECT PRACTICE.

INFORMATION SYSTEMS: AGENCY

The speed at which current electronic technologies can work with information is so tremendous that they are dramatically changing the role of information in society. This is especially true in the human services, which collect, store, manipulate, and communicate large volumes of information in the process of serving clients. Computerized information systems are requiring a reexamination of the role of information in every aspect of social work practice.

By examining manual information systems, it is relatively easy to understand that an information system is simply an organized method for working with information. What

Table 1. Forms, Definitions, and Examples of Information

Form	Definition	Example
Character	A letter, number, or symbol used alone or in combination to represent data	A e 5 121 * @
Data (pl.) Datum (sing.)	The assigned characters that represent facts, entities, or events	79
Information	The meaning put on data by humans through processing	79% error rate
Knowledge	Information in the form of descriptions and relationships	Description: A divorced person cannot be married but can have children. Relationship: Previous violence increases the likelihood of subsequent abuse.
Concept	A generalized idea formed on the basis of knowledge or experience	Feedback, child abuse, poverty

occurs in an electronic information system is relatively difficult to understand, yet the same basic processes exist as in a manual system. In a manual system, humans store, manipulate, retrieve, and communicate information. In most modern information systems, computers perform these same tasks in more complex and sophisticated ways.

This article discusses the history and concepts of electronic information systems and explores their use in social work practice. The development of the information system, its problems, its impact, and issues surrounding its use are also discussed. Unless otherwise indicated, the term "information system" in this article will denote a computerized information system that processes information in electronic form.

Basic Concepts

The word "information" as used in the term "information system" is a generic term that refers to information in its various forms. Table 1 presents definitions and examples of some common forms of information. Pieces of information can be combined into groupings as illustrated by the hierarchical arrangement in Table 2.

The word "system" in "information system" implies that organized and integrated processes are involved in working with information to reach a goal. These processes include capturing, storing, retrieving, manipulating, transferring, and presenting information. The goal of an information system is defined by the user, which indicates that people are one important component of an information system. Information, the inputs and outputs of an information system, is another important component. Manipulating information according to the user's specifications is the core process in an information system. Information manipulation involves logical processes, such as determining whether one value is greater than or lesser than another value, and mathematical processes, such as addition and subtraction. An information system is a system of people, procedures, and equipment—usually computer based—for collecting, manipulating, retrieving, and reporting information.

A computer must be distinguished from an information system. The computer provides the basic power for an information system, just as a motor provides the basic power for a transportation system. A computer is a combination of electronic and mechanical devices that work together to provide the capacity to rapidly store, retrieve, and perform arithmetic and logical operations on data according to programmed instructions. An information system, on the other hand, involves people and their goals, information needs, and the organizations in which these goals and needs exist. Electronic devices other than a computer may be used to

Table 2. Hierarchy of Information Groupings

Database: A collection of data, possibly consisting of records in files, where the data is stored and managed to minimize redundancy and to allow for easy access and manipulation. An agency database usually consists of fiscal, client, and staff files.

$\wedge$
$\wedge$

    File: A grouping of similarly constructed records treated as a unit; for example, a client file.

$\wedge$
$\wedge$

    Record: A set of related data items; for example, a client record.

$\wedge$
$\wedge$

    Data item, data element, or field: A label given one small unit or piece of information; for example, client name, age, or date of birth.

perform information system functions. One example is a printer.

In a computer system, the physical components are called hardware. The instructions that guide and control the operations of the hardware are called computer programs. Computer programs, the procedures for using them, and their accompanying documentation are called software. Computers are used in other systems that do not have information as their input and output. For example, a robotic arm may use human movement as the input and have mechanical movement as the output.

The key component of any information system, but especially of those that require large volumes of stored information, is file or database management technology, which helps the user perform functions such as:

1. Protecting the confidentiality of data by using techniques such as passwords and access codes.

2. Designing forms for entering data.

3. Processing and storing data using simple commands or more sophisticated programming.

4. Designing reports for retrieving and displaying information. Graphics software is often used to produce visually oriented output, such as bargraphs and pie charts.

5. Managing and controlling the internal operations of the system, such as creating new files and regenerating the data after system failure.

Many information systems are built on a commercially available software package called a Database Management System (DBMS), which is purchased separately and then customized to fit the particular needs of the user. Other information systems are custom built to solve specific problems. This results in a more tailored system, but one which may not have the sophisticated features of commercial DBMSs and which may be more difficult to maintain or alter.

Historical Perspective

Computers were developed in the 1940s and early 1950s and became commercially viable in the late 1950s. In the 1950s the first large, expensive, and slow mainframe computers were used to process routine information in specialized areas such as payroll. Data processing (DP) was the term given to the use of computers for these routine applications. Using many computers to distribute DP tasks throughout an organization was called distributed data processing (DDP).

In the 1960s, as many middle-management tasks were computerized, the term management information system (MIS) was used to denote the connection of separate DP operations into a single system of hardware, software, computing technicians, computing managers, and users. As MISs spread throughout organizations, the word management was often dropped from the term MIS.

In the late 1970s, flexible, "user friendly" information systems, which were capable of quickly providing information for "what if" types of questions posed by users, were labeled decision support systems

(DSS). DSS systems typically support complex decision making, such as that which occurs at the policy, top management, and professional client levels.

In the 1980s, artificial intelligence technologies matured to allow for the processing of knowledge (information in the form of relationships and descriptions). One type of knowledge system is particularly relevant for the human services because it is capable of mimicking human expertise in a specialized area. These expert systems use inference mechanisms to extract decisions from large stores of knowledge at skill levels typically relegated to human experts. Information systems technology will continue to develop as more and more people discover the capabilities of electronic information technologies.

Information Systems in Social Work Practice

For this analysis, social work will be divided into five practice areas: policy/community planning, agency management, direct service, client self-help, and education.

Policy/Community Planning. The information needs of social work practice at the policy/community planning level are complex, and much information is collected by agencies to ensure that the services provided match clients' needs in an efficient, effective, and accountable manner. Computerized information systems provide easy access to and selective searching of large volumes of relevant information on a local level or a national level. National networks, sometimes called information utilities, provide specialized information through electronic message systems, bulletin boards, user groups, and bibliographic databases. Some examples are DIALOG (over 180 abstracts, bibliographies, full texts, and statistical databases), AdoptNet (adoption information), ARCNet (information about mental retardation), DeafNet (information for the hearing impaired), and SWAB (an online database abstracting 150 journals in social work and related fields). Users of these information systems can rapidly search for specific pieces of information, post information for general use, or send private electronic messages to other users.

Another function of information systems at the policy/community planning level is to help managers and agency board members cope with the voluminous information they collect. These systems can provide statistical analyses of data, produce models or simulations of complex processes, present graphic displays of complex information, and quickly display the consequences of decision-making preferences.

A third need is for information to support advocacy and fundraising efforts. Information systems can produce sorted mailing labels of persons by specialized interest, send personalized letters, track participants' responses, and produce reports.

Agency Management. The information needed to manage a human service agency is similar to the information needed to manage any organization. As a consequence, a substantial number of computer programs are available. Common programs help perform tasks such as nonprofit accounting, billing, budgeting, inventory, setting goals and objectives, developing workplans, and monitoring work performance. Information systems can also help track client movement through the service delivery system. For example, in a mental health center the information system may contain clients' social, psychological, and physical histories, measures of their level of functioning, a record of their problems, and a record of staff time and effort. These information systems are often the basis of quality assurance programs, program evaluation efforts, and accountability reports to funding sources.

Agencies with information systems that are easy to manipulate have found management data to be extremely useful in policy and planning decisions. For example, the capacity to project quickly what will happen to clients if program funds are reduced has saved many agency programs during the budget allocation or legislative process.

Service Delivery. Information systems that support information needs at the service delivery level are less readily available than management applications. This is partly because social work practice varies by agency and type of client to such an extent that most information systems must be unique or exist in only a few locations. The limited transferability of direct service information systems discourages the investment required to develop them.

Information needs at the service delivery level are of two types: information that helps practitioners manage how they work, and information that supports practitioners' interaction with clients. For a comprehensive overview of direct service delivery applications, see Schwartz (1984) and Hedlund, Vieweg, & Cho (1985).

Managing Practitioners' Work. Several types of information systems help social workers manage their work. For example, computer-administered interviews have been used to gather data from clients with a proficiency equal to or better than that of trained interviewer (Greist et al., 1983). Computerized record keeping can make it easy to complete routine weekly and monthly reports. Information systems can contain staff calendars making it possible to schedule meetings using electronic mail. Scheduling systems can also provide daily listings of client appointments and reminders of important dates, such as client birthdays.

Another area of practitioners' work successfully supported by information systems is tracking and monitoring client services. For example, drug monitoring systems can check the characteristics of a client's background and the guidelines for prescribing drugs to identify potential prescription problems.

Practitioners also need to keep current with developments in the field. Computerized databases, such as the lithium library—which supplies information about lithium as a psychotropic medication—can provide easily searched abstracts of the latest research, and information utilities can play an important role in a practitioner's continuing education.

Supporting Practitioners' Interaction with Clients. One of the greatest needs of social work practitioners is for information that supports their work with clients. Software in this area allows information systems to:

1. Assist in standardized assessment techniques, such as the American Psychiatric Association's *Diagnostic and Statistical Manual* (DSM III).

2. Administer, score, and report the results of psychological tests.

3. Provide information and referral resources immediately by problem, geographic area, or other specification.

4. Educate clients using, for example, Computer Assisted Instruction (CAI).

5. Predict client behavior such as the potential for suicide.

6. Recognize patterns in large numbers of behaviors to assist diagnosis and treatment.

7. Assist in treatment through activities such as the use of computerized games with adolescent clients.

Client Self-Help. Perhaps the sleeping giant in human service information systems is in the area of client self-help. The reason this area may see rapid development is that the number of potential users of self-help software is substantially larger than the number of users of agency and practitioner software. This potential for mass marketing means that it will be financially more rewarding for software vendors to invest their programming resources in self-help products.

The self-help information system market may be similar to the self-help book market, in that faddish and popularized treatments will be developed. However, other more sophisticated self-help software will be designed to help clients educate and treat themselves in areas such as stress reduction, weight control, parenting, and depression. Self-help software programs will have greater potential to help than books because information systems can make sophisticated presentations and can contain monitoring techniques that continuously analyze progress and prescribe remedial work for users.

Clients also need to obtain information about their problems. As the home computer becomes as common as the television, national and local information and referral systems and client self-help groups can provide specific information on almost any human service problem. Electronic self-help groups already exist among clients with computers, for example, users of assistive devices for the disabled. Electronic self-help groups also offer great potential for advocacy at the policy level in that electronic networks can provide the rapid communication necessary for advocacy efforts.

Education. Because information plays a vital role in education, so will information systems technology. The physical searching and browsing of library shelves will be replaced by electronic searches of national databases because it will be less expensive to pay for the electronic transmission of information than for physically transporting a student to a library. Ready access to information and to other electronic tools will focus education on the integration and use of information. For example, with software that helps students outline a subject and control for errors in grammar, spelling, style, and punctuation, the writing of class papers will receive less attention than content and the integration of information.

As information technology continues to be applied to social work practice, additional emphasis will be placed on the information base of practice decisions. Information system tools with this emphasis will be developed and marketed for teaching. For example, simulations of agencies, families, and individuals will allow students to use a trial-and-error approach to decision making. They will receive immediate feedback on the impact of their decisions at the policy, management, and direct practice levels. In summary,

the potential of this technology for social work is great at all levels of practice.

Developing Information Systems

Because information must be used according to certain processes and procedures to solve any problem, developing an information system requires understanding these processes and procedures in such detail that they can be represented to a machine. Processes and procedures that are complex for the trained human mind often become mammoth processes to represent to a computer.

If processes are not adequately represented, however, errors result and the system will not be trusted. An information system requires the trust and cooperation of all involved, because the success of an information system depends on the accurate input of data and on the use of system outputs in decision making.

Steps in the Development Process. Developing an information system requires planning and the investment of significant time and effort as illustrated by the eight-step process shown in Table 3. Buying commer-

(*continued on page 927*)

Table 3. Eight Steps in Developing an Information System

Step 1: Assess Preparedness and Feasibility
Communicate with all staff about the effort
Establish a steering committee
Define the information system's purpose, objectives, development timetables, and responsibilities
Assess commitment of key individuals
Assess the expectations of those affected
Estimate resources for change—money, time, expertise
Estimate improved system impacts (positive and negative)
Prepare and circulate preparedness and feasibility report
Decide to proceed or terminate effort

Step 2: Analysis of Existing System
Identify the major decisions the new information system will support and the information needed to support these decisions
Define the characteristics of the information needed, its source and collection methods
Analyze current and future data input, processing, and output operations and requirements, for example, forms, operations, files, and reports
Describe logical routing or flow of information
Evaluate problems with the existing information system
Review similar efforts and request help from national or state associations
Develop policy and procedural changes as necessary
Prepare and circulate systems analysis report and preliminary design ideas
Decide to proceed or terminate effort

(continued)

Table 3. Continued

Step 3: Conceptual Design
Finalize information system's scope, goals, and objectives
Develop alternative conceptual designs—possible flow and management of data, records, files, and processing functions to meet the information needs
Apply restrictions to possible designs—required and desired data frequency, volume, security, confidentiality, turnaround time; and information system flexibility, reliability, processing and statistical capabilities, growth potential, life expectancy, and tie in with other systems
Apply resources to designs—money, time, expertise
Translate designs into software and hardware configurations
Detail the advantages, disadvantages, and assumptions of alternate designs
Prepare and circulate conceptual design and decide to proceed or terminate effort

Step 4: Detailed Design and Development
Set up controls and technical performance standards
Select the software for the chosen design
Select the hardware to match the software
Design and develop processing operations and procedures, program logic, file definition and structure, indexes, error checks, storage and backup mechanisms
Design input and output forms
Program system
Prepare programming manuals and procedural and instruction manuals

Step 5: System Testing and Agency Preparation
Prepare system operators, users, and others to receive the system
Develop performance criteria and testing plan
Test input/output logic, programming, forms, operational procedures and practices, and the use of outputs in decision making
Educate and train system operators, data users, and others affected

Step 6: Conversion
Develop and approve conversion plan
Incorporate information system into standard operating procedures, for example, performance appraisals, new employee orientation
Reorganize staff and space if necessary
Convert from old to new equipment, new processing methods, and new procedures
Ensure all systems and controls are working

Step 7: Evaluation
Compare system performance with initial system objectives
Relate benefits and costs to initial estimates
Measure satisfaction with the system
Determine if system outputs are used in decision making
Examine if system improved performance, for example, client services

Step 8: Operation, Maintenance, and Modification
Complete standard operating procedures
Prepare backup and emergency plans and procedures
Complete documentation—instructions for adding to, deleting from, or modifying system
Begin Step 1 if additional subsystems are to be developed

Source: D. Schoech, L. L. Schkade, & R. S. Mayers. (1982). "Strategies for Information System Development." *Administration in Social Work, 5*(3), 25–26.

cial software or hiring a vendor may "contract out" some of the activities in some of the steps, especially in the detailed design phase, but all activities must be completed and documented. The information system development process is iterative. Each step builds on and amplifies activities of the previous step. For example, the first step, assessing preparedness and feasibility, must be given repeated consideration throughout the process. Although the development process may appear to be a precise science, at present it is more like a primitive art.

The successful development of an information system depends on many factors, such as the ease of programming a solution. The systems developed are often those that are most feasible rather than those that are most needed. Table 4 identifies the potential problems involved in developing an information system and lists problem indicators. Because one of the major problem areas concerns the selection of software and hardware, this area will be discussed in more detail.

Software and Hardware Selection.
Because software design and development is expensive, the use of commercially available

software can save money initially as well as for future maintenance and enhancements.

The first question to ask is whether a computerized information system is a necessary part of the solution to the problem. Currently, information systems work best with problems that are routine and repetitive. If software and hardware are required, the rule of thumb is to choose the software before choosing the hardware. This advice is hard to follow because hardware is more tangible, vendors prefer to sell hardware, and few vendors understand the human service software currently available.

In talking with vendors about software, it becomes apparent that different vendors use different terminology to describe the same thing. Often, the only way to compare products is to examine the specifications closely and to ignore advertisements, sales talk, and vendor's short demonstrations. National associations such as the National Council of Community Health Centers and the National Association of Area Agencies on Aging are a good source of software listings. Also, ask the vendor for a current list of users and randomly select several to be visited. Be sure that the vendor does not limit the list by

Table 4. Potential Problems in Developing an Information System

I. **Inadequate Overall Planning**
Indicators:
Lack of long-range goals and objectives for information system
Lack of specific system implementation plans
Overreliance on unconnected computer applications
Outgrowing agency's information system in 2 or 3 years
II. **Inadequate Communication, Involvement, and User Preparation**
Indicators:
Lack of well-established communication channels
Lack of a well-functioning, representative steering committee
Isolation of developers and designers from users
Fear that information collected will be misused
Lack of training for all potential users
System developers think the system is great, but users hate it
III. **Lack of Top-Level Commitment and Involvement**
Indicators:
No management control over system developers
Unstable funding
Lack of quality personnel to develop and manage the system
Blaming the computer for management problems
IV. **Inadequate System Management and Location in the Organization**
Indicators:
Computer system controlled by financial department
Power politics played by withholding access to the computer or to information
(continued)

Table 4. Continued

V. Inability to Determine the Cost-Benefit of an Information System
Indicators:
Lack of rules of thumb on when to computerize
Lack of model cost-benefit procedures to follow
Lack of definitions of information system's success
    Some possible measures are:
        Widespread use
        User satisfaction
        Timely, reliable, accurate system output
        Better decision making

VI. Inability to Support the Practitioner/Client Interaction
Indicators:
Inadequate measures of client outcome
Little consistency in the content of clinical records
Social work practice not seen as information based
Practitioners supply information, yet rarely use information system outputs

VII. The Computer Industry Is Always in a State of Rapid Change
Indicators:
Hardware will be dramatically cheaper if one waits
Lack of hardware/software standards
Frequent acquisitions and bankruptcies of computer companies
Frequent job changes among computer personnel

VIII. Difficulty in Obtaining Unbiased Information
Indicators:
Abundance of testimonials, lack of research
Research is outdated before it is disseminated
Most reliable information comes from vendors
Professional associations offer little guidance

IX. Inadequate Documentation
Indicators:
Lack of documentation on the information system's design, use, modification, repair
Not making organizational changes because it is too difficult to change the computer
    system
Inability to function when the computer breaks down
Panic when the system developer/programmer quits

recommending only a few possibilities. Also, check magazines and newsletters for software reviews. The flexibility and growth potential of a particular program are often as important as current performance.

Vendors have been known to attract buyers by advertising products that are not available. Waiting for a key piece of software that was ordered months in advance is a common situation. Vendors can also change products and marketing strategies and leave those waiting stranded. Thus, another rule of thumb is that software does not exist until it is running on the buyer's machine in the manner that the contract specifies.

Buying software can be compared to marriage in that the buyer and vendor enter into a long-term contract, especially if the software solves a substantial number of problems. Once made, software and hardware decisions are difficult and expensive to reverse. Before signing the contract, check out the company well and be sure that the contract is to your liking. If software is custom designed, an experienced lawyer or someone familiar with information system contracts should be consulted. As one clinical director noted, their contract was worth its weight in gold.

Guides To Success. Although many problems in developing information systems are difficult to overcome, overall guidelines for success do exist.

One of the major characteristics of success is adequate preparation and planning. Involvement is also key. Top management must show commitment by guiding the overall effort and placing the development function in a high-level department. Users and others affected must be kept informed and involved throughout the process, because an effective information system ultimately depends on users supporting their decisions with the information produced. Developing an information system should be a gradual process. One module should be implemented at a time, and the total process should be well documented. Continuity of system developers must be assured, but this is difficult with the scarcity and mobility of well-trained staff.

A third rule of thumb that summarizes the guidelines for developing successful information systems is that 10 percent of total resources should be spent on hardware, 40 percent on software, and 50 percent on development, implementation, and training. With current fiscal constraints, many fail to budget adequately for the intangibles associated with the latter component.

If the eight steps in the development process are completed successfully and the above guidelines are followed, many of the problems cited in Table 4 can be overcome. However, everyone involved must be willing to handle the extra work and frustration typically associated with developing an information system.

Impact and Issues

The change of information from handwritten to mechanically printed form had dramatic effects on society. The introduction of movable type by Gutenberg in the early 1400s, for example, is often credited as a cause of the Renaissance in the fourteenth to sixteenth centuries. The change of information from printed to electronic form is predicted to have similar effects.

One way to view this impact is to contrast the coming information society with industrial society. The essence of an industrial society is the capacity to produce mechanical power from other natural resources such as water, coal, and oil. The essence of an information society is the capacity to manipulate and move information in elec-

tronic form. The technologies of an industrial age are motors, systems of gears and levers, and other devices and processes for working with mechanical power. The technologies of an information age are computers, television, satellites, telephones, lasers, and other devices and processes for working with electronic information.

Technologies characterized by a rapid decrease in cost and a rapid increase in capacity potentially have the most impact on society. These two characteristics typify information technology. ENIAC, one of the first computers, cost approximately $400,000 when completed in 1946, occupied the equivalent of a three-bedroom house, weighed 30 tons, and performed 300 manipulations per second. Today, a briefcase-size computer weighing a few pounds that performs 15 million manipulations per second can be purchased for less than $2,000. Computers are predicted to be 1,000 times faster in the 1990s.

At the beginning of a technological revolution, it is difficult to see the impact new technologies will have on society. Those viewing the first steam engine, for example, could hardly envision industrial society. Nevertheless, it is interesting to speculate on the impact of the current technology on human services. This can be viewed from several perspectives: policy/planning, management, direct services, and clients.

Policy/Planning. The major impact of information systems at the policy/planning level will be better control and better use of the vast amount of information available for policy decisions. Because human service policy is developed through citizen boards and legislative bodies, which currently have little expertise in information management technology, qualified staff capable of developing and using information systems are needed. If the gap between policymakers and information technology is not bridged, policy will either be made by technicians or be established independently of the best available information.

The proliferation and connection of agency, state, and national databases will highlight the issues of access, security, confidentiality, and privacy. Access concerns the right of individuals to information and information technology. Security involves the physical protection of information using locks and other physical barriers. Confidentiality concerns the level of restriction placed on information—for example, a person may be able to read but not to change or delete certain parts of a client record. Privacy concerns a client's right to keep personal information secret. Theoretically, policymakers should take a preventive or proactive approach to these issues by establishing overall guidelines addressing the needs of professionals, citizens, and clients alike. However, in the fast-moving field of computers, policymakers typically react only after a situation becomes a severe problem. Thus, some of these issues will be resolved only by a slow step-by-step process with the final decision probably made in court.

New types of human service problems may develop in an information society. Because information is power and good information typically costs money, those with resources can acquire the power of information, leaving the poor and the disadvantaged further behind. Employment is seen as one area in which the issue of access will be played out. The disadvantaged may be destined to work in unskilled service jobs frequently eliminated by automation. Lack of access to technology and information may be a new problem and some traditional social work roles such as information broker may take on increasing importance.

Management. A major impact of information systems at the management level will be what is called the automated office or the integration of text processing, data processing, and telecommunications systems. Moving human service agencies into office automation will highlight existing agency problems. Administrators must determine how quickly to computerize their agencies, knowing that the introduction of new technology may be traumatic for staff in terms of time, effort, and morale.

Key issues will concern overcoming staff resistance to change, job displacement, and how much of the information system budget to allocate for confidentiality and security, especially when this means less money for system development and staff training. Privacy and access issues become more complex when agencies accept tele-

communications to help staff keep in touch with the agency database or to transmit information to funding sources. Because almost all security protection systems have been broken, the choice becomes one of either accepting risk, paying for expensive protection equipment and programming, or continuing to operate inefficiently without telecommunications.

Direct Services. The major impact of information systems at the level of direct services concerns the increasing use of automated data and information to support direct service decision making. It will take time to determine which social work functions are best performed by an expert computer system and which functions are best performed by human experts. One issue will concern the ability of workers to use their professional judgment in overriding computer-generated solutions to problems. For example, if a computer model used by a child welfare worker recommends that a child be withdrawn from the home, but the worker's professional judgment is to leave the child in the home and the child is later abused or killed, are the computer's recommendations confidential or can they be accessed and used against the worker in a malpractice suit?

Another group of issues concerns the role of the social work profession in developing or monitoring self-help software. Should the profession function as a consumer advocate and evaluate self-help software or should a "buyer beware" attitude be taken? Can the social work profession currently determine what is effective self-help treatment?

One privacy issue for direct service practitioners concerns their responsibility for protecting the level of confidentiality agreed to by the client even if client-identifiable information is forwarded to higher levels of the organization or other organizations for nonservice uses—for example, matching client names with bank account information to detect welfare cheaters. If a client is harmed by a breach of confidentiality and the client sues for personal damages, how much responsibility is borne by the practitioner who collected the information for not protecting the client's privacy?

Clients. The major impact of information systems for clients concerns the connection between the client and the service delivery system. This will increase as clients have better access to agency data and especially as agency information systems become accessible to clients through their telephone, television, and computer. For example, clients interactively communicating with agency information systems could access referral sources, complete intake forms, determine their eligibility for services, and use self-education and training programs.

A privacy issue concerns how much client-identifiable information an agency can capture from clients who use agency information systems and what can be done with the information collected. A confidentiality issue is whether an agency can withhold non–client-identifiable information from clients. For example, can agencies restrict access to detailed information on eligibility requirements to limit the number of clients applying for services? Agency information affects clients, yet clients have little input into the development of information systems and are infrequently represented in the debate on these issues.

Conclusion

Because large quantities of information are collected and used at all levels of the human service delivery system, present and future electronic information systems will have a dramatic impact on social work practice. However, some social work direct practice involves decisions so complex that it may take years for information support to be developed and for the resulting issues to be resolved. Nevertheless, even slowly evolving information technologies will add up to major changes in practice as social work enters the information age.

DICK SCHOECH

For further information, see COMPUTER UTILIZATION; INFORMATION SYSTEMS: CLIENT DATA; INFORMATION UTILIZATION FOR MANAGEMENT DECISION MAKING.

References
Greist, J. H., et al. (1983). "Computers and Psychiatric Diagnosis." *Psychiatric Annals, 13*(10), 785–792.
Hedlund, J. L., Vieweg, B. W., & Cho, D. W. (1985). "Mental Health Computing in the 1980s." *Computers in Human Services, 1*(1, 3–34; 2, 1–31).
Schoech, D., Schkade, L. L., & Mayers, R. S. (1982). "Strategies for Information System Development." *Administration in Social Work, 5*(3, 4), 11–26.
Schwartz, M. (Ed.). (1984). *Using Computers in Clinical Practice*. New York: Haworth Press.

For Further Reading
The following journals and newsletters contain helpful articles on the subject of information systems.
Bulletin on Science and Technology for the Handicapped (American Association for the Advancement of Science, Washington, D.C.).
Computers, Environment and Urban Systems (Pergamon Press, Elmsford, N.Y.).
Computers in Human Services (Haworth Press, Binghamton, N.Y.).
Computers in Human Behavior (Pergamon Press, Elmsford, N.Y.).
Computers in Psychiatry/Psychology (New Haven, Conn.).
Computer Use in Social Services Network (Arlington, Tex.).
Micropsych Network (Professional Resources Exchange, Sarasota, Fla.).

INFORMATION SYSTEMS: CLIENT DATA

Two distinct yet related developments make the 1980s unique in the design and use of client data information systems in public welfare. These developments are (1) the emergence of national voluntary data systems for several human service programs, and (2) the increased use of data from agency-based management information systems for research and evaluation. Given the current political climate and continued advances in computer technology, it is likely that these trends will continue.

National Voluntary Data Systems
The Reagan Administration's current policy of shifting the administrative responsibility for many human service programs from the federal to the state level has been accompanied by a significant reduction in federal reporting requirements. As a result, much of the human service program data once gathered, analyzed, and disseminated by the fed-

eral government is no longer available. For example, the Social Services Block Grant, enacted into law as part of the Omnibus Budget Reconciliation Act of 1981 (P.L. 97-35), eliminated the detailed federal reporting requirements mandated under Title XX of the Social Security Act. Similarly, in the field of child welfare, after passage of the Adoption Assistance and Child Welfare Act of 1980 (P.L. 96-272), an expected federal reporting system for child welfare was not implemented by the Reagan Administration.

Instead of mandated federal reporting, the assistant secretary for human development services (HDS), U.S. Department of Health and Human Services, decided to rely on a voluntary reporting system. As a result, the Voluntary Cooperative Information System (VCIS) was established in 1982 with funding assistance from HDS. Managed by the American Public Welfare Association (APWA), VCIS was designed to gather and analyze data voluntarily supplied by public welfare agencies in the areas of child welfare, block grants for social services, and mental retardation and developmental disabilities.

Since fiscal 1982, VCIS has gathered several types of data from public child welfare and social service agencies. In addition to publishing its own reports (American Public Welfare Association [APWA], 1983) on the summary of these data, APWA has shared the national VCIS data with federal agencies and state child welfare and social service agencies to meet their information needs. In 1984, for example, the U.S. Children's Bureau incorporated VCIS child welfare data, along with other data acquired through special projects, into a report to Congress on the status of the implementation of P.L. 96-272. Further, the bureau's research staff have routinely analyzed VCIS data and distributed the findings through the publication of a series of technical bulletins, *Child Welfare Research Notes.* On the whole, the use of VCIS national data at the state level is still limited, although a great deal of potential exists for the use of these unique data by state agency administrators and researchers.

Although VCIS has successfully demonstrated the viability of a voluntary data gathering approach as an alternative to federal reporting requirements, it is not the first attempt to develop national databases for social service programs. Since 1974, for example, the American Humane Association (AHA) has been collecting data on child neglect and abuse from public state agencies through voluntary data gathering. For its National Study on Child Neglect and Abuse Reporting, AHA has routinely collected and analyzed the data and published a statistical summary report each year. Over the years, the AHA data have effectively served the information needs of a variety of professionals, including state protective service agency administrators and social work researchers. The AHA data have been used by many researchers who have attempted to create a better understanding of child neglect and abuse problems (Russell & Trainor, 1984).

The National Reporting Program of the National Institute of Mental Health (NIMH) regularly collects a wide variety of statistical data from mental health facilities across the country. Unlike the national data systems mentioned previously, this voluntary reporting program is managed by the federal government. Using various survey methods, staff of the Survey and Reports Branch of the NIMH Division of Biometry and Epidemiology regularly collect data on patients, services, staffing, and expenditures from such facilities as psychiatric hospitals, community mental health centers, residential treatment centers, and psychiatric facilities operated by the Veterans Administration. The data collected are then analyzed and published in a series of statistical and analytical reports covering different topics. In addition, NIMH staff frequently conduct special analyses of these data to develop articles for publication in professional journals. Over the years, this reporting program has gathered comprehensive mental health data, which have been made available to researchers.

A number of other national data systems also exist. Among these are the National Data Base on Aging developed by the National Association of State Units on Aging and the National Association of Area Agencies on Aging with funding assistance from HDS, the Data Archive on Adolescent Pregnancy/Pregnancy Prevention and Family Planning funded by the U.S. Public Health Service, and the Voluntary Information System for Energy Assistance supported by the Office of Family Assistance in the Social Security Administration. Finally, these national data systems are supported by federal funds and collect data mainly from public agencies on a voluntary basis. There are no data systems on a national scale that gather child welfare or social service data only from voluntary and private agencies. However, it is important to note that voluntary and private agencies providing services through a purchase-of-service agreement generally submit their data to public agencies; thus these data become part of public agency data. For example, VCIS includes data on substitute care and adoption services reported by public child welfare agencies across the country.

Management Information Systems

Nearly 10 years ago, after completing an extensive longitudinal study of children in foster care in New York City, Fanshel and Shinn (1978) noted that

the locus of [future] research should be moved from a university base into the heart of practice and . . . data should be generated on a *routine basis* by service providers as service is delivered, rather than through the vehicle of special research "projects." (p. 501)

They also observed that "much of the fact-gathering undertaken by us was potentially within routine data-gathering capability of agencies" (p. 501). Despite the abundance of human service data that have since become available from state management or client information systems—now generally referred to as management information systems (MISs)—many states still rely on special projects to gather and analyze data for research and evaluation. Some agencies, however, have routinized the use of data from their MISs for research and evaluation purposes, either by management decision or state law. An increased number of researchers, based in both agencies and universities, have become proficient in using MIS data for their inquiries. Data are often downloaded from the mainframe computer to a microcomputer to make statistical manipulations easier. As the cost of installing microcomputers declines and more user-friendly software programs become available at reasonable prices, it is anticipated that more public welfare agencies will acquire microcomputers to support their management, research, and evaluation activities.

One public welfare agency that has developed a system to use MIS data routinely for analytical purposes is the Washington State Department of Social and Health Services. Under its Executive Management Summary Report System, the department routinely downloads mainframe data to a microcomputer that can summarize the data and generate graphs to be included in reports to top agency executives on a regular basis. The systematic downloading of various MIS data to a microcomputer and the extensive use of graphs in management reports make this system unique.

The Permanent Evaluation Information System of the Michigan Department of Social Services provides an example of MIS data being used exclusively for program evaluation and monitoring. Since 1983, this system has routinely generated status reports on various programs based on the summarization of data obtained from a variety of sources, including the agency-based MIS, related national studies, and special client surveys. A unique component of this system is that client outcome information is regularly included in the status reports in addition to the counts of clients served and services provided.

As the public welfare community has become increasingly interested in developing a permanent system of monitoring client outcomes, similar systems have been designed and implemented elsewhere in the country. For example, supported by a grant from HDS, Ramsey County, Minnesota, recently completed a computer-based evaluation information system dedicated solely to monitoring service outcomes. Similar developments have occurred in Colorado, Florida, Illinois, and Texas, to cite only a few. Although most public agency MISs are not dedicated solely to research purposes, MIS data are increasingly used for research and evaluation. As observed by Hoshino and Lynch (1981), secondary analyses of existing data from MISs and other databases are common in social work.

Technological Developments

Recent advances in microcomputer technology, along with the increased availability of software programs, have improved the use of human service data, resulting in new technological developments in the pubic welfare field. For example, on the national level, a significant technological break-through was achieved by the effective use of national VCIS child welfare data for evaluation purposes. APWA has also designed a new evaluation technology—Child Welfare Management Self-Evaluation Technology (CWMSET)—to assist state and local child welfare agencies in the regular monitoring of their program performance. Developed specifically for the data that states are reporting to VCIS, CWMSET is capable of generating, through manual computation or the use of customized software such as CWMSET-SOFT, 37 performance indicators that measure the status of program performance in substitute care and adoption services. These indicators, called CWMSET rates, include substitute care prevalence and incidence rates; entry, new entry, and reentry rates; multiple placement rate; substitute care exit rate; turnover rate; reunification rate; and adoption finalization rate.

CWMSET-SOFT is menu-driven, user-friendly software designed specifically to implement CWMSET technology and can be run on an IBM personal computer (PC) and other microcomputers compatible with IBM-PC hardware. Using this software, state and local child welfare agencies can compute their program indicators and compare them to appropriate national rates. This technology can serve as both a management diagnostic and an analytical tool for agency administrators to determine the strengths and weaknesses of their child welfare programs. Although CWMSET is applicable only to VCIS child welfare data, its concept can be used for other types of aggregate data that are routinely available from public welfare agencies.

Issues and Limitations

Hoshino and Lynch (1981) identified several methodological concerns as unique to the secondary analysis of existing data such as MIS data. These include "the issues of validity and reliability, the emphasis on inductive rather than deductive methods, and the problem of missing data" (p. 335). These concerns are also appropriate for professionals who use data from various national data systems such as VCIS because these systems comprise data primarily gathered from state MISs.

On the whole, the question of validity may not be critical in relation to national

aggregate data because most of these data are straightforward descriptions of facts such as counts and demographic characteristics of clients, types of services provided, and agency expenditures. However, some national data systems include client outcome data. The issue of validity could be a problem here because of the inherent difficulties associated with measuring the outcomes of public welfare services.

The reliability of national data, on the other hand, is tied to the question of how accurately and consistently data are downloaded from the agency's mainframe computer and then reported to national data systems, based on the instructions provided by the operators of these databases. Although VCIS data-gathering activities suggest no reason to doubt the accuracy of agencies' computer work, recent experiences indicate that errors can occur in interpreting the instructions and data specifications included in the data-gathering instrument. Over time, however, it is expected that the reliability of voluntarily gathered data will improve significantly as participating agencies become more familiar with the concept of voluntary data reporting and work cooperatively to meet the required data specifications.

Since most MISs do not exist primarily for research purposes, the involvement of researchers either in the selection of data to be included or in the determination of data collection methodology is generally minimal. It is also true, as Hoshino and Lynch (1981) suggest, that "[i]n secondary analysis, research questions tend to flow inductively from the data, in contrast to the more classical situation in which the research questions determine the types of data collected" (p. 335). Therefore, some researchers (particularly those interested in conducting basic deductive research) are likely to believe that the utility of secondary data is essentially limited to the inductive mode of inquiry and choose to collect their own data based on their research hypotheses. However, as MISs become more sophisticated—with inclusion of service performance and client outcome data (and as recognition of the costliness of original data collection grows)—the reliance of researchers on the routinely gathered data (for example, VCIS data) will increase and special data collection (particularly on a national scale) will become less frequent.

Another problem in the analysis of data from existing systems concerns missing data. Missing data are "facts" not recorded at the time of initial observation. Existing national data, which are based on MIS data from public welfare agencies, have missing data for most data categories. Unfortunately, missing data are not retrievable, so researchers must devise appropriate methods for handling them to minimize their effect. Although several sophisticated approaches are available (Elashoff & Elashoff, 1970; Miller, 1970), the most common method of dealing with missing data in social service research is to omit them from analysis. Unless the extent of missing data is disproportionately large in a given category, this method generally proves sound, although the population size to be included in analysis will be reduced.

One problem that is difficult to solve in a voluntary data-gathering effort is a lack of uniform definitions for certain data items. Although there are more similarities than differences among public welfare agencies in service delivery practice, differences do exist in defining, reporting, and collecting data on the services provided, the clients served, and the cost of services. The operators of most existing national data systems use a standardized data collection instrument. However, consistent with the spirit of voluntary data gathering, they permit participating agencies to define data in accordance with their own practices and procedures. As a result, it is difficult for these data systems to aggregate certain types of data to draw a national picture.

Finally, when analyzing aggregated client data through correlational methods such as regression analysis, researchers must avoid the "ecological fallacy" in interpreting their findings. The ecological fallacy occurs when one makes inferences about the behavior of individuals based on the results of statistical analysis in which the descriptive properties of groups are correlated (Robinson, 1950).

Since Robinson first pointed out a distinct difference between the correlations of data on the attributes of individuals (that is, individual correlations) and the correlations of data on the characteristics of groups (that is, ecological correlations), this fallacy has been widely recognized as one of the methodological errors to be avoided by social researchers. Thus, when the prevalence of foster care is examined using aggregate demographic or economic characteristics of regions or states, the findings should not be used to describe or infer the behavior of individuals. For example, a correlational analysis of the 1982 VCIS child welfare data (aggregated state by state) and female-headed family rates (computed state by state) revealed the existence of a fairly strong correlation between foster care prevalence and the female-headed family status—that is, $r = 0.65$ (AWPA, 1983). This finding only suggests that those states with a larger number of female-headed families had a larger foster care population than those with a smaller number of female-headed families. It cannot be used to infer the behavior of individual female-headed families with respect to foster care.

Ethical Problems

Although data in existing national client data systems for human services contain data that describe the characteristics of individual clients, these data are aggregated and client identifiers are not shown. In addition, most client data systems have developed procedures by which state-specific data can be released to researchers only on approval from state officials. Consequently, the issue of confidentiality is not a major concern for those who analyze aggregate data from these systems. Further, as a recent survey of the National Association for State Information Systems (1982) indicates, public welfare agencies that generate MIS data have developed stringent requirements for safeguarding the privacy of clients and the confidentiality of information gathered from clients. Public welfare agencies are particularly sensitive to the security of computerized client tracking systems that track service recipients on an individualized basis and are enforcing strict procedures whereby only authorized personnel have access to their computer system. On the whole, therefore, serious ethical problems concerning the use of national client data or state MIS data for research and evaluation have not arisen.

It is interesting to note, however, that public welfare agencies regularly release client information, mostly with the informed consent of clients, to other agencies as a matter of administrative routine. The information is generally used to assist agencies in determining eligibility for assistance or in setting payment levels. In addition, client information is frequently computer matched by programs to detect administrative errors or client fraud. The ethical problems related to these practices are still new to social work and are likely to be debated among concerned professionals in the future.

Finally, social work researchers who use existing data from client data systems must be familiar with the Code of Ethics of the National Association of Social Workers, which specifies the ethical principles to which all social workers are expected to conform in their conduct of professional activities. According to Schinke (1981), "As an integral part of social work, [ethics] foster research endeavors which are compatible with the profession's goals and values" (p. 70).

Implications for Social Work

Existing national client data systems and MISs in public welfare agencies provide social work researchers with a wide range of data on clients, services, and service costs. The uses of data from these sources are likely to increase as more social work researchers discover the usefulness of such data for their inquiries and as technologies for data utilization and dissemination (for example, downloading mainframe MIS data or online access to data in national client data systems) continue to improve and become more available. Despite some limitations, the data contained in national data systems or state MISs make possible various analytic activities that are best performed with large quantities of aggregate data.

The types of analysis requiring data from national client data systems or agency-based MISs include longitudinal studies, trends analysis, forecasting and prediction, simulation modeling, and dynamic movement analysis. National client data and MIS data can be used for both macro and micro analyses, as well as for theory building and theory testing, provided that researchers are able to obtain appropriate data for their specific research questions and remain flexible in adjusting their research designs to accommodate the conditions of the data. Had MIS data

been available, Fanshel and Shinn (1978) could have completed their longitudinal investigation of children in foster care in New York City more quickly. In addition to CWMSET, cited earlier, many other data utilization techniques are now available in the field of child welfare (Craft, Epley, & Theisen, 1980; Prosser, 1984). Most of these innovative techniques require a large volume of data that are not easily collected but are available from national client data systems or state MISs.

In terms of theory building, VCIS national data were recently used to develop a Population Flow Paradigm, which is an analytical model for examining the movement of children entering and exiting the substitute care system (Gershenson, 1984). Capable of computing such indicators as substitute care prevalence and incidence rates, recidivism rates, exit rates, and reunification and adoption rates, this paradigm has provided social work researchers with new opportunities for regularly examining the movement of children in the child welfare system and for assessing agency performance. Further, the existence of this model is expected to serve as an incentive for public child welfare agencies to move toward a more uniform collection of data.

Although national client data systems or agency-based MISs were not developed primarily for the benefit of researchers, it is clear that data from these sources will continue to provide social work researchers with ample opportunities for many types of research and evaluation activities. However, because these data systems exist primarily to benefit public welfare agencies, social work researchers must always be sensitive to the needs of agency management in formulating their research designs. It is likely that only those research and evaluation studies that are consistent with the management objectives of the agencies providing the data will gain support and be given access to data stored in national client data systems or state MISs. By carefully formulating their designs to complement agency objectives, social work researchers—through their scientific endeavors—can contribute significantly to the improvement of management and service delivery in public welfare.

TOSHIO TATARA

For further information, see COMPUTER UTILIZA-
TION; INFORMATION SYSTEMS: AGENCY; IN-
FORMATION UTILIZATION FOR MANAGEMENT
DECISION MAKING; PROGRAM EVALUATION;
VALUES AND ETHICS.

References

American Public Welfare Association. (1983).
*Characteristics of Children in Substitute and
Adoptive Care: A Statistical Summary of the
VCIS National Child Welfare Data Base.*
Washington, D.C.: Author.
Craft, J. L., Epley, S. W., & Theisen, W. M.
(Eds.). (1980). *Child Welfare Forecasting.*
Springfield, Ill.: Charles C Thomas, Pub-
lisher.
Elashoff, R. M., & Elashoff, J. D. (1970). "Regres-
sion Analysis with Missing Data." In R. L.
Basco (Ed.), *Data Bases, Computers, and the
Social Sciences* (pp. 198–207). New York:
John Wiley & Sons.
Fanshel, D., & Shinn, E. B. (1978). *Children in
Foster Care: A Longitudinal Investigation.*
New York: Columbia University Press.
Gershenson, C. P. (1984). "Population Flow Anal-
ysis of Social Service Systems." In *Proceed-
ings of the 23rd National Workshop on Wel-
fare Research and Statistics* (pp. 396–401).
Washington, D.C.: U.S. Department of
Health and Human Services.
Hoshino, G., & Lynch, M. M. (1981). "Secondary
Analysis of Existing Data." In R. M. Grin-
nell, Jr. (Ed.), *Social Work Research and
Evaluation* (pp. 333–347). Itasca, Ill.: F. E.
Peacock Publishers.
Miller, R. F. (1970). "Some Ways of Handling
Missing Data—A Case Study." In R. L.
Basco (Ed.), *Data Bases, Computers, and the
Social Sciences,* (pp. 177–197). New York:
John Wiley & Sons.
National Association for State Information Sys-
tems. (1982). *Information Systems Technol-
ogy in State Government.* Lexington, Ky.:
Author.
Prosser, W. R. (1984). "Foster Care Population
Flow Simulation Model." In *Child Welfare
Research Notes* (10, pp. 1–8). Washington,
D.C.: U.S. Children's Bureau.
Robinson, W. S. (1950). "Ecological Correlations
and the Behavior of Individuals." *American
Sociological Review, 15*(3), 351–357.
Russell, A. B., & Trainor, C. M. (1984). *Trends in
Child Abuse and Neglect: A National Per-
spective.* Denver, Colo.: American Humane
Association.
Schinke, S. P. (1981). "Ethics." In R. M. Grinnell,
Jr. (Ed.), *Social Work Research and Evalua-
tion* (pp. 57–70). Itasca, Ill.: F. E. Peacock
Publishers.

For Further Reading

Dery, D. (1981). *Computers in Welfare.* Beverly
Hills, Calif.: Sage Publications.
Fanshel, D. (Ed.). (1980). *Future of Social Work
Research.* Washington, D.C.: National Asso-
ciation of Social Workers.
Ginsberg, L. H. (1983). *The Practice of Social
Work in Public Welfare.* New York: Free
Press.
Schoech, D. (1982). *Computer Use in Human
Services.* New York: Human Sciences Press.
Schuerman, J. R. (1983). *Research and Evaluation
in the Human Services.* New York: Free
Press.
Slavin, S. (Ed.). (1982). *Applying Computers in
Social Science & Mental Health Agencies: A
Guide to Selecting Equipment, Procedures
and Strategies.* New York: Haworth Press.

INFORMATION UTILIZATION FOR MANAGEMENT DECISION MAKING

Basic hallmarks of a rational organization are
the maintenance of records and the use of
information to guide organizational behavior
and performance. Most management paradigms are based on the consumption and use
of information. Drucker (1970) has termed
the modern manager a "knowledge worker,"
thereby suggesting that information is the
principal management resource. Most information received by the manager is unsyste-
matic and comes from a wide variety of
sources, such as conversations with staff,
newspapers, memos, and discussions with
professionals in other organizations (Kaufman, 1973). The focus of this article, however, is on the use of systematically collected
information produced by management information systems and program evaluations.
The perspective is that information from
these sources can and should be used to
improve organizational performance and that
positive outcomes for clients are the central
performance concern. The article explores
the role information plays in management,
the current status of information utilization,
factors that have an influence on information
use, and the principles of effective information management.

Information and the Manager

The purpose of human service management is to contribute to the well-being of the organization and its clients. In this sense, the agenda of managers is the same as that of the front-line worker, but in practice, emphasis is usually placed on the differences, conflicts, and incompatibility of these two positions. As Patti (1984) proposes, "service effectiveness should be the principal criterion of a model of social welfare management practice. This would become the 'bottom line,' much as profit or market share serves this purpose in the business world" (p. 9).

A human service manager contributes to service effectiveness by using skills in program design, managing people, managing resources, and managing information (Rapp & Poertner, 1984). Without negating the human service organization's need for competent staff and more resources, organizational performance can be improved, and improved radically in some cases, by exploiting the power of information. The skillful collection and dissemination of information can create energy and motivation and can direct personnel toward activities that increase organizational performance (Nadler, 1977). Information can also help unify the agendas of organizational units and personnel as they focus their efforts on influencing certain indicators (Rapp & Poertner, 1983).

Peters and Waterman (1982) in their study of successful companies observed:

> We are struck by the importance of available information as the basis for peer comparison. Surprisingly, this is the basic control mechanism in the excellent companies. It is not the military model at all. It is not a chain of command wherein nothing happens until the boss tells somebody to do something. General objectives and values are set forward and information is shared so widely that people know quickly whether or not the job is getting done–and who's doing it well or poorly. (p. 266)

They also observed that the data were never used to "browbeat people with numbers." The data seemed to motivate by themselves. The organizational theorist Mason Haire, as quoted by Peters and Waterman (1982) observed that "what gets measured gets done" (p. 268). He suggested that the simple act of putting a measure on something is tantamount to getting it.

If funds are the lifeblood of an organization, then information is its intelligence. A provocative yet little-realized promise of computerized information systems and program evaluation is that they become a tool whereby the "learning organization" can improve its performance (Rapp & Poertner, 1983). A learning organization is one that takes periodic readings on its performance and makes adjustments so that performance is improved. This requires three elements: (a) the ability for multiple levels of personnel to collect, store, and retrieve performance information in an accurate and timely manner; (b) the ability to access information that would guide the selection of management action; and (c) the ability and motivation of these personnel to change and alter behavior based on the information.

The first element can be termed performance-finding or problem-finding information. Although the literature and curricula on management are replete with content on problem solving, relatively little attention has been devoted to problem finding. Yet a number of observers have argued that problem-finding skills are more potent predictors of successful managers than problem-solving skills (Mackworth, 1969; Livingston, 1971). Problem-finding information can be subsumed under performance finding. The goal is not just to locate inadequate performance but also to locate adequate and superior performance. These instances of accomplishment provide the successful ideas and the opportunity to reward personnel. Performance-finding information is necessary to prevent organizational crises, evaluate staff, and "keep the program ship on course."

The second element involves access to problem-solving information. Performance-finding information tells the manager little about what to do. Problem-solving information helps the manager decide on a course of action or a solution. It could include, for example, information on successful service programs, effective management practices, staff-training packages, or administrative regulations. Sources of problem-solving information range from colleagues and subordinates to journal articles, government publications, and research reports.

The third element focuses attention on the role of the manager. The learning organization requires not only adequate information, but also managers who are skilled and willing to translate information into action. In many cases, it is not a matter of the information being there, nor of mechanically getting the information to the manager; rather, the key element is the manager's ability to exploit it. A study of federal executives, for example, found that 44 percent of the respondents purposely discarded information relevant to their decision making (Caplan, 1975).

Computerized MIS

Computerized management information systems (MISs) are quickly becoming the principal mechanism for providing human service managers with program information. Early development of information systems was prompted by organizational "housekeeping" and reporting demands. Systems were developed to use large mainframe computers to increase the efficiency and accuracy of "getting out the checks" to clients, staff, and other agencies. Other well-established housekeeping functions include maintaining budget records, maintaining lists of provider agencies, and maintaining records of clients (Taber, Anderson, & Rapp, 1975). The large computer systems also allowed top-level administrators to marshal information needed by legislators, federal agencies, and other constituent groups more efficiently. After 20 years, the housekeeping and reporting functions of these systems are well established and well developed.

These benefits to the human service organization have come at great cost. One study estimated that 30 percent of patient day costs in a hospital could be attributed to the demands of information systems (Richart, 1970; Jydstrup & Gross, 1966). These computerized systems have often been burdens to lower-level personnel in human service organizations. These are the personnel who shoulder most of the responsibility for inputting, updating, and correcting the information; yet the systems have not produced benefits for them. Paperwork demands have now reached crisis proportions. The needless collection of information diverts precious time from services, lowers job satisfaction, reduces the likelihood of any information being used (information overload), reduces the accuracy of the information, and, through it all, decreases organizational performance. Lower-level personnel have often trans-

formed their frustration into efforts to sabotage the system (Taber et al., 1975).

These early systems also have been expensive and cumbersome, with redundant demands on organizational personnel. A typical pattern of development in large state human service organizations was to begin computerizing budgets, including payroll, expenditures, and income. Stimulated in part by the trend toward purchase of service, a second system was developed to monitor and reimburse other agencies for services. A third system to capture client records was added. The federal government then required states to document the amount of time workers devoted to specific activities, resulting in a fourth system. This process continued so that in 15 years, a state agency would have 6 to 10 separate systems that could rarely produce integrated reports and that required front-line workers to record identifying characteristics of cases six or seven times for each transaction. Regardless of the benefits, early computer technology was beyond the resources of most medium and small agencies.

The human services are entering a second era in computerized information systems, and it will look very different from the present situation. The coming of the second era is based on two developments. First, microcomputer technology allows small and medium-sized agencies to possess computer capabilities. With adequate software development, such machines will be able to generate reports, do word processing, maintain client records, perform some intake functions, and score standardized tests. Second, it is becoming clearer that information can be used as a management tool to improve agency performance and contribute to improved client outcomes. Business has been using information in this fashion for some time for marketing, scheduling, routing, and investing. Using information to improve program performance is vastly different from current applications in the human services and will be one of the hallmarks of second-era information systems.

The second era will also find computers on the desks of front-line social workers. These machines could be used for maintaining case records and caseload data. They could expedite the completion of forms and reports. They may well replace the file cabinet as the principal storage facility for direct service workers. Computers will not be alien machines or adversaries to these workers but friendly assistants in meeting their responsibilities to the organization and their clients.

Information Use

Despite the prominent role management theory ascribes to managers' use of information, the research suggests that, in practice, managers rarely use the information available to them. The most common complaint of program evaluators is that their results are not used. Weiss (1972) stated that the purpose of evaluation research is to

> . . .improve decision making, lead to the planning of better programs, and so serve program participants in more relevant, more beneficial and more efficient ways. . . . In these terms, the history of evaluation research to date has been disappointing. Few examples can be cited of important contributions to policy and program. (p. 3)

There are myriad examples of the nonuse of evaluations even when the results are clearcut and based on rigorous methodologies (Davis & Salasin, 1975; Rein & White, 1977). Rosenblatt (1968) found that social work practitioners have a low level of knowledge about research and consider it one of the last places to turn as a source of guidance for practice.

In terms of management information systems, even casual observation in most social service agencies shows that managers rarely use systematically collected performance information to direct their operations and inform their decision making (Rapp & Poertner, 1983). The research suggests that managers do not know what information they need or how to purposively use information (Ackoff, 1967). Managers do not engage in an analytic process of determining their information requirements and often delegate this task to information system technicians. The printouts received by managers rarely contain the information that managers need to make day-to-day decisions (Poertner & Rapp, 1980) and tend to obscure rather than illuminate (Janson, 1980).

A statewide study (Rapp, 1982) of a large human service organization found that responding managers occasionally (about 50 percent of the time) distributed reports to subordinates, discussed them with subordi-

nates, and engaged in problem solving with subordinates or superiors. Rarely (less than 50 percent of the time) did the respondents use the reports as a basis for evaluating and rewarding employees; requesting more resources; reallocating resources; revising methods, procedures, or policies; or improving the accuracy of the information. The findings suggest that when databased reports are used, they are likely to be used passively—distributed and discussed, for example. Rarely are the reports used for more aggressive management action, such as acquiring and allocating resources, rewarding employees, or revising procedures.

Factors in Information Use

There is a wide discrepancy between the importance ascribed to managers' use of information and the limited extent to which they use it. Four factors influence whether information is used: (a) organizational culture and contingencies; (b) the content of the information; (c) the format of the information; and (d) the skills, attitudes, and knowledge of the manager.

Organizational Culture. Whether data get interpreted and result in management action partly depends on organizational culture and the contingencies operating in the system. For example, managers of public child welfare agencies frequently receive data on the movement of children into and from foster care. Managers devote time to interpreting this data if superiors question their performance as inadequate or reward them for outstanding performance. Managers probably take action if their evaluations are partly based on the movement of children. In many agencies, however, the match between the data and the organizational contingencies is discrepant except for financial reports. For example, many employee evaluation systems still use dimensions such as punctuality, responsibility, and cooperation to rate employees (Wiehe, 1980) rather than performance related to the organization's mission.

The selection of performance measures has political as well as technical aspects. Organizational personnel tend to find security in broad and vague performance measures and therefore resist measures that are precise and that reflect client outcomes. Without the support of both top-level management and the "people in the trenches," any system of performance measures will be sabotaged and made ineffective. The design of a system must include the involvement of multiple layers of organizational personnel and allow for compromise in the selection of measures. The point is that when data reflect the organizational contingencies, the likelihood of managers spending time interpreting data and acting on it increases.

This dilemma is characteristic of the entire system of human services and contributes to the slow rise in concern about performance information in an organization or unit. As Herzlinger (1977) writes:

A major cause of the problem is the method of financing such organizations. Funding in block grants, which vary with neither volume nor quality of service and which are made before the work is done, does not reward effective and efficient performance and gives managers little incentive to encumber themselves with tighter controls. (p. 84)

Human service organizations are not rewarded for effectiveness, whether it is measured in terms of client satisfaction, client behavior change, or client status change. Administrators are rarely reprimanded or even questioned as to how many clients "improved." Staying within the budget, staying out of the press, and continuing to serve an adequate number of clients seems to suffice. Reports of the federal government are dominated by numbers concerning the number of clients served in various categories, the dollars spent, and the amount of service activity. Rarely do they reflect whether the services produced any benefits to clients. In contrast, businesses need to take careful periodic readings on production, quality control, share of the market, and profits if they are to survive.

Information Irrelevance. A second factor influencing a manager's use of information pertains to the content of the information. Concerning management information systems in the public sector, Herzlinger (1977) observed:

Nonprofit organizations do not lack data; if anything, they enjoy an overabundance of numbers and statistics. Rather, they lack *systematically* provided information to help management do its job. Without good information, it is obviously difficult for managers to make

reasoned and informed decisions, evaluate performance, motivate their employees, and protect the institution against fraud. (p. 81)

Managers do not receive information reflective of agency or program performance and therefore cannot use the information to enhance that performance. Until recently, conceptions of human service performance have been virtually nonexistent. Patti (1984) and Rapp and Poertner (1984) recently proposed virtually identical schema for human service performance. The performance areas are effectiveness, productivity and efficiency, acquisition of resources, and the satisfaction of staff and consumers. The number of clients served or the amount of service provided is the only performance area in which routine reporting is widespread.

Format of Reports. Managers' use of information is also influenced by how the information is presented. Human service managers are extremely busy people with a myriad of responsibilities and tasks. Time is rarely available for reading or contemplating. Yet research reports of a program evaluation usually exceed 50 pages and often exceed 100 pages. Databased reports produced by a management information system usually contain hundreds if not thousands of pieces of data under headings that are often unclear, and the reports provide no meaningful standards for comparing the data. Graphic portrayals of information are rare. In addition, the data are frequently irrelevant to the receiver's place in the organization. What is a local manager to do with data aggregated for an entire state? If information is intended to help managers improve their organization's performance, then that information must be presented in a form that is consonant with the manager's job, resources, and style (Rapp, 1984).

Skills, Knowledge, and Attitudes. The manager is the most powerful factor influencing the use of information. Information is useless unless managers know how to interpret and bring meaning to it and then act on it. Several studies show that certain professional groups have attitudes that discourage the use of data (Friel, Reznikoff, & Rosenberg, 1969; Reznikoff, Holland, & Stroebel, 1967; Rosenberg, Reznikoff, Stroebel, & Erickson, 1967). In this situation, resistance and lack of use would prevail even if all the other factors were facilitative. Training programs in agencies and as part of administrative curricula have not addressed the use of information to improve performance. The literature has few sources that speak directly to techniques for interpreting or using data-based management reports. The result is that such management skills and attitudes are based on a given manager's self-taught, on-the-job training, which, given the normal set of organizational contingencies, is rarely sufficiently developed.

The Effective Information Manager

Despite the largely disappointing current status of information utilization by human service managers, a set of principles for enhancing information utilization is beginning to emerge.

Principle 1. The purpose of the information should be to improve operations. Information gathering, storage, and reporting is a utilitarian enterprise, not an end in itself, and this requires that managers have a clear notion of the organization's mission and that they translate this mission into client outcomes and performance measures. The management information system must be designed to facilitate improvements in the organization's performance. The program evaluation should be designed to answer operations-related questions. Specific mechanisms need to be in place to ensure the connection between information specialists and applied personnel, both executive and field personnel (Rothman, 1980). This principle leads to the second.

Principle 2. Personnel assigned to operations must direct or at least be integrally involved in the design and implementation of the information enterprise. Decisions about the questions to be asked and the information to be collected cannot be delegated to technicians or specialists because their focus is not operations and leaving the design of the system to such technicians would heighten the probability of irrelevancy. The social work manager must be the primary person determining the information requirements.

Principle 3. Support and commitment from top-level administrators are necessary if the information is to be used. Specifically, the executive needs to be committed to improving the agency's performance and to the

value of information to this effort. There is some indication that less than a zealous commitment by the top executive officer can be tolerated if well-placed champions of the information enterprise have operations responsibilities (Patton et al., 1977; Peters & Waterman, 1982).

Principle 4. The content of the information must be consonant with organizational contingencies. Part of the reason for needing top-level support is that this person has considerable influence over the contingencies. A definition of organizational performance is necessary, along with a commitment to enhancing this performance, and supplying contingencies that encourage improved performance. The relationship between organizational contingencies and information is reciprocal, however, and one way to alter contingencies is to change the information collected and stored: "Studies have indicated that individuals, groups, and organizations tend to concentrate their energies and resources in those areas where data are collected, as opposed to those areas where there is no measurement or data collection" (Nadler, 1977, p. 59).

Principle 5. The products of the information enterprise should be formatted in a way that facilitates use. For evaluation research this means that the reports need to be written in nontechnical, clearly understood language and formatted for the specific audience (Rothman, 1980). Management information systems should produce reports characterized by clear labels, graphs, standards, and only the necessary elements (Rapp, 1982). In short, reports generated by evaluators and information systems should help direct and focus management attention and help motivate action.

Principle 6. The utilization of information is enhanced if the environmental/political context is supportive. Patton et al. (1977) found that political factors were the most frequently mentioned determinants of whether the results of evaluation research were used. This finding is not surprising because a primary source of organizational contingencies is the environment in which the agency operates. Davis and Salasin (1975) underscore the importance of the political context when they recommend opportunities for change:

The wise change consultant often will advise delaying the implementation of an idea until events occur which will increase the probability of adoption. Some common events having that effect include the arrival of a new leader, a new budget cycle, crises, new legislation, the availability of exciting and challenging practice techniques, mounting dissatisfaction with conditions, and even seasonal variations. (p. 645)

The political environment should not be viewed as a given, however. In the hands of a skillful manager, information products can be used to alter the environment—to gain support, change the political agenda, and so on.

Principle 7. Information utilization becomes manifest when the manager acts. The link between data and improved organizational performance is the manager's behavior. The information is useless unless it results in the receiver doing something. In general, three types of management activity can occur: (1) the manager can use the data as a basis for rewarding superior performers; (2) the manager can seek to acquire additional resources or reallocate resources in such a way as to facilitate improved performance; (3) the manager may prescribe new behavior by changing policies, procedures, job descriptions, a program's design, or the staff's training. As a basis for the behavioral prescription, the manager locates exemplary performers (staff, team, program) and seeks to incorporate elements of their practice in other units. The manager also locates inadequate performers and seeks to identify obstacles to better performance.

Principle 8. Information utilization for improved performance requires continuous audits of the measures used. The performance measures initially adopted may later be judged to be inadequate or misguided. How mistakes can be made is exemplified by the following:

In 1971, the New York Police Department announced changes in the operations of its narcotics squad. Before, the squad had worked under a quota system with each officer being put under pressure to make at least four arrests a month. The result was that the squad began arresting street corner peddlers, ignoring the complicated and time-consuming cases involving major dealers. The actual amount of drugs confiscated decreased. (Berkley, 1978, p. 310)

The moral of this story is that there are several ways of measuring a given phenomenon and that the selection of a particular measure cannot be a mechanical exercise. A poor selection of measures can lead to a waste of time and cause reduced performance. Therefore, the manager must monitor the measures used.

Principle 9. The only sure way of ensuring that a data set is reasonably accurate is for the manager to use it, regardless of its accuracy. The opposite response occurs frequently, whereby managers excuse the performance reflected by the data because "everyone knows it is inaccurate: the data was entered improperly, the program evaluators did not understand the program, my staff filled out the forms wrong, the computer is wrong. . . ." Many large public agencies routinely initiate data system cleanups. These activities consume large amounts of resources, which then cannot be used to serve clients. The results are always disappointing, leading to next year's cleanup. The best and only method for improving the accuracy of data is for the managers and their staffs to use it as if it were accurate.

Conclusion

The potential of information systems and program evaluations to assist human service managers in their efforts to improve organizational performance is an exciting one. The obstacle to fulfilling this promise is not technological but human and organizational. Management courses in social work and the relevant literature continue to be dominated by content focused on the technology of program evaluation and computers. Similar or perhaps greater attention must be devoted to the manager, through whom data becomes information to be used to improve services to clients.

CHARLES A. RAPP

For further information, see ADMINISTRATION: ENVIRONMENTAL ASPECTS; ADMINISTRATION: INTERPERSONAL ASPECTS; ADMINISTRATION IN SOCIAL WELFARE; INFORMATION SYSTEMS: AGENCY; INFORMATION SYSTEMS: CLIENT DATA.

References

Ackoff, R. (1967). "Management Misinformation Systems." *Management Science, 14*(4).

Berkley, G. E. (1978). *The Craft of Public Administration.* Boston: Allyn & Bacon.

Caplan, N. (1975). "The Use of Social Science Information by Federal Executives." In G. M. Lyons (Ed.), *Social Research and Public Policies* (pp. 46–67). Hanover, N.H.: Dartmouth College Public Affairs Center.

Davis, H. R., & Salasin, S. E. (1975). "The Utilization of Evaluation." In E. L. Struening & M. Guttentag (Eds.), *Handbook of Evaluation Research* (pp. 621–666). Beverly Hills, Calif.: Sage Publications.

Drucker, P. F. (1970). *The Effective Executive*. London, England: Pan Books.

Friel, P. B., Reznikoff, M., & Rosenberg, M. (1969). "Attitudes toward Computers among Nursing Personnel in a General Hospital." *Connecticut Medicine, 33*(May), 307–308.

Herzlinger, R. (1977). "Why Data Systems in Nonprofit Organizations Fail." *Harvard Business Review, 55*(1), 81–86.

Janson, R. L. (1980). "Graphic Indicators of Operations." *Harvard Business Review, 58*(6), 164–170.

Jydstrup, R. A., & Gross, M. J., (1966). "Cost of Information Handling in Hospitals." *Health Services Research, 1*(Winter), 235–271.

Kaufman, H. (1973). *Administrative Feedback*. Washington, D.C.: The Brookings Institution.

Livingston, J. S. (1971). "Myth of the Well-Educated Manager." *Harvard Business Review, 49*(1), 96–106.

Mackworth, H. J. (1969). "Originality." In D. Wolfle (Ed.), *The Discovery of Talent* (pp. 240–278). Cambridge, Mass.: Harvard University Press.

Nadler, D. A. (1977). *Feedback and Organization Development: Using Data-Based Methods*. Cambridge, Mass.: Addison-Wesley Publishing Co.

Patti, R. (1984, March). *In Search of Purpose for Social Welfare Administration*. Paper presented at the Annual Program Meeting of the Council on Social Work Education, Detroit, Mich.

Patton, M. Z., et al. (1977). "In Search of Impact: An Analysis of the Utilization of Federal Health Evaluation Results." In C. H. Weis (Ed.), *Using Social Research in Public Policy Making* (pp. 141–163). Lexington, Mass.: D. C. Heath & Co.

Peters, T. J., & Waterman, R. H. (1982). *In Search of Excellence*. New York: Harper & Row.

Poertner, J., & Rapp, C. (1980). "Information System Design in Foster Care." *Social Work, 25*(2), 114–119.

Rapp, C. (1982). *The Evaluation and Use of Information Services to Area Offices*. Lawrence, Kans.: School of Social Welfare, University of Kansas.

Rapp, C. A. (1984). "Information, Performance and the Human Service Manager of the 1980s: Beyond Housekeeping." *Administration in Social Work, 8*(2), 69–80.

Rapp, C. A., & Poertner, J. (1983). "Organizational Learning and Problem Finding." In M. Dinerman, (Ed.), *Social Work in a Turbulent World* (pp. 76–88). Silver Spring, Md.: National Association of Social Workers.

Rapp, C. A., & Poertner, J. (1984, March). *A Human Service Formulation for Management Education*. Paper presented at the Annual Program Meeting of the Council on Social Work Education, Detroit, Mich.

Rein, M., & White, S. H. (1977). "Can Policy Research Help Policy?" *Public Interest, 49*(3), 119–136.

Reznikoff, M., Holland, C. H., & Stroebel, C. F. (1967). "Attitudes toward Computers among Employees of a Psychiatric Hospital." *Mental Hygiene, 51*(3), 419–425.

Richart, R. H. (1970). "Evaluation of a Medical Data System." *Computer and Biomedical Research, 3*(4), 415–425.

Rosenberg, M., Reznikoff, M., Stroebel, C. F., & Erickson, R. P. (1967). "Attitudes of Nursing Students toward Computers." *Nursing Outlook, 15*(July), 44–46.

Rosenblatt, A. (1968). "The Practitioner's Use and Evaluation of Research." *Social Work, 13*(1), 53–59.

Rothman, J. (1980). *Using Research in Organizations*. Beverly Hills, Calif.: Sage Publications.

Taber, M., Anderson, S., & Rapp, C. A. (1975). *Child Welfare Information Systems*. Urbana, Ill.: University of Illinois.

Weiss, C. A. (1972). *Evaluation Research*. Englewood Cliffs, N.J.: Prentice-Hall.

Wiehe, V. R. (1980). "Current Practices in Performance Appraisal." *Administration in Social Work, 4*(3), 1–12.

INTERGROUP RELATIONS

Intergroup, or "race," relations—an issue of major concern today—was catapulted to center stage after World War II by the 1954 U.S. Supreme Court decision outlawing de jure school segregation. This decision led to numerous confrontations over the means to achieve school integration, such as busing and rezoning, and it also contributed to a resurgence during the 1960s of the civil rights movement. Nonviolent direct actions such as boycotts, sit-ins, marches, and demonstrations were used to attain equal access to jobs, voting, quality housing, and public accommodations.

In many Southern communities, these nonviolent protests were often met with violent resistance in the form of direct physical attacks, shootings, and bombings. In the North, however, black protests often took the violent form of large-scale civil disorders, including arson, looting, and outright guerrilla warfare. Although the civil disorders of the 1960s differed from the "classic" race riots of the past in that they involved mainly clashes between minorities and the police as opposed to clashes between white and black mobs of citizens, they were similar in that they left much destruction of life, limb, and property in their wake.

In 1968 the National Advisory Commission on Civil Disorders (popularly known as the Kerner Commission), appointed by President Lyndon B. Johnson to investigate the causes of ghetto rioting, predicted that the United States was dividing into two societies: one white and the other black. Several unfortunate developments during the 1970s and 1980s appeared to lend credence to this prophecy of increasing racial polarization: (1) the "benign neglect" policies of the Nixon-Ford administrations, (2) back-to-back recessions and double-digit inflation, (3) the disproportionate cuts in programs for the poor made by the Reagan Administration, and (4) the defection of many white liberals to neoconservatism because of sharp differences with minority groups over affirmative action, quotas, preferential college admissions, school busing, community control, and open housing. Thus, in spite of a national commitment to reduce racial and economic inequities, the racial gap in unemployment, poverty, and family income was wider during the first half of the 1980s than it had been a decade earlier. For example, between 1970 and 1982 the ratio of black to white family income fell from 61 to 55 percent, and the jobless rate for blacks rose from 1.7 to 2.4 times greater than that for whites.

Is this widening economic cleavage due to increased prejudice and discrimination on the part of white society? What changes have occurred in the attitudes of white Americans toward people of color? How successful have efforts been to enhance racial integration in schools, housing, employment, and public accommodations? Have increased interracial contacts in these settings reduced or exacerbated intergroup tensions and hostility? What new research insights have been gained about the causes and cures of intergroup conflict? In order to address adequately such questions about recent trends in intergroup relations, we must first provide working definitions of the key concepts involved.

Key Concepts

Intergroup Relations. "Intergroup relations" refers to the various types of contact between subordinate and dominant groups with different physical and cultural characteristics. Before the 1940s, "race relations" was primarily used, but because this terminology identified the "races" mainly as social rather than anthropological classifications and encompassed ethnic as well as racial groupings, it lost some favor (Barron, 1957; Wirth, 1945).

In order to incorporate both the racial and cultural dimensions of intergroup relations, a broader term, "minority group relations," was used to encompass two types of minorities—racial and ethnic. Racial minorities are classifications of subordinate groups based on their physical attributes (primarily skin color), such as blacks, American Indians, and Asian Americans. Ethnic minorities are classifications of subordinate groups based on their cultural attributes (nationality, language, and religion), such as Chinese, Haitians, Puerto Ricans, Irish, Poles, Jews, and Catholics. The term "white ethnics" has been reserved for Northern European nationalities. Although the U.S. government classifies most Hispanics as whites, they will be included here as a racial minority in references to "people of color" because many of them refer to themselves as "browns" or "nonwhites" and because they have had extensive intermixing with nonwhites (for example, Mexican Americans with American Indians and Cubans and Puerto Ricans with Africans). However, when the focus is on cultural attributes (language, religion, or nationality), Hispanics or any other racial minority will be classified as an ethnic minority.

Nevertheless, the term "minority group relations" also has one major shortcoming—its omission of the superordinate group, giving rise to the erroneous implication that its major focus is on interactions among minorities when, in fact, it is on inter-actions between minorities and dominant groups. Superordinate because of their polit-ical and economic superority, dominant groups are often called "majorities" because their numbers frequently exceed those of minorities. But size is only a correlate, not a determinant, of dominant or minority status. Groups may be majorities based on popula-tion size (such as the Bantu in South Africa) yet still constitute minorities because of their political and economic subordination.

Since the 1950s the term "intergroup relations" has had increasing popularity, since it encompasses both the racial and cultural attributes of minority and dominant groups as well as the interactions between them. Although the term "minorities" has recently been expanded to include groups that are discriminated against because of sex, age, physical handicaps, or sexual prefer-ence, it will be applied here only to groups that have been disadvantaged historically be-cause of their race, color, nationality, lan-guage, or religion. Therefore, "intergroup relations" may be operationally defined as contacts between minority and dominant groups of differing physical or cultural at-tributes in which minorities experience vary-ing degrees of racism (prejudice and discrim-ination). The ameliorative connotation of "intergroup relations" refers to activities that are designed to foster positive contact between minority and dominant groups by reducing racism (Lurie, 1972; Williams, 1947). Thus it is necessary also to define operationally two of the key components of intergroup relations: racism and intergroup contacts.

Racism. "Racism" refers to doctrines that assert the inherent superiority of partic-ular racial or ethnic groups over others. It is a form of ethnocentrism that perceives na-tionality, language, and religious minorities as well as racial minorities as "races" and ascribes their subordination to innately infe-rior physical and cultural attributes (Marrett & Leggon, 1979; Schermerhorn, 1970; van den Berghe, 1967; Wilson, 1973).

Racism is manifested mainly through prejudice and discrimination. Although "prejudice" and "discrimination" are often used interchangeably, there are substantive differences between them. "Prejudice" re-fers to negative values and beliefs about minorities, and "discrimination" refers to negative treatment of them (Allport, 1954); the former are hostile attitudes, and the latter are hostile actions or behaviors. Thus, one must distinguish clearly between racist atti-tudes (prejudice) and racist actions (discrim-ination).

One of the biggest misconceptions about intergroup relations is that prejudice and discrimination can only occur jointly (Simpson & Yinger, 1965). But, as Merton (1976) noted, there are four, not two, possible relationships between prejudice and discrim-ination: (1) the presence of both, (2) the absence of both of them, (3) prejudice with-out discrimination, and (4) discrimination without prejudice.

Virtually all the attention of commen-tators on intergroup relations has been on the first two relationships. This undue concentra-tion on the joint presence or absence of prejudice and discrimination makes the latter two relationships—prejudice without dis-crimination and discrimination without prej-udice—appear as anomalies. Prejudice with-out discrimination refers to situations in which prejudiced persons do not "act out" their intolerant attitudes because of such ex-ternal constraints as the threat of formal sanctions (for example, civil rights laws, af-firmative action mandates, or judicial injunc-tions) or the fear of informal sanctions (for example, social ostracism) by unprejudiced colleagues, neighbors, or friends.

Similarly, discrimination without prej-udice occurs when unprejudiced persons manifest discriminatory behavior out of fear of informal sanctions (such as ostracism, harassment, physical assault, property de-struction) from prejudiced colleagues, neigh-bors, and friends; laws, policies, and other formal practices that legitimize or condone intolerant behavior; or ignorance, when indi-viduals are unaware that their actions have discriminatory effects or consequences. This third factor introduces a dimension of dis-crimination that is rarely discussed—its in-dependent variation with motives and intentions. Most observers believe that dis-crimination can only result from prejudiced intentions. But discrimination can also be unintentional—that is, it can emanate from unprejudiced motives or attitudes (Feagin & Feagin, 1978; Friedman, 1975). For example, recent congressional legislation raising the eligible age for retirement at full Social Security benefits from 65 to 68 was enacted solely to increase the solvency of the Social Security Trust Fund for future retirees. Although this policy change was racially neutral in intent, its effect is unintentionally discriminatory against minorities with lower life expectancies than whites—especially black males, whose current life expectancy of 64 years already ensures that most of them will not live long enough to retire at full Social Security benefits.

Institutional Racism. In addition to identifying prejudice and discrimination as two basic components of racism, it is also important to underscore the fact that racism is not limited to individuals but may also result from the policies and activities of institutions and organizations (Carmichael & Hamilton, 1967; Knowles & Prewitt, 1967; Pettigrew, 1975). Thus, there are four forms of racism: (1) individual prejudice, or intolerant attitudes manifested by individuals toward minorities; (2) individual discrimination, or intolerant treatment of minorities by individuals; (3) institutional prejudice, or norms, values, and beliefs in the culture of the dominant society that are deemed superior to the norms, values, and cultural patterns of racial and ethnic minorities—a bias also known as "cultural racism" (Jones, 1972); and (4) institutional discrimination, or laws, regulations, and informal practices of organizations or institutions in the dominant society that produce or maintain differential negative treatment of minorities.

Feagin and Feagin (1978) subdivide institutional discrimination into two types—direct and indirect—based on intentions and motives. "Direct institutional discrimination" refers to bias by organizations or institutions of the dominant group whose intent is to discriminate against minorities. "Indirect institutional discrimination," however, refers to two kinds of unintentional bias: side-effect and past-in-present. "Side-effect discrimination" is used of practices in one institutional area that have a negative impact on minorities because they are linked to direct (intentional) discriminatory practices in another institutional area. For example, direct discrimination in the field of higher education may result in indirect discrimination in another area, such as employment, because minorities were denied equal access to certain educational qualifications.

"Past-in-present discrimination" refers to racially "neutral" practices in an institutional area that indirectly and unintentionally have differentially negative effects on minorities because of past intentional discrimination in the same institutional area. For example, past discriminatory practices that denied minorities equal access to entering certain industries and occupations may prevent them from having sufficient seniority or work experience for promotions to many higher-level positions.

Domination Contacts. Contacts between minority and dominant groups are characterized along two dimensions: (a) extent of domination and (b) extent of integration (Wilson, 1973). Domination encompasses three kinds of superordinate policies toward minorities.

Oppression. Oppression seeks to reduce intergroup hostility and conflict by suppressing most rights and liberties of minorities through force and intimidation. Examples of oppression include slavery in the United States, apartheid in South Africa, and repressive dictatorships.

Accommodation. Accommodation seeks to reduce intergroup hostility and conflict through "reactive" strategies—that is, dilatory concessions, negotiations, and other compromises. Examples of accommodation include laws or edicts that desegregate without integrating, civil rights laws that are passed but not enforced, and token hiring of minorities.

Cooperation. Cooperation seeks to reduce intergroup hostility and conflict through "proactive" strategies—that is, positive initiatives designed to achieve parity for minorities. Examples of cooperation include laws, edicts, or voluntary efforts to achieve racial balance in schools or neighborhoods; and the use of affirmative action goals, timetables, and quotas.

Integration Contacts. Integration refers to the proximity of minority and dominant groups along three dimensions: institutional, cultural, and biological (Gordon, 1964). "Institutional integration" denotes the relative degree of participation and advancement of minorities in the social, economic, and political institutions of the wider society. "Cultural integration" (or "acculturation") refers to the degree to which minority and dominant groups acquire one another's cultural patterns. "Biological integration" (or "amalgamation") refers to the extent of physical mating between minority and dominant groups. Three types of superordinate policies toward minorities concern institutional, cultural, and biological integration.

Separatism. Separatism involves high degrees of institutional exclusion, cultural supremacy, and biological separation. Examples of separatism include apartheid in South Africa, de jure school segregation, de facto residential segregation, and occupational segregation.

Pluralism. Pluralism involves moderate degrees of institutional inclusion and cultural coexistence, and maintains a high degree of biological separation between minority and dominant groups. Examples of pluralism include desegregated school systems, fair housing practices, and observances of the cultural heritage of minorities.

Assimilation. Assimilation involves high degrees of institutional inclusion, acculturation, and amalgamation between minority and dominant groups. Examples of assimilation include "unidirectional acculturation"— that is, minority groups voluntarily or involuntarily adopt the cultural patterns of dominant groups; and "reciprocal acculturation"—that is, minority and dominant groups come to acquire some of each other's cultural patterns.

Recent Trends

The dominant trends and patterns in intergroup relations in the United States in recent decades tend to fall into four categories: (1) shifts in intergroup attitudes, (2) shifts in intergroup conflict, (3) shifts in intergroup accommodation, and (4) shifts in intergroup integration.

Intergroup Attitudes. According to opinion polls and surveys, the United States has experienced a dramatic decline in prejudicial attitudes toward racial minorities over the past 40 years. Between 1942 and 1984, for example, the proportion of whites favoring integrated schools soared from 30 to 90 percent (Smith & Sheatsley, 1984). Similarily, the proportion of whites willing to accept a

black neighbor of comparable economic status on their block jumped from 35 to 84 percent between 1942 and 1972; and the proportion of whites who believe that blacks are inferior to whites fell from 31 to 15 percent between 1963 and 1978 (Pinkney, 1984).

Although such trends seem to show a sharp increase in racial tolerance, many analysts caution against misconstruing them as manifesting a significant decline in racism (Jackman, 1973; Sigall & Page, 1971). In fact, proponents of "modern" or "symbolic" racism contend that antiblack feelings are still pervasive in America, but that socially undesirable "redneck" beliefs have been replaced by intense hostility to racial "symbols," such as busing, affirmative action, quotas, open housing, welfare, and illegal immigration, which can be justified on nonracial grounds. Contemporary racism is difficult to measure because it is often disguised or unconscious. (Kinder & Sears, 1981; McConahay, Hardee, & Batts, 1981; McConahay & Hough, 1976; Ward, 1985).

The continuing significance of racism is also said to be manifested in differential support for broad goals of racial equality and specific measures to achieve them. For example, 9 out of 10 whites favor integrated schools, but only one-fourth support busing to attain that end (Smith & Sheatsley, 1984). Although 93 percent of whites support the right to vote, only 57 percent approve of federal voting rights legislation. And 88 percent approve of equal employment opportunity, but only 62 percent approve of the federal fair employment legislation (Austin, 1976).

Furthermore, a significant decline in prejudicial attitudes does not necessarily mean that there has been a sharp drop in discriminatory behavior (Wicker, 1969). Unfortunately, data on national trends in intolerant behavior are virtually nonexistent because most pollsters and analysts concentrate solely on monitoring intolerant attitudes (Hill, 1984). However, there are data regarding the differential perception of discrimination by whites and blacks. Because whites believe that blacks have made major progress in achieving equality, they perceive very little racial discrimination today. On the other hand, because blacks believe that only limited advances have been made, they perceive a high degree of discrimination.

Although 74 percent of blacks think they are discriminated against in getting white-collar jobs, only 28 percent of whites think blacks are discriminated against in this area. And, whereas 58 percent of blacks think they are discriminated against in trying to get decent housing, only 23 percent of whites agree. Similarly, 45 percent of Hispanics find they are discriminated against in getting decent housing, but only 29 percent of whites agree that this is so. (Harris, 1978). In 1979, 64 percent of all blacks believed there was "a great deal" of racial discrimination in the United States (National Urban League, 1980).

Intergroup Conflict. Since the 1950s the issues that have generated most interracial conflict have been largely sectional. In the South, racial confrontations have focused on school desegregation, public accommodations, and voting rights, whereas intergroup strife in other parts of the country has centered around such issues as police brutality, job discrimination, open housing, immigration, and anti-Semitism (Newman et al., 1978).

In the South the civil rights movement took as its number one priority the dismantling of the "Jim Crow" laws of the 1890s, which required racial separation in almost every realm of life. The major techniques used to accomplish that goal were nonviolent: litigation, negotiation, boycotts, sit-ins, wade-ins, picketing, rallies, and mass marches. The death knell for "separate but equal" public accommodations was rung after a year-long Montgomery, Alabama, bus boycott by the Supreme Court's decision of December 1956 outlawing segregation in public transportation. Two months after the brutal "bloody Sunday" attack by Alabama state troopers on 500 black marchers from Selma to Montgomery on March 7, 1965, the U.S. Congress passed the Voting Rights Bill by an overwhelming margin.

Massive violent and nonviolent resistance by white Southern officials and citizens to the 1954 Supreme Court school desegregation decree had resulted in very little racial integration in public schools for almost a decade. But by the second half of the 1960s, nationwide civil rights demonstrations and protests led to vigorous enforcement efforts by the executive and judicial branches of government. As a result, the proportion of black students attending schools with whites in the South soared from 1 to 39 percent between 1964 and 1968.

In the North, however, the most violent racial confrontations occurred between the police and racial minorities. Over 250 civil disorders erupted in black and Hispanic communities across the nation between 1964 and 1967—and the overwhelming majority were sparked by encounters with the police. And, less than a month after the Kerner Commission issued its report, the assassination of Martin Luther King, Jr., ignited disorders in over 100 communities. During the 1960s, too, several civil rights organizations, notably the Congress of Racial Equality (CORE), used nonviolent techniques to fight employment discrimination in the North. Consequently mass demonstrations and sit-ins were held at numerous construction sites in inner-city areas to protest the paucity of minorities in skilled union jobs. Selective buying campaigns were also leveled against corporations and other businesses that failed to employ adequate numbers of minorities. In addition to protesting busing plans at Northern schools, demonstrations by white citizens were mainly in opposition to various open housing measures. For example, whites in Newark, New Jersey, and Forest Hills, New York, bitterly fought attempts to place low-income housing in their communities, and whites in the all-white Chicago suburb of Cicero launched counterdemonstrations against civil rights marchers in their community.

Because of the sharp growth in their population resulting from high birth rates and immigration (legal and illegal), Hispanics increasingly became the objects of ethnic scapegoating and hostility. This surge was greatest during the 1970s—a decade of back-to-back recessions and double-digit inflation—and Hispanics were vulnerable to charges of taking jobs away from "real" Americans. Thus, in addition to persistent harassment from Immigration and Naturalization Service (INS) agents, many Hispanics were subjected to various forms of hostility and discrimination in their neighborhoods, on the job, in school, and in public facilities. Such widespread mistreatment of Hispanics led to a resurgence of older civil rights groups, such as the League of United Latin

American Citizens (LULAC), and to the formation of more militant organizations, such as the Mexican American Legal Defense and Education Fund (MALDEF), the National Council de la Raza, and the Forum of National Hispanic Organizations.

Another contributory factor in increasing intergroup conflict during the 1970s was the resurgence of anti-Semitism. According to data compiled by the Anti-Defamation League (ADL) of B'nai B'rith, the number of anti-Semitic episodes (that is, verbal and physical assaults on Jewish individuals, organizations, homes, businesses, and synagogues) spiraled from only 49 in 1978 to 829 in 1982, (Perlmutter & Perlmutter, 1982). Because of the geographic distribution of the Jewish population, about two-thirds of these incidents occurred in the Northeast and in California. In part, this rise in religious bigotry can be traced to an expansion of activities by the Ku Klux Klan and neo-Nazi organizations in the North and the South. Klanwatch groups and state advisory committees to the U.S. Commission on Civil Rights have reported increasing numbers of Klan and Nazi sympathizers—if not a rise in actual membership—across the nation. As was true during past economic downturns, these hate groups have succeeded in exploiting the fears of many economically insecure Americans by scapegoating racial and religious minorities (U.S. Commission on Civil Rights, 1983).

Intergroup Accommodation. Most efforts to reduce intergroup conflict have been accommodative, taking the form of partial concessions or compromises. Such accommodation by the dominant group is characterized by five types of responses: (1) establishing study commissions, (2) passing laws with little enforcement, (3) expanding education and training programs, (4) expanding income maintenance programs, and (5) token compliance.

The establishing of high-level study commissions has been a typical response to most of the major racial disorders in the United States—Chicago (1919), Harlem (1935), and Detroit (1943). Thus President Johnson appointed the Kerner Commission in 1967 to study the ghetto disorders of the 1960s. Similarly, in the wake of the assassinations of Dr. King and Robert Kennedy in

1968, he also set up the Eisenhower Commission to study political violence and assassinations. The impact of such study panels is questionable, since in several instances (for example, the Kerner Commission) their recommendations were ignored or rejected by the president who appointed them. Their primary function has been to attempt to reassure the general public and the aggrieved minority that some action is being taken to prevent recurrence of disorders and violence.

A second response has been to enact laws to combat racial and ethnic discrimination but to provide minimal resources for enforcement or to assume a passive role, relying primarily on voluntary compliance. Throughout the 1970s, the U.S. Commission on Civil Rights conducted a series of comprehensive studies on the work of federal agencies charged with enforcing civil rights laws. It concluded that federal civil rights enforcement was characterized by inaction, indifference, and lack of coordination (U.S. Commission on Civil Rights, 1981a). For example, many agencies such as the Equal Employment Opportunity Commission (EEOC) and the Office of Federal Contract Compliance (OFCC) were underfunded and often lacked the status and authority needed to discharge their responsibilities. Overlapping responsibilities of civil rights programs in the departments of Health and Human Services, Education, and Justice also seriously weakened the overall civil rights efforts of the federal government.

A third strategy to reduce intergroup hostility and conflict is to expand education and training programs for minorities. In part, such programs are intended to counter charges that minorities are not denied opportunities because of their race or ethnicity but because of their lack of education and skills. Consequently, a major feature of the War on Poverty was the proliferation of educational and work experience programs: the Job Corps, the Neighborhood Youth Corps, on-the-job training, apprenticeships, classroom training, the Public Employment Program, and the Work Incentive Program (WIN) for welfare recipients. Unfortunately, many minority individuals remained unemployed or underemployed after receiving training in many of these programs. However, many preschool programs (such as Head Start) and college-oriented efforts (such as Upward

Bound, open enrollment, compensatory education, and Basic Opportunity Education Grants) have had greater success in providing upward mobility for many disadvantaged minorities.

The expansion of income maintenance programs has been another strategy for reducing intergroup hostility and conflict. Several analysts contend that one reason for the sharp rise in the welfare rolls during the 1960s and 1970s was an attempt to defuse the momentum of the civil rights movement (Piven & Cloward, 1971). According to this view, because American society was not prepared to provide racial minorities with viable employment opportunities, public assistance programs were expanded (to include food stamps, Medicaid, Supplemental Security Income, and so on) to maintain minorities in a poverty status. Although other factors (such as a vigorous welfare rights movement, periodic recessions, inflation) also contributed to a rise in the number of welfare recipients since the 1960s, the latent function of attempting to defuse racial unrest and interracial conflict must be considered.

A fifth accommodative response to intergroup hostility has been token compliance. Primarily manifested in hiring, enrolling, or promoting a few members of minority groups to give the appearance of full affirmative action compliance, it is also referred to as "window dressing," because the minority individuals may be placed in conspicuous positions (for example, community relations liaison, in front of TV cameras, or as a "visible" receptionist).

Intergroup Integration. Although responses to minority demands for racial equality were predominantly accommodative, until the 1980s the federal government did undertake vigorous actions to achieve racial integration in various aspects of American life. Not only were pioneering antibias laws enacted in the areas of employment, voting rights, public accommodations, housing, and education, but stronger enforcement provisions were added by the legislative, judicial, and executive branches of government. However, gains in some areas were eroded by strong opposition from some administrations to particular desegregation strategies (for example, President Nixon against school busing and President Reagan against affirmative ac-

tion). In fact—in addition to destroying the effectiveness of the U.S. Commission on Civil Rights by appointing a majority of commissioners who vigorously oppose court-sanctioned affirmative action—President Reagan has publicly committed himself to overturning all voluntary and court-ordered affirmative action programs that use quotas. Thus, the momentum toward racial integration slowed during the 1980s (Dunbar, 1984; Pinkney, 1984).

To what extent have governmental antidiscrimination efforts achieved greater integration of racial minorities into American society? Has there been an increase in positive social contacts between whites and minorities?

In order to examine the extent of integration of racial minorities, we will focus primarily on two dimensions: cultural and institutional. "Cultural integration" (or "cultural assimilation") refers to the degree to which minority and dominant groups acquire one another's cultural patterns and "institutional integration" (or "structural assimilation") denotes the degree of participation and advancement of minorities in the economic, political, and social institutions of the dominant society (Gordon, 1964).

The status of cultural integration of racial minorities in America today is best described as "cultural pluralism"—moderate degrees of acculturation coexisting with distinctive customs, languages, and lifestyles. Because blacks were forced to divest themselves of many of their African traditions under slavery, they have adopted more of the cultural features of white Americans than have other nonwhite minorities. Nevertheless, some African customs and characteristics survive in black religion, music, art, cooking, and family life (Blauner, 1972, Herskovits, 1941). Moreover, it should be understood that acculturation is a two-way process. Consequently, white Americans have also acquired many of the cultural patterns of minorities, particularly in the areas of music, art, cooking, and speech. For example, the nationwide break-dancing fad was started by black and Hispanic youth in low-income areas of New York City.

Living on reservations under intense racial exclusion, American Indians were able to retain much of their cultural heritage. But those who left the reservations—currently the majority—were more likely to adopt the culture of white Americans than those who remained. As voluntary immigrants to this country, Hispanics and Asian Americans reflect some of the cultural variations of traditional immigrants. First-generation immigrants are more likely to retain original cultural traditions than are subsequent generations. However, because of continuing racial segregation and discrimination, second- and third-generation Hispanics and Asian Americans are more likely to maintain their cultural distinctiveness than are second- or third-generation European immigrants. Moreover, for second- and third-generation Puerto Ricans and Chicanos, retention of their cultural patterns is also facilitated by geographic proximity, allowing them to return frequently (Graubard, 1981).

The degree of institutional integration of racial minorities today can best be described as "institutional pluralism"—the coexistence of parallel institutions, many of which developed in response to legalized racial segregation. As those barriers fell, some structures were integrated out of existence, especially among black businesses, colleges, and hospitals. For example, mergers of many black and white schools and colleges resulted in the loss of jobs and authority for hundreds of black educators.

Because the main thrust of desegregation efforts has been in education, housing, and employment, the following discussion will focus on these three areas. Unfortunately, however, because of the paucity of relevant data for Hispanics, Asian Americans, and American Indians, much of the assessment will necessarily have to deal with black Americans.

Integration in public schools has increased most in the South, in small to medium-size cities, in cities with relatively small proportions of minorities, and in districts under court orders to desegregate. According to a recent analysis of school integration trends in central city districts of the nation's 100 largest metropolitan areas, the bulk of the increase occurred in the South, leveling off or declining in the North (Farley, 1984). For example, although the proportion of whites attending schools with black students jumped from 11 to 38 percent in the South between 1967 and 1978, the proportion in the North dipped from 37 to 36 percent. Thus, public

schools in the South are more likely to be integrated than those in the North (U.S. Commission on Civil Rights, 1981b). A major reason for continued racial isolation of central city schools in the North was the movement of whites to suburban districts—a movement that is often referred to as "white flight."

Without in-depth analysis of the 1980 census, it is not possible to make a definitive assessment of the extent of residential integration in central city and suburban neighborhoods. However, an analysis of residential segregation for the 25 central cities with the largest black populations in 1980 revealed mixed patterns (Farley, 1984). Neighborhood segregation declined sharply in five cities (Houston, Dallas, Oakland, Jacksonville, and Richmond) between 1970 and 1980, remained virtually unchanged in five cities (New York, Chicago, Washington, D.C., St. Louis, and Newark), and rose in two others (Philadelphia and Cleveland).

Nevertheless, national surveys of blacks and whites suggest that there has been some increase in residential integration during the 1970s. For example, the proportion of blacks reporting contacts with white neighbors jumped from 29 to 38 percent between 1970 and 1978, and the proportion of whites reporting contacts with black neighbors rose from 10 to 16 percent (Harris, 1978).

These surveys also reveal a rise in racial integration in employment. The proportion of blacks with white coworkers went from 59 to 66 percent between 1970 and 1978, and the proportion of whites with black coworkers soared from 32 to 49 percent. Similarly, although the proportion of blacks with white supervisors remained virtually unchanged between 1970 (68 percent) and 1978 (67 percent), the proportion of whites with black supervisors jumped from 6 to 25 percent. Evidently, there was a sharp increase in the number of black managers and foremen with white subordinates during the 1970s.

One of the largest increases in racial contacts occurred in social relationships. The proportion of blacks with white friends rose from 39 to 49 percent, but the proportion of whites with black friends doubled (from 20 to 40 percent) between 1970 and 1978. And the overwhelming majority of these interracial contacts have been positive. Over 90 percent of whites report having pleasant contacts with blacks as coworkers, neighbors, and friends, and 80 percent or more of blacks report having pleasant contacts with whites in these areas (Harris, 1978).

Some of these pleasant social contacts have apparently contributed to a rise in interracial marriages. Between 1970 and 1980, the number of black-white couples spiraled from 65,000 to 166,000, most of them reflecting a sharp increase in the number of black husbands with white wives. In fact, the proportion of interracial couples consisting of black men and white women went from 63 to 72 percent between 1970 and 1980. Thus, the proportion of all black men who were married to white women doubled (from 2 to 4 percent) over that decade. Consequently, although the number of interracial marriages has risen among blacks, they still constitute less than 5 percent of all black marriages (U.S. Bureau of the Census, 1981).

Research on Intergroup Conflict

What research insights have emerged about the sources of and remedies for intergroup conflict? Intergroup relations research tends to fall into three categories based on unit of analysis: individual, group, and institutional. Before the 1960s, most race relations studies were psychological—that is, they focused primarily on the prejudicial attitudes of individuals and groups. Since that time, however, such studies have become more sociological, focusing increasingly on the discriminatory actions of groups and institutions (Pettigrew, 1975).

Sources of Conflict. The popular social-psychological theories of the causes of racial hostility are frustration-aggression, displacement, and projection. According to the frustration theory, racial prejudice results from the inability of dominant group individuals to fulfill important personality needs because of the perceived culpability of racial minorities. Displacement (or "scapegoating") occurs when dominant group individuals transfer hostility from the true source of their frustration (for example, alleged unemployment because of "illegal aliens") to minorities. "Projection," on the other hand, refers to the transference of hostility toward one's in-group to an out-group. Since these may be two-way processes, it is also possible for minority group members to displace or

project their frustrations onto dominant group members (Simpson & Yinger, 1965). But there are many deficiencies in such theories. They fail to explain why specific minorities are singled out and others are not or why—under various social contexts—frustration often does not lead to aggression.

Because of the failure of individual-level theories of racial hostility, group-level theories gained increased currency. These, too, tend to fall into three categories: social, cultural, and situational.

Proponents of social group theories usually attribute intergroup hostility to membership in particular socioeconomic classes. And although most studies of racial attitudes have found increasing levels of education to be correlated with declining levels of racial prejudice, some studies of religious bigotry have found anti-Semitism to rise with increasing education (Perlmutter & Perlmutter, 1982; Stember, 1961). Cultural group theorists, however, focus on conflict between groups arising from membership in different ethnic, religious, or regional groups. Thus, Southerners exhibit more racial prejudice than Northerners, and non-Jews exhibit more prejudice than Jews. Interestingly, although "white ethnics" (that is, Irish, Italians, and Poles) are often reputed to be more prejudiced than white Protestants, most empirical studies have found the reverse to be true—even in the North (Hill, 1975).

Situational group theorists focus on the extent to which the nature and degree of intergroup hostility vary in different group contexts (such as in one's home, in one's neighborhood, in a public facility, in a private club, or at one's place of employment). These studies have found, for example, wide variations in discrimination by highly prejudiced individuals in different group situations (Simpson & Yinger, 1965).

But institutional theorists argue that the major determinants of intergroup hostility are such broad societal factors as urbanization, industrialization, automation, immigration, recessions, inflation, the media, and the sexual revolution. For example, researchers have found direct correlations between hostility and cycles of economic recessions (Simpson & Yinger, 1965; U.S. Commission on Civil Rights [U.S. CCR], 1983). But this thesis fails to explain wide variations in intergroup hostility among different individuals and groups exposed to the same societal forces.

Most social scientists today realize that intergroup prejudice and discrimination cannot be explained sufficiently on only one level—whether individual, group, or institutional. Consequently, contemporary race relations theories attempt to incorporate features from all three levels (Blalock, 1967; Simpson & Yinger, 1965; Wilson, 1973). Unfortunately, however, there is a dearth of empirical studies of race relations that attempt to test these theories using data from individual, group, and institutional levels simultaneously (Hill, 1984).

Conflict Resolution. Research on the resolution of intergroup conflict is sparse in the race relations literature. Most studies have focused more on the causes of racial hostility than on factors responsible for its amelioration. Similarly, there are many more case studies on intergroup strife and discord than there are on intergroup cooperation and harmony. Research on the resolution of racial hostility falls into four categories: (1) studies of programs to reduce individual prejudice, (2) studies of programs to reduce group prejudice, (3) studies of strategies to reduce situational discrimination, and (4) studies of strategies to combat institutional discrimination.

According to syntheses of race relations research by Williams (1947, 1977), Rose (1947), and Simpson and Yinger (1965), the overwhelming majority of studies on conflict resolution have concentrated on educational programs to reduce individual prejudice. These programs have attempted to change prejudicial attitudes through information, persuasion, exhortation, socialization, and individual therapy. On the other hand, programs to combat group prejudice have relied more on widespread media propaganda campaigns and the promotion of interracial contacts in schools, churches, public facilities, and so on.

Educational programs have been most effective in reducing individual prejudice when they place greater emphasis on characteristics that groups have in common rather than on their differences; when they are aimed at individuals with an intermediate attitudinal position rather than those at either extreme; when learners are convinced from the outset that they are not under attack for their opinions; when learners are allowed initial free verbal expression of their hostilities to instructors who maintain an atmosphere of calm objectivity; when information is presented in the context of a group's carrying out its usual social function; and when learners are able to participate actively in gathering the relevant information (Williams, 1947).

Intergroup contacts are likely to be most effective in reducing individual and group prejudice under these conditions: (1) equality of status in the immediate situation; (2) a situation of contact encouraging or requiring mutually interdependent relationships; (3) social norms favoring intergroup association and equalitarian attitudes; (4) characteristics of participants contradictory to negative stereotypes; (5) a setting that promotes intimate rather than distant or casual association (Williams, 1977, p. 274).

Programs to reduce situational discrimination have been most effective in settings that involve mutual cooperation in the attainment of group goals or the accomplishment of group tasks (especially in school, work, and military settings); with cooperating groups that are successful in task performance; with groups that are highly rewarded as such; with groups that display low intragroup competition; with groups that have relatively high rates of participation in decision making; and with groups that encourage the development of competence in all members (Williams, 1977).

Legislation, executive fiat, administrative regulations, confrontation, lobbying, and other constraints have been the primary governmental strategies for reducing discrimination in American institutions. Research studies have revealed that these measures are most effective when authority is clear and explicit, demands accountability, provides legitimacy for obedience, provides strong motivation for compliance, and uses sanctions for noncompliance. On the other hand, threats or demands by minority groups tend to be most effective when goals or objectives are specific rather than diffuse; when minorities are perceived as having the capacity or constituents to carry out its threats; when both groups have a common set of central values and beliefs; and when authorities believe that failure to satisfy all the demands would be more harmful politically than pursuing an alternative course of action (Wilson, 1973).

Social Work Role in Intergroup Relations

In the formative years of the social work profession, social reform was an overriding concern. Thus social workers were in the vanguard of efforts to improve relations between racial, ethnic, and religious groups in America. In 1910, white and black social workers formed the National Urban League as a "bridge" between the races. To combat anti-Semitism and other religious bigotry, social workers were instrumental in setting up such groups as the Anti-Defamation League of B'nai B'rith, the American Jewish Committee, and the National Conference of Christians and Jews. These organizations have relied primarily on education, research, and mediation as strategies for fighting racial and religious bigotry.

However, as the number of social workers spiraled, increasing emphasis was placed on internal professional concerns at the expense of external concerns such as racial inequality. In fact, a major premise of social work practice was that most race relations problems could be resolved by infusing minorities and the poor with "middle-class" values. It soon became evident, however, that these disadvantaged groups already had strong achievement and work ethics and that racism could only be eradicated by changing the attitudes, norms, and actions of victimizing individuals, groups, and institutions.

Thus, it was not coincidental that the community action programs of the War on Poverty were modeled on activist inner-city programs (such as Mobilization for Youth and Haryou-Act) set up by social service professionals. Social workers also provided invaluable assistance to such groups as the National Welfare Rights Organization and La Raza in their efforts to enhance the political and economic clout of minorities and the poor.

Numerous social service organizations adopted a more activist posture during the 1960s. For example, after 100 years of pioneering efforts in social work, the Community Service Society of New York City abandoned its case work practice to focus on institutional change through action research, lobbying, and other forms of advocacy on behalf of the racially and economically disadvantaged. The civil rights movement also produced a wide range of minority caucuses to combat racism within the helping professions. The National Association of Black Social Workers in particular became an important catalyst for institutional reform in social work.

Over the past two decades, many national social service and welfare organizations, notably the National Association of Social Workers, have made important strides toward increasing the profession's responsiveness to the concerns of racial minorities. But much more needs to be done. By sharply increasing the number of minority students and faculty and by making social work education more relevant to contemporary and emerging needs, the profession must insist that schools of social work no longer be unwitting allies of institutional racism. Moreover, social workers must renew their original commitment to the achievement of a just and equitable society for all groups in America (Goodman, 1973).

ROBERT B. HILL

For further information, see AMERICAN INDIANS AND ALASKA NATIVES; ASIAN AMERICANS; BLACKS; HISPANICS; IMMIGRANTS AND UNDOCUMENTED ALIENS; MEXICAN AMERICANS; MINORITIES OF COLOR; PUERTO RICANS; RACIAL DISCRIMINATION AND INEQUALITY; WHITE ETHNIC GROUPS.

References

Allport, G. W. (1954). *The Nature of Prejudice*. Reading, Mass.: Addison-Wesley Publishing Co.

Austin, B. W. (1976). "White Attitudes Toward Black Discrimination." *Urban League Review, 2*(1), 37–42.

Barron, M. L. (1957). *American Minorities*. New York: Alfred A. Knopf.

Blalock, H. M. (1967). *Toward a Theory of Minority Group Relations*. New York: Capricorn Books.

Blauner, R. (1972). *Racial Oppression in America*. New York: Harper & Row.

Carmichael, S., & Hamilton, C. (1967). *Black Power*. New York: Vintage Books.

Dunbar, L. W. (Ed.). (1984). *Minority Reports: What Has Happened to Blacks, Hispanics, American Indians and Other Minorities in the Eighties*. New York: Pantheon Books.

Farley, R. (1984). *Blacks and Whites: Narrowing*

the Gap? Cambridge, Mass.: Harvard University Press.

Feagin, J. & Feagin, C. B. (1978). *Discrimination American Style: Institutional Racism and Sexism.* Englewood Cliffs, N.J.: Prentice-Hall.

Friedman, R. (1975). "Institutional Racism: How To Discriminate Without Really Trying." In T. F. Pettigrew (Ed.), *Racial Discrimination in the United States* (pp. 384–407). New York: Harper & Row.

Goodman, J. A. (1973). *Dynamics of Racism in Social Work Practice.* Washington, D.C.: National Association of Social Workers.

Gordon, M. M. (1964). *Assimilation in American Life.* New York: Oxford University Press.

Graubard, S. (Ed.). (1981). "American Indians, Blacks, Chicanos and Puerto Ricans [Special issue]." *Daedalus, 3*(2).

Harris, Louis, and Associates. (1978). *A Study of Attitudes Toward Racial and Religious Minorities and Toward Women.* Report prepared for National Conference of Christians and Jews, New York.

Herskovits, M. (1941). *The Myth of the Negro Past.* New York: Harper & Bros.

Hill, R. B. (1975). "Who Are More Prejudiced: WASPs or White Ethnics?" *Urban League Review, 1*(1), 26–29.

Hill, R. B. (1981). *Economic Policies and Black Progress: Myths and Realities.* Washington, D.C.: National Urban League.

Hill, R. B. (1984). "The Polls and Ethnic Minorities." *Annals, 472,* 155–166.

Jackman, M. R. (1973). "Education and Prejudice or Education and Response Set?" *American Sociological Review, 38*(3), 327–339.

Jones, J. M. (1972). *Prejudice and Racism.* Reading, Mass.: Addison-Wesley Publishing Co.

Kinder, D. R., & Sears, D. C. (1981). "Prejudice and Politics: Symbolic Racism Versus Racial Threats to the Good Life." *Journal of Personality and Social Psychology, 40*(3), pp. 414–431.

Lurie, W. A. (1972). "Intergroup Relations." In *Encyclopedia of Social Work* (16th ed., pp. 668–676). New York: National Association of Social Workers.

Marrett, C. B., & Leggon, C. (Eds.). (1979). *Research in Race and Ethnic Relations.* Greenwich, Conn.: JAI Press.

McConahay, J. B., & Hough, J. C., Jr. (1976). "Symbolic Racism." *Journal of Social Issues, 32*(2), 23–45.

McConahay, J. B., Hardee, B. B., & Batts, V. (1981). "Has Racism Declined in America?" *Journal of Conflict Resolution, 25*(4), 563–579.

Merton, R. K. (1976). "Discrimination and the American Creed." In R. K. Merton (Ed.), *Sociological Ambivalence and Other Essays*

(pp. 189–216). New York: Free Press. A Division of Macmillan Publishing Co., Inc.

National Urban League, Research Department. (1980). "Initial Black Pulse Findings." *Black Pulse Bulletin, 1.*

Newman, D. K., et al. (1978). *Protest, Politics and Prosperity: Black Americans and White Institutions 1940–75.* New York: Pantheon Books.

Perlmutter, N., & Perlmutter, R. A. (1982). *The Real Anti-Semitism in America.* New York: Arbor House.

Pettigrew, T. F. (Ed.). (1975). *Racial Discrimination in the United States.* New York: Harper & Row.

Pinkney, A. (1984). *The Myth of Black Progress.* New York: Cambridge University Press.

Piven, F. F., & Cloward, R. A. (1971). *Regulating the Poor.* New York: Pantheon Books.

Rose, A. (1947). *Studies in the Reduction of Prejudice.* Chicago: American Council on Race Relations.

Schermerhorn, R. (1970). *Comparative Ethnic Relations.* New York: Random House.

Sigall, H., & Page, R. (1971). "Current Stereotypes: A Little Fading, A Little Faking." *Journal of Personality and Social Psychology, 18*(2), 247–255.

Simpson, G. E., & Yinger, J. M. (1965) *Racial and Cultural Minorities: An Analysis of Prejudice and Discrimination* (3rd ed.) New York: Harper & Row.

Smith, T. & Sheatsley, P. B. (1984). "American Attitudes Toward Race Relations." *Public Opinion, 7*(5), 15–53.

Stember, C. H. (1961). *Education and Attitude Change.* New York: Institute of Human Relations Press.

U.S. Bureau of the Census. (1981). *Statistical Abstract of the United States, 1981* (Table 55, p. 41). Washington, D.C.: U.S. Government Printing Office.

U.S. Commission on Civil Rights. (1981a). *Civil Rights: A National Not A Special Interest.* Washington, D.C.: U.S. Government Printing Office.

U.S. Commission on Civil Rights. (1981b). *With All Deliberate Speed: 1954–19??.* Washington, D.C.: U.S. Government Printing Office.

U.S. Commission on Civil Rights. (1983). *Intimidation and Violence Racial and Religious Bigotry in America.* Washington, D.C.: U.S. Government Printing Office.

Van den Berghe, P. (1967). *Race and Racism: A Comparative Perspective.* New York: John Wiley & Sons.

Wicker, A. W. (1969). "Attitudes Versus Actions: The Relationship of Verbal and Overt Behavioral Responses to Attitude Objects." *Journal of Social Issues, 25*(4), 41–78.

Williams, R. M., Jr. (1947). *The Reduction of*

Intergroup Tensions (Bulletin 57). New York: Social Science Research Council.

Williams, R. M., Jr. (1977). *Mutual Accommodations: Ethnic Conflict and Cooperation.* Minneapolis: University of Minnesota Press.

Wilson, W. J. (1973). *Power, Racism and Privilege: Race Relations in Theoretical and Sociohistorical Perspectives.* New York: Free Press.

Wirth, L. (1945). "The Problem of Minority Groups." In R. Linton (Ed.), *The Science of Man in the World Crisis* (pp. 347–372). New York: Columbia University Press.

INTERNATIONAL SOCIAL WELFARE: COMPARATIVE SYSTEMS

Comparative analysis of social welfare systems assumes special significance in an increasingly complex world. This article includes discussion of (1) comparative analysis, (2) issues in comparative social welfare, (3) selected social welfare services in different countries, and (4) emerging similarities and differences among nations.

A relatively new interdisciplinary and multisystems field, comparative social welfare involves varied orientations, complex dimensions, and differential processes. Estes (1984a) defines comparative social welfare as

a discrete field of inquiry aimed at understanding patterns of national and international social provision that develop in response to the recurrent social risks to which people are exposed irrespective of the social, political, or economic systems under which they live, e.g., poverty, hunger, illness, disability, early death, survivorship. (p. 57)

Comparative social welfare is concerned with the structural differences of various social welfare systems. The study of similarities and differences forms a logical basis for the classification, analysis, and conceptual synthesis of differential systems. Methodologically, although intrinsically related to each other, comparative social welfare differs from international social work: comparative social welfare offers a conceptual and analytical tool, and international social work provides content relating to social work practice in a variety of countries. This view is supported by Falck (1969). Sanders and Pedersen (1984) endorse this distinction:

The term "international" describes the content that is to be taught, whereas the term "comparative" refers to a methodological tool of comparative analysis. . . . It is helpful then . . . to view international as the content or the substance of the knowledge that is taught, and comparative as a conceptual tool (including models and frameworks) used to organize and analyze knowledge. (p. xv)

Eckstein and Apter (1963) observe: "Science begins with the effort to order and classify the objects of the universe. This is the job of comparison, but comparison is not limited to the purely classificatory. It can, and must, be used as a method for determining useful theories" (p. vi). Comparative analysis is thus an essential and useful step in the scientific method. In natural and sociobehavioral sciences, the construction of theoretical and empirical models involves the application of comparative logic, directly or indirectly, at different levels. International social work and comparative social welfare systems are mutually supportive concepts. They provide methodologically consistent foci for analysis. The logic of comparison is primarily based on judgmental rationality; therefore the commonality of cross-cultural experiences, global intersystem linkages, and universal interdependences constitute the base for developing a philosophy of comparative social welfare, which is yet in a nascent phase (Mohan, 1984). Comparative analysis makes dialectical thought possible; also, comparison precedes refutation (Mohan, 1985c).

Social scientists make effective use of comparative designs to study social phenomena cross-culturally. Whiting (1964) developed a technique in which crime could be studied by taking each society as a single case. According to Bacon, Child, and Barry (1963),

Some of the cultural features which may be related to crime show wider variations among societies than within a single society, permitting a more comprehensive test of their significance. Results which are consistent in a number of diverse societies may be applied to a great variety of cultural conditions instead of being limited to a single cultural setting. (p. 291)

Social scientists' application of comparative analysis is particularly visible in comparative politics (Eckstein & Apter, 1963; Kalleberg, 1966; Ward, 1964), comparative social administration (Rodgers, Greve, & Morgan, 1968; Donnison, 1965), and comparative social welfare and social policy (Heidenheimer, Helco, & Adams, 1975; Higgins, 1981; Kahn & Kamerman, 1977; Kaim-Caudle, 1973; Madison 1980; Martin, 1972; Midgley & Hardiman, 1982; Mishra, 1981, 1984, in press; Mohan, 1985a, 1985b; Seigel & Weinberg, 1977; Woodsworth, 1977). Pioneering contributions of Burns (1949, 1956, 1985), Jenkins (1969), Kahn & Kamerman (1975, 1977), Titmuss (1958, 1968, 1974, 1976), Wilensky and Lebeaux (1965), and Wilensky (1975) have stimulated scientific inquiry and understanding in the field of international social work and comparative social welfare. A review of these studies and other comparative researches (Sanders & Estes, 1984) suggests that this extensive area of inquiry is a gold mine of unexplored facts and theories and a challenging opportunity for collaboration. If "social welfare is the care and nurture of the freedom of man" (Grange, 1974, p. 207), comparative social welfare is nothing but transcendence—"a passage toward other beings" (Grange, 1974).

Comparative social welfare analyzes attributive variables of welfare systems. It attempts to unravel the human conditions, policies, institutions, values, resources, methodologies, and delivery systems of various societies, analyzing different dimensions of and approaches to complex social issues and problems. Comparative knowledge implies awareness of the world of different peoples and of historicopolitical processes and arrangements through which varied societies and cultures have sought to live with one another in different places and times. Comparative analysis cannot be a value-free exercise because certain human conditions and societal arrangements are studied within a "comparative-analytic framework" (Mohan, 1985b) that is based on metavalues. If social misery, for example, is the focus of comparative analysis, it involves a critical-evaluative stance for the analysis of such

historicosocietal forces as colonialism, imperialism, and fascism.

Issues in Comparative Social Welfare

As Roman emperor Marcus Aurelius observed in the second century A.D.,

> [Examine] thy own ruling faculty and that of the universe and that of thy neighbour: thy own, that thou mayst make it just; and that of the universe, that thou mayst remember of what thou art a part; and that of thy neighbour, that thou mayst know whether he has acted ignorantly or with knowledge, and that thou mayst also consider that his ruling faculty is akin to thine. (Eliot, 1980, p. 269)

The importance of a cross-national perspective on social welfare is gaining increased recognition, and social scientists are increasingly using this perspective as they become aware of the limitations of their national frames of reference (Madison, 1980). Worldwide experiences with welfare needs, social problems, and populations and with delivery systems and material and nonmaterial resources reflect common concerns pertaining to the social welfare programs and policies. Many of the issues analyzed in the 1980s reveal the failures and advancements of the twentieth-century social welfare systems.

A review of comparative research reveals that comparative social welfare issues fall into three categories: operational, ideational, and quality-of-life issues. Operational issues relate to the methodological, organizational, and structural aspects of different systems (Armer & Grimshaw, 1973; Kaim-Caudle, 1973; Thursz & Vigilante, 1975). Ideational issues relate to conceptual, normative, and cognitive processes (Mishra, 1984; Przeworski & Teune, 1970). Quality-of-life issues involve social indicators relative to the quality of life in different countries (Baster, 1969; Cox, 1970; Drenowski, 1974; Estes, 1984b; Morris, 1979; Myrdal, 1968; Sheldon & Moore, 1968; United Nations [U.N.], 1964). Contemporary comparative issues should be posited in the context of three assumptions:

1. The unity-in-diversity paradigm is useful in efforts to recognize the uniqueness of each comparable unit in a heterogeneous world.

2. The purpose of comparative analysis is humane, neutral, and rational.

3. Comparative scholars deal with relevant issues calling for concerted societal efforts and effective social intervention.

These postulates set forth a frame of reference for analyzing basic issues. The following questions delineate some areas of concern: Has social welfare, as an institution, come of age? Does the sociopolitical environment promote quality-of-life issues? Is the social welfare system functioning effectively? Are there conscious efforts to improve human and societal conditions? Attempts to answer these questions may yield voluminous and pretentious theses in different societies. Comparative analysis, however, seeks to "refute" these "conjectures" (Popper, 1963) in light of the societal context and universal norms.

Thursz and Vigilante (1975) identified five major issues that relate to basic social service needs in nine countries. The issues include: (1) universalism versus selectivity, (2) centralization versus decentralization, (3) public versus voluntary systems, (4) workforce issues, and (5) community care versus institutional care. Most of the issues relative to social services concern social allocations, social provisions, delivery systems, modes of finance, and policy formulation (Gilbert & Specht, 1974).

Obviously, the eligibility, nature and amount of benefits, methods of financing, and administrative organization have served as the guiding reference for the analysis of social provisions (Burns, 1949). Issue analysis, in the comparative field, is a sensitive, tedious, and technical task. A cross-national study, for example, may not present conceptual-methodological problems if it is confined to standard economic indicators. It may, however, turn out to be an awesome task if the subject is human rights. The complexity of variables and their interrelatedness makes the analysis of issues an extremely difficult endeavor. The analysis presented here represents this author's descriptive-analytic perspectives on six important social welfare issues that call for comparative study: (1) crisis of the welfare state and modes of intervention; (2) relative progress of nations; (3) organization and structure of programs, policies, and planning; (4) approaches to social problems; (5) educational and personnel issues; and (6) the problem of values.

Welfare State and Modes of Intervention. Welfare states throughout the world are in disarray. Even the concept of the welfare state is in jeopardy, as Mishra (1984, pp. xiii–xiv) comments:

> The techniques of state intervention in the market economy developed in the postwar years—conveniently labelled as Keynesianism—seem to work no longer. Indeed Keynesian forms of intervention in the economy increasingly appear as a part of the problem rather than the solution. More generally, the effectiveness of state action and therefore also its scope is in question. . . . The legitimacy of the welfare state is in serious doubt.

Mishra (1984) contends that postwar Britain, which once served as a model of the welfare state, has increasingly turned into its opposite and that Fabian reformism, with its piecemeal social engineering, has tended to isolate social welfare from wider structures of society. The reformist programs have not been conducive to cross-national analysis.

Social welfare varies with time and place. It has emerged as a dynamic developmental, institutional force in recent decades; however, it is not yet free of its residual and pejorative character. Although modern, industrially advanced capitalist countries seek more effective alternatives to residual and institutional modes of intervention, the Third World still clings to its pejorative, residual, reformist, and incremental strategies. At issue is the developmental status of the welfare state.

Has social welfare come of age? Titmuss (1963) once observed that welfare state is a term of abuse or an article of faith, depending on one's political beliefs. In many nations, political realities are changing fast, and the politics of comparison influence the modes of intervention selected: "international comparisons are used in the political processes which surround the evolution of domestic policies" (Parker, 1983, p. 7). Because domestic issues in both the East and the West influence the international social climate, comparisons of regional as well as general strategies and resources will strengthen international operations.

International issues, on the other hand, affect domestic policies and programs that call for pragmatic changes. Social welfare systems continue to be in a state of flux.

Politicoeconomic considerations outweigh societal needs, expectations, and commitments.

Relative Progress of Nations. Becker (1968) contends that the idea of progress must be reintroduced into the human sciences and that it must be properly interpreted. The science of people in society, he observes, "must be a superordinate value science; one which has opted for human progress, and which has a clear and comprehensive, compelling idea of what constitutes such progress. The task of such a science would be the incessant implementation of human wellbeing" (p. xiii). Advancement of technology does not ensure human progress and welfare. Nations of the world, both poor and rich, are pursuing scientific goals devoid of human values and the result is a massive global social "illfare." Countries that need to feed the hungry and solace the deprived are spending more and more on guns. A study by Brown (1984) shows that the "guns versus butter" issues have created a dangerous situation: Global military spending has gone up 20 percent in the past four years. Third World countries now spend more on the import of arms than on the import of grain. As a result, many national populations are poorer and hungrier, but better armed. The advanced nations are caught in a superpower conflict that compels them to prepare for "star wars" at the expense of general social well-being. Global progress has become a conflict-ridden strategy rather than a commonly agreed-upon goal.

Organization and Structure. Social welfare programs, according to Romanyshyn (1971), perform three important functions: (1) social provisions, or the quest for social security and social justice, (2) social services, or the quest for an adequate socialization structure, and (3) social action, or the quest for community and a better polity. Most of the issues in contemporary comparative social welfare deal with the functions and performance of social programs. Although policymaking and planning are the conventional processes used to change, implement, and enhance program performances, different societies are resorting to different approaches to accomplish these goals. All these approaches are, however, "caught between so-cial welfare's conservative function of helping to maintain the social system and its innovative function of helping to adapt social institutions to new conditions and higher aspirations for the self-fulfillment of all" (Romanyshyn, 1971, p. 153). Capitalistic and socialistic ideologies have generated conflicting, often counterproductive, organizations and structures, and as a result, concerns relative to social justice and development remain unresolved.

The main issues include the proliferation of weapons of unprecedented destructiveness, extreme population growth, environmental change, extensive resource depletion, and new patterns of disease. These issues have been described by David A. Hamburg of the Carnegie Corporation as the unwanted side effects of rapid scientific and technological changes:

> We see the institutional deficits throughout the world in the prevalence of totalitarian governments, in the absence of strong conflict-resolving mechanisms within and among nations, in the shortcomings of educational and other social institutions in preparing young people adequately for the modern world, in the lack of social support systems to help compensate for changes in family structure, and in the waste of talents, vigor, and health by damage in early life that is preventable. (Carnegie Corporation of New York, 1984, July 13, p. 1)

The emergence of "general" or "personal" social services throughout the industrial world is an example of changing patterns of service—changes affecting fields and activities such as family and child welfare; social services for the young and the aged; social care for the handicapped, frail, and retarded; information and referral services; and community services. This development seems to be taking place, without regard to national ideologies, in most of the industrial societies (Kamerman & Kahn, 1976).

The philosophy underlying the personal social service system, according to Kamerman and Kahn (1976), "holds that a complex technological society is a difficult environment for many of us, and that good government works actively to make life easier for its citizens" (p. 4). This expands the traditional purview of social welfare from five fields (education, health, income maintenance, housing, and employment) to six. The emergence of the "sixth system" (Kahn & Kamerman, 1977) is a fascinating development in comparative social welfare.

In the Third World, Midgley (1985) has found that the social services are subject to incrementalism, inappropriateness, and unequal access. To overcome these problems, he supports the practice of the appropriate redistributive welfare model.

Approaches to Social Problems.

The "new poor" in the United States and Europe and the continuing miseries of the victims of the old feudal-colonial systems in the developing countries represent different global concerns (Mohan, 1972). The commonality of unfulfilled basic needs underscores some of the issues highlighted in the preceding section. However, approaches to social problems and the vulnerable populations vary so widely that a conclusive statement is hard to formulate. Today's world problems are markedly and qualitatively different from those of past centuries. A realistic view of the future compels the social scientists and policymakers of the world's communities to address basic issues (both micro and macro) in a global perspective.

What is sorely lacking among social workers in the international sphere is the ability to empathize with sufferers who are unlike themselves. Though social work's status as a truly international profession is not in question, its methodologies and their crossnational adaptations reflect the consequences of "professional imperialism" (Midgley, 1981). The central issues of the upcoming decades transcend local and regional boundaries. Comparative social welfare theorists need to explore adaptive innovations that can address collective well-being in an increasingly complex world. Gabel (1984) comments:

Society, from local communities to the global commonwealth, has problems. There is nothing new. What is new is the unparalleled complexity, interconnectedness, and danger inherent in these problems as a result of their global scope, as well as the destructive power of today's weapons. In a well-populated, well-armed, and interdependent world, solving a problem locally does not in fact solve the problem: it merely masks a local symptom for a while. To solve our problems, both local and global, we need to take a global ap-

proach. . . . Attempting to solve global problems with local solutions is like the proverbial rearranging of deck chairs on the Titanic. (p. 21)

Educational and Personnel Issues.

International social welfare and social work have largely developed in the era following World War II. The organized efforts of the various divisions of the United Nations (U.N.) and other international agencies have promoted professional education and training by providing technical assistance for social progress. A first step in this direction was taken on December 14, 1946, when the U.N. General Assembly, in resolution 58 (I), authorized the Secretary-General to continue the "urgent and important" advisory functions in the field of social welfare carried on by UNRRA [United Nations Relief and Rehabilitation Administration] including the assignment of social welfare experts and the provision of social welfare fellowships to governments in need of assistance in developing their social welfare programs (U.N., 1950). Social work was recognized as a helping, social, and liaison activity that seeks to:

1) assist individuals, families and groups in relation to the many social and economic forces by which they are affected . . . 2) perform an integrating function for which no other profession is made in contemporary society . . . [and] 3) maximize the resources available in the community for promoting social well-being. (U.N., 1950, pp. 88–89)

The international survey (U.N., 1950) recognized two lines of professional development, each appropriate to a particular type of socioeconomic system:

On the one hand, in those countries whose socio-economic systems are based on private initiative, social work activities tend to be oriented towards the *individual,* and to be conceived in terms of ministering to the individual's unsatisfied needs. On the other hand, in those countries whose socio-economic systems are based on cooperative endeavour, social work activities tend to be regarded as a single aspect of a *collective* effort to create the environmental conditions appropriate to a more or less planned society. (pp. 89–90)

Comparative educational issues of the 1980s and the future emanate from this dual source, a background of mixed yet distinct experiences. Appropriateness of social work models continues to be a major issue (Midgley, 1981). The need to design, organize, and implement curricula reflective of societal needs and problems is a concern of most social work educators having international consciousness. A professional hiatus that apparently exists between practitioners and educators underscores the need to resolve certain professional issues. The issue of transferability of professional skills and international style is only an example (Vigilante, 1985). Besides, such factors as ethnocentrism, ideological bias, individual background, and the overall societal context may posit educational experiences in a counter-productive mold that is less conducive to cosmopolitan and comparative innovations. Social work education has a long way to go to achieve true international status. Although collaborative efforts between the Council on Social Work Education (CSWE) and the International Association of Schools of Social Work (IASSW) are welcomed and encouraged, documentation and analysis of facts that constitute "a solid informational basis for decision making" remain incomplete and pretentious (Kendall, 1984, p. v). Internationalization of social work is, however, entangled with challenging obligations and demanding tasks (Mohan, 1985b).

Problem of Values. Comparative analysis involves contrasts between the value judgments of two or more systems. The problem of values has two ramifications: conceptual and methodological. Conceptually, the relationship of facts and values is an important issue. Becker (1968) contends that "the separation of fact and value is a historical anomaly that has no place in contemporary science" (p. xiii). Second, the problem relates to the theorist's own values and his or her methodology. Hough (1977) has analyzed the impact of Weberian-Parsonian "ideal types" and "pattern variables" on U.S.-Soviet relationships:

> On balance, political science has benefited immensely from the insights of developmental sociology, but in several respects the impact of Weber and Parsons on the discipline has been unfortunate. Specifically, many political scientists have adopted not only the basic analysis of Weber and Parsons, but also its framework: the ideal type as used by Weber and the emphasis upon comprehensive systems analysis found in Parsons. These methodologies, as they have been used in political science, have had a number of negative consequences that are especially potent in the comparison of the Soviet Union and the West. (p. 225)

The application of systems theory has further aggravated this problem. The aspect of systems theory that "has had a most baneful effect upon the Soviet-Western comparison has been the insistence upon the need to define the boundaries between the political system and other social systems" (Hough, 1977, p. 225). Social welfare services are representative of cultural norms and standards of a particular society. Social values regulate individual and group behavior. In comparisons, the use of "ideal" models is politically motivated because comparative politics thrives on this logic.

Comparative analysis is fraught with methodological dilemmas and value-oriented issues. Normative standards applied without regard to cultural patterns create deceptive, faulty, and often dangerous profiles, and the result can be a misguided, politicized, and even vulgar representation of reality. Nevertheless, certain universal values of a high order often guide the sophisticated development of social realities. Thus, a lot of "muddling through" goes on.

The preceding analysis of comparative social welfare issues is not intended to be either exhaustive or comprehensive. It is a broad conceptual outline of basic concerns that generate global discussions on crucial issues.

Selected National Services

The majority of cross-national comparative efforts in social welfare have been impaired by enormous conceptual problems; by problems of missing, incomplete, or otherwise unavailable data; and by the worldwide shortage of researchers and statisticians trained to undertake relevant research (Estes, 1984b). Nevertheless, certain selected data can be usefully compared.

The purview of social welfare in the West is currently limited to six fields: health, education, income maintenance, housing, employment, and personal (or general) social services. The developing nations do seek to fulfill their obligations in these fields, but their resources are too easily consumed by their survival needs. The specter of massive poverty, deprivation, hunger, disease, and war is dehumanizing, and the assumption of social welfare as an institutional function is beyond the resources and capacities of the Third World nations. An overview of selected health and related programs follows.

Health Programs. Characterizations of the World Health Systems (U.S. House, 1984), from most to least extensive in health care coverage, include Sweden, the United Kingdom, the Federal Republic of Germany, Canada, Japan, and Mexico. A summary is given below:

Sweden. The publicly funded, nationally planned, decentralized health insurance program in Sweden constitutes the world's most comprehensive health care system. Salaried physicians and nurses, who are state employees, provide health care through community health centers and hospitals. Cost effectiveness, however, has become an issue. The current trend is to encourage ambulatory instead of inpatient care.

United Kingdom. The National Health Service (NHS) combines centralized planning with decentralized administration and covers the entire population (6 percent of the population is privately insured). The NHS is largely (85 percent) funded by general revenues approved by Parliament. Physicians are paid on a capitation basis, and specialists are hospital employees. The Conservative government has encouraged the growth of insurance and private health services without significantly altering the structure of the NHS.

Federal Republic of Germany. Universal access and quality care characterize the West German health system, which is a complex network of providers, patients, provider associations, and sickness funds. Employer-employee contributions, rather than general revenues (as in the United Kingdom and Sweden), provide funding for health care that covers about 99 percent of the population. Hospitals are managed by public, private, and charitable organizations. A national health care conference, mandated by the German Health Care Cost Containment Act of 1977, regulates the delivery system.

Canada. Universality, comprehensive coverage, ease of access, and public administration characterize the provincial hospitalization and medical care programs that cover 99 percent of the population. The financing is provided by the federal contributions (Medicare) and provincial taxes in a roughly equal proportion. Half of the hospitals are privately owned, and physicians are both salaried and reimbursed. A balance of quality, access, and cost is maintained.

Japan. The eight nonprofit health care plans found in Japan are a mix of both public and private sponsorship representing the system's origins in an employment-based health scheme. The national health insurance plan, with its eight alternatives, is a successful demonstration of Japanese ingenuity. Annually negotiable fee schedules regulate the elected "fee-for-service" and "all inclusive" rates. A point system is used to rate and index medical procedures. Emphasis is being placed on preventive programs, increased cost sharing, and effective processing procedures.

Mexico. The Mexican Institute of Social Security (IMSS) and the national public assistance health program provide health care to about 50 percent of the country's population. The IMSS, funded by employer-employee contributions and general revenues, covers about 15 percent of the population holding steady employment. Mexico's major concerns are primary health problems, locally supported rural clinics, and poverty. "Coplomar" clinics in rural areas offer health services in exchange for about 10 days of voluntary work per year.

The United States. Even without a system for delivery of health care, the vast health resources of the United States thrive despite the confusion resulting from a lack of organized consumer power and egalitarian policy. A congressional comparative study (U.S. House, 1984) concluded:

> Quality, access and cost are three values that shape the health systems of the world. . . . Health systems throughout the world offer us lessons about the tradeoffs amongst values and the alternative outcomes we can expect . . . . [We] provide less health care coverage to our population than any other major industrialized nation in the world. . . . Taking into account the historic, political and economic conditions in the United States, a flexible fee schedule—possibly a hybrid of the mode subscribed to by West Germany and Japan— would be most effective in achieving the optimal balance of quality, access and cost . . . . The emphasis in the United States health care

system is top heavy. We deliver inordinate amounts of care through the most expensively staffed and equipped hospitals. A bottom weighted three-tier system localizes care since the majority of care can be provided through less expensive, more accessible community clinics . . . . High quality, low cost delivery of services is achieved in a number of countries through the localization of primary care . . . . In sum, greater access should be strived for through policies which encourage the containment of costs and maintenance of quality. (pp. 25–28)

Medical and health care is fundamentally a social, not a technical or a commercial, relationship and expresses some of the values of the larger society (Bates, 1983). Britain and the United States, for example, represent two different value and organization systems. Although public responsibility for the sick and poor is a British tradition, the use of a means test based on individual capacity to pay is a typically American approach to social provisions. According to Abel-Smith (1981), the sickness insurance movement in Britain began as a movement launched by consumers for their mutual benefit. In the United States, on the contrary, the Blue Cross medical insurance system was a movement promoted by the service providers.

As health care costs increase and resources become scarce, the efficiency of health care systems are being questioned. Assuming that health care is a major determinant of health status and that its ultimate goal is the improvement of public health, a framework proposed for health statistics by Erickson, Henke, and Brittain (1983) underscores five categories of data in the production process: (1) health care expenditures, (2) health care resources, (3) health services utilization, (4) health insurance, and (5) sources of funding. International comparisons of health data have always been useful in making comprehensive policies. An international health data system based on intranational health concerns will promote comparative research.

Medicine, health, and social systems should be studied beyond narrow boundaries of space and time. Eyles and Woods (1983) feel that "spatial patterns formed by social phenomena are a good starting point for examining the relationships between medicine, health and society" (p. 11). A health

care system is a microcosm of a society's values, institutions, resources, and organization. Eyles and Woods (1983) also see allocations of resources to health care and welfare primarily as a power question; they find that health care policy and the spatial allocation of resources are root questions of power and social justice:

The social Darwinistic values of the market-oriented military dictatorships of Latin America will suggest that it is only 'natural justice' that the richest (the fittest) have the best health care facilities. Thus Escudero (1981) argues that the reemergence of military participation in Argentinian civilian life has led to a lowering of health standards, increases in the rates of mortality and morbidity and the establishment of elitist, commodity-centered health policies. A less extreme but similar view of social justice may be said to underpin USA health care provision. (pp. 226–227)

This situation is also representative of many less developed countries regardless of their political and ideological orientations. Although the major preoccupation of health economists has been the medical profession of the industrialized world, economic evaluation of health care in developing countries is gradually receiving attention (Carrin, 1984).

The health care systems in the Third World are plagued by intranational economic and political problems. Certain countries, such as India, possess advanced medical facilities and subsidized health care, but the access to and quality of social programs is rather limited. Private and public institutions and programs provide health care to millions, yet millions remain unprotected.

Other Services. Policies governing services such as health, education, and housing have a significant influence on international migration (Oberai, 1983). "Meeting basic needs in poor societies hinges crucially upon the degree of equality that can be made to prevail" (International Labor Office [ILO], 1977, p. 67). The meeting of basic needs therefore largely depends on productivity, redistribution of resources, and the provision of social services (ILO, 1977). Social welfare's major task, according to the Cocoyoc Declaration (U.N., 1982), is to redefine the whole purpose of development. This should not be to develop things, but to develop people: "Human beings have basic needs:

food, shelter, clothing, health, education. Any process of growth that does not lead to them, or even disrupts them, is a travesty of the idea of development" (p. 14). A systemic view of health and other basic needs calls for comprehensive, dynamic assessment of global resources and their equitable distribution.

Mental Health Services. Decentralization and fragmentation are labels applied to U.S. mental health care (Mechanic, 1969), which represents a heterogeneous mix of public and private services. Unlike the U.S. system, British mental health services are centrally administered governmental obligations. In Sweden, the tendency has been to localize these services. A historical comparative review of the mental health policy in these countries reveals interesting cycles of social reform (Armour, 1981).

Custodial, somatic treatment approaches and colonial institutions generally constitute mental health care in most of the Third World countries. Psychiatry in India is still practiced in isolation from the community life in old mental hospitals that, with few exceptions, provide obsolete treatment modalities. Affluent patients do, of course, find humane and modern services (Mohan, 1973).

Housing. Like other social services, housing programs reflect the sociopolitical climate of society. European housing problems in the postwar era have been studied extensively (U.N., 1976; McGuire, 1981; Wynn, 1984). Wynn (1984) points out that qualitative deficiencies are emerging as a major focus for new policies after the quantitative deficits have been overcome. Subsidies for house construction followed rent freezes in Western Europe. In Eastern Europe, large-scale construction was stimulated under centrally planned economies. In the 1960s and 1970s, the "boom" growth of urban centers followed:

> In Western Europe, a variety of new forms of subsidy were introduced. In France, new forms of cheap loans for aspiring house purchasers came into effect in conjunction with a radically reformed savings scheme for home purchase. . . . Similar developments occurred in other countries: in West Germany, Netherlands and Denmark, new systems were introduced in the sixties which resulted in a far higher initial subsidy of rents in state aided construction. (Wynn, 1984, p. 2)

Income Maintenance. Analysis of poverty, income distribution, and unemployment has been the major preoccupation of the ILO's World Employment Program (WEP). Beckerman (1979) studied the effectiveness of antipoverty measures in four industrialized countries: Australia, Belgium, Norway, and Great Britain. This WEP study made prebenefit and postbenefit estimates of poverty in terms of the degree of poverty as well as the number of poor people. From the allocative principles perspective, income maintenance programs may be placed in two broad categories: negative income tax programs (guaranteed income) and family or children's allowances. These two approaches are guided by selective and universal principles, respectively. In the United States, the Family Assistance Plan and the Children's Allowances program are the main examples. Gilbert and Specht (1974) point out that more than 60 nations throughout the world, including all of the industrialized West except the United States, offer some form of children's allowances as an *integral* part of their welfare system. The Social Security Act and its provisions have provided major social benefits to the people in the United States.

Cross-national similarities are revealed in income maintenance programs of several Western countries that "seem to use the same basic program ingredients: compensation for work injuries; social insurance for the aged, disabled, and widowed; help in paying medical bills; benefits for the unemployed; and, often, aid to parents of large families" (Heidenheimer et al., 1975, p. 188).

Miscellaneous. Aside from health care, housing, and income maintenance a number of other services, such as recreational and other community services have been studied in an international context (Kaim-Caudle, 1973; Jenkins, 1969; Kahn & Kamerman, 1977; Thursz & Vigilante, 1975). Social services are undergoing a major change in many nations. The crises of the welfare state, faltering economies, political instabilities, and organizational dysfunctions are causing serious problems. Alternative strategies are being developed.

The Swedish Secretariat for Future Studies has recommended that in lieu of raising taxes the government should "levy time" by requiring citizens to work in the community and that no one be permitted to escape the levy. The Secretariat's suggestion was made in a report that analyzed funding for the care of the aged, handicapped, young, or ill (Doyle, 1984).

Social Welfare in the Soviet Union. People's abilities and needs, regardless of the quality and quantity of their labor, have been the main criteria of eligibility in the Soviet welfare system, whose accomplishments are usually underrated in the noncommunist West. Human emancipation in general and social security in particular have been the main general goals of social services through specifics such as improved labor conditions and wages, social insurance, health, sanitation, and new methods of dealing with industrial disputes.

The revolutionary socialist program of 1919 underscored the universal need for social security, public health, and housing. This idea, according to a 1961 program, will eventually accomplish its egalitarian ideals "not through war with other countries but by the example of a more perfect organization of society, by rapid progress in developing progressive forces, the creation of all conditions for the happiness and well-being of man" (Fisher, 1968, p. xv). Notwithstanding the shortcomings of the Soviet total social welfare state, affluent countries such as the United States as well as developing nations of the world have a great deal to learn from the Soviet experiences (Madison, 1968).

Similarities and Differences

The concept of a World Village is helpful in explaining the primordial nature of global tensions and superpower politics. The emerging similarities and differences among nations—in relation to the United States, the world's most powerful, prosperous, and advanced nation—may be viewed in the confluence of this setting. Although prospects of peace, progress, and prosperity tend to unite nations, the pursuit of power and politics perpetually plagues the possibilities of a cohesive world order. Common concerns and basic differences transcend the stereotypical "types" and "blocs." The United States and the Soviet Union may be political foes, but no nation is more serious than these two powers about the survival of the human race. The demise of ideology is no more an issue.

In a comparative-analytic paradigm

(Mohan, 1985a), nations may be classified beyond the traditional dichotomies, such as East-West, Capitalist-Communist, and "Haves-Have nots." However, two dimensions are significant in characterizing similarities and differences: freedom and oppression. Freedom means human liberation, and oppression implies dehumanization caused by racism, inequalities, and social injustice. Because world communities do not have consensus, apparent similarities get blurred in the chaotic mist of ubiquitous oppressive forces.

Emerging similarities and differences among nations seem to cluster around variables such as demographic conditions, patterns of sociocultural living, politico-economic systems, and national ideologies (Mohan, 1985b). Kaim-Caudle (1973) has shown that basic similarities as well as differences exist among ten developed nations in standard of living, electoral support, and ethnic-linguistic background. Dissimilarities, however, exist among most of the 131 member states of the United Nations in respect to their conceptions of social welfare, modes of social intervention, resource distribution, and geopoliticocultural orientations. National uniqueness is the rule.

International social work seeks to promote universal well-being at the expense of chauvinism and regional rivalries. "If nationalism, regionalism, or parochialism is our only concern, social work education as an international force will become fragmented and impotent and no one will benefit," wrote Kendall (1978, p. 190). A superordinate structure of collective will and commitment is an imperative in attempts to eschew the existing inequalities among nations. The progress of nations is being thwarted by population growth, differential rates of economic expansion, global militarism, human rights violations, nuclearization, and erosion of the extended family (Estes, 1984b). To alter social inequalities significantly, Estes (1984b) observes, "will require that each of us, acting as responsible citizens within our own nations *and* as citizens of the world community, accept personal responsibility for engaging in effective actions that will improve the adequacy of national, regional, and global social provision" (p. 167). International social welfare is a moral equivalent of success and progress. All nations aspire to this goal through varied strategies. The advanced nations' obligation is to promote this collective goal without imperialist intent.

Carnoy and Castells (1984) indicate that arms exports to the Third World have become a key factor in the economic growth of an increasing number of industrialized nations—not only the United States and the Soviet Union, but also France, Germany, Israel, Britain, and Brazil. Efforts to "privatize" American society have put pressure on the social wage, and the quality of American life has deteriorated. National greed can create international disorder.

Comparative analysis, promoted through international cooperation, has tremendous potential to lubricate the rusty mechanism of international relations. A wise man suggests: "When dealing with your neighbor, a business rival, or the Soviet Union, the way to get ahead is to get along" (Allman, 1984, p. 25).

BRIJ MOHAN

For further information, see INTERNATIONAL SOCIAL WELFARE ORGANIZATIONS AND SERVICES; INTERNATIONAL SOCIAL WORK EDUCATION.

References

Abel–Smith, B. (1972). "The History of Medical Care." In A. Crichton (Ed.), *Health Policy Making* (pp. 72–80). Ann Arbor, Mich.: Health Administration Press.

Allman, W. F. (1984). "Nice Guys Finish First." *Science, 5*(8), 25–32.

Armer, M., & Grimshaw, A. D. (Eds.). (1973). *Comparative Social Research: Method of Logical Problems and Strategies.* New York: John Wiley and Sons.

Armour, P. K. (1981). *The Cycles of Social Reform.* Washington, D.C.: University Press of America.

Bacon, M. K., Child, I. L., & Barry, H., III. (1963). "A Cross–Cultural Study of Correlates of Crime." *Journal of Abnormal and Social Psychology, 66*(4), 291–300.

Baster, N. (1969). *Level of Living and Economic Growth: A Comparative Study of Six Countries.* Geneva, Switzerland: United Nations Research Institute for Social Development.

Bates, E. M. (1983). *Health Systems and Public Scrutiny: Australia, Britain, and the United States.* New York: St. Martin's Press.

Becker, E. (1968). *The Structure of Evil.* New York: The Free Press.

Beckerman, W. (1979). *Poverty and the Impact of*

Income Maintenance Programmes. Geneva, Switzerland: International Labor Office.

Brown, L. R. (1984). *State of the World.* Washington, D.C.: Worldwatch Institute.

Burns, E. M. (1949). *The American Social Security System.* Boston: Houghton Mifflin Co.

Burns, E. M. (1956). *Social Security and Public Policy.* New York: McGraw–Hill Book Co.

Burns, E. M. (1985). "Welcome to a New Journal." *Journal of International and Comparative Social Welfare, 1*(2), 1–2.

Carnegie Corporation of New York (1984, July 13). Press release summarizing the corporation's annual report.

Carnoy, M., & Castells, M. (1984). "After the Crisis." *World Policy Journal, 1*(3), 495–515.

Carrin, G. (1984). *Economic Evaluation of Health Care in Developing Countries.* New York: St. Martin's Press.

Cox, I. (1970). *The Hungry Half: A Study in the Exploitation of the Third World.* London, England: Laurence and Wishart.

Donnison, D. V. (1965). *Social Policy and Administration: Studies in the Development of Social Services at the Local Level.* London, England: Allen and Unwin.

Doyle, D. P. (1984, April 17). "Sweden: Involuntary Volunteers?" *The Wall Street Journal,* pp. 51–52.

Drenowski, J. (1974). *On Measuring and Planning the Quality of Life.* The Hague, The Netherlands: Mouton.

Eckstein, H., & Apter, D. E. (1963). *Comparative Politics.* New York: Free Press.

Eliot, C. W. (Ed.). (1980). *The Harvard Classics—The Meditations of Marcus Aurelius.* Danbury, Conn.: Grolier Enterprises.

Erickson, P., Henke, K. D., & Brittain, R. D. (1983). "A Health Statistics Framework: U.S. Data Systems as a Model for European Health Information." In A. J. Culyer (Ed.), *Health Indicators* (pp. 117–138). New York: St. Martin's Press.

Escudero, J. C. (1981). "Democracy, Authoritarianism, and Health in Argentina." *International Journal of Health Services, 11,* 559–572.

Estes, R. J. (1984a). "Education for International Social Welfare Research." In D. S. Sanders & P. Pedersen (Eds.), *Education for International Social Work* (pp. 56–86). Honolulu: University of Hawaii School of Social Work and Council on Social Work Education.

Estes, R. J. (1984b). *The Social Progress of Nations.* New York: Praeger.

Eyles, J., & Woods, K. J. (1983). *The Social Geography of Medicine and Health.* New York: St. Martin's Press.

Falck, H. S. (1969). "Teaching of Comparative Social Welfare at the Doctoral Level." In K. Kendall (Ed.), *Teaching and Comparative*

Social Welfare. New York: Council on Social Work Education.

Fisher, H. H. (1968). "Foreword." In B. W. Madison, *Social Welfare in the Soviet Union* (pp. xi–xv). Stanford, Calif.: Stanford University Press.

Gabel, M. (1984). "Planning Diseases." *The Futurist, 18*(5), 21–22.

Gilbert N., & Specht, H. (1974). *Dimensions of Social Welfare Policy.* Englewood Cliffs, N.J.: Prentice–Hall.

Grange, J. (1974). "Social Welfare and the Science of Man: An Existential Approach." In J. M. Romanyshyn (Ed.), *Social Science and Social Welfare* (pp. 197–210). New York: Council on Social Work Education.

Heidenheimer, A. J., Heclo, H., & Adams, C. T. (1975). *Comparative Public Policy: The Politics of Social Choice in Europe and America.* New York: St. Martin's Press.

Higgins, J. (1981). *States of Welfare: A Comparative Analysis of Social Policy.* New York: St. Martin's Press.

Hough, J. F. (1977). *The Soviet Union and Social Science Theory.* Cambridge, Mass.: Harvard University Press.

International Labor Office. (1977). *The Basic Needs Approach to Development.* Geneva, Switzerland: Author.

Jenkins, S. (1969). *Social Security in International Perspective.* New York: Columbia University Press.

Kahn, A. J., & Kamerman, S. B. (1975). *Not For the Poor Alone.* Philadelphia: Temple University Press.

Kahn, A. J., & Kamerman, S. B. (1977). *Social Services in International Perspective.* Washington, D.C.: U.S. Department of Health, Education, and Welfare.

Kaim–Caudle, P. R. (1973). *Comparative Social Policy and Social Security: A Ten Country Study.* New York: Dunellen Publishing Co.

Kalleberg, A. L. (1966). "The Logic of Comparison: A Methodological Note on the Comparative Study of Political Systems." *World Politics, 19*(1), 69–82.

Kamerman, S. B., & Kahn, A. J. (1976). *Social Services in the United States: Policies and Programs.* Philadelphia: Temple University Press.

Kendall, K. A. (1978). *Reflections on Social Work Education: 1950–1978.* Vienna, Austria: International Association of Schools of Social Work.

Madison, B. Q. (1980). *The Meaning of Social Policy – The Comparative Dimension in Social Welfare.* Boulder, Colo.: Westview Press.

Martin, C. W. (Ed.). (1972). *Comparative Social Welfare.* London, England: Allen & Unwin.

McGuire, C. (1981). *International Housing Policies.* Toronto, Canada: Lexington Books.

Mechanic, D. (1969). *Mental Health and Social Policy.* Englewood Cliffs, N.J.: Prentice–Hall.

Midgley, J. (1981). *Professional Imperialism: Social Work in the Third World.* London, England: Wm. Heinemann.

Midgley, J. (1985). "Models of Welfare and Social Planning in Third World Countries." In B. Mohan (Ed.), *New Horizons of Social Welfare and Policy* (pp. 89–108). Cambridge, Mass.: Schenkman Publishing Co.

Midgley, J., & Hardiman, M. (1982). *Social Dimensions of Development: Social Policy and Planning in the Third World.* New York: John Wiley & Sons.

Mishra, R. (1981). *Society and Social Policy.* Atlantic Highlands, N.J.: Humanities Press.

Mishra, R. (1984). *The Welfare State in Crisis.* New York: St. Martin's Press.

Mohan, B. (1972). *India's Social Problems.* Allahabad, India: Indian International Publications.

Mohan, B. (1973). *Social Psychiatry in India: A Treatise on the Mentally Ill.* Calcutta, India: Minerva Publications.

Mohan, B. (1984). "Editorial." *Journal of International and Comparative Social Welfare, 1*(1), p. ii.

Mohan, B. (1985a). *New Horizons of Social Welfare and Policy.* Cambridge, Mass.: Schenkman Publishing Co.

Mohan, B. (1985b). *Toward Comparative Social Welfare.* Cambridge, Mass.: Schenkman Publishing Co.

Morris, M. D. (1979). *Measuring the Conditions of the World's Poor.* New York: Pergamon Press.

Myrdal, G. (1968). *Asian Drama: An Inquiry Into the Poverty of Nations.* New York: Random House.

Oberai, A. S. (1983). *State Policies and Internal Migration.* New York: St. Martin's Press.

Parker, R. (1983). "Comparative Social Policy and the Politics of Comparison." In J. Gandy et al. (Eds.), *Improving Social Intervention* (pp. 3–21). New York: St. Martin's Press.

Popper, K. R. (1959). *The Logic of Scientific Discovery.* London, England: Hutchinson Press.

Popper, K. R. (1963). *Conjectures and Refutations.* London, England: Routledge & Kegan Paul.

Przeworski, A., & Teune, H. (1970). *The Logic of Comparative Social Inquiry.* New York: John Wiley & Sons.

Romanyshyn, J. M. (1971). *Social Welfare: Charity to Justice.* New York: Random House.

Sanders, D. S., & Estes, R. J. (Eds.). (1984). *International Social Welfare—A Selected Bibliography.* New York: Council on Social Work Education.

Sanders, D. S., & Pedersen, P. (1984). *Education for International Social Welfare.* New York: Council on Social Work Education.

Seigel, R. L., & Weinberg, L. B. (1977). *Comparing Public Policies.* Homewood, Ill.: Dorsey.

Sheldon, E., & Moore, W. (Eds.). (1968). *Indicators of Social Change.* New York: Russell Sage Foundation.

Thursz, D., & Vigilante J. L. (Eds.). (1975). *Meeting Human Needs: An Overview of Nine Countries.* Beverly Hills, Calif.: Sage.

Titmuss, R. M. (1958). *Essays on the Welfare State.* London, England: George Allen & Unwin.

Titmuss, R. M. (1963). "The Welfare State: Images and Realities." *Social Service Review, 37*(1), 1–11.

Titmuss, R. (1968). *Commitment to Welfare.* London, England: George Allen & Unwin.

Titmuss, R. (1974). *Social Policy.* London, England: George Allen & Unwin.

Titmuss, R. (1976). *Essays on the Welfare State* (rev. ed.). London, England: George Allen & Unwin.

United Nations. (1964). *Handbook of Household Surveys: A Practical Guide for Inquiries on Level of Living.* New York: Author.

United Nations. (1976). *Human Settlements in Europe: Post–War Trends and Policies.* New York: Author.

United Nations. (1982). *Poverty and Self–Reliance: A Social Welfare Perspective.* New York: United Nations Department of International Economic and Social Affairs.

U.S. House. (1984). *World Health Systems* (Report Presented by Edward R. Roybal, Chairman of the Select Committee on Aging). Washington, D.C.: U.S. Government Printing Office.

Vigilante, J. L. (1985). "Professional Skills, International Style: The Issue of Transferability." *Journal of International and Comparative Social Welfare,* (Spring), 61–71.

Ward, R. E. (1964). *Studying Politics Abroad in the Developing Areas.* Boston: Little, Brown.

Whiting, J. W. M. (1964). "The Cross–Cultural Method." In G. Lindzey (Ed.), *Handbook of Social Psychology: Vol. 1. Theory and Method* (pp. 523–531). Cambridge, Mass.: Addison–Wesley Publishing Co.

Wilensky, H. (1975). *The Welfare State and Equality.* Berkeley, Calif.: University of California.

Wilensky, H., & Lebeaux, C. (1965). *Industrial Society and Social Welfare.* New York: Free Press.

Woodsworth, D. E. (1977). *Social Security and National Policy.* London, England: McGill–Queens University Press.

Wynn, M. (Ed.). (1984). *Housing in Europe.* New York: St. Martin's Press.

INTERNATIONAL SOCIAL WELFARE ORGANIZATIONS AND SERVICES

International social welfare refers to activities by national governments, intergovernmental organizations, voluntary agencies, and associations operating across national boundaries regarding social welfare policy standards, technical assistance, research, and exchange of personnel and information. Direct services is another important component—refugee programs, relief, and intercountry adoptions. International social welfare has come of age in the past 40 years. International advisory services and research and information activities established in the United Nations and in direct intercountry activities have reached every geographical area, although on a modest scale. The activities of nongovernmental agencies and associations and universities have contributed significantly to this social welfare interchange. Funds from all sources have failed to keep pace with requests for services, however. Budget reductions beginning in the late 1970s and extending well into the 1980s have further accentuated the gap between needs and resources for international as well as national social welfare.

International Development

World conditions necessarily set the stage for international cooperation. Examining progress in a global framework, U.N. reports portray a sharp downward trend in development. After 2 decades of sustained growth in the 1960s and 1970s, developing countries have suffered a real setback in the 1980s. The worldwide recession of the early 1980s had a marked effect on social conditions and on social services.

A periodic assessment of progress in development is made by the United Nations in cooperation with specialized international organizations (United Nations, 1984a). Available evidence shows a mixed picture in different regions of the world. In Asia, over the past decade, large groups have improved their standards of living. Elsewhere, for example in Africa, poverty has increased dramatically as severe droughts exacerbated the conditions of extreme poverty for large groups of the population. Some Latin American countries showed deteriorating living conditions for both middle-income groups and the poor.

The recovery experienced by the United States in 1983–1984 was not typical of trends in other countries, particularly in the Third World. These countries were suffering the worst effects of the global recession, with high inflation, debt crises, investment capital in flight, and resultant unemployment and underemployment. Opportunities for migration—a safety valve in earlier years—were disappearing as curbs on migration grew and migrant workers were pressured to return home. Overall, deteriorating economic conditions forced many governments to cut back on social programs. Family planning, education, and health and social welfare services, built up with painstaking care—many through international cooperation—have faced a difficult challenge.

The range of current issues faced by national social welfare programs in different regions of the world was well presented at the Twenty-second International Conference on Social Welfare in Montreal in August 1984. Hepworth's (1984) conference working paper included the views of national councils of social welfare, data from international organizations, and the statements of experts. He reported that criticisms of the welfare state had resulted in increasing decentralization of programs to state and local levels. Yet the needs accentuated by economic conditions— for example, unemployment—made even more critical the role of social welfare in the community. In less-developed countries, where no real safety net exists, minimum benefits (if available) had to be limited to the poorest and most disadvantaged.

Lack of systematic comparative cross-national data limits evaluation of progress in social welfare from an international perspective. In broad-based national development programs, social welfare programs or personal social services are not identified as a sector similar to the health, education, or housing sectors. National accounts and comparative regional studies of expenditures in public services do not identify social welfare costs other than social security. Thus, the relative importance and scope of social welfare in a country's use of national resources cannot be accurately assessed. However, relying on reports of international groups of experts and a few cross-national studies and national reports submitted to international conferences, the inference can be made that, despite cutbacks, social welfare programs have been maintained in every region.

On the positive side, the changing concepts and objectives of development have encouraged international organizations in the 1980s to take fuller account of human resources as a key factor in improving national economics. Robert McNamara (1980, pp. 613–657), then president of the World Bank, in his address to the bank's Board of Governors in 1980, urged investment in the human potential of the poor as not only morally right but sound economics. An effective attack on pervasive poverty required that basic needs be met, particularly through primary education and primary health care. Redesigned packages of community social services could indeed contribute a significant economic return. The annual reports in the 1980s of the World Bank and other large international development organizations confirmed growing support for investment in the social infrastructure. This focus, which has resulted in the establishment or extension of basic services in some developing countries, is reflected in social indicators.

This development is marked in the health sector by a drop in high infant mortality and a reduction in the incidence of common diseases. Other social indicators point to positive changes in literacy rates, educational enrollment, and overall life expectancy. With rising expectations, people have sought to advance opportunities for their children as well as to maintain or strengthen their own situations.

The most impressive and encouraging trend worldwide has been the stability of various social security systems. The continuing economic recession had led to efforts to contain costs after a period of steady expansion in the 1970s. High unemployment, the aging of populations, and inflation meant that some countries changed formulas for calculating benefits, raised ceilings for contributions, and slowed the effect of benefit adjustment mechanisms. Overall, the systems have been well maintained, however, with considerable popular and political support. In the developing world, a few countries even added new features to existing programs. The number of countries with some form of social security has increased from 57 in 1940 to 140 in 1983. The report *Social Security Throughout the World: 1983* (U.S. Department of Health and Human Services, 1984) presents comparative data on current programs.

International Conferences

Through international conferences, the United Nations seeks to focus world attention on specific problem areas. Single-issue international conferences, begun in the 1970s, have continued with considerable benefit to the international social welfare field. Intercountry contacts established earlier through technical cooperation and research were expanded and stabilized in the preparations for and follow-up of major international meetings.

The World Assembly on Aging (WAA), meeting in 1982 in Vienna, Austria, for example, was a historic occasion for both the aging population and the international community. The United States was active in proposing the world assembly and has officially expressed satisfaction with the outcome. Attended by delegates from 121 nations, the conference produced a wealth of information on aging. National reports were submitted as well as summaries of regional technical meetings. The convergence of public and private sector concerns was an outstanding positive achievement for international social welfare. The assembly fulfilled its charge to develop an international plan of action on aging. The objective was to provide member nations and U.N. agencies with guidelines for formulating policies relating to the elderly. The plan—titled the *Vienna International Plan of Action on Aging* (United Nations Center for Social Development, 1982)—is regarded as a highly significant document in providing policymakers everywhere with a framework for future policy development and for the assessment of existing programs.

The Non-Governmental Organizations (NGOs), or voluntary organizations, were unusually active in preparing for WWA and throughout its deliberations. NGOs are called upon repeatedly in the WAA plan of action to join with the public sector in implementing the recommendations. A U.S. Committee on World Aging, representing American national organizations concerned with aging, is actively following up the assembly's recommendations. The plan calls for periodic reports to the United Nations by the member states. Progress in the United States as a result of the assembly's work is reported by the federal government to the United Nations. One of the main accomplishments of WAA has been consciousness raising about the societal implications of aging, particularly in developing countries, and recognition of the urgency of responding to the aging population's needs.

Other international conferences in the 1980s that involved the international social welfare community included the International Conference on Population in Mexico City in 1984 and the U.N. Conference to Review and Appraise the Achievements of the United Nations Decade for Women in Nairobi, Kenya, in 1985. The successful conclusion of the U.N. conference on women attended by representatives of 157 countries marked the emergence of the women's movement as a full-fledged political power. The final report of the conference (United Nations, 1985a) includes proposals concerning the role of women in government, in the workplace, and in their families.

The designation of International Years encourages national and international interest and concern. A report by the United Nations (1984b) lists conferences and special observances. The celebration of the International Year of Disabled Persons in 1983 gave considerable impetus to carrying forward and expanding activities for the disabled. A U.N. Decade for the Disabled 1983–1992 has set the framework for continued cooperation and interchange.

Government and NGO committees in which social welfare experts participate were active in the consideration of issues related to International Youth Year, celebrated in 1985. Plans were also under way for the International Year for Peace in 1986 and the International Year of Shelter for the Homeless in 1987. These international conferences of the 1970s and 1980s have underscored the close link between social welfare and national development.

Conference of Ministers

A landmark in international cooperation was the first U.N. Conference of Ministers Responsible for Social Welfare, held in New York in September 1968. Officials of 96 countries attended, including 61 of ministerial or equivalent rank. In authorizing the conference, the U.N. Economic and Social Council summarized its purpose: to examine the role of social welfare programs in national development and to identify the elements of social welfare functions common to all nations. Specifically, the council asked delegates to draw up principles for social welfare programs, both national and international; recommend ways to promote the training of workers for social welfare programs; and recommend actions that could improve U.N. social welfare programs.

The findings and conclusions of the conference strongly supported preventive and developmental social welfare functions (United Nations, 1969). A reorientation of social welfare toward a developmental approach was seen as essential. There was wide support for the basic responsibility of government to assure the availability and accessibility of social welfare services as a right to a nation's entire population. Gaps were especially noted in rural services and in communitywide programs to provide for needs formerly met by the extended family. The conference emphasized the need to reorient training to the development role of social welfare. Training and preparation of top-level personnel for research, planning, and administration were cited as priorities.

Since the initial conference on ministers in 1968, the concept of social welfare has moved from an essentially remedial approach to a positive and comprehensive approach based on the strength of individuals and groups, rather than their weaknesses. U.N. expert groups and studies (United Nations, 1984d) have addressed the issue of social welfare within a development context. The basic conceptual components of this approach have been identified as (1) a positive orientation toward the development of human potential, (2) a comprehensive understanding of the interrelationship of needs, (3) the relevance of social welfare to all segments of the population, (4) meeting the total needs of the population and enhancing the social relationships and problem-solving capabilities of people through active participation in their communities, and (5) creating or modifying institutional processes for change conducive to national development.

The extensive changes in social welfare policy made since the 1968 conference of

ministers were to be assessed at an interregional consultation scheduled by the United Nations for 1987 in Vienna. Extensive preparatory work was undertaken in the U.N. regions by means of ministerial meetings and U.N. regional commissions, with social welfare systems being reevaluated in light of past experience, current realities, and future prospects. The interregional meeting was expected to update, assess, and synthesize information on current national social welfare systems.

Exchange Programs

To most Americans, the visible evidence of participation in international social welfare is the foreigner who comes to the United States to study and observe American social welfare services. Visitors include officials of welfare ministries, national and state or provincial legislators, social work educators, community planners, and volunteers from nongovernmental services. Local communities in every American state have cooperated in these programs. Community leaders and professionals come to the United States under many different auspices and sometimes through personal resources.

The development of a social welfare work force has had a top priority in international social welfare. The United States—with its many graduate schools of social work, its large public welfare program, and its extensive and unique development of voluntary services—has been a mecca for students from abroad and for experts interested in observing services or consulting with planners and researchers. Bilateral programs between the United States and other countries have operated primarily through the United States Information Agency's (USIA) International Exchange, administered by the Bureau of Educational and Cultural Affairs. The Agency for International Development (AID) also provides opportunities for study in response to requests from individual countries.

The many American voluntary organizations active in international cooperation sponsor international visitors or cooperate in developing study programs. In addition, the international units of federal departments provide programming services. For example, the Office of Human Development Services, International Affairs, in the Department of Health and Human Services, arranges professional programs for visitors coming from a range of sponsoring organizations: the United Nations, the Organization of American States, USIA, AID, national governments, joint technical boards such as the U.S.–Yugoslav Joint Board for Technical Cooperation, the International Council on Social Welfare, and various embassies located in Washington, D.C. As international contacts are extended, many experts and students come to the United States through arrangements made by their own local organizations or through personal professional relationships.

Through, the USIA's international exchange the major channel for exchanging personnel in social welfare and other fields, approximately 8,000 visitors come to the United States annually. The first U.S–sponsored worldwide program was authorized by the Smith-Mundt Act of 1948 and later incorporated in the Fulbright-Hays Act of 1961. The intent is to bring about an interchange of knowledge and skills among prominent persons in education, the arts, public affairs, and other important areas. Social welfare is included as one of the top 10 fields for study and observation. Increasing attention is given to exchanges with Latin America, the newly emerging countries of Africa, and the Far East, which now share the greater part of the exchange grants. Emphasis is placed on professional interests in addition to a general introduction to the United States. Visitors are selected by the American diplomatic missions abroad, and each visitor's program is arranged by one of several programming agencies with which USIA has contracts.

Council of International Programs.

Among the largest U.S. exchange programs in social welfare is one sponsored by the Council of International Programs (CIP), popularly known as the Cleveland Program. Since 1956, CIP has brought more than 5,000 professionals from 110 countries to the United States to share cultural values and technical skills. The disciplines represented in this exchange include social services, education, allied medical and legal professions, youth and recreation leadership, and community development. Through this exchange of people, skills, and service, CIP contributes to increased professional knowledge, promotion

of a positive image of American life, increased understanding of the world's diverse cultures, and furthering world peace through effective cross-cultural communication. CIP has received financial support for 30 years from the U.S. Department of State and more recently from USIA.

CIP local affiliates operate city programs and cooperate with nine universities. Professional programs last 4 to 13 months and include orientation, job experience, and university study. Participants are placed with host families. Local advisory councils assisted by many local volunteers facilitate CIP's operations. The experience features a two-way exchange of knowledge and appreciation of differing values and methodologies.

The thirtieth anniversary of the CIP Program was celebrated at a conference in Berea, Ohio, in August 1985 with the participation of several hundred people from the United States and abroad. With its strong emphasis on the interchange of young people, the CIP conference coincided well with the worldwide celebration of International Youth Year.

International Youth Exchange Initiative.

The President's International Youth Exchange Initiative, created in May 1982 by President Reagan, is USIA's newest exchange program (President's Council for Youth Exchange and the Consortium for International Citizen Exchange, 1983–1984). It represents a partnership between government and private organizations in this country working together to double in 3 years the number of young people exchanged between the United States and Canada, France, the Federal Republic of Germany, Italy, Japan, and the United Kingdom. In 1984, the program was extended to 25 other countries of the world. All programs under the initiative are carried out by not-for-profit organizations in the private sector. Under grant guidelines approved by Congress, USIA holds publicly announced competitions to award funds derived from both the private and public sectors.

In the first year of the initiative, USIA had significant success in obtaining matching funds from other participating governments. Most notable was the financial commitment of the Federal Republic of Germany, which matched the $400,000 spent by the U.S. government in bilateral short-term nonacademic youth exchanges. The West German government also committed $2.5 million annually for a full-scholarship academic-year high school exchange program.

Japan has committed about $250,000 annually to a Diet-Senate youth exchange in which the Japanese government invites 100 American teenagers to Japan for a 3-month study-homestay program. The United States, in turn, invites 47 Japanese students, one for each prefecture in Japan, for a year's academic homestay program. The Italian government is funding 30 American undergraduates for a semester of study in Italy. The United States is reciprocating by funding a semester's stay in the United States for 30 Italian students.

Special features of the initiative program include community workshops on local facilities, services, and traditions. The program seeks to increase local visibility to highlight international cooperation as well as to increase the number of volunteers and host families to support the widened exchange effort.

U.S. Organizations

The United States has a long history of cooperation in international social welfare. Its experts served on the League of Nations Committee on Social Questions. As early as 1942, Latin American experts and trainees came to the United States to study social services in an exchange among the American republics. When the United Nations was formed, social workers in the United States were active in focusing attention on social development and on the need to establish adequate machinery within the United Nations to consider social matters and to provide advisory services in extending social welfare programs. The United States cosponsored the U.N. resolutions in December 1946 to establish the United Nations International Children's Emergency Fund (UNICEF) and to transfer the Technical Advisory Social Welfare Services of the United Nations Relief and Rehabilitation Administration to the United Nations proper, thus providing the basis for an international action program in social welfare.

In the federal government, HHS is the main agency concerned with international social welfare and social development as well

as international health. This international involvement, which has grown substantially in recent years, serves several purposes:

- advancing HHS's domestic goals
- responding to humanitarian concerns such as national disasters and epidemics
- serving the foreign policy and development objectives of the Department of State and AID
- promoting international communication among colleagues to advance knowledge

HHS has a number of bilateral technical cooperation agreements with counterpart ministries around the world. These provide for a wide range of cooperative activities. Extensive support is provided to the U.S. foreign assistance program, and officials and other experts serve on the U.S. delegations to meetings of intergovernmental organizations including the World Health Organization (WHO), the Pan American Health Organization, the U.N. Commission on Social Development, UNICEF, and the International Labor Office (ILO).

The Office of International Affairs in the Office of the Secretary of HHS has overall responsibility for advising the secretary on policy issues and providing staff support for the secretary's involvement in international activities. The director of this office coordinates the many international activities carried on by HHS agencies.

The office of Human Development Services (HDS) in HHS serves as a focal point for cooperative international social welfare activities. An international unit responsible for international social welfare activities has existed for more than 30 years. This unit does initial work on policy development relating to international issues in aging, the family, child welfare and youth services, and overall social development. HDS also provides professional development programs for foreign visitors at the request of the Department of State, AID, and many international nongovernmental agencies. Staff support is provided to the assistant secretary for human development and other officials for participation in technical cooperation missions to other countries as well as international meetings. A series of cooperative international research projects and comparative studies is coordinated by this unit. Special agreements for cooperation and interchange in social welfare and social affairs have been initiated with such countries as Israel and Finland. HDS is also involved in international policy development, program planning, and evaluation through membership of the U.S. delegation to the U.N. Commission on Social Development and expert committees and conferences of the United Nations.

The international staff of the Social Security Administration (SSA), also in HHS, provide similar services with regard to international social security matters. These include training activities as well as participation in the work of various international organizations that conduct programs on social security and technical and administrative research such as ILO, the International Social Security Association, and the Inter-American Conference on Social Security. Development of international social security standards and negotiations on bilateral social security agreements are important SSA functions. SSA's periodic publication *Social Security Programs Throughout the World,* which brings together comparative information on social security systems in all countries, is widely used as a reference by administrators and legislators.

In the Department of State, the Office of Coordinator for Multilateral Development Programs of the Bureau of International Organization Affairs provides major guidance for U.S. participation in international organizations. It thus serves as a liaison in work with the United Nations, the Organization of American States, and other international agencies concerned with social questions.

The many American-based voluntary organizations conducting international programs of service and assistance abroad are widely represented in every region of the world. In July 1984, the major American umbrella agencies—the American Council of Voluntary Agencies for Foreign Services and Private Agencies in International Development—merged to form a new consortium of over 100 private American voluntary organizations engaged in international development. The purpose of the new association—Interaction/American Council for Voluntary International Action—is to enable all these agencies to work together on issues of common concern, as well as to communicate and cooperate more effectively with the public and private sectors. The major areas of activity include development assistance, development education, material resources, migration and refugee affairs, private funding, and public policy–federal relations. The consortium has issued a brochure (Interaction, 1984) directory of members with precise information on its administration, programs, budget, and location of projects. It also publishes a biweekly newsletter on current issues and agency activities and maintains offices in New York and Washington, D.C.

United Nations Agencies

Center for Social Development and Humanitarian Affairs. In the United Nations, the Center for Social Development and Humanitarian Affairs, part of the U.N. Department of Economic and Social Affairs, (CSDHA) is the lead secretariat unit for international social welfare and social development. The extensive program of technical assistance, research, and information launched and carried forward in earlier decades has been drastically cut back because of changes in U.N. leadership and funding as well as shifts in national priorities. The relocation of the center from New York to Vienna in 1978 has limited its active participation in planning for technical cooperation and development activities in the New York headquarters.

Nevertheless, the center has provided major support for the extensive efforts required for the U.N. International Years and U.N. Decades. For example, in preparation for celebration of International Youth Year (IYY) in 1985, the center developed a specific program of measures and activities to serve as a model for international, regional, and national action. An international advisory committee met periodically to develop guidelines and suitable follow-up in the field of youth. The secretary general presented a comprehensive report (United Nations, 1985b) to the U.N. General Assembly on the wide range of activities and conditions involved in worldwide celebration of IYY. The primary emphasis was on concrete plans and programs at the national level. For IYY, 125 countries established national coordinating committees, and the NGO community was extensively involved. Two major studies

(United Nations, 1985c) on the situation of youth in the 1980s, prospects for the year 2000, and guidelines for a global plan of action for youth were completed during IYY.

In the field of aging, the center has actively followed up on the successful World Assembly on Aging and its plan of action. National interest has been maintained in both developing and industrialized countries. An international network for exchanging information is facilitating research and continuing collaboration. The center issues a bulletin on aging five times a year and a new scholarly journal (United Nations, 1985d) has been instituted. A trust fund provides some limited funds for technical cooperation.

A renewed emphasis on the family was an important new direction for the U.N. social development program in the 1980s. A U.N. seminar on the family was convened in Moscow in October 1984. An in-depth series of case studies (United Nations, 1984c) was completed and published by the United Nations late in the same year. The report examines different methods of designing and implementing a comprehensive approach to the delivery of child and family services. The study marks a useful beginning in the work of the center on the role of the family in development. The U.N. Economic and Social Council has authorized an action program of studies and information sharing between countries on developments related to the family.

Economic and Social Council. All social policy and programs at the U.N. are under the aegis of the U.N. Economic and Social Council (ECOSOC), the main body assisting the General Assembly in promoting economic and social development. (Programs and activities of the Center for Social Development and Humanitarian Affairs are authorized by ECOSOC.) ECOSOC has 54 members, 18 of whom are selected by the General Assembly each year for a 3-year term. The United States, the United Kingdom, France, and the Soviet Union have been members since the United Nations was founded. ECOSOC was established to promote higher standards of living, full employment and conditions of economic and social progress and development, social health, international cultural and educational cooperation, and uni-

versal respect for and observance of human rights and fundamental freedom for all.

ECOSOC's standing Commission on Social Development, meeting biennially, develops recommendations on social questions of international significance. It carries overall responsibility for policy related to social development as well as special accountability for areas of the social field not covered by specialized intergovernmental agencies. The agenda of each session of the commission ranges across the whole field of social development. The number of experts on the commission from any one area of the social welfare field is limited. Hence, detailed questions of social welfare administration and policy are usually considered by expert groups authorized by the commission. The reports of such groups have provided guidance to national governments and schools of social work in every part of the world.

Major recommendations from the Commission on Social Development are referred to ECOSOC for approval. Programs requiring authorization or new money are taken up for final General Assembly approval through the assembly's committees. An initiative may be taken by the commission—for example, the new emphasis on the family was developed at the commission session in 1982. The U.N. *Declaration on Social Progress and Social Development* (United Nations General Assembly, 1969) was influenced by the commission before its approval by the General Assembly. The proposal for an interregional consultation to follow up on the Conference of Ministers of Social Welfare was lobbied for vigorously in the commission, approved by ECOSOC, and is being implemented, with plans for convening the meeting in 1987.

Within the constraints of its infrequent meetings, the Commission on Social Development participates in development of U.N. strategies for each decade. Through its review of the *World Social Reports* and other U.N. studies, the commission calls attention to identified social needs and emphasizes the interdependence of social and economic development. It also oversees U.N. work in the preparation and follow-up of sectoral developments—for example, the U.N. Decade of Disabled Persons—and urges government implementation of the relevant U.N. recommendations.

U.N. Regional Commissions. The United Nations has decentralized many of its activities to five regional commissions—the Economic Commission for Europe (ECE), the Economic and Social Commission for Asia and the Pacific (ESCAP), the Economic Commission for Latin America and the Caribbean (ECLAC), the Economic Commission for Africa (ECA), and the Economic and Social Commission for Western Asia (ESCWA). These are located in Bangkok, Thailand; Santiago, Chile; Addis Ababa, Ethiopia; Geneva, Switzerland; and Baghdad, Iraq. The secretariats are staffed by regional officers, and the commissions, which meet annually, have become the major action arms of the United Nations.

All the regions develop their own economic and social programs within guidelines provided by ECOSOC. They have taken the lead in bringing together at the regional level top government members to consider social welfare policy issues. As U.N. resources for technical cooperation have become less available, the regions are reporting more emphasis on data collection and special studies. For example, ECA has completed two studies on social trends, strategies, and action programs undertaken in the African countries in light of the severe crises in Africa in the 1980s. ESCAP has expanded its regional social development data base and its research in special issues while maintaining advisory and technical training services, a popular program well established during its initial years of operation. In Europe—where ECE has limited its work to the economic sphere—an impressive series of regional social welfare seminars has been administered by the U.N. Center for Social Development and the European Center for Social Welfare Research and Training. Seminars covered such issues as the role of social welfare in current economic crises, the needs of the rural elderly, established social services versus new social initiatives, and welfare state developments and the new technology.

The regional commissions and their secretariats serve as a dynamic link between the needs and experiences of national governments and activities at U.N. headquarters. Thus, well in advance of a U.N. global conference, the regions organize the participation of member countries in advisory group discussions, in the collection of data, and in an evaluation of their experiences. To the extent that this activity is carried out effectively, international policies offer practical guidelines for action at both national and international levels.

U.N. Development Program. The U.N. Development Program (UNDP) is the central funding organization for technical cooperation in the U.N. system. More than $1.1 billion was spent for UNDP's overall activities in 1983. Voluntarily funded, it is the world's largest channel for multilateral technical and preinvestment cooperation. It is active in 150 countries and territories and in virtually every economic and social sector. More than 5,000 UNDP-supported projects currently operate at the national, regional, interregional, and global levels. The projects, jointly supported by UNDP and the host country, are aimed at helping developing countries make better use of their assets, improve living standards, expand productivity, and achieve self-reliance. Almost all projects are carried out either by the U.N. Department of Technical Cooperation for Development or by one of the 35 United Nations–related agencies, including specialized agencies such as WHO, ILO, UNESCO, and other U.N. organizations such as the World Food Program. The *Annual Report of the Administrator for 1983* (U.N. Development Program, 1984) provides full data on projects, priorities, and related activities.

UNDP also joins efforts to meet emergency situations. In 1984, the mounting food crisis in Africa was the basis for the U.N. secretary general's initiative for urgent international action. UNDP field officers are serving as centers for operational support for what is expected to be a large-scale, long-term international effort. UNDP has also intensified its collaboration with the Office of the United Nations High Commissioner for Refugees to respond to the issue of development that is necessarily part of the solution of the refugee problem. Collaborative work with the U.N. Children's Fund, the U.N. Fund for Population Activities, the World Food Program is another reflection of the UNDP's concern for social programming. In 1984, a senior advisor was appointed to handle so-called grass-roots and NGO matters. Overall, UNDP is actively pursuing its catalytic and coordinating role as a central funding organization for technical cooperation.

UNICEF. Established by the U.N. General Assembly as the United Nations International Children's Emergency Fund (UNICEF), the agency later changed its main emphasis from emergency work to a program of long-range benefit to children in developing countries. Its name is now simply the United Nations Children's Fund. When the General Assembly designated 1979, which was the twentieth anniversary of the adoption of the Declaration of the Rights of the Child, as the International Year of the Child, UNICEF served as the lead agency coordinating all U.N. activities. The aim of the Year of the Child was to encourage all countries to review their programs for children and enhance support for national and local actions.

UNICEF combines humanitarian and development objectives. It assists countries in planning and expanding services benefiting children and in exchanging experiences; provides funds to strengthen the training of national personnel, including child welfare specialists; and delivers technical supplies, equipment, and other aids. UNICEF assists governments to plan, develop, and extend—in both urban and rural environments—low-cash community-based services, maternal and child health care, and nutrition, education, parenting, and support services for women and girls. UNICEF also provides emergency relief to children and mothers following disasters, civil strife, or epidemics. UNICEF is financed entirely from voluntary contributions, with most of the money coming from governments. Greetings card sales and various fundraising activities as well as contributions, from individuals and organizations produce the balance of the funds. Total expenditures for 1984 were $345 million. The executive board report (UNICEF, 1985) discusses programs and resources.

Since UNICEF was established, social workers have been associated with the program at UNICEF headquarters in New York, in its many field offices, and in urban and rural projects in developing countries throughout the world. In its early years—from the late 1940s through the 1960s—UNICEF proved to be an important resource for national social services in developing countries. Training projects were initiated

and schools of social work strengthened. Over time, UNICEF has extended its collaboration to a range of international and national organizations concerned with meeting the acute needs of children in health, education, food and nutrition, and sanitation. In this broad program development, social services have played a lesser role, partially because of changed priorities in U.N. headquarters and a reduced project development staff in the U.N. unit responsible for social welfare.

The pervasive cutbacks in government services in the 1980s recession created a growing peril for children in developing countries. UNICEF responded by articulating new goals and program guides to be encompassed in a new "Children's Revolution." *Assignment Children* (UNICEF, 1983) discusses these measures in some detail. A series of tested low-cost measures to implement national child survival and development programs was recommended to reduce infant mortality and contribute to the healthy development of children. These included growth surveillance of young children, oral rehydration therapy (providing salt, sugar, and water) for children suffering from diarrhea and other effects of malnutrition, breast feeding and immunization, spacing of births, food supplements, and education of women and girls. Encouraging progress at the national level as a result of these efforts was noted at the 1985 UNICEF executive board meeting. The goal of universal immunization of all children by 1990, as enunciated by the United Nations, was strongly supported at this session of the UNICEF board.

Plans for the 1986 session of the UNICEF executive board called for consideration of a report of priority interest to the social work community. The report—*Children in Especially Difficult Circumstances* (Namazi, 1986)—discusses children endangered by armed conflicts and natural disasters, children endangered by exploitation, and those exposed to abuse and neglect. The report also presents recommendations for UNICEF action.

Other U.N. Agencies and Programs

International cooperation in other major sectors of the social welfare field—health, education, labor, and agriculture—is carried out by specialized U.N. agencies established by intergovernmental agreement. Their activities are coordinated by the U.N. Economic and Social Council. The major specialized agencies are ILO, WHO, the U.N. Educational, Scientific, and Cultural Organization (UNESCO), and the Food and Agriculture Organization (FAO). The impact of their services on improving social conditions in different countries has been an impressive demonstration of the value of international cooperation.

Of special interest to social work are ILO activities in the income security field. In addition to developing standards as set forth in conventions and recommendations, ILO staff have made numerous studies of social insurance and related income security problems. The administrative office provides technical assistance on social security questions, awards fellowships to trainees in a number of other countries, and holds regional seminars.

In June 1982, the 68th International Labor Conference adopted a new international convention (No. 157) revising and updating standards for international social security agreements. This convention, titled "Convention Concerning the Establishment of an International System for the Maintenance of Rights in Social Security" (International Labor Office, 1982), revises an earlier convention (No. 48) adopted by the nineteenth International Labor Conference in 1935. The adoption of this new convention and the standards it establishes largely reflect the considerable progress that has been made in the past 47 years in the development of bilateral and multilateral social security agreements, but it also represents an attempt to take an important new step in the direction of greater international cooperation by governments to protect the social security benefit rights of workers who cross international borders in pursuit of a livelihood.

Office of the High Commissioner for Refugees. From time to time the U.N. General Assembly creates special bodies to carry out social welfare assignments. One of these is the Office of the High Commissioner for Refugees (UNHCR). This office provides international protection to refugees within its mandate, gives assistance to the needy, and seeks permanent solutions to refugee problems by voluntary repatriation, local integration, or resettlement to another country.

UNHCR operations are financed by voluntary contributions. Expenditures under the 1984 General Programs totaled $335.5 million, and expenditures under Special Programs were $96.2 million.

The nature of refugee problems have fundamentally changed since UNHCR was established in 1951. Since the mid-1970s, increasing attention has been given to problems arising from mass movements of people who are forced to seek refuge elsewhere as a result of severe civil disturbances or military conflict in their countries of origin. Some of these mass movements involve hundreds of thousands or even millions of people. At the same time, UNHCR has continued its effective assistance to individual refugees and those who seek asylum, whose problems are as critical as those involved in large-scale resettlement.

The July 1984 Second International Conference on Assistance to Refugees in Africa (ICARA II), called in cooperation with the Organization for African Unity (OAU) and UNHCR, recognized technical and capital infrastructure assistance to countries with refugees or returnees as an important new element of international assistance. Refugee problems have indeed become global. As needs have grown around the world and appear to be of a long-term rather than a temporary nature, efforts are being made through research and evaluation to develop relevant policies based on assessed experience.

The universality of international refugee instruments was considerably strengthened during 1982 with the accession of the People's Republic of China to the United Nations Refugee Convention and Protocol relating to the status of refugees. The inclusion of El Salvador and Guatemala in 1983 brought to 95 the number of states that were party to this instrument.

In December 1982, the General Assembly acted on the continuing great need for international action on behalf of refugees and displaced persons of concern to the High Commissioner. The assembly decided to continue the Office of the High Commissioner for 4 more years from January 1984.

United Nations Relief and Works Agency for Palestine Refugees in the Near East. Another U.N. body in the refugee field is the United Nations Relief and Works Agency for Palestine Refugees in the Near East (UNRWA). Since 1950, the agency has been providing relief, education, training, and health and other services to Arab refugees from Palestine. UNRWA's mandate was expanded in 1967 to include humanitarian assistance on a temporary basis to other displaced persons in serious need as a result of hostilities. The agency's mandate has been extended several times, most recently until June 1987. The total number of Palestine refugees registered with UNRWA was 2,012,636 as of March 1984. The projected budget for 1985 was approximately $231.6 million, with a projected shortfall of $67 million.

The turmoil following Israel's move into Lebanon in 1982 created emergency needs costing millions of dollars as UNRWA attempted to help dislocated Palestine refugees. Schools, churches, and welfare services had to be reestablished, and a housing program had to be developed. As further crises have erupted, UNRWA's financial resources have been severely strained.

UNWRA's operations are financed by voluntary contributions. A special appeal for $13 million was made in 1983 for reconstruction of UNWRA's installations, camp infrastructure, and refugee housing. By early 1985, just over $10 million had been received.

Organization of American States

The Organization of American States (OAS), through its General Secretariat and its specialized organizations, carries on a variety of programs designed to accelerate social development. The approach is comprehensive and multidisciplinary, illustrated by two major projects initiated in 1982–1983. A project in Paraguay on integrated rural development was made possible through joint investment by the Inter-American Development Bank, the International Agricultural Development Fund, and the government of Paraguay. Another important project initiated in the same period was the OAS-Spain Labor Immigration Project involving the international migrant population in a 17-country area. The Caribbean Basin Initiative of the United States was a significant step forward that could potentially lay the groundwork for a new policy of hemispheric coop-

eration if extended to all the American States.

Overall, the OAS program is focused on employment and human resources planning. Areas of activity include vocational training for youth and worker participation in development, occupational safety and work conditions, social organization and participation, development of cooperatives and other forms of group management and community involvement, food security and nutrition, overcoming socially marginal conditions, and research and training facilities.

The work program is carried out through multinational, regional, and national projects. A multinational project on nonconventional training for youth in the Caribbean, which began in July 1983, is being carried forward by an agreement with U.S. AID for cooperation and cofinancing. The goal is to train and ensure the gainful employment of 1,250 young people. Regional projects have included courses for trade union leaders, technical services to improve housing cooperatives, and cooperative schools for rural workers. Advisory services in social security continue to be an important interest, with technical assistance provided each year to a number of member states.

The Inter-American Social Development Center (CIDES)—the main training and research facility of OAS, with headquarters in Buenos Aires, Argentina—offers national and regional courses on contemporary social development problems. Specialized seminars focus on useful methodology to evaluate a country's infrastructure and to prepare and evaluate social projects. The regional training program allows technicians to use fellowships for study in specialized fields in Latin American countries and in Europe.

Advisory services are now available through national projects focused on problems such as the renewal and development of marginal urban areas, on specific components of integrated social development programs, and on a variety of training activities designed to meet national needs. The whole program encourages the development and use of network facilities for interchange in employment, community development, and planning.

The Inter-American Children's Institute, a specialized organization with headquarters in Montevideo, Uruguay, cooperates with member states in the establishment and improvement of social welfare and other services for children, youths, and families. A Pan American Child Congress is held every 4 years to deal with the most important problems of childhood. A significant event was the Meeting of Experts on Adoption of Minors, held in Quito, Ecuador, in March 1983. Following the guidelines drawn at that meeting, actions on behalf of minors and families have been strengthened, and assistance has been provided to organizations in charge of coordinating activities for children in countries that have requested assistance. Cooperation with other national and international agencies continues to intensify, especially with OAS and U.N. agencies. Cooperation has also continued in developing Associations of Friends of the Inter-American Children's Institute, of great importance for the dissemination and promotion of the institute's ideas in the hemisphere. An agreement has been signed with the U.N. Latin American Institute for Prevention of Crime and the Treatment of Criminals, raising to 34 the number of agreements signed with other agencies and institutions.

The Inter-American Commission of Women, through its Permanent Secretariat, provides technical and financial support for specific projects, meetings, and research in education and jobs for women. Attention is given to interinstitutional coordination and the search for additional sources to finance projects requested by member countries. Activities include the development of industrial and support centers, legal services, work on family problems, nutrition, management training, and the establishment of national women's bureaus and seminars for bureau directors. The commission gives priority to projects that have potential impact on national development.

The Pan American Health Organization, through advisory services, workshops, and seminars, is helping to implement a regional plan of action to achieve the goal of health for all in the year 2000. The concept that health is part of the overall development process is emphasized, as well as increased attention to national efforts to encourage community participation. Interagency cooperation has been strengthened at the international and regional levels in a joint approach to health problems in Latin America and the Caribbean.

The Inter-American Indian Institute seeks to coordinate the policies of member countries toward their Indian populations, to stimulate awareness of Indian problems, and to promote research and training to develop Indian communities in the Americas. Specific problems are addressed, such as the condition of Indian groups living in border areas of two or more countries. Interagency agreements facilitate research to gain better knowledge of these groups and to solve their health, economic, and educational problems.

The Inter-American Institute for Cooperation on Agriculture sponsors a number of projects in social development in its broad program to improve agricultural production. Regional rural development projects include substantial social components and rural welfare activities in member countries.

International Voluntary Organizations

International nongovernmental, or voluntary, agencies have activities that complement in many ways the programs operating under intergovernmental and governmental auspices. Some of these organizations have consultative status with the United Nations or its specialized agencies. The activities of such agencies are likely to be closely coordinated with intergovernmental programs.

International bodies with membership in a number of countries include (1) organizations that provide a forum for international discussion and the exchange of information on social welfare subjects, (2) federations of national organizations that provide coordination and the exchange of information, and (3) agencies providing relief and services of an international character. Organizations having consultative status with the United Nations contribute in a significant way to intergovernmental action.

International Council on Social Welfare. Among the international organizations in the first category, the most important is the International Council on Social Welfare (ICSW). The council's leadership role during the past decade has grown as industrialized as well as new countries have sought interchange on effective social policy and practice. Organized in 1928 to promote the exchange of information and experience in social welfare, ICSW now has a membership of 85 national committees and more than 25 international organizations. Nonpolitical, nongovernmental, nondenominational, and nonprofit, the council has become a world organization for the promotion of social development.

The main functions of the council are
■ to provide a worldwide forum for the exchange of knowledge in the social welfare and social development field
■ to support and assist in national social welfare development
■ to act as a link between international nongovernmental and intergovernmental organizations that are concerned with social development issues.

The council has a central secretariat, with a small staff, located in Vienna, Austria. Regional activities are focused in their respective regions. The council also has a world program. Financial responsibility for the organization is based on an assessment similar to that of the United Nations, which uses a comparative scale of capacity among nations. Consequently, countries such as the United States and Canada bear a proportionately larger share of financial responsibility than small developing countries. The ICSW U.S. Committee is based in Washington, D.C., and directed by an elected board of individuals and organizations with a commitment to working for international social welfare through ICSW.

ICSW international conferences, which have an almost unbroken record of biennial global meetings since 1928, provide a unique world forum. For example, 87 countries sent more than 1,200 participants to the twenty-second International Conference held in Montreal in August 1984. At such conferences, administrators, practitioners, researchers, and other individuals concerned with social issues are offered an opportunity to extend their knowledge and exchange their experience with counterparts from other countries. The week-long event includes plenary sessions, special forums, and table discussions examining the conference theme from an overall or specialized perspective such as youths, the aging, or refugees. Workshops, a new feature of the conference, seek to identify suggested solutions to priority needs. A centerpiece for international exchange in social development, the ICSW conference is also the occasion for scheduling a number of other international meetings of a specialized nature, thus maximizing the potential for interchange between countries in the social welfare field. The twenty-third ICSW conference was scheduled for the end of August 1986 in Tokyo, Japan. The Federal Republic of Germany extended an invitation to hold the 1988 meeting in Berlin. The conferences have a heightened importance because no specialized intergovernmental agency for social welfare exists, and ICSW is frequently called on as the main voice of social welfare in the international community.

ICSW gives high priority to regional activities. For example, a working session in Harare, Zimbabwe, established plans for organizing regional and subregional meetings on issues of concern to the people of Africa, such as the training and exchange of social work personnel and action-oriented research. During the summer of 1985, ICSW regional seminars were held in Taipei, Taiwan, for Asia and the Western Pacific; in Lusaka, Zambia, for Africa; and in Turku, Finland, for the European area. The theme of the Turku seminar was The Post-Industrial Age: A Challenge for Social Policy and Action. During 1984, all ICSW regions including North America sponsored regional sessions on the topics of problems and policies related to youth.

The council has expanded its technical assistance. A pilot project launched in Asia has involved national councils on social welfare in Indonesia, Nepal, the Philippines, Sri Lanka, Thailand, Taiwan, and India. Positive results for the national bodies include an expansion in council membership, effective regional networks, and new opportunities for training in management, communications, and programming.

Similar ICSW project activities are now under way in Africa with the cooperation of Botswana, Malawi, Mauritius, Tanzania, Uganda, Zimbabwe, and Zambia. Grants from governments or other organizations in Canada, Australia, the Netherlands, Japan, and the United Kingdom have made possible this valuable extension of ICSW work. Preliminary consultation has been undertaken with member organizations in Latin America and countries in the Caribbean focusing on future project activity to study their national welfare structures and personnel.

Increasingly action-oriented, ICSW had a major role in organizing the activity of nongovernmental organizations for the highly successful World Assembly on Aging, conducting a workshop during the assembly and maintaining active follow-up. ICSW helped prepare for the U.N. Population Conference in Mexico in 1984, for the World Conference to Review and Appraise the Achievements of the United Nations Decade for Women, and for the International Youth Year. It was also involved in the celebration of the International Year of the Child and the International Year of Disabled Persons. ICSW shares its expertise and knowledge on social policies, services, and development with WHO, UNESCO, UNICEF, and the U.N. Center for Social and Humanitarian Affairs. Liaison personnel maintain channels of communication for the organization in New York, Geneva, Rome, and Vienna. This effective cooperation with U.N. bodies is possible because ICSW has consultative status with the United Nations. ICSW has presented views on major social issues before the U.N. Commission on Social Development, the Economic and Social Council, and the General Assembly. It is an excellent illustration of a nongovernmental organization contributing to intergovernmental action in social welfare and development.

Closely associated with ICSW are two other international social welfare organizations, the International Association of Schools of Social Work (IASSW) and the International Federation of Social Workers (IFSW). These three organizations jointly plan their biennial conferences to take place at the same site and within an agreed time frame. The three organizations jointly sponsor an official journal, *International Social Work,* published quarterly.

International Association of Schools of Social Work.
IASSW, founded in 1929, is a worldwide organization of individual schools and associations of schools of social work. Through IASSW, social work educators come together to share common interests, problems, and aims. More than 500 schools of social work and associations of schools in 70 countries are members. IASSW plays a leading role in developing standards of social work education internationally. The biennial International Congress of Schools of Social Work provides an exceptional opportunity for interchange among the worldwide community of social welfare professionals.

The expansion of social work education is well reflected in the second edition of the *World Guide to Social Work Education* (International Association of Schools of Social Work, 1984). This edition carries entries for 74 schools in 61 countries, 24 national and regional associations, and IASSW. The guide provides information to identify differences in national educational systems and in patterns and content of social work education within these systems. The guide also facilitates comparative study of social work education in a global context.

International Federation of Social Workers.
IFSW is made up of the national professional social work associations of 44 countries grouped into 5 regions covering Africa, Asia, Europe, Latin America and the Caribbean, and North America. Founded in 1956, IFSW aims to promote the social work profession through international cooperation and action. It is particularly concerned with professional practice standards, training, ethics, working conditions, and the participation of social workers in social planning and social policy formulation.

The IFSW biennial international symposium is one of a number of means by which IFSW promotes contact among social workers and supports the development and integration of social work theory and practice. At the general meeting in Montreal in 1984 (IFSW, 1985), policy papers adopted or in process included ones on child welfare, health, the elderly, client confidentiality, refugees, peace and disarmanent, education, rural communities, and youth. Different national associations of social workers have responsibility for working on the papers and presenting them. IFSW has also helped prepare for and follow up on the International Years and U.N. Decades.

International Social Security Association.
A major nongovernmental organization working in the social development field is the International Social Security Association (ISSA). Its objective is to protect, promote, and develop social security around the world.

As a worldwide organization, ISSA brings together official agencies responsible for the administration of social security. The association enjoys a special relationship with the International Labor Office and has been granted consultative status by the Economic and Social Council of the United Nations. Affiliate members of ISSA are government departments and central institutions or national federations of institutions that administer social security or any branch of social security. National institutions interested in the development of social security but which have no administrative responsibility are eligible for associate membership. ISSA currently has 252 affiliate members and 70 associate members in 123 countries.

ISSA activities include analysis of problems in social security worldwide, research and documentation, and regional programs especially designed to meet the needs of member organizations in the region. ISSA's outstanding series of publications includes the *International Social Security Review,* the only international quarterly publication in this field that is published in four languages.

A major event of the 1983 ISSA General Assembly was the organization of a roundtable discussion on the role of social security institutions in the development of social services. This theme was not new for ISSA, in that the association had undertaken extensive surveys during the 1960s and early 1970s to ascertain the involvement of social security institutions in providing social services. The roundtable was intended to update this work and examine to what extent the economic recession had had a negative effect on this activity. The agenda comprised a series of national reports on the provision of social services by social security institutions in areas such as programs for the aged (Czechoslovakia), the family (Argentina), the unemployed (the Netherlands), and marginal population groups (Mexico). The principal background report (International Social Security Association, 1983), prepared by Jean Iliovici of the ISSA Secretariat, is a highly useful analysis of the issues covered.

International Federation on Aging.
The International Federation on Aging (IFA) is a nongovernmental nonprofit organization that brings together national associations of

and for elderly people. Since its founding in 1973, IFA has grown from the original 17 organizations based primarily in Europe to 88 organizations in 45 countries on all continents. IFA has consultative status with the United Nations Economic and Social Council, ILO, and WHO. It serves as an international advocate for the well-being of older people and played an active role in promoting and following up on the 1982 U.N. World Assembly on Aging. The IFA program includes promotion of research, services, and the interchange of skills and information.

International Society for Rehabilitation of the Disabled.
The International Society for Rehabilitation of the Disabled is a world federation of voluntary organizations from approximately 80 countries. Its primary purpose is to improve rehabilitation services in all parts of the world and to assist professional workers and laymen toward a better understanding of the needs of the disabled.

League of Red Cross Societies.
Among international voluntary agencies serving as federations of national organizations, the League of Red Cross Societies is widely known. Comprising 135 national Red Cross and Red Crescent organizations, the league provides coordination and clearinghouse and exchange services for its member organizations. In its role as a permanent liaison for national societies, it conducts training institutes and seminars and arranges educational exchanges of Red Cross officials to help strengthen normal peacetime Red Cross activities, including improvements in public health, disaster relief, development of nursing services, and the Red Cross youth movement.

Youth Activities.
Organizations concerned with youth activities that are also pioneers in international cooperation include the Young Men's and Young Women's Christian Associations and the Boy and Girl Scouts.

Service and Relief Programs.
Many international voluntary agencies operate service and relief programs, and several have consultative status with the United Nations. Their services, coordinated with and complementary to intergovernmental activities, are

financed through their national member organizations. For example, International Social Service, with branches and offices in 15 countries, provides skilled services for individuals and families whose problems extend across national boundaries, studies problems underlying migration, and collaborates with organizations having related interests.

The International Union for Child Welfare encourages the development of services for children through studies and surveys, special conferences, and publications. The International Union of Family Organizations stimulates interchange in social programs affecting family life through international conferences and publications. The Catholic International Union for Social Service is active in encouraging high standards of professional social services and professional training of staff.

Other organizations operating service and relief programs include such agencies as the World Council of Churches, representing various Protestant denominations; the International Conference of Catholic Charities; and the World Organization for Rehabilitation through Training (ORT), an agency that promotes vocational training for Jewish people.

International Committee of the Red Cross. The International Committee of the Red Cross (ICRC), the founding body of the Red Cross movement, is a private Swiss organization. As a neutral intermediary, it carries out its work worldwide, mainly in times of armed conflict, internal strife, and the like. Its right to intervene in armed conflicts is embodied in the Geneva Conventions and their Additional Protocols, which are international treaties signed by governments aimed at protecting and assisting the victims of war. Beyond the scope of the Geneva Conventions, ICRC protects and assists political prisoners and their families when permitted by the governments concerned. Through its Central Tracing Agency, ICRC gathers information relating to prisoners, internees, and displaced persons; communicates to the families of captured and missing persons news of their relatives; traces missing persons; reunites members of dispersed families by organizing transfers and repatriations; and issues certificates of captivity and death and ICRC travel papers for refugees and people who are displaced or stateless.

Looking Ahead

The range of activities of these numerous international organizations has demonstrated that social welfare has a role in development. Through United Nations organizations and nongovernmental bodies, social welfare has contributed to international social policy and to social services. It has helped to enhance world awareness of human values and human needs, shared its knowledge and skills, and—at the same time—enlarged its own perspective. To achieve greater impact, this movement needs to be accelerated.

Expansion of intergovernmental social welfare depends on strong support from government representatives serving on U.N. authorizing bodies. This can be achieved through positive initiatives taken by the social welfare leadership in each country. In the nongovernmental sphere, closer coordination of the main social welfare organizations—ICSW, IASSW, and IFSW—in policy formulation and advocacy can make the role of social welfare increasingly visible and more effective in the action plans of world bodies.

DOROTHY LALLY

For further information, see INTERNATIONAL SOCIAL WELFARE: COMPARATIVE SYSTEMS; INTERNATIONAL SOCIAL WORK EDUCATION.

References

Hepworth, H. P. (1984, August). *Social Welfare in a World in Crisis: Perceptions and Responsibilities.* Paper presented at the 22nd International Conference on Social Welfare, Vienna, Austria.
Interaction/American Council for Voluntary International Action. (1984). *Interaction.* New York: Author.
International Association of Schools of Social Work. (1984). *World Guide to Social Work Education.* New York: Council on Social Work Education.
International Federation of Social Workers. (1985). *Minutes of the General Meeting, Montreal 1984.* Geneva, Switzerland: Author.
International Labor Office. (1982). "Convention Concerning the Establishment of an International System for Maintenance of Rights in Social Security." In *Record of Proceedings of the 68th International Labor Conference.* Geneva, Switzerland: Author.
International Social Security Association. (1983). "The Role of Social Security Institutions in the Development of Social Services: Recent Trends and Current Issues." *International Social Security Review, 36*(4), 509–528.

McNamara, R. S. (1980). "Report to the Board of Governors." In *The McNamara Years at the World Bank* (pp. 613–657). Baltimore, Md.: Johns Hopkins University Press.

Namazi, B. (1986). *Children in Especially Difficult Circumstances.* Paper prepared for UNICEF Executive Board, Geneva, Switzerland.

President's Council for Youth Exchange and the Consortium for International Citizen Exchange. (1983–1984). *International Youth Exchange: A Presidential Initiative.* Pueblo, Colo.: Author.

UNICEF. (1983). "A Child Survival and Development Revolution." In *Assignment Children* (pp. 21–31). Geneva, Switzerland: Author.

UNICEF. (1985). *Report to the Executive Board.* New York: Author.

United Nations. (1969). *Proceedings of the International Conference of Ministers Responsible for Social Welfare.* New York: Author.

United Nations. (1984a). *Social Aspects of Development: Report of the Secretary General.* New York: Author.

United Nations. (1984b). *United Nations Conferences and Special Observances* (Reference Paper No. 23). New York: Author.

United Nations. (1984c). *The Family: Models for Providing Comprehensive Services for Family and Child Welfare.* New York: Author.

United Nations. (1984d). *Developmental Social Welfare: A Global Survey of Issues and Priorities—1968–83.* Unpublished report. Vienna, Austria: Author.

United Nations. (1985a). *Report of the Conference to Review and Approve the Achievements of the United Nations Decade for Women: Equality, Development and Peace.* New York: Author.

United Nations. (1985b). *International Youth Year: Participation, Development and Peace.* New York: Author.

United Nations. (1985c). *Guidelines for Further Planning and Suitable Follow Up in the Field of Youth.* New York: Author.

United Nations. (1985d). *U.N. Periodical on Aging.* New York: Author.

United Nations Center for Social Development and Humanitarian Affairs. (1982). *Vienna International Plan of Action on Aging.* Vienna, Austria: Author.

United Nations Development Program. (1984). *Annual Report of the Administrator for 1983.* New York: Author.

United Nations General Assembly. (1969). *Declaration on Social Progress and Development* (Resolution 2542/XXIV). New York: Author.

U.S. Department of Health and Human Services. (1984). *Social Security Programs Throughout the World: 1983.* Washington, D.C.: Author.

For Further Reading

Brandt Commission. (1983). *Common Crisis North–South: Cooperation for World Recovery.* Cambridge, Mass.: M.I.T. Press.

Commission of the European Communities. (1984). *Report on Social Developments: 1983.* Washington, D.C.: European Community Information Services.

Hokenstad, M. C., & Druge, G. S. (1984). *Internationalization of the Social Work Curriculum: A Guide to Resources for Social Work Educators.* Cleveland, Ohio: School of Applied Social Sciences, Case Western Reserve University.

International Association of Schools of Social Work. (1985). *Survival and Development; Choices and Responsibilities; Challenges for Social Work.* Toronto, Canada: University of Toronto.

International Council on Social Welfare. (1984). *Biennial Report 1982/1983.* Vienna, Austria: Author.

International Council on Social Welfare. (1984, August). *Social Welfare in a World in Crisis.* Paper presented at the 22nd International Conference on Social Welfare, Montreal, Canada.

International Council on Social Welfare, International Association of Schools of Social Work, & the International Federation of Social Workers. (1986). *International Social Work.* London, England: Sage Publications.

Organization for Economic Cooperation and Development. (1985). *Social Expenditures 1960–1990: Problems of Growth and Control.* Paris, France: Author.

Stein, H. (1984). "Learning and Doing in International Social Development." In *Proceedings of the 22nd International Conference on Social Welfare* (pp. 52–58). Vienna, Austria: International Council on Social Welfare.

United Nations. (1984). *Basic Facts About the United Nations: 1984.* New York: Author.

United Nations. (1985). *1985 Report on the World Social Situation.* New York: Author.

United Nations. (1985). *Within Our Reach: Highlights of the Economic and Social Work of the United Nations—1945–1985.* New York: Author.

United Nations Children's Fund. (1984). *The State of the World's Children: 1984.* New York: Oxford University Press.

World Health Organization. (1984). *The World of WHO 1982–83: Biennial Report of the Director General to the World Health Assembly and to the United Nations.* Geneva, Switzerland: Author.

INTERNATIONAL SOCIAL WORK EDUCATION

Social work, as a worldwide expression of man's humanity to man, emerged out of centuries of personal benevolence and religious duty. Only in this century, however, has social work become nationally and internationally recognized as a professional discipline requiring special preparation.

Historical Note

Toward the end of the nineteenth century, social reformers and charity organizers in Europe and the United States came to the conclusion that some kind of training was essential for those engaged in helping the poor. Britain led the way in the 1890s with lectures and practical work related to the activities of the Charity Organisation Society and the Women's University Settlement in London. At about the same time in Germany, courses were started by Alice Salomon and others as an outgrowth of the embryonic women's movement. The Charity Organization Society in New York and the Hull House pioneers in Chicago paved the way for the establishment of professional social work education in the United States with short summer courses. The honor of establishing the first clearly defined school of social work, however, goes to a group of social reformers in Amsterdam, the Netherlands, who in 1899 founded the Institute for Social Work Training. The institute provided a 2-year full-time course of theoretical and practical training for men and women who wished to dedicate themselves to what was unequivocally designated as social work (United Nations, 1959).

By 1910, the movement had led to the founding of 14 schools of social work in Europe and the United States. In 1920, the first school in Latin America was opened in Santiago, Chile, through the efforts of the renowned Belgian doctor and social pioneer, René Sand. With the establishment in 1936 of the Tata Institute of Social Sciences in Bombay, India, the road to professional social work education was opened in Asia. South Africa in 1924 and Egypt in 1936 initiated programs of social work education, but it was not until the 1960s that schools or departments of social work came into being in most of Africa.

By that time, the United Nations had become the major motivating force and source of guidance for the establishment of social welfare services and schools of social work in the developing world. From its first meeting in 1947, the Social Commission (now the Commission for Social Development) of the Economic and Social Council was concerned with the preparation of social welfare personnel. An international survey of social work training was requested and completed in 1949 (United Nations, 1950). In 1951, the Social Commission and the Economic and Social Council adopted a resolution that recognized social work as an emerging profession with distinguishable functions and educational requirements. The first two paragraphs of that resolution defined the U.N. commitment:

> The Social Commission, having considered the report entitled *Training for Social Work: An International Survey* and the comments of governments on the suggestions contained therein, recommends the following principles:
> 1. That social work should in principle be a professional function performed by men and women who have received professional training by taking a formal course of social work theory and practice in an appropriate educational institution;
> 2. That these courses, whether provided at universities or special schools of social work, should be of the highest possible quality and should be sufficiently comprehensive to do justice to both the variety and unity of social work. (United Nations, 1951, p. 3)

A wide-ranging program was put into effect to assist governments in the staffing of newly established social welfare services with appropriately qualified personnel. In the 1950s and 1960s, the program—which included expert working groups, international and regional seminars, technical assistance to governments, and international exchange and fellowship opportunities—encouraged a veritable explosion of schools of social work throughout the developing world. The commission also authorized the continuing production of reports on social work training. *Training for Social Work: Third International Survey*, prepared by Dame Eileen Younghusband of the United Kingdom (United Nations, 1959), was a landmark study that contributed greatly to the sound development of new educational programs. It explored the nature of social work and its relationship to such emerging fields as community development; it examined the curriculum content and methods of teaching in social work education; and it discussed the training of auxiliary and other nonprofessional personnel.

The United Nations no longer plays a vital role in the development or strengthening of social work education, but for many years it produced periodic reports on professional and nonprofessional training of personnel for social welfare and social development functions. UNICEF and the International Association of Schools of Social Work (IASSW) also contributed significantly in the 1950s and 1960s to the growth of social work schools in Asia, Africa, and Latin America.

Patterns of Social Work Education

Social work education exists within national educational systems, which may differ in a number of respects from one country to another. There is no universal pattern of social work education, and even within countries a variety of models may coexist comfortably. Patterns of social work education may be described roughly as university and nonuniversity, but within that broad classification there are differences, ranging from the upper cycle of secondary education through several levels of higher, or tertiary, education. There are also substantial differences in the duration of training programs, usually related to the academic level at which the training is offered. A general description of prevailing patterns in each of the major geographical areas provides an overview.

Africa. Social work education in Africa still reflects the influence of the ex-colonial powers—France, Britain, Belgium, and Portugal—plus American varieties. Most of the Francophone, or French-speaking, countries retain the French and Belgian educational pattern: 3-year programs are offered by nonuniversity, postsecondary schools, which grant a certificate or state diploma. Several countries, however, have extended these programs to 4 years, two have established social work courses in national universities, and others have shortened the training to 2 years.

In the Anglophone, or English-speaking, countries, there is a greater degree of diversity. Intermediate and higher-level programs in university and in nonuniversity schools are frequently found in the same country, with the university usually taking responsibility for more advanced training. Egypt has two schools of social work in universities that offer master's and doctoral degrees in addition to a basic 4-year bachelor's degree program, four nonuniversity "higher institutes" that enjoy university status and offer a 4-year program leading to a bachelor's degree, and three nonuniversity "intermediate institutes" that grant a diploma on completion of 2 years of social work training.

Ghana, Kenya, Nigeria, Uganda, Zambia, and Zimbabwe also provide 3- to 4-year undergraduate university programs for higher positions and 1- to 2-year university or nonuniversity courses for front-line workers. Tanzania, which offers a 1-year certificate program and a 3-year diploma course in an independent national institute, is awaiting the development of a program of social work education within its national university. In South Africa, university education for social work has been the pattern from the beginning. A bachelor's degree on completion of 4 years (3 years in several universities) is the basic professional qualification; master's and doctoral degrees may also be earned in several universities.

Asia and the Pacific. Except for a few pockets of British educational influence, undergraduate or graduate university education along American lines prevails in most Asian countries. Again, there are many instances of mixed patterns. India, which might have been expected to follow the British model, took its lead from the Tata Institute of Social Sciences, established in Bombay in 1936 by an American missionary and developed by Indian social workers with master's degrees from leading U.S. schools of social work. Originally an independent educational institution, the institute was accorded full university status with degree-granting privileges in the 1960s. The American pattern—2 years of graduate study leading to a master's degree—was adopted by the Tata Institute and later became the model for subsequent programs in India, all of which were or are now established in universities. As in the United States, social work education in India has recently experienced a downward extension into undergraduate courses of study and an upward extension into doctoral programs. The histories of development in Pakistan and Bangladesh follow the Indian pattern.

Thailand, with one university school of social work, offers a master's degree, but the 4-year bachelor's degree program has always been the basic professional qualification. The Philippines and Korea initially adopted the American master's degree program but later shifted to 4 years of undergraduate education, with the bachelor's degree as the first professional degree; advanced degrees are available in both countries. Japan offers a wide range of programs: 2 years of study in community colleges, 4 years of undergraduate study in a college or university (the most common pattern), and 2 years of postgraduate work in a university for the master's degree. Two universities offer doctoral programs.

Even more complicated arrangements are found in some Asian countries. Indonesia, which inherited the Dutch pattern of nonuniversity schools of social work, provides different levels of education under a variety of auspices: secondary education courses and programs of undergraduate and graduate education in any of 21 university and nonuniversity schools of social work. The highest qualification—master of social work—is awarded by the nonuniversity school of social work related to the Ministry of Social Affairs.

Some schools in countries influenced by the British educational pattern have remained relatively unchanged in their organizational structure; others—usually those with more recently established programs—have combined elements of American and British models. In general, social work qualifications in Australia, New Zealand, Singapore, and Hong Kong consist of a diploma or degree awarded on completion of 3 or 4 years of undergraduate university study. However, Hong Kong has also initiated postsecondary courses in British-style polytechnics, and master's and doctoral programs are becoming available in Australia.

Europe. The considerable diversity in educational traditions and ideologies in Europe hinders easy generalization about schools of social work. Nevertheless, there are certain common as well as distinctive elements. Until recently, schools of social work in continental Europe operated as independent educational institutions under governmental, religious, secular, or political auspices. This remains the most common, although not the only, pattern in Austria, Belgium, Denmark, France, Greece, Italy, the Netherlands, Norway, Portugal, and Switzerland. Although schools in these countries are organized within the framework of tertiary education and frequently have the same admission requirements as universities, they are not equated with universities. The programs, usually 3 to 4 years in duration, are regarded as technical or specialized vocational (professional) training. The qualification awarded is a diploma or the title of social worker.

A new model in Germany bridges the technical and university levels of education. Legislation in the early 1970s transformed the schools of social work, with certain other professional and vocational schools, from secondary-level educational institutions into colleges. These *Fachhochschulen* define their programs as "course[s] of study designed as an alternative to (traditional) university education" (Rao & Kendall, 1984, p. 44). In Italy and Greece, as well, new legislation is altering the status of previously independent schools. The most significant change has occurred in the Nordic countries, where, with some exceptions in Denmark and Norway, schools that were once independent have been fully integrated into the highest level of university education.

There is no single pattern of social work education in the United Kingdom, which provides programs in universities, polytechnics, or colleges of further education. Present programs include 4-year bachelor's degree courses, 1-year postgraduate courses, 2-year courses for graduates, 2-year courses for nongraduates, and 3-year courses for nongraduates. The qualifications awarded include degrees, diplomas, and certificates. The unifying factor in the complicated British system is a process of certification of both courses and students by the Central Council for Education and Training in Social Work (CCETSW). Graduates of approved courses who meet CCETSW standards receive a certificate of qualification in social work (CQSW), which is the nationally accepted credential for professional practice.

University or college social work education is also standard in the Mediterranean countries. A formerly independent institute in Jordan has now become a 2-year junior college of social work. In Lebanon, a former nonuniversity school in the French style has become affiliated with a private university, with the prospect of awarding degrees as well as a diploma. A program of social work education is now offered by a university in Turkey; for many years the only course of study in that country was available through an independent academy sponsored by the ministry responsible for social welfare. Schools of social work in Israel (with the exception of a training institution under the Ministry of Social Welfare) are fully integrated into universities, offering 3-year programs leading to a bachelor's degree as the basic professional qualification. Master's degree programs have been developed, and doctoral education can also be pursued.

Relatively little is known about social work education in Eastern Europe. Schools of social work have been in operation in Poland and Yugoslavia for a number of years. In both countries, the schools were originally organized at the technical, postsecondary level. In 1983, however, Yugoslavia's 6 schools of social work became attached to universities. Social work courses enjoy the same status as those of other university departments, with 2- or 4-year programs leading to a first- or second-level diploma. In Poland, all but 2 of the 16 schools of social work are linked organizationally with medical training. Two years of study there leads to a diploma and the title of social worker. In addition, Poland has recently established a master's degree program in social work at the University of Warsaw. Czechoslovakia, with Poland, pioneered social work education in central Europe and from 1930 was represented on the board of the International Committee of Schools of Social Work (ICSSW). However, the only form of education offered there that might be regarded as social work training is a 2-year program in a secondary school of social law. After a decision some years ago to provide training for the social field, the government of Hungary appointed a team to design a program at the Institute of Sociology of the Hungarian Academy of Sciences. The team has been in communication with IASSW about patterns and programs in other countries, and it is anticipated that some form of social work education will soon be instituted.

Latin America and the Caribbean. The progression of schools of social work from one level of education to another is most clearly exemplified in Latin America. When Dr. René Sand developed the first school of social work in Chile along Belgian lines, social work education in independent schools became the model for all early programs in the rest of Latin America. The most important sponsors were ministries or governmental social welfare agencies, which operated schools of social work in Argentina, Bolivia, Brazil, Colombia, Chile, Ecuador, Guatemala, Mexico, Paraguay, Peru, and Venezuela. In these and in other countries, the Catholic church also established nonuniversity schools. Although this situation in general persisted until 1950, a new pattern first began to emerge in 1944, when an independent school in Costa Rica entered into a loose affiliation with a university; in 1947, the school became an integral part of the university. At about the same time, Panama initiated university social work education by making its school an integral part of the National University. Throughout the 1950s, independent schools in all the Latin American countries began to affiliate in one way or another with universities. By the end of the 1960s, a majority of the nonuniversity schools had adopted the new pattern, which, in the 1970s and 1980s, was followed by full integration into the universities.

Social work education in the early years favored nonuniversity schools, which provided a 3-year course of study (4 years in some countries), or a 4-year program when the school was affiliated with a university; generally, the qualification awarded was the title of social worker. A few countries still offer programs in nonuniversity schools at the intermediate or technical level, but the current pattern throughout the region is five years of university study (four years in some countries). The credential most commonly awarded on completion of a university program is the first degree of *licenciado*. Postgraduate study is developing in several countries, particularly in Brazil, where six master's degree programs and one doctoral program are now being offered. In addition, postgraduate specialization is available in 1-year advanced courses.

The pattern of social work education in Mexico differs somewhat from the rest of Latin America with respect to the ratio of technical to university programs. There are more than 100 schools of social work in Mexico grouped in four zones around the country, with a minimum of 6 schools in each zone. Statistics vary, but at most only 20 programs grant the qualification of *licenciado* following 4 or 5 years of university study. The majority provide 3 years of technical training at the postsecondary level in nonuniversity schools, and the qualification that is awarded on completion translates as "social work technician."

The islands of the West Indies, French-speaking Haiti, and the non-Spanish-language countries at the northern tip of South America are frequently placed in the Caribbean region. The University of the West Indies in Jamaica has functioned as a regional university and the major source of higher education for the islands. Three levels of social work education and training are offered. A 2-year course in the British pattern leads to the professional qualification of a certificate. Graduates of that program who have achieved a prescribed standard may take a third year and earn the degree of bachelor of social work. A regularly scheduled 4-month course designed as a form of in-service training for persons with some social welfare experience operates under the extramural department of the university, which awards a certificate of merit to those who complete the course satisfactorily.

Guyana formerly used the facilities of the University of the West Indies for the preparation of social workers, but in 1970, a 2-year social work program leading to a diploma was established in the department of sociology of the University of Guyana. In 1983, a 4-year bachelor's degree program was instituted as a second level of social work education. Haiti and Suriname have attempted to build their own facilities for qualifying social welfare personnel, but no information is currently available on their educational programs.

North America. For many years, schools of social work in the United States and Canada shared membership in the U.S.–based Council on Social Work Education (CSWE), which served as the accrediting body for social work education in North America. The partnership, which was terminated in 1970, extended beyond quality control, encompassing a broad range of activities designed to promote high standards of professional preparation. Canadian educators also maintained a close collegial relationship with their counterparts in the United Kingdom, but their educational programs were modeled on the 2-year postgraduate university structure developed in the United States. In the 1960s, pressing personnel needs led to a rapid expansion of social work education in Canada, which in turn prompted the Canadian Association of Schools of Social Work to develop a national educational policy establishing the bachelor of social work degree as the basic professional qualification for social work practice. Although schools in the United States were also moving in the direction of undergraduate as well as graduate professional education, the time had come to separate and end the accrediting relationship.

With some variations, the new pattern in Canada consists of 3 or 4 years of undergraduate university study that, upon completion, leads to the first professional degree of bachelor of social work; this may then be followed by a 12- to 18-month graduate program of advanced study for a master of social work degree. Three schools still offer a 2-year master's degree program that, unlike the new 1-year programs, does not require a B.S.W. for entry. Doctoral education has been available for a number of years in one school, and other schools are now considering such programs. Another departure from the prevailing pattern is found in French Canada, where a new type of educational institution has been established that bridges secondary and university education. Called *collèges d'enseignement général et professionel*, these institutions offer nonuniversity 2-year courses of study (including programs in social work education) for entry into either the universities or the labor market.

Social work education in the United States is discussed elsewhere in this encyclopedia, but for purposes of international comparison, a brief note on the current pattern is provided here. Professional social work qualifications are awarded at three levels of education: a bachelor's degree as the first professional credential, granted on completion of 4 years of study in an accredited undergraduate social work program; a master's degree, most often earned in 2 years of study at an accredited graduate school of social work, but also available in a shortened form for students holding an accredited bachelor's degree; and the doctoral degree, requiring 2 or more years of postmaster's study in a graduate school. In addition, advanced courses in various specializations are offered at the postmaster's level in programs of continuing education; students who successfully complete such courses are generally awarded a certificate. At the lower end of the scale, 2-year associate degree programs have been developed in community colleges as technical or auxiliary training for paraprofessionals in human services.

CSWE has established a Foreign Equivalency Determination Service, which assesses foreign social work credentials within the structure and content of U.S. social work education. Knowledge of the history, organization, and content of programs in other countries is needed to ensure appropriate comparisons and equitable judgments. For this purpose, IASSW has produced two editions of the *World Guide to Social Work Education* (1974, 1984), which include historical and descriptive information on representative schools of social work in the member countries. To produce guidelines for the assistance of individual countries, IASSW is also investigating national approaches to equivalency determination.

International Association of Schools of Social Work (IASSW)

The International Committee of Schools of Social Work (ICSSW) and the International Conference of Social Work (ICSW) were born in the course of the first international gathering of philanthropists, charity organizers, social workers, government officials, and others engaged in humanitarian work. When it was convened in Paris in 1928 by Dr. René Sand, more than 3,000 delegates from 42 countries searched for a new and improved approach to "the technique of philanthropy." Social work education was enthusiastically proclaimed as a means to professionalize and get better results from charitable activities.

Dr. Alice Salomon of Germany and Dr.

M. J. A. Moltzer of Holland took the lead in forming ICSSW to give practical expression to the high hopes expressed at the conference. Consequently in 1929, 46 schools in 10 countries became founding members of what is now IASSW. Leadership in this early period, was European, as were most of the activities. One exception, however, was the biennial International Congress of Schools of Social Work, in which educators from the United States and Canada played an important role.

The European network was shattered by World War II. Dr. Salomon, the founding president and secretary, had escaped detention by the Gestapo in Germany before the war but could not reconstitute the governing board or revive the membership from her exile in the United States. Dr. Sand again assumed leadership as president of ICSSW, mobilizing schools of social work in Europe and North America to meet the overwhelming need for social workers—in nonbelligerent as well as war-torn countries—to deal with the tasks of reconstruction and rehabilitation.

Following the death of Dr. Sand in 1953, the secretariat moved to the United States, where it received office space and staff support through CSWE. This arrangement continued until 1971, when sufficient funds became available for an independent secretariat under the direction of Dr. Katherine A. Kendall, who had previously served as a volunteer elected secretary-general while acting in various executive capacities with CSWE. When she retired in 1978, IASSW returned to Europe with Dr. Marguerite Mathieu of Canada as secretary-general. With assistance from the Austrian government, the secretariat was established in Vienna, also home to the International Council on Social Welfare, the European Centre for Social Welfare Research and Training, and U.N. offices related to social welfare.

IASSW is governed by an international board of directors consisting of 41 officers and members, 12 elected and 29 named by national, regional, and international organizations. A general assembly, made up of delegates from all member schools of social work, meets every 2 years in conjunction with the International Congress of Schools of Social Work, electing officers and board members, reviewing reports and board actions, and advising on policies and programs for the association. A primary activity of IASSW through the years has been the provision of an international forum for exploration of issues and common concerns in social work education. The biennial international congress is held in conjunction with ICSW and has concurrent sessions with the International Symposium of the International Federation of Social Workers. Worldwide dissemination of information on trends and developments is also provided through seminars, expert working groups, and publications.

A significant function of the association from its inception has been representation of the interests and expert knowledge of social work education before international and regional bodies. In the early years, ICSSW was involved with the Social Committee of the League of Nations and with the International Labor Office, which established a documentation center for social work education in Geneva. An immediate postwar concern for ICSSW was to find its proper place as a nongovernmental organization related to the United Nations. In 1947, it was granted consultative status by the Economic and Social Council, which led to active participation in the work of the Social Commission and to cooperative activities with the U.N. Secretariat in New York and the European office in Geneva. With the organization of economic commissions (which also handle social questions) in Africa, Asia, Latin America, and the Middle East by the United Nations, IASSW was enabled to extend its collaboration on U.N. projects. IASSW officers and board members also emerged as key figures in U.N. policy and program activities, serving on the Social Commission, as authors of U.N. studies and reports, directors of seminars, consultants to governments, and contributors to the training of social welfare personnel. A similar cooperative relationship was established with UNICEF. IASSW was also granted consultative status by UNESCO, the Council of Europe, and the Organization of American States.

Scarce financial resources have somewhat limited the program possibilities available to IASSW in working with member schools. Nevertheless, much has been accomplished through the work of volunteers, who have organized regional and international seminars, workshops, and consultations in cooperative arrangements involving IASSW and local schools or national and regional associations.

In the 1970s and 1980s, IASSW's leadership role in social work education in the developing world was recognized through grants for special projects awarded by the U.S. Agency for International Development, the Canadian International Development Agency, the Swedish International Development Authority, and the Austrian government. A number of nongovernmental funding agencies and foundations have also contributed to its programs. Basic support comes from annual dues from approximately 450 member schools in 68 countries. Individual associates also contribute through the payment of dues. Despite the paucity of resources, IASSW has had a major impact on social work education, particularly in the Third World.

Current Influences and Future Potentials

Until the mid-1960s, influences on social work education stemmed either directly or indirectly—through the United Nations—from the United States and certain European countries. The great expansion of schools of social work after World War II resulted, as noted earlier, from the commitment of the United Nations and UNICEF, assisted by IASSW, to the staffing of newly established social welfare services by qualified personnel. The use of Western educators as advisers was not only welcomed but insisted on by participating governments, who wanted the best for their countries. In their view, the best came from the West, particularly the United States. Scores of American, British, and Canadian educators were recruited to start or improve schools of social work throughout the developing world.

At the same time, educators in Europe used American casework to revitalize social work education and practice shattered by years of war and isolation. Through the European office of the United Nations and the U.S. Fulbright program, American educators conducted training seminars and served as casework teachers. Social work educators in Latin America—early recipients of the U.S. government's first international technical assistance program—embraced American casework as a better way of working with people than the paternalistic or autocratic and moralistic approach often found in their own countries.

Traffic was anything but one way. Scholarships and fellowships available from international agencies, national governments, and private sources brought social workers from all over the world to schools of social work in the United States, Canada, and the United Kingdom. This helped to internationalize the profession and instill a sense of unity among social work educators. It also served to solidify Western influence on social work education in the developing world, where graduates shared the views of their governments that what was good enough for the great universities of the United States and Britain should certainly be good enough for them. Because social work education was a new departure, they were constrained to use what they had learned rather than explore new patterns of structure and content better suited to their particular circumstances.

In the growing social discontent of the mid-1960s, new influences emerged to revolutionize social work education in Latin America, "decolonialize" schools of social work in Africa and Asia, and broaden the focus of educational programs in the Western world. The underlying forces at work included ideological-political factors, surging nationalism, rejection of foreign influences, repudiation of dependence on Western assistance and leadership, and—perhaps most galling to social workers, an apparent inability to cope with massive and seemingly insoluble problems. Social work educators experienced a crisis of confidence, even a crisis of credibility. In seeking solutions, they looked inward, with the result that there now exist within each region the beginnings of new configurations of social work education more closely related to national and local needs. Latin America has stressed reconceptualization of social work theory and practice, with the process of conscientization as a central element. Asia and Africa have adopted social development or developmental social welfare as key objectives for education and practice and have emphasized educational programs related to indigenous needs and conditions. Thus, Third World countries are attempting to refashion programs of social work education and practice from the ground up and to

contribute to social change, social and rural development, and, in some countries, the liberation of oppressed peoples.

In 1971, IASSW launched a new program in a number of developing countries calling for pilot schools to reexamine their educational programs. A major purpose of the program was to formulate educational objectives appropriate to each particular society, with a strong emphasis on indigenous curriculum development. International and regional seminars scheduled as part of this program brought together faculty members from the different regions to explore problems involved in shaping new patterns of social work education. The experience of regional exchange fostered by IASSW had already led to the establishment in 1965 of the Latin American Association of Schools of Social Work. The African Association for Social Work Education followed in 1971 as a result of a series of expert working groups cosponsored in Africa by IASSW and the United Nations. In 1974, Asian educators involved in the IASSW curriculum development project launched what is now called the Asian and Pacific Association of Social Work Education.

In Europe, too, regional development is a major trend. The European schools came together initially as an ad hoc committee in association with IASSW; by 1980, however, the IASSW European Regional Group for Social Work Education had been established. European diversity will in all likelihood foster the creation of subregional groups as well. German-speaking schools are currently engaged in joint activities, and the Nordic schools have met regularly since the mid-1950s as the Scandinavian (now called the Nordic) Committee of Schools of Social Work to hold seminars and work on common concerns.

Although regional groupings have encouraged the schools to seek and express a new identity—reflected in programs with a greater emphasis on preventive and developmental aspects of social work, innovative field practice, and methodologies directed toward social change—regionalism is not without its problems. Indigenous development that subordinates social work education to extremes of nationalism or sectarianism or a particular ideology cannot long survive as a professional discipline. If parochial concerns become the overriding preoccupation of schools of social work, the inevitable result will be stultified growth. The greatest potential for the future of social work education lies in the fusion of local and global knowledge and experience in meeting human and social needs. Experience may be local, but knowledge knows no national boundaries. In the 1980s, there is welcome evidence that those schools of social work responsibly rooted in their native soil are producing new insights into social work intervention that will add to the store of knowledge for all schools.

The emphasis in Third World schools on national needs and local traditions is definitely a worldwide trend. So, too, is the long-standing debate on social work as an instrument of social change versus social work as treatment of social ills and personal problems. In Europe and North America (particularly the United States), this question has taken on new urgency as a result of attacks on the welfare state. Erosion of public support for governmental assistance to the disadvantaged has led to curtailment of services traditionally staffed by social workers. For the first time, in some countries, social workers are appearing in the ranks of the unemployed. A social climate hostile to the values and functions of social work hampers recruitment into the profession and has increased the attractiveness of private practice rather than agency employment as a career goal for those who enroll in schools of social work. The new pattern of university education for social work in continental Europe has introduced cross-disciplinary programs of social work education, increasing the tension between those who wish to stress preparation for clinical practice and those who see social policy, planning, and administration as more appropriate to a university discipline.

A global review of social work education reveals similarities as well as differences. Historically, programs of social work education, no matter how they are organized, are informed by humanistic values and encompass knowledge of social ills and social provision, understanding of individuals and society in interaction, and methods of intervention into social and human problems. The challenge for the future of international social work education is to make common cause with diversity, accept a pluralistic conception of the role of the social worker, and affirm the values that have characterized social work as a caring profession.

KATHERINE A. KENDALL

For further information, see CONTINUING EDUCATION; INTERNATIONAL SOCIAL WELFARE ORGANIZATIONS AND SERVICES; PROFESSIONAL ASSOCIATIONS: COUNCIL ON SOCIAL WORK EDUCATION; SOCIAL WORK EDUCATION.

References

Rao, V., & Kendall, K. A. (1984). *World Guide to Social Work Education.* New York: Council on Social Work Education, IASSW.

United Nations. (1950). *Training for Social Work: An International Survey* (United Nations Publication Sales No.: 50. IV. II). New York: United Nations.

United Nations. (1951). "Report of the Social Commission." *Economic and Social Council Official Records* (13th Session, Supplement 12, 1950). New York: United Nations.

United Nations. (1959). *Training for Social Work: Third International Survey* (United Nations Publication Sales No.: 59. IV. I). New York: United Nations.

For Further Reading

International Association of Schools of Social Work. (1973). "New Themes in Social Work Education." *Proceedings of the International Congress of Schools of Social Work, 1972.* Vienna, Austria: Author.

International Association of Schools of Social Work. (1974). *World Guide to Social Work Education* (1st ed.). Vienna, Austria: Author.

International Association of Schools of Social Work. (1975). "Education for Social Change: Human Development and National Progress." *Proceedings of the International Congress of Schools of Social Work, 1974.* Vienna, Austria: Author.

International Association of Schools of Social Work. (1977). "Social Realities and the Social Work Response." *Proceedings, International Congress of Schools of Social Work, 1976.* Vienna, Austria: Author.

International Association of Schools of Social Work. (1980). "Discovery and Development in Social Work Education." *Proceedings of the International Congress of Schools of Social Work, 1978.* Vienna, Austria: Author.

Kendall, K. A. (1978). *Reflections on Social Work Education 1950–1978.* Vienna, Austria: International Association of Schools of Social Work.

Smith, M. J. (1965). *Professional Education for Social Work in Britain—An Historical Account.* London, England: National Institute for Social Work Training.

University Grants Commission. (1978). *Review of*

Social Work Education in India—Retrospect and Prospect. New Delhi: Author.

Yiman, A. (1984). *Curricula of Schools of Social Work and Community Development Training Centres*. Addis Ababa, Ethiopia: Association for Social Work Education in Africa.

Younghusband, E. (1978). *Social Work in Britain: 1950–1975* (Vol. 2). London, England: George Allen & Unwin.

INTERVIEWING

Irrespective of practice setting, social workers use interviewing as a major vehicle to accomplish their objectives. Interviewing is the primary mode of influence used by direct practitioners, but administrators and social planners also rely heavily on its techniques in their work. Interviews vary according to purpose and type of setting and may involve individuals, couples, or family units. Interviews are conducted in offices, homes, hospitals, prisons, automobiles, and other diverse settings. Despite the many variables that may be involved, certain factors are essential to *all* effective interviews—among them purpose, structure, direction, and focus.

The purpose of an interview in social work is to exchange information in order to illuminate and solve problems, promote growth, and plan strategies or actions aimed at improving people's quality of life. The structure of an interview varies somewhat from setting to setting, from client to client, and from one phase of the helping process to another. Indeed, skillful interviewers adapt flexibly both to different contexts and to the ebb and flow of each individual session. Thus each interview is unique. Still, effective interviews conform to a general structure, manifest certain properties, and reflect use of the same skills by interviewers.

Initial Interviews

Initial interviews generally involve three phases: (1) establishing rapport (including making introductions), (2) exploring problems and expectations, and (3) negotiating goals and formulating a contract.

Establishing Rapport. A cardinal feature of effective interviews is open communication, which in turn requires at least minimal rapport between the participants. Achieving rapport requires that clients gain trust in the practitioner's helpful intent and goodwill, so that they are willing to risk revealing personal and sometimes painful feelings and information.

Establishing rapport begins with introductions. In making introductions and in addressing clients, it is prudent to use surnames or to determine how clients prefer to be addressed. Although some clients prefer the informality of using first names, it is important to others to be addressed by their surnames. For example, blacks tend to interpret being addressed by their first names as indicative of a lack of respect (Edwards, 1982; McNeely & Badami, 1984).

With many clients, practitioners must surmount formidable barriers before achieving rapport. The majority of clients have had little or no experience with social workers and enter initial interviews with uncertainty and apprehension. Many view having to seek assistance with their problems as evidence of failure, weakness, or inadequacy. Moreover, revealing personal problems is embarrassing and even humiliating for many people, especially those who have difficulty confiding in others. Clients' difficulties in communicating openly tend to be even more severe when their problems involve such socially unacceptable behavior as child abuse, sexual deviations, moral infractions, and criminal behavior.

Cultural factors further compound potential barriers to rapport. Many Asian Americans have been taught not to discuss personal or family problems with outsiders. Revealing problems to others may be perceived as a reflection of personal inadequacy and as a stigma on an entire family. The resultant fear of shame may thus impede communication with such clients. Blacks, American Indians, and Hispanics may experience difficulty in developing rapport with whites because of distrust caused by their history of being exploited or discriminated against by whites.

One means of fostering rapport is a warm-up period. This is particularly important with ethnic minority clients for whom such periods of informal exchange are the cultural norm. Aguilar (1972), for example, has stressed the importance of warm-up periods with Mexican Americans:

When Mexican-Americans meet to negotiate or arrange affairs, the first step is to set the climate or *ambiente*. A preliminary period of warm, informal, personal conversation precedes the discussion of the concerns that brought them together. Jumping into the middle of serious and controversial affairs—as many persons in the United States are inclined to do—seems confusing and even discourteous to most Mexican-Americans. (p. 67)

Hull (1982) has cautioned practitioners about the hazards of not engaging in a warm-up period with American Indians and has clarified the need to proceed at a generally relaxed tempo. Consistent with Hull's observation, Palmer and Pablo (1978) suggested that practitioners who are successful with American Indians are low-key and nondirective. People of Polynesian background also typically expect to begin new contacts with outside persons by engaging in "talk story," which involves warm, informal, and light personal conversation similar to that described by Aguilar.

Warm-up periods are also important in gaining rapport with adolescents. Because they are in a stage of emancipating themselves from adults, adolescents may be wary of practitioners. This tendency is particularly strong among delinquents and those who are rebelling against authority. Moreover, adolescents who have had little or no experience with social workers may view them as adversaries, fearing that their role is to punish or to exercise power over them in some manner.

With the majority of clients a brief warm-up period is sufficient. When special ethnic or age barriers do not apply, introductions and a brief discussion of a timely topic (unusual weather, a current local or national event, or a topic of known interest to the client) adequately foster a climate conducive to exploring the client's concerns. Most clients, in fact, expect to plunge into discussion of their problems early on, and their anxiety level is heightened if practitioners delay getting to the business at hand.

Empathic Responding. Another vital factor that fosters rapport is responses (both verbal and nonverbal) that convey understanding and acceptance of clients' feelings. Empathic responses to clients' verbal and nonverbal messages convey understanding in a form that clients can readily discern. Empathic responses clearly say, "I am with you; I hear and understand what you are saying and experiencing."

Being empathically attuned involves not only grasping clients' immediate and apparent feelings but also identifying the underlying emotions and discovering their meaning, function, and personal significance. To get in touch with camouflaged feelings and meanings, the practitioner must tune in not only to the client's verbal messages but also to more subtle cues—including facial expressions, tone of voice, tempo of speech, and postures and gestures—that may amplify or contradict verbal messages.

Although responding empathically involves attempting to perceive the client's world of experience, the practitioner must avoid being overwhelmed by the client's feelings. "Being with" thus involves focusing intensely on the client's affective state without losing perspective or taking on the client's emotions. Gladstein (1983) argues persuasively that the element of empathy referred to by social psychologists as "emotional contagion" (that is, acquiring the same emotional state as another person) involves an overreaction and can create emotional distress for practitioners, hindering a helping stance.

Practitioners often convey empathy nonverbally through facial expressions and gestures that mirror clients' feelings. They also employ several different types of verbal empathic responses, such as:

1. "I gather you're feeling really discouraged about the whole situation."
2. "At best, it's a miserable and overwhelming situation for you."
3. "You seem to be feeling, 'I'm really confused and have to sort this out so I can take some action.'"
4. "So I take it you felt like a real klutz and wanted to disappear."

The first message is a typical reflective response that pinpoints the feeling (discouragement) and reflects it back to the client. The second message reflects a state of being ("a miserable and overwhelming situation") rather than pinpointing a specific feeling. The third message reflects a feeling (confusion) but puts it in the first person as though the client is expressing the feeling. The last message uses a simile to express a feeling ("like a real klutz"). Practitioners should use varying forms of empathic responses, avoiding such repetitious and shopworn phrases as, for example, "What I hear you saying is . . . ."

Empathic responding can be used for many purposes other than establishing rapport. Hepworth and Larsen (1982) have identified seven additional uses:

- Staying in touch with clients
- Facilitating exploration of problems
- Eliciting feelings expressed nonverbally
- Helping to make confrontations more palatable
- Handling obstacles that are presented by clients
- Managing strong feelings (including hostility)
- Facilitating group discussions.

Because of its versatility, empathic responding may be regarded as the workhorse of interviewing.

A large number of research studies (Truax & Mitchell, 1971) reported that skills in empathic responding are correlated with positive case outcomes. More recent outcome studies (Parloff, Waskow, & Wolfe, 1978), however, have produced somewhat divergent findings. Gladstein (1983) has attributed this divergence to the conceptual complexity of empathy and to the fact that different empathy scales tap different dimensions of empathy. An earlier correlational study (Kurtz & Grummon, 1972) of different empathy scales supports this view. Gladstein (1983) has attempted to unravel some of the conceptual confusion. Nevertheless, experts are still virtually unanimous that empathy is critical to effective interviewing.

Relating as a Genuine Person. Another complex factor that fosters rapport involves the practitioner's sharing of self by relating in a natural, sincere, spontaneous, open and genuine manner. Being authentic or genuine involves relating in such a way that expressions are spontaneous rather than contrived. Practitioners' verbalizations are also congruent with their actual feelings and thoughts. Authentic practitioners thus relate as real persons, expressing and assuming responsibility for their feelings rather than denying them or blaming the client for causing them.

Authenticity also involves being nondefensive and human enough to admit errors to clients. Because they expect clients to lower their defenses and increase their vulnerability by relating openly, practitioners must be models of humanness and openness and avoid hiding behind a mask of "professionalism."

Practitioners who relate genuinely provide clients with an experience that more closely approximates the clients' social worlds than do practitioners who conceal themselves behind a professional facade. They thus facilitate the clients' transfer of openness to the broad arena of interpersonal relationships—a transfer that is generally held to reflect positive growth and achievement of personal and interpersonal potential.

The aspect of genuineness denoted as self-disclosure has been variously defined by different authors (Chelune, 1979). For this discussion it will be defined as the conscious and intentional revelation of information about oneself through both verbal expressions and nonverbal behaviors (for example, by smiling or grimacing at something the client has said or shaking one's head in disbelief). Viewed from a therapeutic perspective, practitioner self-disclosure encourages clients to reciprocate with trust and openness. In fact, numerous research studies (Doster & Nesbitt, 1979) indicate that client self-disclosure is correlated with practitioner self-disclosure.

Being authentic and self-disclosing does not mean that practitioners indiscriminately disclose feelings or focus on their own feelings. In fact, some genuine expressions can be abrasive, inappropriate, and destructive. A general guideline, therefore, is that practitioners should engage in self-disclosure only when doing so is likely to further therapeutic objectives.

Researchers have studied the differential effects of several types of self-disclosure. Danish, D'Augelli, and Hauer (1980) have distinguished between self-involving statements and personal self-disclosing statements. The former include messages that express the practitioner's personal reaction to the client during the course of a counseling session. Examples of this type would be, "As I listened to you just now, I found myself feeling excited about the goals you've set for yourself" or "I want to share with you my reaction to what you just said." By contrast, personal self-disclosing statements shift the focus to the practitioner. These have been subdivided by Danish, D'Augelli, and Brock (1976) into statements that disclose a problem the practitioner had in the past that resembles the client's problem and statements that reveal a current problem that is similar to the client's.

Research findings comparing the effects of the different types of self-disclosures have been mixed (Dowd & Boroto, 1982; McCarty & Betz, 1978; Reynolds & Fischer, 1983). Given the sparse and inconclusive findings, practitioners should be judicious in their use of self-disclosure. Logic suggests that disclosing current problems may undermine clients' confidence and that focusing on the practitioner's problems diverts attention from the client. Self-involving statements, on the other hand, appear to be more relevant to the helping process.

Still another aspect of self-disclosure involves levels of intensity, ranging from superficial to highly personal statements. Giannandrea and Murphy (1973) found that individuals returned for second interviews at a higher rate when the interviewer used moderate rather than high or low levels of self-disclosure. Other studies (Mann & Murphy, 1975; Simonson, 1976) report similar findings.

Practitioner self-disclosure is not, however, the primary mode for fostering client self-disclosure. In fact, Vondracek (1969) found that probing messages elicit greater client self-disclosure than either self-disclosing or reflective messages. Another qualification is that practitioners should exercise discretion in using self-disclosure with psychotic clients. Shimkunas (1972) and Doster, Surratt, and Webster (1975) report that paranoid schizophrenic patients show higher levels of symptomatic behavior (for example, delusional ideation) after personal self-disclosure by practitioners. Superficial self-disclosure, by contrast, did not produce increases in disturbed behavior.

Starting Where the Client Is. A critical concept in establishing and maintaining rapport and psychological contact with clients is starting where the client is. Applying this concept to interviewing involves focusing attention on clients' immediate concerns and emotional states. If, for example, a client is emotionally upset at the beginning of an initial interview, focusing attention on these emotions and related factors tends to reduce distress that might otherwise impede the exploration process. Moreover, responding sensitively to clients' emotions fosters rapport as the client begins to experience the practitioner as a concerned and perceptive person.

The concept of starting where the client is is particularly important in work with ethnic minority clients. These clients usually feel vulnerable and need assurance that it is safe to take chances in new and unknown relationships. Because it will take more time to establish rapport with such clients, practitioners must be careful not to move at too rapid a pace. With many ethnic minority clients, starting where the client is involves a warm-up period.

The concept of starting where the client is also has critical significance with involuntary clients. Because these clients are compelled by external sources to seek help or are institutionalized against their will, they generally enter initial interviews with negative and perhaps hostile feelings. Practitioners should therefore begin by eliciting and focusing on these feelings until they subside. By responding empathically and conveying understanding and acceptance, skillful practitioners often succeed in neutralizing negative feelings, thus enhancing clients' receptivity to exploring their problems. If practitioners fail to deal with clients' negativism, they are likely to encounter persistent sullenness, recalcitrance, and other forms of resistance.

The importance of starting where the client is has been documented by the research findings of Duehn and Proctor (1977). Building on the work of Rosen (1972), these researchers subdivided the concept into two operational components. The first, stimulus-response congruence, refers to the extent to which a practitioner's responses provide feedback to clients that their messages are accurately received. The second, content relevance, involves the extent to which a practitioner's responses are relevant to clients' substantive concerns. Based on analysis of practitioners' performance on these skill components in initial interviews, Duehn and Proctor found higher dropout rates among clients whose interviewers responded more frequently with messages that were not congruent or relevant to the clients' substantive concerns. It thus appears that starting where the client is enhances client satisfaction, fosters continuance, and also greatly facilitates the establishment of a viable working relationship.

Exploring Problems. When clients are ready, it is appropriate to begin exploring problems. Practitioners typically initiate the process with open-ended probing messages (discussed later) such as: "Could you tell me about your situation and how you think I might be helpful?" and "Could you share with me the difficulties you've been having so we can think about them together?"

Clients receiving such messages generally respond by beginning to relate their difficulties. The practitioner's role at this point is to draw out clients, to convey understanding, and to seek the information needed to gain a clear picture of the factors involved in their difficulties. Some clients provide rich information spontaneously or with little assistance. Others may be hesitant, struggle with emotions, or have difficulty expressing themselves.

Furthering Responses. Practitioners use a number of skills to facilitate the process of exploration, often blending two or more in a single response. One type of skill, known as furthering responses, encourages clients to continue verbalizing. Furthering responses include minimal prompts (both verbal and nonverbal) and accent responses, both of which convey attention, interest, and an expectation of the client's continued verbalization. Minimal prompts include short but encouraging responses such as "Yes," "I see," "Mm-hmm," "And?" "But," or "Then what?" Nonverbal furthering messages include head-nodding, facial expressions, and gestures that acknowledge receptivity and commitment to understanding. Accent responses involve repeating, in a questioning tone of voice or with emphasis, a word or short phrase contained in the client's previous message. For instance, if a client says, "I've really had it with the way my supervisor at work is treating me," the practitioner might respond, "Had it?" to prompt further elaboration by the client.

Verbal Following Responses. Another type of skill, called verbal following responses, facilitates communication (and fosters rapport) by providing clients with immediate feedback that their messages have been heard and understood. Verbal following is simply defined as "respond[ing] to client communication rather than asking questions or directing discussion" (Katz, 1979, p. 217). Verbal following messages thus start where the client is and ensure that practitioners maintain close psychological contact with clients.

Paraphrasing is a verbal following response frequently used by practitioners to provide feedback that they have grasped the content of a client's message. Paraphrasing involves using fresh words to restate the client's message concisely. Paraphrasing responses are more apt to focus heavily on the cognitive aspects of client messages (that is, to emphasize situations, ideas, objects, persons) than on the client's affective state (Cormier & Cormier, 1979), although reference may be made to feelings that are obvious. Below are two examples of paraphrasing responses:

> *Client*: I knew retiring would be hard because my life has centered around my work. But it's even worse than I expected. I just don't know what to do with myself.
> *Practitioner*: So it's been even tougher for you than you expected and a real struggle even now.

> *Client*: Yesterday I should've stayed in bed. I wrecked the car, got a ticket, and my date stood me up.
> *Practitioner*: Sounds like yesterday was a real disaster for you. Everything went wrong.

Empathic responding, which was discussed earlier, is another form of verbal following. It differs from paraphrasing by providing feedback that the practitioner is aware of emotions rather than cognitive content. Such messages are critical in effective communication.

Still another form of verbal following involves summarizing responses. Summarizing responses may be used to condense the essential content or feelings of lengthy and complex messages or to make connections between related aspects of separate messages. Summarization is also commonly used at the conclusion of an interview to review its major focal points. Hepworth and Larsen (1982) have discussed at length the various uses of this important skill.

The importance of verbal following skills is shown by their inclusion in all systematic programs designed to teach interviewing skills (Danish, D'Augelli, & Hauer,

1980; Larsen & Hepworth, 1978; Mayadas & O'Brien, 1976; Schinke et al., 1980; Zastrow & Navarre, 1979). Social work instruments designed to evaluate interviewing effectiveness also include items related to this variable (Finn & Rose, 1982; Katz, 1979). Moreover, in a study comparing the pre- and post-training interviewing competence of social work students, Katz (1979) found that verbal following ability was by far the most accurate predictor of how students would be rated. In this regard Katz observed: "Inexperienced interviewers tend to be more patently manipulative and try to get clients moving in a particular direction, while experienced interviewers tend to respond more communicatively to clients' thoughts and feelings." (pp. 216–217)

Both paraphrasing and empathic responding are especially crucial with clients who have limited language facility, including ethnic minority clients and those who are developmentally disabled. Practitioners should be careful not to assume that such clients understand them and vice versa. It is vital to slow down the pace of communication and to be especially sensitive to nonverbal indications of confusion. To avoid embarrassment, such clients sometimes indicate they understand messages when in fact they are perplexed.

With clients who have been culturally conditioned not to discuss personal or family problems with outsiders, practitioners need to make special efforts to grasp intended meanings. Such clients are often unaccustomed to interviews and tend not to discuss their concerns openly. Rather, they may send covert messages and expect practitioners to discern their problems by reading between the lines. Thus, more extensive use of feedback is needed to determine if practitioners' perceptions of intended meanings are "on target." Using feedback in this way can avoid unnecessary, reciprocal misunderstanding. Further, clients generally appreciate practitioners' efforts to reach shared understandings, interpreting patience and persistence as evidence of being respected and valued.

Structuring Responses During the entire process of exploration, practitioners assess the significance of information revealed as their clients discuss problems and interact with the practitioner or with each other. Indeed, judgments about the meaning and significance of fragments of information guide the practitioner in deciding which aspects of a problem are salient and warrant further exploration, how ready a client is for deeper exploration of certain facets of a problem, what patterned behaviors of the client or system interfere with effective functioning, when and when not to draw out intense emotions, and so on. In fact, Proctor (1983) has reported research findings indicating that, during initial and subsequent sessions with clients, "Relatively high proportions of workers' verbalizations were devoted to content guidance—responses in which workers explicitly indicated content areas for discussion with clients" (p. 30).

Content areas relevant for exploration vary from situation to situation. However, clients who belong to certain populations—such as delinquents, unwed mothers, nursing home residents, the mentally retarded, patients in psychiatric institutions, or families in the same stage of life development—generally have many problems in common. Before interviewing clients from populations with which they are unfamiliar, inexperienced practitioners can prepare themselves by drawing up a list of promising problem areas for exploration. This reduces the likelihood of focusing on areas irrelevant to clients' problems and eliciting numerous bits of inconsequential information.

It is important, however, not to follow an outline rigidly or to use it as a crutch. Rigidly structured interviews preclude spontaneity and prevent clients from relating their stories in their own way. As noted earlier, the practitioner's role is to encourage clients to discuss their problems freely and to facilitate the in-depth exploration of any problems that emerge. The flexible use of outlines thus may involve reordering the sequence of topics; modifying, adding, or deleting topics; or abandoning the outline altogether if using it hinders communiciation.

Open- and Closed-Ended Probing Messages Open-ended probing messages are typically used to initiate problem exploration and to begin exploration of selected content areas. Used to initiate exploration, they define a topic but leave clients free to respond in any way they choose. Because they do not limit the client's response, such relatively unstructured probing messages invite expanded verbalization and tend to elicit information rich in self-disclosure. The following are examples of open-ended probing responses:

> Please tell me more about how you reacted when you learned you were going to lose your leg.
>
> Could you tell me about how the two of you decided to get marital therapy?
>
> I'm curious about how your family makes decisions about family activities.

By contrast, closed-ended questions not only define a topic but restrict clients' responses to a few words or to yes and no answers. As such, they are typically used to elicit specific information otherwise not likely to be disclosed. Typical examples of closed-ended questions are:

> How many children did your parents have?
>
> Are you taking any medications?
>
> Who is your landlord?
>
> How long have you lived in this city?

Although closed-ended questions restrict clients' responses and thus yield limited information, in many instances they are essential to fill in gaps in information.

Beginning practitioners typically ask too many closed-ended questions, many of which are inefficient because they block communication or are irrelevant to the helping process. When this occurs, an interview tends to take on the flavor of an interrogation, the practitioner bombarding the client with questions and taking responsibility for maintaining verbalization. In fact, research studies (Finn & Rose, 1982; Schinke et al., 1980) have revealed that experienced and inexperienced social workers are sharply differentiated by their use of closed-ended responses. Beginning social workers use them frequently and open-ended responses infrequently. The reverse is true of experienced social workers.

Seeking Concreteness. Clients (like most people) tend to relate problems and to describe events in general terms (for example, "We fight over everything"). Moreover, in relating feelings they often use vague terms with numerous possible meanings, such as "upset" or "frustrated." Consequently, to achieve precise understanding of problems and communications, practitioners must be skillful in directing exploration toward in-

creasing specificity. Seeking concreteness (also known as "specificity of response") is an indispensable skill for eliciting specific information. Like verbal following, it is included in all systematic skill development programs.

To appreciate fully the critical significance of seeking concreteness, it is important to realize that accurate understanding requires that all possible meanings of a message be reduced to the precise meaning intended by the sender. A client may report, for example, "My husband is cruel." A skillful interviewer will avoid making assumptions about the meaning of the term "cruel" and will instead seek concreteness by using a response such as one of the following:

> In what way is he cruel?
>
> Could you clarify what you mean by cruel?
>
> Would you give me some recent examples of how he is cruel?

By moving toward specificity, the practitioner may determine that "cruel" means withholding companionship or making caustic remarks rather than being physically abusive.

Hepworth and Larsen (1982) have identified and discussed eight categories of responses used to seek concreteness:

- Checking out perceptions to determine if one has accurately interpreted a client's message
- Clarifying the meaning of vague or unfamiliar terms
- Exploring the basis of opinions and conclusions drawn by clients
- Assisting clients to personalize their messages rather than speaking abstractly of focusing on others
- Pinpointing emotions when clients express feelings in vague or general terms
- Shifting the focus from the "there and then" to the "here and now"
- Eliciting details related to significant events.
- Eliciting behavioral details involved in interaction.

The importance of seeking concreteness has been supported by the research of Proctor (1983), whose analysis of the use of structuring responses by experienced social workers during initial and second interviews disclosed a relatively high and constant rate of specificity responses.

Focusing Responses. Because practitioners spend limited time with clients, it is critical that they give direction to interviews by avoiding wandering conversations that consume valuable time. In fact, sharp focusing differentiates effective interviews from social conversations. Focusing skills are also vital because some clients shift rapidly from one topic to another. Without focusing interventions, interviews with such individuals would become fragmented and explorations of topics would be superficial.

Focusing responses typically blend several of the exploring skills discussed previously. After an open-ended response is used to initiate exploration of a topic, furthering responses, verbal following skills (particularly paraphrasing and empathic responding), and responses that seek concreteness are used to elicit the additional information needed to gain full and accurate understanding of the topic. To illustrate this blending, we have borrowed the following example from Hepworth and Larsen's (1982) chapter on focusing skills:

Client (single male, age 20): There has to be something wrong with me, or women wouldn't treat me like a leper. Sometimes I feel like I'm doomed to be alone the rest of my life. I'm not even sure why I came to see you. I think that I'm beyond help.

Practitioner: You sound like you've about given up on yourself—as though you're utterly hopeless; but apparently part of you still clings to hope and wants to try. (Empathic response)

Client: What else can I do? I can't go on like this, but I don't know how many more times I can get knocked down and get back up.

Practitioner: I sense you feel deeply hurt and discouraged at those times. Could you give me a recent example of when you felt you were being knocked down? (Blended empathic and concrete response)

Client: Well, a guy I work with got me a blind date. I took her out, and it was a total disaster. I know I'm no Prince Charming, but you'd think she could at least let me take her home. After we got to the dance, she ignored me the whole night and danced with other guys. Then, to add insult to injury, she went home with one of them and didn't even have the

decency to tell me. There I was, wondering what had happened to her.

Practitioner: Besides feeling rejected, you must have been mad as blazes. When did you first feel you weren't hitting it off with her? (Blended empathic and concrete response)

Client: I guess it was when she lit up a cigarette while we were driving to the dance. I kidded her about how she was asking for lung cancer.

Practitioner: I see. What was it about her reaction then, that led you to believe you might not be in her good graces? (Concrete response)

Client: Well, she didn't say anything. She just smoked her cigarette. I guess I really knew then that she was upset at me. (p. 148)

In the above example, the empathic responses focused on and conveyed concern for the client's distress. Open-ended responses and responses that seek concreteness yielded details of a recent event and valuable clues that the client may be rejected by women because of insensitive and inappropriate social behavior.

Exploring Expectations. At some point during an interview, it is important to determine what the client expects from the helping process and from the practitioner. Clients' expectations vary considerably, sometimes diverging markedly from what practitioners can realistically provide. Unless practitioners are aware of such unrealistic expectations and handle them successfully, clients may be keenly disappointed and discontinue after the initial interview (Aronson & Overall, 1966; Mayer & Timms, 1969; Perlman, 1968; Rhodes, 1977).

Formulating Goals and Negotiating a Contract. After exploring problems adequately, if the problems match the agency's function and clients manifest readiness to proceed in the helping process, it is appropriate to negotiate a contract. Ordinarily, contracting begins by engaging in goal selection, which is introduced by explaining the rationale for formulating goals. Goals are vital because they give direction and purpose to the problem-solving process and serve as criteria of its progress and outcome. They should be mutually negotiated, and clients should be given major responsibility for selecting the goals they perceive as relevant to their problems. Clients who perceive goals as irrelevant tend to self-terminate after the initial interview (Duehn & Proctor, 1977; Epperson, Bushway, & Warman, 1983). Criteria for selecting goals have been discussed at length by Hepworth and Larsen (1982).

After negotiating goals, the focus shifts to defining the participants' roles—a process known as role induction. Clarity about expected roles reduces ambiguity (and hence anxiety) for clients. It also eliminates unnecessary, time-consuming testing behavior by clients seeking to learn what is expected of them or attempting to control the interaction with the practitioner. Moreover, research has indicated that effective role induction fosters clients' continuance in the helping process (Hoehn-Saric et al., 1964).

Both initial interviews and the contracting process conclude with discussions of the means of accomplishing goals and of length and frequency of sessions, who will participate, duration of the helping process, fees, time of the next appointment, provisions for renegotiating the contract, means of monitoring progress, pertinent agency policies and procedures, and other relevant matters. Research has documented the importance of contracting in clients' continuance beyond initial interviews (Seabury, 1976).

Providing Continuity

During the often difficult and always challenging process of attaining goals, it is important to maintain focus on one goal until clients have made sufficient progress to warrant shifting to another. Otherwise, they may jump from one concern to another without achieving significant progress. The burden therefore falls on the practitioner to provide clients with structure and direction. Maintaining focus during single sessions and continuity from one session to the next are critical. To provide continuity, summarizing skills are used to review tasks clients have agreed to implement between sessions and to begin subsequent sessions by discussing their experience in implementing these tasks (Reid, 1978).

Change-Oriented Skills

During the change-oriented phase of the helping process, practitioners use additional interviewing skills to facilitate change, drawing from a wide range of interventions aimed at inducing change. The focus here is on selected interviewing skills, namely additive empathy, interpretation, and confrontation. Before considering these skills, however, it is important to note that all the skills identified earlier are employed during the change-oriented phase, although to a diminished extent. Relationship building, exploration, assessment, goal selection, and contracting are ongoing processes.

Additive Empathy. This skill (also known as expanded empathy) involves empathic responses that go somewhat beyond what clients have expressed, comprising some degree of inference by practitioners. Hence additive empathic responses are moderately interpretive; that is, they interpret clients' feelings, thought patterns, needs, environmental factors, motives, beliefs, and dysfunctional patterns that bear on their difficulties. Insights into the effects of such factors can be extremely valuable to clients with limited awareness of the forces that produce their difficulties.

Additive empathic responses help clients to get in touch with emotions that lie at or slightly beyond the edge of awareness, enabling them to experience feelings more fully and to integrate them into their total experience. Among the additional purposes of additive empathy (Egan, 1975; Hammond, Hepworth, & Smith, 1977; Hepworth & Larsen, 1982) is the expansion of clients' awareness of (1) underlying meanings of feelings, thoughts, and behavior; (2) wants and needs; (3) hidden purposes of behavior; and (4) unrealized strengths and potentialities. (Guidelines to the use of additive empathy and self-instructional exercises and modeled responses are included in the preceding references.)

Interpretation. In recent years, theoreticians and researchers have devoted considerable attention to interpretation, a concept that has generated much controversy over the years. Historically, interpretation has been a primary tool of psychoanalytically oriented practitioners, whereas proponents of several other theories (most notably, client-centered, gestalt, and certain existential theories) have eschewed this technique. Still others (Claiborn, 1982; Levy, 1963) maintain that interpretation is essential to the counseling process regardless of theoretical orientation, and that many behaviors of practitioners (whether intentional or not) perform interpretive functions. Semantic and conceptual confusion has contributed to this divergence in views, but recent writings have tended to sharpen concepts, reducing vagueness and confusion.

Based on Levy's (1963) conceptualization, Claiborn (1982) posits that interpretation, irrespective of theoretical orientation, "presents the client with a viewpoint discrepant from the client's own, the function of which is to prepare or induce the client to change in accordance with that viewpoint" (p. 442). Viewed in this light, interpretation encourages clients to see their problems from a different perspective, with the desired effect of opening up new possibilities for remedial courses of action. This generic view, which emphasizes a discrepant viewpoint, is sufficiently broad to encompass many change-oriented techniques identified in different theories, including reframing (Watzlawick, Weakland, & Fisch, 1974); relabeling (Barton & Alexander, 1981); positive connotation (Palazzoli et al., 1974), redefining problems (Hepworth & Larsen, 1982), positive reinterpretation (Hammond, Hepworth, & Smith, 1977), additive empathy, and traditional psychoanalytic interpretation. The content of interpretations of the same clinical situation thus varies with the theoretical allegiances of practitioners; however, according to the research (Claiborn, 1982), "Interpretations differing greatly in content seem to have a similar impact on clients" (p. 450).

Levy (1963) puts interpretations into two categories, semantic and propositional. Semantic interpretations describe clients' experiences according to the practitioner's conceptual vocabulary (for example, "By 'frustrated,' I gather you mean you're feeling hurt and disillusioned"). Semantic interpretations are thus closely related to additive empathic responses.

Propositional interpretations, on the other hand, involve the practitioner's notions or explanations of causal relationships among factors in clients' problem situations (for example, "When you try so hard to avoid displeasing others, you displease yourself and end up resenting others for taking advantage of you"). Claiborn (1982) presents numerous examples of both types of interpretation as well as comprehensive discussion of

this important topic. Other researchers (Beck & Strong, 1982; Claiborn, Crawford, & Hackman, 1983; Dowd & Boroto, 1982; Feldman, Strong, & Danser, 1982; Milne & Dowd, 1983) have also reported on the comparative effects of different types of interpretation.

Confrontation. This potent technique involves facing clients with factors that contribute to their problems or that block progress toward goal attainment. Confrontation is relevant when clients manifest blind spots to discrepancies or inconsistencies in their beliefs, emotions, or behavior that perpetuate dysfunctional behavior. (A comprehensive analysis of discrepancies and inconsistencies is contained in Hammond, Hepworth, & Smith, 1977, pp. 286–318).

Blind spots to discrepancies, of course, are universal, and an external vantage point enables the practitioner to offer fresh perspectives and corrective feedback. Skillful confrontations, then, are aimed at expanding clients' awareness of forces that underlie resistance to change.

Confrontation, interpretation, and additive empathy are all used to expand clients' awareness of the psychodynamic forces that mediate their behavior. In fact, Egan (1975) maintains that effective confrontation is merely an extension of accurate empathy. Confrontation, however, is used only to assist clients to discover and resolve behaviors that are discrepant with their desired changes and that thus impede progress or threaten to undermine the helping process. By contrast, interpretation and additive empathy are used to expand awareness in diverse therapeutic situations.

Confrontation involves some risk to the helping relationship because clients may interpret confrontations as criticisms, putdowns, or rejections. Consequently, they may react by feeling hurt or hostile or by withdrawing. In extreme instances they may fail to return for additional interviews. It is important, therefore, to couch confrontations in language that indicates helpful intent and goodwill. Confrontations should also be used with discretion, and practitioners should avoid adopting a confrontive style of interviewing because of the risk of inflicting psychological damage on clients (Lieberman, Yalom, & Miles, 1973). In fact, highly skilled practitioners foster self-confrontation (which involves little risk) by drawing clients' attention to issues, behaviors, or inconsistencies they may have overlooked. The following are examples of messages that encourage self-confrontations:

> I can understand you gained some satisfaction when you told your teacher off, but I'm wondering how it made things better for you.

> Let's stop and look at what each of you just did to produce the strain you're feeling now.

> I'm having trouble seeing how the behavior you just described relates to your goal. How do you see it?

Effective direct confrontations embody four elements: (1) expression of concern, (2) reference to the client's goal, belief, or commitment, (3) the discrepant behavior (or absence of behavior), and (4) the probable negative outcomes of the discrepant behavior. The following message (Hepworth & Larsen, 1982, p. 407) illustrates a confrontive response. The numbers following parts of the message correspond to the numbers of elements just cited:

> (To male parolee): Al, I know the last thing you want is to have to return to prison.(2) I want you to stay out too, and I think you sense that. But I have to level with you. (1) You're starting to hang out with the same bunch you got in trouble with before you went to prison. (3) You're heading the same direction you were before, and we both know where that leads.(4)

The risk of putting clients on the defensive or alienating them is reduced by delivering confrontations in a warm, concerned tone of voice that conveys caring. Further, practitioners should be alert to the possible negative reactions following confrontations, responding empathically to reduce defensiveness and to clarify helpful intent. These are but two of numerous guidelines that are important to effective use of confrontations. Other guidelines, as well as skill development exercises and modeled responses are available in works by Egan (1975), Garrett (1982), Hammond, Hepworth, and Smith (1977), and Hepworth and Larsen (1982).

DEAN H. HEPWORTH
JO ANN LARSEN

For further information, see ASSESSMENT IN DIRECT PRACTICE; CONTRACTING AND ENGAGEMENT IN DIRECT PRACTICE; DIRECT PRACTICE IN SOCIAL WORK: OVERVIEW; ETHNIC-SENSITIVE PRACTICE.

References

Aguilar, I. (1972). "Initial Contacts With Mexican-American Families." *Social Work*, *17*(3), 66–70.

Aronson, H., & Overall, B. (1966). "Treatment Expectations of Patients in Two Social Classes." *Social Work*, *11*(1), 35–41.

Barton, C., & Alexander, J. F. (1981). "Functional Family Therapy." In A. S. Gurman & D. P. Kniskern (Eds.), *Handbook of Family Therapy* (403–443). New York: Brunner/Mazel.

Beck, J. T., & Strong, S. R. (1982). "Stimulating Therapeutic Change With Interpretations: A Comparison of Positive and Negative Connotation." *Journal of Counseling Psychology*, *29*(6), 551–559.

Chelune, G. J. (1979). "Measuring Openness in Interpersonal Communication." In G. Chelune & Associates, *Self-Disclosure*. San Francisco: Jossey-Bass.

Claiborn, C. D. (1982). "Interpretation and Change in Counseling." *Journal of Counseling Psychology*, *29*(5), 439–453.

Claiborn, C. D., Crawford, J. B., & Hackman, H. W. (1983). "Effects of Intervention Discrepancy in Counseling for Negative Emotions." *Journal of Counseling Psychology*, *30*(2), 164–171.

Cormier, W., & Cormier, L. (1979). *Interviewing Strategies for Helpers: A Guide to Assessment, Treatment, and Evaluation*. Monterey, Calif.: Brooks/Cole Publishing Co.

Danish, S. J., D'Augelli, A. R., & Brock, G. W. (1976). "An Evaluation of Helping Skills Training: Effects on Helpers' Verbal Responses." *Journal of Counseling Psychology*, *23*(3), 259–266.

Danish, S. J., D'Augelli, A. R., & Hauer, A. L. (1980). *Helping Skills: A Basic Training Program*. New York: Human Sciences Press.

Doster, J. A., & Nesbitt, J. G. (1979). "Psychotherapy and Self-Disclosure." In G. Chelune & Associates, *Self-Disclosure* (pp. 177–224). San Francisco: Jossey-Bass.

Doster, J. A., Surratt, F., & Webster, T. N. (1975, March). "Interpersonal Variables Affecting Pathological Communications of Hospitalized Psychiatric Patients." Paper presented at meeting of Southeastern Psychological Association, Atlanta, Ga.

Dowd, E. T., & Boroto, D. R. (1982). "Differential Effects of Counselor Self-Disclosure, Self-Involving Statements, and Interpretation." *Journal of Counseling Psychology*, *29*(1), 8–13.

Duehn, W. D., & Proctor, E. K. (1977). "Initial Clinical Interaction and Premature Discontinuance in Treatment." *American Journal of Orthopsychiatry, 47*(2), 284–290.

Edwards, A. W. (1982). "The Consequences of Error in Selecting Treatment for Blacks." *Social Casework, 63*(7), 429–433.

Egan, G. (1975). *The Skilled Helper: A Model for Systematic Helping and Interpersonal Relating.* Monterey, Calif.: Brooks/Cole Publishing Co.

Epperson, D. L., Bushway, D. J., & Warman, R. E. (1983). "Client Self-Terminations After One Counseling Session: Effects of Problem Recognition, Counselor Gender, and Counselor Experience." *Journal of Counseling Psychology, 30*(3), 307–315.

Feldman, D. A., Strong, S. R., & Danser, D. B. (1982) "A Comparison of Paradoxical and Nonparadoxical Interpretations and Directives." *Journal of Counseling Psychology, 29*(6), 572–579.

Finn, J., & Rose, S. (1982). "Development of Validation of the Interview Skills Role-Play Test." *Social Work Research and Abstracts, 18*(2), 21–27.

Garrett, A. (1982). *Interviewing: Principles and Methods* (rev. ed.). New York: Family Service America.

Giannandrea, V., & Murphy, K. C. (1973). "Similarity, Self-Disclosure and Return for a Second Interview." *Journal of Counseling Psychology, 20*(6), 545–548.

Gladstein, G. A. (1983). "Understanding Empathy: Integrating Counseling, Developmental, and Social Psychology Perspectives." *Journal of Counseling Psychology, 29*(4), 467–482.

Hammond, D., Hepworth, D., & Smith, V. (1977). *Improving Therapeutic Communication.* San Francisco: Jossey-Bass.

Hepworth, D. H., & Larsen, J. A. (1982). *Direct Social Work Practice: Theory and Skills.* Homewood, Ill.: Dorsey Press.

Hoehn-Saric, R., et al. (1964). "Systematic Preparation of Patients for Psychotherapy—I. Effects on Therapy Behavior and Outcome." *Journal of Psychiatric Research, 2*(4), 267–281.

Hull, G., Jr. (1982). "Child Welfare Services to Native Americans." *Social Casework, 63*(6), 340–347.

Katz, D. (1979). "Laboratory Training to Enhance Interviewing Skills." In F. W. Clark et al. (Eds.), *The Pursuit of Competence in Social Work* (pp. 205–226). San Francisco: Jossey-Bass.

Kurtz, R. R., & Grummon, D. L. (1972). "Different Approaches to the Measurement of Empathy and Their Relationship to Therapy Outcomes." *Journal of Consulting and Clinical Psychology, 39*(1), 106–115.

Larsen, J. A., & Hepworth, D. H. (1978). "Skill Development Through Competency-Based

Education." *Journal of Education for Social Work, 14*(1), 73–81.

Levy, L. H. (1963). *Psychological Interpretation.* New York: Holt, Rinehart & Winston.

Lieberman, M. A., Yalom, I. D., & Miles, M. D. (1973). *Encounter Groups: First Facts.* New York: Basic Books.

McCarty, P. R., & Betz, N. E. (1978). "Differential Effects of Self-Disclosing Versus Self-Involving Counselor Statements." *Journal of Counseling Psychology, 25*(4), 251–256.

McNeely, R. L., & Badami, M. K (1984). "Interracial Communication in School Social Work." *Social Work, 29*(1), 22–25.

Mann, B., & Murphy, K. C. (1975). "Timing of Self-Disclosure, Reciprocity of Self-Disclosure, and Reactions to an Initial Interview." *Journal of Counseling Psychology, 22*(4) 303–308.

Mayadas, N. S., & O'Brien, D. E. (1976). "Teaching Casework Skills in the Laboratory: Methods and Techniques." In *Teaching for Competence in the Delivery of Direct Services* (pp. 72–82). New York: Council on Social Work Education.

Mayer, J. E., and Timms, N. (1969). "Clash in Perspective Between Worker and Client." *Social Casework, 50*(1), 32–40.

Milne, C. R., & Dowd, E. T. (1983). "Effect of Interpretation Style and Counselor Social Influence." *Journal of Counseling Psychology, 30*(4), 603–606.

Palazzoli, M. Selvini, et al. (1974). "The Treatment of Children Through Brief Therapy of Their Parents." *Family Process, 13*(4), 429–442.

Palmer, B., & Pablo, S. (1978). "Community Development Possibilities for Effective Indian Reservation Child Abuse and Neglect Effects." In M. Lauderdale, R. Anderson, & S. Cramer (Eds.). *Child Abuse and Neglect: Issues on Innovation and Implementation* (Vol. 1). Washington, D.C.: U.S. Department of Health, Education, and Welfare.

Parloff, M., Waskow, I., & Wolfe, B. (1978). "Research on Therapist Variables in Relation to Process and Outcome." In S. Garfield & A. Bergin (Eds.), *Handbook on Psychotherapy and Behavior Change* (pp. 233–282) New York: John Wiley & Sons.

Perlman, H. H. (1968). *Persona: Social Role and Responsibility.* Chicago: University of Chicago Press.

Proctor, E. K. (1983). "Variables in the Structuring of Early Treatment." *Social Work Research and Abstracts, 19*(1), 26–33.

Reid, W. J. (1978). *The Task-Centered System.* New York: Columbia University Press.

Reynolds, C. L., & Fischer, C. H. (1983). "Personal Versus Professional Evaluations of Self-Disclosing and Self-Involving Counselors."

Journal of Counseling Psychology, 3(30), 451–454.

Rhodes, S. (1977). "Contract Negotiation in the Initial Stage of Casework." *Social Service Review, 5*(1), 125–140.

Rosen, A. (1972). "The Treatment Relationship: A Conceptualization." *Journal of Clinical Psychology, 38*(3), 329–337.

Seabury, B. A. (1976). "The Contract: Uses, Abuses, and Limitations." *Social Work, 21*(1), 16–21.

Schinke, S. P., et al. (1980). "Developing Intake-Interviewing Skills." *Social Work Research and Abstracts, 16*(4), 29–34.

Shimkunas, A. M. (1972). "Demand for Intimate Self-Disclosure and Pathological Verbalization in Schizophrenia." *Journal of Abnormal Psychology. 80*(2), 197–205.

Simonson, N. R. (1976). "The Impact of Therapist Disclosure on Patient Disclosure." *Journal of Counseling Psychology, 23*(1), 3–6.

Truax, C., & Mitchell, K. (1971). "Research on Certain Therapist Interpersonal Skills in Relation to Process and Outcome." In A. Bergin & S. Garfield (Eds.), *Handbook of Psychotherapy and Behavior Change* (pp. 299–344). New York: John Wiley & Sons.

Vondracek, F. W. (1969). "Behavioral Measurement of Self-Disclosure." *Psychological Reports, 25*(3), 914.

Watzlawick, P., Weakland, J., & Fisch, R. *Change: Principles of Problem Formulation and Problem Resolution.* New York: W. W. Norton & Co.

Zastrow, C., & Navarre, R. (1979). "Using Videotaped Role Playing to Access and Develop Competence." In F. W. Clark et al. (Eds.), *The Pursuit of Competence in Social Work.* San Francisco: Jossey-Bass, 1979.

INDEX

INDEX

(Note: References to entire articles are in **boldface**.)